■ THE RESOURCE FOR THE INDEPENDENT TRAVELER

"The guides are aimed not only at young budget travelers but at the independent traveler; a sort of streetwise cookbook for traveling alone."

—*The New York Times*

"Unbeatable; good sight-seeing advice; up-to-date info on restaurants, hotels, and inns; a commitment to money-saving travel; and a wry style that brightens nearly every page."

—*The Washington Post*

"Lighthearted and sophisticated, informative and fun to read. [Let's Go] helps the novice traveler navigate like a knowledgeable old hand."

—*Atlanta Journal-Constitution*

"A world-wise traveling companion—always ready with friendly advice and helpful hints, all sprinkled with a bit of wit."

—*The Philadelphia Inquirer*

■ THE BEST TRAVEL BARGAINS IN YOUR PRICE RANGE

"All the dirt, dirt cheap."

—*People*

"Anything you need to know about budget traveling is detailed in this book."

—*The Chicago Sun-Times*

"Let's Go follows the creed that you don't have to toss your life's savings to the wind to travel—unless you want to."

—*The Salt Lake Tribune*

■ REAL ADVICE FOR REAL EXPERIENCES

"The writers seem to have experienced every rooster-packed bus and lunar-surfaced mattress about which they write."

—*The New York Times*

"Value-packed, unbeatable, accurate, and comprehensive."

—*The Los Angeles Times*

"[Let's Go's] devoted updaters really walk the walk (and thumb the ride, and trek the trail). Learn how to fish, haggle, find work—anywhere."

—*Food & Wine*

LET'S GO PUBLICATIONS

TRAVEL GUIDES

Australia 8th edition
Austria & Switzerland 12th edition
Brazil 1st edition
Britain & Ireland 2005
California 10th edition
Central America 9th edition
Chile 2nd edition
China 5th edition
Costa Rica 2nd edition
Eastern Europe 2005
Ecuador 1st edition **NEW TITLE**
Egypt 2nd edition
Europe 2005
France 2005
Germany 12th edition
Greece 2005
Hawaii 3rd edition
India & Nepal 8th edition
Ireland 2005
Israel 4th edition
Italy 2005
Japan 1st edition
Mexico 20th edition
Middle East 4th edition
Peru 1st edition **NEW TITLE**
Puerto Rico 1st edition
South Africa 5th edition
Southeast Asia 9th edition
Spain & Portugal 2005
Thailand 2nd edition
Turkey 5th edition
USA 2005
Vietnam 1st edition **NEW TITLE**
Western Europe 2005

ROADTRIP GUIDE

Roadtripping USA **NEW TITLE**

ADVENTURE GUIDES

Alaska 1st edition
New Zealand **NEW TITLE**
Pacific Northwest **NEW TITLE**
Southwest USA 3rd edition

CITY GUIDES

Amsterdam 3rd edition
Barcelona 3rd edition
Boston 4th edition
London 2005
New York City 15th edition
Paris 13th edition
Rome 12th edition
San Francisco 4th edition
Washington, D.C. 13th edition

POCKET CITY GUIDES

Amsterdam
Berlin
Boston
Chicago
London
New York City
Paris
San Francisco
Venice
Washington, D.C.

ROADTRIPPING USA

THE COMPLETE COAST-TO-COAST GUIDE TO AMERICA

EMILIE S. FITZMAURICE EDITOR
JIM FINGAL ASSOCIATE EDITOR
LINDSAY KATHLEEN TURNER ASSOCIATE EDITOR
JULIA REISCHEL AND KATHY H. LEE ORIGINATING EDITORS

RESEARCHER-WRITERS

KATIE BURCH
TABBY GEORGE
KATIE HELLER
ZOILA HINSON
MATTHEW K. HUDSON

THOMAS LAAKSO
DEVIN LYONS-QUIRK
BEN SIRACUSA
ELLI THOMSON

ELIZABETH HALBERT PETERSON AND CHRISTINE YOKOYAMA MAP EDITORS
CHARLOTTE DOUGLAS AND JEFFREY DUBNER MANAGING EDITORS

ST. MARTIN'S PRESS ❧ NEW YORK

HELPING LET'S GO. If you want to share your discoveries, suggestions, or corrections, please drop us a line. We read every piece of correspondence, whether a postcard, a 10-page email, or a coconut. **Address mail to:**

Roadtripping USA
67 Mount Auburn Street
Cambridge, MA 02138
USA

Visit Let's Go at **http://www.letsgo.com,** or send email to:

feedback@letsgo.com
Subject: "Let's Go: Roadtripping USA"

In addition to the invaluable travel advice our readers share with us, many are kind enough to offer their services as researchers or editors. Unfortunately, our charter enables us to employ only currently enrolled Harvard students.

Maps by David Lindroth copyright © 2005 by St. Martin's Press.

Distributed outside the USA and Canada by Macmillan, an imprint of Pan Macmillan Ltd.
20 New Wharf Road, London N1 9RR
Basingstoke and Oxford
Associated companies throughout the world
www.panmacmillan.com

ISBN: 0-312-33569-5
EAN: 978-0312-33569-4
First edition
10 9 8 7 6 5 4 3 2 1

Roadtripping USA is written by Let's Go Publications, 67 Mount Auburn Street, Cambridge, MA 02138, USA.

Let's Go® and the LG logo are trademarks of Let's Go, Inc.
Printed in China

CONTENTS

HOW TO USE THIS BOOK

ORGANIZATION. The book is organized into eight unique routes that will take you from ocean to ocean, from Mexico to Alaska, and to every scenic drive, classic diner, and roadside dinosaur in between. Follow just one route, or choose your own adventure by combining two or more; the **Crossroads** section at the beginning of each chapter lets you know where our routes cross paths. At the beginning of the book, **The Road** and **Essentials** chapters will get you excited for your roadtrip and get you through it in one piece. The black tabs on the side of each page help guide you through.

MAPS. In addition to city maps, *Let's Go Roadtripping USA* includes new vertical route maps to help you navigate the road. Each map plots approximately 200 mi. of the route. The maps are oriented along your path; we've angled the text for easy reading if you rotate the book to north.

SPECIAL FEATURES. *Let's Go Roadtripping USA* includes special features to highlight the road's sights and stories in a way standard coverage can't. **100 Mile Radius** tempts drivers to supplement our routes with sights a bit off the path, while **Beyond the Asphalt** sends readers off the road altogether to experience gorgeous natural sights. **From the Road** includes our researchers' memorable tales, and **In the Passenger Seat** introduces you to characters they met along the way. **The Local Story** gives a closer look at culture and undiscovered gems; **No Work, All Play** is your ticket to the best festivals and celebrations. Finally, whet your appetite for regional cuisine with **Road Food.**

RANKINGS. *Let's Go* lists establishments in order of value, starting with the best. Our absolute favorites are denoted by the 🔥**Let's Go thumbs-up.**

PHONE CODES AND TELEPHONE NUMBERS. Phone numbers in this guide are marked with the ☎ icon. All include the area code and local number. In many cities, all ten digits are required even for local calls; often in more remote areas only the final seven are needed for local calls.

WHEN TO USE IT

ONE YEAR BEFORE. Some national parks' summer accommodations and campgrounds fill up many months in advance. Use our coverage to make your plans and secure your spot.

ONE MONTH BEFORE. Take care of insurance, and write down a list of emergency numbers and hotlines. Make a list of packing essentials (see **Packing**) and shop for anything you are missing. Read through the coverage and make sure you understand the logistics of your itinerary (ferries, distance between gas and rest stops, etc.). Make any reservations if necessary.

2 WEEKS BEFORE. Leave an itinerary and a photocopy of important documents with someone at home. Make sure to check all of the fluids in the vehicle you are planning on taking, as well as making sure the tires are in good shape. It's a good idea to have a tune-up, just in case.

ON THE ROAD. The **Appendix** contains metric conversion tables and a basic introduction to French and Spanish terms, which may come in handy during the portions of the roadtrips that occur in Eastern Canada and Mexico. Arm yourself with a journal, some sunglasses, and plenty of gas, and hit the road!

A NOTE TO OUR READERS. The information for this book was gathered by *Let's Go* researchers from January 2003 through August 2004. Each listing is based on one researcher's opinion, formed during his or her visit at a particular time. Those traveling at other times may have different experiences since prices, dates, hours, and conditions are always subject to change. You are urged to check the facts presented in this book beforehand to avoid inconvenience and surprises.

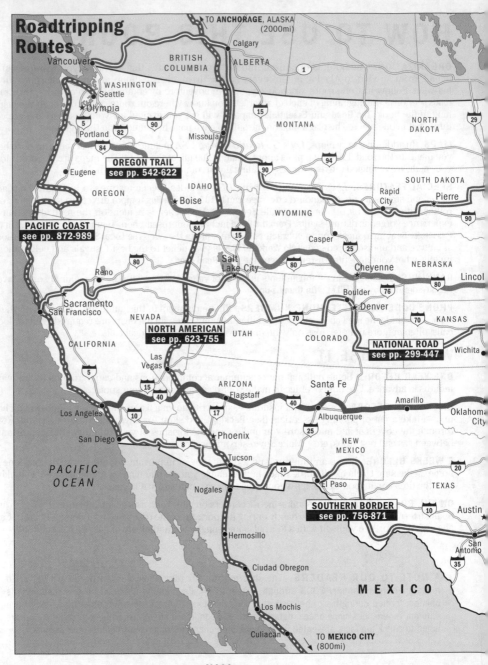

Roadtripping Routes

TO **ANCHORAGE**, ALASKA
(2000mi)

Vancouver
Calgary
BRITISH
COLUMBIA
ALBERTA
①

WASHINGTON
Seattle
★ Olympia
⑤ ⑨⓪ ⑧②
Portland
⑧④
Missoula
MONTANA
NORTH
DAKOTA
②⑨

Eugene
⑨⓪
⑨④
OREGON
IDAHO
⑧④
★ Boise
SOUTH
DAKOTA
Rapid
City
Pierre ★

OREGON TRAIL
see pp. 542-622

WYOMING
⑨⓪

PACIFIC COAST
see pp. 872-989
⑤
⑧④
⑮
Casper
②⑤
⑨⓪

Reno
⑧⓪
Salt
Lake City
★
⑧⓪
Cheyenne
NEBRASKA
⑦⑥
Lincol

Sacramento ★
San Francisco
NEVADA
UTAH
⑦⓪
Boulder
★ Denver
⑦⓪
KANSAS

NORTH AMERICAN
see pp. 623-755

CALIFORNIA
⑤
Las
Vegas
⑮
COLORADO
NATIONAL ROAD
see pp. 299-447
Wichita

ARIZONA
Flagstaff
⑰
⑩
⑮
⑰
⓪
Santa Fe ★
④⓪
Amarillo
Oklahoma
City

Los Angeles
⑩
Albuquerque
②⑤

San Diego
⑧
★ Phoenix
Tucson
NEW
MEXICO
②⓪

PACIFIC
OCEAN
⑩
El Paso
TEXAS

Nogales
SOUTHERN BORDER
see pp. 756-871
⑩
Austin ★

Hermosillo
San
Antonio
③⑤

Ciudad Obregon
M E X I C O

Los Mochis

Culiacan
TO **MEXICO CITY**
(800mi)

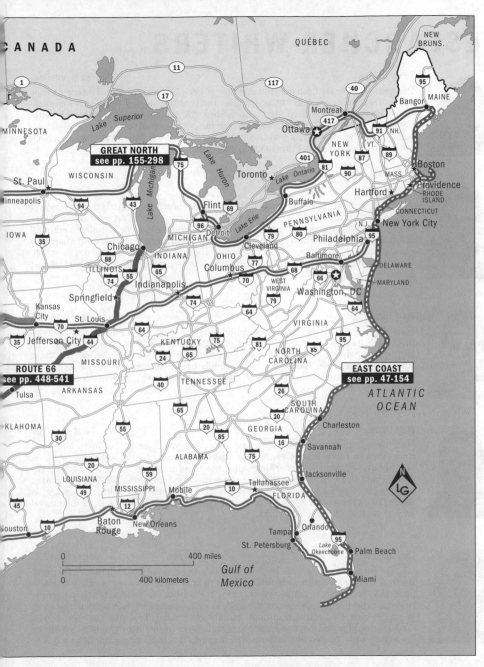

CANADA

QUÉBEC

NEW BRUNS.

MAINE

GREAT NORTH
see pp. 155-298

ROUTE 66
see pp. 448-541

EAST COAST
see pp. 47-154

ATLANTIC
OCEAN

MINNESOTA

Lake Superior

St. Paul

Minneapolis

WISCONSIN

Lake Michigan

Lake Huron

Toronto

Lake Ontario

Montreal

Ottawa

NEW YORK

VT.

NH.

Bangor

Boston

Providence

RHODE ISLAND

MASS.

CONNECTICUT

Hartford

New York City

N.J.

Philadelphia

DELAWARE

MARYLAND

Washington, DC

IOWA

Chicago

Flint

Detroit

Cleveland

Buffalo

PENNSYLVANIA

Baltimore

MICHIGAN

INDIANA

OHIO

Columbus

WEST VIRGINIA

ILLINOIS

Indianapolis

Springfield

Kansas City

St. Louis

Jefferson City

MISSOURI

KENTUCKY

VIRGINIA

NORTH CAROLINA

TENNESSEE

ARKANSAS

Tulsa

OKLAHOMA

LOUISIANA

MISSISSIPPI

Mobile

ALABAMA

GEORGIA

SOUTH CAROLINA

Charleston

Savannah

Jacksonville

Tallahassee

FLORIDA

Houston

Baton Rouge

New Orleans

Tampa

St. Petersburg

Orlando

Lake Okeechobee

Palm Beach

Miami

Gulf of Mexico

0   400 miles

0   400 kilometers

N
LG

RESEARCHER-WRITERS

Tabby George *The North American*

Returning to Let's Go from her stint as editor of *Let's Go: Europe* and *Western Europe 2004,* Tabby was one half of the dynamic duo sent to conquer The North American Route, cruising from Mexico City to Anchorage, AK. With impeccable style and Southern manners, Tabby charmed her way across the continent, all the while ruthlessly pursuing hidden hot spots, sights, and deals. For more of Matt & Tabby's adventures, check out their travel journal at http://roadtrip.letsgo.com.

Katie Heller *Route 66*

Katie Heller got her kicks on Route 66 in the middle of winter, braving the icy winds of Chicago and racing snowstorms across the New Mexico desert. But even cold weather couldn't stop this researcher; Katie experienced life on the road to its fullest, venturing off-road at the Grand Canyon and stopping at every trading post, souvenir shop, and classic motel along the way. Katie also had an uncanny knack for finding the most delicious desserts along the way—her editors appreciated the recipes she sent back almost as much as her good-humored prose.

Zoila Hinson *The East Coast*

Zoila stoically braved deadly insects, debilitating floods, and side mirror-stealing gremlins on her trek up and down the East Coast Route. A New Jersey native, graduate in History and Science, budding Ultimate Frisbee player, and Gemini, she was old hat at researching the Outer Banks, where her family has spent many a summer exploring lighthouses. Zoila enjoys long walks on the beach, which is why we sent her to research just about 2000 miles of beaches.

Matt Hudson *The North American*

Matt brought his trademark humor and swoon-worthy style to the North American route, driving Tabby across a continent (and occasionally crazy) on their zany three-month odyssey. Matt's copywriting skills, honed as an Associate Editor of *Let's Go Europe* and *Western Europe 2003* and as series managing editor in 2004, resulted in painless proofing for his editors—except, of course, for the side-splitting laughter his writing often prompted. For more of Matt & Tabby's adventures, check out their travel journal at http://roadtrip.letsgo.com.

Tom Laakso *The Oregon Trail*

Like the pioneers whose path he followed, Tom persevered through the hardships of the trail, reaching Oregon with plenty of time to spare before winter. A native of Fitchburg, MA, Tom studies astrophysics during the school year and was able to put his celestial expertise to good use on the road, sleeping under the stars beneath the wide, Western skies. Dedicated, thorough, and always upbeat, Tom outdrove tornadoes, tamed the wild jackalope, and blazed new paths over forbidding mountains, charming his editors with detailed illustrations of his exploits and lively prose along the way.

Devin Lyons-Quirk
The Southern Border

The experience of running track and planning total world domination aided Devin in surviving the desert heat of the Southern Border. This hard-to-the-core explorer, raised on the mean streets of San Diego, has an unquenchable thirst for the road, and nothing could keep him down—not even mountain lions, rattlesnakes, cacti, and Southerners unused to seeing people exercising in short running shorts. After having been released from his duties, he promptly took a well-earned surfing break.

Ben Siracusa
The National Road

With an eye for detail, a penchant for history, and an appetite for adventure, Ben was without a doubt the perfect researcher for the National Road. Indefatigable, he took fearlessly to the road in Atlantic City and drove the whole lonely way to San Francisco, churning out a steady stream of meticulous copy that never left his editors wondering about a single little thing. While he took time to marvel at the spectacular landscapes of the parks along the way and even did a little off-road adventuring himself, his solid, well-researched copy earned respect all around.

Elli Thomson
The Great North

Currently working as an IT Engineer, Elli braved the wild animals and big cities of the Great North Route with great resiliency. This came as little surprise, though, since she already had experience fending off bears while working in Glacier National Park. A Montreal fortune teller insisted to her that she was especially lucky, and it later paid off in the form of a free room and a decent-sized white pearl—long story—but we think we're the lucky ones.

Katie Burch
The Pacific Coast

Katie Burch traced the Pacific coast, sending in copy and bumper-sticker sightings that made her editors feel as though they, too, were out on the open road. Katie mastered the art of car cuisine as she searched out pockets of authenticity in Southern California, the land that spawned fast food, freeways, and chain malls. Although happiest tracking down a hidden hike or sapphire-blue cove, Katie reconciled her love of nature with SoCal's car culture—after all, smoggy skies produce the best sunsets.

CONTRIBUTING WRITERS

Ron Evans is a travel writer and the editor of VIA Magazine's Oregon/Idaho issue. He has written articles on driving U.S. 50 through Nevada and biking Oregon's backroads and byways.

Mike Marriner crossed the country in a neon green RV, interviewing self-made men and women for his book, *Roadtrip Nation: A Guide to Discovering Your Path In Life.*

Bryan Di Salvatore is the author of *A Clever Base-Ballist: The Life and Times of John Montgomery.* He lives and writes in Missoula, MT.

John Stilgoe is Orchard Professor in the History of Landscape at Harvard University, and the author of *Outside Lies Magic: Regaining History and Awareness in Everyday Places.*

ACKNOWLEDGMENTS

TEAM ROADTRIP THANKS: Charlotte, for feeding and caring for us; Elizabeth for simultaneously putting up with us and catching our mistakes; Naomi, Jeff, and Max, the other half of the ▇▇ pod, for making work fun; Joanna for all her hard work; and J-Todd for being so clutch in the last days.

EMILIE THANKS: My AEs: Lindsay, for collaboration and thoughtful edits; and Jim, for artsy writing and edgy humor; our ME, Charlotte, for helping to visualize a whole new book and then pulling it all together; Matt & Tabby, for letting me be the boss (and showing me how it should be done); my family, for their constant support and listening; and always, Dan, for everything.

JIM THANKS: Lindsay and Drew, for both doing more work than me at my summer jobs; Emilie and Charlotte, for knowing more LG esoterica than me; Katherine, for bagels and coffee; you know who, for having really crazy curly hair and being all lovely and stuff; the cellar crew, for keeping me sane during the lonely summer months; Jamie Stewart, Jason Molina, and Morrissey, for helping work go along smoothly; my family, for being awesome; Thomas, for graciously offering to sleep on my couch all summer; and the guys at home, for giving me so much roadtrip experience in the first place. Also: hardcore, and kittens.

LINDSAY THANKS: Jim, for awesome work and brilliant ideas—really. Emilie, for fearless leadership, and Charlotte, for flawless style. The polymaths at Magnolia Ave. (all of you, Tali included!) for AWOD awesome-ness and putting up with me. Julia, especially, for keeping me company through all the craziness. Cathy, Paul, Ethan, Alexis, and Rob, for real letters and conversation. Lauren, for understanding and advice and visiting me. Mom and Dad, for everything. Also: fiddles, and ▇Tennessee.

ELIZABETH THANKS: Emilie, Jim, and Lindsay, for all their hard work. Teresa and Emma, for giving me this job. And all the map editors, for making it an awesome summer.

Editor
Emilie S. FitzMaurice
Associate Editors
Jim Fingal, Lindsay Kathleen Turner
Originating Editors
Julia Reischel and Kathy H. Lee
Managing Editors
Charlotte Douglas and Jeffrey Dubner
Map Editors
Elizabeth Halbert Peterson and Christine Yokoyama
Typesetter
Victoria Esquivel-Korsiak

Publishing Director
Emma Nothmann
Editor-in-Chief
Teresa Elsey
Production Manager
Adam R. Perlman
Cartography Manager
Elizabeth Halbert Peterson
Design Manager
Amelia Aos Showalter
Editorial Managers
Briana Cummings, Charlotte Douglas, Ella M. Steim, Joel August Steinhaus, Lauren Truesdell, Christina Zaroulis
Financial Manager
R. Kirkie Maswoswe
Marketing and Publicity Managers
Stef Levner, Leigh Pascavage
Personnel Manager
Jeremy Todd
Low-Season Manager
Clay H. Kaminsky
Production Associate
Victoria Esquivel-Korsiak
IT Director
Matthew DePetro
Web Manager
Rob Dubbin
Associate Web Manager
Patrick Swieskowski
Web Content Manager
Tor Krever
Research and Development Consultant
Jennifer O'Brien
Office Coordinators
Stephanie Brown, Elizabeth Peterson

Director of Advertising Sales
Elizabeth S. Sabin
Senior Advertising Associates
Jesse R. Loffler, Francisco A. Robles, Zoe M. Savitsky
Advertising Graphic Designer
Christa Lee-Chuvala

President
Ryan M. Geraghty
General Manager
Robert B. Rombauer
Assistant General Manager
Anne E. Chisholm

ABOUT LET'S GO

GUIDES FOR THE INDEPENDENT TRAVELER

We believe that travel opens an immense world of opportunities—opportunities to learn from and be enriched by the places you visit, to grow and be challenged by ideas and ways of life different from your own, and to change yourself. In the same vein, we are unapologetically idealistic—we know that travel makes a difference in the lives of our writers and editors, and we believe it can make a difference in our readers and in the world as well. We also recognize that with those opportunities come responsibilities: the responsibility to try to dig deeper than the normal tourist experience, to share what you've learned during your travels, to give back to the communities you visit, and to protect them for future generations. We focus on budget travel not because we think of it as a last resort for the destitute, but because we believe it's the only way to travel. Traveling close to the ground almost always results in a more authentic experience and allows you to interact more directly with the places and people you've gone to see.

BEYOND THE TOURIST EXPERIENCE

To help our readers gain a deeper connection with the places they travel, our researchers give you the heads-up on both world-renowned and off-the-beaten-track attractions, sights, and destinations. They engage with the local culture, writing features on regional cuisine, local festivals, and hot political issues. We've also opened our pages to respected writers and scholars to hear their takes on the countries and regions we cover, and asked travelers who have worked, studied, or volunteered abroad to contribute first-person essays about their experiences. We've increased our coverage of responsible and sustainable travel and share with our readers more opportunities to experience the places they travel.

FORTY-FIVE YEARS OF WISDOM

Let's Go got its start in 1960, when a group of creative and well-traveled students compiled their experience into a 20-page mimeographed pamphlet, which they gave to travelers on charter flights to Europe. Four and a half decades later, we've expanded to cover six continents and all kinds of travel—while still retaining our founders' passionate, idealistic attitude toward the world. Our guides are researched and written entirely by students on shoestring budgets, adventurous and experienced travelers who know that train strikes, stolen luggage, food poisoning, and marriage proposals are all part of a day's work. This year, we're expanding our coverage of South America and Southeast Asia, with brand-new *Let's Go: Ecuador*, *Let's Go: Peru*, and *Let's Go: Vietnam*. Our adventure guide series is growing, too, with the addition of *Let's Go: Pacific Northwest Adventure* and *Let's Go: New Zealand Adventure*. And we're immensely excited about our new *Let's Go: Road-tripping USA*—two years, eight routes, and sixteen researchers and editors have put together a travel guide like none other.

A COMMUNITY OF TRAVELERS

We're a small company, and we stay that way because we believe that a close-knit staff that can lavish individual attention on every title we publish is the recipe for the best travel guides. We love it when our readers become part of the Let's Go community as well—please visit us online (www.letsgo.com), drop us a postcard (67 Mt. Auburn St., Cambridge, MA 02138, USA), or send us an e-mail (feedback@letsgo.com) to tell us about your adventures and discoveries.

THE ROAD

HISTORY

THE FIRST ROADTRIP

For a $50 bet, Horatio Nelson Jackson set out from San Francisco in 1903 to cross the continent by car in 90 days, challenging the belief that the newfangled "horseless carriages" were an unreliable and impractical means of travel. Jackson and his mechanic struck out for New York in a two-cylinder, 20-horsepower Winton Touring Car with a maximum speed of 30 mph. A blowout 15 mi. into their journey was the first of many mechanical disasters encountered along their often-unpaved route tracing the historic Lewis and Clark Trail, but Jackson persevered, winning the hearts of the public and acquiring a goggle-sporting bulldog named Bud along the way. Sixty-three days, 12 hours, and 30 minutes after they began, the triumphant trio crossed the Harlem River into Manhattan. The media raved about the trip's success, and Americans began to reconsider the possibilities of the automobile. And thus, the great American roadtrip was born.

HISTORY OF THE ROAD

"Let us bind the republic together with a perfect system of roads and canals. Let us conquer space..."
–John C. Calhoun, speech before Congress, 1816

THE EARLY ROADS. Although John Calhoun had proposed a cross-country network of roads almost a century before Jackson's trip, in 1903 this "perfect system" was still far from complete. There were roads in most parts of the country, but they were almost universally "unimproved"—that is, made of packed dirt or gravel, wide enough only for a single carriage to pass—and unfit for long trips. Once-flourishing wagon routes, such as the Cumberland Road, had fallen into disrepair as the railroad became the country's dominant means of long-distance travel in the 1850s. The state of roads a traveler could expect to encounter varied widely by region. In the East, rural roads were often indirect, ill-placed, and haphazardly maintained. In the South, where 96% of public roadways were classified as "unimproved" as of 1904, the norm was an unmapped dirt road that would become muddy quagmire during the soggy Southern rains. Farther west, roads were constructed along the edges of rectangular townships and plots of public land. Although the resulting grid system was well-organized, the roads themselves were little more than wagon ruts.

THE FIRST HIGHWAYS. By the early 20th century, the state of America's national roads was changing. With the growing popularity of the automobile, more and more attention was turned toward the quality of the nation's highways. The members of the new **American Automobile Association (AAA,** founded in 1903) began to clamor for improvements as they tried to drive their new vehicles over narrow, bumpy, unpaved roads. In 1908, the association held its first annual National Good Roads Convention to inaugurate the **Good Roads Movement,** which pushed for raised, graded, and ditched highways that wouldn't flood or wash out with every rain. The country's first "good road" appeared in 1909 as a mile of concrete highway outside Detroit, Michigan (not coincidentally the birthplace of the Model T).

In 1913, industrialists Carl Fischer, Frank Seiberling, and Henry Joy envisioned a paved road from coast to coast, and by 1915 their dream had been realized; the **Lincoln Highway,** as it was known, became the first transcontinental American road, stretching almost 3400 mi. from New York to California. The Federal-Aid Road Act of 1916 created a system of federal funding for the local construction. Part of President Franklin D. Roosevelt's New Deal plan to provide employment opportunities during the depression, the Federal Highway Act of 1921 established the Bureau of Public Roads to oversee the laying down of a numbered system of paved, two-lane highways throughout the states, inaugurating the first era of standardized road building nationwide. Eventually the Lincoln Highway became integrated into this growing highway network.

THE ROAD

Throughout the 40s and 50s, highway construction continued steadily as more Americans discovered the joys of the road. During this period, famous cross-continental highways like Route 66 and Route 40 were traveled by hordes of motorists, developing the lore and romance of the national roadtrip. Though a vast improvement over the roads that preceded them, the Federal Aid highways were still two-lane roads. Even as these two-lane highways became vital arteries to the nation, they were made obsolete by the advance of new multi-lane, high-speed Interstates.

HIGH-SPEED INTERSTATES. The Federal-Aid Act of 1944, later cemented in the Federal-Aid Highway Act of 1956, created a National System of Interstate Highways, an interregional system of high-speed routes. As President Eisenhower described, it would "connect by routes, as direct as practicable, the principal metropolitan areas, cities, and industrial centers" of the nation. The Interstate program was touted as the "greatest public works program in history." Designed to measure 42,500 mi. when finished, it would be 30 times as long as the Great Wall of China and would pave a surface area the size of West Virginia. It was a fitting project for transitional post-war America and, in conjunction with the older Federal-Aid and state-run highway projects, would be the capstone of the national effort to make the continent accessible by car. As high-speed Interstates stretched across the nation, they became the preferred routes for drivers seeking direct travel between cities, gradually surpassing slower and more scenic two-lane roads.

Construction of the interstate continued throughout the 60s, as environmental concerns became influential and Cold War tension made national security a high priority. In 1966, the Department of Transportation was formed to "develop and coordinate policies that will provide an efficient and economical national transportation system, with due regard for need, the environment, and the national defense." The Bureau of Public Roads was absorbed into this new department as the **Federal Highway Administration (FHWA).** During the 70s and 80s, Interstate construction reached a state of virtual completion.

THE ROAD TODAY. President Dwight D. Eisenhower's dream of a well-organized Interstate highway system has today been realized; a comprehensive, well-maintained, efficient network connects the cities and states of the US. The plan was originally for the Interstates and the old highways to co-exist, but as the Interstate system began reshape trade routes and became the dominant arteries for transportation, older highways began to be forgotten. On the old highway maps, the Interstates were mapped out in red ink and the two-lane highways and back roads were colored in blue ink, hence the term, **Blue Highways.**

The Blue Highways of America have since come to represent all that is central to the experience of the American roadtrip: the "myth of the road," road culture, romance, diners, and 50s motels with large neon signs. The twisted back roads have come to represent an alternative to the commerce, congestion, anonymity, and pollution that is symbolized by the Interstate system.

Several of the Blue Highways have found their way into legend. **US Route 66,** running from Chicago to Los Angeles, has become synonymous with American road culture. Created by a congressional act in 1925 and continuously paved by 1938, Route 66 saw the westward migration of thousands of families from the Dust Bowl to the greener fields and vineyards of California during the Depression, an exodus depicted in John Steinbeck's *The Grapes of Wrath* (1939). Later, Route 66 would facilitate the movement of thousands more westward-bound, adventure-seeking travelers, as well as the development of the modern service station and motel. All of Route 66 was officially decommissioned by 1985, but the "Main Street of America" remains a standard roadtrip route as well as a pop culture legend.

Another great old highway is **US Route 40,** the "National Road," which spans the 3200 miles from Atlantic City to San Francisco. Sometimes called the "Golden Highway," Route 40 at its creation roughly paralleled the old Lincoln Highway, and at its heyday during the 1950s, was the transcontinental route of choice for many travelers. Although it, like Route 66, has been largely replaced by the modern Interstate system, Route 40 remains, in all its neon light and roadside diner glory, a road culture standard.

More recently, the US Department of Transportation has begun to recognize roads with special historic, scenic, or cultural significance through its **Scenic Byways Program.** Since 1992, the program has funded almost 1500 roadways in 48 states, designating routes as National Scenic Byways or as All-American Roads. Famous and well-loved byways include the Blue Ridge Parkway through the southern Appalachian mountains, the San Juan Skyway in Southern Colorado, and the Pacific Coast Highway, as well as parts of Routes 40 and 66.

HISTORY OF THE CAR

Far from being a new innovation, the automobile that made Horatio Jackson's journey a reality was the result of a gradual process of development. The first **self-propelled vehicle** was a French invention; in 1769, French engineer Nicolas Joseph Cugnot invented a steam-powered military tractor. (Two years later, Cugnot also became the first person to experience a motor vehicle accident, when he drove one of his contraptions into a stone wall.) Some early vehicles also used electrical power. In the mid 1830s, Scottish inventor Robert Anderson put together the first **electric carriage,** and these battery-powered vehicles, clunky and expensive as they were, were the dominant form of car in the US until about 1900.

Around the turn of the century, **gasoline-powered cars** began to outsell other types of vehicles. Largely a result of the late 19th-century innovations of German engineers Karl Benz (as in Mercedes-Benz) and Gottlieb Daimler, these gas-fueled automobiles featured a more powerful and efficient internal combustion engine, the granddaddy of engines used in cars today.

Although Americans like to think of their country as the birthplace of the automobile, the world's first car **manufacturers** were Frenchmen: Rene Panhard and Emile Levassor in 1889, and Armand Peugot in 1891. The first "modern" automobile was also a European creation; in 1901 William Bayback designed a 35-horsepower Mercedes model with a maximum speed of 53 mph. Gasoline-powered automobiles were not manufactured in the US until 1893, when bicycle mechanic brothers Charles and Frank Duryea of Springfield, MA, began to manufacture a small number of expensive limousines. The first car to be mass produced in the US was the Curved Dash Oldsmobile; 425 of these classic vehicles were manufactured in **Detroit** in 1901. Later, Detroit, the hub of American auto manufacturing, would grow to be known as the Motor City, and when **Henry Ford** started manufacturing small, black lightweight cars there for only $850 in 1908, he ignited what would become a nationwide obsession for cars. Suddenly, automobile travel was cheap and available to a wide cross-section of American society.

THE EARLY YEARS. The Ford Model T was only the first car to capture the attention of the American public; its debut marked the beginning of America's love affair with the automobile, and simple, no-frills design of the Model T was rapidly replaced by bigger, fancier, and faster models. By the late 1920s, auto manufacturers were producing ever grander and more stylish cars. Throughout the 50s car size increased, and designs became increasingly less practical; hallmarks of the typical 1950-era automobile include the outlandish **space fins,** and the late 60s saw the advent of the **muscle car.**

These increasingly ostentatious car designs reflected more than just changing styles; they were indications of the changing mentality surrounding the car in American culture. The early Fords were primarily farmers' cars, designed to be efficient and practical. Later, however, the car had become a status symbol and a means of self-expression. Ownership became widespread during America's post-war boom. Teenagers, especially, began to own and show off their automobiles, as earning a driver's license became a major rite of passage into adulthood and independence. It wasn't until the oil embargo and new government safety restrictions of the 1970s that manufacturers and consumers began to rein in their enthusiasm for gas-guzzling automobiles.

Increased car ownership combined with an extensive road network prompted the growth of the residential **suburb,** reshaping the American city from a residential center to a place of industry and helping facilitate the American dream of home ownership. The **fast-food joint,** today an American roadside icon, evolved to its present form in the 1950s (the ubiquitous McDonalds was founded by Ray Kroc in 1954), when long road-trips made eating on the go a necessity. The **drive-in movie theater,** where patrons could watch movies (or amorous teenagers could *not* watch movies) was also a product of America's automobile infatuation, peaking in the 1950s.

TODAY. Today, driving and car culture have evolved into a massive industry as well as a way of life. The road continues to be an shaping force on the American imagination, influencing arts in all media with its political and social ramifications. More than half of US citizens drive automobiles, and there are many more cars than licensed drivers; in 2001, there were 191 million drivers out of 281 million American citizens, who owned 226 million motor vehicles. Americans now drive over two trillion miles a year, and even though the days of the hot rod and the muscle car are over, individuals continue to spend vast amounts of time and money on their automobiles. Meanwhile, the US government continues to pump money into the road infrastructure, spending over $75 billion each year on the highway system.

Indeed, it might be fair to say that cars, like baseball games, are an American obsession. AAA is currently second only to the Catholic church in terms of membership in the US, with more than 45 million members and around 1000 offices. Automobile-themed magazines, like the popular *Car and Driver*, abound, and radio stations feature car-themed shows (such as National Public Radio's *Car Talk*). Clubs like the **Antique Automobile Club of America** (which has over 400 chapters and 60,000 members nationwide), host conferences, shows, festivals, and "meets," at which old-car enthusiasts congregate by the thousands. Established in 1977, the **Society for Commercial Archaeology (SCA)** devotes itself to preserving the sights and symbols of 20th-century roadside culture, publishing a journal and hosting annual conferences and tours.

The automobile in America isn't just a mode of transportation; it's also a status symbol. A driver's license is a sign of coming of age and a red convertible connotes a mid-life crisis. Recently, the giant SUV has become endemic. Almost any American will reminisce fondly about his or her first automobile, and the Sunday after-dinner drive is as American as apple pie. Oh yes, and did we mention the classic American roadtrip?

LIFE ON THE ROAD

ROADTRIP ATTITUDE

What is it that makes a roadtrip different from an average, ordinary vacation? Like the car and the open road, the roadtrip has acquired a specific meaning; the type of roadtrip ingrained in American tradition revolves around the journey and the experience of travel itself. As Robert Pirsig, author of *Zen and Motorcycle Maintenance*

mused, "To live only for some future goal is shallow. It's the sides of the mountain which sustain life, not the top. Here's where things grow."

At one extreme, a roadtrip can be a marathon, a test of endurance, a major undertaking. Visiting all of one sort of thing is a popular way of planning out a trip—taking a tour of America's mystery spots, hitting up all of the missions in California, or visiting all of the lighthouses on the East Coast, for example. Event-based trips are also popular—baseball roadtrips from one stadium to the next are an American tradition, as are "follow your favorite band on tour" roadtrips. Every year people make pilgrimages to large gatherings such as Shakespeare festivals or to watch battles put on by the Society for Creative Anachronism. Fair game, too, are historical tours, such as the Lewis and Clark Trail, and any sort of funky place-name themed trip, like setting out to see both Truth or Consequences, New Mexico and Love, Ohio.

At the other end of the spectrum, a roadtrip can evolve without a concrete goal, only a vague direction and desire for knowledge and experience. The exploration of a specific region or historic two-lane highway is a good way to start out, as is following one of the cardinal directions. This kind of trip, more digressive and languorous, revolves around discovering the lives and culture of the people who live along the way—seeing every historical site, stopping at every diner, mingling at every bar. This is the sort of back-road wandering made famous by Jack Kerouac and William Least Heat-Moon. In *Blue Highways: A Journey into America*, Least Heat-Moon separates the classic roadtrip into two types of experience: the epic roadtrip and the lyrical roadtrip. An epic roadtrip embodies the spirit of adventure, while the a lyrical roadtrip is a journey of personal exploration, the best sort of trip for solo travelers.

ROADTRIP TRADITIONS

FRIENDS. From Bonnie and Clyde to Thelma and Louise, roadtrippers traditionally travel in pairs; roadtrip culture is oriented around the experience of a shared journey. Picking the right friend or friends to bring along requires care, but a trusty companion in the front seat makes the miles go by faster. Bringing a friend also means you have an extra navigator—unless your travel companion of choice, like John Steinbeck's, happens to be a dog.

WHO TO TAKE ALONG:

The Adventurer: Adventurers are outgoing and are not afraid to deviate from pre-arranged plans to see a sight that a complete stranger recommended to them. They are not embarrassed to engage in long conversations with people they've never met before and find out where the locals hang out. The adventurer's motto is: "Sure, sounds like fun."

The Navigator: These godsends couldn't get lost if you blindfolded them and left them in the middle of the forest. They have lodestones in their foreheads, know how to read maps, and yet are not overconfident in their abilities; they know when to ask for directions. The navigator's motto is: "Regardless of whether this *feels* like the right off-ramp, let's make sure just in case."

The Optimist: These positive individuals somehow know how to make changing a tire in the snow on the New Jersey turnpike feel like a rousing good time. They take adversity with a grain of salt and keep the big picture in mind. The optimist's motto is: "Good thing the radiator overheated, otherwise we would never have seen this sunrise."

ROAD ETIQUETTE

A growing concentration of rushed drivers on America's highways means road etiquette is increasingly important. Unfortunately, road rage incidents are no myth. **Tailgating,** gratuitous **horn-honking,** driving with **high beams** on when approaching other cars, **eye contact** with aggressive drivers, and **obscene language and gestures** are all road taboos. On highways with two or more lanes, the left-hand lane (the "fast lane") is for passing, and on any road, it is standard politeness to let faster cars pass. One of the most offensive gestures in the US is extending the middle finger of your left hand. Also known as "giving someone the finger," this gesture is considered not only rude, but obscene.

Because roadtrips mean long times in small spaces, certain standards of car etiquette should probably be established before you go. **Communication** is essential with getting along with people, as is flexibility. **Share,** because other people like candy too, and when all else fails, just **chill out—** take a few breaths, close your eyes, lean back, and feel the wind in your hair.

ROADFOOD

Today, most Interstates and many highways are lined with fast-food joints, but the real richness and variety of American roadfood can best be found at local, non-chain ice-cream parlors, hot dog stands, barbecue pits, delis, and diners.

Diners have historically been places where entire communities congregate to enjoy a home-style meal in a comfortable atmosphere. The first roadside diner, however, was little more than a horse-drawn wagon in 1872. Later diners included the slick, streamlined eateries of the 30s and the Colonial/Mediterranean restaurants in the 60s and 70s. The classic diner, a modular, factory-made structure, still appears along many roadsides, and usually promises warm (if greasy) food, considerate service, and a piping hot cup of coffee.

REGIONAL TREATS

With a little extra attention and a discerning eye, a roadtripper can experience a variety of flavor, ranging from the spicy green chilies of New Mexico to the sweetness of New England maple syrup. Finding such regional delights at their peak quality can end up the highlight of any roadtrip.

RITUALS. Miles of uninterrupted cornfields have inspired an extensive collection of **road games** to eliminate that persistent "are we there yet?" Favorites include I Spy, Twenty Questions, Road Bingo, and the License Plate Game, in which the first player to identify license plates from all fifty states wins. For some ideas, check out www.liveandlearn.com/cargame.html.

There is also a repertoire of **roadtrip superstition.** Details vary by region, but standards include holding your breath while driving past graveyards, across state lines, or through tunnels, making wishes when you see a haywagon or at the end of a tunnel, and raising your feet while crossing bridges or railroad tracks. Another common ritual is the "punchbuggy" game, in which the first person to see a Volkswagon Beetle shouts "punchbuggy!" and punches the ceiling or (in a more risky version) the arm of the person next to him or her. Variations of this classic, taken very seriously by the finest of roadtrippers, include shouting "p-diddle" or extending the ritual to include pink cars, limousines, or cars with one headlight.

NORTHEAST. America's English settlers first landed in the Northeast, combining their staples of meats and vegetables with uniquely American foodstuffs such as turkey, maple syrup, clams, lobster, cranberries, and corn. The results yielded such treasures as Boston brown bread, **Indian pudding,** New England **clam chowder,** and **Maine boiled lobster.** The shellfish are second to none.

SOUTHEAST. Be prepared for some good ol' down-home cookin'. Fried chicken, biscuits, grits, collard greens, and sweet potato pie are some of the highlights of Southeastern cuisine. **Virginia ham** is widely renowned, and ham biscuits provide a savory supplement to lunch and dinner dishes. In addition to the famed collection of animal by-products that make up **"soul food"**—pig's knuckles and ears, hog maws, and chitterlings (boiled or fried pig intestines) among others—Southern cuisine has a strong African and West Indian influence in its sauces and spices.

LOUISIANA. Chefs in New Orleans are among the contry's best, and **creole** or **Cajun** cooking tantalizes the taste buds. Smothered crawfish, fried catfish, **jambalaya** (rice cooked with ham, sausage, shrimp, and herbs), and **gumbo** (a thick stew with okra, meat, and vegetables) are delicacies. The faint of taste buds beware: spicy Cajun and creole cooking can fry the mouth.

TEXAS. From juicy tenderloins to luscious baby back ribs to whole pig roasts, Texans like to slow cook their meats over an open fire, flavoring the meat with the smoke from the burning mesquite or hickory. Eat at any of the state's many **BBQ** joints, though, and they'll tell you that the real secret's in the tangy sauce. For those in the mood for something ethnic, enchiladas, burritos, and fajitas are scrumptious **Tex-Mex** options.

MIDWEST. Drawing on the Scandinavian and German roots of area settlers, Midwest cuisine is hearty, simple, and plentiful. The Scandinavian influence brings **lefse** (potato bread) and the indomitable **lutefisk** (fish jellied through a process of soaking in lye). Breads include German Stollen and Swedish Limpa Rye, complementing an assortment of meats, cheeses, soups, and relishes.

CALIFORNIA. Fresh fruits and vegetables are grown throughout California and the Central Valley; avocado and citrus fruits are trademark favorites. Southern California has more Mexican influences, while the long coastline allows for excellent seafood throughout the state. California is also home to the spiritual mother of all road stops, **In-N-Out** Burger, where you can get a simple and cheap 50s-style burger that has been nowhere near a microwave, heat lamp, or freezer. Do you want a malt with that double-double?

SOUTHWEST. The Mexican staples of corn, flour, and chilies are the basic components of Southwestern grub. Salsa made from tomatoes, chilies, and **tomatillos** adds a spicy note to nearly all dishes, especially cheese- and chicken-filled quesadillas and ground beef tacos. In most Southwest roadfood stops, you can get **green chile,** a spicy extra, on pretty much anything you want.

CANADA. Canadian specialties vary by region. Newfoundland boasts the food with rather unusual names, including **bangbelly** (salt pork in a spiced bun,) **toutons** (salt pork with white raisin bread), **figgy duff** (a raisin pudding), and **Jigg's Dinner** (a large meal prepared in a pot containing salt beef, cabbage, turnips, carrots and potatoes). Smoked salmon is a favorite in British Columbia, and Quebec is well known for its **maple syrup** (served on everything from pancakes to omelettes to meats) and varieties of **poutine,** a tasty combination of french fries, cheese curds, and a thick, dark gravy sauce.

MEXICO. Cuisine in the Puebla region is often topped by the regional specialty, **mole Poblano,** a thick, sweet chocolate sauce served over chicken and turkey. Along with this is served **camotes,** a sweet potato dessert. In Oaxaca, travelers drink coffee *a la olla* (slow cooked with sugar and cinnamon) alongside dishes topped with the local *mole Oaxaqueno,* another sweet *mole* variant cooked with bananas. Foods from the Yucatan are Mayan influenced and consist of meats baked in banana leaves covered by fruit-based sauces.

ROADTRIP CULTURE

LITERATURE

"Afoot and light-hearted, I take to the open road...From this hour, freedom!"
—Walt Whitman, 1856

The roadtrip that you are about to embark on is the stuff of poetry. The journey along the open road in search of a new life, new experiences, and a new understanding of America has fueled the creativity of authors before the first Model T rolled off the assembly line, and generations of writers and poets have found life on the road an incisive place to mount a critique against the fast-paced consumer culture of America.

FICTION

Adventures of Huckleberry Finn (1884) by Mark Twain. A carefree lad's misadventures typify the American roadtrip spirit.

Grapes of Wrath (1939) by John Steinbeck. A Depression-era journey westward.

Lolita (1955) by Vladimir Nabokov. The famous and controversial social critique of American culture, telling the story of Humbert Humbert and his tragic love.

On the Road (1957) and just about everything else written by Jack Kerouac. A Beatnik's odyssey and the seminal text of road literature.

The Getaway (1958) by Jim Thompson. Two bank robbers flee across the country and cut a violent swath across America.

Rabbit Run (1960) by John Updike. The story of Harry "Rabbit" Angstrom's running from his former life and search for new meaning.

Travels with Charley: In Search of America (1962) by John Steinbeck. A veteran writer takes to the road with his dog (Charley) to rediscover his homeland.

In Cold Blood (1966) by Truman Capote. An analysis of a crime and the mystery as to why two men would drive over 400 miles to kill four people who they did not know.

Zen and the Art of Motorcycle Maintenance (1974) by Robert Pirsig. A critique of modern Western values set on a cross-country roadtrip.

Another Roadside Attraction (1971) by Tom Robbins. The story of comedic genius and 1960s counterculture recounting how a troupe of carnies come into the possession of the embalmed body of Jesus Christ. Also check out the classic story of the hitchhiking small-town girl in *Even Cowgirls Get the Blues.*

Blue Highways: A Journey into America (1983) by William Least Heat-Moon. A trip through the backroads of small-town America.

Road Fever (1991) by Tim Cahill. The documentation of an attempt to travel from Tiera del Fuego to the tip of Alaska in 25½ days.

Interstate (1995) by Steven Dixon. The telling and retelling of a father's search for the perpetrators of a seemingly random act of road violence.

Amnesia Moon (1995) by Jonathan Lethem. The post-apocalyptic journey of a boy named Chaos.

Dharma Girl (1996) by Chelsea Cain. A memoir of the the author's move from Southern California to Iowa.

American Gods (2001) by Neil Gaiman. The story of a dark, brooding man named Shadow and his involvement with the battle between the old gods of mythology and the new American Gods.

NON-FICTION & POETRY

A Hoosier Holiday (1916) by Theodore Dreiser. A precursor to the "road novel," this non-fiction work documents a roadtrip Dreiser took with fellow artist Franklin Booth.

The Air-Conditioned Nightmare (1947) by Henry Miller. A non-fiction account of Henry Miller's 1940-1941 journey through America and his criticism of American culture.

Out West (1987) by Dayton Duncan. The account of a man and his Volkswagon trip westward, following the trail of Lewis and Clark.

The Lost Continent: Travels in Small Town America (1990) by Bill Bryson. A search across 38 states for the essence of small-town life.

American Nomad (1997) by Steve Erickson. The non-fiction account of Erickson's continued road journey after covering the 1996 presidential election for Rolling Stone.

Songs for the Open Road: Poems of Travel and Adventure (1999) by The American Poetry & Literacy Project. Collection of 80 poems by 50 British and American poets, about travel and journeys.

Driving Visions (2002) by David Laderman. Discusses the cultural roots of the Road Movie and analyzes its role in literary tradition.

Ridge Route: The Road That United California (2002) by Harrison Irving Scott. An in-depth look at highway construction over the grapevine.

Roadtrip Nation (2003) by Mike Marriner and Nathan Gebhard. A "guide to discovering your path in life," this book focuses on the carpe diem spirit of the roadtrip and explores how you can apply it to your daily life and career.

RV Traveling Tales: Women's Journeys on the Open Road (2003) edited by Jaimie Hall & Alice Zyetz. An anthology of women writers and their experiences living on the road.

FILM

Counterculture, existential, visionary, or just slapstick, classic road movies tell the story of rebels, outlaws, and nomads. If you want to learn just about everything there is to know about the genre, David Laderman explores film's fascination with the road in his in-depth study, *Driving Visions*, describing the genre's "Modernist Engine" in its use of technology as a liberating force and exploring how the film conventions of the road have changed with American culture over the decades.

MOVIES

The Wild One (1954): Marlon Brando and his motorcycle gang, rebelling against whatever you got, terrorize a town and disrupt a motorcycle race.

Bonnie and Clyde (1967): The world's most notorious and romanticized bank robbers, played by Warren Beatty and Faye Dunaway, drive across the Midwest robbing banks during the Great Depression.

Easy Rider (1969): Peter Fonda and Dennis Hopper play two non-conforming bikers searching for America on a motorcycle trek from L.A. to New Orleans.

Two-Lane Blacktop (1971): James Taylor and Dennis Wilson, as "The Driver" and "The Mechanic," drag race their way across the US.

The Blues Brothers (1980): On a mission from God, Jake and Elwood Blues find themselves amongst hundreds of wrecked cars, 106 miles from Chicago, with a full tank of gas, half a pack of cigarettes, in the dark, wearing sunglasses.

National Lampoon's Vacation (1983): The now-classic Griswold family summer vacation journey to Wally-World.

(Sesame Street Presents) Follow That Bird (1985): Big Bird, forlorn and feeling like he does not belong, searches for himself out on the road.

Pee-Wee's Big Adventure (1985): Pee Wee, a loner and a rebel, goes on a cross-country quest to find his stolen bicycle in the basement of the Alamo.

My Own Private Idaho (1991): Gus Van Sant directs this gay interpretation of Henry IV, in which River Phoenix and Keanu Reeves search across the country and across the Atlantic for maternal support.

Highway to Hell (1992): In a retelling of the Orpheus myth, Las Vegas newlyweds have to go to hell and bargain with Satan.

Wild Wheels (1992): Directed by Harold Blank, a documentary on car art in America.

Natural Born Killers (1994): Mickey and Mallory drive Route 666 in this postmodern tale of murder and mayhem.

To Wong Foo, Thanks for Everything! Julie Newmar (1995): Three drag queens drive from New York to Hollywood in an old Cadillac that breaks down in small-town America.

Boys on the Side (1995): An unlikely trio of women drive across the country to L.A. and find common bonds with each other.

Road Trip (2000): Four college students take off cross-country to retrieve a mistakenly mailed incriminating video tape.

Rat Race (2001): A modern *It's a Mad, Mad, Mad, Mad World*.

Y tu Mamá También (2001): Two amorous teenage boys, ditched by their girlfriends, travel by car through Mexico with an older woman in search of a hidden beach.

Crossroads (2002): Starring Britney Spears, a heartbreaking *Künstlerroman* telling the tale of three best friends striving to realize themselves as human beings and as musical artists.

Horatio's Drive: America's First Road Trip (2003): Directed by Ken Burns, the story of the Horatio Jackson, America's first roadtripper.

MUSIC

Traveling music has been around since bards have been writing and singing ballads, and oral poetry of travel dates back beyond Homer. In America, there is a strong folk tradition of travel songs, with artists such as Woodie Guthrie singing Kerouacian tunes about rambling through the dust bowl and living the itinerant life. Distinct from the folk ballad is the "hot rod song" of the early 60s and bands like the Beach Boys or Jan and Dean, primarily about the appeal of fast cars and flashy lifestyles.

THE OLD SCHOOL (PRE-1977)

The Allman Brothers, "Ramblin' Man"

Chuck Berry, "No Particular Place to Go"

Blue Oyster Cult, "The Last Days of May"

Canned Heat, "On the Road Again"

Jim Croce, "I Got a Name"

Deep Purple, "Highway Star"

The Doobie Brothers, "Rockin' Down the Highway"

The Doors, "Roadhouse Blues"

Anything by Bob Dylan

Woody Guthrie, "Hard Travelin'"

Jimi Hendrix, "Crosstown Traffic"

Don McLean, "American Pie"

Willie Nelson, "On the Road Again"

Lynyrd Skynyrd, "End of the Road"

Bob Seger & the Silver Bullet Band, "Against the Wind"

Bruce Springsteen, "Born to Run"

James Taylor, "Traveling Star"

Bobby Troup, "Route 66"

Tom Waits, "The Ballad of Big Joe and Phantom 309"

THE NEW SCHOOL (POST-1977)

AC/DC, "Highway to Hell"

Audioslave, "I am the Highway"

The Apples in Stereo, "Signal in the Sky"

Cake, "The Distance"

Sheryl Crow, "Everyday is a Winding Road"

Depeche Mode, "Behind the Wheel"

Eve 6, "Open Road Song"

Fastball, "The Way"

Sammy Hagar, "I Can't Drive 55"

Judas Priest, "Heading Out To The Highway"

Modest Mouse, "Head South"

Tom Petty, "Travelin'"

Red Hot Chili Peppers, "Road Trippin'"

Smog, "The Hard Road"

Stone Temple Pilots, "Interstate Love Song"

System of a Down, "Highway Song"

George Thorogood and the Destroyers, "Gear Jammer"

U2, "Where the Streets Have No Name"

ON THE WEB

These roadside culture websites list all the funky stuff we know you really want to see along the way. After all, no roadtrip is truly complete without a visit to the two-headed calf of Ft. Cody, NE.

www.driveinmovie.com. The drive-in is not quite a thing of the past; this site lists places where you can still enjoy the big screen from the comfort of your car.

www.roadfood.com. Lists and reviews a variety of road-side eateries, all presumably serving homestyle, greasy, classic American roadtrip food.

www.roadsideamerica.com. A guide to "offbeat tourist attractions," classic American kitsch, and just plain weirdness.

www.wlra.us. This site is entirely devoted to the world's largest roadside attractions, such as the world's largest ball of twine, the world's largest cow skull, and the world's largest watermelon. Who knew?

HOLIDAYS

2005 HOLIDAYS	
January 1	New Year's Day
January 17	Martin Luther King, Jr. Day (US)
February 2-8	Carnaval (MEX)
February 5	Día de la Constitución (MEX)
February 22	Presidents Day (US)
February 24	Día de la Bandera (Flag Day; MEX)
March 25-28	Easter Weekend (CAN, MEX)
March 21	Birthday of Benito Juárez (MEX)
May 1	Día del Trabajo (Labor Day; US, MEX)
May 5	Cinco de Mayo (MEX)
May 23	Victoria Day (CAN)
May 30	Memorial Day (US)
July 1	Canada Day
July 4	Independence Day (US)
September 1	Labor Day (US, MEX)
September 16	Día de la Independencia (MEX)
October 10	Columbus Day (US)
October 10	Canadian Thanksgiving
October 12	Día de la Raza (Columbus Day; MEX)
November 11	Veterans Day (US); Remembrance Day (CAN)
November 20	Día de la Revolución (MEX)
November 27	Thanksgiving (US)
December 25	Christmas Day
December 26	Boxing Day (CAN)

Roadtripping takes many forms and serves many purposes. When my buddy Nathan and I graduated from college, our form was a 31 ft. long neon green funky RV from 1984, and our purpose was to go out and interview people from all walks of life to learn how they got to where they are today. What started out as a roadtrip to figure out what we wanted to do with our lives soon became a documentary on PBS, a nationally released book with Random House, and a program on college campuses across the country that puts other students on their own roadtrips.

While creating *Roadtrip Nation* in the last few years, we've logged more than 14 months on the road, traveled at least 45,000 mi., been to every contiguous state, and met more amazing, eccentric, and brilliant people than we could have ever met inside our comfort zones. And we discovered that when you boil everything down—the photo ops, the scenic drives, the endless cheeseburgers—you discover the real beauty of roadtripping comes from the people you meet along the way.

Without those people, a roadtrip becomes, well, a mere trip. People give your expedition texture. They push you to a deeper level—a level that makes your roadtrip not just a fun vacation, but a change-your-life-forever-experience.

Here's the difference. Imagine a roadtrip in Maine. Some drivers will just coast through, only stopping to eat lobster at some cheeseball restaurant with a big neon sign. Those people miss the chance to meet Manny the lobsterman on the docks. Through him, we were able to spend a day out on his boat, the Jarvis Bay. On that boat, we weren't just in Maine, we were living Maine. We helped bring in the day's catch, downed a few shipyard brews as we watched the sun slip into the Atlantic, and retired to Manny's pad to cook up a few lobster tails. The meal was the best we've ever had, but what we remember the most is Manny.

It might seem tough to find interesting characters on the road, but opportunities pop up with every twist and turn of the journey. Say you get a flat tire on the Texas/Louisiana state line. You pull into the most classic truck stop you've ever seen, and out comes a tattooed 60-year-old man with a cigarette plastered to his mouth, Vietnam vet medals pinned to the mesh on his trucker's hat, and a rough beard grown to cover the scars on his face. Do you sit in the waiting room reading a 3-year-old issue of *Entertainment Weekly* until your tire is neatly primped, or do you hang with "Doc" as he puts the tire back on, learning a bit about him and going out to coffee with him afterwards? If you choose the latter option, you will learn, over a 3hr. cup of coffee at a typical Louisiana diner, that he flew helicopters in Vietnam, sat in a POW camp for months, survived to

go on and get his Ph.D. in electrical engineering from MIT, and now runs his own truck stop because fixing trucks (and big green RVs) is his passion.

Yep, meeting people on the road is where it's at, but HOW do you meet them?

The first rule is Carpe Diem. Seize the Day. It's not just a rule, but also a roadtrip philosophy, a perspective thwack on how you live your life, and an elevation of intensity that milks the experience out of every day. To live the rest of your life at this high pace would be not only tiring, it would be impossible. But while you're on the road for that finite amount of time, you really have nothing to lose. If Manny offers you a day on his boat, you put off your plans to go to Boston. If the founder of Starbucks, who also owns the Seattle Supersonics, offers you tickets to the basketball game that night, you have a quiet, relaxing evening some other time. If the guy who decoded the human genome wants to have coffee with you the next morning, and you're an 8hr. roadtrip away, fire up the engine and drive all night. You can sleep when you get home. Carpe Diem, roadtrip-style.

Secondly, leave your prejudices at home. On the road, nothing is as it seems. The moment you start judging people is the moment you close yourself off from an authentic connection. If we would have seen Doc as some low-level mechanic not worth our time, we would have missed out on one of the best cups of coffee of our lives.

Third, make a project out of it. Wrapping your roadtrip in some creative framework gives you the excuse to get in doors you wouldn't normally be able to open, and meet people you wouldn't normally be able to meet. Our excuse was to film an independent documentary about learning how people got to where they are today. So we interviewed the Lobsterman on his boat, we captured the story of the founder of Starbucks, and we learned where the guy who decoded the human genome was when he was our age. Your project could be doing a coffee table book on the best bakeries in the Pacific Northwest, taking photos of the best breakfast burritos in every state, surfing the northernmost point break in Maine, or finding the best concert venues down the eastern seaboard. Get creative. Open your mind. Put a little twist on things to wrap a mission around your expedition.

The degree of commitment to achieving "the mission" ranges from slacker to obsessive, but by thinking differently about your journey you'll meet people you would have never imagined. And who knows where it could go? I thought I would be in medical school right now.

Mike Marriner crossed the country in a neon green RV, interviewing self-made men and women from the CEO of National Geographic to the head stylist for Madonna. He is a founder of roadtripnation.com and an author of Roadtrip Nation: A Guide to Discovering Your Path In Life. See www.roadtripnation.com/campus/ bring for information on hitting the road with RTN on one of their future roadtrips.

ESSENTIALS

BEFORE YOU GO

ENTRANCE REQUIREMENTS
Passport. Required of all visitors who are not citizens of the US or Canada. Recommended for citizens of the US and Canada visiting Mexico.

Visa. Generally required of all visitors who are not citizens of the US or Canada, but requirement can be waived for residents of certain countries (including Australia, New Zealand, Ireland, and the UK) if staying less than 90 days.

Driving Permit. Required for all those planning to drive. Foreign licenses are accepted, although an **International Driving Permit** (p. 12) may be preferable. A **Vehicle Permit** (p. 13) is required to bring an automobile more than 22km into Mexico from the US.

VITAL DOCUMENTS

PASSPORTS

REQUIREMENTS
Citizens of countries other than the US and Canada need valid passports to enter the US, Canada, and Mexico. Returning home with an expired passport is usually illegal and may result in a fine, or it may not be possible at all. Passports must be valid for at least six months (for visitors to the US or Mexico) or one day (for visitors to Canada) beyond the intended stay. Canadians can enter the US (and vice versa) with proof of citizenship and a photo ID—a driver's license and birth certificate should suffice. Proof of citizenship (such as a birth certificate, naturalization certificate, consular report of birth abroad, or a certificate of citizenship) and a photo ID will allow US and Canadian citizens entrance into Mexico. Your passport, however, is the most convenient method of identification.

NEW PASSPORTS
Citizens of the US, Canada, Australia, Ireland, New Zealand, and the UK can apply for a passport at a passport office or court of law. Many post offices also accept passport applications. Any new passport or renewal applications must be filed well in advance of the departure date, though most passport offices offer rush services for a very steep fee, typically $60-200.

PASSPORT MAINTENANCE
Photocopy the page of your passport with your photo. Carry one copy in a safe place, apart from the original, and leave a copy at home. Consulates recommend that you carry an expired passport or an official copy of your birth certificate in a part of your baggage separate from other documents.

If you lose your passport, immediately notify the local police and the nearest embassy or consulate of your home government. To expedite its replacement, you will need to know all info previously recorded and show ID and proof of citizenship, as well as pay a fee and include a police report. Replacements take approximately 10 days to process, but some consulates offer three-day rush service for an additional fee. A replacement may be valid only a limited time. Any visas stamped in your old passport will be irretrievably lost. In an emergency, some consulates provide immediate temporary traveling papers that will permit you to re-enter your home country.

VISAS
Citizens of some non-English speaking countries need a visa—a stamp, sticker, or insert in your passport specifying the purpose of your travel and the permitted duration of your stay—in addition to a valid passport to enter the US. Canadian citizens do not need to obtain a visa for admission; citizens of Australia, New Zealand, and most European countries (including the UK and Ireland) can waive US visas through the **Visa Waiver Program (VWP).** Visitors qualify if they are traveling only for business or pleasure (*not* work or study), are staying for fewer than 90 days, have proof of intent to leave (e.g., a return plane ticket), possess

an I-94W form (arrival/departure certificate issued upon arrival), are traveling on particular air or sea carriers (most major carriers qualify—contact the carrier for details), and have no visa ineligiblities.

As of October 2004, visitors in the VWP must possess a **machine-readable passport** to be admitted to the US without a visa, although most countries in the VWP have been issuing such passports for some time and many travelers will not need new passports. **Children** from these countries who normally travel on a parent's passport will also need to obtain their own machine-readable passports. Additionally, as of June 2004, all passports issued after October 26, 2004 must have **biometric** identifiers to be used as visa waivers. However, most countries in the VWP are not expected to be able to convert to biometric passports by the deadline, so **even VWP travelers to the US with recently issued passports may have to apply for a visa.** Legislation to extend the biometric deadline to 2006 is under consideration by Congress but has not been passed. See http://travel.state.gov/visa or contact your consulate for a list of countries participating in the VWP as well as the latest info on biometric deadline extensions.

For stays of longer than 90 days in the US, all foreign travelers (except Canadians) must obtain a visa. Visitors to the US under the VWP are allowed to leave and re-enter the US to visit Canada, Mexico, and some neighboring islands, but time spent in those areas counts toward the total 90-day limit. Travelers eligible to waive their visas who wish to stay for more than 90 days must receive a visa before entering the US.

In Canada, citizens of some non-English speaking countries also need a visitor's visa if they're not traveling with a valid green card. Citizens of the US, Australia, Ireland, New Zealand, the UK, as well as many other countries do not need a visa. See http://www.cic.gc.ca/english/visit/visas.html for a list of countries whose citizens are required to hold visas, or call your local Canadian consulate. Visitor's visas cost CDN$75 and can be purchased from the **Canadian Embassy** (☎202-682-1740) in Washington, D.C. US citizens can take advantage of the **Center for International Business and Travel** (**CIBT**; ☎800-929-2428; www.cibt.com), which secures visas to almost all countries for a varying service charge.

If you're planning to travel to Mexico, it's a good idea to check with the nearest Mexican consulate or embassy for exact entry requirements, unless you're a North American tourist visiting for fewer than six months. US citizens can also consult www.pueblo.gsa.gov/cic_text/travel/foreign/foreignentryreqs.html.

MEXICAN TOURIST CARDS

All visitors to Mexico, regardless of nationality, must carry a **tourist card** (**FMT,** Folleto de Migración Turística) in addition to proof of citizenship. Most tourist cards are good for up to 180 days; some, however, are only good for 30 days or less. If you need to leave and re-enter the country during your trip, make sure your tourist card will enable this; you might have to ask for a multiple-entry permit. US and Canadian citizens don't need the tourist card if they are staying in the country for less than 72hr. or intend to stay within the 22km US-Mexico border zone. You can avoid delays by obtaining a card from a Mexican consulate or tourist office before you leave or purchase one when crossing the border. You may need to present your card when exiting the country, so keep it in a safe place.

PERMITS & INSURANCE

Always keep your driver's license on your person, and keep a copy of the car's registration in the glove compartment. It is wise to carry another form of identification, such as a passport, birth certificate, or social security card. Never carry all your forms of ID together; keep them in separate places in case of theft or loss. Make two sets of copies of all important documents before you leave—keep one with you and leave one at home.

INTERNATIONAL DRIVING PERMIT

If you do not have a license issued by a US state or Canadian province or territory, you might want an **International Driving Permit (IDP).** While the US, Canada, and Mexico accept foreign licenses for up to a year, it may ease interaction with police if your license is written in English. You must carry your home license with your IDP at all times. IDPs are valid for a year, and must be issued in the country from which your license originates. To apply, contact the national or local branch of your automobile association.

CAR INSURANCE

While the minimum level varies between states, insurance is required in all states of the US; proof of insurance must be kept in the car at all times.

Insurance costs depend on type of coverage and how big of a "risk" the driver poses, and may vary based on age, sex, driving record, and credit history. Common types of coverage include **liability insurance,** the most standard and most often required type, which protects against the cost of damage to other people or property; **uninsured** or **under-insured motorist insurance,** which protects against damages to you caused by those driving illegally without insurance or without sufficient coverage; and **collision insurance,** which protects against the cost of damage caused to your vehicle in a collision in which you are at fault.

Most US insurance policies cover drivers in Canada as well; check with your provider before departure to obtain proof of coverage. Mexican insurance is available at border crossings. Purchase sufficient coverage (at least equal to your US coverage), as drivers involved in accidents may be detained until all liability is met.

For helpful info about the different types of insurance and statistics on which are required in each state, consult www.autoinsurance-indepth.com.

MEXICAN VEHICLE PERMITS

Crossing into Mexico by land can be as uneventful or as complicated as the border guards want it to be. You may be waved into the country or directed to the immigration office to procure a **tourist card** (see p. 12); carry this with you at all times. You will need to obtain a **vehicle permit** at the border or on the Banjercito website (www.banjercito.com) if you plan to travel farther than 22km past the border. Permits are $22 when you pay with a valid debit or credit card. Those without credit cards will have to provide a cash deposit or bond worth $200-400, depending on the make of the car. Your deposit will be repaid in full when you return across the border, but paying the minimal fee by credit card is strongly advised.

The permit is valid only for the person to whom it was issued unless another driver is approved by the federal registry. To get a permit, you need an original copy and a photocopy of several documents: a **state vehicle registration certificate and vehicle title,** a **tourist entry form** (FME, FMT, FM6, FM3), a **valid driver's license,** and a **passport** or **birth certificate.** If leasing a vehicle, you must provide the **contract** in your name (in duplicate). Regulations change frequently; for updated info, contact a consulate or check the Banjercito website.

Beware those outside the Banjercito office offering quickie permits, as cars without valid paperwork are subject to seizure. Make sure all papers are in order before proceeding; if there is anything amiss when you reach an immigration checkpoint 22km into the interior, you'll have to turn back.

IDENTIFICATION

When you travel, always carry at least two forms of identification on your person, including at least one photo ID; a passport and a driver's license or birth certificate is usually adequate. Never carry all of your IDs together; split them up in case of theft or loss, and keep photocopies of all of them in your luggage and at home.

The **International Student Identity Card (ISIC),** the most widely accepted form of student ID, provides discounts on some sights, accommodations, food, and transport; access to a 24hr. emergency line; and insurance benefits for US cardholders. Applicants must be full-time secondary or post-secondary school students at least 12 years old.

The **International Teacher Identity Card (ITIC)** offers teachers the same insurance coverage as the ISIC and similar, but limited, discounts. For travelers who are 25 years old or under but are not students, the **International Youth Travel Card (IYTC)** provides many of the same benefits.

Each of these identity cards costs US$22 or equivalent. ISIC and ITIC cards are valid for one academic year; IYTC cards are valid for one year from the date of issue. Many student travel agencies issue the cards; for a list of issuing agencies or more info, check with the **International Student Travel Confederation** (ISTC; www.istc.org).

The **International Student Exchange Card (ISE)** is a similar identification card available to students, faculty, and youth 12-26. The card provides discounts, medical benefits, access to a 24hr. emergency crisis line, and the ability to purchase student airfares. The card costs US$25; call ☎800-255-8000 for more info, or visit www.isecard.com.

CUSTOMS

Upon entering the US, Canada, or Mexico, you must declare certain items from abroad and pay a duty on the value of those articles if they exceed the allowance established by the local customs service. Note that goods and gifts purchased at **duty-free** shops abroad are not exempt from duty or sales tax; "duty-free" means that you need not

pay a tax in the country of purchase. Upon returning home, you must declare all articles acquired abroad and pay a duty on the value of articles in excess of your home country's allowance. To expedite your return, make a list of any valuables brought from home and register them with customs before traveling abroad, and be sure to keep receipts for all goods acquired abroad.

It is a very bad idea to take illegal drugs into or out of Mexico. If you have questions, call the Mexican Embassy in the US (☎ 202-728-1600) or contact your embassy or consulate. In northern Mexico, especially along the Pacific coast, expect to be stopped repeatedly by burly, humorless troopers looking for contraband. That innocent-looking hitchhiker you were kind enough to pick up may be a drug peddler with a stash of illegal substances. If the police find drugs in your car, the possession charges will extend to you, and your car may be confiscated. If you carry **prescription drugs** while you travel, have a copy of the prescriptions and a doctor's note accessible at borders. Note that when entering the US from Mexico, you may be hassled by immigration officers if you are a minority or resident alien of the US, or simply have a Latino surname.

EMBASSIES

Contact the nearest embassy to obtain info regarding the visas and permits necessary to travel to the US, Canada, and Mexico. Listings of foreign embassies in the US as well as US embassies abroad can be found at www.embassy-world.com. The **US State Department** (http://travel.state.gov) provides a list of US embassy and consulate websites. The **Canadian Ministry of Foreign Affairs** (www.dfait-maeci.gc.ca/dfait/missions/menu-e.asp) lists the websites of its overseas embassies and consulates. General info for US citizens traveling to Canada can be found at www.amcits.com. See the **Vital Stats** boxes of Mexican cities for info on consulates in Mexico.

MONEY

CURRENCY & EXCHANGE

The currency chart below is based on November 2004 exchange rates between US dollars (US$) and Australian dollars (AUS$), Canadian dollars (CDN$), European Union euros (EUR€), New Zealand dollars (NZ$), and British pounds (UK£). Check the latest exchange rates in a large newspaper, or try a currency converter on websites like www.xe.com or www.bloomberg.com.

US DOLLARS	
AUS$1 = US$0.78	US$1 = AUS$1.34
CDN$1 = US$0.82	US$1 = CDN$1.22
EUR€1 = US$1.28	US$1 = EUR€0.78
NZ$1 = US$0.68	US$1 = NZ$1.46
1 PESO = US$0.09	US$1 = 11.57 PESOS
UK£1 = US$1.84	US$1 = UK£0.54

As a general rule, it's cheaper to convert money in the US than abroad. While currency exchange is available in most airports and border towns, it's wise to bring enough local currency to last for the first 24-72hr. of your trip. When changing money, try to go only to banks that have at most a 5% margin between their buy and sell prices. Since you lose money with every transaction, convert large sums, but no more than you'll need.

If you use traveler's checks or bills, carry some in small denominations (the equivalent of $50 or less) for times when you are forced to exchange money at disadvantageous rates, but bring a range of denominations since charges may be levied per check cashed. Store your money in a variety of forms; ideally, at any given time you will be carrying some cash, some traveler's checks, and an ATM and/or credit card.

TRAVELER'S CHECKS

Traveler's checks are one of the safest and least troublesome means of carrying funds. Check issuers provide refunds if the checks are lost or stolen, and many provide additional services, such as toll-free refund lines abroad, emergency message services, and stolen credit card assistance. American Express and Visa are the most recognized brands. Many banks and agencies sell them for a small commission. They are readily accepted in the US and Canada; in Mexico, however, some businesses are accustomed to cash and will accept no substitute. Ask about refund hotlines and the location of refund centers when purchasing checks, and always carry some cash.

American Express: Checks available with commission at select banks, at all AmEx offices, and

ESSENTIALS

online (www.americanexpress.com; US residents only). American Express cardholders can also purchase checks by phone (☎800-721-9768). For more info, contact AmEx's service centers (☎800-221-7282).

Visa: Checks available at banks worldwide. AAA (p. 31) offers commission-free checks to its members. For the nearest office, call Visa (☎800-227-6811).

Travelex and **Thomas Cook:** Issue Visa traveler's checks. Members of AAA and affiliated automobile associations receive a 25% commission discount on check purchases. In the US and Canada call ☎800-287-7362, in the UK 0800 62 21 01.

CREDIT, DEBIT, & ATM CARDS

Where they are accepted, credit cards are a convenient way to pay your expenses. Credit cards may also offer services such as insurance or emergency help, and are sometimes required to reserve hotel rooms or rental cars. **Mastercard** and **Visa** are the most welcomed; **American Express** cards work at some ATMs and at AmEx offices.

ATMs are widespread in the US, Canada, and Mexico. Depending on the system your home bank uses, you can likely access your personal bank account from the road. ATMs get the same exchange rate as credit cards, but there is often a limit on the amount of money you can withdraw per day (usually around $500). The two major international ATM networks are **Cirrus** (☎800-424-7787; www.mastercard.com) and **Visa/PLUS** (☎800-843-7587; www.visa.com). Most ATMs charge a transaction fee that is paid to the bank that owns the ATM.

Debit cards are as convenient as credit cards but have a more immediate impact on your funds. A debit card can be used wherever its associated credit card company (usually Mastercard or Visa) is accepted, yet the money is withdrawn directly from the holder's checking account. Debit cards often also function as ATM cards and can be used to withdraw cash from associated banks and ATMs throughout the US, Canada, and Mexico. Ask your local bank about obtaining one.

GETTING MONEY

If you run out of money on the road, the easiest and cheapest solution is to have someone back home make a deposit to an account linked to your credit card or ATM card. Failing that, consider wiring money. It is possible to arrange a **bank**

money transfer, which means asking a bank back home to wire money to a bank along your route. This is the cheapest way to transfer cash, but it's also the slowest, usually taking several days or more. Money transfer services like **Western Union** are faster and more convenient than bank transfers—but also pricier. Western Union has many locations worldwide. To find one, visit www.westernunion.com, or call ☎800-325-6000. To wire money within the US using a credit card (Visa, MasterCard, Discover), call ☎800-225-5227. Money transfer services are also available at **American Express** and **Thomas Cook.**

COSTS

The cost of your roadtrip will vary considerably, depending on where you go, how you drive, and where you stay. Significant expenses will include food, lodging, car maintenance, and gasoline. Before you go, spend some time calculating a reasonable daily **budget.** Don't forget to factor in emergency reserve funds (at least $200) when planning how much money you'll need.

FOOD & LODGING

To give you a general idea, bare-bones lodging on the road (camping or sleeping in hostels) starts at about $12 per night, and a basic sit-down meal costs about $5-10. A slightly more comfortable day (sleeping in hostels/guesthouses and the occasional budget hotel, eating one meal per day at a restaurant, going out at night) would cost about $50-65, and for a luxurious day, the sky's the limit. In general, prices vary depending on the region and are usually higher along both costs and around major cities or tourist attractions than in some parts of the South, West, and Midwest. Prices in Canada are similar to those in the US, while food and accommodations in Mexico are significantly cheaper.

GASOLINE

Gas prices in the US have risen steeply over the past year. A gallon of gas now costs about $2 ($0.50 per L), but prices vary widely according to state gasoline taxes. In Canada, gas costs as much as CDN$0.90 per L (CDN$3.40 per gallon). In Mexico, gas prices vary by region, but in most of the country gas is a little more than in the US. It is more than worth your while to shop around for the best price. Gas prices fluctuate quickly, but there are a number of websites entirely devoted to helping you find good gas prices. For average gas prices by state, check out **www.fuelgaugereport.com.** There's also a gas cost calculator: enter the start and end points of your trip, and the make, model, and year of your car to get approximate fuel costs for your roadtrip. Two websites, **www.fuelmeup.com** and **www.gasbuddy.com,** let travelers enter a zip code and then provide high, low, and average gas prices for that zip code, as well as the gas stations at which those prices can be found. However, because both rely on info submitted by other consumers, coverage can be spotty, especially in rural areas.

In general, it is a good idea to fill up your car before entering urban areas. Gas tends to be more expensive in cities, and you never know when you will get stuck in a traffic jam with the fuel needle flirting with empty. Similarly, fill up before entering a large rural stretch of road where there may not be a gas station when you need it.

In some cities, and at night, gas stations require you to **pay before you pump.** At most gas stations in the US, you'll be able to pay with a credit card, either inside the station or at the pump; however,

at some rural stations and in Mexico, you may only be able to pay by cash or check, so carry enough cash to fill up, just in case.

Most gas stations offer gas in three or four **octane levels;** usually, higher octane ratings have a higher price. Octane is the measurement of the "antiknock" quality of the gasoline, or its ability to resist undesired spontaneous combustion due to increased temperature and pressure. Higher octane gas experiences fewer spontaneous explosions, making it easier on your engine. Most cars come with a recommendation for which grade to use. If the recommended grade is not posted on the sticker on the back of the fuel filler door, consult your owner's manual. In Mexico, the national oil company, Petroleos Mexicanos, or **PEMEX,** sells two types of unleaded gasoline: Magna (regular) and Premium (plus).

TIPS FOR SAVING MONEY

Some simpler ways to stay within your budget include searching out opportunities for free entertainment, splitting accommodation and food costs with trustworthy fellow travelers, and buying food

in supermarkets rather than eating out. Camping (see p. 39) is often a good way to save money, as is doing your laundry in the sink (unless this is explicitly prohibited). That said, don't go overboard. Though preserving your budget is important, don't scrimp at the expense of your health or a great travel experience.

TIPPING

In the US, it is customary to tip wait staff and cab drivers 15-20% (at your discretion). Tips are usually not included in restaurant bills, unless you are in a party of six or more. In hotels, porters expect at least a $1 per bag tip to carry your bags. Tipping is less compulsory in Canada; a good tip signifies remarkable service. In Mexico, it can be hard to know what to do. Overly eager tipping can be offensive, but many people make their livings assisting tourists in exchange for tips. In general, anyone who offers a service and then waits around afterward is expecting a tip. In restaurants, waiters are tipped based on the quality of service; good service deserves at least 15%.

TAXES

In the US, sales tax is usually 4-10%, depending on the item and the place. Usually taxes are not included in the prices of items. In many states, groceries are not taxed. In Canada, you'll quickly notice the 7% goods and services tax (GST) and an additional sales tax in some provinces. Visitors can claim a rebate of the GST they pay on accommodations during stays of less than one month and on most goods they buy and take home, so be sure to save your receipts and pick up a GST rebate form while in Canada. To qualify for a rebate, total purchases must reach CDN$200, and the rebate application must be made within 10 months of the date of the purchase. A brochure detailing restrictions is available from local tourist offices or from Revenue Canada, Visitor's Rebate Program, 275 Pope Rd., #104, Summerside, PE C1N 6C6 (☎902-432-5608 or 800-668-4748).

PACKING

When packing for your roadtrip, consider what you'll be doing along the way; pack comfortable clothes and shoes for driving, and if you plan to do a lot of hiking or camping, also consult our **Outdoors** section (see p. 39). You might want to

bring a small cooler for bottled water and road-friendly snacks. Depending on your car and the number of people you are taking with you on your trip, space considerations may vary.

Luggage: In addition to your main pieces of luggage, a **daypack** (a small backpack or courier bag) is useful for storing essentials like your water bottle and copy of Let's Go for on-foot exploration.

Clothing: Whether your route takes you east-west or north-south, count on climates varying by region and elevation. Regardless of the season, those headed to into the great outdoors should bring a waterproof **rain jacket**, sturdy shoes or **hiking boots,** and **thick socks.** Cotton socks are not recommended, as they tend to soak up and retain moisture. Keep the intense sunlight out of your eyes with a wide-brimmed **hat** or **sunglasses.** Those headed to the highlands or to mountainous national parks should pack a wool sweater or medium-weight fleece for the chilly nights. You may also want outfits for going out, and maybe a nicer pair of shoes. Mexican culture values a neat appearance, and visitors are recommended to dress accordingly, especially when dealing with officials at border crossings or military roadblocks. Shorts are rarely worn outside of coastal towns and touristy ruins, and bathing suits are only appropriate on the beach.

Converters and Adapters: In the US, Canada, and Mexico, electricity is 120 volts AC. Appliances from anywhere outside North America will need an adapter (which changes the shape of the plug; $5) and a converter (which changes the voltage; $20-30). Don't make the mistake of using only an adapter (unless appliance instructions state otherwise).

Cellular Phones: A cell phone (p. 35) can be a lifesaver on the road; it is highly recommended that travelers carry one, especially when traveling alone.

Toiletries: Most common toiletries are readily available throughout the US and Canada. Toothbrushes, towels, cold-water soap, talcum powder (to keep feet dry), deodorant, razors, tampons, and condoms may be difficult to find in more rural areas of Mexico. **Contact lenses** are likely to be expensive and difficult to find on the road, so bring extra pairs and enough solution for your entire trip. Carry a copy of your prescription in case you need emergency replacements.

First-Aid Kit: For a basic first-aid kit, pack bandages, pain relievers, antibiotic cream, a thermometer, a Swiss Army knife, tweezers, moleskin, decongestant, motion-sickness remedy, diarrhea or upset-stomach medication (Pepto Bismol or Imodium), an antihistamine, sunscreen, insect repellent, and burn ointment.

Film: Film and developing in the US are affordable (about $10 for a roll of 24 color exposures) and commonly available, so it is relatively easy to develop film while traveling. Less serious photographers may want to buy a disposable camera.

Other Useful Items: For safety purposes, you might consider bringing a **money belt** and **padlock**. Basic **outdoors equipment** (plastic water bottle, compass, waterproof matches, pocketknife, sunglasses, sunscreen, hat) may also prove useful. Quick repairs of torn garments can be done on the road with a needle and thread; also consider bringing electrical tape for patching tears. Other things you're liable to forget are an umbrella, sealable **plastic bags** (for damp clothes, soap, food, and other spillables), an **alarm clock**, safety pins, rubber bands, earplugs, garbage bags, and a small **calculator.**

Important Documents: Don't forget your driver's license and car insurance forms, passport, traveler's checks, ATM and/or credit cards, adequate forms of identification, and photocopies of the aforementioned in case these documents are lost or stolen.

For Your Car: When traveling in the summer or in the desert, bring substantial amounts of **water** (a suggested 5 L per person per day) for drinking and for the radiator. It is also a good idea to carry extra **food.** Make sure you take **good maps** and **sunglasses.** A **compass** and a **car manual** can also be useful. You should always carry a **spare tire** and **jack, jumper cables, extra oil, flares,** a **flashlight,** and **heavy blankets** (in case your car breaks down at night or in the winter). An empty **gas container** in your trunk can come in handy if you need to carry fuel to your car from a distant gas station. Alternatively, a bottle of non-volatile Pennzoil Roadside Rescue **emergency fuel** ($16) can be stored in your trunk and will get you an extra 10 mi. if you run out of gas. For more car-related essentials, see **Car Care on the Road** p. 27.

SAFETY & HEALTH

GENERAL ADVICE

In any type of crisis situation, the most important thing to do is **stay calm.** The emergency numbers in the box below are some of your best resources when things go wrong.

EMERGENCY 911. For emergencies in the US and Canada, dial ☎**911.** This number is toll-free from all phones, including coin phones and cell phones. In a very few remote communities, 911 may not work. If it does not, dial 0 for the operator. In national parks, it is usually best to call the **park warden** in case of emergency. In Mexico, the equivalent to 911 is ☎**060,** but this number is not always answered. On toll (or other major) highways, the **Green Angels** (p. 31) can be reached at ☎818-340-2113.

SPECIFIC CONCERNS

DRUGS & ALCOHOL

In the US, the drinking age is 21; in Canada it is 19, except in Alberta, Manitoba, and Québec, where it is 18. In Mexico it is 18. Most localities restrict where and when alcohol can be sold. Sales usually stop at a certain time at night and are often prohibited entirely on Sundays. Drinking restrictions are particularly strict in the US. The youthful should expect to be asked to show government-issued identification when purchasing any alcoholic beverage.

Driving under the influence is a serious crime in the US, Canada, and Mexico. **Don't do it.** All 50 states, the District of Columbia, and all Canadian provinces have laws defining it a crime to drive with a blood alcohol concentration (BAC) above a certain level, in most cases, 0.08%, which can be achieved with as few as two drinks in one hour. A DUI conviction usually results in license suspension or revocation, and in 30 states, repeat offenders may have their cars taken away. Most states have zero-tolerance laws for those under 21, with severe consequences for those found to have consumed *any* amount of alcohol. In Mexico, drunk drivers will spend time in jail. Additionally, Mexican car insurance does not cover accidents that occur because of impaired driving.

In many states, **open containers** of alcoholic beverages in the passenger compartment of a car will result in heavy fines; a failed breathalyzer test will mean fines, a suspended license, imprisonment, or all three. Drivers under 21 should be aware that they may be convicted of underage possession if any alcohol is present in their vehicle.

Narcotics such as heroin and cocaine are highly illegal in the US and Canada. Though it may be partially decriminalized in some areas of Canada, marijuana is still illegal in most provinces and throughout the US. Contrary to international opinion, **Mexico rigorously prosecutes drug cases.** A minimum jail sentence awaits anyone found guilty of possessing any illegal drug, and Mexican law does not distinguish between marijuana and other narcotics. Even if you aren't convicted, getting arrested and tried in Mexico will be a long and incredibly unpleasant process. If you carry prescription drugs while you travel, keep a copy of the prescription with you, especially at border crossings. A letter from your doctor is advisable if you carry large amounts of prescription drugs.

TERRORISM

In light of the September 11, 2001 terrorist attacks, there is an elevated threat of further terrorist activities in the US. Terrorists often target landmarks popular with tourists; however, the threat of an attack is generally not specific or great enough to warrant avoiding certain places or modes of transportation. Keep aware of developments in the news and watch for alerts from federal, state, and local law enforcement officials. Also, due to heightened security, allow for extra time at border crossings, and be sure you have the appropriate documents. For more info on security threats to the US, visit the US Department of Homeland Security's website at www.dhs.gov.

PERSONAL SAFETY

EXPLORING

To avoid unwanted attention, try to blend in as much as possible. Familiarize yourself with your surroundings before setting out, and carry yourself with confidence. When walking at night, stick to busy, well-lit streets and avoid dark alleyways. If you ever feel uncomfortable, leave the area as quickly and directly as you can.

Crime is mostly concentrated in the cities, but being safe is a good idea no matter where you are. Common sense and a little bit of thought will go a long way in helping you to avoid dangerous situations. Park your vehicle in a garage or well-traveled area and use a steering wheel locking device in larger cities.

Let's Go warns of neighborhoods that should be avoided when traveling alone or at night. There is no sure-fire way to avoid all the threatening situations you might encounter while traveling, but a good **self-defense course** will give you concrete ways to react to unwanted advances. Impact, Prepare, and Model Mugging can refer you to local self-defense courses in the US (☎800-345-5425). Visit the website at www.impactsafety.org for a list of nearby chapters. Workshops (2-3hr.) start at $50; full courses (20hr.) run $350-500.

PROTECTING VALUABLES

Never leave your belongings unattended; crime occurs in even the most demure-looking hostel or hotel. There are a few steps you can take to minimize the financial risk associated with traveling. First, **bring as little with you as possible.** If it's not replaceable, don't bring it on the road. Second, buy a few combination **padlocks** to secure your belongings in your pack or in a hostel locker. Third, be sure to lock your car whenever you park it, even for a few minutes. Keep all bags and especially valuables out of sight, in the trunk, or under your seat. Fourth, **carry as little cash as possible.** Especially in big cities, roadtrippers might want to keep traveler's checks and ATM/credit cards in a **money belt**—not a "fanny pack"—along with passport or ID cards. Fifth, keep a small cash reserve separate from your primary stash.

In large cities **con artists** often work in groups. Beware of certain classics: stories that require money, rolls of bills "found" on the street, mustard spilled (or saliva spit) onto your shoulder to distract you while they snatch your bag. **Never let your passport or bags out of your sight.** Beware of **pickpockets** in crowds. Also, be alert in public telephone booths: if you must say your calling card number, do so quietly; if you punch it in, make sure no one can look over your shoulder.

If you will be traveling with electronic devices, such as a laptop computer or a PDA, check whether your homeowner's insurance covers loss, theft, or damage when you travel. If not, you might consider purchasing a low-cost separate insurance policy. **Safeware** (☎ 800-800-1492; www.safeware.com) specializes in covering computers and charges $90 for 90-day comprehensive international travel coverage up to $4000.

PRE-ROADTRIP HEALTH

Before you leave, write (in your passport or on something else you plan to keep safe and in your car at all times) the names of any people you wish to be contacted in case of a medical emergency, and list any allergies or medical conditions. If you take prescription drugs, consider carrying up-to-date, legible prescriptions or a statement from your doctor stating the medication's trade name, manufacturer, chemical name, and dosage. While traveling, be sure to keep all medication close at hand, and carry a basic **first-aid kit** (see p. 18).

IMMUNIZATIONS

The following vaccines should be kept up to date for travelers over two years old: MMR (measles, mumps, and rubella); DTaP or Td (for diphtheria, tetanus, and pertussis); IPV (for polio); Hib (for *haemophilus* influenza B); and HepB (for Hepatitis B). For recommendations on immunizations and prophylaxis, consult the Centers for Disease Control and Prevention, and check with a doctor for guidance.

INOCULATION REQUIRE-MENTS. The US, Canada, and Mexico do not require visitors to carry vaccination certificates, nor do they require specific vaccinations for entry. Consult your doctor four to six weeks before departure. In addition to **booster shots for measles and tetanus,** consider the following vaccines and prescriptions:

Hepatitis A: Vaccine or immune globulin.

Hepatitis B: Recommended for those who might be exposed to blood or bodily fluids.

Malaria: Chloroquinine tablets is recommended for those traveling in rural areas in southern Mexico.

Rabies: Recommended for those who might have contact with animals, especially those traveling in Mexico.

Typhoid Fever: Recommended for those traveling to rural areas in Mexico.

INSURANCE

Travel insurance covers four basic areas: medical/health problems, property loss, trip cancellation/interruption, and emergency evacuation. Though regular insurance policies may well extend to travel-related accidents, you may consider purchasing separate travel insurance if the cost of potential trip interruption or emergency medical evacuation is greater than you can absorb. Prices for travel insurance generally run about $50 per week for full coverage, while trip cancellation/interruption may be purchased separately at a rate of $3-5 per day depending on length of stay.

Medical insurance (especially university policies) often covers costs incurred abroad; check with your provider. **US Medicare** does not cover foreign travel, though in rare circumstances it pays for care in Canada and Mexico. **Canadian** provincial health insurance plans increasingly do not cover foreign travel; check with the provincial Ministry of Health or Health Plan Headquarters. **Homeowners' insurance** (or your family's coverage) often covers theft during travel and loss of documents up to $500.

ISIC and **ITIC** (see p. 13) provide basic insurance benefits to US cardholders, including $100 per day of in-hospital sickness for up to 60 days and $5000 of accident-related medical reimbursement. (See www.isicus.com for details.) Cardholders have access to a 24hr. helpline for medical, legal, and financial emergencies overseas. **American Express** (☎800-528-4800) grants most cardholders collision, rental theft, and accident coverage of $100,000 on flight purchases made with the card.

INSURANCE PROVIDERS

STA offers a range of insurance plans that can supplement your basic coverage. Other private insurance providers in the US and Canada include: **Access America** (☎800-284-8300; www.accessamerica.com); **Berkely Group** (☎800-797-4514; www.berkely.com); **Globalcare Travel Insurance** (☎800-821-2488; www.globalcare-cocco.com); **Travel Assistance International** (☎800-821-2828; www.europ-assistance.com); and **Travel Guard** (☎800-826-4919; www.travelguard.com).

USEFUL ORGANIZATIONS

The US **Centers for Disease Control and Prevention** (CDC; ☎877-FYI-TRIP; www.cdc.gov/travel) maintains an international travelers' hotline and an informative website. Their comprehensive booklet *Health Information for International Travel* (The Yellow Book), an annual rundown of disease, immunization, and general health advice, is available free online or for $29 via the Public

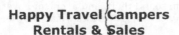

Health Foundation (☎ 877-252-1200; http://bookstore.phf.org). For detailed info on travel health, including a country-by-country overview of diseases (and a list of travel clinics in the US), try the *International Travel Health Guide*, by Stuart Rose, MD ($30; www.travmed.com). For info on medical evacuation services and travel insurance firms, check http://travel.state.gov/medical.html, and for general health info, contact the **American Red Cross** (☎ 800-564-1234; www.redcross.org).

STAYING HEALTHY

Common sense is the simplest prescription for good health on your roadtrip. Drink lots of fluids to prevent dehydration and constipation, and wear sturdy, broken-in shoes and clean socks.

ON THE ROAD

ENVIRONMENTAL HAZARDS

Heat exhaustion and dehydration: Heat exhaustion, characterized by dehydration and salt deficiency, can lead to fatigue, headaches, and wooziness. Avoid it by drinking plenty of fluids, eating salty foods (e.g., crackers), and abstaining from dehydrating beverages (e.g., alcohol, coffee, tea, and caffeinated soda). Continuous heat stress can eventually lead to heatstroke, characterized by a rising temperature, severe headache, and cessation of sweating. Victims should be cooled off with wet towels and taken to a doctor. The risk of heat exhaustion is greatest while traveling through desert areas, where the combination of heat and dryness can result in rapid water loss.

Hypothermia and frostbite: A rapid drop in body temperature is the clearest sign of overexposure to cold. Victims may also shiver, feel exhausted, have poor coordination or slurred speech, hallucinate, or suffer amnesia. *Do not let hypothermia victims fall asleep.* To avoid hypothermia, keep dry, wear layers, and stay out of the wind. When the temperature is below freezing, watch out for frostbite. If skin turns white, waxy, and cold, do not rub the area. Drink warm beverages, get dry, and slowly warm the area with dry fabric or steady body contact.

Sunburn: Always wear sunscreen (at least SPF 30) when outdoors. If you are planning on spending time near water, in the desert, or in the snow, you are at a higher risk of getting burned, even on a cloudy day. If you get sunburned, drink more fluids than usual and apply an aloe-based lotion. Severe sunburns can lead to sun poisoning, a condition that affects the entire body, causing fever, chills, nausea, and vomiting. Sun poisoning should be treated by a doctor.

Air Pollution: While traveling through urban areas, especially Mexico City and greater Los Angeles, air pollution can be a serious problem. Fortunately, many of the possible effects—wheezing, tightness in the chest, bronchitis—tend to reverse themselves once exposure stops. Long-term exposure can result in serious problems such as lung cancer and heart disease. To protect yourself, heed daily pollution warnings. Pollution is often worst during the winter and in early morning.

Altitude Sickness: Many mountainous areas are high enough for altitude sickness to be a concern. Symptoms may include headaches, dizziness, and sleep disruption. To minimize effects, avoid rapid increases in elevation, and allow your body a couple of days to adjust to a new elevation before exerting yourself and take special care when driving. Note that alcohol is more potent and UV rays stronger at high elevations.

INSECT-BORNE DISEASES

Many diseases are transmitted by insects—mainly mosquitoes, fleas, ticks, and lice. Be aware of insects in wet or forested areas, and while hiking or camping. Use an insect repellent that has a 30-35% concentration of DEET (5-10% is recommended for children). Wear long pants and long sleeves (fabric need not be thick or warm; tropic-weight cottons can keep you comfortable in the heat) and consider buying a **mosquito net** for travel in coastal or humid regions. Natural repellents can be useful supplements: taking vitamin B-12 pills regularly can eventually make you smelly to insects, as can garlic pills. Calamine lotion or topical cortisones (like Cortaid) may stop insect bites from itching, as can a bath with half a cup of baking soda or oatmeal. **Mosquitoes**—responsible for malaria, dengue fever, yellow fever, and Japanese encephalitis, among others—can be particularly dangerous in wet, swampy, or wooded areas. **Ticks**—responsible for Lyme and other diseases—can be particularly common in rural and forested regions of the Northeast, the Great Lakes, and the Pacific Northwest.

Malaria: Transmitted by *Anopheles* mosquitoes that bite at night. The incubation period varies anywhere between 10 days and 4 weeks. Early symptoms include fever, chills, aches, and fatigue, followed by high fever and sweating, sometimes with vomiting and diarrhea. See a doctor for any flu-like sickness that occurs after travel in a risk area. To reduce the risk of contracting malaria, use mosquito repellent, particularly in the evenings and when visiting forested areas. Make sure you see a doctor at least 4-6 weeks before a trip to a high-risk area to get up-to-date malaria prescriptions and recommendations. A doctor may prescribe oral prophylactics, like **mefloquine** or **doxycycline.** Be aware that mefloquine can have very serious side effects, including paranoia, psychotic behavior, and nightmares.

Dengue fever: An "urban viral infection" transmitted by *Aedes* mosquitoes, which bite during the day rather than at night. The incubation period is 3-14 days, usually 4-7 days. Early symptoms include a high fever, severe headaches, swollen lymph nodes, and muscle aches. Many patients also suffer from nausea, vomiting, and a pink rash. If you experience these symptoms, see a doctor immediately, drink plenty of liquids, and take fever-reducing medication such as acetaminophen (Tylenol). *Never take aspirin to treat dengue fever.* There is no vaccine available for dengue fever.

Lyme disease: A bacterial infection carried by ticks and marked by a circular bulls-eye rash of 2 in. or more. Later symptoms include fever, headache, fatigue, and aches and pains. Antibiotics are effective if administered early. Left untreated, Lyme can cause problems in joints, the heart, and the nervous system. If you find a tick attached to your skin, grasp the head with tweezers as close to your skin as possible and apply slow, steady traction. Removing a tick within 24hr. greatly reduces the risk of infection. Do not try to remove ticks with petroleum jelly, nail polish remover, or a hot match. Tick bites usually occur in moist, shaded environments and heavily wooded areas. If you are going to be hiking in these areas, wear long pants and sleeves and an insect repellent with DEET.

Other insect-borne diseases: Filariasis is a roundworm transmitted by mosquitoes. Infection causes enlargement of extremities and has no vaccine. **Leishmaniasis** is a parasite transmitted by sand flies. Common symptoms are fever, weakness, and swelling of the spleen. There is a treatment, but no vaccine. **CHAGAS disease (American trypanomiasis)** is a common parasite transmitted by the cone-nose and kissing bugs, which infest mud, adobe, and thatch. Its symptoms are fever, heart disease, and, later on, an enlarged intestine. There is no vaccine and limited treatment. All three diseases are rare and limited to the tropical areas of Chiapas and the Yucatán in Mexico.

FOOD- AND WATER-BORNE DISEASES

Prevention is the best cure; be sure that your food is properly cooked and the water you drink is clean. The tap water in the US and Canada is treated to be safe for drinking; however, in Mexico, contaminated water is enemy number one. Never drink water straight from the tap or from dubious sources, such as water fountains. Be suspicious of the most clever disguise of impure water—the treacherous ice cube. **Drink only purified, bottled water (agua embotellada) with an intact seal.** If you must purify your own water, bring it to a rolling boil (simmering isn't enough) and let it boil for about 30min., or treat it with **iodine drops or tablets.** Poorly cooked food is also a concern. Stay away from salads and uncooked vegetables. Other culprits include raw shellfish, unpasteurized milk and dairy products, and sauces containing raw eggs. Peel fruits and vegetables before eating them. Beware food from markets or street vendors that may have been "washed" in dirty water or fried in rancid oil. Juices, peeled fruits, and exposed coconut slices are all risky.

Traveler's diarrhea (*Turista*): Results from drinking untreated water or eating uncooked foods. Symptoms include nausea, bloating, and urgency. Try quick-energy, non-sugary foods with protein and carbohydrates to keep your strength up. Over-the-counter anti-diarrheals (e.g., Imodium) may counteract the problems. The most dangerous side effect is dehydration; drink 8 oz. of water with ½ tsp. of sugar or honey and a pinch of salt, try caffeine-free soft drinks, or eat salted crackers.

Dysentery: Results from a serious intestinal infection caused by certain bacteria. The most common type is bacillary dysentery, also called shigellosis. Symptoms include bloody diarrhea (sometimes mixed with mucus), fever, and abdominal pain and tenderness. Bacillary dysentery generally only lasts a week, but it is highly contagious. Amoebic dysentery, which develops more slowly, is a more serious disease and may cause long-term damage if left untreated. Dysentery can be treated with the drugs norfloxacin or ciprofloxacin (commonly known as Cipro).

Parasites: Microbes, tapeworms, etc. that hide in unsafe water and food. **Giardiasis,** for example, is acquired by drinking untreated water from streams or lakes. Symptoms include swollen glands or lymph nodes, fever, rashes or itchiness, and digestive problems. Boil water, wear shoes, and eat only cooked food.

Hepatitis A: The symptoms of this viral liver infection, acquired primarily through contaminated water, include fatigue, fever, loss of appetite, nausea, dark urine, jaundice, vomiting, aches, and light stools. Risks are highest in rural areas in Mexico. Ask your doctor about the vaccine (Havrix or Vaqta) or an immune globulin injection (IG; formerly called gamma globulin).

Typhoid Fever: Caused by the salmonella bacterium, typhoid is most common in villages and rural areas in Mexico. While primarily transmitted through contaminated food and water, it may also be acquired by direct contact with an infected person. Early symptoms include fever, headache, fatigue, loss of appetite, constipation, and sometimes a rash on the abdomen or chest. Antibiotics are available, but a vaccination (70-90% effective) is recommended.

OTHER INFECTIOUS DISEASES

Rabies: Transmitted through the saliva of infected animals; fatal if untreated. By the time symptoms (thirst and muscle spasms) appear, the disease is in its terminal stage. If you are bitten, wash the wound thoroughly, seek immediate medical care, and try to have the animal located. A rabies vaccine, which consists of 3 shots given over a 21-day period, is available and recommended for developing-world travel, but is only semi-effective. Rabies is found all over the world, and is often transmitted by dog bite.

Hepatitis B: A viral infection of the liver transmitted via blood or other bodily fluids. Symptoms, which may not surface until years after infection, include jaundice, loss of appetite, fever, and joint pain. It is transmitted through activities like unprotected sex, injections of illegal drugs, and unprotected health work. A 3-shot vaccination sequence is recommended for health-care workers, sexually-active travelers, and anyone planning to seek medical treatment abroad; it must begin 6 months before traveling.

Hepatitis C: Like Hepatitis B, but the mode of transmission differs. IV drug users, those with occupational exposure to blood, hemodialysis patients, and recipients of blood transfusions are at the highest risk, but the disease can also be spread through sexual contact or sharing items like razors and toothbrushes that may have traces of blood on them. No symptoms are usually exhibited, but if they can include loss of appetite, abdominal pain, fatigue, nausea, and jaundice. If untreated, Hepatitis C can lead to liver failure.

AIDS and HIV: For detailed info on Acquired Immune Deficiency Syndrome (AIDS) in North America, call the US Centers for Disease Control's 24hr. hotline at ☎800-342-2437, or contact the Joint United Nations Programme on HIV/AIDS (UNAIDS), 20, ave. Appia, CH-1211 Geneva 27, Switzerland (☎41 22 791 3666; fax 22 791 4187). The Council on International Educational Exchange's pamphlet *Travel Safe: AIDS and International Travel* is posted on their website (www.ciee.org) along with links to other online and phone resources.

Other Sexually Transmitted Infections (STIs): Gonorrhea, chlamydia, genital warts, syphilis, herpes, hepatitis B and C, and other STIs are more common than HIV and can cause serious complications. There is no cure for herpes or the virus that causes genital worts. Both Hepatitis C and syphilis can be fatal if untreated. Though **condoms** may protect you from some STIs, they are far from completely effective. Oral or even tactile contact can lead to transmission. If you think you may have contracted an STI, see a doctor immediately.

OTHER HEALTH CONCERNS

MEDICAL CARE ON THE ROAD

Medical care in the US and Canada is among the best in the world. In case of medical emergency, call ☎911 from any phone and an operator will dispatch paramedics, a fire brigade, or the police as needed. Emergency care is also readily available at any emergency room on a walk-in basis. If you do not have insurance, you will have to pay for medical care. Appointments are required for non-emergency medical services.

In Mexico, the quality of medical care varies directly with the size of the city or town. The same applies to the availability of English-speaking medical practitioners. Medical care in Mexico City is first-class, while care in more rural areas can be spotty. Along with the town clinic or Red Cross, local pharmacies can be sources of medical help. Most pharmacists are knowledgeable about mild illnesses—particularly those that plague tourists—and can recommend shots or medication.

If you are concerned about obtaining medical assistance while traveling, you may wish to employ special services. The *MedPass* from **GlobalCare, Inc.,** 6875 Shiloh Rd. E., Alpharetta, GA 30005, US (☎800-860-1111; www.globalcare.net), provides 24hr. international medical assistance, support, and medical evacuation resources. The

International Association for Medical Assistance to Travelers (IAMAT; ☎ 716-754-4883, in Canada 519-836-0102; www.cybermall.co.nz/nz/iamat) has free membership, lists English-speaking doctors worldwide, and offers info on immunization requirements and sanitation.

Those with medical conditions (such as diabetes, allergies to antibiotics, epilepsy, heart conditions) may want to obtain a **Medic Alert** membership (first year $35, annually thereafter $20), which includes a stainless steel ID tag and a 24hr. collect-call number. Contact the Medic Alert Foundation, 2323 Colorado Ave., Turlock, CA 95382, US (☎ 888-633-4298; www.medicalert.org).

WOMEN'S HEALTH

Unsanitary conditions and even just stretching the distance between pit stops can contribute to **urinary tract (including bladder and kidney) infections.** Over-the-counter medicines can sometimes alleviate symptoms, but if they persist, see a doctor. **Vaginal yeast infections** may flare up in hot and humid climates. Wearing loose-fitting trousers or a skirt and cotton underwear will help, as will over-the-counter remedies like Monistat or Gyne-Lotrimin, which should only be used if you have previously been diagnosed with a yeast infection and have exactly the same symptoms. **Tampons, sanitary pads,** and **contraceptive devices** are widely available in the US and Canada, but may be more difficult to find in Mexico—bring extras of anything you can't live without. **Abortion** is legal in both the US and Canada, but remains illegal in Mexico.

CAR SAFETY

ROAD RULES

While driving, be sure to **buckle up**—seat belts are required by law in many regions of the US and Canada. Children under 40 lb. should ride only in a specially designed car seat, available for a small fee from most car rental agencies, and children under 12 should ride in the backseat. Sleeping in your car is one of the most dangerous (and often illegal) ways to get your rest. *Let's Go* does not recommend hitchhiking under any circumstances, particularly for women and solo travelers, and it is *never* a good idea to pick up hitchhikers.

The **speed limit** in the US varies considerably from region to region. Most urban highways have a limit of 55 mph (89 kph), while rural routes range from 65 mph (104 kph) to 75 mph (120kph). Heed the speed limit; not only does it save gas, but most local police forces and state troopers make use of radar to catch speed demons. The speed limit in Canada is 50 kph (31mph) in cities and 80 kph (49 mph) on highways. On rural highways the speed limit may be 100 kph (62 mph). In Mexico, the speed limit is 100 kph (62 mph) unless otherwise posted. Like most other traffic regulations, it is often ignored. However, as road conditions in Mexico vary, it is a good idea to drive slowly.

Don't tailgate. Most rear-end collisions are a result of following too closely, so use the **two-second rule** to determine a safe following distance—choose a fixed object ahead of you on the road and start counting slowly when the vehicle in front of you passes it. If you reach the object before two seconds, you're following too closely.

Driving at night requires extra caution. Dim your brights so as not to blind any oncoming drivers, and stay alert. Be aware of **weather conditions** and drive appropriately. Try to avoid **driving in fog,** but if you have to, go slowly and keep your headlights on dim or use foglights. In the **rain,** roads get slippery, so it is a good idea to slow down and allow extra time for breaking, especially right after it has started raining and roads are slick with dust and oil. Usually you are required to keep your headlights on while it's raining, even during the day.

Finally, **winter driving** can be especially hazardous; be aware of the temperature and of road conditions. It can be hard to tell if roads are icy (bridges and overpasses can be icy even when the rest of the road is clear), and breaking can take extra time.

BEFORE YOU LEAVE

It is a good idea to have your car checked over by a mechanic a few weeks before you depart, to allow time to fix any problems. Things like worn brakes or strained shock absorbers, while not always in need of immediate replacement, may fail on you after you've put them through the rigor of a long-distance roadtrip.

Fuel-injected vehicles may benefit from a few doses of **fuel system cleaner** both before you go and on the road—though it might cost you $10-15 per

NAPTIME. Even if you don't fall asleep at the wheel, just being sleepy can endanger you by slowing your reaction time and handicapping your driving skills. People typically tire at night and in the mid-afternoon. Crash rates rise during these times, as drowsiness reduces responsiveness, contributes to tunnel vision, and impairs decision-making and concentration. The only antidote for drowsiness is sleep. Slapping yourself, turning the radio up, or sticking your head out the window may entertain you and fellow drivers, but is no substitute for rest. Walking around every couple of hours will make you more a more alert driver, but is also not a reliable solution. You'll be most alert at the wheel if you sleep on a regular schedule in a cool, dark, quiet place. Avoid caffeine and alcohol before bedtime, and try to get some kind of exercise during the day.

bottle (typically, one bottle is dumped into one tank of gas), it is cheaper than having the fuel system overhauled. At the same time, don't consider cleaner a substitute for necessary repairs uncovered during a pre-departure inspection.

In order to make minor repairs on your car, or to keep it moving after a problem, you will need to carry several tools, including a **wrench** (an adjustable wrench can handle many sizes of bolts, but may be too large for small spaces), a **flashlight** or two (a larger flashlight for illuminating things at night, and a smaller **pen light** for slim crevasses), a few good **screwdrivers** with both **Phillips** and **flathead** ends (these should range in size from small to large, and should be long enough to reach down into concealed engine spaces—if your vehicle has star, square or other special screws types, make sure that you have the correct screwdriver on hand), and a couple of different kinds of **pliers** (one for gripping larger items and a narrower needle-nosed pair for reaching into tight spaces).

Other vital items include extra **oil**, extra **coolant**, a **jack**, a **tire iron**, a **full-sized spare tire**, extra **gasoline**, extra **clean water**, a **tire pressure gauge**, **road flares**, **hose sealant**, a **first-aid kit** (see p. 18), **jumper cables**, **fan belts**, extra **windshield washer fluid**, **plastic sheeting**, **string** or **rope**, a larger **tow rope**, **duct tape**, an **ice scraper**, **rags**, a **funnel**, a **spray bottle** filled with **glass cleaner**, a **compass**, **matches**, and **blankets** and **food**. Even if you don't have a tow hitch, or are traveling alone, carry along a tow rope. Having one on hand will make it easier for others to help get you out of your jam.

CAR CARE ON THE ROAD

TIRE CARE

Check your **tire pressure** periodically throughout your trip. Most tires are stamped with the appropriate pressure to which they ought to be inflated. If not, look at the inside of your driver's side door or in your vehicle's owner's manual. The pressure is represented in **PSI** (pounds per square inch). You can use a **tire pressure gauge** to determine the PSI of your tires—this small tool is often shaped like a pen with a metal bulb at one end, and will cost $10-40, depending on the model (digital models are typically priced at the higher end). **Overinflation** and **underinflation** are both dangerous and can contribute to skidding, flats, and blowouts, as well as reducing your gas mileage.

Be aware that climate shifts can have a large impact on tire PSI—make sure to check it after periods of changing temperature. Since hot temperatures will give you inaccurate readings, check the PSI after your tires have cooled down from driving. Regular tire maintenance should also include **tire rotations** every 6000 mi. (9700km). If your tires are worn or bald, consider having them replaced entirely before taking a roadtrip. Tires that are dangerously worn can cause the car to start vibrating violently and make lots of noise.

FLUID, HOSE & FILTER CARE

Long days of driving mean that you will need to change your **oil** and your **oil filter** more frequently than you normally would. Three thousand miles (4800km) should be the absolute maximum distance you drive before you change your oil and oil filter. If conditions are extremely dusty, it may be necessary to change your oil even more frequently. You should check your oil level every few days by taking your vehicle's **dipstick** and sliding it into the engine's oil level test tube. The dipstick will often be resting in this tube, but to get an accurate measurement, wipe it off first and then plunge it in and out of the tube, checking the actual oil level against the level recommended on the dipstick or in your vehicle's owner's manual. Test the level after your vehicle has been at rest for at least several minutes. If your level is low, add more oil.

Dust will also collect in your **air filter** and clog it. Though air filter replacements are normally recommended every 20,000 mi. (32,300km), you will want to have yours inspected during each oil change. Replacement air filters may cost $15-30, but if your filter is dirty, the money will be well spent—your air filter doesn't just sieve the junk out of your air, it also protects your fuel system.

Other essentials you should have inspected before your journey and after hard driving include your **brake fluid, transmission fluid, fuel filter, PCV breather filter** (which filters gases from engine combustion and protects your oil system, and which should be replaced every 30,000 mi. or 48,300km), **automatic transmission filter, spark plugs,** and your **distributor cap** and **rotor.** It is cheaper to replace all of these than it is to fix a single catastrophe caused by ignoring one of them.

Hoses and **belts** are extremely important to monitor for wear and damage—even very small problems with vacuum hoses, for instance, will prevent your vehicle from starting. **Fan belts** are notorious for snapping on travelers in the most remote places. It is worthwhile to carry along a few extra fan belts, but it is even better to get failing belts replaced. Replace any fan belt if it looks loose, cracked, or if it is glazed or shiny. In an emergency, **panty hose** can serve as a very temporary substitute.

CHANGING A FLAT TIRE

To change a tire, you will need at least a **jack,** a sturdy **tire iron** capable of withstanding a couple hundred pounds of pressure, and a **full-sized spare tire.** Park your vehicle securely on level ground with the emergency (hand) brake applied. Turn on your **emergency flashers** to alert other vehicles that you are stalled on the side of the road. At night, it may be helpful to light a couple **road flares,** especially if your vehicle is not entirely off of the road. Place the jack on smooth ground (you may need to lay down a flat board for the jack), and locate the place underneath the vehicle where the jack will do its lifting. There are usually flat panels close to each wheel, perhaps behind it or to its sides. Locate this area, and align it with the jack. Do not pump the jack yet—you will need to loosen the tire's **lugnuts.** If you have a **hubcap,** remove it and set it aside.

Practice changing your tire before you leave—if the lugnuts are fastened too tightly, they may be difficult or impossible for you to loosen on your

own. Choose a lugnut to loosen, place the tire iron against it, and loosen it until it spins freely. After loosening the first lugnut, loosen the lugnut diagonally opposite from it. The third lugnut you loosen should be next to the first. The fourth will be diagonally opposite the third. Repeat this pattern until all of your lugnuts are loose.

Before jacking up the car, make sure your spare tire is on the ground outside the car. Raise the jack slowly and carefully, making sure that your vehicle is stable. Never place anything else underneath the vehicle, or reach under the vehicle while it is propped up by a jack. Use the jack to raise your vehicle far enough for your tire to rotate freely. Once the vehicle is raised, remove the loosened lugnuts and place them in your hubcap or another secure area. Carefully remove the tire.

Take the spare tire and align its holes with the tire studs on the wheel hub. If you can't see the tire's air valve facing you, the tire is probably on backwards. Once the spare tire is resting against the wheel hub, replace the lugnuts in the same order you removed them, and tighten them down with your fingers. Do not use the tire iron yet. Slowly lower your vehicle, remove the jack, and use the tire iron to tighten the lugnuts. Drive slowly for a few hundred feet to make sure that the tire is on correctly. Gradually increase your speed, and make your way down to the next service station to buy yourself another spare.

OVERHEATING

In Mexico, the US, and some parts of Canada, summer days can reach shocking levels of heat. Take **several gallons of clean water** with you—this can be used for drinking or for pouring into your radiator if you experience overheating or loss of coolant. Dedicate about 1½ gallons (5.6L) of water per person per day solely for drinking, and carry an additional few gallons for your radiator. The water should be clean to prevent damage to your radiator—though it is possible to use impure stream or lake water to top off your radiator, you'll need to have the radiator flushed afterwards. Also carry a gallon of **coolant** along with you. Coolant needs to be mixed with water after being poured into the radiator, so don't substitute water with more coolant—take both.

On a hot day, you can help prevent overheating by turning off your **air conditioning** system. This would seem to be exactly the time when you need A/C the most, but the it takes a toll on your vehicle's cooling mechanisms. If your car has a temperature gauge, check it frequently. If not, stop periodically and check for signs of overheating—any sort of boiling noise coming from under your hood is a strong indicator that you need to let the vehicle cool down for a while—and check your hoses for leaks. Turning the **heater** on full blast will help cool the engine. If your car overheats, pull off the road and turn the heater on full force to let the engine blow off its steam. If radiator fluid is steaming or bubbling, turn off the car for 30min. or more. If not, run the car in neutral at about 1500 rpm for a few minutes, allowing the coolant to circulate. Never pour water over the engine and never try to lift a searingly hot hood. Be warned that if you turn on the heater, the heat may actually be enough to melt the plastic fins which cover your car's vents—put them in an open and loose position in case they become trapped later on.

If you open your radiator cap, always wait 45min. or more until the coolant inside of the radiator loses its heat—otherwise, you may be spattered with boiling coolant. Even after waiting, you may still be spattered with warm coolant, so stand to the side whenever opening the cap. Remember that 'topping off' your radiator does not mean filling it completely. Instead, there is probably a tank or reservoir with a filling indicator somewhere near the radiator. Pour a small amount of water and coolant into the radiator (in a 50/50 mixture) and wait for it to work its way into the system and raise the reservoir. Some vehicles need the engine running in order to draw the coolant in.

Coolant leaks are sometimes just the product of overheating pressure, which forces coolant out of the gaps between the hoses and their connections to the radiator. If not, or if there are other holes in the hose, it helps to have **hose sealant** on hand with you. Many hose sealants also double as temporary gas tank sealants and cost between $7-15. If you apply sealant, treat it as a very short-term solution, and get the vehicle to a service station as soon as possible. Drive slowly and keep your heater on to avoid stressing the seal. Always put the radiator cap back on—coolant will erupt from your vehicle if you don't.

BATTERY FAILURES & FLUBS

If you turn the key in the ignition and nothing happens, or if the engine refuses to start, you may have a dead battery. Recharging the battery at a service station may be your only option if your battery is too drawn down—this is why it helps to have the tools on hand to remove your battery (and often the accompanying battery cover) from your vehicle. A **screwdriver** and **wrench** are usually required for this task. However, your first option should be to try and **jump start** your car. This may require waiting for a while on the side of the road with your hood raised, and is one of the reasons why you should always carry **jumper cables.**

Since many batteries are run down through simple carelessness (forgetting to turn off headlights, etc.), it's a good idea to devise a simple system to help you remember to turn off all your lights when leaving the vehicle. Also, many vehicles have lights in places that are not obvious, such as below your rearview mirror. Check these periodically to make sure that they are not on.

To safely jump start your vehicle, position the two cars close to one another while making sure that there is no contact between them. Set the emergency brakes and turn off both engines before you open the hoods. Identify the positive posts on both batteries, and attach the red cable to both posts. Do not let the red clips contact the clips on the black cable. Attach one clip on the black cable to the negative post on the working battery, and then attach the other clip to bare metal on the disabled vehicle's engine frame, as far as possible from the battery—otherwise, the battery's hydrogen gas could ignite. Start the working vehicle, and rev it for a few moments before starting the disabled vehicle. Once both vehicles are running, disconnect the cables in reverse order, starting with the black cable attached to the bare metal. Do not kill the engines or allow the cables to contact one another until they are completely disconnected. Afterwards, drive around for 30min. or more to allow the alternator to recharge the battery.

LEAVING YOUR KEYS IN THE CAR

Lockouts can be particularly troublesome in remote areas, since locksmiths are uncommon and often expensive. Prevent lockouts by keeping a **spare copy** of your vehicle's door key somewhere on your person at all times, perhaps in a money belt. If you do happen to find yourself locked out, it may be possible to get assistance from local police services. Though they may be reluctant to provide assistance if there are other options in the

area, in some towns the police are the only agency with locksmithing equipment. Be prepared to prove your ownership of the vehicle afterwards.

As a very last resort, if you simply cannot wait for the police, many vehicles have **small triangular windows** next to the main roll-down windows, especially in the rear. If you can reach the lock from this window, use a stone or other blunt object to break the glass. Take care not to cut yourself—wrap a cloth around your hand and arm before reaching for the lock. You can temporarily patch the damage with a **plastic sheet** or **tarp** folded over several times until it is quite thick, sealed to the car with **duct tape** on every edge. Keep it taut to resist the wind.

ROAD HAZARDS

SKIDDING

Avoid skids by reducing your speed whenever driving in wet or icy conditions. If you find yourself in a skid, **do not apply the brakes.** This will only make things worse, and may cause your vehicle to roll over and start skidding on its top. Instead, at the beginning of a skid, ease off of both the brake and gas. The most important thing to do is to control the steering wheel. Grip the wheel firmly with both hands. **Steer into the skid.** If you are skidding to the right, then take the wheel and firmly turn it to the right. Once you feel the vehicle straightening out, carefully tug the wheel back toward a straight position. At this point, you may need to press down on the gas pedal a bit to push the vehicle onto its new course.

Afterwards, slow down—you were probably skidding because you were traveling faster than you could safely handle. You may want to pull over and inspect your vehicle for damage. Prioritize a **brake inspection.** Your skid probably sapped a few months off of the life of your brake pads.

BLOWOUTS

You should become familiar with the feel of your car under normal driving conditions—the first sign of a tire rupture will probably involve a change in the way the vehicle feels while you are driving. A deflating tire may not be obvious at first, especially if you have the windows rolled up or are playing loud music. You might notice that the car doesn't turn as easily, or it might feel a bit more wobbly than usual. Pull over to a safe place at the first sign of trouble—make sure that you stop somewhere off the road, away from blind corners, and on level ground. You will feel a tire blowout (or tread separation) right away—the car will suddenly become much more difficult to steer, especially on turns, and you may be tugged in a particular direction.

To handle a tire blowout, absolutely **do not slam on the brakes,** even though this may be your first instinct. A blown tire (especially a blown front tire) will reduce your braking capability, and slamming on the brakes will just send you in an uncontrolled skid—at worst, the car may even roll over. The same advice applies to steering—even though your vehicle may be pulled out of its original direction, don't compensate by wrenching the wheel forcefully the other way around. Instead, grip the wheel firmly while you take your foot off of the gas, steering only enough to keep the vehicle in a straight line or away from obstructions. Let the vehicle come to a complete stop—don't worry about damaging the wheel of the blown tire, since a blowout is an emergency situation, and your safety is more important.

CRITTERS

One of the dangers of driving in rural areas is that the long distances tend to lull you. You might not check the **speedometer** as often as you should, or you might be tempted to gaze at the scenery instead of the road. This may seem safe for stretches at a time, but don't do it—some areas of the US are rife with wildlife such as **deer, moose,** or **bears.** If you aren't paying attention, you could find yourself poised to collide with any one of these creatures.

TRUCKS & GRAVEL

Roads are repaired in sections, so you may find yourself cruising along comfortably on a smooth road when the pavement suddenly ends and your excessive speed sends you slamming into deep potholes and roadside brush. One useful indicator of potential road trouble is the presence of **black tire marks**—these are created by the tag axles of large trucks as they hit dips in the road. If you see these markings, reduce your speed dramatically.

The large number of RVs and trucks on major roads means that there is a chance you could suffer a chipped or cracked windshield from flying debris—if you see a large vehicle trundling toward you on the road, pull as far away from the center as possible and slow down. Pulling toward the center of the road while the approaching vehicle is still somewhat far away may encourage the other driver to slow down, but use this tactic carefully. Hopefully, stones flung in your direction will bounce off if both of you keep it slow. You can take other measures to reduce the risk of rock damage. Consider having **protective covers** placed on your headlights. Though not required, it is good to have a **gas tank cover** placed over your gas tank.

STEEP GRADES

Some parts of the road take you up **steep grades.** Make sure your **brake system** is in good order before you set out, and that your **brake pads** aren't worn. Don't attempt to run up steep hills too quickly—it might cause you to overheat or blow your transmission. On downhill grades, go slower than you typically would, since controlling a skid on a downhill slope is one of the hardest things you should never have to do. Travel slowly in case you meet an oncoming truck—flung gravel will punish reckless speeders. Finally, if you blow a tire on a slope (much more likely when you speed), you will need to keep going until you find a flat and level place to stop, meaning that you might have to absorb damage to your wheels.

INCIDENTS & ACCIDENTS

If you see flashing lights in your rearview mirror, you're being **pulled over.** Slow down and move onto the shoulder as soon as you can. Turn off the engine, keep your hands on the wheel, and wait for an officer to come to your window. Don't fumble for your license and registration until you're asked for it. Excuses usually won't get you out of a ticket, but respect and courtesy go a long way.

If you're involved in an **accident,** even a minor fender-bender, stay calm and call the police. Never move an injured person unless he or she is in danger, but move your car out of traffic if you can. Exchange info with the other driver involved; get the driver's license number, insurance company info, address, phone number, and license plate number, as well as names and contact info for any witnesses. You may need to file an accident report and contact your insurance company.

CAR ASSISTANCE

In addition to **911** service in the US and Canada and, most **automobile clubs** offer free towing, emergency roadside assistance, travel-related discounts, and random goodies in exchange for a modest membership fee. Travelers should strongly consider membership if planning an extended roadtrip. In Mexico, the Secretary of Tourism dispatches the **Green Angels** (☎818-340-2113) to help drivers with car trouble.

American Automobile Association (AAA; ☎800-222-4357; www.aaa.com). Emergency assistance, free trip-planning services, maps, guidebooks, and 24hr. emergency road service anywhere in the US. Free towing and commission-free American Express traveler's cheques from over 1000 offices across the country. Discounts on Hertz car rental (5-20%) and various motel chains and theme parks. Basic membership $45, Associate Membership $12. To sign up, call ☎800-564-6222.

Canadian Automobile Association (CAA), 1145 Hunt Club Rd., #200, Ottawa, ON K1V 0Y3 (☎800-222-4357; www.caa.ca). Affiliated with AAA (see above), the CAA provides the same membership benefits, including 24hr. emergency roadside assistance, free maps and tourbooks, route planning, and various discounts. Basic membership CDN$78. Call ☎800-268-3790 for membership services.

 ROAD INFORMATION. In many states across the nation, dialing ☎**511** will get you helpful info, including details on area traffic, construction projects, road closures, detours, and weather conditions.

GETTING AROUND

NAVIGATING

On most road signs and maps, "I" refers to interstate highways (as in "I-90"), "U.S." (as in "U.S. 1") to US highways, and "Rte." (as in "Rte. 7") to state and local highways. For Canadian highways, "TCH" refers to the **Trans-Canada Hwy.,** while "Hwy." or "autoroute" refers to standard routes.

Most US roads are named with an intuitive **numbering system.** Even-numbered interstates run east-west and odd ones run north-south, decreasing in number toward the south and the west. Except for a few cases, primary (two digit) interstates have unique numbers nationwide. North-south routes begin on the West Coast with I-5 and end with I-95 on the East Coast. The southernmost east-west route is I-4 in Florida. The north-

ernmost east-west route is I-94, stretching from Montana to Wisconsin. Three-digit numbers signify branches of other interstates that often skirt large cities, and generally are numbered by adding a multiple of 100 to the number of its parent interstate (as in I-285, a branch of I-85). Traditionally, if an interstate has three digits that start with an even number, then it is bounded on both ends by other interstates, and if beginning with an odd digit, it meets another interstate at only one end.

A good **map** is a roadtripper's best friend; make sure you have one before starting your journey. *Rand McNally's Road Atlas,* covering all of the US and Canada, is one of the best commercial guides (available at bookstores, gas stations, and online at www.randmcnally.com; $9). Free maps of the interstate and national highway system can be found online from the US Department of Transportation at www.fhwa.dot.gov/hep10/nhs/.

YOUR WHEELS

For a life-changing, classic American roadtrip, any car will do. If you already own one, drive it. Some people think that off-road vehicles like pickup trucks and SUVs are necessary, while others prefer flashy red sportcars. In truth, none of this is true—most of America's roads are paved and accessible by almost any car.

CAR RENTAL

National car rental agencies usually allow you to pick up a car in one city and drop it off in another for a hefty charge, sometimes in excess of $1000. The drawbacks of car rentals include steep prices (a compact car rents for $25-45 per day) and high minimum ages for rentals (usually 25). Some branches rent to drivers ages 21-24 for an additional (steep) fee, but policies vary from agency to agency. **Alamo** (☎800-327-9633; www.alamo.com), **Dollar** (☎800-800-4000; www.dollar.com), **Enterprise** (☎800-736-8222; www.enterprise.com), and **Thrifty** (☎800-367-2277; www.thrifty.com) all rent to ages 21 to 24 for varying surcharges.

Rent-A-Wreck (☎800-944-7501; www.rent-a-wreck.com) specializes in supplying vehicles that are past their prime for lower-than-average prices; a bare-bones compact less than eight years old rents for around $20-25. There may be an additional charge for a **collision and damage waiver (CDW),** which usually comes to about $12-15 per day. Major credit cards (including MasterCard and American Express) will sometimes cover the CDW if you use their card to rent a car; call your credit card company for specifics.

Most US rental companies do not allow customers to take their rental cars into **Mexico;** if you plan on driving in Mexico, make sure your rental company allows it, or drive your own car.

Because it is mandatory for all drivers in the US, check that you are covered by **insurance.** Be sure to ask whether the price includes insurance against theft and collision. Some credit cards cover standard insurance. If you rent, lease, or borrow a car, and you are not from the US or Canada, you will need a **green card** or **International Insurance Certificate** to certify that you have liability insurance that applies abroad. Green cards can be obtained at car rental agencies, car dealerships, and some travel agents and border crossings. Driving a conventional rental on an **unpaved road** is almost never covered by insurance.

Instead of a traditional rental, **Adventures on Wheels,** 42 Rte. 36, Middletown, NJ 07748 (☎800-943-3579; www.wheels9.com), will sell you a motor home, camper, minivan, station wagon, or compact car, organize its registration and insur-

ance, and guarantee that they will buy it back after your travels. Cars with a buy-back guarantee start at $2500. Buy a camper for $6500, use it for six months, and sell it back for $3000-4000. The main office is in New Jersey; there are other offices in L.A., San Francisco, Las Vegas, Denver, Montreal, and Miami. Vehicles can be picked up at one office and dropped off at another.

CAR TRANSPORT SERVICES

Car transport services match drivers with car owners who need cars moved from one city to another. Would-be travelers give the company their desired destination and the company finds a car that needs to go there. Expenses include gas, tolls, and your own living expenses. Some companies insure their cars; with others, your security deposit covers any breakdowns or damage. You must be over 21, have a valid license, and agree to drive about 400 mi. per day on a fairly direct route. More info on auto transport options (including overseas and listings by state) can be found at www.movecars.com. **Auto Driveaway Co.,** 310 S. Michigan Ave., Chicago, IL 60604

(☎800-346-2277; www.autodriveaway.com), and **Across America Driveaway,** 9839 Industrial Dr., Highland, IN 46322 (☎800-677-6686; www.schultz-international.com), are two transport companies.

CAMPERS & RVS

Much to the chagrin of more purist outdoorsmen, the US and Canada are havens for the home-and-stove on wheels known as the recreational vehicle (RV). Most national parks and small towns cater to RV travelers, providing campgrounds with large parking areas and electrical outlets ("full hook-up"). The costs of RVing compare favorably with the price of staying in hotels and renting a car, and the convenience of bringing along your own bedroom, bathroom, and kitchen makes it an attractive option. **Renting** an RV is also a possibility. **Cruise America,** 11 W. Hampton Ave., Mesa, AZ 85210 (☎800-327-7799; www.cruiseamerica.com) rents and sells RVs in the US and Canada. Rates vary widely by region, season (July and August are most expensive), and type of RV, but prices for a standard RV are around $800 per week.

MOTORCYCLES

The revving engine, burly leather, and wind-in-your-face thrill of motorcycling have built up a cult following, but motorcycling is one of the most dangerous ways to experience the open road. Helmets are required in many states and always recommended; wear the best one you can find. Those considering long trips should contact the **American Motorcyclist Association,** 13515 Yarmouth Dr., Pickerington, OH 43147 (☎800-262-5646; www.amacycle.org), the linchpin of US biker culture. And of course, take a copy of Robert Pirsig's *Zen and the Art of Motorcycle Maintenance.*

KEEPING IN TOUCH

BY MAIL

SENDING MAIL

First-class letters sent and received within the US take one to three days and cost $0.37; postcards are $0.23. Priority Mail packages up to 1 lb. generally take two days and cost $3.85, up to 5 lb. $7.70. All days specified denote business

days. For more details, see www.usps.com. For Canadian mailing information, visit Canada Post at www.canadapost.ca. Mexican mail is painfully slow. Anything important should be sent *registrado* (registered mail) or taken directly to the post office, at very least. **Mexpost** promises two-day delivery out of state; it also works with Express Mail internationally to deliver mail quickly and reliably.

RECEIVING MAIL

Mail can be sent to the US, Canada, or Mexico through **Poste Restante or General Delivery** to almost any city or town with a post office. Address letters to:

Elvis PRESLEY
Poste Restante
Post Office Street Address
Memphis, TN 38101 or Kelowna, BC V1Z 2H6
COUNTRY

The mail will go to a special desk in the central post office, unless you specify a post office by street address or postal code. As a rule, it is best to use the largest post office in the area; mail may be sent there regardless of what is written on the envelope. It is usually safer and quicker to send mail express or registered. When picking up mail, bring a form of photo ID, preferably a passport.

SENDING MAIL OVERSEAS

Aerogrammes, printed sheets that fold into envelopes and travel via airmail, are available at post offices. The marking "par avion" is universally understood. The cost is $0.70; a simple postcard is also $0.70. A **standard letter** can be sent abroad in about four to seven business days for $1.50. For packages up to 4 lb., use **Global Priority Mail** for delivery to major locations in three to five business days for a flat rate ($5).

If regular airmail is too slow, **Federal Express** (☎800-247-4747) can get a letter from New York to Sydney in two business days for a whopping $30. By **US Express Mail,** a letter would arrive within four business days and would cost $15.

Surface mail is by far the cheapest and slowest way to send mail. It takes one to three months to cross the Atlantic and two to four to cross the Pacific—appropriate for sending large quantities of items you won't need to see for a while.

BY TELEPHONE

DOMESTIC CALLS

The simplest way to call within the US and Canada is to use a coin-operated **pay phone,** which charges $0.35 for local calls. You can also buy **prepaid phone cards** that carry prepaid phone time. Phone rates tend to be highest in the morning, and lowest Sunday and at night.

US and Canadian phone numbers consist of a seven-digit local number and a three-digit area code. *Let's Go* lists all 10 digits, although often only the final seven are needed for in-city dialing.

The entire Mexican telephone system has been reorganized in the last few years. Now, all local numbers are seven digits (with the exception of those in Mexico City, Guadalajara, and Monterrey, which are eight). Area codes are three digits (two digits where locals numbers are eight digits). *Let's Go* includes all 10 digits, although only the local number is needed for same-code dialing. The area code is always preceded by the national access code, 01. All area codes can be found on the telmex website at **www.telmex.com.**

Before purchasing any calling card, compare rates with other cards, and make sure that it serves your needs (a local phonecard is generally better for local calls, for instance).

CELLULAR PHONES

While pay phones can be found in almost every city and town, you can avoid much of the hassle of scrounging up change or a card by using a cell phone. Cell phone reception is clear and reliable in cities and along major highways throughout most of the US, although in remote areas reception can be spotty. Your provider may also slap on hefty additional roaming or extended area fees of up to $1.25 per min. Call your service provider to check their coverage policies in your destination.

The international standard for cell phones is **GSM,** a system that began in Europe and has spread to much of the rest of the world. Some cell phone companies in the US and Canada use GSM in certain regions (e.g., T-Mobile and AT&T), but most employ other services such as **TDMA, CDMA, I-den,** and **AMPS.** You can make and receive calls in the US and Canada with a GSM or GSM-compatible phone, but you will only get coverage in relatively populated areas, and your phone will only work if it is from North America or if it is a **tri-band** phone. American GSM networks use different frequencies from those used in Europe; a tri-band phone allows you to use both the European 900MHz and 1800MHz frequencies as well as the North American 1900MHz frequency.

If you are using a GSM phone in the US or Canada, you will need a **SIM (subscriber identity module) card,** a country-specific, thumbnail-sized chip that gives you a local phone number and plugs you into the local network. You may need to **unlock** your phone in order to insert a SIM card. Many companies will offer to unlock your phone for fees from $5-50, but call your provider; some will unlock your phone for free upon request. If your provider won't unlock your phone, your best bet is to look online for an unlocking service, but bear in mind that getting your phone unlocked may violate your service agreement. Many SIM cards are prepaid, meaning that they come with calling time included and you don't need to sign up for a monthly service plan. Incoming calls are frequently free. When you use up the prepaid time, you can buy additional cards or vouchers. For more info on GSM phones, check out www.telestial.com, www.orange.co.uk, www.roadpost.com, or www.t-mobile.com.

Renting a cell phone is possible but usually more expensive than a short-term prepaid contract. A good option, especially if you want to make occasional calls over a short period, is to buy a cell phone with a **prepaid contract,** which allows a customer to buy a certain amount of minutes each month. Phones such as those provided by **Ecallplus** (www.ecallplus.com), **AT&T** (www.att.com), or **Verizon** (www.verizon.com) provide this type of service. Before you buy a used cell phone, make sure it is compatible with the service you want.

INTERNATIONAL CALLS

To make international calls from the US or Canada, a **calling card** is probably your cheapest bet. You can often make **direct international calls** from pay phones, but if you aren't using a calling card, you may need to drop your coins as quickly as your words. Where available, prepaid phone cards (see below) and major credit cards can be used for direct international calls, but they are pricey.

In Mexico, the **LADATEL phones** that have popped up all over the country have revolutionized the way Mexico calls. To operate one, you'll need a

PLACING INTERNATIONAL CALLS. To call North America from abroad or to call abroad from the North America dial:

1. The **international dialing prefix.** To dial out of Australia, dial 0011; the Republic of Ireland, Mexico, New Zealand, or the UK, 00; Canada or the US, 011.
2. The **country code**. To call Australia, dial 61; the Republic of Ireland, 353; Mexico, 52; New Zealand, 64; the UK, 44; Canada or the US, 1.
3. The **city/area code.**
4. The **local number.**

colorful **pre-paid phone card,** available at most *papelerías* (stationery stores) or *tiendas de abarrotes* (general stores)—look for the "De venta aquí LADATEL" signs in store windows. Cards come in 30-, 50-, and 100-peso increments.

To use a calling card from Mexico, contact the operator for your service provider by dialing the appropriate toll-free Mexico access number. If your provider does not have a Mexico-specific access code, you should inquire beforehand as to the correct dialing procedures.

TIME DIFFERENCES

North America covers several time zones, ranging from 5-9hr. behind **Greenwich Mean Time (GMT).** Most areas observe Daylight Savings Time, so clocks are set forward 1hr. in the spring and backward 1hr. in the fall.

8AM	9AM	10AM	11AM	NOON
Anchorage	Seattle L.A. Las Vegas	Denver Nogales (Mex.)	Chicago St. Louis Mexico City	Toronto Boston Miami

BY EMAIL & INTERNET

If your email provider won't let you check your e-mail from the web, your best bet for reading email from the road is to use a free **web-based email account** (www.gmail.com and www.yahoo.com are two options). Most public libraries in the US and Canada offer free Internet access, and Internet cafes abound. These cafes can even be found in some of the smaller Mexican towns; expect to pay 10-15 pesos per hour for access. Check the vital stats boxes of major cities for establishments with Internet access. For lists of additional cyber-cafes in the US, Canada, and Mexico, check out www.cypercaptive.com or www.cybercafe.com.

Increasingly, travelers find that taking their **laptop computers** on the road can be a convenient option for staying connected. Laptop users can call an Internet service provider via a modem using long-distance phone cards specifically intended for such calls. They may also find Internet cafes that allow them to connect laptops to the Internet. Travelers with wireless-enabled computers may be able to take advantage of Internet "hotspots" where they can get online for free or for a small fee. Newer computers can detect hotspots automatically; otherwise, websites like www.jiwire.com, www.wi-fihotspotlist.com, and www.locfinder.net can help you find them. For info on insuring your laptop, see p. 20.

ACCOMMODATIONS

HOTELS & MOTELS

HOTELS

Commonly found in the downtowns of cities, hotels were born in the age before cars, when traveling from city to city was difficult and often expensive and lodging was a grand affair suited to the occasion. The hotels came to symbolize the height of sophistication and luxury—to stay in a hotel was emblematic of wealth and class. Though hotels still dominate the downtowns of most major American cities, today many of them are franchises, and brand names like Radisson, Hilton, Ritz-Carlton, Mariott, Hyatt, Sheraton, and the ever-present Holiday Inn appear on street corners from New York to New Orleans. These franchises strive to maintain the old style of city lodging, but some of the unique extravagance of the 19th century has been lost. Most cities still boast at least one lavish independent hotel, usually a relic from this golden age, which is usually the absolute cream of the hotel crop. None of these hotels, of course, are cheap.

Hotel rooms in the US vary widely in cost depending on the region in which the hotel is located. The cheapest hotel single in the Northeast would run about $60 per night, while it is possible to stay for $30 per night in a comparable hotel in the South, West, or Midwest. You'll typically have a private bath and shower, although some cheaper places may offer shared restrooms.

MOTELS

With car culture in the US came a new kind of lodging. As motorists began driving long distances, they began to need places to sleep along the way, and the motor hotel, now universally known as the motel, was born. In the 1910s, organized tent camps and motor cabins appeared along roads to popular destinations. Throughout WWI and the Great Depression, "cottage courts" and "motor courts" replaced tourist camps as the lodging norm on the road. These courts offered stand-alone cabins or "bungalows" for touring visitors, and often featured amenities like gas and food. With the appearance of the interstate, motor courts began to unite their rooms under one roof and package them as "motels."

Just as the grand city hotel had its golden age in the mid-19th century, the motel flourished in the 1950s; colorful names, distinct architecture, idiosyncratic themes, and garish signs lined America's highways, each competing for the attention of the rising tide of roadtrippers. Today's motels are still car-oriented; the horizontal layout of some motels allows guests direct access to cars parked right outside their doors. Interstates are lined with familiar brand names such as Motel 6, Super 8, Comfort Inn, Red Roof Inn, Howard Johnson, Travelodge, Econolodge, Best Western, and Hampton Inn. Most rooms cost between $35 and $60 per night; again, expect to pay more near cities and in the Northeast than in rural areas or the West.

HOSTELS

Hostels are generally dorm-style accommodations, often in large single-sex rooms with bunk beds, though some hostels do offer private rooms for families and couples. They sometimes have kitchens and utensils, bike or moped rentals, stor-

ESSENTIALS

age areas, and laundry facilities. There can be drawbacks: some hostels close during certain daytime "lockout" hours, have a curfew, don't accept reservations, impose a maximum stay, or, less frequently, require that you do chores. For more info about Mexican hostels, contact the Red Mexicana de Alojamiento para Jóvenes (☎5518 1726; www.hostellingmexico.com) or the Asociación Mexicana de Albergues Juveniles, A.C. (☎5564 0333; www.hostels.com.mx), both of which are hosteling organizations affiliated with Hostelling International.

> **A HOSTELER'S BILL OF RIGHTS.** There are certain standard features that we do not include in our hostel listings. Unless we state otherwise, you can expect that every hostel has no lockout, no curfew, a kitchen, free hot showers, some secure luggage storage, and no key deposit.

HOSTELLING INTERNATIONAL

Joining the youth hostel association in your own country automatically grants you membership privileges in **Hostelling International (HI),** a federation of national hosteling associations. HI hostels are scattered throughout the US and Canada and may accept reservations via the **International Booking Network** (www.hostelbooking.com). HI's umbrella organization's web page (www.iyhf.org) lists the web addresses and phone numbers of all national associations. Other hosteling websites include www.hostels.com and www.hostel-planet.com.

Most HI hostels also honor **guest memberships**— you'll get a blank card with space for six validation stamps. Each night you'll pay a nonmember supplement (one-sixth the membership fee) and earn one guest stamp; get six stamps, and you're a member. Most student travel agencies sell HI cards, as does **Hostelling International-Canada (HI-C),** 205 Catherine St. #400, Ottawa, ON K2P 1C3 (☎613-237-7884; www.hihostels.ca).

> **BOOKING HOSTELS ONLINE.** One of the easiest ways to ensure you've got a bed for the night is by reserving online. Click to the **Hostelworld** booking engine through **www.letsgo.com,** and you'll have access to bargain accommodations from Guadalajara to Anchorage with no added commission.

OTHER TYPES OF ACCOMMODATIONS

YMCAS

Young Men's Christian Association (YMCA) lodgings are usually cheaper than a hotel but more expensive than a hostel. Not all YMCA locations offer lodging; those that do are often located in urban downtowns. Many YMCAs accept women and families; most will not lodge those under 18 without parental permission.

YMCA of the USA, 101 N. Wacker Dr., Chicago, IL 60606 (☎888-333-9622 or 800-872-9622; www.ymca.net). Provides a listing of the nearly 1000 YMCAs across the US and Canada, with prices, services, and contact info. Free reservations can be made at www.travel-ys.com.

YMCA Canada, 42 Charles St. East, 9th fl., Toronto, ON M4Y 1T4 (☎416-967-9622; www.ymca.ca). Info on YMCAs in Canada.

YWCA of the USA, Empire State Bldg., #301, 350 Fifth Ave., New York, NY 10118 (☎212-273-7800; www.ywca.org). Publishes a directory ($8) on YWCAs across the USA.

BED & BREAKFASTS

For a cozy alternative to hotel rooms, bed & breakfasts (B&Bs; private homes with rooms available to travelers) range from the acceptable to the sublime. Rooms generally cost $50-70 for a single and $70-90 for a double in the US and Canada, but on holidays or in expensive locations, prices can soar. For more info, check out **Bed & Breakfast Inns Online** (☎615-868-1946; www.bbonline.com), **InnFinder** (☎608-285-6600; www.inncrawler.com), or **InnSite** (www.innsite.com).

UNIVERSITY DORMS

Many colleges and universities open their residence halls to travelers when school is not in session (May-Sept.)—some do so even during term-time. Getting a room may take a couple of phone calls and require advance planning, but rates tend to be low, and many offer free local calls and Internet access. Some universities that host travelers include the University of Texas in Austin, TX (☎512-476-5678), Ohio State University in Columbus, OH (☎614-292-9725), and McGill University in Montréal, QC (☎514-398-6367).

THE OUTDOORS

Camping is probably the most rewarding way to slash travel costs. Considering the number of public lands available for camping in both the US and Canada, it may also be the most convenient. Well-equipped campsites (usually including prepared tent sites, toilets, and water) go for $5-25 per night in the US and CDN$10-30 in Canada. **Backcountry camping,** which lacks all of the above amenities, is often free but can cost up to $20 at some national parks. Most campsites are first come, first served. The **Great Outdoor Recreation Pages** (www.gorp.com) provides excellent general info for travelers planning on spending time outdoors.

Travelers in Mexico who are accustomed to clean and well-maintained campgrounds may be in for a few surprises, as many public camping spots are neither. Privately owned **trailer parks** are relatively common on major routes—look for signs with a picture of a trailer, or the words *parque de trailer, campamento,* or *remolques.* These places often allow campers to pitch tents or sling up a hammock. For those budget-minded individuals traveling along the coast, the hammock is the way to go. Most beach towns in Mexico are dotted with **palapas** (palm-tree huts). For a small fee, open-air restaurants double as places to hang your hat and hammock when the sun sets. At beaches and some inland towns frequented by tourists, **cabañas** (cabins, usually simple thatch-roof huts) are common.

USEFUL RESOURCES

A variety of publishing companies offer hiking guidebooks to meet the educational needs of novice or expert. For info about camping, hiking, and biking, write or call the publishers listed below to receive a free catalog.

Family Campers and RVers/National Campers and Hikers Association, Inc., 4804 Transit Rd., Bldg. #2, Depew, NY 14043 (☎716-668-6242; www.fcrv.org). Membership fee ($25) includes their publication *Camping Today.*

The Mountaineers Books, 1001 SW Klickitat Way, Ste. 201, Seattle, WA 98134 (☎206-223-6303; www.mountaineersbooks.org). Over 600 titles on hiking, biking, natural history, and conservation.

Sierra Club Books, 85 2nd St., 2nd fl., San Francisco, CA 94105 (☎415-977-5500; www.sierraclub.org). Publishes general resource books on camping and women traveling in the outdoors, as well as books on hiking in Arizona, Florida, Arkansas, the Rockies, the California Desert, and Northern California.

Wilderness Press, 1200 5th St., Berkeley, CA 94710 (☎800-443-7227 or 510-558-1666; www.wildernesspress.com). Carries over 100 hiking guides and maps, mostly for the western US.

Woodall Publications Corporation, 2575 Vista Del Mar Dr., Ventura, CA 93001 (☎877-680-6155; www.woodalls.com). Annual campground directories.

NATURE PRESERVES

US NATIONAL PARKS

National Parks protect some of the most spectacular scenery in North America. Though their primary purpose is preservation, the parks also host recreational activities such as ranger talks, guided hikes, marked trails, skiing, and snowshoe expeditions. For more info, contact the **National Park Service,** 1849 C St. NW, Washington, D.C. 20240 (☎202-208-6843; www.nps.gov).

The larger and more popular parks charge a $4-20 entry fee for cars. The **National Parks Pass** ($50), available at park entrances, allows the passport-holder's party entry into all national parks for one year. National Parks Passes can also be bought through the National Park Foundation, P.O. Box 34108, Washington, D.C. 20043 (☎888-467-2757; www.nationalparks.org). For an additional $15, the Parks Service will affix a **Golden Eagle Passport** hologram to your card, which will allow you access to sites managed by the US Fish and Wildlife Service, the US Forest Service, and the Bureau of Land Management. Senior citizens qualify for the lifetime **Golden Age Passport** ($10), which entitles the holder's party to free park entry, a 50% discount on camping, and reductions on various recreational fees. Persons eligible for federal disability benefits can enjoy the same privileges with the free **Golden Access Passport.**

Most national parks have both backcountry and developed **camping.** Some welcome RVs, and a few offer grand lodges. At the more popular parks in the US, reservations are essential, available through MISTIX (☎800-365-2267; http://reservations.nps.gov) no more than five months in advance. Indoor accommodations should be reserved months in advance. Smaller campgrounds often observe first come, first served policies, and many fill up by late morning.

US NATIONAL FORESTS

Often less accessible and less crowded, **US National Forests** (www.fs.fed.us) are a purist's alternative to parks. While some have recreation facilities, most are equipped only for primitive camping—pit toilets and no water are the norm. When charged, entrance fees are $10-20, but camping is generally $3-4 or free. Necessary wilderness permits for backpackers can be obtained at the US Forest Service field office in the area. *The Guide to Your National Forests* is available at all Forest Service branches and the main office (USDA, Forest Service, P.O. Box 96090, Washington, D.C. 20090; ☎ 202-205-1760). This booklet includes a list of all national forest addresses; request maps and other info directly from the forests you plan to visit. Reservations are available for most forests with a one-time $16.50 service fee, but are usually only needed during high season at the more popular sites. Call the National Recreation Reservation Center (☎ 877-444-6777; outside US 518-885-3639; www.reserveusa.com) up to one year in advance.

CANADA'S NATIONAL PARKS

Less touristed than their southern counterparts, these parks boast plenty of natural splendor. Park entrance fees are CDN$3-7 per person, with family and multi-day passes available. Reservations are offered for a limited number of campgrounds for CDN$7. For these reservations or info on the over 40 parks and historical sites in the network, call **Parks Canada** (☎ 888-773-8888) or consult their web page (www.pc.gc.ca). Regional passes are available at relevant parks; the best is the **Great Western Pass,** which covers admission to the parks in the Western provinces for a year (CDN$35 per adult, CDN$70 for groups of seven or fewer).

MEXICO'S PROTECTED LANDS

The Mexican government has nine different categories for its protected public lands, but there are two main divisions. **National Parks** vary greatly in definition, from small urban parks to archaeological sites to volcanoes to desert and forest areas. They are generally oriented toward historical appreciation or recreational purposes. On the other end of the spectrum, **Reserves** are areas of significant biological diversity and are mainly created for the preservation of local wildlife and for the purpose of scientific study. Tourists are often discouraged from exploring these areas.

WILDERNESS SAFETY

Stay warm, stay dry, and stay hydrated. The vast majority of life-threatening wilderness situations can be avoided by following this simple advice. Prepare yourself for an emergency by always packing raingear, a hat and mittens, a first-aid kit, a reflector, a whistle, high energy food, and extra water for any hike. Dress in warm layers of wool or synthetic materials designed for the outdoors; never rely on cotton for warmth, as it is useless when wet. For info about outdoor ailments and basic medical concerns, see **Health,** p. 23.

WILDLIFE

If you are hiking in an area that might be frequented by **bears,** keep your distance. No matter how cute they appear, don't be fooled—bears are powerful and dangerous animals. If you see a bear at a distance, calmly walk (don't run) in the other direction. If the bear pursues you, back away slowly while speaking in low, firm tones. If you are attacked by a bear, get in a fetal position to protect yourself, put your arms over your neck, and play dead. Remain calm and don't make any loud noises or sudden movements. Don't leave food or other scented items (e.g., trash, toiletries, the clothes that you cooked in) near your car or tent. Putting these objects into canisters is now mandatory in some national parks. **Bear-bagging,** hanging edibles and other good-smelling objects from a tree out of reach of hungry paws, is the best way to keep your toothpaste from becoming a condiment. Bears are also attracted to any **perfume,** as are bugs, so cologne, scented soap, deodorant, and hairspray should stay at home.

Poisonous **snakes** are hazards in many wilderness areas of North America and should be avoided. The two most dangerous are coral snakes and rattlesnakes. Coral snakes reside in the Southwestern US and Mexico and can be identified by black, yellow, and red bands. Rattlesnakes live in desert and marsh areas and will shake the rattle at the end of their tail when threatened. Don't attempt to handle or kill a snake; if you see one, back away. If you are bitten, apply a pressure bandage and ice to the wound and immobilize the limb. Seek immediate medical attention for any snakebite that breaks the skin.

In the desert areas of the Southwestern US and Mexico, travelers should also be on the lookout for poisonous **lizards.** The two dangerous types of

LEAVE NO TRACE. The idea behind environmentally responsible tourism is to leave no trace of human presence behind. A camp stove is a safer and more efficient way to cook than using vegetation, but if you must make a fire, keep it small and use only dead branches or brush rather than cutting vegetation. Make sure your campsite is at least 150 ft. (50m) from water supplies or bodies of water. If there are no toilet facilities, bury human waste (but not paper) at least 4" (10cm) deep and above the high-water line, and 150 ft. or more from any water supplies and campsites. Always pack your trash in a plastic bag and carry it with you until you reach the next trash receptacle. For more info on these issues, contact one of the organizations listed below.

Earthwatch, 3 Clock Tower Pl., Ste. 100, Box 75, Maynard, MA 01754 (☎800-776-0188 or 978-461-0081; www.earthwatch.org).

Ecotourism Society, P.O. Box 668, Burlington, VT 05402 (☎802-651-9818; www.ecotourism.org).

National Audubon Society, Nature Odysseys, 700 Broadway, New York, NY 10003 (☎212-979-3000; www.audobon.org).

lizards are Gila monsters and Mexican beaded lizards. Gila monsters are large lizards (around 12-18 in.) with dark, highly textured skin marked by pinkish mottling, and thick, stumpy tails. The Mexican beaded lizard resembles the Gila monster, but with uniform spots rather than bands of color. Both are poisonous, though they are docile in nature and unlikely to bite unless antagonized.

Though often mistakenly thought to be exclusive desert dwellers, **scorpions** can also be found throughout the grassland, savannah, jungle, and forest regions of North America. The coloration of these arachnids (8 legs, not 6) varies greatly, though they are generally brown or black. Scorpions range from the typical 1 in. to the more impressive (and scary) 8 in., and are active mostly at night. Scorpions usually sting in self-defense, and stings are usually excruciatingly painful but not life-threatening, though in Mexico certain lethal scorpions have neurotoxic venom that can

cause symptoms such as blurred vision, difficulty breathing, numbness, muscle twitching, and convulsions. Seek immediate medical attention, as an antivenom can be used to counter the effects.

Mountain regions are the stomping grounds for **moose.** These big, antlered animals have been known to charge humans, so never feed, walk toward, or throw anything at a moose. If a moose charges, get behind a tree. If it attacks, get on the ground in a fetal position and stay still.

Mosquitoes will be your main source of agony during the summer. The volume of mosquitoes after spring thaw can be unbearable without some sort of protection. Though these creatures start cropping up in spring, peak season runs from June through August before tapering off at the approach of fall. Mosquitoes can bite through thin fabric, so cover up with thicker materials. Products with **DEET** are useful, but the mosquitoes can be so ravenous that nothing short of a **mosquito hood** and netting will stop every jab.

OUTDOORS EQUIPMENT

WHAT TO BUY
Good camping equipment is both sturdy and light.

Sleeping Bags: Most sleeping bags are rated by season; "summer" means 30-40°F (around 0°C) at night; "four-season" or "winter" often means below 0°F (-17°C). Bags are made of **down** (warm and light, but expensive; miserable when wet) or of **synthetic** material (heavy, durable; warm when wet). Prices range $50-250 for a summer synthetic to $200-300 for a down winter bag. **Sleeping bag pads** include foam pads ($10-30), air mattresses ($15-50), and self-inflating mats ($30-120). Bring a **stuff sack** to store your bag and keep it dry.

Tents: The best tents are free-standing (with their own frames and suspension systems), set up quickly, and only require staking in high winds. Low-profile dome tents are the best all-around. Worthy 2-person tents start at $100, 4-person at $160. Make sure your tent has a rain fly and waterproofed seams. Other useful accessories include a **battery-operated lantern,** a plastic **groundcloth,** and a nylon **tarp.**

Backpacks: Internal-frame packs mold well to your back, keep a lower center of gravity, and flex adequately to allow you to hike difficult trails, while **external-frame packs** are more comfortable for long hikes over even terrain, as they carry weight higher and distribute it more evenly. Make sure your pack has a strong, padded hip-belt to transfer weight to your legs. Sturdy backpacks cost from $125-420—your pack is an area where it doesn't pay to economize.

Boots: Be sure to wear hiking boots with good **ankle support.** They should fit snugly and comfortably over 1-2 pairs of **wool socks** and a pair of thin **liner socks.** Break in boots over several weeks before you go to spare yourself blisters.

Other Necessities: Synthetic layers, like those made of polypropylene or polyester, and a pile jacket will keep you warm even when wet. A **space blanket** ($5-15) helps retain body heat and doubles as a groundcloth. Plastic **water bottles** are vital; look for shatter- and leak-resistant models. Carry **water-purification tablets** for when you can't boil water. Although most campgrounds provide campfire sites, you may want to bring a small **metal grate** or **grill.** For places that forbid fires, you'll need a **camp stove** (the classic Coleman starts at $50) and a propane-filled **fuel bottle.** Also bring a **first-aid kit, flashlight, pocketknife, insect repellent,** and **waterproof matches** or a **lighter.**

WHERE TO BUY IT

The mail-order/online companies below offer lower prices than many retail stores. A visit to a local camping or outdoors store will give you a sense of the look and weight of certain items.

Campmor, 28 Pkwy., P.O. Box 700, Upper Saddle River, NJ 07458, US (☎888-226-7667; www.campmor.com).

Discount Camping, 880 Main North Rd., Pooraka, South Australia 5095, Australia (☎08 8262 3399; www.discountcamping.com.au).

Eastern Mountain Sports (EMS), 1 Vose Farm Rd., Peterborough, NH 03458, US (☎888-463-6367; www.ems.com).

L.L. Bean, Freeport, ME, US 04033 (☎800-441-5713; www.llbean.com).

Mountain Designs, 51 Bishop St., Kelvin Grove, Queensland 4059, Australia (☎07 3856 2344; www.mountaindesigns.com).

Recreational Equipment, Inc. (REI), Sumner, WA 98352, US (US and Canada ☎800-426-4840, elsewhere 253-891-2500; www.rei.com).

YHA Adventure Shop, 19 High St., Staines, Middlesex, TW18 4QY, UK (☎1784 458625; www.yhaadventure.com).

OTHER CONCERNS

SUSTAINABLE TRAVEL

As the number of travelers on the road continues to rise, the detrimental effect they can have on natural environments becomes an increasing concern. With this in mind, *Let's Go* promotes the philosophy of sustainable travel. Through a sensitivity to issues of ecology and sustainability, today's travelers can be a powerful force in preserving and restoring the places they visit.

Americans are notorious for the pollution generated by their dependence on cars and gas-guzzling SUVs. However, recent EPA reports indicate that air pollution is declining and air quality is improving nationwide. This is due, in part, to improvements in car and fuel technology such as **catalytic converters, cruise control, fuel injection, overdrive transmission,** and **radial tires.** While road-tripping will probably never be the most eco-friendly mode of travel, there are things you can do to maximize the benefits of this technology and reduce pollution from your roadtrip.

Choosing a more **fuel efficient car** can help preserve the environment and your budget. Consider driving a vehicle that makes use of an alternative fuel source or a **hybrid vehicle** that combines the use of an internal combustion engine with an electric motor. Both of these types of vehicles emit dramatically lower levels of pollution and greenhouse gases. For more info on fuel economy, alternate fuel sources, and finding and comparing the comparative gas mileages of different cars, consult www.fueleconomy.gov.

Leaving your car running for a long time means more pollution, so **avoid idling** if you can. Consider parking and going in instead of driving through at fast-food restaurants. Also, newer cars don't need to be warmed up in cold weather by idling. Besides reducing your chances of being stranded on some lonesome highway, **regular tune-ups** diminish pollution from your car and increase fuel efficiency. Maintaining recommended **tire pressure** also improves gas mileage, and be sure to replace your air filter as needed—consult your owner's manual. Another way to maximize fuel efficiency is to **accelerate smoothly and maintain a steady speed.** Here's where cruise control comes in handy. We understand the appeal of the classic tire-squealing, gravel-throwing start, but besides being hard on your tires, it's a waste of fuel. **Be air conditioner savvy.** Limiting air conditioner use can increase fuel efficiency. Additionally, repair air conditioner leaks immediately, as some air conditioners contain ozone-depleting chlorofluorocarbons. **Don't speed.** Not only is speeding illegal and dangerous, but it also wastes fuel. Finally, **bring your friends.** Carpooling means fewer cars on the road, reducing traffic and pollution.

SOLO ROADTRIPPERS

While roadtrips are a great opportunity to spend quality time with your friends, there is a certain romance to flipping the top back and finding your own way across the country. However, any solo traveler is a more vulnerable target of harassment and street theft. As a lone roadtripper, try not to stand out as a tourist, look confident, and be especially careful in deserted or very crowded areas. If questioned, never admit that you are traveling alone. Maintain regular contact with someone at home who knows your itinerary.

INFORMATION SERVICES

Connecting: Solo Traveler Network, 689 Park Rd., Unit 6, Gibsons, BC V0N 1V7, CAN (☎604-886-9099; www.cstn.org). Bimonthly newsletter features going solo tips, single-friendly tips, and travel companion ads. Membership CDN$35.

Travel Companion Exchange (TCE), P.O. Box 833, Amityville, NY 11701, US (☎800-392-1256 or 631-454-0880; www.whytravelalone.com). Subscription $48.

FURTHER READING

Traveling Solo, Eleanor Berman. Globe Pequot ($17).

The Single Traveler Newsletter, P.O. Box 682, Ross, CA 94957, US (☎415-389-0227). 6 issues $29.

WOMEN ROADTRIPPERS

Women taking roadtrips on their own inevitably face some additional safety concerns, but it's easy to be adventurous without taking undue risks. If you are concerned, consider staying in hostels that offer single rooms that lock from the inside or in religious organizations with rooms for women only. **Picking up hitchhikers is never safe,** especially for women traveling alone.

Dress conservatively, especially in rural areas. Expect extra attention in Mexico, where women seldom travel without men. Wearing a conspicuous **wedding band** sometimes helps to prevent unwanted overtures. The best answer to verbal harassment is no answer at all; feigning deafness, sitting motionless, and staring straight ahead will usually be effective. Don't hesitate to seek out a police officer or a passerby if you are being harassed. Memorize the emergency numbers in places you visit, and consider carrying a whistle on your keychain. A self-defense course (see p. 20) will both prepare you for a potential attack and raise your level of awareness of your surroundings. Also be sure you are aware of the health concerns that women face when traveling (see p. 26). **National Organization for Women (NOW;** ☎202-628-8669; www.now.org) can refer women travelers to rape crisis centers and counseling services.

FURTHER READING

Active Women Vacation Guide, Evelyn Kaye. Blue Panda Publications ($18).

The Bad Girl's Guide to the Open Road, Cameron Tuttle. Chronicle Books ($15).

A Journey of One's Own: Uncommon Advice for the Independent Woman Traveler, Thalia Zepatos. Eighth Mountain Press ($17).

GLBT ROADTRIPPERS

US and Canadian cities are generally accepting of all sexualities, and thriving gay, lesbian, bisexual, and transgendered (GLBT) communities can be found in most cosmopolitan areas. Most college towns are also GLBT-friendly. Still, in rural areas homophobia can be rampant, and GLBT travelers should take extra caution. As evidenced by anti-gay legislative measures narrowly defeated in various states and gay-bashing incidents in both countries, homophobia is still all too common.

Mexico's conservative and Catholic traditions makes homosexuality frowned upon at best. Intolerance is especially rampant in more rural areas of the country, where displays of affection may attract violence. More urban areas are generally more accepting of homosexuality; there are fledgling gay-rights movements in Mexico City. However, the best rule of thumb is to avoid public displays of affection at least until you know you are in a safe and accepting environment.

Out and About (www.planetout.com) offers a bi-weekly newsletter and a comprehensive site addressing gay travel concerns. The online newspaper **365gay.com** (www.365gay.com/travel/travelchannel.htm) also has a travel section.

To avoid hassles at border crossings, transgendered travelers should make sure that all of their travel documents consistently report the same gender. Many countries (including the US and Canada) will amend the passports of post-operative transsexuals to reflect their true gender, though governments are generally less willing to amend documents for pre-operative transsexuals and other transgendered individuals.

INFORMATION SERVICES

Gay's the Word, 66 Marchmont St., London WC1N 1AB, UK (☎44 20 7278 7654; www.gaystheword.co.uk). The largest gay and lesbian bookshop in the UK, with fiction and non-fiction titles.

Giovanni's Room, 1145 Pine St., Philadelphia, PA 19107, USA (☎215-923-2960; www.queerbooks.com). An international lesbian/feminist and gay bookstore with mail-order service (carries many of the publications listed below).

International Gay and Lesbian Travel Association, 4331 N. Federal Hwy. 304, Fort Lauderdale, FL 33308, USA (☎800-448-8550; www.iglta.org). An organization of over 1200 companies serving gay and lesbian travelers worldwide.

International Lesbian and Gay Association (ILGA), 81 rue Marché-au-Charbon, B-1000 Brussels, Belgium (☎32 2 502 2471; www.ilga.org). Provides political info, such as homosexuality laws of countries.

FURTHER READING

Damron Men's Travel Guide, Damron Road Atlas, Damron Accommodations Guide, Damron City Guide, and *Damron Women's Traveller.* Damron Travel Guides ($11-19). For info, call ☎800-462-6654 or visit www.damron.com.

Ferrari Guides' Gay Travel A to Z, Ferrari Guides' Men's Travel in Your Pocket, Ferrari Guides' Women's Travel in Your Pocket, and *Ferrari Guides' Inn Places.* Ferrari Publications ($16-20).

The Gay Vacation Guide: The Best Trips and How to Plan Them, Mark Chesnut. Kensington Books ($15).

Gayellow Pages USA/Canada, Frances Green. Gayellow Pages ($16). Also publishes smaller regional editions. Visit Gayellow pages at www.gayellowpages.com.

A Man's Guide to Mexico and Central America. Señor Córdova ($19).

Spartacus 2003-2004: International Gay Guide. Bruno Gmunder Verlag ($33).

MINORITY ROADTRIPPERS

While attitudes in the US and Canada differ drastically from region to region, racial and ethnic minorities sometimes face blatant and, more often, subtle discrimination or harassment. Verbal harassment is now less common than unfair pricing, false info on accommodations, or unfriendly service at restaurants. Report discriminating individuals to a supervisor and establishments to the **Better Business Bureau** (www.bbb.org); contact the police in extreme cases.

In Mexico, nearly all of the population is white, Native American, or a combination of the two. This means that many minority travelers are bound to stick out, particularly when traveling in rural or less touristed parts of the country. In general, the whiter your skin, the better treatment you'll receive; unfortunately, light-skinned travelers are also viewed as wealthier and therefore are more likely targets of crime. Travelers of African or Asian ancestry will likely attract attention.

DIETARY CONCERNS

Most major US and Canadian cities are vegetarian-friendly, especially those on the West Coast. While **vegetarians** should have no problem finding suitable cuisine as they travel, **vegans** may still meet with some confused blank stares, especially along routes through small-town America. *Let's Go* often indicates vegetarian options in restaurant listings; other places to look for vegetarian and vegan cuisine are local health food stores or large natural food chains such as ■**Trader Joe's** and **Wild Oats.** Vegan options are more difficult to find in smaller towns and inland; be prepared to make your own meals. The travel section of the The Vegetarian Resource Group's website (www.vrg.org/travel) has a comprehensive list of organizations and websites geared toward helping vegetarians and vegans on the road. For more info, consult *The Vegetarian Traveler: Where to Stay if You're Vegetarian, Vegan, Environmentally Sensitive*, by Jed and Susan Civic (Larson Publications; $16). Vegetarians will also find numerous resources on the web; try www.vegdining.com, www.happycow.net, and www.vegetariansabroad.com, for starters.

Vegetarians are rare in Mexico, and vegans are almost unheard of. Expect incredulous stares in many places—sometimes from concerned patrons at nearby tables as well as waiters. If pressed, allergies or illness make better alibis. Almost all meals are prepared using animal products, but some popular vegetarian dishes include quesadillas (melted cheese wrapped in tortillas), *chilaquiles* (strips of fried tortillas baked in tomato sauce with cheese and fresh cream), *molletes* (french bread smothered with refried beans

and cheese), *tortas de queso*, and *frijoles* (beans). Be aware that nearly all flour tortillas and many types of beans are prepared with *manteca* (lard). Vegan tourists may have to subsist on corn tortillas and rice. It's a good idea to bring high-calorie snacks (such as protein bars and peanuts).

Travelers who keep **kosher** should contact synagogues in larger cities for info on kosher restaurants; your own synagogue should have lists of Jewish institutions across the nation. You may also consult the restaurant database at www.shamash.org/kosher. The *Jewish Travel Guide* ($16) lists synagogues, kosher restaurants, and Jewish institutions in the US and Canada, and is available from ISBS, 5804 NE Hassallo St., Portland, OR 97213 (☎800-944-6190).

INFORMATION SERVICES

North American Vegetarian Society, P.O. Box 72, Dolgeville, NY 13329, US (☎518-568-7970; www.navs-

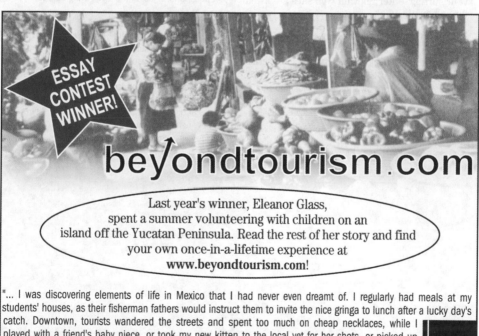
ESSENTIALS

online.org). Publishes *Transformative Adventures, a Guide to Vacations and Retreats* ($15), and the *Vegetarian Journal's Guide to Natural Food Restaurants in the US and Canada* ($12).

Vegetarian Resource Group, P.O. Box 1463, Dept. IN, Baltimore, MD 21203, US (☎410-366-8343; www.vrg.org). Website has a travel section with general info and listings of vegetarian businesses, as well as dining guides for American cities and a formidable collection of links to vegetarian resources on the web.

OTHER RESOURCES

WORLD WIDE WEB

Almost every aspect of budget travel is accessible via the web. Listed here are some sites to start off your surfing; other relevant web sites are listed throughout the book.

ROADTRIP WEBSITES

America's Byways: www.byways.org. Lists Scenic Byways and All-American Roads as well as suggested itineraries through scenic areas.

Information Roadtrip: www.informationroadtrip.com. A nifty tool for your roadtrip research, including links, attractions, planning tips, and suggestions galore.

Roadtrip America: www.roadtripamerica.com. Almost everything you'd want to know before taking a roadtrip, from info on maps and planning to pop culture landmarks to a forum for answers to your roadtrip queries.

Roadtrip Planning: www.roadtripplanning.com. Helpful tips, driving directions, and links to attractions and tourist destinations.

INFORMATION ON THE US & CANADA

CIA World Factbook: www.odci.gov/cia/publications/factbook/index.html. Vital statistics on the US and Canada's geography, government, and people.

Tourism Offices Worldwide Directory: www.towd.com. Lists tourism offices for all 50 states and Canada, as well as consulate and embassy addresses.

US Department of State Guide to Travel and Living Abroad: www.state.gov/travel. Lists travel warnings and has info about laws and considerations regarding passports, visas, and citizens living abroad.

 WWW.LETSGO.COM *Let's Go's* website features valuable advice at your fingertips. Our resources section is full of info you'll need before you hit the road, and our forums are buzzing with advice from other travelers. Visit **http://roadtrip.letsgo.com** to read road journal entries by our researchers Matt and Tabby, who drove from Mexico City to Anchorage during the spring of 2004.

THE EAST COAST

The East Coast Route is a testament to the radical diversity of the regions of the US. Beginning in Bar Harbor, ME, former playground of New England old money, the road traces the Atlantic coast to the lazy tropical splendor of Key West. Begin your journey sipping formal afternoon tea at the Jordan Pond House in **Acadia National Park** (p. 51), and end it wasted away in **Margaritaville** (p. 154).

Starting from the north, U.S. 1 hugs the Maine coast from **Mt. Desert Island** (p. 49) to the **Desert of Maine,** outside Freeport, ME (p. 56)—proof that poor crop rotation and damaging agricultural techniques can have awesome results—and past **Eartha,** the world's largest rotating globe (p. 56), in Yarmouth, ME. The road traces down through New Hampshire and into northern Massachusetts, where you can grab some fried clams in **Essex** (p. 61) before indulging witch-hunt hysteria at the numerous scary museums of **Salem** (p. 64).

Twisting through the cobblestone streets of **Boston** (p. 66), the road visits some colonial history with **Plimoth Plantation** and the surprisingly diminutive **Plymouth Rock** (p. 72). After tracing around the flexed arm of **Cape Cod** and seeing more than a few lighthouses (p. 73), the route heads back through Rhode Island, hitting both **Newport** (p. 78), home of opulent mansions, and **Providence** (p. 80), home of Brown University, the Rhode Island School of Design, and thousands of arty college students.

From there, the road passes through the small towns and gigantic **Indian Casinos** (p. 86) of the Connecticut coast. Stopping for a slice of pizza in **New Haven** (p. 88) and artfully dodging the traffic of New York, it shoots down the Garden State Expressway, straight for **Atlantic City** (p. 91), home to the streets on the Monopoly board and next door to **Lucy the Elephant** (p. 95). After the Cape May-Lewes Ferry into Delaware, the route curves along the Delaware and Maryland coast, through **Assateague Island National Seashore** and into Virginia at the **Chincoteague Wildlife Refuge** (p. 104). Once in Virginia Proper, the road visits the blacksmiths and tanners of **Colonial Williamsburg** (p. 105) and the beer and roller-coasters of **Busch Gardens** (p. 107). From there through Virginia Beach, the road takes flight at **Kitty Hawk** (p. 111) and coasts

through the idyllic Outer Banks of North Carolina. After visiting the actually-not-so-scary **Cape Fear** (p. 115), the road leads to **Myrtle Beach and the Grand Strand** (p. 118), where you can't throw a corndog without hitting a mini-golf course.

ROUTE STATS

Miles: c. 2000

Route: Bar Harbor, ME to Key West, FL.

States: 14; Maine, New Hampshire, Massachusetts, Rhode Island, Connecticut, New York, New Jersey, Delaware, Maryland, Virginia, North Carolina, South Carolina, Georgia, and Florida.

Driving Time: You could drive it in four days, but what fun would that be? Take three weeks to sample the diverse environments of the Atlantic coast.

When To Go: Anytime, though winter brings snow to New England and late summer brings the danger of hurricanes to the South.

Crossroads: The Great North in Mt. Desert Island, ME (p. 156); **The National Road** in Atlantic City, NJ (p. 300); **The Southern Border** in the Everglades, FL (p. 868).

The South brings the historic homes and plantations of **Charleston, SC** (p. 121) and **Savannah, GA** (p. 125). Traveling down the **Cumberland Island National Seashore** in Georgia (p. 130) and the Scenic Rte. A1A along the coast of Florida, most cities have a landmark sight to offer, from the **Fountain of Youth** in St. Augustine (p. 133) and the aquatic **Marineland** (p. 136), to the **International Speedway** at **Daytona Beach** (p. 136) and the **Kennedy Space Center** in **Cape Canaveral** (p. 138). With a stop to party with the celebrities in **South Beach, Miami,** the road leads to the fantastic **Coral Castle** (p. 151). After dodging mosquitoes and alligators in the Everglades, the road drifts south through the paradise of Florida's Keys, passing by the African Queen in **Key Largo** (p. 151) and the six-toed cats of "Papa" Hemingway's house in **Key West** (p. 152).

So whether you prefer drinking tropical beverages in a hammock in Florida or rubbing elbows with the rich and famous in New England, the East Coast Route will give you a chance to sample everything the Atlantic Coast has to offer—don't forget your sunscreen!

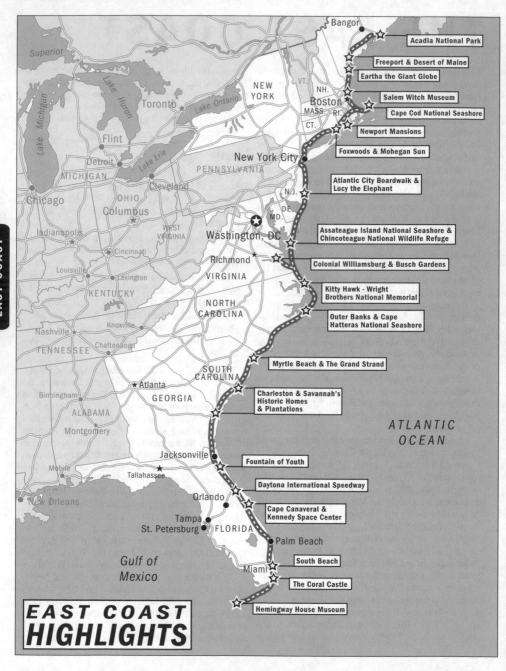

EAST COAST

Acadia National Park

Freeport & Desert of Maine

Eartha the Giant Globe

Salem Witch Museum

Cape Cod National Seashore

Newport Mansions

Foxwoods & Mohegan Sun

Atlantic City Boardwalk & Lucy the Elephant

Assateague Island National Seashore & Chincoteague National Wildlife Refuge

Colonial Williamsburg & Busch Gardens

Kitty Hawk - Wright Brothers National Memorial

Outer Banks & Cape Hatteras National Seashore

Myrtle Beach & The Grand Strand

Charleston & Savannah's Historic Homes & Plantations

Fountain of Youth

Daytona International Speedway

Cape Canaveral & Kennedy Space Center

South Beach

The Coral Castle

Hemingway House Museum

EAST COAST HIGHLIGHTS

Welcome To MAINE

MT. DESERT ISLAND

There's no better place to begin your roadtrip than Mt. Desert Island, where the marvels of the wilderness and the American small town come together. For wilderness, go to Acadia National Park, which harbors some of New England's last protected marine, mountain, and forest environments. To revel in small-town Americana, head to Bar Harbor, the largest of the island's many picturesque towns, or drive between the island's smaller towns, stopping to stroll along the coast and pick up some lobster-to-go.

▣ GETTING AROUND

Mt. Desert Island is shaped roughly like a big lobster claw, 16 mi. long and 13 mi. wide. The claw reaches from the north to the south and is dotted with small towns. The island's only links to the mainland are **Rte. 3,** which runs down the arm of the claw from the north, and the vehicle **ferry** (☎888-249-7245; www.catferry.com) to Yarmouth, Nova Scotia, which leaves from Bar Harbor. The island's main roads are **Rte. 3,** which runs along the coast of the eastern half the island, and **Rte. 102,** which traces the western coast. To the east, on Rte. 3, lies **Bar Harbor,** the island's largest town. **Seal Harbor,** also on Rte. 3, sits on the southeast corner of the island. South on Rte. 198, near the cleft of the claw, is **Northeast Harbor.** Across Somes Sound on Rte. 102 is ruggedly scenic **Southwest Harbor.** At the southern tip of the island, on the west half of the claw, sits the town of **Bass Harbor,** and up the western coast on Rte. 102 lie the hamlets of **Seal Cove, Pretty Marsh,** and **Somesville.**

BAR HARBOR

Bar Harbor is actually a township encompassing 28,800 acres (or 45 sq. mi.) of beautiful land and picturesque districts. Once a summer hamlet for the affluent, the town now welcomes a motley mélange of R&R-seekers, who still enjoy the area's homey antique houses and grand farms. Quaint country churches, small shops, and charming restaurants are also scattered across the area. Downtown Bar Harbor, the most crowded and glitzy part of the island, overflows with fascinating stores, galleries, and museums.

VITAL STATS

Population: 4800

Visitor Info: Chamber of Commerce, 93 Cottage St. (☎888-540-9990). Open June-Oct. M-F 8am-5pm; Nov.-May M-F 9am-5pm. **Info Booth,** 1 Harbor Pl. (☎207-288-5103; www.barharbormaine.com). Open mid-May to mid-Oct. daily 9am-5pm.

Internet Access: The Opera House, 27 Cottage St. (☎207-288-3509). $2.25 first 15min., $0.10 per min. thereafter. Open daily May-June 8am-11pm; July-Oct. 7am-11pm.

Post Office: 55 Cottage St. Open M-F 8am-4:30pm, Sa 9am-noon. **Postal Code:** 04609.

▣ GETTING AROUND

Bar Harbor's streets are all state highways, most of which are known by other names within the town itself. **Rte. 3** runs through Bar Harbor, becoming **Mt. Desert St.** and then **Main St.** On the waterfront, **Cottage St.** and **West St.** run parallel to Mt. Desert St. Both Mt. Desert St. and Cottage St. are home to shops, restaurants, and bars. **Parking** is available on nearly every street, and "parking lots" (simply wider sections of the street), are abundant. All parking is for 2-3hr. and is free. After 6pm, no time limit is in effect.

▣▧ SIGHTS & OUTDOORS

If you're interested in the Wabanaki, Maine's first Native Americans and expert basket weavers, the **Abbe Museum,** 26 Mt. Desert St. (Rte. 3), is the place to go. The original museum is in Acadia Park, and has been restored to its 1928 state since this downtown location opened. (☎207-288-3519; www.abbemuseum.org. Open June to mid-Oct. Su-W 10am-5pm, Th-Sa 10am-9pm; mid-Oct. to June Th-Su 10am-5pm. $4.50; ages 6-15 $2; under 6, Native Americans, and Abbe members free.)

In summer, the historic **Criterion Theatre,** 35 Cottage St., hosts mainstream movies, puppet shows every other Saturday, and the occasional concert. (☎207-288-3441. 2 movies nightly. Box office opens 30min. before show. $7.50, seniors $6.50, under 12 $5.50; balcony seats $8.50.)

In nearby Southwest Harbor is the primary of the two **Mount Desert Oceanarium** locations, at the end of Clark Pt. Rd. near Beal's. The hands-on displays feature sea stars, urchins, cucumbers, anemones, and other creatures. The secondary Oceanarium is located in Hull's Cove at 1351 Rte. 3, just north of the town, and receives rave reviews for its amusing presentations of everything you ever wanted to know about lobsters but were too hungry to ask. Guess the weight of their "big lobster" and win that many pounds of lobster meat. (☎207-244-7330. Open daily mid-May to mid-Oct. 9am-5pm. $8-10, ages 4-12 $6-7.)

On the **Shore Path** are some of the area's largest shorefront "cottages," most dating from the late 1800s or early 1900s. These homes recall the gilded age of Bar Harbor, when only the most rich and famous inhabited the island. The local piers, at the junction of Main and West St., are start points for a variety of excursions into Frenchman Bay. Boat tours of the seven lighthouses in the Mount Desert Island area are available. Foot travelers can head to **Bar Island** at low tide, when a gravel path with tide pools, accessible via Bridge St., is exposed for 2-3hr.

For the adventurous or the aquatically-inclined, **Acadia Bike & Canoe,** 48 Cottage St., rents bikes, canoes, and kayaks, and leads sea kayaking tours. (☎800-526-8615. Open May-Oct. daily 8am-6pm. Inquire for advanced tours or multi-day tours.) **Beal & Bunker** runs ferries from the Northeast Harbor town dock to Great Cranberry Island. (☎207-244-3575. Open late June to early Sept. daily 8am-4:30pm; call for winter hours. 15min.; 6 per day. $12, under 12 $6.) **Bar Harbor Whale Watch,** 1 West St., sets sail several times a day for 2-3hr. tours and offers a refund if no whales are sighted. (☎207-288-2386; www.whalesrus.com. Call ahead for prices and schedules.)

🍴 FOOD

Bar Harbor and the smaller hamlets surrounding it offer good food for the appetite acquired during a day of rambling in that healthy salt air. Whatever you do, don't leave without ordering lobster.

■ **Reel Pizza,** 33 Kennebec Pl. (☎207-288-3828), at the end of Rodick Pl. off Main St. Combination movie theater and pizzeria shows 2 films each evening for $5 and serves up creative pies ($7-19), such as the "Hawaii 5-0" with ham, pineapple, green pepper, and macadamia nuts. The first 3 rows of the "theater" are comfy couches and chairs. Open daily 5pm to end of last screening.

Ben and Bill's Chocolate Emporium, 66 Main St. (☎207-288-3281), near Cottage St. Scoops out 48 flavors of homemade ice cream, including—no kidding—lobster. Cones $3-4. Fudge $12 per lb. Open mid-Feb. to Jan. daily 9am-11:30pm.

Poor Boy's Restaurant, 300 Main St. (☎207-288-4148). Local favorite for good food and great prices. Extensive menu features lobster in no fewer than 10 different incarnations. Catch the early-bird special before 7pm, where everything on the impressive menu is $9. Entrees $10-14. Lobster meal, which might just be the best deal on the island, $16. Open daily 4:30-10pm. Reservations recommended.

Beal's, (☎207-244-3202 or 800-245-7178), in Southwest Harbor, off Main St. at the end of Clark Rd. in Southwest Harbor. Offers lobster on a patio overlooking the pier. Pick a live one from a tank ($9.75 per lb.) and it'll be buttered and red in minutes. Open daily May-Oct. 7am-8pm; Nov.-Apr. 7am-4pm. Seafood sold year-round daily 9am-5pm. Hours vary with weather.

Docksider Restaurant, 14 Sea St. (☎207-276-3965), outside of Bar Harbor in Northeast Harbor. Lobster traps on the wall and the decorative seashells create a clambake atmosphere. Open daily 11am-8:30pm.

Bunny's, 39 Kebo St. (☎207-288-4572). Offers a 2-trip breakfast buffet for $7 for early risers with big appetites. Open 6:30-10:30am.

🏠 ACCOMMODATIONS

Lodging is easy to find in Bar Harbor—it seems that every other building is an inn or a B&B. Affordable accommodations, on the other hand, are another story; grand hotels and even grander prices recall the island's exclusive resort days. More reasonable establishments assemble on Rte. 3 north of Bar Harbor. Hotel and B&B prices can more than double over the course of a week (especially July-Aug.), depending on how busy it is. Book as early as possible to get the best deal.

■ **Bar Harbor Youth Hostel,** 321 Main St. (☎207-288-5587). Perennially popular hostel accommodates up to 30 people in 2 dorm rooms and 1 family room (for 3) with a private bath. Friendly manager gives out free baked goods and discounts on kayak rentals. A book-swap and free movie nights keep travelers entertained. Lockout 10am-5pm. Curfew 11pm. Reservations only with deposit. Open May-Nov. Dorms $21, nonmembers $25; family room $55, nonmembers $65.

Llangolan Inn & Cottages, 865 Rte. 3 (☎207-288-3016; www.acadia.net/llangolan). Some of the best lodging on Rte. 3. Lovely B&B 5 mi. north of the park. The eternally smiley owner makes a delicious free breakfast of muffins, scones, and pumpkin bread. Rooms are immaculate and tastefully decorated; the B&B is cozy without a whiff of tackiness. Inn with 5 rooms (shared bath for 2 rooms) open year-round, 8 cabins open May to mid-Oct. Check-out 10am. Rooms $35-60; cottages with kitchenettes $45-70.

Edenbrook Motel, 96 Eden St. (☎207-288-4975 or 800-323-7819). If you must stay downtown, Edenbrook has rooms at decent prices with a great view. Open mid-May to mid-Oct. Rooms in summer $68-90; low-season $36-60.

Hearthside, 7 High St. (☎207-288-4533). A comfortable, if pricey, hotel nestled on a back street a short walk from downtown. A/C and private bath; some rooms have fireplaces. Rooms in summer $100-150; low-season $70-100.

NIGHTLIFE

Although the surrounding scenery is the town's best offering, roadtrippers looking for nightlife won't be disappointed in Bar Harbor. **Geddy's Pub,** 19 Main St., provides a backwoods backdrop to a nightly dancing frenzy. Weathered wooden signs, beat-up license plates, and moose head trophies look on while tables are moved aside for a DJ and dance floor in the summer. Pub-style dinner ($10-17) is served until 10pm. (☎207-288-5077. Live music daily 7-10pm. No cover. Open daily Apr.-Oct. 11am-1am; winter hours vary.) Also offering good music and good times is the **Lompoc Cafe & Brew Pub,** 36 Rodick St., off Cottage St. Locals adore this evening haunt, which features Bar Harbor Real Ale ($4), a free bocce court, and live jazz, blues, Celtic, rock, and folk on Friday and Saturday nights. (☎207-288-9392. Th open mic. No cover. Open May-Oct. daily 11:30am-1am.)

ACADIA NATIONAL PARK

Roughly half of Mt. Desert Island as well as several other small islands are part of Acadia, New England's only national park. During the summer, the island swarms with tourists lured by thick for-

ests, glacial lakes, tiny islands, and rocky beaches leading up to steep granite cliffs. Fern-shrouded streams and 120 mi. of hiking trails crisscross the rugged coastal terrain.

⊂ VITAL STATS ⊃

Area: 48,000 acres.

Visitor Info: Hulls Cove Visitors Center (☎207-288-5262), off Rte. 3. Open daily mid-June to mid-Sept. 8am-6pm; mid-Apr. to mid-June and mid-Sept. to Oct. 9am-5pm. **Park Headquarters** (☎207-288-3338), on Rte. 233. 3 mi. west of Bar Harbor, near Eagle Lake. Provides visitor info during the low season. Open M-F 8am-4:30pm.

Gateway Town: Bar Harbor (p. 49)

Fees: Weekly pass $10, motorcycles $5.

▐ GETTING AROUND. Though visitors are welcome to drive into Acadia, most of the beauty of the place is off-limits to cars, thanks to John D. Rockefeller. Fearing the island would one day be overrun by automobiles, millionaire Rockefeller funded the creation of 51 mi. of carriage roads, which are now accessible only to hikers and mountain bikes. The best way by car to see Acadia is to drive the **Acadia Byway.**

◢ SIGHTS. A good way to see Acadia is to drive the **Park Loop Rd.** (20 mi.). About 4 mi. south of Bar Harbor on Rte. 3, Park Loop Rd. runs along the shore of the island, where waves crash against vertical cliffs, before eventually making a 27 mi. circuit of the eastern section of the island. Begin your drive on Park Loop Rd. at the Hulls Cove Visitors Center by turning onto the one-way road to Sand Beach. The first stop is **Sieur de Monts Spring,** where over 300 species of flora thrive in the Wild Gardens of Acadia. The original **Abbe Museum,** built in honor of the Native American Wabanaki people, is also here. The next stop is **Sand Beach,** the only sandy beach in the otherwise rocky park. From here you can also take a short hike to see the **Beehive,** a 520 ft. mountain, sculpted by glaciers to resemble a honeycomb. Next, the road passes **Thunder Hole,** where, at three-quarters tide, the air trapped in the narrow granite hollow emits a thunderous howl. At **Wildwood Stables** (☎207-276-3622), a half-mile south of Jordan Pond, tourists can explore Rockefeller's carriage roads via horse and carriage. Farther along the road is Jordan Pond, with the Jordan Pond House at its south-

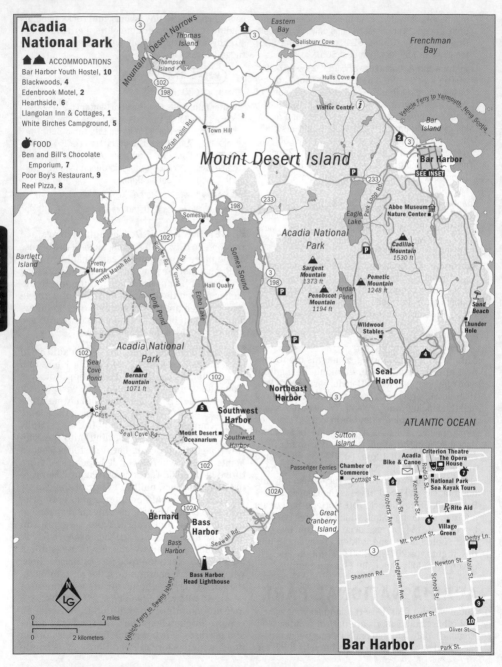

Acadia National Park

▲▲ ACCOMMODATIONS
Bar Harbor Youth Hostel, **10**
Blackwoods, **4**
Edenbrook Motel, **2**
Hearthside, **6**
Llangolan Inn & Cottages, **1**
White Birches Campground, **5**

🍎 FOOD
Ben and Bill's Chocolate Emporium, **7**
Poor Boy's Restaurant, **9**
Reel Pizza, **8**

Eastern Bay

Frenchman Bay

Mountain Desert Narrows

Thomas Island

Thompson Island

Salisbury Cove

Hulls Cove

Vehicle Ferry to Yarmouth, Nova Scotia

Bar Island

Visitor Center

Bar Harbor
SEE INSET

Town Hill

Indian Point Rd.

Mount Desert Island

233

Park Loop Rd.

Abbe Museum Nature Center

Somesville

198

233

Eagle Lake

Acadia National Park

Cadillac Mountain
1530 ft

Bartlett Island

Pretty Marsh

Pretty Marsh Rd.

Beech Hill Rd.

Hall Quarry

Sargent Mountain
1373 ft

198

Pemetic Mountain
1248 ft

Sand Beach

Somes Sound

Penobscot Mountain
1194 ft

Jordan Pond

Thunder Hole

Echo Lake

Long Pond

Wildwood Stables

Acadia National Park

Bernard Mountain
1071 ft

Seal Cove Pond

102

Seal Harbor

Northeast Harbor

3

Seal Cove

Seal Cove Rd.

5

Southwest Harbor

ATLANTIC OCEAN

Mount Desert Oceanarium

Southwest Harbor

Sutton Island

Passenger Ferries

Bernard

102A

Bass Harbor

Bass Harbor

Seawall Rd.

Great Cranberry Island

Bass Harbor Head Lighthouse

N

Vehicle Ferry to Swans Island

0   2 miles
0   2 kilometers

Bar Harbor

Chamber of Commerce
Cottage St.

Acadia Bike & Canoe

Criterion Theatre
The Opera House

7

Rodick St.

National Park Sea Kayak Tours

6

Kennebec St.

Rx Rite Aid

Roberts Ave.

High St.

8

Village Green

Derby Ln.

Mt. Desert St.

Newton St.

9

Ledgelawn Ave.

School St.

Main St.

10

Shannon Rd.

3

Pleasant St.

Oliver St.

Park St.

ern shore. Near the end of Park Loop Rd. is **Cadillac Mountain;** try the detour to the top of the mountain for the best view in the park.

▧ HIKING. Getting out of the car is the only way to see Acadia in full; the park is rife with short yet breathtakingly scenic hikes. **Precipice Trail** (1½ mi.), a popular and strenuous hike, challenges hikers with iron ladders, which are needed to finish off the meandering cliff and ledge trail. **Mt. Champlain/Bear Brook** (2¼ mi.) and the more strenuous **Beehive** (¾ mi.) provide dramatic views of the Atlantic coast. A relatively easy ½ mi. amble along the **Bowl** trail from the summit of Mt. Champlain rewards hikers with views of Sand Beach and Otter Point. A moderate trail circles **Jordan Pond** (3¼ mi.) and offers perspectives of lakes, mountains and forests. Good family hikes can be found on the Bubble Rock (1¼ mi.) or on the North Bubble (1¼ mi.). On the quieter western half of the island there are a variety of breathtaking and less used trails. **Beech Mountain** (½ mi.), is a pleasant trail for amateur hikers. More challenging and not for those afraid of heights (there are many ladders and hundreds of stone steps), is the **Beech Mountain Trail** (1½ mi.) from Echo Lake to the summit.

▨ CAMPING. While solid-roof accommodations cluster in Bar Harbor, quality camping is all over the park, especially on Rte. 102 and Rte. 198. **White Birches Campground,** in Southwest Harbor, on Seal Cove Rd. 1 mi. west of Rte. 102, has 60 wooded sites. (☎207-244-3797 or 800-716-0727. Reservations recommended, especially July-Aug. Open mid-May to mid-Oct. daily 8am-8pm. Sites

$21, with hookup $25.) **Blackwoods,** 5 mi. south of Bar Harbor on Rte. 3., has 300 wooded sites that get crowded in summer. (☎800-365-2267. Open mid-Mar. to Oct. Sites $20; call for low-season rates. No hookups.) A 10min. walk from the ocean, **Seawall,** off Rte. 102A on the western side of the island, 4 mi. south of Southwest Harbor, is more removed than most island campsites, with widely spaced sites and surrounding deep woods. (☎800-365-2267. Open late May to Sept. Sites $14; drive-in and RV sites $20. No hookups.)

▨ BASS HARBOR LIGHTHOUSE
1 mi. before the city of Bass Harbor on Rte. 102A.

On the southern tip of Mt. Desert Island sits Bass Harbor lighthouse, Maine's most-photographed lighthouse. Unfortunately, the coast around the lighthouse is fenced off, making it difficult to get a good picture unless you're on the water.

▨ LEAVING MT. DESERT ISLAND
Follow **Rte. 3** over the bridge to the Main(e)land to begin your cross-country journey, continuing north along Rte. 3 into Trenton.

TRENTON. Trenton has live **lobster pounds** worth stopping by if you'd like to lunch on one of the tasty beasties. (In Maine-speak, a "lobster pound" is a store that sells lobsters.) Your lobster can even be packed for car travel if you need a clawed companion riding shotgun. While in Trenton, check out the **The Great Maine Lumberjack Show** on Bar Harbor Rd. (Rte. 3). In the 1870s, Maine was one of America's largest logging centers. Boastful lumberjacks used to challenge each

YE OLDE ROADTRIP

THE LOCAL STORY

Try roadtripping turn-of-the-century style with Acadia National Park's carriage roads. Already dismayed at automobile's intrusion into the wilderness, John D. Rockefeller built the roads between 1913 and 1940 to provide a motor-free way to explore the island. The carriage roads are broken stone roads that are oriented by signposts and large blocks of granite refered to by locals as "Rockefeller's teeth," which serve as guard rails.

Cars are not permitted on the carriage roads, but bicycles are allowed free of charge. The roads can be accessed from the intersections with the Park Loop Rd. at Bubble Pond, Upper Hadlock Rd., and others. To experience the full early 20th-century roadtrip experience, visitors can rent carriages at **Wildwood Stables.** (Reservations ☎207-276-3622. Preplanned tours $18-22, ages 6-12 $8-9, ages 2-5 $4.50-6. Private carriage charters can also be arranged for up to 4 people.)

other to the "Olympics of the Forest," an event the Great Maine Lumberjack Show reenacts nightly. As seen on ESPN, the 14 events include axe throwing, log rolling, and cross-cut sawing. The show also offers hands-on activities for kids to try. Don't miss the **LumberJills,** a group of women who keep up with (or outlast) their male counterparts. (☎ 207-667-0067; "log" onto www.mainelumberjack.com. Shows mid-June to Aug. nightly at 7pm. Box office opens 6pm.)

▼ APPROACHING ELLSWORTH
Roll into Ellsworth by following **Rte. 3** downhill into town as it becomes **High St.**

ELLSWORTH
Not wanting to be just another "gateway" city, Ellsworth, 17 mi. from Bar Harbor, has come up with the slogan "Crossroads of Downeast Maine." Fuel and stock up here—this town, the largest between Bar Harbor and Bangor, is more of a pit stop than an attraction. The **Stanwood Wildlife Sanctuary,** 289 High St., was built in 1958 as a memorial for Cordelia J. Stanwood, who spent her life establishing herself as a leading ornithologist and wildlife photographer. The homestead on the property was placed on the National Registry of Historic Places in 1973, ensuring no urban expansion would ever invade in the area. The 165 acres of woodland are home to owls and other wildfowl. (☎ 207-667-8460. Open daily May-Oct. 10am-4pm. Trails and grounds open year-round.)

On your right as you drive downhill into town, China Hill, 301 High St., is a popular Chinese restaurant near the eastern entrance to Ellsworth, serving Szechuan, Hunan, Mandarin, Cantonese, and a few American choices. (☎ 207-667-5308. Entrees $8-12. All-you-can-eat buffet Tu and F-Sa nights and all day Su $9-10. Open in summer daily 11am-10pm; low-season Su-Th 11am-9pm, F-Sa 11am-10pm.) Those needing a good night's sleep should consider the Ellsworth Motel, 24 High St., an affordable place to stay on the main road. With 1950s TVs, chartreuse bedrooms and lemon-yellow bathrooms, and a pool, this place is retro but comfortable. (☎ 207-667-4424. Rooms $39-50.)

▼ LEAVING ELLSWORTH
Leaving Ellsworth, take **U.S. 1** heading southwest to Belfast.

BELFAST
On the coast of the Penobscot Bay, Belfast is an ideal base for daytrips to the rest of Waldo County, Acadia, and southern New Brunswick. Its 19th-century history as a major shipping and shipbuilding center is apparent in the beautiful period architecture throughout its downtown. Quaint without being too cutesy, the unique shops and restaurants provide a casual alternative to some of the more touristy towns along the Maine coast.

(**VITAL STATS**)

Population: 6400

Visitor Info: Belfast Information Center, 15 Main St. (☎ 207-338-5900). Open daily 7:30am-8pm.

Internet Access: Belfast Public Library, 106 High St. (☎ 207-288-3884; www.belfast.lib.me.us). Open M 9:30am-8pm, Tu and Th-F 9:30am-6pm, W noon-8pm, Sa 10am-2pm.

Post Office: 1 Franklin St. (☎ 207-338-1820). Open M-F 8am-5pm, Sa 8am-noon. **Postal Code:** 04915.

▛ GETTING AROUND. Belfast sits at the mouth of the **Passagasswakeag River** on the Penobscot Bay. **Main St.** and **High St.** are the main commercial and shopping streets in downtown Belfast; their intersection forms the center of town. Unlimited **parking** is available next to the Visitors Center, in a lot off Washington St.

▣ SIGHTS. A visitor could spend an entire afternoon at the **Penobscot Marine Museum,** at U.S. 1 and Church St. in Searsport. With 11 separate buildings displaying artifacts of 19th-century seafaring life in period buildings, the museum educates visitors about the history of the Penobscot Bay Area. The museum includes an art gallery and features a new exhibit on shipbuilding or the sea each summer. (☎ 207-548-2529; www.penobscotmarinemuseum.org. Open Memorial Day to late Oct. M-Sa 10am-5pm, Su noon-5pm; last admission 4pm. $8, seniors $6, ages 7-15 $3, under 6 free.) Constructed in the mid-1800s with granite from nearby Mount Waldo, Fort Knox was part of a plan to protect the Penobscot River against British invasion. Info panels guide visitors through the **Fort Knox State Historic Site** from the storage vaults to the powder magazine. (Take U.S. 1 to Rte. 178; the fort is the first right. ☎ 207-469-6533. Open May-Oct. 9am-sunset. $3, under 5 free.)

FOOD & ACCOMMODATIONS. The ◼️**Belfast Co-op,** 123 High St., has organic snacks for reasonable prices and a cafe that serves grilled sandwiches, baked goods, and salads, as well as a wide selection of vegan and vegetarian options. (☎ 207-338-2532. Organic pretzels $2.50. Open daily 8am-7pm.) The **Lookout Pub,** 37B Front St., sports a marine theme and a casual bar atmosphere. A delicious mushroom burger with sweet potato fries ($7) makes the establishment vegetarian friendly as well. (☎ 207-388-8999; www.thelookoutpub.com. Open daily 11:30am-10pm.)

Belfast's historic B&Bs occupy the gorgeous houses downtown. (Rooms $75-150, depending on season.) An accommodations pamphlet is available at the Visitors Center downtown. The **Seascape Motel and Cottages,** 2202 Searsport Ave. on Rte. 1, provides one of the best deals in the area. The cottages include full kitchens, and the hotel offers a heated pool and spa, grills, and scheduled activities. (☎ 207-338-2130 or 800-477-0786; www.seascapemotel.com. Rooms from $49.) **Searsport Shores Camping Resort,** 209 W. Main St., in Searsport, provides a cheaper alternative to pricey hotels and B&Bs. Water is available at campsites, but electricity is not. The campground also offers Internet, a ping-pong table, and a pool table. (☎ 207-548-6059. Sites from $20; rental units from $50.)

APPROACHING CAMDEN
Take **U.S. 1 South** about 20 mi. to Camden.

CAMDEN

In the summer, khaki-clad crowds flock to Camden, 100 mi. north of Portland, to dock their yachts alongside tall-masted schooners in Penobscot Bay. Sea life sights dominates the downtown, from the gift shops to the design of restaurants to the large public landing where boaters can dock.

GETTING AROUND. Camden lies 2 mi south of Belfast on **U.S. 1,** which becomes **High St., Main St.,** and finally **Elm St.** as in travels through town. Most restaurants and shops lie around Main St. near the large public green.

SIGHTS. Camden's primary attractions center on water and the outdoors. **Maine Sports,** on U.S. 1 in Rockport, just south of Camden, rents and sells a wide array of sea-worthy vehicles. (☎ 207-236-7120 or 800-722-0826. Open mid-June

to Aug. daily 9am-8pm; Sept. to mid-June M-Sa 9am-6pm, Su 10am-5pm. Single kayaks $35-50 per day; tandems $45-65. Canoes $35-40 per day.) **Ragged Mountain Sports,** 46 Elm St. (☎ 207-236-6664 or 207-596-6895), in downtown Camden, offers daily bike rentals for under $20, bike tours for $45, and kayaking tours for $35-100. **Day tours** are available on a variety of boats at the public dock, with times on display at the Chamber of Commerce. Most boat owners sit at the public landing displaying their signs. (Schooner Olad ☎ 207-236-2323. Schooner Lazy Jack ☎ 207-230-0602. Both $25.) The **Maine State Ferry Service,** 5 mi. north of Camden in Lincolnville, floats to quaint and residential **Islesboro Island.** (☎ 800-491-4883. 30min. 5-9 per day; last return trip 4:30pm. Round-trip $5.25, with bike $10.25. Car and driver $15. Parking $6 per day.) The ferry also has an agency at 517A Main St., on U.S. 1 in Rockland, which runs to Vinalhaven and North Haven. (☎ 207-596-2202. Rates and schedules change with weather; call ahead.)

FOOD & ACCOMMODATIONS. At the ◼️**Camden Deli,** 37 Main St., patrons enjoy gourmet sandwiches from the classic reuben to the veggie focaccia. Two seating areas offer gorgeous ocean views. (☎ 207-236-8343. Open daily 7am-9pm.) At **Cappy's Chowder House,** 1 Main St., friendly waitstaff serve up local seafood specialities (including its signature chowder) and homemade pies. (☎ 207-236-2254. Entrees $10-14. Chowder cup $6, bowl $9. Open daily 11am 11pm.)

VITAL STATS

Population: 5200

Visitor Info: Camden-Rockport-Lincolnville Chamber of Commerce (☎ 207-236-4404 or 800-223-5459; www.camdenme.org), at the public landing. Open mid-May to mid-Oct. M-F 9am-5pm, Sa 10am-5pm, Su 10am-4pm; mid-Oct. to mid-May closed Su.

Internet Access: Camden Public Library, 55 Main St. (☎ 207-236-3440; www.camden.lib.me.us). Open M, W, F-Sa 9:30am-5pm; Tu and Th 9:30am-8pm; Su 1-5pm.

Post Office: 28 Chestnut St. (☎ 207-236-3570). Open M-F 8:30am-5pm, Sa 9am-noon. **Postal Code:** 04843.

The **Good Guest House,** 50 Elm St., has two appealing rooms at reasonable rates. (☎ 207-236-2139. Breakfast included. Room with double bed $60, with king-size bed $70; low-season $80/$90.) **Camden Hills State Park,** 1¼ mi. north of town on U.S. 1, is almost always full in summer. Arrive by 2pm for better chances at securing a spot. This secluded retreat also offers 25 mi. of trails, including a popular lookout from the top of Mt. Battie. (☎207-236-3109, reservations 800-332-1501. Reception 7am-10pm. Reservations $2 per day. Open mid-May to mid-Oct. Sites $20, ME residents $15. Free showers. Day use $3.)

APPROACHING PORTLAND
Take **U.S. 1 South** out of Camden to **I-95 South.** Continue on to **I-295 South,** which leads into Portland.

THE DESERT OF MAINE   95 Desert Rd.
In Freeport, 2 mi. off I-295, Exit 20.

Nestled between Maine's lush forests and its famous coast is...a desert? Maine's "famous natural phenomenon" since 1925, the desert is actually the result of the Tuttle family's mishandling of their family farm through overgrazing, overforesting, and neglecting to rotate crops. These poor techniques caused massive soil erosion that exposed the hidden glacial sand deposit that spread to become the Desert of Maine. Scientists have attested to the authenticity of the phenomenon and it has been documented by Ripley's "Believe It or Not." Today, the **Farm Museum** documents 18th-century farm life in the original Tuttle Barn and narrated trolley tours educate guests about the desert. Visitors can stay overnight at the campgrounds and enjoy air conditioners ($2) and modem access ($1) as well as access to the park. (☎207-865-6962. Open daily 8:30am-5:30pm. Tours 9am-5pm. $7.75, 13-16 $5.25, ages 5-12 $4.25, under 4 free. Sites $21; $7 per extra person.)

EARTHA
In the DeLorme building in Yarmouth off I-95.

The **world's largest rotating globe** and the largest printed representation of the earth, Eartha was finished in July of 1998, stealing the title of world's largest from a globe in Wellesley, MA. Forty-two feet in diameter and weighing 6000 lb., the globe has a circumference of 130 ft., and rotates on an axis at 23.5°, just like the real thing. (Open M-Th 9:30am-6pm, F-Sa 9:30am-7pm, Su 9:30am-6pm.)

PORTLAND

Portland combines the cultural appeal of a large industrial center with excellent opportunities to explore the outdoors. At night, the Victorian architecture in the Old Port Exchange provides a ironic backdrop to Portland's spirited youth culture. Teenagers and 20-somethings gather in bars, restaurants, and cafes near the wharf, and flood the streets, keeping the local nightclubs alive. Outside the city, ferries run to the Casco Bay Islands, while Sebago Lake offers sun and water-skiing.

VITAL STATS

Population: 64,000

Visitor Info: 245 Commercial St. (☎207-772-5800), between Union and Cross St. Open M-F 8am-5pm, Sa 10am-5pm.

Internet Access: Portland Public Library, 5 Monument Sq. (☎207-871-1700). Open M, W, F 9am-6pm; Tu and Th noon-9pm; Sa 9am-5pm.

Post Office: 400 Congress St. (☎207-871-8464). Open M-F 8am-7pm, Sa 9am-1pm. **Postal Code:** 04101.

GETTING AROUND

Downtown Portland rests in the middle of a peninsula jutting into the Casco Bay, along **Congress St.** between **State St.** and **Pearl St.,** and stretches down to the water's edge. A few blocks south of Congress St. along the waterfront lies the **Old Port,** between Commercial and Middle St. These two districts contain most of the city's sights and attractions. **I-295** (off I-95) forms the northwestern boundary of city. Metered **parking** for up to 2hr. is available throughout the city. Garages lie on Pearl St. between Fore and Milk St. ($1.25 per hr.) and Newbury St. ($0.75 per hr.).

SIGHTS

OFFSHORE ISLANDS. With secluded beaches and relatively undeveloped interiors, these islands lie just a ferry ride from the city proper. **Casco Bay Lines,** on State Pier near the corner of Commercial and Franklin St., runs daily to **Long Island,** where waves crash on an unpopulated beach, and **Peaks Island,** as well as other islands. (☎207-774-7871;

www.cascobaylines.com. Long Island: Operates M-Sa 5am-9:30pm, Su 7:45am-9:30pm. Round-trip $8, seniors and ages 5-9 $4. Peaks Island: Operates M-Sa 5:45am-11:30pm, Su 7:45am-11:30pm. $6/$3.) On Peaks Island, **Brad's Recycled Bike Shop** rents bikes. (115 Island Ave. ☎207-766-5631. $5 per hr., $12 per day. Open daily 10am-5pm.)

TWO LIGHTS STATE PARK. Across the Casco Bay Bridge, the Two Lights State Park is a great place for a secluded spot to picnic or walk alongside the shimmering ocean. (From State or York St. go south along Rte. 77 to Cape Elizabeth. ☎207-799-5871; www.state.me.us/doc/parks. $2.50.)

PORTLAND HEAD LIGHT IN FORT WILLIAMS PARK. This functioning lighthouse is a scenic detour worth the time. Families play on the large green spaces of the park, which offers numerous views of the shoreline and nearby islands, including a lighthouse off the coast. Inside is the **Port Head Light Museum,** with a timeline that documents the history of the lighthouse. There is unfortunately no access to the tower. (From Rte. 77 North turn right at the flashing signal onto Shore Rd. and proceed to the park. Open sunrise-sunset. Lighthouse suggested donation. Museum open 10am-4pm. $2, ages 6-16 $1, under 5 free.)

PORTLAND OBSERVATORY. Not only is it the last maritime signal tower in the US, it's also the best view in town. Tours provide a detailed history and an enthusiastic explanation of signalling in general. (138 Congress St. ☎207-774-5561; www.portlandlandmarks.org. Open daily 10am-5pm; last tour 4:40pm. $5, ages 6-16 $4, under 6 free.)

SHIPYARD BREWING CO. While it takes about eight days to brew a batch of beer at the Shipyard Brewing Co., it will only take 30min. to tour the brewery and try the free sample. (86 Newbury St. ☎207-761-0807. Open summer M-F 3-5pm, Sa-Su noon-5pm; winter W-F 3-5pm, Sa noon-5pm. Tours every 30min. Free.)

🎵 ENTERTAINMENT

Signs for theatrical productions are ubiquitous throughout Portland, and schedules are available at the Visitors Center. The **Portland Symphony** presents concerts renowned throughout the Northeast. (☎207-842-0800; www.porttix.com. Tickets through Porttix, 20 Myrtle St. Open M-Sa noon-6pm. Occasional 50% student discount.) Info on

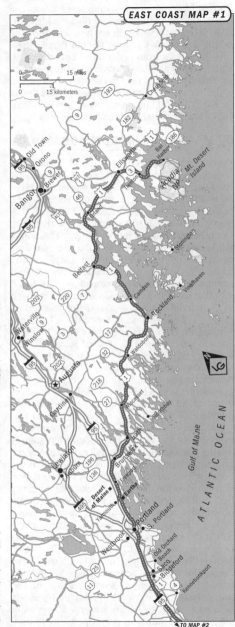
EAST COAST MAP #1

EAST COAST

Portland's jazz, blues, and club scene packs the *Casco Bay Weekly* (www.cascobayweekly.com) and *FACE,* both of which are free. Traditionally on the first Sunday in June, the **Old Port Festival** fills the blocks from Federal to Commercial St. with as many as 50,000 people enjoying free public entertainment. On Friday afternoons from early July to late August, the **Weekday Music Series** (☎207-772-6828) hosts a variety of bands in Post Office Sq. between Middle and Exchange St.

FOOD & ACCOMMODATIONS

Portland's harbor overflows with the fruits of the ocean, but non-aquatic and vegetarian fare isn't hard to find. The **Portland Public Market,** at Preble St. and Cumberland Ave., provides ethnic foods, seafood, and baked goods from over 20 small vendors. (☎207-228-2000; www.portlandmarket.com. Open M-Sa 9am-7pm, Su 10am-5pm.) The homemade, organic pizzas ($8-14) at the **Flatbread Company,** 72 Commercial St., make tasty, healthy treats. The view is a combination of ocean and parking garage, but the hand-painted wall hangings that speak to local causes and huge clay oven in the middle of the floor are ample distraction. (☎207-772-8777 Open summer M-Th 11:30am-10pm, F-Sa 11am-10:30pm; winter M-Th 11:30am-9pm, F-Sa 11:30am-10pm.) **Federal Spice,** 225 Federal St., just off Congress St., seasons wraps and soft tacos (under $6) with fiery Caribbean, South American, and Asian ingredients. The giant chili pepper on the sign tells travelers all they needs to know about the vegetarian-friendly establishment. (☎207-774-6404. Open M-Sa 11am-9pm.)

Portland has some inexpensive accommodations during the winter, but prices jump steeply during the summer, especially on weekends. Lodging in the smaller towns up and down the coast within 30min. of Portland can be a less expensive option. **The Inn at St. John,** 939 Congress St., is not located in an especially appealing neighborhood, but its old-fashioned upscale decor makes it an elegant choice. (☎207-773-6481 or 800-636-9127. Continental breakfast included. Rooms in summer M-Th $70-135, F-Su $115-175; winter $55-100/$60-115.) The closest campground to Portland is **Wassamki Springs,** 56 Saco St., in Scarborough to the south. RVs and brightly colored tents cluster around a lake encircled by sandy beaches. (☎207-839-4276. Reserve 2 weeks in advance, especially July-Aug. Open May to mid-

Oct. 2 person sites with water and electricity $28, with hookup $30, $5 per additional person, lakefront sites $3 extra. Showers free.)

NIGHTLIFE

The Old Port area, known as "the strip"—especially **Fore St.** between Union and Exchange St.—livens up after dark as shops stay open and bars start getting crowded. **Brian Boru,** 57 Center St. provides a mellow pub scene with top-notch nachos for $6. (☎207-780-1506. Su $2 pints. Open daily 11:30am-1am.) **Gritty MacDuff's,** 396 Fore St., brews its own beer (pints $3.50) and entertains a largely local crowd with live music. (☎207-772-2739. Live music Sa-Su nights. Open daily 11:30am-1am.) **Una Wine Bar & Lounge,** 505 Fore St., mixes speciality martinis and serves wine by the taste, glass ($5-10), or bottle. (☎207-828-0300. Tapas $3-15. Open daily 4:30pm-1am.)

Welcome To

NEW HAMPSHIRE

APPROACHING PORTSMOUTH
I-95 South provides the quickest, easiest route from Portland to Portsmouth. There are 2 tolls, $1.50 and $0.50. Exit 7 leads to the center of downtown.

PORTSMOUTH

Although New Hampshire's coastline extends only 13 mi. along the Atlantic Ocean, the state makes the most of its toehold on the water. Once a colonial capital, Portsmouth is one of the nicest seaside towns in New England, with 18th-century architecture recalling its rich history.

GETTING AROUND

State St. (U.S. 1) and **Congress St.** are the two major roads that run northeast-southwest through town. The central intersecting road is **Market St.,** which runs southeast-northwest. The town is best navigated by foot; leave the car in the lot on the corner of Hanover and Market St. ($.50 per hr.).

(*VITAL STATS*)

Population: 21,000

Visitor Info: Greater Portsmouth Chamber of Commerce, 500 Market St. (☎603-436-1118; www.portcity.org). Open M-W 8:30am-5pm, Th-F 8:30am-7pm, Sa-Su 10am-5pm. Info kiosk in Market Sq. Open May to mid-Oct. daily 10am-5pm.

Internet Access: Portsmouth Public Library, 8 Islington St. (☎603-427-1540), at the corner of Middle and State St. Open M-Th 9am-9pm, F 9am-5:30pm, Sa 9am-5pm.

Post Office: 80 Daniel St. (☎603-431-2871). Open M-F 7:30am-5:30pm, Sa 8am-12:30pm. **Postal Code:** 03801.

Seacoast Trolley (☎603-431-6975) runs in summer every hr. from 10am to 5pm, with 14 stops around Portsmouth. ($2.50 partial loop, $5 full loop with reboarding privileges).

⊙ SIGHTS

STRAWBERY BANKE MUSEUM. Modern Portsmouth sells itself with its colonial past, the most characteristic example of which is the Strawbery Banke Museum. Each building has been restored to display the region in various time periods. Museum employees frequent the various houses and shops in garb appropriate to their time period. *(At the corner of Marcy and Hancock St. From there, follow the signs that lead toward the harbor. ☎603-433-1100; www.strawberybanke.org. Open May-Oct. M-Sa 10am-5pm, Su noon-5pm; Nov.-Apr. Th-Sa 10am-2pm, Su noon-2pm. May-Oct. $15, seniors $14, ages 5-17 $10, families $35. Nov.-Apr. $10/$9/$5/ $25. Tickets good for 2 consecutive days.)*

PRESCOTT PARK. Across the street from the Strawbery Banke Museum, Prescott Park runs along the bank of the Piscataqua River. The small, well-tended gardens and lawns offer a pleasant respite with an amazing view. Local productions of shows and musicals go up during the summer.

JOHN PAUL JONES HOUSE. Maintained as it would have been during the 18th century, this house provides another great way to experience colonial and seafaring history. Guides tell visitors about the famous captain's life. *(At the corner of Middle and State St. ☎603-436-8420; www.portsmouthhistory.org. Open late May to mid-Oct. M-Tu and Th-Su 11am-5pm. $6, ages 6-14 $2.50.)*

THE USS ALBACORE. The *USS Albacore* is a research submarine built locally at the Portsmouth Naval Shipyard. Visitors can explore a small museum before taking a guided tour of the sub. *(☎603-436-3680. Open May-Oct. daily 9:30am-5pm; winter hours vary. $5, seniors and military with ID $4, ages 7-17 $2; families $10.)*

NORTH CEMETERY. One of Portsmouth's oldest graveyards, the North Cemetery is the resting place for some of the city's most prominent citizens, including signers of the Declaration of Independence and the U.S. Constitution. **Gravestones by Dusk** offers a 1hr. historical tour of the cemetery. *(☎603-436-5096. Tours daily Apr.-Oct. $10 per person. Times vary; call for reservations.)*

PORTSMOUTH BLACK HERITAGE TRAIL. The Portsmouth Black Heritage Trail offers a different means to experience the city's celebrated history. Plaques throughout the city mark the relevant sites, and brochures are available at the Strawbery Banke Museum Visitors Center, its museum shop, or the Chamber of Commerce.

MUSIC HALL. The Music Hall, a 125-year-old theater, shows mainstream, independent, and foreign films during the summer, as well as live musical and dance performances. Be prepared for the occasional silly twist—those who wear a togas to the *Animal House* showing, for example, get in free. Schedules of movies and events are available outside the theater. *(28 Chestnut St. ☎603-436-2400. Box office open M-Sa noon-6pm or until 30min. after the shows. $8, students and seniors $6.)*

SANDY POINT DISCOVERY CENTER. Popular with bird-watchers, Sandy Point is one of only three points where the public can explore the Great Bay Estuary and has a half-mile boardwalk. The Discovery Center houses exhibits about the estuary's wildlife and runs programs and kayak trips for all ages. In September and October, a replica of a flat-bottomed gundalow boat once used to move lumber in the estuary visits the center. *(89 Depot Rd. South on Rte. 33, in Stratham. ☎603-778-0015; www.greatbay.org. Free.)*

⬛🏠 FOOD & ACCOMMODATIONS

Seafood is a popular Portsmouth mainstay, while a pint of local ale is an after-dinner staple. A local landmark, ◪**The Friendly Toast,** 121 Congress St., is cluttered with ghastly artifacts of the 1950s:

mannequin limbs, pulp novels, Formica, and bad art. Menu items such as the "mission burrito" ($7) are nearly impossible to finish, combining classic breakfast fare with vegetarian and healthy twists. The thick homemade bread is heavenly. (A block and a half from Market Sq. ☎603-430-2154. Breakfast served all day. Entrees $6-8. Open M-Th 7am-11pm, F-Su 7am-9pm.) Semi-inebriated folk trail out the door of nearby pubs and into the street for heavenly burgers and sandwiches at **Gilly's Lunchcart,** 175 Fleet St., into the wee hours of the night. The place is tiny—a row of stools are the only seating—but the food makes up for the inconvenience. (M 11am-6pm "Dog Days" $1 hotdogs. Fries $1.50. Burgers $2.25. Open M 11:30am-6pm, Tu-Su 11:30am-2:00am.) For a lighter option, check out **The Juicery,** 51 Hanover St., which uses all fresh, organic, vegetarian ingredients in wraps, juices, and smoothies. (☎603-431-0693. Juices $3.50-4.25. Wraps $7.25. Smoothies $5.)

Portsmouth isn't budget-friendly when it comes to finding a place to hang your hat; accommodation prices in town are steep. Try **U.S. 1A** south of Portsmouth for typical chain motels. Another alternative is **Camp Eaton,** in York Harbor, about 15 mi. north of Portsmouth off U.S. 1. Although still expensive, the wooded sites are a relative bargain, with immaculate bathrooms and well-kept grounds. (☎207-363-3424. Take U.S. 1 North into York village, take a right onto York St. and follow it to the beach to reach the site. 2-person sites $37, off-season $23. $6 per additional person.)

LEAVING PORTSMOUTH
From downtown, take **U.S. 1 South** to **Miller Ave. (U.S. 1A).** U.S. 1A heads along the shore toward Rye and Hampton Beaches.

RYE AND HAMPTON BEACH

Five miles apart, Rye Beach and Hampton Beach stretch along U.S. 1A down the New Hampshire Coast. Primarily a tourist area, the towns have a number of seafood restaurants, beaches, and lodgings that range from bare minimum motels to elaborate resorts. While Rye Beach has a simple, relatively untouched feel with rocky shores and many private homes, Hampton Beach is the gaudiest beach-front north of the Jersey shore and, for much of the summer, is swarmed with tourists.

VITAL STATS

Population: 5200/15,000

Visitor Info: Hampton Beach Chamber of Commerce Visitor (☎603-926-8717; www.hampton-beach.org), on Ocean Blvd.

Internet Access: Rye Public Library, 581 Washington Rd. (☎603-964-8401), in Rye. Open M, W, F 9am-5pm; Tu and Th 9am-8pm; Sa 9am-3pm.

Post Office: 25 Stickney Terr. (☎603-926-6413) in Hampton. Open M-F 8:30am-5pm, Sa 8:30am-noon. **Postal Code:** 03870.

⌷ GETTING AROUND. U.S. 1A runs along the shore in both towns. In Hampton Beach it becomes one-way heading north, so southbound drivers must take **Ashworth Ave.** Though metered **parking** along the shore costs the same as at North Hampton State Beach, there are lots, particularly along Ashworth Ave., that charge $5-8 for the entire day.

◙ SIGHTS. North of Rye along U.S. 1a, **Odiorne State Park** consists of open fields and a rocky beach more suitable for looking at than for swimming. It features the **Seacoast Science Center,** with exhibits on aquaculture, radar, and a ship-wreck off the coast. Visitors can play a 3-D underwater video game and pick up a free 1hr. audio tour of the seven distinct natural habitats featured in the park. (Open daily 10am-5pm. $3, ages 3-12 $1, under 3 free.) The park also includes the remains of **WWII's Fort Dearborn.** (☎603-436-7406. Open 8am-8pm. $3, under 12 free). For the fisherman, the marina in **Rye Harbor State Park** offers the perfect opportunity to catch a big one. (☎603-436-5294. Parking $4.) Stands there sell whale watching tours and trips around the **Isles of Shoals,** nine islands off the coast that were once popular resort communities. Try **Granite State Whale Watch** (☎603-964-5545 or 800-964-5545; whale watches at 8:30am and 1:30pm) or the **Atlantic Queen II** (☎800-942-5364 or 603-964-5220; half-day fishing 8am, whale watch 1pm). Between Ordiorne State Park and Rye Beach lies **Wallis Sands State Beach,** a relatively unadulterated stretch of sand and surf. (Open daily mid-June to Labor Day 8am-8pm; mid-May to mid-June Sa-Su 8am-8pm. Parking M-F $5, Sa-Su $8.) **North Hampton State Beach** is a thin strip of sandy beach closer to the commercial center of Hampton Beach. Parking is also much steeper on the

pricing—$1 per 40min. **Hampton Beach** lies still farther south along Rte 1A, right in the center of the Hampton Beach madness.

▟▛ FOOD & ACCOMMODATIONS. Along with the henna tattoo stands and arcades, **Ocean Blvd.** is crowded with fast-food joints, burger stands, and pizza parlors. For a sit-down meal, try the **Purple Urchin,** 167 Ocean Blvd., right across from the Visitors Center. While it's a little short on the vegetarian options, it serves up tasty seafood that varies from a Haddock sandwich ($9) to the char-grilled filet mignon. (☎603-929-0800. Open daily noon-10pm.) **Sawasake Thai Cuisine,** 69 Ocean Blvd. (☎603-929-7272), offers decent Thai food served in small dining room. The best deals are the lunch specials ($8), which include an entree, spring roll, crab rangoon, salad, and rice.

Hampton Beach is filled with fairly reasonable hotels and motels that are close to the beach, in the middle of the intense noise and tumult of the boardwalk. For reasonably priced accommodations right on the ocean, try **The Kentville,** 315 Ocean Blvd. in Hampton. With tasteful floral decorations, the rooms include fridges and microwaves or complete kitchens. Many have ocean views. (☎603-926-3950 or 800-992-4297; www.kentvilleontheocean.com. Doubles mid-June to mid-Sept. $109; mid-Sept. to mid-June $59-79.) The strip along Rye Beach has a number of quaint inns, but few budget options. **Rye Beach Motel and Cottages,** on Old Beach Rd., has individual motel rooms with fridges and microwaves and cottages that can be rented by the week. The quiet residential location is perfect for those who want to escape the chaos of the Hampton Beach, but the lack of air conditioning can make the rooms less than comfortable on hot summer days. (☎603-964-5511. Rooms $60. Weekly cottages $445-540 for 1 room; $720 weekly for 5-6 people.)

▞ APPROACHING ESSEX
Take **U.S. 1A** south along the coast until it turns inland and joins **U.S. 1.** Continue on **U.S. 1 South** until Newburyport. There, take **U.S. 1A** south until switching to **Rte. 133 South** in Rowley. Rte. 133 will take you south to Essex, becoming **Main St.** in town.

ESSEX

Tiny Essex is known for two distinctive features: its many antique shops and flea markets, and the legend of Lawrence "Chubby" Woodman who, in 1916, dipped the clam in vegetable oil and cornmeal and invented the fried clam. **The White Elephant,** 32 Main St., and **RC Schonick Antiques,** 67 Main St., are among the towns endless antique shops. On the weekends, deal-hunters flock to **Todd Farm** for anything it's possible to sell. The more historically inclined can head to the **Essex Shipbuilding Museum and Store,** at 66 Main St. and 128 Main St. (☎978-768-7541; www.essexship-buildingmuseum.org. Open Su and W-Sa noon-4pm. $5, students and seniors $3, under 12 free.)

To experience Essex's clamming history, diners can head to **Woodman's,** 121 Main St., to sample delicious fare from the purveyors of Chubby Woodman's legacy. (☎978-768-7541; www.wood-mans.com. Open Su-Th 11am-9pm, F-Sa 11am-10pm.) Across the street is **Tom Shea's,** 122 Main St., whose chowder was voted number one at the 2003 Essex Clamfest. (☎978-768-6931. Open M-Sa 11:30-9:30pm, Su 10am-9:30pm.) Visitors can stay at the town's one and only hotel, the **Essex River House,** 132 Main St., which provides clean rooms and personal service, but requires a seven-day cancellation notice and a one-night non-refundable deposit. (☎978-768-6800. Rooms $89-120).

APPROACHING ROCKPORT
Follow **Rte. 133** east to Gloucester and then take **Rte. 127** east to Rockport.

ROCKPORT

Along with Gloucester, Manchester-by-the-Sea, and Essex, Rockport is one of the main communities of Cape Ann, the self-proclaimed "home of the perfect vacation." Rockport sports small beaches, a house made entirely of paper, and a downtown oriented toward the touristy. There is life outside of the small downtown, however, and exploring it brings out the town's more unique features.

GETTING AROUND

Rte. 127 leads into **Main St.** and **Broadway,** two of the town's central streets. Main St. turns to run along the water and leads into **Mt. Pleasant St.** to

the southeast and **Beach St.** to the northwest. This stretch along the beach is the main commercial and tourist section of town, with numerous restaurants, shops, and accommodations. The intersection of Main St., Mt. Pleasant St., and Bearskin Neck forms **Dock Sq.,** the center of the downtown.

Parking is available in a lot on Main St. about a mile from downtown and across the street from the Sandy Bay Motor Inn. A shuttle runs to downtown. (Runs daily July-Aug. 11am-7pm; Sept.-May Sa-Su only. $1 round-trip.) Visitors can also park in the "residents only lot" between the Town Hall and Granite Savings Bank on Main St. after 6pm or in the metered parking available on most streets.

> **VITAL STATS**
>
> **Population:** 7300
>
> **Visitor Info: Rockport Harbormaster's Office,** 34 Broadway (☎978-546-9589). **Cape Ann Chamber of Commerce,** 33 Commercial St. (☎978-283-1601; www.capeannvacations.com) in Gloucester.
>
> **Internet Access: Rockport Public Library,** 17 School St. (☎978-546-6934). Open M-Th 1-8pm, Sa 10am-5pm, Su 1-6pm.
>
> **Post Office:** 39 Broadway. Open M-F 9am-5pm Sa 8:30am-noon. **Postal Code:** 03870.

SIGHTS

THE PAPER HOUSE. In 1922, Elis F. Stenman, a mechanical engineer from Cambridge, was experimenting with newspapers as a insulation material for his summer cottage. When he noticed how sturdy they were, he used varnish to waterproof them, intending to cover the outside with clapboards. After the walls survived a harsh New England winter with minimal damage, Stenman decided to leave them exposed, and the paper house was born. While it has a wood frame and a normal roof, the walls and the furniture that Stenman continued to add until his death in 1942 are made entirely of newspapers. Stenman used about 100,000 newspapers to make his house: the desk was made of copies of the *Christian Science Monitor*; a grandfather clock consisted of newspapers from 48 state capitals; a writing desk was constructed entirely of papers documenting Charles Lindbergh's flight across the Atlantic. The walls are 215 sheets (or about 1½ in.) thick. Now maintained by Stenman's grandnephew, the paper house has attracted visitors since the 1930s. *(52*

Pigeon Hill. Follow Rte. 127 north to Pigeon Cove, take a left onto Curtis St., and then another left onto Pigeon Hill. The paper house is on the right; there are signs marking the way. ☎978-546-2629. Open Apr.-Oct. daily 10am-5pm. $1.50.)

HALIBUT POINT STATE PARK. Occupying the land around the Babson Farm Quarry off Rte. 127, Halibut Point State Park features a half-mile, self-guided walking tour around the quarry. Brochures leading the tour and explaining its sights are at the Visitors Center, which highlights the history of the park, the artifacts left over from the quarry, and the natural habitat that the park constitutes. Visitors can also follow a path down to a beach of huge rocks, but wear shoes suitable for climbing over stones and exploring tidepools. *(On Gott Ave. Take Rte. 127 north out of downtown Rockport and turn right on Gott Ave. ☎978-546-2997. Open daily 8am-8pm. Parking $2.)*

BEARSKIN NECK. One of the country's oldest artist colonies, Bearskin Neck is now also one of Rockport's most tourist-oriented areas, featuring gift shops, ice-cream stores, and a motel at the end of the small peninsula. Most galleries highlight painting, but a few display sculpture and jewelry. The area got its name in an unfortunately literal manner; a bear was caught and killed by the tide there. *(From Broadway, take a left onto Mt. Pleasant St., then a right onto Bearskin Neck. From Main St., continue on Main St. as it curves right, then left onto Bearskin Neck at Dock Sq. There is not a lot of space to drive, so parking and walking there is easiest.)*

MOTIF NO. 1. A sort of "little fish shack that could," Motif No. 1 is still just a fish shack, but perhaps the most famous fish shack in the world. At the end of a Bearskin Neck wharf, the red fish shack has been the subject of innumerable paintings. Legend has it that the building received its name when artist Lester Hornby saw yet another student drawing featuring this most popular subject—or motif—and christened it "motif no. 1."

FOOD

Rockport is a dry town, so no restaurants or stores sell alcohol, although some allow visitors to bring their own. **Top Dog,** in Bearskin Neck, serves a wide array of dogs—hot dogs, that is—such as the "Chihuahua" (jalapeno peppers, salsa and cheese), the "Golden Retriever" (macaroni and cheese), and the classic "Purebred" for $2.50. Diners get a free meal if they are ordering when the Red Sox hit a home run. (☎978-546-0006; www.topdogrockport.com. Open Su-Th 11am-8pm, F-Sa 11am-9pm.) **The Sunrise Grill,** 18 Beach St., by Front Beach, serves grilled cheese ($4.50) and other American favorites. (☎978-546-9995. Open daily 6am-2pm.) **The Greenery,** 15 Dock Sq., offers light fare in a casual cafe atmosphere. The avocado special (avocado, cheese, veggies, and creamy garlic on pita; $7) is particularly tasty. Try a Yacht Club soda, a Rhode Island favorite. (☎978-546-9593. Open daily 8am-9:30pm.)

ACCOMMODATIONS

Like many towns along the New England coast, Rockport has a plethora of accommodations, most of which are hard on the pocketbook. The recently downsized **Peg Leg Inn,** 18 Beach St., across the street from Front Beach, offers 11 colonial-style rooms with beautiful views of the water. The continental breakfast, accommodating staff, and personal decor in both rooms and the spacious lounge set it apart from most roadside establishments. However, not all of the rooms have A/C, there is a two-night minimum stay, and the regular clientele means that new visitors should call well in advance to book. (☎978-546-2352 or 800-346-2352; www.pegleginn.com. Open Apr.-Dec. Rooms $135-150.) The slightly more reasonable **Turks Head Inn,** 151 South St., lies farther out of town in a residential neighborhood and has more traditional rooms, but also includes beach access and a heated indoor swimming pool. (Take Broadway until it hits Mt. Pleasant St. and turn right onto Mt. Pleasant St., which becomes South St. ☎978-546-3436; www.turksheadinn.com. Open late spring to late fall. Rooms $109.) The **Sandy Bay Motor Inn,** 173 Main St., is conveniently located across the street from the "park and ride" parking lot, with easy access to the shuttle into town. The establishment has rooms with and without kitchenettes that include a sink, stove, fridge, and dishes. The hotel also has a pool and hot tub. (☎978-546-7155. Rooms from $99.)

APPROACHING SALEM
From Rockport, take **Rte. 127** to **U.S. 1A South,** about a 20 mi. drive along the coast.

SALEM

Salem is considered the Halloween headquarters of the world, and though it has more to offer, it isn't trying very hard to free itself from the stereotype. Witch museums, supernatural gift shops and witch-themed restaurants line the streets. The town's history is not limited to the infamous Puritan hysteria, and includes roles as a shipbuilding center and home to author Nathaniel Hawthorne.

VITAL STATS

Population: 40,400

Visitor Info: Salem Visitors Center, 2 New Liberty St. (☎978-740-1650). Free maps, public restrooms, historical displays, and gift shop. Open daily July-Aug. 9am-6pm; Sept.-June 9am-5pm.

Internet Access: Salem Public Library, 370 Essex St. (☎978-531-0100). Open M-Th 9am-9pm, F-Sa 9am-5pm, Su 1:30pm-5pm.

Post Office: 2 Margin St. (☎978-744-4671). Open M-F 8am-5pm, Sa 8am-1pm. **Postal Code:** 01970.

⌐ GETTING AROUND

U.S. 1A enters Salem from the north, turning into **Bridge St. (Rte. 107).** Bridge St. runs parallel to **Essex St.** and **Derby St.,** where many sights are located, and perpendicular to **Washington St.** and **North St. (Rte. 114),** the former which heads south to Essex St. and New Derby St., and the latter which leads to North Salem. Taking **Pleasant St.** south from Bridge St. soon after entering town will take you to the Salem Common, and continuing south will take you to Salem Harbor.

⊙ SIGHTS

SPELLBOUND MUSEUM. The only Salem museum to focus on witchcraft and the supernatural as a legitimate subject apart from the 17th-century hysteria, Spellbound features artifacts from different cultures. Check out vampire killing kits, objects for contacting the spirit world, and a hoodoo (New Orleans voodoo) love spell. The owner is a licensed Ghost hunter with the International Ghost Hunters Society and a member of the International Society for Paranormal Investigators, and leads ghost-hunting tours every night at 8pm from the Visitors Center. (*190 Essex St.*

☎978-745-0138; www.spellboundtours.com. Open Apr.-Oct. daily 10am-5pm; call for winter hours. Tickets not required for walking tours until Oct. $10, students and seniors $7, under 13 $5. Walking tours $13, students and seniors $10, under 12 $7.)

WITCH HYSTERIA. Salem certainly doesn't try to minimize the most infamous event in its history. The **Salem Witch Museum** uses real testimony from contemporary documents in a live-action exhibit called "Witches: Evolving Perceptions" that runs continuously daily from 10am to 5pm. (*Washington Sq.* ☎978-744-1692; www.salemwitchmuseum.com. $6.50, seniors $6, ages 6-14 $4.50, under 5 free.) The **Salem Wax Museum of Witches and Seafarers** displays life-sized statues of major figures from the trials, including Colonel Lieutenant John Hathorne, ancestor of author Nathaniel Hawthorne and supposedly the only person never to regret his involvement. A series of full-scale dioramas documents Salem history. (*288 Derby St.* ☎800-298-2929; www.salemwaxmuseum.com. Open daily 10am-5pm. $6.) The "Hysteria Pass" is available for $10 and grants access to the wax museum and to the **Salem Witch Village,** an indoor re-creation of a 17th-century village. Practicing witches give a tour of the village to help "discover both the myths and facts surrounding the subject of Witchcraft." (*282 Derby St.* ☎978-740-9229; www.salemwitchvillage.net. Open daily 10am-5pm.) The **Witch Dungeon Museum** features still more reenactments of the witch trials and continuously running tours of the dungeon. (*16 Lynde St.* ☎978-741-3570; www.witchdungeon.com. Open daily 10am-5pm.) The **Witch House,** home of witch trial judge Jonathan Corwin, is "Salem's only home with direct ties to the trials." (*310½ Essex St.* ☎978-744-8815; www.salemweb.com/witchhouse. Open daily mid-May to mid-Nov. daily 10am-5pm.) The **Salem Witch Trials Memorial** consists of stones featuring quotations from the trial testimonies. Finish it off twith a trip to the **Witch History Museum,** a tour through a series of animatronic scenes of key moments in the hysteria and trials. (*197-201 Essex St.* ☎978-741-7770; www.witchhistorymuseum.com. Open Apr.-Nov. 10am-5pm. $6.) A combination ticket ($15) is available to the Witch History Museum, the Witch Dungeon Museum and the **New England Pirate Museum.** (*274 Derby St.* ☎978-741-2800; www.piratemuseum.com. Open May-Oct. daily 10am-5pm.)

HOUSE OF THE SEVEN GABLES. The so-called "second most famous house in America," the Turner-Ingersoll Mansion became famous as Nathaniel Hawthorne's "House of the Seven Gables." Costumed guides lead guests through the house, built off of a maritime trade fortune. Admission includes the tour, the gardens, and the waterfront. Guests can also visit the Garden Cafe with a view of the ocean. *(54 Turner St. ☎ 978-744-0991; www.7gables.org. Open daily 10am-5pm; July-Oct. until 7pm. $11, ages 5-12 $6.50.)*

PEABODY ESSEX MUSEUM. In June 2003, this 200-year-old museum reopened after a $215 million expansion that added more than 250,000 sq. ft. of space. Displaying some of its extraordinary collections for the first time, the museum presents a wide array of decorative arts and exhibits on maritime history. *(East India Sq. ☎ 866-745-1876; www.pem.org. Open Su-W and F-Sa 10am-5pm, Th 10am-9pm. $13, under 16 $9.)*

SALEM MARITIME NATIONAL HISTORICAL SITE. Down the waterfront from the witch-oriented section of town, the site is dedicated to Salem's colonial and maritime history. The **Orientation Center** shows a film entitled *To the Farthest Part of the Rich East* every 30min. throughout the day. Guides lead tours of the **1817 Custom House** and a joint tour of the **1762 Derby House** and **1672 Narbonne House.** Visitors can also pick up brochures for the self-guided tour of "Nathaniel Hawthorne's Salem" and to the African-American Heritage Sites in Salem for free. *(193 Derby St. Orientation Center open daily 9am-5pm. Custom house tours daily 10am, 1pm, 3:30pm; Derby and Narbonne House tours daily 11:15am and 2:15pm. $5, ages 6-15 and seniors $3, under 6 free.)*

WALKING TOURS. Salem residents really enjoy showing visitors around. In addition to the self-guided tours of African-American Heritage Sites and major locations in Nathaniel Hawthorne's history and writing, tours abound. The **Spellbound Tour** led by the owner of the Spellbound Museum leaves from outside the Visitors Center. **Salem Historical Tours** offers its own **Haunted Footsteps Ghost Tour** of sites of "documented hauntings" led by guides costumed in period-appropriate attire. *(Tours May-Oct. 8pm; Oct. 8-31 7 and 8pm. $12.50, seniors $10, ages 6-12 $8.)* The company also offers the **Cemetery and Witch Trials Memorial Tour** and **History and Architecture Tour,** which highlights

key historical moments from all time periods and Salem figures such as Alexander Graham Bell and Nathaniel Bowditch. *(Witch Trials tour Su-M and W-Sa 2pm. $7, ages 6-12 $5, seniors $6. History and Architecture tour Su-M and W-Sa 4pm. $7, seniors $6, ages 6-12 $5.)* The **Salem Trolley Tours** provide a more relaxed way to visit a number of major Salem sites, including the Wax Museum, the House of the Seven Gables, and the Witch Dungeon Museum. *(Runs Apr.-Oct. daily 10am-5pm. $10, seniors $9, ages 5-14 $3, under 5 free.)*

🍴 FOOD

Only a few doors down from the Visitors Center and across the street from the Witch History Museum, **Fuel,** 196 Essex St., serves creative fare such as the apple and strawberry salad and tasty santa fe wrap, all made to order for about $5. The cafe also offers fresh juices and a wide array of teas for the discriminating palate (☎ 978-741-0850.) The **Derbydeli Cafe,** 245 Derby St., offers classic deli options like the ham and cheese sandwich in hearty but manageable portions ($4.50) as well as specialty coffees and ice cream. (☎ 978-741-2442. Open daily 7:30am-6pm.) **Finz,** 76 Wharf St., on Pickering Wharf, has a sleek, casual dining room with a bar and lovely view of the ocean and marina. Its menu focuses primarily on an old New England favorite, namely, seafood. Diners particularly recommend the haddock topped with crab meat ($19) and the market-fresh fish. (☎ 978-744-8485. Open daily 11:30am-10pm.)

🏨 ACCOMMODATIONS

Salem has a large number of B&Bs and quaint inns in historic houses, most outside the price range of the budget traveler. The most reasonable option is the **Clipper Ship Inn,** 40 Bridge St., off U.S. 1A, the "only motel in downtown Salem." The 60 larger-than-average rooms include A/C and cable TV, but few extras. Guests must drive themselves into the downtown area—or take a long walk—to reach the most famous attractions. (☎ 978-745-8022. Doubles $120.) Nearby Danvers has a less expensive **Days Inn,** 152 Endicott St. The rooms are less than spectacular but are clean and include many useful amenities. (Take North St. north to Market St. and turn Left on Endicott St. ☎ 978-777-1032 or 978-777-0204. Rooms from $100.)

APPROACHING BOSTON

Take **I-95 West** to **U.S. 1 South,** which merges with **I-93/Rte. 3** as it enters Boston. Take Exit 26B for **Storrow Dr.** heading west and exit left at the sign marked **"Copley Sq./Back Bay."**

BOSTON

For a long time, Boston *was* the United States. In the 17th and 18th centuries—America's formative years—the city played a starring role in the country's fight for independence. In the 19th century, some of America's most influential doers and thinkers called Boston home, unabashedly dubbing it the "Hub of the Universe." In the 20th century, the Biggest Small Town in America experienced the same growing pains sweeping the rest of the nation, including immigration booms, civil rights battles, and problems with urban expansion and renewal. Today, Boston is a restless stew of compact neighborhoods, distinct communities, cultural attractions, and urban parks. While the Freedom Trail is a nice place to start, wandering around Boston's many districts, its jumble of streets, and its (rarely square) squares will give you a better glimpse of this evolving metropolis.

VITAL STATS

Population: 600,000

Visitor Info: Greater Boston Convention and Visitors Bureau (☎617-536-4100; www.bostonusa.com) has a booth at Boston Common, outside T: Park St. Open M-F 8:30am-5pm. Downtown's **National Historic Park Visitor Center,** 15 State St. (☎617-242-5642), has Freedom Trail info and tours. T: State. Open daily 9am-5pm.

Internet Access: Boston Public Library, 700 Boylston St. (☎617-536-5400; www.bpl.org), at T: Copley. Open M-Th 9am-9pm, F-Sa 9am-5pm.

Post Office: 25 Dorchester Ave. (☎617-654-5302), behind South Station at T: South Station. Open 24hr. **Postal Code:** 02205.

GETTING AROUND

Boston is situated on a peninsula jutting into Massachusetts Bay. **I-93/U.S. 1/Rte. 3** runs north-south along the city's eastern edge. The Charles River divides Boston and its neighbor to the north, Cambridge; speedy **Storrow Dr.** and **Memorial Dr.** run along its southern and northern banks.

Boston's heart is the grassy **Boston Common,** sandwiched between **Beacon Hill** to the north, downtown to the south and east, and **Back Bay** to the west. Back Bay is Boston's most navigable area. Major avenues **Beacon St., Commonwealth Ave., Newbury St.,** and **Boylston Ave.** run parallel to Storrow; alternating one-way cross streets are named alphabetically from Arlington to Hereford as you head west. Elsewhere, driving is more complicated. **The Big Dig** still wreaks havoc on the roads of the waterfront, and the labyrinthine cobblestone paths of Boston's colonial downtown are almost impossible to navigate. Luckily for out-of-towners, Boston's metro system, **the T,** is clean, efficient, and cheap ($1.25). For sightseeing in Boston's compact center, it makes the most sense to park and walk. **Parking** garages are pricey (up to $20 per day), but they are often the only option; metered parking is limited and ticketing is relentless. Resident parking permits are required for street parking in many residential neighborhoods.

SIGHTS

THE FREEDOM TRAIL. Passing the landmarks that put Boston on the map, the 2½ mi. red-painted Freedom Trail is a great introduction to the city's history. Start at the **Visitors Center,** where the National Park Service offers free guided tours from the Old South Meeting House to the Old North Church. *(15 State St., opposite Old State House. T: State. ☎617-242-5642; www.nps.gov/ bost. Tours mid-June to Aug. daily 10, 11am, 2pm; mid-Apr. to mid-June M-F 2pm. Arrive 30min. before tour to get a ticket. Limit 30 people per tour.)*

DOWNTOWN. In 1634, colonists designated **Boston Common** as a place for cattle to graze. Today, street vendors, runners, and tourists roam the green and congregate near the **Frog Pond,** a wading pool in summer and an skating rink in winter. *(T: Park St.)* Across Charles St. from the Common is the lavish **Public Garden,** the nation's first botanical garden. Bronze versions of the title characters from the children's book *Make Way for Ducklings* point the way to the **Swan Boats,** graceful paddleboats that float around a quiet willow-lined pond. *(☎617-522-1966. Park open daily dawn-dusk. Boats open Apr. 18-June 19 daily 10am-4pm; June 20-Labor Day daily 10am-5pm; Labor Day-Sept. 6 M-F noon-4pm, Sa-Su 10am-4pm. $2.50, ages 2-15 $1 for a*

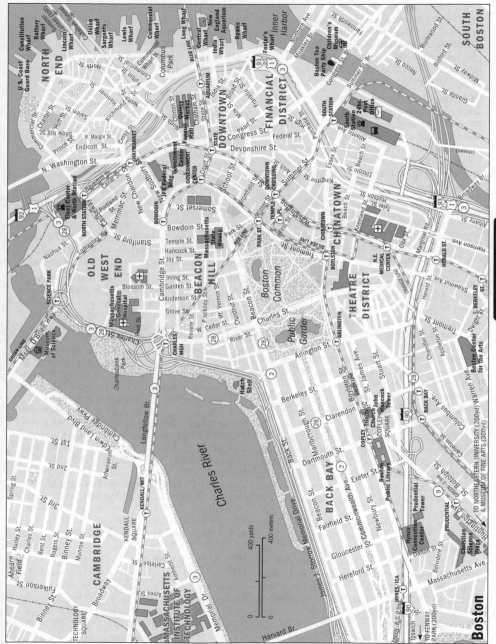

15min. ride.) Steps from the Common is the pedestrian mall at **Downtown Crossing.** The city's biggest budget shopping district is centered on legendary **Filene's Basement,** a chaotic feeding frenzy for bargain hunters. *(426 Washington St. T: Downtown Crossing. ☎617-542-2011; www.filenesbasement.com. Open M-F 9:30am-8pm, Sa 9am-8pm, Su 11am-7pm.)*

BEACON HILL. Looming over the Common is aristocratic Beacon Hill, an exclusive residential neighborhood. Antique shops, pricey cafes, and ritzy boutiques line charming **Charles St.,** the neighborhood's main artery. For generations, the Hill was home to Boston's intellectual, political, and social elite, christened the "Boston Brahmins." For a taste of Brahmin life, visit the **Nichols House,** preserved as it was in the 19th century. *(55 Mt. Vernon St., off Charles St. T: Charles/ MGH. ☎617-227-6993. Open May-Oct. Tu-Sa noon-5pm; Nov.-Apr. Th-Sa noon-5pm. $5, under 12 free. Entrance by tour only.)* Boston was the first city in the US to outlaw slavery, and many African-Americans moved to the Beacon Hill area after the Civil War. The **Black Heritage Trail** is a free 2hr. (1½ mi.) walking tour through Beacon Hill sights important during Boston's abolitionist era. It begins at the foot of Beacon Hill, near the Shaw Memorial, and ends at the **Museum of Afro-American History.** *(46 Joy St. ☎617-725-0022; www.afroammuseum.org. Museum open June-Aug. daily 10am-4pm; Sept.-May M-Sa 10am-4pm. Heritage Trail tours June-Aug. daily 10am, noon, 2pm; Sept.-May by appointment. Both free.)* Also at the foot of the hill is the **Bull & Finch Pub,** 84 Beacon St., the inspiration for the bar in *Cheers.*

WATERFRONT. The Waterfront district refers to the wharves along Boston Harbor from South Station to the North End. The excellent ⧫**New England Aquarium** features cavorting penguins, an animal infirmary, and briny beasts in a four-story tank. *(On Central Wharf at T: Aquarium. ☎617-973-5200; www.neaq.org. Open July-Aug. M-Tu and F 9am-6pm, W-Th 9am-8pm, Sa-Su 9am-7pm; Sept.-June M-F 9am-5pm, Sa-Su 9am-6pm. $16, students and seniors $14, ages 3-11 $9, under 3 free.)* The Long Wharf, north of Central Wharf, is **Boston Harbor Cruises'** departure point for sightseeing cruises and whale-watching. *(☎617-227-4321. Open late May to Sept. Cruises 45min.-90min.; 3 per day; $17, students and seniors $15, under 12 $12. Whale-watches 3hr., $29/$26/$20. Reservations recommended.)*

COPLEY SQUARE. Named for painter John Singleton Copley, Copley Sq. is popular with both lunching businessmen and busy Newbury St. tourists. The square is dominated by H.H. Richardson's Romanesque **Trinity Church,** reflected in the 14 acres of glass used in I.M. Pei's stunning **John Hancock Tower.** *(T: Copley. Church ☎617-536-0944. Open daily 8am-6pm. $4.)* Facing the church, the dramatic ⧫**Boston Public Library** is a museum in disguise; don't miss John Singer Sargent's recently restored *Triumph of Religion* murals. Of the library's seven million books, 128 are copies of *Make Way for Ducklings.* *(☎617-536-5400; www.bpl.org. Open M-Th 9am-9pm, F-Sa 9am-5pm. Free 1hr. tours M 2:30pm, Tu and Th 6pm, F-Sa 11am.)* The 50th floor of the **Prudential Center** mall next door to Copley Sq. is home to the **Prudential Skywalk,** which offers a 360° view from 700 ft. *(T: Prudential. ☎617-859-0648. Skywalk open daily 10am-10pm. $7, seniors and under 10 $4.)* One block north of Copley, fashionable **Newbury St.** is where Boston's trendiest strut their stuff and empty their wallets.

CAMBRIDGE. Separated from Boston by only a small river, Cambridge (pop. 100,000) is often called Boston's "Left Bank" for its liberal politics and bohemian flair. **Harvard Sq.** is, of course, named after **Harvard University.** Student-led tours are the best way to tour the university's dignified red-brick-and-ivy campus and learn about its history and museums. *(Holyoke Ctr. Arcade across Dunster St. T: Harvard Sq. ☎617-495-1573; www.harvard.edu. Tours Sept. to mid-May M-F 10am and 2pm, Sa 2pm; June to mid-Aug. M-Sa 10, 11:15am, 2, 3:15pm.)* Kendall Sq. is home to the **Massachusetts Institute of Technology (MIT),** the world's leading institution dedicated to the study of science. *(Free campus tours begin at the MIT Info Center, 77 Mass. Ave., in Lobby 7. T: Kendall Sq. ☎617-253-1000; www.mit.edu. Tours M-F 10am and 2pm.)* The ⧫**MIT Museum** features cutting-edge technological wonders in dazzling multimedia exhibitions. *(265 Mass. Ave. ☎617-253-4444. Open Tu-F 10am-5pm, Sa-Su noon-5pm. $5; students, seniors, and ages 5-18 $2.)*

🏛 MUSEUMS

If you're planning a museum binge, consider a **CityPass** (www.citypass.com), which covers the JFK Library, MFA, the Museum of Science, Harvard's Museum of Natural History, the Aquarium (see p. 68), and the Prudential Center Skywalk (see p. 68). Passes, available at museums or online, are valid for nine days. ($37, ages 3-17 $26.)

■ **Museum of Fine Arts,** 465 Huntington Ave. (☎617-267-9300; www.mfa.org), in Fenway. T: Museum. The exhaustive MFA showcases artwork from samurai armor to contemporary American art to medieval instruments. The ancient Egyptian and Nubian galleries, Impressionist paintings (the largest collection outside France), and the colonial portrait gallery (includes the painting of George Washington found on the $1 bill) are highlights. Open M-Tu 10am-4:45pm, W-F 10am-9:45pm (Th-F only West Wing open after 5pm), Sa-Su 10am-5:45pm. $15, students and seniors $13, ages 7-17 M-F $6.50. M-Tu after 3pm free, W after 4pm and all day Sa-Su free, Th-F after 5pm $2 off.

■ **Museum of Science,** Science Park (☎617-723-2500; www.mos.org). T: Science Park. Educates and entertains children of all ages with countless cool interactive exhibits. A 5-story OMNI Theater and trippy laser shows are at the Hayden Planetarium. Open July-Aug. M-Th 9am-7pm, F 9am-9pm, Sept.-June M-Th and Sa-Su 9am-5pm, F 9am-9pm. $14, seniors $12, ages 3-11 $11. IMAX or laser show tickets $8.50/$7.50/$6.50.

Isabella Stewart Gardner Museum, 280 Fenway (☎617-566-1401; www.gardnermuseum.org), in Fenway. T: Museum. This astounding private collection remains exactly as eccentric Mrs. Gardner arranged it over a century ago—empty frames even remain where stolen paintings once hung. The Venetian-style *palazzo* architecture draws as much attention as the Old Masters, and the courtyard alone is worth the admission price. Highlights include Titian's *Europa,* the most important Italian Renaissance work in North America. Open Su and Tu-Sa 11am-5pm. Free tours Tu-F 2:30pm. M-F $10, Sa-Su $11; students $5; under 18 and those named "Isabella" free with ID.

🎵 ENTERTAINMENT

The best publications for entertainment listings are the weekly *Boston Phoenix* (free from streetside boxes) and the *Boston Globe* Thursday Calendar section ($0.50). In addition to selling tickets to most major theater shows, **Bostix** sells half-price, day-of-show tickets for select shows from booths at Faneuil Hall and Copley Sq. (☎617-723-5181; www.artsboston.org. Tickets daily 11am. Cash only.) The **Charles Playhouse,** 74 Warrenton St., is home to the performance art of Blue Man Group. (☎617-426-6912. $43-53.) Boston's heart beats at storied **Fenway Park**, where diehard fans cheer on their 2004 World Series Champion Red Sox. The nation's oldest, smallest, and most expensive baseball park, Fenway is home to the Green Monster (the left field wall). (Ticket Office, 4 Yawkey Way, T: Kenmore. ☎617-482-4769. $12-70.) If you're a basketball or hockey fan, head to the **Fleet Center,** 50 Causeway St., T: North Station, which hosts basketball's **Celtics** and hockey's **Bruins.** (☎617-624-1750. Box office open in summer M-F 10am-5pm; in season daily 10am-7pm. Celtics $10-140. Bruins $19-99.)

TOP 10

TAKE ME OUT TO THE BALLGAME

Tiny Fenway Park sells out almost every night, and tickets—the most expensive in baseball—are illegally scalped at up to a 500% markup (though after games start, prices plummet). But fear not: there *are* options for snagging choice seats without parting with a first-born. On game days, the box office sells obstructed-view and standing-room tickets beginning at 9am. (Line up early, especially for Sox-Yankees games.) Obstructed-view seats in the infield are excellent, while standing-room seats offer tremendous views of the field. Risktakers can wait until a few hours before a game, hoping the team will release the seats held for players' families.

Seat quality varies widely. Avoid sections 1-7, unless you enjoy craning your neck. The best "cheap" seats are sections 32-36 (32-33 are down the left-field line in the outfield, close enough to touch the famed Green Monster). Sections 34-36 have perfect sightlines for watching pitches, but some fans emerge lobster-red from the direct sun on their seats.

■ FOOD

Trendy bistros, fusion restaurants, and a globe-trotting array of ethnic eateries have taken their place alongside the long-standing "chowda" shacks, soul-food joints, and welcoming pubs.

DOWNTOWN

The best and most affordable options downtown are the sandwich shops found on almost every corner and the diverse food court inside **Quincy Market** (p. 66). Downtown is also near the fresh seafood shops lining Boston's Waterfront district.

Durgin Park, Quincy Market (☎617-227-2038). T: Government Ctr. Boston's most touristed restaurant has served old New England dishes like fried seafood, Yankee pot roast, and Indian pudding since 1827. Meat entrees $9-13. Open Su-Th 11:30am-midnight, F-Sa 11:30am-1am.

No Name, 15½ Fish Pier (☎617-338-7539). This Waterfront eatery is one of Boston's best, cheapest seafood spots, serving no-frills dishes with fish fresh off the boat. Entrees $7-20. Open M-Sa 11am-10pm, Su 11am-9pm. Cash only.

Legal Sea Foods, 255 State St. (☎617-227-3115), opposite the New England Aquarium. T: Aquarium. Now a small chain, Legal Sea Foods remains Boston's finest seafood restaurant. High-quality cuisine (raw bar $8-9; entrees $18-30) includes the best clam chowder ($3.75-4.50) in the city. Open M-Th 11am-10pm, F-Sa 11am-11pm, Su noon-10pm.

NORTH END

Boston's Italian-American enclave is the place to go for authentic Italian fare, with over 100 restaurants packed into 1 sq. mi. Quality doesn't vary drastically from place to place, but price does. Most establishments line **Hanover St.,** accessible from T: Haymarket. After dinner, try **Mike's Pastry,** 300 Hanover St., or **Modern Pastry,** 257 Hanover St.

Trattoria Il Panino, 11 Parmenter St. (☎617-720-1336), at Hanover St. A romantic North End *trattoria* with gigantic portions of classic fare. Don't miss the *gnocchi alla sorrentina*, potato dumplings garnished with tomato, basil, and mozzarella. *Antipasti* $11-13. Pastas $10-15. Chicken dishes $16-17. Open Su-Th 11am-11pm, F-Sa 11am-midnight. Il Panino also runs the cheaper lunch counter **Il Panino Express,** at 264 Hanover St. Subs and salads $5-8. Open daily 11am-11pm. Cash only.

L'Osteria, 104 Salem St. (☎617-723-7847). Turn left off Hanover St. onto Parmenter St., then right onto Salem St. Serves all the robust Italian favorites found on Hanover St. at lower prices. Pastas $9-15. Chicken dishes $15-16. Open daily 11am-11pm.

Pizzeria Regina, 11½ Thacher St. (☎617-227-0765). Turn left off Hanover St. onto Prince St., then left again onto Thacher St. Since 1926, the North End's best pizza has come gooey, greasy, and always piping hot. Worth the wait. Open M-Th 11am-11:30pm, F-Sa 11am-midnight, Su noon-11pm. Cash only.

CHINATOWN

Chinatown is *the* place for filling and cheap Asian food (not just Chinese) anytime. Stuck between the skyscrapers of the Financial District (take T: Chinatown), the neighborhood is slightly grimy and run-down, but the prices are unbeatable and most places stay open until 3-4am.

Shabu-Zen, 16 Tyler St. (☎617-292-8828), off Beach St. Spartan Shabu-Zen is named for its signature do-it-yourself dish, *shabu-shabu*. Waitresses offer thinly sliced meats and vegetables that you cook in pots of boiling water. 2-person combo plates $10-15. A la carte $5-10. Open Su-W 11:30am-11pm, Th-Sa 11:30am-midnight.

Jumbo Seafood Restaurant, 5-7-9 Hudson St. (☎617-542-2823). Greet your dinner in the tanks by the entrance at the best of Chinatown's Hong Kong-style seafood spots, with huge plates, a light touch, and a glowing velvet mural on the wall. Dinner entrees $10-15. Lunch specials $9-10. Open daily 11am-midnight.

Ginza, 16 Hudson St. (☎617-338-2261). Walk against traffic down Washington St., turn left at the parking lot onto Beach St., head several blocks down to Hudson St., and turn right. Ginza's sushi doesn't come cheap ($3-10), but their sake bombs will ease the pain your bill inflicts. Open M-F 11:30am-2:30pm and 5pm-2am, Sa 11:30am-4pm and 5pm-4am, Su 5pm-2am.

BACK BAY

The diverse eateries of the Back Bay line elegant **Newbury St.**

Kashmir, 279 Newbury St. (☎617-536-1695), at Gloucester St. T: Hynes/ICA. The best Indian food in Boston. Marble floors, traditional carpets, and plush red seats create a setting as light and exotic as the subtle curries ($12-15) and extensive selection of vegetarian dishes. All-you-can-eat buffet M-F 11:30am-3pm ($9), Sa-Su noon-3pm ($12). Open daily 11:30am-11pm.

Parish Café, 361 Boylston St. (☎617-247-4777), near T: Arlington. This lively bar is no secret among locals who crowd tables and barstools to order sandwiches ($9-17) designed by the city's hottest chefs. Open M-Sa 11:30am-1am, Su noon-1am. Bar open until 2am.

SOUTH END

Prices here continue to rise as more Bostonians flock to the hip South End, but the waits and hefty bills are worth it; the restaurants creatively meld flavors and techniques from around the world with amazing results.

Addis Red Sea, 544 Tremont St. (☎617-426-8727), near T: Back Bay. Spicy, curry- and veggie-heavy Ethiopian cuisine in a sophisticated (but casual) setting is not to be missed. Entrees are served utensil-free on traditional *mesob* tables, to be scooped up with spongy *injera* bread. Entrees $9-15. Open M-F 5-11pm, Sa-Su noon-11pm.

The Dish, 253 Shawmut Ave. (☎617-426-7866), at Milford St., near T: Back Bay. Attains the culinary and atmospheric perfection all casual neighborhood eateries aspire to. Upscale decor meets a low-key local clientele and a menu of eclectic comfort food, like Cajun-style meatloaf and cod with lime ginger marmalade. Entrees $11-17. Open daily 5pm-midnight.

Flour, 1595 Washington St. (☎617-267-4300), at Rutland St. Near T: Prudential, Mass. Ave., or Back Bay. Chef/owner Joanne Chang bakes the most mouth-watering cakes, cookies, and pastries ($1-3) in the city, all nothing short of transcendent. Sandwiches $6-7. Open M-F 7am-7pm, Sa 8am-6pm, Su 9am-3pm.

Laurel, 142 Berkeley St. (☎617-424-6711), on the corner of Columbus St. from T: Back Bay. Culinary artistry ($10-20) includes duck confit with sweet potatoes or shrimp and prosciutto ravioli. Open M-Th 11:30am-2:30pm and 5:30-10pm, F 11:30am-2:30pm and 5:30-10pm, Sa 5:30-10pm, Su 11am-2:30pm.

ACCOMMODATIONS

Finding cheap accommodations in Boston is hard. Rates and bookings are highest in summer and during college-crunch times in September, late May, and early June. Reservation services promise to find discounted rooms, even during sold-out periods. Try **Boston Reservations** (☎617-332-4199), **Central Reservation Service** (☎800-332-3026; www.bostonhotels.net), or **Citywide Reservation Services** (☎617-267-7424; www.cityres.com). All rooms in Boston come with a **12.45% room tax.**

HI—Boston Fenway (HI), 575 Commonwealth Ave. (☎617-267-8599), in Fenway. T: Kenmore, lets out on Comm. Ave. The best hostel in Boston, in a former luxury hotel, with 155 bright, airy 3-bed dorm rooms and a penthouse common room with a 360° view of Boston. Private bath and A/C. Same freebies as HI—Boston (below). Check-out 11am. Open June-Aug. Dorms $35, nonmembers $38; private rooms $87/$90.

Oasis Guest House, 22 Edgerly Rd. (☎617-267-2262; www.oasisgh.com), at Stoneholm St., in Back Bay. From T: Hynes/ICA, exit onto Mass. Ave., walking with Virgin Megastore on your left, cross Boylston St., and turn right onto Haviland St.; the next left is Edgerly Rd. This rambling 30-room guesthouse is true to its name, a calm respite from the city. Continental breakfast daily 8-11am. Reservations recommended. May to mid-Nov. Singles $59; doubles with shared bath $69, with bath $89. Mid-Nov. to Apr. $80/$90/$130.

Newbury Guest House, 261 Newbury St. (☎617-437-7666 or 800-437-7668; www.newburyguesthouse.com), between Gloucester and Fairfield St. 32 immaculately clean, bright, and tastefully decorated rooms with private bath and digital cable. Reception 24hr. Check-in 3pm. Check-out noon. Doubles Apr.-Oct. $125-170; Nov.-Mar. $99-125.

HI—Boston (HI), 12 Hemenway St. (☎617-536-1027; www.bostonhostel.org), in Back Bay. From T: Hynes/ICA, walk down Massachusetts Ave., turn right on Boylston St., then left onto Hemenway St. Central location, spotless bathrooms, quiet dorms, and complimentary entrance to museums and dance clubs. Laundry. Free lockers, linen, and kitchen use. Check-in noon. Check-out 11am. Dorms $32-35, nonmembers $35-38.

YMCA of Greater Boston, 316 Huntington Ave. (☎617-927-8040). T: Symphony. Access to world-class athletic facilities and location near Boston's cultural attractions make the surprisingly hefty price tag more palatable. 18+. Breakfast included. Key deposit $5. Reception 24hr. Check-out 11am. Singles $46, with bath $66; doubles $66; quads $96.

NIGHTLIFE

Boston bars and clubs are notoriously strict about age requirements (usually 21+), so bring backup ID. Puritanical zoning laws require that all nightlife shuts down by 2am. The T stops running at

1am, though, so bring extra cash for the taxi ride home, or catch the "Night Owl" bus service, which runs until 2:30am Fridays and Saturdays.

DANCE CLUBS

Most of the city's clubs are located on or near Kenmore Sq.'s **Lansdowne St.**

Avalon, 15 Lansdowne St. (☎617-262-2424). The flashy, trashy grand dame of Boston's club scene, and the closest Puritan Boston gets to Ibiza—that is, not very. World-class DJs, gender-bending cage dancers, and throngs of students pack the giant dance floor. Su gay night. Th-F 19+, Sa-Su 21+. Cover $10-15. Open Th-Su 10pm-2am.

Pravda 116, 116 Boylston St. (☎617-482-7799), in the Theater District. T: Boylston. The caviar, red decor, long lines, and 116 brands of vodka may recall Mother Russia, but capitalism reigns supreme at Pravda, the favored haunt of Boston's yuppified twenty-somethings. 21+. Cover W $15, F-Sa $10. Bars open W-Sa 5pm-2am. Club open W and F-Sa 10pm-2am.

Sophia's, 1270 Boylston St. (☎617-351-7001). From T: Kenmore, walk down Brookline Ave., turn left onto Yawkey Way, then right onto Boylston St. Far from Lansdowne St. in distance and style, Sophia's is a fiery Latin dance club with 4 floors of salsa and merengue. Trendy, international crowd. 21+. Cover $10 after 9:30pm. Open Tu-Sa 6pm-2am.

Axis, 13 Lansdowne St. (☎617-262-2437). The smaller, less popular little sister of Avalon has a similar techno beat and sweaty college crowd. Drag shows M night, hosted by 6 ft. drag diva Mizery. If the dance floor's too hot and heavy, chill upstairs in the chic lounge **ID.** 19+. Cover $7-20. Open M and Th-Sa 10pm-2am.

BARS AND PUBS

Boston's large student population means the city is filled with great bars and pubs. Most tourists stick to the faux Irish pubs around downtown, while the Theater District is the premier afterdark destination of the city's international clique.

Bukowski's Tavern, 50 Dalton St. (☎617-437-9999), in Back Bay off Boylston St. Named for boozer poet Charles Bukowski, the casual feel and 99+ bottles of beer on the wall are a respite from trendy Boylston St.. Pints from $3. Open M-Sa 11:30am-2am, Su noon-2am. Cash only.

Mantra/OmBar, 52 Temple Pl. (☎617-542-8111), downtown. T: Temple Pl. Seductive. Scandalous. Incomprehensible. And that's just the bathroom, which has 1-way mirrored stalls and ice cubes in the urinals.

A French-Indian fusion restaurant by day, Mantra becomes OmBar by night, with a thumping bar downstairs and a smoke-free "hookah den" upstairs. Cocktails $9. Open M-Sa 5:30pm-2am.

Delux Café, 100 Chandler St. (☎617-338-5258), at Clarendon St. 1 block south of T: Back Bay, in the South End. Dine or drink among kooky Elvis shrines, lit-up Christmas trees, and continuously looped cartoons. Cocktails $3.50-5. Open M-Sa 5pm-1am. Kitchen closes 11:30pm. Cash only.

Purple Shamrock, 1 Union St. (☎617-227-2060), by Quincy Market. This faux Irish pub hosts popular Karaoke night Tu 9pm. 21+ after 9pm. Cover Th-Sa $5. Open daily until 2am.

GLBT NIGHTLIFE

For listings of GLBT nightlife, pick up a free copy of the South End-based *Bay Windows*, a gay weekly available everywhere, or check the free *Boston Phoenix* and *Improper Bostonian*. The **South End's** bars and late-night restaurants, accessible from T: Back Bay, are all gay-friendly (sorry ladies, these are mostly for the boys). The sports bar **Fritz**, 26 Chandler St. (☎617-482-4428), and divey **The Eagle**, 520 Tremont St. (☎617-542-4494), are exclusively for gay men. Boston's other gay bar/clubs are the Theater District's **Vapor/Chaps,** 100 Warrenton St. (☎617-422-0862); **Jacque's,** 77-79 Broadway (☎617-426-8902); and **Europa/Buzz,** 51 Stuart St. (☎617-482-3939), which also has evenings for women. In Fenway is the all-encompassing **Ramrod,** 1254 Boylston St. (☎617-266-2986), a Leather & Levis spot that spawned a non-fetish dance club known as **Machine.** Lesbians flock to **Midway Café,** 3496 Washington St. (☎617-524-9038), south of T: Green St.

▶ LEAVING BOSTON

From Back Bay, Take Boylston St. east, turn right on Arlington, and take the first left onto **Stuart St.,** which becomes **Kneeland St.** and leads to the onramp for **Rte. 3 South.**

PLYMOUTH

Despite what textbooks say, the Pilgrims' first step onto the New World was *not* at Plymouth. They stopped first at Provincetown (see p. 76), then promptly left because the soil was inadequate. **Plymouth Rock** is a small stone that has been identified—by a 90-year-old man repeating what his father told him—as the rock on which the Pilgrims disembarked the second time. During the American Revolution it was moved near the courthouse as a symbol of defiance, and broken in the process. In 1880, the two halves were reunited at the foot of North St., and the date 1620 was carved in the rock to commemorate the pilgrims' landing. In 1920, it gained the Greek-style portico that now protects it from the elements.

(VITAL STATS)

Population: 52,000

Visitor Info: Waterfront Tourist Information Center, (☎508-747-7525 or 800-872-1620), on Water St., between Park and Memorial. Tickets for harbor tours and sights like the Plimoth Plantation and Mayflower II. Open daily Apr.-May and Sept.-Nov. 9am-5pm; June 9am-6pm; July-Aug. 9am-9pm. **Plymouth Visitors Center,** 170 Water St. (☎508-747-7525 or 800-872-1620). Open daily Apr.-May and Sept.-Nov. 9am-5pm; June 9am-6pm; July-Aug. 9am-9pm.

Internet Access: Plymouth Public Library, 132 South St. (☎508-830-4250; www.plymouthpubliclibrary.org). Open M-W 10am-9pm, Th 10am-6pm, F-Sa 10am-5:30pm.

Post Office: 6 Main St. Ext. (☎508-746-8175). Open M-F 8:30am-5pm, Sa 8:30am-noon. **Postal Code:** 02360.

⬛ **SIGHTS.** The town is not lacking in ways to celebrate and explore its colonial history. The **Pilgrim Hall Museum,** 75 Court St. contains personal effects, tools, and clothing of the pilgrims. (☎508-746-1620; www.pilgrimhall.org. $6, seniors $5, ages 5-17 $3. $1 AAA discount.) The **1749 Court House,** in Town Sq., has a museum on the first floor and a real courtroom on the second. The court house was the Plymouth court for over 70 years and was home to young attorneys like John Adams and James Otis. (☎508-830-4075. Open late June to early Oct. Free.) There, visitors can pick up brochures for a "Walk Through History," walking tour around the historic Town Sq. The only wax museum dedicated to America's colonial heritage, the **Plymouth National Wax Museum,** 16 Carver St., overlooks Plymouth Rock and features life-size recreations of key moments in colonial history like the signing of the Mayflower compact and the first Thanksgiving. Voice-overs explain the history, while light and

sound effects dramatize the scene. (☎508-746-6468. Open daily July-Aug. 9am-9pm; June and Sept.-Oct. 9am-7pm.)

Continuing along Rte. 3 headed southeast, the historical theme park ⬛**Plimoth Plantation** recreates the Pilgrims' early settlement. In the **Pilgrim Village,** costumed actors play the roles of villagers carrying out their daily tasks, while **Hobbamock's Homesite** represents a Native American village of the same period. (☎508-746-1622. Open Apr.-Nov. daily 9am-5pm. $20, ages 6-12 $12. $2 AAA discount.) Docked off Water St., the **Mayflower II** is a 1950s scale replica of the Pilgrims' vessel, staffed by actors to recapture the atmosphere of the original ship. (Open Apr.-Nov. daily 9am-5pm. $8, ages 6-12 $6. Admission to both sights $22, students $20, ages 6-12 $14. $3 AAA discount.)

◢ APPROACHING CAPE COD
From Plymouth, follow **Rte. 3 South** to the Sagamore Bridge, which crosses the Cape Cod Canal. In the rotary immediately after the bridge, take the second exit—**U.S. 6 East (Mid-Cape Highway).**

CAPE COD

One of New England's premier vacation destinations, this sandy spit draws tourists with its charming small towns and diverse, sun-drenched landscapes—from cranberry bogs and sandy beaches to freshwater ponds and desert-like dunes. Though parts of the Cape are known as a playground of the rich and famous, it can be a great option for budget travelers thanks to free activities like sunbathing and hiking, and a decent hostel and budget B&B system.

▣ GETTING AROUND

Stretching into the Atlantic Ocean south of Boston, Cape Cod resembles a bent arm, with **Falmouth** and **Woods Hole** at its armpit, **Hyannis** at its biceps, **Chatham** at its elbow, the **National Seashore** tattooed on its forearm, and **Provincetown** at its clenched fist. **Upper Cape** refers to the developed area closer to the mainland. Proceeding east from the mainland and curving up along the Cape, you travel **Down Cape** through **Mid-Cape,** finally hitting the **Lower Cape** and the National Seashore.

Running down the center of the Cape, **U.S. 6** is its major highway for those on the move. **U.S. 6a** and **Rte. 28** are more scenic, passing beaches and quaint towns as they meander along the Cape's inner and outer shores, respectively. All three are jammed with vacationers in the summer, especially on Friday and Sunday afternoons.

◤ APPROACHING HYANNIS
From **U.S. 6**, take Exit 6, turning right on **Iyannough Rd. (Rte. 132)**. At the rotary, take the second exit to **Barnstable Rd.**, and follow it to Hyannis center.

HYANNIS

Hyannis is not the Cape Cod most people expect. Though JFK spent his summers in nearby Hyannisport, Hyannis proper is little more than a transportation hub (ferries to Nantucket depart from here) with a depressing Main St. and tacky mall. While it recognizes its place in Kennedy history, it hardly indulges in its past, so don't expect many a quirky museum or historically-oriented shop. **Veterans Park** includes the **Korean War Veterans Memorial** and the **John Fitzgerald Kennedy Memorial.** (Park open 9am-9pm.) Drivers can park and enter for free and from the parking lot can visit **Veteran's Beach** and **Kalmus Beach.** The **John F. Kennedy Museum,** 397 Main St., displays memorabilia and pictures from the former president's life, from his childhood in Massachusetts to his presidency. (Located in Barnstable's Old Town Hall. ☎508-775-3075. Open M-Sa 9am-5pm, Su and holidays noon-5pm. $5, ages 10-16

$2.50.) At Hyannis Harbor, visitors can ride the seven seas on the *Sea Gypsy* through **Pirate Adventures.** The trips on a pirate boat of dubious historical accuracy require 16 passengers, but provide a unique—if bizarre—experience. Face-painting is included. (☎508-430-0202; www.pirateadventurescapecod.com. Reservations required.) **Hy-Line Cruises** offers ferries to Nantucket ($59, ages 5-12 $41) and Martha's Vineyard ($28, ages 5-12 $14), as well as cruises down the Cape Cod Canal (☎508-778-2600 or 800-492-8082. $10-15, ages 5-12 $5-8.)

Hyannis has a lot of pricier restaurant options along Main St., but not many serve the quality or quantity their prices seem to promise. The **Box Lunch,** 357 Main St., offers creative sandwiches and "rollwiches" like the "John Alden" (turkey, cranberry sauce, lettuce, mayonnaise, tomatoes and onions) and a wide variety of vegetarian options all for under $6. Their tasty guacamole sandwich includes avocado, melted swiss, provolone, American, tomatoes, onions and mayonnaise. (☎508-790-5855. Open M-F 10am-4pm, Sa 10am-3pm.) Hyannis is full of cookie-cutter motels and inns. The **Hyannis Travel Inn,** 18 North St., lies across the street from the public parking lot. It has two pools (one indoor, one outdoor) and each room comes with an iron and mini-fridge. (☎508-775-8200. Continental breakfast included. Rooms $70-100). The **Harbor House Inn,** 119 Ocean St., sits across from the marina. The rooms are all efficiencies with kitchenettes. (☎508-771-1880; www.harborhouseinn.net. Rooms Su-Th $189, F-Sa $124).

THE LOCAL STORY

THERE IS A LIGHT THAT NEVER GOES OUT

A tour of Cape Cod's lighthouses is a way to appreciate the area and its seafaring past. The **Chatham Light,** Main St. in Chatham, sits a few miles south of Shore Rd. The light isn't open to the public, but the lookout area provides a gorgeous view of the "Chatham Break," sandbar. A cast iron and brick tower built in 1877, **Nauset Light** was moved from Chatham in 1923. In 1996 it was moved again, this time to rescue it from the erosion of a 60 ft. cliff. (Follow Rte. 6 north to Eastham, take a right onto Nauset Rd., follow Doane Rd. as it splits off, and go left onto scenic Ocean View Dr.) Heading west along Cable Rd. leads to the **Three Sisters,** three wooden towers originally built in 1892. Only the center tower, "The Beacon," survived, but today all three have been restored. Follow Rte. 6 north to Truro to see the **Highland Light.** The grounds include the Highland House Museum, documenting the light's history. (Lighthouse tours 10am-5:30pm. $3, under 12 free.) At the tip of the Cape, Provincetown has several offerings for the lighthouse-lover. Visitors can't enter the **West End Light,** but they can explore the grounds. and nearby **Long Point Light.** Visitors can reach the **Race Point Light** by a 45min. hike from Race Point Beach.

LEAVING HYANNIS
Follow **Main St. (Rte. 28)** east out of Hyannis.

THE ROAD TO CHATHAM

On its way to Chatham, Rte. 28 provides a glimpse of the quintessential Mid-Cape, crossing shallow tidal rivers and wide salt marshes while passing countless cottages, ice-cream shops, clam shacks, and mini golf courses. As it enters Harwichport, Rte. 28 passes **Trampoline Center,** 296 Rte. 28, where you can stretch your legs bouncing on one of the outdoor trampolines set into the ground. (☎508-432-8717. Open in summer daily 9am-11pm. $4.50 per 10min.) If you haven't done enough driving yet, take the wheel at **Bud's Go Karts,** 9 Sisson Rd., on the left just a few doors down. (☎508-432-4964. Open in summer daily 9am-11pm. $5.) Stop at Cape favorite **Bonatt's Bakery,** 537 Rte. 28, for one of their famous meltaway pastries. (☎ 508-432-7199. Open daily 6am-1:30pm.)

APPROACHING CHATHAM
Just outside Chatham, **Rte. 28** enters a rotary heading southeast as **Main St.** and exits it heading north as Old Harbor Rd. Stay straight on Main St. to head into Chatham Center.

CHATHAM

A quaint and lovely town at the 'bend' in Cape Cod, Chatham has a small-town feel while still providing plenty of sights and activities for visitors. The downtown stores offer shopping opportunities, while museums supply a taste of local history. Unlike many towns on the cape, Chatham doesn't feel like it was built specifically for tourists.

VITAL STATS

Population: 6600

Visitor Info: Chatham Chamber of Commerce Visitor Information Center (☎800-715-5567 or 508-945-5199; www.chathaminfo.com), at the intersection of Rte. 28 and 137 in South Chatham.

Internet Access: Eldredge Public Library, 564 Main St. (☎508-945-5170). Open M, W, F-Sa 10am-5pm; Tu and Th 1-9pm.

Post Office: 802 Main St. (☎508-945-6054). Open M-F 9am-4:30pm, Sa 9am-noon. **Postal Code:** 02633.

GETTING AROUND. Main St. is home to most of the shopping and restaurants. Heading left on **Shore Rd.** leads drivers to the ocean. Free public **parking** is easy to come by, including at the Chatham Light (30 min. max), by the Town Hall on Main St., and the Colonial Building Parking Lot just behind Main St. on Stage Harbor Rd.

SIGHTS. The **Old Grist Mill** is a small windmill built in the late 18th century to grind corn. Originally located on Mill Hill off of Stage Harbor, the mill was moved in 1956 to its current location on Shattuck Rd. (From the rotary, take Main St. from the rotary toward the water, take a right on Cross St., then a left on Shattuck. Open July-Labor Day M-F 10am-3pm.) The **Chatham Fish Pier,** on Shore Rd. north of the intersection with Main St., attracts many summer tourists. Visitors watch the fishing fleet bring in haddock, cod, lobster and halibut that they can purchase in local fish markets later that same day. They can also see the **Fisherman's Monument,** built to honor the town's fishing industry. The monument, called the Provider, is a little unusual: an abstraction of an upturned hand is supported by a structure of polls over a base of fish and shellfish in relief. Free parking is available in the upper lot; the lower lot is permit parking only. Run by the Chatham Historical Society, the 250-year-old **Old Atwood House Museum,** 347 Stage Harbor Rd., houses artifacts and pieces of art documenting over two centuries of life in Chatham. Featuring work by local artist Harold Brett, a worldwide seashell collection, and pieces from early trade and industry, the museum offers a truly unique perspective on the town. (☎508-945-2493. Open M-F 1-4pm, Sa 10:30am-12:30pm.) Built from 1818-1820 by the town postmaster for his bride-to-be, the **Josiah Mayo House,** 540 Main St., is maintained as an accurate representation of a home from that era. Furnished with period furniture and accessories, including toys, clothing, and a rope bed, the house offers a great opportunity to learn about early 19th-century life. (Open mid-June to Sept. Tu-Th 11am-4pm.)

The **Chatham Conservation Society,** 104 Crowell Rd., offers and info on several of Chatham's most popular hiking trails (☎508-945-4084. Open daily 2-5pm). **Honeysuckle Ln.** lies off of Stage Harbor Rd. and has several short trails that feature white cedar trees. A small bridge connects to other trails. At the corner of Old Queen Anne Rd. and Training Field Rd., a trail leads to **Bar-**

clay **Pond** before splitting off into several trails that explore a 30 acre area. By **Frost Fish Creek** along Rte. 28, in North Chatham, trails run along a small creek and nearby marshes.

⬛ FOOD. Chatham has some tasty, inexpensive options for hungry diners. The **Anytime Cafe,** 512 Main St., serves pizza and yummy seafood rolls for about $10 and sandwiches for less. (☎508-945-4080. Coffee and pastries available at 9am, full menu from 11:30am.) **Chatham Cookware,** 524 Main St., might sound like Martha Stewart's favorite store, but it's actually a cafe, with a bakery in the front and a soup and sandwich counter in back. The soup is excellent (particularly the Mediterranean eggplant) and the sandwiches are creative reincarnations of old favorites like the "hungry pilgrim" (smoked turkey, cranberry chutney, stuffing, lettuce, tomato, and mayonnaise on country white) for $7. (☎508-945-1250. Open daily 6:30am-6pm.) **Sandi's Diner,** 639 Main St., serves breakfast classics like pancakes and eggs all day and, according to one patron, "the best tuna sandwich in Massachusetts." (☎508-945-0631.)

CAPE COD NATIONAL SEASHORE

As early as 1825, the Cape had suffered so much erosion that the town of Truro required locals to plant beach grass and keep their cows off the dunes. These conservation efforts culminated in 1961, when President Kennedy and the National Park Service created the Cape Cod National Seashore. The seashore spans the Lower and Outer Cape from Provincetown south to Chatham, including six beaches: **Coast Guard** and **Nauset Light,** in Eastham; **Marconi,** in Wellfleet; **Head of the Meadow,** in Truro; and **Race Point** and **Herring Cove,** in Provincetown. Parking at the beaches is expensive. (In summer up to $10 per day.)

Among the best of the seashore's 11 self-guided nature trails are the **Great Island Trail** and the **Atlantic White Cedar Swamp Trail.** The **Great Island Trail,** in Wellfleet, traces an 8 mi. loop through pine forests and grassy marshes and has views of the bay and Provincetown. The **Atlantic White Cedar Swamp Trail,** a 1¼ mi. walk, starts at Marconi Station in south Wellfleet and passes swampy waters and towering trees. There are also three bike trails: **Nauset Trail** (1½ mi.), **Head of the Meadow Trail** (2 mi.), and **Province Lands Trail** (5 mi.). Park rangers at the **National Seashore's Salt Pond Visitors Center,**

at Salt Pond, off U.S. 6 in Eastham, provide maps, schedules for guided tours, and additional information about the park. (☎508-255-3421. Open daily July-Aug. 9am-5pm; Sept.-June 9am-4:30pm.)

Camping in the National Seashore is illegal. Eastham's **Mid-Cape Hostel (HI-AYH),** 75 Goody Hallet Dr., close to the bike path known as the **Cape Cod Rail Trail,** features communal bungalow living in a woodsy location. (From Chatham, follow U.S. 6, take the Rock Harbor Exit at the Orleans Ctr. rotary, turn left onto Bridge Rd., then left again onto Goody Hallet Dr. ☎508-255-2785 or 888-901-2085. Shared bathrooms, kitchen, and BBQ facilities. Bikes $14 per day. 7-day max. stay. Open late June to early Sept. Dorms $19, nonmembers $22.) **Truro Hostel (HI-AYH),** 111 N. Pamet Rd., in Truro, sits on a bluff overlooking the ocean, and offers a large kitchen, porch, and access to Ballston Beach all in a turn-of-the-century Coast Guard station. (From U.S. 6, take the Pamet Rd. exit, which becomes N. Pamet Rd. ☎508-349-3889 or 888-901-2086. Check-in 4-9pm. Check-out 7:30-10am. Curfew 10pm. Reception late June to early Sept. 8-10am and 4-10pm. Dorms $22, nonmembers $25.)

◤ APPROACHING PROVINCETOWN
Continue on **U.S. 6A,** which arrives in Provincetown parallel to **Commercial St.**

PROVINCETOWN

At first glance, Provincetown may seem like a typical Cape Cod village with a slight cosmopolitan twist. What sets it apart is its popularity as one of the premier gay and lesbian communities and vacation spots on the East Coast. The first landing site of the Pilgrims in 1620, Provincetown was a key fishing and whaling center in the 1800s, attracting a large Portuguese population. In the early 20th-century, the town's popularity soared with resident artists and writers like Norman Mailer, Tennessee Williams, and Edward Hopper. Provincetown's tradition of tolerance and open-mindedness soon began to attract the gay community, which now fills the town in summer. Though far from inexpensive, P-town has better options for dining and nightlife than much of Cape Cod.

▣ GETTING AROUND. Commercial St., P-town's main drag—home to art galleries, novelty shops, and trendy bars and eateries—runs along the harbor, centered on **MacMillian Wharf. Standish St.** divides the town into the East and West Ends.

(**VITAL STATS**)

Population: 3400

Visitor Info: Provincetown Chamber of Commerce, 307 Commercial St. (☎508-487-3424; www.ptownchamber.com), on MacMillian Wharf. Open June-Sept. daily 9am-7pm; reduced low-season hours. **Province Lands Visitors Center,** 220 Race Point Rd. (☎508-487-1256), off U.S. 6, at the north end of Cape Cod National Seashore. Open May-Oct. daily 9am-5pm.

Internet Access: Provincetown Public Library, 330 Commercial St. (☎508-487-7094; www.ptown-lib.com). Open M and F 10am-5pm, Tu and Th noon-8pm, W 10am-8pm, Sa 10am-2pm, Su 1pm-5pm.

Post Office: 219 Commercial St. (☎508-487-0368). Open M-F 8:30am-5pm, Sa 9am-noon. **Postal Code:** 02657.

🏳 📐 SIGHTS & OUTDOORS. The **Pilgrim Monument,** the tallest all-granite structure in the US at 253 ft., and the **Provincetown Museum,** on High Pole Hill just north of the center of town, commemorate the Pilgrims' first landing. Hike up to the top of the tower for stunning views of the Cape and the Atlantic. (☎508-487-1310. Open daily July-Aug. 9am-7pm; Apr.-June and Sept.-Nov. 9am-5pm. Last admission 45min. before closing. $7, seniors $5, ages 4-12 $3.50, under 4 free.) A large bas-relief **monument,** in the small park at Bradford and Ryder St. behind the town hall, depicts the signing of the Mayflower Compact on Nov. 11, 1620 in Provincetown Harbor.

Provincetown's miles of shoreline provide spectacular scenery and more than enough space to catch some sun. At **Race Point Beach,** waves roll in from the Atlantic, while **Herring Cove Beach,** at the west end of town, offers calm, protected waters. Directly across from Snail Rd. on U.S. 6, an unlikely path leads to a world of rolling **sand dunes;** look for shacks where writers such as Tennessee Williams, Norman Mailer, and John Dos Passos spent their days. At the west end of Commercial St., the 1¼ mi. **Breakwater Jetty** takes you away from the crowds to a secluded peninsula, where there are two working lighthouses and the remains of a Civil War fort.

Today, Provincetown seafarers have traded harpoons for cameras, but they still enjoy whale-hunting—**whale-watching cruises** rank among P-town's most popular attractions. Most companies guarantee sightings. (3hr. tour $18-20. Discount coupons at the Chamber of Commerce.) **Boston Harbor Cruises Whale Watch** (☎617-227-4321 or 877-733-9425), **Dolphin Fleet** (☎507-349-1900 or 800-826-9300), and **Portuguese Princess** (☎508-487-2651 or 800-422-3188) leave from MacMillian Wharf.

🍴 FOOD. Sit-down meals in Provincetown tend to be expensive. Fast-food joints line the Commercial St. extension (next to MacMillian Wharf) and the Aquarium Mall, farther west on Commercial St. Though the post office theme at the **Post Office Cafe,** 303 Commercial St., is somewhat inconsistently executed, the seafood, pasta, and sandwiches are consistently good. Their clambake special (1¼ lb. lobster and steamers at the daily market price) is the best deal in town. (☎508-487-3892. Entrees $7-20. Open daily 8am-midnight.) **Tofu A Go-Go,** 338 Commercial St., is a casual restaurant with deliciously fresh vegetarian, vegan, and macrobiotic options in hearty portions. Sit on the terrace or get the order to go. (☎508-487-6237. Entrees $5-8. Open June-Aug. daily 11am-9pm; call for low-season hours.) **Karoo Kafe,** 338 Commercial St., is a self-described "fast-food safari," serving up South African and Mediterranean favorites. (☎508-487-6630. Entrees $5-7. Open daily June-Aug. 11am-9pm; Mar.-May and Sept.-Nov. lunch hours only.) **Cafe Edwidge,** 333 Commercial St., serves meals in a candlelit dining room or sleek outdoor terrace, but a casual atmosphere. Though the dinner menu is delicious ($8-22), it's Edwidge's breakfast ($6-10) that draws crowds. (☎508-487-4020. Open late June to Aug. 8am-1pm and 6-10pm; mid-May to late June and Sept. to mid-Oct. Sa-Su 8am-1pm and 6-10pm.)

🏠 ACCOMMODATIONS. Provincetown teems with expensive places to rest your head. ⧫**Somerset House,** 378 Commercial St., is a fun 12-room guesthouse with a very social, sassy atmosphere—and with a motto like "Get Serviced," you'd expect nothing less. (☎508-487-0383 or 800-575-1850. Doubles June-Aug. $110-245; Sept.-May $75-177. Nov.-Apr. 50% off second day. 10% discount with *Let's Go.*) **Dexter's Inn,** 6 Conwell St., just off Bradford St., offers hotel-quality rooms for reasonable prices, plus a lush garden, large sun-deck, and free parking. (☎508-487-1911. Mid-June to mid-Sept. 4-night min. stay. Rooms mid-June to mid-Sept. $75-125; late May to mid-June and mid-Sept. to mid-Oct. $70-90; mid-Oct. to late May $50-65.) **Sunset Inn,** 142 Bradford St., was the inspira-

EAST COAST

tion for Edward Hopper's painting *Rooms for Tourists*. It's lost some of the painting's romance, but has simple, well-kept rooms, plus a "clothing optional" sundeck. (☎508-487-9810 or 800-965-1801. Rooms with shared bath June-Sept. $79-89; Apr.-May and Oct. $59-99.) The only real budget digs are **Outermost Hostel,** 28 Winslow St., with five cramped cottages. (☎508-487-4378. Key deposit $10. Linen $3. Reception 8-9:30am and 5:30-10pm. Open May to mid-Oct. Dorms $20.)

◪ **NIGHTLIFE.** Nightlife in P-town is almost totally GBLT-oriented. The establishments listed are all 21+. **Crown & Anchor,** 247 Commercial St., is a complex with a restaurant, two cabarets, the chill Wave video bar, and the techno-filled Paramount dance club, where the boys flock nightly. (☎508-487-1430. Beer $3-4. Mixed drinks $4-8. Sa "Summer Camp." Cover $10; no cover for Wave. Open summer daily 11pm-1am; low-season Sa-Su 11pm-1am.) Founded in 1798 by gay whalers, the **Atlantic House,** 6 Masonic Pl., just off Commercial St., still attracts its fair share of seamen. Choose from three different scenes: the low-key "little bar"; the Leather & Levis "macho bar"; and the "big room," where you too can be a dancing queen. (☎508-487-3821. Beer $3. Mixed drinks $4. Cover $10. Open daily 9pm-1am. "Little bar" 11am-1am.) The only major club for women is **Vixen,** 336 Commercial St., with a casual bar out front and a steamy dance floor in back. (☎508-487-6424. Cover $5. Bar open daily noon-1am. Club open daily 10pm-1am.) Don't be fooled by the traditional decor at **Governor Bradford,** 312 Commercial St.; the Governor hosts drag karaoke nightly 9:30pm. (☎508-487-2781. Open daily 11am-1am.)

◪ **APPROACHING NEWPORT**
From Provincetown, follow U.S. 6 West. Merge onto Rte. 25 toward I-495/I-195 and take I-195 South to Rte. 24 south and then take Rte 114 south. It becomes Rte 138 and heads into the center of town, changing names again to W. Main Rd. and Broadway.

Welcome To
RHODE ISLAND

NEWPORT

Money has always found its way into Newport. Once a center of trans-Atlantic shipping, the coastal town later became the summer home of America's elite seeking to leave the hustle and bustle of urban life behind. Today, Newport is still a high-priced tourist town, but its numerous arts festivals, extravagant mansions, and natural beauty are reason enough to visit.

⌐ VITAL STATS ⌐

Population: 26,000

Visitor Info: Newport County Convention and Visitors Bureau, 23 America's Cup Ave. (☎401-845-9123 or 800-976-5122; www.gonewport.com), 2 blocks from Thames St., in the Newport Gateway Center. Open Su-Th 9am-5pm, F-Sa 9am-6pm.

Internet Access: Public Library, 300 Spring St. (☎401-849-8720). Open M 11am-8pm, Tu-Th 9am-8pm, F-Sa 9am-6pm. Free.

Post Office: 320 Thames St. (☎401-847-2329.) Open M-F 8:30am-5pm, Sa 9am-1pm. **Postal Code:** 02840.

▛ GETTING AROUND

Running parallel to the shore, **Thames St.** is home to the tourist strip and the wharves, while **Bellevue Ave.** contains many of Newport's mansions. Consider **parking** at the **Newport Gateway Center** ($1 per day) and taking the Rhode Island Public Transit Authority bus. Otherwise, **parking** is an expensive affair. There's free parking along Bellevue Ave., but it's hard to come by. Try the lot at Thames and Touro St. (first 30min $2.25, each additional 30min. $1.75). There's also parking at the Bellevue Gardens Shopping Center on Bellevue near the Tennis Hall of Fame. (first 1hr. free, next 30min. $5, each additional 30min. $3).

◉ SIGHTS

MANSIONS. George Noble Jones built the first "summer cottage" in Newport in 1839, thereby kicking off the creation of an extravagant string of palatial summer estates. Most of the mansions lie south of downtown on Bellevue Ave. A self-guided walking tour or, in select mansions, a guided tour by the **Preservation Society of Newport**

provides a chance to ogle the decadence. *(424 Bellevue Ave. ☎ 401-847-1000; www.newportmansions.org. Open summer daily 9am-5pm; winter M-F 9am-5pm.)* The five largest mansions are **The Elms,** 367 Bellevue Ave., **Chateau-sur-Mer,** 474 Bellevue Ave., **Rosecliff,** 548 Bellevue Ave., the **Marble House,** 596 Bellevue Ave., and **The Breakers,** 44 Ochre Point Ave. Of these, the Marble House, containing over 500,000 cubic ft. of marble, silk walls, and gilded rooms is the must-see. The enormous, ornate Breakers and Elms estates, surrounded by striking formal gardens, are also well worth checking out. *(☎ 401-847-1000. Mansions open M-F 10am-5pm. $10-15 per house, ages 6-17 $4. Combination tickets for 2-5 houses $25-32/$7-11.)*

BEACHES. Newport's gorgeous beaches are frequently as crowded as the streets. The most popular sandy spot is **Easton's Beach,** or First Beach. *(On Memorial Blvd. ☎ 401-848-6491. Parking late May to early Sept. M-F 10am-9pm $8, before 10am $6; Sa-Su $10.)* Other beaches line Little Compton, Narragansett, and the shore between Watch Hill and Point Judith; for details, inquire at the Visitors Center. Starting at Easton's Beach or Bellevue Ave., the **Cliff Walk** traverses Newport's eastern shore as a 3½ mi. walking trail. The Cliff Walk can be accessed along a number of roads that intersect with Bellevue Ave. Most have 4hr. free parking from 6am to 9pm. Wildflowers and rocky shoreline mark one side while mansions border the other. *(www.cliffwalk.com.)*

FORT ADAMS STATE PARK. Fort Adams State Park offers picnic areas and fishing piers. *(South of town on Ocean Dr., 2½ mi. from the Visitors Center. ☎ 401-847-2400; www.fortadams.org. Park open dawn-dusk. Tours daily 10am-5pm. $6, ages 12-18 $5, ages 5-11 $3, under 5 free.)* The park also features the **Museum of Yachting** with an exhibit on America's Cup, chronicling the history of the trophy and the Single Handed Sailor's Hall of Fame. *(☎ 401-847-1018. Open Mid-May to Oct. 10am-5pm. $5, seniors and under 12 $4. AAA discount.)*

OCEAN DRIVE. In the Fort Adams area, Ocean Drive winds along the coast with startling views of the rocky coast and tide pools, as well as luxurious inns and mansions that line Newport's coast. There are plenty of places to pull over to walk along the coast or take a dip, but watch out—private owners do not appreciate trespassing pass-

ersby. Stop at **Brenton Point State Park** to take in the view, play on the open fields, or visit the **Portuguese Navigators Monument,** celebrating the Portuguese explorers who revolutionized modern exploration. The point was chosen because of its resemblance to Sagres, where Prince Henry founded a school of navigation in 1417.

OTHER SIGHTS. The oldest synagogue in the US, the restored **Touro Synagogue** dates back to 1763. *(85 Touro St. ☎ 401-847-4794; www.tourosynagogue.org. Tours July-Aug. Su-F 10am-5pm; call for low-season tour schedule. Last tour begins 30min. before closing. Free.)* The **Tennis Hall of Fame** contains a history of the sport, numerous displays on tennis champions like Arthur Ashe, Althea Bigson, and Billie Jean King, and a colorful exhibit on tennis ball canisters through history. *(194 Bellevue Ave. ☎ 401-849-3990 or 800-457-1144; www.tennisfame.com. Open daily 9:30am-5pm. $8, students and seniors $6, under 16 $4; families $20.)* The **Newport Historical Society** celebrates Newport's colonial history with the **Museum of Newport History** and the **Great Friends Meeting House.** All of their properties are open for 30min. tours from late June to August. *(Newport Historical Society: 82 Touro St. ☎ 401-846-0813. Open Tu-F 9:30am-4pm, Sa 9:30am-noon. Museum of Newport History: 127 Thames St. ☎ 401-841-8770. Open May-Oct. M and W-Sa 10am-5pm, Su 1-5pm; Nov.-Apr. Su 1-4pm, F-Sa 10am-4pm. Great Friends Meeting House: At Farewell and Marlborough St. Open late June to late Aug. Th-Sa 10am-5pm.)* Tours of **Colony House** depart every 30min. from 10am to 3:30pm, while tours of the meeting house and **Wanton-Lyman-Hazard House** depart at 10, 11am, 1, 2, and 3pm. *($4.)*

🎵 ENTERTAINMENT

From June through August, Newport gives lovers of classical, folk, jazz, and film each a festival to call their own. Festival tickets, as well as accommodations, fill up months ahead of time, so start looking early if you want to attend. The **Newport Music Festival** brings classical musicians from around the world for over 60 concerts during two weeks in July. *(☎ 401-846-1133, box office 401-849-0700; www.newportmusic.org. Box office open daily 10am-6pm. Tickets $35-40.)* Bring a picnic to Fort Adams State Park and partake in the festivities of one of the oldest and best-known jazz festivals in the world, the **Newport Jazz Festival.** Also at Fort Adams State Park, folk singers entertain at the **Newport Folk Festival,** where former acts include Bob Dylan, Joan Baez, and the Indigo Girls. (☎ 401-847-3700; www.festivalproductions.net. Tickets $50 per day, under 12 $5.) Over the course of six days in June, the **Newport International Film Festival** (☎ 401-846-9100; www.newportfilmfestival.com.) screens over 70 feature, documentary, and short films in the **Jane Pickens Theater** and the **Opera House Cinema.**

Pubs and clubs line Thames St., making it a happening area at night. Be sure to bring proper ID, as area clubs are very strict. If you are willing to brave the long lines, **The Rhino Bar and Grille's Mamba Room,** 337 Thames St., is the place to dance the night away. (☎ 401-846-0707. Cover $10-20. Open W-Sa 9pm-1am.) **One Pelham East,** 274 Thames St., showcases alternative bands. (☎ 401-324-6111. Live music nightly. Cover $3-20. Open daily 3pm-1am.) Don't be fooled by the name of **The Newport Blues Cafe,** 286 Thames St.; it plays a variety of live music ranging from blues to rock to reggae. (☎ 401-841-5510. Live music after 9:30pm. Cover up to $15. Open daily 6pm-1am. Kitchen closes 10pm.) For a pint ($4) at the best pub in town, head over to **Aidan's,** 1 Broadway. (☎ 401-845-9311. Open daily 11:30am-1am.)

FOOD

While many Newport restaurants are pricey, cheap food can be found with a little extra effort. Your best bet is on **Thames St.,** where inexpensive eateries and ice-cream parlors line the street. A drive north down **W. Main Rd.** reveals typical chains and the **Newport Creamery,** 208 W. Main. Rd., which serves typical American breakfast and lunch fare like pancakes, eggs, and burgers as well as ice cream. (☎ 401-846-2767. Dinner $6-10. Open daily 6:30am-11pm.) The vegetarian-friendly **Panini Grill,** 186 Thames St., offers tasty grilled sandwiches ($5-6), is open to satisfy late-night cravings, and now features low-carb options. (☎ 401-847-7784. Open Su-Th 11am-9:30pm, F-Sa 11am-2am). The **Sandwich Board Deli,** 397 Thames St. (☎ 401-849-5358), has some Newport-themed sandwiches like the Patriot (turkey, Vermont cheddar, bacon, lettuce and tomato) or the Bellevue Ave. (extra lean pastrami with melted Swiss and spicy mustard on marble rye) for about $6. The specialty is the lobster salad roll. Good, hearty breakfasts ($7-8) like the "Portuguese Sailor" (chorizo sausage and eggs) are prepared before your eyes at the **Franklin Spa,** 229 Spring St. (☎ 401-847-3540. Open M-W 6am-2pm, Th-Sa 6am-3pm, Su 7am-1:30pm.)

ACCOMMODATIONS

With over 250 guesthouses and inns scattered throughout the city, small, private lodging abounds in Newport. Those willing to share a bathroom or forego a sea view might find a double for $75. Many hotels and guesthouses book solid two months in advance for summer weekends, especially during the well-known festivals. For less expensive lodging it is best to head out of town a bit. **Rte. 114 (W. Main Rd.)** hosts a variety of chain motels about 4 mi. from Newport. Family-owned **Twin Lanterns,** 1172 W. Main Rd., 7 mi. north of Newport, is relatively inexpensive and offers a homey setting. They currently have eight clean, one-room cabins with two single beds, A/C, TV fridges and private bathrooms, as well as eight tent sites with hot shower facilities. (☎ 401-682-1304 or 866-682-1304. Reservations highly recommended, especially mid-June through Aug. Cabins $40-60; tent sites $15.) A few minutes from Newport's harborfront, the **Newport Gateway Hotel,** 31 W. Main Rd., in Middletown, has clean, comfortable doubles with A/C and cable TV. (☎ 401-847-2735. Rooms Su-Th $65-99, F-Sa $159-195.) **Fort Getty Recreation Area,** on Fort Getty Rd. on Conanicut Island, provides peaceful lodging as well as much needed wallet relief. (☎ 401-423-7211. Showers and beach access. Reservations recommended. Sites $20; RVs $30.)

APPROACHING PROVIDENCE

Driving from Newport, take **Rte. 114 North.** Follow **Rte. 114 North** all the way to **I-195** near East Providence. Take 195 East into Providence (exits 22-a, b, and c).

PROVIDENCE

At the mouth of the Seekonk River, Providence is a compact, easily navigable city. Cobbled sidewalks, historic buildings, and modern sculptures occupy the heart of downtown, while the surrounding area supports a plethora of inexpensive restaurants and shops. The home of two world-class institutes of higher education, Providence seamlessly blends the bustle of a busy state capital with the more laid-back feel of a college town.

(VITAL STATS)

Population: 174,000

Visitor Info: Providence/Warwick Convention and Visitors Bureau, 1 Sabin St. (☎800-233-1636). Open M-Sa 8:30am-5pm. **Roger Williams National Memorial Information Center,** 282 N. Main St. (☎401-521-7266). Open daily 9am-4:30pm.

Internet Access: Providence Public Library, 225 Washington St. (☎401-455-8000). Open M-Th 9am-8pm, F-Sa 9am-5:30pm.

Post Office: 2 Exchange Terr. (☎401-421-5214). Open M-F 7:30am-5:30pm, Sa 8am-2pm. **Postal Code:** 02903.

▐ TRANSPORTATION

I-95 and the **Providence River** run north-south and split Providence into three sections. West of I-95 is **Federal Hill;** between I-95 and the Providence River is **Down City;** and east of Providence is **College Hill,** home to **Brown University** and **Rhode Island School of Design (RISD).** A jaunt down **Benefit St.** in College Hill reveals notable historic sights and art galleries. **Providence Link,** run by the **Rhode Island Public Transit Authority (RIPTA),** has trolleys ($0.50) that run through the city with stops at major sights. Walking—the three main areas are within 15min. of each other—or taking the Providence Link are the best ways to see the city during daylight hours.

◉ SIGHTS

RISD MUSEUM OF ART. The world-renowned **Rhode Island School of Design (RISD)** occasionally shows the work of its students and professors at the ▨**RISD Museum of Art.** The museum's three-floor maze of galleries also exhibits Egyptian, Indian, Impressionist, medieval, and Roman artwork, as well as a gigantic 12th-century Japanese Buddha. From March through November, the third Thursday of each month is **gallery night,** when 24 galleries across the city open their doors for free, with free parking in 11 designated lots. *(224 Benefit St. ☎401-454-6500; www.risd.edu/museum.cfm. Open Su and Tu-Sa 10am-5pm. $8, students $3, seniors $5, ages 5-18 $2.)*

BROWN UNIVERSITY. Established in 1764, Brown University incorporates several 18th-century buildings, including **Carliss-Brackett House,** now the Office of Admission. *(45 Prospect St. ☎401-863-2378; www.brown.edu/admission. Open M-F 8am-4pm. Free 1hr. walking tours M-F 9am-4pm.)*

RHODE ISLAND STATE CAPITOL. From atop college hill, gaze at the stunning marble dome of the Rhode Island State Capitol. *(☎401-222-3938; www.state.ri.us/tours/tours.htm. Open M-F 8:30am-4:30pm. Free tours every hr. M-F 9am-noon. Reservations recommended for groups. Self-guided tour booklets available in room 38 in the basement M-F 8:30am-3:30pm.)*

HISTORICAL SIGHTS. The **John Brown House Museum** is steeped in tranquil elegance. The 1hr. tour includes a brief video introducing the house and the families that have occupied it. *(52 Power St. ☎401-331-8575. Open Su noon-4pm, Tu-Sa 10am-5pm. $7, students and seniors $5.50, ages 7-17 $3; families $18.)* The factory that started the industrial revolution is preserved in Pawtucket at the **Slater Mill Historic Site.** Situated by the rushing Blackstone River, the site has a large waterwheel and working water-powered machinery. *(67 Roosevelt Ave., in Pawtucket, north on I-95. ☎401-725-8638; www.slatermill.org. Open June-Nov. Tu-Sa 10am-5pm; call for winter hours. Continuous 1½hr. tours. $8, seniors $7, ages 6-12 $6, under 6 free.)* In addition to founding Rhode Island, in 1638 Roger Williams founded the *first* **First Baptist Church of America.** Its 1775 incarnation is rarely crowded. Visitors should register with the church office. *(75 N. Main St. ☎401-454-3418; www.fbcia.org. Tours available after Su service. Open M-F 10am-noon and 1-3pm, Sa 10am-noon. Free.)* The **Roger Williams National Memorial** has small, shady green spaces with stations describing the history of Rhode Island and Roger Williams, the separatist who founded the state and forged relationships with the local Narragansett tribes.

MUSEUMS. The **Providence Children's Museum** has interactive fun for all ages and is easily accessible in downtown Providence. *(100 South St. ☎401-273-5437; www.childrenmuseum.org. Open Apr.-Aug. daily 9:30am-5pm; Sept.-Mar. Su and Tu-Sa 9:30am-5pm; open selected F until 8pm. $4.75.)* The **Culinary Archives and Museum** documents over five millennia of food and cooking with exhibits on the development of kitchen gadgets and the

EAST COAST

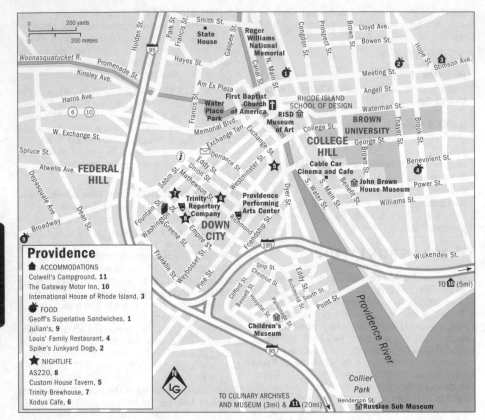

Providence

⌂ ACCOMMODATIONS
Colwell's Campground, **11**
The Gateway Motor Inn, **10**
International House of Rhode Island, **3**

🍴 FOOD
Geoff's Superlative Sandwiches, **1**
Julian's, **9**
Louis' Family Restaurant, **4**
Spike's Junkyard Dogs, **2**

★ NIGHTLIFE
AS220, **8**
Custom House Tavern, **5**
Trinity Brewhouse, **7**
Xodus Cafe, **6**

evolution of Presidential dining and entertaining. *(315 Harborside Blvd. ☎401-598-2805; www.culinary.org. $7, seniors $6, students with ID $3, ages 5-18 $2, under 5 free.)* Visitors can explore a Cold War relic at the **Russian Sub Museum.** Launched in 1956, this diesel-powered Juliett carried four nuclear cruise missiles. *(Collier Point Park at the end of Henderson St. off of Allens Ave. ☎401-823-4200; www.saratogamuseum.org. Open daily 10am-6pm. $8, seniors and military $6, ages 6-17 $5.)*

🎵 ENTERTAINMENT

For film, theater, and nightlife listings, read the *Weekend* section of the *Providence Journal* or the *Providence Phoenix.* Between 10 and 15 summer evenings per year, floating and stationary bonfires spanning the entire length of the downtown rivers are set ablaze during **Water Fire,** a public art exhibition and festival. *(☎401-272-3111; www.waterfire.org. Free.)* The regionally acclaimed **Trinity Repertory Company,** 201 Washington St., typically offers $12 student rush tickets the day of performances. *(☎401-351-4242; www.trinity-rep.com. Box office open M-F 10am-5pm, Sa-Su noon-5pm. Tickets $32-48.)* The **Providence Performing Arts Center,** 220 Weybosset St., hosts high-end productions such as concerts and Broadway musicals. *(☎401-421-2787; www.ppacri.org. Box office open M-F 10am-6pm, Sa noon-5pm. Tickets $26-68. Half-price tickets for students and seniors sometimes available 1hr. before showtimes M-F; call ahead.) For more ticket info, consult **www.ArttixRI.com** or call ☎401-621-6123. The **Cable Car Cinema and Cafe,** 204 S. Main St., shows arthouse and foreign films in a small theater with comfy couches. A friendly staff serves up sandwiches ($4-5) and offers vegan baked goods, ice cream, and beverages. (☎401-272-3970. 2 shows per evening, times vary. $8; M-W students $6. Cafe open M-F 7:30am-11pm, Sa-Su 9am-11pm.)

FOOD

Providence provides a wide variety of delicious, inexpensive culinary options for the budget traveler. **Atwells Ave.,** on Federal Hill just west of downtown, has a distinctly Italian flavor; **Thayer St.,** on College Hill to the east, is home to off-beat student hangouts and ethnic restaurants; and **Wickenden St.,** in the southeast corner of town, has a diverse selection of inexpensive eateries.

Geoff's Superlative Sandwiches, 163 Benefit St. (☎401-751-2248), in College Hill. Attracts a mixed crowd with about 85 creatively named sandwiches ($5-7), such as the "French connection," the "Wacko," and the "Embryonic Journey," Grab a green treat from the huge pickle barrel to complement your meal. Open M-F 8am-9pm, Sa-Su 9:30am-9pm.

Julian's, 318 Broadway (☎401-861-1770), near Federal Hill. A funky eatery with vegetarian options and art on the walls. Wraps and sandwiches $5-8. Dinner entrees $11-22. Live music (usually jazz) Tu and Su. Open M 9am-5pm, Tu-F 9am-1am, Sa 9am-3pm and 5pm-1am, and Su 9am-3pm and 6pm-1am.

Louis' Family Restaurant, 286 Brook St. (☎401-861-5225). Serves eclectic breakfast and lunch fare from omelettes and burgers to vegan chili and the tofu scramble to scores of college students. Homemade art and collages cover the walls, generating a friendly, familiar atmosphere. Open M-Sa 5:30am-3pm.

Spike's Junkyard Dogs, 273 Thayer St. (☎401-454-1459). Frequented by Brown students, Spike's serves pizza and subs along with their hot dog specialties like the Pizza Dog (pizza sauce, mozzarella, and Italian spices) and the German Shephard (sauerkraut and mustard) for under $3. Open M-Tu 11:30am-1:30am, W-Sa 11am-2am, Su 11am-1:30am.

ACCOMMODATIONS

Downtown motel rates make Providence an expensive stay. Rooms fill up well in advance for the graduation season in May and early June. Head 10 mi. south on I-95 to **Warwick** or **Cranston** for cheaper motels, or to **Seekonk, MA** on U.S. 6.

International House of Rhode Island, 8 Stimson Ave. (☎401-421-7181), off Hope St. near the Brown campus. Catering largely to international visitors, this house with stained-glass windows has 3 unique rooms. Fridge, bath and TV in each room, as well as shared kitchen and laundry. Reception Aug.-May M-F 9:30am-5pm; June-July M-F 8:30am-4pm. Reservations required and should be made far in advance. Singles $35; students $35; doubles $60/$45.

The Gateway Motor Inn, 50 Mink St. (☎508-336-8050), on U.S. 6 about 1 mi. after entering Seekonk, MA. Clean, comfortable, unexceptional rooms. Continental breakfast included. Singles $59; doubles $65. $6 per additional person.

Colwell's Campground, 119 Peckham Ln. (☎401-397-4614), in Coventry. From Providence, take I-95 South to Exit 10, then head west 8½ mi. on Rte. 117 to Peckham Ln. One of the closest campgrounds to Providence. Showers and hookups for sites along the Flat River Reservoir, a perfect place to swim or water-ski. Check-in 9am-3pm. Sites $16, with electricity $18.

NIGHTLIFE

Brownies, townies, and RISDs rock the night away at several hot spots throughout town. Something's going on every night at **AS220,** 115 Empire St., between Washington and Westminster St., a non-profit, totally uncensored cafe/bar/gallery/performance space. The chalkboard outside lists the acts and times for performances coming up in the next week. (☎401-831-9327. Cover under $10, usually around $6. Open M-F 10am-1am, Sa 1-6pm and 7pm-1am, Su 7pm-1am.) **Trinity Brewhouse,** 183 Fountain St., behind Trinity Repertory Theatre, offers award-winning beer and a live blues band on Wednesday nights. (☎401-453-2337.; www.trinitybrewhouse.com. Open M-Th 11:30am-1am, F 11:30am-2am, Sa-Su noon-2am.) Head over to the **Custom House Tavern,** 36 Weybosset St., in Down City, to hear local talent perform rock, jazz, or funk. (☎401-751-3630. Open M-Th

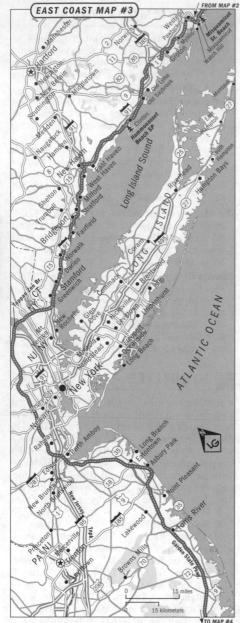

EAST COAST MAP #3

FROM MAP #2

TO MAP #4

11:30am-1am, F 11:30am-1am, Sa 8pm-2am, Su 8pm-1am.) The new **Xodus Cafe,** 276 Westminster St., serves up cocktails in a sleek lounge and hosts regular poetry readings, musical performances, and battling emcees. The cafe is also home to the **Providence Black Repertory Company** (☎401-351-0353; www.blackrep.org), which puts up more formal theatrical performances.

APPROACHING MISQUAMICUT
Follow **U.S. 1** out of Providence along the coast for about 55 mi. to Misquamicut and Watch Hill.

MISQUAMICUT AND WATCH HILL
Far west on the Rhode Island coast lies **Misquamicut State Beach,** a half-mile stretch of crowded sand. (☎401-596-4097. Lifeguards on duty 9am-6pm. Park open 9am-sunset. Parking M-F $12, Sa-Su $14; $7 for RI residents.) Farther down the coast, **Watch Hill Beach** is a favorite with locals. Watch Hill is also home to the **Flying Horse Carousel,** the country's oldest merry-go-round ($1 for outside horse, $0.50 for inside horse), and streets of beautiful old houses. Northeast of Watch Hill, near Narragansett, visitors can explore the small park surrounding the **Point Judith Lighthouse,** but the building itself belongs to the Coast Guard and is off limits. (Follow U.S. 1 North to Rte. 108 in Narragansett and take Point Judith Rd. ☎401-789-0444.) From nearby Galilee, visitors can take the **Block Island Ferry** to the tiny island, only 3 mi. across at its widest point, for a windswept day of biking. Over 200 endangered animal and plant species reside on the island. Don't miss the **Southeast Light,** the highest lighthouse in New England. (☎401-783-4613; www.blockislandferry.com. Round-trip $15.20, children $7.10. Parking available along Great Island Rd. for $7-10 per day.)

Hungry beachgoers might visit the **New Beachway Market,** 656 Atlantic Ave., in Misquamicut, for deli sandwiches ($4-6), drinks, ice cream, and snacks. (☎401-322-0224. Open M-Sa 7am-9pm, Su 7am-7pm.) Visitors to Watch Hill can check out the **Bay Street Deli,** 112 Bay St., for salads and sandwiches. (☎401-596-6606. Open daily 8am-8pm.) The **Ocean View Motel,** 140 Atlantic Ave., in Westerly, has personal if spare rooms, as well as efficiency suites that include a pull-out couch, fridge, and microwave. (☎401-596-7170. Rooms $69-109; suites $79-125.) **Watch Hill Inn,** 38 Bay St., has lovely hotel rooms in the middle of downtown

Watch Hill. (☎401-348-6300 or 800-356-9314. Continental breakfast included. Rooms $125-160.) Nearby Charlestown, off U.S. 1A, is home to **Burlingame State Camp Ground**, 1 Burlingame Park Rd., which has 750 sites, as well as bathroom facilities, a playground, and hiking trails. (☎401-322-7994 or 401-322-7337. Open mid-Apr. to Oct. Sites $20.)

Welcome To CONNECTICUT

🛕 APPROACHING MYSTIC
Follow **U.S. 1** about 10 mi., over the river and through the towns of Pawcatuck and Wequetequock.

MYSTIC

In the days when Herman Melville's white whale Moby Dick became legend, Connecticut's coastal towns were busy seaports full of dark, musty inns packed with tattooed sailors swapping stories. Today, prim-and-proper vacationers and sailing enthusiasts venture to the Connecticut coast seeking brighter, more commodious accommodations and a whale of a good time.

⌐ VITAL STATS

Population: 4000

Visitor Info: Mystic Tourist and Information Center (☎860-536-1641; www.visitmystic.com), Bldg. 1d in Old Mystick Village off Rte. 27. Open mid-June to Sept. M-Sa 9am-6pm Su 10am-5pm; Sept. to early June M-Sa 9am-5:30pm, Su 10am-5pm.

Internet Access: Mystic & Noank Library, 40 Library St. (☎860-536-7721). $0.25 per 15min. Open M-W 10am-9pm, Th-Sa 10am-5pm; mid-June to early Sept. closes Sa 1pm.

Post Office: 23 E. Main St. (☎860-536-8143). Open M-F 8am-5pm, Sa 8:30am-12:30pm. **Postal Code:** 06355.

⬛ GETTING AROUND.
Downtown Mystic lies along **U.S. 1**, which goes by Williams Ave., Roosevelt Ave., and Broadway before becoming **Main St.,** between **Greenmanville Ave. (Rte. 27)** to

the east and the Mystic River to the west. Most attractions lie along Rte. 27 south of I-95, which roughly parallels U.S. 1.

◪ SIGHTS. Located along the Mystic River, **Mystic Seaport,** north of U.S. 1 on Pearl St., offers a look at 18th-century whaling. In the 17 acres of recreated village, actors in period dress entertain visitors with interactive skits, a functioning wood-only shipyard, and three splendid ships. (☎860-973-2767; www.mysticseaport.org. Open daily Apr.-Oct. 9am-5pm; Nov.-Mar. 10am-4pm. $17, seniors $16, ages 6-12 $9.) A few dollars more entitles visitors to a **Sabino Charters** cruise along the Mystic River on an authentic 1908 coal-fired steamboat. (☎860-572-5351. 30min. cruise mid-May to early Oct. daily every 30min. 10:30am-3:30pm $5, ages 6-12 $4. 1½hr. cruise 4:30pm. $10/$9.) The **Mystic Aquarium and Institute for Exploration,** 55 Coogan Blvd., takes visitors underwater through real-time video feeds from marine sanctuaries around the US, and features an impressive collection of seals, penguins, sharks, and beluga whales. (North of Rte. 27 off U.S. 1. ☎860-572-5955; www.mysticaquarium.org. Open Mar.-Nov. daily 9am-6pm; Dec.-Feb. M-F 10am-5pm, Sa-Su 9am-6pm. $16, seniors $15, ages 3-12 $11.) Only 1½ mi. east of downtown, the **Denison Pequotsepos Nature Center,** 109 Pequotsepos Rd., offers excellent bird watching and indoor exhibits about the wildlife that inhabits the 8 mi. of trails. (☎860-536-1216; www.dpnc.org. Visitors Center open M-Sa 9am-5pm, Su 10am-4pm. Park open daily dawn-dusk. $6, seniors and ages 6-12 $4.)

▨▧ FOOD & NIGHTLIFE. The popular **Mystic Pizza,** 56 W. Main St., has been serving its "secret recipe" pizzas for 30 years. The pizzeria's renown stems largely from the 1988 Julia Roberts movie *Mystic Pizza* that was filmed here. (☎860-536-3737. Small pizza $6. Large $11. Open daily 11am-11pm.) Locals recommend **Cove Fish Market,** in a shack on Old Stonington Rd. 1 mi. east of downtown, for its excellent seafood. (☎860-536-0061. Entrees $6-12. Crab-patty burger $3. Open mid-May to early Sept. daily 11am-8pm. Fish market open M-Sa 10am-7pm, Su 10am-6pm.) There are several places to kick back a cold one in Mystic. The younger crowd heads to **Margarita's,** 12 Water St., downtown. (☎860-536-4589. 2-for-1 deals on food W with student ID. Happy hour 4-7pm; $4.50 margaritas. Open Su-Th 4pm-1am, F-Sa 4pm-2am. Kitchen closes M-Th 10pm, F-Su 11pm.)

♦ **ACCOMMODATIONS.** It's almost impossible to find budget-friendly lodgings in Mystic; make reservations well in advance. At the intersection of Rte. 27 and I-95, the **Old Mystic Motor Lodge,** 251 Greenman Ave., offers standard motel rooms with TVs, mini-fridges, microwaves, and a continental breakfast. (☎860-536-9666. Rooms $89-99.) Reasonably priced rooms with TVs, A/C, mini-fridges, and microwaves are available at the **Windsor Motel,** 345 Gold Star Hwy. (Rte. 184), in Groton. (☎860-445-7474. Singles Su-Th $45, F-Sa $75; doubles $55/$85.) Close to Mystic, the **Seaport Campgrounds,** on Rte. 184, offers a pool, mini-golf course, a pond for fishing, and playground area. (☎860-536-4044. Open mid-Apr. to mid-Nov. Sites with water and electricity mid-May to mid-Sept. $33; Apr. to mid-May and mid-Sept. to mid-Nov. $26. $7 per additional adult. Seniors and AAA members 10% discount.)

LEAVING MYSTIC
From Mystic, keep following **U.S. 1** for about 30 mi. to reach Old Saybrook.

DETOUR: CONNECTICUT CASINOS
Follow U.S. 1 to I-395 and take Exit 79A to Rte. 2A East. Mohegan Sun is 1 mi. away, on Mohegan Sun Blvd. Follow 2A to Rte. 2 to reach Foxwoods, 9 mi. farther.

Foxwoods and Mohegan Sun, two tribally owned casinos in southeastern Connecticut, bring sin to the suburbs. Although they each have their own style, their shared tendency toward decadence make them both worth a traveler's while, even if just to gawk. The 4.7 million sq. ft. **Foxwoods** (☎888-287-2369; www.foxwoods.com.) complex contains a casino complete with 6400 slot machines, blackjack, craps, poker, and the other usual suspects, as well as three glitzy hotels, a spa, elaborate nightclubs and adult entertainment, a village for shopping, and fancy restaurants with food from all over the world. The 1450-seat **Fox Theatre** hosts live performances from boxing to

THE LOCAL STORY

FOXWOODS VS. MOHEGAN SUN

Both Foxwoods and Mohegan Sun are huge casino complexes. Both are in the middle of nowhere in eastern Connecticut. So how do the two stack up?

Size: Mohegan Sun has over 300,000 sq. ft. of gambling space, including 6200 slot machines and 300 game tables. Sounds like a lot, but Foxwoods has 20,000 more sq. ft. of gambling space, more than 350 game tables and 6400 slots. Mohegan Sun is plenty big for slower times, but the extra space will make a difference during the crowded summer months.

Navigability: ...or how long before you get lost in the maze of slots and tables. Both offer floor plans to help visitors, but Mohegan Sun's is color coded and significantly easier to read. It also has "Lost Guest" stations for anyone who finds the maps insufficiently helpful.

Accommodations: Neither complex works particularly hard to offer inexpensive lodgings. Their rooms are approximately the same size, though Foxwoods's are divided among the Grand Pequot Tower, Great Ceder Hotel, and Two Trees Inn, the least expensive ($99-210).

Entertainment: Both casinos have theaters for live entertainment. Mohegan Sun has a huge, 10,000-person auditorium for its bigger acts (who have included David Bowie and Simon and Garfunkel), plus the Wolf Den lounges. In contrast, Foxwoods has a significantly more cozy and intimate 1450-person theater for big acts like Mary J. Blige and Patti Labelle.

Food: Both complexes offer a wide array of dining options, though many of the chain restaurants have marked up the prices on their menus. Both also offer huge all-you-can-eat buffets for about $14, probably the best deal in either complex.

pop music; past appearances include Frank Sinatra, Bill Cosby, and the Dixie Chicks. (☎800-200-2882. Prices and performance times vary.)

Mohegan Sun (☎888-226-7711; www.mohegansun.com) offers two of the world's largest casinos: the nature-themed Casino of the Earth and the Art Deco Casino of the Sky. The entire complex is contained in an enormous interconnected structure. While Foxwoods offers classic glamour, Mohegan Sun presents its services, entertainment, lodging, and shopping in tribal packaging, with trees as pillars that change with the seasons and an enormous waterfall.

OLD SAYBROOK

A small town, Old Saybrook has an amazing array of historical homes. The quaint downtown doesn't pander to tourists, but has unique shops, and its sights make for a good afternoon's exploring.

> ## VITAL STATS
>
> **Population:** 10,000
>
> **Visitor Info: Chamber of Commerce,** 146 Main St. (☎860-388-3266; www.oldsaybrookct.com).
>
> **Internet Access: Acton Public Library,** 66 Old Boston Post Rd. (☎401-395-3184). Open M-Th noon-8:30pm, F 9am-5pm, Sa 9am-5pm; in winter also Su 1-5pm.
>
> **Post Office:** 36 Main St. (☎860-388-4479). Open M-F 8:30am-5pm, Sa 8:30am-1:30pm. **Postal Code:** 06475.

GETTING AROUND. Boston Post Rd. (U.S. 1) runs approximately parallel to I-95 in town, and Rte. 154 crosses both and becomes **Main St.** in town. Main St. has most restaurants and shops, while most of the hotels lie along Boston Post Rd.

SIGHTS. Most attractions in Old Saybrook celebrate the town's rich history. **Fort Saybrook Monument Park** lies at the end of Main St. Standing on land once owned by locals tribes, the fort was built in 1636 as the first fortification in southern New England. The land was later acquired by the Connecticut Valley Railroad, and the remains of the roundhouse and turning station are still there. The park consists of 14 acres, more than half of which are marshland. The **Old Saybrook Preservation Society** occupies the **General William Hart House,** 350 Main St. The house was originally built

by William Hart, a general in the Revolutionary War, for his bride in 1767. (☎860-388-2622. Open Su-F 1-4pm.) A walk down Main St. reveals more historic homes and sights; of interest are the **Railroad Station** (finished 1870) and the **Humphrey Pratt Tavern,** built in 1785. Also worth a visit is the **Florence Griswold Museum,** 96 Lyme St., in nearby Old Lyme. In the late 19th-century, Florence Griswold opened her home to boarders, including artist Harry Ward Ranger, who founded an art colony there. Over 200 artists, mostly Impressionists, eventually came and painted at the estate, often inspired by the immediate surroundings. Today, visitors can see both the grounds and much of the art that was created on site. (☎860-434-5542; www.flogris.org. Open Su 1-5pm, Tu-Sa 10am-5pm. $7, seniors and students $6, ages 6-12 $4.)

FOOD. In downtown Old Saybrook, **Caffe Toscana,** 25 Main St., offers tasty sandwiches, wraps, and panini. (☎860-388-1270. Sandwiches $6-7. Open M-F 7am-4pm, Sa 8am-4pm.) **Walt's Food Market,** 178 Main St., sells groceries sandwiches, a selection of homemade soups, and fresh sushi that is delivered daily. The homemade cookies and bread are particularly good. (☎860-388-3308. Open M-F 9am-6pm, Sa 8am-6pm, Su 8am-1pm.) **Pat's Kountry Kitchen,** 70 Mill Rock Rd. off of U.S. 1, serves hearty, home-style meals in a dining room filled with antiques and country kitchen gadgets. The menu features sandwiches, seafood, and classic dinner entrees. Check out the huge collection of teddy bears. (☎860-388-4784. Open Su-Tu and Th-Sa 7am-9pm; closed Su 12:30-2pm).

ACCOMMODATIONS. Boston Post Rd. (U.S. 1) is home to most of the area's motels and hotels. The **Heritage Motor Inn,** 1500 Boston Post Rd., is a family-owned motel with American Colonial decor. (☎860-388-3743. Rooms $78-128). Down the road the recently remodeled **Sandpiper Motor Inn,** 1750 Boston Post Rd., is fairly generic, clean, and well kept, offering Internet access, a heated outdoor pool, and rooms with microwaves and fridges. (☎860-399-7973; www.sandpipermotorinn.com. Continental breakfast included. Rooms $60-150.) For more plush accommodations, try the **Water's Edge Resort and Spa,** 1525 Boston Post Rd. The rooms are decorated in rich, deep colors, and guests have access to the beach and spa facilities. (☎860-399-5901 or 800-222-3901; www.watersedge-resort.com. Rooms $150-400.)

APPROACHING CLINTON
Reach Clinton from Old Saybrook by following **U.S. 1** for about 10 mi.

CLINTON
Founded in 1663, Clinton was the original home of the school that would become Yale University. Still a relatively rural community, much of the town's life centers on outdoor pursuits. The **Clinton Town Beach** at the end of Riverside Ln. is small and uncrowded, offering a volleyball court, basketball net, and playground. (Open daily 9am-5pm. $10.) The **Clinton Chamber of Commerce,** 50 East Main St., provides free maps of the town and a guide to stores and activities. (☎860-669-3889; www.clintonct.com.) Visitors can also pick up *A Walk Through Historic Clinton,* which highlights buildings dating back to the colonial period.

Main St. features several cafes and country-kitchen style restaurants. The **M. Serba Fine Art Cafe,** 95 E. Main St., is located in the home of General Horatio Right and serves a variety of gourmet coffees and lighter fare, such as delicious spinach au gratin. (☎860-669-5062; www.serba.com. Open M-F 8am-6pm, Sa 8pm-8am.) The town also has a few quaint inns, but those looking to pinch pennies should head to the **Clinton Motel,** 163 E. Main St. (☎860-669-8850), or the **Holiday Motel,** 345 East Main St. (☎860-669-2368). Both offer clean if unspectacular rooms with A/C and TV from $50.

HAMMONASSET BEACH STATE PARK
1288 Boston Post Rd. (U.S. 1)
Covering nearly 1000 acres, Hammonasset Beach State Park has a long stretch of beach, two interpretive nature walks, an educational **Nature Center,** and a launch for smaller watercraft. The park is favored by families, and features 560 campsites that are open from the third weekend in May until Columbus Day weekend. (☎877-668-2267, office 203-245-1817; www.reserveamerica.com. Open daily 8am-dusk. Entrance fee $10-14. Sites $15.)

APPROACHING NEW HAVEN
Follow **U.S. 1** 13 mi. west from Clinton.

NEW HAVEN
A city with a bad reputation that has proven hard to drop, New Haven has been working hard to revitalize itself—with impressive results. Home to Yale University, the city still struggles with town-gown tensions, but the new New Haven, particularly the area around Yale's campus, now sustains a healthy assortment of hip bars, trendy boutiques, art galleries, bookstores, and coffeehouses supported by students and townies alike.

VITAL STATS
Population: 124,000

Visitor Info: Greater New Haven Convention and Visitors Bureau, 59 Elm St. (☎203-777-8550; www.newhavencvb.org). Open M-F 8:30am-5pm. **Info New Haven,** 1000 Chapel St. (☎203-773-9494; www.infonewhaven.com). Open M-Th 10am-9pm, F-Sa 10am-10pm, Su noon-5pm.

Internet Access: New Haven Public Library, 133 Elm St. (☎203-946-8130). Open June to mid-Sept. M-Th 10am-6pm, F 10am-5pm; mid-Sept. to May M noon-8pm, Tu-Th 10am-8pm, Sa 10am-5pm.

Post Office: 170 Orange St. (☎203-752-3283.) Open M-F 7:30am-5pm, Sa 8am-noon. **Postal Code:** 06510.

GETTING AROUND

New Haven lies at the intersection of **I-95** and **I-91** and is laid out in nine squares surrounded by radial roads. Main northwest-southeast routes **Chapel St.** and **Elm St.** run one-way in opposite directions along the Yale campus and border **New Haven Green.** Cross streets **College St.** and **Temple St.** frame the green's other edges and host restaurants and bars. At night, don't wander too far from the immediate downtown and campus areas; surrounding neighborhoods, especially south of the green, can be unsafe. **Parking** is available at meters along Chapel ($1 per hr.; 2hr. max.), or in garages on College St. or along Crown St., one block southwest of Chapel ($8-15 per day).

SIGHTS

The majority of the sights and museums in New Haven are located on or near the Yale University campus. Most of the campus buildings were designed in the English Gothic or Georgian Colonial styles, many of them with intricate moldings and a few with gargoyles. The **Yale Visitors Center** faces the New Haven Green and is the starting point for **campus tours.** Bordered by Chapel, College, Grove, and High St., the charming **Old Campus** contains Connecticut Hall, which, raised in

1753, is the university's oldest remaining building. *(149 Elm St. ☎ 203-432-2300; www.yale.edu. Open M-F 9am-4:45pm, Sa-Su 10am-4pm. Free 1¼hr. campus tours M-F 10:30am and 2pm, Sa-Su 1:30pm.)*

STERLING MEMORIAL LIBRARY. Sterling Memorial Library is designed to resemble a monastery—even the telephone booths are shaped like confessionals. The design is not entirely without a sense of humor, though—the Cloister Hall has carved stone corbels portraying sleeping, smoking, and lounging students using the library for anything but studying. *(120 High St., 1 block north of the Yale Visitors Center, on the other side of Elm St. ☎ 203-432-1775. Free Internet. Open June-Sept. M-W and F 8:30am-5pm, Th 8:30am-10pm, Sa 10am-5pm; Sept.-June Su-Th 8:30am-midnight, F 8:30am-5pm, Sa 8:30am-7pm.)*

BEINECKE RARE BOOK AND MANUSCRIPT LIBRARY. Paneled with Vermont marble cut thin enough to be translucent, Beinecke Rare Book and Manuscript Library is a massive modern structure containing 600,000 rare books and manuscripts. The building protects one of the five Gutenberg Bibles in the US and holds an extensive collection of John James Audubon's prints. *(121 Wall St. ☎ 203-432-2977. Open M-Th 8:30am-8pm, F 8:30am-5pm, Sa 10am-5pm. Free.)*

YALE UNIVERSITY ART GALLERY. The Yale gallery holds over 100,000 pieces from around the world, including works by Monet, Van Gogh, Matisse, and Picasso, as well as a sculpture garden. *(1111 Chapel St., at York St. ☎ 203-432-0600. Open Su 1-6pm, Tu-W and F-Sa 10am-5pm, Th 10am-8pm. Audio tours available. Free.)*

PEABODY MUSEUM OF NATURAL HISTORY. The Peabody Museum houses Rudolph F. Zallinger's Pulitzer Prize-winning mural depicting the "Age of Reptiles" in a room containing dinosaur skeletons. Check out the 100 million-year-old 8 ft. turtle and a mummy residing in the "House of Eternity." *(170 Whitney Ave. Exit 3 off I-91. ☎ 203-432-5050. Open M-Sa 10am-5pm, Su noon-5pm. $7, seniors and ages 3-15 $5.)*

YALE CENTER FOR BRITISH ART. The Center for British Art is in the last building designed by architect Louis I Kahn. Having grown out of an alumnus's donation, the museum now houses 2000 paintings, the most complete collection of British art outside of the UK. *(1080 Chapel St. ☎ 203-432-2800; www.yale.edu/ycba. Open Su noon-5pm, Tu-Sa 10am-5pm. Free.)*

AMISTAD MEMORIAL. Those interested in New Haven history should visit the Amistad Memorial. A 14 ft., three-sided sculpture cast in bronze, in front of New Haven City Hall, it stands across the Green from where the Africans involved in the Amistad revolt were held.

EAST ROCK PARK. East Rock Park provides an excellent sunset view of New Haven and Long Island Sound from an overlook 325 ft. above sea level. *(Outside the campus, accessible from East Rock Rd. northeast of the city. ☎ 203-782-4314.)*

⬛ FOOD

For authentic Italian cuisine, work your way along Wooster St., in **Little Italy**, 10min. east of downtown. ⬛**Pepe's**, 157 Wooster St., claims to be the inventor of the American pizza, originally known as "tomato pie." Try a red or white sauce clam "New Haven" pie for $9. *(☎ 203-865-5762. Open M and W-Th 4-10pm, F-Sa 11:30am-11pm, Su 2:30-10pm.)* Then head next door to **Libby's**, 139 Wooster St., for 12 types of cannoli. *(☎ 203-772-0380. Cannoli $1.50-2. Open M and W-Th 11:30am-10pm, F-Sa 11:30am-11pm, Su 11:30am-9pm.)* No condiments are allowed at **Louis' Lunch**, 263 Crown St., one of several establishments claiming to be the birthplace of the burger. Cooked vertically in cast iron grills, these burgers ($4)—and burgers are all they make—are too fine for ketchup. *(☎ 203-562-5507. Open Tu-W 11am-4pm, Th-Sa 11am-2am.)* Indian restaurants dominate the neighborhood southwest of downtown, near **Howe St.** The all-you-can-eat lunch ($8) and lunch entrees ($4-6) at **Tandoor**, 1226 Chaple St., a diner-style restaurant decorated with holiday lights regardless of season, are some of the best deals in town. *(☎ 203-776-6620. Entrees $8-14. Open M-Th 11:30am-10:30pm, F-Su 11:30am-11pm.)*

⬛ ACCOMMODATIONS

Inexpensive lodgings are sparse in New Haven, especially around Yale Parents Weekend (mid-Oct.) and Commencement (early June). Head 10 mi. south on I-95 to **Milford** for affordable motels. **Hotel Duncan**, 1151 Chapel St., located in the heart of Yale's campus, has the most affordable rates in the downtown area. Guests enjoy spacious rooms and ride in the oldest manually operated elevator in the state. *(☎ 203-787-1273. Reservations recommended F-Su. Singles $44-50; doubles $60-70.)*

EAST COAST MAP #4 FROM MAP #3

TO MAP #5

EAST COAST

NIGHTLIFE

The **Yale Repertory Theatre,** 1120 Chapel St. (☎203-432-1234; www.yalerep.org), hosts productions combining professional talent with students at the Yale School of Drama. The **New Haven Symphony Orchestra,** 247 College St., performs at the Shubert Theater year-round. (☎203-562-5666. Box office open M-F 9:30am-5:30pm, Sa 10am-2pm.)

Toad's Place, 300 York St., has hosted gigs by Bob Dylan, the Rolling Stones, and George Clinton. Toad's also features dance parties Wednesday and Saturday nights during the school year. (☎203-562-5694, recorded info 203-624-8623. Box office open daily 11am-6pm; buy tickets at the bar after 8pm. Cover $5-35 for shows, $5 for dance nights. Open Su-Th 8pm-1am, F-Sa 8pm-2am; closed when there is not a show.) **Bar,** 254 Crown St., is a hip hangout, offering a pool table, lounge room, dance floor/theater, five homemade beers brewing at the bar, and brick-oven pizza. The party every Tuesday night attracts a large gay crowd. (☎203-495-8924. Cover Tu $3, Sa $6. Open Su-Tu 4pm-1am, W-Th 11:30am-2:30am, F 11:30am-2am, Sa 5am-2am.) Don't be confused if **Playwright,** 144 Temple St., looks more Sunday morning than Saturday night—its facade and interior were constructed from architectural elements from abandoned Irish and British churches. Inside, it's an Irish pub with a young, energetic vibe. (☎203-752-0450. Live music Th, DJ W and F-Sa. Open Su-Th 11:30am-1am, F-Sa 11:30am-2am.)

LEAVING NEW HAVEN
West of New Haven, U.S. 1 gets congested as it winds past strip malls and discount stores. **I-95,** though no more scenic, is the fastest way out of Connecticut. From downtown New Haven, follow **College St.** three blocks southwest to the I-95 South entrance.

DETOUR: NEW YORK CITY
*Follow **I-95** to New York Exit 1A for Rte. 9A (Henry Hudson Pkwy.), which follows the west side of Manhattan and becomes the West Side Hwy. as it approaches Midtown.*

Though not a car-friendly city by any stretch of the imagination, the City has a lot to offer, and some roadtrippers may choose to visit. Pick up a copy of *Let's Go: New York City* for the most up-to-date info on where to go and what to see in New York.

APPROACHING NEW JERSEY

Bypass most of New York City's traffic by taking exit 21 for **I-287 West** after leaving Connecticut. Cross the **Tappan Zee Bridge,** then take exit 14A onto the **Garden State Pkwy.** To get to Asbury Park from the Garden State Pkwy., take exit 102 to **Rte. 16 East.**

Welcome To NEW JERSEY

ASBURY PARK. Built from the ground up by developer James Bradley, Asbury Park is now best known as the hometown of rocker Bruce Springsteen. Having suffered under economic changes that hurt many Jersey Shore resort towns, Asbury Park has attempted an economic, commercial, and cultural renewal. Most of Asbury Park's attractions center around its role in rock and roll history. With over 2000 pieces, the **Asbury Park Library,** 500 1st. Ave., has the world's largest collection of published material relating to Bruce Springsteen and the E-Street Band. (☎732-774-4221. Open M-W 11am-8pm, Th 9am-5pm, F-Sa noon-5pm). The **Stone Pony,** 913 Ocean Ave., is a landmark rock venue that originally opened in 1974 and reopened in 2000. (☎732-502-0600.) The **Stephen Crane House,** 508 4th. Ave., has nothing to do with rock, but was the teenage home of the author of the *Red Badge of Courage*. The house, currently undergoing renovation, is not open for tours, but hosts occasional readings and lectures. (☎732-775-5682.)

APPROACHING ATLANTIC CITY

Take the **Garden State Pkwy.** south, and then head east on the **Atlantic City Expwy.** to get straight to the heart of Atlantic City.

ATLANTIC CITY

An express train and early cars once brought thousands of East Coast city dwellers to Atlantic City for inexpensive weekend getaways, and later the city gained fame as the home of the *Miss America Pageant* and the source of *Monopoly*'s property names. But the former opulence of Boardwalk and Park Place have faded from neglect and evolved into casino-driven tackiness. Gambling, legalized in the 1970s in an attempt to revive the city, brought mega-dollar casinos to the Boardwalk and restored a flow of tourists, but the casinos appear to have done little for the city itself. Highlights center on the Boardwalk, where blaring announcements invite pedestrians to step into the casinos to try their luck.

VITAL STATS

Population: 41,000

Visitor Info: Atlantic City Visitors Center (☎609-449-7130), on the Atlantic Expwy., 1 mi. after the Pleasantville Toll Plaza. Open daily 9am-5pm. **Atlantic City Convention Center and Visitors Bureau Info Center** (☎888-228-4748; www.atlanticcitynj.com), on the Boardwalk at Mississippi St. Open daily 9:30am-5:30pm; Memorial Day-Labor Day Th-Su until 8pm.

Internet Access: Atlantic City Library, 1 N. Tennessee Ave. (☎609-345-2269). Open M-W 10am-8pm, Th-Sa 9am-5pm.

Post Office: 1701 Pacific Ave. (☎609-345-4212), at Illinois Ave. Open M-F 8:30am-6pm, Sa 8:30am-12:30pm. **Postal Code:** 08401.

GETTING AROUND

Attractions cluster on and around the **Boardwalk,** which runs northeast-southwest along the Atlantic Ocean. Parallel to the Boardwalk, **Pacific Ave.** and **Atlantic Ave.** offer cheap restaurants, hotels, and convenience stores. Atlantic Ave. can be dangerous after dark, and any street farther inland can be dangerous even by day. Getting around is easy on foot on the Boardwalk.

The **Jitney,** 201 Pacific Ave., is basically a small shuttle bus. Jitneys run on four routes to all the casinos and most major points of interest. (☎609-344-8642. $12.50 for 10 tickets or $1.50 in cash per ride). **Rolling Chair Rides** appear along the Boardwalk as frequently as yellow cabs in Manhattan. (☎617-347-7500. $5 for up to 5 blocks.)

Parking is available on some residential streets. Try **Oriental Ave.** at **New Jersey Ave.** near the Garden Pier Historic Museum for free 3hr. parking at easy walking distance from the Boardwalk. Be careful at night: this area is more desolate than other parts of the city. On streets farther from the Boardwalk, such as down Martin Luther King

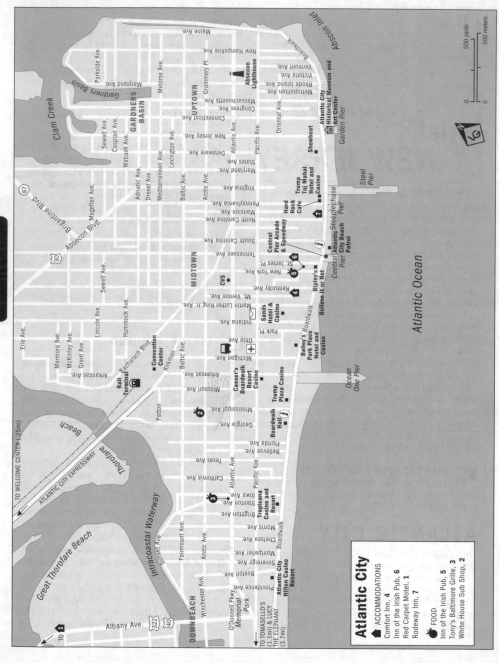

EAST COAST

Atlantic City

▲ ACCOMMODATIONS
Comfort Inn, **4**
Inn of the Irish Pub, **6**
Red Carpet Motel, **1**
Rodeway Inn, **7**

🍴 FOOD
Inn of the Irish Pub, **5**
Tony's Baltimore Grille, **3**
White House Sub Shop, **2**

Atlantic Ocean

Absecon Inlet

Blvd., free parking is unlimited, but be prepared to walk several blocks to the Boardwalk and casinos. Parking lots near the Boardwalk run $5-10.

SIGHTS

THE BOARDWALK. There's something for everyone in Atlantic City, thanks to the Boardwalk. On one side stretches the beach, with its bars and two piers of arcades and amusement rides. The other side is lined with gift shops, surf shops, food stalls selling pizza, funnel cakes, stromboli, and ice cream, the occasional jewelry store, and, of course, the casinos (see p. 94). There's often live music playing, usually paid for by s casino trying to lure in gamblers. Visitors can walk, ride bikes between 6 and 10am, or take advantage of the rolling chairs. Most of the action along this 8 mi. stretch takes place south of the Showboat. Beyond this harried flurry of activity, it's most enjoyable as a quiet walk. Those under 21 play for prizes at the many arcades that line the Boardwalk, including **Central Pier Arcade & Speedway**. It feels like real gambling, but the teddy bear in the window is easier to win than the convertible on display at Caesar's. The pier also has go-karts and paintball. *(At the Boardwalk and Tennessee Ave. ☎609-345-5219. Go-karts single $6, double $14. Must be 12 and 54 in. tall to ride alone. Paintball $3 per 15 shots.)* The historic **Steel Pier** juts into the coastal waters with a ferris wheel that spins riders over the Atlantic. It also offers the rest of the usual amusement park attractions: a roller coaster, a carousel, and games of "skill" aplenty. *(On the Boardwalk at Virginia Ave. ☎609-898-7645 or 866-386-6659; www.steelpier.com. Open daily noon-midnight; call the Taj Mahal for winter hours. Tickets one for $0.75 or 35 for $25. Rides 1-5 tickets.)* When and if you tire of spending money, check out the historic **Atlantic City Beach,** pretty much the only free activity in town. For more water fun, visitors invariably stumble upon at least one of the piers occupied by **Morey's Piers & Raging Waters Waterparks.** *(On the Boardwalk at 25th Ave., Schellenger, and Spencer. ☎609-522-3900 or 888-667-3971; www.moreyspiers.com.)* Just west of Atlantic City, **Ventnor City Beach** offers more tranquil shores.

MUSEUMS. Those looking for a quieter, more cultured way to spend the afternoon can explore the **Atlantic City Art Center,** which displays the work of local and regional artists. *(On Garden Pier at New Jersey Ave. and the Boardwalk. ☎609-347-5837; www.aclink.org/acartcenter. Open daily 10am-4pm. Free.)* On the same pier, the **Atlantic City Historical Museum** contains memorabilia from the history of the "Queen of Resorts," including displays on the *Miss America Pageant, Monopoly,* sand art, and the role of electricity. *(☎609-347-5839; www.acmuseum.org. Open daily 10am-4pm. Free.)*

OTHER SIGHTS. The tallest lighthouse in New Jersey and the third tallest in the nation, **Absecon Lighthouse** ceased operation in 1933. Today, it remains open as a tourist attraction, offering a small museum and the chance to climb to the top for a stunning view of the city and ocean. *(31 S. Rhode Island Ave. Drive northeast on Pacific Ave. from midtown; it's on the left. ☎609-449-1360;*

HIGH DIVING HORSES

Before gambling took over Atlantic City, the main attraction was the high-diving horse act. Atlantic City historian Allen "Boo" Pergament tells the story. William "Doc" Carver, frontiersman, army scout, and friend of famed Buffalo Bill, accidentally fell while crossing the Platte River. Years later, after having delved into the world of Wild West Shows, Doc used his brush with death and decided to train young women and horses to dive from a high platform. Unfortunately, Doc passed away just before his act opened in Atlantic City, but [it] went into the annals of history as the most memorable act in town. Five thousand spectators would end their adventures on the Steel Pier with dread-filled and delighted anticipation as a horse ran up an L-shaped platform to meet a young woman who would jump on its back seconds before it plunged 40 ft. into a pool of water below. From 1929 to 1978, audiences could count on the high-diving horse act every summer.

www.abseconlighthouse.org. Open July-Aug. daily 10am-5pm; Sept.-June M and Th-Su 11am-4pm. Call for winter hours. $5, seniors $4, ages 4-12 $2.) **Ripley's Believe It or Not Museum** may not be quite so historically oriented, but it does feature some pretty freaky artifacts and stories that are, well, hard to believe. *(At New York Ave. and the Boardwalk. ☎ 609-347-2001; www.ripleys.com. Open summer daily 10am-10pm; winter M-F 11am-5pm, Sa-Su 10am-9pm. $11, ages 5-12 $7, under 5 free.)*

🏛 CAINO

All casinos on the Boardwalk fall within a dice toss of one another. The farthest south is the elegant **Hilton**, between Providence and Boston Ave. (☎ 609-347-7111 or 800-257-8677; www.hiltonac.com), and the farthest north is the gaudy **Showboat**, at Delaware Ave. and Boardwalk. (☎ 609-343-4000 or 800-621-0200; www.harrahs.com). Donald Trump's glittering **Trump Taj Mahal Hotel and Casino**, 1000 Boardwalk, (☎ 609-449-1000; www.trumptaj.com), at Virginia Ave., is too ostentatious to be missed; this tasteless tallboy and the rest of Trump's casino holdings have been struggling with financial difficulties. In true *Monopoly* form, Trump owns three other hotel casinos in the city: the recently remodeled Trump Plaza, at Mississippi and the Boardwalk (☎ 609-441-6000 or 800-677-7378; www.trumpplaza.com); Trump World's Fair, on the Boardwalk (☎ 800-473-7829); and **Trump Castle**, on Huron Blvd. at the Marina (☎ 609-441-2000; www.trumpmarina.com). In summer, energetic partiers go to "rock the dock" at Trump Castle's indoor/outdoor bar and restaurant, **The Deck** (☎ 877-477-4697). Many a die is cast at **Caesar's Boardwalk Resort and Casino**, 2100 Pacific Ave., at Arkansas Ave. (☎ 609-348-4411; www.caesarsatlantcity.com). At Indiana Ave., **The Sands** (☎ 609-441-4000; www.acsands.com) stands tall and flashy with its seashell motif. The newest casino in town is **The Borgata** (☎ 866-692-6742; www.theborgata.com), a golden scintillation near the Trump Marina Hotel Casino and Harrah's in the Marina District that has been in the works since 2000. All casinos are open 24hr. and are dominated by slot machines.

🔪 FOOD

Although not recommended by nutritionists, $0.75 hot dogs and $1.50 pizza slices are readily available on the Boardwalk, and there is no shortage of ice-cream parlors. Some of the best deals in town await at the casinos, where all-you-can-eat lunch ($7) and dinner ($11) buffets abound. Tastier, less tacky fare can be found farther from the seashore.

Inn of the Irish Pub, 164 St. James Pl. (☎ 609-345-9613; www.theirishpub.com). Locals lounge downstairs and foreign students and hostelers stay upstairs at this hostel-and-bar combo. Serving hearty pub-style food all night, it's packed with carousers at all hours. Start off with a "20th St. sampler" (buffalo wings, fried mozzarella, potato skins, and chicken thumbs; $7). The daily lunch special (11:30am-2pm) includes a sandwich and a cup of soup for $2. Dinner specials 2-8pm ($6). Domestic drafts $1. Open 24hr. Cash only.

White House Sub Shop, 2301 Arctic Ave. (☎ 609-345-8599, takeout 609-345-1564; www.whitehousesubshop.com), at Mississippi Ave. Sinatra was rumored to have had these immense subs ($4-7 for half, $9-12 for whole) flown to him while on tour. Pictures of sublovers Joe DiMaggio, Wayne Newton, and Mr. T overlook the team making each sandwich to order. Open Su-Th 10am-10pm, F-Sa 10am-11pm. Cash only.

Tony's Baltimore Grille, 2800 Atlantic Ave. (☎ 609-345-5766), at Iowa Ave. Tourists can't resist the old-time Italian atmosphere with personal jukeboxes, not to mention the $3-8 pizza. Seafood platter $12. Open daily 11am-3am. Bar open 24hr. Cash only.

Bill's Gyro and Souvlaki, 1607 Boardwalk (☎ 609-347-2466), near Kentucky Ave. Park in one of the casino lots or on the street. Thousands of customer-signed dollar bills adorn the walls, stools, cash registers, and counter at this bright establishment. The menu offers 24hr. breakfast (eggs $3-5.75), hot and cold sandwiches ($4.45-10), burgers, and dessert. Open 24hr.

🏠 ACCOMMODATIONS

Motels are located 2-6 mi. out of town on U.S. 40 and U.S. 30, as well as in Absecon (8 mi. west of town on U.S. 30). Before dropping in the off season, rates can more than triple the week of the *Miss America Pageant*, usually the second or third week in September.

🛏 **Inn of the Irish Pub**, 164 St. James Pl. (☎ 609-344-9063; www.theirishpub.com), between New York Ave. and Tennessee Ave., near the Ramada Tower. Spacious, clean rooms less than a block from the Boardwalk. Enjoy the porch's rocking chairs and refreshing Atlantic breeze. The down-

🏰 stairs bar offers lively entertainment and a friendly atmosphere. Key deposit $7. Free parking across the street. Doubles with $45-52, with bath $75-90; quads with shared bath $85-99.

Comfort Inn, 154 S. Kentucky Ave. (☎609-348-4000), between Martin Luther King Blvd. and New York Ave., near the Sands. Basic rooms with king-size or 2 queen-size beds and—true to Atlantic City swank—a jacuzzi. Continental breakfast, free parking, and a heated pool. Rooms with ocean views are $20 extra, but come with fridge, microwave, and a bigger jacuzzi. Reserve in advance for weekends and holidays. Singles June-Aug. $100-159; Sept.-May $59-69.

Rodeway Inn, 124 S. North Carolina Ave. (☎609-345-0155 or 800-228-2000), across from the Resorts Casino. Fairly basic motel room fare, but the rates are reasonable and the location is excellent, nestled between the pricier resort casinos and only a bit farther from the Boardwalk. Rooms $50-150.

Red Carpet Motel, 1630 Albany Ave. (☎609-348-3171). A bit out of the way, off the Atlantic Expwy. on the way to town. Be careful in the surrounding neighborhood after dark. Standard, comfy rooms with cable TV and free shuttles to the Boardwalk and casinos. Restaurant in lobby. Doubles $39-59; quads $55-79. Prices can jump to $130 summer weekends.

Shady Pines Campground, 443 S. 6th Ave. (☎609-652-1516), in Absecon, 6 mi. from Atlantic City. Take Exit 12 from the Expwy. This leafy, 140-site campground has a pool, playground, laundry, firewood service, and new showers and restrooms. Call ahead for summer weekend reservations. Open Mar.-Nov. Sites with water and electricity $33.

🔵 **LUCY THE ELEPHANT** 9200 Atlantic Ave. *In Margate City, off the Garden State Pkwy. at Exit 36. Follow signs to Margate and Lucy.*

Originally built in 1881 by land developer James Lafferty as a marketing gimmick, Lucy has always been a sight for the public. It's no wonder; at 65 ft. and 90 tons, she's hardly the average pachyderm. After she fell into disrepair in the 1960s, the Save Lucy Committee convinced the city to donate land for a site and raised $62,000 to restore her and move her two blocks down the beach to her present location. (☎609-823-6473; www.lucytheelephant.org. Open mid-June to Labor Day M-Sa 10am-8pm, Su 10am-5pm; Apr. to mid-June and Sept.-Dec. Sa-Su 10am-5pm. Tours every 30min. $4, children $2. No public parking or restrooms; free street parking.)

🔺 **APPROACHING OCEAN CITY**
From Atlantic City or Margate, the **Garden State Pkwy.** goes over the Longport toll bridge to the north end of the island and becomes **Wesley Ave.**

OCEAN CITY, NJ

Billing itself as "America's favorite family resort," Ocean City balances the busy boardwalk and gaudy excess of beach attractions with an array of cultural activities ranging from a summer concert series to a nature center. While hotels and B&Bs clutter the boardwalk, a few blocks away the town is mostly residential—a nice contrast to some of its rowdier neighbors. The family-oriented atmosphere, however, means that there's not much to do after dark, so it's best to take full advantage of the daytime activities.

(VITAL STATS)

Population: 15,500

Visitor Info: Ocean City Regional Chamber of Commerce (☎609-399-2629 or 800-232-2465), on the Howard Stainton Memorial Causeway. Open M-Sa 9am-5pm, Su 10am-2pm. **Information booth,** on the boardwalk at 8th Ave.

Internet Access: Ocean City Free Public Library, 1735 Simpson Ave. (☎609-399-2434 or 609-399-2143). Open M-F 9am-9pm, Sa 9am-5pm, Su 1-5pm.

Post Office: 859 Ocean Ave. (☎609-399-0475). Open M-F 9am-9pm, Sa 9am-5pm, Su 1-5pm. **Postal Code:** 08226.

📧 GETTING AROUND. The boardwalk stretches 2½ mi. along the beach toward the north end of the island. Most hotels lie between the beach and **Ocean Ave.,** between 1st and 9th St. Downtown centers on **Asbury Ave.** between 6th and 14th St. Public **parking** lots are available near the beach for $10-15, but there is metered parking along Asbury Ave. for up to 4hr. and free parking in some residential areas farther away. All parking fills up quickly in summer.

📷 SIGHTS. In the summer, Ocean City's **beaches** are its best attraction. Those over 11 have to wear **beach tags,** available on the boardwalk at the end of 8th Ave. (Open for swimming June-Labor Day daily 9am-5:30pm; closed 10pm-6am. Beach tag $5 per day, $8 per week.) **Surf Buggy Centers,** at 8th Ave. and Broadway, rents bikes and surreys for seashore exploration. (☎609-399-2468; www.surfbuggycenters.com. Bikes $5-6 per hr., $18 per day; surreys $15 per hr.) The **7th Street Surf Shop,** 654 Boardwalk, rents surfboards and offers lessons. (☎609-391-1700. Surfboards $10 per hr., $30 per day, $75 per week. Credit card or driver's license required.) The **Bayside Center,** 520 Bay Ave., has an environmental center with exhibits on local animals, a lifeguard museum, and models of local buildings. During summer, the center also offers **guided beachwalks,** starting at 59th and Central Ave., to explain natural relics. (Summer ☎609-525-9244, winter 609-525-9301. Open daily 8am-8pm. Beachwalks July-Aug. Tu 9:30am, W 6:30pm. $1, children $0.50.)

The **Ocean City Art Center,** 1735 Simpson Ave., offers classes in everything from dance to pottery and organizes art shows. (☎609-399-7628; www.oceancityartscenter.org. Open M-Th 9am-9pm, F-Sa 9am-4pm.) In the same building, the **Friends of the Ocean City Historical Museum** displays remnants of the Sindia, a large barque that ran aground in Ocean City in 1901, and mannequins in turn-of-the-century outfits suited to the season. (☎609-399-1801. Open May-Oct. M-F 10am-4pm, Sa 1-4pm; June-Aug. also open Th 4-7pm; Nov. M-Sa 1-4pm. Free.) The **Boardwalk Concert Series** at the **Music Pier** runs summers with family-friendly musical acts. (☎609-525-9248. Tickets available at the Music Pier Box Office in the Ocean City Regional Chamber of Commerce.)

⊶ FOOD. Ocean City's boardwalk is lined with storefronts that provide the cheapest, if not the most well-rounded, meals in town, selling pizza and South Jersey favorites like Italian ice (also, redundantly, called "water ice"), funnel cakes, and custard. Downtown, streets are lined with a number of casual, inexpensive eateries. **Kibbitz Down the Shore,** 846 Central Ave., is a New York-style deli dishing out massive portions—the reubens ($7 half, $11 whole) have a full pound of corned beef. Make sure to save room for the blintzes, potato pancakes, rugalach, and hammentash. (☎609-398-0880. Open daily 11am-8pm.) Local favorite **Portobello Ristorante and Pizzeria,** 953 Asbury Ave., serves classic Italian dishes from ravioli ($12) to *pasta al delia* ($17) in an old-world atmosphere. (☎609-399-3278. Open daily 11am-

9:30pm.) While it has little by way of character, **Nags Head Fine Foods,** 801 Asbury Ave., has delicious meals with fresh ingredients. (☎609-391-9080. Sandwiches $6-9. Entrees $10-15. Open M-Sa 11:30am-2pm and 5-8pm.)

⌐ ACCOMMODATIONS. Ocean City has plenty of quaint but pricey B&Bs. For cheaper albeit less luxurious accommodations, there is the **Sun Beach Motor Lodge,** on 9th St. at Wesley Ave., which has basic rooms and amenities as well as an outdoor pool and free morning coffee. (☎609-399-3350; www.sunbeachmotel.com. Rooms in summer $100-150; in low season $55-70.) The **Homestead Hotel,** 805 E. 8th St., offers more distinctive accommodations in a European-style building with views of the city and the ocean. It has an excellent location only a few blocks from the boardwalk. (☎609-391-0200; www.homesteadhotel.info. Rooms in summer $120-140; low season $70-90.)

⊼ APPROACHING CAPE MAY
Follow the tollbooth-laden **Garden State Pkwy.** about 25 mi., as far south as it goes. Watch for signs to **Center City** until you reach **Lafayette St.**

CAPE MAY

At the southern end of New Jersey's coastline, Cape May is the oldest seashore resort in the US, and the money here is no younger. Once the summer playground of Upper East Side New Yorkers, the town still shows signs of affluence in the elegant restaurants of Beach Ave. Meanwhile, the resort's main attraction remains its sparkling white beaches, which are not burdened with the commercialism of more modern beach towns.

⊏ GETTING AROUND

The **Garden State Pkwy.** leads into Cape May from the north, reaching its end at Cape May Harbor. Parallel to the parkway are **U.S. 9** and **Rte. 626.** As Rte. 626 heads south toward the southern tip of the cape, it becomes **Seashore Rd.** and then **South Broadway,** running parallel to **Lafayette St. (Rte. 633).** There is free **parking** at the Cape May City elementary school (on the right heading into town from the north) in summer.

VITAL STATS

Population: 4000

Visitor Info: Welcome Center, 609 Lafayette St. (☎ 609-884-9562). Open daily 9am-4:30pm. **Chamber of Commerce,** 513 Washington St. Mall. (☎ 609-884-5508; www.capemaychamber.com). Open M-F 9am-5pm, Sa-Su 10am-6pm. **Washington Street Mall Information Booth** (☎ 800-275-4278; www.capemaymac.org), at Ocean St. Open summer daily 9:15am-4pm and 6-9pm; call for low-season hours.

Internet Access: Cape May County Library, 30 Mechanic St. (☎ 609-463-6350). Open summer M-Th 8:30am-9pm, F 8:30am-4:30pm, Sa 9am-4:30pm; winter M-F 8:30am-9pm, Sa 9am-4:30pm, Su 1-5pm. **Magic Brain Cybercafe** (see p. 98).

Post Office: 700 Washington St. (☎ 609-884-3578). Open M-F 9am-5pm, Sa 8:30am-12:30pm. **Postal Code:** 08204.

◎ SIGHTS

THE BEACH. Cape May's sands actually sparkle, studded with the famous Cape May "diamonds" (quartz pebbles). A **beach tag** is required for beachgoers over 11, available from roaming vendors or from the **Beach Tag Office.** *(At Grant and Beach Dr. ☎ 609-884-9522. Open for swimming daily 10am-5pm; closed 10pm-6am. Tags required June-Sept. daily 10am-5pm. $4 per day, $11 per week.)* **South End Surf Shop** rents beach necessities. *(311 Beach Ave. ☎ 609-898-0988. Surfboards $15 per day. Driver's license required. Open Apr.-Sept. daily 9am-4pm.)* Those thinking of wave jumping can rent boats, waverunners, and kayaks from **Cape May Watersports.** *(1286 Wilson Dr. ☎ 609-884-8646. Boats $50-60 per 4hr., waverunners $50 per hr.; kayaks $15 per hr. Open daily 8am-dusk.)* **Cape May Seashore Lines** runs four old-fashioned trains per day to attractions along the 26 mi. stretch to Tuckahoe. *(☎ 609-884-2675. $8, children $5.)* Bike the beach with the help of **Shields' Bike Rentals.** *(11 Gurney St. $4 per hr., $9 per day; tandems $10/$30; surreys $24 per hr. Open daily 7am-7pm.)*

CAPE MAY POINT STATE PARK. Those in search of exercise and a view of the seashore can ascend the 199 steps to the beacon of the 1859 **Cape May Lighthouse** in Cape May Point State Park, west of town at the end of the point. The 157 ft. lighthouse was the third built on the site, and the 1893 oil house now serves as gift shop and Visitors Center. Three clearly marked trails commence at the Visitors Center: the red (½ mi.), yellow (1¼ mi.; moderate and flat), and the blue trails (2 mi.; moderate and flat) boast excellent bird watching in the marsh and oceanside dunes. The behemoth bunker next to the lighthouse is a WWII gun emplacement, used to scan the shore for German U-boats. There's a sandy beach available too, but due to dangerous currents swimming is not allowed. *(Lighthouse and museum ☎ 609-884-5404; www.njparksandforests.org. Visitors Center ☎ 609-884-2159. Park open daily dawn-dusk. Lighthouse open Apr.-Nov. daily 9am-8pm; Dec.-Mar. Sa-Su 8am-dusk. Museum open daily 8am-8pm. Visitors Center open daily July-Aug. 8am-8pm; Sept.-June 8am-4:30pm. Lighthouse $5, ages 3-12 $1.)*

WILDLIFE. Due to the unusually close proximity of freshwater ponds adjacent to the oceanside, even migratory birds flock to Cape May for a break from the long southbound flight. Sneak a peek at over 300 types of feathered vacationers at the **Cape May Bird Observatory,** a birdwatcher's paradise. Bird maps, field trips, and workshops are available, along with advice about where to go for the best birdwatching. *(701 E. Lake Dr., on Cape May Point. ☎ 609-884-2736; www.njaudubon.org. Open Su and Tu-Sa 10am-5pm.)* For a look at some larger creatures, including dolphins and whales, **Cape May Whale Watch and Research Center** offers tours. *(☎ 888-531-0055. $17-22, ages 7-12 $8-12.)*

MID-ATLANTIC CENTER FOR THE ARTS (MAC). The MAC runs walking and trolley tours of the city's major historical sites, including the **Emlen Physick Estate,** a Victorian mansion restored to showcase the luxury of the upper classes and the living conditions of their servants. Trolley tours run to the city's west end, east end, and along the beach front and last about 30min. Combination tours with the Physick Estate are available. MAC also runs unique cultural events, such as the **Sherlock Holmes Weekends** and the annual **Victorian Weekends.** *(1048 Washington St. ☎ 609-688-5404 or 800-275-4278; www.capemaymac.org. Tours $6, ages 3-12 $3.)*

CAPE MAY AIRPORT AVIATION MUSEUM. This museum displays vintage aircraft in a WWII-era hangar—the perfect stop for an aviation buff. *(500 Forrestal Rd., at Cape May Airport. Take Exit 4A* off the Garden State Pkwy. and follow signs. ☎609-886-8787; www.usnasw.org. Open summer daily 9am-5pm; winter M-F 8am-4pm, Sa-Su 8am-3pm.)

▓ FOOD

Cape May's cheapest food is the generic pizza and burger fare along **Beach Ave.** Shell out a few more clams for one of the posh beachside restaurants. Crawling with pedestrians hunting for heavenly fudge and saltwater taffy, the **Washington St. Mall** supports several popular food stores and eateries.

The Mad Batter, 19 Jackson St. (☎609-884-5970; www.madbatter.com). Start the morning right with blueberry blintz crepes with warm syrup ($7.50) or one of the array of omelettes ($9). Choose from sandwiches for lunch ($5-10) or steak and seafood ($20-25) for dinner. Open daily 8am-10pm.

Ristorante a Ca Mia, 524 Washington St. Mall (☎609-884-6661). Richly flavored Northern Italian food combines with contemporary American twists to create meals like the crab cake Italiano (breaded and sauteed with spinach and pine nuts; $10.75). Bakery serves homemade baked goods, salads, and gourmet coffees. Open summer daily 11:30am-3pm and 5-10pm; winter closed M-F.

Ugly Mug, 426 Washington St. Mall (☎609-884-3459). Worth battling through the initially suffocating smokescreen. Patrons inhale a New England cup o' chowder ($2.25) or the ever-popular "oceanburger" ($5.75). Free pizza M 10pm-2am. Open M-Sa 11am-2am, Su noon-2am. Hot food served until 11pm.

Magic Brain Cybercafe, 31 Perry St. (☎609-884-8188; www.magicbraincybercafe.com). Spotless new Internet cafe with an amicable staff less than 1 block from the beach. The best place in town to grab a quick caffeine fix and check email. Internet $7 per 30min. Open daily 8am-10pm. Cash only.

▓ ACCOMMODATIONS

Lodgings aren't cheap in Cape May; hotels and Victorian B&Bs along the beach run $85-250 per night. Prices drop farther from the shore. Campgrounds line U.S. 9 just north of Cape May.

Hotel Clinton, 202 Perry St. (☎609-884-3993), at S. Lafayette St. Family-owned establishment with 16 breezy, home-style rooms, the most affordable rates in town, and charismatic Italian proprietors. Reservations recommended. Open mid-June to Sept. Singles $35; doubles $45. Cash only.

Parris Inn, 204 Perry St. (☎609-884-8015). Rents a variety of spacious, comfortable rooms and apartments less than 3 blocks from the beach, most with private baths, A/C, and TV. Open mid-Apr. to Dec. Singles $45-65; doubles $65-125.

Poor Richard's Inn, 17 Jackson St. (☎609-884-3536; www.poorrichardsinn.com). An elegant inn less than 1 block from the beach, in the heart of a line of colorful Victorian homes and B&Bs. Some shared baths. Check-in 1-10pm. Check-out 10:30am. Rooms Memorial Day-Oct. $75-165; low-season $65-150.

Cape Island Campground, 709 U.S. 9 (☎800-437-7443; www.capeisland.com). In a prime seashore location. Connected to Cape May by the Seashore Line. Fully equipped campground features mini-golf, 2 pools, a playground, a store, and laundry facilities. Sites with full hookup $38.

▓ NIGHTLIFE

Appealing to the alternative rock scene, **Carney's,** on Beach Ave. between Jackson and Decatur St., offers nightly entertainment in the summer beginning at 10pm. Themed parties include "Island Tropics" and "Animal House." The "other room" features live jazz, blues, and gospel. (☎609-884-4424. Su jams 4-9pm. Open daily 11:30am-2am.) A chic crowd congregates at **Cabana's,** at the corner of Decatur St. and Beach Ave., across from the beach. You'll have to find a lot of sand dollars if you want an entree ($16-22), but sandwiches and burgers are substantially less ($7-10) and there is no cover for the nightly blues or jazz. (☎609-884-4800; www.cabanasonthebeach.com. Acoustic sessions Sa 4-6:30pm. Open daily noon-2am.)

LEAVING NEW JERSEY: THE CAPE MAY-LEWES FERRY

A ferry runs between Cape May, NJ and Lewes, DE, cutting 2-3hr. off the drive. Driving from the tip of Cape May, take **Rte. 626** over the Cape May Canal, then turn left onto **U.S. 9** (called first **Sandman Blvd.** then **Ferry Rd.**) to the ferry terminal. The transportation is fairly elaborate for a 1½hr. cruise—four viewing decks, multiple lounges with televisions, a children's center with games and activities, and a food court. The ferry often sells out during the summer, so call ahead for reservations ($5 fee). On the Lewes side, the ferry lets out onto **Cape Henlopen Dr.** leading either to **Cape Henlopen State Park** on the left or into the town of **Lewes** on the right. (☎800-643-3779; www.capemaylewesferry.com. Runs Apr.-Nov. and Christmas week. One-way Apr.-Oct. $25 for car and driver; $8 per additional passenger, under 6 free. Nov.-Dec. $20/$6.)

Welcome To **DELAWARE**

LEWES

Explored by Henry Hudson and founded in 1613 by the Dutch, Lewes (pronounced Lewis) was the first town in the first state. Over the years it has attracted colonists, pirates, fishermen, and now summer renters. The city hasn't changed much, maintaining its Victorian houses, quiet streets, and genuine lack of tourist culture. Though Lewes has plotted out a walking tour of its colonial attractions, the main draw—especially for the older and wealthier set—remains its beautiful beach.

(VITAL STATS)

Population: 2900

Visitor Info: Fisher-Martin House Info Center, 120 Kings Hwy. (☎302-645-8073 or 877-465-3937; www.leweschamber.com), off Savannah Rd. Open M-F 10am-4pm.

Internet Access: Lewes Public Library, 111 Adams Ave. (☎302-645-2733), at Kings Hwy. Open M and W-Th 10am-9pm, Tu and F 10am-5pm, Sa 10am-2pm.

Post Office: 116 Front St. (☎302-644-1948). Open M-F 8:30am-5pm, Sa 8am-noon. **Postal Code:** 19958.

▐ GETTING AROUND. Cape Henlopen Dr. (Rte. 19) runs along the coast into Cape Henlopen State Park. **Kings Hwy. (U.S. 9)** runs out from the city and intersects with **U.S. 1.** There is metered public

parking on Front St. ($0.25 per 30min.) from 9am to 6pm, as well as free parking on some residential streets outside the small downtown.

◐ ꕔ SIGHTS & OUTDOORS. Secluded among sand dunes and scrub pines 1 mi. east of Lewes on the Atlantic Ocean is the 4000-acre **Cape Henlopen State Park,** where children frolic in the waves under the watchful eyes of lifeguards. In addition to its expansive beach, the park is home to sparkling white "walking dunes," a 2 mi. paved trail ideal for biking or skating, and a well-preserved WWII observation tower. Campsites are also only a short hike from the beach. (From the north, bypass Savannah Rd. and continue on U.S. 1; signs mark the park on the left. ☎302-645-8983. Park open daily 8am-dusk. Campground open Apr.-Nov. Sites $22, with water $24. Day-use $5 per car.) Bike rentals are free at the **Seaside Nature Center,** the park's museum on beach and ocean wildlife, which also hosts weekly lectures and leads hikes. (☎302-645-6852. Open daily July-Aug. 9am-5pm; Sept.-June 9am-4pm. Bike rental available 9am-3pm; 2hr. limit.)

The Zwaanendael Museum, 102 Kings Hwy., is a bright two-story space filled with relics of maritime history and exhibits on the settlement of Delaware, lighthouses, and shipwrecks. The museum building itself is a replica of the old town hall in Hoorn, Holland. Its name comes from the original name of the town, meaning "Valley of the Swans," and the museum emphasizes Delaware's heritage as a Dutch colony. (☎302-645-1148. Open Su 1:30-4:30pm, Tu-Sa 10am-4:30pm. Free.)

Historic buildings assemble around the **Historical Society Complex,** 110 Shipcarpenter St., near 2nd St. The society runs walking tours of historic Lewes that leave from Ryves Holt House at the corner of 2nd St. and Mulberry St. It has also preserved 12 properties as museums. (☎302-645-7670; www.historiclewes.org. Complex open June-Aug. M and W-F 10am-4pm, Sa 10:30am-noon. Tours May-Oct. Tu and F 3pm. Museum open June-Aug. M-F 10am-4pm, Sa 10am-1pm. Complex $6. Tours $5. Museum $6, under 12 free.)

▞ FOOD. The few restaurants in Lewes cluster primarily on **2nd St.** Once a sea captain's house, **The Buttery,** at 2nd and Savannah St., is the best spot for fine dining and people-watching in Lewes, with a traditional dining room complete with white tablecloths. (☎302-645-7755. Lunch

$7-15. Dinner $18-32. Su brunch 10:30am-2:30pm. Open M-F 11am-2:30pm and 5-9pm, Sa-Su 11am-2:30pm and 5-10pm. Reservations recommended.) Voted "Best Ice Cream" in 2003 by *Delaware Today*, **Kings Homemade Ice Cream Shops,** 201 2nd. St., is the toast (or should we say "topping") of the town. (☎302-645-9425. 1 scoop $2.25, 2 scoops $3.25. Open May-Oct. daily 11am-11pm.) **Books by the Bay Cafe,** 111 Bank St., serves coffee and creative sandwiches like the Reuben by the Sea or the Pilgrim's Feast panini ($5.50). The cafe also includes a small book shop, and the decor is maritime-oriented, with anchor-shaped coat hooks and clean blue and white walls. (Cafe ☎302-644-6571. Bookstore ☎302-645-2304. Breakfast served until 11:30am. Open daily 7am-5pm.) **Cafe Azafran,** 109 Market St., has affordable Mediterranean dishes that creatively combine tastes from various countries, such as the Ricardo's Panini ($5.75) with pesto, artichokes, cheese, roasted peppers, and arugula on Italian bread. (☎302-644-4446. Open daily 6:30am-4:30pm and 6-10pm.) Check out the **Rose and Crown Restaurant and Pub,** 108 2nd St., for great burgers ($5-7) or English specialties like bangers and mash ($13). On weekends come for live blues and rock. (☎302-645-2373. Happy hour 4-6pm; $1 off all drinks. Open daily 11am-1am.)

▐ ACCOMMODATIONS. From the bustle of Lewes's main thoroughfare, escape to the secluded and classy **Zwaanendael Inn,** 142 2nd St. In addition to a central location, the inn offers finely decorated, spacious quarters. (☎302-645-6466; www.zwaanendaelinn.com. Check-in 2pm. Check-out 11am. Rooms in summer $95-260; winter $50-170.) The least expensive accommodations downtown are found at the **Vesuvio Motel,** 105 Savannah Rd., right by the shops of Front St. and 2nd St. The rooms are basic but much cheaper than the town's B&Bs. (☎302-645-2224. Rooms $65-135.)

▐ APPROACHING REHOBOTH BEACH
To reach Rehoboth from Lewes, take **U.S. 9** to **U.S. 1A,** which becomes **Rehoboth Ave.** after 4 mi.

REHOBOTH BEACH

Rehoboth Beach lies between Lewes and Ocean City, both geographically and culturally. While Lewes tends to be quiet and family-oriented and Ocean City attracts rowdy students, Rehoboth balances boardwalk fun with serene, antique B&Bs and family-run guest-houses. Well-heeled Washington families and a growing gay population comprise the beach's summer crowd.

(VITAL STATS)

Population: 1500

Visitor Info: Rehoboth Beach Chamber of Commerce, 501 Rehoboth Ave. (☎302-227-2233 or 800-441-1329; www.beach-fun.com). Open M-F 9am-5pm, Sa-Su 9am-1pm.

Internet Access: Rehoboth Beach Public Library, 226 Rehoboth Ave. (☎302-227-8044). Open M and F 10am-5pm, Tu-Th noon-8pm, Sa 10am-3pm.

Post Office: 179 Rehoboth Ave. (☎302-227-8406), at 2nd St. Open M-F 9am-5pm, Sa 8:30am-12:30pm. **Postal Code:** 19971.

▐ GETTING AROUND

The town's main drag is **Rehoboth Ave.,** which heads straight for the water. Perpendicular to Rehoboth Ave. is **2nd St.,** which turns into **Bayard Ave.** and **Silver Lake Dr.** as it travels south. **Mike's Bikes,** at the corner of Baltimore Ave. and Division St., has bike rentals. ($5 per hr., $14 per half-day. ID required. Open daily 6am-5pm.)

◉▐ SIGHTS & BEACHES

Just south of Rehoboth lies **Dewey Beach,** a favorite with the younger crowd and home to plenty of hotels, motels, and food markets. Farther south is the **Delaware Seashore State Park,** with opportunities for camping, swimming on the ocean and in the bay, and crabbing and clamming without a license. There is also a marina packed with fishing boats and concession stands. (☎302-227-2800; www.destateparks.com. Open Apr.-Nov. daily 8am-4:30pm; Dec.-Mar. M-F 8am-4:30pm. $5.) Slightly north of the park is the **Indian River Life-Saving Station Museum and Historic Site,** 130 Coastal Hwy., in the 1876 building that was one of six life-saving stations built along Delaware's coast to help the victims of shipwrecks. The museum displays photographs and artifacts from the lives and the "surfmen" who once worked there. (☎302-227-0478. Open Memorial

Day-Labor Day daily 10am-5pm.) **Bethany Beach** lies still farther down the Coastal Hwy. and is primarily a summer destination for families seeking a quieter vacation.

FOOD

Rehoboth is known for its high-quality beach cuisine at bargain prices. **Taste,** 122 Rehoboth Ave., is a recent addition to the dining scene and combines cultures to create meals in a brightly colored, casual restaurant. (☎302-226-4250. Entrees $10-16. Appetizers $7-10.) **Cafe Papillon,** 42 Rehoboth Ave., in the Penny Lane Mall, offers light, authentic French fare. Chefs serve fresh crepes ($2.75-7), croissants ($2-3.50), and stuffed baguette sandwiches ($5-8) on a small outdoor patio. (☎302-227-7568. Open July-Oct. daily 8am-11pm; Apr.-June Sa-Su 8am-11pm.) The **Java Beach Coffee House and Cafe,** 167 Rehoboth Ave., serves generously portioned salads, sandwiches, and breakfast sandwiches all day long on the ground floor of an old house. (☎302-226-3377. Free wireless Internet. Open daily 6:30am-10pm.) **Royal Treat,** 4 Wilmington Ave., serves up a stack of pancakes and bacon for just $5.90 and sells ice cream late into the evening. (☎302-227-6277. Open daily June-Aug. 8-11:30am and 1-11:30pm.) **S.O.B's Deli,** 56 Baltimore Ave., assembles classic sandwiches and creatively named "specialty hoagies" like the Pauli, the Slob, and the Fat Bastard (corned beef, pastrami, Swiss cheese and mustard) for $6-8 at a quick and casual counter. (☎302-226-2226. Open daily summer 10am-5pm; winter 11am-3pm.)

ACCOMMODATIONS

Inexpensive lodgings abound in Rehoboth. The **Boardwalk Plaza Hotel,** on Lewes Boardwalk at Olive Ave., offers upscale lodging, complete with parrots in the lobby, Victorian decor, and rooftop and oceanside pools. (☎302-227-7169; www.boardwalkplaza.com. Check-in 3pm. Check-out 11am. Rooms $59-519. 10% AAA, military, and AARP discount in low season.) The comfortable porch at **The Abbey Inn,** 31 Maryland Ave., is just a block away from the attractions of Rehoboth Ave. and gets endorsements from guests who

enjoy its homey atmosphere. (☎302-227-7023. 2-night min. stay. Open late May to early Sept. Singles and doubles with shared bath from $48; triples and quads with shared bath $61; suite with private bath $105. 15% surcharge on weekends.) **The Beach View Motel,** 6 Wilmington Ave., 50 yd. from the boardwalk, has clean, if bland rooms that come with refrigerators, microwaves, and continental breakfast. (☎302-227-2999; www.beachviewmotel.com. Rooms in summer $139-194; in winter $45-139.) **Big Oaks Family Campground,** 1 mi. off U.S. 1 on Rd. 270, offers a rugged alternative to town lodging. (☎302-645-6838. Sites $32.) Camping is also available a few miles south on U.S. 1 at the **Delaware Seashore State Park.** (☎302-539-7202, reservations 877-987-2757. Sites $22, with full hookup $34.)

NIGHTLIFE

Rehoboth party-goers head out early to maximize their time before 1am last calls. The super-casual **Summer House Saloon,** 228 Rehoboth Ave., across from City Hall, is a favorite flirtation spot for a youngish crowd with walls painted with skies and clouds. (☎302-227-3895; www.summerhousesaloon.com. Su 4-8pm half-price daiquiris. Live blues and rock Th 9:30pm-1:30am. DJ and dancing F 9pm-1am. Open May-Sept. M and Sa-Su 4pm-1am, Tu-F 5pm-1am.) Look for live music at **Dogfish Head Brewings & Eats,** 320 Rehoboth Ave., with brewery-style decor and food for those who don't believe in eating light. (☎302-226-2739; www.dogfish.com. Happy hour daily with $2 homemade rum and gin drinks. Live music F-Sa 10pm-1am. Open May-Aug. M-Th 4-11pm, F 4pm-1am, Sa noon-1am, Su noon-11pm; Sept.-Apr. M and Th 4pm-midnight, F 4pm-1am, Sa noon-1am, Su noon-11pm.) As its name implies, **Sydney's Blues and Jazz Restaurant,** 25 Christian St., at the corner of Rehoboth Ave., features nightly musical performances. Weekends spotlight blues, soul, and R&B, Thursday is jazz, and Sunday features cabaret. (☎302-227-1339; www.rehoboth.com/sydneys. Cover varies. Music 8:30pm weekdays, 9:30pm weekends. Open daily 5pm-1am.)

LEAVING REHOBOTH
From Rehoboth, follow **U.S. 1** south, which becomes **Coastal Hwy./Philadelphia Ave.** The journey is about 28 mi. long.

OCEAN CITY, MD

Ocean City is a lot like a kiddie pool—it's shallow and plastic, but can be fun if you're the right age, or just in the right mood. This 10 mi. strip of prime Atlantic beach packs endless bars, all-you-can-eat buffets, hotels, mini-golf courses, boardwalks, flashing neon, and sun-seeking tourists into a thin region between the ocean and the Assawoman Bay. The siren call of senior week beckons droves of recent high-school and college graduates to alcohol and hormone-driven fun, turning O.C. into a city-wide block party in June. July and August cater more to families and professional singles looking for inexpensive fun in the sun.

VITAL STATS

Population: 7200

Visitor Info: Ocean City Visitors Center, 4001 Coastal Hwy.(☎800-626-2326; www.ococean.com), at 40th St. in the Convention Center. Open June-Aug. M-F 8:30am-5pm, Sa-Su 9am-5pm; Sept.-May daily 8:30am-5pm.

Internet Access: Ocean City Public Library (☎410-289-7297), on Coastal Hwy. between 14th and 15th St. Open M-F 9am-5pm, Sa 9am-noon.

Post Office: 7101 Coastal Hwy. (☎410-524-7611). Open M-F 9am-5pm, Sa 9am-noon. **Postal Code:** 21842.

GETTING AROUND

Within Ocean City, numbered streets run east-west across the narrow strip of land linking the ocean to the bay. Numbers increase from south to north. Avenues run vertically north-south

through town, as does the **Coastal Hwy.** The **Boardwalk** parallels the ocean. Most hotels are in the lower numbered streets near the ocean; most clubs and bars are uptown toward the bay. There is free **parking** on many of the island's residential streets, particularly on the bay side of the Coastal Hwy. The Hugh T. Cropper Inlet Lot also lies at the southern end of the island. (Under 30min. free, $1.50 per hr., $0.25 per additional 10min.)

SIGHTS & BEACHES

Ocean City's star attraction is its beautiful **beach.** The wide stretch of surf and sand runs the entire 10 mi. worth of town and can be accessed by taking a left onto any of the numerous side streets off Philadelphia and Baltimore Ave. The breaking waves know no time constraints, but beach-goers are technically limited to 6am-10pm. Located at the corner of Wimcomico St. and the boardwalk, **Ocean City Pier Rides and Amusements** has a huge ferris wheel, a merry-go-round, roller coasters and games for fun stuffed animals. At the inlet, **Trimper's Amusements** offers a slightly smaller ferris wheel, a century-old Hershell carousel, and a tilt-a-whirl. For a larger park, try the **Jolly Roger Amusement Park,** 2901 Coastal Hwy., which includes multiple go-kart tracks, mini-golf, a number of rides, and the huge Splash Mountain water park featuring slides, a large water playground, and a kids' area. (☎410-289-4902; www.jollyrogerpark.com. Splash Mountain day pass $30, under 42 in. $11.) The **Ocean City Life-Saving Station Museum,** at the southern tip of the Boardwalk, contains artifacts from the history of the United States Life-Saving Service, as well as over a hundred different "sands of the world," antique swimsuits, and a mermaid collection. (☎410-289-4991. Open June-Sept. daily 11am-10pm; May and Oct. daily 11am-4pm; Nov.-Apr. Sa-Su 11am-4pm. $3, under 12 $1.)

FOOD

Ocean City's cuisine is plentiful and cheap, but don't expect gourmet quality. **Reflections,** 6600 Coastal Hwy., at 67th St., on the ground floor of the Holiday Inn, offers tableside cooking, a generous buffet, and cheesy decor. (☎410-524-5252. Early-bird dinner entrees $10-

19. Entrees from $20. Open daily 5-10:30pm.) For a something more expensive and a bit healthier, try **Coral Reef Cafe,** 1701 Atlantic Ave., inside the Holiday Inn on the Boardwalk at 17th St. Crab dip with toasted focaccia ($10) and the New Orleans chicken wrap ($9) are just a couple of specialties worth the extra money. (☎410-289-6388; www.ocsuites.com. Open daily June-Sept. 7am-10pm; Oct.-May 7am-9pm.) **Al's Louisiana Kitchen,** 9636 Stephen Decatur Hwy./Rte. 611, at Sunset Ave., serves Cajun-style favorites. Al's blackened catfish with crawfish Louisiana is the house specialty, but the seafood platter ($19) of shrimp, catfish, and oysters is the best deal. (☎410-213-1150. Open daily 6am-10pm.) **Brass Balls Saloon & Bad Ass Cafe,** on the Boardwalk between 11th and 12th St., is known for its $1.25 Jell-O shots (after 10pm). The motto here is "Drink Hearty, Eat Healthy." Breakfast specials like the Oreo waffles ($5.25) or the $7 pizzas seem to defy the latter imperative, though the college crowds can't get enough of the "drink hearty" part. (☎410-289-0069; www.brassballssaloon.com. Open Mar.-Oct. daily 8:30am-2am.) With freshly caught food and a friendly atmosphere, **The Embers,** at 24th St. and Coastal Hwy., boasts the biggest seafood buffet in town. All the clams, oysters, Alaskan crab legs, prime rib, and steak you can eat are $26. (☎410-289-3322 or 888-436-2377; www.embers.com. Open daily 3-10pm.)

ACCOMMODATIONS

The **Atlantic House Bed & Breakfast,** 501 N. Baltimore Ave., at 5th St., offers free bike rentals, a full breakfast buffet, a great location, and, in a 1920s house, a wholesome change of pace from the Ocean City motel trend. They even have complimentary beach chairs, umbrellas, and towels. (☎410-289-2333; www.atlantichouse.com. A/C, cable TV, hot tub, parking. Closed Dec.-Mar. except for Valentine's Day. Rooms June-Sept. $110-225; Oct.-May $75-175.) Just a half-block from the beach, the **Sea Spray Motel,** 12 35th St., may not feature the world's most exciting decor, but it does have a great location and offers a variety of options from motel rooms to efficiencies to full apartments to senior suites that sleep eight. A gas grill is available on premises and all rooms offer cable TV, A/C, and laundry facilities. (☎410-289-6648 or 800-678-5702; www.seaspraymotel.com. Rooms June-Sept. $80-125.) The only in-town camping option is **Ocean City Travel Park,** 105 70th St. There are laundry facilities, showers, and restrooms, but no rec room and virtually no open space. (☎410-524-7601. Sites $27-57.)

■ NIGHTLIFE

When the sun goes down, hard-earned tans glow under the glaring lights of Ocean City's bars and nightclubs. The veteran of the bayside clubs, **Fager's Island,** at 60th St. in the bay, has hordes walking the plank to its island location. Nightly live rock, R&B, jazz, and reggae accompany the selection of over 100 beers. No one seems to know the source of the tradition, but the *1812 Overture* booms at every sunset. Start the week at the Monday night deck party until 2am. (☎410-524-5500. Happy hour Tu-F with half-price drinks and appetizers. Cover before 7pm $5, after 7pm $10. Open daily 11am-2am.) Professional party-goers will no doubt be impressed by **Secrets,** on 49th St., a virtual entertainment mecca and amusement park for adults that works a tiki-bar gone wild motif. This oasis features 10 bars, including two floating bars on the bay. Barefoot partygoers wander from bar to bar, sipping the signature frozen rum runner mixed with piña colada ($6) to the strains of live bands. A magnificent sunset view ushers in early revelers for cocktails in the raft pool. (☎410-524-4900; www.secrets.com. Cover $5-20. Open daily 11am-2am.) A new addition to the Ocean City scene, the **Party Block Complex,** at 17th St. and Coastal Hwy., offers patrons one cover to flirt between four clubs, from the laid-back **Oasis Bar** to the flashy **Rush Club,** which features live hip-hop every Thursday and no cover until 10pm.

■ APPROACHING ASSATEAGUE & CHINCOTEAGUE

From Ocean City, take **U.S. 50 West** to **Rte. 611 South,** right to Assateague Island. Getting from Assateague to Chincoteague is complicated: take **Rte. 376** off of Rte. 611, then head south on **U.S. 113** toward **Snow Hill.** Continue east on **Rte. 12,** which becomes **Rte. 679,** and head north on **Rte. 175.**

ASSATEAGUE & CHINCOTEAGUE

Crashing waves, windswept dunes, wild ponies galloping free—if it sounds like the stuff of a child-hood fantasy, that's because it is. Local legend has it that ponies first came to Assateague Island by swimming ashore from a sinking Spanish galleon. A less romantic and more likely theory is that miserly colonial farmers put their horses out to graze on Assateague to avoid mainland taxes. Whatever their origins, the famous ponies now roam free across unspoiled beaches and forests of the picturesque island, and, on the last Wednesday and Thursday in July, swim from Assateague to Chincoteague during Pony Penning.

VITAL STATS

Population: 4300

Visitor Info: Barrier Island Visitors Center, 7206 National Seashore Ln./Rte. 611 (☎410-641-1441), in Berline, MD. Open daily 9am-5pm. **Chincoteague Chamber of Commerce,** 6733 Maddox Blvd. (☎757-336-6161; www.chincoteague.com), in Chin-coteague. Open M-Sa 9am-4:30pm.

Internet Access: Island Library, 4077 Main St. (☎757-336-3460), in Chincoteague. Open M, W, F-Sa 1-5pm; Tu 10am-5pm; Th 4-8pm.

Post Office: 4144 Main St. (☎757-336-2934). Open M-F 8am-4:30pm, Sa 8am-noon. **Postal Code:** 23336.

▐ GETTING AROUND

Assateague Island is the longer barrier island facing the ocean, while **Chincoteague Island** is nestled between Assateague and mainland Eastern Shore. Maryland and Virginia share Assateague Island, which is divided into three parts: the **Assateague State Park,** the **Assateague Island National Seashore,** and the **Chincoteague Wildlife Refuge,** which is actu-ally on Assateague. Unfortunately, driving the length of Assateague Island is neither permitted nor possible—there aren't roads.

▐ SIGHTS

ASSATEAGUE. The ▧**Chincoteague National Wild-life Refuge** stretches across the Virginia side of the island. Avid bird-watchers flock here to see rare species such as peregrine falcons, snowy egrets, and black-crowned night herons. The **wild pony roundup,** held the last consecutive Wednesday and Thursday in July (after a month-long carnival), brings hordes of tourists to Assateague. During slack tide, local firemen herd the ponies together and swim them from Assateague to Chincoteague Island, where the fire department auctions off the foals the following day. Head to the Visitors Cen-ter, located just inside the refuge, to learn about biking, hiking, walking, and bird and nature tours. Guided wildlife bus tours are also available. *(Tours Memorial Day-Labor Day daily 10am, 1, 4pm. $12, children $8.)* Trails include the 3 mi. pony-popu-lated **Wildlife Loop** *(open 3pm-dusk for cars, all day for pedestrians and bicyclists),* the 1½ mi. **Woodland Trail** *(cars not permitted),* and the quarter-mile **Light-house Trail** *(pedestrians only).* The last leads to the **Assateague Lighthouse,** which visitors can explore Easter weekend to Thanksgiving weekend. *(☎757-336-3696. Open daily Easter-Thanksgiving 9am-5pm. $4, ages 2-12 $2.)* Follow Beach Rd. to its end to find the famous beach and sand dunes. Park rangers request that visitors resist the urge to feed the ponies, who, if overfed by guests, could starve in the winter months when visitors have left the islands. Gawk from a safe distance—the ponies may appear harmless, but they can be tem-peramental. *(8231 Beach Rd. ☎757-336-6122; http://chinco.fws.gov. No pets permitted. Park open daily May-Sept. 5am-10pm; Oct. and Apr. 6am-8pm; Nov.-Mar. 6am-6pm. Visitors Center open daily Memo-rial Day-Labor Day 9am-5pm; Labor Day-Memorial Day 8am-4:30pm. Weekly pass $10 per car.)*

CHINCOTEAGUE. The **Oyster & Maritime Museum** is the only non-profit museum in Chin-coteague. Originally focused on the seafood industry, it's turned its attention to local history. Don't miss the 1865 Barbier & Frenestre first order Fresnel lens from the old Assateague Light-house, one of only 21 in the US. Its light could be seen from 23 mi. away. *(7125 Maddox Blvd. ☎757-336-6117. Open May-Sept. M-Sa 10am-5pm, Su noon-4pm; low-season hours vary. $3, under 13 $1.50, seniors $2. Cash only.)* The **Chincoteague Pony Centre** offers pony rides and showcases vet-erans of the pony swim in shows every night at 8pm. *(6417 Carriage Dr. Heading north on Main St., turn right onto Church St., left onto Chicken City Rd., and right onto Carriage Dr. ☎757-336-2776. Open summer M-Sa 9am-10pm, Su 1-9pm. Rides M-Sa 9am-1pm and 3:30-6pm, Su 1-4pm. $5. Shows $5.)*

FOOD & ACCOMMODATIONS

Visitors eat and sleep on **Chincoteague**. The **Sea Star,** 4121 Main St., serves "gourmet takeout" from a brightly painted booth. The signature sandwiches ($5-6) are delicious and feature plenty of vegetarian options. Painted picnic tables with umbrellas provide attractive seating in good weather. (☎757-336-5442. Open M-Th 11am-6pm, F-Sa 11am-7pm, Su 11am-4pm.) For coffee and pastries, stop by **Main St. Shop & Coffee House,** 4288 Main St. The shop also has quirky clothes, shoes, and houseware in rainbow colors. (☎757-336-6782. Open Easter-Labor Day daily 8:30am-5pm; Labor Day-Thanksgiving Sa-Su 8:30am-5pm.) **AJ's on the Creek,** 6585 Maddox Blvd., specializes in handcut steaks and grilled fish. (☎757-336-5888. Entrees $15-25. Open summer M-Sa 11am-10pm; winter M-F 4-9pm, Sa 4-9:30pm.) For light seafood on the water, try **Shucker's Cafe,** 6186 Landmark Plaza, on Chincoteague Bay. (☎757-336-5145. Open daily 8am-3pm.)

The dazzling **Hampton Inn & Suites,** 4179 Main St., is the newest lodging in town and one of the most luxurious, with continental breakfast, fridges and microwaves in every room, guest laundry, and a free business center. (☎757-336-1616. Rooms June-Aug. from $139; Sept.-May from $79. 10% AAA, AARP discount.) For breathtaking views, head to the waterfront **Island Motor Inn,** 4391 Main St. (☎757-336-3141. Rooms from $125. AAA and senior discount in low season.) **Maddox Family Campground,** across from the Visitors Center, is a sprawling site with a grocery store, arcade, pool, and bath house on site. (☎757-336-3111. For full hookups, reserve at least 3 months in advance. Sites $29-35.) More rugged camping is available on **Assateague State Park.** (Sites $30, with hookup $40.) The **Assateague Island National Seashore** (☎757-336-6122) has cold showers, a cold water source, and chemical toilets.

Welcome To VIRGINIA

APPROACHING WILLIAMSBURG

From Chincoteague, take **U.S. 13 South,** over the bridge-tunnel. Switch to **I-64 West** and get off on the **Colonial Pkwy.** exit to reach Williamsburg.

WILLIAMSBURG

Colonial Williamsburg is a blast from the past—a fife-and-drum corps marches down the streets, and costumed wheelwrights, bookbinders, and blacksmiths go about their business. Travelers who visit in late fall or early spring avoid the crowds, but miss the special summer programs.

VITAL STATS

Population: 12,000

Visitor Info: Colonial Williamsburg Visitors Center, 100 Visitors Center Dr. (☎800-447-8679 or 757-229-1000; www.colonialwilliamsburg.com). Open daily 8:30am-7pm.

Internet Access: Williamsburg Library, 7770 Croaker Rd. (☎757-259-4040). Open M-Th 10am-9pm, F 10am-6pm, Sa 10am-5pm, Su 1-5pm.

Post Office: 425 N. Boundary St. (☎757-229-0838). Open M-F 8am-5pm, Sa 9am-2pm. **Postal Code:** 23185.

GETTING AROUND

The **Colonial Pkwy.** enters Williamsburg from the east, curving south to intersect with **Rte. 5** and **Francis St. Duke of Gloucester St.,** around which Colonial Williamsburg sights cluster, runs parallel to Francis St., one block north. Free all-day public **parking** is available at the Colonial Williamsburg Visitors Center and for periods ranging from 2hr. to all day at lots downtown, near **Merchant's Sq.**

SIGHTS

At **Colonial Williamsburg,** the world's largest living history museum, it's always time to play dress-up, and visitors can partake in the fun by renting costumes inside the Visitors Center. A shuttle runs from the center to the colonial area, though a short walking path is also available. The **Orientation Walking Tour** begins at the shuttle stop and introduces visitors to the main sights of the town.

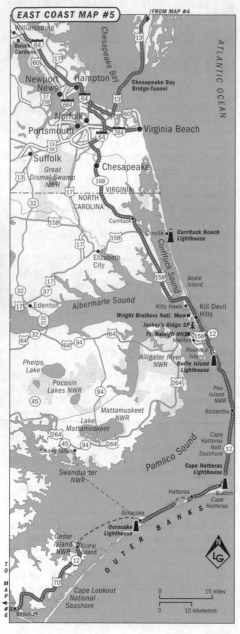

EAST COAST MAP #5

FROM MAP #4

Williamsburg
Busch Gardens
Newport News
Hampton
Chesapeake Bay
Chesapeake Bay Bridge-Tunnel
ATLANTIC OCEAN
Norfolk
Portsmouth
Virginia Beach
Suffolk
Great Dismal Swamp NWR
Chesapeake
VIRGINIA
NORTH CAROLINA
Currituck
Corolla
Currituck Beach Lighthouse
Elizabeth City
Currituck Sound
Bodie Island
Edenton
Albermarle Sound
Kitty Hawk
Kill Devil Hills
Wright Brothers Natl. Mem.
Jockey's Ridge SP
Ft. Raleigh NHS
Manteo
Roanoke Island
Phelps Lake
Alligator River NWR
Bodie Island Lighthouse
Pocosin Lakes NWR
Pea Island NWR
Rodanthe
Mattamuskeet NWR
Lake Mattamuskeet
Cape Hatteras Natl. Seashore
Swanquarter
Cape Hatteras Lighthouse
Pamlico Sound
Swanquarter NWR
Hatteras
Buxton
Cape Hatteras
Ocracoke
Ocracoke Lighthouse
OUTER BANKS
Cedar Island NWR
Cedar Island
TO MAP 6
Cape Lookout National Seashore
Beaufort

0   15 miles
0   15 kilometers

The **Governor's Palace,** at the head of the village green, housed seven colonial governors (as well as two state governors, Patrick Henry and Thomas Jefferson) and has been restored to the state it was in the days of Governor Dunmore, the last of the British colonial governors. Shows go on throughout the day at the reconstructed **Play Booth Theater.** The original was a full indoor theater, but this incarnation was built to resemble open-air English theaters of the day. The **Public Gaol** on Market Sq. teaches visitors about what happened to those colonists who chose a life of crime, stealing a horse or failing to honor the sabbath.

Ever wonder about what a roadtrip was like in the 18th century? Find out at the **Raleigh Tavern,** down Duke of Gloucester St., where tours explain the significance of the tavern in town life as well as accommodations, activities, and entertainment available for tired travelers. On the other end of Duke of Gloucester, **Market Sq.** jolts visitors out of the past with modern-day shops and restaurants.

The tours of the **Capitol** focus on the events and philosophies that led up to the American Revolution and the country's independence. Multi-millionaire John D. Rockefeller financed the initial venture to create Colonial Williamsburg by reconstructing buildings. **Bassatt Hall** was his home in town and is preserved in a 1920s-era style, as it was when he lived here. His wife has lent her name to the **Abby Aldrich Rockefeller Folk Art Museum,** America's first museum devoted to folk art. A visit to Colonial Williamsburg wouldn't be complete without seeing a few artisans at work, including a wheelwright, cobbler, and wigmaker. (☎757-229-1000; www.history.org/history/museums/abby_art.cfm. Most exhibits open daily 9am-5pm. Colonial sampler pass $33, ages 6-17 $16; includes access to over 40 sites, but not the Capitol, the Governor's Palace or the museums. Governor's Key to the City pass $45/$23; includes Capitol, Governor's Palace and museum.)

■ FOOD

The Old Chickahominy House, 1211 Jamestown Rd., 1½ mi. from the historic district on the Williamsburg-Jamestown border, serves plates of Miss Melinda's pancakes with a side of smoked bacon ($8) for breakfast. Later on in the day, Becky's "complete luncheon" ($7) includes Virginia ham, hot biscuits, fruit salad, a slice of homemade pie, and iced tea or coffee. (☎ 757-229-4689. Open M-F 8:30-10:30am and 11:30am-2:30pm, Sa-Su 8:30-10am and 11:45am-2pm.) In **Chowning's Tavern,** on Duke of Gloucester St., quasi-historical dishes like "Ploughman's Pastie" (roasted turkey and melted cheddar cheese in a flaky pastry; $7.25) will have you chowing down George Washington-style. The outdoor garden serves lighter, modern fare until 5pm. After 5pm, the merriment continues as costumed waiters sing 18th-century ballads and challenge guests to card games. (☎ 757-220-7012; http://intranetcwf.org. Cover $3. Open daily 11am-10pm.) **The Cheese Shop,** in Merchant's Sq., is popular for a quick, tasty meal. Doubling as a gourmet food store, the establishment sells fresh sandwiches that can be eaten on the patio out front. (☎ 757-220-1324. Sandwiches $4-6. Open M-Sa 10am-9pm, Su 10am-6pm.) **Berret's,** 199 S. Boundary St., at Merchant's Sq., combines two restaurants in one: the less expensive and more casual **Tap House Grill,** and the pricey and more formal **Berret's Restaurant and Bar.** Start off at the Restaurant with baked escargot ($8), then try the Virginia ham and crab meat combination ($24) for an all-American splurge. (☎ 757-253-1847. Grill: Entrees $12-15. Sides and sandwiches $8-13. Live music in summer Su 6-9pm. Tap House open daily from 4pm. Restaurant and Bar open daily 11:30am-3:30pm and 5:30-10pm.)

ACCOMMODATIONS

Williamsburg has no shortage of chain hotels and motels. Other options include **Bryant Guest House,** 702 College Terr., featuring four rooms with private baths, TV, and limited kitchen facilities in an exquisitely landscaped brick home. The residential location provides a break from the colonial part of town. (From Scotland Rd., turn right onto Richmond Rd., then left onto Dillard St. ☎ 757-229-3320. Singles $35; doubles $45; 5-person suite $75.) For those who can afford it, the **Liberty Rose,** 1022

Jamestown Rd., is a romantic Victorian B&B. (☎ 757-253-1260. Check-in 3pm. Check-out 11am. Rooms from $185.) **Lewis Guest House,** 809 Lafayette St., is a 10min. walk from the historic district, and rents two rooms, including an upstairs unit with private entrance, kitchen, A/C, and shared bath. (☎ 757-229-6116. Rooms $25-35. Cash only.)

LEAVING WILLIAMSBURG
Take **I-64 East** to Busch Gardens.

BUSCH GARDENS
Located 3 mi. east of Williamsburg off I-64.

Busch Gardens puts its own spin on Williamsburg's colonial theme. The park is divided into themed sections such as "Italy," "Germany" and "New France," with appropriate restaurants and rides. A train runs around the park's perimeter from the entrance to New France on the other side, and a skyride provides a view of the park and quicker journey from England to France. The park features four roller coasters: the tame **Apollo's Chariot,** the **Big Bad Wolf,** the **Lock Ness Monster** that includes interlocking loops, and the hanging **Alpengeist.** There are tons of snack stands, but those in search of a heartier meal can try the **Trapper Smokehouse,** which smokes meat on a huge grill and serves up BBQ platters. The **Ristorante della Piazza** offers basic Italian pasta dishes. (☎ 800-343-7946; www.buschgardens.com. Open daily 10am-10pm. $50, ages 3-6 $40. Strollers $10 per day. Lockers $6 per day.)

APPROACHING HAMPTON
Hampton is about 30 mi. west down **I-64.** Exit 267 takes drivers right downtown.

HAMPTON

Perhaps the most fully functional town among a series of vacation resorts, Hampton has a small, compact downtown surrounded by residential homes and chain stores. A relatively quiet town that does not pander to tourists, Hampton serves either as a welcome respite from boardwalks and cheesy sights or a locus of potential boredom.

VITAL STATS

Population: 150,000

Visitor Info: Hampton Visitors Center, 120 Hampton Ln. (☎ 757-727-1102 or 800-800-2202; www.hamptoncvb.com). Open daily 9am-5pm.

Internet Access: Hampton Public Library, 4207 Victoria Blvd. (☎ 757-727-1154; www.hampton.va.us/hpl). Open M-Th 9am-9pm, F-Sa 9am-5pm, Su 1-5pm.

Post Office: 809 Aberdeen Rd. (☎ 757-826-0299). **Postal Code:** 23670.

 GETTING AROUND

Off of the highway, take a left onto **Settlers Landing Rd.,** the main drag through downtown. The **Hampton River** runs between the downtown and the Hampton University campus. There is free **parking** all day in a lot across the street from the Visitors Center, as well as 2hr. parking on many streets downtown. The old park-and-walk is best for exploring the downtown area.

◉ SIGHTS

HAMPTON HISTORY MUSEUM. The museum provides an interactive orientation to the town, from the Kecoughtan tribes to the founding of the city to the present day. Costumed guides lead tours. *(120 Old Hampton Ln. ☎ 757-727-1610. Open M-Sa 10am-5pm. $5, ages 4-12 $4.)*

ART MARKET. The Art Market displays over 20 sculptures throughout downtown Hampton, all for sale for anywhere from $800 to $35,000. Guides to the walking tour are available at the Visitors Center and a number of shops throughout town. *(756 Settlers Landing Rd. ☎ 757-727-1271; www.downtownhampton.com. Free.)*

VIRGINIA AIR AND SPACE CENTER. This interactive, hands-on museum is oriented toward children, but even the stodgiest adult can find something to learn and enjoy. The flight simulator lets visitors step into the cockpit of a number of different jets or do a "wing walk" with slightly less risk than the real thing. The enormous IMAX theater plays films on everything from volcanoes to space travel. *(600 Settlers Landing Rd. ☎ 757-727-0900 or 800-296-0800; www.vasc.org. Open M-W 10am-5pm, Th-Su 10am-7pm with extended hours for the IMAX theater. $8, seniors and military $7.50, children $6.50. IMAX $7.50/$6.50/$6. Simulator $2.)*

SANDY BOTTOM NATURE PARK. Visitors can rent boats and canoes to explore the lake, learn about the local animals and habitats at the **Nature Center,** or go birding at the observation tower. Ten trails run through the park, all marked and most fairly level. *(1255 Big Bethel Rd. ☎ 757-825-4657; www.hampton.gov/sandybottom. Open daily Apr.-Sept. 8am-dusk; Oct.-Mar. 9am-dusk. Nature Center open M-Th 9am-6pm, F-Su 9am-7:30pm. Free.)*

HAMPTON CAROUSEL. This antique carousel, located at the Buckroe Beach Amusement Park from 1921 until the city bought it in 1985, is one of only 70 such carousels still functioning in the US. In addition to being a great ride for kids, it's also an example of American folk art; the horses and oil paintings are all originals. *(On Settlers Landing Rd., across the street from the Virginia Air and Space Center. ☎ 757-727-0900. Open M-W 11:30am-5:30pm, Th-Su 11:30-7:30pm. $1.)*

HAMPTON UNIVERSITY MUSEUM. Founded with the university in 1868, the museum is the nation's oldest institution dedicated to African-American history and currently contains over 9000 artifacts and works of art. *(In the Huntington Bldg. on the Hampton University campus. Follow Settlers Landing Rd. over the Hampton River and take a right onto the Hampton University campus. ☎ 757-727-5308. Open M-F 8am-5pm, Sa noon-4pm.)*

THE COUSTEAU SOCIETY. The U.S. headquarters for the Cousteau Society, the building hosts a small museum about the life and work of Jacques-Yves Cousteau. Although best appreciated by those already somewhat familiar with Cousteau's work, it has several nifty pieces, including the remains of a mechanical, remote-controlled shark named Allison, and one of the claustrophobia-inducing mini-subs Cousteau used to explore the depths from the deck of the *Calypso*. *(710 Settlers Landing Rd. ☎ 757-722-9300 or 800-441-4395. Open M-F 10am-4pm, Su 10am-3pm. Free.)*

🍴 FOOD & ACCOMMODATIONS

Most of Hampton's restaurants are downtown, and nicer options are on **Queens Way. La Bodega Hampton,** 22 Wine St., serves inexpensive sandwiches from basic egg salad ($3.25) to elaborate signature sandwiches like the Buck Roe ($5.50). It also sells gourmet food and a variety of wines, specializing in local vineyards. (☎757-722-8466. Open M-F 7:30am-6pm, Sa 10am-4pm.) **Marker 20,** 21 E. Queens Way, serves microbrews and fresh seafood in a pub atmosphere. (☎757-726-9410; www.marker20.com. Lunch entrees $4-9. Dinner entrees $7-17. Open daily 11am-2am.) For more exotic fare, try **Bahir Dar,** 17 E. Queens Way, a coffee room serving authentic Ethiopian food, including vegetarian options. (☎757-723-0100. Open Su 1-9pm, Tu-Th 11am-11pm, F-Sa 11am-2am.)

Most accommodations in Hampton are generic hotel chains of varying rates and qualities. The **Little England Inn,** 4400 Victoria Blvd., provides three rooms in a sprawling house in a residential neighborhood only a few blocks from Settlers Landing Rd. (☎757-722-0985 or 800-606-0985; www.littleengland-inn.com. Full breakfast included. Rooms $115.) On the other end of the price spectrum is camping at **Sandy Bottom Nature Park,** bounded by I-64, Big Bethel Rd., and Hampton Road Center Pkwy. (☎757-825-4657; www.hampton.gov/sandybottom. Quiet hours 10pm-7am. No electricity or water. No reservations. Sites $10; group sites $30. Cabins $40; $60 deposit.)

🏴 APPROACHING VIRGINIA BEACH

From Hampton, take **I-64** south to **I-264,** which splits into **21st** and **22nd St.** in the downtown area of Virginia Beach.

VIRGINIA BEACH

Virginia's largest city, once capital of the collegiate crowd, is shedding its playground image and maturing into a family-oriented vacation spot. Fast-food, motels, and discount shops abound, but culture now penetrates the plastic veneer.

🧭 GETTING AROUND

In Virginia Beach, east-west streets are numbered and north-south avenues, running parallel to the beach, have ocean names. Prepare to feel like a thimble on a Monopoly board: **Atlantic** and **Pacific Ave.** comprise the main drag. **Arctic, Baltic,** and **Mediterranean Ave.** are farther inland. Municipal **parking** lots on Atlantic Ave. charge $1 per hr.

(VITAL STATS)

Population: 430,000

Visitor Info: Virginia Beach Visitors Center, 2100 Parks Ave. (☎800-822-3224 or 757-491-7866; www.vbfunc.om), at 22nd St. Open daily June-Aug. 9am-8pm; Sept.-May 9am-5pm.

Internet Access: Virginia Beach Public Library, 4100 Virginia Beach Blvd. (☎757-431-3000). Open M-Th 10am-9pm, F-Sa 10am-5pm; Oct.-May also Su 1-5pm. Free.

Post Office: 501 Viking Dr. (☎757-340-0981). Open M-F 7:30am-6pm, Sa 10am-2pm. **Postal Code:** 23452.

🅖 SIGHTS

BACK BAY NATIONAL WILDLIFE REFUGE. Composed of islands, dunes, forests, marshes, ponds, and beaches, this remote national refuge is a sanctuary for an array of endangered species and other wildlife, not to mention tourists tired of Virginia Beach's joyful tackiness. With nesting bald eagles and peregrine falcons, the natural wonderland is open to the public for camping, hiking, fishing, and photography, and features a daily 9am tram tour from Little Island City Park up the road. *(Take General Booth Blvd. to Princess Anne Dr.; turn left, then turn left onto Sandbridge Rd. and continue approximately 6 mi. Turn right onto Sandpiper Rd., which leads to the Visitors Center.* ☎757-721-2412; www.backbay.fws.gov. *Visitors Center open M-F 8am-4pm, Sa-Su 9am-4pm. Closed Dec.-Mar. Sa $5 per car. Tram* ☎757-721-7666 *or* 757-498-2473, www.bbrf.org. *Departs daily 9am, returns 12:45pm. $6, seniors and under 12 $4.)*

FALSE CAPE STATE PARK. False Cape State Park got its name because around the 17th century ships used to touch shore there, mistakenly thinking that they had landed at the nearby Cape Henry (where America's first English settlers landed in 1607). The Back Bay tram stops at False Cape State Park, where there is a 1 mi. trek to the beach. If you miss the 9am daily tram, prepare for a 4 mi. hike or canoe ride. *(4001 Sandpiper Rd. ☎ 757-426-7128 or 800-933-7275, tours 888-669-8368 or 757-480-1999; www.dcr.state.va.us/parks. Campsites $9; reservations necessary.)*

VIRGINIA MARINE SCIENCE MUSEUM.

The Virginia Marine Science Museum houses Virginia's largest aquarium and is home to hundreds of species of fish, including crowd-pleasing sharks and stingrays in two pavilions separated by a walkway. Visitors can get a "bird's eye" view of a marsh habitat and can get up close and personal in the touch tank. The museum also houses a six-story IMAX theater and offers excursions for dolphin observation in summer and whale watching in winter. *(717 General Booth Blvd., 1 mi. drive or 30min. walk south down Pacific Ave., which becomes General Booth Blvd. ☎ 757-425-3474, excursions 757-437-2628; www.vmsm.com. Open daily summer 9am-7pm; off-season 9am-5pm. $12, seniors $11, ages 3-11 $8. Combined museum and IMAX $16/$13/$10. Excursions $12, ages 4-11 $10.)*

FOOD

Cuisine and Co., 3004 Pacific Ave. (☎ 757-428-6700; www.cuisineandcompany.com). This sophisticated eatery serves gourmet lunches and rich desserts in a sleek, clean environment. Treats include creamy tuna melts ($5), a chunky chicken salad ($5.50), and decadent cookies ($8 per lb.). Open Labor Day-Memorial Day M-Sa 9am-8pm, Su 9am-6pm.

The Happy Crab, 550 Laskin Rd. (☎ 757-437-9200). Dine on the screened patio overlooking a small harbor. Early-bird specials (daily 5-6:30pm) offer unbeatable seafood platters ($25) or huge servings big enough to share. Open Mar.-Sept. M-Th 11am-10pm, F-Su 11am-11pm; winter hours vary.

Lunesea, 206 22nd St. (☎ 757-437-4400). This "Key West Cafe" serves a combination of seafood and traditional Mexican fare in a relaxed environment. Diners can sample the fajitas, chimichanga, or the made-at-your-table fresh guacamole from the benches on the front deck. Live music several days of the week and a make-your-own-margarita bar on "hacienda Sundays." M Karaoke. Open M 4:30pm-2am, Tu-Sa 11am-2am.

ACCOMMODATIONS

Angie's Guest Cottage, Bed and Breakfast, and HI-AYH Hostel, 302 24th St. (☎ 757-428-4690; www.angiescottage.com). Barbara "Angie" Yates and staff welcome guests to an old house with great advice on the beach scene. Kitchen, BBQ, ping-pong, and lockers. No A/C. Linen $2. Street parking first come, first served with a $20 deposit for the permit. Reception 9am-9pm. Check-out 10am. Reservations recommended. Open Apr.-Sept. 4- to 9-bed dorms $16.50, nonmembers $20; off-season $12/$15. Private singles $36.

First Landings, 2500 Shore Dr. (☎ 757-412-2300 or 800-933-7275; www.dcr.state.va.us), about 8 mi. north of town on Rte. 60. In the eponymous State Park, beachfront sites thrive on the natural beauty of Virginia's shore. Picnic areas, private swimming on a sprawling beach, a bathhouse, and boat launching areas. The park is very popular; call at least 11 months ahead for reservations. Cabins June-Aug. $85-95; Apr.-May and Sept.-Nov. $65-75.

The Castle Motel, 2700 Pacific Ave. (☎ 757-425-9330). Quite possibly the best bang for your buck as motels go. Spacious, clean rooms come with cable TV, refrigerator, shower and bath, desk, and 2 full beds. The beach is just 2 blocks away. 21+. Check-out 11am. Open May-Oct. Rooms M-F from $69, Sa-Su from $99.

NIGHTLIFE

Closet-sized college bars cluster on "The Block," between 21st and 22nd St., crowded with rowdy party-goers and clubbers enjoying the scene.

Mahi Mah's, 615 Atlantic Ave. (☎ 757-437-8030; www.mahimahs.com), at 7th St. inside the Ramada Hotel. Sushi, wine tastings, live music, and ocean views. Smart crowd. Outdoor band nightly. Happy hour 3-6pm. Open daily 7am-1am.

Chicho's, 2112 Atlantic Ave. (☎ 757-422-6011; www.chichos.com), on "The Block." One of the most popular spots on the strip features gooey pizza ($2.25-3.25), tropical drinks ($5-7), and live rock music M. Open May-Sept. M-Tu 6pm-2am, W-Su noon-2am; Oct.-Apr. M-F 6pm-2am, Sa-Su noon-2am.

Harpoon Larry's, 216 24th St. (☎ 757-422-6000; www.harpoonlarrys.com), at Pacific Ave., serves tasty fish in an everyone-knows-your-name atmosphere. The amicable staff welcomes 20- and 30-somethings to

EAST COAST

a more relaxed atmosphere than the sweat and raging hormones of "The Block." Specials include crab cakes ($7) and rum runners (Tu $2). W $1.50 Coronas with $0.25 jalapeño poppers. Happy hour M-F 7-9pm; $1 domestic drafts and $2 rail drinks. Open May-Sept. daily noon-2am; winter hours vary.

▶ APPROACHING BODIE & KITTY HAWK
From Virginia Beach, take **I-264 West** about 11 mi. to **I-64 East** toward Chesapeake. About 8 mi. down the road, switch to **Rte. 168** south, which will continue southeast onto **U.S. 158.**

$$\mathcal{W}elcome\ \mathcal{T}o$$

NORTH CAROLINA

BODIE & KITTY HAWK

Bodie Island is the most populated, developed, and commercialized of the four islands of the Outer Banks. Kitty Hawk is one of a string of towns along Rte. 12 in the northern half of the island that are heavily trafficked and dense with stores. Farther south on Rte. 12, however, pristine beaches remain undeveloped, as national park status has preserved much of the island's beauty.

VITAL STATS

Population: 3000

Visitor Info: Aycock Brown Welcome Center (☎252-261-4644), Mile 1½ on U.S. 158 in Kitty Hawk. Open daily 9am-5:30pm.

Internet Access: Dare County Library, 400 Mustian St. (☎252-441-4331), in Kill Devil Hills, 1 block west of U.S. 158. Open M and Th-F 9am-5:30pm, Tu-W 10am-7pm, Sa 10am-4pm.

Post Office: 3841 N. Croatan Hwy. (☎252-261-2211), in Kitty Hawk. Open M-F 9am-4:30pm, Sa 10am-noon. **Postal Code:** 27949.

⌂ GETTING AROUND. Bodie is the northernmost of the Outer Banks islands. It is joined to the mainland by **U.S. 158** and serves as a major point of entry over the **Wright Memorial Bridge.** For much of Bodie Island, **Rte. 12 (Beach Rd.)** parallels U.S. 158 (called the **Bypass**). Directions on Bodie Island are usually given in terms of distances in miles from the bridge. Traffic calls for extra caution and travel time, especially on Saturdays and Sundays when the rental homes turn over.

◎ SIGHTS. The **Wright Brothers National Memorial,** Mile 8 on U.S. 158, marks the spot where Orville and Wilbur Wright took to the skies. Exhibits in the Visitors Center document humanity's journey from the first airplane to the first moon landing. Outside, stone markers show the distance of the four flights taken the morning of December 17, 1903. The **Centennial Pavilion,** built in 2003, contains a replica of the plane the brothers used and material from NASA and the US Air Force. (☎252-441-7430. Open daily June-Aug. 9am-6pm; Sept.-May 9am-5pm. $3, under 16 free. Tickets good for 1 week.) Nearby **Jockey's Ridge State Park,** Mile 12 on U.S. 158, includes the east coast's largest naturally occurring sand dune, around 100 ft. high and containing approximately 30 million tons of sand. The museum at the Visitors Center has displays on how dunes form and preservation efforts. (☎252-441-7132. Open daily June-Aug. 9am-7:45pm.; Nov.-Feb. 9am-4:45pm; Mar.-Oct. 9am-5:45pm; Apr. May and Sept. 9am-6:45pm. Free.) The 158 ft. **Currituck Beach Lighthouse,** on the northern tip of the island off the Bypass, was completed in 1875 to fill the final "dark spot" on the state's coast. (☎252-453-4939. Open for climbing daily 10am-5pm). On the other end of the island, also off the Bypass, is the **Bodie Island Lighthouse,** first lit in 1872. Standing 156 ft. high, the lighthouse is painted with a distinctive white and black striped pattern, each stripe 22 ft. thick. Climbing the lighthouse is not permitted, but learn about its history and see a section of the fresnel lens from the Cape Hatteras lighthouse in the Visitors Center. (☎252-441-5711. Open daily 10am-5pm.) **Public beaches** line the beach road. The beaches are free, but parking is limited.

🍴 FOOD. The fun and lively **Chilli Peppers,** Mile 5½ on U.S. 158, specializes in fresh seafood and Tex-Mex. (☎252-441-8081; www.chillippeppers.com. Spicy fish quesadilla $7. Sandwiches from $7. Dinner entrees from $15. Open M-Sa 11:30am-2am, Su 11:30am-10:30pm.) Popular and sometimes crowded, **Tortuga's Lie,** Mile 11 on Beach Rd. in Nags Head, serves Caribbean-influenced seafood, sandwiches, pasta, and grill items in a low-key bar setting. (☎252-441-7299; www.tortugaslie.com. W sushi night. Open daily 11:30am-10pm.) The **Flying Fish Cafe,** Mile 10 on U.S. 158 Bypass, offers American and Mediterranean fare in a warm, classy setting. It also serves espresso and cappuccino beverages and delicious desserts. Check out the sinfully delicious chocolate hurricane ($6), five kinds of chocolate wrapped in a chocolate cylinder. (☎252-441-6894; www.flyingfishcafe.net. Open daily 5-10pm). At Mile 1 on the Beach Rd., the **Rundown Cafe's** food and atmosphere are anything but. The Asian and Caribbean-influenced menu includes delicious coconut shrimp ($16) and the vegetarian *thali,* a platter with six different vegetarian dishes ($12). Save room for the chocolate cookie pie covered in warm fudge ($4). At the rooftop Tsunami Bar, patrons can chill out and grab a drink. (☎252-255-0026. Opens M-Sa 11:30am, Su noon.)

⚑ ACCOMMODATIONS. Most visitors stay in houses rented by the week (weekend rentals are sometimes available in the off-season), which run from one-bedroom cottages to oceanfront mansions. **Outer Banks International Hostel (HI-AYH),** 1004 W. Kitty Hawk Rd., is the best deal in the northern islands. This clean, friendly hostel has 60 beds, two kitchens, A/C, volleyball, shuffleboard, Internet ($5 per 30min.), and laundry. (☎252-261-2294; www.outerbankshostel.com. Linen $2. $16, nonmembers $19; private rooms $15 plus $16/$19 per person; tent sites $17 for 2 adults, $4 per additional person. Tent rental $6.) The **Nettlewood Motel,** 1718 Beach Rd., near Mile 7, offers clean and comfortable rooms with private access to an uncluttered strip of beach. (☎252-441-5039. TV, A/C, heat, refrigerators, and pool. Doubles are equipped with a kitchenette. Mid-June to late Aug. singles M-F $55, Sa-Su $75; doubles $99/$150. Mid-May to mid-June and late Aug. to late Sept. singles $40/$50; doubles $55/$75. Jan. to mid-May and Oct.-Nov. singles $35/$40; doubles $45/$55.)

⚐ APPROACHING ROANOKE ISLAND
Follow **U.S. 158** to **U.S. 64** to the island.

ROANOKE ISLAND

Roanoke Island was the location of the first (failed) English settlement in the New World. A second settlement on the island was established in 1587 and mysteriously disappeared sometime during the next three years. This disappearing col-

ony is the inspiration for a live, musical theatrical extravaganza entitled the **Lost Colony** performed every night in the summer. (☎252-473-3414; www.thelostcolony.org. Shows June-Aug. M-Sa 8:30pm. $16, seniors $15, under 11 $8.) The theater is located on the **Fort Raleigh National Historic Site,** 1409 National Park Rd., which marks the location of the first attempted settlement. The **Fort Raleigh Visitors Center** has information about the colony and multiple daily programs explaining and re-enacting pieces of that history. (☎252-473-2127 or 866-468-7630. Visitors Center open daily June-Aug. 9am-6pm; Sept.-Mar. 9am-5pm.)

Nearby, flowers release their perfumes in the romantic **Elizabethan Gardens,** where visitors can wander among fountains, finely tended gardens, and antique statues, including one of Virginia Dare, the first English child born in the New World. (☎252-473-3234; www.elizabethangardens.org. Open June-Aug. M-Sa 9am-8pm, Su 9am-7pm; low-season hours vary. $6, seniors $5, ages 6-18 $2, under 5 free.) **Manteo** is the island's biggest town, right over the bridge on U.S 64. Facing the Manteo Waterfront, **Roanoke Island Festival Park** (follow signs from the highway), staffed largely by actors in 16th-century garb, features *Elizabeth II,* a replica of a 16th-century English merchant ship. It also includes a settlement site built for Elizabethan soldiers, an art gallery, an interactive museum, and a film depicting native reaction to the European arrival. (☎252-475-1500; www.roanokeisland.com. Park and museum open in summer daily 10am-7pm. Ship open daily 10am-6:30pm. Last admission 6pm. Winter hours vary; park closed Jan.-Feb. $8, students $5, under 6 free.) In summer, students from the **North Carolina School of the Arts** perform jazz and ballet at the park's outdoor pavilion. (Suggested donation $5.)

THE ROAD DOWN CAPE HATTERAS

Following Rte. 12 south off of Bodie Island and over the bridge brings drivers to scenic Hatteras Island, covered almost entirely in parkland. The top half of the island consists of the **Pea Island National Wildlife Refuge,** established in 1938 to preserve the island's unique barrier island habitat. The **Visitors Center** has info about the wildlife and marks the beginning of the **North Pond Wildlife Trail,** which stretches a half mile to the sound. (☎252-987-2394; http://peaisland.fws.gov. Open daily in summer 9am-4pm; winter hours vary.) More intrepid explorers can bike or walk the 4 mi. of service road that encircle the pond and connect back to Rte. 12. Get two shores for the price of one along the 70 mi. expanse of the **Cape Hatteras National Seashore;** one faces the Atlantic Ocean and another looks across the Pamlico Sound to North Carolina's mainland. Dotted with dunes, stunted trees, and stretches of marshland, the park's main appeal is this unique landscape.

Driving south from Hatteras to Ocracoke, the water of the sound reaches out to the horizon to the right, while magnificent, largely empty beaches lie over the dunes on the left. Drivers can pull over at designated areas to take advantage of the free, isolated beaches all along the drive for both swimming and fishing (daytime access only). Numerous boardwalks stretch from the road out over the marshy land toward the sound. Try the **Charles Kuralt Nature Trail,** which affords trekkers a chance to glimpse grackles, pelicans, and the Carolina salt marsh snake. The trail is named for the journalist who invented the television news segment "On the Road." Along the way, drivers can look out to the ocean to marvel at the feared "Graveyard of the Atlantic," the cause of more then 2000 shipwrecks. A shipwrecked barge is visible at low tide across the Pea Island.

US Fish and Wildlife Station, a schooner that went down in August 1933 can be seen from the beach at Ramp 27, north of the town of Avon, and a second schooner that sank in 1878 is still visible from Cape Point, Buxton. At the southern end of Hatteras Island on Rte. 12 lies the **Cape Hatteras lighthouse.** The second lighthouse at this location, it towers at 208 ft., the tallest in the U.S. The old keeper's quarters now house a Visitors Center and museum with info on the light. (☎252-995-4474. Open Memorial Day-Labor Day 9am-6pm; Labor Day-Memorial Day 9am-5pm. $6, children $3.)

A little farther along Rte. 12 lies the **Frisco Native American Museum and Natural History Center,** an interactive museum about the history of the island's first inhabitants. The museum consists mostly of local artifacts, including a dugout canoe discovered on the museum's own grounds. (☎252-995-4400. Open M by appointment, Tu-Sa 11am-5pm. $2, seniors $1.50; families $5.)

OCRACOKE

The southernmost of the Outer Banks islands, Ocracoke is traditionally the most isolated, with only a single tiny town, Ocracoke Village, near the southern tip. Residents are known for their distinctive dialect, or brogue, but the unique way of speaking has begun to deteriorate as the emphasis of the economy has shifted from fishing to tourism. For visitors, the town still represents an amazing escape from the hustle of mainland life.

> **VITAL STATS**
>
> **Population:** 770
>
> **Visitor Info:** (☎252-928-4531), located off of Rte. 12 in town.
>
> **Post Office:** Off Rte. 12, right as you enter town. It's a really small place—you'll find it. **Postal Code:** 27960.

GETTING AROUND. The only way to reach Ocracoke is by ferry. Free ferries run between **Hatteras** and **Ocracoke** (40min., daily 5am-midnight). This ferry is extremely busy from 9am to noon going to Ocracoke and from 3 to 7pm returning. Drivers should be prepared to wait at least 1hr. during these times. To reach the village, drive south on **Rte. 12.** The road will wind through town and into the ferry terminal, also home to a Visitors Center and a free public **parking** lot. Grab a map at the Visitors Center, because none of the roads in town are marked with street names.

Toll ferries run between Ocracoke and **Cedar Island,** east of New Bern on Rte. 12, which becomes U.S. 70. (2¼hr.; $1 per pedestrian, $3 per cyclist, $15 per car. Reservations required.) Toll ferries also travel between Ocracoke and **Swanquarter,** on U.S. 264 (2½hr.). Call ahead for schedules and reservations (general info and reservations ☎800-293-3779; www.ncferry.org).

SIGHTS. Ocracoke is full of tiny shops selling clothes, books, and souvenirs. Those interested in watersports need look no farther than the booths lining Rte. 12 (called the **Irvin Garrish Hwy.**) in town. Visitors can also check out **Ocracoke Lighthouse,** on Lighthouse Rd. The third structure built here in the 1820s, it stands 75 ft. tall. A boardwalk leads to the lighthouse, but no one can go inside. The **Ocracoke Preservation Society Museum,** near the ferry terminal, displays artifacts from life on Ocracoke Island, including a parlor with a cast-iron stove and a kitchen with a hand-pump to reflect the recent installation of running water, circa 1970. It also has a room devoted to the Ocracoke brogue, including a video illustrating the pro-

nunciation, grammar, and vocabulary—
"dingbatters" are non-natives of the island. (☎252-
928-7375. Open M-F 10am-5pm, Sa-Su 11am-4pm).
The **Pony Pasture,** on Rte. 12, acts as the stomping
ground for a herd of semi-wild horses, said to be
descendants of horses left here by shipwrecked
explorers in the 16th or 17th century.

FOOD AND ACCOMMODATIONS.
Occupying a counter along the back wall of Sty-
ron's General Store (est. 1920) at the corner of
Lighthouse and Creek Rd. in Ocracoke, the **Cat
Ridge Deli,** 300 Lighthouse Rd., specializes in Thai-
influenced cuisine. (☎252-928-3354. Wraps around
$6. Open daily summer 10:30am-7pm; low-season
10:30am-5pm. Closed Jan.-Mar.) The **Back Porch
Restaurant,** at Rte. 12 and Back Rd., serves fine,
classic meals in a setting both classy and casual.
(☎252-928-6401. Open daily 5-9:30pm.)

For wood-paneled rooms at some of Ocra-
coke's lowest prices, **Blackbeard's Lodge,** 111 Back
Rd., is a nice option. The swing and rocking chairs
on the porch provide a spot to relax, and the large
lounge downstairs feels like a ship's cabin. (Turn
right off of Rte. 12 just before the boat filled with
seashells. ☎252-928-3421, reservations 800-892-
5314; www.blackbeardslodge.com. Game room,
A/C, cable TV, and pool. Rooms in summer $85-
105; low-season $45-70; apartments and efficien-
cies $60-185.) The bright rooms at the **Sand Dollar
Motel,** 70 Sand Dollar Rd. in Ocracoke, exude a
beach-cabin feel. (☎252-928-5571 or 866-928-5571.
Refrigerators, microwaves, A/C, cable TV, pool,
and breakfast. Open Apr. to late Nov. Rooms in
summer from $80; in low-season from $45.)

APPROACHING BEAUFORT
From Ocracoke, take the ferry at the south of
the island to the mainland. Schedules are available at
the Visitors Center. (☎252-225-3551 or 800-856-
0343). Follow **Rte. 12** south from the ferry to **U.S. 70,**
which leads into Beaufort.

BEAUFORT

A tiny town near Morehead City on Cedar Island,
Beaufort is home to a beautiful, quaint downtown
with a celebrated history. It's not exactly happening, but it's a great spot to spend a quiet weekend.

GETTING AROUND. Turner St. leads south
from **U.S. 70** to the main part of Beaufort, including the historic downtown and the **Beaufort His-**

(**VITAL STATS**)

Population: 3800

Visitor Info: Beaufort Historic Site (☎252-728-
5225), at Turner St. Open M-Sa 9:30am-5pm, Su
noon-4pm.

Internet Access: Carteret County Public Library,
210 Turner St. (☎252-728-2050). Open M-Th
8:30am-9pm, F 8:30am-6pm, Sa 8:30am-5pm.

Post Office: 701 Front St. (☎252-728-4821). Open
M-F 8:30am-5pm, Sa 8:30am-noon. **Postal Code:**
28516.

toric Site. U.S. 70 continues west to **Morehead City**
and the nearest sandy beaches, while **Front St.**
runs along the water downtown and is home to
most of the shops and restaurants. **Free parking** is
available along Front St. and in a lot at the dock.

SIGHTS. The Beaufort Historic Site, at 100
Turner St., features the **Mattie King Davis Art Gallery,** the county's oldest art gallery, and several
restored buildings, including the **Dr. Josiah Davis
House,** an 1854 apothecary, and the **Josiah Bell
House,** home to a Confederate agent. Visitors can
take tours of those homes, as well as two others.
(Art Gallery open M-Sa 10am-4pm. Tours M-Sa 10,
11:30am, 1, 3pm. Tours $6, children $4). The **Beaufort Historical Association** also gives bus tours to the
nearly 100 historical buildings throughout town.
(Tours M, W, and F 11am and 1:30pm; Sa 11am.) A
block or so away lies the **Old Burying Ground,** a
cemetery deeded to the town in 1731. The site has
a pamphlet for a self-guided walking tour of the
burying ground. Most of the graves face east,
apparently because those buried wanted the sun
on their faces the morning of Judgement Day.
(Open daily 8am-5pm.) Those looking for a more
fantastic historical experience can follow the
Ghost Walk, which leads ghost hunters to the **Hammock House,** once owned by Blackbeard, and ends
at the Old Burying Ground. (Tours depart from
Front St. across the street from the Inlet Inn; look
for a flag marked with a red cross. ☎252-342-0715.
$8, under 12 $7. Call ahead.)

The **North Carolina Maritime Museum,** 315 Front
St., features exhibits on Blackbeard, the evolution
of services protecting the coastline, and the origins of indigenous watercraft. (☎252-728-7317;
www.ah.dcr.state.nc.us/sections/maritime. Open
M-F 9am-5pm, Sa 10am-5pm, Su 1-5pm. Free.) It
also has a Repository for Shipwreck Artifacts with

pieces from Blackbeard's flagship, the *Queen Anne's Revenge*, which sank a few miles of off Beaufort's coast. (Open M and W 10am-4pm, F 2-4pm, Sa 1-4pm. $5.) Anyone further nautically inclined can head across the street to the **Harvey W. Smith Watercraft Center** and see small watercraft being handbuilt by experts, as well as displays of tools and the "half-models" used to design ships. **Fort Macon State Park** lies a few miles south of Beaufort at Atlantic City Beach. Constructed from 1826-1834, the fort is a pentagon-shaped structure that was used in both the Civil War and the Spanish American War. Visitors can learn about life in the fort by checking out the soldiers' quarters, the commissary, and the "hot shot furnace," which heated non-explosive cannonballs in order to destroy wooden marine vessels. (Take Rte. 70 south, then head east over the Highrise Bridge and take a left on E. Ft. Macon Rd. which heads right to the fort. ☎ 252-726-3775. Swimming area open daily 10am-5:45pm. Fort open daily 9am-5:30pm. Tours daily every hr. 10am-3pm.)

FOOD. Downtown Beaufort has a generous array of tasty, elegant restaurants. The **Beaufort Grocery Co.**, 117 Queen St., serves delicious sandwiches and classic American entrees like the NY strip steak and the Portabella Wellington. The atmosphere is classy both in the dining room and at the pastry counter. (☎ 252-728-3899; http://beaufortgrocery.com. Sandwiches $7-10. Entrees $18-22. Open daily from 11am; Labor Day-Memorial Day closed Tu.) Step back in time at **The Soda Fountain,** 510 Front St., which serves burgers and deli sandwiches in an early-20th-century-style soda shop, complete with a counter. (☎ 252-728-0933. Open Su and Tu-Sa 7am-4pm.) The **Dock House,** 500 Front St., represents classic waterfront dining: fresh seafood and outdoor seating on the dock. A local crowd favors both the restaurant and the bar. (☎ 252-728-4506. Open daily 11:30am-10pm.)

ACCOMMODATIONS. Beaufort is, impressively, entirely devoid of chain accommodations. One of only two hotels in town, the **Inlet Inn,** 601 Front St., has 35 rooms with porches on the first two floors, fridges, fireplaces, and complimentary continental breakfast delivered daily. (☎ 252-728-3600; www.intlet-inn.com. Rooms in summer $129, on the water $129-144; low-season $59-99/$79-109.) The **Elizabeth Inn,** 307 Front St., houses three homey rooms with private baths in an historic 1857 home. (☎ 252-728-3861; www.theelizabethinn.com. Rooms $75-85.) Furnished exclusively with antiques, the **Captains' Quarters,** 315 Ann St., is a "Bed & Biscuit" located a sprawling Victorian home. Visitors can relax in white wicker chairs and enjoy the complimentary full breakfast prepared by the owners. (☎ 252-728-7711 or 800-659-7111. Rooms in summer $90-110; low season $70-90.)

APPROACHING CAPE FEAR
Take **U.S. 70** to **Rte. 24 West** to Jacksonville and switch to **U.S. 17 South.** U.S. 17 heads right into Wilmington, but drivers should switch to **U.S. Bus. 17** by heading straight instead of turning left at 16th St.

WILMINGTON & CAPE FEAR

Wilmington manages to combine the assets of an economic center with a historic downtown. A shipbuilding center during WWII, Wilmington has been a major shipping location. Recently, Wilmington has served as a locale for movies and TV shows (most famously *Dawson's Creek*) looking for a small-town feel with the amenities of a city.

EAST COAST

VITAL STATS

Population: 76,000

Visitor Info: Cape Fear Coast Convention and Visitors Bureau, 24 N. 3rd St. (☎ 910-458-5538 or 800-222-4757), in the 1892 courthouse. Open M-F 8:30am-5pm, Sa 9am-4pm, Su 1-4pm.

Internet Access: New Hanover County Public Library, 201 Chestnut St. (☎ 910-798-6301). Open M-W 9am-8pm, Th-Sa 9am-5pm, Su 1-5pm.

Post Office: 152 Front St. (☎ 910-313-3293). **Postal Code:** 28401.

GETTING AROUND

Wilmington proper is north of Cape Fear. In town, **Bus. U.S. 17** is called **Market St.** and runs midway through downtown. Downtown is bounded by **Red Cross St.** to the west, **Castle St.** on the east, and **Front St.** along the water. The roads running parallel to Front St. are all numbered and the streets form a grid. **U.S. 421** runs the length of Cape Fear.

Parking is available in three parking decks downtown—two on **2nd St.**, one on **Water St.** They are free on weekends. Metered parking is available on most downtown streets.

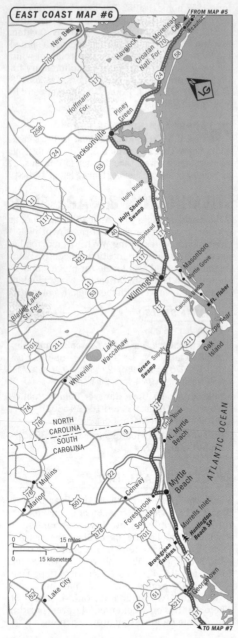

SIGHTS

CAPE FEAR MUSEUM. The museum documents and celebrates all aspects of Cape Fear life—political, cultural, and scientific. Of particular interest are the model of the city during the Civil War and a diorama of the battle of Fort Fisher. For basketball fans, there's an exhibit on native Michael Jordan. *(814 Market St. ☎ 910-341-3450; www.capefearmuseum.com. Open M-Sa 9am-5pm, Su 1-5pm; Labor Day-Memorial day closed M. $5, students and seniors $4, ages 3-17 $1.)*

BELLAMY MANSION MUSEUM. This mansion was the residence of planter John D. Bellamy and is an amazing example of antebellum architecture. The 22-room home has been restored, and two gallery spaces display exhibitions focusing on the arts, historic preservation, and architecture. *(503 Market St. ☎ 910-251-3700; www.bellamymansion.org. Open Su 1-5pm, Tu-Sa 10am-5pm.)*

BURGWIN-WRIGHT MUSEUM HOUSE AND GARDENS. An example of Georgian architecture, the house was built on top of an abandoned jail. The kitchen, in a separate building behind the house, features demonstrations of open hearth cooking. *(224 Market St. ☎ 910-762-0570; www.geocities.com/picketfence/garden/4354. Open Tu-Sa 10am-4pm; last tour 3pm.)*

WILMINGTON RAILROAD MUSEUM. For over 150 years, Wilmington was home to Atlantic Railroads. The railroad museum is at the old transportation headquarters. In addition to memorabilia, pictures, and models, it also contains an old caboose, steam engine, and box car to climb in and explore. *(501 Nutt St. ☎ 910-763-2634. Open mid-Mar. to mid-Oct. M-Sa 10am-5pm, Su 1-5pm; mid-Oct. to mid-Mar. M-Sa 10am-4pm.)*

CAPE FEAR SERPENTARIUM. Visitors can get up close and personal with all kinds of snakes and reptiles, including crocodiles and a 23 ft. long python. The snakes are kept in replicas of their natural habitats, so the experience is as real-life as possible. *(20 Orange St. ☎ 910-762-1669. Open M-F 11am-5pm Sa-Su 11am-6pm. $7, under 2 free.)*

LOUISE WELLS CAMERON ART MUSEUM. Dedicated to North Carolina's artistic heritage, the museum displays the work of artists such as Mary Cassatt. Traditional media are supplemented by decoys and computer-generated art. *(3201 S. 17th St. ☎910-395-5999; www.comeronartmuseum.com. Open Su 10:30am-4pm, Tu-Sa 10am-5pm. $5.)*

BATTLESHIP NORTH CAROLINA. Having served in every major battle of WWII, the *North Carolina* was home to a crew of over 2300. Visitors can climb inside to experience life on a major battleship, from the hospital to the movie theater. The museum provides the history both of the ship itself and of the battle for the Pacific and WWII watercraft. *(Off U.S. 17, south of Wilmington. ☎910-350-1817; www.battleshipnc.com. Open daily 8am-8pm; Last admission 7pm. $9, seniors and military $8, ages 6-11 $4.50, under 6 free.)*

FORT FISHER. Fort Fisher served a major role in the Civil War. The fort was able to withstand the shock of torpedo shells and other blasts because it consisted almost entirely of sand and dirt, but it was finally captured in January 1865. The recreation site has a crowded beach and a number of nature-oriented programs. Also at Fort Fisher is the **North Carolina Aquarium.** The aquarium allows visitors to view and interact with the state's aquatic life. Visitors can touch the animals in the Touch Tanks and see the staff feed the fish, reptiles, and various and sundry sea creatures. *(On U.S. 421 south of Wilmington. Fort ☎910-458-5798. Aquarium ☎910-458-8257. Recreation area open daily 6am-9pm. Historic Site open M-Sa 9am-5pm. Aquarium open daily 9am-5pm. Aquarium $7, seniors and active military $6, ages 6-17 $5.)*

THE LATIMER HOUSE. Built in the popular "Italiante" style, this 1952 home contains period furnishings and artwork, including portraits of the Latimer family. *(126 S. 3rd St. ☎910-762-0492; www.latimerhouse.org. Open M-F 10am-3:30pm, Sa noon-5pm. Walking tours W and Sa 10am.)*

🍴 FOOD

Caffé Phoenix, 9 S. Front St., has a chic, European feel with colorful art for sale on the walls and abundant greenery. The food consists of trendy, Italian-influenced versions of American fare, like the beef tenderloin with wild mushroom risotto and the torta rustica sandwich. (☎910-343-1395. Opens M-Sa 11:30am, Su 10:30am.) **Birds Cafe,** 202 Princess St., serves "chicken with an attitude," most famously, the "stinky chicken" smothered in olive oil and garlic. The restaurant is decorated with (unsurprisingly) chickens—figurines, wooden models, iron-wrought statues, the works. (☎910-762-1414. Entrees $5-7. Open M-F 11am-3pm.) The **Caprice Bistro,** 10 Market St., serves French cuisine at intimate tables. After dinner, diners head upstairs to the sofa bar to relax with cocktails. (☎910-815-0810; www.capricebistro.com. Open M-Th 5pm-10:30pm, F-Sa 5-11pm, Su 5-10pm. Sofa bar open until 2am.)

🏨 ACCOMMODATIONS

Wilmington's best lodging comes in the form of B&Bs; you'll find most of them in the historic downtown area. Though rooms usually cost $100-200 per night, the personalized experience, free breakfasts, unique rooms, convenient location, and riverfront views may make them worth the extra cash. Space is limited, so reserve as far in advance as your plans allow, especially during the summer. **Catherine's Inn,** 410 S. Front St., offers gorgeous rooms, a two-story porch overlooking the Cape Fear River, a sunken garden with a gazebo, a full country breakfast, and warm hospitality. (☎910-251-0863 or 800-476-0723; www.catherinesinn.com. Private bath, off-street parking, Internet, and complimentary wine, beer, and sodas. Check-in 3-5pm. Singles with queen-size bed $80, with king-size bed $85; doubles $100-105/$115-120.) Those who seek less expensive lodging will find nearly every budget chain on **Market St.** between College Rd. and 23rd St. Weekend rates often run $10-20 higher than weekday prices. **Travel Inn,** 4401 Market St., is a single-floor motor court that provides basic rooms with tiny showers for some of the lowest rates available. (☎910-763-8217. Pool, cable TV with free HBO, and A/C. Rooms in summer M-F $35-39, Sa-Su $59-79; in winter from $35. 10% AAA/AARP discount.) The **Carolina Beach State Park,** about 18 mi. south of the city on U.S. 421, offers campsites as well as hiking, picnic areas, and a marina. (☎910-458-8206. Restrooms, hot showers, laundry facilities, water, and grills. No RV hookups. Sites $15.)

🔺 APPROACHING MYRTLE BEACH

Follow **U.S. 17** south. To avoid congestion and traffic lights north of Myrtle Beach, take **Rte. 9** just south of Little River, SC, to **Rte. 31/Carolina Bay Pkwy.**, then use **Rte. 378** to get back on U.S. 17.

Welcome To

SOUTH CAROLINA

MYRTLE BEACH & THE GRAND STRAND

Each summer, millions of Harley-riding, RV-driving Southerners make Myrtle Beach the second-most-popular summer tourist destination in the country. During Spring Break and early June, Myrtle Beach is thronged with rambunctious students on the lookout for a good time. The rest of the year, families, golfers, shoppers, and others partake in the unapologetic tackiness of the town's theme restaurants, amusement parks, and shops. The pace slows significantly on the rest of the 60 mi. Grand Strand. South of Myrtle Beach, Pawley's Island is lined with beach cottages and beautiful private homes.

(VITAL STATS)

Population: 23,000

Visitor Info: Myrtle Beach Chamber of Commerce, 1200 N. Oak St. (☎843-626-7444 or 800-356-3016; www.mbchamber.com), at 12th N. Open M-F 8:30am-5pm Sa-Su 9am-5pm.

Internet Access: Chapin Memorial Library, 400 14th Ave. N. (☎843-918-1275). Open M and W 9am-6pm, Tu and Th 9am-8pm, F-Sa 9am-5pm.

Mini Golf: Absolutely everywhere.

Post Office: 505 N. Kings Hwy. (☎843-626-9533), at 5th Ave. N. Open M-F 8:30am-5pm, Sa 9am-1pm. **Postal Code:** 29577.

▐ GETTING AROUND

Most attractions are on **Kings Hwy./U.S. 17,** which splits into a Bus. Rte. and a bypass 4 mi. south of Myrtle Beach. **Ocean Blvd.** runs along the ocean, flanked on either side by cheap pastel motels. Avenue numbers repeat themselves on both sides of 1st Ave. in the middle of town; note whether the

Ave. is "north" or "south." Also, take care not to confuse north **Myrtle Beach** with the town **North Myrtle Beach,** which has an almost identical street layout. **Rte. 501** runs west toward Conway and I-95. Unless otherwise stated, addresses on the Grand Strand are for Myrtle Beach.

◉ SIGHTS

The boulevard and the beach are both "the strand," and while you're on it, the rule is see and be seen. Fashionable teens strut their stuff, low riders cruise the streets, and older beachgoers showcase their sunburns. Coupons are everywhere—never pay full price for any attraction. Pick up a copy of the *Monster Coupon Book*, *Sunny Day Guide*, *Myrtle Beach Guide*, or *Strand Magazine* at any Visitors Center or hotel.

The colossal **Broadway at the Beach,** at U.S. 17 Bypass and 21st Ave. North (☎843-444-3200 or 800-386-4662), is a sprawling 350-acre complex determined to stimulate and entertain with theaters, a water park, mini golf, 20 restaurants, nightclubs, 100 shops, and other attractions. The info centers and booths sell tickets for major attractions at a discount. Within Broadway, the **Butterfly Pavilion,** the first facility of its kind in the nation, showcases over 40 species of butterflies in free flight. (☎843-839-4444. Open daily 10am-11pm. $26, seniors and ages 3-12 $16.)

South Carolina's most visited attraction is Broadway's **Ripley's Aquarium,** where guests roam through a 330 ft. underwater tunnel and gaze at the ferocious sharks and terrifying piranhas swimming above. (☎843-916-0888 or 800-734-8888; www.ripleysaquarium.com. Open daily 9am-11pm. $18.25, ages 5-11 $10, ages 2-4 $4.25.) There's also a miniature amusement park with a few rides, including a small ferris wheel, carousel, and tea cups. ($1.50 per ticket, $15 for unlimited rides.) The reptile capital of the world is the amazing ▧**Alligator Adventure,** on U.S. 17 in North Myrtle Beach at Barefoot Landing, where visitors are mesmerized by snakes, lizards, and frogs. Don't miss the hourly gator feedings and the park's 20 ft., 2000 lb. resident, Utan—the largest crocodile ever exhibited in the US. (☎843-361-0789. Open daily 9am-10pm. $14, seniors $12, ages 4-12 $9.)

Most visitors to Myrtle Beach putter over to one of the many elaborately themed **mini golf** courses on Kings Hwy. Get behind the wheel (again) at the **NASCAR Speedpark,** across from Broadway at the

Beach on the U.S. 17 Bypass. The park provides seven different tracks, catering to the need for speed, including the difficult, exciting Thunder Road. (☎843-918-8725. Open daily 10am-11pm. Unlimited rides $25, under 13 $15.)

🍴 FOOD

The Grand Strand tempts hungry motorists with over 1800 restaurants serving every type of food in every type of setting imaginable. Massive family-style, all-you-can-eat joints beckon from beneath the glow of every traffic light. **U.S. 17** offers countless steakhouses, seafood buffets, and fast-food restaurants. Seafood, however, is best on **Murrells Inlet**. With license plates covering the walls and ceiling and discarded peanut shells crunching underfoot, the **River City Cafe,** 404 21st Ave. N., celebrates a brand of American informality bordering on delinquency. Peruse the enthusiastic signatures of patrons on tables and walls as you polish off a burger ($3-6), or knock back a $3 beer while sitting at one of the picnic tables on the front porch. (☎843-448-1990. Open daily 11am-10pm.) While most of the restaurants on Broadway at the Beach seem to sacrifice quality fare for elaborate decor, **Benito's,** in the "Caribbean Village" part of the complex, serves up delightful stuffed shells ($10) and delectable calzones ($6) that will make you forget the screaming children and blaring lights outside. (☎843-444-0006. Open daily 11am-10:30pm.) Take a break from Ocean Dr. at **Dagwood's Deli,** 400 11th. Ave. North, where beach bums and businessmen come together to enjoy a "Shag" (ham, turkey, and swiss cheese; $5) or a Philly cheesesteak ($5-7). Be prepared to wait. (☎843-448-0100. Open M-Sa 11am-9pm.)

🏠 ACCOMMODATIONS

There are hundreds of motels lining **Ocean Blvd.,** with those on the oceanside fetching higher prices. Cheap motels also dot **U.S. 17.** From October to March, prices plummet as low as $20-30 a night for one of the luxurious hotels right on the beach. Call the **Myrtle Beach Lodging Reservation Service,** 1551 21st Ave. North, #20, for free help with reservations. (☎800-626-7477. Open M-F 8:30am-5pm.) Across the street from the ocean, the family-owned **Sea Banks Motor Inn,** 2200 S. Ocean Blvd., has immaculate rooms with mini-fridges, cable TV, laundry, and pool and beach

access. The rooms aren't elaborate, but the location is great. (☎843-448-2434 or 800-523-0603. Mid-Mar. to mid-Sept. singles $48; doubles $78. Mid-Sept. to mid-Mar $22/$28.) The **Hurl Rock Motel,** 2010 S. Ocean Blvd., has big, clean rooms with a pool and hot tub and is right across the street from the beach. (☎843-626-3531 or 888-487-5762. 25+. In high season singles $45; doubles $54-89. In low-season from $25/from $28.)

🌙 NIGHTLIFE

The New Orleans-style nightclub district of **Celebrity Sq.,** at Broadway at the Beach, facilitates stepping out with 10 clubs, ranging in theme from classic rock to Latin. Particularly kitschy are the **Hard Rock Cafe,** in a giant fake pyramid guarded by sphinxes, and **Margaritaville,** named for the Jimmy Buffet song. Elsewhere, **Club Millennium 2000,** 1012 S. Kings Hwy. (☎843-445-9630), and **2001,** 920 Lake Arrowhead Rd. (☎843-449-9434), bring clubbers a hot-steppin' odyssey. (21+. Cover varies. Open daily 8pm-2am.)

MURRELLS INLET

Ten miles south of Myrtle Beach lies tiny Murrells Inlet, which stretches along Bus. U.S. 17. The town is famous as a fishing village, and provides day access to its multiple marinas for a reasonable fee. The 9100-acre 🌿**Brookgreen Gardens,** U.S. 17, opposite Huntington Beach State Park south of Murrells Inlet, offer a tranquil respite from the tackiness that dominates Myrtle Beach. Over 500 American sculptures are scattered throughout the grounds beneath massive oaks. Tours of the gardens and wildlife trail are available in addition to summer drama, music, and food programs. (☎843-235-6000; www.brookgreen.org. Open daily 9:30am-5pm. 7-day pass $12, seniors and ages 13-18 $10, under 13 free.)

This "seafood capital" features an array of restaurants for every taste. The fun and casual **Captain's Restaurant**, off Bus. U.S. 17, features Low-Country favorites like the crab casserole and the fried Murrells Inlet creek shrimp (☎843-651-2416. Entrees $15-20. Open M-F 4:30-9pm, Su 11:30am-9pm; summer closed M.) The slightly more expensive **Divine Fish House,** at the Wahoo's Marina, combines classic Southern favorites like fried green tomatoes with more exotic dishes like the banana leaf mangrove grouper and wood duck with a pumpkin walnut muffin. (☎843-651-5800. Entrees $20-25. Open Su-Th 5-10pm, F-Sa 5-10:30pm.) Decorated with a collection of over 3000 hats, **Flo's Place** serves up authentic Cajun cuisine. Make sure to sample the alligator nuggets ($7.25), and yes, they are made with real alligator. (☎843-651-7222; www.flosplace.com. Open daily 11:30am-10pm.) There are basically no budget accommodations in town, so staying in Myrtle Beach or farther south in Georgetown is probably the best bet. **Huntington Beach State Park Campground,** 16148 Ocean Hwy., 3 mi. south of Murrells Inlet on U.S. 17, is located in a diverse environment including lagoons, salt marshes, and a beach. Take advantage of the fishing and boating access and the nature trails. Be careful: gators come within yards of the sites. (☎843-237-4440. Open daily Apr.-Oct. 6am-10pm; Nov.-Mar. 6am-6pm. Sites Apr.-Oct. $12, with water and electricity $25, with full hookup $27; Nov.-Mar. $10/$21/$23. Day-use $4.)

APPROACHING GEORGETOWN
Follow **U.S. 17 South;** it becomes **Church St.** in Georgetown.

GEORGETOWN

Once a critical Southern port city, Georgetown showcases white-pillared 18th-century rice and indigo plantation homes. It might not be the most happening place along the route, but gives visitors a chance to while away an afternoon in the quaint downtown and escape the noise of Myrtle Beach.

(VITAL STATS)

Population: 9000

Visitor Info: Georgetown County Chamber of Commerce, 1001 Front St. (☎843-546-8436 or 800-777-7705; www.georgetownchamber.com). Open daily 9am-5pm.

Internet Access: Georgetown County Library, 405 Cleland St. (☎843-545-330). Open M-Th 9am-8pm, F-Sa 9am-5pm; Sept.-May also Su 2-5pm.

Post Office: 1101 Charlotte St. (☎843-546-5515). **Postal Code:** 29440.

GETTING AROUND. In town, **Church St. (U.S. 17)** runs parallel to the waterfront and to **Front St.,** the main street downtown. Signs will direct drivers to downtown, indicating when to turn left coming from the north.

SIGHTS. Located right next to the Visitors Center, **Kaminski House Museum,** 1003 Front St., is a 1769 house decorated with period English and American furnishings, including examples of Charleston's finest cabinetmaking. Tour guides lead visitors through the home, explaining both the particular history of the home and its place in 18th-century South Carolina life. (☎843-546-7706 or 843-233-0383. Museum open M-Sa 9am-5pm, Su 1-5pm. Tours every hr. M-Sa 10am-4pm, Su 1-4pm. $5, ages 6-12 $2, under 6 free. AAA and AARP discount.) The **Rice Museum,** 633 Front St., presents the history of rice culture in the county and illustrates how dependence on a single agricultural product shaped the era's history. The museum leads a tour through the 1842 Clock Tower building, Kaminski Hardware building, and the Maritime History Museum. (☎843-546-7423; www.ricemuseum.com. Open M-Sa 10am-4:30pm. $4, ages 12-21 $2, under 12 free.)

Swamp Fox Tours and **Remember When Tours** give narrated, tram rides through the historical district, highlighting major points of interest and local stories. (Swamp Fox Tours begin at Visitors Center. ☎843-527-6469; www.georgetown-sc.com. Tours M-F 10am-4pm. $7.50, children $4. Remember When Tours tickets available at the Remember When Coffee Shoppe, 926 Front St., and Riverfront Antique Mall, 929 Front St. Tours daily 10:30am-3:30pm. $8, seniors $7, children $5.) The Visitors Center also has brochures for a self-guided walking tour to major historic sights.

The **Hampton Plantation State Historic Site,** 1950 Rutledge Rd. in McClellanville, off U.S. 17 south of Georgetown, focuses on Low Country rice culture. The tour of the plantation house highlights the architecture of the huge 1750s mansion and cutaway sections of wall and ceiling show its evolution from farmhouse to stately manor. (☎843-546-9361. Park grounds open daily 9am-6pm. Mansion tours daily Memorial Day-Labor Day 11am-4pm; Labor Day-Memorial Day 1-4pm. Last tour at 3pm. Tours $2, age 6-16 $1.)

FOOD & ACCOMMODATIONS. The **Riverside Grille,** 716 Front St., serves up food in a maritime themed restaurant with anchors on the wall and model ships in the window. Diners should check out the signature foot-long Riverdog ($5.25) with cheese, chili, and onions. (☎843-527-4438. Open M-F 11:30am-2:30pm.) The **Front Street Deli**, 809 Front St., features sandwiches and salads in a no-nonsense atmosphere. The large, tasty sandwiches ($4.75) like the BLT or reuben on rye are local favorites. (☎843-546-2008. Open M-Sa 10am-4pm.) The fun **Dogwood Cafe,** 713 Front St., prints its menus on newsprint and features classic Southern fare like the stuffed flounder ($17) and tasty po' boys. (☎843-545-7777. Open M-Th 10am-9pm, F-Sa 10am-11pm.)

Downtown Georgetown is peppered with B&Bs, but for budget options, visitors will have to resort to more generic hotels and motels. The **Harbor Inn,** 600 Church St., has clean, spacious rooms, as well as a large outdoor pool. (☎843-546-5111. Rooms $40-60.) The **Carolinian Inn,** 706 Church St., has many of the same amenities, including fridge, microwave, and pool, but is located on a former plantation. The antebellum architecture of the central building, the lush greenery, and the view over a nearby marsh give the establishment a special charm. (☎843-546-5191; www.carolinianinn.com. Rooms in high season $120-140; low season $60-80.) Just inside town, the **Jameson Inn,** 120 Church St., featuring classy decor and a deluxe continental breakfast with biscuits and gravy, is probably one of the best deals in town. (☎843-546-6090; www.jamesoninn.com. Rooms $70-80. AAA and AARP discount.)

⚑ APPROACHING CHARLESTON

Follow **U.S. 17** over the **Cooper River Bridge** and take the first right. Two more immediate right turns put drivers on **E. Bay St.,** where signs will point to parking, major attractions, and the Visitors Center.

CHARLESTON

Built on rice and cotton, Charleston's antebellum plantation system yielded vast riches now seen in its numerous museums, historic homes, and ornate architecture. An accumulated cultural capital of 300 years flows like the long, distinctive drawl of the natives. Several of the South's most renowned plantations dot the city, while two venerable educational institutions, the College of Charleston and the Citadel, add youthful eccentricity. Horse-drawn carriages, cobblestone streets, pre-Civil War homes, beautiful beaches, and some of the best restaurants in the Southeast explain why Charleston often heads the list of the nation's top destinations.

VITAL STATS

Population: 97,000

Visitor Info: Charleston Visitors Center, 375 Meeting St. (☎843-853-8000 or 800-868-8118; www.charlestoncvb.com), across from Charleston Museum. Open daily Apr.-Oct. 8:30am-5:30pm; Nov.-Mar. 8:30am-5pm.

Internet Access: Charleston Public Library, 68 Calhoun St. (☎843-805-6801). Open M-Th 9am-9pm, F-Sa 9am-6pm, Su 2-5pm.

Post Office: 83 Broad St. (☎843-577-0690). Open M-F 8:30am-5:30pm, Sa 9:30am-2pm. **Postal Code:** 29402.

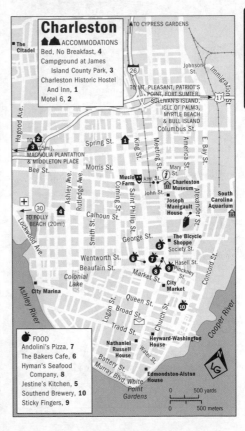

Charleston

ACCOMMODATIONS
Bed, No Breakfast, **4**
Campground at James Island County Park, **3**
Charleston Historic Hostel And Inn, **1**
Motel 6, **2**

FOOD
Andolini's Pizza, **7**
The Bakers Cafe, **6**
Hyman's Seafood Company, **8**
Jestine's Kitchen, **5**
Southend Brewery, **10**
Sticky Fingers, **9**

EAST COAST

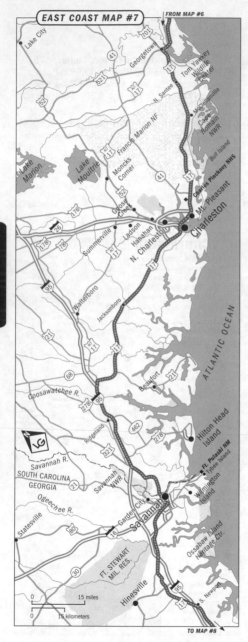

GETTING AROUND

Old Charleston lies at the southernmost point of the 1 mi. wide peninsula below **Calhoun St.** The major north-south routes through the city are **Meeting St., King St.,** and **E. Bay St.** The area north of the Visitors Center is run-down and uninviting. **Savannah Hwy. (U.S. 17)** cuts across the peninsula heading south to Savannah and north across two towering bridges to Mt. Pleasant and Myrtle Beach. There are plenty of metered **parking** spaces, and plenty of police officers giving tickets. The easiest parking is available in the public lots found all over the historic district ($1 per hr.).

The **Downtown Area Shuttle (DASH)** is made up of trolley routes that circle downtown. (Operates daily 8am-11pm. $1, seniors $0.50, disabled $0.25; 1-day pass $3; 3 day $7.) **The Bicycle Shoppe,** 280 Meeting St., between George and Society St. offers bike rental. (☎843-722-8168. $5 per hr., $20 per day. Open M-Sa 9am-7pm, Su 1-5pm.)

SIGHTS

Charleston's historic homes, monuments, churches, galleries, and gardens can be seen by foot, car, bus, boat, trolley, or horse-drawn carriage—or on one of the nine ghost tours. **City Market,** downtown at Meeting St., stays abuzz in a newly restored 19th-century building. (Open daily from about 9am-5pm.)

PLANTATIONS & GARDENS. The 300-year-old **Magnolia Plantation and Gardens** is the most majestic of Charleston's plantations, not to mention the oldest major public garden in the country. Visitors can enjoy the Drayton family's staggering wealth by exploring their 50 acres of gorgeous gardens with 900 varieties of camellia and 250 varieties of azalea. Other attractions include a hedge maze, petting zoo, bike and canoe rental, swamp, and bird sanctuary. *(On Rte. 61, 10 mi. northwest of town off U.S. 17. ☎843-571-1266 or 800-367-3517. Open Feb.-Nov. daily 8am-5:30pm; call for winter hours. Gardens $12, seniors $11, ages 13-19 $9, ages 6-12 $6; with house admission $19/$18/$16/$13; with nature trail $18/$17/$15/$10; with swamp garden $17/$16/$13/$9. Canoes or bikes $5 per 3hr.)* A bit farther down the road, **Middleton Place** is a more manicured plantation with working stables, gardens, house, restaurant, and inn, as well as demonstrations of 18th- and 19th-century crafts. *(4300 Ashley River Rd. On Rte. 61, 14 mi. northwest of downtown. ☎843-556-6020 or 800-782-3608; www.middletonplace.org. Open daily 9am-5pm. Gardens $20, under 16 $12. House tour $10. AAA discount.)* Even farther out, but worth the trip, **Cypress Gardens** lets visitors paddle their own boats out onto eerie, gator-filled swamps. *(3030 Cypress Gardens Rd., off Rte. 52. ☎842-553-0515; www.cypressgardens.org. Open daily 9am-5pm. $9, ages 6-12 $3.)* The 738-acre **Boone Hall Plantation** in Mt. Pleasant features a plantation house, slave cabins, and the gorgeous Avenue of Oaks, a half-mile drive of oaks thickly draped in Spanish moss. There is also a butterfly garden, a duck pond, and a nature trail. *(1235 Long Point Rd. ☎843-884-4371; www.boonehallplantation.com. Open M-Sa 8:30am-6:30pm, Su 1-5pm. $14.50, ages 6-12 $7.)*

CHARLESTON MUSEUM & HISTORIC HOMES. Across the street from the Visitors Center stands the **Charleston Museum,** the country's oldest museum, which contains outstanding exhibits on the Revolutionary War and the Civil War, as well as an exhaustive look into the history of the Low Country. *(360 Meeting St. ☎843-722-2996; www.charlestonmuseum.org. Open M-Sa 9am-5pm, Su 1-5pm. $9, children $4.)* Built in 1772, the **Heyward-Washington House** was home to Thomas Heyward, Jr., a signer of the Declaration of Independence. The house, which was rented to George Washington during his 1791 trip through the South, features timeless American furniture and a lush surrounding garden. Also managed by the Charleston

Museum is the **Joseph Manigault House,** a stunning piece of Neoclassical architecture built in 1803. Be sure to check out the Gate Temple, a gorgeous outdoor vestibule that leads to the front door and porch. *(Heyward-Washington House: 87 Church St. ☎843-722-0354. Joseph Manigault House: 350 Meeting St. ☎843-723-2926. Both houses open M-Sa 10am-5pm, Su 1-5pm. Tours every 30min. 1 house $8, ages 3-12 $4; museum and 1 house $12; museum and 2 houses $18.)* The **Nathaniel Russell House** and **Edmondston-Alston House** are both examples of the late Federal style of architecture, with the former featuring a "free-flying" staircase and masterful iron balconies and the latter a lush garden, stunning views of the Charleston Harbor, and many of the Alston family's personal belongings. *(Nathaniel Russell: 51 Meeting St. ☎843-724-8481. Open M-Sa 10am-5pm, Su 2-5pm. $8, under 6 free. Edmondston-Alston: 21 E. Battery St. ☎843-722-7171 or 800-782-3608. Open Su-M 1:30-4:30pm, Tu-Sa 10am-4:30pm. $10.)*

PATRIOT'S POINT, FORT SUMTER, & FORT MOULTRIE. Climb aboard four naval ships, including a submarine and the aircraft carrier *Yorktown,* in **Patriot's Point Naval and Maritime Museum,** the world's largest naval museum. *(40 Patriots Point Rd. Across the Cooper River in Mt. Pleasant. ☎843-884-2727; www.state.sc.us/patpt. Open daily Apr.-Sept. 9am-6pm, ships close 7:30pm; Oct.-Mar. 9am-5pm, ships close 5:30pm. $12.50, seniors and military $11, ages 6-11 $6.)* From Patriot's Point in Mt. Pleasant, **Fort Sumter Tours** has boat excursions to the National Historic Site where Confederate soldiers bombarded Union

GULLAH FESTIVAL

NO WORK, ALL PLAY

Every Memorial Day weekend, almost 100,000 people come to the small, quiet town of Beaufort, South Carolina, to pay homage to the culture and history that emerged when Africans were shipped to America as slaves many generations ago. Known as the Gullah Festival, the gathering is a five-day celebration of African traditions that has attracted droves of tourists, scholars, and locals since its creation in 1986. African storytellers captivate visitors, who also watch seductive African dance, listen to the harmonizing strains of live gospel and jazz music, and enjoy a multitude of authentic African dishes. A former slave market is memorialized in a special ceremony. Basket-weaving and boat-building exhibitions have also made their way into the festival, showcasing techniques that were used centuries ago. Festival organizers have made a point to reach out to a younger audience in recent years, adding to the schedule a Miss Gullah Pageant and a Gullah Golf Tournament. (For more info, call ☎843-522-1998.)

forces in April 1861. There's a dock at Liberty Square next to the South Carolina Aquarium in Charleston. *(Fort Sumter: ☎ 843-883-3123; www.nps.gov/fosu. Tours: ☎ 843-881-7337. $12, ages 6-11 $6. Allow 25min. before departure time for ticketing and boarding.)* **Fort Moultrie** is the third in a series of forts built at the same location, this one completed in 1809, and the site from which the attack on Fort Sumter was launched to begin the Civil War. *(1214 Middle St. Follow Coleman Blvd. off of U.S. 17 as it becomes 703, and take a right onto Middle St. ☎ 843-883-3123. Open daily 9am-5pm.)*

CHARLES PICKNEY NATIONAL HISTORIC SITE. The site lies on a portion of what was once the property of Charles Pickney, a South Carolina delegate to the 1787 Constitutional Convention and former state governor. The grounds cover 28 acres and feature a ½ mi. history and nature trail, 1828 Low Country cottage, and a museum with exhibits on rice agriculture, plantation life, and the American Revolution in South Carolina. *(1254 Long Point Rd., off U.S. 17 in Mt. Pleasant. ☎ 843-881-5516; www.nps.gov/chpi. Open daily 9am-5pm.)*

BEACHES. Folly Beach is popular with students from the Citadel, College of Charleston, and University of South Carolina. *(Over the James Bridge and U.S. 171, about 20 mi. southeast of Charleston. ☎ 843-588-2426.)* The more exposed **Isle of Palms** extends for miles down toward the less-crowded **Sullivan's Island.** *(Across the Cooper Bridge, drive 10 mi. down U.S. 17 North, and turn right onto the Isle of Palms Connector. ☎ 843-886-3863.)*

SOUTH CAROLINA AQUARIUM. With over 50 interactive exhibits, the aquarium has become Charleston's greatest attraction. Its exhibits showcase aquatic life from the region's swamps, marshes, and oceans. Stare down the fishies at the 330,000-gallon Great Ocean Tank, which contains the nation's tallest viewing window. *(At the end of Calhoun St. on the Cooper River, overlooking the harbor. ☎ 843-720-1990; www.scaquarium.org. Open daily mid-June to mid-Aug. 9am-6pm; mid-Aug. to mid-June 9am-5pm. $14, seniors $12, ages 3-11 $7.)*

BULL ISLAND. To get away from human civilization, take a 30 min. ferry to Bull Island, a 5000-acre island off the coast of Charleston. The boat is often greeted by dolphins swimming in some of the cleanest water on the planet. On the island there are 16 mi. of hiking trails populated by 278 different species of birds. *(Ferries depart from Moore's Landing, off Seewee Rd., 16 mi. north of Charleston off U.S. 17. ☎ 843-881-4582. Departs Mar.-Nov. Tu and Th-Sa 9am and 12:30pm, returns noon and 4pm; Dec.-Feb. Sa 10am, returns 3pm. Round-trip $30, under 12 $15.)*

GIBBES MUSEUM OF ART. One of the best collections in the Southeast, the museum features portraits and miniatures, as well as an extensive collection of Japanese block prints. Rotating exhibits highlight local and regional artists. *(135 Meeting St. ☎ 843-722-2706; www.gibbesmuseum.org. Open Su 1-5pm, Tu-Sa 10am-5pm. $7, seniors, students, and military $6, children $3.)*

▇ FOOD

Charleston has some of the best food in the country. While most restaurants cater to big-spending tourists, there are plenty of budget opportunities to sample the Southern cooking, BBQ, and fresh seafood that have made the Low Country famous.

Hyman's Seafood Company, 215 Meeting St. (☎ 843-723-6000). Since 1890, this restaurant has offered 15-25 kinds of fresh fish daily ($7-15), served in 8 styles. Po'boy sandwich with oyster, calamari, crab, or scallops $7-8. No reservations; expect long waits. Open daily 11am-11pm.

Southend Brewery, 161 E. Bay St. (☎ 843-853-4677). Outstanding ribs ($13-20), eclectic pizzas ($8-10), and home-brewed beers ($3.50)—not to mention the opportunity to color on the tablecloths with crayons—entice many to this 3-story brewhouse. Happy hour daily 4-7pm. Open Su-W 11:30am-10pm, Th-Sa 11:30am-11pm. Bar open until 1am.

Jestine's Kitchen, 251 Meeting St. (☎ 843-722-7224). Serving up some of the best Southern food in Charleston, Jestine's has become a local favorite with its daily blue-plate specials ($7-10) and "blue collar special" (peanut butter and banana sandwich; $3). Open Su 11am-9pm, Tu-Th 11am-9:30pm, F-Sa 11am-10pm.

Andolini's Pizza, 82 Wentworth St. (☎ 843-722-7437), just west of King St. Perfectly hidden from the uber-trendy King St. shoppers, Andolini's is fabulously kitschy, decorated with everything from a kangaroo crossing sign to a huge metal sign for Sunbeam bread. Amazing pizza at unbeatable prices. A large slice with any topping, a salad, and a drink runs $5. Large thin-crust cheese pies $11. Calzones from $5. Open M-Th 11am-11pm, F-Sa 11am-midnight, Su noon-10pm.

Sticky Fingers, 235 Meeting St. (☎843-853-7427). A local chain voted the best barbecue in town on numerous occasions, Sticky Fingers has become a Charleston legend for its mouth-watering ribs ($12-26)—prepared in 5 different ways. The Carolina combo lets diners enjoy ribs, barbecue, chicken, and all the sides for $13. Open M-Sa 11am-11pm, Su 11am-10pm.

The Bakers Cafe, 214 King St. (☎843-577-2694). Delighting local patrons for the past 23 years, this upscale cafe cooks up elegant morning and midday meals. Open daily 8am-3pm.

ACCOMMODATIONS

Motel rooms in historic downtown Charleston are expensive. Cheap motels are a few miles out of the city, around Exits 209-211 on I-26 West in North Charleston, or across the Ashley River on U.S. 17 in Mt. Pleasant.

Charleston's Historic Hostel and Inn, 194 Saint Phillip St. (☎843-478-1446 or 843-853-0846). Located only 3 blocks from the Visitors Center, the hostel includes a common room with Internet access and TV, a fully equipped kitchen, and a warm friendly atmosphere. The brightly painted walls give a fun, funky feel to this historic home, complete with wrap-around front porch. A/C in all rooms. Dorms $15, private rooms with fridge $40.

Bed, No Breakfast, 16 Halsey St. (☎843-723-4450). The only budget option within walking distance of downtown, this charming 2-room inn offers guests an affordable way to stay in the historic heart of the city. Shared bathroom. Reservations recommended. Rooms $60-95. No credit cards.

Motel 6, 2058 Savannah Hwy. (☎843-556-5144), 5 mi. south of town. Be sure to call ahead and reserve one of these clean rooms; the immensely popular motel is often booked solid for days. Rooms Su-Th $44, F-Sa $54; $6 per additional person.

Campground at James Island County Park (☎843-795-4386 or 800-743-7275). Take U.S. 17 South to Rte. 171 and follow the signs. Spacious, open sites. The spectacular park features 16 acres of lakes, bicycle and walking trails, and a small water park. Bike and boat rental. Primitive sites $13; tent sites $19; hookup $26. 10% senior discount.

NIGHTLIFE

With nearby colleges and a constant tourist presence, Charleston's nightlife beats strong. Free copies of *City Paper*, in stores and restaurants, list events. Big-name bands take center stage nightly at the **Music Farm,** 32 Ann St., in the old train station. (☎843-853-3276. Tickets $5-25. Box office open M-F noon-4pm; www.musicfarm.com.) With its hilarious musicians and singing servers, **Pluto Rocks,** 479 King St., makes dueling pianos cool, and is an up-and-coming hot spot. (☎843-722-1088. Dueling pianos F-Sa. Cover F-Sa $3 after 9pm. Open W-Sa 7pm-2am.)

APPROACHING SAVANNAH
Follow **U.S. 17** to **I-95,** and head into the city.

Welcome To **GEORGIA**

SAVANNAH

In February 1733, General James Oglethorpe and a band of 120 vagabonds founded the city of Savannah and the state of Georgia. General Sherman later spared the city during his rampage through the South—some say he found it too pretty to burn, presenting it to President Lincoln as a Christmas gift. Sherman's reaction is understandable to anyone who sees Savannah's stately old trees and Federalist and English Regency houses interwoven with spring blossoms.

GETTING AROUND

Savannah rests on the coast of Georgia at the mouth of the **Savannah River,** which runs north of the city along the border with South Carolina. The city stretches south from bluffs overlooking the river. The restored 2½ sq. mi.

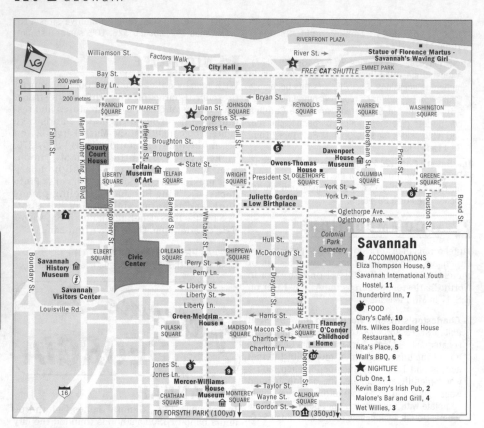

EAST COAST

Savannah

🏠 ACCOMMODATIONS
Eliza Thompson House, **9**
Savannah International Youth
    Hostel, **11**
Thunderbird Inn, **7**

🍴 FOOD
Clary's Café, **10**
Mrs. Wilkes Boarding House
    Restaurant, **8**
Nita's Place, **5**
Wall's BBQ, **6**

⭐ NIGHTLIFE
Club One, **1**
Kevin Barry's Irish Pub, **2**
Malone's Bar and Grill, **4**
Wet Willies, **3**

VITAL STATS

Population: 130,000

Visitor Info: Savannah Visitors Center, 301 Martin Luther King Jr. Blvd. (☎912-944-0455; www.savannahgeorgia.com), at Liberty St. Open M-F 8:30am-5pm, Sa-Su 9am-5pm.

Internet Access: Savannah Public Library, 2002 Bull St. (☎912-652-3600). Open M-Th 9am-9pm, F-Sa 9am-6pm, Su 2-6pm.

Post Office: 2 N. Fahm St. (☎912-235-4610), at Bay St. Open M-F 7am-6pm, Sa 9am-3pm. **Postal Code:** 31402.

downtown historic district, bordered by **E. Broad St., Martin Luther King Jr. Blvd., Gwinnett St.,** and the river, is best explored on foot. Do not stray

south of Gwinnett St.; the historic district quickly deteriorates into an unsafe area. A **parking pass** ($8) allows 2-day unlimited use of all metered parking, city lots, and garages. There is a public **parking** deck across the street from the Visitors Center.

👁 SIGHTS

Most of Savannah's 21 squares contain some distinctive centerpiece. Elegant antebellum houses and drooping vine-wound trees often cluster around the squares, adding to the classic Southern aura. Bus, van, and horse carriage **tours** leave from the Visitors Center, but walking can be more rewarding. (Tours daily every 10-15min. $13-15.)

HISTORIC HOUSES. Two of Savannah's best-known historic homes are the Davenport House and the Owens-Thomas House. Built in 1820, the **Davenport House** is nearly exactly as Isaiah Davenport left it in the mid-19th century, complete with the original furniture, cantilevered staircase, and exemplary woodwork. The **Owens-Thomas House** is similar, but the carriage house, holding artifacts and relating stories about slave life, is free. *(Davenport: 324 E. State St., on Columbia Sq. ☎912-236-8097; www.davenportsavga.com. Open M-Sa 10am-4pm, Su 1-4pm. $7, students with ID and ages 7-18 $3.50. Owens-Thomas: 124 Abercom St., 1 block away on Oglethorpe Sq. ☎912-233-9743. Open M noon-5pm, Tu-Sa 10am-5pm, Su 1-5pm. Tours every 30min.; last tour 4:30pm. $8, seniors $7, students $4, ages 6-12 $2.)* The **Green Meldrim House** is a Gothic Revival mansion that served as General Sherman's Savannah headquarters following his famed "march to the sea." It was from this house that Sherman wrote the famous telegram to President Lincoln, giving him the city as a gift. *(14 W. Macon St., on Madison Sq. ☎912-232-1251. Open Tu and Th-F 10am-4pm, Sa 10am-1pm. Tours every 30min. $5, students $2.)* The **Mercer-Williams House**, once home to songwriter Johnny Mercer, is one of the town's most famous literary sites. Here also lived Jim Williams, accused and acquitted four times of shooting hustler Danny Hansford in the case that inspired *Midnight in the Garden of Good and Evil*. *(429 Bull St. ☎912-236-6352 or 912-238-0208. Open M-Sa 10:30am-4pm, Su 12:30-4pm. Tours $12.50, under 13 $8.)* Literary fans can visit the **Flannery O'Connor Childhood Home,** where the award winner spent 12 years growing up and one year just chilling. *(207 E. Chareton St. ☎912-233-6014. Open Sa-Su 1-4pm. $2.)*

FORT PULASKI NATIONAL MONUMENT. Savannah's four forts once protected the city's port from Spanish, British, and other invaders. The most intriguing, Fort Pulaski National Monument marks the Civil War battle where Union forces first used rifled cannons to decimate the Confederate opposition. *(15 mi. east of Savannah on U.S. 80 East and Rte. 26. ☎912-786-5787. Open daily summer 9am-7pm; off-season 9am-5pm. $3, under 16 free.)*

JULIET GORDON LOW BIRTHPLACE. Girl scouts might want to check out the Juliet Gordon Low Birthplace, the city's first registered historic landmark. Now owned by the Girl Scouts of America, it celebrates the organization, founded in 1912 by Juliet Gordon Low with her niece, Daisy Gordon, as the first scout. *(10 E. Oglethorpe Ave. ☎912-233-4501. Open M-Tu and Th-Sa 10am-4pm, Su 12:30-4:30pm.)*

SAVANNAH HISTORY MUSEUM. Conveniently located in the same building as the Visitors Center, the Savannah History Museum features an excellent overview of Savannah history, including an 1800 cotton gin and memorabilia such as Forest Gump's bench. *(303 Martin Luther King Jr. Blvd. ☎912-238-1779. Open daily 9am-5pm. $4; seniors, students, and active military $3.50; ages 6-11 $3.)*

TELFAIR MUSEUM OF ART. The oldest art museum in the South, the Telfair Museum of Art has a rich collection, including major works by members of the Ashcan school and examples of Regency-era decorative arts. *(121 Barnard St. ☎912-232-1177. Open M noon-4:30pm, Tu-Sa 10am-5pm, Su 1-5pm. $8, children $2.)*

🎵 **ENTERTAINMENT**

Green is the theme of the **St. Patrick's Day Celebration on the River** (☎912-234-0295), a five-day, beer- and fun-filled party that packs the streets and warms celebrants up for the annual **St. Patrick's Day Parade** (☎912-233-4804), the second-largest in the US. During the annual **NOGS Tour of the Hidden Gardens of Historic Savannah** (☎912-238-0248), in late April, private walled gardens are opened to the public, who can join in on a special Southern tea. **First Friday for the Arts** (☎912-232-4903) occurs on the first Friday of every month in City Market, when visitors meet with residents of a local art colony. **First Saturday on the River** (☎912-234-0295) brings arts, crafts, entertainment, and food to historic River St. each month. A free paper, *Connect Savannah*, found in restaurants and stores, has the latest in news and entertainment.

🍴 **FOOD**

Nita's Place, 129 E. Broughton St., is reason enough to come to Savannah. You can read enthusiastic letters from satisfied customers pressed beneath the glass tabletops while you experience fantastic soul food. The dessert-like squash casserole will make you a believer. (☎912-238-8233. Entrees $10-13. Open M-Th 11:30am-3pm, F-Sa

11:30am-3pm and 5-8pm.) **Wall's BBQ,** 515 E. York Ln., in an alley between York St. and Oglethorpe Ave., serves up mouth-watering barbecue in a hole-in-the-wall location. Don't plan on devouring your delicious barbecue sandwich or ribs ($4.50-12) here; most locals know to order and then relish their meal in one of the neighboring squares. (☎912-232-9754. Baked deviled crabs $3. Open Th-Sa 11am-9pm.) **Mrs. Wilkes Boarding House,** 107 W. Jones St., is a Southern institution where friendly folks gather around large tables for homestyle atmosphere and soul food. Fried chicken, butter beans, and biscuits are favorites, and the dining room often fills up quickly. (☎912-232-5997. All-you-can-eat $12. Open M-F 8-9am and 11am-3pm.) **Clary's Café,** 404 Abercorn St., has been serving up some of Savannah's best diner-style breakfasts since 1903. The famous weekend brunch features $4 malted waffles. (☎912-233-0402. Open M-Th 7am-4pm, F 7am-5pm, Sa 8am-5pm, Su 8am-4pm.)

ACCOMMODATIONS

Downtown motels cluster near the historic area, Visitors Center, and Greyhound station. **Ogeechee Rd. (U.S. 17)** has several budget options. **The Eliza Thompson House,** 5 W. Jones St., is the premier B&B in Savannah, located in the heart of downtown, minutes from the city's beautiful, bustling squares. Built in 1847, this historic inn welcomes guests with complimentary wine, coffee, and dessert hours. (☎912-236-3620 or 800-348-9378; www.elizathompsonhouse.com. Reservations recommended. Rooms from $140.) **Thunder-**

bird Inn, 611 W. Oglethorpe Ave., has the least expensive rooms downtown. The modest exterior belies the clean rooms and pleasant, vaguely beach-themed furnishings within. Be careful walking around in the surrounding area as it may become unsafe after dark. (☎912-232-2661. Singles Su-Th $40, F-Sa $50. 5% off with mention of *Let's Go.*) **Savannah International Youth Hostel (HI-AYH),** 304 E. Hall St., is the most affordable option for budget travelers wishing to stay in the historic district. This small bare-bones inn, near an unsafe part of town, offers little more than a bed and a roof but is located only minutes from some of Savannah's greatest sights. (☎912-236-7744. Bike rental $10. Linen $1. Reception 7-10am and 5-11pm; call for late-night check-in. Lockout 10am-5pm. 3-night max. stay. Open Mar.-Oct. Dorms $18; private rooms $35-45.) **Skidaway Island State Park** is 6 mi. southeast of downtown off Diamond Causeway; follow Liberty St. east from downtown until it becomes Wheaton St., turn right on Waters Ave., and follow it to Diamond Causeway. The park has bathrooms, heated showers, electricity, and water. (☎912-598-2300 or 800-864-7275. Open daily 7am-10pm. Sites $18, with hookup $20.)

NIGHTLIFE

The waterfront area on **River St.** brims with endless dining opportunities, street performers, and a friendly pub ambience. At **Kevin Barry's Irish Pub,** 117 W. River St., the Guinness flows and the entire bar reels with live Irish folk music. (☎912-233-9626. Music W-Sa after 8:30pm. Cover $2. Open M-F 2pm-3am, Sa

THE LOCAL STORY

SAVANNAH'S BOOK

The news of Danny Hansford's death spread through the reserved southern city of Savannah like wildfire. When residents discovered that Hansford—a hot-tempered local hustler—had been shot his lover, society antiques dealer Jim Williams at the historic Mercer House in Monterey Square, they could not believe their ears. As is the case with all good hearsay, the story of the murder soon took on many forms, each with a unique perspective. John Berendt, a New York writer, caught wind of the trial and general commotion and recorded it as *Midnight in the Garden of Good and Evil* (1994), an eloquent and fascinating story about the eccentric characters of a this hothouse city, including a scandalous drag queen, a squatter who runs "historic" tours of vacant homes, and the prim and proper ladies of the Married Woman's Card Club. Since the release of "the Book" (as it is called by locals), tourism has skyrocketed, pumping over $100 million into Savannah's economy. Some local spots mentioned include Clary's, 404 Abercorn St., and the Mercer-Williams House, Monterey Square.

11:30am-3am, Su 12:30pm-2am.) If sugary drinks are your pleasure, head to **Wet Willies,** 101 E. River St., for its casual dining and irresistible frozen daiquiris. (☎912-233-5650. Drinks $4-6. Open Su-Th 11am-1am, F-Sa 11am-2am.) Local college students eat, drink, and shop at the restaurants and stores of **City Market,** on Jefferson at W. St. Julian St., the largest Historic District in the US. **Malone's Bar and Grill,** 27 W. Barnard St., delivers dancing, drinks, and live music. The lower floor opens up to a game room, while techno and rap beat upstairs Friday and Saturday nights. (☎912-234-3059. Happy hour 4-8pm. F-Sa top level 18+. Open M-Sa 11am-3am, Su noon-2am. Kitchen closes 1am.) For the best alternative scene and a GBLT-friendly atmosphere check out **Club One,** 1 Jefferson St. near Bay St., where the Lady Chablis, a character featured in *Midnight in the Garden of Good and Evil*, performs. (☎912-232-0200. Cover $3-10. Open M-Sa 5pm-3am, Su 5pm-2am.)

APPROACHING ST. SIMONS ISLAND
Following **U.S. 17 South,** reach the island over the **St. Simons Causeway.** Veer to the right on **Kings Way** to reach downtown and Neptune Park.

ST. SIMONS ISLAND

St. Simons Island has long been a popular resort and vacation destination, with plenty of sun and fun for all. **Neptune Park** is home to the **St. Simons Island Lighthouse.** The second lighthouse built on the island (the first was destroyed during the Civil War), it dates from 1872 and rises 104 ft. (☎912-638-4666. Open M-Sa 10am-5pm, Su 1:30-5pm. $5, ages 6-12 $2.50.) Heading north on Frederica Rd. leads to **Fort Frederica,** a fort established by Georgia founder James Oglethorpe. A movie explains the fort's history and a walking tour leads visitors through the remains of the town to the fort itself. (☎912-638-3639; www.nps.gov/fofr. Open daily 8am-5pm. $5 per vehicle.) Just before the Fort on Frederica Rd. lies **Christ Episcopal Church,** the second-oldest Episcopal parish in the state. Across the street, the **Wesley Memorial Monument** celebrates Revered Charles Wesley, who conducted the parish's first services in February of 1736. (☎912-638-8683. Open daily 2-5pm.) Off Demere Rd. lies the frighteningly named **Bloody Marsh,** where Oglethorpe's men ambushed Spanish troops fighting to retake the island in 1742. Sup-

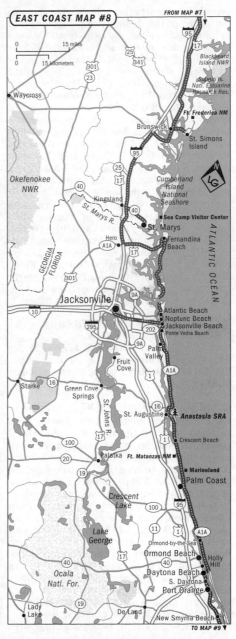

EAST COAST MAP #8

FROM MAP #7

TO MAP #9

EAST COAST

posedly the marsh ran red with their blood during the battle, and Oglethorpe's victory kept the island in British hands. (Open daily 8am-4pm. Free.)

For a quick meal, head to **Waves,** 135 Pier Village Market (☎912-634-4822), which serves "sandwich wraps for the masses," including tasty vegan options ($7). It only has a counter, so head for nearby Neptune Park for a relaxed lunch outdoors. The local favorite **Drener's Village Cafe,** 223 Mallery St., serves basic Southern fare like three-egg omelettes (with grits and biscuits, of course) for about $5. (☎912-634-1217. Open M-F 7:30am-2:30pm, Sa-Su 8am-2:30pm.) The least expensive accommodations on the island are available at **Epworth by the Sea,** a Methodist center that mostly hosts large groups for retreats and other events. Because of this, facilities for tennis and sports are available. (☎912-638-8688; www.epworthbythesea.org. Call ahead. Rooms $48-104.) For accommodations closer to town, try **Queen's Court,** 437 Kings Way, a clean, pretty motel conveniently located only a couple of blocks from the Visitors Center. (☎912-638-8459. Rooms $62-96.)

APPROACHING CUMBERLAND ISLAND

From St. Simon's Island, take **U.S. 17/Rte. 25** to I-95. Follow **I-95 South** about 26 mi. and head east on **Rte. 40** toward **St. Mary's,** turning left on **Kingsland/ St. Mary's Rd.**

CUMBERLAND ISLAND

Off the coast of southeastern Georgia near the tiny town of St. Mary's, Cumberland Island National Seashore remains an astoundingly untouched piece of nature, with herds of wild horses roaming the 36,500 acres of the park. With only 500 people permitted on the island daily, visitors can wander on near-deserted beaches, but be sure to pack a lunch, as only limited water is available on the island. (Day-use $4.) On the southern end of the island, south of where the ferry arrives, **Dungeness,** the former home of Carnegie sibling Thomas and his wife Lucy, now lies in ruins covered in palm trees and ivy. A tour leaves from the Sea Camp dock 30min. after the ferry arrives. The **Ice House Museum,** located in the Carnegie's old ice house, documents the history of the island beginning with early Native American settlers with a focus on the Carnegie residents. (Open daily 8am-4pm. Free.)

Camping is available at the **Sea Camp** campsite, which includes cold water showers and bathrooms, or at a backcountry site. Those planning to camp should get off at the second dock for the half-mile trek to the beach and the shorter walk to the campsite. (Sea Camp sites $4 per person; backcountry sites $2 per person.)

Ferries leave from St. Mary's to two docks on the island. Tickets are sold at the **Visitors Center** on the mainland daily 8:15am-4:30pm. (☎800-817-3421. Ferries depart from St. Mary's Mar.-Nov. daily 9am and 11:45am; Dec.-Feb. Su-M and Th-Sa 9am and 11:45am. Return from Cumberland Island 10am and 4:45pm; Mar.-Sept. additional departure 2:45pm. $12, seniors $9, under 13 $7.) In St. Mary's, near the ferry docks, the **Cumberland Island Mainland Museum,** 169 Osborne St., provides info. (☎912-882-4336. Open daily 1-4pm.)

THE ROAD TO FLORIDA

From St. Mary's, get back on **I-95 South** via Rte. 40 West. After crossing over into Florida, switch to **Rte. 200/A1A** at the town of Hero, traveling east to the coast and curving south. Florida's Rte. A1A begins in Fernandina Beach on Amelia Island and stretches down the barrier islands that line Florida's Atlantic coast. From **Amelia Island,** Rte. A1A heads south through several scenic parks, including the **Amelia Island State Recreation Area, Big Talbot Island State Park,** and **Little Talbot Island State Park.** Drivers will then have to take the auto ferry to the beach troika of Atlantic, Neptune, and Jacksonville beaches.

Welcome To **FLORIDA**

APPROACHING JACKSONVILLE

To enter Jacksonville proper from Jacksonville Beach on A1A, take **Beach Blvd.** west, which becomes **U.S. 90/Rte. 212.** Turn right on **Southside**

Blvd. (Rte. 115), and continue on until turning left onto **Alt. U.S. 90 West/Rte. 10a.**

JACKSONVILLE

At almost 850 sq. mi., Jacksonville is geographically the largest city in the continental US. Without theme parks, star-studded beaches, or tropical environs, Jacksonville struggles to shine through the cluttered tourist offerings of southern Florida. The city, however, still draws visitors with its family-oriented attractions, and its downtown has undergone a massive makeover in preparation for the 2005 Super Bowl.

VITAL STATS

Population: 740,000

Visitor Info: Jacksonville and the Beaches Convention and Visitors Bureau, 550 Water St., Ste. 1000 (☎904-798-9111 or 800-733-2668; www.visitjacksonville.com). Open M-F 8am-5pm.

Internet Access: Jacksonville Main Public Library, 122 N. Ocean St. (☎904-630-2665). Open M-Th 9am-8pm, F-Sa 9am-6pm, Su 1-6pm.

Post Office: 311 W. Monroe St. (☎904-353-3445). Open M-F 8:30am-5pm, Sa 9am-1pm. **Postal Code:** 32202.

▛ GETTING AROUND

Three highways intersect in Jacksonville, making driving the city quick and easy. **I-95** runs north-south, while **I-10** starts in the downtown area and heads west. **I-295** forms a giant "C" on the western half of the city, and **Arlington Expwy.** becomes **Atlantic Blvd. (Rte. 10)** heading to the beach. The St. Johns River snakes throughout the city.

◉ SIGHTS

BEACHES. Miles of uncrowded white sands can be found at **Jacksonville Beach,** as well as neighboring **Atlantic Beach, Neptune Beach,** and **Ponte Vedra Beach.** Fishermen stake out spots on the **Jacksonville Beach Pier,** while golfers take advantage of the more than 20 area golf courses. Free parking lots run all along the beach, but they fill up quickly and there are no bathrooms. The **Boardwalk** is abuzz with activity, from musical festivals to sand-castle building contests. Surfing and volleyball tournaments take place in May. Staple Florida attrac-

tions are nearby, including a dog track, mini golf, go-karts, and a waterpark. *(To reach the Atlantic take Rte. 90/Beach Blvd. or Rte. 10/Atlantic Blvd. east from downtown for about 30min.)*

ANHEUSER-BUSCH BREWERY. Visitors from all over the globe unite under the banner of brewsky at the Anheuser-Busch Brewery Tour. Most are awed by their sneak peak at the brewing process, though all are blown away by the "hospitality room," in which 21+ beer-lovers sample any two of Busch's 12 beers; DDs enjoy free soda and pretzels. *(111 Busch Dr., Exit 360 off I-95, 10min. north of downtown. ☎904-696-8373; www.budweisertours.com. Tours M-Sa every hr. 9am-4pm. Free.)*

TIMUCUAN ECOLOGICAL AND HISTORIC PRESERVE. This preserve contains 46,000 serene acres of saltwater marshes and tidal creeks teeming with fish, dolphins, and eagles. *(Take I-95 North to Rte. 105 heading east (Exit 124A). Signs point to the major sights and the Visitors Center. ☎904-641-7155. Open daily 8am-dusk. Free.)* On St. John's Bluff within the park lies the **Ribault Monument,** marking the spot where, in 1562, French Huguenot Jean Ribault landed to claim the land for King Charles IX. The park contains two historical sights; the first, **Fort Caroline National Memorial,** was the site of a 1565 battle between Spanish and French Huguenot forces—the first armed conflict between European powers over New World settlement. Today, visitors can try their hand at storming a replica of the fort; the less aggressive can peruse the museum's Native American and French artifacts. *(12713 Fort Caroline Rd. ☎904-641-7155. Open daily 9am-5pm. Free.)* The second historical site in the preserve is **Kingsley Plantation,** a former rice plantation that became involved in the lawsuit that eventually voided Florida's state law barring free blacks from owning property. *(Open daily 9am-5pm. Free.)*

CUMMER MUSEUM OF ART AND GARDENS. The beautiful grounds of the museum line the St. Johns River south of downtown. Indoors, Renaissance, Baroque, and American colonial exhibits impress art connoisseurs, while children delight in "Art Connections," the exciting hands-on art education center. *(829 Riverside Ave. ☎904-356-6857; www.cummer.org. Open Su noon-5pm, Tu and Th 10am-9pm, W and F-Sa 10am-5pm. $6, seniors $4, students $3. Tu 4-9pm free. College students with ID free Tu-F after 1:30pm.)*

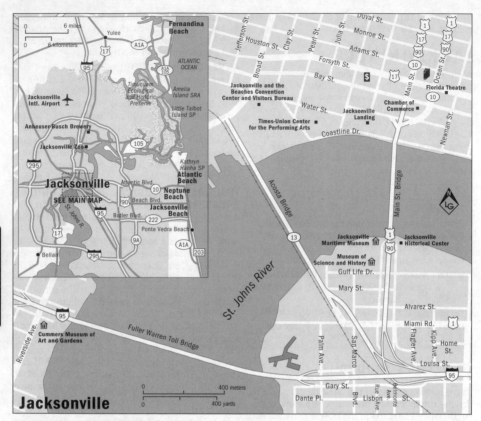

Jacksonville

JACKSONVILLE ZOO AND GARDENS. The Jacksonville Zoo and Gardens houses silverback gorillas, wallabies, and giant anteaters, as well as an education complex. *(Take I-95 Exit 358A to Heckscher Dr. East. Off of Rte. 105. ☎ 904-757-4463; www.jaxzoo.org. Open daily 9am-5pm. $9.50, seniors $8, ages 3-12 $5. 10% AAA discount.)*

HISTORY MUSEUMS. In town, the historically-inclined can visit the **Jacksonville Maritime Museum,** which displays an antique diving helmet and artifacts from the USS *Columbia* used during the Civil War. *(1015 Museum Cir. Unit 2, Southbank Riverwalk Main St. ☎ 904-398-9011; www.jaxmarmus.com. Open M-F 10:30am-3pm, Sa-Su 1-5pm. Free.)* Across the street via a walkway is the **Jacksonville Historical Society,** which has a small museum documenting major phases in city history, including Spanish and English colonial periods and the more recent involvement of Hollywood in the area. *(Open M-Sa 11am-5pm, Su 11am-5pm. Free.)* The **Museum of Science and History,** which sits in the same circle, has a planetarium and a few small exhibits on dinosaurs, local wildlife, and Florida history. *(☎ 904-396-6674; www.themosh.org. Open M-F 10am-5pm, Sa 10am-6pm, Su 1-6pm. $7, ages 3-12 $5, seniors $5.50.)*

♫ ENTERTAINMENT

Acts ranging from Ringo Starr to the Dixie Chicks to Gilbert and Sullivan theater have performed at the historic **Florida Theatre,** 128 E. Forsyth St. (☎ 904-355-2787), built in 1927. The theater hosts more than 300 performances per year; check out www.floridatheatre.com for upcoming shows. A different kind of popular culture thrives at the **Alltel Stadium** (☎904-633-2000), at E. Duval and Haines St., home to the NFL's Jaguars. Much of Jacksonville's nightlife centers on **Jacksonville Landing,** at Main St. and Independent Dr., a riverfront area packed with restaurants, bars, shopping, and live entertainment. (☎904-353-1188. Open M-Th 10am-8pm, F-Sa 10am-9pm, Su noon-5:30pm.) Next door, wolf down some Not 'cho Average Nachos ($8) while taking in the game at **Legends Sports Bar.** During Monday Night Football, you can wash your chips down with $4 pitchers of beer. (☎904-353-4577. Open daily 11am-2am.)

FOOD & ACCOMMODATIONS

Breakfast fans rejoice at **Famous Amos Restaurant,** 375 Atlantic Blvd., where the day's most important meal is deliciously cooked up morning, noon, and night ($2-7). For a more traditional lunch or dinner meal, Famous Amos offers heaping portions of chicken, steak, and stew for $5-10. (☎904-249-3025. Open 24hr.) Locals take a break from the rays at the **Beachside Seafood Market and Restaurant,** 120 N. 3rd St. (Rte. A1A), by 2nd Ave., where the cooks fry up fish sandwiches and baskets ($4-6) using their own fresh catches. (☎904-241-4880. Open M-Sa 11am-6:30pm, Su 11am-5pm.) For an elegant bistro with a casual twist, head over to **Benny's Steak and Seafood,** at Jacksonville Landing, where the mostly local clientele take on the Colossal Cowboy (22 oz. ribeye; $30) and fresh grouper ($19) in the classy interior or on the waterfront deck. (☎904-301-1014. Open Su-Th 11am-10pm, F-Sa 11am-midnight.)

Inexpensive hotels abound along I-95 and on the Arlington Expwy. heading to the ocean. The cheapest options are the chains north of the city off of I-95, where rooms generally run $50-70 in summer and $80-100 in winter. Just steps from the sands of Jacksonville Beach, **Fig Tree Inn Bed and Breakfast,** 185 4th Ave. S, offers five differently themed rooms brimming with antiques. Enjoy your breakfast or afternoon tea on the front porch of this beach-style shingle cottage. (☎904-246-8855 or 877-217-9830. Rooms $75-140.) **Kathryn Abbey Hanna Park,** 500 Wonderwood Dr., in Mayport, has 293 wooded sites near the beach, all with full hookup, along with four cabins with A/C. Twenty miles of bike paths and a water playground are also on site. (☎904-249-

4700. Cabins 2-night min. stay. Reception 8am-9pm. Reservations recommended for cabins. Tent sites $13.50; RVs $18; cabins $34.)

THE ROAD TO ST. AUGUSTINE. Head back to the coast to trek farther down south. The drive down Rte. A1A from Jacksonville Beach stretches right along the coast toward St. Augustine, where it takes a brief jog onto the mainland before heading back out to St. Augustine Beach. Continue on Rte. A1A through St. Augustine.

ST. AUGUSTINE

Spanish adventurer Pedro Menéndez de Aviles founded St. Augustine in 1565, making it the first European colony in North America and the oldest continuous settlement in the US. Thanks to preservation efforts, much of St. Augustine's Spanish flavor remains intact. This city's pride lies in its provincial cobblestone streets, *coquina* rock walls, and antique shops rather than in its token beaches. Forget L.A.'s high-priced plastic surgeons—eternal youth comes cheap around these parts—about $5.75, to be exact, in the form of admission to the famed Fountain of Youth.

VITAL STATS

Population: 12,000

Visitor Info: Visitors Center, 10 Castillo Dr. (☎904-825-1000; www.oldcity.com), at San Marco Ave. Open daily 8:30am-5:30pm.

Internet Access: St. Johns County Public Library, 1960 N. Ponce de Leon Blvd. (☎904-823-2650). Open M-W 9:30am-9pm, Th-F 9:30am-6pm, Sa 9:30am-5pm, Su 1-5pm.

Post Office: 99 King St. (☎904-829-8716). Open M-F 8:30am-5pm, Sa 9am-1pm. **Postal Code:** 32084.

GETTING AROUND

Most of St. Augustine's sights lie within a 10-15min. walk from the hostel and motels. Narrow streets and frequent one-ways can make driving in St. Augustine unpleasant. The city's major east-west routes, **King St.** and **Cathedral Pl.,** run through downtown and become the Bridge of Lions that leads to the beaches. **San Marco Ave.,** or **Avenida Menendez,** runs north-south. **Castillo Dr.** diverges from San Marco Ave.

near the center of town. **Saint George St.,** a north-south pedestrian route, contains most of the shops and many of the sights in town. There is all-day **parking** for $6 at the Visitors Center or for $5 on Cathedral St. between St. George and Crodova St.

Sightseeing Trains, 170 San Marco Ave., shuttle travelers on a red trolley that hits all the major attractions on its 20 stops. (☎904-829-6545 or 800-226-6545. Runs every 15-20min. 8:30am-5pm. 3-day pass $12, ages 6-12 $5.)

👁 SIGHTS

FOUNTAIN OF YOUTH. No trip to St. Augustine would be complete without a trek down beautiful Magnolia Ave. to the **Fountain of Youth,** the legend that sparked Ponce de León's voyage to the New World. A tour navigates the moving, life-sized exhibits that trace hundreds of years of Spanish conquistador history, beginning with the Spanish cross to mark the site of the first landing. To capture the historical significance of the place, take a swig of the sulfury libation and try to ignore the fact that the water now runs through a pipe. *(11 Magnolia Ave. Go right on Williams St. from San Marco Ave. and continue until it dead-ends into Magnolia Ave. ☎904-829-3168 or 800-356-8222. Open daily 9am-5pm. $6, seniors $5, ages 6-12 $3.)*

SPANISH HERITAGE. The oldest masonry fortress in the continental US, **Castillo de San Marcos National Monument** has 14 ft. thick walls built of *coquina*, the local shell-rock. The fort, a four-pointed star complete with drawbridge and moat, contains a museum, a large courtyard surrounded by garrison quarters, a jail, a chapel, and the original cannon brought overseas by the Spanish. *(1 Castillo Dr., off San Marco Ave. ☎904-829-6506. Open daily 8:45am-5:15pm; last admission 4:45pm. Grounds closed noon-5:30am. Occasional tours; call ahead. $5, ages 6-16 $2.)* One of the most significant religious sights in the US is the **Shrine of our Lady de la Leche and Mission of Nombre de Dios,** where the first Mass in the US was held over 400 years ago. A 208 ft. cross commemorates the city's founding, and the shaded lawns make for a peaceful stroll. Casual visitors should be respectful of those there for religious purposes. *(27 Ocean*

St., off San Marco Ave. ☎904-824-2809. Open M-F 8am-5pm, Sa 9am-5pm, Su 9:30am-5pm. Mass M-F 8:30am, Sa 6pm, Su 8am. Donation suggested.)

HISTORICAL SIGHTS. Not surprisingly, the oldest continuous settlement in the US holds some of the nation's oldest artifacts. The **Gonzalez-Alvarez House** is the oldest house on the National Registry of Historic Places. Constructed in the 17th century, the tiny house now serves as a tourist attractions, containing exhibits on the Spanish, British, and American heritage of the area, a museum, and lovely ornamental gardens. In the main rooms, visitors can see floors made of tabby, a building material made of lime, shells, and sand and brought over by slaves from Senegal. *(14 Saint Francis St. ☎904-824-2872; www.oldcity.com/oldhouse. Open daily 9am-5pm; last tour 4:30pm. $7, students and seniors $4; families $14.)* Step into the past at the **Oldest Store Museum,** a former general store showcasing over 100,000 turn-of-the-century items, from a high-wheel bicycle to a Model T. *(4 Artillery Ln. ☎904-829-9729. Open M-Sa 10am-4pm, Su noon-4pm. $5, ages 6-12 $1.50.)* The **Oldest Wooden Schoolhouse** in America also housed the schoolmaster. Visitors can take a step back in time as a teacher and students dressed in period garb describe the Spanish colonial schoolhouse experience. *(14 George St. ☎888-635-7245. Open daily. $3, seniors $2.50, ages 6-12 $2.)* For the best view of the nation's oldest city and its surrounding waters, climb the 219 stairs of the **St. Augustine Lighthouse and Museum,** Florida's oldest lighthouse. Tour the 19th-century tower and keeper's house to learn about marine archaeological studies in the area waters. *(81 Lighthouse Ave. Off Rte. A1A across from the Alligator Farm. ☎904-829-0745; www.stagustinelighthouse.com. Open daily 9am-6pm. Tower, grounds, and house $6.50, seniors $5.50, ages 7-11 $4. House and grounds $4/$3/$2.)*

HISTORIC BUILDINGS. Visitors can take a student-led tour through **Flagler College,** a small liberal arts institution housed in the restored Spanish Renaissance-style **Ponce de Léon Hotel.** Constructed by railroad and Standard Oil tycoon Henry Flagler in 1888, the hotel served as the luxury playground for America's social elite. Celebrity heavyweights such as John Rockefeller and Will Rogers once strolled through the gorgeous interior, much of which was designed by Louis Comfort Tiffany. *(☎904-823-3378; www.fla-*

gler.edu. Tours mid-May to mid-Aug. daily every hr. 10am-4pm. $4, under 12 $1.) In 1947, Chicago publisher and art lover Otto Lightner converted the Alcazar Hotel into the **Lightner Museum** to hold an impressive collection of cut, blown, and burnished glass, as well as old clothing and oddities. Today, the museum's eccentricity remains its highlight, as it houses everything from a stuffed lion to a Russian bath steamroom. *(75 King St. ☎ 904-824-2874; www.lightnermuseum.org. Open daily 9am-5pm; last admission 4:30pm. 18th-century musical instruments play daily 11am-2pm. $8, students and ages 12-18 $2.)*

JUST FOR FUN. Across the Bridge of Lions, the ⛴**St. Augustine Alligator Farm** allows visitors to get up close and personal with some of nature's finest reptiles. The park, which has been delighting visitors since 1893, is the only place in the world where all 23 known crocodilian species live. Check out the white alligator from the Louisiana bayou, who, according to legend, bestows good luck on viewers. *(On Rte. A1A South ☎ 904-824-3337. Open daily 9am-6pm. Presentations every hr. Feeding daily 1:30pm. $14.25, ages 5-11 $8.50. AAA, military, and senior discounts.)* A mouth-watering adventure of a different sort awaits at **Whetstone Chocolates.** Take the self-guided tour through the only chocolate factory in Florida, and enjoy a free sample of their product. *(2 Coke Rd., off State Rd. 312 just east of U.S. 1. ☎ 904-825-1700. Open M-Sa 10am-5:30pm. Free.)*

🍴 FOOD

The bustle of daytime tourists and the abundance of budget eateries make lunch in St. Augustine's historic district a delight, especially among the cafes and bars of **Saint George St.** The **Bunnery Bakery and Cafe,** 121 Saint George St., is an always-packed cafe that leaves patrons in a state of bakery bliss. Locals and tourists flock to the Bunnery for its hearty breakfasts (8-11am; $2-6), like ham and eggs with fried apples and grits and Southern eggs with biscuit and sausage, and then return for delectable panini sandwiches ($4-7) and vegetarian options at lunch (☎ 904-829-6166. Open daily 8am-6pm. No credit cards.) You'll get more BBQ than you can handle at **Scarlett O'Hara's,** 70 Hypolita St., at Cordova St. Monster "Big Rhett" burgers ($6) and full slabs of ribs ($15) are consumed by patrons who will never go hungry again. Live music, usually rock or reggae, entertains nightly out on the porch and in this amusingly rough and tumble environment. (☎ 904-824-6535. Happy hour M-F 4-7pm. Occasional $2 cover. Open daily 11am-12:30am.) At **Pizzalley's,** 117 St. George St., scarf down a piping hot slice ($3) or a tremendous sub ($5-7) in a cramped but worthwhile eatery. (☎ 904-825-2627. Open daily 11am-9pm.)

🏠 ACCOMMODATIONS

🏨 **Pirate Haus Inn and Hostel,** 32 Treasury St. (☎ 904-808-1999 or 877-466-3864), just off Saint George St. From Rte. 16 East, go south on U.S. 1, make a left on King St. and then left on Charlotte St. Hands-down the best place to stay, with spacious dorms, beautiful private rooms, and a great location. Weary travelers are pampered by a common room, Internet access, and a pancake breakfast. Key/linen deposit $5. Parking available in metered lot behind the inn. Reception 8-10am and 6-10pm. Dorms $15, nonmembers $17; private rooms $46. Under 13 free.

Sunrise Inn, 512 Anastasia Blvd. (☎ 904-829-3888). The best option among the many motels along Rte. A1A. A/C, cable TV, phones, and pool. Singles Su-Th $28, F-Sa $38; doubles $33/$43.

Seabreeze Motel, 208 Anastasia Blvd. (☎ 904-829-8122). Clean rooms with refrigerators and pool access. A/C, cable TV, and free local calls. Kitchenettes available. Singles M-F $40, Sa-Su $45, holidays and special events $60; doubles $45/$50/$65.

Anastasia State Recreation Area, 1340a Rte. A1A (☎ 904-461-2033; www.floridastateparks.org/anastasia), 4 mi. south of the historic district. From town, cross the Bridge of Lions and turn left past the Alligator Farm. Nearby, Salt Run and the Atlantic provide great windsurfing, swimming, and hiking. Reception 8am-dusk. Reservations recommended F-Sa. Sites $18, with electricity $20. Day-use $5 per vehicle.

🎭 NIGHTLIFE

St. Augustine supports a variety of bars, many on Rte. A1A and Saint George St. *Folio Weekly* contains event listings. Local string musicians play on the two stages in the **Milltop,** 19½ Saint George St., a tiny yet illustrious bar above an old mill in the restored district. Get a great deal on the bucket of beers—four domestic for $10 or four imports for $12.

(☎904-829-2329. Happy hour 5:30-7:30pm. Music daily 1pm until closing. Cover varies. Open M-Sa 11am-1am, Su 11am-10pm.) Sample your choice of 24 drafts at the **Oasis Deck and Restaurant,** 4000 Rte. A1A South at Ocean Trace Rd. (☎904-471-3424. Gator tail $6. Seafood sandwich $3-7. Happy hour 4-7pm. Live rock or reggae M-Sa 8pm-12:30am, Su 7-11:30pm. Open daily 6am-1am.) Cheap flicks and bargain eats await at **Pot Belly's,** 36 Granada St. Screening just-out-of-theaters movies, this combination pub, deli, and cinema serves a range of sandwiches ($3-6) and brew ($7.50 per pitcher) to the in-house tables, ensuring that viewers never have to miss that crucial moment. (☎904-829-3101. Movie tickets $5. Shows 6:30pm and 8:45pm.)

LEAVING ST. AUGUSTINE
Follow **Rte. A1A South** to Marineland.

MARINELAND 1960 Ocean Blvd.
Off Rte. A1A, a few miles south of St. Augustine.
The world's original oceanarium, Marineland provides an opportunity to get up close and personal with sea creatures. The establishment offers a variety of options for interactions. For $20 on top of the admission price, visitors can touch and feed the dolphins. The several-hour-long **instant trainer program** teaches about dolphin behavior and the hand signals and reward systems used to train dolphins. **Diving and snorkeling** are available in the 450,000 gallon oceanarium for $65 and $35, respectively, including equipment. The establishment's most famous and most intimate sea experience comes in the **dolphin encounter,** a 1½hr. program during which visitors learn about dolphin behavior and spend 20min. waist deep in the pool with them as they swim and play. (☎888-279-9194 or 877-326-7539 for show times and special programs. Open daily 9:30am-4:30pm. $14, children 3-11 $9. AARP and AAA discounts.)

THE ROAD TO DAYTONA BEACH. Along Rte. A1A to Daytona Beach, there are several more state parks and recreation areas, but the biggest draws are the long expanses of sandy beach, virtually all of which are free until hitting **Ormond-by-the-Sea** north of Daytona Beach. Finding parking on the beach is sometimes difficult, but it is often allowed on nearby residential streets.

DAYTONA BEACH

When locals first started auto-racing on the hard-packed sands of Daytona Beach, they were combining two aspects of life that would come to define the town's entire mentality: speed and sand. Daytona played an essential role in the founding of the National Association of Stock Car Auto Racing (NASCAR) in 1947, and the mammoth Daytona International Speedway still hosts several big races each year. While races no longer occur on the sand, 23 mi. of Atlantic coastline still pump the lifeblood of the community.

(VITAL STATS)

Population: 64,000

Visitor Info: Daytona Beach Area Convention and Visitors Bureau, 126 E. Orange Ave. (☎800-544-0415; www.daytonabeachcvb.org), on City Island. Take Rte. A1A South to Silver Beach Rd., take a right, and follow it onto City Island where it becomes Orange Rd. Open M-F 9am-5pm.

Internet Access: Volusia County Library Center, 105 E. Magnolia Ave. (☎386-257-6036). Open M and W 9:30am-5:30pm, Tu and Th 9:30am-8pm, F-Sa 9:30am-5pm.

Post Office: 220 N. Beach St. (☎386-226-2618). Open M-F 8am-5pm, Sa 9am-noon. **Postal Code:** 32115.

GETTING AROUND

I-95 parallels the coast and the barrier island. **Atlantic Ave. (Rte. A1A)** is the main drag along the shore. **International Speedway Blvd. (U.S. 92)** runs east-west from the ocean through the downtown area to the racetrack. Daytona Beach is a collection of smaller towns; many street numbers are not consecutive and navigation can be difficult. To avoid the gridlock on the beach, arrive early (8am) and leave early (around 3pm). Visitors must pay $5 to drive onto the beach, and police enforce the 10 mph speed limit. Free **parking** is plentiful during most of the year but sparse during Spring Break (usually mid-Feb. to Apr.), Speedweek, Bike Week, Biketoberfest, and the Pepsi 400.

SIGHTS

The center of the racing world, the **Daytona International Speedway** hosts the **Daytona 500,** in February. **Speedweek** precedes the legendary race, while the Pepsi 400 heats up the track in early July. Next door, **Daytona USA,** 1801 W. International Speedway Blvd., includes a simulation ride, an IMAX film on Daytona, and a program on NASCAR commentating. The breathtaking **Speedway Tour** is a chance to see the garages, grandstands, and 31° banked turns up close. Included in the admission is a walk through a hall of winning cars, an exhibit on the history of car racing, and the NASCAR IMAX movie. The **Richard Petty Driving Experience** puts fans in a stock car for a 150mph ride-along. (☎386-947-6800, NASCAR tickets 385-253-1223. Open daily 9am-7pm. Tours every 30min. daily 9:30am-5:30pm. $21.50, seniors $18.50, ages 6-12 $15.50. Tours $7. Richard Petty ☎800-237-3889. 16+. $106. Speedway only $7.50. Acceleration alley NASCAR simulator $5.) **Bike Week** (www.bikeweek.com) draws biker mamas for motorcycle duels, and **Biketoberfest** (www.biketoberfest.com) brings them back for more.

For an alternative to the car and beach culture of Daytona Beach, the **Halifax Historical Museum,** 252 S. Beach St., displays memorabilia from early beach racing and Spanish military gear. (☎386-255-6976; www.halifaxhistorical.org. Open Tu-Sa 10am-4pm. $4, children $1.) The **Museum of Arts and Sciences,** 1040 Museum Blvd., combines traditional art, decorative art, natural history and science on display. Check out the **Cuban Museum** for a look into the country's artistic and historical past, visit the planetarium, or see the **Root Family Museum,** which has hundreds of teddy bears on display. (☎386-255-0285; www.moas.org. Open Tu-F 9am-4pm, Sa noon-5pm. $4, under 2 free. Planetarium $3, children $2.)

FOOD

One of the most famous (and popular) seafood restaurants in the area is **Aunt Catfish's,** 4009 Halifax Dr., at Dunlawton Ave., next to the Port Orange Bridge. Order anything that resides under the sea and you're in for a treat, though the lobster and crab receive the most praise. The relaxed atmosphere means diners don't need to dress up, but they might want to call ahead for reservations. (Take Rte. A1A South to Dunlawton Ave., turn right, and follow the road over the bridge; Halifax Dr. is on the right. ☎386-767-4768; www.auntcatfish.com. Entrees $9-15. Salads under $9. Open M-Sa 11:30am-9:30pm, Su 9am-9:30pm.) From frog legs ($10) to flounder ($10), **B&B Fisheries,** 715 E. International Speedway, doesn't mess around

when it comes to serving up some of Daytona's best seafood. Don't worry, landlovers, B&B also dishes out incredible slabs of steak from $10. (☎386-252-6542. Open M-F 11am-8:30pm, Sa 4-8:30pm.) With fanciful decoration, from plants to glass beads on the handle, **The Dancing Avocado Kitchen,** 110 S. Beach St., offers a delicious alternative to the Daytona seafood-and-grill scene. Enjoy the belly dancer sandwich (avocado, hummus, lettuce, tomato, and olives; $5.50) or the signature symphony salad ($6) in this organically delightful eatery. (☎386-947-2022. Open M-Sa 8am-4pm.)

ACCOMMODATIONS

Almost all of Daytona's accommodations cluster on **Atlantic Ave. (Rte. A1A),** either on the beach or across the street; those off the beach offer the best deals. Spring Break and race events drive prices to absurdly high levels, but low-season rates are more reasonable. Almost all the motels facing the beach cost $35 for a low-season single; on the other side of the street it's $25. The **Camellia Motel,** 1055 N. Atlantic Ave. (Rte. A1A), across the street from the beach, is an especially welcoming retreat with cozy, bright rooms, free local calls, cable TV, and A/C. (☎386-252-9963. Reserve early. Singles $30; doubles $35. During Spring Break, singles $100; $10 per additional person. Kitchens $10 extra.) For a truly unique sleeping experience, try the **Travelers Inn,** 735 N. Atlantic Ave. Each of the 22 rooms has a different theme—find the force with Yoda in the *Star Wars* room or rock out with Jimi Hendrix or the Beatles in their rooms. (☎386-253-3501 or 800-417-6466. Singles $29-49; doubles $39-59; $10 per additional person. Kitchens $10 extra.) **Tomoka State Park,** 2099 N. Beach St., 8 mi. north of Daytona in Ormond Beach, has 100 sites under a tropical canopy. Enjoy salt-water fishing, nature trails, and a sculpture museum. Unfortunately, no swimming is allowed. (☎386-676-4050, reservations 800-326-3521. Open daily 8am-dusk. Sites Nov.-Apr. $17; with electricity $19; May-Oct. $11/$13. Seniors half-price. Entrance fee $3.25 per vehicles.)

NIGHTLIFE

When Spring Break hits, concerts, hotel-sponsored parties, and other events answer the call of students. News about these travels fastest by word of mouth, but the *Calendar of Events* and *SEE Daytona Beach* make good starting points. On mellow nights, head to the board-walk to play volleyball or shake your groove-thing at the **Oceanfront Bandshell,** an open-air amphitheater constructed of *coquina* rock. Dance clubs thump along Seabreeze Blvd. just west of N. Atlantic Ave. **Razzle's,** 611 Seabreeze Blvd., caters to the scandalous Spring Break crowd with its high energy dance floors, flashy light shows, and nightly drink specials. (☎386-257-6326. Cover around $5. Open daily 7pm-3am.) **Ocean Deck,** 127 S. Ocean Ave., stands out among the clubs with its live music on the beach and nightly drink specials. Chow down on the "shipwreck" (shrimp, crab, oysters and clams; $10) while grooving to the reggae, jazz, and calypso, with rock on Sundays. (☎386-253-5224. Music nightly 9:30pm-2:30am. 21+ after 9pm. Open daily 11am-3am. Kitchen closes 2am.)

☑ DETOUR: DISNEY WORLD

Take I-4 West to Exit 64 for the Magic Kingdom and MGM Studios, Exit 65 for the Animal Kingdom, or Exit 67 for EPCOT Center.

Disney World is the Rome of central Florida: all roads lead to it. Within this Never-Neverland, theme parks, resorts, theaters, restaurants, and nightclubs all work together to be the embodi-ment of fun. The **Magic Kingdom** is the Disney of your childhood, home to such classics as Space Mountain, It's a Small World, and Pirates of the Caribbean. **EPCOT Center** is home to Future World and the World Showcase, representing the architecture, culture, and monuments of 11 countries. **MGM Studios** is a re-created movie set and hosts the Tower of Terror. **Animal Kingdom's** catchphrase is NAHTAZU: "not a zoo," but it is the site of jungle treks, safaris, and the ecologi-cally mined Kali River Rapids. Besides the four main parks, Disney offers innumerable other attractions with different themes and separate admissions. (☎407-939-6244; www.disney-world.com. 1 park $55, ages 3-9 $44; 2-park Park-Hopper Pass 4-day $129/$104.)

◤ LEAVING DAYTONA BEACH

Follow **U.S. 1 South** towards Cocoa Beach.

THE INDIAN RIVER LAGOON SCENIC HIGHWAY

Heading south on U.S. 1 from Daytona Beach, drivers can jog east on Rte. 406 to the **Merritt Island National Wildlife Refuge.** There, the **Canaveral National Seashore** stretches along the northeast portion of the refuge. Backtracking and heading south on U.S. 1, the scenic drive continue over Rte. 528/A1A onto Cape Canaveral. Rte. A1A stretches south right along the eastern coast of the barrier island, through Cocoa Beach, Mel-bourne, and Palm Bay before becoming a much smaller, narrower road on the way to Sebastian.

COCOA BEACH & CAPE CANAVERAL

Cape Canaveral and the surrounding "Space Coast" were a hot spot during the Cold War. Once the great Space Race began, the area took off—it became the base of operations for every major space exploration, from the Apollo moon landings to the current International Space Sta-tion effort. The towns of Cocoa Beach and nearby Melbourne provide typical beach atmo-sphere. During summer launch dates, tourists pack the area and hotel prices follow NASA into the stratosphere.

⬭ VITAL STATS

Population: 12,500

Visitor Info: Cocoa Beach Chamber of Commerce, 400 Fortenberry Rd. (☎321-459-2200; www.cocoa-beachchamber.com), on Merritt Island. Open M-F 8:30am-5pm. **Space Coast Office of Tourism,** 8810 Astronaut Blvd. (Rte. A1A), #102 (☎407-868-1126 or 800-936-2326). Open M-F 8am-5pm.

Internet Access: Cocoa Beach Public Library, 550 N. Brevard Ave. (☎321-868-1104). Open M-W 9am-9pm, Th 9am-6pm, F-Sa 9am-5pm, Su 1-5pm.

Post Office: 500 N. Brevard Ave. (☎321-783-4800), in Cocoa Beach. Open M-F 8:30am-5pm, Sa 8:30am-noon. **Postal Code:** 32931.

☐ GETTING AROUND. The Space Coast, 50 mi. east of Orlando, consists of mainland Cocoa and Rockledge, oceanfront Cocoa Beach and Cape Canaveral, and Merritt Island. Both **I-95** and **U.S. 1** run north-south on the mainland, while **Rte. A1A (North Atlantic Ave.)** is the beach's main drag. Don't miss ⬛**Ron Jon Surf Shop,** 4151 N. Atlantic Ave., where you'll find two floors of boards, shirts, and sunscreen. (☎321-799-8888. Open 24hr.)

⬛ THE FINAL FRONTIER. All of **NASA's** shut-tle flights take off from the **Kennedy Space Cen-ter,** 18 mi. north of Cocoa Beach on Rte. 3. The **Kennedy Space Center Visitors Complex (KSC)**

pro53vides a huge welcome center, complete with two 3D IMAX theaters, a Rocket Garden, and exhibits on the latest in-space exploration. KSC offers two tours of their 220 sq. mi. grounds. The **Kennedy Space Center Tour** features the three main attractions: the LC 39 Observation Gantry, Apollo/Saturn V Center, and the International Space Station Center. Meet a real space pioneer face-to-face at the daily **Astronaut Encounter,** in which astronauts of the past and present discuss their other-worldly experiences. The **NASA Up Close Tour** provides access to facilities that are restricted on the standard tour. Check out the shuttle launch pad, the gigantic VAB building (where the shuttle is put together), and the Crawler Transporter. Check NASA's **launch schedule**— you may have a chance to watch *Endeavor*, *Atlantis*, or *Discovery* thunder off into the blue yonder above the Cape. A combo package will get you admission to the Visitors Complex and transportation to a viewing area to watch the fiery ascension. The **Cape Canaveral: Then and Now Tour** goes to the first launch site, the Air Force Space and Missile Museum and the Cape Canaveral Lighthouse. (Follow Rte. A1A north as it joins Rte. 528 West onto Merritt Island, then to Rte. 3 North. ☎321-452-2121 or 321-449-4444 for launch info; www.kennedyspacecenter.com. Open daily 9am-7pm. Tours 9am-2:15pm. Standard KSC grounds tour $28, ages 3-11 $18. "Maximum Access" tour, including admission to the Astronaut Hall of Fame, $35/$25. Up Close and Cape Canaveral tour $22/$16. Astronaut encounter $20/$13. Launch combo $17.)

Surrounding the NASA complex, the **Merritt Island National Wildlife Refuge** teems with sea turtles, manatees, wild hogs, and over 300 species of birds. (Take Rte. A1A/528 off Cape Canaveral, over Merritt Island onto the mainland, and take I-95 North to Exit 220. At the end of the exit ramp, take a right on Rte. 406/Garden St. heading east to County Rd. 402 North. ☎321-861-0667. Open daily dawn-dusk. Visitors Center open M-F 8am-4:30pm, Sa-Su 9am-5pm.) **Canaveral National Seashore,** on the northeastern shore of the refuge, covers 67,000 acres of undeveloped beach and dunes. (Take Rte. 406 East off U.S. 1 in Titusville. ☎321-407-867-0677. Open daily Apr.-Oct. 6am-8pm; Nov.-Mar 6am-6pm. Closed 3 days before and 1 day after NASA launches. $5 per vehicle.)

EAST COAST

⚡ FOOD. Bikini contests, live rock and reggae, karaoke, drink specials, and seafood make the pastel-colored **Coconut's on the Beach,** 2 Minutemen Causeway, at Rte. A1A, a popular hangout for kids of all ages. Try the classic crab cake for lunch ($7) or the coconut-crusted mahi-mahi for dinner ($15), while chilling on the deck and ogling surfers. Call for a monthly events schedule. (☎321-784-1422. Key lime pie $3. Open M-Sa 11am-1:30am, Su 10am-1:30am.) Lines for "famous" New York-style pizza stream out the door of **Bizzarro,** 4 1st Ave., off Rte. A1A in Indialantic. (☎321-724-4799. Sicilian slice $1.50. Open M-Th 11am-9pm, F-Sa 11am-11pm, Su noon-9pm.) The **Tea Room,** 6211 N. Atlantic Ave. (Rte. A1A), combines home cookin' and a little TLC to start your day off right. Locals regularly take advantage of the dirt-cheap prices and relaxed, friendly atmosphere (☎321-783-5527. Daily breakfast specials around $3. Pastries $0.50-1.25. Open M-F 7am-2pm, Sa-Su 7:30am-2pm.) Take advantage of the southern Florida location at **Roberto's Little Havana,** 26 N. Orlando Ave., where Cuban favorites are served up in a classy but casual dining room. (☎321-784-1868. Open daily 6am-3pm, Su and Tu-Sa also 5-9pm.)

⚑ ACCOMMODATIONS. Wary of wild teenagers, most hotels in Cocoa Beach rent rooms only to guests who are 21+. Across from the beach, **Motel 6,** 3701 N. Atlantic Ave. (Rte. A1A), offers clean, comfortable rooms at cheaper rates than most accommodations in the area. (☎321-783-3103. A/C, TV, pool, laundry, and shuffleboard. 21+. Singles $43; F-Sa $6 per additional person.) Behind the water tower, the **Dixie Motel,** 301 Forrest Ave., is a family-owned establishment with clean rooms, floor-to-ceiling windows, A/C, cable TV, and a swimming pool. (☎321-632-1600. Laundry available. 21+. Rooms Nov.-Apr. from $55; May-Oct. from $40.) Party-hard teenagers and vacationing families flock to the **Cocoa Beach Comfort Inn,** 3901 N. Atlantic Ave., which offers visitors enormous rooms with all the perks, including pool, A/C, cable TV, coffeemakers, and, in some rooms, a wet bar. (☎321-783-2221. 18+. Rooms Nov.-Apr. from $80; May-Oct. from $60.) The hot pink, wondrously tacky **Fawlty Towers Resort,** 100 E. Cocoa Beach Causeway, includes a heated pool and a tiki bar, though sadly it lacks hilarious British hosts. (☎321-784-3870 or 800-887-3870. Rooms from $75.) Pitch your tent at scenic **Jetty Park Campgrounds,** 400 E. Jetty Rd., at the northern

tip of Cape Canaveral. The sites include sewer hookup, hot showers, laundry facilities, a playground, a swimming beach, a volleyball court, and a dump site (Follow Rte. A1A straight north. ☎321-783-7111. Reserve 3 months ahead, especially before shuttle launches. Sites Jan.-Apr. $19, with water and electricity $23, full hookup $26; May-Dec. $17/$21/$24.)

◥ APPROACHING PALM BEACH & WEST PALM BEACH
From Cocoa Beach, follow **Rte. A1A** South, then take **U.S. 1** South from Ft. Pierce.

PALM BEACH & WEST PALM BEACH

Nowhere else in Florida is the line between the "haves" and the "have-nots" as visible as at the intracoastal waterway dividing aristocratic vacationers on Palm Beach Island from blue-collar residents of West Palm Beach. Five-star resorts and guarded mansions reign over the "Gold Coast" island, while auto repair shops and fast-food restaurants characterize the mainland.

(VITAL STATS)

Population: 10,500/82,000

Visitor Info: Palm Beach County Convention and Visitors Bureau, 1555 Palm Beach Lakes Blvd. (☎561-471-3995; www.palmbeachfl.com). Open M-F 8:30am-5:30pm.

Internet Access: Palm Beach County Library, 3650 Summit Blvd. (☎561-233-2600), in West Palm Beach.

Post Office: 640 Clematis St. (☎561-833-0929), in West Palm Beach. Open M-F 8:30am-5pm. **Postal Code:** 33401.

▭ GETTING AROUND

I-95 runs north-south through the center of West Palm Beach, then continues south to Fort Lauderdale and Miami. **Rte. A1A** also travels north-south, crossing over Lake Worth at the **Flagler Memorial Bridge** to Palm Beach. Large highways cut through urban areas and residential neighborhoods; finding your way around can be a bit confusing. Stick to the major roads like north-south **U.S. 1** (which turns into **S. Dixie Hwy.**), Rte. A1A, east-west **Palm Beach Lakes Blvd.,** and **Belvedere Rd.** The heart of downtown West Palm Beach is **Clematis St.,**

across from the Flagler Memorial Bridge, and **City Place,** 222 Lakeview Ave.; both contain affordable restaurants and nightclubs.

◎ SIGHTS

Perhaps one of West Palm Beach's greatest treasures is the **Norton Museum of Art,** 1451 S. Olive Ave. Well known for its collection of European, American, contemporary, and Chinese art, the museum displays works by Cézanne, Matisse, O'Keeffe, and Pollock. Stop by the central garden, which features its own fountain of youth. (☎561-832-5196; www.norton.org. Open May-Sept. Su 1-5pm, Tu-Sa 10am-5pm; Nov.-Apr. M-Sa 10am-5pm, Su 1-5pm. Tours M-Su 2-3pm. Lectures M-F 12:30-1pm. $8, ages 13-21 $3. Special exhibits $10/$4. Under 13 free. Self-guided audio tour $4.) If you're visiting in early spring, catch the training seasons of the **Montreal Expos** and **Atlanta Braves,** who make their winter home at **Municipal Stadium,** 1610 Palm Beach Lakes Blvd. (☎561-683-6012).

In Palm Beach, just walking around is one of the most enjoyable (and affordable) activities. Known as the "Rodeo Drive of the South," **Worth Ave.,** between S. Ocean Blvd. and Coconut Row, outfits Palm Beach's rich and famous in the threads of fashion heavyweights. Walk or drive along **Ocean Blvd.** to gawk at spectacular mansions owned by celebrities and millionaires. One particularly remarkable complex is **The Breakers,** 1 S. County Rd., a sizable Italian Renaissance resort. Even if you can't afford the bare-minimum $270 price tag for a night of luxury, live vicariously though a guided tour. (☎561-659-8440 or 888-273-2537. Tour W 3pm. $10.)

Of course, a trip to Palm Beach County is incomplete without relaxing on one of its picturesque beaches. Although most of the beachfront property in Palm Beach is private, more public beaches can be found in **West Palm Beach.** Good options on Palm Beach include the popular **Midtown Beach,** 400 S. Ocean Blvd., and **Phipps Ocean Park,** 2185 S. Ocean Blvd. (☎561-585-9203).

▨ FOOD

Clematis St., in downtown West Palm Beach, offers lively options for travelers on the cheap. A mixture of pool hall, sports bar, concert venue, and meat market, ▨**Spanky's,** 500 Clematis St., is West Palm Beach's notoriously fun night spot. Enjoy cold beer (pitchers $5) and tasty bar food in this enormous venue, whose closing time is pretty much whenever customers feel like leaving. Every night is a different theme and drink special, like Island Tuesdays with $0.75 Coronas and $2 Rum Runners. (☎561-659-5669. Beer-battered onion rings $4. Hot wings 12 for $8. Open M-F from 11:30am, Sa from noon, Su from 1pm; closes when the place empties out.) Voted "Best Burger" and "People's Choice" in a recent cook-off, **O'Shea's Irish Pub and Restaurant,** 531½ Clematis St., at Rosemary St., will modify any dish to fit vegetarian needs, though the results have varying success. Locals and those nostalgic for Dublin flock here for the live nightly music, usually Irish rock or folk, and Mrs. O'Shea's $7.50 savory chicken pie. (☎561-833-3865. Open Su-Tu 11am-10pm, W-Th 11am-midnight, F-Sa 11am-1am.) For a respite from West Palm Beach's bar-and-grill scene, **Maision Carlos,** 207 Clematis St., is your best bet. This elegant French and Italian bistro serves both lunch ($7-15) and dinner ($12-25) to its hungry clientele, who savor their pasta and meat under the indoor umbrellas and low-hanging lights. (☎561-659-6524. Open M-Sa 11:30am-2:30pm and 5:30-10pm.)

You won't find a disco or "local bar" anywhere along the ritzy downtown area. You will, however, find **Sprinkles Ice Cream & Sandwich Shop,** 279 Royal Poinciana Way, the best bargain for a hungry stomach. Customers line up for a scoop of homemade ice cream ($3.75) in a hand-dipped cone. (☎561-659 1140. French bread pizza $5.50. Open Su-Th 9am-10pm, F-Sa 9am-11pm.)

⌂ ACCOMMODATIONS

Catering to the rich and famous (with an emphasis on *rich*) who flock to Palm Beach during the winter months, extravagant resorts and hotels are arguably the most notable attraction lining the Gold Coast. Many reasonably priced B&Bs are booked far in advance; reserve a room before you arrive. West Palm Beach is the best bet for an affordable room near the action, but the absolute cheapest options are the chain hotels near the highway. Built in 1922 by a former Palm Beach mayor and elegantly restored in 1990, ◪**Hibiscus House Bed & Breakfast,** 501 30th St., in West Palm Beach, at the corner of Spruce St., is affordable without sacrificing luxury. Sleep in one of nine antique-decorated bedrooms and wake up to a two-course gourmet breakfast served on Waterford crystal. Each room has a terrace, TV, phone, and A/C. (☎561-863-5633 or 800-203-4927. Call ahead for reservations. Rooms Dec.-Mar. $100-270; Apr.-Nov. $75-135.) **Hotel Biba**, 32 Belvedere Rd., in West Palm Beach, is fun, funky, and eclectic. Don't be fooled by its lackluster turquoise exterior; Hotel Biba has become a haven for those budget-conscious travelers with a sense of style. Beautiful bodies lounge on the pool deck and gather in the garden bar for drinks in the evening. (☎561-832-0094. Breakfast included. Rooms Dec.-Mar. $109-129; Apr.-Nov. $79-109.) **Heart of Palm Beach Hotel**, 160 Royal Palm Way, is Palm Beach's most inexpensive hotel, yet still manages to embody the prestige of the nearby beaches and ritzy Worth Ave. (☎561-655-5600. Internet access, refrigerators, TV, heated pool. Call ahead for reservations. Rooms Dec.-Mar. $199-399; Apr.-Nov. $89-169; under 18 free with parents.)

◤ APPROACHING FORT LAUDERDALE
From Palm Beach, follow **U.S. 1 South** into the middle of town.

FORT LAUDERDALE

Over the past two decades, Fort Lauderdale has transformed itself from a city known as a beer-stained Spring Break mecca to the largest yachting center in North America. City streets and highways may be fine for the commoner's transportation needs, but Fort Lauderdale adds another option: canals. Intricate waterways connect ritzy homes with the intracoastal river and, while the elite take to these waterways in multi-million dollar vessels, even mere mortals can cruise the canals via the Water Taxi, an on-the-water bus system. "The Venice of America" also has 23 mi. of beach where Spring Break mayhem still reigns supreme and some of the best shopping in Florida along trendy Las Olas Blvd., making Fort Lauderdale fun even for those who can't afford a yacht.

▢ GETTING AROUND

Fort Lauderdale is bigger than it looks. The city extends westward from its 23 mi. stretch of beach to encompass nearly 450 sq. mi. Streets and boulevards run east-west and avenues run north-south. All are labeled NW, NE, SW, or SE according to quadrant. The two major roads in Fort Lauderdale are **Broward Blvd.** and **Andrews Ave.** The brick-and-mortar downtown centers around **U.S. 1 (Federal**

(VITAL STATS)

Population: 150,000

Visitor Info: Greater Fort Lauderdale Convention and Visitors Bureau, 1850 Eller Dr., #303 (☎954-765-4466 or 800-227-8669; www.sunny.org), in the Port Everglades. Open M-F 8:30am-5pm. **Chamber of Commerce,** 512 NE 3rd Ave. (☎954-462-6000), 3 blocks off Federal Hwy. at 5th St. Open M-F 8am-5pm.

Internet Access: Public Library, 100 S. Andrews Ave. (☎954-357-7444). Open M-Th 9am-9pm, F-Sa 9am-5pm, Su noon-5:30pm.

Post Office: 1900 W. Oakland Park Blvd. (☎954-527-2028). Open M-F 7:30am-7pm, Sa 8:30am-2pm. **Postal Code:** 33310.

Hwy.) and **Las Olas Blvd.,** about 2 mi. west of the oceanfront. Yachts fill the inlets of the **Intracoastal Waterway** between downtown and the waterfront. **The Strip** (a.k.a. Rte. A1A, Fort Lauderdale Beach Blvd., 17th St. Causeway, Ocean Blvd., or Seabreeze Blvd.) runs 4 mi. along the beach between **Oakland Park Blvd.** to the north and Las Olas Blvd. to the south. North-south **I-95** connects West Palm Beach, Fort Lauderdale, and Miami. **Rte. 84/I-75 (Alligator Alley)** slithers 100 mi. west from Fort Lauderdale across the Everglades to small cities on Florida's Gulf Coast. Florida's **Turnpike** runs parallel to I-95.

◉ SIGHTS

When splashing in the crystal-clear waves of the Atlantic, it's easy to forget the city's other notable attractions. Cruising down the palm-lined shore of Beachfront Ave. (Rte. A1A), biking through a nature preserve, or boating through the winding intracoastal canals reveals the less sandy, and lesser-known, side of Fort Lauderdale.

THE WATERFRONT. Fort Lauderdale Beach doesn't have a dull spot on it, but most of the action is between Las Olas Blvd. and Sunrise Blvd. The latest on-the-beach mall, **Las Olas Waterfront,** boasts clubs, restaurants, and bars. *(2 SW 2nd St.)* The **Water Taxi** offers a relaxing way to beat rush-hour traffic and maneuver through town. The friendly captains will steer right up to any Las Olas restaurant or drop you off anywhere along the Intracoastal Waterway or New River. Alternatively, ride the entire route for an intimate view of the colossal houses along the canal. Special packages include a canal pub crawl to Fort Lauderdale's best bars. *(651 Seabreeze Blvd. (Rte. A1A).* ☎*954-467-6677; www.watertaxi.com. Call 30min. before pickup. Runs daily 9am-midnight. $4, seniors and under 12 $2; 1-day unlimited pass $5; 3-day pass $7. Pub crawl $15.)* If traveling with a family or young children, take a tour aboard the tourist-targeted **Jungle Queen.** The captain explains the changing scenery as the 550-passenger riverboat cruises up the New River. *(801 Seabreeze Blvd. At the Bahia Mar Yacht Center, on Rte. A1A, 3 blocks south of Las Olas Blvd.* ☎*954-462-5596; www.jungle-queen.com. 3½hr. tours daily 10am, 2, 7pm. $13.50, ages 2-10 $9.25; 7pm tour $30/$17, dinner included.)* **Water Sports Unlimited** is the best beach spot for watersport equipment rentals and trips. Charter a sailboat or enjoy the serene blue water from above on a parasailing trip. Speed boats and wave runners are also available. *(301 Seabreeze Blvd. (Rte. A1A).* ☎*954-467-1316. Open daily 9am-5pm. Sailing $95 per 2hr. Parasailing $60-70.)*

DRY LAND. Get lost in an oasis of subtropical trees and animals in the middle of urban Fort Lauderdale at **Hugh Taylor Birch State Park.** Bike, jog, canoe, or drive through the 3½ mi. stretch of mangroves and royal palms, or relax by the fresh lagoon filled with herons, gophers, tortoises, and marsh rabbits. There are also areas for picnicking, fishing, birding, and swimming. *(3109 E. Sunrise Blvd., west off Rte. A1A.* ☎*954-564-4521. Open daily 8am-dusk. Gate on Rte. A1A open 9am-5pm. $4 per vehicle, $1 entrance fee. Canoes $5.30 per hr. Cabins and primitive sites available by reservation; call ahead.)* Anointed by Guinness as the "fastest game in the world," with players hurling balls at up to 180 mph, Jai Alai still remains mostly unknown to Americans outside the state of Florida. Take a break from the beach heat and watch a match at **Dania Jai-Alai,** which sports one of the largest *frontons* (courts) in the state. *(301 E. Dania Beach Blvd., off U.S. 1, 10min. south of Fort Lauderdale.* ☎*954-927-2841. Games Su 1pm, Tu and Sa noon and 7:15pm, W-F 7:15pm. General admission $1.50; reserved seats from $2.50.)*

MUSEUMS. Cast your line at the International Game Fishing Association's **Fishing Hall of Fame and Museum,** where a gallery of odd fish, a timeline of American fishing, the inside scoop on fishing hot spots, and an interactive reeling exercise amaze avid fisherman. Check out the large wooden replicas of world-record catches adorning the museum's ceiling, the interactive simula-

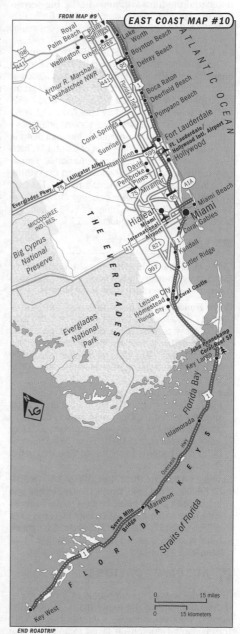

FROM MAP #9

EAST COAST MAP #10

END ROADTRIP

EAST COAST

tions, and the film *Journeys* in the big-screen theater. *(300 Gulf Stream Way, off I-95 at Griffin Rd., Exit 23. ☎ 954-922-4212; www.igfa.org/museum. Open daily 10am-6pm. $6, seniors $4.50, children $4. IGFA members free.)* For a different kind of high-seas adventure, doggy-paddle on over to the **International Swimming Hall of Fame and Museum,** where exhibits on the sport and some of its greatest athletes await. *(1 Hall of Fame Dr. ☎ 954-462-6536; www.ishof.org. Open daily 9am-7pm; back building open 9am-5pm. $3; students, seniors, and military $1; families $5.)* Fort Lauderdale's **Museum of Art** is home to an extensive collection of painter William Glacken's work in addition to remarkable temporary exhibits, which have showcased everything from Surrealism to photojournalism. *(1 E. Las Olas Blvd. ☎ 954-468-3283; www.museumofart.org. Open Su and Tu-Sa 11am-5pm. Tours Sa-Su 1:30pm. $7, seniors $6, children and students $5.)*

🍴 FOOD

Clubs along the strip offer massive quantities of free happy hour grub; wieners, chips, and hors d'oeuvres come on surfboard-sized platters.

The Floridian, 1410 E. Las Olas Blvd. (☎ 954-463-4041). A low-key local favorite serving up french toast ($5), cheeseburgers ($5), and veggie burger platters ($7). Try the house specialty, the Floridian (grilled tuna salad sandwich; $6), with one of the excellent milkshakes ($4), and you might never want to leave. Open 24hr.

Big City Tavern, 609 E. Las Olas Blvd. (☎ 954-727-0307). An elegant eatery in the heart of the Las Olas strip, the refined Big City Tavern creates delectable dishes without the accompanying pretension. Enjoy almond crusted trout ($15) or 12 oz. New York steak ($28) in the brick-lined interior or on the tranquil patio. Open daily 11am-10pm.

Squiggy's N.Y. Style Pizza, 207 SW 2nd St. (☎ 954-522-6655), in Old Town. Whether you're between bars or looking for a treat before heading home, Squiggy's is the place for those late-night munchies. Gooey slices of Sicilian pie ($2, after 8pm $2.50) and $3 beers will certainly satisfy. Open M 11am-11:30pm, Tu-W 11am-3am, Th-Su 11am-4am.

🏠 ACCOMMODATIONS

Thank decades of spring breakers for the abundant hotels lining the beachfront. Motels just north of the strip and a block west of Rte. A1A are the cheapest. Generally, it's easy to find a room at any time of the year. High season runs from mid-February to early April, and many hotels offer low-season deals for under $35. The **Greater Fort Lauderdale Lodging and Hospitality Association,** 1412 E. Broward Blvd., provides a free directory of area hotels. (☎ 954-567-0766. Open M-F 9am-5pm.) The *Fort Lauderdale News* and the *Miami Herald* occasionally publish listings from local residents who rent rooms to tourists in spring. Sleeping on the well-patrolled beaches is illegal. Instead, check out one of the area's outstanding hostels.

Fort Lauderdale Beach Hostel, 2115 N. Ocean Blvd. (☎ 954-567-7275; www.fortlauderdalehostel.com), between Sunrise and Oakland Park Blvd. After a long day at the adjacent beach, backpackers mingle in the tropical courtyard. A/C, ping-pong, grill, free Internet, and free local calls. Breakfast included, some free food available. Free lockers. Free parking. Linen deposit $10. Reception 8:30am-1pm and 5-9pm. Reservations recommended Dec.-June. Dorms $16-18; private rooms $42-59. $5 off 1st night with *Let's Go*.

Floyd's Hostel/Crew House, 445 SE 16th St. (☎ 954-462-0631; www.floydshostel.com). A homey hostel catering to international travelers and boat crews. The owners got engaged thanks to *Let's Go: USA 1995*. Free food, linen, lockers, laundry, and Internet. Passport or American driver's license required. Check-in by midnight or call. 4-bed dorms $18. Private rooms winter $59; summer $40.

Tropic-Cay Beach Hotel, 529 N. Ft. Lauderdale Beach Blvd. (☎ 954-564-5900 or 800-463-2333). Tropic-Cay is hands-down the best deal on the beach. Before heading back to their super clean, extremely large rooms, hard-partying guests return from late-night ruckus to the outdoor patio bar and pool, where fun continues long into the night. Kitchens available. 21+ to rent during Spring Break. Key deposit $10. Doubles Sept.-May $90; May-Sept. $70. $10 per extra person.

Tropi-Rock Resort, 2900 Belmar St. (☎ 954-564-0523 or 800-987-9385), 2 blocks west of Rte. A1A at Birch Rd. A few blocks inland from the beach, this yellow-and-orange hotel provides a resort atmosphere at affordable prices. Lush hibiscus garden with caged birds and Tiki bar. Gym, Internet, tennis courts, free local calls, and refrigerators. Rooms mid-Dec. to Apr. $85-160; Apr. to mid-Dec. $65-105. AAA discount.

🌙 NIGHTLIFE

As any local will tell you, the *real* Fort Lauderdale nightlife action is in **Old Town.** Two blocks northwest of Las Olas Blvd. on 2nd St. near the

Riverwalk district, the 100 yd. of Old Town are packed with raucous bars, steamy clubs, cheap eats, and a stylish crowd. Considerably more expensive, and geared specifically toward tourists, the **Strip** is home to several popular nightspots across from the beach. Most bars have hefty cover charges (from $5) and drink minimums (from $3).

▣ **Tarpon Bend,** 200 SW 2nd St. (☎954-523-3233). Always the busiest place on the block, it's upscale with an ocean-oriented decor. Bottle beers $3-4. "Draft of the month" $1. W ladies drink free until 11pm. Open daily 11:30am-1am or later.

The Voodoo Lounge, 111 SW 2nd St. (☎954-522-0733). A well-dressed and well-known party in lush red VIP rooms, this upscale club offers a more refined approach to fun. The pretentious bouncers and velvet rope may seem out of character for the beach crowd, but this club has something for everyone. Su Drag shows, W Ladies night. F-Sa 21+. Cover F-Sa $10. Open M, W, F-Su 10pm-4am.

Rush Street, 220 SW 2nd St. (☎954-524-1818). A young crowd flocks here, where the truly trendy mingle with the beach bums. All get down on the dance floor, which rocks the house with neon lights and blaring music. No cover. Lunch M-F 11am-2pm. Open M-Th 5:30-10pm, F-Sa 5:30-11pm, Su 4:30-9pm.

Elbo Room (☎954-463-4615), on prime real estate at the corner of Rte. A1A and Las Olas Blvd. The booming sidewalk bar is one of the most visible and packed scenes on the Strip. Casual, fun, and perfect for wandering in roff the street. Live rock music nightly. Open M-Th 11am-2am, F-Sa 11am-3am, Su noon-2am.

⚑ BIENVENIDOS A MIAMI

From Fort Lauderdale, roll down **I-95** into Miami in your pimped-out low-rider.

MIAMI

No longer purely a vacation spot for the "snowbirds," Miami's heart pulses to a beat all its own, infused with a Latin influence fueled by the largest Cuban population this side of Havana. Appearance rules supreme in this city, and nowhere is this more apparent than on the sands of South Beach, where visual delights include Art Deco architecture and tanned beach bodies. South Beach is also host to a hopping nightclub scene, which attracts some of the world's most beautiful people. But it's not all bikinis and sand— Miami is the entry point to the Everglades and the gateway to the Keys.

⸨ VITAL STATS ⸩

Population: 360,000

Visitor Info: Miami Beach Visitors Center, 420 Lincoln Rd. (☎305-672-1270; www.miamibeachchamber.com). Open M-F 9am-6pm, Sa-Su 10am-4pm. **Info booth,** 401 Biscayne Blvd. (☎305-539-2980), downtown outside of Bayside Marketplace. Open daily 10am-6:30pm. **Coconut Grove Chamber of Commerce,** 2820 McFarlane Ave. (☎305-444-7270), in South Beach. Open M-F 9am-5pm. **Greater Miami Convention and Visitors Bureau,** 701 Brickell Ave. (☎305-539-3000 or 800-283-2707), 27th fl. of Barnett Bank Bldg., downtown. Open M-F 9am-5pm.

Internet Access: Miami Public Library, 101 W. Flagler St. (☎305-375-2665), across from the Museum of Art. Open M-W and F-Sa 9am-6pm, Th 9am-9pm, Su 1-5pm.

Post Office: 500 NW 2nd Ave. (☎305-639-4284), downtown. Open M-F 8am-5pm, Sa 9am-1:30pm. **Postal Code:** 33101.

▣ GETTING AROUND

Three highways crisscross the Miami area. **I-95,** the most direct north-south route, merges into **U.S. 1 (Dixie Hwy.)** just south of downtown. **Rte. 836 (Dolphin Expwy.),** a major east-west artery through town, connects I-95 to **Florida's Turnpike.** When looking for addresses, pay attention to the systematic street layout; it's easy to confuse North Miami Beach, West Miami, Miami Beach, and Miami addresses. Streets in Miami run east-west, avenues north-south; both are numbered. Miami divides into NE, NW, SE, and SW quadrants; the dividing lines are **Flagler St.** and **Miami Ave.**

The heart of **Little Havana** lies between SW 12th and SW 27th Ave. One block north of **Calle Ocho (SW 8th St.)** is **W. Flagler St.,** a hub of Cuban business. **Coconut Grove,** south of Little Havana, centers around the shopping and entertainment district on **Grand Ave.** and **Virginia St.** An upscale residential area, **Coral Gables,** rests around the intersection of **Coral Way (SW 24th St.)** and **Le Jeune Rd.,** also known as **SW 42nd Ave.**

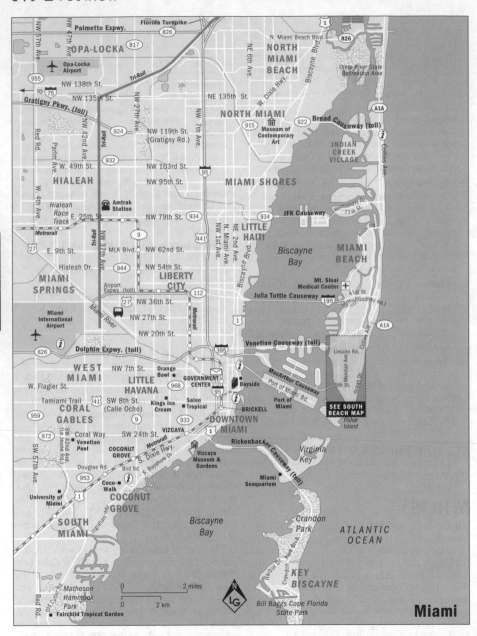

Miami

Several causeways connect Miami to **Miami Beach.** The most useful is **MacArthur Causeway,** which becomes **5th St.** Numbered streets run east-west across the island, increasing as you go north. In South Beach, **Collins Ave. (Rte. A1A)** is the main north-south drag; parallel are club-filled **Washington Ave.** and beachfront **Ocean Ave.** The commercial district sits between 6th and 23rd St. One-way streets, traffic jams, and limited parking make driving around **South Beach (SoBe)** frustrating. Tie on your most stylish sneakers, park the car at one of the garages on 16th, 12th, 13th or 5th St., and enjoy the small island at your leisure.

 When visiting Miami, it's best to avoid Liberty City, which is considered an unsafe area and offers visitors little. When partying in South Beach, stay north of 6th St.; the area quickly deteriorates into an unsafe neighborhood. Also, residents of SoBe—which has long been considered a gay-friendly area—complain that homosexuals are sometimes verbally berated. Be vigilant at all times.

👁 SIGHTS

SOUTH BEACH. South Beach is the reason to come to Miami, namely, to party in the city where the heat is on, all night, on the beach till the break of dawn. The liberal atmosphere, hot bodies, Art Deco design, and sparkling sand make these 17 blocks seem like their own universe. *(Between 6th and 23rd St.)* **Ocean Dr.** is where Miami's hottest come to see and be seen. Bars and cafes cram this tiny strip of land, which is part fashion show and part raging party. The **Art Deco Welcome Center** dispenses free area maps and advice to visitors, houses a free museum, and hosts a lecture series. *(1001 Ocean Dr. ☎ 305-531-3484. For info on lectures check www.mdpl.org. Open M-F 11am-6pm, Sa 10am-10pm, Su 11am-10pm.)* **Walking tours** are also available from the welcome center. These 90min. strolls highlight the revival of the historic Art Deco district. *(☎ 305-672-2014. Tours W and Sa-Su 10:30am; Th 6:30pm. $15, students and seniors $10.)* The **Holocaust Memorial** commemorates the six million Jews who fell victim to genocide in WWII. Gaze at the 42 ft. bronze arm protruding from the ground, whose base is supported by dozens of sculpted figures struggling to escape persecution. *(1933-45 Meridian*

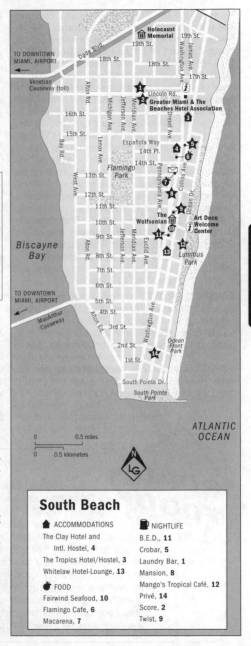

EAST COAST

South Beach

🛏 **ACCOMMODATIONS**
The Clay Hotel and
  Intl. Hostel, **4**
The Tropics Hotel/Hostel, **3**
Whitelaw Hotel-Lounge, **13**

🍴 **FOOD**
Fairwind Seafood, **10**
Flamingo Cafe, **6**
Macarena, **7**

🍸 **NIGHTLIFE**
B.E.D., **11**
Crobar, **5**
Laundry Bar, **1**
Mansion, **8**
Mango's Tropical Café, **12**
Privé, **14**
Score, **2**
Twist, **9**

Ave. ☎ 305-538-1663. Open daily 9am-9pm. Tours available upon request. Free.) Part of Florida International University, **The Wolfsonian** examines the cultural impact of art and design from 1885 to 1945, exhibiting over 70,000 pieces. It includes an exhaustive look at propaganda from WWII, an array of political cartoons, and a series of original Norman Rockwell paintings. (1001 Washington Ave. ☎ 305-531-1001; www.wolfsonian.org. Open Su noon-5pm, Th 11am-9pm, F-Sa 11am-6pm. $5, students and seniors $3.50. Th 6-9pm Free.) Visit the new home of Parrot Jungle Island, on Watson Island in Biscayne Bay. Since 1936, visitors have walked among free-flying parrots, strutting flamingos, and swinging orangutans. Also on site are the Parrot Bowl amphitheater, the Serpentarium, the clay cliffs of Manu Encounter, and the Treetop Ballroom. (1111 Parrot Jungle Tr. From downtown Miami, take the MacArthur Causeway east toward South Beach; Parrot Jungle Tr. is the 1st exit after the bridge. ☎ 305-258-6453; www.parrotjungle.com. Open daily 10am-6pm. $24; seniors, military, and students $22; ages 3-10 $19. Parking $6.)

COCONUT GROVE. A stroll through the lazy streets of **Coconut Grove** reveals an unlikely combination of upscale boutiques and tacky tourist traps. The people-watching is unparalleled at the open-air mall, **CocoWalk,** along Grand Ave. On the bayfront between the Grove and downtown stands **Vizcaya Museum and Gardens.** Built in 1916 for affluent James Deering, the 70-room Italian villa, surrounded by 10 acres of gardens, features antiques, tapestries, and art. (3251 S. Miami Ave. ☎ 305-250-9133; www.vizcayamuseum.com. Open daily 9:30am-5pm; last entry 4:30pm. $10, ages 6-12 $5. $1 off for ISIC holders. Gardens free.)

BAYSIDE. Miami's sleek shopping center hops nightly with street performers. Stores and restaurants cater to cruise ship guests and tourists with money to burn, though a tour through the center and its surrounding statues makes it worthwhile. (On the waterfront, downtown. Open M-Th 10am-10pm, F-Sa 10am-11pm, Su 11am-9pm.)

NORTH MIAMI. The **Museum of Contemporary Art (MOCA),** is known for its often eccentric exhibits and displays. Having played host to Versace dresses and steel drummers alike, MOCA supports uncommon means of artistic expression. (770 NE 125th St. ☎ 305-893-6211; www.mocanomi.org. Open Su noon-5pm, Tu-Sa 11am-5pm. $5, students and seniors $3, under 12 free.)

🎵 ENTERTAINMENT

For the latest on Miami entertainment, check out the "Living Today," "Lively Arts," and Friday "Weekend" sections of the *Miami Herald*. Weekly *Oceandrive, New Times, Street,* and *Sun Post* also list local happenings. *TWN* and *Miamigo,* the major gay papers, are available free in paper boxes along Ocean Dr. **Performing Arts and Community Education (PACE)** manages more than 400 concerts each year (jazz, rock, soul, dixieland, reggae, salsa, and bluegrass); most are free. **Carnaval Miami,** the nation's largest Hispanic festival, fills 23 blocks of Calle Ocho in early March with salsa dancing and the world's longest conga line.

CUBAN CUISINE

ROAD FOOD

Bienvenidos a Miami, where the streets are lined with South American and Cuban restaurants. Knowledge of some common dishes can help guide out-of-towners through *desayuno* (breakfast), *almuerzo* (lunch), and *cena* (dinner). Breakfast options include *huevos rancheros*—fried eggs with spicy salsa. For lunch, try a Cuban sandwich, with ham, roast pork, and Swiss cheese, heated and pressed flat, melting the cheese and making the bread warm and crispy. A favorite dinner choice among Cubans, *boliche* is a beef roast stuffed with *chorizo* (hardened sausage), onions, green peppers, and spices. Argentinian *empanadas* are turnovers filled with ham, beef, or cheese. Don't let the direct translation of *vaca frita* ("fried cow") repulse you. This traditional Cuban dish is slowly roasted beef sautéed with onions, green peppers, and spices. A popular dessert is *flan,* a rich custard made with eggs and baked in a pan of dark, caramelized sugar. For a sweet treat, try *maduros*—caramelized plantains.

FOOD

Four-star restaurants owned by celebrities and chefs are just as prevalent in Miami as four-choice sandwich counters. The South Beach strip along Ocean Dr. houses an eclectic mix of tourist traps like **Hard Rock Cafe,** celebrity favorites like **Joia** and **Tantra,** and booty-shaking pseudo-clubs like **Mango.** Go at least one block inland from the beach to find wallet-pleasing prices.

Macarena, 1334 Washington Ave. (☎305-531-3440), in Miami Beach. Dance your way to wonderful food in an atmosphere that's intimate and festive. This eatery serves up Latin American delights while captivating dancers provide entertainment. *Paella* big enough for 2 ($14, lunch $7) and the best rice pudding ever ($5.50) are savory Spanish delicacies. Wine comes from the restaurant's own vineyards. F-Sa Flamenco dancing, Th ladies night, Sa live salsa. Open for lunch daily 12:30-3:30pm; dinner Su-Tu 7pm-1am, W-Th 7pm-1:30am, F-Sa 7pm-5am.

Fairwind Seafood, 1000 Collins Ave. (☎305-531-0050), across from the Essex House. One of the best-kept secrets in South Beach. Sit out under the canopied porch with flowers and bamboo fans, and try the superb *sashimi* tuna salad with mango salsa ($9.50), seafood pasta ($10.50), or Key Lime Crème Brûlée ($4). Happy hour 4-7pm. Open daily 7am-6am.

Flamingo Cafe, 1454 Washington Ave. (☎305-673-4302), near the Clay Hostel in Miami Beach. Far and away the biggest bang for your buck, this friendly cafe produces huge portions for staggeringly low prices. Breakfast plate (eggs, toast, and meat) $2. Beef tacos and salad $2.75. *Frijoles con queso* $2.75. Lunch specials $5-7. Open M-Sa 7am-9:30pm.

Bissaleh Cafe, 17608 Collins Ave. (☎305-682-2224). Whether you're enjoying the authentic Israeli dips platter ($4) in the chic, lively interior or smoking a hookah ($7) under the midnight moon, Bissaleh's Middle Eastern charm will leave you enchanted. Dairy kosher. Open Su-Th noon-2am, Sa dusk-3am.

King's Ice Cream, 1831 SW 8th St. (☎305-643-1842). Break from the Little Havana heat with a refreshing (and delicious) tropical fruit *helado* (ice cream). Flavors include a regal coconut (served in its own shell), *mamey,* and mango. $1 for a small cup. Open M-Sa 10am-11pm, Su 1-11pm.

ACCOMMODATIONS

Cheap rooms abound in South Beach, and choosing a place to stay is all about attitude. Hostels in Miami Beach are the cheapest option for the solo traveler. If young bohemian isn't your thing, cruise down Collins Ave. to the hot-pink Art Deco hotels. In general, high season for Miami Beach runs late December through mid-March; during the low season, hotels are often quick to bargain. The **Greater Miami and the Beaches Hotel Association,** 407 Lincoln Rd., #10G, can help you find a place. (☎305-531-3553; www.gmbha.com. Open M-F 9am-5pm.) The Miami Beach Visitors Center (see p. 145) can get you the best rates. Camping is not allowed on Miami Beach.

Banana Bungalow, 2360 Collins Ave. (☎305-538-1951), at 23rd St., along the northern edge of the Art Deco district. Banana Bungalow is known as "party central"—the pool and fully stocked bar keep the young and hip crowd occupied all day and long into the night. The activity desk provides opportunities for canoeing, kayaking, and clubbing as well as free guest passes for the club *du jour.* All rooms have A/C and cable TV, though not all the fixtures work. Free coffee, tea, and toast. Game room with pool table and arcade games. Cafe open daily 8am-9:30pm. Internet $0.20 per min. Key/linen deposit $20. 6-bed dorms $17-19; private rooms $67-77; $10 per additional person.

Whitelaw Hotel-Lounge, 808 Collins Ave. (☎305-398-7000). From 7-9pm, bright white leather and chrome greet beautiful people lured in by complimentary cocktails. Down comforters, TV, A/C, refrigerator, free Internet access, and VIP passes to any club in SoBe. Continental breakfast included. Jan.-Mar. doubles $145; Apr.-Dec. $90.

The Tropics Hotel/Hostel, 1550 Collins Ave. (☎305-531-0361), across the street from the beach. Quiet refuge from the intense SoBe scene offers large, comfortable rooms with A/C, private baths, pool access, and an outdoor kitchen, as well as a casual, social common area. Lockers at front desk; none in rooms. Free linen. Laundry. Key deposit $10. Internet access $0.20 per min. Dorms $16; singles or doubles $40-50. ISIC discount. No parking available.

The Clay Hotel and International Hostel (HI-AYH), 1438 Washington Ave. (☎305-534-2988 or 800-379-2529), in the heart of the Art Deco district. This historic Mediterranean-style building, once the center of Al Capone's Miami gambling syndicate and often featured on the TV series *Miami Vice*, now hosts a largely international crowd. Kitchen, laundry, and A/C. Dorms come with phone and fridges; some have TV. Internet $6 per hr. Lockers $1 per day. Key/linen deposit $10. 4- to 6-bed dorms $16 for IYHF members, nonmembers $17; private rooms $43-79.

NIGHTLIFE

Nightlife in the Art Deco district of South Miami Beach starts late (usually after midnight) and continues until well after sunrise. Gawk at models, stars, and beach bunnies while eating dinner at one of Ocean Blvd.'s open cafes or bars, then head down to **Washington Ave.**, between 6th and 18th St., for some serious fun. Miami Beach's club scene is transient; what's there one week may not be there the next. Clubs change character depending on the night of the week, so check beforehand or you may be in for a surprise. Many clubs don't demand cover until after midnight, and often the $20+ door charge includes an open bar. However, even willingness to pay a steep cover is no guarantee of admission. Difficult doormen can prove impossible after 1am, so show up early. Most clubs have dress codes and everyone dresses to the nines, even on so-called "casual" nights. If discos aren't your thing, pull up a stool at one of the frat-boy party bars along the beach.

Mansion, 1235 Washington Ave. (☎305-532-1525; www.mansionmiami.com). An assault on all the senses, the richly decorated Mansion sets the standard among SoBe clubs. The VIP section is littered with celebrities sipping Cristal, and the dance floor is a sea of energy. By midnight lines are around the corner, so arrive early. 21+. Cover around $20. Open daily 10pm-5am.

Crobar, 1445 Washington Ave. (☎305-531-8225). Though no longer the clear winner among Washington Ave. super-clubs, Crobar is no slouch. Always packed, the dance floor is filled with the chic and trendy. Su gay night. 21+. Open daily 10pm-5am.

Mango's Tropical Cafe, 900 Ocean Dr. (☎305-673-4422). All that noise you hear while walking up Ocean Dr. is coming from here. Order a stiff and delicious CoCo-Loco ($7) and stay for a set of live music, concluded by a bar-top dance extraordinaire by alluring waitresses and buffed-up waiters. Not for

the faint of heart, the atmosphere here is party, be it 2pm or 2am. Cover $10-20 at night. Open daily 11am-5am.

Privé, 136 Collins Ave. (☎305-531-5535). The exclusive upstairs lounge area is home to SoBe's best hip-hop party. If you forgot to bring your white linen Armani suit, you'll have a bit more luck at the door here than at some of the other clubs. The Betty Ford party on Th is legendary. Open daily 10pm-5am.

B.E.D., 929 Washington Ave. (☎305-532-9070). The acronym stands for Beverage, Entertainment, and Dining, which pretty much sums up the attraction of this venue. Patrons lounge on sexy king-size beds as they enjoy dinner, drinks, and the atmosphere of silky seduction that oozes from every corner of this SoBe favorite. No cover. Open Su and W-Sa 8pm-5am.

GLBT NIGHTLIFE

South Beach's lively gay scene takes to the street at night in search of the new "it club." The area's gay and mixed clubs are among the city's trendiest, attracting partiers both gay and straight.

Twist, 1057 Washington Ave. (☎305-538-9478). A popular 2-story club with an outdoor lounge, rockin' dance floor, and 6 bars. Straight couples welcome. 21+. Cover varies. Open daily 1pm-5am.

Laundry Bar, 721 Lincoln Ln. North. (☎305-531-7700). Men and women alike flock to the unusual Laundry Bar, where the chic and friendly clientele sips cocktails to DJ-spun beats and the hum of laundry machines. A great place for an early drink before dinner or clubbing. 21+ from 10pm. No cover. Open daily 7am-5am.

Score, 727 Lincoln Rd. Mall (☎305-535-1111). Plenty of style and plenty of attitude. Mostly men frequent this multi-bar hot spot, where a packed dance floor grooves under the watchful eye of Adonis himself. 21+. No cover. Open daily M-Sa 3pm-5am, Su 3pm-2am.

LEAVING MIAMI

Follow **U.S. 1 South** from the center of Miami all the way to the Keys.

DETOUR: THE EVERGLADES

Drive south on U.S. 1 until Florida City. Turn right onto Palm Dr. and follow the signs into the park.

Encompassing the entire tip of Florida, the Everglades span 1.6 million acres of prairies, mangrove swamps, and coral reefs, supporting a number of species found nowhere else in the world. To explore this unique ecosystem, see our coverage in the Southern Border Route (p. 868).

THE CORAL CASTLE 28655 S. Dixie Hwy. *In Homestead, off U.S. 1.*

Latvian immigrant Ed Leedskalnin built the entire Coral Castle by hand in tribute to his 16-year-old fiancée, who jilted him the day before their wedding. Driven by an affection romantic or creepy, Leedskalnin managed to build a tower, a bathtub, thrones for himself and his "Sweet Sixteen," and a nine-ton gate so perfectly balanced that it can be lifted with a single finger. Audio tours lead visitors through the throne room and playground. (☎ *305-248-6345. Open M-Th 9am-6pm, F-Su 9am-7pm. $9.75, seniors $6.50, ages 7-12 $5.)*

KEY LARGO

Over half a century ago, Hollywood stars Humphrey Bogart and Lauren Bacall immortalized the name "Key Largo" in their hit movie. Quick-thinking locals of Rock Harbor, where some scenes were shot, changed the name of their town to Key Largo to attract tourists. It worked. While some visitors still come to see the relics of the movie-making past, more are drawn to Key Largo's greatest natural assets: the coral reefs and the incredible fishing. Pennekamp State Park was the country's first completely underwater park, and divers of all abilities flock to the isle for a glimpse of the reef and the numerous shipwrecks. Don't believe the hype; sharks are scarce here.

VITAL STATS

Population: 12,000

Visitor Info: Key Largo Chamber of Commerce/ Florida Keys Visitors Center, 106000 U.S. 1 (☎ 305-451-1414 or 800-822-1088; www.key-largo.org), Mile 106. Open daily 9am-6pm.

Internet Access: Key Largo Library Branch, 101485 Overseas Hwy. (☎ 305-451-2396), in the Tradewinds Shopping Center. Open M and W 10am-8pm, Tu and Th-Sa 10am-6pm.

Post Office: 101000 U.S. 1 (☎ 305-451-3155), Mile 100. Open M-F 8am-4:30pm. **Postal Code:** 33037.

GETTING AROUND. The **Overseas Hwy. (U.S. 1)** bridges the Keys and the southern tip of Florida, stitching the islands together. Mile markers

section the highway and replace street addresses beginning with Mile 0 at the southernmost point in the continental US, in Key West. Traveling along U.S. 1 can be treacherous due to fast cars and narrow shoulders; beer flows freely in the Keys, and drunk driving is a problem—stay alert.

SIGHTS & OUTDOORS. Key Largo is the self-proclaimed "Dive Capital of the World," and diving instructors advertise on highway billboards. The best place to dive is the nation's first underwater sanctuary, **John Pennekamp Coral Reef State Park,** Mi. 102½. The park extends 3 mi. into the Atlantic Ocean, safeguarding a part of the reef that runs the length of the Keys. (☎ 305-451-1202; www.pennekamp-park.com. $3.50 per vehicle with 1 occupant, 2 occupants $6; $0.50 per additional person.) Stop by the park's **Visitors Center** for maps, boat and snorkeling tour info, and hourly films. To see the reefs, visitors must take their own boats or rent. (☎ 305-451-9570, for reservations 305-451-6325. 18 ft. motor boat $125 per 4hr., $119 per day. Canoes $10 per hr. Deposit required. Open daily 8am-5pm.) **Scuba trips** depart from the Visitors Center. (☎ 305-451-6322. Trips 9:30am and 1:30pm. 2-tank dive $41. Equipment additional; certification and deposit required.) A **snorkeling tour** also allows visitors to experience the depths. (☎ 305-451-6300. Tours 9am, noon, 3pm. $26, under 18 $22. Equipment $5; deposit required.) Head to any local marina to charter a spot on a fishing boat. To avoid paying a commission, hang out on the docks and ask a friendly captain yourself. **Glass Bottom Boat Tours** provides a crystal clear view of the reefs without wetting your feet. (☎ 305-451-1621. Tours 9:15am, 12:15, 3pm. $20, under 12 $12.) At Mile 100 on the ocean side, the Holiday Inn Hotel also offers scuba, snorkel, and boat trips. The best known is the Key Largo Princess, which offers 2hr. glass bottom boat tours. (☎ 305-451-4655. Tours 10am, 1, 4pm. $20, children $10.) Aside from its always-active dock, the hotel has become a tourist destination, as it houses the African Queen, the boat on which Humphrey Bogart and Katherine Hepburn sailed in the movie of the same title.

FOOD. Seafood restaurants of varying price, specialty, and view litter the **Overseas Hwy.** The neighboring island **Islamorada** boasts one of the best seafood restaurants in all the Keys. The **Islamorada Fish Company,** Mile 81½, offers an incredible array of seafood sandwiches ($7-10) and entrees

($13-18). Be sure to taste the legendary Key Lime Pie ($3) when you finish. (☎305-664-9271 or 800-258-2559. Open daily 11am-9pm.) Tucked away on a quiet residential street, **Calypso's,** 1 Seagate Dr., at Oceanbay near Mile 99½, offers delectable Buffalo Shrimp ($7) and an equally delicious dolphin fish sandwich. (☎305-451-0600. Open M and W-Th noon-10pm, F-Sa noon-11pm.) For a scrumptious breakfast, head to **The Hideout Restaurant,** Mile 103½, at the end of Transylvania Ave. on the ocean side. Plate-size pancakes (2 for $3) and not-soon-forgotten raisin toast ($3) feed a heavily local crowd. (☎305-451-0128. Open Su-Th and Sa 11:30am-2pm, F 11:30am-2pm and 5-9pm.) **Mary Mac's Kitchen,** Mile 99, on the bay side, cooks up lunches for its eager patrons, who enjoy famous steak sandwiches ($4-5) and overwhelming hamburgers ($4). The windows feature neon beer signs, and the walls are adorned with license plates. (☎305-451-3722. Open daily 10:30am-5pm.)

ACCOMMODATIONS. Ed and Ellen's Lodgings, 103365 U.S. 1, Mi. 103½, on Snapper Ave., has clean, large rooms with cable TV, A/C, mini-fridges and microwaves. Ed, the humorous and ever-present owner, is tremendously helpful with everything from restaurant suggestions to diving and snorkeling reservations and has information on activities all up and down the Keys. (☎305-451-9949 or 888-333-5536. Doubles $59-79; off-season $49-59. $10 per additional person. Rates increase on weekends, holidays, and in lobster season.) A few lodgings near downtown Key Largo have reasonable rates. The **Bay Cove Motel,** 99446 Overseas Hwy., Mi. 99½, borders a small beach on the bay side of the island. Rooms have cable TV, A/C, and mini-fridges. (☎305-451-1686. Doubles $50-80, depending on season.) Right next door, the waterside **Hungry Pelican,** Mile 99½, features bougainvillea vines, tropical birds, and cozy rooms with double beds, fridges, and cable TV. Use of paddle boats, canoes, and hammocks is free. (☎305-451-3576. Continental breakfast included. Rooms $50-115; $10 per additional person.) Reservations are recommended for the popular **John Pennekamp State Park Campground** (see **Sights,** p. 151). The 47 sites are clean, convenient, and worth the effort required to obtain them. Half are available through advance registration; the others are first come, first served. (☎305-451-1202; www.pennkamppark.com. Showers. 14-day max. stay. Open 8am-dusk. Sites $24, with electricity $26.)

KEY WEST

The small "last island" of the Florida Keys, Key West has drawn a cast of colorful characters since the days of pirates, smugglers, and treasure hunters. Henry Flagler, Ernest Hemingway, Tennessee Williams, Truman Capote, and Jimmy Buffett have all called the quasi-independent "Conch Republic" home. Today, thousands of tourists hop on the Overseas Hwy. to glimpse the past, sample the over 300 bars, and kick back under the sun. The crowd is as diverse as Key West's past; families spend a week enjoying the water, 20-somethings come to party, and a gay population finds a haven of clubs and resorts oriented to them. Key West is as far south as you can get in the continental US. This is the end of the road—enjoy it.

(VITAL STATS)

Population: 25,000

Visitor Info: Key West Welcome Center, 3840 N. Roosevelt Blvd. (☎305-296-4444 or 800-284-4482), just north of the intersection with U.S. 1. A private reservation service. Open M-Sa 9am-7:30pm, Su 9am-6pm. **Key West Chamber of Commerce,** 402 Wall St. (☎305-294-2587 or 800-527-8539; www.keywestchamber.org), in old Mallory Sq. Open M-F 8:30am-6:30pm, Sa-Su 8:30am-6pm.

Internet Access: Key West Library, 700 Fleming St. (☎305-292-3595). Open M and W 10am-8pm, Tu and Th-Sa 10am-6pm.

Post Office: 400 Whitehead St. (☎305-294-2557), 1 block west of Duval St. Open M-F 8:30am-5pm, Sa 9:30am-noon. **Postal Code:** 33040.

GETTING AROUND

Key West lies at the end of **Overseas Hwy. (U.S. 1),** 155 mi. southwest of Miami. The island is divided into two sections; the eastern part, known as **New Town,** harbors tract houses, chain motels, shopping malls, and the airport. Beautiful old conch houses fill **Old Town,** west of White St. **Duval St.** is the main north-south thoroughfare in Old Town; **Truman Ave. (U.S. 1)** is a major east-west route. Driving in town can be difficult; due to limited parking, traversing Key West by bike or moped is more convenient than driving. Parking at the **Park 'N Ride** facility, at Caroline and Grinnell St., is $3 per day. Do not park overnight on the bridges.

For those who prefer riding, the **Conch Tour Train** is a 1½hr. narrated ride through Old Town. (Leaves from Mallory Sq. at 3840 N. or from Roosevelt Blvd., next to the Quality Inn. ☎305-294-5161. Runs daily 9am-4:30pm. $18, ages 4-12 $9.) **Old Town Trolley** runs a similar tour, but you can get on and off through the day at nine stops. (☎305-296-6688. Tours 9am-5:30pm. $18, ages 4-12 $9.)

🄯 SIGHTS

ON LAND. No one should leave Key West without a visit to the ▧**Ernest Hemingway Home,** a Caribbean-style mansion where "Papa" wrote *For Whom the Bell Tolls* and *The Snows of Kilimanjaro.* Take a tour with hilarious guides who relate Hemingway and Key West history, then traipse among 60 descendants of Hemingway's cat, half of which have extra toes. *(907 Whitehead St. ☎305-294-1136; www.hemingwayhome.com. Open daily 9am-5pm. $10, ages 6-12 $6. Free parking across the street.)* Tucked into the ritzy Truman Annex Gated Community, the **Harry S. Truman Little White House Museum** provides a fascinating look at both President Truman and his getaway in Key West, used at various times by John Kennedy, Dwight Eisenhower, and Thomas Edison. *(111 Front St. ☎305-294-9911; www.trumanlittlewhitehouse.com. Open daily 9am-5pm. $10, children $5; includes tour. Grounds of the Truman Annex open 8am-6pm.)* In addition to its serene garden, the **Audubon House** shelters antiques and engravings by John James Audubon. *(205 Whitehead St. ☎305-294-2116; www.audubonhouse.com. Open daily 9:30am-5pm; last admission 4:30pm. $8, students $7.50, seniors $5, ages 6-12 $3.50.)*

ON WATER. The **Mel Fisher Maritime Heritage Society Museum** showcases the discovery and salvage of the Spanish galleon *Atocha*, which sank off the Keys in the 17th century and was uncovered after a 16-year search. The museum also has an entire floor dedicated to the study of the 17th- and 18th-century slave trade. *(200 Greene St. ☎305-294-2633; www.melfisher.org. Open daily 9am-5pm; last admission 4:30pm. $10, students $8.50, ages 6-12 $6.)* The **Key West Shipwreck Historeum Museum** exhibits the remains of the *Isaac Allerton*, the 594-ton ship that sank in 1856. Get a glimpse into the lives of classic adventurers by surveying the original cargo. The museum's **Lookout Tower**, which stands 65 ft. tall, offers one of the best views of the island. *(1 Whitehead St., in Mallory Sq. ☎305-292-8990;*

www.shipwreckhistoreum.com. Open daily 9:30am-5pm. $9, ages 4-12 $4.50, under 4 free.) Down Whitehead St., past the Hemingway House, you'll come to the southernmost point in the continental US at the fittingly named **Southernmost Beach.** A small, conical monument marks the spot: "90 miles to Cuba." At the **Mallory Sq. Dock**, street entertainers and kitsch-hawkers work the crowd, while boats parade in revue during the **Sunset Celebration.** The **glass bottom boat** *Fireball* cruises to the reefs and back. *(☎305-296-6293. 2-2½hr. cruises daily noon, 2, and 6pm. $20, at sunset $25; ages 5-12 $10/$12.50.)*

🍴 FOOD

Expensive trendy restaurants line **Duval St.,** while side streets offer lower prices and fewer crowds.

Blue Heaven, 729 Thomas St. (☎305-296-8666), 1 block from the Caribbean House. Feast on healthy breakfasts with fresh banana bread ($2-9); Caribbean or Mexican lunches ($2.50-10); and heavenly dinners ($9-19). Open M-Sa 8am-3pm and 6-10:30pm, Su 8am-1pm and 6-10:30pm.

El Siboney, 900 Catherine St. (☎305-296-4184). Breaking with the unfortunate Key West tradition of overpriced food, this Cuban establishment serves up heaping mounds of beans, rice, and meat, all for around $7. Open M-Sa 11am-9:30pm.

Rooftop Cafe, 308 Fronts Ave. (☎305-294-2042), at Tifts Ave. This quaint Cuban eatery overlooks tourist trains and skin shows. The chicken bella vista salad ($11) and the steak largo hueso ($12), however, keep patrons' minds on their food. Open daily 9am-11pm.

Karr Breizh Creperie, 512½ Duval St. (☎305-296-1071). Watch as the owner creates an array of French crepes, from banana and apple to Nutella ($4-7), then eat right at the counter. For lighter fare, try goat cheese salad ($6). Open daily 9am-11pm.

Grand Cafe, 314 Duval St. (☎305-292-4816). With its secluded patio and elegant interior, the Grand Cafe provides refuge from the often hectic Duval St. Try one of the gourmet pizzas ($10-12) or garden fresh salads ($5-10). Open daily 11am-11pm.

🏠 ACCOMMODATIONS

Key West is packed virtually year-round, particularly from January through March, so reserve rooms far in advance. **Pride Week** (www.pridefestkeywest.com) each June is particularly busy. In

EAST COAST

Old Town, B&Bs dominate, and "reasonably priced" still means over $50. Some of the guesthouses in Old Town are for gay men exclusively.

■ **Casablanca Hotel,** 900 Duval St. (☎305-296-0815), in the center of town. This charming B&B once hosted Humphrey Bogart and James Joyce. Pool, beautiful courtyards, cable TV, and large bathrooms. Breakfast included. Call ahead for reservations during Fantasy Fest. Rooms Dec.-May $89-200; June-Nov. $79-89.

Caribbean House, 226 Petronia St. (☎305-296-1600 or 800-543-4518). Colorful Caribbean rooms with A/C, cable TV, free local calls, fridge and comfy double beds. Continental breakfast included. Reception 9am-5pm; guests must fax credit card info if planning to arrive later. No reservations for cottages. Winter rooms $69; cottages $89. Summer rooms from $49/$69.

Wicker Guesthouse, 913 Duval St. (☎305-296-4275 or 800-880-4275). Pastel decor, private baths, A/C, and cable TV. Most rooms have kitchenettes. No phones. Kitchen, pool access, and free parking. Breakfast included. Reservations recommended; ask for summer specials. Rooms late Dec. to May $130-150; June-Dec. $89-105.

Eden House, 1015 Fleming St. (☎305-296-6868 or 800-533-5397), just 5 short blocks from downtown. Brightly painted hotel with a hostel-like atmosphere. Clean, classy rooms with bath. Pool, jacuzzi, hammock area, and kitchens. Bikes $10 per day. Happy hour daily 4-5pm. Rooms with shared bath in high season $105; low-season $80.

Boyd's Campground, 6401 Maloney Ave. (☎305-294-1465). Take a left off U.S. 1 onto Macdonald Ave., which becomes Maloney. Sprawls over 12 oceanside acres and provides full facilities. Sites for 2 in winter $45-70, with water and electricity $55-80, full hookup $60-85; in summer $42-60/$52-70/$57-75. $8 per each additional person. Waterfront sites add $6-14.

▲ NIGHTLIFE

The free *Island News,* found in local restaurants and bars, lists dining spots, music, and clubs. Nightlife in Key West revs up at 11pm and winds down in the wee hours. The action centers around upper **Duval St.** Key West nightlife reaches its exultant high in the third week of October's **Fantasy Fest** (☎305-296-1817; www.fantasyfest.net), when decadent floats filled with drag queens, pirates, and wild locals take over Duval St.

■ **The Green Parrot,** 601 Whitehead St. (☎305-294-6133). Though off the beaten path of Duval St., this bar has enough of a reputation to have warranted a nod from *Playboy* as Key West's best bar. A real area hangout; stop by and meet a crowd of local characters. Open daily 11am-late.

Capt. Tony's Saloon, 428 Greene St. (☎305-294-1838). The oldest bar in Key West and reputedly one of Tennessee Williams's preferred watering holes has been serving since the early 1930s. Bras and business cards festoon the ceiling. Live music daily, mostly rock. Open M-Sa 10am-2am, Su noon-2am.

Rick's, 202 Duval St. (☎305-296-4890). An unabashed meat market, Rick's boasts body shots, the cheapest drinks in town, and a hot clientele. Happy hour 3-6pm; $2 longneck Buds. W-Th $7 all-you-can-drink nights. Open M-Sa 11am-4am, Su noon-4am.

Sloppy Joe's, 201 Duval St. (☎305-294-5717). For the best party you'll most likely forget, stop by Hemingway's favorite hangout and be blown away by the house specialty, the Hurricane ($7). Grab the *Sloppy Joe's News* to learn the latest on upcoming entertainment, with a different act every night. 21+. Open M-Sa 9am-4am, Su noon-4am.

Margaritaville, 500 Duval St. (☎305-292-1435). Find your lost shaker of salt in this Jimmy Buffet-inspired bar that specializes in, yes, margaritas ($6). Open daily 10am-2am.

GLBT NIGHTLIFE

Known for its wild, outspoken gay community, Key West hosts more than a dozen fabulous drag lounges, night clubs, and private bars for the gay man's enjoyment. Most clubs welcome straight couples and lesbians, but check with the bouncer. Gay clubs line **Duval St.** south of Fleming Ave. *Celebrate!* covers the gay and lesbian community.

Aqua, 711 Duval St. (☎305-294-0555; www.aquakeywest.com). The hottest drag club in Key West. You're likely to see many wide-eyed tourists checking out the singing beauties.

KWEST MEN, 705 Duval St. (☎305-292-8500), is a sweaty, scandalous dance club, where boys in G-strings gyrate on the dance floor. Drag show nightly 10pm. Tu amateur night. 21+. Open daily 4pm-4am.

The Bourbon Street Pub, 724 Duval St. (☎305-296-1992; www.bourbonstreetpub.com). An alternative to Duval St.'s jock-strap clad waiters, this is a more traditional bar, though still hip. No cover. Open daily 4pm-4am. Sister club **801 Bourbon,** 801 Duval St. (☎305-294-4737) is also popular. Open daily 11am-4am.

THE GREAT NORTH

The Great North Route is a many-splendored thing; the first half of the trip is marked by some of the most hip and vibrant and cities in the US and Canada, while the second half travels through some of the largest and most beautiful National Parks and natural areas in North America. The Great North offers the best of both worlds, whether you enjoy sipping coffee in a cafe in Montréal or Minneapolis-St. Paul, or camping out in the serene wilderness next to the Geysers of Yellowstone or the mineral springs of Banff.

The road begins on the rocky coast of Maine, where it finds its first and largest statue of Paul Bunyan in **Bangor, ME** (p. 163). After traveling through central Maine and northern New Hampshire, the road takes a sweet turn toward **Waterbury, VT,** home of the **Ben & Jerry's Factory** (p. 174) and its ice-cream graveyard of lost and forgotten flavors. The route then heads north across the border into Canada, to the island city of **Montréal** (p. 180), host to McGill university and the "Underground City"—an network of shops and restaurants beneath the city that makes pedestrian travel in the winter much more pleasant.

After seeing Parliament Hill in **Ottawa, ON,** (p. 190), the road passes the **Jell-O Museum** of **LeRoy, NY** (p. 200) on its way to **Niagara Falls** (p. 200), where, in a strange inversion, the American side of the falls has serene parks and wilderness while the Canadian side is all bright lights and consumerism. After this natural wonder, the route travels south around the shore of Lake Erie, offering the opportunity to sample the original buffalo wings at the **Anchor Bar** in **Buffalo, NY** (p. 202). The road along the lake hits both small towns and big cities, visiting the **Rock and Roll Hall of Fame** in **Cleveland, OH** (p. 206) and the **Heidelberg Project** in **Detroit, MI** (p. 213), before crossing over to Michigan's Upper Peninsula via the **Straits of Mackinac** (p. 219).

From there, the road travels past the cheese factories of **Wisconsin** (p. 227) on its way to the Twin Cities, **Minneapolis** and **St. Paul,** home of the **Mall of America** (p. 230) and its indoor roller coaster. Leaving the Twin Cities, the road shifts from the big cities and Great Lakes to the road oddities of the Midwest. Beginning with the **Jeffers Petroglyphs** (p. 235) in western Minnesota, the road finds an unlikely hotbed of roadside sights in western South Dakota, from the bizarre landscape of the **Badlands** (p. 238), to the kitschy animatronic dinosaurs of **Wall Drug** (p. 240), to the man-made wonders of **Mt. Rushmore** (p. 243). From there, the road strikes out of the natural wonders of **Wind Cave** (p. 245) and **Jewel Cave** (p. 245), then north to the gigantic **Crazy Horse Memorial** (p. 245) and the shootouts and casinos of **Deadwood** (p. 246)— what more could a roadie could ask for?

(ROUTE STATS)

Miles: c. 3800

Route: Bar Harbor, ME to Vancouver, BC.

States and Provinces: 15; Maine, New Hampshire, Vermont, Quebec, New York, Pennsylvania, Ohio, Michigan, Wisconsin, Minnesota, South Dakota, Wyoming, Montana, Alberta, and British Columbia.

Driving Time: Two to three weeks minimum; allow four to appreciate the profound natural beauty of the north.

When To Go: While the cold and snow of winter may make camping and driving much more difficult, those who brave the cold can take on some of the best skiing from east to west. Depart in mid-September to watch the leaves change all along the route.

Crossroads: The East Coast in Mt. Desert Island, ME (p. 49); **The North American** in Missoula, MT (p. 705) and Banff National Park, AB (p. 276).

After leaving South Dakota, the journey's theme shifts toward the vast expanses of some of North America's most pristine lands. The road travels through the geysers and mudpots of **Yellowstone, WY** (p. 250), the alpine lakes of the **Waterton-Glacier Peace Park, MT** (p. 265), the springs of **Banff, AB** (p. 276), the Great Divide of **Yoho, BC** (p. 281), and the glaciers of **Glacier National Park, BC** (p. 282), before finding its terminus in **Vancouver, BC** (p. 291).

In Vancouver you can get reacquainted with civilization in art galleries and botanical gardens. Of all you've seen—the best of what the city and the backcountry have to offer—one thing will always stay with you; in the back of your mind, there will always be the lingering question: "Exactly how far *am* I from Wall Drug?"

GREAT NORTH

Welcome To MAINE

MT. DESERT ISLAND

There's no better place to begin your roadtrip than Mt. Desert Island, where the marvels of the wilderness and the American small town come together. For wilderness, go to Acadia National Park, which harbors some of New England's last protected marine, mountain, and forest environments. To revel in small-town Americana, head to Bar Harbor, the largest of the island's many picturesque towns, or drive between the island's smaller towns, stopping to stroll along the coast and pick up some lobster-to-go.

⬚ GETTING AROUND

Mt. Desert Island is shaped roughly like a big lobster claw, 16 mi. long and 13 mi. wide. The claw reaches from the north to the south and is dotted with small towns. The island's only links to the mainland are **Rte. 3,** which runs down the arm of the claw from the north, and the vehicle **ferry** (☎ 888-249-7245; www.catferry.com) to Yarmouth, Nova Scotia, which leaves from Bar Harbor. The island's main roads are **Rte. 3,** which runs along the coast of the eastern half the island, and **Rte. 102,** which traces the western coast. To the east, on Rte. 3, lies **Bar Harbor,** the island's largest town. **Seal Harbor,** also on Rte. 3, sits on the southeast corner of the island. South on Rte. 198, near the cleft of the claw, is **Northeast Harbor.** Across Somes Sound on Rte. 102 is ruggedly scenic **Southwest Harbor.** At the southern tip of the island, on the west half of the claw, sits the town of **Bass Harbor,** and up the western coast on Rte. 102 lie the hamlets of **Seal Cove, Pretty Marsh,** and **Somesville.**

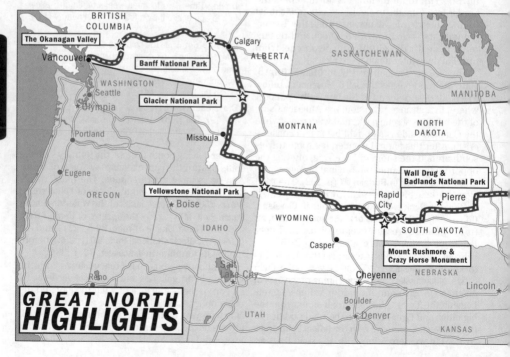

GREAT NORTH HIGHLIGHTS

comes a motley mélange of R&R-seekers, who still enjoy the area's homey antique houses and grand farms. Quaint country churches, small shops, and charming restaurants are also scattered across the area. Downtown Bar Harbor, the most crowded and glitzy part of the island, overflows with fascinating stores, galleries, and museums

GETTING AROUND

Bar Harbor's streets are all state highways, most of which are known by other names within the town itself. **Rte. 3** runs through Bar Harbor, becoming **Mt. Desert St.** and then **Main St.** On the waterfront, **Cottage St.** and **West St.** run parallel to Mt. Desert St. Both Mt. Desert St. and Cottage St. are home to shops, restaurants, and bars. **Parking** is available on nearly every street, and "parking lots" (simply wider sections of the street), are abundant. All parking is for 2-3hr. and is free. After 6pm, no time limit is in effect.

VITAL STATS

Population: 4800

Visitor Info: Chamber of Commerce, 93 Cottage St. (☎888-540-9990). Open June-Oct. M-F 8am-5pm; Nov.-May M-F 9am-5pm. **Info Booth,** 1 Harbor Pl. (☎207-288-5103; www.barharbormaine.com.). Open mid-May to mid-Oct. daily 9am-5pm.

Internet Access: The Opera House, 27 Cottage St. (☎207-288-3509). $2.25 first 15min., $0.10 per min. thereafter. Open daily May-June 8am-11pm; July-Oct. 7am-11pm.

Post Office: 55 Cottage St. Open M-F 8am-4:30pm, Sa 9am-noon. **Postal Code:** 04609.

BAR HARBOR

Bar Harbor is actually a township encompassing 28,800 acres (or 45 sq. mi.) of beautiful land and picturesque districts. Once a summer hamlet for the affluent, the town now wel-

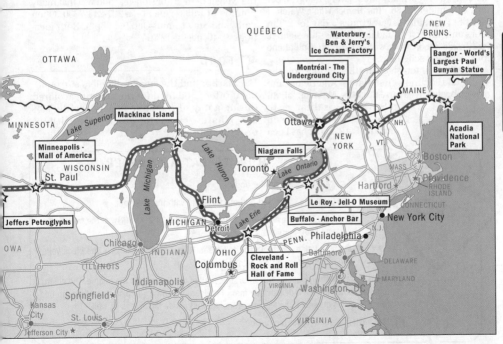

🔲 SIGHTS

Along the **Shore Path** are some of the area's largest shorefront "cottages," most of which date from the late 1800s or early 1900s. These homes are one reminder of the gilded age of Bar Harbor, when only the most rich and famous inhabited Mount Desert Island. The local piers, at the junction of Main St. and West St., are start points for a variety of excursions into Frenchman Bay. Boat tours are available to see seven lighthouses in the Mount Desert Island area. Travelers on foot can head to **Bar Island** at low tide, when a gravel path with tide pools, accessible via Bridge St., is exposed for two or three hours.

For the adventurous or the aquatically-inclined, **Acadia Bike & Canoe,** 48 Cottage St., rents bikes, canoes, and kayaks, and leads sea kayaking tours. (☎800-526-8615. Open May-Oct. daily 8am-6pm. Inquire for advanced tours or multi-day tours.) **Beal & Bunker** runs ferries from the Northeast Harbor town dock to Great Cranberry Island. (☎207-244-3575. Open late June to early Sept. daily 8am-4:30pm; call for winter hours. Every 15min.; 6 per day. $12, under 12 $6.) **Bar Harbor Whale Watch,** 1 West St., set sails several times a day for 2-3hr. tours and offers a refund if no whales are sighted. (☎207-288-2386; www.whalesrus.com. Call ahead for prices and schedules.)

If you're interested in the history of the Wabanaki, Maine's first Native Americans and expert basket weavers, the **Abbe Museum,** 26 Mt. Desert St. (Rte. 3), is the place to go. The original museum is in Acadia Park, and it has been restored to its 1928 state since this downtown location opened. (☎207-288-3519; www.abbemuseum.org. Open June-mid-Oct. Su-W 10am-5pm, Th-Sa 10am-9pm; mid-Oct.-June Th-Su 10am-5pm. $4.50, ages 6-15 $2; under 6, Native Americans, and Abbe members free.)

In summer, the historic **Criterion Theatre,** 35 Cottage St., hosts mainstream movies, puppet shows every other Saturday, and the occasional concert. (☎207-288-3441. Two movies show nightly. Box office opens 30min. before show. $7.50, seniors $6.50, under 12 $5.50; balcony seats $8.50.)

In nearby Southwest Harbor is the primary of the two **Mount Desert Oceanarium** locations, at the end of Clark Pt. Rd. near Beal's. The hands-on display featuring sea stars, urchins, cucumbers, anemones, and other creatures fascinate all ages. The secondary Oceanarium is located in Hull's Cove at 1351 Rte. 3, just north of the town, and receives rave reviews for its amusing presentations of everything you ever wanted to know about lobsters but were too hungry to ask. Guess the weight of their "big lobster" and win that many pounds of lobster meat. (☎207-244-7330. Open daily mid-May to mid-Oct. 9am-5pm. Both locations $8-10, ages 4-12 $6-7.)

🔲 FOOD

Bar Harbor and the smaller hamlets surrounding it offer good food for the appetite acquired during a day of rambling in that healthy salt air. Whatever you do, don't leave without ordering lobster.

ROAD FOOD

HOW TO EAT A LOBSTER

1 Twist claws off the body.

2 Crack the claws and pull out the meat with the little fork.

3 Flip the lobster over, and cut down the center of the tail. Twist the tail off the body and open it up along the cut.

4 Use the little fork to push out the tail meat. Remove and do not eat the black vein (even if your friends tell you it's high in protein).

5 If you don't get easily queasy, pull apart the shell of the body down the middle. The green tomalley is considered a delicacy by many locals–wipe it off if you disagree. Meat can be found in the joints where the legs are attached and inside larger legs as well.

6 Still having trouble? Order the bisque.

Reel Pizza, 33 Kennebec Pl. (☎207-288-3828), at the end of Rodick Pl. off Main St. Combination movie theater and pizzeria shows 2 films each evening for $5 and serves up creative pies ($7-19), such as the "Hawaii 5-0" with ham, pineapple, green pepper, and macadamia nuts. The first 3 rows of the "theater" are comfy couches and chairs. Open daily 5pm to end of last screening.

Ben and Bill's Chocolate Emporium, 66 Main St. (☎207-288-3281), near Cottage St. Scoops out 48 flavors of homemade ice cream, including—no kidding—lobster. Cones $3-4. Fudge $12 per lb. Open mid-Feb. to Jan. daily 9am-11:30pm.

Poor Boy's Restaurant, 300 Main St. (☎207-288-4148). Local favorite for good food and great prices. Extensive menu features lobster in no fewer than 10 different incarnations. Catch the early-bird special before 7pm, where everything on the impressive menu is $9. Entrees $10-14. Lobster meal, which might just be the best deal on the island, $16. Open daily 4:30-10pm. Reservations recommended.

Beal's, (☎207-244-3202 or 800-245-7178), in Southwest Harbor, off Main St. at the end of Clark Rd. in Southwest Harbor. Offers lobster on a patio overlooking the pier. Pick a live one from a tank ($9.75 per lb.) and it'll be buttered and red in minutes. Open daily May-Oct. 7am-8pm; Nov.-Apr. 7am-4pm. Seafood sold year-round daily 9am-5pm. Hours vary with weather.

Docksider Restaurant, 14 Sea St. (☎207-276-3965), outside of Bar Harbor in Northeast Harbor. Lobster traps on the wall and the decorative seashells create a clambake atmosphere. Open daily 11am-8:30pm.

Bunny's, 39 Kebo St. (☎207-288-4572). Offers a 2-trip breakfast buffet for $7 for early risers with big appetites. Open 6:30-10:30am.

ACCOMMODATIONS

Lodging is easy to find in Bar Harbor—it seems that every other building is an inn or a B&B. Affordable accommodations, on the other hand, are another story; grand hotels and even grander prices recall the island's exclusive resort days. More reasonable establishments assemble on Rte. 3 north of Bar Harbor. Hotel and B&B prices can more than double over the course of a week (especially July-Aug.), depending on how busy it is. Book as early as possible to get the best deal.

Bar Harbor Youth Hostel, 321 Main St. (☎207-288-5587). Perennially popular hostel accommodates up to 30 people in 2 dorm rooms and 1 family room (for 3) with a private bath. Friendly manager gives out free baked goods and discounts on kayak rentals. A book-swap and free movie nights keep travelers entertained. Lockout 10am-5pm. Curfew 11pm. Reservations only with deposit. Open May-Nov. Dorms $21, nonmembers $25; family room $55, nonmembers $65.

Llangolan Inn & Cottages, 865 Rte. 3 (☎207-288-3016; www.acadia.net/llangolan). Some of the best lodging on Rte. 3. Lovely B&B 5 mi. north of the park. The eternally smiley owner makes a delicious free breakfast of muffins, scones, and pumpkin bread. Rooms are immaculate and tastefully decorated; the B&B is cozy without a whiff of tackiness. Inn with 5 rooms (shared bath for 2 rooms) open year-round, 8 cabins open May to mid-Oct. Check-out 10am. Rooms $35-60; cottages with kitchenettes $45-70.

Edenbrook Motel, 96 Eden St. (☎207-288-4975 or 800-323-7819). If you must stay downtown, Edenbrook has rooms at decent prices with a great view. Open mid-May to mid-Oct. Rooms in summer $68-90; low-season $36-60.

Hearthside, 7 High St. (☎207-288-4533). A comfortable, if pricey, hotel nestled on a back street a short walk from downtown. A/C and private bath; some rooms have fireplaces. Rooms in summer $100-150; low-season $70-100.

NIGHTLIFE

Although the surrounding scenery is the town's best offering, roadtrippers looking for nightlife won't be disappointed in Bar Harbor. **Geddy's Pub,** 19 Main St., provides a backwoods backdrop to a nightly dancing frenzy. Weathered wooden signs, beat-up license plates, and moose head trophies look on while tables are moved aside for a DJ and dance floor in the summer. Pub-style dinner ($10-17) is served until 10pm. (☎207-288-5077. Live music daily 7-10pm. No cover. Open daily Apr.-Oct. 11am-1am; winter hours vary.) Also offering good music and good times is the **Lompoc Cafe & Brew Pub,** 36 Rodick St., off Cottage St. Locals adore this evening haunt, which features Bar Harbor Real Ale ($4), a free bocce court, and live jazz, blues, Celtic, rock, and folk on Friday and Saturday nights. (☎207-288-9392. Th open mic. No cover. Open May-Oct. daily 11:30am-1am.)

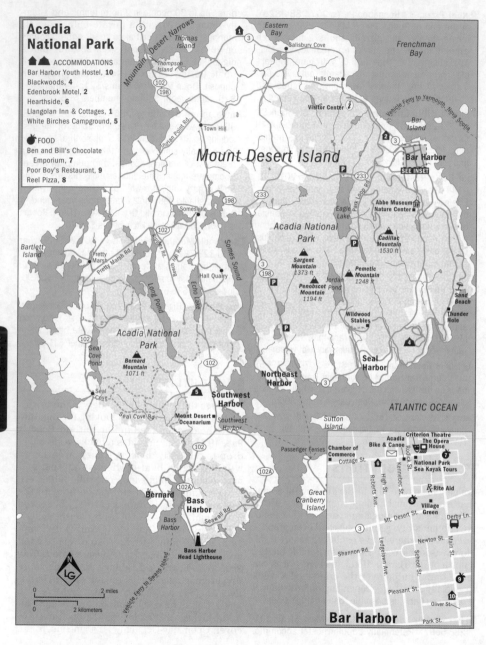

Acadia National Park

▲▲ ACCOMMODATIONS
Bar Harbor Youth Hostel, **10**
Blackwoods, **4**
Edenbrook Motel, **2**
Hearthside, **6**
Llangolan Inn & Cottages, **1**
White Birches Campground, **5**

🍎 FOOD
Ben and Bill's Chocolate Emporium, **7**
Poor Boy's Restaurant, **9**
Reel Pizza, **8**

ACADIA NATIONAL PARK

Roughly half of Mt. Desert Island as well as several other small islands are part of Acadia, New England's only national park. During the summer, the island swarms with tourists lured by thick forests, glacial lakes, tiny islands, and rocky beaches leading up to steep granite cliffs. Fern-shrouded streams and 120 mi. of hiking trails crisscross the rugged coastal terrain.

VITAL STATS

Area: 48,000 acres.

Visitor Info: Hulls Cove Visitors Center (☎ 207-288-5262), off Rte. 3. Open daily mid-June to mid-Sept. 8am-6pm; mid-Apr. to mid-June and mid-Sept. to Oct. 9am-5pm. **Park Headquarters** (☎ 207-288-3338), on Rte. 233. 3 mi. west of Bar Harbor, near Eagle Lake. Provides visitor info during the low season. Open M-F 8am-4:30pm.

Gateway Town: Bar Harbor (p. 157)

Fees: Weekly pass $10, motorcycles $5.

⚑ GETTING AROUND. Though visitors are welcome to drive into Acadia, most of the beauty of the place is off-limits to cars, thanks to John D. Rockefeller. Fearing the island would one day be overrun by automobiles, millionaire Rockefeller funded the creation of 51 mi. of carriage roads, which are now accessible only to hikers and mountain bikes. The best way by car to see Acadia is to drive the **Acadia Byway.**

◉ SIGHTS. A good way to see Acadia is to drive the **Park Loop Rd.** (20 mi.). About 4 mi. south of Bar Harbor on Rte. 3, Park Loop Rd. runs along the shore of the island, where waves crash against vertical cliffs, before eventually making a 27 mi. circuit of the eastern section of the island. Begin your drive on Park Loop Rd. at the Hulls Cove Visitors Center by turning onto the one-way road to Sand Beach. The first stop is **Sieur de Monts Spring,** where over 300 species of flora thrive in the Wild Gardens of Acadia. The original **Abbe Museum,** built in honor of the Native American Wabanaki people, is also here. The next stop is **Sand Beach,** the only sandy beach in the otherwise rocky park. From here you can also take a short hike to see the **Beehive,** a 520 ft. mountain, sculpted by glaciers to resemble a honeycomb. Next, the road

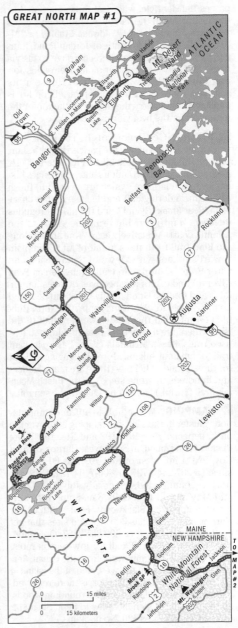

GREAT NORTH MAP #1

GREAT NORTH

passes **Thunder Hole,** where, at three-quarters tide, the air trapped in the narrow granite hollow emits a thunderous howl. At **Wildwood Stables** (☎207-276-3622), a half-mile south of Jordan Pond, tourists can explore Rockefeller's carriage roads via horse and carriage. Farther along the road is Jordan Pond, with the Jordan Pond House at its southern shore. Near the end of Park Loop Rd. is **Cadillac Mountain;** try the detour to the top of the mountain for the best view in the park.

⊠ HIKING. Getting out of the car is the only way to see Acadia in full; the park is rife with short yet breathtakingly scenic hikes. **Precipice Trail** (1½ mi.), a popular and strenuous hike, challenges hikers with iron ladders, which are needed to finish off the meandering cliff and ledge trail. **Mt. Champlain/Bear Brook** (2¼ mi.) and the more strenuous **Beehive** (¾ mi.) provide dramatic views of the Atlantic coast. A relatively easy ½ mi. amble along the **Bowl** trail from the summit of Mt. Champlain rewards hikers with views of Sand Beach and Otter Point. A moderate trail circles **Jordan Pond** (3¼ mi.) and offers perspectives of lakes, mountains and forests. Good family hikes can be found on the Bubble Rock (1¼ mi.) or on the North Bubble (1¼ mi.). On the quieter western half of the island there are a variety of breathtaking and less used trails. **Beech Mountain** (½ mi.), is a pleasant trail for amateur hikers. More challenging and not for those afraid of heights (there are many ladders and hundreds of stone steps), is the **Beech Mountain Trail** (1½ mi.) from Echo Lake to the summit.

⚞ CAMPING. While solid-roof accommodations cluster in Bar Harbor, camping is all over the park, especially on Rte. 102 and Rte. 198. **White Birches Campground,** in Southwest Harbor, on Seal Cove Rd. 1 mi. west of Rte. 102, has 60 wooded sites. (☎207-244-3797 or 800-716-0727. Reservations recommended, especially July-Aug. Open mid-May to mid-Oct. daily 8am-8pm. Sites $21, with hookup $25.) **Blackwoods,** 5 mi. south of Bar Harbor on Rte. 3., has 300 wooded sites that get crowded in summer. (☎800-365-2267. Open mid-Mar. to Oct. Sites $20; call for low-season rates. No hookups.) A 10min. walk from the ocean, **Seawall,** off Rte. 102A on the west side of the island, 4 mi. south of Southwest Harbor, is more removed, with widely spaced sites and surrounding woods. (☎800-365-2267. Open late May to Sept. Sites $14; drive-in and RV sites $20. No hookups.)

 BASS HARBOR LIGHTHOUSE
1 mi. before the city of Bass Harbor on Rte. 102A.

On the southern tip of Mt. Desert Island sits Bass Harbor lighthouse, Maine's most-photographed lighthouse. Unfortunately, the coast around the lighthouse is fenced off, making it difficult to get a good picture unless you're on the water.

⚟ LEAVING MT. DESERT ISLAND
Follow **Rte. 3** over the bridge to the Main(e)land to begin your cross-country journey, continuing north along Rte. 3 into Trenton.

TRENTON. Trenton has live **lobster pounds** worth stopping by if you'd like to lunch on one of the tasty beasties. (In Maine-speak, a "lobster pound" is a store that sells lobsters.) Your lobster can even be packed for car travel if you need a clawed companion riding shotgun. While in Trenton, check out the **The Great Maine Lumberjack Show** on Bar Harbor Rd. (Rte. 3). In the 1870s, Maine was one of America's largest logging centers. Boastful lumberjacks used to challenge each other to the "Olympics of the Forest," an event the Great Maine Lumberjack Show reenacts nightly. As seen on ESPN, the 14 events include axe throwing, log rolling, and cross-cut sawing. The show also offers hands-on activities for kids to try. Don't miss the **LumberJills,** a group of women who keep up with (or outlast) their male counterparts. (☎207-667-0067; "log" onto www.mainelumberjack.com. Shows mid-June to Aug. nightly at 7pm. Box office opens 6pm.)

⚟ APPROACHING ELLSWORTH
Roll into Ellsworth by following **Rte. 3** downhill into town as it becomes **High St.**

ELLSWORTH

Not wanting to be just another "gateway" city, Ellsworth, 17 mi. from Bar Harbor, has come up with the slogan "Crossroads of Downeast Maine." Fuel and stock up here—this town, the largest between Bar Harbor and Bangor, is more of a pit stop than an attraction. The **Stanwood Wildlife Sanctuary,** 289 High St., was built in 1958 as a memorial for Cordelia J. Stanwood, who spent her life establishing herself as a leading ornithologist and wildlife photographer. The homestead on the property was placed on the National Registry of Historic Places in 1973, ensuring no urban expansion would ever invade in the area. The 165 acres of woodland are home to owls and other wildfowl. (☎207-667-8460. Open daily May-Oct. 10am-4pm. Trails and grounds open year-round.)

On your right as you drive downhill into town, **China Hill**, 301 High St., is a popular Chinese restaurant near the eastern entrance to Ellsworth, serving Szechuan, Hunan, Mandarin, Cantonese, and a few American choices. (☎207-667-5308. Entrees $8-12. All-you-can-eat buffet Tu and F-Sa nights and all day Su $9-10. Open in summer daily 11am-10pm; low-season Su-Th 11am-9pm, F-Sa 11am-10pm.) Those needing a good night's sleep should consider the **Ellsworth Motel**, 24 High St., an affordable place to stay on the main road. With 1950s TVs, chartreuse bedrooms and lemon-yellow bathrooms, and a pool, this place is retro but comfortable. (☎207-667-4424. Rooms $39-50.)

◤ APPROACHING BANGOR

To continue through Ellsworth on to Bangor, keep going straight through the stop light, following **Rte. 3** as it turns into **U.S. 1A.**

BANGOR

Bangor is both the "Gateway to Maine" and the "Queen City." The first moniker seems the most apt; due to its central location, Bangor serves as a hub for adventures to Canada, Acadia National Park, Augusta, and the Moosehead Lake region. But that doesn't mean there isn't anything to do in the city itself; Bangor is the economic and cultural center of eastern Maine. The city celebrates its history as the "lumber capital of the world" with museums, monuments, and an annual folk music festival during the autumn. The University of Maine runs an art museum, and downtown Bangor maintains a flourishing arts scene, led by the Bangor Symphony Orchestra, the oldest community orchestra in the US. While easily accessible to tourists, the city is geared primarily toward residents, meaning lower prices and a low-key atmosphere—but problems finding a restaurant open downtown after 6pm.

▣ GETTING AROUND

Rte. 2 runs east-west through the heart of Bangor as **State St.** on the west side of Kenduskeag Stream, and **Hammond St.** on the east side. **Main St.** runs north-south along the Penobscot River, inter-

VITAL STATS

Population: 31,000

Visitor Info: Bangor Region Chamber of Commerce, 519 Main St. (☎207-947-0307; www.bangorregion.com). Open M-F 9am-5pm.

Internet Access: Bangor Public Library, 145 Harlow St. (☎207-947-8336). Open June 19-Sept. 7 M-Th 9am-7pm, F 9am-5pm; Sept. 8-June 20 M-Th 9am-9pm, F 9am-5pm.

Post Office: 202 Harlow St. (☎207-941-2016). Open M-F 7:30am-6pm, Sa 8am-1pm. **Postal Code:** 04401.

secting Hammond St. near the courthouse downtown. **I-95** and **I-395** intersect southwest of the city. There are several free 2hr. **parking** lots located downtown, and parking can also be found on most streets for free.

◉ SIGHTS

Most of the sights in Bangor center around the intersection formed by State, Hammond, and Main St. Walking to the Museum of Art, Maine Discovery Museum, Bangor Museum and Center for History, and Bangor Police Museum is easy, but reaching the Cole Land Transportation Museum and Leonard's Mills requires driving.

UNIVERSITY OF MAINE MUSEUM OF ART. In addition to works by more well-known artists such as Picasso, the museum maintains a permanent collection featuring Maine artists such as Winslow Homer and Andrew Wyeth. Containing over 5700 pieces of art, the museum also organizes a changing calendar of rotating exhibits. *(Norumbega Hall, 40 Harlow St. Walk west down State St. and take a right onto Harlow St. ☎207-561-3350. Open Su 11-5pm, Tu-Sa 9am-5pm. $3.)*

BANGOR MUSEUM AND CENTER FOR HISTORY. The Bangor Museum was born of the work of the Bangor Historical Society and has two locations: one on State St. that offers new exhibitions to showcase issues in Maine history, and the fully restored, 19th-century **Thomas A. Hill House.** The museum also runs several tours including the Mount Hope Cemetery Tour, the Candlelight Ghost Tour, the Downtown Bangor Architectural Tour, and a walking tour of downtown Bangor. *(6 State St. From City Hall, go west down State St.; the museum is just over the 1st bridge on your left.*

GREAT NORTH

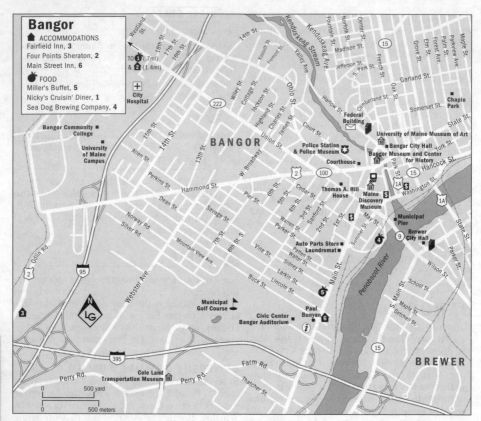

Bangor

🏠 ACCOMMODATIONS
Fairfield Inn, **3**
Four Points Sheraton, **2**
Main Street Inn, **6**

🍎 FOOD
Miller's Buffet, **5**
Nicky's Cruisin' Diner, **1**
Sea Dog Brewing Company, **4**

☎ 207-942-1900. Open Tu-Sa, 10am-4pm. Tours by appointment. Free. Thomas A. Hill House, 159 Union St. From the direction of City Hall, walk southwest down Main St. and take a right on Union St. ☎ 207-942-5766. Open Tu-Sa 10am-4pm. $5, children free.)

COLE LAND TRANSPORTATION MUSEUM.
The museum, spanning more than an acre, houses over 200 vehicles built or used in Maine, as well as Bangor's World War II Memorial and Vietnam Veterans Memorial. Knowledgeable volunteers provide free tours. (405 Perry Rd. Take Odlin Rd. south from Hammond St. to Perry Rd. and turn left. ☎ 207-990-3600. Open daily May to mid-Nov. 9am-5pm. $6, seniors $4, under 19 free. AAA discount.)

LEONARD'S MILLS. A historic reconstruction of a 1790s logging and milling community, the grounds include the **Maine Forest and Logging**

Museum, including a sawmill and log-cabin. "Living history days" are scheduled several times each summer, highlighting blacksmiths and woodsmen and holding events such as ax-throwing. The site also features a picnic ground, amphitheater, and a system of trails. (Located off of Rte. 178 in the Pembascot Experimental Forest. Take Union St. across the Pembascot River into Brewer, then take a left onto Rte. 178 through Brewer and Eddington into Bradley. Be sure to stay on Rte. 178 by veering left when it splits with Rte. 9. ☎ 207-581-2871. Always open. Free. Living history days $7, children $2.)

OTHER SITES. The **Maine Discovery Museum** offers fun learning opportunities for kids. (74 Main St. ☎ 207-262-7200. Open Su noon-5pm, Tu-Sa 9:30am-5pm. $5.50.) The **Police Museum** provides a more adult-oriented view of life in Bangor, with news clippings from the department's history. *(35 Court St. Open M-F 9am-5pm. Free.)*

 Check out the 3700 lb. statue of Paul Bunyan, at Buck and Main St., the largest representation of the legendary logger in the world. Made of steel and reinforced fiberglass, the 31-ft. statue contains a time capsule placed in 1959 to be opened on February 2, 2084 in honor of Bangor's 250th anniversary.

FOOD

A friendly waitstaff welcomes customers to **Miller's Buffet,** 427 Main St., a family restaurant praised by residents for its food and low prices. Miller's assimilates a little bit of everything from seafood ($13) to desserts ($2). The all-you-can-eat lunch buffet ($7) is popular. Miller's adjacent sister restaurant, **The Lion,** is slightly more refined and offers an excellent dinner buffet. (☎ 207-945-6361; www.millersrestaurant.com. Miller's open M-Th 11am-9pm, F-Sa 11am-10pm, Su 11:30am-8pm. The Lion open Tu-Th 5pm-8pm, F-Sa 5pm-9pm.) Overlooking the Pembascot River, the **Sea Dog Brewing Company,** 26 Front St., takes advantage of its locale with a covered deck looking out onto the water. The menu includes seafood from mussels ($7) to salmon ($15), as well as a few vegetarian options. The Sea Dog sundae ($5) is pure Maine decadence—cinnamon ice cream, ginger snaps, and caramel porter sauce. Try the Bluepaw Wheat Ale, made with local blueberries. (Follow May St. off of Main St. toward the river. ☎ 207-947-8004; www.seadogbrewing.com. Th open mic night. Open daily 11:30am-1am.) **Nicky's Cruisin' Diner,** 957 Union St., celebrates its diner character with records and license plates on the walls. Customers seat themselves to order classic American fare such as cold plates, cutlets, and breakfast all day long. Outside there is a takeout window with tuna melts ($7), fajita sandwiches ($6), and ice cream. Wednesday nights classic car owners gather to go cruisin.' (☎ 207-942-2430. Open daily 6am-9pm.)

ACCOMMODATIONS

Bangor has a fair share of hotel and motel chains, with most accommodations on **Odlin St.,** west of downtown near the airport. One of the few non-chain beds in town, the **Main Street Inn,** 480 Main St., features a helpful staff and a location with easy access to downtown Bangor. (☎ 207-942-5285. Continental breakfast included. Singles $45; doubles $51.) Catering to business travel, the **Four Points Sheraton,** 308 Godfrey Blvd., provides above-average sized rooms with little in the way of a view. Guests can get their parking stubs validated at the front desk. (Located in the airport parking lot, adjacent to the rental car lots. ☎ 207-947-6721. Singles July-Oct. from $129; Nov.-June from $109.) The **Fairfield Inn,** 300 Odlin Rd., has a gym, sauna, hot tub, and indoor pool available 24hr. (☎ 207-990-0001. Basic cable and A/C. Continental breakfast included. King-sized beds from $99; 2 double beds from $109. AAA discount.)

LEAVING BANGOR
Leaving Bangor, stay on **State St.** heading west, which becomes **U.S. 2** outside of town.

NEWPORT. Seventy-two miles from Bar Harbor, Newport refers to itself as the "Hub of Maine" because it sits at the intersection of S. 2 and the I-95 freeway. Stop here to enjoy beautiful **Sebasticook Lake. Christie's Campground,** 83 Christie's Campground Rd., 3 mi. east of town, accommodates tents and RVs and provides six comfortable cabins equipped with kitchen, picnic table, porch, and toilet. Christie's also offers fishing, boating, swimming, volleyball, basketball, as well as bike, paddle boat, canoe, and kayak rentals. (☎ 207-368-4645 or 800-688-5141. Open May-Nov. Lakefront sites $15-19, RV hookups $21; cabins $30 per person, 2nd night half-price. Day-use $2.)

THE ROAD TO SKOWHEGAN

About 16 mi. from Newport along U.S. 2, **Canaan's** main attraction is **The Charles Lindbergh Crate Museum,** 241 Easy St. This eccentric museum is a collection of Lindberghabilia displayed inside a giant packing crate—the one in which Charles Lindbergh's famous *Spirit of St. Louis* airplane was shipped back to America after he completed the first solo transatlantic flight in 1927. The museum is in the backyard of Larry Ross, who collected the memorabilia. (Follow Easy St. straight as it goes up a hill and past a trailer park. Look for a small sign on a mailbox. ☎207-474-984; larreb@somtel.com. Open by appointment only. Free.) Enjoy the view by the side of the Kennebec River at the Kennebec Banks Rest Stop, 2 mi. east of Skowhegan on U.S. 2, and take advantage of picnic tables. Near here is also the **Lake George Regional Park,** a great place for swimming, boating, and picnicking and relaxing on a sandy beach. From here it's about 9 mi. west to Skowhegan.

SKOWHEGAN

Skowhegan is the largest city between Bangor and St. Johnsbury, NH, but its biggest claim to fame is that it's the hometown of the **World's Tallest Indian Statue.** From the Chamber of Commerce, it's easy to see the 62 ft. statue tucked among the trees. He was erected by Bernard Langlais in 1969 in honor of Maine's Abnaki Indians and in observance of Maine's 150th year as a state. Sadly, the statue has fallen into disrepair, but the town has rallied around their tallest citizen and is raising funds to "Save the Indian." Also worth a stop in Skowhegan is the **Skowhegan History House,** 66 Elm St., a 1839 Greek Revival homestead turned into a museum of Skowhegan antiques and Civil War artifacts. (☎207-474-6632. Open June-Sept. Tu-F 1-5pm. Donations accepted.) The **Margaret Chase Smith Library,** 56 Norridgewock Ave., is a congressional research library honoring the first female senator. Lining the ceiling is the impressive display of the 95 robes from Ms. Smith's honorary degrees. (☎207-474-7133; ww.mcslibrary.org. Open M-F 10am-4pm.)

If you're driving by in the winter, hit the slopes at **Eaton Mountain Ski Resort,** 89 Lambert Rd. (☎207-474-2666; www.eatonmountain.com). Lights cover the mountain for night skiing, and the base lodge has equipment rentals as well as a restaurant, lounge, and game room.

🔺 APPROACHING FARMINGTON
From Skowhegan, it's about a 30 mi. jaunt along **U.S. 2** to Farmington. U.S. 2 bypasses downtown, so turn right to get onto **Main St.**

FARMINGTON

Farmington is home to the **University of Maine at Farmington,** one of the best public liberal arts colleges in the US. The presence of the college has turned Farmington into the cultural center of the region, but a quiet rural lifestyle still lingers. Farmington is the starting point for thousands who come to see the fall foliage, enjoy the area's many outdoor activities, or head to Sugarloaf Ski Resort, a 40min. drive north.

Downtown Farmington offers several upscale restaurants. **The Granary,** 23 Pleasant St., has a great view; diners sit on an inviting deck and look out onto the forested valley. The restaurant is also home of the **Narrow Gauge Brewing Company.** (Take a left onto Pleasant St. from Main St. ☎207-779-0710. Lunch $6-7. Dinner $13-17. Open M-Sa 11am-10pm, also Su brunch.) **Gifford's Ice Cream,** 293 Main St., is Maine right down to the last gooey drip, with flavors such as Maine Deer Tracks (vanilla, fudge, and peanut butter cup). A "small" cone is a heaping two scoops. (☎207-778-3617; www.giffordsicecream.com. Cones $1.50-2.85.) Motels are generally reasonably priced and located on Rte. 2, mostly on the west side of town.

🔺 LEAVING FARMINGTON
Leaving Farmington, head toward Rangeley by driving north out of town on **Rte. 4.** Be sure to check your gas in Farmington since the next convenient fill-up is in Rangeley, 41 mi. away.

🍴 QUAD M'S CABIN RESTAURANT
476 Fairbanks Rd. (Rte. 4)
2 mi. outside Farmington.

This quiet, log cabin-style country restaurant is a pleasant stop for food and conversation at almost any time of the day. Try your hand at the "Big Quad" for dinner—64 oz. of Black Angus sirloin. If you do manage to finish this hunk of meat, you get the next free. A takeout window also serves ice cream and limited offerings. (☎207-778-2776. Breakfast $3-5. Lunch $4-7. Dinner $9-12. Open M and W-Sa 6am-9pm, Su 6am-7pm.)

THE ROAD TO RANGELEY. Three miles outside the town of Madrid is a turnout where you can park at the base of a charming **waterfall.** Six miles from Madrid, roadtrippers can stretch cramped legs by hiking the **Appalachian Trail** to **Piazza Rock;** from where the trail crosses the road, it's an easy 1½ mi. trek through rolling woodland to an enormous, flat, overhanging boulder that looks suspended in mid-air. There are boulder caves and hidden picnic spots around the rock.

RANGELEY

The Rangeley area is home to 110 lakes and ponds, 150 mi. of snowmobile trails, and an assortment of eccentric artists and inquisitive moose. Rangeley is the largest hamlet on the lakes, and its one major street is the main drag of this pastoral corner of Maine. A 691-acre recreation area located on Rangeley Lake, **Rangeley Lake State Park** offers picnicking, swimming, a boat launch, a playground, hiking trails, restrooms, showers, and forested campsites. (From Rte. 4 take a left on South Shore Dr. The park turn-off is 5 mi. on the right. ☎207-862-3858l; www.campwithme.com. Check-in after 1pm. Check-out before 11am. Curfew 11pm. Open May-Sept. M-F 9am-4pm. Sites $15, non-Maine residents $20. Entrance fee $3, seniors and ages 5-11 $1, under 5 free.) For wintertime roadtrippers, **Saddleback Mountain's** location deep in Maine's snow belt means exceptional snow conditions. Skiers enjoy uncrowded, well-groomed trails, glade skiing, untracked powder, and natural snow trails. The drop of 1830 ft. places this mountain among Maine's largest. (☎207-864-5671; www.saddlebackskiarea.com.)

There are several dining options in Rangeley, but the locals adore the **Red Onion,** 77 Main St., for its Italian fare. Best known for its homemade fresh dough pizza, the Red Onion also serves sandwiches, vegetarian options, lasagna, and chicken parmesan. Meals and pizza are available to go. (☎207-864-5022. Open daily 11am-10pm.)

▰◤ **LEAVING RANGELEY**
Take **Pleasant St.** out of town; it turns into **Rte. 4/16.** Oquossoc is about 7 mi. west of Rangeley.

OQUOSSOC. Oquossoc is little more than a few stores at a crossroads; however, as lodging in the area can cost an arm and a leg, **Oquossoc's Own B&B,** 32 Rangeley Ave., is definitely worth a stop. The best deal around, the B&B has been open year-round since 1980. Repeat customers enjoy its cozy atmosphere and excellent food. Volleyball and croquet are available, as well as a grill for guest use and a living room that serves as a lounge. (7 mi. west of Rangeley along Rte. 4. ☎207-864-5584. Singles $40; doubles $70. Children under 6 free.) The **Bald Mountain Trail** is on Bald Mt. Rd., three-quarters of a mile south of Oquossoc off Rte. 4. Along this 1¾ mi. trail are picnic tables, and a 30 ft. lookout tower gives a 360° view of the surrounding mountains and lakes.

THE ROAD TO RUMFORD

From Oquossoc, head south on Rte 17. **Angel Falls,** 17 mi. south of Oquossoc on Rte. 17, is a scenic hanging falls, and its 90 ft. plummet onto the rocks below is one of the longest drops in the state. A small neighbor of Rumford, **Mexico** is the better of the two for dining. **Mexico Chicken Coop,** 32 Bridge St., has a shabby exterior that hides the good food inside. A family restaurant where chicken is king, the Coop is also known for its fried foods and fresh seafood. (☎207-364-2710. Lunch $3-5. Dinner $10-16. Open M-Th and Su 11am-8pm, F-Sa 11am-9pm.) Head south on **Rte. 17,** turning right after about 1 mi. to go west along **U.S. 2** into Rumford.

RUMFORD

Rumford looks like a city a century past its prime. If you can stand the smell of the Mead paper mill, New England's largest, it's worth seeing the second, shinier giant **Paul Bunyan Statue** along the trip. He stands in front of the **Rumford Chamber of Commerce,** 34 River St., on Rte. 2 just past the bridge. (☎207-364-3241. Open M-F 8am-4pm.) While you're in Rumford, peek over the bridge at the **Penacook Falls,** the tallest falls east of Niagara, with a drop of 180 ft.

Located in a Greek Revival building listed on the National Historic Registry, the small **Hotel Harris,** 25 Hartford St., rents rooms at hostel rates. Equipped for visitors planning an extended stay, rooms include refrigerators, microwaves, coffee pots, sinks, and ▨**8-track players.** Rooms are often used by out-of-towners working in the nearby paper mill, so they are more likely to be available on weekends. (☎207-364-7313. Singles $25; doubles $35.) About 4 mi. west of Rumford on Rte. 2 and the Androscoggin River is **Madison Resort Inn and Camping,** an inn, restaurant, and campground. It includes 60 units of motel rooms, as well as a pool, health club, sauna, waterfront nature trail, canoes, and riverside wooded campsites. (☎207-364-7973 or 800-258-6234; www.madisoninn.com. Live entertainment some evenings. RV hookups but no sewer. Rooms $40-60; sites $25.)

▰◤ **APPROACHING BETHEL**
Follow **U.S. 2** west out of Rumford. At **Newry,** 17 mi. from Rumford, it curves left; follow it, staying on U.S. 2 now going south. It's about 22 mi. to Bethel.

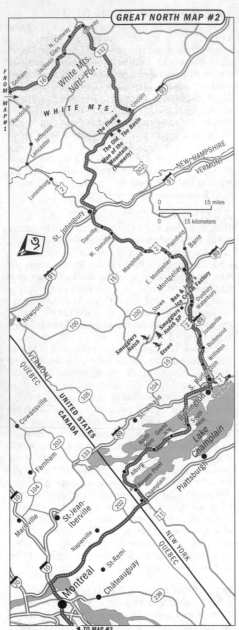

GREAT NORTH MAP #2

GREAT NORTH

ARTIST'S COVERED BRIDGE

Near the turn-off to Sunday River on U.S. 2, there's a picnic area with a covered bridge on the Androscoggin River. Past the ski resort, you'll find the **Artist's Covered Bridge** spanning the river, so called because it's so picturesque.

BETHEL. Bethel is one of Maine's most beautiful mountain villages. Nearby, along U.S. 2, is the **Sunday River Ski Resort** (☎207-824-3000; www.sundayriver.com). Skiers enjoy 126 trails, which are available for hiking and biking in the summer. The **Crossroads Diner and Deli,** on U.S. 2 at Parkway just before the turn-off to downtown, offers daily specials. (☎207-824-3673. Breakfast $3-5. Sandwiches and soups $4-5. Blue-plate dinner specials $6-9. Open Su-Th 5:30am-8pm, F-Sa 5:30am-9pm.) **The Inn at Rostay,** 186 Mayville Rd., has ski cabins with hand-sewn quilts. The inn is the closest motel to Sunday River, and the main house serves a country breakfast for $5 and a three-course dinner for $12. (Located on U.S. 2, 1 mi. east of town. ☎888-754-0072 or 207-824-3111; www.rostay.com. Rooms in winter M-F $50-60, Sa-Su from $100; in summer $60; in spring $45-50.)

LEAVING BETHEL

After Bethel, **U.S. 2** continues west, entering New Hampshire near **Shelburne.**

Welcome To NEW HAMPSHIRE

THE ROAD TO GORHAM. About 16 mi. from Bethel, Shelburne is best known for the **Shelburne Birches,** part of the White Mountain National Forest. The **White Birches Camping Park,** 218 U.S. 2, is a place to camp if you're in a bind, offering tent sites and a pool. (☎603-466-2022. Sites $17; full hookup $27.) If you can stand to drive a bit longer, try the **Moosehead Lake State Park** west of Gorham instead. (☎603-466-2022. Office open 8am-10pm. Sites $11; $5 per additional person.) Leaving Shelburne, continue west along U.S. 2.

APPROACHING GORHAM

Six miles from Shelburne, **U.S. 2** passes through Gorham as **Main St.**

GORHAM

Gorham is the gateway to the **White Mountains National Forest,** set at the crossroads of U.S. 2 and Rte. 16. The railroad capital of the White Mountains, Gorham celebrates its past in the **Train Within a Train** exhibit, 25 Railroad St., behind the info office and playground. Inside an actual granary boxcar, a computerized, miniature Androscoggin Valley train system is fully operational. A variety of railroad paraphernalia can be found in another boxcar as well as in the nearby depot, which also serves as the town's historical museum. (Open daily May-Nov. 1-5pm. Donations requested.) Also near Gorham, 44 clean campsites sit off the highway at **Moose Brook State Park,** 30 Jimtown Rd. The park's great location positions campers between the park and nearby cities. Moose Brook and Perkins Brook run through the campground with walking trails leading along the banks and a swimming and picnic area close by. (1 mi. west of Gorham. Turn north onto Jimtown Rd. and follow it for 1 mi.; the office is on the right. ☎603-271-3628. Check-in 1-8pm. Check-out noon. Open May to mid-Oct. Sites $15 for 2 adults and children; $7.50 per additional adult. No hookups.)

Turkey is the business at **Wilfred's & News Room Pub,** 114 Main St. (U.S. 2), in downtown Gorham, and business is good. The best place to eat in Gorham, Wilfred's serves lunch and dinner. (☎603-466-2380. Entrees $6-10. Open M-Tu and Th-Su 11am-9pm.) Offering clean, simple rooms, the **Gorham Motor Inn,** 324 Main St. (U.S. 2), west of town, is the cheapest accommodation in town. (☎603-466-3381. Rooms $38-48.)

LEAVING GORHAM

Turn left from **Main St.** onto **Rte. 16,** which will take you into the White Mountain National Forest.

THE ROAD THROUGH THE WHITE MOUNTAINS

Driving south from Gorham, Rte. 16 winds its way deep into the **White Mountain National Forest.** Occupying 780,000 acres of national forest maintained by the US Forest Service, the White Mountains provide an immense playground for outdoor enthusiasts. The White Mountains are an attractive destination throughout the year, offering excellent skiing, hiking, camping, canoeing, kayaking, and fishing. The forest also holds geological wonders and provides a refuge for moose and black bears. From Gorham, it's about 30 mi. south to **North Conway,** past Mt. Washington and through the small towns of **Jackson** and **Glen.**

For more info on the area, the **Appalachian Mountain Club (AMC)** operates a Visitors Center in Pinkham Notch (see below). Any unattended vehicle (except vehicles at national forest campground sites) parked on White Mountain National Forest land must display a **parking pass** (☎603-528-8721; $5 per week) sold by the US Forest Service and the AMC as well as the **White Mountain Attraction Center,** off Exit 32 from I-93, in North Woodstock. (☎603-745-8720. Open daily July-Sept. 8:30am-6pm; Apr.-July and Sept. to mid-Oct. 8:30am-5:30pm; mid-Oct. to Apr. 8:30am-5pm.)

PINKHAM NOTCH

Pinkham Notch, New Hampshire's easternmost notch, lies in the shadow of the tallest mountain in the Northeast—the 6288 ft. **Mt. Washington.** Pinkham's proximity to the peak makes it more crowded and less peaceful than some neighboring towns, but secluded areas can still be found not too far off the beaten path. The **AMC's Pinkham Notch Visitors Center** lies between Gorham and Jackson on Rte. 16. (☎603-466-2727; www.outdoors.org. Open daily 6:30am-10pm.) Stretching from just behind the Pinkham Notch Visitors Center all the way up to the summit of Mt. Washington, **Tuckerman's Ravine Trail** demands 4-5hr. of steep hiking each way. Mt. Washington is one of the most dangerous small mountains in the world due to the highly unpredictable weather, including high winds that reach hurricane force frequently. Authorities urge caution when climbing. It has never been recorded to be warmer than 72°F atop Mt. Washington, and the average temperature on the peak is a bone-chilling 26.9°F. The summit also boasts the highest wind speed ever recorded at 231 mph. With proper measures, however, the trek up the mountain is stellar. Those lucky enough to hike on a clear day are rewarded with a view of five states and Canada. A less daunting option is the **Lion's Head Trail,** which diverges from the Tuckerman's Ravine Trail about 2 mi. in.

Adventurous roadtrippers can take the **Mt. Washington Auto Road,** a paved and dirt road that winds 8 mi. to the summit. The road begins 3 mi. north of the Visitors Center on Rte. 16. Owners of vehicles sturdy enough to reach the top receive bragging rights in the form of a free "This Car Climbed Mt. Washington" bumper sticker. (☎603-466-3988. Road open daily June-Aug. 7:30am-6pm; May-June and Sept.-Oct. 8am-5pm. $18 per car; free audio tour included. $7 per additional passenger, ages 5-12 $4.) If you are afraid (or confident) that your car might not make it, tours are available through **Great Glen Stage Tours,** across Rte. 16 from the Auto Road. (☎603-466-2333. Tours daily 8:30am-5pm. $24, seniors $22, ages 5-11 $11.)

Many of the region's lodging options are on or near Mt. Washington. Accessible by car, the **Joe Dodge Lodge,** immediately behind the Pinkham Notch Visitors Center, offers over 100 comfortable bunks, including seven family rooms, as well as a library and living room. (☎603-466-2727. Breakfast and dinner included. Reservations recommended. Rooms in summer $55, under 16 $37; in low-season $52/$34. 2-person private rooms $70-74, for 4 or more $89-97.)

NORTH CONWAY

With its proximity to ski resorts in winter, foliage in the fall, and hiking and shopping year-round, North Conway is one of New Hampshire's most popular vacation destinations. Rte. 16, the traffic-infested main road, is home to outlet stores as well as a variety of smaller local shops. The town of Conway, a little farther south, has fewer touristy shops but excellent meal and lodging options.

> ## (VITAL STATS)
>
> **Population:** 2100
>
> **Visitor Info: Mt. Washington Valley Chamber of Commerce and Visitors Bureau,** P.O. Box 2300 (☎800-367-3364; www.mtwashingtonvalley.org).
>
> **Internet Access: North Conway Public Library,** 2719 White Mtn. Hwy. (☎603-356-2861). Open M-Tu and Th-F 9am-5pm, W 9am-7pm.
>
> **Post Office:** 78 Grove St. (☎603-356-2293). Open M-F 9am-5pm, Sa 9am-noon. **Postal Code:** 03860.

▐ GETTING AROUND. North Conway is about 28 mi. south of Gorham and 5 mi. north of Conway, along **Rte. 16** and **U.S. 302.** In North Conway, Rte. 16 and U.S. 302 merge, running through town as the main drag. Conway sits near the junction of U.S. 302, Rte. 16, **Rte. 112,** and **Rte. 153.**

▟ OUTDOOR ACTIVITIES. Numerous stores in the North Conway area rent outdoor equipment. For ski goods in winter or biking gear during other seasons, **Joe Jones,** 2709 White Mtn. Hwy., in North Conway, has it all. (☎603-356-9411. Open daily July-Aug. 9am-8pm; Sept.-Nov. and Apr.-June Su-Th 10am-6pm, F-Sa 9am-6pm; Dec.-Mar. M-F 8:30am-6pm, Sa-Su 8:30am-8pm. Alpine skis, boots, and poles $20 per day, $36 for 2 days; cross-country equipment $15/$26; snowboards $20/$38. Bikes $25 per day.) A second branch, **Joe Jones North** (☎603-356-6848), lies a few miles north of town on Rte. 302. **Eastern Mountain Sports (EMS),** just north on White Mtn. Hwy. in the lobby of the Eastern Slope Inn, sells camping equipment and rents tents (2-person $15 per day, $20 for 3 days; 4-person $20/$25), sleeping bags ($15/$20), snowshoes, packs, and skis. The knowledgeable staff happily provides first-hand info on climbing and hiking, and offers a summer climbing school. (☎603-356-5433. Open June-Sept. M-Sa 8:30am-9pm, Su 8:30am-6pm; Oct.-May Su-Th 8:30am-6pm, F-Sa 8:30am-9pm.)

▟ FOOD. For sports fans who will appreciate the autographed bats and other sports paraphernalia, **Delaney's,** to the north of town along Rte. 16, is the place to stop. Enjoy a sandwich and fries for $7-11. (☎603-356-7776. Open daily 11:30am-11pm.) A bagful of penny candy from **Zeb's General Store** can help you keep up your energy while exploring the shop, which sells New England staples, from maple syrup to moose memorabilia. Thirsty tourists might partake of the $1 homemade soda. (☎603-356-9294. Open daily mid-June to Dec. 9am-10pm; off-season hours vary.) Adjacent to Olympia Sports in the center of North Conway, **Morning Dew** caffeinates the local populace. This hole-in-the-wall coffee shack offers bagels ($1), juice ($1.50), and the daily paper in addition to a variety of coffees ($1-2.50), teas, and steamers. (☎603-356-9366. Open daily 7am-5pm.) Several miles south in Conway, pink, green, and purple paint decorate the walls and ceilings of **Cafe Noche,** 147 Main St., while colorful paper cutouts flutter through the air. Local patrons recommend the Montezuma Pie (Mexican lasagna; $8.50) or the garden burger ($4.25) among the multitude of authentic Mexican options. (☎603-447-5050. Open daily 11:30am-9pm.)

ACCOMMODATIONS. Located in the heart of Conway and maintained by incredibly friendly folk, the ◪White Mountains Hostel (HI-AYH), 36 Washington St., off Rte. 16 at the intersection of Rte. 153, is kept meticulously clean and environmentally friendly. The hostel has 43 comfy bunks, a kitchen, and common room. Each bed comes with clean linen and a pillow. (☎603-447-1001. Light breakfast included. Laundry $3. Reception 7:30-10am and 5-10pm. Check-out 10am. Reservations recommended. Dorms $22, nonmembers $25; private rooms $48.) The hostel at the beautiful **Cranmore Mt. Lodge,** 859 Kearsarge Rd., in North Conway, has 22 bunks. The lodge is about 2 mi. from downtown, but the living room, pool, jacuzzi, cable TV, refrigerator, and duck pond that are at the disposal of guests justify the trip. Be sure to bring a warm blanket to protect against the nightly temperature drop. (☎603-356-2044 or 800-356-3596. Linens and towel $3. Check-in 3-11pm. Check-out 11am. Dorms $20.)

> If you camp, be aware that **bears** are a threat. Keep food hung and well away from sleeping areas, and do not keep anything food-scented in or near your tent. **Moose** can be a danger for drivers as well, so keep a watchful eye.

LEAVING NORTH CONWAY
From North Conway, take **Rte. 16** 5 mi. south to Conway. In Conway, take a right to head west on **Rte. 112,** also known as **Kancamagus Scenic Hwy.**

THE KANCAMAGUS SCENIC HIGHWAY. The 35 mi. stretch of Rte. 112 between Conway and Lincoln is known as the ◪Kancamagus Scenic Hwy. It requires at least 1hr. to drive, though the vistas typically lure drivers to the side of the road or to one of the many scenic outlooks for a picnic. Check gas at Conway, as none is available for 35 mi., then head west on the clearly marked Kanc to enjoy the scenic splendor all the way to Lincoln.

LEAVING LINCOLN
In Lincoln, **Rte. 112** is also known as **Main St.** From Main St., merge onto **I-93** going north to pass through the Franconia area of the White Mountains on the way to St. Johnsbury.

THE ROAD TO ST. JOHNSBURY

Imposing granite cliffs, formed by glacial movements that began during an ice age 400 million years ago, tower on either side of the **Franconia Notch Pkwy. (I-93)** and create one of the more scenic spots in the White Mountains. Traveling north from Lincoln on I-93, ◪The Flume, Exit 34A on I-93, is a 2 mi. walk cutting through a spectacular granite gorge. Although only 12-20 ft. apart, the moss-covered canyon walls are 70-90 ft. high. Take a leisurely stroll over centuries-old covered bridges and past the 345 ft. **Avalanche Falls.** Tickets can be purchased from the **The Flume Visitors Center,** where a 15min. film acquaints visitors with the landscape and geology of the area. (☎603-745-8391; www.flumegorge.com. Open daily May-June and Sept.-Oct. 9am-5pm; July-Aug. 9am-5:30pm. $8, ages 6-12 $5.) Between Exits 34A and 34B on I-93, visitors can find a well-marked turn-off for **The Basin.** Here a 5-10min. walk will take you to a 20 ft. whirlpool that has been carved out of a massive base of granite by a 15 ft. waterfall.

For years **Franconia,** 10 mi. north of Lincoln, has been well known as the home of the **Old Man of the Mountain,** but in May 2003, the profile fell from its perch. The viewing areas at Exit 34B on I-93 and between Exit 34A and 34B on I-93 are still open and explain the Old Man's fall.

CANNON MOUNTAIN AERIAL TRAMWAY AND NEW ENGLAND SKI MUSEUM
10 mi. north of Lincoln. Take exit 34B off I-93.

The 80-passenger **Cannon Mountain Aerial Tramway,** climbs over 2000 ft. in 7min. and carries visitors to the summit of the **Cannon Cliff,** a 1000 ft. sheer drop into the cleft between Mt. Lafayette and Cannon Mountain. The tram offers unparalleled vistas of Franconia Notch along its ascent. Once at the top, a short walk will bring you to an **observation tower** (over 4200 ft.) overlooking the Notch. (☎603-823-8800. Open daily mid-May to mid-Oct. and mid-Dec. to mid-Apr. 9am-5pm. Trains run every 15min. Round-trip $10, ages 6-12 $6. One-way $8.) In winter, the tram takes skiers up the mountain, which has 58 trails. (Ski pass M-F $34, Sa-Su $45.) Right next to the tramway station sits the one-room **New England Ski Museum,** with old photographs and a display of skis through the ages. (☎603-823-7177. Open daily mid-May to mid-Oct. and mid-Dec. to mid-Apr. noon-5pm. Free.)

GREAT NORTH

Welcome To VERMONT

APPROACHING ST. JOHNSBURY

Head north through Littleton on **I-93**. Soon, you'll cross the Connecticut River to Vermont. Exit for **Rte. 18** (Exit 1) and bear right, then take a left onto **U.S. 2**, also known here as **Portland Rd.**

ST. JOHNSBURY

St. Johnsbury is a town built on a hill with steep streets that resemble those of San Francisco. The booming economy that built St. Johnsbury was based on maple and platform scales. Enduring prosperity, however, has eluded the town—although St. Johnsbury is conveniently located at the junctions of U.S. 2 and U.S. 5, Interstates 91 and 93, and the Maine Central and Canadian Pacific railroads, the economy has never regained its former glory. The upside is that this has protected the town from the clutches of chain stores.

VITAL STATS

Population: 7600

Visitor Info: Northeast Kingdom Chamber of Commerce, 357 Western Ave. (☎802-748-3678 or 800-639-6379; www.nekchamber.com).

Internet Access: St. Johnsbury Athenaeum, 1171 Main St. (☎802-748-8291). Open M and W 10am-8pm; Tu and Th-F 10am-5:30pm, Sa 10am-4:30pm.

Post Office: 1153 Main St. (☎802-748-3301). Open M-F 8am-5pm, Sa 9am-noon. **Postal Code:** 05819.

GETTING AROUND. U.S. 2 comes into town from the east over a bridge and heads uphill to **Main St.,** which is lined with Victorian mansions. Spanning the bottom of the hill is **Railroad St.,** while Main St. covers the top of the hill.

SIGHTS. The **Fairbanks Museum,** 1302 Main St., has one of the nicest collections of impressive odds and ends in New England, hence its affectionate nickname, the "Cabinet of Curiosi-

ties." The museum was given as a gift to the town of St. Johnsbury from Franklin Fairbanks, the inventor of Fairbanks platform scales. The museum now sits in a splendid Victorian mansion, the cornerstone of the **Main St. Historic District.** Inside is a collection of North American wildlife and birds, the Northern New England Weather Center, and artifacts from all over the globe. The creepy-crawliest exhibit is John Hampson's "bug art"—a series of nine painstakingly crafted pieces, such as a portrait of Abe Lincoln, made out of thousands of shimmering bugs. (☎802-748-2372. Open M-Sa 9am-5pm, Su 1-5pm. $5, seniors $4.) A short distance from the intersection of U.S. 2 and Main St. is the **St. Johnsbury Athenaeum, Art Gallery, and Public Library,** 30 Main St. (☎802-748-8291. Open M-F 10am-5:30pm. Free.) Also in downtown St. Johnsbury is the **Octagon** building and annex. The structure now houses offices for the Air Force, army, and marines—there isn't much to tour, but the 1854 building is worth look just for its odd shape. If you are visiting in March or April, you may be lucky enough to see maple syrup being tapped. An alternative to the real thing is to visit the **Maple Grove Farms,** 1052 Portland St., the largest packager of maple syrup in the US. Here, visitors can tour a museum, tasting room, and candy factory. (1 mi. east of town on U.S. 2. ☎802-748-5141; www.maplegrove.com. Open M-F 10am-2pm. In fall 1hr. tours every 15min. $1, under 13 free.)

 The **World's Largest Can of Maple Syrup,** a 10 ft. metallic can emblazoned with the Maple Grove logo, can be found at the Maple Grove Farms.

FOOD & ACCOMMODATIONS. A typical diner, **Anthony's Diner,** 321 Railroad St., serves sandwiches ($5) and dinners. Try the Exploring Salad ($8.25) with Maple Grove Sweet and Sour salad dressing. (☎802-748-3613. Open M-Th 6:30am-8pm, F-Sa 6:30am-8:30pm, Su 7am-4pm.) In the world of inexplicably expensive St. Johnsbury lodging, **Aime's Motel,** 46 Rte. 18, 3 mi. east of St. Johnsbury, offers an affordable alternative. Creekside cabins have large, sparsely decorated rooms and covered porches. (☎802-748-3194 or 800-504-6663. Rooms in fall $87; summer $47-57; in winter and spring $42.)

LEAVING ST. JOHNSBURY
Head west along **Main St.** toward St. John's Academy, then turn right at the signs for **U.S. 2.**

AMERICAN SOCIETY OF DOWSERS
Off U.S. 2 in Danville. 184 Brainerd St.

At the national headquarters of the 4000-member American Society of Dowsers you can observe the art of dowsing, which uses forked sticks or pendulums to find water under the ground. Walking around the backyard labyrinth clears the mind for the necessary "sensitivity and awareness" for proper dowsing. (☎ 802-684-3417. Open M-F 9am-5pm. Membership $35 per year; $53 per family.)

GREAT VERMONT CORN MAZE
From Danville, take Hill St./Badger Hwy. north from the blinking light at Danville, and continue for 5 mi. From North Danville, take McReynolds Rd. (100 ft.), Old North Church Rd. (3 mi.) and Wheelock Rd. (1 mi.).

Spelled out in a cornfield in North Danville is the word "Vermont." For those in the know, the design is just a part of the Great Vermont Corn Maze, 2 mi. of pathways and 5 acres of an a"maize"ingly perplexing cornfield. The first two weekends of October, the Haunted Maze opens in the spirit of Halloween. Victims take a hayride to the site where they walk half a mile through haunted forest and cornfield. A "Starlight Maze" is available for an added challenge. (☎ 802-748-1399. Open daily mid July-Sept. 10am-5pm; early Oct. 10am-4pm and 6-10:30pm. Last entry 1hr. before closing. $7, ages 4-11 $5.)

MAPLE VALLEY COUNTRY STORE & CAFE
19 mi. from Danville, in Plainfield, on U.S. 2.

At this hippie-flavored local hangout, roadtrippers cruising through early should try the breakfast sandwich (tofu, sprouts and tomato; $4.25). Also excellent are the veggie burgers ($3) or the smoothies made with Ben & Jerry's ($3.50-5). The store is also home to a gift shop and serves pizza. (☎ 802-454-8626. Breakfast $2-4. Lunch and dinner $3-9. Open daily 6am-8pm.)

APPROACHING MONTPELIER
U.S. 2 approaches Montpelier about 29 mi. from Danville. Exit U.S. 2 at **Main St.**

MONTPELIER

Chartered in 1781, Montpelier became the capital of Vermont in 1805. For decades, the community has made efforts to restore historical buildings and locally owned businesses. Now, a beautiful capitol dome shines over the city, and the downtown bursts with cafes, markets, and bookstores. Although Montpelier is the smallest state capital, visiting the city is still enjoyable.

VITAL STATS

Population: 8000

Visitor Info: Central Vermont Chamber of Commerce, at Paine Turnpike and Berlin St. (☎ 802-229-5711 or 802-229-4619; www.central-vt.com). Open M-F 9am-5pm.

Internet Access: Kellogg-Hubbard Library, 135 Main St. (☎ 802-223-3338). Open M-Th 10am-8pm, F 10am-5:30pm, Sa 10am-1pm.

Post Office: 87 State St. (☎ 802-229-1718). Open M-F 8am-5:30pm, Sa 8am-2pm. **Postal Code:** 05602.

GETTING AROUND. U.S. 2 skirts the city's southern edge, tracing the north bank of the Winooski River. From the east, a right on **Main St.** leads to downtown. U.S. 2 turns into Main St. briefly, and then continues west as **State St.** Continuing straight after the intersection of U.S. 2 and Main St. puts you on **Memorial Dr.,** which roughly parallels U.S. 2 on the other side of the river.

SIGHTS. The best views of Montpelier and the countryside come from the 54 ft. observation tower in **Hubbard Park,** on Hubbard Park Dr., the highest point in the city. The park has nearly 180 wooded acres for hiking and cross-country skiing. (From Memorial Dr. head north onto Bailey Ave., then turn right on Hubbard Park Dr.) **Morse Farm Maple Sugarworks,** 1168 County Rd., is home to the oldest maple family in Vermont. See the trees and take the tour to learn how many gallons of sap it takes to make syrup. A "creatures exhibit" stars Hoover the pig and Blackberry Muffin the lamb. (Take Main St. 2½ mi. north of town and turn right on County Rd. ☎ 800-242-2740; www.morse-farm.com. Open daily summer 8am-8pm; winter 9am-5pm. Free tours and tastings.)

⧉⧉ FOOD & ACCOMMODATIONS. The **New England Culinary Institute**'s three restaurants in Montpelier are also classrooms; students-in-training spend weeks and months cooking and training in each location. The **Main St. Grill**, 118 Main St., serves American fare at reasonable prices. (☎802-223-3188. Open M-F 11:30am-2pm and 5:30-9pm, Sa 11am-2pm and 5:30-9pm, Su 10am-2pm and 5:30-9pm.) The **Chef's Table**, 118 Main St., is a slightly upscale version of the Main St. Grill. (☎802-229-9202. Open M-F 11:30am-1:30pm and 5:30-9:30pm, Sa 5:30-9:30pm.) **La Brioche**, 89 Main St., lets students experiment with bakery food; they prepare eye-pleasing cakes, pastries, and sandwiches. (☎802-229-0443. Open M-F 7am-7pm, Sa 8am-5:30pm, Su 8am-5pm.) **Sarducci's**, 3 Main St., dishes out Italian cuisine from a wood-burning oven. Food is served on a deck over the Winooski River. (☎802-223-0229. Lunch $6-8. Dinner $8-16. Open M-Sa 11am-10pm, Su 4:30-10pm.)

Betsy's B&B, 74 E. State St., is a Victorian home downtown. Offering bay windows, wood floors, antique furnishings, and oriental rugs, Betsy's has been recognized for its exemplary environmental management. Betsy's serves Vermont breakfasts of blueberry pancakes with maple syrup or omelettes filled with Cabot cheese. (Take a right off Main St. onto E. State St. ☎802-229-0466; www.betsysbnb.com. All rooms with private baths. Rooms $65-105.)

⛑ APPROACHING WATERBURY
Between Montpelier and Waterbury, 12 mi. down the road, **U.S. 2** is a windy drive paralleling **I-89.**

WATERBURY

Waterbury sits on the banks of the Winooski River, where mountain peaks rise on the horizon. Every trip warrants a stop at the ▧**Ben & Jerry's Factory,** 30 Community Dr. Ben & Jerry's premium ice cream all began with two schoolboys running at the back of the pack in gym class. In 1978, armed with diplomas from a $5 ice cream-making correspondence course at Penn State, they converted an abandoned gas station into their first ice cream parlor, launching a double-scoop success story. Whether you're into "Karamel Sutra" or just "Makin' Whoopie Pie," the 30min. tours give you a taste of the founders' passion, ending with free samples. Behind the factory sits the ice cream graveyard, a collection of tombstones for discontinued flavors. (Take Exit 10 from I-89, then go

north for 1 mi. on Rte. 100. ☎802-846-1500. Open daily Nov.-May 10am-5pm; June 9am-5pm; July-Aug. 9am-8pm; Aug.-Oct. 9am-6pm. $3, seniors $2, under 13 free.) The **Ziemke Glass Blowing Studio,** 3033 Stowe Rd. (Rte. 100), is also worth a stop. (☎802-224-6126. Demonstrations M-Tu and Th-Su 10am-5pm. Open daily 10am-6pm.)

Waterbury also offers a collection of hotels, B&Bs, and restaurants, both chain and non-chain. The **Waterbury Tourism Council** runs an info booth on the side of Rte. 100, about a quarter mi. north of the intersection with I-89.

⛑ APPROACHING STOWE
From Waterbury, it's a short but delicious 10 mi. north on **Rte. 100** to Stowe.

STOWE

Stowe curves gracefully up the side of Mt. Mansfield, Vermont's highest peak (4393 ft.). A mecca for outdoor enthusiasts in all seasons, but especially during the winter, the village tries to live up to its aspirations as a ritzy European skiing hot spot. In fact, Stowe has an obsession with all things Austrian; nowhere is this more clear than in the proliferation of Austrian-style chalets and restaurants sprouting off the mountain's road.

╭─ VITAL STATS ─╮

Population: 4300

Visitor Info: Stowe Area Association, 51 Main St. (☎802-253-7321 or 800-247-8693; www.gostowe.com). Open June to mid-Oct. and mid-Dec. to Mar. M-Sa 9am-8pm, Su 9am-5pm; mid-Oct. to mid-Dec. and Apr.-May M-F 9am-5pm.

Internet Access: Stowe Free Library, 90 Pond St. (☎802-253-6145). Open M, W, F 9:30am-5:30pm; Tu and Th 2-7pm; Sa 10am-3pm.

Post Office: 105 Depot St. (☎802-253-7521). Open M-F 7:15am-5pm, Sa 9am-noon. **Postal Code:** 05672.

⬛ GETTING AROUND. Stowe is located 10 mi. north of I-89 Exit 10, 27 mi. southwest of Burlington. The ski slopes lie along **Mountain Rd. (Rte. 108),** northwest of Stowe.

⚑ OUTDOOR ACTIVITIES. In summer, Stowe's frenetic pace drops off some, but it still burns with the energy of outdoor enthusiasts. **Action Outfitters,** 2160 Mountain Rd., can serve nearly all recreation needs. (☎802-253-7975. Open daily May-Oct. 9am-5pm; Nov.-Apr. 8am-6pm. Mountain bikes $16 per half-day, $24 per full day; in-line skates $12/$18; Canoes $25/$30.) Stowe's 5½ mi. asphalt **recreation path** runs parallel to Mountain Rd.'s ascent and begins behind the church on Main St. Perfect for biking, skating, and strolling in summer, the path accommodates cross-country skiing and snowshoeing in winter. A few miles past Smuggler's Notch on Mountain Rd. (Rte. 108), the road shrinks to one lane and winds past huge boulders and 1000 ft. high cliffs.

Fly fishermen should head to the **Fly Rod Shop,** 2½ mi. south of Stowe on Rte. 100, to pick up the necessary fishing licenses, rent fly rods and reels, and enroll in the free fly-fishing classes in the shop's pond. (☎802-253-7346 or 800-535-9763. Open M-F 9am-6pm, Sa 9am-4pm, Su 10am-4pm; Nov.-Mar. until 5pm. Classes W 4-6pm and Sa 9am-11am. Rods and reels $15 per day. Licenses $15 per day.) **Umiak,** on Rte. 100, three-fourths of a mile south of Stowe Center, rents kayaks and canoes in the summer. During the snowy season, Umiak runs moonlight snowshoeing tours with wine and cheese served. (☎802-253-2317. Open daily 9am-6pm; winter hours vary. Snowshoe tours $39. River trips $38. Kayaks $12 per hr., $24 for 4hr.; canoes $18/$34.)

◢ **SKIING.** Every winter, skiers pour onto the Northeast's finest slopes. **Stowe Mountain Resort** (☎802-253-3000 or 800-253-4754; www.stowe.com) offers one-day lift tickets for $60, 48 trails (16% beginner, 59% intermediate, 25% expert), and impressive summer facilities: a golf course and country club, alpine slides, a gondola, a scenic toll road ($16 per car), and a skate park. The hills are alive with cross-country skiing on 60km of groomed trails and 45km of backcountry skiing at the **Von Trapp Family Lodge,** 2 mi. off Mountain Rd., accessed from Luce Hill Rd. Budget travelers beware: lodging prices soar in high season. However, there's no charge to visit, and rentals and lessons are inexpensive. (☎802-253-5719 or 800-826-7000. Trail fee $16. Ski rentals $18. Lessons $15-45 per hr. Ski school package includes all 3 for $40.) **AJ's Ski and Sports,** 350 Mountain Rd., rents equipment. (☎802-253-4593 or 800-226-6257. Skis, boots, and poles: downhill $26 per day, cross-country $15. Snowboard and boots $22. Open winter Su-Th 8am-8pm, F-Sa 8am-9pm; summer daily 9am-6pm.)

For complete info on skiing statewide, contact **Ski Vermont,** 26 State St., P.O. Box 368, Montpelier 05601. (☎802-223-2439; www.skivermont.com. Open M-F 7:45am-4:45pm.) Cheaper lift tickets can be found during low season—before mid-December and after mid-March.

▰▰ **FOOD & NIGHTLIFE.** The ◳**Depot Street Malt Shoppe,** 57 Depot St., is reminiscent of decades past. Sports pennants and vinyl records line the walls, while rock favorites liven up the outdoor patio seating. The cost of a 1950s-style cherry or vanilla Coke has been adjusted for inflation, but prices remain reasonable. (☎802-253-4269. Meals $3-6. Open daily 11:30am-9pm.) Perfect for picnics, **Mac's Deli,** located in Mac's Stowe Market, on S. Main St., has tasty sandwiches, subs,

THE ROCKY ROAD TO STOWE

Rte. 100 features a bona fide food fiesta south of Stowe. Begin at **Ben & Jerry's** and drive north on Rte. 100. The first stop is the Cabot Annex Store, home to **Lake Champlain Chocolates** and the **Cabot Creamery Cooperative.** The annex is bursting at the seams with rich chocolate truffles and Vermont cheddar and provides free samples of both. (☎802-241-4150. Open daily 9am-6pm.) Leave room for **Cold Hollow Cider Mill;** in addition to free samples of cider, jams, and jellies, you can pick up $0.40 doughnuts, crunchy and sweetened with apple nectar. (☎800-327-7537; www.coldhollow.com. Call for a cider-making schedule Sept.-Oct. Open daily 8am-7pm.) Free fudge samples go down easy in the **Waterbury Center** next door. The adjacent **Grand View Winery** offers wine and hard cider sampling for $1. (☎802-456-7012. Tasting daily 11am-5pm.) **Stowe Maple Products** sells home-harvested goods all year. (☎802-253-2508. Open M-Sa 9am-5pm, Su 10am-4pm.)

GREAT NORTH

and wraps ($3-5) made with any of the meats and cheeses in the market's deli selection. Mac's also serves piping hot soups for $2-3. (☎802-253-4576. No seating. Open M-Sa 7am-9pm, Su 7am-8pm.) Fans of little green men and all things not of this planet will enjoy **Pie in the Sky,** 492 Mountain Rd. "Out of This World" pizzas include such works as the "Blond Vermonter" with olive oil, Vermont cheddar, apples, and ham. (☎802-253-5100. Pizza $8-17. Open daily 11:30am-10pm.)

For sports fans, the **Sunset Grille and Tap Room,** 140 Cottage Club Rd., off Mountain Rd., allows its guests to face off at air hockey and pool tables while following sporting events on over 15 TVs. The adjacent restaurant offers barbecue. (☎802-253-9281. Lunch $4-9. Dinner $10-15. Kitchen open daily 11:30am-midnight. Bar open until 2am.) The weekday specials and six homemade microbrews served up in **The Shed,** 1859 Mountain Rd., make this brewery stand out. (☎802-253-4364. Tu night $2.50 pint night. Open daily 11:30am-midnight.)

⚑ ACCOMMODATIONS. Easy access is one of many reasons to stay at the **Stowe Bound Lodge,** 645 S. Main St., located a half mile south of the intersection of Rte. 100 and 108. The friendly owners make travelers feel at ease with their engaging conversation and comfortable common space with a piano and fireplace. (☎802-253-4515. Rooms with shared bath $20 per person.) **Foster's Place,** 4968 Mountain Rd., offers dorm rooms with a lounge, laundry facilities, game room, outdoor pool, and hot tub/sauna in a recently renovated school building. (☎802-253-9448 or 800-330-4880. Reservations recommended. Singles $35-39, with bath $49-59; quads $55. Call for seasonal rates.) A converted 19th-century farmhouse and adjacent motel, the **Riverside Inn,** 1965 Mountain Rd., 2 mi. from town, offers a number of great perks and some of the best rates around. The friendly owners loan out their mountain bikes. (☎802-253-4217 or 800-966-4217. Rooms $39-99.) **Smuggler's Notch State Park,** 6443 Mountain Rd., 8 mi. west of Stowe, just past Foster's Place, keeps it simple with hot showers, tent sites, and lean-tos. The scanty amenities are more than made up for by the natural beauty and seclusion of the park's sites. (☎802-253-4014. Reservations recommended. Open late May to mid-Oct. 4-person sites $14; lean-tos $21. $4 per additional person.)

⚑ LEAVING STOWE
From Stowe, turn around and take **Rte. 100** back to **Waterbury,** then continue west on **I-89** to **Burlington.**

THE ROAD TO BURLINGTON. About 25 mi. separate the Stowe and Burlington. Be sure to notice the art along the road between Exits 12 and 13; on the north side of the road is a set of **granite whale tails** protruding from the hillside. The $100,000 sculpture nearly found a home with the Hartford Whalers hockey team before the team both moved and changed its name. Instead, the tails found their way to I-89. Sculpted by Jim Sardonis, the piece is entitled "Reverence" and is meant to symbolize the fragility of the planet.

⚑ APPROACHING BURLINGTON
I-89 enters Burlington from the east and takes a right turn north of town along Lake Champlain. Take Exit 13 from I-89 into South Burlington and onto **Rte. 7 (Shelburne Rd.).** Follow Rte. 7 north about 2 mi. as it turns into **S. Willard St.,** which will take you into downtown Burlington.

BURLINGTON

Tucked between Lake Champlain and the Green Mountains, the largest city in Vermont offers spectacular views of New York's Adirondack Mountains across the sailboat-studded waters of Champlain. Several colleges, including the University of Vermont (UVM), give the area a youthful, progressive flair. On a warm day, the city resembles a mountain beach town; if you're lucky enough to catch some rays, visit the boardwalk where you can take a boat trip, or visit the brand new ECHO aquarium and science center. On a rainy day, walk along Church St., where numerous cafes offer a taste of middle-class hippie atmosphere and a chance for people-watching, or drive south to Shelburne (see p. 179).

▣ GETTING AROUND

In Burlington, **U.S. 2** is known as **Main St.** The major north-south streets downtown are **St. Paul St., Pine St.,** which is one block to the west of St. Paul, and **Battery St.,** which is to the west next to the lake. **Church St.** also runs north-south but is

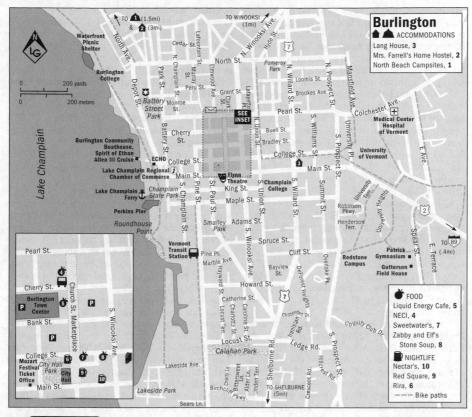

Burlington

🏠 ▲ ACCOMMODATIONS
Lang House, **3**
Mrs. Farrell's Home Hostel, **2**
North Beach Campsites, **1**

🍎 FOOD
Liquid Energy Cafe, **5**
NECI, **4**
Sweetwater's, **7**
Zabby and Elf's
  Stone Soup, **8**

🍷 NIGHTLIFE
Nectar's, **10**
Red Square, **9**
Rira, **6**

--- --- --- Bike paths

GREAT NORTH

VITAL STATS

Population: 39,000

Visitor Info: Lake Champlain Regional Chamber of Commerce, 60 Main St. (☎802-863-3489 or 877-686-5253; www.vermont.org). Open M-F 8am-5pm; May to mid-Oct. also Sa-Su 9am-5pm.

Internet Access: Fletcher Free Library, 235 College St. (☎802-864-7146). Open M-Tu and Th-F 8:30am-6pm, W 8:30am-9pm, Sa 9am-5pm, Su noon-6pm.

Post Office: 11 Elmwood Ave. (☎802-863-6033), at Pearl St. Open M-F 8am-5pm, Sa 8am-1pm. **Postal Code:** 05401.

mainly a pedestrian stretch full of restaurants and shops. Major east-west streets are (from south to north) **Main St., College St., Cherry St.,** and **Pearl St.**

Drivers get 2hr. of free parking in all city-owned garages every day, and garages and meters are free on Sundays. Outdoor parking is available at the corners of Pearl and N. Champlain St., College and Lake St., and St. Paul and Maple St. Indoor parking is available at Cherry St. between N. Winooski Ave. and Church St., College St. between Pine St. and Battery St. (free shuttle), and Main St. and S. Winooski Ave.

👁 SIGHTS

Amateur historians delight in **S. Willard St.,** where **Champlain College** occupies many of the Victorian houses that line the street. The pastoral **City Hall Park,** in the heart of downtown, and **Battery St. Park,** on Lake Champlain near the edge of downtown, provide an escape into the cool shade on hot summer days. With a stunning view across Lake Champlain, the **Burlington Community Boathouse,** at the base of College St., rents sailboats for a cruise on the lake and operates a small snack bar for those who just want to enjoy the view. (☎802-865-3377. Open mid-May to mid-Oct. Rentals open daily 10am-6pm. Sailboats $30-45 per hr.) The **Spirit of Ethan Allen III** runs a narrated, 500-passenger scenic cruise that departs from the boathouse at the bottom of College St. (☎802-862-8300; www.soea.com. Cruises daily late May to mid-Oct. 10am, noon, 2, 4pm. Sunset cruise 6:30pm. $10, ages 3-11 $4. Sunset cruise $13/$5.)

Visitors have the opportunity to discover ecology, culture, and history at **ECHO**, 1 College St., a science center and lake aquarium near the water. The multitude of hands-on exhibits and interactive demos are fun for young and old alike. You can properly meet the critters who keep you company when you take a dip in Lake Champlain. (☎802-864-1848; www.echovermont.org. Open M-W and F-Su 10am-5pm, Th 10am-8pm. $9, students and seniors $8, ages 3-17 $6.)

The **Ethan Allen Homestead** rests northeast of Burlington on Rte. 127 in the Winooski Valley Park. In the 1780s, Allen, his Green Mountain Boys, and Benedict Arnold forced the surrender of Fort Ticonderoga and helped establish the state of Vermont. Today, 1hr. tours tell the story of the daring frontiersman. (☎802-865-4556; www.sover.net/~eahome. Open June-Oct. M-Sa 10am-5pm, Su 1-5pm; Nov.-Apr. Sa 10am-5pm, Su 1-5pm; May daily 1-5pm. $5, seniors $4, ages 5-17 $2.50; families $14.) **Magic Hat Artifactory,** on Bartlett Bay Rd., 3 mi. south of Burlington off Rte. 7, offers brewery tours and free samples. (☎802-658-2739; www.magichat.net. In summer tours W-F 3, 4, 5pm; Sa noon, 1, 2, 3, 4pm. Winter Th-F 3:30 and 4:30pm; Sa noon, 1, 2, 3pm.)

⬛ ENTERTAINMENT

A pedestrian haven for tie-dye seekers, ice-cream lovers, and those seeking a casual pint with friends, **Church St. Marketplace** nurtures off-beat puppeteers and musicians who entertain the crowds at all hours. Pick up a free *Seven Days* newspaper to get the skinny on what's happening around town. In the summer, the **Vermont Mozart**

Festival (☎802-862-7352; www.vtmozart.com) brings Bach, Beethoven, and Mozart to local barns, farms, and meadows. The **Discover Jazz Festival** (☎802-863-7992; www.discoverjazz.com) features over 1000 musicians each year, with past performers including Ella Fitzgerald, Dizzy Gillespie, and Betty Carter. The **Champlain Valley Folk Festival,** located about halfway between Burlington and Middlebury, croons in early August. (☎800-769-9176; www.cvfest.org. Tickets $25-75.) The **Flynn Theater Box Office,** 153 Main St., handles sales for the Folk Festival and the Discover Jazz Festival. (☎802-863-5966; www.flynn-center.org. Open M-F 10am-5pm, Sa 11am-4pm.)

⬛⬛ FOOD & NIGHTLIFE

With approximately 85 restaurants in the **Church St. Marketplace** and its adjacent sidestreets, Burlington is a haven for hungry travelers. A mostly vegetarian cafe, ⬛**Zabby and Elf's Stone Soup,** 211 College St., specializes in hefty meals from the hot and cold bars ($6 per lb.) and sandwiches ($6-7) on freshly baked bread. (☎802-862-7616. Open M 7am-7pm, Tu-F 7am-9pm, Sa 9am-7pm. No credit cards.) At the **Liquid Energy Cafe,** 57 Church St., customers may concoct delicious smoothies ($3-5) from the long list of unconventional ingredients. (☎802-860-7666. Open M-Th 7am-7pm, F-Sa 7am-8pm, Su 9am-7pm.) The **New England Culinary Institute (NECI),** 25 Church St., known for its superb food at very reasonable prices, is a training ground for student chefs. (☎802-862-6324. Entrees from $14. Open for lunch M-Sa 11:30am-2pm; bistro M-Sa 2-4pm, Su brunch 11am-3pm; dinner M-Th 5:30-10pm, F-Sa 5:30-10:30pm, Su 5:30-9:30pm. In winter dinner closes 30min.-1hr. earlier.) At **Sweetwater's,** 120 Church St., incredibly high ceilings and vast wall paintings dwarf those who come for delicious soups ($3-6) and sandwiches ($6-9). When the warm weather rolls around, ask to be seated outdoors. (☎802-864-9800. Open M-F 11:30am-2am, Sa 11:30am-1am, Su 11:30am-midnight. Bar open until midnight.)

With so many colleges in the area, Burlington's nightlife scene is always alive and kicking. **Nectar's,** 188 Main St., rocks with inexpensive food, including the locally acclaimed gravy fries ($3), and nightly live tunes. (☎802-658-4771. Open M-Tu 11am-2:30am, W-F 6am-2:30am, Sa-Su 7am-2:30am.) One of Burlington's most popular night spots, the **Red Square,** 136 Church St., hosts live music nightly. Bands play in the alley if the crowd gets large. (☎802-859-8909. Open daily 4pm-2am.) For a laid-back pint, try **Rira,** 123 Church St., a traditional Irish pub. (☎802-860-9401. Beer $2.50-4.50. Open M-Sa 11:30am-2am, Su 11:30am-1am.)

ACCOMMODATIONS

The Chamber of Commerce has the rundown on area accommodations, which tend toward the more upscale. B&Bs are found in the outlying suburbs. Reasonably priced hotels and guest houses line **Shelburne Rd. (Rte. 7),** south of downtown, and **Main St. (Rte. 2),** east of downtown. ⬛**Mrs. Farrell's Home Hostel (HI-AYH),** 27 Arlington Ct., 3 mi. north of downtown via North Ave. and Heineberg Rd., is a welcoming abode. Six beds are split between a clean, comfortable basement and a lovely "summer cottage." (☎802-865-3730; call 4-6pm. Check-in before 5pm. Dorms $17, nonmembers $20; cottage $40/$43.) For an upscale experience, stay at the **Lang House,** 360 Main St., a four-year-old B&B only a 5-10min. walk from Church St. and downtown. Chefs from the New England Culinary Institute prepare a gourmet breakfast daily, and the view of Lake Champlain from the third-floor rooms is stunning. (☎802-652-2500 or 877-919-9799. Rooms with TV and A/C $135-195.) The **North Beach Campsites,** on Institute Rd., 1½ mi. north of town by North Ave., have 137 sites with access to a pristine sandy beach on Lake Champlain. The beach is open to non-campers and is stellar for picnics. (Take Rte. 127 to North Ave. ☎802-862-0942 or 800-571-1198. Beach open 24hr. for campers; beach parking closes 9pm. Lifeguards on duty daily mid-June to Aug. 10am-5:30pm. Campgrounds open May to mid-Oct. Sites $21, with water and electricity $27, full hookup $29. Showers $0.25 per 5min. $5 parking fee for non-campers. Boat rentals from **Umiak.** ☎802-253-2317. Canoes $15 per hr., kayaks $10-15 per hr. Open daily 10am-5pm.)

DETOUR: SHELBURNE
Take Rte. 7 (Shelburne Rd.) 7 mi. south from South Burlington.

The ⬛**Shelburne Museum,** 7 mi. south of Burlington, houses one of the most impressive collections of Americana in the country. A covered bridge, lighthouse, and 1950s house are displayed beside Degas, Cassat, Manet, Monet, Rembrandt,

and Whistler paintings. (☎802-985-3346; www.shelburnemuseum.org. Open daily mid-May to late-Oct. 10am-5pm. Tickets valid for 2 days $18, ages 6-18 $9; after 3pm $10/$5.) **Shelburne Farms,** 1611 Harbor Rd., just north of the museum., was built in 1886. Within the estate is a castle-like farm and the majestic Inn on Lake Champlain. Today, it is a nonprofit environmental education center and scenic 1400-acre working farm. (☎802-985-8686; www.shelburnefarms.org. Open mid-May to mid-Oct. $6, seniors $5, ages 3-17 $4, under 3 free. Welcome center open daily May-Oct. 9am-5:30pm; Nov.-Apr. 10am-5pm. Rooms at Inn $105-365 in fall; $95-315 in spring.)

Food and accommodations outside the city are available at the **Dutch Mill Motel and Family Restaurant,** 4385 Shelburne Rd. The Dutch Mill built 25 cottages in the mid 1920s, the only accommodations of their kind in the Northeast. The lighted dome shone through the crazy times of prohibition, but a modern motel recently replaced the cottages and a camping area has been added in the back. The restaurant serves eggs ($7) and pancakes all day. (☎802-985-3568; www.dutchmillvt.com or www.shelburnecamping.com. Restaurant open Su and Tu-Sa 7:30am-2pm. Rooms in fall $70 fall; winter-summer $40-42.)

LEAVING BURLINGTON
From **Main St.** in Burlington, turn left on **U.S.2/U.S. 7** (known as the **Ethan Allen Hwy.**). Merge with **I-89 North** for about 6 mi. Take Exit 17 for **U.S. 2 West.**

THE ROAD THROUGH THE CHAMPLAIN ISLANDS

U.S. 2 heads north through the rural Champlain Islands. Nestled between the Adirondacks and Green Mountains, these islands have avoided exploitation, despite the allure of their natural beauty and their prime location between Montréal and Burlington, and still devote their land to farms, orchards, vineyards, and sandy beaches. North of Winooski, the Sandbar Causeway connects to the south end of the Champlain Islands. The northern end of the islands is connected to New York by Rouses Point Bridge, west of Alburg.

SOUTH HERO. This town is known as the "Garden Spot of Vermont" due to an especially long season of agricultural growth. **Grand Isle State Park,** 36 E. Shore Rd. South, offers near-perfect camping, with fireflies outside your tent and the waves of Lake Champlain lapping against the shore. Because South Hero Island is less marshy, not as many bugs pester this campground as in North Hero. (2 mi. north of town on east side of road. ☎802-372-4300; www.vtstateparks.com. 36 lean-to and 120 sites. Showers, RV sites, swimming, fishing, boat ramp, rowboat and kayak rental, volleyball courts, and playground. No hookups. Reception 2-9pm. Sites $13; lean-to $20.)

NORTH HERO

For a short time during the summer, the island hosts the famous **Royal Lipizzaner Stallions.** Originally bred for the exclusive use of the Hapsburg royal family of Austria, the magnificent horses return every summer to North Hero and give spectacular performances under the direction of Colonel Ottomar Herrmann. (☎802-372-6400. Shows Mid-July to Aug. Th-F 6pm, Sa-Su 2:30pm; free open barn other times. $15, seniors $12, ages 6-12 $8, under 6 free. Reservations recommended.)

Called the "Finest General Store on the Planet" in Yankee Magazine, **Hero's Welcome,** 3537 U.S. 2, stocks anything you could ever (or never) need, from slinkies to DVDs, fish bait to film, and a bakery/deli to boot. (☎802-372-4121. Open M-F 7am-7pm, Sa-Su 7am-8pm.) The **North Hero Visitor's Center,** 70 N. Main St., offers info. (☎802-796-3980. Open daily summer 10am-6pm; winter 9am-5pm.)

THE ROAD TO CANADA. The road between the border and Montréal was hit by an ice storm in 1998, scarring the already unimpressive landscape. Skip straight to Montréal along **I-87/Hwy. 15** instead of taking the slower back roads. In all, it's about 65 mi. from North Hero to Montréal.

⚔ LEAVING THE US

See Vital Documents (p. 11) for info on passport, visa, and identification requirements. Don't forget to fill up on gas before you cross into Canada; it's more expensive there. Until entering back into the US, all prices listed are in Canadian dollars.

⛰ APPROACHING MONTRÉAL

To the east of Montréal, Hwy. 15 connects with the Hwy. 10/Hwy. 20 crossing the St. Lawrence River via the Champlain Bridge (Pont Champlain) into Montréal. Merge onto Hwy. 10 as it leaves Hwy. 15. Hwy. 10 takes you downtown on rue Université.

Welcome To **QUÉBEC**

MONTRÉAL

This island city has been coveted territory for over 300 years. Wars and sieges dominated Montréal's early history as British forces strove to wrest it from French control. Today, the only invaders are visitors eager to experience the city's cosmopolitan air. Though only an hour from the US border, Montréal has grown to be the second-largest French-speaking city in the world. Fashion that rivals Paris, a nightlife comparable to London, and international cuisine all attest to the city's prominent European legacy. Whether attracted to Montréal's global flavor or its large student population, it is hard not to be swept up by the vibrancy coursing through the *centre-ville*.

VITAL STATS

Population: 1 million

Visitor Info: Infotouriste, 1001 rue de Square-Dorchester (☎877-266-5687; www.tourisme-montreal.org), on N. Ste-Catherine between rue Peel and Rue Metcalfe. Open daily July-Aug. 8:30am-8pm; Sept.-June 9am-6pm.

Currency Exchange: Custom House, 905 Blvd. Maisonneuve (☎514-844-1414). Open M-F 8:30am-6pm, Sa 9am-4pm. **Calforex,** 1250 rue Peel (☎514-392-9100). Flat $2.75 fee. Open M-W 8:30am-7pm, Th-Sa 8:30am-9pm, Su 10am-6pm; low season Sa 10am-7pm.

Internet Access: Bibliothèque Nationale du Québec, 1700 rue St-Denis (☎514-873-1100). Open M-F 9am-5pm.

Post Office: 685 rue Cathcart (☎514-395-4539). Open M-F 8am-6pm. **Postal Code:** H3B 3B0.

▐ GETTING AROUND

Two major streets divide the city, making getting around simple. The one-way **Blvd. St-Laurent** (also called **"le Main,"** or **"The Main"**) runs north through

Montréal Overview

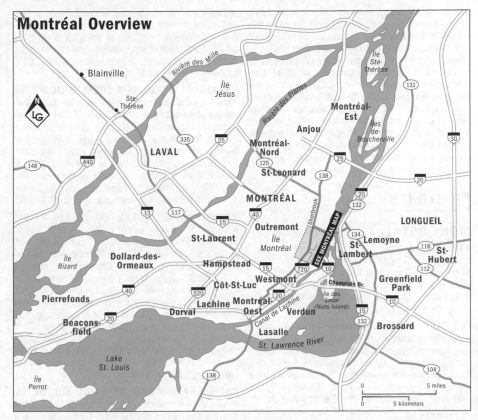

the city, splitting Montréal and its streets east-west. The Main also serves as the unofficial French/English divider; English **McGill University** lies to the west, while **St-Denis,** a street running parallel to St-Laurent, lies to the east and defines the French student quarter (also called the *quartier latin* and the "student ghetto"). **Rue Sherbrooke,** which is paralleled by **de Maisonneuve** and **Ste-Catherine** downtown, runs east-west almost the entire length of Montréal. The **Underground City,** a network of shops and restaurants, runs north-south, stretching from **rue Sherbrooke** to **rue de la Gauchetière** and **rue St-Antoine.** A free map from the tourist office helps navigation.

Parking is expensive and often difficult to find along the streets. Try lots on the city's outskirts for reasonable prices, and consider using the convenient **STM Métro and Bus** (☎514-288-6287; www.stm.info). The four Métro lines and most buses run daily 5:30am-12:30am ($2.25; 6 tickets $9.50; day pass $7; 3-day $14).

NEIGHBORHOODS

When first founded, Montréal was limited to the riverside area of present-day **Vieux Montréal.** It has since evolved from a settlement of French colonists into a cosmopolitan metropolis. A stroll along **rue Ste-Catherine,** the flashy commercial avenue, is a must. European fashion is all the rage, conversations mix English and French, and upscale retail shops intermingle with tacky souvenir stores and debaucherous clubs. Its assortment of peep shows and sex shops has earned it the nickname "Saint-Vitrine" (holy windows).

A small **Chinatown** lines rue de la Gauchetière. At the northern edge of the city's center, **Little Italy** occupies the area north of rue Beaubien between rue St-Hubert and Louis-Hémon. Rue St-Denis, home to the city's elite at the turn of the century, still serves as the **Quartier Latin's** main street. Restaurants of all flavors are clustered along **rue Prince Arthur.** Nearby, **Sq. St-Louis** hosts a beautiful fountain and sculptures. **Blvd. St-Laurent,** north of Sherbrooke, is perfect for walking or biking. Many attractions between **Mont-Royal** and the **Fleuve St-Laurent** (St. Lawrence River) are free. **Le Village,** the gay village, is located along rue Ste-Catherine Est between rue St-Hubert and Papineau.

 # SIGHTS

MONT-ROYAL, LE PLATEAU, & THE EAST

Package tickets *(forfaits)* for the Biodôme, Funiculaire, and Gardens/Insectarium are a decent deal. Tickets are good for 30 days. (Any 2 sights $17, students and seniors $12.75, children 5-17 $8.50. All 3 sights $25/$19/$12.50.)

BIODÔME. The fascinating Biodôme is the most recent addition to Olympic Park. Housed in the former Olympic Vélodrome, the Biodôme is a "living museum" of four complete ecosystems: a Tropical Forest, a Laurentian Forest, a St-Laurent marine ecosystem, and a Polar World. *(4777 av. Pierre-de-Coubertin. M: Viau. ☎514-868-3000; www.biodome.qc.ca. Open daily summer 9am-6pm; off season 9am-5pm. $10.50, students and seniors $8, ages 5-17 $5.25.)*

ST. JOSEPH'S. The dome of **St. Joseph's Oratory,** is the second-highest dome in the world after St. Peter's Basilica in Rome. An acclaimed religious site that attracts pilgrims from all over the globe, St. Joseph's is credited with a long list of miracles and unexplained healings. The **Votive Chapel,** where the crutches and canes of thousands of healed devotees hang for all to see, keeps warm with the heat of 10,000 candles. *(3800 ch. Queen Mary. M: Côte-des-Neiges. ☎514-733-8211; www.saint-joseph.org. Open daily 6am-9:30pm.)*

OLYMPIC PARK. The world's tallest inclined tower *(le Tour Olympique)* is the glory of Olympic Park, built for the 1976 summer games. Take the **Funiculaire** to the top of the tower for a breath-

taking view. *(3200 rue Viau. M: Viau, Pie-IX. ☎514-252-4141. 4 tours daily, 2 in French and 2 in English. Tour $5.50, students and seniors $5, ages 5-17 $4.25. Funiculaire open daily mid-June to early Sept. 9am-9pm; early Sept. to mid-June 9am-5pm. $10, students and seniors $7.50, ages 5-17 $5.)*

BOTANICAL GARDENS & INSECTARIUM. The Japanese and Chinese landscapes at the **Jardin Botanique** showcase the largest *bonsai* and *penjing* collections outside of Asia. The gardens also harbor an **insectarium** of exotic bugs, including at least a dozen fist-sized spiders. *(4101 rue Sherbrooke Est. M: Pie-IX. ☎514-872-1400; www.ville.montreal.qc.ca/jardin or /insectarium. Open daily July-Aug. 9am-6pm; Sept.-June 9am-4pm. $10.50, students and seniors $8, ages 5-17 $4.25.)*

PARC DU MONT-ROYAL. Designed by Frederick Law Olmstead, creator of New York's Central Park, the 127-year-old Parc du Mont-Royal surrounds and includes Montréal's namesake mountain. Though the hike from rue Peel up the mountain is longer than it looks, the view of the city from the observation deck is rewarding. The 30m cross at the summit is a replica of the cross placed there in 1643 by de Maisonneuve, the founder of Montréal. *(M: Mont-Royal or Bus #11. ☎514-844-4928, tour info 514-843-8240. Open daily 6am-midnight. Tours M-F 9am-5pm from Smith House, 1260 ch. Remembrance, between Beaver Lake and Chalet du Mont-Royal.)*

CATHÉDRALE MARIE REINE DU MONDE. A scaled-down replica of St. Peter's in Rome, this Roman Catholic cathedral stirred tensions when it was built in the heart of Montréal's Anglo-Protestant area. *(At René-Lévesque and Cathédrale. ☎514-866-1661. Open M-F 6am-7pm, Sa 7:30am-8:30pm, Su 8am-7pm. Free.)*

MCGILL UNIVERSITY. The McGill University campus extends up Mont-Royal and is composed predominantly of Victorian buildings on pleasant greens. Stop by the **McGill Welcome Center** for a tour. *(Burnside Hall Bldg., Room 115. ☎514-398-6555. Open M-F 9am-5pm; July-Aug. also Sa tours. Call for details.)* The campus includes the site of the 16th-century Native American village of **Hochelaga** and the **Redpath Museum of Natural History.** *(Main gate at rue McGill and Sherbrooke. M: McGill. ☎514-398-4086; www.mcgill.ca/redpath. Open July-Aug. M-Th 9am-5pm, Su 1-5pm; Sept.-June M-F 9am-5pm, Su 1-5pm. Free.)*

THE UNDERGROUND CITY

Not content with being one of the best shopping spots on the planet, Montréal has set its sights lower. Thirty kilometers of tunnels link Métro stops and form the ever-expanding "prototype city of the future," with restaurants, cinemas, theaters, hotels, two universities, two department stores, 1700 businesses, 1615 housing units, and 2000 boutiques. Here, residents bustle through the hallways of this sprawling, mall-like, "sub-urban" city. At the McGill stop lie some of the Underground City's finest and most navigable offerings.

SHOPS. To find the shopping wonderland **Pl. Bonaventure,** follow signs marked "Restaurants et Commerce" through the maze of shops under rue de la Gauchetière Ouest. The Visitors Center supplies maps of the tunnels and underground attractions. *(900 rue de la Gauchetière Ouest. M: Bonaventure. ☎514-397-2325. Shops open daily 9am-9pm.)* The **Promenades de la Cathédrale** take their name from their above-ground neighbor, **Christ Church Cathedral.** *(635 rue Ste-Catherine Ouest. Church ☎514-843-6577. Open daily 8am-6pm. Promenades ☎514-849-9925.)*

VIEUX MONTRÉAL

In the 17th century, struggling with Iroquois tribes for control of the area's lucrative fur trade, Montréal erected walls encircling the settlement. Today, the remnants of those ramparts delineate the boundaries of Vieux Montréal, the city's first settlement, on the stretch of river bank between **rue McGill, Notre-Dame,** and **Berri.** The fortified walls that once protected the quarter have crumbled, but the beautiful 17th- and 18th-century mansions of politicos and merchants have retained their splendor. **Guidatour** leads **walking tours** of Vieux Montréal, departing from the Basilique Notre-Dame-de-Montréal. *(☎514-844-4021 or 800-363-4021; www.guidatour.qc.ca. 1½hr. tours mid-June to late Sept. daily 11am, 1:30, 4pm in English, and 11am in French; late May to mid-June and early Oct. tours Sa-Su only. $13.50, students $11.50, ages 6-12 $5.50.)*

⊠BASILIQUE NOTRE-DAME DE MONTRÉAL. Towering above the Place d'Armes and its memorial to Maisonneuve is the most beautiful church in Montréal. One of North America's largest churches and a historic center for the city's Catholic population, the neo-Gothic **Basilique Notre-Dame de Montréal** has hosted everyone from Québec separatists to the Pope. Don't miss the Sacred Heart Chapel's bronze altarpiece and the sound-and-light spectacular *Et la lumière fut*—"And then there was light." *(110 rue Notre-Dame Ouest. M: Place-D'Armes. ☎514-842-2925; www.basiliquenddm.org. Open M-Sa 8am-5pm, Su 1:30-4pm. $3, ages 7-17 $1. Light show Tu-Th 6:30pm, F 6:30 and 8:30pm, Sa 7 and 8:30pm. $10, seniors $9, ages 1-17 $5.)*

🏛 MUSEUMS

McCord Museum, 690 rue Sherbrooke Ouest (☎514-398-7100; www.mccord-museum.qc.ca). M: McGill or bus #24. The McCord's exhibits range from toys to wedding gowns, lawn ornaments to photographs. Absorbing displays chronicle Montréal's development and quirks. Open M-Sa 10am-6pm, Su 10am-5pm; Oct.-May closed M. $10, seniors $7, students $5, ages 7-12 $3; families $19.

Musée des Beaux-Arts, 1380 and 1379 rue Sherbrooke Ouest (☎514-285-1600; www.mmfa.qc.ca), 5 blocks west of the McGill entrance. The museum's small permanent collection features art from ancient cultures to 20th-century works, including Inuit art. Don't miss the collection of creative decorative arts, which includes an 18th-century French sleigh and a cactus hat stand. Open Su and Tu-Sa 11am-6pm. Tours W and Su 1:30 (French) and 2:30pm (English). Free.

Pointe-à-Callière: Montréal Museum of Archaeology and History, 350 Place Royale (☎514-872-9150; www.pacmusee.qc.ca), off rue de la Commune near Vieux-Port. M: Place d'Armes. This museum and historic site uses the products of 10 years of archaeological digs in an underground tour of the city's past. Open July-Aug. M-F 10am-6pm, Sa-Su 11am-6pm; Sept.-June Tu-F 10am-5pm, Sa-Su 11am-5pm. $10, seniors $7.50, students $6, ages 6-12 $3.50, under 5 free.

Musée d'Art Contemporain, 185 rue Ste-Catherine Ouest (☎514-847-6226; www.macm.org), at Jeanne-Mance. M: Place-des-Arts. Canada's premier modern art museum concentrates on the work of Canadians. Open Su, Tu, Th-Sa 11am-6pm; W 11am-9pm. $6, seniors $4, students $3, under 12 free. W 6-9pm free.

Canadian Centre for Architecture, 1920 av. Baile (☎514-939-7026; www.cca.qc.ca). M: Guy-Concordia or Atwater. Houses one of the world's most important collections of architectural prints, drawings, photographs, and books. Tours Sa-Su 2 (French), 3:30pm (English). Open Tu-W and F-Su 11am-6pm, Th 11am-

9pm. $6, seniors $4, students $3, under 12 free. Th after 5:30pm free.

♫ ENTERTAINMENT

Like much of the city, Vieux Montréal is best seen at night. Street performers, artists, and *chanson-niers* in various *brasseries* set the tone for lively summer evenings of clapping, stomping, and singing along. Real fun goes down on **St-Paul,** near the corner of St-Vincent. For a sweet Sunday afternoon in summer, **Parc Jeanne-Mance** reels with bongos, dancing, and handicrafts.

FESTIVALS & SPORTS

Montréal might be in the running for festival capital of the world. To keep track of the offerings, pick up a copy of *Mirror* (English) or *Voir* (French) in any theater and many bars and cafes. In summer, keep your eyes peeled for *ventes-trot-toirs,* "sidewalk sales" that shut down a major street. In mid-June, Montréal reels from its always-entertaining **Fringe Festival** (☎514-849-3378; www.montrealfringe.ca), with theater, dance, and music events at various spots throughout the Plateau Mont-Royal. It wouldn't be Montréal without high-spirited **Fête Nationale** (☎514-849-2560; www.cfn.org), on St-Jean-Baptiste Day, June 24, a celebration of Quebecois pride through local music performances and cultural events.

Two of Montréal's signature summer festivals draw crowds from all over the world. In early June, the **Mondial de la Bière,** offers tastings of over 300 brands of beer, port, scotch, and whiskey. (☎514-722-9640; www.festivalmondialbiere.qc.ca. $10.) The first week of July, jazz fiends take over the city for the **Montréal International Jazz Festival** (☎514-871-1881; www.montrealjazzfest.com). From Bobby McFerrin to Ray Charles, the show brings together a variety of over 300 performers. A month later, **Divers/Cité** (☎514-285-4011; www.diverscite.org), a gay pride week, rocks the city in and around Emilie-Gamelin Park.

Montréal also has its share of sporting events. Between October and April, hockey's **Canadiens** (aka Les Habitants—"the locals"—or Les Habs) play at the **Centre Bell,** 1250 rue de la Gauchetière Ouest. (☎514-989-2841, tickets 514-790-1245. M: Bonaventure. $23-150.) Get in on the action during the one-day **Tour de l'Île,** an amateur cycling event with over 45,000 participants. (☎514-521-8356.)

THEATER

Montréal lives up to its cultured reputation with a vast selection of theater in French and English. The **Théâtre du Nouveau Monde,** 84 rue Ste-Catherine Ouest, stages French productions. (☎514-878-7878, ticket info 514-866-8668; www.tnm.qc.ca. M: Place-des-Arts. Tickets $36-42.) In mid-July, however, the theater is turned over to the bilingual **Festival Juste pour Rire/Just for Laughs** (☎514-790-4242; www.hahaha.com). The renowned **National Theatre School of Canada,** 5030 rue St-Denis, stages excellent "school plays." (☎514-842-7954; www.ent-nts.qc.ca. Most shows free.) The city's exciting **Place des Arts,** 260 Blvd. de Maisonneuve Ouest (☎514-842-2112; www.pda.qc.ca), at rue Ste.-Catherine Ouest and Jeanne Mance, houses the **Opéra de Montréal** (☎514-985-2258; www.operademontreal.com), the **Montréal Symphony Orchestra** (☎514-842-9951; www.osm.ca.), and **Les Grands Ballets Canadiens** (☎514-849-0269; www.grandsballets.qc.ca). **Théâtre Saint-Denis,** 1594 rue St-Denis (☎514-849-4211), hosts Broadway-style productions. Peruse the *Calendar of Events,* available at tourist offices and newspaper stands, or call **Tel-Spec** for ticket info. (☎514-790-2222; ww.tel-spec.com. Open M-Sa 9am-9pm, Su noon-6pm.) **Admission Ticket Network** has tickets. (☎514-790-1245 or 800-361-459; www.admission.com. Open daily 8am-1am.)

🍴 BON APPÉTIT

In Montréal, chic restaurants rub shoulders with funky cafes, and everyone can find something to fit their taste. **Chinatown** and **Little Italy** boast outstanding examples of their culinary heritage. The western half of **Ste-Catherine** and the area around **Blvd. St-Laurent** north of Sherbrooke offer a large range of choices. By far the best and affordable restaurants cluster on **rue St-Denis.**

Many restaurants, even upscale ones, have no liquor license; head to the nearest *dépanneur* or **SAQ** *(Societé des alcools du Québec)* to buy wine. For further guidance, consult the free *Restaurant Guide,* published by the **Greater Montréal Convention and Tourism Bureau** (☎514-844-5400), which lists over 130 restaurants by type of cuisine.

■ **Restaurant l'Académie,** 4051 rue St-Denis (☎514-849-2249), at the corner of av. Duluth. M: Sherbrooke. An elegant culinary experience where lunchtime indulgence is reasonably priced and the atmosphere is refined without being stuffy. Most recognized for their *moules frites* (steamed mussels; around $10). Open daily noon-10pm.

📖 **Brûlerie St. Denis,** 3967 rue St-Denis (☎514-286-9158). M: Sherbrooke. A fun student cafe where the food and coffee are excellent, the waiters are friendly, and the patrons seem to know each other already. *Café du jour* $1.50. Bagel "Belle Hélène" $4.50. Open daily 8am-11pm.

Étoile des Indes, 1806 Ste-Catherine Ouest (☎514-932-8330), near St-Mathieu. A local favorite for Indian food. Spicy Bangalore *phal* dishes are only for the brave, but the homemade cheese *paneer* plates are for everyone. The Butter Chicken ($10) is phenomenal. Lunch specials including soup $6-9. Dinners $5-15. Open M-Sa noon-2:30pm and 5-11pm, Su 5-11pm.

La Fringale, 312 rue St-Paul Ouest (☎514-842-4491), in Vieux Montréal. Reminiscent of a warmly lit farmhouse, this acclaimed restaurant serves traditional French cuisine with a country air. Entrees $20-35. Open M-F 11am-midnight, Sa-Su 5pm-midnight.

La Crêperie Bretonne le Trishell, 3470 rue St-Denis (☎514-281-1012). M: Sherbrooke. Montréalers have been known to line up for a taste of le Trishell's melt-in-your-mouth crêpes and fondues. Strawberry crêpe $6.75. Open M-W 11:30am-11pm, Th-F 11:30am-midnight, Sa noon-midnight, Su noon-11pm.

La Crème de la Crème Bistro Café, 21 rue de la Commune Est (☎514-874-0723), in Vieux Montréal. A brick cafe on the waterfront that combines Greek cuisine and Provençal decor, La Crème serves tasty baguette sandwiches (with salad; $7-9) and slices of cake ($4). Open June-Sept. daily 11am-midnight; Oct.-June opens at 11am, hours vary with weather.

🏠 ACCOMMODATIONS

The **Infotouriste** (☎877-266-5687) is the best resource for info about hostels, hotels, and *chambres touristiques* (rooms in private homes or small guesthouses). Inquire about B&Bs at the **Downtown Bed and Breakfast Network,** 3458 av. Laval, near Sherbrooke; the managers run their own modest hideaway and maintain a list of 80 other homes downtown. (☎800-267-5180;

www.bbmontreal.qc.ca. Open daily 9am-9pm. Singles $40-75; doubles $45-90.) The least expensive *maisons touristiques* and hotels cluster around **rue St-Denis,** which abuts Vieux Montréal. Canada Day and the Grand Prix in July make accommodations scarce, even outside the city.

📖 **Auberge de Jeunesse, Montréal Youth Hostel (HI-C),** 1030 rue MacKay (☎514-843-3317; www.hostellingmontreal.com). M: Lucien-L'Allier; from the station exit, cross the street and head right. The hostel is on the 1st real street on the left, across from the parking lot. Full bathroom in every room, complete kitchen, laundry, pool tables, Internet, and a *petit café*. Pub crawl Tu and F 8:30pm. Linen $2.30; no sleeping bags. 1-week max. stay. Reception 24hr. Check-in 1pm. Checkout 11am. The 240 beds fill quickly in summer; reservations strongly recommended. Dorms $22, nonmembers $26; private doubles $58/68.

McGill University, Bishop Mountain Hall, 3935 rue de l'Université (☎514-398-6367; www.mcgill.ca/residences/summer). M: McGill. Follow Université along the edge of campus; when the road seems to end in a parking lot at the top of the steep hill, bear right—it is the circular grey stone building with lots of windows. Kitchenettes on each floor. 1000 beds. Free Internet access, common room with TV. Towels and linens provided. Laundry facilities. Full breakfast M-Th 7:30-9:30am $7; continental breakfast $4.50. Reception 7am-10pm; there is a guard for late check-in. Check-in 3pm. Check-out noon. Open mid-May to mid-Aug. Singles $45, students and seniors $40.

Université de Montréal, Residences, 2350 rue Edouard-Montpetit (☎514-343-6531; www.resid.umontreal.ca). Metro: Edouard-Montpetit. Follow the signs up the steep hill. Located in a tranquil, remote neighborhood on the edge of a beautiful campus, the East Tower affords a great view. Free local calls. Laundry facilities. TV lounge. Cafe open M-F 7:30am-2:30pm. Parking $10. Reception 24hr. Check-in noon. Check-out noon. Open mid-May to early Aug. Singles $35; doubles $45. 10% student discount.

Hôtel de Paris, 901 rue Sherbrooke Est (☎514-522-6861 or 800-567-7217; www.hotel-montreal.com). M: Sherbrooke. This European-style 19th-century flat houses pleasant hotel rooms with private bath, TV, telephone, and A/C. Some rooms contain kitchenettes. There are also about 100

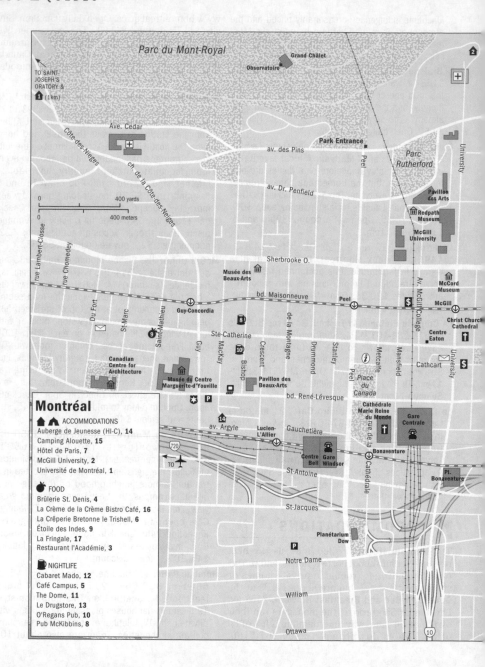

Parc du Mont-Royal

Grand Châlet

Observatoire

TO SAINT-JOSEPH'S ORATORY & **1** (1km)

2

Ave. Cédar

Côte-des-Neiges

ch. de la Côte-des-Neiges

av. des Pins

Park Entrance

Peel

Parc Rutherford

University

Pavillon des Arts

av. Dr. Penfield

Redpath Museum

McGill University

0   400 yards
0   400 meters

rue Lambert-Closse

rue Chomedey

Du Fort

St-Marc

Saint-Mathieu

Sherbrooke O.

Musée des Beaux-Arts

Av. McGill College

McCord Museum

bd. Maisonneuve

Peel

McGill

$

Guy-Concordia

Christ Church Cathedral

Centre Eaton

8

Ste-Catherine

Guy

MacKay

Crescent

Bishop

de la Montagne

Drummond

Stanley

9

10

University

Cathcart

$

Canadian Centre for Architecture

Musée du Centre Marguerite-d'Youville

Pavillon des Beaux-Arts

bd. René-Lévesque

Peel

i

Metcalfe

Mansfield

Place du Canada

P

14

av. Argyle

Lucien-L'Allier

Gauchetière

Cathédrale Marie Reine du Monde

Gare Centrale

720

TO ✈

Centre Bell

Gare Windsor

Bonaventure

St-Antoine

rue de la Cathédrale

Pl. Bonaventure

St-Jacques

Planétarium Dow

P

Notre Dame

William

Ottawa

10

Montréal

◤◤ ACCOMMODATIONS
Auberge de Jeunesse (HI-C), **14**
Camping Alouette, **15**
Hôtel de Paris, **7**
McGill University, **2**
Université de Montréal, **1**

🍎 FOOD
Brûlerie St. Denis, **4**
La Crème de la Crème Bistro Café, **16**
La Crêperie Bretonne le Trishell, **6**
Étoile des Indes, **9**
La Fringale, **17**
Restaurant l'Académie, **3**

🍸 NIGHTLIFE
Cabaret Mado, **12**
Café Campus, **5**
The Dome, **11**
Le Drugstore, **13**
O'Regans Pub, **10**
Pub McKibbins, **8**

GREAT NORTH

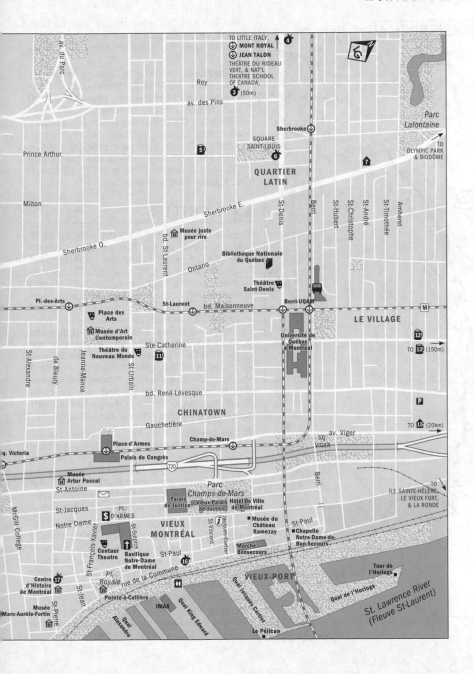

TO LITTLE ITALY,
⊘ MONT ROYAL
⊘ JEAN TALON
THÉÂTRE DU RIDEAU
VERT, & NAT'L
THEATRE SCHOOL
OF CANADA,
3 (50m)

4

Roy

av. des Pins

*Parc
Lafontaine*

Sherbrooke ⊘

SQUARE
SAINT-LOUIS

Prince Arthur

5

6

TO
OLYMPIC PARK
& BIODÔME

QUARTIER
LATIN

7

Milton

Sherbrooke E.

St-Denis
Berri
St-Hubert
St-Christophe
St-André
St-Timothée
Amherst

Sherbrooke O.

bd. St-Laurent

Musée juste
pour rire

Ontario

Bibliothèque Nationale
du Québec

Théâtre
Saint-Denis

Pl.-des-Arts ⊘

St-Laurent

bd. Maisonneuve

Berri-UQAM

M

LE VILLAGE

Place des
Arts

Musée d'Art
Contemporain

Université de
Québec
à Montréal

12

Théâtre du
Nouveau Monde

Ste-Catherine

11

TO **13** (150m)

St-Alexandre
de Bleury
Jeanne-Mance
St-Urbain

bd. René-Lévesque

CHINATOWN

P

Gauchetière

av. Viger

SQ.
VIGER

TO **15** (20km)

q. Victoria

Place-d'Armes ⊘

Champ-de-Mars

Palais de Congrès

720

Musée
Artur Pascal

St-Antoine

Berri

TO
ÎLE SAINTE-HÉLÈNE,
LE VIEUX FORT,
& LA RONDE

*Parc
Champs-de-Mars*

St-Jacques

Palais
de Justice

Vieux Palais
de Justice

Hôtel de Ville
de Montréal

McGill College

Notre Dame

$

PL.
D'ARMES

VIEUX
MONTRÉAL

St-Sulplice
St-Vincent
Jacques-Cartier

Musée du
Château
Ramezay

St-Paul

Centaur
Theatre

Basilique
Notre-Dame
de Montréal

St-François-Xavier

St-Paul

16

■ Chapelle
Notre-Dame-de-
Bon-Secours

Marché
Bonsecours

Centre
d'Histoire
de Montréal

17

Pl.
Royale

rue de la Commune

VIEUX-PORT

Tour de
l'Horloge

St-Jean

Pointe-à-Callière

Musée
Marc-Aurèle-Fortin

St-Pierre

Quai
Alexandra

IMAX

Quai King Edward

Quai Jacques-Cartier

Quai de l'Horloge

*St. Lawrence River
(Fleuve St-Laurent)*

Le Pélican

av. du Parc

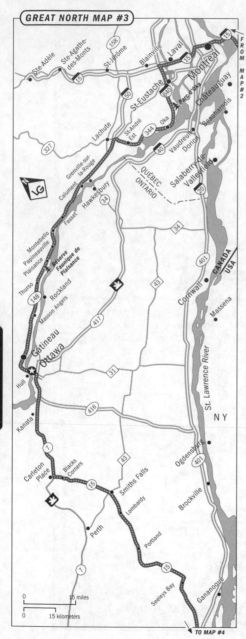

hostel beds, which, while cheaper than the hotel rooms, are not as good a deal as Montréal's other hostels. Linen $3. Single-sex dorms $20; rooms $80-155.

Camping Alouette, 3449 rue de l'Industrie (☎514-450-464-1661 or 888-464-7829; www.campingalouette.com), 30km from the city. Follow Autoroute 20 south, take Exit 105, and follow the signs. The privacy missing from Montréal's bustling hostels is omnipresent at these secluded campsites. Nature trail, pool, laundry facilities, a small store, volleyball courts, a dance hall, and a daily shuttle to and from Montréal (30min., $12 round-trip). Sites for 2 $22, with hookup $33; $2 per additional person.

■ NIGHTLIFE

Combine a loosely enforced drinking age of 18 with thousands of taps flowing unchecked till 3am and the result is the unofficially titled "nightlife capital of North America." Most pubs and bars offer a happy hour (usually 5-8pm) when bottled drinks may be two-for-one and mixed drinks may be double their usual potency. In summer, restaurants often spill onto outdoor patios. Avoid crowds of drunken American college students by ducking into one of the laid-back local pubs along **rue St-Denis** north of Ste-Catherine. Alternatively, *be* a drunken American college student on **rue Ste-Catherine,** especially around **rue Crescent.** Tamer fun can be found in the pedestrian-only section of **rue Prince Arthur** at **rue St-Laurent.**

■ **Café Campus,** 57 rue Prince Arthur (☎514-844-1010; www.cafecampus.com). Unlike the more touristy meat-market discothèques, this hip club gathers a friendly student and 20-something crowd. Su French music, Th "Tabasko" (Latin groove), and the fun and happy Tu Retro. Drinks $4-5.50. Cover $2-15. Open daily 8:30pm-3am.

Pub McKibbins, 1426 rue Bishop (☎514-288-1580). Fine drinks are served in this warmly lit Irish pub. Trophies and tokens ornament the walls and dartboards entertain the crowds, while a fieldstone fireplace warms the quarters in winter. Irish jam nights M-Tu, folk music W, live Irish bands Th-Sa. Open daily 11am-3am; kitchen closes 10pm.

O'Regans Pub, 1224 rue Bishop (☎514-866-8464), south of rue Ste-Catherine. The best fish and chips in town ($9.25). Tartan stools are quickly claimed F-Su for live traditional Irish music. W Celtic jam night. Open daily noon-3am. Kitchen closes 9pm.

The Dome, 32 rue Ste-Catherine Est (☎514-875-5757), at the corner of St-Laurent. Attracts an international crowd to bump and grind to hip-hop and R&B. Cover $5. Open F-Sa 10pm-3am.

GBLT NIGHTLIFE

Most of Montréal's gay and lesbian hot spots can be found in the **gay village,** along rue St-Catherine between St-Hubert and Papineau. While most of the village's establishments cater to men, there are a few lesbian-friendly locales.

Le Drugstore, 1366 rue Ste-Catherine Est (☎514-524-1960). M: Beaudry. A 3-story megaplex basking in the glow of neon lights. Crowd is mostly male, though women are welcome. Open daily 8am-3am.

Cabaret Mado, 1115 St-Catherine Est (☎514-525-7566). M: Beaudry. This cabaret is the home of the wildest drag shows in town. Come Tu for "le Mardi à Mado." Straight-friendly, especially weekends. Drinks $4-5. Cover varies. Open daily 4pm-3am.

LEAVING MONTRÉAL
Getting out of Montréal to the west can be a harrowing experience. The easiest way to reach Saint-Eustache is to take **rue Saint-Antoine,** which merges onto **Hwy. 720.** Take Hwy. 720 2.5km south to **Hwy. 15,** Take Hwy. 15 22km to the northwest until it connects with **Hwy. 344.**

SAINT-EUSTACHE. The area of Saint-Eustache near the highway brims with chain restaurants and shops. Worth seeing is **Old Saint-Eustache,** the heart of the town established in the 18th century. Heritage houses, beautiful riverside surroundings, historical sites, and museums invite further exploration. If you're hungry, try **La Chitarra,** 168 rue St-Louis, which lists an extensive selection of pasta, steak, and seafood. (☎450-974-2727. Entrees $10-17. Open M-F 11:30am-10:30pm, Sa-Su 5pm-midnight.) The only hotel in Saint-Eustache, **L'Auberge Saint-Eustache,** 40 Dubois St., offers 39 rooms that are spacious but sparsely decorated. (From Hwy. 148 North, turn right on Grignon St. and right on Dubois St. ☎514-473-6825. Rooms $70-80.)

LEAVING SAINT-EUSTACHE
Follow **Hwy. 344** out of St. Eustache to Oka.

OKA. A perfectly landscaped town on the banks of the Ottawa River, Oka is home to small diners and ice-cream shops as well as a couple of B&Bs. The cities to the east won't be as well groomed as Oka until you reach Montebello. Take a break from the road here at the **Parc National d'Oka,** 2020 Chemin d'Oka, or spend the night; showers, swimming, boating, and picnicking all await. (☎450-479-8365; www.parcsquebec.com. Open daily May to mid-Oct. 8am-10pm. Sites $22; RVs $31. Day-use $3.50, ages 6-17 $1.50, under 6 free.)

THE ROAD TO MONTEBELLO. Continue along Hwy. 344 heading west. Along this stretch of highway you'll find the **Stretch of Cigs;** the highway runs through an Indian Reservation, so every 20 ft. for about 4 mi. there is stand after stand selling cheap "native cigs" if you're in need of a nicotine fix. Between Grenville and St-Andre-Est, Hwy. 344 and 148 meet up, continuing west as **Hwy. 148.**

AUBERGE L'ETAPE
686 Rte. de Outaouais (Hwy. 344)
Halfway between St-Andre and Grenville.

This brick house dating back to 1862 served as a manse for the minister of St. Mungo's Presbyterian Church. The B&B there today, on the beautiful Ottawa River in quiet Argenteuil county, offers four bedrooms, a living/dining room with fireplace and piano, and a TV/reading room. (☎514-562-5715. Breakfast included. Reservations recommended May-Sept.; $20 deposit. Rooms $35-45.)

MONTEBELLO

In the town of Montebello, be sure to check out **Fairmont le Château Montebello,** 392 Notre Dame St. (Hwy. 148). Château Montebello may just be the world's largest log building; trying to squeeze the whole star-shaped marvel into one picture is challenging. You can wander around the 260 sq. km of lakefront property or call to reserve a tour. To stay at the Château is incredibly pricey, however, starting at $319 per night. (☎819-423-6341 or 800-441-1414; www.fairmont.com.) Be sure not to wash your car before a visit to **Parc Omega,** Hwy. 323 North, since the inevitable deer slobber will ruin the effort; majestic elk, buffalo, and what seem like hundreds of ducks and boars roam free throughout the park, walking right up to your car to lick the window in hopes of a carrot. The 1500 acre enclosed area has a 10km driving loop and walking trails. (Turn onto Hwy. 323 in Montebello,

4km north on left. ☎819-423-5487; www.parc-omega.com. Open daily June-Oct. 9:30am-6pm; Nov.-May 10am-5pm. June-Oct. $13, ages 6-15 $8, ages 2-5 $4; Nov.-May $11/$7/$4.)

Inside, **Le Zouk,** 530 Notre Dame St. (Hwy. 148) looks like a Montebellan wood cabin, but the terrace feels like Jamaican resort, with colorful umbrellas, beach music, and plants. (☎819-423-2080. Lunch $6-8. Dinner $10-15. Open M-Tu 11am-10pm, W-Su 11am-11pm.) Expect a doilied, lace-curtained stay at **Gites des 3D Chez Dodo,** 493 rue Notre-Dame (Hwy. 344), in downtown Montebello. The owners will cook you up a hearty breakfast and then show you the handy wood-carvings they make. Unfortunately, because Montebello is a highway town, the rooms can get noisy at night with passing cars. (☎819-423-5268. Rooms $45-55.) For more info, swing by **Info Touristique,** 502A Notre Dame St. (☎819-423-5602.)

 **FERME ROUGE**　　　1957 Hwy. 148
East of Hull.

Ferme Rouge has live cabaret-style entertainment that includes music, dancing, and 20 different entertainers every night. An all-you-can-eat seafood buffet complements the show. Cheesiness aside, the Ferme Rouge entertains; it has twice won first prize as a tourist attraction in the Outaouais Region. (☎819-986-7013; www.fermerouge.ca. Open Su and W-Sa from 6pm.)

APPROACHING GATINEAU
Enter Gatineau from the east on **Hwy. 148.**

GATINEAU

As of January 1, 2002, the city of Gatineau became an amalgamation of Aylmer, Buckingham, Masson-Angers, Gatineau, and Hull. Don't miss the **Canadian Museum of Civilization,** 100 Laurier St. Housed in a striking sand-dune-like structure across the Alexandra Bridge from the National Gallery, the museum offers life-sized dioramas and architectural re-creations exploring 1000 years of Canadian history. (☎819-776-7000; www.civilization.ca. Open Apr.-Oct. M-W and F-Su 9am-6pm, Th 9am-9pm; low-season hours vary. $10, seniors $7, students $6, ages 2-12 $4; families $22. Th after 4pm free. Su half-price.)

Occupying 356 sq. km northwest of Ottawa, **Gatineau Park** is certainly stop-worthy. Don't miss the spectacular fall foliage. Bikes and a variety of boats are available at Lakes Philippe

and la Pêche. (☎819-827-2020, rentals ☎819-456-3016; www.canadascapital.gc.ca/gatineau. Bikes $8 per hr., $30 per day; boats $10/$30. Open mid-June to Labor Day daily; Sa-Su thereafter.) Additionally, there are three rustic campgrounds within 1hr. of Ottawa: **Lac Philippe Campground,** which offers 248 sites with facilities for family camping, trailers, and campers; **Lac Taylor Campground,** which has 33 semi-rustic sites; and **Lac la Pêche Campground,** with 36 sites accessible only by canoe. (Take Hwy. 5 north and exit at Old Chesea. Check-in 1:30pm. Permit $20-24.)

APPROACHING OTTAWA
Cross the **Alexandra Bridge,** which will take you into the Parliament Hill area of the city.

OTTAWA

Legend has it that in the mid-19th century, Queen Victoria chose Ottawa as Canada's capital by closing her eyes and pointing a finger at a map. In reality, perhaps political savvy, rather than blind chance, guided her to this once-remote logging town. Held by neither the French nor the English, Ottawa was the perfect compromise. Forced to attempt to forge national unity while preserving local identities, Ottawa continues to play cultural diplomat to rest of Canada.

GETTING AROUND

The **Rideau Canal** divides Ottawa into the eastern lower town and the western upper town and is lined with bike paths and walkways. The canal is a major access route and the world's longest skating rink during the winter. West of the canal, Parliament buildings and government offices line **Wellington St.,** a major east-west arteries, running directly into the heart of downtown. **Laurier Ave.** is the only other east-west street permitting traffic from one side of the canal to the other. East of

GREAT NORTH

VITAL STATS

Population: 320,000

Visitor Info: National Capital Commission Information Center, 90 Wellington St. (☎613-239-5000; www.capcan.ca), opposite the Parliament Bldg. Open daily early May to early Sept. 8:30am-9pm; early Sept. to early May 9am-5pm.

Currency Exchange: Custom House Currency Exchange, 153 Sparks St. (☎613-234-6005; www.customhouse.com), behind the tourist office. $2 flat service charge, waived for groups of 5 or more. Open May-Sept. M-Sa 9am-7pm, Su 10am-5pm; Oct.-Apr. M-F 9am-5pm.

Internet Access: Ottawa Public Library, 120 Metcalf St. (☎613-236-0301). Open M-Th 10am-9pm, F noon-6pm, Sa 10am-5pm.

Post Office: 59 Sparks St. (☎613-844-1545). Open M-F 8am-6pm. **Postal Code:** K1P 5A0.

the canal, Wellington St. becomes **Rideau St.,** surrounded by a fashionable shopping district. North of Rideau St., the **Byward Market** hosts a summertime open-air market and most of Ottawa's nightlife. **Elgin St.** runs north-south from Hwy. 417 (the Queensway) to the War Memorial just south of Wellington near Parliament Hill. **Bank St.,** which runs parallel to Elgin three blocks to the west, services the town's older shopping area. **Parking** downtown is hard to find, and Ottawa is notorious for prompt ticketing of vehicles. On weekends, park for free in the World Exchange Plaza, on Queen St. between O'Connor and Metcalfe.

⊙ SIGHTS

THE HUB. Parliament Hill, on Wellington at Metcalfe St., towers over downtown with its distinguished Gothic architecture. The **Centennial Flame** at the south gate was lit in 1967 to mark the 100th anniversary of Confederation. The Prime Minister can be spotted at the central Parliament structure, **Centre Block,** which contains the House of Commons, Senate, and Library of Parliament. Free tours of Centre Block depart every 30min. from the white **Infotent** by the Visitors Center. (☎613-992-4793. Infotent open daily mid-May to mid-June 9am-5pm; mid-June to Aug. 9am-8pm. Tours mid-May to Sept. M-F 9am-8pm, Sa-Su 9am-5pm; Sept. to mid-May daily 9am-3:30pm.)

When Parliament is in session, you can watch Canada's officials debate. (☎613-992-4793; www.parl.gc.ca. Mid-Sept. to Dec. and Feb. to mid-June M-Th 2:15-3pm, F 11:15am-noon. Arrive about 2hr. in advance to obtain passes.) On display behind the library, the bell from Centre Block is one of few remnants of the original 1859-1866 structure that survived a 1916 fire. According to legend, the bell crashed to the ground after chiming at midnight the night of the blaze. Today, daily concerts chime from 53 bells hanging in the Peace Tower. (1hr. concerts June-Sept. M-F 2pm. 15min. concerts Sept.-June M-F noon.)

Those interested in trying to make a statuesque soldier smile should attend the 30min. **Changing of the Guard** on the broad lawns in front of Centre Block. (☎613-993-1811. Late June to late Aug. daily 10am, weather permitting.) At dusk, Centre Block and its lawns transform into the background for **Sound and Light,** which relates the history of the Parliament Buildings and the nation. (☎613-239-5000. Shows mid-May to early Sept.) Several blocks west along Wellington St. stand the **Supreme Court of Canada** and the **Federal Court.** (☎613-995-5361; www.ssc-csc.gc.ca. Open daily June-Aug. 9am-5pm; Sept.-May hours vary. Free tours every 30min.; No tours Sa-Su noon-1pm. Tours alternate between French and English.)

CONFEDERATION SQUARE. East of the Parliament Buildings at the junction of Sparks, Wellington, and Elgin St. stands **Confederation Square** and the enormous **National War Memorial,** dedicated by King George VI in 1939. The structure, a life-size representation of Canadian troops marching under the eye of the angels of liberty, symbolizes the triumph of peace over war. At **Nepean Point,** several blocks northwest of Rideau Centre and the Byward Market, behind the National Gallery of Canada, share a panoramic view of the capital with a statue of explorer Samuel de Champlain.

ROYALTY. The Governor General, the Queen's representative in Canada, resides at **Rideau Hall.** Take a tour of the house, gardens, and art collection—many visitors even run into the Governor General Himself. (1 Sussex Dr. ☎613-991-4422 or 800-465-6890; www.gg.ca. Free 45min. tours 10am-3pm; self-guided tours 3-4:30pm.) See the production of collectors' "loonies" ($1 coins) at the **Royal Canadian Mint.** (320 Sussex Dr. ☎613-993-8990 or

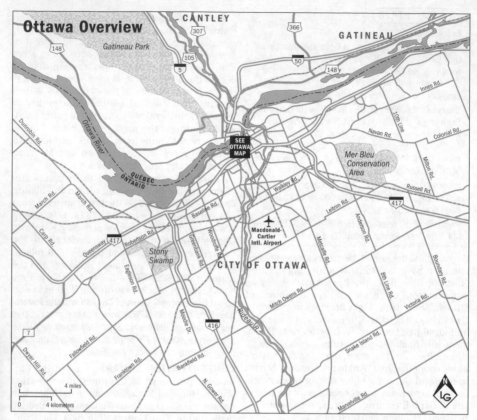

Ottawa Overview

CANTLEY
307
366
GATINEAU
148
Gatineau Park
105
50
148
5
Innes Rd.
Ottawa River
Navan Rd.
10th Line
Colonial Rd.
Duntobin Rd.
SEE OTTAWA MAP
Mer Bleu Conservation Area
Milton Rd.
QUEBEC ONTARIO
Walkley Rd.
Russell Rd.
March Rd.
March Rd.
Baseline Rd.
Leitrim Rd.
417
Carp Rd.
Queensway
417
Robertson Rd.
Woodroffe Rd.
Greenbank Rd.
Macdonald-Cartier Intl. Airport
Anderson Rd.
Metcalfe Rd.
Boundary Rd.
Stony Swamp
CITY OF OTTAWA
8th Line Rd.
Eagleson Rd.
Mitch Owens Rd.
Victoria Rd.
7
Fallowfield Rd.
Moodie Dr.
416
Rideau R.
Snake Island Rd.
Dwyer Hill Rd.
Franktown Rd.
Bankfield Rd.
N. Gower Rd.
Marvelville Rd.

0   4 miles
0   4 kilometers

N
LG

800-276-7714. Tours every 15min. Summer M-F 9am-8pm, Sa-Su 9am-5:30pm; winter daily 9am-5pm. M-F $3, Sa-Su $1.50; children free.)

OUTDOOR ACTIVITIES. Artificial **Dow's Lake,** accessible by the Queen Elizabeth Dr., extends off the Rideau Canal south of Ottawa. **Dow's Lake Pavilion** rents boats, canoes, and bikes in summer and ice skates and sleighs during the winter. *(101 Queen Elizabeth Driveway, near Preston St. ☎613-232-1001. Open mid-May to Sept. daily 8am-8pm.)*

🏛 MUSEUMS

▓ **National Gallery,** 380 Sussex Dr. (☎613-990-1985 or 800-319-2787, tickets or reservations 888-541-8888; www.national.gallery.ca). A glass-

towered building adjacent to Nepean Pt. holds the world's most comprehensive collection of Canadian art. The facade is a reinterpretation of the nearby neo-Gothic Library of Parliament. Don't miss Rideau Chapel, a church reconstructed inside the Gallery. Open May-Oct. M-W and F-Su 10am-5pm, Th 10am-8pm; off season closed M-Tu. Free.

Canadian Museum of Contemporary Photography, 1 Rideau Canal (☎613-990-8257; www.cmcp.gallery.ca), on the steps between the Château Laurier and the Ottawa Locks. Showcases an impressive rotation of temporary exhibits. Open M-W and F-Su 10am-5pm, Th 10am-8pm; off season closed M-Tu. Free.

Canadian War Museum, 330 Sussex Dr. (☎613-776-8600; www.warmuseum.ca). Documents the history of the Canadian armed forces, from colonial skirmishes to UN Peacekeeping missions. See Hitler's armored car and walk through a mock WWI trench. Open M-W and F-Su 9:30am-5pm, Th 9:30am-8pm; mid-Oct. to May closed M. $4, students and seniors $3, children $2, families $9. Th after 4pm free. Su half-price.

Canadian Museum of Nature, 240 McLeod St. (☎613-566-4700; www.nature.ca), at Metcalfe St. A multimedia exploration of the natural world. Open May to early Sept. M-W and F-Su 9:30am-5pm, Th 9:30am-8pm; off-season hours vary. $8, students and seniors $7, ages 3-12 $3.50, families $13. Sa before noon free.

FESTIVALS

Ottawans celebrate everything, even the bitter Canadian cold. All-important **Canada Day,** July 1, involves fireworks, partying in Major's Hill Park, concerts, and merrymaking. During the first three weekends of February, **Winterlude** (☎800-465-1867; www.canadascapital.gc.ca/winterlude) lines the Rideau Canal. Ice sculptures and a working ice cafe illustrate how it feels to be an Ottawan in the winter—frozen. In early May, the **Tulip Festival** (☎613-567-4447 or 800-668-8547; www.tulipfestival.ca) explodes with a kaleidoscope of more than a million buds around Dow's Lake, while pop concerts and other events center on Major's Hill Park. Music fills the air during the **Dance Festival** (☎613-947-7000; www.canadadance.ca), in late June, and the **Jazz Festival** (☎613-241-2633; www.ottawajazzfestival.com), in late July.

FOOD

Ottawa's **Byward Market,** on Byward St. between York and George St., is full of tables displaying produce, plants, and sweet maple syrup. (☎613-562-3325. Open in warmer weather daily 8am-5pm.) York, George, and Clarence St. are packed with cafes, great restaurants, and bars.

◙ **Medithéo,** 77 Clarence St. (☎613-562-2500; www.meditheo.com). Whether it's the alluring atmosphere, the exotic cuisine, or that 3rd glass of sangria ($7), the world looks different from the inside of this unique eatery. Entrees $17-25. Open M-F 11am-11pm, Sa-Su 11am-2am.

◙ **Mamma Grazzi's Kitchen,** 25 George St. (☎613-241-8656). This Italian hideaway is tucked in a stone building in one of the oldest parts of Ottawa.

Thin-crust pizza ($9-15) is worth the wait. Generally open Su-Th 10:30am-10pm, F-Sa 10:30am-11pm.

Byward Café, 55 Byward Market (☎613-241-2555), at George St. Fun pop music and a huge array of savory treats bring both young and old to eat, drink, and relax on the breezy covered patio. Panini sandwiches $4.50. Open daily summer 8am-11pm; winter 8am-6pm.

D'Arcy McGee's Irish Pub, 44 Sparks St. (☎613-230-4433; www.darcymcgees.ca). Whether lured in by the traditional Celtic music or chased in by the traditional Canadian rain, visitors to D'Arcy's are never sorry they came. Hearty pub food $8-15. Live music W. Open Su-Tu 11am-1am, W-Sa 11am-2am.

ACCOMMODATIONS

In downtown Ottawa, economical options exist only if you avoid hotels. Advance reservations are strongly recommended, especially if staying through Canada Day (July 1). **Ottawa Bed and Breakfast** represents 10 B&Bs in the Ottawa area. (☎613-563-0161. Singles $49-54; doubles $59-64.)

◙ **University of Ottawa Residences,** 90 University St. (☎613-564-5400 or 877-225-8664), in the center of campus, an easy walk from downtown. Clean, spacious dorms in a concrete landscape. Parking $10 per day. Check-in 4:30pm. Check-out 10:30am. Open early May to late Aug. Singles $40, students $30; doubles $60/$45.

Ottawa International Hostel (HI-C), 75 Nicholas St. (☎613-235-2595), in downtown Ottawa. The site of Canada's last public hanging,, former Carleton County Jail now "incarcerates" travelers in tiny cells. Kitchen, Internet, laundry, lounges, jail tours, and a friendly, ironic atmosphere. Linen $2.50. Key deposit $2. Parking $5 per day. Reception 24hr. Check-in 1pm. Check-out 11am. Lockout in winter 1-7am. Dorms $20, nonmembers $24; private rooms from $53/$57.

NIGHTLIFE

Many of Ottawa's nightclubs have been bought out recently due to crime (mostly old-fashioned bar brawls). Now that nightspots can serve alcohol until 2am, the capital city is where it's at.

The Honest Lawyer, 141 George St. (☎613-562-2262), near Dalhousie St. If you were to mix an arcade, a college library, and a law office, this cavernous bar is what you'd get. A bowling alley, pool table, and foosball round out this sports bar. The

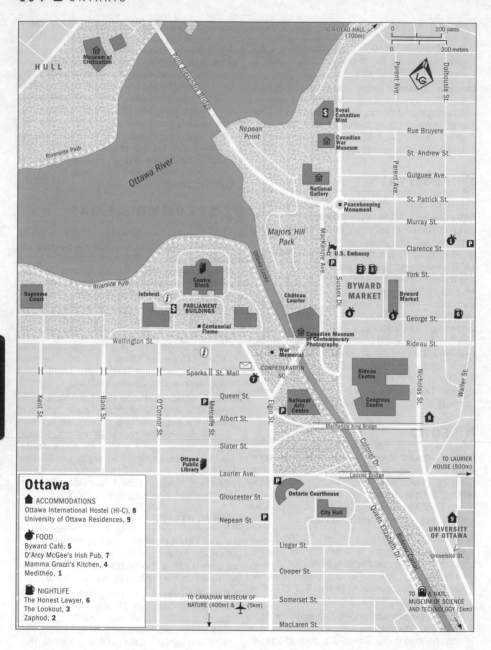

GREAT NORTH

HULL

Museum of Civilization

Ottawa River

Riverside Path

Pont Alexandra Bridge

TO RIDEAU HALL (700m)

0   200 yards
0   200 meters

Nepean Point

Royal Canadian Mint

Canadian War Museum

National Gallery

Peacekeeping Monument

Parent Ave.

Rue Bruyere

St. Andrew St.

Guiguee Ave.

St. Patrick St.

Murray St.

Clarence St.

York St.

Dalhousie St.

Majors Hill Park

MacKenzie Ave.

U.S. Embassy

BYWARD MARKET

Byward Market

George St.

Rideau St.

Riverside Path

Centre Block

Infotent

PARLIAMENT BUILDINGS

Centennial Flame

Supreme Court

Sussex Dr.

Château Laurier

Ottawa Locks

Canadian Museum of Contemporary Photography

Wellington St.

War Memorial

CONFEDERATION SQ.

Sparks St. Mall

Queen St.

Albert St.

Slater St.

Kent St.

Bank St.

O'Connor St.

Metcalfe St.

Elgin St.

National Arts Centre

Rideau Centre

Congress Centre

Nicholas St.

Waller St.

MacKenzie King Bridge

Laurier Ave.

Ottawa Public Library

Gloucester St.

Nepean St.

Ontario Courthouse

City Hall

Colonel Dr.

Laurier Bridge

TO LAURIER HOUSE (500m)

UNIVERSITY OF OTTAWA

Université St.

Rideau Canal

Queen Elizabeth Dr.

Ottawa

ACCOMMODATIONS
Ottawa International Hostel (HI-C), **8**
University of Ottawa Residences, **9**

FOOD
Byward Café, **5**
D'Arcy McGee's Irish Pub, **7**
Mamma Grazzi's Kitchen, **4**
Medithéo, **1**

NIGHTLIFE
The Honest Lawyer, **6**
The Lookout, **3**
Zaphod, **2**

Lisgar St.

Cooper St.

Somerset St.

MacLaren St.

TO CANADIAN MUSEUM OF NATURE (400m) & (5km)

TO & NATL. MUSEUM OF SCIENCE AND TECHNOLOGY (1km)

130 oz. "Beerzooka" is, well, a lot of beer ($35). M $7 all-you-can-eat wings. F-Sa 21+. Open M-F 11:30am-2am, Sa 3pm-2am, Su 6pm-2am.

Zaphod, 27 York St. (☎613-562-1010; www.zaphodbeeblebrox.com), in Byward Market. Named for a character in *The Hitchhiker's Guide to the Galaxy,* this popular alternative rock club shows local musicians. Pangalactic Gargle Blasters $6.50. Live bands W-Sa. Cover $2-10. Open daily 4pm-2am.

The Lookout, 41 York St. (☎613-789-1624), next to Zaphod's on the 2nd floor. A hoppin' gay club with intense dancing. Though the Th evening crowd is mostly male, women flock here on F. Sa is house party night. Open daily noon-2am.

▲ APPROACHING SMITH FALLS
From Ottawa, take **Hwy. 417 (Queensway)** west to **Hwy. 7,** which will meet **Hwy. 15** near Smiths Falls. Hwy. 15 enters Smiths Falls as Union St. from the north at a T-junction with **Cornelia St.** Turn right on Cornelia St. and take a left onto **Elmsley St.**

SMITHS FALLS

Smiths Falls satisfies all the senses—scenic views of Rideau River are easy on the eyes, open stage jams delight the ears, ocal museums offer hands-on displays, and the scent of the local Hershey factory tantalizes the tastebuds. The **Rideau Canal Museum,** 34 Beckwith St., houses five floors of high tech displays, images, and artifacts. Exhibits cover everything from the construction of the factory to modern influences on the local lifestyle. (☎613-284-0505; www.rideau-info.com/museum. Open mid-May to mid-Oct. daily 10am-4:30pm. $3, seniors $2.75, ages 6-18 $2.) The air surrounding **Hershey's Factory,** 1 Hershey Dr., is heavy with the sweet smell of chocolate, tempting sweet teeth well before the entrance to the endless (and unavoidable) gift shop. The self-guided tour has movies and displays on Hershey history. From the elevated viewing level, you can see the production lines turning out thousands of your favorite candies. The best part of the tour? A free full-size chocolate bar sample at the end. (Follow Elmsley St. ½ mi. south until it turns into Queen St.; the factory is on the left. ☎613-283-3300; www.hersheys.com/visit/smithfalls. Open M-F 9am-6pm, Sa 9am-5pm, Su 10am-5pm. Free.)

The **Stardust Cafe,** 6 Russell St. E, is a big dose of 1950s Americana in Ontario. A jukebox stands in the corner and Elvis posters, guitars, and vinyl records plaster the walls. Red bar stools line the diner counter where customers eat standard diner fare such as sandwiches ($4) and chicken, or specialties like schnitzel ($4) and escargot. (☎613-283-8459. Open M-Sa 11am-2pm and 4:30-8pm.) **Montgomery's on Main,** 117 Main St., offers rooms that shine with class. Wholesome breakfasts are served on the sun deck, and the proprietors will pack you a lunch. (☎613-284-0947. Rooms $50-75.)

▲ APPROACHING KINGSTON
Take **Hwy. 15 South** until it merges with Hwy. 401. Take the **Division St.** exit for downtown Kingston.

KINGSTON

The "Limestone City" was chosen for its strategic location as the western gateway to the Thousand Islands, the southern end of the Rideau Canal, and the source of the St-Lawrence River. Kingston was built by the British following the War of 1812. Believed to be impregnable in its day, it was never fired upon. Today, the Fort Henry Guard leads military and domestic re-enactments of the 1860s.

(VITAL STATS)

Population: 120,000

Visitor Info: Information Office, 209 Ontario St. (☎888 855 4555; www.cityofkingston.ca). Open daily summer 9am-9pm; winter 9am-6pm.

Internet Access: Kingston-Frontenac Public Library (☎613-549-8888). Open M-Th 9am-9pm; F-Sa 9am-5pm.

Post Office: 120 Clarence St. (☎613-530-2260). **Postal Code:** K7L 1X7.

■ **GETTING AROUND. Hwy. 15** enters Kingston from the north and meets with **U.S. 2** across the river from downtown. Cross the Lasalle Causeway to get onto **Ontario St.,** which serves as Kingston's main drag, following the waterfront through downtown. **Sir John A. MacDonald Blvd.** marks the western edge of downtown.

◎ ❀ **SIGHTS & FESTIVALS.** Kingston offers several free museums, including the **Correctional Service of Canada Penitentiary Museum,** 55 King St. West. The museum follows the history of Can-

GREAT NORTH MAP #4

GREAT NORTH

ada's federal penitentiary system, detailing the early history of Canadian penitentiaries and showing contraband weapons, escape devices, and punishment equipment. (From Ontario St., turn onto West St. for 1 block, then left onto King St. for 1 mi. ☎613-530-3122. Open May-Sept. M-F 9am-4pm, Sa-Su 10am-4pm; Oct.-Apr. by appointment only.) More light-hearted, the **Original Hockey Hall of Fame,** at York and Alfred St., is hockey's "first hall of fame" and the oldest hall of fame in Canada. Memorabilia from past and present hockey greats, including Wayne Gretzky's Edmonton Oiler rookie sweater, and the oldest hockey sweater, all await. (From Ontario St., turn onto Princess St. After ¾ mi., take a right onto Alfred St. ☎613-544-2355; www.ihhof.com. Open June 15-Labor Day M-Sa 10am-4pm, Su noon-4pm.)

Scare yourself silly on one of the **Haunted Walks of Kingston,** departing from the **Fort Henry National Historic Site,** 200 Ontario St. Just after sunset, these lantern-lit tours wind through Kingston's spooky streets and historic 19th-century fortress, exploring burial grounds ravaged by grave-robbers and the places of public execution. Watch out for the ghost of a murdered young mother-to-be, or the ghosts of the two young lovers killed in Deadman's Bay and eternally reunited on the shores. (☎613-549-6366; www.hauntedwalk.com. Tours daily May 9-June 26 8pm, June 27-Aug. 8 and 9pm, Sept. Oct. 24 8pm. $12, seniors $10, ages 6-12 $5. Reservations strongly recommended.)

Kingston's prosperity still shows in its heavily attended festivals, such as the **Busker's Rendezvous** (www.kingstonbuskers.com) in mid-July when over 100 street performers from all over the world perform downtown. Another major festival is the **Limestone City Blues Festival** (www.kingstonblues.com) at the Grand Theatre stage in Confederation Park during the third week in August, a favorite of Blues Brother Dan Aykroyd.

■ FOOD. Housed in an 1870s building, the **Kingston Brewing Company,** 34 Clarence St., off Ontario St., was the first public house in Ontario to receive a license to brew its own beer and wine on premises. Try the "Dragon's Breath Ale" or "Pooh Lager." Outside, streetside and courtyard patios are fringed with hanging white lights. Daily specials include Indian and Mexican food. (☎613-542-4978; www.kingstonbrewing.com. Entrees $6-12. Tours available. Open daily 11am-2am.) **Darbar,** 479 Princess St., off Ontario St., is one of a host of affordable Indian restaurants and a student favorite. Darbar offers all the usual Indian fare and combinations ($18) such as samosas, chicken bhoona, vegetable curry, naan, papadum, and dessert. (☎613-548-7053. Open Su-Th 11:30am-2pm and 5-9:30pm, F-Sa 11:30am-2pm and 5-10pm.)

⚑ ACCOMMODATIONS. In summer, budget-friendly accommodations in Kingston can be found at **Louise House (HI),** 329 Johnson St., a residence for Queens students September through April and a hostel for summer visitors. (From Ontario St., turn onto Barrie St., left onto Brock St., left onto Division St., and left onto Johnson St. ☎613-531-8237. Laundry, lounge, free local calls. Check-in 4pm. Check-out 11am. Open May-Aug. 20. Dorms $19, non-members $23; singles $25; doubles $40.) During its career days, the 210 ft. *Alexander Henry* was a Canadian Coast Guard ship used primarily as a navigation aid and ice breaker. Today, *Alexander Henry* is busier than most retirees, serving as the **Alexander Henry Ship B&B,** 55 Ontario St., and accommodating over 50,000 guests since 1986. If seasickness isn't a worry, you'll find the place comfortable and hotel-like, though the rooms with single beds are a bit cramped. (☎613-542-2261; www.marmuseum.ca. Check in at the Marine Museum. Parking available at the museum. Continental breakfast 7-9am. Shared baths. Check-in 4:30pm. Check-out 10am. Open May-Oct. Singles $32-55; doubles $32-90.)

◤◣ LEAVING ONTARIO
The route returns to the US over water, crossing the St. Lawrence River and Lake Ontario to **Wolf Island,** and then to Cape Vincent by **ferry.** From Kingston, ferries depart nearly every hour for Wolf Island. (☎613-548-7227. 25 min. May-Oct. 19 per day 6:15am-2am. Free.) On Wolf Island, follow the well-marked signs leading to the next dock. It is a 7 mi./11km drive (about 10-12min.) and the ferry gives about a 20min. buffer period, so you don't need to drive quickly, but the ferry to Cape Vincent is much smaller and space is limited. Ferries depart Wolf Island nearly every hour for Cape Vincent. (☎315-783-0638 or 613-385-2402. 10min. Runs daily 8am-7pm. Car and driver US$8/CDN$12; passengers US$2/CDN$3.) Be prepared to show identification and proof of citizenship upon boarding the ferry and landing in Cape Vincent. See **Vital Documents** (p. 11) for information on passport and visa requirements.

Welcome To NEW YORK

CAPE VINCENT

Cape Vincent is nestled in the scenic **Thousand Island Seaway,** which spans 100 mi. from the mouth of Lake Ontario to the first of the many locks on the St. Lawrence River. Surveys conducted by the US and Canadian governments determined that there are 1864 islands in the seaway, with requirements being that at least 1 sq. ft. of land must sit above water year-round and two trees should grow on it. The islands, which have granite cliffs, shady trees, and sandy beaches, are surprisingly variable for a relatively small region. The region is also a fisherman's paradise, with some of the world's best bass and muskie catches.

Aubrey's Inn, 126 S. James St., serves up some of the best deals in the seaway beside an indoor mural of the Tibbetts Point Lighthouse. (☎315-654-3754. Breakfast $1.50-6. Entrees $7-9. Open daily 7am-10pm.) For roadtrippers with time, Cape Vincent makes a nice base from which to explore the region; the **Tibbetts Point Lighthouse Hostel (HI-AYH),** 33439 County Rte. 6, provides maritime-themed accommodations. At night, the hypnotic rhythm of the waves lulls visitors to sleep in the old keeper's quarters. (Turn west onto Broadway and follow the river 3 mi. ☎315-654-3450. 26 dorm beds, family rooms available. Linen $1. Check-in 5-10pm. Reservations recommended July-Aug. Open mid-May to Oct. Dorms $14, nonmembers $17. No credit cards.) **Burnham Point State Park,** on Rte. 12 East, 4½ mi. east of Cape Vincent, has a wonderful view of the water and three picnic areas among the 49 sites, but lacks a beach and is therefore often one of the less crowded campgrounds. (☎315-654-2324. Showers. Reception late May to early Sept. daily 8am-10pm. Sites $13-19, with electricity $19-23. Boat dockage $6 per day; $2.75 surcharge for each registration. Day-use $6 per car.)

LEAVING CAPE VINCENT
Take Rte. 12 East south to Limerick, then merge onto Rte. 180 West. South of Dexter, turn onto Rte. 3 East.

THE DUCK INN
12260 Rte. 12 East
12 mi. from Cape Vincent, in Chaumont.

The Duck Inn serves home-cooking with daily specials; Friday nights feature fish fries and Saturday nights are prime rib. After you've Ducked Inn for dinner, Duck Out next door for ice-cream sundaes and splits. (Duck Inn ☎315-649-3825. Duck Out ☎315-649-2535. Open daily 11am-10pm.)

OLD MCDONALD'S
26 mi. from Cape Vincent. Turn east onto Smithville Rd. across the street from the Trading Post and follow it for 2 mi.

Old McDonald does have a farm, and on that farm he has a petting zoo, not to mention a Wizard of Oz hayride, cow milking trolley, and pony rides. (☎315-583-5737; www.oldmcdonaldhasa-farm.com. Generally open 10am-5pm. $5. Pony rides $2. Moo Town Trolley Tour $2.)

MR. BALDJAMIAH'S
7512 Rte. 3
59 mi. from Cape Vincent in Pulaski.

This restaurant in a log cabin offers specials for holidays like "Take Your Dog to Work Day" or "Blue T-Shirt Day." No matter what day, the restaurant serves delicious Philly cheesesteaks ($5.50) and $0.20 wings. (☎315-298-6335. Drink specials $4. "Attitude adjustment hour" M-F 4-7pm. Open Apr. to mid-Oct. M-Th 11:30am-9pm, F 11:30am-10pm, Sa noon-10pm, Su noon-8pm.)

APPROACHING OSWEGO
South of Pulaski, turn off **Rte. 3** onto **Rte. 104.**

OSWEGO
This small city offers a wealth of historical attractions. Rebuilt time and again by Britain and the US after attacks, the **Fort Ontario State Historic Site,** 1 E. 4th St., was established in 1949. Today, it has been restored to its 1867-1872 appearance. Costumed interpreters host demonstrations. (☎315-343-4711. Open May-Oct. M-Sa 10am-5pm, Su 1-5pm.) In 1944, 982 refugees fled the Nazi regime from 18 war-torn countries; Oswego became their home for the next 18 months. **Oswego Safe Haven,** 2 E. 7th St., is a non-profit corporation that docu-

ments the lives of the Holocaust refugees who found sanctuary at the Fort Ontario Emergency Refugee Shelter. (☎315-342-3003, www.oswego-haven.org. Open Su 1-5pm, Tu-Sa 10am-5pm. $5, seniors $2, ages 5-12 $2, under 5 free.)

Enjoy your food on a patio with views of the river at the **Whitewater Grille,** 7 Bridie Sq. Featuring Italian and French cuisine, the Grille cooks pizza, burgers, sandwiches, and chicken cordon bleu ($13). Upstairs is the **Stoneledge Ice Cream Parlor.** (☎315-343-9910. Entrees $6-20. Open daily 11am-10pm.) Local art is displayed throughout the **Oswego Inn,** 180 E. 10th St. (☎800-721-7341. Continental breakfast included. Off-street parking available. Singles $45-55; doubles $60-70.)

APPROACHING ROCHESTER
Take **Rte. 104** to **I-590** to **I-490,** which leads into downtown Rochester.

ROCHESTER
Rochester is New York's third-largest urban area, which has allowed it to combine its historic past with an inventive metropolitan present. Few American cities have had such a lasting social and political impact; both Susan B. Anthony and Frederick Douglass spent their most active years in Rochester and are buried now in Rochester's Mount Hope Cemetery. The international corporations of Bausch and Lomb, Eastman Kodak, and Xerox all got their start in Rochester as well.

VITAL STATS

Population: 220,000

Visitor Info: Greater Rochester Visitors Association, 45 East Ave., Ste. 400. (☎585-546-3070 or 800-677-7282; www.visitrochester.com). Open M-F 8:30am-5pm, Sa 10am-4pm, Su 10am-3pm; in summer Sa 9am-5pm.

Internet Access: Rochester Public Library, 115 South Ave. (☎585-428-7300). Open M and Th 9am-9pm, Tu-W and F 9am-6pm, Sa 9am-5pm, Su 1pm-5pm.

Post Office: 1335 Jefferson Rd. (☎585-272-5953). Open M-F 7am-7pm, Sa 8am-2pm. **Postal Code:** 14692.

GETTING AROUND. The **Genesee River** runs through the middle of Rochester. I-490 makes a loop in town; the **Clinton Ave.** exit leads to downtown. **Main St.** runs east-west. A half-mile east of the city center, **Park Ave.** houses many services within the radius of a couple of blocks.

◐ SIGHTS. Susan B. Anthony, a pioneer for women's rights, lived in Rochester during her most politically active years; the **Susan B. Anthony House,** 17 Madison St., still remains standing. It was in this red brick house that she was arrested for voting in 1872. Today, the house is a museum. (From Main St., head west ½ mi., and turn right onto Madison St. ☎585-235-6124; www.susanbanthonyhouse.org. Open Labor Day-Memorial Day Su and W-Sa 11am-4pm; Memorial Day-Labor Day Su and Tu-Sa 11am-5pm. Last tour 1hr. before close. $6, seniors $5, children $3.) The reproduction of Sesame Street at the **Strong Museum,** 1 Manhattan Sq., is among those that have made the museum the nation's leading hands-on history center for families and children. (From Main St., turn south onto S. Clinton Ave. Turn left onto Woodbury Ave. At the next light, cross Chestnut St. into the parking lot. ☎585-263-2700; www.strongmuseum.org. Open M-Th and Sa 10am-5pm, F 10am-8pm, Su noon-5pm. $6, seniors and students $5, ages 2-17 $5, under 2 free.)

In 1888, George Eastman produced a flexible film camera that launched an amateur photography company later known as Eastman Kodak. The **George Eastman House,** 900 East Ave., owns works by over 10,000 photographers and the **world's largest collection of American cameras,** including the first Kodak Brownie and a camera that belonged to Ansel Adams. (☎585-271-3361; www.eastman.org. Open Su 1-5pm, Tu-Sa 10am-5pm, Th 10am-8pm. Tours 10:30am and 2pm. $8, seniors $6, students $5, ages 5-12 $3, under 5 free.) At the thriving **High Falls Entertainment District,** 60 Brown's Race, check out the dazzling laser light show projected on the walls of the river gorge, nightclubs, restaurants and shops. High Falls is also a National Register Historic District with old mills and factories from Rochester's glory days. An 850-ft. Pont-de-Rennes pedestrian bridge sits across the High Falls waterfall. (☎585-325-2030.)

▟▛ FOOD & ACCOMMODATIONS. The restaurants on **Park Ave.** are especially good, offering intimate bistros and sidewalk cafes. Locals congregate at **Jines Restaurant,** 658 Park Ave., amid the uber-modern Art Deco furnishings. Breakfast specials include banana bread french toast. (☎585-

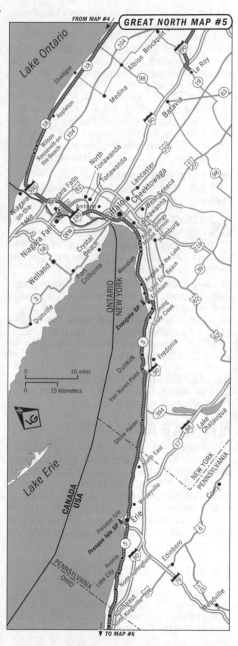

GREAT NORTH

461-1280. Open M-Sa 7am-10pm, Su 7am-8pm.) The inside of **Charlie's Frog Pond,** 652 Park Ave., is funky, with colorful and silly straw-like sculptures on the booths. Paintings from a famous local painter, Ramon Santiago, cover the walls. An eclectic selection of evening specials includes duck with kahlua creme sauce and the more low key "Horny Toad" ($6.50), which is ground beef, an English muffin, and chili and cheese. (☎585-271-1970. Breakfast $4-6. Sandwiches $3-7. Open M-F 7am-9pm, Sa 8am-10pm, Su 8am-3pm.) Affordable lodging near Rochester can be found at chain motels south of town in Henrietta.

🔼 LEAVING ROCHESTER

From **I-390,** turn west onto **Lake Ontario State Pkwy.** which becomes **Rte. 18.**

🔽 DETOUR: JELL-O MUSEUM   23 E. Main St.

Take I-490 West from Rochester, merge onto I-90 West (NY State Thruway) and then exit onto Rte. 19 South. LeRoy is 4 mi. south of the interstate. The gallery is behind the Historic LeRoy House.

The Jell-O factory offers self-guided tours with a guided introduction. Jell-O memorabilia, souvenirs, and trivia are available, and you get a free package of Jell-O when you leave. (☎585-768-7433; www.jellomuseum.com. Open M-F 10am-4pm; May-Oct. also Sa 10am-4pm, Su 1-4pm. $3, ages 6-11 $1.50, under 6 free.)

🔼 APPROACHING NIAGARA FALLS

Continue west on **Rte. 18** to the **Robert Moses Pkwy.,** which heads south into Niagara Falls.

NIAGARA FALLS

Niagara Falls, one of the seven natural wonders of the world, is flat-out spectacular. In an inversion to what you might expect, Niagara on the Ontario side is full of flashy Vegas-style attractions—a trend that horrified many residents over the past couple decades—while the New York side is mainly a park area and something of a ghost town. The giant falls are best viewed from the Canadian side of the Niagara River.

▣ GETTING AROUND

Niagara Falls spans the US-Canadian border. The **Robert Moses Pkwy.** runs along the river to the sights on the US side of the falls. On the US side, **Niagara St.** is the main street, ending in the west at

VITAL STATS

Population: 56,000

Visitor Info: US: Orin Lehman Visitors Center (☎716-278-1796) on Prospect St., in front of the Falls Observation Deck. Open M-F 8am-7pm, Sa-Su 10am-6pm. **CAN: Niagara Falls Tourism,** 5515 Stanley Ave. (☎905-356-6061 or 800-563-2557; www.discovemiagara.com). Open daily 8am-8pm.

Internet Access: Niagara Falls Public Library, 1425 Main St. (☎716-286-4894; www.niagarafalls-publiclib.org). Open M-W 9am-9pm, Th-F 9am-5pm.

Post Office: 615 Main St. (☎716-285-7561). Open M-F 8:30am-5pm, Sa 8:30am-2pm. **Postal Code:** 14302.

the one-way **Rainbow Bridge** to Canada (pedestrians $0.50; cars $2.50). In Canada, **Roberts St. (Rte. 420)** is the main east-west street, and **Stanley Ave.** is the main north-west street, but Clifton Hill is where the attractions are. **Whirlpool Bridge** leads back to the US (no fee). To get there, take Stanley Ave. north and turn right onto **Bridge St.**

Parking is cheaper farther into the city and away from the falls where you can find lots as cheap as $3. In NY, go to **Prospect St.,** where the parking is $10 in winter (no overnight). There are two lots on Goat Island. (Open daily summer 8am-11pm; winter 8am-8pm. $8. Arrive before 8am and you don't have to pay.) The city lots on the Canadian side are expensive. (Open daily 9am-8pm; summer until 11pm. CDN$12-18.) For free parking, use the casino lot on **Kitchener St.** and take the free shuttle to the casino, just a quick walk from the falls.

People Movers buses tourists through the 30km area on the Canadian side of the falls, stopping at attractions along the way. (☎877-642-7275. Runs Mid-June to early Sept. daily 9am-11pm; low-season hours vary. CDN$6, children CDN$3.)

◉ SIGHTS

AMERICAN SIDE. For over 150 years, the ▨**Maid of the Mist** boat tour has entertained visitors with the awe-inspiring (and wet) views from the foot of both falls. (*☎716-284-8897. Open daily 10am-6pm. Tours in summer every 30min. $10.50, ages 6-12 $6.25. $1 for entrance to observation deck only.*) The **Cave of the Winds Tour** hands out souvenir (read: ineffective) yellow raincoats and sandals for a drenching hike to the base of the Bridal Veil Falls, including an optional walk to

Hurricane Deck where strong waves slam down from above. (☎716-278-1730. *Open May to mid-Oct.; hours vary depending on season and weather conditions. Trips leave every 15min. Must be at least 42 in. tall. $8, ages 6-12 $7.*) The **Master Pass**, available at the Visitors Center, covers admission to the Maid of the Mist; the Cave of the Winds Tour; the **Niagara Gorge Discovery Center**, in Prospect Park, which has gorge trail hikes and a simulated elevator ride through the geological history of the falls; the **Aquarium**, which houses the endangered Peruvian Penguin; and the **Niagara Scenic Trolley**, a tour of the park and the best transport between the sights on the American side. *(Master Pass $25, ages 6-12 $18. Discovery Center ☎716-278-1780. $5, children $3. Aquarium: 701 Whirlpool St., across from Discovery Center. ☎716-285-3575; www.aquariumofniagara.org. Open daily July-Aug. 9am-7pm; off season 9am-5pm. $7, children and seniors $5. Trolley ☎716-278-1730. Runs May-Aug. daily 9am-10pm every 10-20min. $5, children $3.)*

CANADIAN SIDE. On the Canadian side of Niagara Falls, **Queen Victoria Park** provides the best view of **Horseshoe Falls**. Starting 1hr. after sunset, the falls are illuminated for 3hr. every night, and a free fireworks display lights up the sky every Friday and Sunday at 10pm in summer. Bikers, inline skaters, and walkers enjoy the 32km **Niagara River Recreation Trail**, which runs from Fort Erie to Fort George and passes many historical sights dating back to the War of 1812. Far above the crowds and excitement, **Skylon Tower** has the highest view of the falls at 520 ft. above ground and 775 ft. above the base of the falls. The tower's **Observation Deck** offers a calming, unhindered vista. *(5200 Robinson St. ☎716-356-2651. Open June-Oct. M-F 8am-11pm, Sa-Su 8am-midnight; Nov.-May daily 9am-11pm. CDN$10, seniors CDN$9, children CDN$6; families CDN$27.)* The **Adventure Pass** includes entrance to the **Maid of the Mist** boat tour; **Journey Behind the Falls**, a tour behind Horseshoe Falls; **White Water Walk**, a long boardwalk next to the Niagara River Rapids; and the **Butterfly Conservatory**, on the grounds of the world-famous Niagara Parks Botanical Gardens. It also offers CDN$2 discounts for the **Spanish Aero Car**, an aerial cable ride over the rapids' whirlpool waters, and all-day transportation on the People Movers. *(www.niagaraparks.com has details and sells passes online. Adventure Pass: CDN$38, children CDN$24. Maid of the Mist: ☎716-357-7393. Open summer*

daily 9:45am-5:45pm. Trips every 15min. CDN$13/CDN$8. Journey ☎716-354-1551. Open in summer daily 9am-7:30pm. CDN$10/CDN$6. Walk ☎716-374-1221. Open summer daily 9am-8pm. Tours available. CDN$8/CDN$5. Conservatory ☎716-358-0025. CDN$10/CDN$6. Open summer daily 9am-7:30pm. Aero Car ☎716-354-5711. Open in summer daily 9am-6:45pm. CDN$11/CDN$7.)

▨ FOOD

Niagara Cumpir, 4941 Victoria Ave., ON, serves a young, hip clientele affordable Mediterranean fare on two patios. (☎905-356-9900. Open Su-W 11am-11pm, Th-Sa 11am-1am). The oldest restaurant in town, **Simon's Restaurant**, 4116 Bridge St., ON, one block from the HI hostel, is still a local favorite, thanks to its huge breakfasts (CDN$6), giant homemade muffins (CDN$0.69), and home-style dinners. (☎905-356-5310. Open M-Sa 5:30am-7pm, Su 5:30am-2pm.) In the US, backpackers and locals alike flock to **The Press Box Restaurant**, 324 Niagara St., for enormous meals at tiny prices. On Monday and Wednesday, feast on $1.25 spaghetti. (☎716-284-5447. Open daily 9am-11pm.)

▨ ACCOMMODATIONS

Niagara is a popular honeymoon destination. In Canada, cheap motels (from CDN$35) advertising free wedding certificates line **Lundy's Ln.**, while moderately priced B&Bs overlook the gorge on **River Rd.** between the Rainbow Bridge and the Whirlpool Bridge.

▨ **Hostelling International Niagara Falls (HI-AYH)**, 4549 Cataract Ave., Niagara Falls, ON (☎905-357-0770 or 888-749-0058; www.hihostels.ca). Just off Bridge St. Remarkable, well-equipped hostel with a laid-back atmosphere and convivial, rainbow-colored interior. Organic vegetable garden, a compost pile, and fair trade organic coffee. Activities include hemp flower pancake breakfasts, Su vegan potluck (6-9pm), and a drum circle. Internet CDN$1 per 15 min. Lockers CDN$2. Linen CDN$2 (free with ISIC). Key deposit CDN$5. Reception summer 24hr., winter 8am-midnight. Check-out 11am. Quiet hours 11pm-7am. Reservations recommended May-Nov. Dorms CDN$19, nonmembers CDN$23; singles $50/$59.

Backpacker's International Hostel, 4219 Huron St., Niagara Falls, ON (☎905-357-4266 or 800-891-

7022; www.backpackers.ca), at Zimmerman Ave. A well-maintained hostel in a historic home with clean and simple dorm rooms. Family-run and owned. Private rooms are a great deal. Bike rentals CDN$15 per day. Free Internet access. Breakfast, bed linens, and parking included. Reception 24hr. with reservation. Dorms CDN$20; singles CDN$50; doubles CDN$65.

Hostelling International Niagara Falls (HI-AYH), 1101 Ferry Ave. (☎716-282-3700), off Memorial Pkwy. Avoid walking alone on Ferry Ave. at night. 38 beds in an old house. Kitchen, TV lounge, and limited parking. Family rooms available. Linens $1.75. Check-in 7:30-9:30am and 4-11pm. Lockout 9:30am-4pm. Curfew 11:30pm; lights-out midnight. Open Feb. to mid-Dec. Dorms $15, nonmembers $18. No credit cards.

APPROACHING BUFFALO
I-190 East takes you across Grand Island and into Buffalo. Take the **Niagara St.** exit.

BUFFALO

At first glance, it seems that Buffalo is characterized by its problems: brutal winters and luckless sports franchises add to the erosion of a blue collar economy, the decaying rust belt industry, and sprawling suburbanization. Do not, however, underestimate this self-proclaimed "All America City;" from the downtown skyline to funky Elmwood Village, Buffalo balances small-town warmth with big-city culture.

VITAL STATS

Population: 280,000

Visitor Info: Visitors Center, 617 Main St. (☎716-852-2356 or 800-283-3256; www.visitbuffalonia-gara.com), in the Theater District. Open daily summer 10am-4pm; winter 10am-2pm.

Internet Access: Buffalo and Erie County Public Library, 1 Lafayette Sq. (☎716-858-8900) at Washington St. Internet access with $1 temporary library membership. Open M-Sa 8:30am-6pm.

Post Office: 701 Washington St. (☎716-856-4603). Open M-F 8:30am-5:30pm, Sa 8:30am-1pm. **Postal Code:** 14203.

GETTING AROUND. The main north-south streets are **Main St., Delaware Ave.,** and **Niagara St.** The main east-west streets are **Clinton St., Broadway St.,** and **Seneca St.** Street **parking** is not difficult to find; most lots run about $5 per day.

SIGHTS. At the **Buffalo Zoo,** 300 Parkside Ave., over 23 acres shelter 1500 exotic and domestic animals. Hands-on summer activities include feeding giraffes and washing elephants. By far the best attraction is Surapa, the painting elephant. (☎716-837-3900; www.buffalozoo.org. Open daily June-Labor Day 10am-5pm; Labor Day-May 10am-4pm. Surapa shows Su-M and F-Sa at 11:30am. $7, seniors $3, ages 2-14 $3.50, under 2 free.) The **Albright-Knox Art Gallery,** 1285 Elmwood Ave., houses a collection of over 6000 modern pieces, including works by Picasso and Rothko. (☎716-882-8700; www.albrightknox.org. Open Su noon-5pm, Tu-Sa 11am-5pm. $8, seniors and students $6, under 13 free; families $12. Sa 11am-1pm free.) Next to the gallery is **Delaware Park,** the center of Buffalo's park system, which was designed by legendary landscape architect Frederick Law Olmsted. Frank Lloyd Wright also designed several important houses in the area. Architecture buffs can take a 2hr. self-guided **walking tour** of historic downtown Buffalo. Pick up the free guide, *Walk Buffalo,* at the Visitors Center.

FOOD. Elmwood Village, up Elmwood Ave. between Virginia and Forest Ave., is full of funky boutiques, coffee shops, and ethnic restaurants. On a busy Friday night in 1964 at the **Anchor Bar,** 1047 Main St., Teressa Bellissimo cooked up an unusual midnight snack for her son's hungry friends. The curiosities were chicken wings, which back then were only used in the stock pot for soup. Thus Buffalo wings were born, and the rest is history. The original restaurant still exists, and today you can enjoy their wings mild, medium, hot, spicy BBQ, or suicidal. Try 10 wings for $8 or a bucket of 50 for $25. (☎716-886-8920. Live jazz F-Sa 9pm-midnight, $2.50. Open M-Th 11am-11pm, F 11am-1am, Sa-Su noon-1am.) **Gabriel's Gate,** 145 Allen St., with its rustic furniture, mounted animal heads, and big chandelier, is a friendly restaurant reminiscent of a saloon. Enjoy the famous "Richmond Ave." burger ($5) or the vegetarian portobello sandwich ($6) on the comfy shaded patio. (☎716-886-0602. Open Su-W 11:30am-midnight, F-Sa 11:30am-2am.)

ACCOMMODATIONS. Budget lodgings are a rarity in Buffalo, but chain motels can be found near the airport and off I-90, 8-10 mi. northeast of downtown. The bright **Hostel Buffalo (HI-AYH),** 667 Main St., is a clean facility with 50 beds in a centrally located neighborhood. The friendly staff makes travelers feel at home and offers free nightly movies. Kitchen and common rooms, pool table, Internet access ($1 per 15min.), free linens, and laundry facilities are available for guest use. (☎716-852-5222; www.hostelbuffalo.com. Reception 24hr. with reservation; otherwise 9-11am and July-Aug. 4-11pm; Sept.-June 5-10pm. Check-out 10am. Reservations recommended in summer. Dorms $20, nonmembers $23; private rooms $50-$65; $10 per additional adult, $5 per additional child.) The old-fashioned rooms at the **Lenox Hotel & Suites,** 140 North St., at Delaware Ave., are only 5min. from Elmwood Village nightlife. (☎716-884-1700; www.lenoxhotelandsuites.com. Cable TV, A/C. Singles from $59; suites $69-119.)

🆔 **NIGHTLIFE.** Downtown bars and clubs are concentrated on **Chippewa St.** and **Franklin St.,** but live music can be found at numerous establishments throughout the city. From Thursday to Saturday the bars are open until 4am, and thousands of Western New Yorkers are out all night. Pick up a copy of *Artvoice* for event listings. Music is burned into the walls at **Nietzsche's,** 248 Allen St., the legendary club where Ani DiFranco and the 10,000 Maniacs got their big breaks. (☎716 886 8539; www.nietzsches.com. Beer on tap from $2.50. Live bands every night. 21+. Open daily noon-4am.) **D'Arcy McGee's Irish Pub and Sky Bar,** 257 Franklin St., is an authentic Irish pub on the first floor, a nightclub on the second, and Buffalo's only open air rooftop lounge on top. Patrons can ride a glass elevator up to the sky bar to relax above the bustling scene below. (☎716-853-3600; www.buffnight.com. 21+. Sky bar cover $2-3 after 10pm. Open daily 11am-4am.) **Club Marcella,** 622 Main St., is a gay nightclub, but clubbers of all persuasions party on its two dance floors. (☎716-847-6850; www.clubmarcella.com. Drag shows W-Th and Su. F-Sa hip-hop. 18+. Cover usually $3. Open W-Su 9pm-4am.)

APPROACHING LACKAWANNA
Take **Rte. 5 West** and exit onto **Ridge Rd.**

LACKAWANNA

In Lackawanna, 6 mi. from Buffalo, the tri-dome of the **Buffalo and Erie County Botanical Gardens,** 2655 South Park Ave., rises like a crown above the green cushion of the surrounding park. Frederick Law Olmsted, the father of modern landscape architecture, designed the surrounding **South Park** in 1888. Events at the gardens include orchid shows, rare plant sales, Buffalo Philharmonic Orchestra concerts, and the annual Hot Luck ethnic food festival during the third week in July. (☎716-827-1584; www.buffalogardens.com. Open M-F 9am-4pm, W 9am-6pm, Sa-Su 9am-5pm. Donations accepted.) The **Our Lady of Victory Basilica and National Shrine,** at South Park Ave. and Ridge Rd., built in 15th- and 16th-century Renaissance style, has copper-topped towers and a huge copper dome. (☎716-828-9433. Gift shop open M-Sa 10am-4pm, Su 9am-4pm. Tours Su 1pm.) The **Grand View Drive-In Movie Theater,** Rte. 5 and Lake St. near Angola, shows new releases. (☎716-549-2450. Shows 9:30 and 11:30pm. $6, ages 6-11 $3.)

The maritime-themed **Hoak's Restaurant,** 4100 Lake Shore Rd., in Athol Springs, has a sunlit patio on Lake Erie. Entrees include char-grilled shrimp skewers ($12) and lake perch ($9.50). Also find traditional favorites—sandwiches, like Hoak's famous steak end on a kummelweck roll ($4.75), and steak specialties. (☎716-627-7988. Open M-Th 11am-11pm, F-Sa 11am-11:30pm, Su noon-11pm.)

DUNKIRK

If you happen to be in town on February 2nd, don't miss **Dunkirk Dave,** the town groundhog who comes out on the special day to forecast the coming of spring. The **Dunkirk Historical Lighthouse and Veterans Park Museum** is located at the end of Point Dr. The keeper's quarters house a museum of war memorabilia as well as lighthouse paraphernalia. (☎716-366-5050. Open Apr.-June M-Tu and Th-Sa 10am-2pm; July-Aug. 10am-4pm; Sept.-Nov. 10am-1pm. $5, ages 4-12 $2.) Just in case you hadn't gotten your daily dose of giant **Carved Indian Heads,** Dunkirk has you covered. In the 1970s, Peter Toth traveled the country carving heads as part of his "Trail of Whispering Giants" project, which now reaches through all 50 states. A gnarly 15 ft. tall giant (Ong-Gwe-Ohn-Weh), on Lakeshore Dr. (Rte. 5) on the west side of town, is carved into an existing tree trunk.

Lodging on beautiful Lake Erie is desirable, but expensive. The **Pines Motel,** 10684 W. Lake Rd., south of town in Ripley, grants a half-mile of private lake access. The rooms are decorated to enhance the natural knotty pine walls. (☎716-736-7463; www.thepineslakeerie.com. June-Aug. singles $60; doubles $66. Apr.-May $40/$48.)

ERIE

The city of Erie and the Great Lake are named after the Erie Indians, who inhabited the region until a fierce battle with the Iroquois in the 1600s. Erie is the third-largest city in Pennsylvania and stands out for having an extensive maritime history and the state's only seashore.

VITAL STATS

Population: 104,000

Visitor Info: Erie Area Convention and Visitors Bureau, 208 E. Bayfront Pkwy. (☎814-454-7191; www.visiteriepa.com). On the harbor next to the Maritime Museum. Open M-F 8:30am-5pm.

Internet Access: Erie County Public Library, 160 E. Front St. (☎814-451-6900). Open M-Th 9am-8:30pm, F-Sa 9am-5pm, Su 1-5pm.

Post Office: 2108 E. 38th St. (☎814-898-7300). Open M-F 8:30am-5pm, Sa 8:30am-12:30pm. **Postal Code:** 16515.

GETTING AROUND. Rte. 5 becomes **6th St.** in the downtown area, divided between **E. 6th St.** and **W. 6th St.** on respective sides of **Perry Sq.,** where 6th St. intersects with **State St.** Leaving town to the east, Rte. 5 becomes **E. Lake Rd.** Numbered streets start on the Erie shore and increase as they go inland (southeast).

SIGHTS. The constantly evolving **Erie Maritime Museum,** 150 East Front St., chronicles local history, including the story of the Battle of Lake Erie during the War of 1812. Particularly interesting is a video of museum staff shooting actual cannons at the sides of a ship they had crafted for that specific purpose. The results are on display with the shells still embedded. (☎814-452-2744; www.brigniagara.org. Open Apr.-Dec. M-Sa 9am-

5pm, Su noon-5pm; Jan.-Mar. Su noon-5pm, Th-Sa 9am-5pm.) The biologically diverse ■**Presque Isle State Park,** on Peninsula Dr., juts out 7 mi. into Lake Erie, covering 3200 acres. Enjoy nature as you swim, hike, bike, fish, wind surf, cross-country ski, or ice skate. Be sure to take a free pontoon boat ride through the lagoons at Misery Bay. (☎814-871-4251. Beaches open Memorial Day to mid-Sept. Open daily summer 5am-11pm; winter 5am-9pm. Pontoon rides 11am, 1, 2pm. Free.)

 Over time, Presque Island has shifted 3 mi. to the east, heading toward New York. To keep the island from drifting away, Erie has employed shoreline management since the 1800s, creating breakwaters to hold the island in place.

FOOD. Perfect for a roadtrip, the **Quaker Steak & Lube Restaurant,** 7851 E. Peach St., revolves around road culture. Outside, full-size cars are displayed on the roof and the walkway, and inside there's even a motorcycle behind the bar and a "convertible room" with a retractable roof. The restaurant serves creatively named dishes, like the LubeBurger ($6.50) and O-Rings Ontenna (short $5, long $10), a stack of onion rings on an onion antenna with a baby moon hubcap. (☎814-836-9464; www.quakersteakand-lube.com. Lunch buffet M-F 11am-2pm; $7.50. Open Su-Th 11am-11pm, F-Sa 11am-midnight.) **El Canelo,** 2709 W. 12th St., serves delicious Mexican fare in a south-of-the-border atmosphere where red brick, sombreros, and Mexican flags abound. Lunch has a shorter menu with the same food for about $2 less. (☎814-835-2290. Combination dinners $5-6. Fajitas $8.75. Open M-Th 11am-10pm, F-Sa 11am-11pm, Su 11am-9pm.)

ACCOMMODATIONS. The Lighthouse Inn, 3704 E. Lake Rd., is a friendly, family-run motel with spacious rooms. (3 mi. east from downtown. ☎814-899-9300; www.erielighthouseinn.com. Restaurant open 8am-2pm. Late Sept. to late May singles M-F $35, Sa-Su $40; doubles $45. Late May to late Sept. singles $45/$60; doubles $55/$70.) The **El Patio Motel,** 2950 W. 8th St., at Peninsula Dr., has white balconies and a pool. Inside, the rooms are a little funky, but they're a great deal for lodging so close to the beautiful Presque Isle. Pool, volleyball, basketball, and shuffleboard are available, as

well as rooms with jacuzzis and kitchenettes. (Right outside the entrance to Presque Isle. ☎ 814-838-9772. Summer singles M-F $39, Sa-Su $79; doubles $49/$89. In winter $29/$49; $39/$59.) People crowd **Sara's Beachcomber Campground,** 50 Peninsula Dr. Since there's no overnight camping in Presque Isle State Park, the location can't be beat. RV Sites are in the woods and tent sites on the beach. (☎ 814-833-4560; www.sarasbeachcomber.com. Check-in 9am. Check-out Su-F 5pm, Sa 1pm. Open Apr.-Oct. Tents $18; RVs $20-22.)

◤ LEAVING ERIE

Take **Rte. 5 West** out of Erie. In Conneaut, take **U.S. 20** to **Rte. 7 North.** From Rte. 7, turn onto **Rte. 531 West** along Lake Rd. Rte. 531 leads through small **Ashtabula** and into **Geneva-On-The-Lake.**

Welcome To OHIO

◤ DETOUR: COVERED BRIDGE FESTIVAL
25 W. Jefferson St.

From Ashtabula, take Rte. 11 to where it meets with Rte. 46. Take Rte. 46 into Jefferson, where it intersects with W. Jefferson St.

Ashtabula County is known for its 16 historical covered bridges. The Covered Bridge Festival during the foliage season is in the second weekend in October and features parades, arts and crafts, antique cars, farmers markets, and van- and self-guided tours. Self-guided tour maps of the bridges are available year-round. (☎ 440-576-3769; www.coveredbridgefestival.org.)

Geneva-On-The-Lake has **America's Oldest Miniature Golf Course** in continuous play.

GENEVA-ON-THE-LAKE

By the end of WWII, Geneva-on-the-Lake was widely known as the playground of Lake Erie. Today, the resort maintains a 1950s ambience, but caters to modern visitors. Chain hotels still have not discovered Geneva-on-the-Lake, where modern go-karts coexist with vintage kiddy rides.

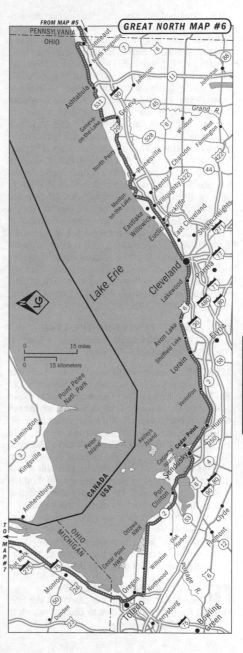

GREAT NORTH MAP #6

GREAT NORTH

Overlooking Lake Erie, the village's first fire station now houses the **Old Firehouse Winery,** 5499 Lake Rd. (Rte. 531), decorated with fire engines and memorabilia. Entrees include Firehouse BBQ ribs (½ rack $11, whole $17), sandwiches ($6), and Mexican dishes. (☎440-466-9300 or 800-862-6751; www.oldfirehousewinery.com. Open Su-Th noon-9pm, F-Sa noon-midnight.) The affordable **Anchor Motel,** 5196 Lake Rd. (Rte. 531), offers whimsical rooms—one room has a photo of a dog underwater wearing scuba gear and a tropical fish-themed toilet bowl cover. The grounds have gas grills and a shaded picnic area. (☎440-466-0726 or 800-642-2978; www.anchormotelandcottages.com. Reservations recommended. Singles M-F $50, Sa-Su $55; doubles $60/$65; cottages with kitchenette $85/$95. 10% *Let's Go* discount.) You can enjoy a complete vacation without leaving the boundaries of the **Indian Creek Camping Resort,** 4710 Lake Rd. East (Rte. 531). The 110 acres feature a game room, a grocery store, a restaurant, swimming pools, fishing lakes, and laundromats. Planned activities include volleyball, basketball, hayrides, and shuffleboard. (☎440-466-8191; www.indiancreekresort.com. Sites with hookup $30; RVs $38.)

LEAVING GENEVA-ON-THE-LAKE
Take **Rte. 531** south from town. In Geneva, **Rte. 531** meets with **U.S. 20 West.**

MENTOR. Mentor and Mentor-On-The-Lake are close enough to Cleveland to take advantage of the big-city lifestyle, yet isolated enough to set aside 800 acres for parkland. **Headlands Beach State Park** is a great destination for sunbathers and sunset-watchers. Mentor's most impressive sight is the **James A. Garfield National Historic Site,** 8095 Mentor Ave. (U.S. 20). President Garfield purchased his farm in 1876, when he was still a congressman, and it was here that he launched his presidential campaign. The home was nicknamed "Lawnfield" by reporters due to the expansive lawn where they often camped before press appearances. (☎440-255-8722; www.wrhs.org. Open May-Oct. M-Sa 10am-5pm, Su noon-5pm; Nov.-Apr. Su noon-5pm, Sa 10am-5pm. $7, seniors $6, ages 6-12 $5, under 6 free. $1 AAA discount.)

APPROACHING CLEVELAND
Take **I-90 West** along the coast of Lake Erie. From I-77, take the **9th St.** Exit to **Euclid Ave.,** which runs into **Public Sq.**

CLEVELAND

Ridiculed for having a river so polluted it caught fire (twice) and branded the "Mistake on the Lake," Cleveland has gone to great lengths over the past decade to correct its beleaguered image. Early in the 90s, new football and baseball stadiums catalyzed the downtown makeover, which reached its zenith in 1995 with the arrival of the Rock and Roll Hall of Fame. Meanwhile, the lake and river were cleaned, the city skyline was redefined, and deserted factories and warehouses were transformed into bustling bars and clubs.

(VITAL STATS)

Population: 480,000

Visitor Info: Cleveland Convention and Visitors Bureau, 3100 Tower City Ctr. (☎216-621-4110 or 800-321-1001; www.travelcleveland.com), in Terminal Tower. Open M-F 10am-4pm.

Internet Access: Cleveland Public Library, 525 Superior Ave. (☎216-623-2904). Open M-Sa 9am-6pm, Su 1-5pm; closed Su in summer.

Post Office: 2400 Orange Ave. (☎216-443-4494, after 5pm 216-443-4096.) Open M-F 7am-8:30pm, Sa 8:30am-3:30pm. **Postal Code:** 44101.

GETTING AROUND

Terminal Tower, in **Public Sq.,** at the intersection of Detroit Ave. and Ontario St., forms the center of downtown and splits the city east and west. Street numbers correspond to the distance of the street from Terminal Tower. To reach Public Sq. from **I-90** or **I-71,** take the Ontario St./Broadway exit. While the downtown area and **University Circle** are relatively safe, the area between the two around 55th St. can be rough and should be avoided at night. **The Flats,** along both banks of the Cuyahoga River, and **Coventry Rd.,** in Cleveland Heights, are the happening spots for food and nightlife.

SIGHTS

DOWNTOWN. The aspirations of a new Cleveland are revealed in the new downtown—a self-declared "Remake on the Lake." A centerpiece is I.M. Pei's glass pyramid housing the ⊠**Rock and Roll Hall of Fame,** where blaring music invites visitors into a dizzying retrospective of rock music.

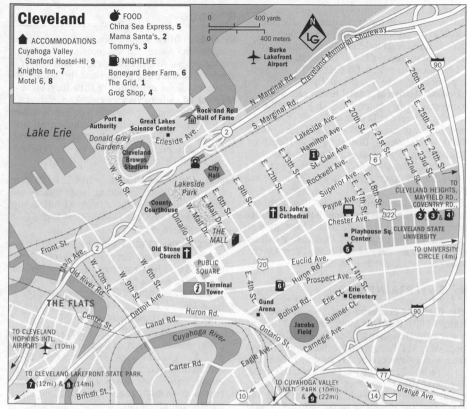

Cleveland

🍎 FOOD
China Sea Express, **5**
Mama Santa's, **2**
Tommy's, **3**

🛏 ACCOMMODATIONS
Cuyahoga Valley
  Stanford Hostel-HI, **9**
Knights Inn, **7**
Motel 6, **8**

🍸 NIGHTLIFE
Boneyard Beer Farm, **6**
The Grid, **1**
Grog Shop, **4**

Take a tour through rock history on the "Mystery Train," listen to the "500 Songs that Shaped Rock and Roll," and ogle memorabilia from Elvis's jumpsuits to Jimi Hendrix's guitar. (*1 Key Plaza.* ☎*614-781-7625; www.rockhall.com. Open M-Tu and Th-Su 10am-5:30pm, W 10am-9pm; June-Aug. also Sa 10am-9pm. $18, students $16, seniors $14, ages 9-11 $11, under 9 free.*) Next door, the **Great Lakes Science Center** educates with interactive exhibits. (*601 Erieside Ave.* ☎*614-694-2000; www.glsc.org. Open Su-Th 9:30am-5:30pm, Sa 9:30am-6:45pm. Science center or OMNIMAX $8, seniors $7, ages 3-17 $6. Both $11/$10/$8.*)

THE WILD SIDE. Cleveland Lakefront State Park is a 14 mi. park near downtown with beaches, bike trails, and great picnic areas. The soft sand at Edgewater Beach beckons sunbathers and swim-

mers. (☎*614-881-8141. Open daily 6am-11pm.*) Another great place to escape the urban jungle are the **Cleveland Metroparks,** which extend into the Cuyahoga Valley. The **Cleveland Metroparks Zoo,** 5 mi. south of downtown on I-71 at the Fulton Rd. exit, allows visitors to walk through the African Savannah and the Northern Trek, catching glimpses of Siberian tigers, red pandas, and hissing cockroaches. One of the zoo's highlights is the Rainforest, which houses Bornean orangutans. (☎*614-661-6500; www.clemtzoo.com. Open daily 10am-5pm. $9, ages 2-11 $4, under 2 free.*)

UNIVERSITY CIRCLE. While much has been made of Cleveland's revitalized downtown, the city's cultural nucleus still lies in **University Circle,** a part of Case Western University's campus, 4 mi. east of the city. The **Cleveland Museum of Art** boasts

GREAT NORTH

a grand hall of armor—part medieval, part Asian—along with a survey of art from the Renaissance to the present. An exceptional collection of Impressionist and modern works is highlighted by nine Picasso pieces. *(11150 East Blvd. ☎614-421-7340; www.clevelandart.org. Open Tu, Th, Sa-Su 10am-5pm; W and F 10am-9pm. Free.)* Nearby, the **Cleveland Museum of Natural History** sends visitors to the stars in the planetarium, while those dreaming of a different kind of sparkle can explore the new gallery of gems. *(1 Wade Oval Dr. ☎614-231-4600; www.cmnh.org. Open June M-Sa 10am-5pm, Su noon-5pm; July-Aug. M and F-Sa 10am-5pm, Tu-Th 10am-7pm, Su noon-5pm; Sept.-May M-Tu and Th-Sa 10am-5pm, W 10am-10pm, Su noon-5pm. $7; students, seniors, and ages 7-18 $5; ages 3-6 $4.)* Reopened in the summer of 2003 after a $40 million renovation, the **Cleveland Botanical Garden** provides a peaceful respite from urban life with traditional Victorian and Japanese gardens. *(11030 East Blvd. ☎614-721-1600. Open Apr.-Oct. M-Sa 9am-dusk, Su noon-dusk. Free.)*

♪ ENTERTAINMENT

The **Cleveland Orchestra** performs at **Severance Hall,** 11001 Euclid Ave. (☎614-231-7300; www.clevelandorch.com. Box office open Sept.-May M-F 9am-6pm, Sa 10am-6pm. Tickets from $25.) **Playhouse Square Center,** 1519 Euclid Ave. (☎614-771-4444), a 10min. walk east of Terminal Tower, is the second-largest performing arts center in the US. Inside, the **State Theater** hosts the **Cleveland Opera** (☎614-575-0900; www.clevelandopera.org) and the **Cleveland Ballet** (☎614-426-2500) from October to June. (Box office open M 10am-5pm, Tu-Su 10am-8pm.)

Football reigns supreme in Cleveland, where the **Browns** grind it out at **Cleveland Browns Stadium.** (☎614-241-5555. Tickets from $25.) Baseball's **Indians** hammer the hardball at **Jacobs Field,** 2401 Ontario St. (☎614-420-4200. Tickets from $5.) If you can't catch a game, the best way to see the field is on a 1hr. **stadium tour.** (☎614-420-4385. Tours Apr.-June and Sept. M-F 1 and 2pm, Sa when the Indians are away every hr. 10am-2pm; mid-June to Aug. M-Sa every hr. 10am-2pm. $6.50, seniors and under 15 $4.50.) The **Cavaliers** hoop it up at **Gund Arena,** 1 Center Ct. (☎614-420-2000). In summer, the WNBA's **Rockers** (☎614-263-7625) play in the same building.

🍴 FOOD

Delis downtown satiate most hot corned beef cravings, but Cleveland has more to offer. A hip, young crowd heads to the cafes and colorful shops of **Coventry Rd.,** in **Cleveland Heights.** Italian crooners fill the sidewalks of **Little Italy,** around **Mayfield Rd.,** where visitors can shop in the tiny stores before settling down to a delicious Italian meal. Over 100 vendors hawk produce, meat, and cheese at the old-world-style **West Side Market,** 1979 W. 25th St., at Lorain Ave. (☎614-771-8885. Open M and W 7am-4pm, F-Sa 7am-6pm.)

Tommy's, 1824 Coventry Rd. (☎614-321-7757), in Cleveland Heights. Tantalizing veggie-friendly cuisine, including a variety of falafel ($5.40-6.10). Entrees from $5. Open M-Th 7:30am-10pm, F-Sa 7:30am-11pm, Su 9am-10pm.

Mama Santa's, 12305 Mayfield Rd. (☎614-231-9567), in Little Italy just east of University Circle. Mama Santa's has kept hordes of college students and courting couples happy for over 40 years with its sumptuous Sicilian pizzas and welcoming atmosphere. Pizzas $5.25-6.25. Open M-Th 11am-10:30pm, F-Sa 11am-11:30pm; closed most of Aug.

China Sea Express, 1507 Euclid Ave. (☎614-861-0188), downtown. Chinese food worth more than its price. A delicious all-you-can-eat lunch buffet is $5.75 and includes wonton soup, lo mein, General Tso's chicken, crab rangoon, and all of the expected Chinese staples. Open Su-Th 11am-9pm, F-Sa 11am-10pm. Buffet served 11am-3pm.

🏠 ACCOMMODATIONS

With hotel taxes (not included in the prices listed below) as high as 14.5%, cheap lodging is hard to find in Cleveland. Prices tend to be lower in the suburbs or near the airport. Most accommodations will not rent to those under 21.

Cuyahoga Valley Stanford Hostel (HI-AYH), 6093 Stanford Rd. (☎330-467-8711), in Peninsula, 22 mi. south of Cleveland in the Cuyahoga Valley National Park. A 19th-century farm house, this idyllic hostel offers clean dorms with a kitchen, living room, and access to trails. Linen $3. Lockout 10am-5pm. Dorms $16.

Motel 6, 7219 Engle Rd. (☎440-234-0990), off Exit 235 on I-71, 15 mi. southwest of the city. Comfy rooms with cable TV and A/C. Located near restaurants, stores, and a park-and-ride lot. 21+. Singles Su-Th $46, F-Sa $56; doubles $52/$62.

Knights Inn, 22115 Brookpark Rd. (☎440-734-4500), at Exit 9 off I-480; take the first 2 rights after the freeway. Standard motel rooms, free local phone calls, continental breakfast. 21+. Singles $40; doubles $45. Weekly rooms $175.

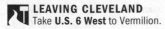 NIGHTLIFE

Most of Cleveland's nightlife centers on the **Flats,** recently transformed into a haven of beer and debauchery. For info on clubs and concerts, pick up a copy of *Scene* or the *Free Times.* The *Gay People's Chronicle* and *OUTlines* are available at gay clubs, cafes, and bookstores.

Grog Shop, 2785 Euclid Heights Blvd. (☎614-321-5588), at Coventry Rd. in Cleveland Heights. A mainstay of Cleveland's alternative music scene. A move to a larger, less dingy location in the summer of 2003 had purists waxing nostalgic about an era lost, but the Grog continues to host the best in underground rock and hip-hop. Cover varies. Open M-F 7pm-2:30am, Sa-Su 1pm-2:30am.

The Grid, 1437 St. Claire Ave. (☎614-623-0113). Entertains a predominantly gay crowd with a space-age dance floor, 4 bars, and male strippers select nights. M karaoke, Tu drag show. 18+. Cover F-Sa $5 after 11pm, ages 18-20 $10. Open M-Sa 5pm-2:30am, Su 4pm-2:30am. Floor open F until 3am, Sa until 4am.

Boneyard Beer Farm, 748 Prospect Ave. (☎614-575-0226), in the Gateway District. Serves over 120 beers from around the world for brew lovers. Skull and crossbones decor, faux cow-skin chairs, and barrels of peanuts make this a great place to enjoy a brew. Beer $3-6.50. Open M-Sa 4pm-2:30am, Su 7pm-2:30am.

LEAVING CLEVELAND
Take **U.S. 6 West** to Vermilion.

VERMILION

Another shipbuilding town, Vermilion is a great place to touch up on your nautical knowledge. At the **Inland Seas Maritime Museum,** 480 Main St. (off U.S. 6), interactive exhibits, model ships, and a 1910 steamship pilot house relate the history of the Inland Seas (code for "Great Lakes"). Harrowing stories tell of shipwrecks, and the original timber of the Brig Niagara is on display. (☎440-967-3467 or 800-893-1485; www.inlandseas.org. Open daily 10am-5pm. $6, seniors $5, students $4.)

The **Main Street Soda Grill,** 5502 Liberty Ave., is a blast from the past. Grab a phosphate ($1), a Coney burger ($3.25), or an egg creme ($1.50), and then marvel at the 1930s memorabilia. (☎440-967-4002. Open Su-Th 11am-9pm, F-Sa 11am-10pm.) The quaint **Lakeland Lodges,** 13115 W. Lake Rd., has a private sandy beach, rooms with kitchenettes, barbecues, volleyball, and badminton in a resort setting. (☎800-475-9690; www.lodges-onthelake.com. Check-in 2pm. Check-out 10am. Reservations recommended; 25% deposit required. Doubles Mid-June to Aug. M-F $74, Sa-Su $89; Apr. to mid-June and Sept. $49/$64.)

APPROACHING SANDUSKY
U.S. 6 enters downtown from the east along **Cleveland Rd.,** then turns into **Washington St.**

SANDUSKY

Though most visit Sandusky just for Cedar Point, the waterfront business district, established in 1818, has one of the most beautiful collections of historic architecture in the Midwest. Along Washington St., between Wayne St. and Jackson St., is **Washington Park,** where you can see Sandusky's floral park and the historic "Boy with the Boot" statue and fountain. Consistently ranked the "best amusement park in the world" by *Amusement Today,* ▓**Cedar Point Amusement Park,** 1 Point Cedar Dr., off U.S. 6, has many of the world's highest and fastest roller coasters. The towering **Top Thrill Dragster** takes the cake in both categories, launching thrill-seekers 420 ft. before plummeting down at 120 mph. Fifteen other coasters, including the enormous **Millennium Force** (310 ft., 90 mph), offer a grand old adrenaline rush. (☎800-237-8386; www.cedarpoint.com. Open daily June-Aug. 10am-11pm; Sept. to early Oct. hours vary. $44, seniors $30, under 4 ft. $22. Parking $8.)

A devoted longtime staff serves customers at **Markley's,** 160 Wayne St., on the corner of Market St., downtown. For lunch, try the Little Sister sandwich platter (bacon cheeseburger, fries, and cole slaw; $5), the specialty for 45 years. They also serve breakfast all day, fresh doughnuts, and pies. (☎419-627-9441. Open Su-Th 6am-2pm, F-Sa 6am-7pm.) The **Mecca Motel,** 2227 Cleveland Rd. (U.S. 6), has lower rates than the chain hotels that surround Cedar Point. The one-floor motel runs shuttle service to Cedar Point and has a free 9-hole mini-golf course and a swimming pool. (☎800-986-3222. Rooms $55-100.)

🏔 LEAVING SANDUSKY

East of downtown, Washington St. becomes **Tiffin Ave.**, which meets **Venice Rd.** and continues as **U.S. 6.** From Venice Rd., take **U.S. 2**, to Port Clinton.

🏔 AFRICAN SAFARI WILDLIFE PARK

Off U.S. 2.   267 Lightner Rd.

The African Safari Wildlife Park is Port Clinton's biggest attraction. The rare white zebras, buffalo, and giraffes are as curious about you as you are about them; activities at the park include rides on camels or ponies and the Pork Chop Downs pig races. (☎419-732-3606; www.africansafariwildlifepark.com. Open mid-Apr. to mid-Oct. daily 9am-7pm; last entry 1hr. before close.)

🏔 LEAVING PORT CLINTON

Between Port Clinton and Toledo, take **U.S. 2** through **Oregon.**

🍴 TONY PACKO'S   1902 Front St.

Located on the river north of I-280.

🏛Tony Packo's was made famous by M*A*S*H star Jamie Farr, whose character Klinger would frequently crave a Packo's dog. The real specialty is the Hungarian hot dogs ($2.50). The wieners are even part of the decor; celebrity-autographed buns line the walls. (☎419-691-6054; www.tonypackos.com. Open daily 11:30am-11pm.)

🏔 APPROACHING TOLEDO

Cross the **Maumee River** into **Toledo** via **Main St. (Rte. 2).**

TOLEDO

The 🏛**Toledo Zoo** is home to over 4700 animals and 700 species, including polar bears, seals, primates, and elephants. Visit the **Hippoquarium** with underwater viewing of Nile River hippos, or go nose to nose with wolves in the Arctic Encounter Wolf Exhibit. (From downtown, take N. Michigan St. (Rte. 25) south past I-75 until it becomes Anthony Wayne Trail. The zoo is 2 mi. ahead. ☎419-385-5721; www.toledozoo.org. Open daily May-Labor Day 10am-5pm; Labor Day-Apr. 10am-4pm. $8.50, ages 2-11 and seniors $5.50, under 2 free.) The Grecian-style marble **Toledo Museum of Art**, 2445 Monroe St., hosts exhibits art from ancient Egypt to the present. (☎800-644-6862; www.toledomuseum.org. Open Su 11am-5pm, Tu-Th and Sa 10am-4pm, F 10am-10pm. Free.)

The historic **Oliver House** near downtown Toledo dates back to 1859 when it served as Toledo's premier hotel. Today, the **Maumee Bay Brewing Company,** 27 Broadway St., is busy running a restaurant and the Toledo Brewing Hall of Fame. Try Walter's burger ($7.30), or the pizzas ($8) for a quick bite. (☎419-241-1253. Open M-Th 11am-10pm, F-Sa 11am-11pm, Su 2-9pm.) There aren't many affordable motels in downtown Toledo, but chain motels starting at $40 are clustered around nearby Maumee to the south near I-475 and I-80/90. The **Classic Inn,** 1821 E. Manhattan Blvd., has typical cheap

---

LAKE ERIE ISLANDS

Many ferry companies run boats to and from the beautiful Lake Erie Islands, complete with gorgeous limestone cliffs, crystal caverns, and historic wineries. You can visit **Kelleys Island State Park** (☎419-797-4530; www.dnr.state.oh.us/parks/parks/lakeerie.htm) and enjoy 6 mi. of hiking trails, nature preserves, fishing access, and swimming beaches. When you realize it's too beautiful to leave, you can stay overnight in the park's campground. Other islands include **Catawba Island** (☎419-797-4530), **Middle Bass Island** (☎419-285-0311), and **South Bass Island** (☎419-285-211). The cheapest ferry can also carry your car over for an additional fee. **Miller Boatline** leaves from the Miller Dock ar Water St. and Crogan on Catawba Island. Be in line 20min. before ferry departure. (☎800-500-2421; www.millerferry.com. $5, ages 6-11 $1, under 6 free; bicycle $2 extra; car $12 extra.)

motel rooms, as well as an outdoor swimming pool, and free deluxe breakfast. (Near the junction of I-75 and I-280. ☎877-428-0475. Singles $40-52; doubles $50-57.)

🖈 LEAVING TOLEDO

There really isn't anything to see between Toledo and Detroit, so don't feel guilty taking the interstate. From downtown, take **Summit St. (Rte. 65 East)** to **I-280,** which connects to **I-75** north of town.

Welcome To MICHIGAN

DETROIT

Long the ugly step-sister of America's big cities, Detroit has nowhere to go but up. Race riots in the 1960s caused a massive flight to the suburbs; the population has more than halved since 1967, turning much of the city into post-industrial wasteland. The decline of the auto industry in the late 1970s added unemployment to the city's ills. Today, the five towers of the riverside Renaissance Center symbolize the hope of a city-wide effort to revitalize downtown. Top-notch museums cluster in the cultural center of the city, while professional sports and a music scene inherited from Motown entertain locals and travelers. Across the river, Windsor, Ontario exudes a cosmopolitan flavor from streets packed with bars and restaurants.

VITAL STATS

Population: 950,000

Visitor Info: Convention and Visitors Bureau, 211 W. Fort St., 10th fl. (☎313-202-1800 or 800-338-7648; www.visitdetroit.com). Open M-F 9am-5pm.

Internet Access: Detroit Public Library, 5201 Woodward Ave. (☎313-833-1000). Open Tu-W noon-8pm, Th-Sa 10am-6pm.

Post Office: 1401 W. Fort St. (☎313-226-8304). Open 24hr. **Postal Code:** 48233.

FROM MAP #6

GREAT NORTH MAP #7

GREAT NORTH

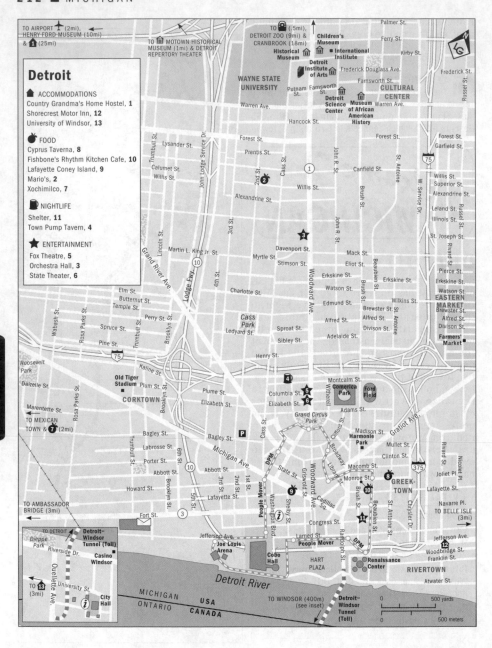

Detroit

🛏 ACCOMMODATIONS
Country Grandma's Home Hostel, 1
Shorecrest Motor Inn, 12
University of Windsor, 13

🍎 FOOD
Cyprus Taverna, 8
Fishbone's Rhythm Kitchen Cafe, 10
Lafayette Coney Island, 9
Mario's, 2
Xochimilco, 7

🍸 NIGHTLIFE
Shelter, 11
Town Pump Tavern, 4

⭐ ENTERTAINMENT
Fox Theatre, 5
Orchestra Hall, 3
State Theater, 6

GETTING AROUND

The Mile Roads are major east-west arteries. **Eight Mile Rd.** is the city's northern boundary. **Woodward Ave.** heads northwest from downtown, dividing city and suburbs into "east side" and "west side." **Gratiot Ave.** flares out northeast from downtown, while **Grand River Ave.** shoots west. **I-94** and **I-75** pass through downtown.

Detroit can be dangerous at night, but it is typically safe during the day. Driving is the best way to negotiate this sprawling city, where good and bad neighborhoods alternate on a whim. Though streets tend to end suddenly and reappear several blocks later, **parking** is relatively easy to find.

SIGHTS

Detroit and the surrounding area allow visitors a chance to explore everything from books to wildlife, while also enjoying the city's public parks.

DETROIT ZOO. Exotic animals like tigers and red pandas roam the suburban grounds of the Detroit Zoological Park. The park includes the National Amphibian Conservation Center and an Arctic Ring of Life exhibit featuring polar bears and a trek through the Tundra. *(8450 W. Ten Mile Rd., just off the Woodward Exit of Rte. 696 in Royal Oak. ☎248-398-0900; www.detroitzoo.org. Open daily May-Oct. 10am-5pm; Nov.-Apr. 10am-4pm. $9, seniors and ages 2-12 $6. Parking $4.)*

CRANBROOK. Fifteen miles north of Detroit in posh Bloomfield Hills, Cranbrook's scholarly campus contains public gardens, several museums, and an art academy. Far and away the best of the lot is the **Cranbrook Institute of Science,** with a planetarium and rotating exhibits emphasizing educational fun. *(39221 N. Woodward Ave. ☎877-462-7262; www.cranbrook.edu. Open M-Th and Sa-Su 10am-5pm, F 10am-10pm. $7, seniors and ages 2-12 $5. Planetarium shows $3, under 2 $1. Bat Zone $3/$1; free with general admission.)*

HEIDELBERG PROJECT. The Heidelberg began as a building painted with pink polka dots. Crazy additions and art installations were added to the building, then to the street. Not long after the expansion, the area became infested with rats and the city shut the project

down for a while, bulldozing several art-enhanced homes and trees. But this didn't stop the artists; the Heidelberg Project has been revitalized, and you can see it today on Heidelberg St. *(Take Gratiot St. northeast from downtown. www.heidelberg.org.)*

BELLE ISLE. The best escape from Detroit is the 1000-acre **Belle Isle,** where a conservatory, nature center, aquarium, maritime museum, and small zoo allow animal lovers to drift from sight to sight. *(3 mi. from downtown via the MacArthur Bridge at the foot of E. Grand Blvd. ☎313-852-4078. Isle accessible daily 6am-10pm. Attractions open 10am-5pm. $2 per sight, ages 2-12 $1. Zoo $3/$1.)*

MUSEUMS

MOTOWN HISTORICAL MUSEUM. The Motown Historical Museum is housed in the apartment where entrepreneur and producer Berry Gordy founded Hitsville, USA, and created the Motown sound. An impressive collection of memorabilia includes the piano used by legendary Motown artists. Downstairs, **Studio A**—where the Jackson 5, Marvin Gaye, and Smokey Robinson recorded—has been meticulously preserved. *(2648 W. Grand Blvd. ☎313-875-2264; www.motownmuseum.com. Open Tu-Sa 10am-5pm. $8, under 13 $5.)*

DETROIT INSTITUTE OF ARTS. The majority of the museum's collection of American art is on tour while renovations continue for the new American Wing, set to open in 2006. However, there's an extensive collection of Flemish art as well as a modern collection that includes works by Picasso, Van Gogh, and Matisse. Among the highlights of the museum is Diego Rivera's monumental mural *Detroit Industry. (5200 Woodward Ave. ☎313-833-7900; www.dia.org. Open Su 10am-5pm, W-Th 10am-4pm, F 10am-9pm, Sa 10am-5pm; 1st F of each month 11am-9pm. Suggested donation $4, students and children $1.)*

HENRY FORD MUSEUM. Housing full-scale planes, trains, and automobiles, the museum explores "100 Years of the Automobile." The impressive display details the cultural changes brought about by cars. On premises is the convertible in which President Kennedy was assassinated, the bus in which Rosa Parks sat up front, and the chair in which Lincoln was shot. *(20900*

GREAT NORTH

Oakwood Blvd., off I-94 in Dearborn. ☎313-271-1620; *www.hfmgv.org. Open M-Sa 9am-5pm, Su noon-5pm. $14, seniors $13, ages 5-12 $10.)*

MUSEUM OF AFRICAN AMERICAN HISTORY. This museum features a poignant core exhibit that begins with the slave trade and moves through African-American history, ending in a bittersweet display of modern African-American culture. *(315 E. Warren Rd.* ☎313-494-5800; *www.maah-detroit.org. Open Su 1-5pm, W-Sa 9:30am-5pm. $5, under 17 $3.)*

DETROIT SCIENCE CENTER. Children can strum a stringless harp or take virtual trips through the rings of Saturn in the planetarium. *(5020 John R St.* ☎313-577-8400; *www.sciencedetroit.org. Open mid-Sept. to early June M-F 9:30am-3pm, Sa-Su 10:30am-6pm; mid-June to early Sept. M-F 9:30am-5pm, Sa-Su 10:30am-6pm. $7, seniors and ages 2-12 $6. IMAX $4.)*

🎵 ENTERTAINMENT

Though the era of Motown has come and gone, a vibrant music scene still dominates the Motor City. The **Detroit Symphony Orchestra** performs at **Orchestra Hall,** 3711 Woodward Ave., at Parsons St. (☎313-962-1000, box office 313-576-5111; www.detroitsymphony.com. Open M-F 10am-6pm. Tickets $10-25. Half-price student and senior rush tickets 1½hr. prior to show.)

Dramatic works are performed in the restored **Theater District,** around Woodward Ave. and Columbia St. The **Fox Theatre,** 2211 Woodward Ave., near Grand Circus Park, features dramas, comedies, and musicals in a 5000-seat theater that occasionally shows epic films. (☎313-983-3200. Box office open M-F 10am-6pm. Tickets $25-100; movies under $10.) The **State Theater,** 2115 Woodward Ave. (☎313-961-5450, tickets 248-645-6666), hosts concerts. Beyond the Theater District, the acclaimed **Detroit Repertory Theater,** 13103 Woodrow Wilson Ave., puts on four productions a year. (☎313-868-1347. Shows Th-F 8:30pm, Sa 3 and 8:30pm, Su 2 and 7:30pm. Tickets from $17.)

Baseball's **Tigers** round the bases at new **Comerica Park,** 2100 Woodward Ave. (☎313-471-2255. Tickets $5-60.) Football's **Lions** hit the gridiron next door at **Ford Field,** 200 Brush St. (☎800-616-7627. Tickets $35-54.) Inside the **Joe Louis Arena,** 600 Civic Center Dr., the 2002 Stanley Cup cham-

pion **Red Wings** play hockey. (☎313-645-6666. Tickets $20-40.) Basketball's **Pistons** hoop it up at **The Palace at Auburn Hills,** 2 Championship Dr. in Auburn hills. (☎248-377-0100. Tickets $10-60.)

FOOD

Although many restaurants have migrated to the suburbs, there are still some options in town. The downtown area doesn't offer much after 5pm, but ethnic neighborhoods provide interesting choices. At **Greektown,** Greek restaurants and bakeries line one block of Monroe St., near Beaubien St. To snag a *pierogi,* cruise Joseph Campau Ave. in **Hamtramck** (Ham-TRAM-eck), a Polish neighborhood northeast of Detroit. **Mexican Town,** just west of downtown, is packed with Mexican restaurants, markets, and nightspots. No one should miss the **Eastern Market,** at Gratiot Ave. and Russell St., an 11 acre produce-and-goodies festival. (☎313-833-1560. Open Sa 4am-5pm.)

Cyprus Taverna, 579 Monroe St. (☎313-961-1550). *Moussaka* ($9) and other Greek specialties in the heart of Greektown. Lunch specials from $5.25. Entrees $9-13. Open Su-Th 11am-1:30am, F-Sa 11am-4am.

Mario's, 4222 2nd St. (☎313-832-6464), downtown. An elegant, old-fashioned Italian eatery. All meals include antipasto platters, salad, and soup. Live bands and ballroom dancing take over on the weekends. Entrees from $16. Open M-Th 11:30am-11pm, F 11:30am-midnight, Sa 4pm-midnight, Su 2-10pm.

Lafayette Coney Island, 118 W. Lafayette St. (☎313-964-8198). Detroit's most famous culinary establishment, Lafayette doles out its coney dogs ($2.10) and chili cheese fries ($2.45) to loyal customers. Open M-Th 7:30am-4am, F-Sa 7:30am-5am, Su 9:30am-4am.

Xochimilco, 3409 Bagley St. (☎313-843-0129). Draws the biggest crowds in Mexican Town with cheap, delicious enchiladas and burrito platters ($5-8). Muraled walls, great service, and warm chips and salsa are just a few of the details that separate Xochimilco (so-she-MIL-co) from its competition. Open daily 11am-2am.

Fishbone's Rhythm Kitchen Cafe, 400 Monroe St. (☎313-965-9600), in Greektown. Brings Mardi Gras to the Motor City, with zydeco music, an oyster bar, and Cajun specialities like deep-fried alligator ($9)and seafood gumbo ($5.25). Open M-F 6:30am-1am, Sa 6:30am-2am, Su brunch 10am-2pm.

ACCOMMODATIONS

Detroit's suburbs harbor a bevy of chain motels. Those near the airport in **Romulus** tend to be pricey, and others along **E. Jefferson Ave.,** near downtown, can be of questionable quality. For a mix of convenience and affordability, look along **Telegraph Rd.** off I-94, west of the city. If the exchange rate is favorable, good deals can be found across the border in **Windsor.**

Country Grandma's Home Hostel (HI-AYH), 22330 Bell Rd. (☎ 734-753-4901), in New Boston, 6 mi. south of I-94 off I-275. Take Exit 11B, turn right, and make an immediate right onto Bell Rd. Worth the trip for the hospitality and respite from urban Detroit. 7 beds, kitchen, free parking. Bring your own linen. Reservations required. Open Apr.-Sept. Dorms $15, nonmembers $18. Cash only.

Shorecrest Motor Inn, 1316 E. Jefferson Ave. (☎ 313-568-3000 or 800-992-9616), ideally located 3 blocks east of the Renaissance Center. Rooms include A/C, fridges, and data ports. Key deposit $20 when paying by cash. Free parking. Reservations recommended. 21+. Singles $69; doubles $89.

University of Windsor, 401 Sunset Ave. (☎ 519-973-7074), in Windsor. Rents functional rooms with refrigerators, A/C, and shared bathrooms from early May to late Aug. Free Internet access and use of university facilities. Singles CDN$32; doubles CDN$37.

Pontiac Lake Recreation Area, 7800 Gale Rd. (☎ 248-666-1020), in Waterford, 45min. northwest of downtown; take I-75 to Rte. 59 West, turn right on Will Lake northbound, and left onto Gale Rd. Huge wooded sites in rolling hills, 4 mi. from the lake. Sites $11. Vehicle permit $4.

FESTIVALS

Detroit's festivals draw millions of visitors. Most outdoor events take place at **Hart Plaza,** a downtown oasis that hugs the Detroit River. A recent and successful downtown tradition, the **Detroit Electronic Music Festival** (☎ 313-393-9200; www.demf.org) lures over a million ravers to Hart Plaza on Memorial Day weekend. Jazz fans jet to the riverbank during Labor Day weekend for the **Ford Detroit International Jazz Festival** (☎ 313-963-7622; www.detroitjazzfest.com), which features more than 70 acts on three stages and interna-

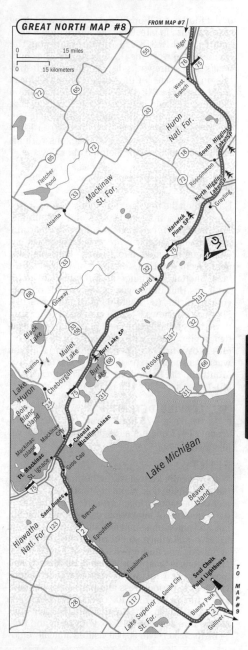

TO MAP #9

tional food at the World Food Court. A week-long extravaganza in late June, the international **Freedom Festival** (☎313-923-7400), celebrates the friendship between the US and Canada. The continent's largest fireworks display ignites the festivities on both sides of the border. **Detroit's African World Festival** (☎313-494-5853) fills Hart Plaza on the third weekend in August for free reggae, jazz, and gospel concerts. The nation's oldest state fair, the **Michigan State Fair** (☎313-369-8250), at Eight Mile Rd. and Woodward Ave., beckons with art and livestock two weeks before Labor Day.

NIGHTLIFE

For info on the trendiest hot spots, pick up a free copy of *Orbit* in record stores and restaurants. The *Metro Times* also has complete entertainment listings. *Between the Lines*, also free, has GLBT entertainment info. Head to **Harmonie Park,** near Orchestra Hall, for some of Detroit's best jazz. **Shelter,** the dance club downstairs in St. Andrews Hall, draws young, hip crowds on nonconcert nights. (☎313-961-6358. St. Andrews 18+. Shelter 21+. Shows F-Su. Tickets $7-12.) On Saturdays, the State Theater (see p. 214), houses **Ignition,** a giant party with alternative dance music. (18+. Cover from $5. Open Sa 9pm-2am.) If all you want is a good pint, try the **Town Pump Tavern,** 100 Montcalm St., behind the State Theater. (☎313-961-1929. Open daily 11am-2am.)

⚔ LEAVING DETROIT
Head onto **I-75 North** toward Flint. Merge off I-75 onto **I-475** and exit at **Saginawa St.,** which will take you into downtown Flint.

FLINT

More recently known as the hometown of independent filmmaker Michael Moore and the subject of the movie *Roger and Me*, Flint has seen the industries of lumbering, carriage-manufacturing, and automobile-building all come and go, and today it still clings stubbornly to life despite its economic ups and downs. One of Flint's major attractions is **Crossroads Village & Huckleberry Railroad,** 6140 Bray Rd., where visitors wander among villagers in period dress and partake of old-fashioned fun. (☎810-736-7100 or 800-648-7275. Open June-Aug. Su, Tu, Th-Sa 10am-5pm, W 10am-8pm. $7, seniors $6, ages 3-12 $5; with train and boat $11/$10/$8.50.) Over 90,000 visitors annually enjoy

the collection of the **Flint Institute of Arts,** which encompasses more than 6,000 works including paintings by John Singer Sargent and Andrew Wyeth, and a **Prancing Horse** sculpture from the Han Dynasty. (☎810-234-1695; www.flintarts.org. Open Su 1-5pm, Tu-Sa 10am-5pm. Free.) The **Robert T. Longway Planetarium,** Michigan's largest planetarium, has Sky Theater planetarium shows and laser shows. (☎810-237-3400; www.longway.org. Open M-F 8:30am-4:30pm. $5, under 12 $4.)

⚔ LEAVING FLINT
Take the **Dort Hwy. (Rte. 54)** north. Near **Clio,** Rte. 54 turns into **Rte. 83,** which heads north toward Frankenmuth.

FRANKENMUTH

Frankenmuth was founded in 1845 by a band of Bavarian missionaries who came to Michigan to convert the Chippewa Indians to Christianity. Today, "Michigan's Little Bavaria" maintains much of its original identity with some of the most authentic Bavarian architecture found anywhere in the US. (There are some exceptions, like the "Bavarian" McDonald's.)

(VITAL STATS)

Population: 4800

Visitor Info: Frankenmuth Visitors Center, 635 S. Main St. (☎989-652-6106 or 800-386-8696; www.frankenmuth.org). Open M-F 8am-5pm, Sa 10am-5pm, Su noon-5pm; June-Aug. Th-Sa until 8pm.

Internet Access: Wickson James E Memorial Library, 359 S. Franklin St. (☎989-652-8323). Open M-Th 9am-9pm, F 9am-5pm, Sa 10am-5pm, Su 1-4pm.

Post Office: 119 N. Main St. (☎989-652-6751). Open M-F 8:30am-5pm, Sa 9am-noon. **Postal Code:** 48734.

⬛ GETTING AROUND. Rte. 83 enters Frankenmuth from the south and becomes **Main St.** in town. The main intersections with Main St. are **Curtis Rd.** and **Genesee St.**

◎ SIGHTS. The holiday season never ends at **Bronner's Christmas Wonderland,** 25 Christmas Ln., the **world's largest Christmas store.** Its European-style marketplace is the size of 1½ football fields, and the landscaped grounds cover 27 acres. Here, you can see 400 nativity scenes from around the world, 200 styles of nutcracker, a replica of the Silent Night Memorial Chapel in Oberndorf, Austria, and Christmas Lane at night with over 10,000 twinkling lights. (☎989-652-9931; www.bronners.com. Open Jan.-May M-Th and Sa 9am-5:30pm, F 9am-9pm, Su noon-5:30pm; June-Dec. M-Sa 9am-9pm, Su noon-7pm.) The **Frankenmuth River Place** shopping area, 925 S. Main St., is set up as a miniature European village. The best part is the nightly "Lights Fantastic" laser show. (☎800-600-0105; www.frankenmuth-riverplace.com.)

🍴 **FOOD.** If you're famished, you might be able to finish the all-you-can-eat dinner ($16) at **Bavarian Inn**, 713 S. Main St., which includes platters of Frankenmuth Chicken and baked dressing, mashed potatoes, *gemuese* (hot vegetable), chicken *nudelsuppe, stollen* (fruit and nut bread), *krautsalat* (cole slaw), and homemade ice cream. Additional German *winer schnitzel, kasseler rippchen, sauerbraten,* or *bratwurst* are available. (☎517-652-9941; www.bavarianinn.com. Open Su-Th 11am-9:30pm, F-Sa 11am-9pm.) The all-you-can-eat chicken meal ($14.50) at **Zehnders,** 730 S. Main St., includes chicken, dressing, noodle soup, cabbage salad, chicken liver pâté, cheese spread with garlic toast, freshly baked breads, mashed potatoes, egg noodles and ice cream. (☎800-863-7999; www.zehnders.com. Open June-Dec. daily 11am-9:30pm; Jan.-May M-F 11am-8pm, Sa-Su 11am-9pm.)

🛏 **ACCOMMODATIONS.** If you'd like to stay in Frankenmuth without paying resort prices, the **Frankenmuth Motel,** 1218 Weiss St., is an affordable option. (☎800-821-5362. Rooms $49-89.) If you've got money burning a hole in your pocket and want the real German experience, stay at the **Bavarian Inn Lodge,** 1 Covered Bridge Ln. The seven-acre building features five pools, indoor mini golf, four tennis courts, two lounges, and nightly entertainment. (Across the covered bridge on Cass River. ☎888-775-6343; www.bavarianinn.com. Rooms high season $120-150; low season $89-109.)

LEAVING FRANKENMUTH
Rte. 83 continues north through fruitful green farms toward **Bay City** as **Rte. 15.**

BAY CITY. Lush pine forests once fueled Bay City's prosperous lumber industry. Though the city's former prosperity is not as evident today, it still boasts several waterfront parks and historic districts. **Midland Street Historic District** is known as the entertainment capital of mid-Michigan and backs up that reputation with over 20 bars, many of which host live jazz and rock music. The Material Girl herself grew up here, adding to the town's street cred. The Friendship Shell amphitheater in **Wenonah Park** hosts fireworks shows and concerts during the summer. (Parking in Delta Planetarium lot. ☎989-893-0343; www.bayartscouncil.org.)

LEAVING BAY CITY
In Bay City, take **Center Ave. (Rte. 15/25)** across the bridge onto **Jenny St.** From Jenny St., turn north onto **Euclid Ave. (Rte. 13),** which becomes **Huron Rd.** and leads toward **Pinconning.**

THE ROAD TO HIGGINS LAKE

North of Bay City, there isn't much to see besides hordes of cheese factory outlets. Huron Rd. (Rte. 13) becomes Main St. as it enters the town of **Standish** to the north. From Standish, take **Rte. 76** northwest toward the town of **Sterling.** This town of is known for its many canoe livery services along Rifle River. **White's Canoe Livery,** 400 Old Rte. 70 (Greenwood Rd.), is the largest paddle-sport and camping operation in Michigan, and offers tubing, kayaking, and rafting, as well as camp-grounds and cabins. (☎989-654-2654; www.whitescanoe.com. Open May-Sept. Su-W 8am-8pm, Th-Sa 8am-10pm. Canoe trips $30-75. Sites $20; cabins $50.)

Taking Rte. 76 instead of the freeway between Standish and West Branch is worth it. Giant pine trees line the stick-straight road, allowing you to see for miles through tunnel-like greenery. If you need a rest, stop at **Coyle's Restaurant,** 3444 Rte. 55, in West Branch. To get to Coyle's, you'll head through their gift shop, filled with Western-style knick-knacks, before you find yourself in the similarly themed restaurant. Coyle's is known around town for their all-you-can-eat buffets; choose a buffet anytime of the day ($5.50-8): breakfast, lunch, or dinner. (☎989-343-9440. Open Su-Th 8am-9pm, F-Sa 8am-10pm.) To continue onto **Higgins Lake,** hop on **I-75** and exit at Roscommon.

ROSCOMMON. Roscommon is a small village on the banks of the Ausable River's South Branch, known nationwide for its clear blue waters. Born a typical lumber town when the railroad made its way through town, Roscommon's main business is now tourism. The **Firemen's Memorial,** 1 mi.

GREAT NORTH

south of Roscommon, a half-mile east of Rte. 18 on County Rd. 103, stands 12 ft. tall. The third weekend in September is the **Michigan Firemen's Memorial Festival** (☎989-275-5880; www.firemens-memorial.org), when thousands of visitors from all over the US come to honor the valiant fire fighters who lost their lives protecting their communities. **North Higgins Lake State Park** and **South Higgins Lake State Park** both have campgrounds, camp stores, and beaches. (☎800-447-2757. Open daily 8am-10pm. Entrance fee $4. Sites $20; cabins $30.)

LEAVING ROSCOMMON
Head north on **I-75** to the **Upper Peninsula** (also known as the U.P.).

HARTWICK PINES STATE PARK
4216 Granger Rd.
Located on Rte. 93 in Grayling, Exit 259 off I-75.
The 9762 acres of Hartwick Pines are home to 49 acres of one of Michigan's last stands of old-growth pine forests. The 1¼ mi. Old Growth Forest Foot Trail leads to the **Logging Museum.** (☎989-348-7068. Grounds open daily 8am-10pm. Museum open daily June-Aug. 9am-7pm; Sept.-Oct. and May 9am-4pm. Sites $15-19, with electricity $23; cabins $40. Day-use $4.)

GAYLORD

In the 1960s, Gaylord recreated itself as an "Alpine Village, and today, the town's main attractions are its Swiss architecture and its status as the Ski Capital of Michigan. In 1965, Gaylord chose Pontresina, Switzerland as its sister city, and Pontresina sent a boulder from the Swiss Alps as a gift to the town. You can see the **Pontresina Stone** on the corner of the courtyard lawn. ⊠**The Cross in the Woods,** 7078 Rte. 68, is one of Michigan's best-known monuments. The cross was inspired by Kateri Tekakwitha, a Native American woman who erected crosses in the woods around the area. This particular cross was crafted from a redwood tree and its crucified Jesus was sculpted by renowned Michigan sculptor Marshall M. Fredericks. The cross stands a truly monumental 55 ft. high and 22 ft. wide. (☎231-238-8973. www.rc.net/gaylord/crossinwoods. Always open. Free.) **The Bottle Cap Museum,** 4977 Sparr Rd., displays a vast collection of historical Coca-Cola memorabilia, including dispensers and coolers dating from 1930-1970. Admission gets you a free Coke. (5

mi. east of Gaylord on Rte. 44, next to the mall. ☎989-732-1931. $2.50, seniors $2, ages 6-12 $1.50, under 6 free. Open W-Sa 11am-5pm.)

La Senorita, 737 W. Main St., cooks fabulous fajitas and presents them, sizzling, at your table ($11-12). Daily lunch specials are only $4.60. (☎989-732-1771. Open M-Sa 11am-10pm, Su noon-10pm. Bar open until midnight.) **The Timberly Motel,** 881 South Otsego, is less Alpine and less pricey than the rest of Gaylord. The rooms are bland, but the beds are new. (☎989-732-5166. Summer singles $48; doubles $58. Winter $38/$42.)

The **Museum of the Cross in the Woods,** in Gaylord, MI, proudly holds the largest collection of nun dolls in the US, which (amazingly) fails to include any of those punching nun puppets.

APPROACHING MACKINAW CITY
To explore downtown, get off I-75 at Exit 337 **(Old U.S. 31/M-108/Nicolet).**

MACKINAW CITY

While in the Mackinac area, be sure to stock up on some of the famously rich and creamy Mackinac fudge, a favorite since 1887. The 5 mi. Mackinac Bridge ("Mighty Mac"), connecting Mackinaw City to St. Ignace in the U.P., is the third-longest suspension bridge in the US.

(VITAL STATS)

Population: 860

Visitor info: Michigan Dept. of Transportation Welcome and Travel Information Center (☎231-436-5566), Nicolet St. off I-75 at Exit 338. Open daily mid-June to Aug. 8am-6pm; Sept. to mid-June 9am-5pm.

Internet Access: Mackinaw Area Public Library, 528 W. Central Ave. (☎231-436-5451). Open M-Tu and Th-F 11am-5pm, W 1-9pm.

Post Office: 306 E. Central Ave. (☎231-436-5526). **Postal Code:** 49701.

GETTING AROUND. I-75 runs through town and across the Mackinac Bridge (toll $2.50). **U.S. 23** enters Mackinaw City from Cheboygan to the east. **Nicolet** and **Huron** are the main north-south streets. **Central Ave.** is the main east-west street and leads west to **Wilderness State Park.**

◙ SIGHTS. A local tradition is the annual **Labor Day Bridge Walk,** where Michigan's governor leads thousands across the bridge from Mackinaw City to St. Ignace. Historic Mill Creek, Fort Michilimackinac, and Fort Mackinac form a trio of State Historic Parks. Colonial enthusiasts should buy a **Combination Pack,** good for seven days from date of purchase, for unlimited admission to all three. ($18, ages 6-17 $10.50. Available at all 3 sights.) Near the bridge in Mackinaw City, **Colonial Michilimackinac Fort** still guards the straits between Lake Michigan and Lake Huron. (☎231-436-4100. Open daily early May to early June and late Aug. to mid-Oct. 9am-5pm; mid-June to late Aug. 9am-6pm. $9, ages 6-17 $5.75.) **Historic Mill Creek,** which includes a working sawmill and nature trails, is located 3½ mi. south of Mackinaw City on U.S. 23. (☎231-436-4100. Open daily early May to mid-Oct. 9am-5pm; mid-July to late Aug. until 6pm. $7, ages 6-17 $4.25.) When you're done enjoying the sights, be sure to take the ferry to Mackinac Island before you cross the Mackinac Bridge to St. Ignace.

▚▐ FOOD & ACCOMMODATIONS. Family-oriented restaurants cluster around Central St., near Shepler's Dock in Mackinaw City. **Cunningham's,** 312 E. Central St., serves homemade pasties ($6.50), pies, and fresh fish. (☎231-436-8821. Dinner specials $8.50. Open daily spring 8am-8pm; summer 8am-10pm; fall 8am-9pm.) At the laid-back **Audie's,** 314 N. Nicolet St. (☎231-436-5744), huge sandwiches ($6.50-8) keep visitors happy. For the best pasties in town, head to the **Mackinaw Pastie & Cookie Co.,** 117 W. Jamet St., which serves six variations of the UP's favorite meat pie. (☎231-436-8202. Open daily 9am-9pm.)

Lakeshore accommodation options abound on U.S. 23, south of the city. The best deals in the area lie across the Mackinac Bridge on **Bus. I-75** in St. Ignace. For an outdoor escape, campers can crash at one of the 600 sites of **Mackinac Mill Creek Campground,** 3 mi. south of town on U.S. 23. The grounds provide beach access, fishing, and trails. (☎231-436-5584. Public showers, pool, and Internet. Sites $15, full hookup $17.50; cabins $40.)

▜ APPROACHING MACKINAC ISLAND
Ferry lines leave Mackinaw City (in summer every 30min. 8am-11pm). **Shepler's** (☎800-828-6157) offers the fastest service. Catamarans operated by **Arnold Transit Co.** are also a fun way to jet to the island. (☎800-542-8528. Round-trip $16, under 16 $8; bikes $6.50.)

MACKINAC ISLAND

Mackinac Island, a 16min. ferry ride from the mainland, has long been considered one of Michigan's greatest treasures. Victorian homes and the prohibition of cars on the heavily touristed island—and the resulting proliferation of horse-drawn carriages—give Mackinac an aristocratic air with a decidedly equine aroma. Travelers flock to the island for its stunning parks, museums, and coastal, old-world charm. Escape the touristy Main St.

THE LOCAL STORY

SAY YA TO DA U.P., EH?

Ask someone from Detroit about Michigan's Upper Peninsula, and you'll detect a whiff of superiority tinged with... is it envy? Certainly they'll deny it—what would a big-city denizen of Mo-town want with the small-town wilderness that lies to the north, on the other side of Lake Michigan and Lake Huron? It's a different world on the peninsula, from the wilderness expanses of of green pine woods and shimmering beaches, right down to the language; "yoopers" have an accent that is half-Canadian, half-Midwestern, and totally unique. To spot a yooper, listen to hear if their "O"s are drawn out "o-o-o"s, they say "da" intead of "the," and use the ubiquitous Canadian "eh" liberally; if so, you've got one. Much of Detroit and below-the-lake Michigan dismisses the U.P., but the yoopers don't mind—they know that the "trolls" living under the Makinac bridge don't know any better.

for a quiet look at what made the island popular in the first place—its beautiful fauna and rolling hills. **Fort Mackinac** is one of the island's main draws. (☎231-436-4100. Open daily early May to mid-June. and late Aug. to mid-Oct. 9:30am-4:30pm; mid-July to late Aug. 9:30am-6pm. $9, ages 6-17 $5.75, under 6 free.) Tickets to the fort also allow access to four museums of island history that are housed in refurbished period buildings. Encompassing 80% of the island, **Mackinac Island State Park** features a circular 8¼ mi. shoreline road for biking and hiking. The invaluable *Mackinac Island Locator Map* ($1) and the *Discover Mackinac Island* book ($2) are available at the **Mackinac Island Chamber of Commerce and Visitors Center,** on Main St. (☎906-847-3783; www.mackinacisland.org. Open daily June-Sept. 8am-6pm; Oct.-May 9am-5pm.)

Hotel rates on the island are exorbitantly high; the mainland is the place to stay. For food, **Mighty Mac,** on Main St., cooks it cheap, with quarter-pound burgers for under $4. (☎231-847-8039. Open daily 8am-8pm.) The **Pink Pony,** also on Main St., serves handmade pastas, fresh salads, and fish dishes under the watchful eyes of the pink-colored horses on the wall. (☎906-847-3341. Entrees from $10. Open daily leaving 8am-10pm.)

ST. IGNACE

Founded in 1671 by Father Marquette and named for St. Ignatius of Loyola, St. Ignace is Mackinaw City's sister city in the Upper Peninsula. Be sure to take a stroll along the **Huron Boardwalk** on the waterfront downtown, where open-air exhibits relate the history of St. Ignace. **Castle Rock** began as the lookout of the Ojibway Indians. The lookout tower rises 200 ft. above St. Ignace with spectacular views of Mackinac Island and Lake Huron. You can also find yet another **Paul Bunyan statue** at Castle Rock. (Exit 348 off I-75, 4 mi. north of the Mackinac Bridge. ☎906-643-8268. $0.50 to climb.) Five minutes from the docks, the **Harbor Light Motel,** 1449 State St. on I-75, rents newly refurbished rooms with cable TV, A/C, and refrigerator. A volleyball net and the occasional bonfire on the beach make this a good bet. (☎906-643-9439. Summer singles $45; doubles $47. Low season $30/$32.)

LEAVING ST. IGNACE
From St. Ignace, head out on **U.S. 2 West.**

SEUL CHOIX POINT LIGHTHOUSE   R.R. 1
From Gulliver, turn south onto County Rd. 432, then turn right onto County Rd. 431.

Hundreds of years ago, a group of French sailors were caught in rough storm on Lake Michigan. Seeking shelter, they landed on the rocky shore and took refuge at what they named Seul Choix, meaning "Only Choice." In 1892, the Seul Choix Point Lighthouse was completed on the harbor and has remained a place of refuge since those early days. (☎906-283-3183. Open daily June to mid-Oct. 10am-6pm. $5.)

MANISTIQUE. The restored iron smelting village of Manistique is now a popular tourist destination on Lake Michigan. The city makes a great base for the many outdoor activities to be found nearby in the Upper Peninsula. The wood and cement **Manistique Boardwalk** lines 2 mi. of Lake Michigan shoreline. In front of the Manistique Visitors Center is yet another **Paul Bunyan statue.** Cool your heels at **Jessie's Sunrise Kitchen,** a friendly little restaurant close to downtown Manistique. Try the Yooper Breakfast (bacon, sausage, ham, potatoes, and pancakes with gravy; $8). If you show up late, the whitefish ($10) is a great lunch or dinner choice. (☎906-341-5284. F fish fry 4-10pm. Su buffet 11am-7pm. Open daily 7am-10pm.)

LEAVING MANISTIQUE
Continue west on **U.S. 2.**

ESCANABA. The **Sand Point Lighthouse** bears little resemblance to a lighthouse. The lighthouse was built in 1867 and operated until 1939, when it was closed because the changing contour of Escanaba Harbor no longer necessitated its use. After that, the lens and lantern were removed and the tower shortened. You can visit the lighthouse and **Delta County Historical Museum** next door. (From U.S. 2, turn east onto Ludington St., then left onto Jenkins Dr. ☎906-786-3763. Open daily June-Aug. 9am-5pm; Sept. 1-4pm.)

The **Swedish Pantry,** 819 Ludington St., is consistently packed with diners eagerly munching on Swedish specialties. The *kroppkakor* (ham dumplings; $7-10) and the *kottbullar* (swedish meatballs with lingonberries; $7-9.50) are worth trying. (☎906-786-9606. Open Su-F 8am-7:30pm, Sa 3am-3pm.) The rooms at the **Hiawatha Motel,** 2400 Ludington St., have comfy beds, as well as free conti-

The arrival of the first cold front in early September marks the departure of thousands of **Monarch Butterflies** from their summer home near Escanaba. The butterflies annually fly over 1900 mi. from Michigan to their winter home near Zitácuaro, Mexico. The dates of migration are unpredictable, but good viewing locations are Peninsula Point and Stonington Peninsula.

nental breakfasts, movie rentals, and rooms with kitchenettes. (At U.S. 2 and Rte. 41. ☎ 800-249-2216. Singles $34-40; doubles $50-60.)

LEAVING ESCANABA
Hop off **U.S. 2** and onto **Rte. 35** toward **Ford River.** It's a long way to the nearest city, so check your gas tank before you set out!

Before Cedar River, Rte. 35 enters the Central Time Zone, where it is 1hr. earlier.

CEDAR RIVER. Cedar River is the only town for 50 mi. between Ford River and Menominee, so if you're hungry, stop for a bite to eat at The **Lighthouse Inn,** N. 8241 Rte. 35. Pictures of Cedar River back in its logging days line the walls of this small restaurant, which gives you the feeling of being inside a Lake Michigan tugboat. The Lighthouse Special (chicken, ham, mushrooms, and swiss cheese on a kaiser roll, $6.50) is a good bet for lunch or dinner. (☎ 906-863-2922. Open daily noon-10pm.) The 678 acres of **J.W. Wells State Park,** N. 7670 Rte. 35, nourish thick, ferny forests that almost look like a Michigan rainforest. The park offers 7 mi. of trails and 3 mi. of sandy beach that line the shore with swimming and picnic areas. (☎ 906-863-9747. Tent sites $15. Day-use $4.)

MENOMINEE. The first inhabitants in Menominee were an Algonquin-speaking Indian tribe known as the "wild rice people;" the name Menominee translates to "wild rice," which once grew abundantly here. Menominee is known for its historic waterfront district, which was for a time the world's greatest lumber shipping port. Take some time to travel down **1st. St.** between 10th and 4th Ave. to see dozens of buildings with unique architecture. Highlights include the bandshell on Doyle Dr., the **Menomi-**

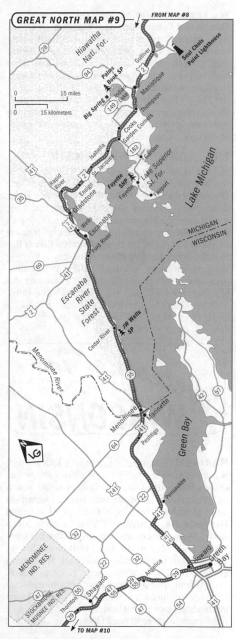

GREAT NORTH MAP #9

FROM MAP #8

GREAT NORTH

TO MAP #10

nee **Abstract Building**, 945 1st. St., and the **Menominee County Historical Museum**, 904 11th Ave. Indian legend holds that the **Spirit Stone** brought luck to whomever made an offering and a wish to the stone. The Indians also believed that when the stone weathered away, the last of the Menominee would have gone to the Happy Hunting Grounds of the Great Spirit. The stone now sits in front of the **Menominee Welcome Center**, 1343 10th Ave. (☎906-863-6496. Open daily 8am-4pm.)

THE ROAD TO WISCONSIN

In Menominee, **Rte. 35** joins **U.S. 41** and crosses the **Interstate Bridge** into **Marinette,** Wi. Between Menominee and Marinette, the Menominee River flows into Green Bay. The surrounding bodies of water provide Menominee and Marinette with boating, fishing, swimming, and even ice boating in the winter. Exhibits at the **Marinette County Historical Society Logging Museum** include a logging camp in miniature and the Evancheck log cabin. Special exhibits honor Queen Marinette and the Menominee Indians. (On Stephenson Island, between Menominee and Marinette. ☎715-732-0831. Open Memorial Day-Labor Day Su noon-4pm, Tu-Sa 10am-4:30pm.)

MARINETTE. Named in honor of a 19th-century Native American trading post owner known as Queen Marinette, Marinette County is the waterfall capital of Wisconsin, with over 14 **waterfalls** located within a one-day drive. U.S. 41 is called **Marinette Ave.** in town. With locations in Marinette, Menominee, and Peshtigo, **The Brothers Three**, 1302 Marinette Ave., is famous for its yummy thin crust pizza made with Wisconsin cheese. (☎715-735-9054. Large $13. Open M-W 11am-10pm, Th-Sa 11am-11pm.) For tourism on the surrounding area, visit the **Wisconsin Travel Information Center**, 1680 Bridge St. (☎715-732-4333; http://travelwisconsin.com. Open M-Sa 8am-4pm.)

LEAVING MARINETTE
From Marinette, take **U.S. 41 South** to **Green Bay.**

NORTHEASTERN WISCONSIN ZOO
4418 Reforestation Rd.
Just north of Green Bay. Exit to City Rd. B (Sunset Beach Rd./School Lane Rd.) into the town of Suamico. Follow Rd. B west for 2 mi. to City Rd. IR (Reforestation Rd.) Turn right and travel 1 mi. to zoo.

Within the Brown County Reforestation Camp, the Northeastern Wisconsin Zoo ("NEW ZOO," as it's called) is home to lions, moose, penguins, and their friends. Together, the zoo and Reforestation Camp make up a 1560 acre recreation area with trails, picnic areas, and trout ponds. (☎920-434-7841; www.co.brown.wi.us/zoo. Open daily Apr.-Oct. 9am-6pm; Nov.-Dec. and Mar. 9am-4pm. $4, seniors $2, ages 3-15 $2, families $12.)

APPROACHING GREEN BAY
Rte. 41 enters Green Bay from the north and borders the city along the west side. To enter downtown, head from the highway onto **Dousman St.** or **Shawano St.** and head east.

GREEN BAY

Green Bay is the oldest settlement in the Midwest, established in 1634 when French fur trappers explored the area. Today, Green Bay is well known for its rowdy, cheese-headed sports fans. In the fall, the city is crowded with Packer football fans trying to get a seat in the revered Lambeau Field. Winter brings hockey season as the Green Bay Gamblers play at the Resch Center.

> **VITAL STATS**
>
> **Population:** 102,000
>
> **Visitor Info: Packer Country Regional Tourism Office,** 1901 S. Oneida St. (☎920-494-9507 or 888-867-3342; www.packercountry.com). Open M-F 8am-4:30pm.
>
> **Internet Access:** 515 Pine St. (☎920-448-4400).
>
> **Post Office:** 300 Packerland Dr. (☎920-498-3892). Open M-F 7:30am-5:30pm, Sa 8am-noon. **Postal Code:** 54303.

GETTING AROUND. I-43 borders the city to the north and east. **Rte. 172** borders Green Bay to the south, completing the loop around the city.

You can sit in the cab of the **World's Largest Steam Locomotive** in the National Railroad Museum.

◙ **SIGHTS.** Bicycling is huge in Wisconsin; the state leads the nation with nearly 1000 mi. of trails. The historic **Fox River Trail** in downtown Green Bay is a great place to start. Once a footpath for Native Americans traveling between their villages, the trail now begins on the east side of the Fox River between E. Mason St. and Walnut St. and ends in Greenleaf, WI. (☎920-448-4466; www.foxrivertrail.org. Day pass $3.)

At the **National Railroad Museum**, 2285 S. Broadway, there are more than 70 trains on display, including one that will take you on a ride around the block. (☎920-437-7623; www.nationalrrmuseum.org. Open M-Sa 9am-5pm, Su 11am-5pm. Rides May-Sept. daily 10, 11:30am, 1, 2:30, and 4pm.) **Heritage Hill State Park**, 2640 S. Webster Ave., has managed to fit four periods of Wisconsin's history into 48 acres. Barter with a fur trader (1672-1825), march alongside soldiers at Fort Howard (1836), get your horse shod at the blacksmith's (1871), or churn butter with the farmers at the Belgian Farm (1905) in one of the 25 historic and reconstructed buildings. (Off Rte. 172. ☎800-721-5150; www.heritagehillgb.org. Open Apr.-Oct. Su noon-4:30pm, Tu-Sa 10am-4:30pm. Tours Sept.-Oct. M-F 1:30pm, Sa 11am and 1:30pm. $7, seniors $6, children $5, under 5 free.)

The old-fashioned **Bay Beach Amusement Park**, 1313 Bay Beach Rd., is your ticket to the days before Six Flags and $60 admission fees. Free admission to the park includes 16 old-fashioned rides at old-fashioned prices. The park also includes concessions, volleyball and softball facilities, and games. (Off I-43 on Webster Ave., on the waterfront of Green Bay. ☎920-391-3671. Open late May to mid-Aug. daily 10am-9pm; late-Aug. daily 10am-6pm; early May and Sept. Sa-Su 10am-6pm. Tickets $0.25)

▓▐ **FOOD & ACCOMMODATIONS.** Located in the old Dousman Street Station, the **Titletown Brewing Company**, 200 Dousman St., has walls lined with authentic pictures of historic Green Bay. Specialties on tap at the brewery are Johnny "Blood" McNally Red Ale and Grandma's root beer. Try the beer-braised pot roast. (☎920-437-2337; www.titletownbrewing.com. Open M-F 11am-10pm, Sa-Su 11am-11pm. Bar open until 2am.) **Kroll's**, at 1658 Main St. and 1990 S. Ridge Rd., has been a long-time local burger favorite. (☎920-468-4422. Open 10:30am-11pm.)

Motels are fewer and more expensive on the east side, though **Days Inn**, 406 N. Washington St. (☎920-435-4484), is the most affordable. Cheaper hotels can be found on the west side closer to the athletic fields. **Motel 6**, 1614 Shawano Ave. (☎920-494-6730), is a decent option. The **Bay Motel**, 1301 S. Military Ave. (City Rte. 41), has clean rooms close to Lambeau Field. The rooms are predictably more expensive on game weekends. (☎920-494-3441. Doubles $40-60.)

◤▐ **APPROACHING WAUSAU-MOSINEE**
Leaving Green Bay, head west through residential areas on **Shawano St.**, which becomes **Rte. 29/ 32 West** outside town. Take Exit 171 to the **Bus. Rte. 51 South** loop to visit Rothschild and the visitor center. To go downtown, take Exit 171 to **Bus. Rte. 51 North** through Schofield, 3 mi. into Wausau.

WAUSAU-MOSINEE

Wausau was founded in 1845 as "Big Bull Falls." At the request of the postmaster, the name was changed to something more appropriate for ladies to write on envelopes, and Wausau and Mosinee were chosen. Today, Marathon County is the world leader in the production of the medicinal root ginseng. Whitewater canoeing and kayaking on the Wisconsin River are also a big attraction.

(VITAL STATS)

Population: 2200

Visitor Info: Wausau/Central Wisconsin Convention & Visitors Bureau, 10204 Park Plaza, Ste. B (☎715-355-8788 or 888-948-4748; www.wausaucvb.com), off Exit 185 on I-39/51 in Mosinee. Open M-F 8am-5pm, Sa-Su 9am-5pm.

Internet Access: Marathon County Public Library, 300 N. 1st St. (☎715-261-7200). Open M-Th 9am-8:30pm, F 9am-5pm, Sa 9am-1pm.

Post Office: 235 Forest St. (☎715-261-4200). Open M-F 8am-5:30pm, Sa 8am-1pm. **Postal Code:** 54403.

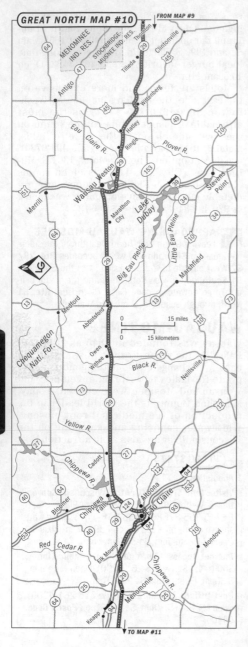

GREAT NORTH MAP #10 → FROM MAP #9

TO MAP #11

GREAT NORTH

FROM MAP #9

▼ TO MAP #11

GETTING AROUND. Rte. 29 enters Wausau from the south, between **Schofield** and **Rothschild.** Southwest of Wausau, **Rte. 29** connects with **Rte. 51.** At the north side of town, Rte. 29 continues to the west and Rte. 51 continues north.

SIGHTS. Changing exhibits at the **Leigh Yawkey Woodson Art Museum,** at Franklin and 12th St., display artwork from around the world. The museum is also home to permanent collections of historic and contemporary paintings and "Birds in Art," a world-class collection of avian art. (☎ 715-845-7010; www.lywam.org. Open Su noon-5pm, Tu-F 9am-4pm, Sa noon-5pm. Free.) **Hsu's Ginseng Enterprise,** T6819 County Hwy. West, specializes in all things ginseng, a medicinal plant. Wisconsin's cool summers and virgin soil produce roots with the size, weight, and shape that buyers desire. (☎ 800-388-3818; www.hsuginseng.com.) **Artsblock** was built around the historic Grand Theater, adding 75,000 sq. ft. of performance space. Three buildings are connected by the new space including the Grand Theater, the Center for the Visual Arts, and Great Hall. Events scheduled include over 15 shows featuring Broadway productions, staged spectaculars, and guest entertainers. (Surrounded by Scott, 4th, Jefferson and 5th St. ☎ 715-842-0988; www.grandtheater.org.)

Rib Mountain, 3605 N. Mountain Rd., is one of the oldest geologic formations on earth, with an observation tower providing views of the entire Wisconsin River Valley. **Granite Peak,** built over 65 years ago, is one of America's oldest ski resorts; expansions over the past three years have made it one of the Midwest's biggest, with 72 runs. (☎ 715-845-2846; www.skigranite-peak.com. Open mid-Nov. to Mar. daily 9am-9pm. Lift ticket $38, ages 6-12 $26, seniors $26.)

FOOD & ACCOMMODATIONS. Walk in the doors (a mine shaft really) of the ■**Wausau Mine Company,** 3904 W. Stewart Ave., and discover that the **Mother Lode Eatery** restaurant and **Rusty Nail Saloon** have been carved to resemble the caverns within the mine, along with original mining artifacts. Try the Virgil Cristo Burger ($6), named after the miner dummy who keeps watch over the bar. (Turn north on Rte. 51/39 junction and exit at Sherman St. Turn left on Sherman St., then right on 28th St., and proceed 1 mi. ☎ 715-845-7304. Open M-F 11am-10pm, Sa-Su 11am-11pm.) Rock music greets patrons of

Hudson's Classic Grill, 2200 W. Stewart Ave., a 50s bar and grill with walls lined with Burma Shave signs. Choose between old-school booths or the outdoor patio and beer garden. Try the spark plugs (jalapeno poppers; $5) for a warm up. (☎715-849-8586. Open Su-Th 11am-11pm, F-Sa 11am-midnight.)

Rooms at the **Nite Inn,** 425 Grand Ave., in Schofield, are available with kitchenettes. (☎715-355-1641; www.niteinninterimlodg.com. Singles $32; doubles $37; 1-room apartment $46; 2-room apartment $52. Under 16 free.)

LEAVING WAUSAU
Take **Stewart Ave.** west from downtown, and merge onto **Rte. 29** at Exit 192. To visit the downtown area, merge onto **Rte. 124 North** and go across the bridge over Chippewa River.

CHIPPEWA FALLS

Chippewa Falls was named one of the top 10 small towns in the U.S. in 1997 and it's easy to see why: museums, gardens, and the Chippewa River make this picturesque city worth visiting. The industrial area is full of historic buildings, including the Chippewa Shoe Factory, which began by producing shoes for lumberjacks and rivermen.

(VITAL STATS)

Population: 13,000

Visitor Info: Chippewa Falls Area Visitors Center, 10 S. Bridge St. (☎715-723-0331 or 888-723-0024; www.chippewachamber.org). Open summer M-F 8am-5pm, Sa 10am-3pm, Su 11am-2pm; winter M-F 8am-5pm.

Internet Access: Public Library, 105 W. Central St. (☎715-723-1146).

Post Office: 212 Bay St. (☎715-726-2500). **Postal Code:** 54729.

GETTING AROUND. Rte. 29 borders Chippewa Falls to the south. Rte. 124 is **Bridge St.** as it comes from the south and crosses the river. It curves north on the other shore, intersecting with Rte. 29 and **Rte. 178,** eventually becoming **N. High St.** and **Jefferson St.**

SIGHTS. The **Old Abe State Trail,** 711 N. Bridge St. (☎800-866-6264; www.wiparks.net), connects Chippewa Falls to Cornell and is open year-round for biking, horseback riding, and cross-country skiing. **Leinenkugel's Brewery,** 1 Jefferson Ave., is Chippewa Falls's oldest business and has been brewing Germanic beer in the North Woods of Wisconsin since 1867. A tour shows the original spring where the brewery got water and the caves where the beer was kept in the days before refrigeration. Before or after the tour, hang out in the recently opened Leinie Lodge and gift shop, where you can also sip your two free beer samples. (☎715-723-5557 or 888-534-6437; www.leinie.com. Open June-Aug. M-Sa 9am-5pm, Su 11am-4pm; Sept.-May M-Sa 9am-5pm. Free 45min. tours every 30min.; last tour 1hr. before close. Reservations recommended.)

Chippewa Falls claims a history of manufacturing and processing dating back to the 1840s, and was the site of Seymour Cray's invention of the supercomputer, the benchmark for speed. At the **Chippewa Falls Museum of Industry & Technology,** 21 E. Grand Ave., displays showcase interactive exhibits on regional industries, photos and documents of Cray's collection, and nanosecond knowledge. (☎715-720-9206; www.cfmit.com. Open Tu-F 1-5pm, Sa 10am-3pm. $3, children $1.) **XMI Neckwear,** 8336 Rte. 178, was founded in New York City in 1986 and expanded production to Chippewa Falls in 1987. Their neckties are frequently worn by Tom Brokaw, David Letterman, and Bryant Gumbel, and the store sells a huge selection of ties at reduced prices. (☎715-723-1999. Open M-F 8am-4pm.)

FOOD & ACCOMMODATIONS. Since 1944, **Olson's Ice Cream Parlor & Deli,** 611 N. Bridge St., has been serving 22 different "Homaid" ice creams made daily in flavors ranging from chocolate chip cookie dough to Dinosaur Crunch. The deli serves sandwiches ($3-4), soups ($2), and salads. (☎715-723-4331. Open daily 10am-9pm.) The **Indianhead Motel,** 501 Summit Ave., has simple rooms with desks, clean beds, and little decoration. (Off Rte. 29 South, east of town. ☎715-723-9171 or 800-306-3049; www.indianheadmotel-chippewa.com. Singles $40; doubles $46.)

APPROACHING EAU CLAIRE
Take **Rte. 124 South** off Rte. 29 and exit onto **Birch St.**

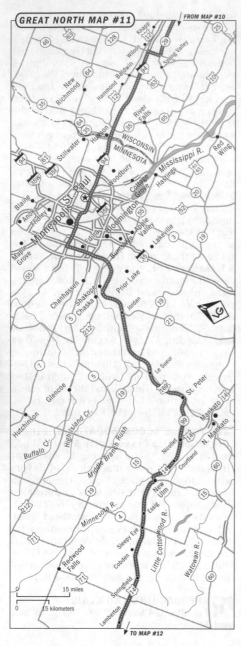

GREAT NORTH MAP #11

FROM MAP #10

TO MAP #12

GREAT NORTH

EAU CLAIRE

Eau Claire (French for "Clear Water") was one of Wisconsin's busiest lumber towns in the 1800s thanks to its location at the junction of the Eau Claire and Chippewa Rivers, which are now lined by bike trails. The **Paul Bunyan Logging Camp**, 1110 Carson Park Dr., welcomes visitors with the **Henry O. Strand Interpretive Center**, a hands-on introduction to Wisconsin's logging industry. The camp's log cabins duplicate the rugged conditions the early settlers faced. (Follow Main St. until it ends at Graham Ave., turn left on Graham, go 2 blocks, and turn right on Lake St. ☎ 715-835-6200. Open Apr.-Sept. daily 10am-4:30pm.) Beneath the towering pines of Carson Park, the exhibits at the **Chippewa Valley Museum** begin with the arrival of the Ojibwe Indians and continue through the lumbering days of settlers from Germany and Norway. (☎ 715-834-7871; www.cvmuseum.com. Open May-Aug. daily 10am-5pm; Sept.-Apr. Su and W-Sa 1-5pm, Tu 1-8pm. $4, children $1.50.)

"Let no one hunger for lack of a better sandwich" is the motto at the **Acoustic Cafe**, 505 South Barstow. The food choices are limited; visit for the hip atmosphere or outdoor seating. (☎ 715-832-9090. Live music 8:30pm. Open M-Th 8am-10pm, F-Sa 8am-midnight, Su 11am-9pm.) **Erbert & Gerbert's**, at 405 Water St. and 3003 London Rd., is a popular sandwich chain, serving unique subs and clubs. (☎ 715-835-9995. Open M-Sa 10:30am-11pm, Su 10:30am-10pm.) Cheap motels can be found around N. Clairemont Ave. and Craig Rd., including the **Highlander Inn**, 1135 W. MacArthur Ave. (☎ 715-835-2261 or 877-568-0773. Rooms $26-60.) On the outside, ▨**Maple Manor**, 2507 S. Hastings Way, is your ordinary motel, but inside it's a quaint B&B. Each room has its own unique flavor; the Wisteria is a vision in purple. (☎ 715-834-2618 or 800-624-3763. Singles $30-40; doubles $40-60.)

LEAVING EAU CLAIRE

Follow **U.S. 12** out of Eau Claire. Just after the small town of **Elk Mound**, turn off U.S. 12 onto **Rte. 29 West** toward Menomonie.

MENOMONIE. Beautiful Menomonie, on man-made Lake Menomonie and the Red Cedar River, was first inhabited by Native Americans. The **Mabel Tainter Theater**, 205 Main St., was built in 1890 in Richardson-Romanesque style. The beautiful Victorian theater has been restored to its original splendor and is now one of the top 10 architecturally significant theaters in the US. (☎715-235-9726. 1hr. tours daily 1, 2, 3, 4pm. 15 min. 'peek tours' offered any time.) If you're in need of a little pick-me-up, **Legacy Chocolates,** 544 S. Broadway, is revered for their high quality truffles, chocolates, and gourmet beverages. The spiel about chocolate being one of nature's most nutritious and easily digested foods makes it hard to resist. (☎715-231-2580; www.legacychocolates.com. Open M-Sa 7am-5:30pm.)

◣ DETOUR: CADDIE WOODLAWN HISTORIC PARK

12 mi. south of Menomonie on Rte. 25, west of Dunnville.

For nearly 70 years, thousands of children have enjoyed reading the adventures of Caddie Woodlawn, the young pioneer girl. The Caddie Woodlawn Historic Park is the site of the original Woodlawn home, made famous in Caddie Woodlawn's granddaughter's books. Many of the buildings and sites mentioned in the book can be seen along Rte. 25 or the Red Cedar Bike Trail. (Open daily spring-fall dawn-dusk.)

◣ DETOUR: BULLFROG'S "EAT MY FISH" FARM
N1321 Bullfrog Rd./566th St.
12 mi. south of Menomonie, 2 mi. Northeast on the trail off of the Dunnville Bridge.

At Bullfrog's, you can enjoy a day fishing at a tranquil stocked trout farm, then grill up your catch and have a picnic next to the pond. Presentations and tours of the fish hatchery and workshops are also offered. (☎715-664-8775; www.eatmyfish.com. Open "casually" daily noon-6pm. Pole rental $2. Fish from $4.50 per lb.)

◤ LEAVING MENOMONIE
Take **Rte. 29 West** toward Spring Valley.

◤ CADY CHEESE
126 Rte. 128
West of Menomonie, ¼ mi. north of intersection of Rte. 29 and Rte. 128 in Spring Valley.

No trip to Wisconsin is complete without a visit to a cheese factory, and Cady Cheese is as good as any. The family-owned and operated business turns out 25 tons of cheese every day. Sample the 100 varieties of cheese and sausages in the gift shop. (☎715-772-4218; www.cadycheese.com. Open Jan.-Apr. daily 9am-5pm; May-Dec. M-F 8:30am-6pm, Sa-Su 9am-5pm.)

◤ APPROACHING HUDSON
Take **Rte. 128 North** to **I-94 West.** Exit onto **Rte. 35,** which becomes **2nd St.** downtown.

HUDSON. At **Lakefront Park** on the St. Croix River, a National Scenic Waterway, you can fish, feed ducks, and sail at the marina. The **Octagon House,** 1004 3rd St., at the corner of Myrtle St., was built in the mid-1800s when eight-sided houses were all the rage. The Victorian complex also includes farm animals, a general store, and a carriage house with a blacksmith and gift shop. (☎715-386-2654. Open May-Oct. and late Nov. to mid-Dec. Su 2-4:30pm, Tu-Sa 11am-4pm. Last tour 30min. before close. $3, ages 13-18 $2, children $1.) From the street, the palm trees of **San Pedro Cafe,** 426 2nd St., exude Caribbean flair. Inside, the aroma of the wood fired oven fills the air. For lunch, try the wood roasted BBQ jerk-pork ($9). Dinner options include the Rasta Pasta ($12) and wood fired pizzas. (☎715-386-4003; www.sanpedrocafe.com. Open M-Th 10:30am-10pm, F 10:30am-11pm, Sa 8am-11pm, Su 8am-10pm.)

◤ APPROACHING THE TWIN CITIES
Take **I-94/U.S. 12 West** into the Twin Cities.

Welcome To MINNESOTA

MINNEAPOLIS & ST. PAUL

Native Garrison Keillor wrote that the "difference between St. Paul and Minneapolis is the difference between pumpernickel and Wonder bread." Indeed, the story of the Twin Cities is one of contrast: St. Paul is a conservative, Irish-Catholic town, while Minneapolis deserves its distinction as a young metropolis. Minneapolis's theaters and clubs rival those of New York, while stately sights such as the capitol and cathedral reside in St. Paul. The growing metropolitan area of the Twin Cities is fueled by families seeking the options Minneapolis and St. Paul can offer as a pair.

VITAL STATS

Population: 380,000/290,000

Visitor Info: Minneapolis Convention and Visitors Association, 250 Marquette Ave. (☎612-335-6000; www.minneapolis.org), in a kiosk at the Convention Center. Publications available M-Sa 6am-10pm, Su 7am-8pm. Desk open M-Sa 8am-4:30pm, Su noon-5pm. **St. Paul Convention and Visitors Bureau,** 175 W. Kellogg Blvd., #502 (☎651-265-4900; www.visitstpaul.com), in the River Centre. Open M-F 8am-4:30pm.

Internet Access: Minneapolis Public Library, 250 Marquette Ave. (☎612-630-6200; www.mplib.org). Open M, W, F 10am-5pm; Tu and Th noon-7pm; Sa 10am-5pm.

Post Office: 100 S. 1st St. (☎612-349-4713), at Marquette Ave. on the river. Open M-F 7am-8pm, Sa 9am-1pm. **Postal Codes** 55401.

GETTING AROUND

Despite one-way streets and skewed numbered grids, the streets are not congested and parking garages are reasonably priced, making driving manageable. Downtown Minneapolis lies about 10 mi. west of downtown St. Paul via **I-94. I-35** splits in the Twin Cities, with **I-35 West** serving Minneapolis and **I-35 East** serving St. Paul. **I-494** runs to the airport and the Mall of America, while **I-394** heads to downtown Minneapolis from the western suburbs. **Hennepin Ave.** and the pedestrian **Nicollet Mall** are the two main roads in Minneapolis; **Kellogg Ave.** and **7th Street** are the primary thoroughfares in St. Paul.

👁 SIGHTS

MINNEAPOLIS

LAKES AND RIVERS. In the land of 10,000 lakes, Minneapolis boasts many of its own; the city contains 22 lakes, 150 parks, and 100 golf courses. **Lake Calhoun,** the largest of the bunch, is a recreational paradise. Scores of inline skaters, bicyclists, and runners loop the lake on all but the coldest days. Ringed by stately mansions, the serene **Lake of the Isles** is an excellent place to commune with Canada geese. Just southeast of Lake Calhoun on Sheridan St., **Lake Harriet** lures the locals with

tiny paddleboats and a bandshell with nightly free concerts in summer. The city maintains 28 mi. of lakeside trails around the three lakes for strolling and biking. **Calhoun Cycle Center,** three blocks east of Lake Calhoun, rents out bikes for exploring the paths. *(1622 W. Lake St. ☎612-827-8231. Open M-Th 10am-8pm, F-Sa 9am-9pm, Su 9am-8pm. $15-25 per half-day, $25-40 per day. Credit card and driver's license required.)* At the northeast corner of Lake Calhoun, **The Tin Fish** offers canoe, kayak, and paddleboat rentals on the side of the restaurant. *(3000 E. Calhoun Pkwy. ☎612-555-1234; www.thetinfish.com. Open M-Sa 11am-9pm, Su 11am-7pm. All boats $10 per hr. $20 deposit, driver's license, or credit card required.)* **Minnehaha Park** offers striking views of the impressive **Minnehaha Falls,** immortalized in Longfellow's *Song of Hiawatha. (Falls are off Minnehaha Ave. at Minnehaha Pkwy.)*

MUSEUMS. The **Minneapolis Institute of Arts,** south of downtown, showcases more than 100,000 art objects spanning 5000 years, including Rembrandt's *Lucretia* and the world-famous *Doryphoros,* Polykleitos's perfectly proportioned man. *(2400 3rd Ave. South ☎612-870-3131; www.artsmia.org. Open Su noon-5pm, Tu-W and Sa 10am-5pm, Th-F 10am-9pm. Free.)* A few blocks southwest of downtown, the world-renowned **Walker Art Center** counts daring exhibits by Lichtenstein, Rothko, and Warhol among its amazing galleries of contemporary art. *(725 Vineland Pl., at Lyndale Ave. ☎612-375-7622; www.walkerart.org.)* Next to the Walker lies the **Minneapolis Sculpture Garden,** the largest urban sculpture garden in the US. The iconic, postcard-friendly **Spoonbridge and Cherry** sculpture joins rotating exhibits in the impressive gardens. The adjacent **Cowles Conservatory** houses an array of plants and an impressive Frank Gehry fish sculpture. *(Garden open daily 6am-midnight. Conservatory open Su 10am-5pm, Tu-Sa 10am-8pm. Free.)* Gehry also holds the honor of having designed the Twin Cities' most unique and controversial structure: the **Weisman Art Museum,** on the East Bank of the U of M campus. The undulating metallic building was the rough draft for his famous Guggenheim in Bilbao, and hosts an inspired collection of modern art, including works by O'Keeffe, Warhol, and Kandinsky. The thought-provoking walk-through apartment replica, by Edward and Nancy Reddin Kienholz, engages all the senses by asking viewers to eavesdrop at each

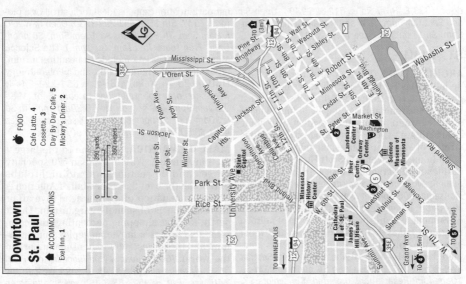

Downtown St. Paul

🍴 FOOD

Cafe Latte, **4**
Cossetta, **3**
Day By Day Cafe, **5**
Mickey's Diner, **2**

▲ ACCOMMODATIONS

Exel Inn, **1**

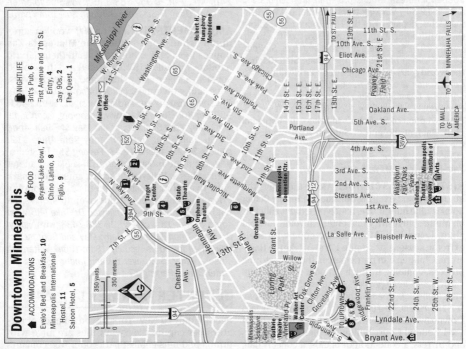

Downtown Minneapolis

▲ ACCOMMODATIONS

Evelo's Bed and Breakfast, **10**
Minneapolis International
Hostel, **11**
Saloon Hotel, **5**

🍴 FOOD

Bryant-Lake Bowl, **7**
Chino Latino, **8**
Figlio, **9**

🎵 NIGHTLIFE

Brit's Pub, **6**
First Avenue and 7th St
Entry, **4**
Gay 90s, **2**
The Quest, **1**

GREAT NORTH

door. *(333 E. River Rd.* ☎ *612-625-9494. Open Su and Sa 11am-5pm, Tu-W and F 10am-5pm, Th 10am-8pm, Sa 11am-5pm. Free.)*

ST. PAUL

ARCHITECTURE. History and architecture define stately St. Paul. Mark Twain said that the city "is put together in solid blocks of honest bricks and stone and has the air of intending to stay." Nowhere is this more evident than along ▧**Summit Ave.,** the nation's longest continuous stretch of Victorian houses, including the childhood home of novelist **F. Scott Fitzgerald** and the Minnesota **Governor's Mansion.** *(Fitzgerald: 599 Summit Ave. Currently a private residence. Governor's Mansion: 1006 Summit Ave.* ☎ *651-297-8177. Tours May-Oct. F 1-3pm. Reservations required. Free.)* Also on Summit Ave., the magnificent home of railroad magnate **James J. Hill**—the largest and most expensive home in the state when it was completed in 1891—offers 1¼hr. tours. *(240 Summit Ave.* ☎ *651-297-2555. Open Su noon-4pm, W-Sa 10am-4pm. Reservations preferred. $8, seniors $7, ages 6-12 $4.)* **Walking tours** of Summit Ave., lasting 1½hr., depart from the Hill House and explore the architectural and social history of the area. *(*☎*651-297-2555. Tours Sa 11am and 2pm, Su 2pm. $4-6.)* Golden horses top the ornate **State Capitol,** the world's largest unsupported marble dome. *(75 Constitution Ave.* ☎ *651-296-3962. Open M-F 9am-5pm, Sa 10am-3pm, Su 1-4pm. Tours every hr. M-F 9am-3pm, Sa 10am-2pm, Su 1-3pm. Free.)* A scaled-down version of St. Peter's in Rome, the **Cathedral of St. Paul,** at the end of Summit Ave., overlooks the capitol. *(239 Selby Ave.* ☎ *651-228-1766. Open M-Th 7am-5:30pm, F 7am-4pm, Sa 7am-7pm, Su 7am-5pm. Tours M, W, F 1pm.)*

HISTORY AND SCIENCE. Along the river, the innovative and exciting ▧**Minnesota History Center** houses nine interactive, hands-on exhibit galleries on Minnesota history that entertain young and old alike. Learn how Minnesotans cope with their extreme seasons or admire Prince's "Purple Rain" attire. Children can participate in the grain-storing process, climbing through a model of a grain elevator. *(345 Kellogg Blvd. West.* ☎ *651-296-6126; www.mnhs.org. Open Su noon-5pm, Tu 10am-8pm, W-F 10am-3pm, Sa 10am-5pm. Free. Pay parking lot.)* Downtown's **Landmark Center** is a grandly restored 1894 Federal Court building replete with towers and turrets, a collection of pianos, a concert hall, and four courtrooms. Out front, **Rice Park,** the old-

est park in Minnesota, is ideal for a stroll or a picnic. *(75 W. 5th St.* ☎ *651-292-3230. Open M-W and F 8am-5pm, Th 8am-8pm, Sa 10am-5pm, Su noon-5pm. Free tours Th 11am, Su 1pm.)* The **Science Museum of Minnesota** includes a beautiful atrium, an exhibit on the human body, and a Paleontology Hall. *(120 W. Kellogg Blvd.* ☎ *651-221-9444; www.smm.org. Open mid-June to early Sept. M-Sa 9:30am-9pm; low season M-W 9:30am-5pm, Th-Sa 9:30am-9pm, Su noon-5pm. $7.50, seniors and ages 4-12 $5.50; with omnitheater $12.50/$9.50.)*

MALL OF AMERICA. Welcome to the largest mall in America. With more than 520 specialty stores and 60 restaurants and nightclubs extending for over 2 mi., the Mall of America is the consummation of an American love affair with all that is obscenely gargantuan. Don't settle for just shopping and eating; the complex also boasts a movie megaplex, an aquarium, and the largest indoor amusement park in the world. *(60 E. Broadway, in Bloomington. From St. Paul, take I-35 West south to I-494 West to the 24th Ave. Exit.* ☎ *952-883-8800; www.mallofamerica.com. Open M-Sa 10am-9:30pm, Su 11am-7pm.)*

AMUSEMENTS. Located on 500 wooded acres in suburban Apple Valley, the **Minnesota Zoo** houses local and exotic animals in their natural habitats, including 15 endangered and threatened species, a Tiger Lair exhibit, and native beavers, lynx, and wolverines. *(13000 Zoo Blvd. Take Rte. 77 South to Zoo exit and follow signs.* ☎ *952-431-9500 or 800-366-7811; www.mnzoo.org. Open June-Aug. daily 9am-6pm; Sept. and May M-F 9am-4pm, Sa-Su 9am-6pm; Oct.-Apr. daily 9am-4pm. $12, seniors $8.25, ages 3-12 $7. Parking $5.)* In Shakopee, even the most daring thrill-seekers can get their jollies at **Valleyfair,** a quality amusement park with five roller coasters and the heart-stopping Power Tower, which drops over 10 stories, as well as a waterpark. *(1 Valleyfair Dr. Take I-35 West south to Rte. 13 West.* ☎ *800-386-7433; www.valleyfair.com. Open June-Aug. daily; May and Sept. select days. Call for hours, usually 10am-10pm; waterpark closes earlier. $32, over 60 and under 48 in. $16, under 3 free. Parking $7.)*

🎵 ENTERTAINMENT

Second only to New York City in number of theaters per capita, the Twin Cities are alive with drama and music. Most parks offer free concerts and shows on summer weekends, while theaters present a wide variety of classical and modern plays during the winter. Music is an important part of the cities—the thriving alternative, pop, and classical music scenes fill out the wide range of cultural options. For more info, read the free *City Pages* (www.citypages.com), available at libraries, most cafes, and newsstands around town.

THEATER

The renowned 🏛**Guthrie Theater,** 725 Vineland Pl., in Minneapolis, adjacent to the Walker Art Center just off Hennepin Ave., draws praise for its mix of daring and classical productions. (☎612-377-2224; www.guthrietheater.org. Season Aug.-June. Box office open M-F 9am-8pm, Sa 10am-8pm, Su hours vary. Tickets $16-44. Students and seniors $5 discount. Rush tickets 15min. before show $12.50; line starts 1-1½hr. before show.) The historic **State Theatre,** 805 Hennepin Ave., the **Orpheum Theatre,** 910 Hennepin Ave. North, and the **Pantages Theatre**, 710 Hennepin Ave., comprise the **Hennepin Theater District** in downtown Minneapolis, with Broadway shows and musical events. (Box office ☎612-339-7007; www.hennepintheaterdistrict.com. Tickets from $15.) For family-oriented productions, the **Children's Theater Company,** 2400 3rd Ave. South, next to the Minneapolis Institute of Arts, comes through. (☎612-874-0400. Season Sept.-June. Box office open in season M-Sa 9am-5pm; summer M-F 9am-4pm. Tickets $15-28; students, seniors, and children $9-22. Rush tickets 15min. before show $11.) The ingenious **Théâtre de la Jeune Lune,** 105 1st St. North, stages critically acclaimed productions in an old warehouse. (☎612-332-3968, tickets 612-333-6200. Open M-F 10am-6pm. Tickets $10-26.) **Brave New Workshop,** 3001 Hennepin Ave., in Uptown, stages satirical comedy shows and improv in an intimate club. (☎612-332-6620; www.bravenewworkshop.com. Box office open M-W 9:30am-5pm, Th-F 9:30am-9pm, Sa 10am-11pm. Tickets $15-22.)

MUSIC

The Twin Cities' vibrant music scene offers everything from opera and polka to hip-hop and alternative. **Sommerfest,** a month-long celebration of Viennese music put on by the **Minnesota Orchestra,** is the best of the cities' classical options during July. **Orchestra Hall,** 1111 Nicollet Mall, in downtown Minneapolis, hosts the event. (☎612-371-5656 or 800-292-4141; www.minnesotaorchestra.org. Box office open M-Sa 10am-6pm. Tickets $15-65. Student rush tickets 30min. before show

$10.) Nearby, **Peavey Plaza,** on Nicollet Mall, holds free nightly concerts and occasional film screenings. The **Saint Paul Chamber Orchestra,** the **Schubert Club,** and the **Minnesota Opera Company** all perform at St. Paul's glass-and-brick **Ordway Center For The Performing Arts,** 345 Washington St., which also hosts touring productions. (☎651-224-4222; www.ordway.org. Box office open M-F 9am-6pm, Sa 11am-5pm, Su 11am-4pm. Tickets $15-85.)

SPORTS

The puffy **Hubert H. Humphrey Metrodome,** 900 S. 5th St., in downtown Minneapolis, hosts baseball's **Minnesota Twins** (☎612-375-7454; www.twinsbaseball.com) and football's **Minnesota Vikings** (☎612-338-4537; www.vikings.com). The NBA's **Timberwolves** (☎612-337-3865; www.timberwolves.com) and WNBA's **Lynx** (☎612-673-8400; www.wnba.com/lynx) howl at the **Target Center,** 601 1st Ave., between 6th and 7th St. in downtown Minneapolis. The NHL team, the **Wild,** takes to the ice at St. Paul's **Xcel Energy Center** (☎651-222-9453; www.wild.com). The soccer craze hits the Midwest with the minor-league **Thunder,** at the **National Sports Center** (☎763-785-5600) in suburban Blaine.

FESTIVALS

In late January and early February, the **St. Paul Winter Carnival,** near the state capitol, cures cabin fever with ice sculptures, ice fishing, skating contests, and an ice palace. On the 4th of July, St. Paul celebrates the **Taste of Minnesota** with fireworks, concerts, and regional and ethnic cuisine from hordes of local vendors. The **Minneapolis Riverfront Fourth of July Celebration and Fireworks** (☎612-378-1226; www.mississippimile.com) is a day for the family with trolley rides, concerts, food, and fireworks. On its coattails rides the 10-day **Minneapolis Aquatennial** (☎612-518-3486), with concerts and art exhibits glorifying the lakes. In the two weeks prior to Labor Day, everyone heads to the nation's largest state fair, the **Minnesota State Fair,** at Snelling and Como St. in St. Paul. (☎651-612-642-2200; www.mnstatefair.org. $8, seniors and ages 5-12 $7, under 5 free.)

🍴 FOOD

The Twin Cities' cosmopolitan vibe is reflected in its many culinary options. Posh restaurants share the streets with intimate cafes. **Uptown** Minneapolis, near Lake St. and Hennepin Ave., offers funky restaurants and bars where the Twin Cities' young professionals meet after work. In downtown Minneapolis, the **Warehouse District**, on 1st Ave. North between 8th St. and Washington Ave., and **Nicollet Mall**, a 12-block pedestrian stretch of Nicollet Ave., attract locals and tourists with shops and simple eateries ranging from burgers to Tex-Mex. While grabbing a bite to eat, check out the statue of **Mary Tyler Moore**, famous for turning the world on with her smile, at Nicollet and 7th St. South of downtown, Nicollet turns into **Eat Street**, a 17-block stretch of international cuisine.

In St. Paul, the upscale **Grand Ave.**, between Lexington and Dale, is lined with laid-back restaurants and bars, while **Lowertown**, along Sibley St. near 6th St. downtown, is a popular nighttime hangout. Near the University of Minnesota (U of M) campus between the downtowns, **Dinkytown**, on the East Bank of the river, and the **Seven Corners** area of the West Bank, on Cedar Ave., cater to student appetites—including late-night cravings.

In the Twin Cities, many forgo restaurants for area cafes (see below). For cook-it-yourself-ers, pick up fresh produce at the **St. Paul Farmers Market**, on Wall St., between E. 4th and 5th St. (☎651-227-6856. Open late Apr. to mid-Nov. Sa 6am-1pm.) Even better is the **Minneapolis Farmers Market**, off 94W at E. Lyndale Ave. and 3rd Ave. North, which offers a wide array of fruits, vegetables, flowers, and crafts in over 450 booths that claim to comprise the "largest open-air market in the Upper Midwest." (☎612-333-1737. Open Sa-Su 6am-1pm.)

MINNEAPOLIS

▨ **Chino Latino**, 2916 Hennepin Ave. (☎612-824-7878), at Lake St., Uptown. Drinks like the signature watermelon *mojito* ($8.50) characterize this trendy Latin-Asian fusion restaurant. Offering entrees for 2 ($13-40), a chic *satay* bar ($7-9), and unusual dishes that often require instruction from the waitstaff, Chino Latino is for the hip. Open daily 4:30pm-1am. Reservations recommended.

Bryant-Lake Bowl, 810 W. Lake St. (☎612-825-3737), at Bryant St. near Uptown. Built in the 1930s, this funky bowling alley/bar/cabaret serves quality food at friendly prices. The "BLB Scramble" (a breakfast dish of eggs and vegetables; $5.50), ravioli, soups, and sandwiches ensure that the stylish patrons throw strikes with pleasantly full stomachs. Bowling $3.75. Entrees $8-15. Open daily 8am-1am.

Loring Pasta Bar, 327 14th Ave. SE (☎612-378-4849; www.loringpastabar.com), in Dinkytown near the U of M campus. The well-decorated restaurant is whimsical and sophisticated, with a menu ranging from potstickers ($7) to pastas ($13-15). Live music nightly. Su night tango DJ. Open M-Sa 11:30am-1am, Su 5:30pm-1am. Kitchen closes earlier.

Figlio, 3001 Hennepin Ave. (☎612-822-1688), at W. Lake St. in the Calhoun Sq. complex, Uptown. Dishing up Italian fare with flair, Twin City residents have awarded Figlio the honor of "Best Late Night Dining" for many years, for its scrumptious sandwiches (from $9) and delicious pastas and pizzas (from $11). Open Su-Th 11:30am-1am, F-Sa 11:30am-2am.

ST. PAUL

Cossetta, 211 W. 7th St. (☎651-222-3476). What began as an Italian market in 1911 now serves quality eat-in or takeout specialities. Try the veal parmigiana ($9) or famous pizza ($11-21). Open Su-Th 11am-9pm, F-Sa 11am-10pm; winter M-Th 11am-9pm, F-Sa 11am-10pm, Su 11am-8pm.

Mickey's Diner, 36 W. 7th St. (☎651-222-5633), at St. Peter St. A 1937 diner on the National Register of Historic Places, Mickey's offers food that outshines its bright history and chrome-and-vinyl decor. Take a spin at a counter stool, or groove to some oldies on the jukebox at each booth (30min. limit). Open 24hr.

Day By Day Cafe, 477 W. 7th St. (☎651-227-0654; www.daybyday.com). Started in 1975 by an alcoholism treatment center, Day By Day now serves the community, with breakfast all day ($4.50-8), as well as lunch and dinner specials ($7.50-9), in its library-like dining room and outdoor patio. Live music F 7-10pm. Open M-Th 6am-8pm, F 6am-10pm, Sa 6am-3pm, Su 7am-3pm. Cash only.

Cafe Latte, 850 Grand Ave. (☎651-224-5687), at Victoria St. More substantial than a cafe, and more gourmet than its prices and cafeteria-style setup would suggest, this cafe/bakery/pizzeria/wine bar is also famous for its wonderful desserts. Chicken-salsa chili ($5), turtle cake ($4), and daily specials fill the 2 spacious floors with hungry locals. Open M-Th 9am-11pm, F-Sa 9am-midnight, Su 9am-10pm.

◤ CAFES

Cafes are an integral part of the Twin Cities' nightlife. Particularly in Uptown Minneapolis, quirky coffeehouses caffeinate the masses and draw crowds as large as those at any bar. Most of these creatively decorated coffeehouses complement their java with some of the cheapest food in town.

🅺 **Uncommon Grounds,** 2809 Hennepin Ave. S (☎612-872-4811), at 28th St., Uptown. The self-described "BMW of coffeeshops" uses secret ingredients to make the tastiest coffees ($2-5) and teas around. With velour booths and relaxing music in a smoke-free interior, this coffeehouse lives up to its name. Open M-F 5pm-1am, Sa-Su 10am-1am.

Pandora's Cup and Gallery, 2516 Hennepin Ave. (☎612-381-0700), at 25th St., Uptown. This 2-story coffeehouse offers great coffee, tasty sandwiches (portobello and swiss $5.25) and Internet access ($1 per 6min.). Hip patrons vie for spots on the retro furniture or on the 2 outdoor patios, sipping espresso and munching on peanut butter and jelly "sammiches" ($2). Open daily 7am-1am.

Vera's Cafe, 2901 Lyndale Ave. (☎612-872-1419), between 29th and Lake St., Uptown. Serves the gay community with its signature "White Zombie" ($4.40), free wireless Internet, and breakfast all day ($5). Regulars return daily for the great java and for the strong community feel. Occasional events on the back patio. Open daily 7am-midnight.

Plan B Coffeehouse, 2717 Hennepin Ave. (☎612-872-1419), between 27th and 28th St., Uptown. This coffeehouse has an intellectual bent, as evidenced by its sign—the periodic table. Animated conversation, artwork, and mismatched furniture. Try the "tripper's revenge" ($3.75). Internet access. Open Su-Th 9am-midnight, F-Sa 9am-1am.

🏠 ACCOMMODATIONS

The Twin Cities are filled with unpretentious, inexpensive accommodations. Minneapolis caters to a younger crowd and consequently has cheaper hotels; St. Paul offers finer establishments for those with thicker wallets. Visitors Centers have lists of **B&Bs,** while the **University of Minnesota Housing Office** (☎612-624-2994; www.umn.edu/housing/offcampus.htm) keeps a list of local rooms ($15-60) that can be rented on a daily or weekly basis. The section of I-494 at Rte. 77, near the Mall of America, is lined with budget chain motels from $40. The nearest private campgrounds are about 15 mi. outside the city; the closest state park camping is in the **Hennepin Park** system, 25 mi. away. Call **Minnesota State Parks** (☎651-296-6157 or 888-646-6367).

Minneapolis International Hostel, 2400 Stevens Ave. South (☎612-522-5000; www.minneapolishostel.com), south of downtown Minneapolis by the Institute of Arts. Clean hostel with a strong community atmosphere. Internet, living room, porch, and patio. Check-in 1pm. Check-out 11am. Reservations recommended. Dorms $19, nonmembers $20; singles $49.

Evelo's Bed and Breakfast, 2301 Bryant Ave. (☎612-374-9656), in south Minneapolis, just off Hennepin Ave. Owners rent out 3 lovingly tended rooms in this 1897 Victorian home. Fresh flowers in each room, continental breakfast, and shared bath. Reservations and deposit required. Singles $55; doubles $70.

Saloon Hotel, 828 Hennepin Ave. (☎612-288-0459; www.gaympls.com), in downtown Minneapolis, between 8th and 9th St. Located above the Saloon nightclub, this hotel offers food, lodging, and entertainment in a venue geared toward the GLBT community, though all are welcome. "The inn that's out" has a colorful lounge with TV and free Internet. Reservations recommended. Singles $44; doubles $50-65.

Exel Inn, 1739 Old Hudson Rd. (☎651-771-5566; www.exelinns.com), in St. Paul off I-94 East, Exit 245. Clean rooms with cable TV and easy access to St. Paul and the Mall of America. Reservations recommended. Singles $45-55; doubles $60-65.

🌙 NIGHTLIFE

Minneapolis's vibrant youth culture feeds the Twin Cities' nightlife. Anchored by strong post-punk influences, the area's thriving music scene has spawned, among others, Soul Asylum, Hüsker Dü, and The Replacements. A cross-section of the diverse nightlife options can be found in the downtown **Warehouse District** on Hennepin Ave.; in **Dinkytown,** by U of M; and across the river on the **West Bank** (bounded on the west by I-35 West and to the south by I-94), especially on **Cedar Ave.** Even the top floor of the **Mall of America** invites bar-hopping until the wee hours. The Twin Cities card hard, however, even for cigarettes.

The Quest, 110 5th St. (☎612-338-3383; www.thequestclub.com), between 1st Ave. North and 2nd Ave. North in the Warehouse District. Once owned by Prince, this upper-class dance club pays homage to His Purple Highness with purple windows and funk. House music draws a young, cosmopolitan crowd. Live salsa M. Cover $5-10. Hours vary.

Brit's Pub, 1110 Nicollet Mall (☎612-332-3908; www.britspub.com), between 11th and 12th St. Patrons can play a game of "lawnboy" ($5 per hr.) on the rooftop garden. 18 different beers, the stilton burger ($9), and fish and chips ($13) add to the English flavor. Open daily 11am-1am.

First Ave. and 7th St. Entry, 701 1st Ave. North (☎612-338-8388; www.first-avenue.com), in downtown Minneapolis. Rocks with the area's best live music several nights a week, including concerts with the hottest rock bands in the nation. Music from grunge to world beat. Cover $6-10, for concerts $6-30. Usually open M-Th 8pm-2am, F-Sa 9pm-3am, Su 7pm-2am.

The Gay 90s, 408 Hennepin Ave. (☎612-333-7755; www.gay90s.com), at 4th St. Claims the 7th-highest liquor consumption rate of all clubs in the nation. This gigantic complex hosts gay and lesbian partiers in its 8 bars and showrooms, though the straight crowd is sizable. Drag shows upstairs Su and Tu-Sa 9:30pm. M-Tu and F-Sa 21+, W-Th and Su 18+. Cover $3-5 after 9pm. Open M-Sa 8am-2am, Su 10am-2am.

LEAVING MINNEAPOLIS
Take **U.S. 169 South** from Minneapolis.

LE SUEUR. Entering Le Sueur along U.S. 169 South, drivers are greeted by a monstrous billboard cutout of the **Jolly Green Giant** and Sprout (his diminutive peapod pal) standing cardboard guard over the valley, much like in the commercials. The valley itself it true to the pictures with green rolling hills covered in bushy trees and farmland. The **Le Sueur Museum,** 709 N. 2nd St., documents the history of the Green Giant. Exhibits, videos, and jolly green statues tell the tale of how the canning company grew from its start in 1903 by C.N. Cosgrove and a few other Le Sueur businessmen, until its purchase in 1979 by the Pillsbury Company. Other exhibits include an old-time drug store and displays on veterinary medicine and pharmaceutical manufacturing. (☎507-665-2050. Open Memorial Day-Labor Day M and F-Su 1pm-4:30pm, Tu-Th 9am-4:30pm; Labor Day-Memorial Day Tu-Th 9am-4:30pm.) The **W.W. Mayo House,** 118 N. Main St. is where Dr. William Worrall Mayo set up his medical practice in 1859. Tours of the house by costumed interpreters tell all about the lives of the two famous families who called it home. (☎507-665-3250. Open mid June-Aug. $3, seniors $2, children $1, under 6 free.)

APPROACHING ST. PETER
U.S. 169 enters St. Peter from the north as **N. Minnesota Ave.** Continue along U.S. 169 as it joins **Rte. 99** and **Rte. 22** along Minnesota Ave.

ST. PETER. St. Peter lures visitors with the beauty and refuge of the Minnesota River Valley and surrounding bluffs. One of Minnesota's oldest cities, St. Peter is built on the rich black soil that makes the surrounding area some of the most fertile farmland in the country. **Gustavus Adolphus College** was founded here in 1876. The 2500 student college is one of the best private liberal arts colleges in the Midwest. It hosts the annual **Nobel Conference** on the first Tuesday and Wednesday of October, the first ongoing educational conference in the U.S. to earn official authorization of the Nobel Foundation. The **Treaty Site History Center,** 1851 N. Minnesota Ave., has exhibits on the region's Native American heritage. (1 mi. north of St. Peter at the intersection of U.S. 169 and Rte. 22 West. ☎507-934-2160. Open Su 1-4pm, Tu-Sa 10am-4pm. $3, under 13 free.) Try the classic Black Angus Burger ($9) or spice things up a bit with the Smoked Rainbow Trout fresh from streams in Idaho at **Whiskey River,** Rte. 99 East. (☎507-934-5600. F Live music, Su brunch. Open M-Sa 6am-1am, Su 9am-1am.)

APPROACHING NEW ULM
South of St. Peter, turn off **U.S. 169** onto **Rte. 99 West** toward **Nicollet.** In Nicollet, Rte. 99 meets **U.S. 14** and continues west to New Ulm as U.S. 14, which enters on **7th St. North** and turns north on **Broadway.**

NEW ULM
German heritage is still evident in the city of "Charm and Tradition," composed of manicured yards and well-kept homes. New Ulm's **August Schell Brewery,** founded in 1860, is the second-oldest family-owned brewery in the US. Today, the fifth generation of Schells brews the acclaimed beer in the building where brewing began over 140 years ago. (Head south on Broadway, and turn west on 18th St. ☎507-354-5528 or 800-770-5020; www.schellsbrewery.com. Open in summer daily 11am-5pm; winter Sa noon-3pm. Gardens open 8am-dusk. Tours summer M-F 2:30, 4pm; Sa-Su 1, 2, 3, 4pm; winter Sa. 1, 2:30pm. $2.) The New Ulm **Glockenspiel,** at 4th

North St. and Minnesota St., guards the city center. Three times each day the stage door slides up and entertains viewers with wood-chip carvings moving mechanically to the chiming bells. The 45 ft. tall clock is one of the world's only free-standing carillon clock towers. (Daily noon, 3, 5pm.) The **Hermann Monument,** at Center St. and Monument St., honors the hero Hermann, who liberated Germany from the Romans. (☎507-359-8344. Open Memorial Day-Labor Day M-F 10am-4pm, Sa-Su 10am-7pm.)

Veigel's Kaiserhoff, 221 N. Minnesota St., has been a New Ulm institution and "home to those famous barbecue ribs" for over 65 years. Their first order of barbecue ribs sold for $0.45, but today you can get an order for $13-15. Jukeboxes sit by each table ready to entertain everyone in the low-ceilinged, cozy dining room, for a quarter. (☎507-359-2071. Open daily 11am-9pm.) The small **Colonial Inn,** 1315 N. Broadway, has 24 basic units with A/C and refrigerators. (☎507-354-3128 or 888-215-2143; www.colonialinn.net. Rooms $45-55.)

THE ROAD TO SLEEPY EYE

From Broadway, **U.S. 14** turns to the west along **Birchwood Dr.** Continue west on U.S. 14. Just after New Ulm you will see your first **Wall Drug** sign, one of many on the trip toward Wall, South Dakota. The landscape also loses its rolling green hills and settles into the flatness that will keep you yawning through several states. The importance of corn in is only made more apparent by the trucks you'll see in small towns near Sleepy Eye, selling ears of corn for as little as $3 for 15 ears. U.S. 14 passes through the heart of Sleepy Eye as Main St.

SLEEPY EYE. Sleepy Eye is named after the Dakota chief with droopy eyelids, Ish Tak Ha Ba. The **Sleepy Eye Depot Museum,** 100 Oak St. NW, displays artifacts from the Sleepy Eye area, included a permanent display of the state champion drum and bugle corps. Beside the Depot Museum is a granite obelisk erected in honor of Chief Sleepy Eye. (☎507-794-5053. Open May-Dec. Tu-Sa 2-5pm.) **Sleepy Eye Lake** features swimming beaches, parks, picnic areas, boat landings, and free campsites. Visitor info is available at the **Sleepy Eye Convention & Visitors Bureau,** 232 E. Main St. (☎507-794-4731 or 800-290-0588; www.sleepyeyeminimall.com. Open M-F 9am-4pm.)

DETOUR: JEFFERS PETROGLYPHS
27160 County Rd. 2
From Sleepy Eye, take U.S. 14 West to U.S. 71 South. Go 3 mi. east on Cottonwood County Rd. 10 and travel 1 mi. south on County Rd. 2.

Jeffers petroglyphs are one of Minnesota's most intriguing artifacts, islands of exposed rock where American Indians carved records nearly 5000 years ago. The rock outcroppings feature buffalo, turtle, thunderbird, and human images frozen in time. (☎507-628-5591. Memorial Day-Labor Day M-F 10am-5pm, Sa 10am-8pm, Su noon-8pm; Sept. and May Su noon-5pm, F-Sa 10am-5pm; Oct.-Apr. by appointment. $4, seniors $3, children 6-12 $2.)

LAURA INGALLS WILDER MUSEUM
330 Eighth St.
In Walnut Grove, 39 mi. down U.S. 14 from Sleepy Eye.

The Laura Ingalls Wilder Museum was built in 1974 at the same time the popular television series "Little House on the Prairie" began. The Ingalls family arrived in Walnut Grove in 1874, when Laura was seven. Their first home was a dugout on the banks of Plum Creek 1½ mi. north of Walnut Grove, where only a depression remains today. The nearby museum complex houses an early settler's home, a chapel, and a depot building that contains original items belonging to the Ingalls family. (☎507-859-2358 or 888-528-7298; www.walnutgrove.org. Open June-Aug. daily 10am-6pm; May and Sept. M-Sa 10am-5pm, Su noon-5pm; Apr. and Oct. M-Sa 10am-4pm, Su noon-4pm. $3, ages 6-12 $1, under 6 free.)

APPROACHING PIPESTONE
Continue west on **U.S. 14** until it intersects with **Rte. 23** 7 mi. past Balaton. Take Rte. 23 South to **Pipestone.** Between **Ruthton** and **Holland** (and northwest of Lake Benton) are futuristic windmills popping up along the Buffalo Ridge.

PIPESTONE. The historic downtown of Pipestone has a decidedly different flavor than any other Midwestern town; many of the buildings having been crafted from the Sioux Quartzite building stone mined in the quarries. The **Pipestone National Monument,** 36 Reservation Ave., provides a relief from the surrounding plains. The monument is a Native American quarry, where visitors can watch the crafting of pipes and carvings. An enjoyable **Circle Tour** (¾ mi.) leads past Winnewissa Falls, Leaping Rock, and

GREAT NORTH

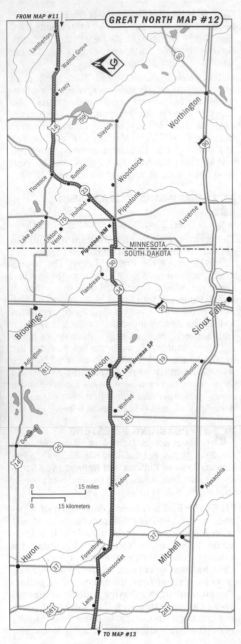

GREAT NORTH MAP #12

Lamberton
Walnut Grove
Tracy
Worthington
Slayton
Woodstock
Ruthton
Florence
Holland
Pipestone
Lake Benton
Eikton
Verdi
Pipestone NM
Luverne

MINNESOTA
SOUTH DAKOTA

Flandreau
Brookings
Sioux Falls
Arlington
Madison
Lake Herman SP
Humboldt
Winfred
DeSmet
Fedora
Alexandria

0   15 miles
0   15 kilometers

Huron
Foresburg
Woonsocket
Mitchell
Lane

▼ TO MAP #13

GREAT NORTH

a marker from the Nicollet Expedition. (☎507-825-5464. Open Memorial Day-Labor Day M-Th 8am-6pm, F-Su 8am-8pm; Labor Day-Memorial Day daily 8am-5pm. $3, under 16 and Native Americans free; families $5.) Constructed in 1888, the **Calumet Inn,** 104 West Main St., is a historic landmark, built from the Sioux Quartzite mined in the nearby quarries. The inn's **restaurant** has been written up in *USA Today* for Minnesota food. Try the Canadian Walleye ($15) and the popular wild rice soup ($3-4) or the cheaper burgers and sandwiches. (☎507-825-5871 or 800-535-7610; www.calumetinn.com. Restaurant open M-F 11am-10pm, Sa 3-10pm. Rooms in summer $79-84; off season $69-72.)

Welcome To SOUTH DAKOTA

THE ROAD TO MADISON

With fewer than 10 people per square mile, South Dakota has the highest ratio of sights to people in all of the Great Plains. Nearly as amusing as any of the sights are the roadside sentinels; this is billboard country. Advertisers appear to have come to the consensus that the drive across the tediously flat interstate would be more bearable for sleepy drivers if they had a little eye candy to entertain. Nothing is safe from becoming a billboard, including old train cars posing the well-worn question "Have you dug Wall Drug?"

APPROACHING MADISON
Follow **Rte. 30** to **Rte. 34.**

MADISON

Madison's proximity to Lake Madison and Lake Herman, the second-most visited state park in South Dakota, make it ideal for a stop. The city is also home to the 1800-student **Dakota State University.** Two miles west of Madison, the **Prairie Village,** at Rte. 34 and Rte. 81, is a living history museum built as a pioneer town. Over 50 buildings have been moved into Prairie Village and restored in their original decor. Attractions include a steam carousel, a sod house, and a working railroad. (☎605-256-3644 or 800-693-

3644; www.prairievillage.org. Open Mother's Day-Sept. daily 10am-5pm. $5. Camping and RV hookups available.)

Any lake in South Dakota is a welcome sight. **Lake Herman,** 23409 State Park Dr., has been a popular campsite for hundreds of years. Before settlers arrived, it was a stopover for Native Americans traveling to nearby quarries. The grounds boast fishing, boating, swimming, hiking, and 72 sites and two cabins with electricity, showers, and dump stations. (☎605-256-5003 or 800-710-2267; www.campsd.com. Open daily May-Sept. 6am-11pm; Oct.-Apr. 6am-9pm. Sites $10, with electricity $13; 4-person cabins $32. Day-use $5 per vehicle.)

THE ROAD THROUGH SOUTH DAKOTA

Just past Howard on Rte. 34/U.S. 81, the pastures populated with bovines are replaced with pastures populated with sheep. The bounteous cornfields and wheat crops are taken over by the wild, untamed grassland—the real backbone of the great plains that stretch across Midwestern states. The only break from the unending plains is the occasional grove of trees standing up like a prairie oasis along the horizon. **Woonsocket** is a small town that springs from nowhere with a little lake in the middle of town. In the lake is an island just big enough for the ensuing gazebo with a walking bridge leading from shore.

WESSINGTON SPRINGS. The **Hathaway Cottage at Shakespeare Garden,** 501 Alene Ave. North, was built in 1932 using plans drawn from a picture postcard of the original cottage at Stratford-on-Avon. In 1995 a thatched roof was added, the only one in South Dakota. (Travel north on Dakota Ave. to 6th St. Go west 3 blocks, and then south 1 block. ☎605-539-1529; www.shakespearegarden.org. Open in summer daily 1-5pm.) The rooms at the **Travelers Motel,** 320 E. Main St. resemble a trailer more than a motel, but they're clean enough and a good stop for tired travelers. (☎605-539-1440. Singles $25; doubles $30.)

⚐ LEAVING WESSINGTON SPRINGS
From Wessington Springs, drive west on **Rte. 34** until you hit **Rte. 45.** Turn left to go south on Rte. 45 until you reach **I-90,** at which point you will turn right to head west again.

THE ROAD TO CHAMBERLAIN

If you wake early in the morning, on the drive west from Wessington Springs you'll find birds and prairie dogs playing chicken in the road. The occasional hill offers sweeping views of flat golden valleys where cows have replaced buffalo that used to roam this area. Once on reservation land, the abundant crops of hay and straw cease and the prairie runs wild. **Lake Sharpe,** created by the Big Bend Dam, makes a great recreation area near Fort Thompson. Two of the larger recreation areas are **Farm Island** and the **Tailrace** area below the dam. Facilities include campgrounds, picnic shelters, swimming beaches, water, showers, electric hookups, and boat ramps.

CHAMBERLAIN

Nearly 200 years ago, the Lewis and Clark expedition spent three days at Camp Pleasant, watching thousands of buffalo graze on the nearby bluffs. One of Chamberlain's main sights is the **Akta Lakota Museum,** on N. Main St. at St. Joseph's Indian School. Akta Lakota means "to honor the people" and the museum honors the Lakota people, offering a living lesson on the Native American way of life. (☎605-734-3452 or 800-798-3452; www.stjo.org. Open Memorial Day-Labor Day M-Sa 8am-6pm, Su 9am-5pm; Labor Day-Memorial Day M-F 8am-5pm. Donations appreciated.)

The **Derby Cafe,** 138 S. Main St., is a relatively new addition to Chamberlain. If you're dying for some music, ask the staff to pick up an instrument; they're all musicians. Friday and Saturday evenings the cafe holds steak dinners, and the rest of the time it serves up breakfast, sandwiches ($3-5), soups, and the best espresso within 100 mi. (☎605-234-1380. Open M-Th 7am-6pm, F-Sa 7am-9pm.) **Alewel's Lake Shore Motel,** 115 N. River St., offers scenic views of the Missouri River's Lake Francis Case. (☎605-734-5566. Continental breakfast included. Open mid-Mar. to mid-Nov.)

THE ROAD TO THE BADLANDS

Continue on **I-90 West;** you know you've reached the interstate as people appear from nowhere and suddenly you're forced to wait in line for gas. Helpful info centers abound along I-90, but most are only accessible from one direction. The **Lewis & Clark** office in Chamberlain at mile marker 264 is accessible from both east and west and is open through December. (☎605-895-2188. Most open mid-May to mid-Sept. daily 8am-6pm.)

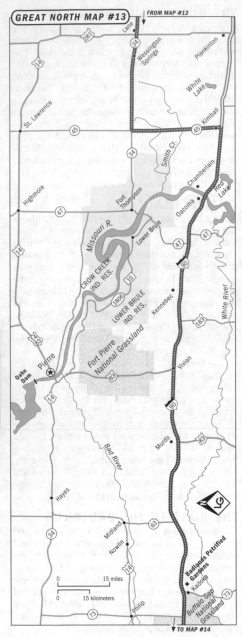

GREAT NORTH

OACOMA. Just west of Chamberlain, Oacoma is a permanent home to only 400 residents, yet has more big chain hotels than some small nations. At the **Pioneer Auto Museum,** I-90 Exit 192, the pride and joy is Elvis's motorcycle. Thirty-nine buildings are packed with over 275 old cars, motorcycles, tractors, and trucks. (☎605-669-2691; www.pioneerautoshow.com. Open Memorial Day-Labor Day 7am-10pm; winter hours vary.) The **1880 Town and Longhorn Ranch,** I-90 Exit 170, showcases a collection of historically correct buildings from an early South Dakota town. The buildings range from Indian relics to the 14-sided barn built in 1919. In the barn are an automated hay and manure system, as well as dozens of antique buggies and horses. A museum houses more valuable collections, including Buffalo Bill memorabilia and a tribute to Casey Tibbs, the 19-time World Champion Rodeo Cowboy. (☎605-344-259 or 605-669-2387. Open daily June-Sept. 6am-dusk; May and Oct. 8am-dusk.)

 About 60 mi. from Oacoma, I-90 enters the Mountain Time Zone, where it is 1hr. earlier.

THE ROAD TO THE BADLANDS

From Oacoma, drive about 130 mi. west on **I-90** until you see an alien landscape emerge from the plains. Right before the Badlands is **Kadoka,** home of the Badlands Petrified Garden., off Exit 152. This indoor museum features a fluorescent mineral exhibit and some impressive prehistoric Badlands fossils. The outdoor park includes the largest petrified trees and logs found in the Badlands Area. (☎605-837-2448. Open daily June-Aug. 7am-7pm; Apr.-May and Sept.-Oct. 8am-5pm. $4.25, ages 6-16 $2, under 6 free.)

THE BADLANDS

The Badlands are nature's sandcastles, minus the beach to sweep them out to sea. When faced with the mountainous rock formations suddenly appearing out of the prairie, early explorers were less than enthusiastic. General Alfred Sully called these arid and treacherous formations "Hell with the fires out," and the French translated the Sioux name for the area, *mako sica,* as *les mauvaises terres:* "bad lands." Late spring and fall in the Badlands offer pleasant weather that can be a relief from the extreme temperatures of mid-summer and winter; however, even at their worst, the Badlands are worth a visit. Deposits of iron oxide lend layers of marvelous red and brown hues to the land, and the moods of the Badlands change with the time, season, and weather. According to geologists, they erode about 2 in. every year. At that, rate they will disappear in 500,000 years—hurry and visit before it's too late. The peaks jut up surprisingly from the flat prairie and drop down sharply without warning from the bluffs.

> **VITAL STATS**
>
> **Area:** 244,000 acres
>
> **Visitor Info: The Ben Reifel Visitors Center** (☎605-433-5361; www.nps.gov/badl), 5 mi. inside the park's northeastern entrance, serves as the park headquarters. Open daily 9am-4pm; extended hours vary. **White River Visitors Center** (☎605-455-2878.), 55 mi. to the southwest, off Rte. 27, in the park's less-visited southern section. Open June-Aug. daily 10am-4pm.
>
> **Gateway Town:** Wall (p. 240).
>
> **Fees:** $10 per vehicle. Comes with a free copy of *The Prairie Preamble* with trail map.

GETTING AROUND

Badlands National Park lies about 150 mi. west Oacoma on I-90. **Driving tours** of the park can start at either end of Rte. 240, which winds through wilderness in a 32 mi. detour off I-90 Exit 110 or 131. A drive along **Rte. 240/Loop Rd.** is an excellent introduction to the entire northern portion of the park. This scenic byway makes its way through rainbow-colored bluffs and around hairpin turns, with numerous turn-offs for views of the Badlands. The gravel **Sage Creek Rim Rd.,** west of Rte. 240, has fewer people and more animals. Highlights are the Roberts Prairie Dog Town and the park's herds of bison and antelope; across the river from Sage Creek campground lies another prairie dog town and popular bison territory.

SIGHTS

The 244,000-acre park protects large tracts of prairie and stark rock formations. The Ben Reifel Visitors Center has an 18min. video on the Badlands as well as info on nearby activities and camping. Park rangers offer free talks daily at 2pm and a

prairie walk daily at 5:30pm from June to August. **Hiking** is permitted throughout the entire park, although officials discourage climbing on the formations and request that you stick to high-use trails. The south unit is mostly uncharted territory, and the occasional path is most likely the tracks of wildlife. Five hiking trails begin off Loop Rd. near the Ben Reifel Visitors Center. The **Notch Trail** (1½ mi., 1½-2hr.) demands surefootedness through a canyon and a willingness to climb a shaky ladder at a 45° angle. Not for the faint of heart, the trail blazes around narrow ledges before making its way to the grand finale: an unbelievable view of the Cliff Shelf and White River Valley. The moderate **Cliff Shelf Nature Trail** (½ mi., 30min.) consists of stairs, a boardwalk, and unpaved paths. It is the best bet for coming face-to-face with wildlife. **Door Trail** (¾ mi., 20min.) cuts through buttes and crevices for spectacular views of the countryside. **Window Trail** (¼ mi., 10min.), more of a scenic overlook than an actual hike, consists of a wheelchair-accessible ramp with a splendid view.

Those interested exploring the area on horseback can check out **Badlands Trail Rides,** 1½ mi. south of the Ben Reifel Visitors Center on Rte. 377. While the trails do not lead into the park, they do cover territory on the park's immediate outskirts. (☎605-309-2028. Open summer daily 8am-7pm. 30min. rides $15; 1hr. rides $20.)

 The Ranch Store, off Exit 131 on the eastern entrance to the Badlands Loop, has the **World's Largest Prairie Dog.** And no, it won't dig tunnels in your backyard or eat your flowers; it's a larger than life 6 ton statue! Out back behind the gift shop, they have the real thing; a maze of prairie dog tunnels populated by hungry dogs. For $0.50 you can buy a bag of peanuts to keep 'em satisfied. (☎605-433-5477. Open June-Sept. daily 7:30am-8pm.)

FOOD

A true South Dakota experience, the **Cuny Table Cafe,** 8 mi. west of the White River Visitors Center on Rte. 2, doesn't advertise because it doesn't need to—the food does all the talking. The restaurant is packed at lunchtime; try the Indian Tacos (home-cooked fry bread piled with veggies, beans, and beef) for $5. (☎605-455-2957. Open daily 5:30am-5:30pm. Cash only.) About 60 mi. north, by the main Visitors Center, the **Cedar Pass Lodge Restaurant** has buffalo burgers ($5.50), fry bread ($2.25), and fantastic views to the north of the Badlands. (☎605-433-5460. Open daily mid-May to Aug. 7am-8:30pm; Sept. 7:30am-7pm; Oct.-May 8am-4:30pm.) The **A&M Cafe,** just 2 mi. south of the Ben Reifel Visitors Center on Rte. 44, outside the park in Interior, is a small, hectic cafe with generous breakfasts ($4-8) and sandwich platters. (☎605-433-5340. Open daily 6:30am-9pm.)

ACCOMMODATIONS

In addition to standard lodging and camping, **backcountry camping** allows an intimate introduction to this austere landscape, but be sure to bring water. Campers are strongly urged to contact one of the rangers at the Visitors Center before heading out and to be extra careful of bison, which can be extremely dangerous. When it comes to indoor accommodations, the two best options are essentially identical. Within the park, the **Cedar Pass Lodge,** 1 Cedar St., next to the Ben Reifel Visitors Center, rents cabins with A/C and showers. (☎605-433-5460; www.cedarpasslodge.com. Reservations recommended. Open mid-Apr. to mid-Oct. Singles $58; $5 per additional person.) The slightly cheaper **Badlands Inn,** at Exit 131 off I-90, south of the Ben Reifel Visitors Center in Interior on Rte. 44, sits outside the park, but all rooms have a wide view of the Badlands and access to an outdoor pool. (☎605-433-5401 or 800-341-8000; www.badlandsinn.com. Open mid-May to mid-Sept. Singles $65; $5 per additional person.) If you'd rather sleep under the stars, the **Sage Creek Campground,** 13 mi. from the Pinnacles entrance south of Wall, is on a flat open field in the prairie with pit toilets and no water. (Take Sage Creek Rim Rd. off Rte. 240. Free.) You pay for view at the **Cedar Pass Campground,** south of the Ben Reifel Visitors Center, which also has more organized sites with water and flush toilets, but no showers. It's best to get there before 6pm in summer, since sites fill before evening. (Sites $10.)

APPROACHING WALL
Wall is located at the junction of **Rte. 240** and **I-90,** to the north of the Badlands.

WALL

Farther down I-90 from the entrance to the Badlands is Wall, world famous for the presence of **Wall Drug** in the town, at 510 Main St. You absolutely can't miss it, because for hundreds of miles the highway is lined with Wall Drug billboards, and Wall Drug signs, largely erected by independent individuals. Signs have be seen on the Paris Metro, the buses of London and rail lines in Kenya, at the Taj Majal and Great Wall of China, and at both poles. At the actual store you can buy just about anything you can imagine that is useless and has your name on it. Opened in 1931, the drug store has turned into a sprawling complex that includes innumerable novelty shops, an arcade, an 80 ft. dinosaur, a guitar and banjo played by a machine, and any number of animatronic figures. (☎605-279-2175; www.walldrug.com. Open daily 6:30am-10pm.) Two blocks south of Wall Drug is the **Buffalo Gap National Grassland Visitors Center,** 708 Main St., whose slogan is, "Anyone can love the mountains, but it takes soul to love the prairie." The 591,000-acre Buffalo Gap National Grassland is one of 20 national grasslands and includes intermingled eroding Badlands. The sweeping sea of grass stretches horizon to horizon and is home to a mixed array of prairie plants and secretive wildlife. There are no established hiking trails, but you can mountain bike, ATV, hunt, fish, and bird-watch in designated areas. (☎605-279-2125. Open daily summer 8am-6pm; winter 8am-4:30pm.)

The Homestead, 113 6th Ave., offers comfortable rooms with cable TV and A/C and a friendly staff. (☎605-279-2303. Rooms $46.) For more town info, contact the **Wall Chamber of Commerce** (☎888-852-9255 or 605-279-2665; www.wall-badlands.com.)

APPROACHING RAPID CITY
From Wall, it's 50 mi. west on **I-90** to Rapid City. Downtown Rapid City is located off I-90's Exit 57.

RAPID CITY

Rapid City's location makes it a convenient base from which to explore the surrounding attractions; Mount Rushmore, Crazy Horse, the Black Hills, and the Badlands are all within an hour's drive of downtown Rapid City. The area welcomes three million tourists each summer, over 50 times the city's permanent population.

VITAL STATS

Population: 60,000

Visitor Info: Rapid City Chamber of Commerce and Visitors Information Center, 444 Mt. Rushmore Rd. North (☎ 605-343-1744; www.rapidcitycvb.com), in the Civic Center. Open M-F 8am-5pm. **Black Hills Visitor Information Center** (☎ 605-355-3700), at Exit 61 off I-90. Open daily June-Aug. 8am-8pm; Sept.-May 8am-5pm.

Internet Access: Rapid City Public Library, 610 Quincy St. (☎ 605-394-4171) at 6th St. Open June-Aug. M-Th 9am-9pm, F-Sa 9am-5:30pm; Sept.-May M-Th 9am-9pm, F-Sa 9am-5:30pm, Su 1-5pm.

Post Office: 500 East Blvd. (☎ 605-394-8600), east of downtown. Open M-F 8am-5:30pm, Sa 8:30am-12:30pm. **Postal Code:** 57701.

⊟ GETTING AROUND. Rapid City's roads are laid out in a sensible grid pattern, making driving along its wide streets easy. **Saint Joseph St.** and **Main St.** are the main east-west thoroughfares and **Omaha St.** is two-way. **Mount Rushmore Rd. (U.S. 16)** is the main north-south route. Many north-south roads are numbered, and numbers increase from east to west, beginning at **East Blvd.**

◪ SIGHTS. Rapid City's Civic Center supplies a glossy brochure and map of the **Rapid City Star Tour,** which leads to 12 free attractions, including a jaunt up Skyline Dr. for a bird's-eye view of the city and the seven concrete dinosaurs of **Dinosaur Park,** as well as a magical trip to **Storybook Island,** an amusement park. In Memorial Park, check out America's larg-est **Berlin Wall Exhibit,** featuring two pieces of the wall. The **Journey Museum,** 222 New York St., traces the history of the Black Hills, detailing the geology, archaeology, and people of the region, with skull castings of a Tyrannosaurus rex, a holographic story tent, and a mercantile trading post. (☎ 605-394-6923; www.journeymuseum.org. Open late May to early Sept. daily 9am-5pm; off season M-Sa 10am-5pm, Su 1-5pm. $6, seniors $5, students $4.) The 8 mi. **Rapid City Recreational Path** runs along Rapid Creek.

▧▨ FOOD & NIGHTLIFE. The **Millstone Family Restaurant,** 2010 W. Main St., at Mountain View Rd., cooks up large portions of chicken ($5.75-8), spaghetti and meatballs ($7.35), and pork ribs ($9). Fill up on the steak and salad bar combo for $8. (☎ 605-343-5824. Open daily 6am-11pm.) **Pauly's Sub Co.,** 2060 W. Main St. west of downtown, shares space with **Java Junkie,** creating a one-stop spot for cheap coffee ($1) and a selection of hot, cold, and vegetarian subs from $2.30. (☎ 605-348-2669. Open M-Sa 10am-9pm, Su 11am-8pm. Java Junkie open M-F 6:30am-7pm, Sa 8am-6pm, Su 8am-4pm.) Nightlife options line **Main St.** between 6th St. and Mt. Rushmore Rd. For a beer as black as the Hills, throw back a Smokejumper Stout ($3) at the **Firehouse Brewing Company,** 610 Main St. The company brews five beers and serves sandwiches, burgers, and salads ($6-10) in the restored 1915 firehouse. (☎ 605-348-1915; www.firehousebrewing.com. Live music Sa-Su. Open M-Th 11am-10pm, F-Sa 11am-11pm, Su 4-9pm. Summer open 1hr. later and Su 11am-10pm.)

GREAT NORTH

IN THE PASSENGER SEAT

WRITING ON THE WALL

Ted Hustead is the third-generation president of Wall Drug, the world's largest drug store. With nearly 200 enticing billboards across South Dakota and countless others across the world, Wall Drug, with its Western memorabilia, clothing, and artwork, has become a major tourist attraction.

"In 1936, my grandmother came up with an idea in the middle of summer... She said, 'Ted, we've got to let the people know that we have a business here, the people that are going past Wall on their way to Mt. Rushmore and Yellowstone on dusty, dirty Highway 14... Let's put up a sign and advertise free ice water; it's 110°.' My grandpa thought it was a little corny, but he was up for trying anything. He hired a couple local people and made a series of signs and put them on the edge of town: 'Slow down the ol' hack—Wall Drug, just across the railroad track. Free ice water.' That summer, they had to hire nine ladies just to wait on all the customers that started pouring into this business..."

ACCOMMODATIONS. Rapid City accommodations are more expensive in summer, and motels often fill weeks in advance, especially during the **Sturgis Motorcycle Rally** in mid-August. Budget motels surround the junction of I-90 and Rte. 59 by the Rushmore Mall. Large billboards guide the way to **Big Sky Motel,** 4080 Tower Rd., 5min. south of town on a service road off Mt. Rushmore Rd. The rooms are very clean and the doubles have great views of Rapid City and the surrounding valley. (☎605-348-3200 or 800-318-3208. Open May-Oct. No phones. Mid-June to mid-Aug. singles $50, doubles $65. Off-season $35-40/$46-55. AAA discount.) **Camping** is available at **Badlands National Park** (see p. 238), **Black Hills National Forest** (see p. 242), and **Custer State Park** (see p. 244).

HOG HEAVEN. Unless you've got a Harley underneath you, the Black Hills are best avoided during the first two weeks in August, when the **Sturgis Rally** takes over the area. Nearly 500,000 motorcyclists roar through the hills, filling up campsites and motels and bringing traffic to a standstill.

THE ROAD TO THE BLACK HILLS

The Lakota called this region Paha Sapa, meaning Black Hills, for the hue that the Ponderosa pines take on when seen from a distance, and thought the region so sacred that they would only visit, but not settle. The Treaty of 1868 gave the Black Hills and the rest of South Dakota west of the Missouri River to the tribe, but when gold was discovered in the 1870s, the US government snatched back 6000 sq. mi. Today, the area attracts millions of visitors with a trove of natural treasures, including Custer State Park, Wind Cave National Park, and Jewel Cave National Monument, while the monuments of Mt. Rushmore and Crazy Horse stand as larger-than-life symbols of the cultural clash that defines the region's history.

BLACK HILLS NATIONAL FOREST

I-90 skirts the northern border of the Black Hills from Rapid City in the east to Spearfish in the west. **U.S. 385** twists from Hot Springs in the south to Deadwood in the north. The beautiful winding routes and dirt Forest Service roads hold drivers to half the speed of the interstate. Winter in the northern area of the Black Hills offers skiing

and snowmobiling. Unfortunately, many attractions close or have limited hours, and most resorts and campgrounds are closed in winter. The Black Hills region holds over 130 attractions—including a reptile farm, a Flintstones theme park, and a Passion play—but the greatest sights are the natural ones. Most of the land in the Black Hills is part of the Black Hills National Forest and exercises the "multiple use" principle—mining, logging, ranching, and recreation all take place in close proximity. The forest itself provides opportunities for backcountry hiking, swimming, biking, and camping, as do park-run campgrounds and tent sites.

In the hills, the **Visitors Center,** on U.S. 385 at Pactola Lake, offers a great view of the lake, a wildlife exhibit with a bald eagle, maps of the area, and details on backcountry camping. (☎605-343-8755. Open late May to early Sept. daily 8:30am-6pm.) In Rapid City there is the **Black Hills Visitor Information Center** (see p. 241). **Backcountry camping** in the national forest is free, allowed 1 mi. away from any campground or Visitors Center and at least 200 ft. off the side of the road (leave your car in a parking lot or pull off). Open fires are prohibited, but controlled fires in provided grates are allowed. Good **campgrounds** include: **Pactola,** on the Pactola Reservoir just south of the junction of Rte. 44 and U.S. 385; **Sheridan Lake,** 5 mi. northeast of Hill City on U.S. 385; and **Roubaix Lake,** 14 mi. south of Lead on U.S. 385. All three have some sites in the winter. All national forest campgrounds are quiet and wooded, offering fishing, swimming, and pit toilets. No hookups are provided. (☎877-444-6777; www.reserveusa.com. $17-20.) The Wyoming side of the forest permits some campfires and horses, and draws fewer visitors. The hostel in **Deadwood** (p. 246) is the cheapest and best indoor accommodation around.

APPROACHING MT. RUSHMORE
Travel from Rapid City through the Black Hills along **U.S. 16.** 4 mi. north of Keystone, turn south onto **Alt. U.S. 16.** In **Keystone,** turn west onto **Rte. 244** which will take you to Mt. Rushmore after 2 mi.

REPTILE GARDENS
5 mi. south of Rapid City on U.S. 16.

Reptile Gardens was opened in the winter of 1937 (four years before Rushmore was completed) by Earl Brockelsby, who noted that the biggest draw

at other attractions was the thrill of seeing a rattle-snake close-up. Reptile Gardens is more fun than your average zoo, with exhibits like "death row" filled with the world's most poisonous snakes, a rare white alligator, giant tortoises, and komodo dragons. (☎605-342-5873 or 800-335-0275; www.reptilegardens.com. Open daily Apr.-Oct. 8am-7pm. $11, ages 5-12 $7, under 5 free.)

RUSHMORE BORGLUM STORY
Alt. U.S. 16 in Keystone

If you'd like to know more about the man behind the mountain, visit the Rushmore Borglum museum. A 22min. movie documents the progress of the mountain and tells the story of Gutzon Borglum. Borglum, who initially encountered opposition from those who felt the work of God could not be improved, defended the project's size, insisting that "there is not a monument in this country as big as a snuff box." (☎605-666-4448; www.rushmoreborglum.com. Open daily May-Sept. 8am-7pm. $7, seniors $6.50, ages 7-17 $3.25, under 7 free; families $20.)

MOUNT RUSHMORE
Mount Rushmore National Memorial boasts the faces that launched a thousand minivans. Historian Doane Robinson originally conceived of this "shrine of democracy" in 1923 as a memorial for frontier heroes; sculptor Gutzon Borglum chose four presidents instead. In 1941, the 60 ft. heads of Washington, Jefferson, Roosevelt, and Lincoln were finished. The **Info Center** details the monument's history and has ranger tours every hour on the half-hour. A state-of-the-art **Visitors Center** chronicles the monument's history and the lives of the featured presidents. (Info center ☎605-574-3198. Visitors center ☎605-574-3165. Both open daily summer 8am-10pm; off season 8am-5pm.) From the Visitors Center, it's half a mile along the planked wooden **Presidential Trail** to **Borglum's Studio.** (Open in summer daily 9am-6pm. Ranger talks every hr.) In summer, the **Mount Rushmore Memorial Amphitheater** hosts a patriotic speech and film at 9pm, and light floods the monument from 9:30 to 10:30pm. (☎605-574-2523; www.nps.gov/moru. Trail lights extinguished 11pm.)

Horsethief Campground lies 2 mi. west of Mt. Rushmore on Rte. 244 in the Black Hills National Forest. President George H. W. Bush fished here in 1993; rumor has it that the lake was overstocked with fish to guarantee presi-

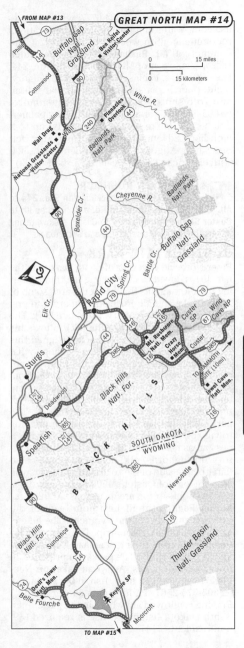

GREAT NORTH MAP #14

GREAT NORTH

dential success. (☎877-444-6777; www.reserve-usa.com. Water and flush toilets. Reservations recommended on weekends. Sites $22.) The commercial **Mt. Rushmore KOA/Palmer Gulch Lodge,** 7 mi. west of Mt. Rushmore on Rte. 244, has campsites, cabins, two pools, spa, laundry, nightly movies, a small strip mall, car rental, and free shuttle service to Mt. Rushmore. (☎605-574-2525 or 800-562-8503; www.palmer-gulch.com. Make reservations early, up to 2 months in advance for cabins. Open May-Oct. Sites June-Aug. $28, May and Sept.-Oct. $24; with electricity $35/$32; cabins $52-60/$44-52.)

▟ LEAVING MT. RUSHMORE
From Mt. Rushmore, backtrack on **Rte. 244** to **Alt. U.S. 16/Iron Mountain Rd.** and head south to **Custer State Park.** The road to Custer is slow, taking drivers through tunnels, curves, and switchbacks.

CUSTER STATE PARK
Peter Norbeck, governor of South Dakota in the late 1910s, loved to hike among the thin, towering rock formations that haunt the area south of Sylvan Lake and Mt. Rushmore. In order to preserve the land, he created Custer State Park. The spectacular **Needles Hwy. (Rte. 87)** follows his favorite hiking route—Norbeck designed this road to be especially narrow and winding so that newcomers could experience the pleasures of discovery. **Iron Mountain Rd. (Alt. U.S. 16)** from Mt. Rushmore to near the Norbeck Visitors Center (see below) takes drivers through a series of tunnels, "pigtail" curves, and switchbacks. The park's **Wildlife Loop Road** twists past prairie dog towns, bison wallows and corrals, and wilderness areas near prime hiking and camping territory. Pronghorns, elk, deer, and ponies also loiter by the side of the road, and often cars will stop for one of Custer's 1500 bison crossings; don't get out—bison are dangerous. At 7242 ft., **Harney Peak** is the highest point east of the Rockies and west of the Pyrenees. The hike is a strenuous 6 mi. round-trip. The 3 mi. **Sunday Gulch Trail** offers the most amazing scenery of all the park's trails. The park also provides 30 lower-altitude trails. At **Sylvan Lake,** on Needles Hwy., you can hike, fish, boat, or canoe. (☎605-575-2561. Paddleboats $4 per 30min.) Fishing is allowed anywhere in the park, but a South Dakota fishing license is required ($9, non-residents $14).

The **Peter Norbeck Visitors Center,** on Alt. U.S. 16, ½ mi. west of the State Game Lodge (where Eisenhower and Coolidge stayed), serves as the park's info center. (☎605-255-4464; www.custer-statepark.info. Open daily Apr.-May and mid-Oct. to Nov. 9am-5pm; June-Aug. 8am-8pm; Sept. to mid.-Oct. 8am-6pm. Weekly entrance pass May-Oct. $12 per vehicle; Nov.-Apr. $6.) The Visitors Center offers info about **primitive camping,** which is available for $2 per night in the **French Creek Natural Area.** Eight campgrounds have sites with showers and restrooms. No hookups are provided; only the **Game Lodge Campground** offers two electricity-accessible sites. (☎800-710-2267. Open daily 7am-9pm. Over 200 of the 400+ sites can be reserved; the entire park fills in summer by 3pm. Sites $13-18.) The **Legion Lake Resort,** on Alt. U.S. 16, 6 mi. west of the Visitors Center, rents mountain bikes. (☎605-255-4521. $10 per hr., $25 per half-day, $40 per day.) The strong granite of the Needles makes for great rock climbing. For more info contact **Sylvan Rocks,** 208 Main St. in Hill City, 20 mi. north of Custer City. (☎605-574-2425. Open in summer M-Tu and Th-Su 8am-10am.)

▟ APPROACHING CUSTER
Custer is off **U.S. 16,** west of Custer State Park.

CUSTER. Custer has plenty of places to refuel after a day of exploration. **The Wrangler,** 302 Mt. Rushmore Rd., is a local family restaurant, serving up dependably good breakfasts ($3-5), deluxe buffalo burgers ($5.25), and dinners ($8-10) on the early side. (☎605-673-4271. Open M-Sa 5am-8pm, Su 6am-8pm.) **Sage Creek Grille,** 607 Mt. Rushmore Rd., downtown, serves upscale food at reasonable prices. Try the delicious salads ($4-8), sandwiches ($7-9), and buffalo and elk burgers for $9. (☎605-673-2424. Open Tu-F 11am-2pm, Th-Sa 5-8pm.) An anomaly among campgrounds, **Fort Welikit,** 24992 Sylvan Lake Rd., has private bathrooms on large sites. (☎605-673-3600 or 888-946-2267; www.blackhillsrv.com. Sites $9 per person; RVs $23, with hookup $27.) The **Shady Rest Motel,** 238 Gordon Rd., sits on the hill overlooking Custer and has homey cabins. (☎605-673-4478 or 800-567-8259. Closed in winter. Singles $60; doubles $65.) The **Rocket Motel,** 211 Mt. Rushmore Rd., in west Custer, has very clean, tastefully furnished rooms with cable TV. (☎605-673-4401. Open Apr.-Oct. Singles from $50; doubles $65.) The **Custer Visitors**

Center, 615 Washington St., supplies helpful info. (☎ 605-673-2244 or 800-992-9819; www.custersd.com. Open mid-May to Aug. M-F 8am-7pm, Sa-Su 9am-6pm; winter M-F 8am-5pm.)

DETOUR: MAMMOTH SITE 1800 U.S. 18
From Custer, take Rte. 89 South to U.S. 18 West.

The Mammoth Site is the only in situ (bones left as found) mammoth fossil display in America. Remains of more than 50 mammoths have been found among other prehistoric animals that were trapped and died in a spring-fed sinkhole. The first remains were discovered in 1974 when excavation began for a housing project. (☎ 605-745-6017; www.mammothsite.com. Open June-Aug. daily 8am-8pm; Sept.-Oct. and Mar.-Apr. daily 9am-5pm; Nov.-Feb. M-Sa 9am-3:30pm, Su 11am-3:30pm.)

DETOUR: WIND CAVE
From Custer, take Rte. 89 South to U.S. 385 South. About 18 mi. from Custer.

In the cavern-riddled Black Hills, the subterranean scenery often rivals the above-ground sites. After the Black Hills formed from shifting plates of granite, warm water filled the cracked layers of limestone. Since then, intricate and unusual structures have formed in the area's prime underground real estate. Bring a sweater on all tours—Wind Cave remains a constant 53°F, while Jewel Cave is 49°F. Wind Cave was discovered by Tom Bingham in 1881 when he heard the sound of air rushing out of the cave's only natural entrance. The wind was so strong, in fact, that it knocked his hat off. Air forcefully gusts in and out of the cave due to changes in outside pressure, informally called "breathing." Scientists estimate that only 5% of the volume of the cave has been discovered. Within the 100 mi. that have been explored, geologists have found a lake over 200 ft. long in the cave's deepest depths. Wind Cave is unique in that it does not house the typical crystal formations of stalagmites and stalactites. Instead, it is known for housing over 95% of the world's "boxwork"—a honeycomb-like lattice of calcite. (☎ 605-745-4600. Tours June-Aug. daily 8:40am-6pm; less frequently in winter. $7-23.) The **Wind Cave National Park Visitors Center** in Hot Springs, can provide more info. (☎ 605-745-4600; www.nps.gov/wica. Open June to mid-Aug. daily 8am-7pm; winter hours vary.)

DETOUR: JEWEL CAVE
From Custer, take U.S. 16 west 13 mi.

Distinguishing itself from nearby Wind Cave's boxwork, the walls of Jewel Cave are covered with a layer of calcite crystal. These walls enticed the cave's discoverers to file a mining claim for the "jewels," only to realize that giving tours would be more profitable. The **Scenic Tour** (½ mi., 1¼hr.; 723 stairs) highlights chambers with the most interesting formations. (In summer every 20min. 8:20am-6pm; in winter call ahead. $8, ages 6-16 $4, under 6 free.) The **Lantern Tour** is an illuminating journey lasting 1¾hr. (In summer every hr. 9am-5pm; in winter call ahead. $8, ages 6-16 $4.) The **Visitors Center** has more info. (☎ 605-673-2288. Open daily June to mid-Aug. 8am-7:30pm; Oct. to mid-May 8am-4:30pm.) The **Roof Trail** behind the Visitors Center is short, but provides a memorable introduction to the Black Hills' beauty while trekking across the "roof" of Jewel Cave.

APPROACHING CRAZY HORSE
Back in Custer you can take **Rte. 385/U.S. 16 North** to the Crazy Horse Memorial.

CRAZY HORSE MEMORIAL
Off Rte. 385/U.S. 16.

In 1947, Lakota Chief Henry Standing Bear commissioned sculptor Korczak Ziolkowski to sculpt a memorial to Crazy Horse. A famed warrior who garnered respect by refusing to sign treaties or live on a government reservation, Crazy Horse was stabbed in the back by a treacherous white soldier in 1877. The Crazy Horse Memorial, which at its completion will be the **world's largest sculpture,** stands in the Black Hills the Lakota hold sacred as a spectacular tribute to the revered Native American leader and warrior. The first blast rocked the hills on June 3, 1948, taking off 10 tons of rock. On the memorial's 50th anniversary, the completed face (all four of the Rushmore heads could fit inside it) was unveiled. With admission prices funding 85% of the cost, Ziolkowski's wife Ruth and seven of their 10 children carry on his work, currently concentrating on the horse's head, which will be 219 ft. high. Part of Crazy Horse's arm is also visible, and eventually, his entire torso and head, as well as part of his horse, will be carved into the mountain.

GREAT NORTH

The memorial, includes the **Indian Museum of North America,** the **Sculptor's Studio-Home,** and the **Native American Educational and Cultural Center,** where native crafts are displayed and sold. The orientation center shows a moving 17min. video entitled "Dynamite and Dreams." (☎605-673-4681; www.crazyhorse.org. Open daily May-Sept. 7am-dark; Oct.-Apr. 8am-dark. Monument lit nightly about 10min. after sunset for 1hr. $9, under 6 free; $20 per vehicle.)

▲ APPROACHING DEADWOOD
Continue on to Deadwood up **Rte. 385/16 North.**

DEADWOOD
Gunslingers Wild Bill Hickok and Calamity Jane sauntered into Deadwood during the height of the Gold Rush in the summer of 1876. Bill stayed just long enough—three weeks—to spend eternity here. At her insistence, Jane and Bill now lie side-by-side in the Mount Moriah Cemetery, just south of downtown, off Cemetery St. ($1, ages 5-12 $0.50.) Gambling takes center stage in this authentic western town—casinos line **Main St.,** and many innocent-looking establishments have slot machines and poker tables waiting in the wings. Children are allowed in the casinos until 8pm. There's live music outside the **Stockade** at the **Buffalo-Bodega Complex,** 658 Main St. (☎605-578-1300), which is packed with throngs of 24hr. gambling spots. **Saloon #10,** 657 Main St., was forever immortalized by Wild Bill's murder. Hickok was shot holding black aces and eights, thereafter infamous to poker players as the "dead man's hand." The chair in which he died is on display, and every summer the shooting is reenacted on location. (☎605-578-3346 or 800-952-9398; www.saloon10.com. Open daily 8am-2am. Reenactments in summer daily 1, 3, 5, 7pm.) Onlookers follow the scene outdoors as **shootouts** happen daily along Main St. (2, 3, 4, 6pm)—listen for gunshots and the sound of Calamity Jane's whip.

Right outside Deadwood is Kevin Costner's new museum **Tatanka: Story of the Bison,** 1 mi. north on Rte. 85, an educational center with a spectacular outdoor sculpture of three riders pursuing bison over a cliff and a view of North Dakota in the other direction. The cafe serves dishes with bison meat for $4-8. (☎605-584-5678; www.storyofthebison.com. Open May 15-Oct. 15 daily 9am-6pm. $6.50, seniors $5.50, children

$4.50.) The **Deadwood History and Information Center,** 3 Siever St., behind Main Street's Silverado, can help with any questions. (☎605-578-2507 or 800-999-1876; www.deadwood.org. Open daily summer 8am-7pm; winter 9am-5pm.)

Even those who lose most of their money at the gambling tables can afford to stay at ◪**Black Hills at the Penny Motel (HI),** 818 Upper Main St. A great kitchen, comfortable beds, super-clean rooms, and a friendly owner await visitors. Free Internet, a book swap, a video club, and private bathrooms are the icing on the cake. (☎605-578-1842 or 877-565-8140; www.pennymotel.com. Bikes $5 per hr., $18 per day. 50% discount for guests. Dorms $13, non-members $16; 1 private room $39. Motel rooms in summer $46-68; winter $29-56.) The **Whistlers Gulch Campground,** off U.S. 85, has a pool, laundry facilities, and showers. (☎605-578-2092 or 800-704-7139. Sites $22; full hookup $33.)

▲ ENTERING WYOMING
Take **U.S. 85 North** to **I-90 West.**

Welcome To WYOMING

SUNDANCE. It's not the Sundance of the film festival, but if you know of Butch Cassidy, then surely you've heard of the Sundance Kid. Visit Sundance to see where he got his name. Sundance sits at the southern foot of the Wyoming Black Hills in the shadow of a mountain named **Wi Wacippi Paha** (Temple of the Sioux). The **Crook County Museum and Art Gallery,** 309 Cleveland St., tells the story of several famous people from Crook County. The museum has displays of some items related to these famous men as well as authentic cowboy guns, saddles, and branding irons, and the Sundance Kid's court records. (☎307-283-3666. Open M-F June-Aug. 8am-8pm; Sept.-May 8am-5pm. Free.) The **Budget Host Arrowhead Motel,** 214 Cleveland St., is the cheapest lodging in town. (☎307-283-3307 or 800-283-4678. Singles $55; doubles $59.) The Black Hills National Forest extends into Wyoming throughout the area, and the **Bearlodge Ranger Station** directs visitors to the west. (☎307-283-1361. Open M-F 7:30am-5pm, Sa 9am-3pm.)

APPROACHING DEVILS TOWER

Devils Tower is a short detour from Sundance 21 mi. along **U.S. 14 West.** Turn north onto **Rte. 24** and follow it 6 mi. to the Visitors Center.

DEVILS TOWER NATIONAL MONUMENT

The massive column that figures so prominently in the myths of Native Americans, geologists, and space aliens is the centerpiece of **Devils Tower National Monument,** the nation's first national monument. Read about the rock and register to climb at the **Visitors Center,** 3 mi. from the entrance. (☎307-467-5283, ext. 20. Open late May to Sept. daily 8am-8pm; Mar. to late May and Oct.-Nov. usually 8am-5pm. Entrance fee $8 per vehicle per week.) The most popular of the several hiking trails, the paved **Tower Trail** (1¼ mi.), loops the monument and provides terrific views of the multi-faceted columns of the tower. The **Red Beds Trail,** a 3 mi. loop, takes hikers up and around the bright red banks of the Belle Fourche River. Hikers can connect with the shorter **Valley View Trail** (½ mi.) for a flat walk through the prairie dog town and the **South Side Trail** (½ mi.), which climbs back to the bluffs of the Red Beds Trail. The park maintains a **campground** near the Belle Fourche River. (☎307-467-5283. Water, bathrooms, grills, picnic tables, and lots of noisy prairie dogs; no showers. Open roughly Apr.-Oct.; call ahead. Sites $12.) The best camping deal around is at the **Devils Tower View Store Campground,** on Rte. 24, a few miles before the monument. There's a great view of the monument and an inexpensive restaurant next door. (Open June-Sept. Sites $9.)

APPROACHING GILLETTE

Take Rte. 24 South to U.S. 14 South. Drive past the scenic **Keyhole State Park and Reservoir** on your way to the interstate; when you get to **I-90** in **Moorcroft,** go west, until you reach Gillette.

GILLETTE

Gillette is Wyoming's fourth-largest city and proudly calls itself the "Energy Capital of the Nation." Gillette is the commercial hub for the oil, gas, and coal industries, as evinced by the facto-

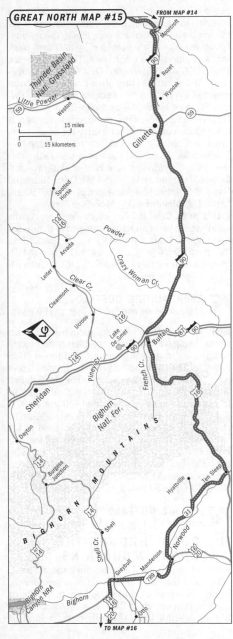

GREAT NORTH MAP #15

FROM MAP #14

TO MAP #16

GREAT NORTH

ries outside the city to the east. Campbell County contains more coal than any other county in Wyoming; about 5% of all US coal lies in the county. ▓Coal mine tours are provided by **RAG Coal West, Inc.** at Eagle Butte Coal Mine, 1810 S. Douglas Hwy. (☎ 800-544-6136 or 307-686-0040. Tours June-Aug. M-F 9 and 11am. Reservations recommended. Free.) The free **Rockpile Museum,** 900 W. 2nd St., rises above the landscape as a symbol of Gillette's history. One hundred years ago it marked the end of the cattle drive for weary cowboys, and today it has exhibits on ranching life. The saddles, rifles, and pioneer items are impressive, as is the video presentation of explosive surface coal mining. (☎ 307-682-5723. Open Memorial Day-Labor Day M-Sa 9am-8pm, Su 12:30-6:30pm; Labor Day-Memorial Day M-Sa 9am-5pm.)

Lula Bell's Cafe, 101 N. Gillette Ave., is no frills eatin' where you can join customers in their cowboy hats. Breakfast doesn't get more basic than "Meat and Eggs" ($5). Later, try the burgers ($4-6), or chicken fried steak. (☎ 307-682-9798. Open M-Sa 5am-9pm, Su 5am-5pm.)

🔺 **APPROACHING BUFFALO**
Between Gillette and Buffalo, jump on **I-90 West.**

BUFFALO. Buffalo has a uniquely historic main street dating back to 1804, complete with bronze sculptures, murals, and an old-fashioned soda fountain. The city is home to one of the west's premier frontier history museums. The **Jim Gatchell Museum,** 100 Fort St., overflows with 15,000 artifacts from Indians, soldiers, and settlers. (☎ 307-684-9331; www.jimgatchell.com. Open mid-Apr. to Dec. daily 9am-6pm. $4, seniors $3, ages 6-16 $2, under 6 free; families $10. The **Stagecoach Inn,** 845 Fort St., may look like a motel from the outside, but inside is a rustic restaurant. The chef cooks up famous soups ($1.50-2.50) and green chili. (☎ 307-684-0713. Open Su 6am-2pm, Tu-Sa 6am-9pm.)

🔺 **LEAVING BUFFALO**
From Buffalo, Take **U.S. 16 West.**

THE ROAD THROUGH THE BIGHORN MOUNTAINS

Relatively uncrowded, the **Bighorn National Forest,** with more than one million acres of grasslands, meadows, canyons, and deserts, may be one of the best kept secrets in the Rocky Mountains. The Bighorns erupt from the hilly pasture land of northern Wyoming, providing a dramatic backdrop for grazing cattle, sprawling ranch houses, and valleys full of wildflowers. Visitors can hike through the woods or follow **U.S. 16** in the south to waterfalls, layers of prehistoric rock, and views above the clouds. A listing of Bighorn's attractions and a map of the area, can be found in *Bighorn Bits and Pieces*, free at all of the Visitors Centers.

From the **Hunter Corrals Trailhead,** move to beautiful **Seven Brothers Lake,** 3 mi. off U.S. 16 on Rd. 19, an ideal base for day hikes into the high peaks beyond. **Cloud Peak Wilderness** offers sheer solitude. Registration at major trailheads is required to enter the Cloud Peak area. The most convenient access to the wilderness area is from the trailheads off U.S. 16, around 20 mi. west of Buffalo. To get to the top of 13,175 ft. Cloud Peak, most hikers enter at **West Ten Sleep Trailhead,** accessible from the town of **Ten Sleep** on the western slope, 55 mi. west of Buffalo on U.S. 16. Ten Sleep was so named because it took the Sioux "ten sleeps" to travel from there to their main winter camps. The **Burgess Junction Visitors Center,** off U.S. 14 about halfway into the area, provides lots of great info and several films on the surroundings. (Open mid-May to Sept. daily 8am-5:30pm.) Thirty-five campgrounds (☎ 877-444-6777; www.reserve.com) fill the forest. There is no fee to camp at the uncrowded **Elgin Park Trailhead,** 16 mi. west of Buffalo off U.S. 16, which promises good fishing along with parking and toilets. **Doyle Campground,** near a fish-filled creek, has 19 sites with toilets and water. Drive 26 mi. west of Buffalo on U.S. 16, then south 6 mi. on Hazelton Rd./County Rd. 3—it's a rough ride. (☎ 307-684-7981. Sites $9.) Many other campgrounds line U.S. 16. Campgrounds rarely fill up in the Bighorns, but if they do free **backcountry camping** (☎ 307-674-2600) is permitted at least 100 yd. from the road.

🔺 **APPROACHING CODY**
When **U.S. 16** reaches **Ten Sleep,** take the cutoff road **Rte. 31 West** to **Manderson,** where you'll turn West onto **U.S. 16** toward **Cody.**

CODY

To this day, as numerous billboards proclaim, Cody *is* Rodeo—a visit to this cowboy town is your best chance to catch the sport.

VITAL STATS

Population: 8800

Visitor Info: Chamber of Commerce Visitors Center, 836 Sheridan Ave. (☎307-587-2297; www.codychamber.org). Open summer M-Sa 8am-6pm, Su 10am-3pm; off season M-F 8am-5pm.

Internet Access: Cody Public Library, 1157 Sheridan Ave. (☎307-527-8820). Open summer M-F 10am-5:30pm, Sa 10am-1pm; winter hours vary.

Post Office: 1301 Stampede Ave. (☎307-527-7161). Open M-F 8am-5:30pm, Sa 9am-noon.

Postal Code: 82414.

⊫ GETTING AROUND. Cody is 54 mi. from Yellowstone National Park along the **Buffalo Bill Cody Scenic Byway,** at the junction of Rte. 120, U.S. 14A, and U.S. 14/16/20. The town's main drag is **Sheridan Ave.,** which turns into **Yellowstone Ave.** west of town.

◙ SIGHTS. Praised for its breathtaking scenery and Western charm, Cody is home to the longest-running rodeo in the US. For 63 straight years, the **Cody Nite Rodeo** has thrilled audiences every night in summer. (☎307-587-5855. Shows June-Aug. 8:30pm. $12-14, ages 7-12 $6-8.) Over 4th of July weekend the town attracts the country's cowboys when the **Buffalo Bill Cody Stampede** rough-rides into town. (☎307-587-5155 or 800-207-0744. $15. Reserve ahead.) There are **daily street gunfights** every afternoon. A street is blocked off and actors in period attire fire blanks at each other in a noisy, smoky skit. (On 12th St. in front of the Irma Hotel. Daily 6pm.) The **Cody Trolley Tour** offers a 1hr. tour of the city, visiting frontier sites and portraying the historical Old West. (☎307-527-7043. $12, over 62 $9, ages 6-12 $6.) **Rafting** trips on the Shoshone provide more energetic diversions. To make arrangements, call **Wyoming River Trips,** 1701 Sheridan Ave., at Rte. 120 and 14. (☎307-587-6661 or 800-586-6661. Open May-Sept. 2hr. trip $22; half-day trip $54.) **Powder River Tours** offers daytrips through Yellowstone National Park and departs from several locations in town. (☎307-527-3677 or 800-442-3682, ext. 114. $60, seniors $54, under 16 $30. Reservations recommended.) For equine adventures, try **Cedar Mountain Trail Rides.** (☎307-527-4966. $20 per 1hr. $100 per day.)

⛏⛏ FOOD & ACCOMMODATIONS. Wyoming license plates in all colors and spicy chili peppers line the walls in the **Noon Break,** 927 12th St., a little chili cafe that's "Taming the Wild Western Pepper." Green or red chili is the best ($3.50-5), but you can also get breakfast, sandwiches ($5.50), or Mexican food. (☎307-587-9720. Open M-Sa 7am-2pm.) **Peter's Cafe and Bakery,** at 12th St. and Sheridan Ave., offers cheap breakfasts (3 buttermilk pancakes $3) and thick subs from $3. (☎307-527-5040. Open M-F 6:45am-8pm, Su 6:45am-4:15pm.) Celebrate the women of the Wild West at **Annie Oakley's Cowgirl Cafe,** 1244 Sheridan Ave., downtown. The $10 Rocky Mountain Oysters appeal to the adventurous traveler. (☎307-587-1011. Burgers $5-8. Sandwiches $5-6. Open summer daily 11am-10pm; winter hours vary.)

Room rates go up in the summertime, but reasonable motels line **W. Yellowstone Ave.** Just a block from downtown, the **Pawnee Hotel,** 1032 12th St., has 18 unique rooms. (☎307-587-2239. Rooms $22-38.) The **Rainbow Park Motel,** 1136 17th St., is a bargain in winter, but prices jump during the summer months. Carpeted, wood-paneled rooms have phone, HBO, and A/C. (☎307-587-6251. Summer singles $75; doubles $82. Winter $34/$43.) **Buffalo Bill State Park** offers two campgrounds on the Buffalo Bill Reservoir. The **North Shore Bay Campground,** is located 9 mi. west of town on U.S. 14/16/20. (☎307-527-6274. Sites $12.)

⚑ LEAVING CODY
Follow the Buffalo Bill Cody Scenic Byway **(U.S. 14/15/20)** west into Yellowstone.

⫸◀ WAPITI LODGE & STEAK HOUSE
On U.S. 14/16/20, in Wapiti.
The Wapiti Lodge & Steak House is a welcome stop on the lonely drive between Cody and Yellowstone. Sit in the Western dining hall, or shoot pool and order from the pub menu at the bar in an Outback setting. "The Duke," a 24 oz. New York Steak ($27), was specially created for and served to John Wayne. (☎307-587-6659. Open daily 7am-10pm. Outback pub open daily 4pm-2am.)

THE ROAD TO YELLOWSTONE

Linking Yellowstone National Park with Cody, WY, the **Buffalo Bill Cody Scenic Byway (U.S. 14/16/20)** bridges the majestic peaks of the Absaroka Mountains (ab-SOR-ka) with the sagebrush lands of the Wyoming plains. This 52 mi. drive winds through the canyon created by the North Fork of the Shoshone River and is a spectacular prelude to Yellowstone. The high granite walls and sedimentary formations of the **Shoshone Canyon** are noticeable from the road, as is the smell of sulfur from the DeMaris springs in the Shoshone River. Once the site of the world's tallest dam, the **Buffalo Bill Dam Visitors Center and Reservoir,** 6 mi. west of Cody, celebrates man's ability to control the flow of water to fit human needs. Built between 1904 and 1910, the Buffalo Bill Dam measures 350 ft. in height. (☎307-527-6076. Visitors Center open daily June-Aug. 8am-8pm; May and Sept. 8am-6pm.) West of the dam, strange rock formations, created millions of years ago by volcanic eruptions in the Absarokas, dot the dusty hillsides. Continuing west to Yellowstone, sagebrush and small juniper trees gradually lead into the thick pine cover of the **Shoshone National Forest,** the country's first national forest. The **East Entrance** to Yellowstone National Park guards the west end of the scenic byway and is closed in winter.

YELLOWSTONE NATIONAL PARK

Yellowstone National Park holds the distinctions of being the largest park in the contiguous US and the first national park in the world. Yellowstone also happens to be one of the largest active volcanoes in the world, with over 300 geysers and over 10,000 geothermal features spewing steam and boiling water from beneath the earth's crust. The park's hot springs are popular among local wildlife; bison and elk gather around the thermal basins for warmth

and easier grazing during the winter months. Today, Yellowstone is recovering from devastating fires that burned over a third of the park in 1988. The destruction is especially evident in the western half of the park, where charred tree stumps and saplings line the roads. Despite the fires, Yellowstone retains its rugged beauty. With the reintroduction of wolves in 1995, all of the animals that lived in the Yellowstone area before the arrival of Europeans still roam the landscape, with the exception of the black-footed ferret.

▣ GETTING AROUND

Yellowstone is huge; both Rhode Island and Delaware could fit within its boundaries. Yellowstone's roads are designed in a figure-eight configuration, with side roads leading to park entrances and some of the lesser-known attractions. The natural wonders that make the park famous (e.g., Old Faithful) are scattered along the **Upper** and **Lower Loops**. Construction and renovation of roads is ongoing; call ahead (☎307-344-7381) or consult the extremely helpful *Yellowstone Today*, available at the entrances and Visitors Centers, to find out which sections will be closed during your visit. Travel through the park can be slow regardless of construction. The speed limit is 45 mph and is closely radar-patrolled; steep grades, tight curves, and frequent animal crossings can also cause driving delays.

The bulk of Yellowstone National Park lies in the northwest corner of Wyoming with slivers in Montana and Idaho. There are five

THE LOCAL STORY

WOLFPACK IS BACK

For many years, the only wolves in Yellowstone were the stuffed pair in the Albright Visitors Center. They, along with all Yellowstone's other wolves, were killed in 1922 when these predators were considered a menace to other wildlife. When gray wolves were declared endangered in 1973, talk of bringing back the wolf population started up. After more than 20 years of debate, 14 wolves from Canada were rereleased into the park in 1995. Today, over 300 wolves roam the area. The reintroduction has undoubtedly meant that some domestic animals have become prey. A wolf compensation trust, brainchild of the Bailey Wildlife Foundation, was established to pay ranchers for losses due to wolves, a shift in economic responsibility that has created broader acceptance. As keystone predators, wolves play an important role within the ecosystem; the overpopulation of herbivores has been reduced and and studies indicate that biodiversity in the ecosystem has increased.

VITAL STATS

Area: 2.2 million acres

Visitor Info: Most regions of the park have their own central Visitors Center. All centers offer general info and backcountry permits, but each has distinct hiking and camping regulations and features special **regional exhibits.** The closest Visitors Center entering the park from the east is **Fishing Bridge** (☎307-242-2450). Open daily late May to Aug. 8am-7pm; Sept. 9am-6pm. The main Visitors Center, **Albright** (☎307-344-2263; www.nps.gov/yell), at Mammoth Hot Springs, features exhibits on the history of Yellowstone and the origins of America's National Parks, along with stuffed examples of natural wildlife. Open daily late May to early Sept. 8am-7pm; early Sept.-May 9am-5pm.

General Park Information: ☎307-344-7381. **Weather:** ☎307-344-2113. **Road Report:** ☎307-344-2117. **Radio Info:** 1610AM.

Gateway Towns: Pahaska to the east, West Yellowstone to the west (p. 256).

Fees: $20 per vehicle.

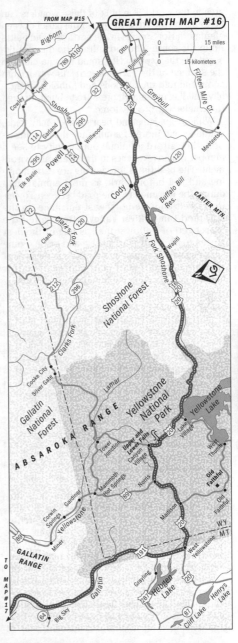

entrances to the park; West Yellowstone, MT, and Gardiner, MT are the most developed entrance points. The East Entrance to the park is 53 mi. west of Cody along **U.S. 14/16/20.** The southern entrance to the park is bordered by **Grand Teton National Park.** The only road within the park open year round is the northern strip between the North Entrance and Cooke City. All other roads are only open from May through October.

👁 SIGHTS

Xanterra (☎307-344-7311) organizes tours, horseback rides, and chuck wagon dinners. These outdoor activities are expensive, however, and Yellowstone is best explored on foot. Visitors Centers give out self-guided-tour pamphlets with maps for each of the park's main attractions ($0.50 including Old Faithful, Mammoth Hot Springs, and Canyon). Trails to these sights are accessible from the road via walkways, usually extending ¼-1½ mi. from the road.

Yellowstone is set apart from other national parks and forests in the Rockies by its **geothermal features**—the park protects the largest geothermic area in the world. The bulk of these wonders can be found on the western side of the park between Mammoth Hot Springs in the north and Old Faithful in the south. The most dramatic thermal fissures are the **geysers.** Hot liquid magma close to the surface of the earth superheats water from snow and rain until it boils and bubbles, eventually building up enough pressure to burst through the cracks with steamy force.

While bison-jams and bear-gridlock may make wildlife seem more of a nuisance than an attraction, they afford a unique opportunity to see a number of native species in their natural environment. The best times for viewing are early morning and just before dark, as most animals nap during the hot midday. The road between Tower-Roosevelt and the northeast entrance, in the untamed **Lamar River Valley,** often called the "Serengeti of Yellowstone," is one of the best places to see wolves, grizzlies, and bison. Some species take to the higher elevations in the heat of summer, so travel earlier or later in the season (or hike to higher regions) to find the best viewing .

Yellowstone can be dangerous. While roadside wildlife may look tame, these large beasts are unpredictable and easily startled. Stay at least 75 ft. from any animal, 300 ft. from bears. Both black bears and grizzly bears inhabit Yellowstone; consult a ranger about proper precautions before entering the backcountry. If you should encounter a bear, inform a ranger. Bison, regarded by many as mere overgrown cows, can travel at speeds of up to 30 mph; visitors are gored every year. Finally, watch for "widow makers"— dead trees that can fall over at any time, especially during high winds.

OLD FAITHFUL AREA. Yellowstone's trademark attraction, ■**Old Faithful,** is the most predictable of the large geysers and has consistently pleased audiences since its discovery in 1870. Eruptions usually shoot 100-190 ft. in the air, occurring every 45min. to 2hr. (average 90min.) and lasting about 1½-5min. Predictions for the next eruption, usually accurate to within 10min., are posted at the Old Faithful Visitors Center. Old Faithful lies in the **Upper Geyser Basin,** 16 mi. south of the Madison area and 20 mi. west of Grant Village. This area has the largest concentration of geysers in the world, and boardwalks connect them all. The spectacular rainbow spectrum of **Morning Glory Pool** is an easy 1½ mi. hike from Old Faithful, and provides up-close-and-personal views of hundreds of hydrothermal features along the way, including the tallest predictable geyser in the world, **Grand Geyser,** and the graceful **Riverside Geyser,** which spews at a 60° angle across the Firehole River. Between Old Faithful and Madison, along the Firehole River, lie the **Midway Geyser Basin** and the **Lower Geyser Basin.** The **Excelsior Geyser Crater,** a large, steaming lake created by a powerful geyser blast, and the **Grand Prismatic Spring,** the largest hot spring in the park, are both located in the Midway Geyser Basin. The basin is about 5 mi. north of Old Faithful and worth the trip. Two miles north is the less developed but still thrilling **Firehole Lake Drive,** a 2 mi. side loop through hot lakes, springs, and dome geysers. Eight miles north of Old Faithful gurgles the **Fountain Paint Pot,** a bubbling pool of hot, milky white, brown, and grey mud. Four types of geothermal activity present in Yellowstone (geysers, mudpots, hot springs, and fumaroles) are found along the trails of the Firehole River. There's a temptation to wash off the grime of camping in the hot water, but swimming in the hot springs is prohibited. You can swim in the **Firehole River,** near Firehole Canyon Dr., just south of Madison Junction. Prepare for a chill; the name of the river is deceptive.

NORRIS GEYSER BASIN. Fourteen miles north of Madison and 21 mi. south of Mammoth, the colorful Norris Geyser Basin is both the oldest and the hottest active thermal zone in the park. The geyser has been spewing hot water at temperatures up to 459°F for over 115,000 years. The area has a half-mile northern **Porcelain Basin** loop and a 1½ mi. southern **Back Basin** loop. **Echinus,** in the Back Basin, is the largest known acid-water geyser, erupting 40-60 ft. every 1-4hr. Its neighbor, **Steamboat,** is the tallest active geyser in the world, erupting over 300 ft. for anywhere from 3-40min. Steamboat's eruptions, however, are entirely unpredictable; the last eruption occurred April 26, 2002, after two years of inactivity.

MAMMOTH HOT SPRINGS. The hot spring terraces resemble huge wedding cakes at Mammoth Hot Springs, 21 mi. to the north of the Norris Basin and 19 mi. west of Tower in the northwest corner of the upper loop. Shifting water sources, malleable travertine limestone deposits, and tem-

Beware: the crust around many of Yellowstone's thermal basins, geysers, and hot springs is thin, and boiling, acidic water lies just beneath the surface. Stay on the marked paths and boardwalks at all times. In the backcountry, keep a good distance from hot springs and fumaroles.

perature-sensitive, multicolored bacterial growth create the most rapidly changing natural structure in the park. The **Upper Terrace Drive**, 2 mi. south of Mammoth Visitors Center, winds 1½ mi. through colorful springs and rugged travertine limestone ridges and terraces. When visiting, ask a ranger where to find the most active springs, as they vary in intensity from year to year. Some go dormant for decades, their structures gradually crumbling, only to revive unexpectedly to build new domes and cascades. In recent years, **Canary Spring**, on the south side of the main terrace, has been extremely active as it expands into virgin forest, killing trees and bushes. Also ask about area trails that provide wildlife viewing. **Swimming** is permitted in the **Boiling River**, 2½ mi. north.

GRAND CANYON. The east side's featured attraction, the **▨Grand Canyon of the Yellowstone,** wears rusty red and orange hues created by hot water acting on the rock. The canyon is 800-1200 ft. deep and 1500-4000 ft. wide. For a close-up view of the mighty **Lower Falls** (308 ft.), hike down the short, steep **Uncle Tom's Trail** (over 300 steps). **Artist Point**, on the southern rim, and **Lookout Point,** on the northern rim, offer broader canyon vistas and are accessible from the road between Canyon and Fishing Bridge. Keep an eye out for bighorn sheep along the canyon's rim. **Stagecoach rides** along the canyon are available at Roosevelt Lodge. *(June-Sept. $8.25, ages 2-11 $7.)*

YELLOWSTONE LAKE AREA. Situated in the southeast corner of the park, **Yellowstone Lake** is the largest high-altitude lake in North America and a protective sanctuary for cutthroat trout. While the surface of the lake may appear calm, geologists have found geothermal features at the bottom. **AmFac** offers lake cruises that leave from the marina at Bridge Bay. *(☎ 307-344-7311. Early June to mid-Sept. 5-7 per day. $9.75, ages 2-11 $5.)* Geysers and hot springs in **West Thumb** dump 3100 gallons of water into the lake per day. Notwithstanding this thermal boost, the temperature of the lake remains quite cold, averaging 45°F during the summer. Visitors to the park once cooked freshly caught trout in the boiling water of the **Fishing Cone** in the West Thumb central basin, but this is no longer permitted. Along the same loop on the west side of the lake, check out the **Thumb Paint Pots,** a field of puffing miniature mud volcanoes and chimneys. On the northern edge of the lake is **Fishing Bridge,** where fishing is prohibited in efforts to help the endangered trout. The sulphurous odors of **Mud Volcano,** 6 mi. north of Fishing Bridge, can be distinguished from miles away, but the turbulent mudpots, caused by the creation of hydrogen sulfide gas by bacteria working on the naturally-occurring sulfur in the spring water, are worth the assault on your nose. The unusual geothermal mudpot, with their rhythmic belching, acidic waters, and cavernous openings, have appropriate names such as **Dragon's Mouth, Sour Lake,** and **Black Dragon's Cauldron.**

◪ OUTDOOR ACTIVITIES

Most visitors to Yellowstone never get out of their cars, and therefore miss out on over 1200 mi. of trails in the park. Options for exploring Yellowstone's more pristine areas range from short day hikes to long backcountry trips. When planning a hike, pick up a **topographical trail map** ($9-10 at any Visitors Center) and ask a ranger to describe the network of trails. Some trails are poorly marked, so be sure of your skill with a map and compass before setting off on more obscure paths. The 1988 fires scarred over a third of the park; hikers should consult rangers and maps on which areas are burned. Burned areas have less shade, so pack hats, extra water, and sunscreen.

In addition to the self-guided trails at major attractions, many worthwhile sights are only a few miles off the main road. The **Fairy Falls Trail** (5¼ mi. round-trip, 2½hr.), 3 mi. north of Old Faithful, provides a unique perspective on the Midway Geyser Basin and up-close views of 200 ft. high Fairy Falls. This easy round-trip trail begins in the parking lot marked Fairy Falls just south of Midway Geyser Basin. A more strenuous option is to follow the trail beyond the falls up **Twin Buttes,** a 650 ft. elevation gain, which turns this trail into a moderate, 4hr. round-trip hike. The trail to the top of **Mount Washburn** (5½ mi. round-trip, 4hr.; 1380 ft. elevation gain) is enhanced by an enclosed observation area with sweeping views of the park's central environs, including the patchwork of old and new forests. This trail begins at Chittenden Rd. parking area, 10 mi. north of Canyon Village, or Dunraven Pass, 6 mi. north of Canyon Village. A more challenging climb to the top of **Avalanche Peak** (4 mi., 4hr.; final elevation 10,568 ft.) starts 8 mi. west of the East Entrance on East Entrance Rd. A steep ascent up several switchbacks opens to stunning panoramas out over Yellowstone Lake and the southern regions of the park, west to the Continental Divide and east to Shoshone National Forest. Wildlife-viewing opportunities in this area are superb. This route is ideal with a second vehicle, negating a return along the same route. There are dozens of extended backcountry trips in the park, including treks to the Black Canyon of the Yellowstone, in the north-central region, and to isolated Heart Lake in the south.

Fishing and **boating** are both allowed within the park. Permits are required for fishing. The park's three native species are catch-and-release only. (Fishing permits $15 per 3 days, $20 per 10 days; ages 12-15 free.) In addition to Yellowstone Lake, popular fishing spots include the Madison and Firehole Rivers; the Firehole is available for fly fishing only. To go boating or even floating on the lake, you'll need a **boating permit**, available at backcountry offices (check *Yellowstone Today*), Bridge Bay marina, and the South, West, and Northeast entrances to the park. (Motorized vessels $10 for 10-day pass; motor-free boats $5.) **Xanterra** rents row boats, outboards, and dockslips at Bridge Bay Marina. (☎ 307-344-7311. Mid-June to early Sept. Rowboats $8 per hr., $36 per 8hr.; outboards $37 per hr.; dockslips $15-20 per night.)

FOOD

Buying food in the park can be expensive; stick to **general stores** at each lodging location. The stores at Fishing Bridge, Lake Village, Grant Village, and Canyon Village sell lunch counter-style food. (Open daily 7:30am-9pm, but times may vary.) For other restaurants, see West Yellowstone (p. 256).

Grizzly Pad Grill and Cabins (☎ 406-838-2161), 315 Main St., on Rte. 212 on the eastern side of Cooke City. Try the Grizzly Pad Special—a milkshake, fries, and large cheeseburger ($8). Alternatively, pick up a sack lunch ($6.50). Open late May to mid-Oct. daily 7am-9pm; Jan. to mid-Apr. hours vary.

Ka-Bar Restaurant (☎ 406-848-9995), on U.S. 89 just as it enters Gardiner. Fixes up a fiery Mexican chipotle steak ($8) and meat-laden pizzas (8 in. $6.75). Don't let the rustic exterior fool you; this is one of the tastiest and most filling places to enjoy dinner after a romp in the park. Open daily 11am-10pm.

Helen's Corral Drive-In (☎ 406-848-7627), a few blocks west on U.S. 89 in Gardiner. Rounds up super ½ lb. buffalo burgers and pork chop sandwiches ($5-8) in a lively atmosphere. Open in summer daily 11am-10pm.

The Miner's Saloon, 108 Main St. (☎ 406-838-2214), on Rte. 212 in downtown Cooke City. The best place to go for a frosty Moose Drool beer ($3). Tasty burgers and fish tacos $6-7. Weekend live music. Open daily noon-10pm. Bar open until 2am.

ACCOMMODATIONS

The park's high season extends roughly from mid-June to mid-September. Lodging within the park can be hard to come by on short notice, but is sometimes a better deal than the motels along the outskirts of the park. During peak months, the cost of a motel room can skyrocket to $100, while in-park lodging remains relatively inexpensive. **Xanterra** controls all accommodations within the park, employing a code to distinguish between cabins: "Roughrider" means no bath, no facilities; "Budget" offers a sink; "Pioneer" has shower, toilet, and sink; "Frontier" is bigger, more plush; and "Western" is the biggest and most comfortable. Facilities are close to cabins without private bath. (☎ 307-344-7311; www.travelyellowstone.com. Rates are based on 2 adults; $10 per additional adult; under 12 free. Reserve in advance.)

Old Faithful Inn and Lodge, 30 mi. southeast of the West Yellowstone entrance, between Madison and Grant on the lower loop. In the heart of key attractions and a masterpiece unto itself. Admire the 6-story central lobby and stone fireplace from the birds-eye vantage of numerous balconies and stairways, all built of solid tree trunks. Constructed in 1904 by architect Robert Reamer as an embodiment of the natural surroundings, it is the quintessential example of "parkitecture." Open mid-May to mid-Sept. Cabins $55; Frontier cabins with bath $81; hotel rooms from $78, with bath $99-136.

Roosevelt Lodge, in the northeast portion of the upper loop, 19 mi. north of Canyon Village. A favorite of Teddy Roosevelt, who seems to have frequented every motel and saloon west of the Mississippi. The lodge provides scenic accommodations and it is located in a relatively isolated section of the park. Open June to early Sept. Roughrider cabins with wood-burning stoves $56; Frontier cabins with bath $91.

Canyon Lodge and Cabins, in Canyon Village at the middle of the figure-eight, overlooks the Grand Canyon of Yellowstone. Less authentic than Roosevelt's cabins, but centrally located and more popular among tourists. Open early June to mid-Sept. Budget cabins with bath $44; Pioneer cabins $59; Frontier cabins $82; Western cabins $119.

Mammoth Hot Springs, on the northwest part of the upper loop near the north entrance. A good base for early-morning wildlife-viewing excursions in the Lamar Valley to the east. Open early May to mid-Oct. Lattice-sided Budget cabins $64; Frontier cabins (some with porches) from $91; hotel rooms $73, with bath $96.

Lake Lodge Cabins, 4 mi. south of Fishing Bridge, southeast corner of lower loop. A cluster of cabins from the 1920s and 50s, all close to Yellowstone Lake. Open mid-June to late Sept. Pioneer cabins $59; Western cabins $119. Next door, **Lake Yellowstone Hotel and Cabins** has yellow Frontier cabins with bath but no lake view for $80.

CAMPING

Campsites fill quickly during the summer months. Call **Park Headquarters** (☎307-344-7381) for info on campsite vacancies. Backcountry camping or hiking permits are free, or $20 for a reserved permit ahead of time from the **Central Backcountry Office,** P.O. Box 168, Yellowstone National Park 82190. (☎307-344-2160. Open daily 8am-5pm.) The seven **National Park Service campgrounds** do not accept advance reservations. During the summer, these smaller campgrounds generally fill by 10am, and finding a site can be frustrating. Their popularity arises from their often stunning locations; most are well worth the effort to secure a spot. Two of the most beautiful campgrounds are **Slough Creek Campground,** 10 mi. northeast of Tower Junction (29 sites; vault toilets; open June-Oct.; $12) and **Pebble Creek Campground** (32 sites; vault toilets; no RVs; open early June to late Sept.; $12). Both are located in the northeast corner of the park, between Tower Falls and the Northeast Entrance, and offer relatively isolated sites and good fishing. Travelers in the

southern end of the park might try **Lewis Lake** (85 sites; vault toilets; open mid-June to early Nov.; $12), halfway between West Thumb and the South Entrance, a rugged campground with several walk-in tent sites that tend to fill up late in the day, if at all. **Tower Falls** (32 sites; vault toilets; open mid-May to late Sept.; $12) between the Northeast Entrance and Mammoth Hot Springs, has sites situated atop a hills, with fine views over mountain meadows. **Norris** (116 sites; water and flush toilets; open late May to late Sept.; $14); **Indian Creek,** between the Norris Geyser Basin and Mammoth Hot Springs (75 sites; vault toilets; open mid-June to mid-Sept.; $12); and **Mammoth** (85 sites; water and flush toilets; $14) are less scenic but still great places to camp. The lodges at Mammoth and Old Faithful have showers, but no laundry facilities.

Xanterra runs five of the 12 developed campgrounds (all $18, except Fishing Bridge RV) within the park: **Canyon,** with 272 spacious sites on forested hillsides, is the most pleasant, while **Madison,** with 277 sites on the banks of the Firehole River, has the advantage of being in the heart of the park's western attractions. **Grant Village** (425 sites) and **Bridge Bay** (432 sites), both near the shores of Yellowstone Lake, are relatively open with little vegetation to provide privacy. Finally, **Fishing Bridge RV** ($32; RVs only) provides closely packed parking spots for the larger motor homes and those desiring full hookups. Canyon, Grant Village, and Fishing Bridge RV have showers ($3; towel rental $0.75) and coin laundry facilities (open daily 7am-9pm). All five sites have flush toilets, water, and dump stations. (Advance reservations ☎307-344-7311, same-day 307-344-7901. Campgrounds usually open mid-May to early Oct., though Canyon has the shortest season, mid-June to mid-Sept. The two largest Xanterra campgrounds, Grant Village and Bridge Bay, are the best bet for last-minute reservations. Group camping is available at Madison, Grant, and Bridge Bay for $47-77 per night; reservations required.)

LEAVING YELLOWSTONE
When you're ready to leave the park, continue north along **Rte. 89,** or head west to the Tower Roosevelt area, then south to **Canyon Village,** the Grand Canyon of Yellowstone. Continue west from Canyon Village along **U.S. 287/20** to exit the park through the West Yellowstone exit.

WEST YELLOWSTONE

Much in West Yellowstone is unsuprisingly park-oriented. The **Museum of the Yellowstone,** on the corner of Canyon St. and Yellowstone Ave., has extensive exhibits on park flora and fauna, earthquakes, fires, and historical development. (☎406-646-1100. Open mid-May to mid-Oct. daily 9am-8pm. $6, children $4.) The **Grizzly and Wolf Discover Center,** 201 S. Canyon St., gives visitors an opportunity view the legendary grizzly bear and gray wolf. The center is home to bears and wolves that are unable to survive on their own in the wild. (☎800-257-2570; www.grizzlydiscoverctr.org. Open June-Aug. daily 8am-8:30pm; Sept. reduced hours. $8, ages 6-12 $4, under 6 free.)

Stockpile provisions at the **Food Round-Up Grocery Store,** 107 Dunraven St. (☎406-646-7501. Open daily summer 7am-10pm; winter 7am-9pm.) The **Running Bear Pancake House,** 538 Madison Ave., at Hayden, has inexpensive breakfasts and sandwiches in a friendly home-town atmosphere. Don't miss the special walnut and peach pancakes, served all day. (☎406-646-7703. Burgers, salads, and sandwiches $5-7. Open daily 7am-2pm.) The **Timberline Cafe,** 135 Yellowstone Ave., prepares travelers for a day tromping through the park with a large salad-and-potato bar and homemade pies. For a real energy meal with all the fixin's, chow down on the home-style chicken fried steak with soup and salad. (☎406-646-9349. Burgers, sandwiches, and omelettes $6-8. Open daily 6:30am-10pm.) At the **Gusher Pizza & Sandwich Shoppe,** at the corner of Madison and Dunraven, food is only half their specialty—partake of the full video game room, pool tables, and casino. (☎406-646-9050. Open daily 11:30am-10:30pm.)

The **West Yellowstone International Hostel,** 139 Yellowstone Ave., at the **Madison Hotel,** provides the best indoor budget accommodations around the park. The friendly staff and welcoming lobby make travelers feel right at home. The kitchen has a microwave and hot water only. (☎800-838-7745. Internet $5 per hr. Open late May to mid-Oct. Dorms $20, nonmembers $23; singles and doubles $27-39, with bath $49-53.) The **Lazy G Motel,** 123 Hayden St., has an affable staff and 15 spacious 1970s-style rooms with queen-size beds, refrigerators, and cable TV. (☎406-646-7586. Reservations recommended. Open May-Mar. Singles $32-48; doubles $40-59, with kitchenette $42-68.)

LEAVING WEST YELLOWSTONE

From West Yellowstone, take **U.S. 191 North** for about 90 mi. to **Bozeman.**

BIG SKY

1 Lone Mountain Trail

Off U.S. 191 45 mi. south of Bozeman.

The world-class ski area **Big Sky** has over 150 trails and short lift lines. The Lone Peak trams reach an altitude of 11,166 ft. for extreme skiing options. (☎800-548-4486. Open daily mid-Nov. to mid-Apr. Lift ticket $59, students and ages 11-17 $47, seniors $30. Rentals $27-39, juniors $19. Snowboards $33.) In summer, scenic **lift rides** soar up Big Sky. (Open June to early Oct. daily 9:45am-5pm. $14, seniors $9, under 10 free.) Full suspension mountain bike rentals are also available ($23 per hr., $46 for 8hr). Equestrians gallop at nearby **Big Sky Stables,** on the spur road off U.S. 191, about 2 mi. before Big Sky's entrance. (☎406-995-2972. Open daily mid-May to early Oct. 1 hr. rides $32; 2hr. rides $52. 1-day notice required.)

BOZEMAN

Surrounded by world-class hiking, skiing, and fishing, Bozeman has recently become a magnet for outdoor enthusiasts. Cowboy hats and pickup trucks are still popular among students at Montana State University (MSU), but the increasing diversity of the student body reflects the cultural vigor of this thriving community.

VITAL STATS

Population: 27,500

Visitor Info: Summer Visitors Center (☎406-586-5421; www.bozemanchamber.com), 1003 N. 7th Ave. Open June-Sept. daily 9am-6pm.

Internet Access: Bozeman Public Library, 220 E. Lamme St. (☎406-582-2400). Open M-Th 10am-8pm, F-Sa 10am-5pm.

Post Office: 32 E. Babcock St. (☎406-586-2373). Open M-F 9am-5pm. **Postal Code:** 59715.

GETTING AROUND. I-90/U.S. 191 enters
Bozeman from the southeast, and U.S. 191
splits off to become **Main St.** in town. Main St.
runs east-west, and has major intersections
with **Rte. 86, 7th Ave.,** and **19th Ave. (Rte. 412)/
McIntosh Ct.**

SIGHTS & OUTDOORS. Get friendly
with dinosaurs and other artifacts of Rocky
Mountain history at the **Museum of the Rockies,**
600 West Kagy Blvd., near the university. Dr.
Jack Horner (the model for *Jurassic Park*'s
Alan Grant) and other paleontologists make
this their base for excavating prehistoric
remains throughout the West. (☎406-994-3466;
www.montana.edu/wwwmor. Open summer
daily 8am-8pm; off season M-Sa 9am-5pm, Su
12:30-5pm. $8, ages 5-18 $4.) Standing on the
site of the old county jail, **The Pioneer Museum,**
317 W. Main St., offers a look at the gallows
and jail cells. (☎406-522-8122; www.pioneer-
museum.org. Open mid-May to mid-Sept. M-Sa
10am-4:30pm; mid-Sept. to mid-May Tu-F
11am-4pm, Sa 1-4pm. Free.)

The warm, shallow **Madison River** makes
tubing a popular, relaxing, and cheap way to
pass long summer days. Rent tubes ($3 per
day) at **Big Boys Toys,** 28670 Norris Rd. (☎406-
587-4747. Canoes $25 per day; windgliders $25
per day. Open daily 8am-6pm.) **Yellowstone
Raft Co.** shoots the rapids of the Gallatin River,
7 mi. north of the Big Sky area on U.S. 191.
Trips meet at the office, between mileposts 55
and 56 on U.S. 191. (☎800-348-4376. Half-day
$39, children $30; full day $79/$63.)

FOOD. Affordable eateries aimed at the
college crowd line **W. College St.** near the university. Now a popular chain throughout Montana, the original **Pickle Barrel** resides at 809
W. College St. Enormous sandwiches with
fresh ingredients and free pickles have drawn
MSU students for years. (☎406-587-2411.
Hefty 9 in. sandwiches $5. Open daily summer
10:30am-10pm; winter 11am-10:30pm.) The
quirky **Cateye Cafe,** 23 N. Tracy Ave., is popular among locals and the college crowd.
(☎406-587-8655. Open M and W-F 7am-
2:30pm, Sa-Su 7am-2pm.) **La Parrilla,** 1533 W.
Babcock St., wraps up just about everything in
their giant 1 ft. tortillas ($5-6), including
homemade barbecue, fiery jambalaya, and

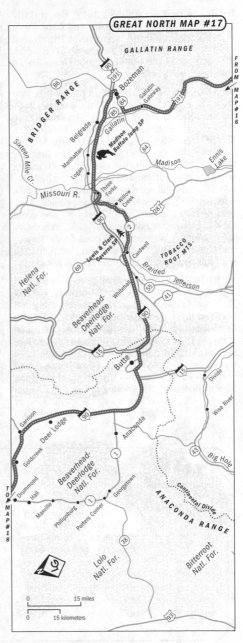

GREAT NORTH MAP #17

GREAT NORTH

fresh seafood. (☎406-582-9511. Open daily 11am-9pm.) **Sweet Pea Bakery and Cafe,** 19 S. Wilson St., cooks up a gourmet lunch and brunch, with dishes like mango chicken salad, for around $8. (☎406-586-8200. Open Su-Tu 7am-3pm, W-Sa 7am-10pm.)

 ACCOMMODATIONS. Budget motels line Main St. and 7th Ave. north of Main. **Bozeman Backpacker's Hostel,** 405 W. Olive St., has a kitchen, three dogs, and the cheapest beds in town. (☎406-586-4659. Laundry facilities. Co-ed dorms $14; private rooms with shared bath $32.) The **Blue Sky Motel,** 1010 E. Main St., offers rooms with microwaves, refrigerators, and cable TV. (☎800-845-9032. Continental breakfast included. Singles $49; doubles $58.) The **Bear Canyon Campground,** 4 mi. east of Bozeman at Exit 313 off I-90, has great views of the surrounding countryside. (☎800-438-1575. Laundry, showers, and pool. Open May to mid-Oct. Sites $16, with water and electricity $21, with full hookup $26; $2 per additional person.)

 NIGHTLIFE. Get the lowdown on music and nightlife from the weekly *Tributary* or *The BoZone.* Locals and travelers thirsty for good beer and great live music head over to the ■**Zebra Cocktail Lounge,** in the basement at Rouse Ave. and Main St. The large selection of beers and the hipster atmosphere always draw a young, cool crowd. (☎406-585-8851. W-Sa DJ or bands. Open daily 8pm-2am.) One of only two non-smoking bars in Bozeman, the **Rocking R Bar,** 211 E. Main St., offers hot drink specials every night. (☎406-587-9355. Free food

W-F 5-9pm. Live music W and Sa. Karaoke Th. Open daily 11am-2am.) Sample some of Montana's best brews at **Montana Ale Works,** 601 E. Main St. (☎406-587-7700. Open Su-Th 4pm-midnight, F-Sa 4pm-1am.)

 LEAVING BOZEMAN
 Take **I-90 West** about 30 mi. to the **Three Forks** exit, and continue west along **Rte. 2.**

 DETOUR: LIVINGSTON
 26 mi east of Bozeman off I-90.

Surrounded by three renowned trout fishing rivers—Yellowstone, Madison, and Gardiner—the small town of Livingston is an angler's heaven; the film *A River Runs Through It* was shot here and in Bozeman. Livingston's Main St. features a strip of early 20th-century buildings, including bars (with gambling), restaurants, fishing outfitters, and a few modern businesses. If fishing's your thing, **Dan Bailey's,** 209 W. Park St. in Livingston, sells licenses and rents gear. (☎406-222-1673 or 800-356-4052. Open M-Sa summer 8am-7pm; winter 8am-6pm. 2-day fishing license $22. Rod and reel $10; waders and boots $10.)

 LEWIS & CLARK CAVERNS
 20 mi. from Three Forks on Rte. 2.

At Lewis and Clark Caverns, visitors can take a tour of the extensive limestone and calcite caves. The tour is 2 mi., with steep grades up 300 ft. to the entrance and stooping and bending required for descending the 600 stairs. Be sure to dress warmly; the caves remain 50°F year-round. (☎406-287-3541. Tours May-Sept. daily 9:15am-6:30pm.)

THE LOCAL STORY

CASHING OUT

Legend has it that cattle rancher Grover Chestnut of Bozeman conceived the best way to ensure visitors to his grave. Before his death, Chestnut allegedly had an ATM installed in his tombstone. He gave debit cards to his heirs and told them that they could withdraw $300 from the grave each week.

APPROACHING BUTTE
In Cardwell, take **Rte. 2** to **I-90** toward Butte.

BUTTE

"A mile high, a mile deep, and a mile wide" is a popular expression about Butte; the city perches 1 mi. high in the Rocky Mountains. One nearby mine reaches 1 mi. deep, and another, the Berkeley Pit, is 1 mi. wide. The ◪**World Museum of Mining,** 155 Museum Way, presents a realistic look at a mining camp in the 1880s. Located on the site of the silver and zinc **Orphan Girl Mine,** the 22-acre museum presents the history of mining in exhibits on hard rock mining, and includes Hell Roarin' Gulch, a town lined with over 50 reconstructed mining camp businesses. Daily tours circle the museum on the Orphan Girl Express mini train, pulled by a 1911 tram engine. (☎406-723-7211; www.miningmuseum.org. Open Apr.-Oct. daily 9am-5pm. $7, seniors $6, ages 13-18 $5, ages 5-12 $2.) The **Dumas Brothel Museum,** 45 E. Mercury St., now offers tours of the three levels of the nation's longest running house of prostitution, including the underground "Cribs" that were sealed up in 1943 and now appear a virtual time capsule. (☎406-494-6908; www.thedumasbrothel.com. Open in summer 10am-5pm. $5, under 12 free but possibly scarred for life.) The **Mineral Museum,** 1300 W. Park St., located on the Montana Tech Campus, displays classic mineral specimens from Butte's underground mines, as well as a 27½ troy-ounce gold nugget and a 400 lb. smoky quartz crystal called "Big Daddy." (☎406-496-4414. Open June-Aug. daily 9am-6pm; May and Sept.-Oct. M-F 9am-4pm, Sa-Su 1-5pm. Free.) The **Mai Wah Museum,** 17 W. Mercury St., was built in honor of the Chinese miners who came to Butte to work the mines. (☎406-723-6731; www.maiwah.org. Open Memorial Day-Labor Day Su 11am-3pm, Tu-Sa 11am-4pm.) **Our Lady of the Rockies,** a 90 ft. statue seated on the Continental Divide, overlooks peaks and valleys for nearly 100 mi. Bus tours leave daily from the Butte Plaza Mall at 3100 Harrison Ave. (☎800-800-5239; www.ourladyoftherockies.com. 2½hr. tours June-Sept. M-Sa 9am-5pm, Su 10am-5pm.)

Located in the historic Uptown district of Butte, the **Finlen Hotel and Motor Inn,** 100 E. Broadway, was opened in 1924 and has been in constant operation ever since. These hotel rooms once housed Copper Kings, and now provide lodging for nostalgic visitors. (☎800-729-5461; www.finlen.com. Singles $40-44; doubles $50-54.)

LEAVING BUTTE
Hop on **I-90 West** toward **Deer Lodge.**

DEER LODGE

Nestled within a sheltered valley, Deer Lodge has always offered gold seekers, ranchers, and settlers the opportunity for a good life. The Clark Fork, Little Blackfoot, Nevada Creek Reservoir and Blackfoot Rivers all flow through the area, promising abundant trout. The **Frontier Museum** has the largest display of cowboy collectibles between Cody and Calgary. The **Old Montana Prison and Montana Auto Museums,** 1106 Main St., is home to both museums and admission covers entrance to both. Deer Lodge is also home to the **Old Montana Prison,** built by inmate labor at the turn of the century. The fortress incarcerated at least one member of Butch Cassidy's Wild Bunch. The **Montana Auto Museum** showcases over 120 classic cars. The collection is sure to make a motorhead drool; offerings include Model Ts, Model As, V-8 Fords, a DeSoto AirFlow, a 1929 Hudson, and a 1903 Ford. Across the street from the Prison, the **Yesterday's Playthings Museum** is Montana's foremost doll and toy museum. (☎406-846-3111; www.pcmaf.org. Open daily summer 8am-8pm; winter 8:30am-5pm. 1½hr. tours daily in summer 10am and 2pm. $9, seniors $8, ages 10-15 $5, under 10 free.)

LEAVING DEER LODGE
Take **I-90/U.S 12** north and west toward **Missoula.**

GARNET GHOST TOWN
Take Bear Gulch Rd. north from I-90/U.S.12

Montana's history claims more than 600 mining camps and towns, many of which vanished almost as quickly as they'd appeared when inhabitants fled to follow rumors of other strikes. Visit Garnet to see a ghost town of a mining camp. (☎406-522-3856. www.montana.com/ghosttown.)

MISSOULA

A liberal haven in a largely conservative state, Missoula attracts new residents every day with its revitalized downtown and bountiful outdoor opportunities. Home to the University of Montana, downtown Missoula is lined with bars and coffeehouses spawned by the large student population. Four different mountain ranges and five major rivers surround Missoula, supporting skiing during the winter and fly fishing, hiking, and biking during the summer.

> ### (VITAL STATS)
>
> **Population:** 57,000
>
> **Visitor Info: Missoula Chamber of Commerce,** 825 E. Front St. (☎406-543-6623; www.explore-missoula.com), at Van Buren. Open late May to early Sept. M-F 8am-7pm, Sa 10am-6pm; early Sept. to late May M-F 8am-5pm.
>
> **Internet access: Missoula Public Library,** 301 E. Main St. (☎406-721-2665). Open M-Th 10am-9pm, F-Sa 10am-6pm. Free.
>
> **Post Office:** 200 E. Broadway St. (☎406-329-2222). Open M-F 8am-5:30pm. **Postal Code:** 59801.

▣ GETTING AROUND

U.S. 93 takes the name of **Reserve St.,** running north through the western part of town. Downtown Missoula lies north of the Clark Fork River, around the intersection of **N. Higgins Ave.** and **Broadway St. (Bus. I-90/Rte. 10).** The University of Montana lies southeast of downtown, accessible by heading south on **Madison St.** from Broadway. Businesses outside of downtown have **parking lots,** and meters are readily available in the downtown area during business hours.

◎ SIGHTS

Missoula's hottest sight is the **Smokejumper Center,** 5765 Rte. 10. It's the nation's largest training base for aerial firefighters who parachute into flaming forests. (Just past the airport, 7 mi. northwest of town on Broadway. ☎406-329-4934. Open daily 8:30am-5pm. Tours May-Sept. every hr. 10-11am and 2-4pm. Free.) The **Carousel,** in Caras Riverfront Park, is a beautiful example of a hand-carved merry-go-round. (☎406-549-8382. Open daily June-Aug. 11am-7pm; Sept.-May 11am-5:30pm. $1, seniors and under 19 $0.50.) **Out to Lunch,** also in Caras Riverfront Park, offers free performances in summer; call the Missoula Downtown Association for info. (☎406-406-543-4238. W 11am-1:30pm.)

Pick up the *Missoula Gallery Guide* brochure at the tourist office for a self-guided tour of Missoula's art galleries. Among them, the **Dana Gallery** at 123 W. Broadway (☎406-721-3154; open M-F 10am-6pm, Sa 10am-4pm), the **Gallery Saintonage** at 216 N. Higgins Ave. (☎406-543-0171; open Tu-F 10am-5:30pm, Sa 10am-4pm), and the **Montana Museum of Art & Culture** on the UM campus (☎406-243-2019; open Tu-Th and Sa 11am-3pm, F 3-7pm) are particularly noteworthy. The **Historical Museum at Fort Missoula,** in Building 322 at Fort Missoula, on South Ave. one block west of Reserve St., displays 22,000 artifacts (☎406-728-3476; www.montana.com/ftmslamuseum. Open summer Su and Tu-Sa 10am-5pm; winter Su and Tu-Sa noon-5pm.)

The **Western Montana Fair and Rodeo,** held at the beginning of August, has live music, a carnival, fireworks, and concession booths. (☎406-721-3247. Open daily 10am-10pm.) Soak your weary feet at the **Lolo Hot Springs,** 35 mi. southwest of Missoula on Rte. 12. The 103°-105°F springs were a meeting place for local Native Americans and were frequented by Lewis and Clark in 1806. (☎406-273-2290 or 800-273-2290. $6, under 13 $4.)

▲ OUTDOOR ACTIVITIES

Nearby parks, recreation areas, and surrounding wilderness areas make Missoula an outdoor enthusiast's dream. Bicycle-friendly Missoula is located along both the Trans-America and the Great Parks bicycle routes, and all major streets have designated bike lanes. **Open Road Bicycles and Nordic Equipment,** 517 S. Orange St., has bike rentals. (☎406-549-2453. $3.50 per hr., $17.50 per day. Open M-F 9am-6pm, Sa 10am-5pm, Su 11am-3pm.) The national **Adventure Cycling,** 150 E. Pine St., is the place to go for info about local trails, including the Trans-America and Great Parks routes. (☎406-721-1776 or 800-755-2453. Open M-F 8am-5pm.) The **Rattlesnake Wilderness National Recreation Area,** 11 mi. northeast of town off the Van Buren St. exit on I-90, and the **Pattee Canyon Recreation Area,** 3½ mi. east of Higgins on Pattee Canyon Dr., are highly recommended for their biking trails.

Alpine and Nordic **skiing** keep Missoulians busy during winter. **Pattee Canyon** has groomed trails conveniently close to town, and **Marshall Mountain** is a great place to learn how to ski, and has night skiing. (☎406-258-6000. $19 per day.) Experienced skiers should check out the extreme **Montana**

Snowbowl, 12 mi. northwest of Missoula, with a vertical drop of 2600 ft. and over 35 trails. (☎406-549-9777 or 800-728-2695. Open Nov.-Apr. daily 9:30am-4pm. Lift tickets $29, children $13.)

The Blackfoot River, along Rte. 200 east of Bonner, is an excellent location to tube or raft on a hot day. Call the **Montana State Regional Parks and Wildlife Office,** 3201 Spurgin Rd., for info about rafting locations. (☎406-542-5500. Open M-F 8am-5pm.) Rent tubes or rafts from the **Army and Navy Economy Store,** 322 N. Higgins. (☎406-721-1315. Tubes $3 per day. Rafts $40 per day, credit card required; $20 deposit. Open M-F 9am-7:30pm, Sa 9am-5:30pm, Su 10am-5:30pm.) **Hiking** opportunities also abound in the Missoula area. The relatively easy 30min. hike to the "M" (for the U of M, not Missoula) on Mount Sentinel, has a tremendous view of Missoula and the surrounding mountains.

The **Rattlesnake Wilderness National Recreation Area,** named for the river's shape (there are no rattlers for miles), is 11 mi. northeast of town, off the Van Buren St. exit from I-90, and makes for a great day of hiking. Other popular areas include **Pattee Canyon** and **Blue Mountain,** south of town. Maps ($6) and info on longer hikes in the Bitterroot and Bob Marshall areas are at the **US Forest Service Information Office,** 200 E. Broadway; the entrance is at 200 Pine St. (☎406-329-3511. Open M-F 7:30am-4pm.) For rentals, stop by **Trailhead,** 110 E. Pine St., at Higgins St. (☎406-543-6966. Tents M-F $10-18; backpacks $9; sleeping bags $5. Open M-F 9:30am-8pm, Sa 9am-6pm, Su 11am-6pm.)

Western Montana is **fly-fishing** country, and Missoula is at the heart of it all. Fishing licenses are required and can be purchased from the **Department of Fish, Wildlife, and Parks,** 3201 Spurgin Rd. (☎406-542-5500), or from sporting goods stores. **Kingfisher,** 926 E. Broadway, offers licenses ($22-67) and pricey fishing trips. (☎406-721-6141. Open daily in summer 7am-8pm; off-season 9am-5pm.)

◥ FOOD

Missoula, the culinary capital of Montana, has a number of innovative, delicious, and inexpensive eating establishments. Head downtown, north of the Clark Fork River along **Higgins Ave.,** and check out the array of restaurants and coffeehouses that line the road. Walk through the gift shop pharmacy to reach **⊠Butterfly Herbs,** 232 N. Higgins Ave., where the classic hummus sandwich ($4), chai milkshake ($3), and organic green salad ($2.50) are exciting alternatives to diner fare.

(☎406-728-8780. Open M-F 7am-6pm, Sa 9am-5:30pm, Su 9am-5pm.) **Worden's,** 451 N. Higgins Ave., is a popular deli, serving a wide variety of world-class sandwiches in three sizes: 4 in. ($4.25), 7 in. ($5.75), and 14 in. ($10.75). You can also pick up groceries while munching. (☎406-549-1293. Open summer M-Th 8am-10pm, F-Sa 8am-11pm, Su 9am-10pm; winter M-Th 8am-9pm, F-Sa 8am-10pm, Su 9am-10pm.) **Eat to Live,** 1916 Brooks St., prides itself on healthy, low-fat meals reminiscent of Mom's home cooking. (☎406-721-2510. Open M-F 11:30am-3pm.) **Tipu's,** 115½ S. 4th St. W., is one of the only all-veggie establishments and the lone Indian restaurant in Montana. (☎406-542-0622. All-you-can-eat lunch buffet $7. Open daily 11:30am-9:30pm.) At **Tacos del Sol,** 422 N. Higgins Ave., get a Mission Burrito for under $4. (☎406-327-8929. Open M-F 11am-7pm.)

◤ ACCOMMODATIONS

There are no hostels in Missoula, but there are plenty of inexpensive alternatives on Broadway. Rooms at the **City Center Motel,** 338 E. Broadway, have cable TV, fridges, and microwaves. (☎406-543-3193. Singles Jan.-Aug. $45, Sept.-Dec. $35; doubles $48-52/$42.) To reach the **Aspen Motel,** 3720 Rte. 200 E., in East Missoula, take I-90 East to Exit 107 and travel ½ mi. east. (☎406-721-9758. Singles $40; doubles with 1 bed $46, with 2 beds $57.) The **Missoula/El-Mar KOA Kampground,** 3450 Tina Ave., just south of Broadway off Reserve St., is one of the best KOAs around, providing shaded tent sites apart from RVs, as well as a pool, hot tub, mini-golf courses, and 24hr. laundry facilities. (☎406-549-0881 or 800-562-5366. Sites for two $21, with water and electricity $25, full hookup $31; cabins $38-43; each additional person $3.)

◢ NIGHTLIFE

The *Independent* and *Lively Times,* available at newsstands and cafes, offer the lowdown on the Missoula music scene, while the *Entertainer,* in the Friday *Missoulian,* has movie and event schedules. College students swarm the downtown bar area around Front St. and Higgins Ave. during the school year. Bars have a more relaxed atmosphere in summer. **Charlie B's,** 420 N. Higgins Ave., draws an eclectic clientele of bikers, farmers, students, and hippies. Framed photos of longtime regulars blot out the walls—park at the bar for 10 or 20 years and join them. Hungry boozers can

GREAT NORTH

weave their way to the **Dinosaur Cafe** at the back of the room for Creole delights. (☎406-549-3589. Open daily 8am-2am.) The popular **Iron Horse Brew Pub,** 501 N. Higgins Ave., always packs a crowd; the patio fills up during summer. (☎406-728-8866. Open daily 11am-2am.) Follow the advice of the "beer coaches" at **The Kettle House Brewing Co.,** 602 Myrtle, one block west of Higgins between 4th and 5th, and "support your local brewery." The Kettle House serves an assortment of beers, including their hemp beer: Bongwater Stout. (2 free samples, then $2.75 per pint. Open M-Th 3-9pm, F-Sa noon-9pm; no beer served after 8pm.)

▶ LEAVING MISSOULA
Take **Broadway** north to its intersection with **U.S. 93 North,** and head out of town and into the quiet mountain country of Western Montana.

▶ NATIONAL BISON RANGE
In Ravalli, take Rte. 200 West. Following the signs, take a right onto Rte. 212 after 5 mi.; the entrance to the park is 5 mi. north, on your right.

The National Bison Range was established in 1908 to save bison from extinction. At one time 30-70 million bison roamed the plains, but after years of hunting the population dropped to less than 1000. The range is home to 350-500 buffalo as well as deer, pronghorn, elk, bighorn sheep, and mountain goats. The 2hr. Red Sleep Mountain self-guided tour offers a view of the Flathead Valley and the best chance for wildlife observation. (☎406-644-2211. Visitors Center open Nov. to mid-May M-F 8am-4:30pm; mid-May to Oct. daily 8am-6pm. Red Sleep Mountain drive open mid-May to mid-Oct. daily 7am-dusk. $4 per vehicle.)

ST. IGNATIUS
Named for the Jesuit Mission for which it is best known, St. Ignatius sits just east of U.S. 93 at the foot of the Mission Mountains on the Flathead Indian Reservation. While there's not much to experience in town, **St. Ignatius Catholic Mission,** the brick building just off of the highway, is worth a look. Built in 1891 at the request of the local Flathead tribe, the mission features 58 frescoes and murals painted by the mission cook, Brother Carignano, that look as though they could have been taken from European cathedrals. (☎406-745-2768. Open daily 9am-8pm. Donation suggested.)

Across the highway from town, Col. Doug Allard's mini-empire constitutes most of the services offered in St. Iggy's, starting with **Col.**

Doug Allard's Indian Museum and Trading Post, which houses traditional native clothing and artifacts, as well as a small display of stuffed (dead) animals. Perhaps most impressive, however, is the World Champion Stick Game Tournament Trophy, replete with actual sticks, that Col. Allard himself has awarded to various stick game luminaries. (☎406-745-2951. Open daily 9am-5pm. Free.) The best restaurant around is none other than **Col. Doug Allard's Original Buffalo Ranch Cafe,** in the large log building with the stuffed white buffalo in the display case over the entrance. Here you can ponder the history and struggle of the Flathead Indian Reservation buffalo herd, the last naturally wild herd in the world, while digging into a delicious Montana Buffalo Hump Roast ($14), BBQ Buffalo Sandwich ($7), or Buffalo Stew. (☎406-745-5100. Open daily 6:30am-9pm.) For a quick bite, head to **The Malt Shop,** 101 1st. St., where burgers and dogs ($1-5) or tasty sandwiches are washed down by a huckleberry milkshake ($3) that is delightful. (☎406-745-3501. Open M-Sa 10:30am-10pm, Su 11:30am-9pm.)

◉ NINEPIPES MUSEUM OF EARLY MONTANA
40962 U.S. 93
In Charlo, directly on U.S. 93. Look for the large log cabin-style buildings.

Chronicling the histories and traditions of the nearby Ninepipes Refuge and the surrounding area, the museum displays photographs and artifacts of Native Americans, trappers, miners, loggers and frontiersfolk. Fine Native American beadwork and dioramas depicting life in the Old West make this roadside attraction worth investigating. (☎406-644-3435. Open Su and W-Sa 11am-5pm. $4.) Adjacent **Ninepipes Lodge and Restaurant** offers lodging and dining for the road-weary. (☎406-644-2588. Singles $72; doubles $78. Restaurant open Su-Th 9am-9pm, F-Sa 9am-10pm.)

▶ APPROACHING POLSON
Follow **U.S. 93** (Main St.) north through town, around the courthouse rotary, and on out to the west shore of beautiful Flathead Lake, which the highway follows straight to Polson, on its southwestern corner.

POLSON & FLATHEAD LAKE
On the southern side of Flathead Lake, Polson has a small town's share of outdoor activities and art, but the real reason to stop here is the

⊠Miracle of America Museum, 58176 U.S. 93. With displays of old posters, uniforms, motorcycles, and weapons, the museum is the life's work of proprietor Gil Mangels. A re-created general store, saddlery shop, barber shop, soda fountain, and gas station sit among such oddities as an 1898 sheep-powered treadmill. The museum celebrates Live History Day the third weekend in July. (☎406-883-6804. Open June-Sept. daily 8am-8pm; Oct.-May M-Sa 8am-5pm, Su 2-6pm. $4, ages 3-12 $1.) Fresh fruit stands line **Flathead Lake,** the largest natural lake west of the Mississippi. Renowned for fresh cherries and fresher fish, U.S. 93 between Polson and Kalispell skirts the western edge of the lake. The waters near Polson have some of best Class II and Class III rafting around, and the **Flathead Raft Co.,** 1501 U.S. 93, prepares visitors for the experience. The famous Buffalo Rapids of the Lower Flathead River are especially good at folding your raft in half and tossing your shipmates overboard. (☎406-883-5838 or 800-654-4359; www.flatheadraftco.com. $40, seniors $36, ages 8-12 $32.) A local secret, **Blacktail Mountain Ski Resort** (☎406-844-0999; www.blacktailmountain.com), in Lakeside, is one of the newest ski areas in the country, built for affordable family skiing. The lone ski lodge is a welcome break from the crowded ski resorts that so many tourists make their destination—you won't find lift lines here.

M&S Meats (☎406-844-3414 or 800-454-3414; www.shopworks.com/msmeats), 86755 U.S. 93, is worth a stop for some of the best jerky you'll ever taste ($18 per lb.). Jerky and sausage come in beef or buffalo. Most lodging on the lake is expensive, but there are some affordable options. **Edgewater Motel,** 7140 U.S. 93, in Lakeside, has rooms available as apartments or with kitchenettes and lake frontage with docks. (☎406-844-3644 or 800-424-3798. Open in summer. Singles from $60.) The **Cherry Hill Motel,** 1810 U.S. 93, offers clean and comfortable rooms just north of the museum. (☎406-883-2737. Singles $60; doubles $76.)

APPROACHING KALISPELL
Drive up **U.S. 93** north to **Kalispell.**

KALISPELL

Nestled between the ski-haven Big Mountain and gorgeous Flathead Lake, Kalispell mixes rampant outdoorsmanship with the art and culture of the largest urban center of northwestern Montana. While it may not take long to get a feel for the town proper, Kalispell is a gateway to the wilderness adventures of the Montana countryside.

(VITAL STATS)

Population: 15,000

Visitor Info: Chamber of Commerce, 15 Depot Park (☎406-758-2800), in Depot Park, on Main St. at Center St. Open M-F 8am-5pm.

Internet Access: Flathead County Library, 247 1st Ave. E. (☎406-758-5819), 1 block off of Main St. (U.S. 93). Open M-Th 10am-8pm, F 10am-5pm, Sa 11am-5pm.

Post Office: 350 N. Meridian Rd., (☎406-755-6450), right off of U.S. 2 west of Main St., at 3rd St. Open M-F 9am-5pm, Sa 9am-2pm. **Postal Code:** 59904.

GETTING AROUND. Kalispell is laid out in a grid centered on the intersection of **Main St. (U.S. 93)** and **Idaho St. (Rte. 2),** the older highway around which the town's businesses first developed. Numbered avenues flank Main St., increasing in number as they move out in both directions, with East and West designating their orientation. Numbered streets count southward from **Center St.,** while streets north of Center bear state names. **Street parking** is free, but limited to two hours.

SIGHTS. Museums, small stores, and galleries give the downtown area around Main St. more character than most towns of this size. **The Hockaday Museum of Art,** 302 2nd Ave. E., houses a collection of art inspired by Glacier National Park, along with rotating exhibits of nationally renowned and emerging artists. (☎406-755-5268. Open M-Sa 10am-6pm, Su noon-4pm. $5.) The **Conrad Mansion National Historic Site Museum,** 6 blocks east of Main St. on 4th St. E., shows 26 beautifully furnished rooms in their original 1895 condition, along with pleasant gardens and a Victorian gift shop. (☎406-755-2166; www.conradmansion.com. Open daily 10am-5pm. $8.) **The M,** 124 2nd Ave. E., displays the history and culture of Northwestern Montana. (☎406-756-8381; www.yourmuseum.org. Open Tu-Sa 10am-5pm. $6.)

FOOD. A variety of chain restaurants line U.S. 93 and U.S. 2, but a few local eateries provide a moment of escape from corporate greed and oppression. **Bojangles Diner,** 1319 U.S. 2 W., is a 50s style throwback replete with a jukebox and trains.

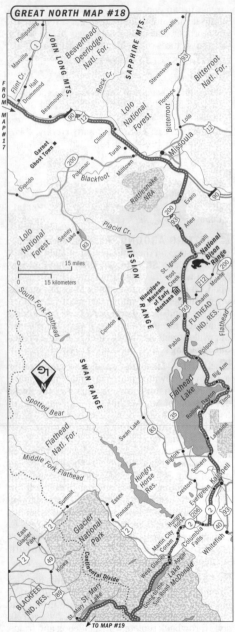

GREAT NORTH MAP #18

GREAT NORTH

(☎406-755-3222. Breakfasts $3-10. Burgers and sandwiches $5-6, dinners $7-11. Open daily 6am-8pm.) **D.G. Barley's Brewhouse & Grill,** 285 North Main St., at the junction of U.S. 93 and U.S. 2, serves up Southwestern fare worthy of any cowgirl in a kitschy, glam-ranch atmosphere. (☎406-756-2222. Steaks $13-17. Salads $7-9. Burgers $7-9. Open Su-Th 11am-10pm, F-Sa 11am-11pm.) **Avalanche Creek Restaurant & Coffeehouse,** 38 1st Ave. E., specializes in some of the valley's finest soups ($3-5), salads ($4-6), and sandwiches ($4-6) in a setting of the work of local artists. (☎406-257-0785. Open M-F 7am-5pm, Sa 9am-5pm.)

ACCOMMODATIONS. A few chain motels such as **Motel 6** and **Super 8** dot the sides of Main St. (U.S. 93) on the south side of town, just past the courthouse. Older, privately-run endeavors crop up along **Idaho St.** (U.S. 2), heading east. The █**Kalispell Grand Hotel,** 100 Main St., has provided the finest "frontier hotels" have to offer since 1912, with vintage architecture and ambiance blending seamlessly with high-speed Internet and jetted bathtubs. (At 1st St. ☎800-858-7422; www.kalispellgrand.com. Singles $76-125; doubles $83-125.) **Blue & White Motel,** 640 E. Idaho St., 6 blocks east of Main St., spruces up the motel experience with an indoor swimming pool, sauna, and jacuzzi available year-round. (☎800-382-3577. Singles $62; doubles $78.)

LEAVING KALISPELL
Head east on **E. Idaho St. (U.S. 2)**.

BIG SKY WATERSLIDES
At the intersection of U.S. 2 and Rte. 206.
Big Sky Waterslides is the place to cool down. Some of the waterpark's ten waterslides require innertubes to navigate 360° turns while others steeply drop 50 ft. The park also has a mini-golf course. (☎406-892-5025; www.bigskywaterslide.com. Open daily 10am-8pm. $18, seniors and under 10 $14. Discounted twilight rate from 4pm.)

HUNGRY HORSE. Hungry Horse is the "Friendliest Dam Town in the West." The small town of was named after two starving horses, Tex and Jerry, who survived the bitter winter of 1900. The impressive Hungry Horse Dam controls the flow of the Flathead River.

THE HUCKLEBERRY PATCH
On U.S. 2 East.

The Huckleberry Patch specializes in huckleberry products including jams, syrups, and fudge. For a treat, try the huckleberry milkshakes ($3). The restaurant serves homecooked meals; try the huckleberry waffle ($4.50) or burger. (☎406-387-4000 or 800-527-7340. Burger $5.50. Restaurant open in summer daily 8am-3pm.)

GLACIER NATIONAL PARK

Glacier National Park makes up most of the Waterton-Glacier Peace Park; although technically one park, Waterton-Glacier is actually two distinct areas: the small Waterton Lakes National Park in Alberta, and the enormous **Glacier National Park** in Montana. Waterton-Glacier transcends international boundaries to encompass one of the most strikingly beautiful portions of the Rockies. The massive Rocky Mountain peaks span both parks, providing sanctuary for endangered bears, bighorn sheep, moose, mountain goats, and gray wolves. Perched high in the Northern Rockies, Glacier is sometimes called the "Crown of the Continent," and the alpine lakes and glaciers shine like jewels. The *Waterton Glacier Guide*, provided at any park entrance, has dates and times of trail, campground, and border crossing openings.

VITAL STATS

Area: 1.2 million acres

Visitor Info: Logan Pass Visitors Center (☎406-888-7800; www.nps.gov/glac/home.htm), at the summit of Going-to-the-Sun Rd.

Gateway Towns: West Glacier, St. Mary

Fees: $10 per vehicle.

GETTING AROUND

Linking West Glacier and St. Mary, **Going-to-the-Sun Rd.,** the only road through the park, is a spectacular 52 mi. scenic drive climbing 3000 ft. through cedar forests, mountain passes, and arctic tundra. (Allow 2-3hr. or more. Closed in winter.) **U.S. 2** skirts the southern border of the park. At "Goat Lick," about halfway between East and West Glacier, mountain goats traverse steep cliffs to lap natural salt deposits. **U.S. 89** heads north along the east edge of the park through St. Mary.

HIKING

Most of Glacier's scenery lies off the main roads and is accessible only by foot. An extensive trail system has something for everyone, from short, easy day hikes to rigorous backcountry expeditions. Stop by one of the Visitors Centers for maps with day hikes. Beware of bears and mountain lions. Familiarize yourself with the precautions necessary to avoid an encounter, and ask rangers about wildlife activity.

Avalanche Lake (4 mi. round-trip, 3hr.) is a breathtaking trail and by far the most popular day hike in the park. Starting north of Lake McDonald on the Going-to-the-Sun Rd., this moderate hike climbs 500 ft. to picture-perfect panoramas.

Iceberg Lake (7 mi., 5 hr.), begins at the trailhead at the Swiftcurrent Motor Inn in Many Glacier. The trail climbs steeply for the first ½ mi., then inclines more gradually. The lake rivals the beauty of any in the world, circled by mountains with turquoise blue water and icebergs that float in the lake year-round.

Trail of the Cedars (¾ mi. loop, 20min.) begins at the same trailhead as Avalanche Lake and is an easy walk that also has a shorter, wheelchair-accessible hike.

Grinnell Glacier Trail (11 mi. round-trip, 7hr.) passes near several glaciers and follows along Grinnell Point and Mt. Grinnell, gaining a steady and moderate 1600 ft. Trailhead at the Many Glacier Picnic Area.

Hidden Lake Nature Trail (3 mi. round-trip, 2hr.), beginning at the Logan Pass Visitors Center, is a short and modest 460 ft. climb to a lookout of Hidden Lake and a chance to stretch your legs while winding along the Going-to-the-Sun Rd.

OUTDOOR ACTIVITIES

Opportunities for bicycling are limited and confined to roadways and designated bike paths; cycling on trails is strictly prohibited. Although the Going-to-the-Sun Rd. is a popular route, only experienced cyclists with appropriate gear and legs of titanium should attempt this grueling ride; the sometimes nonexistent road shoulder can create hazardous situations. The **Inside North Fork Rd.,** which runs from Kintla Lake to Fish Creek on the

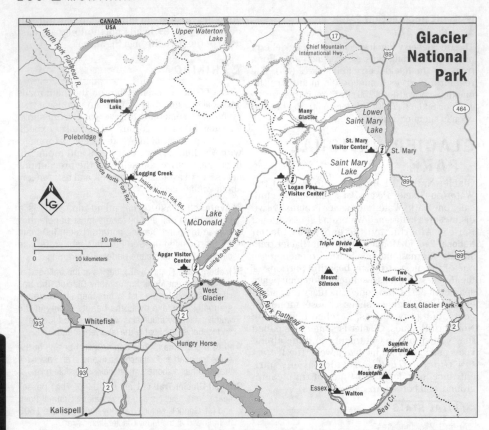

Glacier National Park

west side of the park, is good for **mountain biking**, as are the old logging roads in the Flathead National Forest. Equestrian explorers should check that trails are open; there are steep fines for riding closed trails. **Trail rides** from **Mule Shoe Outfitters** (2hr.; May to early Sept. every 2hr. 8:30am-3:30pm; $45) are available at Many Glacier (☎406-732-4203) and Lake McDonald (☎406-888-5121).

The **Glacier Park Boat Co.** (☎406-257-2426) runs **boat tours** ($10-12) that explore Glacier's lakes. **Glacier Raft Co.**, in West Glacier, leads trips down the middle fork of the Flathead River. (☎800-235-6781. Half-day $40, under 13 $30; full-day trip with lunch $65/$48.) You can rent **rowboats** ($10 per hr.) at Lake McDonald, Many Glacier, Two Medicine, and Apgar; **canoes** ($10 per hr.) at Many Glacier, Two Medicine, and Apgar; **kayaks** ($10 per hr.) at

Apgar and Many Glacier; and **outboards** ($17 per hr.) at Lake McDonald and Two Medicine. No permit is needed to fish in the park, and limits are generally high. Some areas, however, are restricted, and certain species may be catch-and-release. Pick up *Fishing Regulations*, available at Visitors Centers for info.

■ FOOD

Polebridge Mercantile Store (☎406-888-5105), on Polebridge Loop Rd. a quarter-mile east of N. Fork Rd., has homemade pastries ($1-3) as splendid as the surrounding peaks. Gas, gifts, and pay phones are also available. (Open daily June-Sept. 8am-9pm; Oct.-May 8am-6pm.) Next door, the **Northern Lights Saloon** serves cheeseburgers ($5-6) and all-

Montana-brewed cold pints ($3) in a log cabin with tree trunks for bar stools. (☎406-888-5669. Kitchen open June-Sept. M-Sa 4-9pm, Su 9am-noon and 4-9pm; bar open until midnight.) Sample Montanan delicacies at the **Whistle Stop Restaurant**, in East Glacier, best known for its omelettes and huckleberry french toast. (☎406-226-9292. Open mid-May to mid-Sept. daily 7am-9pm.)

▌ ACCOMMODATIONS

Visitors planning overnight backpacking trips must obtain the necessary **backcountry permits.** With the exception of the **Nyack/Coal Creek** camping zone, all backcountry camping must be done at designated campsites equipped with pit toilets, tent sites, food preparation areas, and food hanging devices. (June-Sept. overnight camping $4 per person, ages 9-16 $2; Oct.-May no fees. For an additional $20, reservations are accepted beginning in mid-Apr. for trips between June 15 and Oct. 31.) Pick up a free and indispensable *Backcountry Camping Guide* from Visitors Centers or the **Backcountry Permit Center**, next to the Visitors Center in Apgar, which also has valuable info for those seeking to explore Glacier's less-traveled areas. (Open daily May-June and mid-Sept. to Oct. 8am-4pm; July to mid-Sept. 7am-4pm.)

Staying indoors within Glacier is expensive, but several affordable options lie just outside the park boundaries. On the west side of the park, the small, electricity-less town of **Polebridge** provides access to Glacier's remote and pristine northwest corner. From Apgar, take Camas Rd.

north, and take a right onto the poorly marked gravel Outside North Fork Rd., just past a bridge over the North Fork of the Flathead River. (Avoid Inside North Fork Rd.—your shocks will thank you.) From Columbia Falls, take Rte. 486 north. To the east, inexpensive lodging is just across the park border in **East Glacier.** The distant offices of **Glacier Park, Inc.** (☎406-756-2444; www.glacierparkinc.com) handle reservations for all in-park lodging.

Brownies Grocery (HI-AYH), 1020 Rte. 49 (☎406-226-4426), in East Glacier Park. Check in at the grocery counter and head up to the spacious hostel. Kitchen, showers, linens, laundry, and a view of the Rockies. Internet $1.75 per 15min. Key deposit $5. Check-in by 9pm. Reservations recommended; credit card required. Open May-Sept., weather permitting. Dorms $13, nonmembers $16; private singles $18/$21; doubles $26/$29; family rooms for 4-6 $38/$41; tent sites $10.

North Fork Hostel, 80 Beaver Dr. (☎406-888-5241), in Polebridge. The wooden walls and kerosene lamps are reminiscent of a hunting retreat. Showers and beautiful fully equipped kitchen, but no flush toilets. During the winter, old-fashioned wood stoves warm frozen fingers. Internet $2 per 20min. Canoe rentals $20 per day; mountain bikes $15; snowshoes $5; nordic ski equipment $5. Linen $2. Check-in by 10pm. Check-out noon. Call ahead, especially in winter. Dorms $15, teepees $10 per person; cabins $30; log homes $65.

Backpacker's Inn Hostel, 29 Dawson Ave. (☎406-226-9392), in East Glacier. 14 clean beds in co-ed rooms. Hot showers. Sleeping bags $1. Open May-Sept.

BEWARE OF THE BEAR SPRAY

FROM THE ROAD

Bear spray that is sold to ward off attacking bears is actually a very powerful form of pepper spray. Contrary to the belief of more than a few tourists, bear spray is not the ursine equivalent of bug spray—I used to sell the stuff, and I can't tell you how many parents I've seen mist down their children before a hike or tourists who have walked out the store to "try it out" on passersby. It's not pretty—and I know. During the summer I was working in Glacier National Park, a careless security guard had the safety lock pulled off his can of bear spray. After extinguishing our campfire, he proceeded to trip over a bench and spray himself and me directly in the face. I hit the ground, feeling like I was breathing fire, and heaved for the next 20min.; the guard ran off with a bloody nose. The moral of the story: don't use your bear spray on anyone but a bear.

—*Elli Thomson*

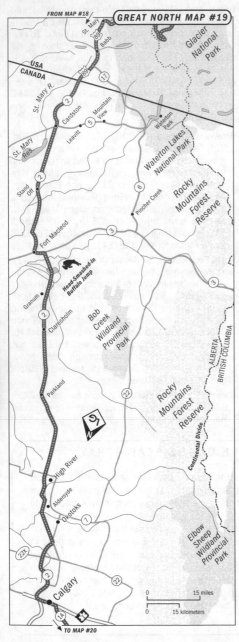

FROM MAP #18

GREAT NORTH MAP #19

St. Mary
Babb
Glacier National Park
USA
CANADA
St. Mary R.
Cardston
Mountain View
Waterton Park
Leavitt
Waterton Lakes National Park
St. Mary Res.
Stand Off
Pincher Creek
Rocky Mountains Forest Reserve
Fort Macleod
Head-Smashed-In Buffalo Jump
Granum
Bob Creek Wildland Provincial Park
Claresholm
ALBERTA
BRITISH COLUMBIA
Parkland
Rocky Mountains Forest Reserve
Continental Divide
High River
Aldersyde
Okotoks
Elbow Sheep Wildland Provincial Park
Calgary
0   15 miles
0   15 kilometers
TO MAP #20

TO MAP #20

Dorms $10; private rooms with queen-size bed and full linen $20-30.

Swiftcurrent Motor Inn (☎406-732-5531), in Many Glacier Valley. One of the few budget motels in the area. All cabins share bath. Open early June to early Sept. 1-bedroom cabins $43; 2-bedroom $53.

LEAVING GLACIER NATIONAL PARK
From St. Mary, take **U.S. 89 North.**

CATTLE BARON SUPPER CLUB
At the intersection of U.S. 89 and road to Many Glacier in Babb.

The Cattle Baron Supper Club might just be the nicest surprise you'll ever find in the middle of nowhere; inside the beautiful dining room, complete with murals and an enormous pine tree that grows right through the middle of the building, waiters in tuxedos serve amazing steaks ($23-26). They may be expensive, but they've been known to convert vegetarians. (☎406-732-4033. Open daily 5-10pm. Bar open until midnight.)

LEAVING THE US
Take U.S. 89 North to the **Piegan/Carway Border Crossing** (open daily 7am-11pm). In Canada, U.S. 89 becomes **Hwy. 2,** heading north to **Cardston.** See **Vital Documents** (p. 11) for info on passport and visa requirements.

Welcome To ALBERTA

CARDSTON
Cardston, located in the Lee Creek Valley where the foothills of the Rockies meet the Great Plains, is a convenient place to stay halfway between nearby Glacier/Waterton Lakes National Park and Calgary. There are several worthwhile attractions in town, including the **Fay Wray Fountain,** which honors the hometown girl who rose to fame next to the immortal King Kong. The **Remington Carriage Museum,** 623 Main St., houses over 250 horse-drawn vehicles, the largest collection in North America. (☎403-653-5139; www.remingtoncentre.com. Open

daily mid-May to mid-Sept. 9am-6pm, mid-Sept. to mid-May 10am-5pm. $6.50, seniors $5.50, ages 7-17 $3, under 7 free.)

Cardston's hotels are pricey; a cheaper and friendlier option is to stay at one of the town's many B&Bs. **Temple Sunset View,** 221 3rd St. East, welcomes guests with beautiful gardens and a patio with a fabulous view. Giant Canadian breakfasts of pancakes, eggs, bacon, and toast with homemade jelly will get you going in the morning. (☎403-653-3539. Singles $35; doubles $45.)

THE ROAD TO FORT MACLEOD. From Cardston, **Hwy. 2** is a straight shot all the way to Calgary. The road north from Cardston might just be flatter than South Dakota. Keep on the lookout for locusts dive-bombing your car and delicate little white butterflies reenacting the Boston massacre on your bumper. By the time you arrive in Fort Macleod, your car will be covered in such a thick iridescent sheen of butterfly dust that it won't be much of a surprise if it sprouts wings and flies from the parking lot.

FORT MACLEOD. Fort Macleod, southern Alberta's oldest settlement, preserves Canada's past in its many wood frame buildings from the 1890s and its brick and sandstone structures from the 1900s. At the ▨**The Fort Museum of the North-West Mounted Police,** 219 25th St., mounties circle the fort on horseback on their Musical Ride. (☎403-553-4703; www.nwmpmuseum.com. Open Mar.-Dec. and July-Aug. $7.50, seniors $7, ages 12-17 $5.50, ages 6-11 $4.50; families $22.) The yellow stucco cottages of the **Kozy Motel,** 433 Main St., sport red trim and flower baskets in the windows. All rooms include refrigerators. (☎403-553-3115. Singles $45-50; doubles $50-65; suites $70-85.)

HEAD-SMASHED-IN BUFFALO JUMP *Located 18km from Fort MacLeod on Hwy. 785.*

For over 10,000 years, Native Americans stampeded buffalo off strategically placed sandstone cliffs. Legend has it that this particular buffalo jump got its name from a young brave who wanted to witness the falling buffalo. Standing in the shelter of an overhanging ledge, he was trapped by the mounting bodies. When his people came to collect the buffalo, they found him with his skull crushed by the weight of the buffalo, and named the place "Head-Smashed-In."

Today you can visit the jump, no longer in active use, and an impressive interpretive center. (☎403-553-2731; www.head-smashed-in.com. Open daily in summer 9am-6pm; in fall and winter 10am-5pm.)

HIGH RIVER. The best way to see High River is to follow the 14km **Happy Trails** pathway system, which winds by a number of murals that transform the concrete walls of downtown shops into historical works of art. Exhibits at the **Museum of the Highwood,** 406 1st St. SW, are rotating, but some of the quirky themes include "Hair's to You" a century of women's hairstyles, or "Polo, the Galloping Game." Local history and reference material is also archived here. (☎403-652-7156. Open summer M-Sa 10am-5pm, Su 12:30-5:30pm; winter Su and Tu-Sa noon-4pm. $2.50, students and seniors $2, under 13 free.) The food is as unique as the atmosphere at the **Railroad Cafe,** 406 1st St. SW, at the Museum of Highwood, which is actually built into the dining car of an old train. Try the brie and cucumber sandwiches ($6.75) or a chicken mango quesadilla. (☎403-652-7156. Open M 10am-2pm, Tu-Sa 10am-4pm, Su 11am-4pm.)

CALGARY

Mounties founded Calgary in the 1870s to control Canada's flow of illegal whisky, but oil made the city what it is today. Petroleum fuels Calgary's economy and explains why the city hosts the most corporate headquarters in Canada outside of Toronto. As the host of the 1988 Winter Olympics, Calgary's dot on the map grew larger; already Alberta's largest city, this thriving young metropolis is the second fastest-growing in all of Canada.

VITAL STATS

Population: 950,000

Visitor Info: Calgary Chamber of Commerce, 100 6th Avenue SW (☎403-750-0400). Open M-F 8am-4:30pm.

Internet Access: Calgary Public Library, 616 Macleod Trail SE (☎403-260-2600). $2 per hr. Open M-Th 10am-9pm, F-Sa 10am-5pm; mid-Sept. to mid-May also Su 1:30-5pm.

Post Office: 207 9th Ave. SW (☎403-974-2078). Open M-F 8am-5:45pm. **Postal Code:** T2P 2G8.

GREAT NORTH

▣ GETTING AROUND

Calgary is 126km east of Banff along the **Trans-Canada Hwy. (Hwy. 1).** It's divided into quadrants: **Centre St.** is the east-west divider; the **Bow River** splits the north and south. Avenues run east-west; streets north-south. Derive cross streets from the first digit of the street address: 206 7th Ave. SW, for example, would be found on 7th Ave. at 2nd St.

◉ SIGHTS

CALGARY TOWER. To get your bearings quickly, take a trip up the Calgary Tower. The 191m tower, built in 1967, was the first of its kind. Now the tower has a grill, observation terrace, and revolving dining room. *(101-9th Ave. SW. ☎403-266-7171; www.calgarytower.com. Open in summer M-F 6:30am-10:30pm, Sa-Su 7am-10:30pm; winter M-F 7am-10pm, Sa-Su 8am-10pm. $10, ages 2-17 $7, under 2 free.)*

OLYMPIC LEFTOVERS. For two glorious weeks in 1988, the world's eyes were on Calgary for the Winter Olympics. Almost 20 years later, the world has moved on, but the city still clings relentlessly to its Olympic stardom. Visit the **Canada Olympic Park** and its looming ski jumps and twisted bobsled and luge tracks. The **Olympic Hall of Fame** honors Olympic achievements with displays, films, and a ▧**bobsled simulator.** *(10min. northwest of downtown on Hwy. 1. ☎403-247-5452. Open in summer daily 8am-9pm; in winter M-F 9am-9pm, Sa-Su 9am-5pm. $10 ticket includes chair-lift and entrance to ski-jump buildings, Hall of Fame, and icehouse. Tours $15.)* In summer, the park opens its hills and a lift to **mountain bikers.** *Mountain biking daily May-Oct. 9am-9pm. Roadway pass $9 for cyclists. Front-suspension bike rental $12 per hr., $31 per day.)* Keep an eye out for ski-jumpers, who practice at the facility year-round. The miniature mountain (113m vertical) also opens up for recreational **downhill skiing** in winter. The **Olympic Oval,** an enormous indoor speed-skating track on the University of Calgary campus, remains a major international training facility. Speedskaters work out in the early morning and late afternoon; sit in the bleachers and observe the action for free. *(☎403-220-7890; www.oval.ucalgary.ca. Public skating hours vary. $4.75, children and seniors $2.75. Skate rental $5.)*

PARKS AND MUSEUMS. Devonian Gardens is one of the world's largest indoor parks, spanning three levels of the Toronto Dominion Square and housing 20,000 plants. A visit to the peaceful gardens will reveal waterfalls and fountains in the Sun Garden, flower-banked pathways in the Quiet Garden, or fish and turtles to feed. *(317-7 Ave. SW. ☎403-268-5207. Open daily 9am-9pm. Free.)* Footbridges stretch from either side of the Bow River to **Prince's Island Park,** a natural refuge only blocks from the city center. In July and August, Mount Royal College performs **Shakespeare in the Park.** *(☎403-240-6908. Call for shows and times.)* Calgary's other island park, **St. George's Island,** is accessible by the river walkway to the east or by driving. It houses the **Calgary Zoo,** including a botanical garden and children's zoo. For those who missed the Cretaceous Period, life-sized plastic dinosaurs are also on exhibit. *(Parking off Memorial Dr. on the north side of the river. ☎403-232-9300. Open daily 9am-5pm. $15, seniors $13, ages 13-17 $9, ages 3-12 $6.50.)*

STAMPEDE. The more cosmopolitan Calgary becomes, the more tenaciously it holds on to its frontier roots. The Stampede draws one million cowboys and tourists each July for world-class steer wrestling, bareback and bull-riding, and pig races. The festival spills into the streets from early in the morning (free pancake breakfasts all around) through the night. *(Stampede Park is just southeast of downtown, bordering the east side of Macleod Trail between 14th Ave. SE and the Elbow River. ☎800-661-1767; www.calgarystampede.com. $11, seniors and ages 7-12 $6, under 7 free.)*

▣ FOOD

The small ▧**Thi-Thi Submarine,** 209 1st St. SE, manages to pack in two plastic seats, a bank of toaster ovens, and the finest Vietnamese submarines in Calgary. Most meaty subs are sub-$5; the veggie sub is an unreal $2.25. *(☎403-265-5452. Open M-F 10am-7pm, Sa-Su 10:30am-5pm.)* A generational anomaly and worthy destination, ▧**Peter's Drive In,** 219 16th Ave. NE, is one of the city's last remaining drive-ins. Hordes of chummy patrons attest to the swell quality. Drive in or walk to the service window. Famous milkshakes are under $3 and burgers are under $4. *(☎403-277-2747. Open daily 9am-midnight.)* **Take**

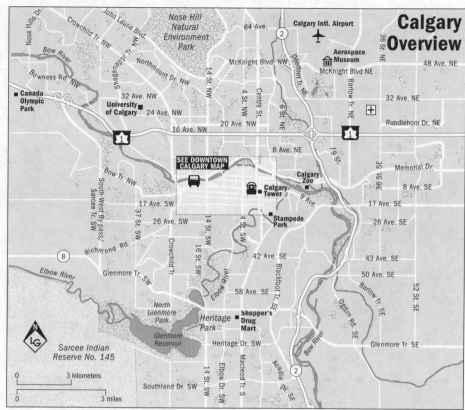

Calgary Overview

10 Cafe, 304 10th St. NW, became a local favorite by offering dirt-cheap, high-quality food. All burgers are under $5.75, and the menu also serves Chinese food, most under $8. (☎403-270-7010. Open M-F 9am-4pm, Sa-Su 8:30am-3pm.) **Wicked Wedge,** 618 17th Ave. SW, serves large, topping-heavy pizza ($3.75) to Calgary's post-party scene. (☎403-228-1024. Open M-Th and Su 11am-midnight, F-Sa 11am-3am.)

ACCOMMODATIONS

Busy and sometimes impersonal, **Calgary International Hostel (HI),** 520 7th Ave. SE, near downtown, has some nice accessories; the clean kitchen, lounge areas, laundry, and backyard with barbecue are pluses. (☎403-269-8239. 120 beds. Dorms $22, nonmembers $26; private rooms $75/$83.) The **University of Calgary,** in the ex-Olympic Village in the NW quadrant, is popular with conventioneers and often booked solid. (Coordinated through **Cascade Hall,** 3456 24th Ave. NW. ☎403-220-3203. Rooms available May-Aug. Shared rooms $25 per person; singles $34-100.) The **YWCA,** 320 5th Ave. SE, has two recently renovated residential floors. (☎403-232-1599. Women only. 150 beds available. Singles from $40; doubles $50; triples $130; quads $140. Seniors 10% discount.)

NIGHTLIFE

Nightgallery Cabaret, 1209B 1st St. SW, has a large dance floor and a diverse program of music attracts clubbers. Enjoy house at "Sunday Skool."

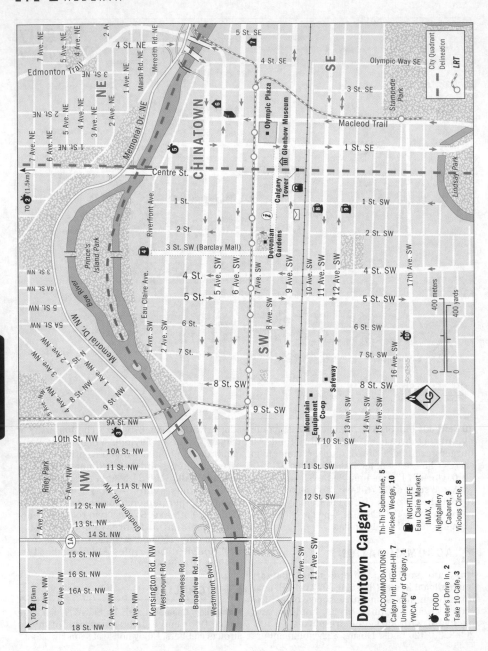

Downtown Calgary

ACCOMMODATIONS
Calgary Intl. Hostel-HI, **7**
University of Calgary, **1**
YWCA, **6**

FOOD
Peter's Drive In, **2**
Take 10 Cafe, **3**
Thi-Thi Submarine, **5**
Wicked Wedge, **10**

NIGHTLIFE
Eau Claire Market
IMAX, **4**
Nightgallery
Cabaret, **9**
Vicious Circle, **8**

City Quadrant
Delineation
LRT

(☎403-264-4484; www.nightgallerycabaret.com. Reggae-Dub on M draws a slightly older crowd. Open daily 8pm-3am.) A very relaxing bar, **Vicious Circle,** 1011 1st St. SW, offers a solid menu, colored mood lights, and a disco ball, plus pool tables, couches, eclectic art, and TV. Kick back on the summer patio seating and sample one of the 140 different martinis. (☎403-269-3951. Happy hour all night Su. Live music W. Open M-Th 11:30am-1am, F 11:30am-2am, Sa-Su noon-2am.) At the **Eau Claire Market IMAX,** 132 200 Barclay Parade SW, pit your imagination against a large-screen feature that claims to be bigger. (☎403-974-4629. Box office open M-F 11:30am-10pm, Sa-Su 10:30am-10pm. IMAX films $10.50, seniors $8.50, under 13 $7.50; nightly double feature $15.)

APPROACHING CANMORE

From Calgary, take **Rte. 1** (marked by the Maple Leaf sign) all the way west to Lake Louise. West of Calgary is about 30 mi. of flat land with no mountains in sight, but just west of Cochrane, the Rockies pop up, a misty vision in the distance. The road climbs uphill into pine trees with views of bare valleys and rolling hills laid out in front of the looming peaks.

CANMORE. Canmore got its start over 100 years ago, when miners were lured to the valley by rich coal deposits. Worldwide attention turned to the sleepy town in 1988, when the Nordic skiing events of the Winter Olympic Games were held here. Effort has been put into creating the charming downtown area, which today offers a walk past family shops and homey restaurants. The **Canmore Museums,** 907 7th Ave., include a Geoscience Center with ancient stones and bones, the historic North West Mounted Police Barracks, and artifacts from local mines. (☎403-678-2462; www.cmags.org. Open daily mid-May to mid-Sept. 9am-5pm; mid-Sept. to mid-May Su and Tu-Sa noon-4pm.) The **HI Canmore,** on Indian Flats Rd., offers plush accommodations, but the beds are closely packed. (☎403-678-3200; info@alpineclubofcanada.ca. Internet, laundry, linens. Reservations required. 4- to 6-bed co-ed dorms.)

BANFF TOWNSITE

Less townsite than chic resort, Banff nestles fine dining and luxury lodgings just below majestic, snow-capped peaks. A stroll downtown reveals decadent sweet shops and jewelry boutiques

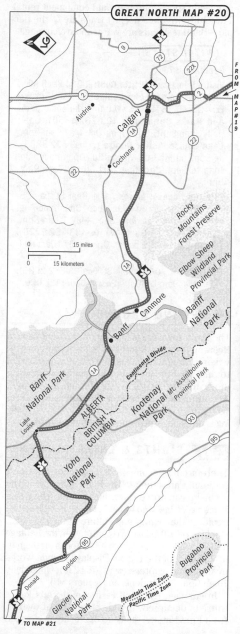

GREAT NORTH MAP #20

GREAT NORTH

TO MAP #21

alongside sports outfitters and equipment rental. The chilly weather doesn't translate to the people—Banff residents are warm and welcoming.

VITAL STATS

Population: 7000

Visitor Info: Banff Visitor Centre, 224 Banff Ave., includes **Banff/Lake Louise Tourism Bureau** (☎403-762-8421; www.banfflakelouise.com) and **Parks Canada** (☎403-762-1550). Open daily June-Sept. 8am-8pm; Oct.-May 9am-5pm. **Lake Louise Visitor Centre** (☎403-522-3833), at Samson Mall on Village Rd. Open daily mid-June to Sept. 8am-6pm; Oct. to mid-June 9am-5pm.

Internet Access: Library, 101 Bear St. (☎403-762-2611). Sign up in advance. Open June-Aug. M-Sa 10am-8pm; daily Sept.-May 10am-8pm. **Cyber Web,** 215 Banff Ave. (☎403-762-9226). $3 per 15min., $8 per hr. Open daily 10am-midnight.

Post Office: 204 Buffalo St. (☎403-762-2586). Open M-F 9am-5:30pm. **Postal Code:** T0L 0C0.

GETTING AROUND

The Banff townsite is located off the **Trans-Canada Highway (Hwy. 1). Banff Ave.** leads to downtown, where restaurants, shops, and bars reside. Parallel to and west of Banff Ave. is **Bear St.,** where the movie theater and the Whyte Museum are located. Accommodations scatter the downtown area, with pricier options clustered closer to town. **Parking** is ample in and around the downtown area.

SIGHTS & ENTERTAINMENT

There are numerous outdoor activities in Banff National Park (see p. 276), but a quiet day in the townsite can prove rewarding as well. The **Whyte Museum of the Canadian Rockies,** 111 Bear St., explores the history and culture of the Canadian Rockies over the last two centuries in the **Heritage Gallery,** while temporary exhibits focus on the natural history of the region. Displays include works by Canadian painters. (☎403-762-2291. Open daily 10am-5pm. $6, students and seniors $4.)

In summer, the **Banff Festival of the Arts** keeps tourists occupied. A wide spectrum of events, from First Nations dance to opera, are performed

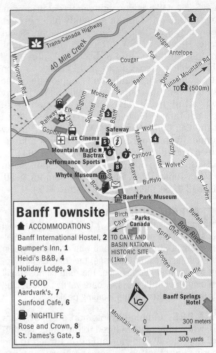

Banff Townsite

♠ ACCOMMODATIONS
Banff International Hostel, **2**
Bumper's Inn, **1**
Heidi's B&B, **4**
Holiday Lodge, **3**

♣ FOOD
Aardvark's, **7**
Sunfood Cafe, **6**

♫ NIGHTLIFE
Rose and Crown, **8**
St. James's Gate, **5**

from May to mid-August. Some shows are free; stop by the Visitors Center for a schedule. The **Banff Mountain Film Festival,** in the first week of November, screens films and videos that celebrate mountaineers. (For times and info, call ☎403-762-6301.) **Lux Cinema Centre,** 229 Bear St. (☎403-762-8595) shows Hollywood hits.

OUTDOOR ACTIVITIES

There are countless outdoor opportunities in Banff National Park (see p. 276). Before you head out, however, you'll need to rent equipment in town. Here are several options:

Mountain Magic Equipment, 224 Bear St. (☎403-762-2591). One of the few places in Banff to rent packages for Telemark ($25 per day) and mountaineering ($50 per day). They also offer the usual bike, ski, and snowboard rentals. Open daily Apr.-Nov. 9am-9pm; Dec.-Mar. 8am-9pm.

Bactrax Rentals, 225 Bear St. (☎403-762-8177). Rents mountain bikes for $6-10 per hr., $22-36 per day. Bike tours $15 per hr. including all equipment. Ski packages from $16 per day; snowboard packages $28. 20% HI discount. Open daily Apr.-Oct. 8am-8pm; Nov.-Mar. 7am-10pm.

Performance Sports, 208 Bear St. (☎403-762-8222). Rents tents ($20-26 per day), fishing gear ($16-30 per day), cross-country ski or snowshoe packages ($12 per day, $31 for 3 days), avalanche packages ($23 per day), and snow or rainwear ($8-17 per day). 10% HI or Real Big Adventures discount. Open daily July-Aug. 9:30am-8pm; Sept.-June 10am-6pm.

Wilson Mountain Sports (☎403-522-3636) in the Lake Louise Samson Mall. Rents bikes ($15 per hr., $35 per day) and camping and fishing gear. Mountaineering ($35 per day) and rock climbing packages ($15 per day). Open daily mid-June to Sept. 9am-9pm; Oct. to Apr. 8am-8pm; May to mid-June 9am-8pm.

🍴 FOOD

Like everything else in town, Banff restaurants tend toward the expensive. The Banff and Lake Louise hostels serve affordable meals in their cafes ($3-10). **Sunfood Cafe,** 215 Banff Ave., is a relaxed vegetarian cafe hidden upstairs in a touristy mall. (☎403-760-3933. Veggie burger with the works $6.25. Open M-Sa 11am-9pm.) **Aardvark's,** 304A Caribou St., does big business selling pizza after the bars close. It's often standing-room-only as hungry revelers jostle for a spot. (☎403-762-5500 or 762-5509. Small-ish slices of pizza $3. Small pie $6-9; large $13-21. Buffalo wings $5 for 10. Open daily 11am-4am.)

🏠 ACCOMMODATIONS

Finding a cheap place to stay in Banff has become increasingly difficult; the number of visitors soars into the millions every year. Townsite residents offer rooms in their homes, occasionally at reasonable rates ($75-140; in winter $60-100). Check the list at the back of the *Banff and Lake Louise Official Visitor Guide,* available free at the Visitors Centers. The hostel does provide an alternative to camping and several inns in town run on the not-so-expensive-compared-to-everything-else side. For more options, stop by the Banff tourist office, which supplies free accommodations guides, replete with general price rankings. For more options inside the park, see p. 278.

Banff International Hostel (**HI;** ☎403-762-4122), 3km uphill from Banff Townsite on Tunnel Mountain Rd. This monster hostel sleeps 215 and has 3 lounges and kitchens. Laundry and hot showers. Check-in 3pm. Check-out 11am. Dorms $26-27.50, nonmembers $30-32.

Bumper's Inn (☎403-762-3386 or 800-661-3518; www.bumpersinn.com), at the corner of Banff Ave. and Marmot St. This cozy, quiet inn is 1.5km from downtown and offers large, comfortable suites with an outdoor courtyard. Rooms $60-135, depending on the number of people and season.

The Holiday Lodge, 311 Marten St. (☎403-762-3648), on Marten St. between Elk St. and Moose St. This quaint inn has heritage home decor and private baths with showers. Rooms with double or queen-size beds in summer $50; in winter $70.

THE LOCAL STORY

THINGS THAT GO BANFF IN THE NIGHT

Bear sightings are common in the Canadian Rockies, but one grizzly bear gave Banff residents a reminder of whose park it really is. Known as Bear 16 (numbers are used to discourage personification), this ursine vagabond moved into town, disrupting everyday activity by foraging in front lawns and lazing in the road, blocking traffic. Bear 16 finally crossed the line when the scent from a bakery lured him too close to human territory. The park staff ultimately relocated Bear 16 to the Calgary Zoo. While most travelers are eager to see the area's wildlife, few want as intimate a confrontation as Bear 16 offered. To avoid a close encounter, the safest bet is to talk, sing, or yodel loudly while hiking, especially on windy days or near running water. The number of bear attacks actually ranks low among all park animals; dozens of visitors are bitten each year by rodents pursuing human food. The most dangerous Banff animals, however, are people—cars are the most common cause of death for wildlife in the park.

Heidi's B&B, 214 Otter St. (☎403-726-3806), between Wolf and Caribou St., 3 blocks away from downtown. Comfortable rooms have private baths and tubs with jets. Rooms in summer from $90; in winter from $55.

◪ NIGHTLIFE

For some real wildlife, check out Banff's bars. Check the paper or ask at the Visitors Center to find out which nightspots are having "locals' night," featuring cheap drinks. **Banff Ave.** hosts more bars, restaurants, kitschy gift shops, and banks than there are mountains.

◪ **Rose and Crown,** 202 Banff Ave. (☎403-762-2121), upstairs at the corner of Caribou St. Ample room for dancing, and pool-playing ($1.25), even on busy nights. Living room for watching sports and live music every night at 10pm. Happy hour M-F 3:30-6:30pm. Cover Sa $2. Su Jam Night with happy hour 9pm-close. Open daily 11am-2am.

St. James's Gate, 205 Wolf St. (☎403-762-9355). A laid-back Irish Pub with friendly staff. Ask the bartenders which of the 32 beers on tap to try. Live jigs and reels F-Sa. Open daily 11am-2am.

BANFF NATIONAL PARK

Banff is Canada's best-loved and best-known natural park, with 6641 sq. km of peaks, forests, glaciers, and alpine valleys. It also holds the title of Canada's first National Park, declared so only days after the Canadian Pacific Railway's completion in 1885. The park's name comes from Banffshire, Scotland, the birthplace of two Canadian Pacific Railway financiers who convinced Canada's first Prime Minister that a "large pecuniary advantage" might be gained from the region, telling him that "since we can't export the scenery, we shall have to import the tourists." Their plan worked to a fault, but streets littered with gift shops and chocolatiers cannot mar the the wilderness outside of the Banff townsite. Outdoors lovers arrive with mountain bikes, climbing gear, and skis, but a trusty pair of hiking boots remains the park's most widely-used outdoor equipment. Banff's natural beauty, along with the laid-back attitude it affords, have turned the Banff Townsite (see p. 273) into one of Canada's youngest towns.

(see p. 273)

VITAL STATS

Area: 1.6 million acres.

Visitor Info: Banff Visitor Centre, 224 Banff Ave. (see p. 273).

Gateway Towns: Banff, Lake Louise

Fees: $5, seniors $4, ages 6-16 $2.50.

▣ GETTING AROUND

Banff National Park hugs the Alberta side of the Alberta/British Columbia border, 128km west of Calgary. The **Trans-Canada Hwy. (Hwy. 1)** runs east-west through the park, connecting it to Yoho National Park (p. 281) in the west. The **Icefields Pkwy. (Hwy. 93)** connects Banff with Jasper National Park to the north and Kootenay National Park to the southwest. Civilization in the park centers on the towns of **Banff** and **Lake Louise,** 58km apart on Hwy. 1. The more serene **Bow Valley Pkwy. (Hwy. 1A)** parallels Hwy. 1 from Lake Louise to 8km west of Banff, offering excellent camping, hosteling, sights, and wildlife. The southern portion of Hwy. 1A is restricted at night in late spring and early summer to accommodate wildlife. **Parking** in Banff National Park is plentiful.

◉ SIGHTS

The **Banff Park Museum National Historic Site** is western Canada's oldest natural history museum, with rooms of stuffed specimens dating to the 1860s. (☎403-762-1558. Open daily mid-May to Sept. 10am-6pm; Oct. to mid-May 1-5pm. Tours daily in summer 3pm; in winter Sa-Su only. $2.50, seniors $2, children $1.50.) Banff National Park would not exist if not for the **Cave and Basin Mineral Springs,** once rumored to have miraculous healing properties. The **Cave and Basin National Historic Site,** a refurbished bath house built circa 1914, is now a small museum detailing the history and science of the site. Access to the low-ceilinged cave containing the original spring is inside the building. Five of the pools are the only home of the park's most endangered species: the small Banff Springs snail, *Physella johnsoni.* (☎403-762-1566. Open summer daily 9am-6pm; in winter M-F 11am-4pm, Sa-Su 9:30am-5pm. Tours at 11am. $2.50, seniors $2, children $1.50.) The **springs** are southwest of the city on Cave Ave. For an actual dip in the hot water, follow the sulfurous smell to the Upper Hot Springs pool, a 40°C (104°F) sulfurous cauldron on Mountain Ave. (☎403-762-1515. Open daily mid-May to mid-Oct. 9am-11pm; mid-Oct. to mid-May Su-Th 10am-10pm, F-Sa 10am-11pm. Swimsuits $1.50, towels $1.25, lockers $0.50. In summer $7.50, seniors and children 3-17 $6.50; in winter $5.50/$4.50/$15.)

⚡ OUTDOOR ACTIVITIES

A visitor sticking to paved byways will see a tiny fraction of the park and the majority of the park's visitors. Those interested in the endless outdoor options can hike or bike on more than 1600km of trails. Grab a free copy of the *Mountain Biking and Cycling Guide* or *Dayhikes in Banff* and peruse trail descriptions at information centers. For still more solitude, pick up *The Banff Backcountry Experience* and an overnight **camping permit** at a Visitors Center and head out to the backcountry. ($6 per person per day.) Be sure to check with the rangers at the information center for current weather, trail, and wildlife updates.

HIKING
Two easy trails are within walking distance of Banff Townsite, but longer, more rigorous trails abound farther away. The best escapes are found in the backcountry.

Fenland (2km, 1hr.). Follow Mt. Norquay Rd. to the outskirts, look for signs across the tracks on road's left side. This flat, easy trail crosses area shared by beaver, muskrat, and waterfowl, but is closed for elk calving in late spring and early summer.

Tunnel Mountain (2.5km, 2hr.). Follow Wolf St. east from Banff Ave., and turn right on St. Julien Rd. to reach the head of the steep, moderately difficult trail. Provides a dramatic view of the **Bow Valley** and **Mt. Rundle.** Tunnel Mountain has the distinction of being the Rockies' smallest mountain. Not that it matters.

Aylmer Pass (26.5km round-trip, 8hr.) This strenuous trail leaves from the shore of Lake Minnewanka on Lake Minnewanka Rd. (the extension of Banff Ave. across the Trans-Canada from town). Parking just above tour boat area. A steep climb to the summit yields a panoramic view of the lake and surrounding scenery. The trail can be abridged by hiking only 11.6km to the lookout, cutting the final 250m ascent.

Johnston Canyon (5.5km). West of the Norquay Interchange on Hwy. 1, then 18km along the Bow Valley Pkwy. (Hwy. 1A). A very popular moderate-to-strenuous half-day hike. A catwalk along the edge of the deep limestone canyon runs 1.1km over the thundering river to the canyon's lower falls, then another 1.6km to the upper falls. The trail continues for a rugged 3.2km to seven blue-green cold-water springs, known as the **Inkpots,** in a valley above the canyon. More than 42km of trails beyond the Inkpots are blissfully untraveled and punctuated with campgrounds roughly every 10km.

Sulphur Mountain (5.5km, 2hr.). Winds along a well-trodden trail to the peak, where a spectacular view awaits; the **Sulphur Mountain Gondola** doesn't charge for the 8min. downhill trip. (☎403-762-2523. Uphill $19, ages 6-15 $9.50, under 6 free.) The **Panorama Restaurant** (☎403-762-7486), perched atop the mountain, serves breakfast ($10) and lunch buffets ($13) from mid-May to mid-August.

BACKCOUNTRY
Backcountry trekking is the way to see Banff as the masses cannot. Banff's wild backcountry, replete with mind-boggling scenery, belies the civilized tourist trap that the townsite has become. Amateurs and experts alike should beware of dangerous and changing conditions on strenuous trails that do not receive as much maintenance as more accessible routes; consult park rangers for information. Trails to ask about include **Egypt Lake** (12.5km one-way, 2 days), **Twin Lakes** (9km one-way, 2 days), **Mystic Pass** (37km, 3 days), **Skoki Loop** (34km, 3 days), **Assiniboine Loop** (55km, 4 days), **Sawback Trail** (74km, 5 days), and **Mystic Pass-Flint's Park-Badger Pass Trail** (76km, 5 days).

BIKING
Biking is permitted on public roads, highways, and certain trails in the park. Spectacular scenery and a number of hostels and campgrounds make the **Bow Valley Pkwy. (Hwy. 1A)** and the **Icefields Pkwy. (Hwy. 93)** perfect for extended cycling trips. Every other store downtown seems to rent bikes; head to **Bactrax** or **Performance Sport** (see **Equipment Rental,** p. 274) for HI discounts. Parks Canada publishes a free *Mountain Biking and Cycling Guide* that describes trails and roadways where bikes are permitted; pick up a copy at bike rental shops or Visitors Centers.

WATERSPORTS
Fishing is legal in most of the park during specific seasons, but live bait and lead weights are not. Get a **permit** and check out regulations at the info center. (7-day permit $6.) **Bourgeau Lake,** a 7km hike in, is home to a particularly feisty breed of brook

GREAT NORTH

trout. Closer to the road, try **Herbert Lake,** off the Icefields Pkwy., or **Lake Minnewanka,** on Lake Minnewanka Rd. northeast of Banff. Lake Minnewanka Rd. passes **Johnson Lake,** where shallow warm water makes a perfect swimming hole.

Hydra River Guides runs whitewater rafting trips along the Kicking Horse River. (☎403-762-4554 or 800-644-8888; www.raftbanff.com. Up to Class V rapids. $90, HI members $76; includes lunch, transportation, and gear.) **Blast Adventures** leads half-day inflatable kayak trips on the rowdy Kananaskis River. (☎403-609-2009 or 888-802-5278; www.blastadventures.com. $64 per person including transportation, gear, and snacks.)

ACCOMMODATIONS

Mammoth modern hostels in Banff and Lake Louise anchor a chain of cozier hostels from Calgary to Jasper. Rustic hostels provide more of a wilderness experience (read: no electricity or flush toilets), and often have some of the park's best hiking and cross-country skiing right in their backyards. Wait-list beds become available at 6pm, and the larger hostels try to save a few stand-by beds for shuttle arrivals. Beds go quickly, especially during the summer, so make your reservations as early as possible. Reservations can be made through the southern **Alberta HI administration.** (☎866-762-4122; www.hostellingintl.ca.) Free reservations are held until 6pm, but can be guaranteed until later with a credit card. Because of a recent move towards centralizing the administration of these hostels, information regarding prices, closures, and facilities is currently in flux.

Rampart Creek Wilderness Hostel (HI), 34km south of the Icefield Centre. Close to several world-famous ice climbs (including Weeping Wall, 17km north), this hostel is a favorite for winter mountaineers and anyone who likes a rustic sauna after a hard day's hike. Wood-burning sauna, full-service kitchen. 12-bed co-ed cabins Su-Th $18, nonmembers $22; F-Sa $21/$25.

Castle Mountain Wilderness Hostel (HI), in Castle Junction, 1.5km east of the junction of Hwy. 1 and Hwy. 93 south, between Banff and Lake Louise. One of the hardest hostels to find, Castle Mountain offers a quieter alternative to the hubbub of its big brothers. Comfortable common area with huge bay windows. Friendly staff, hot showers, kitchen, laundry, electricity, and volleyball. Check-in 5-10pm; check-out 10am. Dorms Su-Th $18, nonmembers $22; F-Sa $21/$25.

Mosquito Creek Wilderness Hostel (HI), 103km south of the Icefield Centre and 26km north of Lake Louise. Across the creek from the Mosquito Creek campground. Close to the Wapta Icefield. Enormous living room with wood stove, wood-burning sauna, kitchen, and pump water. 16-bed co-ed cabins Su-Th $18, nonmembers $22; F-Sa $21/$25.

CAMPING

A chain of campgrounds stretches between Banff and Jasper. Extra-large, fully hooked-up grounds lie closer to the townsites; for more trees and fewer vehicles, try more remote sites farther from Banff and Lake Louise. At all park campgrounds, a **campfire permit** (includes firewood) is $4. Sites are first come, first served; go early. The sites below are listed from south to north and have no toilets or showers unless otherwise noted.

Tunnel Mountain Village, 4km from Banff Townsite on Tunnel Mountain Rd. With nearly 1200 sites, this is a camping metropolis. Trailer/RV area has 321 full RV sites, Village 2 has 188 sites, and Village 1 houses a whopping 618. Fires allowed in Village 1 only; all villages have showers. Village 2 is open year-round; 1 and 3 closed Oct. early May. Sites $17, with electricity $21; full RV sites $24.

Two Jack, 13km northeast of Banff, across Hwy.1. 381 main sites ($13) have no showers or disabled access; 80 lakeside sites ($17) do. Open mid-May to Aug.

Johnston Canyon, 26km northwest of Banff on Bow Valley Pkwy. 140 sites. Access to Johnston Canyon Trail (see p. 277). Showers. Open mid-June to mid-Sept. Sites $17.

Protection Mountain, 15km east of Lake Louise and 11km west of Castle Junction on the Bow Valley Pkwy. (Hwy. 1A). 89 spacious sites (14 trailer) in a basic campground. Open late June to early Sept. Sites $13.

Lake Louise, 1½km southeast of the Visitors Center on Fairview Rd. On Bow River, not the lake. Plenty of hiking and fishing awaits. Showers. 189 trailer sites with electricity, open year-round. 220 tent sites, open mid-May to Sept. Tent sites $17; RV sites $21.

Mosquito Creek, 103km south of the Icefield Centre and 26km north of Lake Louise. 32 sites with hiking access. Pit toilets. Sites $10.

Rampart Creek, 147km north of Banff, 34km south of the Icefield Centre, across the highway from Rampart Creek hostel and amazing ice climbing. Pit toilets. Open late June to Aug. Sites $10.

LAKE LOUISE TOWNSITE

The highest community in Canada (1530m), Lake Louise and the surrounding glaciers have often passed for Swiss scenery in movies and are the emerald in the Rockies' tiara of tourism. The lake was named in 1884 in honor of Queen Victoria's daughter, and its beauty is nothing short of royal.

VITAL STATS

Population: 1200

Visitor Info: Lake Louise Visitor Centre (☎403-522-3833), at Samson Mall on Village Rd. Open daily mid-June to Sept. 8am-6pm; Oct. to mid-June 9am-5pm. **Banff/Lake Louise Tourism Bureau,** in Banff (see p. 273).

Internet Access: The Depot (☎403-522-3870), in the Samson Mall. Open daily 6:30am-7pm.

Post Office: Mail services at The Depot (see above). **Postal Code:** TOL 1E0.

GETTING AROUND

The townsite's center, to the right off Hwy. 1/Hwy. 93, is literally that—a small shopping center with a few restaurants and a market. After a brief stop, it's best to push on to the lake, where the hardest task is escaping fellow gawkers at the posh, though aesthetically misplaced, **Chateau Lake Louise.** The chateau's canoe rentals are an unheard of $30 per hr. (☎403-522-3511. Room rates vary with the season, but are often prohibitively expensive.) **Parking** is ample in the city center and at motels and campsites around the lake.

OUTDOOR ACTIVITIES

The **Lake Louise Sightseeing Lift,** up Whitehorn Rd. and across the Trans-Canada Hwy. from Lake Louise, cruises up **Mt. Whitehorn.** (☎403-522-3555; www.skilouise.com. Open daily May 9am-4pm; June and Sept. 8:30am-9pm; July and Aug. 8am-6pm. $19, students and seniors $17, ages 6-12 $9, under 6 free. To enjoy breakfast at the top, add $2; for lunch, add $6.)

HIKING

If you don't want to succumb to the town's prices, you can view the water and its surrounding splendor from several hiking trails that begin in the

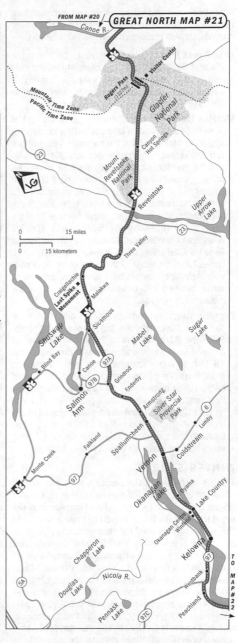

GREAT NORTH MAP #21
FROM MAP #20

GREAT NORTH

neighborhood and climb along the surrounding ridgelines. But be warned, with beauty comes crowds; expect masses of tourists (and bears).

Lake Agnes Trail (3.5km, 2½hr. round-trip), and the **Plain of Six Glaciers Trail** (5.5km, 4hr. round-trip) both end at teahouses and make for a lovely, if sometimes crowded, day hike with views down to the Lake. Open daily in summer 9am-6pm.

Moraine Lake, 15km from the village, at the end of Moraine Lake Rd. and off Lake Louise Dr. (no trailers or long RVs). Moraine lies in the awesome **Valley of the Ten Peaks,** opposite glacier-encrusted **Mt. Temple.** Join the multitudes on the **Rockpile Trail** for an eye-popping view of the lake and valley and a lesson in ancient ocean bottoms (10min. walk to the top). To escape the camera-wielding hordes, try one of the lake's more challenging trails, either **Sentinel Pass** via Larch Valley (6km one-way, 5-6hr.), with stunning views from flower-studded meadows, or **Wenkchemna Pass** via Eiffel Lake (10km one-way, full day), which carries hikers the length of the Valley of the Ten Peaks with incredible views in both directions. Be sure to arrive before 10am or after 4pm to see the view instead of the crowds.

Paradise Valley, depending on which way you hike it, can be an intense day hike or a relaxing overnight trip. From the **Paradise Creek Trailhead,** 2.5km up Moraine Lake Rd., the loop through the valley runs 18.1km through subalpine and alpine forests and along rivers (7½hr.; elevation gain 880m). One classic backpacking route runs from Moraine Lake up and over **Sentinel Pass,** joining the top of the Paradise Valley loop after 8km. A **backcountry campground** marks the mid-point from either trailhead. Grizzly activity often forces the park wardens to close the area in summer; check with the wardens before hiking in this area.

WINTER SPORTS

Winter activities in the park range from world-class ice climbing to ice fishing. Those 1600km of hiking trails make for exceptional **cross-country skiing** (**Moraine Lake Rd.** is closed to vehicle traffic in the winter, and is used for cross-country skiing, as are the backcountry trails), and three allied resorts offer a range of **skiing and snowboarding** opportunities from early November to mid-May. All have terrain parks for snowboarders. Shuttles to all the following three resorts leave from most big hotels in the townsites, and Banff and Lake Louise hostels typically have ticket and transportation **discounts** available for guests. Multi-day passes good for all three resorts are available at

the **Ski Banff/Lake Louise** office, 225 Banff Ave. (☎403-762-4561), in Banff, and at all resorts. Passes include free shuttle service and an extra night of skiing at Mount Norquay.

Sunshine Mountain (☎403-762-6500, snow report 760-7669; www.skibanff.com). Spreading across 3 mountains, with the most snowfall (9.9m) in the area, this mountain attracts loyal followers to its 3168 acres. Lift tickets $56; seniors, students under 24, and ages 13-17 $46; ages 6-12 $20.

Lake Louise (☎403-522-3555, snow report 403-762-4766; www.skilouise.com). The 2nd-largest ski area in Canada (4200 ski-able acres), with amazing views, over 1000m of vertical drop, and the best selection of expert terrain. Some simpler slopes cover plenty of the mountain. Lift tickets $59; students under 25 and seniors $47; ages 6-12 $15.

Mt. Norquay (☎403-762-4421). A local's mountain: small, and close to town. F night-skiing and 2-5hr. tickets. Lift tickets $47; students, ages 13-17, and over 55 $37; ages 6-12 $16. Night-skiing $23/$21/$12.

🍴🏨 FOOD & ACCOMMODATIONS

There are more food options in Banff than Lake Louise, so if you plan to dine out, it's best to stay in the city. The town's main shopping center, however, has a grocery and a few restaurant options. The **Village Market** (☎403-522-3894), in the Samson Mall, has fresh produce and the basics. **Laggan's Deli,** in Samson Mall, is always crowded. Thick sandwiches ($4-5) or fresh-baked loaves ($3) are always favorites. (☎403-522-2017. Open daily June-Sept. 6am-8pm; Oct.-May 6am-7pm. Cash or traveler's checks only.) The **Lake Louise Village Grill & Bar Family Restaurant & Lounge,** also in the Samson Mall, is as versatile as its name suggests, with steaks ($12-21), breakfast options, sandwiches, and Chinese food. (☎403-522-3879. Salads $5-12. Sandwiches and burgers $7-11. Chinese entrees $14-17. Open daily 11am-9pm.)

There are several campsites near Lake Louise (see p. 278), and one hostel in town. **Lake Louise International Hostel (HI),** 500m west of the Visitors Center in Lake Louise Townsite, on Village Rd. toward the Park Warden's office, is ranked fourth in the world by HI, and rightly so. More like a resort than a hostel, it boasts a reference library, a stone fireplace, two full kitchens, a sauna, and a quality cafe. (☎403-522-2200. Hub for mountaineering tours. Private rooms available. Internet $2 per 20min.

Check-in 3pm. Check-out 11am. Dorms $26, nonmembers $30.) There are also a handful of inns directly in Lake Louise, but they tend to be pricey. The posh **Lake Louise Inn,** 210 Village Rd., has an indoor swimming pool, suites with kitchens and fireplaces, and several in-house restaurants. (☎403-522-3791 or 800-661-9237; www.lakelouise.com. Rooms from $100.)

Welcome To BRITISH COLUMBIA

YOHO NATIONAL PARK

A Cree expression for awe and wonder, Yoho is the perfect name for this park. It sports some of the most engaging names in the Rockies, such as Kicking Horse Pass, named after Captain John Hector who was kicked in the chest by his horse. Driving down Yoho's narrow pass on Hwy. 1, visitors can see geological forces: massive bent and tilted sedimentary rock layers exposed in sharply eroded cliff faces, and rock bridges formed by water that has carved away the stone. Beneath these rock walls, Yoho overflows with natural attractions, including the largest waterfall in the Rockies—Takakkaw Falls—and paleontolologically illuminating 500 million-year-old fossils.

VITAL STATS

Area: 325,000 acres.

Visitors Info: Yoho National Park Visitor Centre (☎250-343-6783), in Field on Hwy. 1. Open daily in summer 8am-7pm; in spring and fall 9am-5pm; winter 9am-4pm.

Gateway town: Field.

Fees: $6, seniors $4.50, children $3.

GETTING AROUND

The park lies on the **Trans-Canada Hwy. (Hwy. 1),** next to Banff National Park. Within Yoho is the town of **Field,** 27km west of Lake Louise on Hwy. 1. **Parking** is available at campsites and most lookout points and trailheads.

SIGHTS

The **Great Divide** is both the boundary between Alberta and BC as well as the Atlantic and Pacific watersheds. Here a stream forks with one arm flowing 1500km to the Pacific Ocean, and the other flowing 2500km to the Atlantic via the Hudson Bay. It is also the site of the **Burgess Shale,** a layer of sedimentary rock containing imprints of the insect-like, soft-bodied organisms that inhabited the world's oceans prior to the Cambrian Explosion. Discovered in 1909, the unexpected complexity of these 505 million-year-old specimens changed the way paleontologists thought about evolution. Larger, clumsier animals known as humans have since lobbied to protect the shale from excessive tourism: educational hikes led by the **Yoho-Burgess Shale Foundation** are the only way to see it. (☎800-343-3006. July to mid-Sept. only. Call ahead. Full-day, 20km hike $45, under 12 $25.) A steep 6km loop to the equally old and trilobite-packed **Mt. Stephen Fossil Beds** runs $25. For easier sightseeing, follow the 14km of the Yoho Valley Rd. to views of the **Takakkaw Falls,** Yoho's most splendid waterfall, and the highest-altitude major falls in the Canadian Rockies.

HIKING

The park's six **backcountry campgrounds** and 400km of trail make for an intense wilderness experience, with countless quickly accessed trails exhibiting scenery equal to and beyond that of the larger parks. Before setting out, pick up **camping permits** ($6 per person per day), maps, and the free *Backcountry Guide to Yoho National Park* at the Visitors Center. Whiskey Jack Hostel (see p. 282) is also well stocked with trail info. The park's finest terrain is in the Yoho Valley, accessible only after the snow melts in mid- to late summer.

Iceline Trail (via Little Yoho 19.8km, via Celeste Lake 17km). Starts at the hostel. Takes hikers through forests of alder, spruce, and fir before leading them above the treeline, over glacial moraines, and past the striated rock and icy pools of Emerald Glacier. Moderate.

Emerald Triangle (21.5km round-trip). The route travels through the Yoho Pass to the Wapta Highline trail, Burgess Pass, and back to the start. Most of the journey is above treeline with breathtaking views over much of Yoho's diverse landscape. Moderate.

Mt. Hunter Lookout to Upper Lookout (12.8km one-way). Cuts through lower altitudes, with a nice view of Kicking Horse and Beaverfoot valleys. Moderate.

Wapta Falls (4.8km round-trip). The trailhead is not marked on Hwy. 1 for westbound traffic as there is no left-turn lane. Continue 3km to the west entrance of the park, turn around, and come back east. Highlights include the Kicking Horse River's 30m drop. The least ambitious and least spectacular of the hikes. Easy.

FOOD

The most convenient food stop in Yoho, and potentially a sit-all-day-stop, is the ◤**Truffle Pigs Cafe and General Store,** on Stephen Ave. in Field, which sells basic foodstuffs, microbrews, wine, and camping supplies. Local crafts line the walls, and the owners peddle sandwiches ($4.25), breakfast ($4.50-7), and delicious dinners. (☎250-343-6462. Has the only **ATM** in the area. Open daily in summer 8am-10pm; in winter M-Sa 10am-7pm.)

ACCOMMODATIONS

With one of the best locations of the Rocky Mountain hostels, the ◤**Whiskey Jack Hostel (HI),** 13km off Hwy. 1 on the Yoho Valley Rd., blurs the line between civilization and nature. It offers a kitchen, plumbing, propane light, access to Yoho's best high-country trails, and the splendor of the Takakkaw Falls from the porch. Reserve through the Banff Hostel. (☎403-762-4122. Open mid-June to mid-Oct., depending on snow. Dorms Su-Th $18, nonmembers $22; F-Sa $21/$25.)

The four official **frontcountry campgrounds** offer a total of 200 sites, all accessible from the highway. All sites are first come, first served, but only Monarch and Kicking Horse fill up regularly in summer. ◤**Takakkaw Falls Campground** is situated beneath mountains, glaciers, and the magnificent falls 14km up curvy Yoho Valley Rd. It offers only pump water and pit toilets, and campers must park in the Falls lot and haul their gear 650m to the peaceful sites. (35 sites. Open late June until snow. Sites $13.) **Hoodoo Creek,** on the west end of the park, has kitchen shelters, hot water, flush toilets, a nearby river, and a playground. (30 sites. Open June to early Sept. Sites $13.) **Monarch Campground** sits at the junction of Yoho Valley Rd. and Hwy. 1. (46 sites and 10 walk-ins. Open late June to early Sept. Sites $13.) **Kicking Horse,** another kilometer up Yoho Valley Rd., has toilets and is wheelchair accessible. (86 sites. Hot showers.

Open mid-May to mid-Oct. $18.) Reserve one of two backcountry **alpine huts** through the Alpine Club of Canada. (☎403-678-3200. $16.)

LEAVING YOHO NATIONAL PARK
Leave Yoho traveling west on **Hwy. 1.** Golden is a bit south of the intersection with **Hwy. 95.**

GOLDEN. Surrounded by six national parks (Glacier, Yoho, Banff, Jasper, Kootenay, and Mount Revelstoke), Golden is a convenient base for regional exploration and outdoor activities. At the foot of Kicking Horse Ski Mountain, the **Kicking Horse Hostel,** 518 Station Ave., matches its location with ski-lodge decor, complete with skis and snowshoes hanging from the walls. (☎250-344-5071. Kitchen, free linens. Co-ed dorms $25.)

APPROACHING GLACIER NATIONAL PARK
Take **Hwy. 95 North** to **Hwy. 1 West.**

GLACIER NATIONAL PARK

This aptly named national park (not to be confused with the Glacier National Park in Montana) is home to over 400 monolithic ice floes that cover one-tenth of its 1350 sq. km area. The jagged peaks and steep, narrow valleys of the Columbia Range not only make for breathtaking scenery but also prevent development in the park. In late summer, brilliant explosions of mountain wildflowers offset the deep green of the forests. In the winter, more literal explosions shake the calm of the valleys—scientists fire 105mm shells into mountain sides to create and observe controlled avalanches.

(VITAL STATS)

Area: 333,000 acres

Visitor Info: Rogers Pass Information Centre (☎250-837-7500), on Hwy. 1 in Glacier.

Gateway Town: Roger

Fees: $5, seniors $4.25, under 16 $2.50.

▐ GETTING AROUND. Glacier is 350km west of Calgary and 723km east of Vancouver. There are no roads in the park other than the **Trans-Canada Highway (Hwy. 1),** from which all trailheads depart.

 Glacier National Parks straddles two time zones; after the Rogers Pass you enter the Pacific Time Zone, where it is 1hr. earlier.

■ **HIKING.** More than 140km of rough, often steep trails lead from the highway, inviting mountaineers to attempt the unconquerable. While the highway works its way through the park's lush valleys, a majority of the area in the parkland lies above the treeline, providing for incredibly steep, high altitude, highly beautiful hikes. Leaving from the info center, the **Abandoned Rails Trail** (1.25km one-way, 1hr.) follows the 1885 Canadian Pacific Railway bed over the top of historic Rogers Pass. From the Beaver River Trailhead, **Copperstain Trail** (16km one-way, 6hr.) leads uphill through alpine meadows. This trail is often combined with the longer Beaver Valley Trail to create a four-day backpacking loop. The challenging **Balu Pass Trail** (10km round-trip, 4hr.) begins at the west edge of Rogers Centre parking lot, near Rogers Pass Information Centre. The Ursus Major and Ursus Minor peaks provide the best chance of seeing wildlife. This trail is prime bear habitat; check with park wardens before embarking. **Hermit Trail** (3km one-way, 2hr.) climbs nearly 800m into the Hermit Glacier, hanging high over Rogers Pass.

■ **CAMPING.** Glacier has two recently rebuilt campgrounds: **Illecillewaet** (ill-uh-SILL-uh-way-et), 3.5km west of Roger's Pass (60 sites; open late June to early Oct.; $16), and smaller **Loop Brook,** another 3km west on Hwy. 1. (20 sites; open July-Sept.; $16) Both offer toilets, kitchen shelters with cook stoves, and firewood. The park has no vehicle-accessible sites until late June; **Canyon Hot Springs** (see below) is the closest alternative for drivers. Backcountry campers must purchase a **backcountry pass** from the Parks Canada office in Revelstoke (☎205-837-7500; $8 per day) or from the Rogers Pass Information Centre.

 LEAVING GLACIER NATIONAL PARK
Follow **Hwy. 1 West** to Revelstoke.

 CANYON HOT SPRINGS
On Hwy. 1

At Canyon Hot Springs, two spring water swimming pools simmer at 26°C and 40°C (86°F and 106°F) to ease aching muscles. (☎250-837-2420; www.canyonhotsprings.com. Open daily July-Aug. 9am-10pm; May-June and Sept. 9am-9pm. $6.50, seniors and ages 4-14 $5.50, under 4 free. Sites $22, with water and electricity $30. Free showers.) The neighboring **Apex Raft Company**

runs 2-4hr. whitewater rafting tours on the Illecillewaet River's Class II-III rapids. (☎888-232-6666; www.apexrafting.com. $74, under 17 $62.)

REVELSTOKE

Located on both the Columbia River and the Canadian Pacific Railway, Revelstoke was born as a transfer station for boats and trains. Although still largely a stopover for travelers to the Rockies, Revelstoke is finally coming into its own. Revelstoke's laid-back social life complements the physical rigors of the area. Excellent hostels, free and surprisingly lively outdoor entertainment in the town center, and extensive outdoor pursuits make Revelstoke a welcoming destination.

VITAL STATS

Population: 7500

Visitor Info: Visitors Centre (☎205-837-3522; www.revelstokecc.bc.ca), at the junction of Mackenzie and Victoria Rd. Open daily July-Aug. 9am-6pm; May-June 9am-5pm. **Parks Canada** (☎205-837-7500), at Boyle Ave. and 3rd St. Open M-F 8:30am-noon and 1-4:30pm.

Internet Access: Revelstoke Public Library, 600 Campbell Ave. (☎205-837-5095). Open Tu noon-8pm, W noon-7pm, Th 10am-4pm, F 10am-5pm.

Post Office: 307 W. 3rd St. (☎205-837-3228). Open M-F 8:30am-5pm. **Postal Code:** V0E 2S0.

■ **GETTING AROUND**

Revelstoke is on the **Trans-Canada Hwy. (Hwy. 1),** 285km west of Banff. The town is easily navigated on foot or by bike, hence the lack of traffic and abundance of **parking** spaces downtown. **Mt. Revelstoke National Park** lies just east of town on Hwy. 1. Most of the town is on the east bank of the river, and **Victoria Rd.** is the main street that curves parallel to the highway.

■ **SIGHTS**

Revelstoke Railway Museum, 719 W. Track St., off Victoria Rd., tells of the construction of the Trans-Canada line, which was completed a few miles from Revelstoke in 1885. Other exhibits include a steam engine and a passenger car. (☎877-837-6060; www.railwaymuseum.com. Open daily July-Aug. 9am-8pm; May-June and

Sept. 9am-5pm; Apr. and Oct. M-Sa 9am-5pm; Nov. M-F 9am-5pm; Dec.-Mar. M-F 1-5pm. $6, seniors $5, ages 7-16 $3, under 7 free.) The mechanical marvels of the **Revelstoke Dam** comprise one of North America's largest hydroelectric developments. (☎205-837-6515. Open daily mid-June to mid-Sept. 8am-8pm, May to mid-June and mid-Sept. to mid-Oct. 9am-5pm.)

The town also hosts a blues festival during the third weekend in June, a lumberjack competition in early July, and a railroad festival in August.

▐▌ OUTDOOR ACTIVITIES

SUMMER ACTIVITIES

A relaxing aquatic experience can be found with **Natural Escapes Kayaking,** 1115 Pineridge Crest. (☎205-837-2679; www.naturalescapes.ca. $25 per 2hr., $40 for 2hr. lesson and tour.) The 140 bolted routes on Begbie Bluffs offer exceptional **sport climbing** (from the small parking area almost 9km down 23 South from Hwy. 1, the bluffs are a 10min. walk; take the left fork). Rogers Pass and the surrounding peaks offer a limitless amount of year-round opportunity to hone one's mountaineering skills. **Glacier House Resort** has a large range of equipment rentals and trips year-round. (☎205-827-9594; www.glacierhouse.com. Canoe rentals $30 per half-day, $40 per day. Mt. Revelstoke guided day hike $85 per day.)

WINTER SPORTS

Winter in Revelstoke brings 60-80 ft. of powder, and excellent downhill skiing. **Powder Springs Resort** is only 5km outside town and maintains one chairlift and 21 trails with a 1000 ft. vertical drop on the bottom third of Mt. MacKenzie. (☎800-991-4455; www.catpowder.com. Lift tickets $28-32.) The **Powder Springs Inn,** 200 3rd St. W. (☎205-837-5151; www.catpowder.com), offers Ski & Stay packages for as little as $30 per day and rents skis for $20 per day. The **SameSun Backpacker Lodge** (see below) also offers lift-ticket packages. **Parks Canada** offers excellent advice and brochures on area nordic trails and world-class backcountry skiing. They also provide info on area snowmobiling, as can **Great Canadian Snowmobile Tours,** by Frisby Ridge, 6km north of town on West Side Rd. (☎205-837-5030 or 877-837-9594; www.snowmobilerevelstoke.com. Snowmobiles $210-300 per day.)

MT. REVELSTOKE NATIONAL PARK

Adjacent to town, Mt. Revelstoke National Park furnishes convenient and satisfying access to nature with its astounding scenery. It is a favorite of mountain bikers and hikers. The park requires a **National Parks Permit** ($5, seniors $4.25, under 16 $2.50) that can be purchased at the **Parks Canada Office** in Revelstoke. The park is too tiny to offer extensive backcountry opportunities, but does boast two backcountry campgrounds, **Eva Lake,** a 6km hike, and **Jade Lake,** a 9km hike. (Each has 4 sites. No pumped water. Jade Lake is equipped with a bear pole. Open July-Sept. Sites $8 per person.) Two boardwalks off Hwy. 1 on the east side of the park access the trails. **Skunk Cabbage Trail** (1.3km, 30min.) leads through acres of stinking perfection: skunk cabbage plants tower at heights of over 1.5m. **Giant Cedars Trail** (500m, 15min.) has majestic, over-600-year-old trees growing around babbling brooks. **Meadows in the Sky Parkway** (Summit Rd.) branches off Hwy. 1 about 1.5km east of town, leading to a 1km hike up Mt. Revelstoke to subalpine meadows.

▐▌ FOOD

The town's market is **Cooper's Supermarket,** 555 Victoria St. (☎205-837-4372. Open daily 8am-9pm.)

▨ **Luna Taverna,** 102 2nd St. East (☎205-837-2499). Titanic helpings of Greek and Mediterranean fare. Appetizers run $6-8, full meals $12-18. Staying at SameSun Lodge earns free cheesecake. Open Tu-Sa 11am-2pm and 5-9pm.

Woolsey Creek Cafe, 212 Mackenzie Ave. (☎205-837-5500). Offers meals in a relaxed, toy-strewn atmosphere. Internet access $1 per 10min. Breakfast $5-8. Lunch and dinner $6-15. $5 pints. Open M-Th and Su 7:30am-11pm, F-Sa 7:30am-midnight.

Chalet Deli and Bakery, 555 Victoria St. (☎205-837-5552), across the parking lot from Cooper's. This bakery is also a lunch spot with a hot deli, pizza by the slice ($2.50), fresh baked bread (loaves $2), and sandwiches ($4.50). Open M-Sa 6am-6pm.

Main Street Cafe, 317 Mackenzie Ave. (☎205-873-6888) at 3rd St. Serves breakfast ($5-8) and sandwiches ($5-6) at a pleasant downtown patio. Open daily July 8am-9pm; Aug.-June 8am-5pm.

ACCOMMODATIONS

 SameSun Backpacker Lodge, 400 2nd St. West (☎877-562-2783; www.samesun.com). The friendly staff hosts a lively youth hostel scene and a more sedate older crowd in the private rooms. Several kitchens, full bathrooms, living room with TV, and a constant mellow soundtrack. Free pool table and backyard BBQ. Internet $1 per 10 min. Reception 24hr. Dorms $20; singles $39-43.

Martha Creek Provincial Park, 22km north of Revelstoke on Hwy 23. Beach and a boat launch. The campground tends to be full of RVs, so get there early if you want a good spot. Open Apr.-Oct. Sites $14.

Williamson's Lake Campground, 1818 Williamson Lake Rd. (☎888-676-2267; www.williamsonlakecampground.com), 5km southeast of town on Airport Way. Farther from the highway than competitors, next to a peaceful swimming hole. Laundry and general store. Reception 8am-9:30pm. Open mid-Apr. to Oct. Sites $16; RVs $20. Free showers.

 LEAVING REVELSTOKE
Follow **Hwy. 1 West** 74km to Sicamous.

👁 **ENCHANTED FOREST**
Between Revelstoke and Sicamous on Hwy. 1.
Looking slightly out of place among pines and ferns, over 350 colorful, slightly kitschy, concrete figurines of fairy-tale creatures inhabit a lush, old-growth forest. Also on-site is British Columbia's tallest tree house. Nearby fish ponds and beaver dams are accessible via row boat. (☎866-944-9744; www.enchantedforestbc.com. Open daily June-Aug. 8am-dusk; May and Sept. 9am-5pm. $6.50, ages 3-15 $5, under 3 free.)

 On Hwy. 1 at Craigellachie, the **Last Spike Monument** stands in honor of the completion of the transcontinental Canadian Pacific Railway; the last spike was pounded in here on November 7th, 1885.

SICAMOUS. The houseboat capital of Canada and gateway to the nearby Shuswap Lakes, Sicamous is also home to the the the **D Dutchman Dairy,** a tasty pit stop. Savor 40 flavors of ice cream (2 scoops $3.25) and wander around the petting zoo to see llamas, cows and calves, donkeys, and a camel. (Open daily 8am-9pm. Cash only.)

LEAVING SICAMOUS
Continue south on **Hwy 97A** through the Okanagan Valley to **Kelowna.**

THE ROAD THROUGH THE OKANAGAN VALLEY

The road enters Okanagan Valley, or "Canada's California," known for its bountiful fruit harvests. The valley lures visitors with summer blossoms, ample sun, plentiful wineries, and tranquil lakes. The **Okanagan Connector** (Hwy. 97C) links the valley to Vancouver in a 4hr. drive, making it a popular vacation destination among sun-starved coastal British Columbians. In the winter, **Big White** and **Apex Mountain** ski resorts both attract skiers and snowboarders looking to avoid long lines and pricey lift tickets at Whistler.

KELOWNA

In the heart of the Okanagan Valley, Kelowna (kuh-LOW-nuh) is one of Canada's richest agricultural regions and a popular tourist destination. The town's fruit stands, wineries, and independent shops draw thousands every summer. In the winter, those not skiing in Whistler find the slopes of Big White Ski Resort equally rewarding.

VITAL STATS

Population: 108,000

Visitor Info: Tourism Kelowna, 544 Harvey Ave. (☎250-861-1515; www.tourismkelowna.org). Open May-Sept. M-F 8am-7pm, Sa-Su 9am-7pm; Oct.-Apr. M-F 8am-5pm, Sa-Su 10am-3pm.

Internet Access: Okanagan Regional Library Kelowna Branch, 1380 Ellis St. (☎250-762-2800) Open M and F-Sa 10am-5:30pm, Tu-Th 10am-9pm.

Post Office: 101-591 Bernard Ave. (☎250-868-8480). Open M-F 8:30am-5:30pm, Sa 9am-5pm. **Postal Code:** V1Y 7G0.

GETTING AROUND

Kelowna lies on **Hwy. 97** at the eastern shore of Okanagan Lake. Hwy. 97, known as **Harvey Ave.** in town, runs east-west across the lake and bisects the town. In the east, Hwy. 97 becomes the **Okanagan Hwy.** and curves north, intersecting **Hwy. 33** by the golf course. The floating bridge across the lake is one-of-a-kind in Canada.

GREAT NORTH

⑤ SIGHTS

PARKS & BEACHES. The sun is Kelowna's main attraction, warming Okanagan parks and beaches for an average of 2000hr. per year. **City Park** and **Waterfront Park**, on the west end of downtown, are popular hangouts. **Boyce Gyro Park**, on Lakeshore Rd. south of the Okanagan Bridge, features beach volleyball. **Kelowna Parasail Adventures** transforms patrons into living kites, floating them high above the lake. (1310 Water St. at the docks of Grand Okanagan Resort north of City Park. ☎ 250-868-4838; www.parasailcanada.com. Open daily May-Sept. 9am-dusk. $50.) Take a sail around the lake with **Go With the Wind Cruises.** (On Waterfront Walkway. ☎ 250-763-5204; www.gowiththewind.com. $25 per hr. Open daily May-Sept. 9am-6pm.)

KELOWNA MUSEUM. The museum houses a regional artifacts, including those of the Okanagan and other First Nations. (470 Queensway Ave. ☎ 250-763-2417; www.kelownamuseum.ca. Open Tu-Sa 10am-5pm. Suggested donation $2, children $1.)

WINE & FRUIT. Over the past few years, the Okanagan Valley has become the center of the Canadian wine industry. Kelowna and the surrounding area is home to 12 of the valley's wineries, all of which offer tastings. Contact the Visitors Center or call **Okanfana Wine Country Tours** at ☎ 250-868-9463 for a complete list of tours. Wine and cheese parties are common at the **Okanagan Wine Festival** for ten days in early October, for four days at its lesser counterpart in late April, and for three days at the **Icewine Festival** in late January. (☎ 250-861-6654; www.owfs.com. Events $15-65 each.) **Mission Hill,** overlooking the west bank of Okanagan Lake, is one of Kelowna's most respected wineries, offering tours of an underground wine cavern, bell tower, and outdoor amphitheater, and tastes of four wines. (1730 Mission Hill Rd. Cross the bridge west of town, turn left on Boucherie Rd., and follow the signs. ☎ 250-768-6448; www.missionhillwinery.com. Open daily 10am-5pm; July-Sept. until 7pm. Tours daily Oct.-Apr. 11am, 1, 3pm; May-June and Sept. every hr. 11am-4pm; July-Aug. every 30min. 10am-5pm. $5.) **Kelowna Land and Orchard,** the town's oldest family-owned farm, offers a 45min. hayride that explains farming techniques. The tour finishes at the orchard's farm stand. (3002 Dunster Rd., off KLO Rd. on E. Kelowna. ☎ 250-763-1091; www.k-l-o.com. Open daily Apr.-Oct.

9am-4pm; call for winter hours. Tours June-Aug. 11am, 1, 3pm; Apr.-May and Sept.-Oct. 11am and 3pm. $6.50, students $3, under 12 free.)

⚠ OUTDOOR ACTIVITIES

Equipment rental is available at **Sports Rent,** 3000 Pandosy St. (☎ 250-861-5699; www.sportsrentkelowna.com. Mountain bikes from $23; in-line skates $11; kayaks $30; canoes $35. Open daily May-Sept. 9am-6pm; Oct.-Apr. 9am-8pm.)

HIKING & BIKING

While Kelowna's main attraction is Okanagan Lake, surrounding areas offer excellent opportunities for off-road fun. Ponderosa pines dominate this hot and dry landscape. **Knox Mountain,** just north of the city, features many hiking trails as well as a paved road to the summit. Hike, bike, or drive to the top for a spectacular view of Kelowna and Okanagan. While you're there, don't pass up a chance to check out one of the city's natural secrets, **⧉Paul's Tomb.** A secluded gravel beach named for the grave of one of Kelowna's early settlers, it's only a 2km walk or bike from either the trailhead at the base of the mountain or the one at the lookout halfway up.

Bear Creek Regional Park's 20km of trails include a challenging hike that ascends to the canyon rim to view the city and lake. Much of the large and popular **Okanagan Mountain Provincial Park** was ravaged by a voracious 2003 wildfire, leaving large portions of the park closed. Ask at the Visitors Center for updates on its opening status.

Another biking trail is the **Kettle Valley Railbed,** which passes through scenic **Myra-Bellevue Provincial Park** and the stunning **Myra Canyon** and then through the only desert in western Canada. The railbed through Myra Canyon stretches 12km, but the bike trail continues all the way to Penticton.

In addition, there are 18 regional parks within a 40km radius of Kelowna, providing everything from picnic areas to swim spots, and in some cases nature and hiking trails. Highlights include the **Mission Creek Regional Park,** with over 12km of hiking trails and a connection to the **Mission Creek Greenway,** with 7km of trails leading to the waterfront; and **Glen Canyon Regional Park,** offering hikes along the old concrete flume and the cliff edges.

WINTER SPORTS

In the winter, downhill skiing is the most popular outdoor activity in the Okanagan Valley. **Big White Ski Resort** offers 15 lifts serving over 100 trails throughout 7355 acres of terrain. The resort completed a $130 million expansion at the beginning of the 2004 season, adding two new chairlifts and a state-of-the-art terrain park. (On a clearly marked access road off Hwy. 33, east of town. ☎250-765-3101; www.bigwhite.com. Open mid-Nov. to late Apr. Lift tickets $56, ages 13-18 $48. Night skiing $16. Ski rental $28; snowboards $35.) Those preferring a smaller, less crowded mountain should head to **Crystal Mountain,** with 22 trails and an 800 ft. drop located at the top of Glenrosa Rd., 10min. from the Westbank overpass of Hwy. 97. (☎250-768-5189; www.crystalresort.com. Open mid-Nov. to mid-Dec. Sa-Su 9am-3:30pm; mid-Dec. to mid-Jan. daily 9am-3:30pm; mid-Jan. to Mar. Th-Su 9am-3:30pm. $34, ages 13-17 $27. Ski rental $26; snowboards $30; snowshoes $15.)

CLIMBING

The area around Kelowna boasts numerous spots for climbers. Along the KVR, in the Myra-Bellevue Provincial Park are the **Boulderfields,** with six main areas and 25 independent walls, almost all of advanced difficulty. **Idabel Lake,** lying near Okanagan Falls on Rte. 33 off Hwy. 97, boasts the best bouldering routes in the area. Unfortunately, the most popular climbing in the area at **Kelowna Crags,** by Chute Lake Mountain Park, has been closed since the area was decimated by a 2003 forest fire. When open, the area offers climbs of a range of difficulties, as well as a trail to the top for spectators to see the lake vista and relax in well-worn chairs constructed from stones. (Follow Lakeshore Ave. to Chute Lake Rd. Follow the road for 2 mi. after it becomes a dirt road, 1 mi. after the sign marking the edge of Kelowna.)

FOOD

Kelowna overflows with fresh produce. Find juicy delights at the stands outside town along **Benvoulin Rd.** and **KLO Rd.,** or head south on **Lakeshore Dr.** to the pick-your-own cherry orchards. **Bernard Ave.** is lined with restaurants and cafes.

The Bohemian Bagel Cafe, 363 Bernard Ave. (☎250-862-3517; www.vtours.com/boh). Rich breakfast and lunch offerings in a colorful atmosphere on the main drag. Try mango-chutney turkey salad ($7), homemade bread and soup ($5), or a unique sandwich (from $5). Open Su 9am-1pm, Tu-F 7:30am-2:30pm, Sa 8:30am-2:30pm.

The Pier Marina Pub & Grill, 2035 Campbell Rd. (☎250-769-4777), just across the floating bridge outside Kelowna. This unassuming joint serves up hot and heaping lunches—calamari ($7), burgers with lots of fixings ($8), and chowder ($5)—along with dinners at a steal, including an $11 12 oz. sirloin steak. Open M-W and Su 11am-midnight, Th-Sa 11am-1am.

Le Triskell Creperie, 467 Bernard Ave. (☎250-763-5151). This long, narrow restaurant with Parisian artwork manages to emulate the essence of a sidewalk bistro. Open M-W 9am-2pm, Th-F 9am-2pm and 5-10pm, Sa 10am-2pm and 5-10pm.

Tripke Bakery Konditorei & Cafe, 567 Bernard Ave. (☎250-763-7666). Grab a loaf of health bread ($3.15) before taking off for an outdoor adventure. Open M-Sa 8am-5:30pm.

▗ ACCOMMODATIONS

Warm, dry summer days attract thousands, so make reservations, even at campgrounds. If everything is full, there are inns and chain hotels along **Lakeshore Dr.** and **Hwy. 97** in either direction.

Kelowna International Hostel (HI), 2343 Pandosy St. (☎250-763-6024; www.kelowna-hostel.bc.ca). Only 1 block from the beach in a colorfully painted home. This laid-back hostel is a budget paradise with super-friendly hosts, comfortable lounge, and daily activities. Pancake breakfast included. Internet $1 per 30min. Reception 7am-11pm. Dorms $19, nonmembers $20; private rooms $40.

SameSun Backpacker's Lodge, 245 Harvey Ave. (877-562-2783; www.samesun.com), just across the floating bridge. This lively hostel features keg parties and BBQs almost every summer night. For daytime fun, join a bike trip to Mission Creek ($20) or spend the day on the SameSun houseboat ($27). Key deposit $5. Dorms $20-24; private rooms $49-57.

By the Bridge B&B, 1942 McDougall St. (☎250-860-7518; www.villagenet.ca/bythebridge), at the east end of Okanagan Lake Bridge, minutes from the beach and downtown. Cozy rooms, private baths, and a continental breakfast including freshly baked bread, jam, and fruit. Check-out 11am. Singles $49-69; doubles $59-79; triples $79-89; quads $89-99.

Bear Creek Provincial Park, (☎800-689-9025 or 494-6500), 9km north of Hwy. 97 on Westside Rd. Day use/picnic area and camping. Shaded lakeside sites, 400m of Okanagan lake shore, boat launch, and a walking trail along the creek and waterfront. Sites $22.

 **LEAVING KELOWNA**
Continue south on scenic **Hwy. 97** to Penticton.

PENTICTON

Indigenous peoples named the region between Okanagan and Skaha Lakes Pen-tak-tin, "a place to stay forever." Today, Penticton is known more commonly as the "Peach City," complete with a giant peach on the waterfront that would make Roald Dahl proud. Penticton is more than an agricultural mecca, however; the city bustles with tourists and fruit harvesters during the summer.

VITAL STATS

Population: 41,000

Visitor Info: Penticton Wine and Information Center, 888 W. Westminster Ave. (☎800-663-5052; www.penticton.org), at Power St. Free Internet. Open July-Sept. daily 8am-8pm; Oct.-June M-F 9am-6pm, Sa-Su 10am-5pm.

Internet Access: Penticton Public Library, 785 Main St. (☎250-492-0024). Open M, W, F-Sa 10am-5:30pm; Tu and Th 10am-9pm; in winter also Su 1-5pm.

Post Office: 56 W. Industrial Ave. (☎250-492-5769). Open M-F 8:30am-5pm. **Postal Code:** V2A 6J8.

GETTING AROUND

Penticton lies at the junction of **Hwy. 3** and **Hwy. 97,** at the southern extreme of the Okanagan Valley. **Okanagan Lake** borders the north end of town, while smaller **Skaha Lake** lies to the south. **Main St.** bisects the city from north to south, turning into **Skaha Lake Rd.** as it approaches the lake.

SIGHTS

S.S. SICAMOUS AND S.S. NARAMATA.

While lounging on the beachfront, meander over to the *S.S. Sicamous* and *S.S. Naramata,* restored steel-hulled ships from 1914 that transported goods and passengers to the communities along the Okanagan. Tours offer a window into the leisure and luxury of the early Okanagan Valley; for those truly intrigued, the Sicamous also hosts a musical about life on board the ship. Just adjacent is the small but fragrant and calming **Rose Garden** in which to sit or stroll. (*1099 Lakeshore Dr.* ☎250-492-0403; www.sssicamous.com. Open daily June-Sept. 9am-9pm; Apr.-May and Oct.-Dec. 15 9am-6pm; Jan. 15-Mar. 9am-5pm. $5.)

SUMMERLAND. Just 12 mi. north of Penticton on Hwy. 20, the town of Summerland is home to ornamental gardens and the preserved portion of the 1910 **Kettle Valley Steam Railway** today operating as a tourist attraction. The 1½hr. tour provides views of vineyards and the highest bridge on the original railway. (*Take Hwy. 97 to Summerland exit. Follow Prairie Valley Rd. then turn right on Doherty Ave.* ☎877-494-8424; www.kettlevalleyrail.org. Tour runs May to early Oct. M and Sa-Su 10:30am and 1:30pm; July-Sept. also Th-F. $16, students $14.)

PENTICTON MUSEUM. The museum chronicles the history of Penticton's gold trails and the Kettle Valley Railway, as well as First Nations history, preserved in over 8000 artifacts. (*785 Main St., same building as the library.* ☎250-490-2451. Open July-Aug. M-Sa 10am-5pm; Sept.-June Tu-Sa 10am-5pm. Suggested donation $2, children $1.)

OUTDOOR ACTIVITIES

LAKEFRONT. In the summer, the Penticton tourist trade revolves around **Lake Okanagan** and **Lake Skaha.** Youths gravitate toward Skaha Lake Park to the south and to the summer afternoon pastime of tubing down the Okanagan River canal from Lake Okanagan to Lake Skaha. **Coyote Cruises** rents tubes for $11 and provides a free shuttle for the return. (*215 Riverside.* ☎250-492-2115. Open daily late June to Sept. 10am-6pm.) **Pier Water Sports,** just beyond the Peach on the beach pier, rents more water vessels for those with an active spirit and a few extra bucks. (*45 N. Martin St.* ☎250-493-8864. Jet skis $83 per hr.; canoes $16 per hr.; kayaks $19 per hr. Banana boat rides $10.)

HIKING & BIKING. Although the lakes are the star attractions, those looking for land-based adventures will not be disappointed. Visit **Munson Mountain,** an extinct volcano with "PENTICTON" spelled out in letters 50 ft. high and 30 ft. wide, for a bird's eye view of the valley. *(Take Vancouver Ave. north of town, turn right on Tupper Ave. then left on Middle Bench Rd., to Munson Mt. Rd. The road takes you within minutes of the summit.)* Bikers, walkers, and runners will enjoy dozens of pathways and trails in the city and surrounding hills, many of which offer panoramic views of the lakes. The abandoned tracks of the **Kettle Valley Railway (KVR)** run through Penticton and along both sides of Okanagan Lake and are the site of the Trans-Canada Trail in this area. Traveling north, you'll pass through orchards, vineyards, and wineries, all with a fantastic view of the lake. Those looking for a daytrip from Penticton can travel 21km at a gradual ascent to Glenfir, or 41km to Chute Lake. For a short, moderate hike, follow the trail on the western side of the river channel to Sage Mesa for stunning views. *(Take Vancouver Ave. north to the intersection with Vancouver Pl. ☎ 250-496-5220; www.kettlevalleytrail.com.)*

CLIMBING. The **Skaha Bluffs,** southeast of town on Valley View Rd., feature some of Canada's best rock climbing. For hikers and spectators, there are trails throughout the park. Check out *Skaha Rock Climbs,* by Howie Richardson, for detailed info on climbs. **Skaha Rock Adventures** offers guide and instructional services. *(113-437 Martin St. ☎ 250-493-1765; www.skaharockclimbing.com. Open M-F 9am-5pm. Guided climbing $115.)*

SKIING. Apex Mountain Resort offers the best downhill skiing in the area. Apex has downhill, cross-country, and night skiing on over 60 runs with a 2000 ft. vertical drop. They also boast a halfpipe and terrain park for boarders and an extensive glade area for the adventurous. In the summer, ski slopes become a dream come true for mountain bikers. *(Off Green Mtn. Rd. west of Penticton on Hwy. 3. ☎ 877-777-2739; www.apexresort.com. Night skiing W and F-Sa 4:30-9:30pm. Lift tickets $48, ages 13-18 $39, ages 8-12 $29. Rental equipment $29/$16/$13. Night skiing $12.)*

🍴 FOOD

The **Penticton Farmers Market,** 100 Block Main St., in Gyro Park, sells local produce and baked goods. *(☎ 250-770-3276. Open June-Oct. Sa 8:30am-noon.)* You can't miss fruits and vegetables at family stands (look for signs on the side of the road) both north and south of town on Hwy.

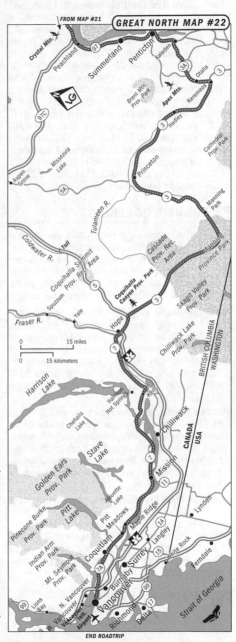

FROM MAP #21 — GREAT NORTH MAP #22

END ROADTRIP

GREAT NORTH

97 and 3A. At **Il Vecchio Delicatessen,** 317 Robinson St., locals line up daily for delicious sandwiches at incredible value. (☎250-492-7610. Homemade soup $2.15. Open M-Sa 8:30am-6pm.) **The Dream Cafe,** 67 Front St., recently moved to a larger space to accommodate the audiences for weekly live music. The cafe is an intimate and colorful organic oasis with light sandwiches and dinners; try the gypsy spring salad rolls ($5.25), or the mango roasted chicken sandwich. (☎250-490-9012. Open daily 9am-11pm; Nov.-Mar. closed M.) **Isshin Japanese Deli,** 101-449 Main St., is a local favorite, serving affordable, fresh sushi and heaping noodle dishes. (☎250-770-1141. Open M-Th 11:30am-2:30pm and 5-9pm, F 11:30am-2:30pm and 5-10pm, Sa noon-2:30pm and 5-10pm.)

⌂ ACCOMMODATIONS

Penticton is a resort city year-round; cheap beds are few and far between. It's essential to make reservations in summer. If possible, avoid the hotels that lurk along Skaha Lake Rd. and take advantage of the beautiful hostel. Campgrounds along Skaha Lake are costly and often tightly packed.

Penticton Hostel (HI), 464 Ellis St. (☎250-492-3992). A large, well-maintained hostel with rooftop solar panels for hot water. Only a 10min. walk to the beach. Comfortable lounge, TV room and patio. Bikes $24 per day. Laundry $2. Reception 8am-noon and 5-10pm. June-Sept. dorms $19, nonmembers $23; singles $29. Oct.-May dorms $17/$21/$33.

Riordan House, 689 Winnipeg St. (☎250-493-5997; www.icontext.com/riordan). Busily decorated rooms in a historic Penticton home. Scrumptious "Okanagan breakfast" of fresh muffins and cobbler made from local peaches. Shared baths. Bikes $15 per day. Singles $50; doubles with TV and fireplace $60-95.

Okanagan Lake Provincial Park, (☎250-494-6500 or 800-689-9025), 24km north of town on Hwy. 97. 168 sites total on 2 campgrounds (North and South, with a connecting walking trail). The North park is more spacious, with a good swimming beach. Free firewood and showers. Reservations recommended. Sites $22.

↑T LEAVING PENTICTON
In Kaleden, turn west onto **Hwy. 3A.** In Keremeos, turn west onto the **Crowsnest Hwy. (Hwy. 3).**

HOPE

Despite its fame as the Chainsaw Carving Capital of Canada, visitors will find quiet Hope, halfway between Penticton and Vancouver, a tranquil stay. Hope's location at the intersection of several highways ensure easy arrival and departure. Seven hikes of various lengths and difficulties begin in or near town. The lush **Rotary Trail** (20min.), on Wardle St., is a casual walk with views of the Fraser and Cocquihalla Rivers. **Mt. Hope Lookout** (45min.) offers an impressive view of the town and surrounding area. This trail continues past the Lookout to become the **Mt. Hope Loop** (4hr. round-trip). The hike begins at intersection of Hwy. 1 and **Old Hope Princeton Way,** off the dirt road behind the picnic tables. Pause for a pleasant diversion at **Kawkawa (aka Suckers) Creek,** off Union Bar Rd., enhanced in 1984 to aid the late summer and mid-fall salmon spawning. The boardwalk along the creek leads to a swimming hole. For biking, hiking, fishing, and hunting needs, stop by **Cheyenne Sporting Goods,** 267 Wallace St. (☎605-869-5062. Open M-Sa 8:30am-5:30pm.) The **Visitors Centre,** 919 Water Ave., provides the riveting, self-guided **Rambo Walking Tour** (*First Blood* was filmed here) in addition to sharing info on Fraser River Canyon and Manning Park. (☎605-869-2021 or 800-435-5622; www.destinationhopeandbeyond.com. Open July-Aug. daily 8am-8pm; June M-F 9am-5pm, Sa-Su 8am-6pm; Sept.-May M-F 8am-4pm.)

Locals feast on generous portions of homemade cherry pie ($3.50 per slice) at the **Home Restaurant,** 665 Old Hope Princeton Hwy. (☎605-869-5558. Open daily 6am-11pm.) The **Blue Moose Cafe,** 322 Wallace St., offers Internet ($0.10 per min.) and a variety of coffees ($1.65), smoothies ($4), and beers. (☎605-869-0729; www.bluemoosecafe.com. Open M-F 8am-10pm, Su 9am-10pm.) **Holiday Motel,** 63950 Old Yale Rd., features an outdoor swimming pool, playground, volleyball court, and fire pit. (☎605-869-5352. Rooms with cable TV from $40; tent sites $19; RVs $22.) Campers can head for the big trees at the spacious and secure **Coquihalla Campsite,** 800 Kawkawa Lake Rd., off 6th Ave. on the east side of town along the banks of the Coquihalla River. (☎888-869-7118. Open Apr.-Oct. Sites $17; river sites $20; RVs $23.)

✈ APPROACHING VANCOUVER
Head west toward Vancouver along **Hwy. 7.**

≦ DETOUR: OTHELLO-QUINTETTE TUNNELS
A 10min. drive east of Hope along Kawkawa Lake Rd. Follow the signs right on Othello Rd. off Kawkawa Lake Rd. and right again on Tunnel Rd.

In the **Coquihalla Canyon Recreation Area,** the Othello-Quintette Tunnels, blasted through solid granite, provide evidence of the daring engineering that led to the opening of the **Kettle Valley Railway** in 1916. The railway has since been turned into an easy walking path, allowing hikers to walk through the dark tunnels leading to narrow bridges over rapids that shoot through the gorge. These tunnels have served as the backdrop to many Hollywood adventure films.

VANCOUVER

Last stop: Vancouver. The largest city in British Columbia and the third-largest city in Canada, on paper Vancouver may sound like an overwhelming, over-bustling metropolis. But while Vancouver's size is evident in its mind-blowing mix of sights, restaurants, and cultural events, the city's residents know that the British Columbian wilderness is just a short drive, hike, or paddle away. Surrounded on three sides by water and closely hemmed in by the Coast Mountain Range, Vancouver can never stray too far from its humble logging-town roots, no matter how urban it may become. This mix of big-city benefits with easily accessible outdoor adventure makes for a unique destination for the budget traveler and a fitting end to any Great Northern roadtrip.

(VITAL STATS)

Population: 2 million

Visitor Info: 200 Burrard St. (☎604-683-2000; www.tourismvancouver.com), on the plaza level near Canada Place. Open daily 8:30am-6pm.

Internet Access: Vancouver Public Library, 350 W. Georgia St. (☎604-331-3600). Open M-Th 10am-9pm, F-Sa 10am-6pm, Su 1-5pm.

Post Office: 349 W. Georgia St. (☎604-662-5725). Open M-F 8am-5:30pm. **Postal Code:** V6B 3P7.

⎘ GETTING AROUND

Vancouver lies in the southwestern corner of mainland British Columbia. It is divided into distinct regions, mostly by waterways. South of the city flows the Fraser River and to the west lies the Georgia Strait, which separates the mainland from Vancouver Island. **Downtown** juts north into the Burrard Inlet from the main mass of the city and **Stanley Park** goes even farther north. The **Lions Gate** suspension bridge over Burrard Inlet links Stanley Park with North and West Vancouver (West Van), known collectively as the **North Shore;** the bridges over **False Creek** south of downtown link downtown with **Kitsilano** ('Kits') and the rest of the city. West of Burrard St. is the **West End. Gastown** and **Chinatown** are just east of downtown. The **University of British Columbia (UBC)** lies to the west of Kitsilano on Point Grey. **Hwy. 99** runs north-south from the US-Canada border through the city along **Oak St.,** through downtown, then over the Lions Gate bridge. It joins temporarily with the **Trans-Canada Hwy.** (Hwy. 1) before splitting off again and continuing north to Whistler. The Trans-Canada enters from the east, cuts north across the Second Narrows Bridge to the North Shore, and ends at the Horseshoe Bay ferry terminal. Most of the city's attractions are grouped on the peninsula and farther west. The area east of Gastown, especially around **Hastings** and **Main St.,** should be avoided late at night if possible.

Roadtrippers may want to consider using the **Park n' Ride** system (☎604-953-3333; www.translink.bc.ca), or free parking lots at major transit hubs where you can leave your car for the day and take public transit into town.

◉ SIGHTS

▧VANCOUVER ART GALLERY. This gallery hosts fantastic temporary exhibitions and a varied collection of contemporary art and design from the West Coast. *(750 Hornby St., in Robson Sq. ☎604-662-4700; www.vanartgallery.bc.ca. Open Apr.-Oct. M-W and F-Su 10am-5:30pm, Th 10am-9pm; call for hours Nov.-Mar. $15, seniors $11, students $10, under 12 free. Th 5-9pm pay-what-you-can. 2-for-1 HI discount.)*

VANDUSEN BOTANICAL GARDEN. Some 55 acres of a former golf course have been converted into an immense garden featuring 7500 species from six continents. An international sculpture collection is interspersed with the plants, while more than 60 species of birds can be seen in areas such as the Fragrance Garden, Children's Garden, Bonsai House, Chinese Medicinal Garden, or the Elizabethan Maze, which is planted with 3000 pyramidal cedars. Daily tours are given at 2pm; alternatively, follow a self-guided tour tailored to show the best of the season. The Flower & Garden Show is the first weekend of June. *(5251 Oak St., at W 37th Ave.* ☎*604-257-8665; www.vandusengarden.org. Open daily June-Aug. 10am-9pm; mid-Aug. to Sept. and May 10am-8pm; Oct.-Mar. 10am-4pm; Apr. 10am-6pm. Apr.-Aug. $7.50, seniors $5.20, ages 13-18 $5.70, ages 6-12 $3.90, under 6 free.)*

CHINATOWN. Southeast of Gastown, the neighborhood bustles with restaurants, shops, bakeries, and **the world's narrowest building** at 8 W. Pender St. In 1912, the city expropriated all but a 1.8m (6 ft.) strip of Chang Toy's property in order to expand the street; he built on the land anyhow, and today the building is a symbol of Chinatown's perseverance. The serene **Dr. Sun Yat-Sen Classical Chinese Garden** maintains imported plantings, carvings, and rock formations in the first full-size garden of its kind outside China. *(578 Carrall St.* ☎*604-662-3207; www.vancouverchinesegarden.com. Open daily May to mid-June 10am-6pm; mid-June to Aug. 9:30am-7pm; Sept. 10am-6pm; Oct.-Apr. 10am-4:30pm. Tours every hr. 10am-6pm. Admission to part of the garden is free, while another section is $8.25, students $5.75, seniors $6.75, under 5 free.)* Don't miss the sights, sounds, smells, and tastes of the weekend, when vendors set up stands selling nearly anything at the **night market** along Keefer St. east of Main. *(F-Su 6:30-11pm.)* Chinatown is relatively safe, but its surroundings are some of Vancouver's less savory sections.

BLOEDEL FLORAL CONSERVATORY. Go from the tropics to the desert in 100 paces inside this 43m diameter triodetic geodesic dome, constructed of Plexiglas bubbles and aluminum tubing. The conservatory, maintained at a constant 18°C (65°F), is home to 500 varieties of exotic plants and 150 birds. The conservatory is located inside beautiful Queen Elizabeth Park, whose ele-

vation also affords views of downtown Vancouver. *(1 block east of Cambie and 37th Ave.* ☎*604-257-8584. Open Apr.-Sept. M-F 9am-8pm, Sa-Su 10am-9pm; daily Oct. and Feb.-Mar. 10am-5:30pm; daily Nov.-Jan. 10am-5pm. $4.25, seniors 4 $2.90, ages 13-18 $3.10, ages 6-12 $2.)*

UNIVERSITY OF BRITISH COLUMBIA (UBC). The high point of a visit to UBC is the breathtaking **Museum of Anthropology.** The high-ceilinged glass and concrete building houses totems and other massive carvings, highlighted by Bill Reid's depiction of Raven discovering the first human beings in a giant clam shell. *(6393 NW Marine Dr.* ☎*604-822-5087; www.moa.ubc.ca. Open June-Sept. M and W-Su 10am-5pm, Tu 10am-9pm. $9, students and seniors $7, under 6 free. Tu after 5pm free.)* Across the street, caretakers tend to **Nitobe Memorial Garden.** Consistently rated in the top five North American Shinto gardens, the Nitobe is a peaceful spot designed for meditation. *(*☎*604-822-9666; www.nitobe.org. Open daily mid-Mar. to mid-May 10am-5pm; mid-May to Aug. 10am-6pm; Sept.-Oct. 10am-5pm. $3, seniors $1.75, students $1.50, under 6 free.)* The **Botanical Gardens** are a collegiate Eden encompassing eight gardens in the central campus, including the largest collection of rhododendrons in North America. *(6804 SW Marine Dr.* ☎*604-822-9666; www.ubcbotanicalgarden.org. Same hours as Nitobe Garden. $5, seniors $3, students $2, under 6 free. Both Nitobe and the Botanical Gardens $6.)*

STANLEY PARK. Established in 1888 at the tip of the downtown peninsula, the 1000-acre **Stanley Park** is a testament to the foresight of Vancouver's urban planners. The thickly wooded park is laced with cycling and hiking trails and surrounded by an 10km **seawall** promenade popular with cyclists, runners, and in-line skaters. *(*☎*778-257-8400. A free shuttle runs between major destinations throughout the park late June to Sept. every 30min. 10am-6:30pm.)* The **Lost Lagoon,** brimming with fish, birds, and the odd trumpeter swan, provides a utopian escape from the skyscrapers. Nature walks start from the **Nature House,** underneath the Lost Lagoon bus loop. *(Walks* ☎*604-257-8544. 2hr. Su 1-3pm. $5, under 12 free. Nature House open June-Aug. F-Su 11am-7pm.)* The park's edges feature restaurants, tennis courts, a running track, swimming beaches staffed by lifeguards, and an outdoor theater, the **Malkin Bowl.** *(*☎*604-687-0174.)* For

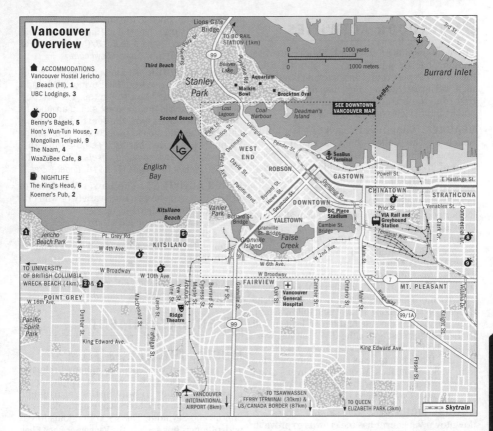

Vancouver Overview

🏠 **ACCOMMODATIONS**
Vancouver Hostel Jericho Beach (HI), **1**
UBC Lodgings, **3**

🍴 **FOOD**
Benny's Bagels, **5**
Hon's Wun-Tun House, **7**
Mongolian Teriyaki, **9**
The Naam, **4**
WaaZuBee Cafe, **8**

🍸 **NIGHTLIFE**
The King's Head, **6**
Koerner's Pub, **2**

warm, chlorinated water, take a dip in the **Second Beach Pool.** *(Next to Georgia St. park entrance.* ☎*604-257-8371. $4.40, seniors $3.10, ages 13-18 $3.30, ages 6-12 $2.25. Towels $2; lockers $0.25.)*

🖼**VANCOUVER AQUARIUM.** The aquarium, on Stanley Park's eastern side not far from the entrance, features exotic aquatic animals with a focus on the British Columbia coastline. BC, Amazonian, and other ecosystems are skillfully replicated. Dolphin and beluga whales demonstrate their advanced training and intelligence, and the new Wild Coast exhibit allows visitors to get a close-up view of marine life, including otters and seals. Outside the aquarium, an orca fountain by sculptor Bill Reid glistens blackly. *(*☎*604-659-3474; www.vanaqua.org. Open daily July-*

Aug. 9:30am-7pm; Sept.-June 10am-5:30pm. Shows every 2hr. 10am-5:30pm. $17, students and seniors $13, ages 4-12 $9.50, under 4 free.)

H.R. MACMILLAN SPACE CENTRE. Housed in the same circular building as the **Vancouver Museum,** the space center runs a motion-simulator ride, planetarium, solar observatory and exhibit gallery, as well as two laser-light rock shows every Friday and Saturday night, starting at 9:30pm. *(1100 Chestnut St.* ☎*604-738-7827; www.hrmacmillanspacecentre.com. Open daily July-Aug. 10am-5pm; Sept.-June closed M. $14, students and seniors $11. Laser-light show $9.35. Vancouver Museum* ☎*604-736-4431; www.vanmuseum.bc.ca. Open June-Sept. M-W and F-Su 10am-5pm, Th 10am-9pm; Sept.-June closed M. $10, seniors $8, under 19 $6.)*

◪ OUTDOOR ACTIVITIES

Three mountains on the North Shore provide a stunning backdrop to the city's skyline, bringing the locals out year-round. In winter, all three offer night skiing and heavier snow than mountains farther from the ocean. In summer, all offer hiking and beautiful views of the city from the top.

BEACHES. Vancouver has kept its many beaches clean. Follow the western side of the Stanley Park seawall south to **Sunset Beach Park,** a strip of grass and beach extending all the way along **English Bay** to the Burrard Bridge. The **Aquatic Centre,** at the southeast end of the beach, is a public facility with a sauna, gym, and 50m indoor pool. (1050 Beach Ave. ☎ 604-665-3424. Generally open M-Th 9am-4:20pm and 8-10pm, F 9am-4:20pm and 8:20-9pm, Sa 10am-9pm, Su 1-9pm. $4, ages 13-18 $3, ages 6-12 $2.) **Kitsilano Beach** ('Kits'), across Arbutus St. from Vanier Park, is a favorite for tanning and beach volleyball (the water is a bit cool for swimming). For fewer crowds, more kids, and free showers, visit **Jericho Beach** (head west along 4th Ave. and follow signs). A cycling path at the side of the road leads uphill to the westernmost end of the UBC campus. West of Jericho Beach is the quieter **Spanish Banks;** at low tide the ocean retreats almost 1km, allowing long walks on the flats. Most of Vancouver's 31km of beaches are patrolled by lifeguards from late May to Labor Day between 11:30am and 9pm.

GROUSE MOUNTAIN. The ski hill closest to downtown Vancouver has the crowds to prove it. The slopes are lit for skiing until 10:30pm from mid-November to mid-April. The very steep and well-traveled 2.9km **Grouse Grind Trail** is a popular hiking trail among Vancouverites in the summer; it charges straight up 853m to the top of the mountain but rewards its hikers with a beautiful view of downtown and beer ($5). The Skyride back down costs $5. (☎ 604-984-0661; www.grousemountain.com. Lift tickets $42, seniors and ages 13-18 $30, under 13 $18. Tramway $27, seniors $24, ages 13-18 $15, ages 5-12 $10.)

CYPRESS BOWL. Cypress Bowl in West Vancouver provides a less crowded ski alternative. It boasts the most advanced terrain of the local mountains on its 23 runs, at prices close to Grouse Mtn. A few minutes before the downhill area, the 16km of groomed trails at Hollyburn cross-country ski area are open to the public. In summer, the cross-country trails have hiking and berry-picking. (Go west on Hwy. 1 and take Exit 8/Cypress Bowl Rd. ☎ 604-922-0825; www.cypressbowl.com.)

MOUNT SEYMOUR. At Mount Seymour Provincial Park, trails leave from Mt. Seymour Rd. and a paved road winds 11km to the top. The Mt. Seymour ski area has the cheapest skiing around. Its marked terrain is also the least challenging, although the spectacular backcountry is preferred by many pro snowboarders. (☎ 604-986-2261; www.mountseymour.com. Lift tickets $34, ages 13-18 $28, seniors $24, ages 6-13 $18, under 6 free.)

OTHER ACTIVITIES. The Lower Mainland of British Columbia hosts a huge variety of wild critters, including mule deer, black bears, wolves, cougars, and more than a few bird species. Indian Arm is an ideal spot for fishing, diving, and kayak-camping. The **Deep Cove Canoe and Kayak Center** in North Vancouver offers 2hr. canoe and kayak rentals. (2156 Banbury Rd. ☎ 778-929-2268; www.deepcovekayak.com. Reservations suggested in summer. Open Apr.-Oct. 9am-9pm.)

♫ ENTERTAINMENT

MUSIC, THEATER, & FILM

The renowned **Vancouver Symphony Orchestra** (☎ 604-876-3434; www.vancouversymphony.ca) plays September to May in the refurbished **Orpheum Theatre** (☎ 604-665-3050), at the corner of Smithe and Seymour. The VSO often joins forces with other groups such as the **Vancouver Bach Choir** (☎ 604-921-8012; www.vancouverbachchoir.com).

Vancouver has a lively theater scene. The **Vancouver Playhouse Theatre Co.** (☎ 604-873-3311), at Dunsmuir and Georgia St., and the **Arts Club Theatre** (☎ 604-687-1644; www.artsclub.com), on Granville Island, stage low-key shows, often including local work. **Theatre Under the Stars** (☎ 604-687-0174; www.tuts.bc.ca) puts on outdoor musicals in the summer in Stanley Park's Malkin Bowl. The world-famous improvisational theater company **Theatresports League** (☎ 604-687-1644; www.vtsl.com) performs competitive improv, comedies, and improv jam sessions at the Arts Club New Revue Stage on Granville Island.

The **Ridge Theatre,** 3131 Arbutus, shows arthouse, indie, European, and vintage film double features. (☎ 604-738-6311; www.ridgetheatre.com. $5, seniors and children $4.) The **Hollywood Theatre,** 3123 W. Broadway, shows arthouse, documentaries, and second-run mainstream double features for less than other theaters downtown. (☎604-515-5864; www.hollywoodtheatre.ca. Films $6, seniors and under 14 $3.50.)

SPORTS

One block south of Chinatown on Main St. is **BC Place Stadium,** 777 S. Pacific Blvd., home to the CFL's **BC Lions** and the world's largest air supported dome. (☎604-669-2300; www.bcplacestadium.com. Tickets from $15.) The NHL's **Vancouver Canucks** (www.canucks.com/gm) call nearby **GM Place** home. The **Vancouver Canadians** play AAA baseball in Nat Bailey Stadium, at 33rd. Ave. and Ontario, opposite Queen Elizabeth Park. For tickets and info call **Ticketmaster** at ☎604-280-4400 or visit www.ticketmaster.ca.

FESTIVALS

Vancouver's diverse cultural makeup brings festivals of all shapes and sizes to the city. As with almost everything else, buying tickets in advance for these festivals often results in reduced prices.

Chinese New Year will fall on Feb. 9, 2005 and Jan. 29, 2006. Fireworks, music, and dragons in the streets of Chinatown and beyond.

Alcan Dragon Boat Festival (☎604-696-1888; www.adbf.com). Late June. Traditional food and dance from around the world and dragon boat racing on False Creek. $10, seniors and children $8.

Vancouver International Jazz Festival (☎604-872-5200 or 888-438-5200; www.jazzvancouver.com). Late June to early July. Draws over 500 performers and bands for 10 days of jazz, from acid to swing. Free concerts in Gastown, at the Roundhouse on Davie St., and around Granville Island. Other events $10-60.

Vancouver Folk Music Festival (☎604-602-9798 or 800-985-8363; www.thefestival.bc.ca). Performers from around the world give concerts and workshops the 3rd weekend of July. Tickets $40-55 per day, weekend $130. Discounts for seniors and children.

Celebration of Light (☎604-738-4304; www.celebration-of-light.com). Late July to early Aug. Pyrotechnists light up the sky over English Bay on Sa and W nights. Hundreds of thousands gather to watch, closing off downtown streets and crowding Kitsilano beaches.

Holy Pride! (☎604-687-0955; www.vanpride.bc.ca). Late July to early Aug. This is Vancouver's gay and lesbian festival. Events include dances, parties, games, music, and a parade.

Vancouver International Film Festival (☎604-683-3456; www.viff.org). Late Sept. to early Oct. This event showcases movies from over 50 countries with over 500 screenings, with emphasis on Canadian films, East Asian films, and documentaries. Tickets $6-8.

FOOD

The diversity and excellence of Vancouver's cuisine makes the rest of BC seem positively provincial. Vancouver's **Chinatown** and the **Punjabi Village** along Main and Fraser, around 49th St., both serve cheap, authentic food. Every type of world cuisine, from Vietnamese noodle shops to Italian cafes to succulent- yet-cheap sushi, is represented along **Commercial Dr.,** east of Chinatown.

Restaurants in **downtown** compete for the highest prices in the city. The **West End** caters to diners seeking a variety of ethnic cuisines (check out the globe-spanning lineup on Denman St.), while **Gastown** lures tourists fresh off the cruise ships. Many cheap establishments along Davie and Denman St. stay open around the clock. Dollar-a-slice, all-night **pizza places** pepper downtown.

WEST END, DOWNTOWN, & GASTOWN

■ **Subeez Cafe,** 891 Homer St. (☎604-687-6107), at Smithe, downtown. Serves hipster kids in a cavernous setting. The eclectic menu includes vegetarian gyoza ($7.50), organic beef burgers ($10), and breakfast all day. Lengthy wine list, large bar, and home-spun beats (DJs W and F-Sa 9pm-midnight). Weekly specials. Entrees $7-15. Open M-F 11:30am-1am, Sa 11am-1am, Su 11am-midnight.

■ **The Dish,** 1068 Davie St. (☎604-689-0208). Prides itself on creative dishes with fresh, natural ingredients. Vegetarian sandwiches and entrees are available, including the roasted veggie wrap ($5) and the lentil stew on rice ($6.50). Carnivores will not be disappointed with the deli-style sandwiches ($5-6) and entrees like curry chicken on rice ($6.50). Open M-Sa 7am-10pm, Su 9am-9pm.

La Luna Cafe, 117 Water St. (☎604-687-5862), in Gastown. Loyal patrons swear by the coffee, roasted

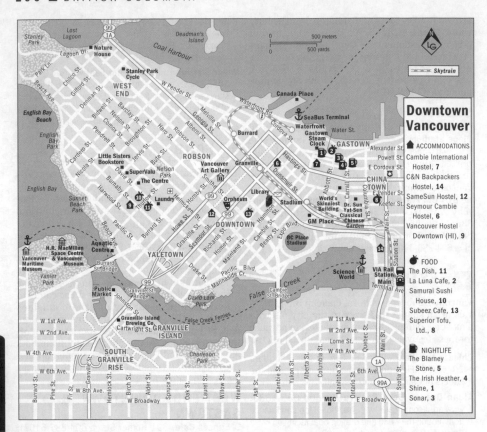

Downtown Vancouver

🏠 ACCOMMODATIONS
Cambie International
    Hostel, **7**
C&N Backpackers
    Hostel, **14**
SameSun Hostel, **12**
Seymour Cambie
    Hostel, **6**
Vancouver Hostel
    Downtown (HI), **9**

🍎 FOOD
The Dish, **11**
La Luna Cafe, **2**
Samurai Sushi
    House, **10**
Subeez Cafe, **13**
Superior Tofu,
    Ltd., **8**

🍷 NIGHTLIFE
The Blarney
    Stone, **5**
The Irish Heather, **4**
Shine, **1**
Sonar, **3**

on site. Cheap, satisfying sandwiches ($4-6) and homemade soups ($4). Internet $1 per 15min. Open M-F 7:30am-5pm, Sa 10am-5pm.

Samurai Sushi House, 1108 Davie St. (☎604-609-0078). A range of cheap sushi options makes this Japanese restaurant a backpackers' favorite. Lunch specials include salad, soup, and sushi for $7. Open M-Th and Su 11am-midnight, F-Sa 11am-1am.

COMMERCIAL DRIVE & EAST VANCOUVER

Mongolian Teriyaki, 1918 Commercial Dr. (☎604-253-5607). Diners fill a bowl with four types of meat, veggies, 16 sauces, and noodles, and the chefs cook eand serve it with miso soup, rice, and salad for $4 (large bowl $6). Open daily 11am-9:30pm.

WaaZuBee Cafe, 1622 Commercial Dr. (☎604-253-5299), at E. 1st St. Sleek, metallic decoration, ambient music, huge murals, and an enormous wine list. Entrees such as spinach and ricotta lagnoilotti pasta or Thai prawns run $11-16. Chicken, lamb, beef, tuna and veggie burgers $9-11. Open M-F 11:30am-1am, Sa 11am-1am, Su 11am-midnight.

KITSILANO

🏮 **The Naam,** 2724 W. 4th Ave. (☎604-738-7151; www.thenaam.com), at MacDonald St. One of the most diverse vegetarian menus around, with great prices to boot. Beautifully presented entrees such as Crying Tiger Thai stir fry ($9) and several kinds of veggie burgers (under $7). Tofulati dairy-free ice cream $3.50. Live music 7-10pm. Open 24hr.

Benny's Bagels, 2505 W. Broadway (☎604-731-9730). Benny's can start, end, or continue your day with beer ($3), bagels ($1.35, $6 fully-loaded), and sandwiches and melts ($5.50-7.50). Open M-Th and Su 7am-1am, F-Sa 24hr.

CHINATOWN

The prettiest are usually the priciest in Chinatown and adjacent **Japantown.** Lively afternoons make this a better place for lunch than dinner.

Hon's Wun-Tun House, 268 Keefer St. (☎604-688-0871). This award-winning Cantonese noodle-house is the place to go. Over 300 options make reading the menu take as long as eating from it. Noodle bowls $4-8. Open M-Th and Su 8:30am-9pm, F-Sa 8:30am-10pm. Cash only.

Superior Tofu, Ltd., 163 Keefer St. (☎604-682-8867; www.superiortofu.com). This deli-style vegetarian restaurant's menu revolves around homemade tofu and soy milk. Open 5:30am-6pm daily.

ACCOMMODATIONS

Vancouver B&Bs are an option for couples or small groups (singles from $45; doubles from $55). **HI hostels** are good for clean and quiet rooms; some non-HI options can be seedy or rowdy.

DOWNTOWN & WEST END

Vancouver Hostel Downtown (HI), 1114 Burnaby St. (☎604-684-4565 or 888-203-4302), in the West End. Sleek and clean 225-bed facility in a quiet neighborhood between downtown, the beach, and Stanley Park. Library, kitchen, Internet ($4 per hr.), lockers, laundry ($3), rooftop patio. Free pub crawls M and W; frequent tours of Granville Island. Travel agency in the lobby. Reception 24hr. Reservations recommended June-Sept. Dorms $20-26, nonmembers $24-29; doubles $59-63/$68-72.

SameSun Hostel, 1018 Granville St. (☎604-682-8226; www.samesun.com), at the corner of Nelson, next to Ramada Inn. Funky, laid-back, technicolor hangout in an area with great nightlife. Internet, pool table, free lockers (bring your own lock) laundry ($2). Dorms $23, nonmembers $27; doubles $53/$60, with bath $60/$65.

C&N Backpackers Hostel, 927 and 1038 Main St. (☎604-682-2441 or 888-434-6060; www.cnnbackpackers.com). At the 1038 location, cheap meal deals with the **Ivanhoe Pub** ($2.50 breakfast all day) make living above the bar a bargain, but across the street is a quieter location. Laundry $2. Bikes $10 per day. Reception 8am-10:30pm. Dorms $16; doubles $40. Weekly dorms $90; doubles $240. Monthly rates available in winter.

Seymour Cambie Hostel, 515 Seymour St. (☎604-684-7757 or 877-395-5535; www.cambiehostels.com). The quieter of 2 downtown Cambie hostels. Movie nights (M and Su), soccer games (July-Sept.), free tours of Granville Island Brewery (Tu noon, 2, 4pm). Internet $4 per hr. Breakfast $2.50. Free lockers (bring your own lock). Laundry $2. 4-person dorms $20; doubles $23; private rooms $45. Oct.-June $3 less.

GASTOWN

Cambie International Hostel, 300 Cambie St. (☎877-395-5335; www.cambiehostels.com). The Cambie offers easy access to the busy sights and sounds of Gastown (including those of the bar downstairs) in one of the older buildings in the neighborhood. No kitchen, but continental breakfast included. Common room, Internet access ($4 per hr.), and laundry ($2). Pool tables in the pub. Reception 24hr. Dorms $22; singles $43. Oct.-May $3 less.

KITSILANO & ELSEWHERE

Vancouver Hostel Jericho Beach (HI), 1515 Discovery St. (☎888-203-4303), in Jericho Beach Park. Follow 4th Ave. west past Alma and bear right at the fork. Practically on the beach with a great view across English Bay. 280 beds In 14-person dorm rooms. 10 4-bed family rooms. Cafe (breakfasts $6; dinner $7-8), kitchen, TV room, free linen. Laundry $2.50. Parking $3 per day. Open May-Sept. Dorms $20, nonmembers $24; family rooms $50-60.

UBC Lodgings, 5959 Student Union Blvd. (☎604-822-1000; www.ubcconferences.com), at Gage Towers on the UBC campus. In the 17-story towers behind the student center. TV lounges, shared microwave and fridge, pubs and food on campus. Internet $10 per day. Free linen. Laundry $2.50. Open May-Aug. Singles $24-84. 10% HI/ISIC discount.

CAMPING

Capilano RV Park, 295 Tomahawk Ave. (☎604-987-4722; www.capilanorvpark.com), at foot of Lions Gate Bridge in North Van. Reception 8am-9pm. 2-person sites $28-30; full RV sites from $46. 10% AAA/CAA discount.

Richmond RV Park, 6200 River Rd. (☎800-755-4905; www.richmondrvpark.com), near Holly Bridge in Richmond, a 30min. drive from Vancouver. Follow the Westminster Hwy. west into Richmond from Hwy. 99, turn right on No. 2 Rd., then right on River Rd. Limited privacy. Open Apr.-Oct. 2-person sites $17; RVs from $25. 10% AAA/CAA discount.

Hazelmere RV Park and Campground, 18843 8th Ave. (☎604-538-1167; www.hazelmere.ca), in Surrey, a 45min. drive from downtown. Close to the US/Canada border. Off Hwy. 99A, head east on 8th Ave. Quiet sites on the Campbell River, 10min. from the beach. 2-person sites $23; full RV sites $31. $3 per additional person. Showers $0.25 per 5min.

ParkCanada, 4799 Hwy. 17 (☎604-943-5811), in Delta 30km south of downtown, near Tsawwassen ferry terminal. Take Hwy. 99 south to Hwy. 17, then go east for 2.5km. The campground, located next to a waterslide park, has a pool. 2-person sites $19; RVs from $21. $2 per additional person. Showers free.

 NIGHTLIFE

Vancouver's nightlife centers on dance clubs playing beats and DJs spinning every night. Pubs are scattered through the city's neighborhoods. The weekly *Georgia Straight* (www.straight.com) publishes comprehensive event listings, restaurant reviews, and coupons. *Discorder* (http://discorder.citr.ca) is the unpredictable monthly publication of the UBC radio station CITR.

GASTOWN

☒ The Irish Heather, 217 Carrall St. (☎604-688-9779; www.irishheather.com). The 2nd-highest seller of Guinness in BC, this true Irish pub and bistro serves up memories of the Emerald Isle to a clientele of regulars. Full 20 oz. draughts ($6.10), mixed drinks ($6.50), and bangers and mash or fish and chips will keep those eyes smiling. Lots of veggie dishes, too. Entrees $13-16. Live music Tu-Th 8pm-close. Open M-Th noon-11pm, F-Sa noon-midnight.

Sonar, 66 Water St. (☎604-683-6695; www.sonar.bc.ca). Party-goers crowd onto this popular beat factory's large dance floor. Long lines weekends, but a visit to www.clubvibes.com will get you on the guest list. International DJs spin house (W), techno (F), and hip-hop (Sa). Open W 9pm-2am, F-Sa 9pm-3am.

Shine, 364 Water St. (☎604-408-4321; www.shine-nightclub.com), in the basement. Named the "sexiest club in Canada" in 2001 by *Flare Magazine,* this ultra-hip club draws in crowds with its sleek decor and nightly specials. M electro-funk, Tu hip-hop, W reggae, Th 80s, F-Sa hip-hop/pop, Su house (also gay night). Beer and mixed drinks $6-8. Cover Su-Th $3, F-Sa $10. Open M-Tu 10pm-2am, W-Th 9pm-2am, F-Sa 9pm-3am, Su 9pm-2am.

The Blarney Stone, 216 Carrall St. (☎604-687-4322). For a more raucous Irish experience, join the mostly university crowd for live music by Killarney, a Celtic-rock band that has played here 4 nights a week for 20 years. Cover F-Sa $7. Open W-Sa 7pm-2am.

KITSILANO

The King's Head, 1618 Yew St. (☎604-738-6966), at 1st St. Cheap drinks, cheap food, relaxing atmosphere, and a great location near the beach. Bands play acoustic sets nightly at 9pm on a tiny stage. Daily drink specials. $3.50 pints. Open M-F 9am-1am, Sa 8am-1am, Su 8am-midnight.

Koerner's Pub, 6371 Crescent Rd. (☎604-822-0983), in the basement of the Graduate Student Building on UBC campus. Owned and operated by the Graduate Student Society, this is the place to meet sexy brains. Mellow M with live music and open jam. Pints $5. Open M-F noon-1am, Sa 4pm-1am.

THE NATIONAL ROAD

If cross-country's the name, the National Road is your game. This route cuts across the middle of the country, from sea to shining sea. For the first stretch, you'll follow the **Old National Road,** much of which is today's **U.S. 40.** Construction on this road began in 1811, and the road reached its original terminus, **Wheeling, WV** (p. 328) by 1818. By 1833, it had been extended to **Vandalia, IL** (p. 344); from the start of the route to Vandalia, **Old National Road Markers**, as well as **Madonna of the Trails** (p. 328) statues, are still visible on the roadsides.

> ### ROUTE STATS
>
> **Miles:** c. 3000
>
> **Route:** Atlantic City, NJ to San Francisco, CA.
>
> **States:** 14; New Jersey, Pennsylvania, Delaware, Maryland, West Virginia, Ohio, Indiana, Illinois, Missouri, Kansas, Colorado, Utah, Nevada, and California.
>
> **Driving Time:** Give yourself three to four weeks to begin to experience what the road has to offer.
>
> **When To Go:** Almost any time you feel like taking off for California. Go in winter and ski in Colorado (but keep in mind that driving conditions can be treacherous) or go in summer and explore the wilderness along the way (but keep in mind that prices and temperatures are higher). The bottom line? Just go.
>
> **Crossroads: The East Coast** in Atlantic City, NJ (p. 91); **Route 66** in St. Louis, MO (p. 470); **The Oregon Trail** in Independence, MO (p. 544); **The North American** in Ely, NV (p. 693); **The Pacific Coast** in San Francisco, CA (p. 941).

Start your trip in **Atlantic City, NJ**—check out **Lucy the Elephant** (p. 304), but don't spend all your quarters at the slots here; save some for **Reno, NV** (p. 416), still 2700 mi. down the road. From here, continue on to **Philadelphia** (p. 305), revered by some as the birthplace of the nation and revered by more as the birthplace of the **cheesesteak sandwich,** before passing through **Baltimore** (p. 315). Soon enough you'll enter the foothills of the **Blue Ridge Mountains.** Stop at scenic **Harpers Ferry National Historic Park** (p. 322) before rolling through Ohio and into Indiana, home of the world's only **National Cookie Cutter Museum** (p.

338) and the world-famous **Indianapolis Motor Speedway** (p. 340). Continue, officially passing into the West under the arch at **St. Louis** (p. 346) and then through Missouri, home state of ragtime legend **Scott Joplin** (in **Sedalia,** p. 355). Next is Kansas, home of the **world's largest hairball** (p. 373). By now, you'll be on **U.S. 50,** another famous continent-crosser, paralleling the historic **Lincoln Highway.** It's a long, straight shot to Colorado, and then from **Denver** (p. 379) up into the mountains, winding through the **Rocky Mountains National Park** (p. 387) and some of the nation's best skiing at **Vail** (p. 391). This area also hosts unparalleled opportunities for summertime activities, including rafting and mountain biking.

The stunning scenery continues into Utah; our route takes you through **Moab** (p. 399), gateway to the spectacular formations of **Arches National Park** (p. 400), and then north to **Salt Lake City** (p. 405) and its namesake **Great Salt Lake.** From there, it's on to northern Nevada, where U.S. 50 is known as **"The Loneliest Road,"** tracing the route of the short-lived **Pony Express** (p. 415). The road here is a black ribbon winding across the desert, broken by the occasional cow, cactus, or mining town. You'll pass **Great Basin National Park** (p. 410) and then Reno—"biggest little city in the world"—before the welcome blue oasis of **Lake Tahoe** (p. 419), which somehow offers pristine wilderness and **casino-sponsored debauchery** (p. 422) side-by-side. Continuing west, you'll come down from the **Sierra Nevada** into California's Central Valley. **Berkeley** (p. 429), is a bibliophile's dream and home to **Chez Panisse** (p. 430), the birthplace of California Cuisine. Go west, young roadtripper, until you can go west no more, ending your journey in **San Francisco** (p. 432). Watch the sun set over the **Golden Gate Bridge** (p. 435), a grand end to a grand transcontinental roadtrip.

Welcome To **NEW JERSEY**

ATLANTIC CITY

An express train and early cars once brought thousands of East Coast city dwellers to Atlantic City for inexpensive weekend getaways, and later the city gained fame as the home of the *Miss America Pageant* and the source of *Monopoly*'s property names. But the former opulence of Boardwalk and Park Place have faded from neglect and evolved into casino-driven tackiness. Gambling, legalized in the 1970s in an attempt to revive the city, brought mega-dollar casinos to the Boardwalk and restored a flow of tourists, but the casinos appear to have done little for the city itself. Highlights center on the Boardwalk, where blaring announcements invite pedestrians to step into the casinos to try their luck. .

⬛ GETTING AROUND

Attractions cluster on and around the **Boardwalk,** which runs northeast-southwest along the Atlantic Ocean. Parallel to the Boardwalk, **Pacific Ave.** and **Atlantic Ave.** offer cheap restaurants, hotels,

(VITAL STATS)

Population: 41,000

Visitor Info: Atlantic City Visitors Center (☎609-449-7130), on the Atlantic Expwy., 1 mi. after the Pleasantville Toll Plaza. Open daily 9am-5pm. **Atlantic City Convention Center and Visitors Bureau Info Center** (☎888-228-4748; www.atlanticcitynj.com), on the Boardwalk at Mississippi St. Open daily 9:30am-5:30pm; Memorial Day-Labor Day Th-Su until 8pm.

Internet Access: Atlantic City Library, 1 N. Tennessee Ave. (☎609-345-2269). Open M-W 10am-8pm, Th-Sa 9am-5pm.

Post Office: 1701 Pacific Ave (☎609-345-4212), at Illinois Ave. Open M-F 8:30am-6pm, Sa 8:30am-12:30pm. **Postal Code:** 08401.

and convenience stores. Atlantic Ave. can be dangerous after dark, and any street farther inland can be dangerous even by day. Getting around is easy on foot on the Boardwalk.

The **Jitney,** 201 Pacific Ave., is basically a small shuttle bus. Jitneys run on four routes to all the casinos and most major points of interest. (☎609-

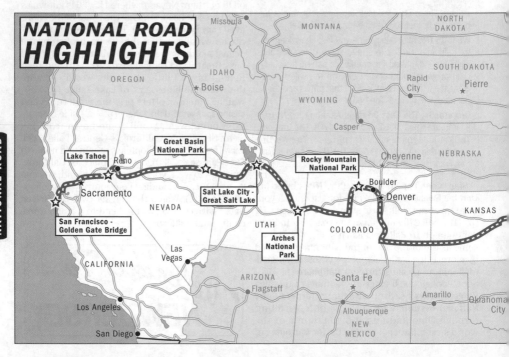

344-8642. $12.50 for 10 tickets or $1.50 in cash per ride). **Rolling Chair Rides** appear along the Boardwalk as frequently as yellow cabs in Manhattan. (☎617-347-7500. $5 for up to 5 blocks.)

Parking is available on some residential streets. Try **Oriental Ave.** at **New Jersey Ave.** near the Garden Pier Historic Museum for free 3hr. parking at easy walking distance from the Boardwalk. Be careful at night: this area is more desolate than other parts of the city. On streets farther from the Boardwalk, such as down Martin Luther King Blvd., free parking is unlimited, but be prepared to walk several blocks to the Boardwalk and casinos. Parking lots near the Boardwalk run $5-10

👁 SIGHTS

THE BOARDWALK. There's something for everyone in Atlantic City, thanks to the Boardwalk. On one side stretches the beach, with its bars and two piers of arcades and amusement rides. The other side is lined with gift shops, surf shops, food stalls selling pizza, funnel cakes,

stromboli, and ice cream, the occasional jewelry store, and, of course, the casinos (see p. 303). There's often live music playing, usually paid for by s casino trying to lure in gamblers. Visitors can walk, ride bikes between 6 and 10am, or take advantage of the rolling chairs. Most of the action along this 8 mi. stretch takes place south of the Showboat. Beyond this harried flurry of activity, it's most enjoyable as a quiet walk. Those under 21 play for prizes at the many arcades that line the Boardwalk, including **Central Pier Arcade & Speedway**. The pier also has go-karts and paintball. *(At the Boardwalk and Tennessee Ave. ☎609-345-5219. Go-karts single $6, double $14. Must be 12 and 54 in. tall to ride alone. Paintball $3 per 15 shots.)* The historic **Steel Pier** juts into the coastal waters with a ferris wheel that spins riders over the Atlantic. It also offers the rest of the usual amusement park attractions: a roller coaster, a carousel, and games of "skill" aplenty. *(On the Boardwalk at Virginia Ave. ☎609-898-7645 or 866-386-6659; www.steelpier.com. Open daily noon-midnight; call the Taj Mahal for winter hours. Tickets one for $0.75 or 35 for $25. Rides 1-5 tickets.)* When and if you tire of spending

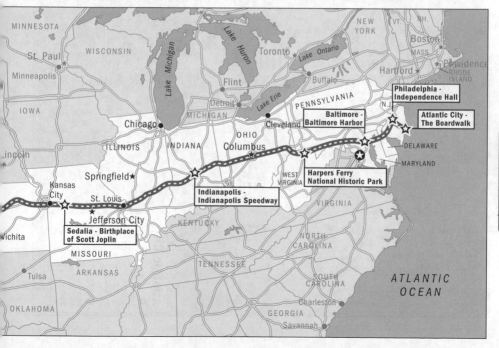

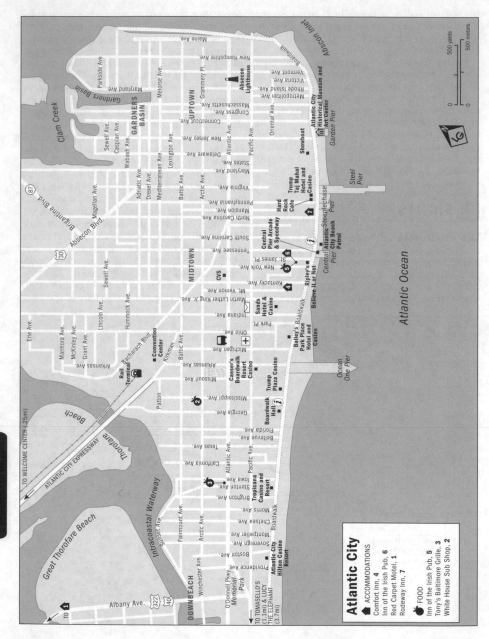

Atlantic City

▲ ACCOMMODATIONS
Comfort Inn, 4
Inn of the Irish Pub, 6
Red Carpet Motel, 1
Rodeway Inn, 7

● FOOD
Inn of the Irish Pub, 5
Tony's Baltimore Grille, 3
White House Sub Shop, 2

money, check out the historic **Atlantic City Beach,** pretty much the only free activity in town. For more water fun, visitors invariably stumble upon at least one of the piers occupied by **Morey's Piers & Raging Waters Waterparks.** *(On the Boardwalk at 25th Ave., Schellenger, and Spencer.* ☎609-522-3900 or 888-667-3971; www.moreyspiers.com.*)* Just west of Atlantic City, **Ventnor City Beach** offers more tranquil shores.

MUSEUMS. Those looking for a quieter, more cultured way to spend the afternoon can explore the **Atlantic City Art Center,** which displays the work of local and regional artists. *(On Garden Pier at New Jersey Ave. and the Boardwalk.* ☎609-347-5837; www.aclink.org/acartcenter. Open daily 10am-4pm. Free.)* On the same pier, the **Atlantic City Historical Museum** contains memorabilia from the history of the "Queen of Resorts," including displays on the *Miss America Pageant, Monopoly,* sand art, and the role of electricity. *(☎609-347-5839; www.acmuseum.org. Open daily 10am-4pm. Free.)*

OTHER SIGHTS. The tallest lighthouse in New Jersey and the third tallest in the nation, Absecon Lighthouse ceased operation in 1933. Today, it remains open as a tourist attraction, offering a small museum and the chance to climb to the top for a stunning view of the city and ocean. *(31 S. Rhode Island Ave. Drive northeast on Pacific Ave. from midtown; it's on the left.* ☎609-449-1360; www.abseconlighthouse.org. Open July-Aug. daily 10am-5pm; Sept.-June M and Th-Su 11am-4pm. Call for winter hours. $5, seniors $4, ages 4-12 $2.)* Ripley's Believe It or Not Museum may not be quite so historically oriented, but it does feature some pretty freaky artifacts and stories that are, well, hard to believe. *(At New York Ave. and the Boardwalk.* ☎609-347-2001; www.ripleys.com. Open summer daily 10am-10pm; winter M-F 11am-5pm, Sa-Su 10am-9pm. $11, ages 5-12 $7, under 5 free.)*

🏛 CAINO

All casinos on the Boardwalk fall within a dice toss of one another. The farthest south is the elegant **Hilton,** between Providence and Boston Ave. (☎609-347-7111 or 800-257-8677; www.hiltonac.com), and the farthest north is the gaudy **Showboat,** at Delaware Ave. and Boardwalk. (☎609-343-4000 or 800-621-0200; www.harrahs.com). Donald Trump's glittering **Trump Taj Mahal Hotel and Casino,** 1000 Boardwalk, (☎609-449-1000; www.trumptaj.com), at Virginia Ave., is too ostentatious to be missed; this tasteless tallboy and the rest of Trump's casino holdings have been struggling with financial difficulties. In true *Monopoly* form, Trump owns three other hotel casinos in the city: the recently remodeled Trump Plaza, at Mississippi and the Boardwalk (☎609-441-6000 or 800-677-7378; www.trumpplaza.com); Trump World's Fair, on the Boardwalk (☎800-473-7829); and **Trump Castle,** on Huron Blvd. at the Marina (☎609-441-2000; www.trumpmarina.com). In summer, energetic partiers go to "rock the dock" at Trump Castle's indoor/outdoor bar and restaurant, **The Deck** (☎877-477-4697). Many a die is cast at **Caesar's Boardwalk Resort and Casino,** 2100 Pacific Ave., at Arkansas Ave. (☎609-348-4411; www.caesarsatlaticity.com). At Indiana Ave., **The Sands** (☎609-441-4000; www.acsands.com) stands tall and flashy with its seashell motif. The newest casino in town is **The Borgata** (☎866-692-6742; www.theborgata.com), a golden scintillation near the Trump Marina Hotel Casino and Harrah's in the Marina District that has been in the works since 2000. All casinos are open 24hr. and are dominated by slot machines.

🍴 FOOD

Although not recommended by nutritionists, $0.75 hot dogs and $1.50 pizza slices are readily available on the Boardwalk, and there is no shortage of ice-cream parlors. Some of the best deals in town await at the casinos, where all-you-can-eat lunch ($7) and dinner ($11) buffets abound. Tastier, less tacky fare can be found farther from the seashore.

Inn of the Irish Pub, 164 St. James Pl. (☎609-345-9613; www.theirishpub.com). Locals lounge downstairs and foreign students and hostelers stay upstairs at this hostel-and-bar combo. Serving hearty pub-style food all night, it's packed with carousers at all hours. Start off with a "20th St. sampler" (buffalo wings, fried mozzarella, potato skins, and chicken thumbs; $7). The daily lunch special (11:30am-2pm) includes a sandwich and a cup of soup for $2. Dinner specials 2-8pm ($6). Domestic drafts $1. Open 24hr. Cash only.

White House Sub Shop, 2301 Arctic Ave. (☎609-345-8599, takeout 609-345-1564; www.whitehousesubshop.com), at Mississippi Ave. Sinatra was rumored to have had these immense subs ($4-7 for half, $9-12 for whole) flown to him while on tour. Pictures of sub-lovers Joe DiMaggio, Wayne Newton, and Mr. T overlook the team making each sandwich to order. Open Su-Th 10am-10pm, F-Sa 10am-11pm. Cash only.

Tony's Baltimore Grille, 2800 Atlantic Ave. (☎609-345-5766), at Iowa Ave. Tourists can't resist the old-time Italian atmosphere with personal jukeboxes, not to mention the $3-8 pizza. Seafood platter $12. Open daily 11am-3am. Bar open 24hr. Cash only.

🏠 ACCOMMODATIONS

Motels are located 2-6 mi. out of town on U.S. 40 and U.S. 30, as well as in Absecon (8 mi. west of town on U.S. 30). Before dropping in the off season, rates can more than triple the week of the *Miss America Pageant,* usually the second or third week in September.

📷 Inn of the Irish Pub, 164 St. James Pl. (☎609-344-9063; www.theirishpub.com), between New York Ave. and Tennessee Ave., near the Ramada Tower. Spacious, clean rooms less than a block from the Boardwalk. Enjoy the porch's rocking chairs and refreshing Atlantic breeze. The downstairs bar offers lively entertainment and a friendly atmosphere. Key deposit $7. Free parking across the street. Doubles with $45-52, with bath $75-90; quads with shared bath $85-99.

Comfort Inn, 154 S. Kentucky Ave. (☎609-348-4000), between Martin Luther King Blvd. and New York Ave., near the Sands. Basic rooms with king-size or 2 queen-size beds and—true to Atlantic City swank—a jacuzzi. Continental breakfast, free parking, and a heated pool. Rooms with ocean views are $20 extra, but come with fridge, microwave, and a bigger jacuzzi. Reserve in advance for weekends and holidays. Singles June-Aug. $100-159; Sept.-May $59-69.

Rodeway Inn, 124 S. North Carolina Ave. (☎609-345-0155 or 800-228-2000), across from the Resorts Casino. Fairly basic motel room fare, but the rates are reasonable and the location is excellent, nestled between the pricier resort casinos and only a bit farther from the Boardwalk. Rooms $50-150.

Red Carpet Motel, 1630 Albany Ave. (☎609-348-3171). A bit out of the way, off the Atlantic Expwy. on the way to town. Be careful in the surrounding neighborhood after dark. Standard, comfy rooms with cable TV and free shuttles to the Boardwalk and casinos.

Restaurant in lobby. Doubles $39-59; quads $55-79. Prices can jump to $130 summer weekends.

📷 LUCY THE ELEPHANT 9200 Atlantic Ave. *In Margate City, off the Garden State Pkwy. at Exit 36. Follow signs to Margate and Lucy.*
Originally built in 1881 by land developer James Lafferty as a marketing gimmick, Lucy has always been a sight for the public. It's no wonder; at 65 ft. and 90 tons, she's hardly the average pachyderm. After she fell into disrepair in the 1960s, the Save Lucy Committee convinced the city to donate land for a site and raised $62,000 to restore her and move her two blocks down the beach to her present location. (☎609-823-6473; www.lucytheelephant.org. Open mid-June to Labor Day M-Sa 10am-8pm, Su 10am-5pm; Apr. to mid-June and Sept.-Dec. Sa-Su 10am-5pm. Tours every 30min. $4, children $2. No public parking or restrooms; free street parking.)

🏁 LEAVING ATLANTIC CITY

U.S. 40 has a humble and unlabeled beginning. Take **Pacific Ave.** southwest until it curves right onto **Albany St. (U.S. 40).**

MAYS LANDING. Eighteen miles along U.S. 40 from Atlantic City is well-maintained Mays Landing. Note the American Hotel on your left and the courthouse on your right, both built in the late 1830s. The American Hotel now forms part of the **public library,** 40 Farragut Ave., which offers free Internet access. (☎609-625-2776. Open M-Th 9am-9pm, F-Sa 9am-5pm.) A bit more homey than area diners, **Ye Old Mill Street Pub,** 6033 W. Main St., is a good choice for grub. (☎609-625-2466. Lunch $3-5. Open M-Sa 11:30am-midnight, Su 1pm-midnight.)

WOODSTOWN. Sixty-four miles from Atlantic City, U.S. 40 passes through Woodstown. Architecturally interesting buildings line Woodstown's leafy main streets. Locals congregate under chef photographs at the **Woodstown Diner,** 16 E. Ave. (☎856-769-1140. Breakfast $1.75-6.50. Lunch $4.50-7. Dinner $5-16. Open daily 6am-10pm.)

THE ROAD TO CAMDEN. Leaving Woodstown, keep left to stay on **U.S. 40.** When you see the exit to the right for **U.S. 40/Delaware Memorial Bridge,** stay straight. One mile ahead, turn right on **U.S. 130,** and head north to Camden. Along U.S. 130, you'll pass small **Penn's Grove.** One of several depressed towns along the New Jersey shore,

Penn's Grove has little to it; most buildings are boarded up. Turning left onto Main St., about a half-mile into town on U.S. 130, takes you to the center of town, and then to the water.

APPROACHING CAMDEN
Keep left as **U.S. 130** merges with **I-295.** Take Exit 23 and stay on U.S. 130 North even when a sign for Camden directs you elsewhere. U.S. 130 North then joins with **U.S. 30 West.** When they split, go west on U.S. 30 toward the Benjamin Franklin Bridge, and follow it into Camden. Take the exit for Camden Business District/Rutgers University and follow signs for the waterfront.

CAMDEN
While for years Camden languished like its smaller counterparts farther down the shore, a revitalization program introduced a little over a decade ago has yielded results. Although much of Camden is not safe for tourists, the waterfront area is a pleasant exception, offering attractions that, while a bit expensive, are worth a stop. Camden fought a long battle to host the Navy's most decorated battleship, which was in service until the early 1990s and has been moored here since 2001. Visitors can take a 1½hr. tour of the prize, docked next to the Tweeter Center just south of the aquarium, at the **USS New Jersey Naval Museum and Veterans Memorial.** Tours offer a look at life on a modern battleship, complete with weapons and radio rooms, officers' quarters, and a mess area. (☎866-877-6262; www.bb62museum.org. Open daily 9am-5pm. $12.50, ages 6-11 and seniors $8, veterans and military personnel free.) Also in the waterfront area is the **New Jersey State Aquarium and Camden Children's Garden,** 1-3 Riverside Dr. The aquarium features live seal exhibitions, penguin feedings, and a carefully monitored opportunity to touch a shark. (☎856-365-3300. Open mid-May to mid-Sept. daily 9:30am-5:30pm; mid-Sept. to mid-May M-F 9:30am-4:30pm, Sa-Su 10am-5pm. $14, students and seniors $12, ages 3-11 $11. Garden only $5, children $3.) The destinations are all within walking distance of each other, and a free shuttle bus runs regularly.

If you're looking for food close to the waterfront, there are a few options in and nearby the aquarium. Although it has cafeteria-style tray service, the atmosphere at the **Crossroad Cafe,** 1 Port Center, across from the aquarium, is classy. (☎856-365-1700. Hot daily specials $4.75. Sand-wiches $4-4.75. Open M-F 7am-3pm.) Otherwise, the **Riverview Cafe,** at the aquarium, offers burgers and fried fare, and there is a similar stand at the **USS New Jersey Naval Museum.** The best place to sleep is across the river in Philadelphia; Camden's waterfront is a daytime destination, and attractions close by 6pm.

APPROACHING PHILADELPHIA
Follow signs for **U.S. 30** to get on **Federal St.** heading away from the waterfront. After crossing **Broadway,** turn left onto the **Ben Franklin Bridge.** Take the exit for **Independence Hall** to access the central attractions.

Welcome To
PENNSYLVANIA

PHILADELPHIA
With his band of Quakers, William Penn founded the City of Brotherly Love in 1682. But it was Ben, not Penn, who transformed the town into the metropolis it is today. Benjamin Franklin, ingenious American ambassador and inventor, almost single-handedly built Philadelphia into an American colonial capital. Today, sightseers will eat up Philly's historic attractions, world-class museums, and architectural accomplishments—not to mention the native cheesesteaks and the endless culinary offerings of the city's ethnic neighborhoods.

GETTING AROUND

The construction of **I-676** and **I-95** through Philadelphia's center has made navigating the already-challenging grid of one-way streets and alleys even more difficult. I-676 runs east-west through the **Center City** area, which is bordered by I-95 on the east and I-76 just across the Schuylkill River. Within the city, numbered north-south streets ascend in value from the **Delaware River** on the east past the **Schuylkill River** on the west, and serve as good reference points. The first street is **Front St.;** the others follow consecutively from 2nd to 69th.

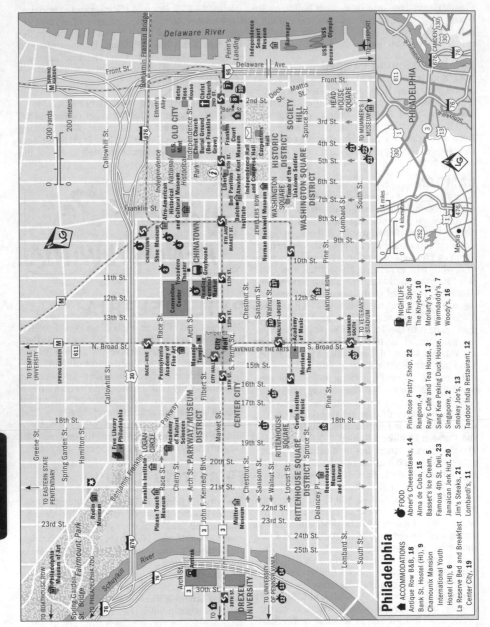

NATIONAL ROAD

Philadelphia

▲ ACCOMMODATIONS
Antique Row B&B, **18**
Bank St. Hostel (HI), **9**
Chamounix Mansion
International Youth
Hostel (HI), **6**
La Reserve Bed and Breakfast
Center City, **19**

● FOOD
Abner's Cheesesteaks, **14**
Alma de Cuba, **15**
Basset's Ice Cream, **5**
Famous 4th St. Deli, **23**
Jamaican Jerk Hut, **20**
Jim's Steaks, **21**
Lombardi's, **11**

Pink Rose Pastry Shop, **22**
Rangoon, **4**
Ray's Cafe and Tea House, **3**
Sang Kee Peking Duck House, **1**
Singapore, **2**
Smokey Joe's, **13**
Tandoor India Restaurant, **12**

■ NIGHTLIFE
The Five Spot, **8**
The Khyber, **10**
Moriarty's, **17**
Warmdaddy's, **7**
Woody's, **16**

Seeing attractions in the historic district is best done on foot. There is no shortage of expensive **parking** lots (about $11 per day) in Center City. Outside of the area around the convention center and Independence Hall, lot prices get somewhat cheaper, and virtually all lots offer day-long specials if you are in by 9 or 10am and out by 6pm. There is a somewhat cheaper lot ($5-11) on Race St. between 10th and 9th St. Metered spots ($1 per hr.) also exist throughout the city except in the immediate area of **Independence Mall.** Also, while most Center City meters give you 2hr., the spots at the Delaware River end of Chestnut and Market St. up above **Penn's Landing** offer 4hr. time slots.

 SIGHTS

INDEPENDENCE MALL

Often referred to as the birthplace of the nation, this historic area of downtown Philadelphia is home to the city's most time-honored attractions, all must-sees for anyone passing through.

INDEPENDENCE NATIONAL HISTORICAL PARK. A small green framed by Market, Walnut, 2nd, and 7th St., the park is home to several historical buildings. At night, the **Lights of Liberty Show** relates the story of the American Revolution in a breathtaking way. A 1hr., half-mile tour through the park—with an elaborate audio program—narrates the events while an impressive $12 million laser light show illuminates five key sites in the downtown area. (Park ☎215-597-8974 or 215-965-2305. Open daily June-Aug 9am-6pm; Sept.-May 9am-5pm. Light Show starts at the PECO Energy Liberty Center at 6th and Chestnut St. ☎877-462-1776; www.lightsofliberty.org. Tu-Sa, times vary. $17.76, seniors and students $16, ages 6-12 $12.)

INDEPENDENCE HALL & VISITORS CENTER. Instead of wandering blindly through the park, begin your trip down American history memory lane at the newly renovated and impressive Visitors Center (see p. p. 307). They dispense detailed maps and brochures, offer a small exhibit detailing each historical site, and provide electronic trip-planners that cater to the desires of each individual visitor. Revolutionary history abounds at **Independence Hall,** one of the most popular of Philadelphia's historic landmarks. After Thomas Jefferson drafted the Declaration of Independence, the delegates signed the document here in 1776 and reconvened in 1787 to ink their names onto the US Constitution. Today, knowledgeable park rangers lead visitors on a brief but informative tour through the nation's first capitol building. (On Chestnut St. between 5th and 6th St. Open daily 9am-5pm. Free tours every 15min. Tickets distributed at the Visitors Center.)

CONGRESSIONAL SIGHTS. The US Congress first assembled in nearby **Congress Hall.** While soaking up the history, visitors can rest in plush Senate chairs. (At Chestnut and 6th St. Open daily 9am-5pm.) The First Continental Congress united against the British in **Carpenters' Hall,** now a mini-museum heralding those responsible for such architectural achievements as Old City Hall and the Pennsylvania State House. (320 Chestnut St. ☎215-925-0167. Open Mar.-Dec. Su and Tu-Sa 10am-4pm; Jan.-Feb. Su and W-Sa 10am-4pm.)

LIBERTY BELL & CONSTITUTION CENTER. While freedom still rings in Philadelphia, the **Liberty Bell** does not; the bell, today at the **Liberty Bell Pavilion,** cracked in 1846 on George Washington's birthday. (On Market St., between 5th and 6th St. ☎215-597-8974. Open daily 9am-5pm. Free.) The stunning, modern **National Constitution Center** provides visitors with an in-depth look at the significant history of the American Constitution. (525 Arch St., in Independence National Historical Park. ☎215-409-6600 or 866-917-1787; www.nationalconstitutioncenter.org. Open daily 9:30am-5pm. 17min. multimedia presentation prior to entrance; last showing 4:10pm. $6, seniors and under 12 $5.)

OTHER SIGHTS. The rest of the park preserves residential and commercial buildings of the Revolutionary era. On the northern edge of the Mall, a white building replicates the size and location of Ben Franklin's home in **Franklin Court.** The original abode was unsentimentally razed by the statesman's heirs in 1812 in order to erect an apartment complex. The home features an underground museum, a 20min. movie, a replica of Franklin's printing office, and a working post office—the first post office in the nation and the only one not to fly the American flag, as there wasn't one in 1775. *(318 Market St., between 3rd and 4th St. ☎ 215-965-2305. Open summer daily 9am-5pm. Free.)* On a more somber note, a statue of the first American president and army general presides over the **Tomb of the Unknown Soldier,** in Washington Sq., where an eternal flame commemorates the fallen heroes of the Revolutionary War. Adjacent to the house where Jefferson drafted the Declaration of Independence, the **Balch Institute for Ethnic Studies at the Philadelphia Historical Society** affords an academic glimpse into America's social history, including the plight of African slaves and of Japanese Americans during WWII. *(1300 Locust St. ☎ 215-732-6200; www.balchinstitute.org. Open M-Tu and Th-F 1-5:30pm, W 1-8:30pm. $6; students and seniors $3. Sa 10am-noon free.)*

SOCIETY HILL

Society Hill proper begins on Walnut St., between Front and 7th St., east of Independence Mall. As at Independence Mall, history presides over 200-year-old townhouses and cobblestone walks illuminated by electric "gaslights." Flames don't have a chance in **Head House Square,** at 2nd and Pine St., which holds the distinction of being America's oldest firehouse and marketplace and now houses restaurants and boutiques. Bargain hunters can test their skills at the outdoor crafts fair. *(☎ 215-790-0782. Open June-Aug. Sa noon-11pm, Su noon-6pm. Free workshops Su 1-3pm.)* Each January, sequin- and feather-clad participants join in a rowdy New Year's Day Mummer's parade. South of Head House Sq., the **Mummer's Museum** swells with the glamour of old costumes. *(1100 S. 2nd St., at Washington Ave. ☎ 215-336-3050; www.riverfrontmummers.com/museum.html. Open May-Sept. Su noon-4:30pm, Tu 9:30am-9:30pm, W-Sa 9:30am-4:30pm; Oct.-Apr. Su noon-4:30pm, Tu-Sa 9:30am-4:30pm. Free string band concerts Tu 8pm. $3.50; students, seniors, and under 12 $2.50.)*

CENTER CITY

As the financial hub of Philadelphia, Center City barely has enough room to accommodate the professionals who cram into the area bounded by 12th, 23rd, Vine, and Pine St. Rife with activity during the day, the region retires early at night.

ART & ARCHITECTURE. The country's first art museum and school, the **Pennsylvania Academy of Fine Art** has permanent displays of artwork by Winslow Homer and Mary Cassatt, while current students show their theses and accomplished alumni get their own exhibits each May. *(118 N. Broad St., at Cherry St. ☎ 215-972-7600; www.pafa.org. Open Su 11am-5pm, Tu-Sa 10am-5pm. 45-60min. tours M-F 11:30am-1:15pm, Sa-Su noon-1:45pm. $5, students and seniors $4, ages 5-18 $3. Special exhibits $8/$7/$5.)* Presiding over Center City, the granite and marble **City Hall** took 30 years to build (a bit longer than the expected 5 years) and is currently undergoing a $125 million cleaning project. It remains the nation's largest working municipal building and, until 1908, it reigned as the tallest building in the US, aided by the 37 ft. statue of William Penn at its peak. A law prohibited building anything higher than Penn's hat until entrepreneurs overturned it in the mid-1980s. A commanding view of the city still awaits visitors in the building's tower. *(At Broad and Market St. ☎ 215-686-2840. Open M-F 9:30am-4:30pm. City Hall tour daily 12:30pm, ends at the tower 2pm. Tower Tour daily every 15min. 9:15am-4:15pm. 5 people per tour. Reservations recommended. $1.)*

RITTENHOUSE SQUARE

Masons of a different ilk left their mark in the brick-laden **Rittenhouse Square District,** a ritzy neighborhood southeast of Center City. This part of town cradles the musical and dramatic pulse of the city, housing several performing arts centers.

RITTENHOUSE MUSEUMS. For the best results, digest lunch completely before viewing the bizarre and often gory medical abnormalities displayed at the highly intriguing **Mütter Museum.** Among the potentially unsettling fascinations are a wall of skulls and human horns. The museum also contains an exhibit on infectious diseases from the Black Death to HIV and displays a Level 4 biohazard suit. *(19 S. 22nd St. ☎ 215-563-3737, ext. 211; www.collphyphil.org/muttpg1.shtml. Open daily 10am-5pm. $9; seniors, students, and ages 6-18 $6.)* Just south of the square, the more benign **Rosenbach Museum and Library** displays the original manuscript of Joyce's *Ulysses*. The collected illustrations of Maurice Sendak are among rotating exhibits. *(2010 Delancey St. ☎ 215-732-1600; www.rosenbach.org. Open Su, Tu, and Th-Sa 10am-5pm, W 10am-8pm. 1hr. tours Su and Tu-Sa 11am-4pm, W 6:30pm. $8, students and seniors $5.)*

PARKWAY & MUSEUM DISTRICT

BENJAMIN FRANKLIN PARKWAY. Once nicknamed "America's Champs-Élysées," the Benjamin Franklin Parkway has seen better days. Of the city's five original town squares, **Logan Circle** was the sight of public executions until 1823 but now delights hundreds of children who frolic in its **Swann Memorial Fountain.** Designed by Alexander Calder, the fountain represents the Wissahickon Creek, and the Schuylkill and Delaware Rivers— the three bodies of water surrounding the city.

SCIENCE MUSEUMS. A modern assemblage of everything scientific, the interactive **Franklin Institute** would make the old inventor proud. A skybike allows visitors to pedal across a tightrope suspended nearly four stories high. (At 20th St. and Ben Franklin Pkwy. ☎ 215-448-1200; www.fi.edu. Open daily 9:30am-5pm. $12.75, seniors and ages 4-11 $10. IMAX Theater $8. Museum and IMAX $16, children $13.) Part of the Institute, the newly renovated **Fels Planetarium** flashes lively laser shows on Friday and Saturday nights. (222 N. 20th St. ☎ 215-448-1388. $6, seniors and ages 4-11 $5. Exhibits and laser show $12.75/$10.50. Exhibits and both shows $14.75/$12.50.) Opposite Fels, the **Academy of Natural Sciences** allows budding archaeologists to try digging up fossils. (1900 Ben Franklin Pkwy., at 19th St. ☎ 215-299-1000; www.acnatsci.org. Open M-F 10am-4:30pm, Sa-Su 10am-5pm. $9, seniors and military $8.25, ages 3-12 $8. $1 AAA discount.) For a little family fun, visit the **Please Touch Museum,** where kids can romp in the Alice In Wonderland Funhouse, play mini golf in the Science Park, or hone broadcasting skills in the Me On TV workshop. (210 N. 21st St. ☎ 215-963-0667; www.pleasetouchmuseum.org. Open daily 9am-4:30pm. $9. Su 9-10am free.)

ART MUSEUMS. Sylvester Stallone may have etched the sight of the **Philadelphia Museum of Art** into the minds of movie buffs everywhere when he bolted up its stately front stairs in Rocky (1976), but it is the artwork within that has earned the museum its fine reputation. The world-class collection includes Asian, Egyptian, and decorative art. (At Benjamin Franklin Pkwy. and 26th St. ☎ 215-763-8100; www.philamuseum.org. Open Tu, Th, Sa-Su 10am-5pm; W and F 10am-8:45pm. Tours daily 10am-3pm. Live jazz, fine wine, and light fare F 5:30-8:30pm. $9; students, seniors, and ages 5-18 $7. Su free.) A cast of The Gates of Hell outside the **Rodin Museum** guards the portal of human passion, anguish, and anger in the most extensive collection of the sculptor's works this side of the Seine. One of the original casts of The Thinker (1880) marks the museum entrance. (At Benjamin Franklin Pkwy. and 22nd St. ☎ 215-763-8100; www.rodinmuseum.org. Open Su and Tu-Sa 10am-5pm. Suggested donation $3. 1hr. audio tour $5.)

FAIRMOUNT PARK. Philly's finest outdoor opportunities can be found in the resplendent Fairmount Park. The faux-Grecian ruins by the waterfall behind the Museum of Art are the abandoned **Waterworks,** built between 1819 and 1822. Free tours of the Waterworks' romantic architecture, technology, and social history meet on Aquarium Dr., behind the art museum. (☎ 215-685-4935; www.fairmountwaterworks.org. Open Sa-Su 1-3:30pm.) Farther down the river, Philadelphia's place in the rowing world is evidenced by a line of crew clubs forming historic **Boathouse Row.** The Museum of Art hosts tours of Boathouse Row on Wednesday and Sunday, as well as trolley tours to mansions in Fairmount Park. The area near Boathouse Row is also the city's most popular in-line skating spot. In the northern arm of Fairmount Park, trails follow the secluded Wissahickon Creek for 5 mi., as the concrete city fades to a distant memory. The **Japanese House and Garden** is designed in the style of a 17th-century shoin; the authentic garden offers the utmost in tranquility. (Off Montgomery Dr. near Belmont Ave. ☎ 215-878-5097; www.shofuso.com. Open May-Oct. Tu-F 10am-4pm, Sa-Su 11am-5pm; call for seasonal hours. Free 30-45min tour. $2.50, students and seniors $2.) Some neighborhoods surrounding the park are not safe, and the park is not safe at night.

♫ ENTERTAINMENT

Old City, the area framed by Chestnut, Vine, Front and 4th St., comes alive for the **First Friday** celebration, when art galleries, museums, and restaurants open their doors to entice visitors with free food. (☎ 800-555-5191; www.oldcity.org. 1st F of each month.) The **Academy of Music,** at Broad and Locust St., was modeled after Milan's La Scala and hosts the six annual productions of the **Pennsylvania Ballet.** (☎ 215-551-7000; www.paballet.org. Tickets $20-85.) The **Philadelphia Orchestra** performs from September to May at the stunning **Kimmel Center,** 260 S. Broad St. (☎ 215-790-5800 or 215-893-1999; www.kimmelcenter.org. Box office

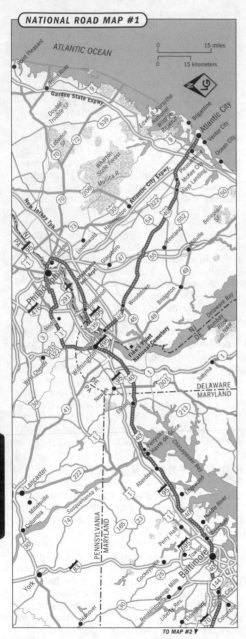

NATIONAL ROAD MAP #1

ATLANTIC OCEAN

open daily 10am-6pm and until performance begins. $5 tickets go on sale at the Locust St. entrance F-Sa 45min. before show. $8 student rush tickets Tu and Th 30min. before show.)

With 5000 seats under cover and 10,000 on outdoor benches and lawns, the **Mann Music Center,** on George's Hill near 52nd and Parkside Ave. in Fairmount Park, hosts big-name entertainers like Tony Bennett and Willie Nelson, as well as jazz and rock concerts. (☎215-546-7900, tickets 215-893-1999; www.manncenter.org. Tickets available at the Academy of Music box office. Pavilion seats $10-32. Free lawn tickets for June-Aug. orchestra concerts available from the Visitors Center, at 16th and JFK Blvd., day of a performance.) **The Trocadero,** 1003 Arch St., at 10th St., at 120 years old, is the oldest operating Victorian theater in the US and hosts local as well as big-name bands. (☎215-922-5486; www.thetroc.com. Advance tickets through Ticketmaster. Box office open M-F noon-6pm, Sa noon-5pm. Tickets $6-16.) The **Robin Hood Dell East,** on Ridge Ave. near 33rd St. in Fairmount Park, brings in top names in pop, jazz, and gospel in July and August. During the school year, theatrical entertainment bustles as the students of the **Curtis Institute of Music,** 1726 Locust St., (☎215-893-5252; www.curtis.edu.) give free concerts.

Baseball's **Phillies** (☎215-463-1000; www.phillies.com) play at the new **Citizens Bank Park,** on Pattison Ave. between 11th and Darien St. Football's **Eagles** (☎215-463-5500l; www.philadelphiaeagles.com) play at **Lincoln Financial Field,** at Broad St. and Pattison Ave. Across the street, fans fill the **First Union Center** to watch the NBA's **76ers** (☎215-339-7676; www.sixers.com) and the NHL's **Flyers** (☎215-755-9700; www.philadelphiaflyers.com).

🍴 FOOD

Street vendors represent the heart of Philadelphia culinary tradition, hawking cheesesteaks, hoagies, cashews, and soft pretzels. Ethnic eateries cluster in several specific areas: hip **South St.,** between Front and 7th St.; **18th St.** around Sansom St.; and **2nd St.,** between Chestnut and Market St. The nation's third-largest Chinatown is bounded by 11th, 8th, Arch, and Vine St., and offers vegetarian restaurants. The quintessential Philly cheesesteak rivalry squares off at 9th and Passyunk Ave., in South Philadelphia; **Pat's King of Steaks** (☎215-468-1546; www.patskingof-steaks.com; open 24hr.), the legendary founder of

TO MAP #2 ▼

the cheesesteak, faces the larger, more neon **Geno's Steaks.** (☎215-389-0659; www.genosteaks.com. Open 24hr.).

Fresh fruit and other foodstuffs pack the crowded streets of the immense **Italian Market,** which spans the area around 9th St. below Christian St. Philadelphia's original farmers market (since 1893), the **Reading Terminal Market,** at 12th and Arch St., across from the Pennsylvania Convention Center, is the largest indoor market in the US. Stocking diverse food, the market is a fabulous lunch spot. (☎215-922-2317; www.readingterminalmarket.org. Open M-Sa 8am-6pm. Amish merchants open W-Th 8am-3pm, F-Sa 8am-5pm.)

HISTORIC DISTRICT

Famous 4th St. Delicatessen, 700 S. 4th St. (☎215-922-3274), at Bainbridge St. This deli rivals New York's finest. A landmark since 1923, it has earned its reputation by serving hot corned beef sandwiches ($7.50). Open M-Sa 8am-6pm, Su 8am-4pm.

Jim's Steaks, 400 South St. (☎215-928-1911; www.jimsteaks.com), at 4th St. Though the place looks a little run-down on the outside, Jim's bustles with activity. Customers arrive in droves for the Philly hoagie ($3.50 5) and fries ($1.25), and pass the time in line by inspecting the wall of fame. Open M-Th 10am-1am, F-Sa 10am-3am, Su noon-10pm.

Pink Rose Pastry Shop, 630 S. 4th St. (☎215-592-0565; www.pinkrosepastry.com), at Bainbridge St. Serves up a wide selection of homemade delicacies at tables graced with fresh flowers. The sour cream apple pie ($4.50) is unforgettable. Open M-Th 8am-10pm, F 8am-11pm, Sa 9am-11pm, Su 9am-10pm.

CHINATOWN

✿ Singapore, 1006 Race St. (☎215-922-3288), between 10th and 11th St. Health-conscious food fanatics flock to this restaurant for the vegetarian roast "pork" with black bean sauce ($6.50) or the tofu with vegetables ($7). Open daily 11am-11pm.

Rangoon, 112-114 9th St. (☎215-829-8939), between Cherry and Arch St. Simple pink and plastic decor belies the complex, spicy scents of Burmese cuisine wafting onto the sidewalk. The crisp lentil fritters ($9) and tasty mint kebab ($9) earn this place its reputation as one of the best. Open daily 11:30am-9:30pm.

Sang Kee Peking Duck House, 238 9th St. (☎215-925-7532), near Arch St. Locals pack the large dining room for the extensive menu. Entrees $6-10. Open Su-Th 11am-11pm, F-Sa 11am-midnight.

Ray's Cafe and Tea House, 141 N. 9th St. (☎215-922-5122). Ideal for quick snacks on the run or spending quiet time curled up with your favorite read. Delectable dishes such as bok choy ($7) or rice noodle soup ($7) are for hungrier folk. For lighter fare, the mango bubble tea ($3), smooth and light, is excellent. Open M-Th 9am-9:30pm, F 9am-10:30pm, Sa 11:30am-10:30pm, Su 11:30am-9pm. Cash only.

CENTER CITY

✿ Jamaican Jerk Hut, 1436 South St. (☎215-545-8644), near Broad St. This tropical paradise brightens a bleak block. While chefs jerk Negril garlic shrimp ($15) to perfection, Bob Marley tunes jam in the backyard veranda. The vegetable stir fry, over a bed of jasmine rice and 2 fried bananas ($7-9), is sure to please. Live music F-Sa 7pm; cover $2. Open M-Th 11am-10pm, F-Sa 11am-11pm, Su 5-10pm.

Alma de Cuba, 1623 Walnut St. (☎215-988-1799; www.almadecubarestaurant.com), near Rittenhouse Sq. Trendy spot for hot Latin food. Try the *sancocho de pollo* soup (coconut-chicken broth with poached chicken slices, yucca, carrots, cilantro, peas, and lime juice; $6). Happy hour M-F 5-7pm. Live Cuban jazz W 9pm-midnight. Salsa Su 8pm. Open M-Th 5-11pm, F-Sa 5pm-midnight, Su 5-10pm.

Bassett's Ice Cream (☎215-925-4315), in Reading Terminal Market at 12th and Arch St. Established in 1861, Bassett's is the oldest ice creamery in the state, and some say the best in the nation. Originals like tomato ice cream join classics such as peach, mocha chip, and rum raisin all excellent. 2 scoops $2.50, 3 scoops $3.25. Open M-Sa 8am-6pm.

Lombardi's, 132 S. 18th St. (☎215-564-5000; www.lombardisoriginalpizza.com), off Rittenhouse Sq. between Sansom and Chestnut St. Established in 1905, this hometown favorite uses a coal oven to cook its crusts to perfection. Original pizza with fresh mozzarella, basil, and homemade meatballs $16. Fresh salads $6-8. Pastas $7-11. Open M-W 11:30am-4pm and 5-10pm, Th-F 11:30am-4pm and 5-11pm, Sa 11:30am-11pm, Su 11:30am-10pm. Cash only.

UNIVERSITY CITY

✿ Tandoor India Restaurant, 106 S. 40th St. (☎215-222-7122), between Chestnut and Walnut St. Northern Indian cuisine with bread fresh from the clay oven. Lunch buffet 11:30am-3:30pm ($6). Dinner buffet 4-10pm ($9). 20% student discount with valid ID. Open daily 11:30am-10:30pm.

NATIONAL ROAD

Smokey Joe's, 210 S. 40th St. (☎215-222-0770), between Locust and Walnut St. Hearty meals at student-friendly prices make this a popular UPenn bar and restaurant. The Franklin Field Deal offers a burger and a choice of soup, chicken tenders, cheesefries, mozzarella sticks, poppers, chicken fingers, wings, or nachos, plus refills on soda, for only $9.50. Open daily 11am-2am; closed 2nd week of Aug.

Abner's Cheesesteaks, 3813 Chestnut St. (☎215-662-0100; www.abnerscatering.com), at 38th St. Local fast food in a bright, spacious, and cleaner-than-average joint attracts the professional set for lunch and tipsy UPenn students deep into the night. Cheesesteak, large soda, and fries $6.20. Open Su-Th 11am-midnight, F-Sa 11am-3am.

ACCOMMODATIONS

Aside from the two hostels, inexpensive lodging in Philadelphia is uncommon. If reserved a few days in advance, comfortable rooms close to Center City can be had for around $60. The motels near the airport at Exit 9A on I-95 sacrifice location for taffordable rates. The personable proprietors at **Antique Row Bed and Breakfast** and **La Reserve** (see p. 312) will recommend rooms if theirs are full. **Bed and Breakfast Connections/Bed and Breakfast of Philadelphia,** in Devon, PA, books rooms in Philadelphia and southeastern Pennsylvania. (☎215-610-687-3565; www.bnbphiladelphia.com. Open M-F 9am-5pm. Reserve at least 1 week in advance; registration fee $10. Singles $60-90; doubles $75-250.) Most hotels and hostels listed are not parking-friendly; park in a lot or plan to pay meters.

🏛 **Chamounix Mansion International Youth Hostel (HI-AYH),** 3250 Chamounix Dr. (☎215-878-3676 or 800-379-0017; www.philahostel.org), in West Fairmount Park. Take I-76 West to Exit 339, take a left on Belmont, a left on Ford Rd., and a left on Chamounix Rd. Dorms in a converted mansion. Kitchen, laundry, TV/VCR, and bikes. Free parking. Internet $1 per 5min. Linen $3. Check-in 8-11am and 4:30pm-midnight. Lockout 11am-4:30pm. Curfew midnight. Dorms $15, nonmembers $18.

🏛 **Bank Street Hostel (HI-AYH),** 32 S. Bank St. (☎215-922-0222 or 800-392-4678; www.bankstreethostel.com). Off Market St. Social hostel in an alleyway between 2nd and 3rd St. in the historic district. Offers A/C, a big-screen TV, free coffee and tea, laundry facilities, kitchen, and pool table. 70 beds. Internet access

$1 per 4min. Linens $3. Lockout 10am-4:30pm. Curfew Su-Th 12:30am, F-Sa 1am. Dorms $18, nonmembers $21. Cash only.

Antique Row Bed and Breakfast, 341 S. 12th St. (☎215-592-7802; www.antiquerowbnb.com). Enchanting traditional B&B amid colonial rowhouses. The owner offers restaurant referrals and serves her own hearty breakfast. 4 apartments for longer visits with TV, utilities, and laundry. Rooms $75-100.

La Reserve (Bed and Breakfast Center City), 1804 Pine St. (☎215-735-1137; www.centercitybed.com). Take I-676, to the 23rd St. Exit and bear right. 10 blocks down, turn left on Pine. Personable owner gives Philly advice. Breakfast included. Doubles $80-130.

🦟 NIGHTLIFE

Check the Friday *Philadelphia Inquirer* for entertainment listings. The free Thursday *City Paper* and the Wednesday *Philadelphia Weekly* have weekly listings. A diverse club crowd jams to ive music on weekends along **South St.** toward the river. Many pubs line **2nd St.** near Chestnut St., close to the Bank St. hostel. Continuing south to Society Hill, especially near **Head House Sq.,** an sliolder crowd fills dozens of streetside bars and cafes. **Delaware Ave.,** or **Columbus Blvd.,** running along Penn's Landing, has become a hot spot full of nightclubs and restaurants that attracts droves of yuppies and students. Gay and lesbian weeklies *Au Courant* (free) and *PGN* ($0.75) list events. Most bars and clubs that cater to a gay clientele congregate along **Camac, S. 12th,** and **S. 13th St.**

The Khyber, 56 S. 2nd St. (☎215-238-5888; www.thekhyber.com). A speakeasy during Prohibition, the Khyber now legally gathers a young crowd to listen to a range of punk, metal, and hip-hop music. The ornate wooden bar was shipped over from England in 1876. Vegetarian sandwiches $3. Happy hour M-F 5-7pm. Live music daily 10pm. Cover $10. Open daily 11am-2am. Cash only.

Warmdaddy's (☎215-627-8400; www.warmdaddys.com), at Front and Market St. Entrees are pricey, but Bayou dreamers eat up this Cajun club renowned for blues. Music and reduced entrees Su 3pm. $5 cover for Th midnight happy hour. Live music summer 7pm; winter 8:30pm. Cover F-Sa $10; varies during the week. Open Tu-Th 5:30pm-1am, F-Sa 7pm-2am.

The Five Spot, 5 S. Bank St. (☎215-574-0070), off Market St. between 2nd and 3rd St. The classic lounge encourages hearty drinking, while the cramped dance floor hosts swingers of all abilities. Th Latin dancing with free lessons. F-Sa DJ spins modern, rap, and R&B. 21+. Cover $5. Dress well. Open daily 9pm-2am.

Moriarty's, 1116 Walnut St. (☎215-627-7676; www.moriartysrestaurant.com), near 11th St. and the Forest theater. This Irish pub draws a healthy crowd late into the night with a quiet, comfortable bar scene. Over 20 beers on tap, ESPN on the TV, and private booths galore. Grolsch $2 pints daily 3-5pm and midnight-2am. Open Su noon-2am, kitchen closes midnight; M-Sa 11am-2am, kitchen closes 1am.

Woody's, 202 S. 13th St. (☎215-545-1893; www.woodysbar.com), at Walnut St. An outgoing gay crowd frequents this lively club with a free cyber bar, coffee bar, and dance floor. Happy hour daily 5-7pm. M karaoke. Tu Big Gay Divas night. Lunch daily noon-3:30pm; dinner daily 4-11pm. Bar open M-Sa 11am-2am, Su noon-2am. Cash only.

LEAVING PHILADELPHIA
Take **I-76** west to Exit 339 for **City Ave./U.S. 1 South.** Continue down U.S. 1 across **I-476** toward **Media, PA.** Exit for **Rte. 252.** To get to Media, after 11 mi. on Rte. 252, turn left onto **Providence Rd.** Proceed 1½ mi. and take a right on **State St.**

MEDIA. Architecturally eclectic restaurants and shops, many of which date from the 19th century line State St., Media's main drag. As you enter town, notice the **armory** on State St. just after Monroe St., still in use by the Army National Guard. A large stone bank marks the center of town at **Veterans Sq.,** and two blocks to the north stands Media's most significant architectural attraction, the **courthouse,** built in four stages from 1851-1929. Restaurants in Media are not overly expensive, but don't come expecting cheap eats. For a light bite, check out the **Coffee Club,** 214 W. State St., near Orange St., which offers coffee, pastries, smoothies, wraps, sandwiches, and several vegetarian selections. (☎610-891-6600. Sandwiches $4-5. Open M-Th 7am-5pm, F-Sa 8am-10pm, Su 8:30am-1pm. Cash only.) Only small towns have places like **D'Ignazio's Towne House,** 117 Veterans Sq., at Baltimore Ave., where homemade pasta ($10) and steaks ($12-17) are served in rooms lit by antique lamps and covered with old paintings and ornaments. (☎610-566-6141. Open M-Sa for lunch and dinner, Su dinner only; closed Sa July-Aug. Call for hours.) The brick and wood of **Iron Hill Brewery and Restaurant,** 30 E. State St., stand out among the old buildings of Media. Sample the selection of self-made brews. (☎610-627-9000. House wines or pints $2. Wings $0.25. Wood-oven pizza $8-11. Happy hour M-Th 5-7pm. Open M-Sa from 11:30am, Su from 11am. Closing varies.)

LEAVING MEDIA
Take **Baltimore Ave.** west out of town. It becomes the **Baltimore Pike** and merges onto **U.S. 1** 1½ mi. from town. Follow U.S. 1 out of Media for 9 mi., then turn left on **U.S. 202 (Concord Pike)** heading south.

DETOUR: BRANDYWINE BATTLEFIELD PARK
Instead of turning south on U.S. 202, continue straight on U.S. 1 for 1½ mi.; the park is on the right.

The Brandywine Battlefield Park is 10½ mi. from Media on a small section of the 10 sq. mi. area where a critical Revolutionary War battle took place. Your ticket gets you into the two houses on the site, inhabited by "living artifacts"—men costumed as the Marquis de Lafayette and George Washington, who adopt accents and tell their life stories. (☎602-459-3342; www.ushistory.org/brandywine. Open Su noon-5pm, Tu-Sa 9am-5pm. $5, seniors $3, ages 6 17 $2.50. Cash only.)

APPROACHING WILMINGTON
Continue on **U.S. 202 (Concord Pike)** 1½ mi. past I-95 and turn right onto **N. Market St.**

Welcome To **DELAWARE**

WILMINGTON

Plunged into depression when its industry dried up and moved elsewhere, Delaware's largest city has recently begun to rebuild. An outlet mall, restaurants, and upscale housing now brighten up the once-decrepit downtown and riverfront areas.

▣ GETTING AROUND. In the city's center, numbered streets run east-west, starting at the southern end with **Front St.** and running from 2nd to 15th St., then continuing with 16th St. on the

(VITAL STATS)

Population: 73,000

Visitor Info: Greater Wilmington Convention and Visitors Bureau, 100 W. 10th St. (☎302-652-4088; www.visitwilmingtonde.com), at Market and Orange St. Open M-F 9am-5pm. **Info Center,** on I-95 south (☎302-737-4059). Open daily 8am-8pm.

Internet Access: Wilmington Library (☎302-571-7400), at 10th and Market St., downtown. Open M-Th 9am-8pm, F 9am-5pm, Sa 11am-3pm.

Post Office: 1101 N. King St. (☎800-275-8777), at 11th St. downtown. Open M-F 5am-6:30pm, Sa 5am-3pm. **Postal Code:** 19801.

other side of the Brandywine River. Major north-south roads in the downtown area include **Walnut St., King St.,** and **Market St.** To the west, restaurants crowd on north-south **Union St.** and **Lincoln St.** Take **Pennsylvania Ave.** from the city center for easy access to these streets. **Parking** is limited downtown; feed the meters or park in a lot. Elsewhere, free street parking is generally available.

◎ SIGHTS. Less touristy and more unique than the riverfront attractions are the city's two "outdoor museums," the Hagley Museum and Library and the Nemours Mansion, which together tell the story of the DuPont family and the DuPont industrial conglomerate's 200-year history in the area. The **Hagley Museum and Library,** on Rte. 141, is a 235-acre site containing the mills where the DuPont company manufactured blasting powder for over a century. Visitors often flock to the large mansion, but the real draw is the live demonstration of how the powder mills worked. This site is a bit time-consuming; wait to board a shuttle bus (every 30min.) or walk, as driving is not permitted on the grounds. (North of Wilmington. Turn right off U.S. 202 onto Rte. 141. ☎302-658-2400; www.hagley.lib.de.us. Tours Mar.-Dec. daily 9:30am-4:30pm; Jan.-Mar. M 1:30pm, Sa-Su 9:30am-4:30pm. $11, students and seniors $9, ages 6-14 $4; families $30. AAA discount.) The ritzy **Nemours Mansion and Gardens,** 1600 Rockland Rd., shows a more glamorous side of DuPont than the Hagley mills. Tour this 300-acre imitation Versailles, former home of Alfred DuPont, a founder of the DuPont corporation. (☎302-651-6912. Tours May-Dec. Su 11am, 1, 3pm; Tu-Sa 9, 11am, 1, 3pm. $10. Reservations recommended.)

▤ ► FOOD & ACCOMMODATIONS. Restaurants can be found in two areas: **Union** and **Lincoln St.,** and the **Trolley Square District,** up Delaware Ave. **Mrs. Robino's,** 520 N. Union St., is a great pit-stop specializing in no-frills Italian cooking. (☎302-652-9223; www.mrsrobinos.com. Pasta $6-11. Platters $7-12. Open M-Th 11am-9pm, F-Sa 11am-10pm, Su noon-9pm.) For typical Irish pub fare, try **Kelly's Logan House,** 1701 Delaware Ave., in Trolley Square, which dates back to the Civil War. (☎302-652-9493; www.loganhouse.com. Appetizers $5-9. Burgers $7-9. Pasta $10. Open M-Sa 11:30am-11:00pm.)

Chain hotels and motels dominate the northern approach to the city; some cheaper motels lie south of the city on **Dupont Hwy.** (Rte. 13) in **Newcastle,** but you get what you pay for. A slight cut above the rest in this area is the **Delaware Motel and Trailer Park,** 235 S. DuPont Hwy., south of the city, near the junction of Rte. 13 and U.S. 40. (☎302-328-3114. Rooms $40.)

► LEAVING WILMINGTON
Proceed down **King St.** After crossing **E. 2nd St.,** take a left onto **Bus. Rte. 13 South.** Follow signs for **U.S. 13,** which joins **U.S. 40 West.**

► APPROACHING HAVRE DE GRACE
39 mi. from Wilmington, turn left on **Otsego Rd.** at the sign for Havre de Grace.

HAVRE DE GRACE

Located where the Susquehanna River meets the Chesapeake Bay, Havre de Grace is home to residents who once made their living by fishing and building boats. Both industries remain, though more for the benefit of tourists than for commercial purposes. At the corner of Lafayette and Concord St. in the southeast corner of town is the **Concord Point Lighthouse.** Short and stubby, this lighthouse, while officially decommissioned in 1975, still illuminates the port. Next door, an active wooden boat-building shop is located at the back of the small **Havre de Grace Maritime Museum.** (☎410-939-4800. Open June-Aug. daily 11am-5pm; Sept.-May M and F-Su 11am-5pm. Boat building Tu 6-9:30pm. $2, students and seniors $1.)

A local favorite, **La Cucina,** 103 N. Washington St., acts as a pizza parlor and a gourmet Italian restaurant. Identity crisis aside, it is a good place for both a quick bite and a relatively inexpensive sitdown meal. (☎410-939-1401. New York-style pizzas $8-15. Pastas $7-11. Open M-Th 10:30am-10pm, F-Sa 10:30am-11pm, Su noon-9pm.)

ABERDEEN

Just 2½ mi. past Havre de Grace lies the town of Aberdeen, which Baltimore Orioles fans know as the hometown of their beloved **Cal Ripken, Jr.,** who broke Lou Gehrig's record for most consecutive baseball games ever played. Equipment from the earliest days of baseball guides visitors through the evolution of the sport at the **Ripken Museum,** 3 W. Bel Air Ave. in the former Aberdeen City Hall. Photos and memorabilia from the legendary Ripken family give the journey a face and a story. (From U.S. 40, turn right onto W. Bel Air Ave. ☎410-272-2325; www.ripkenmuseum.com. Open M-F 9am-5pm, Sa 11am-4pm. Hours may vary; call ahead. $3, seniors $2, students $1.) "Real" is the best word to describe the ◪**US Army Ordnance Museum,** on the Aberdeen Proving Ground; there are few photos or replicas, just real guns, real mortars, and real tanks. (After passing the checkpoint, take a left at the 4th light and then an immediate right into the parking lot in front of the tanks. ☎410-278-3602. Open daily 9am-4:45pm.)

Two quirky roadside diners occupy the Aberdeen Area. The **New Ideal Diner,** on U.S. 40 just past Bel Air Ave, is prettied up as a chrome and metal railway car. The building is a 1952 "O'Mahony" type, built elsewhere and moved to this site. The diner specializes in seafood; its prices are on the high side. (☎410-272-1880. Seafood up to $18. Open daily 6am-8pm.) The 14-page menu at the chrome-and-neon **White Marsh Double T Diner,** 10741 Pulaski Hwy. (U.S. 40), is sure to have something you want. While not the cheapest, this is one of the better diners on this stretch of U.S. 40. (In White Marsh, MD, at the corner of Ebenezer Rd. ☎410-344-1020. Burgers $5-8. Open 24hr.)

LEAVING ABERDEEN
Cross the Baltimore Beltway and follow **U.S. 40.**

ROSEDALE. Diners and motels abound on this stretch of the road, but tiny Rosedale is home to a pleasing pair. The chrome **Happy Day Diner,** 8302 Pulaski Hwy., has a more limited selection than the White Marsh, but the food is cheaper. (☎410-687-2129. Open M-F 6am-10pm, Sa-Su 24hr.) **Duke's Motel,** 7905 Pulaski Hwy., offers the cheapest accommodations around. (☎410-686-0400. Key deposit $5. Singles $45; doubles $50.)

APPROACHING BALTIMORE
Stay on **U.S. 40** as it crosses **I-895/I-95.** About 1½ mi. past the beltway, veer right, following signs for **U.S. 40/Orleans St.**

BALTIMORE

Stuck between the North and the South and nicknamed the "Charm City" for its mix of small-town hospitality and big-city flair, Baltimore offers visitors eclectic museums, big-city markets, and a lively restaurant and bar scene. Visitors flock to the touristy Inner Harbor at the base of downtown, but most residents live and work elsewhere in the city. Birthplace of the *Star-Spangled Banner*, Baltimore lies just north of the nation's capital and is home to two major sports teams that provide year-round spectacle.

VITAL STATS

Population: 650,000

Visitor Info: Baltimore Area Visitors Center, 100 Light St. (☎877-225-8466 or 410-837-7024; www.baltimore.org). Open daily 9am-6pm.

Internet Access: Enoch Pratt Free Library, 400 Cathedral St. (☎410-396-5430). Open M-W 10am-8pm, Th 10am-5:30pm, F-Sa 10am-5pm; Sept.-May also Su 1-5pm.

Post Office: 900 E. Fayette St. (☎410-347-4202). Open M-F 7:30am-10pm, Sa 8:30am-5pm. **Postal Code:** 21233.

GETTING AROUND

Baltimore lies 35 mi. north of Washington D.C. and about 150 mi. west of the Atlantic. **U.S. 40** runs east-west through the northern end of downtown, while the **Jones Falls Expressway (I-83)** cuts into Baltimore from the north. The **Baltimore Beltway (I-695)** and a series of other ring roads circle

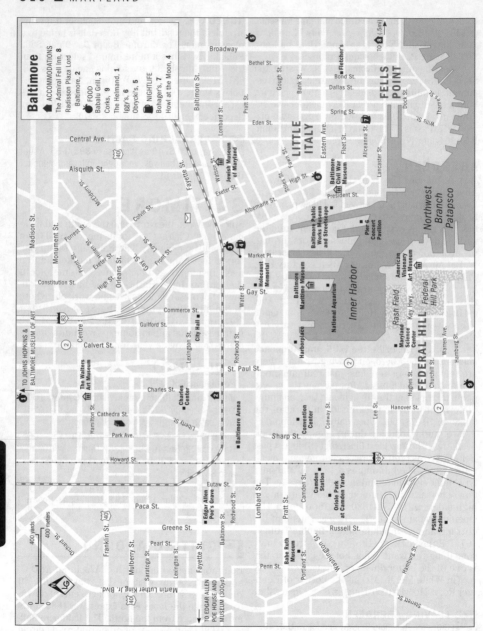

Baltimore

▲ **ACCOMMODATIONS**
The Admiral Fell Inn, 8
Radisson Plaza Lord
Baltimore, 2

● **FOOD**
Babalu Grill, 3
Corks, 9
The Helmand, 1
Iggy's, 6
Obrycki's, 5

■ **NIGHTLIFE**
Bohager's, 7
Howl at the Moon, 4

the city, which lies just off north-south **I-95**. Within the city, streets have directionality based on their relationship to east-west **Baltimore St.** and north-south **Charles St.** The main arteries serving the Inner Harbor and downtown Baltimore are mostly one-way and include **Charles St.** which runs north, and **St. Paul St./Light St.**, which runs south (both intersect U.S. 40). **Pratt St.** runs east, **Lombard St.** runs west, and both end at **Rte. 144/Frederick Rd.**

The best bet for **parking** is to bring a roll of quarters, as meters are plentiful but hungry (generally $1 per hr.), with many enforced 24hr. Garages are easy to find throughout downtown and are most expensive near the Inner Harbor (up to $12 daily). A long stretch of 4hr. parking meters lies along Key Hwy. just south of the Inner Harbor; take St. Paul St. south past the Inner Harbor and turn left on Key Hwy. In **Little Italy,** there is a lot on Albemarle St., just north of Eastern St. ($7 flat rate).

👁 SIGHTS

Commercial shopping and touristy restaurants crowd the **Inner Harbor,** home to the National Aquarium. An excursion to the Johns Hopkins University campus and nearby Druid Hill Park escapes the glitz (and grime) of the city. And just roaming the different neighborhoods and myriad small museums has its own rewards. Baltimore sights are spread into several clusters, so your best bet is to drive to an area, park, and walk.

▓ THE NATIONAL AQUARIUM. The National Aquarium is perhaps the one thing, besides its murder rate, that sets Baltimore apart from all other major American cities. Though a visit to the outdoor sea pool to watch slap-happy seals play is free to the general public, it is worth the time and money to venture inside. The eerie **Wings in the Water** exhibit showcases 50 species of stingrays in an immense backlit pool. In the steamy **Tropical Rainforest,** parrots and a pair of two-toed sloths peer through the dense foliage in a 157 ft. glass pyramid. At the **Marine Mammal Pavilion,** dolphins perform every hour on the half-hour. *(Pier 3, 501 E. Pratt St. ☎410-576-3800; www.aqua.org. Open M-Th 9am-5pm, F-Sa 9am-8pm, Su 9am-7pm. $17.50, seniors $14.50, ages 3-11 $9.50, under 3 free.)*

BALTIMORE MARITIME MUSEUM. Several ships, most of which belong to the Baltimore Maritime Museum, grace the harbor by the aquarium. Visitors clamber through the interior of the **USS Torsk,** the intricately painted submarine that sank the last WWII Japanese combat ship. You can also board one of the survivors of the Pearl Harbor attack, the Coast Guard cutter **Roger B. Taney,** and ascend the octagonal **lighthouse** on Pier 5. For these historic sites and more, purchase the **Seaport Day Pass,** which grants access to the **Maritime Museum,** the **Museum of Industry,** Baltimore's **World Trade Center,** and the **USS Constellation**—the last all-sail warship built by the US Navy. Water taxi service to and from attractions is included. *(Piers 3 and 5. ☎410-396-3453; http://baltomaritimemuseum.org. Open Su-Th 10am-5:30pm, F-Sa 10am-6pm; in winter Su and F-Sa 10:30am-5pm. Boats stay open 1hr. later than ticket stand. $6, seniors $5, ages 5-13 $3. Seaport Day Pass $16/$13.50/$9.)*

FEELING CRABBY?

A long-time Maryland favorite, crab cakes are deep- or pan-fried patties of lump crabmeat and batter that together form a delectable entree. Most restaurants in the Baltimore area serve crab cakes. The quality and size of said cakes vary widely among restaurants, and diners often pay up to $15 for just 2 crab cakes! *Let's Go* recommends making these simple homemade crab cakes instead.

Ingredients: 1 lb. backfin crab meat; 1 egg, beaten; 8 crumbled saltine crackers; 2 tbsp. mayonnaise; 1 tsp. mustard; dash Worcestershire sauce

Carefully remove all cartilage from the crab meat. Put meat in a bowl and set it aside. Mix together all other ingredients. Gently mix in crab meat. Shape into 6 crab cakes. Put crab cakes on a plate, cover with wax paper, and refrigerate for an hour. In a large frying pan, heat about 1-2 tbsp. of vegetable oil. Sauté until golden brown (about 2-3min. per side). Serve crab cakes on a bed of greens with Hollandaise sauce and an ice cold beer.

ROAD FOOD

NATIONAL ROAD

WALTERS ART MUSEUM. Spanning 50 centuries in three buildings, the Walters Art Museum houses one of the largest private art collections in the world. The ancient art features sculpture, jewelry, and metalwork from Egypt, Greece, and Rome, and is the museum's pride and joy. Byzantine, Romanesque, and Gothic art are also on display. At the **Hackerman House,** an exquisite mansion attached to the Walters, rooms filled with dark wooden furniture, patterned rugs, and plush velvet curtains display art from China, Korea, Japan, and India. *(600 N. Charles St. ☎410-547-9000; www.thewalters.org. Open Su and Tu-Sa 10am-5pm, 1st Th of every month 10am-8pm. Tours W noon and Su 1:30pm. $8, seniors $6, students $5, under 19 free. Free Sa 10am-1pm and 1st Th of every month.)*

EDGAR ALLAN POE HOUSE. Horror pioneer Edgar Allan Poe was born in 1809 in what is now a preserved historical landmark in the heart of a run-down neighborhood. The house contains period furniture and exhibits relating to Poe, all impeccably maintained by a staff eager to regale visitors with Poe stories. Steer clear of the neighborhood at night. *(203 N. Amity St., near Saratoga St. 2nd house on the right. ☎ 410-396-7932; www.eapoe.org. Open Apr.-July and Oct.-Dec. W-Sa noon-3:45pm; Aug.-Sept. Sa noon-3:45pm. $3, under 13 $1.)*

JOHNS HOPKINS UNIVERSITY. Approximately 3 mi. north of the harbor, prestigious Johns Hopkins University (JHU) radiates out from 33rd St. JHU was the first research university in the country and is currently a world leader in medicine, public health, and engineering. The campus was originally the Homewood estate of Charles Carroll, Jr., the son of the longest-lived signer of the Declaration of Independence. One-hour campus tours begin at the **Office of Admissions** in Garland Hall. *(3400 N. Charles St. ☎410-516-8171; www.jhu.edu. Tours Sept.-May M-F 10am, noon, 3pm. For summer hours, call ☎410-516-5589.)* One mile north of the main campus, the **Evergreen House** is an exercise in excess—even the bathroom of this elegant mansion is plated in 23-carat gold. Purchased in 1878 by railroad tycoon John W. Garret, the house, along with its collections of fine porcelain, impressive artwork, Tiffany silver, and rare books, was bequeathed to JHU in 1942. *(4545 N. Charles St. ☎410-516-0341. Open M-F 10am-4pm, Sa-Su 1-4pm. Tours every hr. 10am-3pm. $6, seniors $5, students $3.)*

ENTERTAINMENT

Much of Baltimore's finest entertainment can be enjoyed free of charge. At **Harborplace,** street performers are constantly amusing tourists with magic acts and juggling during the day. On weekend nights, dance, dip, and dream to the sounds of anything from country to calypso. The **Baltimore Museum of Art,** 10 Art Museum Dr., offers free summer jazz concerts in its sculpture garden. (☎410-466-0600. May-Sept. Sa 7pm.) More jazz can be found several times a week from May to October at the canvas-topped **Pier 6 Concert Pavilion,** 731 Eastern Ave. (☎410-625-3100. Tickets $15-30.) For a more private performance from local artists and some big names, **Fletcher's,** 701 S. Bond St., features everything from rock to rap to blues. (☎410-558-1889. Open Su-Th 5pm-2am, F-Sa 4pm-2am.) Zydeco fans gather at **Harry's,** 1200 N. Charles St., a Vegas-style bar and performance space. (☎410-685-2828. Shows F-Sa. Cover $3-10. Open F 11am-2am, Sa 2pm-2am.)

The **Theater Project,** 45 W. Preston St., near Maryland St., experiments with theater, poetry, music, and dance. (☎410-752-8558. Box office open 1hr. before shows; call to charge tickets. Shows Su 3pm, Th-Sa 8pm. $15, seniors $10.) The **Arena Players,** the first black theater group in the country, performs comedy, drama, and dance at 801 McCullough St., at Martin Luther King, Jr. Blvd. (☎410-728-6500. Box office open M-F 10am-2pm. Tickets from $15.) The **Showcase of Nations Ethnic Festivals** celebrate Baltimore's ethnic neighborhoods, featuring a different culture each week.

The beloved **Baltimore Orioles** play ball at **Camden Yards,** at the corner of Russell and Camden St. (☎410-685-9800. Tickets $7-50.) The expansion-team Baltimore **Ravens,** successors to the defunct Baltimore Colts, matured fast enough to win the 2001 Super Bowl. They play in **Ravens Stadium** (☎410-481-7328; www.ravenszone.net).

FOOD

If you're blowing through Baltimore with some cash to burn, forget the touristy, overpriced eateries that crowd the Inner Harbor and head to some of Baltimore's more-upscale choices, scattered throughout the city. Be sure not to leave without a taste of the region's famous ◼**crab cakes.**

⬧ **Corks,** 1026 S. Charles St. (☎410-752-3810). A hidden retreat specializing in a vast array of strictly American wines and fine contemporary American cuisine infused with classic French techniques and Asian influences. Semi-formal attire. Appetizers $10-15. Entrees $24-30. Open M-Th 5-10pm, F-Sa 5-11pm, Su 5-9:30pm.

Obrycki's, 1727 E. Pratt St. (☎410-732-6399). Fresh, fabulous seafood since 1944. Crab cake sandwiches $15. Dinner entrees $13-29. Open M-Sa 11:30am-11pm, Su 11:30am-9:30pm.

Iggy's, 410 S. High St. (☎410-685-6727), near Little Italy. From U.S. 40, head south on Broadway to Eastern and turn right. Local favorite serves sandwiches ($5) and soups ($3) from its long counters. Free but limited street parking. Open M-Sa 7am-2:30pm.

Babalu Grill, 32 Market Pl. (☎410-234-9898), in Power Plant Live. Popular appetizers include Cuban-style turnovers with seasoned beef and avocado salsa ($6). Babalu turns into a hot salsa club at night ($5 cover 10-11pm, $10 cover after 11pm). Open for lunch Tu-F 11:30am-2:30pm; dinner M-Th 5-10pm, F-Sa 5-11pm, Su 4-9pm. Club open Th-Sa 10pm-2am.

The Helmand, 806 N. Charles St. (☎410-752-0311). This unassuming Afghan restaurant is the best in town, with dishes like *kaddo borani* (pan-fried and baked pumpkin in a yogurt-garlic sauce; $3). Entrees up to $10. Vegetarians have options, and desserts satisfy every sweet tooth. Open Su-Th 5-10pm, F-Sa 5-11pm.

🏠 ACCOMMODATIONS

Hotels dominate the Inner Harbor, and budget lodgings elsewhere are hard to find. Amanda's Bed and Breakfast Reservation Service, 1428 Park Ave., reserves B&Bs. (☎800-899-7533; www.bedandbreakfast-maryland.com. Open M-F 10am-5pm. Rooms from $65.) There are motels on **Washington Blvd.,** 4-10 mi. south of the downtown area. To get there from downtown, take Light St. west to Conway St. Turn left to get on I-395 South, following it to I-95 South. Take Exit 50A onto Caton Ave. and turn right on Washington Blvd.

Radisson Plaza Lord Baltimore, 20 W. Baltimore St. (☎410-539-8400 or 800-333-3333), between Liberty and Charles St. A national historic landmark built in 1928, this is the oldest hotel in Baltimore. Rooms are large though sometimes shabby, but the location—6 blocks from the Inner Harbor—and historic flavor are

unbeatable. Fitness center. Parking $25 per night. Reservations recommended. Rooms $129-209. 10% AAA discount.

The Admiral Fell Inn, 888 S. Broadway (☎410-522-7377 or 866-583-4162; www.harbormagic.com), at Thames St. A portal to the past with themed rooms that include canopied beds and armoires. Unlimited Internet access $4 per day. Parking $15 per night. Rooms $169-259. 10% AAA discount.

Capitol KOA, 768 Cecil Ave. North (☎410-923-2771 or 800-562-0248), in Millersville, between D.C. and Baltimore. Take U.S. 50 East to Rte. 3 North. Bear right after 8 mi. onto Veterans Hwy., turn left under the highway onto Hog Farm Rd., and follow the signs. Mostly RVs, some cabins, and a small wooded area for tents. Pool, volleyball courts, and bath/shower facilities. Open Mar. 25-Oct. 1-room cabins $58; 2-room cabins $67; sites for 2 $33, with water and electricity $39, with full hookup $44. $5 per additional person.

White Elk Motel, 6195 Washington Blvd. (☎410-796-5151), in Elkridge, 10 mi. south of downtown. While a bit out of the way, a landscaped entrance and cottage inn-style rooms with bathtubs make this a comfy place. Singles $50; doubles $53.

🎭 NIGHTLIFE

Nightlife in Mount Vernon tends more toward classic bars populated by an older and more sophisticated set, while Fells Point and Power Plant Live are home to the college and 20-something scene. Be aware of the 1:30am last call.

Bohager's, 701 S. Eden St., between Spring and Eden St. in Fells Point, is a tropical paradise for college students and folks who drink like them. Patrons jive to the sounds of DJs' island and house mixes under a retractable dome in the most debauched club in Baltimore. (☎410-563-7220 Open M-F 11:30am-2am, Sa-Su 3pm-2am.) **Howl At The Moon,** 34 Market Pl., in Power Plant Live, is an dueling-piano bar where the crowd runs the show. All songs are by request, and sing-alongs are frequent. (☎410-783-5111. Cover $7. Open Tu-Th and Sa 7pm-2am, F 5pm-2am.)

🚗 LEAVING BALTIMORE

The route out of Baltimore follows the old **National Road,** or **Rte. 144,** which is not U.S. 40. From down town, get on **Lombard St.** heading west and take a soft left to proceed on Rte. 144 West.

NATIONAL ROAD

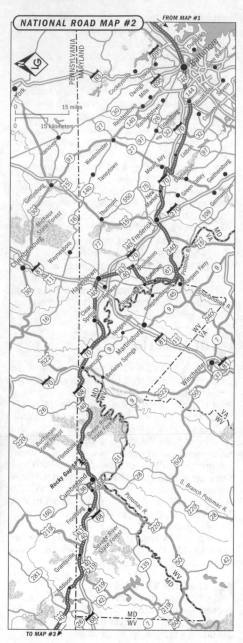

NATIONAL ROAD MAP #2 · FROM MAP #1 · TO MAP #3

ELLICOTT CITY

Ten miles from Baltimore, Frederick Rd. (Rte. 144) becomes Main St. as it crawls into Ellicott City, an old Quaker mill town nestled into an idyllic hillside. The most memorable experience of your stop here may be just marveling at the city's physical location on the descending Patapsco River. Today, antique shops in equally antique buildings line the brick sidewalks along Main St. Housed in the oldest railroad terminal in America, the **B&O Railroad Station Museum,** 2711 Maryland Ave., at Main St., relates the history of the area's railroad and its role in the Civil War. (☎410-461-1945; www.ecbo.org. Open M and F-Sa 11am-4pm, Su noon-5pm.) The **Visitors Center,** 8267 Main St., has info on walking tours. (In the basement of the post office; enter off Hamilton St. ☎410-313-1900. Open M-F 10am-5pm, Sa-Su noon-5pm.)

Shopkeepers in Ellicott City get lunch at **Sorrento's,** 8167 Main St., which serves up burgers ($2), subs ($4-9) and large cheese pizzas ($7.50). The bar upstairs offers the same food with a bit more atmosphere. (☎410-465-1001. Open M-Th 11am-9pm, F-Sa 11am-10pm, Su 11am-8pm. Bar open from 4pm.) Not particularly congruent with the rest of town but still a good option is **La Palapa Grill & Cantina,** 8307 Main St., featuring *burritos grandes* ($10-12), fajitas ($15), and seafood specialties ($15-17) in a large, colorful dining room. (☎410-465-0070; www.lapalapagrill.com. Open Su-Th 11am-9pm, F-Sa 11am-10:30pm.)

THE ROAD TO FREDERICK

Notice the National Road/Cumberland Road markers on the way out of town. It is along this stretch that the route begins exploring towns that grew up on the National Road. The road becomes two-lane and rural, with few lights or services through the least densely populated area yet. The gradual hills signal the approach of the Appalachian Mountains. **Rte. 144 (Frederick Rd.)** flirts with **U.S. 40** after leaving Baltimore; stay on Rte. 144 and proceed around the rotary to pass through the small town of Lisbon.

▶ APPROACHING NEW MARKET
After Lisbon, **Rte. 144** curves and stops at a T-intersection. Turn right on **Rte. 27,** following signs for **Mt. Airy.** Turn left on **E. Ridgeville Blvd.,** which becomes the **Old National Pike** after about 1½ mi.

NEW MARKET. The self-proclaimed "antiques capital of Maryland," lies on the old National Road. Older than most of the towns on the road, with several buildings dating from the 1700s, New Market has become a center for antique shops, each with its own specialty. Shopkeepers here seem to have found the good life; most stores only open on weekends. The town guide lists the specialties of the various shops. During the week, supplies can be found at the tourist-oriented **General Store,** 26 W. Main St. (☎301-865-6313. Open M-Tu and Th-F 9am-5pm, Sa-Su 9am-6pm.)

LEAVING NEW MARKET
Leave on **Main St.** About 3 mi. past New Market, fork right at the sign for "To West 40." Stay west on **Rte. 144,** which is **E. Patrick St.** in Frederick.

FREDERICK

Frederick lies at the southeastern corner of a region littered with Civil War sites. Like neighboring Harper's Ferry (see p. 322), the city was at the center of the battle lines, alternately occupied by Union and Confederate forces. Modern-day Frederick has a pleasant, well-kept downtown with an assortment of boutiques and pricey but good food.

(VITAL STATS)

Population: 53,000

Visitor Info: Frederick Visitors Center, 19 E. Church St. (☎301-228-2888 or 800-999-3613; www.cityoffrederick.com). Open daily 9am-5pm.

Internet Access: C. Burr Artz Library, 110 E. Patrick St. (☎301-694-1630), downtown. Open M-Th 10am-9pm, F-Sa 10am-5pm, Su 1-5pm.

Post Office: 201 E. Patrick Street (☎800-275-8777), between East and Caroll St. Open M-F 8am-6pm, Sa 8am-2pm. **Postal Code:** 21701.

GETTING AROUND. Rte. 144, the old National Road, runs one-way west through Frederick, where it is known as **Patrick St.** At the center of town it intersects the main north-south thoroughfare, one-way **Market St.** Shops and restaurants congregate on these streets and surrounding blocks. To head east, use **South St.,** just south of Patrick St., or **Church St.,** one block north.

Most streets have 2hr. parking meters, but **parking** can be tight. There are several garages in town, including one off E. Patrick St. by the library (M-F $1 per hr., $5 max.; Sa-Su all-day $1) and another off Church St. by the Visitors Center.

SIGHTS. Civil War history is well preserved in Frederick. The **National Museum of Civil War Medicine,** 48 E. Patrick St., focuses on "immersion exhibits," seven life-sized dioramas with accompanying audio that depict battlefield medical scenes. (☎301-695-1864; www.civilwarmed.org. Open M-Sa 10am-5pm, Su 11am-5pm. $6.50; seniors, military, and students $6; ages 10-16 $4.50; under 10 free.) Recreated after floods, the house and gardens of the **Barbara Fritchie House & Museum,** 154 W. Patrick St., hearken back to the days when Fritchie championed the efforts of Union soldiers. According to legend, as General Stonewall Jackson marched into town, a 95-year-old Fritchie waved her Union flag. Today this site exhibits original furnishings, documents, and clothing. (☎301-698-0630. Open Apr.-Sept. M and Th-Sa 10am-4pm, Su 1-4pm.) The **Mt. Olivet Cemetery,** 515 S. Market St., has graves from the Civil War era, including those of Francis Scott Key, the author of the national anthem, and Thomas Johnson, the first governor of Maryland. (Head south from Patrick St. on Carroll St., turn right onto South St., then left onto Market St. ☎301-662-1164. Open daily dawn-dusk.) For those less into Civil War lore, **Wonder Book and Video,** 1306 W. Patrick St., is a worthwhile stop, with 30 aisles of books packed floor to ceiling. Comics and videos are also available. (2½ mi. west of town, in the Golden Mile Marketplace. ☎301-694-5955. Open daily 10am-10pm.)

FOOD & ACCOMMODATIONS. Frederick offers simple yet enjoyable dining options. A local favorite, family-owned **Nido's,** 111 E. Patrick St., serves Italian fare with homemade sauces. (☎301-624-1052. Pastas $7-11. Entrees $8-21. Open M-Th 11:30am-2:30pm and 4:30-9:30pm, F-Sa 11:30am-10pm, Su 3-9pm. Reservations recommended on weekends.) At the **Mountain View Diner,** 1300 W. Patrick St., customers can see the Blue Ridge Mountains off to the west as they enjoy a California chicken salad ($9) or burger. (☎301-696-1300. Entrees $9-19. Open M-Th 7:30am-11pm, F-Sa 7:30am-midnight, Su 7:30am-10pm.)

NATIONAL ROAD

The best bet for budget lodging in Frederick is **Masser's Motel,** 1505 W. Patrick St., 3¼ mi. west of the town center, which offers simple, dated rooms, some with microwaves and fridges. (☎301-663-3698. Singles $37; doubles $42.)

LEAVING FREDERICK

Head west on **W. Patrick St. (Rte. 144).** Proceed ½ mi. to the intersection with **Jefferson St.,** and make a soft left at the sign for **U.S. 340 West.**

HI-AYH HARPERS FERRY LODGE

19123 Sandy Hook Rd. *18 mi. from Frederick, in Knoxville. Turn left onto Keep Tryst Rd. and take your 1st right on Sandy Hook Rd.*

Backpackers, passing travelers, and scouting troops all find respite at the homey ⚑**Harpers Ferry Lodge** hostel, situated near the route as well as the C&O Canal and Appalachian Trails. Housed in a single-level building, it has a fully equipped kitchen, showers, laundry, and lounge/library. For $5 extra, indulge in the all-you-can-eat pancake breakfast. (☎301-834-7652; www.harpersferryhostel.org. Reception Mar. 14-Nov. 14 7-9am and 6-10pm. Lockout 9am-6pm. Reserve ahead. Dorms $15-18; tent sites $9 per person.)

THE ROAD TO HARPERS FERRY. Continuing west on U.S. 340 past Keep Tryst Rd., this pretty stretch of road parallels the old C&O Canal, through rolling woods and fields, and veers briefly into Virginia before entering West Virginia.

APPROACHING HARPERS FERRY

At the sign for Harpers Ferry, turn left to enter the **Harpers Ferry National Historic Park** or right to enter the town of Harpers Ferry on **Washington St.**

HARPERS FERRY

A bucolic hillside town overlooking the Shenandoah and Potomac rivers, Harpers Ferry earned its fame when a band of abolitionists led by John Brown raided the US Armory in 1859. Although Brown was captured and executed, the raid brought the issue of slavery into the national spotlight. Brown's adamant belief in violence as the only means to overcome the problem of slavery soon gained credence, and the town became a major theater of conflict, changing hands eight times during the Civil War. Today, Harpers Ferry attracts more mild-mannered guests who come to enjoy the surrounding wilderness.

VITAL STATS

Population: 300

Visitor Info: Jefferson County Convention and Visitors Bureau (☎304-535-2627; www.jeffersoncountycvb.com), on Washington St., just off U.S. 340. Open daily summer 9am-6pm; winter 9am-5pm. **Cavalier Heights Visitors Center** (☎304-535-6298; www.harpersferryhistory.org), off U.S. 340, inside Harpers Ferry National Historic Park entrance. Open daily 8am-5pm. **Historic Town Area Visitor Information Center,** (☎304-535-6298; www.harpersferryhistory.org), on Shenandoah St., near High St. Open daily 8am-5pm.

Post Office: 1010 Washington St. (☎304-535-2479). Open M-F 8am-4pm, Sa 9am-noon. **Postal Code:** 25425.

GETTING AROUND

Harpers Ferry lies just south of the Potomac River and is surrounded on three sides by Harpers Ferry National Historic Park. **U.S. 340** runs just south of town; most attractions are located on **Washington St.,** which runs east-west through town. **Parking** is generally free at Washington St. establishments but is not permitted on the streets of the **Lower Town** area of the National Historic Park; visitors must park at the Cavalier Heights Visitors Center unless they are staying at accommodations with parking within walking distance of town. Shuttles leave the lot for town every 10min.; the last pickup is at 6:45pm.

SIGHTS

The **Harpers Ferry National Historic Park,** comprising most of historic Harper's Ferry, consists of several museums, all of which are included with admission to the park. The park also offers occasional reenactments of Harpers Ferry's history. (☎304-

535-6298. Open daily summer 8am-6pm; winter 8am-5pm. 3-day admission $5 per car; $3 per pedestrian, bike, or motorcycle.) The shuttle from the parking lot stops at **Shenandoah St.,** where a barrage of replicated 19th-century shops greets visitors. The **Dry Goods Store** displays clothes, hardware, liquor, and groceries that would have been sold over 100 years ago. Check out the 1850s price list to compare prices then and now. The **Harpers Ferry Industrial Museum,** on Shenandoah St., describes the methods used to harness the powers of the Shenandoah and Potomac Rivers and details the town's status as the terminus of the nation's first successful rail line. The once-unsung stories of the area captivate visitors at **Black Voices from Harpers Ferry,** at the corner of Shenandoah and High St., where well-trained actors play fettered slaves expressing their opinions of John Brown and his raid. Next door on High St., the plight of Harpers Ferry's slaves is further elaborated in the **Civil War Story.** Informative displays detail the importance of Harpers Ferry's strategic location. A ticket is required for some exhibits.

The **John Brown Museum,** on Shenandoah St., just beyond High St., is the town's most captivating historical site. A 30min. video chronicles Brown's raid of the armory with a special focus on the moral and political implications of his actions. A daunting, steep staircase hewn into the hillside off High St. follows the **Appalachian Trail** to **Upper Harpers Ferry,** which has fewer sights but is laced with interesting historical tales. Allow 45min. to ascend past **Harper's House,** the restored home of town founder Robert Harper, and **St. Peter's Church,** where a pastor flew the Union Jack during the Civil War to protect the church. Just a few steps uphill from St. Peter's lie the archaeological ruins of **St. John's Episcopal Church,** which was built 1852 and used as a hospital and barracks during the Civil War before being abandoned in 1895.

OUTDOOR ACTIVITIES

Pick up trail maps at the park's Visitors Center before setting off into the wilderness. The moderate difficulty **Maryland Heights Trail,** located across the railroad bridge in the Lower Town of Harpers Ferry, winds 4 mi. through steep Blue Ridge Mountains that include precipitous cliffs and crumbling Civil War-era forts. The strenuous 7½ mi. **Loudon Heights Trail** starts in Lower Town off the Appalachian Trail and leads to Civil War infan-

try trenches and scenic overlooks. For less strenuous hiking, the 2½ mi. **Camp Hill Trail** passes by the Harper Cemetery and ends at the former Stoner College. History dominates the **Bolivar Heights Trail,** starting at the northern end of Whitman Ave.

The **Chesapeake & Ohio Canal** towpath, off the end of Shenandoah St. and over the railroad bridge, serves as a reminder of the town's industrial roots and is the departure point for a day's bike ride to Washington, D.C. The **Appalachian Trail Conference,** 799 Washington St., at Jackson St., offers deals on hiking books and trail info. (☎304-535-6331; www.appalachiantrail.org. Open mid-May to Oct. M-F 9am-5pm, Sa-Su and holidays 9am-4pm; Nov. to mid-May M-F 9am-5pm. Membership $30, seniors and students $25.)

River & Trail Outfitters, 604 Valley Rd., 2 mi. out of Harpers Ferry off U.S. 340, in Knoxville, MD, rents canoes, kayaks, inner tubes, and rafts. They also organize everything from scenic daytrips to placid rides down the Shenandoah River ($21) to wild overnights. (☎301-695-5177; www.rivertrail.com. Canoes $55 per day. Raft trips $50-60 per person, under 17 $40. Tubing $32 per day.) At **Butt's Tubes, Inc.,** on Rte. 671 off U.S. 340, adventurers can buy a tube for the day and sell it back later. (☎800-836-9911; www.buttstubes.com. Open M-F 10am-3pm, last pickup 5pm; Sa-Su 10am-4pm, last pickup 6pm. $12-20.) Equestrian activities in the area include a variety of recreational trips offered through **Elk Mountain Trails.** (☎301-834-8882; www.elkmountaintrails.com. $20-68. Cash only.)

At the **Appalachian Trail Regional Headquarters and Information Center,** 799 Washington St., a 10 ft. relief map shows the whole trail, and more sedentary visitors can take a virtual hike. Volunteers are available to answer questions. Maps are for sale at the trail shop. On weekdays, park on Washington St. in front of the old school. On weekends, park in the lot behind the offices off Storer College Pl. (☎304-535-6331; www.appalachiantrail.org. Open M-F 9am-5pm except holidays; mid-May to Oct. also open Sa-Su and holidays 9am-4pm.)

FOOD

Harpers Ferry has sparse offerings for hungry hikers on a budget. U.S. 340 welcomes fast-food fanatics with various chain restaurants. The historic area, especially High St. and Potomac St., caters to the lunch crowd with either burgers and fries or salads and steaks but vacates at dinner-

NATIONAL ROAD

time. Nearby Charles Town's ◨**La Mezzaluna Cafe,** Somerset Village Ste. B3, serves surprisingly delicious Italian favorites in a spacious setting. Pasta entrees ($9-14) come with a house salad. (Off U.S. 340, 5min. from Harper's Ferry. ☎304-728-0700. Lunch Tu-Sa 11am-3pm; dinner Su 2:30-9pm, Tu-Th 4-9pm, F-Sa 4-10pm.) Across the street from the Hillside Motel, the **Cindy Dee Restaurant,** 19112 Keep Tryst Rd., at U.S. 340, fries enough chicken ($5) to clog all your arteries. The homemade apple dumplings ($2.75) are delectable. (☎301-695-8181. Open daily 7am-9pm.) Amid the colonial architecture of E. German St., the **Mecklinburg Inn,** 128 E. German St., provides rock 'n' roll and Rolling Rock ($1.75) on open mic night every Tuesday from 9pm to midnight. (☎301-876-2126. Happy hour M-F 4:30-6:30pm. 21+ after 5pm. Open M-Th 3pm-12:30am, F 3pm-1:30am, Sa 1pm-2am, Su 1pm-12:30am. Cash only.) **The Anvil,** 1270 Washington St., serves delightfully non-greasy pub food for lunch, and fresh fish, beef, and filets for dinner; vegetarian items are also available. Don't miss the slot machines in the "gaming room" behind the door opposite the bar. (☎304-535-2582. Open Su and W-Sa 11am-9pm.) For lighter fare, **Jumpin Java Coffee,** 1274 Washington St., serves breakfast and light lunch accompanied by funky tunes. (☎304-728-0195. Sandwiches $3-6. Bagels and wraps $2-5. Open Su 9am-4pm, Tu-Th 7am-4:30pm, F 7am-7pm, Sa 8am-5:30pm. Cash only.)

⌂ ACCOMMODATIONS

There are B&Bs located in town as well as in nearby Charles Town (west of Harpers Ferry on U.S. 340). The HI-AYH Harpers Ferry Lodge (see p. 322) is 2 mi. east of town. Fishing fanatics might try **Anglers Inn,** 867 Washington St., with mariner decor and fly-fishing packages available. All rooms come with a private bath. (☎304-535-1239; www.theanglersinn.com. Rooms $95-115.) The **Hillside Motel,** 19105 Keep Tryst Rd., 3 mi. from town in Knoxville, MD, has 19 clean rooms inside a beautiful stone motel. (☎301-834-8144. Singles $40; doubles $50. Less in winter.) The charming **Harpers Ferry Guest House,** 800 Washington St., is ideally located in the center of the historic district. (☎304-535-6955. Rooms M-Th $75, F-Su $95.) Without a doubt, the most splendid views of the rivers and mountains can be had at the historic **Hilltop House Hotel,** 400 E. Ridge St., which sits on a cliff within walking distance of sights and

attractions. Although the rooms are somewhat worn, the views more than compensate. Ask about weekend murder mystery group parties. (☎304-535-2132 or 800-338-8319; www.hilltophousehotel.net. Rooms $70-155.)

Camp along the **C&O Canal,** or in one of the five Maryland state park campgrounds within 30 mi. of Harpers Ferry. (Ranger station ☎301-739-4200.) **Greenbrier State Park,** on U.S. 40 E off Rte. 66, has 165 campsites and outdoor recreation near a lake. (☎301-791-4767 or 888-432-2267; http://reservations.dnr.state.md.us. Reservations required. Open May-Sept. Sites $20, with hookup $25.)

THE ROAD TO HAGERSTOWN

The road to Antietam Battlefield from Harpers Ferry is fantastically beautiful, winding its way north through the Blue Ridge Mountains. Head east on **U.S. 340** from Harpers Ferry for about 4½ mi., passing into Virginia and then Maryland. Cross Harpers Ferry Rd. and turn right on **Keep Tryst Rd.** Take your first right onto **Sandy Hook Rd.,** which becomes **Harpers Ferry Rd.** Continue on Harpers Ferry Rd. approximately 13 mi. until you reach **Sharpsburg.** Harpers Ferry Rd. through this section can be dangerous; it is quite narrow and there are a number of unsigned sharp curves. Avoid driving this stretch at night or in snowy conditions. In Sharpsburg, turn right at the second stop sign onto **Main St.,** and follow Main St. east out of town, where it becomes **Rte. 34** en route to Boonsboro. **Newcomer House,** 8422 Shepardstown Pike, 1 mi. from Sharpsburg, is a 1790s residence that now houses a private collection of Civil War memorabilia, including a signed copy of the Emancipation Proclamation. (☎301-432-0300. Open daily, hours vary. $3, families $5.) Rte. 34 leads into the town of **Boonsboro.** Turn left here onto **Alt. U.S. 40** to continue toward Hagerstown.

Welcome To **MARYLAND**

◉ **ANTIETAM NATIONAL BATTLEFIELD**
18 mi. from Harpers Ferry. From Main St. in Sharpsburg, take a left onto S. Church St. (Rte. 65).

The day of the Civil War battle of Antietam, September 17, 1862, is said to have been the single bloodiest day in US history. The battle killed 23,110 soldiers but stopped General Lee's advance into the north and eventually led to the Emancipation Proclamation. Inside the park, a stone observation tower offers a view of the expansive fields and nearby farmhouses. There are several fairly flat hiking trails through the area; the Visitors Center offers info on vegetation and wildlife. A driving tour of the battlefield leads through the fields and past the major sites of the battle. To begin, stop at the **Antietam National Battlefield Visitors Center,** which handles the admission fee and distributes a driving guide. A short film plays every 30min. Ranger tours run throughout the day from the Visitors Center. (☎301-432-5124. Open daily summer 8:30am-6pm; winter 8:30am-5pm. Call ahead for a schedule. $5 per car.)

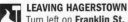

APPROACHING HAGERSTOWN
Continue on **Alt. U.S. 40** through **Funkstown.** Alt. U.S. 40 becomes **Frederick St.** As you come into Hagerstown, make a soft left onto **Baltimore St.** and take the next right onto **Locust St.,** which runs 1 block east of the center of town.

HAGERSTOWN. Once a principal town on the C&O Railway, Hagerstown remains the capital of this region of Maryland and is home to a symphony orchestra, art museum, and small theater. For sheer quantity of food, **Ryan's,** on U.S. 40 just west of town, takes the cake and barely dents the wallet, offering an all-you-can eat buffet that includes steak. (☎301-766-4440. Dinner after 4pm; $8. Weekday lunch 10:45am-4pm; $6. Drinks not included. Open Su-Th 10:45am-9:30pm, F-Sa 10:45am-10pm.) A pleasant family eatery, **Richardson's Restaurant,** 710 Dual Hwy. (U.S. 40), serves classy cuisine. Dinner entrees include New York strip steak ($12) and chicken Parmesan ($9) and come with soup and salad. (☎301-733-3660. Open M-Th 7am-9pm, F-Sa 7am-10pm.)

LEAVING HAGERSTOWN
Turn left on **Franklin St.** and head out of town.

THE ROAD TO CUMBERLAND
In the town of **Clear Spring,** notice signs showing the covered wagons that passed through here on their way west. From Clear Spring, merge into **I-70.** Nineteen miles from Hagerstown, U.S. 40 and I-70 become one; although this stretch of road lies on the interstate, it has views of forests and rugged mountains. Several times along this stretch there appears the option to take an exit for "Scenic 40," which usually ends up returning you to I-70 after a short detour. About 60 mi. from Hagerstown, idyllic **Rocky Gap State Park,** tucked away in the no-man's-land between Hagerstown and Cumberland, offers fishing, boating, and swimming in beautiful blue Lake Habeeb. (Take Exit 50 and follow the signs. ☎888-432-2267; http://reservations.dnr.state.md.us. Sites $23, with electricity $28; 4-person cabins $40.)

APPROACHING CUMBERLAND
Take Exit 43C ("Downtown") from **I-70.**

CUMBERLAND. The site of the National Road, C&O Canal, and several railroads, Cumberland once served as the gateway to the west. The **C&O Canal National Historic Park Visitors Center,** 13 Canal St., explains the significance of the waterway, which ran to Washington, D.C. (☎301-722-8226. Open daily 9am-5pm. Free.) The restored **Western Maryland Scenic Railroad,** 13 Canal St., runs to Frostburg and back. The views from the train beat most of what you would see stuck behind your dashboard. (☎800-872-4650; www.wmsr.com. Trains depart 11:30am May-Sept. Su and Th-Sa; Oct. daily; Nov.-Dec. Sa-Su. $19, seniors $17, under 13 $10.) Convenient to the attractions, second-story **Kramers Deli,** 13 Canal St., sells wraps ($6) with names like King Creole and Cajun Johnny. (☎301-722-8004. Subs $3-6. Open M-F 10am-8pm, Sa 10am-7pm, Su 10am-7pm.) The best bet for lodging in the area is the **Slumberland Motel,** 1262 National Hwy. (Alt. U.S. 40), 6 mi. west of Cumberland in Lavale. (☎301-729-2880 or 877-273-6874. Singles $50; doubles $55.)

LEAVING CUMBERLAND
In Cumberland, **Greene St.** ends at a marker indicating the start of the National Road. Turn left, then take your first right to cross the river. Take a left on **Mechanic St.,** which curves right onto **Frederick St.** Cross Liberty St. and take a left on **Centre St.,** which becomes **Alt. U.S. 40 West;** follow this out of town toward Lavale.

 TOLL HOUSE
6¾ mi. west of Cumberland, in Lavale.

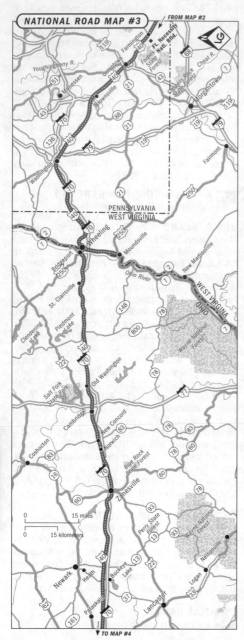

NATIONAL ROAD MAP #3 ◄ FROM MAP #2

PENNSYLVANIA
WEST VIRGINIA

▼ TO MAP #4

The first visible tollhouse on this road, Maryland's only surviving tollhouse is perched at a high point from which the toll collector could see people coming. (Open Sa-Su 1:30-4:30pm. Free.)

FROSTBURG. While parts of Main St. remain empty, Frostburg still has a few worthwhile attractions. The nearby campus of **Frostburg State University** supplies the town with cultural events and a student population. At the **Thrasher Carriage Museum,** 19 Depot St., a collection of horse-drawn carriages reminds visitors that, in the days before the automobile, those heading west along this route settled for much slower transportation. The variety of carriages represents the diversity of their owners, from the milkman to the president. (From U.S. 40, take a right onto Depot St. ☎301-689-3380; www.thrashercarriagemuseum.com. $3, children $1. Open Su and W-Sa 10am-3pm.) Standing amid the empty storefronts of Main St., the **Princess Restaurant,** 12 W. Main St. (Alt. U.S. 40), at Broadway St., feels like a step into the past. A BLT sets you back $2, a grilled pepper steak $5. (☎301-689-1680. Desserts $2. Open M-Sa 6am-8pm.)

◉ PENN ALPS 125 Casselman Rd.
Off Alt. U.S. 40, near Grantsville.

The Penn Alps Area, besides offering a selection of local arts and crafts and a restaurant, showcases local history. **Stanton's Mill** looks rickety for a reason; it has stood here since 1797 and was still in operation as late as 1990. The nearby **Casselman River Bridge** also dates back to the beginning of the 19th century. This beautiful stone arch was in use from 1813 to 1932. Also in the area, a collection of old buildings houses artists in residence at the **Spruce Forest Artisanal Village.** It's serious work—artists undergo a strict selection process to win a coveted spot in the village. (☎301-895-3332. Mill open daily 10am-6pm. Village open May-Oct. M-Sa 10am-5pm and by appointment.)

Welcome To **PENNSYLVANIA**

ADDISON. The town of Addison, 3 mi. from the Maryland border, is a sleepy collection of homes along what used to be the busy National Road.

Nearby lies the **Addison Toll House,** with an original toll sign. (☎814-395-3550. Tours mid-May to mid-Sept. Su 1:30-4pm or by appointment).

◉ FORT NECESSITY NATIONAL BATTLEFIELD
Near Farmington, just off U.S. 40.

Leave those Civil War sites behind and jump back to the French and Indian War. This battlefield, much more tranquil and less touristed than Gettysburg, includes a reproduction of the original stockade fort, the Mt. Washington Tavern, and Braddock's Grave. While the notion of entering the West in Pennsylvania seems a bit farfetched, the stockade bears witness to the fact that this wooded area was once the frontier. The tavern has an exhibit on the National Road along with period furnishings. (Open daily 9am-5pm. $3.)

◤ DETOUR: KENTUCK KNOB AND FALL-INGWATER
Turn right at the sign for Kentuck Knob onto Chalk Hill-Ohiopyle Rd. The house is 5¾ mi. down the road.

Contemporary architect Frank Lloyd Wright chose a beautiful site at **Kentuck Knob** to construct a house, three years before his death. Part of an 80-acre estate, the home is postmodern architecture writ large. Steeply priced tours explore the house and sculpture garden, which are currently owned by a British couple. (☎724-329-1901. Open Su and Tu-Sa Mar.-Dec. 9am-4pm; Jan.-Feb. 11am-3pm. 1½ hr. tours Tu-F $10, ages 6-18 $8; Sa-Su $15/$12.) Down the way, the world-renowned **Fallingwater,** "the most famous private residence ever built" exemplifies Wright's organic architecture, striking a balance with the landscape. (☎724-329-8501; www.wpconline.org/fallingwaterhome.org. Open Mar.-Nov. Su and Tu-Sa 10am-4pm.)

◤ APPROACHING UNIONTOWN
Follow **U.S. 40** around Uniontown; take the exit for **West 40/Bus. U.S. 40/Main St. Uniontown.** At the bottom of the ramp, turn right to proceed 1 mi. to downtown Uniontown on **Main St. (Bus. U.S. 40).**

UNIONTOWN. Little has changed since Uniontown, the county seat, served as a provisioning stop on the National Road; today, the town remains primarily service-oriented. At **Meloni's,** 105 W. Main St. (Bus. U.S. 40), hearty entrees come at moderate prices, with the full orchestral suite of *The Godfather* tossed in for ambience. (☎724-437-0820. Pasta $5-8. Open M-Th 11am-10pm, F-Sa 11am-11pm, Su noon-9pm.) Two miles west of Uniontown, the **MG Motel,** 7909 National Pike (U.S. 40), offers small, neat rooms, some with TVs. (☎724-437-0506. Singles $42; doubles $47.)

◤ LEAVING UNIONTOWN
Proceed west on **Main St.** until **Bus. U.S. 40** turns into **U.S. 40 West.**

◉ SEARIGHT TOLL HOUSE
On U.S. 40, 5 mi. west of Uniontown.

Cheery folks from the Fayette County Historical Society manage this brick toll house, one of two left in Pennsylvania. See where the travelers of yore had to pay for their passage or else face iron gates. (☎412-439-4422. Open mid-May to mid-Oct. Su and Tu-Sa 10am-4pm. $1.)

◤ APPROACHING BROWNSVILLE
Follow the signs indicating the **original National Road** into Brownsville.

BROWNSVILLE. Brownsville, 12 mi. from Uniontown, once served as a junction between the National Road and the Monongahela River heading to Pittsburgh; in the 1940s more freight went down this river than any other river in the world. Considerably less busy today than in its days of glory, Brownsville is home to two interesting attractions: the 1830s-era Flatiron Building and the Nemacolin Castle. The **Flatiron Building and Frank L. Melaga Art Museum,** 69 Market St., looks like a clothes iron and houses a small gift shop with National Road-related memorabilia. It also contains a one-room museum of paintings by Frank Melaga, a Brownsville native who painted signs for local businesses as well as emotional portraits of area workers and coal miners. (From U.S. 40, turn left at the light for Market St.; the building is down the hill on the right. ☎724-785-9331. Open M-Sa 11am-5pm, Su noon-6pm.) Built in three stages, **Nemacolin Castle's** unassuming exterior hides a neat collection of 22 rooms, each furnished differently and with different architectural styles from 150 years of American history. (From U.S. 40, turn left just before the Market St. light onto Brashear St. ☎724-785-6882. Open Jun.-Aug. Su and Tu-Sa 11am-5pm; Mar.-Oct. Sa-Su 11am-5pm. $7, under 13 $3.)

◤ LEAVING BROWNSVILLE
Continue through Brownsville, following the **National Road** markers across the Monongahela River and rejoining **U.S. 40** after about 3 mi.

NATIONAL ROAD

MADONNA OF THE TRAIL
On U.S. 40, 8 mi. from Brownsville.

This 16 ft. statue is one of 12 Madonnas of the Trail (the first of five along the National Road). Erected in 1928 by the Daughters of the American Revolution as a monument to "pioneer mothers of the covered wagon days," the expression of this pinkish-colored granite statue evokes steadfastness and determination.

 HILL'S TAVERN AT CENTURY INN
2175 E. National Pike (U.S. 40)
In Scenery Hill, 11 mi. from Brownsville.

Once host to Andrew Jackson, this tavern, built in 1794, remains active as a B&B and elegant restaurant. If you head inside, check out the flag from the Whiskey Rebellion. Lunch items include peanut soup ($3), Welsh rarebit ($7) and rainbow trout ($9). Dinner takes a heftier bite out of the wallet; entrees are $17-34. (☎412-945-6600. Open daily for lunch noon-3pm; dinner M-Th 4:30-8pm, F-Sa 4:30-9pm, Su 3:30-7pm.)

WASHINGTON

While at first Washington may appear remarkably similar to Uniontown, the city has a few attractions scattered in and around the downtown area. Check out the majestic US capitol-style **County Courthouse** at the corner of Main and Beau St. At the **Pennsylvania Trolley Museum,** 1 Museum Rd., an earlier era lives on; visitors can ride restored vintage streetcars down a 3 mi. track. (Take I-79 north and Exit 49 for "Meadow Lands," then follow the blue signs for the museum. ☎724-228-9256 or 877-728-7655; www.pa-trolley.org. Open Memorial Day-Labor Day daily 11am-5pm; Apr.-Dec. Sa-Su 11am-5pm. $6, seniors $5, ages 2-15 $3.50.) Visitors to the **LeMoyne House,** 49 E. Maiden St. (U.S. 40), can see where runaway slaves hid and learn about Dr. LeMoyne, the staunch abolitionist who ran this stop on the Underground Railway. (☎724-225-6740; www.wchspa.org. Open Tu-F 11am-3:30pm. $4, students $2.) Visitor info is available at the **Washington County Tourism Promotion Agency,** 273 S. Main St., north of the railroad tracks. (☎724-227-5520 or 800-531-4114; www.washpatourism.org. Open M-F 9am-4:30pm.)

The **New Tower Restaurant and Lounge,** 680 W. Chestnut St. (U.S. 40), caters to townies and travelers looking for a quick no-fuss bite. (☎724-222-5952. Breakfast $3-6. Dinner with 2 sides and a salad $8-10. Open Su 7am-8pm, Tu-Th 7am-10pm, F-Sa 7am-11pm.) Washington has very few motels, but fortunately, the chains that cluster on **W. Chestnut St. (U.S. 40)** at the exits for I-70, 2 mi. west of town, offer rooms for as low as $38 per night. Just outside the city, the **Washington PA KOA,** 7 KOA Rd., has laundry, a game room, and a pool. (Off Vance Station Rd. Follow signs off U.S. 40/U.S. 19. ☎724-225-7590 or 800-562-0254. Sites $20, with hookup $27; cabins $36.)

 LEAVING WASHINGTON
Take **Main St.** north and turn left on **Chestnut St.,** which becomes **U.S. 40.**

THE ROAD TO WHEELING. Seven miles from Washington, visible on the north side of U.S. 40, is the **S-Bridge.** Part of the original National Road, the bridge was originally built in an S-shape because the river was at an angle to the road and masons found it easier to construct straight arches over a river than to build them at angles. Seventeen miles from Washington, the road leaves Pennsylvania and enters West Virginia; 9 mi. later, U.S. 40 turns right to head into Wheeling. On your way into town, notice the **Madonna of the Trail** monument, commemorating pioneer women, on your right. From here, U.S. 40 takes a long, scenic route around the hills to get to downtown Wheeling.

 APPROACHING WHEELING
To get to downtown quickly, get on **I-70 West** at one of the several places it intersects **U.S. 40.**

WHEELING

Once a thriving economic and political capital of the western part of Virginia and then West Virginia, Wheeling today retains a warm, small-town feel. The **Kruger Street Toy and Train Museum,** 144 Kruger St., displays 20,000 toys in a gorgeous restored Victorian-era schoolhouse. (☎304-242-8133. Open June-Oct. Su-M and W-Sa 10am-6pm; Nov.-Dec. daily 10am-6pm; Jan.-May Su and F-Sa 10am-6pm. $8, students $5, seniors

$7, ages 10-17 $5.) Why does West Virginia exist? The answer is found at the **West Virginia Independence Hall,** 1528 Market St., which narrates the history of the division between the regions of Richmond and Wheeling. The building marks the site where West Virginia become a state with Wheeling as its original capital. (Proceed south on Main St. to 16th St., and turn left. ☎304-238-1300. $3, students $2. Open daily 10am-4pm; Jan.-Feb. closed Su.) From Main St. (at 10th St.), you can view the **Wheeling Suspension Bridge,** just south of the current I-70/U.S. 40 bridge. Built in 1849 to carry the National Road across the Ohio River, this 1010 ft. suspension bridge opened 34 years before the Brooklyn Bridge. Visitor info is available at the Wheeling Convention and Visitors Bureau, 1401 Main St. (☎800-828-3097; www.wheelingcvb.com. Open M-F 9am-5pm, Sa 10am-3pm, Su noon-4pm.)

Buy fresh fish or have it cooked for you at ▨**Coleman's Fish Market,** at 22nd and Market St., which serves up fried and steamed delicacies. (Behind Centre Market. ☎304-232-8510. Chicken platter $2.30. Oyster sandwich $1.60. Open M-Tu 10am-5:30pm, W-Th 8:30am-5:30pm, F 8:30am-7pm, Sa 8:30am-5:30pm.)

▧ **DETOUR: FORMER WEST VIRGINIA PENITENTIARY** 818 Jefferson Ave.
From downtown Wheeling, take Rte. 2 (Main St./ Chapline St. in Wheeling) south 12 mi. to Moundsville, then turn left on 8th St.; the penitentiary is 2 blocks ahead.

If you can't wait until Alcatraz (2577 mi. ahead), head down to Moundsville to tour this Civil War-era structure where West Virginia still conducts its Mock Prison Riot training. (☎304-845-6200; www.wvpentours.com. Open Apr.-Nov. Su and Tu-Sa 10am-4pm. $8, seniors $7, ages 6-12 $5.)

◤ **LEAVING WHEELING**
Take **Market St.** north to the ramp for **I-70 West.** Take the first exit (Exit 0) for **U.S. 40 West.**

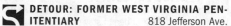
Welcome To **OHIO**

THE ROAD TO CAMBRIDGE. The road enters Ohio 1 mi. from Wheeling. Continue straight ahead on Main St., even though there is not a "U.S. 40" sign for close to 2 mi. In **Bridgeport,** the homey and scenic **Hillside Motel,** 54481 National Road (U.S. 40), is an excellent place to spend the night; each of the 13 rooms has a different shape and size. (☎740-645-9111. Non-smoking rooms available. Singles $35; doubles $44.

CAMBRIDGE

Cambridge was and still is at the heart of a glass-producing region; several factories in town offer tours. Like many other cities along the route, Cambridge has taken full advantage of its position along the National Road, and its Main St. retains a quaint charm. Three glass factories around Cambridge offer visitors the opportunity to see the craftsmanship that comprises the backbone of Cambridge's industry. **Mosser Glass Inc.,** 9279 Cadiz Rd. (U.S. 22 East), is the largest operational glass factory in Cambridge. (☎740-439-1827. Open M-F 8:30am-3:30pm.) **Boyd's Crystal Art Glass,** 1203 Morton Ave., may look tiny from the outside, but inside workers are busy producing specialty glass. (From U.S. 40, turn left onto 11th St., which becomes Morton Ave. ☎740-439-2077. Open June-Aug. M-F 7am-3:30pm, Sa 9am-1pm.) The **Degenhart Paperweight and Glass Museum,** on Highland Hills Rd. at U.S. 22 and I-77, has glass samples from different companies and periods of time, each with informative explanations. (From town, take U.S. 22 east until you see the museum on your left, just before the I-77 exits. ☎740-432-2626. Open Apr.-Dec. M-Sa 9am-5pm, Su 1-5pm. $1.50, seniors $1, under 18 free.) The **National Road Heritage Market,** 738 Wheeling Ave., sells an assortment of "made in Ohio" products, and the owner provides a wealth of knowledge about the Cambridge region. (☎740-432-8789 or 866-334-6446. Open M-Sa 10am-7pm, Su noon-5pm.)

▨**Theo's Restaurant,** 632 Wheeling Ave. (U.S. 40), serves delightfully cheap and non-greasy food. Their best-known specialty is the Coney Island Hot Dog ($1), which is perfectly accompanied by a wedge of pie ($1.50) baked fresh in-house. (☎740-432-3878. Chicken gyro $4. BBQ $6-7. Steak $9. Open M-Sa 10am-9pm.) For accommodations, chain motels lie just south from the center of town on Southgate Pkwy. (Rte. 209), or try the cozy and family-run **Budget Inn,** 6405 Glenn Hwy. (U.S. 40), 2 mi. west of town. (☎740-432-2304. Non-smoking rooms available. Singles $30; doubles $35.)

 LEAVING CAMBRIDGE
Follow **U.S. 40 West** through town.

 JOHN AND ANNIE GLENN HISTORIC SITE   68 W. Main St.
On U.S. 40 8 mi. west of Cambridge, in New Concord.
At this small museum, the town of New Concord memorializes its hero, John Glenn. Learn the story of this small-town Ohioan, US senator, and astronaut as you explore different facets of American history. (☎740-826-3305; www.johnglennhome.org. Open Apr.-Labor Day Su 1-4pm, W-Sa 10am-4pm; Labor Day to mid-Nov. W-Sa 10am-3pm. $5, seniors $4, ages 6-12 $2.)

 NATIONAL ROAD/ZANE GREY MUSEUM
                                              8850 E. Pike (U.S. 40)
In Norwich. Look for the large sign for "Baker's Motel" across U.S. 40, then turn left into the museum.
All the bits and pieces of National Road history come together at the ▨**National Road/Zane Grey Museum.** With an extensive diorama, the museum highlights some sights already passed along the route, such as the Searight Toll House and the Hill Tavern, and previews what is yet to come. For kicks, also check out the world's largest vase. (☎740-872-3143. Open May-Sept. M-Sa 9:30am-5pm, Su noon-5pm. $6, students $2, under 6 free.)

ZANESVILLE

Zanesville has become famous among National Road fanatics as the home of the famous Y-bridge, which was rebuilt in 1984 to replace the original 1902 bridge. From **Zane's Landing Park,** roadtrippers can ride the **Lorena Sternwheeler** down the Muskingam River, accompanied by "riverboat music" and dinner at night. (Take Market St. west until it ends at the park. ☎740-455-8883 or 800-246-6303. Cruises June-Sept. daily 1 and 2:30pm; Sept. to mid-Oct. Sa-Su 1 and 2:30pm. $6, seniors $5, ages 2-12 $3. Dinner cruises W and Sa 6 and 8pm. $30.) Quirky and cool, the old **Masonic Temple,** 38 N. 4th St., features great tile flooring and old frosted-glass doors. Ask the elevator operator to give you a ride in the 100-year-old elevator and show you the 6th floor ballroom. As you leave

town on U.S. 40, just after the Y-bridge, take the first left on Pine St. and then turn left on Grandview Ave., following signs for **"Y-Bridge Overlook."**

The original incarnation of a roadside favorite, ▨**Classic Denny's,** 4990 E. Pike, has a regular Denny's menu, but the interior features red and white leather seats with chrome finishing that look like they came right out of your grandfather's Chevy. (☎740-588-9310. Open 24hr.) Other dining establishments include **Nicol's Restaurant,** 730 Putnam Ave., where home-style entrees are less than $7 (except the T-bone steak) and lunch specials with soup or salad are $4. Don't forget Nicol's homemade ice cream ($2) to finish off your meal. (From Main St. or Market St., turn left onto 4th St. or 5th St., turn left at Canal St., and then take your first right onto Putnam Ave. ☎740-452-2577. Open daily 7am-8pm. Cash only.) Staying in Zanesville can be surprisingly expensive. Hotels cluster around the U.S. 40 junction with I-70 about 7 mi. east of town, and there are a number of other chains downtown. Your best bet is to stay elsewhere; the **Budget Inn** near Cambridge (see above) and the **Homestead Motel** near Columbus (see p. 331) are both inexpensive and comfortable.

 LEAVING ZANESVILLE
Continue out of town on **Main St. (U.S. 40),** bearing left on the Y-bridge to stay on U.S. 40.

THE ROAD TO COLUMBUS

It's about 50 mi. along U.S. 40 from Zanesville to Columbus, but there are several worthwhile stops along the way. About 20 mi. from Zanesville, north of Newark, is the **Dawes Arboretum,** 7770 Jacksontown Rd., where visitors can walk or drive a 1-2½ mi. tour through trees carefully grouped into clusters on beautifully landscaped grounds. (Turn right onto Rte. 13 and head north 1½ mi.; the arboretum is on the left. ☎740-323-2355 or 800-443-2937; www.dawesarb.org. Open daily dawn-dusk. Free.) Twenty-three miles from Zanesville, the **Buckeye Central Scenic Railroad,** on U.S. 40, offers 10 mi. rides on old railroad cars through the farmlands of Ohio. (☎740-366-2029 or 740-928-3827. Memorial Day-Oct. Su 1 and 3pm. $7, ages 2-11 $5, under 2 free.) Food and lodging are available in the **Buckeye Lake** area, just south of U.S. 40. The hungry shouldn't miss **Catfish Charley's,** 11048 Hebron Rd. (Rte. 79), a no-frills pizza place in Buckeye Lake Village. (☎740-928-7174. All-you-can-eat pizza and salad $5. Calzones $5. Open Su-

Th 11am-10pm, F-Sa 11am-11pm.) Located in a pretty area near the village of Buckeye Lake, the well-maintained **Buckeye Lake/Columbus East KOA,** 4460 Walnut Rd., offers shaded tent sites, a pool, laundry, and a miniature golf course. (☎740-928-0706. Open Apr.-Oct. Sites $26, with full hookup $36-40; 1-room cabins $48; 2-room cabins $59.) Better than most area motels, **The Homestead Motel,** 4182 E. Main St. (U.S. 40), 7 mi. from downtown Columbus, has exceedingly spacious, well-lit rooms with impressive furnishings. (☎614-235-2348. Singles $35; doubles $40.)

APPROACHING COLUMBUS

Soon after entering Bexley, **U.S. 40** leaves Main St. and veers to the right onto **Drexel St.** for ¾ mi. before turning left onto **Broad St.** to continue its trek downtown. The sign for U.S. 40 is small and hard to see; if you miss the turn, **Main St.** will also take you into downtown, albeit on a slightly less scenic path.

COLUMBUS

Rapid growth, huge suburban sprawl, and some gerrymandering have nudged the population of Columbus beyond that of neighboring cities. Columbus has refused to let its size affect its character, however—the city is still without glitz, fame, pretentiousness, or smog. Friendly neighborhoods, down-to-earth residents, and impressive museums make Columbus a pleasant stop on any roadtrip.

VITAL STATS

Population: 710,000

Visitor Info: Greater Columbus Visitors Center, 111 S. 3rd St. (☎614-221-2489 or 800-345-4386; www.surpriseitscolumbus.com), on the 2nd fl. of City Center Mall. From Broad St. (U.S. 40), turn left onto 3rd St. Open M-Sa 10am-8pm, Su noon-6pm.

Internet Access: Columbus Metropolitan Library, 96 S. Grant Ave. (☎614-645-2275). Open M-Th 9am-9pm, F-Sa 9am-6pm, Su 1-5pm.

Post Office: 850 Twin Rivers. (☎800-275-8777). Open M-F 8am-7pm, Sa 8am-2pm. **Postal Code:** 43215.

GETTING AROUND

Columbus is easy to navigate but can be frustrating to get around, as left turns are rarely permitted, especially during rush hour. The city is laid out in an easily navigable grid. **High St.,** running north-south, and **Broad St. (U.S. 40),** running east-west, are the main thoroughfares. High St. heads north from the towering office complexes downtown to the lively galleries and restaurants in the **Short North,** continuing on to Ohio State University (OSU). South of downtown lies the historic German Village.

There is little free **parking** available in Columbus except on evenings and weekends at certain meters. Lots downtown tend to be expensive ($12 per day) but are less elsewhere. Meters proliferate on almost every street but time limits and prices vary widely. Restaurants on High St. tend not to have parking of their own; park at meters, on adjacent streets, or in municipal lots. Watch for "permit parking only" signs in nearby residential areas.

> NPR here (90.5 FM) plays great funky driving music during non-news hours.

SIGHTS

OSU AND VICINITY. Ohio State University (OSU) lies 2 mi. north of downtown. **The Wexner Center for the Arts** was the first public building designed by controversial Modernist Peter Eisenman. The museum is under renovation and scheduled to reopen in the fall of 2005, but until then much of its avant-garde collection is scattered throughout various venues across the city. Performance spaces host dance, music, and theater productions. (*1871 N. High St. ☎614-292-3535; www.wexarts.org. Open Feb.-June Su noon-6pm, Tu-W and F-Sa 10am-6pm, Th 10am-9pm. $3, students and seniors $2. Th 5-9pm free. Films $5, students and seniors $4, under 12 $2. Call for info on other locations.*)

MUSEUMS. The **Columbus Museum of Art** displays a growing collection of contemporary American art. Other highlights include a collection of local folk art and a great children's exhibit that allows kids to walk into a Dutch studio. Don't miss the giant "ART" sign towering right behind the museum. (*480 E. Broad St. ☎614-221-6801; www.columbusmuseum.org. Open Su, Tu-W, F-Sa 10am-5:30pm; Th 10am-8:30pm. $6; students, seniors, and ages 6-18 $4. Th free. Parking $3.*) The submarine-shaped **Center of Science and Industry**

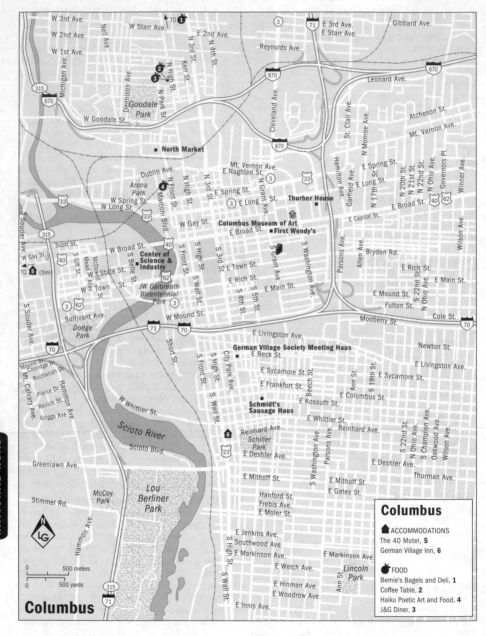

W 3rd Ave.
W 2nd Ave.
W 1st Ave.
W Starr Ave.
TO 1
E 2nd Ave.
3
E 3rd Ave.
E Starr Ave.
Gibbard Ave.
Reynolds Ave.
Leonard Ave.
670
Neil Ave.
Michigan Ave.
N 3rd St.
N 4th St.
315
670
Dennison Ave.
N High St.
Kerr St.
2
3
N Park St.
Goodale Park
Cleveland Ave.
St. Clair Ave.
N Monroe Ave.
Atcheson St.
Mt. Vernon Ave.
W Goodale St.
670
Hamilton Ave.
Garfield Ave.
E Spring St.
E Long St.
N 17th St.
N 20th St.
N 21st St.
N 22nd Ave.
N Ohio Ave.
Governors Pl.
Winner Ave.
North Market
Mt. Vernon Ave.
E Naghten St.
Dublin Ave.
33
Arena Park
4
N High St.
N 3rd St.
N Grant Ave.
E Spring St.
E Long St.
Thurber House
E Broad St.
E Capital St.
40
62
Wilson Ave.
33
W Spring St.
W Long St.
Marconi Blvd.
N Front St.
3
E Long
33
S Souder Ave.
315
Scott St.
W Gay St.
S High St.
S 3rd St.
Columbus Museum of Art
E Broad St.
First Wendy's
S Grant Ave.
S Washington Ave.
Parsons Ave.
Allen Ave.
Bryden Rd.
E Rich St.
E Main St.
W Gay St.
40
TO 5 (5mi)
W Broad St.
40
Center of Science & Industry
62
McDowell
Mead St.
S Belle St.
S Gift St.
State St.
W State St.
S High St.
S Wall St.
S 3rd St.
S 4th St.
E Town St.
E Rich St.
E Main St.
E Mound St.
Fulton St.
S 22nd St.
N Ohio Ave.
Cole St.
62
W Town St.
W Alley
JW Galbreath Bicentennial Park
3
Mooberry St.
70
Sullivant Ave.
3
62
W Mound St.
71
70
Dodge Park
70
E Livingston Ave.
Mound St.
Coolidge Dr.
Buchanan Dr.
Pierce Dr.
Renick St.
Hammon Ave.
Griggs Ave.
Mt. Calvary Ave.
Short St.
German Village Society Meeting Haus
E Beck St.
Newton St.
E Livingston Ave.
City Park Ave.
S High St.
S Wall St.
S Front St.
E Sycamore St.
E Frankfort St.
Beech St.
Ann St.
S 18th St.
E Sycamore St.
E Columbus St.
W Whittier St.
Scioto River
Schmidt's Sausage Haus
E Kossuth St.
S 22nd St.
N Ohio Ave.
S Champion Ave.
Oakwood Ave.
Wilson Ave.
Scioto Blvd.
E Whittier St.
Reinhard Ave.
Reinhard Ave.
6
Schiller Park
S Washington Ave.
Parsons Ave.
E Deshler Ave.
23
E Deshler Ave.
Thurman Ave.
Greenlawn Ave.
E Mithoff St.
E Mithoff St.
E Gates St.
Stimmel Rd.
McCoy Park
Lou Berliner Park
Hanford St.
Frebis Ave.
E Moler St.
E Jenkins Ave.
Southwood Ave.
E Markinson Ave.
E Markinson Ave.
Lincoln Park
Hammon Ave.
N
LG
0   500 meters
0   500 yards
Lincoln Park
E Welch Ave.
S High St.
E Hinman Ave.
E Woodrow Ave.
S Wall St.
Ann St.
315
71
E Innis Ave.

Columbus

Columbus

▲ **ACCOMMODATIONS**
The 40 Motel, **5**
German Village Inn, **6**

🍴 **FOOD**
Bernie's Bagels and Deli, **1**
Coffee Table, **2**
Haiku Poetic Art and Food, **4**
J&G Diner, **3**

NATIONAL ROAD

(COSI) allows visitors to explore space from the safety of an armchair, create their own short stop-animation films, and enjoy arcade games like Pong, Centipede, and Space Invaders. A seven-story Extreme Screen shows action-packed films. *(333 W. Broad St. Take Broad St. (U.S. 40) west past High St.; the museum is on the left just after crossing the river. ☎ 614-228-2674; www.cosi.org. Open M-Sa 10am-5pm, Su noon-6pm. $12, seniors $10, ages 2-12 $7. Extreme Screen $6. Combination ticket $17/$15/$10.)* Nearby, James Thurber's childhood home, the **Thurber House,** guides visitors through the major events of the famous *New Yorker* writer's life. It also serves as a literary center, hosting seminars with authors like John Updike. *(77 Jefferson Ave., off E. Broad St. From Broad St., turn right on Jefferson Ave. just past I-71. ☎ 614-464-1032. Open daily noon-4pm. Free. Tours Su $2.50, students and seniors $2.)*

ARTS DISTRICT. The **Short North Arts District** is rife with galleries ready for browsing. On the first Saturday of each month from 6 to 10pm, the district is packed with an eclectic crowd for the free **Gallery Hop Night.** The eccentric **Gallery V** exhibits contemporary paintings and sculptures along with handcrafted jewelry. *(694 N. High St. ☎ 614-228-8955. Open Tu-Sa 11am-5pm. Free.)* The **Thomas R. Riley Galleries** specialize in elaborate glass sculptures. *(642 N. High St. ☎ 614-228-6554. Open Su noon-5pm, Tu-Sa 11am-6pm. Free.)*

GERMAN VILLAGE. For some good Germanica, march down to the **German Village,** south of Capitol Sq. This area, first settled in 1843, is now the largest privately funded historical restoration in the US, full of stately homes and beer halls. At **Schmidt's Sausage Haus,** lederhosen-clad waitresses serve Bavarian specialities like huge sausage platters ($9.25-10.25) while traditional oompah bands (Schnickel-Fritz, Schnapps, and Squeezin' 'n' Wheezin') lead polkas. *(240 E. Kossuth St. ☎ 614-444-6808. Polkas Th 7-10pm, F-Sa 8-11pm; in summer also W 7-10pm. Open M-Th 11:30am-10pm, F-Sa 11:30am-11pm, Su 4-10pm.)* One block west, **Schmidt's Fudge Haus** concocts savory fudge and chocolate delicacies named for local celebrities. *(220 E. Kossuth St. ☎ 614-444-2222. Open M-Th noon-4pm, F-Sa noon-7pm, Su noon-3pm.)* The **German Village Society Meeting Haus** provides info on local happenings. *(588 S. 3rd St. ☎ 614-221-8888. Open M-F 9am-4pm, Sa 10am-2pm; reduced winter hours.)*

OTHER SIGHTS. About 10 mi. north of downtown, the surreal **Field of Corn** contains 109 concrete ears of corn, each 7 ft. tall, that pay homage to the town's agrarian roots and suggest a subtle indictment of modern development. *(4995 Rings Rd. Always open. Free.)* The **Franklin Park Conservatory and Botanical Garden** cultivates lush greenery from various parts of the world and is a good break from whatever the weather happens to be in Ohio. *(1777 E. Broad St., off Rte. 745 in Dublin. ☎ 614-645-8733; www.fpconservatory.org. Open Su and Tu-Sa 10am-5pm; 1st W of month 10am-8pm. $5, students and seniors $3.50, ages 2-12 $2.)*

🎵 ENTERTAINMENT

Four free weekly papers available in shops and restaurants—*The Other Paper*, *Columbus Alive*, *The Guardian*, and *Moo*—list arts and entertainment options. The 2002 National Champion **Ohio State Buckeyes** play football in the historic horseshoe-shaped **Ohio Stadium.** Major League Soccer's **Columbus Crew** (☎ 614-447-2739) kicks off at **Crew Stadium.** Columbus's brand-new NHL hockey team, the **Blue Jackets** (☎ 614-246-3350), plays winter games in Nationwide Arena. The **Clippers,** a minor league affiliate of the NY Yankees, swing away from April to early September. (☎ 614-462-5250. Tickets $5-8.)

If you're feeling bored, Columbus has a sure cure: rock 'n' roll. Bar bands are a Columbus mainstay, and it's hard to find a bar that doesn't have live music on the weekend. Bigger national acts stop at the **Newport,** 1722 N. High St. (☎ 614-228-3580. Tickets $5-40.) To see smaller alternative and local bands, head to **Little Brothers,** 1100 N. High St. (☎ 614-421-2025. 18+. Cover $5-30. Open daily 8pm-2am.) Beer chugging and pool playing replace traditional study techniques at the **Library,** 2169 N. High St., a bar that attracts a mix of locals and students. (☎ 614-299-3245. Beer $2-3. Open M-Sa 3pm-2:30am, Su 7pm-2:30am.) South from Union Station is the **Brewery District,** where barley and hops have replaced coal and iron in the once industrial area.

🍴 FOOD

By far the best place for budget eats in Columbus is the **North Market,** 59 Spruce St., in the Short North Arts District. Vendors hawk their wares from every corner of this restored marketplace, offering a variety of wines, meats, cheeses, fruits, prepared ethnic foods, and food-related items, from sushi to barbecue to fresh produce. (Take High St. north to Spruce St. and turn left. ☎614-463-9664; www.northmarket.com. Open Su noon-5pm, Tu-F 9am-7pm, Sa 8am-5pm. Some merchants open M 9am-5pm.) Also worth a stop if you're not sick of fast food by now is **Wendy's First Restaurant,** 257 E. Broad St., at the corner of 5th St. Dave Thomas started Wendy's on this corner in 1969, and the restaurant now houses a Wendy's museum with old ads, articles, and pictures of Dave. (☎614-464-4656. Open M-F 10am-8pm, Sa 10am-7pm, Su 11am-6pm.) **High St.** is lined with a variety of cafes and coffee shops, all tasty and reasonably priced.

J&G Diner, 733 N. High St. (☎614-294-1850), in the Short North District. Amid provocative paintings of a green-clad bombshell, this diner serves filling Belgian waffles ($4) and "hippie" ($6.50) or "rabbi" ($7.50) omelettes. Open M-F 10:30am-10pm, Sa 9am-10pm, Su 9am-9pm.

Coffee Table, 731 N. High St. (☎614-297-1177), next door to the J&G Diner. Provides the espresso fix for an eclectic crowd and seems to have an Elvis infatuation. Drinks from $1.55. Open M-Th 7am-midnight, F 7am-10pm, Sa 8am-10pm.

Bernie's Bagels and Deli, 1896 N. High St. (☎614-291-3448). Serves healthy sandwiches ($3-5) and all-day breakfast in a subterranean dive, with live music nightly. Open daily 11am-2:30am.

Haiku Poetic Art and Food, 800 N. High St. (☎614-294-8168). Sushi chefs produce their edible art amid chic Japanese decor. Noodle dishes ($10-13), such as *udon tempura,* might just inspire poetry. Open M-Th 11am-11pm, F-Sa 11am-midnight, Su 4-10pm.

ACCOMMODATIONS

Those under 21 will have a hard time finding accommodations in Columbus; a city ordinance prevents hotels from renting to underaged visitors. Nearby suburbs are your best bet to dodge the ban. From mid-June to mid-August, **OSU** offers cheap, clean rooms on North Campus with A/C, free local calls, private bathrooms, microwaves, and fridges, close to endless nightlife and food options. (☎614-292-9725. Rooms $36-44.) The recently remodeled **German Village Inn,** 920 S. High St., close to downtown, offers clean, well-appointed rooms with cable TV, A/

C, and free local calls. (☎614-443-6506. 21+. Rooms $60; $6 per additional person.) **The 40 Motel,** 3705 W. Broad St. (U.S. 40), 5 mi. from downtown Columbus, has bright rooms and the largest neon sign in the city of Columbus. Even if you don't stay, be sure to see the sign and its changing daily message. (☎614-276-2691 or 800-331-8223. Singles $42; doubles $44. 2-night special Sa-Su $55.)

LEAVING COLUMBUS
From **Broad St.,** proceed west out of the downtown area on **U.S. 40.**

THE ROAD TO SPRINGFIELD. There is little to see once you move beyond Columbus until you reach Springfield. U.S. 40 mostly bypasses the tiny towns; you can take "Old U.S. 40" for brief stretches to pass through **Summerford** and **South Vienna,** ending up back on U.S. 40. Thirty-seven miles west of Columbus, in Harmony, OH, the Rainbow Industry Company displays a **giant roadside balloon.**

SPRINGFIELD

A town proud of its manufacturing heritage, Springfield continues to flourish as the site of private Wittenberg University, the Clark County Seat, and the gateway to Buck Creek State Park.

VITAL STATS

Population: 65,000

Visitor Info: Springfield Area Convention and Visitors Bureau, 333 N. Limestone St., #201 (☎937-325-7621 or 800-803-1553; www.springfield-clark-countyohio.info). From North St. (U.S. 40 West), turn right on Limestone St. Open M-F 8am-5pm.

Internet Access: Clark County Public Library, 201 S. Fountain Ave. (☎937-328-6903). From North St. (U.S. 40 West), turn left on Fountain Ave. Open M-F 9am-9pm, Sa 9am-6pm, Su 1-5pm.

Post Office: 150 N. Limestone St. (☎937-323-6498). Open M-F 8am-6pm, Sa 8am-1pm. **Postal Code:** 45501.

GETTING AROUND. In Springfield, **U.S. 40 West** becomes **North St.** and runs one-way through town. One block south, U.S. 40 East runs the other way as **Columbia St.** The two are intersected by **Limestone St.,** which runs one-way north, and **Fountain Ave.,** which runs one-way south.

⑤ SIGHTS. The **Heritage Center of Clark County,** 117 S. Fountain Ave., exhibits cars, surgical instruments, steamrollers, fire trucks—all full-size and made right in Springfield—in a built-on addition to a restored marketplace. The marketplace also houses a large National Road history museum, complete with a refurbished Conestoga wagon. (☎937-324-0657. Open Tu-Sa 9am-5pm. Free.) A collection of paintings by mostly American artists adorns the vibrant pastel-toned walls of the respectably sized **Springfield Museum of Art,** 107 Cliff Park Rd. The museum also sponsors amateur and professional contests and displays the entries in an exhibition hall. (From North St., turn right on Fountain Ave., cross the small bridge and then take an immediate left onto Cliff Park Rd. ☎937-325-4673. Open Su 2-4pm, Tu and Th-F 9am-5pm, W 9am-9pm, Sa 9am-3pm. Free.)

From North St., head south two blocks to High St. to see the **Westcott House,** 1340 E. High St. (☎888-701-6300). This Frank Lloyd Wright home, long in private hands, is scheduled to open to the public for tours in 2005. The small campus of **Wittenberg University** lies just north of the downtown area. To get there, turn right on Fountain Ave. and continue into the College Hill neighborhood, where old homes have been converted to frat houses and student dorms.

◼︎⋔ FOOD & ACCOMMODATIONS. For food, locals recommend **Station One,** 325 N. Fountain Ave. This grungy local bar serves sandwiches ($3-5), subs ($4-7), and pizza. (☎937-324-3354. Drive-through service available. Open M-Sa 11am-2am, Su 3pm-2am. Kitchen closes 9pm.) About 3 mi. from downtown, **The Drake Motel,** 3200 E. Main St. (U.S. 40), offers spacious, clean rooms. (☎937-325-7334. Singles $38; doubles $40.)

◤ APPROACHING DAYTON
In Springfield, continue on **North St.,** following signs for **U.S. 40 West.** 2 mi. from Springfield, U.S. 40 West merges with **Rte. 4 South.** When they split 1 mi. later, stay on Rte. 4. 9 mi. from Springfield, **Rte. 4** merges with **I-70 West.** Take I-70 West 2 mi. to **I-675 South.** Continue to Exit 13 for **U.S. 35 West.** Take U.S. 35 West to the exit for Main St./Jefferson St./ Rte. 48, and follow signs for **Rte. 48 North** into town.

DAYTON

Dayton, whose economy still revolves around the sprawling Wright-Patterson Air Force Base, has attempted to take advantage of the centennial of the first human flight (2003) to reinvent itself as a tourist destination. Most sights and attractions in the area have to do with aviation or aviators.

(VITAL STATS)

Population: 166,000

Visitor Info: Dayton/Montgomery County Convention and Visitors Bureau, 1 Chamber Plaza, Ste. A (☎937-226-8211), at 5th and Main St. Open M-F 8am-5:30pm.

Internet Access: Dayton Metro Library, 215 E. 3rd St. (☎937-227-9500), at the corner of St. Clair. Open M-Th 9am-9pm, F-Sa 9am-5:30pm; Sept.-May also Su 1-5pm.

Post Office: 1111 E. 5th St. (☎937-227-1122). Open M-F 7am-6pm, Sa 8am-2pm. **Postal Code:** 45401.

▐▀ GETTING AROUND. I-75 runs north-south through the city just west of the downtown area. **U.S. 35,** a controlled-access highway for much of its length, runs east-west at the base of downtown. **Rte. 48** runs primarily on **Main St.** north-south through the center of downtown. Numbered streets run east-west perpendicular to Main St., and **Monument Ave.** is one block north of **1st St.**

⑤ SIGHTS. At the ◪**United States Air Force Museum at the Wright-Patterson Air Force Base,** 1100 Spaatz St., 2800 visitors pouring through the museum every day marvel at 300 aircraft, dating from the beginning of human flight onwards as the latest models fly overhead. Also onsite is the **National Aviation Hall of Fame.** Allow at least 2hr. to explore; it is dense and there is a lot to see. Arrive early (especially on weekends) to sign up to see the extra-special Presidential Aircraft and Development/Test Flight Hangars. (Follow I-70 East to I-675, take Exit 15 for the Col. Glenn Hwy., and follow the signs. ☎937-255-3286; www.wpafb.af.mil/ museum. Open daily 9am-5pm. Free.)

More aviation fun is on display at the **Dayton Aviation Heritage National Historical Park: Wright-Dunbar Interpretive Center & Aviation Trail Visitors Center,** 22 S. Williams St., which relates the story of the Wright Brothers and of 19th-century African-American poet Paul Laurence Dunbar, who lived

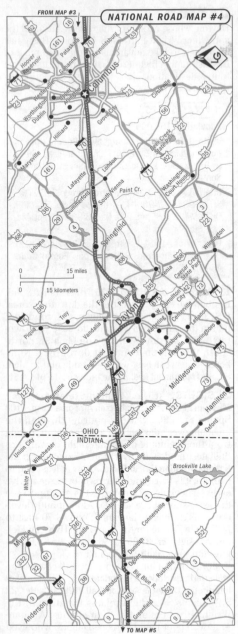

in West Dayton and worked closely with the brothers. (From 3rd St., turn left onto S. Williams St. ☎ 937-225-7705. Open daily 8am-5pm. Free.)

Perhaps a better bet for the Wright Brothers story is the **Wright Brothers Aviation Center in Carillon Historical Park,** where the saga is told in more intricate detail by a vivid display, experienced guides, and actual items belonging to the Wright Brothers, including their 1903 plane. (☎ 937-293-2841. Open Apr.-Oct. Su noon-5pm, Tu-Sa 9:30am-5pm. $5, seniors $4, ages 3-17 $3.)

Arts enthusiasts (and those tired of aviation paraphernalia) will appreciate the **Dayton Art Institute,** 456 Belmont Park N. The American art spanning from the 18th century to the present is particularly noteworthy. In addition to some more contemporary pieces, the institute displays Peter Rothermel's magnificent *King Lear* (1858). Also on display are smaller collections of Asian, African, European, and Native American art. (From Jefferson St., take a left on Monument Ave. Cross the bridge and turn right onto Riverview Ave., then take your first left on Belmont Park N. ☎ 937-223-5277; www.daytonartinstitute.org. Open M-W and F-Su 10am-4pm, Th 10am-8pm. Free.)

At **Sunwatch Prehistoric Indian Village,** 2301 W. River Rd., archaeologists have reconstructed an Indian village. This site dates back about 500 years before anything else along the road, and the interactive layout explains the logic of archaeology. (From Edwin C. Moses Blvd. downtown, turn left and proceed southwest past the I-75 exits, and take a left onto W. River Rd. ☎ 937-268-8199; www.sunwatch.org. Open Su noon-5pm, Tu-Sa 9am-5pm. $5, ages 6-17 and seniors $3.)

▓▐ FOOD & ACCOMMODATIONS. Cheap eats congregate on **Broad St.** near Dayton University. For standard pub fare, try **Flanagan's Pub,** 101 E. Stewart St., near Broad St., where a small lunch crowd enjoys a beer with the regulars. (☎ 937-228-5776. Burgers $3-5. Grilled cheese $2.75. Open M-Sa 11am-10pm.) **Chipotle,** 1211 Brown St., north of Stewart St., serves burritos and tacos ($5) to college kids. (☎ 937-222-2238. Open daily 11am-10pm.)

For accommodations, some of the cheapest rates in town are found at the **Econolodge,** 2140 Edwin C. Moses Blvd., just west of I-75 Exit 51. (☎ 937-223-0166. Continental breakfast included. Rooms from $40.) Another slightly cheaper option is the **Cross Country Inn,** 9325 N. Main St. (Rte. 48),

8 mi. outside the city, offering spotless, almost luxurious rooms. (In Englewood, behind the Comfort Inn. ☎937-836-8339. Non-smoking rooms available. Singles $39-46; doubles $46-53.)

◥ DETOUR: ENGLEWOOD METROPARK

Instead of continuing straight onto Rte. 48/U.S. 40, turn right to head east on U.S. 40 by the Englewood Dam to the "East Park" entrance on your left.

The only of Dayton's 24 "metroparks" to be listed in the state of Ohio's guide to natural areas, Englewood's lofty greenery provides a shaded opportunity to get off the road before heading into the fairly nature-less Indiana stretch. The park has three small waterfalls and several miles of flat hiking trails, as well as fishing and canoeing. Maps are available inside the park. (☎937-890-7766; www.metroparks.org. Open daily 8am-dusk.)

◥ LEAVING DAYTON

Head north on **Rte. 48**, which joins **U.S. 40 West** for a brief stretch, and then take a left at the **National Road/U.S. 40** sign.

THE ROAD TO RICHMOND. Thirty-eight miles from downtown Dayton, the road enters Indiana. Fill up your tank here; there are few gas stations for the next 28 mi. Also note **Madonna of the Trail** statue in Richmond; look to your right by 22nd St. and U.S. 40, at the entrance to Glen Miller Park.

 Between Apr. and Oct., set your watch 1hr. back at the border. Nov.-Mar., the time changes at the Illinois border.

RICHMOND

Ohio may have been the beginning of the Midwest, but you'll know you've reached America's heartland when you come to Richmond. Flat and full of chain establishments and wide open road, the "gateway to eastern Indiana" feels like America in all its small-town glory. A stop at the **Indiana** Football Hall of Fame, 815 N. A St., might evoke fond (or perhaps not-so-fond) memories of high-school gym class. Eight high-school football coaches mortgaged their homes in the 1970s to buy this building, which honors the best players and coaches from Indiana high schools. The walls of the aging museum's rooms are filled with photographs of high-school teams, hall of fame members, and winners of the college scholarships that the center awards each year. (☎765-966-2235. Open M-F 10am-4pm. $1, ages 14-16 $0.50.)

Richmond residents lament the loss of most local eateries, but it's still possible to catch a bite of local flavor. Low-key and mellow **Little Sheba's,** 175 Fort Wayne Ave., is best known in town as a sandwich place with fun names like "Stupid Idiot" (ham, turkey, roast beef, feta, and veggies) or "Hot Mama." (☎765-962-2999. F-Sa night spaghetti $7-9. Open M-Th 11am-9pm, Fri. 11am-10pm, Sa 11am-10pm.) Expect little decor and a simple menu at the unpretentious **Main Street Diner**, 1600 E. Main St. (U.S. 40), where a chef salad bowl is $6 and omelettes are $3-6. (☎765-962-7041. Open M-F 6:30am-2pm, Sa 6:30am-2pm, Su 8am-2pm. Cash only.) Richmond offers two budget-friendly hotels. On the way into town, the **Holiday Motel,** 3004 E. Main St., offers comfortable rooms, and the price is right. (☎765-962-3561. Non-smoking rooms available. Some rooms with microwaves and refrigerators. 21+ to rent. Singles $25; doubles $35.) Rooms are small but clean at the **Richmond Motel,** U.S. 40 East, 5 mi. from Richmond in Centerville. A nice pair of owners recently took over and renovated this place, giving it a new paint job. (☎765-855-5616. Non-smoking rooms available. Breakfast included. Singles $25; doubles $35.)

THE ROAD TO INDIANAPOLIS

The stretch of U.S. 40 from Richmond to Knightstown, including **Centerville** and **Cambridge City,** forms part of Indiana's **"Antique Alley."** Webb's **Antique Mall,** 200 W. Union St., in Centerville, hosts a warehouse-sized collection of antique merchants (85,000 sq. ft. in all), with multiple booths filled with signs, plates, books, clothing, records, furniture, and everything else that you didn't know you needed. (At the traffic light, turn right on Morton St., then take a left on Union St. ☎765-855-5551; www.webbsantiquemalls.com. Open daily Mar.-Nov. 8am-6pm; Dec.-Feb. 9am-5pm.) Six sisters native to Cambridge City helped turn pottery into an American art form, and a small collection of their work remains on display at the **Museum of Overbeck Art Pottery,** in the Cambridge City Public Library, 33 W. Main St. (U.S. 40). The pieces, housed in glass cases, are small and intricately detailed. (☎ 765-478-3335. Open M-Sa 10am-noon and 2-5pm, or by appointment. Free.)

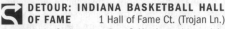 **DETOUR: INDIANA BASKETBALL HALL OF FAME** 1 Hall of Fame Ct. (Trojan Ln.)
Turn right in Ogdon onto Rte. 3 North, and turn right at the Shell Station; the museum is on the left.

High-school basketball is to Hoosiers (people from Indiana) as high-school football is to people elsewhere—very serious. This large museum glorifies hoops and honors the best Indianans to play the game. (☎ 765-529-1891. Open Su 1-5pm, Tu-Sa 10am-5pm. $4, seniors $3, children $2.)

NATIONAL COOKIE CUTTER MUSEUM
224 E. Main St. (U.S. 40)
In Knightstown, 34 mi. from Richmond.

Said to be North America's "King of Copper Cookie Cutters" (say *that* three times fast), coppersmith Michael Bonne crafts cookie cutters in all shapes and sizes, from cows to teeth to pumpkins. At the back of the specialty store that sells Bonne's work, a small set of glass cases displays cookie cutters through the ages. (☎ 765-345-7831. Open M-Sa 9am-5pm. Free.)

TRUMP'S TEXACO MUSEUM
39 N. Washington St.
From U.S. 40, turn right on Washington St. and continue 1 block to the corner of Brown and Washington St.

Stare at this corner long enough and you might think life jumped back 50 years. Made to look like an actual Texaco station, this outdoor/indoor museum has three pumps outside and genuine Texaco memorabilia inside, including signs, oil cans, and an old cash register. To go inside, you'll need an appointment; call ☎ 765-533-3453.

 **APPROACHING INDIANAPOLIS**
From U.S. 40, when you reach the beltway, head north on **I-465** to the next exit for I-70. Follow **I-70 West** to Exit 111, and take that exit for **Ohio St.**

INDIANAPOLIS

Surrounded by flat farmland, Indianapolis feels like a model Midwestern city. Locals shop and work all day among downtown's skyscrapers

before returning to the sprawling suburbs. Life ambles here—until May, that is, when 400,000 spectators overrun the city and the road warriors of the Indianapolis 500 claim the spotlight.

VITAL STATS

Population: 780,000

Visitor Info: Indianapolis Convention and Visitors Association, 1 RCA Dome, Ste. 100. (☎ 317-639-4282; www.indy.org). Open M-F 8:30am-5pm.

Internet Access: Indianapolis/Marion County Interim Public Library, 202 N. Alabama St. (☎ 317-269-1700). Open M-Tu 9am-9pm, W-F 9am-6pm, Sa 9am-5pm; Sept.-May also Su 1-5pm.

Post Office: 125 W. South St. (☎ 317-464-6804). Open M 7:30am-5pm, Tu-F 8am-5pm, Sa 8am-noon. **Postal Code:** 46204.

GETTING AROUND

While most attractions are within several miles of the city center, be prepared to drive. Indianapolis does not lend itself well to walking, except around downtown. The downtown, called **Center City,** is in the middle of the city, and is marked by a dense cluster of skyscrapers. **Washington St.** divides city north-south; **Meridian St.** divides it east-west. They meet just south of Monument Circle downtown. **I-465** circles the city, while **I-70** cuts through the city east-west. Outside the beltway (I-465) both east and west of the city, **Washington St.** is **U.S. 40.** Metered **parking** is abundant almost everywhere along Indianapolis's wide, straight streets, including downtown and near Circle Centre Mall.

SIGHTS

While Indianapolis is best known for being the home of the Indy 500, there's plenty to do in the city for those less interested in fast cars, thanks to an assortment of parks and museums.

MUSEUMS. Near the park entrance, the **Eiteljorg Museum of American Indians and Western Art,** features an impressive collection of art depicting the Old West, including works by Georgia O'Keeffe and Frederick Remington. The museum also offers a collection of Native American artifacts from across the US. (*500 W. Washington St. ☎ 317-636-9378; www.eiteljorg.org. Open Su noon-5pm, Tu-Sa 10am-5pm; May-Sept. also M 10am-5pm. Tours*

TO SPEEDWAY ❶ & ❷ (4mi)

16th St.

❸

15th St.

Ransom St.

14th St.

13th St.

Cora St.

Drake St.

12th St.

Smith St.

Crispus Attucks Museum

11th St.

YMCA

10th St.

❻

9th St.

St. Clair

St. Joseph St.
Sahm St.

Walnut St.

Public Library
(opens 2006)

❼

CANAL
WALK
DISTRICT

North St.

Veterans
Memorial
Plaza

Michigan St.

Indiana War
Memorial

Indiana University
Purdue University
Indianapolis

Vermon St.

Allegheny St.

Tippecanoe
St.

University
Park

New York St.

Military
Park

Indiana
State Museum

State
Library

Eiteljorg
Museum

Washington
Ave.

WHITE RIVER
STATE PARK

Indiana
State Capitol

Federal
Building

Ohio St.

Market St.

Monument
Circle

Indianapolis
Indians
Ball Park

Washington St.

Court St.

IU, INDIANAPOLIS ZOO,
WHITE RIVER GARDENS
I-465

Maryland St.

Artsgarden

Chesapeake St.

RCA
Dome

Georgia St.

Jackson Pl.

Union
Station

South St.

Henry St.

Merrill St.

McCarty St.

Wyoming St.

Ray St.

Morris St.

Kansas St.

16th St.

15th St.

14th St.

13th St.

12th St.

11th St.

10th St.

Puryear St.

MASSACHUSETTS
AVENUE ARTS
DISTRICT

St. Clair

❽

North St.

James Whitcomb
Riley Home

Michigan St.

New York St.

Miami St.

❾

Interim
Public
Library

Market
Square

Wabash St.

Market Square
Arena

Market St.

Washington St.

WHOLESALE
DISTRICT

Pearl St.

Louisiana St.

Lord St.

Fletcher
Ave.

South St.
Empire St.

Henry St.

Stevens St.

McCarty St.

Buchanan St.

Prospect St.

❿

⓫

Morris St.

Sanders St.

NATIONAL ROAD

Indianapolis

🏠🏠 **ACCOMMODATIONS**
Indiana State Fair Campgrounds, 5
Motel 6, 1
Methodist Tower Inn, 3
Renaissance Tower Historic Inn, 7

🍎 **FOOD**
The Abbey, 6 & 8
Bazbeaux Pizza, 9
Don Victor's, 11
Shapiro's, 10
Union Jack Pub, 2 & 4

daily 1pm. $7, seniors $6, students and ages 5-17 $4.) Next door, the **Indiana State Museum** lets visitors follow the "Hoosier Heritage Trail" through in-depth exhibits on Indiana history—so in-depth, in fact, that it starts off with the beginning of the earth and wraps up with profiles of Indiana's famous citizens, from Larry Bird to Axl Rose. *(650 W. Washington St. ☎317-232-1637; www.indianamuseum.org. Open M-Sa 9am-5pm, Su 11am-5pm. $7, seniors $6.50, children $4. IMAX $8.50/$7/$6.)*

Kids will get a kick out of the fun-filled **Indianapolis Children's Museum,** the largest children's museum in the world. *(3000 N. Meridian St. ☎317-334-3322; www.childrensmuseum.org. Open Mar.-Aug. daily 10am-5pm; Sept.-Feb. closed M. $9.50, seniors $8, children $4.)* It may be far from downtown, but the **Indianapolis Museum of Art** offers nature trails, a historic home, botanical gardens, a greenhouse, and a theater. The interior includes American, African, and Neo-Impressionist works. *(1200 W. 38th St. ☎317-923-1331; www.ima-art.org. Open Su noon-5pm, Tu-W and F-Sa 10am-5pm, Th 10am-8:30pm. Free. Special exhibits $5.)*

Chronicling the history of the Crispus Attucks High School, formed in 1927 to educate African-Americans in Indianapolis, the **Crispus Attucks Museum** is well done and understated. *(1140 Dr. Martin Luther King, Jr. St., on the Crispus Attucks Middle School campus. Look for the sign indicating the visitor entrance; enter the office and ask to be let in. ☎317-226-2430. Open M-F 10am-2pm.)*

RACING ATTRACTIONS. The country's passion for fast cars reaches fever pitch during the **500 Festival,** an entire month of parades and hoopla leading up to race day at the **Indianapolis Motor Speedway.** The festivities begin with time trials in mid-May and culminate with the "Gentlemen, start your engines" of the **Indianapolis 500** the Sunday before Memorial Day. Tickets for the race go on sale the day after the previous year's race and usually sell out within a week. In quieter times, buses full of tourists drive around the 2½ mi. track at slightly tamer speeds. *(4790 W. 16th St., off I-465 at the Speedway Exit. ☎317-481-8500; www.indy500.com. Track tours daily 9am-4:40pm. $3, ages 6-15 $1. Festival info ☎317-636-4556.)* The **Speedway Museum,** at the south end of the infield, displays **Indy's Hall of Fame** and a large collection of cars that have tested their mettle on the storied track over the years. *(☎317-484-6747. Open daily 9am-5pm. $3, ages 6-15 $1.)*

OTHER SIGHTS. A majestic stained-glass dome graces the marble interior of the **State House.** *(200 W. Washington St., between Capitol and Senate St. ☎317-233-5293. Open M-F 8am-4pm. 1hr. tours 2-5 per day. Free.)* No sports fan should miss the **NCAA Hall of Champions,** which covers all 28 college sports. Relive the passion of the Final Four in the March Madness Theater and try your hand at hitting a clutch shot in the 1930s-style gymnasium. *(700 W. Washington St. ☎317-735-6222; www.ncaa-hallofchampions.org. Open M-Sa 10am-5pm, Su noon-5pm. $7, students $4, under 6 free.)* Animal lovers should check out the seemingly cageless **Indianapolis Zoo,** which holds large whale and dolphin pavilions. *(1200 W. Washington St. ☎317-630-2001; www.indyzoo.com. Open daily June-Aug. 9am-5pm; Sept.-May 9am-4pm. $10.75, seniors $7.75, ages 2-12 $6.75. Parking $3.)*

♫ ENTERTAINMENT

The **Walker Theatre,** 617 Indiana Ave., a 15min. walk northwest of downtown, used to house the headquarters of African-American entrepreneur Madame C.J. Walker's beauty enterprise. Today, the landmark hosts arts programs, including the biweekly **Jazz on the Avenue.** *(☎317-236-2099. Tours M-F 9am-5pm. Jazz F 6-10pm. $5.)* The **Indianapolis Symphony Orchestra** performs from late June to August in the **Hilbert Circle Theater** on Monument Circle. *(☎317-639-4300; www.indyorch.org. Box office open M-F 9am-5pm, Sa 10am-2pm.)* Sports fans have far more to be thankful for than just the speedway. Basketball lovers watch the **Pacers** hoop it up at the **Conseco Fieldhouse,** 125 S. Pennsylvania St. *(☎317-917-2500. Tickets $10-92.)* The WNBA's **Indiana Fever** take over in the summer. *(☎317-239-5151. Tickets $8-90.)* Football's **Colts** take to the gridiron at the **RCA Dome,** 100 S. Capital Ave. *(☎317-239-5151.)*

🍴 FOOD

Ethnic food stands, produce markets, and knick-knack vendors fill the spacious **City Market,** 222 E. Market St., a renovated 19th-century building. *(☎317-630-4107. Open M-W and F 6am-6pm, Th 6am-8pm, Sa 6am-4pm.)* Moderately priced restaurants cluster in Indianapolis's newly constructed **Circle Centre,** 49 West Maryland St. *(☎317-681-8000).* **Massachusetts**

Ave. is home to some of the liveliest restaurants and bars in town; in the summer, crowded outdoor patios fill with diners every night.

Bazbeaux Pizza, 334 Massachusetts Ave. (☎317-636-7662), and 832 E. Westfields Blvd. (☎317-255-5711). Serves Indianapolis's favorite pizza, from $11. Construct your own wonder ($6) from a choice of 53 toppings. Open Su-Th 11am-10pm, F-Sa 11am-11pm.

The Abbey, 771 Massachusetts Ave. (☎317-269-8426), and 923 Indiana Ave. (☎317-917-0367). A popular coffee shop, offering wraps, sandwiches ($6-7), and vegetarian options. Sip cappuccinos ($2.25) in velvet chairs. Open M-Th 8am-midnight, F 8am-1am, Sa 11am-1am, Su 11am-midnight.

Don Victor's, 1032 S. East St. (☎317-637-4397). The best Mexican food in town. Burrito and enchilada platters ($6), as well as more authentic dishes such as *menudo* and *pozole.* The 2-person Fiesta Platter ($21) is a good way to sample various dishes. Open Su-Th 11am-9pm, F-Sa 11am-10pm.

Shapiro's, 808 S. Meridian St. (☎317-631-4041). Take Meridian St. south past South St. When it diverts right onto Madison St., take a quick right on Henry St. and then a quick left to get back on Meridian St. According to legend, the "busiest lunch place downtown." 100 years of practice have given Shapiro's ample time to turn food production into a science. Open daily 6:30am-8pm.

Union Jack Pub, 6225 W. 25th St. (☎317-243-3300), and 924 Broad Ripple Ave. (☎317-257-4343). For 25th St. location, from I-465, take Exit 16A for Crawfordsville Rd. east and turn left onto High School Rd., then right onto 25th St. Loads of race memorabilia, rows of drivers' helmets, and an Indy racecar. Extensive pub menu, including specialty pizzas. Open M-W 11am-11pm, Th-Sa 11am-midnight, Su noon-11pm.

ACCOMMODATIONS

Budget motels line the I-465 beltway, 5 mi. from downtown. Make reservations a year in advance for the Indy 500, which drives rates up drastically in May.

Motel 6, 6330 Debonair Ln. (☎317-293-3220), at Exit 16A off I-465. Clean, pleasant rooms with A/C and cable TV. Singles $29-35; doubles $35-40.

Methodist Tower Inn, 1633 N. Capitol Ave. (☎317-925-9831). Large rooms with TV and A/C are occa-

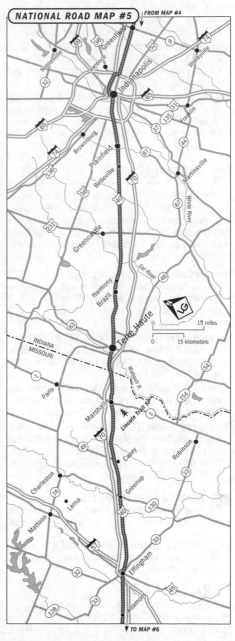

NATIONAL ROAD MAP #5 — FROM MAP #4 — TO MAP #6

sionally hard to come by but the cheapest ones near downtown. A short walk from Monument Circle. Singles $63; doubles $67.50; $5 per additional person.

Renaissance Tower Historic Inn, 230 E. 9th St. (☎317-261-2652 or 800-676-7786). Reasonable rates for luxurious rooms with cable TV, A/C, kitchenettes, and stately canopy beds. Rooms $59.

Indiana State Fair Campgrounds, 1202 E. 38th St. (☎317-927-7520). 170 sod-and-gravel sites, mostly packed by RVs. To get close to nature, go elsewhere. Especially busy during the state fair. Sites $16; full hookup $19.

🐾 NIGHTLIFE

Somewhat bland by day, the Broad Ripple area, 6 mi. north of downtown at College Ave. and 62nd St., transforms into a center for nightlife after dark. Partiers fill the clubs and bars and spill out onto the sidewalks until about 1am on weekdays and 3am on weekends.

The Jazz Cooker, 925 E. Westfield Blvd. (☎317-253-2883). Heats up when the Steve Ball Trio begins jamming. The attached **Monkey's Tale** is a relaxed bar. Live music F-Sa 7-10pm. Bar open M-Sa until 3am, Su until 12:30am.

Vogue, 6259 N. College Ave. (☎317-255-2828). The hottest club in town. Hosts national acts. Shows 8pm; call for schedule. 21+. Cover $3-5; ladies free F. Open W 9pm-3am, F-Sa 10pm-3am.

Patio, 6308 N. Guildford (☎317-233-0799). Live music every night. The place for local and alternative acts. 21+. Cover around $5. Open daily 9pm-close.

The Slippery Noodle, 372 S. Meridian St. (☎317-631-6974), downtown. The oldest bar in Indian and one of the country's best venues for nightly live blues. 21+. Cover Th-Sa $5. Open M-F 11am-3am, Sa 12:30pm-3am, Su 4pm-12:30am.

🎌 **LEAVING INDIANAPOLIS**
Take **Washington St.** west of downtown; it becomes **U.S. 40** once you cross the beltway (I-465).

🎌 **APPROACHING TERRE HAUTE**
U.S. 40 becomes **Wabash Ave.** and leads directly into Terre Haute.

TERRE HAUTE

Terre Haute was once called the "crossroads of America" by virtue of its existence at the junction of U.S. 40 and U.S. 41. Deceptively large, the city today retains only a shadow of its former importance. Industries, including that responsible for Clabber Girl Baking Powder, power the area close to downtown, but outlying areas have become a little more run-down. During the school year, the **Children's Science and Technology Museum,** 523 Wabash Ave., takes its weather-related exhibits on the road to give children hands-on science education. During the summer, those exhibits, along with the museum's permanent collection of interactive teaching tools, are on display here. (☎812-235-5548. Open Tu-Sa 9am-4pm. $3, children $2.50.) Quite a bit of self-glorification goes on at the **Clabber Girl Museum,** 900 Wabash Ave., at 9th St., which preaches about Hulman & Co.'s wonderful and benevolent deeds not only for the American homemaker but also for the citizens of Terre Haute. Demonstrations show the baking powder manufacturing process, and on display are an eclectic collection of old telephones, an early 20th-century kitchen, and goods at the "country store." (☎812-478-7223; www.clabbergirl.com. Open M-F 10am-6pm, Sa 10am-3pm. Free.) At **St. Mary-of-the-Woods College's Providence Center,** 1¾ mi. from Terre Haute, a site for spiritual retreats, a simple **"Christian labyrinth"** awaits visitors. (Turn right to head north on Rte. 150. Proceed 2¾ mi. to the sign for St. Mary-of-the-Woods College on the left. Turn left and proceed 1 mi. to the main entrance on the right. Follow signs for Owens Hall and the labyrinth. ☎812-535-4531. Open daily dawn-dusk. Free.)

For a refreshing change from the usual American fare, try **Gerhardt's Bierstube,** 1724 Lafayette Ave., where German music complements menu items like wienerschnitzel ($13) and *kassler rippchen* (porkchop; $13). (From downtown, take 7th St. north to Lafayette Ave. and turn right. ☎812-466-9249. Open Su 4-9pm, Tu-Th 11am-2pm and 4-9pm, F 11am-2pm and 4-10pm, Sa 4-10pm.) Clean and cheap, the ◪**Midtown Motel,** 400 S. 3rd St., is comfortable, spacious, and close to both U.S. 40 and the center of town. (☎812-232-0383. Singles $30; doubles $35, with additional person $38.)

🎌 **LEAVING TERRE HAUTE**
Hop on **U.S. 40 West.** 1¼ mi. past 3rd St., there is an unlabeled curve—follow it around to the left.

Welcome To ILLINOIS

 If you are traveling between Nov. and Mar., you enter the Central Time Zone, where it is 1he. earlier, as you cross the border.

APPROACHING MARSHALL
5 mi. from Terre Haute, **U.S. 40** merges with **I-70.** The signed National Road diverges here but rejoins U.S. 40 in about 2½ mi. 14½ mi. from Terre Haute, turn left at the sign for **Marshall/Historic National Road** to enter the town of Marshall on the National Road, which runs through town as **Archer St.**

MARSHALL. The small town of Marshall is home to the **Lincoln Trail State Park,** perfect for a bit of out-of-car relaxing on a sunny day. This 1000-acre rustic, wooded park offers flat hiking through American beech woods, fishing, picnicking, and inexpensive camping around a 146-acre lake. (From the center of town, head south on Rte. 1 for 3 mi. ☎217-826-2222. No swimming. Primitive tent sites $7; car-access sites $8; full hookup $11.) An alternative the busy chain eateries by the interstate, **Bishop's Cafe,** 710 Archer Ave., caters to a crowd that prefers home cooking from scratch. Locals come for the baskets ($4-7), which include a sandwich with fries and slaw. Drivers can grab an early breakfast here before pushing westward. (☎217-826-9933. Omelettes $3-5. Open M-Sa 5am-1:30pm, Su 6am-2pm.) Interesting (but not cheap) **Archer House,** 717 Archer Ave., at Rte. 1, is the oldest hotel in the state of Illinois. Built in 1841, this B&B was originally a stagecoach stop on the National Road. The inside has been beautifully furnished by its owner. (☎217-826-8023. Not generally open for public tours. Rooms from $100.)

LEAVING MARSHALL
Continue out of Marshall on **Archer Ave.;** it rejoins **U.S. 40** 2 mi. west of Rte. 1.

THE ROAD TO EFFINGHAM
On your way from Marshall, notice the 1828 stone arch bridge about half a mile west of town, remarkably still in use. Continuing west, follow the sign for the National Road (Rte. 121) heading into **Greenup.** Following Rte. 121, you'll pass over a single-lane covered wooden bridge over the Embarras (say "um-braw") river, built in the late 1990s to the specifications of one originally built by Abe and Thomas Lincoln. After the bridge, proceed to the "dead end," which dumps you back on U.S. 40 toward Effingham.

DETOUR: LINCOLN LOG CABIN STATE HISTORIC SITE
400 S. Lincoln Hwy. Rd. In Lerna, 13½ mi. north of Greenup and U.S. 40. Follow the signs from Greenup, taking Rte. 130 North.
At this "living history" museum and working 1840s farm, actors play members of the Lincoln family and their wealthy neighbors, the Sargeants. The long detour is worth it; after all, Illinois is nicknamed the "Land of Lincoln." (☎217-345-1845; www.lincolnlogcabin.org. Open Apr.-Oct. Su and W-Sa 9am-5pm; Nov.-Mar. until 4pm. Free.)

APPROACHING EFFINGHAM
The signed National Road leads to **Jefferson Ave.** and **3rd St.** in downtown Effingham. Alternatively, U.S. 40 becomes **W. Fayette St.** in Effingham.

EFFINGHAM
Though surprisingly cosmopolitan for its rural location, Effingham moves at an easy, slow pace. Locals reside in the proud shadow of a 198 ft. high steel cross erected on the outskirts of town.

VITAL STATS

Population: 12,000

Visitor Info: Effingham Chamber of Commerce, 408 W. Fayette St. (☎217-342-4147). Open M-F 8am-5pm. **Convention and Visitors Bureau,** 210 E. Jefferson St. (☎217-342-5310 or 800-772-0750), inside City Hall at the corner of 3rd St. Open M-F 8am-noon and 1-5pm.

Internet Access: Helen Matthes Library, 100 E. Market Ave. (☎217-342-2464). Take 3rd St. north from Fayette Ave. and turn left at the sign. Open M-Th 10am-7pm, F 10am-5pm, Sa 10am-1pm.

Post Office: 210 N. 3rd St. (☎800-275-8777), 3 blocks north of Fayette St. Open M-F 7:30am-5:30pm, Sa 8:30am-12:30pm. **Postal Code:** 62401.

GETTING AROUND. Main east-west streets in Effingham include **Fayette Ave. (U.S. 40), Jefferson Ave.,** and **Washington Ave.,** each of which is lined with shops and restaurants. Jefferson Ave.

runs one-way east between Banker St. and 3rd St., while Washington Ave. runs one-way west. The main north-south thoroughfare through the center of town is **3rd St. (Rte. 45).** At the western edge of downtown is **Keller Dr.** (Henrietta St. on the other side of Fayette Ave.), another main drag. There is free 2hr. street **parking** in the downtown area; most other establishments have parking lots.

◨ **SIGHTS.** Effingham is well endowed in the way of quirky roadtrip attractions. The more than 20 pristine-condition Corvettes at the ◪**Mike Yager Mid-America Designs Corvette Museum,** 1 Mid America Pl. (off Rte. 45), is enough to make most teenaged boys (and middle-aged men) drool. Looking at the walls is almost as fun as the cars; the airplane hangar-sized garage is set up with 1950s- and 60s-style wall decorations and storefronts. Ask about **Funfest,** an annual event in which 8000 cars descend on the town for some adult-only partying. (Take 3rd St. north 3 mi. to the museum on the right. ☎217-347-5591. Open M-Sa 8am-5pm; occasionally closed to rotate cars. Free.)

It's visible from U.S. 40 on the way out of town, but for the full experience, you have to drive to the ◪**Cross at the Crossroads,** off Pike Ave. On the outskirts of Effingham, this giant 181-ton steel cross stands a whopping 198 ft. tall and 113 ft. across, surrounded by black stone monuments representing each of the ten commandments. Quite simply, this "world's biggest" has to be seen to be believed. (Take Fayette St. west out of downtown, turn left on Raney St., then right on Pike Ave. ☎217-347-2846; www.crossusa.org. Visitors Center open daily 9:30am-8pm.) In the center of town, the old Art Deco **Heart Theatre,** at the corner of 3rd and Jefferson St., still shows movies. (☎217-342-5555. Movies generally M-Th 7pm, F-Sa 4:15 and 7pm. $3, before 6pm $2.)

▨▐ **FOOD & ACCOMMODATIONS.** Some of the best grub in town is served at local recommended **El Rancherito,** 1313 Keller Dr. Huge portions of sizzling hot, authentic, non-greasy Mexican food guarantee stuffed and satisfied customers. Try a skillet of mouth-watering fajitas ($9.50) or one of the combination dinners ($5-8)— *relleno,* burrito, or enchilada. (Take W. Fayette Ave. heading west out of downtown and turn right on Keller Dr. ☎217-342-4753. Lunch $3.50-6. Open Su-Th 11am-10pm, F-Sa 11am-11pm.) For a pleth-

ora of steak varieties ($8-14), stop by **Niemerg's Steak House,** 1410 W. Fayette Ave. A smattering of other options include fish dinner specials ($7-9), eggs ($2), and the special "country-fried chicken dinner" ($5). Lunch ($3-4) is served from 10:15am to 2pm. (☎217-342-3921. Open daily 6am-2am.)

Roadtrippers looking for a night's lodgings in Effingham might try the **Paradise Inn,** 1000 W. Fayette Ave. (U.S. 40), which offers standard, well-maintained rooms in a convenient location. (☎217-342-2165. Singles $33; doubles $38.) The cheapest rates are found at the **Abe Lincoln,** at the corner of Henrietta St. and Fayette Ave. Rooms are cramped, but some come with kitchenettes. (☎217-342-2165. Singles $28; doubles $35.)

▛ **APPROACHING VANDALIA**
Follow **U.S. 40** through several turns as it makes its way west out of Effingham. The giant cross is to the left after you turn right off Henrietta St. and onto the **Old National Road. U.S. 40** turns right in Vandalia; proceed straight at the "National Road" sign 1 block on **Gallatin Ave.** until you reach the **Madonna of the Trails Statue.** This statue marks the original end of the 591 mi. National Road from Cumberland, Maryland, to Vandalia.

VANDALIA

It's hard to believe that tiny Vandalia was the original end of the National Road and once the capital of Illinois. Relics of this golden age exist, however, in the form of the majestic state house and Madonna of the Trails Statue. The **Vandalia State House State Historic Site,** 315 W. Gallatin St., is located at the corner of 3rd St. Abraham Lincoln first served as a state representative at this imposing white-painted brick building, which was the Illinois State House from 1836-1839. The simply furnished interior is open for tours, and across the street is tiny **Lincoln Park,** complete with a statue of a young Abraham Lincoln. (☎618-283-1161. Open Mar.-Oct. Su and W-Sa 9am-5pm; Nov.-Feb. until 4pm. Suggested donation $2, under 17 $1.) Two blocks from the State House, the **Evans Public Library,** 215 S. 5th St., houses the life mask of Abraham Lincoln made by Leonard Volk. While a reproduction of Volk's mask is on display at the State House, the real (and eerie) thing sits in the "Lincoln Room" at the back of the library. (☎618-283-2824. Open M-Th 9am-7pm, F-Sa 9am-5pm.)

LEAVING VANDALIA
Follow **U.S. 40 West** out of town. Turn left to go south on **Rte. 127,** toward Carlyle.

DETOUR: RICHARD W. BOCK SCULPTURE MUSEUM

2½ mi. from U.S. 40 in Greenville. Turn right to go north on Rte. 127 into Greenville, and follow signs for Greenville College. The museum is on College St. just before the intersection with Spruce St.

This museum, in Greenville College's oldest building, houses around 300 sculptures and 500 sketches and drawings by sculptor Richard Bock, who worked closely with Frank Lloyd Wright. (☎618-664-6724; www.greenville-chamber.com/bock.htm. Open by appointment.)

CARLYLE LAKE

Carlyle Lake is second only to Chicago as the most-visited place in Illinois. State parks and campsites operated by the US Army Corps of Engineers encircle the large man-made lake, each with its own combination of camping, sailing, fishing, hunting, boating, and swimming facilities. Strong winds make the lake especially suitable for sailing. The small county seat of Carlyle, at the southwest corner of the lake, serves park users.

VITAL STATS

Population: 3400

Visitor Info: Carlyle Lake Visitors Center, 801 Lake Rd. (☎618-594-5253). Head east off Rte. 127 at the sign. Open in summer daily 10am-6pm; limited hours during the rest of the year.

Internet Access: Case-Halstead Library, 571 Franklin St. (☎618-594-5210), at 6th St. Open M-Th noon-8pm, F-Sa 9am-2pm.

Post Office: 1080 Fairfax St. (☎618-594-3322), at 11th St. Open M-F 8:30am-5pm, Sa 9am-11pm. **Postal Code:** 62231.

GETTING AROUND. Carlyle Lake occupies three counties; primary access points include those near the towns of **Carlyle, Keyesport,** and **Boulder.** Eldon Hazlet State Park is 4 mi. north of Carlyle off **Rte. 127.** The **Dam West, Dam East,** and **McNair** areas lie just north of the town of Carlyle, while the **Coles Creek** facility and **South Shore State Park** both lie on the southeastern shore of the lake between Carlyle and Boulder.

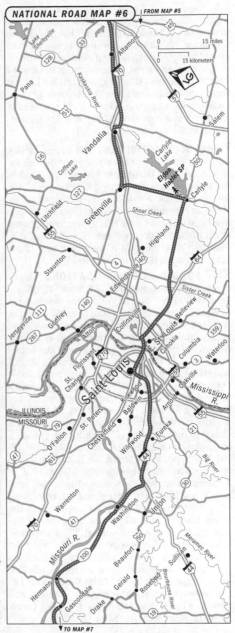

NATIONAL ROAD MAP #6 — FROM MAP #5

TO MAP #7

NATIONAL ROAD

In the town of Carlyle, **Rte. 127** runs north-south through downtown as **12th St.;** since getting to most places requires turning off Rte. 127 before this point, check out directions in advance to avoid having to backtrack. All north-south streets in town are numbered, from 1st St. in the east to 24th St. in the west. **U.S. 50** joins with Rte. 127 and runs north-south above **Franklin St.,** joining Franklin St. on the way out of town. Most restaurants and services are concentrated along Franklin St. or **Fairfax St.,** one block north.

♫ OUTDOOR ACTIVITIES. The largest facility operated by the Illinois Department of Natural Resources, **Eldon Hazlet State Park** attracts families for summer lakeside getaways. Park day use is free, and the lake is stocked with farm-reared fish. Hunting is permitted in winter. (From Rte. 127, head east on Hazlet Park Rd., approximately 4 mi. north of the Carlyle town center. ☎ 618-594-3015. Visitors Center open M-F 8am-noon and 12:30-4pm. Swimming pool $4, under 16 $3).

▚▐ FOOD & ACCOMMODATIONS. Windows at the **Dockside Diner,** 5 Resort Dr., offer a good view of the boats moored in the nearby lake. Relatively new, with a log-cabin exterior, the diner was built to accommodate the growing tourist and boater crowd. The varied dinner menu includes a reuben or "dockside dog" ($6), entrees like home-made lasagna ($9), and the "Jack Daniels Steak," which tops the menu at $15. (☎ 618-594-4657. Open Su-Th 6am-9pm, F-Sa 6am-10pm.) For a nicer dinner that won't empty your wallet, try **Patrick's,** 870 Franklin St., at 9th St., an Irish pub slightly more elegant than most. Meat and fish dishes like pork chops ($11), prime rib ($13-22), and baked roughy ($12.50) fill the menu. (☎ 618-594-8115. Open Su-W 4-9pm, Th 11am-2pm and 4-9pm, F 11am-2pm and 4-10pm, Sa 4-10pm.)

Campsites are mostly scattered near the lake, with a few abutting the lakefront directly; these offer shady trees and gorgeous views across the water. Only 65 sites allow reservations, and the rest are first come, first served. Sites are often sold out on summer weekends in June and July. (☎ 618-594-3015. Sites $7, with hookup $11; cabins $35.) Two campgrounds here are run by the U.S. Army Corps of Engineers: **Coles Creek,** with 148 campsites, a beach, showers, and laundry, and **McNair,** with 32 sites and a beach. (Coles Creek sites $12-24. McNair sites $10.)

At the **Sunset Motel,** 1631 Franklin St., each room is different. A fair number of the guests are permanent; be prepared for a casual, noisy atmosphere. (☎ 618-594-4838. Singles $34; doubles $40, with kitchenette $46.) Many things are green at the **Motel Carlyle,** 570 12th St., from the light green doors to the dark green carpet. It offers 19 comfy rooms surrounding a parking lot. (☎ 618-594-8100 or 866-594-8102. Singles $48; doubles $52.)

▐▜ LEAVING CARLYLE
Take **12th St. (U.S. 50/127)** north out of the center of town. 1 mi. from the town center, turn left to get on **U.S. 50 West.** 30 mi. outside Carlyle, U.S. 50 West joins with **I-64 West** toward St. Louis.

▐▜ APPROACHING ST. LOUIS
Take **I-64/U.S. 50 West** through Illinois toward St. Louis. At the large highway split, when the downtown buildings and arch are already visible, stay left for **South I-55/West I-70/I-64/St. Louis.** Take the exit for the **Martin Luther King Jr. Memorial Bridge** toward downtown St. Louis and cross over the mighty Mississippi River, just north of the famous arch.

 In Missouri, minor state routes have letters, not numbers. From your cell phone, you can contact the State Highway Patrol at *55.

ST. LOUIS

Directly south of the junction of three rivers—the Mississippi, Missouri, and Illinois—St. Louis marks the transition between the Midwest and the West. The soaring Gateway Arch pays homage to America's westward expansion, while only a couple of miles south, the Anheuser-Busch Company churns out Budweiser, the most American beer of them all. Innovative musicians crowd bars and cafes, influenced by St. Louis blues and ragtime players of the past. Sprawling and diverse, St. Louis offers visitors city life with a frontier feel.

(VITAL STATS)

Population: 348,000

Visitor Info: Visitors Center, 308 Washington Ave. (☎314-241-1764; www.explorestlouis.com), at Memorial Blvd. Open daily 9:30am-4:30pm. Branch inside **America's Convention Center** (☎314-342-5160), at the corner of 7th St. and Washington Ave. Open M-F 8:30am-4pm, Sa 9am-2pm.

Internet Access: St. Louis Central Library, 1301 Olive St. (☎314-241-2288). Open M 10am-9pm, Tu-F 10am-6pm, Sa 9am-5pm.

Post Office: 1720 Market St. (☎314-436-4114). Open M-F 8am-8pm, Sa 8am-1pm. **Postal Code:** 63101.

▐ GETTING AROUND

U.S. 40/I-64 runs east-west through the center of the metropolitan area, while **I-70, I-44 (U.S. 50),** and **I-55** all run to downtown from other outlying areas. Downtown is defined as the area east of **Tucker Blvd.** between **Martin Luther King** and **Market St.,** which divides the city north-south. Numbered streets parallel the Mississippi River, increasing to the west. St. Louis is a real neighborhood city, with attractions and restaurants concentrated in several distinct areas. The historic **Soulard** district borders the river south of downtown. **Forest Park** and **University City,** home to **Washington University** and old, stately homes, lie west of downtown. The Italian neighborhood called **The Hill** rests south of these. St. Louis is also a driving town; **parking** comes easily and wide streets and interstates allow for fast-moving traffic (most of the time).

◉ SIGHTS

JEFFERSON EXPANSION MEMORIAL. At 630 ft., the ▨**Gateway Arch**—the nation's tallest monument—towers gracefully over all of St. Louis and southern Illinois, serving as a testament to the city's historical role as the "Gateway to the West." The ground-level view is impressive, and the arch frames downtown beautifully from the Illinois side, but the 4min. ride to the top in quasi-futuristic elevator modules is more fun. Waits are shorter after dinner or in the morning, but are uniformly long on Saturday. Beneath the arch, the underground **Museum of Westward Expansion** adds to the appeal of the grassy park complex known as the Jefferson Expansion Memorial. The museum radiates out in a semi-circle from a statue of a surveying Jefferson, celebrating the Louisiana Purchase and Westward expansion. (☎*314-982-1410; www.gatewayarch.com. Museum and arch open daily summer 8am-10pm; winter 9am-6pm. Tram $8, ages 13-16 $5, ages 3-12 $3. Museum free.)*

DOWNTOWN. It's a strike either way at the **International Bowling Museum and Hall of Fame** and the **St. Louis Cardinals Hall of Fame Museum,** which share a home across from Busch Stadium. The mildly amusing bowling museum traces the largely speculative history of the sport and allows visitors to bowl, while the baseball museum exhibits memorabilia from the glory days of St. Louis hardball. The museum also offers stadium tours. (*111 Stadium Plaza.* ☎*314-231-6340. Open Apr.-Sept. daily 9am-5pm, game days until 6:30pm; Oct.-Mar. Su and Tu-Sa 11am-4pm. Museums or stadium tour $6, ages 5-12 $4; both $8.50/$7.50.)* Historic **Union Station,** 1 mi. west of downtown, houses a shopping mall, food court, and entertainment center in a magnificent structure that was once the nation's busiest railroad terminal. (*At 18th and Market St.* ☎*314-421-6655; www.stlouisunionstation.com. Open M-Sa 10am-9pm, Su 10am-6pm.)* "The Entertainer" lives on at the **Scott Joplin House,** just west of downtown near Jefferson St., where the ragtime legend tickled the ivories and penned classics from 1900 to 1903. The 45min. tour delves into Joplin's long-lasting influence on American music. (*2658 Delmar Blvd.* ☎*314-340-5790. Tours Apr.-Oct. M-F every 30min. 10am-4pm, Su noon-5pm; Nov.-Mar. also Sa 10am-4pm. $2.50, ages 6-12 $1.50.)*

SOUTH OF DOWNTOWN. Soulard is bounded by I-55 and 7th St. In the early 1970s, the city proclaimed this area a historic district due to its former populations of German and East European immigrants, many of whom worked in the breweries. Today, it is an attractive, tree-lined neighborhood packed with 19th-century brick townhouses. The district surrounds the bustling **Soulard Farmers Market,** where fresh, inexpensive produce abounds. (*730 Carroll St. From downtown, travel south on Broadway or 7th St. to Lafayette.* ☎*314-622-4180. Open W-Sa 7am-7pm; hours vary among merchants.)* At the end of 12th St., the **Anheuser-Busch Brewery,** the largest brewery in the world, produces the "King of Beers." The 1½hr. tour

NATIONAL ROAD

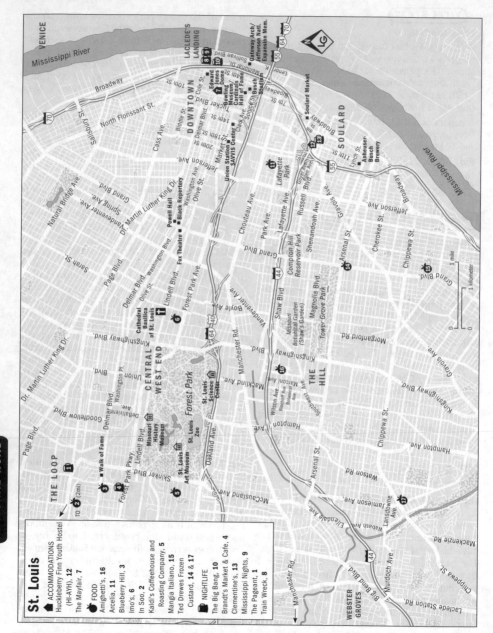

St. Louis

▲ ACCOMMODATIONS
Huckleberry Finn Youth Hostel
(HI-AYH), **12**
The Mayflair, **7**

◆ FOOD
Amighetti's, **16**
Arcelia, **11**
Blueberry Hill, **3**
Imo's, **6**
In Soo, **2**
Kaldi's Coffeehouse and
Roasting Company, **5**
Mangia Italiano, **15**
Ted Drewes Frozen
Custard, **14 & 17**

◆ NIGHTLIFE
The Big Bang, **10**
Brandt's Market & Cafe, **4**
Clementine's, **13**
Mississippi Nights, **9**
The Pageant, **1**
Train Wreck, **8**

includes a glimpse of the famous Clydesdales and two beer samples. *(1127 Pestalozzi St., at 12th and Lynch St. Take bus #40 "Broadway" south from downtown. ☎ 314-577-2626; www.budweisertours.com. Tours June-Aug. M-Sa 9am-5pm, Su 11:30am-5pm; Sept.-May M-Sa 9am-4pm, Su 11:30am-4pm.)*

The internationally acclaimed 79 acre **Missouri Botanical Garden** thrives north of Tower Grove Park on grounds left by entrepreneur Henry Shaw. The Japanese Garden is guaranteed to soothe the weary traveler. *(4344 Shaw Blvd. From downtown, take I-44 west. ☎ 800-642-8842; www.mobot.org. Open daily 9am-5pm; June-Aug. also M 9am-8pm. Tours daily 1pm. $7, seniors $5, under 12 free.)* **Grant's Farm,** the former home of President Ulysses S. Grant, is now a zoo. The tram-ride tour crosses terrain inhabited by over 1000 free-roaming animals, including elephants, zebras, and more of Anheuser's Clydesdale collection. *(3400 Grant St. Take I-55 west to Reavis Barracks Rd. and turn left onto Gravois. ☎ 314-843-1700; www.grants-farm.com. Open mid-May to Aug. Su 9:30am-4pm, Tu-F 9am-3:30pm, Sa 9am-4pm; Sept.-Oct. W-F 9:30am-2:30pm, Sa-Su 9:30am-3:30pm; early Apr. to early May Su 9:30am-3:30pm, W-F 9am-3pm, Sa 9am-3:30pm. Free. Parking $5.)*

FOREST PARK. Forest Park contains three museums, a zoo, a 12,000-seat amphitheater, a grand canal, and countless picnic areas, pathways, and flying golf balls. Marlin Perkins, the late host of TV's *Wild Kingdom,* turned the **St. Louis Zoo** into a world-class institution, featuring black rhinos, Asian elephants, and a top-notch penguin and puffin habitat. *(☎ 314-781-0900; www.stlzoo.com. Open daily June-Aug. 8am-7pm; Sept.-May 9am-5pm. Free. Children's Zoo $4, under 2 free.)* Atop **Art Hill,** a statue of France's Louis IX, the city's namesake, raises his sword in front of the **St. Louis Art Museum,** which contains masterpieces of Asian, Renaissance, and Impressionist art. *(☎ 314-721-0072; www.slam.org. Open Tu-Th and Sa-Su 10am-5pm, F 10am-9pm. Tours Su and W-Sa 1:30pm. Free. Special exhibits usually $10, students and seniors $8, ages 6-12 $6. F free.)* The **Missouri History Museum** focuses on the state's cultural heritage and has a small exhibit on the 1904 World's Fair. *(Located at Lindell and DeBaliviere St. ☎ 314-454-3124; www.mohistory.org. Open M and Su and W-Sa 10am-6pm, Tu 10am-8pm. Free. Special exhibits usually $5, seniors and students $4. Tu 4-8pm free.)* The **St. Louis Science Center** features an Omnimax theater, a planetarium, and over 700 interactive exhibits. Program the behavior of a virtual fish or build your own arch. *(5050 Oakland Ave. ☎ 314-289-4444; www.slcs.org. Open early June to Aug. M-Th and Sa 9:30am-5:30pm, F 9:30am-9:30pm, Su 11:30am-5:30pm; Sept.-May M-Th and Sa 9:30am-4:30pm, F 9:30am-9:30pm, Su 11:30am-4:30pm. Free. Omnimax $7, seniors and ages 2-12 $6. Planetarium $6/$5.)*

CENTRAL WEST END. From Forest Park, head east a few blocks to gawk at the Tudor homes of the Central West End. The vast **Cathedral Basilica of St. Louis** showcases varying architectural styles; visitors enjoy the intricate ceilings and mosaics depicting Missouri church history. *(4431 Lindell Blvd. ☎ 314-533-0544. Open daily summer 7am-7pm; low-season 7am-dusk. Tours M-F 10am-3pm, Su after noon Mass. Call to confirm hours.)* At a shrine of a different sort, monster truck enthusiasts pay homage to **Bigfoot,** the "Original Monster Truck," who lives with his descendants near the airport. *(6311 N. Lindbergh St. ☎ 314-731-2822. Open M-F 9am-6pm, Sa 9am-3pm. Free.)* Northwest of the Central West End, the sidewalks of the **Loop** are studded with gold stars on the **St. Louis Walk of Fame,** which features local luminaries from Maya Angelou to Ike and Tina Turner. *(6504 Delmar Blvd. ☎ 314-727-7827; www.stlouiswalkoffame.org.)*

OTHER SIGHTS. The slightly surreal ▓**City Museum** is constructed from salvaged parts of area buildings and contains wonderful amalgam of architectural styles. The outdoor "Monstrocity," made entirely of recycled parts, includes two planes, a fire truck, a ferris wheel, sky tunnels, and a gothic tower with gargoyles, is far and away the coolest playscape ever. *(701 N. 15th St., downtown. ☎ 314-231-2489; www.citymuseum.org. Open Sept.-May Su 11am-5pm, W-F 9am-5pm, Sa 10am-5pm; June-Aug. Su 11am-5pm, Tu-Th 9am-5pm, F 9am-1am, Sa 10am-1am. Main museum $7.50; museum and "Monstrocity" $10; museum and skate park $10.)* **Six Flags St. Louis** reigns supreme in the kingdom of amusement parks. The brand-new "Xcalibur" catapults thrill-seekers 113 ft. into the air while spinning in circles, and the "Boss" wooden roller coaster features a 570° helix. *(30min. southwest of St. Louis on I-44 at Exit 261. ☎ 636-938-4800. Hours vary by season. $39, seniors and under 48 in. $24.)*

NATIONAL ROAD

🎵 ENTERTAINMENT

Founded in 1880, the **St. Louis Symphony Orchestra** is one of the country's finest. **Powell Hall,** 718 N. Grand Blvd., holds the 101-member orchestra in acoustic splendor. (☎ 314-534-1700. Performances late Sept. to early May Th-Sa 8pm, Su 3pm. Box office open mid-Aug. to late May M-Sa 9am-5pm and before performances; late May to mid-Aug. M-F 9am-5pm; tickets $10-95, students half-price.)

St. Louis offers theatergoers many options. The outdoor **Municipal Opera,** also known as the "Muny," presents hit musicals on summer nights in Forest Park. (☎ 314-361-1900. Box office open June to mid-Aug. daily 9am-9pm. Tickets $8-54.) Productions are also regularly staged by the **St. Louis Black Repertory,** 634 N. Grand Blvd. (☎ 314-534-3807), and by the **Repertory Theatre of St. Louis,** 130 Edgar Rd. (☎ 314-968-4925). The **Fox Theatre,** 537 N. Grand Blvd., was originally a 1930s movie palace, but now hosts Broadway shows, classic films, and country and rock music stars. (☎ 314-534-1111. Open M-Sa 10am-6pm, Su noon-4pm. Tours Tu, Th, Sa 10:30am. Tu $5, Th and Sa $8; under 12 $3. Call for reservations.) **Metrotix** (☎ 314-534-1111) has tickets to most area events.

A St. Louis ordinance permits gambling on the river for those over 21. The **President Casino on the Admiral** floats below the Arch on the Missouri side. (☎ 314-622-1111 or 800-772-3647; www.presidentscasino.com. Open M-Th 8am-4am, F-Su 24hr. Entry tax $2.) On the Illinois side, the **Casino Queen** claims "the loosest slots in town." (☎ 618-874-5000 or 800-777-0777; www.casinoqueen.com. Open daily 9am-7am.) Parking for both is free. The **St. Louis Cardinals** play at **Busch Stadium.** (☎ 314-421-3060. Tickets $9-55.) The **Rams,** formerly of L.A., take to the field at the **Edward Jones Dome.** (☎ 314-425-8830. Tickets $40-49.) The **Blues** hockey team slices ice at the **Savvis Center** at 14th St. and Clark Ave. (☎ 314-843-1700. Tickets from $15.)

🍴 FOOD

In St. Louis, the difference of a few blocks can mean vastly different cuisine. The area surrounding **Union Station,** at 18th and Market St. downtown, is being revamped with hip restaurants and bars. The **Central West End** offers coffeehouses and outdoor cafes. A slew of impressive restaurants awaits just north of Lindell Blvd. along **Euclid Ave.**

St. Louis's historic Italian neighborhood, **The Hill,** southwest of downtown and just northwest of Tower Grove Park, produces plenty of inexpensive pasta. Cheap Thai, Philippine, and Vietnamese restaurants spice the **South Grand** area, at Grand Blvd. just south of Tower Grove Park. Coffee shops and unique restaurants cluster on **University City Loop,** on Delmar Blvd. between Skinker and Big Bend Blvd.

🍽 **Blueberry Hill,** 6504 Delmar Blvd. (☎ 314-727-0880), on the Loop. Eclectic rock 'n' roll restaurant with 9 different rooms including the "Elvis Room." Walls decked with record covers, Howdy Doody toys, a *Simpsons* collection, and giant baseball cards. Call ahead to find out if Chuck Berry is playing; he usually jams in the "Duck Room" 1 W each month. Big, juicy burgers $5. Live bands F-Sa and some weeknights 9:30pm. 21+ after 9pm. Cover $4-15. Kitchen open daily 11am-9pm.

🍽 **In Soo,** 8423 Olive Blvd. (☎ 314-997-7473). Home to some of the best pot stickers ($5) and vegetable mooshu ($9) you'll ever taste. Open M and Su and W-Sa 11:30am-10pm.

Ted Drewes Frozen Custard, 4224 S. Grand Blvd. (☎ 314-352-7376), and 6726 Chippewa St. (☎ 314-481-2652), on Rte. 66. *The* place for the St. Louis summertime experience since 1929. Those who make it through the line are rewarded by the "chocolate chip cookie dough concrete shake," ($1.70-3.80). Open May-Aug. daily 11am-midnight; Chippewa St. location also Sept.-Dec. and Feb.-May 11am-11pm.

Mangia Italiano, 3145 S. Grand Blvd. (☎ 314-664-8585). Fresh pasta made on site ($5-9). A hand-painted mural and mismatched tables add flair. Jazz weekend nights. Kitchen open M-F noon-10pm and Sa-Su 12:30-10:30pm. Bar open until 3am.

Amighetti's, 5141 Wilson St. (☎ 314-776-2855). Probably St. Louis's most famous sandwich place, serving the "special sandwich" (small $5.50, large $3.40) for 3 generations. Adjoining gelateria and bakery. Pasta $3.50/$6, salads $3.50/$6. Sandwich shop open Tu-F 7:30am-6pm, Sa 7:30am-5:30pm; in summer Tu-F until 7pm. Bakery open Tu-Sa 7:30am-3pm, gelateria open Su 11am-4pm, Tu-F 11am-2:30pm.

Arcelia, 2001 Park Ave. (☎ 314-231-9200). Big combination platters ($5.50-10.25) feature usual suspects like burritos and enchiladas, but this bustling Mexican eatery also offers more authentic dishes such as *mole de pollo* and *menudo*. Open M-Th 10am-2pm and 5-10pm, F-Su 10am-10pm.

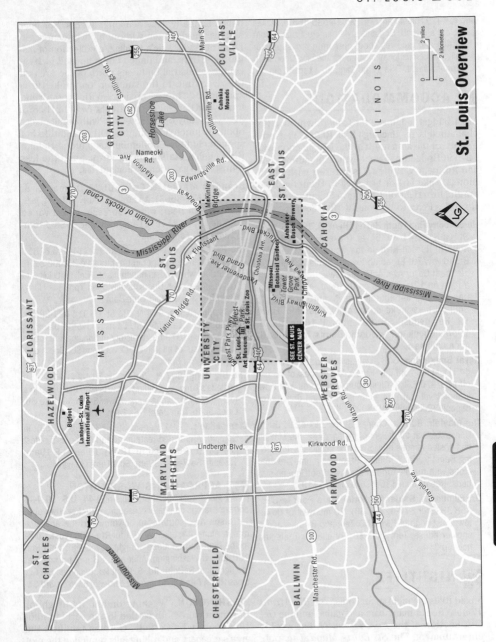

St. Louis Overview

Imo's, 4479 Forest Park Ave. (☎314-535-4667). Makes the city's favorite St. Louis-style thin-crust pizza (from $6.40) and receives shout-outs from rap superstar Nelly. Numerous locations through the city. Open M-Th 11am-midnight, F-Sa 11am-1am, Su 11am-11pm.

ACCOMMODATIONS

Most budget lodging is far from downtown. For chain motels, try **Lindbergh Blvd. (U.S. 67)** near the airport, or the area north of the I-70 junction with I-270 in Bridgeton, 5 mi. beyond the airport. **Watson Rd.** near Chippewa is littered with cheap motels. Take I-64 or I-44 west to Hampton Blvd. South., turn right on Chippewa St., and cross the River des Peres to Watson Rd. (Rte. 366).

Huckleberry Finn Youth Hostel (HI-AYH), 1908 S. 12th St. (☎314-241-0076), at Tucker Blvd., 2 blocks north of Russell Blvd. in the Soulard District. Take Broadway/7th St. south toward Soulard, turn right just past Geyer Ave. onto Allen Ave., and then take a right on 12th St.; it's on the right. A full kitchen, free parking, unbeatable prices, and proximity to Soulard bars make dorm rooms tolerable. Linen $2. Key deposit $5. Reception 8-10am and 6-10pm. Check-out 9:30am. Dorms rooms $19, nonmembers $21.

Royal Budget Inn, 6061 Collinsville Rd. (☎618-874-4451), in Fairmont City, Illinois, 20min. east of the city off I-55/I-70 Exit 6. Clean, purple-lit rooms with a Taj Mahal flavor make for an unusual budget option. Key deposit $2. Rooms $40.

The Mayfair, 806 St. Charles St. (☎314-421-2500). Constructed at the height of the Jazz Age, the Mayfair has hosted famous musicians and politicians, from Irving Berlin to Harry Truman. Standard rooms are spacious with marble-topped sinks and soft queen-size beds. Rooms from $109; suites from $119.

Dr. Edmund A. Babler Memorial State Park (☎636-458-3813 or 877-422-6766), 20 mi. west of downtown, just north of Hwy. 100. Tent and RV sites and a shower house. Tent sites $8; RV sites with electric hookup $14.

NIGHTLIFE

Music rules the night in St. Louis. The *Riverfront Times* (free at many bars and clubs) and the *Get Out* section of the *Post-Dispatch* list weekly entertainment. The *St. Louis Magazine,* pub-

lished annually, lists seasonal events. For beer and live music, often without a cover charge, St. Louis offers **Laclede's Landing,** a collection of restaurants, bars, and dance clubs housed in 19th-century industrial buildings north of the Arch on the riverfront. In the summer, bars take turns sponsoring "block parties," with food, drink, music, and dancing in the streets. (☎314-241-5875. 21+. Generally open 9pm-3am, with some places open for lunch and dinner.) Other nightlife hot spots include the bohemian **Loop** along Delmar Blvd., **Union Station** and environs, and the less touristy and gay-friendly **Soulard** district.

Brandt's Market & Cafe, 6525 Delmar Blvd. (☎314-727-3663). A Loop mainstay, offering jazz, along with beer, wine, espresso, and a varied menu. Open M-Th 11am-midnight, F-Sa 11am-1am, Su 11am-10pm.

The Pageant, 6161 Delmar Blvd. (☎314-726-6161). Line up early for a spot in the fantastic 33,000 sq. ft. nightclub, which hosts national acts. Call for ticket and cover prices. 18+. Doors usually open 7pm. The classy **Halo Bar** is open daily 5pm-3am.

Mississippi Nights, 914 N. 1st St. (☎314-421-3853), at Laclede's Landing. St. Louis's favorite place for music since 1979 has a history of bringing in the best national acts of all genres. Cover from $6. Doors usually open 7 or 8pm.

The Big Bang, 807 N. 2nd St. (☎314-241-2264), at Laclede's Landing. Dueling pianists lead the crowd in a rock 'n' roll sing-along show. Cover Su-Th $3, F-Sa $6. Open Su-Th 7pm-3am, F-Sa 5pm-3am.

Clementine's, 2001 Menard St. (☎314-664-7869), in Soulard. A crowded restaurant and St. Louis's oldest gay bar (established in 1978). Open M-F 10am-1:30am, Sa 8am-1:30am, Su 11am-midnight.

APPROACHING WASHINGTON

Head west out of St. Louis on **I-44/U.S. 50.** I-44 entrance ramps can be accessed from **Tucker Blvd.** or **S. Jefferson Ave.** south from downtown to the entrance ramps. From I-44, take Exit 251 for **Rte. 100 West.** Curve to the right and continue straight at the light onto Rte. 100 toward Washington. After about 8 mi., turn right at the light onto **S. Point Rd.** S. Point Rd. becomes 5th St.; cross Rte. 47 and head into the center of town on **3rd St.**

WASHINGTON. Washington and its neighbor Hermann were both settled in the early to mid-19th century by Catholic German families; the area's greenery and rolling hills reminded them of

Germany's Rhine Valley. Today, some industry in Washington continues, including the manufacture of corncob pipes at the Missouri Meerschaum Company. Washington is also home to the **Washington Historical Society Museum,** at the corner of 4th and Market St. (☎636-239-0280; www.historicalwashmo.org. Open Mar.-Dec. Su noon-4pm, Tu-Sa 10am-4pm.) The best part town is **Cowan's,** 114 Elm St., which feels like a very large living room. The spaghetti and meatball dinner ($7) comes bottomless with salad and toast. Finish up with a piece of homemade pie. (At the corner of 2nd St. Take Market St. or Jefferson St. to 2nd St. and turn left. ☎636-239-3213. Sandwiches $5.50-7. Open M and W-Sa 6am-8pm, Su 6am-7pm.)

APPROACHING HERMANN
Leaving Washington, take **Jefferson St.** to **Rte. 100 West.** Rte. 100 becomes **1st St.** before joining with **Rte. 19** and turning south onto **Market St.**

HERMANN

Surrounded by Missouri wineries, Hermann also depends heavily on tourism for revenue; tourist-oriented development of this picturesque valley (centered on the area's German heritage) has made it the "B&B capital of Missouri." The artifacts on display at the **Historic Hermann Museum,** 312 Schiller St., chronicle the history of early German immigrants to this area, and the **Deustche Market** inside sells works by local artisans. (Take Market St. to 4th St. and turn left; it's on the corner of 4th in the old German School. ☎573-486-2017. Open Apr.-Oct. Su and Tu-Sa 10am-4pm.) On the way out of Hermann is a sign for the **Stone Hill Winery** off to the right; the largest winery in Missouri, Stone Hill lets visitors tour the grounds and caves where the wine ages, and tours relate the history of the winery and the story of Hermann. (☎573-486-2221 or 800-909-9463; www.stonehillwinery.com. Open M-Th 8:30am-7pm, F-Sa 8:30am-8pm, Su 10am-6pm. $1.50.)

On Rte. 100 headed into town, the **Rivertown Restaurant,** 222 E. 1st St., offers ravenous roadtrippers old-fashioned cooking amidst kitsch. (☎573-486-3298. Sandwiches $1.60-5. Steaks $8-12. Open M 7am-2pm, Tu-Sa 7am-8pm, Su 7am-1pm.)

Accommodations are generally expensive in touristy Hermann. To find the most suitable B&B, call or stop by the **Visitors Center,** 312 Market St. (☎573-486-2744 or 800-932-868; www.hermannmo.com. Open Apr.-Oct. M-Sa 9am-5pm, Su 11am-4pm; Nov.-Mar. M-Sa 9:30am-4pm, Su 11am-4pm.) Also try the **Hermann Motel,** 112 E. 10th St., at Market St., which offers pleasant rooms. Non-smoking rooms are available. (☎573-486-3131. Continental breakfast included. Rooms $42-70.)

THE ROAD TO JEFFERSON CITY. From Hermann, Rte. 100 meanders along the scenic Missouri River, passing numerous wineries. It does test driving skills a bit, as it runs up and down roller-coaster hills; not all curves requiring a reduction in speed are labeled. Forty-two miles from Hermann, the road rejoins U.S. 50 near the town of **Linn;** turn right here to head west on **U.S. 50** to Jefferson City.

APPROACHING JEFFERSON CITY
Follow **U.S. 50** all the way into downtown Jefferson City, where it becomes the **Whitton Expwy.** To access downtown, turn right onto **Adams, Monroe, Madison, Jefferson,** or **Broadway St.**

JEFFERSON CITY

As one might expect from the capital of Missouri, Jefferson City is refreshingly relaxed and low-key. Because there's virtually no industry, government is the main business in town, and even it operates at a slow pace—the Missouri legislature has been known to spend seven years on the passage of a bill. Situated above the Missouri River, the tall capitol building is the focal point of downtown.

VITAL STATS

Population: 40,000

Visitor Info: Jefferson County Convention and Visitors Bureau, 213 Adams St. (☎573-632-2820 or 800-769-4183; www.visitjeffersoncity.com), just north of High St. Open M-F 8am-5pm.

Internet Access: Missouri River Regional Library, 214 Adams St. (☎573-634-2464), off High St. Open M-Th 9am-9pm, F-Sa 9am-5pm, Su 1-5pm.

Post Office: 131 W. High St. (☎573-636-4186), across from the capitol building. Open M-F 8am-4:30pm, Sa 9am-noon. **Postal Code:** 65101.

GETTING AROUND. Jefferson City is surprisingly easy to navigate. **U.S. 50,** called **Whitton Expwy.** in town, runs east-west just south of the downtown area. North of U.S. 50 lie **McCarty St., High St.** (so named because of its hilltop location), and **Main St./Capitol Dr.** North-south streets through downtown are named for the first six U.S. Presidents, although unfortunately not in order. **Missouri Blvd. (Bus. U.S. 50)**, a major thoroughfare, runs parallel to U.S. 50 west of downtown and then north-south within the downtown area itself. **U.S. 54** runs north-south through the entire area. Street **parking** is available and sometimes metered.

◎ SIGHTS. The ■Missouri State Capitol Building overlooks the Missouri River from High St. Informative tours run through this early 20th-century building, explaining Missouri's government and showcasing the plush legislative floor when the legislature is not in session. The highlight of the tour is the visit to the Thomas Hart Benton mural on the third floor, which gives considerable insight into Missouri's history. (☎573-751-4127. Open daily 8am-5pm. Tours every hr. 8am-11am and 1-4pm. Free.) Near the capitol, the **Missouri Governor's Mansion**, 100 Madison St., allows visitors to tour the first floor of the first family's home, a brick mansion on a bluff overlooking the Missouri River. (☎573-751-7929; www.missouri-mansion.org. Tours Tu and Th every 30min. 10-11:30am and 1-2:30pm; no tours Aug. and Dec. Reserve 24hr. in advance. Free.)

Five centuries worth of veterinary medicine are on display at the **Veterinary Museum**, 2500 Country Club Dr. Visitors can learn about instruments, animal specimens, diseases, and surgery. (Take U.S. 50 west out of town 2½ mi. to the exit for Rte. 179, turn right at the bottom of the ramp, and take the next right onto Country Club Dr. ☎573-636-8737. Open W-F noon-4pm, Sa by appointment. Free.)

▛▛ FOOD & ACCOMMODATIONS. The usual assortment of chain restaurants is laid out along Missouri Blvd., but more flavorful food is abundant in Jefferson City. Small and homey, ■Woolly Llama's, 616 E. High St., has no regular menu; what owner-operator-llama-lover Cindy Borgwordt serves depends on what she buys that morning at the farmers market. Super-fresh fruit, vegetables, and meat make for unusually delicious sandwiches ($2.50-4.50), soups ($1.50-3.50), and salads. (☎573-636-0040. Open M-F 10am-3pm.) **Bone's Lounge**, 210 Commercial Ave., is really two restaurants in one; the carpeted ground floor serves hearty sit-down meals in a conventional atmosphere, while upstairs is a bar, with neon decorations, plastic furnishings, and a younger clientele. (Take High St. to Monroe St., head north ½

block; Commercial St. is the alley on your left. ☎573-636-8955. Sandwiches $4-7. Steak and seafood $10-15. Open daily 11am-1am.) If you do nothing else while passing through town, indulge in a few scoops of freshly made ice cream at **Central Dairy**, 610 Madison St., a long-standing Jefferson City landmark. (☎573-635-6148. Open M-Sa 8am-6pm, Su 10am-6pm.)

Most accommodations, including an assortment of chain motels, lie on U.S. 54 just south of downtown. Unusually comfortable beds, clean rooms, bright lights, and powerful showers at the ■Budget Motel, 1309 Jefferson St., make for a pleasant night in "Jeff City." Rooms have fridges and non-smoking rooms are available. (☎573-636-6167. Singles $34; doubles $39.)

▛ LEAVING JEFFERSON CITY
Take **U.S. 50 West** out of town (from downtown, take **Broadway** or **Jefferson St.** south to **Whitton Expwy.** and turn left). It soon becomes a 4-lane highway. Push that pedal and head for California.

CALIFORNIA. Twenty-three miles from Jefferson City, California is one of the many towns along this stretch of road that feature attractive centers, river overlooks, or residential areas. U.S. 50, however, does not pass through those stretches of town. Services like fast food and gas concentrate on the highway, but the good stuff—like **Burger's Smokehouse**, 32819 Rte. 87—is found a little way off the road. Burger's cures hams and other meats, which they sell around the world and right out of their factory store. (Turn left to head south on Rte. 87. Proceed 2¾ mi. and turn left at the sign. ☎573-796-3134 or 800-203-4244.)

◉ MACLAY HOME
In Tipton, turn right off U.S. 50 at the sign for Rte. B and head into town. Cross the railroad tracks; it's just ahead on the left.

The Maclay descendants kept this 1858 home intact in early 20th-century style until turning it over to a non-profit foundation that oversees its preservation. (☎660-433-2101. Tours May-Oct. on the 2nd and 4th Su of each month 2-4pm, or by appointment. $3, under 13 $1.)

 In Tipton, as you pass the intersection with Rte. 5, notice the water tower ahead. It's white with a bulbous, black 8-ball for a top.

APPROACHING SEDALIA

Take **U.S. 50** into town. You can turn right on **Ohio Ave.** to reach the downtown historic district or left on **U.S. 65** to access motels and other sites.

SEDALIA

Most of the year, Sedalia, at the junction of U.S. 65 and U.S. 50, is a quiet, well-to-do city with a relaxed and laid-back air. But Sedalia is also the permanent home of the Missouri State Fair, and for 11 days every August, city and country dwellers, numbering over 345,000, pour into town, filling Sedalia's hotels, bars, and restaurants.

(VITAL STATS)

Population: 20,000

Visitor Info: The Chamber of Commerce, 600 E. 3rd St. (☎660-826-2222; www.visitsedailamo.com), inside the reconstructed Katy Depot. Open M-F 9am-5pm; summer also Sa 10am-3pm. **Visitor Info Caboose,** on the west side of U.S. 65 just south of U.S. 50. Open M-F 10am-3pm.

Internet Access: Sedalia Public Library, 219 W. 3rd St. (☎660-827-7323), at Kentucky St. Open M and W-F 9am-6pm, Tu 9am-7pm, Sa 9am-5pm.

Post Office: 405 E. 5th St. (☎800-275-8777), at Washington Ave. Open M-F 8am-5:30pm, Sa 8am-noon. **Postal Code:** 65301.

GETTING AROUND. U.S. 50 is known as **Broadway Blvd.** and runs east-west through the entire area (where 8th St. would be). North of Broadway on **Ohio Ave.** and the surrounding streets lies the downtown historic district. The Missouri State Fairgrounds and State Fair Community College lie along **16th St.** (south of Broadway) to the west. **Limit Ave. (U.S. 65)** runs north-south through the area and is home to many motels, chain hotels, and chain restaurants. Free on-street **parking** is generally plentiful.

SIGHTS. Ragtime was born and bred in Sedalia thanks to native son Scott Joplin. That heritage returns each year in the form of concerts at the **Scott Joplin Ragtime Festival,** held each June. The rest of the year, pick up ragtime music and memorabilia at the **Scott Joplin Ragtime Store,** 321 S. Ohio St. (☎660-826-2271 or 866-218-6258; www.scottjoplin.org. Hours vary; call for info.) Well done and worth a brief stop, the **Daum Museum of Contemporary Art,** 3201 W.

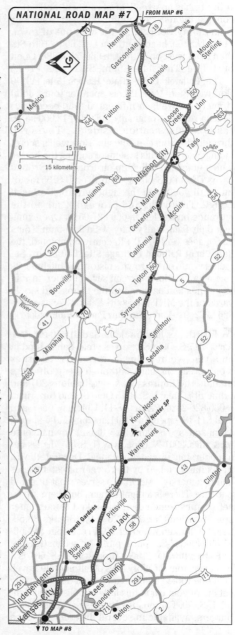

NATIONAL ROAD MAP #7 FROM MAP #6

TO MAP #8

16th St., has an excellent permanent collection considering its size and location. (At State Fair Community College, on the way out of town. From U.S. 50, head south on U.S. 65 to 16th St., then head west on 16th St. ☎660-530-5888. Open Su 1-5pm, Tu-F 11am-5pm, Sa 1-5pm. Free.)

The **Bothwell Lodge State Historic Site**, 19349 Bothwell State Park Rd., is open for tours; John Homer Bothwell, an influential (and eccentric) Sedalia resident, originally built this 12,000 sq. ft. castle as his vacation residence. Tours run through the house, disclosing Bothwell's secret hiding places and his system of cooling the house, which entailed pulling up air from underground caves. (From U.S. 50, head north on U.S. 65 for 6¼ mi. until you reach the right turn for Bothwell Lodge. Turn right and proceed ½ mi. to the entrance on the left. ☎660-827-0510. Open summer daily 9am-4pm; winter W-Sa 9am-5pm. Tours $2.50, ages 6-12 $1.50.) Recently completed, the **Katy Depot Railroad Heritage Site**, 600 E. 3rd St., includes info on the town's history, highlighting its role as a junction between several different railroad lines and as home to the shops and stockyards of the MKT (Missouri-Kansas-Texas ☎660-826-2222; free) and Missouri Pacific Railroads.

▓ FOOD. As laid-back as Sedalia itself, **Del-Amici**, 317 S. Ohio St., serves great Italian food in an attractive, relaxing setting. Most favorites won't break the bank, although menu offerings include the impressive steak diablo ($20) and prime rib. (Take U.S. 50 to Ohio St. and turn right. ☎660-826-2324. Pastas $8-11. Chicken, beef, and veal $11-18. Open Tu-Th 11am-2pm and 5-9pm, F 11am-2pm and 5-10pm, Sa 5-10pm.) Town favorite **McGrath's**, 2901 W. Broadway (U.S. 50), dishes out a moderately priced, good meal. Decorated with items hand-picked by the owner at estate sales and flea-markets, McGrath's serves meat-oriented pub fare. There is a regular menu but there are no set recipes—each dish is cooked to customer specifications. (☎660-826-9902. Steaks $8.50-24.50. Chicken $7.50-11.50. Fresh fish $11.50-15.50. Open M-Sa 5pm-10pm.) The squat structure of **Eddie's Drive-In**, 115 W. Broadway (U.S. 50), is a holdover from the glory days of automobile travel. Don't be fooled by the name—you don't actually eat out of your car at this little establishment right off U.S. 50. Famous for its fresh-ground steakburgers, available in several different varieties

($1.70-5), Eddie's also has "broasted" chicken ($4-8). Apparently, "broasted" means "fried." (☎660-826-0015. Open M-Sa 7:30am-8pm.)

▛ ACCOMMODATIONS. Sedalia offers a range of accommodations; unfortunately, many aren't very well maintained, and rates approximately double during fairtime and the Scott Joplin Ragtime Festival. Just south of the intersection with U.S. 50, **Motel Memory**, 1000 S. Limit Ave. (U.S. 65), offers basic rooms that are aging but clean, and include microwaves and refrigerators. (☎660-827-7333. Singles $33; doubles $37; triples $42.) Although accommodations at the **Sho-Me-Kort Motel**, 1217 S. Limit Ave., are not spotless, rooms come with couches and microwaves. (On U.S. 65 just south of the intersection with U.S. 50. ☎660-826-2488. Non-smoking rooms available. Singles $34; doubles $38.) At the landmark **Hotel Bothwell**, 103 E. 4th St., at Ohio St., rooms come in all shapes, sizes, and prices. All rooms are ornately furnished and some even feature fireplaces. (Singles $49; family suites $94; owners' suites $129.)

▛ LEAVING SEDALIA
Take **Broadway Blvd. (U.S. 50)** west from town.

▛ KNOB NOSTER STATE PARK
18 mi. from Sedalia. Take the exit for Rte. 23. At the top of the ramp, turn left, and proceed straight for 1¼ mi. to the park entrance on the right.

With its mixture of prairie and second-growth forest, this park caters to naturalists and equestrians. Camping is available. Reserve sites at the Missouri Centralized Reservation System, online at www.mostateparks.com. (☎877-422-6766. Visitors Center open M-F 8am-4:30pm, Sa-Su 9am-4:30pm. Staffed M-F 8am-12:30pm and 1:30-4:30pm. Sites $8, with electricity $14, with full hookup $17.)

◉ OLD WARRENSBURG COURTHOUSE
302 N. Main St.
Take the exit for Missouri Rte. 13, turn left at the top of the ramp, and turn right at Young St. (Bus. U.S. 50). To reach the town center, proceed 2 blocks to the blinking light at Holden St. and turn left.

A speech given at the courthouse in Warrensburg as part of the 1870 Old Drum Trial gave rise to the phrase "Man's best friend is his dog." On a monument on the courthouse lawn, the pathos-filled speech has been faithfully inscribed for all to read; the monument is topped by a statue of the famous dog, "Old Drum" himself. (Tours of the courthouse M-Sa 1-4pm. $3, students free.)

POWELL GARDENS   1609 NW U.S. 50
On the north side of U.S. 50.

Colorful, carefully sculpted flowerbeds surround bridges and mini waterfalls at Powell Gardens. Concentrated into three small sites, the grounds take visitors from the heat of the prairie to the comfort of the shaded rock and waterfall garden. Driving is not permitted in the gardens. (☎816-697-2600; www.powellgardens.org. Open daily Apr.-Oct. 9am-6pm; Nov.-Mar. 9am-5pm. $6, seniors $5, ages 5-12 $2.50.)

APPROACHING INDEPENDENCE
Stay left at the Colburn Rd. Exit to remain on **Rte. 291.** Proceed 3½ mi. to the light at **23rd St.,** and turn left. Drive 2 mi. just past the light at Noland St. and turn right onto **S. Main St.**

INDEPENDENCE

Now in the shadow of larger Kansas City, Independence is the hometown of President Harry S. Truman. During the era of westward expansion, this city stood on the edge of a vast wilderness; Independence was the last waystation for pioneers seeking a new life. Today, modernized antebellum estates and thriving hundred-year-old businesses let this suburb maintain its legacy.

(VITAL STATS)

Population: 113,000

Visitor Info: Tourist Information Center and Truman Home Ticket Center (☎816-254-9929), at Main St. and Truman Rd. Open M-F 8:30am-5pm.

Internet Access: Mid-Continent Public Library, South Independence Branch, 13700 E. 35th St. (☎816-461-2050). Open M-Th 9am-9pm, F 9am-6pm, Sa 9am-5pm.

Post Office: 301 Lexington St. (☎816-521-3608). Open M-F 8am-5pm, Sa 8am-noon. **Postal Code:** 64050.

⬛ GETTING AROUND

Downtown Independence remains the practical center of the city. **Exit 12** from **I-70** leads to **Noland Rd.,** a busy strip of gas stations and fast-food joints. Follow this road for about 3 mi., then go left onto **Walnut St.** A right onto either **Main** or **Liberty St.** will lead to the central square formed by Liberty, Lexington, Main, and Maple St. All four of these streets are lined with free **parking** and surround the Jackson County Courthouse, the historical nexus of Independence.

⬛ SIGHTS

In the center of downtown stands the **Jackson County Courthouse,** where a young Harry Truman worked as a judge just a few yards from his first job at Clinton's Drugstore. The building houses offices now, but its statue-filled courtyard is a

KATY TRAIL

Nationwide, there has been a movement to convert old railroad rights-of-way into hiking trails. The largest such project is the 225 mi. Katy Trail, which runs along the trackbed of the Missouri-Kansas-Texas Railroad. "Katy" comes from K-T (Kansas-Texas), the name by which the railroad was known.

The Katy Trail, like the Katy Railroad before it, passes through the farms, wineries, hills, and flatlands of Missouri. One way to sample the Katy Trail is to park at the trailhead near the Katy Depot in Sedalia and head west through mostly residential areas of Sedalia. Like the other towns along the trail, Sedalia grew up near where the MKT chose to locate its shops and stockyards. Unlike many towns on the trail, Sedalia has survived. For a more picturesque section of the trail, head north 1 mi. from the town of Hermann on Rte. 19, to McKittrick. This part of the trail has views of the lofty bluffs above the river, including the town of Hermann itself. (☎800-334-6946, or stop by Katy Depot in Sedalia.)

BEYOND THE ASPHALT

NATIONAL ROAD

Independence

▲ ACCOMMODATIONS
American Inn, **1** & **2**
Budget Host Inn, **3**
Serendipity Bed and Breakfast, **5**

● FOOD
Clinton's Soda Fountain, **7**
Dave's Bakery and Deli, **6**
Stephenson's Apple Farm
    Restaurant, **4**

great start at visiting the city's historical sites. Nearby, at the corner of Osage St., the **National Frontier Trails Museum,** 318 W. Pacific St., is filled with history and a few genuine artifacts from the days of Manifest Destiny. Exhibits explain the significance of three major trails that began in Independence—the Santa Fe, the California and the Oregon. (☎816-325-7575; www.frontiertrailsmuseum.com. Open M-Sa 9am-4:30pm, Su 12:30-4:30pm. $4, seniors $3.50, ages 6-17 $2.50.)

Back up Main St. at the corner of Truman Rd., the **Truman Home Ticket Center** houses the Tourist Information Center. Tours of Truman's home, at 219 Delaware Rd., depart from here following a short introductory video. The video itself notes that "few memorable events took place at 219 Delaware"; the tour should probably be reserved for real enthusiasts. (☎816-254-9929. Tours Labor Day-Memorial Day Su and Tu-Sa every 15min.

9am-4:45pm. $3.) The sidewalk outside the center is the starting point for **Pioneer Trails Adventures.** These wagon rides through town are guided by the Wrangler, an in-character driver and storyteller. (☎816-456-4991 or 816-254-2466; www.pioneertrailsadventure.com. Tours $6-20.)

The graves of President Truman and his wife, his preserved office, and the legendary "The Buck Stops Here" are all on display at the **Truman Presidential Library and Museum,** 500 U.S. 24. Galleries focus on the different crises of the Truman administration, presenting multi-perspective analyses of its most controversial decisions, especially the use of atomic weapons in Japan. (Head north up Liberty St. past U.S. 24, turn left onto Mechanic St., and go five blocks west. ☎816-833-1225; www.trumanlibrary.org. Open M-W 9am-5pm, Th 9am-9pm, F-Sa 9am-5pm, Su noon-5pm. $7, seniors $5, ages 6-18 $3.)

FOOD

Independence has a number of fine restaurants, but **Clinton's Soda Fountain,** 100 Maple St., shines as one of the most delicious, and certainly the most interesting, options. Located right in Independence Sq., Clinton's provided a young Harry Truman with his first job and now serves double-duty as a historical site. The result is great food in an old-fashioned atmosphere; patrons can still order soda fountain phosphates ($1.30). The menu features a variety of excellent sandwiches, all for less than $5. Customers can finish their meals with a milkshake ($4-5) or Harry's Favorite ($3.70), a butterscotch sundae with chocolate ice cream. (☎816-833-2046. Open M-F 8:30am-6pm, Sa 10am-6pm.) Also worth a stop is **Dave's Bakery And Deli,** 214 Maple St., a block west of Independence Sq. The deli's futuristic look is delightfully out of place in historic downtown Independence. Home-baked confections almost seem anachronistic here, but they're still delicious. The deli sandwiches ($3.50) are made fresh, with spectacular breads baked right in the store. (☎816-833-2046. Open M-F 6am-5pm, Sa 7am-3pm.)

Stephenson's Apple Farm Restaurant, 16401 U.S. 40, is south of I-70 on Noland Rd. The red barn building and low wooden rafters are only the beginning of its rural style, with appetizers such as fritters, livers ($5.50), and gizzards ($5) on the menu. City-slickers needn't fear though, as the entrees are a bit less exotic. Hickory-smoked chicken is the house specialty, with other options including hickory-smoked ham or ribs, and pork chops. (From Noland Rd., go left down U.S. 40 and take a right onto Lees Summit Rd.; Stephenson's parking lot is immediately on the left. ☎816-373-5400. Entrees $13-18. Open summer M-Sa 11am-10pm, Su 10am-9pm; winter M-Th 11am-9pm, F-Sa 11am-10pm, Su 10am-9pm.)

ACCOMMODATIONS

Hotels are cheaper and easier to find just outside of Independence. Exit 18 off I-70 has fine budget options. Beautiful, historic, and overrun with greenery, the **Serendipity Bed and Breakfast,** 116 Pleasant Ave., is three blocks west of Liberty St. Keeping with the Victorian-era decor, breakfast is served by candlelight. (☎800-203-4299 or 816-833-4719; www.bbhost.com/serendipitybb. Check-in 4-9pm. Singles $45-70; doubles $80-85.)

Cheaper options include two **American Inn** locations: Woods Chapel Rd., off Exit 18 from I-70, and 4141 S. Noland Rd. Rooms are clean and reasonably well maintained, but this budget chain will only rent to those under 21 if they are 50 mi. from their home address. (Woods Chapel Rd. ☎816-228-1080. S. Noland Rd. ☎816-373-8300. Singles $40-$50.) The **Budget Host Inn,** 15014 U.S. 40, south of I-70, is another convenient choice for less expensive lodging, with clean, if slightly worn, rooms. (☎816-373-7500 or 800-283-4678. Singles $35.)

APPROACHING KANSAS CITY

From downtown Independence, return to **Noland Rd.** via **Walnut St.** and drive approximately 3 mi. south. Ramps onto **I-70** are very well marked. **I-70** passes hrough the northern part of Kansas City, close to downtown. **Exit 3a** feeds onto **The Paseo,** which is a large road parallel to, and a bit east of **Main St.**

KANSAS CITY

With more boulevards than Paris and more fountains than Rome, Kansas City looks and acts more European than one might expect from the "Barbecue Capital of the World." When Prohibition stifled most of the country's fun in the 1920s, Mayor Pendergast let the good times continue to roll. The Kansas City of today maintains its blues-and-jazz reputation in a metropolis spanning two states.

(VITAL STATS)

Population: 150,000

Visitor Info: Convention and Visitors Bureau of Greater Kansas City, 1100 Main St., #2200 (☎816-221-5242 or 800-767-7700; www.vis-itkc.com), on the 22nd fl. of the City Center Sq. Bldg. Open M-F 8:30am-5pm. **Missouri Tourist Information Center,** 4010 Blue Ridge Cut-Off (☎816-889-3330 or 800-877-1234). Follow signs from Exit 9 off I-70. Open daily 8am-5pm, except on days when the Chiefs are playing at home.

Internet Access: Kansas City Public Library, Central Branch, 14 10th St. (☎816-701-3414). **Plaza branch,** 301 51st St. (☎816-701-3575). **Westport branch,** 118 Westport Rd. (☎816-701-3635).

Post Office: 315 W. Pershing Rd. (☎816-374-9100). Open M-F 8am-8pm, Sa 8:30am-3:30pm. **Postal Code:** 64108.

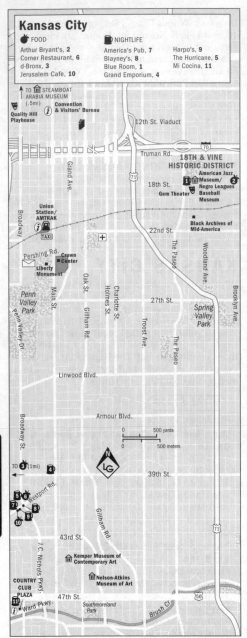

Kansas City

● FOOD

Arthur Bryant's, **2**
Corner Restaurant, **6**
d-Bronx, **3**
Jerusalem Cafe, **10**

● NIGHTLIFE

America's Pub, **7**
Blayney's, **8**
Blue Room, **1**
Grand Emporium, **4**

Harpo's, **9**
The Hurricane, **5**
Mi Cocina, **11**

GETTING AROUND

Though Kansas City is laid out in a relatively simple grid, car travel can be very frustrating due to the tangle of one-way streets and turning-only lanes. Only east-west streets are numbered, with numbers increasing as one travels south. **Main St.**, which runs north-south and divides the city in two, is in fact two one-way streets located a block apart from each other. Large pay-garages are available in the downtown area, but virtually every street has free or metered **parking** on the shoulder, so travelers may prefer to drive to each site rather than park and walk.

SIGHTS

18TH & VINE HISTORIC DISTRICT. The entire 18th & Vine Historic District pays tribute to great jazz musicians who lived and played here in the early 20th century. The **American Jazz Museum** brings the era back with music listening stations, neon dance hall signs, and paraphernalia ranging from Ella Fitzgerald's eyeglasses to Louis Armstrong's lip salve. In the same building, the **Negro Leagues Baseball Museum** documents the athletic feats of 1920s African-American ballplayers and the racism that once divided baseball and society. The museum is dominated by an indoor diamond manned by statues of a Negro League Dream Team. (*1616 E. 18th St. Jazz museum ☎816-474-8463; www.americanjazzmuseum.com. Baseball museum ☎816-474-8453; www.nlbm.com. Both open Su noon-6pm, Tu-Sa 9am-6pm. Single museum $6, under 12 $2.50; both museums $8/$4.*)

NELSON-ATKINS MUSEUM OF ART. This museum features one of the best East Asian art collections in the world and a sculpture park with 13 pieces by Henry Moore. The museum is under renovation until further notice, so call ahead. (*4525 Oak St., 3 blocks northeast of Country Club Plaza. ☎816-561-4000; www.nelson-atkins.org. Open Su noon-5pm, Tu-Th 10am-4pm, F 10am-9pm, Sa 10am-5pm. Live jazz inside the Rozzelle Court Restaurant F 5:30-8:30pm. Free walking tours Sa 11am-2pm, Su 1:30-3pm. Admission is free while the construction is going on, except for special exhibits.*)

KEMPER MUSEUM OF CONTEMPORARY ART.

Gigantic, malformed spiders adorn the lawn and outer walls of the Kemper Museum of Contemporary Art, a great alternative to more traditional museums. Inside, other works both more and less orthodox than the arachnids are on display in cool white galleries. *(4420 Warwick Blvd., off Main St. just north of the Country Club Plaza. ☎ 816-753-5784; www.kemperart.org. Open Su 11am-5pm, Tu-Th 10am-4pm, F-Sa 10am-9pm. Free.)*

STEAMBOAT ARABIA MUSEUM.

In 1856, the steamboat Arabia struck a fallen tree and vanished at the bottom of the Missouri River, along with its impressive international cargo. Preserved in the mud, these 19th-century wonders have since been excavated and restored. Delicate glassware, lovely pottery, clothing, and a vast array of other antebellum objects are now on display at the Treasures of the Steamboat Arabia Museum. Functioning parts of the ship chug away on a life-sized re-creation of the steamer's deck, complete with enormous paddlewheel. *(400 Grand Blvd., next to the City Market. ☎ 816-471-4030; www.1856.com. Open M-Sa 10am-5:30pm, Su noon-5pm. $9.75, seniors $9.25, ages 4-12 $4.75.)*

COUNTRY CLUB PLAZA.

The Country Club Plaza, or just the Plaza, is a shopping and dining district and a lovely re-imagining of Suavely, Spain. The result is wonderfully bizarre, as shoppers share sidewalks with medieval gargoyles and advertisements compete for space with tiled mosaics. Filled with Old-World charm and hip cafes, the Plaza hums with life in early evening. *(Along 47th St., between Main and Madison St. Free concerts May-Sept. Th 5-8pm and Sa-Su 2-5pm.)*

CROWN CENTER.

Headquarters of Hallmark Cards, the Crown Center contains myriad restaurants and shops. It is also home to the children's **Coterie Theatre,** which features games, a maze, and theater technology demonstrations, as well as performances. During the winter, the **Ice Terrace** is Kansas City's only public outdoor ice-skating rink. On the third level of the center, see how cards and accessories are made at the **Hallmark Visitors Center.** Pershing St. and the Crown Center area are dominated by an enormous WWI **Liberty Monument,** which sits on a grassy hill overlooking Union Station. A vast frieze is built into the hillside, depicting the horrors of war on the right and the pleasures of peace on the left. *(2405 Grand Ave., 2 mi. north of the Plaza near Pershing Rd. Crown Center ☎ 816-274-5916. Coterie Theatre ☎ 816-474-6785. $8, under 18 $6. Ice Terrace ☎ 816-274-8412. Rink open Nov.-Dec. Su-Th 10am-9pm, F-Sa 10am-11pm; Jan.-Mar. daily 10am-9pm. $5, under 13 $4. Skate rental $1.50. Hallmark Visitors Center ☎ 816-274-3613, recording 816-274-5672; hallmarkvisitorscenter.com. Open M-Г 9am-5pm, Sa 9:30am-4:30pm; closed early Jan.)*

🎵 ENTERTAINMENT

From September to May, the **Missouri Repertory Theatre,** at 50th and Oak St., stages American classics. *(☎ 816-235-2700; www.missourirep.org. Tick-*

THE LOCAL STORY

NATIONAL AGRICULTURAL HALL OF FAME

This museum contains a vast hodgepodge of farming artifacts and a farmers hall of fame, but the real attractions are the special events.

In the "lineman's rodeo," which takes place around Labor Day, competitors must navigate a series of electrical poles closely spaced. About 600 people participate in teams of three, grouped by skill level, and thousands come to watch as the linemen go from pole to pole, stringing and taking down wire and performing other tasks like rescuing injured linemen (dummies). They are judged on their speed, accuracy, and safety. In another event, competitors plow fields with 18th-century farm machinery. (630 Hall of Fame Dr., in Bonner Springs, 16 mi. from Kansas City, MO. Turn left off Rte. 40 at the sign for the Center, or take I-70 to Exit 223. ☎ 913-721-1075; www.aghalloffame.com. Open summer M-Sa 9am-5pm, Su 1-5pm; winter hours vary. Special events are ongoing; call for more info. $6.50, seniors $5, ages 5-16 $3.)

ets $10-48. $3 off for students and seniors.) **Quality Hill Playhouse,** 303 W. 10th St., produces off-Broadway plays and revues from September to June. The box office is located at 912 Baltimore Ave., Ste. 200. (☎816-421-1700. Box office open M-F 9am-5pm. Tickets $22. $2 off for students and seniors.) From late June to mid-July, the **Heart of America Shakespeare Festival** (☎816-531-7728; www.kcshakes.org) in Southmoreland Park, at 47th and Oak St., puts on free shows.

Sports fans stampede into Arrowhead Stadium, at I-70 and Blue Ridge Cutoff, home to football's **Chiefs** (☎816-920-9400 or 800-676-5488; tickets $51-70) and soccer's **Wizards** (☎816-920-9300; tickets $12-17). Next door, Kauffman Stadium houses the **Royals,** Kansas City's baseball team. (☎816-921-8000 or 800-676-9257. Tickets $5-22.)

⚡ FOOD

Kansas City's specialty is its unusually tangy barbecue. The **Westport** area, at Westport Rd. and Broadway St. just south of 40th St., has eclectic cafes and coffeehouses. Ethnic eateries cluster along **39th St.** just east of the state line. The **City Market** area has Asian grocery stores and open-air produce markets at the intersection of 5th and Walnut St. (Open Su-F 9am-4pm, Sa 6am-4pm.)

🍴 **Arthur Bryant's,** 1727 Brooklyn Ave. (☎816-231-1123). The grand-daddy of KC barbecue and a perennial candidate for best barbecue in the country. Bryant's "sandwiches" ($9) are a carnivore's delight—wimpy triangles of bread

drowning in pork perfection. Open M-Th 10am-9:30pm, F-Sa 10am-10pm, Su 11am-8:30pm.

d-Bronx, 3904 Bell St. (☎816-531-0550), at 39th St. A New York deli in Middle America, d-Bronx has over 35 kinds of subs (half $4-6, whole $8-12) and powdered sugar brownies ($1.50). Open M-W 10:30am-9pm, Th 10:30am-10pm, F-Sa 10:30am-11pm.

Jerusalem Cafe, 431 Westport Rd. (☎816-756-2770). Patrons enjoy primarily vegetarian Mediterranean fare while playing backgammon. Pita sandwiches ($6-7) complement unusual appetizers, such as stuffed grape leaves (under $5). Relax upstairs in the Nargila Coffee-House. Open M-Sa 11am-10pm, Su noon-8pm.

Corner Restaurant, 4059 Broadway St. (☎816-931-6630), in the heart of Westport. A greasy spoon famous for its all-day breakfasts, including plate-sized pancakes ($2-3). Weekday lunch specials $6. Open daily 7am-3pm.

🛏 ACCOMMODATIONS

The least expensive lodgings lie near the interstates, especially I-70, and toward Independence. Downtown hotels tend to be on the pricey side.

American Inn (☎800-905-6343) dominates the KC budget motel market with locations at 4141 S. Noland Rd. (☎816-373-8300); Woods Chapel Rd. (☎816-228-1080), off I-70 at Exit 18; 1211 Armour Rd. (☎816-471-3451), off I-35 at Exit 6B. The rooms are large and pleasant. A/C, cable TV, and outdoor pools. Singles and doubles from $40.

Interstate Inn (☎816-229-6311), off I-70 at Exit 18. A great deal if you get one of the walk-in singles or dou-

NATIONAL ROAD

THE LOCAL STORY

CROSSROADS ARTS DISTRICT

Each gallery in this up-and-coming neighborhood has a different feel, a testament to Kansas City's surprisingly varied arts scene. Don't miss "First Fridays," a night of gallery openings, fun, and food on the First Friday of each month—one of Kansas City's newest and hippest social scenes. Within the large neighborhood, galleries concentrate on Wyandotte and Baltimore St. between 18th and 20th St., but you might not see their entrances—many aren't well labeled. Pick up a copy of *The Review* (available at most of the galleries), a thick arts newspaper with reviews of each gallery's shows. Many of the galleries sell art; others offer studio and exhibition places only. The key to seeing interesting things is to ask around once you get inside one of the galleries; gallery owners and workers are often more than happy to show interested visitors studio spaces, discuss the latest shows, and point you to other galleries. (Open 7-9pm on the 1st F of each month. Free.)

bles. 21+. Singles from $29; doubles $44. More for non-smoking rooms.

Lake Jacomo (☎816-795-8200), 22 mi. southeast of downtown. From I-70, take Rte. 291 South to Colbern Rd.; Lake Jocomo is 2 mi. down the road. Lots of water activities, 33 forested campsites, and a marina. Sites $10, with electricity $15, with electricity and water $18, full hookup $22.

NIGHTLIFE

In the 1920s, jazz musician Count Basie and his "Kansas City Sound" reigned at the River City bars. Twenty years later, saxophonist Charlie "Bird" Parker spread his wings and soared, asserting Kansas City's prominence as a jazz music roost to be reckoned with. The restored **Gem Theater,** 1615 E. 18th St., stages old-time blues and jazz. From October to April, the Jammin' at the Gem concert series swings in a serious fashion. (☎816-842-1414. Box office open M-F 10am-4pm.) Across the street, the **Blue Room,** 1600 E. 18th St., cooks four nights a week with some of the smoothest local acts in town. (☎816-474-2929. Cover F-Sa $5. Open M and Th 5-11pm, F 5pm-1am, Sa 7pm-1am.) The **Grand Emporium,** 3832 Main St., twice voted the best blues club in the US, has live music five nights a week. (☎816-531-1504. Live music M and W-Sa. Cover up to $15, depending on act. Open M and Sa noon-2am, Tu-F 11am-2am.) For something besides jazz, bars and nightclubs cluster in **Westport.**

Blayney's, 415 Westport Rd. (☎816-561-3747). Canned R&B on the dance floor, live music on the outdoor deck. Cover $2-6. Open Tu-Th 8pm-3am, F 6pm-3am, Sa 5pm-3am.

America's Pub, 510 Westport Rd. (☎816-531-1313). Kansas City's bachelorette party headquarters. While the dance floor is usually packed, the elevated barstools provide a chance to relax. Th $1 drinks. Cover $6. Open W-Sa 8pm-3am.

The Hurricane, 4048 Broadway St. (☎816-753-0884). Hosts everything from open mic (M) to hip-hop (Th). Cover $5-10. Open M-F 3pm-3am, Sa-Su 5pm-3am.

Harpo's, 4109 Pennsylvania Ave. (☎816-753-3434). The keystone of Westport nightlife. The live music and $0.25 beer on Tu attract college students ready to party. Cover Tu and Sa $2-3. Open daily 11am-3am.

Mi Cocina, 620 W. 48th St. (☎816-960-6426). The place to see and be seen in Kansas City. Trendy Latin

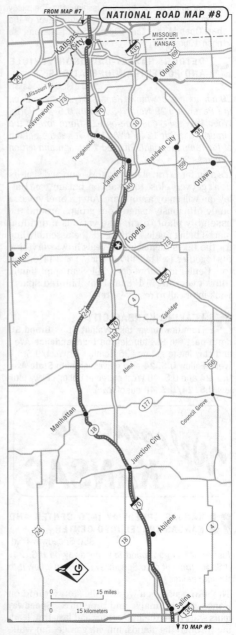

FROM MAP #7 **NATIONAL ROAD MAP #8**

0   15 miles

0   15 kilometers

▼ TO MAP #9

NATIONAL ROAD

music accompanies couture-clad fashionistas. The pricey Mexican food is generally overlooked in favor of the bar. Open M-Th 11am-10pm, F-Sa 11am-3am, Su noon-10pm.

⬛ DETOUR: HARLEY-DAVIDSON VEHICLE AND POWERTRAIN OPERATIONS

11401 N. Congress St.

20 mi. north of downtown Kansas City. Head north on the Paseo to I-29 North/I-35 North/U.S. 71 North. When they split, continue on I-29 North toward the airport. Take Exit 12 for NW 112th St.; at the bottom of the ramp turn right. Proceed 1 mi. and turn left on Congress St.

It's a bit far to travel for a factory tour, and visitors don't get very close to the action, but any true Harley fan will enjoy a stop here. After a brief video, a guide officiously ushers tour groups around the assembly plant to glimpse various individual pieces being made. At the end, the assembly line for the bikes themselves reveals how everything fits together. (☎414-343-7850 or 877-883-1450. Visitors Center and store open M-F 8am-3pm. 45min. tours every hr. M-F 8am-1pm. Limited space; walk-in or call to reserve. Free.)

⬛ LEAVING KANSAS CITY

From downtown, take **Walnut St.** or **Grand St.** north past 6th St., turn left on **Independence Ave.**, and stay left to get on I-35 South/I-70 West/U.S. 24 West. Follow **U.S. 24** as it curves left onto **State Ave.** U.S. 24 and U.S. 40 West merge at College Pkwy.; follow **U.S. 24/U.S. 40** out of town.

Welcome To
KANSAS

⬛ KANSAS SPEEDWAY INFO CENTER AND KANSAS TRAVEL INFO CENTER

350 Speedway Blvd.

Just after you go around the speedway on U.S. 24/U.S. 40, turn left onto Speedway Blvd. and follow it to the info center.

The info center is a worthwhile stop for info on Kansas towns, maps, and brochures. **Speedway tours** start from the info center and last 1hr., leading through the stands, infield, garage, fan walk,

and track. Sadly, visitors can't drive around the track. (☎913-328-3327. Info center open daily 9am-5pm. Tours generally offered daily at 10am and 2pm, but call ahead. $10, children $5.)

⬛ APPROACHING LAWRENCE

Follow **U.S. 40** into Lawrence City limits. To get downtown, proceed straight across the bridge, and when U.S. 40 turns right onto 6th St., continue straight onto **Vermont St.**

LAWRENCE

Forty miles from Kansas City, Lawrence was founded in 1854 by anti-slavery advocates to ensure that Kansas became a free state. Now home to the flagship University of Kansas (KU), Lawrence is a good-times college town, fully equipped with excellent restaurants and a happening musical scene.

> ### ⬛ VITAL STATS
>
> **Population:** 80,000
>
> **Visitor Info: Lawrence Visitors Center,** 402 N. 2nd St. (☎785-865-4499 or 888-529-5267; www.visitlawrence.com), at Locust St. Open Apr.-Sept. M-F 8:30am-5:30pm, Su 1-5pm; Oct.-Mar. M-Sa 9am-5pm, Su 1-5pm.
>
> **Internet Access: Lawrence Public Library,** 707 Vermont St. (☎785-843-3833; www.lawrencepubliclibrary.org). Public terminals located downstairs. Open M-F 9am-9pm, Sa 9am-6pm, Su 2-6pm.
>
> **Post Office:** 645 Vermont St. (☎785-843-1681). Open M-F 8am-5:30pm, Sa 9am-noon. **Postal Code:** 66045.

⬛ GETTING AROUND

Almost everything of interest is found along **Massachusetts St.** or parallel **Vermont** and **New Hampshire St.** Numbered streets run east-west. Vermont and New Hampshire St. are thick with free 2hr. **parking** lots, making driving in Lawrence an easy and pleasant experience. Watch the arrows on the meters at slanted parking spots; it can be confusing to figure out which one goes with which car.

⬛ SIGHTS

The Wild West was in full swing in Lawrence during the bleeding Kansas days, giving the city quite a bit of fascinating history. The **Uni-**

versity of Kansas Watkins Community Museum of History, 1047 Massachusetts St., features several floors of Lawrence lore, including an exhibit on the abolitionist activist John Brown. (☎785-841-4109. Open Tu-W 10am-6pm, Th 10am-9pm, F 10am-5pm, Sa 10am-4pm. Suggested donation $3.) The main attractions, however, are two tours through downtown Lawrence. A 1½hr. driving tour, **Quantrill's Raid: The Lawrence Massacre,** beginning at 1111 E. 19th St., traces the events leading up to the slaughter of over 200 men by pro-slavery vigilantes on August 21, 1863. The second tour, **House Styles of Old West Lawrence,** provides a look at 19th-century homes. There are walking (45min.) and driving (25min.) variations; pick up a map at the Visitors Center.

For the more refined, the **Spencer Museum of Art,** 1301 Mississippi St., is home to a small but impressive collection of paintings, sculpture, and glasswork from medieval and Renaissance Europe, as well as medieval Japan and Dynastic China. (☎785-864-4710. Open Su noon-5pm, Tu-W and F-Sa 10am-5pm, Th 10am-9pm. Free.)

▚ FOOD

Downtown Lawrence features both traditional barbecue joints and health-conscious offerings. The **Free State Brewing Company,** 636 Massachusetts St., was the first legal brewery in Kansas. This local hangout brews over 50 beers annually and always has at least five on tap. (☎785-843-4555. Beer $2.50. Sandwiches $6. Pasta $8-10. M $1.25 beer. Open M-Sa 11am-midnight, Su noon-11pm.) **Jefferson's,** 743 Massachusetts St., promotes "Peace, Love and Hotwings" along with its entrees, all under $7. Unleash your artistry on a dollar bill and add it to the thousands already gracing the walls. (☎785-832-2000. Open M-W 11am-10pm, Th-Sa 11am-11pm, Su noon-10pm.)

Between meals, it's possible to have pretty much any conceivable combination of fruit in a glass down at the **Juice Stop,** 812 Massachusetts St. Sports-named smoothies all sell for $3.90, be it the Hat Trick or the Half-pipe. (☎785-331-0820. Open M-F 8am-9pm, Sa 9am-8pm, Su 10am-8pm.) The **Wheatfields Bakery and Cafe,** 904 Vermont St., serves large sandwiches ($6.50) on French bread, olive loaf, or focaccia. (☎785-841-5553. Open M-Sa 6:30am-8pm, Su 7:30am-4pm.)

▟ ACCOMMODATIONS

Inexpensive motels are hard to come by in Lawrence. The best place to look is around Iowa and 6th St., just west of the KU campus. Three blocks from downtown, the **Halcyon House Bed and Breakfast,** 1000 Ohio St., is extremely close to local attractions and good parking. (☎785-841-0314. Rooms $49.) The traditional **Westminster Inn and Suites,** 2525 W. 6th St., offers many amenities, including a pool, to make stays more comfortable. (☎785-841-8410. Breakfast included. Singles M-Th $49, F-Su $55; doubles $59/$65. $5 AAA discount.) The **Virginia Inn,** 2903 W. 6th St., offers large rooms with microfridges, right in the downtown area. (☎785-843-6611. Singles $50.) A more luxurious but rather expensive stay is available at the **Eldritch Hotel,** at the corner of 7th and Massachusetts St. The two-room suites are *very* comfortable. (☎785-749-5011 or 800-527-0909. Rooms $89-235.)

▚ NIGHTLIFE

The rowdy saloon-goers of Lawrence's past have come and gone, but late-night fun is still available; yesterday's cowboys have been replaced by college students. The place to be for live music, ▨**The Bottleneck,** 737 New Hampshire St., hosts local acts and big-name artists. There's a show every night except Thursday, when Retro Dance Night takes hold. (☎785-841-5483. Cover up to $10, depending on show. Open daily from 3pm.) For live music and a neighborhood bar atmosphere, head down to well-equipped **Jazzhaus,** 926½ Massachusetts St. (☎785-749-3320. Cover after 9pm $2-8; Tu $1.50, but no live music. Open daily 4pm-2am.) Across the street from each other and under one management, the **Jackpot Saloon and Music** and the **Replay Lounge,** 943 Massachusetts St., serve multiple facets of the clubbing community. The Replay is dark and low-ceilinged, with a bar and pinball, while the Jackpot is open, bright and sociable. Both put on a variety of musical acts. (Jackpot ☎785-832-1085. Shows daily. 21+. Open daily from 4pm. Replay ☎785-749-7676. Shows weekly. 21+ after 10pm. Open daily from 3pm.)

NATIONAL ROAD

LEAVING LAWRENCE
Follow **6th St. (U.S. 40)** west out of town. 22½ mi. from Lawrence, exit to stay on **U.S. 40;** it joins Rte. 4 and I-70 headed west into Topeka.

TOPEKA

The capital of Kansas, Topeka is essentially a vast tract of plazas and strip-malls. Though this arrangement has led to a particularly high density of fast-food joints and gas stations, intriguing restaurants and sights are still hidden throughout the city. Topeka displays its state pride at several historic sights that memorialize its role in the abolition and civil rights movements.

⎛ VITAL STATS ⎞

Population: 112,000

Visitor Info: Topeka Convention and Visitors Bureau, 1275 Topeka Blvd. (☎800-235-1030; www.topekacvb.com). Open M-F 9am-5pm.

Internet Access: Topeka and Shawnee County Public Library, 1515 10th Ave. (☎785-580-4400; www.tscpl.org), at the corner of Washburn Ave. Open M-F 9am-9pm, Sa 9am-6pm, Su noon-9pm.

Post Office: 424 S. Kansas Ave. (☎785-295-9178). **Postal Code:** 66603.

▐ GETTING AROUND

Much of Topeka is a rough grid of four-lane roads—definitely a driver's city. **Topeka Blvd.** is the city's major north-south artery, with numerous restaurants and hotels. **Gage Blvd.,** a few blocks west, is a haven of gas stations and fast food. The majority of Topeka's sights lie on or near one of these two main roads, which are connected by east-west streets. Many of these end in residential cul-de-sacs, but **10th St.** to the north and **29th St.** to the south both span the full distance.

Parking in Topeka is plentiful and free in most areas; virtually every building has its own lot, so there is no need to park on the street. Downtown is the exception; visitors to the city center may have to find spaces along the curb, which can be hard to come by. Many of these spaces are free, though they often have 2hr. time restrictions.

◉ SIGHTS

Most of Topeka's sights are not focused around one region, so a good bit of driving is necessary to see them all. In the center of Topeka is the **Kansas**

State Capitol, at the corner of 10th Ave. and Jackson St. (☎785-296-3966. Tours M-F every hr. 9am-3pm, except noon. Free.) The new **Brown v. Board National Historic Site,** at the intersection of Monroe and 15th St., is dedicated to the groundbreaking Supreme Court decision that ruled school segregation unconstitutional. Built in a former elementary school, the museum is filled with photographs chronicling the history leading up to and resulting from the decision. In the powerful Hall of Courage exhibit, visitors pass through a narrow corridor of gigantic screens, which blast footage of jeering crowds denouncing newly admitted black students. (Follow 10th St. to Topeka Blvd. and proceed south to 15th St. ☎785-354-4273. Open daily 9am-5pm. Free.)

The **Kansas Museum of History,** 6425 6th St., is a guide to the history of Kansas, from prehistoric native life to 20th-century developments. Rotating special exhibits highlight particular time periods and events. (Drive north on Topeka Blvd. to 6th St., then proceed east to the very end of the road. ☎785-272-8683; www.kshs.org. Open Su 1-5pm, Tu-Sa 9am-5pm. $4, seniors $3, students $2.)

In addition to lions, giraffes, and other exotic animals, the **Topeka Zoological Park,** 635 Gage Blvd., has an indoor rainforest where visitors share the pathways with monkeys, birds, turtles, and other small jungle creatures. (☎785-368-9143. Open daily 9am-5pm. $4.50, ages 3-12 $3.)

Proceeding south to Forbes Field Airport will bring you to the **Combat Air Museum,** a hangar that houses combat planes from many eras. (☎785-862-3303; www.combatairmuseum.org. Open M-Sa 9am-4:30pm, Su noon-4:30pm; last admission 3:30pm. $6, ages 6-17 $4.)

◼ FOOD

Topeka is home to several fine restaurants, though finding them can be a bit of challenge; like much in this city, they are scattered across countless strip-malls. The ▨**Blind Tiger Brewery and Restaurant,** 417 37th St., east of Topeka Blvd., is named for the stuffed tigers which were sometimes used to advertise Prohibition-era speakeasies. The microbrewery and restaurant are separated only by a low wall, so the buzz of the bar blends softly into the dim, trendy eating area. Menu offerings include a range of salads, vegetarian options, and appetizer specialties such as the "tiger tips" (smoked ribs) and "tiger wings" (buffalo wings with house sauce). Finish it all off with

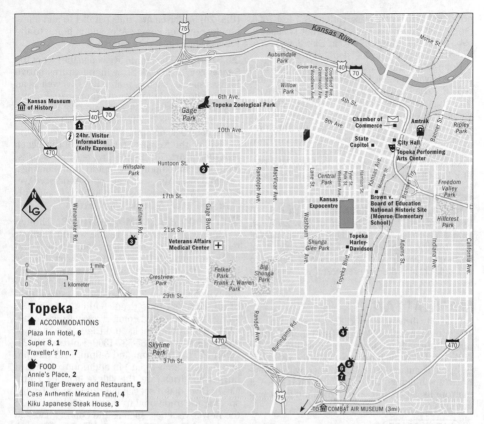

Topeka

ACCOMMODATIONS
Plaza Inn Hotel, 6
Super 8, 1
Traveller's Inn, 7

FOOD
Annie's Place, 2
Blind Tiger Brewery and Restaurant, 5
Casa Authentic Mexican Food, 4
Kiku Japanese Steak House, 3

a Prohibition Float, made with root beer brewed right in the building. (☎785-267-7527; www.blindtiger.com. Appetizers from $6. Pasta from $11. Grill entrees from $8. Restaurant open Su-Th 11am-9pm, F-Sa 11am-10pm. Lounge open Su-Th 11am-1am, F-Sa 11am-2am.)

Food preparation is a spectacle at **Kiku Japanese Steak House,** 5331 22nd Pl., in the Fairlawn Plaza off Fairlawn Rd. Chefs cook food hibachi style at your table. (☎785-272-6633. Appetizers $3-10. Entrees from $11. Open M-F 11:30am-1:30pm and 4:30-10pm, Sa-Su noon-10pm. Reservations recommended.) A local favorite, **Annie's Place,** 4014 Gage Center Dr., is located in the Gage Center Plaza off Gage Blvd. Whether you desire a hot dog ($3.75) or three-cheese quiche ($7.25), Annie's provides. The in-house bakery sells fabulous pies for $8-12. (☎785-273-0848. Open M-Sa 11am-10pm, Su 11am-9pm.) **Casa Authentic Mexican Food,** 3320

Topeka Blvd., south of 29th St., is a pleasant family restaurant with private booths and well-priced Mexican meals. The combination dinners are an excellent bargain, complete with an entree such as the house chili ($7.65) as well as salad or soup. (☎785-266-4503. Open M-Th 11am-10pm, F-Sa 11am-11pm, Su 11:30am-10pm.)

ACCOMMODATIONS

Hotels cluster near the highway exits, but some of the nicest and least expensive accommodations are closer to downtown. The **Plaza Inn Hotel,** 3880 Topeka Blvd., is located just south of 37th St. Though it looks like every other budget hotel on the outside, the rooms are spacious, pleasant, and well priced. (☎785-266-4591. Singles from $39; doubles from $44.) Nearby, the **Traveller's Inn,** 3846 Topeka Blvd., offers great deals and an outdoor pool. (☎ 785-267-1222, reservations 877-524-7666. Singles $35; doubles $40.) A safe bet is **Super 8,** 5968 10th Ave., right off I-70 at Exit 356. (☎ 785-273-5100. Singles from $50; doubles from $55.)

Road-weary travelers can spend evenings fishing and swimming at **Lake Shawnee Campground,** 3435 E. Edge Rd. Though there are many more RV sites than tent sites, only tents have the option of being right on the water's edge. (Follow 29th St. east to the edge of Topeka, then go south on Croco Rd.; E. Ridge Rd. is a short distance down to the right. ☎ 785-267-1156. Electrical hookups at most sites. Mid-Apr. to mid-Oct. tent sites $14; RVs $15; Mid-Oct. to mid-Apr. $11/$14. Showers free.)

🚶 APPROACHING MANHATTAN

Take **I-70** to **Exit 358A** and hop on **U.S. 75 North.** Proceed 2 mi. to the exit for **U.S. 24 West,** toward Manhattan. The speed limit on this section of U.S. 24 soon becomes 70 mph. On the outskirts of Manhattan, **Poyntz Ave.** appears running parallel to **U.S. 24.** Entering the city is easiest if you get on this road as soon as possible.

MANHATTAN

A little city thriving around Kansas State University and an inexplicable number of indoor shopping centers, Manhattan proclaims itself "The Little Apple." While it may seem like the *really* little apple compared to its big brother, within Manhattan's borders are many hallmarks of a metropolis: an art museum, a zoo, and great restaurants.

(VITAL STATS)

Population: 45,000

Visitor Info: Manhattan Convention and Visitors Bureau, 501 Poyntz Ave. (☎ 785-776-8829; www.manhattancvb.org). Open M-F 8am-5pm.

Internet Access: Manhattan Public Library, 629 Poyntz Ave. (☎ 785-726-4741). Open M-Th 9am-8:30pm, F 9am-6pm, Sa 9am-5:30pm, Su 1-5:30pm.

Post Office: 2307 Tuttle Creek Blvd. (☎ 913-776-8851). **Postal Code:** 66502.

🏢 GETTING AROUND.

Businesses and official buildings are located along **Poyntz Ave.,** which degenerates into a mess of highway intersections to the east. Unfortunately, this area is the only way to reach the lodgings on **Tuttle Creek Blvd.**

(U.S. 24). Anderson Ave. runs parallel to and a few blocks north of Poyntz Ave. and is home to the Kansas State University campus.

◉ SIGHTS.

The prairie lives on in the city at the **Sunset Zoo,** 2333 Oak St., which features native Kansas species such as prairie dogs, as well as an exotic red panda and snow leopard. (Follow Poyntz Ave. past Sunset Ave. and take a right on Oak St. ☎ 785-587-2737; www.sunsetzoo.com. Open daily 9:30am-5pm. $4, ages 3-12 $2.) At the far end of the Kansas State campus, the **Beach Museum of Art,** 701 Beach Ln., exhibits works, including contemporary sculpture and paintings. (From Sunset Ave., turn right onto Anderson Ave. ☎ 785-532-7718; www.k-state.edu/bma. Open Su 1-5pm, Tu-F 10am-5pm, Sa 1-5pm. Free.)

🍽 FOOD & ACCOMMODATIONS.

Though a number of restaurants reside within Manhattan's shopping centers, others can still be found walking through the downtown area. **Harry's Uptown,** 418 Poyntz Ave., serves satisfying entrees at steep prices. Unorthodox sandwiches such as the Wild Mushroom Philly are the best deals. Best of all, Harry's offers tired roadies a chance to lounge in upholstered comfort away from the sterility of shopping malls and the sticky vinyl of worn car seats. (☎ 785-537-1300. Entrees $13-24. Open M-Th 11am-2pm and 5-9pm, F 11am-2pm and 5-10pm, Sa 5-10pm.) In addition to standard burger-and-fries fare, the **Village Inn,** 204 Tuttle Creek Blvd., has a special flair for crepes. Try the spectacular traditional fruit crepe ($6), or one of the newer varieties, such as the country sausage crepe. (☎ 785-537-3776. Open Su-Th 5am-10pm, F-Sa 5am-1pm.) At **The Sirloin Stockade,** 325 Poyntz Ave., roadtrippers can fulfill meat cravings without spending too much. All-you-can-eat options run pretty much all day, with different deals in effect at various times, often for as little as $6. (☎ 785-776-0516. Open M-Th 11am-9pm, F 11am-10pm, Sa 8am-10pm, Su 8am-9pm.)

Those in need of a good night's sleep might consider **The Cottage at Cedar Meadows Bed and Breakfast,** 15955 Cedar Meadows Rd., in Wamego, an elegant stay easily reached by backtracking east on U.S. 24. (☎ 785-456-8654; www.thecottagebnb.com. Rooms $79-139.) Chain hotels are abundant in Manhattan, and good bargains include the **Motel 6** at Tuttle Creek Blvd., which has an outdoor pool. (☎ 785-537-1022. Singles Su-Th $40, F-Sa $50; doubles $50/$56.)

LEAVING MANHATTAN

Take **Rte. 18 West** out of town. 8¼ mi. from Manhattan, Rte. 18 exits to the right. Take that exit and fork right to rejoin **I-70** heading west, and then take Exit 300 for Junction City attractions.

JUNCTION CITY

The ✪**Geary County Historical Society Museum,** 530 N. Adams St., has the usual set of historical exhibits, but what makes it a must-visit is its live demonstration of historic undergarments, entitled "Undercover Story." Middle-aged and elderly women parade in period undergarments dating from the 1880s through the 1920s as the museum director narrates. (☎ 785-238-1666. Open Su and Tu-Sa 1-4pm. Call Museum Director Gaylynn Childs in advance of your visit to arrange for "Undercover Story." Free.) Be sure to check out Freedom Park and the Atomic Cannon, just south of I-70 at Exit 301. A climb up a shadeless switchback trail leads to the **atomic cannon,** designed during the Cold War to launch nuclear shells but never used. Fort Riley was the headquarters of the US Cavalry until it was disbanded in 1950.

Across the Kansas River in Fort Riley, visitors can learn about the cavalry's role in war and in the expansion of the American frontier at the aging **US Cavalry Museum.** A 28-stop, 10 mi. driving tour around the rest of the 19th-century buildings of the fort and past a small herd of buffalo is also possible. Pick up the driving tour guide at the Cavalry Museum, where the tour starts. Entrance to the museum requires passing through a military police checkpoint—bring photo ID and proof of car registration and insurance. (☎ 785-239-2737. Open M-Sa 9am-4:30pm, Su noon-4:30pm. Free.)

APPROACHING ABILENE

From I-70, take **Exit 275** and turn **left** onto **Rte. 15,** which becomes **Buckeye** in town.

ABILENE

Though most recently known as the birthplace of President Dwight D. Eisenhower, Abilene began as a cowtown. The town remains prosperous today thanks to industry on its outskirts, and many young families can be seen strolling through the city park or splashing in the town pool. With a small but entertaining collection of sights and museums, Abilene is a good place for a stopover.

VITAL STATS

Population: 6500

Visitor Info: Abilene Convention and Visitors Bureau, 201 NW 2nd St. (☎ 785-263-2231; www.abilenekansas.org). Open M-Sa 8am-6pm, Su 10am-4pm.

Internet Access: Abilene Public Library, at NW 4th St. and Broadway. Open M-W 9am-6pm, Th noon-7pm, F 9am-5pm, Sa 9am-noon.

Post Office: 217 N. Buckeye (☎ 785-263-2691), at 3rd St. Open M-F 8am-4:30pm, Sa 9am-11:30pm.
Postal Code: 67410.

GETTING AROUND. Buckeye (Rte. 15) is the major north-south axis stretching from I-70 into town. Numbered streets run east-west and count up in both directions from **1st St.,** at the central east-west axis. For example, an address on NW 2nd St. is west of Buckeye and one block north of 1st St., while one on SE 4th St. is east of Buckeye and three blocks south of 1st St.

SIGHTS. The museum at the **Eisenhower Center,** 200 SE 4th St., at Buckeye, focuses on Eisenhower's military and presidential careers as well as the work of his wife, Mamie. Newly revised and updated, the museum remains a glorification of Ike's presidency, but some newer exhibits call into question some elements of Ike's legacy. Other attractions include the family's 19th-century home and a Visitors Center that shows an hourly movie. Researching at the **Presidential Library** requires an application; call for more info. (☎ 877-746-4453; www.eisenhower.archives.gov. Museum and Visitors Center open summer daily 8am-5:45pm. $5, seniors $4.50, under 16 $1, students free.)

Housed inside the County History Museum, the **Museum of Independent Telephony,** 412 S. Campbell St., displays examples of telephone technology dating from the 1880s to today, including switchboards, switching stations, and some foreign equipment. (From Buckeye turn left on SE 3rd St. and proceed past the Eisenhower Center. Follow Campbell St. around to the right. ☎ 785-263-2681. Open summer M-Sa 10am-8pm, Su 1-5pm; winter M-Sa 10am-5pm, Su 1-5pm. $3.)

Just south of the Eisenhower Center, **Old Abilene Town,** on SE 6th St., recreates the Abilene of cowtown days with replicas of 19th-century buildings and gunfight reenactments.

NATIONAL ROAD

(☎785-263-1868. Buildings open M-F 9am-4pm, Sa 9am-5pm, Su 12:30-5pm. Stagecoach rides Sa 10am-5pm, Su 12:30-5pm. $3. Reenactments Sa-Su 11:30am, 1:30, 3:30pm.) Live specimens greet visitors at the **Greyhound Hall of Fame,** 407 S. Buckeye, where you can learn about greyhounds (the dog, not the bus) and racing. (☎800-932-7881; www.greyhoundhalloffame.com. Open daily 9am-5pm. Free.)

⛏️🍴 FOOD & ACCOMMODATIONS. You'll probably hear about the ⭐**Brookville Hotel,** 105 E. Lafayette Dr., even before you arrive in Abilene. There is only one item on the menu at this Midwestern institution—"One-half Skillet Fried Chicken" ($12, ages 3-11 $7), served family style with relishes, cole slaw, mashed potatoes, creamed corn, biscuits, and ice cream—and boy is all of it good! (Take Buckeye 1 block north of I-70 to Lafayette Dr. and turn right. ☎785-263-2244; www.brookvillehotel.com. Open Su 11am-2:30pm and 5-7:30pm, Tu-F 5-8pm, Sa 11am-2pm and 4:30-8pm.) The historic **Kirkby House Restaurant,** 205 NE 3rd St., serves classy Midwestern fare in a high-ceilinged Victorian home. Come for casual Fridays, when a barbecue platter is only $10, or reserve the table in the tower for a romantic night. (☎785-263-7336; www.kirby-house.com. Sandwiches and salads $7-8. Seafood $15. Steak $19-24. Open M-Sa 11am-2pm and 5-8pm, Su 11am-2pm.)

A friendly couple runs the **Diamond Motel,** 1407 NW 3rd St., which has comfortable rooms in a residential area. (☎785-263-2360. Refrigerators and central A/C. Non-smoking rooms available. Singles $33-36; doubles $40-48. AAA discount.) The **Budget Lodge Inn,** 101 NW 14th St., is the budget option in town. (☎785-263-3600. Singles $25; doubles $30; larger rooms for up to 4 people $42.)

APPROACHING SALINA
Take **Buckeye (Rte. 15)** for about 5 mi. Turn right onto **1700 Ave.,** at the "Salina 19" sign. **1700 Ave.** becomes **Country Club Rd.** in Salina. Curve left onto **Marymount Rd.,** take your first right onto **E. Iron Ave.,** and drive 1¾ mi. into the center of downtown, the intersection with **Santa Fe Ave.**

 Half a mile after you turn onto Santa Fe. Ave., notice the grinning all-metal **Muffler Man** on your left.

SALINA

Salina (pop. 46,000), not to be confused with the Salinas, CA of Steinbeck fame, is a mid-sized town that has little to offer besides decent lodging. The educational **Smoky Hill Museum,** 211 W. Iron Ave., presents the history of the Smoky Hill region, which spans central Kansas from Salina to the south. (☎785-826-7414; www.smokyhillmuseum.org. Open Su 1-5pm, Tu-F noon-5pm, Sa 10am-5pm. Free.) At the **Rolling Hills Zoo,** 625 N. Hedville Rd., 65 acres of Kansas prairie have been transformed into the "naturalistic habitats" of exotic animals. Although there don't seem to be that many animals, the grounds are pretty and this "prairie oasis" surpasses many urban zoos. Pay the extra $2 for the tram or be prepared to walk across the unshaded park. (Follow I-135 or 9th St. north to I-70, take Exit 244 and head south 2 mi. to the zoo. ☎785-827-9488; www.rhrwildlife.com. Open daily June-Aug. 8am-5pm; Sept.-May 9am-5pm. $8, ages 2-12 $5, seniors $7.)

It may look like a deli, but **Martinelli's Little Italy,** 158 S. Santa Fe Ave., between Walnut St. and E. Iron Ave., is actually a whole Italian restaurant. (☎785-826-9190. Open M-Sa 11am-10pm, Su 11am-4pm.) **Capers,** 109 N. Santa Fe Ave., is a trendy half-coffee, half-sandwich place. The funky furnishings invite lingering, while the country music reminds you that you're in Kansas, not Starbucks. Large deli sandwiches, panini, and wraps are all $6. (☎785-823-7177. Open M-Sa 7am-6pm.) For accommodations, the **Travelers Lodge,** 245 S. Broadway, offers clean, comfortable rooms, with refrigerators and microwaves. (☎785-827-9351. Outdoor pool. Singles $30; doubles $33-40.) Nearby, the **Village Inn,** 453 S. Broadway, has rooms with refrigerators. (☎785-827-4040. Outdoor pool. Singles $33; doubles $40.)

LEAVING SALINA
Follow **Iron Ave.** west, turn right on **College St.,** then left on **State St.** 7 mi. past Broadway, turn left to continue on State St., which becomes **Rte. 140.**

THE ROAD TO ELLSWORTH

Gas gets progressively more expensive as you move from Salina toward Great Bend; fill up earlier rather than later. **Kanopolis Lake** has four separate camping facilities, together providing about 380 sites. You can swim in the lake at the Venango and Langley Point Areas. (19 mi. east of Salina, take Rte. 141 South for about 6 mi.; the park entrance is on the right. ☎ 785-546-2565. Park entrance fee $5-6. Camping permit $10.) The huge, creviced, mushroom-shaped rocks at ◪**Mushroom Rock State Park** are truly unique; the natural sculptures resemble petrified UFOs on top of stone landing posts. (On I-135 at State St. 23 mi. from Salina, turn left onto 25th Rd., then left again after 1 mi. onto Ave. K. ☎ 785-546-2565. No camping.)

APPROACHING ELLSWORTH
From **Rte. 140,** take **Rte. 156** into town and bear right to get onto **Douglas Ave.**

ELLSWORTH. Texas Longhorn cattle were once herded through the lawless streets of Ellsworth, and the town's main street, **Douglas Ave.,** has purposely preserved itself as it was in the 1870s. To see the haunts of today's recreational cowboys, start at **Drovers Mercantile,** 119 N. Douglas Ave., which sells hats, boots, and spurs. (☎ 785-472-4703; www.droversmercantile.com. Open M-Sa 10am-5pm.) At the **Hodgden House Museum Complex,** 104 W. Main St., off Douglas Ave., a set of preserved buildings recall Ellsworth's history as a cowtown. (☎ 785-472-3059. Open Tu-Sa 9am-5pm.)

LEAVING ELLSWORTH
Leave Ellsworth on **Rte. 156.** Outside of Great Bend, fork right to get on **U.S. 56 West.**

GREAT BEND. Great Bend serves mainly as a support city for the region's dominant industry, agribusiness. U.S. 56 runs straight through the area; head north on **Main St.** to reach downtown shops and businesses, or continue west on U.S. 56 to reach chain motels and restaurants or to leave town. The **Kansas Quilt Walk,** 1400 Main St., in Courthouse Sq., surrounds the sidewalk, and showcases Kansan quilt patterns from the late 19th and early 20th centuries. The **Visitors Center,** 3111 10th St., west of downtown, is around the rear side of the Convention Center, through an unmarked doorway. (☎ 620-792-2750; www.greatbend.com/visitor. Open M-F 8:30am-5pm.) **Delgado's Restaurant,** 2210 10th St., is a good bet for Mexican fare. (☎ 620-793-3786. Open M-F 11am-2pm and 5-8:30pm.) Breakfast and lunch are offered at the cute, one-room **Granny's Kitchen,** 925 10th St. (☎ 620-793-7441).

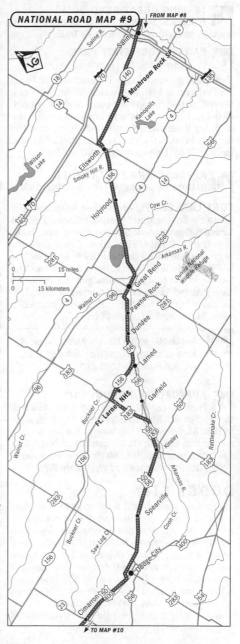

NATIONAL ROAD MAP #9   FROM MAP #8

▶ TO MAP #10

LEAVING GREAT BEND

Follow **U.S. 56 West.** From Great Bend to Kinsley, U.S. 56 aligns with the **Santa Fe Trail.**

PAWNEE ROCK STATE PARK

In Pawnee Rock. Turn right onto Centre St.

Pawnee Rock was a major landmark on the Santa Fe Trail, rising high above this flat area. It once served as both a lookout point and a signpost. Erosion and development have shortened the rock, but it must have been wonderful to view it as the only break in the vast, uncultivated landscape. (☎785-272-8681. Open daily 8am-dusk. Free)

APPROACHING FORT LARNED

In **Larned,** stay straight to drive on **Rte. 156.**

FORT LARNED. This fort used to defend the Santa Fe Trail against "hostile Indians." The **Fort Larned National Historic Site** consists of nine 1860s-era stone buildings. The officers' quarters have been recreated, but otherwise there isn't much to see here. (☎620-285-6911. Open daily June-Aug. 8am-6pm; Sept.-May 8:30am-5pm. $3, under 16 free.) At the **Santa Fe Trail Center,** on Rte. 156, exhibits explore the Santa Fe Trail. (☎620-285-2054. $4, students $2.50, children $1.50.)

The **Middle of the US** is in Kinsley, where a large road sign reads "New York City 1561 mi.; San Francisco 1561 mi."

APPROACHING DODGE CITY

From Fort Larned, continue along **Rte. 156** until the junction with **Rte. 183;** take Rte. 183 back south to **U.S. 56.** Follow U.S. 56 through Kinsley, where it merges with **U.S. 50.** On the outskirts of Dodge City, fork left to get on **Bus. U.S. 50 West,** the main drag of Dodge City (known in town as **Wyatt Earp Blvd.**)

DODGE CITY

Dodge City was and still is the most famous cowtown of the west. Silhouettes of cowboys on horses welcome visitors driving into town, and the smell of beef hangs in the air. This is the dusty heart of meat-packing country, and the factories still provide the town with its economic base 125 years after Dodge City served as a frontier post. While it can be hard to separate what's real from what's just for show, you'll find that local residents display a genuine pride in Dodge that is independent of all the cowboy hoopla.

(VITAL STATS)

Population: 25,000

Visitor Info: Dodge City Convention and Visitors Bureau, 400 W. Wyatt Earp Blvd. (☎620-225-8186; www.visitdodgecity.org). Open summer daily 8:30am-6:30pm; winter M-F 8:30am-5pm.

Internet Access: Dodge City Public Library, 1001 2nd Ave. (☎620-225-0248), up the hill at Elm St. Open M-W 9am-6pm, Th 9am-8pm, F 9am-6pm, Sa 10am-5pm, Su 1-5pm.

Post Office: 700 Central Ave. (☎800-275-08777). Open M-F 8:30am-5pm, Sa 9am-noon. **Postal Code:** 67801.

GETTING AROUND. Dividing east and west at **Central Ave, Wyatt Earp Blvd. (Bus. U.S. 50),** runs east-west through the entire area and is the reference point for most directions. Downtown Dodge lies north of Wyatt Earp Blvd. between Central Ave. and **5th Ave.;** Boot Hill lies on **Front St.,** next to Wyatt Earp Blvd. between 3rd and 5th Ave.

SIGHTS. The **Boot Hill Museum,** on Front St., between 3rd and 5th Ave., is a 1950s-era re-creation of Dodge City's legendary frontier. While some locals lament that the museum has gone downhill, it is still Dodge's main attraction. (☎620-227-8188; www.boothill.org. Open summer daily 8am-8pm; winter M-F 9am-5pm, Su 1-5pm. $8, seniors and students $7.50.) Located 4 mi. east of town on U.S. 400, the wooden **Coronado Cross** marks the spot where the Spanish explorer Coronado supposedly crossed the Arkansas River in 1541 in search of the mythical "Cities of Gold." On your way back, check out **Fort Dodge,** which once guarded the Santa Fe Trail.

FOOD & ACCOMMODATIONS. As the name suggests, **Casey's Cowtown,** 503 E. Trail St., serves steak ($10-17) in all shapes and sizes. Place settings here automatically include a steak knife, but Casey's also offers chicken, seafood, and salads. (Take 1st. south across the railroad tracks and turn left on Trail St. ☎620-227-5225. Open M-Sa 11am-10pm.) Authentic and spicy Mexican food brings south-of-the-border flavor to the Sunflower State at **Casa Alvarez,** 1701 W. Wyatt Earp Blvd. (☎620-225-7164. Fajitas $10. Combo plates $5.50-7.50. Open M-Th 10:30am-2pm and 5-9pm, F-Sa 11am-9:30pm, Su 10am-8pm.)

The **Astro Motel,** 2200 W. Wyatt Earp Blvd., has well-maintained, clean, rooms with refrigerators and microwaves. (☎620-227-8146. Continental breakfast included. Singles $36; doubles $44. The **Bel Air Motel,** 2000 E. Wyatt Earp Blvd. is a single-level motel with basic rooms. (☎620-227-7155. Singles $26; doubles $29.)

⚔ GETTING THE HELL OUT OF DODGE
Wyatt Earp Blvd. (Bus. U.S. 50 West) rejoins U.S. 50/U.S. 400 West outside of town. Take **U.S. 50** toward Garden City.

THE ROAD TO GARDEN CITY. During the 50-year period when this area was part of the **Santa Fe Trail,** continuous passage by wagons scarred the land with deep ruts. Check them out off the side of U.S. 50/400 on your way out of Dodge City. Twenty-eight miles west of the city, pull off at the marked overlook for a good view of cattle, farms, and lots of grass.

⚔ APPROACHING GARDEN CITY
U.S. 50 turns north just outside of Garden City; head straight into town on **Fulton St.;** it rejoins U.S. 50 after **Holcomb.**

GARDEN CITY. Though it has a large population, Garden City doesn't cater much to tourists. The **Finney County Historical Museum,** 403 S. 4th St., is the home of the ◢**world's largest hairball.** At the **Finney Game Refuge** (☎316-276-9400), on Rte. 83, a large bison herd roams; call ahead for a driving tour. **Hannah's Corner Restaurant,** 2605 N. Taylor, is a neighborhood hangout in the shadow of a beef packing plant. Besides a large breakfast selection and cheap sandwiches ($3-6), it also offers meaty dinners ($6-12). (☎620-276-8044. Open Su 6am-1:30pm, Tu-Th 5:30am-8pm, F-Sa 5:30am-9pm.)

The **World's Largest Hairball** is the size of a small bowling ball. Try picking it up; weighing only about a third of its original 55 lb. when it came out of the cow's stomach, it's still quite heavy. To see it, visit the **Finney County Historical Museum** in Garden City, KS. (☎316-272-3664. Open summer M-Sa 10am-5pm, Su 1-5pm; winter daily 1-5pm. Free.)

⚔ LEAVING GARDEN CITY
Take **Fulton St.** and turn right on **Main St.** Follow Bus. U.S. 50 as it turns left on **Kansas** and then right onto **Taylor.** Turn left on **Mary St.** Proceed 2 mi. and turn right on **Jones Ave.** to get to **Holcomb.**

HOLCOMB. This town became infamous as the site of grisly murders depicted in Truman Capote's *In Cold Blood.* The house where the murders took place is on the outskirts of town; you may be able to find it, but people live there and won't want to be disturbed. Holcomb is also home to the **world's largest beef-packing plant,** IBP.

⚔ LEAVING HOLCOMB
Follow **Jones Ave.** 1 mi. past Ron's Convenience Store, then turn left on **U.S. 50.**

> After Holcomb, U.S. 50 passes from the Central Time Zone to the Mountain Time Zone, where it is 1hr. earlier.

▦ HAMILTON COUNTY MUSEUM
At Gates St. and E. Ave. A, in Syracuse.
Though the entrance of this museum is so unassuming that you might miss it, the spacious interior is impressive. Old collections of everything from pens to stuffed birds to typewriters that once belonged to people in town are now on display. Don't miss the giant mammoth tusk, discovered just outside of town. (☎620-384-7496. Open summer M-F 1-5pm; winter M-W 10am-4pm. Free.)

Welcome To **COLORADO**

LAMAR
Thirty-two miles inside the state border, Lamar may be in Colorado, but it doesn't resemble the mountainous terrain depicted in postcards and license plates. As the buzzing flies constantly remind you, Lamar, like much of west Kansas, is cow country. This region is known as "Big Timbers" after the giant cottonwood trees that once stood on the banks of the Arkansas River. The **Big Timbers Museum,** 7515 U.S. 50, focuses on the settlement of the area. (☎719-336-2472. Open daily summer 10am-5pm; winter 1:30pm-4:30pm. Free.) At the northwest corner of Main and Beech St. by the Welcome Depot, the familiar **Madonna of the Trail** returns for a final, fleeting visit.

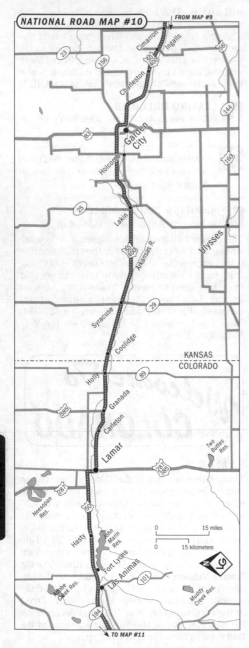

NATIONAL ROAD MAP #10

FROM MAP #9

KANSAS
COLORADO

0   15 miles
0   15 kilometers

TO MAP #11

Nicer than most family restaurants, big, friendly **Blackwell Station,** 1301 S. Main St., serves good old-fashioned American food. (☎719-336-7575. Steaks $8-17. Seafood $6-14. Lunch specials $6. Open M-Th 11am-9pm, F-Sa 11am-9:30pm, Su 11am-2pm.) North of town on U.S. 50, truckers and farmers flock to the **Ranchers Restaurant at Lamar Truck Plaza,** 33110 County Rd., for a smoke and heaping portions of food. They call the all-you-can-eat soup and salad bar a "spreader," because it is presented on the back of an old manure spreader. (☎719-336-3445. Open 24hr.) On the upscale side, the spacious rooms at **El Mar Budget Host Motel,** 1210 S. Main St., have comfortable furnishings. (☎719-336-4331. Heated pool. Rooms $38-43.) Basic rooms at the **Passport Inn,** 113 N. Main St., lack some of the amenities or furnishings found at more expensive places, but are otherwise solid. (☎719-336-7746. Singles $32-35; doubles $40.)

LEAVING LAMAR
Follow **U.S. 50 West** out of Lamar.

JOHN MARTIN RESERVOIR STATE PARK
21 mi. from Lamar, in Hasty.

This dusty state park surrounds a reservoir and dam. Small Lake Hasty offers swimming opportunities. Two campsites operate in the park, the slightly shaded **Hasty Campground** (full hookup $16) and the totally shadeless **Point Campground** (sites $12), which offers better views of the reservoir but no facilities. You can swim, water-ski, or jet-ski here (rentals available in town), and have a good chance of glimpsing a prairie dog, but the mountains ahead have much prettier surroundings. (☎719-829-1801. Park entrance fee $5.)

APPROACHING LA JUNTA
Continue past the fort on **Rte. 194.** After 6½ mi., follow signs to get on **U.S. 50 West.** Turn left off U.S. 50 onto **Colorado Ave.**

LA JUNTA. The ▇**Koshare Indian Museum,** 115 W. 18th St., is *the* reason to stop in La Junta. Along the entire route there are countless museums about the "settlement" of the west, but this museum is devoted to the people who were already here. At the back of the building is the original 1949 *Kiva,* a log-roofed theater in which today's Koshare Indian Dancers perform a couple of times per week in June and July. (☎719-384-4411; www.koshare.org. Open June-Aug. daily 10am-5pm; Sept.-May Su and Tu-Sa

12:30-4:30pm. $4, students and seniors $3. Shows $5/$3; includes museum admission.) The crowded and kitschy **Copper Kitchen,** 116 Colorado Ave., offers a large variety of breakfast and lunch options. (☎ 719-384-7216. Breakfast $1-5. Lunch $3-6.) The **Bamboo Panda,** 313 Colorado Ave., is clean, bright, and generous with its portions. (☎ 719-384-9880. Lunch specials $5.25. Open M-Sa 11am-9:30pm, Su 11am-9pm.)

APPROACHING PUEBLO
About 58 mi. from La Junta, U.S. 50 and Rte. 96 join. When they split 3 mi. later, take the exit for **Rte. 96 (4th St.)** into the center of Pueblo.

PUEBLO
A longtime steel town, Pueblo is often shunned by residents of more mountainous regions for its flatness and supposed lack of sophistication. Once Colorado's second-largest city, today much of the steel business is gone. But Pueblo has a hip side; new restaurants have opened, artists have moved into old warehouse spaces, and preservation efforts have created some interesting sights. The **Rosemount Museum,** 419 W. 14th St., is Pueblo's only really worthwhile sight. More like a castle than a home, this 37-room Victorian mansion is decked out with an elegant original interior. (4 blocks west of Santa Fe Ave. at Greenwood St. ☎ 719-545-5290; www.rosemount.org. Open Feb.-Dec. Tu-Sa 10am-4pm. $6, under 20 $4.)

Don't let the "diner" in the name fool you at the **Steel City Diner and Bakeshop,** 121 W. B St. Run by a couple who met while training at the Culinary Institute of America, this place has an innovative menu with items like wild mushroom ravioli and Colorado lamb sirloin. Although expensive, a meal here has quality that far exceeds the cost. (Take Union Ave. south to B St. and turn right. ☎ 719-295-1100. Entrees $13-22. Open Tu 11am-2pm, W-Sa 11am-2pm and 5-9pm.) The **Traveler's Motel,** 1012 N. Santa Fe Ave., is a bare-bones motel with gaudy concrete interiors. (☎ 719-543-5451. Laundry. Singles $27; doubles $39.)

LEAVING PUEBLO
Take **I-25 North** from downtown Pueblo to Exit 101 for **U.S. 50 West.** Proceed 35 mi. to Cañon City.

CAÑON CITY
For Coloradans, the mountain town of Cañon City will always be associated with prisons; Colorado's first territorial prison was here, and there are still several correctional facilities in the area. Going back several hundred million years, dinosaurs were also plentiful in these parts, and many sets of fossilized remains have been discovered, especially in the area of Florissant National Monument. Today, as other mountain regions have become more touristed, so has Cañon City, a great base from which to explore the surrounding area.

┌─── **VITAL STATS** ───────────────

Population: 15,000

Visitor Info: Cañon City Chamber of Commerce, 403 Royal Gorge Blvd. (☎ 719-275-2331; www.canyoncitycolorado.com), at 4th St. Open M-F 8am-5pm. The chamber also operates 2 **visitor "cabins"** (☎ 719-269-1777), located on either side of U.S. 50 at the outskirts of town. Approaching Cañon City from Pueblo, turn right at Dozier Ave. Open summer daily 8am-6pm.

Internet Access: Cañon City Public Library, 516 Macon Ave. (☎ 719-269-9020). Open M-Th 9:30am-7pm, F 9:30am-5pm, Sa 9:30am-2pm.

Post Office: 1501 Main St. (☎ 719-275-6877). Open M-F 8:30am-5:30pm, Sa 9am-noon. **Postal Code:** 81212.

GETTING AROUND. U.S. 50 runs east-west through the entire area and is known as **Royal Gorge Ave.** The town itself mostly lies north of U.S. 50 in an easily navigable downtown area; numbered streets head north from U.S. 50. **Royal Gorge** is about 10 mi. west of Cañon City on U.S. 50.

SIGHTS & OUTDOORS. At the western edge of downtown, the **Museum of Colorado Prisons,** 201 N. 1st St., presents a series of cells highlighting disciplinary methods, famous riots, prison breaks, and individual prisoners. An actual gas chamber is located in the front yard. Ghost walks in Cañon City meet at the museum. (☎ 719-269-3015; www.prisonmuseum.org. Open summer daily 8:30am-6pm; winter F-Su 10am-5pm. Ghost walks F-Su 6:45pm. $6, seniors $5, children $4. Ghost walks $8, children $5.) The **Royal Gorge Route Train Ride,** 401 Water St., provides a 2hr., 24 mi. train ride through the Royal Gorge. While not cheap, the luxury train is a good way to kick back and enjoy the canyon. (Take 3rd St. south to Santa Fe Depot at Water St. ☎ 303-569-2403 or 888-724-5748. Runs mid-June to mid-Aug. daily 9:30am, 12:30pm, 3:30pm; dinner trains Sa 7pm. Coach $27, children $17; first class $47/$37. Dinner train $70. Locomotive ride $95. Reservations recom-

NATIONAL ROAD

mended.) **Tunnel Drive,** a 2 mi. trail through three tunnels, offers views of the Arkansas River. It's best explored in early morning when the reflections off the river are brilliant. (Head west on U.S. 50 past the prison; it's on the left. Drive back ½ mi. to the trailhead and parking.)

🛶 RAFTING. The Arkansas River, which the route has followed more or less since Kansas, reaches a hilly point around Cañon City where it produces some fantastic rapids. Four companies based in and around the city offer rafting excursions: **Adventure Quest Expeditions** (☎719-269-9807 or 888-448-7238; www.aqerafting.com); **Raft Masters,** 2315 E. Main St. (☎800-568-7238; www.raftmasters.com); **Whitewater Adventure Outfitters,** 50905 U.S. 50 West (☎719-275-5344 or 800-530-8212; www.waorafting.com); and **Echo Canyon River Expeditions,** 45000 U.S. 50 West (☎800-595-3246; www.raftecho.com).

🍴🛏 FOOD & ACCOMMODATIONS. Judy's Restaurant, 1208 S. 9th St., has an extensive, creative breakfast, vegetarian, fish, and meat menu full of fresh ingredients. (☎719-269-1111. Breakfast $2-5. Lunch $5-8. Dinner $9-17. Open M-Sa 9am-10pm, Su 9am-9pm. Bar open until 2am.)

Motels line U.S. 50 near downtown as well as E. Main St., south of U.S. 50. It's good to reserve ahead, especially on weekends. **The Knotty Pine Motel,** 2990 E. Main St., 2 mi. east of downtown, has clean rooms in a red wooden structure that matches the natural "decor" of the area. (☎719-275-0461. Refrigerators and microwaves. Summer singles $40-45; doubles $55-60. Winter $34/$39-46.) Shag carpets and bright colors invoke the 70s at the **Pioneer Motel,** 201 Main St., where rooms are basic but clean. (☎719-269-1745. Singles $34-52; doubles $50-78; quads $54-78.)

◀ DETOUR: ROYAL GORGE PARK
Take U.S. 50 West 10 mi. from Cañon City.

Years ago it was free to walk over the Royal Gorge Bridge, the world's highest suspension bridge, but today they charge an exorbitant price. Admission for the amusement-park-style area includes an incline railway down to the bottom of the gorge or an aerial tram above it; jumping out over the area in a harness is $15 extra. The scenery from the air is spectacular, but to just see the bridge, park in the parking lot and take the trail (near the entrance gate) down to an overlook. (☎888-333-5597; www.royalgorgebridge.com. Open daily 10am-6:30pm; summer 7am-dusk. $20, ages 4-11 $16.)

▲ APPROACHING COLORADO SPRINGS
A bit of backtracking is required here—from Cañon City, follow **Royal Gorge Blvd. (U.S. 50)** back east out of town to the junction with **Rte. 115 North,** which becomes **Nevada Ave.** in town.

COLORADO SPRINGS

Once a resort town frequented only by America's elite, Colorado Springs has grown to be the second most-visited city in Colorado. When early gold seekers discovered bizarre red rock formations here, they named the region Garden of the Gods, in part due to a Ute legend that the rocks were petrified bodies of enemies hurled down

THE LOCAL STORY

BENT'S OLD FORT

Traveling through the Rocky Mountains, U.S. 50 parallels the famous Santa Fe Trail along the Arkansas River. The trail served as the key trade route from Independence, MO, to Santa Fe, NM, in the 1830s and 40s. The highlight of the trail is Bent's Old Fort, once the largest outpost in the region and the trade hub between the US and Mexico. Today, the fort has been rebuilt as it was in its heyday. Rising amid cottonwood groves, the thick adobe walls are impressive. Inside, blacksmith and carpenter demonstrations, storerooms, sleeping quarters, a kitchen, a billiards room, and stables provide glimpses into the past. Reenactments set the fort abuzz year-round. In mid-June, youngsters dress like trappers, traders, craftsmen, Native Americans, and soldiers. On August 1st, a reenactment of Col. Kearny's "Army of the West," destined for war with Mexico, passes through. (On U.S. 194, 13 mi. west of Las Animas, CO. ☎719-383-5010. $3, under 13 $2.)

from the sky. Today, the US Olympic Team continues the quest for gold here, while jets from the US Air Force Academy roar overhead.

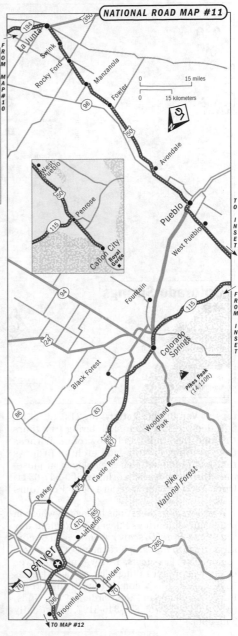

NATIONAL ROAD MAP #11

───────────
| VITAL STATS |
───────────

Population: 360,000

Visitor Info: Colorado Springs Chamber of Commerce, 515 S. Cascade Ave. (☎719-635-7506). Open M-F 8:30am-5pm; summer also Sa-Su 9am-5pm.

Internet Access: Penrose Public Library, 20 N. Cascade Ave. (☎719-531-6333). Open M-Th 10am-9pm, F-Sa 10am-6pm, Su 1-5pm.

Post Office: 201 E. Pikes Peak Ave. (☎800-275-8777), at Nevada Ave. Open M-F 7:30am-5:30pm, Sa 8am-1pm. **Postal Code:** 80903.

▣ GETTING AROUND

Colorado Springs is laid out in a grid of broad thoroughfares. **Nevada Ave.** is the main north-south strip from which numbered streets ascend moving westward. **I-25** from Denver cuts through downtown, dividing **Old Colorado City** from the eastern sector of the town, which remains largely residential. **Colorado Ave.** and **Pikes Peak Ave.** run east-west across the city. Just west of Old Colorado City lies **Manitou Springs** and the **Pikes Peak Area.** Colorado Ave. becomes **Manitou Ave.** as it extends into Manitou Springs and serves as the main street through town.

◉ ⚠ SIGHTS & OUTDOORS

Olympic hopefuls train with some of the world's most high-tech equipment at the **US Olympic Complex,** 1750 E. Boulder St., at the corner of Union St. The best times to get a glimpse of athletes in training are 10-11am and 3-4pm. (☎719-578-4792 or 888-659-8687. Open M-Sa 9am-5pm, Su 10am-5pm. Tours M-Sa.) The **Pioneer's Museum,** 215 S. Tejon Ave., recounts the settling of the city. (☎719-385-5990. Open Su 1-5pm, Tu-Sa 10am-5pm; in winter closed Su. Free.)

Just north of Lake St., the **World Figure Skating Museum and Hall of Fame,** 20 1st St., traces the history, art, and science of skating through film and photos and boasts an extensive collection of medals and skating outfits. (☎719-635-5200. Open M-F 10am-4pm, Sa 10am-4pm. $3, seniors and ages 6-12 $2.) Pot-

NATIONAL ROAD

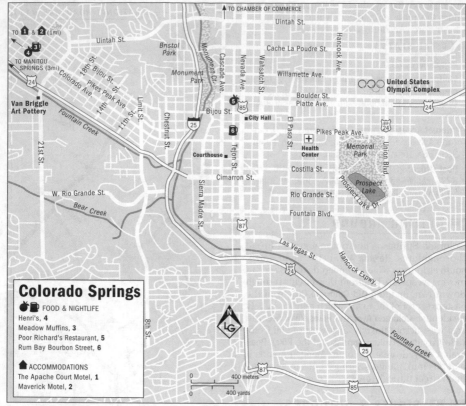

Colorado Springs

🍎🍴 FOOD & NIGHTLIFE
Henri's, **4**
Meadow Muffins, **3**
Poor Richard's Restaurant, **5**
Rum Bay Bourbon Street, **6**

🏠 ACCOMMODATIONS
The Apache Court Motel, **1**
Maverick Motel, **2**

ters at **Van Briggle Pottery,** on 21st St. (Rte. 24), demonstrate their skill during free tours through the studio and showroom. Witness the spinning, casting, and etching process that has produced pieces displayed in museums throughout the world. (☎800-847-6341. Open M-Sa 8:30am-5pm, Su 1-5pm. Free tours M-Sa.)

If you want to do serious hiking anywhere in the Colorado Springs/Pikes Peak Region, buy the *Pikes Peak Discovery Atlas,* which contains detailed topographical maps of the whole region. **Pikes Peak Tours,** 3704 W. Colorado Ave., offers whitewater rafting trips on the Arkansas River, as well as a combo tour of the US Air Force Academy and the Garden of the Gods. (☎719-633-1181 or 800-345-8197. Open daily 8am-5pm.)

 Sam's, a bar at **Rum Bay Bourbon Street** in Colorado Springs, is officially the **world's smallest bar,** according to the *Guinness Book of World Records.*

🍴🍷 FOOD & NIGHTLIFE

Students fill the outdoor tables in front of the cafes and restaurants lining **Tejon Ave.**

🥗 **Poor Richard's Restaurant,** 324½ N. Tejon Ave. (☎719-632-7721). A popular local hangout with great New York-style pizza (from $12), sandwiches ($6), and salads ($5-6). W live bluegrass. Th Celtic. Open Su-Tu 11am-9pm, W-Sa 11am-10pm.

🥗 **Savelli's,** 301 Manitou Ave. (☎719-685-0440). Cheery waitresses bring out cooked-to-order Italian food. The pasta ($5-9) is tasty, but the specialty here is the pizza ($5-17), which comes in baked-in, gourmet, and stone-baked varieties. Open M-Sa 11am-9pm, Su noon-9pm.

Organic Earth Cafe, 1124 Manitou Ave. (☎719-685-0986). Consisting of a 1904 Victorian Tea Room, the Future Earth Room, and Fairy Tale Rose Gardens bordering Fountain Creek, this cafe also features special events every night of the week. Amazing list of smoothies and plant shakes ($4-5). Open M-Th 9am-midnight, F-Su 9am-2am.

Henri's, 2427 W. Colorado Ave. (☎719-634-9031). Henri's has served *chimichangas* ($7.50) and a wide variety of *cervezas* for over 50 years. *Tacos al carbone* ($8.50) are a popular favorite. Drop in for a margarita during happy hour (M-Th 4pm-8pm, F 3pm-8pm) or check out the strolling *mariachi* singers F-Sa night. Open Su-Th 11am-9pm, F-Sa 11am-10pm.

Rum Bay Bourbon Street, 20 N. Tejon St. (☎719-634-3522), a multi-level bar and club complex with 6 clubs included under one cover charge ($5). The main Rum Bay Club features Top 40, Masquerade is a disco club, Copy Cats is a karaoke bar, and Fat City is a lounge with live blues. Rum drinks $6-7. Th ladies night. 21+ after 8pm. Rum Bay open Tu-Sa 11am-2am. All other clubs open Th-Sa 6pm-2am.

Meadow Muffins, 2432 W. Colorado Ave. (☎719-633-0583). Wagons hanging from the ceiling were used *Gone With The Wind,* and the windmill-style fan was in *Casablanca.* Tu-Sa live music. W karaoke. Sa ladies night. 21+ after 8pm. Open daily 11am-2am.

ACCOMMODATIONS

Motels line **Nevada Ave.** near downtown, but the best options can be found farther west in and around Manitou Springs. Campgrounds lie in the mountains flanking Pikes Peak, about 30min. from Colorado Springs. Campgrounds clutter Rte. 67, 5-10 mi. north of **Woodland Park,** which lies 18 mi. northwest of the Springs on U.S. 24. Try **Colorado, Painted Rocks,** or **South Meadows,** near Manitou Park. (Generally open May-Sept. Sites $12-14.) Unless otherwise posted, you can camp on national or forest property for free if you are at least 500 ft. from a road or stream. The **Pikes Peak Ranger District Office,** 601 S. Weber St., has maps. (☎719-636-1602. Open M-F 8am-4:30pm.)

Beckers Lane Lodge, 115 Beckers Ln. (☎719-685-1866), at the south entrance of the Garden of the Gods. Clean rooms with microwaves and fridges. Outdoor pool and barbecue area. Rooms $40-50.

Ute Pass Motel, 1123 Manitou Ave. (☎719-685-5171). Guests can take advantage of the indoor hot tub or settle into the hammock on the upper deck, or barbecue and picnic on the lower deck next to Fountain Creek. Kitchens available. Laundry. Summer, singles $55; doubles $75-90. Winter $35/$50.

The Apache Court Motel, 3401 W. Pikes Peak Ave. (☎719-471-9440). Pink adobe rooms with microwaves and fridges. Common hot tub. Rooms $37-59.

Maverick Motel, 3620 W. Colorado Ave. (☎719-634-2852 or 800-214-0264). An explosion of pastels. Rooms come with fridge and microwave. Singles $40; 2-room units $45-55.

Eleven Mile State Recreation Area (☎719-748-3401 or 800-678-2267), off County Rd. 90 from U.S. 24. Farther afield, visitors may camp on Lake George reservoir. Pay showers and laundry. Reception M-F 7:30am-4:30pm. Sites $12, with electricity $16.

☛ APPROACHING DENVER

Take **Cimarron (U.S. 24)** west from downtown or east from Old Colorado City to **I-25 North.** For the first part of the drive, an unbroken chain of Rocky Mountains greets drivers on the left, while on the right are the plains. Proceed about 68 mi. north to Denver. For downtown and sights, take Exit 210A for **U.S. 40/Colfax Ave.**

DENVER

In 1858, the discovery of gold in the Rocky Mountains brought a rush of eager miners to northern Colorado. After an excruciating trek through the plains, the desperados set up camp before heading west into "them thar hills." Overnight, Denver became a flourishing frontier town. Recently named the number one sports town in America, Denver also boasts the nation's largest city park system, brews the most beer of any metropolitan area, and has the most high-school and college graduates per capita. However, the city's greatest characteristic is its atmosphere—a unique combination of urban sophistication and Western grit.

NATIONAL ROAD

VITAL STATS

Population: 550,000

Visitor Info: Denver Visitors Bureau, 918 16th St. (☎303-892-1505: www.denver.org), in the 16th St. Mall. Open June-Aug. M-F 9am-5pm, Sa 9am-1pm; Sept.-May M-F 9am-5pm.

Internet Access: Public Library, 10 W. 14th Ave. (☎303-865-1363). Open M-W 10am-9pm, Th-Sa 10am-5:30pm, Su 1-5pm.

Post Office: 951 20th St. (☎303-296-4692). Open M-F 7am-10:30pm, Sa-Su 8:30am-10:30pm. **Postal Code:** 80202.

▐ GETTING AROUND

Running north-south, **Broadway** slices Denver in half. About 2½ mi. east of Broadway, **Colorado Blvd.** is another north-south thoroughfare. Running east-west, **Colfax Ave. (U.S. 40),** is the main north-south dividing line. Both named and numbered streets run diagonally in the downtown area; east of Broadway and west of Downing Ave., only those above 20th Ave. run diagonally. In the rest of the city, numbered avenues run east-west, increasing as you head north. Named streets run north-south. Many of the avenues on the eastern side of the city become numbered streets downtown. Downtown (specifically the 16th St. Mall), is the social, culinary, and entertainment center.

Parking in Denver varies greatly from one area to the next; it can be expensive and difficult in LoDo (the neighborhood extending from Wynkoop St. to Larimer Sq., between Speer Blvd. and 20th St.), while there are generally a plethora of empty meters elsewhere in and out of downtown. At night, avoid the west end (Colfax Ave., Federal Blvd., S. Santa Fe Blvd.), the Capitol Hill area (on the east side of town beyond the Capitol) and 25th-34th St. on the west side of the Barrio.

◉ SIGHTS

Many of the best sights in Denver center on downtown, which makes touring on foot easy. One of the best tour deals around, the **Cultural Connection Trolley** visits over 20 of the city's main attractions. The easiest place to begin a tour is along the 16th St. Mall, near the Mall

Ride stops, but the tour can be joined at many attractions; look for the trolley sign. (☎303-289-2841. Buses depart June-Aug. daily every hr. 8:30am-4:30pm. $16, under 13 $8.)

COLORADO STATE CAPITOL. The Capitol Building is a sensible place to start a visit to the Mile High City—marked by a small engraving, the 15th step leading to the building's entrance sits one mile above sea level. (☎303-866-2604. Open M-F 7am-5:30pm. 30min. tours M-F 9am-3:30pm.)

DENVER ART MUSEUM. Near the Capitol stands the Denver Art Museum (DAM), a unique seven-story "vertical" museum. The DAM houses a world-class collection of Native American art and pre-Colombian artifacts. (100 W. 14th Ave. Pkwy. ☎720-865-5000; www.denverartmuseum.org. Open Su noon-5pm, Tu and Th-Sa 10am-5pm, W 10am-9pm. Daily tours of special exhibits; call for times. $6, students, seniors, and ages 13-18 $4.50.)

SIX FLAGS. Make a splash at the Island Kingdom water park at Six Flags Elitch Gardens, across the freeway from Mile High Stadium. The Boomerang, Mind Eraser, and the Flying Coaster keep thrill-seekers screaming. (At Elitch Cir. and Speer Blvd. ☎303-595-4386. Open June-Aug. daily 10am-10pm; spring and early fall Sa-Su, call for hours. $36, seniors and under 4 ft. $21.)

OCEAN JOURNEY. Denver's brand new aquarium guides visitors through two spectacular underwater exhibits: the **Colorado River Journey,** descending from the Continental Divide to the Sea of Cortez in Mexico, and the **Indonesian River Journey,** emptying from the volcanic Barisan Mountains in Sumatra into the South China Sea. The aquarium houses over 15,000 exotic marine creatures, including several species of sharks, sea otters, and the magnificent Napoleon wrasse. (700 Water St. ☎303-561-4450 or 888-561-4450; www.oceanjourney.org. Open daily June-Aug. 10am-6pm; Sept.-May 10am-5pm. $15, seniors and ages 13-17 $13, ages 4-12 $7.)

DENVER MUSEUM OF NATURE AND SCIENCE. This gigantic museum hosts a variety of exhibits, including the Hall of Life and the Prehistoric Journey room. Ride the skies in the museum's digital **Gates Planetarium**. (2001 Colorado Blvd., at Montview St. ☎800-925-2250; www.dmns.org. Open daily 9am-5pm. $9; students and seniors $6. IMAX and museum $13/$9. Planetarium and museum $13/$9.)

Denver

TO
70
RED ROCKS (15 mi),
& AIRPORT

TO BLACK AMERICAN
WEST MUSEUM (90yd)

E. 22nd Ave.

Downing St.

Clarkson St.

300 yards

300 meters

Court
Pl.

Tremont Pl.

24th St.

23rd St./Park Ave.

Benedict
Fountain
Park

Glenarm Pl.

California St.

Welton St.

22nd St.

21st St.

E. 20th Ave.

E. 19th St.

E. 18th Ave.

E. 17th Ave.

E. 16th Ave.

Pearl St.

Pennsylvania St.

Logan St.

Grant St.

Sherman St.

Lincoln St.

Broadway

Cleveland Pl.

Cheyenne

Court Pl.

Glenarm Pl.

Tremont Pl.

Welton St.

Ogden St.

Emerson St.

Clarkson St.

Washington St.

E. Colfax Ave.

Molly Brown
House

Corona St.

Ogden St.

Emerson St.

Clarkson St.

E. 14th Ave.

Colorado History Museum

TO (1mi)

NIGHTLIFE
The Church, 12
El Chapultepec, 5
Fado Irish Pub, 3
Foxhole Lounge, 4

State Capitol

i

RTD Civic
Center
Station

Civic
Center
Park

Bannock St.

ELLSWORTH AVE. (1.1mi)
(150yd), &
(300yd),

Brown
Palace
Hotel

Federal
Bldg.

Curtis St.

Champa St.

Stout St.

20th St.

19th St.

18th St.

17th St.

16th St.

Arapahoe St.

Lawrence St.

Larimer St.

Market St.

Blake St.

Wazee St.

Wynkoop St.

Wewatta St.

Delgany St.

Museum of
Western Art

Coors Field

TO 4 (300yd)

P

7

Union
Station

2

3

5

i

RTD Market St.
Bus Terminal

WRITER
SQUARE

LARIMER
SQUARE

P

P

6

P

16th St. Mall

Skyline Park

15th St.

14th St.

13th St.

Firefighter's
Museum

US Mint

Colfax Ave.

Delaware St.

Denver Performing
Arts Complex

Colorado
Convention
Center

Greek Amphitheater

Denver Art Museum

Byers/Evans House
Denver History Museum

12th St.

Speer Blvd.

Speer Blvd.

Klamath St.

Pepsi
Center

Cherry Creek

Speer Blvd.

Auraria Pkwy.

Student
Union

UNIVERSITY
OF COLORADO -
DENVER

Library &
Media Center

St. Elizabeth's

Metropolitan
State College

Community
College of
Denver

287

TO 10 (500yd)

9

Osage St.

Mariposa St.

Lipan St.

14th Ave.

Curtis St.

W. Colfax Ave.

13th St.

FOOD
Benny's Restaurant and
Cantina, 13
The Buckhorn Exchange, 10
Domo, 9

Mercury Cafe, 7
Wazee Lounge & Supper
Club, 6
Wynkoop Brewery, 2

ACCOMMODATIONS
Broadway Plaza Motel, 11
Budget Host Inn, 1
Hostel of the Rocky Mtns.
(HI-AYH), 8

1

8

10

NATIONAL ROAD

LG

0
300 yards
0
300 meters

COORS BREWERY. Located in nearby Golden, this is the world's largest one-site brewery. Free tours take visitors through the brewing process and provide free samples. *(Take I-70 West to Exit 264, head west on 32nd Ave. for 4½ mi., then turn left on East St. and follow the signs. ☎303-277-2337. 1½hr. tours every 30min. M-Sa 10am-4pm.)*

COLORADO HISTORY MUSEUM. Interesting exhibits document Colorado's multi-faceted history, including a series of intricate historical dioramas made by the WPA in the 1930s. *(1300 Broadway, at 13th St. ☎303-866-3682. Open M-Sa 10am-4:30pm, Su noon-4:30pm. $5, seniors and students $4.50, children $3.50.)*

BLACK AMERICAN WEST MUSEUM. Denver resident Paul W. Stewart had a lifelong desire to tell the public about a fact that was "not recorded in history books"—that one of every three cowboys was black. The small museum, mostly a collection of photos with brief explanations, details the role black Americans played in settling the west. There are also exhibits about Justina Ford, an early 20th-century physician to Denver's poor and minority residents. *(3091 California St. ☎303-292-2566. Open June-Aug. daily 10am-5pm; Sept.-May W-F 10am-2pm, Sa-Su 10am-5pm. $6, seniors $5.50, ages 5-12 $4.)*

MUSEO DE LAS AMERICAS. This museum exhibits work by Latin American artists, including photographers, painters, and fabric makers. *(861 Santa Fe Dr., between 8th and 9th St., south of downtown. ☎303-571-4401. Open Tu-Sa 10am-5pm. $4, seniors and students $3.)*

▲ OUTDOOR ACTIVITIES

Denver has more public parks per square mile than any other city, providing prime space for bicycling, walking, or lolling. **Cheesman Park,** at 8th Ave. and Humboldt St., offers picnic areas, manicured flower gardens, and a view of snow-capped peaks. **Confluence Park,** at Cherry Creek and the South Platte River, lures bikers and hikers with paved riverside paths. Free live music is the name of the game at **Confluence Concerts,** along the banks of the South Platte. (☎303-455-7192. July to early Aug. Th 6:30-8pm.) One of the best parks for sporting events, **Washington Park,** at Louisiana Ave. and Downing St., hosts impromptu volleyball and soccer games on summer weekends. Wide

paths for biking, jogging, and in-line skating encircle the park, and the two lakes in the middle are popular fishing spots. At **Roxborough State Park,** (☎303-973-3959) visitors can hike and ski among rock formations in the **Dakota Hogback** ridge. Take U.S. 85 South, turn right on Titan Rd., and follow it 3½ mi. (Open dawn-dusk.)

Forty miles west of Denver, the road to the top of **Mount Evans** (14,264 ft.) is the **highest paved road** in North America. Take I-70 W to Rte. 103 in Idaho Springs. (☎303-567-2901. Open late May to early Sept. $10.)

♫ ENTERTAINMENT

The **Denver Performing Arts Complex (DPAC),** at Speer Blvd. and Arapahoe St., is the largest arts complex in the nation. DPAC is home to the Denver Center for the Performing Arts, Colorado Symphony, Colorado Ballet, and Opera Colorado. (Call ☎303-893-4100 or 800-641-1222 for tickets M-Sa 10am-6pm.) The **Denver Center Theater Company** (☎303-893-4000) offers one free Saturday matinee per play. In the intimate **Geminal Stage Denver,** 2450 W. 44th Ave., every seat is a good one. (☎303-455-7108. Shows F-Su. Tickets $14-18.) The **Bluebird Theater,** 3317 E. Colfax Ave. (☎303-322-2308), is an old theater-turned-music venue.

Denver's baseball team, the **Colorado Rockies,** plays at **Coors Field,** at 20th and Blake St. (☎303-762-5437 or 800-388-7625. Tickets $4-41.) Football's **Denver Broncos** play at the **Mile High Stadium,** 2755 W. 17th Ave. (☎720-258-3333), which is used by soccer's **Colorado Rapids** (☎303-299-1599) during the spring and summer. The NBA's **Denver Nuggets** and the NHL's **Colorado Avalanche** share the state-of-the-art **Pepsi Center,** 1000 Chopper Cir. (☎303-405-1100).

❀ FESTIVALS

Every January, Denver hosts the nation's largest livestock show and one of the biggest rodeos, the **National Western Stock Show & Rodeo,** 4655 Humboldt St. Cowboys compete for prize money while over 10,000 head of cattle, horses, sheep, and rabbits compete for "Best of Breed." Between big events, all sorts of oddball fun take place, including western battle re-creations, monkey sheep herders, and rodeo clowns. (☎303-295-1660; www.nationalwestern.com. Tickets $10-20.)

The whole area vibrates during the **Denver March Pow-Wow** (☎303-934-8045; www.denver-marchpowwow.org), at the Denver Coliseum, when over 1000 Native Americans from all over North America dance in full costume to the beat of the drums. During the first full week of June, the **Capitol Hill People's Fair** (☎303-830-1651; www.peoplesfair.com), is one of the largest arts and crafts festivals in Colorado. Originally named to celebrate Denver's dual personalities as the Queen City of the Plains and the Monarch Metropolis of the Mountains, **The Festival of Mountain and Plain: A Taste of Colorado** (☎303-295-6330; www.atasteofcolorado.com) packs Civic Center Park on Labor Day weekend.

FOOD

Downtown Denver offers a full range of cuisines, from Russian to traditional Southwestern. Al fresco dining and people-watching are available along the **16th Street Mall**. Gourmet eateries are located southwest of the Mall on **Larimer St.** Sports bars and trendy restaurants occupy **LoDo**. Outside of downtown, **Colorado Blvd.** and **6th Ave.** also have their share of posh restaurants. **E. Colfax Ave.** offers a number of reasonably priced ethnic restaurants, including Greek and Ethiopian cuisine. You may wonder what sort of delicacies "Rocky Mountain oysters" are, especially given Denver's distance from the ocean. Fear not; these salty-sweet bison testicles, sold at the Buckhorn Exchange (see below), do not hail from the sea.

Mercury Cafe, 2199 California St. (☎303-294-9281), at 22nd St. Decorated with a new-age flair, the Merc specializes in home-baked wheat bread and reasonably priced soups ($2-3), salads ($6-9), enchiladas ($5.50-7), and vegetarian specials. Live bands provide music in the dining room, while the upstairs dance area hosts free swing and tango lessons Su and Th. Open Tu-F 5:30-11pm, Sa-Su 9am-3pm and 5:30-11pm. Dancing Su and Tu-Th until 1am, F-Sa until 2am. Cash only.

Domo, 1365 Osage St. (☎303-595-3666; www.domorestaurant.com). Take Colfax Ave. to Osage St. (east of I-25) and head south 1 block. One of the top Japanese restaurants in the nation. Filling tradi-

tional dishes ($15-23) are served in the outdoor Japanese garden or airy interior. For a rare treat, try the wanko sushi, a country-style sushi mixed with vegetables and served on large platters (3 courses $22.25.) Open Th-Sa 11am-2pm and 5-10pm.

Benny's Restaurant and Cantina, 301 E. 7th Ave. (☎303-894-0788). A local favorite for cheap, tasty Mexican food, including their trademark breakfast burritos ($4.25) and fish tacos ($7). Open M-F 8am-10pm, Sa-Su 9am-11pm.

Wazee Lounge & Supper Club, 1600 15th St. (☎303-623-9518), in LoDo. The black-and-white tile floor, Depression-era wood paneling, and a mahogany bar create a unique bohemian ambience at this laid-back diner. Wazee's award winning pizza ($6-8) and strombolis ($8) are popular favorites. Happy hour M-F 4-6pm. Open M-Sa 11am-2am, Su noon-midnight.

Wynkoop Brewery, 1634 18th St. (☎303-297-2700), at Wynkoop St., in LoDo. Colorado's first brewpub serves beer ($2) and homemade root beer, along with full lunch and dinner menus including "big mouth" burgers and "two-fisted" sandwiches ($7-8). 20 pool tables, dart lanes, and shuffleboard. An independent improv troupe performs downstairs Th-Sa (☎303-297-2111). Happy hour M-F 3-6pm. Free brewery tour Sa 1-5pm. Kitchen open M-Sa 11am-2am, Su 11am-midnight.

The Buckhorn Exchange, 1000 Osage St. (☎303-534-9505; www.buckhorn.com). Take Colfax Ave. to Osage St. and head south 3 blocks. Denver's oldest restaurant is famous for its hunting-themed walls, crowded with the heads of several hundred game animals—deer, buffalo, chipmunks, even a two-headed calf—as well as a large gun collection. Carnivores will delight in mammoth meat portions. Open for lunch M-F 11am-2pm; dinner M-Th 5:30-9pm, F-Sa 5-10pm, Su 5-9pm.

ACCOMMODATIONS

Inexpensive hotels line **E. Colfax Ave.,** as well as Broadway and Colorado Blvd.

Hostel of the Rocky Mountains (HI-AYH), 1530 Downing St. (☎303-861-7777), off E. Colfax Ave. Take 14th Ave. east of the Capitol and turn left on Downing St. The best value in Denver. Internet $1 per 10min. Breakfast included. Linen $2. Key deposit $5. Reception 7am-11:30pm. Dorms $19; rooms $40. The **B&B of the Rocky Mountains,** next door, shares the same management. Quieter than the hostel, spacious rooms have shared baths. Rooms $40-55.

Broadway Plaza Motel, 1111 Broadway (☎303-893-0303), south of the Capitol. Clean rooms near downtown. Free HBO. Singles $45-55; doubles $55-65.

Budget Host Inn, 2747 Wyandot St. (☎303-458-5454). Comfortable rooms conveniently located near Six Flags Elitch Gardens. $15 off Six Flags tickets. Singles from $46; doubles from $56.

Cherry Creek State Park, 4201 S. Parker Rd. (☎303-699-3860), in Aurora, an urban area situated around Cherry Creek Lake. Take I-25 to Exit 200, then head north for about 3 mi. on I-225 and take the Parker Rd. Exit. Pine trees provide limited shade. Boating, fishing, swimming, and horseback riding available. Arrive early. Open May-Dec. Sites $12, with electricity $18.

◢ NIGHTLIFE

Downtown Denver, in and around the 16th St. Mall, is an attraction in itself. A copy of the weekly *Westword* gives the lowdown on LoDo, where much of the action begins after dark.

◣ El Chapultepec, 1962 Market St. (☎303-295-9126), at 20th St. A be-boppin' jazz holdover from the Beat era of the 50s. Live music nightly from 9pm. No cover. Open daily 8am-2am. Cash only.

The Church, 1160 Lincoln St. (☎303-832-3528). In a remodeled chapel complete with stained-glass windows and an elevated altar area, the Church offers 4 full bars, a cigar lounge, and a weekend sushi bar. Th 18+, F-Su 21+. Cover $5-15 after 10pm. Open Su and Th 9pm-2am, F-Sa 8pm-2am.

Fado Irish Pub, 1735 19th St. (☎303-297-0066). Built in Ireland and brought to Denver piece by piece, Fado's is as authentic a pub as you'll find. Open M-F 11:30am-2am, Sa-Su 10am-2am.

Foxhole Lounge, 2936 Fox St. (☎303-298-7378). A popular gay club, this is the place to be on Su nights, so get there early or expect to wait. Open Th-F 8pm-2am, Sa-Su 2pm-2am.

◤ LEAVING DENVER
Take **I-25 North** to Exit 217 for **U.S. 36 West,** the **Denver-Boulder Turnpike.**

BOULDER

The 1960s have been slow to fade in Boulder. A liberal haven in an otherwise conservative region, the city brims with fashionable coffee shops, teahouses, and juice bars. Boulder is home to both the central branch of the University of Colorado (CU) and Naropa University, the only accredited Buddhist university in the US. Seek spiritual enlightenment through meditation workshops at Naropa, or pursue a physical awakening through Boulder's incredible outdoor activities, including biking, hiking, and rafting along Boulder Creek.

⌐VITAL STATS

Population: 95,000

Visitor Info: Boulder Chamber of Commerce and Visitors Service, 2440 Pearl St. (☎303-442-1044; www.boulderchamber.com.), at Folsom. Open M-Th 8:30am-5pm, F 8:30am-4pm.

Internet Access: University of Colorado Information (☎303-492-6161), in the University Memorial Center (UMC). Open summer M-F 7am-10pm, Sa 9am-11pm, Su noon-10pm; term-time M-F 7am-11pm, Sa 9am-midnight, Su noon-11pm.

Post Office: 1905 15th St., at Walnut St. (☎303-938-3704). Open M-F 7:30am-5:30pm, Sa 10am-2pm. **Postal Code:** 80302.

◢ GETTING AROUND

Boulder is a small, manageable city. The most developed area lies between **Broadway (Rte. 7/Rte. 93)** and **28th St. (Rte. 36),** two busy north-south streets. Broadway, 28th St., Arapahoe Ave. and Baseline Rd. border the **University of Colorado (CU)** campus. The area around the school is known as **the Hill.** The pedestrian-only **Pearl Street Mall,** between 9th and 15th St., is lined with cafes, restaurants, and posh shops. Most streets in the commercial areas of Boulder have **parking** meters. On weekends, park for free in city lots (meters are free only on Su). Be alert for bicyclists. Avoid meandering around the Hill alone after dark.

◢ ◣ SIGHTS & OUTDOORS

The **◣Dushanbe Teahouse,** 1770 13th St., was built by artists in Tajikistan, and then was piece-mailed from Boulder's sister city of Dushanbe. The building is leased to a private restauranteur, who lays out a scrumptious spread from cultures spanning the globe. (☎303-442-4993. Tea $2-4. Lunch $7-9. Dinner $9-12. Open for lunch M-F 8am-3pm; tea time 3-5pm; dinner Su-Th 5-9pm, F-Sa 5-10pm.) The intimate **Leanin' Tree Museum,** 6055 Longbow

Dr., presents an acclaimed collection of over 200 paintings and 80 bronze sculptures. (☎303-530-1442, ext. 299; www.leanintreemuseum.com. Open M-F 8am-4:30pm, Sa-Su 10am-4pm. Free.) Minutes away, **The Celestial Seasonings Tea Company,** 4600 Sleepytime Dr., lures visitors with tea samples and tours of the factory, including the Peppermint Room. (☎303-581-1202. Open M-Sa 9am-4pm, Su 11am-4pm. Tours every hr. Free.)

Due to its proximity to the mountains, Boulder's supports many outdoor activities. Starting at **Scott Carpenter Park,** hiking and biking trails follow Boulder Creek to the foot of the mountains. **Chautauqua Park** has many trails varying in length and difficulty that climb up and around the Flatirons. From the auditorium, the **Enchanted Mesa/McClintock Trail** (2 mi.) is an easy loop through meadows and ponderosa pine forests. A more challenging hike, **Greg Canyon Trail** starts at the Baird Park parking lot and rises through the pines above Saddle Rock, winding back down the mountain past Amphitheater Rocks. Before heading into the wilderness, grab a map at the entrance to Chautauqua Park. Beware mountain lions.

▓ FOOD

The streets on **the Hill,** which surround CU, as well as those along the Pearl St. Mall, burst with good eateries, natural food markets, and colorful bars. Boulder nearly has more options for vegetarians than meat-eaters. Twice a week from April through October, Boulder shuts down 13th St. between Canyon and Arapahoe for a **Farmers Market.** (Open Apr.-Oct. W 5-8pm, Sa 8am-2pm.) A standout among sandwich shops, ▩**Half Fast Subs,** 1215 13th St., makes over 90 oven-baked subs. Cheesesteak, meat specialty, stuffed, and vegetarian subs galore ride at ridiculously inexpensive prices ($3.50-5). All 7 in. subs are $3.75 during happy hour. (☎303-449-0404. Happy hour M-F 5-7pm. Open Su-W 11am-10pm, Th-Sa 11am-1:30am.) Fill up on tasty noodle and rice bowls, salads, and sushi at **Moshi Moshi Bowl,** 1628 Pearl St., all for under $5. (☎303-565-9787. Open M-Th 11am-8pm, F 11am-9pm, Sa noon-8pm.) **Cafe Prasad,** 1904 Pearl St., serves a full menu of vegan and organic sandwiches and baked goods, along with organic juice and smoothies. (☎303-447-2667. Live music F 7-8:30pm. Open daily 11am-8pm.)

♫ ENTERTAINMENT

An exciting street scene pounds through both the Mall and the Hill; the university's kiosks have the lowdown on happenings. From June to August, find live music and street performances on Pearl St. Mall. (Tu and Th-F noon-1:30pm.) From late June to early Aug., the **Colorado Shakespeare Festival** draws over 50,000 people, making it the third-largest festival of its kind. (☎303-492-0554; www.coloradoshakes.org. Tickets $10-50. $5 student and senior discount.) The **Colorado Music Festival** performs July through August. (☎303-449-2413; www.coloradomusicfest.org. Lawn seats $5.) The local indie music scene is on display at the popular **Fox Theater and Cafe,** 1135 13th St. (☎303-447-0095; www.foxtheater.com).

▐ ACCOMMODATIONS

With a great location right on the Hill next to the CU campus, **Boulder International Hostel,** 1107 12th St., at College Ave., is the best deal in town. Youthful travelers fill the spacious downstairs lobby to watch cable TV and surf the Internet. (☎303-442-0522. Laundry. Internet $2 per 30min. Linen $5. Key deposit $10. 3-day max. stay in dorms during the summer. Reception 8am-11pm. Lockout 10am-5pm. Dorms $17; singles July-Sept. $49 first night, $39 each additional night. Reduced rates in winter.) Located 2 mi. west of Boulder off Canyon Blvd./Hwy. 119, **Boulder Mountain Lodge,** 91 Four Mile Canyon Dr., is in the mountains, yet just 5min. from downtown. Guests are treated to clean rooms at great rates, as well as a hot tub by the stream. (☎303-444-0882 or 800-458-0882. Summer singles $68; doubles $88. Winter $53/$68.)

Chautauqua Association, off Baseline Rd. at the foot of the Flatirons, has lodge rooms as well as private cottages. (Turn at the Chautauqua Park sign and take Kinnikinic to Morning Glory Dr. ☎303-442-3282, ext. 11. Reception June to early Sept. M-F 8:30am-7pm, Sa-Su 9am-5pm; Sept.-May M-F 8:30am-5pm, Sa-Su 9am-3pm. Reserve months in advance. In summer rooms $57-102; 1-bedroom suites $84-114; 2-bedroom cottages $119-139; 3-bedroom cottages $144-159. Small additional charge for stay fewer than 4 nights.)

Camping info for **Arapahoe/Roosevelt National Forest** is available from the **Boulder Ranger District,** 2140 Yarmouth Ave., just off of Rte. 36 to the north of town. (☎303-541-2500, reservations 877-444-6777. Open mid-May to early Sept. M-Th 8am-4:30pm, F 8am-5:30pm, Sa 9am-3pm; Sept. to mid-May M-F 8am-5pm. Most sites have water, none have electric hookups. Open mid-May to Oct. Sites $13). **Kelly Dahl**, 17 mi. west on Hwy. 119, is the closest campground to Boulder. Their 46 sites lie among pine trees and picnic tables with open views of the Continental Divide. For a more primitive, quieter camping experience, **Rainbow Lakes** lies 6½ mi. north of Nederland off Hwy. 72; turn at the Mountain Research Station (CR 116) and follow the dirt road for 5 mi. (No water. Sites $7.)

NIGHTLIFE

The city overflows with nightlife hot spots, each with its own unique spin. For bluegrass, funk, and the best brews in Boulder (try the "kind crippler"), head to ◪**Mountain Sun Pub and Brewery**, 1535 Pearl St. (☎303-546-0886. Acoustic performances Su 10pm-1am. $2 pints daily 4-6pm and 10pm-1am. Open M-Sa 11:30am-1am, Su noon-1am.) A Boulder classic, **The Sink**, 1165 13th St., still awaits the return of its one-time janitor, Robert Redford, who quit his job and headed to California in the late 1950s. Students fill the place for late-night drinking and great pizzas amid wild graffiti and low ceilings. (☎303-444-7465. Burgers $6-8. Open M-Sa 11am-2am, Su noon-2am; food served until 10pm.) **The West End Tavern**, 926 Pearl St., has a rooftop bar with a downtown. (☎303-444-3535. Draft beers $3-4. Open M-Sa 11am-11pm, Su 11:30am-11pm. Bar open until 1:30am.) **The Library Pub**, 1718 Broadway, boasts the largest outdoor patio in Boulder. Punk, hard rock, and reggae fans flood in for live music Thursday through Saturday. (☎303-443-2330. Happy hour 4-6pm and 9-11pm. Open daily noon-2am.)

LEAVING BOULDER
Take **28th St.** north from Boulder to **U.S. 36 West.** Allow 1-1¼hr. from Boulder to **Estes Park,** and another 30min. to get into **Rocky Mountain National Park** itself. Fill up in Boulder, where gas is much cheaper than in Estes Park. Unfortunately, gas gets even more expensive beyond the park—the next gas spot with decent prices is Kremmling.

ESTES PARK

This town is called Estes Park because "park" is mountain lingo for "valley." The **Stanley Hotel**, 333 Wonderview Ave., found itself in

The route through Rocky Mountain National Park from Estes Park to Grand Lake is closed from mid-Oct. to June. If you are traveling during this time, you will need to head back out to Estes Park and take Rte. 7 to Rte. 72 to Rte. 119 down to I-70.

the spotlight as the "Overlook Hotel" in the film adaptation of Stephen King's novel *The Shining*, and in several movies, including "Dumb and Dumber." (☎970-586-3371 or 800-976-1377; www.stanleyhotel.com. Tours daily 11am and 2pm. $5, children $2. Rooms $150-180. Parking $3.) The **Estes Park Area Historical Museum**, 200 4th St., offers a detailed account of the town's history. (☎970-586-6256. Open May-Oct. M-Sa 10am-5pm, Su 1-5pm; Nov.-Apr. Su 1-5pm, F-Sa 10am-5pm. $2.50, children $1.)

Locals flock to **The Notchtop Bakery & Cafe**, 459 E. Wonderview, for "natural foods and brews." Breads, pastries, and pies are baked fresh every morning. (In the upper Stanley Village Shopping Plaza, east of downtown off Rte. 34. ☎970-586-0272. Soups $4. Sandwiches and wraps $6-7. Open daily 7am-5pm.) In the heart of downtown, **Local's Grill**, 153 E. Elkhorn Ave., is a self-proclaimed "world-famous gathering place." Customers crowd the front patio for gourmet sandwiches ($5-8) and pizza. (☎970-586-6900. Open M-Th 11am-9pm, F-Su 11am-10pm.) The intimate seating area at **Sweet Basilico Cafe**, 401 E. Elkhorn Ave., overflows with patrons seeking focaccia bread sandwiches ($6) and freshly made pastas ($7-10) of every kind. (☎970-586-3899. Open June-Sept. M-F 11am-10pm, Sa-Su 11:30am-10pm; Oct.-May Su and Tu-Sa 11am-2:30pm and 4:30-9pm.) The tidy, dorm-style rooms at **The Colorado Mountain School**, 341 Moraine Ave., are open to travelers unless booked by mountain-climbing students. (☎970-586-5758. Reception June-Sept. daily 8am-5pm; winter hours vary. Dorms $25 per person.) **Saddle & Surrey Motel**, 1341 S. Saint Vrain (Rte. 7), offers clean and comfy rooms. (☎800-204-6226. Heated outdoor pool and spa. Microwave, fridge, and cable TV. Singles $45-70; doubles $50-99.)

APPROACHING THE PARK
From Estes Park, take **U.S. 34 West** into the park.

ROCKY MOUNTAIN NATIONAL PARK

Of all the US national parks, Rocky Mountain National Park is closest to heaven, with over 60 peaks exceeding 12,000 ft. A third of the park lies above the treeline, and Longs Peak tops off at 14,255 ft. Here among the clouds, the alpine tundra ecosystem supports bighorn sheep, dwarf wildflowers, and arctic shrubs interspersed among granite boulders and crystal lakes.

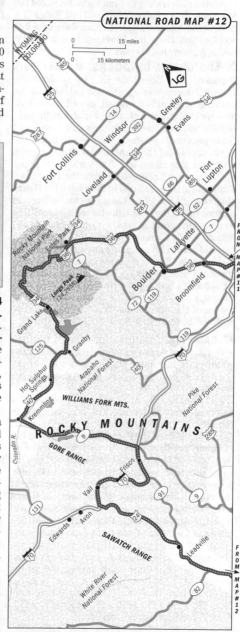

VITAL STATS

Area: 266,000 acres

Visitor Info: Park Headquarters and Visitors Center (☎ 970-586-1206), 2½ mi. west of Estes Park on Rte. 36, at the Beaver Meadows entrance to the park. Open daily mid-June to late Aug. 8am-9pm; Sept. to mid-June 8am-5pm.

Gateway Towns: Estes Park (p. 386), Grand Lake (p. 388).

Fees: Weekly pass $15 per car, $5 per motorbike. Backcountry camping permit $10 for 3 days.

GETTING AROUND. U.S. 36 and **U.S. 34** both lead into Rocky Mountain National Park. **U.S. 36** is the main route into the park; it's about 2 mi. shorter than U.S. 34 and passes the **Beaver Meadows Visitors Center,** the campgrounds at Moraine Park and Glacier Basin, and the trailheads at Sprague Lake and Bear Lake. **U.S. 34,** less crowded, passes the Aspenglen campground, provides access to Old Fall River Rd., and goes by the smaller **Fall River Visitors Center.**

The star of the park is **Trail Ridge Rd. (U.S. 34),** a 48 mi. stretch that rises 12,183 ft. above sea level into frigid tundra. The round-trip drive takes roughly 3hr. by car. Beware of slow-moving tour buses and people stopping to ogle wildlife. The road is sometimes closed or inaccessible—especially from October to May—for weather. Heading west, steal a view of the park from the boardwalk along the highway at **Many Parks Curve. Rainbow Curve** and the **Forest Canyon Overlook** offer impressive views of the vast tree-carpeted landscape. The 30min. **Tundra Communities Trail** provides a once-in-a-lifetime-look at the fragile alpine tundra. Signposts along the paved trail explain local geology and wildlife. The **Lava Cliffs** attract crowds, but are worth the hassle. After peaking at **Gore Range,** a mighty 12,183 ft. above sea level, Trail Ridge Rd. runs north to the **Alpine Visitors Center.**

A wilder alternative to Trail Ridge Rd. is **Old Fall River Rd.** The road intersects Trail Ridge Rd. behind the Alpine Visitors Center. **Bear Lake Rd.,** south of Trail Ridge Rd., leads to the most popular hiking trails within the park.

SIGHTS & OUTDOORS. Moraine Park Museum, off of Bear Lake Rd., 1½ mi. from the Beaver Meadows entrance, has exhibits on the park's geology and ecosystem, as well as comfortable rocking chairs with a view of the mountains. (☎970-586-1206. Open in summer daily 9am-5pm.) Numerous trailheads lie in the western half of the park, including the **Continental Divide** and its accompanying hiking trail. The park's most popular trails are all accessible from the Bear Lake Trailhead at the south end of Bear Lake Rd. **Flattop Mountain** (4½ mi., 3hr.), the most challenging and picturesque of the Bear Lake hikes, climbs 2800 ft. to a vantage point along the Continental Divide. **Nymph** (½ mi., 15min.), **Dream** (1 mi., 30min.), and **Emerald Lakes** (1¾ mi., 1hr.) are a series of three glacial pools offering inspiring glimpses of the surrounding peaks. Forking left from the trail, **Lake Haiyaha** (2¼ mi., 1¼hr.) includes switchbacks through dense sub-alpine forests and superb views of the mountains. A scramble over the rocks at the end grants a view of Lake Haiyaha.

CAMPING. Visitors can camp a total of seven days anywhere within the park. In the backcountry, the maximum stay increases to 14 days during the winter. All five **national park campgrounds** are $18 in the summer, while winter sites are $12 unless otherwise noted. A backcountry camping permit (3-day pass $10, 7-day pass $15) is required in summer. On eastern slopes, permits are available from the **Backcountry Permits and Trip Planning Building,** near the park headquarters. (☎970-586-1242. Open daily mid-May to late Oct. 7am-7pm; Nov. to mid-May 8am-5pm.) The only national park campground on the western side of the park is **Timber Creek,** 10 mi. north of Grand Lake. Campsites can also be found in the surrounding **Arapaho National Forest** (☎970-887-4100). **Stillwater Campground,** west of Grand Lake on the shores of Lake Granby, has 127 tranquil sites. (Open year-round. Sites $16, with water $19, with full hookup $21.) **Green Ridge Campground,** on the south end of Shadow Mountain Lake, is also a good bet with 78 sites. (Open mid-May to mid-Nov. Sites $13.) For both sites, reserve at ☎877-444-6777 or www.reserveusa.com.

APPROACHING GRAND LAKE
Turn off **U.S. 34** at the sign for Grand Lake and stay right at the fork in the road.

GRAND LAKE

Grand Lake, the "snowmobile capital of Colorado," offers spectacular cross-country routes. It is also the jumping-off point for several hiking trails. **Lake Verna** (7 mi., 3½hr.), starts at the East Inlet Trailhead at the far east end of Grand Lake. This moderate hike gains a total of 1800 ft. in elevation as it passes **Adams Falls** and **Lone Pine Lake** and rewards hikers with open views of **Mount Craig** before re-entering the forest. The culmination of the hike is an overlook of the lake. (To get to the North Inlet and East Inlet Trailheads, turn off U.S. 34 at the sign for Grand Lake and stay left at the fork in the road for W. Portal Rd.) The North Inlet Trailhead is accessible off a dirt road to the left. The East Inlet Trailhead lies at the end of the road; proceed straight onto CR 339 and the trailhead is to the left. **Deer Mountain** (6 mi. round-trip, 3hr.), leaving from Deer Mountain Trailhead, is a moderate hike with a 1000 ft. rise. The light foliage affords views of the Rockies all the way up.

At the far end of town, **Pancho and Lefty's,** 1120 Grand Ave., has an outdoor patio overlooking Grand Lake and a bar large enough to fit most of its residents. Try the *rellenos fritos* ($11) and wash it all down with a margarita. (☎970-627-8773. Live music W 8pm, Sa 9pm. Open daily June-Sept. 11am-11pm; Sept.-June 11am-8pm.) A Grand Lake tradition, the **Chuck Hole Cafe,** 1119 Grand Ave., has served its famous reuben sandwiches ($6-8) for over 65 years. (☎970-627-3509. Open daily 7am-2pm.) **Mountain Inn,** 612 Grand Ave., serves mouthwatering chicken fried steak. (☎970-627-3385. Live music in summer Sa 12:30-4pm. Open M-F 5-10pm, Sa-Su 11:30am-2:30pm and 5-10pm.) The hand-built pine **Shadowcliff Hostel (HI-AYH),** 405 Summerland Park Rd., perches on a cliff. (☎970-627-9220. Kitchen, showers, wood burning stove. Internet $3 per day. Linen $2. 6-day min. stay for cabins. Make cabin reservations as far as 1 year in advance. Open June-Sept. Dorms $14, nonmembers $18. Rooms with shared bath $45; $10 per additional person. 6- to 8-person cabins $100.) Cozy rooms and the only heated indoor pool in Grand Lake await at **Sunset Motel,** 505 Grand Ave., which boasts a yellow front and baby-blue trim. (☎970-627-3318.

Summer singles $60; doubles $90. Winter $40/ $60.) **Bluebird Motel,** 30 River Dr., on Rte. 34, 2 mi. west of town, overlooks Shadow Mountain Lake and the Continental Divide. Many rooms have fridge; others have kitchenettes. (☎970-627-9314. Singles $30-55; doubles $50-75.)

LEAVING GRAND LAKE
Continue west on **U.S. 34** to **U.S. 40 West.**

HOT SULPHUR SPRINGS RESORT AND SPA
25 mi. from Grand Lake.

This tranquil spot, where signs exhort you to keep quiet, is fed by natural mineral hot springs, ranging from 98° to 112°. Visitors can walk up and down small sets of stairs between 18 pools. Food facilities are limited, so pack a lunch. The motel-style rooms are small, but clean, comfortable, and quiet, with log-style wooden furniture. (☎970-725-3306. Open daily 8am-10pm. Hot springs $15.50. Private bath $12 per hr. Rooms $98-108.)

KREMMLING. Forty-two miles from Grand Lake, Kremmling offers few cultural attractions or restaurants; the area serves primarily as a regional base for outdoor sports. **Mad Adventures,** on U.S. 40 east of town, will outfit you for class I-III rafting on the Colorado River. (☎970-726-5290; www.madadventures.com. Half-day trips $40, ages 4-11 $35; full day $59/$49.) Bike rentals are available at **Motion Sports,** 208 Eagle Ave. (☎970-724-9067. Bikes $15 per day. Open Su and Tu-Sa; hours vary.) The **Moose Cafe,** 115 W. Park Ave., serves all-day breakfast and lunch. (☎970-724-9987. Breakfast $3.50-8.50. Hot sandwiches $6-7.50. Open daily 6am-2pm.) **Bob's Western Motel,** 110 W. Park Ave., has a variety of basic rooms. (☎970-724-3266. Singles $39; doubles $57.)

LEAVING KREMMLING
Take **Rte. 9 South** toward I-70.

DETOUR: TROUGH ROAD
2 mi. south of town, turn right onto Trough Rd. Trough Rd., while unpaved, is an extraordinarily smooth, all-vehicle-capable road. It ascends gradually for 8½ mi. to a turn-off at the aptly named **⚑Inspiration Point,** providing a stupendous view of the impossibly steep Gore Canyon and the headwaters of the Colorado River, which slice through the canyon far below. This is one of the best driving views of the trip.

DETOUR: LOWER CATARACT LAKE TRAIL AND WHITE RIVER NATIONAL FOREST
Take Rte. 9 for 12½ mi. south of U.S. 40, and turn right onto Heeney Rd. 30. After 5 mi., turn right on Cataract Creek Rd. The campground is 2 mi. along the road, and the trailhead is ¾ mi. farther. This route is not recommended in wintertime.

This road winds around the far side of a lake for 18 mi. before meeting back up with Rte. 9. The lake is magnificent, surrounded by sloping hills on all sides and the higher rocky peaks off in the distance to the south. There are seven mostly sunny open-area lakeside campgrounds operated by the National Forest Service (168 slots total; sites $9), and several are accessible from Rte. 9 and Heeney Rd. 30. The highlight of the area is the wonderful **Lower Cataract Loop Trail** and neighboring **Cataract Creek Campsite** (entrance fee $5). There are four primitive drive-in camping sites ($13) in a quiet spot, filled with tall trees and mountain views. About as isolated as it gets for drive-in camping, this is a perfect spot sleep under the stars.

APPROACHING FRISCO
Take **Rte. 9 South** until it joins with **I-70 West,** and follow I-70 for 3 mi. to Exit 203 for **Rte. 9 South/Frisco.**

FRISCO

The mountains stare from all sides at the droves of tourists who come to Frisco to bike the paved and mountain trails in the area or to ski at nearby Breckenridge. Downtown, expensive restaurants and sport shops cater to seasonal visitors.

VITAL STATS

Population: 2000

Visitor Info: Summit County Visitors Center, 916 Summit Blvd. (☎800-530-3099; www.summitchamber.org). Open daily 9am-5pm.

Internet Access: Frisco-Summit County Library, 0037 County Rd. 1005 (☎970-779-5555). Take Summit Blvd. south of Main St. Open M-Th 9am-9pm, F-Sa 9am-5pm, Su 1-5pm.

Post Office: 25 W. Main St. (☎800-275-8777), at Madison. Open M-F 8:30am-5pm, Sa 9am-12:30pm. **Postal Code:** 80443.

GETTING AROUND. Frisco is extremely easy to navigate. **I-70** borders the area to the northwest. **Summit Blvd. (Rte. 9),** home to motels,

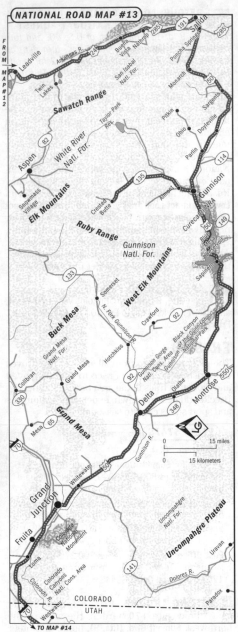

NATIONAL ROAD MAP #13

Wal-Mart, Safeway, and other large stores, runs north-south along the eastern edge of town from I-70 to Main St. before turning to head southeast. **Main St.,** the town's main commercial street, houses restaurants, smaller lodging establishments, and local stores. It runs east-west from I-70 on the west to Summit Blvd. on the east. **Parking** in town is free, but there is a 2hr. limit for cars parked on Main St.; if you plan to hike or bike, use the free lots at the designated trailheads.

SIGHTS & OUTDOORS. The **Frisco Historic Park,** 120 Main St. contains the Frisco Schoolhouse Museum and wood and stone buildings that tell the town's story. (☎970-668-3428. Open in summer Su and Tu-Sa 11am-4pm; winter Tu-Sa 11am-4pm. Free.) In the summer, Frisco, Breckenridge, and surrounding Summit County are a biking heaven, with some 70 mi. of paved trails and many more of mountain paths. A popular moderate route circles **Dillon Reservoir** (18 mi.). Miles of hiking trails crisscross the area and go up into the mountains. A fun, moderately challenging climb, the hike up 1350 ft. **Mount Royal** (4 mi. round-trip; 2-3hr.) offers great views of Lake Dillon and Frisco below. (To get to the trailhead, take Main St. west, and just before the entrance to I-70, turn left into the parking lot for the Tenmile Canyon Trailhead. Park and follow the bike path ½ mi. southeast along the mountain's base.) Bike rentals are available at **Wilderness Sports,** 400 Main St. (☎970-668-8804. Bikes $18-38 per day; helmet included. Open in summer M-F 8:30am-6pm, Sa-Su 8am-6pm.) Another good place is **All Seasons Sports,** 720 Granite St. at Summit Blvd., one block south of Main St. (☎970-668-5599. Bikes $15-35 per day. Open in summer daily 8:30am-6:30pm.)

SKIING. Summit County offers some of Colorado's best skiing; **Copper Mountain, Breckenridge,** and **Keystone** resorts all lie within short driving distance of Frisco. Breckenridge (☎970-453-5000 or 800-789-7669; www.breckenridge.com) is 9 mi. south of Frisco on Rte 9. One of the most popular ski resorts in the country, Breckenridge has a 3400 ft. vertical drop, 139 trails, the best halfpipe in North America, and 2043 acres of skiable terrain made accessible by 25 lifts. In the summer, most mountains offer hiking, biking, and various other outdoor activities; consult the **Breckenridge Activities Center,** 137 S. Main St., at Washington St. details. (☎970-453-5579 or 877-864-0868. Open daily 9am-5pm.)

✄ FOOD. Busy **Lazaroni's Pizzeria,** 106 3rd Ave., serves up the usual Italian flavors. (☎970-668-3773. Subs $7-13. Pizza $7.50-19. Open daily 11:30am-9pm.) Across from Wal-Mart, **Claim Jumper,** 805 N. Summit Blvd., is an old-fashioned family restaurant with a homey atmosphere and good variety. (☎970-668-3617. Extensive breakfast menu $3-7. Sandwiches $6-9. Entrees $10-15. Open M-Th 6am-9pm and Su F-Sa 6am-10pm.)

⌂⌂ ACCOMMODATIONS & CAMPING. The friendly owners of **█Just Bunks,** 208 Teller St., welcome visitors to plush bunks in the furnished basement. Comfortable nooks abound in their living room, shared full kitchen, and tranquil garden area. (At 2nd St., 2 blocks south of Main St. ☎970-668-4737. 1 co-ed room with 4 bunks. Reserve in advance. Dorms $25-30.) **New Summit Inn,** on Dillon Dam Rd., has narrow rooms with refrigerators and mountain views. (Take Summit Blvd. one block south from I-70. ☎970-668-3220. Hot tub. Rooms winter $64-100; summer $44-59.) The **Snowshoe Motel,** 521 Main St., has modern rooms in the center of Frisco. (☎970-668-3444. Hot tub and sauna. Rooms winter $75-125; summer $42-75.)

South of Frisco, in Breckenridge, you can find reasonably priced, smoke-free accommodations at the **█Fireside Inn (HI-AYH),** 114 N. French St., two blocks east of Main St., at the corner of Wellington Rd. The indoor hot tub is great for après-ski. (☎970-453-6456; www.firesideinn.com. Breakfast $3-6. Reception daily 8am-9:30pm. Summer dorms $25; private rooms $65. Winter dorms $38/$180.) A number of campgrounds around Dillon Reservoir are operated by the U.S. Forest Service. **Heaton Bay Campground,** on Dillon Dam Rd., has 72 shady spots northwest of the reservoir with water and outhouse style toilets. "D" loop is the quietest. (☎877-444-6777; www.reserveusa.com. 10-day max. stay. Advance reservations only. Sites $13.) **Prospector Campground** has 107 sites on the east side of the reservoir. The "E" loop in Prospector is the quietest. (Take Rte. 9 south out of Frisco to Swan Mountain Rd. and turn left. ☎877-444-6777; www.reserveusa.com. Shady, with water and outhouse style toilets. 10-day max. stay. Advance reservations only. Sites $12.)

⚐ LEAVING FRISCO

Take **Main St.** to **I-70 West.** Take Exit 176 for Vail.

VAIL

The largest one-mountain ski resort in all of North America, Vail has ritzy hotels, swank saloons, and sexy boutiques, but it's the mountain that wows skiers with its prime snow and back bowls. According to local folklore, the Ute Indians treasured the area's rich supply of game, but became so upset with the white settlers that they set fire to the forest, creating the resort's open terrain.

(VITAL STATS)

Population: 4500

Visitor Info: Vail Visitors Center, S. Frontage Rd. (☎800-525-3875), in Vail Village. Open daily summer 8am-7pm; winter 8am-6pm.

Internet Access: Vail Public Library, 292 W. Meadow Dr. (☎970-479-2184). Open M-Th 10am-8pm, F 11am-6pm, Sa-Su 11am-6pm.

Post Office: 1300 N. Frontage Rd. West. (☎970-476-5217). Open M-F 8:30am-5pm, Sa 8:30am-noon. **Postal Code:** 81657.

█ GETTING AROUND. Greater Vail consists of **East Vail, Vail Village, Lionshead Village, Cascade Village,** and **West Vail.** Vail Village and Lionshead Village, which are the main centers of action, are pedestrian-only; visitors must **park** in garages off S. Frontage Rd., which are free in summer.

◉ SIGHTS. The **Ski Hall of Fame** is housed in the **Colorado Ski Museum,** on the third level of the Vail Transportation Center. It captures the history of the sport and includes a fascinating section on the 10th Mountain Division and its training around Vail for the rigors of fighting in the mountains of Italy during WWII. (☎970-476-1876. Open June-Sept. and Nov.-Apr. Su and Tu-Sa 10am-5pm. $1, under 12 free.) In the summer, the **Gerald R. Ford Amphitheater,** at the east edge of Vail Village, presents outdoor concerts, dance festivals, and theater productions. (☎970-476-2918. Box office open M-Sa noon-6pm. Lawn seats $15-40; Tu free.) Next door in the lovely **Betty Ford Alpine Gardens,** view the peaceful meditation and rock gardens. (☎970-476-0103. Open May-Sept dawn-dusk. Tours M, Th, Sa 10:30am. Free.) The **Vilar Center for the Arts,** in Beaver Creek, hosts shows from Shakespeare to Broadway. (☎970-845-8497 or 888-920-2787. Box office open M-Sa 11am-5pm.)

⚠️🔥 SKIING & OUTDOOR ACTIVITIES. Not even the glamorous people and glitzy hotels of the village can overshadow Vail's main attraction—its **skiing**. Though the mountain has a reputation for being pricier than some of its more down-to-earth neighbors, affordable lift tickets are still available, and the mountain's 193 trails, 34 lifts, 5,289 skiable acres, and seven legendary back bowls are certainly worth it. (☎ 800-892-8062; www.vail.com.) Before slaloming, visit **Ski Base,** 610 W. Lionshead Cir., for equipment. (☎ 970-476-5799. Skis, poles, and boots from $14 per day. Snowboard and boots from $20 per day. Open in winter daily 8am-7pm.) The store becomes **Wheel Base Bike Shop** in the summer. (Bikes $15 per day; mountain bikes from $27 per day. Open in summer daily 9am-6pm.) The **Eagle Bahn Gondola** in Lionshead and the **Vista Bahn Chairlift,** part of Vail Resort, whisk hikers and bikers to the top of the mountains. (☎ 970-476-9090. Open daily 8:30am-4:30pm. Eagle Bahn open summer Su-W 10am-4pm, Th-Sa 10am-9pm; winter F-Su 10am-4pm. Day pass $17, ages 65-69 and 5-12 $10, seniors $5. Bike haul $29. Vista Bahn open mid-July to early Sept. F-Su 10am-4pm.) During the summer months, enjoy the **Eagle Bahn Gondola Twilight Ride.** (Runs Th-Sa 5-9pm. Free.)

🍴🍸 FOOD & NIGHTLIFE. You'll never need to cook breakfast in Vail as long as the griddle is hot at **DJ's Classic Diner,** 616 W. Lionshead Plaza, on the west end of Lionshead Village. During the winter, locals ski in 'round the clock to warm up to DJ's crepes ($4-6), omelettes ($4-5), and pasta frittatas from $7.50. (☎ 970-476-2336. Open summer M-Th and Sa-Su 7am-1pm, F 10pm-3am; winter M 7am-1pm, Tu 7am-midnight, W-Sa 24hr., Su midnight-1pm.) Right in the heart of Vail Village, **The Red Lion,** Hanson Ranch Rd. and Bridge St., was built by its owners as a hotel—but they had so many children there were no rooms left for guests. It serves succulent barbecue brisket ($13) and ribs. (☎ 970-476-7676. Nightly drink specials. Open from 11am.) With Alabama-style barbecue, **Moe's Original BBQ,** 675 W. Lionshead Cir., is "A Southern Soulfood Revival." Their box lunches ($8-9) with pulled pork or smoked chicken along with two sides might be the best deal in town. (☎ 970-479-7888. Open M-Sa 11am-sellout.)

With two clubs, three floors, four bars, and seven decks, **The Tap Room & Sanctuary,** 333 Bridge St. in Vail Village, attracts all types. While the Tap Room caters to those looking for good rowdy fun, the Sanctuary upstairs is for those in search of a classier nightclub. (☎ 970-479-0500. Tap Room open daily 10am-2am. Sanctuary open Tu-Sa 8pm-2am.) **Garfinkel's,** 536 E. Lionshead Cir., orders patrons to "Ski hard, party harder." (☎ 970-476-3789. Meals $8-11. Restaurant open June-Sept. and Nov.-Apr. daily 11am-10pm. Bar open until 2am.)

♖ ACCOMMODATIONS. The phrase "cheap lodging" is not part of Vail's vocabulary. Rooms rarely dip below $175 per night in winter, and summer lodging is often equally pricey. **Lionshead Inn,** 705 W. Lionshead Cir., has great deals on luxury accommodations. With an exercise room, game room, hot tub, fireplace lounge, and free Internet, the inn also offers plush robes and down comforters on every bed and balconies in every room. Call for lower walk-in rates and book online for 50% off during the summer. (☎ 970-476-2050 or 800-283-8245; www.lionsheadinn.com. Continental breakfast included. Singles from $59-79.) The **Roost Lodge,** 1783 N. Frontage Rd., in West Vail, provides affordable lodging. The rooms are impressively clean and include breakfast, cable TV, fridge, microwave, and access to a jacuzzi, sauna, and heated indoor pool. (☎ 970-476-5451 or 800-873-3065. Continental breakfast in winter. Singles summer from $59; winter $109-129.) Located in Eagle, about 30 mi. west of Vail, **The Prairie Moon,** 738 Grand Ave., offers some of the cheapest lodging near the resort. (☎ 970-328-6680. Singles $30-55; doubles $45-65.) The **Holy Cross Ranger District,** right off I-70 at Exit 171 (follow signs), provides info on summer campgrounds near Vail. (☎ 970-827-5715. Open M-F 8am-5pm.)

🅰️ APPROACHING LEADVILLE
Take **I-70 West** to Exit 171 for **U.S. 24 South.**

LEADVILLE

Leadville's biggest claim to fame is that it marks the beginning of a cluster of **"fourteeners"** (mountain peaks over 14,000 ft.), which attract hikers and thrill-seekers from far and wide. The **National Mining Hall of Fame and Museum,** 120 W. 9th St., showcases the mining that resulted when the 59ers headed to Colorado in search of gold. The best part of the museum is the second floor, featuring a recreated mine and a set of dioramas. (☎ 719-486-1229; www.leadville.com/miningmuseum. Open May-Oct. daily 9am-5pm; Nov.-Apr. M-Sa 10am-4pm. $6, ages 6-11 $3.) The **Healy House and Dexter Cabin Museum,** 912 Harrison Ave., date from the first decades of the town's founding. Dexter Cabin was the lavish 1879 mountain hideaway of Colorado's first millionaire, James Dexter, while Healy House is an 1878 Greek Revivial home kept in good shape. (☎719-486-0487. Open June-Aug. daily 10am-4:30pm; Sept. Sa-Su 10am-4:30pm. $4, ages 6-16 $2.50.) The **Mineral Belt Trail,** a 12½ mi. all-season paved loop, circles the town, following old railroad rights of way and paths through California and Slaughterhouse Gulches. Along the way it passes the remnants of several old mines, tunnels, and shafts.

Tracks Coffee Company, 714 Harrison Ave. (U.S. 24), feels like a European ski lodge. The cafe by day and bar by night serves quality sandwiches ($6), large salads ($5-7), and individual gourmet pizzas ($7) to hungry hikers. (☎719-486-0284. Open daily 7am-midnight.)

LEAVING LEADVILLE
Follow **U.S. 24 East,** heading south.

BUENA VISTA. A family-oriented community that has attracted migrants from Colorado's Front Range, Buena Vista offers easy access to the fourteeners, hot springs, and rafting opportunities in the summer, and snowmobiling and cross-country skiing in the winter, though it lacks the cultural opportunities of slightly larger Salida just down the road. One of the nicest resorts in Colorado, the **Cottonwood Hot Springs Inn and Spa,** 18999 CR 306, steams the stress away with four soaking pools of varied sizes, shapes, and temperatures, a 112° hot tub, and cold pools. (☎719-395-6434. Open daily 8am-midnight. Clothing optional. No children after dark. $10, F-Su $15.)

LEAVING BUENA VISTA
About 2 mi. south of Buena Vista get on **U.S. 285 South** and turn left onto **Rte. 291.**

SALIDA

Residents are proud of what they consider to be Colorado's last unspoiled mountain town. Though tourists have yet to discover Salida, the artists have; excellent galleries congregate on several streets. Salida's downtown district is today composed of galleries, restaurants, and outlets catering to outdoor enthusiasts. The Arkansas River, home to excellent rafting, abuts one end of town.

GETTING AROUND. Rte. 291 runs along the northeastern edge of town along the Arkansas River. It is called **Grand Ave.** as it approaches town, **1st St.** in downtown, and **Oak St.** as it heads south

VITAL STATS
Population: 5500
Visitor Info: Salida Chamber of Commerce, 406 U.S. 50 (☎719-539-2068). Open M-Sa 9am-5pm.
Internet Access: Salida Regional Library, 405 E St. (☎719-539-4826). Open M-F 9am-8:30pm, Sa 9am-5:30pm, Su 1-5pm.
Post Office: Salida Main Post Office, 310 D St. (☎800-275-8777), at 3rd St. Open M-F 7:30am-5pm, Sa 8:30am-noon. **Postal Code:** 81201.

to **U.S. 50.,** which is also known as **Rainbow Blvd.** and runs east-west at the southern edge of town. Lettered streets run northeast-southwest between U.S. 50 and the Arkansas River, while numbered streets parallel the river, starting with 1st St., running northwest-southeast.

SIGHTS & OUTDOORS. In the last decade Salida has seen a new gallery or two open each year, leading some locals to wonder if it might be on its way to becoming the best little art town in America. Salida's 15 or so **downtown galleries** concentrate on 1st St. between E and G St.

Salida is a stopping point on the **Monarch Crest Trail,** a 28 mi., 4½hr. grueling mountain bike trail from Salida to Monarch Pass that includes 14 mi. along the Continental Divide. Bike rentals are available at **Otero Cyclery,** 104 F St. (☎719-539-6704. Full suspension bikes $40 per day; crusiers $5 per hr. Open M-Sa 9am-6pm, Su 10am-5pm.) While there are **rafting** companies located all along the Arkansas River, Salida is particularly convenient to **Brown's Canyon,** a relaxing section of the Arkansas River. Thrill-seekers also use Salida as a jumping-off point to head east 60 mi. to the more challenging Royal Gorge (see p. 376). **Whitewater Voyagers,** 105 E. U.S. 50, leads trips that leave at 9am and 1:30pm. (☎800-539-4447; www.whitewatervoyagers.com. Open 7am-10:30pm. Brown's Canyon half-day $35, under 15 $29; full day $69/$55. Royal Gorge trips $54 half-day, full day $89.) A number of **hiking** trails run through the Salida area, and it also serves as a good base from which to hike the fourteeners.

FOOD & ACCOMMODATIONS. At **Laughing Ladies,** 128 W. First St., Napa Valley-trained chefs serve "California-inspired nouveau cuisine" at a high-end but not high-priced downtown fixture. Local artists exhibit work on the walls, and gourmet lunch sandwiches ($5.50-6.25) and dinner entrees ($14-17) like molasses barbecued quail are delicious. (☎719-539-6209. Open M 11am-2:30pm and 5-8pm, Th 5-8pm, F-Sa 11am-2:30pm and 5-8:30pm, Su 9am-2pm and 5-8pm.) At **Fiesta Mexicana,** 1220 E. U.S. 50, heaping portions of fresh, authentic Mexican fare will leave you stuffed. (☎719-539-5203. Entrees $11-13. Combo plates $8-9.50. Open Su-Th 11am-10pm, F-Sa 11am-11pm.) For old-fashioned country home cooking, try **Country Bounty,** 413 U.S. 50 West, where even oatmeal is made fresh-to-order. (☎719-539-3546. Breakfast $3-7. Sandwiches $5-10. Entrees $9-15. Open daily 6am-9pm.)

The best deal in town, the **Motel Westerner,** 7335 U.S. 50 West, offers clean, no-frills rooms with refrigerators and microwaves, but no A/C. (☎719-539-2618. Singles $28; doubles $32.50; quads $35. Reservations recommended in summer.) Most rooms at the **Budget Lodge,** 1146 U.S. 50 East, are quite small and the walls are thin, but the owner is friendly and the price is right. (☎719-539-6695 or 877-909-6695. Summer singles $35-38; doubles $45; twins $50-55. Winter $32-35/$35-38/$40-45.)

LEAVING SALIDA
From downtown, head away from the river to **U.S. 50** and turn right. About 5 mi. west of town, fork right and then turn left to stay on **U.S. 50 West.**

THE ROAD TO GUNNISON

Fifteen miles from Salida, the scenic road meanders through deep shades of green. There are lots of bikers here; pay careful attention. The **Monarch Park Campground,** one of many in the San Isabel National Forest, has small, flat sites in a dense spruce forest. (20 mi. from Salida, 1 mi. off U.S. 50. 36 sites with toilets and water. 14-day max. stay. Open mid-June-Aug. Sites $12.) Gentler than other area resorts (with a 1200 ft. vertical drop), the **Monarch Ski and Snowboard Area** has five lifts that cater to groups and families. (21 mi. from Salida, turn right at the sign. ☎888-996-7669; www.skimonarch.com. Open in winter daily 9am-4pm. Lift ticket $44, seniors $26, ages 7-12 $17.) Twenty-three miles from Salida, U.S. 50 crosses the Continental Divide at **Monarch Pass** (11,312 ft.).

GUNNISON. Gunnison is ideal for an afternoon rest stop. The **Pioneer Museum,** 803 E. Tomichi Ave. (U.S. 50), has a large collection of western hats and a garage of about 50 antique cars. (☎970-641-4530. Open mid-May to mid-Sept M-Sa 9am-5pm, Su 1-5pm. $7, ages 6-12 $1.) The **Gunnison**

National Forest Office, 216 N. Colorado Ave., has info on area forest service lands including Crested Butte. (☎970-641-0471. Open M-F 7:30am-4:30pm.) As U.S. 50 curves left at the western edge of town, look left for the **giant white "W"** carved into W Mountain—the "W" is for Western State College, located in Gunnison. ▨**Farrells' Restaurant,** 310 N. Main St., serves sandwiches ($5-6) and fresh breads to patrons on the shady back patio and garden. (☎970-641-2655. Open M-F 7am-3pm.)

DETOUR: CRESTED BUTTE
27 mi. north of Gunnison via Rte. 135.
Crested Butte was settled by miners in the 1870s. The coal was exhausted in the 1950s, but a few years later the steep powder fields began attracting skiers. Thanks to strict zoning rules, the historic downtown is a throwback to early mining days. Three miles north of town, **Crested Butte Mountain Resort,** 12 Snowmass Rd., offers over 800 acres of bowl skiing. (☎800-544-8448. Open mid-Dec. to mid-Apr. Lift ticket around $50.) In summer, Crested Butte becomes the mountain biking capital of Colorado. During the last week of June, the town hosts the **Fat Tire Bike Festival** (www.ftbw.com), four days of biking, racing, and fraternizing. In 1976, a group of cyclists rode from Crested Butte to Aspen, starting what is now the oldest mountain biking event in the world. Every September, experienced bikers repeat the trek over the 12,705 ft. pass to Aspen and back during the **Pearl Pass Tour,** organized by the **Mountain Biking Hall of Fame,** 331 Elk Ave. (☎970-349-1880).

APPROACHING CURECANTI
The **Curecanti National Recreation Area** begins along **U.S. 50** starting 120 mi. from Salida.

CURECANTI NATIONAL RECREATION AREA

While you wouldn't know it just by looking, the large bodies of water in this area are man-made, created by dams on the Gunnison River. Curecanti is primarily used for fishing, boating, sailing, and horseback riding. Inexpensive boat tours and hiking trails are also popular, offering views of the Gunnison River Canyon and Dillion Pinnacles—spires created by erosion of volcanic mudflows. The moderately strenuous **Dillon Pinnacles Trail** (4 mi.) ascends 600 ft. to an up-close view of a large set of spires. (Trailhead off U.S. 50, 5½ mi. west of the Elk Creek Visitors Center.) If you have time, the strenuous **Curecanti Creek Trail** (4 mi.) goes down into the upper Black Canyon and then along the tumbling Curecanti Creek. (11 mi. west of Elk Creek Visitors Center, turn right onto Rte. 92, and continue 5¾ mi. to the Pioneer Point Trailhead.) Along the way, you have the chance to see peregrine falcons and golden eagles. At the end, look across the Morrow Point Reservoir to view the 700 ft. Curecanti Needle. **Morrow Point Boat Tours** leave from Pine Creek Boat Dock, 12 mi. west of Elk Creek Visitors Center. The 1½hr. ride rushes through the upper Black Canyon. (☎970-641-2337. Runs in summer F-Su 9 and 11:30am. $10, ages 2-12 $5. Reservations recommended.) **Elk Creek Marina** offers boat rentals and guided fishing trips. (Elk Creek Marina ☎970-641-0707. Lake Fork Marina ☎970-641-3048. Boat rentals $13-35 per hr., $60-185 per day. Fishing trips from $275.)

Due to its climate and low-lying location, camping in Curecanti tends not to be as picturesque as that in the National Parks or in the Forest Service sites near Heeney and Twin Lakes. On the other hand, campsites are generally convenient to the road and easily obtained. Curecanti's four major campsites, primarily sheets of asphalt, turn into a city of RVs in the summer, and offer water, toilets, grills, and picnic tables. The most developed of the campgrounds, **Elk Creek** and **Lake Fork,** have showers. (☎970-641-2337. Sites $10.)

APPROACHING BLACK CANYON
Turn right at the sign for **Rte. 347/Black Canyon** and go 6 mi. to **Black Canyon National Park.**

BLACK CANYON NATIONAL PARK

Native American parents used to tell their children that the light-colored strands of rock streaking through the walls of the Black Canyon were hairs of a blond woman—if they got too close to the edge they would get tangled and fall. The Gunnison River slowly carved the 53 mi. canyon, crafting a steep 2500 ft. gorge. Christened by President Clinton in 1999, Black Canyon is the nation's youngest national park.

GETTING AROUND. The Black Canyon lies 15 mi. east of the town of **Montrose.** The **South Rim** is easily accessible by a 6 mi. drive off U.S. 50 at the end of Rte. 347; the wilder **North Rim** can only be reached by an 80 mi. detour around the canyon followed by a gravel road from Crawford off Rte.

(**VITAL STATS**)

Area: 30,000 acres

Visitor Info: South Rim Visitors Center (☎970-249-1914, ext. 423; www.nps.gov/blca), on South Rim Dr. Free wilderness permits. Open daily summer 8am-6pm; winter 8:30am-4pm.

Gateway Town: Montrose (p. 396).

Fees: $7 per vehicle.

92. This road is closed in winter. The **East Portal Rd.,** accessed from South Rim Rd. near the park entrance, takes you down to the East Portal, inside the canyon at the side of the river. This is a good spot for a picnic.

The spectacular 8 mi. **South Rim Road** traces the edge of the canyon, and boasts jaw-dropping vistas including the spectacular **Chasm View,** where you can peer 2300 ft. down the highest cliff in Colorado and across to the streaked Painted Wall. For an even better view of the Painted Wall—arguably the most impressive in the park—head to the **Painted Wall View** overlook.

HIKING. Paths into the canyon follow drainage gullies, and as such are worn but not marked. A drainage is by nature wide at the top and narrow at the bottom, so it is easy to find your way down but harder to find your way back. Setting up cairns (piles of rocks) is permitted, but you must knock them down on your return. Leave early in the morning to avoid the afternoon heat.

A couple of hiking routes skirt the edge of the canyon and provide an in-depth experience than the overlooks. The moderate **Oak Flat Loop Trail** (2 mi.) begins near the Visitors Center and gives a good sense of the terrain below the rim. When it comes down to it, however, dropping over the edge of the canyon and reaching the roaring river is where it's really at. From the South Rim, you can scramble down the popular **Gunnison Route,** which drops 1800 ft. over 1 mi. Allow 1-1½hr. for the treacherous descent, and even longer for the climb out. If you're feeling courageous, tackle the more difficult overnight **Tomichi** or **Warner Routes.** A free wilderness permit (from the South Rim Visitors Center) is required for inner-canyon routes, and you are advised to check-out on your return. Bring at least one gallon of water per person, per day, more if it's hot.

OUTDOOR ACTIVITIES. Not surprisingly, the sheer walls of the Black Canyon make for a **rock climbing** paradise. This rock is not for begin-

NATIONAL ROAD

ners or the faint of heart, and all climbers must register at the Visitors Center. For a relaxed, insider's view of the canyon, call ahead to reserve a **rafting** trip with **Gunnison River Expeditions.** (☎970-249-4441. $200. Reserve ahead.)

Anglers from all over Colorado trek to the Black Canyon to practice the art of **fly fishing.** Gunnison River Expeditions runs fly-fishing float trips in the Black Canyon (1 day $650 for 2 people) and 1-day walk-wade trips on the Gunnison ($275.) **Gunnison Gorge National Conservation Area** is a particularly popular stretch of the river. Non-motorized boaters have access to the area via the Chukar Boater Put-In and the Gunnison Forks Boater Take-Out. The only land access is by hiking one of four trails from the rim of the gorge. The access roads are rough; some, especially Bobcat Rd., require 4WD, and others are impassable when wet.

◢ CAMPING. The **South Rim Campground** has 102 sites with pit toilets, charcoal grills, and water. (Sites $10, with hookup $15.) If you're feeling adventuresome, turn right from the entrance to the South Rim park and head down the 16% grade of E. Portal Rd. to find tent sites at the base of the canyon. (Water, toilets, grills. Sites $10.) In the canyon, unimproved campsites lie along a beach beside the river. Eleven hike-in only campsites are available in the **Gunnison Gorge National Conservation Area** northwest of Montrose. (☎970-240-5300. 2-night max. stay. Sites $10. Day-use $5.)

MONTROSE

Fifteen miles west of the Black Canyon, the quiet, community of Montrose serves as both the center of a farming region and a gateway to the spectacular beauty of southwest Colorado. Amidst the sounds of "nature music" at the **Ute Indian Museum,** 17253 Chipeta Rd., you can learn the history of the Ute people. Though they once inhabited much of present-day Colorado and Utah, today the Utes have only a small reservation at the southern end of the state. (Take U.S. 550 south to the museum on your right. ☎970-249-3098. Open mid-May to Oct. M-Sa 9am-4:30pm, Su 11am-4:30pm. $3, seniors $2.50, ages 6-16 $1.50.)

Sicily's Italian Restaurant, 1135 E. Main St. (U.S. 50), offers solid Italian food. The comfy, garden-like atmosphere extends to the porch, where pretty flowers fail to block out the noise on Main St. (☎970-240-9199. Pasta $8-11. Entrees $14-19. Open daily in summer 11am-10pm; closing times vary the rest of the year.) For tasty sandwiches

($5) and delightful omelettes ($6), head to the **Daily Bread Bakery and Cafe,** 346 Main St. (☎970-249-8444. Open M-Sa 6am-3pm.) **Camp Robber Cafe,** 228 Main St., caters to locals with its Southwestern flair. Try the specialty Green Chile Pistachio Crusted Pork Medallions at $16.50 or the Cilantro Quesadilla for $9. (☎970-240-1590. Open Su 9am-2pm, Tu-Sa 11am-3pm and 5-9pm.) Many inexpensive motels line E. Main St. (U.S. 50) east of downtown Montrose. At **Western Motel,** 1200 E. Main St., a pool, hot tub, and continental breakfast make the rooms a deal. (☎800-445-7301. Doubles and family units available. Reception 24hr. Checkout 10am. Singles in summer from $50; in winter $35.) The prices at **Traveler's B&B Inn,** 502 S. 1st St., can't be beat in Montrose, although, despite the name, no breakfast is served. (☎970-249-3472. Singles $34, with bath $34-36; doubles $42.)

◢◣ APPROACHING GRAND JUNCTION
U.S. 50 becomes **5th St.** entering Grand Junction.

GRAND JUNCTION

Grand Junction takes its name from its seat at the junction of the Colorado and Gunnison Rivers and the nexus of the Río Grande and Denver Railroads. Today, the name aptly describes Grand Junction's role as a transportation hub for the masses heading to southern Utah and the Colorado Rockies. If you need big-city services, Grand Junction is a good place to stop; the next stop with a population over 10,000 is Salt Lake City.

ⓘ VITAL STATS

Population: 42,000

Visitor Info: Grand Junction Visitors Bureau, 740 Horizon Dr. (☎970-244-1480 or 800-962-2547; www.grandjunction.net.). Head east to 7th St., turn left, then turn right on Horizon Dr. Open daily May-Sept. 8:30am-8pm; Oct.-Apr. 8:30am-5pm.

Internet Access: Mesa County Library, 530 Grand Ave. (☎970-243-4442). Open M-Th 9am-9pm, F-Sa 9am-5pm; Sept.-May also Su 1-5pm.

Post office: 241 N. 4th St. (☎970-244-3400). Open M-F 7:45am-5:15pm, Sa 10am-1:30pm. **Postal code:** 81501.

▣ GETTING AROUND. Grand Junction lies on the **Colorado River** near **I-70.** In town, streets run north-south, increasing in number from west to east, and avenues run east-west. **Grand Ave.** is a main artery, running one block north of **Main St.**, also the location of many establishments. **North Ave. (U.S. 6)** runs one block north of Grand Ave.

◢ SIGHTS. There are lots of **sidewalk sculptures** in downtown Grand Junction; don't miss the dinosaur riding a bicycle at 3rd and Main St.—it bridges millions of years of Grand Junction history. The **Museum of Western Colorado,** at 5th St. and Ute Ave., has several excellent exhibits, including one on the famous Alfred Packer, tried and convicted of cannibalism, as uncovered by modern forensic techniques. See Bill Cody's 1881 gun and head up the Educational Tower for a 360° view of Grand Junction and surroundings. (☎970-242-0971. Open May-Sept. M-Sa 9am-5pm, Su noon-4pm; Oct.-Apr. Tu-Sa 10am-3pm. $5.50, seniors $4.50, ages 3-12 $3.)

▲ OUTDOOR ACTIVITIES. The Grand Junction area has a smorgasbord of outdoor activities close to town and even more within an hour's drive. Biking, hiking, river running, hunting, and fishing guides can be hired through **Fruita Outdoor Adventures** (☎970-260-5848). The best hiking around Grand Junction awaits in the **Colorado Canyons National Conservation Area** just west of the Colorado National Monument. Pollock, Rattlesnake and Knowles Canyons all feature beautiful hikes. (Take I-70 to Exit 19 and head south 1¼ mi. to Kings View Estates subdivision. Follow the Kings View Rd. west and look for signs to the trailhead.) East of Grand Junction, the Book Cliffs overlook the town. The **Mt. Garfield Trail** is a great option for a short hike to amazing views of this otherworldly rockscape. The hike gains 2000 ft. over 1½ mi., taking about 1¼hr. up and 45min. down. Wild horses are sometimes visible from the top during winter and early spring. (To reach the trailhead, take Exit 42 from I-70 and travel south on 37 Three-tenths Rd. to G Seven-tenths Rd. Take a right and go west just under 2 mi. to 35 Five-tenths Rd. Turn right and cross I-70 to the trailhead.)

Three main trail areas draw mountain bikers around Grand Junction: the Kokopelli area, the 18-Mile Rd. area, and the Tabeguache area. A bevy of mountain bike shops offer advice and rent bikes. Downtown, **Ruby Canyon Cycles,** 301 Main St., is a full-service bike shop with full-day rentals. (☎970-241-0141. Hard-tail bikes $7 per hr., $25 per day; full-suspension $8/$35. Open M-F 9am-6pm, Sa 9am-5pm.) Out toward the Visitors Center on North Ave., **Board and Buckle**

Ski and Cyclery, 2822 North Ave., rents bikes at $25 per day. (☎970-242-9285. Open in summer M-F 9am-6pm, Sa 9am-5pm. Winter ski rentals 7am-7pm.)

▼ FOOD. Thursday nights in summer see downtown transformed into the **Farmer's Market Festival,** with local produce, live music, and extended Main St. restaurant hours. (☎970-245-9697. Th 4:30-8pm.) South of downtown, **Ying Thai,** 757 U.S. 50, serves great Thai in a homey setting. (☎970-245-4866. Lunch $6. Dinner $9-15. Open Tu-F 11am-2pm and 5-9pm, Sa 5-9pm.) Massive, mouth-watering breakfasts ($4-8) are the specialty at **Crystal Cafe,** 314 Main St., but hot lunches ($5.50-7) and decadent baked goods don't fall short. (☎970-242-8843. Open M-F 7am-1:45pm, Sa 8am-noon.)

☗ ACCOMMODATIONS. Between 3rd and 4th St., **Hotel Melrose,** 337 Colorado Ave., offers historic rooms in the heart of the city. In addition to dorms, there are private rooms. (☎800-430-4555; www.hotelmelrose.com. Reception 9am-1pm and 4-10pm. Check-out 11am. Dorms $20; singles $35, with bath $50; doubles from $65. Reduced rates off-season.) **Daniel's Motel,** 333 North Ave., rents clean rooms, some with kitchenettes. (☎970-243-1084. Check-out 10am. Singles $30-45; doubles $45-55.) Camping is available at **Fruita State Park,** 10 mi. west of town, off Exit 19 from I-70. (☎800-678-2267. 80 sites with showers and hookups. Park entrance fee $4. Sites $10-16.)

▣ NIGHTLIFE. The presence of Mesa State College lends Grand Junction's nightlife a youthful enthusiasm, and weekend nights see crowded bars. **Rockslide Restaurant and Brew Pub,** 401 S. Main St., joins the avalanche of microbreweries blanketing the nation. The Big Bear Stout comes in a half-gallon growler for $8.50. (☎970-245-2111. Half-price appetizers M-F 4-6pm. Open daily 10am-midnight.) **The Sports Page,** 103 N. 1st St., is a typical sports bar right down to the jerseys on the walls. (☎970-241-4010. Happy hour M-F 4-6pm and 10pm-midnight. Local bands W. Live band or DJ F-Sa. Open M-Th 4pm-midnight, F-Sa 4pm-2am, Su 4-11pm.) Set in a converted theater, the **Mesa Theater,** 538 Main St., features live music summer weekends. (☎970-241-1717; www.mesatheater.com. W under 21. Th college night with R&B. Cover Th $6, F-Sa $12-50. Open W 8-11:30pm, Th 9pm-2am, F-Sa 8pm-1am, Su hours vary.)

LEAVING GRAND JUNCTION
Proceed north on **5th St.** 3 blocks past Main St. to **Grand Ave.,** and turn left. At the intersection with 1st St. head straight onto **Broadway/Rte. 340** (Grand Ave. becomes Broadway). After about 1 mi., turn left onto **Monument Rd.** at the sign for the monument.

COLORADO NATIONAL MONUMENT

Sitting on the outskirts of Grand Junction, Colorado National Monument is a 32 sq. mi. sculpture of steep cliff faces, canyon walls, and obelisk-like spires wrought by the forces of gravity, wind, and water. The monument was established in 1911, largely due to the efforts of John Otto, who blazed most of the trails used today and badgered the government to protect this dreamworld of rock.

> **VITAL STATS**
>
> **Area:** 20,500 acres.
>
> **Visitor Info: Visitors Center** (☎970-858-3617; www.nps.gov/colm), 4 mi. east of the western entrance. Open daily June to early Sept. 8am-6pm; early Sept.-May 9am-5pm.
>
> **Gateway Town:** Fruita, Grand Junction (p. 396).
>
> **Fees:** $5 per vehicle.

GETTING AROUND. For those without time to explore on foot, the 23 mi. **Rim Rock Dr.** runs along the edge of red canyons across the mesa top between the two entrances, providing views of awe-inspiring rock monoliths, the Book Cliffs, Grand Mesa, and the city of Grand Junction. From many of the overlooks, the striated mesa is visible in the distance, rising like a series of mini-mountains. The best overlooks include the colorful **Coke Ovens,** a little over halfway into the road. A bit beyond that, aptly-named Grand View provides a panoramic look back into the multiple layers of the canyon. The next overlook, Independence Monument, offers a view of the park's highest free-standing rock formation. Its solid capstone has prevented it from eroding as quickly as the sandstone of the canyon walls.

HIKING. Although Rim Rock Dr. provides breathtaking views, the trails that crisscross the monument are the only way to fully appreciate the scope and scale of this canyon country. Unlike some of the parks in the Southwest, the monument allows off-trail backcountry hiking. There are a number of short walks that whisk hikers away from the road and immerse them in the terrain. The **Window Rock Trail** (½ mi. round-trip) leaves from a trailhead on the campground road and offers expansive vistas through piñon-juniper woodland over the Grand Valley, as well as views of Monument Canyon, Wedding Canyon, and many of the monument's major rock formations. **Ottos Trail** and **Coke Ovens Trail** (1 mi. round-trip) are gentle and offer good views of monoliths and the Coke Ovens, respectively. The 1½ mi. **Devil's Kitchen Trail** begins off the park drive just past the east entrance, and drops into No Thoroughfare Canyon and Devils Kitchen, a natural grotto surrounded by enormous upright boulders.

There are a number of options for longer hikes in the monument, making for a good overnight stop. Most of these trails are fairly primitive and marked with cairns. The moderately strenuous 6 mi. **Monument Canyon Trail** is popular because it allows hikers to view eerie, skeletal rock formations up close. The trail descends 600 ft. from the mesa top to the canyon floor and then wanders amid giant rocks, including Independence Monument, Kissing Couple, and the Coke Ovens, until it emerges on Rte. 340 (Broadway/Redlands Rd.).

CAMPING. Backcountry camping is free and allowed anywhere over a quarter-mile from the roads and 100 yd. from the trails. A required permit is available at the Visitors Center. **Saddlehorn Campground,** a half-mile north of the Visitors Center, offers 50 beautiful, secluded sites on the mesa's edge. (☎970-858-3617. Water and bathrooms. No showers. Sites $10.)

LEAVING THE NATIONAL MONUMENT
Proceed out the west entrance and turn left at the T-intersection onto **Rte. 340** toward Fruita. Go 2½ mi. to **I-70 West.** Take Exit 202 for **Rte. 128 South.**

THE ROAD TO MOAB. After the road crosses the Colorado River, towering, reddish rocky cliff formations radiate out on all sides as the road winds through a canyon along the banks of the river. After rounding a corner about 4 mi. past the bridge, you see the first of the area's hallmark red spires. Rte. 128 dead-ends at U.S. 191; from here, turn left to go 2½ mi. to Moab.

MOAB

Moab, about 70 mi. from the Colorado/Utah border, first flourished in the 1950s, when uranium miners rushed to the area and transformed the town into a gritty desert outpost. Today, the mountain bike has replaced the Geiger counter, as outdoors enthusiasts rush into town eager to bike the slickrock, raft whitewater rapids, and explore Arches and Canyonlands National Parks.

VITAL STATS

Population: 5000

Visitor Info: Moab Information Center, 3 Center St. (☎435-259-8825 or 800-635-6622), at corner of Main St. Open daily June-Sept. 8am-9pm; Nov.-Dec. 9am-5pm; Jan.-Feb. 9am-5pm; Mar. 8am-7pm; Apr.-May and Oct. 8am-8pm.

Post Office: 50 E. 100 North (☎435-259-7427). Open M-F 8:30am-5:30pm, Sa 9am-1pm. **Postal Code:** 84532.

GETTING AROUND. Moab sits 30 mi. south of **I-70** on **U.S. 191,** just south of the junction with **Rte. 128.** The town center lies 5 mi. south of the entrance to Arches National Park and 38 mi. north of the turn-off to the Needles section of Canyonlands National Park. U.S. 191 becomes **Main St.** for 5 mi. through downtown.

SIGHTS. The **Dan O'Laurie Canyon Country Museum,** 118 E. Center St., highlights the Native Americans who lived here, the 1950s Uranium boom, and the geology of the area. (☎435-259-7985. Open summer M-Sa 1-8pm; winter M-Th 3-7pm, F-Sa 1-7pm. $2, under 12 free; families $5.) About 15 mi. south, **Hole N' The Rock,** 11037 S. U.S. 191, is not quite what the name purports. Earlier in the century, a couple blasted a set of cozy, cavernous rooms for themselves out of entrada sandstone; today, you can tour the unique, naturally climate-controlled home. (Take U.S. 191 South 15½ mi. from Moab. ☎435-686-2250. Open daily summer 8am-8pm; winter 9am-5pm. 10min. tours every 12-15min. $4.25, ages 6-12 $2.25.)

OUTDOOR ACTIVITIES. Mountain biking and **rafting,** along with nearby national parks, are the big draws in Moab. The well-known **Slickrock Trail** (10 mi.) rolls up and down the slickrock (actually sandstone) outside of Moab. The trail has no big vertical gain, but is technically difficult and temperatures often reach 100°F. **Rim Cyclery,** 94 W. 100 North, rents bikes and has trail info. (☎435-259-5333. Open Su-Th 9am-6pm, F-Sa 8am-6pm. Bikes $32-50 per day; includes helmet.) Countless rafting companies are based in Moab. **OARS/North American River Expeditions,** 543 N. Main St., offers the best guides on the river. (☎435-259-5865 or 800-342-5938. Half-day $36, ages 5-17 $27; includes snacks and a natural history lesson.) **Western River Expeditions** also offers good deals. (☎435-259-7019 or 800-453-7450. Half-

THE LOCAL STORY

LIKE A CHICKEN WITH ITS HEAD CUT OFF

Clutching the bird in one hand, the farmer in faded dungarees picks up the wood handle of the gleaming axe. He holds the chicken firmly against the worn chopping block and with one clean, smooth motion, brings the blade slicing down across the rough skin of its scrawny neck. Blood spurts across his bare forearm as he releases the mass of twitching feathers and flailing feet. In a second, the beast is on its feet and races around the farmyard—for two years! When Mike, The Headless Chicken, was beheaded in Fruita, CO, sometime in the middle of the last century, things didn't go exactly as planned. Rather than falling to the ground, dead as a doornail after a run-in with a farmer's axe, Mike managed to survive for more than two years. His amazed owners fed him with a medicine dropper and Mike toured the country to rave reviews. Today, all that remains of Mike's legend are the tales told by Fruita old-timers and a piece of sculpture in downtown Fruita, depicting the illustrious Mike in full stride.

day $37, full-day $49; children $29/$37; includes lunch.) Outfitters arrange horseback, motorboat, canoe, jeep, and helicopter expeditions.

⬛ FOOD. Retro booths at the ⬛**Moab Diner and Ice Cream Shoppe,** 189 S. Main St., might take you back to the 1950s, but with veggie specials and tasty green chili ($4-10), the food won't. (☎435-259-4006. Open Su-Th 6am-10pm, F-Sa 6am-10:30pm.) ⬛**EklectiCafe,** 352 N. Main St., offers delicious pastries, coffee drinks, breakfasts ($3-7), and lunch options ($4-8). Locals perform music on Sunday mornings to an audience crunchier than the bacon. (☎435-259-6896. Open Su 7:30am-1pm, M-Sa 7:30am-2:30pm.) The **Peace Tree Juice Cafe,** 20 S. Main St., will cool you off with a smoothie or fresh juice ($2.50-5). (☎435-259-6333. Open Su-Th 9am-5pm, F-Sa 9am-9pm.) Adding a little Fifth Ave. flair to an otherwise Western town, **Breakfast at Tiffany's,** 90 E. Center St., offers almond French toast and catfish and eggs. (☎435-259-2553. Open M-F 7am-3pm, Sa-Su 7am-7:30pm. Cash only.)

⬛ ACCOMMODATIONS. Chain motels clutter Main St., but rooms in Moab are not cheap and fill up fast from April to October, especially on weekends. **Lazy Lizard International Hostel,** 1213 S. U.S. 191, is 1 mi. south of Moab. The owners of this well-maintained hostel will give you the lowdown on the area, while the kitchen, VCR, laundry, and hot tub draw a mix of college students, backpackers, and aging hippies. (☎435-259-6057. Reception 8am-11pm, but late arrivals can be arranged. Check-out 11am. Reservations recommended for weekends in

the spring and fall. Dorms $9; private rooms from $22; cabins sleeping up to 6 $27-47; tent sites $6.) At **Hotel Off Center,** 96 E. Center St., a block off Main St., the owners offer lavish rooms accented by such eclectic items as a miner's hat, and a Victrola. (☎435-259-4244. Open Mar.-Nov. Dorms $12; singles $39; doubles $49.)

The Moab area features 1000 campsites, so finding a place to sleep shouldn't be a problem. **Goose Island, Hal Canyon, Oak Grove, Negro Bill,** and **Big Bend Campgrounds,** all on Rte. 128, sit on the banks of the Colorado River 3-9 mi. northeast of downtown Moab. Many sites are shaded. (☎435-259-2100. Fire pits but no hookups or showers. Water is available at Negro Bill at the intersection of U.S. 191 and Rte. 128. Sites $10.) The secluded **Up the Creek Campground,** 210 E. 300 South, is a short walk from downtown and caters solely to tent camping. (☎435-259-6995. 20 sites. Showers. Open Mar.-Oct. $10 per person.)

⬛ APPROACHING ARCHES
Head north on **U.S. 191,** passing the junction with Rte. 128. The entrance is 5 mi. north of Moab.

ARCHES NATIONAL PARK

Here, thousands of sandstone arches, spires, pinnacles, and fins tower above the desert floor in overwhelming grandeur. Some arches are so perfect in form that early explorers believed they were constructed by a lost civilization. Deep red sandstone, green piñon pines and juniper bushes, and a strikingly blue sky combine in an unforgettable palette of colors. While most visi-

100 MILE RADIUS

OLYMPIAN FOR A DAY

With a range of camps that take place at the same facilities that hosted the 2002 Winter Olympics, summer at **Olympic Park** has its own highs for the adrenaline junky. Ski jumper wannabes can take a crash course in freestyle aerial thanks to the park's **Flight School and Aerial Jumping Arena,** which includes multiple bungee jumping stations and a 750,000 gallon splash pool. The steepest ramp launches wetsuit-clad skiers and snowboarders some 60 ft. into the thin mountain air before they cannon-ball into the water below. 1988 Olympian Chris "Hatch" Haslock is on hand to teach you the tricks that qualify you as totally fearless and just shy of insane. (Open June-Sept. Su and Tu-Sa from 12:30pm. $40 per session.) If soaring and flipping aren't your thing, the Comet awaits on solid ground. This **Olympic bobsled** ride hurtles through 15 curves over ¾ mi. at a screaming 70 mph top speed. (☎435-658-4206; www.olyparks.com. Open late May to late Aug. Tu-Sa 1-4pm.)

tors come in the summer, 100°F temperatures make hiking difficult; bring at least one gallon of water per person per day. The weather is best in the spring and fall when temperate days and nights provide a more comfortable stay. In the winter, white snow creates a brilliant contrast to the red arches. While the striking red slickrock around Arches may seem like attraction enough, the real points of interest here lie off the paved road. Load up on water and sunscreen and seek out the park's thousands of natural arches, each one pinpointed on the free map and guide passed out at the fee collection booth. The most popular hike in the park leads to the oft-photographed **Delicate Arch.** The trail (3 mi., 2½hr.) leaves from the Wolfe Ranch parking area and climbs 480 ft. To view the spectacular Delicate Arch without the 3 mi. hike, take the **Delicate Arch Viewpoint Trail,** which begins in the Viewpoint parking area. This 300 ft. trail takes around 15min. and is wheelchair accessible. **Tower Arch** (3½ mi., 2-3hr.) can be accessed from the trailhead at the Klondike Bluffs parking area via Salt Valley Rd. This moderate hike explores one of the remote regions of the park, and is a good way to escape crowds. Salt Valley Rd. is often washed out—check at the Visitors Center before departing.

The park's only campground, **Devil's Garden,** has 52 excellent campsites nestled amid piñons and giant red sandstone formations. The campsite is within walking distance of the Devil's Garden and Broken Arch trailheads; however, it is a long 18 mi. from the Visitors Center. (☎435-719-2299. Bathrooms and water. No wood-gathering. 1-week max. stay. Sites $10.) If the heat becomes unbearable at Arches, the aspen forests of the **Manti-La Sal National Forest** (☎435-259-7155) offer a respite. Take Rte. 128 along the Colorado River and turn right at Castle Valley, or go south from Moab on U.S. 191 and turn to the left at the Shell Station. There are a number of campgrounds here including **Warner Lake,** where beautiful sites sit 4000 ft. above the national park and are invariably several degrees cooler. (Sites $10.) **Oowah Lake,** a 3 mi. hike from the Geyser Pass Rd., is a rainbow trout haven. Fishing permits are available at stores in Moab and at the Forest Service Office, 62 E. 100 North, for $5 per day.

🔺 LEAVING ARCHES
Take **U.S. 191 North** 27 mi. to **I-70 West,** then proceed 17 mi. to Exit 162 **(Rte. 19).**

GREEN RIVER

The town of Green River, 52 mi. from Moab, straddles the calm section of the waterway famous for its raging rapids to the north and south. An oasis in the vast desert traversed by the interstate, Green River once acted as a robber's roost, a remote desert hideout for the Wild Bunch and other outlaws. Today Green River is a center for rafting the Green and Colorado Rivers and melon farming. If you're in town for the August harvest or the September festival that follows, the watermelon and cantaloupe can't be missed.

(VITAL STATS)

Population: 860

Visitor Info: Green River Visitors Center, 885 E. Main St. (☎435-564-3526), in the John Wesley Powell Museum. Open daily June-Aug. 8am-8pm; Sept.-May 8am-5pm.

Internet Access: Green River City Library, 85 S. Long St. (☎435-562-3349). Open M-F 10am-6pm.

Post Office: 20 E. Main St. (☎435-564-3329). Open M-F 8:30am-noon and 1-4:30pm, Sa 8:30-11:30am. **Postal Code:** 84525.

▐▀ GETTING AROUND. Green River lies along I-70 just east of its intersection with **U.S. 191,** 185 mi. southeast of Salt Lake City. **Main St.,** the only road in town, runs between two exits off I-70.

◙ SIGHTS. While outdoor activities steal the show in Green River, the **John Wesley Powell Museum,** 885 E. Main St., captivates history buffs with Colorado River lore and a slideshow with narrated excerpts from Powell's journals. Artifacts from his expedition line the museum, including a replica of his boat, the *Emma Dean.* (☎435-564-3427. Same hours as Visitors Center. $2.)

🅰 OUTDOOR ACTIVITIES. Predictably, the town's grandest offering is the river itself, and rafting trips depart frequently from late spring through early fall. Two reputable local outfitters are **Moki Mac River Expeditions,** 100 S. Sillman Ln. (☎435-564-3361 or 800-284-7280), and **Holiday Expeditions,** 1055 E. Main St. (☎801-266-2087 or 800-624-6323). Both offer daytrips on the Green River for about $55 as well as multiday trips on the Green, the Colorado, and other area rivers. Holiday expeditions combine rafting with biking.

To see the terrain from the banks rather than the river, try the **Green River Scenic Drive** along Hastings Rd. This drive traces the river through Gray Canyon for almost 20 mi., offering biking, hiking, swimming, and camping. The drive starts from Hastings Rd., off Main St. east of downtown and the Powell Museum. Turn north on Hastings Rd. 8 mi. out at Swasey Beach; the pavement ends and the road stays just above the river for the rest of the drive, ending at a rock formation that resembles Queen Nefertiti.

Thanks to an uplift 40-60 million years ago and the subsequent forces of erosion, the spectacular topography of the **San Rafael Swell** is a wonderland for hikers, backpackers, and bikers. This kidney-shaped area, located off I-70 19 mi. west of Green River, has been designated a Wilderness Study Area (WSA) by the Bureau of Land Management (BLM) and is up for inclusion in the National Park system as a National Monument, though the decision is still pending. The Visitors Center in Green River provides info on road conditions and a free guide to the **San Rafael Desert Loop Drive,** which begins just south of town and follows the river to **Horseshoe Canyon,** an extension of Canyonlands National Park. It then links with Rte. 24 to skirt the edge of the saw-tooth ridge that marks the eastern rim of the swell, called **San Rafael Reef,** before intersecting with I-70. **Backcountry camping** is usually allowed (check with the BLM in advance), and developed sites are available at **Goblin Valley State Park,** south of the swell near Temple Mountain and Crack Canyon just off Rte. 24.

Crystal Geyser, about 10 mi. south of town, erupts every 14-16hr. for about 30min. at a time, shooting a jet of water 80-100 ft. high. Environmental purists may be surprised to learn that the phenomenon owes its origin to the oil extraction industry; the geyser formed in 1936 after a petroleum test well was drilled on the riverbank. To reach the geyser, drive east on Main St. over I-70 and turn left onto the frontage road. After 2¾ mi., turn right and continue 4½ mi. to the geyser.

▇▐ FOOD & ACCOMMODATIONS. Ben's Cafe, 115 W. Main St., dishes out ample portions of Mexican and American fare as jukebox tunes fill the air. Bargain breakfasts range $3.75-7, while lunch runs $5-8. (☎ 435-564-3352. Open daily summer 7am-11pm; winter 7am-10pm.) For the second-best option in town, head to **Ray's Tavern,** right

FROM THE ROAD

SUNSET HIKE TO DELICATE ARCH

Approaching Moab, I suddenly found myself plunged into a sea of red. Red dust, red rocks, red canyons and red spires took over the view, and the expanse became more scenic as my car rounded each corner. I reached Moab and headed north to one of Utah's best-known short hikes—the Sunset Hike to Delicate Arch.

As the sun began to meander toward the horizon, yellows and reds and purples began to reflect brilliantly off the red rock. A pair of crows settled on top of the arch, adding black to the otherwise solid-red expanse. Lightning and accompanying rain far in the distance produced the soft colors of an early-evening rainbow on a piece of sky visible directly through the arch itself. As the sun set, we started back down the slickrock. We began to notice billowing clouds at multiple levels of sky, some forming their own white arches in the sky as if to complement the red ones down below. Rain on two sides of the sky and the final traces of sunset on a third produced a brilliant alpenglow on the fourth, and the vast sea of red rock became transformed into greens, reds, and purples. The last of the light vanished just as we reached our cars. During the drive out, red arches became black silhouettes against the still slightly luminescent blue sky, while the distant twinkling lights of Moab and the pairs of headlights switchbacking down to the highway filled the void between the fading sky and the black canyon walls.

—Ben Siracusa

(A moderately strenuous 1hr. hike. Allow 25min. to drive from the park entrance to the trailhead. Ambient light lasts about 30min. after the sunset; bring a flashlight.)

next door at 26 S. Broadway. Rafting t-shirts adorn the walls above diners helping themselves to ½ lb. burgers and pizzas ($9-14) at tree-trunk tables. (☎435-564-3511. Open daily 11am-10pm.) During the harvest in August, look for **stands** along Main St., where fresh fruit is $0.17 per lb.

Main St. is lined with budget motels. One of the cheapest is **Budget Inn,** 60 E. Main St. Located across the street from the Green River Community Park, the inn offers Internet access, large rooms with queen-size beds, cable TV, and A/C units. (☎435-564-3441. Reception 24 hr. Singles $24-29; doubles $5 more.) **Robbers Roost Motel,** 225 W. Main St., offers clean, basic rooms with shower/bath combinations. (☎435-564-3452. Outdoor pool. Reception 7am-2am. Check-out 10:30am. Singles $29; doubles $39. Less in winter.) **Green River State Park,** 145 S. Green River Blvd., has 40 grassy sites and showers. (☎435-564-3633. No hookups. Check-in 3pm. Check-out 2pm. Sites $14.)

APPROACHING PRICE

Take **I-70 West** to **U.S. 191 North/U.S. 6 West.** At **Wellington** exit U.S. 191/6 to take the 78 mi. Scenic Backcountry Byway through **Nine-Mile Canyon.** (The marked turn-off for Silver Creek Rd. toward Nine-Mile Canyon is 51 mi. from I-70.) If you're not up for the strenuous drive, take U.S. 191 North to **U.S. 40 West** in **Duchesne.** Take Exit 243 for Bus. U.S. 6 through Price.

PRICE. Sixty-three miles from Green River, the route passes through Price, whose attractions include prehistoric displays and nearby outdoor sights. The **College of Eastern Utah's Prehistoric Museum,** 155 E. Main St., displays fossils and skeletons from the Cleveland-Lloyd Quarry, and has exhibits on Nine-Mile Canyon and prehistoric life in Utah. (☎435-637-5060. Open Apr.-Sept. daily 9am-6pm; Oct.-May M-Sa 9am-5pm. Free.) The **Log Palace Restaurant,** 150 N. Hospital Dr., serves American fare in a log cabin. (From the center of town, head north one block to turn left on Rte. 100 North. ☎435-636-0779. Breakfast $3-8. Sandwiches $5-9. Open M-Th 6am-2pm and 5-9pm, F 6am-2pm and 5-10pm, Sa 6am-10pm, Su 8am-6pm.)

LEAVING PRICE

Head west on **Rte. 100.** After going over the viaduct, take **U.S. 6 West/U.S. 191 North** through Helper.

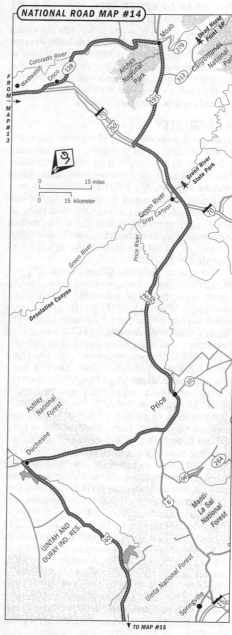

NATIONAL ROAD MAP #14

Moab

Dead Horse Point SP.

Colorado River

Westwater   Cisco   128   191   313   Canyonlands National Park

Arches National Park

FROM MAP #13

70   50

Green River State Park

Green River Gray Canyon

Price River

Green River

Desolation Canyon

95   70

10   Price

Ashley National Forest

Duchesne

UINTAH AND OURAY IND. RES.   40

96   264

6   Manti-La Sal National Forest

Uinta National Forest

Springville   15

0   15 miles
0   15 kilometer

▼ TO MAP #15

NATIONAL ROAD

THE ROAD TO HEBER CITY. Follow **U.S. 191** north as it forks off to the right. A designated scenic byway, this section runs through the **Ashley National Forest** and **Uintah and Ouray Indian Reservations.** At Duchesne, turn right off of U.S. 191 to follow **U.S. 40** west to Heber City. The latter 30 mi. of the trip to Heber City are more attractive then the earlier ones, as you enter the Uinta National Forest and pass the **Strawberry Reservoir.**

HEBER CITY

This farming community, 125 mi. from Price, lies in the shadow of its wealthier neighbor, Park City. U.S. 40 runs north-south through town as Main St. Heber Valley is home to the **Heber Valley Historic Railroad,** 450 S. 600 West. Using railcars that used to run through the area, this scenic railroad goes into Provo Canyon (3hr. round-trip). A shorter trip to Soldier Hollow (1½hr.) as well as one-way trips are available. (☎435-654-5601; Provo Canyon $24, seniors $21, children $14; Soldier Hollow $16/$13/$10.)

The upscale, delicious ▓**Snake Creek Grill,** 650 W. 100 South, seems somewhat out of place in this down-home, farming community. Eclectic main dishes ($11-20) include the chef's special, ten-spice salmon with red curry Japanese noodle stir fry ($18), as well as starters ($4-10) like grilled asparagus with shallot-black pepper vinaigrette. (☎435-654-2133; www.snakecreekgrill.com. Open Su 5:30-8:30pm, W-Sa 5:30-9:30pm) The less fancy but still decent **Wagon Wheel Cafe,** 220 N. Main St., serves tasty food at reasonable prices. (☎435-654-0251. All-day breakfast $2-7. Sandwiches $4-6. Entrees $8-14. Open daily 6:30am-10pm.) Located in Park City, about 15 mi. north of Heber City, ▓**Base Camp Park City,** 268 Historic Main St., is a dazzling, state-of-the-art hostel offering 70 affordable beds. Also included are free Internet, free parking, discounts on selected Main St. restaurants, a spectacular movie/DVD theater, and free transportation to Deer Valley, The Canyons, and Park City ski areas. (Take U.S 40/U.S. 189 north to Park City and turn left on Rte. 248. ☎435-655-7244 or 888-980-7244; www.parkcitybasecamp.com. Make reservations by phone or on-line far in advance during ski season. Summer dorms $25; private rooms $80. Winter $35/$120.) Unlike in Park City, where Base Camp is the only budget option, affordable accommodations abound in Heber City. The **Alpine Lodge,** 90 N. Main St., has solid, older rooms with comfortable, homey furnishings. (☎435-654-0231. Singles $36; doubles $42, with kitchenettes $49-59. Senior and AAA discounts.) At the **Bear Mountain Motel,** 425 S. Main St. (U.S. 40), roadtrippers can expect to find spacious, comfortably furnished, clean rooms with refrigerators. (☎435-654-2150. Summer singles $46; doubles $57. Winter $32-38/$42.)

THE ROAD TO BIG COTTONWOOD CANYON

If you have plenty of time and a yen to see more dirt roads and parklands, get to Salt Lake City by driving through **Wasatch Mountain State Park,** which leads through Big Cottonwood Canyon and offers scenic vistas and access to excellent hiking trails. This route is passable for 2WD vehicles in dry conditions; it is not recommended in wet conditions. Guardsman Pass is closed to all vehicles in winter. If conditions are iffy, skip this route and follow U.S. 40 to I-80 West heading into the city.

To go through the park, head west out of Heber City on Rte. 100 South (Rte. 113) and continue into the town of **Midway.** Two blocks west of Center St. in Midway, turn right at the sign for Rte. 224. Follow **Rte. 224** until it ends up on **Homestead Dr.** and the **Watsatch Mountain State Park Visitors Center.** Turn right at the sign to stay on Rte. 224. Continue past the **Pine Creek Campground.** After the road becomes dirt, travel 7.5 mi. to **Guardsman Pass,** forking left at the sign for **Brighton.** Continue west on **Rte. 152** through the **Big Cottonwood Canyon.** Rte. 152 runs about 14 mi. through the canyon, between Brighton and the outskirts of Salt Lake City. The drive itself offers great views of the canyon, even if you choose not to stop, making the dirt road worthwhile.

BIG COTTONWOOD CANYON

Spanning over 22,000 acres, Big Cottonwood Canyon (emergency within park ☎435-654-1791; $5 per vehicle), includes parts of the Wasatch Mountains. While the area is perhaps best known for the skiing offered in the winter, summertime travelers will find an array of forested camping areas and recreational opportunities like a golf course and hiking trails. More spectacular hiking, however, lies just over Guardsman Pass in Big Cottonwood Canyon. Trails here include the **Mill B South Fork** to Lake Blanche, Florence, and **Lillian,** which is strenuous but not technically challenging and offers great canyon and lake views. An easy hike (½ mi.) to the second bridge, leads to a shaded bench by the water with a view of the canyon. The Mill B South Fork Trailhead is on the left, 9½ mi. from the stop sign at the bottom of the road to Guardsman Pass. The **Wetland Loop** (¾ mi.), a flat interpretive trail, takes you around wetlands at the edge of Brighton and explains their ecosystem.

Little Deer Creek Campground (☎435-654-3961) has 17 shady tent sites ($11) with water and flush toilets but no electricity or showers. **Pine Creek Campground** in Oak Hollow Loop, has 40 secluded tent sites in open areas surrounded by trees. (☎801-322-3770. Water, showers, picnic tables, and grills. Gates open 8am-10pm. Reservations recommended; $7 fee. Sites $17.)

APPROACHING SALT LAKE CITY
After leaving the forest, turn right onto **Rte. 190**. Go 1½ mi. and take **I-215 West** to **I-15 North** to Exit 310, following the signs to downtown **Salt Lake.**

SALT LAKE CITY

Salt Lake City has long been a welcome sight for travelers. Tired from five grueling months of travel, Brigham Young looked out across the Great Salt Lake and proclaimed: "This is the place." In this desolate valley, he believed that his band of Mormon pioneers had finally found a haven where they could practice their religion. To this day, Salt Lake City remains dominated by Mormon influence. The Church of Jesus Christ of Latter-Day Saints owns the tallest office building downtown and welcomes visitors to Temple Square, the epicenter of the Mormon religion. Despite its commitment to preserving tradition, Salt Lake is rapidly attracting high-tech firms and droves of outdoor enthusiasts.

VITAL STATS

Population: 180,000

Visitor Info: Salt Palace Convention Center and Salt Lake City Visitors Bureau, 90 S. West Temple (☎801-534-4902; www.visitsaltlake.com), in Salt Palace Convention Center. Open M-F 8:30am-6pm, Sa-Su 9am-5pm.

Internet Access: Salt Lake Public Library, 209 E. 500 South (☎801-524-8200). Open M-Th 9am-9pm, F-Sa 9am-6pm, Su 1-5pm.

Post Office: 230 W. 200 South (☎800-275-8777). Open M-F 8am-5pm, Sa 9am-2pm. **Postal Code:** 84101.

GETTING AROUND

Like most in cities in Utah, Salt Lake City's streets follow a grid system. Brigham Young designated **Temple Square** as the heart of downtown. Street names increase in increments of 100 and indicate how many blocks east, west, north, or south they lie from Temple Sq.; the "0" points are **Main St.** (north-south) and **South Temple** (east-west). State St., West Temple, and North Temple are 100 level streets. Occasionally, streets are referred to as 13th South or 17th North, which are the same as 1300 South or 1700 North. Local address listings often include two cross streets.

ON THE EDGE

It was the one section I didn't bother to read. I had dutifully memorized survival-book sections on runaway camels and alien abduction. The chapter on what to do if your car is hanging off the edge of a cliff, though, struck me as contrived. If your car's hanging off a cliff, I thought, you're screwed. Next page. Driving down the dirt road through Nine-Mile Canyon on the way from Vernal to Price, a car appeared around a blind corner. We swerved right, into a ditch. The front right tire hit a boulder and the rear of the car swung right, slamming canyon wall as we skidded across the road. I closed my eyes before we came to rest, tilted backwards at a 45° angle, the right front tire 2 ft. off the ground. A second elapsed. I opened the door and got out, slowly, deliberately. I looked down—100 ft. Later the car would be winched back onto the road, loaded onto a truck, and taken away. Life would go on, a little more real.

—*Evan North*

FROM THE ROAD

Salt Lake City

▲ ACCOMMODATIONS
The Avenues Hostel
(HI-AYH), **3**
City Creek Inn, **2**
Ute Hostel
(AAIH/Rucksackers), **11**

● FOOD
Orbit, **6**
Red Iguana, **1**
Ruth's Diner, **8**
Sage's Cafe, **10**

■ NIGHTLIFE
Bricks, **5**
Club Axis, **4**
DV8, **7**
Zipperz, **9**

For example, a building on 13th South (1300 South) might be listed as 825 E. 1300 South, meaning the cross street is 800 East (8th East). Metered **parking** spots are usually available and inexpensive. ($0.25 per 20min.)

🔵 SIGHTS

LATTER-DAY SIGHTS. The majority of Salt Lake City's sights are sacred to the Church of Jesus Christ of Latter-Day Saints, and free. The seat of Mormon authority and the central temple, **Temple Square** is the symbolic center. The square has two **Visitors Centers,** north and south. Visitors can wander the flowery ten-acre square, but the temple is off-limits to non-Saints. Tours leave from the flagpole every 10min. *The Testaments,* a film detailing the coming of Jesus Christ to the Americas (as related by the Book of Mormon), is screened at the **Joseph Smith Memorial Building.** *(☎ 800-537-9703. Open M-Sa 9am-9pm. Free.)* Temple Sq. is also home to the **Mormon Tabernacle** and its famed choir. Weekly rehearsals and performances are free. In the summer, there are frequent free concerts at **Assembly Hall** next door. *(Assembly Hall ☎ 800-537-9703. Organ recitals Su 2-2:30pm, M-Sa noon-12:30pm; in summer also M-Sa 2-2:30pm. Choir rehearsals Th 8-9:30pm. Choir broadcasts Su 9:15am.)*

The **Church of Jesus Christ of Latter Day Saints Office Building** is the tallest skyscraper in town. The elevator to the 26th floor grants a view of the Great Salt Lake to the west opposite the Wasatch Range. *(40 E. North Temple. ☎ 801-240-3789.*

Observation deck open M-F 9am-4:30pm.) The church's genealogical materials are accessible and free at the Family Search Center, 15 E. South Temple, in the Joseph Smith Memorial Building. The actual collection is housed in the Family History Library. (35 N. West Temple. ☎ 801-240-2331. Center open M-Sa 9am-9pm. Library open M 7:30am-5pm, Tu-Sa 7:30am-10pm.)

CAPITOL HILL. At the northern end of State St., Utah's **State Capitol** features beautiful grounds, including a garden that changes daily. *(☎ 801-538-3000. Open M-F 8am-5pm. Tours M-F 9am-4pm.)* Down State St., **Hansen Planetarium** has free exhibits and laser shows. *(15 S. State St. ☎ 801-531-4925. Open M-Th 9am-9pm, F-Sa 9:30am-midnight, Su 1-5pm. Laser show $6. Science show $4.50.)*

PIONEER MEMORIAL MUSEUM. In Salt Lake City, "Pioneer" refers to those who came to Utah with Joseph Smith and in the 20 years thereafter (1847-1869) to help found the Mormon Church. This huge museum has hundreds of photographs and hand-crafted personal items. The jewels of the museum are several sets of "character dolls," and a 1902 horse-drawn steam fire engine. *(300 N. Main St., across Columbus St. from the State Capitol. ☎ 801-538-1050. Open M-Sa 9am-5pm; June-Aug. also Su 1-5pm. Free.)*

OTHER MUSEUMS. Visiting exhibits and a world art wow enthusiasts at the expanded **Utah Museum of Fine Arts,** on the University of Utah campus. *(☎ 801-581-7332. Open M-F 10am-5pm, Sa-Su noon-5pm. Free.)* Also on campus, the **Museum of Natural History** focuses on the history of the Wasatch Front. *(☎ 801-581-6927. Open M-Sa 9:30am-5:30pm, Su noon-5pm. $4, ages 3-12 $2.50, under 3 free.)* The **Salt Lake Art Center** displays art and documentary films. *(20 S. West Temple. ☎ 801-328-4201. Open Su 1-5pm, Tu-Th and Sa 10am-5pm, F 10am-9pm. Suggested donation $2.)*

RED BUTTE GARDEN AND ARBORETUM. In the hills above the city, the arboretum offers 4 mi. of hiking trails with views of wildlife, the Red Butte Canyon, and wildflowers. The garden offers an outdoor summer concert series. *(300 Wakara Way., on the University of Utah campus. ☎ 801-581-4747; www.redbuttegarden.com. Open May-Sept. M-Sa 9am-8pm, Su 9am-5pm; Apr. and Oct. daily 9am-5pm; Nov.-Mar. Su and Tu-Sa 10am-5pm. $5; students, seniors, and children $3.)*

CITY CREEK CANYON. City Creek Canyon offers scenic picnicking and recreation close to the city. The one-way 5¾ mi. drive climbs 1300 ft. Picnicking pavilions must be reserved in advance. *(Head east into the Avenues neighborhood and take B St. north. ☎ 801-596-5065. Open daily 8am-10pm; last entry 8pm. Open to vehicles on even-numbered days, bicycles on odd-numbered days, and pedestrians all the time. $2.50. Picnic pavilions $2.50-3.)*

🎵 ENTERTAINMENT

Salt Lake City's sweltering summer months are filled with frequent evening concerts. Every Tuesday and Friday at 7:30pm, the **Temple Square Concert Series** presents a free outdoor concert in Brigham Young Historic Park, with music ranging from string quartets to acoustic guitar. (☎ 801-240-2534. Call for a schedule.) The **Utah Symphony Orchestra** performs in Bereaving Hall, 123 W. South Temple. (☎ 801-533-6683. Office open M-F 10am-6pm. Tickets Sept. to early May $15-40. Limited summer season; call 1 week in advance.)

The free *City Weekly* lists events and is available at bars, clubs, and restaurants. Famous for teetotaling, the early Mormon theocrats made it illegal to serve alcohol in a public place. Hence, all liquor-serving institutions are "private clubs," serving only members and "sponsored" guests. To get around this law, most bars and clubs charge a "temporary membership fee"—essentially a cover charge. Nonetheless, Salt Lake City has an active nightlife, centering on S. West Temple and the run-down blocks near the railroad tracks. **Bricks,** 200 S. 600 West, is the city's oldest and largest dance club. (☎ 801-238-0255. Separate 18+ and 21+ areas. Cover $5-7. Open daily 9:30pm-2am.) **Club Axis,** 100 S. 500 West, features VIP lounges, a jungle-themed bar, and multiple dance floors. (☎ 801-519-2947; www.clubaxis.com. F gay/alt. lifestyle night, W and Sa dress to impress. Separate 18+ and 21+ areas. Cover $5-7. Open W-Sa 10pm-2am.) At six stories, **DV8,** 115 S. West Temple, hosts live acts Monday through Thursday for all ages. (☎ 801-539-8400. F-Sa club nights 21+. Cover $5-7. Club open F-Sa 9pm-2am; call for M-Th times.) A diverse mix of Salt Lake City's gay and lesbian crowd flocks to the classy **Zipperz,** 155 W. 200 South, to sip martinis ($4.75) in wingchairs and groove on the dance floor. (☎ 801-521-8300. 21+. Cover $5-6. Open Su-Th 2pm-2am, F-Sa 5pm-2am.)

⬛ FOOD

Good, cheap restaurants are sprinkled around the city and its suburbs. If you're in a hurry downtown, **ZCMI Mall** and **Crossroads Mall,** both across from Temple Sq., have standard food courts.

⬛ **Sage's Cafe,** 473 E. 300 South (☎801-322-3790). This organic, vegan cafe is a hotbed of culinary innovation. Calling themselves "culinary astronauts," talented chefs produce delectable dishes. Try the basil and macadamia nut pesto pasta dish for $13. Sugar- and oil-free meals available. Weekday lunch buffet $6.75. Open Su 9am-9pm, W-Th 5pm-9:30pm, F 5pm-10pm, Sa 9am-10pm.

⬛ **Ruth's Diner,** 2100 Emigration Canyon Rd. (☎801-582-5807; www.ruthsdiner.com). The best breakfasts in town and a bar with live music at night. Originally run out of a trolley car, Ruth's is the 2nd-oldest restaurant in Utah and has been a Salt Lake landmark for 70 years. Huge portions, delicious omelettes like the "Rutherino" ($6-7), and brownie sundaes ($6) help it outlast rivals. Open daily 8am-10pm.

Red Iguana, 736 W. North Temple (☎801-322-4834), across the bridge from downtown in the bright orange building. This popular eatery serves up authentic pre-Colombian Mexican food, including burritos, enchiladas, tacos ($5-7), and combo plates ($10-12). Open M-Th 11am-10pm, F-Sa 11am-11pm, Su noon-9pm.

Orbit, 540 W. 200 South (☎801-322-3808; www.orbitslc.com), close to the dance clubs in the old industrial district. With a sports bar and patio seating, Orbit boasts sleek decor and a diverse clientele. Sandwiches $7-10. Dinner entrees $10-16. Pizzas $8-10. Open M-W 11am-11pm, Th-F 11am-1am, Sa 10am-1am, Su 10am-10pm.

⬛ ACCOMMODATIONS

Affordable chain motels cluster at the southern end of downtown, around 200 West and 600 South, and on North Temple.

City Creek Inn, 230 W. North Temple (☎801-533-9100; www.citycreekinn.com), a stone's throw from Temple Sq. 33 immaculate ranch-style rooms for the cheapest rates downtown. Singles $53; doubles $64. AAA discount.

Ute Hostel (AAIH/Rucksackers), 21 E. Kelsey Ave. (☎801-595-1645 or 888-255-1192), near the inter-section of 1300 South and Main St. Free tea and coffee, parking, linen. Reception 24hr. Reservations accepted in advance with pre-payment, recommended July-Sept. and Jan.-Mar. Dorms $15; singles $25; doubles $35. Cash only.

The Avenues Hostel (HI-AYH), 107 F St. (☎801-359-3855), a 15min. walk from Temple Sq. in a residential area. Free parking, a new entertainment system, 2 kitchens, and mountain bike rentals ($10 per day; $100 deposit). Key deposit $5. Reception 7:30am-noon and 4-10:30pm. Reservations recommended July-Aug. and Jan.-Mar. Dorms $17; doubles $36.

⬛ LEAVING SALT LAKE CITY

From downtown, take **600 North** west to **I-15 South,** and take the first exit for **I-80 West.**

⬛ GREAT SALT LAKE

Take Exit 104 for access to the south shore; there is also a scenic overlook from the highway about 3½ mi. past the exit, near milepost 101. To get to the island, take Exit 335 from I-15 and follow signs to the causeway.

The Great Salt Lake is so salty that only blue-green algae and brine shrimp can survive in it. The salt content varies from 5-27%, providing the unusual buoyancy credited with keeping the lake free of drownings. Decaying organic material on the lake shore gives the lake its pungent odor, which locals prefer not to discuss. **Antelope Island State Park,** in the middle of the lake, is a favorite for visitors. (☎801-625-1630. Open daily 7am-10pm; winter dawn-dusk. Vehicles $8, bicycles and pedestrians $4.) There are two options for visiting the south shore. **Saltair** is located just across from the exit and has and a souvenir shop. The beach itself is nearly non-existent, but many tourists use this spot to access the water. (☎801-250-4388. Open May-Sept. daily 9am-9pm.) About 1½ mi. west of Saltair is the **Great Salt Lake State Marina,** the starting point for cruises on the lake. (☎801-252-9336. $12-18; dinner cruises $29-48.)

THE ROAD TO DELTA

After you visit the lake, get back on I-80 West to Rte. 36 toward **Tooele.** Rte. 36 runs across a sparsely populated area of the state, ending about 88 mi. from Salt Lake City. As Rte. 36 ends, follow signs for U.S. 6 West to Delta. Gasoline is available in the tiny town of **Lynndyl** if you need to fill up before cutting across the 94 mi. no-man's-land in the western part of the state. In the town of Tooele, **Melina's,** 29 N. Main St., has captured the hearts of locals with its central location. (☎ 801-843-8700. Burritos $3-7. Mixed dinner platters $5-8. Steak and seafood $5-12. Open M-Sa 11am-10pm.) The dunes are open for enjoyment at the **Little Sahara Recreation Area,** just over 100 mi. from Salt Lake City, the dunes are open for enjoyment. Primitive camping is available. The day-use fee ($8) lasts until 2pm the next day, regardless of arrival time. (Turn off U.S. 6, head about 6 mi. on a dirt road to the Visitors Center, and turn right at the sign. ☎ 435-433-5965. Visitors Center open F 1-10pm, Sa 9am-10pm, Su 8am-6pm. Sites $8.)

APPROACHING DELTA

About 5 mi. outside of Delta, a sign "To U.S. 50" leads to U.S. 50 East; ignore this sign. Entering Delta, **U.S. 6** and **U.S. 50 West** merge; follow them ½ mi. west to the town center. U.S. 6/50 is known as **Main St.**

DELTA

Delta is the largest in a cluster of desert towns near a wide section of the Sevier River, and the largest outpost until Ely, NV, 170 mi. west. The **Great Basin Museum,** 328 W. 100 North, has a collection of local memorabilia as well as exhibits on mining and geology. Outside is an exhibit on the Topaz Internment Camp, where Japanese Americans were held during WWII. Don't miss the 3D map which shows the roadtrip route from Green River to the Nevada border. (☎ 435-864-5013. Open M-Sa 10am-4pm. Free.) Visitor info is available at the **Delta City Chamber of Commerce,** 80 N. 200 West. (☎ 435-864-4316. Open M-F 8:30am-3pm.)

Locals leave their own mugs for their daily coffee at **Top's City Cafe,** 313 W. Main St. (☎ 435-864-2148. Sandwiches $5-6. Dinner entrees $8-12. Steak $14-17. Open summer M-Sa 6am-10pm, Su 7am-9pm; winter closes 1hr. earlier.) Much more than the name implies, **The Pizza House,** 69 S. 300 East, serves filling Italian and American food at refreshingly cheap prices. (☎ 435-864-2207. Open M-Th 11am-9:30pm, F-Sa 11am-10pm.) Roadtrippers may want to catch up on rest before the long ride across the emptiness of Utah at the ⬛**Budget Motel,** 75 S. 350 East, which offers unusually high-quality rooms for the price. Other highlights here include A/C, powerful showers, and a noon checkout time. (☎ 435-864-4533. Singles $30; doubles $33. $2 AAA discount.) Small but homey, the

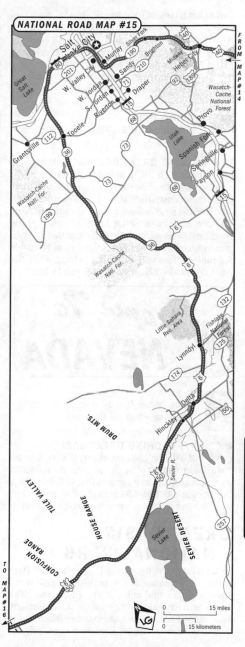

NATIONAL ROAD MAP #15

FROM MAP #14

Salt Lake City
Murray
Silver Fork
Brighton
Midway
Heber City
Great Salt Lake
W. Valley City
Sandy
W. Jordan
S. Jordan
Riverton
Draper
Wasatch-Cache National Forest
Tooele
Utah Lake
Provo
Grantsville
Spanish Fork
Springville
Payson
Wasatch-Cache Natl. For.
Wasatch-Cache Natl. For.
Little Sahara Rec. Area
Fishlake National Forest
Lynndyl
Delta
Hinckley
DRUM MTS.
Sevier R.
TULE VALLEY
HOUSE RANGE
CONFUSION RANGE
Sevier Lake
SEVIER DESERT

TO MAP #16

0   15 miles
0   15 kilometers

NATIONAL ROAD

Deltan Inn Motel, 347 E. Main St., has minimal furnishings, thin walls, refrigerators, and microwaves. (☎ 435-864-5318. Singles $29; doubles $32.)

Don't forget to fill up on gas before leaving Delta—there are miles and miles and miles between here and the next pump!

LEAVING DELTA
Take **Main St. (U.S. 6/50)** west out of town, following signs for Ely.

THE ROAD TO GREAT BASIN. The last gas is 6 mi. west of Delta, in **Hinckley.** A long, straight road stretches across the desert, and lonely mileposts count down the 83 mi. to the Nevada border. Much of the road is flat, and part goes through the lakebed of ancient Sevier Lake. Eventually, the road begins its ascent into the mountains. When you emerge on the other side, the road is visible for miles before you. Gambling is legal when the road crosses into Nevada, 89 mi. from Delta.

Welcome To **NEVADA**

As the border, U.S. 6/50 enters the Pacific Time Zone, where it is 1hr. earlier.

APPROACHING GREAT BASIN
Just after the cattle guard exactly 3 mi. from the state border, turn left at the sign for Great Basin National Park. Turn left at the stop sign onto **Rte. 487.** Turn right at the junction with **Rte. 488** in the town of **Baker.** Turn right. The park lies an additional 5 mi. down this road.

GREAT BASIN NATIONAL PARK

Established in 1986, Great Basin National Park preserves ancient glaciers, prehistoric pine trees, diverse fauna, and miles of unrefined trails. The basin area extends through much of Nevada, and is so named because no precipitation falling in the region reaches the ocean. Eastern Nevada's Snake

Range forms the spine of the park, with various creeks, lakes, and forest spreading out from its peaks. Despite the desolation of the area's vast desert stretches, high alpine areas created by the towering ranges support a surprising ecological diversity, including rare species such as the ancient bristlecone pine and the mountain lion.

VITAL STATS

Area: 77,100 acres.

Visitor Info: Great Basin National Park Visitors Center (☎ 775-234-7331; www.nps.gov/grba), at the end of Rte. 488. Open daily May-Oct. 7:30am-5:30pm; Nov.-Apr. 8am-4:30pm.

Gateway towns: Baker, Ely (**p. 412**).

Fees: No entrance fee. Lehman Caves $2-8.

GETTING AROUND

Only one paved road, **Rte. 488,** enters the park, running west to the **Visitors Center** and providing access to all four of the park's developed campgrounds along the way. Improved gravel roads grant access to the park's northern reaches and central drainage, while a high-clearance dirt road ventures into the park's southern mountains. **Ely** bills itself as a gateway to the park and offers most comforts, but the town of **Baker** (5 mi. from the Visitors Center) and the **Border Inn** (13 mi. from the park on U.S. 6/50) also provide basic services.

SIGHTS

Beginning just down the hill from the Visitors Center, the paved **Wheeler Peak Scenic Drive** winds 12 mi. to 10,000 ft. Laden with sharp curves and switchbacks, the road demands caution and takes 25-40min. one-way. As the road climbs, it passes first through greasebrush and sagebrush, then piñon pines and junipers, then ponderosa pines, white fir, and mountain mahogany, and finally through spruce, limber pine, and high alpine aspen groves. As late as June, snowbanks line the summit area and make the warm desert weather at the base a pleasant memory. **Mather Overlook** features an awe-inspiring view of jagged **Wheeler Peak** and **Wheeler Glacier;** in the other direction, the road stretches across the flat basin you crossed on your way west to the park. For a closer view of the peak, stop at **Wheeler Peak Overlook.**

NATIONAL ROAD

Because much of the park remains undeveloped, exploring its far reaches requires good hiking boots, plenty of water, several days of food, and strong legs. Luckily, for those not enthusiastic about hauling a burly pack through the backcountry, the park's other most notable features, **Bristlecone Groves, Lexington Arch,** and **Lehman Cave,** are accessible via shorter excursions.

LEHMAN CAVE. Absalom Lehman came across these splendid caves in 1885, and soon he was charging visitors for the pleasure of exploring them by candlelight. The caves continue to delight travelers with their fantastic formations. The Park Service prohibits self-guided tours, offering three varieties of **guided tours:** entrance into the first room only, the Gothic Palace; a 1hr. tour of the Gothic Palace, Lodge Room, and Inscription Room; and a 1½hr. tour of the entire accessible cave including the spectacular **Grand Palace Room.** The cave remains cool at 50°F all year, a refreshing break from the sun in the summer months; just be sure to bring an extra layer. (☎ 775-234-7331, ext. 242. Tours mid-June to mid-Aug. every 30min. 8am-4:30pm; Sept.-May every 2hr. 9am-3pm. 30min. tour $2, under 12 free; 1hr. tour $6/$3; 1½hr. tour $8/$4. Reservations recommended. No children under 5 permitted on the Grand Palace tour.)

LEXINGTON ARCH. A mammoth, six-story limestone sculpture in the wild southeast section of the park, Lexington Arch is evidence of nature's powerful craftsmanship. The 3½ mi. round-trip hike switches back and forth up several hundred feet before paralleling a drainage back to the base of the arch. The majority of the trail, which gains a total 820 ft., sits on Forest Service land, so dogs are welcome. (Drive south 12 mi. from the intersection of Rte. 487 and 488 through Garrison, UT, to the sign for Lexington Arch. Follow the rough, high-clearance dirt road nearly 12 mi. to the trailhead.)

BRISTLECONE PINE GROVE. The Great Basin Bristlecones, gnarled but beautiful trees, are the world's oldest living organisms. Bristlecones regularly grow high on mountain slopes where no other trees can survive by deadening themselves until more hospitable times allow then to flourish. Although there are several Bristlecone groves throughout the park, the grove below Wheeler Peak offers the easiest access. Follow the Wheeler Peak Scenic Drive to the end and take the trail (2¾ mi. round-trip) from **Bristlecone Trailhead** to the trees. Tours of the grove depart from the trailhead at 10am daily during the summer.

▨ OUTDOOR ACTIVITIES

For the experienced **spelunker,** the park contains extensive limestone caverns. Exploring them requires a permit from the Park Service, acquired two weeks in advance and with proof of significant prior caving experience. Although cycling in the park is limited to roads, **mountain bikers** will relish excellent riding at the BLM's **Sacramento Pass Recreation Site,** east of the park along U.S. 6/50. Some of the best trails in the area explore Black Horse Canyon, northeast of the park, accessible off of U.S. 6/50 via the marked forest road, three quarters of a mile south of Sacramento Pass.

Several trails along the Wheeler Peak Scenic Drive grant ample opportunities to stretch weary legs. For a less crowded jaunt, try the longer trails departing from the Baker Creek Trailhead. The **Mountain View Nature Trail** (30min.) begins at the Rhodes Cabin next to the Visitors Center and provides a brief glimpse into park ecology and geology for those pressed for time. Stop by the Visitors Center for an informative trail guide. The **Alpine Lakes Loop Trail** (2¾ mi. round-trip; 1½-2½hr.) climbs a heavily used trail that allows quick access to two scenic lakes, Stella and Teresa, as well as views of Wheeler Peak, which looms overhead. The trailhead is at the end of Wheeler Peak Scenic Drive. The only day hike flagged for winter use, **Lehman Creek Trail** (7 mi. round-trip; 4-6hr.) hugs the babbling creek for much of its course, with over 2000 ft. in elevation change through a range of Great Basin habitats. This trail departs from the end of Wheeler Peak Scenic Drive or either of the Lehman Creek campgrounds.

▨ FOOD

Catering to those unwilling to trek to Baker or pack their own grub, the Visitors Center's **Lehman Caves Cafe** serves breakfast ($5), sandwiches ($5), and ice cream, and peddles park memorabilia. (☎ 775-234-7221. Open daily June-Aug. 8am-5pm; Apr.-May and Sept.-Oct. 8am-4pm.) For a more substantial menu, check out **T&D's** restaurant, bar, and convenience store in the center of Baker. The store stocks grocery and camping essentials, and the restaurant serves breakfasts (F-Su; $3-4), sandwiches and burgers ($4-7), and Mexican food. (☎ 775-234-7264. Store open daily 8am-7pm. Restaurant open M-Th 11am-9pm, F-Su 7am-9pm.)

CAMPING

Four developed campsites accommodate Great Basin visitors in addition to several primitive sites along Snake and Strawberry Creeks and nearly unlimited backcountry camping. All four developed campgrounds cost $10 per night per vehicle and are first come, first served. **Wheeler Peak Campground** (9890 ft.) offers scenic sites nestled among aspen groves and alpine meadows in the shadow of 13,000 ft. Wheeler Peak. Access to the sites is at the end of the serpentine Wheeler Peak Scenic Dr., a road not recommended for vehicles over 24 ft. (37 sites. Pit toilets and potable water. Open June-Sept.) Following the graded gravel road south from Rte. 488 leads to **Baker Creek Campground** (7530 ft.), a serene spot on the banks of Baker Creek. (32 sites. Pit toilets and potable water. Open May-Oct.) **Upper** (24 sites; open May-Oct., try sites 17-24 for a more removed and spacious stay) and **Lower** (11 sites) **Lehman Creek Campgrounds,** close to the Visitors Center and Lehman Caves, guard the banks of Lehman Creek along the first 3 mi. of the Wheeler Mountain Scenic Dr. Both campgrounds crowd quickly, so arrive early. Both sites have pit toilets and potable water. Both Upper Lehman and Wheeler Creek Campgrounds host evening ranger talks during summer months. Scenic **primitive camping,** which offers pre-dug fire pits, rewards those willing to travel gravel roads. **Snake Creek Rd.,** 5 mi. south of Baker along Rte. 487, follows the fertile watershed Snake Creek area and allows easy access to six primitive sites. **Strawberry Creek Rd.,** 3 mi. from the U.S. 6/50 and Rte. 487 junction, leads to four primitive sites along Strawberry Creek.

Motels are rare, but the **Border Inn,** straddling the Utah/Nevada border along U.S. 6/50, proffers sizeable rooms with miniature TVs and VCRs. (☎ 775-234-7300. Singles $31-33.) For four walls and a mattress somewhat closer to the mountains, try the **Silver Jack Motel,** at 14 Main St., in Baker. (☎ 775-234-7323. Singles $37-42.)

DETOUR: LAS VEGAS
In Majors Place, hang a left off U.S. 6/50 for the 255 mi. trek south on the U.S. 93.

It's not a daytrip by any stretch, but Las Vegas (see The North American Route, p. 685) offers a glittery change of scenery from the Nevada desert.

APPROACHING ELY
Entering Ely, U.S. 6 heads left; stay on **U.S. 50.**

ELY

With a lonely 70 mi. of U.S. 6 separating Ely (rhymes with "really") and the entrance to Great Basin National Park, this mining town hardly fits the profile of a typical "gateway" city, but its barren surroundings and the convergence several highways make Ely the locus of much trans-Nevadan traffic. In the beginning of the century, development of the area's copper resources brought an influx of residents and a railroad system, but today's Ely is a shadow of its old self. Remnants of past glory remain—like the stately Nevada Hotel and Casino, once the state's tallest building.

((VITAL STATS))

Population: 4000

Visitor Info: White Pine County Chamber of Commerce, 636 Autland St. (☎ 775-289-8877). Open M-F 9am-5pm.

Internet Access: White Pine County Library, 900 Campton St. (☎ 775-289-3737), 1 block south of Autland St. Open M-Th 9am-6pm, F 9am-5pm; 1st and 3rd Sa of each month 10am-2pm.

Post Office: 2600 Bristlecone Ave. (☎ 775-289-9276). Open M-F 8:30am-5pm, Sa 10am-2pm. **Postal code:** 89301.

[GETTING AROUND. U.S. 6, 50, and **93** meet in Ely and radiate toward Reno, Las Vegas, Utah, Idaho, and California. Approaching the town from the southeast, U.S. 50 runs along **Great Basin Blvd.** before turning west onto **Aultman St.,** Ely's main drag, lined with restaurants, shops, banks, casinos and budget motels. Great Basin Blvd. serves as the division between numbered north-south streets with an east and west designation. Lettered streets run east-west, east of Great Basin Blvd.

◎ SIGHTS. In 1983, the railroad through East Ely shut down, leaving behind an office and depot full of old equipment and records. Relics from the depot are on display at the **Nevada Northern Railway Museum,** 1100 Ave. A, in East Ely. A tour goes through the restored office building and well-informed guides share their knowledge of the railroad, town, and surrounding region. There's also a train ride on the old line, pulled by a 93-year-old coal-fired locomotive. Or you can drive a locomotive 14 mi. yourself—$550 for the steam locomotive, $300 for the diesel. (Where U.S. 50 turns left onto Aultman St., turn right and then left onto 11th St. East. ☎775-289-2085 or 866-407-8326; www.nevadanorthernrailway.com. Open M-F 8am-5pm, and some weekends. Tours free. Train rides M-F 1 per day, Sa-Su 2 per day. $12-35, ages 4-12 $8-18. No train Tu.) The **White Pine Public Museum,** 2000 Aultman St., displays artifacts and a hodgepodge of paraphernalia from stuffed birds to telegraph equipment. (☎775-289-4710. Hours vary; call ahead. Free.)

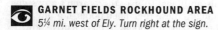 **FOOD & ACCOMMODATIONS.** Aultman St. has several steak-and-potatoes chop houses, including restaurants in the downtown casinos. The **Red Apple Family Restaurant,** 2060 Aultman St., serves up substantial portions of classic American food. The menu is limited, but what they make is tasty. (☎775-289-8585. Breakfast $2-7. Sandwiches and burgers $4-6. Meat entrees $7-13. Reduced prices for seniors and children under 12. Open daily 6am-10pm.) **La Fiesta,** on McGill Hwy., prepares lunch (11am-3pm; $6.25-6.75) and the $10 Taquitos La Fiesta. (☎775-289-4112. Open daily 11am-9:30pm.) For a change of pace, **Twin Wok,** 700 Great Basin Blvd., offers Chinese and Japanese cuisine. Try Mandarin entrees ($8-10) or pricier ($11-15) hibachi selections. (☎775-289-3699. Open daily 11am-10pm.)

Many of Ely's 17 hotels and motels are located on Aultman St. Far and away the best is the grand **Hotel Nevada,** 501 Aultman St., a relic from another era. Many rooms are shrines to celebrities who have stayed here, like Mickey Rooney and Wayne Newton. (☎775-289-6665 or 888-406-3055. Singles $30-38; doubles $40-48.) **The Rustic Inn,** 1555 Aultman St., is one of the cheapest in town, with clean rooms kept by friendly owners. (☎775-289-6797. Singles from $25; doubles from $35.)

LEAVING ELY
Follow **Aultman St. (U.S. 50)** west out of town. Gas between Ely and Fallon is expensive, but don't forget to fill up—the next chance is 77 mi. away.

GARNET FIELDS ROCKHOUND AREA
5¼ mi. west of Ely. Turn right at the sign.

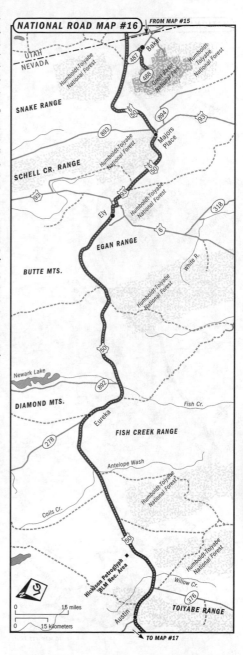

NATIONAL ROAD MAP #16   FROM MAP #15

UTAH
NEVADA
Baker
487
488
Great Basin National Park
Humboldt-Toiyabe National Forest
Humboldt-Toiyabe National Forest

SNAKE RANGE

50
894
93
893
Majors Place

SCHELL CR. RANGE
Humboldt-Toiyabe National Forest
50
93
318

Ely
Humboldt-Toiyabe National Forest
6

EGAN RANGE

BUTTE MTS.
Humboldt-Toiyabe National Forest
White R.

50

Newark Lake
892
Fish Cr.

DIAMOND MTS.
Eureka

FISH CREEK RANGE
278
Antelope Wash

Humboldt-Toiyabe National Forest

Coils Cr.

50

Hickison Petroglyph BLM Rec. Area

0   15 miles
0   15 kilometers

Willow Cr.
376
Austin
TOIYABE RANGE

TO MAP #17

NATIONAL ROAD

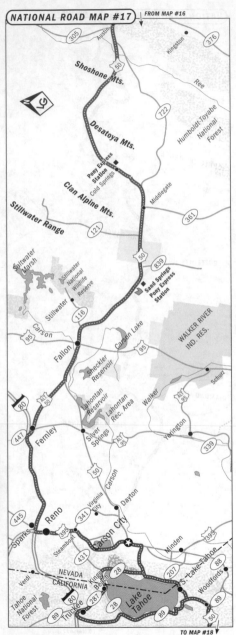

TO MAP #18 ▼

"Pockets" in volcanic rock were created by quickly-cooling lava; carefully break these rocks open and with luck, red garnet will shine inside. The top of the Garnet Hill affords a good view of the goldish-colored pit mine and waste dumps in Ruth, a by-product of the region's mining.

EUREKA

Eureka boomed in population and wealth after the discovery of silver in the area. The mine boom quickly busted, however, leaving behind a smattering of late 1870s buildings and little else. Today a bit of mining remains, but Eureka has never regained its 19th-century prosperity. U.S. 50, known as Main St., runs straight through the center of town. The **Eureka County Sentinel Museum,** 10 N. Monroe St., contains the printing press that produced the local *Eureka Sentinel,* a daily from 1871 to 1960. The original wall, papered with decaying posters from the Opera House and old news stories, is fascinating. (☎ 775-237-5010. Open May-Oct. daily 10am-6pm; Nov.-Apr. Tu-Sa 9am-5pm.) The **Eureka Courthouse,** 10 S. Main St., is a restored, elegant courthouse. Ask someone to show you the old jail at the back of the building. (Open M-F 8am-noon and 1-5pm.) Nevadan artists focusing on the display their work at the **Opera House,** 31 S. Main St. (☎ 775-237-6006. Open M-F 8am-noon and 1-5pm.)

At **D.J.'s Drive-In and Diner,** 509 S. Main St., a message board flashes cheesy sayings. This burger-and-sandwich joint serves sandwiches ($3-6) and rib, seafood, or chicken dinners ($7-8) as well as a pizzas and ice cream. (☎ 775-237-5356. Open daily 10am-10pm.) The **Sundown Lodge,** 60 N. Main St., offers dark, clean rooms. Call ahead. (☎ 775-237-5334. Singles $33; doubles $38-41.)

THE ROAD TO AUSTIN

At the **Hickison Petrogylph Recreation Area,** 45 mi. from Eureka, a free interpretive guide discusses a short loop trail, which leads to prehistoric designs carved into rock faces. The designs, somewhat harder to see than those at Grimes Point, consist mostly of curved lines. (Turn right onto a ¾ mi. dirt road to reach the site. ☎ 775-635-4000.) Surrounded by mountains and isolated from civilization, **Spencer Hot Springs,** 58 mi. from Eureka, is worth a stop. While the springs are well known to locals and legal to use, there aren't any signs pointing to these rock-lined pools, nor any gate-keepers asking for money. A bit of a drive down a dirt road, **Toquima Cave,** carved into volcanic rock, is filled with prehistoric art, including painted pictographs and carved petroglyphs. (From U.S. 50, turn left onto Rte. 376. Proceed ¼ mi. and turn left onto the dirt road. To reach the Hot Springs, turn left onto an unlabeled dirt road after 5½ mi. and continue 1½ mi. To get to Toquima Cave, continue straight for 12 mi. and then turn left at the sign.)

AUSTIN

While still the only sign of civilization for miles around, Austin has dwindled significantly since its days as a major mining camp. It is a good 2hr. drive from Austin to Fallon, however, so Austin makes a good place for a fill-up, food, or an overnight stop. A developed network of mountain biking trails goes through the nearby **Toiyabe National Forest.** Trails range in difficulty and distance; pick up a trail guide and forest service map at the **Austin Ranger District Office,** just west of town (☎ 775-964-2671. Open M-F 8am-4:30pm) or the **Chamber of Commerce,** located on the second floor of the Austin Courthouse (☎ 775-964-2200; open M-F 9am-5pm). Rent bikes at **T-Rix Mountain Bikes,** 270 Main St. (☎ 775-964-1212). Based on a Roman design, three-story **Stokes Castle** was built as a luxury summer home. Today, it is a ruin just west of the Chevron Station; turn left on Castle Rd.

Austin offers few dining options; for a decent meal the **International Bar and Cafe,** 59 N. Main St., is the place to go. (☎ 775-964-9905. Breakfast $3-6. Sandwiches and burgers $5-6. Dinner entrees $7.50-19. Open daily 6am-9:30pm.) Austin's motels lie adjacent on U.S. 50. **Lincoln Motel,** 60 N. Main St., provides minimalist rooms with thin walls. (☎ 775-964-2698. Singles $30; doubles $37.) **Mountain Motel,** 41 N. Main St., has more cramped rooms and, like Lincoln, thin walls. (☎ 775-964-1102. Rooms $35-45.)

 LEAVING AUSTIN
Follow **U.S. 50 West** out of town.

 COLD SPRINGS PONY EXPRESS STATION
51 mi. from Austin on U.S. 50, 1½ mi. past Cold Springs.

Most people skip this site and check out the one at Sand Springs farther down the road, which doesn't require a long hike in the treeless desert. But die-hard history buffs will appreciate a look at the station, which, probably because of its isolation, is in the best condition of remaining Pony Express stations. The short stone walls of the former station enclose the several rooms that once made it up; after a 1½ mi. hike, visitors can walk around the inside, now overgrown with bushes, and read about the site on small plaques.

 MAVERICK AND GOOSE. In the 25 mi. between Sand Springs and Fallon, watch (or listen) for Navy jets overhead; Fallon is the home of the **Naval Fighters Weapons School,** a.k.a. "Top Gun."

FALLON

The self-proclaimed "Oasis of Nevada," Fallon is at the center of a fertile farming region, created when the Newlands Project built two dams and a canal, bringing water to the desert. Fallon's farmers grow delicious produce, especially canataloupe. While artifacts are few at the **Churchill County Museum,** 1050 S. Maine St., this local history museum has extensive displays on the natural history and northwestern Nevada. Highlights include a display on Hidden Cave as well as a large mineral and rock collection. (☎ 775-423-3677. Open Mar.-Oct. M-Sa 10am-5pm, Su noon-5pm; Nov.-Apr. closes 4pm. Free.)

At **La Fiesta,** 60 W. Center St., friendly waiters in tuxedo shirts and bow-ties serve delicious, well-made Mexican food in spotlessly clean surroundings. (From U.S. 50, head south 1 block on Maine St. and turn right. ☎ 775-423-1605. Open M-Th 11am-10pm, F-Su 11am-11pm.) Also a good choice is **Armando's Ristorante Italiano,** 301 S. Maine St. This typical Italian and American hybrid serves pizza, pasta, subs, and steak—and, oddly enough, Krispy Kreme donuts. (☎ 775-428-1198. Sandwiches $6-7. Pizza $5-21. Open M-F 6am-10pm, Sa-Su 7am-10pm.) Roadtrippers looking for a night's lodging will find cool, clean rooms and an outdoor pool at the **Western Motel,** 125 S. Carson St. (1 block west of Maine St., turn left on Carson St. ☎ 775-423-5118. Singles $37; doubles $41.)

 APPROACHING RENO
Head west out of Fallon on **U.S. 50.** 9½ mi. west of town, the road divides; take **Alt. U.S. 50** to I-80 and Reno. Take Exit 13 off I-80 an turn left onto **Virginia St.** to reach the casino towers.

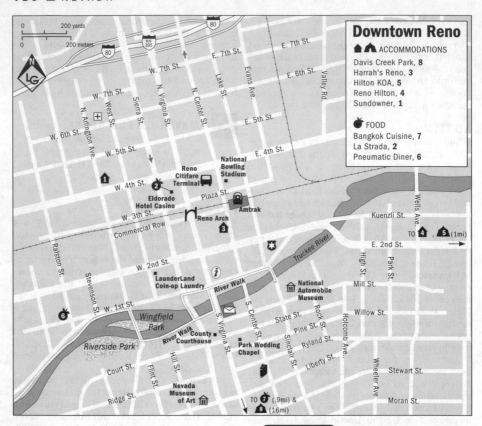

Downtown Reno

▲▲ ACCOMMODATIONS

Davis Creek Park, **8**
Harrah's Reno, **3**
Hilton KOA, **5**
Reno Hilton, **4**
Sundowner, **1**

🍎 FOOD

Bangkok Cuisine, **7**
La Strada, **2**
Pneumatic Diner, **6**

RENO

With decadent casinos only a die's throw away from snow capped mountains, Reno embodies both the opportunist frenzy and the natural splendor of the West. Catering to those interested in making a fast buck or saying a quick vow, the self-proclaimed "biggest little city in the world" has earned a reputation for its crazed gamblers and delirious lovers.

GETTING AROUND

Most major casinos are downtown between **West** and **Center St.** and **2nd** and **6th St.** The neon-lit streets are heavily patrolled, but don't stray far east of the city center at night. **Virginia St.** is Reno's main drag; south of the **Truckee River** has cheaper accommodations, outlying casinos, and strip mall after strip mall. **Sparks,** a few miles northeast along I-80, has several casinos frequented by locals. The *Reno/Tahoe Visitor Planner,* avail-

VITAL STATS

Population: 180,000

Visitor Info: Reno-Sparks Convention and Visitors Authority, 1 E. 1st St. (☎800-367-7366; www.reno-laketahoe.com), on the 2nd fl. of the Cal-Neva Bldg. Open M-F 8am-5pm.

Internet Access: Washoe County Library-Downtown Reno Branch, 301 S. Center St. (☎775-327-8300. Open M 10am-8pm, Tu-Th 10am-6pm, F and Su 10am-5pm.

Post Office: 50 S. Virginia St. (☎775-786-5936). Open M-F 8:30am-5pm. **Postal code:** 89501.

able at info kiosks throughout the city, has a local map and is a helpful city guide. Most of the downtown casinos offer free **parking** for patrons in their garages; at busy times, crowded garages can take up to 15min. to get in and out of. If you're in a hurry, downtown surface lots charge $2-3.

👁 🌸 SIGHTS & FESTIVALS

There's far more to Reno culture than just nightlife. Roadtrippers won't want to miss the 🏛**National Automobile Museum,** 10 Lake St. South. By far the best car collection along the roadtrip route, it boasts rare cars, early model years, and one-of-a-kind prototypes from the private collection of the late gambling magnate Bill Harrah. (☎ 775-333-9300. Open M-Sa 9:30am-5:30pm, Su 10am-4pm. Free 1½hr. tours M-Sa 10:30am and 1:30pm, Su 12:30pm. $8, seniors $7, children $3.) The newly reopened **Nevada Museum of Art,** 160 W. Liberty St., is in a striking structure inspired by the Black Rock Desert. Rotating exhibits feature artists like Diego Rivera, Edward Hopper, and Dennis Oppenheim. (☎ 775-329-3333. Open Su, Tu-W, F 11am-6pm; Th 11am-8pm. $7, students and seniors $5, ages 6-12 $1, under 6 free.) After hearing that a diseased cottonwood tree needed to be cut down, a local family commissioned woodcarvers to transform the trunk's four branches into trout. The result was the **Truckee River Trout Tree,** a unique and intricate piece of public art. (From downtown, take either 4th or 2nd St. west about ½ mi., turn left on Keystone Ave., and keep right.)

The renowned annual **Reno Rodeo** (☎ 775-329-3877; www.renorodeo.com) gallops in for eight days in late June. Reno heats up with the popular **Artown** festival (☎ 775-322-1538; www.renoisartown.com), every July. The event features dance, jazz, painting, and theater, almost all for free. August roars in with the chrome-covered, hot-rod splendor of **Hot August Nights** (☎ 775-356-1956; www.hotaugustnights.com), a celebration of classic cars and rock 'n' roll. In September, the **Great Reno Balloon Race** (☎ 775-826-1181), in Rancho San Rafael Park, and the **National Championship Air Races** (☎ 775-972-6663; www.airrace.org), at Reno/Stead Airport, draw international contestants who take to the sky as spectators look on. Nearby Virginia City hosts **Camel Races** (☎ 775-847-0311) during the weekend after Labor Day, in which both camels and ostriches scoot about town.

🍴 FOOD

The cost of eating out in Reno is low, but the food quality doesn't have to be. Casinos offer all-you-can-eat buffets and next-to-free breakfasts. Escaping these giants is worthwhile, as inexpensive eateries outside of the mainstream abound.

🏛 **Pneumatic Diner,** 501 W. 1st St. (☎ 775-786-8888, ext. 106), at the corner of Ralston and W. 1st St. in the Truckee River Lodge. This funky diner is a subversive melting pot fighting against the hegemony of casinos. All-natural ingredients make up a menu with nods to Italian, Mexican, French, and Middle Eastern food. Beverage concoctions

THE LOCAL STORY

THIS PARTY BITES!

Today, memorials honoring the Donner Party are ubiquitous in Truckee. Their tragic story began in April 1846, when a group of Midwesterners (led by George Donner) set off for California. The ill-fated party took a "shortcut" advocated by explorer Lansford Hastings, who had never actually seen the route. They hacked through the wilderness, losing cattle and wagons along the way. When they finally rejoined the trail, they were weeks behind. By late October the group arrived at Truckee Meadows, exhausted, demoralized, and running out of food. When they reached Truckee (now Donner) Lake November 4, snow was already on the ground. The party made three attempts to cross the Sierras and was finally forced to settle around the lake. The thaw they hoped for never came, and, trapped by 22 ft. of snow, many resorted to cannibalism before the snows cleared in April 1847. Only 47 of the initial 89 survived. Today, an Annual Donner Party Hike (☎ 916-587-2757) reenacts the fateful journey every October (meal not included).

(try the Snoopy, $1.50-4), breakfast ($1.50-6.50), and sandwiches satisfy. Open M-F 11am-11pm, Sa 9am-11pm, Su 7am-11pm.

Bangkok Cuisine, 55 Mt. Rose St. (☎ 775-322-0299), near the corner of S. Virginia St. Delicious Thai food served and an elegant setting, a welcome respite from Reno's steaks and burritos. Huge menu with soups ($4-7), noodles ($8-12), fried rices ($8-12) and curries ($8-10). Open M-Sa 11am-10pm.

Victorian Buffet, 407 N. Virginia St. (775-329-4777), inside the Silver Legacy. Huge domed ceiling with replica mining tower makes this casino feel more like Las Vegas than others in Reno. Carving station, seafood, pizza, desserts, and lots of fresh fruit. Open daily 7:30am-2pm and 4:30-9pm, F-Sa until 10pm.

La Strada, 345 N. Virginia St. (☎ 775-348-9297), in the Eldorado Hotel. Award-winning northern Italian cuisine in the heart of the Eldorado. Pastas made fresh daily ($10-20) as well as beef and fish entrees ($13-24). Open daily 5-10pm.

ACCOMMODATIONS

While weekend prices at casinos are usually high, weekday rates and off-season discounts mean great deals. **Eldorado,** 345 N. Virginia (☎ 800-648-5966 or 775-786-5700) and **Silver Legacy,** 407 N. Virginia St. (☎ 800-687-7733 or 775-325-7401), offer good deals along with their central locations and massive facilities. Rates can drop to $35, but generally hover around $60 for a single. Be advised—heterosexual prostitution is legal in most of Nevada (though not in Reno), which may be reflected in some motels' low rates. Prices below don't include Reno's **12% hotel tax.**

Harrah's Reno, 219 N. Center St. (☎ 800-427-7247 or 775-786-5700), between E. 2nd St. and Commercial Row. 2 towers of luxurious rooms, 7 restaurants, pool, and health club leave little to be desired. 65,000 sq. ft. casino draws crowds with Reno's highest table limits. Sammy's Showroom and the Plaza host top performers. Free valet parking. Rooms M-Th from $49, F-Su from $89.

Reno Hilton, 2500 E. 2nd St. (☎ 800-648-5080 or 775-789-2000), off Hwy. 395 at the Glendale exit. More than 2000 elegant rooms, a 9000-seat outdoor amphitheater, driving range, 50-lane bowling center, health club and spa, and shopping mall make the Hilton Reno's biggest. Press your luck in the casino, or for something even more stomach-churning check out the Ultimate Rush reverse bungee. Rooms $35-149.

Sundowner, 450 N. Arlington Ave. (☎ 800-648-5490 or 775-786-7050), between W. 4th and W. 5th St. This working man's casino represents the meat and potatoes of Reno's gambling industry. No frills, but the rooms are clean and come with everything you'd expect, such as A/C and telephones. Pool, hot tub, and jacuzzi. Rooms Su-Th from $26, F $50, Sa $70.

Truckee River Lodge, 501 W. 1st St. (☎ 800-635-8950 or 775-786-8888), at the corner of Ralston St. A short walk from the slots. Non-smoking joint and against everything typically Reno. Rooms with kitchenettes and cable TV. Rents bikes and arranges all kinds of outdoor adventures. Weekly rates available. Doubles Su-F $48, Sa $70; 2-bedroom suites $120/$160.

CAMPING

Campers can drive to the woodland campsites of **Davis Creek Park.** (18 mi. south on U.S. 395 to Rte. 429, then follow the signs ½ mi. west. ☎ 775-721-4901. Volleyball courts and trout-packed Ophir Creek Lake. Showers and toilets on site. Sites $15, additional car $5.) To get closer to the action, bunk down in the urban jungle at the **Hilton KOA,** 2500 E. 2nd St., next to the Hilton. There's no grass, but campers have access to the Hilton's pool, tennis courts, and fitness center. (☎ 888-562-5698 or 775-789-2147. Hookups $27-38.)

NIGHTLIFE

Reno is a giant adult amusement park; its casinos the main attractions. Knowing what's good for business, casinos offer free gaming lessons. The most popular games and minimum bets vary between establishments, but slots are ubiquitous. Drinks are usually free if you're gambling, but alcohol's inhibition-dropping effects can make betting a bad experience. Almost all casinos offer live nighttime entertainment, but few shows are worth the steep admission prices. **Harrah's,** 219 N. Center St. (☎ 775-786-3232), is an exception, carrying on a dying tradition with its **Night on the Town** in Sammy's Showroom. Starting at $39, Harrah's offers dinner at one of its restaurants and a performance by its critically acclaimed performers. At **Circus Circus,** 500 N. Sierra, a small circus on the midway above the casino floor performs "big top" shows. (☎ 775-329-0711. Every 30min. M-Th 11:30am-11:30pm, F-Su 11:15am-11:45pm).

APPROACHING CARSON CITY
Head east from Virginia St. to **U.S. 395 South.**

CARSON CITY

At the crossroads of traffic bound for the Lake Tahoe region and home to three large casinos, this former mint town lacks the quaint, homey feel of other small capital cities. Thirty miles from Reno and only 10 mi. from Lake Tahoe, it's a good overnight stop before a day of outdoor exploration. Occupying part of the building that once contained a US Mint, the **Nevada State Museum,** 600 N. Carson St., highlights distinct aspects of Nevada's past and present: silver mining and the resulting ghost towns, animal and plant life of the desert, and Native Americans that inhabited this area. There is an emphasis on the prehistoric past, with a good exhibit on earth history. (☎ 775-687-4810. Open daily 8:30am-4:30pm. $3, seniors $2.50, under 18 free.) Railroad buffs won't want to miss the **Nevada State Railroad Museum,** 2180 S. Carson St., which showcases a collection of cars and engines from the historic Virginia & Truckee Railroad, as well as hosting lectures and an annual railroad symposium. (☎ 775-687-6953. Open daily 8:30am-4:30pm. $4, seniors $3, under 18 free.)

At **Red's Old 395 Grill,** 1055 S. Carson St., covered wagons, horses, and sleighs hang suspended from the ceiling. Patrons devour delicious, non-greasy barbecue or sip one of the 52 beers on tap. (☎ 775-887-0395. Lunch $5-8. Wood-fired pizza $7-8. Dinner entrees $12-18. Open M-Th 11am-9:30pm, F-Sa 11am-10:30pm, Su 9am-9:30pm.) **B'Sghetti's,** 318 N. Carson St., serves tasty pasta. Upbeat service and an easygoing atmosphere attract everybody to this pub-style Italian restaurant. (☎ 775-887-8879. Soups, salads, sandwiches $7-10. Pasta $7-12. Open M-Th 11am-9pm, F-Sa 11am-10pm, Su 4-9pm.) Carson City has the usual set of casino hotels and motels, but rooms fill fast on weekends, especially during events. Even the dingiest lodgings are pricy at peak times. Motels line Carson St. throughout town. **The Best Value Inn,** 2731 S. Carson St., offers basic rooms with refrigerators, nature posters, and comfy chairs. (☎ 775-882-2007. In summer singles $39-44; doubles $48-50. In winter rooms $30-43.) At the **Round House Inn,** 1400 N. Carson St., rooms have lots of furniture, large closets, and comfy beds. (☎ 775-882-3446. Rooms Su-Th $36, F-Sa from $55.)

APPROACHING LAKE TAHOE
U.S. 50 merges with Rte. 28 on the eastern edge of the lake before heading into **S. Lake Tahoe.**

Welcome To **CALIFORNIA**

LAKE TAHOE

Coming over the Sierra Nevada Mountains from Carson City, the green-blue of Lake Tahoe is a welcome sight indeed. The vast lake stretches for miles, surrounded by rugged peaks. In a town without an off-season, visitors can try their luck at everything from keno to kayaking, but no matter the reason for visiting, the centerpiece and constant in every experience remains the lake itself, the highest alpine lake in North America.

VITAL STATS

Population: 24,000 (S. Lake Tahoe, CA)

Visitor Info: Lake Tahoe Basin's Taylor Creek Visitors Center (USFS; ☎ 530-543-2674), north of South Lake Tahoe on Rte. 89. Open mid-June to late Sept. daily 8am-5:30pm; late May to mid-June and Oct. Sa-Su 8am-4pm.

Internet Access: South Lake Tahoe Branch Library, 1000 Rufus Allen Blvd. (☎ 530-573-3185). Open Tu-W 10am-8pm, Th-Sa 10am-5pm.

Post Office: 1046 Al Tahoe Blvd. (☎ 800-275-8777). Open M-F 8:30am-5pm, Sa noon-5pm. **Postal Code:** 96151.

GETTING AROUND

Lake Tahoe is divided into two main regions, **North Shore** and **South Shore.** The North Shore includes **Tahoe City,** CA, and Incline Village, NV, while the South Shore comprises **South Lake Tahoe,** CA, and Stateline, NV. Most establishments listed here are in South Lake Tahoe, as U.S. 50 passes directly through the city. Food, lodging, and attractions are plentiful around the lake, so check out North Shore attractions as well. **Lake Tahoe Blvd. (U.S. 50)** is the main drag of South Lake Tahoe and Stateline. At the west end of town, Rte. 89 traces the lake's western shore. Major streets in town include **Ski Run Blvd., Wildwood Ave.,** and **Park Ave.**

If you want to **loop the lake** (2½hr. min., plus stops), you can circumnavigate all but about 16 mi. of the shore by heading north on **Rte. 28** to **Rte. 89 South** back to U.S. 50 in the town of South Lake Tahoe. This route, once named "The Most Beautiful Drive in America," provides spectacular views, but bypasses the busiest section of the lake.

■ HIKING

Hiking is a great way to explore the Tahoe Basin. Always bring a jacket and drinking water. Ask where the snow has (or has not) melted—it's usually not all gone until July. After decades of work, the 165 mi. **Tahoe Rim Trail** has finally been completed. The trail, which circles the lake along the ridge tops of Lake Tahoe Basin, welcomes hikers, equestrians, and, in most areas, mountain bikers. Camping is allowed on most of the trail, though permits are required in the Desolation Wilderness. Hiking is moderate to difficult. On the western shore, the route comprises part of the Pacific Crest Trail. Popular trailheads include **Spooner Summit,** at the U.S. 28/50 junction and **Tahoe City,** off Rte. 89 on Fairway Dr.

SOUTH SHORE. The southern region of the basin offers moderate to strenuous hiking trails; stop by the Taylor Creek Visitors Center (see p. 419) for maps and more info. For many visitors, picturesque **Emerald Bay** is an essential stop. This crystal-clear pocket of the lake is home to Tahoe's only island and most photographed sight—tiny, rocky Fannette. **Emerald Bay State Park,** from which you can access the Bayview Trail into Desolation Wilderness, offers hiking and biking trails of varying difficulty, along with camping and rock climbing. *(Entrance fee $3.)* Possibly the most popular South Shore Trail, the **Eagle Falls Trail** offers a short 1 mi. moderate hike into Desolation Wilderness to **Eagle Lake.** A strenuous trail continues past Eagle Lake several miles to a series of other lakes surrounded by the Velma Mountains. Accessible from D.L. Bliss State Park and ending up at Vikingsholm is one of the best hikes in Tahoe, the **Rubicon Point Trail,** which wraps 5½ mi. around Emerald Bay. If you make it the full 5½ mi., you can take a shuttle back to D.L. Bliss; inquire at the park Visitors Center for details. Permits are required for hikes into Desolation Wilderness, and

there is a fee for overnight camping. Day hikers can self-issue free permits from any of the eastern trailheads. Those looking for a more leisurely excursion can enjoy the nature trails around the Taylor Creek Visitors Center, 3 mi. north of South Lake Tahoe on Rte. 89. The **Lake of the Sky Trail** (½ mi. round-trip) is dotted with informative signs about the lake's origins, its early inhabitants, and current wildlife. The centerpiece of the Visitors Center, however, is the **River Profile Chamber,** which features a cross-section of a Tahoe creek.

NORTH SHORE. At 10,778 ft., **Mount Rose** is one of the tallest mountains in the region as well as one of the best climbs. The panoramic view from the summit offers views of the lake, Reno, and the Sierra. The 12 mi. round-trip trek starts out as an easy dirt road but ascends switchbacks for the last couple of miles. Take Rte. 431 north from Incline Village to reach the trailhead. The **Granite Chief Wilderness,** west of Squaw Valley, is a spectacular outdoor destination; its hiking trails and mountain streams wind through secluded forests in 5000 ft. valleys to the summits of 9000 ft. peaks. The **Alpine Meadows Trailhead,** at the end of Alpine Meadows Rd. off Rte. 89 between Truckee and Tahoe City, and the **Pacific Crest Trailhead,** at the end of Barker Pass Rd. (a.k.a. Blackwood Canyon Rd.), grant access to the wilderness.

EAST SHORE. The **Marlette Lake Trail** begins at Spooner State Park, NV, at the junction of U.S. 50 and Rte. 28. The hike climbs 5 mi. through the moderately difficult terrain of the aspen-lined North Canyon to Marlette Lake.

⚠ OUTDOOR ACTIVITIES

BIKING. Miles of excellent trials and killer views make Tahoe a mountain biking hot spot. The lake's premier ride is the **Flume Trail,** in Nevada State Park. *($5 entrance fee.)* The trail begins near the picnic area at Spooner Lake. This 23 mi. single-track loop has magnificent views of the lake from 1500 ft. off the deck. **Flume Trail Mountain Biking** rents bikes and runs bike shuttles to favorite trails. *(At Spooner Lake.* ☎ 775-749-5349. *Bikes $34-49 per day. Shuttles $10-15. Open daily May-June 9am-6pm; July-Aug. 9am-7pm; Sept.-Oct. 9am-5pm.)* Other tire trials include **Mr. Toad's Wild Ride,** a 3 mi., 2200 ft. descent south of South Lake Tahoe off Rte. 89, and **McKinney/Rubicon Road,** a loop ride to difficult peaks that climbs off Rte. 89 north of

Tahoma. For rentals in South Lake Tahoe check out **South Shore Bike & Skate.** *(1056 Ski Run Blvd.* ☎ *775-541-7272. Mountain bikes $25-45 per day.)* Cyclists can cover parts of the Lake Tahoe loop; the **Pope-Baldwin Bike Path** on the South Shore runs parallel to Rte. 89 for over 3 mi. past evergreen forests until it joins the **South Lake Tahoe Bike Path** (via bike lanes on U.S. 50), which goes through South Lake Tahoe and into Nevada.

ROCK CLIMBING. There are many climbs in Lake Tahoe, but proper safety precautions and equipment are a must. Inexperienced climbers can try bouldering in **D.L. Bliss State Park.** A host of popular climbing spots are scattered along the South Shore; the super-popular **Ninety-Foot Wall** at Emerald Bay, **Twin Crags** at Tahoe City, and **Big Chief** near Squaw Valley are some of the more famous area climbs. **Lover's Leap,** in South Lake Tahoe, is an incredible (and crowded) route spanning two giant cliffs. East of South Lake Tahoe, off U.S. 50, the **Phantom Spires** have amazing ridge views, while **Pie Shop** offers serious exposure.

WINTER ACTIVITIES. With its world-class alpine slopes, knee-deep powder, and luxuriant (or notorious) California sun, Tahoe is a skier's mecca. There are 15 ski resorts in the Tahoe area. Visitors Centers provide info, maps, free publications like *Ski Tahoe* and *Sunny Day,* and coupons. All the major resorts offer lessons and rent equipment. For the best slopes, try **Squaw Valley,** site of the 1960 Olympic Winter Games, or **Heavenly.** *(Squaw Valley:* ☎ *775-583-6985 or 888-766-9321; www.squaw.com. Heavenly: 775-586-7000; www.skiheavenly.com.)* One of the best ways to enjoy Tahoe's pristine snow-covered forests is to cross-country ski. **Spooner Lake** offers 57 mi. of machine-groomed trails and incredible views. *(At the junction of U.S. 50 and Rte. 28.* ☎ *775-749-5349. $19, children $3.)* **Tahoe X-C** maintains 40 mi. of trails for all abilities winding through North Shore forests. *(2 mi. northeast of downtwn Tahoe City on Dollar Hill off of Rte. 28.* ☎ *775-583-5475. $18, mid-week $13; children $6.)* Snowshoeing is easier to pick up than cross-country skiing, and equipment is available at many sporting goods stores for about $15 per day. Check local ranger stations for ranger-guided winter snowshoe hikes.

BEACHES. Many beaches dot Lake Tahoe. Parking generally costs $3-7; bargain hunters should leave cars in turnouts on the main road and walk to the beaches. On the North Shore, **Sand Harbor Beach** has gorgeous granite boulders and clear waters that attract swimmers, sunners, snorklers, and boaters to its marina. The parking lot often fills by late morning. *(2 mi. south of Incline Village on U.S. 28. Parking $5.)* **Tahoe City Commons Beach** contains a playground for kids, a sandy beach for sunbathing, and pristine lake waters for swimming. *(In the heart of Tahoe City just off North Lake Blvd.)* Boats, jet-skis, wakeboards, and waterskis can be rented at **Tahoe Water Adventures.** *(120 Grove St., next to the beach.* ☎ *775-583-3225.)*

The West Shore offers **Meeks Bay,** family-oriented and equipped with picnic tables, volleyball courts, BBQ pits, campsites, and a store. *(10 mi. south of Tahoe City.)* **D.L. Bliss State Park** is home to **Lester Beach** and **Calawee Cove Beach** on striking Rubicon Bay. It's also the trailhead for the Rubicon Trail. *(17 mi. south of Tahoe City on Rte. 89. Parking here is $5 and limited, so check at the Visitors Center or park on the road and walk.)*

Baldwin Beach, on the South Shore, and neighboring **Pope Beach,** near the southernmost point of the lake off Rte. 89, are shaded expanses of shoreline popular with South Lake Tahoe crowds. It's easy to find a parking spot on the highway and avoid the fee. For kayak tours, lessons, and rentals check out **Kayak Tahoe.** *(3411 Lake Tahoe Blvd., near the intersection of Johnson Blvd. and Lake Tahoe Blvd.* ☎ *775 544 2011. Singles $50 per day; tandems $75 per day. Tours $45-75. Lessons $32-155.)*

Nevada Beach is close to the casinos and offers a sandy sanctuary with a view of sun-kissed mountains. *(On the east shore, 3 mi. north of South Lake Tahoe off U.S. 50.)* **Zephyr Cove Beach** hosts a young crowd keen on beer and bikinis. This beach offers boat rentals, jet-skis, parasailing, and towel-side cocktail service. *(On U.S. 50, 8 mi. south of the intersection with Rte. 28.)*

OTHER LAKES. Many lakes are accessible from hiking routes and may offer a bit more privacy than Tahoe. **Angora Lakes,** a pair of mountain lakes accessible by car except for a final half-mile walk, are popular with families. *(Take Rte. 89 North from S. Lake Tahoe for 3 mi. Turn left onto Fallen Leaf Rd. Proceed 2 mi. and turn left onto Tahoe Mountain. Rd. Continue half a mile and turn right onto Forest Service Rd. #1214. The parking area is 3 mi. up. Open daily 6am-10pm. Free.)*

NATIONAL ROAD

FOOD

Sprouts Natural Foods Cafe, 3123 Harrison Ave. (☎530-541-6969), at the intersection of Lake Tahoe Blvd. and Alameda Ave. Natural foods in unnaturally large portions. Try the breakfast burrito with avocados ($5), the tasty smoothies ($3-3.75), or a shot of wheat grass ($2). Open daily 8am-10pm.

The Red Hut Cafe, 2723 Lake Tahoe Blvd. (☎530-541-9024), and 22 Kingsbury Grade (☎530-588-7488). Friendly staff has been dishing out homestyle cooking since 1959 at this Tahoe original. Waffles piled with fruit and whipped cream $5.75. Avocado burgers $6.50. Open daily 6am-2pm. No credit cards.

Lakeside Beach Grill, 4081 Lakeshore Blvd. (☎530-544-4050), on the beach between Park and Stateline Ave. Tasty menu and spectacular views. Try one of the inventive entrees ($7-11), like the calamari burger. Open daily June-Sept. 11am-7pm.

Orchid Thai, 2180 Lake Tahoe Blvd. (☎530-544-5541). Terrific fare including vegetarian options like the Pad Basil Garden ($7) or crispy tofu ($4). Carnivores are sated with Pottery Shrimp ($11) and a wide range of curries ($7-13). Open M-Sa 11am-10pm, Su 3-10pm.

ACCOMMODATIONS

On the South Shore, the blocks bordering U.S. 50 on the California side of the border support the bulk of the area's motels. Glitzy and cheap, motels in South Lake Tahoe can be had for next to nothing mid-week. Accommodations are more expensive along the North Shore. Fall and spring around the lake are the most economical times to visit.

Tahoe Valley Lodge, 2214 Lake Tahoe Blvd. (☎800-669-7544 or 530-541-0353; www.tahoevalleylodge.com). The immaculate rooms take the mountain motif to an extreme. Reception 24hr. Singles $95; doubles $125.

Royal Inn, 3520 Lake Tahoe Blvd. (☎530-544-1177). Clean rooms with queen-size beds and cable TV. Heated pool and laundry facilities. Singles Su-Th $28-35; doubles $39-49. Weekends and holidays see greatly inflated rates. Don't be bashful about mentioning *Let's Go*—you may be handsomely rewarded.

Doug's Mellow Mountain Retreat, 3787 Forest Ave. (☎530-544-8065). Coming from the north turn left onto Wildwood Rd. west of downtown Stateline and take a left on Forest Ave.; it's the 6th house on the left.

Easygoing Doug supplies a modern kitchen, BBQ, and fireplace in a woodsy house in a residential neighborhood. Internet $5 per hr. Linen included. Dorms $15; private rooms $25. Discounts for stays over a week.

Best Tahoe West Inn, 4107 Pine Blvd. (☎800-700-8246 or 530-544-6455), off Park Ave. Within walking distance of the casinos but closer to the beach. Modern rooms are chock full of amenities. Pool, jacuzzi, and sauna on the premises. Reception 7am-11pm. Rooms June-Aug. $54-99; Sept.-May $34-89.

CAMPING

The Taylor Creek Visitor Center (see p. 419) provides up-to-date info on camping. Campgrounds ring the lake; **Rte. 89** is rife with sites between Tahoe City and South Lake Tahoe. Sites can be booked on weekends in July and August, so it pays to reserve in advance; call the **California State Parks Reservation Center** (☎800-444-7275) or the **National Recreation Reservation System** (☎877-444-6777; www.reserveusa.com). Backcountry camping is allowed in designated wilderness areas with a permit from the Forest Service.

Nevada Beach (USFS; ☎775-588-5562), off U.S. 50, 10½ mi. south of the junction with Rte. 28. Sites here are more rustic but benefit from being well spaced near a peaceful, family-oriented beach. 54 sites. Water, no showers. Sites $20-22.

Fallen Leaf Lake (USFS; ☎530-544-0426). Take Rte. 89 for 3 mi. north of U.S. 50 and turn left onto Fallen Leaf Rd. 206 sites by Fallen Leaf Lake. Reserve well in advance via NRRS. Sites $18.

D. L. Bliss State Park (CA; ☎530-525-7277), off Rte. 89, 10½ mi. north of U.S. 50. Access to Lester Beach and trailheads for the Rubicon and Lighthouse Trails. Grills, water, flush toilets, and showers. Open late-May to Sept. Sites $15-19; $5 per additional vehicle.

NIGHTLIFE

Nightlife in South Lake Tahoe centers around casinos, which are busy 24/7. To get in, you must be 21 and have a government-issued photo ID.

Caesar's Palace, 55 U.S. 50 (☎888-829-7630 or 775-588-3515). Large casino, restaurants, and clubs. **Club Nero** (☎775-586-2000) is a hotspot for dancing and drinking, with M $1 drinks, Tu Latino night, and W wet t-shirt contests and free admission for ladies. Th-Sa ladies night with free admission and well drinks until midnight. Su $1 drafts. Cover $5-25. Open daily from 9pm.

Harrah's (☎800-427-7247 or 775-588-6611), U.S. 50. Glamour and glitz go wild in this slot machine heaven replete with restaurants, bars, and cocktail lounges. Home to **Altitude Nightclub** (☎775-586-6705), which hosts its fair share of foam parties. Cover $5-25. Open M-Tu and Th-Sa from 9pm.

The Brewery, 3542 Lake Tahoe Blvd. (☎530-544-2739). Stop in and try one of the 7 microbrews on tap. Pizzas (from $10) come crammed with toppings. Laid-back atmosphere makes this spot a favorite for locals. Open Su-Th 11am-10pm, F-Sa 11am-2am.

THE ROAD TO PLACERVILLE

Leaving Lake Tahoe, the route follows the spectacularly scenic **U.S. 50 West** through the high granite cliffs and tall conifers of **El Dorado National Forest**. Let your car be checked for fruit at the agricultural inspection near the California border.

Continuing westward, the road enters **Gold Country** around Placerville. After gold was found in California in 1849, "gold fever" brought a stampede of over half a million prospectors over the next decade. Five years after the big discovery, the panning gold was gone, and miners dug deeper and deeper into the rock. All but a few mines were abandoned by the 1870s. These days, remnants of the Gold Rush attract tourists who feed the area's economy; there's no shortage of historical landmarks or restored towns. Strung throughout the tawny Sierra foothills, "Gold Rush Towns" are relaxed and dotted with the relics of the Gold Rush era.

◤ SLY PARK   4771 Sly Park Rd.
From U.S. 50, take the exit for Sly Park Rd. Turn left and proceed 4¼ mi.

At Sly Park a heavily wooded pine forest shades dark sandy beaches around a pristine lake. Mountain bikers enjoy the 8½ mi. loop trail around the water, while the lake offers a lovely place to swim or take out a small boat. Though the views are less spectacular than Tahoe's, there isn't a more comfortable place to camp than on Sly Park's natural pine beds. (☎530-644-2545; www.eid.org. Reserve ahead for weekend camping; $7 fee. Open daily 6am-10pm. Sites $16-$21. Day-use $7.)

PLACERVILLE

In its Gold Rush prime, Placerville was the third-largest town in California. Today, restaurants and shops fill its restored, historic downtown. Beyond downtown, however, chain stores dominate and Placerville's Gold-Rush charm is nowhere to be found. Relative to other Gold Country towns, Placerville is less concerned with historic fame and more comfortable as a contemporary town.

⌐ VITAL STATS ⌐

Population: 9000

Visitor Info: Chamber of Commerce, 542 Main St. (☎530-621-5885). Open M-F 9am-5pm.

Internet Access: El Dorado County Library, 345 Fair Ln. (☎530-621-5540). Open M-W 10am-8pm, Th-Sa 10am-5pm.

Post Office: 3045 Sacramento St. (☎530-642-5280). Open M-F 8:30am-5pm, Sa 8:30am-noon. **Postal Code:** 95667.

◨ **GETTING AROUND.** Between Sacramento and Lake Tahoe on **U.S. 50,** Placerville is positioned to snare campers, boaters, and skiers. Most streets, like **Main St.,** run parallel to U.S. 50 to the north. **Rte. 49** bisects the town, running north to Auburn (10 mi.), and south to Calaveras County.

◨▱ **SIGHTS & ENTERTAINMENT.** Placerville was once known as "Hangtown, USA," as it doled out speedy justice at the end of a rope. Now the **Historic Hangman's Tree,** 305 Main St., is a friendly neighborhood bar (hangout?) with a replica of a hanged man (George) outside, and a ghost (Willy) inside. The old-fashioned bar keeps old-fashioned hours. (☎305-622-3878. Open M-Sa 6am-10pm, Su 6am-5pm.) The hills around Placerville are filled with fruit. Drivers can tour the apple orchards and wineries off U.S. 50 in the area known as ▨**Apple Hill;** the fall is particularly busy with events, concerts, and apple-picking. A complete listing and map of orchards is available from the Visitors Center and at many orchards. **Larsen Apple Barn** (☎530-644-1415) has 12 varieties of apples and a large picnic area. Most orchards are open only September through December, but **Boa Vista Orchards,** 2952 Carson Rd. (☎530-622-5522), stays open year-round, selling fresh pears and cherries from a huge open barn.

For free wine tasting, try **Lava Cap Winery,** 2221 Fruitridge Rd. (☎530-621-0175. Open daily 11am-5pm.) Also visit **Madroña Vineyards,** 2560 High Hill Rd. (☎530-644-5948), or the sophisticated **Boeger Winery,** 1709 Carson Rd. (☎530-622-8094. Open daily 10am-5pm.) June visitors should not miss **Brewfest** (☎530-672-3436), when hordes of locals pony up $20 for a small tasting glass and wander to over 30 downtown businesses for free beer. Streets close and there's a band on every block.

▓ FOOD & ACCOMMODATIONS. Those seeking a *Dukes of Hazzard* experience should saunter into ☜**Poor Red's,** on El Dorado's Main St., 5 mi. south of Placerville on Rte. 49. The bar and dining room of this BBQ joint are always packed. Their famous two-glass "Golden Cadillac" ($6) is responsible for 3% of American consumption of galliano. (☎530-622-2901. Sandwiches $6. Entrees $9-17. Open M-Sa 5pm-11pm, Su 2-11pm.) The historic **Cozmic Cafe and Bar,** 594 Main St., dates from 1859. It may look unexceptional, but the back has seating in a walk-in mine shaft. (☎530-642-8481. Sandwiches $5-6. Smoothies $3.50-5. Th movie night, F open mic, Sa live band. Open M-W 7am-3pm, Th 7am-8pm, F-Sa 7am-11pm, Su 8am-3pm.) **Sweetie Pies,** 577 Main St., is known for its huge cinnamon buns, full lunches (sandwiches $6), and breakfast menu ($4-7). Homemade pie by the slice ($3.25) is delicious. (☎530-642-0128. Open M-W 6:30am-4pm, Th-Su 7am-9pm.)

One of the best deals in town, the **National 9 Inn,** 1500 Broadway, has spotless new rooms, cable TV, A/C, and comfortable king beds. (☎530-622-3884. Singles $49; doubles $55-75.) **Camping** is plentiful in the Eldorado National Forest, east of town. **Sand Flat,** 3800 ft., has 29 sites and is on U.S. 50, 28 mi. east of town. (Vault toilets, water. No reservations. Sites $12.) **Dispersed camping** is free and does not require a permit, although campfire permits are required for fires and stoves.

⚡ APPROACHING SACRAMENTO
Follow **U.S. 50,** which merges with **Bus. I-80** to become a freeway. Exit for **10th St.** to downtown.

SACRAMENTO

California's more glamorous cities often overshadow the state capital. Best known for its politics and agriculture, Sacramento is also the nation's most diverse city, not to mention the home of a vibrant arts scene and excellent cuisine.

The city was the central outpost for the gold-seekers who flooded the area in the 1850s, and over the next century, mansions and suburban bungalows paved the way for future residents Ronald Reagan and Arnold Schwarzenegger.

⸢ VITAL STATS ⸣

Population: 400,000

Visitor Info: Old Sacramento Visitors Center, 1002 2nd St. (☎916-442-7644). Open M-Th and Su 10am-5pm, F-Sa 9am-6pm.

Internet Access: Sacramento Public Library, 828 I St. (☎916-264-2700), between 8th and 9th St. Open M and F 10am-6pm, Tu-Th 10am-9pm, Sa 10am-5pm, Su noon-5pm.

Post Office: 801 I St. (☎916-556-3415). Open M-F 8am-5pm. **Postal Code:** 95814.

▐ GETTING AROUND

Sacramento is at the center of the **Sacramento Valley.** Five major highways converge on the capital: **I-5** and **Rte. 99** run north-south, with I-5 to the west, **I-80** runs east-west between San Francisco and Reno, and **U.S. 50** and **Rte. 16** bring traffic westward from Gold Country. Downtown, numbered streets run north-south and lettered streets run east-west in a grid. The street number on a lettered street corresponds to the number of the cross street (2000 K St. is near the corner of 20th St.). The capitol building, parks, and endless cafes and restaurants occupy the area around **10th St.** and **Capitol Ave.** Old Sacramento is located just west of downtown, on the Sacramento River. Exercise caution at night downtown.

◉ SIGHTS

Since the Gold Rush, Sacramento has been more of a pit stop on the way to the lakes and mountains in the east than a destination in itself, but the city's numerous historical sights and museums have been growing in popularity.

GOVERNMENT BUILDINGS. Debates about the budget and water shortages, as well as a considerable amount of Arnold-spotting, occur daily in the elegant **State Capitol.** *(At 10th St. and Capitol Ave. ☎916-324-0333. 1hr. tours depart daily every hr. 9am-4pm. Free tickets distributed in Room B27.)* Colonnades of palm trees and grassy lawns transform **Capitol Park** into a shaded oasis in the middle of downtown's busy bureaucracy. The **State Historic Park Governor's Mansion** was built in 1877, and its faded, weathered exterior makes it look not a year younger. The mansion served as the residence of California's governor and his family until then-governor Ronald Reagan opted to rent his own pad. *(At 16th and H St. ☎ 916-324-0539. Open daily 10am-4pm. Tours every hr. $2, under 16 free.)*

OLD SACRAMENTO. This 28-acre town of early 1800s buildings attracts nearly five million visitors annually and has been refurbished to its late 19th-century appearance. Today, tourists tread wooden planked sidewalks, browsing gift shops or eating at restaurants. Attractions include a restored riverboat, California's first theater, and a military museum. The 100,000 sq. ft. **California State Railroad Museum** exhibits 23 historic locomotives, half of which you can walk through, and is regarded as the finest railroad museum in North America. *(125 I St. ☎ 916-445-6645. Open daily 10am-5pm. $4, under 17 free. 1hr. train rides from the Train Depot in Old Sacramento Apr.-Sept. Sa-Su. $6, ages 6-12 $3, under 6 free.)*

CALIFORNIA HISTORY. Sutter's Fort was the only remaining property of John Sutter after the rest were overrun by goldseekers. These days, busloads of tourists and local school children come to see the restored fort and its educational exhibits. *(2701 L St. ☎ 916-445-4422. Open daily 10am-5pm. $4, ages 6-16 $1, under 5 free.)* At the **California State History Museum**, multimedia exhibits include a virtual trip on a 1936 bus with a video of immigrant stories. *(1020 O St. ☎ 916-653-0563. Open Su noon-5pm, Tu-Sa 10am-5pm. $5, ages 6-13 $3, seniors $4, under 6 free.)*

CROCKER ART MUSEUM. This small museum packs in excellent art with permanent works by Brueghel, Rembrandt, and David, as well as large rotating exhibits. What makes the Crocker stand out, however, is its contemporary Californian art, including pieces by local burnout artist Robert Arneson. *(216 O St. ☎ 916-264-5423; www.crocker-artmuseum.org. Open Su, Tu-W, F-Sa 10am-5pm; Th 10am-9pm. Tours available; book a week in advance. $6, seniors $4, ages 7-17 $3, under 7 free.)*

SACRAMENTO ZOO. Chimps, giraffes, lions, white tigers, and an albino alligator are among the nearly 400 critters at the Sacramento Zoo. It sits in an eucalyptus-filled park and emphasizes protec-

tion of endangered species and the recreation of natural habitats. *(On William Land Park Dr. off I-5 at the Sutterville Exit. ☎ 916-264-5885; www.sac-zoo.com. Open daily Nov.-Jan. 10am-4pm; Feb.-Oct. 9am-4pm. $6.75, ages 3-12 $4.50, under 3 free.)*

⚡ OUTDOOR ACTIVITIES

The **American River** winds through Sacramento, and its rushing waters make **river rafting** an opportunity for adventure seekers. Rent rafts at **American River Raft Rentals,** 11257 S. Bridge St., in Rancho Cordova, 14 mi. east of downtown on U.S. 50. (Exit on Sunrise Blvd. and take it north 1½ mi. to the American River. ☎ 916-635-6400. Open daily 9am-6pm; rentals available until 1pm. 4-person rafts $38; kayaks $27. $2 launch fee. Return shuttle $3.50 per person.) The **American River Recreation Trail and Parkway,** spanning over 30 mi. from Discovery Park to Folsom Lake, is a nature preserve with a view of the downtown skyline. Hundreds of people cycle, jog, swim, fish, hike, and ride horses along the paths every day. You can enter the trail in Old Sacramento or at designated points along the river. **Folsom Lake State Recreation Area,** 25 mi. east on I-80 (take Douglas Blvd.), hosts a giant 11,000-acre reservoir perfect for swimming, boating, fishing, and wake-boarding. Over 100 mi. of trails wind through the surrounding hills. (☎ 916-988-0205. Open daily 6am-10pm. $2-6 per car.)

🎵 ENTERTAINMENT

In summer, Sacramento bustles with free afternoon concerts and cheap food. The Friday *Sacramento Bee* contains a supplement called *Ticket*, which gives a rundown of events. For music and activities, check free weeklies, such as *Sacramento News and Review* and *Inside the City. Alive and Kicking* has music and arts schedules.

If you're visiting Sacramento in the spring, scream alongside the **Sacramento Kings** fans, reputed to be the loudest in the NBA, at the Arco Arena, 1 Sports Pkwy. (Tickets ☎ 916-649-8497, 530-528-8497, or 209-485-8497.) Minor league baseball fans can catch the **Sacramento Rivercats,** at Raley Field, 400 Ballpark Dr., in West Sacramento. (Tickets ☎ 800-225-2277. Early Apr.-Sept.)

Second Saturday Art Walk (www.sacramento-second-saturday.org). On the 2nd Sa of each month,

NATIONAL ROAD

art galleries in Sacramento stay open late, allowing art lovers to wander and check out the scene. Pick up a copy of the *Sacramento News and Review* for a list of participating galleries. Free.

Friday Night Concert Series (☎916-442-2500), in Cesar Chávez Park, at 10th St. and I St. Live bands (rock, blues, jazz, folk, and pop), food stands, and beer gardens. In summer F 5-9pm. Free.

Dixieland Jazz Jubilee (☎916-372-5277; www.sacjazz.com). Over 100 bands play every Memorial Day weekend in Old Sac, attracting thousands.

Shakespeare Lite (☎916-442-8575), in St. Rose of Lima Park, at 7th St. and K St. Comedic versions of the Bard's work. June to mid-July Th noon-1pm.

California State Fair (☎916-263-3000; www.bigfun.org). This classic fair doesn't skimp on spinning rides, fairway food, or pig races. Mid-Aug. to early Sept. Tickets $7, seniors $5, children $4.50.

▧ FOOD

Food in Sacramento is plentiful and good, thanks to a hip midtown, immigrant populations, and a Californian culinary inventiveness. Many eateries are concentrated on **J St.** or **Capitol Ave.** between 19th and 29th St. The stretch of **Fair Oaks Blvd.** between Howe and Fulton St. is home to restaurants of all price ranges. Old Sacramento is filled with more expensive and gimmicky restaurants.

▧ **Zelda's Pizza,** 1415 21st St. (☎916-447-1400), at N St. A local favorite. Posters of Italy and Christmas lights enliven this windowless joint. Open M-Th 11:30am-2pm and 5-10pm, F 11:30am-2pm and 5-11:30pm, Sa 5-11:30pm, Su 5-10pm.

Ernesto's, 1901 16th St. (☎916-441-5850; www.ernestosmexicanfood.com), at the corner of S St. Dishes out upscale Mexican food at reasonable prices. Extensive vegetarian menu. Huge burritos ($7-9), quesadillas ($7), and salads ($6-8). Open Su-W 11am-10pm, Th 11am-11pm, F-Sa 9am-midnight.

Cafe Bernardo, 2726 Capitol Ave. (☎916-443-1189; www.cafebernardo.com), at 28th St. In earth tones and stainless steel, Cafe Bernardo serves sandwiches ($6-8), salads ($2-7), and soups ($2-4). Outdoor seating. Open Su-Th 7am-10pm, F-Sa 7am-11pm.

The Fox and Goose, 1001 R St. (☎916-443-8825), at 10th St. Situated in a huge brick factory, the Fox and Goose blends English public house with American alternative culture. Primarily a brunch spot. Open mic nights and live music Th-Sa. Open M-F 7am-2pm and 5:30pm-midnight, Sa-Su 8am-2am.

▧ ACCOMMODATIONS

Sacramento has many hotels, motels, and B&Bs, but advance reservations are always a good idea. **W. Capitol Ave.** has many cheap hotels, but they can be on the seedy side, so investigate first. Within Sacramento proper, **16th St.** has hotels and motels. Rates fluctuate, but standard chain hotel and motel rooms usually go for $50-150 per night.

▧ **Sacramento Hostel (HI-AYH),** 900 H St. (☎916-443-1691; reservations 800-909-4776, ext. 40), at 10th St. Built in 1885, this pastel Victorian mansion looks more like a B&B than a hostel. Huge modern kitchen, 3 living rooms, library, laundry, TV/VCR, and a selection of video rentals ($1). Dorm-style rooms are immaculate. Family, couple, and single rooms available. Parking $5 per night. Check-in 7:30-9:30am and 5-10pm. Check-out 9:30am. Lock-out 10am-5pm. Curfew 11pm. Dorms $21-23, nonmembers $24-26.

Courtyard by Marriott, 4422 Y St. (☎916-455-6800), at the UC Davis Medical Center. A full-fledged hotel at a relatively low price. Rooms have cable TV and high-speed Internet connections. Doubles from $74.

Vagabond Inn Midtown, 1319 30th St. (☎916-454-4400; www.vagabondinn.com), between M and N St. Low rates, moderately sized well-kept rooms, and above average amenities. Rooms have cable TV, phone, Internet, and free newspapers. Continental breakfast included. Doubles from $48.

▧ NIGHTLIFE

Capital-dwellers slink about in brass- and mahogany-lined bars and coffeehouses. Sacramento's midtown entertainment venues, on the other hand, afford a view of city residents who have a few more body-piercings than their representatives in the government. Nightclubs are scattered around Sacramento's periphery.

▧ **True Love Coffeehouse,** 2406 J St. (☎916-492-9002; www.truelovesacto.com). A quirky alternative hangout. A small stage hosts unusual entertainment, from movie screenings to waffle night. Check out the shaded patio. Some performances $6-7. Open Su-Th 5pm-midnight, F-Sa 5pm-2am.

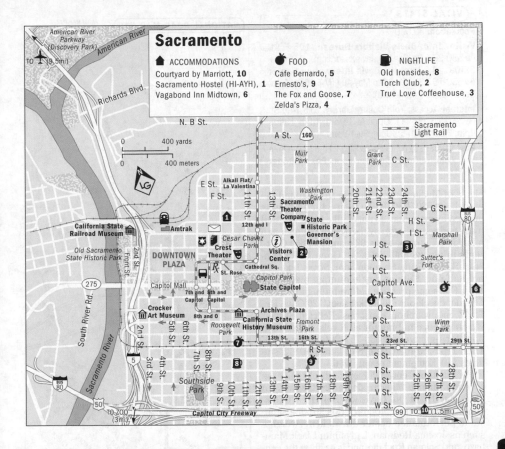

Sacramento

♠ ACCOMMODATIONS
Courtyard by Marriott, **10**
Sacramento Hostel (HI-AYH), **1**
Vagabond Inn Midtown, **6**

🍎 FOOD
Cafe Bernardo, **5**
Ernesto's, **9**
The Fox and Goose, **7**
Zelda's Pizza, **4**

🍺 NIGHTLIFE
Old Ironsides, **8**
Torch Club, **2**
True Love Coffeehouse, **3**

Sacramento Light Rail

Old Ironsides, 1901 10th St. (☎916-443-9751; www.theoldironsides.com), at S St. The first bar to get its liquor license after Prohibition, Old Ironsides is has 2 rooms, one for grooving and one for boozing. Lipstick DJ Tu. Open mic W. Live music Th-Sa (cover $5-10). Open M-F 11am-1:30am, Sa-Su 6pm-1:30am.

Torch Club, 904 15th St. (☎☎916-443-2797; www.the-torchclub.com), at I St. The ultimate blues and blue-grass venue in town. Live bands play every night. 21+. Cover varies. Open daily 10am-2am.

APPROACHING DAVIS
Take **Bus. I-80/U.S. 50 West** until it merges with **I-80.** To enter Davis, about 14 mi. from Sacramento, exit at **Richards Blvd. Northd,** following signs for downtown.

DAVIS

Davis prides itself on higher education, agriculture, and two-wheeled transportation. Davis's residents own more bicycles per capita than any other US city, and several intersections feature bike-specific traffic lights. The diverse students of University of California at Davis (UCD) shape the unique character of the town, and activity centers on the campus and adjacent downtown.

◎ SIGHTS. Of the UC schools, the **University of California at Davis** is the largest in square miles and also tops the list in agriculture and viticulture (vine cultivation). Step into nature at the **UCD Arboretum** on Putah Creek, which features trees and

VITAL STATS

Population: 60,000

Visitor Info: Davis Visitors Bureau, 105 E St. (☎530-297-1900; www.davisvisitor.com). Open M-F 8:30am-4:30pm. **UC Davis Information Center** (☎530-752-2222). Open May-Aug. M-F 10am-4pm; Sept.-Apr. M-F 8am-7pm.

Internet Access: Yolo County Library, 315 14th St. (☎530-757-5591). Open M 1-9pm, Tu-Th 10am-9pm, F-Sa 10am-5:30pm, Su 1-5pm.

Post Office: 2020 5th St. (☎800-275-8777). Open M-F 7am-5:30pm, Sa 9am-4pm. **Postal Code:** 95616.

plants of Mediterranean climate from around the world. (☎530-752-4880. Open 24hr.) Davis is marked by more than 40 mi. of bike trails. For trail maps and ratings, stop by the Visitors Bureau or a bike shop in town. **Ken's Bike and Ski,** 650 G St., rents bikes. (☎530-758-3223. Open M-F 10am-8pm, Sa 9am-7pm, Su noon-5pm. Street bikes $6 per half-day, $10 per day; mountain bikes $14/$28.) For some practice before hitting the rocks outside, check out the **Rocknasium,** 720 Olive Dr., Ste. Z, in a warehouse just past Redrum Burger, which offers climbing for all levels, including a bouldering cave. (☎530-757-2902. Open M-F 11am-11pm, Sa 10am-9pm, Su 10am-6pm. $12, students $10. Equipment rental $8/$6.)

For cultural entertainment, check out the recently opened **Mondavi Center for the Arts,** on Mrak Hall Dr. at Old Davis Rd. Built for UCD by wine tycoon Robert Mondavi, this striking sandstone performance center draws heavyweights such as Joshua Redman, Ladysmith Black Mambazo, and Salman Rushdie, and is easily at the center of cultural enrichment in Davis. (Box Office at 1 Shields Ave. ☎530-754-2787; www.mondaviarts.org. Open M-F 10am-6pm, Sa noon-6pm, and 1hr. before performances. Tickets $20-50.)

🍴 FOOD & ACCOMMODATIONS. Wednesday nights in summer bring locals to Central Park (at 3rd and C St.) for the renowned **Davis Farmers Market.** (☎530-756-1695; www.davisfarmersmarket.org. Open year-round Sa 8am-1pm; Oct.-Mar. W 2-6pm; Apr.-Sept. W 4:30-8:30pm.) Davis is rife with ethnic restaurants and quirky cafes. The downtown area between E and G St. south of 3rd St. is always a sure bet for a slice of pizza, a vegetarian smorgasbord, or a cup of joe. The **Davis Food Co-op,** 620 G St., has organic pro-

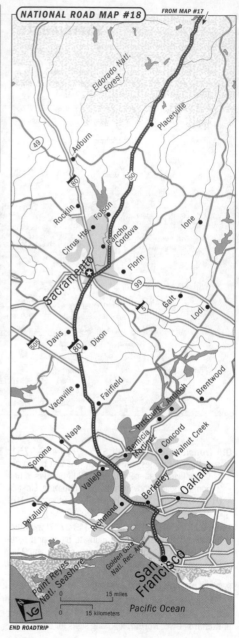

NATIONAL ROAD MAP #18   FROM MAP #17

Eldorado Natl. Forest

Placerville

49

Auburn

80   50

Rocklin   Folsom

Citrus Hts.   Rancho Cordova   Ione

Sacramento   Florin

99

Galt

5   Lodi

505   Davis   Dixon   80

Vacaville   Fairfield   Brentwood

Napa   Pittsburg Antioch

Benicia   Concord   Walnut Creek
Martinez

Sonoma   Vallejo   Berkeley   Oakland

Petaluma   Richmond

Point Reyes Natl. Seashore   Golden Gate Natl. Rec. Area   San Francisco

0   15 miles

0   15 kilometers   Pacific Ocean

END ROADTRIP

duce, fresh deli foods, international wines, and offers 15min. of free Internet access. (☎530-758-2667. Open daily 8am-10pm.) The **Crepe Bistro**, 234 E St., a Davis legend, is in the middle of downtown and is staffed by longtime, tattooed Davis residents who know their crepes. (☎530-753-2575. Open M-F 10:30am-10pm, Sa-Su 9:30am-10pm.) **Redrum Burger**, 720 Olive Dr., is a 50s-style diner with a bizarre history. True carnivores come for the full 1 lb. burgers ($9). Ostrich burgers ($5.50) add a twist, and super-thick milkshakes ($3.70) complement patties of any kind. (☎530-756-2142. Open daily 10am-10pm.)

Motels in Davis do not come cheap, and during university events rooms are scarce. **University Park Inn**, 1111 Richards Blvd., off I-80 at the Richards Blvd. exit, is six blocks from campus. It has 45 spotless rooms with cable TV, refrigerators, A/C, and a pool. (☎530-756-0910. Continental breakfast included. Doubles $75-85. AAA discount.) The **University Inn Bed and Breakfast**, 340 A St., near Central Park, has the feel of a country home in the middle of town. (☎530-756-8648. Doubles $65, with breakfast $78.)

⬛ NIGHTLIFE. At night, students party at **The Graduate**, 805 Russell Blvd., in the University Mall. Popular Friday evenings attract swarms of students with drink specials. The walls usually reverberate with mainstream pop and hip-hop, but The Graduate can be hit-or-miss; beware line-dancing nights. (☎530-758-4723. Open daily 10:30am-2am.) An older and more sophisticated crowd gathers at **Sophia's Thai Bar**, 129 E St., a tiny bar with tropical decor, aquariums, outdoor seating, and occasional live music. (☎530-758-4333. Open M-Sa 5pm-2am, Su 5-10pm.) South of 3rd St., G St. also houses many bars.

APPROACHING FAIRFIELD
Exit I-80 at **N. Texas St.**, and follow it south until it turns west onto **Texas St.**

FAIRFIELD. Fairfield's most roadtrip-worthy attraction is the **Jelly Belly Factory**, 1 Jelly Belly Ln. While waits can be unbearably long in the summer, the 35min. tour, an artful mix of actual observation of the factory floor and video presentations, leaves you sugar-high and jelly bean enlightened. They even sweeten the deal with a small bag of free jelly beans. Don't miss the opportunity to buy "Belly Flops" at the factory store, irregularly sized jelly beans that go for cheap. (From downtown take Pennsylvania Ave. south to Rio Vista Rd. (Rte. 12), turn right, and exit at Chadbourne Rd. Turn left on Courage Dr. and then left onto N. Watney Way. ☎800-953-5592. Open daily 9am-5pm. Free.) Offering food a little less sugary and more substantial is **Joe's Buffet**, 834 Texas St., near Jackson St. When you order a sandwich at this old-style delicatessen, they slice the fresh meat right onto it; the sloppy result is fantastic. (☎707-425-2317. Open M-Sa 10am-4pm.)

APPROACHING BERKELEY
Continue straight onto **W. Texas St.** to get back onto **I-80** toward Berkeley. About 15 mi. past the Carquinez Bridge, take the **University Ave.** exit to downtown Berkeley and the UC Berkeley (Cal) campus.

BERKELEY

Famous as an intellectual center and a haven for iconoclasts, Berkeley lives up to its reputation. Although the peak of its political activism occurred in the 1960s and 70s—when students attended more protests than classes—UC Berkeley continues to foster an alternative atmosphere. The vitality of the population infuses the streets, which overflow with hip cafes and top-notch bookstores. Telegraph Ave., with its street-corner soothsayers, hirsute hippies, and itinerant musicians, remains one of the town's main draws.

⬭ VITAL STATS

Population: 100,000

Visitor Info: Berkeley Convention and Visitor Bureau, 2015 Center St. (☎510-549-7040; www.visitberkeley.com), at Milvia St. Open M-F 9am-5pm. **UC Berkeley Visitors Center,** 101 University Hall (☎510-642-5215; www.berkeley.edu), at the corner of University Ave. and Oxford St. Open M-F 8:30am-4:30pm.

Internet Access: UC Computer, 2569 Telegraph Ave. (☎510-649-6089). Open M-Sa 10am-6pm.

Post Office: 2000 Allston Way (☎510-649-3155), at Milvia St. Open M-F 9am-5pm, Sa 10am-2pm. **Postal Code:** 94704.

▣ GETTING AROUND

To prevent people from using residential streets as cut-offs to bypass traffic-filled main streets, Berkeley installed rows of planters to interrupt many streets. Use main streets to navigate as closely to your destination as possible before cutting in. The heart of town, **Telegraph Ave.**, runs south from the UC Berkeley Student Union, while the **Gourmet Ghetto** north of campus hosts California's finest dining. **Parking** can be expensive, and meters often offer only 1hr. The best option is to park in residential neighborhoods south of downtown, where you are allowed 2hr. free parking on weekdays and unlimited free parking on Saturday, Sunday, or after 7pm. There are some cheaper garages away from Telegraph Ave.

◉ SIGHTS

In 1868, the private College of California and the public Agricultural, Mining, and Mechanical Arts College united as the **University of California.** The 178-acre university in Berkeley was the first of nine U of C campuses, so by seniority it has sole right to the nickname "Cal." The campus is bounded on the south by Bancroft Way, on the west by Oxford St., on the north by Hearst Ave., and on the east by Tilden Park. Enter through **Sather Gate** into **Sproul Plaza**, both sites of celebrated sit-ins and bloody confrontations with police. Tours leave from **Sather Tower,** the tallest building on campus; its observation level offers a great view. (Open M-F 10am-4pm. $2.) ◪**Berkeley Art Museum (BAM)**, 2626 Bancroft Way, is most respected for its 20th-century American and Asian art. BAM is also associated with the **Pacific Film Archive.** (☎510-642-0808; www.bampfa.berkeley.edu. Open Su and W-Sa 11am-7pm. Adults $8; students, seniors, disabled, and ages 12-17 $5. 1st Th of each month free.) You haven't really visited Berkeley until you've strolled along **Telegraph Ave.**, lined with cafes, bookstores, and used clothing and record stores. For off-campus fun, check out the **Takara Sake USA Inc.,** 708 Addison St., where visitors can learn the history and science of sake making and sample 15 different types of Japan's fire-water. (☎510-540-8250; www.takarasake.com. Open daily noon-6pm. Free.)

When you're ready to get out of town, Berkeley is happy to oblige. In the pine and eucalyptus forests east of the city lies the beautiful anchor of the East Bay park system—**Tilden Regional Park.** Hiking, biking, running, and riding trails criss-cross the park and provide impressive views of the Bay Area. (Take Spruce St. to Grizzly Peak Blvd. to Canon Ave. ☎510-635-0135. Open daily dawn-dusk.) Also inside the park, the small, sandy beach at **Lake Anza** is a popular swimming spot during the hottest summer days. (☎510-843-2137. Open summer 11am-6pm. $3, seniors and children $2.)

▨ FOOD

Berkeley's **Gourmet Ghetto,** at Shattuck Ave. and Cedar St., is the birthplace of California Cuisine. The north end of **Telegraph Ave.** caters to student appetites and wallets, with late-night offerings along **Durant Ave.** A growing number of international establishments are helping to diversify the area. **Solano Ave.** to the north is great for Asian cuisine while **4th St.** is home to some more upscale (but cheaper than Gourmet Ghetto) eats. The birthplace of California Cuisine, ◪**Chez Panisse**, 1517 Shattuck Ave., was opened by chef Alice Waters in 1971. Alice still prepares the nightly fixed menu (4 courses; $50-75) in the downstairs restaurant. Upstairs, the more casual cafe serves similar, but less expensive fare. (☎510-548-5525, cafe 548-5049; www.chezpanisse.com. Entrees $15-20. Reservations strongly recommended. Cafe open M-Th 11:30am-3pm and 5-10:30pm, F-Sa 11:30am-3:30pm and 5-11:30pm. Restaurant open for dinner M-Sa; seatings at 6-6:30pm and 8:30-9:30pm.) ◪**Café Intermezzo**, 2442 Telegraph Ave., is a veggie-lover's paradise, serving heaping salads with homemade dressing, huge sandwiches on freshly baked bread, and tasty soups, all at delicious prices. (☎510-849-4592. Open daily 10am-10pm.) North of Cedar St., **César**, 1515 Shattuck Ave., is a great place for savory tapas ($3-12), *bocadillos* (small sandwiches on french bread; $5-7), desserts ($4-5), and a long list of spirits. (☎510-883-0222. Open daily noon-midnight. Kitchen closes Su-Th 11pm, F-Sa 11:30pm.) An icon of Berkeley gastronomic life, **Yogurt Park,** 2433 Durant Ave., just west of Telegraph Ave., serves huge portions made daily. (☎510-549-2198; 510-549-0570 for daily list of flavors. Open daily 10am-midnight.) For Ethiopian cuisine, try **The Blue Nile,** 2525 Telegraph Ave. Sip *mes* (honey wine; $2) while eating *injera* bread with your fingers (☎510-540-6777. Open Su and Tu-Sa 5-10pm. Reservations recommended.)

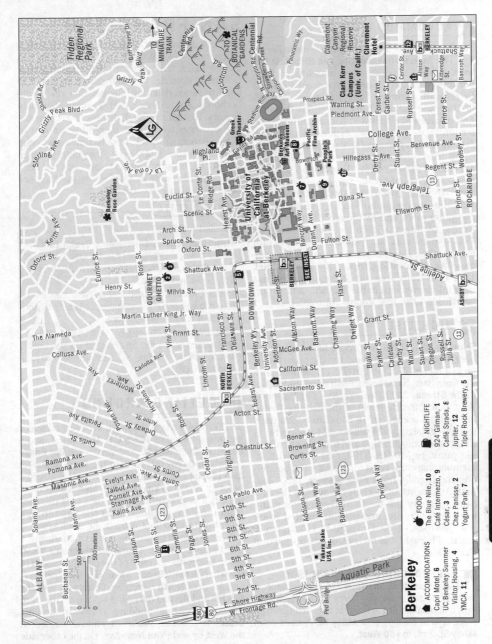

Tilden Regional Park

TO MINIATURE TRAIN
Centennial Rd.
TO BOTANICAL GARDENS
Centennial Dr.

Grizzly Peak Blvd.

Cyclotron Rd.

Strawberry Creek Rd.

N. Canyon Rd.

Canyon Rd.

Stadium Rimway

Panoramic Wy.

Claremont Canyon Regional Reserve

Claremont Hotel

Golf Course Dr.

Grizzly Peak Blvd.

Shasta Rd.

Grizzly Peak Blvd.

Sterling Ave.

Keith Ave.

La Loma Ave.

Highland Pl.

Greek Theater

Gayley Rd.

Berkeley Art Museum

Pacific Film Archive

Peoples Park

Bowditch St.

Prospect St.

Warring St.
Piedmont Ave.

Clark Kerr Campus (Univ. of Calif.)

Forest Ave.
Garber St.

College Ave.

Hillegass Ave.

Derby St.

Benvenue Ave.

Stuart St.

Regent St.

Prince St.

Woolsey St.

Center St.
Alston Way
Kittredge St.
Bancroft Way

Shattuck Ave.

Russell St.

Prince St.

ROCKRIDGE

Telegraph Ave.

Berkeley Rose Garden

Le Conte Ave.
Ridge Rd.

Euclid St.

Scenic St.

Arch St.

Spruce St.

Oxford St.

Hearst Ave.

University of California at Berkeley

Bancroft Wy.

Durant Ave.

Dana St.

Fulton St.

Ellsworth St.

Haste St.

Regent St.

Eunice St.

Rose St.

Henry St.

Milvia St.

GOURMET GHETTO

Shattuck Ave.

Oxford St.

DOWNTOWN

Center St.

Shattuck Ave.

SEE INSET

BERKELEY

Adeline St.

ASHBY

Martin Luther King Jr. Way

Vine St.
Grant St.

Francisco St.
Delaware St.

Berkeley Wy.

University Ave.

Addison St.

Alston Way

Bancroft Way

Charning Way

Dwight Way

Grant St.

The Alameda

Collusa Ave.

Carlotta Ave.

Monterey Ave.

Hopkins St.

Acton St.

Lincoln St.

McGee Ave.

California St.

Sacramento St.

Blake St.

Parker St.

Carleton St.

Derby St.

Ward St.

Oregon St.

Russell St.

Stuart St.

Julia St.

NORTH BERKELEY

Hearst Ave.

Peralta Ave.

Ramona Ave.
Pomona Ave.

Masonic Ave.

Curtis St.

Ordway St.
Acton St.
Santa Fe Ave.

Virginia St.

Chestnut St.

Bonar St.
Browning St.
Curtis St.

Cedar St.

Dwight Way

Evelyn Ave.
Talbut Ave.
Cornell Ave.
Stannage Ave.
Kains Ave.

San Pablo Ave.

10th St.
9th St.
8th St.
7th St.
6th St.
5th St.
4th St.
3rd St.
2nd St.

Addison St.

Alston Way

Bancroft Way

Dwight Way

Solano Ave.

ALBANY

Buchanan St.

Marin Ave.

Harrison St.

Gilman St.

Camelia St.

Page St.

Jones St.

Takara Sake USA Inc.

Ped Bridge

Aquatic Park

E. Shore Highway
W. Frontage Rd.

580
80

500 yards
500 meters

Berkeley

▲ ACCOMMODATIONS
Capri Motel, **6**
UC Berkeley Summer
Visitor Housing, **4**
YMCA, **11**

● FOOD
The Blue Nile, **10**
Café Intermezzo, **9**
César, **3**
Chez Panisse, **2**
Yogurt Park, **7**

■ NIGHTLIFE
924 Gilman, **1**
Caffè Strada, **8**
Jupiter, **12**
Triple Rock Brewery, **5**

NATIONAL ROAD

ACCOMMODATIONS

There are few cheap accommodations in Berkeley. The **Berkeley-Oakland Bed and Breakfast Network** (☎510-547-6380; www.bbonline.com/ca/berkeley-oakland) coordinates great East Bay B&Bs with a range of rates (singles $50-150; doubles $60-150). No-frills motels line **University Ave.** between Shattuck and Sacramento St.; ritzier joints are downtown, especially on **Durant Ave. UC Berkeley Summer Visitor Housing** has simple dorms, shared baths, and free Internet access. (☎510-642-4108. Parking $6 per day. Open June to mid-Aug. Singles $53; doubles $68. 7th night free.) The **YMCA,** 2001 Allston Way, has a communal kitchen, shared bath, computer room, and TV lounge. Use of pool and fitness facilities is included. (☎510-848-6800. 18+. 10-night max. stay; special application for longer stays. Reception daily 8am-9:30pm. Singles $39; doubles $49; triples $59.) **Capri Motel,** 1512 University Ave., at Sacramento St., has tasteful rooms with cable TV, A/C, and fridge. (☎510-845-7090. 18+. Rooms from $85.)

NIGHTLIFE

Jupiter, 2181 Shattuck Ave., features a huge beer garden, live music, and terrific pizza for $8. (☎510-843-8277. Open M-Th 11:30am-1am, F 11:30am-2am, Sa noon-2am, Su noon-midnight.) **Caffè Strada,** 2300 College Ave., at Bancroft Way, is a glittering jewel of the caffeine-fueled intellectual scene. (☎510-843-5282. Open daily 6:30am-midnight.) **924 Gilman,** 924 Gilman St., is a legendary all-ages club and a staple of California punk. (☎510-524-8180. Cover $5 with $2 membership card, good for 1 year.) The boisterous and friendly **Triple Rock Brewery,** 1920 Shattuck Ave., north of Berkeley Way, was the first (and to many the best) of Berkeley's many brewpubs. Try the award-winning Red Rock Ale. (☎510-843-2739. Open Su-W 11:30am-midnight, Th-Sa 11:30am-1am. Rooftop garden closes 9pm.)

APPROACHING SAN FRANCISCO

Head south on **Shattuck Ave.,** past downtown Berkeley. Just after crossing Derby St., Shattuck forks right onto **Adeline St.;** follow that fork, and turn right ¼ mi. later at the light onto **Ashby St.** Proceed down Ashby St. 2 mi. to **I-80 West.**

SAN FRANCISCO

If California is a state of mind, then San Francisco is euphoria. Welcome to the city that will take you to new highs, leaving your mind spinning, your tastebuds tingling, and your calves aching. The dazzling views, daunting hills, one-of-a-kind neighborhoods, and laid-back, friendly people fascinate visitors. Though smaller than most "big" cities, the city manages to pack an incredible amount of vitality into its 47 sq. mi., from its thriving art communities and bustling shops to the pulsing beats in some of the country's hippest nightclubs and bars. For more coverage of the City by the Bay, see 📖*Let's Go: San Francisco.*

> **VITAL STATS**
>
> **Population:** 777,000
>
> **Visitor Info: California Welcome Center** (☎415-956-3493; www.sfvisitor.org), on Pier 39 at the Great San Francisco Adventure. Open Su-Th 9am-9pm, F-Sa 9am-10pm.
>
> **Internet Access:** At the California Welcome Center (see above). For complete listings of Internet cafes in SF, check www.surfandsip.com.
>
> **Post Office:** 170 O'Farrell St. (☎415-956-0131), at Stockton St., in the basement of Macy's. Open M-Sa 10am-5:30pm, Su 11am-5pm. **Postal Code:** 94108.

GETTING AROUND

San Francisco sits at the junction of several major highways, including **I-280, U.S. 101, Hwy. 1,** and **I-80.** From the east, **I-80** runs across the **Bay Bridge** (westbound-only toll $3) into the **South of Market Area (SoMa)** and then connects with U.S. 101 just before it runs into **Van Ness Ave. Market St.,** one of the city's main thoroughfares, runs on a diagonal from the **Ferry Building** near the bay through downtown and to the **Castro** in the southwest.

Neighborhood boundaries get a bit confusing; a good map is a must. Touristy **Fisherman's Wharf** sits at the northeast edge of the city. Just south of the wharf is **North Beach,** a historically Italian area, and south of North Beach lies **Chinatown.** Wealthy **Nob Hill** and **Russian Hill** round out the northeast of the city. Municipal buildings cluster in the **Civic Center,** which lines Market St. and is bounded on the west by wide Van Ness Ave. On the other side of Van Ness Ave. is hip **Hayes Valley.** Retail-heavy **Union Square** is north of Market St. and gives way in the west to the rougher **Tenderloin.**

The **Golden Gate Bridge** stretches over the Bay from the **Presidio** in the city's northwest corner. Just south of the Presidio, **Lincoln Park** reaches westward to the ocean, while vast **Golden Gate Park** dominates the western half of the peninsula. Near Golden Gate Park sits the former hippie haven of **Haight-Ashbury.** The trendy **Mission** takes over south of 14th St. The diners and cafes of the "gay mecca" of the **Castro** dazzle on Castro and Market St., northwest of the Mission. On the opposite side of the city, the skyscrapers of the **Financial District** crowd down to the **Embarcadero.**

Parking in San Francisco is rare and expensive even where legal, and zealous cops dole out tickets mercilessly. You can stow your car all day in the residential **Richmond** or **Sunset Districts,** south of Golden Gate Park, but watch signs indicating weekly street-cleaning times. To park near a popular area, your best bet may be a parking garage.

When parking facing uphill, turn front wheels away from the curb, and, if driving a standard, leave the car in first gear. If your car starts to roll, it will stop when the tires hit the curb. When facing downhill, turn the wheels toward the curb and leave the car in reverse. *Always* set the emergency brake.

SIGHTS

FISHERMAN'S WHARF & THE BAY

Piers 39 through 45 provide access to San Francisco's most famous and touristy attractions. Easily visible from the waterfront is Alcatraz Island.

ALCATRAZ. In its 29 years as a maximum-security federal penitentiary, **Alcatraz** harbored a menacing cast of characters, including Al "Scarface" Capone and George "Machine Gun" Kelly. There were 14 separate escape attempts. Only one man is known to have survived crossing the Bay; he was recaptured. On the rock, the cell-house audio tour immerses visitors in the infamous days of Alcatraz. A **Park Ranger tour** can take you around the island and through its 200 years of occupation, from a hunting and fishing ground for Native Americans to a Civil War outpost to a military prison, a federal

prison, and finally a birthplace of the Native American civil rights movement. Now part of the **Golden Gate National Recreation Area,** Alcatraz is home to diverse plants and birdlife. *(Take the Blue and Gold Fleet from Pier 41. ☎415-773-1188, tickets 415-705-5555. Ferries 9:30am and every 30min. 10:15am-4:15pm; arrive 20min. early. $9.25, seniors $7.50, ages 5-11 $6. Reservations recommended. Audio tours $4, ages 5-11 $2. Park Ranger tours free. "Alcatraz After Dark" $20.75, seniors and ages 12-17 $18, ages 5-11 $11.50; call for times and availability. Other boating companies run shorter boats around the island for $10.)*

GHIRARDELLI SQUARE. Ghirardelli Sq. is a mall in what used to be a chocolate factory. No golden ticket is required to gawk at the **Ghirardelli Chocolate Manufactory's** vast selection of goodies, or the **Ghirardelli Chocolate Shop and Caffe,** with drinks, frozen yogurt, and a smaller selection of chocolates. Both hand out **free samples,** but the Caffe is usually less crowded. *(Mall 900 N. Point St. ☎415-775-5500. Stores open M-Sa 10am-9pm, Su 10am-6pm. Ghirardelli Chocolate Manufactory ☎415-771-4903. Open Su-Th 10am-11pm, F-Sa 10am-midnight. Soda fountain open Su-Th 10am-11pm, F-Sa 10am-midnight. Chocolate Shop and Caffe ☎415-474-1414. Open M-Th 8:30am-9pm, F 8:30am-10pm, Sa 9am-10pm, Su 9am-9pm.)*

MARINA & FORT MASON

■ **PALACE OF FINE ARTS.** With its open-air domed structure and curving colonnades, the Palace of Fine Arts was originally built to commemorate the opening of the Panama Canal, testifying to San Francisco's recovery from the 1906 earthquake. *(On Baker St., between Jefferson and Bay St. next to the Exploratorium. Open daily 6am-9pm. Free.)* The **Palace of Fine Arts Theater,** located directly behind the rotunda, hosts dance and theater performances and film festivals. *(☎415-563-6504; www.palaceoffinearts.com.)*

FORT MASON. Fort Mason Center is home to some of the most innovative and impressive cultural museums and resources in San Francisco. The array of outstanding attractions seem to remain unknown to both tourists and locals, making it a quiet waterfront counterpart to the tourist blitz of nearby Fisherman's Wharf. On the first Wednesday of every month all museums are free and open until 7pm. The grounds are also the headquarters of the **Golden Gate National Recreation**

Area. *(The park is at the eastern portion of Fort Mason, near Gashouse Cove.* ☎ *415-441-3400, ext. 3; www.fortmason.org.)*

NORTH BEACH

WASHINGTON SQUARE. Washington Sq., bordered by Union, Filbert, Stockton, and Powell St., is North Beach's *piazza*, a pretty, not-quite-square, tree-lined lawn. The wedding site of Marilyn Monroe and Joe DiMaggio, the park fills every morning with *tai chi* practitioners. By noon, sunbathers, picnickers, and bocce-ball players take over. **St. Peter and St. Paul Catholic Church**, beckons sightseers to take refuge in its dark nave. *(666 Filbert St.)* Turn-of-the-century San Francisco philanthropist and party-girl Lillie Hitchcock Coit donated the **Volunteer Firemen Memorial** in the middle of the square.

COIT TOWER. Also built by Lillie Hitchcock Coit, the Coit Tower stands 210 ft. high and commands a spectacular view of the city and the Bay. During the Depression, the government's Works Progress Administration employed artists to paint the colorful and subversive murals in the lobby. *(☎ 415-362-0808. Open daily 10am-7pm. Elevator $3.75, seniors $2.50, ages 6-12 $1.50, under 6 free.)*

CITY LIGHTS BOOKSTORE. Beat writers came to national attention when Lawrence Ferlinghetti's City Lights Bookstore (est. 1953) published Allen Ginsberg's *Howl*, which was banned in 1956 and then subjected to an extended trial at the end of which a judge found the poem "not obscene." City Lights has expanded since its Beat days and now stocks wide selection of fiction and poetry, but it remains committed to publishing young poets and writers under its own label. *(2261 Columbus Ave.* ☎ *415-362-8193. Open daily 10am-midnight.)*

CHINATOWN

WAVERLY PLACE. Find this little alley and you'll want to spend all day gazing at the incredible architecture. *(Between Sacramento and Washington St. and between Stockton St. and Grant Ave.)* The fire escapes are painted in pinks and greens and held together by railings cast in intricate Chinese patterns. **Tien Hou Temple** is the oldest Chinese temple in the US. *(125 Waverly Pl.)*

ROSS ALLEY. Once lined with brothels and opium dens, today's **Ross Alley** has the look of old Chinatown. The narrow street has stood in for the Orient in such films as *Big Trouble in Little China, Karate Kid II,* and *Indiana Jones and the Temple of Doom.* Squeeze into a doorway to see fortune cookies being shaped at the ■**Golden Gate Cookie Company.** *(56 Ross Alley.* ☎ *415-781-3956. Bag of cookies $3, with "funny," "sexy," or "lucky" fortunes $5. Open daily 10am-8pm.)*

NOB HILL & RUSSIAN HILL

THE CROOKEDEST STREET IN THE WORLD. The famous curves of **Lombard St.**—installed in the 1920s so that horse-drawn carriages could negotiate the extremely steep hill—serve as an icon of SF. From the top, pedestrians and passengers enjoy the view of city and harbor. The view north along Hyde St. isn't too shabby either. *(Between Hyde and Leavenworth St. at the top of Russian Hill.)*

GRACE CATHEDRAL & HUNTINGTON PARK. The largest Gothic edifice west of the Mississippi, **Grace Cathedral** is Nob Hill's stained-glass studded crown. Inside, modern murals mix San Franciscan and national historical events with saintly scenes. The altar of the AIDS Interfaith Memorial Chapel celebrates the church's "inclusive community of love." *(1100 California St., between Jones and Taylor St.* ☎ *415-749-6300; www.gracecathedral.org. Open Su-F 7am-6pm, Sa 8am-6pm. Tours M-F 1-3pm, Sa 11:30am-1:30pm, Su 1:30-2pm. Suggested donation $3.)* Outside, the building looks onto the turf and trees of **Huntington Park,** equipped with a park and playground.

UNION SQUARE & THE TENDERLOIN

MAIDEN LANE. When the Barbary Coast (now the Financial District) was down and dirty, Union Sq.'s **Morton Alley** was dirtier. Around 1900, murders on the Alley averaged one per week and prostitutes waved to customers from second-story windows. After the 1906 earthquake and fires destroyed most of the brothels, merchants moved in and renamed the area **Maiden Ln.** in hopes of changing the street's image. It worked. Today, the pedestrian-only street that extends two blocks from Union Sq.'s eastern side is as virtuous as they come and makes a pleasant place to stroll or sip espresso while sporting your new Gucci shades.

GOLDEN GATE BRIDGE & THE PRESIDIO

GOLDEN GATE BRIDGE. When Captain John Fremont coined the term "Golden Gate" in 1846, he meant to name the harbor entrance to the San Francisco Bay after the mythical Golden Horn port of Constantinople. In 1937, however, the colorful name became permanently associated with Joseph Strauss's copper-hued engineering masterpiece—the Golden Gate Bridge. Built for $35 million, the bridge stretches across 1¼ mi. of ocean, its towers looming 65 stories above the Bay. It can sway up to 27 ft. in each direction during high winds. On sunny days, hundreds of people take the 30min. walk across. The views from the bridge are amazing, as well as from the Vista Point in Marin County just after the bridge. To see the bridge itself, it's best to get a bit farther away; Fort Point and Fort Baker in the Presidio, Land's End in Lincoln Park, and Mt. Livermore on Angel Island all offer spectacular views on clear days.

PRESIDIO. When Spanish settlers forged their way up the San Francisco peninsula from Baja California in 1769, they established *presidios*, or military outposts, as they went. San Francisco's Presidio, the northernmost point of Spanish territory in North America, was dedicated in 1776.

LINCOLN PARK & OCEAN BEACH

COASTAL TRAIL. The Coastal Trail loops around the interior of Lincoln Park for a scenic and sometimes hardcore coastal hike. The entrance to the trail is not well marked, so be careful not to mistakenly tackle a much more difficult cliffside jaunt. The path leads first into **Fort Miley**, a former army post. Near the picnic tables rests the **USS San Francisco Memorial.** The USS *SF* sustained 45 direct hits in the battle of Guadalcanal on November 12-13, 1942. Nearly 100 men died in the clash, but the ship went on to fight in ten more battles. *(Trail begins at Pt. Lobos and 48th Ave. Free.)* The Coastal Trail continues for a 3 mi. hike into **Land's End,** famous for its views of both the Golden Gate Bridge and the "sunken ships" that signal treacherous waters below. Biking is permitted on the trail, although parts contain stairs and bumpy terrain better suited to mountain bikes. From Land's End, onlookers have the option to hike an extra 6 mi. into the Presidio and on to the arches of Golden Gate Bridge. For hikers and bikers who aren't so inclined, the walk along **El Camino Del Mar** originates close to the Coastal Trail but runs farther in from the shore. Enjoy the forested views the **Palace of the Legion of Honor** before finishing "The Path of the Sea" at **China Beach.** *(Begins at Pt. Lobos and Sea Rock Dr.)*

BEACHES. Swimming is permitted but dangerous at scenic **China Beach** at the end of Seacliff Ave. on the eastern edge of Lincoln Park. Adolph Sutro's 1896 **bathhouse** lies in ruins on the cliffs. Cooled by ocean water, the baths were capable of packing in 25,000 occupants at a time. **Ocean Beach,** the largest and most popular of San Francisco's beaches, begins south of Point Lobos and extends down the northwestern edge of the city's coastline. The undertow along the point is dangerous, but die-hard surfers brave the treacherous currents and the ice-cold water anyway.

GOLDEN GATE PARK

Take your time to enjoy this park. Museums (see p. 440) and cultural events pick up where the lush flora and fauna leave off, and athletic opportunities abound. The park has a municipal golf course, equestrian center, sports fields, tennis courts, and stadium. On Sundays, park roads close to traffic, and bicycles and in-line skates come out in full force. The **Visitors Center** is in the Beach Chalet on the western edge of the park. (☎415-751-2766. Open daily 9am-7pm.) **Surrey Bikes and Blades,** 50 Stow Lake Dr., in Golden Gate Park, rents equipment. (☎415-668-6699. Bikes from $6 per hr., $21 per day. Skates $7/$20. Open daily 10am-dusk.)

GARDENS. The **Garden of Fragrance** is designed especially for the visually impaired; all labels are in Braille and the plants are chosen specifically for their textures and scents. Near the Music Concourse off South Dr., the **Shakespeare Garden** contains almost every flower and plant ever mentioned by the Bard. *(Open daily dawn-dusk; in winter closed M. Free.)* The **Japanese Cherry Orchard,** at Lincoln Way and South Dr., blooms intoxicatingly the first week in April. Created for the 1894 Mid-Winter Exposition, the elegant **Japanese Tea Garden** is a serene collection of wooden buildings, small pools, graceful footbridges, carefully pruned trees, and lush plants. *(☎ 415-752-4227. Open daily summer 8:30am-6pm; winter 8:30am-5pm. $3.50, seniors and ages 6-12 $1.25. Free summer 8:30-9:30am and 5-6pm; winter 8:30-9:30am and 4-5pm.)*

NATIONAL ROAD

San Francisco

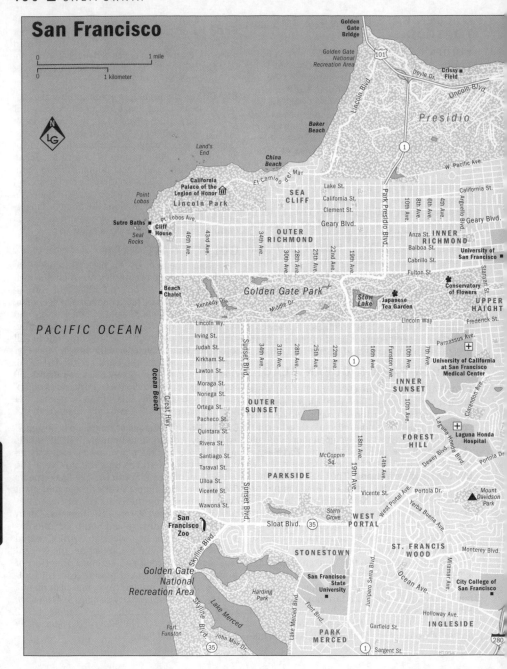

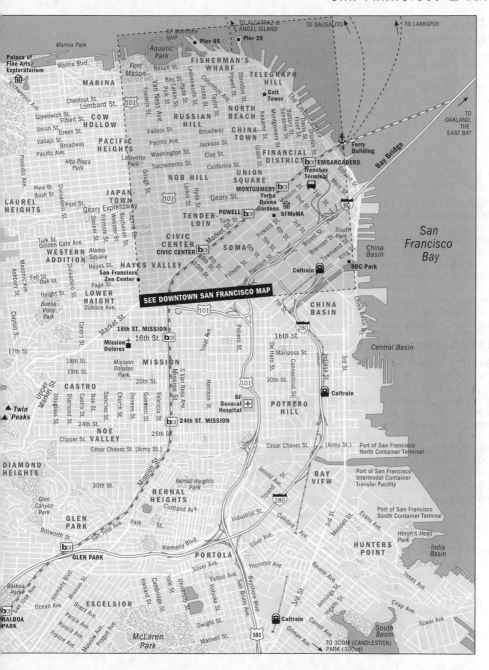

TO ALCATRAZ &
ANGEL ISLAND
TO SAUSALITO
TO LARKSPUR

SF Maritime
NHP
Pier 45
Pier 39

Marina Park
Palace of
Fine Arts/
Exploratorium
Aquatic
Park
FISHERMAN'S
WHARF
TELEGRAPH
HILL

Marina Blvd.
Fort
Mason
Beach St.

Richardson Ave.
Bay St.
Coit
Tower

MARINA
Chestnut St.
Lombard St.

Van Ness Ave.
Larkin St.
Hyde St.
Leavenworth St.
Jones St.
Taylor St.
Stockton St.
Powell St.
Columbus Ave.
Mason St.

RUSSIAN
HILL
NORTH
BEACH

Greenwich St.
Filbert St.
Polk St.
Franklin St.

COW
HOLLOW
Union St.
Green St.

Vallejo St.
Broadway
Broadway
CHINA-
TOWN

PACIFIC
HEIGHTS
Pacific Ave.
Pacific Ave.
Jackson St.
Grant St.
Kearny St.
Montgomery St.
Sansome St.
Battery St.
Front St.
Davis St.
Drumm St.
The Embarcadero

FINANCIAL
DISTRICT
Ferry
Building

Presidio Ave.
Alta Plaza
Park
Lafayette
Park
Washington St.
Clay St.
Sacramento St.
California St.

Pine St.
Bush St.
NOB HILL
UNION
SQUARE
EMBARCADERO
Transbay
Terminal

LAUREL
HEIGHTS
Geary Expressway
JAPAN-
TOWN
Post St.
Geary St.
Larkin St.
Hyde St.
MONTGOMERY
Yerba
Buena
Gardens
2nd St.
Mission St.

Golden Gate Ave.
Turk St.
Masonic Ave.
Divisadero St.
Steiner St.
Webster St.
Fillmore St.
Buchanan St.
Laguna St.
TENDER-
LOIN
POWELL
SFMoMA
Howard St.
4th St.
3rd St.

WESTERN
ADDITION
Alamo
Square
Turk St.
CIVIC
CENTER
CIVIC CENTER
SOMA
Folsom St.
5th St.
6th St.
7th St.
Bryant St.
Brannan St.
Townsend St.
King St.
South
Park

Ashbury St.
Fell St.
Oak St.
Hayes St.
Page St.
HAYES VALLEY
San Francisco
Zen Center
10th St.
9th St.
8th St.
Harrison St.
Caltrain
SBC Park
China
Basin

San
Francisco
Bay

LOWER
HAIGHT
Haight St.
Buena
Vista
Park
Duboce Ave.
Market St.

Clayton S.
SEE DOWNTOWN SAN FRANCISCO MAP
CHINA
BASIN

17th St.
16th ST. MISSION
16th St.
Mission
Dolores
16th St.
16th St.
Central Basin

Upper Market St.
Castro St.
18th St.
19th St.
Mission
Dolores
Park
MISSION
20th St.
Treat Ave.
Potrero St.
Mariposa St.
De Haro St.
20th St.
Connecticut St.
Indiana St.
3rd St.

CASTRO
Douglass St.
Diamond St.
Noe St.
Sanchez St.
Church St.
Dolores St.
Guerrero St.
Valencia St.
Harrison St.
S Van Ness Ave.
Mission St.
SF
General
Hospital
POTRERO
HILL
Caltrain

Twin
Peaks
24th St.
NOE
VALLEY
Clipper St.
24th ST. MISSION
25th St.
César Chávez St. (Army St.)
César Chávez St. (Army St.)
Port of San Francisco
North Container Terminal
BAY
VIEW

DIAMOND
HEIGHTS
Glen
Canyon
Park
30th St.
Bernal Heights
Park
BERNAL
HEIGHTS
Cortland Ave.
Port of San Francisco
Intermodal Container
Transfer Facility

GLEN
PARK
Bosworth St.
San Jose Ave.
Park
St.
Industrial St.
Jerrold Ave.
Toland St.
Oakdale Ave.
3rd St.
Mendell St.
Evans Ave.
Port of San Francisco
South Container Terminal
Heron's Head
Park
India
Basin

GLEN PARK
Alemany Blvd.
PORTOLA
Silver Ave.
Silver Ave.
HUNTERS
POINT
Innes Ave.
Crisp Ave.

Balboa
Park
Ocean Ave.
Alemany Blvd.
Mission St.
Brazil Ave.
Persia Ave.
Russia Ave.
Thornton Ave.
Felton Ave.
Yale St.
Cambridge St.
Harvard St.
University St.
Holyoke St.
San Bruno Ave.
Bayshore Blvd.
Revere Ave.
Thomas Ave.
3rd St.
Jennings St.
Ingalls St.
Carroll Ave.
Gilman Ave.
South
Basin
Spear Ave.

BALBOA
PARK
San Jose Ave.
EXCELSIOR
Moscow St.
Prague St.
France Ave.
Dwight St.
Mansell St.
McLaren
Park
Caltrain
TO 3COM (CANDLESTICK)
PARK (300yd)

NATIONAL ROAD

FINANCIAL DISTRICT

TRANSAMERICA PYRAMID. Certain areas of the Financial District's architectural landscape rescue it from the otherwise banal functionalism of the business area. The leading lady of the city's skyline, the Transamerica Pyramid, is, according to new-age sources, directly centered on the telluric currents of the Golden Dragon Ley line between Easter Island and Stonehenge. Planned as an architect's joke and co-opted by one of the leading architectural firms in the country, the building has earned disdain from purists and reverence from city planners. (*600 Montgomery St., between Clay and Washington St.*)

JUSTIN HERMAN PLAZA. When not overrun by skateboarders, the Plaza is home to bands and rallyists who sometimes provide lunch-hour entertainment. U2 rock star Bono was arrested here in 1987 for spray painting "Stop the Traffic— Rock and Roll" on the fountain. Recently, the plaza has been the starting point for Critical Mass, a pro-bicyclist ride that takes place after 5pm on the last Friday of every month. If you happen to be around on a rare hot day, walk through the inviting mist of the **Vaillancourt Fountain** to cool off.

JAPANTOWN & PACIFIC HEIGHTS

SAINT DOMINIC'S ROMAN CATHOLIC CHURCH. Churchgoers and architecture buffs appreciate Saint Dominic's towering altar, carved in the shape of Jesus and the 12 apostles. With its imposing stone and Gothic feel, St. Dominic's is a must see, especially its renowned shrine of **Saint Jude,** skirted by candles and intricately carved oak. (*2390 Bush St., at Steiner St. Open M-Sa 6:30am-5:30pm, Su 7:30am-9pm. Mass M-F 6:30, 8am, 5:30pm; Sa 8am and 5:30pm; Su 7:30, 9:30, 11:30am, 1:30, 5:30, 9pm candlelight service.*)

FUJI SHIATSU & KABUKI SPRINGS. After a rigorous day hiking the hills, reward your weary muscles with an authentic massage at **Fuji Shiatsu.** (*1721 Buchanan Mall, between Post and Sutter St. ☎ 415-346-4484. $41-44.*) Alternatively, head to the bathhouse at **Kabuki Hot Springs** to relax in the sauna and steam-room, or enjoy the *Reiki* treatment to heal, rejuvenate and restore energy balance. (*1750 Geary Blvd. ☎ 415-922-6000; www.kabukisprings.com. Open daily 10am-10pm. M-F before 5pm $15, after 5pm and Sa-Su $18. Men only M, Th, Sa; women only Su, W, F; co-ed Tu.*)

CIVIC CENTER

ARCHITECTURE. Referred to as "The Crown Jewel" of American Classical architecture, **City Hall** reigns supreme over the Civic Center, with a dome to rival St. Paul's cathedral and an area of over 500,000 sq. ft. (*1 Dr. Carlton B. Goodlett Pl., at Van Ness Ave. ☎ 415-554-4000. Open M-F 8am-8pm, Sa-Su noon-4pm.*) The seating in the $33 million glass-and-brass **Louise M. Davies Symphony Hall** was designed to give audience members a close-up view of performers. Its **San Francisco Symphony** is highly esteemed. (*201 Van Ness Ave. ☎ 415-552-8000; tickets ☎ 415-431-5400. Open M-F 10am-6pm, Sa noon-6pm.*) The recently renovated **War Memorial Opera House** hosts the **San Francisco Opera Company** and the **San Francisco Ballet.** (*301 Van Ness Ave., between Grove and McAllister St. Box office at 199 Grove St. ☎ 415-864-3330. Open M-Sa 10am-6pm and 2hr. before each show.*)

MISSION

MISSION DOLORES. Founded in 1776, the **Mission Dolores** is thought to be the city's oldest building. Bougainvillea, poppies, and birds-of-paradise bloom in its cemetery, which was featured in Hitchcock's *Vertigo*. (*3321 16th St., at Dolores St. ☎ 415-621-8203. Open May-Oct. daily 9am-4:30pm; Nov.-Apr. 9am-4pm. Adults $3, ages 5-12 $2.*)

MISSION MURALS. A walk east or west along 24th St., weaving in and out of the side streets, reveals magnificent murals. Continuing the Mexican mural tradition made famous by Diego Rivera and Jose Orozco, the murals have been a source of pride for Chicano artists and community members since the 1980s. Standouts include the political murals of **Balmy Alley,** off 24th St. between Harrison and Folsom St., a three-building tribute to guitar god **Carlos Santana** at 22nd St. and Van Ness Ave., the face of **St. Peter's Church** at 24th and Florida St., and the **urban living center** on 19th St. between Valencia and Guerrero St.

CASTRO & NEARBY

THE CASTRO. Stores throughout the area cater to gay-mecca pilgrims, with everything from rainbow flags and pride-wear to the latest in BGLT books, dance music, and trinkets of the unmentionable variety. Many local shops, especially on colorful **Castro St.,** also double as novelty galleries. Discover just how anatomically correct Gay Billy is at **Does Your Father Know?**, a one-stop kitsch-and-camp overdose. To read up on gay history and culture, try at **A Different Light Bookstore.**

WALKING TOURS. For a tour of the Castro that includes sights other than biceps and abs, check out **Cruisin' the Castro.** Trevor Hailey, a resident since 1972, is consistently recognized as one of SF's top tour leaders. Her 4hr. walking tours cover Castro life and history from the Gold Rush to today. (☎ 415-550-8110; www.webcastro.com/castrotour. Tours Tu-Sa 10am. $40; lunch included. Reservations required.)

HAIGHT-ASHBURY

FORMER CRIBS. The former homes of counter-culture legends still attract visitors. From the corner of Haight and Ashbury St., walk just south of Waller St. to check out the house occupied by the **Grateful Dead** when they were still the Warlocks. (710 Ashbury St.) Look across the street for the **Hell's Angels** house. If you walk back to Haight St., go right three blocks, and make a left on Lyon St., you can check out **Janis Joplin's** abode. (122 Lyon St., between Page and Oak St.) Cross the Panhandle, continue three blocks to Fulton St., turn right, and wander seven blocks toward the park to see where the Manson "family" planned murder and mayhem at the **Charles Manson** mansion. (2400 Fulton St., at Willard St.)

SAN FRANCISCO ZEN CENTER. Appropriately removed from the havoc of the Haight, the **San Francisco Zen Center** offers a peaceful retreat. The temple is called Beginner's Mind Temple, so don't worry if you don't know where to begin looking for your *chi*. The best option for most is the Saturday morning program, which includes a mediation lecture at 8:45am followed by activities and lunch. (300 Page St., at Laguna St. ☎ 415-863-3136. Office open M-F 9:30am-12:30pm and 1:30-5pm, Sa 9am-noon. Sa morning program $6.)

🏛 MUSEUMS & GALLERIES

MARINA

Exploratorium, 3601 Lyon St. (☎ 415-563-7337 or 415-561-0360; www.exploratorium.edu). The Exploratorium can hold over 4000 people, and when admission is free usually does. Over 650 displays—including miniature tornadoes, computer planet-managing, and giant bubble-makers—explain the wonders of the world. On the 2nd W of each month Nov.-Mar., the Exploratorium hosts avant-garde **art cocktail nights** that feature Bay Area artists, a DJ, and bar. Open June-Aug. daily 10am-6pm; Sept.-May Su and Tu-Sa 10am-5pm. $12; students, seniors, disabled, and ages 9-17 $9.50; ages 4-8 $8. 1st W of each month free. Tactile Dome $15; includes general admission.

FORT MASON

Museum of Craft and Folk Art, Bldg. A. (☎ 415-775-0990; www.mocfa.org). The MOCFA brings together crafts and functional art from past and present, showcasing everything from 19th-century Chinese children's hats to war-time commentary made through lightbulbs. Open Su and Tu-F 11am-5pm, Sa 10am-5pm. $4, students and seniors $3, under 18 free. Free Sa 10am-noon and 1st W of each month 11am-7pm.

African-American Historical and Cultural Society Museum, Bldg. C, (☎ 415-441-0640). Displays historic artifacts and artwork, modern works, and a permanent collection by local artists. Open Su and W-Sa noon-5pm. $3, seniors and students 12 $1, under 12 free. 1st W of each month free.

SF Museum of Modern Artists Gallery, Bldg. A., 1st fl. (☎ 415-441-4777). Over 1200 Bay Area artists show, rent, and sell work here. Monthly curated exhibits are downstairs, while most other pieces are sold upstairs. Every May, the gallery hosts a benefit sale—all works half-price. Open Tu-Sa 11:30am-5:30pm. Free.

NOB HILL & RUSSIAN HILL

San Francisco Art Institute, 800 Chestnut St. (☎ 415-771-7020 or 800-345-7324; www.sfai.edu). The oldest art school west of the Mississippi, the Institute is lodged in a converted mission and has produced a number of American greats including Mark Rothko, Ansel Adams, Imogen Cunningham, Dorothea Lange, and James Weeks. To the left as you enter is the **Diego Rivera Gallery,** 1 wall of which is covered by a huge 1931 Rivera mural. Open daily June-Aug. 9am-8pm; Sept.-May 9am-9pm.

Cable Car Powerhouse and Museum, 1201 Mason St. (☎ 415-474-1887). After the steep journey up Nob Hill, you'll understand the development of the vehicles celebrated here. The modest building is the working center of San Fran's cable car system. Look down on 57,300 ft. of cable whizzing by or learn about the cars, some of which date back to 1873. Open daily Apr.-Oct. 10am-6pm; Nov.-Mar. 10am-5pm. Free.

NATIONAL ROAD

UNION SQUARE

Martin Lawrence Gallery, 366 Geary St. (☎415-956-0345). Displays works by pop artists like Warhol and Haring, who once distributed his work for free to New York commuters in the form of graffiti; it now commands upwards of $13,000 in print form. Also houses studies by Picasso and America's largest collection of work by Marc Chagall. Open Su 10am-7pm, M-Th 9am-8pm, F-Sa 9am-10pm. Free.

Hang, 556 Sutter St. (☎415-434-4264; www.hangart.com). Works hang from the exposed ceiling beams of this chrome warehouse. An annex recently opened directly across the street. Open Su M-Sa 10am-6pm, Su noon-5pm. Free.

TENDERLOIN

509 Cultural Center/Luggage Store, 1007 Market St. (☎415-255-5971) and 1172 Market St. (☎415-865-0198). Presents performing arts, exhibitions, and education initiatives. The often-graphic art exhibits probably won't be grandma's favorites. Regular events include comedy open mic (Tu 8pm), improv music concerts (Th 8pm), and a theater festival each June. (Suggested donation $6-10 each.) Next door to 509, the **Cohen Alley** houses a third venue for the area's creative talent; the alley is leased to the Luggage Store, which has made it an artistic showcase.

LINCOLN PARK

California Palace of the Legion of Honor (☎415-863-3330; www.legionofhonor.org), in the middle of Lincoln Park. A copy of Rodin's *Thinker* beckons visitors into the grand courtyard, where a little glass pyramid recalls another Paris treasure, the Louvre. A thorough catalogue of masters, from medieval to modern, hangs inside. Just outside the Palace, a **Holocaust memorial** depicts a single, hopeful survivor looking out through a barbed-wire fence to the beauty of the Pacific. Open Su and Tu-Sa 9:30am-5pm. $8, seniors $6, ages 12-17 $5, under 12 free. Tu free.

GOLDEN GATE PARK

California Academy of Sciences, 55 Concourse Dr. (☎415-750-7145; www.calacademy.org), on the east side of the park at 9th Ave. Houses several museums specializing in different fields of science. The **Steinhart Aquarium,** home to over 600 aquatic species, is livelier than the natural history exhibits. Shark feedings M-W and F-Su 10:30am, 12:30, 2:30, 4:30pm. Open ocean fish feedings daily 1:30pm. Penguin feedings daily 11:30am and 4pm. At the **Natural History Museum,** the Earthquake Theater shakes visitors. Open June-Aug. daily 9am-6pm; Sept.-May 10am-5pm. Combined admission $8.50; seniors, students, and ages 12-17 $5.50; ages 4-11 $2. 1st W each month free (open until 8:45pm). The **Morrison Planetarium** re-creates the heavens with sky shows M-F 2pm. $2.50/$1.25.

SOMA

San Francisco Museum of Modern Art (SFMOMA), 151 3rd St. (☎415-357-4000; www.sfmoma.org), between Mission and Howard St. Holds 5 floors of art, with an emphasis on design, and is home to the largest selection of 20th-century American and European art this side of New York. Open Sept.-May M-Tu and F-Su 11am-5:45pm, Th 11am-8:45pm; June-Aug. M-Tu and F-Su 10am-6pm, Th 10am-9pm. 4 free gallery tours per day. $10, seniors $7, students $6, under 13 free. Th 6-9pm half-price. 1st Tu of each month free.

Yerba Buena Center for the Arts, 701 Mission St. (☎415-978-2787; www.yerbabuenaarts.org). The center runs an excellent theater and gallery space, with programs emphasizing performance, film, viewer involvement, and local work. It is surrounded by the **Yerba Buena Rooftop Gardens,** a vast expanse of concrete, fountains, and foliage. Open Su and Tu-Sa 11am-6pm. $6, students and seniors $3. Th free.

♫ ENTERTAINMENT

MUSIC

The distinction between bars, clubs, and live music venues is hazy in San Francisco. Almost all bars will occasionally have bands, and small venues have rock and hip-hop shows. Look for the latest live music listings in *S.F. Weekly* and *The Guardian*. Hard-core audiophiles might snag a copy of *Bay Area Music (BAM)*.

Café du Nord, 2170 Market St. (☎415-861-5016), between Church and Sanchez St. in the **Castro.** Live music nightly—from pop and groove to garage rock. M Night Hoot showcases local singing and songwriting. Happy hour 6-7:30pm; martinis and cosmos $2.50. 21+. Cover $5-10 after 8:30pm. Open Su-Tu 6pm-2am, W-Sa 4pm-2am.

Justice League, 628 Divisadero St. (☎415-440-0409; www.ticketweb.com), at Hayes St. in the **Lower Haight.** Live hip-hop is hard to find in San Francisco, but the Justice League fights ever onward for a good beat. M reggae and dub, W soul night. 21+. Cover $5-25. Open daily 9pm-2am.

Bottom of the Hill, 1233 17th St. (☎415-626-4455; www.bottomofthehill.com), between Missouri and Texas St. in **Potrero Hill.** Intimate rock club with tiny stage is the last best place to see up-and-comers before they move to bigger venues. Most Su afternoons feature local bands and all-you-can-eat barbecue. 21+. Cover $5-10. Open M-Th 8:30pm-2am, F 3pm-2am, Sa 8:30pm-2am, Su hours vary.

The Fillmore, 1805 Geary Blvd. (☎415-346-6000; www.thefillmore.com), at Fillmore St. in **Japantown.** Bands that pack stadiums often play at the legendary Fillmore, the foundation of San Francisco's 1960s music scene. Tickets $15-40.

DANCE

▨ **Alonzo King's Lines Contemporary Ballet** (☎415-863-3360; www.linesballet.org), in **Hayes Valley.** Dancers combine elegant classical moves with athletic flair to the music of great living jazz and world music composers. Tickets $15-25.

▨ **Oberlin Dance Company,** 3153 17th St. (☎415-863-9834; www.odctheater.org), between South Van Ness and Folsom St. in the **Mission.** Mainly dance, but occasional theater space with gallery attached. Box office open W-Sa 2-5pm.

California Contemporary Dancers, 530 Moraga St. (☎415-753-6066; www.ccdancers.org), in the **Sunset.** The all-woman modern dance company brings together the best of widely diverse dance and musical traditions to create exciting, innovative performances.

THEATER

Downtown, **Mason St.** and **Geary St.** constitute "Theater Row," the city's center for theatrical entertainment. **TIX Bay Area,** located in a kiosk in Union Sq. at the corner of Geary and Powell St., is a Ticketmaster outlet. (☎415-433-7827; www.theaterbayarea.org. Open Su 11am-3pm, Tu-Th 11am-6pm, F-Sa 11am-7pm.)

Magic Theatre (☎415-441-8822; www.magictheatre.org), in Fort Mason Center, stages international and American premieres. A famous landmark, **The Orpheum,** 1192 Market St. (☎415-512-7770), at Hyde St. near the Civic Center hosts big Broadway shows. **Geary Theater,** 415 Geary St. (☎415-749-2228; www.act-sfbay.org), at Mason St. in Union Sq. is home to the renowned **American Conservatory Theater,** the jewel in SF's theatrical crown. The ▨**Castro Theatre,** 429 Castro St. (☎415-

621-6350; www.thecastrotheatre.com), near Market St., shows eclectic films, festivals, and double features, some featuring live organ music.

SPORTS

Home to the five-time Super Bowl champion **49ers** (☎415-468-2249, tickets 415-656-4900; www.sf49ers.com), 3COM Park, also known as **Candlestick Park,** sits right on the ocean, resulting in trademark gusts that led to one of the lowest homerun averages in baseball back when the Giants played there. The **Giants** play at the **Pacific Bell Park,** 24 Willie Mays Plaza (☎415-972-2000 or 888-464-2468; www.sfgiants.com), in SoMa.

✹ FESTIVALS

If you can't find a festival going on in San Francisco, well, you just aren't trying hard enough. Cultural, ethnic, and queer special events take place year-round. For two consecutive weekends in April, the Japanese **Cherry Blossom Festival** (☎415-563-2313) lights up the streets of Japantown with hundreds of performers. The oldest film festival in North America, the **San Francisco International Film Festival** shows more than 100 international films of all genres over two weeks. (☎415-561-5022; www.sffs.org. Most $9.) If film's your thing, you may also want to check out the **San Francisco International Gay and Lesbian Film Festival** (☎415-703-8650; www.frameline.org), California's second-largest film festival and the world's largest gay and lesbian media event. The $6-15 tickets go fast. It takes place during the 11 days leading up to **Pride Day** (☎415-864-3733; www.sfpride.org). The High Holy Day of the queer calendar, Pride Day celebrates with a parade and events downtown starting at 10:30am.

For a bit of high culture, consider the free **San Francisco Shakespeare Festival,** every Saturday and Sunday in September in Golden Gate Park. (☎415-865-4434. Shows 1:30pm, but arrive at noon for a seat.) You'll find guilt-free chocolate heaven at the **Ghirardelli Square Chocolate Festival** (☎415-775-5500; www.ghirardellisq.com) in early September, when proceeds go to Project Open Hand. The oldest in America, **San Francisco Blues Festival** attracts some of the biggest names in the business. (☎415-979-5588; 3rd weekend in Sept. in Fort Mason.) Finally, the leather-and-chains gang lets it all hang out at the **Folsom Street Fair,** Pride

Day's raunchier, rowdier little brother. (☎415-861-3247; www.folsomstreetfair.com; on Folsom St. between 7th and 11th St.)

FOOD

Strolling and sampling the food in each neighborhood is an excellent way to get a taste for the city's diversity. For the most up-to-date listings of restaurants, try the *Examiner* and the *S.F. Bay Guardian*. The glossy *Bay Area Vegetarian* can also suggest places to graze.

Pier 39 and **Fisherman's Wharf** overflow with eateries that charge high rates for average food. Tourists may feel compelled to try some clam chowder and sourdough bread.

San Francisco's **Chinese cuisine** is widely held to be unsurpassed outside of Asia, but it can be difficult to distinguish the excellent restaurants from the mediocre. **Chinatown** is filled with cheap restaurants whose sheer number can baffle even the savviest of travelers. Some locals claim that Chinese restaurants in the **Richmond** are better than those in Chinatown. **Clement St.,** between 2nd and 12th Ave., has the widest variety.

In **North Beach's** tourist-friendly restaurants, California cuisine merges with the bold palate of Italy, inspiring *delicioso* dishes that blend tradition and innovation. In the **Financial District,** corner cafes vend Mediterranean grub at rock-bottom prices. Pedestrian side streets are packed with outdoor bistros. The dominance of Mexican specialties and gigantic burritos is undeniable in the **Mission,** but the area also houses homey diners, quirky vegan-friendly cafes (along **Valencia St.**), and Middle Eastern, Italian, and Thai cuisine. Campy diners and posh cafes dominate the nearby **Castro's** culinary offerings, where little is as cheap as in the Mission.

FISHERMAN'S WHARF

Pat's Café, 2330 Taylor St. (☎415-776-8735), between Chestnut and Francisco St. With playful yellow swirls on the building's facade, Pat's bright decor welcomes diners to a hearty home-cooked meal like mom would make. Burgers, sandwiches, and big breakfasts $5-10. Open M and Th-Su 5:30-9pm, Tu-W 7:30am-3pm.

CHINATOWN

▨ **Chef Jia,** 925 Kearny St. (☎415-398-1626), at Pacific St. Insanely cheap and delicious food. A local

crowd comes for lunch and dinner specials ($4.80) or the celebrated signature dishes, such as rolling lettuce chicken with pine nuts ($9). Open M-F 11:30am-10pm, Sa-Su 5-10pm. No credit cards.

Golden Gate Bakery, 1029 Grant Ave. (☎415-781-2627), in Chinatown. This tiny bakery's moon cakes, noodle puffs, and vanilla cream buns (all $0.75-1.50) draw long lines. Open daily 8am-8pm.

NORTH BEACH

▨ **L'Osteria del Forno,** 519 Columbus Ave. (☎415-982-1124), between Green and Union St. Acclaimed Italian roasted and cold foods, plus homemade breads. Terrific thin-crust pizzas (slices $2.50-3.75) and focaccia sandwiches ($5-6.50). Open Su-M and W-Th 11:30am-10pm, F-Sa 11:30am-10:30pm.

Mario's Bohemian Cigar Store Café, 566 Columbus Ave. (☎415-362-0536), at the corner of Washington Sq. The Beats frequented this laid-back cafe, which still serves first-rate grub. Hot focaccia sandwiches ($7-8.50). Open daily 10am-11pm.

NOB HILL & RUSSIAN HILL

Zarzuela, 2000 Hyde St. (☎415-346-0800), at Union St. in Russian Hill. Spanish homestyle cooking and a festively upscale setting make *chorizo al vino* ($4-7) the highlight of the evening. Entrees $8-14. Open Tu-Th 5:30-10pm, F-Sa 5:30-10:30pm.

Sushigroove, 1916 Hyde St. (☎415-440-1905), between Union and Green St. Without a full kitchen, this chic, inexpensive sushi-*sake* joint (most sushi and *maki* $3-7) serves up a lot of rolls (many vegetarian) but nothing that has seen the inside of an oven. Open Su-Th 6-10pm, F-Sa 6-10:30pm.

UNION SQUARE & THE TENDERLOIN

▨ **Le Colonial,** 20 Cosmo Pl. (☎415-931-3600; www.lecolonialsf.com), off Post St. between Taylor and Jones St. Exquisite French-Vietnamese cuisine in a stunning French-inspired building. The veranda, with its high white adobe walls, ivy-clad lattice, and overhead heating lamps, offers the best opportunity to revel in the architecture and down signature mojitos ($8). Entrees $20-33. Open Su-W 5:30-10pm, Th-Sa 5:30-11pm. Lounge open from 4:30pm.

▨ **The California Culinary Academy,** 625 Polk St. (☎415-216-4329), between Turk and Eddy St. Academy students cook behind a window visible from the high-ceilinged Carême dining room. The Tu-W *prix-fixe* 3-course lunch ($16) or dinner ($24) indulges patrons with ambitious and extremely successful culinary combinations. Wine pairings with each course are a steal at $5 total. The Th-F grand buffet lunch ($22) or dinner ($38) draws large crowds; reserve 1 week ahead. Open Tu-F 11:30am-1pm and 6-8pm.

SOUTH OF MARKET AREA (SOMA)

▨ **The Butler and the Chef Cafe,** 155A S. Park Ave. (☎415-896-2075; www.thebutlerandthechef.com), between Bryant, Brannan, 2nd, and 3rd St. Advertising itself as San Francisco's only authentic French bistro, this stellar reproduction of a Parisian street cafe serves breakfast crepes ($4-10) and baguette sandwiches ($7). Open Tu-Sa 8am-4:30pm.

HAIGHT-ASHBURY

▨ **Pork Store Cafe,** 1451 Haight St. (☎415-864-6981), between Masonic Ave. and Ashbury St. A breakfast place that charges itself very seriously with the mission to fatten you up—they proudly stock only whole milk. The 2 delicious healthy options ("Tim's Healthy Thursdays" and "Mike's Low Carb Special"; each $7) pack enough spinach, avocado, and salsa to hold their own against the Piggy Special ($7). Open M-F 7am-3:30pm, Sa-Su 8am-4pm.

Kate's Kitchen, 471 Haight St. (☎415-626-3984), near Fillmore St. Start your day off right with one of the best breakfasts in the neighborhood (served all day), like the "Farmer's Breakfast" or the "French Toast Orgy" (with fruit, yogurt, granola, and honey; $7.50). It's often packed, so sign up on a waiting list outside. Open M 9am-2:45pm, Tu-F 8am-2:45pm, Sa-Su 8:30am-3:45pm. No credit cards.

MISSION & THE CASTRO

▨ **Taquería Cancún,** 2288 Mission St. (☎415-252-9560), at 19th St. Additional locations: 3211 Mission St. (☎415-550-1414) and 1003 Market (☎415-864-6773). Delicious burritos (grilled chicken upon request; $4) and scrumptious egg dishes served with chips and salsa, small tortillas, and choice of sausage, ham, or salsa ($5). Open Su-Th 9am-1:45am, F-Sa 9am-3am.

▨ **Mitchell's Ice Cream,** 688 San Jose Ave. (☎415-648-2300), at 29th St. This takeout parlor gets so busy that you have to take a number at the door. With a list of awards almost as long as the list of flavors (from caramel praline to Thai iced tea), Mitchell's will chocolate dip any scoop. Cone $2.10. Pint $5.10. Open daily 11am-11pm.

Nirvana, 544 Castro St. (☎415-861-2226), between 18th and 19th St. Playfully concocted cocktails such as "nirvana colada" and "phat margarita" ($8-9) complement Burmese cuisine with a twist (from $8). Open M-Th 4:30-9:30pm, F-Sa noon-10:30pm, Su noon-9:30pm.

▐▜ ACCOMMODATIONS

For those who don't mind sharing a room with strangers, many San Francisco hostels are homier and cheaper than budget hotels. Book in advance if at all possible, but since many don't take reservations for summer, you might have to just show up or call early on your day of arrival. B&Bs are often the most comfortable and friendly, albeit expensive, option. Beware that some of the cheapest budget hotels may be located in areas requiring extra caution at night.

HOSTELS

▨ **San Francisco International Guesthouse,** 2976 23rd St. (☎415-641-1411), in the **Mission.** Look for the blue Victorian with yellow trim near the corner of Harrison St. With hardwood floors, wall tapestries, and comfortable common areas, this hostel feels like the well-designed (but totally clean) room of your tree-hugger college roommate. Passport with international stamps "required." Free Internet. 5-night min. stay. No reservations, but chronically filled to capacity. All you can do is try calling a few days ahead of time. Dorms $16; doubles $32.

▨ **Adelaide Hostel and Hotel,** 5 Isadora Duncan (☎877-359 1915; www.adelaidehostel.com), at the end of a little alley off Taylor St. between Geary and Post St. in **Union Square.** The bottom 2 floors, recently renovated with fresh paint and new furniture, entice a congenial international crowd. Try to avoid the top 2 floors until they undergo renovations. 4-day max. stay. Check-out 11am. Reserve online or by phone. Dorms $22; rooms from $65.

▨ **Green Tortoise Hostel,** 494 Broadway (☎415-834-1000; www.greentortoise.com), off Columbus Ave. at Kearny St. in **North Beach.** A ballroom preceded this super-mellow and friendly pad, allowing today's laid-back, fun-seeking young travelers to hang out amid abandoned finery in the spacious common room. Free sauna. Breakfast and dinner (M, W, F) included. Key deposit $20. 10-day max. stay. Reception 24hr. Check-out 11am. Reservations recommended. Dorms $19-22; private rooms $48-60. No credit cards.

Fort Mason Hostel (HI-AYH), Bldg. #240 (☎415-771-7277; sfhostel@norcalhostels.org), in **Fort Mason.** The

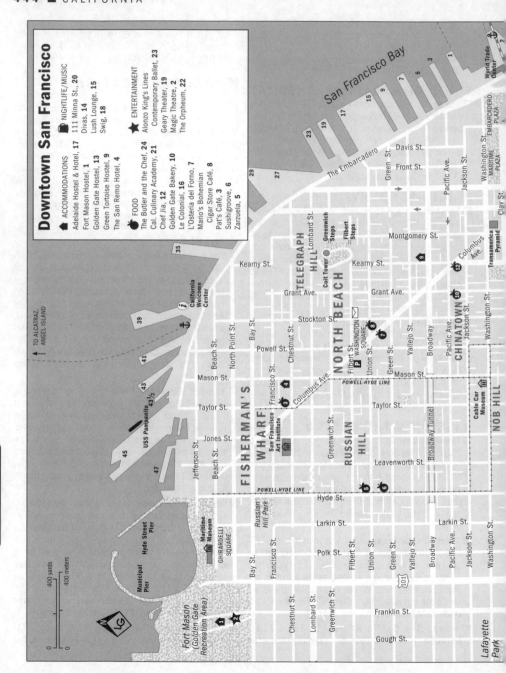

Downtown San Francisco

San Francisco Bay

World Trade Center

MARITIME PLAZA

EMBARCADERO PLAZA

The Embarcadero

Davis St.

Front St.

Green St.

Pacific Ave.

Jackson St.

Washington St.

Clay St.

Transamerica Pyramid

Columbus Ave.

Montgomery St.

Kearny St.

Grant Ave.

Broadway

Pacific Ave.

Jackson St.

Washington St.

CHINATOWN

Cable Car Museum

NOB HILL

Broadway Tunnel

Stockton St.

WASHINGTON SQUARE

Filbert St.

Union St.

Green St.

Vallejo St.

Mason St.

Taylor St.

POWELL-HYDE LINE

NORTH BEACH

Coit Tower

TELEGRAPH HILL

Lombard St.

Greenwich Steps

Filbert Steps

Kearny St.

Grant Ave.

Columbus Ave.

Chestnut St.

Powell St.

Francisco St.

Beach St.

North Point St.

Bay St.

California Welcome Center

USS Pampanito

Hyde Street Pier

Municipal Pier

Maritime Museum

GHIRARDELLI SQUARE

Russian Hill Park

FISHERMAN'S WHARF

San Francisco Art Institute

Mason St.

Taylor St.

Jones St.

Beach St.

Jefferson St.

RUSSIAN HILL

Greenwich St.

Leavenworth St.

POWELL-HYDE LINE

Hyde St.

Larkin St.

Polk St.

Filbert St.

Union St.

Green St.

Vallejo St.

Larkin St.

Franklin St.

Gough St.

Bay St.

Francisco St.

Chestnut St.

Lombard St.

Greenwich St.

Fort Mason
(Golden Gate
Recreation Area)

Lafayette Park

TO ALCATRAZ,
ANGEL ISLAND

TO ALCATRAZ, ANGEL ISLAND

400 yards
400 meters

101

NATIONAL ROAD

35

39

41

43

43½

45

47

29

27

23

19

17

15

9

7

5

3

1

hostel is at the corner of Funston and Pope St. past the administrative buildings. Beautiful surrounding forest and wooden bunks provide a campground feel. Not a place for partiers—strictly enforced quiet hours (11pm) and no smoking or alcohol. Movies, walking tours, dining room, and parking. Laundry (wash $1, dry $1). Check-in 2:30pm. Reserve weeks in advance. Dorms $22.50-29, under 13 $15-17.

HOTELS & GUESTHOUSES

▨ **The San Remo Hotel,** 2237 Mason St. (☎415-776-8688; www.sanremohotel.com), between Chestnut and Francisco St. in **Russian Hill.** Built in 1906, this pension-style hotel features small but elegantly furnished rooms with antique armoires, bedposts, lamps, and complimentary backscratchers. Shared bathrooms with brass pull-chain toilets. Check-out 11am. Reservations recommended. Rooms $50-70.

▨ **Hayes Valley Inn,** 417 Gough St. (☎415-431-9131, reservations 800-930-7999; www.hayesvalley-inn.com), just north of Hayes St. in **Hayes Valley.** European-style B&B with small, clean rooms, shared bath, and lace curtains. Bedrooms range from charming singles with daybeds to extravagant turret rooms with wraparound windows and queen-size beds. All rooms have cable TV, phone, and private sink. Breakfast included. Check-in 3pm. Check-out 11am. Singles $47; doubles $53-66; turret rooms $63-71.

▨ **The Red Victorian Bed, Breakfast, and Art,** 1665 Haight St. (☎415-864-1978; www.redvic.com), west of Belvedere St. in the **Upper Haight.** Inspired by the 1967 "Summer of Love," proprietress Sami Sunchild nurtures guests. Reception 8am-9pm. Check-in 2-5pm or by appointment. Check-out

11am. Reservations strongly recommended, especially if you desire a specific room. Rooms $86-200.

San Francisco Zen Center, 300 Page St. (☎415-863-3136; www.sfzc.org), near Laguna St. in the **Lower Haight.** Even if rigorous soul-searching is not for you, the Zen Center offers breezy, unadorned rooms whose courtyard views instill a meditative peace of mind. All meals included in the discounted weekly (10% off) or monthly (25% off) rates. Rooms $66-120.

Golden Gate Hotel, 775 Bush St. (☎415-392-3702 or 800-835-1118; www.goldengatehotel.com), between Mason and Powell St. in **Union Square.** A positively charming B&B, with a staff as kind and solicitous as the rooms are plush and inviting. Continental breakfast and afternoon tea (4-7pm) included. Reservations recommended. Doubles $85, with bath $115.

◧ NIGHTLIFE

Nightlife in San Francisco is as varied as the city's personal ads. Everyone from the "shy first-timer" to the "bearded strap daddy" can find places to go on a Saturday (or Tuesday) night. The spots listed below are divided into bars and clubs, but the lines get blurred in SF after dark, and even cafes hop at night. Check out the nightlife listings in the *S.F. Weekly, S.F. Bay Guardian,* and *Metropolitan.* All clubs listed are 21+. San Francisco is not a particularly friendly city to underagers.

Politics aside, nightlife alone is enough to earn San Francisco the title of "gay mecca." Generally, the boys hang in the **Castro** neighborhood, while the girls gravitate to the **Mission** (on and off Valencia St.); all frolic along **Polk St.** (several blocks

THE LOCAL STORY

LSD, FROM THE MAN TO THE PEOPLE

In 1938, Albert Hoffman synthesized a compound called d-Lysergic Acid Diethylamide (LSD). The new drug was said to cure psychosis. In the early 50s, the CIA adopted LSD for Operation MK-ULTRA, a series of mind-control experiments. Writers Ken Kesey, Allen Ginsberg, and the Grateful Dead's Robert Hunter were first exposed to acid as subjects in government experiments. The CIA soon abandoned the unpredictable hallucinogen, but Kesey, a Stanford graduate student, made it his mission to share it with the world. The hippies in the Haight were among LSD's first adherents. Amateur chemists began producing the compound, and intellectuals like Timothy Leary and Aldous Huxley advocated its use as a means of mind expansion. In 1966, the drug was made illegal, and Kesey's Merry Pranksters hosted the first public Acid Test, immortalized in Tom Wolfe's *The Electric Kool-Aid Acid Test.* Acid became part of youth culture, juicing up rallies and love-ins across the country.

north of Geary Blvd.), and in **SoMa**. Polk St. can seem seedy and SoMa barren, so keep a watchful eye. Most clubs and bars below are gay-friendly.

BARS & LOUNGES

Noc Noc, 5574 Haight St. (☎415-861-5811), near Fillmore St. in the **Lower Haight.** This lounge, creatively outfitted as a modern cavern, seems like the only happening place before 10pm—neo-hippies mingle at high-backed bar stools, or relax on the padded floor cushions. Open daily 5pm-2am.

111 Minna St. (☎415-974-1719), at 2nd St. in **SoMa.** A funky gallery by day, hipster groove-spot by night. The bar turns club W 5-10pm for a crowded night of progressive house music. Cover $5-15. Gallery open M-F noon-5pm. Bar open Tu 5-9pm, W 5-11pm, Th-F 5pm-2am, Sa 10pm-2am.

Lush Lounge, 1092 Post St. (☎415-771-2022; www.thelushlounge.com), at Polk St. in **Nob Hill.** Oh-so-lush, with ample vegetation and sassy classic Hollywood throwback decor. Kick back as the best in 80s nostalgia, from ABBA to Madonna, streams through the speakers. Open daily 4pm-2am; in summer M-Tu from 5pm. No credit cards.

Swig, 561 Geary St. (☎415-931-7292; www.swig-bar.com), between Taylor and Jones St., in **Union Square.** With an artful, intimate back room and an upstairs smoking lounge this recently opened bar has already entertained Eminem, D12, and the Wallflowers. Open daily 5pm-2am.

CLUBS

El Rio, 3158 Mission St. (☎415-282-3325), between César Chavez and Valencia St. in the **Mission.** Each area in this sprawling club has its own bar, but the patio is center stage for the young urbanites who play cards and smoke cigars. Diverse queer and straight crowd. W and Sa live Bay area bands. Th "Arabian Nights," F world music. Su live salsa (mainly GLBT) 3-8pm; salsa lessons 3-4pm. Cover M $2, Th after 10pm $5, Su $7. Open M 5pm-1am, Tu-Sa 5pm-2am, Su 3pm-midnight. No credit cards.

Pink, 2925 16th St. (☎415-431-8889), at S. Van Ness Ave. in the **Mission.** With new French owners, this venue plays it chic. Pink satin and gossamer draperies lend a lounge feel weekdays but expect clubbers F-Sa. DJs spin a mix of world music, soulful house, Cuban jazz, and Afro beats. Cover $5, F-Sa $10. Open Su and Tu-Th 9:30pm-2am, F-Sa 9:30pm-3am.

GLBT NIGHTLIFE

Divas, 1081 Post St. (☎415-928-6006; www.divassf.com), at Polk St. in the **Tenderloin.** With a starlet at the door and a savvy pin-striped madam working the bar, this transgender nightclub is simply fabulous. Tu Talent night. F-Sa drag show. Cover $7-10. Open daily 6am-2am. No credit cards.

The Bar on Castro, 456 Castro St. (☎415-626-7220), between Market and 18th St. An urbane **Castro** staple with padded walls and dark plush couches perfect for eyeing the stylish young crowd, or scoping the techno-raging dance floor. Open M-F 4pm-2am, Sa-Su noon-2am. No credit cards.

SF Badlands, 4121 18th St. (☎415-626-0138), near Castro St. in the **Castro.** Strutting past the sea of boys at the bar, cruise a circular dance floor where the latest Top 40 divas shake their thangs. Cover F-Sa $2. Open daily 2pm-2am. No credit cards.

Wild Side West, 424 Cortland Ave. (☎415-647-3099), at Wool St., in **Bernal Heights.** The oldest lesbian bar in SF is a favorite for women and men. The backyard jungle has benches, fountains, and statues by patrons. Open daily 1pm-2am. No credit cards.

ROUTE 66

Route 66 is *the* roadtrip. Born of America's love affair with the automobile, 66 is the final resting place of classic car culture. From its lakeside beginnings in **Chicago, IL** (p. 450), it's about 2400 mi. of flashy signs and lonely two-lane road to the glistening Pacific waters and bustling boardwalks of **Santa Monica, CA** (p. 537).

Route 66 is one of the most famous American roads. Known variously as the **"Main Street of America,"** the **"Mother Road,"** and the **"Will Rogers Highway,"** Route 66 appeared in Steinbeck's *The Grapes of Wrath* (the term "Mother Road" comes from here), has been memorialized in song by Bobby Troup, and—most importantly—has been driven by millions. Continuously paved by 1938, over the subsequent decades the road saw the westward migration of thousands of families heading to California, looking to escape the dust and poverty of the Great Depression. It also

spawned the development of the motel, the drive-through, and, of course, the assortment of mom-and-pop businesses that sprang up along the way.

While Route 66 was eventually eclipsed by the many-laned sterility of the Interstate Highway and officially decommissioned in 1985, the road is experiencing a revival in the form of thousands of modern-day migrants who seek to re-create the classic journey of generations past. Purists fear the influx of tourists may result in higher prices and loss of character route-wide, but the roadtripper needn't worry—whether you're searching for yourself or just good burger and a cheap motel room, Route 66, in all its neon-lit glory, delivers.

From Chicago, which offers world-class **skyscrapers** (not to mention **deep-dish pizza**), our route follows the original as closely as possible, through the rolling countryside of Illinois and Missouri, home to **Henry's Rte. 66 Emporium and Rabbit Ranch**

(p. 469), and one hell of a milkshake at **Ted Drewes Frozen Custard** (p. 475) in **St. Louis.** From here, the next stop is **Meramec Caverns** (p. 478)—if the caverns' reputation as Missouri's biggest tourist attraction doesn't reach you, the sheer number of signs surely will. After passing the oddly Gothic **Jasper County Courthouse** (p. 482), it's on to the lonely, dusty plains of Oklahoma, where traffic is sparse, cows are many, and almost every town has a street (or at least a park) named for **Will Rogers.** Route 66 passes through El Reno, OK, where **Johnnie's Grill** (p. 494) proudly cooks up the **world's largest hamburger** each May, before traversing **Texas** and entering **New Mexico,** where you, too, can stay in **"Tucumcari tonight"** at the **Blue Swallow Motel** (p. 502).

Route 66 then cuts a magnificent swath across **New Mexico** and **Arizona,** through miles and miles of scrubby desert, where skies are blue and sweeping, and colorful little trading posts line the road, peddling Navajo crafts, road snacks, and, of course, Route 66 souvenirs. The road passes through **Santa Fe** (p. 504), where Spanish colonial architecture, Native American influence, and

---

ROUTE STATS

Miles: c. 2400

Route: Chicago, IL to Santa Monica, CA.

States: 8; Illinois, Missouri, Kansas, Oklahoma, Texas, New Mexico, Arizona, and California.

Driving Time: You could spend forever cruisin' the lonely backroads of the Southwest, but allow at least three weeks to savor 66.

When To Go: Summer in the desert is hot. Very, very, very hot. Summertime highs in Needles, CA, can reach 120°F. We leave you with this; go when you wish.

Crossroads: The National Road in St. Louis, MO (p. 346); **The North American** in Kingman, AZ (p. 683); **The Pacific Coast** in Santa Monica, CA (p. 900).

---

green chiles come together in one spicy, delicious mix, and continues on through charming **Albuquerque** (p. 509), the stunning and **scenic pueblo country** of Arizona, and the one and only **Petrified Forest National Park** (p. 518). Take it easy in **Winslow, AZ** (p. 520) before reaching **Flagstaff,** where you can consider taking a brief jaunt off 66 to visit the

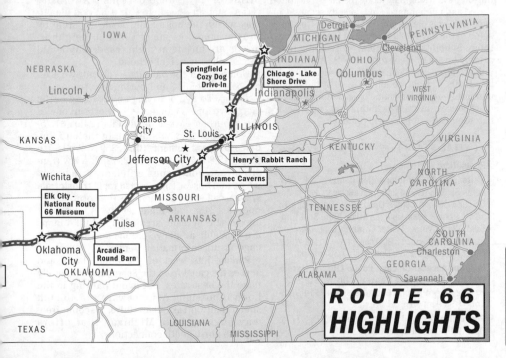

Springfield - Cozy Dog Drive-In

Chicago - Lake Shore Drive

Henry's Rabbit Ranch

Meramec Caverns

Elk City - National Route 66 Museum

Arcadia-Round Barn

ROUTE 66 **HIGHLIGHTS**

ROUTE 66

Grand Canyon (p. 524). Continue across the punishing Mojave Desert toward **Los Angeles** (p. 537), the sprawling city of the stars. Finally, the near-perfect roadtrip reaches its near-perfect end at **Santa Monica** (p. 537); after a day at the on the roller coasters, dip your toes in the ocean, kick back on the pier, and watch the sun set over the Pacific.

Welcome To ILLINOIS

CHICAGO

From its start on Adams St. to where Joliet Rd. escapes the city, Chicago's portion of Rte. 66 takes drivers through the city's latest and greatest, as well as its tried and true. From the renowned museums and shopping along the lakefront to the varied and vibrant music and comedy scenes, Chicago's charms please almost any visitor. Retaining some of the flavor of its industrial legacy, Chicago today is both a contemporary city and a place acutely aware of its historical roots. A symbol of industrialized city life in middle America since the late 1800s, Chicago continues to wear the mantle admirably—travelers can expect to find a city of many voices, diverse neighborhoods, and spectacular food and entertainment options.

VITAL STATS

Population: 2.9 million

Visitor Info: Visitor Information Center, 77 E. Randolph St. (☎312-744-2400), at Michigan Ave. in the Chicago Cultural Center. Open M-W 10am-7pm, Th 10am-9pm, F 10am-6pm, Sa 10am-5pm, Su 11am-5pm. **Water Works Visitor Center,** 163 E. Pearson St. (☎312-742-8811), at Michigan Ave. in the Water Tower Pumping Station. Open daily 7:30am-7pm.

Internet Access: Chicago Public Library, Harold Washington Library Center, 400 S. State St. (☎312-747-4999), at Congress. Open M-Th 9am-7pm, F-Sa 9am-5pm, Su 1-5pm.

Post Office: 433 W. Harrison St. (☎800-275-8777). Open 24hr. **Postal Code:** 60607.

■ GETTING AROUND

Chicago has overtaken the entire northeastern corner of Illinois, running north-south along 29 mi. of the southwest Lake Michigan shorefront. The city sits at the center of a web of interstates, rail lines, and airplane routes. And of course, depending on how you look at it, Chicago is the origin or terminus of **Old Rte. 66.** The flat, sprawling city's grids usually make sense to drivers. At the city's center is the **Loop,** Chicago's downtown business district and the public transportation hub. The block numbering system starts from the intersection of **State** and **Madison St.,** increasing by about 800 per mile. The Loop is bounded loosely by the **Chicago River** to the north and west, **Wabash Ave.** to the east, and **Congress Pkwy.** to the south. South of the Loop, east-west street numbers increase toward the south. A good map is essential for navigating; pick one up free at the tourist office or any Chicago Transit Authority (CTA) station—see below. It is a good idea to stay within the boundaries made apparent by tourist maps, as many Chicago neighborhoods are unsafe at night; especially avoid the South Side neighborhood.

Competition for parking in downtown Chicago is ferocious, and parking lot prices are extreme. To avoid driving and parking in the city, daytrippers can leave their cars in one of the suburban park-and-ride lots (24hr. $1.75-10.75, depending on station). In the city, the **Chicago Transit Authority (CTA),** 350 N. Wells, 7th fl. (☎312-836-7000 or 888-968-7282; www.transitchicago.com), runs efficient trains, subways, and buses. The **elevated rapid transit train system,** called the **El,** encircles the Loop. The El operates 24hr. Late-night service is infrequent and unsafe in many areas. Helpful CTA maps are available at many stations and at the Chicago Visitor Information Center.

Parking lots west of the South Loop and across the canal from the **Sears Tower** generally have the best rates, but avoid parking in the Loop if possible. Also, beware the 45 mph speed limit on **Lake Shore Drive,** a scenic freeway hugging Lake Michigan that offers express north-south connections.

Chicago Overview

Lake Michigan

Mount Prospect

Rand Rd.

Northwest Hwy.

W Golf Rd.

W Golf Rd.

Evanston

Northwestern University

Dempster St.

Skokie

Milwaukee Ave.

N. Caldwell Ave.

W Peterson Ave.

Kennedy Expwy.

Rosemont

Chicago O'Hare International Airport

Tri-State Tollway

Mannheim Rd.

Norridge

Irving Park Rd.

Pulaski Rd.

Milwaukee Ave.

Chicago R. North Branch

Ashland Ave.

Lincoln Ave.

Lake Shore Dr.

Lincoln Park

SEE DOWNTOWN CHICAGO MAP

Schiller Park

Franklin Park

Elmhurst

W Lake St.

S 1st Ave.

Harlem Ave.

Oak Park

Hillside

Eisenhower Expwy.

CHICAGO

W North Ave.

Cicero Ave.

Western Ave.

CHICAGO

Grant Park

Indiana Ave.

Cicero

W Ogden Ave.

Cermak Rd.

Burnham Park

W 22nd St.

Tri-State Tollway

Archer Ave.

W 47th St.

W Garfield Blvd.

Dan Ryan Expwy. E

Dr. M.L. King Jr. Dr.

Michigan Ave.

University of Chicago

Stevenson Expwy. N

Ronald J. Bredasal Memorial Blvd.

Chicago Midway Airport

Marquette Park

W 55th St.

Ashland Ave.

Halsted St.

Jackson Park

Rainbow Park

Bedford Park

Bridge-view

Burbank

W 79th St.

Western Ave.

Pulaski Rd.

W 79th St.

Chicago Skyway (toll road)

S Lake Shore Dr.

79th St.

Sanitary Drainage and Ship Canal

87th St.

Calumet Park

Kingery Hwy.

Archer Ave.

Crooked Ck. Woods

Calumet Sag Channel

W 95th St.

Oak Lawn

W 95th St.

E 95th St.

Torrence Ave.

Archer Ave.

S LaGrange Hwy.

Southwest Hwy.

Alsip

Calumet Park

Wolf Lake

Lake George Cline

Indianapolis Blvd.

Calumet River

Orland Park

Tri-State Tollway

Cicero Ave.

Dixie Hwy.

Calumet City

Hammond

W 159th St.

E 159th St.

W 162nd St.

Governors Hwy.

Crawford Ave.

Western Ave.

Halsted St.

Southwest Hwy.

ILLINOIS | INDIANA

0 — 4 miles

0 — 4 kilometers

👁 SIGHTS

Only a fraction of Chicago's eclectic attractions are revealed by tourist brochures, bus tours, and strolls through the downtown area. Chicago's sights range from well-publicized museums to undiscovered back streets, from beaches and parks to towering skyscrapers, and to see it all requires some off-the-beaten path exploration. Fortunately, Chicago is one of a growing number of cities worldwide to have a **Greeter** program (☎312-744-8000; www.chicagogreeter.com), where a volunteer staff of knowledgeable Chicagoans will show you around.

THE LOOP

TOURS. Nearly leveled in the Great Fire of 1871, Chicago embraced the skyscraper as it rebuilt. Visitors can view the architecture via **walking tours** organized by the **Chicago Architecture Foundation**. Highlights of the 2hr. tours include Louis Sullivan's arch, classic windows, and Mies van der Rohe's revolutionary skyscrapers. *(224 S. Michigan Ave. ☎312-922-8687; www.architecture.org. Historic skyscraper tours May-Oct. M and Sa-Su 10am and 2:30pm, Tu-F 10am. Modern skyscraper tours May-Oct. M and Sa-Su 11am and 1:30pm, Tu-F 1:30pm. $12 for 1 tour, $18 for both.)*

SEARS TOWER. A few blocks west on Jackson, the **Sears Tower** is undoubtedly Chicago's most immediately recognizable landmark. The tower is the second-tallest building in the world (first, in the minds of Chicagoans), standing 1454 ft. tall. On a clear day, visitors to the 103rd floor **Skydeck** can see three states. *(233 S. Wacker Dr.; enter on Jackson. ☎312-875-9696; www.sears-tower.com. Open daily May-Sept. 10am-10pm; Oct.-Apr. 10am-8pm. Lines usually at least 1hr. $9.50, seniors $7.75, children $6.75.)*

THE PLAZA. The **Bank One Building and Plaza** is one of the world's largest bank buildings, luring gazes skyward with its diamond-shaped, diagonal slope. Back on the ground, Marc Chagall's vivid mural *The Four Seasons* lines the block and defines a public space used for concerts and lunchtime entertainment. The mosaic is a fabulous sight at night, when it is lit by various colored bulbs. Two blocks north, the Methodist **Chicago Temple,** the world's tallest church, sends its Babel-esque steeples heavenward. *(77 W. Washington St., at the corner of Clark and Washington St. ☎312-236-4548. Tours M-Sa 2pm, Su after mass. Free.)*

STATE STREET. State and Madison St., the most famous intersection of "State Street, that great street," forms the focal point of the Chicago street grid as well as another architectural haven. Louis Sullivan's beloved **Carson Pirie Scott** store is adorned with ironwork and an extra-large Chicago window. Sullivan's other masterpiece, the **Auditorium Building,** sits several blocks south at the corner of Congress St. and Michigan Ave. Once Chicago's tallest building, it typifies Sullivan's obsession with form and function, housing a hotel and an opera house with some of the world's finest acoustics.

MUSEUMS

 For a museum blitz with easy parking, visit the Field Museum, the Shedd Aquarium, and the Adler Planetarium, which all share on-street metered parking and a designated parking lot ($12) near downtown.

🏛 ART INSTITUTE OF CHICAGO. It's easy to feel overwhelmed in this expansive museum, whose collections span four millennia of art from Asia, Africa, Europe, and beyond. Make sure to see Chagall's stunning *America Windows*—the artist's stained glass tribute to the country's bicentennial—as well as Wood's *American Gothic*, Hopper's *Nighthawks*, and Monet's *Haystacks*. *(111 S. Michigan Ave., at Adams St. in Grant Park. ☎312-443-3600. Open M and W-F 10:30am-4:30pm, Tu 10:30am-8pm, Sa-Su 10am-5pm. $10, students and children $6, under 6 free. Tu free.)*

FIELD MUSEUM OF NATURAL HISTORY. Sue, the largest T. Rex skeleton ever unearthed, towers over excellent geology, anthropology, botany, and zoology exhibits. Other highlights include Egyptian mummies, Native American halls, and a dirt exhibit. *(1400 S. Lake Shore Dr., at Roosevelt Rd. in Grant Park. ☎312-922-9410. Open daily 9am-5pm. $8; students, seniors, and ages 3-11 $4; under 3 free.)*

MUSEUM OF SCIENCE AND INDUSTRY. This museum features the Apollo 8 command module, a full-sized replica of a coal mine, and a host of interactive exhibits on topics from DNA to

North Ave.

Second City

TO WRIGLEY
FIELD (3mi)

TO
(1mi)

Chicago
Historical
Society

Burton Pl.

International
Museum of
Surgical Science

TO LINCOLN PARK
(1mi)

W. Schiller St.

La Salle St.

Goethe St.

Division St.

Elm St.

Cedar St.

Bellevue Pl.

Oak St.
Beach

Oak St.

Locust St.

Rush St.

Walton St.

Delaware Pl.

E. Chestnut

Chicago Water
Tower

Wells St.

Franklin St.

Hudson Ave.

Sedgwick St.

Orleans St.

Larabee St.

Huron St.

La Salle St.

Clark St.

Dearborn St.

State St.

Wabash Ave.

Michigan Ave.

John Hancock
Bldg. and
Observatory

Water Tower Place

Pearson St.

Chicago Ave.

Superior St.

Museum of
Contemporary Art

Terra
Museum

Erie St.

Ontario St.

Ohio St.

Grand Ave.

Illinois St.

W. Hubbard St.

Merchandise
Mart

Kinzie St.

Wrigley
Building

Tribune
Tower

E. North Water St.

St. Clair St.

Fairbanks Ct.

Olive
Park

Ohio St.

Navy Pier

Outer
Harbor

Downtown Chicago

⌂ ACCOMMODATIONS

Arlington House, **1**
Cass Hotel, **5**
Hostelling International
  Chicago (HY-AYH), **10**
Hotel Wacker, **3**
House of Blues Hotel, **8**
International House, **11**

🍎 FOOD

Ed Debevic's, **4**
Giordano's, **2**
Lou Malnati's, **7**
Lou Mitchell's, **9**
Pizzeria Uno, **6**

N. Lake Shore Dr.

N. Kingsbury St.

Chicago River

Wacker Dr.

S. Water St.

E. Lake St.

Field Bd.

Chicago River

Lake St.

Franklin St.

Canal St.

Clinton St.

Wacker Dr.

State of
Illinois Building

Randolph St.

City Hall

Daley
Plaza

Goodman
Theatre

Chicago
Cultural
Center

E. Randolph Dr.

Lake
Michigan

Washington St.

Northwestern
Station

Monroe St.

Union
Station

Civic Opera House
(Lyric Opera)

Madison St.

Bank One Plaza

THE LOOP

Chicago Temple

Carson Pirie
Scott

E. Monroe Dr.

Shubert
Theater

Symphony
Center

Art Institute
of Chicago

Petrillo
Music Shell

Monroe
Harbor

Grant Park

Sears Tower
and Observ.

Adams St.

Board of
Trade

Jackson Blvd.

Monadnock Building

Chicago
Architecture
Foundation

E. Jackson Dr.

Van Buren St.

Chicago Board
of Options
Exchange

Congress Pkwy.

290

Harrison St.

Harold
Washington
Library

Fine Arts Building

Auditorium Theater

Congress Dr.

Spertus Museum

Columbia
College

Buckingham
Fountain

Chicago
Harbor

W. Polk St.

E. 8th St.

9th St.

E. 11th St.

E. Balbo Dr.

Columbus Dr.

S. Wells St.

Roosevelt Rd.

Chicago River

South Branch

Canal St.

Clinton St.

E. 13th St.

E. 14th St.

Michigan Ave.

Wabash Ave.

Indiana Ave.

State St.

Clark St.

S. Lake Shore Dr.

Field Museum
Of Natural
History

John G. Shedd
Aquarium

Solidarity Dr.

Adler
Planetarium

W. 14th St.

TO
COMISKY PARK,
MUSEUM OF SCIENCE
& INDUSTRY, HYDE PARK,
U. OF CHICAGO

Soldier
Field

Burnham
Park
Harbor

0   300 yards

0   300 meters

the Internet. Stop by the Yesterday's Main Street exhibit for a scoop at the 1920s-style ice-cream parlor. (*5700 S. Lake Shore Dr., at 57th St. in Hyde Park. Direct access to indoor parking garage on Cornell Dr., just before 57th St. $8 per day. ☎ 773-684-1414. Open daily June-Aug. 9:30am-5:30pm; Sept.-May 9:30am-4:30pm. $9, seniors $7.50, under 11 free; with Omnimax $15/$12.50/$10.*)

MUSEUM OF CONTEMPORARY ART
(MCA). The beautiful view of Lake Michigan is the only unchanging feature in the MCA's ultra-modern exhibition space. Pieces from the outstanding permanent collection rotate periodically. Call to see what is on display—their collection includes works by Calder, Warhol, Javer, and Nauman. (*220 E. Chicago Ave., 1 block east of Michigan Ave. ☎ 312-280-2660. Open Su and W-Sa 10am-5pm, Tu 10am-8pm. $8, students and seniors $6, under 12 free. Tu free.*)

TERRA MUSEUM OF AMERICAN ART.
Wedged between the posh shops on N. Michigan Ave., this is one of few galleries to showcase exclusively American art from colonial times to the present. Exhibits include works from Hopper, Inness, and the celebrated Hudson River School. (*664 N. Michigan Ave. Between Huron and Erie St. ☎ 312-664-3939. Open Su noon-5pm, Tu 10am-8pm, W-Sa 10am-6pm. Tours Su and Sa noon and 2pm, Tu-F noon and 6pm. Free.*)

MUSEUM OF HOLOGRAPHY. This unconventional museum explores the wild world of holograms, including fantastic hologram pictures of famous

people. (*1134 W. Washington Blvd., just west of the Loop. ☎ 312-226-1007. Open Su and W-Sa 12:30-4:30pm. $5, under 12 $3.*)

INTERNATIONAL MUSEUM OF SURGICAL SCIENCE. A sculpture of a surgeon holding his wounded patient marks the entrance to this unique museum, a harrowing journey through the history of surgery. Highlights, if they can be so called, include a fascinating collection of gallstones and bladderstones. (*1524 N. Lake Shore Dr., at North Ave. ☎ 312-642-6502. Open Su and Tu-Sa 10am-4pm. $6, students and seniors $3. Tu free.*)

OAK PARK
Gunning for the title of the most fantastic suburb in the US, Oak Park is the Chicago sight for any architecture aficionado or Wright buff, or just anyone looking for a quiet detour among some of America's most drool-worthy homes. Easily accessible from Rte. 66, Oak Park offers a leisurely walking or driving excursion at the **Oak Park Visitors Center,** 158 N. Forest Ave., which offers both metered parking and garage parking for $0.20 per hr. (10 mi. west of downtown. Take I-290 West to Harlem St. ☎ 708-848-1500 or 888-625-7275; www.visitoakpark.com. Open daily summer 10am-5pm; winter 10am-4pm.)

UNITY TEMPLE. When Frank Lloyd Wright designed this cubical church, he declared it the beginning of modern architecture. Striking in both its aesthetic and its utility, the building features an interior that employs receding planes and builds in wood trim to guide the eye. (*875 Lake St., 1 mi. north on Harlem Ave. From I-290, turn east on Lake*

THE LOCAL STORY

A STICKY SITUATION

With the laying of Rte. 66 and the increase in traffic, the land south of St. Louis became prime real estate. On the eve of Rte. 66, the *St. Louis Times* bought up a parcel of land along the Meramac River, and sold off chunks of in the new Times Beach community. Rte. 66 was the sole access road to the community, as well as the only paved road around. To combat the summer dust raised, the town's board contracted Russell Bliss, a waste oil hauler who offered to spray their streets with the oil he was transporting. The oil kept the dust down, Bliss kept down transport costs, and kids loved to play in the stuff. Not until 1982 did the EPA reveal—and residents learn—that Bliss's oil in fact came from a chemical company unbeknownst to Bliss and contained Dioxin, a leading ingredient in Agent Orange. Although the federal government ultimately offered to buy out the Times Beach community to dissuade residents from staying, the controversy divided and ultimately destroyed the town.

for ½ mi. to Kenilworth Ave. On-street metered parking. ☎708-383-8873; www.unitytemple-utrf.org. Open Mar.-Nov. M-F 10:30am-4:30pm, Sa-Su 1-4pm; Dec.-Feb. daily 1-4pm. Tours M-F by appointment, Sa-Su 1, 2, 3pm. $6 seniors and students under 22 with ID $4, under 5 free.)

FRANK LLOYD WRIGHT HOME AND STUDIO.
Frank Lloyd Wright's house showcases the evolution of his creative ideas, from conception to reality. Visitors can see not only the studio where he planned his work, but also his house, which was the constantly evolving subject of his architectural experimentation. (951 Chicago Ave. From Rte. 66, go north to Chicago Ave., and head east for 3 blocks. ☎708-848-1606. Open daily 10am-5pm. 45min. tours M-F 11am, 1, 3pm; Sa-Su every 20min. 11am-3:30pm. $9, seniors and under 18 $7. Combination interior/exterior tour $14/$10.)

ERNEST HEMINGWAY BIRTHPLACE AND MUSEUM.
Throughout the year, fans flock to the Ernest Hemingway Birthplace and Museum to take part in the many events honoring the novelist (including a birthday lecture and champagne/cake reception every July 21st). The museum features photos of Hemingway, his childhood diaries, and other memorabilia. (339 N. Oak Ave. ☎708-848-2222. On-street parking. Open Su and Th-F 1-5pm, Sa 10am-5pm. $7, seniors and students $5.50.)

OTHER SIGHTS

MAGNIFICENT MILE. Chicago's glitzy shops along N. Michigan Ave. between the Chicago River and Oak St. magnificently drain the wallet. Several of these retail stores were designed by the country's foremost architects and merit a look. The plain **Chicago Water Tower** and **Pumping Station** stick out at the corner of Michigan and Pearson Ave. Built in 1867, these were the sole structures in the area to survive the Great Chicago Fire. Across Pearson St., expensive, trendy stores pack **Water Tower Place,** the first urban shopping mall in the US. One block north, the **John Hancock Building** rockets toward the sky in black steel and glass.

NAVY PIER. Big, bright, and always festive, Navy Pier captures the carnival spirit 365 days a year. No small jetty, the 1 mi. long pier has it all: a concert pavilion, dining options, nightspots, sightseeing boats, a spectacular ferris wheel, a crystal garden with palm trees, an Omnimax theater, and a Shakespeare theater. From here, explorers can rent bicycles to navigate the Windy City's streets. Free trolleys run from here to State St.; consider taking advantage of reasonable parking rates here, and ride to get a close-up of downtown. (600 E. Grand Ave. ☎312-595-7437 or 800-595-7437; www.navypier.com. Bike rental open daily June-Sept. 8am-11pm; May 8am-8pm; April and Oct. 10am-7pm. $9 per hr., $36 per day.)

ADLER PLANETARIUM. Aspiring astronauts can discover their weight on Mars, read the news from space, and explore a medieval observatory. (1300 S. Lake Shore Dr., on Museum Campus in Grant Park. ☎312-922-7827. Open daily 9:30am-4:30pm. Sky show daily every hr. Admission and sky show $13, seniors $12, ages 4-17 $11. Special exhibits $5 extra. Sky show $5.)

SHEDD AQUARIUM. The **world's largest indoor aquarium** has over 6600 species of fish in 206 tanks. The Oceanarium features beluga whales, dolphins, seals, and other marine mammals in a giant pool that appears to flow into Lake Michigan. See piranhas and tropical fish of the rainforest in the "Amazon Rising" exhibit or get a rare glimpse of seahorses in the oceanarium exhibit "Seahorse Symphony." Also, check out the sharks at the new "Wild Reef" exhibit. (1200 S. Lake Shore Dr., in Grant Park. ☎312-939-2438. Open June-Aug. Su-W and F-Sa 9am-6pm, Th 9am-10pm; Sept.-May M-F 9am-5pm, Sa-Su 9am-6pm. Feedings M-F 11am, 2, 3pm. Combined admission to Oceanarium and Aquarium $21, seniors and ages 3-11 $15. Oceanarium tour $3.)

THE LAKE. ■Lincoln Park extends across 5 mi. of lakefront on the north side with winding paths, natural groves of trees, and asymmetrical open spaces. The **Lincoln Park Zoo** is usually filled with children fascinated by the zoo's caged gorillas and lions. (☎312-742-2000; www.lpzoo.com. Open daily 10am-5pm; in summer Sa-Su until 7pm. Free.) Next door, the **Lincoln Park Conservatory** is a veritable glass palace of plants from varied ecosystems. (☎312-742-7736. Open daily 9am-5pm. Free.) **Grant Park,** covering 14 lakefront blocks east of Michigan Ave., follows the 19th-century French park style: symmetrical and ordered with corners, a fountain, and wide promenades. The Grant Park Concert Society hosts free summer concerts in the **Petrillo Music Shell.** (520 S. Michigan Ave. ☎312-742-4763.) Colored lights illuminate **Buckingham Fountain** from 9 to 11pm. On the north side,

Lake Michigan lures swimmers and sun-bathers to **Lincoln Park Beach** and **Oak St. Beach.** Beware, though: the rock ledges are restricted areas, and swimming from them is illegal. Although the beaches are patrolled 9am-9:30pm, they can be unsafe after dark. The **Chicago Parks District** has further info. (☎ *312-742-7529.*)

ENTERTAINMENT

The free weeklies *Chicago Reader* and *New City*, available in many bars, record stores, and restaurants, list the latest events. The *Reader* reviews all major shows with times and ticket prices. *Chicago* magazine includes theater reviews alongside exhaustive club, music, dance, and opera listings. *The Chicago Tribune* includes an entertainment section every Friday. *Gay Chicago* provides info on social activities as well as other news for the area's gay community.

THEATER

One of the foremost theater centers of North America, Chicago's more than 150 theaters feature everything from blockbuster musicals to off-color parodies. Downtown, the recently formed **Theater District** centers on State St. and Randolph and includes the larger venues in the city. Smaller theaters are scattered throughout Chicago. Most tickets are expensive. Half-price tickets are sold on the day of performance at **Hot Tix Booths,** 108 N. State St., and on the 6th floor of 700 N. Michigan Ave. Purchases must be made in person. (☎312-977-1755. Open M-F 10am-7pm, Sa 10am-6pm, Su noon-5pm.) **Ticketmaster** (☎312-559-1212) supplies tickets for many theaters; ask about discounts at all Chicago shows. The "Off-Loop" theaters on the North Side put on original productions, with tickets usually under $18. Both Gary Sinise and John Malkovitch got their start at the ▨**Steppenwolf Theater,** 1650 N. Halsted St. (☎312-335-1888; www.steppenwolf.org). The **Goodman Theatre,** 170 N. Dearborn St. (☎312-443-3800; www.goodmantheatre.org), presents consistently solid original works. **Bailiwick Repertory,** 1225 W. Belmont Ave. (☎312-773-327-5252; www.bailiwick.org), is a mainstage and experimental studio space.

COMEDY

Chicago boasts a plethora of comedy clubs. The most famous, ▨**Second City,** 1616 N. Wells St. (☎312-642-8189; www.secondcity.com), at North

Ave., spoofs Chicago life and politics. Alums include Bill Murray, John Candy, and John Belushi. Most nights a free improv session follows the show. Next door at **Second City Etc.,** 1608 N. Wells St., a group of up-and-coming comics offers still more laughs. (☎312-642-6514. Tickets $18. Shows for both M-Th 8:30pm, F-Sa 8 and 11pm, Su 8pm. Box office open daily 10:30am-10pm. Reservations recommended for weekend shows.) Watch improv actors compete to bust your gut at **Comedy Sportz,** 2851 N. Halsted, where two teams of comedians create sketches based on audience suggestions. (☎773-549-8080. Tickets $17. Shows Th 8pm, F-Sa 8 and 10:30pm.)

DANCE, MUSIC, & OPERA

Ballet, comedy, live theater, and musicals are performed at **Auditorium Theatre,** 50 E. Congress Pkwy. (☎312-922-2110; www.auditoriumtheatre.org. Box office open M-F 10am-6pm.) From October through May, the sounds of the **Chicago Symphony Orchestra** resonate throughout **Symphony Center,** 220 S. Michigan Ave. (☎312-294-3000; www.chicagosymphony.org). **Ballet Chicago** pirouettes throughout theaters in Chicago. (☎312-251-8838; www.balletchicago.org. Tickets $12-45.) The acclaimed **Lyric Opera of Chicago** performs from September through March at the **Civic Opera House,** 20 N. Wacker Dr. (☎312-332-2244; www.lyricopera.org). While other places may suck your wallet dry, the **Grant Park Music Festival** affords a taste of the classical for free. From mid-June through late August, the acclaimed **Grant Park Symphony Orchestra** plays a few free evening concerts per week at the Grant Park **Petrillo Music Shell.** (☎312-742-4763; www.grantparkmusicfestival.com. Usually W-Su; schedule varies.)

FESTIVALS

The city celebrates summer on a grand scale. The first week in June, the **Blues Festival** celebrates the city's soulful music. The **Chicago Gospel Festival** hums and hollers in mid-June, and Nashville moves north for the **Country Music Festival** at the end of June. In early July, the **Taste of Chicago** festival cooks for eight days. Seventy restaurants set up booths with endless samples in Grant Park, while crowds chomp to the blast of big-name bands. The Taste's fireworks are the city's biggest. (Food tickets $0.50 each.) The ¡**Viva Chicago!** Latin music festival steams up in late August, while the **Chicago Jazz Festival** scats over Labor Day weekend. All festivals center on the Grant Park Petrillo Music Shell. The Mayor's Office's **Special Events Hotline** (☎312-744-3370; www.ci.chi.il.us/special-events/festivals.htm) has more info.

The regionally famous **Ravinia Festival** (☎312-847-266-5100; www.ravinia.org), in the northern suburb of Highland Park, runs from late June to early September. During the festival's 14-week season, the Chicago Symphony Orchestra, ballet troupes, folk and jazz musicians, and comedians perform. On certain nights, the Orchestra allows free lawn admission with student ID. (Shows 8pm, occasionally 4:30 and 7pm; call ahead. Lawn seats $10-15, others $20-75.)

SPORTS

The National League's **Cubs** step up to bat at **Wrigley Field,** 1060 W. Addison St., at N. Clark St. (☎773-404-2827; www.cubs.com. Tickets $10-22.) The **White Sox,** Chicago's American League team, swing on the South Side at **Comiskey Park,** 333 W. 35th St. (☎312-674-1000. Tickets $12-24.) The **Bears** of the NFL play at the renovated **Soldier Field,** 425 E. McFetridge Dr. (☎888-792-3277. Tickets $45-65.) The **Bulls** have won three NBA championships at the **United Center,** 1901 W. Madison, just west of the Loop. (☎312-943-5800. Tickets $30-450.) Hockey's **Blackhawks** skate onto United Center ice when the Bulls aren't hooping it up. (☎312-455-4500. Tickets $25-100.) **Sports Information** (☎312-976-4242) has info on sporting events.

FOOD

Chicago's many culinary delights, from pizza to po' boy sandwiches, are among its main attractions. One of the best guides to city dining is the monthly *Chicago* magazine, which includes an extensive restaurant section, indexed by price, cuisine, and quality. It can be found at tourist offices and newsstands throughout the city.

PIZZA

Lou Malnati's, 439 N. Wells St. (☎800-568-8646; www.loumalnatis.com), between Illinois and Hubbard downtown. A Chicago mainstay for 30 years. Lou used to be in business with the founders of Pizzeria Uno's, but in the mid-70s, irreconcilably divided over recipes, the two went their separate ways. Today rivalry remains fierce over whose pies are Chicago's finest. Lou's is a local sports memorabilia-themed chain with bubbling deep-dish masterpieces. There are over 20 other

ROUTE 66 MAP #1

ROUTE 66

branches throughout the city and suburbs. Pizzas $4.50-20. Open M-Th 11am-11pm, F-Sa 11am-midnight, Su noon-10pm.

▨ **Giordano's,** 730 N. Rush St. (☎312-951-0747), 1 block west of Michigan and 1 block south of Chicago St. The home of the famous stuffed crust. A stuffed pizza, with heaps of cheese and other toppings sizzling inside it, is $11-22 and takes 30min. to prepare. For the less adventurous, the "not less famous" thin crust pie ($7-21) is another satisfying option. Lines can be long, but customers can pre-order while they wait. Call for other locations throughout the city and surrounding suburbs. Open M-Th 11am-midnight, F-Sa 11am-1am, Su noon-midnight.

Pizzeria Uno's, 29 E. Ohio St. (☎312-321-1000), at the corner of Wabash and Ohio St. It may look like any other Uno's, but this is where the legacy of deep-dish began in 1943. Pizza (large $20) takes 45min. to prepare, but the world-famous pies have a made-from-scratch taste worth the wait. Individual-sized pies ($5) only take 25min. If lines are too long, head up the street to **Pizzeria Due,** 619 N. Wabash Ave. (☎312-943-2400)—just the same, minus the mozzarella sticks and plus a terrace. Uno open M-F 11:30am-1am, Sa 11:30am-2am, Su 11:30am-11:30pm. Due open Su-Th 11am-1:30am, F-Sa 11am-2:30am.

Gino's East of Chicago, 633 N. Wells (☎312-988-4200), at Ontario, 7 blocks west of Michigan Ave. Valet parking ($7), or on-street metered parking available. The writing on the wall proclaims this the best pizza around. Make your own mark on the customer-decorated walls under the faux starry sky while you munch appetizers ($5-8), deep dish or thin crust pie ($10-20), pasta ($9), or cookies ($1). Open M-Th 11am-9pm, F-Sa 11am-11pm, Su noon-9pm.

THE LOOP

▨ **Lou Mitchell's,** W. Jackson St. (☎312-939-3111), at the corner of Jefferson St., ½ mi. west of the start start of Rte. 66. Recently inducted into the restaurant hall of fame, this retro diner has been stuffing faithful customers for over 75 years. Start the day with "the world's finest cup of coffee" ($1.50) or end with a piece of homemade pie. Lines are long but move fast. Female customers—and persistent men—get free Milk Duds and excellent doughnut holes while they wait. Cash only. Open M-Sa 5:30am-3pm, Su 7am-3pm.

RIVER NORTH

▨ **Ed Debevic's,** 640 N. Wells St. (☎312-664-4993), at Ontario, across from Gino's East Pizza.

Valet parking ($7) or on-street metered parking. With a dedicated Rte. 66 room, poodle-skirted waitresses who dance on the counter-tops, and an embankment of gumball machines, this 50s-60s diner is worth the slight trip off the highway. Appetizers from $3. Burgers $7. Shakes $4. Open Su-Th 11am-9pm, F-Sa 11am-11pm.

SOUTH SIDE

Dixie Kitchen and Bait Shop, 5225 S. Harper St. (☎773-363-4943), in Hyde Park. Metered lot across the street. Tucked in a parking lot on 52nd St., Dixie's looks like a garage sale exploded. This place is as tasty for the eye as the gullet—coffee cans, bottles, signs, and even a gas pump decorate the walls. Free plastic alligators come with the kids meal. Fried green tomatoes ($5) and oyster po' boy sandwiches ($8) are among Dixie's southern highlights. Fried catfish $10, blackened voodoo beer $2. Open Su-Th 11am-10pm, F-Sa 11am-11pm.

Manny's Coffee Shop & Deli, 1141 S. Jefferson St. (☎312-939-2855; www.mannysdeli.com), 1 block east of Rte. 90, off the Madison St. exit. Free parking out back. In business since 1942, this enormous and locally worshipped kosher coffee shop serves up huge and affordably priced servings of everything from Salisbury steak ($7.25) to chop suey ($7.25) to veggie burgers ($4.50). Open M-Sa 5am-4pm.

GREEKTOWN

The Parthenon, 314 S. Halsted St. (☎312-726-2407), on the west side of the street between Jackson and Van Buren. Free valet parking. Look in the window around dinner time to see meat slowly roasting on a spit. The staff converses in Greek, murals transport you to the Mediterranean, and the food wins awards. The Greek Feast family-style dinner ($17 per person) has everything from saganaki (flaming goat cheese) to baklava. Open Su-F 11am-1am, Sa 11am-2am.

LINCOLN PARK

Cafe Ba-Ba-Reeba!, 2024 N. Halsted St. (☎773-935-5000), just north of Armitage. Valet parking $7, limited on-street parking. Hard to miss with its colorful facade and bustling interior, the sprawling Ba-Ba-Reeba pleases with unbeatable tapas ($4-8) and hearty Spanish paellas ($10-15 per person). Open for lunch Sa-Su noon-5pm; dinner Su-Th 5-10pm, F-Sa 5pm-midnight. Reservations recommended.

BUCKTOWN/WICKER PARK

Kitsch'n on Roscoe, 2005 W. Roscoe (☎773-248-7372), at Damen Ave. in Roscoe Village. On-street parking on side streets. "Where kitsch meets cool in Roscoe Village." Vinyl seats, 50s memorabilia, and a decade-themed menu add vintage spice to this breakfast and lunch hot spot. Enjoy "Jonny's Lunch Box" (soup, sandwich, fruit, and a snack cake served in a lunch box; $6.50) on campy theme tables. Open Su 9am-3pm, Tu-Sa 9am-10pm.

Earwax Cafe, 1564 N. Milwaukee St. (☎773-772-4019), north of the Loop off of I-90, at Damen St. On-street metered parking. The cafe is decorated inside and out in tasteful circus paraphernalia, with giant posters, ornate booths, and a giant dragon head mounted on the wall. Scrumptious and quick veggie options for breakfast (served all day; $3-7), lunch, and dinner menus (appetizers $4-7; entrees $7-9). Open M-Th 8am-noon, F 8am-1pm, Sa-Su 10am-noon.

WRIGLEYVILLE

Mia Francesca, 3311 N. Clark St. (☎773-281-3310), 1 block north of the intersection of Clark and Belmont. Valet parking ($7) or limited on-street parking. An urban trattoria specializing in Northern Italian cuisine. Eat in one of the two busy dining rooms or escape to the courtyard and coachhouse in the back, but don't miss the fried calamari ($5). Entrees $10-20. Call for other locations. Open Su-Th 5pm-10:30pm, F-Sa 5pm-11pm. Reservations recommended.

OAK PARK

Petersen's Emporium, 1100 Chicago Ave. (☎708-386-6131; www.petersenicecream.com), 2 blocks west of Forest St. on Chicago Ave. On-street parking. Historic Petersen's has been dishing up rich homemade ice cream ($4) since 1919. Complete breakfast, lunch, and dinner menu. Sandwiches ($7), burgers ($6) and a pastry case. Open summer Su-Th 7am-10pm, F-Sa 7am-midnight; off-season daily 7am-10pm.

▚ ACCOMMODATIONS

It is easy to find a cheap, convenient place to rest your head at one of Chicago's many hostels. The motels on **Lincoln Ave.** in Lincoln Park are accessible and moderately priced. Motel chains off the interstates, about 1hr. from downtown, are out of the way and more expensive (from $35), but are an option for late-night arrivals. **At Home Inn Chicago** (☎800-375-7084) offers a reservation and referral service for many downtown B&Bs. Most have a two-night minimum stay, and rooms average around $120. Chicago has a **15% tax** on most accommodation rates.

Hostelling International Chicago (HI-AYH), 24 E. Congress Pkwy. (☎312-360-0300; www.hichicago.org), off Wabash St. in the Loop. The location offers easy access to the major museums during the day, but be careful on the deserted streets of the Loop at night. Student center, library, kitchen, and organized activities give the hostel a lively social atmosphere. Laundry and Internet. Reservations recommended. Dorms $29, nonmembers $37.50.

Arlington House, 616 W. Arlington Pl. (☎773-929-5380). A giant renovated nursing home, this 300+ bed hostel is so full in the summer that it's a scramble to get one of their 140+ dorm beds. Private and double rooms are also available, but get pricey fast with extra guests. Kitchen, TV room, laundry ($1.75), and Internet ($1 per 4min.) ensure a comfortable and lively stay. Close proximity to a plethora of bars and clubs. Reservations recommended; international guests have priority for dorm beds. Dorms $24; private rooms with shared bath from $54.

House of Blues Hotel, 330 N. Dearborn St. (☎312-245-0333). An eclectic mix of Gothic, Moroccan, Indian, and American folk art influences make this unique hotel a visual feast. Excellent service and prime location near entertainment and food. Spacious, vibrant rooms come with even bigger bathrooms. TV, VCR, CD player, in-room Internet Access. Free music F-Sa in lobby bar. Gym access $15. Rooms from $129.

International House, 1414 E. 59th St. (☎773-753-2270), in Hyde Park off Lake Shore Dr., at the corner of 59th and Blackstone on the University of Chicago Campus. Student roadtrippers will feel right at home in the tidy if teeny University dorm rooms. Don't wander off campus at night. Students only. Laundry, Internet, coffee shop, tennis courts, game room, and weight room access. Reservations recommended. Single with shared bath $52; doubles $82.

Hotel Wacker, 111 W. Huron St. (☎312-787-1386), at the corner of N. Clark St. On-street metered parking available. A giant green, formerly neon sign on the corner makes this place easy to find. Do not be put off by the slightly institutional look of downstairs; rooms are clean, comfortable, and, considering the downtown location, very reasonable. TV, A/C in summer. Key and linen deposit $5. Reception 24hr. Singles $55; doubles $65. $5 per additional person.

Cass Hotel, 640 N. Wabash Ave. (☎312-787-4030 or 800-227-7850; www.casshotel.com), just north of the Loop. Reasonable rates and a location near the Magnificent Mile make this recently renovated, modest hotel a favorite of the budget-conscious roadie looking to be near the action. The $2 breakfast at the cafe downstairs is a great deal. Parking $26 per day. Reservations recommended. In summer singles $84; doubles $104. In winter singles $64; doubles $79.

🎵 NIGHTLIFE

"Sweet home Chicago" takes pride in the innumerable blues performers who have played here. Jazz, folk, reggae, and punk clubs throb all over the **N. Side.** The **Bucktown/Wicker Park** area stays open late with bars and clubs. Aspiring pickup artists swing over to **Rush St.** and **Division St.** Full of bars, cafes, and bistros, **Lincoln Park** is frequented by singles and young couples, both gay and straight. The vibrant center of gay culture is between 3000 and 4500 **North Halsted St.** For more upscale raving and discoing, there are plenty of clubs near **River North,** in Riverwest, and on Fulton St.

BARS AND BLUES JOINTS

🏅 **The Green Mill,** 4802 N. Broadway Ave. (☎773-878-5552). Founded as a Prohibition-era speakeasy, Mafiosi-to-be can park themselves in Al Capone's old seat. This authentic jazz club draws late-night crowds after other clubs shut down. The cover-free jam sessions on weekends after main acts finish are reason enough to chill until the wee hours. Cover $5-15. Open M-Sa noon-5am, Su noon-4am.

Kingston Mines, 2548 N. Halsted St. (☎773-477-4647). One of the oldest clubs in town, this is the place to see big names. Mick Jagger and Bob Dylan have been known to frequent this raucous blues joint. Live blues on 2 stages daily from 9:30pm. Cover $8-15. Open Su-F 8pm-4am, Sa 8pm-5am.

The Hideout, 1354 W. Wabansia Ave. (☎773-227-4433). Nestled in a municipal truck parking lot, this is the insider's rock club. Some weekends, the lot fills with "kid's shows" for families still able to rock. Arrangements with a record company have established the club as one of the best places to catch rising alt-country acts. Cover Tu-F $5-10. Open M 8pm-2am, Tu-F 4pm-2am, Sa 7pm-3am.

B.L.U.E.S., 2519 N. Halsted St. (☎773-528-1012). Crowded and intimate. Albert King, Bo Diddley,

Wolfman Washington, and Dr. John have played here. Live music every night 9:30pm-2am. 21+. Cover M-Th $6-8, F-Sa $8-10. Open Su-F 8pm-2am, Sa 8pm-3am.

DANCE CLUBS

Berlin, 954 W. Belmont Ave. (☎773-348-4975). Anything goes at Berlin, a gay-friendly mainstay of Chicago's nightlife. Crowds pulsate to house/dance music amid drag contests and disco nights. W ladies night. 21+. Cover F-Sa $5 after midnight. Open M-F 4pm-4am, Sa 2pm-5am, Su 4pm-2am.

Funky Buddha Lounge, 728 W. Grand Ave. (☎312-666-1695). Trendy, eclectic dance club where hip-hop and funk blend with leopard and velvet decor. W soul and r&b night. Cover $10 for women, $20 for men. Free before 10pm. Open M-W 10pm-2am, Th-F 9pm-2am, Sa 9pm-3am, Su 6pm-2am.

The Apartment, 2251 N. Lincoln Ave. (☎773-348-5100). Sit on sofas in front of the fireplace and play Playstation 2, lounge in the master bedroom, or chat in the faux kitchen. A bathtub of beer keeps the good times rolling. No cover. Open W-Th 9pm-2am, F-Sa 9pm-3am.

🚗 LEAVING CHICAGO

Just west of the Art Institute of Chicago on Adams St., an unimposing road sign marks the beginning of "The Mother Road," **Rte. 66.** To begin at the very beginning, follow Lake Shore Dr. to Jackson St., head south on Jackson St., and begin facing west on Adams St. Follow **Adams St.** west until you hit **Ogden St.,** then angle left on **Ogden St.,** and continue 10 mi. to **Harlem Ave.** Turn left on **Harlem Ave.** and drive ½ mi., then turn right onto **Joliet Rd.** Rte. 66 is well marked through these parts—look for the brown-and-white signs by the roadside leading you down "Historic Route 66." To follow the original Rte. 66 alignment, follow **Joliet Rd.** for 7 mi. until it merges with **I-55** where Rte. 66 has been paved over.

🍴 RIVERSIDE FAMILY RESTAURANT

3422 S. Harlem Ave. *At Lawton St. in Riverside. From Rte. 66, head right at S. Harlem Ave. when you turn off Ogden St.*

Run by the Stanga family for over 20 years, this family-style diner serves giant portions of Czech food for cheap, cheap, cheap. Enormous plates of wienerschnitzel, duck, or pork come with a side of dumplings, mashed or boiled potatoes, and your choice of sauerkraut, apple sauce, cabbage, or beets, plus dessert and a bottomless cup of coffee—all for an astounding $6-8. (☎ 708-442-0434. Open Su 11am-7pm, Tu-Sa 11am-8pm.   Cash   only.)

👁 THE SPINDLE AND OTHER SCULPTURES
In Berwyn. From the intersection of Harlem Ave. and Ogden St., continue north 17 mi. on Harlem Ave. Chicago is a rough place to have a car. Just check out the 50 ft. tower of eight impaled cars in the middle of the Cermak Plaza parking lot. Don't miss the flattened VW on the wall as you enter from Harlem Ave., or the various glass-encased sculptures around the parking lot's edge.

🚩 APPROACHING LEMONT
Continue on **I-55 South/Rte. 66.** Exit I-55 on **S. Lemont St.** at Exit 271A and drive south on Lemont St. for 3 mi. Head west after crossing the bridge, and follow the road around to **Main St.**

LEMONT
This town, 6 mi. south of where Joliet Rd. joins I-55, offers a surprisingly interesting historic district. Almost out of place in its grandeur atop the hill overlooking Lemont, the lavishly carved **Hindu Temple of Greater Chicago,** 10915 Lemont Rd., is a fully functioning religious and community center for the Hindus of Chicago. (1¼ mi. north of downtown Lemont. ☎ 630-972-0300. Open daily 9am-9pm; in winter open until 8pm.) Thousands of cookie jars of all shapes and sizes are on display in the **Cookie Jar Museum,** 111 Stephen St. (☎ 630-257-5012). Tragically, none of them contain cookies. Call Lucille, founder and proprietor, in the early evening for appointments to visit the museum.

At the same location for 75 years, in the various guises of pharmacy and convenience store, **Budnik's,** 400 Main St. (☎ 630-257-6224), sells everything from golf balls to lotto tickets, and all with that old-time general store feeling. **Lemont Lanes Bowling Alley,** 1015 State St., may look like your typical ball-hurling venue, but locals flock here for a hearty, dirt-cheap breakfast of champions. (☎ 630-257-1994. Omelettes $5. 4 pancakes $3.50. Open Tu-Sa 7am-9pm. Cash only.) **Nick's Tavern,** 221 Main St., is the home of the Nickburger ($5), and features colored hanging lights, holographic wallpaper behind the bar, and figurines from JFK to giant hamburgers. (☎ 630-257-6564. Open M-Sa 10am-midnight. Grill open until 10:30pm.)

🚩 LEAVING LEMONT
Leave Lemont the only way you can: south on **I-55.** To continue following Rte. 66, exit I-55 8 mi. south of Lemont, at Exit 269. Head south on **Joliet Rd.,** following the Historic Rte. 66 markers.

THE ROAD TO JOLIET. If you're running low on gas or peanuts, 4 mi. down the road is strip mall heaven, but continue toward Joliet for anything more than necessities. Joliet Rd. is marked as Rte. 53, but every mile or so, you should see the easily distinguishable Historic Rte. 66 markers. Call it pre-emptive, but 9 mi. south from picking up Joliet Rd. you'll find the **Illinois State Police.** Hit the gas too hard here, and you might find yourself a quarter-mile down the road quicker than you expected, at one of Joliet's most well-known landmarks, the **Department of Corrections.**

JOLIET
Entering Joliet from the north, Rte. 7/53 brings you through a quaint, historic neighborhood before shuttling you out through more developed areas. For lunch or a tour of the Rte. 66 welcome center, stick to the north side of Joliet, though supermarkets, gas stations, and banks abound farther south. Folks at the **Joliet Historical Museum and Welcome Center,** 214 N. Ottawa St., are only too happy to share the stories of the blue Cadillacs in the lobby. The Rte. 66 memorabilia collection is showcased as part of the official **Joliet Route 66 Welcome Center.** Entrance to the welcome center (and Rte. 66 gift shop) is free (☎ 815-722-7225. Open Su noon-5pm, Tu-Sa 10am-5pm. Tours Tu-Sa 11am and 3pm. Joliet Historical museum $5, seniors and students with ID $4, children $3.) A restored vaudeville theater guarded by massive second-story columns, the **Rialto Square Theatre,** 102 N. Chicago St., was designed to resemble the Hall of Mirrors at Versailles. (☎ 815-726-6600. Box office open M-F 9am-5pm, Sa 9am-noon.)

Follow the lunch crowd to the **Sandwich Shoppe,** 79 N. Chicago St., for subs ($4) or salads ($4). (☎ 815-723-8071. Open M-F 11am-2pm.) If **Home Cut Donuts,** 815 Jefferson St., has got the fullest parking lot in town at any hour of the day, it's because their donuts are cheap and delicious. (☎ 815-727-3511. Donuts $0.50, 12 for $5.50. 50 donut holes $6. Open 24hr.) For something besides milkshakes and burgers, indulge in the elegant ambience of red velvet curtains, high ceilings, and tiled floors at **Barolo,** 158 N.

Chicago St. This reasonably priced option serves a seasonal vegetable and spinach salad ($8), ciabatta panini ($8), and veal ($10) in an upscale setting. (☎815-722-1744. Open M-Th 11:30am-2pm and 5-9pm, F 11:30am-2pm and 5-10pm, Sa 5-10pm.) Low-cost lunches, prepared by culinary arts students at Joliet Junior College, are available across the lobby from the Historical Society at the **Renaissance Room,** 214 N. Ottawa St. Wednesday and Friday feature an all-you-can-eat lunch buffet for $7. (☎815-280-1561 or 815-280-1443. Su champagne brunch buffet $9. Open M-F 11am-1:30pm, Sa by reservation only, Su 10am-2pm.)

LEAVING JOLIET
Take **Ottowa St.** left, following signs for **Rte. 6 West, Rte. 53 South,** and **Rte. 66.**

CHICAGOLAND SPEEDWAY AND ROUTE 66 RACEWAY
1 mi. east off Rte. 66 at Laraway Rd., 3½ mi. south of Joliet.

Racecar enthusiasts can watch the pros get their kicks at the Chicagoland Speedway, which sits on 930 acres and seats over 75,000. Rte. 66 Raceway, Chicagoland's sister track, is nearby. If you want to see a race, reserve well in advance. (☎815-727-7223; www.chicagolandspeedway.com.)

MIDEWIN NATIONAL TALLGRASS PRAIRIE
30071 S. Rte. 53
In Wilmington, 13 mi. south of Joliet, 3¾ mi. south of the VA cemetery.

The forest service is attempting to transform these former army TNT testing grounds back into 19,000 acres of prairie featuring non-motorized recreational and interpretation areas. The process is still ongoing; progress and current trail availability are posted on the website. (☎815-423-6370; www. fs.fed.us/mntp.)

WILMINGTON. Nothing says Rte. 66 like a giant green man holding a rocketship—the Gemini Giant—watching over your car while you eat. At the **Launching Pad Drive-In,** at the corner of Daniels St. and Rte. 66, Rte. 66 wallpaper and map-covered tabletops let you trace your path while enjoying tasty eats. Launching Pad was inducted into the Route 66 Hall of Fame June 10, 2000. (☎815-476-6535; www.launchingpadrt66.com. Hamburgers $1. "Route 66

Burger" $3. Open daily 9am-10pm. Cash only.) In summer, Mr. Van Duyne of the **Van Duyne Motel,** 107 Bridge St., offers canoe trips ($30) up the river and opens his Rte. 66 memorabilia-lined balcony for cookouts and socializing. Clean rooms in the motel each come with mini-fridge, microwave, cable TV, and a private bathroom. (1 mi. south of central Wilmington. ☎815-476-2801. Singles $40.)

BRAIDWOOD. Rte. 66 continues south through Braidwood, 4 mi. south of Wilmington. Elvis, Marilyn, James Dean, and Betty Boop welcome you to the parking lot of the **Polka Dot Drive-In,** 222 N. Front St., and walls full of smiling celebrity faces rain kitschy benevolence onto this chrome and checkered 50s diner, which was originally located in a white bus decorated with rainbow polka dots. Stop by the first Saturday in August for the annual Rte. 66 roadster cruise. (☎815-458-3377. Outdoor seating available. Burgers $1.45. Chicken $7.20. Open daily summer 11am-9pm; off-season 11am-8pm.) Right across the tracks is the clean and comfortable **Braidwood Motel,** 120 N. Washington St. Rooms have refrigerators and cable TV. (☎815-458-2321 Singles $30; doubles $36.)

RIVIERA RESTAURANT
5650 Rte. 53
1 mi. north of Gardner.

"Al Capone passed gas here in 1932" proclaims the sign above the lofty men's toilet, and Gene Kelly danced through the parking lot on his way to Hollywood, declaring he would be famous one day. Step into the underground grotto of stalactites and tiki-lights and enjoy frog legs (market price) the way Mama used to make them. (☎815-237-2344. Open Su 4-9pm, Tu-Th 5-9pm, F-Sa 5-10pm.)

CURLEY'S
114 Depot St.
In Gardner, 29 mi. south of Joliet.

If you felt stifled as a child, start your defiant wall-scribbling pilgrimage at **Gino's** in Chicago (see p. 458) and find your next haven at **Curley's,** 114 Depot St. In this ancient beer-meets-arts and crafts establishment, you can write on the walls. (☎815-237-8060. Beer $2. Mixed drinks $2.50. Daily drink specials. Open M 3pm-1:30am, Su and Tu-Sa 11am-1:30am.) Also check out neighboring partner establishment **Marks Brothers Grill.**

APPROACHING DWIGHT

Heading south from Gardner, watch for turns in the road; they are all marked by the little brown signs on the right. 3 mi. south of Gardner, take a right onto **Rte. 53** and go over the railroad tracks, then follow the signs directing you left on **Rte. 66.** 37 mi. south of Joliet, the road jogs left so that it is right next to the railroad tracks, bypassing a stretch of motels and gas stations to the north of **Dwight.**

DWIGHT

Another railroad town over the tracks, Dwight prides itself on its refurbished windmill. As you pass through the south end of town (Rte. 66 mainly bypasses downtown), the **Becker Marathon Gas Station** on the left dates back to 1932. To see downtown Dwight, head east toward the railroad tracks and the leafy median marking Main St.

The garish "Mother Road" decorations on the outside don't quite match the cozy-country-kitchen interior of the **Old 66 Family Restaurant,** 105 S. Old 66, 2 mi. south of town. This restaurant is obviously the local favorite, and the atmosphere is worth the prices. (☎815-584-2920. Burgers $3. Chicken bucket $8. Open Su-Th 5am-9pm, F-Sa 5am-10pm.) Housed in a stately storefront on Main St., the **Hotel Frances,** 114 Main St., is primarily patronized by long-term guests and Dwight residents. Rooms are clean, if tiny and somewhat spartan and institutional. (☎815-584-2163. Singles and doubles $25. Cash up-front only.) The **Classic Inn Motel,** 15 E. Northbrook Dr. (☎815-584-1200.), 1 mi. north of Dwight, off Rte. 66, has comfortable rooms with private bath and TV.

THE ROAD TO PONTIAC

Continue south on what is now marked "Old 66," following the well-marked brown "Historic Rte. 66" signs. There are a number of turns, but they are all well marked. For much of the way, Rte. 66 runs parallel to I-55, although there are a few stretches where drivers can still race the railroad unrivaled. Even where Rte. 66 has been paved over or routed under I-55, divergent rows of telephone poles peeling off into the distance reveal the old path of the Mother Road. Eight and a half miles south of Dwight, follow the Rte. 66 signs to the left, diverging from I-55 to follow the railroad.

You might not know you were in it until you were out of it, but the **Standard Oil Company Gas Station** (with sign proudly proclaiming 87 mi. from Chicago, 2361 from L.A.), at the south end of Odell, is the winner of the "Best Preservation Project on all of Rte. 66" award. Don't roll in on an empty tank—you can fill up on 66 memorabilia, but not on gas. The Rte. 66 "Turn Out" signs in **Cayuga** lead to an abandoned stretch of road and a photo op of an old **Meramec Caverns barn-side sign.**

PONTIAC

Pontiac was once voted one of the ten best towns in America under 25,000 inhabitants by *Time* magazine. Famed for its ornate courthouse and extensive veterans memorials, Pontiac has several elegant swinging bridges abutting the Chatauqua recreation area. The **Humiston Woods Nature Center** has a variety of restored and original prairie habitats, including trails for walking, bird-watching, cross-country skiing, watersports, and picnicking. **Humiston Pool at Chautauqua Park** dates from 1926. The **Pontiac Visitors Center,** 120 W. Howard St., has a wealth of maps and friendly folk, who will tell you that "Pontiac has three swinging bridges, and we're a swinging town!" Ask nicely and they'll even give you a letter opener. When they did the same for Congressman John Shimkus, he made sure to include it in his 15-page list of gifts received for his Congressional financial-disclosure form, which also included 21 calendars, a bumper sticker from a displeased citizen, sausage, and 12 jars of horseradish. (1 mi. east of Rte. 66, at the corner of Mill St. ☎815-844-5847. Open M-F 8am-5pm.)

Heinz Hanekamp's tidy **Downtowner Motel,** 100 N. Main St., is decorated in Bavarian style, yet its neat striped carpets and dark wood paneling give it a 70s-retro feel. It is the oldest motel in town, and certainly the hippest. Each room has a mini-fridge, TV, heat, and A/C. Be sure to check out the back side of the motel, above the granite yard, for an impressive mural of Pontiac. (☎815-844-5102. Reception 7am-midnight. Singles $40; doubles $45.) When Rte. 66 was rerouted away from the railroad tracks, the whole **Old Log Cabin Food and Spirits** building, just off the northbound side of Rte. 66, was jacked up and turned around to keep it facing the road. Decorated with discarded telephone poles by the founding Selotis brothers in the early 1920s, today the log cabin is one of the dining highlights of the road, putting kitsch to shame with its genuine laid-back reverence for the old road, and extremely friendly and road-knowledgeable staff. (☎815-842-2908. Shockingly bright bottles of Route 66 Pop $1.50. Open M-Tu 5am-4pm, W-Sa 5am-8pm.)

LEXINGTON. Farther up Rte. 66, Lexington has two banks, a post office, and Internet access at the public library, but no stop in Lexington would be complete without a stop at the **Shake Shack,** 512 W. Main St. The red-and-white checked interior with surprisingly low counter stools is the home of the "world's greatest milkshakes" ($1.80 for the biggest small you've ever seen, $2.30 for a large) and an unparalleled collection of kerosene lamps. (☎309-365-3005. Open daily summer 9am-10pm; winter 9am-9pm. Cash only.) The **Koch Depot,** 322 W. Main St., sells an assortment of Rte. 66 memorabilia. (☎309-365-3516. Rte. 66 signs $5. Rte. 66 hats $5. Open M-Sa 10am-5pm, Su 1-5pm.)

◤ APPROACHING BLOOMINGTON
Following **Rte. 66** toward Bloomington requires close attention to the signs. Heading south from Towanda, follow Rte. 66 through the stops, and left onto **Henry St.** through a suburban area. After ¼ mi., turn left onto **Linden St.**, take right on **Willow St.**, followed by another left. Don't worry; this is all well signed. Rte. 66 curves right onto **Veterans Pkwy.**, but going straight instead will lead into downtown Bloomington.

BLOOMINGTON & NORMAL

The "twin cities" of Bloomington and Normal, about 127 mi. from Chicago, are home to an array of food and lodging establishments, as well as a significant student population, thanks to the presence of **Illinois State University** in Normal and **Illinois Wesleyan University** in Bloomington. It's still 2321 mi. to Los Angeles, but if driving is already getting you down, take advantage of the **Constitution Trail,** a joint Bloomington/Normal recreational venture, including over 20 mi. of trails throughout the two cities. The **Clover Lawn Estate,** 1000 E. Monroe St., built for Supreme Court Justice and longtime Lincoln associate David Davis, displays the elegant home and lifestyle of one of Illinois's most celebrated politicians. (☎309-828-1084. Tours W-Sa 9am-4pm. Suggested donation $2, children $1.) The majestic **Ewing Manor,** at the corner of Towanda Ave. and Emerson St. (☎309-829-6333; www.ewingmanor.ilstu.edu), looms like a castle above the surrounding wooded area. Although visitors can tour the manor only by appointment, in the summer locals gather for a Shakespeare festival put on in the theater out back. The manor has two lovely gardens, one Japanese and the other inspired by Shakespeare.

Playboy ranked **Pub II,** 102 N. Linden St., among its top 100 campus bars. With sports posters galore and video games, Pub II doesn't disappoint the fun-loving crowd. (☎309-452-0699. ½ lb. burger $3. Chicago hot dog $2.50. Open summer M-Sa 11am-1am, Su 4pm-1am; winter M-Sa 11am-1am, Su noon-1am.) Standard chain motels are found around Normal and Bloomington, particularly to the north near Normal. For a break from roadside digs, visit stately, antique-laden **Davis Manor,** 1001 E. Jefferson St., across from the David Davies Mansion in Bloomington. (☎309-829-7703. Rooms with shared bath $45.)

◤ APPROACHING SHIRLEY
From Bloomington, take **Center St.** through town, following the signs toward I-55. 4 mi. south of where Bloomington and Normal meet, things get tricky. Rte. 66 effectively doubles back on itself, finally heading south again on **Beich Rd.,** parallel to I-55. Just hold on tight and follow the signs.

SHIRLEY

Signs advertise no services in Shirley, 8½ mi. south of Bloomington, but keep going to reach the gem of the area, which lies about 4 mi. south on Rte. 66, in Funk's Grove. **Funk's Grove** produces some of the finest maple sirop in the midwest. And yes, they do mean "sirop"—according to the FDA, "sirop" with an "i" means it's 100% natural. To buy the sweet stuff, continue half a mile south of Funk's Grove to the small store. (☎309-876-3360 or 309-874-3720. Open by chance or appointment.) Turn west at the "Sirop" sign and follow the signs toward Funk's Grove to reach the peaceful **Funk's Grove Church and Cemetery,** 1 mi. off Rte. 66. Behind the 1864 church is a modest monument to the more than 50 Irish immigrants who came to Illinois in the 1850s to help construct the Chicago and Alton Railroad. Across the road, in the **Church of the Templed Trees,** felled trunks form the pews and stumps the altar of an outdoor sanctuary.

The friendly folks at the **Sugar Grove Nature Center** will show you everything you ever wanted to know about making sugar. The center is closed in winter, but trails are available winter and summer during daylight hours for hiking, picnicking, birdwatching, and cross-country skiing. When the stars are right, an observatory is open for public stargazing. (Head right at the "Sirop" arrow 4 mi. south of Shirley, on Funk's Grove Rd. and take a right at Funk's Grove Church sign. ☎309-874-2174; www.funksgrove.org.)

☉ DIXIE TRUCKER'S HOME AND ROUTE 66 HALL OF FAME

The road curves to the right at Shirley; continue straight to the junction of I-55 and U.S. 136.

This epic truck stop, dating from 1928, is for everyone from the truck-wannabes to the real deal. The Dixie serves up burgers ($6), sandwiches ($5), and a hearty buffet ($7) 24-7. You can check out the company over the years in the **Route 66 Hall of Fame,** and end your visit with a complimentary polaroid of you alongside your rig. (☎309-874-2323. Open 24hr.)

THE ROAD TO LINCOLN. Past the truck stop and hall of fame, continue south through the town of **Atlanta,** 19 mi. south of Bloomington. **Sherman's Curiosity Shop,** 108 New Race St., is worth a stop for the antique obsessed. (☎219-648-2121. Open Su 1-5pm.) The road hits **Lawndale** 23 mi. south of Bloomington and then enters Lincoln.

LINCOLN. The only town to be named for Abraham Lincoln during his lifetime, the town of **Lincoln** is home to a white gilt courthouse and refurbished movie theater. (Shows $6; before 6pm $5.) There are campsites at **Camp-a-While,** 1779 1250 Ave., 1¼ mi. north of Lincoln, 2 mi. west of Rte. 66. Keeping in mind what the countryside looks like around here (flat, open, and with few trees), Camp-a-While affords about as much privacy as you can hope for. Sites include hookups, hot showers, laundry, and laptop Internet hookup. (☎217-732-8840. Sites $10; RVs $20. Electricity $2.)

◤ APPROACHING SPRINGFIELD

Pass through **Broadwell,** and **Elkhart.** At **Williamsville,** turn right on **Elm St.** About 1 mi. later turn right. Turn right again, and follow I-55 to Exit 105, passing through **Sherman,** then **Springfield.**

SPRINGFIELD

Springfield is the birthplace of Abe Lincoln *and* the corn dog—it doesn't get much more American than that. Lincoln-mania is clearly the tourist focus of the town, but business—primarily the running of the state—gets done here, amidst the dated storefronts of 5th St. and under the domes of the stately legislative buildings. Springfield also honors its portion of Rte. 66; the city is home to the "International Route 66 Mother Road Festival," as well as several classic diners.

⬭ VITAL STATS

Population: 111,000

Visitor Info: Springfield Convention and Visitor's Bureau, 109 N. 7th St. (☎217-789-2360). Open M-F 8am-5pm.

Internet Access: Lincoln Public Library, 326 S. 7th St. (☎217-753-4900). Open June-Aug. M-Th 9am-9pm, F 9am-6pm, Sa 9am-5pm; Sept.-May M-Th 9am-9pm, F 9am-6pm, Su noon-5pm.

Post Office: 411 E. Monroe St. (☎800-275-8777), at Wheeler St. Open M-F 7:45am-5pm. **Postal Code:** 62701.

▛ GETTING AROUND

Getting around in Springfield is fairly simple. **N. Grand Ave.** is one of the city's main thoroughfares, running east-west through town. Streets run north-south and are numbered; main streets include **5th St.,** which borders the Lincoln Neighborhood and Oak Park Cemetery, and **7th St. N. Grand Ave.** is known as **N. Grand Ave. West** west of the intersection with **5th St.** and **N. Grand Ave. East** east of the intersection. There is plenty of on-street metered **parking** available in Springfield, as well as public lots near many sights.

☉ SIGHTS

The sleepy state capital plays curator to the 16th president's legacy; many of Springfield's sights revolve around Lincoln's life and family. For variety, there are also Rte. 66-related attractions, and a few oddball sights.

THE LINCOLN NEIGHBORHOOD. Bringing together North and South (Springfield), Lincoln's old haunts in the center of town have been turned into a pedestrian-only pilgrimage site, where Lincoln-o-philes can take Park Service tours of Lincoln's home and neighborhood. Tickets are free in the Visitors Center. (☎217-492-4241 Ext. 244; www.nps.gov/liho. Open daily 8:30am-5pm; extended summer hours. Parking $2; closes at 6pm. On-street metered parking also available.)

Springfield

ACCOMMODATIONS
Henry Mischler House, **13**
KOA Campground, **6**
Mr. Lincoln's Campground, **4**
The Pear Tree Inn, **5**

FOOD
Boyd's New Generation Family
  Restaurant, **2**
Cafe Brio, **12**
Cozy Dog Drive-In, **3**
Krekel's Custard, **1**
Trout Lily Cafe, **11**

NIGHTLIFE
Brewhaus, **7**
Central Jazz Station, **9**
Underground City Tavern, **10**

Capital Airport
J. David Jones Pkwy
Browning Rd.
Lincoln Tomb
Taintor Rd.
Veterans Pkwy Ext
State Fair Grounds
Veterans Pkwy
Sangamon Ave.
Shea's Gas Station Museum
Lincoln Park
Peoria Rd.
Museum of Funeral Customs
Robin Roberts Stadium
North Grand Ave.
North Grand Ave.
Dirksen Pkwy
Monument Ave.
Walnut St.
MacArthur Blvd.
Jefferson St.
97
Madison St.
5th St.
7th St.
Clear Lake Rd.
36
72
SEE INSET
Governor St.
Lawrence Ave.
6th St.
9th St.
Cook St.
66
Monroe St.
Washington Park
Chatham Rd.
Illini Rd.
1st St.
2nd St.
Public Library
South Grand Ave.
Fast Track Laundry Center
Taylor Ave.
Laurel St.
Ash St.
Cherry Rd.
55
72
29
Veterans Pkwy
Wabash Ave.
Parks St.
Robbins Rd.
Westchester
Adlai Stevenson Dr.
Lake Springfield
TO 6 (6mi)
72
72
Mather's Rd.
Prairie Crossing
N
LG
0   3 miles
0   3 kilometers
Spaulding Orchard Rd.
4
Lake Springfield
55

INSET — THE LINCOLN NEIGHBORHOOD
Madison St.
Jefferson St.
Chamber of Commerce
Washington St.
Old State Capitol
7
1st St.
2nd St.
4th St.
5th St.
6th St.
7th St.
9th St.
Adams St.
8
IL State Historical Society
10
Adams St.
8th St.
12
11
Monroe St.
Lincoln Library
Lincoln Home National Historic Site
Capitol Ave.
Illinois State Capitol
Lincoln Home Visitor Center
THE LINCOLN NEIGHBORHOOD
Jackson St.
Executive Mansion
P
13
Edwards St.
Edwards St.
Cook St.
P
Dana Thomas House
8th St.
Lawrence Ave.

THE DANA-THOMAS HOME. Built in 1902, the stunning home was one of Frank Lloyd Wright's early experiments in Prairie Style and features the largest collection of original furniture and art glass of any Wright structure. Tours explain of the house and the eccentric millionaire who lived there. *(301 E. Lawrence Ave., 6 blocks south of the Old State Capitol at 4th and Lawrence. ☎217-782-6776. Open Su and Tu-Sa 9am-4pm. Tours approximately every 20min. Parking lot behind the museum. Suggested donation $3, under 17 $1.)*

LINCOLN TOMB. The final resting place of Honest Abe, Mary Todd Lincoln, and three of the Lincoln children is here, under a statue-endowed obelisk in the Oak Ridge Cemetery. *(1500 Monument Ave. ☎217-782-2717. Open daily Mar.-Oct. 9am-5pm; Nov.-Feb. 9am-4pm.)*

SHEA'S GAS STATION MUSEUM. Looking as though Rte. 66 exploded onto one happy and eclectic lot of signs, car parts, and memorabilia, this mini-museum just north of Springfield proper is worth a pit stop. *(2075 Peoria Rd. ☎217-522-0475. Open Tu-F 7am-4pm, Sa 7am-noon; closed during the Illinois State Fair. Free.)*

OTHER SIGHTS. For a break from the upbeat, the **Museum of Funeral Customs** features a history of American embalming and funeral customs, including a variety of caskets and embalming tools. *(1440 Monument Ave. ☎217-544-3480. Open Su 1-4pm, Tu-Sa 10am-4pm. $3, children $1.50.)* The **Illinois State Museum** has everything you ever wanted to know about Illinois, heralded from the outside by a replica of an Alaskan Tlingit totem pole, complete with its own Lincoln tribute topping. *(502 S. Spring St. ☎217-782-7386; www.museum.state.il.us. Open M-Sa 8:30am-5pm, Su noon-5pm.)* In 1858, Lincoln delivered his famous "House Divided" speech at the **Old State Capitol;** the building is open for tours today. *(☎217-785-7961. Open Mar.-Oct. daily 9am-5pm; Nov.-Feb. Tu-Sa 9am-4pm.)*

■ FOOD

Springfield offers a surprising array of dining options, ranging from classic American to Italian to southern home cooking. Springfield is also home to several classic Rte. 66 diners and fast-food joints; even if you're just passing through, these are ones you shouldn't miss.

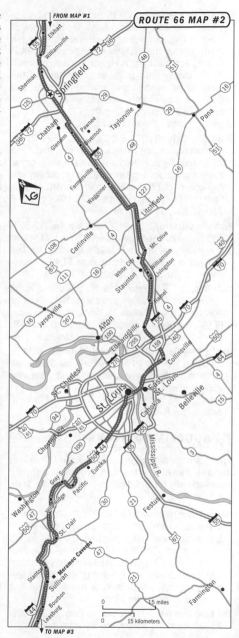

ROUTE 66

❦ **Cozy Dog Drive-In,** 2935 5th St. (☎217-525-1992; www.cozydogdrivein.com). The birthplace of the corn dog and one of the all-time greats of the road. Run by the Waldmire family since 1949. Brother Bob Waldmire is an artist, and is responsible for innumerable maps and caricatures of the road—spend enough time driving the route and Bob's art is pleasantly unavoidable. Pick up postcards ($0.50), maps, a Cozy Dog ($1.50), or other greasy goodies. Open M-Sa 8am-8pm.

Trout Lily Cafe, 218 S. 6th St. (☎217-391-0101; www.troutlilycafe.com). Purple and yellow exterior and the Curious George themed murals provide coziness inside and out. An excellent selection of specialty and drip coffees ($2.50), quiche, and salads ($4), plus Springfield's special buttercake ($1.50). Open M-F 7am-4:30pm, Sa 9am-3pm.

Krekel's Custard, 2121 N. Grand Ave. (☎217-525-4952). Eat-in, eat-out, or drive-thru, the shakes and burgers here are legendary. Milkshakes from chocolate and vanilla to lemon and pineapple $1.40. Cheeseburgers $1.90. Open M-Sa 10:30am-7:30pm.

Cafe Brio, 524 E. Monroe St. (☎217-544-0574), at the corner of 6th St. Excellent upscale Tex-Mex cuisine for reasonable prices. Salads $5. Fantastic chicken tacos ($10). Oozy-gooey chocolate yum $6. Open M-Th 11am-10pm, F-Sa 11am-11pm, Su 11am-3pm.

Boyd's New Generation Family Restaurant, 1831 S. Grand Ave. East (☎217-544-9866). The South rises again in this homestyle southern cookery, featuring whole catfish ($7), or nuggets ($6) for the faint of heart. Su all-you-can-eat buffet $9. Open M-Th 7am-3pm, F 7am-7pm, Su 1-5pm.

ACCOMMODATIONS

There are cheap lodgings off I-55 and U.S. 36 on **Dirksen Pkwy.** Rooms downtown should be reserved early for holiday weekends and the **State Fair** in mid-August.

Henry Mischler House (☎217-525-2660; www.mischlerhouse.com). The 19th-century home of dry goods merchant Henry Mischler has been turned into a colorful B&B in 1930s boarding house-meets-quirky Victorian-manor style by super-friendly proprietor Roger Schmitz. Rooms individually decorated, with private baths. Breakfast included. Rooms from $75.

The Pear Tree Inn, 3190 S. Dirksen Pkwy. (☎217-529-9100). For all the comfort and less price, head to the end of the Dirksen Pkwy. row of motels. Breakfast, cable TV, and free local calls. Rooms from $40.

Mr. Lincoln's Campground, 3045 Stanton Ave. (☎217-529-8206) off Stevenson Dr. RV hookups, tent sites, and a limited number of private cabins. Reception 8am-8pm; in winter until 6pm. Cabins not open in winter. Sites $16, with hookup $21; cabins with A/C $25.

KOA Campground, 5775 W. Farm 140 (☎217-498-7002). The sites are fairly close together, but the campground is removed from the road in the sweeping countryside south of Springfield. Reception 24hr. Open Apr.-Nov. Sites $16; RVs $23; cabins $28.

◎ NIGHTLIFE

Locals crowd around the bar and lounge in wooden booths in the **Brewhaus,** 617 E. Washington St., one of the most popular and laid-back nightspots around. (☎217-525-6399. Beer $1-3. Mixed drinks $5. Open M-F 7am-1am, Sa 8am-1am, Su 5pm-1am.) The **Underground City Tavern,** 700 E. Adams St., is a lounge of surprise and sophistication underneath the Hilton, featuring live music weekends. (☎217-789-1530. Mixed drinks $3.50-6. Sandwiches $8. Cover varies. Open M-F 2pm-3am, Sa noon-3am, Su noon-midnight.) Way upstairs, on the 30th floor, **Central Jazz Station** has a stunning view of Springfield that cannot be topped. (☎217-789-1530. Live music F-Sa. Open M-Th 5pm-11pm, F-Sa 5pm-3am, Su 7pm-3am.)

◤ LEAVING SPRINGFIELD
Follow **Rte. 66** south out of Springfield on **5th St.,** past the Cozy Dog. Heading south, there is an unavoidable stretch of **I-55**—follow the signs.

THE ROAD TO LITCHFIELD

From Springfield, the bevy of towns on the way south to St. Louis pride themselves on their Rte. 66 status, and many still host restaurants that hearken back to the days of Mother Road glory. Directly south of Springfield, **Glenarm, Pawnee,** and **Divernon** are all home to necessities like gas, mom-and-pop diners, and chain motels. Eight miles south of Springfield is the turnoff for the **Sugar Creek Covered Bridge,** a scenic picnic area next to an out-of-use covered bridge.

Continue on Rte. 66 and keep an eye out about 12 mi. south of Springfield for a giant banner proclaiming **"Start the day with Pork"** on the west side of the road. A half-mile beyond that is a **giant tribute to Abraham Lincoln**—he's perched in a wagon, absorbed in a book, axe in a tree nearby. Driving past the giant Lincoln, head left at the T and then back onto I-55, just until Exit 80, approximately 1 mi., which will lead straight into **Divernon.**

Just over 3 mi. south of Divernon, turn west at the faded sign on Montgomery and follow it up over I-55. Take the frontage road south 1 mi. to reach **Punkie's Palace,** 20 mi. south of Springfield., where travelers enjoy a decadent night's rest in the motel's precious gem-themed rooms. Rooms are pricey, but include dinner, breakfast, all-night snacking, and the run of a luxurious antique-filled home. (☎217-227-3701 or 217-227-3733; www.punkies-palace.com. Rooms $100-130.)

As Rte. 66 climbs over I-55 at **Farmersville,** 10 mi. south of Divernon, keep an eye out for old 66 standby **Art's Restaurant and Motel.** These days, the restaurant goes by the name of **Gloria's Formerly Art's,** at Exit 72 off I-55. Gloria prides herself on her supersized portions, so get ready for the hearty meal that awaits, then sleep it off at the newly renovated rooms next door. (☎217-277-3566. Entrees $8. Gigantic truckers' breakfast $6. Open Su-M 7am-3pm, Tu-Sa 7am-8pm. Motel singles $30-35; doubles $70-75.)

Along Rte. 66 3 mi. south of **Waggoner,** keep an eye out for **Frances Marten's Our Lady of the Highways Shrine.** Erected in 1956, the statue of the Virgin Mary prays for the road safety of those who pass under her gaze. A series of Burma Shave style signs leading southward spells out the Hail Mary.

APPROACHING LITCHFIELD
7½ mi. south of the Shrine, Rte. 66 heads up over I-55, so that I-55 is now to the west of the road. At **Litchfield,** drivers have the choice to head straight through town on the 1940-1977 alignment of Rte. 66, or diverge to the left on the older alignment, dating from 1930-1940. The newer alignment leads to chain motels and fast food, while the older alignment passes the **Skyview Drive-In** and the **Ariston Cafe.**

LITCHFIELD
Litchfield is a town proud to be on Rte. 66. The **Sky View Drive-In,** on the Rte. 66 1930-1940 alignment, just north of Union St., still shows movies for $1 during the summer months, just like the in days of old. (☎217-324-4451. Call for showtimes.) Numer-ous annual celebrations include an April reenact-ment of 1800s life, and a July International Chili Society district cook-off. Nearby **Lake Lou Yaeger** offers beachfront, watersports availability, camp-grounds, and playgrounds.

The **Ariston Cafe,** located at the corner of Rte. 66 and Union St., on the 1930-1940 align-ment, has been serving roadies since the 1920s, and since 1935 at this spot. (☎217-324-2023; www.ariston-cafe.com. Appetizers $5. Entrees $7-15. Open M-F 11am-10pm, Sa 4-10pm, Su 11am-9pm.)

THE ROAD TO STAUNTON
Leaving Litchfield at the southern end of town, either follow the newer alignment of Rte. 66 all the way through town, or take the old alignment 2 mi. until it joins the newer segment. Six miles south of Litchfield, turn left toward the town of **Mt. Olive,** a town proud to be the final resting place of Mary "Mother" Jones, and "General" Alexander Bradley, both instrumental in the fight for the rights of mine workers, in the **Union Miners Cemetery.** Approximately 10½ mi. south of central Litchfield, Rte. 66 reaches a T inter-section; take a left to rejoin the old route, and continue on over I-55. Thirteen miles from Litchfield is **Staunton.** Lara's Sweet Nuthin's, 319 W. Main St., in Staunton is worth the breakfast stop for all things sweet, costing near to nuthin'. (☎618-635-2844. Softball-sized cinnamon buns $1. Strudel $1. Open Tu-Sa 5:30am-5:30pm.)

HENRY'S RTE. 66 EMPORIUM AND RABBIT RANCH
1107 Old Rte. 66, *Just south of Staunton, at the corner of Rte. 66 and Madison St.*

"Hare it is!" proclaim the signs, as if you could miss the two giant tractor trailers out front with the galloping camels and "Humpin' to Please" painted on them. Henry's Emporium defines the joy of Rte. 66 culture—18 rabbits and one Rte. 66 enthusiast extraordinare hop amongst the eclectic and ever-expanding col-lection of memorabilia. Rich Henry has worked and lived on Rte. 66 all his life, and has projects in the works to improve his empo-rium. Drive by and check out the latest, includ-ing an upcoming "Rabbit Ranch" and the "Meramec Cabins" of Staunton. (☎618-635-5655; www.henrysroute66.com. Open daily 9am-4pm or whenever Rich Henry is around.)

THE ROAD TO HAMEL

Continue on Rte. 66 from Henry's Emporium another 10 mi. to the town of **Hamel.** Just north of Hamel, on the eastern side of I-55 is a repainted sign for the famous **Meramec Caverns** of Stanton, MO, so proudly advertised near Pontiac and so happily jibed by Rich Henry. Across Rte. 66 from the Meramec Barn is **St. Paul's Church,** where the neon blue cross at the top has been lighting road-trippers' ways for years.

EDWARDSVILLE. Seven miles south of Hamel is the town of Edwardsville, home of the **Southern University of Illinois.** Gas and amenities abound in town, including a new library and some excellent eating and lounging options. **Sacred Ground Cafe,** 233 N. Main St., is a student-friendly coffee shop offering ample space to relax with a book, spread out over a board game, or just gobble down some health food. Veggie options are available. (☎618-692-4150. Wraps, salads, quiche, or panini $4. Open daily 7am-11pm.) Chalkboards at the **Stagger Inn Again,** 104 E. Vandalia St., proclaim specials and quips, and the wooden bar, checkered floors, and spacious dining area with frequent live music invite diners in for a night out or a lunch on the go. (☎618-656-4221. Sandwiches or staggerburgers $4-6. Open M-W 11am-1am, Th 11am-2am, F-Sa 11am-2:30am, Su 3pm-1am.)

 LUNA CAFE   201 E. Chain of Rocks Rd. *5 mi. south of Edwardsville, in Mitchell.*

Rumor has it that Al Capone used to come to this legendary old Rte. 66 bar, still tucked under a blinking vintage neon sign, when he feared foul play in St. Louis. (☎618-931-3152. Hamburgers $3. Drinks $2-3. M and Th free wings. Open Su-F 7am-2am, Sa 7am-3am.)

> Collinsville is home to the **World's Largest Catsup Bottle,** a giant painted water tower dating from 1949.

COLLINSVILLE. Take I-55 south to Rte. 159 south to get to downtown Collinsville, and head south on Morrison St. as your hamburger dreams materialize over the horizon. Pick up your catsup postcards and catsup paraphernalia at **Ashmond's Drugs** on Main St. As you head down Main St., keep an eye to the left for an ancient Bull Durham Tobacco sign painted on a brick wall. For a taste of the extraordinary, stop into **Bert's Chuckwagon BBQ,** 207 E. Clay St. On the outside of the A-frame building is a giant modern mural of Biblical scenes (check out Mary's mirrored eyes) painted by the owner's sons. Inside is tasty barbecue ($3 rib tips, $10 full side) and Tex-Mex. (☎618-344-7993.)

▼ LEAVING COLLINSVILLE
Take **Main St.** west to **St. Louis Rd.,** which will turn into **Collinsville Rd.** Take **I-255 North** to **I-55 South/I-70 West,** which will take you toward St. Louis.

◉ CAHOKIA MOUNDS
Outside Collinsville, off of I-55 South/I-70 West. Don't be fooled; they're not in Cahokia.

And you thought San Francisco had hills. These giant grassy knolls are the remnants of the prehistoric Native American city of Cahokia. No one is quite sure what to make of them, although archaeologists are fairly certain some were burial mounds. "Monks Mound," the largest Indian mound north of Mexico, is named for Trappist Monks who set up camp on top of the mound in the 1800s. (☎618-345-4999. Open Su and W-Sa 9am-5pm. Extended summer hours; call for more info. Suggested donation $2, children $1.)

Welcome To MISSOURI

ST. LOUIS

Directly south of the junction of three rivers—the Mississippi, Missouri, and Illinois—St. Louis marks the transition between the Midwest and the West. The Gateway Arch pays homage to America's westward expansion, while only a couple of miles south, the Anheuser-Busch Company churns out Budweiser, the most American beer of them all. Innovative musicians crowd bars and cafes, influenced by great St. Louis blues and ragtime players of the past. Sprawling and diverse, St. Louis offers a taste of city life with a frontier feel.

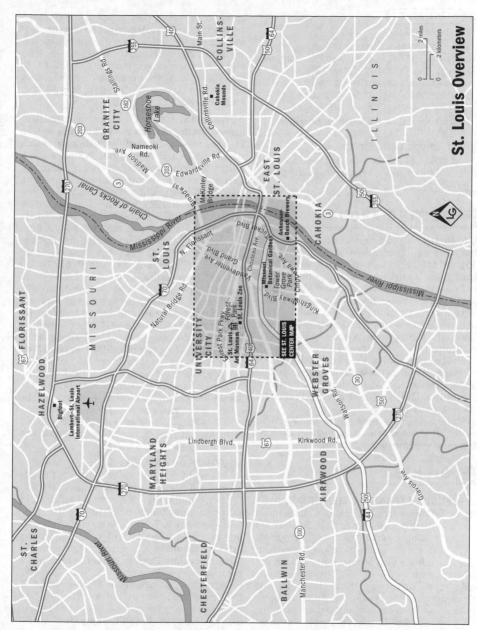

St. Louis Overview

2 miles
2 kilometers

LG

COLLINS-VILLE
Main St.
Stallings Rd.
GRANITE CITY
Horseshoe Lake
Collinsville Rd.
Cahokia Mounds
Nameoki Rd.
Madison Ave.
Edwardsville Rd.
McKinley Bridge
Broadway
Chain of Rocks Canal
Mississippi River
EAST ST. LOUIS
CAHOKIA
Anheuser-Busch Brewery
Tucker Blvd.
Choteau Ave.
ILLINOIS
Mississippi River
ST. LOUIS
N. Florissant
Grand Blvd.
Vandeventer Ave.
Missouri Botanical Garden
Tower Grove Park
Kingshighway Blvd.
Chippewa
Iowa Ave.
Natural Bridge Rd.
FLORISSANT
MISSOURI
HAZELWOOD
Lambert–St. Louis International Airport
Bigfoot
UNIVERSITY CITY
Forest Park Pkwy.
Forest Park
St. Louis Art Museum
St. Louis Zoo
SEE ST. LOUIS CENTER MAP
WEBSTER GROVES
Watson Rd.
MARYLAND HEIGHTS
Lindbergh Blvd.
Kirkwood Rd.
KIRKWOOD
Gravois Ave.
ST. CHARLES
Missouri River
CHESTERFIELD
BALLWIN
Manchester Rd.

VITAL STATS

Population: 348,000

Visitor Info: Visitors Center, 308 Washington Ave. (☎314-241-1764; www.explorestlouis.com), at Memorial Blvd. Open daily 9:30am-4:30pm. Branch inside **America's Convention Center** (☎314-342-5160), at the corner of 7th St. and Washington Ave. Open M-F 8:30am-4pm, Sa 9am-2pm.

Internet Access: St. Louis Central Library, 1301 Olive St. (☎314-241-2288). Open M 10am-9pm, Tu-F 10am-6pm, Sa 9am-5pm.

Post Office: 1720 Market St. (☎314-436-4114). Open M-F 8am-8pm, Sa 8am-1pm. **Postal Code:** 63101.

▣ GETTING AROUND

U.S. 40/I-64 runs east-west through the center of the entire metropolitan area, while **I-70, I-44 (U.S. 50),** and **I-55** all run to downtown from other outlying areas. Downtown is defined as the area east of **Tucker Blvd.** between **Martin Luther King** and **Market St.,** which divides the city north-south. Numbered streets parallel the Mississippi River, increasing to the west. St. Louis is a real neighborhood city, with attractions and restaurants concentrated in several distinct areas. The historic **Soulard** district borders the river south of downtown. **Forest Park** and **University City,** home to **Washington University** and old, stately homes, lie west of downtown. The Italian neighborhood called **The Hill** rests south of these.

St. Louis is also a driving town; **parking** comes easily, and wide streets and interstates allow for fast-moving traffic (most of the time).

◉ SIGHTS

JEFFERSON EXPANSION MEMORIAL. At 630 ft., the ▨**Gateway Arch**—the nation's tallest monument—towers gracefully over all of St. Louis and southern Illinois, serving as a testament to the city's historical role as the "Gateway to the West." The ground-level view is impressive, and the arch frames downtown beautifully from the Illinois side, but the 4min. ride to the top in quasi-futuristic elevator modules is more fun. Waits are shorter after dinner or in the morning, but are uniformly long on Saturday. Beneath the arch, the underground **Museum of Westward Expansion** adds to the

appeal of the grassy park complex known as the Jefferson Expansion Memorial. The museum radiates out in a semi-circle from a statue of a surveying Jefferson, celebrating the Louisiana Purchase and Westward expansion. (☎ 314-982-1410; www.gatewayarch.com. Museum and arch open daily summer 8am-10pm; winter 9am-6pm. Tram $8, ages 13-16 $5, ages 3-12 $3. Museum free.)

DOWNTOWN. It's a strike either way at the **International Bowling Museum and Hall of Fame** and the **St. Louis Cardinals Hall of Fame Museum,** which share a home across from Busch Stadium. The mildly amusing bowling museum traces the largely speculative history of the sport and allows visitors to bowl, while the baseball museum exhibits memorabilia from the glory days of St. Louis hardball. The museum also offers stadium tours. (111 Stadium Plaza. ☎ 314-231-6340. Open Apr.-Sept. daily 9am-5pm, game days until 6:30pm; Oct.-Mar. Su and Tu-Sa 11am-4pm. Museums or stadium tour $6, ages 5-12 $4; both $8.50/$7.50.) Historic **Union Station,** 1 mi. west of downtown, houses a shopping mall, food court, and entertainment center in a magnificent structure that was once the nation's busiest railroad terminal. (At 18th and Market St. ☎ 314-421-6655; www.stlouisunionstation.com. Open M-Sa 10am-9pm, Su 10am-6pm.) "The Entertainer" lives on at the **Scott Joplin House,** just west of downtown near Jefferson Ave., where the ragtime legend tickled the ivories and penned classics from 1900 to 1903. The 45min. tour delves into Joplin's long-lasting influence on American music. (2658 Delmar Blvd. ☎ 314-340-5790. Tours Apr.-Oct. M-F every 30min. 10am-4pm, Su noon-5pm; Nov.-Mar. also Sa 10am-4pm. $2.50, ages 6-12 $1.50.)

SOUTH OF DOWNTOWN. Soulard is bounded by I-55 and 7th St. In the early 1970s, the city proclaimed this area a historic district due to its former populations of German and Eastern European immigrants, many of whom worked in the breweries. Today, it is an attractive, tree-lined neighborhood packed with 19th-century brick townhouses. The district surrounds the bustling **Soulard Farmers Market,** where fresh, inexpensive produce abounds. (730 Carroll St. From downtown, travel south on Broadway or 7th St. to Lafayette. ☎ 314-622-4180. Open W-Sa 7am-7pm; hours vary among merchants.) At the end of 12th St., the **Anheuser-Busch Brewery,** the largest brewery in the world, produces the "King of

Beers." The 1½hr. tour includes a glimpse of the famous Clydesdales and two beer samples. *(1127 Pestalozzi St., at 12th and Lynch St. Take bus #40 "Broadway" south from downtown. ☎314-577-2626; www.budweisertours.com. Tours June-Aug. M-Sa 9am-5pm, Su 11:30am-5pm; Sept.-May M-Sa 9am-4pm, Su 11:30am-4pm.)*

The internationally acclaimed 79-acre **Missouri Botanical Garden** thrives north of Tower Grove Park on grounds left by entrepreneur Henry Shaw. The Japanese Garden is guaranteed to soothe the weary traveler. *(4344 Shaw Blvd. From downtown, take I-44 west. ☎800-642-8842; www.mobot.org. Open daily 9am-5pm; June-Aug. also M 9am-8pm. Tours daily 1pm. $7, seniors $5, under 12 free.)* **Grant's Farm,** the former home of President Ulysses S. Grant, is now a zoo. The tram-ride tour crosses terrain inhabited by over 1000 free-roaming animals, including elephants, zebras, and more of Anheuser's Clydesdale collection. *(3400 Grant St. Take I-55 west to Reavis Barracks Rd. and turn left onto Gravois. ☎314-843-1700; www.grantsfarm.com. Open mid-May-Aug. Su 9:30am-4pm, Tu-F 9am-3:30pm, Sa 9am-4pm; Sept.-Oct. W-F 9:30am-2:30pm, Sa-Su 9:30am-3:30pm; early Apr. to early May Su 9:30am-3:30pm, W-F 9am-3pm, Sa 9am-3:30pm. Free. Parking $5.)*

FOREST PARK. Forest Park contains three museums, a zoo, a 12,000-seat amphitheater, a grand canal, and countless picnic areas, pathways, and flying golf balls. Marlin Perkins, the late host of TV's *Wild Kingdom*, turned the **St. Louis Zoo** into a world-class institution, featuring black rhinos, Asian elephants, and a top-notch penguin and puffin habitat. *(☎314-781-0900; www.stlzoo.com. Open daily June-Aug. 8am-7pm; Sept.-May 9am-5pm. Free. Children's Zoo $4, under 2 free.)* Atop **Art Hill,** a statue of France's Louis IX, the city's namesake, raises his sword in front of the **St. Louis Art Museum,** which contains masterpieces of Asian, Renaissance, and Impressionist art. *(☎314-721-0072; www.slam.org. Open Tu-Th and Sa-Su 10am-5pm, F 10am-9pm. Tours Su and W-Sa 1:30pm. Special exhibits usually $10, students and seniors $8, ages 6-12 $6. F free.)* The **Missouri History Museum** focuses on the state's cultural heritage and has a small exhibit on the 1904 World's Fair. *(Located at Lindell and DeBaliviere St. ☎314-454-3124; www.mohistory.org. Open M and Su and W-Sa 10am-6pm, Tu 10am-8pm. Free. Special exhibits usu-*

ally $5, seniors and students $4. Tu 4-8pm free.) The **St. Louis Science Center** features an Omnimax theater, a planetarium, and over 700 interactive exhibits. Program a virtual fish, gape at visual tricks, and build your own arch. *(5050 Oakland Ave. ☎314-289-4444; www.slcs.org. Open early June to Aug. M-Th and Sa 9:30am-5:30pm, F 9:30am-9:30pm, Su 11:30am-5:30pm; Sept.-May M-Th and Sa 9:30am-4:30pm, F 9:30am-9:30pm, Su 11:30am-4:30pm. Free. Omnimax $7, seniors and ages 2-12 $6. Planetarium $6/$5.)*

CENTRAL WEST END. From Forest Park, head east a few blocks to gawk at the Tudor homes of the Central West End. The vast **Cathedral Basilica of St. Louis** boasts intricate ceilings and mosaics depicting Missouri church history. *(4431 Lindell Blvd. ☎314-533-0544. Open daily summer 7am-7pm; low-season 7am-dusk. Tours M-F 10am-3pm, Su after noon Mass. Call to confirm hours.)* At a shrine of a different sort, monster truck enthusiasts pay homage to **Bigfoot,** the "Original Monster Truck," who lives with his descendants near the airport. *(6311 N. Lindbergh St. ☎314-731-2822. Open M-F 9am-6pm, Sa 9am-3pm. Free.)* Northwest of the Central West End, the sidewalks of the **Loop** are studded with gold stars on the **St. Louis Walk of Fame,** which features local luminaries from Maya Angelou to Ike and Tina Turner. *(6504 Delmar Blvd. ☎314-727-7827; www.stlouiswalkoffame.org.)*

OTHER SIGHTS. The slightly surreal ◪**City Museum** is constructed from salvaged parts of area buildings and contains wonderful amalgam of architectural styles. The outdoor "Monstrocity," made entirely of recycled parts, includes two planes, a fire truck, a ferris wheel, sky tunnels, and a gothic tower with gargoyles, is far and away the coolest playscape ever. *(701 N. 15th St., downtown. ☎314-231-2489; www.citymuseum.org. Open Sept.-May Su 11am-5pm, W-F 9am-5pm, Sa 10am-5pm; June-Aug. Su 11am-5pm, Tu-Th 9am-5pm, F 9am-1am, Sa 10am-1am. Main museum $7.50; museum and "Monstrocity" $10; museum and skate park $10.)* **Six Flags St. Louis** reigns supreme in the kingdom of amusement parks. The brand-new "Xcalibur" catapults thrill-seekers 113 ft. into the air while spinning in circles, and the "Boss" wooden roller coaster features a 570° helix. *(30min. southwest of St. Louis on I-44 at Exit 261. ☎636-938-4800. Hours vary by season. $39, seniors and under 48 in. $24.)*

VENICE

Mississippi River

Broadway

LACLEDE'S LANDING

Gateway Arch/
Jefferson Natl.
Expansion Mem.

Mississippi River

North Florissant St.

DOWNTOWN

Edward
Jones
Dome

Bowling
Museum/
Cardinals
Hall of Fame

Busch
Stadium

Soulard Market

SOULARD

Cass Ave.

Jefferson Ave.

Union Station
SAVIS
Center

Lafayette
Park

Anheuser-
Busch
Brewery

Natural Bridge Ave.

Page Blvd.

Grand Blvd.

Spring Ave.

Dr. Martin Luther King Dr.

Powell Hall

Black Repertory

Fox Theatre

Chouteau Ave.

Park Ave.

Lafayette Ave.

Russell
Blvd.

Compton Hill
Reservoir Park

Shenandoah Ave.

Arsenal St.

Cherokee St.

Chippewa St.

Sarah St.

Page Blvd.

Delmar Blvd.

Olive St.

Lindell Blvd.

Forest Park Ave.

Shaw Blvd.

Missouri
Botanical Garden
(Shaw's Garden)

Magnolia Blvd

Tower Grove Park

Grand Blvd.

Cathedral
Basilica
of St. Louis

Kingshighway Blvd.

CENTRAL
WEST END

Forest Park

Manchester Blvd.

Vandeventer Ave.

Boyle Ave.

Marconi Ave.
Botanical
Ave.

THE
HILL

Kingshighway Blvd.

Dr. Martin Luther King Dr.

Goodfellow Blvd.

Delmar Blvd.

Union Pl.

Washington Pl.

Ave.

DeBaliviere Ave.

Missouri
History
Museum

St. Louis
Zoo

St. Louis
Art Museum

St. Louis
Science
Center

Mackland Ave.

Oakland Ave.

Wilson Ave.

Southwest Ave.

Hampton Ave.

Chippewa St.

THE LOOP

Lindell Blvd.

Skinker Blvd.

Forest Park Pkwy.

Morganford Rd.

Gravois Ave.

Kingshighway Blvd

Walk of Fame

TO 2 (2mi)

McCausland Ave.

Arsenal St.

Watson Rd.

Chippewa St.

Hampton Ave.

Manchester Rd.

Ellendale Ave.

Jamieson Ave.

Lansdowne Ave.

Mackenzie Rd.

Wabash Ave.

Big Bend Blvd

Laclede Station Rd.

Manchester Rd.

WEBSTER
GROVES

Murdoch Ave.

Chippewa St.

1 mile

1 kilometer

St. Louis

▲ ACCOMMODATIONS
Huckleberry Finn Youth Hostel
(HI-AYH), **12**
The Mayfair, **7**

🍴 FOOD
Amighetti's, **16**
Arcelia, **11**
Blueberry Hill, **3**
Imo's, **6**
In Soo, **2**
Kaldi's Coffeehouse and
Roasting Company, **5**
Mangia Italiano, **15**
Ted Drewes Frozen
Custard, **14 & 17**

🎵 NIGHTLIFE
The Big Bang, **10**
Brandt's Market & Cafe, **4**
Clementine's, **13**
Mississippi Nights, **9**
The Pageant, **1**
Train Wreck, **8**

♫ ENTERTAINMENT

Founded in 1880, the **St. Louis Symphony Orchestra** is one of the country's finest. **Powell Hall,** 718 N. Grand Blvd., holds the 101-member orchestra in acoustic splendor. (☎314-534-1700. Performances late Sept. to early May Th-Sa 8pm, Su 3pm. Box office open mid-Aug. to late May M-Sa 9am-5pm and before performances; late May to mid-Aug. M-F 9am-5pm. Tickets $10-95, students half-price.)

St. Louis offers theatergoers many options. The outdoor **Municipal Opera,** also known as the "Muny," presents hit musicals on summer nights in Forest Park. (☎314-361-1900. Box office open June to mid-Aug. daily 9am-9pm. Tickets $8-54.) Productions are also regularly staged by the **St. Louis Black Repertory,** 634 N. Grand Blvd. (☎314-534-3807), and by the **Repertory Theatre of St. Louis,** 130 Edgar Rd. (☎314-968-4925). The **Fox Theatre,** 537 N. Grand Blvd., was originally a 1930s movie palace, but now hosts Broadway shows, classic films, and country and rock music stars. (☎314-534-1111. Open M-Sa 10am-6pm, Su noon-4pm. Tours Tu, Th, Sa 10:30am. Tu $5; Th and Sa $8; under 12 $3. Call for reservations.) **Metrotix** (☎314-534-1111) has tickets to most area events.

A St. Louis ordinance permits gambling on the river for those over 21. The **President Casino on the Admiral** floats below the Arch on the Missouri side. (☎314-622-1111 or 800-772-3647; www.presidentscasino.com. Open M-Th 8am-4am, F-Su 24hr. Entry tax $2.) On the Illinois side, the **Casino Queen** claims "the loosest slots in town." (☎618-874-5000 or 800-777-0777; www.casinoqueen.com. Open daily 9am-7am.) Parking for both is free. The **St. Louis Cardinals** play at **Busch Stadium.** (☎314-421-3060. Tickets $9-55.) The **Rams,** formerly of L.A., take to the field at the **Edward Jones Dome.** (☎314-425-8830. Tickets $40-49.) The **Blues** hockey team slices ice at the **Savvis Center** at 14th St. and Clark Ave. (☎314-843-1700. Tickets from $15.)

▨ FOOD

In St. Louis, the difference of a few blocks can mean vastly different cuisine. The area surrounding **Union Station,** at 18th and Market St. downtown, is being revamped with hip restaurants and bars. The **Central West End** offers coffeehouses and outdoor cafes. A slew of impressive restaurants awaits just north of Lindell Blvd. along **Euclid Ave.**

St. Louis's historic Italian neighborhood, **The Hill,** southwest of downtown and just northwest of Tower Grove Park, produces plenty of pasta. Cheap Thai, Philippine, and Vietnamese restaurants spice the **South Grand** area, at Grand Blvd. just south of Tower Grove Park. Coffee shops and restaurants cluster on **University City Loop,** on Delmar Blvd. between Skinker and Big Bend Blvd.

▨ **Blueberry Hill,** 6504 Delmar Blvd. (☎314-727-0880), on the Loop. Eclectic rock 'n' roll restaurant with 9 different rooms including the "Elvis Room." Walls decked with record covers, Howdy Doody toys, a *Simpsons* collection, and giant baseball cards. Call ahead to find out if Chuck Berry is playing; he usually jams in the "Duck Room" 1 W each month. Big, juicy burgers $5. Live bands F-Sa and some weeknights 9:30pm. 21+ after 9pm. Cover $4-15. Kitchen open daily 11am-9pm.

▨ **In Soo,** 8423 Olive Blvd. (☎314-997-7473). Home to some of the best pot stickers ($5) and vegetable moo-shu ($9) you'll ever taste. Open M and Su and W-Sa 11:30am-10pm.

Ted Drewes Frozen Custard, 4224 S. Grand Blvd. (☎314-352-7376), and 6726 Chippewa St. (☎314-481-2652), on Rte. 66. The place for the St. Louis summertime experience since 1929. Those who make it through the line are rewarded by the "chocolate chip cookie dough concrete shake," ($1.70-3.80). Open May-Aug. daily 11am-midnight; Chippewa St. location also Sept.-Dec. and Feb.-May 11am-11pm.

Mangia Italiano, 3145 S. Grand Blvd. (☎314-664-8585). Fresh pasta made on site for $5-9. A hand-painted mural and mismatched tables add flair. Jazz weekend nights. Kitchen open M-F noon-10pm and Sa-Su 12:30-10:30pm. Bar open until 3am.

Amighetti's, 5141 Wilson St. (☎314-776-2855). Probably St. Louis's most famous sandwich place, serving the "special sandwich" (small $5.50, large $3.40) for 3 generations. Adjoining gelateria and bakery. Pasta $3.50/$6, salads $3.50/$6. Sandwich shop open Tu-F 7:30am-6pm, Sa 7:30am-5:30pm; in summer Tu-F until 7pm. Bakery open Tu-Sa 7:30am-3pm, gelateria open Su 11am-4pm, Tu-F 11am-2:30pm.

Arcelia, 2001 Park Ave. (☎314-231-9200). Big combination platters ($5.50-10.25) feature usual suspects like burritos and enchiladas, but this bustling Mexican eatery also offers more authentic dishes such as *mole de pollo* and *menudo.* Open M-Th 10am-2pm and 5-10pm, F-Su 10am-10pm.

Kaldi's Coffeehouse and Roasting Company, 700 De Mun Ave. (☎314-727-9955), in Clayton. From downtown, take I-64 West to Exit 34B: Clayton Rd./Skinker Blvd. Proceed straight for Clayton Rd. and take a right onto De Mun Ave. An eclectic crowd sips espresso drinks (from $1) and munches on fresh baked goods, and veggie delights. Hummus plate $4.50. Open daily 7am-11pm.

Imo's, 4479 Forest Park Ave. (☎314-535-4667). Makes the city's favorite St. Louis-style thin crust pizza (from $6.40) and receives shout-outs from rap superstar Nelly. Numerous locations through the city. Open M-Th 11am-midnight, F-Sa 11am-1am, Su 11am-11pm.

ACCOMMODATIONS

Most budget lodging is far from downtown. For chain motels, try **Lindbergh Blvd. (U.S. 67)** near the airport, or the area north of the I-70 junction with I-270 in Bridgeton, 5 mi. beyond the airport. **Watson Rd.** near Chippewa is littered with cheap motels. Take I-64 or I-44 west to Hampton Blvd. South., turn right on Chippewa St., and cross the River des Peres to Watson Rd. (Rte. 366).

Huckleberry Finn Youth Hostel (HI-AYH), 1908 S. 12th St. (☎314-241-0076), at Tucker Blvd., 2 blocks north of Russell Blvd. in the Soulard District. Take Broadway/7th St. south toward Soulard, turn right just past Geyer Ave. onto Allen Ave., and then take a right on 12th St.; it's on the right. A full kitchen, free parking, and proximity to Soulard bars make dorm rooms tolerable. Linen $2. Key deposit $5. Reception 8-10am and 6-10pm. Check-out 9:30am. Dorms rooms $19, nonmembers $21.

Royal Budget Inn, 6061 Collinsville Rd. (☎618-874-4451), in Fairmont City, Illinois, 20min. east of the city off I-55/I-70 Exit 6. Clean, purple-lit rooms with a Taj Mahal flavor make for an unusual budget option. Key deposit $2. Rooms $40.

The Mayfair, 806 St. Charles St. (☎314-421-2500). Constructed at the height of the Jazz Age, the Mayfair has hosted famous musicians and politicians, from Irving Berlin to Harry Truman. Standard rooms are spacious with marble-topped sinks and soft queen-size beds. Rooms from $109; suites from $119.

Dr. Edmund A. Babler Memorial State Park (☎636-458-3813 or 877-422-6766), 20 mi. west of downtown, just north of Hwy. 100. Tent and RV sites and a shower house. Tent sites $8; RV sites with electric hookup $14.

 NIGHTLIFE

Music rules the night in St. Louis. The *Riverfront Times* (free at many bars and clubs) and the *Get Out* section of the *Post-Dispatch* list weekly entertainment. The *St. Louis Magazine*, published annually, lists seasonal events. For beer and live music, often without a cover charge, St. Louis offers **Laclede's Landing,** a collection of restaurants, bars, and dance clubs housed in 19th-century industrial buildings north of the Arch on the riverfront. In the summer, bars take turns sponsoring "block parties," with food, drink, music, and dancing in the streets. (☎314-241-5875. 21+. Generally open 9pm-3am, with some places open for lunch and dinner.) Other nightlife hot spots include the bohemian **Loop** along Delmar Blvd., **Union Station** and environs, and the less touristy and gay-friendly **Soulard** district.

Brandt's Market & Cafe, 6525 Delmar Blvd. (☎314-727-3663). A Loop mainstay, offering live jazz, along with beer, wine, espresso, and a varied menu. During the summer, specials are served outside, while musicians jam in the dark interior. Open M-Th 11am-midnight, F-Sa 11am-1am, Su 11am-10pm.

The Pageant, 6161 Delmar Blvd. (☎314-726-6161). Line up early for a spot in the fantastic 33,000 sq. ft. nightclub, which hosts national acts. Call for ticket and cover prices. 18+. Doors usually open 7pm. The classy **Halo Bar** is open daily 5pm-3am and features live DJs.

Mississippi Nights, 914 N. 1st St. (☎314-421-3853), at Laclede's Landing. St. Louis's favorite place for music since 1979 has a history of bringing in the best national acts of all genres. Cover from $6. Doors usually open 7 or 8pm.

The Big Bang, 807 N. 2nd St. (☎314-241-2264), at Laclede's Landing. Dueling pianists lead the crowd in a rock 'n' roll sing-along show. Cover Su-Th $3, F-Sa $6. Open Su-Th 7pm-3am, F-Sa 5pm-3am.

Train Wreck, 720 N. 1st St. (☎314-436-1006), at Laclede's Landing. This multi-level entertainment center includes a nightclub, restaurant, and sports bar. Alternative cover bands F-Sa nights. Cover $3. Open Su-Th 11am-10pm, F-Sa 11am-3am.

Clementine's, 2001 Menard St. (☎314-664-7869), in Soulard. A crowded restaurant and St. Louis's oldest gay bar (established in 1978). Open M-F 10am-1:30am, Sa 8am-1:30am, Su 11am-midnight.

LEAVING ST. LOUIS

From downtown St. Louis, hop on **I-44** going west.

THE ROAD TO PACIFIC

Heading south from St. Louis, the terrain of the Ozark Mountains becomes increasingly steep, frequently bringing the road through cut-away cliffs and over high passes. On either side of the route, cliffsides fall away sharply—be careful, as the route is narrow and frequently traveled by giant tractor trailers. Follow I-44 to Exit 266, 23½ mi. south of St. Louis, to visit **Rte. 66 State Park** and the former **Times Beach Community.** (Continue on I-44 to Exit 261, at **Eureka,** and follow **Old Rte. 66** to Pacific.

PACIFIC. Pacific is home to the **Old Rte. 66 Flea Market,** where everything you ever needed (and a whole heck of a lot you never did) awaits. (☎636-257-8333. Sa-Su 8am-5pm.) Roadtrippers in Pacific stop for their munchies at **Monroe's Rte. 66 Diner,** 409 E. Osage St., where Rte. 66 memorabilia entertains the eyes while heaping portions of meatloaf ($5.45) or the Rte. 66 Skillet ($4.75) please the palate. (☎636-257-7866. Open M-F 6am-7:30pm, Sa-Su 7am-2pm.)

APPROACHING GRAY SUMMIT

Head west along **W. Osage St. (Bus. I-44).** Join I-44 briefly, crossing over I-50 and onto **Rte. 100.**

GRAY SUMMIT. In Gray Summit, I-44 and the old alignment of Rte. 66 rejoin. Although ancient signs herald its arrival several miles earlier, the **Diamonds Restaurant and Inn,** constructed in 1928 on this spot, has now been turned into the **Tri-County Truck Stop,** where giant servings and Rte. 66 memorabilia will fuel hungry drivers. (Breakfast all day $5. Burgers $3-5. Open M 5am-2pm, Tu-Su 5am-9pm.) The **Shaw Nature Reserve,** across from the Diamond Restaurant signs, provides miles of trails; wildflower gardens and the former home of a Confederate Colonel are located at this extension of the Missouri Botanical Garden. (☎636-451-3512. Grounds open daily 7am-dusk. Visitors Center open M-F 8am-4:30pm, Sa 9am-5pm.)

THE ROAD TO STANTON

Continuing along Rte. 66, you'll cross over the highway 6¾ mi. from Gray Summit and continue parallel to the railroad tracks. Eleven miles south

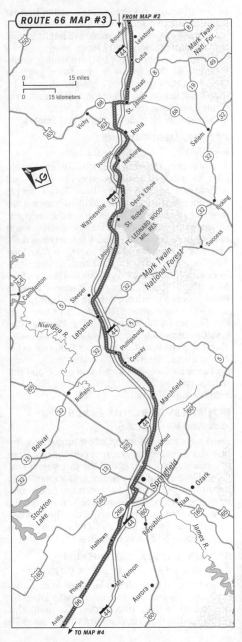

ROUTE 66 MAP #3 — FROM MAP #2

TO MAP #4

ROUTE 66

of Grey Summit on Rte. 66, the **Indian Harvest** store, in the two giant blue-and-white teepees along the west side of the road, will fulfill visitors' buffalo sausage, jerky, and jewelry needs.

Half a mile later, cross I-44, continuing southwest into **St. Clair.** One mile from town, just past the intersection with Rte. 30, head north over I-44, then head left on the outer road, and cross over again 9 mi. later, following the increasingly frequent signs for Meramec Caverns into **Stanton.**

 MERAMEC CAVERNS
South of Stanton; follow the signs.

The Meramec Caverns are virtually unmissable after the miles of advertisements on barns and billboards. Reputedly where Jesse James and his gang once hid their loot, the 26 mi. of caverns are now one of Missouri's biggest tourist attractions. Other cave-side attractions include riverboat and mining tours. (☎573-468-3166. Caverns open daily Mar. 9am-5pm; Apr. and Sept. 9am-6pm; May-June 9am-7pm; July-Labor Day 8:30am-7:30pm; Nov.-Dec. 9am-4pm. Tours every 30min. $14, ages 5-11 $7, under 5 free.) Nearby, the **Meramec Caverns Motel** provides riverfront lodging adjacent to Missouri's favorite caves. (☎537-468-4215. Open Apr.-Oct. Singles $42; doubles $55.) The **Meramec Caverns Campground** has comfortable, shaded sites along the river, at the mouth of the caverns. Amenities include restrooms and showers, a supply store, a concession stand, and canoe and raft rentals. (☎573-468-3166. Open Apr.-Oct. Sites $12, with hookup $16.)

 RIVERSIDE REPTILE RANCH
Near Meramec Caverns.

Don't miss one of Missouri's best attractions, the best thing ever to happen to a petting zoo. Here you can stroke a snake, test the jaw strength of baby alligators with your finger, get wrapped up in a Burmese python, or just watch the scaly creatures from behind glass—just keep an eye out for Zeus, the giant American alligator who paddles the grounds. (☎573-927-6253. Open daily 10am-7pm. $6, ages 5-12 $5, under 5 free.)

 JESSE JAMES WAX MUSEUM
Along old Rte. 66 just south of the caverns.

This memorial to the legendary bandit explores such questions as whether James was killed by his cousin in 1882, or whether the man who resurfaced in Stanton claiming to be James 70 years later was the robber. (☎573-927-5233. Open June-Aug. daily 9am-6pm; Sept.-Oct. and Apr.-May Sa-Su 9am-5pm. $6, ages 5-11 $2.50, under 5 free.)

THE ROAD TO LEASBURG. From Stanton, follow Rte. 66 into **Sullivan,** crossing right onto Rte. 185. Motels and gas stations cluster along the west side, while fast-food restaurants assemble to the east. To continue on Rte. 66, follow **Elmont St.** right, then turn left at the stop sign as you enter town. Follow the outer road south from Sullivan to reach the next small towns; **Bourbon** is 5¼ mi. south of Sullivan and 5½ mi. later is **Leasburg.**

LEASBURG

Located in **Onondaga Caves State Park,** just south of Leasburg, the Onondaga Caves feature an active river and spring. Camping is permitted in the park at the recently renovated **Onondaga Caves Campgrounds,** which offer showers, restrooms, laundry, and general store facilities. (Head left off Rte. 66 at the Route 66 Inn, through Leasburg, following signs for the caves. ☎573-345-6576. Visitors Center open daily 10am-4pm. Cave tours Mar.-Oct. daily 9am-5pm. $9, ages 13-19 $7, ages 6-12 $5, under 6 free. Sites $7, with hookup $12. Call for availability and opening dates.)

At the turn-off for the caves, the **Route 66 Inn,** 247 Rte. (Rte. 66), actually a restaurant, is another incarnation of the Rte. 66 bar featuring mozzarella sticks and burgers. (☎573-245-6683. Open M-Th noon-1am, F-Sa noon-1:30am, Su 1pm-1am.) On busy nights, it seems like every car in town pulls up in front of homey **Ike's Chat'n'Chew,** 2344 Rte. H. (☎573-245-6268. Steak, potatoes, and salad $8. Open daily 8am-6pm.) Continue on Rte. 66 to Cuba, 5½ mi. beyond the Leasburg turn-off.

CUBA. Missouri Hick Barbecue, 913 E. Washington St., at the entrance to Cuba, is decorated with saddles and farm equipment and provides welcome break from diners and highway fare. (☎573-885-6791. Open summer Su-Th 11am-9pm, F-Sa 11am-10pm; winter Su-Th 11am-8pm, F-Sa 11am-9pm.) Nearby, the **Wagon Wheel Motel,** 901 E. Washington St., offers deals almost as good as when the motel opened in 1934. (☎573-885-3411. Singles $13-16; doubles $18.)

ST. JAMES WINERY   540 Sidney St.
Roughly 14 mi. south of Cuba, turn right on Jefferson St. (Rte. 68) and then right onto Sidney St.

The area south of Cuba is traditionally grape country, and the roadside is lined with winery advertisements. Just north of St. James, the St. James Winery offers 15min. tours, wine samples every day, and excellent grape juice for drivers. (☎800-280-9463. Open daily 11am-4pm. Free.)

APPROACHING ROLLA
In St. James, head right at **Jefferson St. (Rte. 68)**, crossing I-44. Go west on the outer road, and 8½ mi. later, turn left on **Bishop Ave. (U.S. 63)** into Rolla.

ROLLA

Touted as Missouri's "center of everything," Rolla is home to classic diners, quirky motels, and a university, and is convenient to outdoor attractions. Rolla's stretch of Rte. 66 is truly unique; few other places can stretch from Stonehenge at one end of town to the Totem Pole Trading Post at the other.

(VITAL STATS)

Population: 16,000

Visitor Info: Rolla Chamber of Commerce & Visitors Center, 1301 Kingshighway St. (☎573-364-3577; www.rollachamber.org). Open M-F 8am-5pm, Sa 9am-3pm; May-Oct. also Su 1-5pm.

Internet Access: Rolla Public Library, 900 Pine St. (☎573-364-2604). Open M-Th 9am-9pm, F-Sa 9am-5pm, Su 1:30-5pm.

Post Office: 501 W. 8th St. (☎573-364-1775). Open M-F 7:45am-5:15pm, Sa 8:30am-12:30pm. **Postal Code:** 65401.

GETTING AROUND. Rte. 66 cuts through town on **U.S. 63,** which is known as **Bishop Ave.** and runs north-south. Numbered streets run east-west through downtown, starting at Bishop Ave. To reach downtown, head east on **10th St.** or south on **Pine St.,** which runs parallel to Bishop Ave. a few blocks to the east. **Kingshighway St.** heads west from U.S. 63, becoming **Martin Springs Dr.** in the west and running parallel to **I-44.**

SIGHTS. Be sure to check out the **Route 66 Nostalgia Gift Shop,** 12601 Bishop Ave., just in case you've still got holes in your 66 memorabilia collection. The adjoining **Route 66 Motors** showcases old cars, most available for purchase. (☎573-265-5200. Open M-Sa 9am-5pm.) Compare your wheels to 66 roadsters of the past at **Memoryville USA,** 220 Bishop Ave., an antique automobile restoration shop and museum. Memoryville has a reputation for giving new life to outdated cars; an array of shiny, polished, classics, enough to delight any true auto fan, is on display in the museum. (☎573-364-1810. Museum open M-F 9am-6pm, Sa-Su 9am-5:30pm. Shop open daily 9am-4:30pm. $3.50, seniors $3, ages 6-12 $1.50.) For a break from the automobile, head over to the **Stonehenge Replica,** at 14th St. and Bishop Ave., on the campus of the University of Missouri at Rolla. Approximately 160 tons of granite went into the giant rock structure. It's smaller than the original but includes features the original lacked, such as an opening through which the North Star can be seen. (☎573-341-4111. Open daily dawn-dusk. Free.) Leaving Rolla, don't miss the historic **Totem Pole Trading Post,** 1413 Martin Springs Dr. A well-known Rte. 66 landmark, the Trading Post has been offering gas and souvenirs since 1933. (☎573-364-3519. Open daily 7:30am-9pm.)

FOOD & ACCOMMODATIONS. At **Granny's Saw Mill,** at the corner of 9th and Pine St., let Granny fill you up with giant pancakes ($1.50) or a ½ lb. burger ($3.50). On Saturdays, a hearty breakfast buffet ($5.50) is also offered. (☎573-364-8383. Open M-F 5am-2pm, Sa 5am-1:30pm.) A movie theater-turned-restaurant, the **All Star Sports Bar and Grill,** 1100 N. Pine St., serves satisfying portions of appetizers, pastas, and steaks during the day and occasionally hosts live musical acts at night. (In the historic Uptown Theater. ☎573-368-3000. Open M-Sa 11am-1am, Su noon-midnight.) For a night of quirky elegance, **Zeno's Motel and Steakhouse,** 1621 Martin Springs Dr., offers a motel-meets-antique shop atmosphere, with an adjoining steakhouse for excellent in-house dinner. The Scheffer family has been running this establishment since the 1950s. Nearly all the antiques decorating the rooms and lobby are for sale. (☎573-364-1301. Entrees $10-20. Singles from $50; doubles from $62. AAA and AARP discount.)

Motels cluster along **Martin Springs Dr.** on the western edge of Rolla. The rock bottom rates, however, are on the south side of the city at **Budget Deluxe Motel,** 1908 N. Bishop Ave., which offers clean, adequate rooms. (☎573-364-4486. Singles from $20; doubles from $31.)

LEAVING ROLLA
Veer southwest off of **Kingshighway St.** onto **Martin Spring Dr.,** which runs parallel to I-44.

THE ROAD TO ST. ROBERT

Eight miles south of Rolla on Rte. 66, **Vernelle's Motel** offers small, dark, and clean wood-panelled rooms straight out of the glory days of Rte. 66. All rooms have A/C and cable TV. (☎573-762-2798. Singles from $25; doubles from $35).

Although the road becomes narrow and relatively unmarked, follow its curves across the one-lane bridge and through the backwoods of ramshackle log cabins. For one more check on the list of Missouri Caves, the **Onyx Mountain Caves** are 12 mi. south of Rolla, in Newburg. (Cross I-44 and head north on the N. Outer Rd. 1 mi. from I-44 Exit 169. ☎573-762-3341. Open summer daily 8am-6pm; spring and fall daily 8am-5pm; winter Su and Th-Sa 9am-4pm. $5.75, ages 5-12 $3.75.) Continuing south, the route climbs through the Ozark hamlets of **Doolitle,** named for WWII ace Jimmy Doolittle, and **Devil's Elbow,** where bridges cross the Big Piney River and the highway winds over hills and below river bluffs. Just before the bridge over the Big Piney River, about 20 mi. southwest of Rolla, head left across the highway and detour over the creek and steel-trussed bridge. In the afternoon, the light on the rear canyon wall is breathtaking. Just over 2 mi. after detouring through Devil's Elbow, rejoin the highway, heading left, and follow it into **St. Robert** and **Waynesville.**

ST. ROBERT. Small St. Robert is home to several roadside classics. **Jack's Route 66 Diner,** 126 St. Robert Blvd., serves up sandwiches ($3-5), dinner plates ($3), and shakes ($3) from a blinding chrome and red pleather interior. (☎573-336-8989. Open daily 6am-midnight.) The **Sweetwater BBQ,** 14076 Rte. Z, makes mouthwatering BBQ from the small cabin on a hill at the northeastern entrance to St. Robert—a fantastic break from diner food. (Take Exit 163 from I-44 and head east on S. Outer Rd. ☎573-336-8830. Takeout available. Open daily 11am-8pm.) The **Deville Motor Inn,** 461 Old Rte. 66, is another Rte. 66 standard with a restaurant, pool, and clean cinderblock rooms. (☎573-336-3113. Singles from $45; doubles from $48.)

APPROACHING LEBANON

Stay on Rte. 66 continuing through to **Waynesville,** passing over I-44 and veering left at the Y on the west edge of town. Follow the south outer road from Exit 153, steering right on Rte. 17 to the intersection with Rte. P and Rte. NN. 2 mi. later, head right to **Laquey** on P, then left at the Y in town onto Rte. AA.

Head right at Rte. AB; **Hazelgreen** is 9 mi. down the road, and **Sleeper** beyond that. At the junction with Rte. F, 13 mi. later, turn north, crossing I-44, and heading into **Lebanon.**

LEBANON. For a change from burgers, swing by **Goss's Meats and Deli,** at the corner of Adams and Commercial St. in the older part of Lebanon. Fresh deli meats, made-to-order sandwiches, and gourmet deli products are all available. (☎417-588-9300. Open M-F 8am-6pm, Sa 8am-5pm.) One of the best lodging options on this stretch of road is the **Munger Moss Motel,** a holdout from the glory days of the old road. Pass through at night, and the glowing red, blue, yellow and green blinking sign beckons siren-like for drivers to wash up on her shores. Each pleasantly furnished room has hand-quilted bedspreads, and many are decorated in Rte. 66 memorabilia, all for the cost of your standard roadside budget motel. The gift shop also has a great selection of tasteful Rte. 66 memorabilia. (☎417-532-3111. Call ahead for reservations. Singles from $40; doubles from $47.)

APPROACHING SPRINGFIELD

Leaving Lebanon, turn right at the junction with **Rte. W,** then left onto the outer road. 13 mi. later, in **Phillipsburg,** cross to the south side of the interstate, following **Rte. CC** south. Veer right in **Marshfield,** 12 mi. later, then jog left onto **Rte. OO.** Continue across the junction with Rte. B on the way to Springfield.

SPRINGFIELD

The largest city in southern Missouri, and hometown of Brad Pitt and golfer Payne Stewart, grows out of the surrounding cattle fields. As Rte. 66 enters town from the northeast, the stretch of fast-food restaurants, cheap motels, and gas stations are in stark contrast to the old-time heart of downtown, where the ghost of Wild Bill Hickock seems as hearty as the multiplicity of coffee shops, swanky bars, and hip restaurants.

GETTING AROUND

Downtown Springfield is just south of I-44. **U.S. 160** is known as **S. Campbell Ave.** in the city; running north-south, this is one of Springfield's main thoroughfares. Other major streets include **Sunshine St.,** which is labeled E. Sunshine St. or W. Sunshine St. depending on its direction from Cam-

VITAL STATS

Population: 150,000

Visitor Info: Springfield Convention and Visitors Bureau, 815 St. Louis St. (☎800-678-8767; www.springfieldmo.org). Open M-F 8am-5pm.

Internet Access: Springfield-Greene County Library Center, 4653 S. Campbell St. (☎417-874-8110). Open M-Sa 8am-9pm, Su 1-5pm.

Post Office: 500 W. Chestnut Expwy. (☎417-864-0199). Open M-F 7:30am-5:30pm. **Postal Code:** 65801.

bell Ave., and the **Chestnut Expwy.,** which runs east-west north of Sunshine St. Springfield has abundant on-street **parking,** and free public lots.

🎮 SIGHTS

More than just retail, **Bass Pro Shops,** 1935 S. Campbell Ave., is an outdoorsman's amusement park—indoors. The store includes acres of merchandise, plus an aquarium, a firing range, a four-story waterfall, a restaurant, an espresso bar, a museum, and its own McDonalds. (☎417-887-7334. Open M-Sa 7am-10pm, Su 9am-6pm.) Although the owners of Bass Pro Outlets donated the land, **Wonders of Wildlife, the American National Fish and Wildlife Museum,** 500 W. Sunshine St., is not affiliated with the store. The museum features live animals swimming below and flying overhead, with exhibits that emphasize conservation. (☎888-521-9497; www.wondersofwildlife.org. Open daily 9am-6pm. $11.25, children $7.25.)

Just north of Springfield, **Fantastic Caverns,** 4872 N. FR 125, can be toured by jeep-drawn tram. (☎417-833-2010; www.fantasticcaverns.com. Open daily 8am-dusk. $17, ages 6-12 $9.50, under 6 free.) Trade in your old paperbacks at the **Well-Fed Head,** 331 S. Campbell Ave., which buys, sells, and trades books, including a small amount of foreign language literature. (☎417-832-9333. Open M-Sa 11am-9pm, Su 11am-6pm.)

🍴🍷 FOOD & NIGHTLIFE

Springfield's streets are studded with quirky coffeehouses, hearty cafes, and a few laid-back bars.

Casper's, 600 W. Walnut St. (☎417-866-9750). Don't be deceived by the bland exterior—inside Casper's chili-haven is a riot of blue, orange, and most colors in between. The same cook has been dishing out chili ($2.50-3) since 1966. Open Sept.-May M-F 10:30am-4pm; closed June-Aug.

South Avenue Pizza and The Bar Next Door, 305-307 South Ave. (☎417-831-5551). Long and lanky bar and restaurant on downtown's main strip, featuring pizza ($10-20) and abundant veggie options. Live music Tu-Sa. Restaurant open M-Th 11am-10pm, F 11am-11pm, Sa noon-11pm. Bar open Tu-Sa until 1:30am, M until 10pm.

Rasta Grill, 319 W. Walnut St. (☎417-831-7221). Blue walls and fish create an underwater vibe for unusual, excellent Caribbean cuisine. Thai Chicken Burrito $7. Smoothies $3.50. Entrees, with vegetarian options $7-9. Open M-Th 11am-10pm, F-Sa 11am-1am.

Mudhouse Downtown Coffeehouse, 323B S. Ave. (☎417-832-1720). They roast their own beans (espresso $1.50), throw their own ceramics, and make smoothies ($3) and sandwiches ($5). Live music F. Open M-F 7am-midnight, Su 8:30am-11pm.

Magic Beans Coffee and Gallery, 1211 E. Cherry St. (☎417-869-1968). At this hip establishment, chill to live music, swap moves over the occasional chess set, or groove into the wee hours. Open daily 5pm-3am.

Nonna's Italian American Cafe, 306 South Ave. (☎417-831-1222). Cheery yellow, art-bedecked walls add to the family atmosphere of this bistro. Entrees $6-7. Open daily 11am-4:30pm.

Joe's Repair Shop and Saloon, 2251 E. Kearney St. (☎417-862-7100). An old-style saloon updated with a "shoe tree" (leave a pair if you're feeling generous), free pool, karaoke, and the famed "wall-eye Wednesday." Full bar. Appetizers $4. Sandwiches $7. Open M-Sa 11am-1:30am, Su 11am-midnight.

🏨 ACCOMMODATIONS

The chocolate chip cookies next to each bed sum up the decadence of the Victorian **Walnut St. Inn,** 900 E. Walnut St., located in Springfield's historic district. (☎417-864-6346. Rooms $89-169.) Just pretend not to see the blue hallmark of America's biggest chain motel at the **Rail Haven Best Western,** 203 S. Glenstone Ave.; this well-kept motel has ties to the motor courts of Old 66. (☎417-866-1963. Singles from $39; doubles from $44.) Another well-priced option, the **Marigold Inn,** 2006 S. Glenstone, has quirky lobby decorations and wood furnishings in each room. (☎866-881-2833. Singles from $44; doubles from $52.) On the western edge of town, the **Springfield KOA Kampground,** 5775 W. Farm Rd. 140, has over 60 sites, some with full hookup. (☎800-562-1228 or 417-831-3645. Sites from $18, with hookup from $23; cabins $40-50.)

LEAVING SPRINGFIELD
Leave Springfield on **W. Chestnut Expwy.** This road becomes **Rte. 266;** follow it westward.

THE ROAD TO CARTHAGE. The road from Springfield south to Carthage is one of the most untouched stretches of Missouri's Rte. 66; decrepit stone buildings with swinging Rte. 66 signs stand among functioning cattle ranches. There are few points of interest before the Jasper County Courthouse of Carthage rises out of the cattlefields. Follow Rte. 266 out of Springfield, passing through **Halltown,** 16 mi. down the road, and follow Rte. 66 straight where Rte. 96 diverges. Two miles later, cross Rte. 96 and head right over the creek and bridge through **Spencer,** turning left when the back road crosses Rte. 96.

APPROACHING CARTHAGE
Follow **Rte. 66/96** until it becomes **Central Ave.** Turn left on **Main St.** and continue to Courthouse Sq.

CARTHAGE

Miles of cattle and little else give way to the chateau-like turrets of the Jasper County Courthouse in elegant but diminutive Carthage. Cathaginians proudly trace their history parallel to the rise and fall, and rise again, of ancient Carthage, and pride themselves on being emblematic of Missouri's contentious position in the Civil War—Carthage was the site of the very first battle.

VITAL STATS

Population: 13,000

Visitor Info: Chamber of Commerce, 107 E. 3rd St. (☎417-358-2373; www.visit-carthage.com). Open M-F 8:30am-5pm.

Internet Access: Carthage Public Library, 612 S. Garrison Ave. (☎417-237-7040), at the corner of 7th St. Open M-W 9am-8pm, Th-F 9am-6pm, Sa 9am-4pm.

Post Office: 226 W. 3rd St. (☎417-358-2307). Open M-F 8am-4:40pm, Sa 8:30am-noon. **Postal Code:** 64836.

GETTING AROUND. Rte. 66/96 comes into Carthage from the east and runs just north of downtown as **Central Ave.** Numbered streets, starting with **2nd St.** one block south of Central Ave., run east-west through the western part of town. In the eastern section, east-west streets take the names of trees; **Oak St.** is two blocks south of Central Ave. A main north-south drag, **Rte. 571** is known as **Garrison Ave.** Carthage has on-street **parking** and public lots throughout town.

SIGHTS. Downtown Carthage centers on the spired, castle-like **Jasper County Courthouse.** Down the street at the **Carthage Civil War Museum,** 205 Grant St., army figurines and mannequins portray Carthage's role in Missouri politics and the first battle of the Civil War. (☎417-237-7060. Open M-Sa 8:30am-5pm, Su 1-5pm. Free.) More local history is on display at **Kendrick Place,** at Garrison Ave. and Rte. V, north of town, where period-garbed guides take you through a pioneer home dating from the 1850s, outlining Carthage history, the role of the town in the Civil War, and life during the late 1800s. (☎417-358-0636. Open Mar.-Dec. Tu-Sa 10am-5pm; Jan.-Feb. until 4pm. Free.)

FOOD & NIGHTLIFE. A spacious 50s-style diner, pink-Cadillac booths included, the **Carthage Deli,** 301 S. Main St., features diner favorites as well as Italian sodas and espresso drinks. (☎417-358-8820. Sandwiches $4. Open M-F 7am-5pm, Sa 8am-4pm.) **Babe's Drive-Thru,** 1220 Oak St. at the corner of Baker St., still abides by the tradition of fresh meat delivered every day, old-style shakes, hand-cut onion rings, and the famed "Chubby Cheese" double cheeseburger. (☎417-358-0003. Open M-Sa 10am-9pm, Su 11am-7pm.) Leather booths, pool tables, and an overhead flying circus make **Jim's Place,** 325 E. 4th St., the hippest nightspot around, with a full bar, and munchie menu. (☎417-358-8549. Appetizers $5. Burgers $2. Pizza $5. Live music on weekends. Open M-Sa 8am-1:30am. Cash only.) The relaxed **Stone's Throw Dinner Theater,** 796 S. Stone Ln. (Rte. 66), presents comedies, mysteries, and dramas. (☎417-358-9665. Hours vary by show; call ahead. $20, seniors $18, students and children $16.)

ACCOMMODATIONS. At the **Grand Avenue B&B,** 1615 Grand Ave., each room is themed according to a different 19th-century author; lounge in the Mark Twain room, or recline in the Louisa May Alcott. (☎888-380-6786. Breakfast included. Rooms $79-$99.) The **Best Budget Inn,** 13011 Rte. 96, offers comfy rooms overlooking a mini-lake on the eastern entrance to Carthage. (☎417-358-6911. Rooms from $45.) The **KOA Campground,** 5775 W. Farm Rd. 140, offers guests a pool, laundry facilities, telephones, a softball field, a basketball court, and grills. (☎800-562-1228 or 417-831-3645. Sites $18-$30; cabins $33-50.)

LEAVING CARTHAGE
From **Central Ave.,** turn left on **Garrison Ave.,** then right on **Oak St.,** Bear left at the Y on the western edge of town.

JOPLIN. Joplin is noted for its **Thomas Hart Benton mural** in the Municipal Building at 3rd and Broadway. The **Joplin Museum Complex,** in Schifferdecker Park at the corner of Old Rte. 66 and Schifferdecker Ave., contains a glorified rock collection and a salute to the area's mining past. (☎417-623-1180. Open Su 2-5pm, Tu 10am-7pm, W-Sa 10am-5pm. $2.) The **Red Onion Cafe,** at the corner of 4th and Virginia St., is an island in the sea of fast food. (☎417-623-1004. Salads $5-7. Gourmet sandwiches $5-8. Open M-Th 11am-8pm, F-Sa 11am-9pm.) **Wok & Roll,** at 7th and Wall St., in and old Rte. 66 gas station, has been converted into the classiest of the Chinese buffets lining the streets. (☎417-782-6400. Lunch buffet $6. Dinner buffet $8. Open daily 11am-9pm.)

The stretch from Joplin to Afton will take you over three states in record time. Consequently, many area businesses have toll-free numbers to keep their customers from paying out of state long-distance charges.

Welcome To KANSAS

THE ROAD THROUGH KANSAS
Follow 7th St. out of Joplin and head right at the "Rte. 66 Next Right" sign onto an ancient alignment featuring white Rte. 66 shields on the narrow stretches of concrete. Be careful on the rises over railroad tracks, where oncoming traffic is difficult to see. Where bustling I-44 heads straight from Missouri to Oklahoma, Rte. 66 pays a mere 14 mi. tribute to southeastern Kansas. **Galena** and **Baxter Springs,** the two principle Kansas stops along the route, were once known for their cattle; Baxter Springs was in fact "The First Cow Town in the West." After the cattle trade declined, Kansas's rich mineral deposits kept them afloat, helping the area produce more than half the world's industrial metals in the early 20th century.

APPROACHING GALENA
Coming from the old alignment, head left at the T-intersection with **Main St.,** then turn right on **7th St.**

GALENA. The most notable meal option in town is the **Up in Smoke BBQ,** 418 Main St. This small BBQ restaurant, located in an old Rte. 66 filling station, uses only home-prepared ingredients and claims the **world's only train locomotive BBQ smoker.** (☎620-783-5106. Open M-W 11am-6pm, Th-Sa 11am-7pm.) The surprisingly comfortable **Galena Motel,** 918 E. 7th St., rents well-furnished rooms each with carpeting, microwave, refrigerator, TV, A/C and heating. (☎620-783-5428. Singles from $35; doubles from $45. Cash only.)

EISLER BROS. OLD RIVERTON STORE
In Riverton. From Galena, follow 7th St. west 3 mi.
Eisler Bros. is located in a neat, cheery, red and white roadside shack right along Historic Rte. 66 in Riverton. Part deli, part grocery store, part Rte. 66 souvenir shop, Eisler Bros. has been serving a little bit of everything from knickknacks to fresh produce since 1925. (☎620-848-3330. Open M-Th 7:30am-8pm, F-Sa 7:30am-9pm, Su 12:30-7pm.)

APPROACHING BAXTER SPRINGS
Cross over at the junction with Rte. 400, heading straight and then the left, passing an old white trussed bridge along the way. Entering town, veer left, then right on **Aron Ln.,** which turns immediately into **Military Ave.**

LITTLE BRICK INN & CAFE ON THE ROUTE
1101 Military Ave.
In Baxter Springs. Veer left after the junction with Rte. 400, passing a white trussed bridge. In town, turn right on Aron Ln. which turns into Military Ave.

Located in the Baxter National Bank, which was once robbed by Jesse James, the **Cafe on the Route** is a long-standing Rte. 66 eatery, with upscale dining and downscaled prices, featuring salads ($6), pasta ($6-8), and meat entrees ($8-14). **The Little Brick Inn,** upstairs, offers spacious rooms, each with private bath and TV. (☎877-223-3466. Restaurant open M-Th 11am-2:30pm and 4-8pm, F-Sa 11am-2:30pm and 4-8:30pm, Su 11am-2pm. Rooms $50-80. Breakfast included.)

Welcome To OKLAHOMA

THE ROAD TO MIAMI. Leaving town, to stay faithful to the old alignment, head left on **Roberts,** swinging right to detour behind the businesses and then merging left again onto **U.S. 69.** Heading into Oklahoma, Rte. 66 joins U.S. 69. Go through **Quapaw,** 4 mi. over the border, and then pass into **Commerce,** Mickey Mantle's hometown. Locals will be happy to point out the little house where Mickey, the Commerce Comet, grew up.

MIAMI. Don't blow your cover by mispronouncing Miami, 11½ mi. from Commerce. Properly said, it's "My-AM-uh." Check out **Waylan's Ku-Ku Hamburgers,** 915 N. Main St. The remnants of a 1960s chain, Waylan's yellow and green cuckoos are the last of their breed and still serve up burgers ($2-4) as well shakes, malts, and sundaes. (Open M-Th 10am-11pm, F-Sa 10am-midnight.) Locals recommend **Milagros Mexican Restaurant,** 103 E. Central St. Enter the den of fajitas ($9) and Mexican specialties ($5.50) via the office lobby next door. (Open M-Sa 11am-8:30pm.)

THE ROAD TO VINITA. At the west end of Miami, turn south on U.S. 69, continuing straight through Narcissa, 6 mi. later. There is little to stop for in **Afton,** 6½ mi. later, although a decent night's sleep can be had at the **Grand Lake Country Inn Motel,** 21751 S. U.S. 69 (Rte. 66), which includes friendly management, and in-room microwaves, fridges, and coffeemakers. (☎918-257-8313. Singles $33.) Continue on U.S. 69 into Vinita.

ROUTE 66

VINITA

Entering Vinita from the north, the first major attraction is the **Will Rogers Rodeo Grounds** to the left. Instead of following Rte. 66 all the way through town, be sure to stop by the **World's Largest McDonalds.** Spanning the Will Rogers Expressway, the giant glass paean to fast food includes McMeeting rooms, McGiftshops, and McBathrooms, in addition to all your McFood needs. (Head left by the Rodeo and follow the road for about ½ mi. Turn right just before the overpass. ☎918-256-5571. Open daily 5:30am-midnight.)

The **Clanton Cafe,** 319 E. Illinois St., has offered more unique meal options since 1927, including Vinita's famed "Calf Fries" (cow testicles; $5), as well as tamer cow-part options. (☎918-256-9053. Burgers $2-4. Open M-F 5:30am-8pm, Su 11am-2pm.) The **Starlight Bakery & Cafe,** 107 W. Canadian St., with Starbucks coffee and T.J. Cinnamon's sticky buns ($1.50), and Boar's Head Meats might not be exactly home-grown, but the sandwiches, from roasted veggie and mozzarella ($5) to maple glazed honey ham ($5), speak for themselves. (☎918-256-4306. Open M-Sa 6:30am-2pm, Su 8am-2pm.) Each room in **Deward & Pauline's Motel** has (fake) flowers on the table, as well as a microwave, fridge, coffeemaker, and cable TV. (☎918-256-6492. Singles from $28; doubles from $34.)

THE ROAD TO CLAREMORE

In the heart of downtown Vinita, head left on **Wilson St.** Leave town on Rte. 66, following it southwest through the mini-town of **White Oak.** At the northern edge of **Chelsea,** 11 mi. beyond White Oak, the **Heartland Motel,** 325 Layton St. (Rte. 66), attached to the owner's home, has its own homey look in peach and green decor. (☎918-789-3443. Singles from $28; doubles from $39.)

⊙ TOTEM POLE PARK

9 mi. from Chelsea, in Foyil. Turn east at the northern end of town on Rte. 28A, following the road for approximately 4 mi. to get to the park.

One of the stranger attractions along the Oklahoma stretch, artist Ed Galloway's masterpiece in the middle of the prairie is a meadow of brightly colored totem poles, including the **world's largest totem pole,** at 90 ft., birdbaths, and an 11-sided **"Fiddle House"** (it used to hold over 300 fiddles) that now serves as the museum and Visitors Center. (☎918-342-9149. Open daily 11am-3pm. Free.)

CLAREMORE

What Abe Lincoln is to Illinois, cowboy/entertainer Will Rogers is to Oklahoma, and Claremore is command central of Rogers mania. The Will Rogers Memorial Museum sits on Will Rogers Blvd., next to Rogers State University, while Will Rogers sculptures and memorials line the streets. The town is of sufficient size to find any necessities or luxuries, and includes a veritable oasis of antique stores lining Will Rogers Blvd., all the while maintaining its early Sooner look.

VITAL STATS

Population: 16,000

Visitor Info: Claremore Convention and Visitors Bureau, 419 W. Will Rogers Blvd. (☎918-341-8688; www.claremore.org). Open M-F 8:30am-5pm.

Internet Access: Will Rogers Library, 1515 N. Florence St. (☎918-341-1564). Open M-Tu 9:30am-8pm, W-Th 9:30am-6pm, F-Sa 9:30am-5pm.

Post Office: 400 W. 9th St. (☎918-343-8917). Open M-F 8am-5pm, Sa 9am-noon. **Postal Code:** 74017.

⌐ GETTING AROUND. Rte. 65 runs northeast-southwest through Claremore as **Lynn Riggs Blvd.,** and streets are arranged in an easily navigable grid system south of Rte. 65. Numbered streets run roughly east-west through the city, while avenues run north-south. **Will Rogers Blvd.,** one of the city's major streets, runs one block southwest of 4th St. **Parking** is not generally a problem in downtown Claremore.

◙ SIGHTS. Will Rogers fanfare is everywhere in Claremore, and if he was merely a name when you entered town, he'll be a downright friend when you leave. At the **Will Rogers Memorial Museum,** 1720 W. Will Rogers Blvd., the Will Rogers statue out front watches over Claremore from high on the hill to the northeast of town. Inside, constant video reels and a barrage of paintings, clippings, and photographs pay homage to the life of Oklahoma's favorite son. (☎800-324-9455. Open daily 8am-5pm. Suggested donation.) At the **Will Rogers Birthplace Ranch,** 2 mi. east of Oologah, the white log cabin where Will Rogers grew up has been largely preserved. The view from atop the hill remains quietly breathtaking, peopled only with the horses, goats, and even a peacock that wander the grounds. (Head northwest on Will Rogers Blvd. and take Rte. 88 12 mi. north toward Oologah. ☎918-275-4201. Open daily dawn-dusk. Suggested donation.) If you haven't found yourself spelling out Oklahoma in song yet, a visit to the **Lynn Riggs Memorial,** 121 N. Weenonah St., will give you a kickstart. Riggs wrote **Green Grow the Lilacs,** upon which Rogers and Hammerstein based their smash hit *Oklahoma!* (☎918-627-2716. Open M-F 9am-noon and 1-4pm. Free.) The **J.M. Davis Arms & Historical Museum,** 333 N. Lynn Riggs Blvd., features an impressive collection of things that kill, from guns to samurai swords to fearsome longhorn horns. The museum also features Native American artifacts and varieties of artwork, which do not kill. (☎918-341-5707. Open M-Sa 8:30am-5pm, Su 1-5pm. Free.)

FOOD & ACCOMMODATIONS.
Unusual variety characterizes the cooking at the **Hammett House,** 1616 W. Will Rogers Blvd. Pies ($3) come in flavors like Lemon Pecan and Sour Cream Raisin, and their lamb and turkey fries (cousins to calf fries) have a thankful resemblance to chicken. (☎918-341-7333. Sandwiches and salads $6. Entrees $10-20. Open Tu-Sa 11am-9pm.) On the western outskirts of town, the **Big Bopper 1950s Ice Cream Shop,** 774½ S. Lynn Riggs Blvd., pays homage to the poodle-skirt decade with a selection of Edy's Ice Cream (single scoop $1.75), and pie in winter. (Open summer M-Sa 11am-10pm; winter Tu-Sa 1-9pm.)

The **Claremore Motor Inn,** 1709 N. Lynn Riggs Blvd., has well-kept rooms. (☎918-342-4545. Singles from $35; doubles from $45.) On the way to the Will Rogers Birthplace Ranch, **Hawthorn Bluff Campground,** 9¾ mi. north of Claremore, is minimally developed, with swimming and basic sites. (☎918-443-2319. Sites $14, with electricity $18.)

LEAVING CLAREMORE
Follow **Will Rogers Blvd.** west to **Rte. 66,** turn left, and continue west on Rte. 66.

 In Catoosa, about 11 mi. beyond Claremore, the main attraction is a **giant blue whale,** once a water-slide and now merely a picnic area and roadside gawking point.

APPROACHING TULSA
Just past Catoosa, head right on **Ford Ave.** 1 mi. past **Spunky Creek,** then left on Cherokee St. at

---

THE LOCAL STORY

JESSE AGAIN!

Legendary outlaw Jesse James was shot to death by Robert Ford in April 1882, the story goes. Or, rather, so the story went until J. Frank Dalton appeared in a Lawton, OK newspaper in 1949. The 100-year-old Dalton claimed to be the outlaw, and that the corpse buried in Kearny, MO was actually a man named Charlie Bigelow. According to Dalton, the shooting of Charlie Bigelow was set up to allow him to escape the law and live in peace.

Dalton's claim was not the first of its kind, and skeptics have continued to try to find holes in his story. Several uncanny pieces of evidence lend credence to Dalton's story. First, the story goes that James was standing on a chair adjusting a painting on the wall when he was shot. Standing over 6 ft., many question that he would have stood on a chair. Second, James's mother claimed not to know the corpse until she was taken aside by his acquaintances, after which she identified the body as her son. Also, some years after the James shooting, Jesse's brother Frank James went into business with Robert Ford, his brother's supposed murderer. Further, Dalton's body had many scars that James's was said to have. Dalton said that members of his gang had agreed not to divulge the secret until they were 100 years old. Dalton sent a reporter to find his gang's former cook. The cook refused to speak to Dalton, and so the reporter returned empty-handed. Dalton said he had just been testing the reporter, and gave him a password. When the reporter told the cook, he came immediately. Although skeptics have forensic evidence indicating that the body buried in Kearny is James's, before Dalton's death at 103 he made many "Jesse again" about the legendary killing of Jesse James.

the T-intersection 2 mi. later. Head left under the interstate, continuing about 1 mi. to **11th St.** Turn right on 11th St., following it into and through Tulsa.

TULSA

Though Tulsa is not Oklahoma's political capital, it is in many ways the state's center of commerce and culture. First settled by Creek Native Americans arriving on the Trail of Tears, Tulsa's location on the banks of the Arkansas River made it an optimal trading outpost. Contemporary Tulsa's Art Deco skyscrapers, French villas, Georgian mansions, and large Native American population reflect its varied heritage. Rough-riding motorcyclists and slick oilmen have recently joined the city's cultural mix.

> **(VITAL STATS)**
>
> **Population:** 390,000
>
> **Visitor Info: Tulsa Convention and Visitors Bureau,** 2 W. 2nd St., #150 (☎918-585-1201 or 800-558-3311; www.visittulsa.com). Open M-F 8am-5pm.
>
> **Internet Access: Tulsa Public Library,** 400 Civic Center (☎918 596 7977), at 4th St. and Denver Ave. Open M-Th 9am-9pm, F-Sa 9am-5pm; Sept.-Apr. also Su 1-5pm.
>
> **Post Office:** 333 W. 4th St. (☎918-732-6651). Open M-F 7:30am-5pm. **Postal Code:** 74103.

GETTING AROUND

Tulsa is divided into 1 sq. mi. quadrants. Downtown surrounds **Main St.** (north-south) and **Admiral Blvd.** Numbered east-west streets ascend to the north or south of Admiral Blvd. Named avenues run north-south in alphabetical order; those named after Western cities are west of **Main St.,** while Eastern cities lie to the east.

SIGHTS & FESTIVALS

Perched amid the Osage Hills, 2 mi. northwest of downtown, the **Thomas Gilcrease Museum,** 1400 Gilcrease Museum Rd., houses the world's largest collection of Western American art, as well as 250,000 Native American artifacts and certified original copies of the Articles of Confederation and the Declaration of Independence. (Take the Gilcrease Rd. exit off I-244. ☎918-596-2700; www.gilcrease.org. Open Su and Tu-Sa 10am-4pm.) The **Philbrook Museum,** 2727 S. Rockford Rd., close to downtown, presents tasteful exhibits of Native American and international art in a renovated Italian Renaissance villa. (☎800-324-7941. Open Su 11am-5pm, Tu-W and F-Sa 10am-5pm, Th 10am-8pm. $5, students $3.) In 1964, Oral Roberts had a dream in which God commanded him to "Build me a University," and thus one of Tulsa's biggest tourist attractions was born. The ultramodern spectacle of **Oral Roberts University,** 7777 S. Lewis Ave., rises out of the Oklahoma plains 6 mi. south of downtown, between Lewis and Harvard Ave. Visitors are greeted by the giant "Praying Hands" sculpture at the Canning Entrance. At the **Visitors Center,** in the golden Prayer Tower, tourists experience multimedia presentations on Roberts's life. (☎800-678-8876; www.oru.edu. Open June-Aug. M-Sa 9am-5pm, Su 1-5pm; Sept.-May M-Sa 10am-4:30pm, Su 1-4:30pm.)

Tulsa thrives during the **International Mayfest** (☎918-582-6435) in mid-May. August brings both **Jazz on Greenwood,** which includes ceremonies and concerts at Greenwood Park, 300 N. Greenwood Dr., as well as the **Intertribal Powwow,** at the Tulsa Fairgrounds Pavilion, which attracts Native Americans and thousands of onlookers for a three-day festival of food, crafts, and nightly dance contests. (☎918-744-1113. $5, families $16.)

FOOD

Tulsa has the usual fast-food chains lining I-44, but if it's real food you're after, skip these and head for the more original establishments scattered over town—don't miss **Weber's Root Beer,** a local favorite, in the orange shack on Peoria Ave. Classier food is available downtown, though many restaurants cater to businesspeople and close at 2pm on weekdays and altogether on weekends.

Brook Restaurant, 3401 S. Peoria Ave. (☎918-748-9977), in an old movie theater. Classic Art Deco appeal with a traditional menu of chicken, burgers, and salads ($6-8) complemented by an extensive list of signature martinis ($4.50-5.25). Open M-Sa 11am-1am, Su 11am-11pm.

In the Raw Sushi Bar, 3321 S. Peoria Ave. (☎918-744-1300). Serves fresh sushi in unorthodox combos. Candy roll $7. Rainbow roll $20. Open for lunch Tu-F 11:30am-2pm; dinner Tu-Th 5-10pm, F-Sa 5-11pm.

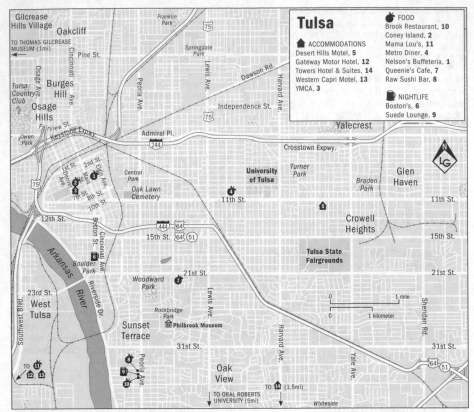

Tulsa

🍎 FOOD
Brook Restaurant, 10
Coney Island, 2
Mama Lou's, 11
Metro Diner, 4
Nelson's Buffeteria, 1
Queenie's Cafe, 7
Raw Sushi Bar, 8

🏠 ACCOMMODATIONS
Desert Hills Motel, 5
Gateway Motor Hotel, 12
Towers Hotel & Suites, 14
Western Capri Motel, 13
YMCA, 3

🍺 NIGHTLIFE
Boston's, 6
Suede Lounge, 9

Metro Diner, 3001 E. 11th St. (☎918-592-2616), on Rte. 66 on the way into town. In an old 66 filling station, the Metro has chrome and 50s kitsch diner appeal, with an *I Love Lucy* theme. Salads, sandwiches, and dinner entrees $4-10. Homemade pies $2. Open Su-Th 6am-10pm, F-Sa 6am-midnight.

Mama Lou's, 5688 W. Skelly Dr. (☎918-445-1700), just off I-44. All-day breakfast. 3 hot cakes, 3 eggs, 3 strips of bacon, and 3 sausage links $4.35. 24hr.

Nelson's Buffeteria, 514 S. Boston Ave. (☎918-584-9969). Has stood by its "It has to be good" motto since 1929, serving up breakfast (2 scrambled eggs, hash browns, biscuit and gravy; $3) and their famed chicken fried steak ($6). Open M-F 6am-2pm.

Coney Island, 123 W. 4th St. (☎918-587-2821). A chain that started on the East Coast and migrated westward but has become a Tulsa tradition. The origi-

nal is on 4th and Cherokee, where they have been serving the little all-beef wieners since 1926. 3 Coneys plus drink $4. Open M-Sa 10am-8pm.

Queenie's Cafe, 1834 Utica Sq. (☎918-749-3481). Excellent sandwiches ($5-6) and baked goods like the Mt. St. Helen's Fudge Torte ($3.50 per slice) and signature Linzer cookies. Open M-F 7am-7pm, Sa 8am-6pm, Su 9am-2pm.

🏠 ACCOMMODATIONS

Decent budget accommodations are scarce downtown. The **Desert Hills Motel,** 5220 E. 11th St. (Rte. 66), offers clean, if dimly lit rooms, although non-smoking options are limited. (☎918-834-3311. Singles from $32.) The best deal in town can be found at the crowded **YMCA,** 515 S. Denver Ave., where a pool, track, weight rooms, racquetball courts, TV, and laundry are all available. (☎918-583-6201. Deposit $20. Rooms $20.) Budget motels are plentiful off I-44 on the east and west sides of town. Designed like a medieval fortress, the **Towers Hotel & Suites,** 3355 E. Skelly Dr., has stone-walled rooms with bathroom chandeliers and whirlpools, for the ultimate luxuries in budget castle living. (☎918-744-4263. Singles from $41; doubles from $51.) Under vintage signs, the **Gateway Motor Hotel,** 5600 W. Skelly Dr., rents recently renovated rooms of varying quality. (☎918-446-6611. Singles $26-33; doubles $35.) Almost 9 mi. out of town on Rte. 66, the vintage sign on the **Western Capri Motel,** 5320 W. Skelly Dr. (☎918-446-2644), advertises clean rooms starting at $30 for singles and $35 for doubles.

◾ NIGHTLIFE

Check out the free *Urban Tulsa*, at local restaurants, and *The Spot* in the Friday *Tulsa World* for up-to-date specs on arts and entertainment. Bars line an area known as **Brookside,** along S. Peoria Ave., and 15th St. east of Peoria. At the **Suede Lounge,** 3340 S. Peoria Ave., a martini lounge/champagne bar, imbibe your lip-smacking libation while watching beautiful people dance to a combination of live music and canned tunes. (☎918-743-0600. 23+. Cover up to $10. Open Tu-Sa 7pm-2am.) A true Tulsan sports bar and grill, **Boston's,** 1738 Boston Ave., serves up everything from chips and salsa ($3) to chicken fried steak ($8), all accompanied by eclectic tunes. On Tuesdays enjoy "Red Dirt" music, a distinctive Oklahoman sound. (☎918-583-9520. Cover $5. Open M-F 11am-2am.)

APPROACHING SAPULPA
Follow **11th St.** southwest. Curve left passing **Denver Ave.,** as 11th St. turns into **12th St.** A quarter mile later, turn left and cross the river. Continue on **Southwest Blvd.** toward Sapulpa. Follow Southwest Blvd. until it becomes **Francoma Rd.** Rte. 66 heading into Sapulpa is also known as **Mission St.;** turn right on Mission St., following the railroad tracks.

SAPULPA. The classic Norma's Diamond Cafe has been reopened as **Diamond Bart's Cafe,** 408 N. Mission St., still featuring breakfast all day and burgers with genuine diner appeal. (☎918-248-4111. Bacon cheeseburger $5. Open Su 9am-3pm, Tu-Th 7am-3pm, F-Sa 7am-9pm.) Farther up Mission St., the blue bubbliness of **HappyBurger,** 215 N.

Mission St., has been leaving customers giddy with grease since the early 1950s. (☎918-224-7750. Burgers $1.50. Open M-F 10:30am-7pm.)

LEAVING SAPULPA
1 mi. after turning onto Mission St. at the northeastern edge of Sapulpa, turn right onto **Dewey St.** Follow Rte. 66 out of Sapulpa through **Kelleyville** and **Bristow.**

RUSS'S RIBS 223 S. Main St.
Along Rte. 66, in Bristow.

Rte. 66 is the main street of Bristow, where life seems relatively unconcerned with the Mother Road. Russ's Ribs, however, displays its Rte. 66 pride with hand-stenciled 66 shields and vintage signs. Sample some of the excellent BBQ, such as the rib sandwich for $3.50. (☎918-367-5656. Open M-Th 10:30am-7pm, F-Sa 10:30am-8pm.)

STROUD. A Rte. 66 classic, the **Rock Cafe,** 114 W. Main St., once the town's Greyhound stop, features multi-ethnic cuisine—crepes ($4.50), and *jagersnitzal* and *spaetzle* ($6.50)—in a stone cabin built from local rock. (☎918-968-3990. Open daily 6am-9pm.) Rooms at the **Skyliner Motel,** 717 W. Main St., beneath the dazzling vintage sign, are clean and cheap. (☎918-968-9556. Singles $35; doubles $45.) Equally nice accommodations can be found across the street at the **Sooner Motel,** 412 N. 8th St. (☎918-968-2595. Singles from $32; doubles from $36.)

GARWOOLY'S GAME ROOM 1023 Broadway
Along Rte. 66, in Davenport.

At the eastern end of town, Garwooly's covers the nightlife bases with a dim, divey, dining area, squeaky clean chrome and tile ice-cream parlor, and adjoining checkered dance floor. (☎918-377-2230. Indian Taco $4. Chicken fried steak $6. Open M-Sa 10am-9pm.)

CHANDLER

Chandler, the next small town along the route, is home to the **Lincoln County Historical Society Museum,** 719 Manvel St., which displays a complete Oklahoma pioneer history, period clothing, a 19th-century buggy, and a flush-toilet outhouse from 1902. (☎405-258-2425. Open M-F 9:30am-4pm, Sa by appointment.)

The fare at **Granny's Country Kitchen** is baked fresh at 1:30am every morning. Tuesdays feature all-you-can-eat spaghetti, and Wednesdays are

ROUTE 66 MAP #5 FROM MAP #4

taco days (both from 4-8pm) for $3.50. (☎405-258-2890. Open M-Sa 6am-8pm, Su 6am-3pm.) The **Lincoln Inn Motel,** 740 E. 1st St., offers snug wooden duplexes, which have faced Rte. 66 for the last 62 years. (☎405-258-0200. Singles $35; doubles $43.)

LEAVING CHANDLER
Rte. 66 becomes **Manvel St.** in Chandler. Follow it as it curves left, heading west toward **Warwick.**

READ RANCH
6 mi. west of Chandler on Rte. 66. Head north at the signs.

Guided trail rides and "Miss Stephanie's" beef brisket create the illusion of Old West living, but if that isn't enough, rise early to feed the petting zoo "varmints" before breakfast. (☎405-258-2999; www.readranch.com. Sites $8, with hookups $16; private bunkhouse with no running water $35. Day-use $5, children $3, under 3 free.)

LUTHER. At the west end of Luther, the **Tres Suenos Vineyards,** 19691 E. Charter Oak Rd., offers free tours and tastings, if your car can handle the miles of red clay gravel roads leading up to it. (☎405-277-7089. Open Th-Sa noon-6pm or by appointment.) Three miles west of Luther on Rte. 66, **DJ's BBQ,** a low-profile old roadhouse with a giant pink and blue pig on top, caters to roadsters and beer-drinkers while priding itself on being suitable for the whole family. (☎405-277-6400. Beer $1.50. Full chicken dinner $6. Open Tu-Th 11am-9pm, F-Sa 11am until the party stops.)

ARCADIA
Arcadia's main attraction is the **Round Barn.** Originally built in 1898, the structure has undergone significant reconstruction, and now the bottom level is a museum, while upstairs is rented for dances and events. But as curator Luther Robinson will point out, it's no place for a square dance. (☎405-396-2761. Open Su and Tu-Sa 10am-5pm.)

The Old West lives in the grey wooden exterior of **Hillbillee's Cafe and Bed & Breakfast,** 208 E. Rte. 66. The Cafe serves three square meals a day, and the B&B features six themed rooms including Doc Holliday's, Shady Lady's, Duke's, Miss Kitty's, and the Bunkhouse, each decorated in Western memorabilia. Although the Old West never had luxury like this, some similarities ring true—while there are private baths and some rooms have TVs, none have telephones. Pool and hot tub are available for guest use in the spring and summer. (☎405-396-2982; www.hillbillees.com. Omelettes $5. Fried chicken dinner for 4 $15. Live music F-Sa. Cafe open M-Th 11am-9pm, F 11am-10pm, Sa 8am-10pm, Su 8am-3pm. Rooms from $65.)

EDMOND

On the way into Edmond on Rte. 66, check out the **Bob Jenni Nature Center,** 4601 E. 2nd St., which has a wide array of creepy crawlers for your viewing pleasure (or dismay), highlighting natural conservation and Oklahoma wildlife. (☎405-340-8105. Open Su and Th-Sa 10am-6pm. $2, children $1.)

Lodging is plentiful in Edmond, and cheaper than the chain motel alternatives in Oklahoma City. **Stafford Inn,** 1809 E. 2nd St., rents elegant brick-walled rooms with jacuzzis and king-size beds. (☎838-730-9162. Continental breakfast included. Singles $44; doubles $49.) **Broadway Suites,** 1305 S. Broadway, provides excellent value with suites or kitchenette units, as well as VCRs for $10 per night and guest laundry. (☎800-200-3486. Kitchenette units $37; suites $75.)

APPROACHING OKLAHOMA CITY
From Edmond on **Rte. 66,** turn left at Broadway, following the **Memorial Rd.** exit, and go left at the stop.

OKLAHOMA CITY

In the late 1800s, Oklahoma's capital was a major transit point on cattle drives from Texas to the north, and today its stockyards are a fascinating window into a world not often seen by outsiders. Lying along the Santa Fe Railroad, the city was swarmed by over 100,000 homesteaders when Oklahoma was opened to settlement in 1889, and it continues to celebrate American westward expansion at one of the nation's largest museums devoted to the West.

VITAL STATS

Population: 506,000

Visitor Info: Oklahoma City Convention and Visitors Bureau, 189 W. Sheridan Ave. (☎405-297-8912 or 800-225-5652; www.okccvb.org), at Robinson St. Open M-F 8:30am-5pm.

Internet Access: Oklahoma City Public Library, 131 Dean McGee Ave. (☎405-231-8650). Open M and W-F 9am-6pm, Tu 9am-9pm, Sa 9am-5pm.

Post Office: 305 NW 5th St. (☎800-275-8777). Open M-F 7am-9pm, Sa 8am-5pm. **Postal Code:** 73102.

GETTING AROUND. Oklahoma City is constructed as a nearly perfect grid. **Santa Fe Ave.** divides the city east-west, and **Reno Ave.** slices it north-south. Cheap and plentiful **parking** makes driving by far the best way to get around. Some areas of the city are unsafe at night; be careful around Sheridan Ave. and Walker St.

SIGHTS. Monday is the time to visit the **Oklahoma City Stockyards,** 2500 Exchange Ave. (☎405-235-8675), the busiest in the world. Cattle auctions (M-Tu) begin at 8am and may last into the night. Visitors enter free via a catwalk over cow pens and cattle herds from the parking lot northeast of the auction house. The auction is as Old West as it gets; beware of tight jeans and big hair.

THE LOCAL STORY

ROADSIDE ORIGINAL

Wanda Queenans the curator of the Route 66 Museum in Elk City, OK.
I grew up listening to stories about Indians. My folks, they had a store on the Cheyenne Reservation. I listened to their stories, and I never thought anything about Indians, but we moved up here from around Carter, OK, and the man I married, you know, he knew some of the Indians around here. And they began bringing us items and we'd buy from 'em. We finally got so much we couldn't sell where we were located. So we would take it out West and sell and then we bought land and built [on Rte. 66] at that time it was just a two-lane road. In the early 1950s, they came in and put another 2-lane south of that one. And then we had the kachinas made by an... Indian, a welder. They stood at our store for over 40 years. We had a lot of parking places. They'd stop and come in the store and buy. We had all kinds of people stop. And then in the middle 70s, I think it was, I-40 was opened up. And I lost my business that way. I sold out gradually. . . I've been with the National Rte. 66 museum for nearly five years now.

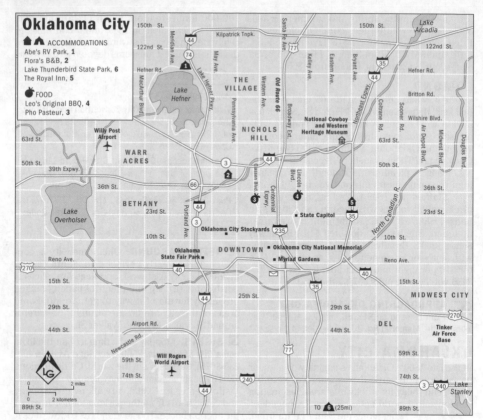

Oklahoma City

🏠🏠 ACCOMMODATIONS
Abe's RV Park, **1**
Flora's B&B, **2**
Lake Thunderbird State Park, **6**
The Royal Inn, **5**

🍎 FOOD
Leo's Original BBQ, **4**
Pho Pasteur, **3**

Plant lovers should make a bee-line for **Myriad Gardens,** 301 W. Reno Ave., with 17 acres of vegetation ranging from desert to rainforest or cross the **Crystal Bridge,** a 70 ft. diameter glass cylinder, perched over a tropical ravine. (☎405-297-3995. Gardens open daily 7am-11pm. Free. Crystal Bridge open M-Sa 9am-6pm, Su noon-6pm. $5, students and seniors $4, ages 4-12 $3.) The **National Cowboy and Western Heritage Museum,** 1700 NE 63rd St., the city's most popular tourist attraction, features an extensive collection of Western art and exhibits on rodeo, Native Americans, and frontier towns. (☎405-478-2250; www.nationalcowboymuseum.org. Open daily 9am-5pm. $8.50, seniors $7, ages 6-12 $4, under 6 free.)

The **Oklahoma City National Memorial,** at 5th and Harvey St., downtown, is a haunting remembrance to the victims of the 1995 bombing of the Murrah Federal Building. Outside lies the Field of Empty Chairs (one for each of the 168 victims), a stone gate, and a reflecting pool. Indoors, a museum tells the story of the bombing through photographs, videos, and testimonials. (☎405-235-3313. Museum open M-Sa 9am-6pm, Su 1-6pm. $7, seniors $6, students $5, under 6 free.)

📲 **ENTERTAINMENT.** Oklahoma City nightlife is growing by leaps and bounds—head to **Bricktown** to get into the thick of it all. **The Bricktown Brewery,** 1 N. Oklahoma St., at Sheridan Ave., brews five beers daily. (☎405-232-2739. Live music Tu and F-Sa 9pm. Upstairs 21+. Cover $5-15 during live music. Open Su-M 11am-10pm, Tu-Th 11am-midnight, F-Sa 11am-1:30am.) **City Walk,** 70 N. Oklahoma St., houses seven clubs. Enjoy the tropical Tequila Park, line dance inside the City Limits, or sing along at Stooge's piano bar. (☎405-232-9255. Cover $5-8. Open Th-Sa 8pm-2am.)

Oklahoma City hosts the **Red Earth Festival** (☎405-427-5228), the country's largest celebration of Native American culture. Early summer finds the annual **Charlie Christian Jazz Festival** entertaining music lovers. Call the Black Liberated Arts Center, Inc. (☎405-424-2552) for more info. The **Cox Business Convention Center** (☎405-236-8666) hosts art fairs and dance competitions. Fall visitors catch the **World Championship Quarter Horse Show** (☎405-948-6800) in mid-November.

⛏ FOOD. Oklahoma City contains the largest cattle market in the US, and beef tops most menus. Most downtown eateries close early in the afternoon after they've served business lunchers. Restaurants with longer hours lie east of town on **Sheridan Ave.** in the Bricktown district and north of downtown along **Classen Blvd.** and **Western Ave.** Asian restaurants congregate around the intersection of Classen and NW 23rd St. **Pho Pasteur**, 2800 N. Classen Blvd., #108, has Vietnamese and Chinese food in a classy setting. (☎405-524-2233. Noodle soups $5. Open daily 9am-9pm.) Everyone's fighting for the rights to the late Leo's recipes at **Leo's Original BBQ**, 3631 N. Kelley St., a classic hickory smoking outfit in the northwest reaches of town. (☎405-424-5367. Beef sandwich and baked potato $4.20. Open M-Sa 11am-9pm.)

⛏ ACCOMMODATIONS. Ten minutes from downtown and 5min. from a huge mall and plenty of eateries, **Flora's B&B**, 2312 NW 46th St., has two traditional rooms available. (☎405-840-3157. Doubles $70.) Other cheap lodging lies along the interstate highways, particularly on I-35 north of the I-44 junction. **The Royal Inn**, 2800 S. I-35, south of the junction with I-40, treats roadtrippers to modest rooms and free local calls. (☎405-672-0899. Singles $35; doubles $45.) Behind a strip mall, the 172 sites of **Abe's RV Park**, 12115 I-35 Service Rd., have a pool, laundry, and showers. (Take southbound Frontage Rd. off Exit 137 and proceed ¼ mi. to the red and white "RV" sign. ☎405-478-0278. Open daily summer 8am-8pm; low season 8am-6pm. Sites $23.) A more scenic option, **Lake Thunderbird State Park** offers campsites near a beautiful lake fit for swimming and fishing. (Take I-40 East to Exit 166 and go south 10 mi. until the road ends. Make

a left and drive 1 mi. ☎405-360-3572. Office open M-F 8am-5pm; host for late or weekend arrivals. Sites $8-10, with water and electricity $16-$23; huts $45. Showers available.)

⚑ LEAVING OKLAHOMA CITY
Take **I-44 West** through **Bethany.**

THE ROAD TO EL RENO

On the west end of **Bethany,** watch for an old steel trussed bridge. Head left across the highway here, and immediately swing right onto the frontage road to cross the bridge and continue on Rte. 66. If you're in the mood for nature, continue straight instead of turning onto the frontage road and check out water-sports at **Lake Overholser.** Otherwise, continue on to **Yukon;** you'll know you've hit town when the giant Yukon's Best Flour sign towers above you, and **Garth Brooks Blvd.** may tip you off that you've stumbled into the hometown of the King of Country himself. Park your pickup truck and rest your broken heart at the **Green Carpet Inn,** 10 E. Main St., where the floral floor coverings compete with riotous striped curtains and tropical bedspreads. But happily this translates into clean rooms at great rates. (☎405-350-9900 or 800-583-0290. Singles $29; doubles $33.)

EL RENO

Located at the intersection of Rte. 66 and the old Chislom Trail, El Reno has a rich history and the buildings to back it up, as well as a location convenient to outdoor activities such as boating and fishing on nearby Lake El Reno. *Rain Man* was filmed here, and a sign was added to the Big Eight Motel that read "Amarillo's Finest" to match the movie's setting. The Big Eight is all but gone (it's been renamed the Deluxe Inn by new management), but Dustin Hoffman fever still runs high.

(VITAL STATS)

Population: 16,000

Visitor Info: El Reno Convention and Visitors Bureau, 206 N. Bickford St. (☎888-535-7757; www.elreno.org). Open M-F 9am-5pm.

Internet Access: El Reno Carnegie Library, 215 E. Wade St. (☎405-262-2409). Open M-Th 9am-7pm, F 9am-5pm, Sa 9am-1pm.

Post Office: 203 N. Evans Ave. (☎800-275-8777). Open M-F 8:30am-5pm, Sa 9-11am. **Postal Code:** 73036.

ROUTE 66

OKLAHOMA
TEXAS

0   15 miles

0   15 kilometers

TO MAP #7 ▼

GETTING AROUND. El Reno is laid out in a simple grid; most streets run east-west, while most avenues run north-south. **U.S. 40** runs just south of town, while **Bus. U.S. 40** splits off to become **Sunset Dr.**, a major road, in town. **U.S. 81** enters El Reno from the north, turning into **Choctaw Ave.** on its way through town; downtown is centered on the intersection of Choctaw Ave. and Sunset Dr. **Parking** is generally plentiful.

SIGHTS. On the way into El Reno, two immediate right turns down a tree-lined avenue bring you to **Fort Reno,** 7107 W. Cheyenne St., originally a military camp monitoring the local Cheyenne and Arapaho populations. Troops from the fort, including two companies of Buffalo Soldiers, oversaw the first great Land Run, making sure no Sooners crossed the line too, well, soon. The fort was the birthplace of Black Jack, the riderless black horse in JFK's funeral, and also served as a German POW camp in WWII. A Visitors Center provides info on the remaining buildings. (4 mi. west of downtown El Reno on Rte. 66. ☎ 405-262-3987. Open M-F 10am-5pm, Sa-Su 10am-4pm.)

The truly lucky will pass through El Reno on the first Saturday in May, for **Onion Fried Burger Day,** when Johnnie's cranks out the **World's Largest Hamburger,** an 800 lb. onion fried burger bonanza.

FOOD & ACCOMMODATIONS. Check out the countertop at **Sid's Diner,** 300 S. Choctaw Ave., one block south of U.S. 81, for photos of Dustin Hoffman. While you're there, enjoy the steak and shake special for $4.50. (☎ 405-262-7757. Open daily 7am-8:30pm.) Try the fajitas at **Oscar's,** 316 S. Choctaw, just down Choctaw from Sid's. Lunch specials (M-F 11am-3pm) are excellent, with fajita plates from $6.50 and enchiladas for $5.50. (☎ 405-422-3739. Open M-Sa 11am-9pm.) El Reno is also famous as home of the scrumptious "Onion Fried Burger" at **Johnnie's Grill,** 301 S. Rock Island St. Grilled onions are pressed into the burger patty and cooked together. (☎ 405-262-4721. Onion fried burger $2.10, or 5 for $8.50. Open M-Sa 6am-9pm, Su 11am-8pm.) **Jube's Drive-In,** 1220 Sunset Dr., still has the old car-side "ordermatics," from which to call in your order for "charburgers" with hickory sauce. (☎ 405-262-0194. Burger $1.80. Open daily 6am-9pm.)

El Reno's best lodging deal is at the **Economy Express**, 2851 S. U.S. 81, where clean and spacious rooms come with microwaves, refrigerators, couches, dressers and TVs. (☎405-262-1022. Singles from $32; doubles from $38.)

LEAVING EL RENO
Continue on the frontage road through **Bridgeport.**

THE ROAD TO WEATHERFORD

Just off Rte. 66 along U.S. 281 under I-40, the **Hinton Country Inn** follows true Rte. 66 style, combining a gas station, convenience store, and motel. (☎405-542-3198. Singles from $42.) For a brief and happy rest stop, take a departure from Rte. 66, following U.S. 281 5 mi. south of I-40 through Hinton to the **Red Rock Canyon State Park**, where basic campsites await in the heart of the canyon. (☎405-542-6344. Open M-F 8am-5pm.) Driving past **Hydro,** the structure on the right used to be **Lucille's,** a landmark filling station and market that was sold on e-Bay following Lucille's death in 2000.

WEATHERFORD. Weatherford is extremely proud of native son Thomas P. Stafford—the 18th man in space. The **Stafford Air and Space Museum**, Exit 84 from I-40, includes replicas and artifacts of air and space travel from the Wright brothers plane to the actual desk that responded to Apollo 13's infamous report, "Houston, we have a problem here." (☎580-772-6143; www.staffordairandspacemuseum.com. Open daily 9am-5pm. $5, under 18 free.) On the way into Weatherford, the much-advertised **Cherokee Trading Post,** 6101 NE Service Rd., sells bulk goods, but the better treat is next door at the cafe, where a quarter-pound ostrich burger costs $5, and a buffalo burger (less fat than chicken) runs $6. (☎580-323-5524. Open Su-Th 7am-10pm, F-Sa 8am-11pm.)

CLINTON

Clinton's provenance reflects relations between settlers and Native Americans in the Great Plains. Deeded the land by the federal government, the Native Americans that had been condensed into the area were prohibited from selling more than half of their 160-acre allotments. Determined to found a town in the rich valley, J.L. Avant and E.E. Blake secretly bought half allotments from four different men, and in 1902 the amalgamated town was dubbed Clinton for Judge Clinton Irwin

VITAL STATS

Population: 9000

Visitor Info: Clinton Chamber of Commerce, 101 S. 4th St. (☎580-323-2222; www.clintonok.org). Open M-F 9am-5pm.

Internet Access: Clinton Public Library, 751 Frisco Ave. (☎580-323-2165). Open M and W 9am-6pm, Tu and Th 9am-6pm, F 9am-5pm, Sa 9am-1pm.

Post Office: 212 S. 11th St. (☎508-323-0712.) Open M-F 8am-4:30pm, Sa 9-11am. **Postal Code:** 74103.

GETTING AROUND. Clinton is centered on the intersection of **Bus. I-40** and **U.S. 183.** I-40 runs just south of downtown. In town, U.S. 183 is known as **Cox St.,** and Bus. I-40 is called **Gary Blvd.,** one of the city's main drags. Numbered streets run north-south, starting with **1st St.** in the east.

SIGHTS. Play Godzilla or Gulliver—depending on your mood—to the miniature golf re-creation of Rte. 66 at the **McLain Rogers Park,** at the corner of 10th and Bess Rogers St., or enjoy the waterslide. The **Cheyenne Cultural Center,** 2250 NE Rte. 66, displays work by Cheyenne craftspeople and artists, providing a sense of Cheyenne regional history, art, and culture. (☎580-323-6224. Open Tu-Sa 10am-5pm.) Finally, don't miss the **Oklahoma Rte. 66 Museum,** 2229. W. Gary Blvd. The state's tribute to Rte. 66 traces the road decade by decade. Also at the museum is the **"World's Largest Curio Cabinet,"** filled with Rte. 66 souvenirs. (☎580-323-7866. Open M-Sa 9am-7pm, Su 1-6pm. Arrive 1hr. before closing. $3, seniors $2.50, ages 6-18 $1, under 6 free.)

FOOD & ACCOMMODATIONS. Check in for a little heartbreak and hang up your blue suede shoes at the **Best Western Trade Winds Courtyard Inn,** 2128 Gary Blvd., where the King himself rocked around the clock each time he came through Clinton. Now a Best Western franchise, Elvis's favorite Clinton motel is still under the same management as it was during his reign, and lodgers can rent his room, with original furnishings. (☎800-321-2209 or 580-323-2610. Singles from $45; doubles $49; Elvis Suite $85.) Rooms at the **Relax Inn,** 1116 S. 10th St., aren't ritzy, but they're clean, adequate, and dirt cheap. (☎580-323-1888. Rooms from $22.50.) At the **Glancy Motel,** 217 Gary Blvd., the giant red vintage sign and the 70s-style wrought iron indicate the age of the motel, but rooms are comfortable enough. (☎580-323-0112. No non-smoking singles. Singles $18.50; doubles $25.)

LEAVING CLINTON
Follow old **Rte. 66,** paralleling I-40 West.

THE ROAD TO ELK CITY. On the way to Elk City along Rte. 66, you'll pass through **Foss,** little more than a dusty ghost town. Five miles north of town, an incongruous man-made reservoir provides opportunities for lakeside camping, swimming, water sports and boat rentals. Later on, **Canute** has few diversions to slow your cross-country progress, but the local **KOA Campground,** off I-40 exit 50, offers a general store, pool, and laundry facilities. (☎580-592-4409. Store open daily in summer 8am-9pm; in winter 8am-7pm. Sites $17, RVs $29; cabins $40.)

ELK CITY

Although Elk City's biggest—in all senses—attraction is heralded by a giant neon Rte. 66 sign at the west end of town, the small historic downtown is relatively unconcerned with the tourist traffic just to the north and offers an assortment of homey dining and loitering options, in no-frills settings with no-frills prices. Meanwhile, the standard bevy of fast-food regulars lines Rte. 66.

(VITAL STATS)

Population: 10,500

Visitor Info: Elk City Chamber of Commerce, 1016 Airport Industrial Rd. (☎800-280-0207; www.elkcitychamber.com). Open M-F 9am-5pm.

Internet Access: Elk City Carnegie Library, 221 W. Broadway (☎580-225-0136). Open M, W and F 10am-6pm; Tu and Th 10am-9pm; Sa 10am-2pm.

Post Office: 101 S. Adams Ave. (☎508-225-0294), at Broadway Ave. Open M-F 8:30am-4:30pm, Sa 9am-11am. **Postal Code:** 73644.

⌐ GETTING AROUND. Streets in Elk City form a grid; avenues run north-south, while streets are numbered and run east-west. An exception to this is **Broadway Ave. (Bus. I-40),** which runs east-west one block south of **3rd St.,** both major Elk City thoroughfares, and **parking** in the area is usually easy to find.

◑ SIGHTS. The **National Rte. 66 Museum,** right along Rte. 66, is Elk City's pride and joy. The museum features a map of the road made out of t-shirts, plus state-by-state displays of the history of Rte. 66. Two giant Kuchina dolls guard the grounds, and the exterior of the museum recreates an Old West Rte. 66 townscape. Next door, the **Old Town Museum** features regional history, including a display on Elk City's own Miss America 1981, Susan Powell, and a rotating display of local collections. (Both museums ☎580-225-6266. Open M-Sa 9am-5pm, Su 2-5pm. Rte. 66 Museum $4. Old Town Museum $2.50, under 12 free. Combination ticket $5, students $4.)

▤⌐ FOOD & ACCOMMODATIONS. The French Silk Pie at the ◪**Country Dove Tea Room,** 610 W. 3rd St., is well worth the stop. If you feel the need to justify it with a meal, the soups and sandwiches are also local legends. (☎580-225-7028. Open M-Sa 11am-2pm.) One of the old Rte. 66 roadhouses, **The Flamingo Restaurant,** 2010 W. 3rd St., features chicken fried steak ($4.50) and an extensive salad bar. (☎580-225-3412. Open M-Sa 6am-9pm, Su 7am-9pm.) At **Nita's Coffee House and Antiques,** 218 W. Broadway, the comfy chairs, big-screen TV, Internet access, and coffee drinks are excellent cover for catching the latest local gossip. (☎580-225-1778. Latte $2.25. Open daily 7:30am-6pm.) The wooden trellises of **Lupe's Cocina y Cantina,** 905 N. Main St., seclude diners enjoying chicken chalupas ($6), and chicken fried steak. (☎580-225-7109. Open M-F 11am-10pm, Sa 4-10pm.) Satiate sweet teeth at **The Sugar Shack,** 521 S. Main St.; although their main gig is decorating cakes, the peanut butter fudge and enormous cinnamon rolls ($1.50) are also delightful. (☎580-243-2253. Open Tu-F 9am-5pm, Sa 9am-3pm.)

Super-cheap accommodations line the entrance to Elk City from the east; the **Budget Inn,** 2611 E. Rte. 66, rents well-furnished rooms, some with full-wall photo murals. (☎580-225-5612. Rooms from $25.) Rooms at the **Budget Host Inn,** 2000 W. 3rd St., all come with whimsical wallpaper and pink and black tiling around the sink area. A limited number of rooms with microwaves and refrigerators are available at no extra charge. (☎580-225-1811. Singles from $26; doubles from $40.)

APPROACHING SAYRE

From Elk City, follow **3rd St.** out of town. Continue on **Rte. 66** 4½ mi., then turn right onto the 2-lane north frontage road. Turn left at the T, crossing over I-40 onto the south side frontage road and, ½ mi. later, cross onto the north side again, continuing west. 3 mi. later, turn right at the stop sign onto **Bus. I-40** (unmarked). Continue for 1½ mi., then turn left on **4th St.** Cross the north fork of the Red River, into **Sayre**.

SAYRE

Worth a stop as you pass through Sayre is the **RS & K Railroad Museum,** 411 N. 6th St. Like a railroad annex to Santa's workshop, Shirley and Ray Killian's garage whirs, whistles, toots, and chugs with the hundreds of miniature trains. (☎580-928-3525. Open M-F 9am-9pm or when the Killians are home. Knock on the front door for a tour.)

From roping to resting, the **Flying W Guest Ranch,** 1000 N. 4th St., will take care of all your cowboy fantasies. Deer, turkey, and quail run wild, and trail riders can visit the largest buffalo killing site in the southern plains. (☎800-928-8864. Trail rides $25-110. Call for campsite rates.) Heading down 4th St., keep an eye peeled **The Picket Fence,** 1402 N. 4th St. Sandwiches are gourmet, and the baked potatoes ($4) are excellent. (☎580-928-9997. Club sandwich $5. Open Su-F 11am-2pm.) The **Western Motel,** 315 NE Rte. 66, on the eastern edge of town, rents spartan but clean rooms. (☎580-928-3353. Rooms from $28.)

LEAVING SAYRE

1½ mi. west of town, take a right just before the overpass onto the 2-lane road, just before the park. Continue ¼ mi. before turning left on **Old Rte. 66,** then continue straight where the road diverges. Curve right, onto the frontage road; 14¾ mi. later, exit for **Texola.**

TEXOLA. Follow tumbleweeds through the ghost town of Texola. On the western edge of town, an ever-so-truthful sign reads "There's no other place like this place anywhere near this place, so this must be the place." Folks congregate at the **Hitchin' Post,** on Rte. 66, for beer ($1.50) and pool. (☎580-526-9911. Open "almost daily" noon-2am.) Another favorite is the delicious BBQ at **Windmill Restaurant,** across the interstate. (☎580-526-3965. Sandwich $3. Open Tu-Sa 6:30am-9pm.)

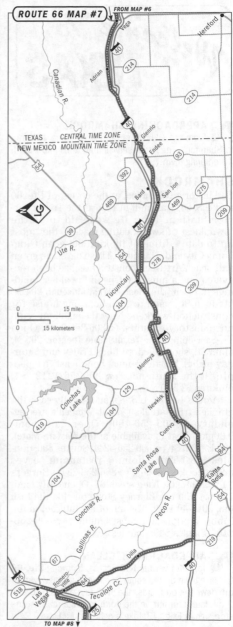

ROUTE 66 MAP #7 — FROM MAP #6

TO MAP #8

ROUTE 66

Welcome To TEXAS

APPROACHING SHAMROCK
From the Oklahoma border, continue 13½ mi. to Shamrock. The south service road turns into **Bus. I-40** entering town.

SHAMROCK
The historic **U-Drop Inn,** at the corner of Rte. 66 and U.S. 83, was built in 1936 as the Tower Service Station. The cafe was said to be the "swankiest of swank eating places," the "most up-to-date edifice of its kind between Oklahoma City and Amarillo." These days, the green and peach Art Deco construction has been renovated into a museum. One of the oldest buildings in town, the **Pioneer West Museum**, 204 N. Madden St., used to be a boarding house for construction workers. Now the small museum hosts history exhibits. (☎806-256-3941. Open Tu-Sa 1-5pm.) The **Texan Movie Theater,** 205 N. Main St., shows feature films Friday and Saturday nights, but there must be at least five people in the audience. (☎806-256-1212. $4, children $2.50.)

Across I-40 on U.S. 83, and slightly east, the chicken fried steaks ($7) at **Mitchell's** are legendary. (☎806-256-1900. Open daily 6am-9:30pm.) Rest is available at the **Western Motel,** 104 E. 12th St. (☎806-256-3244. Singles $36; doubles $38.) The adjoining restaurant serves home-cooked meals. (☎806-256-2342. Burgers $4.50. Chicken fried steak $7. Open daily 6am-10pm.) Rub the Blarney Stone outside the **Irish Inn,** 301 I-40 East. The inn offers Internet in the lobby, a pool, and guest laundry. (☎806-256-2106. Singles $49; doubles $63.)

APPROACHING MCLEAN
Jog left over the **I-40** access, following **Rte. 66** to leave town on the south frontage road. Just over 14 mi. down the oad, cross the interstate at Exit 146 and 2 mi. later turn left on the north frontage road. At the stop sign at Exit 143, take a right into **McLean.**

MCLEAN
More exciting than the flat tire this actual combination would produce, the **Devil's Rope Museum,** dedicated jointly to barbed wire and Rte. 66, features over 2550 different types of barbed wire, a history of cattle brands, a wall tracing the evolution of the American cowboy and the **Texas Old Rte. 66 Association and Museum**. (Entering town on Rte. 66, turn left on Kingsley St. ☎806-779-2225. Open Feb.-Dec. 15 Tu-Sa 10am-4pm. Free.) Farther down Rte. 66 in the heart of McLean, the **McLean-Alanreed Area Museum** has an area ranching exhibit, a memorial to local veterans, and history of McLean and Alanreed. (☎806-779-2731. Open W-Sa 10am-4pm. Free.) Leaving town, glance to the south for a bright orange old Phillip's 66 service station, and remember to gas up.

The **Red River Steakhouse,** 101 Rte. 66 West, is a blend of barn and saloon, with a tin roof, concrete floor, and giant cans of beans and license plates along the walls. (☎806-779-8940. Chicken fried steak $7. Burgers $4. Open Tu-Sa 11am-9pm.) Virtually next door on Rte. 66, the **Cactus Inn** offers singles and suites including kitchenettes, couches, and TVs. (☎806-779-2346. Singles $35; suites $45.)

THE ROAD TO AMARILLO
One mile west of McLean, take a left before the overpass. Ten miles later, cross under to the far side of I-40, then take a left on **Johnson Ranch Rd.** Continue on the south frontage road through **Alanreed.** Three miles north of Rte. 66 at Exit 128, the **Lake McClellan Campsite** offers bottom-of-the-canyon camping for $12 per night. Two miles beyond Exit 128, at Exit 134, cross to the south frontage road. Three miles later, head left over I-44.

The stretch between McLean and Amarillo holds little appeal, as you pass through **Jericho** and into **Groom** 11 mi. beyond Exit 134. Continue on the south frontage road through **Lark** and **Conway.**

The **largest cross** in the Northern Hemisphere is on the roadside near Groom.

APPROACHING AMARILLO
7 mi. beyond Conway, cross to the north side of the road, and turn left on the north frontage road. As this turns into **Farm Market Rd. 2575,** go straight until **FM 1912,** and turn right. When FM 1912 intersects **U.S. 60 (Amarillo Blvd.)** and **Bus I-40,** go left.

AMARILLO

Named for the yellow clay of nearby Lake Meredith, Amarillo began as a railroad construction camp in 1887 and evolved into a Texas-size truck stop. After years of cattle and oil, Amarillo is now the prime overnight stop for motorists en route from Dallas, Houston, or Oklahoma City to Denver and other Western destinations.

(VITAL STATS)

Population: 170,000

Visitor Info: Amarillo Convention and Visitors Bureau, 401 S. Buchanan St. (☎806-374-8474; www.amarillo-cvb.org). Open M-F 8am-5pm. **Texas Travel Info Center,** 9700 I-40 East (☎806-335-1441), at Exit 76. Open daily 8am-6pm.

Internet Access: Amarillo Public Library, 413 E. 4th Ave. (☎806-378-3054). Open M-Th 9am-9pm, Sa 9am-6pm, Su 2-6pm.

Post Office: 505 E. 9th Ave. (☎806-468-2148). Open M-F 7:30am-5pm. **Postal Code:** 79105.

▣ GETTING AROUND. Amarillo sprawls at the intersection of **I-27, I-40,** and **U.S. 87/287. Rte. 335 (the Loop)** encircles the city. **Rte. 66** runs east-west through town as **Amarillo Blvd.** parallel to I-40. Very much a driver's city, Amarillo is fairly easy to navigate, and **parking** is abundant.

▣ SIGHTS. The largest history museum in the state of Texas, the **Panhandle-Plains Historical Museum,** 2401 4th Ave., in nearby Canyon, displays an impressive collection of "cowboy" art as well as a replicated pioneer town and working oil derrick. (☎806-651-2244; www.panhandleplains.org. Open summer M-Sa 9am-6pm, Su 1-6pm; low season M-Sa 9am-5pm, Su 1-6pm. $4, seniors $3, ages 4-13 $1.) The **American Quarter Horse Heritage Center and Museum,** 2601 I-40 East, at Exit 72B, presents the heroic story of "America's horse." Try your hand at a galloping steed on the museum's mechanical horse ride. (☎806-376-5181 or 888-209-8322. Open M-Sa 9am-5pm, Su noon-5pm. $4, seniors $3.50, ages 6-18 $2.50.) At **Cadillac Ranch,** Stanley Marsh III planted ten Cadillacs—model years 1948 to 1963—at the same angle as the Great Pyramids, and as one local notes, "they didn't take root, neither." Get off I-40 at the Hope Rd. Exit, 9 mi. west of Amarillo, cross to the south side of I-40, turn right at the end of the bridge, and drive half a mile down the highway access road.

▣▐ FOOD & ACCOMMODATIONS. At **Dyer's BBQ,** on I-40 at Georgia, find heaping portions and a friendly vibe. The rib plate includes ribs, potato salad, cole slaw, baked beans, apricots, and onion rings for $8—sharing is advised. (☎806-358-7104. Open M-Sa 11am-10pm, Su 11am-9pm.) For a taste of West Texas Mexican fare, head to the most popular joint in town, **Tacos Garcia,** 1100 S. Ross. Try the Laredo platter (3 beef flautas with rice, beans, and guacamole; $7), and satisfy your sweet tooth with flaky, fresh *sopapillas*—a pastry covered in sugar and honey—three for $3. (☎806-371-0411. Open M 10:30am-9:30pm, Tu-Sa 10:30am-10pm, Su 10:30am-3:30pm.)

Amarillo provides over 4000 beds for travelers to leave their boots under. Budget motels proliferate along the entire stretch of I-40, I-27, and U.S. 87/287 near town. Prices rise near downtown. One popular option is the **Big Texan Motel,** 7701 I-40 East, adjacent to the **Big Texan Steak Ranch,** which promises a free 72 oz. steak dinner, if you can eat it in under an hour. (☎806-372-5000. Singles $45; doubles $65.) **KOA Kampground,** 1100 Folsom Rd., has a pool in summer. (Take I-40 to Exit 75, head north to Rte. 60, then go east 1 mi. ☎806-335-1792. Laundry and coffee. Reception daily June-Aug. 8am-10pm; Sept.-May 8am-8pm. Sites $20, with water and electricity $27, with full hookup $28.)

▤ DETOUR: PALO DURO CANYON
23 mi. south of Amarillo; take I-27 to Exit 106 and head east on Rte. 217.

Twenty-three miles south of Amarillo, Palo Duro Canyon, known as the "Grand Canyon of Texas," spans 20,000 acres of breathtaking beauty. The 16 mi. **scenic drive** through the park begins at the headquarters. Rangers allow backcountry hiking, but the majority of visitors stick to interconnected marked trails. Temperatures in the canyon frequently climb to 100°F; bring at least two quarts of water. The park headquarters, just inside the park, has trail maps and info on park activities. (☎806-488-2227. Open daily summer 7am-10pm; winter 8am-5pm. $3, under 12 free.) The official play of Texas, the musical ▨**Texas Legacies,** performed in Pioneer Amphitheater, 1514 5th Ave., is not to be missed. With the canyon as its backdrop, the epic drama includes a tree-splitting lightning bolt. (☎806-655-2181. Shows in summer M-Tu and Th-Su 8:30pm. Tickets $11-26, under 12 $5-23.) **Old West Stables,** a quarter-mile farther along, rents horses and saddles. (☎806-488-2180. Rides Apr.-Oct. 10am, noon, 2, 4pm; June-Aug. 10am, noon, 2, 4, 6pm. $20 per hr. Reservations recommended.)

LEAVING AMARILLO

Follow **Amarillo Blvd.** through town. For the original old Rte. 66, head right onto **Indian Hill Rd.** just before the I-40 overpass into a residential neighborhood. Continue 4½ mi. to the T, then head right, following the north frontage road toward **Bushland,** 13 mi. down the road, and Wildorado, 7 mi. later.

WILDORADO. If hunger or a snooze should take you, Wildorado is a surprising oasis. The decrepit, almost unreadable sign for "Jessie's Cafe" hides what is today **Randy's of Wildorado,** 708 W. I-40, an elegant lunchtime eatery and genuine upscale dining establishment, featuring fresh seafood. (☎806-426-3287. Pan-fried red snapper $19. Portobella "steak" bruschetta $4. *Tazza de crema* $6. Open M 11am-2pm, Tu-Th 11am-9pm, F-Sa 11am-9:45pm.) Next door, the brightly painted, low-slung **Royal Inn** has rooms with floral wallpaper. (☎806-426-3315. Singles $29; doubles $36.)

APPROACHING VEGA
12 mi. past Wildorado on **Rte. 66,** head left on **Bus I-40** after crossing over the road to enter Vega.

VEGA. The folks in Vega take great pride in being on an original alignment of Rte. 66. Dot Leavitt, proprietess of **Dot's Mini Museum,** 105 N. 12th St. (☎806-267-2367), has seen—and collected—it all. The outbuildings next to her house contain a voluminous and eclectic collection of memorabilia, including a room full of cowboy hats. Self-professed to be "Rte. 66-obsessed" she'll gladly chat with passersby. Entering town on Rte. 66, pass through the stoplight—locals just call it "the" stoplight, with no further qualifiers, as it's the only one in the county. Just past the light, at the **Vega Motel,** 1005 Vega Blvd., 1940s architecture affords each customer his or her own carport, and the owners have decorated the rooms with original furnishings. (☎806-267-2205. Singles $35; doubles $42.)

ADRIAN. As they say in Adrian, 15½ mi. beyond Vega, "When you're here, you're halfway there!" From the sign across from the **Midpoint Cafe,** on Rte. 66, it's 1139 mi. to either end of the Mother Road. (☎866-538-6379. Open M-F 8am-4pm, Sa 8am-3pm, Su 8am-2pm.) Entering town from the east, an old pickup truck with a star-spangled "66" greets visitors next to the **Antique Ranch,** 106 E. Rte. 66. The restaurant and adjoining antique store have the best BBQ around. (☎806-538-9944. Sandwich $2.50. Open M-F 10am-7pm.)

THE ROAD TO TUCUMCARI
Continue on the frontage road into ghost-town **Glenrio,** where original Rte. 66 buildings are still hanging on, including a sign for the "First Hotel in Texas" from the west, or "Last Hotel in Texas" from the east. The sign's seen better days, though; now it just advertises "Texas." At Gruhlkey Rd., Exit 18, get on westbound I-40, and continue into **New Mexico.** There's not much to see between the eastern New Mexico border and the first town of any size, San Jon. Entering on the interstate, the **New Mexico Visitors Center,** on the north side, has every map you could ever need. If you use the restrooms, you can press a button on your way out approving or condemning the facilities.

At the border you cross into the Mountain Time Zone, where it is 1hr. earlier.

Continue on the I-40 to Exit 369, heading right at the stop on the exit, then immediately left on the frontage road. In tiny **Endee,** notice the "Cafe Motel" sign, the remnants of the town's old tourist court. Continue on the frontage road through the unobtrusive town of **Bard.** Then, continue on through **San Jon** in the Rte. 66 tradition, for "Tucumcari tonight!" Ten miles south of San Jon on Rte. 469, the **Caprock Amphitheater** puts on open-air summer productions.

APPROACHING TUCUMCARI
Continue on the south frontage road from San Jon. 21 mi. down the road, head right under the interstate and then join **I-40 West.** Get off at Exit 335 and enter Tucumcari on **Tucumcari Blvd.**

TUCUMCARI

The road between Amarillo and Albuquerque is a long one, and in the heyday of Rte. 66, Tucumcari made its name as the town with 2000 rooms for weary travelers. "Tucumcari Tonight" became a popular slogan for travelers, and the wall-to-wall motels lining Tucumcari Blvd. do not disappoint. The strip of neon signs lights up the night—recent renovation and Rte. 66 preservation efforts have brought attention to signs like the Blue Swallow, the bluebird of happiness to drivers for decades.

VITAL STATS

Population: 6000

Visitor Info: Tucumcari/Quay County Chamber of Commerce, 404 W. Tucumcari Blvd. (☎505-461-1694; www.tucumcarinm.com). Open M-F 8am-noon and 1-5pm.

Internet Access: Tucumcari Public Library, 602 S. 2nd St. (☎505-461-0295). Open M 9:30am-7pm, Tu-F 9:30am-5:30pm, Sa 9am-1pm.

Post Office: 222 S. 1st St. (☎505-461-0370). **Postal Code:** 88401.

GETTING AROUND. Tucumcari sits just north of **I-40**; **U.S. 54** runs into town from the north. **Bus. U.S. 54** is known as **Tucumcari Blvd.** in town and is home to the city's famous motel strip. Getting around is fairly simple; streets run north-south and are numbered, while avenues run east-west. Most establishments have parking lots; **parking** is plentiful almost everywhere.

SIGHTS. The **Tee Pee Trading Post,** 924 E. Tucumcari Blvd., has been peddling "damn fine stuff" to Rte. 66 travelers from inside a concrete tee pee since the 1940s. (☎505-461-3773. Open M-Sa 8:30am-6pm, Su 8:30am-7pm.) The **Tucumcari Historical Museum,** 416 S. Adams Ave., is a 1903 schoolhouse overflowing with historical artifacts from the region. (☎505-461-4201. Open summer M-Sa 9am-6pm; winter Tu-Sa 9am-5pm.) Dinosaur enthusiasts should swing by the **Mesalands Dinosaur Museum,** at 1st and Laughlin St. As one of the world's foremost paleontological sights, Tucumcari's main attraction is a dinosaur museum featuring touchable bronze castings of beasts and bones. (☎505-461-2466. Open Tu-Sa Mar. 15-Oct. 15 noon-8pm; Oct. 16-Mar. 14 noon-5pm. $5, students and seniors $3.) **Ute Lake State Park,** in Logan, NM, just north of Tucumcari on U.S. 54, is a narrow glistening strip of natural beauty. Camping is available. (☎505-487-2284. Sites $8.) Movies at the early 1930s **Udon Theater,** 123 S. 2nd St., are $4.50 for adults, $3.50 for children.

FOOD. Tucumcari's motel magnificence comes with unvarnished but satisfying meal options that have been around as long as the route itself. The whimsical and fittingly excellent **La Cita Restaurant,** 812 1st St., is under the giant pink-and-blue sombrero at the corner Tucumcari Blvd. The Route 66 landmark shades some of the best green chili chicken enchiladas ($3) for miles. (☎505-461-0949. Open 11am through "dinner time.") **Del's Restaurant,** 1202 E. Tucumcari Blvd., is hard to miss, well advertised by the huge cow atop its sign. (☎505-461-1740. Open M-Sa 7am-9pm.)

THE LOCAL STORY

TUCUMCARI TONIGHT—AND YESTERDAY

The name "Tucumcari" is also a point of local pride. It is based on a Native American legend involving two young men who were fighting for the hand of a young woman named Kari, daughter of the chief. Kari loved one of the young men, Tocom, and despised the other, Tonopah. The chief needed to pick a successor for himself and husband for his daughter, so he set the two men to duel for the honor. When the despised suitor stabbed Tocum, Kari ran out and killed her lover's murderer, then killed herself. The chief, learning of the tragedy, killed himself, and with his dying breath, pronounced "Tocum-Kari."

Thus, the name became a symbol of undying love and valor. The plateau upon which the struggle took place—Tucumcari Mountain—is visible to the south of town. Less romantic epitomologists claim the name derives from the Comanche word "tuka-mukari," meaning "Signal Peak."

ACCOMMODATIONS. Tucumcari is known for its legendary "2000 Rooms," and the motel strip along Rte. 66 provides. The **Blue Swallow Motel,** 815 E. Rte. 66 Blvd., is perhaps Rte. 66's most celebrated motel. The pink motel with bright blue carports, in traditional tourist court fashion, has airy, well-decorated rooms, and, according to the sign under the giant neon swallow, "100% refrigerated air." (☎505-461-9849; www.blueswallowmotel.com. Singles $30; doubles $34.) For a higher-budget budget option, the **Best Western Pow Wow Inn,** 801 W. Tucumcari Blvd., is one of the original Rte. 66 tourist courts, although its been refashioned and redecorated to be a sterile version of its former self. (☎505-461-0500. Rooms $54. AAA discount.) Budget travelers will appreciate the **Relax Inn,** where decor and prices are stuck in the 70s. (☎505-461-3862. Singles from $17; doubles from $22.) The **Dream Catcher Bed and Breakfast,** 307 E. High St., has slightly cluttered rooms for regular prices, but the upstairs attic—like a sleepover at Grandma's with old beds scattered around dorm-style—is a great bargain at $15 per night. (☎505-461-2423. Singles $65; doubles $85.)

 LEAVING TUCUMCARI
Follow **Tucumcari Blvd.** west as it joins **I-40.**

 TIP   There's gas in Cuervo, but it's best to fill up before leaving Tucumcari. Passersby are few along some of the road, and the vultures would be only too happy for the company.

THE ROAD TO SANTA ROSA

Between Tucumcari and Santa Rosa, the expanses are large and the distractions few. The few towns along the way have long since faded after being bypassed by the interstate, but the long stretches of open road are lovely. From I-40 west of Tucumcari, exit at Palomas, heading across the highway to the south side, and then continue until the spooky narrow tunnel brings you out on the north side. Continue on the north side through **Montoya,** following Rte. 66 signs to cross over to the south side again. Cross over yet again past Montoya, when the road gives you no choice, and then continue on through **Newkirk** and **Cuervo,** if they haven't already crumbled to dust.

APPROACHING SANTA ROSA
Pick up **I-40** past Cuervo leading into Santa Rosa at Exit 277, where Rte. 66 joins with **Bus. I-40.**

SANTA ROSA

Halfway between Albuquerque and Amarillo, Santa Rosa is an oasis amidst the arid surrounds. Less gaudy than neighboring Tucumcari, but near enough to be competition, the city has equal claim to Old 66, with a main drag lined with ancient motels and friendly diners. Santa Rosa got its start as a ranching community, and grew under the propriety of Don Celso Baca, an officer in Kit Carson's brigade. Santa Rosa's principal draw is its lakes; the Blue Hole and Perch Lake both host some of the state's best scuba diving.

VITAL STATS

Population: 2800

Visitor Info: Santa Rosa Visitors Center, 486 Parker Ave. (☎505-472-3763). Open M-F 9am-5pm.

Internet Access: Moise Memorial Public Library, 208 5th St. (☎505-472-3101). Open M-F 10am-6pm, Sa 9am-noon.

Post Office: 120 S. 5th St. (☎505-472-3734), at Rte. 66. Open M-F 8:30am-5pm, Sa 9:45-11:45am. **Postal Code:** 88435.

GETTING AROUND. Unlike many other cities along the route, Santa Rosa is not laid out in a grid. **Rte. 66,** also known as **Will Rogers Dr.,** runs east-west through the city and is the principal road. Streets are numbered starting in the west, and run roughly northwest-southeast through town. **Parking** is readily available. Continue on Rte. 66 over the crest of the hill to get the full effect of Santa Rosa's magnificent perch.

SIGHTS & FESTIVALS. At the north end of Santa Rosa, drool over wheels peppier than yours at the awesome Santa Rosa **Route 66 Auto Museum,** 2766 Will Rogers Dr. Inside are a collection of lovingly restored roadsters and exhibits paying homage to a past of drive-throughs, cruisin', and back-seats. (☎505-472-1966. Open M-Sa 7:30am-7pm, Su 10am-7pm. $5, under 12 free.) In the middle of an arid desert, Santa Rosa is blessed with 13 lakes and watering holes. The most famous is the **Blue Hole,** which draws scuba fanatics with its 80 ft. depth, clarity, and constant 64°F temperature. To reach the Blue Hole from Rte. 66, turn left on Lake Dr., and left again on Blue Hole Rd. This will also take you directly past **Park Lake,** which features an enormous water slide. Northeast of town on Rte. 91, **Santa Rosa Lake** was built to ease the flooding of the Pecos River so cowboys could ford their cattle. The lake boasts camping, fishing, and watersports.

Santa Rosa also hosts a number of festivals. **Santa Rosa Days,** during Memorial Day weekend, draws over 40 softball teams for a tournament, in addition to hosting an arts and crafts fair, pony rides, amusement rides, and goat roping. The **Guadalupe County Fair,** during the first weekend in August, features a pet parade, flower show, barbecue, rodeo, chili cook-off, and horseshoe contest. **Santa Rosa de Lima Fiestas,** the third weekend in September, includes *mariachis* and a fiesta dance. Also in September, the **Route 66 Festival** includes a street dance, hot rod contest, Show & Shine Car Show, and parade.

▐▊▐ FOOD & ACCOMMODATIONS. On the eastern edge of Rte. 66's jaunt though town, the **Route 66 Restaurant,** 1819 Rte. 66, at the top of the hill, has been feeding roadies since the 1950s. The interior is a testimony to the town's road-fever. (☎505-472-9925. Entrees $3-7. Open M-Sa 6am-9pm.) **Joseph's Cafe,** 865 Rte. 66, with landmark **Fat Man** billboards, is a Rte. 66 legend—the hungry look forward to it for miles, and weary travelers can relax with a margarita within easy walking distance of a bevy of motels. (☎505-472-3361. Entrees $6-13. Open daily 6am-10pm.) The laid-back and hearty **Comet Drive-In,** 217 Parker Ave., serves to drive-through and eat-in customers. (☎505-472-3663. Entrees $3-8. Open Su and Tu-Sa 9am-9pm.) For a more upscale setting, the airy and comfortable **Lake City Diner,** 101 4th St., held a law office, dentist, and finance company when it was built in 1901, and now offers dishes chicken fettucine ($8) and delicious sandwiches ($6). (☎505-472-5253. Open M-F 11am-9pm, Sa 5-9pm.)

Like Tucumcari's, Santa Rosa's stretch of Rte. 66 is lined with vintage motels offering decent rooms at very reasonable rates. The giant sunny beacon of the **Sun N' Sand Motel,** 1120 Rte. 66, leads to comfortable rooms. (☎505-472-5268. Singles $29; doubles $35.) Rooms at the **Sunset Motel,** 929 Rte. 66, are spare, but offer even better prices. (☎505-472-2607. Singles $23; doubles $31.)

▐▊ LEAVING SANTA ROSA
Follow **Rte. 66** out of Santa Rosa as it curves to the right, and join **I-40** heading west. Get off at Exit 256, and take **U.S. 84** north through **Dilia** and **Romeroville.** Although it isn't on Rte. 66, heading 3 mi. east from Romeroville on **I-25** will bring you to the *other* Las Vegas—Las Vegas, New Mexico.

THE ROAD TO LAS VEGAS

From Santa Rosa, all the way heading south and west to the New Mexico border, civilization is sparse. This stretch of the country is one of the most beautiful on Rte. 66. It's also one where you should get you gas whenever you can; you never know where the next stop will be. From Santa Rosa, the road heads north to Las Vegas—New Mexico, not Nevada, your wallet will be glad to know—then west toward Santa Fe. The terrain grows increasingly mountainous, and many of the roadside towns along the way are tiny reservation communities. Why the dramatic detour off the interstate, just to end up back in Albuquerque? Like so much of Rte. 66, it was all about politics. During the mapping of the road, an outgoing governor with rivals in the town of Moriarty decided to thwart the town by bypassing it completely with the extravagant loop through Santa Fe. Only later did alignments head in a gas-efficient, but far less interesting, straight line.

LAS VEGAS

Unlike its northern namesake, this Las Vegas supplies in history what it lacks in razzle and dazzle. In 1899, Las Vegas was the biggest city in the New Mexico territory, and it flourished when the railroad was routed through town at the turn of the century. Las Vegas's light dimmed during the Great Depression and the construction of new rail lines. What remains today is a town frozen in time, with nine historic districts and 900 buildings on the National Register of Historic Places. The **City of Las Vegas Museum and Rough Riders Memorial Collection,** 727 Grand Ave., chronicles the history of the "Rough Riders," the US Cavalry regiment involved in the Spanish-American war. In addition to Rough Riders artifacts and local history paraphernalia, the museum also includes an annotated photo display of the hanging of the notorious Black Jack, reported to have said to the priest ministering to him: "Padre, make it snappy. I haven't much time. I have to be in hell and eat dinner with the Devil at noon." Due to a mistake with the rope tension, his head was "cut plumb off." (☎505-454-1401. Open M-F 9am-noon and 1-4pm, Sa 10am-3pm; May-Oct. also Su noon-4pm.)

Estella's Cafe, 148 Bridge St., offers the best Mexican food in town. (☎505-454-0048. Entrees $4-7. Open M-W 11am-3pm, Th-Sa 11am-8pm.) **The Plaza Drug Store,** 178 Bridge St., serves ice cream cones ($1.05) from the old-fashioned soda fountain. (☎505-425-5221. Open daily 8am-6pm.) In addition to being a fully stocked liquor store, bar, and dance club, **Dick's Deli,** 705 Douglas Ave., makes sandwiches to be reckoned with. (☎505-425-8261. Deli open M-F 10am-10pm, Sa 10am-11:30pm. Club open until 2am.) **Charlie's Spic and Span Bakery and Cafe,** 715 Douglas Ave., has a full espresso bar and fresh baked goods daily. Breakfast is served all day. (☎505-426-1921. Open M-Sa 6:30am-5:30pm, Su 7am-3pm.) Budget motels can be found all along **Grand Ave.,** between I-25 Exits 343 and 347. The **Town House Motel,** 1215 Grand Ave., has clean rooms. (☎505-425-6717. Singles $34; doubles $44.) Next door, the **Sunshine Motel,** 1201 Grand Ave., has pleasant rooms at similar prices. (☎505-425-3506. Singles $28; doubles $32.)

🚗 LEAVING LAS VEGAS
Take **I-25** back to where you left **Rte. 66,** then follow Rte. 66 into **Pecos,** turning left onto **Rte. 50** in "downtown" Pecos.

🏔 PECOS WILDERNESS AREA & HISTORICAL PARK
Off Rte. 50, near the town of Pecos.

The **Pecos Wilderness** protects 233,667 acres of high country in the heart of the Sangre de Cristo Mountains, punctuated by the second-highest peak in New Mexico, 13,103 ft. **Trunchas Peak.** Winters are long and snowy, but from late spring to early autumn this is an ideal spot for backcountry hiking. The upper Pecos River is the premier trout-fishing site in the Southwest, so don't be surprised to find campgrounds crowded with Texan fishermen. Once you get a few miles into the backcountry, you'll find yourself alone amid beautiful mountains, forests, and rivers. In 1625, Spanish colonists established an elaborate adobe mission on the wealthy **Pecos Pueblo.** In 1680, the inhabitants of the pueblo joined a united Indian force against the Spanish and, having killed the priest and destroyed the church, built a ceremonial kiva in the convent of the mission. The power of Pecos Pueblo gradually declined through disease, con-

flict and migration, but the ruins of the mission, later rebuilt, and the pueblo are still accessible. Stop in at the **Visitors Center** on Rte. 66 just a few miles before the town of Pecos for more information. (☎505-757-6414. Open M-F 8am-5pm.)

🚗 LEAVING PECOS
From **Rte. 50,** rejoin **I-25** at **Glorieta,** continuing on to Exit 294, 10¼ mi. down the road. Take the north frontage road to Santa Fe.

🍴 THE BOBCAT BITE
On the frontage road, between Glorieta and Santa Fe.

The **■Bobcat Bite** could easily be missed, but shouldn't be. Every car in town is generally parked outside this pink adobe roadhouse, constructed in 1954, and if you've got a hankering for a hunk of meat, or just a fantastic taste of New Mexico's finest green chili, you're in the right place. (☎505-983-5319. Green chili cheeseburger $5.25. Open W-Sa 11am-7:50pm.)

SANTA FE

Tourists may have replaced conquistadors in the Southwest's playground for the rich and famous, but the winding streets of beautiful low adobe buildings, the exquisite museums, and the distinctive artsy feel bring to life a time long forgotten in much of the rest of the region. Founded by the Spanish in 1608, Santa Fe's prime location at the convergence of the Santa Fe Trail, an old trading route running from Missouri, and the Camino Real ("Royal Road"), which originates in Mexico City, has always brought commerce and bustle. In recent years, Santa Fe's popularity has skyrocketed, leading to an influx of gated communities, ritzy restaurants, and California millionaires. In many spots, prices have risen accordingly, but Santa Fe's architecture, museums, and scenery make the bargain hunt well worth the time.

▣ GETTING AROUND

The streets of downtown Santa Fe seem to wind and wander without rhyme or reason. It is helpful to think of Santa Fe as a wagon wheel, with the **Plaza** in the center and roads leading outwards like spokes. **Paseo de Per-**

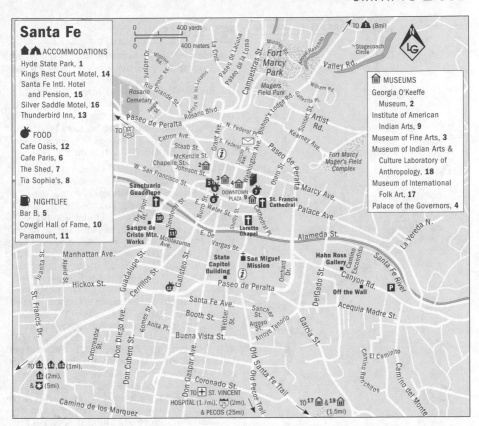

Santa Fe

▲▲ACCOMMODATIONS
Hyde State Park, **1**
Kings Rest Court Motel, **14**
Santa Fe Intl. Hotel
and Pension, **15**
Silver Saddle Motel, **16**
Thunderbird Inn, **13**

🍎 FOOD
Cafe Oasis, **12**
Cafe Paris, **6**
The Shed, **7**
Tia Sophia's, **8**

📷 NIGHTLIFE
Bar B, **5**
Cowgirl Hall of Fame, **10**
Paramount, **11**

🏛 MUSEUMS
Georgia O'Keeffe
Museum, **2**
Institute of American
Indian Arts, **9**
Museum of Fine Arts, **3**
Museum of Indian Arts &
Culture Laboratory of
Anthropology, **18**
Museum of International
Folk Art, **17**
Palace of the Governors, **4**

(Map labels: TO ▲ (8mi), Stagecoach Circle, Valley Rd., Fort Marcy Park, Murales Rd., Arroyo Rancho, Paseo de Lacuna, Paseo de la Loma, Campestras St., la Cruz, Mission Rd., Juniper Dr., Piñon Rd., Rio Grande St., Rosario Cemetary, Alegre St., Paseo de Peralta, TO 84/285, Magers Field Park, William Rd., Bishop's Lodge Rd., Gallecita Pl., Sunset St., Artist Rd., Kearney Ave., Fort Marcy Mager's Field Complex, N. Federal Pl., Grant Ave., Catron Ave., S. Federal Pl., Staab St., McKenzie St., Chapelle St., Johnson St., W. San Francisco St., Lincoln Ave., Washington Ave., Otero St., Paseo de Peralta, Marcy Ave., Palace Ave., Sanctuario Guadalupe, Burro St., Water St., Sleepy St., Cathedral Pl., St. Francis Cathedral, DOWNTOWN PLAZA, E. San Francisco St., De Fouri St., Sandoval St., Montezuma Ave., Sangre de Cristo Mtn. Works, E. De Vargas St., Loretto Chapel, Alameda St., La Vereda N., Santa Fe River, Manhattan Ave., Alarid St., Juanita St., Guadalupe St., De Vargas St., State Capitol Building, San Miguel Mission, Orchard Dr., Hahn Ross Gallery, Camino Escondido, Canyon Rd., Off the Wall, Hickox St., St. Francis Dr., Cerrillos St., Galisteo St., Paseo de Peralta, DelGado St., Santa Fe Ave., Booth St., Webber St., Sanchez St., Arroyo St., Arroyo Tenorio, Garcia St., Acequia Madre St., El Caminito, Camino del Monte, Don Diego Ave., Gomes St., Anita Pl., Buena Vista St., Camino Ranchitos, Catoreador St., Don Cubero Ave., Don Gaspar Ave., Coronado St., Old Santa Fe Trail, Old Pecos Trail, TO ✚ ST. VINCENT HOSPITAL (1.7mi), 25 (2mi), & PECOS (25mi), TO 17 🏛 & 18 🏛 (1.5mi), Camino de los Marquez, TO 13, 14, 15 (1mi), 16 (2mi), & ✚ (5mi))

0 — 400 yards
0 — 400 meters

VITAL STATS

Population: 62,000
Visitor Info: Visitor Info Center, 491 Old Santa
Fe Trail (☎505-875-7400 or 800-545-2040).
Open daily 8am-6:30pm; off season until 5pm.
Santa Fe Convention and Visitor's Bureau,
201 W. Marcy St. (☎800-777-2489). Open M-
F 8am-5pm.

Internet Access: Santa Fe Public Library, 145
Washington Ave. (☎505-955-6781). Open M-
Th 10am-6pm, F-Sa 10am-6pm, Su 1-5pm.

Post Office: 120 S. Federal Pl. (☎505-988-
6351), next to the courthouse. Open M-F
7:30am-5:45pm, Sa 9am-1pm. **Postal Code:**
87501.

alta forms a loop around the downtown area,
and the main roads leading out toward I-25
are **Cerrilos Rd., St. Francis Dr.,** and **Old Santa
Fe Trail.** Except for the museums southeast of
the city center, most upscale restaurants and
sights in Santa Fe cluster within a few blocks
of the downtown Plaza and inside the loop
formed by the Paseo de Peralta. Narrow
streets make driving troublesome; park your
car and pound the pavement. The downtown
area is compact and lined with interesting
shops, restaurants, and sights, and the Plaza
area is restricted to pedestrians. You'll find
parking lots abundant at decent rates, and
metered spaces line the streets near Plaza
and **Canyon Rd.**

● SIGHTS

The grassy **Plaza de Santa Fe** is a good starting point for exploring the museums, sanctuaries, and galleries of the city. Since 1609, the plaza has been the site of religious ceremonies, military gatherings, markets, cockfights, and public punishments—now it shelters ritzy shops and packs of loitering tourists. **Historic walking tours** leave from the blue doors of the Palace of the Governors on Lincoln St. (May-Oct. M-Sa 10:15am. $10.)

MNM MUSEUMS. Sante Fe is home to six imaginative, world-class museums. Four are run by **The Museum of New Mexico.** They all keep the same hours and charge the same admission. A worthwhile four-day pass includes admission to all four museums and can be purchased at any of them. (☎ 505-827-6463; www.museumofnewmexico.org. Open Su and Tu-Sa 10am-5pm. $7, under 16 free. 4-day pass $15. Museum of Fine Arts and Palace of the Governors—are both free F 5-8pm.) Inhabiting a large adobe building on the northwest corner of the plaza, the **Museum of Fine Arts** dazzles visitors with the works of major Southwestern artists, as well as contemporary exhibits of controversial American art. (107 W. Palace Ave. ☎505-476-5072. Open daily 10am-5pm.) The **Palace of the Governors** is the oldest public building in the US and was the seat of seven successive governments after its construction in 1610. The *haciendas* palace is now a museum with exhibits on Native American, Southwestern, and New Mexican history and an interesting exhibit on Jewish Pioneers. (On the north side of the plaza. ☎505-476-5100.) The most distinctive museums in town are 2½ mi. south of the Plaza on Old Santa Fe Trail. The fascinating **Museum of International Folk Art** houses the Girard Collection, which includes over 10,000 handmade dolls, doll houses, and other toys. Other galleries display ethnographic exhibits. (706 Camino Lejo. ☎505-476-1200.) Next door, the **Museum of Indian Arts and Culture Laboratory of Anthropology** displays Native American photos and artifacts. (710 Camino Lejo. ☎505-476-1250.)

OTHER PLAZA MUSEUMS. The popular **Georgia O'Keeffe Museum** attracts the masses with the artist's famous flower paintings, as well as some of her more abstract works. The collection spans her entire life and demonstrates her versatility. (217 Johnson St. ☎505-946-1017. Open daily

TO MAP #9

10am-5pm. $8, under 17 and students with ID free. F 5-8pm free. Audio tour $5.) Downtown's **Institute of American Indian Arts Museum** houses an extensive collection of contemporary Indian art with an intense political edge. (108 Cathedral Pl. ☎ 505-983-8900. Open M-Sa 9am-5pm, Su noon-5pm. $4, students and seniors $2, under 16 free.) The **New Mexico State Capitol** was built in 1966 in the form of the Zia sun symbol. The House and Senate galleries are open to the public, and the building contains an impressive art collection. (5 blocks south of the Plaza on Old Santa Fe Trail. ☎ 505-986-4589. Open M-F 7am-7pm; June-Aug. also Sa 8am-5pm. Free tours M-F 10am and 2pm.)

CHURCHES. Santa Fe's Catholic roots are evident in the Romanesque **St. Francis Cathedral,** built from 1869 to 1886 under the direction of Archbishop Lamy to help convert Westerners to Catholicism. (213 Cathedral Pl., 1 block east of the Plaza on San Francisco St. ☎ 505-982-5619. Open daily 7:30am-5:30pm.) The **Loretto Chapel** was the first Gothic building west of the Mississippi River. The church is famous for its "miraculous" spiral staircase. (207 Old Santa Fe Trail., 2 blocks south of the cathedral. ☎ 505-982-0092. Open M-Sa 9am-5pm, Su 10:30am-5pm. $2.50, seniors and children $2.) About five blocks southeast of the plaza lies the **San Miguel Mission,** at the corner of DeVargas St. and the Old Santa Fe Trail. Built in 1610 by the Tlaxcalan Indians, the mission is the oldest functioning church in the US. Also in the church is the San Jose Bell, the oldest bell in the US, made in Spain in 1356. (☎ 505-988-9504. Open M-Sa 9am-5pm, Su 10am-4pm; may close earlier in winter. $1.)

GALLERIES. Santa Fe's most successful artists live and sell their work along **Canyon Rd.** For about 1 mi., the road supports galleries displaying all types of art and many indoor/outdoor cafes. (To reach their galleries, depart the Plaza on San Francisco Dr., take a left on Alameda St., a right on Paseo de Peralta, and a left on Canyon Rd. Most galleries are open 10am-5pm.) The **Hahn Ross Gallery's** work is hip, enjoyable, and expensive. (409 Canyon Rd. ☎ 505-984-8434. Open daily 10am-5pm.)

🏔 OUTDOOR ACTIVITIES

The nearby **Sangre de Cristo Mountains** reach heights of over 12,000 ft. and offer countless opportunities for hikers, bikers, skiers, and snow-boarders. The **Pecos** and **Río Grande Rivers** are playgrounds for kayakers, rafters, and canoers. Before heading into the wilderness, stop by the **Public Lands Information Center,** 1474 Rodeo Rd., near the intersection of St. Francis Rd. and I-25, to pick up maps, guides, and friendly advice. (☎ 505-438-7542 or 877-276-9404; www.publiclands.org. Open M-F 8am-5pm; winter until 4:30pm.) The Sierra Club Guide to *Day Hikes in the Santa Fe Area* and the Falcon Guide to *Best Easy Day Hikes in Santa Fe* are good purchases for those planning to spend a few days hiking.

The closest **hiking** trails to downtown Santa Fe are along Rte. 475 on the way to the Santa Fe Ski Area. On this road, 10 mi. northeast of town, the **Tesuque Creek Trail** (4 mi., 2hr.) leads through the forest to a flowing stream. The best **skiing** is 16 mi. northeast of downtown, at **Ski Santa Fe.** In the towering Sangre De Cristo Mountains on Rte. 475, the ski area operates six lifts, servicing 43 trails on 600 acres of terrain with a 1650 ft. vertical drop. (☎ 505-982-4429. Open late Nov. to early Apr. daily 9am-4pm. Lift tickets $45, teens $37, children and seniors $33. Rental packages from $18.)

🎵 ENTERTAINMENT

Old verse and distinguished acting invade the city each summer when **Shakespeare in Sante Fe** raises its curtain. The festival shows plays in an open-air theater on the St. John's College campus from late June to late August. (Tickets available at show or call ☎ 505-982-2910. Shows F-Su 7:30pm. Reserved seating tickets $15-32; lawn seating is free, but a $5 donation is requested.) The **Santa Fe Opera,** on Opera Dr., 7 mi. north of Santa Fe on Rte. 84/285, performs outdoors against a mountain backdrop. Nights are cool; bring a blanket. (☎ 800-280-4654 or 877-999-7499; www.santafeopera.org. Shows July W and F-Sa; Aug. M-Sa. Performances begin 8-9pm. Tickets $20-130; rush standing-room tickets $8-15.) The **Santa Fe Chamber Music Festival** celebrates the works of Baroque, Classical, Romantic, and 20th-century composers in the **St. Francis Auditorium of the Museum of Fine Arts** and the **Lensic Theater.** (☎ 505-983-2075, tickets 505-982-1890; www.sfcmf.org. Mid-July to mid-Aug. Tickets $16-40, students $10.)

In the third week of August, the country's largest and most impressive **Indian Market** floods the plaza. The **Southwestern Association** for **Indian Arts** (☎505-983-5220) has more info. Don Diego de Vargas's peaceful reconquest of New Mexico in 1692 marked the end of the 12-year Pueblo Rebellion, now celebrated in the three-day **Fiesta de Santa Fe** (☎505-988-7575). Held in mid-September, festivities begin with the burning of the *Zozobra* (a 50 ft. marionette) and include street dancing, processions, and political satires. The *New Mexican* publishes a guide and a schedule of events.

FOOD

Even fly-bys through Santa Fe should take a time-out to sample some of the best food the Southwest has to offer. Green chili is New Mexico's specialty, and most dishes come with the offer to have them smothered in the zesty sauce. Take them up on it, but the spiciness can vary, so keep your personal temperature gauge in mind. The **Santa Fe Farmers Market,** near the intersection of Guadalupe St. and Paseo de Peralta, has fresh fruits and vegetables. (☎505-983-4098. Open late Apr. to early Nov. Tu and Sa 7am-noon. Call for indoor winter location and hours.)

▧ **Tia Sophia's,** 210 W. San Francisco St. (☎505-983-9880). It looks and feels like a diner, but as the long waits will testify, the food is exceptional. The most popular item is the Atrisco plate ($6)—chile stew, cheese enchilada, beans, *posole*, and a *sopapilla.* Open M-Sa 7am-2pm.

▧ **Cafe Oasis,** 526 Galisteo St. (☎505-983-9599), at Paseo de Peralta. Take a break from the bustle of the city at this laid-back restaurant where the food is organic and artistic expression is a way of being. Creative dishes range from veggie enchiladas ($10.75) to *Samari* stir-fry ($13.50). Breakfast served all day. Live music nightly. Open M-W 10am-midnight, Th-F 10am-2am, Sa 9am-2am, Su 9am-midnight.

Cafe Paris, 31 Burro Alley (☎505-986-9162). The black forest cake is dreamy and the lemon tart ($4) inspires joy, but no one will notice behind a cappuccino ($4) as big as your head. Open Su and Tu-Sa 8am-5pm.

The Shed, 113½ E. Palace Ave. (☎505-982-9030), up the street from the Plaza. Feels like a garden. Lots of vegetarian dishes, like quesadillas ($6) and excellent blue corn burritos ($8.75). Meat-eaters will enjoy the amazing chicken enchilada verde ($10.75). Open M-Sa 11am-2:30pm and 5:30-9pm.

♔ ACCOMMODATIONS

Hotels in Santa Fe tend toward the expensive side. As early as May they become swamped with requests for rooms during **Indian Market** and **Fiesta de Santa Fe.** Make reservations early. In general, the motels along **Cerrillos Rd.** have the best prices, but even these places run $40-60 per night. Downtown, B&Bs dot most corners, but unless your budget is liberal, steer clear. Nearby camping is pleasant during the summer and easier on the wallet. Two sites for free primitive camping are **Big Tesuque** and **Ski Basin Campgrounds** on national forest land. These campgrounds are both off Rte. 475 toward the Ski Basin and have pit toilets.

Santa Fe International Hostel and Pension, 1412 Cerrillos Rd. (☎505-988-1153). Easily accessible, with a fully stocked kitchen, Internet ($2 per day) laundry, and a sitting room. Guests perform one 10min. task each morning. Check-in by 11pm. Check-out by noon. Dorms $14, nonmembers $15; private rooms $25.

Thunderbird Inn, 1821 Cerrillos Rd. (☎505-983-4397). Slightly closer to town than most and an excellent value. Large rooms with A/C and cable TV, some with fridges and microwaves. Reception 24hr. Summer singles $50-55; doubles $55-60. Winter $39-44/$44-49.

Kings Rest Court Motel, 1452 Cerrillos Rd. (☎505-983-8879). Pleasant rooms in this old tourist court come with their own carport, as well as cable TV. Summer singles $48; doubles $60. Winter $36/$45.

Silver Saddle Motel, 2810 Cerrillos Rd. (☎505-471-7663). Beautiful adobe rooms with cowboy paraphernalia have A/C and cable. Reception 7am-11:30pm. Summer singles $67; doubles $72. Winter $45/$50.

Hyde State Park Campground (☎505-983-7175), 8 mi. from Santa Fe on Rte. 475. Over 50 sites with water, pit toilets, and shelters. Sites $10, hookup $14.

NIGHTLIFE

Santa Fe nightlife tends to be more mellow than in nearby Albuquerque. The **Cowgirl Hall of Fame,** 319 S. Guadalupe St., has live hoe-downs that range from bluegrass to country. (☎505-982-2565. Sa-Su ranch breakfast. Happy hour 3-6pm and midnight-1am. 21+ after midnight. Cover under $3. Open M-F 11am-2am, Sa 8:30am-2am, Su 8:30am-midnight.) **Paramount,** 331 Sandoval St., is the only dance club in Santa Fe. (☎505-982-8999. Live music Su, Tu, Th. Sa dance. 21+. Cover $5-7, Sa $5-20. Open M-Sa 9pm-2am, Su 9pm-midnight.) **Bar B,** 330 Sandoval St., has futuristic decor and live music. (☎505-982-8999. Cover $2-7. Open M-Sa 5pm-2am, Su 5pm-midnight.)

LEAVING SANTA FE
Exit Santa Fe on **Cerillos Rd.** Drive 4¼ mi. and then merge into **I-25.** Follow the interstate to Exit 276, and then take the east frontage road toward Exit 267, passing **La Cienega,** 4½ mi. farther, and **Algodones.**

DETOUR: COCHITI PUEBLO
At Exit 264 off the interstate, go west, turning right onto Rte. 16; go 8 mi. and then right onto Rte. 22. Take a left into the Cochiti Pueblo Reservation, and then a right onto Forest Rte. 266. The parking area is 5 mi. from the turnoff.

An excellent spot for picnicking, The **Kasha-Katuwe Tent Rocks Natural Monument** has two easy trails through magnificent slot canyons and towering tent rock formations; one (20min. round-trip) leads up to a small cave, the other (40min. round-trip), has a steep climb up a well-marked path at the end, but leads hikers to a spectacular view. Nearby, the **Cochiti Lake Campground** is high on the pueblo, with lake access. (☎505-761-8700. Monument open summer 7am-6pm; winter 8am-5pm. $5 per vehicle. Sites $5, with hookup $10.)

BERNALILLO. The **Coronado State Monument,** 485 Kuaua Rd., has recreated Indian ruins and a reconstructed Kiva. The small museum has original murals from the Kiva and town walls. (☎505-867-5351. Open M and W-Su 8:30am-4:30pm. $3, under 16 free.) **The Coronado Campground,** just north of Rte. 66 entering town, is a good place to sleep. (☎505-980-8250. Sites $8, with hookup $11, RV sites $18.) The **Range Cafe,** 925 Camino del Pueblo, offers upscale meals ($6-10), and the "world's best brownie" ($2). (☎505-867-1700. Open Su-Th 7:30am-9pm, F-Sa 7:30am-9:30pm.)

APPROACHING ALBUQUERQUE
Continue along the south frontage road from **Bernalillo** through **Alameda** into Albuquerque.

ALBUQUERQUE

Albuquerque, where citizens still refer to Central Ave. as Rte. 66, is full of history and culture, with ethnic restaurants, offbeat cafes, and raging night-clubs. The University of New Mexico is responsible for the town's young demographic, while the Hispanic, Native American, and gay and lesbian communities contribute cultural vibrancy and diversity to New Mexico's largest city.

VITAL STATS

Population: 450,000

Visitor Info: Albuquerque Visitors Center, 401 2nd St. NW (☎505-842-9918; www.abqcvb.org), 3 blocks north of Central Ave. in the Convention Center. Open M-F 9am-5pm. **Old Town Visitors Center,** 303 Romano St. NW (☎505-243-3215), in the shopping plaza west of the church. Open daily Apr.-Oct. 9am-5pm; Nov.-Mar. 9:30am-4:30pm.

Internet Access: Albuquerque Public Library, Main Branch, 501 Copper NW (☎505-768-5141). Open M and W-Sa 10am-6pm, Tu 11am-7pm.

Post Office: 1135 Broadway NE (☎505-346-8044), at Mountain St. Open M-F 7:30am-6pm. **Postal Code:** 87101.

GETTING AROUND

Rte. 66 in Albuquerque is known as **Central Ave.,** and is the main thoroughfare of the city, running through all its major neighborhoods. Central Ave. runs east-west and **I-25** runs north-south; the two divide Albuquerque into quadrants. All downtown addresses come with a quadrant designation: NE, NW, SE, or SW. The campus of the **University of New Mexico (UNM)** spreads along Central Ave. from University Ave. to Carlisle St. **Nob Hill,** the area of Central Ave. around **Carlisle St.,** features coffee shops, bookstores, and galleries. **Downtown** lies on Central Ave. between **10th St.** and **Broadway. Old Town Plaza** sits between **San Felipe, North Plaza, South Plaza,** and **Romero,** off Central Ave.

SIGHTS

OLD TOWN. When the railroad cut through Albuquerque in the 19th century, it missed Old Town by almost 2 mi. As downtown grew around the railroad, Old Town remained untouched until the 1950s, when the city realized that it had a tourist magnet right under its nose. Just north of Central Ave. and east of Río Grande Blvd., the adobe plaza looks today much like it did over 100 years ago, save for the ubiquitous restaurants, gift

Albuquerque

🏕🏠 ACCOMMODATIONS
Coronado Campground, **1**
Rte. 66 Youth Hostel, **6**
Sandia Mountain Hostel, **2**

🍎 FOOD
Graze, **3**
Java Joe's, **7**
El Norteño, **4**

📷 NIGHTLIFE
Banana Joe's Island Party, **8**
Burt's Tiki Bar, **9**
Guild Cinema, **5**

PARADISE HILLS

Boca Negra Canyon

LOS RANCHOS DE ALBUQUERQUE

Rio Grande Blvd.

85

Paseo del Norte

Ventura St.

TO BERNALILLO (8mi), (15mi), & SANTA FE (48mi)

25

Academy Rd.

Petroglyph National Monument Visitor Center

Montaño Rd.

Rio Grande Nature Center

Montgomery Blvd.

EAST SIDE

San Mateo Blvd.

Carlisle Blvd.

Wyoming Blvd.

Eubank Blvd.

Coors Blvd.

Unser

Rio Grande

4th St.

2nd St.

Edith Blvd.

12th St.

Indian Pueblo Cultural Center

Menaul Blvd.

San Pedro Blvd.

UPTOWN

40

TO GALLUP (133mi)

OLD TOWN

Mountain Rd.

Lomas

SEE INSET

DOWNTOWN

MLK

Blvd.

Indian School Rd.

40

Constitution Ave.

Juan Tabo Blvd.

UNIVERSITY

University of New Mexico

Aquarium & Botanic Garden

HIST 66

Rio Grande Zoo

SEE INSET

Central Ave.

SEE INSET

Lomas Blvd.

Presbyterian Hospital

Zuni Blvd.

NOB HILL

Ta Lin Market

HIST 66

40

TO 2 (10mi)

Ceasar Chavez Blvd.

Coors Blvd.

National Hispanic Cultural Center

Broadway

25

University Blvd.

Gibson Blvd.

Louisiana Blvd.

Pennsylvania Blvd.

N LG

45

ℹ

✈ Albuquerque Intl. Airport

47

TO TRUTH OR CONSEQUENCES (130mi)

0   2 miles
0   2 kilometers

Central Ave.

Central Ave.

Harvard Dr.
Cornell Dr.
Stanford Dr.
Columbia Dr.
Princeton Dr.
Vassar Dr.
Girard Blvd.
Dartmouth Dr.
Richmond Dr.
Bryn Mawr Dr.
Wellesley Dr.
Tulane Dr.
Carlisle Blvd.
Amherst Dr.
Hermosa Dr.
Solano Dr.
Aliso Dr.
Morningside Dr.
Montclaire Dr.
Sierra Dr.
Graceland Dr.

3   4 5

0   300 meters
0   300 yards

Old Town Albuquerque

San Felipe Plaza

Albuquerque Children's Museum

National Atomic Museum

Mountain Rd.

LodeStar Astronomy Center

Rio Grande Blvd.

Charlevoix St.

Albuquerque Museum

19th St.

Museum of Natural History & Science

Church St.

ℹ

Plaza Don Luis

North Plaza

San Felipe de Neri Church

OLD TOWN PLAZA

Tiguex Park

Turquoise Museum

South Plaza

HIST 66

Romero St.

San Felipe St.

Old Town Rd.

Central Ave.

N LG

Rattlesnake Museum

Marble Ave.

20th St.

19th St.

18th St.

0   200 meters
0   200 yards

Lomas Blvd.

HIST 66

Downtown Albuquerque

Lomas Blvd.

Fruit Ave.

6th St.
5th St.
4th St.
3rd St.

N LG

Roma Ave.

11th St.

10th St.

8th St.

7th St.

Marquette Ave.

2nd St.

MLK Blvd.

HIST 66

Kent Ave.

Tijeras Ave.

Public Library

Copper

Telephone Pioneer Museum

ℹ

6   Central Ave.

Park Ave.

7

Gold Ave.

8

9

11th St.
10th St.
9th St.
8th St.
7th St.
6th St.
5th St.
4th St.

Silver Ave.

Lead Ave.

Coal Ave.

1st St.

HIST 66

Iron Ave.

0   200 meters
0   200 yards

ROUTE 66

shops, and jewelry vendors. Although a tourist trap, Old Town is an architectural marvel, and a stroll through it is worthwhile. **Walking tours** of Old Town meet at the Albuquerque Museum. *(1hr. tours Su and Tu-Sa 11am. Free with admission.)* On the north side of the plaza, the quaint **San Felipe de Neri Church** has stood the test of time, dating back to 1706. *(Open daily 9am-5pm. Accompanying museum open M-Sa 10am-4pm.)* A cluster of museums and attractions surrounds the plaza. To the northeast, the **Albuquerque Museum** showcases New Mexican art and history. The comprehensive exhibit on the Conquistadors and Spanish colonial rule is a must-see for anyone interested in the history of the area. *(2000 Mountain Rd. NW. ☎505-243-7255. Open Su and Tu-Sa 9am-5pm. Tours of the Sculpture Garden Tu-F at 10am. $3, seniors and children $1.)* No visit to Old Town would be complete without seeing the **Rattlesnake Museum,** which lies just south of the plaza. With over 30 species ranging from the deadly Mojave to the tiny Pygmy, this is the largest collection of live rattlesnakes in the world. *(202 San Felipe NW. ☎505-242-6569. Open M-Sa 10am-6pm, Su 1-5pm. $2.50, seniors $2, under 18 $1.50.)* Just outside the main Old Town area, Spike and Alberta, two statuesque dinosaurs, greet tourists outside the **New Mexico Museum of Natural History and Science.** Inside, interactive exhibits take visitors through the history of life on earth. The museum features a five-story dynatheater, planetarium, and simulated ride through the world of the dinosaurs. *(1801 Mountain Rd. NW. ☎505-841-2802. Open daily 9am-5pm; Sept. closed M. $5, seniors $4, children $2; with Dynatheater ticket $10/$8/$4.)*

UNIVERSITY MUSEUMS. The University of New Mexico has a couple of museums on campus that are worth a quick visit. The **University Art Museum** features changing exhibits that focus on 20th-century New Mexican paintings and photography. *(Near the corner of Central Ave. and Cornel St. ☎505-277-4001. Open Tu-F 9am-4pm. Free.)* The **Maxwell Museum of Anthropology** has excellent exhibits on the culture and ancient history of Native American settlement in the Southwest. *(On University Blvd., just north of MLK Blvd. ☎505-277-5963. Open Tu-F 9am-4pm, Sa 10am-4pm. Free.)*

CULTURAL ATTRACTIONS. The **Indian Pueblo Cultural Center** has a commercial edge, but still provides a good introduction to the history and culture of the 19 Indian Pueblos of New Mexico. The center includes a museum, store, and restaurant. *(2401 12th St. NW. ☎505-843-7270. Museum open daily 9am-4:30pm. Art demonstrations Sa-Su 11am-2pm. Native American dances Sa-Su 11am and 2pm. $4, seniors $3, students $1.)* The **National Hispanic Cultural Center** has an art museum with exhibits that explore folk art and representations of Hispanic social and cultural life in America. *(1701 4th St. SW, at the corner of Bridge St. Open Su and Tu-Sa 10am-5pm. $3, seniors $2, under 16 free.)* During the first week of October, hundreds of aeronauts take flight in hot-air balloons during the **Balloon Festival.** Beneath a surreal sky filled with the colorful giants, the entire city enjoys a week of barbecues and musical events.

◤ OUTDOOR ACTIVITIES

Rising a mile above Albuquerque to the northeast, the sunset-pink crest of the **Sandía Mountains** gives the mountains their name, which means "watermelon" in Spanish. The crest beckons to New Mexicans, drawing thousands to hike and explore. One of the most popular trails in New Mexico, **La Luz Trail** (7½ mi. one-way) climbs the Sandía Crest, beginning at the Juan Tabo Picnic Area. (From Exit 167 on I-40, drive north on Tramway Blvd. 9¾ mi. to Forest Rd. 333. Follow Trail 137 for 7 mi. and take 84 to the top.)

The Sandía Mountains have excellent mountain biking trails. Warm up on the moderate **Foothills Trail** (7 mi.), which skirts along the bottom of the mountains, just east of the city. The trail starts at the Elena Gallegos Picnic Area, off Tramway Blvd. The most popular place for biking is at the **Sandía Peak Ski Area,** 6 mi. up Rte. 536 on the way to Sandía Crest. Bikers can take their bikes up the chairlift and then ride down on 35 mi. of mountain trails and rollers, covering all skill levels. (☎505-242-9133. Helmets required. Chairlifts run June-Aug. Sa-Su 10am-4pm. Full-day lift ticket $14; single ride $8. Bikes $38 per day.)

Sandía Peak Ski Area, only 30min. from downtown, is a serviceable ski area for those who can't escape north to Taos or south to Ruidoso. Six lifts service 25 short trails (35% beginner; 55% intermediate; 10% advanced) on 200 skiable acres. The summit (10,378 ft.) tops a vertical drop of 1700 ft. (☎505-242-9133. Snowboards allowed. Annual snowfall 125 in. Open mid-Dec. to mid-Mar. daily 9am-4pm. Full-day $38, ages 13-20 $32, seniors and under 13 $29.) There are also excellent cross-country skiing trails in the **Cibola National Forest;** the North Crest and 10K trails are popular.

🍴 FOOD

A diverse ethnic community, hordes of hungry interstate travelers, and one big load of green chiles render the cuisine of Albuquerque surprisingly tasty. The area around **UNM** is the best bet for inexpensive eateries. A bit farther east, **Nob Hill** is a haven for yuppie fare, including avocado sandwiches and iced cappuccinos.

Java Joe's, 906 Park Ave. SW (☎ 404-765-1514), 1 block south of Central Ave. This lively, casual restaurant has hearty wraps ($5), sandwiches ($5.50), salads ($4-5), and great breakfast burritos ($3). Lots of vegetarian dishes and occasional live music. Open daily 6:30am-3:30pm.

El Norteño, 6416 Zuni (☎ 505-256-1431), at California. A family-run establishment renowned as the most authentic and varied Mexican joint in town. The shrimp roasted with garlic is a treat, and the vast repertoire runs from chicken *mole* ($8) to *caldo de res* (a beef stew) to beef tongue ($7-9). Lunch buffet M-F 11am-2pm ($6). Open daily 8:30am-9pm.

Graze, 3128 Central Ave. SE (☎ 505-268-4729). Patrons are encouraged to eat what they like from the eclectic menu without the limits of conventional courses. Highly seasonal menu. Chic but friendly; smallish servings. Stuffed pepper with a goat cheese and truffle sauce $9. Open Tu-Sa 11am-11pm.

🏠 ACCOMMODATIONS

Cheap motels line **Central Ave.,** even near downtown. Though many of them are worth their price, be sure to evaluate the quality before paying. During the October **Balloon Festival,** rooms are scarce; call ahead for reservations.

Route 66 Youth Hostel, 1012 Central Ave. SW (☎ 505-247-1813), at 10th St. Friendly hostel located between downtown and Old Town. Dorm and private rooms are simple but clean. Key deposit $5. Reception 7:30-10:30am and 4-11pm. Check-out 10:30am. 10 easy chores required. Dorms $14; singles $20; doubles $25, with bath $30.

Sandía Mountain Hostel, 12234 Rte. 14 North (☎ 505-281-4117), in nearby Cedar Crest. Take I-40

East to Exit 175 and go 4 mi. north on Rte. 14. Only 10 mi. from the Sandía Ski Area, this wooden building offers a living room with fireplace and kitchen, plus a family of donkeys out back. Hiking and biking trails are across the street. Linen $1. Coin-op laundry. Dorms $14; private cabins $32; sites $8.

Coronado Campground (☎ 505-980-8256), about 15 mi. north of Albuquerque. Take I-25 to Exit 242 and follow the signs. A pleasant campground on the banks of the Río Grande. Adobe shelters offer a respite from the heat. Toilets, showers, and water available. Open M and W-Su 8:30am-5pm; self-service pay station after hours. Tent sites $8, with shelters and picnic tables $18; full hookup $18-20.

🍸 NIGHTLIFE

Albuquerque is an oasis of interesting bars, jamming nightclubs, art film houses, and university culture. Check flyers posted around the university area for live music shows or pick up a copy of *Alibi*, the free local weekly. Most nightlife huddles on and near **Central Ave.,** downtown and near the university; **Nob Hill** establishments tend to be the most gay-friendly. **Burt's Tiki Bar,** 313 Gold St. SW, is situated a block south of the Central Ave. strip of clubs, and the difference shows in its friendlier, more laid-back atmosphere. Surf and tiki paraphernalia line the walls and ceiling, while anything from funk to punk to live hip-hop takes the stage. (☎ 505-247-2878. Live music Tu-Sa and occasionally Su-M. No cover. Normally open Tu-Sa 9pm-2am.) **Banana Joe's Island Party,** 610 Central Ave. SW, is the largest club in Albuquerque. With six bars, a tropical patio, a concert hall, and one big dance floor, Banana Joe's brings nightlife to the masses. Nightly live music ranges from reggae to flamenco. (☎ 505-244-0024. DJ downstairs Th-Sa. Happy hour 5-8pm. 21+. Cover Th-Sa $5. Open Su and Tu-Sa 5pm-2am.) The offbeat **Guild Cinema,** 3405 Central Ave. NE, runs independent and foreign films. (☎ 505-255-1848. Open M-Th at 4:30, 7pm, F-Su at 2, 4:30, 9:15pm. $7; students, seniors, and all shows before 5pm $5.)

🚗 LEAVING ALBUQUERQUE
Here the old route joins with the interstate; follow **Rte. 66** west out of Albuquerque on **I-40.**

👁 PETROGLYPH NATIONAL MONUMENT
To reach the park itself, take I-40 to Unser Blvd. (Exit 154) and follow the park signs. To see the nearby

volcanoes, take Exit 149 off I-40 and follow Paseo del Volcán to a dirt road. The volcanoes are 4¼ mi. north of the exit.

Just outside Albuquerque, this national monument features more than 20,000 images etched into lava rocks between 1300 and 1680 by Pueblo Indians and Spanish settlers. The park encompasses much of the 17 mi. **West Mesa,** a ridge of black basalt boulders formed as a result of volcanic activity 130,000 years ago. The most accessible petroglyphs can be found via three short trails at **Boca Negra Canyon,** 2 mi. north of the Visitors Center. The **Rinconada Canyon Trail,** 1 mi. south of the Visitors Center, has more intricate rock art and is an easy 2½ mi. desert hike along the base of the West Mesa. (☎505-899-0205. Park open daily 8am-5pm. M-F $1, Sa-Su $2.)

THE ROAD TO ACOMA PUEBLO

The scenery from Albuquerque is glorious, but the road is often isolated and poorly maintained. Follow I-40 west 38 mi. to **Los Lunas,** Exit 126, passing the historic **Rio Puerco** bridge at Mile 24. Head left on Rte. 6 for 2¼ mi. and turn right on the narrow passage over the railroad tracks. This stretch of road leading to Mesita, approximately 9 mi. later, is potholed, frequently unpaved, and largely unappealing to the underbelly of your car, but the view of the mesas above the winding stretches of old road is quite appealing for anyone with a taste for the Southwest and the open road. Follow the dirt road until it crosses I-40, 8 mi. after picking it up, and continue west on the north frontage road.

Mesita, 1 mi. later, was founded in the late 1800s; the town's old mission is still standing, as are the remains of many old buildings throughout the town, and the traditional intentions of the founders remain in the moratorium on tourist photography in the town.

Continue 5½ mi. from Mesita to the junction with **Rte. 124,** turning west onto 124. Rising up the hill through **Laguna,** try a stretch of the old road through the village by turning left and continuing west up the hill. This segment rejoins the road a half-mile later. Turn left when you rejoin Rte. 124, just across from the transfer station. The town of Laguna was founded in 1699 by Spanish missionaries, and the mission in the town dates from that year, although it fell into disrepair after the Pueblo revolt of 1680, and was restored in the 1930s.

Continue on Rte. 124, snaking through the mesas and along the bottoms of canyons, passing through **Paraje** 5 mi. farther down the road, then **Budville** and **Cubera.** Follow Rte. 124 through **Villa de Cubero** and **San Fidel** and cross to the south side of I-40 in **McCartys.**

 Villa de Cubero was where Ernest Hemingway holed up to write The Old Man and the Sea, although little is left to suggest its role as literary foil to Hemingway's ocean.

ACOMA PUEBLO AND SKY CITY
Turn off the south frontage road 1 mi. beyond McCartys; take the bus to the pueblo.

Arguably the oldest continuously inhabited area in North America, **Sky City,** on the **Acoma Pueblo,** peers over the edge of the high mesa. Accessible only by a narrow staircase, the Sky City avoided Spanish rule until 1599, when its residents were brutally enslaved by Don Juan de Onate. Between seven and 13 families live on the mesa, which lacks electricity and running water, year-round. Perched high above the rocky world below, the **San Esteban Rey Mission** on the pueblo is a gravity-defying architectural feat and a stunning example of Southwestern pueblo architecture. Visitors must buy a bus pass at the Visitors Center below to ride up to the pueblo with a guide. Photographs are prohibited unless you buy a photography pass, and video cameras are forbidden. Bring cash if you plan on ascending the pueblo, as resident native artists often lay out their renowned hand painted pottery. All are welcome September 2 for the Harvest Dance and Annual Feast of San Estevan at Old Acoma. (☎505-470-4966. Open daily except July 10-13 and 1st or 2nd weekend of Oct. Tours daily April-Oct. 8am-6pm; Nov.-Mar. 8am-5pm. Last tour 1hr. before closing. $10, seniors $9, children $7. Photography pass $10.)

APPROACHING GRANTS
From the south frontage road leading from McCartys, pass under **I-40** after 5½ mi. Cross onto the north side and continue into Grants, entering on **Santa Fe Ave.**

GRANTS

Though largely overlooked in the shadow of Gallup 60 mi. to the west, today Grants serves as an excellent base for numerous activities in the area, offering cheap lodging and great bang for the buck eats. Grants first appeared on the map when the three Grant brothers were given a contract to build the Santa Fe railroad through the area. After the railroad boom, Grants became a shoot-'em-up Old West town, and population scraped as low as 350. Grants got its big chance in 1950 when a Navajo named Paddy Martinez overheard some prospectors in a cafe discussing a valuable yellow mineral they called carnotite, and recognized the rock as abundant near his sheep pastures outside of town. Grants became a mining town, and the Uranium wealth made the town glow until the last of the mines was tapped out in the 1980s.

(VITAL STATS)

Population: 8800

Visitor Info: Grants Chamber of Commerce, 100 N. Iron Ave. (☎505-287-4802; www.grants.org), in the New Mexico Mining Museum. Open M-Sa 9am-4pm. **El Malpais Info Center** (☎505-783-4774), 23 mi. south of I-40 on Rte. 53. Open daily 8:30am-4:30pm.

Internet Access: Mother Whiteside Memorial Library, 525 High St. (☎505-287-7927). Open M-F 9am-5pm, Sa 9am-3:30pm.

Post Office: 816 W. Santa Fe Ave. (☎505-287-3143.) Open M-F 8:50am-5pm, Sa 8:30am-noon. **Postal Code:** 87020.

⊏ GETTING AROUND. Although streets in Grants are laid out erratically, getting around is fairly simple; **Rte. 66** runs through the center of town as **Santa Fe Ave.;** most attractions, food, and accommodations can be found along this strip. **I-40** runs just south of town, parallel to Santa Fe Ave. **Parking** is usually easy to come by.

◖ SIGHTS. Grant's mining history is panned out in the **New Mexico Mining Museum,** 100 N. Iron Ave., where you can almost feel yourself glow as you descend a restored mine shaft under the museum. The elevator even descends extra-slowly to create the illusion of being far beneath the basement location. (☎505-287-4802. Open M-Sa 9am-4pm. $3, students and seniors $2, under 6 free.) The volcanic past of the Grants area has created an abundance of interesting natural phenomena. **Malpais National Monument,** south of town on Rte. 53, is home to at least 17 mi. of lava tube caves, ice caves, spatter cones, and rugged ter-

rain. Miles of hiking lead to sandstone bluffs, natural arches, ancient Native American trade routes, and over 30 volcanic craters. Despite its spectacular landscape, the monument does not receive the traffic of some of its neighbors, making it a perfect spot to escape the crowds and head into some true wilderness. Continuing on Rte. 53, the **Ice Caves,** 12000 Ice Caves Rd., are a collapsed lava tube forming a cave that remains 31°F year-round. Admission to the ice caves also includes admission to the **Bandera Volcano,** a maw of fire 10,000 years ago, now a gaping hole. Tickets to the attractions can be purchased at the converted logging saloon and dance hall, now the **Old Time Trading Post.** (☎888-423-2283; www.icecaves.com. Open daily 8am-1hr. before sunset. $8.)

◪ FOOD. As mottoes go, everything's bigger in Texas, but that overlooks the **Uranium Cafe,** 519 W. Santa Fe Ave. Their inch-thick yellow cakes ($3) overlap the plate onto the table; eat two and they're free. The smaller Silver Yellow Cakes are still generously dinner-plate-sized, an inch thick and a deal at $1.75 for enough breakfast for a boy scout troop. Burgers are also "Uranium size." (☎505-876-6003. Open M-F 7am-2pm, Sa 8am-2pm.) **El Cafecito,** 820 E. Santa Fe Ave., is hands-down the best Mexican food in town, with prices that can't hurt. (☎505-285-6229. Entrees $1.50-6. Open M-F 7am-9pm, Sa 7am-8pm.) The **Monte Carlo,** 721 W. Santa Fe Ave., has excellent variety and budget-minded prices on its extensive menu of New Mexican cuisine, seafood, steak, and salads. (☎505-287-9250. Breakfast $2-5. Lunch and dinner $5-13. Open daily 7am-10pm.) The **Canton Cafe,** 1212 W. Santa Fe Ave., serves above-average all-you-can-eat buffet Chinese food. (☎505-287-8314. Buffet $7. Open daily 11am-9pm.)

◖ ACCOMMODATIONS. Entering town on Santa Fe Ave., look to the left for chain accommodations, which cluster with the fast-food joints at the east end of town. Continuing west on Santa Fe Ave., Grants has a neon strip to rival Santa Rosa and Tucumcari. Several of the original Rte. 66 motels are still great budget options. The **Sands Motel,** 112 McArthur, lauded through billboards west of town, and has its own mini-strip coming from the east. Rooms come with microwaves, refrigerators, and the pleasure of knowing your motel was the favorite of an Elvis impersonator and the last traveling American troubadour.

(☎505-287-2996. Singles from $31; doubles from $38.) Just east on Santa Fe Ave., the **Southwest Motel,** 1000 E. Santa Fe Ave., rents rooms almost as nice, but without the microwave and fluorescent glory. (☎505-287-2935. Singles $20; doubles $35.) Across the street, rooms at the **Desert Sun Motel,** 1121 E. Santa Fe Ave., are clean and pleasant. (☎505-287-7925. Singles $20; doubles $25.)

LEAVING GRANTS
Leaving Grants, follow **Rte. 122** through the suburb of Milan. Continue south 9½ mi. to **Prewitt.**

THOREAU
Although signs as far east as Albuquerque advertise a multitude of jewelry and souvenir stops, one of the best places to splurge is in the tiny town of Thoreau (pronounced "Threw"). Less blazingly publicized than the stores clustering around the Continental Divide, the **Navajo Cooperative Store,** 23 1st St., has jewelry, clothing, and other souvenirs, and profits from the store go toward supporting **The Gathering Place,** a community-based non-profit organization run by Navajo to provide community services. (Take the Thoreau exit, heading north into town ¼ mi. Turn right at the stop sign just over the bridge, then right again and under the overpass. ☎505-862-8075. Open M 8:30am-5pm, Tu-F 8:30am-6:30pm, Sa 9am-5pm.)

Across the underpass from the Navajo Coop, **Mel and Dee's,** at 1st and Lenore St., offers traditional dishes with a twist, such as Navajo Burgers (two patties on fry bread; $5). (☎505-862-7712. Open M-F 11am-8pm, Sa 11am-6pm.) Five miles west of town is the **Continental Divide;** rain falling east of the line makes its way to the Atlantic, while rain falling on the west ends up in the Pacific.

RED ROCK STATE PARK
Just east of Gallup.

Red Rock State Park provides camping and hiking opportunities. The park's museum features kachina dolls, pottery, blankets, jewelry, and regional art. During the warmer months Red Rock is the site of concerts, rodeos, and motorcycle races; call ahead to make sure the park is open for camping. (☎505-722-3829; rrsp@ci.gallup.nm.us. Campground ☎505-863-1329. Museum open M-Sa 8am-4:30; June-Aug. also Su. Trading post with basic food supplies and camping registration open daily 8:30-4:30. Sites $10; RVs $18.)

GALLUP
At the intersection of Rte. 66 and U.S. 666, Gallup has enough attractions to fill a day. Native American vendors fill parking lots, and "trading posts" crammed with silversmithing and local turquoise line the downtown streets. If you can overlook the gaudy signs and ubiquitous turquoise vendors, the landscape and proximity to the Petrified Forest National Park make Gallup a worthwhile stop.

⌐ VITAL STATS

Population: 20,000

Visitor Info: Gallup Visitors Center, 701 Montoya Blvd. (☎505-863-4909 or 800-242-4282; www.gallupnm.org), just off Rte. 66. Open daily 8am-5pm; June-Aug. until 6pm. **Gallup Chamber of Commerce,** 103 Rte. 66 (☎505-722-2228). Open M-F 8:30am-5pm.

Internet Access: Octavia Fellin Library, 115 W. Hill St. (☎505-836-1291). Open M-Th 9am-8pm, F-Sa 10am-6pm.

Post Office: 500 S. 2nd St. (☎505-863-3491). Open M-F 8:30am-5pm, Sa 10am-1:30pm. **Postal Code:** 87301.

⌐ GETTING AROUND. Almost all you need to know about getting around in Gallup is that **Rte. 66,** the city's main drag, runs parallel to and south of **I-40.** Numbered streets run roughly north-south; **2nd St.** is also a main thoroughfare, known as N. 2nd St. north of its intersection with Rte. 66 and S. 2nd St. south of the intersection.

◉ SIGHTS. For a small town, Gallup has its share of local attractions, both in town and the surrounding areas. In addition to supplying all the info on Gallup you could ever want, the **Gallup Chamber of Commerce** also houses the town's **Navajo Code Talker Museum,** 103 Rte. 66, paying tribute to the over 400 Navajo whose "code" was never broken by enemy forces during WWII. The museum details the conception of using the Navajo language as the base for a military code through the Navajo involvement in WWII, and finally Ronald Reagan's declaration of August 14 as "National Navajo Code Talkers Day." (☎505-722-2228. Open M-F 8am-5pm.) The **Gallup Cultural Center,** 201 Rte. 66, houses the Storyteller Museum, Kiva Cinema, Angela's Cafe con Leche, the Ceremonial Gallery, the Wisdom Keeper Book Store/Gift Shop, and seasonal artist presentations.

ROUTE 66

FROM MAP #8

ROUTE 66 MAP #9

Fort Wingate

Rehobeth State Park

Gallup

Allison

264

Mentmore

NEW MEXICO
ARIZONA

Mamelito

Lupton

Houck

Sanders

Chambers

Navajo

0   15 miles

0   15 kilometers

Petrified Forest National Park

Sun Valley

Holbrook

Joseph City

Winslow

Little Colorado R.

Two Guns

▼ TO MAP #10

R O U T E   6 6

(☎505-863-4131. Open M-Sa 8am-8pm.) The **Gallup Historical Society** 300 Rte. 66 (☎505-863-1363), tells the story of Gallup as the site of a huge coal deposit, drawing miners and families to paymaster David Gallup's new town. **Gilbert Ortega's,** 3306 Rte. 66 (☎505-722-6666), does a bustling trade; you will get used to it, as the Ortega empire covers everything from jewelry to tacos and extends far down the road toward Arizona. This branch has a stunning selection of turquoise jewelry and the **world's largest turquoise nugget.** For an amazing selection of turquoise jewelry and other locally produced goods, **Richardson's Trading Company and Cash Pawn, Inc.,** 222 Rte. 66 (☎605-722-4762), does brisk business in goods purchased from, and pawned by, local artists and citizens.

🍴 FOOD. For westbound travelers, **Earl's Restaurant,** 1400 Rte. 66, at the east end of town, has been a first stop in town since the 1940s, with food and prices to show why. (☎505-863-4201 or 505-863-3285. Entrees $5-10. Open M-Th 6am-9pm, F-Sa 6am-9:30pm, Su 7am-9pm.) A local favorite, **The Ranch Kitchen,** 3001 Rte. 66, 2 mi. west of town on Rte. 66, dishes up hearty portions of inventive Mexican and American cuisine, like the popular smoked trout omelette ($7), or traditional Native American lamb stew ($7) with fry bread. (☎505-722-2537. Open daily summer 7am-10pm; Oct.-Mar. 7am-9pm.) **Angela's Cafe con Leche,** in the Greyhound station on Rte. 66 downtown, has a variety of gourmet coffee drinks, as well as fresh salads ($6-7), daily soup offerings ($2-3), sandwiches ($6), and quiche ($6). The cafe also hosts live music. (☎505-722-7526. Open M-Th 8:30am-5pm, F 8:30am-9pm.) Located on a section of the old alignment, **Virgie's,** 2720 Rte. 66, is topped with an awesome blinking beacon of Rte. 66 splendor and has popular Mexican dishes, all reasonably priced. (☎505-863-5152. Fajitas $7.50. Open M-Sa 7am-10pm.)

🏠 ACCOMMODATIONS. At the east end of town, Rte. 66 is lined with dirt cheap motels (emphasis on the dirt). Without a doubt, though, the best lodging in Gallup is the sprawling **El Rancho Hotel and Motel,** 1000 Rte. 66. Legend has it that the hotel was built for the brother of film pioneer D.W. Griffith. Conflicting stories claim that Griffith actually had no brother; the man claiming to be R.E. Griffith was little more than a master trickster. The motel does have cinematic claim to fame, though; it has been the longtime lodging choice of celebrities passing through or on location, and most have had a room or a dish in the restaurant named after them. (☎505-863-9311. Singles from $52; doubles from $61.) A good bet for those watching their bottom line is the **El Capitaine Motel,** 1300 Rte. 66, with clean, well-maintained rooms. (☎505-863-6828. Singles from $38; doubles from $42.) The historic **Roadrunner Motel,** 3012 Rte. 66, also offers clean, reasonable rooms on the eastern edge of town. (☎505-863-3804. Rooms from $36.)

LEAVING GALLUP
Approximately 9 mi. west of town on **Rte. 66,** 3½ mi. past the I-40 overpass, head left on **Rte. 118.** Follow the south frontage road 4 mi., under I-40, and then curve right over the railroad tracks.

THE ROAD TO ARIZONA
The tiny old town of **Manuelito** is 15 mi. out of Gallup. The view leaving town is stunning and expansive; a riverbed cuts away on one side, and snow-capped mountains rise on the far side of the tracks. Between Gallup and Holbrook, attractions and gas are few and far between, although curio shops virtually wallpaper the strip. As **Ortega Family** stores lead you into Arizona, the scenery levels to board flat until reaching the colorful terrain of the Painted Desert and the Petrified Forest. The land sinks away dramatically in places, indicating the riverbeds that prehistorically covered the area. At the end of the road is **Holbrook.**

The first of its kind, the **Historic Route 66 Association of Arizona,** P.O. Box 66, Kingman, AZ 86402, sponsors an annual "Route 66 Fun Run" the first weekend in May, starting in Seligman and ending in Topock/Golden Shores. The race is open to all legal vehicles with wheels. Call ☎928-753-5001 for more info.

Welcome To **ARIZONA**

If you're traveling between April and October, you'll enter the Pacific Time Zone as you cross into Arizona, where it is 1hr. earlier. November-March there is no change here.

CHIEF YELLOWHORSE TRADING POST
Along Rte. 66, near Lupton, AZ, and the border.

As you enter Arizona, the land is dramatically empty; however, should the area's natural splendor become overwhelming, Rte. 66 does not fail to disappoint. Just as you pass through absolute nothingness toward the Arizona border, the Chief Yellowhorse Trading Post is a gaudy and sudden oasis of yellow signs and flags. Straddle the state line in the gift-store hogan or take a miniature tour of replica cave dwellings and see a real live buffalo. (☎928-688-2463. Open M-F 9am-5pm.)

THE ROAD TO PETRIFIED FOREST
The Chief Yellowhorse Trading Post is just the first in an unending slew of trading posts stretching from the Arizona line. Just past the border, the **Painted Cliffs Welcome Center** will outfit roadtrippers with maps and info. (☎928-688-2448. Open M-F 8am-5pm.) Just east of the Welcome Center, cross under I-40 to the south frontage road. Continue 5½ mi. to join I-40 at Exit 354. Three miles later in **Houck,** is another Ortega jewelry metropolis, **Indian City,** and **Chee's Indian Store** (☎928-688-2433) in its shadow. The adjacent fry bread stand has fresh Indian Tacos ($5) and fry bread with honey, sugar, or cheese ($2). Three and a half miles farther down the road, the **Ft. Courage Trading Post** also includes a post office and a 1960s pancake house serving everything from tacos to ice cream. (☎928-688-2723. Restaurant open daily 6:30am-6:30pm. Post office open M-F 8:30am-12:30pm and 1-5pm, Sa 9am-noon.)

From Houck, follow the interstate 1½ mi. to the Pine Springs Road Exit (346). For the next 7 mi., original Rte. 66 is a nasty piece of potholed dirt road, often with little shoulder, so you might stay on the interstate to the Sanders Exit (339). The brave (or foolish) who take the dirt frontage road can find age-old **Querino Trading Post,** which stocks everything from shampoo to ice cream. Follow the dirt road 6¼ mi., or stay on I-40 to Exit 341.

At Exit 341, follow the north frontage road 2 mi. to **Sanders,** home to the pink, white, and chrome **Route 66 Diner and Pizza Shack,** on the south side of the interstate. This roadside classic serves shakes

($1.70) and cobblers ($2), hearty breakfasts, sandwiches, lunch and dinner plates, not to mention pizzas. (☎928-688-2537. Open M-F 7am-8pm.) One of the few gas stations along this stretch of route.

Gas is also available in **Chambers,** 6 mi. from Sanders at the junction of I-40 and Rte. 191. Chambers has offered respite to many a stranded traveler with the **Best Western Chieftain Motel,** the only motel for miles. The adjacent restaurant provides non-fast-food meals. (☎800-657-7632. Breakfast included. Singles $87; doubles $93. Restaurant open daily 6am-8pm.) Continue through **Navajo,** where gas is available at the 24hr. Texaco station.

◤ **APPROACHING PETRIFIED FOREST**
Take Exit 311 (6½ mi. past **Navajo**) from **I-40**.

PETRIFIED FOREST NATIONAL PARK

Spreading over 60,000 acres, the Petrified Forest National Park looks like the aftermath of a prehistoric Grateful Dead concert—an enormous tie-dyed desert littered with rainbow-colored trees. Some 225 million years ago, when Arizona's desert was swampland, volcanic ash covered the logs, slowing their decay. Silica-infused water seeped through the wood, and the silica crystallized into quartz, combining with iron-rich minerals to produce rainbow hues. Colorful sediment was laid down in this floodplain, creating the stunning colors that stripe the park's badlands.

╭─ **VITAL STATS** ─────────────────╮

Area: 93,500 acres

Visitor Info: Painted Desert Visitors Center (☎928-524-6228), off I-40 at the north entrance to the park. Open daily June-Aug. 7am-7pm; Sept.-May 8am-5pm.

Gateway towns: Gallup (p. 515), Sun Valley (p. 519), Holbrook (p. 519).

Fees: Weekly pass $10 per vehicle.

╰──────────────────────────────────╯

▣ **GETTING AROUND.** Roughly speaking, the park can be divided into two parts: the northern Painted Desert and the southern Petrified Forest. A 28 mi. road connects the two sections. With lookout points and trails at intervals along the road, driving from one end of the park to the other is a good way to take in the full spectrum of colors

and landscapes. An entrance station and Visitors Center welcomes visitors to both ends of the park, and a restaurant is located at the northern end.

◩ **SIGHTS.** Most travelers opt to drive the 28 mi. park road from north to south. From the north, the first stop is **Tiponi Point.** From the next stop at **Tawa Point,** the **Painted Desert Rim Trail** (½ mi. one-way) skirts the mesa edge above the Lithodendron Wash and the Black Forest before ending at **Kachina Point.** The panoramas from Kachina Point are among the best in the park, and the point provides access to the **Painted Desert Wilderness,** the park's designated region for backcountry hiking and camping. As the road crosses I-40, it enters the Petrified Forest portion of the park. The next stop is the 100-room **Puerco Pueblo.** A short trail through the pueblo offers viewpoints of nearby petroglyphs. Many more petroglyphs may be seen at **Newspaper Rock,** but at a distance. The road then wanders through the eerie moonscape of **The Tepees,** before arriving at the 3 mi. **Blue Mesa** vehicle loop. The **Long Logs** and **Giant Logs Trails,** near the southern Visitors Center, are littered with fragments of petrified wood. Both trails are less than 1 mi. and fairly flat but travel through the densest concentration of petrified wood in the world. Don't pick up the petrified wood—it's already scared enough. Also, taking fragments is illegal and traditionally unlucky. At the southern end of the park, near U.S. 180, the **Rainbow Forest Museum** provides a look at petrified logs up close and serves as a Visitors Center. (☎928-524-6822. Open daily June-Aug. 7am-7pm. Free.)

▨ **CAMPING.** A free permit is required for overnight camping; permits can be obtained at the **Painted Desert Visitors Center** and **Rainbow Forest Museum.** Water is available at the Visitors Centers and at the Painted Desert Inn. In case of emergency, call the ranger dispatch (☎928-524-9726).

▦ **STEWART'S PETRIFIED WOOD**
Take Exit 303 from I-40.

Although removing petrified tree bits from the park is strictly prohibited, a number of curio shops west of the park hawk bits of rock. Some even offer "petrified rocks straight from the factory." The most entertaining of these shops by far is Stewart's Petrified Wood. Just keep an eye out for the giant dinosaurs munching on mannequins. If you get to the school bus perched on a cliff, mannequin poised to sail off the edge, you've gone just a bit too far. Charles and Gazell Stewart have used every kooky advertising ploy to lure visitors into their rock shop—from the papier-mâché dinos to the ostrich pen next door. The store features rock products and fossils. (☎800-414-8533; www.petrifiedwood.com. Open daily 9am-dusk.)

SUN VALLEY. Between the Stewart's rock haven and Holbrook, the only town of note is the cluster of buildings in Sun Valley, at Exit 294. Auto service and food are available here, and the weary may want to pull into the **Painted Desert Lodge,** at Exit 294, which offers basic rooms. (☎928-524-9753. Singles $34; doubles $37.) The **Sun Valley RV Park** has RV sites for $20, and shelters for tenters.

HOLBROOK

All of the Rte. 66 attractions of the surrounding miles converge on tiny Holbrook. Every curio shop hawks petrified wood and Rte. 66 schlock, and the town may have more giant plastic dinosaurs and Rte. 66 murals per capita than anywhere else on the planet. Founded in 1882, Holbrook has always been a tourist mecca, first as home to one of the first Fred Harvey railroad restaurants, and later as a Rte. 66 stopping point, where tourists could hunker down in concrete teepees.

On the eastern approach into Holbrook along Rte. 66, the first of the giant plastic dinosaurs since Stewart's Petrified Wood Store line the highway, beckoning curious visitors into the **International Petrified Forest, Dinosaur Park,** and **Museum of the Americas,** 1001 Forest Dr. Guests can visit the extensive pottery collection and small dinosaur bone collection of the Museum of the Americas, and take a short looping drive among the scattered dinos. (☎928-524-9178 or 928-524-9315. Open daily dawn-dusk. $5.) **Julien's Roadrunner Shop,** 109. W. Hopi Dr., has Rte. 66 trinkets galore, as well as a great collection of signs and t-shirts. (☎928-524-2388. Open M-Sa 8am-5:30pm.) For a sense of local history, the **Navajo County Courthouse and Museum,** on Rte. 66 at the corner of E. Arizona St. and Navajo Blvd., has a small museum including a frightening and claustrophobic jail cell. (☎928-524-6558. Open daily 8am-5pm.)

When *Glamour* wanted a picturesque small-town diner for a photo shoot, **Joe and Aggie's Cafe,** 120 W. Hopi Dr., fit the bill. But you'd have to ask owners Stanley and Alice Gallegos if the models indulged in the hearty Mexican cuisine. (☎928-524-6540. Open M-Sa 7am-8pm.) Across

the street, **Romo's Cafe,** 121 W. Hopi Dr., is less intimate but just as popular for its Mexican specialties. (☎928-524-2153. Open M-F 9am-8pm, Sa 10am-8pm.) On the west end of Hopi Dr., the concrete teepees of the **Wigwam Motel** are preserved in the memories of many a traveler exactly as they are today. Rooms are surprisingly comfortable, each with private bath. (☎928-524-3048. Singles from $40.) If the Wigwams won't fit your budget, the **Holbrook Inn,** 235 W. Hopi Dr., has affordable rooms within teepee eyeshot. (☎928-524-3809. Singles $22.)

▐▌ LEAVING HOLBROOK
In Holbrook, turn right on **Hopi Dr.** to continue on **Rte. 66** ¾ mi. to the interstate. Take **I-40 West.**

▐▀▌ GERONIMO TRADING POST
Exit 290 from I-40, 3¾ mi. west of Holbrook
The historic Geronimo Trading Post, with geode pillars and a stand of gaudy teepees, has been luring roadtrippers in for postcards, gems, jewelry, and petrified wood for years. (☎928-288-3241. Open daily summer 7am-7pm; winter 8am-5pm.)

THE ROAD TO WINSLOW

At Exit 277, take the north frontage road through **Joseph City.** Half a mile west of town, turn south over I-40 on the access road, and 1 mi. later head westbound on the south frontage road. The giant **"Here it Is"** sign of the **Jackrabbit Trading Post,** 5½ mi. down the road at Exit 269, should be familiar—remember Henry Rich's Rabbit Ranch "Hare it is" signs (see p. 469) back in Stanton, IL? The photo-op with the giant plastic rabbit is too good to be missed. The store sells the usual Rte. 66 paraphernalia. (☎928-288-3230. Open M-Sa 7:30am-dusk, Su noon-dusk.)

Two miles east of **Winslow** at Exit 257 off I-40, the **Homolovi Ruins State Park** offers easy walks among pueblo ruins, as well as a beautiful campground with 52 sites, restrooms, and showers. (Visitors Center ☎928-289-4106. Open daily 8am-5pm. Campground ☎928-289-4106. Open daily; water hookups Mid-April to mid-Oct. only. Sites $12, with hookup $19. Day-use $5 per vehicle.)

▐▌ APPROACHING WINSLOW
To continue into **Winslow,** follow the south frontage road and head north on **Bus. I-40** into town; follow **3rd St.** through town.

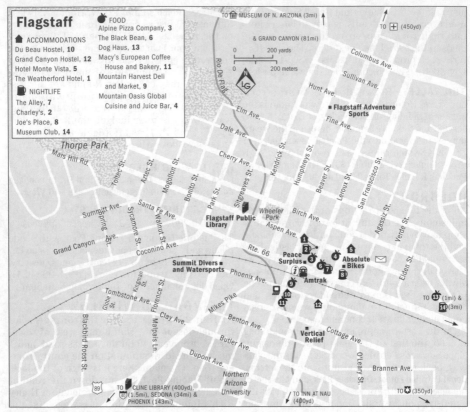

Flagstaff

ACCOMMODATIONS
Du Beau Hostel, **10**
Grand Canyon Hostel, **12**
Hotel Monte Vista, **5**
The Weatherford Hotel, **1**

NIGHTLIFE
The Alley, **7**
Charley's, **2**
Joe's Place, **8**
Museum Club, **14**

FOOD
Alpine Pizza Company, **3**
The Black Bean, **6**
Dog Haus, **13**
Macy's European Coffee
House and Bakery, **11**
Mountain Harvest Deli
and Market, **9**
Mountain Oasis Global
Cuisine and Juice Bar, **4**

WINSLOW

If you don't already know that Winslow was inspiration for the Eagles song "Take it Easy," the folks in Winslow won't let you forget it. "Standing on a corner in Winslow, AZ; such a fine sight to see" has been taken to the extreme, with an entire intersection and three out of the four corners dedicated to that happy moment. If you can possibly get away from the Eagles-mania, Winslow is a small, leisurely paced town, with one amazing hotel and a few small restaurants. Follow the crooning of Don Henley for everything you need to be standing on a corner in high style; **Roadworks Gifts and Souvenirs,** 101 W. 2nd St., pumps Eagles music onto the infamous corner, and sells a full variety of "Standin' on the corner" memorabilia. (☎928-289-5423. Open daily 8am-7pm.) The **Old Trails Museum,** 212 N. Kinsley Ave., or "Winslow's

Attic," is the repository for every sort of historical Winslow knickknack, including Anasazi artifacts, souvenirs from the La Posada Hotel, and Santa Fe Railroad memorabilia. (☎928-289-5861. Open Apr.-Oct. Tu-Sa 1-5pm; Nov.-Mar. Tu, Th, Sa 1-5pm.) The ancient but newly renovated **Winslow Theater,** 115 Kinsley Ave. (☎928-289-4100), shows feature flicks nightly at 7pm, with Saturday and Sunday matinees at 3pm.

The **Highway Diner,** 320 E. 2nd St., is a tiny family-run shed that has been offering cheap, home-cooked vittles for decades. (☎928-289-3629. Burritos $1.25. Hamburgers $2.50. Open when someone's there.) Nearby, the **La Posada Hotel,** 303 E. 2nd St., is a sprawling hacienda of tiled elegance. At roughly the same price as some higher-end motels, a stay here includes plush rooms, some with their own balconies, landscaped outdoor patios, a decadent downstairs lounge, a game room, and a library. On site is an excellent restaurant, where prices reflect the high quality of the food. (☎928-289-4366; www.laposada.org. Checkout noon. Singles $80, with balcony $90; doubles $100.) The **Motel 10,** 725 W. 3rd St., at the west end of town, has well-maintained rooms. (☎928-289-3211. Singles from $31; doubles from $33.)

LEAVING WINSLOW
Turn right onto **I-40 West** at the edge of town and continue toward Flagstaff.

Meteor City, 11¾ mi. from Winslow, is home to the **World's Largest Rte. 66 Mural** and the **World's Largest Dreamcatcher.**

METEOR CRATER
20 mi. west of Winslow.

At Meteor Crater, visitors drive up the side of the first proven meteor impact site and scale the ridge of the crater, 2½ mi. in diameter. A museum on the rim details the story of the crater, including how its resemblance to the moon has made it a training ground for Apollo Astronauts. (☎928-289-2362. Open daily May 15-Sept. 15 6am-6pm; Sept. 16 May 14 8am-5pm. Tours 9:15am and 2:15pm, weather permitting. Closed-toed shoes required. $12, seniors $11.) There's an RV park and gas station by the park entrance. (☎928-289-4002.)

About 14 mi. from the crater, keep an eye to the south side of the road for the remnants of the **Twin Arrows Trading Post,** now just two giant arrows sticking into the ground.

APPROACHING FLAGSTAFF
At Exit 211, go north on the frontage road and follow it through **Winona** to the northeast end of **Flagstaff.** Turn left on U.S. 89, 15¾ mi. after the turn-off.

FLAGSTAFF

Born on the 4th of July, Flagstaff began as a rest stop along the transcontinental railroad; its mountain springs provided precious refreshment along the long haul to the Pacific. These days, Flagstaff is still a major stopover on the way to the Southwest's must-sees. Trains plow through town 72 times a day, while travelers pass through on their way to the Grand Canyon, Sedona, and the Petri-

fied Forest, all within a day's drive. The energetic citizens welcome travelers to their rock formations by day and their breweries by night. Many have wandered into town with camera in hand and ended up settling down; retired cowboys, earthy Volvo owners, New Agers, and serious rock climbers comprise much of the population.

VITAL STATS

Population: 53,000

Visitor Info: Flagstaff Visitors Center, 1 E. Rte. 66 (☎928-774-9541; www.flagstaff.com), in the Amtrak station. Open daily Memorial Day-Labor Day 7am-7pm; Labor Day-Memorial Day 8am-5pm.

Internet Access: Cline Library (☎928-523-2171), on the NAU campus. Take Riordan Rd. east from Rte. 66. Open M-Th 7:30am-10pm, F 7:30am-6pm, Sa 10:30am-5pm, Su noon-10pm.

Post Office: 104 N. Agassiz St. (☎928-779-3559). Open M-F 9am-5pm, Sa 9am-1pm. **Postal Code:** 86001.

GETTING AROUND

The downtown area revolves around the intersection of **Leroux St.** and **Rte. 66.** The Visitors Center, both hostels, and a number of inexpensive restaurants lie within a half-mile of this spot. **S. San Francisco St.,** a block east of Leroux St., hosts many outdoors shops. Split by Rte. 66, the northern area of Flagstaff is more touristy and upscale, while the area south of the tracks is down-to-earth, housing hostels and vegetarian eateries.

SIGHTS

LOWELL OBSERVATORY. In 1894, Percival Lowell chose Flagstaff as the site for an astronomical observatory and spent the rest of his life here, devoting himself to the study of heavenly bodies and culling data to support his theory that life exists on Mars. The Lowell Observatory, where he discovered Pluto, doubles as a tribute to his genius and as a high-powered research center sporting five mammoth telescopes. During the day, admission includes tours of the telescopes, as well as a museum with hands-on astronomy exhibits. If you have stars in your eyes, come back at night for an excellent program about the night sky and constellations. (*1400 W. Mars Hill Rd., 1*

ROUTE 66

mi. west of downtown off Rte. 66. ☎928-774-3358; www.lowell.edu. Open daily Nov.-Mar. noon-5pm; Apr.-Oct. 9am-5pm. Evening programs Nov.-Mar. F-Sa 7:30pm; Apr.-May and Sept.-Oct. W and F-Sa 7:30pm; June-Aug. M-Sa 8pm. $4, students and seniors $3.50, ages 5-17 $2. AAA discount.)

SUNSET CRATER VOLCANO NATIONAL MONUMENT. The crater encompassed by Sunset Crater Volcano National Monument appeared in AD 1065. Over the next 200 years, a 1000 ft. cinder cone took shape as a result of eruptions. The self-guided **Lava Flow Nature Trail** wanders 1 mi. through the surreal landscape surrounding the cone, 1½ mi. east of the Visitors Center, where gnarled trees lie uprooted amid the rocky black terrain. The Visitors Center, 12 mi. north of Flagstaff on U.S. 89, has more info. (☎928-526-0502. Open summer daily 8am-6pm; off season 8am-5pm. $3, under 16 free; includes admission to Wupatki.)

WUPATKI NATIONAL MONUMENT. Wupatki has some of the Southwest's most scenic Pueblo sites, situated 18 mi. northeast of Sunset Crater along a stunning road with views of the Painted Desert. The Sinagua moved here in the 11th century, after the Sunset Crater eruption forced them to evacuate the land to the south. Archaeologists speculate that in less than 200 years, droughts, disease, and over-farming led the Sinagua to abandon these houses. Five empty pueblos face the 14 mi. road from U.S. 89 to the Visitors Center. Another road to the ruins begins 30 mi. north of Flagstaff, on U.S. 89. The largest and most accessible, Wupatki, on a half-mile round-trip loop from the Visitors Center, rises three stories. The spectacular **Doney Mountain Trail** rises half a mile from the picnic area to the summit. Get info and a trail guide brochure at the Visitors Center. Backcountry hiking is not permitted. (Visitors Center ☎928-526-0502. Open daily summer 8am-6pm; winter 9am-5pm. Campgrounds ☎928-526-0866. Open May-Oct. Sites $12.)

ARTS & FESTIVALS. North of town near the museum, the **Coconino Center for the Arts** houses exhibits, festivals, performers, and even a children's museum. (☎928-779-2300.) In the second weekend of June, the annual **Flagstaff Rodeo** comes to town with competitions, barn dances, a carnival, and a cocktail waitress race. Competitions and events go on from Friday to Sunday at the Coconino County Fair Grounds. (On Rte. 89A

just south of town; ask at the Flagstaff Visitors Center for details.) On the 4th of July, the town celebrates its birthday with street fairs, live music, outdoor barbecues, a parade, and, of course, fireworks. On Labor Day, the **Coconino County Fair** digs its heels into Flagstaff with rides, animal competitions, and carnival games. **Theatrikos,** a local theater group, stages plays year-round. (11 W. Cherry Ave. ☎928-774-1662; www.theatrikos.com.)

OTHER SIGHTS. Buy or trade a new or used read for the road at **Starlight Books.** (15 N. Leroux St. ☎928-774-6813. Open M 10am-5pm, Tu-Th 10am-6pm, F-Sa 10am-8pm, Su noon-3pm.) Everything you ever wanted to know about the history of Northern Arizona is on display at the **Museum of Northern Arizona,** which features pottery, kachinas, and jewelry. (3 mi. north of downtown Flagstaff on U.S. 180. ☎928-774-5213. Open daily 9am-5pm. $5, seniors $4, students $3.) At the **Arizona Historical Society Pioneer Museum,** history buffs can peruse displays covering the social and cultural history of Northern Arizona, housed in the former Coconino Country Hospital for the Indigent. (2340 N. Fort Valley Rd. ☎928-774-6272. Open M-Sa 9am-5pm. $3. 1st Sa each month free.)

⚠ OUTDOOR ACTIVITIES

With the northern **San Francisco Peaks** and the surrounding **Coconino National Forest,** Flagstaff offers numerous options for the outdoorsman. Due to the 7000+ ft. altitude, bring plenty of water, regardless of the season. In late spring and summer, rangers may close trails if the potential for fire gets too high. The mountains occupy national forest land, so **backcountry camping** is free.

SKIING

The **Arizona Snowbowl** operates four chairlifts and a tow rope and maintains 32 trails. Majestic **Humphrey's Peak** (12,633 ft.) is the backdrop for the Snowbowl, though the skiing takes place from 11,500 ft. off of **Agassiz Peak.** With an average snowfall of 260 in. and a vertical drop of 2300 ft., the Snowbowl rivals the big-time resorts of the Rockies and easily outclasses its Arizona competition. (Take U.S. 180 about 7 mi. north to the Fairfield Snowbowl turn-off. ☎928-779-1951; www.arizonasnowbowl.com. Open daily 9am-4pm. Lift tickets $40, ages 8-12 $22.) **Equipment rental** is available on the mountain. (Ski package $20-30 per day; snowboards $27 per day.)

HIKING

In the summer, these peaks attract hikers and bikers aplenty. The Coconino National Forest has many trails for hikers of all abilities. Consult the **Peaks Ranger Station**, 5075 N. U.S. 89A (☎928-526-0866), for trail descriptions and possible closures. For the more energetic hiker, the **Elden Lookout Trail** is ideal for jaw-dropping mountain-top views. The trail climbs 2400 ft. in only 6 mi. (round-trip); it is demanding, but worth it for the view. The trail begins at the Peaks Ranger station. The most popular trail in the area is the hike to **Humphrey's Peak**, Arizona's highest mountain. This 9 mi. round-trip begins in the first parking lot at the Snow Bowl ski area. For a longer hike, the moderate to strenuous 17½ mi. round-trip **Weatherford Trail** offers excellent opportunities for bird- and animal-spotting. The trailhead can be found next to Schultz Tank, about 7 mi. from Flagstaff.

MOUNTAIN BIKING

Flagstaff promises excellent mountain biking. The **Schultz Creek Trail** leads bikers into an extensive network of trails in the San Francisco Mountains. Take U.S. 180 north to Schultz Pass Rd. (Forest Service Rd. 420) and park in the dirt lot just as the road becomes unpaved. The trail climbs north along the bottom of a ravine and after almost 4 mi. splits into **Sunset Trail** heading south and **Little Elden Trail** heading east. Sunset Trail climbs through the woods before cresting and descending along **Brookbank Trail** down glorious single-track dropoffs and switchbacks. This 4 mi. stretch spits out riders bearing sloppy grins of satisfaction onto Forest Service Road 557. This road can either be used to ride 4 mi. back to the trailhead or to access renowned and more technical **Rocky Ridge Trail**, which leads to the same trailhead.

🍴 FOOD

Flagstaff will make epicurean roadtrippers happy with its diverse selection of eateries; vegetarian, organic, and just-plain-good food abounds here. Those accustomed to the traditional roadtrip hamburger and hot dog, however, will also find satisfaction among the restaurants of Flagstaff.

Macy's European Coffee House and Bakery, 14 S. Beaver St. (☎928-774-2243), behind Du Beau Hostel. A cheery and earthy hangout serving only vegetarian food and excellent vegan selections. $4-7 specials change daily. Get there early and start the day with a bowl of granola ($4) and a cup of fresh-roasted coffee. Open Su-Th 6am-8pm, F-Sa 6am-10pm. Food served until 1hr. before close. Cash only.

Mountain Harvest Deli and Market, 6 W. Phoenix (☎928-779-4485). A variety of smoothies, fresh juices, and sandwiches ($4-7) supplement an organic bonanza of groceries, bulk foods, and homeopathy. Open M-Sa 8am-8pm, Su 9am-7pm.

The Black Bean, 12 E. Rte. 66 (☎928-779-9905). Enormous, creatively stuffed wraps like veggie parmesan, thai peanut chicken or tofu, or La Baja, featuring chicken, guacamole, and mango-pineapple salsa ($3-5). Open M-Sa 11am-9pm, Su noon-8pm.

Dog Haus, 1302 Rte. 66 (☎928-774-3211). The ultimate in drive-thru hot dog ($2-$3) and hamburger ($2-3) fare. Open M-Th 7am-10pm, F-Sa 7am-11pm, Su 8am-10pm.

Mountain Oasis Global Cuisine and Juice Bar, 11 E. Aspen St. (☎928-214-9270). Offers a pleasant, softly lit eating area with live classical guitar on F during the summer. A wide variety of food from around the world, including vegetarian, vegan, and organic options. Open Su-Th 11am-9pm, F-Sa 11am-10pm; may close early if business is slow.

Alpine Pizza Company, 7 Leroux St. (☎928-779-4109). Comfortably worn-in wood panelling sets the mountain-town tone of this eatery. Pool tables, foosball, and neon beer ads are standard; newspapers with scrawled public commentary as wallpaper in the men's room are anything but. Small pizza $8. Happy hour Tu-Th 4-8pm. Open daily 11am-10pm.

🏠 ACCOMMODATIONS

Cheap motels line Rte. 66 entering town, but there are great inexpensive lodging deals for almost as cheap in the heart of downtown.

The Weatherford Hotel, 23 N. Leroux St. (☎928-779-1919). The oldest hotel in Flagstaff, dating from 1898, the Weatherford has 8 large rooms with balconies and bay windows. No TVs or in-room phones. Reservations recommended. Rooms $55.

Du Beau Hostel and **Grand Canyon Hostel** (☎800-398-7112 for DuBeau, ☎888-442-2696 for Grand Canyon), 2 blocks apart on San Francisco and Beaver St., behind the train station. Jointly managed and offering the same amenities, these are 2 of the best hostels in the Southwest. Spotless, with free breakfast, Internet ($2 per 30min.), kitchens, and BBQ areas. Dorms in old motel rooms, averaging 8 beds to a room, with private baths. Dorms $14-16; private rooms $28-35.

Hotel Monte Vista, 100 N. San Francisco St. (☎928-779-6971 or 800-545-3068; www.hotelmonte-vista.com), downtown. Feels like a classy hotel, with quirky decor and a faux peeling-brick lounge used in the filming of *Casablanca*. Private rooms named for the movie stars they once slept start at $60 weekdays.

CAMPING

Free backcountry camping is available around Flagstaff in designated areas. Pick up a map from the **Peaks Ranger Station,** 5075 N. U.S. 89A (☎928-526-0866), to find out where. All backcountry campsites must be located at least 200 ft. away from trails, waterways, wet meadows, and lakes. For more info, call the **Coconino National Forest Line.** (☎928-527-3600. Open M-F 7:30am-4:30pm.)

Lakeview Campground, on the east side of Upper Lake Mary, 11½ mi. south on Lake Mary Rd. (off I-17 south of Flagstaff). Surrounded by a pine forest. Drinking water and pit toilets. No reservations. Open May-Oct. $10 per vehicle per night.

Pinegrove Campground (☎877-444-6777; www.reserveamerica.com), 5 mi. south of Lakeview at the other end of Upper Lake Mary. Set in a similarly charming locale, with drinking water and flush toilets. $12 per vehicle.

Ashurst/Forked Pine Campground, on both sides of Ashurst lake (a smaller, secluded lake on Forest Rd. 82E). Turn left off Lake Mary Rd., across from Pine Grove Campground. Water and flush toilets on-site, and the fishing is stupendous. 64 sites are available on a first come, first served basis. $10 per vehicle.

NIGHTLIFE

Charley's, 23 N. Leroux St., plays live jazz and blues in the Weatherford Hotel, one of the classiest buildings in town. (☎928-779-1919. Happy hour 5-7pm. Open daily 11am-10pm. Bar open until 1am.)
Joe's Place, at the corner of San Francisco and Rte. 66, hosts indie bands on weekend nights. (☎928-774-6281. Happy hour 4-7pm. Open daily 11am-1am.) **The Alley** plays to a similar crowd and sees many out-of-towners. (☎928-774-7929. Happy hour M-Sa 3-7pm; Su free nacho bar. Open daily 3pm-1am.) If country is your thang, check out the **Museum Club,** a.k.a. the **Zoo,** 3404 E. Rte. 66, the premier spot for honky-tonk action. Five live trees support the building, constructed in 1918. (☎928-526-9434. Cover $3-5. Open daily 11am-3am.)

LEAVING FLAGSTAFF
From Flagstaff, curve left on **Rte. 66** under the rail tracks, and right ½ mi. later. After 4¼ mi., join **I-40 West.**

THE ROAD TO WILLIAMS
Just about every town from Flagstaff to Peach Springs claims to be the "Gateway to the Grand Canyon," but the area has a desolate beauty that can make it a destination in and of itself. Follow I-40 for 5½ mi., take Exit 185 for **Bellemont,** and head north on the frontage road. After 2 mi., the road enters the **Kaibab National Forest,** and 1¾ mi. beyond that turns to dirt; the pavement resumes 3 mi. later. **Parks** is 1 mi. beyond the start of the paved road. Just to the south side of Rte. 66, the **Parks General Store** is also the local gas station, antique shop, post office, hair-dresser, massage parlor, gunsmith, chain-saw sharpening stop, real estate office, and video rental. (☎928-635-1310. Open daily summer 6:30am-6:30pm; winter 7am-6pm. Post office open M-F 8am-noon and 1-6pm, Sa 9am-noon.) Next door is the **Ponderosa Forest RV Park,** offering woodland sites for tents and campers, with showers, laundry, and propane. (☎520-635-0456. Sites $13, with hookup $19.)

MAURICE'S MOTEL AND CAFE
On Rte. 66, ¾ mi. west of Parks.
Historic Maurice's Motel and Cafe is now a B&B where guests can board their horses while they take their own R&R. The horse-themed rooms are small and a little worn, but offer the price of chain motels, with much more character and a paddock of miniature (and regular sized) horses outside the back door. (☎928-635-2116. Rooms $55.)

DEER FARM PETTING ZOO
6752 E. Deer Farm Rd.
At Exit 171, 6 mi. down the road from Parks, take a left on Deer Farm Rd., the north frontage road.
The Deer Farm Petting Zoo gives friendly deer, donkeys, and reindeer the opportunity to maul your pockets as you circulate among the animals and the small children feeding them. (☎928-635-4073 or 800-926-3337. Open daily 9am-6pm. $6.)

WILLIAMS
The closest town to the South Rim of the Grand Canyon, Williams bills itself as the "Gateway to the Grand Canyon." This fortunate geography ensures a steady flow of tourists, and Williams offers small-town America with trees instead of cacti and the leisurely pace of country living.

VITAL STATS

Population: 3000

Visitor Info: Williams Visitors Center and Chamber of Commerce, 204 W. Railroad Ave. (☎928-635-4061). Open daily 8am-5pm.

Internet Access: Williams Library, 113 S. 1st St. (☎928-635-2263). Open Tu-Th 9am-noon, 1-5pm, and 6-8pm, F 9am-noon and 1-5:30pm, Sa 9am-1pm.

Post Office: 120 S. 1st St. (☎928-635-4572). Open M-F 9am-4:30pm. **Postal Code:** 86046.

GETTING AROUND. Getting around in Williams is relatively easy, as **Rte. 66** runs through downtown. One block south of Rte. 66 is **Railroad Ave.,** another main drag. Streets in Williams are numbered and run north-south, while most avenues run east-west. Most of Williams's downtown is centered between Railroad Ave. and Rte. 66 between **1st** and **4th St.;** free **parking** is found just south of Railroad Ave. between 1st and 2nd St.

SIGHTS. The **Grand Canyon Railroad** departs from the Williams railroad depot for the Grand Canyon at 10am daily, arriving 3hr. later, and returning later that day. (☎800-863-0546 or 800-635-4061 for info. Tickets $55-140.) Grand Canyon National Park entrance tickets can be purchased here. For info on the Grand Canyon, see below.

Pete's Rte. 66 Gas Station Museum, 101 E. Rte. 66, has every kind of Rte. 66 car memorabilia crammed into a corner garage gas station. (☎928-635-2675. Open M and W-Su 9am-8pm.) For more small-town America, check out the **Cowpuncher's Reunion Rodeo** during

GRAND CANYON NATIONAL PARK

100 MILE RADIUS

Extending from Lake Powell, UT through Arizona to to Lake Mead, NV, the Grand Canyon captures the imagination of any who stroll to its edge. First, there's the space: 277 mi. long and over 1 mi. deep, the Canyon overwhelms the human capacity for perception. Then, there's the color: the shifts in hue translate to millions of years of geologic history. Finally, there's the river: the chaotically creative force behind most of the Southwest's beautiful landforms is on full display. The Canyon's South Rim, located at the eastern end of the park, is its most accessible and scenic point.

Sights and services concentrate in Grand Canyon Village, at the west end of Park Entrance Rd. The **Canyon View Information Plaza** (☎800-858-2808; www.grandcanyon.com), across from Mather Point, is the one-stop center for Grand Canyon info. The plaza stocks copies of *The Guide* (an essential), other pamphlets, and plenty of information on the park's challenging day and overnight hikes. The steep **Bright Angel Trail** (up to 18 mi. round-trip, 1-2 days) and the strenuous **South Kaibab Trail** (7 mi. one-way, 4-5hr. descent), head for the canyon floor from the South Rim. Trips to the floor and back cannot be undertaken in one day; consult the rangers for reasonable and safe hikes. For other ways to see the Canyon, **Bright Angel** and **Maswik Lodges** handle reservations for mule rides, river rafting, plane tours, and more. (☎928-638-2631. Open daily 6am-8pm.) Free **shuttle buses** run to eight rim overlooks along Hermit Rd. (closed to cars in summer). Avoid walking along the road; the **Rim Trail** (12 mi. one-way, 4-6hr.) is safer and more scenic.

Food and accommodations cluster on the west side of the Village. During the summer, everything on two legs or four wheels converges here as well. If you plan to visit at this time, make reservations well in advance for lodging (☎928-638-2631) or campsites (☎800-365-2267). Compared to the six million years it took the Colorado River to carve the Grand Canyon, however, the year it will take you to get indoor lodging near the South Rim is nothing. (From Williams, take Rte. 64 60 mi. north through Kaibab National Forest, then turn left on S. Entrance Rd. Weekly Park entrance pass $20 per car including passengers.)

ROUTE 66

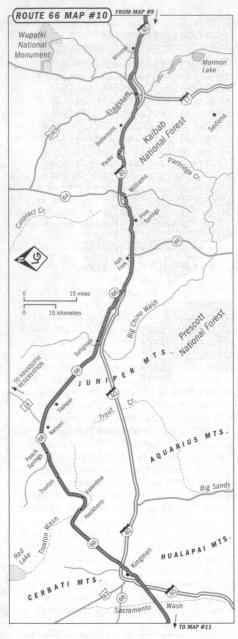

ROUTE 66 MAP #10 FROM MAP #9

Wupatki National Monument

Mormon Lake

Winona

Flagstaff

Kaibab National Forest

Sedona

Bellemont

Parks

Partridge Cr.

Williams

Pine Springs

Cataract Cr.

Ash Fork

0   15 miles
0   15 kilometers

Big Chino Wash

Prescott National Forest

Seligman

J U N I P E R   M T S.

TO HAVASUPAI RESERVATION

Yampai

Trout   Cr.

Nelson

AQUARIUS MTS.

Peach Springs

Big Sandy

Truxton

Valentine

Truxton Wash

Hackberry

Red Lake

HUALAPAI MTS.

Kingman

CERBATI MTS.

Sacramento   Wash

TO MAP #11

ROUTE 66

the first weekend in August, or the **Cool Country Cruise-In & Rte. 66 Festival** during the third weekend in August.

FOOD. At the east end of town, **Pancho McGillicuddy's Mexican Cantina and Espresso Bar,** 141 Railroad Ave., is your "standard" Mexican-Irish blend, although the food seems to favor the south-of-the-border side of the family. Generous portions and daily lunch specials ($5-6) are excellent deals. (☎928-635-4150. Entrees $6-10. Open M-F 11am-10pm, Sa-Su 10am-10pm.) **Rod's Steakhouse,** 301 Rte. 66, is a tribute to steak, from the steer-shaped menus based on the 1940s originals to the beef-themed walls. (☎928-635-2671. Lunch $5-6. Dinner $8-9. Open M-Sa 11:30am-9:30pm.) **Cruisers,** 233 W. Rte. 66 (☎928-635-2445), has the old Rte. 66 cars out front and the vintage signs inside to verify it as one of the great Rte. 66 diners. **Twister's 50's Soda Fountain,** 417 E. Rte. 66, is half 66 gift shop, half glittering chrome soda fountain, with sparkling vintage cars out front. (☎928-635-0266. Ice cream $1.40. Burgers $5. Open daily summer 8am-10pm; winter 8am-8pm.) At the **Pizza Factory,** 214 W. Rte. 66, the pies are homemade and hearty. (☎928-635-3009. Open daily 11am-9:30pm.) The **Sultana,** 301 W. Rte. 66, used to be host to the town's speak-easy in the basement; today the bar is a dark and cavernous pub. (☎928-635-2021. Open daily 10am-1am.)

ACCOMMODATIONS. The **Red Garter Bed and Bakery,** 137 W. Railroad Ave., has guests staying in rooms once belonging to the town madams, now transformed from brothel to classy B&B. (☎928-635-1484; www.redgarter.com. Rooms $85-120.) The **Rte. 66 Inn,** 128 E. Rte. 66, may not look like the most historic motel around, but it has been accommodating guests in sweet pastel rooms with elegant white wood furnishings since the 1930s. Rooms today include TVs, microwaves and fridges. (☎928-635-4791. Singles $22-50; doubles $22-50. 25% discount at Cruisers Restaurant.) The **Red Lake Hostel,** 8 mi. north of Williams on Rte. 64, has spartan but affordable rooms in a converted motel. The common room has a microwave and a refrigerator, and outdoor BBQ facilities are available. (☎928-635-4753. Reception Su-Th 6am-8pm, F-Sa 6am-9pm. Dorms $11; private rooms $33; tent sites $10; RVs $14.) The **Williams Circle Pines KOA,** 5333 Rte. 64, offers reliable camping options with mini-golf, bicycle rentals, game room, heated indoor pool and two spas, nightly family movies, and seasonal activities like an outdoor cafe, horseback riding, and weekend evening hayrides. The campsite also organizes Grand Canyon tours. (☎928-635-2626 or 800-562-9379. Open Mar.-Oct. Sites from $20; RVs from $27; cabins $38-$45.) Tenters can find comfortable and shady spots with primitive facilities and water in the **Kaibab National Forest** (☎928-635-5607).

LEAVING WILLIAMS

Follow **Rte. 66** out of town and continue 1¾ mi. west, then take **I-40 West** for 16½ mi.

THE ROAD TO SELIGMAN. Leave the interstate at Exit 146, and take a right through **Ash Fork.** Those in need of beautification need look no further than the 1960 DeSoto parked on the roof of the **DeSoto Salon,** 314 W. Lewis Ave., where Joe DeSoto and family will make you as glamorous as their giant rooftop hood-ornament. (☎928-637-9886. Open W-Sa 9am-5pm.) From Ash Fork, rejoin I-40 for 4¾ mi. to Exit 139 and take a right on **Crookton Rd.** Continue for about 17 mi. to the Rte. 66 celebration that is **Seligman,** and turn left at the T-intersection.

SELIGMAN

The Rte. 66 enthusiasm in Seligman is hard to hide. The town was founded at the junction of the main line of the Santa Fe Railroad, and when Rte. 66 was routed along the main street of the town, tourist accommodations flourished. When I-40 cut the town off the main thoroughfare, local residents were quick to react; Seligman was where the **Arizona Route 66 Association**—the nation's first—was founded to bring fame back to the road as a destination rather than a thoroughfare. Rte. 66 through Seligman is crowded with outrageous Rte. 66 kitsch. **Delgadillo's Rte. 66 Gift Shop, Museum, and Visitor Center,** 217 E. Rte. 66, Angel Delgadillo's still semi-functioning barber shop, is lined with memorabilia from appreciative travelers worldwide; add your business card to the wall. (☎928-422-3352. Open daily 8am-6pm.) **The Rusty Bolt Gift Shop,** 115 E. Rte. 66, is hard to miss, roofed in dressed-up mannequins and pumping Eagles cover tunes into the otherwise quiet street. (☎928-422-0106. Open daily summer 8am-8pm; winter 8am-6pm.)

The cuisine at the **Road Kill Cafe,** 592 W. Rte. 66, may not be exactly true to the name, but the decor certainly seems to be. Enjoy a foot-high pile of onion rings ($6), or the meat of your choice ($7-15) in the company of an entire herd of dead things on the walls. (☎928-422-3554. Open daily 7am-10pm.) Juan Delgadillo's (brother to Angel) **Sno Cap Ice Cream Shop,** 301 E. Chino Ave., decorated year-round in holiday decorations, prides itself on serving "Dead Chicken" and offers "Get your Gas here." For the less adventurous, it's still a world-class ice-cream stop. At the **Rte. 66 Inn,** 500 W. Rte. 66, rooms are pleasantly decorated with TVs and doilies. (☎928-422-3204. Singles $47; doubles $52.) The **Deluxe Inn,** 203 E. Chino, a 1932 motel, has spacious rooms with wood furnishings and nature photography lining the walls. (☎928-422-3244. Singles from $32; doubles from $35.)

IN THE PASSENGER SEAT

SAVING 66

Angel Delgadillo is a Seligman native. Once, over 9000 cars passed through Seligman daily along Rte. 66; simply crossing the street was a treacherous event. After I-40 was built in 1978, Mr. Delgadillo's daughter recalls that she could have lain in the street for hours without a worry.

My father wanted to make Rte. 66 a historic highway, to bring businesses back. On I-40, people were getting from Point A to point B real quick, but they weren't seeing anything. My parents drove down to Kingman and called a meeting in February of 1987. Fifteen people showed up, and formed the Historic Rte. 66 Association of Arizona. They lobbyed the Arizona legislature to make it an Arizona historic highway, so that it was maintained. This also started the signage. People started traveling the road. But he had no clue that the whole world would respond. Now, he's semi-retired. He was the town barber, but now he only works for the 'Rte. 66-er.'

ROUTE 66

⛟ LEAVING SELIGMAN
Follow **Rte. 66** ever-westward out of Seligman and on toward **Peach Springs.**

◑ GRAND CANYON CAVERNS
On Rte. 66, 24 mi. from Seligman, at Mile 115.

A giant green plastic dinosaur guards the entrance to Grand Canyon Caverns, the largest registered dry cavern in the US. Tours of the enormous rooms, 210 ft. underground, are led by guides eager to point out the unique features of this one-time fallout shelter, including a mummified cat and enough toilet paper for three weeks of nuclear fallout. (☎928-422-3223 or 928-713-2671; www.gccaverns.com. 45min. tours daily every 30min. $12, ages 5-12 $8. Flashlight tours $15/$10. Explorer's tour $45; reservations recommended.) **The Grand Canyon Cavern Restaurant,** conveniently located at the entrance to the caverns, serves diner cuisine cafeteria-style. (Entrees $2-7.) The pink, 70s-inspired rooms at **Grand Canyon Caverns Inn,** also at the caverns' entrance, are the most affordable option for miles in either direction. Rooms come with VCRs, and reception stocks movies. The motel also offers bike rentals and has a full convenience store.(Singles $49; doubles $54. Bikes $4 per hr., $15 per half-day, $25 per day.)

◸ DETOUR: HAVASUPAI RESERVATION
3 mi. from the Caverns, follow signs for Supai and the Havasupai Reservation, 60 mi. north on Rte. 18. Follow the road north approximately 60 mi., ending in a series of narrow hairpin turns down to the canyon rim and the trailhead down to the village of Supai and the Supai waterfalls.

The southwest corner of the Grand Canyon has been long overlooked in favor of the commercialized South Rim, but hikers and off-the-beaten path enthusiasts have begun to bring recognition to the hike down the canyon into the town of Supai. The hike is a demanding trek 2 mi. down the canyon wall, followed by 8 mi. along the floor. The arid landscape of the canyon rim and floor suddenly gives way to a bright green oasis of shade and grass as you draw near the village. Two miles down the path from the village is an astounding sight—three waterfalls in succession, of clear blue-green water. The village of **Supai** has a few resources for hikers, including two small stores, a cafe, a small lodge, and a post office. Visitors do best to pack in whatever food they can carry; prices in the can-yon reflect the fact that supplies are brought in by mule or helicopter. (Supai Store ☎928-448-2951. Open daily 8am-5:30pm.)

The **cafe** provides basic fare, such as pancakes, eggs, and hamburgers, at reasonable prices. (☎928-448-2591. Open daily 7:30am-5:30pm; extended summer hours.) The **lodge** offers rooms for visitors who book well in advance, and the **campgrounds** 2 mi. beyond the village have spaces next to a clear stream between two waterfalls. (☎928-448-2121. Camping reservations M-F 9am-3pm. Register in Supai tourist office 5:30am-5pm. Camping $20 entry fee plus $10 per person.) Visitors can hire mules to carry in bags. (Mules leave 10am from the Hualapai Hilltop, 7am from the campgrounds. $75 one-way.) Visitors can also ride in on horseback. (Pickup 10am on Hualapai Hilltop, or 7am from the campground. $75 one-way.)

⛟ APPROACHING PEACH SPRINGS
From the Grand Canyon Caverns, continue west along **Rte. 66;** from the intersection of Rte. 66 and Rte. 18, it's just over 6 mi. to **Peach Springs.**

PEACH SPRINGS
The headquarters of the Hualapai Tribe and once the western terminus of the Santa Fe Railroad, Peach Springs has few offerings, save the **Hualapi Lodge,** the base for the **River Runners,** a rafting outfitter offering day trips on the Colorado River. (☎888-255-9550 or 888-216-0076. Trips Mar.-Oct. $265 per person; includes round-trip transport, food, helicopter uplift, life jackets, and a souvenir mug.) Peach Springs also prides itself on having the only access road directly into the bottom of the Grand Canyon. Get directions at the lodge.

The **Diamond Creek Restaurant** has an excellent variety of offerings, from chicken-fried steak to trout almondine and the best fry bread around. (☎928-769-2800. Entrees $5-12. Open daily 6am-9pm.) The new and adjoining **Hualapai Lodge,** 900 Rte. 66, has comfortable and relatively upscale spacious rooms at budget prices. (☎888-255-9550. Rooms $75; $10 per extra person.)

THE ROAD TO KINGMAN. Along Rte. 66 from Peach Springs, the road is expansive and empty, save for would-be towns along, or just off, the main road. **Truxton,** 9½ mi. beyond Peach Springs, and **Valentine,** 9 mi. farther on, are quickly passed. Drivers might speed through **Hackberry,** 5 mi. beyond Valentine, with as little notice, save for the

Hackberry Visitor Center & General Store, a roadside store surrounded by vintage cars offering Rte. 66 memorabilia and souvenirs. (☎928-769-2605. Open daily summer 7am-7pm; winter 10am-5pm.) From here, it's a little over 23 mi. to Kingman.

KINGMAN

Kingman has always prided itself on being a transportation town; the railroad and Rte. 66 running straight through Kingman brought in voyagers a plenty, including Clark Gable and Carole Lombard, who were married in the Old Courthouse. The town is as Rte. 66 enthusiastic as any, hosting the Rte. 66 Fun Run the first weekend in May.

VITAL STATS

Population: 20,000

Visitor Info: Powerhouse Visitors Center, 120 W. Rte. 66. (☎866-427-7866; www.kingmanchamber.org). Open daily Mar.-Nov. 9am-6pm; Dec.-Feb. 9am-5pm.

Internet Access: Kingman Public Library, 3269 N. Burbank St. (☎928-629-2665). Open M 10am-6pm, Tu 9am-8pm, W-F 9am-6pm, Sa 9am-5pm.

Post Office: 1901 Johnson Ave. (☎928-753-2480). Open M-F 8:30am-5:30pm, Sa 9am-noon. **Postal Code:** 86401.

GETTING AROUND. Most avenues in Kingman run east-west, while streets are numbered and run north-south (though just north of the downtown area some streets also run east-west). **Rte. 66** enters Kingman from the northeast and is known in town as **Andy Devine Ave.;** many of the city's sights and establishments lie along this road. Downtown centers on the area near **4th St., Beale St.,** and Andy Devine Ave., and **parking** is readily available in most of the city.

SIGHTS. A converted 1907 power station that hosts a decent Rte. 66 gift shop, the **Powerhouse Visitors Center,** 120 W. Rte. 66, now serves as Kingman's Visitors Center. The top floor houses an extensive, lovingly curated Rte. 66 museum, while downstairs a small theater shows Rte. 66 documentaries on demand. Road buffs can while away the hours in the Rte. 66 of Arizona Reading Room upstairs. (☎928-753-9889. Open daily Mar.-Nov. 9am-6pm; Dec.-Feb. 9am-5pm.) At the **Mojave Museum of History and Arts,** 400 W. Beale St., displays focus on the development of the area, arts

and Indian culture, and the life and career of actor Andy Devine, a native of Kingman. An outdoor display highlights a 19th-century Santa Fe Caboose as well as wagons, mining equipment, and farm machinery. (☎928-753-3195. Open M-F 9am-5pm, Sa-Su 1-5pm. $3, children $0.50.)

FOOD & ACCOMMODATIONS. The easily spotted **Mr. D'z Route 66 Diner,** 105 E. Andy Devine Ave., is a pink, green, and chrome tribute to the kitschy Rte. 66 diner, serving breakfast, lunch and dinner. (☎928-718-0066. Breakfast from $3.50. Sandwiches from $2.50. Open daily 7am-9pm.) The scents of home-baked goodies and gourmet coffee waft irresistibly from the **Oldtown Coffeehouse,** 616 E. Beale St., tempting visitors inside. (☎928-753-2244. Open M-F 7am-6pm, Sa 8am-5pm.) **El Palacio,** 401 Andy Devine Ave., is the local Mexican cantina of choice, with hearty entrees like the guacamole quesadilla from $5-8. (☎928-718-0019. Open daily 11am-9pm.)

The historic **Hotel Brunswick,** 315 E. Andy Devine Ave., offers a variety of rooms, ranging from austere singles with shared bathrooms to expansive suites. (☎928-718-1800. Breakfast included. Singles from $25; suites $115.) Guests at the **Hilltop Motel,** 1901 E. Andy Devine Ave., will find basic, clean rooms. (☎928-753-2198. Reservations recommended. Singles $36-55; doubles $85.)

LEAVING KINGMAN
From downtown Kingman, turn left on **Rte. 66** just before the Mojave Museum. Approximately 5 mi. later, take a right under the I-40 onto **Oatman Hwy.,** and ½ mi. later, head left to continue west.

THE ROAD TO OATMAN

The road between Kingman and Oatman is an intense series of hair-raising switchbacks along cliffsides in an otherworldly landscape of craggy peaks and undulating valleys. Check your gages and make sure the sun won't be in your eyes before you embark; after dark, the unlit roads are downright treacherous. Twenty miles west of Kingman, 49er wannabes can tour **Gold Road's** now-defunct mines running directly under Rte. 66. A variety of tours are available, from 1hr. basic tours to "extended" and "extreme" tours lasting 2½-4hr. and including a meal. There are also trail rides, stagecoach tours, and Outlaw Adventure Hummer Tours. When you're done, the gift shop stocks t-shirts proudly proclaiming "Rte. 66—Been on it, Been under it!" (☎928-768-1600. Open daily 10am-5pm. Tours $16-20.) Fare at the next-door **Prospector Cafe** is creatively named in mining terms. (☎928-768-6030. Open daily 10am-5pm.)

OATMAN

Harleys and burros vie rather bizarrely for the right of way in Oatman, and local leather-clad bikers stage mock-gunfights in the heart of town between the kettle-corn and ice-cream stands every weekend. (Sa-Su 1:30 and 3:30pm in the center of town.) The town was originally founded to support nearby mining interests, and became the traditional last stop before venturing across the Mojave, but the road leading to the town was later bypassed in favor of a looping but flatter by-way. Today, seasonal festivities include a January "bed race," July 4th of July Sidewalk "Egg-Fry at High Noon," September "Gold Camp Days," Labor Day "International Burro Biscuit Toss," and December "Christmas Bush Festival." Oatman displays its own Wild West version of hospitality at the **"Oatman Visitors Center,"** an open-faced ancient outhouse, but the display in the Gold Mine next door answers more questions about the town. Across the street, the **Oatman Jail** at the west end of town displays various instruments of imprisonment as well as photos and clippings about the town.

Oatman was named in honor of the Oatmans, a pioneer family ambushed by Indians on their way west. Olive, one of the Oatman daughters, and her sister Mary were taken captive, and their brother was left for dead. Mary died in captivity, but Olive was rescued by the US Army at age 14. The namesake **Olive Oatman Restaurant and Saloon,** 171 Main St., has heaping Navajo tacos, specialty peach fry bread, and live music on the weekends. (☎928-768-1891; www.oatmangold.com/olive. Entrees $5-8. Open daily 8:30am-4:30pm.) Unfortunately, the only lodging in town and for 20 mi. in either direction, the **Oatman Hotel,** 181 Main St. (☎928-768-4408), is currently under renovation; call ahead for re-opening dates. Downstairs, the colorful bar wall-papered in dollar bills caters to locals and tourists alike in Old West saloon style.

 LEAVING OATMAN
2 mi. beyond Oatman, bear left at the Y and continue south and west on **Rte. 66.**

THE ROAD TO CALIFORNIA

The town of **Golden Shores,** 18½ mi. beyond Oatman, has the basics for the traveler in need, but the hint of palm trees and the scent of impending California along the banks of the Colorado River

impel most roadsters onward. Five miles beyond Golden Shores at **Topock** (the Mojave word for "bridge"), take Exit 1 to join **I-40** heading west into the promised land of Rte. 66 travelers—California.

 About 30 mi. southeast of Topock, near Lake Havasu City, is **London Bridge,** which was dismantled in the 1960s, as it was unable to support London traffic. It was later moved and reassembled in Arizona. Should you not believe this, take I-40 East from Topock and head south on Rte. 95 to see for yourself.

From the perilous stretches of deserted road across the Mojave to the luscious greenery of coastal Southern California, California's Rte. 66 embodies the journey that has drawn everyone from the Joad family to starry-eyed starlets westward. The **Moabi Regional Park,** off I-40 about 2 mi. from the border, offers a chance to cool off a little in the Colorado River, and provides alternatives to the nondescript motels of nearby Needles. (☎760-326-3831. Entrance fee $6. Sites $12, with hookup $20. Peninsula sites $18/$35. Day-use $4.)

If you're traveling between November and March, you'll enter the Pacific Time Zone as you cross into California, where it is 1hr. earlier. April-October there is no change here.

APPROACHING NEEDLES
Approaching Needles on **I-40,** exit approximately 10½ mi. from the border into town, taking a right onto **Broadway** and following as it swings into town. The original alignment of **Rte. 66** actually cuts away to the left of the interstate, and then veers right again to enter town on Broadway.

NEEDLES

Needles, famed for its unrelenting summer heat, is the modern Old West counterpart of Oatman, with wide streets lined with dingy motels and truck stops. Needles was also the birthplace of comic-strip artist Charles Schulz, and is the home of his character "Spike." The iconic **Rte. 66 Motel,** 91 Desnok St. (☎760-326-3611), might look familiar as the backdrop for several scenes from the film adaptation of the *Grapes of Wrath*. Rooms currently rent on a strictly monthly basis, but the management is thinking of changing the policy; call to check current policy and rates.

It's a pretty long, deserted stretch after Needles, so eat your fill here; the **California Pantry,** 2411 Needles Hwy., has the widest variety of offerings in town, with an ample menu of salads ($6), burgers ($6), sandwiches, dinners ($7-10), and fresh pies. (☎760-326-5225. Open daily 5am-10pm.) The **Wagon Wheel,** 2420 Needles Hwy., is the ultimate truck-stop, with meals ranging from a truck-size half-pound burger down to the all-you-can eat salad bar. (☎760-326-4361. Open daily 5am-10pm.) At **Lucy's Mexican Restaurant,** 811 Front St., Lucy herself serves up popular Mexican fare just off Rte. 66. (☎760-326-4461. Entrees $4-8. Open Su and Th-Sa 11am-8pm.) The **Hungry Bear,** 1906 Needles Hwy., is a classic family-style diner with booths upholstered in Rte. 66 fabric. Trucker-worthy entrees like pork chops and club sandwiches run $6-12. (☎760-326-2988. Open Su-Th 5:30am-9pm, F-Sa 5:30am-9:30pm.) Motel offerings in town tend toward the seedy but inexpensive. Clean rooms can be found at the **Royal Palms Motel,** 1910 Needles Hwy.(☎760-326-3881. Singles $25-39; doubles $29-49.)

LEAVING NEEDLES
It's a lonely road across the desert to Barstow; fill up on gas before leaving Needles! From Broadway, head left onto **Needles Hwy.** after crossing the tracks. Continue until **Park Rd.,** then turn left and join **I-40** ½ mi. farther. Six miles down I-40, exit at the U.S. 95/Searchlight/Vegas exit and take a right on **Rte. 66.**

THE ROAD TO AMBOY
Approximately 2 mi. down Rte. 66, an eclectic roadside stand operates seasonally, guaranteed to satisfy any taste—giant signs advertise fresh jerky, olives, pistachios, and mangos. Thirteen miles after turning off the interstate, head west toward **Goffs** at the railroad tracks onto Goffs Rd. There's little to see in Goffs (pop. 23), save for the tumbleweeds and a historic schoolhouse, now a museum of historical photographs and negatives, as well as written and oral histories of the desert. (☎760-733-4360. Open select weekends.)

The town of **Fenner,** another 9½ mi. down the road, is even smaller than Goffs but has the only gas station for miles. Five miles past Fenner, head right at the T, 2 mi. later passing through **Essex,** which has little besides a small auto-repair shop.

ROY'S CAFE AND MOTEL
23 mi. beyond Essex, in Amboy.

Roy's is somewhere between comic and picturesque, with the bright 1950s-era sign vying for customer attention with what must be imaginary competition. The vintage motel cottages—without phones or televisions—are comfortable and quiet, and the cafe serves breakfast and lunch, albeit at prices that reflect Amboy's isolation. (☎760-733-4263. Open daily 8am-3pm. Sandwiches $5. Ice cream $2. Rooms $50.)

AMBOY CRATER
On Rte. 66, about 4 mi. west of Amboy.

Heading west from Amboy, the rising mountains on the north side of the road are countered by an equally surprising geological feature to the south—a volcanic crater set back from the road across a volcanic field. A modest hike up the walls of Amboy Crater affords not only a view of a depression of caked mud inside the crater, but also a vista of surrounding plains and mountains.

LUDLOW. Until 1988, Ludlow residents had to dial an operator to place a call, and incoming calls were placed through an operator to numbers Ludlow 1, 2, 3, etc. Different extensions had distinctive rings, and it was up to residents to decipher their ring and determine when to pick up. A veritable metropolis in the desert hinterlands, Ludlow now offers a 24hr. gas station and mini-mart as well as the modest but tasty **Ludlow Cafe,** which caters to folks on the go with telephones in most booths. (☎760-733-4501. Entrees $4-8. Open daily 6am-9pm.) Rooms for those in need are available at the **Ludlow Motel.** (☎760-733-4338, or inquire at the Chevron Station. Singles $50; doubles $52.)

LEAVING LUDLOW
Just before the gas station, restaurant, and motel, take a right on **Crucero Rd.,** under I-40, then head left to go 27 mi. west to **Newberry Springs.**

NEWBERRY SPRINGS
Newberry Springs is home to the now semi-famous **Bagdad Cafe,** 46548 National Trail Hwy., inspiration for the movie of the same title. (☎760-257-3101. Entrees $4-9. Open Su-Th 7am-7pm, F-

ROUTE 66 MAP #11

FROM MAP #10

TO MAP #12

Sa 7am-8pm.) Lodging in town is scarce, but for the wayfarer who happens to end up in Newberry Springs at nightfall, **The Barn** has dancing "every so often," and $2 will get you a country-line dancing lesson from genuine cowfolk on Tuesday nights. Drinks are cheap (beer $2), as are cups of locally grown and specialty flavored pistachios ($1), like salted, smoked, and garlic. (☎ 760-257-4110. Open daily 10am-10pm.) The motel part of the **Newberry Mountain R.V. and Motel Park,** 47800 National Trails Hwy., is yet to be resurrected, but the RV park is up and running, with a man-made lake and a paddle boat. (☎ 760-257-0066. Showers, laundry. Reception 8am-10pm. Sites $13; RVs $18-20.)

🏛 **DAGGETT MUSEUM** 33703 2nd St.
West of Newberry Springs on Rte. 66.

What used to be the mining and railroad town of Daggett is now largely dried up, but the Daggett Museum offers a rustic look at the town's past, with displays covering everything from barbed wire to beaded purses and the folks who owned them. (☎ 760-254-2629. Open Sa-Su 1-4pm.)

APPROACHING BARSTOW
About 2 mi. down **Rte. 66** from Daggett, curve left onto the **Nebo Rd. access,** and then right onto the highway. At the Marine Corps exit, 4½ mi. down the road, turn left at the exit under **I-40,** and then right on **E. Main St.,** and right on **Montara Rd.** into **Barstow.**

BARSTOW

Barstow, a classic rest-stop town of inexpensive motels and fast-food chains, may be what the Joad family was hoping for as they crossed into California. Downtown streets are lined with small shops, and the Italian Renaissance-style railroad depot adds Old World grandeur to this desert thru-way, a gateway to the California desert.

VITAL STATS

Population: 23,000

Visitor Info: Barstow Chamber of Commerce, 409 E. Fredricks St. (☎ 760-256-8617), off Barstow Rd. Open M-F 10am-4pm.

Internet Access: Barstow Public Library, 304 Buena Vista St. (☎ 760-256-4850). Open M and W noon-8pm, Tu, and Th-F 10am-6pm, Sa 9am-5pm.

Post Office: 425 S. 2nd Ave. (☎ 760-256-9304). Open M-F 9am-5pm, Sa 9am-noon. **Postal Code:** 92311.

GETTING AROUND. Barstow sits at the junction of **I-15** and **I-40** and at the convergence of a number of California state routes. Most avenues run north-south; streets run east-west. Downtown centers on the intersection of **1st Ave.** and **Main St. (Rte. 66)**, which is known as W. Main St. or E. Main St. on the respective sides of 1st Ave. **Barstow Rd.** parallels 1st. Ave. a few blocks east.

SIGHTS. In the Casa del Desierto Train Station, a piece of pseudo-Italian Renaissance architecture, the **Route 66 Mother Road Museum**, 681 N. 1st Ave., focuses on the development of Rte. 66 from a collection of old trails to the epic "Mother Road." (☎ 760-255-1890. Open F-Su 11am-4pm. Free.) The **Mojave River Valley Museum**, 207 E. Virginia Way, traces the history of the area. (☎ 760-256-5452. Open daily 11am-4pm. Free.)

Eight miles north of Barstow lies the arid beauty of the **Rainbow Basin Natural Area.** Hikers investigate the colorful canyon by day or gaze at a sky unpolluted by city lights at night. Nearby **Owl Canyon Campground** offers primitive camping. (Head north on N. 1st St., take a left onto Fort Irwin Rd. and continue for 7 mi., then turn left onto Fossil Bed Rd. Follow the signs down this dirt/gravel road for 3 mi. ☎ 760-256-8313, www.ca.blm.gov/barstow. Sites $6.) For info, contact the **California Desert Information Center,** 831 Barstow Rd. (☎ 760-255-8760; www.caohwy.com/c/caldesic. Open daily 9am-5pm.)

The ghost town of **Calico** is a collection of touristy craft stores and mini-attractions like "Calico Woodworking" and the "Mystery Shack." The nearby campground has exposed gravelly sites from $18. (On Ghost Town Rd. off I-15, 10min. north of Barstow. ☎ 800-862-2542. $6, children $3)

FOOD. Every restaurant chain imaginable has a branch on Main St., but Barstow's local cuisine may be more promising. The aroma of savory dishes fills the festive and oddly decorated dining room of **Rosita's Mexican American Food,** 540 W. Main St. (☎ 760-256-9218. Dinner $6-15. Lunch specials Tu-F under $5. Open Su 11am-8pm, Tu-Sa 11am-9pm.) For some hearty Italian food, head to **DiNapoli's Firehouse Italian Eatery,** 1358 E. Main St. Traditional pizzeria fare is served in a refurbished old-fashioned firehouse, complete with the front of a fire engine and a fire pole. (☎ 760-256-1094. Dinner entrees $8-15. Open Su-Th 11am-9pm, F-Sa 11am-10pm.) The world-class donuts at the **Star-light Donut Shop,** 101 W. Main St., are only a prelude to their list of 24hr. offerings, including ice cream, eggrolls, tamales, hot dogs, burgers, and croissants. (☎ 760-256-5974.)

ACCOMMODATIONS. E. Main St. offers an endless line of motels. Prices fluctuate depending on the season, day of the week, and whether Vegas accommodations are full. The **Desert Inn,** 1100 E. Main St., is a newly renovated motel with HBO and A/C. (☎ 760-256-2146. Singles $27; doubles-quads $30.) The massive sign for **El Rancho Motel,** 112 E. Main St., advertises the clean rooms of the white-and-green cottage motel, where the building's history is the main draw. (☎ 760-256-2401. Singles $33; doubles $38.) Just up the street, the **Route 66 Motel,** 195 W. Main St., constructed in 1922, features round beds and ancient alarm clocks inside the stucco cottage-like units, with vintage cars and signs decorating the outside. (☎ 760-256-7866; www.route66motelbarstow.com. Singles from $27; doubles from $37.)

LEAVING BARSTOW
Leaving Barstow, follow **Rte. 66** through **Hodge** and on to **Helendale.**

EXOTIC WORLD   29053 Wild Rd.
In Helendale. Take a right on Indian Trails Rd., and follow it for 1½ mi. over the railroad tracks to the first left on Wild Rd. Follow Wild Rd. 2½ mi. to the concrete gates of Exotic World.

The principal claim to fame of Helendale is Exotic World, **"Home of the Movers & Shakers Burlesque Hall of Fame & Strippers Museum."** An incredible paean to the all-but-lost art of the strip-tease, the walls are lined with photographs of stars like Tempest Storm. If you're lucky, Miss Dixie Evans herself, the Burlesque Marilyn, will be on hand to show you around. She was once sued by the Marilyn Monroe estate for her impersonations, but the lawsuit was dropped when it garnered her too much fame. Exotic World is also home to the Best in Burlesque Miss Exotic World Contest and Striptease Reunion. (☎ 760-243-5261; www.exoticworld.org. Open daily 10am-4pm.)

VICTORVILLE

Four miles beyond Helendale, Victorville offers little long-term diversion, but is home to a few excellent holes-in-the wall as well as the **California Rte. 66 Museum,** 16849 Rte. 66. Worth a stop and nicely down-to-earth, the museum holds an impressive

ROUTE 66

? Three miles beyond Helendale, "Fry Pan" Miles Mahan's monument to friendly wanderers and hoboes, **Hula Ville,** has been mostly relocated to the museum in Victorville, but parts of the original remain here by the side of the road.

collection of Rte. 66 memorabilia coupled with a refreshing array of modern artistic takes on the Old Road. (☎ 760-951-0436. Open M and Th-Sa 10am-4pm, Su Su 11am-3pm. Free.)

Spaghetti Eddie's Too, 14096 Greentree Blvd., is budget travel heaven—an all-you-can-eat rotating daily menu of hearty Italian specialties from spaghetti to manicotti and chicken cacciatore. (☎ 760-241-1332. Lunch buffet $6. Dinner buffet $9. Entrees $4-8. Open M-F 11am-9pm, Sa-Su 7am-noon.) Produce, ranging from cactus to eggplant to mangos, is fresh, ripe, and dirt cheap at the **Fruteria Quality Produce Shed,** 15176 7th St. (☎ 760-245-3037. Open daily 9am-5pm.) Inexpensive lodging options are scarce in Victorville, though chain motels are abundant at the west end of town and along I-15. The horse on the sign outside the **New Corral Motel,** 14643 7th St., doesn't light up anymore, but the rooms are adequate. (☎ 760-245-9378. Singles $40; doubles $50.)

🏍 LEAVING VICTORVILLE
Take **7th St.** out of town, then pick up **I-15 South** toward **San Bernardino.**

🛏 SUMMIT INN 5970 Mariposa Rd.
On the eastbound side of I-15, in Oak Hills; take the exit just before Oak Hills.

The historic Summit Inn offers an impressive menu of locally grown ostrich everything (from omelettes to burgers; $7-8) and exotically flavored milkshakes (date shakes $3) in a pleasant old diner on the summit of Cajon Pass. (☎ 760-949-8688. Open M-Th 6am-8pm, F-Su 6am-9pm; summer open 1hr. later.)

🏍 APPROACHING SAN BERNARDINO
Follow **I-15** over the mountainous **Cajon Pass** 6¾ mi. Head right at the **Cleghorn Rd.** exit, then curve left 6½ mi. farther on, heading left to join the interstate. Almost 2 mi. beyond that, bear right onto the ramp southbound. Immediately shift into the left lane for Exit 215 to San Bernardino. As soon as the highway splits, exit for Devore and take a left at the T. Take a right at the Y, and just a few miles beyond, head

under the railroad trestle. Continue on **Rte. 66** into San Bernardino, 7 mi. farther.

SAN BERNARDINO

Self-billed as the hub of the Inland Empire, San Bernardino is also proud of its Rte. 66 heritage, annually hosting the nation's largest Rte. 66 event. The city is rife with corporate franchises, offering inexpensive food and lodging for passersby.

VITAL STATS

Population: 182,000

Visitor Info: San Bernardino Convention and Visitors Bureau, 201 N. E St. #103 (☎ 909-889-3980). Open M-Th 7:30am-5:30pm, F 7:30am-4:30pm.

Internet Access: San Bernardino Public Library, 555 W. 6th St. (☎ 909-381-8201). Open M-W 10am-8pm, Th-Sa 10am-6pm.

Post Office: 390 W. 5th St. (☎ 800-275-8777), downtown. Open M-F 8am-5pm. **Postal Code:** 92401.

📠 GETTING AROUND. Although traffic in San Bernardino may be a little overwhelming for road-trippers used to the open stretches of Arizona desertway, getting around in San Bernardino is relatively simple; the city is laid out in a grid, with numbered streets running north-south and lettered streets east-west. **Rte. 66** enters the city from the north on **I-15,** becoming **Mt. Vernon Ave.** in town. The area along Mt. Vernon Ave. (Old Rte. 66) can be unsafe, especially at night, so stick to the north end of town or **Hospitality Ln.,** which crosses Waterman Ave. just north of I-10.

📷 SIGHTS. Will Rogers performed his last show at the historic **California Theater,** 562 W. 4th St. (☎ 909-885-5152), along with luminaries like Buster Crabbe and Rita Hayworth. Today, the theater is home to the California Theater of Performing Arts, which hosts popular musicals and shows. Don't miss the giant Will Rogers mural outside. San Bernardino also hosts the **Rte. 66 Rendezvous Weekend** (www.route-66.org.), a Rte. 66 cruisin' weekend open to all vehicles made between 1900-1973, and any model Viper, Corvette, or Prowler. The **original McDonald's** once stood at 1398 N. E St., but don't expect 15-cent burgers anymore. The only thing offered at this half-hearted historic site is a growing display of Golden Arches memorabilia and Happy Meal toys.

FOOD. Modest from the outside but lined with tributes to James Dean and Elvis, **Molly's,** 350 N. D St., at Court St., has healthy options with just enough creativity to draw in the out-of-towners. (☎909-888-1778. Entrees $4-6. Open M-F 6am-3pm, Sa 7am-2pm, Su 7:30am-2pm.) Family owned and run since 1937, **Mitla's,** 602 Mt. Vernon Ave., has enormous Mexican specialties, many for rock-bottom prices. (☎909-888-0460. Open Su 9am-8pm, Tu-W 9am-2pm and 4:30-8pm, Th-F 9am-9pm, Sa 9am-8pm.) **Rosa Maria's,** 4202 N. Sierra Way, serves quick, delicious Mexican food. Dispose of the house favorite "Garbage Burrito" for $4.25. (☎909-881-1731. Open daily 10am-5pm.) Nearby Redlands also offers cafes and restaurants. A favorite is **The Royal Falconer,** 106 Orange St., a British pub with pool tables and heaping burgers. Try the Irish Nachos ($6), french fries with everything on top. (☎909-307-8913. Open daily 11:30am-2am. Kitchen open until 10pm.)

Lodging prices do not include the 10% accommodations tax. At the **Guesthouse Inn,** 1280 S. E St., the rooms have fridges and continental breakfast. (☎909-888-0271. Singles $50; doubles $60.) **Motel 6,** 1960 Ostrems Way, off Rte. 215, is near California State University, San Bernardino. (☎909-887-8191. Singles M-F $38, Sa-Su $47; doubles $44/$53.) The three-star **Hilton San Bernardino,** 285 E. Hospitality Ln., is well priced as the chain goes, and offers the amenities of an upscale hotel. (☎909-889-0133. Rooms $100-130.)

LEAVING SAN BERNARDINO
From San Bernardino, head out of town on 5th St. as it turns into Foothill toward **Fontana,** 5½ mi. out of town.

THE ROAD TO GLENDORA
In summer, juice mongers operate from inside the giant orange on the south side of the road in **Rancho Cucamonga.** Just a few miles ago, towns were as hard to come by as water in the stretch of punishing Mojave Desert across eastern California. From San Bernardino onto L.A., however, the urban sprawl of countless strip-mall towns blend together in one commercialized, chain-brand happy stretch of suburbia that might send east-west roadies into population density shock. Those with an itch for the ocean might consider hitting I-10 to power onto the beach, bypassing the urban sprawl leading into Los Angeles. Persevering through the sprawl, **Upland** is home to the

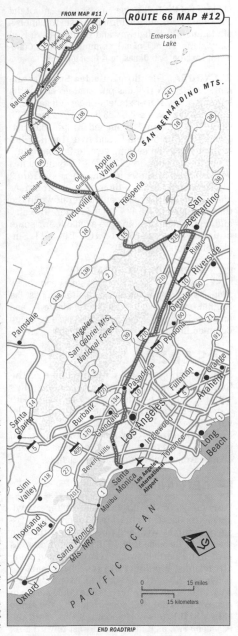

FROM MAP #11

ROUTE 66 MAP #12

END ROADTRIP

Madonna of the Trail statue, marking the end of the National Road, and Californian cousin to Illinois's Madonna of the Highway and Burma Shave Hail Mary signs. From Upland, continue through **Claremont, Laverne, San Dimas,** and **Glendora.**

GLENDORA. Glendora's **Golden Spur Restaurant,** 1223 E. Rte. 66, has pink-and-green booths lending a Roy Rogers-meets-Bogart elegance to the pricey menu. (☎626-963-9302. Frog legs $20. Open M-F 11:30am-3:15pm and 5-10pm, Sa-Su 4-10pm.) At Rte. 66 and Grand Ave., **The Hat Restaurant** has been serving "world-famous" pastrami for decades. (☎626-857-0017. Sandwiches $4.30. Open M-Sa 9am-1am, Su 10am-1am.) Those wishing to keep their distance from L.A. and the end of the road can hunker down in the **Glendora Motel,** 316 W. Rte. 66, where the airy and aqua-themed rooms are available for some of the best prices around. (☎626-914-3211. Singles $39; doubles $45.)

🏲 APPROACHING PASADENA
Count down the video rental stores and coffeeshops as the road winds through the **Azusa,** past the **Foothill Drive-In,** and through **Duarte, Monrovia,** and **Arcadia.** 1 mi. after entering Arcadia, take a right onto **Colorado Blvd.** and follow it into Pasadena.

PASADENA

For the nation, Pasadena is the home of the Rose Bowl; for Californians, it is a serene, ritzy suburb. Old Town combines historic sights with a lively entertainment scene, and wide boulevards lined with trendy eating and shopping options, sidestreets of world-class museums, and graceful architecture make Pasadena a welcome change from its noisy downtown neighbor.

🄵 GETTING AROUND

Pasadena sits on the northeast edge of the sprawling metropolis that is L.A. **Rte. 66** approaches Pasadena from the west and runs east-west through the city as **Colorado Blvd. I-210** parallels Colorado Blvd. to the north; downtown Pasadena and many attractions, including **Old Town Pasadena,** lie between I-210 and Colorado Blvd. Avenues in Pasadena run north-south; streets and boulevards run east-west. On the west edge of the city, the **Arroyo Pkwy. (I-110)** runs north-south. It turns into the **Pasadena Fwy.** as it heads southwest toward L.A., serving as the major route between the cities.

VITAL STATS

Population: 134,000

Visitor Info: Convention and Visitors Bureau, 171 S. Los Robles Ave. (☎626-795-9311; www.pasadenacal.com). Open M-F 8am-5pm, Sa 10am-4pm.

Internet Access: Pasadena Central Library, 285 E. Walnut St. (☎626-744-4066). Open M-Th 9am-9pm, F-Sa 9am-6pm, Su 1-5pm.

Post Office: 967 E. Colorado Blvd. (☎626-432-4835). Open M-F 8:30am-5pm. **Postal Code:** 91106.

👁 SIGHTS

Besides sports, Pasadena's main draw is **Old Town Pasadena,** bordered by Walnut St. and Del Mar Ave., between Pasadena Ave. and Arroyo Pkwy.

▦ NORTON SIMON MUSEUM OF ART. Rivaling the much larger Getty Museum in quality, this world-class private collection chronicles Western art from Italian Gothic to 20th-century abstract. (411 W. Colorado Blvd., at Orange Grove Blvd. ☎626-449-6840; www.nortonsimon.org. Open M, W-Th, Sa-Su noon-6pm, F noon-9pm; $6, seniors $3, students with ID and under 18 free.)

ROSE BOWL. In the gorge that forms the city's western boundary stands Pasadena's most famous landmark. The 90,000-seat stadium is home to the annual college football clash on New Year's Day between the champions of the Big Ten and Pac 10 Conferences. (1001 Rose Bowl Dr. ☎626-577-3100; www.rosebowlstadium.com.) The Bowl also hosts an enormous monthly **flea market** that attracts upwards of 2000 vendors, selling nearly one million items. (☎323-560-7469. Held the 2nd Su of each month 9am-4:30pm. Admission 5-7am $20, 7-8am $15, 8-9am $10, 9am-3pm $7.)

ARTS. The **Pasadena Playhouse** fostered the careers of William Holden, Dustin Hoffman, and Gene Hackman. Founded in 1917 and restored in 1986, it offers some of L.A.'s finest theater. (39 S. El Molino Ave., between Colorado Blvd. and Green St. ☎626-356-7529.) At the **Pasadena Museum of California Art,** displays feature California art, architecture, and design from 1850 to the present. (490 E. Union St. ☎626-568-3665. Open Su and W-Sa 10am-5pm, F 10am-8pm. $6, seniors and students with ID $4. 1st F of the month 5-8pm free.)

SCIENCES. Some of the world's greatest scientific minds do their work at the **California Institute of Technology (Caltech).** Founded in 1891, Caltech has amassed a faculty that includes several Nobel laureates and a student body that prides itself both on its staggering collective intellect and its loony practical jokes. *(1201 E. California Blvd., about 2½ mi. southeast of Old Town. ☎ 626-395-6327. Tours M-F 2pm.)* **NASA's Jet Propulsion Laboratory,** about 5 mi. north of Old Town, executed the journey of the Mars Pathfinder. *(4800 Oak Grove Dr. ☎ 818-354-9314. Free tours by appointment.)*

🍴 FOOD

Eateries line **Colorado Blvd.** from Los Robles Ave. to Orange Grove Blvd. in Old Town. The restaurants and sights around the boulevard make it pleasant and walkable.

📷 Fair Oaks Pharmacy and Soda Fountain, 1516 Mission St. (☎ 626-799-1414), at Fair Oaks Ave. in South Pasadena. From Colorado Blvd., go south 1 mi. on Fair Oaks Ave. to Mission St. This old-fashioned drug store has been serving travelers since 1915. Hand-dipped shakes and malts $4.25. Sandwiches $5.50. Soda fountain open M-F 11am-9pm, Sa 11am-10pm, Su 11am-8pm. Lunch counter open Su-F until 5pm, Sa until 8pm.

Pita! Pita!, 927 E. Colorado Blvd. (☎ 626-356-0106), 1 block east of Lake Ave. Never has a flatbread deserved so many exclamation points. Free appetizers of green olives, yellow pepper, and toasted pita. Spicy chicken pita $6. Lamb kebab with salad, rice, and beans $8. Open Su-Th 11am-9pm, F-Sa 10am-10pm.

Pie 'n Burger, 913 E. California Blvd. (☎ 626-795-1123), just east of S. Lake Ave., near Caltech. A classic 1963 diner, complete with Formica counters and friendly waitresses. Burgers ($5.50) and pies (19 varieties; $3.15-3.65) are the things to order. Open M-F 6am-10pm, Sa 7am-10pm, Su 7am-9pm.

🛏 ACCOMMODATIONS

The apartment-like **Saga Motor Hotel,** 1633 E. Colorado Blvd., offers pleasant peach-decorated rooms. It's pricy, but only marginally so for the step up in quality. (☎ 626-795-0431. Singles from $66; doubles from $72.) At the **Astro Motel,** 2818 E. Colorado Blvd., zany 70s bedspreads, floral wallpaper, carved bedsteads and antique glass lamps lend chaotic comfort to a colorful budget options. (☎ 626-449-3370. Singles $45; doubles $58.)

🔼 LEAVING PASADENA
Continue west on **Colorado Blvd.,** following it straight through town and toward the bridge over the Arroyo Seco. Join the **Arroyo Pkwy.** south and take the **Pasadena Freeway** southwest into the heart of L.A.

LOS ANGELES

In a city where nothing seems to be more than 30 years old, the latest trends demand more respect than the venerable. Many come to this historical vacuum to make (or re-make) themselves. And what better place? Without the tiresome duty of bowing to the gods of an established high culture, Angelenos indulge in a style of their own. Cruise through and watch the sun set over the Pacific in Santa Monica or stay to see the sights and the stars; either way, it's one hell of a show.

🔳 GETTING THROUGH LOS ANGELES

Rte. 66 across Los Angeles is fairly intact—from the **Pasadena Freeway,** take **Sunset Blvd.** to **Figueroa,** heading right and driving just one block before turning right again onto **Sunset.** Turn left on **Manzanita** as it becomes **Santa Monica Blvd.** and cruise into the sunset. For complete coverage of Los Angeles, including more the sights, food, nightlife, and entertainment than you could possibly see, eat, or experience on your way to the beach, see **The Pacific Coast Route,** p. 872.

SANTA MONICA

Finally—the Pacific! After mile upon mile of open road, from the shores of Lake Michigan across flat Oklahoma plains and through the Arizona desert, Santa Monica awaits on the edge of the dazzling blue expanse. But Santa Monica is known as much for its shoreside scene as its shore; the promenade and the pier are popular destinations..

🔳 GETTING AROUND

Rte. 66 enters Santa Monica from the east on **Santa Monica Blvd.** Just north of the boulevard, the **Santa Monica Freeway (I-10)** runs west from L.A. to the **Pacific Coast Hwy.** Car-free **Third St. Promenade** heads north from **Broadway** to **Wilshire Blvd.** Much of Santa Monica is best seen by foot or bike, **park** in one of the lots near the Third St. Promenade; most are free for 2hr. and then $1 each additional 30min. The **Santa Monica Place Mall** has free parking for up to 3hr. ($3 flat fee after 5pm). Downtown streets have meters ($0.50 per hr.), and all-day beach parking is usually available ($6-10).

TO MAGIC MOUNTAIN

TO VENTURA (30mi)

SAN FERNANDO VALLEY

VERDUGO MOUNTAINS

LA CRESCENTA

BURBANK

GLENDALE

CANOGA PARK

Van Nuys Airport

Roscoe Blvd.

Golden State Fwy.

Sepulveda Blvd.

San Fernando Rd.

CALABASAS

Sherman Way

Victory Blvd.

Tampa Ave.

VAN NUYS

Burbank Blvd.

Van Nuys Blvd.

Vineland Ave.

Burbank Intl. Airport

Topanga Canyon Blvd.

Ventura Blvd.

Ventura Fwy.

Ventura Fwy.

WOODLAND HILLS

Mulholland Dr. (Dirt)

Skirball Cultural Center

SHERMAN OAKS

Mulholland Dr.

STUDIO CITY

Universal Studios Hollywood

L.A. Zoo

Griffith Park

Hollywood Sign

Santa Monica Mts. NRA

Topanga State Park

BEL AIR

WEST HOLLYWOOD

Hollywood Bowl

Hollywood Blvd.

Santa Monica Blvd.

Melrose Ave.

SANTA MONICA MOUNTAINS

WESTWOOD

BEVERLY HILLS

WILSHIRE DISTRICT

Malibu Creek State Park

PACIFIC PALISADES

UCLA

Sunset Blvd.

CENTURY CITY

Wilshire Blvd.

Olympic Blvd.

L.A. DOWN-TOWN

BRENTWOOD

Santa Monica Blvd.

San Diego Fwy.

Santa Monica Fwy.

USC

Pacific Coast Hwy.

MALIBU

Topanga State Beach

Will Rogers State Beach

Santa Monica Blvd.

CULVER CITY

La Brea Ave.

Crenshaw Blvd.

Exposition Park

MLK Blvd.

Vermont Ave.

Western Ave.

Malibu Lagoon State Beach

SANTA MONICA

Santa Monica State Beach

Lincoln Blvd.

Pacific Ave.

Venice Blvd.

Marina Fwy.

Harbor Fwy.

VENICE

Venice Beach

Marina del Rey

Manchester Ave.

Los Angeles Intl. Airport (LAX)

INGLEWOOD

WATTS

Playa del Rey

Imperial Hwy.

HAWTHORNE

Avalon Blvd.

Santa Monica Bay

Dockweiler Beach

Vista del Mar Blvd.

Sepulveda Blvd.

Rosecrans Ave.

COMPTON

El Segundo

PACIFIC OCEAN

Manhattan Beach

Hawthorne Blvd.

Artesia Blvd.

San Diego Fwy.

0   5 miles

0   5 kilometers

Hermosa Beach

Sepulveda Blvd.

TORRANCE

Western Ave.

Redondo Beach

Pacific Coast Hwy.

N7

RANCHO PALOS VERDES

B St.

Palos Verdes Dr.

SAN PEDRO

Metropolitan Los Angeles

LA CAÑADA
FLINTRIDGE

Mt. Wilson
5,710ft

Mt. Wilson
Observatory

Monrovia Peak
5,412ft

Pine Mountain
454ft

San Gabriel
Res.

Angeles
National
Forest

Silver Mountain
3,391ft

Mt. Harvard
5,440ft

Mt. Bliss
3,725ft

San Gabriel Cyn. Rd.

Genoa Mtn. Rd.

Morris
Res.

San Dimas
Experimental
Forest

Descanso
Gardens

Glendale Fwy.

210

Rose
Bowl

Washington Blvd.

PASADENA

Sierra Madre Blvd.

Santa Anita Ave.

Foothill Blvd.

GLENDORA

Ventura Fwy.

134

Colorado Blvd.

210

Foothill Fwy.

39

Huntington Gallery
and Gardens

Caltech

Huntington Dr.

ARCADIA

SAN
DIMAS

110

Pasadena Fwy.

SAN
GABRIEL

Rosemead Blvd.

Live Oak Ave.

BALDWIN
PARK

Arrow Hwy.

210

SAN MARINO

Peck Rd.

605

39

COVINA

Grand Ave.

Raging
Waters

ALHAMBRA

Valley Blvd.

ROSEMEAD

Ramona Blvd.

San Bernardino Fwy.

10

CHINATOWN

10

Atlantic Blvd.

MONTEREY
PARK

19

Valley Blvd.

Glandora Ave.

N8

CITY OF
INDUSTRY

POMONA

71

60

60

60

Santa Ana Fwy.

EAST L.A.

Azusa Ave.

Pomona Fwy.

60

5

605

WHITTIER

Orange Fwy.

57

Slauson Ave.

19

72

Colima Rd.

Hacienda Blvd.

Fullerton Rd.

142

HUNTINGTON
PARK

N8

Whittier Blvd.

Chino Hills
State Park

710

Firestone Blvd.

DOWNEY

La Habra Blvd.

90

Century Fwy.

42

La Mirada Rd.

Imperial Hwy.

Beach Blvd.

Harbor Blvd.

Nixon
Library

105

ORANGE
COUNTY

Long Beach Fwy.

Rosecrans Ave.

NORWALK

FULLERTON

Alameda St.

PARAMOUNT

Alondra Blvd.

5

Riverside Fwy.

Artesia Fwy.

91

91

91

ANAHEIM

91

Gardena Fwy.

19

Lakewood Blvd.

CERRITOS

57

55

Atlantic Ave.

LAKEWOOD

Bellflower Blvd.

605

Knotts Berry
Farm

Lincoln Ave.

Arrowhead
Pond

Carson St.

Disneyland

Edison Intl.
Field of
Anaheim

Costa Mesa (Newport) Fwy.

710

Long Beach
Municipal
Airport

Willow St.

Valley View St.

Beach Blvd.

Katella Ave.

103

1

LONG
BEACH

Pacific Coast Hwy.

405

GARDEN
GROVE

22

5

Longbeach
Aquarium

Ocean Blvd.

U.S. Naval
Weapons
Station

Garden Grove Fwy.

1st St.

SANTA
ANA

Queen Mary

Belmont
Shores

San Diego Fwy.

Bolsa Chica Rd.

39

Brookhurst St.

Euclid St.

Los
Angeles
Harbor

FERRY TO
CATALINA ISLAND

Sunset
Beach

1

Warner Ave.

FOUNTAIN
VALLEY

405

TO COSTA MESA (2mi) &
NEWPORT BEACH (8mi)

TO IRVINE (2mi) &
SAN DIEGO (70mi)

ROUTE 66

TO PACIFIC
PALISADES (2mi),
MALIBU (8mi)

Montana Ave.

Idaho Ave.

Washington Ave.

California Ave.

3rd St.

23rd St.

26th St.

Franklin St.

Wilshire Blvd.

Lincoln Park
Wilshire Blvd.

Douglas Park

Santa Monica State Beach

Ocean Ave.

3rd St. Promenade

2nd St.

4th St.

5th St.

6th St.

7th St.

Lincoln Blvd.

9th St.

11th St.

12th St.

Euclid St.

14th St.

15th St.

16th St.

17th St.

18th St.

19th St.

20th St.

Arizona Ave.

Santa Monica Blvd.

26th St.

Centinela Ave.

Santa Monica Pier Aquarium

Santa Monica Place

Broadway

Colorado Ave.

Bergamot Station Arts Center

Santa Monica Pier & Pacific Park

Int'l. Chess Park

Main St.

Memorial Park

Cloverfield St.

SANTA MONICA

Olympic Blvd.

Michigan Ave.

Santa Monica Fwy.

Perry's Beach Rentals

Bicknell Ave.

Pacific St.

Strand St.

Pico Blvd.

Bay St.

Grant St.

Pacific St.

Pearl St.

Delaware Ave.

Virginia Ave.

Kansas Ave.

Santa Monica Bay

Boardwalk

Ocean Front Walk

Main St.

2nd St.

3rd St.

4th St.

5th St.

6th St.

7th St.

11th St.

Euclid St.

14th St.

Santa Monica College

Cloverfield Blvd.

California Heritage Museum

OCEAN PARK

Ocean Park Blvd.

Oak St.

Hill St.

Ashland Ave.

20th St.

26th St.

Speedway

Neilson Way

Banard Wy.

Marine St.

Dewey St.

5th St.

6th St.

7th St.

Museum of Flying

Santa Monica Airport

Rose Ave.

Flower Ave.

Penmar Golf Course

23rd St.

Dewey St.

Warren Ave.

Hampton Dr.

Sunset Ave.

Vernon Ave.

Indiana Ave.

Brooks Ave.

Broadway Ave.

Westminster Ave.

Lake St.

Brooks Ave.

VENICE

Electric Ave.

Abbot Kinney Blvd.

California Ave.

Oakwood Ave.

Shell Ave.

Linden Ave.

Lincoln Blvd.

Palms Blvd.

Palms Blvd.

Vienna Wy.

Carlton Wy.

Wallgrove Ave.

Bundy Dr.

Grand Blvd.

N Venice Blvd.

Victoria Ave.

Lucille Ave.

Venice Blvd.

Penmar Ave.

Venice Canals

Pacific Ave.

Mildred Ave.

Marr St.

Oxford Dr.

Thatcher Ave.

Yale Ave.

Stanford Ave.

Del Rey Ave.

Venice Fishing Pier

Washington Blvd.

Via Dulce

Panay Wy.

Palawan Wy.

Admiralty Way

Princeton Dr.

Washington Blvd.

E

D

C

Venice Beach Boardwalk

Santa Monica

▲ ACCOMMODATIONS

Los Angeles / Santa Monica Hostel, **2**

Ocean Lodge Hotel, **7**

Pacific Sands Motel, **3**

🍴 FOOD

Big Dean's "Muscle-In" Cafe, **6**

Bread & Porridge, **1**

Fritto Misto, **5**

Mariasol, **4**

(VITAL STATS)

Population: 87,000

Visitor Info: Santa Monica Visitors Center, 395 Santa Monica Pl. (☎310-393-7593; www.santamonica.com). Open daily 10am-6pm.

Internet Access: Santa Monica Public Library, 1234 5th St. (☎310-451-8859). Temporary location; main branch under renovation until 2006. Open M-Th 10am-9pm, F-Sa 10am-5:30pm.

Post Office: 1248 5th St. (☎310-576-6786), at Arizona Blvd. Open M-F 9am-6pm, Sa 9am-3pm. **Postal Code:** 90401.

⌗ SIGHTS

Filled with gawkers and hawkers, the area on and around the carnival pier is the hub of tourist activity. The fun spills over to lively **Third St. Promenade.** Farther inland, along Main St. and beyond, are galleries, design shops, and museums.

THIRD STREET PROMENADE. Cars are prohibited on this ultra-popular three-block stretch of mosaic art tiles, fashionable stores, movie theaters, and lively restaurants. The Promenade truly heats up when the sun sets, the ocean breeze kicks in, and the ivy-lined mesh dinosaur sculptures. On Wednesday and Saturday mornings, the area becomes a **Farmers Market** selling flowers and produce, with Saturdays featuring exclusively organic products. *(Between Broadway and Wilshire in downtown Santa Monica. Exit off 4th St. from I-10.)*

SANTA MONICA PIER & PACIFIC PARK.
The famed pier is the heart of Santa Monica Beach and home to the carnivalesque Pacific Park. Adrenaline addicts over 4 ft. tall can twist and turn on the five-story West Coaster or soar 100 ft. above the ocean in the first solar-powered Ferris wheel. *(☎310-458-8900; http://santamonicapier.org. Pier open 24hr. Park open summer Su-Th 11am-11pm, F-Sa 11am-12:30am; in winter hours vary, so call ahead.)*

▧ FOOD

Giant, colorful table umbrellas sprouting from sidewalk patios along Third St. Promenade and Ocean Ave. punctuate Santa Monica's upscale eating scene. Menus nod to (deep-pocketed) health buffs, offering organic and vegetarian choices.

▨ **Fritto Misto,** 601 Colorado Ave. (☎310-458-2829), at 6th St. "Neighborhood Italian Cafe" with cheery waitstaff lets you create your own pasta (from $6). Vegetarian entrees $8-12. Open M-Th 11:30am-10pm, F-Sa 11:30am-10:30pm, Su 11:30am-9:30pm.

Big Dean's "Muscle-In" Cafe, 1615 Ocean Front Walk (☎310-393-2666). You don't need to venture far for the "burger that made Santa Monica famous" ($7). Veggie burgers $5. Happy hour M-F 4-8pm. Open M-F 10am-dark, Sa-Su 10:30am-dark.

Mariasol, 401 Santa Monica Pier (☎310-917-5050). Prime sunset views accompany your meal. Friendly *mariachi* band. Locals recommend the *campechana* ($12), a combination of shrimp, octopus calamari, and ceviche. Appetizers $6-14. Entrees $9-15. Open Su-Th 10am-10pm, F-Sa 10am-11pm. Reservations recommended for 2nd fl. dining room.

Bread & Porridge, 2315 Wilshire Blvd. (☎310-453-4941). Prides itself on exceptional service and an egalitarian division of labor—dishwashers, busboys, servers, cashiers, and cooks all rotate jobs and share tips. Pancakes $6-8. Omelettes $10. Sandwiches and entrees $8-13. Open M-F 7am-2pm, Sa-Su 7am-3pm.

▛ ACCOMMODATIONS

Accommodations in Santa Monica range from cheap oceanfront hostels to expensive oceanfront hotels. The closer you stay to the beach, the more you dish out. Depending on the hostel/hotel, the tax on your room may be 8.5% or 14%. The best budget option in Santa Monica is the new and airy ▨**Los Angeles/Santa Monica Hostel,** 1436 2nd St., which has prime access to the beach and Santa Monica hot spots. The hostel sponsors tours and activities, and has Internet access, video games, nightly movie showings, library, self-service kitchen, laundry, and a travel store. (☎310-393-9913. Check-in 2pm-midnight. Dorms $27, non-members $30; private rooms from $60.) The rooms of the **Pacific Sands Motel,** 1515 Ocean Ave., are at the epicenter of what's happening. (☎310-395-6133. Rooms from $105.) Similarly pleasant rooms are available at the **Ocean Lodge Hotel,** 1667 Ocean Ave., just a block from the beach. (☎310-451-4146. Singles from $150; doubles from $175.)

Sink your toes in the sand, ride the ferris wheel on the pier, take a picture next to the plaque on the grass at Ocean Ave. and Santa Monica Blvd., and dip your feet in the Pacific. You've finished "the Journey," the Mother Road, the Will Rogers Highway, the Main Street of America.

THE OREGON TRAIL

You learned about it in history class, and maybe spent hours honing your bison-hunting, river-fording, and epitaph-writing skills at the computer game simulation, but this is your chance to drive the real thing. Stretching 2000 glorious miles from Independence, MO, to Oregon City, OR, our route traces the path of the pioneers across the prairies of Kansas, over the mountain passes of Wyoming, and along the Columbia River in Oregon.

The Oregon Trail follows a route rich in history. By the mid-1860s, over 300,000 pioneers had emigrated from the crowded east to the fertile valleys of the West Coast. While the original journey, a four- to six-month undertaking, offered settlers the opportunity to stake claims in new lands, it also posed great risks. One in ten people traveling the trail died en route, many claimed by cholera. Wagons were full and space was limited; most travelers walked. Barefoot. Today's travels are

ROUTE STATS

Miles: c. 2000

Route: Independence, MO, to Oregon City, OR.

States: 6; Missouri, Kansas, Nebraska, Wyoming, Idaho, and Oregon.

Driving Time: Nine days minimum; ideally, allow between two and three weeks to appreciate the scenic drives and historic landmarks of the trail.

When To Go: Pioneers started in mid-spring. You, however, benefit from roads, so you could set off almost any time you want. Heed your forerunners; avoid the mountains in winter, when snow makes some stretches impassable. Watch for late-summer tornadoes in the plains.

Crossroads: The National Road in Independence and Kansas City, MO/KS (p. 359); **The North American** in Twin Falls, ID (p. 696).

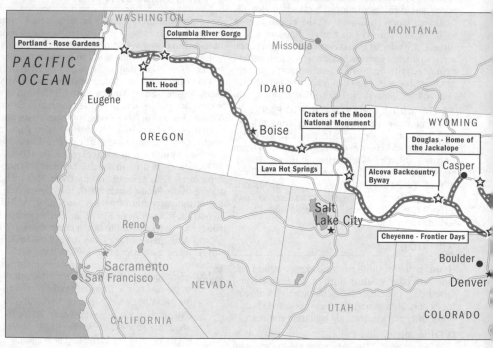

less treacherous, but reminders of pioneers past still line the way, including famous **Alcove Spring** (p. 555), **Chimney Rock** (p. 565), **Scottsbluff** (p. 566), and, of course, **Independence Rock** (p. 579)—make it here by July 4th, and you'll be in Oregon before the winter. The route also crosses the original **Pony Express** trails, pathways of daring young adventurers who embodied the roadtrip spirit.

But the modern Oregon Trail offers far more than just historical sights. From sprawling **Kansas City** (p. 546) in the East, through laid-back **Boise** (p. 600), to funky, hip **Portland** (the microbrewery capital of North America and home to some of the most stunning rose gardens around; p. 616) in the West, the cities that line the road are varied and vibrant. Many revel in their Wild Western heritage; **Douglas, WY** (p. 570) bills itself as the **"Jackalope Capital of the World,"** while **Cheyenne, WY** (p. 572) celebrates **Frontier Days** with rodeos, parades, and square dances each July. Others take full advantage of their natural resources, offering everything from kiteboarding (**Hood River, OR;** p. 613) to mountain climbing (**Enterprise and Joseph;** p.

607) to natural hot springs (**Lava Hot Springs, ID;** p. 588). Like the towns along the way, the Oregon Trail's landscape is just about as varied as it gets. From the sweeping prairies of Kansas and Nebraska, you'll climb into the towering Rocky Mountains of southern Wyoming (don't miss the scenic **Alcova Backcountry Byway;** p. 576), pass through the spectacularly bizarre rock formations of **Craters of the Moon National Monument** (p. 592) in Idaho, and follow the beautiful **Columbia River Gorge** (p. 611) along the waterfalls that line the **Historic Columbia River Highway** (p. 616) from The Dalles to Portland.

The Oregon Trail isn't a big-city route by any stretch of the imagination, so don't expect megamalls or cosmopolitan downtowns. Instead, prepare for the tiny hamlets that line the rural highways of the Great Plains and Rocky Mountains—places where motel rooms and ice-cream cones are cheap, owners are friendly, stoplights are few, and cows are plentiful. Fortunately, even the tiniest towns aren't completely devoid of attractions, and the open road between them has an appeal of its own. And, of course, near Alliance, NE, you'll

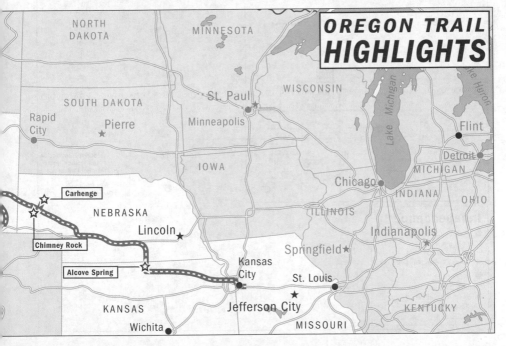

pass by what is perhaps the epitome of all roadtrip culture—delightfully wacky **Carhenge** (p. 565), modeled after England's famous Stonehenge, constructed entirely out of old automobiles.

It's a long, arduous road, but the views along the way are unparalleled, far better than any computer game or textbook. Pack up your wagon and get going—Oregon awaits!

INDEPENDENCE

Every authentic Oregon Trail trip begins in Independence, hometown of Harry S. Truman. During the era of westward expansion, this city stood on the edge of a vast wilderness, truly the last way-station for pioneers. The romantic sense of journey lingers, between the hills of the East and the prairies of the Midwest. Modernized antebellum estates and hundred-year-old businesses allow this suburb to remain a trailhead to the West.

GETTING AROUND

Downtown Independence is the center of the city. **Exit 12** from **I-70** leads to **Noland Rd.**, a strip of gas stations and fast-food joints. Follow this road about 3 mi., then go left on **Walnut St.** A right onto

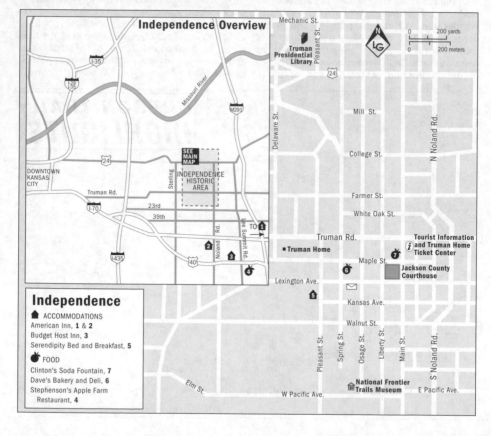

Independence

🛏 ACCOMMODATIONS
American Inn, **1** & **2**
Budget Host Inn, **3**
Serendipity Bed and Breakfast, **5**

🍴 FOOD
Clinton's Soda Fountain, **7**
Dave's Bakery and Deli, **6**
Stephenson's Apple Farm Restaurant, **4**

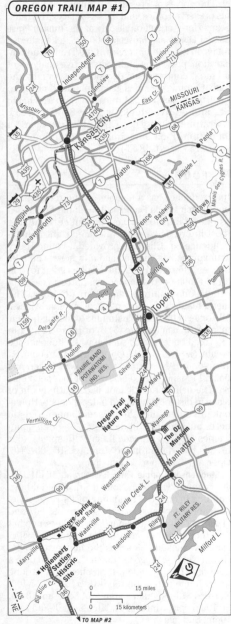

OREGON TRAIL MAP #1

VITAL STATS

Population: 113,000

Visitor Info: Tourist Information Center and Truman Home Ticket Center (☎816-254-9929), at Main St. and Truman Rd. Open M-F 8:30am-5pm.

Internet Access: Mid-Continent Public Library, South Independence Branch, 13700 E. 35th St. (☎816-461-2050). Open M-Th 9am-9pm, F 9am-6pm, Sa 9am-5pm.

Post Office: 301 Lexington St. (☎816-521-3608). Open M-F 8am-5pm, Sa 8am-noon. **Postal Code:** 64050.

either **Main** or **Liberty St.** will lead to the central square formed by Liberty, Lexington, Main, and Maple St. These streets are lined with free **parking** and surround the Jackson County Courthouse.

👁 SIGHTS

In the center of downtown stands the **Jackson County Courthouse,** where a young Harry Truman worked as a judge just a few yards from his first job at Clinton's Drugstore. The building houses offices now, but its statue-filled courtyard is a great start at visiting the city's historical sites. Nearby, at the corner of Osage St., the **National Frontier Trails Museum,** 318 W. Pacific St., is filled with history and a few genuine artifacts from the days of Manifest Destiny. Exhibits explain the significance of three major trails that began in Independence—the Santa Fe, the California and the Oregon. (☎816-325-7575; www.frontiertrailsmuseum.com. Open M-Sa 9am-4:30pm, Su 12:30-4:30pm. $4, seniors $3.50, ages 6-17 $2.50.)

Back up Main St. at the corner of Truman Rd., the **Truman Home Ticket Center** houses the Tourist Information Center. Tours of Truman's home, at 219 Delaware Rd., depart from here following a short introductory video. The video itself notes that "few memorable events took place at 219 Delaware"; the tour should probably be reserved for real enthusiasts. (☎816-254-9929. Tours Labor Day-Memorial Day Su and Tu-Sa every 15min. 9am-4:45pm. $3.) The sidewalk outside the center is the starting point for **Pioneer Trails Adventures.** These wagon rides through town are guided by the Wrangler, an in-character driver and storyteller. (☎816-456-4991 or 816-254-2466; www.pioneertrailsadventure.com. Tours $6-20.)

The graves of President Truman and his wife, his preserved office, and the legendary "The Buck Stops Here" are all on display at the **Truman Presidential Library and Museum,** 500 U.S. 24. Galleries focus on the different crises of the Truman administration, presenting multi-perspective analyses of its most controversial decisions, especially the use of atomic weapons in Japan. (Head north up Liberty St. past U.S. 24, turn left onto Mechanic St., and go five blocks west. ☎ 816-833-1225; www.trumanlibrary.org. Open M-W 9am-5pm, Th 9am-9pm, F-Sa 9am-5pm, Su noon-5pm. $7, seniors $5, ages 6-18 $3.)

▧ FOOD

Independence has a number of fine restaurants, but **Clinton's Soda Fountain,** 100 Maple St., shines as one of the most delicious, and certainly the most interesting, options. Located right in Independence Sq., Clinton's provided a young Harry Truman with his first job and now serves double-duty as a historical site. The result is great food in an old-fashioned atmosphere; patrons can still order soda fountain phosphates ($1.30). The menu features a variety of excellent sandwiches, all for less than $5. Customers can finish their meals with a milkshake ($4-5) or Harry's Favorite ($3.70), a butterscotch sundae with chocolate ice cream. (☎ 816-833-2046. Open M-F 8:30am-6pm, Sa 10am-6pm.) Also worth a stop is **Dave's Bakery And Deli,** 214 Maple St., a block west of Independence Sq. The deli's futuristic look is delightfully out of place in historic downtown Independence. Home-baked confections almost seem anachronistic here, but they're still delicious. The deli sandwiches ($3.50) are made fresh, with spectacular breads baked right in the store. (☎ 816-833-2046. Open M-F 6am-5pm, Sa 7am-3pm.)

Stephenson's Apple Farm Restaurant, 16401 U.S. 40, is south of I-70 on Noland Rd. The red barn building is only the beginning of its rural style, with appetizers such as fritters, livers ($5.50), and gizzards ($5) on the menu. City-slickers needn't fear though, as the entrees are a bit less exotic. Hickory-smoked chicken is the house specialty. (From Noland Rd., go left down U.S. 40 and take a right onto Lees Summit Rd.; Stephenson's parking lot is immediately on the left. ☎ 816-373-5400. Entrees $13-18. Open summer M-Sa 11am-10pm, Su 10am-9pm; winter M-Th 11am-9pm, F-Sa 11am-10pm, Su 10am-9pm.)

▧ ACCOMMODATIONS

Hotels are cheaper and easier to find just outside of Independence. Exit 18 off I-70 has fine budget options. Beautiful, historic, and overrun with greenery, the **Serendipity Bed and Breakfast,** 116 Pleasant Ave., is three blocks west of Liberty St. Keeping with the Victorian-era decor, breakfast is served by candlelight. (☎ 800-203-4299 or 816-833-4719; www.bbhost.com/serendipitybb. Check-in 4-9pm. Singles $45-70; doubles $80-85.)

Cheaper options include two **American Inn** locations: Woods Chapel Rd., off Exit 18 from I-70, and 4141 S. Noland Rd. Rooms are clean and reasonably well maintained, but this budget chain will only rent to those under 21 if they are 50 mi. from their home address. (Woods Chapel Rd. ☎ 816-228-1080. S. Noland Rd. ☎ 816-373-8300. Singles $40-$50.) The **Budget Host Inn,** 15014 U.S. 40, south of I-70, is another convenient choice for less expensive lodging, with clean, if slightly worn, rooms. (☎ 816-373-7500 or 800-283-4678. Singles $35.)

◪ APPROACHING KANSAS CITY
From downtown Independence, return to **Noland Rd.** via **Walnut St.** and drive approximately 3 mi. south. Ramps onto **I-70** are very well marked. **I-70** passes hrough the northern part of Kansas City, close to downtown. **Exit 3a** feeds onto **The Paseo,** which is a large road parallel to, and a bit east of **Main St.**

KANSAS CITY

With more boulevards than Paris and more fountains than Rome, Kansas City looks and acts more European than one might expect from the "Barbecue Capital of the World." When Prohibition stifled most of the country's fun in the 1920s, Mayor Pendergast let the good times continue to roll. The Kansas City of today maintains its blues-and-jazz reputation in a metropolis spanning two states.

▣ GETTING AROUND

Though Kansas City is laid out in a relatively simple grid, car travel can be very frustrating due to the tangle of one-way streets and turning-only lanes. Only east-west streets are numbered, with numbers increasing as one travels south. **Main St.,** which runs north-south and divides the city in two, is in fact two one-way streets located a block

OREGON TRAIL

VITAL STATS

Population: 150,000

Visitor Info: Convention and Visitors Bureau of Greater Kansas City, 1100 Main St., #2200 (☎816-221-5242 or 800-767-7700; www.vis-itkc.com), on the 22nd fl. of the City Center Sq. Bldg. Open M-F 8:30am-5pm. **Missouri Tourist Information Center,** 4010 Blue Ridge Cut-Off (☎816-889-3330 or 800-877-1234). Follow signs from Exit 9 off I-70. Open daily 8am-5pm, except on days when the Chiefs are playing at home.

Internet Access: Kansas City Public Library, Central Branch, 14 10th St. (☎816-701-3414). **Plaza branch,** 301 51st St. (☎816-701-3575). **Westport branch,** 118 Westport Rd. (☎816-701-3635).

Post Office: 315 W. Pershing Rd. (☎816-374-9100). Open M-F 8am-8pm, Sa 8:30am-3:30pm. **Postal Code:** 64108.

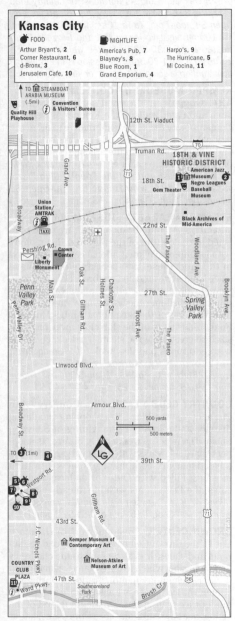

Kansas City

🍎 FOOD
Arthur Bryant's, **2**
Corner Restaurant, **6**
d-Bronx, **3**
Jerusalem Cafe, **10**

🍸 NIGHTLIFE
America's Pub, **7**
Blayney's, **8**
Blue Room, **1**
Grand Emporium, **4**

Harpo's, **9**
The Hurricane, **5**
Mi Cocina, **11**

apart from each other. Large pay-garages are available in the downtown area, but virtually every street has free or metered **parking** on the shoulder, so travelers may prefer to drive to each site rather than park and walk.

👁 SIGHTS

18TH & VINE HISTORIC DISTRICT. The entire 18th & Vine Historic District pays tribute to great jazz musicians who lived and played here in the early 20th century. The **American Jazz Museum** brings the era back with music listening stations, neon dance hall signs, and paraphernalia ranging from Ella Fitzgerald's eyeglasses to Louis Armstrong's lip salve. In the same building, the **Negro Leagues Baseball Museum** documents the athletic feats of 1920s African-American ballplayers and the racism that once divided baseball and society. The museum is dominated by an indoor diamond manned by statues of a Negro League Dream Team. (*1616 E. 18th St. Jazz museum ☎816-474-8463; www.americanjazzmuseum.com. Baseball museum ☎816-474-8453; www.nlbm.com. Both open Su noon-6pm, Tu-Sa 9am-6pm. Single museum $6, under 12 $2.50; both museums $8/$4.)*

NELSON-ATKINS MUSEUM OF ART. This museum features one of the best East Asian art collections in the world and a sculpture park with 13 pieces by Henry Moore. The museum is under renovation until further notice, so call ahead.

(4525 Oak St., 3 blocks northeast of Country Club Plaza. ☎ 816-561-4000; www.nelson-atkins.org. Open Su noon-5pm, Tu-Th 10am-4pm, F 10am-9pm, Sa 10am-5pm. Live jazz inside the Rozzelle Court Restaurant F 5:30-8:30pm. Free walking tours Sa 11am-2pm, Su 1:30-3pm. Admission is free while the construction is going on, except for special exhibits.)

KEMPER MUSEUM OF CONTEMPORARY ART. Gigantic, malformed spiders adorn the lawn and outer walls of the Kemper Museum of Contemporary Art, a great alternative to more traditional museums. Inside, other works both more and less orthodox than the arachnids are on display in cool white galleries. *(4420 Warwick Blvd., off Main St. just north of the Country Club Plaza. ☎ 816-753-5784; www.kemperart.org. Open Su 11am-5pm, Tu-Th 10am-4pm, F-Sa 10am-9pm. Free.)*

STEAMBOAT ARABIA MUSEUM. In 1856, the steamboat Arabia struck a fallen tree and vanished at the bottom of the Missouri River, along with its impressive international cargo. Preserved in the mud, these 19th-century wonders have since been excavated and restored. Delicate glassware, lovely pottery, clothing, and a vast array of other antebellum objects are now on display at the Treasures of the Steamboat Arabia Museum. Functioning parts of the ship chug away on a life-sized re-creation of the steamer's deck, complete with enormous paddlewheel. *(400 Grand Blvd., next to the City Market. ☎ 816-471-4030; www.1856.com. Open M-Sa 10am-5:30pm, Su noon-5pm. $9.75, seniors $9.25, ages 4-12 $4.75.)*

COUNTRY CLUB PLAZA. The Country Club Plaza, or just the Plaza, is a shopping and dining district and a lovely re-imagining of Suavely, Spain. The result is wonderfully bizarre, as shoppers share sidewalks with medieval gargoyles and advertisements compete for space with tiled mosaics. Filled with Old-World charm and hip cafes, the Plaza hums with life in early evening. *(Along 47th St., between Main and Madison St. Free concerts May-Sept. Th 5-8pm and Sa-Su 2-5pm.)*

CROWN CENTER. Headquarters of Hallmark Cards, the Crown Center contains myriad restaurants and shops. It is also home to the children's **Coterie Theatre,** which features games, a maze, and theater technology demonstrations. During the winter, the **Ice Terrace** is Kansas City's only public outdoor ice-skating rink. On the third level of the center, see how cards and accessories are made at the **Hallmark Visitors Center.** Pershing St. and the Crown Center area are dominated by an enormous WWI **Liberty Monument,** which sits on a grassy hill overlooking Union Station. A vast frieze is built into the hillside, depicting the horrors of war on the right and the pleasures of peace on the left. *(2405 Grand Ave., 2 mi. north of the Plaza near Pershing Rd. Crown Center ☎ 816-274-5916. Coterie Theatre ☎ 816-474-6785. $8, under 18 $6. Ice Terrace ☎ 816-274-8412. Rink open Nov.-Dec. Su-Th 10am-9pm, F-Sa 10am-11pm; Jan.-Mar. daily 10am-9pm. $5, under 13 $4. Skate rental $1.50. Hallmark Visitors Center ☎ 816-274-3613, recording 816-274-5672; hallmarkvisitorscenter.com. Open M-F 9am-5pm, Sa 9:30am-4:30pm; closed early Jan.)*

♫ ENTERTAINMENT

From September to May, the **Missouri Repertory Theatre,** at 50th and Oak St., stages American classics. (☎ 816-235-2700; www.missourirep.org. Tickets $10-48. $3 off for students and seniors.) **Quality Hill Playhouse,** 303 W. 10th St., produces off-Broadway plays and revues from September to June. The box office is located at 912 Baltimore Ave., Ste. 200. (☎ 816-421-1700. Box office open M-F 9am-5pm. Tickets $22. $2 off for students and seniors.) From late June to mid-July, the **Heart of America Shakespeare Festival** (☎ 816-531-7728; www.kcshakes.org) in Southmoreland Park, at 47th and Oak St., puts on free shows.

Sports fans stampede into Arrowhead Stadium, at I-70 and Blue Ridge Cutoff, home to football's **Chiefs** (☎ 816-920-9400 or 800-676-5488; tickets $51-70) and soccer's **Wizards** (☎ 816-920-9300; tickets $12-17). Next door, Kauffman Stadium houses the **Royals,** Kansas City's baseball team. (☎ 816-921-8000 or 800-676-9257. Tickets $5-22.)

▰ FOOD

Kansas City's speciality is its unusually tangy barbecue. The **Westport** area, at Westport Rd. and Broadway St. just south of 40th St., has eclectic cafes and coffeehouses. Ethnic eateries cluster along **39th St.** just east of the state line. The **City Market** area has Asian grocery stores and open-air produce markets at the intersection of 5th and Walnut St. (Open Su-F 9am-4pm, Sa 6am-4pm.)

▨ **Arthur Bryant's,** 1727 Brooklyn Ave. (☎ 816-231-1123). The grand-daddy of KC barbecue and a perennial candidate for best barbecue in the country. Bryant's "sandwiches" ($9) are a carnivore's delight–wimpy triangles of bread drowning in pork perfection. Open M-Th 10am-9:30pm, F-Sa 10am-10pm, Su 11am-8:30pm.

d-Bronx, 3904 Bell St. (☎816-531-0550), at 39th St. A New York deli in Middle America, d-Bronx has over 35 kinds of subs (half $4-6, whole $8-12) and powdered sugar brownies ($1.50). Open M-W 10:30am-9pm, Th 10:30am-10pm, F-Sa 10:30am-11pm.

Jerusalem Cafe, 431 Westport Rd. (☎816-756-2770). Patrons enjoy primarily vegetarian Mediterranean fare while playing backgammon. Pita sandwiches ($6-7) complement unusual appetizers, such as stuffed grape leaves (under $5). Relax upstairs in the Nargila Coffee-House. Open M-Sa 11am-10pm, Su noon-8pm.

Corner Restaurant, 4059 Broadway St. (☎816-931-6630), in the heart of Westport. A greasy spoon famous for its all-day breakfasts, including plate-sized pancakes ($2-3). Weekday lunch specials $6. Open daily 7am-3pm.

ACCOMMODATIONS

The least expensive lodgings lie near the interstates, especially I-70, and toward Independence. Downtown hotels tend to be on the pricey side.

American Inn (☎800-905-6343) dominates the KC budget motel market with locations at 4141 S. Noland Rd. (☎816-373-8300); Woods Chapel Rd. (☎816-228-1080), off I-70 at Exit 18; 1211 Armour Rd. (☎816-471-3451), off I-35 at Exit 6B. The rooms are large and pleasant. A/C, cable TV, and outdoor pools. Singles and doubles from $40.

Interstate Inn (☎816-229-6311), off I-70 at Exit 18. A great deal if you get one of the walk-in singles or doubles. 21+. Singles from $29; doubles $44. More for non-smoking rooms.

Lake Jacomo (☎816-795-8200), 22 mi. southeast of downtown. From I-70, take Rte. 291 South to Colbern Rd.; Lake Jocomo is 2 mi. down the road. Lots of water activities, 33 forested campsites, and a marina. Sites $10, with electricity $15, with electricity and water $18, full hookup $22.

NIGHTLIFE

In the 1920s, jazz musician Count Basie and his "Kansas City Sound" reigned at the River City bars. Twenty years later, saxophonist Charlie "Bird" Parker spread his wings and soared, asserting Kansas City's prominence as a jazz music roost to be reckoned with. The restored **Gem Theater,** 1615 E. 18th St., stages old-time blues and jazz. From October to April, the Jammin' at the Gem concert series swings in a serious fashion. (☎816-842-1414. Box office open M-F 10am-4pm.) Across the street, the **Blue Room,** 1600 E. 18th St., cooks four nights a week with some of the smoothest local acts in town. (☎816-474-2929. Cover F-Sa $5. Open M and Th 5-11pm, F 5pm-1am, Sa 7pm-1am.) The **Grand Emporium,** 3832 Main St., twice voted the best blues club in the US, has live music five nights a week. (☎816-531-1504. Live music M and W-Sa. Cover up to $15, depending on act. Open M and Sa noon-2am, Tu-F 11am-2am.) For something besides jazz, bars and nightclubs cluster in **Westport.**

Blayney's, 415 Westport Rd. (☎816-561-3747). Canned R&B on the dance floor, live music on the outdoor deck. Cover $2-6. Open Tu-Th 8pm-3am, F 6pm-3am, Sa 5pm-3am.

America's Pub, 510 Westport Rd. (☎816-531-1313). Kansas City's bachelorette party headquarters. While the dance floor is usually packed, the elevated barstools provide a chance to relax. Th $1 drinks. Cover $6. Open W-Sa 8pm-3am.

The Hurricane, 4048 Broadway St. (☎816-753-0884). Hosts everything from open mic (M) to hip-hop (Th). Cover $5-10. Open M-F 3pm-3am, Sa-Su 5pm-3am.

Harpo's, 4109 Pennsylvania Ave. (☎816-753-3434). The keystone of Westport nightlife. The live music and $0.25 beer on Tu attract college students ready to party. Cover Tu and Sa $2-3. Open daily 11am-3am.

Mi Cocina, 620 W. 48th St. (☎816-960-6426). The place to see and be seen in Kansas City. Trendy Latin music accompanies couture-clad fashionistas. The pricey Mexican food is generally overlooked in favor of the bar. Open M-Th 11am-10pm, F-Sa 11am-3am, Su noon-10pm.

◤ DETOUR: HARLEY-DAVIDSON VEHICLE AND POWERTRAIN OPERATIONS

11401 N. Congress St.

20 mi. north of downtown Kansas City. Head north on the Paseo to I-29 North/I-35 North/U.S. 71 North. When they split, continue on I-29 North toward the airport. Take Exit 12 for NW 112th St.; at the bottom of the ramp turn right. Proceed 1 mi. and turn left on Congress St.

It's a bit far to travel for a factory tour, and visitors don't get very close to the action, but any true Harley fan will enjoy a stop here. After a brief video, a guide officiously ushers tour groups around the assembly plant to glimpse various individual pieces being made. At the end, the assembly line for the bikes themselves reveals how everything fits together. (☎414-343-7850 or 877-883-1450. Visitors Center and store open M-F 8am-3pm. 45min. tours every hr. M-F 8am-1pm. Limited space; walk-in or call to reserve. Free.)

⚑ LEAVING KANSAS CITY
The easiest way to leave Kansas City is to take **Broadway St.** north. Right before reaching the Missouri River, take the ramp to **I-70 West.**

Welcome To **KANSAS**

THE ROAD TO LAWRENCE. The road on the way to Lawrence is an uninspiring stretch of I-70 about 25 mi. long. Tollbooths are in effect in this area, so keep quarters ready. Lawrence can be reached by either Exit 202 or 204 off I-70. Exit 202 provides the more direct approach. Follow the exit through the tolls and straight through the intersection with **2nd St.,** as the exit ramp becomes **McDonald Rd.** Continue south until it intersects with **6th St.** Turn left, and drive east to **Massachusetts St.**

LAWRENCE
Forty miles from Kansas City, Lawrence was founded in 1854 by anti-slavery advocates to ensure that Kansas became a free state. Now home to the flagship University of Kansas (KU), Lawrence is a good-times college town, fully equipped with excellent restaurants and a happening musical scene.

▣ GETTING AROUND

Almost everything of interest is found along **Massachusetts St.** or parallel **Vermont** and **New Hampshire St.** Numbered streets run east-west. Vermont and New Hampshire St. are thick with free 2hr. **parking** lots, making driving in Lawrence an easy

---

VITAL STATS

Population: 80,000

Visitor Info: Lawrence Visitors Center, 402 N. 2nd St. (☎785-865-4499 or 888-529-5267; www.visit-lawrence.com), at Locust St. Open Apr.-Sept. M-F 8:30am-5:30pm, Su 1-5pm; Oct.-Mar. M-Sa 9am-5pm, Su 1-5pm.

Internet Access: Lawrence Public Library, 707 Vermont St. (☎785-843-3833; www.lawrencepubliclibrary.org). Public terminals located downstairs. Open M-F 9am-9pm, Sa 9am-6pm, Su 2-6pm.

Post Office: 645 Vermont St. (☎785-843-1681). Open M-F 8am-5:30pm, Sa 9am-noon. **Postal Code:** 66045.

---

and pleasant experience. Watch the arrows on the meters at slanted parking spots; it can be confusing to figure out which one goes with which car.

◎ SIGHTS

The Wild West was in full swing in Lawrence during the bleeding Kansas days, giving the city quite a bit of fascinating history. The **University of Kansas Watkins Community Museum of History,** 1047 Massachusetts St., features several floors of Lawrence lore, including an exhibit on the abolitionist activist John Brown. (☎785-841-4109. Open Tu-W 10am-6pm, Th 10am-9pm, F 10am-5pm, Sa 10am-4pm. Suggested donation $3.) The main attractions, however, are two tours through downtown Lawrence. A 1½hr. driving tour, **Quantrill's Raid: The Lawrence Massacre,** beginning at 1111 E. 19th St., traces the events leading up to the slaughter of over 200 men by pro-slavery vigilantes on August 21, 1863. The second tour, **House Styles of Old West Lawrence,** provides a look at 19th-century homes. There are walking (45min.) and driving (25min.) variations; pick up a map at the Visitors Center.

For the more refined, the **Spencer Museum of Art,** 1301 Mississippi St., is home to a small but impressive collection of paintings, sculpture, and glasswork from medieval and Renaissance Europe, as well as medieval Japan and Dynastic China. (☎785-864-4710. Open Su noon-5pm, Tu-W and F-Sa 10am-5pm, Th 10am-9pm. Free.)

▧ FOOD

Downtown Lawrence features both traditional barbecue joints and health-conscious offerings. The **Free State Brewing Company,** 636 Massachusetts St., was the first legal brewery in Kansas. This local hangout brews over 50 beers annually and always has at least five on tap. (☎ 785-843-4555. Beer $2.50. Sandwiches $6. Pasta $8-10. M $1.25 beer. Open M-Sa 11am-midnight, Su noon-11pm.) **Jefferson's,** 743 Massachusetts St., promotes "Peace, Love and Hotwings" along with its entrees, all under $7. (☎ 785-832-2000. Open M-W 11am-10pm, Th-Sa 11am-11pm, Su noon-10pm.)

Between meals, it's possible to have pretty much any conceivable combination of fruit in a glass down at the **Juice Stop,** 812 Massachusetts St. Sports-named smoothies all sell for $3.90, be it the Hat Trick or the Half-pipe. (☎ 785-331-0820. Open M-F 8am-9pm, Sa 9am-8pm, Su 10am-8pm.) The **Wheatfields Bakery and Cafe,** 904 Vermont St., serves large sandwiches ($6.50) on French bread, olive loaf, or focaccia. (☎ 785-841-5553. Open M-Sa 6:30am-8pm, Su 7:30am-4pm.)

ACCOMMODATIONS

Inexpensive motels are hard to come by in Lawrence. The best place to look is around Iowa and 6th St., just west of the KU campus. Three blocks from downtown, the **Halcyon House Bed and Breakfast,** 1000 Ohio St., is extremely close to local attractions and good parking. (☎ 785-841-0314. Rooms $49.) The traditional **Westminster Inn and Suites,** 2525 W. 6th St., offers many amenities, including a pool, to make stays more comfortable. (☎ 785-841-8410. Breakfast included. Singles M-Th $49, F-Su $55; doubles $59/$65. $5 AAA discount.) The **Virginia Inn,** 2903 W. 6th St., offers large rooms with microfridges, right in the downtown area. (☎ 785-843-6611. Singles $50.) A more luxurious but rather expensive stay is available at the **Eldritch Hotel,** at the corner of 7th and Massachusetts St. The two-room suites are *very* comfortable. (☎ 785-749-5011 or 800-527-0909. Rooms $89-235.)

NIGHTLIFE

The rowdy saloon-goers of Lawrence's past have come and gone, but late-night fun is still available; yesterday's cowboys have been replaced by college students. The place to be for live music, ▧**The Bottleneck,** 737 New Hampshire St., hosts local acts and big-name artists. There's a show every night except Thursday, when Retro Dance Night takes hold. (☎ 785-841-5483. Cover up to $10, depending on show. Open daily from 3pm.) For live music and a neighborhood bar atmosphere, head down to well-equipped **Jazzhaus,** 926½ Massachusetts St. (☎ 785-749-3320. Cover after 9pm $2-8; Tu $1.50, but no live music. Open daily 4pm-2am.) Across the street from each other and under one management, the **Jackpot Saloon and Music** and the **Replay Lounge,** 943 Massachusetts St., serve multiple facets of the clubbing community. The Replay is dark and low-ceilinged, with a bar and pinball, while the Jackpot is open, bright and sociable. Both put on a variety of musical acts. (Jackpot ☎ 785-832-1085. Shows daily. 21+. Open daily from 4pm. Replay ☎ 785-749-7676. Shows weekly. 21+ after 10pm. Open daily from 3pm.)

APPROACHING TOPEKA
From Lawrence, drive to the northern end of **Massachusetts St.** and head west on **6th St.** until the intersection with **McDonald Rd.** Head north on McDonald Rd., which will lead through the tolls and back onto **I-70,** toward Topeka. I-70 runs through the northern edges of Topeka; the most convenient way to enter the city is via Exit 361A. **Topeka Blvd.** is not directly accessible from the ramp but is very well marked. Exit 358B leads directly to **Gage Blvd.**

TOPEKA

The capital of Kansas, Topeka is essentially a vast tract of plazas and strip-malls. Though this arrangement has led to a particularly high density of fast-food joints and gas stations, intriguing restaurants and sights are still hidden throughout the city. Topeka displays its state pride at several historic sights that memorialize its role in the abolition and civil rights movements.

GETTING AROUND

Much of Topeka is a rough grid of four-lane roads—definitely a driver's city. **Topeka Blvd.** is the city's major north-south artery, with numerous restaurants and hotels. **Gage Blvd.,** a few blocks west, is a haven of gas stations and fast food. The majority of Topeka's sights lie on or near one of these two main roads, which are connected by east-west streets. Many of these end in residential cul-de-sacs, but **10th St.** to the north and **29th St.** to the south both span the full distance.

Parking in Topeka is plentiful and free in most areas; virtually every building has its own lot, so there is no need to park on the street. Downtown is the exception; visitors to the city center may have to find spaces along the curb, which can be hard to come by. Many of these spaces are free, though they often have 2hr. time restrictions.

(VITAL STATS)

Population: 112,000

Visitor Info: Topeka Convention and Visitors Bureau, 1275 Topeka Blvd. (☎800-235-1030; www.topekacvb.com). Open M-F 9am-5pm.

Internet Access: Topeka and Shawnee County Public Library, 1515 10th Ave. (☎785-580-4400; www.tscpl.org), at the corner of Washburn Ave. Open M-F 9am-9pm, Sa 9am-6pm, Su noon-9pm.

Post Office: 424 S. Kansas Ave. (☎785-295-9178). **Postal Code:** 66603.

👁 SIGHTS

Most of Topeka's sights are not focused around one region, so a good bit of driving is necessary to see them all. In the center of Topeka is the **Kansas State Capitol,** at the corner of 10th Ave. and Jackson St. (☎785-296-3966. Tours M-F every hr. 9am-3pm, except noon. Free.) The new **Brown v. Board National Historic Site,** at the intersection of Monroe and 15th St., is dedicated to the groundbreaking Supreme Court decision that ruled school segregation unconstitutional. Built in a former elementary school, the museum is filled with photographs chronicling the history leading up to and resulting from the decision. In the powerful Hall of Courage exhibit, visitors pass through a narrow corridor of gigantic screens, which blast footage of jeering crowds denouncing newly admitted black students. (Follow 10th St. to Topeka Blvd. and proceed south to 15th St. ☎785-354-4273. Open daily 9am-5pm. Free.)

The **Kansas Museum of History,** 6425 6th St., is a guide to the history of Kansas, from prehistoric native life to 20th-century developments. Rotating special exhibits highlight particular time periods and events. (Drive north on Topeka Blvd. to 6th St., then proceed east to the very end of the road. ☎785-272-8683; www.kshs.org. Open Su 1-5pm, Tu-Sa 9am-5pm. $4, seniors $3, students $2.)

In addition to lions, giraffes, and other exotic animals, the **Topeka Zoological Park,** 635 Gage Blvd., has an indoor rainforest where visitors share the pathways with monkeys, birds, turtles, and other small jungle creatures. (☎785-368-9143. Open daily 9am-5pm. $4.50, ages 3-12 $3.)

Proceeding south to Forbes Field Airport will bring you to the **Combat Air Museum,** a hangar that houses combat planes from many eras. (☎785-862-3303; www.combatairmuseum.org. Open M-Sa 9am-4:30pm, Su noon-4:30pm; last admission 3:30pm. $6, ages 6-17 $4.)

🍴 FOOD

Topeka is home to several fine restaurants, though finding them can be a bit of challenge; like much in this city, they are scattered across countless strip-malls. The ▨**Blind Tiger Brewery and Restaurant,** 417 37th St., east of Topeka Blvd., is named for the stuffed tigers which were sometimes used to advertise Prohibition-era speakeasies. The microbrewery and restaurant are separated only by a low wall, so the buzz of the bar blends softly into the dim, trendy eating area. Menu offerings include a range of salads, vegetarian options, and appetizer specialties such as the "tiger tips" (smoked ribs) and "tiger wings" (buffalo wings with house sauce). Finish it all off with a Prohibition Float, made with root beer brewed right in the building. (☎785-267-7527; www.blindtiger.com. Appetizers from $6. Pasta from $11. Grill entrees from $8. Restaurant open Su-Th 11am-9pm, F-Sa 11am-10pm. Lounge open Su-Th 11am-1am, F-Sa 11am-2am.)

Food preparation is a spectacle at **Kiku Japanese Steak House,** 5331 22nd Pl., in the Fairlawn Plaza off Fairlawn Rd. Chefs cook food hibachi style at your table. (☎785-272-6633. Appetizers $3-10. Entrees from $11. Open M-F 11:30am-1:30pm and 4:30-10pm, Sa-Su noon-10pm. Reservations recommended.) A local favorite, **Annie's Place,** 4014 Gage Center Dr., is located in the Gage Center Plaza off Gage Blvd. Whether you desire a hot dog ($3.75) or three-cheese quiche ($7.25), Annie's provides. The in-house bakery sells fabulous pies for $8-12. (☎785-273-0848. Open M-Sa 11am-10pm, Su 11am-9pm.) **Casa Authentic Mexican Food,** 3320 Topeka Blvd., south of 29th St., is a pleasant family restaurant with private booths and well-priced Mexican meals. The combination dinners are an excellent bargain, complete with an entree such as the house chili ($7.65) as well as salad or soup. (☎785-266-4503. Open M-Th 11am-10pm, F-Sa 11am-11pm, Su 11:30am-10pm.)

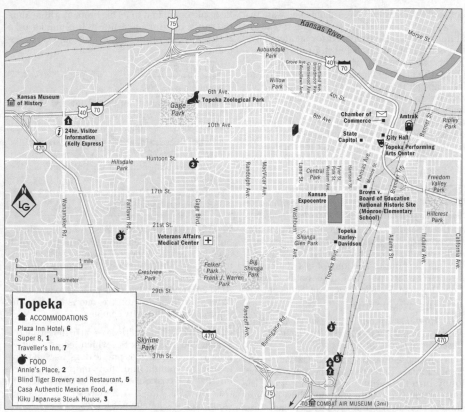

Topeka

🏠 ACCOMMODATIONS
Plaza Inn Hotel, **6**
Super 8, **1**
Traveller's Inn, **7**

🍎 FOOD
Annie's Place, **2**
Blind Tiger Brewery and Restaurant, **5**
Casa Authentic Mexican Food, **4**
Kiku Japanese Steak House, **3**

🏠 ACCOMMODATIONS

Hotels cluster near the highway exits, but some of the nicest and least expensive accommodations are closer to downtown. The **Plaza Inn Hotel,** 3880 Topeka Blvd., is located just south of 37th St. Though it looks like every other budget hotel on the outside, the rooms are spacious, pleasant, and well priced. (☎785-266-4591. Singles from $39; doubles from $44.) Nearby, the **Traveller's Inn,** 3846 Topeka Blvd., offers great deals and an outdoor pool. (☎785-267-1222, reservations 877-524-7666. Singles $35; doubles $40.) A safe bet is **Super 8,** 5968 10th Ave., right off I-70 at Exit 356. (☎785-273-5100. Singles from $50; doubles from $55.)

Road-weary travelers can spend evenings fishing and swimming at **Lake Shawnee Campground,** 3435 E. Edge Rd. Though there are many more RV sites than tent sites, only tents have the option of being right on the water's edge. (Follow 29th St. east to the edge of Topeka, then go south on Croco Rd.; E. Ridge Rd. is a short distance down to the right. ☎785-267-1156. Electrical hookups at most sites. Mid-Apr. to mid-Oct. tent sites $14; RVs $15; Mid-Oct. to mid-Apr. $11/$14. Showers free.)

🔼 LEAVING TOPEKA

To leave the city, follow **Topeka Blvd.** north through downtown and over the Kansas River. Signs indicate **U.S. 24,** which leads west to Manhattan.

THE ROAD TO MANHATTAN

U.S. 24 is a stretch of shining roadtrip glory. The confusion of the interstate gives way to an empty two-lane shot across the Kansas prairie, and the gently curving road and rolling landscape feel custom-made for cranked-down windows and cranked-up volume. Drivers should be aware that U.S. 24 is the main street for several tiny towns along the way. Be prepared for sudden speed drops; the limit swings between 70 and 20 mph.

This particular strip of road follows the original Oregon Trail rather closely, so it is rife with **historical markers.** These big brown signs, found in their own little alcoves beside the road, point out significant locations in the lives of the Oregon Trail travelers, the original roadtrippers. On the eastern outskirts of **St. Mary's,** stop by **Froggy's,** 311 W. Bertrand Ave., for delicious breakfasts and supercheap daily grill specials. (☎785-437-6733. Open M-Sa 8am-9pm, Su noon-3pm.)

OREGON TRAIL NATURE PARK
From U.S. 24, follow signs right down Schoemaker Rd.; turn left at the end onto Oregon Trail Rd.

At the Oregon Trail Nature Park, a pavilion, restrooms, and a gigantic cylindrical mural serve as the launching point for a series of walking trails through the prairie. The longest is a 30min. hike through the "Sea of Grass" to an outlook. (Open daily May-Sept. 7am-9pm; Oct.-Apr. 8am-6pm.)

THE OZ MUSEUM   511 Lincoln Ave.
From U.S. 24, turn left on Lincoln Ave. shortly after crossing the into Wamego city limits. The Oz Museum is 6 blocks up on the right.

This new museum is dedicated to Oz paraphernalia of all kinds. Enter through the dull and dreary lobby into the technicolor brightness of the museum proper, where you can follow a re-creation of Dorothy's journey while marveling at first editions of Baum's novel, props from the movie, memorabilia from the stage production, and all sorts of other artifacts from the Land of Oz. (☎866-458-8686; www.ozmuseum.com. Open M-Sa 1-5pm, Su noon-5pm. $7, ages 4-12 $4.)

APPROACHING MANHATTAN
On the outskirts of Manhattan, **Poyntz Ave.** appears running parallel to **U.S. 24.** Entering the city is easiest if you get on this road as soon as possible, thus avoiding the unpleasant snare of highway intersections at the eastern edge of the city.

MANHATTAN

A little city thriving around Kansas State University and an inexplicable number of indoor shopping centers, Manhattan proclaims itself "The Little Apple." While it may seem like the *really* lit-

tle apple compared to its big brother, within Manhattan's borders are many hallmarks of a metropolis: an art museum, a zoo, and great restaurants.

VITAL STATS

Population: 45,000

Visitor Info: Manhattan Convention and Visitors Bureau, 501 Poyntz Ave. (☎785-776-8829; www.manhattancvb.org). Open M-F 8am-5pm.

Internet Access: Manhattan Public Library, 629 Poyntz Ave. (☎785-726-4741). Open M-Th 9am-8:30pm, F 9am-6pm, Sa 9am-5:30pm, Su 1-5:30pm.

Post Office: 2307 Tuttle Creek Blvd. (☎913-776-8851). **Postal Code:** 66502.

GETTING AROUND. Businesses and official buildings are located along **Poyntz Ave.,** which degenerates into a mess of highway intersections to the east. Unfortunately, this area is the only way to reach the lodgings on **Tuttle Creek Blvd. (U.S. 24). Anderson Ave.** runs parallel to and a few blocks north of Poyntz Ave. and is home to the Kansas State University campus.

SIGHTS. The prairie lives on in the city at the **Sunset Zoo,** 2333 Oak St., which features native Kansas species such as prairie dogs, as well as an exotic red panda and snow leopard. (Follow Poyntz Ave. past Sunset Ave. and take a right on Oak St. ☎785-587-2737; www.sunsetzoo.com. Open daily 9:30am-5pm. $4, ages 3-12 $2.) At the far end of the Kansas State campus, the **Beach Museum of Art,** 701 Beach Ln., exhibits works, including contemporary sculpture and paintings. (From Sunset Ave., turn right onto Anderson Ave. ☎785-532-7718; www.k-state.edu/bma. Open Su 1-5pm, Tu-F 10am-5pm, Sa 1-5pm. Free.)

FOOD & ACCOMMODATIONS. Restaurants reside within Manhattan's shopping centers; others can be found through the downtown area. **Harry's Uptown,** 418 Poyntz Ave., serves satisfying entrees at steep prices. Unorthodox sandwiches such as the Wild Mushroom Philly are the best deals. (☎785-537-1300. Entrees $13-24. Open M-Th 11am-2pm and 5-9pm, F 11am-2pm and 5-10pm, Sa 5-10pm.) In addition to standard burger-and-fries fare, the **Village Inn,** 204 Tuttle Creek Blvd., has a special flair for crepes. Try the spectacular traditional fruit crepe ($6), or one of the newer varieties, such as the country sausage crepe. (☎785-537-3776. Open Su-Th 5am-10pm, F-Sa 5am-1pm.) At **The Sirloin Stockade,** 325 Poyntz Ave., road-trippers can fulfill meat cravings without spending too much. All-you-can-eat options run pretty much all day, with different deals in effect at various times, often for as little as $6. (☎785-776-0516. Open M-Th 11am-9pm, F 11am-10pm, Sa 8am-10pm, Su 8am-9pm.)

Those in need of a good night's sleep might consider **The Cottage at Cedar Meadows Bed and Breakfast,** 15955 Cedar Meadows Rd., in Wamego, an elegant stay easily reached by backtracking east on U.S. 24. (☎785-456-8654; www.thecottagebnb.com. Rooms $79-139.) Chain hotels are abundant in Manhattan, and good bargains include the **Motel 6** at Tuttle Creek Blvd., which has an outdoor pool. (☎785-537-1022. Singles Su-Th $40, F-Sa $50; doubles $50/$56.)

LEAVING MANHATTAN
To leave Manhattan, simply follow **Tuttle Creek Blvd.** north. Outside of the city, it drops the name and becomes **U.S. 24** again.

THE ROAD TO MARYSVILLE
This winding 40 mi. jaunt north begins on **Tuttle Creek Blvd. (U.S. 24 West);** switch to **U.S. 77 North** after driving by Tuttle Creek Lake. The early portion of the drive is less thrilling than the ride between Topeka and Manhattan, but there is a scenic alternative to the last leg. Just past the towns of Waterville and Blue Rapids, **Tumbleweed Rd.** appears, leading west. This dirt road is marked only by a small sign pointing the way to **Alcove Spring,** so it is easy to miss; the **Alcove Spring Historic Marker** 100 yd. south of the turn is easier to spot than the road itself,. Tumbleweed Rd. arcs through the wooded hills of the countryside, where wild turkeys are more plentiful than cars.

Signs at the few intersections point the way to Alcove Spring and Marysville. The 15 mi. ride over the dusty, steep road can take some time, but ends up on **Linden St.** A right here leads back to **U.S. 77,** just a few minutes from Marysville.

ALCOVE SPRING
Tumbleweed Rd. ends on E. River Rd. after a short distance. Follow the signs for about 5 mi. to the Alcove Spring Historic Site.

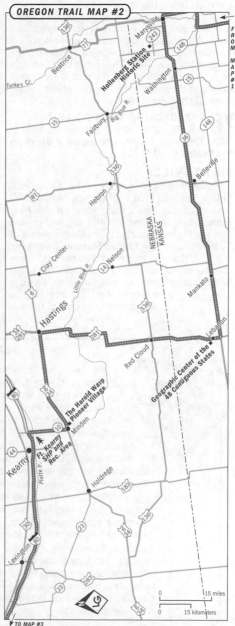

OREGON TRAIL MAP #2

TO MAP #3

Carvings left in the stone by the emigrants still exist at Alcove Spring, which was once a popular camping site for wagon trains on the Oregon Trail. Beyond this historic significance, the area is quiet and serene—a nice place to sit and watch the dragonflies for a while. The spring itself can only be reached on a foot, but the trail is well-maintained and only takes a few minutes to walk. (Open daily dawn-dusk. Free.)

APPROACHING MARYSVILLE

U.S. 77 passes directly through the heart of Marysville; follow it to the intersection of **Broadway** and **Central St. (U.S. 36).**

MARYSVILLE

Pretty and quiet, Marysville is the last outpost before the long haul to Hastings, Nebraska. It was once the first major stop on the **Pony Express,** and the town proudly remembers the daring of these romantic riders. In the center of Marysville, the **Pony Express Museum,** 106 8th St., contains the barn that served as the first home station where courier-riders slept. The other half of the museum details the short, thrilling history of the Pony Express. On display are a copy of the rid-

ers' noble oath never to drink, swear, or fight, and a bulletin seeking young men "willing to risk death daily." (☎ 785-562-3825. Open M-Sa 10am-5pm, Su noon-4pm. $2, ages 4-12 $0.50) The **Marysville Chamber of Commerce,** 101 N. 10th St. (☎ 785-562-3101), has more info for visitors.

Penny's Diner, 1127 Pony Express Hwy., is an all-around great place located in a shiny metallic box of a building that could be straight from 50s sci-fi. Check out the custom omelettes, which start at $5. (☎ 785-562-1234. Breakfast under $7. Lunch and dinner under $8. Open 24hr.) The **Wagon Wheel Cafe,** 703 Broadway St., is right in the heart of Marysville's brick-paved downtown. The menus are mock newspapers, so patrons can read about the history and attractions of Marysville and the surrounding region while they wait to order. In true Kansas style, the Wagon Wheel offers a full BBQ dinner ($9) with brisket, hashbrowns, beans, and cole slaw. (☎ 785-562-3784. Appetizers from $2.75. Sandwiches from $2. Entrees from $6.50.) To the east, Center St. is renamed **Pony Express Hwy.,** where most accommodations can be found. The **Oak Tree Inn,** 1127 Pony Express Hwy., has excellent, reasonably priced rooms. In addition to an exercise center and hot tub, it shares its lot

FROM THE ROAD

THE OZ EXPRESSWAY

I had been cruising uneventfully through the Kansas prairie for hours when my car began trying to commit suicide—pulling itself into the path of the 18-wheelers in the opposite lane, and veering tragically toward a roadside ditch. I hadn't any idea what was causing this worrisome phenomenon until finally I drove by a tree, a rare occurrence in these parts, and noticed that it was bending over in a way that trees, generally, do not. I realized it was wind whipping my car about, and when the road swung north, I caught a disturbing view of a black and apocalyptically boiling sky. With trepidation, I switched on my radio. The part of the world containing northern Kansas and southern Nebraska was coming to an end. Tornado sightings. Reports of 2 in. hail stones. Rising waters. I remembered hearing a few towns back about a Nebraskan town that had been utterly destroyed by a tornado just weeks before. A "Welcome to Nebraska!" sign flashed by me as I entered the ominously named town of Red Cloud. Unable to piece together where the storm was, I called my dad, frantically asking him to see what he could find out. He alerted me, to my relief, that the storm was mostly in the Lincoln area, to my northeast—"except", he added as an aside, "for a purple patch on the border, dead south of Hastings." Purple, I learned, is radar map code for Death. I looked at my map. *I* was dead south of Hastings. Uh oh. I tore north at a thoroughly illegal speed as lightning flickered more or less continuously around me, but fortune was at my side, and I reached Hastings without being thrown over the rainbow. I'd escaped, but in the weeks to come, I never turned my radio off again.

—Tom Laakso

with Penny's Diner, which offers breakfast discounts to Oak Tree guests. (☎785-562-1234. Singles $64; doubles $65.) Nearby, the **Best Western Surf Motel,** 2105 Center St., offers comfortable rooms and amenities including an exercise room, whirlpool, and game room. (☎785-562-2354. Singles $52; doubles $57; triples $61; quads $66.)

LEAVING MARYSVILLE
Sticking with the Oregon Trail, take **Central St.** west out of Marysville; it becomes **U.S. 36 West.**

THE ROAD TO HASTINGS
U.S. 36 is a dead-straight, dead-flat burn through 100 mi. of northern Kansas farmland. At the town of **Lebanon,** the route turns north onto **U.S. 281.** From there, it is a 40 mi. journey across the Kansas-Nebraska border to the city of **Red Cloud** (birthplace of writer Willa Cather), then another 40 mi. to **Hastings.** The road is long, but cloud-chasing passes the time away.

HOLLENBERG STATION HISTORIC SITE
2889 23rd Rd.
Follow U.S. 36 12 mi. west of Marysville. Head north on Rte. 148 for about 5 mi. In Hanover, Rte. 243 will be on the right, and leads to the station's driveway.

Hollenberg Station was a store and rest stop for Oregon Trail travelers that also served as a Pony Express relay station. The **Visitors Center** has a gallery on pioneer life and opens onto a short trail lined with little info stations. The path sometimes has demos on the art of trail cooking—a fine skill for roadtrippers past and present. Still solid after all these years, the station at the end of the trail is open for exploration, including the stuffy attic where Pony Express riders could rest on their dash westward. (☎785-337-2635. Open Su 1-5pm, W-Sa 10am-5pm. $3, students and seniors $2.)

THE GEOGRAPHIC CENTER OF THE US
About 1 mi. after turning onto U.S. 281 North, take a 1 mi. detour up Rte. 191.

In the middle of the Kansas prairie, a stone monument marks the geographic center of the United States. Established in 1898 by government surveyors, the site became the "historical" center of the contiguous states after Alaska and Hawaii joined the Union in 1959.

APPROACHING HASTINGS
Getting into the city of Hastings is easy. **U.S. 281** bends to the east after passing the Hastings city limits, then immediately takes a sharp turn to the left. At this point it changes its name to **Burlington Ave.;** this road runs through the center of Hastings.

HASTINGS
To those who don't look too hard, Hastings is a typical residential city, but beneath its suburban skin, Hastings is a funky place fit for any roadtripper. The birthplace of Kool-Aid, home to a great summer festival, and a haven of cheap hotels—it doesn't get much better than that.

VITAL STATS
Population: 24,000

Visitor Info: Visitors Center, 100 N. Shore Rd. (☎402-461-2370), off Burlington Ave. near the northern edge of the city. Open M-F 10am-5pm.

Internet Access: Hastings Public Library, 517 4th St. (☎402-461-2346; www.hastings.lib.ne.us). Open M-Th 9am-9pm, F 9am-6pm, Sa 9am-5pm.

Post Office: 900 E. South St. (☎402-463-3107). **Postal Code:** 68901.

GETTING AROUND. Burlington Ave. is Hastings' main drag and runs north-south through the city. Numbered streets run east-west very close together, so almost everything is found on some easy-to-locate corner.

SIGHTS. If it's evening, be sure to visit **Fisher Fountain,** at the corner of Denver and 12th St. Lighting concealed in the fountain creates amazing illuminated water displays every night between Mother's Day and Labor Day.

Otherwise, the **Hastings Museum of Natural and Cultural History,** at Burlington Ave. and 14th St., can provide an entire day of entertainment. The main floor is a hall of stuffed wildlife from all over the world, while the upper level extends the same treatment to birds. Best of all is the **Kool-Aid Museum,** which traces the evolution of the sugary, colorful beverage from its origins (1927), through its development into the Kool-Aid kid (a geeky mascot with knee socks), and its final maturation into the jolly Kool-Aid man we all know and love. There are also planetarium shows and documentaries. (☎402-461-4629 or 800-508-4629; www.hastingsmuseum.org. Open M 9am-5pm, Tu-Sa 9am-8pm, Su 10am-6pm. Museum and planetarium $6, ages 3-12 $4. Super-screen films $7/$5.50. Combined admission $11/$8.50.)

▟▛ FOOD & ACCOMMODATIONS. Big Dally's Deli, 801 2nd St., offers exactly 50 different sandwiches, not one of them over $6. (☎402-463-7666. Open daily 7:30am-3:30pm.) Tucked into a plaza at the intersection of Burlington Ave. and 4th St., **Mr. Goodcent's** breaks the chain of burger and steak shops; pastas and subs dominate. The chicken parmesan pasta ($4.30) is excellent. (☎402-463-3848. Appetizers $1-2. Entrees $3-5.30. Open Su-Th 10am-9pm, F-Sa 10am-10pm.)

Three cheap but great hotels are found along U.S. 281 just after entering Hastings. The **Rainbow Motel,** 1000 W. J St., has amazingly comfortable and well-furnished singles. (☎402-463-2989. Singles $40.) The **X-L Motel,** at the intersection of U.S. 281 and U.S. 6, has large, clean rooms, as well as a pool, sauna and laundry facilities. (☎800-341-8000. Singles $31-35; doubles $40.) Finally, the **Midlands Lodge,** 910 W. J St., has a heated pool, continental breakfast, and full-sized refrigerators. (☎402-463-2428. Singles $32; doubles $38.)

▟▛ LEAVING HASTINGS
At the southern border of Hastings, **U.S. 281 North** takes an abrupt right turn. A left turn at this intersection leads to **U.S. 6.** Follow this road west to leave Hastings and head toward Kearney. Immediately west of the Harold Warp Pioneer Village, the route to Kearney turns north along **Rte. 10** toward **I-80.** From there, it's about 15 mi. to Kearney.

◎ HAROLD WARP PIONEER VILLAGE
In Minden, 30 mi. down U.S. 6, at the intersection with Rte. 10.

Mr. Warp's collection of planes, cars, dolls, newspapers, medical instruments, and handicrafts almost certainly provides the king of all timelines. Twenty-six buildings, some of them hangar-sized, house relics from almost every aspect of life. The chronological organization is meant to provide a tour of "mankind's progress since 1830." An official **Pioneer Village Hotel** sits next door for visitors

who want to see everything. A single day's admission is good for extended visits—ask for details at the ticket office. (☎308-832-1181; www.pioneervillage.org. Open daily 8am-7pm. $9, ages 6-12 $4.)

◣ DETOUR: FT. KEARNEY 1020 V Rd.
10 mi. up Rte. 10, take Link 50a west to the fort.

Fort Kearney State Historical Park and Recreation Area is a reconstruction of Fort Kearney, which evolved from a wilderness protection post into a busy rest stop for 49ers and the Pony Express. The fort was abandoned after the Civil War, but the smithy, stockade, and powder magazine are open to visitors. The grounds take a few minutes to explore, but the recreation area to the east has plenty to offer: over 150 acres for hiking and exploring and **campsites** with electrical hookups. For a few weeks in early spring, sandhill cranes flock here on their way north. Pick up a pass to the park in the Visitors Center. (☎308-865-5305. Visitors Center open daily 9am-5pm. Pass $3.)

▟▛ APPROACHING KEARNEY
Get off **I-80** at Exit 272. This will lead to **2nd Ave.** in southern Kearney.

KEARNEY

Home to part of the University of Nebraska, Kearney is by no means a big city, but sometimes, especially around the shops and bars on Central Ave., it still feels like one. There are fewer people, perhaps, and the buildings are smaller, but the chic coffee shops, chatting shoppers, and sense of fun are very much the same. Beyond the confines of this downtown area, Kearney returns to the serenity of rural Nebraska, but within those few blocks a happening college town is made.

▐ GETTING AROUND

While Kearney has a logical layout, it still proves a little quirky. Avenues run north-south, while streets run east-west. **Central Ave.** is the axis of the city. To the east, avenues are numbered, while to the west they are lettered. All streets are numbered, starting with 1st St. in the south.

◎ SIGHTS

Kearney is home to one of the most spectacular, not to mention coolest, historical monuments on the Oregon Trail: **☒The Great Platte River Road Archway Monument,** 3060 1st St. The archway spans all four lanes of I-80 just east of Kearney, its towers spreading huge metallic wings. After driving under it, continue a few more miles to Exit 272 and backtrack east on 1st St. to the parking lot. Visitors don headphones and ride up to the "trail" contained by the arch. Displays chronicle the evolution of I-80 from Oregon Trail to Union Pacific Railroad to modern highway. (☎308-877-511-2724; www.archway.org. Open daily 7am-6pm. $10, seniors $8.50, ages 13-18 $6, ages 6-12 $3.)

(VITAL STATS)

Population: 27,000

Visitor Info: Kearney Visitors Bureau, 17 2nd Ave. (☎308-237-3178 or 800-652-9435; www.kearney-coc.org). Open M-F 8am-6m, Sa 9am-5pm, Su 1-4pm.

Internet Access: Kearney Public Library, 2020 1st Ave. (☎308-233-3282). Open M-Th 8:30am-9pm, F-Sa 8:30am-6pm.

Post Office: 2401 Ave. E (☎308-234-4814), at the corner of 23rd St. Open M-F 8am-5pm, Sa 9am-11:30am. **Postal Code:** 66847.

Back in town, the **Museum of Nebraska Art,** 2401 Central Ave., is dedicated to works and artists connected to Nebraska. Despite its limited scope, the museum contains a great variety of pieces, including fiber art and wall hangings. The first floor contains an entire gallery of paintings by the naturalist John James Audubon. (☎308-865-8559. Open Su 1-5pm, Tu-Sa 11am-5pm. Free.)

The **Trails and Rails Museum,** 710 11th St., is just a few blocks west. Though the museum does have a gallery on railways and a train in the yard, the real attraction is a set of historic buildings transported to this site to be viewed together. The buildings are only loosely related by era, but each is interesting in its own right. The structures include a 19th-century schoolhouse, a freighters' hotel, a log cabin, and the region's first frame house. (☎308-234-3041; www.bchs.us. Open Memorial Day-Labor Day M-Sa 10am-6pm, Su 1-5pm. $2.)

◼ FOOD

Despite its location near the city limits, it's almost impossible to miss **Pane Bello,** 5004 2nd Ave. The restaurant is painted in retro earth colors—burnt orange and olive green. Delicious sandwiches ($3.50-6.30) compete with flatbread pizzas ($8.50) for customer affection, but the Peasant Lunch—cheese, a baguette, and fruit for less than $3—is the real winner. (☎308-233-3677. Open M-F 6:30am-9pm, Sa 7am-9pm, Su 7:30am-9pm.) Watch for the sign for **The Cellar,** 3901 2nd Ave., which lurks beside a cluster of businesses. Though the food is not unusual, diners recline in a peaceful, candlelit atmosphere. (☎308-236-6541. Appetizers $2-7. Entrees $7-16. Open M-Sa 11am-11pm.) A trendy spot in the midst of Kearney's downtown

---

THE PLAINS ARE ALIVE...

NO WORK, ALL PLAY

For the past 15 years, the small Nebraskan town of Hastings has broken its usual suburban quiet and let music roll across the prairies. For three days in June, the annual Cottonwood Festival rocks with acts from jazz to Louisiana Cajun, folk, Celtic, and blues. This is no Woodstock, however—it's a jugglers-and-barbecue family party on a city-wide scale. The music may take over the summer nights, but during the day the Cottonwood resembles a huge county fair, packed with a giddy mixture of families, pets, cotton candy vendors, hot dog and funnel cake stands, and art demos, which even the most hardcore music fans seem to enjoy.

The young festival is ever-evolving. This year offered, for the first time, a "Songwriters Stage" showcased folk musicians, while another stage thundered beneath the lively, rhythmic feet of jigging Irish stepdancers. Next year promises some new innovations to keep the festival alive and well. (☎402-461-2368.; www.cottonwood-festival.org. Tickets $8.)

shopping district, **Black Sheep Coffee Roasters,** 2309 Central Ave., serves iced drinks and coffees and is nice place to relax; a titan-sized chessboard helps the process along. Don't miss the sinful Ghirardelli shake ($3), a chocolate/white chocolate/caramel rush. (☎308-338-0577. Open M-W 8am-5:30pm, Th 8am-8pm, F 8am-5:30pm and 7:30-11pm, Sa 10am-5:30pm and 7-11pm.) **Tex's Cafe,** 23 21st St., is homey and informal. Though the chicken fried steak dinner is tempting, check out the changing nightly specials. Dinners, complete with entree and sides, are $6.25. (☎308-234-3949. Open M-F 6am-4pm, Sa 6am-1pm.)

■ ACCOMMODATIONS

Hotels line **2nd Ave.,** which eclipses Central Ave. as the busiest thoroughfare. The **Midtown Western Inn,** 1401 2nd Ave., is one of the friendliest hotels around, with great rooms to boot. The A/C and pool help keep summer heat at bay, but the greatest amenity of all is the recliner in each room. (☎308-237-3153; www.midtownwesterninn.com. Singles $42; doubles $48.) **The AmericInn,** 215 Talmadge Rd., near the south end of 2nd Ave., offers large rooms, a beautiful indoor pool, continental breakfast, and a game room. (☎308-234-7800; www.americinn.com. Singles $65; doubles $75.) At the **Budget Motel South,** 411 2nd Ave., roadtrippers can find clean, functional rooms at low rates as well as an indoor pool and sauna. (☎308-237-5991. Singles $42.50; doubles $45.)

■ NIGHTLIFE

Kearney offers a small but nonetheless enjoyable selection of nightlife. The microbrewery at **Thunderhead Brewing,** 18 21st St., just off of Central Ave., won a gold medal at the World Beer Cup this year. Thunderhead also hosts free, local music from Thursday to Saturday. The classy building is a great place to have a drink, play pool, and catch a show. (☎308-237-1558. Restaurant open daily 10am-10pm. Bar open until 1am.) In true college-town style, **The Roman,** 2004 Central Ave., serves pizza until 12:30am and offers daily $1 drink specials. (☎308-233-5173. Open Tu-Sa 5pm-1am.)

■ LEAVING KEARNEY

Leaving Kearney is as easy as getting in. Just follow **2nd Ave.** south, then take the ramp onto **I-80.**

THE ROAD TO NORTH PLATTE

U.S. 30 traverses over 100 mi. between Kearney and North Platte, and none of them are very scenic. Endless freight trains chug along beside the highway, screening the view to the south for many miles. The monotony is periodically broken by small towns, but most of these consist of towering industrial complexes. Some drivers may enjoy the simple, rustic feel of these lands, but others may prefer to shoot straight to North Platte via I-80. A pair of larger towns, **Lexington** and **Cozad,** straddle U.S. 30; I-80 runs south of both, but has exits leading almost directly to their borders.

LEXINGTON

Lying about 30 mi. northwest of Kearney, little Lexington is still the largest town on the road. Within its borders, the odd and entertaining **Dawson County Historical Museum,** 805 Taft St., houses some highly irregular objects: the remains of Big Al (a former resident mammoth), the McCabe Aeroplane with its lens-shaped wings, and a set of 3-D jigsaw puzzles assembled by a native of the area. (☎308-324-5340; www.dawsoncountyne.net/dcmuseum. Open M-Sa 9am-5pm. Free.)

Enjoy seriously cheap lunch specials at the **A&D Cafe,** 604 N. Washington St. (Head north up Washington St. from U.S. 30; A&D is on the right, just a block up. ☎308-324-5990. Open daily 6am-3pm.) For something quick, check out **Kirk's Nebraskaland Restaurant,** off I-80 Exit 237, south of town. Kirk's serves a lot of highway traffic, so it has a little of everything. Entrees come with a salad and side for $8-10. (☎308-324-6641. Appetizers $4-7. Open M-Th and Su 6am-midnight, F-Sa 6am-1am.)

The few motels in Lexington are on **Plum Creek Pkwy.,** which links I-80 to town. Approaching from U.S. 30, Plum Creek Pkwy. is the large road to the south which crosses the bridge over the Platte River. Find fine rates and pleasant rooms at the **Gable View Inn,** 2701 Plum Creek Pkwy. (☎308-324-5595. Singles $36; doubles $41.) The nearby **Minute Man Motel,** 801 Plum Creek Pkwy., has good rates, similar rooms, and alliteration. (☎308-324-5544. Singles $38; doubles $42.)

OREGON TRAIL

THE 100TH MERIDIAN MUSEUM
206 8th St.

In Cozad. Head north from U.S. 30 past the 100th Meridian sign. After a few blocks you intersect 8th St.

Cozad founder John Cozad was struck by the grand sound of "100th Meridian." Though he vanished after a shooting, the museum honors the meridian that gave birth to the town. It contains local artifacts, such as photos of early residents. (☎308-784-1100. Open M-F 10am-5pm. Free.)

APPROACHING NORTH PLATTE
U.S. 30 passes through tiny **Gothenburg, Brady,** and **Maxwell** before North Platte. On the eastern edge of North Platte, U.S. 30 turns north suddenly, changing name to **Rodeo Rd.** To reach the town center, continue straight instead, trading U.S. 30 for **E. 4th St.,** the biggest of the town's east-west roads. For Buffalo Bill's ranch and Cody Park, follow U.S. 30.

NORTH PLATTE

Last stop in the Wild West and the home of Buffalo Bill Cody himself, North Platte glories in its cowboy heritage, naming everything it can in honor of those fondly remembered times: Cody Park, Rodeo Rd., and the Wild West Arena, for example. Though lacking in nightlife, North Platte parties in its own way—Western style, of course. The Nebraskaland Days festival is the greatest incarnation of this spirit, spanning 12 days in early June and stirring up an Old West fury of rodeos and parades, crowning the whole affair with the Miss Rodeo Pageant.

VITAL STATS

Population: 24,000

Visitor Info: North Platte Convention and Visitors Bureau, 219 S. Dewey St. (☎308-532-4729 or 800-955-4528; www.visitnorthplatte.com). Open M-F 8am-5pm.

Internet Access: North Platte Public Library, 121 W. 4th St. (☎308-535-8036). Open M and Th 9am-9pm, Tu-W and F-Sa 9am-6pm.

Post Office: 1302 Industrial Ave. (☎800-275-8777). Open M-F 7:30am-5:30pm, Sa 8:30am-noon. **Postal Code:** 69101.

GETTING AROUND

The major roads of North Platte form a cross. **4th St.** runs east-west and **Jeffers St.** runs north-south. Most accommodations are on 4th St.; most food is on Jeffers or **Dewey St.,** which runs parallel to Jeffers St. one block to the west. There is a cluster of sites to the northwest on **Buffalo Bill Ave.,** which joins 4th St. on the western edge of the city.

SIGHTS

North Platte manages to squeeze a huge park, the home of an American legend, and a colossal rail station into its modest borders. This impressive feat well deserves a day's pilgrimage. **Cody Park,** 1400 N. Jeffers St., at the corner of U.S. 30 and Jeffers, is a fusion of campground, zoo, and amusement park, home to everything from a merry-go-round to peacocks. The Wild West monument forms the park's entrance, commemorating Buffalo Bill's very first rodeo, the Old Glory Blowout. (☎800-955-4528. Open daily dawn-dusk. Primitive sites $5.) The highlight of the **Lincoln County Historical Museum and Village,** 2403 N. Buffalo Bill Ave., is an exhibit on the North Platte Canteen, an organization run by local women during WWII that provided food and supplies to soldiers passing through the area. (From U.S. 30, turn right on Buffalo Bill Ave. ☎308-534-5640. Open May-Labor Day M-Sa 9am-7pm, Su 1-5pm; Labor Day-Oct. M-Sa 9am-5pm, Su 1-5pm. $3.)

Farther up Buffalo Bill Ave. is **Scout's Rest,** once Buffalo Bill's home and now the **Buffalo Bill State Historical Park,** 2921 Scout's Rest Ranch Rd. William 'Buffalo Bill' Cody was a Pony Express Rider, an army scout, and a spectacular showman. It was here that he laid his head when his world-traveling Wild West Show was between tours. The ranch in back has a collection of advertisements for the shows and a small theater where surviving footage of the performances can be watched. (☎308-535-8035; www.nypc.state.ne.us/cody.html. Open Memorial Day-Labor Day daily 9am-5pm; Labor Day-Memorial Day M-F 10am-4pm. Nebraska State Parks Permit $3.)

Just off 4th St. sits the **North Platte Area Children's Museum,** 314 N. Jeffers Ave. Designed for children, each room of this museum reflects a dif-

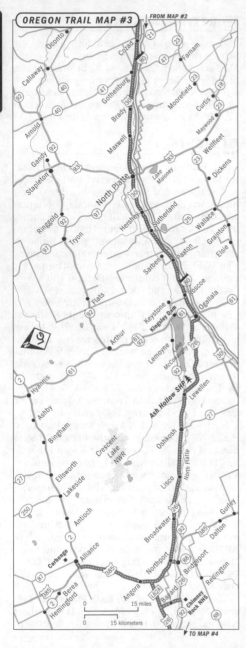

OREGON TRAIL MAP #3 FROM MAP #2

0 15 miles

0 15 kilometers

▼ TO MAP #4

ferent facet of educational entertainment. (☎308-532-3512. Open Su 1-5pm, W 10am-3pm, Th 10am-7pm, F 10am-3pm, Sa 10am-5pm. $2.50.)

Older children (and adults) may enjoy viewing **Bailey Yard,** a titanic Union Pacific train yard that through which pass over 10,000 cars every day. There is a **Visitors Center** hidden about 2 mi. west of town on Front St. This little street runs parallel to 4th St., one block north; take Willow St., which links 4th St. and Front St. directly, then proceed west on Front St. until the sign for the Visitors Center, which will be on the right side of the road. (☎308-532-4729. Open 24hr. Free.)

🍴 FOOD

In the heart of steak country, North Platte is unabashedly a meat-eater's city. Still, non-carnivores needn't worry; options exist at fair prices.

The Brick Wall, 507 N. Dewey St. (☎308-532-7545). In addition to the usual burgers and fries, The Brick Wall offers a respectable vegetarian menu of salads ($7), stir-fries ($7), and pasta ($7.50). Old high-school yearbooks are sealed into the tabletops. Open M-Th 8am-4pm, F-Sa 8am-4pm and 5-9pm.

The Cedar Bowl Touchdown Club, 1100 S. Jeffers St. (☎308-532-5720). A Huskers football museum as much as a restaurant: pictures, pennants and memorabilia adorn the walls. Step in to talk sports and grab an appetizer combo plate ($7). Open M-Sa 10:30am-1am, Su 11am-1am.

Little Mexico Restaurant, 104 N. Jeffers St. (☎308-534-3052). 11 styles of taco start at just $2. Eat in the private wooden stalls or the bustling open space in the building's center. Fajitas $7. Enchiladas $6. Appetizers $6-10. Open daily 11am-10pm.

Main Street Cafe, 517 N. Dewey St. (☎308-534-0922). Though there is a small sandwich menu, the real fun comes with joining the cafeteria-style line to see what's dished out from behind the counter—kind of like elementary school, but with much better food. Entrees usually $5-6. Open M-F 7am-2:30pm.

🏠 ACCOMMODATIONS

North Platte is graced with a cluster of very well priced motels. Cody Park (p. 561) in the north part of town also offers primitive campsites ($5).

Rambler Motel, 1420 Rodeo Rd. (☎308-532-9290), on the edge of town, near Scout's Rest.

The Rambler offers amazingly low rates for pleasant, quiet rooms, each with fridge and microwave. Outdoor pool. Singles $28; doubles $35.

Blue Spruce Motel, 821 S. Dewey St. (☎308-534-2600), downtown. Rooms unusually large and well-furnished for the price. Singles $36; doubles $49.

Traveler's Inn, 602 E. 4th St. (☎308-534-4020; www.bestvalueinn.com). A slightly upscale option with discounts for AAA members, seniors and military personnel. Singles $40; doubles $55.

Husker Inn, 721 E. 4th St. (☎308-534-6960). Well-priced facilities are simple and clean. Singles $33; doubles $35.

LEAVING NORTH PLATTE
Travelers have the option of taking **U.S. 30** or **I-80.** Following **Jeffers St.** south leads directly to I-80. To the north, Jeffers St. intersects **Rodeo Rd.,** which becomes **U.S. 30** outside the city limits.

THE ROAD TO OGALLALA
The 50 mi. stretch from North Platte to Ogallala is less than an hour's drive, even on U.S. 30. The South Platte River follows the road between the two cities, providing a peaceful and scenic route. Truly impressive drives, however, await on the other side of Ogallala.

Between North Platte and Ogallala, U.S. 30 passes from into the Mountain Time Zone, where it is 1hr. earlier.

OLE'S BIG GAME STEAKHOUSE
On Oak St. off U.S. 30 in Paxton.

Beef's on the menu at ◪**Ole's,** but every other kind of animal is up on the wall. Ole's collection of hunting trophies includes the heads of a giraffe and an African elephant; however, even these are eclipsed by the full body of a gigantic polar bear that Ole took down himself. The food is just as impressive: burger-and-steak beefhouses are in endless supply in the Midwest, but Ole's still manages to stand out. The hamburgers (cow or buffalo; from $5) are thick and delicious, and the steaks (from $10) are no different. Skip a meal in North Platte if you have to; showing up at Ole's hungry is worth your while. (☎308-239-4500. Open daily 10am-midnight.)

APPROACHING OGALLALA
U.S. 30 simply becomes **1st St.,** making the approach to Ogallala as easy as possible.

OGALLALA
The name is quite melodic after the first few stumbling tries—Ogallala, the city of Lake McConaughy. Like many of its neighbors, Ogallala basks in its rambunctious Old West heritage, but for visitors, Ogallala's primary attraction is the peaceful serenity of the lake; the waters north of town are lined with beaches, fishing holes, campsites, and the first of western Nebraska's stunning hills.

《VITAL STATS》

Population: 5000

Visitor Info: Ogallala Visitors Center, 204 E. A St. (☎308-284-4066). Open M-F 8am-5pm.

Internet Access: Goodall City Library, 203 W. A St. (☎308-284-4354). Open M-Th 9am-8pm, F-Sa 9am-5pm.

Post Office: 301 N. Spruce St. (☎800-275-8777). Open M-F 8am-4:30pm, Sa 9am-11am. **Postal Code:** 69153.

⬛ GETTING AROUND. Ogallala's street layout can be a bit confusing. **1st St. (U.S. 30)** forms the central artery, running east-west through the city. Parallel streets increase sequentially as one travels north. **Spruce St.,** cutting north-south, is the other key trafficway. Streets parallel to Spruce St. are lettered, but they come in pairs; one block east of Spruce is **East A St.,** one block west is **West A St.** As a result, East E St. and West E St. are nowhere near each other—in fact, they're 10 blocks apart.

◪ SIGHTS. The single largest attraction is **Lake McConaughy,** "Big Mac." Rte. 61 runs northeast from town to the eastern end of the lake. Visitors are required to have a Nebraska State Parks sticker ($3) on their cars, available at the **Visitors Center,** 1475 Rte. 61, a quarter-mile before reaching the lake. Beyond the Visitors Center, the road leads over the magnificent Kingsley Dam, a colossal feat of engineering. From there, 5 mi. of shoreline present myriad possibilities: boating, fishing, swimming, camping, or just relaxing on the beach. There is even an eagle observation post, though the birds are only present during winter months. (☎308-284-8800. For more info on eagle viewing, call ☎308-284-2332. Primitive sites $5, with camping pad $10. Full hookup $18.)

There are also a few sights in the city itself, clustered conveniently in the **Front Street Arcade** off 1st St. This strip of buildings is a re-created Old West main street, complete with hitching-post parking spots. The **Petrified Wood Gallery,** 519 E. 1st St., contains a large collection of this wood-turned-stone, much of it brightly colored and spectacularly patterned. (☎308-284-4488 or 800-658-4390; www.petrifiedwoodgallery.com. Open M-Sa 10am-7pm.) Next door, the **Crystal Palace Revue** always seems to find itself at the center of a (staged) shootout, after which lovely young ladies put on old-style song-and-dance show that tells the story of Ogallala and surrounding lands. (☎308-284-6000. Shows daily Memorial Day to mid-August from 7:15pm. $4.25, ages 5-12 $2.75.)

⬛ FOOD. Like the city itself, dining establishments in Ogallala are steeped in the character of the Old West. Part of the Crystal Palace scene, the **Front Street Steakhouse,** 519 E. 1st St., is easily the most interesting place to eat in downtown Ogallala. "Local favorites" include the Ogallala Steak Sandwich and the Crystal Palace Steak Sandwich for $6.50. (☎308-284-6000. Appetizers $3-7. Sandwiches $5-7. Entrees $8-12. Open daily 11am-9pm.) Lively **Hoke's Cafe,** 302 E. 1st St., is a small-town diner with far more character than most big-time equivalents. The decor is that of automobile worship—pictures and models are everywhere. (☎308-284-4654. Steaks $15. Country-style dinners $9. Hot sandwiches $7-8. Open Su 6am-1pm, Tu-Sa 6am-1pm and 5-8pm.) **Spruce Street Sandwich Shop,** 12 N. Spruce St., offers 32 different sandwiches ($4.50-7.50), as well as a more adventurous guacamole burger. (☎308-284-4879. Open Tu-F 8am-7pm, Sa 8am-4pm.)

⬛ ACCOMMODATIONS. Those who prefer not to camp at the lake still have in-town options, including the usual clump of chain motels off I-80, at the south end of Spruce St. **The Plaza Inn,** 311 E. 1st St., features individually themed rooms, such as the Hollywood room and the Whirlpool room. All have microwaves and refrigerators. (☎308-284-8416. Singles $35; $5 per additional person. Whirlpool room $60.) Just across the South Platte River on Spruce St. is the **Grey Goose Lodge,** 201 Chuckwagon Rd., a fine hotel with very comfortable rooms and nice facilities, including an indoor pool. (☎308-284-3623 or 800-573-7148. Singles $69; doubles $74; triples $79; quads $84.)

◤ LEAVING OGALLALA
Take **East A St.** north, following signs toward Lake McConaughy until it merges into **Spruce St.** Head north for several miles to the junction with Rte. 61 and U.S. 26, then turn left and go west on **U.S. 26.**

THE ROAD TO SCOTTSBLUFF

Beyond Ogallala, U.S. 26 abandons the prairies of the Midwest, beginning the incredibly scenic 120 mi. route to Scottsbluff. The first half of the road weaves through the hills around Lake McConaughy; the second half runs beneath the mighty rock formations of western Nebraska.

✴ WINDLASS HILL & ASH HOLLOW
On U.S. 26. Windlass Hill is 12 mi. northwest of Ogallala; Ash Hollow and the Visitors Center are 2½ mi. farther on U.S. 26.

Windlass Hill is named for the legend that wagons had to be lowered down its slope with a winch, though no evidence of such a device survives. The hill is quite steep, though, and visitors should be prepared for a climb. The view from the top over the lonely ravines of western Nebraska is lovely. Down the road at Ash Hollow is a small Visitors Center and the Ash Hollow Cave. Most Oregon Trail sites are only about 150 years old; this cave has been inhabited for six millennia. Artifacts from the cave are also on display, dating from the prehistoric era all the way to the mid-19th century, when trappers and pioneers used the cave for shelter. (☎308-778-5651. Open Su and Tu-Sa 10am-4pm. Nebraska State Parks Permit $3.)

◤ APPROACHING BRIDGEPORT
About 50 mi. northwest of Ash Hollow, **U.S. 26** turns south and crosses the North Platte River into Bridgeport.

BRIDGEPORT

There isn't much to Bridgeport beyond a main street. The town's primary attraction are **Courthouse Rock** and **Jail Rock,** the first of the bizarre stone formations that mark the end of the first leg of the Oregon Trail. Less celebrated and less spectacular than Chimney Rock or Scotts Bluff, both are best viewed from Main St.—continue south on Main St. for 4 mi. A quick historical diversion is available at the **Pioneer Trails Museum,** on Main St. at the north end of town. (☎308-262-0108. Open M-Sa 9am-6pm, Su 1-6pm. Free.)

Luckily, a good, cheap hotel and restaurant are right on Main St.. **Aunt Bee's Family Restaurant,** 1024 Main St., is stylish and inexpensive; a novelty clock collection fills the dining room. (☎308-262-0234. Sandwiches $2-4.50. Open M-Tu 6am-4pm, W-F 6am-8pm, Sa 6am-2pm, Su 11am-1:30pm.) **The Bridgeport Inn,** 517 Main St., is a prince among budget motels. Huge and well-furnished, the rooms look like they're from a considerably higher price bracket. (☎308-262-0290. Singles $42.50; doubles $49.50.) Tourist info can be found at the **Bridgeport Chamber of Commerce,** 428 Main St. (☎308-262-1825. Open M-F 6am-9pm, Sa 8am-3pm.)

LEAVING BRIDGEPORT
Returning up Main St. onto **U.S. 26** and crossing the North Platte River leads to the junction with **U.S. 385;** this road leads to Alliance. (To continue along the Oregon Trail, Stay on U.S. 26; from here it's a straight shot to Gering and Scottsbluff.)

ALLIANCE AND CARHENGE
30 mi. north of Bridgeport. Take U.S. 385 to 3rd St., the main street of Alliance. Take 3rd St. east 3 mi. and turn north on Rte. 87. Carhenge is 3 mi. north.

The real reason for visiting Alliance is ◪**Carhenge,** a monument exactly alike England's Stonehenge—except constructed entirely out of cars. Maybe profound, maybe a junkyard, definitely worth seeing. Surrounding the automobile monoliths is an outdoor gallery of stacked cars, automobile towers, a dinosaur car, and a vehicle-turned–salmon; it really must be seen to be believed.

The Brownstone, 1203 W. 3rd St., has good food and a menu that mixes the eccentric with the everyday, offering burgers, sandwiches, ostrich steaks ($8), and, for the truly ravenous, a bacon-wrapped filet mignon. (☎308-762-5259. Appetizers $3-5. Entrees $6-11. Open M-Th 6am-9pm, F-Sa 6am-10pm.) **Kim & Dale's Restaurant,** 123 E. 3rd St., is a family restaurant that serves up liver ($5), veal ($5.50), and rainbow trout ($10), among other options. (☎308-762-7252. Open M-Sa 6am-9pm, Su 6am-8pm.) The **West Way Motel,** 1207 W. 3rd St., maintains comfortable rooms and gives vouchers for a free breakfast at the nearby Brownstone. (☎308-762-4040. Singles $34; doubles $39.) The slightly more worn **Rainbow Motel,** 614 W. 3rd St., has refrigerators and microwaves as well as guest laundry facilities. (☎308-762-4980. Singles from $25; doubles from $32.) For more info, visit the **Alliance Chamber of Commerce,** 124 W. 3rd St. (☎308-762-1520. Open daily 8:30am-5pm.)

LEAVING ALLIANCE
Head west on **3rd St.** to the junction with **Rte. 385** and return south. There's a shortcut to Chimney Rock: rather than return to Bridgeport and U.S. 26, head west on **Link 62A,** just south of Angora. Then go south on **U.S. 26** to Bayard and Chimney Rock.

BAYARD. U.S. 26 passes through Bayard, where not much is worth a stop besides **Pizza Point,** 106 E. 2nd St., a hometown pizza joint offering personal pizzas ($3) for the solo road-tripper or large pizzas ($9.70) for families. Also worth noting are the classic and delightfully greasy $1 corndogs. (☎308-586-2255. Open M-Sa 11am-9pm, Su 4-8pm.) Bayard also serves as the jumping-off point for the **Oregon Trail Wagon Train,** 2 mi. south of Bayard and 1 mi. east on Oregon Trail Rd. This service gives travelers with time and money a chance to experience life on the trail. Covered wagon treks wind through the Chimney Rock area, where "pioneers" cook over campfires. The four-day trek includes horseback riding, riflery, a Pony Express delivery, and an Indian raid. For something less time-consuming, chuckwagon cookouts with a short wagon tour are also available. (☎308-586-1850; www.oregontrailwagontrain.com. 24hr. trek $200, children $175; 4-day trek $575/$475; cookouts $18.95/$9.50. All activities by reservation only; call ahead for dates.)

CHIMNEY ROCK NATIONAL HISTORIC SITE
Head south on U.S. 26 from Bayard, then turn west on Rte. 92. Follow the signs over dirt roads to the Visitors Center.

Western Nebraska was once a vast, high-elevation plain of clay and volcanic ash. As wind and water wore the surface down to present-day levels, caps of harder stone resisted the erosion, protecting the ash underneath. Thus Chimney Rock was formed, a delicate spire of vulcan material topped with stone. Visible for miles around, the Chimney was one of the best-known landmarks along the Oregon Trail, mentioned in surviving diaries more than any other landmark. Today, due to prairie conservation efforts and the threat of rattlesnakes, visitors are asked to stay at the Visitors Center rather than approach the rock. A closer look is achieved by driving farther down the dirt road, which terminates close to the rock near a cemetery dedicated to the pioneers. (☎308-586-

2581; www.nps.gov/chro. Visitors Center open Memorial Day-Labor Day daily 9am-5pm; Labor Day-Memorial Day Su and Tu-Sa 9am-5pm. $3.)

APPROACHING SCOTTSBLUFF
From Chimney Rock, it's only 20 mi. west along **U.S. 26** to Scottsbluff. To go straight to the city, stay on **U.S. 26,** which runs through northwest Scottsbluff. It connects directly to **20th St.** in the eastern part of the city and **Ave. I** in the north.

The fastest way to the Scotts Bluff monument, however, is via **Rte. 92** through Gering. Rte. 92 diverges from U.S. 26 a few miles west of Scottsbluff near Melbeta. It then goes through Gering, where it intersects **10th St.,** and continues west to the monument.

SCOTTSBLUFF

Scottsbluff, Gering, and the intermediary region of Terrytown all lie in the shadow of Scotts Bluff, the towering rock formation that gives the largest of the cities its name. The cities themselves support a downtown and some restaurants worth exploring, but the bluffs dominate the skyline; man-made attractions just can't compete with nature in this case. Unlike Chimney Rock, Scotts Bluff can be scaled and explored.

VITAL STATS

Population: 15,000

Visitor Info: Scotsbluff/Gering United Chamber of Commerce, 1517 Broadway (☎308-632-2133; ww.scottsbluffgering.net). Open M-F 8am-5pm.

Internet Access: Scottsbluff Public Library, 1809 3rd Ave. (☎308-630-6250). Open M-Th 9am-8pm, F-Sa 9am-6pm, Su 2-5pm.

Post Office: 112 W. 20th St. (☎800-275-8777). Open M-F 8:30am-4:30pm, Sa 9:15am-11am. **Postal Code:** 69361.

GETTING AROUND

Scottsbluff is the big city of western Nebraska but shares many of its services and much of its bustle with the smaller city of Gering to the south. The two also share the same main street, which changes its name at the border. In Gering it's called **10th St.;** in Scottsbluff, **Broadway.** This road is the largest and most direct link between the two. Unless noted, all listings are in Scottsbluff.

The north-south roads in Scottsbluff are all avenues. To the west of Broadway they are lettered; to the east, numbered. The east-west roads are streets, and are all numbered. **1st St.** is near the Gering border, and street numbers increase heading north. Don't confuse these with 10th St. in Gering, which runs north-south and becomes Broadway at the Scottsbluff city limits.

SIGHTS

The city's name sums up its attractions well; **Scotts Bluff National Monument** is one of the largest, and the most accessible, of the rock formations along this part of the trail. At the base of the bluff, the **Visitors Center** presents Oregon Trail history. The bluff can be scaled by car, shuttle, or the 1½ mi. **Saddle Rock Trail,** which is steep and winding but worth the effort, cutting up the cliff face and straight through the rock to the other side of the bluff. For pioneers, Pony Express riders, and roadtrippers, this marks the first third of the trail. (3 mi. west of Gering on Rte. 92. ☎308-436-4340. Open daily 8am-7pm. $5 per car. Trail maps $0.50.)

For more local history, head to the **North Platte Valley Museum,** at 11th and J St. in Gering. The museum has relics from and dioramas of 19th-century pioneer life as well as Native American culture. Also check out the wall diagramming the evolution of the Nebraska license plate. (Head south on 10th St. in Gering; after the sign, turn right onto Overland Trails Rd. for parking. ☎308-436-5411; www.npvm.com. Open M-F 9am-4pm, Sa-Su 1-4pm. $3, ages 5-12 $1. AAA discount.)

The **Riverside Zoo,** 1600 S. Beltline, is home to a white tiger and two African lions, as well as a moose and a red panda. (☎308-630-6236. Open Mar.-Nov. daily 9:30am-4:30pm; Dec.-Feb. Sa-Su 10am-4pm. $2.50, seniors $2, ages 5-12 $1.)

Located east of town at Lake Minatare is **Nebraska's only lighthouse.** Yup, lighthouse. Head east for 11 mi. on U.S. 26, then north for another 9 mi. on Stone Gate Rd. Once at the lake, a short jaunt down The Point Rd. leads to the structure, which, needless to say, seems a little lost.

ENTERTAINMENT

Although Scottsbluff doesn't have the bumpin' nightlife of a larger city, good fun is out there. **Theatre West Summer Repertory,** 1601 E. 27th St. at the back of the Nebraska Community College Campus, puts on a varied series of shows each summer. (☎308-632-2226. Box office open M-F 9am-4pm, Sa 1-5pm.) Fun, offbeat, and for almost everyone, **Pelini's Jazz and Comedy Club,** 15 E. 16th St., has musical nights, improv shows, stand-up comedy, and even puppetry acts. This "family nightclub" has a non-alcoholic bar in addition to the usual drinks. (☎308-632-6800. Hours vary depending on shows; call ahead.)

FOOD

Scotty's, 618 E. 27th St. (☎308-635-3314). The epitome of American dining. Burgers ($0.90), hot dogs ($0.95), and glorious french fries ($0.90). Bacon double cheeseburger $2.40. Open June-Aug. Su-Th 10am-10:30pm, F-Sa 10am-11:30pm; Sept.-May Su-Th 10am-10pm, F-Sa 10am-11pm.

Wonderful House Restaurant, 829 Ferdinand Plaza (☎308-632-1668). Conventional Chinese fare. Lunch special (11am-3pm) $5.25-5.50 with entree, egg roll, crab rangoon, rice, and fortune cookie. Appetizers $4-7.50. Entrees $7-19. Open M-Th 11am-9:30pm, F-Sa 11am-10pm, Su 11am-9pm.

Bush's Gaslight Restaurant & Lounge, 3315 N. 10th St. (☎308-632-7315), in Gering. Pleasant for relaxing, with a dining room fireplace and comfortable lounge. Chicken, seafood, and steak entrees at moderate to expensive prices. Appetizers $3-10. Entrees $9-40. Restaurant open Su-Th 4:30-9pm, F-Sa 4:30-11:30pm. Lounge open daily 4pm-12:30am.

Prime Cut, 305 W. 27th St. (☎308-632-5353). Impersonal production-line ordering is redeemed by full steak dinners for less than $8. Chicken, sausage, and salad meals available. Old tools and pho-

tographs add antiquity. Open Su-Th 11am-9pm, F-Sa 11am-10pm.

ACCOMMODATIONS

Scottsbluff has a decent selection of hotels and motels, though they're rather scattered. Chain accommodations can be found along **E. 20th St.** and **Ave. I,** near U.S. 26.

Sands Motel, 814 W. 27th St. (☎308-632-6191). Functional rooms and some of the best rates in town. Singles from $32; doubles from $34.

Lamplighter American Inn, 606 E. 27th St. (☎308-632-7108). Quite nice for its low price; spacious rooms, indoor hallways, and an indoor pool. Singles $40; doubles $43.

Microtel Inn, 1130 M St. (☎308-436-1951), in Gering. Unbeatable location, just minutes from the Scotts Bluff monument. Pool and fitness center. Single-bed suites (with kitchenette) $65; 2-bed rooms $60.

Capri Motel, 2424 Ave. I (☎308-635-2057). Travelers approaching Scottsbluff from U.S. 26 will find this spot easily, just down Ave. I. Pleasant and clean rooms at good rates. Singles $35; doubles $35.

Riverside Campground, 1600 S. Beltline (☎308-630-6236), right next to the zoo. Showers and bathrooms. Gates closed 11pm-5am. Primitive sites $5, with water $10. Full hookup $15.

LEAVING SCOTTSBLUFF
Take **Broadway** north to its end, and turn right (west) on **27th St.** Follow 27th until it merges with **U.S. 26,** heading toward Wyoming.

THE ROAD TO GUERNSEY

The journey into Wyoming isn't much more than 60 mi., but the road is lined with wayside stops and small towns: Mitchell, Torrington, Lingle, and Ft. Laramie. Better yet, the landscape showcases the American west in all its glory, with wild untamed hills and meadows, rough grass, and horses 'till Guernsey.

TORRINGTON

Small enough that many drivers might blast on through, Torrington has some roadtripper-friendly spots worth stopping for. The **Homesteader's Museum,** 495 Main St. (U.S. 85), is a good place to stretch your legs and learn some history. The museum displays quite a collection of cowboy paraphernalia, focusing on the Homestead period, after the era of overland emigration. (☎307-532-5612. Open Memorial Day-Labor Day, M-W 9:30am-4pm, Th-F 9:30am-7pm, Sa noon-6pm, Su noon-4pm; Labor Day-Memorial Day M-F 9:30am-4pm. Free.)

Vi's Diner, 1500 E. Valley Rd. (U.S. 26), offers large portions of delightfully fast, greasy, classic roadtrip fare. The all-day breakfast menu is fairly cheap (complete breakfast $5.50) and big enough to keep your pedal-foot going strong all day. (☎307-532-2740. Open M-F 6am-10pm, Sa-Su 24hr.) An unbeatable spend the night before the long haul to Guernsey or Cheyenne is the ◪**Oregon Trail Motel,** 710 E. Valley Rd. (U.S. 26). One of the best deals on the trail, the motel has clean, comfortable, air-conditioned rooms at amazing rates. (☎307-532-2101. Rooms from $20.)

 West of Torrington along U.S. 26 is the town of Lingle. Watch out here; U.S. 26 takes a 90-degree turn with little fanfare.

WESTERN HISTORY CENTER 2308 U.S. 26
Exactly 5 mi. outside Lingle. Watch for the sign.
A sort of archaeological display gallery, the Western History Center showcases mammoth remains, 10,000-year-old arrowheads, and fossils dating as far back as the Cretaceous Period. Rotating on-loan exhibits display everything from international doll collections to ornamental swords, providing an exciting alternative to numerous Oregon Trail museums. (☎307-837-3052. Open M-Sa 10am-4pm, Su 1-4pm. $1.50.)

FORT LARAMIE NATIONAL HISTORIC SITE 965 Gray Rocks Rd.
Follow the signs from the town of Ft. Laramie (pop. 256: according to the sign, "250 good people and 6 sore heads"). The fort is a few miles south of town along Gray Rocks Rd. (Rte. 160).
Fort Laramie was a critical outpost along the overland trails, serving as a central base for the US Army during its violent clashes with tribes led by Red Cloud, Crazy Horse, and Sitting Bull. The Visitors Center provides an informative video on Ft. Laramie's role in these events and is also the starting point for self-guided tours. Audio headsets and guided tours are also available. Sights include the fully restored cavalry

barracks, the captain's quarters, and "old Bedlam"—the bachelor's dormitory. In all, one of the most extensive historical sites along the trail. The **Soldier's Bar** sells (soft) drinks for just $1, served in chilled bottles by a barkeep in 19th-century attire. (☎307-837-2221; www.nps.gov/fola. Grounds open daily dawn-dusk. Visitors Center open daily 8am-7pm. $3.)

APPROACHING GUERNSEY
11 mi. west of Ft. Laramie, **U.S. 26** becomes **Whalen St.,** the center of Guernsey.

GUERNSEY

Guernsey divides two different landscapes; just beyond the town, the Rocky Mountains rise suddenly into view. Nineteenth-century travelers often considered Guernsey's Register Cliff the real marker of the Rockies' borders. Between the names carved into the cliffs long ago and the beauty of Guernsey State Park, the town maintains the adventurous feel of something new.

VITAL STATS

Population: 1150

Visitor Info: Guernsey Visitor Center, 90 S. Wyoming Rd. (☎307-836-2715). Open M-Sa 9am-7pm, Su noon-4pm.

Internet Access: North Platte County Public Library, Guernsey Branch, 108 S. Wyoming Rd. (☎307-836-2816). Open M and W noon-7pm, Tu and Th noon-5pm, F noon-4pm, Sa 9am-11am.

Post Office: 401 S. Wyoming Rd. (☎307-836-2804). Open M-F 8:30am-5pm. **Postal Code:** 82214.

GETTING AROUND. U.S. 26 runs through the center of Guernsey as **Whalen St.** Most sights and establishments line the main drag of **Wyoming Ave.** south of the intersection with Whalen St.

SIGHTS. At **Oregon Trail Ruts State Historic Site,** off Wyoming Ave. about 1 mi. down rough dirt roads, a short climb through the wooded hills reveals deep scars left in the rock by the thousands of wagons that traversed the Oregon and Mormon Trails. Two miles farther down Wyoming Ave. is **Register Cliff,** a soft, sheer face where pioneers sometimes carved their names. (☎307-836-2334. Open daily dawn-dusk. Free.)

Just west of town on U.S. 26, Rte. 317 heads north. A few miles up this road is **Guernsey State Park,** with 8500 acres of cliffs, forested hills, and reservoir waters. A drive through the park is rewarding, but swimming, boating, and camping are also available. The winding road leads to the Visitors Center, which has a few historical displays and explains of the formation of the strata in the cliffs. (☎ 307-836-2334. Visitors Center open mid-May to Labor Day daily 10am-6pm. Day visitors must vacate the park by 10 pm. $4 per car, $2 for Wyoming residents. Camping $12/$6.)

🍴🛏 FOOD & ACCOMMODATIONS. Rob's Riverview Restaurant, 501 W. Laramie St., off U.S. 26 at the west end of town, has nature-inspired decor and huge windows overlooking the North Platte. Titan burgers (½ lb. $6) are available, as well as entrees like the croissant sandwich and the honey mustard melt. Those on the go can grab a sandwich, chips, fruit, and two cookies for just $3. (☎ 307-836-2191. Entrees $5.50-7. Open daily 6am-10pm.) For a sit-down dinner, try the **Trail Inn,** 27 N. Wyoming Ave., which offers Mexican, American, and Italian dishes. The Trash Can Special ($7.65), includes 10 different types of food. (☎ 307-836-2010. Appetizers $1.50-5. Entrees $4-9. Open Su 11am-2pm, Tu-Sa 11am-10pm.)

Those looking for places to stay needn't leave U.S. 26. The **Bunkhouse Motel,** on U.S. 26, has a fridge in every room and a BBQ pit for guest use. (☎ 307-836-2356. Singles $44; doubles $50.) The simple, clean rooms at **Sagebrush Motel,** 151 W. Whalen St., come with microwaves and refrigerators. (☎ 307-836-2331. Singles $32; doubles $37.)

🚩 LEAVING GUERNSEY
Whalen St. leads west, becoming **U.S. 26** again outside of town.

THE ROAD TO DOUGLAS. From Guernsey, U.S. 26 lasts another 15 mi. before terminating at I-25, but the road is glorious; just beyond Guernsey the mountains to the west rise into view, filling the skyline with their purple majesty. Little can inspire wanderlust like a long, straight road that vanishes toward distant peaks. At the junction with I-25, turn north to complete the 43 mi. to Douglas, jackalope capital of the world.

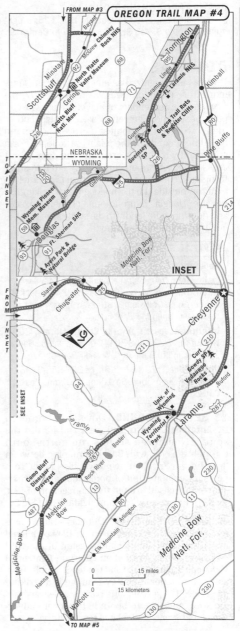

APPROACHING DOUGLAS
From I-25, Exit 135 leads to **Bus. I-25;** a right from here onto **S. 4th St.** leads directly to **Center St.** and downtown.

DOUGLAS
Douglas is recognized as an overland trails landmark, the setting of Owen Wister's *The Virginian*, and the descendant of Ft. Fetterman. The city puts these honors gracefully aside though, choosing to wear a more majestic crown: home and breeding grounds of the mighty jackalope. For a supposedly reclusive creature, the deer-rabbit cross-breed shows up surprisingly often in store fronts and gift shops. One even stands sentinel on a hilltop outside the town along U.S. 30. Skeptics, beware: Douglas is proud of its chimeric mascot and does not take kindly to the suggestion that the creature is, just maybe, a myth.

VITAL STATS

Population: 5300

Visitor Info: Douglas Area Chamber of Commerce, 121 Brownfield St. (☎307-358-2950; www.jackalope.org), just off Center St. a few blocks west of downtown. Open M-F 8am-5pm.

Internet Access: Converse County Library, 300 Walnut St. (☎307-358-3644). Open M and Sa 9am-2pm, Tu and Th 9am-8pm, W and F 9am-6pm.

Post Office: 129 N. 3rd St. (☎307-358-9358). Open M-F 8am-5pm, Sa 10am-12:30pm. **Postal Code:** 82633.

⌐ GETTING AROUND. Douglas is bordered by **Antelope Creek** to the west and I-25 to the south. Numbered streets run north-south through the city, with **Bus. I-25** running between 3rd and 5th St. The downtown area, home to a pleasant combination of bookshops and barbershops, is focused around the intersection of **Center St.,** a main east-west thoroughfare, and **3rd St.**

◙ SIGHTS. The first of Douglas's famed antlered rabbits was "discovered" in 1939 by a local taxidermist. Today, a giant version of the wild creature stands, horned and alert, in **Centennial Jackalope Square,** at 3rd and Center St. Noble, fearsome, and taller than any man, he is a striking presence. The surrounding park is a pleasant picnic spot, and an info booth in the square advertises local events and relates town history.

The **Pioneer Memorial Museum,** 400 W. Center St., in the state fairgrounds, is the king of local history museums, with expansive displays on cowboy, Native American, and domestic pioneer life, and a gift shop. One gallery is dedicated to area cowboys, displaying the tools and weapons of their dusty but romantic profession. Most impressive is the Native American gallery, showcasing earthenware, weavings, and, oddly enough, a teepee used in the movie *Dances With Wolves.* (☎307-358-9288. Open M-F 8am-5pm, Sa 1-5pm. Free.)

It's a bit of a drive from the city itself, but the **Ft. Fetterman Historic Site** tells an interesting chapter in the story begun at Ft. Laramie. A short video, a museum, and a few surviving buildings recall this fort's central role in the "Great Sioux War" that ensued when Red Cloud, Crazy Horse, and others struck against the miners invading the Black Hills. The attacks led to the abandonment of all the forts along the Bozeman Trail except one—Ft. Fetterman. Though smaller than Ft. Laramie, Fetterman was closer to the action and played a more pivotal role in that legendary conflict. (☎307-358-2864 or 307-684-7629. Open daily Memorial Day-Labor Day 9am-5pm. $2, Wyoming residents $1.)

▓⌐ FOOD & ACCOMMODATIONS. The dark side of Douglas is its glut of chain restaurants, but fortunately, a few independent spots still remain. The crowds that pack **The Koop,** 108 N. 3rd St., testify to the fine food offered here. Don't be fooled by the generic menu; the burgers ($4-8) are truly delicious, and the curly fries are the stuff of culinary legend. Shakes, malts, and floats ($2-3) finish meals off right. (☎307-358-3509. Open M-F 6am-3pm, Sa 7am-2pm.) **La Costa,** 1600 E. 2nd St., offers an extensive menu, with sections for chicken, meat, and egg dishes, along with the expected enchiladas, burritos and tostadas. House specials include the *Polla a la Crema* ($10), chicken sauteed in peppers and onions served with a special sauce, rice, and beans. (☎207-235-6599. Entrees $7-11. Open M-Th 11am-10pm, F-Sa 11am-10:30pm, Su 11am-9pm.)

The handful of independently run accommodations in Douglas congregate on **E. Richards St.,** south of downtown off 4th St. One of the best is the **4 Winds Motel,** 615 E. Richards St. Remodeled by new owners, this motel is sparkling clean. Several sizes of rooms are available, allowing those with smaller (or larger) wallets to find something to their satisfaction. (☎307-358-2322. Singles from

$37; doubles $44.) The **Morton Mansion Bed and Breakfast** is a worthwhile stay for travelers with a little money to spare. The building, which is listed on the historic register, has a pleasantly open, airy feeling with a nicely understated decor. The seven rooms all have private baths. (☎307-358-2129. Rooms $65-125.) The **Plains Motel**, 841 S. 6th, has simple but cheap rooms in a location close to the fast-food and gas stations of E. Richards St. (☎307-358-4484. Singles $32; doubles $34.)

 **LEAVING DOUGLAS**
From Douglas, turn around and head south on **I-25** toward Cheyenne.

> ❗ The going gets pretty rough in the not-so-distant future, and the **Alcova Backcountry Byway** (see p. 576) is nearly impossible in winter. If your car can't handle the driving, or it's winter, head on through Douglas, continuing west on **I-25** through Casper and picking up the route at **Alcova** (see p. 577).

DETOUR: AYRES NATURAL BRIDGE
From Douglas, continue heading west along I-25 North. After about 10 mi., take Exit 151 and head 5 mi. south along the road to the bridge.

La Prele Creek still flows beneath the arch it carved into the narrow band of rock that once blocked its path. Far from the highway, and enclosed on either side by great red cliffs, the little park surrounding the bridge is idyllic; at the top of the narrow path which leads onto the bridge, the only sounds are birdsong and water flow. (☎307-358-3532. Open Apr.-Oct. daily 8am-8pm. Free. Some camping permitted; consult the caretaker.)

THE ROAD TO CHEYENNE. It's hard to turn south on I-25, away from the Rockies, but the 75 mph blast through these stony fields is still a lot of fun. It takes a bit of backtracking from Douglas to get to Cheyenne; follow I-25 back south, past the junction with U.S. 26, and 81 mi. farther south, through the towns of Wheatland and Chugwater, to Cheyenne—in all, a 124 mi. drive.

APPROACHING CHEYENNE
To get into Cheyenne, stay on **I-25** through the periphery of the city until it divides: I-25 will continue straight south, while **U.S. 85/87** will peel off to the south

---

THE LOCAL STORY

BIGFOOT

The Oregon Trail was plagued by river crossings, bad weather, and cholera. This wasn't quite bad enough, apparently, as pioneers managed to create a special boogie man of their own. Starr Wilkerson was a true giant, reportedly 6'8" and almost 300 lb. Unkindly nicknamed Bigfoot, Starr was something of an outcast. Hoping to escape the region (and the nickname), he hired himself out as a driver to a pioneer family. As his journey began, he found himself falling in love with the family's daughter—however, she was smitten with another, and trouble soon set in. Tensions mounted between Starr and his rival and broke loose one night when the two were left alone. Starr was shot during the fight but still managed to kill the other man and fled camp, joining a renegade band of Indians and terrorizing the region.

The rest of the ill-fated party chose to spend the winter in on the trail rather than proceed to Oregon through the snow. When spring came, they were heading back to the trail when they encountered Starr once more. The object of Starr's affection angrily rejected him, and when his band slaughtered the entire party, Bigfoot's legend was born. It is rumored that sometime later Bigfoot was slain, but legend also has it that he asked his killer not to tell anyone he was dead. With his end never told, Bigfoot's true whereabouts went unknown, and he became a phantom, blamed for misfortune and seen hiding behind the trees and bushes in bloodthirsty wait.

east. Follow this road until it becomes **Central Ave.**, and once you've crossed **E. Pershing Ave.** you'll be in the central downtown area.

CHEYENNE

"Cheyenne," the name of the Native American tribe that originally inhabited this region, was once considered a prime candidate for the name of the whole Wyoming territory. The moniker was vetoed by the notoriously priggish Senator Sherman, who pointed out that the pronunciation of Cheyenne closely resembled that of the French word *chienne*, meaning "bitch." Once one of the fastest growing frontier towns, Cheyenne may have slowed down a bit, but its historical downtown area still exhibits traditional Western charm, complete with simulated gunfights.

VITAL STATS

Population: 53,000

Visitor Info: Cheyenne Visitors Center, 121 W. 15th St. (☎307-778-3133 or 800-426-5009; www.cheyenne.org), on the 1st fl. of the Cheyenne Depot at the end of Capitol Ave. Open May-Sept. M-F 8am-7pm, Sa 9am-5pm; Oct.-Apr. M-F 8am-5pm, Su 11am-5pm,

Internet Access: Laramie County Public Library, 2800 Central Ave. (☎307-634-3561). Open M-Th 10am-9pm, F-Sa 10am-6pm; Sept. 15-May 15 also Su 1-5pm.

Post Office: 4800 Converse Ave. (☎800-275-8777). Take Lincolnway east, then head north on Converse Ave. past Dell Range Blvd. Open M-F 7:30am-5:30pm, Sa 7am-1pm. **Postal Code:** 82009.

GETTING AROUND

Three streets run parallel to each other through downtown—**Carey Ave., Capitol Ave.,** and **Central Ave.** Perpendicular to these streets are a series of numbered roads, increasing from south to north. Downtown is roughly between **Lincolnway** (which is where 16th St. should be) and **Pershing Ave.,** just north of 30th St. Free 2hr. **parking** is are available downtown, but finding a place can be difficult. Visitors should claim a spot, and then walk.

SIGHTS

During the last full week of July, make every effort to attend the one-of-a-kind **Cheyenne Frontier Days,** a 10-day festival of non-stop Western hoopla, appropriately dubbed the "Daddy of 'Em All." The town doubles in size as tourists arrive from all over to see the world's largest outdoor rodeo competition and partake of the free pancake breakfasts, parades, big-name country music concerts, and square dancing. The USAF Thunderbirds always stop by, too. (☎307-778-7222 or 800-227-6336; www.cfdrodeo.com. Rodeo tickets $10-22.)

Even in the absence of the Frontier Days celebration, the Wild West never dies in Cheyenne, thanks to the efforts of the **Cheyenne Gunslingers.** Summer nights thunder with gunfire as these cowboys fight it out and tell terribly corny jokes in the park at 16th St. and Carey Ave. (☎307-653-1028. Gunfights June-July M-F 6pm, Sa noon. Free.)

The **Cheyenne Street Railway Trolley** guides visitors through historic downtown Cheyenne, with stops at museums and parks along the way. Tours begin hourly at the Cheyenne Depot, at 15th St. and Capitol Ave. (☎307-778-3133. M-F 10am-4pm, Sa 10am and 1:30pm. $8, children $4; with museum admission $14.) Whether you take the trolley tour or not, the stained-glass windows and gold-leafed rotunda of the **Wyoming State Capitol Building,** at Capitol Ave. and 24th St., are worth checking out. Self-guided tour brochures are available, but the building is sometimes closed due to governmental necessity. (☎307-777-7220. Open M-F 8:30am-4:30pm. Free.)

The **Old West Museum,** 4610 N. Carey Ave., in Frontier Park north of downtown, houses an extensive collection of Western memorabilia, including the third-largest carriage collection in the world. A new exhibit considers the wild history of the Frontier Days festival, from its founding in 1897 to the tragic death of world rodeo champion Lane Frost at the horns of a bull in 1989. (☎307-778-7291; www.oldwestmuseum.org. Open summer M-F 8:30am-5:30pm, Sa-Su 9am-5pm; winter M-F 9am-5pm, Sa-Su 10am-5pm. $5.)

≋ FOOD

While Cheyenne seems to sprout fast-food establishments from every corner, it only offers a smattering of non-chain restaurants with reasonably priced cuisine.

Sanford's Grub and Pub, 115 E. 17th St. (☎307-634-3381). Sanford's swelled from humble beginnings as "a few guys drinking beer and watching reruns" to a huge restaurant with a menu so long it has a table of contents. Sandwiches and burgers ($7-8) with bizarre names (Pants on Fire burger, Hobo Sandwich) as well as pies ($7-7.50). 55 beers on tap, 132 different liquors. Check out the game room downstairs. Open daily 11am-10pm.

Zen's Bistro, 2606 E. Lincolnway (☎307-635-1889; www.zensbistro.com). Vegan and vegetarian fare is complemented by a liquid menu with an unending selection of coffees ($1.25-4), teas, and Italian sodas. The glittering front room and patio house the restaurant; the back hosts shows and readings. Open M-F 7am-10pm, Sa 9am-10pm, Su 11am-10pm.

Driftwood Cafe, 200 E. 18th St. (☎307-634-5304), at Warren St. Mom-and-pop atmosphere to match dirt-cheap homestyle cooking. For local flavor, check out the two-cheese, bacon-mushroom Cheyenne Burger ($4.85). Slice of pie $2. Open M-F 7am-4pm.

Luxury Diner, 1401A W. Lincolnway (☎307-638-8971). Easy to spot in its fire engine-red dining car, which was in full service in the 1900s. Breakfast platters ($5-9) sport names like the Conductor, Engineer, and Caboose. Platters of chops, chicken, or fish $6-8. Open daily 6am-4pm.

▟ ACCOMMODATIONS

As long as your visit doesn't coincide with Frontier Days, during which rates skyrocket and vacancies disappear, it's easy to land a cheap room here among the plains and pioneers. Seven budget motels are located on E. Lincolnway alone, within the downtown area. **The Ranger Motel,** 909 W. 16th St., has comfortable modern rooms with cable TV, microwaves, and fridges. (☎307-634-7995. Singles from $24.) South of Cheyenne on I-25, the **Terry Bison Ranch,** 51 I-25 Service Rd. East, offers four-person cabins with kitchenettes, two-man bunkhouses, RV sites and tent sites. The ranch has its own restaurant and runs bus tours to view the local bison herds. (☎307-

634-4171. Office open daily 8am-8pm. Tents $15; bunkhouses $40; cabins $80. Bison tours $10, ages 4-12 $5. Call ahead for departure times.) Renting rooms at fantastically low rates, the **Pioneer Hotel,** 209 W. 17th St., is located in a charming old building. It couldn't be any closer to the action, but the rooms are starting to show their age. (☎307-634-3010. Singles $20, with bath $23; doubles $22/$25.)

▟ NIGHTLIFE

True to its Wild Western past (and present), Cheyenne is home to several rowdy nightspots. At the **Outlaw Saloon,** 3839 E. Lincolnway, at the intersection with Ridge Rd., live country music pours over the dance floor and leaks out to the patio, where there's always a good game of sand volleyball to be played. (☎307-635-7552. Free dance lessons Tu and Th 7:30-8:30 pm. Happy hour with free food M-F 5-7pm. Live music M-Sa 8:30pm. Open M-Sa 2pm-2am, Su noon-10pm.) The rowdy **Cowboy Out South Saloon,** 312 S. Greeley Hwy., hosts rambunctious dancing, crazed eating contests, and plenty of live music over the course of the night. (Take Central Ave. south across I-80; it's on the immediate right. ☎307-637-3800. Live music Tu-Sa 9pm-1:30am. Open daily 11am 2am.) Drink and be merry at the **Crown Bar,** 222 W. 16th St. at the corner of Carey Ave., or drop downstairs for the games, lounge, and techno dance floor of the **Crown Underground.** (☎307-778-9202. Live music upstairs Sa. Bar open M-Sa 11am-2pm, Su 11am-10pm. Underground open W and F-Sa 9pm-2am.)

THE ROAD TO LARAMIE

I-80 provides a quick, straight, uneventful, shot between Cheyenne and Laramie. Rte. 210, **Happy Jack Rd.,** is much more relaxed and scenic. Almost exactly 20 mi. from Cheyenne, the road turns a corner and, for the first time since Missouri, the view doesn't stretch endlessly over plains; it finally feels like the mountains. Camp, fish and hike at **Curt Gowdy State Park,** 24 mi. west of Cheyenne on Happy Jack Rd.; there's also an archery range. (☎307-632-7946. $4 per car. Camping $12. Half price for Wyoming residents. No swimming.) Happy Jack Rd. stretches, in all, for about 40 mi., and then rejoins I-80, heading into Laramie.

▟ VEDAUWOO

28 mi. from Cheyenne on Happy Jack Rd., take a left onto Vedauwoo Rd., just past the Medicine Bow

National Forest sign. Note that this road is 8 mi. long, dirt, and bumpy. It may be faster to continue down Happy Jack Rd. to I-80 and backtrack east to Exit 329.

Named for the towering, curved rock formations that fill it, Vedauwoo (from the Arapaho word meaning "earthborn spirits") is a spectacular sight and destination for rock climbers. Families hike around the spirits' feet, while hardcore climbers scale the sheer neck and shoulders of the stone titans. (☎307-745-2300. $5 per car. Camping $10.)

At the junction of Happy Jack Rd. and I-80 is the **Summit Rest Area**, at 8640 ft. the highest point on I-80. There's a memorial to Henry Joy, first president of the Lincoln Highway Association, which constructed the nation's first intercontinental road. From about the same spot, a craggy Abe Lincoln gazes down from the Lincoln Monument.

DETOUR: AMES MONUMENT
From Exit 323, I-80 heads west toward Laramie. Head 6 mi. east on I-80 instead, to Exit 329 and follow the dirt roads over 2 mi. to the monument.

At the end of a dirt road through the Wyoming hills sits, oddly enough, a 60 ft. pyramid. This is the **Ames Monument,** built by the Union Pacific Railroad to honor brothers who contributed much to the effort to build a transcontinental rail line. Its seemingly random location was once the highest point on that line at 8247 ft., before the railroad was shifted elsewhere. (Always open. Free.)

APPROACHING LARAMIE
Exit 313 and 316 from **I-80** both lead into the city; 313 opens on **3rd St.** near town, while 316 leads to **Grand Ave.,** which runs first past the University of Wyoming, then on to intersect 3rd St. downtown.

LARAMIE
Laramie is the home of the academic cowboy; the museums of the University of Wyoming mix with the Wild West heritage that the city shares with Cheyenne. The heart of Laramie, though, lies in its downtown, a pleasant jumble of antique shops, vintage clothing stores, and rare book sellers.

GETTING AROUND. Laramie's two critical roads are **3rd St.,** which runs north-south, and **Grand Ave.,** which runs east-west. The few blocks around their intersection comprise downtown.

VITAL STATS

Population: 27,000

Visitor Info: Laramie Chamber of Commerce, 800 3rd St. (☎800-445-5303; www.laramie-tourism.org). Open M-F 8am-5pm.

Internet Access: Albany County Library, 310 8th St. (☎307-721-2580). Open M-Th 10am-8pm, F-Sa 1-5pm.

Post Office: 152 5th St. (☎307-721-8837). Open M-F 8am-5:15pm, Sa 9am-1pm. **Postal Code:** 82070.

North of their intersection along 3rd St. are most motels, and east along Grand Ave. are municipal buildings and the University of Wyoming. There's free 2hr. **parking** along most streets downtown.

◘ SIGHTS. There are many museums in Laramie, thanks mainly to the University of Wyoming. Despite its name, the **Geological Museum,** at 11th and Lewis St., is a natural history museum. The centerpiece is a fossilized Apatosaur skeleton. In its shadow is Big Al, one of the world's most complete Allosaurus skeletons. (☎307-766-4218; www. uwyo.ede/geomuseum. Open M-F 8am-5pm, Sa-Su 10am-3pm. Free.)

The bizarre architecture of the **Centennial Complex,** 2111 Willet Dr., contains two of UW's best museums. The **American Heritage Center** is primarily a research center, but has a gallery area displaying a bit of its collection. Western pop culture fills much of the space; exhibits on Western films and TV shows surround the saddles of Hopalong Cassidy and the Cisco Kid. (Take Grand Ave. to 22nd and head north, then east on Willet Dr. ☎307-766-4114; www.uwyo.edu/ahc. Open June-Aug. M-F 7:30am-4:30pm, Sa 11am-5pm; Sept.-May M-F 8am-5pm, Sa 11am-5pm. Free.) Across the lobby is the **University of Wyoming Art Museum.** Exhibits are ever changing, drawing from both traveling selections and the university's own private collection. (☎307-766-6622; www.wyo.edu/artmuseum. Open M-Sa 10am-5pm, Su 1-5pm. Free.)

The Wyoming Children's Museum and Nature Center is a zoo/playground fusion. One room serves as a pioneer play village, while the other holds turtles, frogs, giant salamanders and one glowering owl. (☎307-745-6332; www.wcmnc.org. Open Tu-Th 9am-noon and 3-5pm, Sa 9am-1pm. $3.)

A Pioneer Village and theater are on the grounds of the **Wyoming Territorial Park,** 975 Snowy Range Rd., but the main attraction is the **Territorial Prison,** which once held Butch Cassidy and other famed outlaws, remembered in the restored jail's Hall of Infamy. Cassidy was pardoned after a year and a half; he promised the governor he would never rob a bank again. Keeping his promise, he robbed trains instead. (From 3rd St., head east on Clark St. ☎307-745-6161; www.wyoprison-park.org. Grounds open daily June 26-Aug. 10am-5pm. Museum open daily June-Aug. 10am-5pm; May and Sept. 10am-3pm. Village open June-Aug. W-Su 11am-5pm. $5, ages 12-17 $2.50.)

FOOD & NIGHTLIFE. Laramie is quite hospitable to the vegetarian. The menu at **Jeffrey's Bistro,** 123 Ivinson St., at the corner of 2nd St., lists a number of salad-meals ($8), or you can customize one of your own. (☎307-742-7046. Entrees $6-11. Open M-Sa 11am-9pm.) **Sweet Melissa's,** 213 1st St., right downtown, is a purely vegetarian establishment, with some vegan items as well. Exotic nachos make up much of the appetizer menu ($4-8), while the entrees ($6-8) include lentil loaf, quiche, and eggplant parmesan. (☎307-742-9607. Open M-Sa 11am-9pm.) At the very core of downtown is **Grand Avenue,** 301 Grand Ave., at the corner of 3rd St. This quiet and peaceful establishment serves gourmet pizzas ($10) and calzones ($5-6). The "plain" has sausage, pepperoni, and mushrooms, and it only gets more interesting from there. (☎307-721-2909. Pastas $7-10. Open Tu-Sa 11am-9pm.) Downtown Laramie isn't a crazed club-hopping strip, but the **Buckhorn Bar,** 114 Ivinson St., puts on a good showing with two levels of games (video and otherwise), music and booze. (☎307-742-3554. Live music upstairs F-Sa. 21+. No cover. Open daily 10am-2am.)

ACCOMMODATIONS. Unfortunately, Laramie is not a city of low-price motels. It does, however, have one of the more *interesting* motels around. An army of statues, including bears, horses, cowboys, and a few dinosaurs, monitors the parking lot of the **Gas Lite Motel,** 960 3rd St. The rooms are pleasant and quite large. (☎307-742-6616. Summer singles $55; doubles $65. Winter $45/$55.) **The University Inn,** 1720 Grand Ave., has rooms in a residential neighborhood near the university. (☎307-721-8855. Singles from $50.) One of the best prices in the downtown area is found at the **Ranger Motel,** 453 3rd St. The rooms are spacious and well equipped, with fridges and microwaves. A discount liquor store adjoins the office. (☎307-742-6677. Summer singles $42; doubles $46. Winter $34/$38.)

LEAVING LARAMIE
Head north along **3rd St.** Beyond the city limits, this road becomes **U.S. 30/287,** which arcs northwest toward Sinclair and Rawlins.

THE ROAD TO MEDICINE BOW

The drive along U.S. 30 is an easy-going (and stunningly scenic) 55 mi. roll along a saddle between distant mountain ridges. The road is mostly uninterrupted, passing through tiny **Bosler** 20 mi. along and marginally larger **Rock River** about 20 mi. later.

Five miles west of Rock River, **Marshal Rd.** heads north for almost 8 mi. toward the **Como Bluffs** and the legendary **Dinosaur Graveyard.** After its discovery, the area seemed to be endless source of fossilized North American dinosaurs, even yielding one of the largest skeletons ever unearthed, nearly 70 ft. long. There isn't much to see here beyond the cliffs themselves, however, and it's a dusty, bumpy 8 mi. back to the highway. A bit farther down U.S. 30 from the Marshal turn-off, at the paved road's closest approach to the bluffs, a marker honors the grounds.

MEDICINE BOW. Owen Wister published his novel *The Virginian* in 1902, and suddenly Medicine Bow, one of the book's settings, was famous. In 1909, the mayor had the ⚐**Virginian Hotel,** 404 Lincoln Hwy., built in Wister's honor. Fifty empty miles stretch from Medicine Bow to the Backcountry Byway, and from there it's 64 serviceless miles to Alcova—if you're not ready to undertake that journey yet, The Virginian is a great place to stop and stay, or eat. Each of the rooms is decorated with its own style and color scheme, and highlights include thick carpets, frilled bedspreads, and a few canopied beds or clawed bathtubs—all available at competitive budget prices. The **Virginian Restaurant and Saloon** serves country-style dinners ($8-9) like chicken fried steak and calf liver. The saloon is located in the adjoining room, but drinks can be brought right to the table by request. There is also a formal dining room open to guests, though reservations are appreciated. (☎307-379-2377. Restaurant open daily 6am-8pm. Singles with shared bath $22; doubles $25; suites with bed, sitting room, and bath $45. Suite, champagne, and shrimp dinner combo $108.) There is also an adjoining motel with $45 rooms. For true Wister enthusiasts, across the street from the Virginian is the **Medicine Bow Museum.** (☎307-379-2383. Open M-Sa 10am-5pm, Su 1-5pm.)

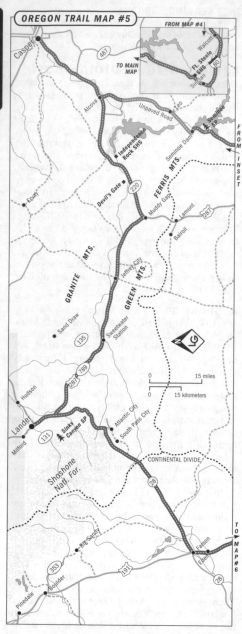

OREGON TRAIL MAP #5

FROM MAP #4

TO MAIN MAP

FROM INSET

TO MAP #6

Casper

487

Walcott

Ft. Steele SHS

Sinclair

80

Alcova

Unpaved Road

Leo

Seminoe SHS

Independence Rock SHS

Seminoe Dam

FERRIS MTS.

Seminoe Mts.

"Ecce"

Devil's Gate

220

Muddy Gap

Lamont

287

Bairoil

GRANITE MTS.

Jeffrey City

GREEN MTS.

Sand Draw

135

Sweetwater Station

789

287

Hudson

Lander

131

Sinks Canyon SP

Milford

Atlantic City

South Pass City

CONTINENTAL DIVIDE

Shoshone Nat'l. For.

28

Big Sandy

Farson

Eden

28

353

Boulder

191

Pinedale

0   15 miles

0   15 kilometers

THE ROAD TO SINCLAIR

The 50 mi. stretch along U.S. 30 and I-80 to Sinclair is marked only by the sight of **Elk Mountain** rising to the south. The town of **Hanna** is located a bit north of U.S. 30, 19 mi. west of Medicine Bow, but it has little to offer travelers. Eighteen miles farther west, U.S. 30 meets I-80; from there it's just over 10 mi. to Sinclair and the Backcountry Byway. A little east of Sinclair, off I-80's Exit 228, are the ruins of **Fort Steele,** an early outpost in the area. The bridge tender's house provides historical background, and a short walk across the river leads to the ruins themselves. (☎307-320-3073. Open May-Nov. 15 daily 9am-7pm.) Take Exit 221 into **Sinclair.** The town shares its name with the gas station and is also home to that company's enormous refinery. The flames spouting from one of its stacks can be seen from miles away. For the not-to-be-missed Backcountry Byway, follow the exit past the refinery, straight through the cluster of houses until 10th St., where you should turn off the main road. This turn is easy to miss, so watch for signs advertising the Wyoming Backway.

ALCOVA BACKCOUNTRY BYWAY

The Oregon Trail did not take this path; the rather large Seminoe Mountains stood in the way. Nevertheless, the scenery makes it a worthy path for Oregon Trail roadtrippers. High-altitude snows can make the road impassable to cars during the winter. Though chained tires may be able to handle the passage, the byway is an advised route only between May and November. Even during the summer months, the road is a slow-going 64 mi. devoid of services; be prepared for a several-hour ride over dirt roads, far from civilization.

The first miles of the route follow the North Platte River through a deepening gorge, the Seminoe Mountains rising rather forbiddingly ahead. After about 20 mi., beyond a hairpin turn, a huge sand dune provides quite a sight, but watch out for the sands which spill across the road's surface.

About 4 mi. farther is **Seminoe State Park,** where a reservoir offers good fishing and boating, and a serene campsite. All manner of wildlife live in and around the reservoir area, even rare mountain lions and bald eagles. The park is divided into several regions, two of which—the North and South Red Hills—can be reached directly from the Byway. (☎307-777-6323; www.wyobest.org. $4 per car. Sites $12, half-price for Wyoming residents.)

Beyond the park, the road becomes steep and winding. The route is hardly crowded, but avoid driving behind others, as cars stir up dust clouds once the pavement ends. The next several miles are the best place to pull off; scenic vistas are everywhere, surveying the mountains and the river flowing down from them. After this the road narrows and passes into deep forests for several miles. A 4 mi. downhill stretch past rock spires completes the mountainous leg of the journey.

At the bottom of the slope is **Miracle Mile,** the slightly misnamed 5 mi. of stream known for its blue-ribbon trout. The fishing ground is formed by **Kortes Dam,** which can be reached by following a 3 mi. detour. This side route breaks off of the main road just past the bridge over Miracle Mile. There is little to do at the dam, but the sight of the giant concrete wall is impressive enough.

The most spectacular parts of the Byway have passed, but the remaining 35 mi. have a harsh appeal, a rocky plain broken by larger formations such as **Dome Rock.** At the end is the town of Alcova, sitting beneath the Alcova Dam.

ALCOVA

A legend of sorts drives Americans to get in cheap cars and cruise across their country in search of a secret, small-town America hidden somewhere along the lesser highways. Many journeys never reach the gleaming general store and friendly diner, maybe because this romantic other America doesn't really exist—but Alcova comes pretty close. The town is on the northern end of the Seminoe Mountains, and the surrounding lakes and rivers are full of campgrounds and fishing spots.

Locals congregate at the **Sunset Bar & Grill,** 22250 W. Rte. 220, at the bottom of the Riverview Inn's hill. It's open late, so the lonely moonlight driver can stop for a sandwich, a drink, or a conversation. (☎307-472-3200. Appetizers $3-7. Sandwiches $5-6. Dinners under $10. Open M-Th 9am-midnight, F 9am-2am, Sa 8am-2am, Su 8am-midnight.) Eight brand new cabins with full kitchens, propane grills, and a maid service that will pick up supplies at the local store are the highlights of the ◨**Inn at Alcova,** located right at the intersection of the Backcountry Byway with Rte. 220. The thematically decorated cabins can house up to six comfortably, but can be rented by one. (☎307-234-2066; www.sloanesatalcova.com. Office in Sloanes General Store next door. Singles $65; doubles $80; triples $90.) With a rocky cliff at its back

and the Gray Reef Reservoir spread out before it, the **Riverview Inn,** 22258 W. Rte. 220, is heartbreakingly scenic. Its traditional motel rooms are very comfortable and sparkling new. (☎307-472-3200. Office in the Sunset Grill down the hill. Laundry. Singles $54; doubles $64.)

◤▮ LEAVING ALCOVA
From Alcova, it's 30 mi. east along **Rte. 220** back to Casper. This city is a bit off the route; it's also possible to skip Casper entirely and head to Lander by continuing along Rte. 220 West. Roadtrippers opting to continue west should be sure to stock up on food (and probably catch some sleep) around Alcova, as it's a ways to the next major town along the route.

CASPER

Casper is one of the largest cities in Wyoming. But while Cheyenne a haven for gunslingers and Laramie a hipster hot spot, Casper struggles to find any sort of character. Nevertheless, pockets of good times still thrive. While it's too small to be called a proper downtown, there *is* a stretch of E. 2nd St. that treats visitors right; it has three old movie theatres complete with flashing marquees, a set of record and bookshops, and the four-story western superstore, Lou Talbert Ranch Outfitters. The city's attempts to kindle historical pride have resulted in the construction of the new National Historic Trails Interpretative Center.

⟮ VITAL STATS ⟯

Population: 50,000

Visitor Info: Casper Visitor Center, 500 N. Center St. (☎307-234-5311; www.casperwyoming.org). Open M-F 8am-6pm, Sa-Su 10am-6pm.

Internet Access: Natrona County Library, 307 E. 2nd St. (☎307-237-4935). Open M-Th 10am-7pm, F-Sa 10am-5pm, Su 1-5pm.

Post Office: 150 E. B St. (☎307-577-6480). Open M-F 8am-6pm, Sa 9am-noon. **Postal Code:** 82604.

▮ GETTING AROUND

Casper's haphazard design makes for nightmarish driving. The city is laid out around **Center St.,** which cuts north-south through the city. **1st St.** runs east-west through the downtown area, with parallel streets increasing in number as one goes south. North of 1st. St., the roads are lettered. **Yel-**

lowstone Hwy. is home to a number of establishments. Unfortunately, it is almost impossible to follow, even with a map, as it does not stay in line with the city's rough grid, frequently breaking off and restarting several block later, only to merge into another road and vanish again.

◉ SIGHTS

In this land of the Wild West and Oregon Trail, the **Nicolaysen Art Museum,** 400 E. Collins St., is an escape into the present. Featuring primarily contemporary artists, the rotating galleries spotlight both locals and famed masters like Andy Warhol. In the same building (through an Alice-in-Wonderland mini-door) is the **Discovery Center,** a workshop where children and their parents can experiment. (☎307-235-5247. Most exhibits remain for 90 days. Open Su and Tu-Sa 10am-5pm. Free.) The upper level of the complex houses the **Wyoming Science Center.** (☎307-261-6130. Open Su and Tu-Sa 10am-5pm. $2, under 13 $1.)

Up in the hills and above the city, the **National Historic Trails Interpretative Center,** 1501 N. Poplar St., lies on the northern end of the road. Despite the dull name, the Interpretive Center is among the best of Oregon Trail museums. A monument to each of the major overland trails—California, Oregon and Mormon—stands in the parking lot. Painted paths lead past miniaturized landmarks such as Chimney Rock, Ft. Laramie and the Ayres Bridge; it's a 1min. condensation of the journey thus far. Once inside, the trails vanish, but a major gallery presents the history, challenges, and people of the Oregon, California and Mormon Trails, and the Pony Express. A full-motion river crossing simulation is available upon request, so you can feel the pain of the pioneers you heartlessly killed playing the Oregon Trail computer game back in the 90s. (From Center St. head west along Collins St. to Poplar St. ☎301-261-7700. Open Apr.-Oct. daily 8am-7pm; Nov.-Mar. Tu-Sa 9am-4:30pm. $6, seniors $5, students $4, ages 6-17 $3, ages 3-5 $1.)

Fort Caspar, 4001 Fort Casper Rd., may have been less significant than some of its counterparts, but it still gets the last laugh; while many other forts are in ruins, Caspar survives, reconstructed by the WPA in the 30s. A museum relates the history of the structure, which was built to guard the developing railroads from attack. A reconstruction of Brigham Young's Mormon Ferry is also on the grounds. (☎307-235-8462. Open June-Aug. M-Sa 8am-7pm, Su noon-7pm; May and Sept. M-Sa 8am-5pm, Su noon-5pm; Oct.-Apr. M-F 8am-5pm, Su 1-4pm. $2, ages 6-17 $1.)

Spiritrider Wagon Train, 5897 S. Twelve Mile Rd., can give Casper visitors an authentic Oregon Trail experience, offering customized tours ranging from half-day wagon rides to week-long camping adventures. Though the company is very accommodating, it is best to call ahead. The week-long trip tours the Hole-in-the-Wall area, covering 55 mi. Much shorter, the Chuckwagon Jamborees are nights of outdoor food and Western fun that run throughout the summer. (☎307-472-5361; www.spiritrider-wagontrain.com. 1-week trip $1500, ages 7-17 $900. Scheduled according to demand. Jamborees summer Tu-F $25, ages 7-17 $13, under 7 $5. Call ahead for meeting locations.)

◥ FOOD

The **Western Grill,** 2333 E. Yellowstone Hwy., meets every requirement of a great restaurant; it's inexpensive, friendly, and has character. The menus, decorated with children's drawings, feature specialty pancakes and grill options for breakfast, as well as a variety of cheap dinners ($6-8). It also provides a great service to scurvy-suffering roadtrippers by selling individual pieces of fruit. (☎307-234-7061. Open M-Sa 5:30am-8:30pm, Su 5:30am-2pm.) **Daddy O's,** 128 E. 2nd St., has an atmosphere cool enough to back up its name. Photos of ballparks share wallspace with team pennants. The specialty is the deep-dish pizza ($7-16), which comes with three default toppings. There are 15 beers on the menu as well as a few wines. (☎307-473-5588. Appetizers $4-6. Salads $6-7. Entrees $11-14. Open Tu-Sa 11am-8:30pm.) Down the street at **Eggington's,** 229 E. 2nd St., the breakfast menu, (under $6), includes the Fruits of the Forest Waffle, which has fruit both baked in and piled on top. Lunch features the Beefeater ($7.50), the herb-dusted ahi steak ($8), or other such sandwiches. (☎307-265-8700. Open M-Sa 6am-2:30pm, Su 7am-2:30pm.)

⌂ ACCOMMODATIONS

For the most part, Casper's accommodations fall into two classes: cheap but very basic, or pleasant but rather expensive. The biggest exception to this rule is the **Sage and Sand Motel,** 901 W. Yellowstone Hwy., where the rooms are large and clean, some with thematic decor. (☎307-237-2088. Laundry. Rooms from $35.) The **National 9 Showboat Motel,** 100 W. F St., off N. Center St., has prices just beyond the budget range, but its distinctly non-budget services, such as cable, indoor hallways, and continental breakfast, justify them. Watch out for the 9am check-out. (☎307-235-2711. Singles from $45; doubles from $57.) The **Virginian Motel,** 830 E. A St., a block north of Yellowstone Hwy., has clean, functional rooms for the lowest prices in the area. (☎307-266-3959. Singles $30; doubles $34.) Those planning to stay in the area for a while will find good weekly rates at the **Yellowstone Motel,** 1610 E. Yellowstone Hwy. The rooms are fairly basic, though a few large, kitchen-equipped rooms are also for rent. (☎307-234-9174. Rooms from $39; suites from $65. Weekly rooms $145.)

LEAVING CASPER
Take **Center St.** to **9th St.** and head west to **Rte. 220.** It's 30 mi. back to Alcova and then a pretty long jaunt to Lander.

THE ROAD TO LANDER
Continuing along Rte. 220, this is a 125 mi. drive through the Sweetwater Valley. Though there are no real full-service towns along the way, gas and some food is available at **Muddy Gap Junction,** a little more than 40 mi. from Alcova, and in **Jeffrey City,** 23 mi. farther. It's by no means a boring drive; the valley has mountain views on both sides, and some geologically and historically significant sights lie along the way. At **Muddy Gap Junction,** 12 mi. past Devil's Gate, the Oregon Trail turns northwest. Turn left onto **U.S. 287 (Rte. 789).**

The road then continues through Jeffrey City before plunging sharply downhill for several miles into a wilderness of plateaus and red cliffs. About 75 mi. past Muddy Gap, there is a junction with Rte. 28; bear right, remaining on U.S. 287. From here, it is less than 10 mi. to Lander.

INDEPENDENCE ROCK
Along Rte. 220, 24 mi. west of Alcova.

This huge and strangely smooth hill of stone was the halfway marker for pioneers heading toward Oregon. If it was reached by Independence Day, then the journey was on schedule to beat the winter. The steep rock can still be scaled, yielding an impressive view of the Sweetwater Valley. The rock-top is gigantic, but if you search hard enough, names can be found carved into the stone, bearing dates as early as 1850. There are few modern additions to the site—just bathrooms and informative plaques. (Open dawn-dusk. Free.)

DEVIL'S GATE
About 5 mi. west of Independence Rock (and visible from it).

Though the trails never passed through it, Devil's Gate was an impressive landmark associated with the Rock. Native legend held that a spirit had once terrorized the Sweetwater Valley in the form of a monstrous tusked beast. When daring warriors assaulted the creature, it tore the cliffs open in fury, forming the Gate. The historic site doesn't actually lead to the opening itself, but commands an excellent view of the gap. A little walkway loop through the grass is lined with plaques detailing the history of the spot. (Open dawn-dusk. Free.)

APPROACHING LANDER
U.S. 287 becomes **E. Main St.** within city limits. Go straight through the intersection where **Rte. 789** breaks away to the east, and you'll find yourself on the western end of **Main St.,** which heads west.

LANDER
With the celebrated wilderness of Shoshone National Forest all around it, the city of Lander is easy to overlook. But while the tourist industry revolves around the forests and mountains, Lander's main street is still very much alive. The town's three llama breeders may be located elsewhere, but businesses of every other variety have found their way to Main St. Outdoor adventure suppliers, a military surplus store, and a smoked meat shop lead the charge of browsable stops. A small caravan of hot-dog stands has even moved in to feed those wandering the long road.

(VITAL STATS)

Population: 6900

Visitor Info: Lander Chamber of Commerce, 160 N. 1st St. (☎307-332-3892 or 800-433-0662; www.landerchamber.org). Open June-Aug. M-F 9am-5pm, Sa 9am-2pm; Sept.-May M-F 9am-5pm.

Internet Access: Fremont County Public Library, 451 N. 2nd St. (☎307-332-5194). Open M-Th 10am-9pm, F-Sa 10am-4pm.

Post Office: 230 Grand View Dr. (☎307-332-2126), off E. Main St. Open M-F 8am-5:30pm, Sa 10am-1pm. **Postal Code:** 82520.

⬛ GETTING AROUND. Lander's main street is **Main St.,** appropriately enough. **Parking** is available on Main St. itself, but vacant spots can be in short supply. It may be easier to just leave your car on the side streets; Main St. is short enough that it can all be seen in a single stroll.

⬛ SIGHTS. While Main St. may be the best in-city attraction, the wild outskirts contain **Sinks Canyon State Park.** From Main St., head south on 5th St., which becomes Rte. 131. Seven miles down this road is the **Rise,** a hillside from which a stream erupts to form the Popo Agie (which is Crow for "Grass River"). Trout food vending machines stand next to the overlook. A quarter-mile farther up the road and upstream are the Sinks, where the raging Popo Agie vanishes abruptly underground on its way to the Rise. The sight is truly bizarre; the river runs down into a little hollow, then simply stops. Geologists are not entirely sure how the underground flow works, but it is believed that the waters seep through a whole system of fissures in the soft rock. The **State Park Visitors Center,** 3079 Sinks Canyon Rd., is right next to the Sinks overlook, providing an overview of the area and its wildlife. (☎307-332-6333. Open summer daily 9am-6pm.)

Beginning 4 mi. north of the town limits but extending for millions of acres beyond is the **Wind River Reservation** of the Arapaho and Shoshone Tribes. Powwows and Sundances are still performed, and visitors may watch. Events are scheduled throughout the summer; for specific dates, contact the Lander Chamber of Commerce.

⬛ FOOD & NIGHTLIFE. A whole string of restaurants lines Main St. **Mom's Malt Shop,** 351 Main St., is simple and delicious. Eat inside or the under umbrellas in the outdoor garden. The sandwiches are inexpensive ($2-4) and varied; try the Polish Dog, especially with the fried pickles. (☎307-332-5535. Sides $1-3. Open M-F 7am-4pm, Sa 7am-2pm.) A little more expensive but still excellent is the **Gannett Grill,** 126 Main St. The patio is popular, but the interior is oddly fascinating with its decor of rancher hieroglyphics. Salads ($4-5) include the Mad Greek and Hail Caesar. (☎307-332-8228. Open daily 11am-10pm.) The menu of the expensive but insanely stylish **Cowfish,** 148 Main St. consists of two sections: Cow, and Fish, though there is also a Pigs & Chickens classification. Occasionally the two worlds intersect, as with the cow-crustacean ($23), a fillet/

shrimp meal. (☎307-332-8227; www.landerbar.com. Appetizers $6-7. Cow $15-23. Fish $10-18. Open M-F 5-10pm, Sa-Su 8am-2pm and 5-10pm.) A little Lander nightlife can be found at the **Global Cafe,** 360 Main St., where shows span genres from folk to punk. Before the music, chill in the game room or patio and sample the smoothies. (☎307-332-7900; www.landerglobalcafe.com. Open Su and W-Sa 3-11pm.)

⬛ ACCOMMODATIONS. The **Downtown Motel,** 569 Main St., advertises itself as The Place With Flowers, and so it is. The rooms, while devoid of flowers, are clean and comfortable. (☎307-332-3171 or 800-900-3171. Rooms from $44.) Unusually large rooms can be found at the **Maverick Motel,** 808 Main St. The free laundry room is a great service for drivers who find that their laundry bags, or backseats, are full. (☎307-332-2300 or 877-622-2300. Singles $45; doubles $49.) Lander also has an excellent B&B in the **Blue Spruce Inn,** 677 S. 3rd St. The four carefully furnished rooms are all individually decorated and named; the Brass Room is a classical alternative to Wyoming's ubiquitous cowboy decor. A pleasant, bookish den unites the four rooms and their guests. (☎307-332-8253; www.bluespruceinn.com. Each room has private bath. Singles $70; doubles $85.)

⬛ DETOUR: LOOP ROAD
Take 5th St. south from Main St. in Lander. This becomes Rte. 131, which feeds into Sinks Canyon. From there, the Loop Road is the only available path. It terminates on Rte. 28, 30 mi. south of Lander.

An alternative to the monotony of the interstate, the Loop Road punishes automobiles with 30 mi. of switchbacks, ledge-riders and washed-out roads. The first few miles lead through **Sinks Canyon,** where the Popo Agie vanishes underground, only to resurrect itself miraculously a few hundred yards away. The **Shoshone National Forest** follows. Hikers can pause at Bruce's Lot to hike the Middle Fork trail up to **Popo Agie Falls;** those who love their car's shocks can then turn around. Beyond here the road scissors up the cliff-face in a series of dusty switchbacks. Well over 10 tiers and 6 mi. later it climbs over the last of the rocks onto level ground. The trials are over; a minor high-altitude paradise awaits. Miles of evergreen forests surround preposterously blue mountain lakes. By the time the road reaches 9500 ft., the snow-capped Wind River Mountains are gloriously close. Take that, Interstate Highway Commission.

LEAVING LANDER
Head east on **Main St.** and back south on **U.S. 287** to return to the junction with **Rte. 28.** Take Rte. 28 southwest toward Rock Springs.

THE ROAD TO ROCK SPRINGS
It's a long, lovely 120 mi. to Rock Springs with few pitstops along the way, and even longer if the Loop Road is substituted for the first leg of Rte. 28. South on Rte. 28, the snowy Wind River Range rises and recedes in the rearview mirror. The town of **Farson** is located at the junction of Rte. 28 and U.S. 191; beyond, heading south on U.S. 191, this segment of road follows the famed South Pass that made wagon travel through the mountains possible. It may seem broad and flat, but the **Continental Divide** lies just a few miles beyond the intersection. It is announced with little fanfare, just a small sign, but represents an important landmark, both geologically and for the Oregon Trail, indicating the completion of the first ascent. The diffuse town of **Eden** is 4 mi. down the road, and **Rock Springs** is 34 mi. beyond that. This road passes through the Red Desert. Herds of wild horses and pronghorn antelope inhabit the area, perhaps spotted by fortunate drivers.

DETOUR: SOUTH PASS CITY
South of Lander, a dirt turn-off leads toward South Pass City; from South Pass City the road continues for another 5 mi. before rejoining Rte. 28.

Along this short dusty road stands the crumbling **Carissa Gold Mine.** South Pass City lived the short life of a gold boom community, springing up in 1867 only to be left a ghost town within 10 years. It was bought by the state before it fell into total ruin though, and 30 of the original 300 buildings have been restored, refurnished, and opened to visitors. (☎307-332-3684. Open daily mid-May to Sept. 9am-6pm. $2, Wyoming residents $1.)

It was a South Pass City legislator who introduced the bill that made Wyoming the first state or territory to allow women to vote and hold public office.

THE FARSON MERC
At the intersection of Rte. 28 and U.S. 191.

"Home of the Big Cone," The Merc is widely famous for its ice cream and 80-year-old building. The cones have been served to locals and travelers from all over the world, even astronaut training crews. Sizes span from the not-so-small Baby Bear ($1.80) to the Devil's Tower ($6.80), one colossus of a cone. (☎307-273-9020. Hours vary.)

APPROACHING ROCK SPRINGS
Entering Rock Springs, **Rte. 191** becomes **Elk St.**

ROCK SPRINGS
Though the arid beauty of the Red Desert and its wild horses surrounds the city, Rock Springs itself is not so attractive. A loop of corporate-dominated highways arcs around residential areas and a Historic Downtown which is now home to gambling dens and a few interesting shops. The city does come alive during the last few days of July for its Red Desert Roundup rodeo. For the rest of the year, it serves as a convenient base-of-operations for expeditions to the Flaming Gorge.

VITAL STATS

Population: 19,000

Visitor Info: Rock Springs Chamber of Commerce, 1897 Dewar Dr. (☎307-362-3771). Open M-F 8am-5pm. Brochure room open 24hr.

Internet Access: Rock Springs Public Library, 400 C St. (☎307-352-6667), in the downtown Historic Downtown District. Open M-Th 10am-9pm, and alternating F and Sa 10am-5pm.

Post Office: 2829 Commercial Way (☎307-362-9792). Open M-F 8am-6pm, Sa 9am-2pm. **Postal Code:** 82901.

GETTING AROUND. The streets of Rock Springs are not easily navigable; grab a street map from the info booth at the Chamber of Commerce. **Rte. 191** enters the city from the north and becomes **Elk St.,** one of the city's main thoroughfares. A little ways into the city it intersects **Center St.,** which runs roughly southwest-northeast. In the western half of the city, Center St. becomes busy **Noland Dr.,** home to the Chamber of Commerce and leading to I-80. The Historic Downtown District can be reached by taking Elk St. south past Center St. until it becomes **A St.**

SIGHTS. A number of dinosaur museums cluster along the Oregon Trail in Nebraska and Wyoming, but none surpass the **Western Wyoming Community College Natural History Museum,** 2500 College Dr. The museum itself is a collection of archaeological finds from the area, but it also sponsors the set of full (cast) skeletons spread across campus. A triceratops, a tyrannosaurs, and the marine monster plesiosaur are among the best of the set. A map of skeleton locations is available in the main lobby of the campus or at the museum. (☎307-382-1666 or 307-382-1600. Open daily 9am-10pm. Free.) Sharing its building with the public library, **The Community Fine Arts Center,** 400 C St., showcases local and state artists in rotating exhibits. The permanent collection includes works by a handful of famed artists, including Norman Rockwell. (☎307-362-6212. Open M-Tu 10am-6pm, W 10am-9pm, Th 10am-6pm, and alternating F and Sa 10am-5pm. Free.) The **Rock Springs Historical Museum** is located at the corner of Broadway and B St. in the Historic Downtown District. (☎307-362-3138. Open Memorial Day-Labor Day M-Sa 10am-5pm; Labor Day-Memorial Day Su and W-Sa 10am-5pm.)

▓▐▐ FOOD & ACCOMMODATIONS. Rock Springs is home to every imaginable branch of the fast-food industry. Most of these swarm around I-80 exits. Other options are regrettably hard to find. The **Broadway Burger Station,** 628 Broadway St., serves hamburgers from a menu laden with Elvis references. Sit at a gleaming silver counter or sparkly red seats straight from the fifties. The final, eyebrow-raising touch comes from the animated neon sign, which endlessly raises Marilyn's skirt. (☎307-362-5858. Burgers $4-8. Sandwiches $4-5. Shakes and malts $2-3. Open M-Th 9am-8pm, F 9am-9pm, Sa 9am-8pm.) Hanging birds and monkeys, ceramic inlaid tables, and psychedelic murals make **Fiesta Guadalajara,** 19 Elk St., a fun place to dine. The combo dishes ($8-9), which come with rice and beans, also make it a pretty good deal. (☎307-382-7147. Appetizers $4-6. Entrees $6-9. Open M-Th 11am-9pm, F-Sa 11am-10pm, Su noon-8pm.)

There is also a glut of chain hotels surrounding I-80's burn through Rock Springs at the western end of **Dewar Dr.** Outside this area, the **Cody Motel,** 75 Center St., has clean and well-furnished rooms with fridge/microwave combinations. (☎307-362-6675. Singles $34.) Back near I-80 is the moderately priced but quite pleasant **Inn at Rock Springs,** 2518 Foothill Blvd., which intersects Dewar Dr. west of I-80. Some of the large rooms come with couches and other amenities, and a guest room with both pool and

pool tables raises the comfort level considerably. (☎307-362-9600. Breakfast included. Singles $49; doubles $59.)

▐▀ LEAVING ROCK SPRINGS
Take **Noland Dr.** west to **I-80,** which leads to Green River and Flaming Gorge.

◣ DETOUR: FLAMING GORGE NATIONAL RECREATION AREA
To follow the western edge of the gorge, take Rte. 530 south from Green River; the junction with Rte. 530 is off Flaming Gorge Way, immediately after getting off I-80 at Exit 91. The eastern border can be skirted via U.S. 191, off I-80 Exit 99 between Rock Springs and Green River.

Seen at sunset, the contrast between the red canyons and the aquamarine water of the Green River makes the landscape of the Flaming Gorge area appear to glow. Legislation was passed in 1963 to dam the river, and the resulting body of water is now home to the **Flaming Gorge National Recreation Area,** to which boating and fishing enthusiasts flock every summer. The area is large enough to spill into the northern reaches of Utah, but its northern tip is just south of the town of Green River. The scenic drive south into the area is thus a serious undertaking, but a shorter jaunt down one edge is also possible. Much of the drive winds past a sprawling reservoir and forested hills, as well as the vivid red cliffs that give the valley its name. Elk, antelope, and bighorn sheep call the land home; these animals may not frequent the highway loop, but a turn onto one of the many lesser roads may lead to a sighting.

The two main highways, U.S. 191 and Rte. 530, meet in Utah near **Red Canyon,** but plenty of activities can be found spread out along the gorge area borders. More than 20 campgrounds are found throughout, and the region also features numerous hiking and biking trails. Adventures such as rafting are possible. The Rock Springs and Green River Chambers of Commerce can provide maps of the area and phone numbers for individual campsites and marinas in the area and sell passes required for park entrance. (Flaming Gorge Ranger District: ☎435-784-3445; www.fs.fed.us. Offices in Manile, UT. $2 per car. 16-day pass $5.)

⛏ APPROACHING GREEN RIVER
Much of the city is laid out along **Flaming Gorge Way,** which is a loop between I-80 Exits 91 and 89. Take Exit 91 to reach the city.

GREEN RIVER
Though not overflowing with attractions, Green River, right in the shadow of Rock Springs, is a peaceful town and a relaxing rest stop. The tip of the long **Flaming Gorge National Recreation Area** is just south of town, and this scenic area defines the town and much of its economy. Green River also houses the **Sweetwater County Historical Museum,** 3 E. Flaming Gorge Way, an interesting mix of Oregon Trail info, dinosaur remains, and esoteric branches of history such as the Mormon War. (☎307-872-6435 or 307-352-6715. Open M-Sa 10am-6pm. Free.) More visitor info is available at the **Green River Chamber of Commerce,** 541 E. Flaming Gorge Way. (☎307-875-5711. Open M-F 8:30am-5:30pm, Sa 9am-5pm.)

Flaming Gorge Way is home to many of Green River's restaurants. **Buckaroo's Family Restaurant,** 580 E. Flaming Gorge Way, is a rope-and-boot adorned diner with some pleasantly inexpensive meals. Several under $4 choices—The Wild West, The Billy the Kid and so forth—are supplemented by larger, more expensive dinners ($6-15) for the hungry driver. (☎307-875-2246. Sandwiches $4-7. Open daily 6am-10pm.) All-day breakfasts and a large supply of moose paraphernalia abound at the **Krazy Moose,** 211 E. Flaming Gorge Way. Omelettes ($5-6) are some of the best offerings, though the large salad list ($5-7) is also impressive. (☎307-875-5124. Breakfast $6-7. Open M-Th 6am-9pm, F-Sa 6am-10pm, Su 7am-7pm.) **Penny's Diner,** 1170 W. Flaming Gorge Way, right off the interstate, is fast, greasy, and prime roadtrip material. Root beer floats ($2) taste miraculous after a dusty day on the road. (☎307-825-3500. Breakfast under $7. Sandwiches under $6. Dinner under $8. Open 24hr.)

The same stretch of road also offers a strip of great motels. The least expensive and most convenient of these is the **Mustang Motel,** 550 E. Flaming Gorge Way, which has enormous rooms for a budget establishment. Rooms include refrigerators and microwaves. (☎307-875-2468. Singles $32; doubles $37.) The **Coachman Inn,** 470 E. Flaming Gorge Way, right next door, is another good bet; though slightly more expensive, it also has large,

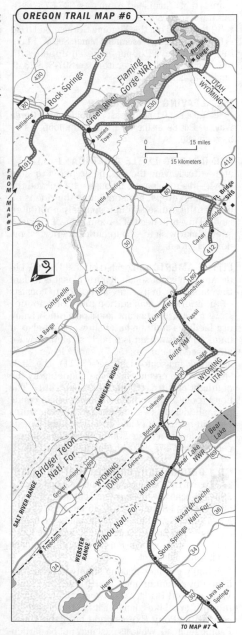

OREGON TRAIL MAP #6

TO MAP #7

comfortably furnished rooms. (☎307-875-3681. Summer singles $38; doubles $40. Winter $32/ $38.) Rounding out this Flaming Gorge motel triad is the comfortable **Western Inn Motel,** 890 W. Flaming Gorge Way. Rooms come equipped with microwaves and refrigerators. (☎307-875-2840. Singles $34; doubles $38.)

▲ LEAVING GREEN RIVER
Take Exit 91 at the east end of **Flaming Gorge Way,** or Exit 89 at the west end of the loop to hop back on **I-80.**

THE ROAD TO LITTLE AMERICA. Immediately after leaving the city, be prepared to slow down—the road passes through a tunnel and the speed limit drops. For some time the ride is an uneventful cruise through sparsely populated lands. Drivers in need of a room, a meal, or just a stretch may wish to stop in Little America, 23 mi. down the road.

LITTLE AMERICA. Located off I-80 Exit 68, Little America is not so much a town as it is a giant travelers' oasis. In its entirety, the "town" consists of an enormous gas station and convenience store, a hotel, a restaurant, and a post office. Laundry facilities and non-hotel showers are also at hand. The restaurant is a fairly straightforward affair, serving burgers ($6-7), sandwiches ($6-7) and steak and seafood entrees ($8-11). The $0.35 soft-serve ice cream cones are undoubtedly the highlight of town. (Restaurant open 24hr.) The hotel rooms, well furnished and in perfect condition, all include TVs, and the two-person suites contain refrigerators and coffee makers. Guests have access to a heated outdoor pool and fitness center. (☎307-875-2400. Singles $66; suites $90.)

◤ DETOUR: FORT BRIDGER HISTORIC SITE
From Little America, continue west on I-80. Exit 39 leads north toward Kemmerer, but the fort is a bit farther down I-80 off Exit 34, 35 mi. west of Little America. Turn left at the end of the ramp and head 2 mi. to the Fort Bridger State Historic Site. The fort is located right at the border of the town of Ft. Bridger, 2 mi. south of the exit.

Originally a money-making supply depot established by mountain men Jim Bridger and Louis Vasquex, Fort Bridger was eventually bought by the military. Like many of its counterparts, it served the Pony Express and later the Union Pacific Railroad. While its past may not be particularly tumultuous, the fort is remarkably well-preserved. One of the 18 standing buildings is a two-story Victorian home that housed the commanding officer; both floors are open for viewing. At the far end of the wooded grounds is a small museum that illustrates the fort's transformation over time. Those who pass by during Labor Day weekend will be treated to the **Mountain Man Rendezvous,** a festival of 19th-century crafts and demonstrations. Don't miss the tomahawk throwing contest. (☎307-782-3842. Grounds open daily 7am-8pm. Museum open May-Sept. daily 8:30am-5:30pm; Oct. to mid-Nov. and mid-Mar. to Apr. Sa-Su 8:30am-5:30pm.)

THE ROAD TO KEMMERER. From Exit 39 off **I-80,** take **Rte. 412** to proceed north. This stretch of driving is a flat and peaceful cruise away from the hills and mountains for a bit. There is little to disturb the relaxing drive; the only town along the way is **Carter,** a tiny blip on the map 7 mi. north of the interstate. Fifteen miles past Carter the road ends; take **U.S. 189** 14 mi. north to the town of Diamondville and on to Kemmerer.

▲ APPROACHING KEMMERER
U.S. 189 joins **U.S. 30** shortly before reaching Diamondville. The roads turn sharply left at the border; watch the signs carefully. Having made this turn, follow **U.S. 30** into Kemmerer.

KEMMERER

Southwestern Wyoming is a pretty and peaceful place, and Kemmerer is no exception. The town's center is a genuine village green, and its sleepy downtown charm remains largely unblemished by corporate invasion. This is somewhat ironic, considering that one of the area's hometown businesses spawned the modern department store giant, J.C. Penney.

▣ GETTING AROUND.
Kemmerer is laid primarily along **U.S. 30,** which runs south-north, changing its name to **Central Ave.** in Diamondville, then **Coral St.** at the Kemmerer line, then to **Pine Ave.** deeper in Kemmerer. **Parking** is generally available on the streets or in private lots.

◉ SIGHTS.
Kemmerer is the home of the original J.C. Penney department store. Once known as The Golden Rule, the mother of all J.C. Penney stores still operates at the intersection of J.C. Penney Dr. and Pine Ave. Just a few shopfronts down is the **Penney Homestead,** 107 J.C. Penney Dr., now

OREGON TRAIL

VITAL STATS

Population: 2700

Visitor Info: Kemmerer/Diamondville Chamber of Commerce, 800 Pine Ave. (☎307-877-9761), in Herschler Triangle Park. Open M-Th 9am-5pm, F 9am-3pm.

Internet Access: Lincoln County Library, 519 Emerald St. (☎307-877-6961), at the corner of Beech St. Take Emerald St. up the hill from Pine Ave. Open M-W 10am-8pm, Th-F 10am-6pm, Sa 10am-2pm.

Post Office: 318 Sapphire St. (☎307-877-3432). Open M-F 8:30am-5pm, Sa 9am-noon. **Postal Code:** 83101.

a museum. The lower floor contains artifacts and photos from the founder's life, while the upstairs has been preserved in its original state. (☎307-877-3164. Open June-Labor Day M-Sa 9am-5:30pm. Free.) More local history is preserved in the **Fossil Country Frontier Museum,** 400 Pine Ave., which, in addition to the usual artifacts, offers an account of the Golden Rule Store's transformation into the J.C. Penney of today. Visitors can descend into a coal mine replica to learn about the dangerous but ingenious techniques the miners used to plunder area shafts. (☎307-877-6551; www.hamsfork.net/~museum. Open June-Aug. M-Sa 9am-5pm; Sept.-May M-Sa 10am-4pm. Free.)

🍴 **FOOD.** Despite its name, the **Busy Bee,** 919 Pine Ave., is crowded with cows. There are hundreds of them, in porcelain, wood, and Far Side comic strip form. The menu is small, but the offerings are well priced and excellent; jalapeno swiss and garlic burgers aren't found at just any cafe. (☎307-877-6820. Sandwiches $2. Burgers $4-5. Open M-F 5:30am-2pm, Sa 7am-2pm, Su 7am-noon.) For a little more variety, there's **Bootlegger's Steakhouse and Grill,** 817 S. Main St., off Pine Ave. just south of Herschler Triangle Park. The usual burgers and sandwiches ($5-8) are supplemented by specialties like catfish ($13) and pasta with chicken ($10). Also worthwhile are the baskets ($7-9), which come with shrimp, chicken fingers, or ribs. The whole place basks in the antique glory of old Coca-Cola advertisements. (☎307-828-3067. Appetizers $5-7. Seafood $11-18. Open M-F 11:30am-2pm and 5-8:30pm, Sa 5-8:30pm.)

🏠 **ACCOMMODATIONS.** Kemmerer's lodgings are mostly budget motels, all comfortable and reasonably priced. The **Downtown Motel,** 902 Pine Ave., has some of the cheapest rooms in town, equipped with fridges and stoves. (☎307-877-3710. Singles $31; doubles $37. Cash only.) The **New Antler Motel,** 419 Coral St., offers a whole range of rooms ranging from functional to family-sized. (☎307-877-4461. Reception 9am-9pm. Singles $32-46; doubles $38-50; triples $65.) Right on the Kemmerer/Diamondville line is the **Fairview Motel,** 61 U.S. 30/189. The rooms here are big and quite well equipped, with large TVs, microwaves, and fridges. Though it's a bit farther from downtown, weary travelers will be pleased by the sight of this motel, the first they will see in Kemmerer. (☎307-877-3938. Rooms from $50.)

🏁 **LEAVING KEMMERER**
Follow **Pine St.** north through the city; on the outskirts of town it becomes **U.S. 30.**

THE ROAD TO MONTPELIER. This substantial 75 mi. drive returns to the hills and ravines of mountain country, so there is much to marvel at along the way. Sharp crosswinds can arise as the road descends between hills, and the whole area is popular with deer, so drivers should be especially alert. Roughly 15 mi. farther, U.S. 30 swings north at the Sage junction. From there, it passes Cokeville. Eleven miles past Cokeville is the junction with Rte. 80—be sure to stay on U.S. 30. Just beyond the junction, the road passes into Idaho, and 20 mi. farther is Montpelier.

👁 **FOSSIL BUTTE NATIONAL MONUMENT**
Turn off U.S. 30 10 mi. west of Kemmerer

Four miles from the turn-off to the monument, the **Fossil Butte National Monument Visitors Center** serves as a base-of-operations, offering info about the area before you set off on one of two hikes through fossil territory. A quick film outlines the vast array of creatures that have been preserved in the now-dry fossil lake. A mural-filled gallery comprises the rest of museum, which displays fossils and replicas of some of the finds, most dating from roughly 50 million years ago. The former location of a community of fossils can be reached on foot via the **Historic Quarry Trail** or the **Fossil Lake Trail.** The former is a geology hike through an abandoned quarry, showing off the rock strata. This moderately strenuous hike is about 2½ mi. and rises 600 ft. in elevation. The other hike is only about 1½ mi. long with a 300 ft. rise, winding through a nearby aspen grove. Note that while the Fossil Lake Trail departs from the Visitors Center, the Historic Quarry trailhead is back down the road a short way; a small parking area marks it. (☎307-877-4455; www.nps.gov/fobu. Open daily summer 8am-7pm; winter 8am-4:30pm. Free.)

Welcome To IDAHO

📍 **APPROACHING MONTPELIER**
U.S. 30 becomes **4th St.**; follow it into town.

MONTPELIER

Built over the famous Oregon Trail rest stop of Clover Creek, Montpelier has long provided rest for weary travelers. The heavily commercialized intersection of U.S. 30 and U.S. 89 is balanced out by the open and sunny downtown blocks of Washington St., which feature an old theater, an ice-cream parlor, and sidewalk benches held up by smiling bears. The mid-20th century aura is given a pleasant jolt by some of the older buildings; one bank here was robbed of almost $17,000 by Butch Cassidy. He escaped unscathed, though a valiant deputy gave chase on a bicycle.

📠 **GETTING AROUND. U.S. 30** in Montpelier is also known as **4th St.**, and is one of Montpelier's two main drags. The other is **Washington St. (U.S. 89)** which runs

roughly north-south, perpendicular to 4th St. **Parking** is readily available in Montpelier, and most establishments have their own lots.

◎ **SIGHTS.** Montpelier's major tourist draw is the ▣**National Oregon/California Trail Center,** 300 N. 4th St. This is no ordinary museum, but a westward journey led by in-character guides. After watching a film on the trails of Idaho, a guide will take you through a gunshop, wagon yard, and mercantile, outlining along the way what to bring (and not to bring) on your trip, and what tricks are out there to help you survive the arduous 2000 mi. journey to the Oregon territory. From there, mount the wagons, which buck and creak through the darkness as tales of the trail are narrated. Finally, climb out at the Clover Creek camp and hear more stories about life on the trail while learning how to make a wagon wheel rug and jack a cart out of the mud. On the way out, a huge and finely detailed woodcut of the trail through Idaho has captured the features of a hundreds of

BEYOND THE ASPHALT

ROADTRIP SUBTERRANEA

The potato isn't the only Idaho attraction that comes from underground—the state has a fascinating landscape of lava flows, falls, and caves. In 1907, a hunter stumbled instead upon one of these caves near Monpelier. The entrance was later expanded by the WPA, forming today's spectacular Minnetonka Cave. Walkways, lighting, and 448 stairs now lead 1800 ft. into the earth. The tour is full of geological wonders, from spectacular stalactites and stalagmites to oddities like Kermit's Castle and the Seven Dwarves. Guides point out spiral rocks, bat roosts, and the hidden Devil's Office plummet that solo explorers might miss. And, just to make the cave-exploring experience more intense, the lights are turned out at the end of the path. The darkness that falls is absolute—hands in front of faces may as well not be there. The cave naturally remains a chilly 40°F, so coats are in order year-round. (☎435-245-4422. 70min. tours daily every 30min. 10am-5:30pm. $5, ages 6-15 $4.)

people, animals and landmarks in vivid color. (☎208-847-3800. Open May-Sept. daily 10am-5pm. $6, seniors $5, ages 5-12 $4.)

◢↑ FOOD & ACCOMMODATIONS. Montpelier's downtown burger and ice cream stands are supplemented by some full-power restaurants out on U.S. 30. The **Cabin Smokehouse BBQ,** 194 N. 4th St., adds "mesquite-smoked" to the burger-and-steak fare of the West. (☎208-841-1824. Appetizers $3-8. Sandwiches $3-8. Ribs $10-17. Open M-Th 8am-10pm, F-Sa 8am-11pm, Su 8am-10pm.) It's unclear if **Butch Cassidy's Restaurant,** 230 N. 4th St., is Old Western or cynically modern in style; the cowboy decor clashes amusingly with the satirical books and bottles of Grey Poupon left in each booth. (☎208-847-3501. Sandwiches $5-7. Entrees $10-18. Open daily 6am-10pm.)

The busy U.S. 30/89 intersection comes to the rescue for sleepy drivers, home to a series of cheap but pleasant motels. **The Budget Motels,** 240 N. 4th St., has titanic budget rooms with stoves and refrigerators. The rooms are a bit older and show some wear but are in good shape overall. (☎208-847-1273. Rooms from $25.) The **Three Sisters Motel,** 112 S. 6th St., at the corner of Washington St., has smaller rooms that include refrigerators and microwaves. (☎208-847-2324. Singles from $25; $5 per additional person.) Recently renovated and under new management, the **Park Motel,** 745 Washington St., is clean and well furnished. It also has an ideal location on the edge of downtown. (☎208-847-1911. Summer singles $40; doubles $45. Winter $30/$40.)

◤↑ LEAVING MONTPELIER
To the west, **4th St.** becomes **U.S. 30** again, heading on toward Soda Springs.

THE ROAD TO SODA SPRINGS

This is just a short 27 mi. drive down U.S. 30, broken only by the farms of Georgetown, 10 mi. from Montpelier. The road is part of the **Oregon Trail/Bear Lake Scenic Byway,** and the landscape is appropriately picturesque. The desert land slowly recedes, and sage brush is gradually replaced with small evergreen trees. The route returns to desert soon enough, so, like the timber-starved pioneers, enjoy the trees while they're around. At least you won't have to cook your food with oxen dung when the trees have vanished.

◤↑ APPROACHING SODA SPRINGS
Like most of these smaller cities, Soda Springs's major road is **U.S. 30;** just continue along it until you enter the city limits. Here, U.S. 30 is known as **2nd South.**

SODA SPRINGS

A hundred springs once rose from these grounds, until a city was built over them. Ironically, the most spectacular of those remaining is the man-made Soda Springs Geyser. Greenways weave through the downtown, allowing the Idaho wilderness to infiltrate the sidewalks.

⟨VITAL STATS⟩

Population: 3000

Visitor Info: Soda Springs Chamber of Commerce, 9 W. 2nd South (☎888-399-0888 or 208-537-4964), inside City Hall. Open M-F 8am-12pm.

Internet Access: Soda Springs Public Library, 149 S. Main St. (☎208-547-2606). Open M-Th 10am-8pm, F 10am-5pm.

Post Office: 220 S. Main St. (☎208-547-3794). Open M-F 8:30am-5pm, Sa noon-2pm. **Postal Code:** 83276.

▣ GETTING AROUND. Whoever chose the street names in Soda Springs was perhaps a bit misguided. **Main St.** runs north-south and forms a cross with **Hooper Ave.** All other streets are numbered: parallel to and west of Main St. is **1st West,** to the east is **1st East;** parallel and to the south of Hooper is **1st South,** to the north is **1st North.** Worse, they are divided in half at the axis streets, so there is W. 1st South as well as S. 1st West, and so on. The result is that it is shockingly easy to get lost in this very small city. Be vigilant.

◎ SIGHTS. Naturally, Soda Springs's greatest attraction is its namesake. The springs still rise from **Geyser Park,** though the **Soda Springs Geyser** is the real thriller. The geyser was actually created when drillers, trying to find a source for a heated swimming pool, struck a pressurized chamber. Today, it is capped for control and allowed to erupt at the stroke of each hour. Geyser Park is also the trailhead for the **Soda Springs Pathway.** Two miles of easy-going trail cut through downtown and then into the surrounding wetlands. The trail stops at **Octagon Park,** at the corner of Hooper Ave. and Main St. The eight-sided pavilion in the center of the park makes for good picnicking. From here, the path continues north to **Hooper Springs Park,** ending in a secluded grove. Beneath a small wooden pavilion, the springs well into a low pool, easily accessible for drinking. The water is naturally carbonated and bitter, but clear and cool. Wise pioneers flavored it with sugar and syrup, but the bold still knock it back straight. (To reach Hooper Springs by car, take Hooper Ave. east to 3rd East, then north to Government Dam Rd., and head west a few hundred yards. ☎208-547-4356. All open daily dawn-dusk. Free.)

The **Enders Building,** 76 S. Main St., also home to the Enders Hotel, is something of an attraction itself, its lobby spectacularly preserved in original 1917 form. The second floor is a museum of local history, and barber chairs, saddles, and relics are spread throughout. The collection's prize is the revolver used by the Sundance Kid; look for it at the bottom of the hallway display case. (☎208-547-4980. Open M-Sa 6am-10pm, Su 7am-9pm. Free.)

⚑ FOOD. While small, Soda Springs still has its share of fast food along the highway; other options are hard to find but still excellent. **Caribou Mountain Pizza and Grill,** 59 W. 2nd South, in a plaza off U.S. 30, offers the ultimate in budget dining: all-you-can-eat. Unlimited salad and soup ($6) are available all day, while the lunch buffet (11am-1:30pm; $6) has pizza, wings and other all-you-can-eat miracles. (☎208-547-4575. Open summer M-Sa 11am-10pm; winter M-Th 11am-9pm, F-Sa 11am-10pm.) In the Enders Building is the **Geyser View Restaurant,** 76 S. Main St. The Geyser Burger ($7) and Geyser Chicken ($6) are sure bets, but interesting items like Cajun sausage pasta ($7) are also available. (☎208-547-4980. Steaks $10-15. Open M-Sa 6am-10pm, Su 7am-9pm.)

⚑ ACCOMMODATIONS. The 30 rooms of the **Enders Hotel,** in the Enders Building, 76 S. Main St., are small but share the antique loveliness of the building at large (and the hallways of the museum). The Anniversary and Honeymoon suites are perfect for the romantic pair—or the loner in need of opulence. The former contains the writing desk of a Confederate general, while the latter houses an original English bed from the 19th century. Both are ornate, even spectacular. (☎208-547-4980. All rates include $5 breakfast voucher good at the Geyser View Restaurant downstairs. Rooms $65-95; Anniversary Suite

$175; Honeymoon Suite $195.) For the more financially restrained, a handful of budget motels line 2nd S. Very well-priced rooms can be found at the **Caribou Lodge & Motel,** 110 W. 2nd South. (U.S. 30). There are a range of rooms, but even the smallest are comfortably arranged and paneled in light, cheery wood. Free coffee is available all morning. (☎208-547-3377. Reception 7am-10pm. Singles from $32; doubles $42.) The **JR Inn,** 179 W. 2nd South, has big rooms of standard budget-motel style, all clean and pleasantly furnished. (☎208-547-3366. Singles $42; doubles $52; triples $69.)

⚑ LEAVING SODA SPRINGS
Take **2nd South (U.S. 30)** west toward the next watery town, Lava Hot Springs.

THE ROAD TO LAVA HOT SPRINGS. From one set of springs to the next is an utterly empty stretch of U.S. 30; a few hills and the occasional cow are the standouts. The land suddenly soars spectacularly up on either side of the road as the route reaches Lava Hot Springs. Twenty-one miles past Soda Springs is a sign announcing the "world-class" hot springs of Idaho. Take the left here and suddenly you'll find yourself in the town.

LAVA HOT SPRINGS

Glittering, expensive, and fun, Lava Hot Springs embodies all the wonder and all the hustle of a resort city. The hot pools and the excitement of the river tubing course delight the hordes of tourists who come from all over the nation to experience the naturally heated waters.

(VITAL STATS)

Population: 520

Visitor Info: Bannock County Historical Center, 110 E. Main St. (☎208-776-5254). Open daily noon-5pm.

Internet Access: South Bannock Public Library, Lava Hot Springs Branch, 33 E. Main St. (☎208-776-5301). Open M and W 1-5pm, Tu and Th 1-6pm, Sa 10am-2pm.

Post Office: 45 Center St. (☎208-776-5680). Open M-F 9am-noon and 1-4:30pm. **Postal Code:** 83246.

⚑ GETTING AROUND. Lava Hot Springs is laid out along the **Portneuf River,** south of **U.S. 30.** Conveniently, most of the town's attractions lie along **Main St.,** which runs east-west through town. In a town of Lava Hot Springs's size, **parking** is rarely a problem; however, things can get crowded when summer visitors arrive.

◪ SIGHTS. The naturally heated waters (104-112 °F) of the **Lava Hot Springs,** 430 E. Main St., have been in use for centuries, long before the Europeans arrived. Once hailed for their curative powers, today there is no doubt that the springs have, at the very least, calming powers. The pools are set off the road in a pleasant and tree-strewn complex. (☎ 208-776-5221; www.lava-hotsprings.com. Open Apr.-Sept. daily 8am-11pm; Oct.-Mar. Su-Th 9am-10pm, F-Sa 9am-11pm. Day pass M-Th $5, ages 3-11 and seniors $4.50; F-Su $7/ $6.50. Single entry F-Su $5.50/$5.) Tubing is allowed on the Portneuf River. The access point is on the eastern end of town, behind the picnic pavilion. The stream runs swiftly under Main St.'s bridge and along the highway before reaching the dismount. Stands up and down Main St. compete to rent tubes and life jackets for a few dollars.

Some non-water-based entertainment can be found at **Baker Ranch Wagon Rides,** 11716 S. Dempsey Creek Rd., south from 4th St. A 40min. mountain wagon ride, powered by draft horses, breaks for a creek-side dinner before the evening return trip. The whole experience requires only about 3hr. (☎ 208-776-5684. Reservations required. Operates Memorial Day-Sept. $21, ages 4-13 $16.)

⛺ FOOD. Ye Ole Chuckwagon Restaurant, 211 E. Main St., has great hamburgers and sandwiches ($4-8) and a respectable array of vegetarian options ($3-5). The Old West motif is thorough, reaching even to the glasses, which are transparent cowboy boots. (☎ 208-776-5141. Entrees $7-15. Open daily 7am-midnight.) **Johnny's,** 78 E. Main St., rose literally from the ashes of the old Silver Grill Cafe to become the elegantly subdued restaurant it is now. Tempting desserts ($1.25-4.25) such as cheesecake and German chocolate cake round off the extensive menu. (☎ 208-776-5421. Open Su-Th 6:30am-9pm, F-Sa 6:30am-10pm.) Two other little shops branch from a single building, serving the casual snackers of Lava Hot Springs. The **Lava Java Coffee House,** 34 E. Main St., is a hip place with a list of coffees and teas for just $1-3.50. Cold drinks like iced coffees and smoothies are all $3-4. (☎ 208-317-8747. Open Su-F 8am-5pm, Sa 8am-8:30pm.) For ice cream, skip through the hallway to the **Riverwalk Ice Cream Shoppe,** where three-scoop cones are only

$3.50, as are banana splits. (☎ 208-776-5117. Open M-W 9am-7:30pm, Th 11am-9pm, F 11am-10:30pm, Sa 10am-10:30pm, Su noon-7:30pm.)

⛩ ACCOMMODATIONS. Most accommodations in Lava Hot Springs are on the expensive side, though a few budget rooms can be found with a bit of searching. The **Aura Soma Lava** complex, 97 N. 2nd East, is the pinnacle of lodgings in Lava Hot Springs. Its smaller motel rooms are only the beginning; there are also four cabins of various sizes and equipment spread throughout the complex, not to mention a private hot pool. The staff also offers massages. (☎ 208-776-5800 or 800-757-1233. Massages $35 per 30min., $60 per 1hr. Rooms $69, with hot tub $79; cabins $89-175.) A pleasant, if slightly humbler, stay can be had at the **Lava Spa Motel,** 359 E. Main St. This spot has a range of room sizes, some of which have hot tubs if you're willing to pay for them. (☎ 208-776-5589. Rooms in summer from $55; in winter from $50.) The **Home Hotel & Motel** and **Tumbling Waters Motel,** 306 E. Main St., jointly managed, have some budget options. Rooms in Tumbling Waters come with pool passes. (☎ 208-776-5507; www.homehotel.com. Rooms from $35.)

THE ROAD TO POCATELLO. From downtown Lava Hot Springs, take **Main St.** to **Center St.,** which leads back to **U.S. 30.** This drive will be relaxing, even if the hot springs weren't; it's a completely uneventful jaunt through a mountain saddle, only about 30 mi. long. Twelve miles out of Lava Hot Springs, U.S. 30 meets **I-15;** take I-15 north for another 18 mi.

⛰ APPROACHING POCATELLO
Exits 67 through 71 from **I-15** all lead into Pocatello and its northern neighbor, Chubbuck. Area attractions are reached most easily via Exit 67, which blends conveniently into the major thoroughfare of **5th Ave.** at the southern tip of the city.

POCATELLO

A giant by mountain area standards, Pocatello draws students and thrill-seekers from all over eastern Idaho and western Wyoming, as well as vacationers from all points who come to see the Hot Springs and Yellowstone Park. This endless flux of visitors, fused with the student population of Idaho State Univer-

OREGON TRAIL MAP #7   FROM MAP #6

sity, gives Pocatello a surprisingly diverse and happening feel for a small city in the heart of the rural potato state.

> **VITAL STATS**
>
> **Population:** 51,000
>
> **Visitor Info: Tourist Information Center,** 2695 S. 5th St. (☎208-233-7333). Open summer M-F 9am-6pm, Sa-Su 10am-4pm; winter M-F 10am-4pm. **Greater Pocatello Chamber of Commerce,** 343 W. Center St. (☎208-233-1525; www.pocatelloidaho.com). Open M-F 8am-5pm.
>
> **Internet Access: Marshall Public Library,** 113 S. Garfield Ave. (☎208-232-1263). Open M-Th 9am-9pm, F-Sa 9am-6pm.
>
> **Post Office:** 730 E. Clark St. (☎208-785-6579), off 5th Ave. Open M-F 8am-5:30pm, Sa 10:30am-2:30pm. **Postal Code:** 83204.

GETTING AROUND

Pocatello is long and narrow, running from the southeast to the northwest in a band between the **Portneuf River** and **I-15.** At the southeast end is **Ross Park,** home to a number of Potacello's attractions. This part of the city is dominated by **5th Ave.,** which runs past restaurants and Idaho State University. Most establishment have lots, so **parking** in the area is easy. Around the center of the city, 5th Ave. ends, running into busy **Yellowstone Ave.** The **Historic Old Town** area, Pocatello's downtown, is south of the train tracks parallel to 5th Ave. **Benton St.** is the most direct route from 5th Ave. to downtown; **Center St.** is larger, but runs one way *from* downtown to 5th Ave. This particular region is small and easily traversed by foot. North of the Pocatello is the suburb of **Chubbuck;** the two are linked by Yellowstone Ave. Another cluster of hotels and restaurants is gathered on Chubbuck's southern border, where **I-86** divides the two cities.

SIGHTS

Lovely greenery and an aquatic center make for good summer lazing at **Ross Park,** at the south end of 5th Ave., which also features three major attractions. Historic Fort Hall became part of reservation territory in the 1860s, so enthusiasts built a full reproduction in Pocatello, the **Fort Hall Replica.** The replica buildings

OREGON TRAIL

are furnished to recall frontier life, though two of the largest rooms house mini-museums on pioneer and Native American life in the area. (☎208-234-1795. Open Memorial Day-Labor Day daily 10am-6pm; mid-April to Memorial Day and Sept. Tu-Sa 10am-2pm. $1.50, ages 6-11 and seniors $1.25.) Next door, the **Bannock County Historical Museum,** 3000 Alvord Loop, in Upper Ross Park, displays relics from Pocatello's past. The medicinal room is especially interesting, with its jars of Dragon's Blood and Ethereal Oil—no further explanation offered by the yellowed labels. (☎208-233-0434. Open Memorial Day-Labor Day daily 10am-6pm; Labor Day-Memorial Day Tu-Sa 10am-2pm. $1, children $0.50.) Only North American wildlife is kept at the **Pocatello Zoo,** 2900 S. 2nd St., on the edge of Ross Park, but the lack of lions isn't a serious loss: bighorn sheep, grizzly bears, coyotes, and cougars still roam the cages. One vast and impressive enclosure contains elk, buffalo, and pronghorn antelope in natural habitats. Keep an eye out for the friendly marmot, who is allowed to roam the grounds freely. (☎208-234-6196. Open Apr. to mid-June daily 9am-5pm; mid-June to Labor Day daily 10am-5pm; Labor Day-Oct. Sa-Su 10am-4pm. $2.50, seniors $2, ages 6-11 $1.50, ages 3-5 $0.75.)

Larger, scarier, but considerably more extinct fauna can be visited at the impressive **Idaho Museum of Natural History,** on the Idaho State campus at the intersection of 5th Ave. and Dillon St. The skeleton of a monstrous *Bison latifrons* is the museum's main prize, the 8 ft. horns being the largest of any bison in history. The new "Dinosaur Times" exhibit has partial remains and full murals, though the most interesting piece may be the tooth whorls of an ancient shark. (☎208-282-3317; http://imnh.isu.edu. Open Memorial Day-Labor Day M 4-8pm, Tu-F 10am-4pm, Sa noon-4pm; Labor Day-Memorial Day Tu-Sa until 3pm. $5, seniors $4, students $3, ages 4-11 $2.) The Historic Preservation Commission has a self-guided walking tour of the **Downtown Historic District,** focusing on the architecture and history behind the late 19th- and early 20th-century buildings; pick up a pamphlet at the Chamber of Commerce. The downtown area is also a great place for exploring—herbalists, record stores, skate shops and other hole-in-the-wall establishments abound.

◪🏠 FOOD & ACCOMMODATIONS

Potacello's best restaurants are scattered all over town. Vine-covered **Buddy's,** 626 E. Lewis St., just north of 5th Ave. on the edge of the Idaho State campus, serves classic Italian meals to a family crowd and a few college regulars. (☎208-233-117. Pasta $14-16. Pizza and calzones from $10. Open M-Sa 11am-midnight.) **Tastee Treat,** 1555 S. 5th Ave., is the proud home of the spaceburger, the sea-space burger, and the Tom burger, offering all the delicious greasiness of classic road fare without the production line taste and character of actual fast food. The ice cream alone draws in hordes of customers, and why not, at just $1.25 for the largest size? (Hamburgers under $3. Open M-Th 11am-10pm, F-Sa 11am-11pm.) Class exudes from the brick walls of the **The Continental Bistro,** 140 S. Main St., downtown. The menu also has an upscale slant; sandwiches ($7-9) include crab and avocado, while the pastas ($7.50-9) feature Thai shrimp curry. (☎208-233-4433. Open M-Sa 11am-10pm.) At the **Shanghai Cafe,** 247 E. Center St., patrons dine on delicious lunch specials beneath romantic painted lanterns. The cafe mixes the low price of some Chinese food dives with the lovely interior of a high-end restaurant. (☎208-233-2036. Combination plates $5.50-6.50. Weekday lunch specials $4. Appetizers $4-6. Entrees $6.50-9. Open M and W-Th 11:30am-10pm, F 11:30am-midnight, Sa 2:30pm-midnight, Su 2:30-9pm.)

With almost nothing to choose from but chain hotels near the highway exits, the budget traveler would be doomed to an unhappy fate were it not for the **Thunderbird Motel,** 1415 S. 5th Ave., which consists, luckily, of many buildings and many clean, spare rooms. (☎208-232-6330. Laundry. Singles $38; doubles $44.)

▣ NIGHTLIFE

There's no cohesive feel to Pocatello nightlife, but that just means there are more ways to party. **Club Charleys,** 331 E. Center St., puts resident band Charleys Angels on the stage the fourth weekend of every month, while hip-hop DJs run things the rest of the time. (☎208-232-9606. Dancing F-Sa. Open M-Sa 5pm-2am, Su 7pm-2am.) **5 Mile Inn,** 4828 Yellowstone Ave., in Chubbuck, is a strictly country den. Eastern-types can experience the full power of a Western hoe-down. (☎208-237-9950 Live music F-Sa 9pm-1am. Food specials nightly. Open daily 11am-2am. Kitchen closes M-Th 10pm.) The **First National Bar,** 232 W. Center St., becomes a house of blues in the downtown area when there's someone around to play. (☎208-233-1516. Cover $5 or less. Open M-Sa 11am-2am, Su noon-6pm.)

LEAVING POCATELLO

From the southern half of the city, the easiest escape is to take **5th St.** south to the junction with **I-15** and head north.

THE ROAD TO CRATERS OF THE MOON. It's almost 80 mi. to Arco, and another 17 to the Craters Monument. The first 21 mi. are fairly boring interstate travel, passing through the **Ft. Hall Reservation.** After this stretch is past, take Exit 93 to **U.S. 26 West.** Food and lodging for those in need can be found in **Blackfoot.** The next bit of road is strangely attractive; the land is remarkably flat, punctuated only by isolated, dome-like hills. Winds can tear across the flatlands, buffeting smaller cars. Thirty-five miles of this lead to the convergence of **U.S. 20** and U.S. 26. Follow them west, crossing the mournfully named Big Lost River. From the bridge, it is 16 mi. to Arco. U.S. 20/26 becomes Front St., then makes a 90° turn, becoming **Grand Ave.** in Arco. Continue about 17 mi. to the entrance to the park.

CRATERS OF THE MOON

Millennia-old volcanic activity left a bizarre mark upon central Idaho. An early visitor to the lava fields declared them "the strangest 75 sq. mi. on the North American continent." This lunar-like landscape of ashy plains and twisted rock is now the Craters of the Moon National Monument. Motels and food aren't available in the park, so those looking for a little more comfort or just some hiking supplies will want to visit the nearby city of Arco, the first American city to be lit by nuclear power.

GETTING AROUND

Craters of the Moon is divided into three areas. The first and smallest is the **Developed Area,** where paved roads lead past several of the more impressive craters, and through some of the more spectacularly grotesque formation clusters. The second region is the **Wilderness Area,** where only a

---

VITAL STATS

Area: 715,000 acres

Visitor Info: Craters of the Moon Visitors Center, (☎208-527-3257), just inside the park. Open daily Memorial Day-Labor Day 8am-6pm; Labor Day-Memorial Day 8am-4:30pm. **Arco Chamber of Commerce,** 159 N. Idaho St. (☎208-527-8977). Open M-F 8am-5pm.

Gateway Town: Arco

Fees: Weekly pass $5 per car.

---

few dirt paths disturb the natural order. The majority of the park is dominated by the **Backcountry Area;** crossed by rough, unmaintained roads, scorched in the summer and snowed under in the winter, the backcountry is not hospitable to the average driver and vehicle. The only access to the park is about 17 mi. west of Arco on **U.S. 20/26.** Immediately inside is the **Visitors Center.** Displays on the volcanic history of the area and the sparse wildlife population serve as a good launch to any exploration. Maps of the park can be obtained here. Anyone planning to camp in the Wilderness Area should obtain a free backcountry permit.

Arco, home to the nearest food and accommodations, is just 17 mi. east on U.S. 20/26, and the easy driving in this area means that less than 20min. separate city and park. In Arco, most services are located right on the highway, which takes the names of **Grand Ave.** and **Front St.** within city limits. Note that the highway takes a 90° turn in the middle of town; watch the signs carefully.

SIGHTS

The easiest way to visit the attractions of the developed portions of the park is to follow the 7 mi. loop road, which departs from the Visitors Center and winds past many of the park's most spectacular sights. Each has its own parking lot, with short trails leading through each area. The **North Crater Flow** is a lumpy field of cooled lava which has taken on fantastic shapes. The smooth (pahoehoe) and rough (aa) lavas produce an unlikely variety of forms. The path here is paved, mostly flat, and only a quarter-mile long. Just a few yards down is the **North Crater Trail,** a steep, rocky path that leads to a volcanic vent. The full trail is 1½ mi. in each direction; the vent, however, is only half a mile up the trail. Next along the loop road is **Devil's Orchard.** The infernal name refers to the sharp chunks of a shattered volcano that litter the area, as well as the sharp clusters of Witch's

Broom which have grown upon the gnarled trees. The trail through the orchard is a half-mile loop of broad, flat sidewalk. At **Inferno Cone,** a tall hill of black cinder overlooks many volcanic miles from the edge of the loop road. The hike up is short but extremely steep, and the path is unpaved. The wind-raked crown is an achievement, commanding the surrounding wasteland from high above.

Some of the most popular attractions of the monument are the caves of the **Blue Dragon Flow.** These are actually lava tubes, tunnels that formed when rivers of molten rock hardened on the surface. The four open caves are completely wild, with no artificial lighting, pathways, or guides. Three of them require flashlights to explore fully. **Dewdrop Cave** is actually just a deep hole scraped into the earth. Explorers are allowed to enter without a flashlight. The largest of the caves is **Indian Tunnel,** whose multiple roof openings let in a lot of light; most of it, as a result, can be seen without a flashlight. Exploring **Beauty Cave,** on the other hand, requires light. Spelunkers will probably enjoy **Boy Scout Cave** the most of all; after you round a bend, the light gives out entirely, while the ceiling and the floor bend to meet each other. Reaching the end requires a bright light and a bent back. ($0.50 cave guides available from a box at the start of the ½ mi. caves trail.)

Between Inferno Cone and the caves is a side road breaking off of the main loop, leading to the Tree Molds trailhead. From here the **Wilderness Trail** winds into the hills and craters south of the developed area. Though not very steep, this trail is long (about 5½ mi. into the wilderness before petering out), often difficult to follow through the sage brush, and brutally exposed to the sun. Hikers wishing to follow this trail to **Echo Crater** (about 4 mi. away) and beyond should wear hiking shoes and carry ample sunscreen and water.

FOOD

Food in the area is largely monopolized by the city of Arco. In addition to restaurants, Arco has a few grocery stores where water and other goods can be bought before any long term wilderness expeditions. With a big green rocking chair out front, **Pickle's Place,** 440 S. Front St., is easy to identify. Home of the atomic burger ($4-5), Pickle's also dishes out classic breakfasts ($4-5) in plentiful portions. (☎208-527-9944. Open daily June-Aug. 6am-11pm; Sept.-May 6am-10pm.) Forego the pizza; the monster sandwiches at the **Deli Sandwich**

Shop, 119 Grand Ave., are a fine deal. Twenty options range in size from 4 in. ($2.90) to 24 in. ($11.90). Yard long (and larger) giants can be made upon request. (☎208-527-3757. Open daily 8am-8pm.) Chicken and ribs are grilling in the backyard at **Grandpa's Southern Bar-B-Q,** 434 W. Grand Ave. Grab a seat on the front porch for a killer pork sandwich ($5) and small-town hospitality. (☎208-527-3362. Dinners $7-13. Open summer daily 11am-8pm; winter Th-Sa 11am-8pm.)

ACCOMMODATIONS

Right next to the Visitors Center is a 50-site campground, accommodating tents and RVs. The grounds have toilets, water and grills. A tip for tent campers: site #13 is considered one of the best, as it is private and nicely shielded from the wind. ($10 per car. No hookups.) A great adventurous camping opportunity (not to mention a free night's stay) is available in the Wilderness Area. The required backcountry pass is free and available at the Visitors Center. Campsites in the Wilderness Area are completely primitive and unmarked; it is recommended that each camper bring a gallon of water for each day spent there.

Like meals, beds and roofs aren't available in the park, but in nearby Arco. Don't let the rather dilapidated sign fool you; the **Arco Inn Motel,** 540 W. Grand Ave., is a great place to stay. The rooms sparkle with cleanliness, and at 300 sq. ft., even the singles are huge. (☎208-527-3100. Singles $34; doubles $40.) The **D-K Motel,** 316 S. Front St., offers rooms ranging from family rooms to economy singles, all comfortable and equipped with microwaves, refrigerators, and coffeemakers. (☎208-527-8282. Singles $33; doubles from $47.) The rooms are small but pleasant at the **Lost River Motel,** 405 Highway Dr., off Front St. near the east edge of town. The refrigerators and microwaves add comfort, as do the deep recliners and motel hot tub. (☎208-527-3600. Reception daily 8am-11pm. Rooms from $35.)

LEAVING CRATERS OF THE MOON
There is only one road in and out; return to the Visitors Center and **U.S. 20/26.** Head west to reach Twin Falls.

THE ROAD TO TWIN FALLS

Nearly 100 mi. long, this stretch of road is punctuated by a few small towns. Immediately after leaving the Craters of the Moon National Monument, the road becomes steep, winding, and edged by cliffs, so expect fluctuating speed limits. This settles down about 15 mi. later, when the lava fields are left behind. Twenty-four miles beyond the monument's exit is **Carey,** a tiny place. From here, the most direct route to Twin Falls is to continue south on U.S. 26, but the Shoshone Ice Caves and several other attractions lie north along U.S. 20 and Rte. 75. From Carey, head west on **U.S. 20,** passing through another micro-town, **Picabo.** Twenty miles after turning onto U.S. 20, turn south on **Rte. 75,** passing through **Shoshone** on the way to Twin Falls.

👁 SHOSHONE ICE CAVES   1561 Rte. 75
12 mi. south of the junction with U.S. 20.

Like Minnetonka Cave, the Ice Caves are kept naturally cool—these at a freezing 26-32°F. Unlike Minnetonka, however, the Ice Caves have fallen prey to tourist baiting; the entrance is flanked by garish statues of Native Americans and dinosaurs, and the grounds are dominated by a gift shop/antique store. The cave itself is 1700 ft. long and drops down 125 ft. total, an impressive geological formation. Tours require about 45min. and depart every hr. in the morning and evening, and every 30min. in the afternoon. (☎208-886-2058. Open daily 8am-8pm. Tours daily from 9am; last tour 7pm. $6, seniors $5.50, ages 5-14 $3.75.)

🍴 MANHATTAN CAFE
Just off Rte. 75 in Shoshone, 17 mi. south of the caves.

The Manhattan Cafe is a fantastic place for breakfast. In addition to a page-long list of pancakes, sausages and omelettes, there's the Everyday Special—sausage or bacon, two eggs, and unlimited pancakes for $4.75. Lunch options run from inexpensive steaks ($7-11) to Chinese noodles ($7) to the Manhattan Mega Meal, a mere pound of beef. Also note the glory of the old but fully-functional Ms. Pac-Man machine. (☎208-886-2142. Open M-Th 6am-10pm, F-Sa 6am-10:30pm, Su 6am-10pm.)

🔺 APPROACHING TWIN FALLS
From Shoshone, continue south via **U.S. 93.** It is 23 mi. to the Snake River and Twin Falls. Stay on U.S. 93 past the junction with I-84. The highway will cross the long **Perrine Bridge,** spanning the deep blue gash of the **Snake River Canyon.** As soon as the you cross the bridge, you'll be in Twin Falls.

TWIN FALLS

Twin Falls is like wherever you're from, only more so. The Chili's is at the mall across the street from The Outback Steakhouse, a block north of Barnes & Noble, which has a Starbucks inside. Target is next to OfficeMax, behind Arby's and Applebee's. In the first mile of Twin Falls, there is a Sonic Burger, two McDonald's, three Subways, and a Burger King. Beyond the prepackaged glow, however, there lies a quiet and charming city that offers easy access to the outdoors; whitewater rafting trips run from Centennial Park, bike and running trails wend along the gorge, and waterfalls shine up and down the river.

VITAL STATS

Population: 35,000

Visitor Info: Visitor Center, 858 Blue Lakes Blvd. N. (☎208-733-9458), just across the bridge. Open Mar.-Oct. daily 9am-5pm.

Internet Access: Cyber Center, 1180 Blue Lakes Blvd. N. (☎208-734-1300). High-speed Internet access with a friendly and knowledgeable staff and snack bar. $5.50 per hr. Open M-Th 8am-7pm, F-Sa 8am-10pm.

Post Office: 253 2nd Ave. West. (☎800-275-8777), right off of Shoshone St. (Rte. 74) from U.S. 93. Open M-Sa 9am-5pm. **Postal Code:** 83301.

🖹 **GETTING AROUND.** U.S. 93 joins up with U.S. 30 outside Twin Falls, becoming **Addison Ave.** U.S. 30 splits off, heading southeast through downtown and eventually becoming **Kimberly Rd.,** while U.S. 93 goes on for a few blocks, takes a left, becoming **Blue Lakes Blvd. N.** Newer businesses and developments lie along Blue Lakes Blvd., while older, privately run eateries and accommodations tend to sit back on Kimberly Rd. The town's third main thoroughfare, **Shoshone St.** (Rte. 74), runs downtown diagonally southwest from the intersection of Blue Lakes and Addison.

Downtown Twin Falls is organized in a logical numbered grid—just not any logic you're familiar with. **Main Ave.** and **Shoshone St.** intersect, forming an X by which all of downtown is oriented. Avenues run northwest-southeast, numbered in both directions by their distance from Main Ave.; streets run northeast-southwest, numbered relative to Shoshone St. Both avenues and streets can be marked with any of the cardinal directions.

Designation changes when the street or avenue crosses either of the two main roads. Thus, 3rd St. South does not become 3rd St. North, but 3rd St. East as it crosses Main St., while, four blocks northwest, 3rd St. West becomes 3rd St. North.

◢ SIGHTS. Twin Falls has a variety of attractions for the outdoorsman, outdoorswoman, and outdoorschild in all of us. Closest to the city proper are the mighty **Shoshone Falls**—the "Niagara of the West" which are actually 50 ft. longer than the real thing. The falls are best viewed in the spring, when snowmelt swells the Snake River and the flow has not yet been diverted to provide summertime irrigation and power. (Follow Blue Lakes Blvd. to the major intersection with Falls Ave., head east on Falls Ave., and take a left onto 3300 East Rd. after 3 mi. ☎ 208-736-2265. Open daily 7am-10pm. $3 per car.) Nearby is **Twin Falls.** The title is an anachronism now, as one of the falls has vanished in the name of electric power. The other rages onward, though, and in the summer can be wider and wilder than Shoshone Falls. (From Falls Ave., head east for a little under 2 mi. and turn left on 3500 East Rd. ☎ 208-736-2265. Open daily 8am-dusk. Free.)

Snake River Canyon, north of town, is a giant hole in the earth. The **I.B. Perrine Bridge,** a $10 million effort completed in 1976, is the longest span bridge in the west. From it, Snake River Canyon displays its impressive 500 ft. drop to the golf courses below. **Centennial Waterfront Park,** on the south rim next to the Visitor Center, half a mile west of the bridge, offers impressive views and enough historical information to complement any picnic. If you'd like to experience the canyon from a slightly different angle, **Idaho Guide Service,** 563 Trotter Dr. (☎ 888-734-3246; www.idahoguideservice.com.), off of Elizabeth Blvd. from Blue Lakes, runs a variety of water tours, from 3hr. motor boat tours to five-day whitewater rafting adventures. If you'd rather get high than wet, **Reeder Flying Service,** 644 Airport Loop (☎ 208-733-5920), west of U.S. 93 on the north rim of the canyon, flies helicopter tours of the canyon and the falls for as low as $25 per person.

The **Herrett Center for Arts and Science,** at the College of Southern Idaho North Entrance, just off of North College Rd. from Blue Lakes Blvd., is home to the **Faulkner Planetarium,** considered to be one of the best in the world. The Herrett Center also features exhibits on stone tools, contemporary art, and the ecology of rainforests, among

THE LOCAL STORY

HOW CAN IT FEEL SO GOOD TO BE SO EVEL?

On September 8th, 1974, daredevil Evel Knievel put Twin Falls on the map by attempting to jump the Snake River Canyon on a rocket-powered motorcycle. To the astonishment of those with no knowledge of physics, he failed.

A crowd of over 30,000 packed the canyon for days prior to the event in a makeshift tent city, and millions of Americans tuned their TV sets to see just how far a man can fly--or fall. As Knievel's rocket-powered Harley hit the massive dirt ramp at the edge of the south rim, his parachute prematurely deployed, setting him down comfortably at the bottom of the canyon.

While the event constituted little more than a national footnote, Twin Falls tells a different story. According to residents watching the jump, Knievel's fans destroyed sections of the canyon park, intentionally setting fire to picnic tables and restrooms, costing the town and damaging the canyon environment.

Whatever the true story is, "Evel Knievel's In-Famous Leap," as locals remember it, remains a defining event in the history of Twin Falls. The dirt ramp Knievel used is still visible to the east of Blue Lakes Blvd. on the south rim.

other things. (☎ 208-733-9554, ext. 2655; www.csi.edu/Support/Museum/Faulkner/welcome.html. Open in summer Su and Tu-Sa 1-9pm; reduced winter hours. Free. Planetarium shows $4.) **Historic Old Town** celebrated its 100th year in 2004. The downtown area sports the lovely **City Park,** which hosts free concerts each Thursday night in summer at the Bandshell.

≣🛈 FOOD & ACCOMMODATIONS. Chain restaurants with glossy menus and perky waitstaff line **Blue Lakes Blvd.** on the north side of town, but smaller operations can be found away from the highway. Of these, **The Depot Grill,** 545 Shoshone St. South, has drawn the local crowd since 1927 with its classic diner decor and smorgasbord lunches. (☎ 208-733-0710. Sandwiches $2-4. Burgers $3-5. Seafood $7-10. Steaks $9-15. Open 24hr., except Su night.) At **Crowley's Soda Fountain,** 144 S. Main Ave., thirsty patrons choose from malts and shakes ($2-5), smoothies ($3), Italian sodas ($3) and phosphates ($1-2). Sandwiches ($2-6) and wraps ($6.25) make for light meals. (☎ 208-733-1041. Open M-Sa 10am-5pm.)

Similarly, Blue Lakes Blvd. also has an abundance of motels. The **Old Towne Lodge,** 248 2nd Ave. West, a few blocks off Addison Ave., offers large, bright rooms at some of the best rates in town. (☎ 208-733-5630. Singles $30; doubles $35.) Another fine option is **El Rancho Motel,** 380 W. Addison Ave. Impossible to miss with its flashing tri-tone neon sign, El Rancho has a handful of clean rooms, complete with refrigerator, microwave, and coffee maker. (☎ 208-733-4021. Singles $32; doubles $37.) The **Monetery Motor Inn,** 433 W. Addison Ave., has nice rooms and nicer bathrooms; the latter are dazzling white and have the blessing of a full tub. (☎ 208-733-5151. Microwaves and refrigerators. Singles $35-40; doubles $45-55.)

🌄 LEAVING TWIN FALLS
Addison Ave. runs west out of town, becoming **U.S. 30.** This portion of the highway is known as the **Thousand Springs Scenic Byway.**

THOUSAND SPRINGS SCENIC BYWAY

The verdant roads of this scenic byway run from Twin Falls to their terminus in the sweetly named town of Bliss. The entire trip is scarcely over 40 mi., but there is a great deal to see, do, and raft down in that distance. Almost immediately after leaving Twin Falls the road sweeps past **Filer,** and,

after 12 mi., enters the willowy town of **Buhl.** With the exception of the mountain passes, this is some of the first territory to support groves of full-sized trees in many, many miles.

 From Buhl, a detour (17 mi. each way) leads to the ridiculous geological formation of **Balanced Rock,** a 40 ft. wide stone supported on a natural pillar just 3 ft. across. In the center of Buhl, turn left onto Main St., following it for 1 mi. Take a right at the end, then an immediate left, following the signs. Continue along for 4 mi., then bear right at the fork. The road passes through farmland, plummeting suddenly into a gorge. When it re-emerges, the unlikely stone will be above the road to the right.

Some 15 mi. beyond Buhl, the highway returns to Snake River and passes the **Thousand Springs.** Many white waterfalls pour from the green-bearded cliffs across the river; the sight feels more Amazonian than Idahonian. There are no overlooks or side roads; have cameras at the ready.

Two miles past this lush terrain, true fossil enthusiasts can make a detour into the dry and dusty fossil cliffs of the region. The well-marked drive to the **Hagerman Fossil Beds National Monument** off U.S. 30 is less than 3 mi., ending at the Snake River Overlook. The boardwalk allows visitors to peer across the river to the stratified rock where fossils were once mined. Across the street is the start of the 3 mi. **Emigrant Trail,** a narrow and grassy footpath that follows the Oregon Trail very closely, even passing some ruts near the end. The trail ends up the road at the Oregon Trail lookout, so be prepared to have someone pick you up, or to walk back. Long pants are also advised, because even if the rattlesnakes and scorpions aren't looking for trouble, the deer ticks probably are.

HAGERMAN

Four miles farther west on U.S. 30 is Hagerman itself, and the **Hagerman Fossil Beds National Monument Visitor Center,** 221 N. Front St. (U.S. 30). The Visitors Center has little to offer, but if you want to see an example of something pulled out of the fossil beds, stop by and see the Hagerman horse skeletons. Twenty full skeletons were found in the area, and are believed to have been a form of North American zebra.

If you're looking for grub, try the **Snake River Grill,** 611 Frogs Landing. Owner Kirt Marten once hosted the television show *Cooking on the Wild Side,* now bringing his skill to this restaurant. Sandwiches ($7-8) and entrees ($13-20) feature locally caught fish like sturgeon and catfish, along with the usual chicken fried steak and ribs. However, how can you say no to alligator? (☎208-837-6227. Open M-Th 7am-9pm, F-Sa 7am-9:30pm, Su 7am-9pm.) For some cheaper options, there is **Larry & Mary's Restaurant,** 141 State St. The Chili Burger ($6.25) is a delicious house specialty. (☎208-837-6475. Open Su 5am-3pm, Tu-Sa 5am-8:30pm.) One of the few lodging options along the way is the **Hagerman Valley Inn,** 661 Frogs Landing, where pleasant rooms include microwaves and refrigerators and are the same price for one person or 10. (☎208-837-6196. Rooms $53.)

DETOUR: MALAD GORGE STATE PARK
Just north of Hagerman on U.S. 30, turn right at the large green sign beside an otherwise unlabeled road reading "Billingsley Creek Lounge and Retreat." 2½ mi. after leaving the highway, take a left onto Ritchie Rd.; this leads to Malad Gorge State Park.

This park can be viewed almost entirely by driving around its 3 mi. road. Built around the deep and narrow cleft of the Malad Gorge, this park is stunning—unfortunately, though, it runs right under the interstate. The main attraction is **Devil's Washbowl,** a green pool below the waterfall that is carving the gorge out of the rock. The spot can be viewed from an bridge spanning the gorge; from there, it is possible to hike right along the edge, among the many birds that flit over and into the cleft. (☎208-837-4505. Open daily 7am-10pm. $4 per vehicle.)

BLISS. Less than 8 mi. along U.S. 30 from Hagerman, Bliss is the last stop on the Thousand Springs Byway, the gateway back to the interstate. Those looking to sleep or eat before returning to the 75 mph speedway have a final handful of options here. The **Oxbow Restaurant,** Main St., is a great roadtripper spot right off the highway. Breakfasts feature the pleasing oddity of the Pancake Sandwich ($5.50), while lunches include burgers and sandwiches. (☎208-352-4250. Lunch $5-7. Dinner $7-9. Open 24hr.) The **Amber Inn Motel,** at the junction of I-84 and U.S. 30, has simple but spacious and pretty bedrooms along indoor hallways. The prices are also quite attractive. (☎208-352-4441. Singles $32; doubles $37.)

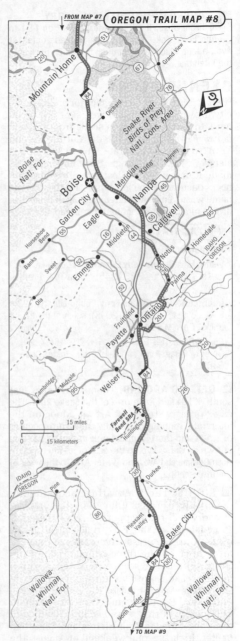

OREGON TRAIL MAP #8

FROM MAP #7

TO MAP #9

APPROACHING GLENNS FERRY
From Bliss, it's just under 20 mi. on **I-84** to Glenns Ferry. Take Exit 121, which feeds onto **1st Ave.,** a loop which leads through town then back onto the interstate.

GLENNS FERRY

Glenns Ferry is strangely quiet for an interstate city. Down on the Snake River, slow and broad here, the town feels like a scene from *Huckleberry Finn*—or from the days of the Oregon Trail, to be more accurate. The river is not as sleepy as it looks, though. Swift undercurrents made it one of the hardest river crossings pioneers once faced; the ferry that gave the town its name wasn't built until after the golden spike was driven into the intercontinental railroad.

(VITAL STATS)

Population: 1600

Visitor Info: Glenns Ferry Chamber of Commerce, 7 E. 1st Ave. (☎208-366-7345). Open Tu-F 11am-4pm.

Internet Access: Glenns Ferry Public Library, 298 S. Lincoln St. (☎208-366-2045), south of the train tracks. Open M-Sa 1-5pm.

Post Office: 108 E. 2nd Ave. (☎208-366-7329). Open M-F 8am-1pm and 2-4:30pm. **Postal Code:** 83623.

GETTING AROUND. Glenns Ferry lies just south of **I-84** and just north of the **Snake River.** The city's primary street, **1st Ave.,** is a loop off the interstate, running diagonally through the center of town and then joining back up with I-84. It is known as E. 1st Ave. to the east of its intersection with **Commercial Ave.** and W. 1st Ave. to the west of the intersection.

SIGHTS. The frustrating, occasionally deadly river crossing faced by the original Oregon Trail roadtrippers is remembered at **Three Island Crossing Park,** right on the banks of the ford. The grassy riverbanks of the park look down on the three islands rising from the Snake River where it widens, which helped make it possible for pioneers to ford the water. Also of aid to the pioneers were Shoshone, Bannock, and Paiute tribesmen. The history of this relationship is detailed in the park's **Oregon Trail History and Education Center.** In the second weekend of August, the crossing is recreated; a column of Native Americans, pioneers, horses, and wagons brave the currents. (Take Commercial Ave. south from 1st Ave. and across the train tracks, turning left onto Madison when Commercial Ave. ends. The park is a short distance down the road, on the left. ☎208-366-2394. $4 per car. Center open daily 9am-4pm. Free. Recreation festival $7. RV sites available; inquire at center.)

FOOD & ACCOMMODATIONS. Dining is limited in the city, but what there is won't disappoint. Right on the banks of the Snake River is the **Carmela Restaurant,** 1289 Madison Ave., easily recognized by the godzilla-sized quail casting its shadow on the driveway. The restaurant serves pastas, steaks and seafood, and the vineyards outside have produced 10 of their own wines ($4-7). The salads ($8-10) are also excellent. (☎208-366-2313. Appetizers $2-9. Entrees $13-21. Open summer M-Sa 11am-9pm, Su 10am-8pm; winter M-F 11am-8pm, Sa-Su 11am-9pm.) **Hanson's Cafe,** 201 E. 1st Ave., serves the enormous 1 lb. Grande Rancher ($8). (☎208-366-9983. Sandwiches $3-6. Open summer M-Th 7am-10pm, F-Sa 7am-11pm, Su 8am-3pm; winter M-Sa closes 1hr. earlier.)

Glenns Ferry has a handful of motels located conveniently along the 1st Ave. loop. These lodgings include a pleasant (and pleasantly inexpensive) B&B, **The Great Basin Bed and Breakfast,** 265 E. 1st Ave. There are four rooms, three of which share a bathroom. All have their own unorthodox style; one is dedicated to the unlikely hero of Kitty Wilkins, self-declared Queen of Horses. (☎208-366-7124. Rooms from $55, with bath from $65.) **Hanson's Hotel,** 201 E. 1st St., is hard to spot, hidden behind trees and the Hanson's Cafe. It's worth finding though, with eight rooms ringing a garden. All rooms include refrigerators. (☎208-366-2587. Singles $35; $5 per additional person.) The cheapest stay in town is at the **Redford Motel,** 97 N. Elmore Ave., at the corner of 1st Ave., where rooms are clean, if spare. All rooms have refrigerators. (☎208-366-2421. Singles $30; doubles $40.)

APPROACHING MOUNTAIN HOME
From downtown Glenns Ferry, continue west along **1st Ave.** until it rejoins **I-84.** Head west for 25 mi. to Mountain Home. Take Exit 95 from I-84; this lets onto **American Legion Blvd.,** which passes directly into the downtown area.

MOUNTAIN HOME

Up in the high deserts, Mountain Home lives symbiotically with the Mountain Home Air Force Base. Jets rip over the borderlands, where training exercises and battle lab tests are performed. Though this will excite aviators and conspiracy theorists, the base is largely closed for security reasons, and the main attraction around the city is the nearby state park, which offers activities ranging from sand skiing to desert stargazing.

(VITAL STATS)

Population: 11,000

Visitor Info: Desert Mountain Visitor Center, 2900 American Legion Blvd. (☎208-587-4464), off I-84 Exit 95. Open summer daily 9am-5pm. **Mountain Home Chamber of Commerce,** 205 N. 3rd East (☎208-587-4334). Open M-F 9am-5pm.

Internet Access: Mountain Home Public Library, 790 N. 10th East (☎208-587-4716; www.mhlibrary.org). Open M-F 10am-7pm, Sa 9am-5pm.

Post Office: 350 N. 3rd East (☎208-587-1413). Open M-F 8:30am-5pm, Sa 9:30-11:30am. **Postal Code:** 83647.

GETTING AROUND. Mountain Home's two primary roads are **American Legion Blvd.**, which runs from **I-84** westward into the center of town, and **Main St.**, which runs southeast-northwest, meeting American Legion Blvd. at a T-junction in the middle of town. The streets around the intersection follow a system: the first direction indicates the direction of the street, while the second number gives what half of the street you're on.

OUTDOOR ACTIVITIES. The **Bruneau Dunes State Park** is Mountain Home's center for recreation. Two large sand dunes spread over 600 acres of the park; at 470 ft., the larger of the two is the tallest in North America. The 15,000-year-old dunes can be played upon and, when the fall weather cools them, skied down. The natural but only 50-year-old lakes at their base support bass and bluegill; fishing is allowed. Clear desert nights leave the stars intensely bright and staggeringly numerous. They can be seen lying on your back—or through the public observatory built beneath the dunes. The telescope, named **Obsession,** is no backyard kit, but a 25 in. automated piece of sophisticated optical machinery. **Camping,** both tent and RV, is allowed in a range of sites across the park. (Fol-

low Main St. south from American Legion Blvd., merging into Rte. 51. After 14 mi., take a left onto Rte. 78; 2 mi. down that road is the turn-off for the park. ☎208-366-7919. Park gates open 7am-10pm. Visitors Center open daily 8am-4:30pm. $4 per vehicle. Telescope open Mar.-Nov. F-Sa starting at dusk. $3, under 6 free. Camping $17; full hookup $21.)

FOOD & ACCOMMODATIONS. Food in Mountain Home is simple—mainly delis and cafes. Boxy and covered in red, white, and blue checking, **Grinde's Diner,** 550 Air Base Rd., is the epitome of American road culture as it was in years past. Two pages' worth of sandwiches ($5.50-6.50) can be served up swiftly, or heavy and juicy meat dinners ($6-12) can be savored after a long day's drive—or, as the sign proclaims, just cool off with a lemonade. (Take Main St. south to Rte. 51 and Air Base Rd. ☎208-587-5611. Open Su and Tu-Sa 7am-11pm.) A couple from Birmingham immigrated out to Idaho some years back, and brought Alabama's hush puppies with them. **Charlie's Top Hat Barbecue,** 145 N. 2nd East, features all kinds of Southern barbecue plates ($7) from all kinds of animals. Oysters and froglegs comprise the seafood portion of the menu. (☎208-587-9223. Sandwiches $4-6. Open M-Sa 11am-9pm.) The **Dilly Deli,** 190 E. 2nd North, and its pickle mascot serve nicely for a quick afternoon sandwich. Choices range from peanut butter and jelly ($2.50) to the three-meat, three-cheese Triple Hitter ($8.50). (☎208-587-0885. Open M-Sa 10:30am-4pm.)

Mountain Home's budget lodgings are located around the downtown area, where American Legion Blvd. meets Main St. Clean, simple, microwave-bearing rooms are available at the **Towne Center Motel,** 410 N. 2nd East, off American Legion Blvd. (☎208-587-3373. Summer singles $40; doubles $50. Winter $35/$50.) **Motel Thunderbird,** 910 Sunset Strip, has smaller, functional rooms for low prices. Watch for the blinking sea-anemone light on the sign. (Follow N. 2nd East north to U.S. 30. ☎208-587-7927. Rooms from $34.)

APPROACHING BOISE

Follow **U.S. 30** out of Mountain Home—just take **Main St.** northwest. U.S. 30 merges with **I-84** en route to Boise. From I-84 Exit 54 feeds directly onto **Broadway;** proceed straight through a commercial strip until you reach **Front St.** in downtown Boise.

BOISE

Built along the banks of the Boise River, Idaho's surprisingly cosmopolitan capital straddles the boundary between desert and mountains. A network of parks protects the natural landscape of the river banks, creating a greenbelt perfect for walking, biking, or skating. Most of the city's sights cluster in the ten-block area between the capitol and the river, making Boise extremely navigable. A revitalized downtown offers a vast array of ethnic cuisine as well as a thriving nightlife.

(VITAL STATS)

Population: 186,000

Visitor Info: Boise Visitors Center, 245 8th St. (☎208-344-5338), Boise Centre Bldg., in the Grove. Open M-Sa 10am-4pm. Branch at 2676 Vista Ave. (☎208-385-0362), between I-84 Exit 53 and Capitol Ave. Open M-F 9am-5pm, Sa-Su 9am-2pm. **Boise National Forest Visitor Info Center,** 1249 S. Vinnell Way (☎208-373-4007). Open M-F 7:45am-4:30pm.

Internet Access: Boise Public Library, 715 S. Capitol Blvd. (☎208-384-4340; www.boisepublicli-brary.org). Open M-Th 10am-9pm, F 10am-6pm, Sa 10am-5pm; June-Aug. also Su noon-5pm.

Post Office: 750 W. Bannock St. (☎800-275-8777), north of Main St. **Postal Code:** 83701.

⊫ GETTING AROUND

Boise is fairly large, but the heart of the action is the pedestrian-only **Grove,** a segment of **8th St.** between **Main St.** and **Front St.** There are two other important downtown thoroughfares: **Grove St.,** which runs between Main and Front St., and **Capitol Blvd.,** which runs between 8th and **6th St.**

Driving in Boise is easy, thanks to large streets, a well-timed light system, and generally well-planned traffic flow, but **parking** is difficult; roadside parking spots are viciously competitive downtown, and most are strictly metered. Drivers will probably save themselves quarters and a good chunk of their sanity by sacrificing some money to one of the area garages and then walking.

👁 SIGHTS

The **Boise Tour Train** begins and ends in Julia Davis Park and covers approximately 75 city sights in 1¼hr. At the end of the ride during the summer, there is the option of taking a trolley to the Boise

River, where a raft will continue the tour. (☎208-342-4796; www.boisetours.net. Tours Memorial Day-Labor Day M-Sa 10am-3pm, Su noon-3:45pm; Sept. Su and W-Sa noon-3pm; May and Oct. Sa-Su 1-2:30pm. $7.50, seniors $7, ages 3-12 $5. Train and river combo tours Memorial Day-Labor Day Su noon and 2:30pm, W-Sa 11:15am and 1:45pm. $30/$27.50/$17.)

JULIA DAVIS PARK. The logical starting point for exploring Boise is the beautiful **Julia Davis Park.** A paddleboat pond, tennis courts, and a bandshell make this an entertaining place, while the alabaster pavilion and rose-garden make it one for summer romance. (Myrtle St. and Capitol Blvd. ☎208-384-4240.) To learn about Idaho and the Old West at your own pace, stroll through the **Idaho Historical Museum,** which showcases a replica 19th-century bar complete with a display of a two-headed calf. A reproduction of a Chinese temple from the days of railroad construction contains an amazingly complex, layered gilt carving recovered from an actual shrine. (610 Julia Davis Dr. ☎208-334-2120. Open Su 1-5pm, Tu-Sa 9am-5pm; Nov.-Apr. closed Su. $2, ages 6-18 $1.) The **Boise Art Museum** displays an impressive collection of contemporary, international, and local works while offering educational programs and tours. (670 Julia Davis Dr. ☎208-345-8330; www.boiseartmuseum.org. Open June-Aug. M-W and F-Sa 10am-5pm, Th 10am-8pm, Su noon-5pm; Sept.-May closed M. $10, under 18 free. Th half-price.)

BIRDS OF PREY CENTER. Far more impressive than the average zoo, the **World Center for Birds of Prey** is a research center and raptor breeding ground. Arrowslit windows open into the chambers, giving an unintrusive view of the fierce birds. The Harpy Eagle and giant Eagle Owl are two of the most striking creatures among a regal flock. (566 W. Flying Hawk Ln. From I-84, take Exit 50, go south on S. Cole St., and turn right. ☎208-362-8687. Open daily Mar.-Oct. 9am-5pm; Nov.-Feb. 10am-4pm. $4, seniors $3, ages 4-16 $2, under 4 free.)

BASQUE MUSEUM. The last remnant of Atlantis, perhaps, is preserved at the The **Basque Museum and Cultural Center,** dedicated to the culture of the Basques, an Iberian peninsula ethnicity with a language related to no other, which prompted the unlikely theory that they descended from the citizens of Atlantis. Many Basque younger sons, seeking land, emigrated to the American West to become herders. This museum recalls their heritage in Western Europe and their

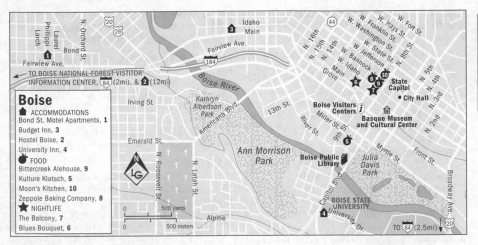

Boise

♦ ACCOMMODATIONS
Bond St. Motel Apartments, **1**
Budget Inn, **3**
Hostel Boise, **2**
University Inn, **4**
● FOOD
Bittercreek Alehouse, **9**
Kulture Klatsch, **5**
Moon's Kitchen, **10**
Zeppole Baking Company, **8**
★ NIGHTLIFE
The Balcony, **7**
Blues Bouquet, **6**

lonely lives in the Idaho pasture lands. The grounds include a gallery of Basque art and a replica of a Basque herder's house. (*611 Grove St. ☎208-343-2671. Open Tu-F 10am-4pm, Sa 11am-3pm. Suggested donation.*)

OTHER SIGHTS. In the **Alive for Five** series, live music infuses The Grove every Wednesday from May to September starting at 4:30pm. (*☎208-472-5200; www.downtownboise.org.*) The **Capitol City Market** takes over 8th St. between Main and Bannock St. every Saturday morning in the summer. Stroll through for a look at local produce and crafts. Bikers, runners, and skaters enjoy the **Boise River Greenbelt,** 25 mi. of asphalt and grass pathway following the Boise River. If you're disdainful of land-lubbing, throw a tube or kayak into the river; they can be rented and put into the water at **Baker Park,** at the southeast end of the Greenbelt. (*☎208-384-4240 or 208-343-6564; www.cityof-boise.org/parks.*) The 28-year-old **Boise Shakespeare Festival** hits town from June to September. (*Theater on Warm Springs Ave., the eastern continuation of Idaho St. ☎208-336-9221; www.idahoshakespeare.org. Tickets Su-Th $18-26, F-Sa $24-32.*)

🍴 FOOD

Although Idaho is world-renowned for potatoes, Boise offers hungry roadtrippers much more than spuds. Beyond its selection of potato wedges, the city is home to numerous restaurants of varying cuisines. The downtown area bustles with delis, coffee shops, ethnic eateries, and stylish bistros.

Kulture Klatsch, 409 S. 8th St. (*☎208-345-0452*). This hip, multicultural eatery has an extensive veggie menu, with vegan alternatives on request, as well as a juice and smoothie bar. Live music (Tu-Th 8-10pm, F-Sa 9-11pm, Su 11am-1pm) including jazz, classical guitar, folk, and rock. Breakfast $4-7. Lunch specials $5-6. Dinner $7-9. Open M 7am 3pm, Tu Th 7am 10pm, F 7am-11pm, Sa 8am-11pm, Su 8am-3pm.

Zeppole Baking Company, 217 N. 8th St. (*☎208-345-2149*). Puts together gourmet sandwiches ($2-3) on famous freshly baked bread. Soup, salad, and sandwich combos $4-5. A whole slew of fresh pastries under $2. Open M-F 7am-5pm, Sa 7:30am-4pm.

Moon's Kitchen, 815 W. Bannock St. (*☎208-447-8383*). Vintage diner and cluttered gift shop has churned out 14 magnificent flavors of shakes, malts and floats since 1955. Shakes $4. Breakfast $4.50-7. Burgers $6-8. Open M-F 7am-3pm, Sa 8am-3pm, Su 9am-2pm.

Bittercreek Alehouse, 246 N. 8th St. (*☎208-345-1813*). Casual yet trendy spot in downtown Boise. Serves burgers and pitas ($6-9) as well as chowder, skewers, and other more interesting choices. Wide and varied drink list. 21+ after 10pm. Open daily 11am-10pm. Bar open until 1 or 2am.

🏠 ACCOMMODATIONS

Lodgings are surprisingly hard to come by in downtown Boise; though some options are scattered around the city's center, others are farther away. A few motels line **Fairview Ave.,** the continuation of Front and Grove St. west of town. Info on area RV **camping** is available at the Boise National Forest Visitor Info Center (see p. 600).

■ **Hostel Boise (HI-AYH),** 17322 Can-Ada Rd. (☎208-467-6858), 15-20min. from downtown Boise. Take Exit 38 off I-84 and turn right onto Garrity Blvd., which turns into Can-Ada Rd. This country home has mountain views and campfires. Internet $1 per 15min. Linen $1.50. Check-in 5-10:30pm. 3-night max. stay. Dorms $17, HI members $14; private rooms $31, $35 for 2.

■ **Bond Street Motel Apartments,** 1680 N. Phillippi St. (☎208-322-4407 or 800-545-5345), off Fairview Ave. Beautiful, furnished studio and 1-bedroom apartments with kitchens. Pots, pans, dishes—even the kitchen sink is included. Reception M-F 8am-5pm. Reservations recommended. Studios $44; 1-bedroom apartments $50.

Budget Inn, 2600 Fairview Ave. (☎208-344-8617). One of the finer budget motels along the Oregon Trail. Bright and attractive rooms with coffeemakers, refrigerators, and microwaves. Closer to downtown than almost any other lodging. Singles $35; doubles $47.

University Inn, 2360 University Dr. (☎208-345-7170 or 800-345-5118), next to Boise State University. Take 9th St. south and follow signs. Cable TV and high-speed Internet; pool and 2 hot tubs. Continental breakfast included. Singles $52-59; doubles $57-62.

NIGHTLIFE

The nightlife-starved roadtripper will find fulfillment in Boise; musicians perform regularly on **Main St.,** while vendors from nearby restaurants hawk food and beer. On the second floor of the Capitol Terrace at **The Balcony,** 150 N. 8th St., DJs spin nightly with ten TVs surrounding the dance floor. All kinds of people gather at the gay-friendly bar to dance, relax on the outdoor terrace, and play pool. "Industria" brings Goth style in on Sundays. (☎208-336-1313. Happy hour 2-7pm. Live music M 9-11. 21+. Cover F-Sa $3. Open daily 2pm-2am.) Cheap drinks and live music draw locals to **Blues Bouquet,** 1010 Main St. (☎208-345-6605; www.blues-bouquet.com. $1-2 drink specials every night. Free swing lessons M 8pm. 21+. Cover F-Sa $5. Open M-F 1pm-2am, Sa 8pm-2am, Su 7pm-2am.) Serving food and a variety of drinks, the **Bittercreek Alehouse** (see p. 601) is also a popular Boise nightspot.

LEAVING BOISE
Take **Front St. (U.S. 20/26)** heading west from downtown, and merge left onto **I-84 West.**

THE ROAD TO PARMA. It's 42 mi. from Boise to Parma, starting out on **I-84.** The interstate leads out of Boise through its busy suburbs, so the driving can be crowded and rather hectic. After 28 mi., take Exit 26 out of this mess, following **U.S. 20/26** away from the interstate. From here the drive is all sunny fields and groves, meandering 14 mi. through the tiny town of **Notus** and on to Parma.

PARMA

Off U.S. 20/26 in Parma is the replica of **Fort Boise.** The original fort was swept away when the Boise River flooded in 1853. Though the exact location of the original isn't known, it was probably somewhere northwest of where the ring of walls stands today. Enclosed within is a local history museum that displays relics from an old church to pages from local high-school yearbooks. (☎208-722-5138. Open June-Aug. F-Su 1-3pm. Free.)

Beyond the fort, Parma is mostly residential, with a few agricultural businesses. Quick food is available at the **Frosty Palace,** at the corner of 9th and Grove St. (U.S. 26/20), a real greasy roadtrip stop, with apple-red Chevy convertibles painted on the walls. The forearm-length hotdogs ($3.10) are supposedly the largest in the world. (☎802-722-7007. Open M-Th 11:30am-9pm, F-Sa 10:30am-10pm, Su 11:30am-9pm.) The **Court Motel,** 712 Grove St., has cheap rooms with colorful decor and framed magazine spreads on the wall. (☎208-722-6734. Laundry. Singles $37; doubles $46.)

THE ROAD TO ONTARIO. From Parma, continue north along **U.S. 20/26.** Six miles from town, be sure to follow the road west; going straight leads into northern Idaho, away from the trail. As soon as the road has made the turn, it crosses the **Snake River** into Oregon, where you'll be greeted by the city of **Nyssa, Thunдеregg Capitol of the World.** About 8 mi. after crossing the border, U.S. 20/26 veers away. Continue straight onto **Rte. 201;** from here it's just a few miles to the city of Ontario.

Welcome To OREGON

APPROACHING ONTARIO
SW 4th Ave. will bear right, leaving **Rte. 201** soon after the city limits. Turn here to reach downtown Ontario.

 Between Ontario and Baker City, Rte. 201/I-84 passes into the Pacific Time Zone, where it is 1hr. earlier.

ONTARIO

After passing over the Snake River into Oregon, a well-deserved rest is in order. Ontario, a quiet city of 11,000 people, is the best of the border towns for that job. The city's major sight is the **Four Rivers Cultural Center,** 676 SW 5th St., which explains the historical relationships between the various ethnicities that have settled the West, including Native Americans, Europeans, Hispanics, and Japanese. (☎541-889-8191 or 888-211-1222; www.4rcc.com. Open M-Sa 10am-5pm. $4; ages 4-6, students, and seniors $3.) Info on other attractions in Ontario and the vicinity is available at the **Ontario Chamber of Commerce,** 676 SW 5th Ave., in the same building. (☎541-889-8012 or 888-889-2012. Open M-F 8am-5pm.)

Places to eat aren't hard to find in Ontario. In spite of its name, **Rusty's Pancake and Steakhouse,** 14 NW 1st St., is a great place for chicken dishes ($7-11). Of course, pancakes are on the menu, from basic ($1.75) to fruit-filled ($7). All kinds of burgers ($1.75-8) are also available. (☎541-889-7200. Sandwiches $6-10. Open daily 7am-10pm.) A relaxed and chatty aura emanates from **DJ's Family Restaurant,** 625 E. Idaho Ave., drawing from the mix of counter seating and big, conversation-inducing tables. All sorts of pastas are available, or stick with hamburgers ($6-8) and sandwiches ($5-7), both generously proportioned. (☎541-889-4386. Entrees $7-9. Open daily 6am-11pm.) Chain lodgings can be found up and down SW 4th Ave., with some budget establishments mixed in. The **Oregon Trail Motel,** 92 E. Idaho Ave., has the cheapest rooms in town, which come with refrigerators and microwaves, as well as colorful bedspreads. (☎541-889-8633. Singles $30; doubles $42. Senior discount.) Attractive wood paneling adds some flair to the spacious and clean rooms of the **Ontario Inn,** 1144 SW 4th Ave. (☎541-823-2556; www.the-ontarioinn.com. Microwaves and refrigerators. Singles $40; doubles $50.)

LEAVING ONTARIO
Return west on **4th Ave.** to **Rte. 201** and head north along the Snake River.

THE ROAD TO BAKER CITY. Rte. 201 is an attractive bit of road, if you can find it; after leaving the city it twists confusingly; watch the signs carefully at these intersections. After this it wanders along the Snake River beneath crumbling, rocky cliffs and hills. There are no towns right on the road, so the scenery is utterly uninterrupted. Less than 30 mi. from Ontario, Rte. 201 rejoins I-84 just southeast of Farewell Bend State Park; from Farewell Bend, it's about 45 mi. to Baker City.

FAREWELL BEND STATE PARK
3 mi. from the junction of Rte. 201 and I-84. Take Exit 353 from I-84.

After over 300 mi. on the Snake River, pioneers had to leave the assurance of fresh water and trek northwest to the Columbia River. Farewell Bend State Park marks one of the first truly wooded spots that the trail has seen; the shade of the pines foreshadows the evergreen slopes to the north, beyond Flagstaff Hill. The isolated campsites of Farewell Bend make it a relaxing place to sleep, and the verdant grounds are a grand escape from a sun-baked car. (☎503-378-6305. Open daily 6am-10pm. Entrance fee $3 per car. Tent sites $15, with hookup $17. Non-camper showers $2.)

APPROACHING BAKER CITY
From **I-84,** take Exit 304. This feeds onto the east end of **Campbell St.** in Baker City.

BAKER CITY

Baker City was a gold boom town, built by the prospectors in search of the legendary Blue Bucket Mine. The lucky will arrive here in mid-July during the annual Miners' Jubilee, when covered wagons and local children march through the streets in a patriotic parade. The town is pleasant any time of the year, however; the old-fashioned main street is lined with little businesses and a tiny brook runs through the park by the library—small-town America to the core.

GETTING AROUND. There are only two roads of any importance to a Baker City visitor. **Campbell St.,** running west from I-84 Exit 304, is the city's fast-food and hotel zone, and home to buildings such as the Visitors Center and the library. At the end of Campbell St. is north-south **Main St.,** Baker City's downtown strip. **Parking** is plentiful, except during the Miners'

(VITAL STATS)

Population: 9800

Visitor Info: Visitor Info Center, 490 Campbell St. (☎541-523-5855), just west of the junction with I-84. Open M-F 8am-5pm; in summer also Sa 8am-4pm, Su 9am-2pm.

Internet Access: Baker County Public Library, 2400 Resort St. (☎541-523-6419 or 866-297-1239; www.bakercountylibrary.org), just north of the intersection of Campbell and Main St. Open M-Th 10am-8pm, F 10am-5pm, Sa 10am-4pm, Su noon-4pm.

Post Office: 1550 Dewey Ave. (☎800-275-8777). Open M-F 8:30am-5pm. **Postal Code:** 97814.

Jubilee, when parking vanishes, traffic swells, roads close, and hotels fill while jacking up their rates.

◙ **SIGHTS.** Baker's central attraction is the misleadingly named **Oregon Trail Regional Museum,** 2480 Grove St., off Campbell St. Those weary of pioneer memorials need not fear, as this is a museum *along* the Trail, not *about* it. An interesting jumble of objects is spread throughout, from a case of Nazi relics to a scale model used in the production of *Paint Your Wagon,* which was filmed nearby. The most impressive gallery is the Cavin-Warfel Collection, several rooms of gems and mineral formations which the Smithsonian once offered to buy. The crystal-in-crystal "phantoms" are mysteriously beautiful, and the giant thundereggs are impressive products of nature. (☎541-523-9308. Open daily 9am-5pm; last entry 4:15pm. $5, seniors $4.50, under 17 free.) An actual Oregon Trail museum is outside of town on Flagstaff Hill, at the **National Historic Oregon Trail Interpretive Center,** 22267 Rte. 86. The museum begins on a reproduction of a stretch of the trail, complete with pioneers, oxen, wagons and roadside graves. The rest of the museum is a stark look at the trail. (Take I-84 to Exit 302 and follow the signs for 5 mi. ☎541-523-1843; www.oregontrail.blm.gov. Open daily Apr.-Oct. 9am-6pm; Nov.-Mar. 9am-4pm. $5, ages 6-17 and seniors $3.50.)

The annual **Miners' Jubilee** takes its name from Baker City's mining heritage, but the huge three-day party has little to do with mining beyond a metal detecting contest and the cartoonish miner and donkey that cavort across shop windows. A parade and carnival are the centerpieces, while bronc-riding, a bed race through downtown, and a

Main St. dance add unorthodox entertainment. The schedule of events changes every year, but the festival always starts on the third Friday in July and runs through the following weekend.

▓ **FOOD.** The hungry can find food in Baker City around Campbell and Main St. An electric train chugs through **Sumpter Junction Restaurant,** 2 Sunset Ln., at Campbell St. The kitchen serves tasty burgers and sandwiches ($6-7.50) as well as a small selection of Mexican cuisine. (☎541-523-9437. Open daily 6am-10pm.) **Barley Brown's Brewpub,** at the corner of Main and Church St., has an ever-popular menu of pasta ($8-14), hearty sandwiches ($7-8) and salads ($3-10). However, surely no one could resist the temptation of something known as the Death Burger, named for its "killer onions." (☎541-523-4266. Open M-Sa 4-11pm.) The **Chamealeon Cafe,** 1825 Main St., has simple but satisfying sandwich-and-salad lunches. It has also created its own signature sandwich, Aunt Caroline's Pork Loin sandwich—naturally, a secret recipe. (☎541-523-7977. Sandwiches $4-7. Salads $6-8. Open M-W 11am-3pm, Th-Sa 11am-9pm.)

▐ **ACCOMMODATIONS.** Baker City sports the usual array of chain accommodations and budget motels on the outskirts of downtown, but it also has few more unusual establishments. The **Eldorado Inn,** 695 Campbell St., is not actually made of gold, but its adobe walls and red roofs put forth an attractive Spanish ambience. The clean and pleasant rooms are also decorated Iberian-style, and guests have access to an indoor pool. (☎541-523-6494. Continental breakfast included. Singles $43; doubles $47.) The **Geiser Grand Hotel,** 1996 Main St., was built in the late 19th century, when it served the rich and famous. It later fell into disrepair but was restored at multi-million dollar expense. Today the Geiser Grand drips with opulence—crystal chandeliers, silk damask, and gilt mirrors. (☎541-523-1889 or 888-434-7374. Rooms from $79.) For a lower price, try the **Bridge Street Inn,** 134 Bridge St., off the south end of Main St. Fewer dollars doesn't mean less comfort; rooms are spacious, clean, and come with refrigerators and microwaves. (☎541-523-9424. Continental breakfast included. Singles $35; doubles $40.)

▐▲ **APPROACHING LA GRANDE**
Head east on Campbell St. to **I-84** and take the westbound lane toward La Grande, 29 mi. to the north. The easiest way to enter La Grande from I-84 is

to get off at the **Island Ave.** exit and follow Island Ave. southwest to **Adams Ave.**

LA GRANDE

La Grande is the gateway into the evergreen wilderness of the Pacific Northwest. It lies between the two arcs of the Wallowa Whitman National Forest, with the Blue Mountains to the west and the Wallowa Mountains to the east. The Grande Ronde river, proclaimed a near-paradise by some pioneers, flows nearby. La Grande is in some ways overshadowed by its environment; it's hard to walk down Main St. without noticing the nearby hills rising into mountains.

VITAL STATS

Population: 12,500

Visitor Info: Union County Chamber of Commerce, 102 Elm St. (☎541-963-8588; www.visitla-grande.com), off Adams Ave. Open M-F 9am-5pm; Memorial Day-Labor Day also Sa 9am-3pm.

Internet Access: La Grande Public Library, 1006 Penn Ave. (☎541-962-1339). Open M 10am-8pm, Tu-F 10am-6pm.

Post Office: 1202 Washington Ave. (☎800-275-8777). Open M-F 8:30am-5pm. **Postal Code:** 97850.

GETTING AROUND. Getting around is a matter of knowing your bearings relative to **Adams Ave.** and **Washington Ave.** These two roads run parallel to each other one block apart, cutting the city in half from southeast to northwest. Most motels and restaurants are on or just off these streets, as is La Grande's downtown. Free **parking** is available on the edges of both streets.

OUTDOOR ACTIVITIES. The closest spot to experience the great outdoors is **Hilgard Junction State Park,** off I-84 Exit 252, about 7 mi. west of La Grande. The park stretches right along the interstate, but the surrounding mountains swallow it behind a convenient ridge, hiding it from view. This is an ideal camping spot, with sites right along the high grass that grows on the banks of the **Grand Ronde,** a clear and gentle stream ideal for summer wading. With no electrical hookups, the nights are dark and silent (except for the growl of the occasional speed demon over the ridge), custom-built for stargazing, campfires, and deep mountain sleeps. (☎541-962-1352. Sites $9.) There's more space to skip merrily among the

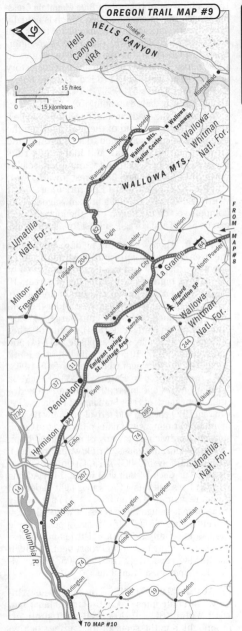

OREGON TRAIL MAP #9

TO MAP #10

trees a bit west of Hilgard, at **Blue Mountain Crossing Oregon Trail Interpretive Park,** which is actually much more park than interpretation; trails roll through the hills, lined with panels and signs offering information on the trials of the emigrants in these parts. Some weekends feature living history actors. (Head west on I-84 to Exit 248 and follow the signs for 3 mi. ☎541-963-7186. Open Memorial Day-Labor Day daily 8am-8pm. $5.)

In general, the roads around La Grande can be a scenic attraction in and of themselves. Even the interstate becomes a scenic tour. Narrower and slower than in Wyoming and Idaho, **I-84** runs through amazingly lush and verdant landscapes north of La Grande. **Rte. 237** (west toward Cove) and **Rte. 82** (north toward Enterprise) are other worthwhile drives. Even if a broken wagon wheel compels you on to Oregon City, the journey itself can be a wildland voyage, at least for a little while.

FOOD. There's a smattering of restaurants in the area around Adams and Washington Ave., downtown, as well as a fast-food oasis at each of the town's highway exits. **Ten Depot Street,** 10 Depot St., is a downtown restaurant and sometime music hall. For appetizers, consider the emu meat ($8); lunch offers the emu burger ($7.50), and dinner the emu steak ($16). Plenty of other options are available, such as pastas ($11-14) and sandwiches ($7.50-10), which include the lentil pecan burger for vegetarian diners. (☎541-963-8766. Appetizers $6-15. Entrees $11-33. Open M-Sa 5-10pm.) A vast and international menu is the distinguishing mark of **Foley Station,** 1114 Adams Ave. Charsiu BBQ chicken and teriyaki cashew beef sit in ethnic harmony with falafel pitas and the Cajun sausage sandwich. Enjoy any of these in addition to the restaurant's classy brick walls and sleek wood chairs. (☎541-963-7473. Open daily 7am-10pm.) The **Cock 'n' Bull Villa Roma,** 1414 Adams Ave., in Pat's Alley, is a Christmas-light bedecked Italian restaurant. The entrees ($9-11) are mostly pasta based, though there is also a wide selection of sandwiches ($5.50-7.50). Menu toppers include the Cock & Bull and Pork & Bird sandwiches, which are simply turkey and roast beef, and ham and turkey, respectively. (☎541-963-0573. Open M-Th 11am-2pm, F-Sa 11am-9pm.)

ACCOMMODATIONS. The numerous windows and balconies of the ⊠**Stange Manor Inn,** 1612 Walnut St., fill this B&B with sunlight, moonlight, and the scent of the gardens below.

The four rooms, all elegant, range from singles to multi-room micro-apartments with fireplaces. All have private baths. (Take Penn Ave. west from Washington Ave; Walnut St. is a few blocks west of the steep hill. ☎541-963-2400; www.stangmanor.com. Breakfast included. Rooms $98-115.) One of La Grande's best budget motels is the **Royal Motor Inn,** 1510 Adams Ave. The rooms have very comfortable chairs and beds, as well as full desks. (☎541-963-4154 or 800-990-7575; www.royalmotorinn.com. Singles $35; doubles $40.) The **Stardust Motel,** 402 Adams Ave., has a romantic name and cheap rooms. (☎541-962-7143. Outdoor Pool. Singles $33; doubles $44.)

LEAVING LA GRANDE
To head toward Enterprise and Joseph, take **Adams Ave** to **Island Ave.** and continue east. Island becomes **Rte. 82.,** leading into **the Wallowa Mountains.**

While the road into the Wallowa Mountains and the towns at the end of it offer some of the most stunning scenery along the trail, it's a long 75 mi. drive, and a bit out of the way. To skip this section and continue west, take **I-84** to Pendleton—see p. 608.

HELL'S CANYON SCENIC BYWAY

This is a serious departure from the Oregon Trail, but a highly worthy one. About 75 mi. through gorges, alongside rivers, and up into foothills of the Wallowa Mountains, this drive is a chance to immerse yourself in northwestern greenery after long, hard, dusty days on the trail. The road has been declared the **Hell's Canyon Scenic Byway,** though that particular formation is many miles to the east.

Right outside of La Grande, Rte. 82 passes through Island City. Be very careful of the signs here; the road turns at a busy intersection, and it's easy to go wrong the way. The first 25 mi. are gentle valley driving through the towns of **Imbler** and **Elgin.** In Elgin, the road turns (watch the signs carefully), and begins a serious climb. Here the ride becomes winding, steep, and wonderful. After riding a gorge for few miles, the road descends, following the water and passing **Wallowa Wayside Park.** After rising a bit, the route passes through the towns of **Wallowa** and **Lostine** before entering **Enterprise.**

ENTERPRISE & JOSEPH

The towns of Enterprise and Joseph, situated in the Wallowa Mountains, are a powerhouse pair. The two are separated by about 6 mi. of Rte. 82, practically on the slopes of the ferociously craggy Wallowas, which blaze on clear days with snow and evergreen. The Eagle Cap Wilderness spreads through the mountains south of Joseph, and much of Joseph's little area is consumed by bike rental shops, fly-fishing stores, and hiker suppliers. The rest of Main St. is a combination of galleries, bookstores, craft shops, bronze statues, and an uncanny number of restaurants. Enterprise is bigger, grayer, duller, but full of motels and necessities, while Joseph is small, bright and slightly eccentric; sleep in the former, play in the latter.

VITAL STATS

Population: 1900/1000

Visitor Info: Wallowa Mountains Visitors Center, 88401 Rte. 82 (☎541-426-5546; www.josephoregon.com). Open M-F 8am-5pm; in summer also Sa 8am-5pm. **Wallowa County Chamber of Commerce,** 115 Tejaka Ln. (☎541-426-4622 or 800-585-4121), off Rte. 82 on the west edge of Enterprise, across the street from the Visitors Center. Open M-F 8am-5pm.

Internet Access: Enterprise Public Library, 101 NE 1st St. (☎541-426-3906). Open M noon-6pm, Tu-Th 10am-6pm, F noon-6pm, Sa 10am-2pm.

Post Office: 201 W. North St. (☎541-426-5980), in Enterprise. Open M-F 9am-4:30pm. **Postal Code:** 97828.

GETTING AROUND

Maneuvering this two-town mountain complex is actually quite easy. Enterprise and Joseph exist primarily along **Rte. 82.** This road enters Enterprise from the west, and runs east under the guise of **North St.** It then turns south under the name **River St.** From the outskirts of Enterprise it continues 6 mi. to Joseph, where it becomes **Main St.** At the south end of Joseph, simply follow the signs out of town, proceeding a quick 6 mi. to **Wallowa Lake,** the main gateway to the **Eagle Cap Wilderness.** Free **parking** is everywhere in both towns, and practically endless around the popular lake.

OUTDOOR ACTIVITIES

Fun in this area revolves around its mountain wildlands. **Eagle Cap Wilderness** is gigantic at 650,000 acres, and even that is dwarfed by the encompassing **Wallowa-Whitman National Forest.** It is almost impossible to explore it fully, but those attempting the feat can get a start at the **Wallowa Mountains Visitors Center,** which provides info on trailheads, car loops, camping areas, wildlife, and almost anything else visitors are interested in. Giant maps of the entire region are available for $6. One of the more popular, most easily accessible outdoor areas is **Wallowa Lake,** 72214 Marina Ln., a state park nearly engulfed by the surrounding National Forest. It is 6 mi. from Joseph; simply take Main St. south and follow the signs. The large lake itself is open for swimming and boating, both very popular summer activities. With no day-use fee, the mountain beach is a happening place.

Hikers can find a few of Eagle Cap's trailheads in Wallowa Lake's southern picnic grounds, leading up into the mountains along the Wallowa River. These are serious trails; the Visitors Center in Enterprise can provide maps and information on current weather and trail conditions. Campsites are numerous, but still crowded; reservations can be made up to nine months in advance, and may become necessary in the peak months of the summer. In all, 121 sites with hookups and 89 tent sites are available. There is also one deluxe cabin and two yurts, which are small domed cabins with carpet, heating, and lighting. (☎541-432-4185. Open for day-use 6am-9pm. May-Sept. sites $17, with hookup $21; yurts $29; cabin $79. Oct.-Apr. sites $13, with hookup $17; yurts $29; cabin $58. Day-use free.)

The peaks around Wallowa Lake aren't reserved for battle-hardened climbers. Mt. Howard (8200 ft.) is scaled by the **Wallowa Lake Tramway;** gondolas roll quietly up the mountainside, allowing riders sweeping vistas over the lake and valleys below. The peak is well developed, with numerous lookouts and a system of easily accessible short trails. The summit and royal purple trails are excellent, with their dramatic views of neighboring snow-capped peaks. The chipmunk-like rodents that live on the mountain have gotten used to the generosity of human visitors. (☎541-432-5331; www.wallowlaketramway.com. Open daily July-Aug. 10am-5pm; Memorial Day to late September 10am-4pm. $19, ages 3-10 $12.)

In the last days of July, the **Chief Joseph Days Rodeo** tears Joseph apart; the four-day event includes dances, parades and outdoor food. Traditional rodeo events are jazzed up with comedy rodeo acts and the new Wildest Ride contest. (☎ 541-432-1015; www.chiefjosephdays.com. $8-15, separate tickets for each day's events.)

⤳ FOOD

Dining establishments abound in Joseph; the number of restaurants crammed onto so short a street is staggering. Enterprise has a more modest selection.

Toma's, 301 S. River St. (☎ 541-426-4873), in Enterprise. Brown brick and a weathered tile exterior lend a solid look to Toma's, which offers entrees from shellfish to shrimp to beef. Salads ($2-7) and homemade soups are fast and cheap, and breakfast ($3-7) is a also good deal. Appetizers $3-5. Entrees $9-16. Open daily 6am-9pm.

Embers Brew House, 206 N. Main St. (☎ 541-232-2739), in Joseph. A modern spot with metallic decor and plenty of vegetarian options. A healthy selection of salads ($4-8) is followed up by vegetarian pizzas, calzones (from $8), and the dinner-sized Veggie Tray ($8). All sorts of other pizzas and calzones. Appetizers $4-8. Beer $3. Open daily 11am-10pm.

Friends Restaurant, 107 N. River St. (☎ 541-426-5929), in Enterprise. A tiny but delicious diner hiding at the corner of Main and River St. Serves some of the best burgers in many miles. Su rotisserie day, W pita day, F fried shrimp day. Sandwiches $4-5. Entrees $7-13. Open daily 6am-9pm.

Cheyenne Cafe, 209 N. Main St. (☎ 541-432-6300), in Joseph. A friendly cafe atmosphere meets friendly low prices. Big breakfasts are available for all-night drivers, and generously portioned lunch combos ($4-9) keep them going through a day of hiking, too. Sandwiches $4-6. Open M-Sa 6am-2pm, Su 7am-2pm.

◪ ACCOMMODATIONS

The surest bet for available lodgings is in Enterprise, though Joseph isn't complete devoid of places to sleep. A little tourist village clusters near Lake Wallowa, but this place is crowded and touristy. Surprisingly, one of the area's best motels is right in downtown Joseph, at the **Indian Lodge Motel,** 201 S. Main St. The 16 units can fill fast in the summer, which is understandable due to their

large size and large TVs. (☎ 541-432-2651 or 888-286-5484; www.eoni.com/~gingerdaggett/. Summer singles $37; doubles $46-52. Winter $32/$37-42.) One of the less expensive Enterprise stays is the **Country Inn,** 402 W. North St. Here, frilled pastel blankets are matched by the curtains tied back with huge pink ribbons. The rooms aren't huge, but still have plenty of room for refrigerators and coffeemakers. (☎ 541-426-4986. Rooms from $48.) The **Ponderosa Motel,** 102 E. Greenwood St., off River St., has carefully decorated rooms filled with artfully rustic wood furniture, right down to the headboards. Rooms include coffeemakers, microwaves and refrigerators. (☎ 541-426-3186. Singles $65; doubles $72.)

◪ LEAVING ENTERPRISE AND JOSEPH

The return journey to La Grande is the same as the approach; take **Rte. 82** east through Joseph and Enterprise, then 75 mi. back to La Grande. From La Grande, take I-84 west to Pendleton.

THE ROAD TO PENDLETON

Several dramatic changes take place over the 50 mi. stretch of I-84 from La Grande to Pendleton. After wandering past the lush mountains of the Hilgard area, the road begins to drop, eventually leading to a 6 mi. descent into the Columbia River Valley, a dry, dusty region much like area before the trail reached the Blue Mountains. There is little along the way but the tiny towns of **Kamela** and **Meacham.** A campground is maintained at **Emigrant Springs State Park,** off Exit 234; one of the last forested landscapes before the drop into the valley. The park is fairly basic, but the sites themselves offer showers and electrical hookups. (☎ 800-551-6949. Sites $14, with hookup $16; cabins $20-35. Non-camper showers $2.)

PENDLETON

Between the Cascades and the Blue Mountains, Pendleton is a harsh return to the hot dust that has marked much of the trail thus far. Pioneers were no less disillusioned as they left the fertility of the Grande Ronde for this unforgiving valley. Although the city struggles to win the hearts of travelers today, Pendleton's colorful history gives it a strange and darkly fascinating character.

◪ GETTING AROUND. The **Umatilla River** runs east-west through Pendleton, and the majority of the city lies south of the river. The city is also bisected by north-south **Main St.** All roads have a

> ### VITAL STATS
>
> **Population:** 17,000
>
> **Visitor Info: Pendleton Chamber of Commerce,** 501 S. Main St. (☎541-276-7411; www.pendleton-chamber.com). Open M-Th 8:30am-5pm, F 10am-5pm; Memorial Day-Labor Day also Sa 9am-4pm.
>
> **Internet Access: Pendleton Public Library,** 502 SW Dorion Ave. (☎541-966-0210). Open M-Th 10am-8pm, F-Sa 10am-5pm.
>
> **Post Office:** 104 SW Dorion Ave. (☎800-275-8877). Open M-F 9am-5pm, Sa 10am-1pm. **Postal Code:** 97801.

double designation giving their positions relative to these two dividers: NW, SE, etc. The city is fairly narrow, and long east-west roads are all one-way, so expect to do a lot of looping. To prevent confusion, the streets names are arranged alphabetically from the river: **Byers, Court, Dorion** and so on.

◪ SIGHTS. A system of tunnels evolved in Pendleton over the years, burrowing between the numerous brothels and saloons that sprung up here; at one point there were as many as 32 bars and 18 houses of ill-repute. This whole sordid and fascinating history is on display through ◪**Pendleton Underground Tours,** 37 SW Emigrant Ave., which leads visitors through the completely restored and redecorated underground establishments. Tours showcase a card room, ice-cream parlor, Chinese quarters and an opium den, as well as Cozy Rooms bordello, among other locations. (☎541-276-7330 or 800-226-6398; www.pendletonundergroundtours.org. Reservations required; call ahead. $10, under 5 free.)

Pendleton also preserves another facet of local history at the **Tamastslikt Cultural Institute,** off I-84 Exit 216, east of Pendleton, an interpretative center dedicated entirely to the history and future of the tribes of the Umatilla Reservation. The nautilus-shaped floor plan spirals through three sections, beginning in the coyote theatre, where a show relates the legends of the trickster, Ispilyay, the Coyote. From there, elaborate displays and many recordings provide a brief but detailed history of the Natitayt. (☎800-654-9453; www.tamastslikt.com. Open daily 9am-5pm. $6; students, children and seniors $4.)

This city has been home to the rocking **Pendleton Round-Up** rodeo since 1910. If you happen to be in town mid-September, don't miss the bronco-

riders, clowns, and Happy Canyon Indian Pageant. The rest of the year, visit the **Round-Up Hall of Fame,** inside the giant Round-Up grounds on the west on Court Ave. Plaques recall every champion in every event from every year, and half of the hall is filled with portraits of the annually elected Rodeo Queen and Happy Canyon Princess. Chemulwick (War Paint), one of the great horses of the rodeo, has been stuffed and memorialized, honored alongside the men who rode him. (☎541-278-0815. Open May-Oct. M-Sa 10am-4pm. Free.) The **Pendleton Woollen Mills,** 1307 SE Court Pl., offers a 15min. tour that breezes through every step of the wool manufacturing process from carding and spinning to the final weaving. (☎541-276-6911 or 800-568-3156; www.pendleton-usa.com. Tours M-F 9, 11am, 1:30, 3pm. Free.)

▧ FOOD. Restaurants cluster around the nexus of Main St., Court Ave. and Dorion Ave. **Como's Italian Eatery,** 39 SE Court Ave., is a tiny spot at the core of downtown serving standard, well-priced entrees ($4-8) like spaghetti or ziti. Sample Italian sweets ($0.50-3) beneath an entertaining display of postcards and pasta boxes. (☎541-278-9142. Open summer M-Th 9am-8pm, F 9am-9pm; winter M-Th 9am-7:30pm, F 9am-8pm.) A giant plastic Betty Boop smiles over the sidewalk of the **Main Street Diner,** 349 S. Main St. The usual breakfast fare ($3-7) complements a few more adventurous lunch options, including the Hula Hoop Burger ($6), a combination of ham, pineapple and sweet and sour sauce. (☎541-278-1952. Sandwiches $3-7. Open daily 7am-3pm.) At **The Hut,** 1400 SW Dorion Ave., patrons dine in the brightly lit, window-side booths or submerge themselves in the dim, deeply cushioned side room. (☎541-276-0756. Appetizers $2-6. Sandwiches $5-6.50. Entrees $7-17. Open M-Sa 11am-9pm.)

▧ ACCOMMODATIONS. Pendleton's accommodations are straightforward and ordinary, with one notable exception. The **Working Girls Motel,** 37 SW Emigrant Ave., is euphemistically named for the former brothel it occupies, one of the 18 that once operated in Pendleton. The rooms are decorated with antiques recovered from the era; no occupants under 18 are allowed. (☎541-276-0730. Rented through Pendleton Underground Tours. Shared bathrooms. Rooms $60; suite $75.) Clean and attractively decorated rooms are available at the **Tapadera Inn,** 105 SE Court Ave. Though the inn is right downtown, cleverly placed walls and

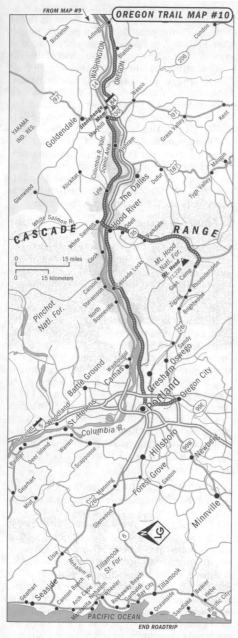

FROM MAP #9

OREGON TRAIL MAP #10

END ROADTRIP

outer walkways shield the rooms from noise and traffic. (☎541-276-3231. Reception M-Sa 7am-10pm, Su 8am-10pm. Singles $51; doubles $56.) One of Pendleton's cheapest stays is found at the **Economy Inn,** 201 SW Court Ave., which offers large rooms and a well-maintained outdoor swimming pool. (☎541-276-5252. Rooms from $37.)

LEAVING PENDLETON
Take **Emigrant Ave.** west to **I-84** and head west on the interstate for the long road to The Dalles.

THE ROAD TO THE DALLES. Make sure you have plenty of gas before leaving Pendleton; the road to The Dalles is 125 mi. long, winding through the brown land of the Columbia River Gorge. The rolling yellowish plains are reminiscent of Kansas and Nebraska for the first leg of the journey. At the 50 mi. mark, the south side of the road is lined for a short distance with perfectly square groves of trees. Fifteen miles beyond these forests, the road joins the Columbia River itself. On the Oregon side, I-84 snakes right along the wide ribbon of water all the way to the Dalles.

APPROACHING THE DALLES
From **I-84,** Exit 87 leads to the eastern end of **2nd Ave.,** the main street of The Dalles. Exit 85 also lets onto 2nd Ave., closer to downtown. Exits 84 and 83 open onto the west end of town.

THE DALLES
The Dalles, a pleasant if unremarkable river city, is the central point in a broad spiral of unusual attractions spread through the area. It was an important nexus for Oregon Trail travelers: here, so close to the end, it became possible, if not easy, to float a wagon to Oregon City. The Dalles's greatest attraction is the **Columbia Gorge Discovery Center and Wasco County Museum,** 5000 Discovery Dr., a double museum on the outskirts of town. The Wasco County Museum contains the usual displays on Native American, missionary, and military life on the Western frontier. Unlike many similar museums, it tells the history of the area right up to the present day. The Columbia Gorge Discovery Center features an indoor gorge, teeming with (stuffed) animals and loud with (recorded) birdsong. (Head west on I-84 to Exit 82 and follow the signs. ☎541-296-8600; www.gorge-discovery.org. Open daily 9am-5pm. $6.50, seniors $5.50, ages 6-16 $3.) For more info on area attractions, swing by **The Dalles Area Chamber of Com-**

merce, 404 W. 2nd St. (☎541-296-1688; www.thedalleschamber.com. Open M-F 8:30am-5pm; Memorial Day-Labor Day also Sa 9am-4pm, Su 10am-3pm.)

Restaurants congregate in the downtown area, well advertised and easy to find. One of the best is **Cafe Solara,** 107C E. 2nd St., in the Columbia Court. Though it's a full restaurant, the small tables and couches make it feel more like a college town coffee shop. Pita pizzas ($6-10) and foot-long wraps are both customizable. Salads ($3-5) and quiche are also on the menu. (☎541-298-4786. Open M-Sa 8am-8pm.) The hungry can jump off Exit 83 to **Cousins' Restaurant,** 2116 W. 6th St., which supports claims of "homestyle entrees" with a meatloaf dinner and a turkey and cranberry sauce plate. A none-too-subtle country atmosphere is created by the dancing farm animal statues outside and a door which moos, oinks, bleats, or crows when opened. (☎541-298-2771. Breakfast $5-11. Sandwiches $5-9. Entrees $7-13. Open daily 6am-10pm.) Accommodations in the Dalles are fairly standard; look for the chains around Exit 83, along W. 6th St. Budget options are dispersed throughout the city. **The Inn at The Dalles,** 3550 SE Frontage Rd., sits atop a ridge. Giant windows give all its rooms glorious panoramas of the river, bridge, and dam. (Take a left immediately after getting off I-84 Exit 87. ☎541-296-1167. Singles $40; doubles $45.) The **Oregon Motor Motel,** 200 W. 2nd Ave., downtown, is conveniently located and offers clean, well-priced rooms with fridges and microwaves. (☎541-296-9111. Singles from $40; doubles from $42.)

LEAVING THE DALLES

Head east via **2nd St.** to the Exit 87 on-ramps, just east of town. Follow the signs toward the interstate, but drive right past the ramps; the road will then proceed across the Columbia River into Washington by way of the **Dalles Bridge.** After the bridge, go west on **Rte. 14,** into Washington State. Between The Dalles and Portland, you'll be driving in the heart of the Columbia River Gorge Scenic Area.

COLUMBIA RIVER GORGE NATIONAL SCENIC AREA

Stretching 75 stunning miles from The Dalles to Portland, the Columbia River Gorge carries the river to the Pacific Ocean through woodlands, waterfalls, and canyons. While driving through offers spectacular vistas, roadtrippers should consider heading off-road via one of the area's many hiking or biking trails.

> **VITAL STATS**
>
> **Area:** 292,500 acres
>
> **Visitor Info: USDA Forest Service Columbia River Gorge National Scenic Area Visitor Center,** 902 Wasco St., Ste. 200, (☎541-308-1700), in Hood River. Open M-F 8am-4:30pm. **Columbia Gorge Interpretive Center,** 9990 SW Rock Creek Dr. (☎800-991-2338; www.columbiagorge.org.), in Stevenson, WA, on Rte. 14. Open daily 10am-5pm. $6, ages 13-18 and seniors $5, ages 6-12 $4.
>
> **Gateway Towns:** The Dalles (p. 610), Portland (p. 616).

GETTING AROUND

The Columbia River Gorge is traversed by several major highways: **I-84** and **U.S. 30** on the Oregon side, and **Rte. 14** in Washington. Attractions on the Washington side of the Columbia can be reached by crossing the river at the **Bridge of the Gods;** 11 mi. west of Hood River, take Exit 44 through Cascade Locks and follow the signs ($1 toll).

SIGHTS

Two miles beyond the Bridge of the Gods turn-off is the **Bonneville Dam Visitor Center.** The center has a deck for viewing the generators; though only their outer shells can be seen, their furious internal spinning can be heard and even felt through the glass. Below, windows have been built into the walls, so it is possible to see fish swimming upstream through the "fish ladders," maze-like structures built around the dam that allow the spawning creatures to continue upstream. (☎541-374-8820. Open daily 9am-5pm. Free.) **Beacon Rock** lies 7 mi. west of the dam. Named by Louis and Clark, this titan boulder juts vertically from the water's edge. Across the street is **Beacon Rock State Park,** a hillside campground and start of the Hamilton Mountain Trail. (☎509-427-8265. Open daily 8am-dusk for day use. Sites $16.)

HIKING

There is a huge array of trails in the Gorge area. For maps and information, visit the Visitors Center in Hood River. The forest service also has comprehensive website that contains maps, descriptions, difficulty ratings, and directions to trailheads for many area trails, at www.fs.fed.us/r6/columbia/forest/recreation/trails.

Pacific Crest Oregon (16 mi. one-way). From I-84, take Exit 44 at Cascade Locks and follow the signs to the Bridge of the Gods. The trail leads from a parking lot on the left before the bridge. This longer trail passes the canyons containing Eagle and Herman Creeks, then passes around the base of 3 small mountains. Closed in winter. Moderate.

Dog Mountain Trail (3 mi. round-trip). The trailhead is marked by a large sign, located off Rte. 14 about 14 mi. east of Stevenson, 1 mi. west of the Bridge of the Gods. This short trail is steep and rocky, but offers great vistas of Mt. Adams, Mt. Hood and Mt. St. Helens. Closed in winter. Moderate.

Angel's Rest (4½ mi. one-way). From I-84, take Exit 35 onto the Historic Columbia River Hwy. and go 7 mi. west. This trail leads through mossy, fern-filled forests, past one of the last falls in the chain, and up a ridge with excellent views. Open Mar.-Dec. Moderate.

Catherine Creek (1¼ mi. round-trip). From Bingen (across the river from Hood River), head east for 4½ mi. on Rte. 14. Turn north onto County Rd. 1230 and proceed for 1½ mi. The paved trail passes through meadows that bloom with 90 species of wildflower Feb.-July. Easy.

🚴 BIKING

Bike trails also lace the gorge, though info on them is not quite as readily available as it is for foot trails. **Discover Bicycles,** 116 Oak St., in Hood River, sells maps in addition to renting out bikes. (☎541-386-4820; www.discoverbicycles.com. Open daily summer 9am-6pm; winter 9am-7pm. Cruisers $5 per hr., $25 per day; road bikes $6/$35; mountain bikes with front suspension $6/$35, with full suspension $8/$45.) The **Post Canyon** area is home to a system of freeride trails and has become very popular with stunt and downhill riders. To reach the canyon, go west on Cascade St. in Hood River all the way to its end and turn left. Follow Country Club Rd. for 1¼ mi., then turn right onto Post Canyon Rd. For more info on freeriding in the canyon, visit www.gfra.org.

Surveyor's Ridge (23¾ mi. round-trip, 3-5hr.). Take Rte. 35 south from Hood River for 31 mi., turn east onto FS 44, and follow it for 3½ mi. to the trailhead. This loop rides the edge of a ridge, offering great views. The final leg of the loop is along FS 17. Open late spring to late fall.

Three Lake Tour (9¼ mi. one-way, 2½-4hr. round-trip). Take 13th St. in Hood River south to Rte. 281 and continue south, turning west onto Portland Dr. The road will pass through the intersection with Country Club Rd. and become Binns Hill Rd. Follow Binns Hill Rd. for ¼ mi., then turn left onto Kinsley Rd. This leads to the trailhead beside Green Point Upper Reservoir. The end, along Waucoma Ridge, provides fine views. Open summer-fall. Easy to moderate.

Mosier Twin Tunnels (4½ mi. one-way, 1hr.). A segment of the Historic Columbia River Hwy. too narrow for cars, between Hood River and Mosier. Offers mainly an on-road ride, with views of the river and the tunnels. Parking $3. Easy to moderate.

▧ DETOUR: MARYHILL MUSEUM & STONEHENGE MEMORIAL

After crossing the Columbia River, turn left to go east on Rte. 14 instead of continuing west. The museum is 15 mi. east of The Dalles, along Rte. 14, and the memorial is 3 mi. east of the museum.

Two unusual sights can be found east of The Dalles. The first is the **Maryhill Museum,** built in the planned home of the wealthy Mr. Sam Hill, who tried to build an experimental community here in the early 20th century. Hill was friends with Queen Marie of Rumania, granddaughter of both Queen Victoria of England and Tsar Alexander II of Russia. The museum displays artifacts from her court, including her golden court gown with spectacular train, and a reproduction of her coronation crown. The third floor has a series of sets from the Theatre de la Mode of post WWII France. These miniature city-scapes and dolls were meant to revitalize the fashion industry while making due with the extremely limited materials available in the wartime economy. The lower floor has a collection of ornate chess pieces and a gallery of Rodin sculptures, including one of the smaller casts of his famous *The Thinker.* (☎541-773-3733. Open mid-Mar. to mid-Nov. daily 9am-5pm. $7, seniors $6, ages 6-16 $2.)

The nearby **Stonehenge WWI Memorial** imitates not the famous ruins, but the full stone structure as it was once believed to have been. The names of 13 men of Klickitat County killed in combat are inscribed on the stones. Pacific Highway visionary Sam Hill is reported to have lamented, after having been told (erroneously) that Stonehenge was an altar for human sacrifice, how tragic it was that men still sacrificed each other in war after so many years. (☎541-773-3733. Grounds open daily 7am-10pm.)

APPROACHING HOOD RIVER

Rte. 14 runs about 20 mi. west from The Dalles turn-off to Bingen. Take the **toll bridge** ($0.75) over the Columbia River back to Oregon. Follow the signs onto **I-84**, but you won't really have to travel on it; the on-ramp flows right into the off-ramp that leads into Hood River. Turn left to enter the center of Hood River.

HOOD RIVER

Built along the Oregon bank of a wide and windy bend of the Columbia River, Hood River has evolved from a center for traditional sports into the windsurfing and kiteboarding capital of the Northwest. While low-tech activities are as popular as ever, the figures cruising gloriously over the water give Hood River its extreme reputation.

VITAL STATS

Population: 6000

Visitor Info: Hood River Visitor Center, 405 Portway Ave. (☎541-386-2000 or 800-366-3530), in the Expo Center. Open M-F 9am-5pm, Sa-Su 10am-5pm.

Internet Access: Hood River County Library, 601 State St. (☎541-285-2525). Open M-Th 8:30am-8:30pm, F-Sa 8:30am-5:30pm.

Post Office: 408 Cascade St. (☎800-275-8777). Open M-F 8:30am-5pm. **Postal Code:** 97031.

GETTING AROUND. Hood River is an easy city to drive in, except for the occasional busy intersection regulated only by four-way stop signs. North-south streets are numbered, increasing from east to west. The most important east-west streets are **Cascade St.** and **Oak St.,** both close to the interstate. There is plenty of metered **parking** on the street sides ($0.25 per 3½hr.).

SIGHTS & OUTDOOR ACTIVITIES. Hood River is the home station of the **Mount Hood Railroad,** 110 Railroad Ave., at the intersection of Cascade and 1st St. The excursion train, composed of early 20th-century Pullman coaches and a red caboose, winds through a valley, providing a narrated historic and scenic tour with a brief stop in the town of Parkdale. Dinner and brunch trains, in authentic restored dining cars, provide a meal to supplement the peaceful countryside ride. Specialty trips like the Train Robbery ride are also offered occasionally; call ahead for dates. (☎541-386-3556 or 800-872-4661; www.mthoodrr.com. Excursion train $23, seniors $21, ages 2-12 $15. Brunch train $57. Dinner train $70.)

Trails wrap all around Hood River in the **Columbia River Gorge National Scenic Area;** the windsurfing and kiteboarding opportunities, however, are almost completely located in the city itself. The most important area in the windsurfing world is **Port Marina Park,** left off I-84 Exit 64, which contains the facilities for most of the windsurfing/kiteboarding schools. North of downtown Hood River is **The Hook,** a cape which forms a windy but sheltered cove where beginners often train, safe but with stiff breeze in their sails (or kites).

Several companies rent equipment and provide instruction for the levels of windsurfers and kiteboarders. **Big Winds,** 207 Front St., at the east end of Oak St., offers 2hr. introductory windsurfing lessons to teach the basics, and an additional 2hr. of free rentals. Kiteboarders have a 1½hr. intro class out of the water to learn how to control a kite; most water lessons are one-on-one. (☎514-386-6086; www.bigwinds.com. Windsurfing intro lesson $55. Rentals $55 full package, $35 for just board or rig. Kiteboarding intro lesson $85. Open daily 8am-6pm.) **Hood River Water Play,** based out of Port Marina Park, provides a 6hr. windsurfing introductory class. Free sailing at the beginners' beach is available upon completion of the intro class. Four more levels of class are available after that, as well as private lessons. There are six levels of kiteboarding instruction: two basic, two intermediate and two advanced. Each pair can be taken together. (☎541-386-9463; www.hoodriverwaterplay.com. Windsurfing intro class $139, successive levels $85-95 for 2-3hr. classes. Kiteboarding intro class $139.)

FOOD. Little cafes and lunch shops cluster in Hood River, so finding somewhere to eat after a day of windsurfing is easy. **Full Sail Brewing,** 506 Columbia St., has made a name for itself winning a number of beer-fest awards. The beers—including the well-named Rip Curl—are sold at the brewery by the pint ($3), and even by the keg. A menu of mostly smoked and grilled meats is also available. (☎888-244-2337; www.fullssailbrewing.com. Meals $5.50-7.50. Open daily noon-8pm; in summer until 9pm.) The young and hip breakfast at **Jean's @ 110,** 110 5th St. Morning dishes include mini quiches ($3) and coconut-banana french toast ($7); many of the items are organic. The restaurant also serves dinner starting at 7pm on Friday nights. (☎541-386-8755. Red chili *posole* $6. Chicken and parmesan salad $8. Open M-Tu and Th-Su 8am-3pm, F also from 7pm.) For a sandwich, salad, or giant multi-hot dog sandwich, try **Bette's Place,** 1 Oak Mall, at the corner of 5th St. Sandwiches include standard ham and turkey, as well as the Gobbler ($7), a turkey, avocado and cranberry sauce creation. The many salads ($6-7.50) include shrimp, oriental, and mandarin orange, as well as cottage cheese and fruit. (☎541-386-1880. Burgers $6-7. Open daily 5:30am-3pm.)

⌐ ACCOMMODATIONS. Hood River accommodations can be expensive, and the smaller motels fill up quickly. The **Bingen School Inn,** one block north of the intersection of Cedar St. and Rte. 14 in Bingen, is cheap and friendly, though it's separated by a toll bridge from Hood River. The converted schoolhouse offers both huge private rooms and clean, dorm-style bunks. The old gymnasium is open for basketball and volleyball players, and the cafeteria is now a television lounge and open kitchen. (☎509-493-3363. Linen $3. Check-in 6-9pm. Dorms $16; private room doubles Su-Th $40, F-Sa $45. $10 per additional person. $40 per night for over 2 nights, even on weekends.) The astoundingly cheap prices at the **Lone Pine Motel,** 2429 Cascade Ave., make it a popular stay, though finding a room here is not always possible. The rooms are clean and well kept, if slightly older, and some retain their lovely wood flooring. (☎541-387-8882. Rooms $25-60. Weekly rooms $125.) **Praters Motel,** 1306 Oak St., is a bit more expensive, though still cheaper than many places in town, and provides excellent gorge views from its alabaster building. Its seven rooms are all decorated in the same pretty, unspoiled white as the exterior, and come with refrigerators and microwaves. (☎541-386-3566. Rooms in summer $44-64; in winter $40-55.)

⚔ APPROACHING MOUNT HOOD
From Hood River, take Oak St. east until it runs into State St., then drive south on **Rte. 35.** it's just over 40 mi. to the intersection with **U.S. 26,** a central point in the arc of area campsites and trailheads.

MOUNT HOOD

Mt. Hood dominates the northwestern skyline of the entire Columbia River Gorge area. Fumaroles and steam vents near the top mark this as a recently active volcano, but that's no deterrent for thousands of outdoors enthusiasts who gravitate to the snowy horn of the mountain. The lower slopes offer easy hiking, while, for the daring, the high-altitude timberline trails wind their way toward the summit. Snow clings to the upper reaches almost year-round, so skiers and snowboarders will feel right at home, even in July.

(VITAL STATS)

Elevation: 11,235 ft.

Visitor Info: Hood River Ranger District Station, 6780 Rte. 35, (☎541-352-6002). Northwest Forest Passes. Open daily 8am-4:30pm; Labor Day-Memorial Day closed Sa-Su.

Gateway towns: Hood River (p. 613), Government Camp.

Fees: Northwest Forest Pass required for some hiking; $5 per day, $30 per year.

⌐ GETTING AROUND

Rte. 35 runs east of Mt. Hood, allowing access to many of the area's trailheads and campsites. Near the southeast edge of the mountain, Rte. 35 meets **U.S. 26,** which leads to the other major trails and camps. Restaurants, motels, and stores can be found in the touristy village of **Government Camp,** which lies on U.S. 26 just east of the intersection with Rte. 35. The town lies on a single road off the highway, **Government Camp Loop.**

◉ SIGHTS

Six miles up a road just east of Government Camp stands the historic **Timberline Lodge,** built by hand in 1937 under the New Deal's Works Progress Administration. The arched hallways are well worth touring for their unorthodox architecture; the timber pillars are meant to represent the pioneers, and the wrought-iron and carvings represent Native Americans. Paintings of wildflowers pay tribute to the other forms of life thriving on the mountain. Timberline's **Magic Mile** express lift carries passengers above the clouds for spectacular views of the mountains and ridges north, though if it's sunny, extra elevation doesn't improve on the view from the Timberline Lodge road. (☎503-622-7979; www.timberlinelodge.com. $8 per person, over 3 people $6 per person. Lift runs whenever the ski lifts are running.)

In the summer, the **Mount Hood Ski Bowl** opens its **Action Park,** which features Indy Kart racing, batting cages, mini-golf ($5), an alpine slide ($7), helicopter rides ($20), horseback riding ($25 per hr.), and bungee jumping ($25). Day passes are available for $16-45, covering different attractions. (☎503-222-2695; www.skibowl.com. Open M-Th 11am-6pm, F 11am-7pm, Sa-Su 10am-7pm.) The Ski Bowl maintains 40 mi. of **bike trails** ($5 trail permit), and **Hurricane Racing** rents mountain bikes from mid-June to October. ($10 per hr., $32 per day; trail permit included.)

🎿 HIKING

Hiking trails circle Mt. Hood; simple maps are posted around **Government Camp.** Maps detailing trailhead locations and the required Northwest Forest Pass are available at the Mt. Hood Ranger District Station. **Timberline Mountain Guides** (☎541-312-9242; www.timberlinemtguides.com), based out of Timberline Lodge, guides summit climbs for $375.

Mirror Lake Trail (6 mi. round-trip, 2-3hr.). Trailhead at a parking lot off U.S. 26, 1 mi. west of Government Camp. A popular day hike, this trail winds its way to the beautiful Mirror Lake. Easy to moderate.

Trillium Lake Loop (4½ mi. round-trip, 1-2hr.). Trailhead in the day-use area of the Trillium Lake Campground. A lakeside trail offering wildlife-viewing and alpine wetlands. Easy to moderate.

Elk Meadows North Trail (7 mi. one-way). Trailhead 25 mi. south of Hood River along Rte. 35, across the highway from the Polallie parking area. This trail rises sharply into the meadows around Mt. Hood, giving spectacular views of the mountain. Campsites are sheltered in the trees at the meadows' edge. Moderate to strenuous.

🍴 FOOD

Government Camp is small and touristy, but its restaurants are still fairly priced. Eight home-brewed ales are on tap at the **Mt. Hood Brewing Co.,** 87304 E. Government Camp Loop, for $4 per pint. Entrees ($12-19) include lots of meat and fish—bratwurst, ribs, halibut, and the specialty Ginger Soy Grilled Beef Tenderloin ($19). Creatively named pizzas like the Goofus Bug, Squirrel Tail Streamer and the Golden Badger are $10-13. (☎503-272-3724; www.mthoodbrewing.com. Open Su-Th noon-

10pm, F-Sa noon-11pm.) The **Huckleberry Inn,** 88611 Bus. U.S. 26, serves generous portions of classic fare. Entrees are straightforward but hearty. (☎503-272-3325. Burgers $6-8. Salads $4.50-8. Open 24hr.)

🏠 ACCOMMODATIONS

Most campgrounds in **Mt. Hood National Forest** cluster near the junction of U.S. 26 and Rte. 35, though they can also be found along the length of both highways on the way to Portland or Hood River. To reach **free camping** spots near the mountain, take the sign toward Trillium Lake (a few miles east of Government Camp on U.S. 26), then follow a dirt road to the right half a mile from the entrance with sign "2650 131," and make a left toward "Old Airstrip." Campsites with fire rings line the abandoned runway. For a more expensive, less outdoorsy experience, stay in a hotel in **Government Camp,** or camp on the mountain. (☎877-444-6777. Sites $9.)

Lost Lake Resort (☎541-386-6366; www.lostlakeresort.org). From Rte. 35, turn east onto Woodworth Dr., right onto Dee Hwy., and then left on Lost Lake Rd. (Forest Service Rd. 13). Sites with water and toilets. A 3 mi. hike around the lake provides views of Mt. Hood. Rent a canoe ($8 per hr.), or fish in the trout-stocked lake. 121 sites. Sites $15; RV sites without electricity $18; cabins $45-100.

Trilium Lake, off U.S. 26, less than 2 mi. west of the Rte. 35/U.S. 26 intersection. The lakeside is beautiful, but the paved, popular sites are close together in some spots. Sites $14-16. Firewood $5.

Still Creek, 1 mi. west of Trillium Lake, off US 26. Generally less crowded than Trillium Lake; even when full, the thickly wooded grounds are quieter, as the sites are more widely spaced than those at the lake. Potable water, toilets, few RVs. Sites $14-16.

Huckleberry Inn, 88611 Bus. U.S. 26, (☎503-227-2335), at the edge of Government Camp. This pretty mountain resort becomes a good deal if enough people are involved. TVs in rooms. Coin-op laundry. Doubles $72; 6-person rooms $101; 10-person rooms $128; suite with kitchen and living room $149.

🚗 LEAVING MOUNT HOOD
Though **U.S. 26** will lead right to Portland, this route circumvents the last bit of the Oregon Trail, as

OREGON TRAIL

well as the western end of the **Columbia Gorge Scenic Area,** which may be the most beautiful stretch along the entire trail. To return to Hood River and Scenic Area, just take **Rte. 35** heading north.

THE ROAD TO PORTLAND

The western regions of the Columbia Gorge Scenic Area are its best; dusty hills give way to evergreen ridges and narrow towers of rock. A number of attractions dot the Washington side of the river, but the greatest draw is the narrow, wooded **Historic Columbia River Hwy.,** on the Oregon side of the waters. A little more than 5 mi. west of Hood River along I-84 is **Viento State Park,** a small park nestled between the highway and the river. This hidden set of campsites, off Exit 56, has water, toilets and showers. (☎541-374-8811. Tent sites $14; RVs $16. Showers $2.) Continuing on, the Historic Columbia River Hwy. leads below a mossy cliff over which flow **seven waterfalls,** five of which are visible right from the road. Unfortunately, the narrow road can be heavy with traffic, and the parking areas below the falls pack in the summer. A slow speed limit and the road's remarkable proximity to the falls mean there's no need to fight for a parking spot; rolled down windows are a perfectly acceptable and dazzling way to marvel at this bit of the world. The first waterfall along the drive is **Horsetail,** a tall, gracefully narrow cataract. Three miles farther is the best of waterfalls, **Multnomah.** Cascading 620 ft. from Larch Mountain, this is the second-highest year-round waterfall in the US. Just beyond are the gentle **Wahkeena Falls,** rolling down a rocky slope after a short free fall. Beyond these lie **Bridal Veil** and **Latourell.** From there, the road winds up to the overlook at Crown Point, then returns to **I-84** at Exit 22, near Corbett. Seventeen miles farther west are the borders of Portland.

APPROACHING PORTLAND

Continue along **I-84** 9 mi. to Exit 1, exit here, and continue straight through the stop lights. You'll reach the intersection with **NE Grand Ave.** and then **NE Martin Luther King Jr. Blvd.** Turn south down MLK Jr. Blvd. to **Burnside St.,** the city's central road.

PORTLAND

With over 200 parks, the pristine Willamette River, and snow-capped Mt. Hood in the background, Portland is an oasis of natural beauty. In the rainy season, Portland's residents flood pubs and clubs, where musicians often strum, sing, or spin for free. Improvisational theaters are in constant production, and the brave can chime in at open mic nights all over town. A fitting (near) end to any roadtrip, Portland embodies a fascinating convergence of the filthy alleyways of every American city and the progressive pubs that represent the green-minded youth of the new millennium.

VITAL STATS

Population: 540,000

Visitor Info: Visitor Information Center, 701 SW 6th St. (☎877-678-5263; www.travelportland.com), in Pioneer Courthouse Sq. Open M-F 8:30am-5:30pm.

Internet Access: Multnomah County Library, 801 SW 10th St. (☎503-988-5234; www.multcolib.org). Open M-Th 9am-9pm, F-Sa 9am-6pm, Su 1-5pm.

Post Office: (☎800-275-8777), on Burnside St. Open M-F 7:30am-6:30pm, Sa 8:30am-5pm. **Postal Code:** 97208.

■ GETTING AROUND

Portland, the biggest city on the trail, feels huge. It is divided into four smaller chunks by the north-south **Willamette River** and east-west **Burnside St.** All streets bear a SW, NW, NE or SE prefix, except for Burnside St., which is just "East" or "West." The river can be crossed by a series of bridges. The **Burnside Bridge** is undoubtedly the most convenient, located near Exit 1.

In southwest Portland, the rectangle enclosed roughly by Burnside St., **4th St.** and **13th St.,** extending south for about ten blocks, is known as **downtown. Old Town,** in northwest Portland, encompasses most of the city's historic sector. Some areas in northwest and southwest Portland around W. Burnside St. are best not walked alone at night. To the north, **Nob Hill** and **Pearl District** feature recently revitalized homes and many of the hippest shops in the city. Southeast Portland contains parks, factories, local businesses, and residential areas. A rich array of cafes, theaters, and restaurants lines **Hawthorne Blvd. Williams Ave.** frames "the North." North and Northeast Portland are chiefly residential, punctuated by a few parks and the **University of Portland.** The east side of the city is decidedly easiest for driving. Here, one-way-south **Martin Luther King Jr. (MLK Jr.) Blvd.,** runs right alongside the river. One block west is its one-way-north twin, **Grand Ave.** The whole area is an incredibly easy-to-maneuver grid, except for **Sandy Blvd.** which winds indiscriminately through the eastern city.

Parking in the east side of the city is plentiful and free, while parking in the western half is very competitive, growing ever more so toward downtown. Parking between the River and SW/NW 11th St. is metered ($1 per hr.; 3hr. limit) from 8am to 6pm Monday through Saturday; a lot of money can be saved by traveling in the evening, or on Sundays. Parking generally is free west of 11th or 12th St. Roadtrippers might want to consider parking and taking advantage of the eco-friendly city's excellent public transportation system.

👁 SIGHTS

WASHINGTON PARK

Fewer than ten blocks west of downtown is the sprawl of Washington Park, a woodland tract encompassing many of Portland's acclaimed gardens. Head west on Burnside St., past 23rd Ave., take a left on Tichner, and turn right at the first intersection onto Kingston Ave. It will eventually reach a T-junction, which is the center of the gardens area.

ROSE GARDEN. To the left after the park entrance is the main entrance to the Rose Garden. The summer blossoms flower in all colors of the rainbow, from dusky red to a watery blue-violet. A sea of blooms arrests the eye, validating Portland's reputation as the City of Roses. *(400 SW Kingston St. ☎ 503-823-3636. Open daily 5am-10pm. Free.)*

JAPANESE GARDENS. Portland's scenic Japanese Gardens, spread across five acres, are reputed to be the most authentic this side of the Pacific Spread. Wandering amid the flora delicately entangling the wood and stone walkways, it is nearly impossible to tell what is arranged and what has grown naturally. *(611 SW Kingston Ave., across the street from the Rose Gardens. ☎ 503-223-1321. Open Apr.-Sept. M noon-7pm, Tu-Su 10am-7pm; Oct.-Mar. M noon-4pm, Tu-Su 10am-4pm. Tours Apr.-Oct. daily 10:45am and 2:30pm. $6.50, seniors $5, students $4, under 6 free.)*

HOYT ARBORETUM. The Hoyt Arboretum, perched at the crest of the hill above the other gardens, features 200 acres of trees. Twelve miles of trails run through the forest, which is home to trees from as far away as the Tierra del Fuego,

south of the Antarctic Circle. *(4000 Fairview Blvd. Take Kingston Ave. to Knights Ave. and turn right, then turn right on Fairview Blvd. ☎ 503-228-8733; www.hoytarboretum.org. Visitors Center open daily 9am-4pm. Tours Apr.-Oct. Sa-Su 2pm. Free.)*

OREGON ZOO. African savannah and rainforest enclosures contain the most exotic of the zoo's creatures, except for the Asian elephants, while the vast Great Northwest and Pacific Shores habitats are home to sea lions and leopards. *(4001 SW Canyon Rd. ☎ 503-220-2493; www/oregonzoo.org. Gates open daily Apr. 15-Sept. 15 9am-6pm; Sept. 16-Apr. 14 9am-4pm. Grounds close 1hr. later. $9, seniors $7.50, ages 3-11 $6.)*

OTHER GARDENS AND PARKS

CLASSICAL CHINESE GARDENS. The largest Ming-style gardens outside of China, the Classical Chinese Gardens occupy a full city block. The large pond and ornate decorations invite a meditative stay. A branching, mosaic-flagged path passes through the intricately bound plants, stones, streams and structures. The only thing more beautiful than the buildings are their names: Moon-locking Pavilion, Painted Boat in Misty Rain, and the Hall of Brocade Clouds. *(At NW 3rd Ave. and Everett St. ☎ 503-228-8131; www.portlandchinesegarden.org. Open daily Apr.-Oct. 9am-6pm; Nov.-Mar. 10am-5pm. $7, seniors $6, students $5.50, under 5 free.)*

FOREST PARK. Joined to the northern edge of Washington park, Forest Park spans 5000 acres, large enough that it suffers from the August fire season like all the great tracts of Western forest. The woods, crisscrossed by 74 mi. of trails, trace Portland's far western edge.

THE GROTTO. In the far-eastern regions of Portland is the Catholic forest-sanctuary known as the Grotto. The towering pines of this quiet, uncrowded forest shelter recessed statues of saints, including a *pieta* set into a shrine hewn in the cliff-face overhead. Take the elevator up to the top, where a monastery sits beside a silent lake. *(At NE 85th St. and Sandy Blvd. Drive east on I-84 to Exit 5. From the ramp, turn right onto Multnomah St., then right again on 82nd St. After about 1 mi., take a 3rd right onto Sandy Blvd. ☎ 503-254-7371; www.thegrotto.org. Grounds open daily summer 9am-8:30pm; winter 9am-5:30pm. Lower level free. Elevator tokens $3, ages 6-11 and seniors $2.50.)*

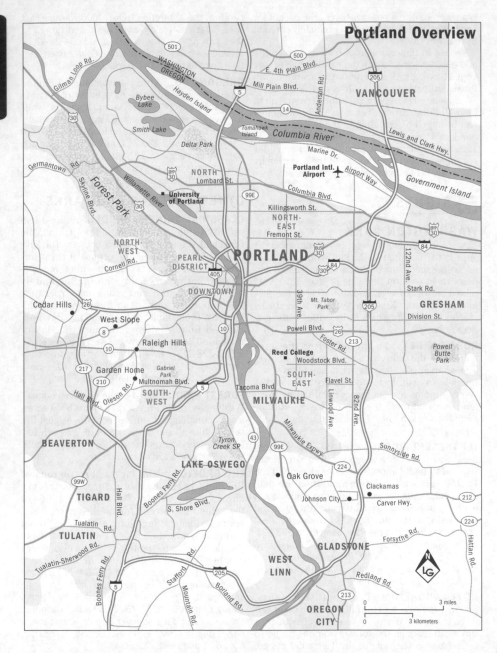

Portland Overview

501
500
E. 4th Plain Blvd.
205
WASHINGTON
OREGON
Gilman Loop Rd.
Mill Plain Blvd.
5
Anderson Rd.
VANCOUVER
Hayden Island
Bybee Lake
14
30
Smith Lake
Tomahawk Island
Columbia River
Marine Dr.
Lewis and Clark Hwy.
Delta Park
Germantown Rd.
Portland Intl. Airport
Airport Way
Government Island
Forest Park
Willamette River
BUS 30
NORTH
Lombard St.
Columbia Blvd.
Skyline Blvd.
University of Portland
99E
Killingsworth St.
BYP 30
NORTH-WEST
NORTH-EAST
Fremont St.
84
Cornell Rd.
PEARL DISTRICT
405
BUS 30
30
84
122nd Ave.
Cedar Hills
26
DOWNTOWN
Stark Rd.
West Slope
10
205
GRESHAM
8
39th Ave.
Mt. Tabor Park
Division St.
10
Raleigh Hills
Powell Blvd.
26
213
Powell Butte Park
217
Garden Home
Gabriel Park
Foster Rd.
Reed College
Woodstock Blvd.
210
Multnomah Blvd.
5
SOUTH-EAST
Hall Blvd.
Oleson Rd.
SOUTH-WEST
Tacoma Blvd.
Flavel St.
82nd Ave.
MILWAUKIE
Linwood Ave.
BEAVERTON
43
Tyron Creek SP
99E
Milwaukie Expwy.
Sunnyside Rd.
LAKE OSWEGO
224
99W
Boones Ferry Rd.
Oak Grove
212
TIGARD
Hall Blvd.
S. Shore Blvd.
Clackamas
Carver Hwy.
Johnson City
224
Tualatin Rd.
TULATIN
Forsythe Rd.
Hattan Rd.
Tualatin-Sherwood Rd.
Boones Ferry Rd.
Stafford Rd.
GLADSTONE
Mountain Rd.
Borland Rd.
205
WEST LINN
Redland Rd.
N
5
213
OREGON CITY

0   3 miles
0   3 kilometers

MUSEUMS

PORTLAND ART MUSEUM. The Portland Art Museum (PAM) sets itself apart from the rest of Portland's burgeoning arts scene on the strength of its collections, especially those of Asian and Native American art. *(1219 SW Park St., at Jefferson St. ☎ 503-226-2811; www.portlandartmuseum.org. Open summer Su noon-5pm, Tu-W and Sa 10am-5pm, Th-F 10am-8pm; winter Su noon-5pm, Tu-Sa 10am-5pm. $15, students and seniors $13, ages 5-18 $6.)*

OREGON MUSEUM OF SCIENCE AND INDUSTRY. Hands-on exhibits occupy both the young and the old at the Oregon Museum of Science and Industry (OMSI). Attractions include computer construction exhibits, a stuffed sabertooth cat, and a giant ear that can be walked through. Planetarium, Omnimax and laser shows are offered here, as well as tours of the *USS Blueback* submarine. *(1945 SE Water Ave. Follow MLK Jr. Blvd. south past Hawthorne St., take a right onto Clay St., and a left onto Water St. Parking is beyond the giant OMSI sign. ☎ 503-797-4000; www.omsi.edu. Omnimax ☎ 503-797-4640. Planetarium ☎ 503-797-4610. U.S.S. Blueback ☎ 503-797-4624. Museum open mid June to Labor Day daily 9:30am-7pm; Labor Day to mid-June Su and Tu-Sa 9:30am-5:30pm. Blueback open in summer daily 10am-5:40pm. Museum and Omnimax admission each $8.50, ages 3-13 and seniors $6.50. 40min. Combination admission to the museum, an Omnimax film and either the planetarium, laser show, or sub $18/$14. Blueback tours $5.)*

DOWNTOWN

▧ POWELL'S CITY OF BOOKS. Downtown on the edge of the northwest district is Powell's gargantuan bookstore, a cavernous establishment holding almost a million new and used volumes, more than any other bookstore in the US. The bookish vaults are so large that the rooms are color coded to help browsers find their desired title among four floors of books. *(1005 W. Burnside St. ☎ 503-228-4651 or 800-878-7323. Open daily 9am-11pm.)*

PIONEER COURTHOUSE. The still-operational Pioneer Courthouse is the centerpiece of the **Pioneer Courthouse Square.** Since opening in 1983, it has become "Portland's Living Room." Tourists and urbanites of every ilk hang out in the brick quadrangle. *(715 SW Morrison St., at 5th Ave. and Morrison St. Events hotline ☎ 503-525-3738.)*

♪ ENTERTAINMENT

Portland's major daily newspaper, the *Oregonian*, lists upcoming events in its Friday edition, and the city's favorite free cultural reader, the *Wednesday Willamette Week*, is a reliable guide to local music, plays, and art. The **Oregon Symphony Orchestra**, 923 SW Washington St., plays classics from September to June. On Sundays and Mondays, students can buy $5 tickets one week before showtime. (☎ 503-228-1353 or 800-228-7343. Box office open M-F 9am-5pm; in symphony season also Sa 9am-5pm. Tickets $17-76; "Symphony Sunday" afternoon concerts $20, students $14.) **Noon Tunes,** at Pioneer Courthouse Sq., presents a potpourri of rock, jazz, folk, and world music. In the evenings, blues drift through the square in the **Live After 5** series. (☎ 503-223-1613. July-Aug. Noon Tunes Tu and Th at noon; Live After 5 Th 5pm. Subject to change.)

Portland Center Stage, in the Portland Center for Performing Arts at SW Broadway and SW Main St., stages classics, modern adaptations, and world premiers. (☎ 503-274-6588. Late Sept.-Apr. Tickets $25-55.) The **Bagdad Theater and Pub,** 3702 SE Hawthorne Blvd., shows second-run mainstream films and has an excellent beer menu. (☎ 503-288-3286. Pub open M-Sa 11am-1am, Su noon-midnight. 21+ after 9pm.) Basketball fans can watch the **Portland Trailblazers** at the **Rose Garden Arena,** 1 Center Ct. (☎ 503-321-3211; for tickets ☎ 503-224-4400; www.rosequarter.com).

❋ FESTIVALS

Portland's premier summer event is the ▧**Rose Festival** (☎ 503-227-2681; www.rosefestival.org), which lasts the entirety of June. A starlight parade and the nation's second-largest floral parade are the central highlights; finding a spot for the rose parade requires an early morning stake-out, at latest. Carnivals, local rodeo courts and naval ships all come to the city along with a massive visitor influx; expect severe room shortages during the early part of June. In early July, the three-day ▧**Waterfront Blues Festival** (☎ 800-973-3378; www.waterfrontbluesfest.com) draws some of the world's finest blues artists. The **Oregon Brewers Festival,** on the last full weekend in July, is the continent's largest gathering of independent brewers, making for one incredible party at Waterfront Park. Buy the (required) mug and tokens to fill it up. (☎503-778-5917; www.oregonbrewfest.com. Under 21 must be accompanied by parent. Mug $3; beer tokens $1 each.) Between the beginning of March and Christmas Eve, the segment of NW 1st St. that runs beneath Burnside is taken over every Saturday (and, oddly, Sunday) by the **Portland Saturday Market.** Vendors ply their wares in an open-air market. (☎503-222-6672; www.portland-saturdaymarket.com. Open Sa 10am-5pm, Su 11am-4:30pm.) The **Northwest Film Center,** 1219 SW Park Ave., hosts the **Portland International Film Festival** in the last two weeks of February, with 100 films from 30 nations. (☎503-221-1156. Box office opens 30min. before each show. $7, students and seniors $6.)

FOOD

Eating in Portland need never be dull; vegan and vegetarian food abounds, most menus are quirky and original, and restaurant decor runs the gamut from the abstract to the blasphemous. Some of the best eateries are found in the southeast (around 30th and Belmont St.), and in the northwest (around 20th and Irving St.).

■ **The Roxy,** 1121 SW Stark St. (☎503-223-9160). Giant crucified Jesus with neon halo, pierced waitstaff, and quirky menu. Drink plenty, so you have an excuse to use the mighty Gaysha Starr Imperial Toilet. Burgers $5-8. Sandwiches $5-6.50. Open Su and Tu-Sa 24hr.

■ **Muu-Muu's Big World Diner,** 612 NW 21st Ave. (☎503-223-8169), at Hoyt St. Artful goofiness—the name of the restaurant was drawn from a hat—amidst red velvet curtains and gold upholstery. Appetizers $3.50-6.50. Entrees $7.50-14. Open M-F 11:30am-1am, Sa-Su 10am-1am.

Nicholas Restaurant, 318 SE Grand Ave. (☎503-235-5123), between Oak and Pine St. Phenomenal Mediterranean food and atmosphere. Sandwiches $5-6. Open M-Sa 11am-9pm, Su noon-9pm.

Calendula, 3257 Hawthorne Blvd. (☎503-235-6800; www.calendula-cafe.com). A completely vegan restaurant with indoor, sidewalk, and balcony seating. The creative menu offers walnut burgers and lots of vegan pancakes. Appetizers $3-7. Entrees $8-13. Open daily 5-10pm; Sa-Su also 10am-3pm.

Laughing Planet Cafe, 3320 SE Belmont St. (☎503-235-6472). Burritos (from $2.25) can be custom-built. Quesadillas ($3-6) and vegan burgers (grain or soy; $4-6) are sold alongside the smoothies ($3.25). Open M-Sa 11am-10pm, Su 11am-9pm.

IN THE PASSENGER SEAT

HAIR OF THE DOG

Hair of the Dog Brewing Company produces what might just be the best beer in a city known for its microbreweries. Let's Go took a tour of the small-scale brewery from co-owner Alan Sprints and got the skinny on the brewing process. (4509 SE 23rd Ave. ☎503-232-6585; www.hairofthedog.com.)

LG: Are you more interested in consistency, or do you prefer experimenting?

A: I enjoy when people like using our beer for celebrating special events and special occasions...it makes me feel good. If it wasn't for people that enjoyed drinking the beer, brewing it wouldn't be so much fun.

LG: What about the name of the brewery, "Hair of the Dog?"

A: Originally, the term literally referred to using the hair of a dog that bit you to help heal the bite. They'd chase a dog down, cut off some of its hair, [then] wrap it around the wound. And that helped chase away the evil spirit.

LG: And that's also for a hangover?

A: Yes, the term later became used in reference to curing a hangover—drinking some of the "hair of the dog" you had the night before (more beer).

LG: Do these beers, having a higher alcohol content, give drinkers a stronger hangover?

A: All I know is we've generated quite a few hangovers.

LG: Oh yeah...? [Feels forehead and eyes the empty glass warily.]

A: Whether the hangovers are worse or not, I don't know. We only use quality ingredients, so you should have a quality hangover.

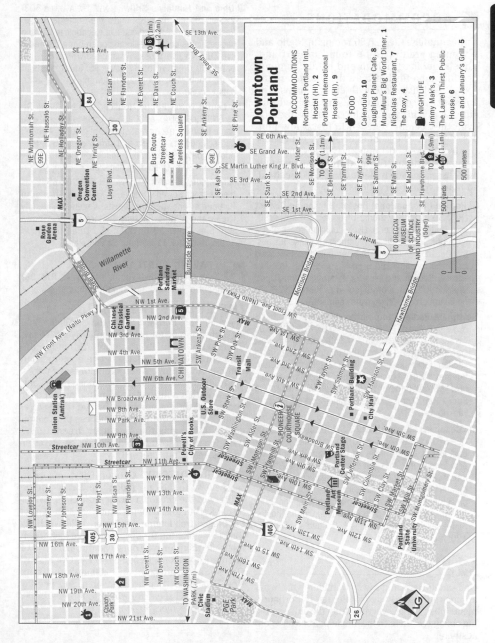

Downtown Portland

ACCOMMODATIONS
Northwest Portland Intl.
Hostel (HI), **2**
Portland International
Hostel (HI), **9**

FOOD
Calendula, **10**
Laughing Planet Cafe, **8**
Muu-Muu's Big World Diner, **1**
Nicholas Restaurant, **7**
The Roxy, **4**

NIGHTLIFE
Jimmy MaK's, **3**
The Laurel Thirst Public
House, **6**
Ohm and January's Grill, **5**

🏠 ACCOMMODATIONS

Unfortunately, the $20-30 rooms of Idaho and Wyoming are not to be found in Portland. Those looking for high-end establishments need look no further than the blocks around Exit 1, which are rife with classy chains. The cheapest accommodations are located outside of downtown, in the suburbs; luckily, even they can be reached in just a few minutes by car. These budget spots, especially the few hostels, fill quickly. All accommodations in Portland fill up during the summer months, particularly during the Rose Festival, so make your reservations early.

🏅 **Portland International Hostel, Hawthorne District (HI),** 3031 SE Hawthorne Blvd. (☎503-236-3380; www.portlandhostel.org). Lively common space and a huge porch define this environmentally conscious hostel. Outdoor stage with Th open mic draws a crowd from the building and area. Free wireless Internet access. Kitchen and laundry. Reception 8am-10pm. Check-out 11am. Dorms (co-ed available) $16-19, nonmembers $19-22; private rooms $36-42.

Northwest Portland International Hostel (HI), 1818 NW Glisan St. (☎503-241-2783; www.2oregonhostels.com), at 18th Ave. on the west side of the river. This snug Victorian building has a kitchen, lockers, laundry, and a small espresso bar. Internet $1 per 16min. 34 dorm beds (co-ed available). Street parking permits available. Reception 8am-11pm. Dorms $16-19, nonmembers $19-22; private doubles $36-59.

McMenamins Edgefield, 2126 SW Halsey St. (☎503-669-8610 or 800-669-8610), in Troutdale. Take I-84 East to Exit 16; turn right off the ramp. Beautiful 38-acre former farm is a posh escape that keeps 2 hostel rooms. Brewery, vineyards, 18-hole golf course, movie theater, and several restaurants. Live acoustic music on summer nights. No TVs or phones. Reception 24hr. Call ahead in summer; no reservations for the hostel. Single-sex dorms $20; singles $50; doubles from $85-120; family rooms for 6 $200.

🍸 NIGHTLIFE

Once an uncouth and rowdy frontier town, always an uncouth and rowdy frontier town. Portland's nightclubs cater to everyone from the clove-smoking college aesthete to the nipple-pierced neo-goth aesthete.

🏅 **Ohm and January's Grill,** 31 NW 1st Ave. (☎503-223-9919), at Couch St., under the Burnside Bridge. Restaurant and club dedicated to electronic music and unclassifiable beats. Weekends often bring big-name live DJs. Th live music. W spoken-word with live band. Su drum 'n' bass. Cover $5. Music starts at 9pm. Open M-Th 10am-2pm, starting F open 24hr. until 2am Su.

The Laurel Thirst Public House, 2958 NE Glisan St. (☎503-232-1504), at 30th Ave. Local talent makes a name for itself in 2 intimate rooms of groovin', boozin', and schmoozin'. Burgers and sandwiches $5-8. Free pool all day Tu. Free happy hour show 6-8pm. Cover after $2-5 8pm. Open daily 9am-2am.

Jimmy Mak's, 300 NW 10th Ave. (☎503-295-6542), 3 blocks from Powell's Books, at Flanders St. Jam to Portland's renowned jazz artists. Vegetarian-friendly Greek and Middle Eastern dinners $8-17. Shows 9:30pm. Cover $3-6. Open M 11am-3pm, Tu-W 11am-1am, Th-F 11am-2am, Sa 6pm-2am.

🚩 LEAVING PORTLAND
Take **MLK Jr. Blvd.** south. It becomes **Rte. 99,** leading out of Portland and into the suburbs.

THE END OF THE TRAIL
The road from Portland to Oregon City is the final leg of the journey for pioneers and drivers. Today, the roughly 10 mi. from central Portland to the limits of Oregon City have become a suburban commercial sprawl. After a mile or so of parks, the road becomes a strip of car dealerships and fast food. It's a little disappointing, perhaps, or perhaps all the entrepreneurs behind those storefronts are signs of the giant success of the emigrants in bringing the American Dream to the west. **Rte. 99,** also known in this area as **McLoughlin Blvd.,** leads into Oregon City.

⊕ OREGON CITY. Oregon City was once home to the only federal land office in the entirety of the Oregon Territory; travelers had little choice but to end their journey here. The **End of the Oregon Trail Interpretive Center,** 1726 Washington St., is great fun for those who have just driven the route themselves. Tours lead through a trio of mammoth wagons. (☎503-657-9336. Open Mar.-Oct. M-Sa 9:30am-5pm, Su 10:30am-5pm. Tours Nov.-Feb. M-Sa 3 per day 11am-4pm, Su 2 per day noon-4pm. Call ahead for winter tour times. $7.50, ages 5-12 $5, seniors $6.50.)

THE NORTH AMERICAN

This is the big one. Spanning three countries and over 5000 mi., the North American Route is roadtripping-gone-extreme-sport. To put this distance in perspective, that's one-fifth of the circumference of the earth. For those whose wanderlust can't be sated by a cross-country Sunday drive the North American can satisfy every desire.

Cities? Try Mexico City, Guadalajara, Tucson, Phoenix, Las Vegas, Edmonton and Anchorage. Outdoor sights? The North American has Nat-Soo-Pah Hot Springs, Shoshone Falls, Snake River Canyon, Bald Mountain, and Sawtooth National Recreation Area—and that's just in Idaho.

The route begins in **Mexico City,** a megalopolis of 26 million. See the Diego Rivera mural that New York missed in the **Palacio de Bellas Artes** (p. 628), and explore Mexico's pre-Columbian past at the **Templo Mayor** (p. 627). From there the road swoops into **Zitácuaro** to catch the **Monarch Butterflies,** before arriving in **Guadalajara** (p. 647), cradle of mariachi music and the Mexican hat dance. We won't need to tell you what to do at the **Sauza Factory** in **Tequila** (p. 653)—just don't get back on the road afterward. Bronze your body on the beaches of Mazatlán before detouring to **Alamos** (p. 660), a silver-mine ghost town. Next, the road makes a run for the border, leaving restless **Nogales, Mex.** for its American cousin, **Nogales, AZ.**

Once in the US, the route takes on **Tucson** (p. 670) and **Biosphere 2** (p. 675) before returning to biosphere 1 (Earth). Sleek, modern **Phoenix** (p. 675) is home to **Heard Museum** (p. 676) and Frank Lloyd Wright's **Taliesin West** (p. 679). The North American gets its kicks (briefly) on **Route 66** in **Kingman** (p. 683), before pondering the mind-boggling engineering of the 726 ft. **Hoover Dam** (p. 684).

Play the tables in Las Vegas if you're feeling lucky, or—if you really want to gamble—get hitched at the **Little White Wedding Chapel** (p. 685). Northern Nevada is an empty stretch of open road, save for **Chuck and Bessie's Stage Stop** (p. 694), an old-time gas station, diner, and oasis of convenience in the desert. You'll know

you've entered Idaho when the desert turns to rocky peaks. **Hailey** and **Ketchum** are small towns with big mountains—ski or bike down the slopes of **Bald Mountain** (p. 699). Montana's roads wind under big sky, and **Missoula** (p. 705) is a funky college town surrounded by an outdoors paradise.

> ## ⌐ ROUTE STATS ⌐
>
> **Miles:** c. 5600; 1500 in Mexico, 1600 across the US, and 2500 in Canada and Alaska.
>
> **Route:** Mexico City, D.F., to Anchorage, AK.
>
> **States and Provinces:** 16; Distrito Federal, Estado de México, Michoacán, Jalisco, Nayarit, Sinaloa, Sonora, Arizona, Nevada, Idaho, Montana, British Columbia, Alberta, Yukon Territory, and Alaska.
>
> **Driving Time:** Although four weeks is enough time to cross the continent, you'll want at least seven or eight to see a few things along the way.
>
> **When To Go:** For those planning to travel the entire length, late spring is the best time to begin. Many sights and services along the Alaska Highway don't open until mid-June and close down in the fall, so time your roadtrip accordingly.
>
> **Crossroads: The Southern Border** in Tucson (p. 781) and Phoenix, A7 (p. 771); **Route 66** in Kingman, AZ (p. 529); **The National Road** in Ely, NV (p. 412); **The Oregon Trail** in Twin Falls, ID (p. 594); **The Great North** in Missoula, MT (p. 259) and Banff, AB (p. 273).

Crossing into Canada, the route winds across the continental divide into ritzy **Banff** (p. 713) and sails through the scenic **Icefields Parkway** (p. 721). Escape to the indoors—although it may not seem like it—at the **world's largest mall** (p. 726). Farther north, **Dawson Creek, BC** (p. 729) is Mile 0 of the **Alaska Highway,** which will carry you north past aquamarine lakes and glacier-sharpened peaks en route to **Haines Junction** and **Kluane National Park** (p. 739). Entering Alaska, the road passes through the **Mat-Su Valley** (p. 746) before descending into park-filled **Anchorage** (p. 747).

It's a long road, but its rewards are many. So go on; we dare you.

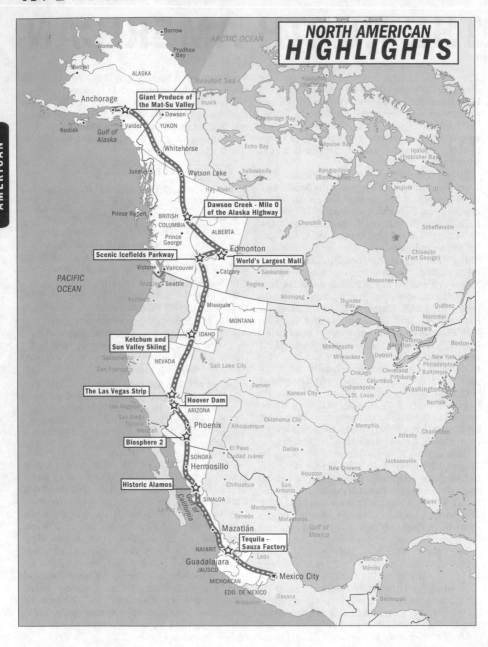

MEXICO: MEXICO CITY TO NOGALES

Welcome To MEXICO

MEXICO CITY

Welcome to one of the most populous and colorful cities in the world. With 26 million people in residence, the city houses one quarter of Mexico's entire population. Incredibly, its large size does not diminish the hospitality of its people. In the city, Mexicans refer to the megalopolis as **el D.F.** (deh-EFF-ay, short for **Distrito Federal;** its residents are called *chilangos*), but to the rest of the country, it is simply **México**, a testament to the city's size and importance.

VITAL STATS

Population: 26 million

Visitor Info: Infotur, Amberes 54 (☎55 5525 93 80), at Londres in the Zona Rosa, M: Insurgentes (Line 1). Helpful staff speaks English. Info booths around town. Open daily 9am-7pm.

Internet Access: Museo Tecnológico, Bosque de Chapultepec (☎55 5229 40 00, ext. 90266). Open daily 9am-5pm. Free.

US Embassy: Paseo de la Reforma 305 (☎55 5080 20 00; www.usembassy-mexico.gov).

Post Office: Lázaro Cárdenas at Tacuba (☎55 5521 73 94), across from the Palacio de Bellas Artes. Open for stamps and *lista de correos* (window 3) M-F 8am-6pm, Sa 9am-4pm, Su 9am-noon. **Mexpost** inside. Open M-F 9am-4pm, Sa 9am-2pm. **Postal Code:** 06002.

GETTING AROUND

Mexico City extends outward from the *centro* roughly 20km to the south, 10km to the north, 10km to the west, and 8km to the east, though there is much debate about where the city actually begins and ends. A rectangular series of routes **(Circuito Interior)** and a system of thoroughfares **(Ejes Viales)** help to make cross-city travel manageable. Of these, the **Eje Central,** commonly known as **Lázaro Cárdenas,** is the central north-south route. A good map of the city's major routes is essential. *Guía Roji Ciudad de México* (110 pesos), a comprehensive street atlas, is a valuable aid for anyone planning to stay in the city for some time. You can also pick up its little sibling, the **mini-Guía Roji** (60 pesos).

At a more local level, the city is difficult to know well; even most *chilangos* don't have it all down pat. What's more, many different neighborhoods use the same street names—more than 300 streets are named for Benito Juárez. Still, it is only a matter of cardinal directions and trial and error before you've mastered the basics of this megalopolis. The most important thing is to know the name of the *colonias* (neighborhoods). Mexico City has over 350 such *colonias;* **Col. Polanco, Zona Rosa, Col. Roma,** and **Col. Juárez** are some of the most touristed. Orient yourself using monuments, museums, *glorietas* (rotaries), and cathedrals.

Parking garages (designated by an **E** for *"estacionmiento publico"*) are everywhere (4-8 pesos per hr.). Avoid valet parking; cars sometimes wind up with the wrong person. Street parking is difficult to find, and vandalism and theft are common. If you return to an empty space, locate the nearest police depot to find out whether your vehicle has been towed or stolen. If anything is missing from the car and you suspect that the police tampered with it, call **LOCATEL** (☎55 5658-11 11).

SIGHTS

Once the nucleus of the Aztec Empire, and later the central command post of Cortés, the thriving capital of Mexico showcases the best of contemporary Mexican art and culture against the backdrop of Spanish-influenced architecture and ancient Aztec ruins. Most museums are closed on Mondays and are free on Sundays. Often, students and teachers with a current ID can get in free or

Metropolitan Mexico City

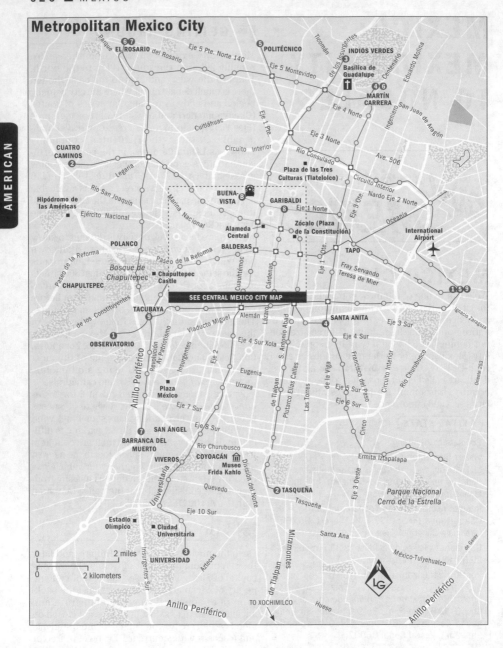

Parque del Rosario
⑥⑦ EL ROSARIO
Eje 5 Pte. Norte 140
⑤ POLITÉCNICO
Ticomán
de los Insurgentes
③ INDIOS VERDES
Eduardo Molina
Centenario
Eje 5 Montevideo
Basílica de Guadalupe †
Ingeniero
San Juan de Aragón
④⑥ MARTÍN CARRERA
Eje 4 Norte
Cuitláhuac
Eje 1 Pte
Eje 3 Norte
Circuito Interior
Río Consulado
Ave. 506

CUATRO CAMINOS ②
Legaría
Río San Joaquín
Circuito Interior
Nardo Eje 2 Norte
Eje 3 Ote.

Hipódromo de las Américas ■
Ejército Nacional
Marina Nacional
Plaza de las Tres Culturas (Tlatelolco) ■
Oceanía

BUENA-VISTA Ⓑ
GARIBALDI
⑧
Eje 1 Norte
International Airport ✈

POLANCO
Paseo de la Reforma
Alameda Central ■
Zócalo (Plaza de la Constitución) □
Eje 1 Ote.

Bosque de Chapultepec
Paseo de la Reforma
BALDERAS
Cuauhtémoc
Cárdenas
TAPO
Fray Servando Teresa de Mier

CHAPULTEPEC
Chapultepec Castle ■
de los Constituyentes
SEE CENTRAL MEXICO CITY MAP
Eje 1 Pte.
①⑤⑨
Ignacio Zaragoza

TACUBAYA ⑨
Alemán
Lázaro
SANTA ANITA ④
Eje 3 Sur
Oriente 353

① OBSERVATORIO
Anillo Periférico
Revolución Av. Patriotismo
Viaducto Miguel
Eje 4 Sur Xola
S. Antonio Abad
Eje 4 Sur
Francisco del paso
Circuito Interior
Río Churubusco

Insurgentes
Eje 2
Eugenia
Urraza
de Tlalpan
Plutarco Elías Calles
de la Viga
Las Torres
Eje 5 Sur
Eje 6 Sur
Plaza México ■
Eje 7 Sur

SAN ÁNGEL
Eje 8 Sur
Cinco
BARRANCA DEL MUERTO ⑦
Río Churubusco
VIVEROS
COYOACÁN 🏛
Ermita Iztapalapa

Universitaria
Museo Frida Kahlo
Quevedo
División del Norte
② TASQUEÑA
Tasqueña
Parque Nacional Cerro de la Estrella

Santa Ana
Estadío Olímpico ■
Ciudad Universitaria ■
Eje 10 Sur
Aztecas
Miramontes
México-Tlayehualco
de Garay

③ UNIVERSIDAD
de Tlalpan

0 ___ 2 miles
0 ___ 2 kilometers
Insurgentes Sur

N
LG

Anillo Periférico
TO XOCHIMILCO
Hueso
Anillo Periférico

for a reduced rates; unfortunately, most archaeological sites and some major museums only offer these discounts to Mexican nationals. There is often a fee for those who wish to carry cameras.

CENTRO HISTÓRICO

On the city's main plaza, known as the **zócalo**, the Aztec **Templo Mayor**, the **Catedral Metropolitana**, and **Palacio Nacional** sit serenely side by side. The architecture suits the eclectic nature of the people; there are street vendors hawking everything from hand-woven bags to batteries, soldiers sporting AK-47s, political protestors, homeless people, and hordes of picture-snapping tourists.

THE ZÓCALO. Officially known as Plaza de la Constitución, the *zócalo* is the principal square of Mexico City. Now surrounded by imposing colonial monuments, the plaza was once the center of Tenochtitlán, the Aztec island-capital. Southwest of the Templo Mayor—the Aztecs' principal place of worship (*Teocalli* in Náhuatl)—was the Aztec marketplace and major square. The space was rebuilt and renamed several times, becoming Plaza de la Constitución in 1812.

CATEDRAL METROPOLITANA. The very first cathedral built in New Spain, the Catedral Metropolitana (begun in 1524 and completed in 1532) sits on the site of the main Aztec temple. Inside, **Altar de Perdón** and **Altar de los Reyes** are decadently covered in gold and offset with paintings, including Juan Correa's murals on the sacristy walls. The chapels honoring the Virgin of Guadalupe are worth a good look. (☎ 55 5510 04 40, ext. 101. Information desk open daily 8am-4pm. No flash photography. Chorus and sacristy tours M-F 11am-2pm and 4-7pm, Sa 11am-1pm and 4-7pm. Bell tower tours M-Sa 8am-6pm, Su 9:30am-6pm. Free cathedral tours Sa 10:30am-1:30pm. Free. Chorus, sacristy, and bell tower tours 10 pesos.)

TEMPLO MAYOR. When Cortés defeated the Aztecs in 1521, one of the first things he did was destroy their main center of worship, the *Teocalli*. He took stones from the plaza and its main temple (the Templo Mayor) to build his magnificent cathedral across the street. Though the temple and surrounding plaza were eventually paved and almost forgotten, they were rediscovered by Metro workers in 1978. The site was extensively excavated, revealing layers of pyramids. Today, a catwalk leads through the outdoor ruins. One of the highlights is the **Great Pyramid,** the remains of a

twin temple, dedicated to Tlaloc (god of rain) and Huitzilopochtli (god of war). At the far end of the ruins, the **Museo del Templo Mayor** takes you on a tour through Aztec civilization. The museum's greatest treasure is the sculpture of **Coyolxauhqui,** goddess of the moon and mother of Huitzilopochtli. An English audio guide is worth every *centavo* if you don't read Spanish. (*On the corner of Seminario and República de Guatemala, between the cathedral and the Palacio Nacional. ☎ 55 5542 49 43. Open Su and Tu-Sa 9am-5pm. 37 pesos; bring exact change. Audio guides 30 pesos.*)

PALACIO NACIONAL. Stretching the entire length of the enormous *zócalo*, the Palacio Nacional occupies the site of Moctezuma's palace. Some of the ruins of the palace are on display inside. Rebuilt several times throughout the centuries, the modern *palacio*, which houses the president's administration, was constructed with stones from the original. The *palacio*'s biggest attractions are the **Diego Rivera murals** in the main staircase and along the western and northern walls. Rivera spent 22 years sketching and painting *Mexico Through the Centuries*. The recently renovated **Museo del Recinto de Homenaje,** on the second floor, is dedicated to the revered Mexican president Benito Juárez. The **Museo del Recinto Parlamentario,** on the second floor of the courtyard, displays political artifacts. Don't leave without visiting the **gardens** at the back of the palace, where immaculate landscaping highlights flowers and cacti from all over Mexico. (*On the east side of the zócalo. Palacio open daily 9am-5pm. Tours M-F 10am-4pm. ID required. Free. Tours 60-70 pesos. Both museums open Su 10am-5pm, Tu-F 9am-5pm, Sa 10am-5pm. Free.*)

SUPREMA CORTE DE JUSTICIA. Four murals painted by José Clemente Orozco in the 1940s cover the second-floor walls of the court, which was built in 1929 where the southern half of Moctezuma's royal palace once stood. (*On the corner of Pino Suárez and Corregidora. ☎ 55 5522 15 00. Open M-F 8am-4:30pm. ID required. Free.*)

MUSEO NACIONAL DE LAS CULTURAS. Originally built in 1731 by Spanish architect Juan Peinado to house the *Real Casa de la Moneda* (Royal Mint), the building was turned into an anthropology museum by order of Emperor Maximilian in 1865. In 1964, the vast collection of prehispanic artifacts was moved to Chapultepec and the museum was converted into a series of colorful exhibits designed promote understanding of different world cultures. *(Moneda 13, just behind the Palacio Nacional. ☎ 55 5521 14 90, ext. 226. Open Su and Tu-Sa 9:30am-5:45pm. Free.)*

THE ALAMEDA

The museums, libraries, and historical buildings around the Alameda are worthy of any cultural capital. Best of all, the Alameda has been cleaned up, and emergency call buttons help make it a much safer area.

ALAMEDA CENTRAL. Today's downtown park was originally an Aztec marketplace and later the site where heretics were burned during the Inquisition. Don Luis de Velasco II created the park in 1592 for the city's elite. The park takes its name from its rows of shady *álamos* (poplars). At the center of the Alameda's southern side is the **Monumento a Juárez,** a marble monument constructed in 1910 to honor the beloved president. *(The Alameda is serviced by 4 Metro stations: M: Bellas Artes (Lines 2, 8), at Hidalgo and Eje Lázaro Cárdenas; M: San Juan de Letrán (Line 8), 1 block from the Torre Latinoamericana; M: Juárez (Line 3), on Balderas 1 block from the park; and, in a less safe area, M: Hidalgo (Lines 2 and 3) at Hidalgo and Paseo de la Reforma.)*

■ PALACIO DE BELLAS ARTES. The middle two floors of this gorgeous Art Nouveau palace are covered by the work of celebrated Mexican muralists. The best-known is a mural on the third floor by Diego Rivera. John D. Rockefeller commissioned Rivera to paint a mural for New York City's Rockefeller Center. Rivera was dismissed from the project when Rockefeller discovered the Soviet flag and a portrait of Lenin in the foreground. The Mexican government asked Rivera to recreate the work; the 1934 result was *El Hombre, Controlador del Universo.* A Marxist vision of revolution, the mural shows man at the controls of a massive industrial apparatus. Rivera did more than keep the portrait of Lenin; he also added a less-than-flattering picture of Rockefeller. *(Juárez and Eje Central, by the park. M: Bellas Artes (Lines 2, 8). ☎ 55 5512 25 93 or 55 5521 92 51, ext. 152, 153, and 154. Open Su and Tu-Sa 10am-6pm. Ticket booth open M-Sa 11am-7pm, Su 10am-7pm. Info booth open daily 9am-9pm. 30 pesos; under 12, students, and teachers free.)*

■ MUSEO NACIONAL DE ARTE. The museum houses the city's most comprehensive collection of Mexican art. Paintings and sculptures dating from 1550 through 1954 are organized chronologically and explained in Spanish. In front is the equestrian statue of Carlos IV of Spain, *El Caballito,* sculpted by Manuel Tolsá. A plaque explains, "Mexico preserves it as a monument of art"—not in honor of the king. *(Tacuba 8, ½ block from Bellas Artes. M: Bellas Artes (Lines 2, 8). ☎ 55 5130 34 60. Open Su and Tu-Sa 10:30am-5:30pm. Free tours noon and 2pm. 30 pesos; students, teachers, under 13, and disabled free. Su free.)*

■ MUSEO MURAL DIEGO RIVERA. Also known as Museo de la Alameda, this fascinating building holds Diego Rivera's 1947 masterpiece, *Sueño de una Tarde Dominical en la Alameda Central.* A key points out famous figures woven into the work: Frida Kahlo, Antonio de Santa Anna, and Hernán Cortés (with his hand covered in blood), among others. Exhibits on Rivera's life and a chart listing his works and their locations, line the walls. One exhibit explains the attack on the painting by 100 university students the morning of June 4, 1948. Ignacio Ramírez was originally depicted holding up the words "God does not exist," an excerpt from a speech he had given in 1836; students blotted out "does not exist," leaving just "God." Rivera allowed the phrase to be left out when the mural was repaired. Upstairs is a modern art exhibit. *(Colón and Balderas, at the end of the Alameda farthest away from Bellas Artes. M: Hidalgo (Lines 2 and 3). ☎ 55 5512 07 59. Open Su and Tu-Sa 10am-6pm. 10 pesos, students free. Su free.)*

■ MUSEO FRANZ MAYER. In the small, sunken Plaza de Santa Veracruz, the restored Hospital de San Juan de Dios houses a beautiful international collection of applied arts. Fliers in English explain parts of the collection. The upstairs library specializes in rare books. Although anyone can enter it, only researchers with credentials can use the books. The courtyard cafe alone is worth the price of admission. *(Hidalgo 45. M: Hidalgo (Lines 2 and 3) or Bellas Artes (Lines 2, 8). ☎ 55 5518 22 66; museo@franzmayer.org.mx. Museum open Su, Tu, Th-Sa 10am-5pm; W 10am-7pm. 20 pesos, students 10 pesos, under 12 and over 70 free. Tu free. Tours 10 pesos. English fliers 2 pesos. Entrance to just the cafe and library 5 pesos.)*

TORRE LATINOAMERICANA. Measuring 182m and 44 stories tall, the Torre is one of the largest buildings in the city. The tower's top-floor observatory commands a startling view of the sprawling city. *(Lázaro Cárdenas and Madero. M: San Juan de Letrán (Line 8). Observatory open daily 9:30am-10pm. 40 pesos.)*

NEAR THE MONUMENTO A LA REVOLUCIÓN

MONUMENTO A LA REVOLUCIÓN AND MUSEO NACIONAL DE LA REVOLUCIÓN. In the early 1900s, President Porfirio Díaz planned this site as the seat of Congress, but progress halted as Revolutionary fighting paralyzed the city streets. Architect Carlos Obregón Sanacilia changed the plans, and instead made a monument to the overthrow of Díaz and his congress. In each of the four supporting columns lies the body of one of Mexico's Revolutionary heroes. The museum under the monument covers Mexican history from 1857 to 1938. Sunday is the only day you can climb to the top of the monument. *(At Plaza de la República. M: Revolución (Line 2). ☎ 55 5546 21 15. Open Su and Tu-Sa 9am-5pm. Call ahead to arrange a tour. 12 pesos, students and children 6 pesos. Su free.)*

MUSEO DEL CHOPO. The modern, relatively tourist-free Chopo displays the works of rising Mexican artists. For 12 years running, the museum has proudly hosted a show of gay and lesbian photography, sculpture, and painting. *(Dr. Enrique González Martínez 10. M: Revolución (Line 2). ☎ 55 5546 12 45; www.chopo.unam.mx. Open Su and Tu-Sa 10am-2pm and 3-7pm. 6 pesos, students 3 pesos; under 10 free. Tu free. Free tours.)*

BOSQUE DE CHAPULTEPEC

The Chapultepec area is home to fabulous museums, myriad hiking paths, and charming streetside vendors. Renting a bike is the best way to see the whole park (rentals by the anthropology museum), though boat rides are the most relaxing. The liveliest time to visit is on Sunday, when families flock to open-air concerts and enjoy free admission to the zoo and museums.

The Chapultepec area is divided into three sections. The first section is the busiest, with the most museums, sights, and people. The second section has fewer tourists and more locals, and is generally less busy. The third section has the fewest attractions but features the water parks El Rollo and Atlantis. It is also the least safe, with hardly any security guards. The park is an adventure in itself. It spans 2100 acres and has been the oldest and biggest urban park in the Americas since the Aztec emperor Moctezuma established it

in the 15th century. *(Section 1: M: Chapultepec (Line 1), by the Niños Héroes monument and museums. Section 2: M: Constituyentes (Line 7). Section 3: take an "El Rollo" pesero from M: Constituyentes. Park open daily 5am-4:30pm.)*

SECTION ONE

▨ MUSEO NACIONAL DE ANTROPOLOGÍA. To visit all 23 halls, be prepared to walk 5km. Besides holding Mexico's most impressive archaeological and ethnographic treasures, this museum is the biggest in all of Latin America. As you enter on the right side of the ground floor, an introduction to anthropology precedes chronologically arranged galleries tracing the histories of central Mexican groups, from the first migration to America through the Spanish Conquest. In the **Sala México** stands the museum's crown jewel, the huge Sun Stone, known as the **Aztec Calendar.** In the center you can see the god Xiuhtecuhtli sticking out his huge tongue, which doubles as a sacrificial knife. *(Paseo de la Reforma and Gandhi. Take an "Auditorio" pesero (2 pesos) southwest on Reforma and get off at the 2nd stop after entering the park. ☎ 55 5553 63 86. Open Su and Tu-Sa 9am-7pm. Call ahead for a free tour for groups of 5 or more. 37 pesos. Audio guides in English 60 pesos.)*

▨ MUSEO NACIONAL DE HISTORIA. Housed in the Castle of Chapultepec, once home of the hapless Emperor Maximilian, this museum exhaustively narrates the history of Mexico since the Spanish Conquest. An immense portrait of King Ferdinand and Queen Isabella of Spain greets visitors in the first room. Galleries contain displays on Mexican economy and society during the War for Independence, the Porfiriato, and the Revolution. *(Walk up the hill directly behind the Niños Héroes monument to the castle. ☎ 55 5241 31 14 or 5241 31 15. Open Su and Tu-Sa 9am-4:15pm; last admission 4pm. 37 pesos; under 13, over 30, students, teachers, and disabled free.)*

MONUMENTO A LOS NIÑOS HÉROES. In 1847, as US troops invaded Mexico City during the Mexican-American War, military academy cadets had to protect the last Mexican stronghold in the capital, Chapultepec Castle. Legend has it that as the troops closed in, the last six teenagers left alive wrapped themselves in a Mexican flag and threw themselves from the castle wall rather than surrender. The six white pillars of this monument honor the boy heroes. *(On the east side of the park; follow the signs or look for the gigantic white pillars.)*

Central Mexico City

⌂ ACCOMMODATIONS
Casa de los Amigos, **1**
Hostal Moneda, **7**
Hostel Catedral (HI), **6**
Hotel Avenida, **4**
Hotel Calvin, **2**
Hotel Manolo I, **3**
Hotel Rioja, **5**

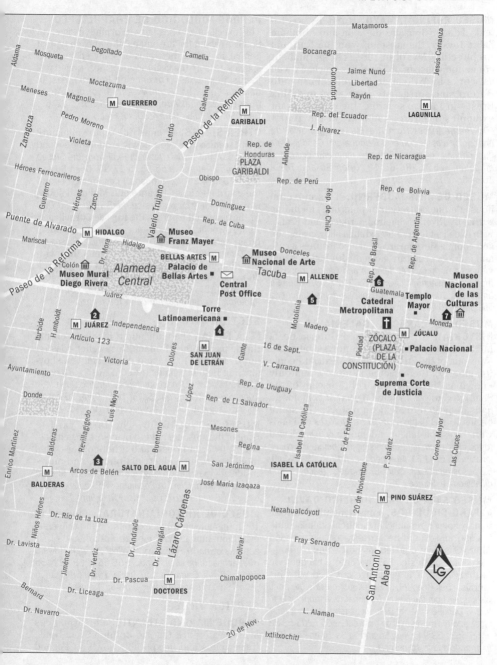

NORTH AMERICAN

Matamoros

Bocanegra

Aldama
Mosqueta
Degollado
Camelia
Jaime Nunó
Libertad
Rayón
Comonfort
Jesús Carranza

Moctezuma

Meneses
Magnolia
M GUERRERO
Galeana
Rep. del Ecuador
J. Álvarez
M LAGUNILLA

Zaragoza
Pedro Moreno
Violeta
Lerdo
M GARIBALDI
Allende
Rep. de Nicaragua

Héroes Ferrocarileros
Paseo de la Reforma
Rep. de Honduras
PLAZA GARIBALDI
Rep. de Bolivia

Guerrero
Héroes
Zarco
Obispo
Rep. de Perú
Rep. de Chile
Rep. de Argentina

Valerio Trujano
Domínguez
Rep. de Cuba

Puente de Alvarado
Mariscal
M HIDALGO
Hidalgo
Museo Franz Mayer 🏛
Rep. de Brasil

Dr. Mora
BELLAS ARTES **M**
Donceles
Museo Nacional de Arte 🏛
Tacuba
M ALLENDE
6
Guatemala
Museo Nacional de las Culturas 🏛

Paseo de la Reforma
Colón 🏛
Museo Mural Diego Rivera
Alameda Central
Palacio de Bellas Artes ■
✉ **Central Post Office**
5
Catedral Metropolitana
Templo Mayor ■
7

Juárez
Torre Latinoamericana ■
Motolinía
Madero
✝
Moneda

Iturbide
Humboldt
2
M JUÁREZ
Independencia
4
16 de Sept.
ZÓCALO (PLAZA DE LA CONSTITUCIÓN)
M **ZÓCALO**

Artículo 123
Victoria
M
SAN JUAN DE LETRÁN
Gante
Dolores
V. Carranza
Piedad
■ **Palacio Nacional**

Ayuntamiento
López
Rep. de Uruguay
Isabel la Católica
5 de Febrero
Suprema Corte de Justicia ■
Corregidora

Donde
Rep. de El Salvador

Enrico Martínez
Balderas
Luis Moya
Revillagigedo
Buentono
Mesones
Regina
Correo Mayor
Las Cruces

3
Arcos de Belén
SALTO DEL AGUA **M**
San Jerónimo
ISABEL LA CATÓLICA
20 de Noviembre
P. Suárez

Niños Héroes
M
BALDERAS
José María Izaqaza
M

Dr. Río de la Loza
Nezahualcóyotl
M **PINO SUÁREZ**

Dr. Lavista
Jiménez
Dr. Vertiz
Dr. Andrade
Dr. Borragán
Lázaro Cárdenas
Bolívar
Fray Servando

Bernard
Dr. Pascua
Dr. Liceaga
M
DOCTORES
Chimalpopoca
San Antonio Abad

Dr. Navarro
L. Alaman
N
LG

20 de Nov.
Ixtlilxochitl

MUSEO RUFINO TAMAYO. Built by architects Teodor González de León and Abraham Zabludovsky, the museum won the National Architecture Award in 1981. The permanent collection consists of Tamayo's work, as well as works by Willem de Kooning, Fernando Botero, and surrealists Joan Miró and Max Ernst—in Tamayo's words, "the most relevant examples of international art of our time." *(Down the street from the Museo Nacional de Antropología at the corner of Reforma and Gandhi. Walk through the trees as you leave the main entrance of the museum. ☎ 55 5286 65 19. Open Su and Tu-Sa 10am-6pm. 15 pesos. Su free.)*

MUSEO DE ARTE MODERNO. This museum houses a fine collection of paintings, including works by Rivera, Siqueiros, Orozco, and Kahlo, with excellent temporary exhibits showcasing up-and-coming Mexican artists. It also features a cafe and outdoor sculpture garden with benches and views of the park. *(At Reforma and Gandhi, opposite the Museo de Antropología. ☎ 55 5211 83 31. Open Su and Tu-Sa 10am-6pm. 15 pesos; students, teachers, and under 10 free. Su free.)*

MUSEO DEL CARACOL (GALERÍA DE HISTORIA). Officially Museo Galería de la Lucha del Pueblo Mexicano por su Libertad (Museum of the Struggle of the Mexican People for Liberty), the museum is more commonly known as Museo del Caracol (Museum of the Snail) because of its spiral design. It contains 12 halls dedicated to Mexican history. The spiral begins with Hidalgo's *Grito de Dolores* and ends with the establishment of democracy. *(On the road to the castle, turn right at the sign just before the castle itself. ☎ 55 5241 31 44. Open Su and Tu-Sa 9am-4pm. 32 pesos; under 13, over 60, students, teachers, and disabled free. Su free.)*

MUSEO SALA DE ARTE PÚBLICO DAVID ÁLFARO SIQUEIROS. Famed muralist, Revolutionary soldier, republican, fanatical Stalinist, anti-fascist, and would-be Trotsky assassin David Álfaro Siqueiros donated his house and studio to the people of Mexico 25 days before his death in January 1974. The walls are covered with his murals. *(Tres Picos 29, at Hegel, just outside the park. Walk uphill from the Museo Nacional de Antropología to Rubén Darío. On the left, Tres Picos forks—follow it for 1 block and the museum is on the right. ☎ 55 5203 58 88 or 55 5531 33 94. Open Su and Tu-Sa 10am-6pm. Call to arrange a tour. 10 pesos.)*

PARQUE ZOOLÓGICO DE CHAPULTEPEC. This excellent zoo has very informative signs (in Spanish) about the life and habitat of each type of animal, including the status of some endangered species. Be sure the visit the zoo's most prized residents, its pandas. *(Entrance on Reforma, east of Calzada Chivatito. From M: Auditorio, head away from the National Auditorium. ☎ 55 5553 62 63. Open Su and Tu-Sa 9am-4:30pm. Free.)*

OTHER SIGHTS. A 9min. ride on the miniature **Tren Escénico** takes you slowly around the second section of the park. *(Down the hill from the Museo de Historia Natural. ☎ 55 5515 17 90. Open Su and W-Sa 10am-4:30pm. 5 pesos.)* **Los Pinos,** beyond the guard booth at Chivatito and Molino del Rey, is the presidential residence. *(☎ 55 5267 80 00.)* At the heart of the park is the **Lago de Chapultepec.** Rent rowboats to experience of the park's oddly green water. *(Rentals daily 7:30am-4pm. 20 pesos per hr. ID required.)* For an organic connection with pre-hispanic Mexico, seek out **El Sargento,** a 700-year-old Ahuehuete tree that is over 40m tall and 12.5m in circumference. *(Between Audiorama and the Fuente de la Templanza.)*

SECTION TWO

🖾 LA FERIA. The undisputed highlight of this theme park is the Montaña Rusa roller coaster, but there's lots to see and do, including a show starring Beluga whales. *(☎ 55 5230 21 31 or 55 5230 21 21; www.feriachapultepec.com.mx. Open M-Th 10am-6pm, F 10am-7pm, Sa-Su 10am-9pm. 10 pesos, not including ride tokens. Beluga show 10 pesos.)*

MUSEO TECNOLÓGICO. The large yard in front of the museum holds a planetarium, a model solar-powered house, and a helicopter—plus models of trains, electrical plants, and more. Inside are exhibits on engines, cars, ships, and an Internet room. *(Next to Papalote. ☎ 55 5229 40 00, ext. 90266 and 90267. Open daily 9am-5pm. Free.)*

MUSEO DE HISTORIA NATURAL. Opened in 1964, this museum has exhibits on the universe, evolution, humanity, the origin of life, and other aspects of natural history. *(Follow the signs toward what appear to be circus tents. ☎ 55 5515 68 82 or 55 5515 63 04. Open Su and Tu-Sa 10am-5pm. 17.5 pesos, students and teachers 9 pesos. Tu free.)*

SECTION THREE

PARQUE MARINO ATLANTIS. Performances at the waterpark feature dolphins, sea lions, trained birds, and, inexplicably, cowboys. Pet and feed the dolphins, or, better, come on the weekend to swim with the dolphins and sea lions. (☎ 55 5271 86 18, 5273 3176, or 55 5277 16 82; www.parqueatlantis.com.mx. Open Sa-Su and holidays 10am-7pm. Dolphin feeding 3:30pm; only the 1st 20 people allowed. Up to 8 people at a time over 6 years old may swim with dolphins and sea lions from 9:30am-2pm.)

PARQUE ACUÁTICO EL ROLLO. Fun waterslides are one of the highlights of this attraction. (☎ 55 5515 13 85. Open Sa-Su and holidays 10am-6pm. 85 pesos, children 36-48 in. tall 50 pesos, children under 36 in. tall free.)

TLATELOLCO

Archaeological work has shown that the city of Tlatelolco ("Mound of Sand" in Náhuatl) existed long before the Aztec capital of Tenochtitlán. By 1473, the Tlatelolco king, Moquíhuix, had built his city into a trading center coveted by Aztec ruler Axayácatl. Tension mounted over territorial boundaries, and soon the Aztecs geared up for attack. The Aztec warriors proved too powerful for Moquíhuix, and Tlatelolco was absorbed.

PLAZA DE LAS TRES CULTURAS. Tlatelolco's central square recognizes the three cultures that have occupied it: Aztec, colonial Spanish, and modern Mexican. A plaque in the southwest corner explains: "On August 13, 1521, heroically defended by Cuauhtémoc, Tlatelolco fell to Hernán Cortés. It was neither a triumph nor a defeat, but the painful birth of the *mestizo* city that is the Mexico of today." More than 400 years later, the plaza witnessed another bloody event: the Tlatelolco Massacre of October 2, 1968. (At the corner of Lázaro Cárdenas and Ricardo Flores Magón, 13 blocks north of the Palacio de Bellas Artes. M: Tlatelolco (Line 3), and take the González exit. Turn right on González, walk 3 blocks east to Cárdenas; turn right and walk up 1 block.)

PIRÁMIDE DE TLATELOLCO. In the plaza, parts of the Pyramid of Tlatelolco (also known as the **Templo Mayor**) and its ceremonial square remain dutifully well kept. At the time of the conquest, the base of the pyramid extended from Insurgentes to the Iglesia de Santiago. The pyramid was second in importance only to Teocalli, and its summit reached nearly as high as the skyscraper to the south. During the Spanish blockade of Tenochtitlán, the Aztecs heaved freshly sacrificed bodies of Cortés's forces down the temple

steps. Nearby is the **Templo Calendárico "M,"** an M-shaped building used by the Aztecs to keep time. (M: Tlatelolco (Line 3). Open daily 8am-6pm. Free.)

COYOACÁN

The Toltecs founded Coyoacán (Place of the Skinny Coyotes) between the 10th and 12th centuries. Well maintained and peaceful today, Coyoacán merits a visit for its museums, or simply for a stroll in beautiful Plaza Hidalgo or the neighboring Jardín Centenario. The neighborhood centers on Plaza Hidalgo, which is bounded by the cathedral and the Casa de Cortés. Calle Carrillo Puerto splits the two parks, running north-south just west of the church.

▓ MUSEO FRIDA KAHLO. Works by Rivera, Orozco, Duchamp, and Klee hang in this restored colonial house, the birthplace and home of Surrealist painter Frida Kahlo (1907-1954). Kahlo's disturbing work and traumatic life story have gained international fame since her death, and she is today regarded as one of Mexico's greatest artists. At 18, Kahlo was impaled by a post during a trolley accident, breaking her spine, rendering her infertile, and confining her to a wheelchair for much of her life. Married twice to the celebrated muralist (and philanderer) Diego Rivera, Kahlo was notorious for her numerous affairs with both men and women, most famously with Leon Trotsky—whom she later plotted to kill. Kahlo's work, as well as portraits of her painted by other artists, fill two rooms. The rest of the museum is a walk-through of the house as it was when Frida and Diego lived there. Kahlo's ashes are in a jar in the back of the studio. (Londres 247. M: Coyoacán (Line 3). ☎ 55 5554 59 99. Open Su and Tu-Sa 10am-6pm. Tours in Spanish. 30 pesos, students with ID 20 pesos.)

MUSEO CASA DE LEÓN TROTSKY. After Stalin expelled Leon Trotsky from the USSR in 1927, he wandered in exile until Mexico's president Lázaro Cárdenas granted him political asylum at the suggestion of Trotsky's friends, muralist Diego Rivera and painter Frida Kahlo. Trotsky arrived with his wife in 1937, and Diego Rivera and Frida Kahlo lent them their house, Casa Azul (now the Museo Frida Kahlo, above). Eventually, they relocated to this house on Churubusco. Bullet holes riddle the interior walls, relics of an attack on Trotsky by muralist David Álfaro Siqueiros on May 24, 1940. Fearing further violence, Trotsky, a self-proclaimed "man of the people," installed bullet-proof doors and hired a team of bodyguards.

Despite precautions, he was eventually assassinated by a Spanish communist posing as a friend-of-a-friend, who buried an ice pick in his skull. *(M: Coyoacán (Line 3). ☎55 5658 87 32. Open Su and Tu-Sa 10am-5pm. 20 pesos, students 10 pesos.)*

IGLESIA DE SAN JUAN BAUTISTA. The church, between Plaza Hidalgo and Jardín Centenario, was begun in 1560 and rebuilt between 1798 and 1804. The interior is elaborately decorated with gold and bronze, and the roof supports five beautifully painted frescoes, depicting scenes taken from the New Testament. *(M: Coyoacán (Line 3). Open M 5:30am-7:30pm, Tu-Sa 5:30am-8:30pm.)*

MUSEO NACIONAL DE LAS CULTURAS POPULARES (MNCP). The MNCP houses temporary exhibits about contemporary culture in Mexico. Learn about agriculture, crafts, and art by indigenous children. *(On Hidalgo by the Plaza Hidalgo, 2 blocks east of Plaza Hidalgo. M: Coyoacán (Line 3). ☎55 5554 86 10. Open Su 10am-8pm, Tu-Th 10am-6pm, F-Sa 10am-8pm. Free.)*

SAN ÁNGEL

Near Coyoacán is another well-heeled (if is less bohemian) neighborhood, San Ángel. Ten kilometers south of the city center, San Ángel's great museums, majestic colonial buildings, and narrow cobblestone streets are a refreshing change of pace. *(M: M. A. Quevedo (Line 3). Head west on Quevedo, away from the big Santo Domingo bakery, for 3 blocks; when it forks, take a left onto La Paz, and continue along the Parque de la Bombilla. For a more direct route, take one of the buses traveling Insurgentes with a "San Ángel" sign.)*

PARQUE DE LA BOMBILLA. The centerpiece of this park is the **Monumento al General Álvaro Obregón,** which honors one of the Revolutionaries who united against Victoriano Huerta, the militaristic dictator who seized power in 1913. The main statue accurately depicts Obregón, who lost an arm during the Revolution. A separate statue of the severed limb stands on the lower level of the monument. In 1920, Obregón became the first president of the post-Revolutionary era, but he later died, assassinated by a religious fanatic.

MUSEO DE ARTE CARRILLO GIL. Inside the dull grey building is one of the capital's most interesting collections of art. It includes works by the big three muralists—Siqueiros, Orozco, and Rivera—but only their paintings on canvas, not the famed murals. The top two floors house rotating exhibits. *(Revolución 1608. ☎55 5550 39 83. Open Tu-Su 10am-6pm. Free.)*

MUSEO ESTUDIO DIEGO RIVERA Y FRIDA KAHLO. These two buildings were the home of Mexican art's royal couple, Diego Rivera and Frida Kahlo, from 1934 to 40. Rivera lived in the pink house until his death in 1957, and his wife Frida stayed in the blue house until returning to her home in Coyoacán in the early 1940s. The museum shows a small collection of Rivera's work and photographs, as well as displays on the artists' lives. On the top floor, you can see where and how Rivera worked—his leftover paints are still lying around. *(At Altavista and Diego Rivera, 5 blocks up Altavista from Revolución. Look for the pink and blue pair, with a cactus fence. ☎55 5550 15 18. Open Su and Tu-Sa 10am-6pm. 10 pesos. Su free.)*

MUSEO SOUMAYA. This museum's pride and joy is its vast collection of Rodin sculptures, the third most important in the world. There is also a collection of Mexican portraits from the 18th and 19th centuries, colonial Mexican art, and paintings by Tamayo. *(In Plaza Loreto, a small shopping mall, at Revolución and Río Magdalena. ☎55 5616 37 31 or 5616 37 61; www.soumaya.com.mx. Open M and Th-Su 10:30am-6:30pm, W 10:30am-8:30pm. 10 pesos, students 5 pesos. Su-M free.)*

OTHER SIGHTS. Across the street from the Iglesia del Carmen is the **Centro Cultural,** which borders lovely **Plaza del Carmen.** Besides hosting changing art exhibits and plays, it's a good source of info on local happenings. *(☎55 5616 12 54. Open M-Sa 10am-8pm, Su 10am-7pm.)* One block up Madero is **Plaza San Jacinto,** at San Francisco and Juárez, which fills on Saturdays with shoppers scoping out pricey arts and crafts at the **Bazar del Sábado.** One block past Casa de Risco on Juárez lies the beautiful **Iglesia de San Jacinto,** a 16th-century church with a magnificent golden altar and a peaceful courtyard. *(Open daily 8am-8pm.)*

CIUDAD UNIVERSITARIA (CU)

UNIVERSIDAD NACIONAL AUTÓNOMA DE MÉXICO. The National Autonomous University of Mexico, or **UNAM,** is the largest university in Latin America, with a staggering enrollment of over 100,000. The original University of Mexico was established in 1553; modern UNAM came into existence at the turn of the century. The Ciudad Universitaria campus was dedicated in 1952, one of the greatest achievements of President Miguel Alemán. Designed by famous architects like Félix Candela and Juan O'Gorman, the campus contains over 26km of paved roads, 430,000 sq. m. of greenery, and four million planted trees. The campus shuttle system is a necessity; UNAM's size makes it difficult to navigate by foot. *(M: Universidad (Line 3). www.unam.mx.)*

CENTRO CULTURAL UNIVERSITARIO (CCU).

Films, plays, concerts, and temporary art shows abound in UNAM's modern facilities. A big booth in the center of the complex has stacks of fliers with info about what is going on at the CCU and all over the city. Most events of interest to tourists take place in the Centro Cultural Universitario (CCU—not to be confused with CU). This large, modern complex houses the performance spaces **Teatro Juan Ruíz de Alarcón, Foro Sor Juana Inés de la Cruz, Sala Miguel Covarrubias,** and **Sala Carlos Chavez,** which regularly hosts big-name concerts and music festivals, and the artsy movie theaters **Sala José Revueltas, Sala Julio Bracho,** and **Sala Netzahualcóyotl.** *(Insurgentes Sur 3000. Teatro Juan Ruíz de Alarcón* ☎ *55 5665 6583. Sala José Revueltas* ☎ *55 5622 70 21. Sala Julio Bracho* ☎ *55 5665 28 50. Sala Netzahualcóyotl* ☎ *55 5665 07 09. Ticket booth open Su 10am-1:30pm and 4:30-6:30pm, Tu-F 10am-2pm and 5-8pm, Sa 10am-1:30pm and 4:30-7:30pm. Theater tickets 100 pesos, students 50 pesos. Movie tickets 30 pesos, students 15 pesos. Concert tickets 60-150 pesos, students 30-75 pesos.)*

LIBRARY. A huge mosaic by Juan O'Gorman wraps around the university library, to the left of the Jardín Central. You could spend hours trying to interpret the mosaic, which depicts Aztecs, eagles, the Olympic rings, a constellation wheel, and a huge atom, among other things. Across the grass from the library is the **Museo Universitario de Ciencias y Artes (MUCA),** which features large temporary exhibits. Opposite the museum entrance is the university's administrative building, graced by a 3D Siqueiros mosaic on the south wall that shows students studying at desks supported by society. *(Library* ☎ *55 5622 1659. Open daily 8:30am-9:30pm. Museo de Ciencias y Artes* ☎ *55 5622 02 73 or 55 5622 02 06. Open Sept.-June M-F 10am-7pm, Sa 10am-6pm. Tours daily 11am-5pm. Free.)*

ESTADIO OLÍMPICO. The stadium, built in the 1950s, was designed to resemble a volcano with a huge crater, and real hardened lava coats the ground upon which it is built. The impressive mosaic over the entrance to the stadium was created by Diego Rivera using large colored rocks. Today, the stadium is home to UNAM's popular professional *fútbol*-playing **Pumas.** *(On the opposite side of Insurgentes Sur from the Jardín Central; cross via the footbridge.* ☎ *55 5622 04 95.)*

CUICUILCO ARCHAEOLOGICAL ZONE.

A bit south of the CCU is the archaeological zone of Cuicuilco. The centerpiece, **El Gran Basamento,** was built between 800 and 150 BC. The area served as a ceremonial center with a population of around 20,000, making it the largest central settlement in Mesoamerica before the rise of Teotihuacán. Measuring 110m in diameter and 25m in height, the pyramid was built in eight different stages with altars at its summit. The area was abandoned when the volcano **Xitle** erupted around AD 100, coating 8 sq. km of surrounding land in a layer of lava. On a clear day, the summit affords a faint view of Xitle to the south and much larger Popocatépetl to the east. *(At Insurgentes Sur and Anillo Periférico, south of CU. From M: Universidad (Line 3), take exit A, B, or C, and take any "Cuicuilco" or "Villa Olímpica" pesero (2 pesos) to the entrance on the west side of Insurgentes Sur. To return, take any "CU Metro" pesero.* ☎ *55 5606 97 58. Open daily 9am-5pm. Tours in Spanish M-F 9am-1:30pm Free.)*

XOCHIMILCO

In Xochimilco ("so-she-MIL-co"; Place of the Flower Growing), there are two things to do. The first is what everyone does: cruise the **floating gardens** of Xochimilco in a hand-poled *chalupa.* The second is far less known—the **Museo Dolores Olmedo** houses an impressive Rivera collection and the largest Kahlo collection in Mexico.

▓ THE FLOATING GARDENS. In the Aztecs' brilliantly conceived system, *chinampas* (artificial islands) were made by piling soil and mud onto floating rafts. These rafts were held firm by wooden stakes until the crops planted on top sprouted roots, reaching through the base of the canals. They became fertile islands, supporting several crops per year. Though polluted today, the canals still bear the waterborne greenery planted centuries ago. Multicolored **chalupa** boats crowd the maze of canals, ferrying passengers past a floating market of food, flowers, and music. *(M: Tasqueña (Line 2). Take the tren ligero (1.5 pesos) to the "Xochimilco" stop; numerous "Embarcadero" signs and boat owners will direct you. Private boats 140-160 pesos per hr.; a shared boat one-way 10 pesos.)*

⊠MUSEO DOLORES OLMEDO. This museum, once the estate of the beautiful Dolores Olmedo Patiño, features the art collection she amassed throughout her life. As the long-time lover of Diego Rivera, she is the subject of many of his paintings. The collection holds 144 of these canvases, including a series of 25 sunsets painted from Olmedo's Acapulco home in 1956, the year before Rivera's death. Perhaps even more impressive, the 25 paintings by Frida Kahlo, much of whose work is held abroad or in private collections, make this the best Kahlo collection in all of Mexico. *(Av. México 5843. M: Tasqueña (Line 2). Ride the tren ligero (trolleybus; 1.5 pesos; follow the "correspondencia" signs) in the "Embarcadero" direction. Exit the "La Noria" stop on the left, turn left at the corner, turn left again at the next corner, and walk straight. ☎ 55 5555 12 21 or 55 5555 08 91; www.museodoloresolmedo.com. Open Su and Tu-Sa 10am-6pm. 30 pesos, students and teachers 15 pesos. Su free.)*

🎵 ENTERTAINMENT

The amazing ⊠**Ballet Folklórico de México** performs regional dances at the Palacio de Bellas Artes (see p. 628). Their exciting and vivacious performances combine *indígena* dancing with more formal aspects of traditional ballet. Many concerts, mostly orchestral works, also occur here. Attending a Bellas Artes performance is the only way to see the **Tiffany crystal curtain,** which weighs 21,228kg and depicts the volcanoes Popocatépetl and Ixtaccíhuatl. The **ticket office** sells tickets for these and other performances throughout the city. An **info booth,** up the stairs next to the ticket booth, supplies details on these performances. *(☎ 55 5512 25 93 or 55 5521 92 51 ext. 152, 153, and 154. Dance performances and concerts at various times throughout the week. No children under 5, no shorts or sport clothing. Tickets 100-400 pesos.)*

The **Auditorio Nacional,** 50 Av. Paseo de la Reforma, is *the* concert venue in Mexico City; the hottest music groups in the world come to play. *(☎ 55 5280 9250; www.auditorio.com.mx.) Fútbol* fans fill the **Estadio Azteca,** Calz. de Tlalpan 3465, Mexico's largest stadium, by the thousands for popular matches. Take a *pesero* or *tren ligero* (trolleybus) from M: Tasqueña. *(☎ 55 5617 80 80 or 55 5617 15 16; www.esmas.com/estadioazteca. Tickets 55 5325 90 00; www.ticketmaster.com.mx. Season runs Oct.-July. Tickets 50-1200 pesos. Tours Su-W and F-Sa 10am-5pm, Th 4 and 5pm. 10 pesos,*

under 5 free.) Plaza México, on Insurgentes Sur, is Mexico's principal bullring, seating 40,000 fans. *(M: San Antonio (Line 7). ☎ 55 5611 44 13. Professional fights July-Nov. Sa; novillada (novice) fights Nov.-Feb. Sa. Tickets from 40 pesos.)*

🍴 FOOD

Options for meals fall into six basic categories: very cheap (and sometimes risky) vendor stalls scattered about the streets; fast, inexpensive, *taquerías;* slightly more formal *cafeterías;* more pricey and decorous Mexican restaurants; locally popular US-style eateries; and expensive international fare. **VIPs** and **Sanborn's,** popular with middle-class Mexicans, run hundreds of restaurants throughout the capital. Vegetarians will have more to eat here than anywhere else in Mexico; the bright orange chain **Super Soya** has soy versions of Mexican and US fast-food favorites. For fresh produce and meats, try **La Merced,** Circunvalación at Anaya, east of the *zócalo,* the mother of all markets. (Open daily 8am-7pm.)

CENTRO HISTÓRICO

Most of the *centro's* restaurants serve traditional Mexican food. Locals offset throngs of tourists, keeping prices lower than in Zona Rosa, but not as low as near Revolución. After the Zona Rosa, this is the best place for vegetarian fare.

⊠ **Balcón del Zócalo,** 5 de Mayo y Zócalo (☎55 5521 21 21), right off the *zócalo.* Songbirds in white cages and pink hanging plants decorate this 6th-floor patio cafe, which overlooks the entire *zócalo.* Try the breakfast buffet (7am-noon; 100-120 pesos) or lunch buffet (1-5pm; 120-130 pesos), or order from the extensive menu. Entrees 60-140 pesos. Open daily 7am-11pm.

⊠ **Café Tacuba,** Tacuba 28 (☎55 5518 49 50), 1 block from Bellas Artes. Vaulted ceiling, stained glass, *azulejo* tiles—the gorgeous interior complements this restaurant's storied history (it hosted numerous wedding feasts, including Diego Rivera's; Anthony Quinn movie buffs may recognize it as well) and well-prepared Mexican dishes. Menu in English and Spanish. *Antojitos* (appetizers) 22-69 pesos. Entrees 54-198 pesos. Open daily 8am-11:30pm.

Restaurantes Vegetarianos del Centro, Madero 56 (☎55 5521 68 80), upstairs, 1½ blocks from the *zócalo.* Also at Mata 13 (☎55 5510 01 13), between 5 de Mayo and Madero. 3 locations lie to

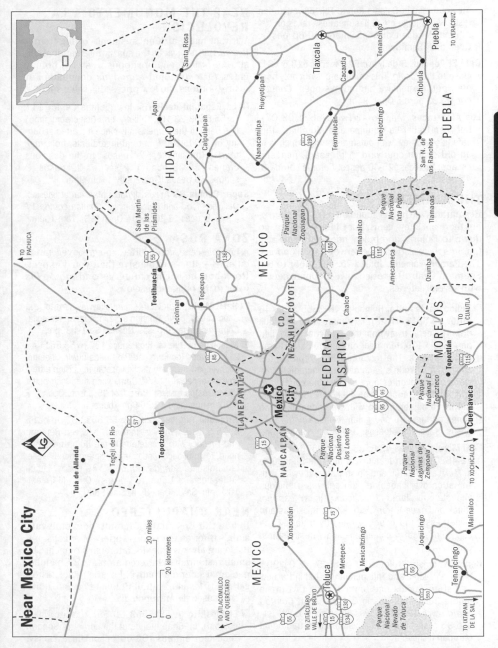

Near Mexico City

the south and in Colonia Roma. This all-vegetarian restaurant's large menu has meatless takes on traditional Mexican dishes. Salads 40-60 pesos. Open daily 8am-8pm.

Café El Popular, 5 de Mayo 52, (☎55 5518 60 81) close to the *zócalo*. This small cafe is not only popular, but inexpensive and always open. *Comida corrida* 33 pesos. Open 24hr.

Los Alcatraces, Madero 42 (☎55 5521 08 07), between Isabel La Católica and Motolinía. This cafe is one of few with outside seating, which is in an old church courtyard. A pleasant, peaceful escape. Breakfast 25-40 pesos. *Comida corrida* 3-45 pesos.

THE ALAMEDA

Restaurants are not as abundant as in the *centro*, but there are a few gems. For Chinese cuisine, go down to Dolores and Independencia. Some restaurants there also have better vegetarian options. The **Parque Alameda,** Juárez 75, next door to the Sheraton Centro Histórico, is a shopping center with several eateries.

◧ **Fonda Santa Anita,** Humboldt 48 (☎55 5518 46 09 or 55 5518 57 23). M: Juárez (Line 3). Walk down Balderas away from the Alameda. Head right on Artículo 120, turn right on Humboldt, and continue ½ block. The restaurant has represented Mexico in 5 World's Fairs and has incredible versions of old favorites from all over the country. At least one vegetarian option every day. Go between 2-4pm to be serenaded with traditional Mexican songs on the harp and guitar. *Comida corrida* 45 pesos. Specials 65 pesos. Open daily 10am-7pm.

◧ **El Moro,** Cárdenas 42 (☎55 5512 0896 or 55 55 18 4580). M: San Juan de Letrán (Line 3). Indulge in Mexican tradition and finish your night with conversation over chocolate and *churros*. Delicious chocolate available in *mexicano* (light), *español* (thick and sweet), *francés* (medium thickness and sweetness), and *especial* (slightly bitter). Each cup comes with 4 cinnamon-sugary pastry strips. Open 24hr.

Centro Naturista, Dolores 10 (☎55 5512 01 90), between Juárez and Independencia behind a new age store. Locals and tourists pack this place before 3pm, when the food is freshest. *Comida corrida* with 1, 2, or 3 *guisados* (dishes; 28, 31, and 35 pesos). Vegetarian variations of traditional Mexican dishes.

NEAR THE MONUMENTO A LA REVOLUCIÓN

Without many affluent residents or big tourist draws, this area lacks the snazzy international cuisine of other neighborhoods. Instead, homey cafes, *torterías*, and *taquerías* dominate. For hearty portions and low prices, this is the spot.

◧ **La Especial de París,** Insurgentes Centro 117 (☎55 5703 23 16). This *nievería* (ice cream shop) has been in the same family since it started scooping in 1921. 100% natural ingredients, from *malteadas* (milkshakes; 24 pesos) to the delicious crepes (22-25 pesos). 2 scoops 22 pesos, 3 scoops 30 pesos. Open daily 11am-9pm.

Super Cocina los Arcos, Ignacio Mariscal at Iglesias. Delicious food and quick service. *Comida corrida* 17 pesos. Entrees 12-30 pesos. Open M-Sa 7am-10pm.

ZONA ROSA

A hipster scene, good coffee, and great vegetarian cuisine—all less expensive than you'd expect. Rock-bottom-cheap cafeterias and *taquerías* cater to the budget-conscious.

◧ **Saint Moritz,** Genova 44, in an alleyway, next to Java Chat. Cheap, basic lunch in a clean, spartan cafeteria. *Comida corrida* 20 pesos. Open M-Sa 1-4:30pm.

El Mesón de la Huerta, Río Pánuco 137 (☎55 5511 48 91), between Río Ebro and Río Guadalquivir. Cheerful, bright-yellow decor and solid vegetarian cuisine attract crowds, especially 12:30-3pm, when the lunch buffet (50 pesos) is tastiest. Breakfast 25 pesos. Open M-F 8:30am-noon and 12:30-6pm (buffet only).

Vegetariano Yug, Varsovia 3 (☎55 5533 32 96 or 55 5525 53 30; www.yug.com.mx), between Reforma and Dresde, with a cafeteria in the Roma neighborhood. Tasteful decor and creative, "international" vegetable dishes. *Comida corrida* 42-49 pesos. Lunch buffet upstairs 1-5pm (53 pesos). Open M-F 7am-10:15pm, Sa 8:30am-8pm, Su 1-8pm.

NEAR CHAPULTEPEC

Inside the Bosque de Chapultepec, sidewalk stands offer an enormous variety of snacks, but these are always risky for a foreign stomach. The small restaurants cluttered around M: Chapultepec are a safer alternative. For the ritzier tastes, get *antojitos* in beautiful Colonia Polanco, north of the Museo de Antropología.

◧ **El Kioskito** (☎55 5553 30 55; kioskito@mexico.com), on Chapultepec at the corner of Sonora. Succulent entrees (50-60 pesos) in a classy, relaxed atmosphere with a tiled fountain and old city photos. You can also eat at the adjoining taco counter. Open daily 8am-9pm.

Vegetariano, Veracruz 3 (☎55 5286 88 27), at Acapulco, facing M: Chapultepec. One of the few places offering both meat and vegetarian dishes—the staff is happy to point out what's what. Try the soup. *Comida corrida* 26 pesos. Open daily 10am-8pm.

COYOACÁN

If you crave great coffee, cheesecake, or pesto, spend an afternoon at one of the outdoor cafes or *taquerías* that line the cobbled streets of Coyoacán. For excellent, inexpensive meals, try the **Indoor Market** on Hijuera, just south of Plaza Hidalgo. Heavily frequented by locals, these tiny restaurants serve home-cooked food at delicious prices. (Open M-Sa 9am-9pm.)

El Guarache (☎55 5554 45 06), by the Jardín Centenario. Bask in the beauty of the nearby coyote fountain at this classy cafe. *Comida corrida* (M-F only) 40 pesos. Entrees 50-70 pesos. *Antojitos* 22-45 pesos. Open daily 9am-10pm.

El Jarocho (☎55 5554 54 18), at Allende and Cuauhtémoc. Follow the smell of freshly ground coffee. Straight from Veracruz, Jarocho has been serving some of the city's best java since 1953. Cappuccino, mochas, and hot chocolate 6-8 pesos. Open daily 7am-midnight.

VegeTaco, Carrillo Puerto 65 (☎55 5659 75 17 or 5658 93 11), past the other taco joints. Create a meal of vegetarian tacos (6 pesos each) or enjoy a combination *platillo* (33-59 pesos). Open daily 10am-8pm.

SAN ÁNGEL

Though some restaurants here are too hip (and too expensive) for their own good, quite a few homey establishments sell solid, reasonably priced food. Great lunch deals can be found in the very stylish Plaza Jacinto.

La Mora, Madero 2 (☎55 5616 20 80). Quaint views of the plaza pair with traditional Mexican *comida corrida* (30 pesos). Open daily 8am-6pm.

La Finca Café Solo Dios (☎55 5550 33 02), on Madero right off Plaza San Jacinto. This hole-in-the-wall coffee stand only serves 100% Mexican-grown beans from Chiapas. Delicious mochas, espresso, and hot chocolate 8-14 pesos. Kilos of Chiapan coffee beans start at 60 pesos. Open daily 8:30am-8:30pm.

ACCOMMODATIONS

Mexico City is home to over 1000 hotels; rooms abound in the *centro histórico* and near the Alameda Central. The best budget bargains are near the Monumento a la Revolución on Plaza de la República. Beware of any hotel marked "Hotel Garage," where clientele enter rooms directly from the garage for an illicit rendezvous. Some budget hotels charge according to the number of beds, not per person, and beds tend to be large enough for two. If you don't mind snuggling, sharing a bed can save major pesos. Always ask to see a room before you accept it; this is easiest to do after check-out time (noon-3pm).

CENTRO HISTÓRICO

The accommodations in the *centro histórico* come in all shapes and sizes: busy hostels filled with international youth, tranquil hotels in historic buildings, and ritzier modernized hotels. Best of all, you're right in the *centro* of things, with spectacular sights within walking distance. Although the quiet of the streets at night is a huge change from the bustle of the day, nighttime activity is on the rise, and the government has been improving safety conditions at night as well.

Hostel Catedral (HI), Guatemala 4 (☎55 5518 17 26 or 55 5518 10 65; www.hostelcatedral.com), behind the cathedral. The place to be for young internationals. Guests snack at the bar in the spacious lobby or surf the web (20 pesos per hr.). Shared kitchen, washing machine (20 pesos), pool table, and lockers (padlocks 20 pesos). Bulletin boards display ads for work, apartments, and parties. Simple and clean dorms 100 pesos, nonmembers 120 pesos; doubles 240 pesos.

Hostal Moneda, Moneda 8 (☎55 5522 58 21 or 800 221 72 65; www.hostalmoneda.com.mx), between the Palacio Nacional and the Templo Mayor. Kitchen, laundry (35 pesos), Internet, elevator, TV room, lockers, rooftop bar and cafe, and a friendly, international vibe. Breakfast included. 5- and 6-bed dorms 100 pesos; 3- and 4- bed dorms 110 pesos; singles 180 pesos; doubles 480 pesos.

Hotel Rioja, 5 de Mayo 45 (☎55 5521 83 33, 55 5521 82 73, or 55 5518 38 52), 3 blocks from the *zócalo*. Clean, comfortable, cool, and in a great location. Singles 130-140 pesos, with windows 150-160 pesos; doubles 160-230 pesos/170-260 pesos.

THE ALAMEDA

There may be more and better offerings in the *centro*, but that does not mean that there is nowhere to stay in the Alameda. The area has been cleaned up, but as with most places in D.F., remember to be careful at night.

Hotel Avenida, Eje Lázaro Cárdenas 38 (☎55 5518 10 07 or 55 5518 10 09), right down the street from Bellas Artes. Inside it is clean and secure. Its busy-street location is safer at night, if a bit noisy. Singles 170-180 pesos; doubles 220-270 pesos.

Hotel Manolo I, Moya 111 (☎55 5521 37 39, 55 5521 77 09, or 55 5521 77 49), near Arcos de Belén. A little out of the way, but definitely a good choice. The hotel is a burst of color off dingy streets. Elevator, clean rooms with king-size bed, phone, TV, and large bath. Doubles 190 pesos.

Hotel Calvin, José Azueta 33 (☎55 5521 79 52 or 55 5521 13 61; fax 55 5512 48 28), at the corner of Independencia. Just 50m from the Alameda Central with room service, TV, and telephone in each room. Singles 150-160 pesos; doubles 230-250 pesos, with jacuzzi 250 pesos; suites 330 pesos.

NEAR THE MONUMENTO A LA REVOLUCIÓN

Hotels near the Monumento a la Revolución are quieter than their counterparts in the *centro* or the Alameda. It is easy to find a cheap, nice room and, although the area itself does not offer much to do, the location—right between the Alameda and the Zona Rosa—is tops.

Casa de los Amigos, Mariscal 132 (☎55 5705 05 21). Once the home of painter José Clemente Orozco, the Casa now houses backpackers, grad students, and eco-warriors from all over the world. Library, lounge, kitchen, and laundry. Breakfast 20 pesos. Quiet hours 10pm-8am. No drugs or alcohol. 4-day min. stay. 3-weeks max. stay, except for Casa volunteers and students. Dorms 80 pesos; singles 100-200 pesos; doubles 180-250 pesos.

NIGHTLIFE

Hundreds of bars and nightclubs enliven the side-streets of Mexico's capital. For the most current information, consult the publications *Tiempo Libre* (7 pesos) and *Ser Gay* (for gay entertainment; free), or ask locals. Women venturing out alone will likely be approached by men offering drinks, dances, and much more. In light of Mexico City's sometimes staggering crime statistics, both men and women should go out with friends.

CENTRO HISTÓRICO

Although the *centro* is known for being quiet at night, the emerging nightlife scene now offers both tourists and locals some great places to go.

■ **La Gioconda,** Filomena Mata 18-E (☎55 5518 78 23), between Madero and 5 de Mayo. Sit back with your cup of coffee (12 pesos), beer (20-32 pesos), or tequila (40-60 pesos) and relax in this friendly, bright cafe/bar. Attracts Mexicans and international clientele of all ages. Great atmosphere and friendly staff. Blues band Sa 9pm-midnight. Open daily 1pm-midnight.

La Casa Del Sol, 5 de Febrero 28 (☎55 1054 68 40), upstairs. Restaurant, bar, and dance club: something for everybody. Live music and karaoke. Beer from 20 pesos. Open M-Th 10am-9pm, F-Sa 10am-4am.

Salon Baraimas, Filomena Mata 7 (☎55 5510 44 88), between Tacuba and 5 de Mayo. Dance and learn salsa (40 pesos per class). Beer 30 pesos. Cover 45 pesos. Open Th-Sa 9pm-3:30am.

PLAZA GARIBALDI

Wandering *mariachis* and roving *ranchero* bands play as tourists, locals, vendors, and children mingle here. Surrounding nightclubs aggressively lure crowds; though they advertise no cover, per-drink prices are astoundingly high. Your best bet is to find a table at one of the open-air cafes, where you can order cheap beers (12 pesos) or try *pulque*, an alcoholic drink made from the maguey cactus (14-70 pesos). If you're hungry, don't miss the **Mercado de Alimentos San Camilito**, on the northwest corner of the plaza. This indoor market contains dozens of small, inexpensive eateries. Most will feed you quite well for around 30 pesos.

The plaza is at the intersection of Lázaro Cárdenas (Eje Central) and Rep. de Honduras, north of the Alameda. From M: Bellas Artes (Lines 2, 8), walk three blocks away from the Palacio de Bellas Artes on Cárdenas; Garibaldi will be on your right. Exercise caution, and especially avoid wandering beyond the plaza to the back streets, which are considerably less charming. The best time to visit is in the evening, between 8pm and midnight on Friday or Saturday.

ZONA ROSA

Home to some of the republic's fanciest discos and highest cover charges, on weekend nights the Zona Rosa can feel like the center of the universe. US-sports-bar-themed **Yarda's** and **Freedom** attract the young and moneyed set. High covers at most clubs makes club-hopping prohibitively expensive. Dress codes are relaxed, but sneakers are out. After a wild night, hop in an all-night *pesero* on Reforma or Insurgentes Sur (5 pesos).

Cantina las Bohemias, Londres 142 (☎55 5207 43 84), at Amberes. Small, cozy, and populated with *mariachis.* A great escape. Beer 20 pesos. Tequila 40-75 pesos. *Antojitos* 30-70 pesos. Entrees 80-160 pesos. Open M-Sa 1pm-1am.

Cielo Rojo, Genova 70 (☎55 5525 54 93). A huge menu of mixed drinks, live salsa music, and a dance fl. make this a great place to be. Beer 25 pesos.

Escándalo, Florencia 32 (☎55 5525 74 26). Great for salsa and merengue lovers. Live music. Beer 25 pesos. Cover 90 pesos. Open Th-Sa 8am-4am.

⚔ LEAVING MEXICO CITY

Follow **Paseo de la Reforma** southwest out of the city center, passing through Chapultepec Park. At the edge of the city it becomes **Mex. 15,** heading toward Toluca. As is nearly always the case, opting to take the toll (*cuota*) road is worth the few pesos.

THE ROAD TO TOLUCA. Mex. 15 winds through 66km (41 mi.) of heart-wrenching, jaw-dropping, hyphen-inducing mountainscape as it whisks you slowly toward your destination. Be advised that the road is extremely winding, and that long stretches of cliffside do not have guardrails. Driving at night is usually a bad idea, but this route in particular should not be attempted at night by those without parachutes.

⚔ APPROACHING TOLUCA

Outside Toluca, **Mex. 15** becomes **Paseo Tollocan.** Follow it to **Av. M. Hidalgo,** which heads straight for Toluca's Alameda Central.

TOLUCA

Toluca ("Those who bow their heads" in Náhuatl), has progressed from small town anonymity to the capital of the State of Mexico and a major center of commerce and industry. Stunning architecture, a host of cultural attractions and famously tasty *antojitos* make Toluca worth a stop.

> ### VITAL STATS
>
> **Population:** 475,000
>
> **Visitor Info:** Urawa 100, Ste. 110 (☎722 212 60 48), at Paseo Tollocan, 6 blocks northeast of the bus station in the large yellow municipal building.
>
> **Internet Access:** Available at the *portales* (shopping center).
>
> **Post Office:** Hidalgo 300 (☎722 214 90 68), 2 blocks east of Juárez. Open M-F 8am-3pm, Sa 9am-1pm. **Postal Code:** 50141.

⌐ GETTING AROUND. The *zócalo*, cathedral, and *portales* constitute the *centro* and are bounded by **Hidalgo** on the south, **Lerdo de Tejada**

THE LOCAL STORY

A NIGHT ON THE PUEBLO

You've spent hours conjugating verbs and rolling your r's, but you still don't fit in. What you need is something that no 7th-grade Spanish teacher could teach—the slang necessary for a night out on the town. Incorporate these into your vocab and watch as your *gabacho* (gringo) status fades away.

The night begins when you head out *al antro* (to the disco). Once there, don't be a *codo* (tightwad)—grab a *chupe* (drink) or a *chela* (beer) and comment on how *chido* or *padre* (cool) the place is—*fresas* (snobs) prefer the phrase *de pelos*. Of course, keep your eyes peeled for *papacitos* (studs) and *mamacitas*—women that are *buenísima* (very fine). Perhaps you'll *echarle perros* (compliment or flatter), *ligar* (hook up), and—if you are *cachondo* (horny)—maybe you'll *fajar* (make out/get down with) a fellow discotechie. The next day, if you're not too *crudo* (hung over), swap stories of the previous night with your friends. If they're telling tales, bring them back in line with a *"¡No mames, buey!"* (Get off it!). As you relate your own night, let everyone know how *alumbrado* (lit up/drunk) you were.

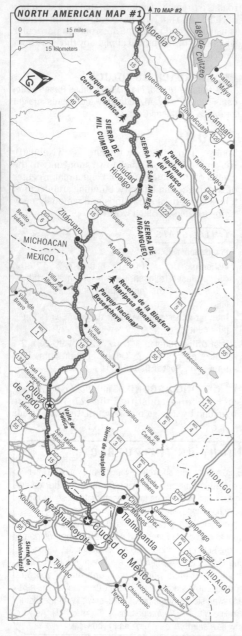

NORTH AMERICAN MAP #1 ▲ TO MAP #2

E GETTING AROUND. The *zócalo*, cathedral, and *portales* constitute the *centro* and are bounded by **Hidalgo** on the south, **Lerdo de Tejada** on the north, **Juárez** on the east, and **Bravo** on the west. **Independencia** parallels Hidalgo one block to the north and forms the south side of the *zócalo*. **Morelos** runs parallel to Hidalgo one block to the south. Address numbers on Hidalgo increase in either direction away from the center of the *portales*. **Parking** is readily available on Hidalgo and side streets (8 pesos per hr.).

G SIGHTS. Toluca's excellent museums are organized and maintained by the Centro Cultural Mexiquense, but the real attraction is the ◼**Cosmovitral**, where half a million tiny pieces of colored glass convey the struggle among the forces of the universe. If you can take your eyes off the walls, the building holds a **botanical garden** of plants from all over the world thoroughly labeled in Spanish. (☎722 214 67 85. Open daily 10am-6pm. 10 pesos, children 5 pesos.) The **Centro Cultural Mexiquense**, 8km outside town, houses a library and three museums. **Museo de Culturas Populares** is a beautifully restored *hacienda* with a large collection of Mexican folk art, including an impressive Metepec Tree of Life, a large tree-like object composed of clay figurines. **Museo de Antropología e Historia** displays all manner of Mexican artifacts, from figurines of pre-Hispanic cultures to early printing presses and cars. Exhibits at the **Museo de Arte Moderno** include paintings by Diego Rivera and Rufino Tamayo. (From the *zócalo*, take Hidalgo west out of the city center and turn left onto Blvr. Las Torres Solidaridad. Entrance to the park will be on the right at Blvr. Lic. Jesus Reyes Heroles. Open Su and Tu-Sa 10am-6pm. Museums 5 pesos each; combination ticket 10 pesos. Su and W free.)

⚑ FOOD & ACCOMMODATIONS. A variety of decent, inexpensive restaurants hover around *portales* for your enjoyment. At ◼**Cafe Hidalgo,** Hidalgo 229A, assorted baked goods complement the *comida corrida* (40 pesos). (☎722 215 27 93. Open daily 8:30am-10:30pm.) **Restaurant Lambiant,** Hidalgo 231, provides stiff competition with tasty *frijoles*, entrees (20-36 pesos), and coffees. (☎722 215 33 93. Open daily 9am-9pm.)

Toluca has an abundance of hotels on and around Hidalgo. Parking overnight at any of the lots will cost around 150 pesos, but is a safer bet than leaving your ride on the street. **Hotel**

Parking across the street. Singles 70 pesos; doubles 110 pesos; triples 150 pesos.) **Hotel La Casa del Abuelo,** Hidalgo 404, glows with a warm pink decor. (☎722 213 36 42. Singles 250-350 pesos; penthouse 450 pesos.)

THE ROAD TO MORELIA

Follow **Mex. 15 (Hidalgo)** out of town and into the countryside. Rolling farmlands and mountain roads alternate with identical roadside towns. Mex. 15 runs through the center of **Zitácuaro,** the site of a bustling market where you can find everything you never thought you needed. Rolling down Mex. 15, you'll see most of what there is to see of **Ciudad Hidalgo.** Outside of the barrage of shops, there are opportunities for outdoor adventure, be it spelunking through the **Grutas de Ziranda** or hiking around **Laguna Larga,** a series of lovely *presos* (man-made lakes). In either case, leave your car behind in one of the parking lots and take a short bus ride into the wilderness. (To get to the bus terminal, head south on Hidalgo one block and turn right on Morelos.) From Ciudad Hidalgo, it's a straight 80km to Morelia.

MORELIA

The state capital, Morelia displays the proud traditions of Michoacán culture and history. Museums, art exhibits, theater, dance productions, and concerts create a vibrant cultural scene, fueled by the city's sizeable student population. In the *centro*, vendors sell traditional textiles and wooden crafts alongside bootleg cassettes and spare blender parts. Nearby stand rose-colored stone arcades and grand, white-washed houses, relics of Morelia's colonial magnificence. Its eclectic art and lively downtown make Morelia one of the most vital cities in the country and an important part of Mexico's colonial heritage.

📠 GETTING AROUND

Mex. 15 turns into **Acueducto** as it enters Morelia; it intersects with major east-west route **Madero** just east of the *zócalo*. **Morelos** is the main road running north-south, with "Nte." or "Sur" indicating its relationship to Madero. **Parking** is hard to come by on the major streets, but lots begin to crop up more regularly two blocks away from the *centro*, especially on side streets Juárez and Domínguez, with standards rates around 8 pesos per hr.

(VITAL STATS)

Population: 575,000

Visitor Info: Galería de Turismo, Nigromante 79 (☎443 312 80 82), west of the *zócalo* in the castle-like building on the right. Some English spoken. Open M-Sa 9am-7pm, Su 10am-2pm.

Internet Access: Internet Imas, at the corner of Galeana and Allende, 1 block from the *zócalo*. 15 pesos per hour. Open daily 8:30am-9pm.

Post Office: Madero Ote. 369 (☎443 312 05 17), in the Palacio Federal, 5 blocks east of the cathedral. Open M-F 8am-4pm, Sa 9am-1pm. **Postal Code:** 58000.

🗿 SIGHTS

Packed with museums and cultural centers, Morelia is a history buff's dream. Many of its famous buildings are ornamented in a style peculiar to the city—imitation Baroque, identifiable by a flat decorative motif on pilasters and columns. Check out the cathedral for an impressive example.

CASA DE LA CULTURA. A gathering place for artists, musicians, and backpackers, the Casa houses a bookstore, art gallery, theater, palatial inner courtyard, and lovely cafe. Ask for the weekly schedule of cultural events. Unfortunately, the Museo de la Máscara has closed indefinitely, taking with it a set of disturbing devil masks. *(Morelos Nte. 485, northeast of the zócalo.)*

CONSERVATORIO DE LAS ROSAS. Built in the 18th century to protect and educate widows and poor or orphaned Spanish girls, the building and its rose-filled courtyard now houses Morelia's premiere music school, the oldest in the Americas. Check with the conservatory's Public Relations office or with the Casa de la Cultura for performance schedules. *(Tapía 334, north of the tourist office. ☎443 312 14 69. Open M-F 8am-8pm, Sa 8am-2pm. Public Relations office open M-F 9am-4pm.)*

CATHEDRAL. Overlooking the *zócalo*, the massive cathedral has a stunning interior graced by vaulted ceilings, chandeliers, tapestries, and stained-glass windows. The oldest treasure inside is the 16th-century *Señor de la Sacristía*, an image of Christ sculpted out of dry corn cobs and orchid nectar. *(Open daily 5:30am-8:30pm. Masses Su every hr. 6am-noon and 6-8pm.)*

Morelia Overview

MUSEO MICHOACANO. This museum houses exhibits on the ecology, archaeology, anthropology, history, and art of Michoacán. Learn more about why parts of Michoacán tried to secede from Mexico after the Revolution, during the Cristero Rebellion, then peruse artifacts, including Franciscan monks' crosses, punctuated with spikes for penitence. *(Allende 305, at the zócalo. ☎443 312 04 07. Open Su 9am-2pm, Tu-Sa 9am-7pm. 30 pesos, seniors and under 14 free. Su free.)*

MUSEO DE MORELOS. Originally bought by José María Morelos, the parish priest who led the Independence movement after Hidalgo's death, this 19th-century building houses a museum detailing Morelos's martyrdom, including maps of his campaigns and a rare image of him as a priest. *(Morelos Sur 323, southeast of the cathedral. ☎443 313 85 06. Open daily 9am-7pm. 22 pesos. Su free.)*

CASA NATAL DE MORELOS. A civic building rather than a museum, the "Birthplace of Morelos" holds glass cases that preserve Morelos's wartime cartography and letters. Also notable are the murals by Alfredo Zalce. *(Corregidora 113. ☎443 312 27 93. Open M-F 9am-8pm, Sa-Su 9am-7pm. Free.)*

CASA DE LAS ARTESANÍAS. This *casa*, occupying part of the **Ex-Convento de San Francisco,** is a huge crafts museum and retail store, selling colorful macramé *huipiles*, straw airplanes, pottery, carved wooden furniture, and guitars. *(On Humboldt, east of the zócalo. ☎443 312 12 48. Open M-Sa 10am-3pm and 5-8pm, Su 10am-4:30pm. Free.)*

BOSQUE CUAUHTÉMOC. The *bosque* lets you lose yourself among trees and fountains. A **mini amusement park** with bumper cars and a train entertains the young and young at heart.

The **Museo de Historia Natural,** in the southeast corner of the *bosque*, is a tiny museum with rotating exhibits on the flora and fauna of Michoacán, past and present, and their uses. On the eastern side of the *bosque* is the **Museo de Arte Contemporaneo Alfredo Zalce,** which displays works in all media by that Zalce—one of Michoacán's most celebrated artists—as well as temporary exhibits of contemporary art. *(To get to the bosque, take a "Ruta Rojo" combi (3.5 pesos) from behind the cathedral on Allende. Amusement park open daily 11:30am-7:30pm. Train 3 pesos. Museo de Historia ☎443 312 0044. Open daily 10am-6pm. 5 pesos. Museo de Arte ☎443 312 54 04. Open Su and Tu-Sa 10am-2pm and 4-8pm. Free.)*

PARQUE ZOOLÓGICO BENITO JUÁREZ. Founded in 1970, this is one of the largest (and most pleasant) zoos in Mexico. Animals reside in natural settings rather than tiny cages. The Friday tour at 8pm includes dinner. *(Take a maroon combi south on Nigromante or a pink "Santa María" combi from in front of the tourist office (3.5 pesos). ☎443 314 04 88. Open M-F 10am-5pm, Sa-Su 10am-5:30pm. 12 pesos, children 6 pesos. F tour 100 pesos.)*

OTHER SIGHTS. At the eastern end of Madero is the city's most recognizable landmark, the statue of **Las Tarascas,** which shows three bare-breasted indigenous women making an offering to the heavens. Nearby is **El Acueducto,** built in the 18th century to meet the city's water needs. Though no longer functional, it is a magnificent sight in the evenings.

🎵 ENTERTAINMENT

The Casa de la Cultura and tourist office carry event listings. Music and theater draw crowds to **Teatro Morelos** (☎443 314 62 02), at Camelina y Ventura Pte., and to **Teatro Ocampo** (☎443 312 37 34), on the corner of Ocampo and Prieto. (Tickets 20-80 pesos.) **Corral de la Comedia,** Ocampo 239, at Prieto one block north of Madero, presents comedies written and performed by local artists. (☎443 312 00 01. Performances Su 7:30pm, Th-Sa 8:30pm. 60 pesos.) The **Planetario,** on Ventura Pte. at Ticateme, in the Centro de Convenciones, has standard planetarium fare. (Take the "Ruta Rojo #3" *combi* from Allende/Valladolid, and watch for the convention center on the right. ☎443 314 24 65 Shows Su 6:30pm; Tu-Sa 1, 5, 7pm. 20 pesos.)

Young people flock to the colonial charm of 🌙**El Rincón de los Sentidos,** Madero Pte. 485, where tables with tall chairs upstairs overlook the band below. (☎443 312 29 03. Beer 18-26 pesos. Mixed drinks from 35 pesos. Live music and cover F-Sa 8pm-midnight. Open Su-W 8am-midnight, Th-Sa 8am-2am.) **Las Musas,** Obeso 290, is more appropriate for a romantic rendezvous, as troubadours belt out *mariachi* classics. (☎443 317 43 12. Beer 25 pesos. Live music Th-Sa 10pm-2:30am. Cover Tu-Sa 30 pesos. Open daily 8pm-3am.) If you prefer a more intense club scene, writhe with twenty-somethings to the latest pop tunes beneath the video screens at **XO Club,** Ramírez 100. (☎443 324 07 65. Open bar F. Cover men 50 pesos, women 10 pesos. Open W-Sa 10pm-3am.) Clubs here have short lives, so ask around for the latest.

HOLDING COURT

(THE LOCAL STORY)

Eastern Michoacán's beautiful landscape is filled not only with vast coniferous forests and rolling hills, but also, during November and December, over 250 million Monarch Butterflies. Each October, the diminutive creatures begin their journeys from all over the US and Canada and gather just north of Zitácuaro. Some scientists say the mass migration is a relic of the ice ages, when southward travel was necessary for reproduction; others insist that even now monarch reproduction is impossible in all but the warmest of climates. Whatever the reason, the sight is stupendous. The butterflies blanket trees, leaving not a single patch of bark visible.

The best place to be a part of the annual convergence is at the Santuario de Mariposas El Rosario, one of only two butterfly sanctuaries open to the public. From just past Zitácuaro (on Mex. 15 between Toluca and Ciudad Hidalgo), turn right onto Mex. 14 and head north 25km. The entrance fee of 15 pesos is well worth it.

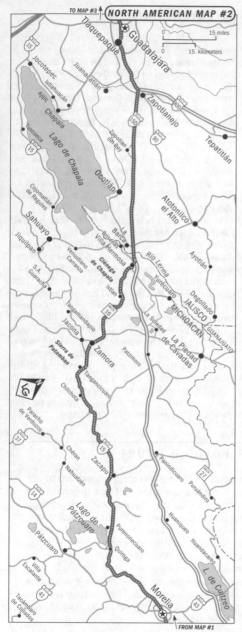

📑 FOOD

It's a breeze to find good, cheap food in Morelia. In some places, almost every street has a family-run restaurant offering *comida corrida* (usually around 20 pesos) in the afternoon. The best deals are around the bus station. Restaurants on the *zócalo* are pricier but stay open later.

📑 Trico, Valladolid 8, 2nd fl. (☎ 443 313 42 32). Elegantly colonial but economical, Trico lures businessmen in suits and families in jeans. Vegetarian options available. Huge breakfasts (39-50 pesos) and regional specialties. Open daily 8am-9pm.

Alborada, Lejarza 36 (☎ 443 313 01 71), right off Madero. A bakery in front and kitchen in back. The *comida corrida* (42 pesos) is mouth-watering. Limitless trips to the salad bar. Breakfasts 20-25 pesos. Open M-Sa 8am-4:30pm. Bakery open M-Sa 8am-9pm.

Super Tortas Homero (☎ 443 333 06 73), at Allende and Abasolo. Great *tortas* (17-28 pesos) draw long lines. Open daily 9am-7pm.

El Tragadero, Hidalgo 63 (☎ 443 313 00 92). Packed with artificial flowers and old images of Morelia. High wood beam ceiling lends a nice feel. Very filling *comida corrida* 37 pesos. Large helpings of local specialties like *caldo tlalpeño* or *sopa tarasco* 26 pesos. Open Su 7:30am-8pm, M-Sa 7:30am-11pm.

📑 ACCOMMODATIONS

Unfortunately, budget hotels with weekend vacancies are about as rare as jackrabbits in Morelia. Moderately priced hotels are all over, but for a real bargain (and a better chance at an empty bed), the IMJUDE hostel is worth extra distance.

IMJUDE Villa Juvenil Youth Hostel, Chiapas 180 (☎ 443 313 31 77; villaju@prodigi.net.mx), at Oaxaca. Go west on Madero Pte., turn left on Cuautla for 6 blocks, then turn right on Oaxaca and continue 4 blocks to Chiapas. Neat 4-person single-sex dorms, communal baths, and a red-tiled lobby with TV. Sports facilities (except pool) can be used with permission. Linen deposit 50 pesos. Reception 7am-11pm. Lockout 11pm. Dorms 60 pesos.

Posada Don Vasco, Vasco de Quiroga 232 (☎ 443 312 14 84), 2 blocks east and 1½ blocks south of the cathedral. Spacious rooms off a pretty stone-arched courtyard have cable TV, phone, carpeting, purified water, and clean, green baths. Singles 198 pesos; doubles 227 pesos; triples 255 pesos.

Hotel Mintzicuri, Vasco de Quiroga 227 (☎443 312 06 64). Railings overflowing with flowers enclose cozy, wood-paneled rooms named for *michoacano* towns and equipped with phones and cable TV. Very popular with Mexican tourists, so call ahead. Singles 206 pesos; doubles 232 pesos; triples 283 pesos.

Hotel el Carmen, Ruiz 63 (☎443 312 17 25), across the courtyard from Casa de la Cultura. Clean, stylish accommodations. Rooms are slightly cramped but have spotless bathrooms, high-beamed ceilings, cable TV, phone, and hardwood furniture. Thin walls can make the rooms a bit noisy. Singles 190-220 pesos; doubles 250 pesos.

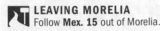

LEAVING MORELIA
Follow **Mex. 15** out of Morelia.

HUERTA COLORINES
Between Morelia and Quiroga on Mex. 15.

The ornate wooden furniture, stained-glass hanging lamps, and carrot-shaped bottle openers make this bar and *restaurante* a unique place to stop. It serves delicious Mexican fare, cold Coronas, and chips with four varieties of sauces to satisfy all tastes. (☎443 330 25 14. Quesadillas 24 pesos. Entrees 30-83 pesos. Open daily 8am-6pm.)

QUIROGA. You'll see more cowboy boots and wooden guitars along the main street of Quiroga than should fit in any one-horse town. The city revolves around its famed **market,** with shops specializing in everything from leather goods and ornate pottery to embroidered linens and cow-shaped candles. The main street and site of the market, Av. Vasco de Quiroga, is right off **Mex. 15,** and parking in front of one of the many shops is easy and relatively safe during the day.

APPROACHING GUADALAJARA
As you near the city limits **Mex. 15** overlaps with **Mex. 80;** they become **Cardenas** downtown. A right turn on **Av. Colon** will take you right to the *centro.*

GUADALAJARA

More Mexican than Mexico itself, Guadalajara is the crossroads of the republic. Here, in the capital of Jalisco state and the country's second-largest city, north meets south, colonial meets modern, and traditional meets cutting-edge. The city has spawned many of Mexico's most marketable icons: bittersweet *mariachi* music, *jarabe tapatío* (Mexican hat dance), and tequila. Founded in 1532 by Nuño de Guzmán, the most brutal of the *conquistadores*, Guadalajara was born in bloodbath; most of the region's *indígenas* were slaughtered, and few pre-Hispanic traditions survived. In the years following, the city served as the capital of Mexico and a key battleground in the Revolution. Today, Guadalajara entices natives and tourists with its parks, museums, plazas, and stately colonial architecture. Meanwhile, the Universidad de Guadalajara, the second-oldest in Mexico, keeps Guadalajara young and colorful with a measure of intellectual sophistication.

VITAL STATS

Population: 8 million

Visitor Info: State Office, Morelos 102 (☎33 3668 16 00 or 800 363 22 00), in Plaza Tapatía. Open M-F 9am-8pm, Sa-Su 9am-1pm. Branch in the Palacio de Gobierno. Open daily 9:30am-3pm.

Internet Access: Librería de Porrua Hnos., Juárez 16 (☎33 3521 28 30). 10 pesos per hr. Open daily 8am-8pm.

US Consulate: Progreso 175 (☎33 3825 22 99). Open M-F 8:30am-noon and 2-3pm.

Post Office: (☎33 3614 74 25), on Carranza between Manuel and Calle Independencia. Open M-F 8am-6:30pm, Sa 9am-1pm. **Postal Code:** 44100.

GETTING AROUND

The cities of **Tlaquepaque, Zapopan,** and **Tonalá** are all seamlessly joined to the Guadalajara metropolitan area. The heart of the city is the *centro histórico* around **Plaza Tapatía** and **Plaza de la Liberación.** The two major streets, **Calzada Independencia** and **Hidalgo/República** (known as República east of Calzada Independencia, and Hidalgo to the west), divide Guadalajara into quadrants. Streets change names at the borders of these quadrants. Note that in addition to Calzada Independencia, Guadalajara has a Calle Independencia, crossing the city east-west just north of the *centro.* **Parking** lots abound, most charging around 8 pesos per hour; they are a much better idea than trying your luck on the street.

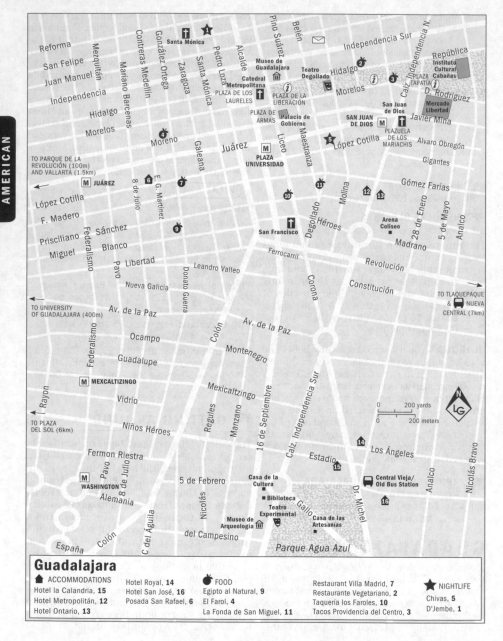

Reforma
San Felipe
Juan Manuel
Independencia
Hidalgo
Morelos

Contreras
González Ortega
Mezquitán
Mariano Barcenas

Santa Mónica
Pedro Loza
Zaragoza
Santa Mónica

Alcalde

Pino Suárez
Belén

Independencia Sur

Santa Mónica

Museo de Guadalajara
Catedral Metropolitana
PLAZA DE LOS LAURELES

Teatro Degollado
Hidalgo
Morelos

República
Instituto Cultural Cabañas
PLAZA TAPATÍA
D. Rodríguez

Calz. Independencia N.

PLAZA DE LA LIBERACIÓN
PLAZA DE ARMAS
Palacio de Gobierno

San Juan de Dios
SAN JUAN DE DIOS
Mercado Libertad
Javier Mina

Moreno
Galeana
Juárez
Liceo
Maestranza
López Cotilla

PLAZA UNIVERSIDAD

PLAZUELA DE LOS MARIACHIS
Alvaro Obregón
Gigantes

López Cotilla
F. Madero
Priscíliano Sánchez
Miguel
Blanco
Libertad
Pavo
Nueva Galicia

JUÁREZ

8 de Julio
E. G. Martínez

Federalismo

Donato Guerra

Leandro Valleo

Ferrocarril
San Francisco
Degollado
Héroes
Molina
Gómez Farías
28 de Enero
5 de Mayo
Analco

Arena Coliseo
Madrano

Corona
Revolución
Constitución

TO PARQUE DE LA REVOLUCIÓN (100m) AND VALLARTA (1.5km)

TO UNIVERSITY OF GUADALAJARA (400m)

TO PLAZA DEL SOL (6km)

TO TLAQUEPAQUE & NUEVA CENTRAL (7km)

Av. de la Paz
Ocampo
Guadalupe

Rayon
Federalismo

Colón
Montenegro
Av. de la Paz

MEXCALTIZINGO
Vidrio
Niños Héroes

Regules
Manzano
Mexcaltzingo
16 de Septiembre
Calz. Independencia Sur

Fermon Riestra
WASHINGTON
Alemania

8 de Julio
Pavo

5 de Febrero
Nicolás
del Campesino

Casa de la Cultura
Biblioteca
Teatro Experimental
Museo de Arqueología

Gallo
Estadio
Los Ángeles
Dr. Michel

Central Vieja/ Old Bus Station
Casa de las Artesanías

Analco
Nicolás Bravo

España
Colón
C del Águila

Parque Agua Azul

0   200 yards
0   200 meters

N
LG

Guadalajara

ACCOMMODATIONS
Hotel la Calandria, **15**
Hotel Metropolitán, **12**
Hotel Ontario, **13**
Hotel Royal, **14**
Hotel San José, **16**
Posada San Rafael, **6**

FOOD
Egipto al Natural, **9**
El Farol, **4**
La Fonda de San Miguel, **11**
Restaurant Villa Madrid, **7**
Restaurante Vegetariano, **2**
Taquería los Faroles, **10**
Tacos Providencia del Centro, **3**

NIGHTLIFE
Chivas, **5**
D'Jembe, **1**

The poorer *colonias* (neighborhoods) of Guadalajara can be dangerous any time of day. Travelers should keep to lighted streets and take a car or taxi after dark. Women travelers may wish to avoid Calzada Independencia after dark, as the street attracts raucous, drunken men and supports a thriving prostitution trade at all hours. Neighborhoods tend to be significantly more dangerous to the east of Calzada Independencia.

👁 SIGHTS

A town of monuments, Guadalajara has perfected the concept of "the plaza." The city's many shopping malls spill over into wide public spaces, packed with *mariachis*, tourists, vendors, and street performers. That said, many of the city's finer sights are in its less chaotic *alrededores*—Zapopan's cathedral, Tonalá's market, Tequila's blue agave, and the picturesque towns around Lake Chapala. The tourist office sells a pamphlet called *Puntos de Interés* (5 pesos), complete with maps, sites, and suggested walks.

THE CENTRO

PLAZA DE LA LIBERACIÓN. Abuzz with activity, the plaza is the center of historic Guadalajara. Horse-drawn carriages line up near the Museo Regional, waiting to cart you around the city. *(45min., 120 pesos.)* The spacious plaza, with its bubbling fountain and large Mexican flag, is surrounded by the cathedral, Museo Regional, Palacio de Gobierno, and Teatro Degollado. Military personnel ceremonially retire the colors daily at 7pm. An enormous sculpture depicts Hidalgo breaking the chains of servitude in commemoration of his 1810 decree abolishing the slave trade, which was signed in the Palacio de Gobierno.

CATEDRAL METROPOLITANA. Facing Teatro Degollado across Plaza de la Liberación, the cathedral was begun in 1561 and completed 60 years later. After an 1848 earthquake destroyed its original towers, ambitious architects replaced them with much taller ones. Fernando VII of Spain donated the cathedral's 11 richly ornamented altars in appreciation of Guadalajara's aid during the Napoleonic Wars. One is dedicated to Our Lady of the Roses and gave Guadalajara its nickname, "City of Roses." Inside the sacristy is the famed *Assumption of the Virgin*, by 17th-century painter Bartolomé Murillo. The towers, known as *cornucopías*, can

NORTH AMERICAN MAP #3

TO MAP #4

FROM MAP #2

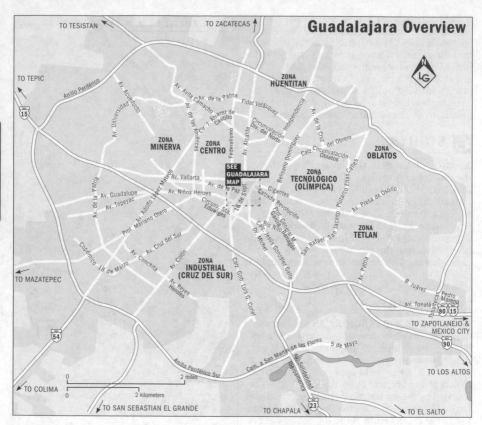

Guadalajara Overview

TO TESISTAN
TO ZACATECAS
TO TEPIC
TO MAZATEPEC
TO COLIMA
TO SAN SEBASTIAN EL GRANDE
TO CHAPALA
TO EL SALTO
TO LOS ALTOS
TO ZAPOTLANEJO & MEXICO CITY

ZONA HUENTITAN
ZONA MINERVA
ZONA CENTRO
ZONA OBLATOS
ZONA TECNOLÓGICO (OLÍMPICA)
ZONA TETLAN
ZONA INDUSTRIAL (CRUZ DEL SUR)

SEE GUADALAJARA MAP

0   2 miles
0   2 kilometers

NORTH AMERICAN

be climbed with the permission of the administrators, who are holed up in the side of the building facing Teatro Degollado. Descend beneath the altar (take the steps on the right-hand side) where the remains of three cardinals and two bishops keep one another company. The 60m jaunt up the tower affords the best view in town. *(Open daily 7:30am-7:30pm.)*.

PALACIO DE GOBIERNO. The palace, built in 1751, served as the headquarters of renegade governments under Hildago from 1810 to 1811 and Juárez in 1858. Today, several José Clemente Orozco murals grace the Palacio. Climb to the roof for a great view. *(Open M-F 9am-8pm. Guided tours available in English.)*

INSTITUTO CULTURAL CABAÑAS. Once known as the Hospicio Cabañas, this building was constructed in 1801 to house an orphanage. The huge structure served as an art school and a military barracks before acquiring its present status as an exhibition/performance/office space. Orozco murals decorate the chapel, which was otherwise finished in 1845. The striking *El Hombre de Fuego* (The Man of Fire), a dramatic reversal of heaven and hell that tops off Orozco's portrait of Mexican history, peers down from the dome. *(Hospicio and Cabañas, 3 blocks east of Independencia. Open Su 10am-3pm, Tu-Sa 10am-6pm. 8 pesos, students 4 pesos, under 12 free. Su free. Camera rights 10 pesos; no flash.)*

MUSEO REGIONAL DE GUADALAJARA. In the old San José seminary, this museum chronicles the history of western Mexico—starting with the Big Bang—with art on display as well. Artsy and educational movie screenings, plays, and lectures take place in the museum's auditorium. Inquire within or at the tourist office. *(Liceo 60 at Hidalgo, on the north side of Plaza de la Liberación.* ☎ *33 3614 9957. Open Su 9am-5pm, Tu-Sa 9am-5:30pm. 30 pesos, seniors and under 12 free. Su free.)*

TEATRO DEGOLLADO. Catch a performance by the Ballet Folklórico (see below) for a good look at breathtaking Teatro Degollado, named for former governor Santos Degollado. Built in 1856, the Neoclassical structure has gold arches, an allegory of the seven muses, and, on the ceiling, an interpretation by Gerardo Suárez of Dante's *Paradiso. (On the east end of Plaza de la Liberación.)*

PLAZUELA DE LOS MARIACHIS. Immediately after you sit down in this crowded plaza, roving *mariachis* will pounce, using every trick in their bag to separate you from your pesos. Prices for songs range from 20 to 35 pesos. *Mariachis* play deep into the night, but beware: late night the Plazuela becomes a stage for roving unsavories, who may use other methods to acquire pesos. *(On the south side of San Juan de Dios, the church with the blue neon cross on Independencia at Mina.)*

PARQUE AGUA AZUL. If you're tired of congested city streets, take a stroll in this 168,000 sq. m park, which features aviaries, orchids, a butterfly house, and a sports complex. *(South of the centro on Calzada Independencia. Open Su and Tu-Sa 10am-6:30pm. 6 pesos, children 4 pesos.)*

NORTH OF THE CENTRO

ZOOLÓGICO GUADALAJARA. You wouldn't know it from hanging around the Plaza Tapatiá, but ecological wealth surrounds Guadalajara. The zoo boasts over 360 species from around the world. At the far end is a spectacular view of the deep Barranca de Huentitán ravine. *(Continue north on Calzada Independencia past Plaza de Toros, and drive 1.5km to the entrance of the zoo from the bus stop on Independencia.* ☎ *33 3674 44 88. Open Su and W-Sa 10am-6pm. 25 pesos, children 15 pesos.)*

CENTRO DE CIENCIA Y TECNOLOGÍA. The center houses a planetarium, exhibits on stars and rocks, and a garden of sculpted plants. *(A 10min. drive from the zoo.* ☎ *33 3674 4106 or 3674 3978. Open Su and Tu-Sa 9am-7pm. Museum 4 pesos. Planetarium 6 pesos.)*

🎵 ENTERTAINMENT

Guadalajara is known for its cultural sophistication and dizzying variety of entertainment options. Check the listings in *The Guadalajara Weekly, Ocio, Vuelo Libre,* and the kiosks and bulletin boards in places like Instituto Cultural Cabañas to keep abreast of all the happenings—from avantgarde film festivals to bullfights. Dazzling the world with precise dance, intricate garb, and amusing antics, the University of Guadalajara puts on ▓**Ballet Folklórico** in **Teatro Degollado** (see p. 651). Tickets are available on the day of the performance or one day in advance. (Performances every Su 10am. Box office open daily 10am-1pm and 4-7pm. Tickets 50-150 pesos.)

🍴 FOOD

Guadalajara has plenty of budget eateries, as well as many expensive, upscale restaurants serving international cuisine. *Birria* is the hearty local dish of stewed meat (usually pork) in tomato broth, thickened with cornmeal and spiced with garlic, onions, and chiles. *Tortas ahogadas,* another local specialty, differ from the standard *torta* with a pork rind filling and special sauce slathered on top, soaking what's often slightly stale bread. After your meal, quench your thirst with an Estrella beer, brewed *clara dorada* (golden clear) right in Guadalajara. **Mercado Libertad,** on Calle Independencia, next to the plaza, is a sensory overload. You can find anything here, from *birria* to fried chicken to live animals. (Open daily 6am-8pm.)

▓ **Restaurant Villa Madrid,** Cotilla 553 (☎ 33 3613 42 50). Employees convert heaping piles of fruit into delicious smoothies and huge *licuados* (25 pesos). *Tostadas* (34 pesos), burritos (36 pesos), and everything else served with lots of sides. Open M-F 12:30-9pm, Sa 12:30-8pm.

La Fonda de San Miguel, Guerra 25 (☎ 33 3613 08 09). Completed in 1694, La Fonda de San Miguel was once Santa Teresa de Jesús, the oldest convent in the city. It has since been flawlessly restored, leaving a gently arched colonade filled with caged birds. *Enchiladas carmelitas* 37 pesos. *Crepas del convento* 37 pesos. *Tacos sonorenses* 40 pesos. Open Su-M 8am-6pm, Tu-Sa 8am-midnight.

Egipto al Natural, Sánchez 416 (☎ 33 3613 62 77). Formerly Restaurant Acuarius. The name has changed but loyal customers insist that the traditional budget-friendly, vegetarian cuisine has not. Vegetarian *comida corrida* 35 pesos. Juice 10 pesos. Open M-Sa 10am-6pm.

Tacos Providencia del Centro, Morelos 86 (☎33 3613 99 14), next to the tourist office. A full range of tacos and other *botanas* in a beautifully refurbished building. *Tacos al pastor* 4.5 pesos, *sopa de tortilla* 25 pesos. Open M-Sa 8am-8pm, Su 10am-6pm.

Taquería los Faroles, Corona 250 (☎33 3613 4723), at Sánchez. Tempts hordes of locals with every type of taco imaginable (4-7 pesos). Try excellent *quesadillas* with homemade tortillas (10 pesos) or famous *torta ahogada* (15 pesos). Open daily 7am-midnight.

Restaurante Vegetariano, Hidalgo 112 (☎33 3614 54 47), to the left of the black-painted window. A wide array of vegetarian foods, including salads (13-15 pesos). Sandwiches 7-10 pesos. Quesadillas 6-8 pesos. Open Su 9am-5pm, M-Sa 9am-7pm.

El Farol, Moreno 466, 2nd fl. (☎33 3613 6349), at Galeana. The friendly owner makes a mean *chile relleno*. Complimentary *buñuelo*, a fried dough dessert doused with syrup. Entrees 20-40 pesos. Tacos 5 pesos. Beer 12-16 pesos. Open daily 10am-8pm.

ACCOMMODATIONS

Guadalajara is full of cheap places to stay. Unfortunately, some bargain accommodations are plagued by typical big city problems—24hr. traffic, poor room quality, and prostitution. The best values are around the old bus station, a 5min. drive south of Plaza Tapatía (Take Calzada Independencia Sur to Dr. Michel.) Regardless of where you stay, call ahead; many places fill up early in the day. Hotels advertising that they cater to families are declaring themselves prostitution-free.

Hotel San José, 5 de Febrero 116 (☎33 3619 28 11; sanjose7@jal1.telmex.net.mx), just down the street from the old bus station. A cut above the rest. Tiled surfaces and potted palms make the hectic world outside fade away. All rooms with TV and private bath. Singles 180-210 pesos; doubles 220-250 pesos.

Hotel la Calandria, Estadio 100 (☎33 3619 65 79), off Dr. Michel just before the old bus station. The wood paneling and brass detail are indicative of the care shown here. Very clean rooms come with private bath and fan. Singles 115 pesos, with TV 135 pesos; doubles 150 pesos/170 pesos.

Hotel Metropolitán, Calz. Independencia Sur 278 (☎33 3613 24 58). A paradise of bland sterility. Rooms with comfortable beds, TV, fan, and neatly tiled bathrooms open onto a pleasant, sky-lit courtyard lobby. Beware of windows facing the street, a major bus route. Singles 130 pesos; doubles 150-220 pesos.

Hotel Royal, Los Ángeles 115 (☎33 3619 84 73 or 3650 09 14), off Dr. Michel north of the old bus station. Clean rooms with TV, private baths, and fans. Singles 110 pesos; doubles 160 pesos.

Posada San Rafael, Cotilla 619 (☎33 3614 91 46). Renovated with an eye to the building's 19th-century charms, this former monastery is a cut above standard Guadalajara fare. Stone walls keep the city at bay. Singles 180 pesos, with TV and remodeled bath 250 pesos; doubles 230 pesos/280 pesos.

Hotel Ontario, Calz. Independencia Sur 137 (☎33 3617 80 99), across from Hotel Metropolitán. Ontario pleases the traveler who wants to be in the thick of it. Simple rooms with private baths. Singles 90 pesos; doubles 110 pesos.

NIGHTLIFE

Guadalajara's extensive nightlife has something to please any partier. Bars and chill cafes cluster near the *centro;* trendy clubs line Av. Vallarta.

Chai, Vallarta 1509 (☎33 3615 94 26). Uber-trendy locals lounge on the terrace or on huge couches as MTV is projected on the walls. Iced lattes 15 pesos. Gourmet sandwiches 35-42 pesos. Open M-Th 9am-midnight and F-Sa 9am-1am.

D'Jembe, Loza 221 (☎33 3849 88 35), between San Felipe and Reforma. Dig the sand floor and the Africa-inspired rhythms and decor. Open daily noon-3am.

La Marcha, Vallarta 2648 (☎33 3615 89 99), at Los Arcos. Fancy art, fountains, and pretension galore. Dress to impress in this 19th-century mansion. Cover men 140 pesos, women 90 pesos.

Bombay Lounge, Hidalgo 2111 (☎33 3630 60 72). A mammoth, multi-tiered disco with raj stylings and a DJ on every floor. Patrons groove to pretty much any kind of dance music. Open daily 9pm-3am.

Chivas, Cotilla 150 (☎33 3613 16 17), near the corner of Delgollado. Home base of Guadalajara's gay scene, the bar's many small tables are crowded with patrons nursing beers (12 pesos). Tequila 30 pesos. Lesbian-friendly. Open daily 5pm-3am.

LEAVING GUADALAJARA

Head south from the *centro* and you'll eventually make it to **Cardenas,** where a right will take you back to **Mex. 15** and out of Guadalajara.

ZAPOPAN. Once a small town, Zapopan, just west on Mex. 15, would now blend easily into the Guadalajara metropolitan area if it weren't for its stunning plaza and giant, famous **Basílica de la Virgen de Zapopan,** erected after a local peasant's vision of the Virgin. The altar holds **Our Lady of Zapopan,** a small cornstalk figure made by *indígenas* in the 16th century. Her healing powers are commemorated by decades worth of *ex votos*, small paintings on sheet metal offering a visual testimony of the cured. The **Sala de Arte Huichal,** on one side of the cathedral, displays indigenous art and handicrafts. (Open daily 9am-2pm and 4-7pm.) Both the Basílica and Sala are situated around **Plaza de las Américas,** where 28 lances represent the nations of the Americas. The market next to the fountain and plaza is the best place to grab a cheap taco or roast chicken.

TEQUILA

Surrounded by gentle mountains and prickly, blue-green *agave* plants stretching as far as the eye can see, Tequila has been dedicated solely to the production and sale of its namesake liquor since the 17th century. The town is home to 16 tequila distilleries, and nearly every business in town is linked to alcohol in some way; tourism sustains t-shirt and souvenir shops, as well as numerous liquor stores in the *centro* and along the route just outside of town. Although it's touristy, Tequila is lots of fun and makes a great stop on the way to Tepic.

VITAL STATS

Population: 40,000

Visitor Info: Tourism Board Module, Plaza Principal across from the Palacio Municipal. Open daily 10am-4pm. The **Museo de Tequila,** Corona 34 (☎374 742 24 11), 1 block off the plaza, has maps.

GETTING AROUND.
All the distilleries are surprisingly close to the town's **Plaza Principal,** the terminus of the long exit road from **Mex. 15.** The giant José Cuervo and Sauza plants are right next to each other two blocks north of the plaza on a street that starts off as **Corona;** this and several other streets in town change names. Street **parking** is available, though many businesses have lots.

SIGHTS.
There's not much to do here other than drink or take a **Tequila Factory Tour.** Or maybe you came for the opera? The tourist office runs tours from their module on the plaza (every hr. 11am-3pm; 25 pesos). A better option may be to head straight to the **Sauza** factory tour, rumored to be the best. Join in at the factory or trek to the tour's official start: 50m down the highway past the entrance to Tequila at Rancho Indio, where a demonstration of blue *agave* cultivation precedes a visit to the factory. (☎374 742 00 13. Tours M-F 11am, 12:30pm, 2:45, 4pm. 35 pesos.) To see the factory in action, try to arrive early, and avoid *siesta* (2-4pm). One block back toward the plaza is the less impressive **José Cuervo** factory. (Tours M-Sa every hr. 10am-2pm. English tours 10am and noon. 30 pesos, students 15 pesos.) For the price of a few shots, you'll learn more than you wanted to know about *agave*, the distillation and aging processes, and the history of the liquor. Throughout the tour, guides will ply you with tequilas and margaritas. The **Museo Nacional de Tequila,** Corona 34, teaches more tequila history with bilingual signs and a gift shop. (☎374 742 2410. Open Su and Tu-Sa 10am-5pm. 15 pesos, children and students 7 pesos.) The **Museo Familia Sauza,** Rojas 22, in the old Sauza family mansion, can be toured. (Open M-F 10am-1:30pm, Sa-Su 10am-4:30pm. Tours every 30min. Donation suggested.)

For the first 12 days of December, Tequila celebrates its **Feria Nacional del Tequila.** Each of the town's factories claims one day, on which it holds rodeos, concerts, cockfights, fireworks, and other festivities. And of course, there are always plenty of drinks to go around.

FOOD & ACCOMMODATIONS.
Cheap restaurants pack the area around the bus station; roast chicken is a local favorite. Dine at **Avicola,** Gorjón 20, where 30 pesos will buy you half a bird, tortillas, and salsa. (Open daily 7:30am-4pm.) For more ambience, try **Resturant Bar el Sauzal,** Juárez 45, between Gorjón and Cuervo, right by the plaza. (Steak 40 pesos. Quesadillas 18 pesos. Beer 13 pesos. Open daily 11am-2am.) Taco stands cluster on the right-hand side of the church.

Even some hotels in town are tequila-themed, including **Hotel Posada del Agave,** Gorjón 83, on the way to the Plaza. Rooms decorated in tiles painted with *agave* plants have private baths, cable TV,

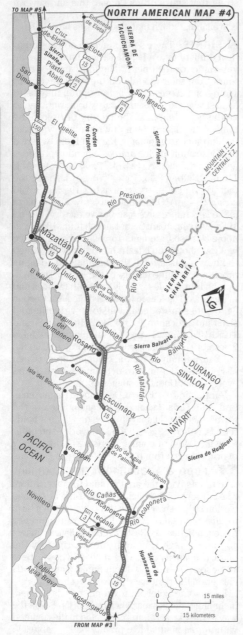

and fans. (☎374 742 07 74. Singles 180 pesos; doubles 250 pesos.) **Hotel San Francisco,** next to the cathedral, is a clean, comfortable sanctuary. All rooms have private baths and fans. (☎374 742 17 57. Singles 170 pesos; doubles 230 pesos.)

LEAVING TEQUILA
Once you've sobered up, head back to **Mex. 15**.

Between Tequila and Ixtlán del Río, Mex. 15 enters the Mountain Time Zone, where it is 1hr. earlier.

IXTLÁN DEL RÍO
Between Tequila and Tepic on Mex. 15. The town itself stretches along Av. Hidalgo.

Ixtlán, or "place of obsidian," is one of Mexico's earliest settlements. Excavated tombs demonstrate the familial burial and the ceramics that characterize early Ixtlán period (300 BC-AD 300). During its the Middle Ixtlán period (AD 750-1110) the Aztatlán built the stone altars marked by stone colonnades on this site. The Aztatlán culture worshipped the four elements, and each altar was dedicated to a god representing one of the elements. The stepped circular pyramid has a unique shape and a recognizable dedication; a close examination of the walls reveals spirals that symbolize moving air and the wind god Ehecatl. The **Museum,** to the left as you enter, sets out other aspects of the culture, as well as the significance of this site in the context of the region. (Open daily 8am-5pm. 23 pesos; students, seniors, and teachers free. Su free.) The **Tourist Office,** Hidalgo Pte. 672, offers brochures on the archaeological site and the town itself. (☎374 243 56 39. Open M-F 9am-6pm, Sa-Su 10am-2pm.)

TEPIC

Called *Tepique* (the Place Between the Hills) by pre-Hispanic inhabitants, Tepic became a center for trade and commerce under Spanish rule in the 16th and 17th centuries. Now home to the Nayarit state government, the city is still a crossroads as well as a haven of slow-paced cafes and shady green parks. Situated 170km 280km south of Mazatlán, Tepic links Guadalajara (230km to the southeast) with the Nayarit beaches via **Mex. 15.** To the north, **Plaza Principal** (officially called the *centro histórico*) is dominated by the cathedral on one end and the Palacio Municipal on the other. The **Museo Amado Nervo,** Zacatecas 284 Nte., celebrates the works of the poet in the house where he was born. (☎311 212 26 52. Open M-F 9am-2pm and Sa-Su 10am-1pm.) The **Museo Emelia Ortiz,** Lerdo 192 Pte., displays the caricatures and *indígena*-inspired art of the Tepic natives as well as local contemporary art. (☎311 212 26 52. Open M-Sa 9am-7pm. Free.) The **Casa Museo de Juan Escutia,** Hidalgo 71 Ote., celebrates the lives of the *niños héroes,* particularly the "Niño Héroe de Chapultepec," one of the group of military cadets who died fighting off US invaders. (☎311 212 33 90. Open M-F 9am-2pm and 4-7pm, Sa 10am-2pm.) The **state capitol** lies at México and Abasolo, a gracefully domed structure dating from the 1870s.

Most tourist services lie on or near México, the town's main drag. Tepic's tons of fruits, fish, and coffee flow through the capital and into most restaurants. **Restaurant Vegetariano Quetzalcóatl,** on León Nte. at Lerdo, four blocks west of Plaza Principal, hosts a popular buffet (Tu-Sa 1pm; 45 pesos) in its leafy courtyard. (☎311 212 99 66. Open Tu-Sa 8:30am-5:30pm.) For cheap food, go to **Restaurant Tirayán,** Zaragoza 20, half a block down from the intersection with Veracruz. (Egg breakfasts 18 pesos. Fish filets 31 pesos. *Tostadas* 10 pesos. Open daily 8am-9pm.) If you want to be above the masses, then **La Gloria,** upstairs at México and Lerdo Altos next to the cathedral, offers more refined fare and incredible views of the plaza. (☎311 847 0464. *Filete miñón* 80 pesos. Open daily 8am-11pm.) ⧉**Hotel Morelia,** Morelia 215, has a lush courtyard and clean, simple rooms. (☎311 216 60 85. Singles 70 pesos; doubles 90 pesos. Pri-vate baths 20 pesos extra.) Next door, **Hotel Pasadena California,** Morelia 215, is slightly cheaper and offers similarly basic rooms. (☎311 212 91 40. Singles 60 pesos, with bath 80 pesos.)

ACAPONETA. Off of Mex. 15 2hr. out of Tepic, **Av. Morelos** runs through the few businesses that make up Acaponeta on its way to a small, pleasant *zócalo*. There's not much to the town, and even less in the way of tourism, but it can make a nice rest stop if you're not in any particular hurry. For a truly authentic dining experience, head to the center of town, where the family that runs **El Asadero de Tochos,** impossible to miss in the tiny main plaza, cooks up whatever local dishes meet their fancy that day. (Tacos 20 pesos. Whole roast chicken 45 pesos. Open daily 10am-10pm.) At **Motel Cadenales,** Morelos 50, take advantage of free parking, comfortable rooms, and the Internet cafe (15 pesos per hr.) next door. (☎325 252 0777. Check-out noon. Singles 300 pesos; doubles 350 pesos; triples 400 pesos; quads 450 pesos.) When you're ready to ramble, hop back on to **Mex. 15.**

MAZATLÁN

Mazatlán has a storied history of 17th-century Spanish gold shipping and foreign blockades. None of this seems to matter, however, to the tourists that now blockade the city's streets in search of golden sands and sunshine. Mazatlán is the perfect place to combine sleepy sun-filled days with debaucherous tequila-drenched nights.

¡TEQUILA TIME!

The best tequila bears a label boasting its content: 100% agave. Plants take 8 to 12 years to mature, when their huge centers (called *piñas*—pineapples—for their appearance) weigh 35-45kg. The *piñas* are harvested and then cooked for up to 36hr. in enormous traditional ovens. *Piñas* are then chopped and mixed with water, and the pulp that's strained off is used for rugs, animal food, and stuffing furniture. The remaining mixture is fermented in tubs. Only 10% of the mixture actually becomes tequila. Be thankful for yeast fermentation—in the past, options included naked workers sitting in the vats or throwing in a piece of dung wrapped in cloth. The tequila then goes through two distillations to lower the alcohol content. In the factory, you can sip tequila after its first distillation, with an alcohol content as high as 80%. Afterwards it is aged in oak barrels—the longer the process, the smoother the taste. All of this can only happen here: it's against the law to produce tequila anywhere but Jalisco and a few surrounding areas.

(VITAL STATS)

Population: 500,000

Visitor Info: Sábalo at Tiburón (☎ 669 916 51 60; fax 669 916 51 66), in the pinkish Banrural building past El Cid resort. Open M-F 9am-5pm.

Internet Access: Telefona Automática de Pacífico, Flores 810 (☎ 669 981 71 59), in the *centro.* 15 pesos per hr. Open daily 8:30am-9:30pm.

US Consular Agency: Playa Gaviotas 202 (☎ 669 916 58 89), in Hotel Playa Mazatlán.

Post Office: (☎ 669 981 21 21), on Flores at Juárez, across from the *zócalo.* Open M-F 8am-6pm, Sa 9am-1pm. **Postal Code:** 82000.

GETTING AROUND

Mazatlán is divided into **Old Mazatlán,** home to the *zócalo* and budget hotels and restaurants, and the **Zona Dorada,** home to the highrise hotels and big-money entertainment. **Paseo Claussen** follows the boardwalk along the beach and connects the two sides of town. **Parking** in the Old City gets tricky the farther in you go, but finding parking along the beach is rarely a problem.

SIGHTS

Most of Mazatlán's sights revolve around its lovely coastline and endless sunshine.

BEACHES. Mazatlán's famous beach stretches 16km from Olas Altas, well past the Zona Dorada. North of Old Mazatlán, along del Mar, is **Playa Norte.** Its small waves and lack of activity make it a tranquil stretch of sand. As you approach the Zona Dorada, the beach gets cleaner, the waves grow larger, and Playa Norte eases into **Playa las Gaviotas.** Past Punta Sábalo, in the lee of the islands, is **Playa Sábalo,** where excellent waves and golden sand enthrall crowds of sun-worshippers. As Playa Sábalo recedes to the north, crowds thin rapidly. In most places, boogie boards *(40 pesos)* and sailboats *(500 pesos per hr.)* are available. Drive north of the Zona Dorada on Sábalo to nearly deserted **Playa Bruja** (Witch Beach), with beautiful sand and 1-2m waves. Camping is permitted, but exercise caution after dark and camp in groups whenever possible.

EL FARO. For a 360° view of Mazatlán and the sea, climb El Faro, the second-tallest lighthouse in the world. The 30min. hike is almost unbearable in the summer; ascend in the early morning or late evening to avoid the heat. *(South of Old Mazatlán.)*

TOWER DIVERS. Mazatlán's tower divers perform acrobatic and dangerous plunges into rocky surf from an 18m high ledge. Dives take place during the day, but be warned that divers will not perform unless they pull in a sufficient amount of money beforehand. The best time to watch is 10-11am and 4:30-6:30pm, when tour buses arrive and tourists fork over their pesos, allowing others to see dives for free. For great viewing stand just south of the towers. *(On Claussen, south of Zaragoza and north of La Siesta Hotel.)*

ISLAS VENADOS. For those itching to escape the beaches, Islas Venados (Deer Island) is a relatively deserted strip of land with fine diving. Catamaran boats leave from the Agua Sports Center. *(At El Cid Resort in Zona Dorada. ☎ 669 913 33 33, ext. 341. Boats depart daily 10am, noon, 2pm. Round-trip 100 pesos.)*

MAZAGUA. Waterpark mania hit Mazatlán with Mazagua, north of the Zona Dorada near Puerta Cerritos. Splash in the wave pool or shoot down slippery slides. *(☎ 669 988 00 41. Open Mar.-Oct. daily 10am-6pm. 80 pesos, under 4 free.)*

ACUARIO MAZATLÁN. One of the largest aquariums in Latin America keeps sharks and other feisty fish (up to 250 breeds in all) in a slew of cloudy tanks, and features performing sea lions and birds. *(Av. de los Deportes 111, off Av. del Mar, 1 block back from the beach; the turn-off is marked with a blue sign. ☎ 669 981 78 15. Open daily 9:30am-6pm. 50 pesos, ages 5-10 25 pesos.)*

TEATRO ÁNGELA PERALTA. The newly restored and luxurious theater hosts an impressive variety of cultural programs. *(At Carnaval and Libertad near Plazuela Machado. ☎ 669 982 44 47; www.teatroangelaperalta.com. 5 pesos.)*

MUSEO CASA MACHADO. This 19th-century mansion is filled with relics from Mazatlán's glory days as the state capital. The museum's collection of spectacularly gaudy old *Carnaval* costumes makes it worth a visit. *(Constitución 79, just off Plazuela Machado. ☎ 669 982 14 40. Open daily 10am-6pm. 20 pesos, children 10 pesos.)*

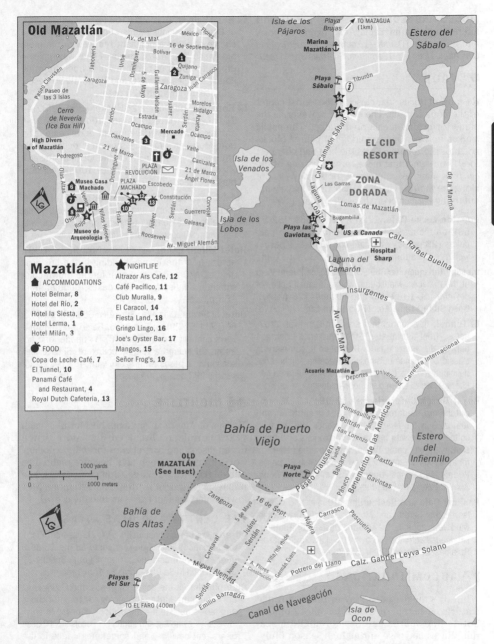

Old Mazatlán

Av. del Mar
México
Flores
16 de Septiembre
Bolívar
Quijano **1**
Zúniga **2**
Zaragoza
Juan Carrasco
Juárez
Guillermo Nelson
5 de Mayo
Domínguez
Uribe
Jaboneria
Paseo Claussen
Zaragoza

Paseo de
las 3 Islas

Cerro
de Nevería
(Ice Box Hill)

Morelos
Hidalgo
Estrada
Ocampo
Serdán
Juárez
Arriba
Mercado
Ocampo

High Divers
■ of Mazatlán
Canizales **3**
Valle
Pedregoso
21 de Marzo
Canizales
21 de Marzo
Ángel Flores
PLAZA
REVOLUCIÓN

**Museo Casa
Machado** **6**
PLAZA
MACHADO
Constitución **13**
Escobedo
Nevería
Olas Altas
17 **10**
Serdán
Guerrero
Corvajal
Galeana

Museo de
Arqueología
Osuna
Rojo
Niños Héroes
Trias
Carnaval
Juárez
Roosevelt

Av. Miguel Alemán

Mazatlán

NIGHTLIFE

ACCOMMODATIONS
Hotel Belmar, **8**
Hotel del Río, **2**
Hotel la Siesta, **6**
Hotel Lerma, **1**
Hotel Milán, **3**

FOOD
Copa de Leche Café, **7**
El Tunnel, **10**
Panamá Café
   and Restaurant, **4**
Royal Dutch Cafeteria, **13**

Altrazor Ars Cafe, **12**
Café Pacífico, **11**
Club Muralla, **9**
El Caracol, **14**
Fiesta Land, **18**
Gringo Lingo, **16**
Joe's Oyster Bar, **17**
Mangos, **15**
Señor Frog's, **19**

Isla de los
Pájaros
Playa
Brujas
TO MAZAGUA
(1km)
Estero del
Sábalo

Marina
Mazatlán

Playa
Sábalo
Tiburón

14
15 **16**

EL CID
RESORT

Calz. Camarón Sábalo

ZONA
DORADA

Las Garzas
Laguna
Loaiza

Lomas de Mazatlán

de la Marina

Bugambilia

Playa las
Gaviotas
18
US & Canada

Calz. Rafael Buelna

Hospital
Sharp

Laguna del
Camarón

Insurgentes

Av. de Mar

Carretera Internacional

19

Acuario Mazatlán
Deportes
Universidad

Isla de los
Venados

Isla de los
Lobos

Bahía de Puerto
Viejo

Ferrusquilla
Beltrán
San Lorenzo
Pánuco
Fuerte
Baluarte
Piaxtla
Benemérito de las Américas
Gaviotas

Estero
del
Infiernillo

OLD
MAZATLÁN
(See Inset)

Playa
Norte

Paseo Claussen

0   1000 yards
0   1000 meters

Bahía de
Olas Altas

Zaragoza
5 de Mayo
16 de Sept.
Juárez
Serdán
G. Nájera
Carrasco
Pesqueira

Villa/tribuite
Germán Evers
A. Flores
Constitución

Miguel Alemán
Potrero del Llano
Calz. Gabriel Leyva Solano

Serdán
Amado
Carnaval
Emilio Barragán

Playas
del Sur

TO EL FARO (400m)

Canal de Navegación

Isla de
Ocon

MUSEO ARQUEOLÓGICO. This small but interesting museum displays clay figurines, rocks, and dioramas. *(Osuna 72, between the centro and Olas Altas. Open M-F 10am-6pm, Su 10am-3pm. Free.)*

🍴 FOOD

Restaurant prices soar closer to the tourist center of the Zona Dorada. The *centro*, however, is the place for quality meals on a budget. The **public market,** between Juárez and Serdán, three blocks north of the *zócalo*, serves the best and cheapest food. For something more formal, try one of the *centro*'s many restaurants or, for the view, a spot along the *malecón* in Olas Altas. Don't leave without trying **Pacífico** beer, the pride of Mazatlán.

Copa de Leche Café, 1220 A Sur (☎669 982 57 53), on the *malecón*. Wake up to eggs and pancakes (28 pesos) with *café con leche* (13 pesos) well into the afternoon. Open daily 7:30am-11pm.

Mesón Marisquero (☎669 982 82 26), on Puerto Viejo at the *malecón*. Marisquero whips up small doses of *ceviche* (10-13 pesos) and *tostadas* (28 pesos). Open Su-Th 11am-11pm, F-Sa 11am-1am.

El Tunnel, in a tunnel that starts at Carnaval 1207, across from the theater. Great ambience upstaged only by the amazing food. Dedicated to (pre)serving classic Sinaloense cuisine, this place has dished out delicious *gorditas* (9 pesos) since 1945. *Agua de horchata* 9 pesos. Open daily noon-midnight.

Royal Dutch Cafeteria (☎669 981 43 96; roydutch@mzt.megared.net.mx), at Constitución and Juárez. Only the freshest baked goods and the best coffee in town, with free refills. The owners also run a **B&B** with A/C, cable TV, movies, and extremely comfortable rooms. Strudel 22 pesos. Sandwich 25 pesos. Rooms 450 pesos. Open M-F 9am-9pm, Sa noon-3pm. Cafeteria closed June-Sept.

Panamá Cafe and Restaurant, at Juárez and Canizales, also at Serdán and Morelos. Gusty A/C will whirlwind your appetite for amazing pastries or authentic *sinaloense antojitos* (33 pesos). Salads 25-35 pesos. Breakfast 25 pesos. Open daily 7am-10pm.

🏠 ACCOMMODATIONS

While it's most fun to stay in the mid-range waterfront hotels of Olas Altas, more budget hotels line Juárez and Serdán in Old Mazatlán. Rates may rise during high season (July-Aug. and Dec.-Apr.).

🏠 **Hotel Belmar,** Olas Altas 166 (☎669 985 11 12), at Osuna. Spacious rooms with baths come with a choice of either a poignant sea view or the more pragmatic TV and A/C combo. Either way, enjoy a dip in the pool or curl up with a book from the library. Singles with A/C and TV from 250 pesos, with ocean view from 320 pesos.

🏠 **Hotel del Río,** Juárez 2410 Nte. (☎669 982 44 30). Clean white halls and rooms hung with antique cowboy propaganda are a welcome relief from Mazatlán's relentless nautical decor. Pleasant management, plus a central location. Reserve 2 or 3 days in advance. Singles 100 pesos; doubles 120 pesos.

Hotel Lerma, Bolívar 622 (☎669 981 24 36), at Serdán. Spacious rooms and ceiling fans make the heat bearable. Free parking. Singles from 70 pesos, with bath from 90 pesos; doubles from 100 pesos.

Hotel Milán, Canizales 717 (☎669 985 34 99), across from the Telmex building in the business district. A/C and TV make up for the brown color scheme. Singles from 140 pesos; doubles from 163 pesos.

Hotel la Siesta, Olas Altas Sur 11 (☎669 981 26 40 or 800 711 52 29), at Escobedo. Tiered wooden walkways connect rooms with A/C, TV, phone, and hot water, set around a verdant courtyard. Singles high season 351 pesos, with ocean view 468 pesos; low season 293 pesos/304 pesos.

🌙 NIGHTLIFE

Masses of American students hit Mazatlán each year to drink and break curfew. More than a dozen discos and bars clamor for *gringo* dollars. Cover prices are steep and, because nightclubs cut deals with package-tour companies, the unpackaged tourist is often charged more. Mellower entertainment exists around the *centro*.

THE CENTRO AND OLAS ATLAS

Altrazor Ars Cafe, Constitución 517, across from Plazuela Machado. Local Gen-Xers come for the 15 peso beer and live music at 8:30pm nightly. Snacks 20 pesos. Open M-Sa 9am-2am, Su 4pm-1am.

Club Muralla, at the corner of Venus and Osuna, just uphill from the Museo Arqueológico. Look for chairs and tables outside the anonymous doorway to enjoy low-stakes gambling and sports TV. Locals sip 10 peso beers, eat *ceviche,* and sometimes dance to live bands on weekends. Open daily noon-2am.

Café Pacífico, Constitución 501 (☎669 981 39 72), across from Plazuela Machado. A "classic pub" with an assortment of animal skins, rifles, and stained-glass windows. The cool interior and 10 peso beers attract a fun crowd of locals seeking respite from the Mazatlán sun. Marlin burritos 50 pesos. Open daily 10am-2am.

ZONA DORADA

Gringo Lingo, Playa Gaviotas 313 (☎669 913 77 37; www.gringolingo.com.mx), across from the Hotel Sábalo. Live music attracts a young crowd. Burgers 40-58 pesos. Th live rock music. Open daily noon-1am.

Mangos, Playa Gaviotas 403 (☎669 916 00 44), set off from the street toward the beach. Filled with a young and trendy crowd. *Margaritas de mango* are the house specialty (single 32 pesos, double 54 pesos). Dress code prohibits tennis shoes, flip flops, and shorts; it is enforced at the management's discretion. No cover. Open Su-Th noon-12:30am, F-Sa noon-4am.

Joe's Oyster Bar, Playa Gaviotas 100 (☎669 983 53 53), next to Los Sábalos Hotel. Beachfront location make this a good place to put away a few beers before hitting the club scene. 2 beers for 30 pesos. Cover 30 pesos; includes one beer. Open daily 11am-3am.

Fiesta Land (☎669 984 16 66), on Sábalo towards the southern end of the Zona Dorada. A grouping of several nightspots. **Valentino's** is a disco with Euro-trash pretensions. **Bora-Bora** is a beach club by day and disco by night. **Cantabar** is part of Valentino's and features karaoke. **Bali Hai** is a sports bar and **Maui** is a snack bar. All operate as separate entities—you usually have to pay to get into each one separately. Cocktails 30-35 pesos. Cover up to 150 pesos. Bora-Bora open daily 9pm-4am. Valentino's open daily 9pm-3am.

El Caracol (☎669 913 33 33, ext. 3245), in the El Cid Hotel on Sábalo. A premier 4-level dance club, with crazy lights rising from the floor. Beer and mixed drinks 30-40 pesos. No cover. Open daily 9pm-2am.

Señor Frog's (☎669 985 11 10), on Paseo del Mar. The beach resort restaurant whose empire extends from Tijuana to Cancún was born 30 years ago in Mazatlán. Fajitas 65-130 pesos. 110 pesos for a 1 yd. long (868ml) mixed drink. There may be a cover on busy nights. Open daily 11am-2am.

◤ LEAVING MAZATLÁN

From Paseo Claussen, **Av. Benemerito de las Americas** leads back inland to **Mex. 15D.** From there, it's an uneventful 230km to Culiacán.

CULIACÁN

Due to the traffic to seaside destinations, Culiacán (pop. 600,000) has become the second most popular tourist site in Sinaloa. Unfortunately, this isn't the only traffic that passes through Culiacán; the city, nicknamed "little Medellín," is believed to be one of the three centers of Mexico's drug trade. Extra effort has kept the *centro* beautiful, and what little artistic wealth falls to Sinaloa is gathered here, making a stop worthwhile. The city centers on the south side of Río Tamazula; follow the signs from **Mex. 15** to the *centro*. The city's shrine to **Jesús Malverde,** on Independencia, a 19th-century bandit whose Robin Hood-esque practices led to his execution in 1909, is its most exciting attraction. (From the *centro*, head west toward Bravo until you reach Madero as it runs along the train tracks; follow this away from the *centro* until it turns into Independencia.) Just off the Plaza Obregón, **Museo de Arte Sinaloa,** at Rafael Buelna and Paliza, houses the work of artists such as Diego Rivera, López Saenz, and Frida Kahlo in its air-conditioned chambers. (☎667 715 55 41. Open Su 11am-5pm, Tu-Sa 10am-3pm and 5-7pm. 5 pesos, students and children 3 pesos. Su free.) The **Tourist Office** is located at Insurgentes and Barraza. (Open M-F 8am-3pm and 5-7pm.)

For cheap food, try **Tacos Ranas,** at the corner of Morelos and Flores, where 3 *tacos al pastor* cost 15 pesos. (Open M-Sa 9am-9pm.) A great view of the Plaza Obregón and good food come together at **Los Antiguos Portales de Culiacán,** Paliza Nte. 574. (☎667 752 19 78. Fajitas 69 pesos. Open daily noon-10pm.) A two-city chain, **Panamá Café,** Francisco Villa Ote. 51, at Parque de Revolución, serves pastries, coffee, and good *comida típica* in a family-style restaurant. (☎667 716 83 50. Enchiladas 33 pesos. Salads 25-35 pesos. Open daily 7am-10pm.) While the area between Bravo and Obregón is safe, other parts of Culiacán can be dangerous, especially at night. Cheap, but not exactly central, **Hotel Louisiana,** Villa Ote. 478, is a high-security hotel with few perks. (☎667 713 91 52. Singles 100 pesos; doubles 120 pesos.) **Hotel Santa Fe,** Hidalgo Pte. 243, greets visitors with an icy A/C blast. Rooms have cable TV, phone, and well-maintained baths. (☎667 715 17 00. Singles 240 pesos; doubles 270 pesos; triples 300 pesos.)

LOS MOCHIS

Back on Mex. 15, Los Mochis was founded and developed by US expats, first as a utopian experiment and later as part of a sugar-growing enter-

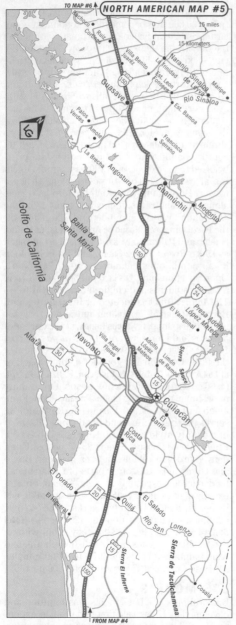

NORTH AMERICAN

NORTH AMERICAN MAP #5

TO MAP #6

FROM MAP #4

prise. The city's US colonial roots are visible in the monotonous grid of wide streets and modern buildings. Though its sugar days are over, Los Mochis continues to be an important link between the coast and the interior, funneling goods and backpackers into the mountains. A large collection of trees and plants grows in the 16-hectare **Parque Sinaloa,** which used to be the private gardens of Benjamin Johnston, owner of the American-run sugar operation in Los Mochis in the 1920s. (Walk to the end of Castro and turn left; the entrance is about half a block down Rosales.) The **tourist office,** on Ordóñez and Allende, is next to the Palacio de Gobierno in the Unidad Administrativa; use the entrance off Ordóñez and turn right. (☎668 815 10 90. Open M-F 9am-4pm.)

The place for excellent grub is **Tacos la Cabaña de Doña Chayo,** Obregón 99, at the corner of Allende, where the absurdly large size of the tacos justifies the price. (☎668 818 54 98. Tacos 13 pesos. Quesadillas 13 pesos. Open daily 8am-1am.) Sanitized, air-conditioned escape from reality is best found at **Chic's,** outside the mall at Obregón and Rosales. (Salads 32-35 pesos. Open daily 7am-10:30pm.) Most decent hotel rooms in Los Mochis cost around 200 pesos. **Hotel Lorena**, Obregón 186, comes furnished with A/C, TVs, purified water, clean baths, and a view. (☎668 812 68 47; fax 668 812 02 39. Singles 225 pesos; doubles 305 pesos; triples 345 pesos.)

NAVOJOA. Straddling the sometimes awkward line separating the newer, developed small cities from older rural townships, Navojoa is one of several waypoints suggestive of as-of-yet-unrealized potential. While passing through, there are a couple of worthwhile eateries. The cool and spacious **Casa Blanca Restaurant Bar,** Pesqueira 605 Nte., offers fine dining at a reasonable price. (☎642 421 35 48. Steak 100-140 pesos. Salmon 100 pesos. Open daily 1-10:30pm.) If you need to stay the night, or if you're using Navojoa as a base from which to explore nearby Alamos, several small, privately run hotels and motels stand ready to offer their services. **Hotel California,** Pesqueira 413, spoils guests with free parking, cable TV, A/C, laundry facilities, and a complimentary continental breakfast. (☎642 421 28 78. Check-out 1:30pm. Singles 220 pesos; doubles 260 pesos.)

◄ DETOUR: ALAMOS

Alamos lies 50km east of Navojoa on Son. 13. As you come into town, Son. 13 becomes Madero.

You'll reach a fork in the road at the bronze statue of Benito Juárez; the left branch leads to Plaza Alameda, the commercial center, and the right branch to Plaza de Armas in the historic district.

Founded in 1531, Alamos was relatively ignored until silver was discovered there in 1683. For nearly 100 years, Alamos produced more silver than any area in the world, but when the veins ran dry, the boomtown shrank to ghost-town proportions. Over the last 50 years, wealthy Americans and Canadians have taken an interest in the town, particularly in the mansions left behind by silver tycoons. Thanks to their funds, Alamos has returned to its glory days—the refurbished haciendas and cobblestone streets give the city a feel unlike any other in northwest Mexico. One of the grandest homes in town was constructed in 1720 and revamped in the 19th century, when it became the home of José María Almada, owner of one of the world's richest silver mines. **Hotel los Portales** now occupies most of the building, including Don Almada's foyer and courtyard. Other impressive homes can be found around the cathedral, including **Casa de los Tesoros, Hotel la Mansión, Casa Encantada,** and **Las Delicias.** You can tour the swanky **Hacienda de los Santos,** a series of colonial homes turned into a five-star hotel. (Tours depart daily 1pm from the main entrance at the corner of Molina and Gutiérrez. 10 pesos.)

The town's cathedral, **La Parroquia de la Purísima Concepción,** occupies a commanding position on Plaza de Armas. The town jail and the Mirador offer excellent views. To get to the jail, walk along Madero west of the center of town and follow the signs. **Museo Costumbrista,** the yellow-and-white building across from Las Palmeras in the Plaza de Armas, has exhibits on Alamos's history. (☎647 428 00 53. Open Su and W-Sa 9am-6pm. 10 pesos, students and children 5 pesos.) The Alamos **Tourist Office,** Juárez 6, under Hotel los Portales on the west side of the Plaza de Armas, has maps and info. (☎647 428 04 50. Open M-F 10am-3pm.)

For a view of the Plaza de Armas and distant foothills, eat at **Restaurant Las Palmeras,** Cárdenas 9, northeast of the Plaza de Armas. (☎647 428 00 65. Breakfast 25-40 pesos *Antojitos* 20-35 pesos. Open daily 7am-10pm.) Unless you strike silver on your way into town, you'll probably have to pass on the *hacienda* hotels.

CIUDAD OBREGÓN. Less than a century old, Obregón is the product of the 1910 construction of Alvaro Obregón Dam. The city's urban planning is

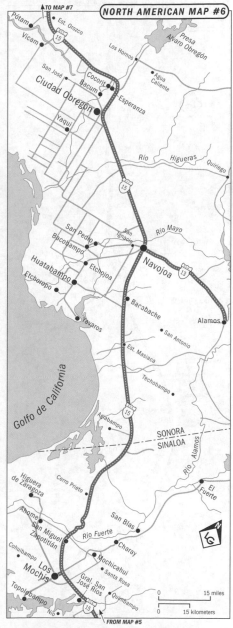

NORTH AMERICAN MAP #6

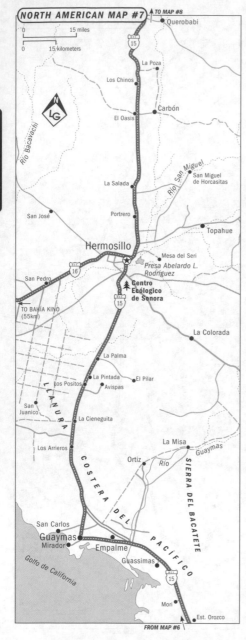

apparent in its wide, well-maintained streets and spacious business lots. **Mex. 15** becomes **Av. Miguel Alemán** in the city, and parking along the street is usually safe and convenient. **El Cortijo,** Miguel Alemán 201, between Nainari and Allende, serves sizzling steaks (80-120 pesos) among rod-iron chandeliers. (☎ 644 415 23 43. Seafood 90-150 pesos. Open Su 11am-7pm, M-Sa noon-midnight.) There are a host of chain motels in the city, but more economical options exist as well. Free parking makes **Motel Cuenca de Sol,** Miguel Alemán 141, worth the extra pesos. It has clean rooms with phones, A/C, and TVs. (☎ 644 414 11 44. Singles 357 pesos; doubles 410 pesos.)

GUAYMAS

Nobody is quite sure what "Guaymas" means—the two most popular suggestions are "to shoot arrows at the head" and "tree toad." Founded in the 18th century, the town of San José de Laguna de San José de Guaymas teetered on the verge of destruction by local Seri Indians, but persevered thanks to the vigorous trade out of its harbor. At once one of Mexico's busiest ports and a luxury tourist destination, modern Guaymas is a lively city full of unexpected opportunities and extreme hospitality a mere 10min. drive away from San Carlos's beachside haven.

VITAL STATS

Population: 120,000

Visitor Info: (☎ 622 224 41 14), at Av. 6 and Calle 19. There is also an air-conditioned booth (☎ 622 222 44 00) at Av. Serdán between Calle 24 and Calle 25. Open daily 9am-6pm.

Internet Access: OmniRed, on Serdán between Calle 15 and Calle 16. 10 pesos per hr. Open daily 9am-11pm.

Post Office: (☎ 622 222 07 57), on Av. 10 between Calle 19 and Calle 20. Open M-F 9am-3pm, Sa 9am-1pm. **Postal Code:** 85400.

GETTING AROUND. Guaymas's *centro* is the area surrounding the chaotic main strip, **Serdán,** beginning at **Calle 10** and ending at **Calle 29.** Running perpendicular to Serdán are numbered *calles*. The waterfront begins at **Calle 20,** two blocks south of Serdán at **Av. 11** (the *malecón*), and Serdán itself continues along the sea after **Calle 24. Parking** in Guaymas is not a problem, as most businesses have parking lots. Women should avoid walking alone more than two blocks south of Serdán or east of Calle 25 after dark.

⬡ **SIGHTS.** Guaymas's **beaches,** popular with both tourists and locals, are located to the north in **San Carlos** (see p. 663) and **Miramar.** Also in Miramar, **Perlas del Mar de Cortéz** cultivates pearls aplenty, and offers free tours of the facilities. (Tours M-F every hr. 9am-3pm, Sa 9am-11pm.)

🍴 **FOOD.** Seafood is the specialty in Guaymas. Pricey local favorites include *cahuama* (manta ray steaks) and *ostiones* (oysters) in a garlic and chile sauce. For those on a tighter budget, **Mercado Municipal,** on Calle 20 one block from Serdán, sells fresh produce, and an abundance of *comida corrida* joints dot Serdán. **Restaurant Bar Los Barcos,** on Malecón between Calle 21 and Calle 22, offers the very finest in seafood. (☎ 622 222 76 50. Mexican surf and turf 165 pesos. *Camarones empanizados* 122 pesos. Open daily 10am-8pm.) Despite its name, **Las 1000 Tortas,** Serdán 188, between Calles 17 and 18, is not just for *torta*-lovers. They also serve delicious *burritos de machaca* (3 for 33 pesos), *bistec ranchero* (40 pesos), and quesadillas. (Open daily 8am-11pm.) **S. E. Pizza Buffet,** on Serdán at Calle 20, serves an Italian buffet (28 pesos) in a dining hall with Disney images and framed posters of American cars on the walls. (Open daily 11am-11pm.)

🏠 **ACCOMMODATIONS.** Heat and humidity conspire to create the perfect micro-climate for the proliferation of roaches, fleas, gnats, and other vermin, making otherwise adequate budget hotels somewhat uncomfortable. It may be worth your while to pay the extra pesos for A/C and frequent fumigation. **Motel Santa Rita,** Serdán 590, at Calle 9, has large, sparkling-clean rooms with A/C, TV, and phone. It's a good pick for a quiet, bug-free night of shut-eye. (☎ 622 224 19 19. Singles 300 pesos; doubles 400 pesos; triples 500 pesos.) **Casa de Huéspedes Marta,** at Av. 9 and Calle 13, offers clean and tidy rooms with bathrooms and fans. While parking prices vary with the season, they are always economical. (☎ 622 222 83 32. Singles 90 pesos; doubles with A/C 100 pesos. TV with cable 50 pesos.) Small rooms equipped with fans and an *agua purificada* dispenser await at **Casa de Huéspedes Lupita,** 125 Calle 15, two blocks south of Serdán. (☎ 622 222 19 45. Singles 80 pesos, with bath 110 pesos, with A/C 160 pesos; doubles with bath, cable TV, and A/C 200 pesos.)

📷 **NIGHTLIFE.** Guaymas has its share of bars, but travelers hunting for more than a bottle of Pacífico find their entertainment on the road to San Carlos. **El Rincón Bohemio,** Carretera Internacional Km 1982, is far more understated than Hotel Flamingos, in which it resides. (☎ 622 221 31 61. Live music Th-Sa 9pm-2am.) For a more up-to-date version of cool, roadtrippers can drive down Carretera to **Equs;** besides being the hottest disco around, Equs is also a sushi bar. (☎ 622 221 30 32. Disco open daily 9pm-2am.) For a quieter evening, **The Friends' Club,** on Av. Rodríguez at Calle Abelardo, offers pool tables. (☎ 622 222 00 53. Pool 20 pesos per hr. Open daily 6pm-2am.)

SAN CARLOS

Once San Carlos (pop. 2500) was just a dusty road in the desert north of Guaymas; now, condos, hotels, and malls sprout like wildflowers to accommodate the growing tourist influx. San Carlos greets visitors with a lush country club, Sonora's only five-star hotel, and the largest, shallowest artificial shipwreck in the world. **Playa San Francisco,** parallel to the freeway from Guaymas, is the most easily accessible beach. The sands are rocky, but the water is pleasant. Drive up to **El Mirador Escénico,** a vista atop a steep road, which affords views of Tetakawi and the secluded coves of **Playa Piedras Pintas.** A dirt road near the gate to Costa Del Mar leads to ⬛**Playa Los Algodones** (Cotton Beach), so named because the soft sand is compared to cotton. Marine flora and fauna make their home in the Sea of Cortés, attracting divers eager to catch a glimpse of the underwater brilliance and fishermen eager to catch dinner. Near the town is **San Pedro Nolasco Island,** a popular dive site. **El Mar Diving Center,** off Beltrones, rents scuba gear and sea kayaks (US$30) and leads guided dives (US$75 per person for 2 people) around the island. (☎ 631 226 04 04. Open Mar.-Oct. daily 7am-6:30pm; Nov.-Feb. M and W-Su 7:30am-5:30pm. AmEx/MC/V.) The US-run **Surface Time,** 1 Edificio Villa Marina near the Plaza de las Glorias, rents charter boats and arranges licenses and equipment for **fishing.** (☎ 622 226 18 88, US 480-897-2300; surfacetime@cox.net. Open daily 7am-7pm.) To go it alone, pick up a fishing license (58 pesos per day) at the **Secretaria de Pesca** on Beltrones just before the turn-off to Plaza Las Glorias. (Open 9am-3pm.) For more info about the town, wander over to **Hacienda Tours,** on Beltrones just before El Mar Diving Center. (☎ 622 226 13 14. Open M-F 9am-5pm, Sa 9am-2pm.)

While most restaurants are expensive, a few places cater to the peso-pincher. Local expats start the day with breakfast (44 pesos) and fabu-

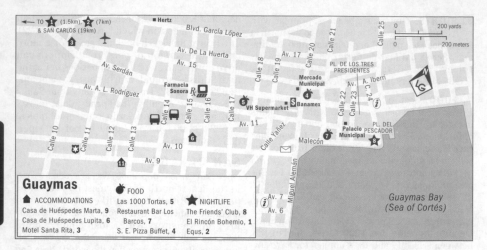

Guaymas

♠ ACCOMMODATIONS		🍎 FOOD		★ NIGHTLIFE	
Casa de Huéspedes Marta, **9**		Las 1000 Tortas, **5**		The Friends' Club, **8**	
Casa de Huéspedes Lupita, **6**		Restaurant Bar Los		El Rincón Bohemio, **1**	
Motel Santa Rita, **3**		Barcos, **7**		Equs, **2**	
		S. E. Pizza Buffet, **4**			

lous malts (25 pesos) at **Jax Snax** (☎622 226 02 70), on Beltrones. **Blackie's,** on Beltrones past the Motel Creston, features steaks and seafood. (Open Su and Tu-Sa noon-11pm. MC/V.) **Mamac-ita's Cafe,** also on Beltrones, serves "healthy food," including fruit and yogurt plates for 35 pesos. (☎622 229 50 21. Salads 25-40 pesos. Juices 10-15 pesos. Open M-Sa 7am-2pm.) San Carlos is full of hotels, none of which suit budget travelers. For lodging, the best bet for free parking is **Motel Cre-ston,** across the street from Jax Snax, which is an easy walk to the beach. Sparkling rooms have two beds, A/C, and bath. (☎622 226 00 20. Doubles 450 pesos; 50 pesos per additional person.) For those wise enough to pack a tent, **El Mirador RV Park,** on the road to El Mirador Escénico, provides full hookups with a glistening pool, free modem access, table games, showers, and two new tennis courts. (US$15 per day, US$120 per week.)

CENTRO ECOLÓGICO DE SONORA

Take Rosales south out of the city for 5km and follow the signs.

More than your token neighborhood zoo, the Cen-tro is host to an impressive array of animal life, a mini-aquarium (complete with outdoor sea lions), hundreds of plant species, and groundbreaking biological research. A clearly marked walkway dotted with water fountains, shady benches, restrooms, and a wading pool guides visitors through the exhibits and affords a spectacular view of Hermosillo and its surrounding moun-tains. The most spectacular feature of Centro

Ecológico is its incredible collection of cacti— over 340 species are labeled and displayed throughout the animal exhibits and just outside the main pavilion. Keep your eyes peeled for the rare *cina* and *biznaga*, from which candy is made, and the *maguey bacanora*, the cactus that is the source of those tequilas you've been down-ing. (☎622 250 12 25. Open summer Su and Tu-Sa 8am-6pm; winter Su and Tu-Sa 8am-5pm. 20 pesos, ages 4-12 and students 10 pesos.)

HERMOSILLO

Once an indigenous settlement named Pitic (meaning "where two rivers meet"), modern Her-mosillo is a sprawling center of commerce and education. The capital of Sonora attracts visitors with imposing government palaces, beautiful murals, huge manicured parks, a glorious cathe-dral, and an ecological research center and zoo. Not all of Hermosillo is so alluring, however. The crowded, dusty roads of the *centro* scream with the activity of urban life, and, by sundown, little more than garbage lines the streets. Although parts of the city can be unsavory, those who spend a day here are in for a pleasant surprise.

GETTING AROUND. Mex. 15 becomes **Blvd. Vildosola** as it enters the city. Most of the activity in Hermosillo occurs inside the *centro* to the west, the area bordered by **Rosales** on the west, **Juárez** on the east, **Serdán** on the south, and **Encinas** on the north. Hermosillo has broad roadways and ample **parking** at most establishments.

VITAL STATS

Population: 1 million

Visitor Info: (☎800 716 25 55 or US 800-476-6672), on the 3rd fl. of Centro de Gobierno at Cultura and Comonfort. Go south on Rosales over the highway, turn right, and drive 1 block west to the big pink building on the right. Open M-F 8am-3pm.

US Consulate: Calle Monterrey 141 (☎662 289 35 00). Open M-F 8am-4:30pm.

Internet Access: C@fe Internet, Morelia 109C (☎662 213 13 68), between Garmendia and Guerrero. An excellent connection for 10 pesos per hr. Open M-Sa 9am-9pm. **Suministros Computacionales VETA,** Monterrey 86 (☎662 212 79 87 or 622 213 59 87), between Pino Suárez and Rosales. 15 pesos per hr. Open M-Sa 9am-6pm.

Post Office: (☎662 212 00 11), on Elías Calles at Rosales. Open M-F 9am-3pm, Sa 9am-1pm. **Postal Code:** 83000.

◯ **SIGHTS.** Hermosillo's two architectural wonders grace opposite sides of the tree-lined Plaza Zaragoza. On the far side of the plaza lie the cross-capped yellow spires of the **Catedral de la Asunción,** while the grey-and-white **Palacio de Gobierno** looms nearer to the center of town. A chapel has stood on the site of the Catedral since 1777, but the current cathedral was only completed in 1908. The main attraction of the Palacio is a series of murals commissioned in the 1980s depicting key periods in Sonora's history. On Rosales just before Encinas, a long staircase to the right leads to the **Museo Regional de Historia.** The museum has two main rooms, containing an exhibit on Sonora's pre-history (including two perfectly preserved mummies recovered in Yécora) and information about the town's intense growth during the 19th century, a period of social, political, and economic change. (Open M-Sa 9am-1pm. Free.)

◯ **FOOD.** Like most major cities, Hermosillo offers a wide range of dining options, the best of which feature local specialties like *carne asada* and that most Sonoran of dishes, *cabrito* (baby goat). For cheap refueling, head for taco and torta places around Serdán and Guerrero. If you feel brave, the food counters lining **Mercado Municipal** on Elías Calles, between Matamoros and Guerrero, cook up tasty and cheap *antojitos.* Most are sufficiently sanitary, but avoid uncooked vegetables. **Xochimilco,** Obregón 51, proclaims "If you come to Hermosillo and don't eat at Xochimilco

Hermosillo

🏠 ACCOMMODATIONS
Hotel Washington, D.C., 5
Hotel San Alberto, 7
Hotel Suites Kino, 9

🍴 FOOD
Fonda Chapala, 3
Los Magos, 1
Restaurant Jung, 2
Xochimilco, 10

★ NIGHTLIFE
El Grito, 8
La Biblioteca, 4
Napy's, 6

then you might as well never have come at all." Specializing in Sonoran *carne asada*, Xochimilco has set the standard since 1949. (Walk down Rosales and, after crossing the highway, turn right. Continue past the green school building and turn left; the restaurant is 400m ahead on the right. ☎662 250 40 89; restaurantxochimilco.tripod.com Open daily noon-9pm. MC/V.)

Los Magos, Madrid 32, claims to be *la casa del cabrito*, and despite its hokey, saloon-themed decor, the locals seem to agree. Kid parts go for 42-136 pesos. (☎662 213 91 99. Open M-Sa noon-9pm.) Mexican oldies blare while middle-aged men drown their sorrows in 40 oz. bottles of Tecate at **Fonda Chapala,** on Guerrero between Sonora and Oaxaca. Chicken, fish, or meat comes fried to crispy perfection and is served with french fries, *frijoles*, tortillas, salad, and a drink. (☎662 212 39 92. Open Su 8am-2pm, M-Sa 8am-10pm.) Attached to a health-food store, **Restaurant Jung,** Niños Héroes 75, at Encinas, serves as the perfect retreat for vegetarians. Particularly noteworthy is the 75 peso all-you-can-eat breakfast buffet, featuring everything from *burritos de hongos* to hotcakes. (☎662 213 28 81. Open Su 9am-5pm, M-Sa 7:30am-8pm.)

⨶ ACCOMMODATIONS. In Hermosillo, low prices tend to come at the expense of cleanliness, with only a few exceptions. ◪**Hotel Washington, D.C.,** Dr. Noriega 68 Pte., between Matamoros and Guerrero, is almost too good to be true, with comfy beds, sparkling rooms, warm showers, A/C, and English-language advice. (☎662 213 11 83. Rooms with queen-size bed 160 pesos; rooms with 2 single beds 175 pesos; 20 pesos per additional person.) Hang out with business travelers around the pool table and restaurant/bar at **Hotel Suites Kino,** Suárez 151 Sur. All rooms have cable TVs, A/C, phones, and bathrooms. (☎800 711 54 60 or 662 213 31 83; www.hotelsuiteskino.com. Free parking and pool. Reservations recommended. Singles from 300 pesos; doubles from 395 pesos.) **Hotel San Alberto,** at Rosales and Serdán, is an oasis with A/C, rustic furniture, magazines, TV, and phone. (☎662 213 18 40. Free parking and pool. Singles 324 pesos; doubles 344 pesos.)

⬛ NIGHTLIFE. As a university town, Hermosillo has a vibrant nightlife. Shoot pool, watch sports, or surf the Internet at **La Biblioteca,** on Rosales at Dr. Noriega. (☎662 212 47 50. Beer 18 pesos. Tequila 25 pesos. Internet from 15 pesos per hr. Pool from 25 pesos. Open M-Sa 10am-2am.) For local music, try

El Grito, Suárez 72, which offers all the *Norteño* you can handle. (☎662 217 53 37. Open daily 10am-2pm.) **Napy's,** Matamoros 109, between Dr. Noriega and Morelia, is a club scene. After 9pm, food service stops, couples hit the dance floors, and friends cheer them on with 50 peso pitchers of Tecate. (☎662 213 28 70. F-Sa live salsa. Open daily 10am-2am.)

◪ DETOUR: BAHÍA KINO
Bahía Kino is 107km west of Hermosillo, at the end of the two dusty lanes of Mex. 16.

This 20km stretch of glistening sand, brilliant blue water, and radiant sun, is home to a pair of beach towns on the beautiful Sea of Cortés. **Kino Viejo,** a quiet fishing village, lies down the road from **Kino Nuevo,** a 4km strip of posh homes. Diving, fishing, and sailing entertain adventurous travelers, while soft, sandy beaches and gentle waves beckon those looking to relax. In general, beaches are better in Kino Nuevo. To rent **diving** equipment or hire a guide, call Carlos Montes (☎662 260 89 01 or 662 269 28 96) or find him at Islandía Marina on weekends. **Fishing** trips can be arranged with Ernesto Hínojosa (☎662 242 03 20). **Museo de los Seris,** on Mar de Cortés at Progreso in Kino Nuevo, offers an air-conditioned refuge and info about an indigenous fishing tribe. (Open Su and W-Sa 9am-4pm. 3 pesos, children 2 pesos.) For more about Kino's offerings, stop by the **tourist office** in Kino Nuevo, next to the police station. (☎662 242 04 47. Open Su and Th-Sa 9am-5pm.)

Jorge's Restaurant, at Mar de Cortés and Alicante, toward the end of Kino Nuevo, offers all the *mariscos* your heart might desire. (☎662 242 00 49. Open daily 9am-10pm.) Safe and comfortable lodgings are plentiful on the beachfront—find a free *palapa* and set up camp. For those who prefer mattresses to sand, Kino's version of "budget" awaits at **Hotel Posada del Mar,** on Mar de Cortés at the beginning of Kino Nuevo. (☎662 242 01 55. Singles 360 pesos; 70 pesos per additional person.)

NOGALES

There's a restless energy to Nogales. Tension builds near the border, where gaudy souvenir shops vie for the daytripper's dollar. The city welcomes many by morning, but says goodbye to the vast majority well before nightfall. It's hard to imagine why anyone would stay longer; Nogales lacks the pleasant parks and *zócalos* that characterize many Mexican cities, and competition for

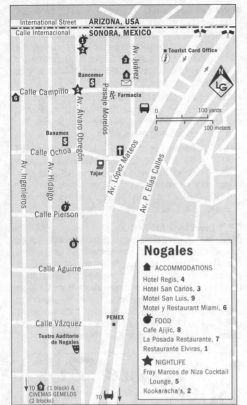

International Street **ARIZONA, USA**
Calle Internacional **SONORA, MEXICO**

Av. Juárez
■ Tourist Card Office
(i)

Bancomer
[S]

Calle Campillo [S]
Rx Farmacia

Av. Álvaro Obregón
Pasaje Morelos

0 — 100 yards
0 — 100 meters

Banamex
[S]
Calle Ochoa

Av. Ingenieros
Av. Hidalgo
Yajar

Av. López Mateos
Av. P. Elías Calles

Calle Pierson

Nogales

Calle Aguirre
♠ ACCOMMODATIONS
Hotel Regis, 4
Hotel San Carlos, 3
Motel San Luis, 9
Motel y Restaurant Miami, 6

PEMEX
■
Calle Vázquez
🍴 FOOD
Cafe Ajijic, 8
Teatro Auditorio
de Nogales
La Posada Restaurante, 7
Restaurante Elviras, 1

★ NIGHTLIFE
Fray Marcos de Niza Cocktail
Lounge, 5
Kookaracha's, 2

▼TO 9 (1 block) &
CINEMAS GEMELOS
(2 blocks)   TO ⟶ ▼

border business and the swelling population have meant heightened crime levels. But if you do get stuck here, you'll be able to soak up the ambience of a classic Mexican border town, where everyone is trying to get somewhere else.

(VITAL STATS)

Population: 250,000

Visitor Info: (☎ 631 312 06 66), next to the immigration center. Open daily 9am-5pm.

US Consulate: (☎ 631 313 4820), Calle San Jose.

Internet Access: Yajar, upstairs at the corner of Morelos and Ochoa. 20 pesos per hr. **Amigos en Red,** López Mateos 258 (☎ 631 312 39 78). 30 pesos per hr. Open M-F 9am-9pm, Sa-Su 11am-8pm.

Post Office: Juárez 52 (☎ 631 312 12 47). Open M-F 8am-5:30pm. **Postal Code:** 84001.

GETTING AROUND

Nogales stretches up into chaotic hillside *barrios*, but the grid of the small **primer cuadro** area, where tourists spend most of their time, is fairly easy to navigate. **Calle Internacional** is the first street running east-west, parallel to the iron fence which marks the border. **López Mateos** heads southwest across the grid, merging with Juárez, Morelos, and, eventually, Obregón. Shadowing López Mateos to the east is **Elías Calles,** the northeast-bound road. The tourist office cautions that the *barrios* on both sides of the *primer cuadro* are unsafe and should be given a wide berth. **Parking** can be found on and around Mateos.

SHOPPING

Despite the half-hearted attempts of the tourist bureau to pass off the statue of Juárez, the industrial park, and even the border crossing as attractions, there isn't much in Nogales. Most Arizonans who come over do so in search of bargain pharmaceuticals and Mexican trinkets, either around Obregón, Campillo, and Morelos, or in a more genteel, air-conditioned setting like the El Greco building at the corner of Obregón and Pierson. Merchandise is priced in anticipation of haggling, so confidence and knowledge of the goods can get you great deals. Shops farther from the border on Obregón are less aimed at the tourist crowd.

ENTERTAINMENT

Cinemas Gemelos, Obregón 368 (☎ 631 312 50 02), between González and Torres (not to be confused with the chain store of the same name further up Obregón), shows recent American films dubbed or subtitled in Spanish (40 pesos). For those seeking a bit of culture, the spacious modern **Teatro Auditorio de Nogales,** Obregón 286 (☎ 631 312 41 80), between Vázquez and González, seats just under 1000 and stages theatre, music, dance, and other events. Call or visit for showtimes and prices; the calendar is posted on the door.

If Tequila calls, answer from Nogales. Right after lunch, the bars on **Obregón** open their doors, and by 10pm on Friday or Saturday, walking through the crowds of bar-goers is nearly impossible. Dance the night away and down tequila shots (US$2) at **Kookaracha's,** Obregón 1, or chill with a *cerveza* (US$2) on the balcony. (☎ 631 312 47 73. Open bar W US$15. Open W and F-Sa 9pm-3am.) **Fray Marcos**

de Niza Cocktail Lounge, at Obregón and Campillo, is a relaxed bar with comfy leather couches and baseball on a big-screen TV. (☎631 312 11 12. Beer US$2. Open daily 11am-1am.)

🍴 FOOD

Nogales is home to high-priced restaurants catering to daytrippers from the US. If tourist pricing is driving you crazy, do as the locals do and head for the **plaza** on López Mateos at Ochoa, where vendors hawk fruits and *tortas* for rock-bottom prices. For an economical meal, look no further than the makeshift counters off Obregón, where locals sell traditional *antojitos* (5-20 pesos).

Restaurante Elviras, Obregón 1 (☎631 312 47 43). Elviras is curiously alluring; it offers a peaceful courtyard just yards from an international border and sits next to a club that shatters its tranquility from 8pm onwards. There's lots of space inside; the decor stays just on the right side of kitsch. Traditional Mexican dishes, steak, and seafood specialties, including award-winning *pescado elvira*. Entrees US$9-15. Open daily 9am-11pm. MC/V.

La Posada Restaurante, Pierson 116 (☎631 312 04 39), west of Obregón. Bustling, family-run place, with the father figure sternly presiding and greeting the locals who come for a hearty breakfast. Omelettes and egg dishes 25-40 pesos. Open daily 7:30am-10pm.

Cafe Ajijíc, Obregón 182 (☎631 312 50 74). The terrace features tiled tables, a picturesque fountain, and live musicians. Less memorable for the food than for the huge selection of coffees (15-22 pesos). Entrees 50-60 pesos. Open daily 8am-midnight. MC/V.

🏠 ACCOMMODATIONS

Nogales's position on the border guarantees it more visitors than might otherwise be expected, and at times its accommodations can be stretched thin. High demand has heightened the quality of what's available; unfortunately, it has also raised prices. The most obvious concentration of "budget" hotels is near the border crossing on **Juárez;** options further afield may have more vacancies.

Motel y Restaurant Miami (☎631 312 54 50 or 631 312 54 70), on Ingenieros at Campillo. Friendly place offers large rooms with clean bath, TV, telephone, and overly enthusiastic A/C. Restaurant attached. The rooms on the upper floors have views out over the town to the border fence and beyond. Singles 300 pesos; doubles 320 pesos. 50 pesos per additional person.

Motel San Luis (☎631 312 4170 or 631 312 40 35; fax 631 312 40 60), at the corner of González and Ingenieros. Clearly indicated by signs from Elías Calles and Obregón. Arranged around a central courtyard, this motel offers rooms similar to the lodgings crowded along Juárez in a less-touristed part of town. Singles 320 pesos; doubles 355 pesos. MC/V.

Hotel Regis (☎631 312 51 81, 631 312 55 80, or 631 312 55 09), between Internacional and Campillo. A/C, phone, and TV. Reservations required. Singles 375 pesos; doubles 400 pesos. MC/V.

Hotel San Carlos, Juárez 22 (☎631 312 13 46 or 631 312 14 09; fax 312 15 57), between Internacional and Campillo. Spacious rooms have A/C, cable TV, high-pressure showers, and phones. Mingle with locals watching TV in the lobby. Reservations recommended. Singles 250 pesos; doubles 290 pesos. MC/V.

✖ LEAVING MEXICO

The easiest border crossing is on **Avenida Calles.** American customs and immigration officials keep a close eye on this border; hour-long delays are not uncommon, and wave-throughs unheard of. Inspectors question Americans about contraband and may also inspect for illegal immigrants. Non-US citizens should be aware of their visa status to ensure that there will be no problem with admittance; see p. 11 for more info on obtaining a US visa. The border crossing is open daily 6am-10pm.

Welcome To ARIZONA

NOGALES, AZ

Nogales is as American as apple pie—if instead of apple, you used jalapeño peppers and a tortilla instead of instead of pie crust. Although the Mexican side of the city boasts over 250,000 people, the American district weighs in at only 20,000. Signs are bilingual or Spanish-only, half the TV stations are Mexican, and even the highway mileage signs are done Mexican-style; all distances are given in kilometers. Nogales lies at the southern terminus of **I-19,** which continues into Mexico as **Mex. 15,** and splits with its commercial doppelganger, "Business I-19," a.k.a. **Grand Ave.,** for the length of the town. The two merge north of town, and are linked by shopping-mall-lined **Mariposa Rd. Rte. 82** connects Nogales to smaller communities in Arizona's southeastern pocket, branching off of Grand Ave. near northern downtown and leading to **Tombstone** (see p. 786) and **Bisbee** (see p. 787).

If you're craving release from the tyranny of the burrito, check out **Sweets 'n' Subs,** 1855 N. Grand Ave., a combination bakery and sub shop. The enormous ham-and-cheese sub is only $3. (☎520-281-4299. Open M-F 6am-6pm, Sa 6am-5pm.) Budget accommodations in Nogales are a bit dodgy. The chain motels along Mariposa and Grand Ave. are inexpensive, though fairly colorless. An independent option, **Time Motel,** on Grand Ave., provides TV, A/C, phone, and a pool at budget prices. (☎520-287-0702. In summer singles $32; doubles $36. In winter singles $36; doubles $40.)

 LEAVING NOGALES
Follow **Grand Ave.** north out of town to **I-19.**

 TUMACACORI NATIONAL HISTORIC PARK
Take Exit 29 off of I-19.

The park preserves the ruins of a Franciscan mission dating back to 1795. Frequently ravaged by the Apache, the church was rebuilt in 1822, but the cemetery is the original. (☎520-398-2341. Open daily 8am-5pm. $3.)

TUBAC. The first European settlement in Arizona, Tubac was settled in 1752 by Spanish soldiers and bears remains from earlier Native American habitation. Today, a short hop off **I-19** at exit 34, the town proffers dozens of shops selling Latin American goods. The original **Presidio** built by those Spanish soldiers of yore has been preserved as a state historical park. (☎520-398-2252. Open daily 8am-5pm. $3, ages 7-13 $1.)

 MISSION SAN XAVIER DEL BAC
Take the San Xavier exit (Exit 92) off I-19.

Built by the Franciscan brothers in the late 1700s, this is the northernmost Spanish Baroque church in the Americas, and the only such church in the US. Located on the Tohono O'odham Indian Reservation, there were few opportunities and fewer funds to restore it until the late 20th century. In the early 90s, a local group gathered money in order to preserve and protect this site; since then, the mortar has been restored, frescoes have been retouched, and the statuary has been cleaned of centuries of soot and desert sand. The dazzling result is worthy of its nickname, "white dove of the desert." (☎520-294-2624. Open daily 8am-6pm; masses held daily. Donations accepted.)

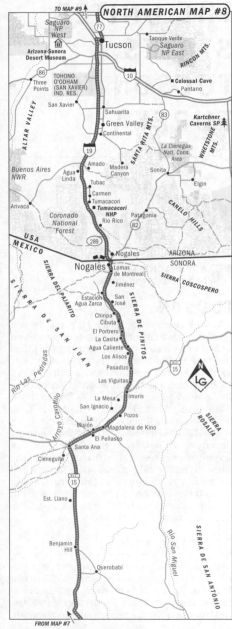

NORTH AMERICAN MAP #8

THE UNITED STATES: TUCSON TO EUREKA

Welcome To **ARIZONA**

┌─ **VITAL STATS** ─┐

Population: 490,000

Visitor Info: Tucson Convention and Visitors Bureau, 130 S. Scott Ave. (☎520-624-1817 or 800-638-8350), near Broadway Blvd. Open M-F 8am-5pm, Sa-Su 9am-4pm.

Internet Access: University of Arizona Main Library, 1510 E. University Blvd. Open Sept.-May M-Th 7:30am-1am, F 7:30am-9pm, Sa 10am-9pm, Su 11am-1am; June-Aug. M-Th 7:30am-11pm, F 7:30am-6pm, Sa 9am-6pm, Su 11am-11pm.

Post Office: 1501 S. Cherry Bell. Open M-F 8:30am-8pm, Sa 9am-1pm. **Postal Code:** 85726.

▲ APPROACHING TUCSON
I-19 runs right into downtown Tucson.

TUCSON

A little bit country, a little bit rock 'n' roll, Tucson (TOO-sahn) is a city that carries its own tune and a bundle of contradictions. Mexican property until the Gadsden Purchase, the city shares many of its south-of-the-border characteristics with such disparate elements as the University of Arizona, the Davis-Monthan Airforce Base, McDonald's, and Southern Baptism. Boasting mountainous flora beside desert cacti and art museums next to the war machines of the Pima Air and Space museum, the city nearly defies categorization. In the last several years, a reenergized downtown core has attracted artists and hipsters, while families and retirees populate sprawling suburbs. Tucson offers the conveniences of a metropolis without the nasty aftertaste, and better tourist attractions than almost any other Southwestern city.

▐ GETTING AROUND

Just east of **I-10,** Tucson's downtown area surrounds the intersection of **Broadway Blvd.** and **Stone Ave.** The **University of Arizona** lies 1 mi. northeast of downtown at the intersection of **Park Ave.** and **Speedway Blvd.** Avenues run north-south, streets east-west; because some of each are numbered, intersections such as "6th and 6th" exist. Speedway, Broadway, and **Grant Rd.** are the quickest east-west routes through town. To go north-south, follow **Oracle Rd.** through the heart of the city, **Campbell Ave.** east of downtown, or **Swan Rd.** farther east. The hip, young crowd swings on **4th Ave.** and on **Congress St.,** both with small shops, quirky restaurants, and a slew of bars. Tucson is accustomed to bustle and, like most of the Southwest, **parking** is not an issue. Leaving your car at a meter is generally a low-risk venture.

◉ SIGHTS

UNIVERSITY OF ARIZONA. Lined with cafes, restaurants, galleries, and vintage clothing shops, **4th Ave.** is an alternative magnet and a great place to take a stroll. Between Speedway and Broadway Blvd., the street becomes a shopping district with increasingly touristy shops. Lovely for its varied and elaborately irrigated vegetation, the University of Arizona's mall sits where E. 3rd St. should be, just east of 4th Ave. The **Center for Creative Photography,** on campus, houses various changing exhibits, including the archives of Ansel Adams and Richard Avedon. (☎520-621-7968. Open M-F 9am-5pm, Sa-Su noon-5pm. Archives available to the public by appointment only. Free.) The **Flandrau Science Center** dazzles visitors with a public observatory and a laser light show. (On Cherry Ave. at the campus mall. ☎520-621-7827. Open M-Tu 9am-5pm, W-Sa 9am-5pm and 7-9pm, Su noon-5pm. $3, under 14 $2. Shows $5, seniors and students $4.50, under 14 $4.) The **University of Arizona Museum of Art** offers

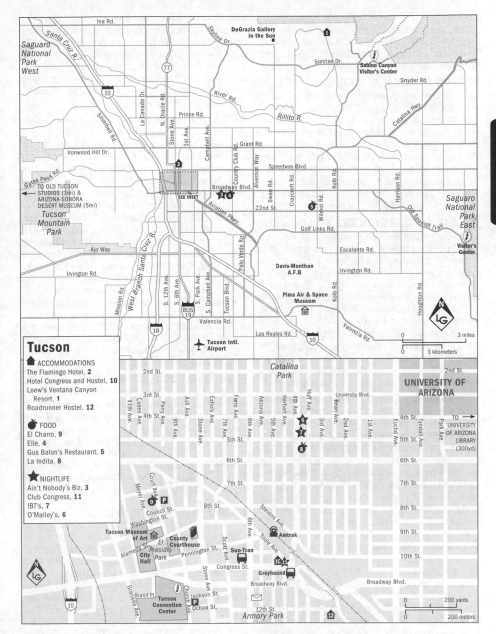

Ina Rd.

Santa Cruz R.

Saguaro National Park West

DeGrazia Gallery in the Sun

Skyline Dr.

Sunrise Dr.

Sabino Canyon Visitor's Center

Snyder Rd.

77

River Rd.

La Canada Dr.

N. Oracle Rd.

Silverbell Rd.

Prince Rd.

Rillito R.

Catalina Hwy.

Stone Ave.

1st Ave.

Campbell Ave.

Grant Rd.

Ironwood Hill Dr.

TO OLD TUCSON STUDIOS (3mi) & ARIZONA-SONORA DESERT MUSEUM (5mi)

Gates Pass Rd.

Speedway Blvd.

Country Club Rd.

Alvernon Way

Swan Rd.

Craycroft Rd.

Kolb Rd.

Harrison Rd.

Old Spanish Trail

Saguaro National Park East

Visitor's Center

Tucson Mountain Park

SEE INSET

Broadway Blvd.

Aviation Pkwy.

22nd St.

Wilmot Rd.

Golf Links Rd.

Ajo Way

Irvington Rd.

West Branch Santa Cruz R.

Palo Verde Ave.

Escalante Rd.

Davis-Monthan A.F.B

Irvington Rd.

Mission Rd.

S. 12th Ave.

S. 6th Ave.

S. Park Ave.

S. Campbell Ave.

Tucson Blvd.

Pima Air & Space Museum

Kolb Rd.

Houghton Rd.

BUS 19

Valencia Rd.

10

Tucson Intl. Airport

Los Reales Rd.

10

Valencia Rd.

0   3 miles

0   3 kilometers

Tucson

ACCOMMODATIONS
The Flamingo Hotel, **2**
Hotel Congress and Hostel, **10**
Loew's Ventana Canyon Resort, **1**
Roadrunner Hostel, **12**

FOOD
El Charro, **9**
Elle, **4**
Gus Balon's Restaurant, **5**
La Indita, **8**

NIGHTLIFE
Ain't Nobody's Biz, **3**
Club Congress, **11**
IBT's, **7**
O'Malley's, **6**

Catalina Park

2nd St.

University Blvd.

2nd St.

UNIVERSITY OF ARIZONA

3rd St.

11th Ave.

Queen Ave.

Perry Ave.

Ash Ave.

9th Ave.

Stone Ave.

Echols Ave.

7th Ave.

6th Ave.

5th Ave.

Arizona Ave.

Herbert Ave.

4th Ave.

3rd Ave.

Bean Ave.

2nd Ave.

1st Ave.

Euclid Ave.

Tyndall Ave.

5th Ave.

Park Ave.

4th St.

3rd St.

4th St.

4th St.

TO UNIVERSITY OF ARIZONA LIBRARY (300yd)

5th St.

Huff Ave.

6th St.

7th St.

8th St.

Court Ave.

Meyer Ave.

Council St.

Stevens Ave.

9th St.

Amtrak

10th St.

Washington St.

Tucson Museum of Art

El Presidio Park

County Courthouse

City Hall

Alameda St.

Pennington St.

Scott Ave.

Sun-Tran

Stone Ave.

Church Ave.

6th Ave.

Toole Ave.

Congress St.

Greyhound

Broadway Blvd.

Broadway Blvd.

Branif Pl.

Granada Ave.

Tucson Convention Center

Jackson St.

Ochoa St.

12th St.

Armory Park

0   200 yards

0   200 meters

visitors modern American and 18th-century Latin American art, as well as the sculpture of Jacques Lipchitz. The best student art is exhibited here. *(1031 N. Olive Rd.* ☎*520-621-7567. Open M-F 10am-3pm, Su noon-4pm. Free.)*

TUCSON MUSEUM OF ART. This major attraction presents impressive traveling exhibits in all media to supplement its permanent collection of American, Mexican, and European art. Houses in the surrounding and affiliated Presidio Historic Block boast an impressive collection of Pre-Columbian and Mexican folk art as well as art of the American West. *(140 N. Main Ave.* ☎*520-624-2333. Open M-Sa 10am-4pm, Su noon-4pm; Memorial Day-Labor Day closed M. $5, seniors $4, students $3, under 13 free. Su free.)*

DEGRAZIA GALLERY IN THE SUN. Stepping through the ornate iron doors of this old-fashioned pueblo home reveals the artistic world of Ettore "Ted" DeGrazia. The home itself, wonderfully spacious and colorful, breathes life into the paintings that adorn the walls. Wander the grounds before entering the gallery; wooden sculptures and sun-bleached metalwork are scattered throughout the cactus garden. Don't miss the chapel, dedicated to the Virgin Guadalupe, where the open-air simplicity complements the humility of the murals. *(6300 N. Swan Rd., about ¼ mi. north of Sunrise Rd.* ☎*800-545-2185; www.degrazia.org. Open daily 10am-3:45pm. Free.)*

SIGHTS ON WEST SPEEDWAY. As Speedway Blvd. winds its way west from Tucson's city center, it passes by a variety of sights. The left fork leads to **Old Tucson Studios,** an elaborate Old West-style town constructed for the 1938 movie *Arizona* and used as a backdrop for Westerns ever since, including many John Wayne films and the 1999 Will Smith blockbuster *Wild Wild West.* It's open year-round to tourists, who can stroll around in the Old West mock up, view gun fight reenactments, and, if fortunate, watch the filming of a current Western. *(*☎*520-883-0100. Open daily 10am-6pm; winter sometimes closed M. Call ahead; Old Tucson is occasionally closed for group functions. $15, seniors $13.50, ages 4-11 $9.50.)* Those opting to take the right fork will eschew the Wild Wild West for the merely wild West; less than 2 mi. from the fork lies the **Arizona-Sonora Desert Museum,** a first-rate zoo and nature preserve. The living museum recreates a range of desert habitats

and features over 300 kinds of animals. A visit requires at least 2hr., preferably in the morning before the animals take afternoon siestas. *(2021 N. Kinney Rd. Follow Speedway Blvd. west of the city as it becomes Gates Pass Rd., then Kinney Rd.* ☎*520-883-2702; www.desertmuseum.org. Open daily Mar.-Sept. 7:30am-5pm; Oct.-Feb. 8:30am-5pm. $9-12, ages 6-12 $2.)*

CAVES. Kartchner Caverns State Park is enormously popular, filled with magnificent rock formations and home to over 1000 bats. This is a "living" cave, which contains water and is still experiencing the growth of its formations. The damp conditions cause the formations to shine and glisten in the light. Taking a tour is the only way to enter the cave. *(Located 8 mi. off I-10 at Exit 302.* ☎*520-586-4100. Open daily 7:30am-6pm. 1hr. tours every 30min. 8:30am-4:30pm. Entrance fee $10 per vehicle. Tours $14, ages 7-13 $6. Reservations strongly recommended.)* Near Saguaro National Park East, **Colossal Cave** is one of the only dormant (no water or new formations) caves in the US. A variety of tours are offered; on Saturday evenings, a special ladder tour through otherwise sealed-off tunnels, crawlspaces, and corridors can be arranged. *(*☎*520-647-7275. Open mid-Mar. to mid-Sept. M-Sa 8am-6pm, Su 8am-7pm; mid-Sept. to mid-Mar. M-Sa 9am-5pm, Su 9am-6pm. $7.50, ages 6-12 $4. Ladder tour $35.)*

PIMA AIR AND SPACE MUSEUM. This museum chronicles aviation history from the days of the Wright brothers to its modern military incarnations. While exhibits on female and African-American aviators are interesting, the main draw is a fleet of decommissioned warplanes. *(*☎*520-574-0462. Open summer daily 9am-5pm; winter M-F 7am-3pm, Sa-Su 7am-5pm. $7.50, seniors $6.50.)* Tours of the **Davis-Monthan Air Force Base** are also offered. *(M-F 5 per day. $5, ages 6-12 $3.)*

▓ OUTDOOR ACTIVITIES

North of the desert museum, the western half of **Saguaro National Park** (Tucson Mountain District) has hiking trails and an auto loop. The **Bajada Loop Drive** runs less than 9 mi., but passes through some of the most striking desert scenery the park has to offer. The paved nature walk near the **Visitors Center** presents some of the best specimens of Saguaro cactus in the Tucson area. *(*☎*520-733-5158. Open daily 8:30am-5pm.)* There are a variety of hiking trails through Saguaro West; **Sendero Esperanza Trail,** beginning at the Ez-kim-in-zin picnic area, is the mildest approach to the summit of **Wasson Peak** (4687 ft.), the highest in the Tucson Mountain Range. The **Hugh Norris Trail** is a slightly longer, more strenuous climb to the top. Mountain biking is permitted only around the **Cactus Forest Loop Drive** and **Cactus Forest Trail,** at the western end of the park near the Visitors Center. The trails in Saguaro East are much longer than those in the western segment of the park.

Northeast of downtown Tucson, the cliffs and desert pools of **Sabino Canyon** provide an ideal backdrop for picnics and day hikes. Locals beat Tucson heat by frolicking in the water holes. No cars are permitted in the canyon, but a shuttle bus makes trips through it. (Take Speedway Blvd. to Swan Rd. to Sunrise Dr. The entrance is at the cross of Sunrise Dr. and Sabino Canyon Rd. ☎520-749-2861. Runs July-Nov. every hr. 9am-4pm; Dec.-June every 30min. dawn-dusk. $6, ages 3-12 $2.) The National Forest's **Visitors Center** lies at the canyon's entrance. (☎520-749-8700. Open M-F 8am-4:30pm, Sa-Su 8:30am-4:30pm.)

🔥 FOOD

Like any good college town, Tucson brims with inexpensive, tasty eateries. Cheap Mexican dominates the culinary scene, but every style of cooking is represented.

- **Elle,** 3048 E. Broadway Blvd. (☎520-327-0500). Cool classical jazz resonates through this stylish eatery. Enjoy mouth-watering chicken penne ($12) in elegant, yet welcoming, surroundings. Open M-F 11:30am-10pm, Sa 4:30-10pm.

- **El Charro,** 311 N. Court Ave. (☎520-622-5465), at the corner of Franklin and Court St., just north of downtown. Tucson's oldest Mexican restaurant—arguably the oldest in the US—is so popular that the USS Tucson submarine has named its galley "El Charro Down Under." Be prepared for a wait for dinner. Entrees $10-12. Open Su-Th 11am-9pm, F-Sa 11am-10pm.

- **Gus Balon's Restaurant,** 6027 E. 22nd St. (☎520-748-9731), just west of Wilmot. This classic diner serves up Tucson's best breakfast ($4-5) all day with heaping plates of eggs, fried potatoes, and toast. Lunch and dinner feature classics like roast sirloin ($5), grilled country ham ($6), and assorted sandwiches ($2-4). The pies lining one wall are an irresistibly sweet temptation ($1.50 per slice). Open M-Sa 7am-9pm.

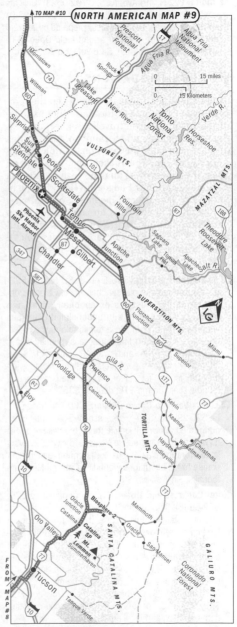

NORTH AMERICAN MAP #9

La Indita, 622 N. 4th Ave. (☎520-792-0523). Delights customers with traditional Mexican cuisine ($3-9) served on tortillas. The food is still prepared by *la indita* herself, providing a bit of added kick. Open M-Th 11am-9pm, F 11am-6pm, Sa 6-9pm, Su 9am-9pm.

ACCOMMODATIONS

There's a direct correlation between the temperature in Tucson and the warmth of its lodging industry to budget travelers; expect the best deals in summer, when rain-cooled evenings and summer bargains are consolation for the midday scorch. **The Tucson Gem and Mineral Show,** the largest of its kind in North America, is an added hazard for budget travelers. Falling at the end of January and beginning of February, the mammoth event fills up most of the city's accommodations for its two-week run and drives prices up considerably. Unless you've made arrangements in advance, this is a bad time to drop in on Tucson.

Roadrunner Hostel, 346 E. 12th St. (☎520-628-4709). Located in a pleasant house a few blocks from downtown, the hostel is exceptionally clean and friendly. Wows guests with unparalleled amenities such as a giant 52 in. TV, a formidable movie collection, free high-speed Internet access, purified water, free coffee and tea, and swamp cooling. Apr.-Sept. international guests get 2 free additional nights when they pay for the first 2. Free lockers, linen, towels, and laundry soap. Dorms $18; doubles $35.

Loews Ventana Canyon Resort, 7000 N. Resort Dr. (☎520-299-2020). A quintessential 5-star hotel 5 mi. north of downtown off Oracle Rd. At the base of an 80 ft. waterfall, the incredible Ventana delivers on every level—from its relaxing spa to its championship golf course to the beautiful surrounding Catalina Mountain foothills. Singles from $95.

Hotel Congress and Hostel, 311 E. Congress (☎520-622-8848). Conveniently located across from the bus and train stations, this hotel and hostel offers superb lodging to night-owl hostelers. Downstairs, Club Congress booms until 1am on weekends, making it rough on early birds. Private rooms come with bath, phone, vintage radio, and ceiling fans. The cafe downstairs serves great salads and omelettes. Dorms $17. June-Aug. singles $29; doubles $38. Sept.-Nov. and May $49/$53. Dec.-Apr. $68/$82. 10% discount for students, military, and local artists.

The Flamingo Hotel, 1300 N. Stone Ave. (☎520-770-1901). Houses not only guests, but also Arizona's largest collection of Western movie posters. There are dozens of rooms available, from the Kevin Costner room to the Burt Lancaster suite—both with A/C, cable TV, telephones, and pool access. Laundry facilities on-site. May-Aug. singles $24; doubles $29. Sept.-Nov. all rooms $49. Dec.-Apr. $75.

CAMPING

In addition to the backcountry camping available in the Saguaro Park and Coronado Forest (both inside and outside the Pusch Ridge Wilderness), there are a variety of other camping options. **Gilbert Ray Campground** (☎520-883-4200), just outside Saguaro West along the McCain Loop Rd., offers campsites ($7) with toilets and drinking water, and is in easy reach of the city as well as all the Speedway sights. **Catalina State Park** (☎520-628-5798), north of Tucson on Oracle Rd., features $10 tent sites fully equipped with hot showers, water, and toilets. Picnic sites are available. Camping areas flank Sky Island Scenic Byway at Mt. Lemmon; an added perk of these sights is their temperate climate. All campgrounds charge a $5 road access fee in addition to the camping costs. **Spencer Canyon** (sites $12) and **Rose Canyon** (sites $15) have potable water and toilets, while **Molino Basin** and **General Hitchcock** have toilets but no potable water (both $5). Call the **Santa Catalina Ranger District** (☎520-749-8700) for more info.

NIGHTLIFE

The free *Tucson Weekly* is the local authority on nightlife, while the weekend sections of the *Star* or the *Citizen* also provide good coverage. Throughout the year, the city of the sun presents **Music Under the Stars,** a series of sunset concerts performed by the **Tucson Symphony Orchestra** (☎520-792-9155). For **Downtown Saturday Nights,** on the first and third Saturday of each month, Congress St. is blockaded for a celebration of the arts with outdoor singers, crafts, and galleries. Every Thursday, the **Thursday Night Art Walk** lets you mosey through downtown galleries and studios. For more info, call **Tucson Arts District** (☎520-624-9977). UA students rock 'n' roll on **Speedway Blvd.,** while others do the two-step in clubs on **N. Oracle.** Young locals hang out on **4th Ave.,** where most bars have live music and low cover charges.

Club Congress, 311 E. Congress St. (☎520-622-8848), has DJs during the week and live bands on weekends, and is the venue for most of the indie music coming through town. The friendly hotel staff and a cast of regulars make it an especially good time. M is 80s night with $0.80 drinks. Cover $3-5. Open daily 9pm-1am.

O'Malley's, 247 N. 4th Ave. (☎520-623-8600). A good spot with decent bar food, pool tables, and pinball. As its name implies, this is a better place to nurse your pint of Guinness than it is to get your groove on. Cover Th-Sa varies. Open daily 11am-1am.

IBT's (☎520-882-3053), on 4th Ave. at 6th St. The single most popular gay venue in Tucson, IBT's can be hard to spot—there is no sign and the is door unmarked. Once you've seen the stucco building halfway down the block, however, there's no mistaking it. It pumps dance music in its classic club environment to a weekend capacity crowd. W and Su drag shows wow audiences. Open daily 9am-1am.

Ain't Nobody's Biz, 2900 E. Broadway Blvd. (☎520-318-4838), in a shopping plaza. The little sister of its Phoenix namesake, and the big mama of the Tucson lesbian scene. A large bar, 'Biz' attracts crowds of all backgrounds and has some of the best dancing in Tucson. Open daily 11am-1am.

◤◤ **LEAVING TUCSON**
From downtown, follow **Speedway Blvd.** to **N. Oracle Rd.,** which becomes **Rte. 77 North.**

◤ **DETOUR: BIOSPHERE 2**
32540 S. Biosphere Rd. *From Oracle Junction, follow Rte. 77 about 10 mi. to E. Biosphere Rd., then follow the signs.*

This massive three-acre laboratory looks and feels like it is indeed independent of planet Earth, which scientists affectionately call Biosphere 1. Concrete, glass, and 500 tons of steel construct and close off this sealed ecosystem, which houses five biomes—a desert, a marsh, a savanna, a rainforest, and even an ocean. Ultra-high technology powers and sustains Biosphere 2, from the two dome-like "lungs" managing air pressure to the wave machine keeping the 700,000 gallons of water moving through the reefs of the ocean biome. Perhaps best known for the 1991 experiment that examined whether a crew of men and women could survive in a closed environment, the center now focuses on education and research. (☎520-838-6200; www.bio2.edu. Open daily 8:30am-3:30pm. $13, ages 13-17 $9, ages 6-12 $6, under 6 free.)

◤◤ **APPROACHING FLORENCE**
In Oracle Juction, leave **Rte. 77** for **Rte. 79.** Once in Florence, turn left onto **Butte Ave (Rte. 287),** and then right onto **Main St.**

FLORENCE. As Rte. 87 rolls into Florence, it passes a sign that reads "State Prison: do not stop for hitchhikers." That, in a nut shell, is the town of Florence. Home to Arizona's largest state prison, the town has a long penal history. The **Pinal County Historical Museum,** 712 S. Main St., documents this history in grisly detail, displaying a collection of hangman's nooses, a two-seater from a gas chamber, and photos of criminals put to death. (☎520-868-4382. Open Sept.-July 14 Su noon-4pm, Tu-Sa 11am-4pm.) Florence also boasts the historic **Pinal County Courthouse,** at 5th and Main St., whose tower looms over the town. Outrageously teal, the **Blue Mist Motel,** 40 S. Pinal Pkwy., off Rte. 79, tries to live up to its name. While the color scheme may be a bit intense, the rooms are affordable, comfortable, and clean. (☎520-868-5875. Singles $45.)

◤◤ **APPROACHING PHOENIX**
After leaving Florence, take **Rte. 79 North** to Florence Junction, then merge onto **U.S. 60 West.** In the thick of the Phoenix suburbs, get onto **I-10 West.** Take Exit 148 to **Washington St.,** which heads into the heart of Phoenix.

PHOENIX

Anglo settlers named their small farming community Phoenix, believing that their oasis had risen from the ashes of ancient Native American settlements. The 20th century has seen this unlikely metropolis live up to its name; the expansion of water resources, the proliferation of the railroad, and the introduction of air-conditioning have fueled Phoenix's ascent to the ranks of America's leading urban centers. Shiny highrises now crowd the business district, while a vast web of six-lane highways and strip malls surrounds the downtown area. Phoenix's rise has not been easy, though; its greatest asset, the sun, is also its greatest nemesis. The scorching heat and arid landscape put a damper on expansion, as water is always in short supply. During the balmy winter, tourists, golfers, and businessmen flock to enjoy perfect temperatures, while in summer, the visitors flee, and the city crawls into its air-conditioned shell as temperatures exceed 100°F and lodging prices plummet.

(VITAL STATS)

Population: 1.3 million

Visitor Info: Phoenix and Valley of the Sun Convention and Visitors Center (☎ 602-254-6500 or 877-225-5749, recorded info 602-252-5588; www.phoenixcvb.com). Downtown location: 2nd and Adams St. Open M-F 8am-5pm.

Internet Access: Burton Barr Central Library, 1221 N. Central Ave. (☎ 602-262-4636). Open M-Th 10am-9pm, F-Sa 9am-6pm, Su noon-6pm.

Post Office: 522 N. Central Ave. (☎ 800-275-8777). Open M-F 8:30am-5pm. **Postal Code:** 85034.

▐ GETTING AROUND

The intersection of **Central Ave.** and **Washington St.** marks the center of downtown. Central Ave. runs north-south, Washington St. east-west. One of Phoenix's peculiarities is that numbered avenues and streets both run north-south; avenues are numbered sequentially west from Central Ave., while streets are numbered east. Think of Central Ave. as the heart of town; facing north, the first road to your right is **1st St.,** the first to your left is **1st Ave.** Large north-south thoroughfares include **7th St., 16th St., 7th Ave.,** and **19th Ave.,** while **McDowell Rd., Van Buren St., Indian School Rd.,** and **Camelback Rd.** are major east-west arteries.

Greater Phoenix includes smaller, independent municipalities that sometimes have different street-naming schemes. The many large asphalt **parking lots** charge around $7 per day. Street parking is also readily available and generally safe.

NEIGHBORHOODS

Driven by dirt-cheap desert land and flat landscape, urban sprawl has gotten out of control in Phoenix. Once a series of independent communities, the numerous townships of "the Valley of the Sun" now bleed into one another in a continuous chain of strip malls, office parks, slums, and super-resorts. The de facto unification of all the disparate neighborhoods has not, however, resulted in homogenization or equalization— some are magnets for tourists and money, others for illegal immigrants and crime. Since many of the most happening locales are located outside of the downtown proper, it's useful to get acquainted with some of Phoenix' outer townships.

Just to the east of downtown Phoenix and south of the Salt River lies **Tempe,** the town that lays claim to both the third-largest university in

the US and the nightlife to prove it. Don't make the mistake of leaving town without experiencing at least one night as a Sun Devil. East of Tempe, the suburban paradise of **Mesa** stretches out along Rte. 202. Tamer than its collegiate neighbor, Mesa is home to one of the largest Mormon colonies outside of Utah as well as a host of cheap eats and chain motels. **Scottsdale,** north of Mesa and northeast of downtown, is the playground of the (sometimes idle) rich. The very sound of the name conjures up images of expensive cars, immaculate homes, and world-renowned resorts. With its pricey accommodations and great sights, Scottsdale is a great place to visit (from Tempe).

◉ SIGHTS

▨**THE HEARD MUSEUM.** Renowned for its presentation of ancient Native American art, the Heard Museum also features exhibits on contemporary Native Americans. There are many interactive and traveling exhibits, some of which are geared toward children. Named after notable benefactors, galleries include the Sandra Day O'Connor Gallery, which houses an exhibit on the museum's founders, and the Barry Goldwater Gallery, which displays photography of the Southwest. The museum occasionally sponsors lectures and Native American dances. (*2301 N. Central Ave., 4 blocks north of McDowell Rd.* ☎ *605-252-8840, recorded info 602-252-8848. Open daily 9:30am-5pm. Free tours at noon, 1:30, and 3pm. $7, seniors $6, ages 4-12 $3, Native Americans with status cards free.*)

THE PHOENIX ART MUSEUM. This museum showcases art of the American West, including paintings from the Taos and Santa Fe art colonies. The permanent collection houses pieces by the *Tres Grandes* of Mexican art (Orozco, Siquiros, and Riviera) as well as works by noted American artists Jackson Pollock and Georgia O'Keeffe. Every major European and American movement has representatives on display. (*1625 N. Central Ave., at McDowell Rd.* ☎ *602-257-1880. Open Su, Tu-W, and F-Sa 10am-5pm, Th 10am-9pm. $7, students and seniors $5, ages 6-18 $2. Free on Th and after 4:15pm.*)

THE ARIZONA SCIENCE CENTER. Interactive science exhibits are supplemented by an IMAX theater and a planetarium. Slot the whole day if you're going with children. (*600 E. Washington St.* ☎ *602-716-2000. Open W-F 10am-5pm, M-Tu and Sa-Su 10am-9pm. $8, ages 4-12 and seniors $6. IMAX or planetarium $3.*)

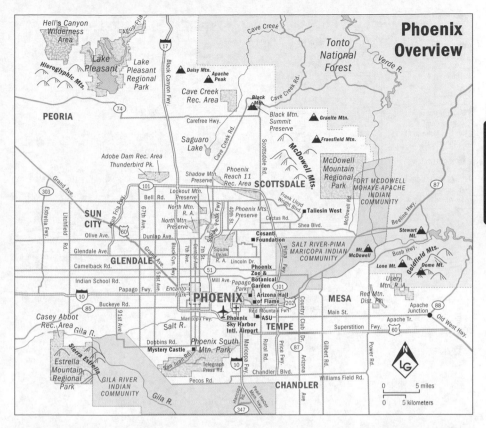

Phoenix Overview

PAPAGO PARK AND ENVIRONS. The **Desert Botanical Garden,** in Papago Park, 5 mi. east of downtown, grows a colorful collection of cacti and other desert plants, many of which are hard to find in the wild. *(1201 N. Galvin Pkwy. ☎ 602-941-1225, recorded info 602-481-8134. Open daily May-Sept. 7am-8pm; Oct.-Apr. 8am-8pm. $7.50, students with ID $4, seniors $6.50, ages 5-12 $3.50.)* The park has spectacular views of the desert along its hiking, biking, and driving trails. If you spot an orangutan amid the cacti, either it's a mirage or you're in the **Phoenix Zoo,** home to South American, African, and Southwestern critters. *(455 N. Galvin Pkwy. ☎ 602-273-1341. Open daily Sept.-May 9am-5pm; June-Aug. 7am-9pm. Sept.-May $12, seniors $9, children $5; June-Aug. $9/$7/$5.)* The **Hall of Flame Museum of Firefighting,** just outside the southern exit of Papago Park, features antique fire engines and other firefighting equipment. *(6101 E. Van Buren St. ☎ 602-275-3473. Open M-Sa 9am-5pm, Su noon-4pm. $5, ages 6-17 $3, ages 3-5 $1.50.)* Still farther east of the city, in Mesa, flows the **Salt River,** one of the last remaining desert rivers in the US. **Salt River Recreation** arranges tubing trips. *(☎ 602-984-3305. Open May-Sept. daily 9am-4pm. Tube rental $9.)*

MYSTERY CASTLE. For those interested in astounding Southwestern architecture, the striking **Mystery Castle** is worth the 5 mi. trip from downtown. Built in small increments over 15 years (ca. 1930), this home is a spectacular example of the creative use of space. Laugh along with the tour guides as they provide tidbits about the peculiarities of this masterpiece. *(800 E. Mineral Rd. Go south on Central Ave., and take a left on Mineral Rd. just before the*

Phoenix

🏠 ACCOMMODATIONS
Metcalf House, **7**
YMCA Downtown
  Phoenix, **9**

🍎 FOOD
5 & Diner, **6**
Gourmet House of
  Hong Kong, **4**
Los Dos Molinos, **11**
La Tolteca, **10**

🍺 NIGHTLIFE
Ain't Nobody's Biz, **2**
Char's Has the Blues, **1**
Mr. Lucky's, **8**
The Willow House, **3**

0   600 yards
0   600 meters

TO ① (2mi)   Monte Vista Rd.   E. Monte Vista Rd.

Heard
Museum

E. Palm Ln.

TO ② (2mi)

E. Coronado Rd.

Phoenix
Art Museum

TO ④ (1mi)

E. McDowell Rd.

E. Brill St.

W. Willetta St.

E. Willetta St.

Burton
Barr
Central
Library

W. Culver St.

Papago Freeway

TO PAPAGO PARK (5mi)
& ⑥ (6mi)

Portland St.   E. Portland St.

Roosevelt St.   Roosevelt St.

⑦

Garfield St.

McKinley St.

TO ⑧ (4.3mi)

McKinley

Pierce St.

Fillmore St.

Taylor St.

2nd Ave.

Fillmore St.

Taylor St.

Polk St.

9th Ave.

7th Ave.

5th Ave.

3rd Ave.

1st Ave.

Central Ave.

3rd St.

5th St.

7th St.

1st St.

10th Ave.

Grand Ave.

University
Park

Phoenix
Museum
of History

Woodland

Arizona
Center

Phoenix
Union
Municipal
Center

TO ⑩ (100yd)
& ✚ (1.5mi)

Van Buren St.

Central
Bus Station

Van Buren St.

Monroe St.

Bureau of Land
Management Office

Herberger
Theater
Center

11th Ave.

9th Ave.

Adams St.

Orpheum
Theater

Renaissance
Square

Phoenix and
Valley of the Sun
Convention and
Visitors Center

Museum
of History

HERITAGE
SQUARE

Phoenix
Civic
Plaza

Arizona
Science
Center

Washington St.

Arizona Hall of
Fame Museum

CESAR
CHAVEZ
PLAZA

PATRIOT'S
SQUARE

Symphony
Hall

E. Washington St.

Jefferson St.

Jefferson St.

Jefferson St.

Jackson

Madison

TO ⑪ (5mi)
& THE MYSTERY
CASTLE (7mi)

America
West Arena

Bank One
Ballpark

E. Jackson St.

9th Ave.

7th Ave.

6th Ave.

5th Ave.

4th Ave.

1st St.

3rd St.

7th St.

Union
Station
Amtrak

Jackson St.

South Mountain Park entrance. ☎ *602-268-1581. Open Oct. to mid-June Th-Su 11am-4pm. $5, seniors $4, ages 5-14 $2.)*

ARCHITECTURE. Taliesin West was built as the winter camp of Frank Lloyd Wright's Taliesin architectural collective. Later in life he lived here full-time, and now it serves as a campus for an architectural college run by his foundation. The beautiful compound, entirely designed by the master, seems to blend naturally into the surrounding desert, and includes a studio, a Chinese cinema, and a performance hall. *(Corner of Frank Lloyd Wright Blvd. and Cactus St.* ☎ *602-860-2700; www.franklloydwright.org. Open Sept.-June daily 9am-4pm. 1hr. or 1½hr. guided tours required. Tours $12.50-16, students and seniors $10-14, ages 4-12 $4.50.)* One of the last buildings he designed, the **Gammage Memorial Auditorium** stands in the Arizona State University campus in Tempe. Its pink-and-beige earth tones blend with the surrounding environment. *(At Mill Ave. and Apache Blvd.* ☎ *602-965-3434. 20min. tours daily in winter.)*

One of Wright's students liked Scottsdale so much he decided to stay. **Cosanti** is a working studio and bell foundry designed by the architect and sculptor Paolo Soleri. The buildings here fuse with the natural landscape even more strikingly than those at Taliesin West, and visitors are allowed to wander the grounds freely. Arriving early in the day (9am-noon) allows guests to watch the casting of the bronze wind bells for which Cosanti is famous. *(6433 Doubletree Rd. Traveling north on Scottsdale Rd., turn left on Doubletree Rd.; it will be on your left in about 5 blocks. Open M-Sa 9am-5pm, Su 11am-5pm. Suggested donation.)*

♫ ENTERTAINMENT

Phoenix offers many options for the sports lover. NBA basketball action rises with the **Phoenix Suns** (☎ 480-379-7867) at the **America West Arena,** while the **Arizona Cardinals** (☎ 480-379-0101) provide American football excitement. The 2002 World Series Champions **Arizona Diamondbacks** (☎ 480-514-8400) play at the state-of-the-art **Bank One Ballpark,** complete with a retractable roof, an outfield swimming pool, and "beer gardens." (☎ 480-462-6799. Tickets start at $6. Special $1 tickets available 2hr. before games; first come, first served.)

▧ FOOD

While much of the Phoenix culinary scene seems to revolve around shopping mall food courts and expensive restaurants, rest assured that hidden jewels can be found. Downtowners feed mainly at small coffeehouses, most of which close on weekends. **McDowell** and **Camelback Rd.** offer a (small) variety of Asian restaurants. The **Arizona Center,** an open-air shopping gallery at 3rd and Van Buren St., features food venues, fountains, and palm trees. Sports bars and grilles hover around the America West Arena and Bank One Ballpark. Tempe's residents fill up on bar food in the many hybrid resto-bars that cater to college kids, while both Scottsdale and Mesa have affordable options hidden in their bourgeois swankness or Mormon sobriety. The *New Times* (☎ 602-271-4000) makes extensive restaurant recommendations.

DOWNTOWN PHOENIX

Los Dos Molinos, 8646 S. Central Ave. (☎ 602-243-9113). From downtown, head south on Central Ave. Go very far, and once you're sure you've gone too far, go farther. Once you leave the barrio, it comes up suddenly on your right. One look and you'll know why you've made the trip; Los Dos Molinos is lively, colorful, and fun. Locals flock here on weekends, filling the indoor restaurant and the colorful courtyard, and spilling onto the street. Come early; they don't take reservations. Enchiladas $3.50. Burritos $5.25-7. Open Tu-F 11am 2:30pm and 5 9pm, Sa 11am 9pm.

5 & Diner, 5220 N. 16th St. (☎ 602-264-5220), with branches dotting the greater metro area. 24hr. service and all the sock-hop music that one can stand. Vinyl booths, smiley waitstaff, and innumerable jukeboxes teach you what the 50s *could* have been. Burgers go for $6-7 and sandwiches are $5-7. You can get the best milkshakes in town for only $3-4. Afternoon blue plate specials (M-F 11am-4pm, $3-6) change daily, but are always a great deal. Outdoor seating with view of scenic N. 16th St. available.

Gourmet House of Hong Kong, 1438 E. McDowell Rd. (☎ 602-253-4859). For those who think that quality Chinese food doesn't exist between the Mississippi and the West Coast, this no-frills restaurant will impress. 40 kinds of soup, noodle dishes, and Hong Kong specialties (chicken feet!) are unceremoniously dished out. No non-smoking section. Entrees $5-7. Lunch specials $3-5. Takeout available. Open M-Th 11am-9:30pm, F-Sa 11am-10:30pm, Su 11am-9pm.

La Tolteca, 1205 E. Van Buren St. (☎602-253-1511). A local favorite, this unassuming cafeteria-style restaurant/Mexican grocery serves up uncommercialized Mexican fare in *grande* portions. Familiar dishes are offered alongside specialties like *cocido* soup ($5) and refreshing *horchata,* a sweet milk and rice drink ($1-2). Big burritos $3-4. Dinner plates $5-6. Open daily 6:30am-9pm.

TEMPE

■ **Dos Gringos Trailer Park,** 216 E. University (☎480-968-7879). The best atmosphere in Tempe, bar-none. Dos, as it's affectionately known, draws a diverse clientele with its open, laid-back feel and its inexpensive yet tasty Mexican food. Deals include a Hangover Special ($5.25), and countless meals for under $6. Open M-Sa 10am-1am, Su noon-1am.

■ **Long Wong's,** 701 S. Mill Ave. (☎480-966-3147). Serving up 6 different flavors, Wong's has the best wings in town ($6 for 6, $9 for 12). A hybrid bar/restaurant run by a young staff with an animated spirit. Half-price wings happy hour M-F 4-8pm. Cover $1-5, depending on the act (mostly local). 21+ in the bar. Takeout available. Open Su-Th 10:30am-11pm, F-Sa 10:30am-12:30am.

SCOTTSDALE

Greasewoods Flats, 27500 N. Alma School Rd. (☎480-585-9430). With an extremely eclectic mix of patrons, the Flats dishes out classic American cuisine at reasonable prices, including succulent hamburgers for $6-8. Rub elbows with hippies, bikers, yuppies, bohos, and everything in between. Open M-F 10am-11pm, Sa 10am-midnight, Su 10am-10pm.

Sugar Bowl Ice Cream Parlor & Restaurant, 4005 N. Scottsdale Rd. (☎480-946-0051). Get out of the heat and into this fun and flavorsome ice-cream parlor, where the sundaes are piled high and thick ($3-5). Open M-Sa 11am-11pm, Su 11am-10pm.

MESA

Ripe Tomato Cafe, 745 W. Baseline Rd. (☎480-892-4340). The biggest, fluffiest omelettes ($6) this side of the desert fill up the entire plate. Eat inside or out, but bring your appetite. Open daily 6am-2:30pm.

Bill Johnson's Big Apple, 950 E. Main St. (☎480-969-6504). The sawdust on the floor fits right in at this country-western restaurant, where the food is almost as good as the Old West decor. Pick from a large selections of steak, and sample the tangy homemade BBQ sauce. Kids eat free W. Open daily 6:30am-10pm.

🏠 ACCOMMODATIONS

Budget travelers should consider visiting Phoenix during July and August when motels slash their prices by as much as 70%. In the winter, when temperatures drop and vacancies are few, prices go up; make reservations if possible. The reservation-less should cruise the rows of motels on **Van Buren St.** east of downtown, toward the airport. Parts of this area can be unsafe; **guests should examine a motel thoroughly before checking in.** Although they are more distant, the areas around Papago Fwy. and Black Canyon Hwy. are loaded with motels and may present some safer options.

Greater Phoenix contains some of the nation's best luxury and high-end resort hotels. Although during the high season they are out of reach to most budget travelers, during the baking summer those who brave the intimidating high-end hotels will find empty rooms and ready deals. If you can stand the heat, you can live like the beautiful people, if only for a night or two. More affordable accommodations are limited, especially in Tempe/Mesa, and tend to take the form of generic, albeit respectable, chain motels.

As an alternative, **Mi Casa Su Casa/Old Pueblo Homestays Bed and Breakfast,** P.O. Box 950, Tempe 85280, arranges stays in B&Bs throughout Arizona, New Mexico, southern Utah, southern Nevada, and southern California. (☎800-456-0682. Open M-F 9am-5pm, Sa 9am-noon. $45 and up.)

DOWNTOWN PHOENIX

Metcalf House (HI-AYH), 1026 N. 9th St. (☎602-254-9803), a few blocks northeast of downtown. Look for the house with lots of foliage out front. The ebullient owner, who gushes helpful advice about the area, fosters a lively community in this decorative house. Evening gab sessions are common on the front porch. The neighborhood has seen better days, so the coin lockers available in the dorms are probably a good idea. Bikes for rent, and discounts to some city sights included in the price. Chores required. Check-in 7-10am and 5-10pm. Dorms $15.

ExtendedStay America, 7345 W. Bell Rd. (☎623-487-0020; www.extendedstay.com), at 73rd Ave. Also in **Scottsdale,** 15501 N. Scottsdale Rd. (☎480-607-3767), and in **Mesa,** 455 W. Baseline Rd. (☎480-632-0201). This chain caters to business travelers. Steep prices for nightly accommodation, but a bargain at the weekly rate. Immaculate rooms have kitchen-ettes and Internet hookups. Rooms $55. Weekly rooms $279.

YMCA Downtown Phoenix, 350 N. 1st Ave. (☎602-253-6181). Another option in the downtown area, the YMCA provides small, single-occupancy rooms and shared bathrooms. Various athletic facilities. A small supply of women's rooms available. Ask at the desk about storing valuables. 18+. Open daily 9am-10pm. Rooms $30. Weekly rooms $119.

TEMPE

Mission Palms, 60 E. 5th St. (☎480-894-1400; www.missionpalms.com). At the base of the Tempe's Hayden Butte, this deluxe hotel is a steal in the summer for $99 per night (with prices more than doubling in the winter). Choose among the smorgasbord of amenities at your fingertips (2 hot tubs, a pool, health club, tennis center, and standard laptop Internet hookups) to pass the time, all the while knowing that raucous Mill Ave. is merely a minute's walk away.

Best Western Inn of Tempe, 670 N. Scottsdale Rd. (☎480-784-2233; www.innoftempe.com), next to U.S. 60 and Scottsdale Dr. Overall, a very well-kept hotel with a friendly staff, this branch of the chain has digital cable and laptop Internet hookups in every room. Rooms in summer from $59; in winter $99.

Super 8 Motel, 1020 E. Apache Blvd. (☎480-967-8891; www.super8.com). Chain with digital cable standard in every room. Consistently has some of the best rates in town. Continental breakfast included. Rooms Apr.-Aug. $39; Sept.-Mar. $49. Weekly rooms $190/$250.

Days Inn Tempe, 1221 E. Apache Blvd. (☎480-968-7793; www.daysinn.com). A chain combining tidy rooms with no-frills prices. Pool. Rooms in summer $49; in winter $79.

SCOTTSDALE

Econolodge, Scottsdale on Fifth, 6935 5th Ave. (☎480-994-9461). Clean rooms and low prices for the location make this branch of the national chain a deal. Singles $55.

MESA

Best Western Dobson Ranch Inn & Resort, 1666 S. Dobson Rd. (☎480-831-7000 or 800-528-1356; www.dobsonranchinn.com), 1 block south of U.S. 60 on Baseline Rd. Advertised as the best resort in the

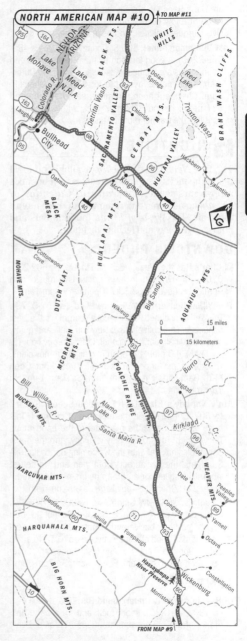

NORTH AMERICAN MAP #10

area, the Ranch is a great alternative for exceptional value at a low cost. 2 pools, a restaurant and massive banquet facilities. Rooms in summer from $55.

Lost Dutchman Motel, 560 S. Country Club Dr. (☎480-969-2200). A good location by many restaurants and clean rooms are the best reasons to stay at the Dutchman. Kitchenettes available for $3 extra. Check-in 3pm. Check-out noon. Summer rates hover around $37 per night and $159 per week, with winter rates doubling the warmer months' prices.

◤ NIGHTLIFE

The free *New Times Weekly*, available on local magazine racks, lists club schedules for Phoenix's after-hours scene. The *Cultural Calendar of Events* covers area entertainment in three-month intervals. *The Western Front*, found in bars and clubs, covers gay and lesbian nightlife.

DOWNTOWN PHOENIX

◪ **Char's Has the Blues,** 4631 N. 7th Ave. (☎602-230-0205). Char's hosts local jazz acts. Live music from 9pm. 21+. Cover Tu-Sa $3-7. Open daily 8pm-1am.

The Willow House, 149 W. McDowell Rd. (☎252-0272). This self-proclaimed "artist's cove" combines the best aspects of chic coffeehouse, New York deli, and quirky musicians' hangout. No alcohol. Coffee happy hour (2-for-1) M-F 4-6 pm. M is open mic night for musicians, Th is open mic for poetry. Live music from 8pm. Open M-Th 6am-midnight, F 6am-1am, Sa 7am-1am, Su 7am-midnight.

Ain't Nobody's Biz, 3031 E. Indian School Rd. #7 (☎602-224-9977), in the east end of the mall. This large lesbian bar is the big sister of the eponymous Tucson club. Top 40 hits play regularly, and the many pool tables mix well with the welcoming dance floor. F-Sa nights, the bar attracts both men and women of vibrant lifestyles for a sure-to-be-memorable experience. 21+. Open M-F 4pm-1am, Sa-Su 2pm-1am.

Mr. Lucky's, 3660 NW Grand Ave. (☎602-246-0687), at the corner of 36th Ave. and Indian School Rd. Don your biggest belt buckle and favorite pair of Wranglers for a night of good ol' country two-steppin'. Try to arrive before 9pm on F and Sa. Age restrictions vary. Cover $5. Open W-Th 7pm-1am, F 5pm-3am, Sa 7pm-3am.

TEMPE

◪ **Beeloe's Cafe & Underground Bar,** 501 S. Mill Ave. (☎480-894-1230). Food, rock, and art are the hallmarks of the hip yet unpretentious Beeloe's. Every night of the week offers special deals to go with the live music. Happy hour M-F 4-7pm. 21+. Cover F-Sa $4. Open daily 4pm-1am.

Mill Cue Club, 607 S. Mill Ave. (☎480-858-9017). For those looking to mingle in style, welcome home. The leather sofas in the corner complement the dark-paneled walls and the rows of pool tables in the back. Try a 20 oz. Long Island Iced Tea ($3.50) to liven up your night. Happy hour 2-7pm. A DJ spins hits Tu-Sa. 21+. No cover. Open daily 2pm-1am.

◤ LEAVING PHOENIX

From downtown, take **Van Buren St.** west to **Grand Ave.,** which becomes **U.S. 60** as it heads northwest out of the city.

◤ HASSAYAMPA RIVER PRESERVE

3 mi. before Wickenburg on U.S. 60 on the left. Look for a small sign and a gated dirt road leading to the Preserve Headquarters.

The 5 mi. stretch of the Hassayampa River that flows just south of Wickenburg is one of the last examples of undisturbed river ecology in Arizona. A variety of well-maintained and clearly marked trails allow for pleasant exploration of the vibrant habitat, home to a wide variety of wildlife, especially birds. Brochures and info are available at the **Preserve Headquarters,** but going it alone is not overly problematic. (Open Su and W-Sa 8am-5pm. Suggested donation $5. Free parking.)

WICKENBURG

Wickenburg just barely manages to outperform typical highway junction towns, offering a few legitimate sights to accompany the standard motels and diners. Of these, most compelling is the **Desert Caballeros Western Museum,** 21 N. Frontier St., at the intersection of Rte. 60 and U.S. 93, which displays a variety of art and artifacts depicting the Old West and all things cowboyish. (☎928-684-2272. Open M-Sa 10am-5pm, Su noon-4pm. $6, seniors $4.50, under 16 $1.) A pleasant walking tour brings the town's quirky history to life. Pick up maps at the **Chamber of Commerce,** 216 N. Frontier St., behind the museum. (Open daily 9am-5pm.) Particularly visit-worthy is the ◪**Jail Tree,** a mesquite tree over 200 years old that served as the town jail from 1863 to 1890. Of the hundreds of outlaws chained to the tree during its tenure, none ever escaped. It still stands just across Tegner St. from the museum.

Of the many small, independent eateries in town, the locals declare **Charley's Steakhouse,** 1187 W. Wickenburg Way (the western extension of Rte. 60), to be the best. Serving tender ribeye steaks ($17), Charley's provides an authentic Southwestern steakhouse experience. (☎928-684-2413. Open Tu-Sa 5-9pm.) A variety of chain motels line Rte. 60 and U.S. 93, but most are on the pricey side, charging around $60 per night for a single. If you're determined to catch some shuteye, try the **Super 8 Motel,** 975 N. Tegner St., west of U.S. 93. Authentic cowboy gear in the lobby and tastefully decorated rooms break the sterile monotony of the motel chain. (☎928-684-0808. Singles $65; doubles $70.)

◤▐ LEAVING WICKENBURG
Follow **N. Tegner St.** north out of town, where it becomes **U.S. 93.**

THE ROAD TO KINGMAN. For a 50 mi. stretch beginning 20 mi. north of Wickenburg, U.S. 93 becomes the scenic **Joshua Forest Pkwy.** Distant mountains frame this desert landscape marked by granite cliffs, boulder fields, sandy creeks, and, of course, plenty of Joshua Trees.

◤▐ APPROACHING KINGMAN
West of Kingman, **U.S. 93** intersects **I-40.** I-40 East heads toward the Grand Canyon (see feature, p. 6). U.S. 93 North and 1-40 West head toward Kingman. Take Exit 53 and turn right off the ramp for a brief stint on fabled **Rte. 66,** known in Kingman as **Andy Devine Ave.**

KINGMAN

Kingman has always prided itself on being a transportation town; the railroad and Rte. 66 running straight through Kingman brought in voyagers a plenty, including Clark Gable and Carole Lombard, who were married in the Old Courthouse. The town is as Rte. 66 enthusiastic as any, hosting the annual Rte. 66 Fun Run, from Seligman to Kingman and on to Topock/Golden Shores, the first weekend in May every year.

◰ GETTING AROUND. Most avenues in Kingman run east-west, while streets are numbered and run north-south (though just north of the downtown area some streets also run east-west). Many of the city's sights and establishments lie along **Andy Devine Ave. (Rte. 66).** Downtown cen-

ters on the area near **4th St., Beale St.,** and Andy Devine Ave., and **parking** is readily available in most of the city.

◪ SIGHTS. A converted 1907 power station that hosts a decent Rte. 66 gift shop, the **Powerhouse Visitors Center,** 120 W. Rte. 66, now serves as Kingman's Visitors Center. The top floor houses an extensive, lovingly curated Rte. 66 museum, while downstairs a small theater shows Rte. 66 documentaries on demand. Road buffs can while away the hours in the Rte. 66 of Arizona Reading Room upstairs. (☎928-753-9889. Open daily Mar.-Nov. 9am-6pm; Dec.-Feb. 9am-5pm.) At the **Mojave Museum of History and Arts,** 400 W. Beale St., indoor displays focus on the development of the area, arts and Indian culture, and the life and career of actor Andy Devine, a native of Kingman. An outdoor display highlights a 19th-century Santa Fe Caboose as well as wagons, mining equipment, and farm machinery. (☎928-753-3195. Open M-F 9am-5pm, Sa-Su 1-5pm. $3, children $0.50.)

▚▐ FOOD & ACCOMMODATIONS. Mr. D'z Route 66 Diner, 105 E. Andy Devine Ave., is a pink, green, and chrome tribute to the kitschy Rte. 66 diner, serving breakfast, lunch and dinner. (☎928-718-0066. Breakfast from $3.50. Sandwiches from $2.50. Open daily 7am-9pm.) The scents of home-baked goodies and gourmet coffee waft irresistibly from the **Oldtown Coffeehouse,** 616 E. Beale St., tempting visitors inside. (☎928-753-2244. Open M-F 7am-6pm, Sa 8am-5pm.) **El Palacio,** 401 Andy Devine Ave., is the local Mexican cantina of choice, with hearty entrees like the guacamole quesadilla from $5-8. (☎928-718-0019. Open daily 11am-9pm.)

The historic **Hotel Brunswick,** 315 E. Andy Devine Ave., offers a variety of rooms, ranging from austere singles with shared bathrooms to expansive suites. (☎928-718-1800. Breakfast included. Singles from $25; suites $115.) Guests at the **Hilltop Motel,** 1901 E. Andy Devine Ave., will find basic, clean rooms. (☎928-753-2198. Reservations recommended. Singles $36-55; doubles $85.)

LEAVING KINGMAN
From downtown, follow **Beale St.** west to **U.S. 93 North.**

DETOUR: LAUGHLIN, NV
Hop on U.S. 68 West from U.S. 93 a few miles north of Kingman. U.S. 68 merges with Rte. 95. Turn right at the Laughlin Bridge to cross into Nevada.

For a preview of Vegas action before the real thing, diehards can hop across the border to Laughlin, the brainchild of Gaming Hall of Fame inductee Don Laughlin. Today, Laughlin is one of the hottest gambling spots in the country (the outside temperature hit 125°F in 1994), but it's easy to keep cool at **Don Laughlin's Riverside Resort,** 1650 S. Casino Drive, on the left just past the bridge. A variety of newer corporate-run hotels and casinos have elbowed their way into the Laughlin market, but only the original captures the spirit of entrepreneurship that started it all. (☎702-298-2535; www.riversideresort.com. Rooms with 2 queen beds from $27, with a view of the river $37.) When you've had your fun or emptied your pockets, retrace your steps back to U.S. 93 North.

HOOVER DAM
70 mi. north of Kingman on U.S. 93; it's the big, concrete dam that prevents your car from tumbling 726 ft. into the Colorado River.

Built to subdue the flood-prone Colorado River, this ivory monolith took 5000 men five years of seven-day weeks to construct. By the time of the dam's completion in 1935, 96 men had died. Their labor rendered a 726 ft. colossus that now shelters precious agricultural land, pumps big voltage to Vegas and L.A., and furnishes a watery playground amid the sagebrush and mountains. It is a spectacular engineering feat, especially given the comparatively primitive state of heavy excavation equipment at the time of its construction. The scaled-down tours and **Interpretive Center** explore the dam's history. (☎866-291-8687. Open daily 9am-5pm. Self-

guided tours with short presentations $10, seniors $8, ages 7-16 $4. Parking on the Nevada side costs $5; free on the Arizona side.)

Welcome To NEVADA

From April to October, Arizona and Nevada are in the same time zone. November through March, you'll be crossing from the Mountain Time Zone into the Pacific Time Zone, where it is 1hr. earlier.

BOULDER CITY
The only city in Nevada where gambling is illegal, Boulder City feels more like a piece of Arizona that got stuck on the wrong side of the dam. Originally populated by the workers constructing the nearby Hoover Dam, Boulder City straddles U.S. 93—here called the Nevada Hwy.—as it enters Nevada, a last reminder of small-town charm before the Kingdom of Sin. The closest thing to an attraction in town is **Boulder Dam Hotel,** 1305 Arizona St., housing the small **Hoover Dam Museum** (☎702-293-3510; www.boulderdamhotel.com), which chronicles the construction of the dam and the people who made the desert bloom.

There are several locally owned diners in the center of town, but don't leave without trying the ▓**Southwest Diner,** 825 Nevada Hwy., which serves delicious specialty sandwiches ($6-7.25) and tasty milkshakes ($2.25-4). Sit inside, among the ice-skate strewn, hometown decor, or order from the drive-through. (☎702-293-1537. Entrees $8-9. Open Su-Th 6am-8pm, F-Sa 6am-9pm.) Due to its proximity to the Hoover Dam, Boulder City has a range of accommodation options. The **Flamingo Inn Motel,** 804 Nevada Hwy., is a great bargain, with comfortable rooms that include TVs and refrigerators. (☎702-293-3565. Rooms $35-44.)

APPROACHING LAS VEGAS
Getting into Las Vegas is not nearly as difficult as getting out with gas money in your wallet. Take **U.S. 93** to Exit 75 and turn left onto **N. Las Vegas Blvd.**

LAS VEGAS

Rising out of the Nevada desert, Las Vegas is a shimmering tribute to excess. Those who embrace it find the actualization of a mirage, an oasis of vice and greed, and one very, very good time. This playground town was founded on gambling, whoring, and mob muscle. These days, however, it's rather family-oriented. Lavish hotels on the Strip recreate Paris, New York, Venice, ancient Egypt, and medieval England in an attempt to entice visitors to their poker tables and nightclubs. Sleeping (and decision-making) can be nearly impossible with sparkling casinos, cheap gourmet food, free drinks, and spectacular attractions everywhere. Nowhere else do so many shed inhibitions and indulge with such abandon. Know thy tax bracket; walk in knowing what you want to spend and get the hell out once you've spent it. In Las Vegas, there's a busted wallet and a broken heart for every garish neon light.

VITAL STATS

Population: 1.6 million

Visitor Info: Las Vegas Convention and Visitors Authority, 3150 Paradise Rd. (☎702-892-0711), 4 blocks from the Strip in the big pink convention center. Up-to-date info on headliners, shows, hotel bargains, and buffets. Open M-F 8am-5pm.

Internet Access: Clark County Library, 1401 E. Flamingo Rd. (☎702-507-3400). 15min. free. Open M-Th 9am-9pm, F-Su 10am-6pm.

Post Offices: 301 E. Stewart Ave. (☎702-385-8944), downtown. Open M-F 8:30am-5pm. **Postal Code:** 89101.

GETTING AROUND

Las Vegas has two major casino areas. The **downtown** area, around **2nd** and **Fremont St.,** has been converted into a pedestrian promenade. Casinos cluster together beneath a shimmering space-frame structure covering over five city blocks. The other main area is the **Strip,** a collection of mammoth hotel-casinos along **Las Vegas Blvd.** Parallel to the east side of the Strip and in its shadow is **Paradise Rd.,** also lined with casinos. As in any city with a constant flux of money, some areas of Las Vegas are unsafe, so remain on well-lit pathways and don't wander too far from major casinos

and hotels. Valeting your car at a major casino and sticking to Fremont St. are safe bets. The neighborhoods just north of Stewart St. and west of Main St. downtown are especially dangerous.

Despite, or perhaps as a result of, its reputation, Las Vegas has a **curfew.** Those under 18 are not allowed unaccompanied in most public places Sunday through Thursday from 10pm to 5am and Friday through Saturday from midnight to 5am. Laws are even harsher on the Strip, where no one under 18 is allowed unless accompanied by an adult from 9pm to 5am Monday through Friday and 6pm to 5am on the weekends. **The drinking and gambling age is a strictly enforced 21.**

👁 SIGHTS

Before casinos inject you full of glitz and suck you dry of greenbacks, explore some of the simpler oddities of the city. Fans of classical music and kitsch will be delighted by the renovated **Liberace Museum,** 1775 E. Tropicana Ave., which displays the showman's velvet, rhinestone, fur, and suede stage costumes. (☎702-798-5595. Open M-Sa 10am-5pm, Su 1-5pm. $12, students and seniors $8, under 12 free.) Silly exhibits at the **Guinness World Records Museum,** 2780 S. Las Vegas Blvd., showcase repulsive and intriguing human oddities and display record-setting events on video. (☎702-792-3766. Open daily 9am-8pm. $6.50, students and seniors $5.50, ages 5-12 $4.50.) Way out in Primm Valley along I-15 near the Cali border, the **Desperado Roller Coaster** is the tallest and fastest bad-boy in the Vegas area, and one of the best coasters on the West Coast. (☎800-248-8453. Open Su-Th 11am-8pm, F-Sa 11am-midnight. $7.)

From 3min. drive-through whirlwinds to elaborate fantasy-themed extravaganzas, the **Little White Wedding Chapel,** 1301 Las Vegas Blvd., is a mainstay of the city's matrimonial traditions. Vegas luminaries like Frank Sinatra and Liberace as well as celebrities Michael Jordan and Britney Spears have been hitched here. The drive-through wedding tunnel begins at a romantic $40 (plus a donation to the minister) and possibilities only end with the imagination. (☎702-382-5943. No reservations required for drive-through services. Have your marriage license ready. Open 24hr.)

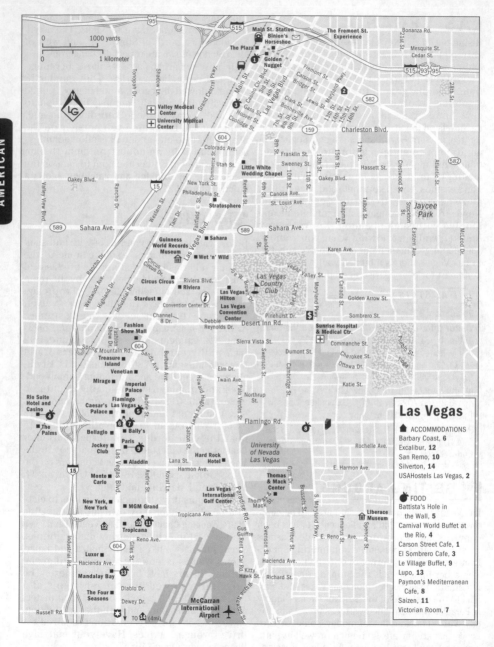

NORTH AMERICAN

Las Vegas

▲ **ACCOMMODATIONS**
Barbary Coast, **6**
Excalibur, **12**
San Remo, **10**
Silverton, **14**
USAHostels Las Vegas, **2**

🍴 **FOOD**
Battista's Hole in the Wall, **5**
Carnival World Buffet at the Rio, **4**
Carson Street Cafe, **1**
El Sombrero Cafe, **3**
Le Village Buffet, **9**
Lupo, **13**
Paymon's Mediterranean Cafe, **8**
Saizen, **11**
Victorian Room, **7**

🏛 CAINO

Casinos spend millions of dollars attracting big spenders, and they do this by fooling guests into thinking they are somewhere else. Efforts to bring families to Sin City are evident everywhere, with arcades and roller coasters at every turn. Still, Vegas is no Disneyland. With the plethora of steamy nightclubs, topless revues, and scantily clad waitresses serving up free liquor, it's clear that casinos' priorities center on the mature, mon-eyed crowd. Casinos, bars, and some wedding chapels are open 24hr., so whatever your itch, Vegas can usually scratch it. Almost every casino resort has a full casino, several restaurants, a club or two, a buffet, a feature show, and other attrac-tions. Look for casino "funbooks" that feature deals on chips and entertainment. **Gambling is illegal for those under 21.**

THE STRIP

The undisputed locus of Vegas's surging regenera-tion, the Strip is a fantasyland of neon, teeming with people, casinos, and restaurants. The nation's 10 largest hotels line the legendary 3½ mi. stretch of Las Vegas Blvd., named an "All-Ameri-can Road" and "National Scenic Byway." Don't let the glitter dupe you—this shimmering facade was built on gamblers' losses.

Mandalay Bay, 3950 S. Las Vegas Blvd. (☎702-632-7777; www.mandalaybay.com). Undoubtedly Vegas's hippest casino, Mandalay Bay tries to con-vince New York and L.A. fashionistas they haven't left home. With all the swank restaurants and chichi clubs, gambling seems an afterthought. Shark Reef has 100 aquatic beasts from all over the globe, including 15 shark species. House of Blues hosts some of Vegas's best music.

Bellagio, 3600 S. Las Vegas Blvd. (☎702-693-7444; www.bellagio.com). The world's largest 5-star hotel, made famous in the remake of *Ocean's Eleven.* Houses a gallery of fine art and a beautifully main-tained floral conservatory that changes with the sea-sons. Spend your winnings on Prada, Hermes, Gucci, or other bling in the Via Bellagio Shops. Muscle your way up for a view of the spectacular fountains, where water is propelled several stories into the air during free water ballet shows, set to Italian opera songs.

Venetian, 3355 S. Las Vegas Blvd. (☎702-414-1000; www.venetian.com). Singing gondoliers serenade pas-

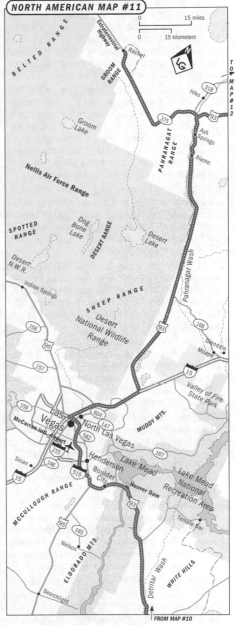

NORTH AMERICAN MAP #11

sengers on the 3 ft. deep chlorinated "canal" that runs through this casino. The Guggenheim Hermitage Museum presents modern artwork. For those who dig the representational, there's Madame Tussaud's wax museum. Elaborate architectural replicas of Venetian plazas, bridges, and towers adorn the exterior. Fine restaurants and upscale shops line the canals.

Caesar's Palace, 3570 S. Las Vegas Blvd. (☎ 702-731-7110; www.caesars.com). At Caesar's, busts abound; some are plaster while others are barely concealed by the low-cut get-ups of cocktail waitresses. Few are real. The pricey Forum Shops lead the high-end shopping craze at Strip casinos. With constant construction and ever-changing attractions (including Celine Dion), Caesar's continues to set the standard for excitement.

Luxor, 3900 S. Las Vegas Blvd. (☎ 702-262-4000; www.luxor.com). This architectural marvel recreates the majestic pyramids of ancient Egypt in opaque glass and steel. Non-gambling diversions include an IMAX Theater, a full-scale replica of King Tut's Tomb, Club Ra, and the Blue Man theater.

Paris, 3655 S. Las Vegas Blvd. (☎ 702-946-7000; www.parislasvegas.com). From restaurants that look like French outdoor cafes to replicas of the Arc de Triomphe, the French Opera House, and even the Eiffel Tower, this themed resort adds a Parisian *je ne sais quois* to Las Vegas glam.

The Mirage, 3400 S. Las Vegas Blvd. (☎ 702-791-7111; www.mirage.com). Arguably the casino that began Vegas's reincarnation in the early 90s. Shelters 8 bottlenose dolphins and a garden of white tigers and lions. A volcano that puts science fair projects to shame erupts every 15min.

MGM Grand, 3799 S. Las Vegas Blvd. (☎ 702-891-1111; www.mgmgrand.com). A huge bronze lion guards Las Vegas's largest hotel (5000 rooms), which echoes the green glamour of the Emerald City from *The Wizard of Oz.* Cowardly and brave felines dwell in the Lion Habitat. The MGM often hosts world-class sporting events and concerts.

New York-New York, 3790 S. Las Vegas Blvd. (☎ 702-740-6969; www.nynyhotelcasino). Towers mimic the Manhattan skyline and re-create the Big Apple. Walk under a replica of the Brooklyn Bridge or visit Coney Island to ride the Manhattan Express (open daily 11am-11pm, $12), the wildest ride on the Strip.

Treasure Island (TI), 3300 S. Las Vegas Blvd. (☎ 702-894-7111; www.treasureisland.com). Refurbished and fully embracing the wave of pirate chic, this once-tired casino is trying to reinvent itself as an "in" spot for young crowds. See the *Sirens of TI* for a sultry sea battle in one of Vegas's most skin-baring free outdoor shows. Shows daily at 7, 8:30, 10pm and 1:30am.

Circus Circus, 2880 S. Las Vegas Blvd. (☎ 702-734-0410; www.circuscircus.com). While parents run to card tables and slot machines downstairs, children watch free circus acts and spend their quarters in the enormous video game arcade upstairs. Adventuredome, inside the hotel complex, is the one of the world's largest indoor theme parks. Rides include a roller coaster and a towering free-fall machine.

Stratosphere, 2000 S. Las Vegas Blvd. (☎ 800-998-6937; www.stratospherehotel.com). World-class dining and a theme park sit at the highest point in Vegas and one of the tallest observation decks in the world, on top of this futuristic-looking resort.

 CASINO TIPPING. Gamblers are served free cocktails; $1 is the standard tip for servers. Leave at least $1 per person for the drink server and bussers at a buffet. Many players reward a good table-game dealer with a $1 tip next to their main bet.

DOWNTOWN AND OFF-STRIP

The tourist frenzy that grips the Strip is less noticeable in "old" Downtown Vegas. **Glitter Gulch** offers smaller hotels, cheaper alcohol and food, and some serious gambling, with table game limits as low as $1. The family atmosphere that the Strip tries to cultivate is lacking here; the feel is grittier, and the focus is on gaming. Years of decline were reversed with Las Vegas's city-wide rebound and the 1995 opening of the **Fremont Street Experience.** Now there's a protective canopy of neon, and construction of a pedestrian promenade has furthered the area's renaissance. Despite the renewal, don't stray far from Fremont St. at night.

Golden Nugget, 129 Fremont St. (☎ 702-385-7111; www.goldennugget.com). An outpost of Strip-like class downtown, this 4-star hotel charms gamblers with marble floors, elegant chandeliers, and high-end gambling. Without the distractions of roller coasters and replicas, the Golden Nugget stands for what Vegas used to be.

Binion's Horseshoe, 128 Fremont St. (☎ 702-382-1600). The Binion family brought their love of high-stakes gaming from Texas. A place to learn the tricks of the trade by observation rather than playing, this casino has been the site of the World Series of Poker—a serious gambler's paradise. Come at night to watch the large poker room in full swing, where tourists take on local hustlers, usually unsuccessfully. High craps odds, single-deck blackjack, and a willingness to honor almost any bet are Horseshoe hallmarks.

Palms, 4321 W. Flamingo Rd. (☎702-942-7777; www.palms.com). Owned by thirty-something marketing genius George Maloof, who is on his way to becoming the next casino mogul, the Palms is the ultimate venue to spot celebrities and party with the young and beautiful. The Skin Pool Lounge has swings and cabanas to enjoy before you hit the bars and clubs.

♫ ENTERTAINMENT

Vegas entertainment revolves around the casinos. Casino-sponsored productions feature marvels such as waterfalls, explosions, fireworks, and casts of hundreds (including animals). You can also see Broadway plays and musicals, individual entertainers in concert, and critically acclaimed performance art. All hotels have city-wide ticket booths in their lobbies. Check out some of the ubiquitous free show guides—*Showbiz, Today in Las Vegas, What's On*—for summaries of shows, times, and prices. For a more opinionated perspective, try one of the independent weeklies—*Las Vegas Mercury, City Life, Las Vegas Weekly,* or *Neon,* the *Las Vegas Review-Journal's* weekly entertainment supplement. It's worth setting aside some money to see one of Vegas's most elaborate shows. There is also plenty of free entertainment, but lounge singers and dancers are nothing compared to some of these big-ticket performances.

Cirque du Soleil's creative shows—*O, Mystère,* and *Zumanity*—are awe-inspiring but bank-busting ($93.50-150). Performed at the Bellagio, ◪*O* is easily the best of the three, with agile performers suspended above a moving pool. **Mystère,** at Treasure Island, is almost as impressive, and often has $60 discount seats. ◪**Blue Man Group,** at the Luxor, pushes the limits of stage entertainment with unique percussion and audience participation. Las Vegas's step into more than just the spectacular, the show is postmodern performance art without snobbishness ($75-85). Those looking for an illusionist will be thrilled by **David Copperfield** (appearing often at MGM; $90-100) and **Lance Burton** (at the Monte Carlo; $65-75). For a cheap laugh, **Second City,** at the Flamingo, is an impro-

visation show featuring some of the country's best up-and-coming comedians ($20). The group inspired the show Saturday Night Live, and many company members went on to write or perform for the show. For a performance by one of the musical stars who haunt the city, such as **Celine Dion** (at Caesar's Palace), **Gladys Knight** (at Flamingo), or **Wayne Newton** (at Stardust), you'll have to fork over at least $50. Incredible impersonator/singer/dancer **Danny Gans** entertains at The Mirage ($100).

⚒ FOOD

From swanky eateries run by celebrity chefs to gourmet buffets, culinary surprises are everywhere in Las Vegas, and usually at a great price. Inexpensive does not always mean low-quality in this town, since food operations are a major part of casino marketing. Be sure to check the marquees of major hotels for specials. $0.99 shrimp cocktails and $5 prime rib can always be found somewhere. Long lines for a buffet are generally a good sign, since the food tends to be fresher.

◪ **Le Village Buffet,** 3655 Las Vegas Blvd. (☎702-946-7000), in the **Paris.** French cuisine at 5 stations, each representing a different region. Begin with heaps of fresh shellfish and cheeses and then order fresh fruit crepes. Beef and veal sit at carving stations, while a pastry chef prepares more than 40 *gateaux.* Breakfast $14. Lunch $18. Dinner $24. Open daily 7am-10pm.

◪ **Carnival World Buffet,** 3700 W. Flamingo Rd. (☎702-222-7757), at the **Rio.** The line can be long, but the 12 themed food stations, from sushi to Mexican, delight those who wait. Breakfast $13. Lunch $16. Dinner $25. Open daily 7am-10pm.

Victorian Room, 3595 S. Las Vegas Blvd. (☎702-737-7111), in **Barbary Coast.** Home to the best night-owl breakfast special (midnight-7am; full breakfast $3) and excellent Chinese food. Also serves pasta, steak, and seafood. Fast, friendly service around the clock. Entrees $7-20. Open 24hr.

Carson Street Cafe, 129 Fremont St. (☎702-385-7111), in the **Golden Nugget.** Exhaustive menu features salads, burgers, pasta, steak, and even Korean kalbi and Japanese udon. Save room for one of the dozens of homemade desserts. Locals love the bread pudding. Entrees $7-24. Open 24hr.

El Sombrero Cafe, 807 S. Main St. (☎ 702-382-9234). Where locals go for authentic Mexican food. Small room, huge portions, friendly staff. Their combination plates offer a lot of food for a little money ($9-11). Lunch $7. Open M-Sa 11am-9:30pm.

Paymon's Mediterranean Cafe, 4147 S. Maryland Pkwy. (☎ 702-731-6030). Some of the best Mediterranean food in the city. Try the delicious combo plate with hummus, tabouli, and stuffed grape leaves ($10), or a big falafel and hummus pita bread sandwich ($6). Attached to **The Hookah Lounge.** Open M-Th 11am-1am, F-Sa 11am-3am, Su 11am-4pm.

Battista's Hole in the Wall, 4041 Audrie St. (☎ 702-732-1424), behind the Flamingo. 33 years' worth of celebrity photos, novelties from area brothels, and the head of "Moosolini" (the fascist moose) adorn the walls. Generous portions; many diners share. An accordion player adds to the charm. Dinner ($18-34) includes all-you-can-drink wine. Open Su-Th 4:30-10:30pm, F-Sa 4:30-11pm.

Saizen, 115 E. Tropicana Ave. (☎ 702-739-9000), in **San Remo.** Meticulous owners are known to use only the best ingredients, giving it the reputation as the best sushi bar on the Strip. Entrees $10-24. Open daily 5:30pm-midnight.

Lupo, 3590 S. Las Vegas Blvd. (☎ 702-740-5522), in **Mandalay Bay,** beside classy nightspots and dining options. Celebrity chef Wolfgang Puck's first Italian restaurant. Pizzas and salads ($11) are well presented. Open M-Th 5-10pm, F 5-11pm, Sa 11:30am-4pm and 5-11pm, Su 11:30am-4pm and 5-10pm.

ACCOMMODATIONS

Room rates in Las Vegas fluctuate; a room that costs $30 during a slow period can cost hundreds during a convention weekend. **Vegas.com** (www.vegas.com) has some of the best rates. Local, free publications such as *What's On In Las Vegas, Today in Las Vegas, 24/7, Vegas Visitor, Casino Player, Tour Guide Magazine, Best Read Guide,* and *Insider Viewpoint of Las Vegas* list discounts, coupons, general info, and schedules of events. If you get stuck, call the **Room Reservations Hotline** (☎ 800-332-5333).

Strip hotels are at the center of the action and within walking distance of each other, but their inexpensive rooms sell out quickly. A number of motels cluster around **Sahara Rd.** and **South Las Vegas Blvd.** Motels also line **Fremont St.,** though

this area is a bit desolate at night; if you want to stay downtown, it is best to stay in one of the casinos in the **Fremont Street Experience** (see Casinos, p. 688) itself. Inexpensive motels also stretch along the southern end of the **Strip,** across from ritzy Mandalay Bay. In the room rates listed below, the **hotel taxes of 9%** (11% for downtown Fremont St.) are not included.

■ **Barbary Coast,** 3595 S. Las Vegas Blvd. (☎ 702-737-7111), at Flamingo St. The best location on the Strip, mere minutes from Bally's. Large rooms and low table limits draw a young crowd. Restaurants, bars, and casino floor always buzzing. Rooms Su-Th $49-79, F-Sa $69-129.

■ **Excalibur,** 3850 S. Las Vegas Blvd. (☎ 702-597-7777), at Tropicana Ave. The best value of the major resorts. This King Arthur-themed castle features 2 pools, a spa and fitness center, a casino and poker room, and a monorail station to Luxor and Mandalay Bay. Many of the 4000 rooms have been recently renovated. Rooms Su-Th $49-79, F-Sa $79-129.

San Remo, 115 E. Tropicana Ave. (☎ 800-522-7366). Just off the Strip, a smaller, quieter version of the major players. Delicious prime rib draws an older crowd. Live entertainment nightly, featuring the "Showgirls of Magic" ($39). Rooms usually Su-Th $45, F-Sa $70.

Silverton, 3333 Blue Diamond Rd. (☎ 800-588-7711; www.silvertoncasino.com). This Old West mining town-themed gambling den has new rooms and a fishing store. Free Las Vegas Blvd. shuttle until 10pm. Doubles Su-Th $35-45, F-Sa $69; $10 per additional person. RV hookups $23-30. $3 energy charge.

USAHostels Las Vegas, 1322 Fremont St. (☎ 800-550-8958 or 702-385-1150; www.usahostels.com). Though it's far from the Strip in a dreary section of downtown, this hostel's laid-back staff keeps guests comfy and entertained. Sparsely furnished rooms. Free trips including a champagne limo tour of the Strip. Pool, hot tub, laundry, and billiard room. International passport, proof of international travel, or out-of-state college ID required. Dorms Su-Th $15-19, F-Sa $17-21; suites $40-42/$40-49. Prices roughly $3 higher in the summer and peak holidays. ISIC discount.

LEAVING LAS VEGAS

Cashing out of Vegas is only as difficult as keeping your finger off of the blinking "Draw" button. Hop on I-15 North. U.S. 93 splits off 25mi. outside Vegas, where open road separates the ka-ching! of Vegas's casinos from the quiet desert towns to the north.

◤ LAKE MEAD
Take Lake Mead Blvd. (Rte. 147) from I-15 east 14 mi. Follow Rte. 147 to Rte. 167, which frames the western shore of the lake. There's a $5 fee to enter the recreation area.

The largest reservoir in the US and the site of the country's first national recreation area, Lake Mead was created by the construction of the Hoover Dam across the Colorado River in the 1930s. Despite diminished water levels due to drought, the lake is a water recreation haven with nearly 500 mi. of shoreline. First-time visitors to the lake will benefit from a trip to the **Alan Bible Visitors Center,** 4 mi. east of Boulder City, and its informative brochures and maps. (☎ 702-293-8990. Open daily 8:30am-4:30pm.) For maps and abundant info about area services, pick up the *Desert Lake View* at one of the several ranger stations dotting Lake Mead's shores. Backcountry hiking and camping is permitted in most areas. Those who cast their line can expect bites from large striped bass; the area around Boulder Beach is particularly promising. Lake Mead is sustained by the multitude of weekend adventurers driving pickup trucks with jet skis in tow. Park service-approved outfitters rent boats along the shores; visit www.funonthelake.com for more info. **Boulder Beach** is accessible by Lakeshore Dr., off U.S. 93. (☎ 800-752-9669. Jet skis $50 per hr., $270 per day. Fishing boats $55/ $100.)

Alongside the Park Service **campsites** ($10), there are RV parks (most of which have become mobile home villages), marinas, restaurants, and occasionally motels. More remote, **Echo Bay Resort** offers motel and camping options. (☎ 800-752-9669. Singles overlooking the lake $85; doubles $100; RV hookups $18.) Its restaurant, **Tale of the Whale,** is decorated in nautical motifs and cooks up $6 burgers and numerous daily specials.

◤ DESERT NATIONAL WILDLIFE REFUGE
West of U.S. 93 between Las Vegas and Alamo.

The largest wildlife preserve in the continental U.S., Desert National Wildlife Refuge fills 1.5 million acres of land west of U.S. 93. The administrative offices are in Alamo, 4 mi. south of town. The road runs straight and flat for most of the length of the eastern border of the refuge, providing a sweeping sense of the undeveloped desert.

ALAMO

Unlike its Texan namesake, Alamo, Nevada seems mostly forgotten. The town lies west of U.S. 93 on 1st South Ave. and Broadway, although beyond the two highway-side motels and the rest stop, there isn't much to see. The town is best treated as a place to hang your hat before moseying down the road. If you do get stuck, however, there are a few historic sites. The **Earl Wadsworth Home,** on 1st South Ave., one block west of U.S. 93, was owned by one of the first Mormon families in Lincoln County, and is a good example of the 1920s early Vernacular-style home. Next door is the **Delamar Ice House,** which was built around 1890 in the mining town of Delmar and relocated to Alamo in 1920. The **Alamo School,** west of U.S. 93 on Broadway, was built by a group of volunteers in 1917 in the "Classic Box" style, presumably on purpose.

The closest Alamo comes to having a restaurant is the **Windmill Ridge Neighborhood Bakery & Cafe,** 151 Broadway, half a block west of U.S. 93, which serves buttermilk pancakes ($3), sandwiches ($5-12), and country salads ($3-8), among other classic American favorites. (☎ 775-725-3685. Open Su-Th 8am-8pm, F-Sa 8am-9pm.) There are two motels in Alamo, and both are easily visible from the highway. The attention to detail paid at **Alamo Meadow Lane Motel,** 300 U.S. 93 North, such as built-in Kleenex dispensers, extra towels, and hyper-pressurized showers, works with the clean 70s decor to ensure a very-Brady motel experience. (☎ 888-740-8009 or 775-725-3371; fax 725-3372. Check-out 11am. Singles $38; doubles with 1 king-size bed $42, with 2 twin beds $46.) The **Chevron station** on U.S. 93 acts as the town gathering spot, with a supermarket, deli, and bank. (Open daily 5am-10pm.)

◤ DETOUR: RACHEL AND AREA 51
40 mi. west of U.S. 93 on Hwy. 375, "The Extraterrestrial Highway.

World-famous for its proximity to Area 51, Rachel (pop. 99) has extraterrestrial mystique, and that's about it. Dusty roads stretch across barren land, where the odd trailer home dots the mountain-streaked horizon. You won't get lost in Rachel, as any vantage point in town allows a view of any

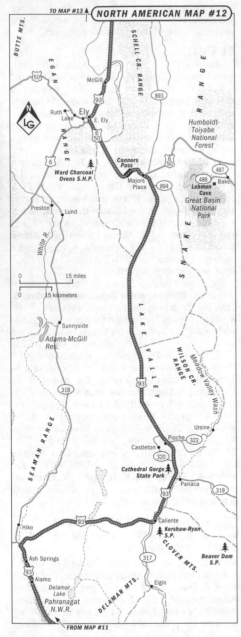

other. The only place to go is the **Little A'Le'Inn,** a family-owned inn and diner where flying saucers and little green men set the mood alongside NRA bumper stickers. To satisfy your Area 51 paraphernalia needs, look no further—the inn sells t-shirts ($18) and bumper stickers. (☎ 775-729-2515; www.aleinn.com. Breakfast $3-8. Sandwiches $4-6. "World Famous Alien Burger" $3.75. Diner open daily 8am-10pm. Rooms $42.)

CALIENTE

Just south of Great Basin National Park (see p. 410) on U.S. 93, you'll discover the true small-town Nevadan experience, where the three-block stretch of road that makes up downtown Caliente features an old-fashioned grocery and a quaint diner, both next to a pawn shop. Caliente was named for its natural hot springs. The town's most breathtaking man-made site is the **Union Pacific Railroad Station,** built in 1923 and originally a hotel, train depot, and restaurant. Now, the building houses City Hall and the library. Nearby outdoor attractions, within driving distance, include Kershaw-Ryan State Park, Beaver Dam State Park, and **Cathedral Gorge State Park** (see p. 692).

You'll spot several motels on the road into town, but none compare to the bargain luxury of **Caliente Hot Springs Motel and Spa.** The welcoming staff takes meticulous care to ensure the comfort of its guests, as evidenced by the motel's clean and homey rooms, replete with kitchenettes, cable TV, and spa tubs, as well as three Roman bathhouses, private rooms with family-size tubs where patrons can soak in hot mineral water. Guests bathe for free, and non-guests are welcome to use the tubs for $5. (☎ 888-726-3777; www.calientehotspringsmotel.com. Regular rooms $45; rooms with spa tubs $55.) Fuel up now—there's an 80 mi. stretch of desert between here and the next service area.

CATHEDRAL GORGE STATE PARK

Just off of U.S. 93 to the west, between Pioche and Panaca.

The land of Cathedral Gorge has been in use since 10,000 BC, when nomadic Native American tribes hunted, gathered, and picnicked there. More recently, it has become an idyllic retreat from the frenzied pace of Las Vegas. The **Regional Information Center,** at the park entrance, has brochures covering the flora and fauna of the park, walking tours, and geological and cultural history. (☎775-728-4460. Open daily 9am-4:30pm.) The park also has a 22-site **campground.** (Showers and flush toilets available Apr.-Nov. No Reservations. Campsites $14. Entrance fee $4.)

🚩 APPROACHING ELY
U.S. 93/50 descends into town on **Great Basin Blvd.** When 93 and 50 split, turn left on **Aultman St.** (U.S. 50) to access downtown Ely.

ELY

With a lonely 70 mi. of U.S. 6 separating Ely (rhymes with "really") and the entrance to Great Basin National Park, this mining and gaming town hardly fits the profile of a typical "gateway" city, but its barren surroundings and the convergence of several highways make Ely the locus of much trans-Nevadan traffic. In the beginning of the century, development of the area's copper resources brought an influx of residents and a railroad system, but, with its natural resources significantly depleted, today's Ely is a shadow of its old self. Remnants of past glory—like the stately Nevada Hotel and Casino, once the tallest building in the state—still line Ely's main drag.

(VITAL STATS)

Population: 4000

Visitor Info: White Pine County Chamber of Commerce, 636 Autland St. (☎775-289-8877). Open M-F 9am-5pm.

Internet Access: White Pine County Library, 900 Campton St. (☎775-289-3737), 1 block south of Autland St. Open M-Th 9am-6pm, F 9am-5pm; 1st and 3rd Sa of each month 10am-2pm.

Post Office: 2600 Bristlecone Ave. (☎775-289-9276). Open M-F 8:30am-5pm, Sa 10am-2pm.
Postal Code: 89301.

F GETTING AROUND. U.S. 6, 50, and **93** meet in Ely and radiate toward Reno, Las Vegas, Utah, Idaho, and California. Approaching the town from the southeast, U.S. 50 runs along **Great Basin Blvd.** before turning west on **Aultman St.,** Ely's main drag, lined with restaurants, shops, casinos and countless budget motels. Great Basin Blvd. serves as division between numbered north-south streets with an east and west designation. Lettered streets run east-west, east of Great Basin Blvd.

🔆 **SIGHTS.** In 1983, the railroad through East Ely shut down, leaving behind an office and depot full of well-preserved old equipment and records. Relics from the depot are still on display at the **Nevada Northern Railway Museum,** 1100 Ave. A, in East Ely. A tour goes through the restored office building and, while there are few especially showy exhibits, the well-informed guides eagerly share their knowledge of the railroad, town, and surrounding region. There is also a train ride on the old line, pulled by a 93-year-old coal-fired locomotive. Or you can drive a locomotive 14 mi. yourself—$550 for the steam locomotive, $300 for the diesel. (Where U.S. 50 turns left onto Aultman St., turn right instead and then turn left onto 11th St. East. ☎775-289-2085 or 866-407-8326; www.nevadanorthernrailway.com. Open M-F 8am-5pm, and some weekends. Tours free. Train rides M-F 1 per day, Sa-Su 2 per day. $12-35, ages 4-12 $8-18. No train Tu.) The **White Pine Public Museum,** 2000 Aultman St., displays artifacts from local inhabitants and a hodgepodge of paraphernalia from stuffed birds to telegraph equipment. They also have a collection of over 1000 dolls, with 300 on display. (☎775-289-4710. Hours vary; call ahead. Free.)

🍴 **FOOD & ACCOMMODATIONS.** Aultman St. has several steak-and-potatoes chop houses, including restaurants in the downtown casinos. The **Red Apple Family Restaurant,** 2060 Aultman St., serves up substantial portions of classic American food. While the menu is limited, what they do make is quite tasty. (☎775-289-8585. Breakfast $2-7. Sandwiches and burgers $4-6. Meat entrees $7-13. Reduced prices for seniors and children under 12. Open daily 6am-10pm.) **La Fiesta,** on McGill Hwy., prepares lunch specials (11am-3pm; $6.25-6.75) and the $10 Taquitos La Fiesta. (☎775-289-4112. Open daily 11am-9:30pm.) For a change of pace, **Twin Wok,** 700 Great Basin Blvd., offers both Chinese and Japanese cuisine. Try the Mandarin entrees ($8-10) or slightly pricier ($11-15) hibachi selections. (☎775-289-3699. Open daily 11am-10pm.)

Many of Ely's 17 hotels and motels are located on Aultman St. Far and away the best is the grand **Hotel Nevada,** 501 Aultman St., a relic from another era. Many rooms are shrines to celebrities who have stayed here, like Mickey Rooney and Wayne Newton. (☎775-289-6665 or 888-406-3055. Singles $30-38; doubles $40-48.) **The Rustic Inn,** 1555 Ault-

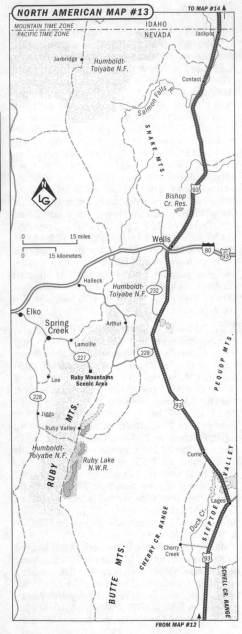

NORTH AMERICAN MAP #13

TO MAP #14 ↑

MOUNTAIN TIME ZONE
PACIFIC TIME ZONE

IDAHO
NEVADA

Jackpot

Jarbridge

Humboldt-
Toiyabe N.F.

Contact

Salmon Falls R.

S N A K E   M T S.

93

Bishop
Cr. Res.

0 _____ 15 miles

0 _____ 15 kilometers

Wells

80   93

Halleck

Humboldt-
Toiyabe N.F.   232

Elko

Spring
Creek

Arthur

Lamoille

227   229

Lee

Ruby Mountains
Scenic Area

228

Jiggs

Ruby Valley

R U B Y   M T S.

Humboldt-
Toiyabe N.F.

Ruby Lake
N.W.R.

P E Q U O P   M T S.

93

Currie

S T E P T O E   V A L L E Y

Lages

Duck Cr.

C H E R R Y   C R.   R A N G E

B U T T E   M T S.

Cherry
Creek

93

SCHELL CR. RANGE

FROM MAP #12

man St., is one of the cheapest in town, with clean rooms kept by friendly owners. (☎ 775-289-6797. Singles from $25; doubles from $35.)

LEAVING ELY
Hop back on **U.S. 93 North.**

CHUCK & BESSIE'S STAGE STOP
In Lages Junction, at U.S. 93 and Alt. U.S. 93

One of the only remaining family-owned gas stations in Nevada, the Stage Stop has been offering visitors a little bit of everything for 37 years, although gas and a snack might be the only things that are advisable to accept. The diner cooks up chicken-fried steak burgers ($6) and sandwiches ($3-5). There's a convenience store and bar on the premises, and a game of pool will set you back a quarter. The owners describe their two rooms as "nothing fancy," and warn that during hunting season (generally Oct.-Feb.) they're booked months ahead. (☎ 775-591-0397; stagestop@Inett.com. Breakfast $1-5. Diner and convenience store open M-Sa 7am-7pm, Su 7am-3pm. Room with 1 bed $18; room with 2 beds $28; RV hookups $7.)

WELLS

The pioneers—including the Donner party—who passed through what is now Wells seeking gold in the West had no idea what that dusty patch of land would later become: a dusty patch of land with some motels on it. While you're passing through, it's worth the little time it takes to check out **Historic 7th St.,** a block of defunct 19th-century businesses intermingled with still-operational endeavors. If you crave a bite or a bet, **4-Way Cafe, Bar & Casino,** 1440 6th St., just off of I-80 and U.S. 93, serves a huge selection around the clock. (☎ 775-752-3344. Breakfast $3-9. Steaks $8-18. Mexican entrees $7-9. Open 24hrs.) For those who have yet to win gas money at blackjack, **RestInn Suites Motel,** 1509 E. 6th St., at I-80 and U.S. 93, across from 4-Way Cafe, has clean rooms with queen-size beds and kitchenettes. (☎ 775-752-2277. Singles $35; doubles $40.)

DETOUR: RUBY MOUNTAINS AND ELKO
40 mi. west of Wells on I-80.

While countless other Nevadan towns have decayed, Elko (pop. 34,000) has charted a different course. The West's three most prosperous industries—mining, ranching, and gaming—have enabled Elko's sharp ascent. Now, 1993's "Best Small Town in America" proudly serves as the commercial and political heart of northern Nevada, welcoming visitors from across the country thanks to its new airport. Elko celebrates cowboy culture with museums, exhibits, and annual events. The **Western Folklife Center,** 501 Railroad St., is perhaps the premier national institution devoted to the subject. (☎775-738-7508. Open Tu-Sa 10am-5pm.) The nearby **Ruby Mountains** are the primary playground for Elko's wilderness fanatics. To reach the Rubies, take either 12th St. or 5th St. to the Lamoille Hwy. For info on outdoor activities, contact the **Forest Service,** 2035 Last Chance Rd., and be sure to grab a copy of their guide to the mountains. (☎775-738-5171. Open M-F 7:30am-4pm.) The recreational use officer at the Elko **BLM Office,** 3900 E. Idaho St., will fit wilderness itineraries to visitors' needs, and give advice about popular, yet untrammeled, outdoors sites. (☎775-753-0200. Open M-F 7:30am-4:15pm.) Relatively new to the recreation scene, **South Fork State Recreation Area,** 10 mi. south of Elko, off Rte. 228, boasts a large reservoir, campgrounds, and hiking.

JACKPOT. Little more than a strip of casinos and a few scattered homes, Jackpot caters to Idahoan farmers looking to blow their seed money in vain hopes of beating the odds. Even if you're just passing through on your way to points north, pop into **Barton's Club 93 Casino,** 1002 U.S. 93. Proudly displaying of old-school *Star Wars* props and memorabilia (a full-size Storm Trooper watches you eat, Darth Vader guards the entrance to the buffet, and Jedi Master Yoda gazes disconsolately at Han Solo, forever suspended in carbonite in the lobby), Barton's also has the best room rates in town and a **buffet** ($11) worth stopping for. (☎800-258-2937. Breakfast $2-8. Sandwiches $5-6.) After you've lost your last dollar to the Silver State, climb back on **U.S. 93** and look toward the peaceful life of Idaho on the horizon.

Welcome To IDAHO

As you cross into Idaho, you'll also enter the Mountain Time Zone, where it is 1hr. later.

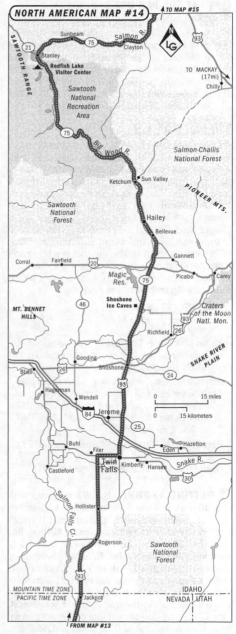

▲ NAT-SOO-PAH HOT SPRINGS
3 mi. east of U.S. 93, just over the Idaho line.
The huge natural hot spring swimming pool sets Nat-Soo-Pah apart from other campgrounds. Clean, pleasant picnicking and tent sites make it a great choice for the outdoorsman looking to spend the night. (☎208-655-4337. Open M-F noon-10pm, Sa-Su 10am-10pm. Hot spring pool $5. Sites $12 for 2 people, $1 per additional person.)

TWIN FALLS

Twin Falls is like wherever you're from, only more so. The Chili's is at the mall across the street from The Outback Steakhouse, a block north of Barnes & Noble, which has a Starbucks inside. Target is next to OfficeMax, behind Arby's and Applebee's. In the first mile of Twin Falls, there is a Sonic Burger, two McDonald's, three Subways, and a Burger King. Beyond the prepackaged glow, however, there lies a quiet and charming city that offers easy access to the outdoors; whitewater rafting trips run from Centennial Park, bike and running trails wend along the gorge, and waterfalls shine up and down the river.

(VITAL STATS)

Population: 35,000

Visitor Info: Visitor Center, 858 Blue Lakes Blvd. N. (☎208-733-9458), just across the bridge. Open Mar.-Oct. daily 9am-5pm.

Internet Access: Cyber Center, 1180 Blue Lakes Blvd. N. (☎208-734-1300). High-speed Internet access with a friendly and knowledgeable staff and snack bar. $5.50 per hr. Open M-Th 8am-7pm, F-Sa 8am-10pm.

Post Office: 253 2nd Ave. W. (☎800-275-8777), right off of Shoshone St. (Rte. 74) from U.S. 93. Open M-Sa 9am-5pm. **Postal Code:** 83301.

▐ GETTING AROUND. U.S. 93 joins up with **U.S. 30** outside Twin Falls, becoming **Addison Ave.** U.S. 30 splits off, heading southeast through downtown and eventually becoming **Kimberly Rd.,** while U.S. 93 goes on for a few blocks, takes a left, becoming **Blue Lakes Blvd. N.** Newer businesses and developments lie along Blue Lakes Blvd., while older, privately run eateries and accommodations tend to sit back on Kimberly Rd. The town's third main throroughfare, **Shoshone St.** (Rte. 74), runs downtown diagonally southwest from the intersection of Blue Lakes and Addison.

Downtown Twin Falls is organized in a logical numbered grid—just not any logic you're familiar with. **Main Ave.** and **Shoshone St.** intersect, forming an X by which all of downtown is oriented. Avenues run northwest-southeast, numbered in both directions by their distance from Main Ave.; streets run northeast-southwest, numbered relative to Shoshone St. Both avenues and streets can be marked with any of the cardinal directions. Designation changes when the street or avenue crosses either of the two main roads. Thus, 3rd St. South does not become 3rd St. North, but 3rd St. East as it crosses Main St., while, four blocks northwest, 3rd St. West becomes 3rd St. North.

◪ SIGHTS. Twin Falls has a variety of attractions for the outdoorsman, outdoorswoman, and outdoorschild in all of us. Closest to the city proper are the mighty **Shoshone Falls**—the "Niagara of the West" which are actually 50 ft. longer than the real thing. The falls are best viewed in the spring, when snowmelt swells the Snake River and the flow has not yet been diverted to provide summertime irrigation and power. (Follow Blue Lakes Blvd. to the major intersection with Falls Ave., head east on Falls Ave., and take a left onto 3300 East Rd. after 3 mi. ☎208-736-2265. Open daily 7am-10pm. $3 per car.) Nearby is **Twin Falls.** The title is an anachronism now, as one of the falls has vanished in the name of electric power. The other rages onward, though, and in the summer can be wider and wilder than Shoshone Falls. (From Falls Ave., head east for a little under 2 mi. and turn left on 3500 East Rd. ☎208-736-2265. Open daily 8am-dusk. Free.)

▧Snake River Canyon, north of town, is a giant hole in the earth. The **I.B. Perrine Bridge,** a $10 million effort completed in 1976, is the longest span bridge in the west. From it, Snake River Canyon displays its impressive 500 ft. drop to the golf courses below. **Centennial Waterfront Park,** on the south rim next to the Visitor Center, half a mile west of the bridge, offers views and enough historical information to complement any picnic. If you'd like to experience the canyon from a different angle, **Idaho Guide Service,** 563 Trotter Dr. (☎888-734-3246; www.idahoguideservice.com.), off of Elizabeth Blvd. from Blue Lakes, runs water tours, from 3hr. motor boat tours to five-day whitewater adventures. If you'd rather get high than wet, **Reeder**

Flying Service, 644 Airport Loop (☎208-733-5920), west of U.S. 93 on the north rim of the canyon, flies helicopter tours of the canyon and the falls for as low as $25 per person.

The **Herrett Center for Arts and Science,** at the College of Southern Idaho North Entrance, just off of North College Rd. from Blue Lakes Blvd., is home to the ☒**Faulkner Planetarium,** considered to be one of the best in the world. The Herrett Center also features exhibits on stone tools, contemporary art, and the ecology of rainforests, among other things. (☎208-733-9554, ext. 2655; www.csi.edu/Support/Museum/Faulkner/welcome.html. Open in summer Su and Tu-Sa 1-9pm; reduced winter hours. Free. Planetarium shows $4.) **Historic Old Town** celebrated its 100th year in 2004. The downtown area sports the lovely **City Park,** which hosts free concerts each Thursday night in summer at the Bandshell.

▚▐ FOOD & ACCOMMODATIONS. Chain restaurants with glossy menus and perky wait-staff line **Blue Lakes Blvd.** on the north side of town, but smaller operations can be found away from the highway. Of these, **The Depot Grill,** 545 Shoshone St. South, has drawn the local crowd since 1927 with its classic diner decor and smorgasbord lunches. (☎208-733-0710. Sandwiches $2-4. Burgers $3-5. Seafood $7-10. Steaks $9-15. Open 24hr., except Su night.) At **Crowley's Soda Fountain,** 144 S. Main Ave., thirsty patrons choose from malts and shakes ($2-5), smoothies ($3), Italian sodas ($3) and phosphates ($1-2). Sandwiches ($2-6) and wraps ($6.25) make for light meals. (☎208-733-1041. Open M-Sa 10am-5pm.)

Similarly, Blue Lakes Blvd. also has an abundance of motels. The **Old Towne Lodge,** 248 2nd Ave. West, a few blocks off Addison Ave., offers large, bright rooms at some of the best rates in town. (☎208-733-5630. Singles $30; doubles $35.) Another fine option is **El Rancho Motel,** 380 W. Addison Ave. Impossible to miss with its flashing tri-tone neon sign, El Rancho has a handful of clean rooms, complete with refrigerator, microwave, and coffee maker. (☎208-733-4021. Singles $32; doubles $37.) The **Monetery Motor Inn,** 433 W. Addison Ave., has nice rooms and nicer bathrooms; the latter are dazzling white and have the blessing of a full tub. (☎208-733-5151. Microwaves and refrigerators. Singles $35-40; doubles $45-55.)

▐ LEAVING TWIN FALLS
Unlike **Evel Knievel** (see feature, p. 595), **U.S. 93** succesfully leaps the Snake River Canyon as it heads north out of town.

SHOSHONE. Halfway between here and there, Shoshone doesn't offer many attractions beyond its historic downtown area, west off Rte. 26, which has a few buildings from the early 20th century and a quaint park. If you've got extra car space, there are several antique stores on the way in and out of town, which sell old saddles, wagon wheels, horse-drawn carriages, and, for a still-unidentified reason, bath tubs. The town is best treated as a rest stop, not a destination. The **Manhattan Cafe,** 133 S. Rail St., is a classic diner and souvenir shop, where locals choose from red-booth or counter seating. (☎208-886-2142. Burgers $4-7. Entrees $8-11. Open Su-Th 6am-9pm, F-Sa 6am-10pm.)

▐ LEAVING SHOSHONE
Rte. 75 heads north out of Shoshone, and so do you.

◉ SHOSHONE ICE CAVES   1561 Rte. 75
17 mi. north of Shoshone on Rte. 75.
Maintaining freezing temperatures year-round, the caves make a great way to beat the Idaho heat in summer months. The attached museum has local gems and minerals and Native American artifacts, while the gift shop takes care of all your ice cave gift-giving needs. (☎208-886-2058. Open daily 8am-8pm. Tours daily from 9am; last tour 7pm. $6, seniors $5.50, ages 5-14 $3.75.)

BELLEVUE

Just south of Hailey and Sun Valley along Rte. 75, the log-cabin gas stations, rod-iron street lamps, and local artisan shops of Bellevue only hint at the charm of this serene mountain town. Much of Bellevue was built in the late 19th century, when the town served as the affluent center of a thriving mining district. A jaunt down Main St. will reveal **The Wood Connection,** constructed in 1884, and **Glenn's Grocery,** housed in a building from 1910, both of which feature an architectually distinct usage of corbel-table ornamentation. The **Bellview Museum,** a white house on the east side of Main St., chronicles the area's history through a series of photographs. Contact Teresa Bergin (☎208-788-4013) to arrange an appointment.

There are many affordable dining options along Main St., but locals flock to **Taqueria Al Pastor,** 321 S. Main St., where "tacos al pastor" are stuffed with onions, pork, cilantro, lime, and, upon request, pineapple. (☎208-578-2300. Entrees $6-12. Open M-Sa 11am-10pm, Su 10am-6pm.) **High Country Motel and Cabins,** 765 S. Main St., has log-cabin decor, roomy suites, and cable TV. (☎800-692-2050 or 208-788-2050. Singles $69; doubles $76.)

HAILEY

By 1884, only five years after its founding, Hailey boasted a dozen casinos, 18 saloons, a Red Light district, and weekly dances organized by its own secret society. While the town of today is more family-friendly, it has not lost its festive spirit. When the sun sets in the valley, resort employees return home to Hailey, where outdoor bars are set against the same heavenly peaks as neighboring Ketchum, but host a more down-to-earth crowd.

VITAL STATS

Population: 7000

Visitor Info: Hailey Chamber of Commerce, 13 W. Carbonate (☎208-788-2700; www.visithailey-idaho.com). Open M-F 10am-5pm.

Internet Access: Hailey Public Library, 7 W. Croy St. (☎208-788-2036), at the corner of Croy St. and S. Main St. $2 per 2hr. Open M, W, F-Sa 10am-6pm; Tu and Th noon-8pm.

Post Office: 820 S. Main St. (☎208-788–2276). Open M-F 9am-5pm, Sa 9am-2pm. **Postal Code:** 83333.

⊟ GETTING AROUND. Hailey sits just 11 mi. south of Ketchum and Sun Valley on Hwy. 75, which becomes **Main St.** The downtown area centers on S. Main St., with numerous restaurants and bars. Motels and resorts hover around Main St. as well, on either side of the business district. **Parking** is ample in town and at hotels.

◎⚐ SIGHTS & ENTERTAINMENT. Most skiers and outdoor enthusiasts head to Ketchum and Sun Valley, but if you don't plan to hit the slopes, there are several points of interest in town. The **Blaine County Historical Museum,** 218 N. Main St., addresses various facets of the area's history, including the development of its transportation system, local politics, period

attire, and its famous literary sons— Ezra Pound and Ernest Hemingway. (☎208-788-1801. Open Memorial Day-Oct. 15.) The **Ezra Pound Association** (☎208-788-2071) is restoring the home of Ezra Pound, who was born in Hailey in 1885 and became a famous poet and critic.

The **Company of Fools** (☎208-578-9122; www.companyoffools.org) acting troupe plays in the **Liberty Theater,** 110 N. Main St., and is dedicated to "the magic, mystery, and wonder of life."

⚑ FOOD. At **Smoky Mountain Pizza & Pasta,** 200 S. Main St., patrons eat oven-fresh pies on the patio, where pinwheels catch the cool mountain breeze. (☎208-578-0667. Small salads $3, large $6-8. Medium specialty pizza $16, large $19. Open M-Sa 11am-10pm, Su noon-9pm.) Locals pack into the **Red Elephant Saloon,** 107 S. Main St., right at 5pm to take advantage of the full bar and daily specials. (☎208-788-6047. Burgers and sandwiches $7-10. Pasta $16-18. Open Su-Th 5-11pm, F-Sa 5pm-midnight.) Owned by famous resident Demi Moore, **Shorty's Diner,** 126 S. Main St., launches full-throttle into the past, with classic decor and American fare like fish and chips ($7), milkshakes, and pies. (☎208-578-1293. Open M-Sa 7am-4pm, Su 8am-4pm.)

⚐ ACCOMMODATIONS. At the **Hailey Hotel,** 201 S. Main St., a popular outdoor bar and low room rates make up for communal bathrooms. (☎208-788-3140. Rooms $40.) **The Hitchrack,** 619 S. Main St., is a recently renovated motel with a gas station and grocery store on its premises. (☎208-788-1696; fax 208-788-5751. Rooms $45-65.) The **Airport Inn,** 820 4th Ave. South, has express breakfast delivery, an outdoor hot tub, and free wireless hookups. (☎208-788-2477; www.taylorhotel-group.com. Singles and doubles $73.)

KETCHUM & SUN VALLEY

In 1935, Union Pacific heir Averill Harriman sent Austrian Count Felix Schaffgotsch to scour the western US for a site to develop into a ski resort that would rival Europe's best. The Count settled on Ketchum and Sun Valley was quickly recognized as a world-class ski resort. In peak months, traffic extends for miles in each direction. Skiing reigns supreme in winter; long summer days are filled with biking, hiking, kayaking, and fishing.

(**VITAL STATS**)

Population: 5300

Visitor Info: Chamber of Commerce/Visitors Center, (☎208-726-3423 or 800-634-3347; www.visitsunvalley.com), at 4th and Main St., in Ketchum. Open in peak season daily 9am-6pm; hours vary during spring and fall.

Internet Access: Community Library, 415 Spruce Ave. (☎208-726-3493). Open M and Sa 9am-6pm, Tu and Th noon-9pm, W 9am-9pm, F 1-6pm.

Post Office: 151 W. 4th St. (☎208-726-5161). Open M-F 8:30am-5:30pm, Sa 11am-2pm. **Postal Code:** 83340.

GETTING AROUND. Rte. 75 runs through the center of Ketchum under the clever guise of **Main St. Parking** is not difficult—there are plenty of spaces in front of businesses and along the streets downtown. If you plan to ski, there's free parking at **Dollar Mountain** and the River Run plaza side of **Bald Mountain.** On the Warm Springs side of Bald Mountain, parking is very limited, so park at the Presbyterian Church on Warm Springs Rd., and catch a **KART bus** from there. (☎208-726-7576. Runs daily 7:20am-midnight. Free.)

OUTDOOR ACTIVITIES. The **Wood River and Sun Valley trail system,** south of town, consists of over 20 mi. of paved paths. The trail begins in Bellevue and continues through Ketchum and Sun Valley, passing by ski slopes and historic sites. The *Wood River Trails* pamphlet, available at the Visitors Center, has more info. Visible for miles, **Bald Mountain,** or "Baldy," is a beacon for serious skiers. Two plazas serve Baldy, River Run on the north side of town and Warm Springs on the south side. Whereas mostly advanced skiers are on Bald Mountain, the gentle slopes of **Dollar Mountain** are perfect for beginners. (☎800-786-8259, ski conditions 800-635-4150. Lift ticket $59, under 12 $32.)

The **Sawtooth National Recreation Area** (**SNRA**; see p. 701) is renowned for its stunning mountain bike trails, which traverse the canyons and mountain passes of the SNRA. Beware: trails might be snowbound or flooded well into July. Take a high-speed quad chairlift to the top of Bald Mountain and ride down on a mountain bike during summer months. (☎208-622-2231. Open in summer daily 9am-3:45pm. $15 per ride, $20 per day.) Inquire about trail conditions and rent gear at **Formula Sports,**

460 N. Main St. (☎208-726-3194. Bikes from $12 per 4hr., $18 per day. Tandems $20/$30. Skis $18-40.) **The Elephant's Perch,** 280 East Ave., at Sun Valley Rd., has a complete stock of outdoor gear. (☎208-726-3497. Open daily 9am-6pm. Bikes $12 per 4hr., $20 per day. Backpacks $15 per day. Sleeping bags $25 per day. Tents $20 per day. Nordic and telemark ski packages $15-30 per day.)

Ketchum locals soak their weary legs in one of several **hot springs.** Melting snow and rain can bury the springs underwater, rendering them inaccessible in spring and early summer. The springs are safe for swimming once the current subsides in July. The Chamber of Commerce has suggestions on which pools are safe and accessible. One of the more accessible, non-commercial springs is **Warfield Hot Springs,** on Warm Springs Rd., 11 mi. west of Ketchum. A commercial alternative to these pools can be found at **Easley Hot Springs,** 12 mi. north of Ketchum on Rte. 75. (☎208-726-7522. Open Su noon-5pm, Tu and Th-Sa 11am-7pm, W 11am-5pm. $5.50, children $4.50, seniors $4.) For the best info on **fishing,** including equipment rentals, stop by **Silver Creek Outfitters,** 500 N. Main St. (☎208-726-5282. Open M-Sa 9am-6pm, Su noon-5pm. Rods, waders, and boots $15 per day.)

FOOD. Ketchum's small confines bulge with over 80 restaurants, but cheap eats beyond fast-food can be hard to find. **Lefty's Bar & Grill,** 231 6th St. East, at the corner of 6th St. and Washington, one block west of Main St., may be your best bet, where burgers ($4-6) and hoagies ($4-5) come at the right price. (☎208-726-2744. Open daily 11:30am-10:30pm.) The **Roosevelt Tavern & Grille,** in the Historic Slavery's Building at the corner of Main St. and Sun Valley Rd., offers all-day appetizers including quesadillas ($7), calamari ($8), and smoked chicken pizza ($9). (☎208-726-0051. Lunch $7-10. Dinner entrees $14-20. Open daily 11:30am-10pm. Lunch served 11:30am-5pm.) **Johnny G's Subshack,** 371 Main St., serves delicious subs (under $5) including the Club Tahiti and the Middle School Madness—a toasted stack of turkey, bacon, and cheddar. (☎208-725-7827. Open M-F 11am-4pm, Sa noon-3pm.)

ACCOMMODATIONS. From early June to mid-October, camping is the best option for cheap sleeps. Check with the **Ketchum Ranger**

Station, 206 Sun Valley Rd., just outside of Ketchum on the way to Sun Valley. (☎208-622-5371. Open daily 8:30am-noon and 1-5pm.) **Boundary Campground,** 3 mi. northeast of town on Trail Creek Rd. past the Sun Valley resort, is closest to town and has nine wooded sites near a creek, plus restrooms, water, and a picnic area. (Sites $11.) There are free primitive dispersed campsites farther along Trail Creek. Up Rte. 75 into the SNRA lie scenic camping spots; the cheapest ($10) are **Murdock** (11 sites) and **Caribou** (7 sites). They are, respectively, 2 and 3 mi. up the unpaved North Fork Rd., which begins as a paved road to the right of the Visitors Center. **North Fork** (29 sites; $11) and **Wood River** (30 sites) are 8 mi. north of Ketchum, along Rte. 75. For North Fork, take the first campground road north of SNRA headquarters; Wood River is 2 mi. farther north. Enjoy great views in town at the **Lift Tower Lodge,** 703 S. Main St. (☎208-726-5163 or 800-462-8646. Rooms $66-90.)

🌙 **NIGHTLIFE.** Beer cans grace the walls of **Grumpy's,** 860 Warm Springs Rd., a flavorful local hangout. (32oz. goblet of beer $3.25. PBR $1. Open daily 11am-10pm.) Head downstairs to the **Cellar Pub,** 400 Sun Valley Rd., near Leadville Ave., for a young crowd, excellent burgers and bangers, and inventive pints like the "straight jacket." (☎208-622-3832. Open daily 5pm-2am.) Sip stiff drinks for 100 pennies on Sunday and Tuesday at **Whiskey Jacques,** 251 Main St. (☎208-726-5297. Live music 9:30pm-2am. Cover $3-5. Open daily 4pm-2am.)

🏔 **LEAVING SUN VALLEY**
Though the 60 mi. of **Rte. 75** from Sun Valley to Stanley twist and turn, the only mistake you could make would be to drive off of the side of a mountain.

STANLEY

Named for Captain John Stanley, who led a team of 23 prospectors to the area in 1863, Stanley (pop. 69) still appeals to the explorer within. The brisk breeze that sails through its picturesque mountain peaks taunts visitors with whispers of the untamed wilderness beyond. There's something for everyone, and most of it centers on the **Sawtooth National Recreational Area** (**SNRA;** see p. 701). Topographical maps ($4) of the SNRA and trail books ($6-20) are available at **McCoy's Tackle and Gift Shop,** on Ace of Diamonds St. McCoy's also sells sporting goods, fishing tackle, and licenses. (☎208-774-3377. Open June-Sept. daily 8am-8pm; off-season hours vary.) **Sawtooth Adventure Rentals,** on Rte. 75 in Lower Stanley, rents kayaks and rafts. (☎866-774-4644. Open May-Sept. Kayaks $25-50. Rafts $75.) The cheapest way to enjoy area waters is to visit the **hot springs** just east of Stanley. **Sunbeam Hot Springs,** 10 mi. east of Lower Stanley on Rte. 75, triumphs over the rest, though high water can wash out the springs temporarily.

Before exploring the SNRA, stock up on food and gas, as well as fishing licenses, at **Jerry's Country Store and Motel,** on Rte. 75 in Lower Stanley. (☎208-774-3566 or 800-972-4627. Open M-Sa 8:30am-9pm, Su 9am-7pm.) Locals rave about the $5 deli sandwiches at **Papa Brunee's,** on Ace of Diamonds St., downtown. (☎208-774-2536. Pizza

---

THE SUN VALLEY ALSO RISES

THE LOCAL STORY

Ernest Hemingway's love affair with both rugged outdoor sports and wealthy celebrities fits Ketchum's dualistic spirit. After spending many vacations hunting and fishing in the Sawtooth Range, the author built a cabin in Sun Valley where he died from a self-inflicted gunshot wound on July 2, 1961. While Hemingway's house is off-limits, there are a number of sites in town that commemorate the author. His grave is located in the **Ketchum Cemetery,** just north of town on Rte. 75. The **Ketchum-Sun Valley Heritage and Ski Museum** displays exhibits on Hemingway's life. (180 1st St. East, at Washington Ave. ☎208-726-8118. Open M-F 11am-5pm, Sa 1-4pm. Times vary in winter.) A bust of Hemingway is tucked away in a shady spot along the river at the **Hemingway Memorial,** about 1 mi. outside of Sun Valley on the way to Boundary Campground (see Accommodations, above). Each year on Hemingway's birthday, July 21, the community library hosts a lecture (☎208-726-3493).

$4-20. Open daily 11am-10pm.) The local watering hole is the **Rod and Gun Club Bar,** on Ace of Diamonds St. This authentic western bar has pool tables, a dance floor, and live weekend music. (☎208-774-9920. 21+. Open daily 8pm-2am.) Stanley is a true gateway city, and its main lodging house caters to both the SNRA-adventure-seeker and the exhausted roadtripper. With its incredible location and comfy rooms, the ⊠**Mountain Village Resort,** just off Rte. 75, makes for an ideal getaway. Self-sufficient in nearly every way, the resort offers a restaurant, bar, grocery store, laundromat, and gas station on site. Suites come with kitchenettes and VCRs, and appointment-based use of the resort's hot springs is free. The lounge serves up sandwiches and burgers ($7-9) and classic hunting lodge fare. Enjoy a draft beer ($3-5) or stiff mixed drink ($4-6) beside the fire. The **Mountain Village Mercantile** sells groceries and hunting gear. (☎208-774-3661; www.mountainvillage.com. Laundry $1. Lounge kitchen open daily 6am-9pm. Store open daily 6am-8pm. Check-in 3pm. Check-out 11am. Doubles summer $80; winter $68. Suites with 2 bedrooms, kitchenette, and bath $121.) At **Danner's Log Cabin Motel,** on Rte. 21, ex-mayor and Stanley history buff Bunny Danner rents cabins built by goldminers in 1939. The office, built in 1906, was the first building in town and originally served as the ranger station. (☎208-774-3539. Cabins in summer $55-125; in spring and fall $42-80.)

SAWTOOTH NATIONAL RECREATION AREA

Established by Congress in 1972, the **Sawtooth National Recreation Area (SNRA)** sprawls over 756,000 acres of National Forest, including 217,000 untouched acres. The park is home to four mountain ranges with more than 40 peaks over 10,000 ft.; the Sawtooth and White Cloud Mountains tower above the landscape in the north, while the Smokey and Boulder Mountains dominate the southern horizon. Over 300 mountain lakes and the headwaters of four of Idaho's major rivers are interspersed through the forest.

◧ **GETTING AROUND.** The **Sawtooth Scenic Byway** (Rte. 75) spans 60 mi. of National Forest land between Ketchum and Stanley, crossing the Galena Pass at 8701 ft. Pause at the **Galena Overlook,** 31 mi. north of Ketchum, for a view of the park. There are **parking** lots at both the SNRA

(**VITAL STATS**)

Area: 756,000 acres.

Visitor Info: Stanley Ranger Station (☎208-774-3000). 3 mi. south of Stanley on Rte. 75. Offers maps, SNRA passes, and outdoor advice. Open in summer M-Sa 8am-4:30pm; off-season M-F 8:30am-4:30pm. **Redfish Lake Visitors Center** (☎208-774-3376). Offers educational programs on wildlife and geology. Open mid-June to early Sept. daily 9am-5pm; late May to mid-June Sa-Su 9am-5pm. **Sawtooth National Recreation Area (SNRA) Headquarters,** 6 mi. north of Ketchum off Rte. 75 (☎208-727-5013 or 800-260-5970). Stocks info on the hot springs, area forests, and trails. SNRA maps $6-7, trail guides $14-18. Open daily mid-June to Aug. 8am-5pm; off-season 9am-3:30pm.

Gateway Town: Stanley

Fees: No entrance fee.

Headquarters and the Stanley Ranger Station. From either location, you can purchase a parking pass that allows you to park in designated areas at trailheads. ($5 for 3 days; annual pass $15.)

⚡ **OUTDOOR ACTIVITIES.** The rugged backcountry of the SNRA is perfect for hiking, boating, fishing, and mountain biking. Pick up a map and inquire about trail conditions at SNRA Headquarters before heading into the park, particularly in early summer, when trails may be flooded (much of the backcountry stays buried in snow well into the summer). **Watch out for black bears;** ranger stations have info about necessary precautions.

Redfish Lake is the source of many trails. Some popular, leisurely hikes include those to **Fishhook Creek** (excellent for children), **Bench Lakes,** and the **Hell Roaring Trail.** The long, gentle loop around **Yellow Belly, Toxaway,** and **Petit Lakes** is a moderate overnight trip suitable for novices. Two miles northwest of Stanley on Rte. 21, the 3 mi. Iron Creek Rd. leads to the trailhead of the 5½ mi. **Sawtooth Lake Hike.** A steep 4 mi. hike to **Casino Lakes** begins at the Broadway Creek trailhead southeast of Stanley. For boat tours of the lake, head for **Redfish Lake Lodge Marina.** (☎208-774-3536. Open in summer daily 7am-8:30pm. 1hr. tours $8, ages 6-12 $5; $32 min. Paddleboats $5 per 30min. Canoes $10 per hr., $50 per day. Outboards $15/$50/$80.) Companies in **Stanley** rent the equipment necessary for outdoor adventuring—see p. 700.

NORTH AMERICAN

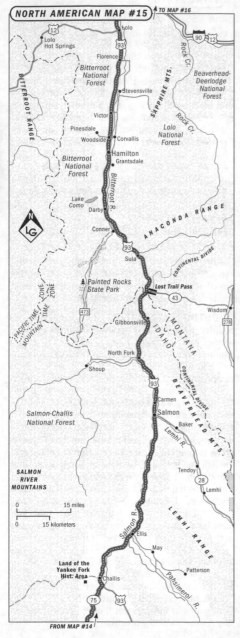

NORTH AMERICAN MAP #15 ↑ TO MAP #16

FROM MAP #14

The Sawtooths have miles of mountain bike trails, but check a map; riding is allowed in National Forest areas but prohibited in the Sawtooth Wilderness. **Riverwear,** on Rte. 21 in Stanley, rents bikes. (☎208-774-3592. Open daily 7am-10pm. Bikes from $17 per day.) The 18 mi. **Fischer/ Williams Creek Loop** is the most popular biking trail, ascending to an elevation of 8280 ft. Beginners will enjoy riding the dirt road that leads to the North Fork campgrounds from the Visitors Center. This gorgeous passage parallels the North Fork of the Wood River for 5 mi. before branching off into other narrower and steeper trails for more advanced riders. The steep **Boulder Basin Rd.,** 5 mi. from SNRA headquarters, leads to pristine Boulder Lake and an old mining camp.

CAMPING. The SNRA boasts 33 campgrounds throughout the park; consult a ranger for help selecting (and locating) a campsite. **Alturas Lake,** 21 mi. south of Stanley on Rte. 75 (the turnoff is marked about 10 mi. north of Galena Pass), has three campgrounds with fishing and swimming. (Vault toilets and water. 55 sites $11-13.) The area around **Redfish Lake,** 5 mi. south of Stanley off Rte. 75, is a scenic but sometimes overcrowded spot. The eight campgrounds are close to Stanley and many trailheads. (Sites $11-13.) East on Rte. 75, past the town of Stanley, sites are available along the wild **Salmon River.** (Water available; no hookups. Sites $11.) One of the best campgrounds is **Mormon Bend,** 8 mi. east of Stanley on Rte. 75, with 15 sites near whitewater rafting. Other inviting spots are **Casino Creek,** 8 mi. east of Stanley on Rte. 75; the **Salmon River Campground,** 9 mi. east of Stanley on Rte. 75; and **Upper and Lower O'Brien,** 2 mi. past Sunbeam Dam. In most areas, a trailhead pass, available at the Stanley Ranger Station, is required for parking.

LAND OF THE YANKEE FORK MUSEUM
Right off Rte. 75, between Stanley and Challis.
Founded in 1992, the Yankee Fork Museum is dedicated to the history of mining in the area. The collection includes a horse-hide coat, vintage gowns, a horse-drawn buggy, and a stamp mill. One large exhibit is dedicated to Sammy Holman, a Harvard-educated lawyer who wandered west after the death of his fiancée. The friendly volunteers who run the museum share their experiences in addition to the material on display. (☎208-838-2201. Open summer daily 8am-6pm; winter M-F 9am-5pm. Donations appreciated.)

APPROACHING CHALLIS

Just before Challis, **Rte. 75** intersects U.S. 93. Take **U.S. 93 North** to the intersection with **Main St.** in Challis.

CHALLIS. The tiny town of Challis was established in the late 19th century, and hasn't grown much since. Situated at the convergence of Rte. 75 and U.S. 93 to the east, **Main St.,** is home to most of the businesses in town. While there's not much to see in Challis, it does make a great rest stop for lunch. **Antonio's Pizza and Pasta,** at the corner of 5th and Main St., has an all-you-can-eat salad bar ($6), pasta dinners ($7-10), and delicious pizza. (☎ 208-879-2210. Pizza $4-18. Open M-Th 11am-9pm, F-Sa 11am-10pm, Su noon-9pm.) At the **Village Inn Motel,** off U.S. 93 on the way into town, log-style cabins come with TVs, phones, and kitchenettes. (☎ 208-879-2239; fax 879-2813. Singles $46; doubles with 1 bed $54, with 2 beds $65.)

SALMON. Farther north along U.S. 93, the ranching town of Salmon makes the perfect base for exploring the surrounding mountain area. Seventeen miles down Rte. 28 are the county's newly renovated **hot springs,** which are free and open to the public, with new pools, changing rooms, and bathrooms. Locals claim that Sacagawea was born in the area. For more information about outdoor activities, visit the **Visitors Center,** 200 Main St. (☎ 208-756-2100. Open M-F 10:30am-4pm.)

Stop at **Bertram's Brewery and Restaurant,** 101 S. Andrews St., to sip a homebrewed beer ($2-4) among the Tiffany-lamp adorned tables under a pink tiled ceiling. (☎ 208-756-3391. Burgers $6-8. Entrees $11-18. Open Su-Th 11am-9pm, F-Sa 11am-10pm.) An enormous fish welcomes you to **Salmon River Coffee Shop,** 608 Main St., established in 1961, where sandwiches go for $3-6 and specialty potatoes run $1-4. (☎ 208-756-3521. Entrees $8-11. Steaks $9-17. Open daily 5am-9pm.) The **Stagecoach Inn Motel,** 201 U.S. 93, has riverside views, a heated swimming pool, and complimentary continental breakfast. (☎ 208-756-2919. Summer singles $61; doubles $65. Winter rooms $54.)

NORTH FORK. While it may not have everything you need, it does have everything you're gonna get. A self-contained roadside cluster where motel registration is located inside the general store that doubles as the post office and is connected to the cafe, North Fork is the epitome of the roadtripper's rest stop. Don't plan to stop in North Fork on

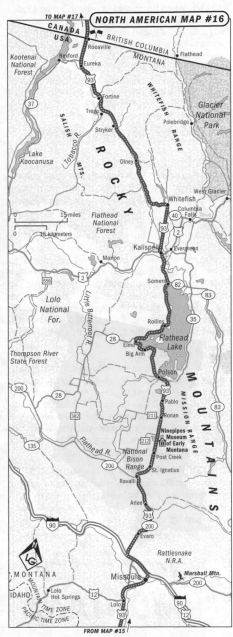

NORTH AMERICAN

Tuesday, when the town (i.e., the store and cafe) is closed. The **North Fork General Store** sells groceries, rents movies, and can fulfill your North Fork memorabilia needs. Motel registration happens at the counter. (☎208-865-2412. Open Su-M and W-Sa 7am-8pm. Singles $40; doubles $47.) With three separate menus for breakfast, lunch, and dinner, **The North Fork Cafe** offers surprising culinary variety. (☎208-865-2412. Breakfast $4-10. Entrees $6-15. Open Su-M and W-Sa 7am-8pm.)

LOST TRAIL HOT SPRINGS RESORT
8321 U.S. 93
Between North Fork and Hamilton on U.S. 93.

For over a century, the Gallogly hot springs have served wearied travelers, their journeys ranging from late 19th-century treks across the Continental Divide to present-day American roadtrips. With affordable, secluded cabins, private and shared hot spring baths, a hot spring-fed swimming pool, a jacuzzi and sauna, a convenience store, and a serene mountain setting, the resort leaves little to desire. The restaurant is adorned with a fire place and Christmas lights, which cast soft glows on the rustic hunting lodge decor. (☎800-825-3574. Burgers and sandwiches $3-8. Dinner entrees $10-19. Hours vary by season. Doubles $55; cabins with jacuzzi and kitchenette $95; tent sites $10.)

HAMILTON

From its origins as a timber town providing lumber to nearby mining operations, Hamilton has emerged as the heart of the surrounding Bitterroot Valley. With a collection of small boutique stores in the downtown area complementing the abundance of outdoor recreational activities available in the valley, Hamilton thrives as both a point of departure and a destination.

⌐ GETTING AROUND. In Hamilton, **U.S. 93** becomes **1st St.,** with numbered streets increasing as you move west. **Main St.** runs east-west and constitutes the downtown area. Businesses have ample **parking,** and street parking is not a problem.

VITAL STATS

Population: 4000

Visitor Info: Bitterroot Valley Chamber of Commerce, 105 E. Main St. (☎406-363-2400), behind the Safeway. Open M-F 8am-5pm.

Internet Access: Internet Coffee Station, 117 N. 4th St. (☎406-375-0290), across from the post office. $6 per hr. Open M-F 7:30am-5:30pm.

Post Office: 150 N. 4th St. (☎406-363-1445), in the downtown area. Open M-F 8:30am-5:30pm, Sa 10am-noon. **Postal Code:** 59840.

◪ SIGHTS. Within the municipal boundaries of Hamilton, a few 19th-century buildings enliven the small-town atmosphere. The **Daly Mansion** was built in the 1880s as the summer home of Marcus Daly, one of Montana's original Copper Barons. The sprawling Georgian Revival estate displays 25 bedrooms amidst the grounds that were once a part of Daly's 22,000 acre Bitterroot Stock Farm. (☎406-363-6004. Open Apr. 15-Oct. 15 daily 10am-4pm. $7.) **Ravalli County Museum,** 205 Bedford St., resides in the turn-of-the-century building formerly occupied by the Ravalli County Courthouse, displaying a variety of exhibits of local art, history, and culture. (☎406-363-3338. Open M and Th-Sa 10am-4pm, Su 1-4pm. $5). The surrounding valley offers outdoor activities from horseback riding to rafting to scenic flights; contact the Chamber of Commerce for more information.

◪⌂ FOOD & ACCOMMODATIONS. What dining in Hamilton lacks in variety, it makes up for in predictability. **BJ's Family Restaurant & Lounge,** 900 N. 1st St., is renowned throughout the Greater Hamilton area for homemade pizzas ($9-11) and lasagnas ($7). (☎406-363-4650. Open Su-Th 6:30am-10pm, F-Sa 6:30am-11pm.) For mouthwatering steaks and burgers, head to **Naps Grill,** 220 N. 2nd St., one block west of 1st St. (☎406-363-0136. Open M-Sa 11am-8pm.) **Coffee Cup,** 500 S. 1st St., has great homemade meals ($7-12) and delicious pies ($3) served amid a charming antique country decor. (☎406-363-3822. Open daily 6am-10pm.)

There are chain hotels and motels along **1st St.,** but smaller, privately owned operations are worth checking out if they have vacancies. **Bitterroot Motel,** 408 S. 1st St., has well-kept rooms at the lowest prices in town. (☎406-363-1142. Singles $36; doubles $43.) Nearby **Deffy's Motel,** 321 S. 1st

St., provides another alternative. (☎406-363-1142. Singles $37; doubles $48.) **Comfort Inn,** 1113 N. 1st St., has an on-site convenience store (open 24hr.) and casino (open 8am-2am), along with the usual amenities of upscale motels. (☎406-363-6600. Singles $57; doubles $59.)

APPROACHING MISSOULA

A few miles outside Missoula **U.S. 93** and **U.S. 12.** merge, only to split again when entering the city. Follow U.S. 12 as it becomes **Brooks St.,** then turns left onto **Higgins St.,** heading right into downtown.

MISSOULA

A liberal haven in a conservative state, Missoula attracts new residents with its revitalized downtown and bountiful outdoors opportunities. Home to the University of Montana, downtown Missoula is lined with bars and coffeehouses serving the large student population. Four different mountain ranges and five major rivers surround Missoula, supporting skiing during the winter and fly fishing, hiking, and biking during the summer.

(VITAL STATS)

Population: 57,000

Visitor Info: Missoula Chamber of Commerce, 825 E. Front St. (☎406-543-6623; www.explore-missoula.com). Open late May to early Sept. M-F 8am-7pm, Sa 10am-6pm; early Sept. to late May M-F 8am-5pm.

Internet Access: Missoula Public Library, 301 E. Main St. (☎406-721-2665). Open M-Th 10am-9pm, F-Sa 10am-6pm.

Post Office: 200 E. Broadway St. (☎406-329-2222. Open M-F 8am-5:30pm.) **Postal Code:** 59801.

GETTING AROUND

U.S. 93 takes the form of **Reserve St.,** running north thought the western part of town. Downtown Missoula lies north of the Clark Fork River, around the intersection of **N. Higgins Ave.,** and **Broadway St.** (Bus. I-90/Rte. 10). The University of Montana (UM) lies southeast of downtown, accessible by heading south on **Madison St.** from Broadway St. Businesses outside of downtown have **parking** lots, and meters are readily available in the downtown area during business hours.

SIGHTS & ENTERTAINMENT

Missoula's hottest sight is the **Smokejumper Center,** 5765 Rte. 10., the nation's largest training base for smokejumpers, aerial firefighters who parachute into flaming, remote forests. (Just past the airport, 7 mi. northwest of town on Broadway St. ☎406-329-4934. Open daily 8:30am-5pm. Tours May-Sept. every hr. 10-11am and 2-4pm. Free.) The **Carousel,** in Caras Riverfront Park, is a beautiful example of a hand-carved carousel. (☎406-549-8382. Open daily June-Aug. 11am-7pm; Sept.-May 11am-5:30pm. $1, seniors and under 19 $0.50.) **Out to Lunch,** also in Caras Riverfront Park, offers free performances in the summer; call the Missoula Downtown Association for more info. (☎406-406-543-4238. W 11am-1:30pm.)

Pick up the *Missoula Gallery Guide* brochure at the tourist office for a self-guided tour of Missoula's art galleries. Among them, the **Dana Gallery** at 123 W. Broadway St. (☎406-721-3154; open M-F 10am-6pm, Sa 10am-4pm), the **Gallery Saintonage,** at 216 N. Higgins Ave. (☎406-543-0171; open Tu-F 10am-5:30pm, Sa 10am-4pm), and the **Montana Museum of Art & Culture** on the UM campus (☎406-243-2019; open Tu-Th and Sa 11am-3pm, F 3-7pm) are particularly noteworthy. The **Historical Museum at Fort Missoula,** in Building 322 at Fort Missoula, on South Ave. one block west of Reserve St., displays 22,000 artifacts covering the history Missoula County. (☎406-728-3476; www.montana.com/ftmslamuseum. Open Su and Tu-Sa summer 10am-5pm; winter noon-5pm.)

The **Western Montana Fair and Rodeo,** held at the beginning of August, has live music, a carnival, fireworks, and concession booths. (☎406-721-3247. Open daily 10am-10pm.) You can soak your weary feet at **Lolo Hot Springs,** 35 mi. southwest of Missoula on Hwy. 12. The 103-105°F springs were an ancient meeting place for local Native Americans and were frequented by Lewis and Clark in 1806. (☎406-273-2290. $6, under 13 $4.)

OUTDOOR ACTIVITIES

Nearby parks, recreation areas, and surrounding wilderness areas make Missoula an outdoor enthusiast's dream. Bicycle-friendly Missoula is located along both the Trans-America and the Great Parks bicycle routes, and all major streets have designated bike lanes. **Open Road Bicycles and Nordic Equipment,** 517 S. Orange St., has bike rentals. (☎406-549-2453. $3.50 per hr., $17.50 per day. Open M-F 9am-6pm, Sa 10am-5pm, Su 11am-3pm.) The national **Adventure Cycling,** 150 E. Pine St., is the place to go for info about local trails, including the Trans-America and Great Parks routes. (☎406-721-1776 or 800-755-2453. Open M-F 8am-5pm.) The **Rattlesnake Wilderness National Recreation Area** (see below) and the **Pattee Canyon Recreation Area,** 3½ mi. east of Higgins on Pattee Canyon Dr., are highly recommended for their biking trails.

Skiing keeps Missoulians busy during winter. **Pattee Canyon** has groomed trails conveniently close to town, and **Marshall Mountain** is a great place to learn how to downhill ski, with night skiing and free shuttles from downtown. (☎406-258-6000. $19 per day.) Experienced skiers should check out the **Montana Snowbowl,** 12 mi. northwest of Missoula, with a vertical drop of 2600 ft. (☎406-549-9777 or 800-728-2695. Open Nov.-Apr. daily 9:30am-4pm. Lift pass $29, children $13.)

The Blackfoot River, along Rte. 200 east of Bonner, is a great place to tube or raft on a hot day. Call the **Montana State Regional Parks and Wildlife Office,** 3201 Spurgin Rd., for information about rafting locations. (☎406-542-5500. Open M-F 8am-5pm.) Rent tubes or rafts from the **Army and Navy Economy Store,** 322 N. Higgins Ave. (☎406-721-1315. Tubes $3 per day. Rafts $40 per day; $20 deposit; credit card required. Open M-F 9am-7:30pm, Sa 9am-5:30pm, Su 10am-5:30pm.) **Hiking** opportunities also abound in the Missoula area. The relatively easy 30min. hike to the "M" (for the U of M, not Missoula) on Mount Sentinel, has a tremendous view of Missoula and the mountains.

The **Rattlesnake Wilderness National Recreation Area,** named after the shape of the river (there are no rattlers for miles), is 11 mi. northeast of town, off the Van Buren St. exit from I-90, and makes for a great day of hiking. Other popular areas include **Pattee Canyon** and **Blue Mountain,** south of town. Maps ($6) and information on longer hikes in the Bitterroot and Bob Marshall areas are available at the **US Forest Service Information Office,** 200 E. Broadway; the entrance is at 200 Pine St. (☎406-329-3511. Open M-F 7:30am-4pm.) For equipment rentals, stop by **Trailhead,** 110 E. Pine St., at Higgins Ave. (☎406-543-6966. Tents M-F $10, Sa-Su $18. Backpacks $9. Sleeping bags $5. Open M-F 9:30am-8pm, Sa 9am-6pm, Su 11am-6pm.)

Western Montana is **fly-fishing** country, and Missoula is at the heart of it. Licenses are required and can be purchased from the **Department of Fish, Wildlife, and Parks,** 3201 Spurgin Rd. (☎406-542-5500), or from sporting goods stores. **Kingfisher,** 926 E. Broadway St., offers licenses ($22-67) and pricey guided trips. (☎406-721-6141. Open daily summer 7am-8pm; off-season 9am-5pm.)

🍴 FOOD

Missoula, the culinary capital of Montana, boasts a number of innovative, delicious, and thrifty eating establishments. Head downtown, north of the Clark Fork River along **Higgins Ave.,** and check out the array of restaurants and coffeehouses that line the road. Walk through the gift shop pharmacy to reach ✎**Butterfly Herbs,** 232 N. Higgins Ave., where the classic hummus sandwich ($4), chai milkshake ($3), and organic green salad ($2.50) are exciting alternatives to normal diner fare. (☎406-728-8780. Open M-F 7am-6pm, Sa 9am-5:30pm, Su 9am-5pm.) **Worden's,** 451 N. Higgins Ave., is a popular local deli, serving a wide variety of world-class sandwiches in three sizes: 4 in. roll ($4.25), 7 in. ($5.75), and 14 in. ($10.75). You can also pick up groceries while munching. (☎406-549-1293. Open summer M-Th 8am-10pm, F-Sa 8am-11pm, Su 9am-10pm; winter M-Th 8am-9pm, F-Sa 8am-10pm, Su 9am-10pm.) **Eat to Live,** 1916 Brooks St., prides itself on serving healthy, low-fat meals reminiscent of Mom's home cooking. (☎406-721-2510. Open M-F 11:30am-3pm.) **Tipu's,** 115½ S. 4th St. West, functions as one of the only all-veggie establishments and the lone Indian restaurant in Montana. (☎406-542-0622. Lunch buffet $7. Open daily 11:30am-9:30pm.) At **Tacos del Sol,** 422 N. Higgins Ave., get a Mission Burrito for under $4. (☎406-327-8929. Open M-F 11am-7pm.)

🏠 ACCOMMODATIONS

There are no hostels in Missoula, but there are plenty of inexpensive alternatives along Broadway. Rooms at the **City Center Motel,** 338 E. Broadway, have cable TV, fridges, and microwaves. (☎406-543-3193. Jan.-Aug. singles $45; doubles $48-52. Sept.-Dec. singles $35; doubles $42.) To reach the **Aspen Motel,** 3720 Rte. 200 East, in East Missoula, take I-90 East to Exit 107 and travel a half-mile east. (☎406-721-9758. Singles $40; doubles with 1 bed $46, with 2 beds $57.) The **Mis-**

soula/El-Mar KOA Kampground, 3450 Tina Ave., just south of Broadway St. off Reserve St., is one of the best KOAs around, providing shaded tent sites away from RVs. (☎406-549-0881 or 800-562-5366. Pool, hot tub, mini-golf courses, and 24hr. laundry facilities. Sites for 2 $21, with water and electricity $25, full hookup $31. Cabins $38-43; each additional person $3.)

⚑ NIGHTLIFE

The *Independent* and *Lively Times*, available at newsstands and cafes, offer the lowdown on the Missoula music scene, while the *Entertainer*, in the Friday *Missoulian*, has movie and event schedules. College students swarm downtown bars around **Front St.** and **Higgins Ave.** during the school year. **Charlie B's,** 420 N. Higgins Ave., draws an eclectic crowd of bikers, farmers, students, and hippies. Framed photos of longtime regulars line the walls; park at the bar for 10 or 20 years in order to join them. Hungry boozers can weave their way to the **Dinosaur Cafe** at the back of the room for Creole culinary delights. (☎406-549-3589. Open daily 8am-2am.) The popular **Iron Horse Brew Pub,** 501 N. Higgins Ave., always packs a crowd. The large patio fills up during the summer months. (☎406-728-8866. Open daily 11am-2am.) Follow the advice of the "beer coaches" at **The Kettle House Brewing Co.,** 602 Myrtle, one block west of Higgins between 4th and 5th St., and "support your local brewery." The Kettle House serves a delectable assortment of beers, including their aptly named hemp beer: Bongwater Stout. (2 free samples; then $2.75 per pint. Open M-Th 3-9pm, F-Sa noon-9pm; no beer served after 8pm.)

⚑ LEAVING MISSOULA

Take Broadway St. north to its intersection with **U.S. 93 North,** and head out of town and into the quiet mountain country of Western Montana.

⚑ NATIONAL BISON RANGE

In Ravalli, take Rte. 200 West. Following the signs, take a right onto Rte. 212 after 5 mi.; the entrance to the park is 5 mi. north, on your right.

The National Bison Range was established in 1908 in an effort to save the dwindling number of bison from extinction. At one time 30-70 million roamed the plains, but after years of hunting the population dropped to less than 1000. The range is home to 350-500 buffalo as well as deer, prong-horn, elk, bighorn sheep, and mountain goats. The 2hr. **Red Sleep Mountain** self-guided tour offers a spectacular view of the Flathead Valley and the best chance for wildlife observation. (☎406-644-2211. Visitors Center open mid-May to Oct. daily 8am-6pm; Nov. to mid-May M-F 8am-4:30pm. Red Sleep Mountain drive open mid-May to mid-Oct. daily 7am-dusk. $4 per vehicle.)

ST. IGNATIUS

Named for the Jesuit Mission for which it is best known, St. Ignatius sits just east of U.S. 93 at the foot of the Mission Mountains on the Flathead Indian Reservation. While there's not much to experience in town, **St. Ignatius Catholic Mission,** the large brick building just off the highway, is worth a look. Built in 1891, the mission features 58 beautiful frescoes and murals painted by the mission cook, Brother Carignano, that look as though they could have been taken from the walls of European cathedrals. (Open daily 9am-8pm. Donations optional.) Across the highway from town, Colonel Doug Allard's mini-empire constitutes most of the services offered in St. Iggy's, starting with **Col. Doug Allard's Indian Museum and Trading Post,** which houses traditional native clothing and artifacts, as well as a small display of stuffed things you can shoot (deer, bear, and wolf) and their equally shot offspring. Perhaps most impressive, however, is the World Champion Stick Game Tournament Trophy, replete with actual sticks, that Col. Allard himself has awarded to such stick game luminaries as Chauncey Beaverhead (1st place, 1996), and the inimitable team including Chuck and Sarah Twoteeth and Dude Smith (3rd place, 1995). This is true. (☎406-745-2951. Open daily 9am-5pm. Free.)

The best restaurant around is none other than **Col. Doug Allard's Original Buffalo Ranch Cafe,** in the large log building with the stuffed white buffalo in the display case over the entrance. Here you can ponder the history and struggle of the Flathead Indian Reservation buffalo herd, the last naturally wild herd in the world, while digging into a delicious Montana Buffalo Hump Roast ($14), BBQ Buffalo Sandwich ($7), or Buffalo Stew. (☎406-745-5100. Open daily 6:30am-9pm.) For a quick bite, locals head to **The Malt Shop,** 101 1st. St., where a regionally delightful huckleberry milkshake ($3) washes down burgers and dogs ($1-5) or tasty sandwiches. (☎406-745-3501. Open M-Sa 10:30am-10pm, Su 11:30am-9pm.)

NINEPIPES MUSEUM OF EARLY MONTANA 40962 U.S. 93
Directly on U.S. 93 in Charlo, MT. Look for the large log cabin-style buildings.
Chronicling the history and traditions of the nearby Ninepipes Refuge and the surrounding area, the museum displays photographs and artifacts of Native Americans, trappers, miners, loggers and frontiersfolk and the lives they led in the settling of Montana. Fine Native American beadwork and dioramas depicting Old West life make this roadside attraction worth a peek. (☎406-644-3435. Open Su and W-Sa 11am-5pm. $4.) Adjacent **Ninepipes Lodge and Restaurant** offers lodging and fine dining for those weary from the road. (☎406-644-2588. Restaurant open Su-Th 9am-9pm, F-Sa 9am-10pm. Singles $72; doubles $78.)

POLSON & FLATHEAD LAKE

An hour south of Kalispell, on the southern side of Flathead Lake, Polson has a small town's share of outdoor activities and art, but the real reason to stop here is the amazing ■**Miracle of America Museum,** 58176 U.S. 93. With displays of old posters, uniforms, motorcycles, and weapons, the museum is the life's work of proprietor Gil Mangels. A recreated general store, saddlery shop, barber shop, soda fountain, and gas station sit among such oddities as an 1898 sheep-powered treadmill, an automated toboggan, and the largest buffalo ever killed in Montana. The museum celebrates **Live History Day** the third weekend in July. (☎406-883-6804. Open June-Sept. daily 8am-8pm; Oct.-May M-Sa 8am-5pm, Su 2-6pm. $4, ages 3-12 $1.) Fresh fruit stands line **Flathead Lake,** the largest natural lake west of the Mississippi. Renowned for fresh cherries and fresher fish, the lake is on U.S. 93 between Polson and Kalispell. Polson has some of best Class II and Class III rafting around, and the **Flathead Raft Co.,** 1501 U.S. 93, helps prepare you for the experience. The famous Buffalo Rapids of the Lower Flathead River are especially good at folding your raft in half and tossing your shipmates overboard. (☎406-883-5838 or 800-654-4359; www.flatheadraftco.com. $40, seniors $36, ages 8-12 $32.) A local secret, **Blacktail Mountain Ski Resort** (☎406-844-0999; www.blacktailmountain.com), in Lakeside, is one of the newest ski areas in the country, built for affordable family skiing. The lone ski lodge is a welcome break

IN THE PASSENGER SEAT

AMERICAN MIRACLES

Gil Mangels is the founder of the Miracle of America Museum in Polson, MT.

LG: You have quite an impressive collection here. What's your favorite piece?
A: That's going to be a tough choice. Motorcycles have been a strong hobby of mine for years. We have over 40 antique and vintage motorcycles here on display. The bear carving in the lobby by John Clarke has got to be a favorite; he was a deaf mute who overcame a handicap to make beautiful art. We hope that everybody who comes into the museum can take something away from that.
LG: Where do you find this stuff?
A: Well, the military vehicles we get from the government; our non-profit status has made us eligible to receive helicopters and planes. Since 9/11 things have tightened up, but we've always followed the letter of the law and they trust us. Some people read about us and will send us things. I'm a machinist by trade, and sometimes I'll trade machine work for artifacts. We don't have much money to spend on acquiring new pieces, but we save what we can to use for the museum. A while ago I was told that I needed a root canal that would cost around $900 or so. I waited as long as I could, then I finally had the tooth pulled for $100. The way I figured, "So I have fewer teeth to chew with, I've got $800 to buy things." I got these three-wheeled roller skates today. Did you see the spring shoes? I thought they'd go great with them...
LG: And indeed they do.

from the crowded ski resorts that so many tourists make their destination—you won't find any lift lines here.

M&S Meats, 86755 U.S. 93 (☎406-844-3414 or 800-454-3414; www.shopworks.com/msmeats), is definitely worth a stop for some of the best jerky you'll ever taste ($18 per pound and nothing like that gas station junk). Jerky and sausage come in beef or buffalo. For the most part, lodging on the lake is expensive. **Edgewater Motel,** 7140 U.S. 93, in Lakeside, has affordable rooms available as apartments or with kitchenettes and lake frontage with docks. (☎406-844-3644 or 800-424-3798. Open in summer. Singles from $60.) If you need another day to take in the overwhelming collection, **Cherry Hill Motel,** 1810 U.S. 93, offers clean and comfortable accommodations just north of the museum. (☎406-883-2737. Singles $60; doubles $76.)

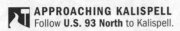

APPROACHING KALISPELL
Follow **U.S. 93 North** to Kalispell.

KALISPELL

Nestled between the ski-haven Big Mountain and gorgeous Flathead Lake, Kalispell mixes rampant outdoorsmanship with the art and culture of the largest urban center of northwestern Montana. While it may not take long to get a feel for the town, Kalispell is a gateway to the endless wilderness adventures of the Montana countryside.

VITAL STATS

Population: 15,000

Visitor Info: Chamber of Commerce, 15 Depot Park (☎406-758-2800), in Depot Park, on Main St. at Center St. Open M-F 8am-5pm.

Internet Access: Flathead County Library, 247 1st Ave. East (☎406-758-5819), 1 block off of Main St. (U.S. 93). Open M-Th 10am-8pm, F 10am-5pm, Sa 11am-5pm.

Post Office: 350 N. Meridian Rd. (☎406-755-6450), right off of U.S. 2, at 3rd St. Open M-F 9am-5pm, Sa 9am-2pm. **Postal Code:** 59904.

GETTING AROUND. Kalispell is laid out in a neat grid centered on the intersection of **Main St. (U.S. 93)** and **Idaho St. (Rte. 2)**, the older highway around which the towns businesses first developed. Numbered avenues flank Main St., increasing in number as they move out in both directions, with East and West designating their orientation. Numbered streets count southward from **Center St.,** while streets north of Center bear State names. **Street parking** is free, but limited to 2hr.

SIGHTS. Kalispell is not so much about seeing as experiencing, though a couple of decent museums and a variety of small stores and galleries give the downtown area around Main St. more character than most towns of this size. **The Hockaday Museum of Art,** 302 2nd Ave. East, two blocks east of Main St. at 3rd St., houses a permanent collection of art inspired by and related to Glacier National Park, along with rotating exhibits of nationally renowned and emerging artists. (☎406-755-5268. Open M-Sa 10am-6pm, Su noon-4pm. $5.) The **Conrad Mansion National Historic Site Museum,** six blocks east of Main St. on 4th St. East, shows 26 furnished rooms in original 1895 condition, along with gardens and a Victorian gift shop. (☎406-755-2166; www.conradmansion.com. Open daily 10am-5pm. $8.) **The M,** 124 2nd Ave. East, two blocks off of Main St. on 1st St., displays exhibits on the history and culture of northwestern Montana. (☎406-756-8381; www.yourmuseum.org. Open Tu-Sa 10am-5pm. $6.)

FOOD. A variety of chain restaurants line U.S. 93 and U.S. 2, but a few local eateries provide a moment of escape from corporate delight. **Bojangles Diner,** 1319 U.S. 2 West, is a 50s-style throwback replete with a jukebox and trains. (☎406-755-3222. Breakfasts $3-10. Burgers and sandwiches $5-6. Dinners $7-11. Open daily 6am-8pm.) **D.G. Barley's Brewhouse & Grill,** 285 N. Main St., at the junction of U.S. 93 and U.S. 2, serves up Southwestern fare worthy of any cowgirl in a kitsch, glam-ranch atmosphere. (☎406-756-2222. Steaks $13-17. Salads $7-9. Burgers $7-9. Open Su-Th 11am-10pm, F-Sa 11am-11pm.) **Avalanche Creek Restaurant & Coffeehouse,** 38 1st Ave. East, serves some of the valley's finest soups ($3-5), salads ($4-6), and sandwiches ($4-6) in a dining room adorned with the work of local artists. (☎406-257-0785. Open M-F 7am-5pm, Sa 9am-5pm.)

ACCOMMODATIONS. Chain motels, like **Motel 6** and **Super 8** dot the sides of Main St. (U.S. 93) on the south side of town, just past the courthouse. Older endeavors crop up along **Idaho St.** (U.S. 2), heading east. For those willing to splurge, ■**Kalispell Grand Hotel,** 100 Main St., at 1st St., has provided the finest "frontier hotels" have to offer since 1912, with vintage architecture and ambience blending with high-speed Internet and jetted bathtubs. (☎800-858-7422; www.kalispellgrand.com. Singles $76-125; doubles $83-125.) **Blue & White Motel,** 640 E. Idaho St., 6 blocks east of Main St., spruces up the motel experience with an indoor swimming pool, sauna, and jacuzzi available year-round. (☎800-382-3577. Singles $62; doubles $78.)

LEAVING KALISPELL
Head north on **Main St. (U.S. 93)** for the 20min. ride to Whitefish. U.S. 93 enters Whitefish as **Spokane Ave.** At **2nd St.** it takes a left and crosses the Whitefish River.

WHITEFISH

Originally known as "Stumptown" for the seemingly endless fields of felled trees that once covered the landscape of this logging town, Whitefish has today emerged as a beautiful, resort-esque small town.

VITAL STATS

Population: 5500

Visitor Info: Chamber of Commerce/Visitors Center, 520 E. 2nd St. (☎406-862-3501; www.whitefishchamber.org). Open M-F 9am-5pm.

Internet Access: Montana Coffee Traders, 5810 U.S. 93 (☎406-862-7633; www.coffeetraders.com). Free Internet (20min. max.) and a variety of coffee blends. Open M-Th and Sa 7am-6pm, F 7am-10:30pm, Su 9am-5pm.

Post Office: 424 Baker Ave. Open M-F 9am-5pm, Sa 11am-2pm. **Postal Code:** 59937.

 GETTING AROUND. Numbered streets run east-west through town, increasing south. **Central Ave.** runs parallel to Spokane Ave. one block to the west, constituting the downtown area. Street **parking** is free and readily available.

 SIGHTS. The best way to experience Whitefish is to stroll the downtown area and explore the variety of small shops and boutiques. **The Whitefish Museum,** 500 Depot St., inside the train depot, presents fascinating railroad and community artifacts

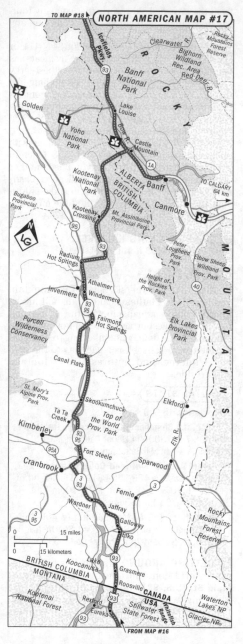

and information, along with the gem of Great Northern Railway Locomotive 181 restored to its 1950s condition. (☎406-862-0067. Open M-Sa 11am-6pm. Free.) **Big Mountain Resort** (☎406-862-2900), north of town via Wisconsin Ave., offers a variety of outdoor activities, from hiking and biking to skiing or rafting.

FOOD & ACCOMMODATIONS. A stroll around downtown Whitefish reveals a variety of great restaurant choices. At **The Wrap & Roll Cafe,** 224 Spokane Ave., try a Thai peanut veggie wrap ($6) or the Fatty Supreme ($5), a burrito stuffed with beans, rice, cheese, salsa, and sour cream. (☎406-862-7447. Open M-Sa 11am-9pm.) The **Moon Thyme Cafe,** 235 Baker Ave., serves buffalo burgers ($5-8), veggie burgers ($7), and tuna salad ($6), in addition to daily specials such as grilled salmon sandwiches. (☎406-863-9061. Open daily 11:30am-3:30pm.) The outdoor section at **Truby's Wood Fired Pizza,** 115 Central Ave., provides the perfect spot to people-watch while enjoying a Ragin' Cajun, Thai, or Fungus Among Us pizza. (☎406-862-4979. Pizza $6-18. Open M-Th 11am-10pm, F-Sa 11am-midnight, Su 4-10pm.)

The **Downtowner Motel,** 224 Spokane Ave., has a workout room (daypass $5), tanning salon, sauna, and outdoor jacuzzi. (☎406-862-2535 or 888-325-2535; www.downtownermotel.cc. Bunks $20. Summer singles $48; doubles $52. Winter $65/$72.) **The Garden Wall Inn Bed & Breakfast,** 504 Spokane Ave., is run by a pair of gourmet chefs who know how to treat their guests right, with beautiful baths and delicious breakfasts prepared each morning. (☎406-862-3440 or 888-530-1700; www.gardenwallinn.com. Singles $115-145; doubles $135.) **Chalet Motel,** 6430 U.S. 93, has great rates, clean rooms, and a 24hr. on-site restaurant. (☎406-862-5581 or 800-543-8064; www.whitefishlodging.com. Singles $82; doubles $87.)

DETOUR: GOING-TO-THE-SUN ROAD
The road begins in West Glacier, 30 mi. east of Whitefish. Take U.S. 93 South to Rte. 40 East to U.S. 2 East.

One of the most spectacular scenic drives in the US, the 52 mi. **Going-to-the-Sun Road** climbs 3000 ft. through cedar forests, mountain passes, and arctic tundra as it crosses Glacier National Park (see p. 265). The views from opposite sides of the road are very different, so driving back along the route to West Glacier is anything but boring. (3-6hr. round-trip from West Glacier. Closed in winter. $10 per car.)

EUREKA

In 1904, the Great Northern Railroad was rerouted through the Tobacco Plains, and the settler influx that followed spawned the small town of Eureka. While the Kutenai Indians were the original inhabitants of the valley, the real cowboy and Indian squabbles occurred much later during Prohibition, when bootleggers and "the dry squad" fought for control of the alcohol flowing across the Canadian border. After a fire and a series of dry seasons in the 1920s, the lumberjacks and minters skipped town, leaving Eureka to grow into the quaint settlement of today. U.S. 93 turns into Dewey Avenue, which hosts the downtown area. South of 1st St., Dewey Ave. runs into the **Riverside Park.** The park contains the town's **Historical Village,** replete with log cabins, a train caboose, wagons, a pioneer church, and an old school.

The creative entrees at **Cafe Jax,** 207 Dewey Ave., are as enticing as the town's history, which is chronicled on the back page of the menu. (☎406-297-9084. Mexican entrees $7-8. Chicken salad $7. Open M-Sa 7am-3pm, Su 8am-4pm.) Experience the small-town charm of specialty burgers, pizza, and gyros without leaving your car at **Big E's Drive-In,** 1210 U.S. 93 North. (☎406-297-3249. Open daily 7am-9pm.) **Montana Chilly Willies,** 204 Dewey Ave., serves homemade soups and salads but is best known for its gigantic single-scoop cones ($2). Try the huckleberry or Moose Tracks ice cream. (☎406-297-2896. Open M-F 7:30am-6pm, Su 10am-4pm.) The **Creek Side Motel and RV Park,** 1333 U.S. 93 North, on the right as you drive into town, has comfortable rooms with kitchens and cable TV available, 12 RV hookups, and 25 sites with shower and laundry facilities. (☎406-297-2361. Singles $43; doubles $49. Camping and RV rates vary by season.)

LEAVING THE US
U.S. 93 crosses quietly into Canada just north of Roosville, MT. See **Vital Documents** (p. 11) for information on passport, visa, and identification requirements. The **border crossing** is open 24hr.

CANADA AND ALASKA: KOOTENAY TO ANCHORAGE

Welcome To
BRITISH COLUMBIA

KOOTENAY NATIONAL PARK

Kootenay National Park hangs off the Continental Divide on the southeast edge of British Columbia, bordering Alberta. Most roadtrippers travel through Kootenay to Banff National Park on the majestic Banff-Windermere Hwy. (Hwy. 93). Kootenay's biggest attraction is its lack of visitors; unlike Banff and Jasper, Kootenay has not been developed at all. The only civilization is found at the Radium Hot Springs, on the park's western border. The park's stately conifers, alpine meadows, and pristine peaks hide in Banff's shadow, allowing travelers to experience the true solitude of the Canadian Rockies.

⌷ GETTING AROUND

Kootenay lies southwest of Banff and Yoho National Parks. **Hwy. 93** runs through the park from the **Trans-Canada Hwy.** in Banff to **Radium Hot Springs** at the southwest edge of the park, where it joins **Hwy. 95.** The 95km **Banff-Windermere Highway (Hwy. 93)** forms the sinuous backbone of Kootenay. Stretching from Radium Hot Springs to Banff, the highway follows the Kootenay and Vermilion Rivers, passing glacier-enclosed peaks, dense stands of virgin forest, and green, glacier-fed rivers. The wild landscape of the Kootenay

Valley remains unblemished but for the ribbon of road. **Parking** is readily available in Radium, and at overlooks and trailheads throughout the park.

(VITAL STATS)

Area: 350,000 acres

Visitor Info: Park Information Center and **Tourism BC Info Centre,** 7556 Main St. West (Parks Canada ☎ 250-347-9505, Tourism BC 250-347-9331), in Radium. Open daily July-Aug. 9am-7pm; Sept.-June 9am-4pm. **Kootenay Park Lodge** (☎ 403-762-9196), 63km north of Radium. Open July-Aug. daily 9am-8pm; June and early Sept. reduced hours. **Park Administration Office** (☎ 250-347-9615), on the access road to Redstreak Campground. Open in winter M-F 8am-noon and 1-4pm. In an **emergency,** call the **Banff Park Warden** (☎ 403-762-4506).

Gateway Towns: Radium, Banff

Fees: No entrance fee.

👁 SIGHTS

The park's main attraction is **Radium Hot Springs,** named after the radioactive element detected there in trace quantities. The crowded complex is responsible for the traffic and towel-toting tourists just inside the West Gate. Natural mineral waters fill two swimming pools—a hot one for soaking at 40°C (104°F; open 9am-11pm) and a cooler one for swimming at 27°C (80°F; open noon-9pm). The hot pool is wheelchair accessible. (☎ 250-347-9485. In summer $6.25, children and seniors $5.25; in winter $5.25/$4.75, group and family rates available. Lockers $0.25. Towel rental $1.25. Swimsuit rental $1.50.) The **Lussier Hot Springs,** in Whiteswan Lake, Provincial Park offer a more natural alternative to Radium's lifeguards and ice-cream vendors. The springs flow directly from the bank into the Lussier River, and rock walls form shallow pools that trap the water at varying temperatures. To find this diamond in the rough, turn onto the rough dirt logging road 66km south of Radium and follow it for 17km.

🏔 HIKING

One of the hot springs' most astounding and therapeutic powers is their ability to suck travelers out of the woods, leaving Kootenay's many longer hiking trails uncrowded. The **Rockwall Trail** in the north of the park is the most popular backcountry area in Kootenay. All **backcountry** campers must stop at a Visitors Center for the hiking guide, which has maps, trail descriptions, and topographical profiles, and sells a mandatory **wilderness pass** ($6 per person per night, $38 per year). A number of shorter trails lead right off Hwy. 93 about 15km from the Banff border.

Marble Canyon Trail (750m, 15min.). Many tourists enjoy this short path, which traverses a deep limestone gorge cut by Tokumm Creek before ending at a roaring waterfall.

Paint Pots Trail (1.6km, 30min.), 3.2km south of Marble Canyon on U.S. 93. This trail leads to springs rich in iron oxide. Tourist-heavy.

Stanley Glacier Trail (5.5km, 4hr.). Starts 3.5km from the Banff entrance and leads into a glacier-gouged valley, ending 1.6km from the foot of Stanley Glacier. This moderately difficult trail is considered the "best day hike in the park."

Kindersley Pass (16.5km). The 2 trailheads at either end of the route, Sinclair Creek and Kindersley Pass, are less than 1km apart on Hwy. 93, about 10km inside the West Gate entrance. The strenuous trail climbs more than 1000m to views of the Columbia River Valley in the west and the crest of the Rockies in the east.

⚡ FOOD

There is little affordable food in Kootenay, with the exception of a basic staples at **Kootenay Park Lodge.** Radium supports some inexpensive eateries on Main St. The best selection of groceries in town is at **Mountainside Market,** 7546 Main St. East, right next to the Park Information Center. (☎250-347-9600. Open M-Sa 9am-9pm, Su 9am-8pm.)

🛏 ACCOMMODATIONS

The **Misty River Lodge (HI),** 5036 Hwy. 93, is the first left after you exit the park's West Gate. It offers bike rentals for $10 per day. (☎250-347-9912. Dorms $17, nonmembers $22; private rooms with bath $42/$65.) There's also a **B&B** upstairs. (Rooms $69-79. 10% HI discount.) Downtown, Radium features over 30 other motels, with high-season doubles from $45. The **Gateway Motel,** on Hwy. 93 just past the center of town to the right, has cozy rooms and a friendly staff. (☎250-347-9655 or 800-838-4238. All rooms non-smoking. Singles $50-60; doubles $55-65.)

The park's only serviced campground is **Redstreak,** on the access road that departs Hwy. 95 near the south end of Radium Hot Springs, which boasts 242 sites, including 50 fully serviced sites and 38 with electricity only. The grounds feature toilets, firewood, and playgrounds. Arrive early to secure a spot. (Free showers. Open mid-May to mid-Oct. Sites $17; RVs $22.) **McLeod Meadows,** 27km north of the West Gate entrance on Hwy. 93, offers more solitude and wooded sites on the banks of the very blue Kootenay River, as well as access to hiking trails. (Open mid-May to mid-Sept. Sites $13.) From September to May, snag one of the seven free winter sites at the **Dolly Varden** picnic area, 36km north of the West Gate entrance, which offers free firewood, water, toilets, and a shelter. Ask at Visitors Centers for details on **Crooks Meadow,** available for groups (75 people max.), and with cheap unserviced camping ($8) in the nearby Invermere Forest District.

⚑ APPROACHING BANFF

Follow **Hwy. 93** from Kootenay to the **Trans-Canada Hwy. (Hwy. 1),** and you'll find the Banff National Park townsite.

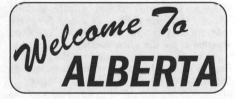

Welcome To ALBERTA

BANFF TOWNSITE

Less townsite than chic resort, Banff nestles fine dining and luxury lodgings just below majestic, snow-capped peaks. A stroll downtown reveals decadent sweet shops and jewelry boutiques alongside sports outfitters and equipment rental. The chilly weather doesn't translate to the people—Banff residents are warm and welcoming.

▣ GETTING AROUND

The Banff townsite is located off the **Trans-Canada Highway (Hwy. 1). Banff Ave.** leads to downtown, where restaurants, shops, and bars reside. Parallel to and west of Banff Ave. is **Bear St.,** where the movie theater and the Whyte Museum are located.

VITAL STATS

Population: 7000

Visitor Info: Banff Visitor Centre, 224 Banff Ave., includes **Banff/Lake Louise Tourism Bureau** (☎403-762-8421; www.banfflakelouise.com) and **Parks Canada** (☎403-762-1550). Open daily June-Sept. 8am-8pm; Oct.-May 9am-5pm. **Lake Louise Visitor Centre** (☎403-522-3833), at Samson Mall on Village Rd. Open daily mid-June to Sept. 8am-6pm; Oct. to mid-June 9am-5pm.

Internet Access: Library, 101 Bear St. (☎403-762-2611). Sign up in advance. Open June-Aug. M-Sa 10am-8pm; daily Sept.-May 10am-8pm. **Cyber Web,** 215 Banff Ave. (☎403-762-9226). $3 per 15min., $8 per hr. Open daily 10am-midnight.

Post Office: 204 Buffalo St. (☎403-762-2586). Open M-F 9am-5:30pm. **Postal Code:** T0L 0C0.

Accommodations scatter the downtown area, with pricier options clustered closer to town. **Parking** is ample in and around the downtown area.

🎯 🎵 SIGHTS & ENTERTAINMENT

There are numerous outdoor activities in Banff National Park (see p. 715), but a quiet day in the townsite can prove rewarding as well. The **Whyte Museum of the Canadian Rockies,** 111 Bear St., explores the history and culture of the Canadian Rockies over the last two centuries in the **Heritage Gallery,** while temporary exhibits focus on the natural history of the region. Displays include works by Canadian painters. (☎403-762-2291. Open daily 10am-5pm. $6, students and seniors $4.)

In summer, the **Banff Festival of the Arts** keeps tourists occupied. A wide spectrum of events, from First Nations dance to opera, are performed from May to mid-August. Some shows are free; stop by the Visitors Center for a schedule. The **Banff Mountain Film Festival,** in the first week of November, screens films and videos that celebrate mountaineers. (For times and info, call ☎403-762-6301.) **Lux Cinema Centre,** 229 Bear St. (☎403-762-8595) shows Hollywood hits.

🧗 OUTDOOR ACTIVITIES

There are countless outdoor opportunities in Banff National Park (see p. 715). Before you head out, however, you'll need to rent equipment in town. Here are several options:

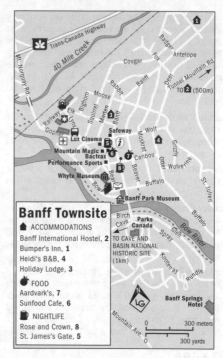

Banff Townsite

♠ ACCOMMODATIONS
Banff International Hostel, **2**
Bumper's Inn, **1**
Heidi's B&B, **4**
Holiday Lodge, **3**

🍴 FOOD
Aardvark's, **7**
Sunfood Cafe, **6**

🍸 NIGHTLIFE
Rose and Crown, **8**
St. James's Gate, **5**

Mountain Magic Equipment, 224 Bear St. (☎403-762-2591). One of the few places in Banff to rent packages for Telemark ($25 per day) and mountaineering ($50 per day). They also offer the usual bike, ski, and snowboard rentals. Open daily Apr.-Nov. 9am-9pm; Dec.-Mar. 8am-9pm.

Bactrax Rentals, 225 Bear St. (☎403-762-8177). Rents mountain bikes for $6-10 per hr., $22-36 per day. Bike tours $15 per hr. including all equipment. Ski packages from $16 per day; snowboard packages $28. 20% HI discount. Open daily Apr.-Oct. 8am-8pm; Nov.-Mar. 7am-10pm.

Performance Sports, 208 Bear St. (☎403-762-8222). Rents tents ($20-26 per day), fishing gear ($16-30 per day), cross-country ski or snowshoe packages ($12 per day, $31 for 3 days), avalanche packages ($23 per day), and snow or rainwear ($8-17 per day). 10% HI or Real Big Adventures discount. Open daily July-Aug. 9:30am-8pm; Sept.-June 10am-6pm.

Wilson Mountain Sports (☎403-522-3636) in the Lake Louise Samson Mall. Rents bikes ($15 per hr., $35 per day) and camping and fishing gear. Mountaineering ($35 per day) and rock climbing packages ($15 per day). Open daily mid-June to Sept. 9am-9pm; Oct. to Apr. 8am-8pm; May to mid-June 9am-8pm.

🍴 FOOD

Like everything else in town, Banff restaurants tend toward the expensive. The Banff and Lake Louise hostels serve affordable meals in their cafes ($3-10). **Sunfood Cafe,** 215 Banff Ave., is a relaxed vegetarian cafe hidden upstairs in a touristy mall. (☎403-760-3933. Veggie burger with the works $6.25. Open M-Sa 11am-9pm.) **Aardvark's,** 304A Caribou St., does big business selling pizza after the bars close. It's often standing-room-only as hungry revelers jostle for a spot. (☎403-762-5500 or 762-5509. Small-ish slices of pizza $3. Small pie $6-9; large $13-21. Buffalo wings $5 for 10. Open daily 11am-4am.)

🏠 ACCOMMODATIONS

Finding a cheap place to stay in Banff has become increasingly difficult; the number of visitors soars into the millions every year. Townsite residents offer rooms in their homes, occasionally at reasonable rates ($75-140; in winter $60-100). Check the list at the back of the *Banff and Lake Louise Official Visitor Guide,* available free at the Visitors Centers. The hostel does provide an alternative to camping and several inns in town run on the not-so-expensive-compared-to-everything-else side. For more options, stop by the Banff tourist office, which supplies free accommodations guides, replete with general price rankings. For more options inside the park, see p. 719.

Banff International Hostel (HI; ☎403-762-4122), 3km uphill from Banff Townsite on Tunnel Mountain Rd. This monster hostel sleeps 215 and has 3 lounges and kitchens. Laundry and hot showers. Check-in 3pm. Check-out 11am. Dorms $26-27.50, nonmembers $30-32.

Bumper's Inn (☎403-762-3386 or 800-661-3518; www.bumpersinn.com), at the corner of Banff Ave. and Marmot St. This cozy, quiet inn is 1.5km from downtown and offers large, comfortable suites with an outdoor courtyard. Rooms $60-135, depending on the number of people and season.

The Holiday Lodge, 311 Marten St. (☎403-762-3648), on Marten St. between Elk St. and Moose St. This quaint inn has heritage home decor and private baths

with showers. Rooms with double or queen-size beds in summer $50; in winter $70.

Heidi's B&B, 214 Otter St. (☎403-726-3806), between Wolf and Caribou St., 3 blocks away from downtown. Comfortable rooms have private baths and tubs with jets. Rooms in summer from $90; in winter from $55.

🌃 NIGHTLIFE

For some real wildlife, check out Banff's bars. Check the paper or ask at the Visitors Center to find out which nightspots are having "locals' night," featuring cheap drinks. **Banff Ave.** hosts more bars, restaurants, kitschy gift shops, and banks than there are mountains.

🏆 Rose and Crown, 202 Banff Ave. (☎403-762-2121), upstairs at the corner of Caribou St. Ample room for dancing, and pool-playing ($1.25), even on busy nights. Living room for watching sports and live music every night at 10pm. Happy hour M-F 3:30-6:30pm. Cover Sa $2. Su Jam Night with happy hour 9pm-close. Open daily 11am-2am.

St. James's Gate, 205 Wolf St. (☎403-762-9355). A laid-back Irish Pub with friendly staff. Ask the bartenders which of the 32 beers on tap to try. Live jigs and reels F-Sa. Open daily 11am-2am.

BANFF NATIONAL PARK

Banff is Canada's best-loved and best-known natural park, with 6641 sq. km of peaks, forests, glaciers, and alpine valleys. It also holds the title of Canada's first National Park, declared so only days after the Canadian Pacific Railway's completion in 1885. The park's name comes from Banffshire, Scotland, the birthplace of two Canadian Pacific Railway financiers who convinced Canada's first Prime Minister that a "large pecuniary advantage" might be gained from the region, telling him that "since we can't export the scenery, we shall have to import the tourists." Their plan worked to a fault, but streets littered with gift shops and chocolatiers cannot mar the wilderness outside of the Banff townsite. Outdoors lovers arrive with mountain bikes, climbing gear, and skis, but a trusty pair of hiking boots remains the park's most widely-used outdoor equipment. Banff's natural beauty, along with the laid-back attitude it affords, have turned the Banff Townsite (see p. 713) into one of Canada's youngest towns.

VITAL STATS

Area: 1.6 million acres.
Visitor Info: Banff Visitor Centre, 224 Banff Ave. (see p. 713).
Gateway Towns: Banff, Lake Louise
Fees: $5, seniors $4, ages 6-16 $2.50.

GETTING AROUND

Banff National Park hugs the Alberta side of the Alberta/British Columbia border, 128km west of Calgary. The **Trans-Canada Hwy. (Hwy. 1)** runs east-west through the park, connecting it to Yoho National Park (p. 281) in the west. The **Icefields Pkwy. (Hwy. 93)** connects Banff with \ National Park to the north and Kootenay National Park to the southwest. Civilization in the park centers on the towns of **Banff** and **Lake Louise,** 58km apart on Hwy. 1. The more serene **Bow Valley Pkwy. (Hwy. 1A)** parallels Hwy. 1 from Lake Louise to 8km west of Banff, offering excellent camping, hosteling, sights, and wildlife. The southern portion of Hwy. 1A is restricted at night in late spring and early summer to accommodate wildlife. **Parking** in Banff National Park is plentiful.

SIGHTS

The **Banff Park Museum National Historic Site** is western Canada's oldest natural history museum, with rooms of stuffed specimens dating to the 1860s. (☎403-762-1558. Open daily mid-May to Sept. 10am-6pm; Oct. to mid-May 1-5pm. Tours daily in summer 3pm; in winter Sa-Su only. $2.50, seniors $2, children $1.50.) Banff National Park would not exist if not for the **Cave and Basin Mineral Springs,** once rumored to have miraculous healing properties. The **Cave and Basin National Historic Site,** a refurbished bath house, is now a small museum detailing the history and science of the site. Access to the cave containing the original spring is inside the building. Five of the pools are the only home of the park's most endangered species: the small Banff Springs snail, *Physella johnsoni.* (☎403-762-1566. Open summer daily 9am-6pm; in winter M-F 11am-4pm, Sa-Su 9:30am-5pm. Tours at 11am. $2.50, seniors $2, children $1.50.) The **springs** are southwest of the city on Cave Ave. For a dip in the hot water, follow the sulfurous smell to the Upper Hot Springs pool, a 40°C (104°F) sulfurous cauldron on Mountain

Ave. (☎403-762-1515. Open daily mid-May to mid-Oct. 9am-11pm; mid-Oct. to mid-May Su-Th 10am-10pm, F-Sa 10am-11pm. Swimsuits $1.50, towels $1.25, lockers $0.50. In summer $7.50, seniors and children 3-17 $6.50; in winter $5.50/$4.50/$15.)

OUTDOOR ACTIVITIES

A visitor sticking to paved byways will see a tiny fraction of the park and the majority of the park's visitors. Those interested in the outdoors can hike or bike on more than 1600km of trails. Grab a free copy of the *Mountain Biking and Cycling Guide* or *Dayhikes in Banff* and peruse trail descriptions at information centers. For still more solitude, pick up *The Banff Backcountry Experience* and an overnight **camping permit** at a Visitors Center and head out to the backcountry. ($6 per person per day.) Check with rangers at the info center for weather, trail, and wildlife updates.

HIKING

Two easy trails are within walking distance of Banff Townsite, but longer, more rigorous trails abound farther away. The best escapes are found in the backcountry.

Fenland (2km, 1hr.). Follow Mt. Norquay Rd. to the outskirts, look for signs across the tracks on road's left side. This flat, easy trail crosses area shared by beaver, muskrat, and waterfowl, but is closed for elk calving in late spring and early summer.

Tunnel Mountain (2.5km, 2hr.). Follow Wolf St. east from Banff Ave., and turn right on St. Julien Rd. to reach the head of the steep, moderately difficult trail. Provides a dramatic view of the **Bow Valley** and **Mt. Rundle.** Tunnel Mountain has the distinction of being the Rockies' smallest mountain. Not that it matters.

Aylmer Pass (26.5km round-trip, 8hr.) This strenuous trail leaves from the shore of Lake Minnewanka on Lake Minnewanka Rd. (the extension of Banff Ave. across the Trans-Canada from town). Parking just above tour boat area. A steep climb to the summit yields a panoramic view of the lake and surrounding scenery. The trail can be abridged by hiking only 11.6km to the lookout, cutting the final 250m ascent.

Johnston Canyon (5.5km). West of the Norquay Interchange on Hwy. 1, then 18km along the Bow Valley Pkwy. (Hwy. 1A). A very popular moderate-to-strenuous half-day hike. A catwalk along the edge of the deep limestone canyon runs 1.1km over the thundering river to the canyon's lower falls, then another 1.6km to the upper falls. The trail continues for a rugged 3.2km to seven blue-green cold-water springs, known as the **Inkpots,** in a valley above the canyon. More than 42km of trails beyond the Inkpots are blissfully untraveled and punctuated with campgrounds roughly every 10km.

Sulphur Mountain (5.5km, 2hr.). Winds along a well-trodden trail to the peak, where a spectacular view awaits; the **Sulphur Mountain Gondola** doesn't charge for the 8min. downhill trip. (☎403-762-2523. Uphill $19, ages 6-15 $9.50, under 6 free.) The **Panorama Restaurant** (☎403-762-7486), perched atop the mountain, serves breakfast ($10) and lunch buffets ($13) from mid-May to mid-August.

BACKCOUNTRY

Backcountry trekking is the way to see Banff as the masses cannot. Banff's wild backcountry, replete with mind-boggling scenery, belies the civilized tourist trap that the townsite has become. Amateurs and experts alike should beware of dangerous and changing conditions on strenuous trails that do not receive as much maintenance as more accessible routes; consult park rangers for information. Trails to ask about include **Egypt Lake** (12.5km one-way, 2 days), **Twin Lakes** (9km one-way, 2 days), **Mystic Pass** (37km, 3 days), **Skoki Loop** (34km, 3 days), **Assiniboine Loop** (55km, 4 days), **Sawback Trail** (74km, 5 days), and **Mystic Pass-Flint's Park-Badger Pass Trail** (76km, 5 days).

BIKING

Biking is permitted on public roads, highways, and certain trails in the park. Spectacular scenery and a number of hostels and campgrounds make the **Bow Valley Pkwy. (Hwy. 1A)** and the **Icefields Pkwy. (Hwy. 93)** perfect for extended cycling trips. Every other store downtown seems to rent bikes;

IN THE PASSENGER SEAT

OUT OF THE FLYING PLANE, INTO THE FIRE

While most people run from wildfires, Mark Wright is part of the elite group of aerial firefighters who jump right on in.

LG: How did you start jumping?
A: I started working for the Helena National Forest as a summer job. Among other things, one of the things they train you to do is put out fires. So I started out as a young firefighter putting my way through college. The "problem" is that it gets in your blood and you become addicted to it. After four years of firefighting through college, I got a teaching degree and ended up continuing to fight fires in my summers off. I've been doing it for the past 27 years.

LG: What does smokejumper training involve?
A: To be a smokejumper, you need recommendations and a minimum of two years' firefighting experience. Many people apply and only a limited number get selected to go through rookie training, which is over a month long. I would compare it to boot camp. They start their morning with calisthenics, go through daily training, and have to pass physical fitness tests... they need to make a minimum of 15 jumps before they're allowed in a fire.

LG: What happens in a typical fire?
A: Smokejumpers are initial attack, so we get calls right when the fire is detected and still fairly small. One of the great advantages smokejumpers have is that we are on an airplane above the fire with the door off. We take a good look at the terrain and see what the fire behavior is. People coming from the ground can only see smoke and don't know what they're getting into. Before we even jump out of the plane, we check for safety zones to see which ways we can approach the fire, pinpoint safe jump spots that are close to the fire but not endangering ourselves, and look for routes out of the fire. After we land in parachutes, we pack it up to put in a safe spot. The plane flies over and drops our cargo, which contains chainsaws, tools, water, freeze-dried food—everything we'll need to fight the fire and camp overnight.

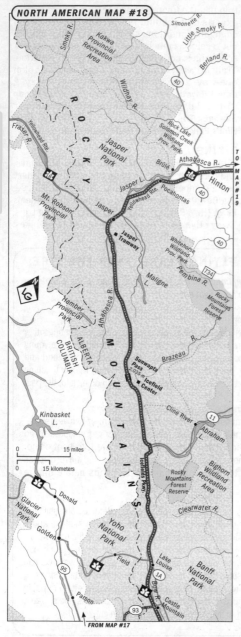

NORTH AMERICAN MAP #18

FROM MAP #17

head to **Bactrax** or **Performance Sport** (see **Equipment Rental,** p. 714) for HI discounts. Parks Canada publishes a free *Mountain Biking and Cycling Guide* that describes trails and roadways where bikes are permitted; pick up a copy at bike rental shops or Visitors Centers.

WATERSPORTS

Fishing is legal in most of the park during specific seasons, but live bait and lead weights are not. Get a **permit** and check out regulations at the info center. (7-day permit $6.) **Bourgeau Lake,** a 7km hike in, is home to a particularly feisty breed of brook trout. Closer to the road, try **Herbert Lake,** off the Icefields Pkwy., or **Lake Minnewanka,** on Lake Minnewanka Rd. northeast of Banff. Lake Minnewanka Rd. passes **Johnson Lake,** where shallow warm water makes a perfect swimming hole.

Hydra River Guides runs whitewater rafting trips along the Kicking Horse River. (☎403-762-4554 or 800-644-8888; www.raftbanff.com. Up to Class V rapids. $90, HI members $76; includes lunch, transportation, and gear.) **Blast Adventures** leads half-day inflatable kayak trips on the rowdy Kananaskis River. (☎403-609-2009 or 888-802-5278; www.blastadventures.com. $64 per person including transportation, gear, and snacks.)

⛏ ACCOMMODATIONS

Mammoth modern hostels in Banff and Lake Louise anchor a chain of cozier hostels from Calgary to Jasper. Rustic hostels provide more of a wilderness experience (read: no electricity or flush toilets), and often have some of the park's best hiking and cross-country skiing right in their backyards. Wait-list beds become available at 6pm, and the larger hostels try to save a few stand-by beds for shuttle arrivals. Beds go quickly, especially during the summer, so make your reservations as early as possible. Reservations can be made through the southern **Alberta HI administration.** (☎866-762-4122; www.hostellingintl.ca.) Free reservations are held until 6pm, but can be guaranteed until later with a credit card. Because of a recent move towards centralizing the administration of these hostels, information regarding prices, closures, and facilities is currently in flux.

⛺ **Rampart Creek Wilderness Hostel (HI),** 34km south of the Icefield Centre. Close to several world-famous ice climbs (including Weeping Wall, 17km north), this hostel is a favorite for winter mountaineers and anyone who likes a rustic sauna after a hard day's hike. Wood-burning sauna, full-service kitchen. 12-bed co-ed cabins Su-Th $18, nonmembers $22; F-Sa $21/$25.

■ **Castle Mountain Wilderness Hostel (HI),** in Castle Junction, 1.5km east of the junction of Hwy. 1 and Hwy. 93 south, between Banff and Lake Louise. One of the hardest hostels to find, Castle Mountain offers a quieter alternative to the hubbub of its big brothers. Comfortable common area with huge bay windows. Friendly staff, hot showers, kitchen, laundry, electricity, and volleyball. Check-in 5-10pm; check-out 10am. Dorms Su-Th $18, nonmembers $22; F-Sa $21/$25.

Mosquito Creek Wilderness Hostel (HI), 103km south of the Icefield Centre and 26km north of Lake Louise. Across the creek from the Mosquito Creek campground. Close to the Wapta Icefield. Enormous living room with wood stove, wood-burning sauna, kitchen, and pump water. 16-bed co-ed cabins Su-Th $18, nonmembers $22; F-Sa $21/$25.

CAMPING

A chain of campgrounds stretches between Banff and Jasper. Extra-large, fully hooked-up grounds lie closer to the townsites; for more trees and fewer vehicles, try more remote sites farther from Banff and Lake Louise. At all park campgrounds, a **campfire permit** (includes firewood) is $4. Sites are first come, first served; go early. The sites below are listed from south to north and have no toilets or showers unless otherwise noted.

Tunnel Mountain Village, 4km from Banff Townsite on Tunnel Mountain Rd. With nearly 1200 sites, this is a camping metropolis. Trailer/RV area has 321 full RV sites, Village 2 has 188 sites, and Village 1 houses a whopping 618. Fires allowed in Village 1 only; all villages have showers. Village 2 is open year-round; 1 and 3 closed Oct. early May. Sites $17, with electricity $21; full RV sites $24.

Two Jack, 13km northeast of Banff, across Hwy.1. 381 main sites ($13) have no showers or disabled access; 80 lakeside sites ($17) do. Open mid-May to Aug.

Johnston Canyon, 26km northwest of Banff on Bow Valley Pkwy. 140 sites. Access to Johnston Canyon Trail (see p. 716). Showers. Open mid-June to mid-Sept. Sites $17.

Protection Mountain, 15km east of Lake Louise and 11km west of Castle Junction on the Bow Valley Pkwy.

(Hwy. 1A). 89 spacious sites (14 trailer) in a basic campground. Open late June to early Sept. Sites $13.

Lake Louise, 1½km southeast of the Visitors Center on Fairview Rd. On Bow River, not the lake. Plenty of hiking and fishing awaits. Showers. 189 trailer sites with electricity, open year-round. 220 tent sites, open mid-May to Sept. Tent sites $17; RV sites $21.

Mosquito Creek, 103km south of the Icefield Centre and 26km north of Lake Louise. 32 sites with hiking access. Pit toilets. Sites $10.

Rampart Creek, 147km north of Banff, 34km south of the Icefield Centre, across the highway from Rampart Creek hostel and amazing ice climbing. Pit toilets. Open late June to Aug. Sites $10.

LAKE LOUISE TOWNSITE

The highest community in Canada (1530m), Lake Louise and the surrounding glaciers have often passed for Swiss scenery in movies and are the emerald in the Rockies' tiara of tourism. The lake was named in 1884 in honor of Queen Victoria's daughter, and its beauty is nothing short of royal.

(VITAL STATS)

Population: 1200

Visitor Info: Lake Louise Visitor Centre (☎403-522-3833), at Samson Mall on Village Rd. Open daily mid-June to Sept. 8am-6pm; Oct. to mid-June 9am-5pm. **Banff/Lake Louise Tourism Bureau,** in Banff (see p. 713).

Internet Access: The Depot (☎403-522-3870), in the Samson Mall. Open daily 6:30am-7pm.

Post Office: Mail services at The Depot (see above). **Postal Code:** TOL 1E0.

GETTING AROUND

The townsite's center, to the right off Hwy. 1/ Hwy. 93, is literally that—a small shopping center with a few restaurants and a market. After a brief stop, it's best to push on to the lake, where the hardest task is escaping fellow gawkers at the posh, though aesthetically misplaced, **Chateau Lake Louise.** The chateau's canoe rentals are an unheard of $30 per hr. (☎403-522-3511. Room rates vary with the season, but are often prohibitively expensive.) **Parking** is ample in the city center and at motels and campsites around the lake.

⚠ OUTDOOR ACTIVITIES

The **Lake Louise Sightseeing Lift,** up Whitehorn Rd. and across the Trans-Canada Hwy. from Lake Louise, cruises up **Mt. Whitehorn.** (☎403-522-3555; www.skilouise.com. Open daily May 9am-4pm; June and Sept. 8:30am-9pm; July and Aug. 8am-6pm. $19, students and seniors $17, ages 6-12 $9, under 6 free. To enjoy breakfast at the top, add $2; for lunch, add $6.)

HIKING

If you don't want to succumb to the town's prices, you can view the water and its surrounding splendor from several hiking trails that begin in the neighborhood and climb along the surrounding ridgelines. But be warned, with beauty comes crowds; expect masses of tourists (and bears).

Lake Agnes Trail (3.5km, 2½hr. round-trip), and the **Plain of Six Glaciers Trail** (5.5km, 4hr. round-trip) both end at teahouses and make for a lovely, if sometimes crowded, day hike with views down to the Lake. Open daily in summer 9am-6pm.

Moraine Lake, 15km from the village, at the end of Moraine Lake Rd. and off Lake Louise Dr. (no trailers or long RVs). Moraine lies in the awesome **Valley of the Ten Peaks,** opposite glacier-encrusted **Mt. Temple.** Join the multitudes on the **Rockpile Trail** for an eye-popping view of the lake and valley and a lesson in ancient ocean bottoms (10min. walk to the top). To escape the camera-wielding hordes, try one of the lake's more challenging trails, either **Sentinel Pass** via Larch Valley (6km one-way, 5-6hr.), with stunning views from flower-studded meadows, or **Wenkchemna Pass** via Eiffel Lake (10km one-way, full day), which carries hikers the length of the Valley of the Ten Peaks with incredible views in both directions. Be sure to arrive before 10am or after 4pm to see the view instead of the crowds.

Paradise Valley, depending on which way you hike it, can be an intense day hike or a relaxing overnight trip. From the **Paradise Creek Trailhead,** 2.5km up Moraine Lake Rd., the loop through the valley runs 18.1km through subalpine and alpine forests and along rivers (7½hr.; elevation gain 880m). One classic backpacking route runs from Moraine Lake up and over **Sentinel Pass,** joining the top of the Paradise Valley loop after 8km. A **backcountry campground** marks the mid-point from either trailhead. Grizzly activity often forces the park wardens to close the area in summer; check with the wardens before hiking in this area.

WINTER SPORTS

Winter activities in the park range from world-class ice climbing to ice fishing. Those 1600km of hiking trails make for exceptional **cross-country skiing** (**Moraine Lake Rd.** is closed to vehicle traffic in the winter, and is used for cross-country skiing, as are the backcountry trails), and three allied resorts offer a range of **skiing and snowboarding** opportunities from early November to mid-May. All have terrain parks for snowboarders. Shuttles to all the following three resorts leave from most big hotels in the townsites, and Banff and Lake Louise hostels typically have ticket and transportation **discounts** available for guests. Multi-day passes good for all three resorts are available at the **Ski Banff/Lake Louise** office, 225 Banff Ave. (☎403-762-4561), in Banff, and at all resorts. Passes include free shuttle service and an extra night of skiing at Mount Norquay.

Sunshine Mountain (☎403-762-6500, snow report 760-7669; www.skibanff.com). Spreading across 3 mountains, with the most snowfall (9.9m) in the area, this mountain attracts loyal followers to its 3168 acres. Lift tickets $56; seniors, students under 24, and ages 13-17 $46; ages 6-12 $20.

Lake Louise (☎403-522-3555, snow report 403-762-4766; www.skilouise.com). The 2nd-largest ski area in Canada (4200 ski-able acres), with amazing views, over 1000m of vertical drop, and the best selection of expert terrain. Some simpler slopes cover plenty of the mountain. Lift tickets $59; students under 25 and seniors $47; ages 6-12 $15.

Mt. Norquay (☎403-762-4421). A local's mountain: small, and close to town. F night-skiing and 2-5hr. tickets. Lift tickets $47; students, ages 13-17, and over 55 $37; ages 6-12 $16. Night-skiing $23/$21/$12.

▦ FOOD & ACCOMMODATIONS

There are more food options in Banff than Lake Louise, so if you plan to dine out, it's best to stay in the city. The town's main shopping center, however, has a grocery and a few restaurant options. The **Village Market** (☎403-522-3894), in the Samson Mall, has fresh produce and the basics. **Laggan's Deli,** in Samson Mall, is always crowded. Thick sandwiches ($4-5) or fresh-baked loaves ($3) are always favorites. (☎403-522-2017. Open daily June-Sept. 6am-8pm; Oct.-May 6am-7pm. Cash or traveler's checks only.) The **Lake Louise**

Village Grill & Bar Family Restaurant & Lounge, also in the Samson Mall, is as versatile as its name suggests, with steaks ($12-21), breakfast options, sandwiches, and Chinese food. (☎403-522-3879. Salads $5-12. Sandwiches and burgers $7-11. Chinese entrees $14-17. Open daily 11am-9pm.)

There are several campsites near Lake Louise (see p. 719), and one hostel in town. **Lake Louise International Hostel (HI),** 500m west of the Visitors Center in Lake Louise Townsite, on Village Rd. toward the Park Warden's office, is ranked fourth in the world by HI, and rightly so. More like a resort than a hostel, it boasts a reference library, a stone fireplace, two full kitchens, a sauna, and a quality cafe. (☎403-522-2200. Hub for mountaineering tours. Private rooms available. Internet $2 per 20min. Check-in 3pm. Check-out 11am. Dorms $26, nonmembers $30.) There are also a handful of inns directly in Lake Louise, but they tend to be pricey. The posh **Lake Louise Inn,** 210 Village Rd., has an indoor swimming pool, suites with kitchens and fireplaces, and several in-house restaurants. (☎403-522-3791 or 800-661-9237; www.lakelouise.com. Rooms from $100.)

THE ROAD TO JASPER

From the jagged cliffsides and towering evergreens, Hwy. 93 carries you into a country of sweeping vistas and icy mountain climes. The **Icefields Pkwy.** began in the Great Depression as a work relief project. The 230km parkway is one of the most beautiful rides in North America, heading north from Lake Louise in Banff National Park to Jasper Townsite in Jasper National Park. Drivers may struggle to keep their eyes on the road as they skirt stunning peaks, aquamarine lakes, and roadside glaciers.

The Icefields Pkwy. has 18 **trails** into the wilderness and 22 **scenic points** with spectacular views. **Bow Summit,** 40km north of Lake Louise, is the Parkway's highest point (2135m); from there, a 10min. walk leads to a view of fluorescent, aqua **Peyto Lake.** Free maps and hiking info are available at the **Icefield Centre,** 132km north of Lake Louise. (☎780-852-6288. Open May to mid-Oct. daily 9am-5pm; July-Aug. until 6pm.) The Icefield Centre lies in the shadow of the tongue of the **Athabasca Glacier.** This gargantuan ice floe is one of six major glaciers that flow from the 200 sq. km **Columbia Icefield,** the largest accumulation of ice and snow in the Canadian Rockies. Visitors can also drive close and take a 10min. walk up piles of glacial debris onto the glacier's mighty toe. The trail onto the glacier is limited to a very small "safe zone." **Do not wander onto the glacier on your own.** For more geological tidbits, sign up for an **Athabasca Glacier Icewalk.** (☎780-852-3803. Tours mid-June to mid-Sept. 3hr. tour $45, ages 7-17 $23.)

There aren't many food options on the glacier; visitors shop in Lake Louise (see p. 720) or Yoho (see p. 281) before heading to the icefield. It's hard to resist the bragging rights of having camped on a glacier. **Columbia Icefield,** 109km south of the townsite, lies close enough to the Athabasca Glacier to intercept an icy breeze. A difficult and steep access road makes the sites tents-only. (22 sites and 11 walk-ins. Dry toilets and pay phones. Open mid-May to mid-Oct. Sites $10.) **Columbia Icefield Chalet,** located in the Icefield Centre, has mountain- and glacier-view rooms. The lodging comes at a high price, however, and rooms are comfortable but not exactly posh. (☎877-423-7433; icefield@brewster.ca. Rooms with glacier views $120-205, with mountain views $110-185.)

JASPER TOWNSITE

A smaller and less glitzy version of Banff, Jasper offers the charm of a medium-sized resort town without the showiness that comes with catering to world-class jetsetters. The downtown area is perfect for leisurely strolls and window shopping, and the mountains that loom overhead ensure the scenery never grows plain. While the town can get expensive during high season, camping abounds and the large grocery store downtown sells fresh bagels and baked goods. Jasper is just as beautiful as Banff, but its laid-back atmosphere makes the mountain village feel less exotic and more homey.

▛ GETTING AROUND. The Jasper Townsite is near the center of the park at the intersection of **Hwy. 16,** which runs east-west through the northern reaches of the park, and the **Icefields Pkwy. (Hwy. 93).** Much like Banff, Jasper is arranged around two parallel streets, **Connaught Dr.** to the east and **Patricia St.** to the west. Patricia St. is one-way with traffic flowing northward. Most of the restaurants in town, the information center, and the post office are on these two streets. The hostels and campgrounds are several kilometers out from town. Public **parking** is abundant downtown, with lots on almost every block of Connaught Dr.

NORTH AMERICA

VITAL STATS

Population: 5000

Visitor Info: Park Information Centre, 500 Connaught Dr. (☎780-852-6176). Open daily mid-June to early Sept. 8am-7pm; early Sept. to late Oct. and late Dec. to mid-June 9am-5pm.

Internet Access: Soft Rock Cafe (see **Food,** below). $2 per 15 min. The **library,** 500 Robson St. (☎780-852-3652), charges $5 per hr. Open M-Th 11am-9pm, F-Sa 11am-5pm.

Post Office: 502 Patricia St. (☎780-852-3041), across from the townsite green. Open M-F 9am-5pm. **Postal Code:** T0E 1E0.

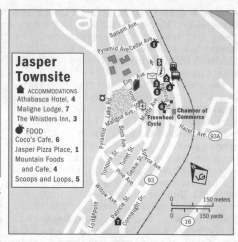

Jasper Townsite

🏠 ACCOMMODATIONS
Athabasca Hotel, 4
Maligne Lodge, 7
The Whistlers Inn, 3

🍴 FOOD
Coco's Cafe, 6
Jasper Pizza Place, 1
Mountain Foods and Cafe, 4
Scoops and Loops, 5

◎ **SIGHTS.** A stroll downtown reveals gift shops, restaurants, and Internet cafes, and can make for a fun afternoon. There are also varied outdoor activities in Jasper National Park (see p. 723). For ski and bike rental, try **Freewheel Cycle,** 618 Patricia Ave. (☎780-852-3898; www.freewheeljasper.ca. Mountain bikes $8 per hr., $24 per day, $32 overnight. Snowboards $28 per day. Watch for twin-tip ski demo deals. Open summer daily 9am-9pm; spring and fall 9am-6pm; call for winter hours.) **Jasper International Hostel** (p. 724) also rents mountain bikes. ($8 per half-day, $15 per day. Snowshoes $8 per day.)

🍴 **FOOD.** Prices in Jasper range from the affordable to the outrageous. However, cheap options can be found and lots of places feature good lunch deals. **Mountain Foods and Cafe,** 606 Connaught Dr., offers a wide selection of sandwiches, salads, home-cooked goodies, and takeout lunches for the trail. (☎780-852-4050. Turkey focaccia sandwich and assorted wraps $7.50. Fantastic breakfast special for $5.50. Open daily 8am-6pm.) **Jasper Pizza Place,** 402 Connaught Dr., offers free delivery in the area. (☎780-852-3225. Large wood-oven pizzas $9-13. Sandwiches $3-8. Open daily 11am-midnight.) A small, vegetarian-friendly spot, **Coco's Cafe,** 608 Patricia St., serves homemade soups, baked goods, and smoothies. (☎780-852-4550. Open daily summer 7am-8pm; winter 7am-6pm.) Not just an ice-cream parlor, **Scoops and Loops,** 504 Patricia St. also serves sushi. (☎780-852-4333. Sandwiches $3-4. Sushi $3-7. Open M-Sa 10am-11pm, Su 11am-11pm.)

🏠 **ACCOMMODATIONS.** Camping in Jasper National Park (see p. 724) or staying in one of the park hostels (see p. 724) is much cheaper than trying to find digs in the townsite. The **Jasper Home Accommodation Association** (www.stayinjasper.com) offers an economical alternative to Jasper resorts by operating a website that sets travelers up with private renters and B&Bs. With newly renovated, Victorian rooms and a restaurant, sports lounge, and nightclub on site, **Athabasca Hotel,** 510 Patricia St., leaves little to desire. (☎780-852-4955 or 877-542-8422; www.athabascahotel.com. Prices vary with season, but generally range $60-80.) At **The Whistlers Inn,** 105 Miette Ave., in the heart of downtown, the rooftop hot tub looks over downtown to the mountains beyond. (☎780-852-3361 or 800-282-9919; www.whistlersinn.com. Rooms in summer from $150; in winter from $65.) **Maligne Lodge,** 900 Connaught Dr., just south of the downtown area, offers roomy suites, parking, and guest jacuzzis. Summer prices and rooms for individuals can be high, but low-season doubles are affordable. (☎780-852-3143 or 800-661-1315; www.decorehotels.com. In summer singles from $159, doubles $180. In winter $79/$89. Ask about discounts and specials.)

JASPER NATIONAL PARK

Northward expansion of the Canadian railway system led to further exploration of the Canadian Rocky Mountains and the 1907 founding of Jasper, the largest of the National Parks in the region. The area went virtually untouristed until 1940, when the Icefields Pkwy. paved the way for the masses to appreciate Jasper's astounding beauty. In summer, caravans of RVs and charter buses line the highway jostling for the chance to take photos of surprisingly fearless wildlife.

GETTING AROUND

The northernmost and largest of the four national parks, Jasper sits northeast of Banff on **Icefields Pkwy. (Hwy. 93).** Hwy. 93 runs north-south through Jasper National Park while Hwy. 16 runs east-west. There is plenty of **parking** at lookouts and trailheads, as well as at the visitor center.

OUTDOOR ACTIVITIES

Jasper National Park offers excellent day hiking. This means nature writ large and exotic wildlife that includes bears and bighorn sheep. Short walks make the postcard-perfect scenery of the Canadian Rockies accessible. For more info, stop by the Visitors Center for a copy of their *Summer Hiking* pamphlet and trail condition updates. As a supplement to hiking, check out **The Jasper Tramway** (☎ 780-852-3093), just past the hostel on Whistlers Rd., 4km south of the townsite on Hwy. 93. Climbing 973m up Whistlers Mountain, the tramway leads to a panoramic view of the park and, on clear days, far beyond it. (Open daily Apr. 13-May 17 and Oct. 9:30am-4:30pm; May 18-June 25 and Sept. 9:30am-9pm; June 26-July 8:30am-10pm. $19, ages 5-14 $9.50, under 5 free.) **Sun Dog Tours** offers a shuttle from town and tram ride to the top. (☎ 780-852-4056; fax 780-852-9663. $24.)

Path of the Glacier Loop (1.6km, 45min.). The trailhead is 30km south of the townsite; take Hwy. 93 to 93A to the end of the bumpy, twisty, and often closed 15km Mt. Edith Cavell Rd. One of the 2 paths features **Mt. Edith Cavell,** the glacier-laden peak named after an English nurse executed by the Germans during World War I. An easy path

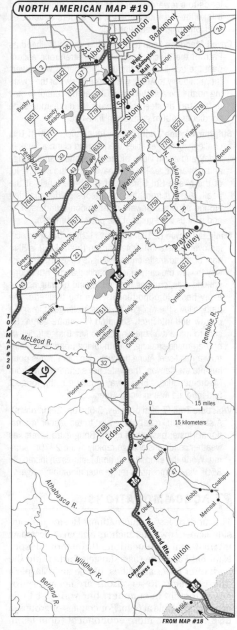

leads to a rewarding view of a glacier receding into a lake littered with icebergs. No trailers or vehicles over 6m long. Open June-Oct.

Cavell Meadows Loop (8km, 3-6hr.). Same trailhead as Path of the Glacier Loop. A more strenuous ascent past the tree line and through a carpet of wildflowers (from mid-July to Aug.), with striking views of the towering north face and the Angel Glacier. Be careful to stay on the trail as steep cliffs make for dangerous slide conditions. 400m gain. Open June-Oct.

Sulphur Skyline Trail (9.6km round-trip, 4-6hr.). This challenging hike enables the hardy to climb a peak in a day and attain views of the limestone Miette Range and Ashlar Ridge. The trail leaves from the parking lot of the Miette Hot Springs. If you have lunch at the peak, guard it from the courageous golden-mantled ground squirrels. Beware of afternoon thunderstorms and serious wind gusts at the peak. 700m gain.

Maligne Canyon (2.1km one-way, 1-2hr.). The spectacular, over-touristed Maligne Canyon (mah-LEEN) is 8km east of the townsite on the Maligne Lake Rd. The best way to view the canyon is by parking at the 5th Bridge parking area, crossing the bridge, and bearing right at every possible opportunity. From the trailhead, the path follows the Maligne River as it plunges through a narrow and intricately sculpted limestone gorge. Be sure to make it all the way to the first Bridge for views of the ground-shaking, breath-taking upper waterfall— truly a must-see. Along the walk, look for springs pouring into the Canyon. The water flows underground from Medicine Lake, 15km away, making it the longest underground river in North America.

Whistlers Trail (7.9km one-way; 3-5hr. up, 2-3hr. down). A strenuous hike beginning next to the Jasper International Hostel basketball court. Bring extra layers, as weather conditions change rapidly at the 2470m summit. Worth the effort; the summit features an incredible 360° view of mountain range after mountain range.

▣ ACCOMMODATIONS

The modern Jasper International Hostel, just outside Jasper Townsite, anchors a chain of **Hostelling International (HI)** locations throughout Jasper National Park. The rustic hostels farther into the park offer fewer amenities, but lie amid Jasper's finest scenery. Reservations are necessary for most hostels in summer, but wait-list beds become available at 6pm. For couples or groups, a **B&B** may prove more economical (doubles in summer $40-130; in winter $30-95). Many are in town near the train station; ask for a list at the park information center or the bus depot.

Jasper International Hostel (HI; ☎ 760-852-3215 or 877-852-0781), known as Whistlers Hostel. 3km up Whistlers Rd. from its intersection with Hwy. 93, 4km south of the townsite. Closest hostel to the townsite. Attracts gregarious backpackers and cyclists. 88 often-full beds (get ready to share—it's possible to have as many as 43 roommates). 2 private rooms available with at least 2 people. Curfew 2am. Dorms $18; nonmembers $23.

Maligne Canyon Hostel (HI), on Maligne Lake Rd. north of the Maligne Canyon parking lot, 11km east of town off Hwy. 16. Small, recently renovated cabins (24 beds) sit on bank of Maligne River, with access to the Skyline Trail and the Maligne Canyon. Manager is on a first-name basis with several local bears. Electricity, fridge, pay phone, potable water. Reception 5-11pm. Open Oct.-Apr. Dorms $13, nonmembers $18.

Mt. Edith Cavell Hostel (HI), 12km up Edith Cavell Rd., off Hwy. 93A. Cozy quarters heated by wood-burning stoves. Propane light, spring water (filter in the newly-painted kitchen), private wash area, firepit, and the best smelling outhouses in the park. Road closed in winter, often until late June, but the hostel is open to anyone willing to pick up the keys at Jasper International Hostel and ski uphill from the highway. Check-in 5-11pm. 32 beds. Dorms $13, nonmembers $18.

Athabasca Falls Hostel (HI), on Hwy. 93 just south of the 93-93A junction, 32km south of the townsite. A hostel in a quiet setting that still has the comforts of town: electricity, email, and ping pong. However, the only running water around is the beautiful Athabasca Falls, which are a 500m stroll away. Propane heat. 40 beds in 3 cabins. Dorms $13, nonmembers $18.

Beauty Creek Hostel (HI), on Hwy. 93, 87km south of the townsite. On the banks of the glacier-fed Sunwapta River and close to the Columbia Icefields, south of the 3.2km Stanley Falls trailhead. Poetry on the outhouse walls and views of the valley from the solar shower. Check-in 5-11pm. Dorms $12, nonmembers $17.

▣ CAMPING

These government-run campgrounds are listed from north to south. Most are primitive sites with few facilities. All are popular and first come, first served. Call the Park Information Center (☎ 760-852-6176) for details. Fire permits are $4. All except Pocahontas also offer kitchen shelters.

Pocahontas, Hwy. 16 at the north edge of the park, 44km northeast of the townsite. Closest to Miette Hot Springs. 130 sites and 10 walk-in tent sites. Flush toilets. Open mid-May to mid-Oct. Sites $13.

Snaring River, on Hwy. 16, 16km north of Jasper Townsite. Right on the river. Come early for choice spots. 56 sites and 10 walk-in tent sites, dry toilets. Open mid-May to late Sept. Sites $10.

Whistlers, on Whistlers Rd., 3km south of the townsite off Hwy. 93. This 781-site behemoth is the closest campground to Jasper Townsite and has all the amenities. Public phones, dump station. Open early May to mid-Oct. Sites $15; RV hookups $24. Free showers.

Wapiti, on Hwy. 93, 3.8km south of Whistlers, along the Athabasca River. Plentiful brush separates tenters from RVers. Pay phone, sani-dump, coin-op showers, and electric RV sites. Mid-June to early Sept. 362 sites; $15-18. Oct. to early May 91 sites; $13-15.

LEAVING JASPER
Either end of town will connect you to **Hwy. 16 East** for the 4hr. jaunt to Edmonton.

THE ROAD TO EDMONTON
Leaving the mountains behind, the prairie lands of Alberta seem to stretch on forever, occasionally punctuated by a small industrial town or truck-driver's rest stop. In the shadow of the Canadian Rockies, **Hinton** remains true to its industrial origins as a coal-mining and logging town. Those interested in learning more about the industries that helped build the early Canadian economy should visit the **Natural Resource Interpretive Park,** along Hwy. 16, just past the shopping center, for detailed explanations of forestry, mining, and the railroads that connected Hinton's resources to developing urban centers. To the east, Edmonton soon emerges: a capital city nestled in the secluded reaches of western Canada.

APPROACHING EDMONTON
Hwy. 16 will take you straight into Edmonton, but **Hwy. 16A,** diverging just outside of the city limits, connects to **Stony Plain Dr.** and is closer to the downtown area and most motels.

EDMONTON
This popular destination hosts the Canadian Finals Rodeo and is home to the world's largest shopping mall. Museums attract children and art lovers, while the Saskatchewan River Valley draws hikers and bikers. The happening strip on Whyte Ave. transforms Edmonton into an urban oasis near the overpowering splendor of the neighboring Rockies.

GETTING AROUND
Edmonton's streets run north-south, and avenues run east-west. Street numbers increase to the west, and avenues increase to the north. The first three digits of an address indicate the nearest cross street; 10141 88 Ave. is on 88 Ave. near 101 St. A river divides the city along a northeast-southwest axis. The river can only be bridged on certain streets: from west to east they are 149th St., Hwy.

BEYOND THE ASPHALT

FLOUR POWER
Passing by the many lakes and streams in the Rockies, you may notice that they have an unusual color. When looking at the swimming-pool turquoise or glowing blue color of these bodies of water, you might wonder if this is some kind of gimmick perpetuated by the park wardens to bring in the tourists. Many years ago, one visitor to Lake Louise claimed that he had solved the mystery of the beautiful water: it had obviously been distilled from peacock tails. Turns out he was a bit off the mark. The actual cause of the color is "rock flour." This fine dust is created by the pressure exerted by the glacier upon rocks trapped within the ice; the resulting ground rock powder is washed into streams and lakes in the glacial meltwater. Suspended particles in lakes and streams trap all colors of the spectrum except for the vibrant blues and greens that are reflected back for your visual pleasure.

VITAL STATS

Population: 1 million

Visitor Information: Edmonton Tourism, Shaw Conference Centre, 9797 Jasper Ave. (☎780-496-8400 or 800-463-4667), on Pedway Level. Open M-F 8:30am-4:30pm. Also at **Gateway Park** (☎780-496-8400 or 800-463-4667), on Hwy. 2 south of town. Open summer daily 8am-8pm; winter M-F 8:30am-4:30pm, Sa-Su 9am-5pm. **Travel Alberta** (☎780-427-4321 or 800-252-3782) is open M-F 7am-7pm, Sa-Su 8:30am-5:30pm.

Internet Access: Dow Computer Lab, at the Odyssium (see **Sights,** below); free with admission. Edmonton Public library, 7 Sir Winston Churchill Sq. (☎780-496-7000). 1hr. free. Open M-F 9am-9pm, Sa 9am-6pm, Su 1-5pm.

Post Office: 9808 103A Ave. (☎800-267-1177), adjacent to the CN Tower. Open M-F 8am-5:45pm. **Postal Code:** T5J 2G8.

2, 109th St., 101st Ave., and Yellowhead Trail. The **city center** is off-center at 105 St. and 101 Ave. **Parking** is ample in and around the downtown area.

ⓖ SIGHTS

WEST EDMONTON MALL. The $1.3 billion **world's biggest mall** engulfs the area from 178 St. to 170 St. between 90 Ave. and 87 Ave. Far more than just a shopping center, it contains the world's largest indoor wave pool, an amusement park, miniature golf, exotic animals, over 800 stores, an ice-skating rink, 110 eateries, a full-scale replica of Columbus' *Santa Maria,* indoor bungee jumping, a casino, a hotel, a dolphin show, and swarms of teenagers. Just remember where you parked. (☎*780-444-5200 or 800-661-8890; www.wested-mall.com. Open M-F 10am-9pm, Sa 10am-6pm, Su noon-6pm. Amusement park open later.)*

FORT EDMONTON PARK. The fort proper sits at the far end of the park, serving as a 19th-century office building for Alberta's first capitalists, the fur traders of the Hudson Bay Company. Between the fort and the park entrance are three streets—1885, 1905, and 1920 St.—bedecked with period buildings decorated to match the streets' respective eras. (*On Whitemud Dr. at Fox Dr. ☎780-496-8787; www.gov.edmonton.ab.ca/fort. Open mid-May to late June M-F 10am-4pm, Sa-Su 10am-6pm; late June to early Sept. daily 10am-6pm; rest of Sept.*

wagon tours only M-Sa 11am-3pm, Su 10am-6pm. $8.25, seniors and ages 13-17 $6.25, ages 2-12 $4.50, families $26.)

ODYSSIUM. The reincarnated Space and Science Centre appeals to all ages with exhibits on the human body and the environment, including a **Gallery of the Gross** and a hands-on **Crime Lab.** Housed in a building shaped like a spacecraft, the largest **planetarium dome** in Canada uses 23,000 watts of audio during its laser light shows. Challenge yourself on the timed balance board or at one of the many logic game stations. The **IMAX theater** makes the planetarium seem like a child's toy. (*11211 142 St. ☎780-451-3344; www.odyssium.com. Open summer daily 10am-9pm; winter Su-Th 10am-5pm, F-Sa 10am-9pm. Day pass includes planetarium shows and exhibits: $10, students and seniors $8, ages 3-12 $7; families $39. General admission and IMAX show $16/$13/$11/$60.)*

RIVER VALLEY. The best part of Edmonton would have to be the longest stretch of urban parkland in Canada. Edmonton's **River Valley** boasts over 50km of easy to moderate paved multi-use trails and 69km of granular and chip trails for hiking and cycling. Any route down the river leads to the linked trail system; pick up a map at the Ranger Station. (*12130 River Valley Rd. ☎780-496-2950. Open daily 7am-1am.)*

🎭 ENTERTAINMENT

The **Edmonton Oilers,** the local NHL franchise, remain in an extended rebuilding period following their Wayne Gretzky-led Stanley Cup runs of the 1980s. But this is Canada, and it is hockey. The Oilers play at 11230 110th St. (☎780-451-8000; www.edmontonoilers.com. Season Oct.-April.)

"Canada's Festival City" (www.festival-city.com) hosts some kind of celebration year-round. The **Jazz City International Music Festival** (☎780-432-7166) packs 10 days with club dates and free performances by top international and Canadian jazz musicians. Around the same time is a visual arts celebration called **The Works** (☎780-426-2122). In August, the **Folk Music Festival** (☎780-429-1899), considered one of the best in North America, takes over Gallagher Park. All the world's a stage for the mid-August **Fringe**

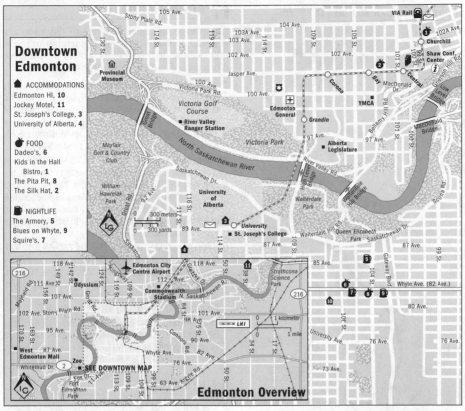

Downtown Edmonton

ACCOMMODATIONS
Edmonton HI, **10**
Jockey Motel, **11**
St. Joseph's College, **3**
University of Alberta, **4**

FOOD
Dadeo's, **6**
Kids in the Hall
Bistro, **1**
The Pita Pit, **8**
The Silk Hat, **2**

NIGHTLIFE
The Armory, **5**
Blues on Whyte, **9**
Squire's, **7**

Edmonton Overview

NORTH
AMERICA

Theater Festival (☎ 780-448-9000), when top alternative music and theater pours from parks, stages, and streets. This is the high point of Edmonton's festival schedule, and 500,000 travelers come to the city just to find the Fringe.

FOOD

Both a capital city and a college town, Edmonton offers cheap and diverse culinary options.

Dadeo's, 10548 Whyte Ave. (☎ 780-433-0930). Spicy Cajun and Louisiana-style food far from the bayou at this funky 50s diner. Su brunch 10am-2pm. M-Tu $7 po' boys. Open M-Th 11:30am-11pm, F-Sa 11:30am-midnight, Su 10am-10pm.

The Silk Hat, 10251 Jasper Ave. (☎ 780-425-1920). The oldest restaurant in Edmonton maintains enough character and sass to top the competition. This diner in the heart of downtown serves a huge array of food, from seafood to veggie-burgers ($6.25) to breakfast all day. Open M-F 7am-8pm, Sa 10am-8pm.

The Pita Pit, 8109 104 St. (☎ 780-435-3200), near Whyte Ave. Delicious pitas, fast-food style. Souvlaki $5.25. Students don't pay sales tax. Open M-W 11am-3am, Th-Sa 11am-4am, Su noon-3am.

Kids in the Hall Bistro, 1 Sir Winston Churchill Sq. (☎ 780-413-8060), in City Hall. This lunchroom is truly one-of-a-kind. Every employee, from waiter to chef, is a young person hired as part of a cooperative community service project. Entrees $5-10. Sandwiches $5-7. Takeout available. Open M-F 8am-4pm.

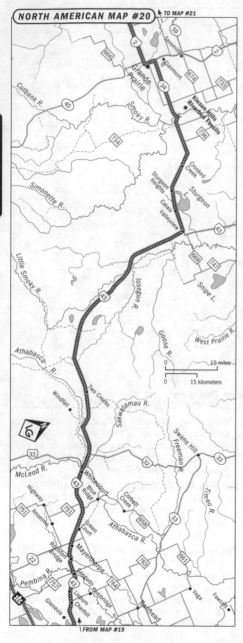

ACCOMMODATIONS

Affordable accommodations in Edmonton are generally easy to come by. Remember to make reservations in the summer, however, when the city's many festivals bring hordes of visitors.

Edmonton International Youth Hostel (HI), 10647 81 Ave. (☎ 780-988-6836). Just around the corner from the clubs, shops, and cafes of Whyte Ave. Facilities include a kitchen, game room, lounge, laundry, and backyard. Dorms $20, nonmembers $25; semi-private rooms $22/$27.

St. Joseph's College, 89 Ave. (☎ 780-492-7681), at 114 St.The rooms here are smaller than those at the university. Huge lounges, rec room, library, laundry, and close proximity to sports facilities. Reception M-F 8:30am-4pm. Call ahead; the 60 dorms often fill up quickly. Rooms available early May to late Aug. Singles $33, with full board $43.

University of Alberta, 87 Ave. (☎ 780-492-4281), between 116 and 117 St. Generic dorm rooms. Dry cleaning, kitchen, Internet access ($1 per 10min.), convenience store, and buffet-style cafeteria downstairs. Check-in 4pm. Reservations recommended. Rooms available late May to Aug. Singles $33.

Jockey Motel, 3604 118 Ave. (☎ 780-479-5981 or 800-843-7703). Offers comfortable rooms with cable TV, coin-operated laundry machines, and a convenient downtown location. Singles and doubles $59.

NIGHTLIFE

While it may not be Montreal, Edmonton's nightlife scene would make any Canadian proud. College students and twenty-somethings pour into town at night, and keep bars and clubs hopping every day of the week.

Squire's, 10505 82 Ave. (☎ 780-439-8594), lower level by Chianti. Popular with college kids. Drink specials. Open M-Tu 7pm-3am, W-Su 5pm-3am.

The Armory, 10310 85 Ave. (☎ 780-432-7300). This well-known dance club shows Edmonton's younger crowd how to party. M is Ladies Night, with $1 highballs until 11pm. Th is "Lowball" Night, with $2.50 highballs. Open M and Th-Sa 9pm-2am.

Blues on Whyte, 10329 82 Ave. (☎ 780-439-5058). Live blues and R&B from top-notch performers every night; Sa afternoon jam starts at 3pm. This joint may deserve its reputation as a biker bar; these blues are anything but sedate. Open daily 10am-3am.

LEAVING EDMONTON
18th Ave. will connect you to **Hwy. 16 West**. Just outside the city, **Hwy. 43** leads north towards Grande Prairie and Dawson Creek.

GRANDE PRAIRIE

Grande Prairie is a fur-trading post turned modern city, and a popular highway rest stop. The large chain motels that spring up around the outskirts of town speak to the city's location at the intersection of Hwy. 43 and 40, as well as its position as a gateway to the Alaska Highway. Don't let the flow of tourist traffic speed your departure too much, however; the city has a quiet charm that isn't easily discovered in just one day.

VITAL STATS

Population: 40,000

Visitor Information: Grande Prairie Regional Tourism Association, 11330 106 St. (☎780-539-7688; www.northernvisitor.com). **Centre 2000,** 330 106 St. (780-513-0240; www.centre200.ca).

Internet Access: Grande Prairie Public Library, 9910 99 Ave. (780-532-3580). Open M-Th 10am-9pm, F-Sa 10am-6pm, Su 2-5pm.

Post Office: 9831 100 Ave. Open M-Sa 8am-9pm, Su 10am-7pm. **Postal Code:** T8V 0T0

GETTING AROUND. The city center is organized around the intersection of **100th St.** and **100th Ave.** Avenues in town run east-west with numbers increasing as you head north, while streets run north-south and numbers increase as you drive west. **Parking** is easy to find and free.

SIGHTS. The **Grande Prairie Museum & Heritage Discovery Centre** is housed in two separate buildings: the museum resides at the corner of 102 Ave. and 102 St. and the discovery center makes up the bottom level of the tourism office (see above). The museum consists of ten buildings from Grande Prairie's first settlement days. They house over 48,000 artifacts, including fossils and arrowheads. The Discovery Centre is only a few years old, and is a modern counterpart to the museum's antique exhibits. It employs video displays to teach the region's history, and proudly exhibits Piper, an animatronic Pachyrhinosaurus dinosaur. (☎780-532-5482; www.grandeprairiemuseum.org. Open Sept.-May daily 8:30am-4:30pm. $3, under 18 $2, under 6 free.)

FOOD. Grande Prairie offers the standard fast-food fare and several grocery stores, all easily visible from the highway. Head downtown for locally owned diners and cafes. **Java Junction,** 9926 100 Ave., has delicious brunch options and exotic specialty brews. (☎780-539-5070. Coffee $1.50-4. Sandwiches $5. Open Su-F 7:30am-5:30pm, Sa 9am-4:30pm.) For amazing dessert, don't miss **Bricco's Cafe,** 10006 101 Ave., which also serves an array of tasty diner fare. (☎780-513-1313. Desserts $4-6. Egg salad sandwich $4.50. Open M-F 6:30am-9pm, Sa 8am-6pm.)

ACCOMMODATIONS. A drive down Hwy. 43 reveals a number of chain hotels. The **Lodge Motor Inn,** 10909 100 Ave., has clean rooms at reasonable rates. (☎780-539-4700 or 800-661-7874; info@lodgemotorinn.com. Singles $70; doubles $72.) There are 29 **campgrounds** in or around town. For details on facilities and locations, head to the Grande Prairie Regional Tourism Office. **Clairmont Park,** 5 mi. north of Grande Prairie on the east side of Clairmont Lake, offers water, firewood, and a playground. (Fully serviced sites $17; non-serviced sites $10.) **Pipestone Creek Park & Campground,** a 25min. drive west of town, displays the skull of a Pachyrhinosaurus and boasts some of the most concentrated dinosaur remains in Canada. The grounds are unserviced but there is a shower house. (Sites $15.)

Welcome To
BRITISH COLUMBIA

 From April to October, at the border you enter the Pacific Time Zone, where it is 1hr. earlier.

DAWSON CREEK

First settled in 1890, Dawson Creek was just another pip-squeak frontier village of a few hundred people among the canola fields of Peace River. Then came the Alaska Hwy., built during World War II in preparation for a possible Japa-

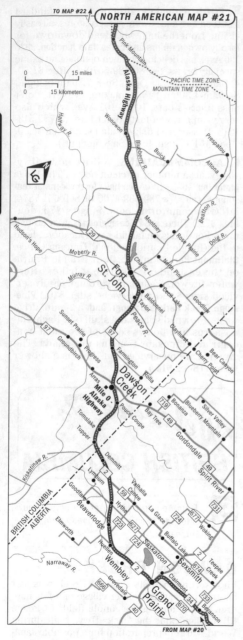

TO MAP #22

NORTH AMERICAN MAP #21

FROM MAP #20

nese invasion, followed shortly by an invasion of an entirely new brigade: senior citizens with a motor homes. The 13,000-odd residents are serious about their home's role as the Mile 0 anchor of the Alaska Hwy., and visitors who pause to enjoy the town's history and hospitality can easily get caught up in the enthusiasm.

VITAL STATS

Population: 13,000

Visitor Info: Visitors Center, 900 Alaska Ave. (☎250-782-9595), next to the big red grain elevator. Open May 15-Labor Day daily 8am-7pm; Labor Day-May 14 Tu-Sa 9am-5pm.

Internet Access: Public Library, (☎250-782-4661), at 10 St. and McKellar Ave. 1hr. free. Open Tu-Th 10am-9pm, F 10am-5:15pm, Sa 1:30-5:15pm.

Post Office: (☎250-782-9429), at 104th Ave. and 10th St. Open M-F 8:30am-5pm. **Postal Code:** V1G 4E6.

GETTING AROUND

Northwest of Grande Prairie along **Hwy. 43/Hwy. 2,** the town is laid out like a grid, with avenue numbers decreasing as you travel south. **8 St.** runs north-south through town and intersects **Alaska Ave.,** the onramp to the **Alaska Hwy.,** in the downtown area. The visitor center is just northwest of this intersection. **Parking** is abundant in town.

SIGHTS

This town boomed during construction. Literally. On February 13, 1943, 60 cases of exploding dynamite leveled the entire business district save the **COOP** building, now Bing's Furniture, opposite the Mile 0 post. Travelers cruising through Dawson Creek can't miss the photo-ops at **Mile 0 Cairn** and **Mile 0 Post.** Both commemorate the birth of the Alaska Hwy. within a stone's throw of the Visitors Center. The **Art Gallery** in the old grain elevator next door displays a photo essay on the Alaska Hwy. creation saga. (☎250-782-2601. Open June-Aug. daily 9am-5pm; Sept.-May Tu-Sa 10am-noon and 1-5pm.) The **Pioneer Village,** 1km west of Mile 0, is a re-creation of Dawson Creek life from the 1920s to the 40s, with antique farm equipment, an antler carver hard at work, nine gardens, and a play area for children. (☎250-782-7144. Open May-Aug. daily 8am-8pm. Donation requested.)

Travel 10km out of town to reach the highland marshes of ▧McQueen's Slough, which is filled with a broad spectrum of birds. In early August, the town plays host to the **Fall Fair & Stampede** (☎250-782-8911), with a carnival, fireworks, chuckwagon races, and a professional rodeo. Take Hwy. 49 east from the Visitors Center, turn left onto Rd. 3. (Rolla Rd., not to be confused with Parkhill Dr., which is also marked "Rolla Rd.," and which is still in town), and take the second left at the driveway across from the binocular signpost.

▧ FOOD

Cheap and hearty food is easy to come by here. Pick up a loaf for the road at the **Organic Farms Bakery**, 1425 97th Ave. Breads are baked fresh from local grain and start at $2; cakes and cookies are also available. (From the Visitors Center, drive west along Alaska Ave. and take a right at 15th St. You can't miss it; the building is huge. ☎250-782-6533. Open F 9:30am-5:30pm, Sa 9am-4pm.)

Alaska Cafe & Pub (☎250-782-7040), "55 paces south of the Mile 0 Post" on 10th St. Excellent burgers and fries from $7. The pub offers live music nightly at 9pm (mostly country), and travelers can sing at M night karaoke amidst stuffed cougars, elk, and marmots. Open Su-Th 10am-10pm, F-Sa 11am-11pm. Pub open daily noon-3am.

PotBelly Deli, 1128 102nd. Ave. (☎250-782-5425). Eating too many sandwiches ($5.50) will give your tummy some chub too, but you won't regret it. Each night, a new international cuisine inspires the chef. Open M-F 10am-7pm, Sa 10am-5pm.

Mile One Cafe (☎250-782-7144), 1km west of Mile 0. Select your entree from the chalkboard as you relive 1940s Dawson Creek in the Pioneer Village. Open Su and Tu-Sa 8am-7pm.

▧ ACCOMMODATIONS

Dawson Creek has a plethora of accommodation options for budget travelers.

Alaska Hotel, on 10th St. (☎250-782-7998), located above the Alaska Cafe & Pub, 1½ blocks from the Visitors Center. Those willing to trade a few amenities for bargain prices, great location, and an off-beat aura should head straight for these historic digs. The comfortable rooms are carefully decorated, some with pictures of Marilyn Monroe and Elvis. Shared bath; no TV or phone. Singles $32; doubles $37.

Voyageur Motor Inn, 801 111th Ave. (☎250-782-1020), facing 8th Ave. This motel offers motoring voyagers cable TV, phones, and fridges in sterile, boxy rooms. Singles $45; doubles $50.

Inn On The Creek, 10600 8th St. (☎250-782-8136), close to downtown. Folks willing to spend more can get all sorts of services here, like cable TVs, fridges, and microwaves. Singles $55-65; doubles $60-70.

Mile 0 Campground (☎250-782-2590), 1km west of Alaska Hwy., adjacent to the Pioneer Village. Popular but RV-laden. Free showers. Coin laundry $1.25. Sites $12; RV hookups $17.

Alahart RV Park, 1725 Alaska Ave. (☎250-782-4702), at the intersection with the John Hart Hwy. Campers can also head to this convenient site for a dump station and laundry. The friendly owners rival the Visitors Center for maps and suggestions on entertainment and food. Free showers. Sites $10; RV hookups $20.

▧ LEAVING DAWSON CREEK
Take **Alaska Ave.** up to the **Alaska Hwy. (Hwy. 97)** to head north.

THE ROAD TO FORT ST. JOHN. The Alaska Hwy. between Dawson Creek and Fort St. John (76km and about 45min. up the Alaska Hwy.) offers little more than cows and rolling hills. It runs through a region that is more concerned with industry (natural gas and timber) than tourism. Ride a 10km loop of the Old Alaska Hwy. over the curved **Kiskatinaw Bridge** (the only original timber bridge still in existence), 28km from Dawson Creek, and you'll appreciate the condition of the new highway.

TAYLOR & FORT ST. JOHN. In early August, gold-grubbers converge 20km south of Fort St. John in **Taylor** to pan for prizes and fame at the **World Invitational Gold Panning Championships** (☎250-789-3392) in Peace Island Park. The **Visitors Center,** 9923 96th Ave., at 100th St., is adjacent to the park and museum. (☎250-785-3033. Open June-Aug. M-F 8am-8pm, Sa and Su 9am-6pm; Sept.-May M-F 8am-5pm.) The people of Fort St. John take deep pride in their gargantuan **North Peace Leisure**

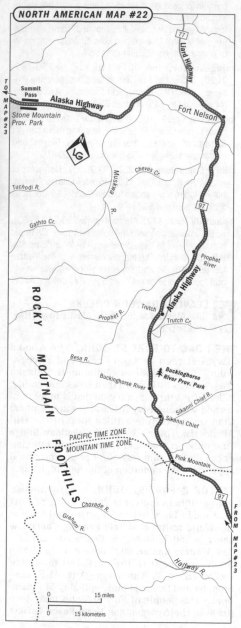

NORTH AMERICAN MAP #22

Pool, containing every imaginable aquatic delight, with a wave pool, sauna, hot tub, water slide, and steam room. (☎250-787-8178. $5, ages 13-18 $3.85, under 13 $2.75.)

If you didn't set your watch back before Dawson Creek, it's time now. From November to March the Alaska Hwy. passes into the Pacific Time Zone about 130km past Fort St. John.

THE ROAD TO FORT NELSON

You're on the Alaska Hwy., and you know it. You can almost feel the last vestiges of civilization scurry off into the surrounding conifers. Soaring, snow-capped mountains, crisply running streams, and tranquil lakes await you in bear country. The road you're on will lead you to the end of the world; all you have to do is follow. At Mile 160, the **Sikanni River RV Park** has full amenities in a mountain setting. Grassy tent sites along the river have picnic tables and fire pits. (☎250-774-1028. Toilets, laundry. Sites $12; full RV sites $19. Free showers.) The best sites for more rustic camping along the way are at **Buckinghorse Provincial Park,** 27km from Sikanni, along the river, although they are not particularly private. (Pit toilets. Sites $12.)

FORT NELSON

Over 450km north of Dawson Creek, Fort Nelson is a bastion of natural resource extraction. The **Fort Nelson Heritage Museum,** across the highway from the Visitors Center, features an impressive collection of stuffed game, as well as remnants from the era of highway construction. (☎250-774-3536. Open daily 9am-6pm. $3, ages 6-16 and seniors $2.) The **First Nations Craft Center** is on 49th Ave. From 50th St., off 50th Ave. South, take a right on 49th Ave.; it's on the right. (☎250-774-3669. Open M-F 8:30am-4:30pm.) The **Visitors Center,** in the Recreation Centre/Curling Rink on the west edge of town, provides daily **ki road reports.** (☎250-774-6400. Open daily May-Sept. 8am-8pm.)

There aren't many choices for dining in Fort Nelson. **Dan's Pub,** at the southern end of town, offers nightly drink specials, pool, and an extensive menu. (☎250-774-3929. 19+ after 8pm. Open M-Th 11am-12:30am, F-Sa 11am-1:30am, Su 11am-midnight.) The **Blue Bell Restaurant,** opposite Dan's in the Blue Bell Inn, serves a $5 breakfast. (☎250-774-3550. Open M-Sa 6am-9pm, Su 8am-

4pm.) Rest at the **Mini-Price Inn,** 5036 51st Ave. West, one block off the highway near the Visitors Center. (☎250-774-2136. No phones. Cable TV. Singles $45; doubles $50. Kitchenettes $5 extra.) The **Almada Inn** is by the CIBC Bank off the Alaska Hwy. (☎250-774-2844. Breakfast included. Singles $69; doubles $79.) The **Westend Campground,** across from the Visitors Center, has dusty sites in a pretty, wooded area, but the place is more RV-oriented than tent friendly. (☎250-774-2340. Laundry: wash $2, dry $1 per 30min. Sites $17; RV hookups $22. Showers $1 per 9min.)

THE ROAD TO WATSON LAKE

Small towns, usually composed of one gas pump, one $50 motel, and one cafe, pock the remainder of the highway to Watson Lake. Fortunately for the driver, scenery improves dramatically a few miles out of Fort Nelson.

STONE MOUNTAIN
150km north of Fort Nelson on Alaska Hwy.

Driving west on the highway, naked Stone Mountain appears. **Summit Lake** lies below the highest summit on the highway (1295m). Neighboring **Stone Mountain Campground** makes a superb starting point for hiking. (Composting outhouse, firewood, water. Sites $12.) The steep **Summit Peaks Trail** begins across the highway from the campground, ascending 5km along a ridgeline to the breathtaking crest. A more moderate trail climbs 6km to the alpine Flower Springs Lake. Each hike takes about 5hr. round-trip. A 70km loop leads from Km 632 of the Alaska Hwy. through the craggy MacDonald Creek Valley and back out the Wokkpash Valley Gorge. Gas and accommodations are available roadside 7km past the lake.

TOAD RIVER CAFE
On Alaska Hwy.

The **Toad River Cafe** has some 5900 hats dangling from the ceiling. Don't miss out on your chance at a warm cinnamon bun, made from homemade bread. Tasty burgers start at $7. (☎250-232-5401. Internet $0.20 per min. Open summer daily 6:30am-10pm; winter 7am-9pm.)

MUNCHO LAKE. Fifty kilometers north of Toad River, Muncho Lake Provincial Park delights even the weariest drivers. Muncho ("big lake" in Tagish) is a 7 mi. long azure mirror. **Strawberry Flats Provincial Campground** and **MacDonald Provincial**

Campground, 8km farther on, have the best camping in the area with sweet lakefront sites. (Pit toilets, fire wood, water. Sites $12.) If you don't want to camp, stay at the **Muncho Lake Lodge,** 10km north of Strawberry Flats. Rooms are well kept, and the service is good. (☎250-776-3456. Singles $45; tent sites $14; RV sites $16.)

LIARD RIVER HOT SPRINGS. Near the 775km mark of the Alaska Hwy. are the Liard River Hot Springs. These two naturally steamy and sulfurous pools are a phenomenal place to sooth a driver's derriere. The park service manages campsites and free day-use of the springs. (Reservations ☎800-689-9025. Water, toilets, firewood. Gates closed 11pm-6am. Sites $15.) About 10km after Liard Hot Springs, a rough, 3km gravel road thwarts RVs and leads to the hidden and largely untouristed **Smith River Falls.** Watch carefully for the turn-off sign. A steep trail with rickety staircases leads right to the base of the huge cascade, and grayling can be fished from the Smith River with a permit. For permit info, contact **BC Parks** at ☎250-787-3407.

 In the Yukon, ☎911 may not work outside the Whitehorse area; call ☎867-667-5555.

WATSON LAKE

Switchbacking between the Yukon and British Columbia, the Alaska Hwy. winds through tracts of young forest. Just after it crosses into the Yukon for the second time, at Km 1021, the highway runs through Watson Lake, site of the zany **Sign Post Forest.** In the 1940s, a homesick WWII Army G.I. posted the mileage from Watson to his hometown of Danville, Illinois. The 50,000 signs that subsequent travelers put up make this site a gigantic, mind-boggling oddity. The **Visitors Center** is hidden inside this forest of signs, along the Robert Campbell Hwy. (☎867-536-7469. Open May-Sept. daily 8am-8pm.) If finding the distance to your hometown fails to capture your attention, call for mountain bluebirds on **Wye Lake** from the 3km boardwalk trail running from the Town Center to Wye Lake Park. Watson Lake also lures passers-by with the **Northern Lights Centre** opposite the Visitors Center, which dispenses explanations for aurora borealis. (☎867-536-7827; www.watsonlake.net. Call ahead for hours. 50min. shows 6 times daily. $10; seniors and students $9; children

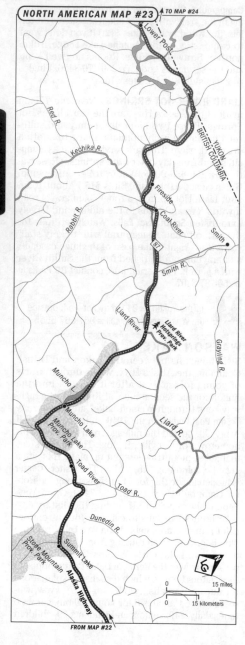

NORTH AMERICAN MAP #23

$6. Exhibits free.) The **Liard Canyon Recreation Site** on **Lucky Lake,** 8km east of town, makes for great picnicking and swimming. A 2km trail down the canyon is a relaxing and scenic stroll.

Hardcore travelers **fish** for dinner. In midsummer, grayling swim in the back eddies of tiny streams west along the Alaska Hwy., and both **Lucky Lake** (5½km east of town) and **Hour Lake** (at the east end of town behind the RCMP) are full of rainbow trout. Check in at the Visitors Center to purchase the appropriate permits. Other than what you can pull out of the lake, dining options in town are restricted to highway fare. The **Pizza Place,** at the **Gateway Motor Inn,** is a somewhat pricey gem. Medium specialty pies start at $15, but ambitious eaters go right for the $22 "Yukoner," loaded with all manner of meats and vegetables. For the tighter budget, meals from the grill range $6.50-9. (☎ 867-536-7722. Open daily 6:30am-10pm.) Accommodations in Watson Lake are plentiful but pricey. **Watson Lake Campground,** 3km west of town along the highway and then 4km down a well-marked gravel road, has primitive sites ideal for tenting. ($8 camping permit only.)

▲ DAWSON PEAKS RESORT
260km west of Watson Lake on Alaska Hwy.

A beautiful resort on Teslin Lake, the Dawson Peaks Resort dishes up delectable burgers in its restaurant ($7) and offers a number of accommodation choices to suit whatever kind of lodging you feel like at the moment. (☎ 867-390-2244. Open daily 7:30am-10pm. Toilets, firewood, water. Sites $10; full RV sites $18; canvas tent platforms $35; private cabins $82. Showers $2.) The friendly hosts can help you get out the door and into the water with **river runs** (4-5 days, $400), guided **fishing charters** ($50 per hr.), and rented canoes ($8 per hr.) and powerboats ($25 per hr.).

TESLIN

Teslin tells its story at **George Johnston Museum,** on the Alaska Hwy. at the west end of town. Born in Alaska in 1889, George Johnston was a Tlingit man who ran a trap line and a general store while experimenting with photography on the side. Johnston left a series of stunning photographs documenting Tlingit life in Teslin from 1910 to 1940. The museum also displays a moose skin boat, Teslin's first automobile (bought by

Johnston when the town was roadless), and an excellent video about the Alaska Hwy.'s effect on native culture. (☎867-390-2550. Open daily mid-May to early Sept. 9:30am-5:30pm. $4, students and seniors $3.50, children 6-15 $2, families $10.)

RV travelers bond over food and the free house boat rides at **Muklak Annie's,** 7km east of Teslin. There's nothing miniature about a mini-salmon plate ($15) or kids' portion ($9), but the big-eaters can pay $19 for loads of salmon, all-you-can-eat salad, fresh rolls, coffee, and dessert. Ribs, pork chops, and burgers are also served on the checked cloths in the gift shop-decor dining hall. (☎867-667-1200. Open daily 7am-9pm. Free campsite, house boat ride, RV wash, and water fill-up with meal. Showers $4. Cabins with shared bath $40.)

🏔 LEAVING TESLIN
From Teslin, the 183km (2hr.) drive to White-horse is interspersed with a few gas stops and provincial campgrounds, but not much else.

◀ DETOUR: CARCROSS
100km past Teslin, exit the Alaska Hwy, for Hwy. 8 (Tagish Rd.), which runs 30km to Carcross. Leaving Carcross, hop on the Klondike Hwy. North (Hwy. 2) to head to Whitehorse.

Carcross, shortened from "Caribou Crossing," perches between Bennett and Nares Lakes, surrounded by snow-capped peaks. Pick up *White-horse Area Hikes and Bikes* at the bus depot. The most popular area hike is the **Chilkoot Trail,** a moderately difficult three to five-day adventure beginning at Skagway and ending at the far end of Lake Bennett. The lake's two sandy **beaches** are popular in July and August. Overlooking the town, **rough mining roads** snake around Montana Mountain. To access them, follow Hwy. 2 south and take the first right after crossing the bridge. Take the first left and drive until the washout. From there, it's all on foot to astounding views. (21km round-trip, 8hr. including drive.) The adventurous can play in the sand of an exposed glacial lake bottom in the world's smallest desert, **Carcross Desert,** 3km north of town on the highway.

Nine kilometers north of town, the **Cinnamon Cache** is a culinary gem tucked away among Dall sheep and bluebirds. Homemade cinnamon buns, survival cookies for the trail (both $2.50), hot pies, and soup and sandwiches make tummies happy. (☎867-821-4331. Open Feb.-Sept. daily 7am-7pm.) The **Spirit Lake Wilderness Resort,** 10km north of town on Hwy. 2, has lakeside accommodations and rents canoes for $8 per hour. (☎867-821-4337. Free showers, toilets, coin laundry. Tent sites $14, with electricity $20; cabins on the jade-colored lake $72 for 1-2 people, $81 for 3-4 people.)

🏔 APPROACHING WHITEHORSE
Arriving in Whitehorse is somewhat of a relief from the highway towns to the east; honest-to-goodness services, restaurants, and lodgings provide the first glimmer of selection you'll have seen for a ways, and you'll never have been more excited to see a town with more than one street. The town sits south of the **Alaska Hwy.,** and the exit, **Two Mile Hill Rd.,** will carry you straight into the downtown.

THE LOCAL STORY

BRIGHT LIGHTS, NO CITY

Many travelers come to the Yukon to get away from the bright lights and noise of the big city only to fall under the spell of the most awesome of natural light shows: the aurora borealis (northern lights). Some Native Americans believed these colored clouds and arcs were the torches of spirits, lighting the way to heaven for those who had died. Scientists, however, credit solar flares hitting the earth, sweeping streams of electrically charged particles into the atmosphere. As the earth's magnetic field deflects these particles toward the poles, the particles enter the atmosphere and begin to glow. Oxygen atoms create brilliant yellow-green and burning red hues, ionized nitrogen particles cast a blue hue, while neutral nitrogen creates purplish-red. But scientific explanations can't detract from the supernatural mystery of the northern lights. A few onlookers claim to be able to even *hear* the lights overhead, although no scientist has yet to record these sounds or come up with an explanation. Some Inuit tribes interpreted these noises as the whisperings of the spirits. So prick up your ears as you next stare skyward, and you may discover that no matter how far away you think you've gotten from civilization, you may still face bright lights and noise.

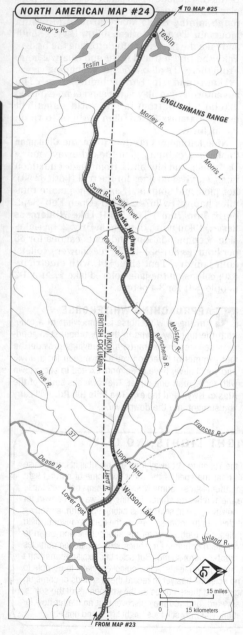

NORTH AMERICAN MAP #24

TO MAP #25

Glady's R.

Teslin

Teslin L.

ENGLISHMANS RANGE

Morley R.

Morris L.

Swift R.

Swift River

Alaska Highway

Rancheria

YUKON
BRITISH COLUMBIA

Meister R.

Rancheria R.

Blue R.

37

Frances R.

Dease R.

Upper Liard

Liard R.

Watson Lake

Lower Post

Hyland R.

0   15 miles

0   15 kilometers

FROM MAP #23

WHITEHORSE

Whitehorse was born during the Klondike Gold Rush, when the gold-hungry used it as a layover on their journey north. Miners en route to Dawson City coined the name, claiming that whitecaps on the rapids downstream resembled galloping stallions. The capital of the Yukon shifted from Dawson to here in 1953, and now the majority of government employees—and 70% of the territory's residents—call Whitehorse home. The town is clogged with acres of RVs during the summer, and an adventurous roadtripper's best bet is to head into the surrounding wilderness.

VITAL STATS

Population: 24,000

Visitor Info: Tourism and Business Centre, 100 Hanson St. (☎867-667-3084), off 1st Ave., at 2nd Ave. Open mid-May to mid-Sept. daily 8am-8pm; late Sept. to early May M-F 9am-5pm.

Internet Access: Whitehorse Library, 2071 2nd Ave. (☎867-667-5239), at Hanson. Free 30min. Internet access twice daily; reserve in advance or stop in for first-come, first-served 15min. of access. Open M-F 10am-9pm, Sa 10am-6pm, Su 1-9pm.

Post Office: 211 Main St. (☎867-667-2485), in the basement of Shopper's Drug Mart. Open M-F 9am-6pm, Sa 11am-4pm. **General delivery** at 300 Range Rd. (☎867-667-2412). **Postal Code:** For last names beginning with the letters A-L it's Y1A 3S7; for M-Z it's Y1A 3S8.

⌐ GETTING AROUND

Whitehorse lies 1500km northwest of Dawson Creek, BC, along the **Alaska Hwy.,** which becomes **Two Mile Hill Rd.** and then **4th Ave.** as it enters town from the north. Bounded on the east by the Yukon River, the city is an oblong grid of numbered avenues running north-south, with **2nd Ave.** and **4th Ave.** being the primary thoroughfares. Streets run east-west, with **Main St.** in the center of town. **Parking** meters line the blocks near Main St., while more distant business generally have parking lots.

👁 SIGHTS

YUKON BERINGIA INTERPRETIVE CENTRE.
Huge woolly mammoths, saber-toothed tigers, and other Ice Age critters make you realize how rough the north's first settlers had it. (*On the*

Alaska Hwy., 2km northwest of the Robert Service Way junction. ☎867-667-8855; www.beringia.com. Open daily mid-May to June and Sept. 9am-6pm; July-Aug. 8:30am-7pm; Oct. to early May Su 1-5pm and by appointment. $6, seniors $5, students $4.)

WHITEHORSE FISHWAY. If you think you're a weary traveler, meet the chinook salmon who swim 27,740km upstream before reaching the fish ladder—designed to save them from death by dam. You're most likely to see them climbing the 370m ladder from late July through August. (2.4km from town, over the bridge by the S.S. Klondike. ☎867-633-5965. Open June Su and W-Sa 10am-6pm; early July to early Sept. daily 8:30am-9pm.)

VISUAL ARTS. Government patronage and an inspired population make Whitehorse an epicenter of the arts. The Yukon Government's **collection** is housed throughout the administrative and public spaces of the capital. (☎867-667-5264.) Pick up a free *ArtWalk* brochure at the Visitors Center, or at the nonprofit, Yukon-artwork-adorned **Captain Martin House Gallery.** (305 Wood St. ☎867-667-4080. Open summer M-F 10am-8pm, Sa 10am-5pm, Su noon-5pm; winter M-Sa 11am-5pm; closed Jan.) The Yukon's only public art museum, the **Yukon Arts Centre Art Gallery,** shows Canadian contemporary art. (300 College Dr., Yukon College. ☎867-667-8578. Open June-Aug. M-F 11am-5pm, Sa-Su noon-5pm; Sept.-May Tu-F 11am-5pm, Sa-Su 1-4pm. $3, students and seniors $2, under 12 free. Su free.)

OUTDOOR ACTIVITIES

HIKING

There seem to be more trails than people around Whitehorse. **Kluane National Park** (see p. 740) beckons from the west, but there is plenty of accessible day hiking near town. Both *Whitehorse Area Hikes and Bikes* ($19), published by the **Yukon Conservation Society,** and the *Whitehorse Area Hikes* map ($10) are available at **Mac's Fireweed Books,** 203 Main St. (☎867-668-2434. Open daily 8am-midnight.) Good hikes include those to Grey Mountain, Lookout Hill, and Miles Canyon Trail Network. Discover where to spot a golden eagle with the aid of the **Yukon Bird Club** (☎867-667-4630) or take a free birding trip in summer.

WATER ACTIVITIES

The **M.V. Schwatka,** on Miles Canyon Rd. off Robert Service Way, floats folks on a relaxing, 2hr. historical ride through Miles Canyon. (☎867-668-

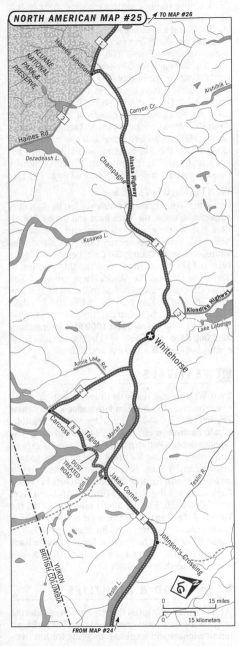

NORTH AMERICAN MAP #25 ↗ TO MAP #26

FROM MAP #24

4716. Cruises daily June to early Sept. 2pm; in July also 7pm tour. $21, ages 2-10 $10.50, under 2 free.) **Up North Boat and Canoe Rentals,** 103 Strickland St., lets you paddle 25km to Takhini River or take a longer trip. (☎ 867-667-7035; www.upnorth.yk.ca. 4hr. trip $30 each for 2 or $60 solo; includes transportation.) An eight-day trip on the Teslin River costs $200, but you can rent sea kayaks and canoes by the day ($30-35). The waterways around **Sanfu Lake** (1½hr. south of Whitehorse on Atlin Rd.) are ideal for kayaking. **Tatshenshini Expediting,** 1602 Alder St., leads intense whitewater rides. (Take the Alaska Hwy. north 2km, turn left on Birch, and left again on 15th St., which becomes Alder. ☎ 867-633-2742. Full day $115.)

WINTER ACTIVITIES

In winter, Whitehorse is criss-crossed by 300km of **snowmobile trails. Up North Boat and Canoe Rentals** (see p. 738) rents snowmobiles and skis. Whitehorse is also a **cross-country skiing** paradise. The **Whitehorse Cross Country Ski Club,** beside Mt. McIntyre, off Hamilton Blvd. near the intersection of Two Mile Hill and the Alaska Hwy., grooms 50km of world-class trails; 5km of trails are lit at night. (☎ 867-668-4477. Day pass $9, under 19 $4; 3 days $22; 5 days $35.) In February, "the toughest race in the world," the **Yukon Quest 1000 Mile International Sled Dog Race** (☎ 867-668-4711), follows Gold Rush routes between Whitehorse and Fairbanks.

❄ FESTIVALS

Two Whitehorse festivals draw crowds from all over the world: the **Yukon International Storytelling Festival** (☎ 867-633-7550) in May, and the **Frostbite Music Festival** (☎ 867-668-4921) in February. The **Commissioner's Potlatch** gathers indigenous groups and visitors in June for traditional dancing, games, artistry, and a feast. Locals, transients, and native artists perform for free at noon with **Arts in Lepage Park** on weekdays. (At Wood St. and 3rd Ave. ☎ 867-668-3136. From June to mid-Aug.) Call the **Yukon Arts Centre Theatre** (☎ 867-667-8574; www.yukonartscentre.org) for stage updates. The **Yukon River** hosts the popular **Rubber Duckie Race** on Canada Day, July 1. (☎ 867-668-7979. $5 per duck. Proceeds go to charity.)

🍴🍷 FOOD & NIGHTLIFE

While Whitehorse gives the impression of catering only to the fast food-craving Alaska Hwy. driver, hip musicians and tourists hungering for the frontier will find good grub, too. Top-quality fruits and veggies can be found at **The Fruit Stand,** at 2nd Ave. and Black St. (Open in summer M-Sa 10:30am-7pm.) **Alpine Bakery,** 411 Alexander St., between 4th and 5th Ave., turns out exquisite bread. (☎ 867-668-6871. Open M-Sa 8am-6pm; in winter closed M.) Those looking for bars can choose from a variety on Main St. Most have live music, and the scene varies from 20-year-old pop fans at the **Lizard Lounge** to classic rock at the **Roadhouse Saloon** to Canadian rock at the **Capitol Hotel.**

■ **The Talisman Cafe,** 2112 2nd Ave. (☎ 867-667-2736). Decorated with local art. Vegetarians, ethnic food lovers, and carnivores will all leave happy. Heaps of fresh food ranging from Mexican to Middle Eastern for $10-14. Open daily 9am-8pm.

■ **Klondike Rib and Salmon Barbecue,** 2116 2nd Ave. (☎ 867-667-7554). In an old wall-tent structure, these down-home folks will call you "sweetie" and serve you friendly-like. Worth its weight in (Yukon) gold, try the rich salmon-dip lunch ($13). Open May-Sept. M-F 11:30am-9pm, Sa-Su 5-9pm.

Sam and Andy's, 506 Main St. (☎ 867-668-6994), between 5th and 6th Ave. Tex-Mex on a jumpin' patio. Generous build-your-own fajitas are mid-range entrees ($13). You can save money by ordering the veggie version. "Thrifty Thursdays" mean $1 drafts, $2 pints. Open M-Sa 11am-11pm, Su 11am-10pm.

Midnight Sun Coffee Roaster, 4168 4th Ave. (☎ 867-633-4563). Offers every coffee drink under the sun ($3-8) to sip among stained-glass art in comfy chairs or in funky outdoor booths. Internet $3 per 30min., $5 per hr. Open M-F 7am-10pm; later on weekends.

Little Japan, 2157 2nd Ave. (☎ 867-668-6620). Affordable sushi (5 salmon rolls $6.50) and western fare for the squeamish (small $15 "Meatzza" pizzas are quite big). Open M-F 6:30am-9pm, Sa-Su 11am-9pm.

🏠 ACCOMMODATIONS

Interchangeable motels around town charge upwards of $70, but fear not; the hostel and campground options are superb.

■ **Hide on Jeckell Guesthouse,** 410 Jeckell (☎ 867-633-4933), between 4th and 5th Ave., 1 block from Robert Service Way. Stay in the continent-themed room of your choice and pick your endangered species-labeled bed. Amenities include coffee, kitchen, bikes, Internet, local calls, linens, and lockers. 22 beds, 6 rooms. Dorms $20.

Beez Kneez Bakpakers Hostel, 408 Hoge St. (☎867-456-2333), off 4th Ave., 2 blocks from Robert Service Way. Weary backpackers find refuge in this hostel equipped with Internet, BBQ deck, washer ($2) and dryer ($2). Dorms $20 each; private rooms $50.

Robert Service Campground (☎867-668-3721), 1km from town on Robert Service Way along the Yukon River. Home for students who tan on the lawn and gear up for hikes. Food trailer, firewood ($2), drinking water. 68 sites. Gates open 7am-midnight. Open late May to early Sept. Tent sites $14. Showers $1 per 5min.

Takhini Hot Springs (☎867-633-2706). Follow the Alaska Hwy. northwest from downtown 10km, turn right on N. Klondike Hwy., and left after 6.5km onto Takhini Hot Springs Rd. Drive 10km to the end. Restaurant, horseback riding ($20 per hr.). 88 sites with showers. Pools open May-Sept. daily 10am-10pm. Sites $12.50, with electricity $15. Day-use $4-5.50.

Roadhouse Inn, 2163 2nd. Ave. (☎867-667-2594), at Black St. An affordable downtown alternative to pricier tourist havens. Rooms are straightforward and simple. The saloon next door keeps the taps flowing until 2am. Motel units start at $45 for singles; doubles from $50. Hotel units with cable TV $10 more.

LEAVING WHITEHORSE
Try to have a destination the day you leave Whitehorse; it's a long 600km to Tok, and the points between can fill up quickly in summer months. When you're ready for the great outdoors, **2nd Ave.** will take you back to **Two Mile Hill Rd.** and the **Alaska Hwy.**

KWADAY DAN KENJI TRADITIONAL CAMP
A few minutes east of the village of Champagne, 70km west of Whitehorse and 88km east of Haines Junction on the Alaska Hwy.

Visit a traditional camp of the Champagne people, recently constructed with the help of local elders, and enjoy a mug of fresh brewed tea ($1.25). **Camping** facilities have pit toilets and fresh water, and there is a guided tour of the traditionally made shelters and animal traps. (Shop with artifacts and local crafts open daily May-Oct. 9am-7:30pm. Sites $10. Day-use $10, children $6.)

HAINES JUNCTION
The gateway to Kluane National Park, tiny Haines Junction (pop. 800) is often called the Yukon's best-kept secret. Except for holiday weekends, the town is relatively free of many tourists. Instead, it makes a quiet and quaint jumping off point for wilderness exploration.

VITAL STATS

Population: 800

Visitor Info: See **Kluane National Park,** p. 740.

Internet Access: Haines Junction Community Library, (☎868-634-2215), in the Yukon Government Administration Bldg. Open Tu-F 1-5pm, Sa 2-5pm.

Post Office: Haines Junction PO (☎800-267-1177). Open M-Th 9am-5pm, F 9am-1pm. **Postal Code:** Y0B 1L0.

NORTH AMERICA

■ **GETTING AROUND.** Haines Junction is 158km west of Whitehorse on the **Alaska Hwy. (Hwy. 1)** at the eastern boundary of Kluane National Park. The tiny downtown centers on Alaska Hwy., with restaurants, bars, and the library adorning its flanks. Parallel to Alaska Hwy. to the east is **Backe St.** and to the west **Luciana St. Parking** is ample and easy to find in town.

■ **OUTDOOR ACTIVITIES.** If you've got the cash, outdoor guides are invaluable for area information, bear security, and navigation skills. In addition to guiding services, **PaddleWheel Adventures,** directly down the road from the Village Bakery, arranges flightseeing over the glaciers, hike-out helicopter rides to the **Kluane Plateau,** and full-day rafting trips on the Class III and IV rapids of the **Blanchard** and **Tatshenshini Rivers.** They also rent the gear you'd need to explore the park on your own, including tents, packs, and bear spray. (☎867-634-2683. Flightseeing $95 per person for 30min. flight over the Kaskawulsh. Rafting $100 per person including lunch. Bikes $25 per day, canoes $25. Guides $150 per day for up to 6 people and $25 per additional person; fishing guides $150 per day for one person.) Call **Kluane Ecotours** for custom-fitted hiking, canoeing, or kayaking guides. (☎867-634-2626. $85 per person; minimum $150 per day.)

■ **FESTIVALS.** Reserved little Haines Junction lets it all hang out in late June for back-to-back festivals. During the second weekend in June, music-loving rowdies from all over the area gather for "the function at the junction" to hear northern artists perform at the **Alsek Music Festival** (☎867-634-2520). Ask about the Kidzone for children.

■ **FOOD.** Most Haines Junction restaurants offer standard highway fare. But the ▓**Village Bakery** breaks the trend, offering fresh veggie dishes, beefy sandwiches, and tray upon tray of fudge and sweets. Also served are substantial soups with bread ($3.50), sourdough cheese dogs ($2.25), sushi (F only; $4.50 for 5 pieces), and espresso fudge ($1.75). Make reservations to enjoy live music and salmon–BBQs ($13.50) on Monday nights. (☎ 867-634-2867. Open daily May-Sept. 7am-9pm.) "We got it all"—the motto of **Madley's General Store**—is an understatement. Here you can find star fruit, tackle, hardware, a butcher block, and anything else you didn't know you needed. (☎ 867-634-2200. Open daily May-Sept. 8am-9pm; Oct.-Apr. 8am-6:30pm.)

Ⓡ **ACCOMMODATIONS.** Most people come to camp, so accommodations in Kluane National Park (see p. 740) are optimal. If you'd rather be close to town, however, the **Stardust Motel** is just 1km north of town on the Alaska Hwy., and offers spacious rooms with satellite TV and private bath. (☎ 867-634-2591. No phones. Kitchenettes extra. Reservations recommended. Open mid-May to mid-Sept. Singles $55; doubles $65.)

KLUANE NATIONAL PARK

Dizzyingly massive glaciers spill off of huge mountains and keep going for kilometers, wedging into the surrounding forests like waves of cold crystal. Lakes thick with fish speckle unbroken tracts of raw forest wilderness, and bears mingle with Dall Sheep beneath soaring eagles. Kluane doesn't shy from natural spectacle—together with Glacier National Park, the adjacent Wrangell-St. Elias National Park in Alaska, and Tatshenshini/Alsek Provincial Park in BC, Kluane is part of one of the world's largest protected wilderness areas. Canada's massive mountain range, the St. Elias Mountains, divides into two separate ranges within the park. The smaller Kluane Range runs right along the Alaska Hwy. The soaring giants of the Icefield Range, including Canada's highest peak, Mt. Logan (5959m), and the most massive non-polar ice fields in the world are separated from the Kluane range by the Duke Depression. The ice-blanketed mountains of Kluane's interior are a haven for experienced expeditioners, but their remoteness renders two-thirds of the park inaccessible to humbler hikers. Fortunately, the northeastern section of the park (bordering the Alaska Hwy.) offers splendid, accessible backpacking, rafting, biking, fishing, and day hiking. Many routes follow original Southern Tutchone and Tlingit Trails and old mining roads left over from Kluane's brief fling with the Gold Rush in 1904-1905.

⟮ VITAL STATS ⟯

Area: 5.4 million acres

Visitor Information: Kluane National Park Visitor Reception Centre (☎ 867-634-7207; www.parkscanada.gc.ca/kluane), on Logan St. in Haines Junction, at Km 1635 on the Alaska Hwy. Registers overnight visitors and provides wilderness permits, fishing permits, topographical maps ($12), and trail and weather info. Open May-Sept. daily 9am-7pm; Oct.-Apr. M-F 10am-noon and 1-5pm. **Sheep Mountain Information Centre** lies 72km north of town at Alaska Hwy. Km 1707. Registers hikers headed for the northern area of the park, sells hiking guides for $1, and rents bear canisters. Open daily May-Labor Day 9am-5pm. Overnight registration until 4:30pm.

Gateway Town: Haines Junction (p. 739)

Fees: Wilderness permit $5 per day. Fishing permit $5 per day.

▣ **GETTING AROUND**

Kluane's 22,015 sq. km are bounded by the **Kluane Game Sanctuary** and the **Alaska Hwy.** to the north, and the scenic **Haines Hwy. (Hwy. 3)** to the east. Beyond **Haines Junction,** there is also access to trails in the north of the park from **Sheep Mountain,** 72km northwest of Haines Junction on the Alaska Hwy. **Parking** is available in town and at trailheads.

▨ **HIKING**

Kluane's trails are varied and very accessible. The Visitors Centers are great sources for trail maps, information, and conditions. A $1 pamphlet lists about 25 trails and routes ranging from 500m to 96km. Routes, as opposed to trails, are not maintained, do not have marked paths, are more physically demanding, and require backcountry navigation skills. Overnight visitors must register and pay at one of the Visitors Centers ($5 per night for adults), and use bear-resistant food canisters, which the park rents for $5 per night (with $150 cash or credit refundable deposit).

Dezadeash River Loop (DEZ-dee-ash; 5km). The trailhead is downtown at the day-use area across from Madley's on Haines Rd. This flat, forested trail will disappoint anyone craving steepness, but it makes for a nice stroll. Easy.

Auriol Loop (15km, 4-6hr.; 400m gain). The trail begins 7km south of Haines Junction on Haines Rd. and cuts through boreal forest, leading to a subalpine bench just in front of the Auriol Range. Divided by a primitive campground halfway along, this is a popular overnight trip, although it can easily be hiked in a day without heavy packs. Moderate.

King's Throne Route (10km round-trip, 1220m gain). Rewarding day hike with a panoramic view begins at Kathleen Lake day-use area (see p. 742). Difficult.

Sheep Creek Trail (10km round-trip, 430m gain). Down a short gravel access road just north of the Visitors Center for **Sheep Mountain.** This satisfying day hike gives you a good chance to see Dall sheep during the summer months. An easy 500m jaunt up to **Soldier's Summit** starts 1km north of the Sheep Mountain Info Centre and leads to the site where the Alaska Hwy. was officially opened on Nov. 20, 1942. Moderate.

Backcountry Treks. Backcountry hiking can quickly become a dangerous and challenging enterprise in the undeveloped, glaciated Kluane interior. Be sure to carry twice as much food as you expect to need, buy the proper topographic maps, and always consult rangers before you head out. Don't underestimate the bears, either. **Donjek** and **Kaskawulsh Glaciers** are the most accessible to backcountry travelers—consult the Visitors Center for more detailed advice on specific approaches. Extreme.

When hiking in bear country, use bear bells or belt out tunes to avoid running into a surprised and grumpy bear.

⚠ OUTDOOR ACTIVITIES

WATER ACTIVITIES. Anglers can put the park's reputation for plentiful fishing to the test at **Kathleen Lake,** home to lake and rainbow trout (catch and release only), grayling, and rare freshwater Kokanee salmon (usually in season mid-May to early June). Less-crowded **St. Elias Lake** is an easy 3.5km hike from the trailhead, 60km south of Haines Junction on Haines Rd. **Pine Lake,** the popular territorial campground, is a good spot to put in a canoe for a paddle, as it is less windy than Kathleen Lake. Fishing here requires a Yukon permit from Madley's, while Kluane waters require a National Parks fishing permit, available at the Visitors Center in Haines Junction (see p. 739). Be sure to pick up the *Yukon Fishing Regulations Summary Booklet* for free from the Visitors Center to avoid any uncomfortable incidents.

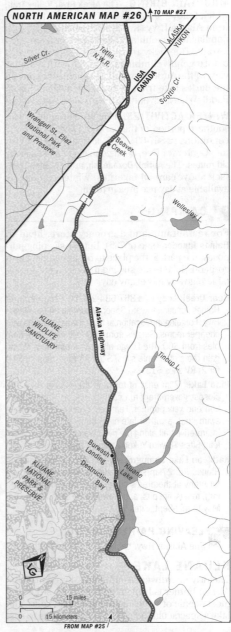

NORTH AMERICAN MAP #26 ↑ TO MAP #27

NORTH AMERICA

Silver Cr.

Teslin N.W.R.

USA CANADA

ALASKA YUKON

Scottie Cr.

Wrangell-St. Elias National Park and Preserve

Beaver Creek

Wellesley L.

KLUANE WILDLIFE SANCTUARY

Alaska Highway

Tincup L.

Burwash Landing

Destruction Bay

Kluane Lake

KLUANE NATIONAL PARK & PRESERVE

0   15 miles
0   15 kilometers

FROM MAP #25

MOUNTAIN BIKING. The **Alsek River Valley Trail,** which follows a bumpy old mining road for 14km from Alaska Hwy. Km 1645 to Sugden Creek, is popular with mountain bikers who crave rugged terrain. The rocky road crosses several streams before gently climbing to a ridge with a stellar view of the Auriol Mountains. More insider tips on the park's bike-friendly trails are available from PaddleWheel Adventures (see p. 739).

WINTER ACTIVITIES. For winter use of the southern portion of the park, call ahead for snow conditions (☎867-634-7207) and stop by the Visitors Center for free, detailed maps of **cross-country ski routes.** The **Auriol, Dezadeash,** and **St. Elias Trails** (see above) are all favorites. Winter camping is available at day-use area in town.

CAMPING

For restaurants and a grocery store, head to **Haines Junction** (see p. 739). But for sleeping purposes, the park is the place to be, as camping by a gorgeous lake beats staying in a clean-but-forgettable highway motel any day.

Bear Creek Lodge (☎867-634-2301), 11km north of Haines Junction toward Sheep Mountain on the Alaska Hwy. Forgoing the location in town rewards visitors with cheaper rooms. Singles from $50 (without bath); doubles from $60. The Lodge also offers **camping** at bargain rates on simple sites. Sites $5 for 1 person, $10 for 2; RV sites $15.

Pine Lake, 7km east of town on the Alaska Hwy. The closest government-run campground to Haines Junction and very popular. Features a sandy beach with a swim float, a pit for late-night bonfires, and a snazzy interpretive trail along the river. Water, firewood, pit toilets. Sites $8 with Yukon camping permit only.

Kathleen Lake Campground, on National Park land off Haines Rd. 27km south of Haines Junction. The base for many of the area's hikes. Water (boil before drinking), toilets, fire pits, and firewood. 39 sites. Open mid-May to mid-Sept. Sites $10.

LEAVING HAINES JUNCTION
The **Alaska Hwy.** beckons; continue northwest.

KLUANE LAKE

The drive northwest from Haines Junction to the Alaska border is broken up by tiny pit stops, the most scenic of which lie along Kluane Lake. The lake's spectacular aquamarine color is due to suspended "glacial flour" particles in the water that reflect blue light waves. Spanning 478 sq. km, Kluane Lake is the largest in the Yukon.

Congdon Creek Campground, at Km 1723 on the Alaska Hwy., is the nicest campground before the US border, with a long stone beach for evening strolls and romantic mountain views. Prime lakeside sites fill up early. Be warned—sometimes the camp shuts down from mid-July to September due to the ripening soapberries and the bears which eat them. (80 sites. Water, pit toilets, firewood. Sites $8 with Yukon camping permits.) If lake spots at the territorial campground are all taken or you prefer showers and laundry, stop 6km short of Congdon at the **Cottonwood RV Park and Campground.** Melt away your woes in the hot tub ($4 for 30min.) or on the mini-golf course. (No phone. Dry RV sites $18; full hookup $24.)

BURWASH LANDING. Near the shores of Kluane Lake on the Alaska Hwy., Burwash Landing is home to the **world's largest gold pan** at the **Kluane Museum of Natural History.** This noisy museum plays animal sound effects to accompany the Yukon's largest wildlife display and a collection of Southern Tutchone garb. The mammoth teeth are enormous. (☎867-841-5561. Open daily late May and early Sept. 10am-6pm; June-Aug. 9am-9pm. $3.75, seniors $3.25, ages 6-12 $2.) Stop at Kluane First Nation's **Dalan Campground** for secluded campsites on the lake. (☎867-841-4274. 25 sites. Wood, water, pit toilets. Sites $10.) The **Burwash Landing Resort** offers rooms with TV and private bath. Campers and RVs are welcome on the lawn or parking lot. The lakeside resort houses a **diner** that serves up hefty $7 sandwiches. (☎867-841-4441. Open summer daily 7am-11pm. Singles $70; doubles $80; RV sites $18. Showers $4.)

PINE VALLEY BAKERY AND RV
At Km 1845 of Alaska Hwy., between Burwash and Beaver Creek.

Break up monotonous mountain-viewing miles and grab some grub, gas, tire repair, or relatively cheap lodging at this busy jack-of-all-trades stop. Showers are also available. (☎867-862-7407. Open mid-May to mid-Sept. 24hr. Rooms from $50.)

BEAVER CREEK. The westernmost community (Km 1935 of the Alaska Hwy.) in Canada is by far the liveliest of all these roadside wonders. Get a sales pitch about Beaver Creek offerings, such as the oddly shaped church, at the **Visitors Center.** (☎867-862-7321. Open daily summer 8am-8pm.) Most of what you need can be found at the log **1202 Motor Inn,** from camping (dry sites $10; RV sites $15) and motel rooms ($35 for "plain jane" with shared bath; $65 for the works) to a grocery store, a restaurant with giant sandwiches ($6.50-8), and an ATM. (☎800-661-0540. Open daily 6:30am-1am.) A heated indoor **pool** is open in summer. Lodging is a steal at the **Beaver Creek Hostel** in the **Westmark Inn,** which has a bar and rec room. (☎867-862-7501. Open May-Sept. Rooms $22.)

LEAVING CANADA

Past Beaver Creek, 20 mi. of highway and prime moose-viewing wilderness separate US and Canadian customs and immigration, although several signs and landmarks are at the **official border** on the 141st meridian. From the border it's 92 mi. (2hr.) to Tok.

Welcome To
ALASKA

At the border, you cross into the Alaska Time Zone, where it is 1hr. earlier.

TETLIN NATIONAL WILDLIFE REFUGE

Southwest of the Alaska Hwy., between the border and Tok.

A tremendous chunk of wetlands and boreal forest comprises the **Tetlin National Wildlife Refuge,** providing limited access to hiking, boating, fishing, and hunting. Roadside pullouts unravel sweeping views of prime moose and waterfowl habitat. The sod-roofed **Visitors Center,** 10 mi. west of the Canadian border, is a good starting point to learn more about the Tetlin's ecology, hunting regulations, and fishing conditions. Fishing conditions are updated regularly and are posted outside after hours. (☎907-778-5312. Open May 15-Sept. 15 daily 8am-7:30pm.)

The refuge maintains two free campgrounds along the Alaska Hwy., the **Lakeview Campground** (Mile 1249) and the larger **Deadman Lake Camp-**

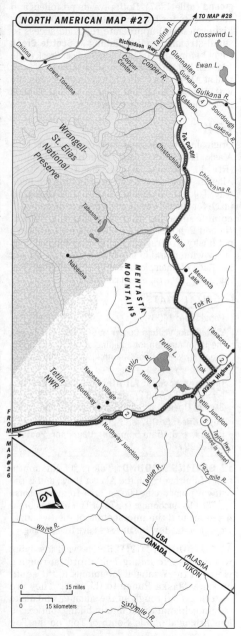

ground (Mile 1257). Both provide pit toilets and lake access for boaters, but lack potable water. Fishermen will appreciate roadside access to small-stream grayling fishing at **Scottie Creek** (right before Mile 1233½) and **Gardiner Creek** (Mile 1246½). **Hidden Lake,** accessible through a 1 mi. trail at Alaska Hwy. Mile 1240, is stocked annually with rainbow trout, but swamp gas and lilypads make shoreline fishing a challenge.

TOK

Originally a base camp for the construction of the Alaska Hwy. (Rte. 2) and Glenn Hwy./Tok Cutoff (Rte. 1), Tok (TOKE) calls itself "Main Street Alaska." Like most small towns along the highway, Tok is now summer tourist-oriented and no place for the RV-shy; it plays the role of state welcome center for motorists entering Alaska. Named in honor of a WWII US Army battalion's pet husky, Tok revives its affection for sled dogs every winter, and in late March hosts the annual the **Race of Champions** (☎907-883-6874), the final major dog race on the Alaska circuit.

(VITAL STATS)

Population: 1400

Visitor Info: Visitors Center (☎907-883-5773), in the large Alaskan log building at the Alaska and Glenn Hwy. junction. Open mid-May to mid-Sept. daily 8am-7pm.

Internet Access: All Alaska Gifts & Crafts (☎907-883-5081), at the junction. $3 per 30min. Open May-Sept. daily 7:30am-10pm.

Post Office: (☎907-883-2025), at the junction. Open M-F 8:15am-5pm, Sa 10am-3pm. **Postal Code:** 99780.

 GETTING AROUND. Tok is 206 mi. southeast of Fairbanks on the Alaska Hwy., and is the halfway point on the 600 mi. drive from **Whitehorse** (p. 736) to **Anchorage** (p. 747). The town is organized around the intersection of the two highways, and the few businesses have free **parking.**

 OUTDOOR ACTIVITES. The vast low-lying wetlands surrounding Tok afford far-ranging views of the Wrangell Mountains to the south and the Alaska Range to the west. They are waterlogged throughout the summer, and make for poor hiking or mountain biking, but excellent **fishing** abounds. South of Tok, on the Tok

Cutoff (Rte. 1), the **Tok River Overflow** (Mile 103½) and the **Little Tok River** (Mile 104½) harbor grayling in their clear, tiny pools. Farther south, **Mineral Lake** (Mile 91) has decent grayling and northern pike fishing. Anglers without a boat might try going after the grayling in the lake's outlet stream. Access to the Mineral Lake itself is through a half-mile trail on the left side of the road heading south.

 FOOD. Follow your nose to a truly colossal grilled meal at the bustling **Gateway Salmon Bake,** on the Alaska Hwy. at the east end of town. Try a buffalo or salmon burger for lunch ($7.25). For dinner, choose between salmon, halibut, or reindeer sausage—all of which come with salad bar, chowder, baked beans, sourdough rolls, and drinks. The whole huge deal costs $17-18. (☎907-883-5555. Open mid-May to mid-Sept. daily 11am-9pm.) Plate-sized sourdough pancakes ($2.50 each) and reindeer sausage ($1.25) send out enticing aromas at **Sourdough Campground,** 1½ mi. down Tok Cutoff. (☎907-883-5543. Cafe open daily 7-11am.) Locals and tourists converge at **Fast Eddy's** for heaping portions. Specialty burgers are $6 and endless trips to the well-stocked fruit and veggie salad bar are $8. (☎907-883-4411. Open daily 6am-midnight.) **Three Bears Food Center,** across from the Visitors Center, is a grocery and hardware store. (☎907-883-5195. Open summer daily 7am-11pm; winter M-Sa 8am-9pm, Su 8am-7pm.)

 ACCOMMODATIONS & CAMPING. Tok is overrun with pricey motels and crowded RV parks. Two dependable alternatives are the pair of state campgrounds directly outside of town. The **Tok River State Recreation Site,** 4 mi. east of town on the Alaska Hwy., offers 43 wooded sites. (Pit toilets. Water must be boiled. Firewood $5. Sites $10.) **Eagle Trail State Park** is quieter, but has more bugs. An overlook trail (3 mi.) leads up into the hills for a fantastic view of the Tok River valley and the Alaska Range foothills. (Pit toilets. Water must be boiled. Firewood $5. Sites $10.) Find quiet beds at the **Tok International Youth Hostel,** 8 mi. towards Delta Junction on the Alaska Hwy., then left on Pringle Rd. This peaceful site, in the midst of a pine forest, has simple wall-tent bunk accommodations. Bring your own bedding. (☎907-883-3745. $10, nonmembers $13.) Those wishing to stay in town can pitch their tent at one of the numerous **RV parks** along the Alaska Hwy. (Sites $12-14.) **Young's Motel,** a roadhouse at the east end of town, has some of the lowest rates in Tok, although that isn't saying much. (☎907-883-4411. Singles $80; doubles $89.)

LEAVING TOK
Heading out of Tok, the Alaska Hwy. (Rte. 2) runs north to Fairbanks. Instead, hop on the **Tok Cut-off (Rte. 1)** for the ride toward Anchorage.

THE ROAD TO GLENNALLEN. The stretch of Glenn Hwy. running from Tok to Glennallen rattles drivers with switchbacking mountain roads and rapid elevation changes. Streams and fishing holes attract swarms of anglers, and the tree cover periodically breaks to reveal glacial peaks and endless vistas. But the end is near; Anchorage approaches, so start using up your film.

GLENNALLEN

Positioned strategically at the intersection of the Glenn and Richardson Hwy., Glennallen has dubbed itself the "Hub of Alaska." This exciting epithet notwithstanding, the romanceless supply depot is also referred to as the "Glennallen RV Park"—once summer hits, so do the caravans, and the whole town flushes with enough motorhomes to swamp the roads. The surrounding marshland lends itself more to mosquito-hunting than hiking, and much of it is privately-owned anyhow. Still, though Glennallen doesn't offer much in the way of outdoor adventure, its location is prime—it sits near the access road into **Wrangell-St. Elias National Park** (Nabesna Rd., 75 mi. to the north; the turn-off for the Edgerton Hwy. is 32 mi. south on the Richardson Hwy.), as well as roads leading to great **salmon fishing** on the Copper River and its tributaries. (**Gakona,** a tiny hamlet home to salmon fishing trip operations, is 15 mi. to the north.) The waves of RVs ensure a full stock of food and gear at competitive (for Alaska) prices. Obtain info on Wrangell-St. Elias and the surrounding area at the **Greater Copper River Valley Visitors Center,** at the intersection of the Glenn and Richardson Hwy. at the east end of town. (☎907-822-5558. Open May 15-Sept. 15 daily 8am-7pm.)

The only supermarket in the region is **Park's Place Groceries,** 1 mi. west of the Glenn Hwy. junction. (☎907-822-3334. Open M-Sa 7am-11pm, Su 9am-11pm.) Several roadside cafes serve up classic highway fare in town, but the **Trailside Grill,**

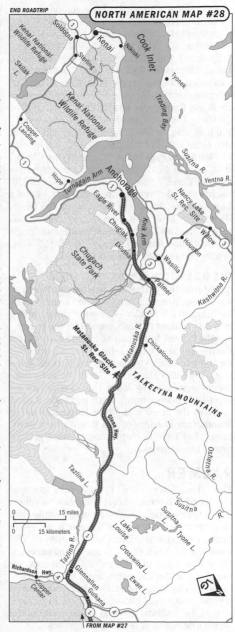

END ROADTRIP

NORTH AMERICAN MAP #28

FROM MAP #27

NORTH AMERICA

located half a mile north of the junction on the Richardson Hwy., earns local approval. Munch on a huge grilled sandwich ($9) or load up at the $6 all-you-can-eat salad bar. (☎907-822-4448. Open daily 6am-10pm.) Glenallen's closest state-run campground is the **Dry Creek State Recreation Site**, 5 mi. north of town on the Richardson Hwy. (Pit toilets and water. Firewood $5. Sites $10.) **Northern Nights Campground and RV Park**, ½ mi. west of the Glenn Hwy. junction, has 25 tightly packed RV and tent sites. (☎907-822-3199. Water and pit toilets. Sites $12; RVs $20. Showers $3, non-guests $5.) **The Sports Page** offers "Cabins on the Glenn," at Mile 187 of the Glenn Hwy., and lets tenters use their unfilled RV sites. (☎907-822-5833. Sites $10. Cabins $70. Showers $5, free with stay.) **Carol's B&B**, on the right side of Birch St. off the Glenn Hwy. about 1 mi. west from the junction, dishes up a "true Alaskan breakfast" with sourdough pancakes and moose sausage. (☎907-822-3594. Singles $65; doubles from $80.)

THE ROAD TO PALMER. The Glenn Hwy. heads into the **Matanuska-Susitna (Mat-Su) Valley.** Three mountain ranges—the Chugach, Talkeetna, and the Alaska—converge and plummet into this verdant flatland, named for the two rivers that drain here into the Knik Arm of the Pacific Ocean's Cook Inlet. The long summer daylight produces extremely large vegetables (e.g., 100+ lb. cabbages). The valley is famous for its produce (look for the Alaska Grown label—it's everywhere), both legal and illegal: those in the know claim that **Matanuska Valley Thunderfuck** is some of the world's best marijuana. *Let's Go* does not recommend getting totally thunderfucked.

PALMER

The Glenn Hwy. (Rte. 1) rolls into the tiny hamlet of Palmer, the heart of the Mat-Su Valley. This low-key agricultural community is a pleasant stop for travelers weary of the rough-and-ready bush and highway culture of the interior. The town has a 1950s feel, and is unexciting except at State Fair time, but the rolling farmlands are bucolic, and the Talkeetna and Chugach Mountains overlooking the Valley entice adventure-seekers with hiking, biking, and skiing. In autumn, stop at the Visitors Center to get an eyeful of the region's defensive lineman-sized legumes.

VITAL STATS

Population: 4300

Visitor Info: 723 S. Valley Way (☎907-745-2880). Open daily May to mid-Sept. 8am-6pm.

Internet Access: Palmer Public Library, 655 S. Valley Way (☎907-745-4690).

Post Office: 500 S. Cobb St. (907-745-5051). Open M-F 10am-5:30pm, Sa 9am-noon. **Postal Code:** 99645.

GETTING AROUND. Most visitor services are clustered near the intersection of the **Glenn Hwy.** and the **Palmer-Wasilla Rd.**, which leads 12 mi. west to the town of Wasilla.

SIGHTS & ENTERTAINMENT. Palmer's claim to fame is the **Alaska State Fair** (☎907-745-9827), held every August over the 11 days preceding Labor Day on the extensive fairgrounds at Mile 40 of the Glenn Hwy. This family-oriented festival has awarded ribbons to mastodonic vegetables larger than many children; past winners have included a 303 lb. squash and a 347 lb. pumpkin. Don't miss out on the exhibits on livestock, baking, and quilting, among other local pastimes. (☎907-745-4827. Open M-F noon-10pm, Sa and Su 10am-10pm. $8, youths and seniors $5.)

The **Reindeer Farm** on the Bodenburg Loop Rd. lets visitors come up close to reindeer with tours and petting areas that are sure to delight children and ironic adults. (☎907-745-4000. Open daily 10am-6pm. $5.) The **Musk Ox Farm**, at Mile 50 of the Glenn Hwy., offers the same activities for the heftier muskoxen, and gives you the opportunity to be a Friend of the Musk Ox, like Alex Trebek or Olivia Newton-John. (☎907-745-4151. Open daily 10am-6pm. $8.) For a flavor of more traditional Palmer agriculture, your best bet is to bypass the admission fees and take a drive on the **Famer Loop Rd.**, off the Glenn Hwy. at Mile 51. While rambling through Palmer's oldest farmed countryside, make sure to watch for farm stands selling fresh produce in harvest season.

HIKING. Several popular, challenging trails snake their way into the lower Chugach Mountains, south of town. **Lazy Mountain** (5 mi., 3-5 hr.; 2600 ft. gain) is a steep, rewarding hike through lush deciduous forest and across alpine ridgeline to the summit of the 3720 ft. peak. From this lofty vantage point, hikers can gaze across the breadth of the Matanuska Valley out to the mountains on its ridges. The eroded dirt trail is very slippery in wet weather. To reach the trailhead, follow the Glenn Hwy. to Mile 41 and turn left on W. Arctic Ave. After crossing the Matanuska River, turn left on to Clark-Wolverine Rd., then right on to Huntly Rd. The trail begins at the dead-end.

The full-day **Pioneer Ridge-Knik River Trail** (10 mi.; 5120 ft. gain) winds up to the Chugach Range's towering Pioneer Peaks, from which a splendid panorama of the entire town and valley unfurls. This difficult day hike ascends through alder thickets until the tree line at 3200 ft., then climbs a steep ridge onto a wide alpine tundra bench, opening up to very photogenic vistas. North and South Pioneer Peaks loom above the ridge and should only be attempted with technical gear. The trailhead is a bit more than 3½ mi. down the Knik River Rd., off the Old Glenn Hwy. (W. Arctic Rd.).

▓ FOOD. ▓**Vagabond Blues,** 642 S Alaska St., four blocks from the Visitors Center, is Palmer's artsy alternative to agriculture. This bar and restaurant has an entirely homemade vegetarian menu that changes daily (sandwiches $5-8), live music, and an open wall for local upstart artists. Try the soup, salad, and bread served on handmade pottery for $6. All dishes and tiled artwork are made by a local potter and are for sale. (☎907-745-2233. Live music F and Sa 8-11pm; cover varies. Open M-Th 7am-9pm, F-Sa 8am-11pm, Su 9am-5pm.) **La Fiesta,** 132 W. Evergreen St., near the Visitors Center, serves good Mexican food, with a solid selection of Mexican beers as well. (☎907-746-3335. Open daily 11am-10pm.) Eat like the farmers do with fresh, locally grown produce at the **Matanuska Farm Market,** at Mile 38 of the Glenn Hwy. (Open daily July-Sept.)

▓▓ ACCOMMODATIONS & CAMPING. For info on **B&Bs** in the area (from $50-60), contact the Visitors Center. After hours, they leave a list of available rooms out front next to the courtesy phone. If you want to delay the jaunt to Anchorage, try the **Alaska Choice Inn Motel,** at Mile 40 off the Glenn Hwy., across from the fairgrounds. All rooms—the cheapest in Palmer—come with cable and microwave, and in a few lucky ones, kitchenettes. (☎907-745-1505. Rooms in summer $70-80; in winter $55-65.) One mile down W. Arctic Rd., at Mile 44 of the Glenn Hwy., lies the **Matanuska River Park Campground,** with wooded tent sites and riverfront

natural trails. Flush toilets, hot showers ($0.50 per minute) and city water add a touch of luxury to the best campground in town. (From the Visitors Center, head north on S. Valley Way, then turn right at E. Arctic Ave., which becomes the Old Glenn Hwy. ☎907-745-9631. Sites $12.) Farther from town, at Mile 37 of the Glenn Hwy., **Kepler Family Park** has tent sites and canoeing potential. (☎907-745-0429. Canoes $6 per hr. Sites $10.)

◉ EKLUTNA VILLAGE HISTORICAL PARK
Mile 26 of Glenn Hwy. about ½ mi. off the Eklutna Exit.

The park houses the remains of a Dena'ina (or Tanaina) village that dates back to 1650. Russian missionaries arrived at the close of the 18th century. The park shows the confluence of Russian Orthodox and Athabascan traditions. Today, the Orthodox tradition is alive and well among the natives in Eklutna. After visitors pass through the displays in the Heritage House, they are free to walk around the park or take a 30min. tour guided by a community religious leaders. Small, colorful spirit houses dot the park. Tradition dictates that families erect a spirit house over the grave of a loved one, paint it in the loved one's favorite colors, and fill it with the deceased's possessions. Visitors may also stop by the two St. Nicholas Russian Orthodox churches, both of which are still in use. (Open M-Sa 10am-6pm. $5.)

▓ APPROACHING ANCHORAGE
The **Glenn Hwy. (Rte. 1)** slides into the city from the east, becoming **5th Ave.** as it hits town.

ANCHORAGE

Alaska's foremost urban center is home to two-fifths of the state's population. Anchorage overwhelms all other towns and surprises those visitors expecting little more than a frontier outpost. The city reigns as the travel and commercial nucleus of the entire North, and in many ways determines the future for a state that has moved swiftly ainto modernity. Long winters are softened by a mild coastal climate, and long summer days persuade dusk to linger past midnight.

It's impossible to pigeon-hole such a diverse city—waves of immigration, intermarriage, and close ties to eastern Asia spice up the population, and people's politics diverge in every direction. Perhaps you didn't come to Alaska seeking highrises and granite-studded cityscapes, but spend some time here, and you just might join those who came for a vacation and stayed for good.

VITAL STATS

Population: 260,000

Visitor Info: Alaska Convention and Visitor's Bureau (☎907-274-3531; www.anchorage.net), located in 2 buildings at the same site: a Log Cabin and the Downtown Visitor Information Center, both on W. 4th Ave. at F St. Open daily June-Aug. 7:30am-7pm; Oct.-Apr. 9am-4pm; May and Sept. 8am-6pm.

Internet Access: Z.J. Loussac Library (☎343-2975), at 36th Ave. and Denali St. Free. Open M-Th 10am-8pm, F-Sa 10am-6pm.

Post Office: 344 W. 3rd Ave. (☎907-279-9188). Open M-F 10am-5:30pm. **Postal Code:** 99510.

▐ GETTING AROUND

Anchorage sprawls across some 50,000 acres of the Anchorage Bowl, framed by military bases to the north, the Chugach Mountains to the east, and the Cook Inlet to the west and south. Downtown Anchorage is laid out in a simple grid, roughly modeled on the layout of Washington, DC: numbered avenues run east-west, with addresses designated east or west from **C St**. North-south streets are lettered alphabetically to the west and named alphabetically to the east of **A St**. "Midtown" Anchorage is a largely commercialized area south of downtown, east of Minnesota Dr. and west of the Seward Hwy. The **University of Alaska Anchorage** and **Alaska Pacific University** lie on 36th Ave., off Northern Lights Blvd. on the eastern edge of the city, toward the Chugach Mountains. **Parking** meters line most of the major streets, and parking lots ($6 per day; $2 min.) crop up all over the city.

◉ SIGHTS

▧ **ANCHORAGE MUSEUM OF HISTORY AND ART.** With a tremendous collection of Native and non-Native artwork and a fascinating gallery on Alaska's rough history, this museum tops all the others in the state. Exhibits on Native Alaskan artifacts, Inuit drawings, and art mingle with national and international works. The museum contains one of the larg-est collections of works by Sydney Laurence, Alaska's foremost Impressionist. The Alaska Gallery traces the land's human history from the Ice Age to the present. *(121 W. 7th Ave., at A St. ☎907-343-4326 or 907-343-6173; www.anchorage-museum.org. Open May 15-Sept. 15 M-W and F-Su 9am-6pm, Th 9am-9pm; Sept. 16-May 14 Su 1-5pm, Tu-Sa 10am-6pm. Tours daily 10, 11am, 1, 2pm. 1hr. films daily 11am and 3pm. $6.50, seniors and military $6, under 18 $2.)*

▧ **THE ALASKA NATIVE HERITAGE CENTER.** Informative displays guide visitors through 11 Alaskan native traditions, complemented by daily cultural shows, storytelling, and dances. Learn how each tradition has sustained itself, from prehistory to contemporary times. Outside, tour recreated village sites, including clothing, tools, and flora from each of the state's five major native regions. All proceeds go back to the tribes. *(8800 Heritage Ctr. Dr. ☎907-330-8000 or 800-315-6608; www.alaskana-tive.net. From the Glenn Hwy., take the 1st right off the North Muldoon exit. Open daily 9am-6pm. Dance and music performances throughout the day. $21, ages 7-16 $16, under 7 free. Discounts for AAA members, Alaska residents, Alaska Natives, and seniors.)*

HISTORIC ANCHORAGE. Enthused volunteers from **Anchorage Historic Properties** take visitors on a 2hr. exploration of downtown's historic sites and explain Anchorage's pioneer history. From the **Historic City Hall** and the Visitor's Center, stops include the Art Deco **4th Avenue Theatre**, the eclectic **Cyrano's Playhouse**, Anchorage's first permanent building (the **Wendler Building**), the **Holy Family Cathedral**, and the **Historic Anchorage Hotel**, home for many years to artist Sydney Laurence. Other stops include the **Alaska Statehood Monument**, the **Old Federal Building**, and the **Kimball Building**, which housed Anchorage's first dry goods store. Tours begin in the lobby of the Historic City Hall. *(524 W. 4th Ave. ☎907-274-3600; www.anchoragehistoricproperties.org. Tours June-Aug. M-F 1-3pm. $5, ages 5-12 $1.)*

RESOLUTION POINT & CAPTAIN COOK MONUMENT. This monument is dedicated to British explorer Captain James Cook who, in 1778, anchored his ship *HMS Resolution* in the inlet that now bears his name. In addition to a life-size statue of the captain, this little park is given character by the sweeping views of the Cook Inlet, Mt. Susitna, and on clear days, Mt. McKinley. Be on the lookout for Beluga whales in the spring and fall. *(At 3rd Ave. and L St.)*

IMAGINARIUM. Perfect for kids young and old who have had enough of the wildlife and outdoors, hands-on activities and interactive programs make the Imaginarium worth a visit. Exhibits include a reptile hall, marine life area, planetarium, bubble lab, and several Alaska-related features. *(737 W. 5th Ave., Ste. G, between H and G St. ☎ 907-276-3179; www.imaginarium.org. Open M-Sa 10am-6pm, Su noon-5pm. $5, ages 2-12 and seniors $4.50. AAA discount.)*

ALASKA ZOO. If you didn't see Alaska's animals in the wild, you can spot them at the Alaska Zoo. Find seals, fox, musk ox, moose, and four kinds of bears among the zoo's residents. Binky the Polar Bear mauled a tourist here in 1994 and remains something of a local hero years after his death. *(4731 O'Malley Rd. Turn toward mountains off Seward Hwy., or take Minnesota Rd., which becomes O'Malley. ☎ 907-346-2133 or 907-346-3242. Open M, W-Th, Sa-Su 9am-6pm; Tu and F 9am-9pm. Education programs in summer Tu 6-9pm. $9, seniors $8, ages 12-17 and students $5, ages 3-11 $4.)*

TONY KNOWLES COASTAL TRAIL. Walk, skate, or bike the trail, an 11 mi. track that skirts Cook Inlet on one side and the backyards of Anchorage's upper crust on the other. Named for Alaska's popular and long-serving governor, this is one of the best urban bike paths in the country. On long summer days, residents of Anchorage stream down the trail en masse, basking in pleasant views of Mt. Susitna, the Knik Arm, and Mt. McKinley. Pick up the trail at the end of 2nd Ave., near H St., or at Elderberry Park, near 5th Ave. and L St., on the west edge of downtown. The coastal trail's southern terminus is at **Kincaid Park,** a haven for cross-country runners and mountain bikers in summer. Nordic skiers take over after snowfall. In addition to the Coastal Trail, nearly 40 mi. of trails connect the city's green spaces.

EARTHQUAKE PARK. In 1964, nearly 75 homes were destroyed when the Good Friday Earthquake took a bite out of the cliff and spat it into Cook Inlet. Now marked by a park, the former cliff-side features an interpretive display on the most powerful tremor recorded in North America. At 9.2 on the Richter scale, the earth-quake rattled Anchorage and much of southcentral Alaska for up to 5min., and evidence of the destruction can be found throughout the city. Devastation aside, the park also offers an unobstructed views of the inlet, downtown skyscrapers, and the Chugach mountains. *(Take Northern Lights Blvd. west toward the airport and away from the mountains; the park is just past Satellite Dr. on the right. Free.)*

DELANEY PARK. This park strip, which separates downtown from midtown Anchorage, first served as a firebreak between the city and the wilderness. It subsequently became Anchorage's first airstrip and later, as the city expanded, a popular park, home to many of the city's festivals. Today, residents use the park for frisbee, picnics, or to enjoy the midnight sun in summer. Delaney Park also has a rose garden and memorials to Alaska's veterans and Dr. Martin Luther King, Jr. *(Takes up the area from A to P St. between 9th and 10th Ave.)*

SATURDAY MARKET. Locals and tourists vie for bargains on arts and crafts, on Saturdays from 10am to 6pm mid-May through mid-September. *(At 3rd Ave. and E St. ☎ 907-272-5634; www.anchoragemarkets.com.)*

◪ OUTDOOR ACTIVITIES

Anchorage's central location makes it easy to use as an exploration base. "Sleeping Lady," the locals' fond name for **Mt. Susitna,** watches over Anchorage from across the Cook Inlet. Legend has it that this marks the resting spot of an Athabascan maid who dozed while awaiting her lover's return from war. When peace reigns again in the world, she will awake. In the meantime, the great outdoors awaits. From mountain peaks to coastal waters, travelers are never more than a quick ride from amazing outdoor activities. East of Anchorage, the **Chugach Range** offers hiking and biking in the summer, and downhill, backcountry, and cross-country skiing in the winter. North of town, the Matanuska Valley has cross-country skiing, whitewater rafting, and more glaciers to hike. Farther north, on the George Parks Hwy. (Rte. 3), Talkeetna links to **Denali.** Just 30min. south along the **Seward Hwy.** (Rte. 1), skiing awaits at **Girdwood;** the drive past the tidal bores of **Turnagain Inlet** shouldn't be missed. The Kenai River sup-

NORTH AMERICA

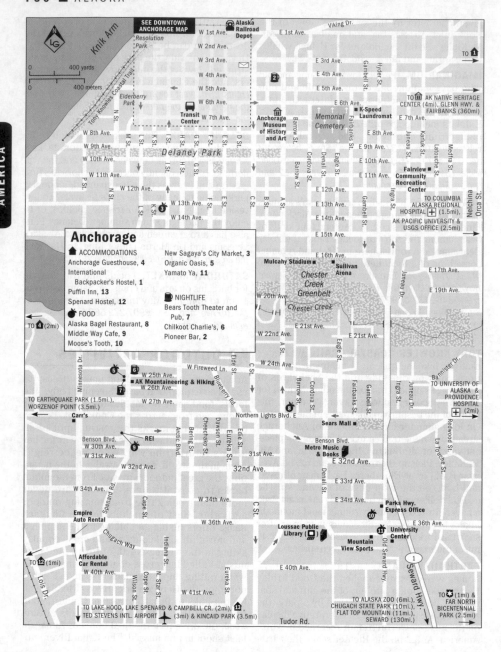

SEE DOWNTOWN ANCHORAGE MAP

Knik Arm

Resolution Park

Alaska Railroad Depot

W 1st Ave.   E 1st Ave.   Viking Dr.

W 2nd Ave.

W 3rd Ave.   E 3rd Ave.

W 4th Ave.   E 4th Ave.

W 5th Ave.   E 5th Ave.

W 6th Ave.   E 6th Ave.

Elderberry Park

Tony Knowles Coastal Trail

Transit Center

W 7th Ave.

Anchorage Museum of History and Art

K-Speed Laundromat

Memorial Cemetery

TO AK NATIVE HERITAGE CENTER (4mi), GLENN HWY. & FAIRBANKS (360mi)

E 7th Ave.

E 8th Ave.

W 8th Ave.   E 9th Ave.

W 9th Ave.   E 10th Ave.

W 10th Ave.   E 11th Ave.

Fairview Community Recreation Center

W 11th Ave.

Delaney Park

W 12th Ave.

TO COLUMBIA ALASKA REGIONAL HOSPITAL (1.5mi), AK PACIFIC UNIVERSITY & USGS OFFICE (2.5mi)

W 13th Ave.   E 13th Ave.

W 14th Ave.   E 14th Ave.

E 15th Ave.

E 16th Ave.

Mulcahy Stadium

Sullivan Arena

E 17th Ave.

E 19th Ave.

TO (2mi)

Anchorage

🏠 **ACCOMMODATIONS**
Anchorage Guesthouse, **4**
International
  Backpacker's Hostel, **1**
Puffin Inn, **13**
Spenard Hostel, **12**

🍴 **FOOD**
Alaska Bagel Restaurant, **8**
Middle Way Cafe, **9**
Moose's Tooth, **10**

New Sagaya's City Market, **3**
Organic Oasis, **5**
Yamato Ya, **11**

🍸 **NIGHTLIFE**
Bears Tooth Theater and
  Pub, **7**
Chilkoot Charlie's, **6**
Pioneer Bar, **2**

Chester Creek Greenbelt

Chester Creek

E 21st Ave.

W 20th Ave.

W 22nd Ave.

TO UNIVERSITY OF ALASKA & PROVIDENCE HOSPITAL (2mi)

W 24th Ave.

W Fireweed Ln.

W 25th Ave.
AK Mountaineering & Hiking
W 26th Ave.

W 27th Ave.

Northern Lights Blvd. E

TO EARTHQUAKE PARK (1.5mi), WORZENOF POINT (3.5mi).

Carr's

Sears Mall

Benson Blvd.
W 30th Ave.
W 31st Ave.

REI

Benson Blvd.
Metro Music & Books

E 32nd Ave.

W 32nd Ave.

32nd Ave.

E 33rd Ave.

E 34th Ave.

W 34th Ave.

W 34th Ave.

Parks Hwy. Express Office

Empire Auto Rental

W 36th Ave.

Loussac Public Library

E 36th Ave.

University Center

TO (1mi)

Affordable Car Rental

W 40th Ave.

Mountain View Sports

W 41st Ave.

TO LAKE HOOD, LAKE SPENARD & CAMPBELL CR. (2mi), TED STEVENS INTL. AIRPORT (3mi) & KINCAID PARK (3.5mi)

Tudor Rd.

TO ALASKA ZOO (6mi), CHUGACH STATE PARK (10mi), FLAT TOP MOUNTAIN (11mi), SEWARD (130mi).

TO (1mi) & FAR NORTH BICENTENNIAL PARK (2.5mi)

ports great fishing near **Cooper Landing.** Hikes near Exit Glacier, flightseeing trips, and a ramble through the **Kenai Fjords National Park** add further persuasions to venture south.

WATERSPORTS

Nancy Lake State Recreation Area, just west of the Parks Hwy. (Rte. 3) near Mile 67¼ and just south of **Willow,** is well known for its **canoeing.** The **Lynx Lake Loop** takes one to two days, weaving through 8 mi. of lakes and portages with designated campsites along the way. The loop begins at Mile 4½ of the Nancy Lake Pkwy., at the Tanaina Lake Canoe Trailhead. For **canoe rental,** call or visit **Tippecanoe** at the S. Raleigh Campground in the Nancy Lake State Recreation Area. (☎907-495-6688; www.paddlealaska.com. Open mid-May to mid-Sept. Sa and Su 8:30am-5:30pm, M-F call for hours. Canoes $20 for 8hr., $27 for full-day, $72 for 2 days, $78 for 1 week; full-week rate includes portage devices.)

Lifetime Adventures (☎907-746-4644; www.lifetimeadventures.net) leads guided **whitewater rafting** trips down Eagle River, 10 min. from Anchorage in Chugach State Park. **NOVA Riverrunners** (☎800-746-5753; www.novalaska.com) runs Class III, IV, and V whitewater rafting trips down the Matanuska River.

Those looking for **surfing,** Alaska-style, should check out the bore tides in **Turnagain Arm.** *Let's Go* recommends that visitors view this unusual tidal phenomenon from the safety of the Seward Hwy. overlooks, and leave the surfing to the experts. **Bird Point,** at Mile 95, provides the optimal spot to witness the tide, which occurs about 2hr. after low tide in Anchorage. Check tide tables for exact times, and be extremely cautious if you venture toward the water.

Although some of the world's best **fishing** is just south in the Kenai Peninsula, Anchorage also boasts of some pretty decent angling. With lakes dotting the city and a criss-cross of creeks, this is a great place to wet your line. Everyone else thinks so, too—"combat fishing", where anglers stand shoulder to shoulder and several deep, is the norm. Join the masses and fish for Alaska salmon at **Ship Creek,** which runs just north of downtown near the train depot, or for pink and silver salmon at **Bird Creek,** just south on the Seward Hwy. Check the **Alaska Department of Fish and Game** for regulations and licenses (☎907-349-4687; www.state.ak.us/local.akpages/fish.game) or visit the **Alaska Public Lands Information Center.** After a

successful trip, have experts at **New Sagaya's Midtown Market** (see p. 753) prepare and ship your catch anywhere you choose.

HIKING

In 1969, a grassroots organization headed by a 19-year-old asked for and received almost every square inch it proposed for the 495,000-acre **Chugach State Park.** The name originates from a native tribe, the Cuatit, that lived in the area. Russian traders recorded the name as Chugatz or Tschugatskoi, and subsequent explorers referred to the mountain range as the Chugach. The park, the second-largest state park in Alaska, surrounds the city on three sides and has enough land and trails to keep an avid hiker busy for years. Check out the **Park Headquarters** (☎907-345-5014) in the Potter's Section House at Mile 115 of the Seward Hwy. to learn about fees and usage information. The park also maintains a **Public Information Center** downtown, 550 W. 7th Ave. Suite 1260. (☎907-269-8400. Open M-F 10am-5pm.)

Reservations for the park's several public use cabins can be filled up to 6 months in advance. Visitors can either call the Public Information Center or contact the state of Alaska or the US Forest Service, both of which run cabins in the area. (State of Alaska: www.state.ak.us; follow links to "Recreational Services." US Forest Services: call ☎800-280-2267 or visit www.reserveusa.com. Prices run $25-40 per night, depending on cabin.) Visitors to Chugach can retreat into nature on 25 established **day hiking** trails, which leave from different points in Anchorage and along the Glenn and Seward Hwy. **Parking** is available at trailhead lots for $5.

Hikers need to bring the proper gear to travel safely in this region. If you have any doubts, contact info centers or park rangers.

SKIING & SNOWBOARDING

Skiing and **snowboarding trails** weave around and through Anchorage. **Alyeska Ski Resort** is a short drive away along the Seward Hwy. (Rte. 1), offering world-class terrain. An easy drive from the city, **Hatcher Pass** to the north and **Turnagain Pass** to the south both promise some of the best backcountry skiing in the region. North of Wasilla and Palmer, the best alpine skiing in the Hatcher Pass area is off of **Archangel Road.** For more backcountry skiing thrills within the city limits, seek out the **Hilltop Ski Area,** 7015 Abbott Rd. (☎907-346-1446;

www.hilltopskiarea.org) and **Alpenglow**, Mile 7 Arctic Valley Rd. (☎907-428-1208; www.skialpenglow.com), north on the Glenn Hwy. to Arctic Valley Rd. and through Fort Richardson. Check at **AMH** and **REI** for conditions and avalanche info.

Hundreds of skiers from the Anchorage bowl stop at **Kincaid Park** (☎907-343-6397), the largest cross-country skiing area in the US, situated at the end of Raspberry Rd. and the Tony Knowles Coastal Trail, near the Ted Stevens International Airport. Nearly 20km of lighted trails, including many that meet World Cup standards, meander through this urban oasis. Nordic skiers frequent a set of hillside trails, including the Lighted Loop. To reach them, take Seward Hwy. east to the Dimond exit (toward the mountains), which turns into Abbott Rd., and follow it for about 3 mi.

🎵 ENTERTAINMENT

While Anchorage lacks the off-beat ambiance spicing up local culture elsewhere in Alaska, it does have some big city elegance with a frontier touch. The Visitors Center has a calendar of events. Friday's *Anchorage Daily News* features *8*, its weekend entertainment section.

Cyrano's Off Center Playhouse, 413 D St., (☎907-274-2599; www.cyranos.org), between 4th and 5th Ave. Contains a cafe, a bookshop, the stage of the **Eccentric Theatre Company,** and a cinema that screens foreign and art films. Voted "Best Live Theater" by the *Anchorage Daily News.* Storytellers spin Alaskan tales here on summer afternoons, amid poetry readings and film discussion groups. Check the cafe for the events schedule. Theater in summer M-Tu and F-Su 7pm; in winter Th-Su 7pm. Tickets $15, students $10.

Alaska Center for Performing Arts, 621 W. 6th Ave. (☎907-263-2900 or 800-478-7328; www.tickets.com.), main entrance at Town Square Park. The center brings world-class opera, music, dance, and theater to this impressive three-theater facility. The Sydney Laurence and Discovery Theatres show films on the state's abundant wildlife and scenery. Beautiful Alaskan Native art adorns the lobby.

Alaska Experience Theater, 705 W. 6th Ave. (☎907-276-3730 or 907-272-9076; www.alaskaexperiencetheatre.com), across from the Transit Center. Tourists flock here for the state's top film attraction, "Alaska the Greatland," a 40min. presentation of Alaskan culture, wilderness, and fauna projected on a 180°

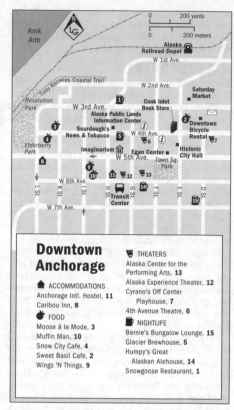

Downtown Anchorage

♠ ACCOMMODATIONS
Anchorage Intl. Hostel, **11**
Caribou Inn, **8**

🍴 FOOD
Moose á la Mode, **3**
Muffin Man, **10**
Snow City Cafe, **4**
Sweet Basil Cafe, **2**
Wings 'N Things, **9**

🎭 THEATERS
Alaska Center for the Performing Arts, **13**
Alaska Experience Theater, **12**
Cyrano's Off Center Playhouse, **7**
4th Avenue Theatre, **6**

🍸 NIGHTLIFE
Bernie's Bungalow Lounge, **15**
Glacier Brewhouse, **5**
Humpy's Great Alaskan Alehouse, **14**
Snowgoose Restaurant, **1**

omniscreen. The three-story high theater's **earthquake exhibit** rumbles for a full 15 fun-filled minutes. Open in summer 9am-9pm; winter noon-6pm. Movie every hr. Earthquake exhibit every 20min. Movie $8, ages 5-12 $4. Exhibit $6/$4. Combo ticket $12/$7.

4th Avenue Theatre, 630 4th Ave. (☎907-257-5009; www.4thavenuetheater.com), 1 block from the Log Cabin Visitors Center. Within a restored 1940s Art Deco decor, floor to ceiling bronze murals embellish the first million-dollar building in Anchorage (1947), and one of few buildings to survive 1964 earthquake. Trolley tours of the historic downtown area leave from here on the hour ($10). The theater also offers a trolley tour and dinner ($22), and a dinner buffet and comedy show F 5:30-8pm ($17).

Mulcahy Stadium, at 16th St. and Cordova St., hosts the **Anchorage Bucs** (☎907-561-2827) and the **Anchorage Glacier Pilots** (☎907-274-3627), who play summer league baseball against other Alaskan teams such as the Kenai Oilers, the Mat-Su Miners, and the Fairbanks GoldPanners. Featuring some of the best college talent in the nation, Mulcahy comes from a tradition of sports heroes, including Mark McGwire, John Olerud, and Tom Seaver, all of whom played here before making it big. When the Bucs are the home team, tickets are $4-7, ages 6-17 half-price. The Glacier Pilots offer $4-6 tickets, $2 for students, $1 for kids over 5, and free for those under 5 or for kids with little league caps. The **Anchorage Aces** smash, crunch, and check their opponents at nearby Sullivan Arena during the Ice Hockey season.

❄ FESTIVALS

The popular summer **Mayor's Midnight Sun Marathon** sends runners around the margins of downtown Anchorage and miles of forest. Check www.mayorsmarathon.com for the latest info. As in most Alaskan towns and cities, the **summer solstice** is a big event here, and Anchorage celebrates with a festival on the weekend closest to the solstice. **Spirit Days** (www.spiritdays.org), in late June, celebrate Native Alaskan heritage with traditional drumming, singing, and dancing. In late February, the annual **Fur Rendezvous**, brings a winter carnival to Anchorage with events including dog sled racing, ice sculpture, a masquerade ball, and a traditional pelt auction.

🍴 FOOD

Anchorage presents the most affordable and varied culinary fare in the state. **Great Harvest Bread Company,** 570 E. Benson Blvd. in Benson Mall, stocks excellent fresh bread with new selections daily. Loaves run $4-7, but hefty slices with butter and honey are free. (☎907-274-3331. Open M-Sa 7am-6pm.) The ubiquitous **Carr's** supermarkets sell groceries around town, including at 1340 Gambell St.; on Seward Hwy. between 13th and 14th Ave.; at 600 Northern Light Blvd at the Mall; and 24hr. in the Aurora Village Shopping Center, 1650 W. Northern Lights Blvd.

🔲 **Moose's Tooth,** 3300 Old Seward Hwy. (☎907-258-2537). Named for one of Denali's mountain neighbors, this relaxed joint serves pizzas (personal $9) and brews ($3.75) as hearty as the climbers who come here. Try the chicken ranch pizza. Hot bands usher in new brews the 1st Th of every month. Be prepared to wait; it's popular. Open M-Th 11am-midnight, F-Sa noon-1am, Su noon-midnight.

🔲 **Sweet Basil Cafe,** 335 E St. (☎907-274-0070), centrally located near the Public Lands Office and Information Center. The owner-chefs must wake up bright and early to bake their fresh pastries, breads, and pastas. Killer vegetable and fruit juices ($3.50) and smoothies ($3-5). Lunch offerings range from fish tacos to cajun sausage ($6-7). Open M-F 8am-3pm, Sa 9am-4pm.

🔲 **Yamato Ya,** 3700 Old Seward Hwy. (☎907-561-2128), at 36th St., next to New Sagaya's Midtown Market. Numerous awards claim the Kusano family makes the best sushi in town, and the packed place attests to this. Seafood, vegetable, chicken, and steak dishes available. Lunch under $10. Dinners are $9-12 and include soup, salad, and rice. Open M-F 11am-3pm, Sa 4-10pm.

🔲 **Middle Way Cafe,** 1200 W. Northern Lights Blvd. (☎907-272-6433), at Spenard Rd. next to REI in the Northern Lights Shopping Center. Locals pack this place for its terrific homemade sandwiches and wraps, salads, and soups for lunch. The combo with half a sandwich and soup or salad is a deal ($7). Everything under $10. Many vegetarian options. Cafe open M-F 7am-6:30pm, Sa 8am-6:30pm, Su 9am-5pm. Kitchen open M-Sa 10am-4:30pm.

Snow City Cafe, 1034 W 4th St. (☎907-272-2489), at L St. Art-bedecked and a local favorite. One of the best breakfasts in town, served until 4pm. Local grub such as reindeer sausage and salmon cakes. Omelettes $8-10. Live music F-Sa. Open mic Su 7-11pm, traditional Irish music "seisiuns" W 7-11pm. Open daily 7am-4pm, W and Su also 7-11pm.

New Sagaya's City Market, 900 W. 13th St. (☎907-274-6173), at L St. This trendy specialty market has been serving Anchorage since 1973. Gourmet-variety pizza, wraps, sandwiches, salads and Asian cuisine all under $10. Other amenities include an espresso bar, freshly baked treats, super-fresh fruits and vegetables, and other groceries. ATM inside. Indoor and patio seating. Open M-Sa 6am-10pm, Su 8am-9pm. Also try **New Sagaya's Midtown Market,** 3700 Old Seward Hwy. at 36th St. (☎907-561-5173 or 800-764-1001). The same deal, but with a large seafood section. Overnight FedEx service available for fish you've caught or bought here. Same hours.

Alaska Bagel Restaurant, 113 W. Northern Lights Blvd., Ste. L (☎907-276-3900). 30 varieties of bagels from apple cinnamon to sun-dried tomato, with new flavors debuting regularly. Complicate your bagel with sandwich concoctions ($7), and a number of bagel specialties such as the bagel pocket or bagel dog ($4). Open M-F 6am-2pm, Sa 7am-2pm, Su 8am-2pm.

Organic Oasis, 2610 Spenard Rd. (☎907-277-7882), across the shopping center from Bear's Tooth. A vegan and vegetarian paradise that began as a wholesale grocery club. All meals served with soup or salad. Juices and smoothies are pricey, but worth it. Bills itself as the only "healthy nightclub" in Anchorage with live music Tu-Sa and open mic on Tu nights. Open M 11:30am-7pm, Tu 11:30am-10:30pm, W and Th 11:30am-9pm, F and Sa 11:30am-10pm.

Muffin Man, 817 W. 6th Ave. (☎907-279-6836), at I St. in the Historic Alaska Art Tile Building. A small and colorfully tiled Art Deco eatery with solid sandwiches ($5-9) salads ($9-10), and many vegetarian options ($5-8). Breakfast also served. Muffins and scones baked daily ($2). Open summer M-F 6am-3pm, Sa-Su 7am-2pm; winter M-F 7am-3pm.

Wings 'N Things, 529 I St. (☎907-277-9464), between 5t and 6th Ave. Serving up Anchorage's original wings since 1983. Indoor and deck seating. Try your chicken wings mild, medium, hot, barbecue, or "nuke." Single, double, triple, or bucket portions. Open M-W 9am-3pm, Th-Sa 9am-10pm.

Moose á la Mode, 360 K St. (☎907-274-4884), at 4th Ave. Enjoy an ice cream in the summer or a hot drink in the winter. Large tables and comfortable chairs perfect for reading, writing, pensive reflection, or musing. Open in summer M-F 7am-11pm, Sa 10am-11pm, Su 1-11pm; in winter closes 5pm.

ACCOMMODATIONS

Anchorage has a number of large hostels, some with more drawbacks than others. Hotels, B&Bs, and even "cheap" motels are expensive, especially downtown. Try **Alaska Private Lodgings** (☎888-235-2148; open M-Sa 9am-6pm) or the **Anchorage reservation service** (☎907-272-5909) for out-of-town B&Bs (from $80). Tent options are available at some of the hostels and outside of town; make sure you're not on private or military land. Several campgrounds and RV parks within the city offer semi-urban camping. Pick up a free copy of *Camping in the Anchorage Bowl* at the Visitors Center for crowded in-town options, or head to nearby **Chugach State Park** (see p. 751).

Anchorage Guesthouse, 2001 Hillcrest Dr. (☎907-274-0408). More expensive than other hostels in the area, but worth the cost. Guests take pride in the elegant kitchen and common area and gladly earn their keep with chores. Owner Andy holds in-house concerts for guests and will talk politics if you're up for a discussion. No alcohol. Bikes $2.50 per hr., $20 per day. Breakfast included (7-10am). Internet $2 per 15 min. Laundry $3. Key deposit $5. 1-week max. stay. In summer dorms $28; private rooms $74. In winter $25/$64.

Spenard Hostel, 2845 W. 42nd Pl. (☎248-5036, www.alaskahostel.org). Originally a commune, this friendly house still retains its original character and

---

BEYOND THE ASPHALT

LET'S MUSH

The celebrated Iditarod, "The Last Great Race" begins in Anchorage on the first weekend in March. Over the course of 9-15 days, over 1000 sled dogs and their mushers traverse a northwesterly trail over two mountain ranges, along the Yukon River, and across the frozen Norton Sound to the town of Nome on the Bering Sea. Officially, the route length is cited as 1049 mi., but the 49 is purely symbolic, in honor of Alaska's status as the 49th state; the real distance is closer to 1100 mi.

The Iditarod ("a far-off place" in Ingalik) Trail began as a dog sled route used to bring supplies to snow-bound gold-rush boom towns. The race commemorates the 1925 rescue of Nome, when sled drivers relayed 300,000 units of life-saving diphtheria serum to town. The first race, in 1967, was a 27 mi. jaunt; today, up to 70 contestants speed each year from Anchorage to Nome, competing for a $450,000 purse. For more info, contact the Iditarod Trail Committee (www.iditarod.com), or visit the headquarters at Mile 2.2 Knik Rd. in Wasilla.

eclectic clientele without sacrificing cleanliness. Highlights include 3 lounges, kitchens, big yard, BBQ facilities, and Internet ($1 per 10min.). 6-day max. stay. Reception 9am-1pm and 7-11pm. Chore requested; free stay for 3hr. work. Guests may also opt to camp in the yard. Call ahead in the summer. Dorms $16 with cash or check, $17 with credit card; private rooms $64.

International Backpackers Hostel, 3601 Peterkin Ave. (☎907-274-3870). A bit of a trek from town and in an older-looking neighborhood, but clean. BBQ facilities and free parking. Bike rental $10 per day. Towels $1 (with $5 deposit). Laundry $3. Key deposit $10. Dorms $15. Tent sites $10; $2 per additional person.

Puffin Inn, 4400 Spenard Ave. (☎907-243-4044 or 800-478-3346, www.puffininn.net), southeast of downtown, near the airport. This clean and modern hotel has a range of rooms available. Some rooms with refrigerators and microwaves. Continental breakfast included. Fitness center and laundry services. Rooms $99-159. $10 AAA discount.

Caribou Inn, 501 L St. (☎907-272-0444), at 5th Ave. Small, clean B&B minutes from the Coastal Trail and within walking distance of downtown locations. Full breakfast in main dining room. Cable TV in all rooms. Kitchenettes in double rooms. Free parking. Rooms in summer from $79; in winter from $45.

Anchorage International Hostel (HI), 700 H St. (☎907-276-3635; www.alaska.net/~hianch), near the Transit Center. The only downtown hostel, and one of the very few reasonably priced accommodations in that area. While its location is key, this place lacks the usual ambiance of a HI hostel. Kitchen. Internet $2.25 per 15 min. Wash and dry $1 each. Key deposit $5. Curfew 1am. No parking at hostel, but street parking available. Dorms $20, non-members $23; family rooms $50/$55.

NIGHTLIFE

Microbrews gush from Anchorage's taps like oil through the Pipeline, fueling a nightlife that can be either laid-back or rowdy, depending on your preference. Nibble an olive at trendy martini bars, dance to lively rhythms at honky-tonk dives, or carouse at establishments anywhere between the two. All bars are 21+ unless otherwise noted. *The Anchorage Press,* a free alternative weekly, has a listing and description of bars and dance clubs.

Bears Tooth Theater and Pub, 1230 W. 27th St. (☎907-276-4200), at Spenard St. This brew-pub theater offers an alternative to the standard scene. Catch recent and classic flicks while enjoying your favorite pint ($3.75). Pizza $2.50 per slice. A balcony for those under 21. $3 cover for movie. Box office open M-Sa at 11am, Su at noon. Grill open daily from 4pm. Call for latest movie listings.

Chilkoot Charlie's, 2435 Spenard St. (☎907-272-1010), at Fireweed St. "Koots" is an Anchorage institution. Usually the place to begin a wild night out, but with 10 different themed bars you might not go far. $1 drink specials until 10pm. Cover $3-6. Open Su-Th 10:30am-2:30am, F-Sa 11am-2:30am.

Pioneer Bar, 739 W 4th. Ave. (☎907-276-7996), near the corner of A St., downtown. 2 pool tables, dart boards, and shuffleboard start to go unnoticed as the weekend nights wear on and the drinks keep coming. Beers $3. Open daily 10am-2am.

Bernie's Bungalow Lounge, 626 D St. (☎907-276-8808), between 6th and 7th St. Relax in a swingback chair as you sip your lemon-drop martini ($5) or puff on a cigar ($3-10). Frequented by the young and retro. Stylin' outdoor patio and lawn (summer only, of course). Live music or DJ Th-Sa. Open daily summer noon-2am; winter 3pm-2am.

Humpy's Great Alaskan Alehouse, 610 6th Ave. (☎907-276-2337), between F and G St. across from the Alaska Center for Performing Arts. This bar teems with locals enjoying the largest draught selection in Alaska. Live music nightly. Open daily 11am-2am.

Glacier Brewhouse, 737 W. 5th Ave. (☎907-274-2739), near G St. Upscale and crowded brewery and restaurant where, as they claim, "Alaskans meet Alaskans." Or at least where the cruise ship crowd comes to meet. Open M 11am-11pm, Tu-Th 11am-11:30pm, F-Sa 11am-midnight, Su noon-11pm.

Snowgoose, 717 W. 3rd Ave. (☎907-277-7727), at G St. The Sleeping Lady Brewing Co. churns out pints as locals and tourists alike take in the views from the outdoor deck. Open in summer 11:30am-sunset.

THE SOUTHERN BORDER

Only the strong survived in the Old West, but you won't need spurs and a sawed-off shotgun to make it through this route—just a lot of water and a working air-conditioner. You will get to experience *both* a dry heat and a wet heat on the way from the Wild West to the deep South, as you travel from the semi-desert of San Diego to the semi-tropics of Florida, on the way visiting the starkly beautiful monuments and national parks that the borderlands have to offer.

From San Diego, home of the **San Diego Zoo** (p. 760) and **Sea World** (p. 761), the road cuts through less-touristed Southern California, sampling small towns along Old Route 80 and visiting the not-so-

ancient pyramid at the **"Official Center of the World!"** (p. 766) on its way to Arizona. Dodging cacti and tortoises, the road crosses the California border at **Yuma, AZ** (p. 767), the mother of all truck stops, and continues through the desert to the **Painted Rocks Petroglyph Site** (p. 769), where ancient spirals and pictures are inscribed on boulders. The road stops in hip **Phoenix, AZ** (p. 771) and the mysterious **Casa Grande Ruins** (p. 777) before striking south to the Wild West town of **Tombstone, AZ** (p. 786) and the **Tucson, AZ** (p. 781). After heading north to the ancient **Gila Gliff Dwellings** (p. 793), the road curves back south to **Hatch, NM,** the Chili Capital of the World (p. 796), where you can buy flaming hot chili peppers by the 40 lb. bag.

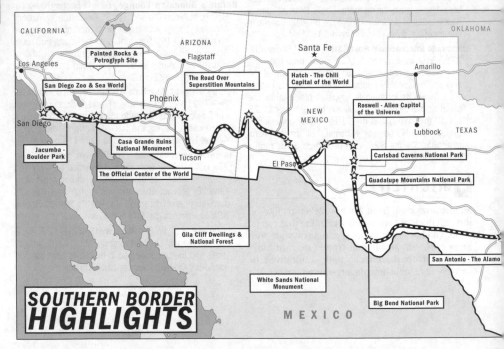

SOUTHERN BORDER HIGHLIGHTS

Crossing the Rockies, the route becomes more populated by parks and monuments. Duck test missiles at White Sands Missile Base while you sand-surf the dunes of **White Sands National Monument** (p. 801). The vistas outside **Ruidoso, NM,** up the sublime **Sierra Blanca** Mountains (p. 803), are the most beautiful of the trip. You might get carried away at **UFO Festival** in **Roswell, NM** (p. 805). Then pay homage at the **Shrine of the Miracle Tortilla** in Lake Arthur, NM (p. 806).

Farther down the road, the highway descends into the cool limestone grottoes of **Carlsbad Caverns,** where at dusk 250,000 bats swarm out of the caves at a rate of 6000 bats per minute (BPM). That's a lot of bats.

The road leads back to **Guadalupe Mountains National Park** (p. 808) and **Big Bend National Park** (p. 811), where you can leave the car to chill out with scenic vistas and mountain lions. Driving through the Lone Star State, where the oil derricks are big and the eat-it-all-and-you-don't-have-to-pay steak plates are bigger, the road makes its not-quite last stand at **The Alamo** in **San Antonio, TX** (p. 817), where your stolen bike is hidden in the basement.

From there, you'll have no problem in **Houston** finding the **Johnson Space Center** (p. 827), the NASA center for the International Space Station.

ROUTE STATS

Miles: c. 2700

Route: San Diego, CA to the Everglades, FL.

States: 8; California, Arizona, New Mexico, Texas, Louisiana, Mississippi, Alabama, and Florida.

Driving Time: Two weeks will get you there, but you'll want four to catch all the scenic sights.

When To Go: Prices will be higher in the winter, but it will be much, much hotter in the summer. Basically, it depends on whether or not your A/C works.

Crossroads: The Pacific Coast in San Diego, CA (p. 874); **The North American** in Phoenix (p. 675) and Tucson, AZ (p. 670); **The East Coast** in the Everglades, FL (p. 150).

The road takes on a new character in the Bayou, heating up in **Avery Island,** home of Tabasco (p. 838) and two-stepping through the French Quarter in **New Orleans, LA** (p. 841). The highway

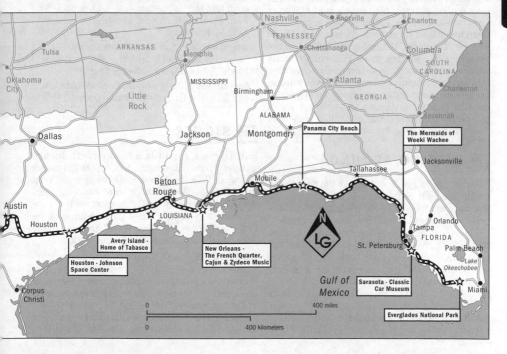

hugs the Gulf of Mexico, passing through "Florida's Forgotten Coast" on the way to **Panama City Beach,** heart of the "Redneck Riviera" (p. 859), and visiting the mermaids at **Weeki-Wachee** (p. 864) on its way to the **Everglades** (p. 868).

From San Diego's animal parks to Florida's swamplands, the Southern Border offers nature's most beautiful wonders, not to mention quite a few wonders of the road. Bring your Texas-sized appetite for adventure and leave behind your winter coats, because the Southern Border is hot!

SAN DIEGO

The natives call it "America's Finest City," and visitors pulling into this picturesque port will soon understand why. In a state where every other town has staked its claim as paradise, San Diego may be Southern California's best return on the promises of a golden state. Year-round sunny weather encourages abundant gardens, inviting beaches, and friendly demeanors. Downtown San Diego is pleasant, but to truly enjoy the majesty of the city, escape the hustle and bustle in favor of the more natural settings of Balboa Park, Old Town, and, of course, the world-class beaches.

⊟ GETTING AROUND

To enter San Diego from **I-5,** take the **Civic Center** or **4th Ave.** exit. Downtown is just south of the freeway, and its grid layout is easily navigable—one-way streets alternate direction every block.

The epicenter of San Diego tourism is historic **Balboa Park.** Northwest of the park is stylish **Hillcrest,** the city's gay enclave with great shopping and restaurants. The reinvigorated **Gaslamp Quarter** sits in the southern section of downtown between 4th and 6th St. and contains signature theaters and nightclubs, as well as fine restaurants. Just north of downtown in the southeast corner of the I-5 and I-8 junction lies a little slice of

old Mexico known as **Old Town.** Discriminating travelers may find Old Town's touristy kitsch a bit contrived, but the fantastic Mexican food and lively scene make this place worth a visit. San Diego has two major bays: **San Diego Bay,** formed by **Coronado Island,** south of downtown, and **Mission Bay,** to the northwest. A jaunt up the coast leads to the swanky tourist haven of **La Jolla.** Farther up the coast are the relaxed, sun-soaked beach communities of the **North County.**

Parking lots are scattered throughout the downtown area and all charge around $5 per hr. If you plan to shop, parking at Horton Plaza (San Diego's gigantic outdoor mall) is free with validation in one of the mall's stores (3hr. max.).

(VITAL STATS)

Population: 1.2 million

Visitor Info: International Visitor Information Center, 1040 West Broadway (☎ 619-236-1212; www.sandiego.org), at Harbor Dr. Open M-Sa 9am-5pm; June-Aug. also Su 10am-5pm. **La Jolla Visitor Center,** 7966 Herschel Ave. Open Sept.-Oct. and Apr.-May M-F 11am-5pm, Sa 10am-6pm, Su 10am-4pm; Nov.-Mar. M-Th 11am-4pm, F 11am-5pm, Sa 10am-6pm, Su 10am-4pm; June-Aug. M-Sa 10am-7pm, Su 10am-7pm.

Internet Access: San Diego Public Library, 820 E St. (☎ 619-236-5800). Open M and W noon-8pm, Tu and Th-Sa 9:30am-5:30pm, Su 1-5pm.

Post Office: 2535 Midway Dr. Open M 7am-5pm, Tu-F 8am-5pm, Sa 8am-4pm. **Postal Code:** 92186.

⊙ SIGHTS

San Diego's world-famous attractions are extremely varied, enough to keep any traveler engaged. Pick the free weekly *Reader* for local event listings. The **San Diego 3-for-1 Pass** ($89, ages 3-9 $63) offers unlimited admission for five consecutive days at discounted rates to three of the city's premier sights—Sea World, the San Diego Zoo, and the San Diego Wild Animal Park.

DOWNTOWN. San Diego's downtown attractions are concentrated in the corridor that includes its business, Gaslamp, and waterfront districts. The steel-and-glass **San Diego Museum of Contemporary Art** encases 20th-century works, including those of Andy Warhol and a wall that looks as though it breathes, which is as weird as

TO OLD TOWN

TO ① & HILLCREST

San Diego Zoo

Spanish Village Art Center

Museum of Art

Museum of Man

Timkin Gallery

Visitor Info Center

San Diego Intl. Airport

Maple St.

Laurel St.

El Prado

Spreckels Organ Pavilion

Ruben H. Fleet Space Center

Kalmia St.

House of Pacific Relations

163

Juniper St.

Automotive Museum

Casa de Balboa Museums

Balboa Park Gardens

Curlew St.

Albatross St.

Brant St.

Front St.

Ivy St.

Aerospace Museum

TO OCEAN BEACH

Laurel St.

Union St.

San Diego Fwy.

Hawthorn St.

6th Ave.

Balboa Dr.

8th Avenue Dr.

Pan-American E.

Presidents W.

Park Blvd.

Balboa Park

Pacific Hwy.

India St.

Kettner Blvd.

Grape St.

Fir St.

Cabrillo Fwy.

U.S. Naval Medical Center

LITTLE ITALY

Elm St.

Date St.

Balboa Stadium

Russ Blvd.

Medea

Berkeley

Maritime Museum

Star of India

Cedar St.

Beech St.

Ash St.

1st Ave.

2nd Ave.

3rd Ave.

4th Ave.

5th Ave.

6th Ave.

7th Ave.

8th Ave.

9th Ave.

10th Ave.

11th Ave.

12th Ave.

San Diego City College

Santa Fe Amtrak Depot

A St.

Museum of Contemporary Art

B St.

C St.

City Hall

Copley Symphony Hall

163

163

SOUTHERN BORDER

5

Pacific Hwy.

Harbor Dr.

B Street Pier

C St.

Broadway Pier

Harbor Excursions

International Visitor Information Center

Greyhound

Broadway

E St.

13th St.

14th St.

15th St.

16th St.

17th St.

94

Navy Pier

Kettner Blvd.

State St.

Union St.

Pantoja Park

③

Horton Plaza Center

F St.

G St.

5

Tuna Harbor Park

GASLAMP QUARTER

163

Market St.

Island Ave.

SEE INSET

Seaport Village

San Diego Convention Center

8th Ave.

J St.

K St.

L St.

Embarcadero Marina Park

Harbor Dr.

Imperial Ave.

Horton Plaza Center

E St.

④

F St.

San Diego Harbor

5

3rd Ave.

4th Ave.

5th Ave.

6th Ave.

7th Ave.

G St.

Market St.

GASLAMP QUARTER

⑥

Bike Tours

Island Ave.

Coronado Island

75

TO CORONADO ISLAND

San Diego

it sounds. *(1001 Kettner Blvd. ☎619-234-1001. Open M-Tu and Th-Su 11am-5pm. Free.)* By day, the charm of the **Gaslamp Quarter** lies in its fading history, with antique shops, Victorian buildings, and trendy restaurants. The **Gaslamp Quarter Foundation** offers guided walking tours as well as a museum. *(410 Island Ave., at William Heath Davis House. ☎619-233-4692; www.gaslampquarter.org. Museum open Su and Tu-Sa 11am-3pm. 2hr. walking tours Sa 11am. Suggested donation $3. Tours $8, students and seniors $6, under 12 free. Self-guided tour maps $2.)* Like most old buildings in San Diego, the **Horton Grand Hotel** is supposedly haunted. Believers may catch a glimpse of Wild West lawman Wyatt Earp. *(311 Island Ave. ☎619-544-1886. Tours W at 3pm. Free.)* Spanish for "dock," the **Embarcadero** has boardwalk shops and museums that face moored windjammers, cruise ships, and the occasional naval destroyer. The jewel of San Diego's redevelopment **Horton Plaza**, at Broadway and 4th Ave., a pastel, open-air, multi-level shopping center.

BALBOA PARK. It would take several days to see all of Balboa Park's museums. Most of them reside within the resplendent Spanish colonial-style buildings that line El Prado St. These ornate structures, several of which were designed for exhibits in 1916 or 1936, were originally intended to last two years. The **Balboa Park Visitors Center** sells park maps and the **Passport to Balboa Park,** which allows admission into 13 of the park's attractions. *(1549 El Prado St. From I-5, merge onto Rte. 163 North and take the Balboa Park Exit. ☎619-239-0512; www.balboapark.org. Maps $0.50. Passport $30. Open daily summer 9am-4:30pm; winter 9am-4pm.)* Creationists beware: the **Museum of Man** dedicates an entire floor to the 98.4% of DNA we share with chimpanzees. The real treat, however, is on the outside: the gleaming Spanish mosaic tiles of the museum's much-photographed tower and dome. *(On the west end of the park. ☎619-239-2001; www.museumofman.org. Open daily 10am-4:30pm. $6, seniors $5, ages 6-17 $3. 3rd Tu of each month free. Special exhibits $8.)* At the east end of Balboa Park, the **Natural History Museum** exhibits stuffed mammals and birds. Live insects and arthropods enhance the displays of standard fossils. *(☎619-232-3821; http://www.sdnhm.org. $9, seniors $6, ages 6-17 $5. 1st Tu of each month free.)* The **Aerospace Museum** displays 24 full-scale replicas and 44 original planes,

as well as information on aviation history and the International Space Station project. *(2001 Pan American Plaza. ☎619-234-8291; www.aerospacemuseum.org. Open daily 10am-4:30pm; extended summer hours. $8, seniors $6, ages 6-17 $3. 4th Tu of each month free.)* The **Reuben H. Fleet Space Theater and Science Center** houses interactive exhibits and the world's first hemispheric Omnimax theater. *(1875 El Prado Way. ☎619-238-1233; www.rhfleet.org. Open daily 9:30am-8pm. $6.75, with Omnimax show $11.50; seniors $6/$8.50; ages 3-12 $5.50/$9.50. 1st Tu of each month free.)* The small, ultra-modern **Museum of Photographic Arts (MOPA)** features contemporary photography. Its film program ranges from cult classic film festivals to more serious cinematic works. *(☎619-238-7559; www.mopa.org. Open M-W and F-Su 10am-5pm, Th 10am-9pm. $6, students $4. 2nd Tu of each month free. Films $5/$4.50.)* The **San Diego Museum of Art** has a collection ranging from ancient Asian to contemporary Californian works. *(☎619-232-7931; www.sdmart.org. Open Su and Tu-Sa 10am-6pm, Th 10am-9pm. $8, seniors and students $6, ages 6-17 $3. Special exhibits $2-20.)* The fragrant **Botanical Building** looks like a giant, wooden birdcage. The orchid collection is particularly striking among the murmuring fountains. *(2200 Park Blvd. ☎619-235-1100, tour info 235-1121. Open M-W and F-Su 10am-4pm. Free.)* Constructed in 1937, the **Old Globe Theater** is the oldest professional theater in California. *(☎619-239-2255; www.theoldglobe.org.)*

⧉ SAN DIEGO ZOO. With over 100 acres of exquisite fenceless habitats, this zoo deserves its reputation as one of the finest in the world. Its unique "bioclimatic" exhibits group animals and plants by habitat. The legendary panda exhibit is the most timeless feature of the park, and the zoo invests over one million dollars a year on panda habitat preservation in China. The educational 40min. double-decker bus tour covers about 75% of the zoo. Although seats on the upper deck are popular, trees can obstruct views and the seats are in the sun; the lower deck is a better choice. *(2920 Zoo Dr., in Balboa Park. ☎619-234-3153; www.sandiegozoo.org. Open daily late June to early Sept. 9am-10pm; early Sept. to late June 9am-dusk. $20, with 35min. bus tour and 2 tickets for the aerial tramway $32; ages 3-11 $12/$20.)*

OLD TOWN. In 1769, Father Serra, supported by Spanish infantry, established the first of 21 missions that would line the California coast in the area now known as Old Town. The remnants of this early settlement have become a tourist mainstay. (*To reach Old Town, take the Old Town Exit from I-5 North.*) The most popular of the area's attractions, the **State Park's** early 19th-century buildings contain museums, shops, and restaurants. **Seely Stable** houses a huge museum of 19th-century transportation, namely of the horse and carriage variety. (☎ 619-220-5427. *Open daily 10am-5pm. Tours every hr. 11am-2pm.*) The **Whaley House** stands on the site of San Diego's first gallows and is one of two **official haunted houses** recognized by the State of California. (*2482 San Diego Ave. ☎ 619-298-2482, tours 619-293-0117. Open daily 10am-4:30pm; last entry 4pm. $5, seniors $4, ages 3-12 $2.*) Across the street is **Heritage Park,** a group of 150-year-old Victorian buildings. Four are open to the public. (☎ 858-565-3600.) The adobe walls of the **Serra Museum** were raised at the site of the original fort and mission in 1929. (*In Presidio Park. ☎ 619-279-3258. Open June-Aug. Su and Tu-Sa 10am-4:30pm; Sept.-May F-Su 10am-4:30pm. $5, seniors and students $4, ages 6-17 $2.*)

CORONADO ISLAND. A slender 7 mi. strip of hauled sand known as the "Silver Strand" tethers the lovely peninsula of Coronado Island to the mainland down near Imperial Beach. The area is perfect for strolling and browsing. Beach babes frolic in the waves that break along the southern shore, while outdoor lovers jog and bike along paved trails. The birthplace of American naval aviation, the **North Island Naval Air Station** comprises the northern chunk of the island. Also among the island's many military enterprises is the training area of the elite **Navy SEAL** (sea, air, and land) special forces teams. Coronado's most famed sight is its Victorian-style **Hotel Del Coronado,** one of America's largest wooden buildings. The long white verandas and the vermilion spires of the "Del" were built in 1888. It has since become one of the world's great hotels (rooms start at $270 per night), hosting 10 presidents and one blonde bombshell—Marilyn Monroe's 1959 *Some Like it Hot* was filmed here. Built in 1969, the graceful **Coronado Bridge** guides cars to Coronado along I-5.

SEA WORLD. Since the 190 acre park opened on March 21, 1964, Sea World has welcomed more than 100 million guests. The A-list star here is the behemoth killer whale Shamu, whose signature move is a cannonball splash that soaks anyone in the first 20 rows. The original Shamu died long ago, but each of his 10 successors has proudly borne the moniker. In addition, there are animals from all walks of sea life in their natural habitats, including penguins, polar bears, and sharks. Try the ray petting pool and Shipwreck Rapids, Sea World's first-ever adventure ride. (*From I-5, take the Sea World Dr. Exit and turn west toward the park. ☎ 619-226-3901. Open daily summer 9am-11pm; winter 10am to varying closing hours. $50, ages 3-9 $40. Parking $7, RVs $9.*)

BEACHES. San Diego's younger population flocks to these communities by the surf for the hopping nightlife. It is said that home-grown and earthy **Ocean Beach (O.B.)** is what the world would be like if the hippies had lasted past the 70s. Anglers can cast from the Western Hemisphere's longest fishing pier. Farther north, at the corner of W. Mission Bay Dr. and Mission Blvd., **Mission Beach** is a people-watcher's paradise. Belmont Park, a combination amusement park and shopping center, draws a youthful crowd. **Pacific Beach** and its boisterous Garnet Ave. is home to the best nightlife. Ocean Front Walk is packed with joggers, cyclists, and the usual beachfront shops.

LA JOLLA. Pronounced *la-HOY-a*, this affluent seaside locality houses few budget accommodation options, but offers some of the finest public beaches in the San Diego area. (*Take the Ardath Exit west from I-5.*) **La Jolla Cove** is popular with scuba divers, snorkelers, and brilliantly colored Garibaldi goldfish. Wander south along the cliffs to a striking semi-circular inlet known as **The Children's Pool,** whose inhabitants are a famously thriving community of sea lions. Some of the best breaks in the county can be found at **Tourmaline Beach** and **Wind 'n Sea Beach.** However, these are notoriously territorial spots, so outsiders might be advised to surf elsewhere. **La Jolla Shores** has gentle swells ideal for new surfers, boogie boarders, and swimmers. Nearby, the ■**Birch Aquarium at the Scripps Institute of Oceanography** has great educational exhibits including a tank of oozing jellyfish, a large collection of seahorses, and a 70,000-gallon kelp and shark tank. (*2300 Expedition Way. ☎ 858-534-3474; http://aquarium.ucsd.edu. Open daily 9am-5pm. $9.50, students $6.50, ages 3-17 $6. Parking $3.*) The visually stunning **San Diego Museum of Contemporary Art** shares its rotating collection of

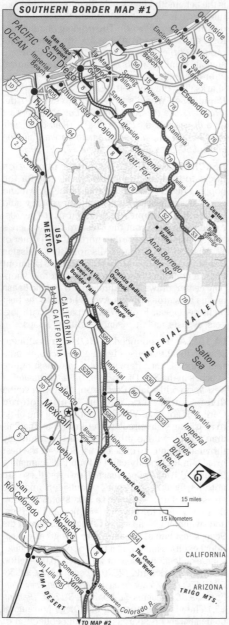

SOUTHERN BORDER MAP #1

pop, minimalist, and conceptualist art from the 1950s with the downtown branch. *(700 Prospect St. ☎858-454-3541. Open M-Tu and F-Su 11am-5pm, Th 11am-7pm. $6; students, seniors, and ages 12-18 $2. 1st Su and 3rd Tu of every month free.)* Be sure to check out the terraces and buttresses of **Geisel Library** at the **University of California San Diego (UCSD),** a space-age structure endowed by La Jolla resident Theodore Geisel, better known by his middle name as the late and beloved children's books author, Dr. Seuss. *(☎858-534-2208. Open M-F 7am-9pm, Sa-Su 7am-5:30pm.)*

ESCONDIDO. Escondido (pop. 125,000) lies 30 mi. north of San Diego amid rolling, semi-arid hills that blossom with wildflowers in the spring. A look at the free-roaming endangered species of the 2100-acre **San Diego Wild Animal Park** is an essential part of any trip to San Diego. The highlight of the park is the large enclosures where many species roam freely. Rhinos, giraffes, gazelles, and tigers can all be found on the park plains. The open-air Wgasa Bush Line Railway, a 1hr. monorail safari, travels through four created habitat areas; sit on the right if possible. *(From I-15, take the Via Rancho Pkwy. ☎619-747-8702; www.wild-animalpark.org. Open daily from 9am; closing times vary by season. Rail tours June-Aug. 9:30am-9pm; Sept.-May 9:30am-4pm. $26.50, ages 3-11 $19.50. Parking $6.)*

🍴 FOOD

With its large Hispanic population and proximity to Mexico, San Diego is renowned for its exemplary Mexican cuisine. **Old Town** serves some of the best authentic Mexican food in the state. San Diego also offers a spectacular assortment of ethnic and more traditional eateries. Good restaurants cluster downtown along **C St., Broadway Blvd.,** and in historic **Gaslamp Quarter.** The best food near Balboa Park and the zoo is in nearby **Hillcrest** and **University Heights.**

La Especial Norte, 664 N. Rte. 101 (☎760-942-1040), in the center of Leucadia. In a town of excellent Mexican cuisine, this is quite possibly the best. The food is so good that the San Diego Coast lifeguards rent the restaurant for their annual banquet. Try the Mexican shrimp cocktail or the tortilla soup. Entrees $6-8. Open daily 10am-10pm.

Casa de Bandini, 2754 Calhoun St. (☎619-297-8211). An Old Town institution set in a Spanish-

SOUTHERN BORDER

style architectural landmark built in 1829. Superb food and boisterous music. The colossal combo plates ($5-8) and heavyweight margaritas ($4-7) are the stuff of legend. Open M-Th 11am-9:30pm, F-Sa 11am-10pm, Su 10am-9:30pm.

■ **The Corvette Diner,** 3946 5th Ave. (☎619-542-1001), in Hillcrest. The ultimate flashback to the days of nickel milkshakes, this 50s-style diner has more chrome than Detroit and more neon than Las Vegas. Greasy-spoon classics and unique creations like the Rory Burger (peanut butter and bacon burger; $7). A DJ spins oldies every night (6-9pm) while costumed waitresses give as much lip as service. Open Su-Th 11am-10pm, F-Sa 11am-midnight.

Pizza Port, 135 N. Rte. 101 (☎858-481-7332), in the center of Solana Beach. This surf-themed pizza parlor and microbrewery offers some of the coast's best grub and grog. After the sun sets, the bar fills up with laid-back surfer types discussing the finer points of the day's swell. Open daily 7am-2am.

Kono's Surf Club, 704 Garnet Ave. (☎858-483-1669), across from the Crystal Pier in Pacific Beach. Identifiable by the line stretching for a block out the door, Kono's is a surfer's shrine. Try the huge Egg Burrito #3, which includes bacon, cheese, potatoes, and sauce ($4). Open M-F 7am-3pm, Sa-Su 7am-4pm.

Kansas City Barbecue, 610 W. Market St. (☎619-231-9680), near Seaport Village. The location of *Top Gun's* Great Balls of Fire bar scene. While the wooden piano remains, all that's left of Goose and Maverick is an abundance of autographed posters and neon signs. Vegetarians will find themselves in the Danger Zone in this barbecue-slathered meatfest. Entrees $9-16. Open daily 11am-2am. Kitchen closes 1am.

ACCOMMODATIONS

Rates predictably rise on weekends and during the summer season. Reservations are recommended. There is a popular cluster known as **Hotel Circle** (2-3 mi. east of I-5 along I-8), where summer prices begin at $60 for a single and $70 for a double during the week. Several beaches in North County, as well as one on Coronado, are state parks and allow camping.

■ **USA Hostels San Diego,** 726 5th Ave. (☎619-232-3100 or 800-438-8622; www.usahostels.com), between F and G St. This colorful Euro-style fun house fits in well with the rocking atmosphere of the Gaslamp district. Hosts frequent par-

ties and pub crawls ($4). Pancake breakfast included. Dinner $4. Linen, lockers, and coin-op laundry. International passport or student ID required. Dorms $19-21; private rooms $46-50.

■ **San Diego Downtown Hostel (HI-AYH),** 521 Market St. (☎619-525-1531; www.sandiegohostels.org), at 5th Ave., in the heart of Gaslamp. Quiet, impeccably clean, and close to popular attractions and clubs. Airy common room with kitchen and pool table and communal bathrooms. 4- to 6-bed dorms $20, nonmembers $23; doubles $45-50/$48-43.

International House at the 2nd Floor, 4502 Cass St. (☎858-274-4325), in Pacific Beach and 3204 Mission Bay Dr. (☎858-539-0043), in Mission Beach. Excellent service, clean and bright rooms, comfortable beds, and 2 great beach locations. Internet. Out-of-state ID or international passport required. Breakfast included. 28-day max. stay. Dorms $20, with student ID $18. Weekly rooms $110.

Ocean Beach International (OBI), 4961 Newport Ave. (☎619-223-7873 or 800-339-7263). Clean rooms near the beach. Proof of international travel in the last 6 months required. Pancake breakfast included. Free BBQ Tu and F night. 29-day max. stay. 4- to 6-bed dorms $18-20; doubles $40-43.

San Elijo Beach State Park (☎760-753-5091), off Rte. 101, south of Cardiff-by-the-Sea. Over 170 sites (23 with RV hookups) on seaside cliffs. Laundry and showers. Tent sites; $12 RVs $18.

South Carlsbad Beach State Park (☎760-438-3143), off Carlsbad Blvd., near Leucadia. Over 100 sites near beautiful beaches with good surfing. Laundry and showers. Tent sites $12; RVs $18.

NIGHTLIFE

Nightlife in San Diego is scattered across distinct pockets of action. Posh locals and party-seeking tourists flock to the **Gaslamp Quarter.** The **Hillcrest,** next to Balboa Park, draws a young, largely gay crowd to its clubs and eateries. Away from downtown, the beach areas (especially **Garnet Ave.** in Pacific Beach) are loaded with clubs, bars, and cheap eateries. The definitive source of entertainment info is the free *Reader,* found in shops, coffeehouses, and Visitors Centers. Listings can also be found in the *San Diego Union-Tribune's* Thursday "Night and Day" section. You can spend a more sedate evening at one of San Diego's excellent theaters, such as the **Balboa Theatre,** 225

Broadway Ave. (☎609-544-1000), and the **Horton Grand Theatre,** 444 4th Ave. (☎619-234-9583), both downtown. The **La Jolla Playhouse,** 2910 La Jolla Village Dr., presents shows on the UCSD campus. (☎858-550-1010; www.lajollaplayhouse.com.)

🎵 **Croce's Top Hat Bar and Grille** and **Croce's Jazz Bar,** 802 5th Ave. (☎619-233-4355), at F St. in the Gaslamp. Ingrid Croce, widow of singer Jim Croce, created this rock/blues bar and jazz bar side-by-side on the 1st fl. of the Keating building. Live music nightly from 8:30pm. Cover $5-10; includes 2 live shows. Top Hat open F-Sa 7pm-1:30am. Jazz bar open daily 5:30pm-12:30am.

Pacific Beach Bar and Grill and **Club Tremors,** 860 Garnet Ave. (☎858-483-9227), one of the only dance clubs in Pacific Beach. Live DJ packs the 2-level dance floor with a young and oh-so-hip crowd. The Bar and Grill has respectable food, more than 20 beers on tap, and live music on Su. Cover $5 if you enter through Club Tremors, but the same club is accessible through the Grill for free. Club open Tu-Sa 9pm-1:30am; bar open 11am-1:30am; kitchen closes midnight.

Canes Bar and Grill, 3105 Ocean front Walk (☎858-488-1780 or 858-488-9690), in Mission Beach. One of the best live music venues in the city, this beachside bar has unbeatable sunset views from the terrace. DJ and dancing every night. Open daily 11am-2am.

The Casbah, 2501 Kettner Blvd. (☎619-232-4355; www.casbahmusic.com). Eddie Vedder of the alternative rock legend Pearl Jam owns this intimate nightspot. Cover varies. 21+. Call ahead or check online for a schedule, as sometimes tickets sell out.

The Flame, 3780 Park Blvd. (☎619-295-4163), in Hillcrest. One of the most popular lesbian dance clubs in the nation. 21+. Open daily 5pm-2am.

▶️ LEAVING SAN DIEGO
From central San Diego, hop on **I-8 East.** In the outskirts of town, exit onto **Rte. 78 North** to begin your journey east.

RAMONA

Located on Rte. 78 in the foothills of the Cuyamaca Mountains, this ranching community centers around horses. Don't miss the **Ramona Rodeo** in May, and the **Country Fair** days in August. For more info, contact the **Ramona Chamber of Commerce,** 960 Main St. (☎760-689-1311). Ramona is also known for its antiques, art, history and wine. The **Woodward Museum,** 645 Main St., offers a taste of historic Ramona. (☎760-789-7644. Open Th-Su 1-4pm.) At the **Ramona Antique Mall,** 872

Main St., vendors sell wares that range from Pepsi artifacts to fine jewelry. (☎760-789-7816. Open M-Sa 10am-5pm, Su 11am-5pm.)

Grab a home-cooked meal at the **Kountry Kitchen,** 826 Main St. (☎760-788-3200; open M-W 5am-3pm, Th and Sa-Su 5am-8:30pm, F 5am-9pm), or outfit yourself in western wear at the **Branding Iron,** 629 Main St. (☎760-789-5050).

▶️ DUDLEY'S BAKERY   30218 Rte. 78
In Santa Ysabel, located at the junction of Rte. 78 and Rte. 79.

A tiny pit-stop 17 mi. past Ramona, Santa Ysabel offers some of the world's best baked goods. Half of the town is 🍞**Dudley's Bakery,** known across San Diego County for the fresh breads it distributes daily. Stop and buy a loaf ($2.35) or try the tasty fruit bars ($2.75) and other assorted pastries. (☎800-225-3348. Convenient public restrooms. Open Su and W-Sa 8am-5pm.)

JULIAN

Apple pie, gold, and the outdoors are the most visible attractions of this mountain village nestled in San Diego's back country. Relive Julian's Old West history through a carriage ride, or by visiting the **Julian Pioneer Museum,** right behind the Julian Town Hall on Main St. (Open Apr.-Nov. Su and Tu-Sa 10am-4pm. $2.) Those looking for an educational adventure should take an interactive tour of the **Eagle Mine,** where visitors can explore 1000 ft. of tunnels and pan for gold. (☎760-765-0036. Open daily. Call ahead for times. Tours $8.)

The **Town Hall,** 2129 Main St. (☎760-765-1857), distributes helpful information about the town, shows local art, and is a good place to start your tour. For food in Julian, visit the 🍴**Miner's Diner & Soda Fountain,** 2134 Main St. Housed in an 1886 building, this old-fashioned soda shop holds true to its roots. The brickwork is still visible behind the 1950s soda fountain, while the opposite wall houses a collection of antique merchandise. Don't miss their displays of license plates. (☎760-765-3471. Breakfast $4-7. Lunch $6-7.) The **RongBranch Restaurant & Boar's Head Saloon,** 2722 Washington St., serves up family dining in an old-fashioned saloon atmosphere. (☎760-765-2265. Entrees $8-24. Open daily 11am-9pm. Saloon open until midnight.) For buffalo lovers and the buffalo-curious, the bison-themed **Buffalo Bill's,** at the corner of 3rd and B St., serves up buffalo burgers ($7.25). Buffalo meat has one-fourth the fat of beef, so chow down guilt-free. (☎760-765-3471. Sandwiches $4-

7.) It would be a tragedy to leave town without a slice of Julian's apple pie, made freshly from the surrounding orchards. Many places on Main St. serve the all-American dessert by the slice for under $3. **Mom's Apple Pies Etc.,** 2219 Main St., is a great place to get your piece of the pie. (☎ 760-765-2472.)

✂ DETOUR: ANZA BORREGO DESERT STATE PARK
200 Palm Canyon Dr.

Follow Rte. 78 past the S2 turn-off to S3. Take S3 North into Borrego Springs, Then hang a right (west) on Borrego Springs Rd. At Christmas Circle, take Palm Canyon Dr. west all the way to the Visitors Center.

This desert preserve is the largest, and arguably the finest, state park in the California State Park system. With seemingly endless desert expanses to explore, Anza Borrego showcases not only the vitality of the desert but also its ecological and geological diversity. The Palm Canyon hike from the Visitors Center is relatively easy, and pays off with the chance to cool down in the palm groves and wading pools of the canyon. More secluded desert sights include **Font's Point** (the desert's answer to the Grand Canyon), the strange shapes of the nearly lifeless **Badlands, Blair Valley,** and the **wind caves.** Camping is available nearby at the **Palm Canyon Campground,** or off S2 at the **Tamarisk Grove Campground.** Backcountry camping is also allowed anywhere in the park. Encompassed by the park, the small town of **Borrego Springs** is an intimate community of desert rats.

✂ DETOUR: CUYAMACA RANCHO STATE PARK

Take Rte. 79 10 mi. south from Julian.

Shady oak canyon groves, wildflower fields, miles of trails, and pint-sized Lake Cuyamaca fill Cuyamaca Rancho State Park. Stop at the **Park Headquarters and Museum,** 12551 Hwy. 79, to pick up info on trails and camping. (☎ 760-765-0755 Open M-F 8:30am-4:30pm, Sa-Su and holidays 10am-4pm.) Green Valley and Paso Picacho both offer beautiful mountain camping. (☎ 800-444-7275. Sites $15; in low season $12. Cabins $27.) When you're ready to leave, backtrack to the intersection of Rte. 79 and the Sunrise Hwy.

THE SUNRISE HIGHWAY

This scenic drive carves through the oak canyons and pine peaks of the Cuyamaca and Laguna Mountains, which stand as a formidable barrier between the coast and the desert. On Rte. 79, 4 mi.

outside Julian, stop at the **vista point** to overlook the desert and mountains of the area. About 3 mi. farther on Rte. 79, turn left to take the scenic **Sunrise Highway,** which roams through the ashen wasteland remaining from the 2002 pine fire, then up into the pine forests of the Laguna Mountains, where breathtaking desert vistas allow for nearly infinite views east. Be sure to stop at the **Desert View Picnic Area** (6000 ft.) for an unbeatable panoramic photo-op. Eventually, the road winds its way out of the forests and back to **Old Rte. 80** and **I-8 East,** which run roughly parallel.

JACUMBA. In 1922 Bert Vaughn, mayor of San Diego, got insider info that Jacumba would be getting a border crossing, so he bought the town. Jacumba never got its crossing, but it did get one of Rte. 80's most interesting sights; Vaughn built a 70 ft. tower on the edge of the mountains overlooking the desert floor. In the 1930s artist W.T. Ratliffe noticed how nearby boulders resembled actual and mythological creatures. He spent the next two years with a mallet and chisel carving mysterious creatures into the surrounding rock. The result is **Boulder Park** (a.k.a. the **Mystery Cave**), where visitors can wander through carvings of Ratliffe's fantasy. The gift store and the friendly owner offer a wealth of roadtrip info. (☎ 619-766-1612. Open daily 8:30am-sunset. $2.50.)

OCOTILLO. After leaving Jacumba, **Old Rte. 80** intersects with **I-8** and you will want to continue along I-8 East. I-8 passes through Ocotillo, a town named for the large, seemingly lifeless, and altogether viciously spiny desert shrub. The ocotillo only bears leaves and flowers immediately after rainfall; since chances are that no rain is coming this way anytime soon, there's no use waiting around. The town is only good for gassing up for the long desert trek ahead. After Ocotillo, continue back along **Rte. 80** to El Centro.

EL CENTRO. El Centro's motto, "where the sun spends its winters," sounds charming and is a much better alternative to "where the sun bakes the hell out of everything in the summer." Since the freeway bypasses this town, the lack of tourism means there are many inexpensive accommodations on **Adams Ave.** (which becomes Rte. 80). Most of these are rented out during the week by nomadic farmhands or county officials. Near the courthouse, the **La Hacienda Family Restaurant,** 841 W. Main St., serves a filling dinner for under $5. Try the taco plate ($4.50): three homemade tacos, rice, and beans. (☎760-353-8118. Open Tu-Th 7am-8pm, F-Sa 7am-9pm.) The **Ranch House Motel**, 808 Adams Ave., welcomes visitors to a lush oasis in the surrounding concrete jungle. The clean and comfortable 15 units are booked nearly every night, so call ahead. (☎760-352-5571. Singles $25; doubles $30.)

THE ROAD TO YUMA. From El Centro, return to **Rte. 80** and head east. This expanse of asphalt is no ordinary backroad highway. The roadway, along with other remaining segments of Old Rte. 80, stands as a testament to the old days—before freeways catapulted travelers across the country in record time—when only Rte. 80 ran through the deserts between San Diego and Phoenix. Nine miles down this road, the highway passes through the tiny community of **Holtville**. As with most Imperial Valley towns, the Holtville community has close ties to agriculture. Leaving Holtville, you can return to **I-8 East** by traveling east on **Rte. 115**.

SECRET DESERT OASIS

1 mi. north of the Holtville/Rte. 115. Exit off I-8, just before the I-8 overpass, turn left onto Evan Hewes Rd., and follow it for about 1 mi. until it crosses the aqueduct. On the right are two bathrooms and a ring of palms surrounding the fountain, spring, spa, and pond.

Refresh yourself in a hot springs worthy of the word "oasis." Surrounded by desert on all sides, the ◪**Secret Desert Oasis'** warm waters are inviting year-round to all those who can find them. Geothermal activity warms the water here, and a fountain caps the source, shooting the water into a spa area perfect for relaxing. An undeveloped pond surrounded by palms creates a mini-paradise.

> **?** The reason for the abundance of sparsely populated towns in this region goes back to the days when steam engines used to roar across the tracks that now parallel the freeway. In the desert heat, trains needed to stop for water about every 6 mi., and every stop required a new town. Today, the towns still appear on the map, but you'll be hardpressed to find anything in them other than ancient junk yards full of cars whose trip into this desert was their last.

THE IMPERIAL DUNES

Exit I-8 on Grays Well Rd., and enter the Imperial Sand Dunes Recreation Area. Continue down the road for about 2 mi., past the campground ($10 per week); down the hill lies a section of the old planks.

If the shifting sands and lifeless rolling slopes of the Imperial Dunes remind you of another planet, they should. These sands appeared as the desert planet Tatooine in the classic movie *Star Wars*, and have been featured in many other films. Today, thousands of buggies and motorcycles zip across the dunes each year, but before it served as a racing grounds, the area presented a formidable obstacle. Winds and migrating dunes quickly erased any trail, while soft sands slowed travelers to a crawl—if they didn't stop them entirely.

With the invention of the automobile, people became even more interested in finding a passage over these sands. The answer came in 1916, with a piece of desert ingenuity—the plank road. Thousands of wooden boards held together by metal bands traversed the dunes, effectively creating a boardwalk for Model Ts. This innovation lasted until 1926, when the paved road that became Rte. 80 was constructed. A piece of the historic old plank road still remains in the desert.

THE CENTER OF THE WORLD

In Felicity. Exit I-8 on Sidewinder Rd., then go north and immediately west to find the spot.

The last town before entering Arizona, Felicity boasts two things: a rip-off gas station, and ◪**The Official Center of the World!** This title was originally made up by the writer of a children's book, but was officially set in stone in 1985, and tours are now given of the granite pyramid where this point resides. Admission comes with a photograph and a commemorative certificate. Outside, stare in wonder at a span of wall (in a pink that matches the pyramid) that commemorates great moments in French aviation, casualties of the Korean War, the entire 1949 class of Princeton University, and the genealogical history of the Taylor family. Michelangelo's Arm of God (from the Sistine Chapel) sets the local solar time at a giant sundial, while stairs from the Eiffel Tower sit nearby, awkwardly leading to nowhere but the desert sky. (☎760-572-0100. Open Thanksgiving-Easter daily.)

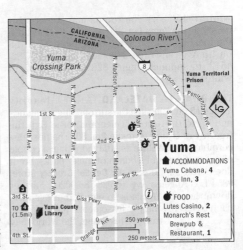

Yuma
♠ ACCOMMODATIONS
Yuma Cabana, 4
Yuma Inn, 3

🍎 FOOD
Lutes Casino, 2
Monarch's Rest
Brewpub &
Restaurant, 1

Welcome To ARIZONA

 Nov.-Mar., you pass into the Mountain Time Zone, where it is 1hr. later. Apr.-Oct. there is no change here.

YUMA

The mother of all truck stops, Yuma sits smack dab in the middle of nowhere. Far from San Diego and equally distant from Tucson, it has been a pit stop for weary travelers for centuries, first used by Spanish explorers, and then as a river-crossing site for gold miners traveling to California.

VITAL STATS

Population: 83,000

Visitor Info: 377 S. Main St. (☎800-293-0071; www.visityuma.com), at the corner of Giss Pkwy. Open Nov.-Apr. M-F 9am-6pm, Sa 9am-4pm, Su 10am-1pm; May-Oct. M-F 9am-5pm, Sa 9am-2pm.

Internet Access: Yuma Public Library, at the corner of Giss Pkwy. and 4th St. Free.

Post Office: 333 S. Main St., unit C (☎928-783-2124). **Postal Code:** 85365

🚗 **GETTING AROUND.** To hit Yuma's main drag, exit I-8 at 4th St. and head south. Most hotels and fast-food chains are ahead on **4th Ave.,** while the **Yuma Crossing State Historic Park** and other useful stops lie east on **Giss Pkwy.** The **Ocean-to-Ocean Bridge,** now closed to traffic, once served as the crossing point over the Colorado River for Rte. 80, the region's now-paved-over artery to the Pacific.

🏛 **SIGHTS.** Legend holds that the infamous prison in the **Yuma Territorial Prison State Historic Park,** 1 Prison Hill Rd., was home to some of the West's most ruthless bandits. In 1876, the inmates were forced to construct the walls that would confine them in the heart of the scorching desert. Tour what remains of the cell blocks and guard tower, and visit the museum, perching atop a hill overlooking the Colorado River and Ocean-to-

Ocean Bridge. If you don't want to spend your money on jail time, visit the free park below the prison. (Take I-8 to Exit I, head east on Giss Pkwy., and turn at Prison Hill Rd. ☎928-782-2192. Open daily 8am-5pm. Tours $4.)

🍴 **FOOD.** Pool and dominos are still played in **Lutes Casino,** 221 S. Main St., as fiercely as they have been since 1920. As you devour your great, if somewhat greasy, meal for under $5 (mostly burgers and sandwiches), you can amuse yourself pondering the truly wacky decor. Why is a moose head mounted to the ceiling, and whose leg is that sticking out of the wall? (☎928-782-2192. Entrees $3.25-5.25. Open M-Th 9am-8pm, F-Sa 9am-9pm, Su 10am-6pm.) A few years ago an Englishman with a taste for brewing left his homeland for the warmer climate of the Arizona Desert. Today, he sells homemade brew in **Monarch's Rest,** 130 S. Main St., an English-style pub, which offers countryside classics like shepherd's pie ($10) and bangers and mash ($13). On weekends (Th-Sa) the pub's a lively late-night spot. (☎928-728-7494. Lunch $6-7. Dinner $8-13. Th night $1 drafts and live DJ. Open M-W 4-9pm, Th-Sa 11am-1am.)

🏠 **ACCOMMODATIONS.** The tropically themed **Yuma Cabana,** 2151 S. 4th Ave., is a resort by truck stop standards. Spacious, clean, and cool rooms come with continental breakfast. (Exit I-8 at 4th Ave., and continue south for about 2 mi.; the Cabana is on the left. ☎520-783-8311. In summer singles $28; doubles $40. In

SOUTHERN BORDER

winter $45/$55.) The rooms may seem a bit musty at the **Yuma Inn,** 260 S. 4th Ave., but both the location and price are unbeatable. (Exit I-8 on 4th Ave., and drive 2 blocks south. ☎ 928-782-4512. In summer singles $28; doubles $35. In winter $40/$45.)

THE ROAD TO DATELAND. After leaving Yuma, **I-8** cuts through the surrounding farmlands and up to the narrow Telegraph Pass. Exit the freeway at **Ligurta** to rejoin **Rte. 80.** The next discernible town, **Wellton,** is little more than a couple of gas stations and a bunch of trailer parks, but it does offer supplies at the **Del Sol Grocery Store,** 9854 Los Angeles Ave. (☎ 928-785-9020). Farther down the road, **Tacna** is so empty that even the palm trees are lonely. Why someone planted palm trees in this desert, the world may never know. In **Mohawk,** Rte. 80 again has no other option but to join up with I-8. Don't worry about missing Mohawk; it won't mind.

DATELAND. One might assume that Dateland is named after the numerous date trees. But here, as often happens on the backroads of America, logic fails. The name is derived from WWII-era General Datelan, who commanded a military base in the area. The dates came later, and with their arrival, the second "d" was added to the name. The gift shop tells about the wonders of the palm tree fruit, but visitors should actually experience it, in the form of the Dateland date milkshake. The ▨**Dateland Palms Village Restaurant** serves up shakes ($2.70) and other date treats, in addition to a full diner menu. The best treat in town is the prickly pear cactus milkshake ($2.70), refresh-

WAYS TO STAY COOL IN THE DESERT

TOP 10

10 Find an oasis. It works in every cartoon you have ever seen; just make sure it isn't a mirage. Try the oasis located off I-8 just outside Holtville.

9 Buy seat covers. If your car doesn't already have cloth seats, get covers. The vinyl, plastic, or leather will roast your rear.

8 Have a cactus milkshake. Your thorny desert friend makes a great treat. Try one at the Dateland Palms Restaurant.

7 Use your body's own A/C: sweat. Don't be afraid to sweat. In cars without A/C, try the method of rolling up the windows to build up a good sweat, then roll them down to feel delightfully cool as the sweat evaporates.

6 Find some shade. Escaping the sun can lower the temperature a dozen degrees. Try the misting benches in the shade of the Boyce Thompson Arboretum outside Superior, AZ.

5 The Colorado River runs straight through Yuma, AZ and other desert cities. Its cool waters are popular with watersports enthusiasts across the West.

4 Turn up the heat. It sounds paradoxical, but if your car is having trouble, turn on the heating system to help keep the engine from overheating. A little uncomfortable warmth is cooler than being stranded in the desert.

3 Find a cave. The Southwest desert is littered with interesting subterranean features. The air in Tuscon's Colossal Cave is always a cool, dry 70°.

2 Drink from a cactus—it really works. Some types of catci have a water reservoir inside. Choose wisely, though; some types of catci are protected in many states.

1 Come back in winter. Desert rats call winter visitors snowbirds, but there's no shame in visiting when the weather is the best.

SOUTHERN BORDER

ingly thornless and delicious. (I-8 at Milepost 67. ☎928-454-2772. Entrees $5-6. Open M-Sa 8am-10pm, Su 9am-10pm.)

 LEAVING DATELAND
From Dateland, follow **Ave. 64** north, back under the freeway and into the desert. This side stint takes you off the beaten path and through some of the immeasurably small desert towns of the region. Turn right onto Palmas Rd. to get to Horn and Hyder.

> In Arizona many stop lights lack the green "turn arrows," and when they do have the turn arrow, it follows the normal green light for through-going traffic instead of coming before it as it does in California.

HORN & HYDER. The barely discernible towns of **Horn** and **Hyder** remain from the days of Camp Horn and Camp Hyder, where military men like General Patton would run drills in the desert in preparation for WWII. Reportedly, Patton believed that if his troops could survive these conditions, combat in Europe would seem easy.

THE ROAD TO THE PAINTED ROCKS

More adventurous roadies should take the 18 mi. dirt road to the 🖼**Painted Rocks Petroglyph Site.** While the rocks and washboard of the 18 mi. route may bounce drivers until they're battered and bruised, with reasonable driving, cars should come out no worse for the wear. A mile into the dirt drive, signs point you right onto Rocky Point Dr. and show the way to **Gila Dam,** 17 mi. away. As the road begins to wreathe and dip its way through mesquite washes, the first saguaro cacti salute the arrival of dusty travelers. The road climbs a volcanic hillside, and the bright green of the Arizona cacti contrasts with the jet black stone. At mile 13 a sign advises that there are primitive road conditions, but aside from a wash that sometimes floods, the road deteriorates no more. The last few miles proceed past farmland. In the last mile a crossroads offers three options. Take the rightmost, and the pavement quickly returns. Painted Rocks Petroglyph Site National Monument is on the right.

👁 **PAINTED ROCKS PETROGLYPH SITE**
Take the dirt road route above, or from I-8, drive 14 mi. down Painted Rocks Rd.

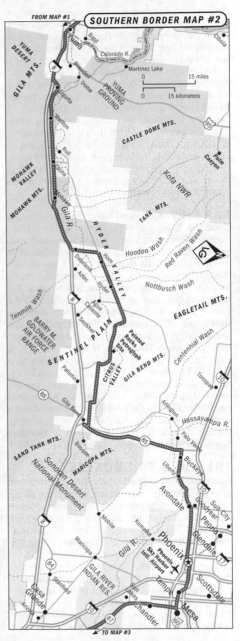

SOUTHERN BORDER

This national monument showcases one of the best collections of prehistoric Native American art in existence. Centuries ago, the Native Americans of the area found a pile of boulders standing alone on the flat desert land and concluded it must be of spiritual importance. They inscribed hundreds of spirals, creatures, and figures, whose complex meanings can be loosely interpreted using guides available at the site. De Anza, the Mormon Battalion, Kit Carson, and many other pioneers passed by and left their own inscriptions. About 1 mi. west of Painted Rock Dam Road on Rocky Point Rd., the **Petroglyph Campground** offers the chance to spend the night under the incredible desert stars at this sacred site, but has no running water and only one pit toilet.

GILA BEND. Gila Bend has definitely seen better days. Once the proud crossroads joining Yuma, Phoenix, and Tucson, today the old town doesn't get a passing glance from motorists whizzing by on I-8. Gila Bend features a fine assortment of gas stations, a good mechanic, and a laundromat, but otherwise it has little to offer. The one attraction that seems to have withstood the test of time is the **Space Age Outer Limits Hotel and Restaurant**, 401 E. Pima Ave. The **Outer Limits Restaurant** offers the best Mexican and American cuisine available in Gila Bend. (Entrees $7-8. Open daily 5am-10pm.) Attached to the restaurant, a giant UFO perches on the top of the hotel lobby, and the inside of this craft features an impressive space-themed mural. The attention to detail is painstaking—even the pool heater is shaped like a crash-landed satellite. After change of ownership, the motel is now officially named the **Best Western Space Age Motel.** (☎928-683-2273. Rooms $69-79.)

THE ROAD TO BUCKEYE

Gila Bend goes as quickly as it came, and as you pass the decaying old military jets in front of the Gila Bend air strip, you enter the desert expanses again, this time on **Rte. 85.** This dangerous two-lane road has more than its share of speeding trucks, so it's best to exit at **Woods Rd.,** 13 mi. outside Gila Bend, to reconnect with Rte. 80. Hidden amidst farmland are the remains of old bridges that were used to protect this artery to the west from flash floods. Now, people just allow the barely used road to wash out. The road narrows 23 mi. from Gila Bend and crosses a steel truss bridge that has begun to rust. While passing over

this relic, look right to see the Gillespie Dam, washed out during the flooding of 1993. The road then climbs to reveal the Gila River Valley, before descending into the Valley of the Sun.

Forty miles into the journey, old Rte. 80 again joins Arizona Rte. 85. Go left, but only briefly. Take a right at the stop sign onto **Buckeye Rd.** and follow it to the town that bears this name.

BUCKEYE

Mainly a farm town, Buckeye bears the dubious distinction of being the largest town between Yuma and Phoenix. Halfway through the town, the highway bears left, but travelers should stay on Monroe St. About 200 yd. down the road stands a monolithic hobo. **Hobo Joe,** the mascot of the Hobo Joe's restaurant chain, was erected here in memory of the Hobo Joe's owner, Marvin Ransdell. Contrary to appearances, this hobo is a rookie to the road, standing only since 1989.

Good food can be found at **Mercy's Mexican Restaurant,** 919 Monroe St. Don't be fooled by its strip mall location and barren walls; this little mom-and-pop joint is as good as Mexican gets. The à la carte items are under $2, but small. For something more substantial, the combination plates ($6-7) are huge. (On the right just before the highway bends halfway through town. ☎623-386-5115. Open M-Th 10am-2pm, F 10am-7pm, Su 9am-2pm.) At the **☒Ranchhouse,** 1009 E. Monroe St., each wrangler gets his or her own plot of land complete with ranchero-style two-room bungalow. John Wayne would be proud. It has the best value around, but rooms fill up; call ahead. (Continue on Monroe St. when the highway turns. It's on the right, 100 yd. from Hobo Joe. ☎663-386-4207, ext. 213. Singles $35; doubles $50.)

■ APPROACHING PHOENIX

Soon after leaving Buckeye, the suburbs of Phoenix start to spring up. The best way to access the city while avoiding the freeways is to follow in the tracks of Rte. 80 yet again.

Follow **Buckeye Rd.** until it crosses Yuma Rd. Turn right (east) on **Yuma Rd.,** which becomes Buckeye Rd. again as it meets up with **Rte. 85** and will take you straight into Phoenix.

As you near downtown Phoenix, take a left (north) on **17th Ave.,** a small street immediately after the 19th Ave. stoplight. One block later, you'll cross under the railroad. With the golden dome of the state capital immediately to the left and the skyscrapers of Copper

Sq. to the right, Rte. 80 leads to the heart of beautiful downtown Phoenix. Take a right on **Van Buren St.** This road will take you right through Copper Sq., Phoenix's shaded and well-landscaped downtown.

PHOENIX

Anglo settlers named their small farming community Phoenix, believing that their oasis had risen from the ashes of ancient Native American settlements. The 20th century has seen this unlikely metropolis live up to its name; the expansion of water resources, the proliferation of the railroad, and the introduction of air-conditioning have fueled Phoenix's ascent to the ranks of America's leading urban centers. Shiny high-rises now crowd the business district, while a vast web of six-lane highways and strip malls surrounds the downtown area. Phoenix's rise has not been easy, though; its greatest asset, the sun, is also its greatest nemesis. The scorching heat and arid landscape put a damper on expansion, as water is always in short supply. During the balmy winter, tourists, golfers, and businessmen flock to enjoy perfect temperatures, while in summer, the visitors flee, and the city crawls into its air-conditioned shell as temperatures exceed 100°F and lodging prices plummet.

(VITAL STATS)

Population: 1.3 million

Visitor Info: Phoenix and Valley of the Sun Convention and Visitors Center (☎ 602-254-6500 or 877-225-5749, recorded info 602-252-5588; www.phoenixcvb.com). Downtown location: 2nd and Adams St. Open M-F 8am-5pm.

Internet Access: Burton Barr Central Library, 1221 N. Central Ave. (☎ 602-262-4636). Open M-Th 10am-9pm, F-Sa 9am-6pm, Su noon-6pm.

Post Office: 522 N. Central Ave. (☎ 800-275-8777). Open M-F 8:30am-5pm. **Postal Code:** 85034.

GETTING AROUND

The intersection of **Central Ave.** and **Washington St.** marks the center of downtown. Central Ave. runs north-south, Washington St. east-west. One of Phoenix's peculiarities is that numbered avenues and streets both run north-south; avenues are numbered sequentially west from Central Ave., while streets are numbered east. Think of Central Ave. as the heart of town; facing north, the first road to your right is **1st St.,** the first to your left is **1st Ave.** Large north-south thoroughfares include **7th St., 16th St., 7th Ave.,** and **19th Ave.,** while **McDowell Rd., Van Buren St., Indian School Rd.,** and **Camelback Rd.** are major east-west arteries.

Greater Phoenix includes smaller, independent municipalities that sometimes have different street-naming schemes. The many large asphalt **parking lots** charge around $7 per day. Street parking is also readily available and generally safe.

NEIGHBORHOODS

Driven by dirt-cheap desert land and flat landscape, urban sprawl has gotten out of control in Phoenix. Once a series of independent communities, the numerous townships of "the Valley of the Sun" now bleed into one another in a continuous chain of strip malls, office parks, slums, and super-resorts. The de facto unification of all the disparate neighborhoods has not, however, resulted in homogenization or equalization—some are magnets for tourists and money, others for illegal immigrants and crime. Since many of the most happening locales are located outside of the downtown proper, it's useful to get acquainted with some of Phoenix' outer townships.

Just to the east of downtown Phoenix and south of the Salt River lies **Tempe,** the town that lays claim to both the third-largest university in the US and the nightlife to prove it. Don't make the mistake of leaving town without experiencing at least one night as a Sun Devil. East of Tempe, the suburban paradise of **Mesa** stretches out along Rte. 202. Tamer than its collegiate neighbor, Mesa is home to one of the largest Mormon colonies outside of Utah as well as a host of cheap eats and chain motels. **Scottsdale,** north of Mesa and northeast of downtown, is the playground of the (sometimes idle) rich. The very sound of the name conjures up images of expensive cars, immaculate homes, and world-renowned resorts. With its pricey accommodations and great sights, Scottsdale is a great place to visit (from Tempe).

SIGHTS

THE HEARD MUSEUM. Renowned for its presentation of ancient Native American art, the Heard Museum also features exhibits on contem-

SOUTHERN BORDER

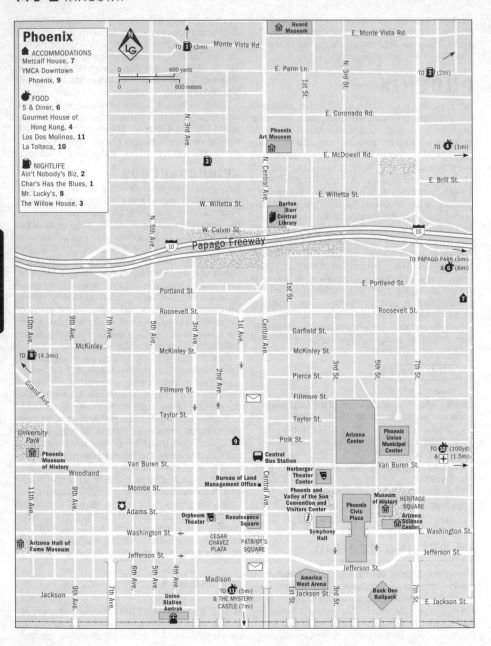

Phoenix

🏠 **ACCOMMODATIONS**
Metcalf House, **7**
YMCA Downtown
  Phoenix, **9**

🍎 **FOOD**
5 & Diner, **6**
Gourmet House of
  Hong Kong, **4**
Los Dos Molinos, **11**
La Tolteca, **10**

🍷 **NIGHTLIFE**
Ain't Nobody's Biz, **2**
Char's Has the Blues, **1**
Mr. Lucky's, **8**
The Willow House, **3**

N
LG

0   600 yards
0   600 meters

Heard Museum

TO **1** (2mi)

Monte Vista Rd.

E. Monte Vista Rd.

E. Palm Ln.

TO **2** (2mi)

E. Coronado Rd.

N. 3rd Ave.

N. 3rd St.

1st St.

Phoenix Art Museum

E. McDowell Rd.

TO **4** (1mi)

3

E. Brill St.

N. Central Ave.

E. Willetta St.

W. Willetta Ave.

E. Willetta St.

Burton Barr Central Library

N. 5th Ave.

W. Culver St.

10

Papago Freeway

TO PAPAGO PARK (5mi) & **6** (6mi)

10

Portland St.

E. Portland St.

Roosevelt St.

1st St.

Roosevelt St.

7

10th Ave.

9th Ave.

7th Ave.

5th Ave.

3rd Ave.

1st Ave.

Central Ave.

Garfield St.

McKinley

McKinley St.

McKinley St.

3rd St.

5th St.

7th St.

TO **8** (4.3mi)

Grand Ave.

Fillmore St.

2nd Ave.

Pierce St.

Fillmore St.

Taylor St.

Taylor St.

University Park

Polk St.

9

Arizona Center

Phoenix Union Municipal Center

TO **10** (100yd) & ✚ (1.5mi)

Phoenix Museum of History

Van Buren St.

Central Bus Station

Van Buren St.

Woodland

11th Ave.

9th Ave.

Monroe St.

Bureau of Land Management Office

Herberger Theater Center

Phoenix and Valley of the Sun Convention and Visitors Center

Museum of History

HERITAGE SQUARE

Adams St.

Orpheum Theater

Renaissance Square

Phoenix Civic Plaza

Arizona Science Center

Washington St.

CESAR CHAVEZ PLAZA

Symphony Hall

E. Washington St.

Arizona Hall of Fame Museum

Jefferson St.

PATRIOT'S SQUARE

Jefferson St.

Jefferson St.

6th Ave.

5th Ave.

4th Ave.

Madison

America West Arena

Bank One Ballpark

Jackson

9th Ave.

7th Ave.

Union Station Amtrak

TO **11** (5mi) & THE MYSTERY CASTLE (7mi)

Jackson St.

1st St.

3rd St.

7th St.

E. Jackson St.

porary Native Americans. There are many interactive and traveling exhibits, some of which are geared toward children. Named after notable benefactors, galleries include the Sandra Day O'Connor Gallery, which houses an exhibit on the museum's founders, and the Barry Goldwater Gallery, which displays photography of the Southwest. The museum occasionally sponsors lectures and Native American dances. (2301 N. Central Ave., 4 blocks north of McDowell Rd. ☎ 605-252-8840, recorded info 602-252-8848. Open daily 9:30am-5pm. Free tours at noon, 1:30, and 3pm. $7, seniors $6, ages 4-12 $3, Native Americans with status cards free.)

THE PHOENIX ART MUSEUM. This museum showcases art of the American West, including paintings from the Taos and Santa Fe art colonies. The permanent collection houses pieces by the *Tres Grandes* of Mexican art (Orozco, Siquiros, and Riviera) as well as works by noted American artists Jackson Pollock and Georgia O'Keeffe. Every major European and American movement has representatives on display. (1625 N. Central Ave., at McDowell Rd. ☎ 602-257-1880. Open Su, Tu-W, and F-Sa 10am-5pm, Th 10am-9pm. $7, students and seniors $5, ages 6-18 $2. Free on Th and after 4:15pm.)

THE ARIZONA SCIENCE CENTER. Interactive science exhibits are supplemented by an IMAX theater and a planetarium. Slot the whole day if you're going with children. (600 E. Washington St. ☎ 602-716-2000. Open W-F 10am-5pm, M-Tu and Sa-Su 10am-9pm. $8, ages 4-12 and seniors $6. IMAX or planetarium $3.)

PAPAGO PARK AND ENVIRONS. The **Desert Botanical Garden,** in Papago Park, 5 mi. east of downtown, grows a colorful collection of cacti and other desert plants, many of which are hard to find in the wild. (1201 N. Galvin Pkwy. ☎ 602-941-1225, recorded info 602-481-8134. Open daily May-Sept. 7am-8pm; Oct.-Apr. 8am-8pm. $7.50, students with ID $4, seniors $6.50, ages 5-12 $3.50.) The park has spectacular views of the desert along its hiking, biking, and driving trails. If you spot an orangutan amid the cacti, either it's a mirage or you're in the **Phoenix Zoo,** home to South American, African, and Southwestern critters. (455 N. Galvin Pkwy. ☎ 602-273-1341. Open daily Sept.-May 9am-5pm; June-Aug. 7am-9pm. Sept.-May $12, seniors $9, children $5; June-Aug. $9/$7/$5.) The **Hall of Flame Museum of Firefighting,** just outside the southern exit of Papago Park, features antique fire engines and other firefighting equipment. (6101 E. Van Buren St. ☎ 602-275-3473. Open M-Sa 9am-5pm, Su noon-4pm. $5, ages 6-17 $3, ages 3-5 $1.50.) Still farther east of the city, in Mesa, flows the **Salt River,** one of the last remaining desert rivers in the US. **Salt River Recreation** arranges tubing trips. (☎ 602-984-3305. Open May-Sept. daily 9am-4pm. Tube rental $9.)

MYSTERY CASTLE. For those interested in astounding Southwestern architecture, the striking **Mystery Castle** is worth the 5 mi. trip from downtown. Built in small increments over 15 years (ca. 1930), this home is a spectacular example of the creative use of space. Laugh along with the tour guides as they provide tidbits about the peculiarities of this masterpiece. (800 E. Mineral Rd. Go south on Central Ave., and take a left on Mineral Rd. just before the South Mountain Park entrance. ☎ 602-268-1581. Open Oct. to mid-June Th-Su 11am-4pm. $5, seniors $4, ages 5-14 $2.)

ARCHITECTURE. **Taliesin West** was built as the winter camp of Frank Lloyd Wright's Taliesin architectural collective. Later in life he lived here full-time, and now it serves as a campus for an architectural college run by his foundation. The beautiful compound, entirely designed by the master, seems to blend naturally into the surrounding desert, and includes a studio, a Chinese cinema, and a performance hall. (Corner of Frank Lloyd Wright Blvd. and Cactus St. ☎ 602-860-2700; www.franklloydwright.org. Open Sept.-June daily 9am-4pm. 1hr. or 1½hr. guided tours required. Tours $12.50-16, students and seniors $10-14, ages 4-12 $4.50.) One of the last buildings he designed, the **Gammage Memorial Auditorium** stands in the Arizona State University campus in Tempe. Its pink-and-beige earth tones blend with the surrounding environment. (At Mill Ave. and Apache Blvd. ☎ 602-965-3434. 20min. tours daily in winter.)

One of Wright's students liked Scottsdale so much he decided to stay. **Cosanti** is a working studio and bell foundry designed by the architect and sculptor Paolo Soleri. The buildings here fuse with the natural landscape even more strikingly than those at Taliesin West, and visitors are allowed to wander the grounds freely. Arriving early in the day (9am-noon) allows guests to watch the casting of the bronze wind bells for which Cosanti is famous. (6433 Doubletree Rd. Traveling north on Scottsdale Rd., turn left on Doubletree Rd.; it will be on your left in about 5 blocks. Open M-Sa 9am-5pm, Su 11am-5pm. Suggested donation.)

♫ ENTERTAINMENT

Phoenix offers many options for the sports lover. NBA basketball action rises with the **Phoenix Suns** (☎480-379-7867) at the **America West Arena,** while the **Arizona Cardinals** (☎480-379-0101) provide American football excitement. The 2002 World Series Champions **Arizona Diamondbacks** (☎480-514-8400) play at the state-of-the-art **Bank One Ballpark,** complete with a retractable roof, an outfield swimming pool, and "beer gardens." (☎480-462-6799. Tickets start at $6. Special $1 tickets available 2hr. before games; first come, first served.)

🍴 FOOD

While much of the Phoenix culinary scene seems to revolve around shopping mall food courts and expensive restaurants, rest assured that hidden jewels can be found. Downtowners feed mainly at small coffeehouses, most of which close on weekends. **McDowell** and **Camelback Rd.** offer a (small) variety of Asian restaurants. The **Arizona Center,** an open-air shopping gallery at 3rd and Van Buren St., features food venues, fountains, and palm trees. Sports bars and grilles hover around the America West Arena and Bank One Ballpark. Tempe's residents fill up on bar food in the many hybrid resto-bars that cater to college kids, while both Scottsdale and Mesa have affordable options hidden in their bourgeois swankness or Mormon sobriety. The *New Times* (☎602-271-4000) makes extensive restaurant recommendations.

DOWNTOWN PHOENIX

Los Dos Molinos, 8646 S. Central Ave. (☎602-243-9113). From downtown, head south on Central Ave. Go very far, and once you're sure you've gone too far, go farther. Once you leave the barrio, it comes up suddenly on your right. One look and you'll know why you've made the trip; Los Dos Molinos is lively, colorful, and fun. Locals flock here on weekends, filling the indoor restaurant and the colorful courtyard, and spilling onto the street. Come early; they don't take reservations. Enchiladas $3.50. Burritos $5.25-7. Open Tu-F 11am-2:30pm and 5-9pm, Sa 11am-9pm.

5 & Diner, 5220 N. 16th St. (☎602-264-5220), with branches dotting the greater metro area. 24hr. service and all the sock-hop music that one can stand. Vinyl booths, smiley waitstaff, and innumerable jukeboxes teach you what the 50s *could* have been. Burgers go for $6-7 and sandwiches are $5-7. You can get the best milkshakes in town for only $3-4. Afternoon blue plate specials (M-F 11am-4pm, $3-6) change daily, but are always a great deal. Outdoor seating with view of scenic N. 16th St. available.

Gourmet House of Hong Kong, 1438 E. McDowell Rd. (☎602-253-4859). For those who think that quality Chinese food doesn't exist between the Mississippi and the West Coast, this no-frills restaurant will impress. 40 kinds of soup, noodle dishes, and Hong Kong specialties (chicken feet!) are unceremoniously dished out. No non-smoking section. Entrees $5-7. Lunch specials $3-5. Takeout available. Open M-Th 11am-9:30pm, F-Sa 11am-10:30pm, Su 11am-9pm.

La Tolteca, 1205 E. Van Buren St. (☎602-253-1511). A local favorite, this cafeteria-style restau-

---

BEYOND THE ASPHALT

DELUGE

The word *monsoon* is more evocative of Southeast Asia than Arizona, but the seasonal storms that batter the southern part of the state are aptly named. June in Arizona brings stereotypical desert weather: heat, sun, more heat, more sun. Perhaps only a single lonely cloud mars the perfect blue sky in Tucson in late June, but come the 4th of July, it's joined by a regular posse of precipitation. The monsoonal flow arrives in July and August. Though temperatures remain high, daily thunderstorms pop up and pour down. Due to the lack of moisture in the desert, vast quantities of dust are taken up into the clouds, producing intense static electricity and some of the most spectacular lightning in the world. The storms are also extremely localized; it is possible to cross the street in Tucson and go from sunshine into driving rain. Although the storms are beautiful from indoors, both the faint of heart and those who faint in the heat should consider visiting southern Arizona in the winter months.

rant/Mexican grocery serves up uncommercialized Mexican fare in *grande* portions. Familiar dishes are offered alongside specialties like *cocido* soup ($5) and refreshing *horchata,* a sweet milk and rice drink ($1-2). Big burritos $3-4. Dinner plates $5-6. Open daily 6:30am-9pm.

TEMPE

🍴 **Dos Gringos Trailer Park,** 216 E. University (☎480-968-7879). The best atmosphere in Tempe, bar-none. Dos, as it's affectionately known, draws a diverse clientele with its open, laid-back feel and its inexpensive yet tasty Mexican food. Deals include a Hangover Special ($5.25), and countless meals for under $6. Open M-Sa 10am-1am, Su noon-1am.

🍴 **Long Wong's,** 701 S. Mill Ave. (☎480-966-3147). Serving up 6 flavors, Wong's has the best wings in town ($6 for 6, $9 for 12). Bar/restaurant run by a young staff. Half-price wings happy hour M-F 4-8pm. Cover $1-5, depending on the act (mostly local). 21+ in the bar. Takeout available. Open Su-Th 10:30am-11pm, F-Sa 10:30am-12:30am.

SCOTTSDALE

Greasewoods Flats, 27500 N. Alma School Rd. (☎480-585-9430). With an extremely eclectic mix of patrons, the Flats dishes out classic American cuisine at reasonable prices, including succulent hamburgers for $6-8. Rub elbows with hippies, bikers, yuppies, bohos, and everything in between. Open M-F 10am-11pm, Sa 10am-midnight, Su 10am-10pm.

Sugar Bowl Ice Cream Parlor & Restaurant, 4005 N. Scottsdale Rd. (☎480-946-0051). Get out of the heat and into this fun and flavorsome ice-cream parlor, where the sundaes are piled high and thick ($3-5). Open M-Sa 11am-11pm, Su 11am-10pm.

MESA

Ripe Tomato Cafe, 745 W. Baseline Rd. (☎480-892-4340). The biggest, fluffiest omelettes ($6) this side of the desert fill up the entire plate. Eat inside or out, but bring your appetite. Open daily 6am-2:30pm.

Bill Johnson's Big Apple, 950 E. Main St. (☎480-969-6504). The sawdust on the floor fits right in at this country-western restaurant, where the food is almost as good as the Old West decor. Pick from a large selections of steak, and sample the tangy homemade BBQ sauce. Kids eat free W. Open daily 6:30am-10pm.

🏠 ACCOMMODATIONS

Budget travelers should consider visiting Phoenix during July and August when motels slash their prices by as much as 70%. In the winter, when temperatures drop and vacancies are few, prices go up; make reservations if possible. The reservation-less should cruise the rows of motels on **Van Buren St.** east of downtown, toward the airport. Parts of this area can be unsafe; **guests should examine a motel thoroughly before checking in.** Although they are more distant, the areas around Papago Fwy. and Black Canyon Hwy. are loaded with motels and may present some safer options.

Greater Phoenix contains some of the nation's best luxury and high-end resort hotels. Although during the high season they are out of reach to most budget travelers, during the baking summer those who brave the intimidating high-end hotels will find empty rooms and ready deals. If you can stand the heat, you can live like the beautiful people, if only for a night or two. More affordable accommodations are limited, especially in Tempe/Mesa, and tend to take the form of generic, albeit respectable, chain motels.

As an alternative, **Mi Casa Su Casa/Old Pueblo Homestays Bed and Breakfast,** P.O. Box 950, Tempe 85280, arranges stays in B&Bs throughout Arizona, New Mexico, southern Utah, southern Nevada, and southern California. (☎800-456-0682. Open M-F 9am-5pm, Sa 9am noon. $45 and up.)

DOWNTOWN PHOENIX

Metcalf House (HI-AYH), 1026 N. 9th St. (☎602-254-9803), a few blocks northeast of downtown. Look for the house with lots of foliage out front. The ebullient owner, who gushes helpful advice about the area, fosters a lively community in this decorative house. Evening gab sessions are common on the front porch. The neighborhood has seen better days, so the coin lockers available in the dorms are probably a good idea. Bikes for rent, and discounts to some city sights included in the price. Chores required. Check-in 7-10am and 5-10pm. Dorms $15.

ExtendedStay America, 7345 W. Bell Rd. (☎623-487-0020; www.extendedstay.com), at 73rd Ave. Also in **Scottsdale,** 15501 N. Scottsdale Rd. (☎480-607-3767), and in **Mesa,** 455 W. Baseline Rd. (☎480-632-0201). This chain caters to business travelers. Steep prices for nightly accommo-

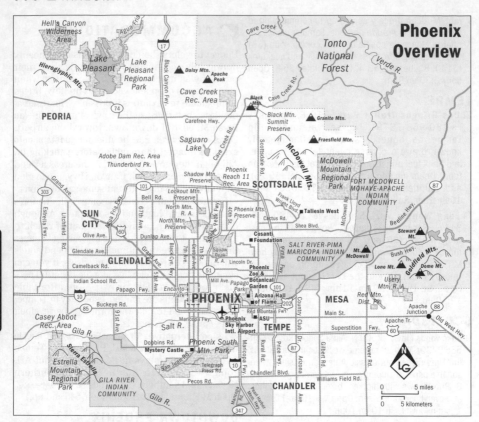

Phoenix Overview

dation, but a bargain at the weekly rate. Immaculate rooms have kitchenettes and Internet hookups. Rooms $55. Weekly rooms $279.

YMCA Downtown Phoenix, 350 N. 1st Ave. (☎602-253-6181). Another option in the downtown area, the YMCA provides small, single-occupancy rooms and shared bathrooms. Various athletic facilities. A small supply of women's rooms available. Ask at the desk about storing valuables. 18+. Open daily 9am-10pm. Rooms $30. Weekly rooms $119.

TEMPE

Mission Palms, 60 E. 5th St. (☎480-894-1400; www.missionpalms.com). At the base of the Tempe's Hayden Butte, this deluxe hotel is a steal in the summer for $99 per night (with prices more than doubling in the winter). Choose among the smorgasbord of amenities at your fingertips (2 hot tubs, a pool, health club, tennis center, and standard laptop Internet hookups) to pass the time, all the while knowing that raucous Mill Ave. is merely a minute's walk away.

Best Western Inn of Tempe, 670 N. Scottsdale Rd. (☎480-784-2233; www.innoftempe.com), next to U.S. 60 and Scottsdale Dr. Overall, a very well-kept hotel with a friendly staff, this branch of the chain has digital cable and laptop Internet hookups in every room. Rooms in summer from $59; in winter $99.

Super 8 Motel, 1020 E. Apache Blvd. (☎480-967-8891; www.super8.com). Chain with digital cable in every room. Consistently has some of the best rates in town. Continental breakfast included. Rooms Apr.-Aug. $39; Sept.-Mar. $49. Weekly rooms $190/$250.

Days Inn Tempe, 1221 E. Apache Blvd. (☎480-968-7793; www.daysinn.com). A chain combining tidy rooms with no-frills prices. Pool. Rooms in summer $49; in winter $79.

SCOTTSDALE

Econolodge, Scottsdale on Fifth, 6935 5th Ave. (☎480-994-9461). Clean rooms and low prices for the location make this branch of the national chain a deal. Singles $55.

MESA

Best Western Dobson Ranch Inn & Resort, 1666 S. Dobson Rd. (☎480-831-7000 or 800-528-1356; www.dobsonranchinn.com), 1 block south of U.S. 60 on Baseline Rd. Advertised as the best resort in the area, the Ranch is a great alternative for exceptional value at a low cost. 2 pools, a restaurant and massive banquet facilities. Rooms in summer from $55.

Lost Dutchman Motel, 560 S. Country Club Dr. (☎480-969-2200). A good location by many restaurants and clean rooms are the best reasons to stay at the Dutchman. Kitchenettes available for $3 extra. Check-in 3pm. Check-out noon. Summer rates hover around $37 per night and $159 per week, with winter rates doubling the warmer months' prices.

🔍 NIGHTLIFE

The free *New Times Weekly*, available on local magazine racks, lists club schedules for Phoenix's after-hours scene. The *Cultural Calendar of Events* covers area entertainment in three-month intervals. *The Western Front*, found in bars and clubs, covers gay and lesbian nightlife.

DOWNTOWN PHOENIX

📷 Char's Has the Blues, 4631 N. 7th Ave. (☎602-230-0205). Hosts local jazz. Live music from 9pm. 21+. Cover Tu-Sa $3-7. Open daily 8pm-1am.

The Willow House, 149 W. McDowell Rd. (☎252-0272). This self-proclaimed "artist's cove" combines the best aspects of chic coffeehouse, New York deli, and quirky musicians' hangout. No alcohol. Coffee happy hour (2-for-1) M-F 4-6 pm. M is open mic night for musicians, Th is open mic for poetry. Live music from 8pm. Open M-Th 6am-midnight, F 6am-1am, Sa 7am-1am, Su 7am-midnight.

Ain't Nobody's Biz, 3031 E. Indian School Rd. #7 (☎602-224-9977), in the east end of the mall. This lesbian bar is the big sister of the eponymous Tucson club. Top 40 hits play, and pool tables mix well with the welcoming dance floor. F-Sa nights, the bar attracts both men and women for a memorable experience. 21+. Open M-F 4pm-1am, Sa-Su 2pm-1am.

Mr. Lucky's, 3660 NW Grand Ave. (☎602-246-0687), at the corner of 36th Ave. and Indian School Rd. Don your biggest belt buckle and favorite pair of Wranglers for a night of good ol' country two-steppin'. Try to arrive before 9pm on F and Sa. Age restrictions vary. Cover $5. Open W-Th 7pm-1am, F 5pm-3am, Sa 7pm-3am.

TEMPE

📷 Beeloe's Cafe & Underground Bar, 501 S. Mill Ave. (☎480-894-1230). Food, rock, and art are the hallmarks of the hip yet unpretentious Beeloe's. Every night of the week offers special deals to go with the live music. Happy hour M-F 4-7pm. 21+. Cover F-Sa $4. Open daily 4pm-1am.

Mill Cue Club, 607 S. Mill Ave. (☎480-858-9017). For those looking to mingle in style, welcome home. The leather sofas in the corner complement the dark-paneled walls and the rows of pool tables in the back. Try a 20 oz. Long Island Iced Tea ($3.50) to liven up your night. Happy hour 2-7pm. A DJ spins hits Tu-Sa. 21+. No cover. Open daily 2pm-1am.

🔼 LEAVING PHOENIX

Continuing on Van Buren St. will take you through the seedy motel district, but the neighborhood quickly improves as the road passes the zoo and the surrounding red rock formations. A gas-lamp-lit bridge crosses the river into the trendy, upscale college town of Tempe as the road becomes Mill St.

Stay left as **Mill St.** becomes **Apache St.** and passes ASU. Apache St. becomes **Main St.** as it enters Mesa. Turn right (south) on **Country Club Dr.,** which becomes **Arizona Ave.** and leaves the major metropolitan area. Arizona Ave. becomes **Rte. 87.** Follow the well-labelled signs to the Casa Grande Ruins.

⊙ CASA GRANDE RUINS   1100 Ruins Dr.
Outside of Coolidge.

The nation's first archaeological preserve, the **📷Casa Grande Ruins National Monument** is also one of the most perplexing. Built around 1350 by the Hohokam people, the four-story structure is almost all that remains of one of North America's most advanced peoples. Mystified Spanish explorers called it Casa Grande ("great house"). The great house stood in the

Phoenix Basin as part of a vast, innovative civilization. The walls of the house face the four cardinal points of the compass, and a circular hole in the upper west wall aligns with the setting sun during the summer solstice. The park features a small Visitors Center and self-guided trails through the ruins. (☎ 520-723-3172. Open daily 8am-5pm. $3.)

APPROACHING FLORENCE

Turn left where **Rte. 87** ends and follow this street until the intersection with **Butte Ave.** Access to **Rte. 79** lies down Butte Ave., but the historic district of Main St. lies straight past this crossroads.

FLORENCE. As Rte. 87 rolls into Florence it passes a sign that reads "State Prison: do not stop for hitchhikers." That, in a nut shell, is the town of Florence. Home to Arizona's largest state prison, the team has a long penal history. The **Pinal County Historical Museum,** 712 S. Main St., documents this history in grisly detail, displaying a collection of hangman's nooses, a two-seater from a gas chamber, and photos of criminals put to death. (☎ 520-868-4382. Open Sept.-July 14 Su noon-4pm, Tu-Sa 11am-4pm.) Florence is also home to the historic **Pinal County Courthouse,** at 5th and Main St., whose tower looms over the town. Outrageously teal, the **Blue Mist Motel,** 40 S. Pinal Pkwy., off Rte. 79, tries to live up to its name. While the color scheme may be a bit intense, the rooms are affordable, comfortable, and clean. (☎ 520-868-5875. Singles $45.)

BOYCE THOMPSON ARBORETUM

37615 U.S. 60

3 mi. before Superior. After leaving Florence, take Rte. 79 North to Florence Junction and merge onto U.S. 60 East, heading toward Superior.

Nestled in the gorge created by Queen Creek lies the shady hollow of the ⬛Boyce Thompson Arboretum State Park. Founded in the mid-1920s, the botanical garden features plants from the world's deserts. Just a bunch of cacti? Think again. In addition to a large selection of domestic and exotic cacti, the gardens exhibit everything from the Australian Outback to the tropics to the native Sonoran desert. The 3201 different plant species attract wildlife from around the world, including a diverse selection of birds. The tall trees and misting benches assure enjoyable trails in any season. (☎ 520-689-2811; www.arboretum.ag.arizona.edu. Open daily 8am-5pm. $6, children $3.)

SUPERIOR

At the base of the Superstition Mountains sits the still-active mining community of Superior. The local copper smelter looms over the village, an imposing monument to the ore that runs this city. Superior has seen better days, but classic Old West facades maintain its mining-town character. The biggest attraction in Superior, ironically, is the ⬛World's Smallest Museum, 1111 West U.S. 60. This 15 ft. long museum displays everything from mining equipment to guns, from a 1984 Compaq computer to a Barry M. Goldwater bobble-head. In an American society obsessed with the biggest and the best, it's nice to know that the smallest can still capture popular attention. Outside, the museum has an assortment of fountains made from old junk. One fountain is made from wheelbarrows and miscellaneous rusted farming equipment, while another is forged entirely from old tires, including a huge tractor tire at the base. (On the right as you enter Superior from U.S. 60 East. ☎ 520-689-5857 Open Su-M and W-Sa 8am-2pm.)

The museum is attached to the **Buckboard City Cafe,** 1111 West U.S. 60. Choose from traditional breakfast fare, hamburgers, sandwiches, salads, soups, and Mexican food. Try the Sweat-hog (spicy wrap with sausage; $6.25) or the Ye Ole Standby (burger; $4.58), both local favorites. (☎ 520-689-5800. Open daily 6am-3pm.)

THE ROAD THROUGH THE SUPERSTITIONS

Leaving Superior on U.S. 60 (⬛Gila Pinal Scenic Road) takes you into the heart of the **Superstition Mountains.** Saguaros give way to oaks as the road winds up the rust-colored walls of the majestic canyon. An impressive bridge arches high above Queen Creek's riparian groves—a feat of engineering that is only upstaged by the quarter-mile long Queen Creek Tunnel penetrating the canyon's high precipices near the summit. When the climb levels off, the road finds itself in a mountaintop valley speckled with oak trees. The aptly named **Oak Flat Campground** offers a chance to explore the red boulder formations and oak groves of these heights. (On the right 10 mi. outside Superior. Free.)

As the road descends toward the mining communities of Globe and Miami, the **Gila Pinal Scenic Road** abruptly ends as the magnificent mountains are replaced by barren hillsides stripped clean of any life by the drills and bulldozers of the mining industry. From U.S. 60 East, turn left onto Broad St. to visit downtown Globe.

GLOBE-MIAMI. The history of these two small conjoined mountain towns is inextricably tied to the mineral deposits that lace the surrounding mountain walls. A quick stop at the **Gila County Historical Museum,** 1330 N. Broad St., reveals the impact mining has had on this community. (Open M-F 10am-4pm, Sa 11am-3pm.) **Joe's Broad Street Grill,** 247 S. Broad St., sits in the heart of Globe's historic district, in the building that was once the Globe's first schoolhouse. This cafe serves excellent Italian food (pastas $7) and handmade burgers ($5), hot off the grill, also come highly recommended. (From U.S. 60 East take a left on Broad St.; it's on the left after Sycamore St. ☎928-425-6269. Open M-F 6am-2:30pm, Sa 6am-2pm.) Inexpensive rooms are located right off U.S. 60 at the **Willow Motel,** 792 N. Willow St. (☎928-425-4573. Singles $18; doubles $28.)

◉ BESH-BA-GOWAH ARCHAEOLOGICAL PARK

From U.S. 60 take Broad St. until it ends at the railroad tracks, then go left on Jess Hayes St. for ½ mi.; the park is up the hill on the left.

Besh-Ba-Gowah advertises itself as a different kind of ruin. Unlike most archaeological sites, this one encourages interaction, even allowing you to climb a narrow ladder to the second story of the pueblo. Also unlike other ruins, Besh-Ba-Gowah is almost entirely reconstructed; few actual archaeological artifacts still remain on the site. If you don't mind the facsimile, then you'll enjoy the intricate walls, multi-storied buildings, and recreated settings. The adjoining **Besh-Ba-Gowah Museum** houses actual artifacts and relates the natural history of the area. The name means "place of metal" and was given to the early mining towns of Globe and Miami by the Apache. (☎928-425-0320. Museum open daily 9am-5pm. Park open daily 9am-6pm. $3, seniors $2, under 11 free.)

THE ROAD TO MAMMOTH. From Globe, turn right (south) onto **Rte. 77.** This road will take you up into the mountains through a canyon known as Carson's Pass, named for Kit Carson's march through this region on his way to California in the late 1800s. Rte. 77 then descends following the

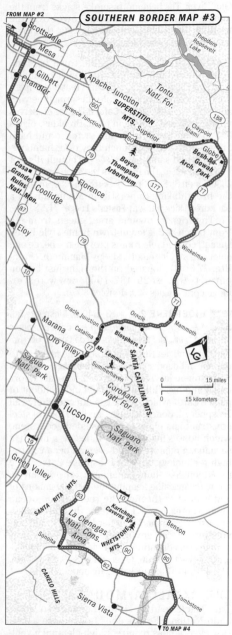

SOUTHERN BORDER MAP #3

FROM MAP #2

TO MAP #4

SOUTHERN BORDER

Gila River. The behemoth smoke stacks from the mining operation in **Winkelman** tower over the foothills, but aside from ore deposits, this town has little to offer besides gas.

MAMMOTH. The next sizable town is Mammoth, the self-proclaimed wildflower capital of Arizona. The prairies and foothills that encompass the town come alive with color in springtime with adequate rainfall. **Alicia's Cafe,** 337 Rte. 77, serves up Mexican and American food. Breakfast plates ($4.50) come with a tortilla or toast and hash browns or beans. For lunch they offer hamburgers ($2) and sandwiches ($4). Though it's not much to look at, the food hits the spot. (☎ 520-487-2380. Open Su 8am-3pm, Tu-Sa 8am-8:30pm.) With the breathtaking Superstition Mountains as a backdrop, kick back at **Foster's Lodge,** 712 N. Rte. 77. The friendly owners greet guests from the front porch at this small-town home-style hotel. Quaint, comfortable rooms provide the peace and quiet of a stay in remote, sleepy Mammoth. (From Rte. 77 South, located on the right just as you enter town. ☎ 520-487-1904; www.foster-lodge.com. Singles $29; doubles $35.)

[] BIOSPHERE 2   32540 S. Biosphere Rd.
17 mi. from Mammoth, turn left onto Biosphere Rd., drive ¼ mi., and take a slight left on Copper Hills Rd.
Farther south on Rte. 77 is Oracle, the host city to the "earth-bound space ship" **Biosphere 2,** 32540 S. Biosphere Rd. This massive 3.2-acre laboratory looks and feels like it is indeed independent of planet Earth, which scientists affectionately call Biosphere 1. Concrete, glass, and 500 tons of steel construct and close off this sealed ecosystem, which houses five biomes—a desert, a marsh, a savanna, a rainforest, and even an ocean. Ultra-high technology powers Biosphere 2, from the two dome-like "lungs" managing air pressure to the wave machine keeping the 700,000 gallons of water moving through the reefs of the ocean biome. Perhaps best known for the 1991 experiment that examined whether humans could survive in a closed environment, the center now focuses on education and research. (☎ 520-838-6200; www.bio2.edu. Open daily 8:30am-3:30pm. $13, ages 13-17 $9, ages 6-12 $6, under 6 free.)

THE CATALINA MOUNTAINS

The Oracle road to Mount Lemmon in Coronado National Forest does not require a 4x4. However, it does require a high-clearance vehi-

cle. Any vehicle can easily make the first 4 mi. of road to Peppersauce Canyon Campground ($10 per night). Immediately after that the road hits its worst terrain as large mounds and pits appear in the road 9 mi. from the summit. The 27 mi. dirt road climbs from around 2000 to 8000 ft. Gates can be locked during the winter or due to harsh conditions, so check with the Forest Service before embarking. To drive the route, follow the signs from Oracle to **Oracle State Park.** Pass the park and continue down this road until it forks and becomes dirt. Take the right fork, and for the rest of the journey remain on the main trail. It ends at **Control Road,** half a mile south of Summerhaven.

Roadtrippers unable or unwilling to undertake the arduous yet rewarding ascent from Oracle to the summit of Mt. Lemmon should at least trek the developed Catalina Rte. into a lofty, pine-studded paradise. In both temperature and terrain, the nearly mile-high climb is equivalent to a transcontinental journey from Mexico to Canada. Every 1000 ft. change in elevation witnesses a metamorphosis that parallels a 300 mi. drive northward. As the road blasts through impressive granite formations and snakes along canyon walls, the temperature drops nearly 30° and the Sonoran desert gives way to a Douglas Fir forest.

Nearing the summit, the highway hugs the ridgeline so that the impressive vistas of the surrounding desert valleys are visible on both sides of the roadway. Stopping at one of the many turnouts or picnic areas for a picture is a must. At 8000 ft., **Inspiration Rock Picnic Ground** offers the brave a chance to take a few steps out onto a giant granite precipice and gaze down at the miniature Tucson Valley below. At the top lies the teensy hamlet of **Summerhaven,** where a public restroom makes up half of the buildings in the town, and **Mt. Lemmon Ski Valley** (☎ 520-576-1321). The drive is 30 mi. each way, and extensive road work could mean delays, but the refreshing climate and views make it worthwhile. The Forest Service offers campsites along the way, with **Rose Canyon Campground,** on the shores of a lovely lake, being the most popular. (☎ 520-749-8700. $14 per vehicle.)

APPROACHING TUCSON
From Oracle continue on **Rte. 77 South.** At Oracle Junction it merges with Rte. 79 and continues its descent into Tucson's valley.

TUCSON

A little bit country, a little bit rock 'n' roll, Tucson (TOO-sahn) is a city that carries its own tune and a bundle of contradictions. Mexican property until the Gadsden Purchase, the city shares many of its south-of-the-border characteristics with such disparate elements as the University of Arizona, the Davis-Monthan Airforce Base, McDonald's, and Southern Baptism. Boasting mountainous flora beside desert cacti and art museums next to the war machines of the Pima Air and Space museum, the city nearly defies categorization. In the last several years, a reenergized downtown core has attracted artists and hipsters, while families and retirees populate sprawling suburbs. Tucson offers the conveniences of a metropolis without the nasty aftertaste, and better tourist attractions than almost any other Southwestern city.

VITAL STATS

Population: 490,000

Visitor Info: Tucson Convention and Visitors Bureau, 130 S. Scott Ave. (☎520-624-1817 or 800-638-8350), near Broadway Blvd. Open M-F 8am-5pm, Sa-Su 9am-4pm.

Internet Access: University of Arizona Main Library, 1510 E. University Blvd. Open Sept.-May M-Th 7:30am-1am, F 7:30am-9pm, Sa 10am-9pm, Su 11am-1am; June-Aug. M-Th 7:30am-11pm, F 7:30am-6pm, Sa 9am-6pm, Su 11am-11pm.

Post Office: 1501 S. Cherry Bell. Open M-F 8:30am-8pm, Sa 9am-1pm. **Postal Code:** 85726.

☞ GETTING AROUND

Just east of **I-10,** Tucson's downtown area surrounds the intersection of **Broadway Blvd.** and **Stone Ave.** The **University of Arizona** lies 1 mi. northeast of downtown at the intersection of **Park Ave.** and **Speedway Blvd.** Avenues run north-south, streets east-west; because some of each are numbered, intersections such as "6th and 6th" exist. Speedway, Broadway, and **Grant Rd.** are the quickest east-west routes through town. To go north-south, follow **Oracle Rd.** through the heart of the city, **Campbell Ave.** east of downtown, or **Swan Rd.** farther east. The hip, young crowd swings on **4th Ave.** and on **Congress St.,** both with small shops, quirky restaurants, and a slew of bars. Tucson is accustomed to bustle and, like most of the Southwest, **parking** is not an issue. Leaving your car at a meter is generally a low-risk venture.

◉ SIGHTS

UNIVERSITY OF ARIZONA. Lined with cafes, restaurants, galleries, and vintage clothing shops, **4th Ave.** is an alternative magnet and a great place to take a stroll. Between Speedway and Broadway Blvd., the street becomes a shopping district with increasingly touristy shops. Lovely for its varied and elaborately irrigated vegetation, the University of Arizona's mall sits where E. 3rd St. should be, just east of 4th Ave. The **Center for Creative Photography,** on campus, houses various changing exhibits, including the archives of Ansel Adams and Richard Avedon. (☎520-621-7968. Open M-F 9am-5pm, Sa-Su noon-5pm. Archives available to the public by appointment only. Free.) The **Flandrau Science Center** dazzles visitors with a public observatory and a laser light show. (On Cherry Ave. at the campus mall. ☎520-621-7827. Open M-Tu 9am-5pm, W-Sa 9am-5pm and 7-9pm, Su noon-5pm. $3, under 14 $2. Shows $5, seniors and students $4.50, under 14 $4.) The **University of Arizona Museum of Art** offers visitors modern American and 18th-century Latin American art, as well as the sculpture of Jacques Lipchitz. The best student art is exhibited here. (1031 N. Olive Rd. ☎520-621-7567. Open M-F 10am-3pm, Su noon-4pm. Free.)

TUCSON MUSEUM OF ART. This major attraction presents impressive traveling exhibits in all media to supplement its permanent collection of American, Mexican, and European art. Houses in the surrounding and affiliated Presidio Historic Block boast an impressive collection of Pre-Columbian and Mexican folk art as well as art of the American West. (140 N. Main Ave. ☎520-624-2333. Open M-Sa 10am-4pm, Su noon-4pm; Memorial Day-Labor Day closed M. $5, seniors $4, students $3, under 13 free. Su free.)

DEGRAZIA GALLERY IN THE SUN. Stepping through the ornate iron doors of this old-fashioned pueblo home reveals the artistic world of Ettore "Ted" DeGrazia. The home itself, wonderfully spacious and colorful, breathes life into the paintings that adorn the walls. Wander the grounds before entering the gallery; wooden sculptures and sun-bleached metalwork are scat-

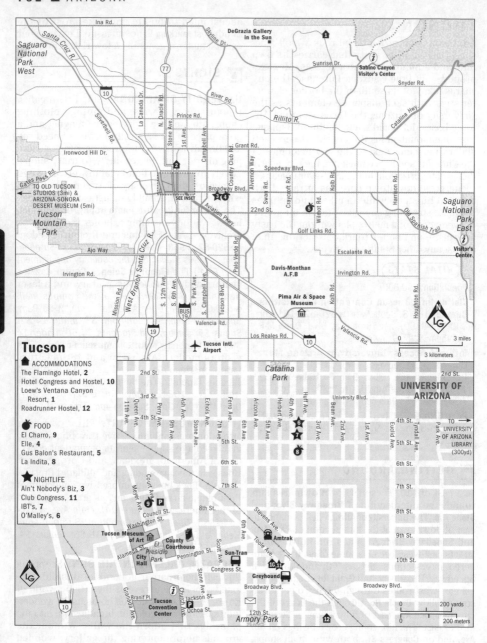

Tucson

ACCOMMODATIONS
The Flamingo Hotel, **2**
Hotel Congress and Hostel, **10**
Loew's Ventana Canyon
   Resort, **1**
Roadrunner Hostel, **12**

FOOD
El Charro, **9**
Elle, **4**
Gus Balon's Restaurant, **5**
La Indita, **8**

NIGHTLIFE
Ain't Nobody's Biz, **3**
Club Congress, **11**
IBT's, **7**
O'Malley's, **6**

tered throughout the cactus garden. Don't miss the chapel, dedicated to the Virgin Guadalupe, where the open-air simplicity complements the humility of the murals. *(6300 N. Swan Rd., about ¼ mi. north of Sunrise Rd.* ☎ *800-545-2185; www.degrazia.org. Open daily 10am-3:45pm. Free.)*

SIGHTS ON WEST SPEEDWAY. As Speedway Blvd. winds its way west from Tucson's city center, it passes by a variety of sights. The left fork leads to **Old Tucson Studios,** an elaborate Old West-style town constructed for the 1938 movie *Arizona* and used as a backdrop for Westerns ever since, including many John Wayne films and the 1999 Will Smith blockbuster *Wild Wild West.* It's open year-round to tourists, who can stroll around in the Old West mock up, view gun fight reenactments, and, if fortunate, watch the filming of a current Western. *(☎ 520-883-0100. Open daily 10am-6pm; winter sometimes closed M. Call ahead; Old Tucson is occasionally closed for group functions. $15, seniors $13.50, ages 4-11 $9.50.)* Those opting to take the right fork will eschew the Wild Wild West for the merely wild West; less than 2 mi. from the fork lies the **Arizona-Sonora Desert Museum,** a first-rate zoo and nature preserve. The living museum recreates a range of desert habitats and features over 300 kinds of animals. A visit requires at least 2hr., preferably in the morning before the animals take afternoon siestas. *(2021 N. Kinney Rd. Follow Speedway Blvd. west of the city as it becomes Gates Pass Rd., then Kinney Rd.* ☎ *520-883-2702; www.desertmuseum.org. Open daily Mar.-Sept. 7:30am-5pm; Oct.-Feb. 8:30am-5pm. $9-12, ages 6-12 $2.)*

CAVES. Kartchner Caverns State Park is enormously popular, filled with magnificent rock formations and home to over 1000 bats. This is a "living" cave, which contains water and is still experiencing the growth of its formations. The damp conditions cause the formations to shine and glisten in the light. Taking a tour is the only way to enter the cave. *(Located 8 mi. off I-10 at Exit 302.* ☎ *520-586-4100. Open daily 7:30am-6pm. 1hr. tours every 30min. 8:30am-4:30pm. Entrance fee $10 per vehicle. Tours $14, ages 7-13 $6. Reservations strongly recommended.)* Near Saguaro National Park East, **Colossal Cave** is one of the only dormant (no water or new formations) caves in the US. A variety of tours are offered; on Saturday evenings, a special ladder tour through otherwise sealed-off tunnels, crawlspaces, and corri-

dors can be arranged. *(☎ 520-647-7275. Open mid-Mar. to mid-Sept. M-Sa 8am-6pm, Su 8am-7pm; mid-Sept. to mid-Mar. M-Sa 9am-5pm, Su 9am-6pm. $7.50, ages 6-12 $4. Ladder tour $35.)*

PIMA AIR AND SPACE MUSEUM. This museum chronicles aviation history from the days of the Wright brothers to its modern military incarnations. While exhibits on female and African-American aviators are interesting, the main draw is a fleet of decommissioned warplanes. *(☎ 520-574-0462. Open summer daily 9am-5pm; winter M-F 7am-3pm, Sa-Su 7am-5pm. $7.50, seniors $6.50.)* Tours of the **Davis-Monthan Air Force Base** are also offered. *(M-F 5 per day. $5, ages 6-12 $3.)*

◩ OUTDOOR ACTIVITIES

North of the desert museum, the western half of **Saguaro National Park** (Tucson Mountain District) has hiking trails and an auto loop. The **Bajada Loop Drive** runs less than 9 mi., but passes through some of the most striking desert scenery the park has to offer. The paved nature walk near the **Visitors Center** presents some of the best specimens of Saguaro cactus in the Tucson area. *(☎ 520-733-5158. Open daily 8:30am-5pm.)* There are a variety of hiking trails through Saguaro West; **Sendero Esperanza Trail,** beginning at the Ez-kim-in-zin picnic area, is the mildest approach to the summit of **Wasson Peak** (4687 ft.), the highest in the Tucson Mountain Range. The **Hugh Norris Trail** is a slightly longer, more strenuous climb to the top. Mountain biking is permitted only around the **Cactus Forest Loop Drive** and **Cactus Forest Trail,** at the western end of the park near the Visitors Center. The trails in Saguaro East are much longer than those in the western segment of the park.

Northeast of downtown Tucson, the cliffs and desert pools of **Sabino Canyon** provide an ideal backdrop for picnics and day hikes. Locals beat Tucson heat by frolicking in the water holes. No cars are permitted in the canyon, but a shuttle bus makes trips through it. (Take Speedway Blvd. to Swan Rd. to Sunrise Dr. The entrance is at the cross of Sunrise Dr. and Sabino Canyon Rd. ☎ 520-749-2861. Runs July-Nov. every hr. 9am-4pm; Dec.-June every 30min. dawn-dusk. $6, ages 3-12 $2.) The National Forest's **Visitors Center** lies at the canyon's entrance. *(☎ 520-749-8700. Open M-F 8am-4:30pm, Sa-Su 8:30am-4:30pm.)*

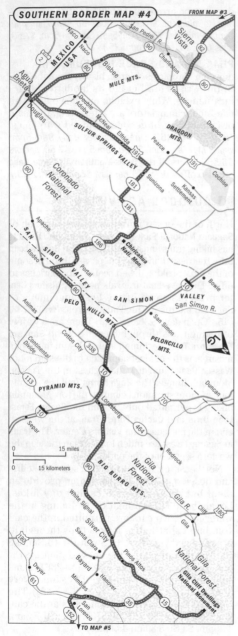

SOUTHERN BORDER MAP #4

FROM MAP #3

SOUTHERN BORDER

TO MAP #5

FOOD

Like any good college town, Tucson brims with inexpensive, tasty eateries. Cheap Mexican dominates the culinary scene, but every style of cooking is represented.

Elle, 3048 E. Broadway Blvd. (☎520-327-0500). Cool classical jazz resonates through this stylish eatery. Enjoy mouth-watering chicken penne ($12) in elegant, yet welcoming, surroundings. Open M-F 11:30am-10pm, Sa 4:30-10pm.

El Charro, 311 N. Court Ave. (☎520-622-5465), at the corner of Franklin and Court St., just north of downtown. Tucson's oldest Mexican restaurant—arguably the oldest in the US—is so popular that the USS Tucson submarine has named its galley "El Charro Down Under." Be prepared for a wait for dinner. Entrees $10-12. Open Su-Th 11am-9pm, F-Sa 11am-10pm.

Gus Balon's Restaurant, 6027 E. 22nd St. (☎520-748-9731), just west of Wilmot. This classic diner serves up Tucson's best breakfast ($4-5) all day with heaping plates of eggs, fried potatoes, and toast. Lunch and dinner feature classics like roast sirloin ($5), grilled country ham ($6), and assorted sandwiches ($2-4). The pies lining one wall are an irresistibly sweet temptation ($1.50 per slice). Open M-Sa 7am-9pm.

La Indita, 622 N. 4th Ave. (☎520-792-0523). Delights customers with traditional Mexican cuisine ($3-9) served on tortillas. The food is still prepared by *la indita* herself, providing a bit of added kick. Open M-Th 11am-9pm, F 11am-6pm, Sa 6-9pm, Su 9am-9pm.

ACCOMMODATIONS

There's a direct correlation between the temperature in Tucson and the warmth of its lodging industry to budget travelers; expect the best deals in summer, when rain-cooled evenings and summer bargains are consolation for the midday scorch. **The Tucson Gem and Mineral Show,** the largest of its kind in North America, is an added hazard for budget travelers. Falling at the end of January and beginning of February, the mammoth event fills up most of the city's accommodations for its two-week run and drives prices up considerably. Unless you've made arrangements in advance, this is a bad time to drop in on Tucson.

Roadrunner Hostel, 346 E. 12th St. (☎520-628-4709). Located in a pleasant house a few blocks from downtown, the hostel is exceptionally clean and friendly. Wows guests with unparalleled amenities such as a giant 52 in. TV, a formidable movie collection, free high-speed Internet access, purified water, free coffee and tea, and swamp cooling. Apr.-Sept. international guests get 2 free additional nights when they pay for the first 2. Free lockers, linen, towels, and laundry soap. Dorms $18; doubles $35.

■ **Loews Ventana Canyon Resort,** 7000 N. Resort Dr. (☎520-299-2020). A quintessential 5-star hotel 5 mi. north of downtown off Oracle Rd. At the base of an 80 ft. waterfall, the incredible Ventana delivers on every level–from its relaxing spa to its championship golf course to the beautiful surrounding Catalina Mountain foothills. Singles from $95.

Hotel Congress and Hostel, 311 E. Congress (☎520-622-8848). Conveniently located across from the bus and train stations, this hotel and hostel offers superb lodging to night-owl hostelers. Downstairs, Club Congress booms until 1am on weekends, making it rough on early birds. Private rooms come with bath, phone, vintage radio, and ceiling fans. The cafe downstairs serves great salads and omelettes. Dorms $17. June-Aug. singles $29; doubles $38. Sept.-Nov. and May $49/$53. Dec.-Apr. $68/$82. 10% discount for students, military, and local artists.

The Flamingo Hotel, 1300 N. Stone Ave. (☎520-770-1901). Houses not only guests, but also Arizona's largest collection of Western movie posters. There are dozens of rooms available, from the Kevin Costner room to the Burt Lancaster suite—both with A/C, cable TV, telephones, and pool access. Laundry facilities on-site. May-Aug. singles $24; doubles $29. Sept.-Nov. all rooms $49. Dec.-Apr. $75.

CAMPING

In addition to the backcountry camping available in the Saguaro Park and Coronado Forest (both inside and outside the Pusch Ridge Wilderness), there are a variety of other camping options. **Gilbert Ray Campground** (☎520-883-4200), just outside Saguaro West along the McCain Loop Rd., offers campsites ($7) with toilets and drinking water, and is in easy reach of the city as well as all the Speedway sights. **Catalina State Park** (☎520-628-5798), north of Tucson on Oracle Rd., features $10 tent sites fully equipped with hot showers, water, and toilets. Picnic sites are available. Camping areas flank Sky Island Scenic Byway at Mt. Lemmon; an added perk of these sights is their temperate climate. All campgrounds charge a $5 road access fee in addition to the camping costs. **Spencer Canyon** (sites $12) and **Rose Canyon** (sites $15) have potable water and toilets, while **Molino Basin** and **General Hitchcock** have toilets but no potable water (both $5). Call the **Santa Catalina Ranger District** (☎520-749-8700) for more info.

NIGHTLIFE

The free *Tucson Weekly* is the local authority on nightlife, while the weekend sections of the *Star* or the *Citizen* also provide good coverage. Throughout the year, the city of the sun presents **Music Under the Stars,** a series of sunset concerts performed by the **Tucson Symphony Orchestra** (☎520-792-9155). For **Downtown Saturday Nights,** on the first and third Saturday of each month, Congress St. is blockaded for a celebration of the arts with outdoor singers, crafts, and galleries. Every Thursday, the **Thursday Night Art Walk** lets you mosey through downtown galleries and studios. For more info, call **Tucson Arts District** (☎520-624-9977). UA students rock 'n' roll on **Speedway Blvd.,** while others do the two-step in clubs on **N. Oracle.** Young locals hang out on **4th Ave.,** where most bars have live music and low cover charges.

Club Congress, 311 E. Congress St. (☎520-622-8848), has DJs during the week and live bands on weekends, and is the venue for most of the indie music coming through town. The friendly hotel staff and a cast of regulars make it an especially good time. M is 80s night with $0.80 drinks. Cover $3-5. Open daily 9pm-1am.

O'Malley's, 247 N. 4th Ave. (☎520-623-8600). A good spot with decent bar food, pool tables, and pinball. As its name implies, this is a better place to nurse your pint of Guinness than it is to get your groove on. Cover Th-Sa varies. Open daily 11am-1am.

IBT's (☎520-882-3053), on 4th Ave. at 6th St. The single most popular gay venue in Tucson, IBT's can be hard to spot—there is no sign and the is door unmarked. Once you've seen the stucco building halfway down the block, however, there's no mistaking it. It pumps dance music in its classic club environment to a weekend capacity crowd. W and Su drag shows wow audiences. Open daily 9am-1am.

Ain't Nobody's Biz, 2900 E. Broadway Blvd. (☎520-318-4838), in a shopping plaza. The little sister of its Phoenix namesake, and the big mama of the Tucson lesbian scene. A large bar, 'Biz' attracts crowds of all backgrounds and has some of the best dancing in Tucson. Open daily 11am-1am.

THE ROAD TO TOMBSTONE

After passing through the small town of **Vail**, there is no other option but to jump on the freeway. Take **I-10 East** for 3 mi. to the next exit: **Rte. 83**, the **Patagonia-Sonoita Scenic Hwy.** This road rambles through mesquite washes and juniper scrubland while making its way toward the high country. Twenty-four miles from the interstate, near the town of Sonoita, it arrives in Arizona's wine country, where a few scattered wineries offer wine tasting down back roads. Despite the images of sunlit vines and lush grape groves this invokes, this area is mostly just open highland prairies.

Little Sonoita, at the crossroads of Rte. 82 and Rte. 83, is just that—a crossroads. The four corners of the intersection offer a bank, a cafe, a gas station, and a pizza place. The aptly named **Sonoita Crossroads Cafe**, 3172 Hwy. 83, fuels up passersby with gourmet coffees and classic American cuisine in a relaxed coffeeshop atmosphere. (☎520-455-5189. Breakfast $2-6. Lunch $4-6. Open M-F 8am-2pm, Sa-Su 8am-1pm.)

To continue on, turn onto **Rte. 82 East** at the crossroads. Take Rte. 82 all the way to Rte. 80, then take **Rte. 80 South** to Tombstone.

TOMBSTONE

Long past its glory days as the largest city between the Mississippi River and the Pacific, Tombstone has abandoned its dangerous Old West history for a more sanitized Disney version of cowboy living. The city offers a little bit of everything—as long as it's a shot of rot-gut or a gunfight re-enactment.

VITAL STATS

Population: 1500

Visitor Info: City of Tombstone Visitor and Information Center, 317 Allen St. (☎520-457-3929; www.cityoftombstone.com), at 4th St. Open M-F 9am-4pm, Sa-Su 10am-4pm.

Internet Access: Gitt Wired (☎520-457-3250), at 5th and Fremont St. $0.15 per min. Open daily 7am-5pm.

Post Office: 100 N. Haskell Ave. **Postal Code:** 85638.

GETTING AROUND. Rte. 80 rolls through Tombstone one block east of downtown **Allen St.** From Rte. 80 South, turn right at the infamous O.K. Corral to hit historic Tombstone. For **park-** **ing,** stow your wheels in the dirt lot on the east side of town between 3rd and 4th St., or turn west off Rte. 80 onto 3rd St. and then left onto Allen St., where more free parking is ahead on the right. All attractions are within a few short blocks of these parking areas.

SIGHTS. Tombstone has turned the shootout at the **O.K. Corral,** on Allen St. next to City Park, into a year-round tourist industry, inviting visitors to view the barnyard where Wyatt Earp and his posse kicked some serious outlaw butt. (☎520-457-3456. Open daily 9am-5pm. $2.50.) Next door at the **Tombstone Historama,** Vincent Price narrates the town's history as a plastic mountain revolves on stage and a dramatization of the gunfight is shown on a movie screen. (☎520-457-3456. Open daily 9am-5pm. $2.50.) The site of the longest poker game in Western history (8 years, 5 months, and 3 days), the **Bird Cage Theater,** at 6th and Allen St., is named for the suspended cages that once held prostitutes. It now houses a sensationalist museum. (☎505-457-3421. Open daily 8am-6pm.) If the cowboy hype and tall tales are not your style, visit the **Tombstone Courthouse State Historic Park,** at 3rd and Toughnut St. The impressive old building that tried to bring law to the lawless is now a museum offering the most scientific account of what really happened at high noon at the O.K. Corral. Visitors have the chance to crack a safe and see the historic gallows. (☎520-457-3311. Open daily 8am-5pm. $2.50, children $1.) The actual tombstones of Tombstone—the results of all that gunplay—rest in the **Boothill Cemetery,** just outside of town on Rte. 80 North. (☎800-457-3423. Open daily 7:30am-6pm. Free.)

For something a little less high-noon and a little more horticulture, the **Rose Tree Museum,** 4th and Toughnut St., shelters the **World's Largest Rose Tree.** (☎520-457-3326. Open daily 9am-5pm. $2.)

FOOD & ACCOMMODATIONS. Once the "Bucket of Blood Saloon" where Virgil Earp was shot from the second-story window, **The Longhorn Restaurant,** 501 E. Allen St., has considerably cleaned up its act. Today, it's a boisterous family restaurant. Try the "too tough to die burger" ($11). Less legendary burgers and sandwiches cost around $6, while dinner plates like roast beef or meatloaf are

Historic Bisbee

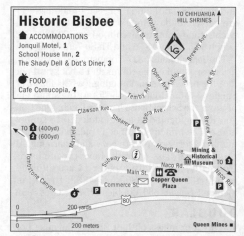

⌂ ACCOMMODATIONS
Jonquil Motel, **1**
School House Inn, **2**
The Shady Dell & Dot's Diner, **3**

🍎 FOOD
Cafe Cornucopia, **4**

TO CHIHUAHUA
HILL SHRINES

Queen Mines ■

$11. (☎ 520-457-3405. Open daily 8am-8pm.) Named for "the girl who loved Doc Holiday and everyone else," **Big Nose Kate's Saloon,** 417 Allen St., is an authentic Old West saloon with live honky-tonk music. The ghost of "the swamper" is said to haunt these halls searching for his lost cache of silver, left here when the building was still The Grand Hotel. Check your weapons at the door. (☎ 520-457-3107. Lunch from $7. Open daily 11am-midnight.) Named after the "angel of the mining camps" who devoted her life to clean living and public service, **Nellie Cashman's Restaurant,** on 5th St. off Allen St., is less Old West and a bit more down-home. (☎ 520-457-2212. Hamburgers from $6. Open daily 7:30am-9pm.)

Removed from the giddyup-in' ruckus of Allen St., the **Larian Motel,** at 5th St. and Rte. 80., offers rooms named for famous outlaws, vigilantes, or ruffians. (☎ 520-457-2272; www.tombstonemotels.com. Singles $40-45; doubles $45-59.)

 Driving north on Rte. 191 the **Dragoon Mountains** rise up out of the valley to the left. This range shares its name with the US Dragoons, an army rapid reaction force responsible for chasing Apaches and bandits from 1832 to 1861. Also in these eastern mountains, deep in the canyons, stood the Cochise Stronghold, where Geronimo and other Apaches took refuge and plotted raids.

 **LEAVING TOMBSTONE**
Continue on **Rte. 80 South** to Bisbee.

BISBEE

This rough and tumble mining-town-turned-artist-colony is famous for its eccentricity. Old miners give tours of prosperous shafts while deadheads groove outside bohemian cafes and galleries. The Victorian-style houses that line the narrow streets could as easily be out of a European town as they are part of this Old West settlement. Some hail it as a land where time stands still, but Bisbee seems more like a community where time accumulates; the Western frontier, the gold rush, the 1950s, the summer of love, and the postmodern age are all alive and well here.

(VITAL STATS)

Population: 6090

Visitor Info: Chamber of Commerce, 31 Subway St. (☎ 520-432-5421). Enter on Naco Rd. and continue straight until it becomes Subway St. Open M-F 9am-5pm, Sa-Su 10am-4pm.

Internet Access: Copper Queen Library, 6 Main St. (☎ 520-432-4232). Open M noon-7pm, Tu and Th-F 10am-5pm, W 10am-7pm, Sa 10am-2pm.

Post Office: Copper Queen, 6 Main St. (☎ 520-432-2052). Open M-F 8:30am-4:30pm. **Postal Code:** 85603.

🔳 GETTING AROUND. The streets of Bisbee are labyrinthine and almost entirely unnavigable. Get a map—you'll still be lost, but you'll feel better. The town's tiny alleys were designed for hooved travel, so the sooner you ditch your car and take to the street, the better off you'll be. **Parking** is available on the left just entering town on **Naco Rd.** Another lot can be found by following Naco Rd. straight onto tiny Subway St. past the Visitors Center and turning right onto Tact St. The lot is adjacent to the wrought-iron angels.

◎ SIGHTS. Copper mining built Bisbee, and, although the industry ceased in 1943, you can still learn about it on educational 1¼hr. tours at the **Queen Mines,** on the Rte. 80 interchange entering Old Bisbee. (☎ 866-432-2071. Tours daily at 9, 10:30am, noon, 2, and 3:30pm. $12, ages 4-15 $5.) After exploring the bowels of Bisbee's mines, you'll welcome the heavenly experience of the **Chihuahua Hill Shrines.** A 20min. hike over rocky ground leads to two shrines, the first Buddhist and the second Mexican Catholic. The Catholic shrine is exceptional in its complexity. It includes numerous statues of the Madonna as well as dioramas of the Saints' lives and a towering cross. The more understated Buddhist shrine features several works of rock art in addition to innumerable prayer flags and pictures of the last two Dalai Lamas. (Head up Brewery Ave.; there is a grocery store on the right. Behind the store are two staircases; take the left one. Next, turn left and briefly follow a concrete driveway. Before the private property sign, turn right off the paved road. At the cross, follow the trail up.) For a retrospective view on the area, visit the **Mining and Historical Museum,** 5 Copper Queen. This Smithsonian-affiliated museum highlights the discovery of Bisbee's copper surplus and the lives of the fortune-seekers who extracted it. (☎520-432-7071. Open daily 10am-4pm. $4, seniors $3.50, under 3 free.)

🍴 FOOD. Cheap eateries line the main drags of downtown. Most have classic American fixings for around $5-9. With fresh sandwiches and crisp salads, ◪**Cafe Cornucopia,** 14 Main St., is the best of Bisbee's many cafes. The quaint establishment, hollowed out of a turn-of-the-century structure, features a small dining room with a pink and brick Old West facade. The chicken salad sandwich ($6) will knock your socks off, and don't miss the tangy cilantro cole slaw. They also serve smoothies ($4) and soups ($4) in a bread bowl. (☎520-432-4820. Open M and Th-Su 10am-5pm.)

🏠 ACCOMMODATIONS. Time travel back to the 50s at ◪**The Shady Dell,** 1 Douglas Rd., where you can stay in one of eight restored vintage trailers, complete with authentic period furnishings including propane stoves, refrigerators, and electric percolators. Each one of the sleek aluminum trailers is unique, and some even have original black-and-white TVs with vintage movie collections or phonographs. RV hookups are also available. (From Rte. 80 East, drive past historic Bisbee and take a left before the rotary. ☎520-432-3567; www.theshadydell.com. No children under 10. Reservations required. Trailers $35-75.) On the grounds you'll also find the unique **Dot's Diner** in a 1957 trailer. A visit to Dot's means fighting the walls for elbow room, but the cozy family kitchen evokes the original atmosphere of diner eating. Space is so snug you can practically reach over

and help the staff along. Classic breakfasts ($3) are served all day along with hamburgers, sandwiches, and Southwestern food. (☎520-432-5882. Lunch $4-5. Open M-Tu and Th-Su 7am-3pm.)

The **Jonquil Motel,** 317 Tombstone Canyon Rd., has clean, smoke-free rooms and a backyard perfect for barbecues or lounging. (☎520-432-7371. Singles $40-55; doubles $55-75.) At the south end of town, the **School House Inn,** 818 Tombstone Canyon Rd., is located in a remodeled 1918 schoolhouse. The principal's office is palatial, while the numbered classrooms are cozy and charming. All rooms, regardless of grade, have private baths. Ironically, no children under 14 are allowed. (☎520-432-2996 or 800-537-4333. Breakfast included. Singles $60; doubles $75-85; suites $95.)

DOUGLAS

Twenty-four miles south of Bisbee, the quiet border town of Douglas sits at the intersection of Rte. 80 and Rte. 191. While Rte. 80 runs through the center of town, Rte. 191 makes a run for the border toward Mexican neighbor Agua Prieta. Stores swarm around Rte. 80 (rechristened **G Ave.** for municipal purposes), and most city services lie off this thoroughfare on **10th St.** For a trip back to the Old West, visit the **John Slaughter Ranch.** John Slaughter, the ranch's eponymous owner, was a Louisiana native who joined the Confederate army during the Civil War. After the war, he left the South for Arizona to become a rancher and lawman, and by the 1880s was voted the Marshal of Tombstone. He proceeded to shoot or prosecute (in no particular order) Tombstone's worst. Slaughter's ranch buildings are now a museum where visitors can get a sense of historic living. (To the east, 15th St. becomes the Geronimo Trail, which leads 15 mi. to the ranch. ☎520-558-2474. Open Su and W-Sa 10am-3pm. $3, children $0.50.)

For more tourist info, consult the **Visitors Center,** 1125 Pan American Rte., near the border on the town bypass route. (☎888-315-9999. Open M-F 8am-5pm, Sa 8am-1pm.) The **Grand Cafe,** 119 G Ave., features a shrine to Marilyn Monroe and offers tasty Mexican food for under $7. (From Rte. 80, follow the signs for the Douglas Historic District; the cafe is on the right a few blocks down. ☎520-364-2344. Open M-Sa 10am-10pm.) Across the street is the **Gadsden Hotel,** 1046 G. Ave., an extravagant, yet cheap hotel. Established in 1907, this opulent palace hails itself as "the last of the grand hotels." The white marble staircase, 14K gold-topped marble pillars, and a ridiculously ornate lobby support the claim. While the rooms may not be as luxurious as the great hall, a stay at the Gadsden delivers high-society living at low prices. (☎520-364-4481; www.gadsdenhotel.com. Rooms with double bed $45; with 2 double beds or a queen $50.)

AGUA PRIETA

A far cry from the extreme poverty and sleaze of some Mexican border towns, Agua Prieta is an authentic, unadulterated taste of small-city Mexico. While there really isn't much to see, a quick hop over the border is worth the cultural experience and the Mexican food. Not the least bit touristy, the only street vendors you'll see in Agua Prieta are those selling *helado* (ice cream), *fruta* (fresh fruit), and *agua fresca* (juice and soda). The city is laid out with *avenidas* running north-south and *calles* running east-west. The best Mexican food can be found on **Avenida 4.** Don't miss the **Plaza** at Calle 5 and Avenida 4, site of many a fiesta. The town also features beautiful churches.

The border crossing is located on **Calle 3.** It is easiest to park your car on the American side of 3rd St. and walk across. If you decide to drive, be prepared to wait in lines returning through the crossing (see **Mexican Tourist Cards,** p. 12). If you're planning on roadtripping though Mexico, this is a great place to start; Agua Prieta marks the beginning of the **Janos Highway,** the shortest route to Mexico City from the US.

ELFRIDA. From Douglas, **U.S. 191 North** leads to Elfrida. Dubbed "the heart of the valley," this town is really nothing more than a farm town with a few local haunts. It is, however, one of the last chances for services for a long while.

Beware, there are no services in the Chiricahua area between the hamlet of Sunizona and the town of Portal, so be ready to travel at least 60 mi. without filling up. (Fortunately, Rte. 191 boasts some of the cheapest gas in southeastern Arizona.)

APPROACHING CHIRICAHUA NATIONAL MONUMENT

14 mi. north of Elfrida, merge right onto **Rte. 181** and follow the clearly labeled signs to Chiricahua National Monument, 26 mi. down the road.

CHIRICAHUA NATIONAL MONUMENT

Over 25 million years ago, the Turkey Creek Caldera spewed forth thick, white-hot ash that settled over the Chiricahua area. Since then, the powers of erosion have sculpted the fused-ash rock into peculiar formations that loom over the landscape and awe those who walk among them. The massive stone spires, weighing hundreds of tons and often perched precariously on small pedestals, inspired the Apaches to call the area "Land of the Standing-Up Rocks," and the pioneers to dub it "Wonderland of Rocks." Whatever you call it, it's nothing short of spectacular. The geological magnificence here could be the sun-bleached cousin of Zion or Bryce Canyons, yet it happily lacks their popularity, allowing visitors to indulge in peace and tranquility.

All of the park, except for a strip around the main road, is federally designated wilderness; no biking or climbing is permitted. The **Visitors Center** is just beyond the entrance station. (☎504-824-3560, ext. 104. Open daily 8am-5pm. $5.)

▣ **GETTING AROUND.** Extending from the park's entrance station to Massai Point at the back of the park is the **Bonita Canyon Drive,** an incredibly scenic 8 mi. trek that is not to be missed. Begin the drive at the Bonita Canyon Campground. From there, the road squeezes through the narrow gap between the towering granite walls of Bonita Canyon and then ascends to pine-studded Massai Point at the mountain's crest. A short interpretive nature trail encircles the peak and also serves as the starting point for the more demanding Echo Canyon Trail and other trails into the wilderness.

◪ **HIKING.** There is a bountiful selection of day hikes in the monument. Keep in mind that many combinations are possible, since several loops and spurs provide flexibility. From the parking lot on Massai Point, the ▧**Echo Canyon Trail** (1½ mi.) leads through an impressive cluster of formations before meeting with the **Hailstone** and **Upper Rhyolite Trails.** Take Hailstone and later the moderate **Ed Riggs Trail,** a 3½ mi. loop and a quick return to the parking lot. For a longer loop, continue down the pine forest of the Upper Rhyolite Trail (1 mi.). The trail meets the **Sarah Deming Trail** (1½ mi.), which steeply ascends the opposite face of the canyon to the highest point of the hike. You can either hike the **Heart of Rocks Scenic Loop,** which offers a spectacular passage through the monument's rock formations, or continue immediately along **Big Balanced Rock Trail** (1 mi.), which winds across ridge tops. There is also a half-mile spur leading to the aptly named **Inspiration Point,** which affords a commanding view of the canyons below. The return trip follows the **Mushroom Rock Trail** and **Ed Riggs Trail** (together about 2 mi.), with more forest and fewer views than the Echo Canyon Trail. The whole loop, without the Heart of Rocks Loop or the Inspiration Point Trail, clocks in around 7½ mi. and takes 4-5hr. To get info and maps for more trails, check the Visitors Center.

CAMPING. Although no backcountry camping is allowed along the trails, there is an established campground inside the park. The well-equipped **Bonita Canyon Campground** features toilets, picnic grounds, water, and easy access to the park trails, but no showers. (☎504-824-3560. 24 sites. 14-day max. stay. Sites $12.)

THE ROAD OVER THE CHIRICAHUA MOUNTAINS

The best way to get from southeastern Arizona to New Mexico is over the Chiricahua Mountains. This road promises awe-inspiring vistas and mind-blowing geological formations, but it degenerates into a rough dirt road as it crests the mountains. The road is not maintained for winter travel, but otherwise is acceptable for almost any vehicle (though at times it's very bumpy). Check with the Coronado Forest Douglas Ranger District office (☎520-364-3468) for information on road conditions and safe driving. **Pinery Canyon Rd.,** located opposite the entrance to Chiricahua National Monument, is the gateway to the Chiricahua wilderness. The 19 mi. trek meanders through the pine forests of the Chiricahua canyons before making its way up to the impressive ridgeline and descending into Portal. The first mile is one of the roughest, which makes it easy to decide whether or not to take this adventure up front. The road forks many times, so follow the well-labeled signs to Portal, staying on **Forest Rd. 42.**

There are many sites around the road where camping is indicated by the clearing of shrubbery near a turnout, but the superior **Pinery Canyon Camp** lies 10 mi. in and offers amenities like picnic tables and fire rings for the right price: free.

When the dusty back road ends 5 mi. from Portal at the **Portal-Paradise Rd.,** and that double yellow line welcomes you back to pavement and civilization, the sense of accomplishment for surviving the 1hr. trek is very satisfying, even if you and your car come out of it wearing a thin white layer of the Chiricahuas.

CAVE CREEK
East of the Chiricahua National Monument, on Pinery Canyon Rd.

As it enters the Cave Creek area, Pinery Canyon Rd. passes a few campgrounds that are much more developed than the ones on top of the mountain, but amenities like toilets require you to pay for the site ($10 per vehicle). The picturesque canyons and giant boulder formations of Cave Creek are worth some exploration before continuing down to the desert below. The **Cave Creek Visitors Center** will welcome you to this serene natural paradise and has an excellent view of the boulder-topped canyon walls which bear a striking resemblance to Yosemite National Park's Half Dome in California. (Open M and Th-Su 9am-4:30pm.)

PORTAL. Leaving the gorgeous meadows and towering canyon walls of Cave Creek, the road descends through the village of Portal. The **Portal Peak Lodge** and attached store is a welcome relief to those who have traveled too far without services, but aside from this general store, there is very little before the road returns to the desert expanses. (☎520-558-2223; www.portalpeak-lodge.com. Office open daily 9:30am-7:30pm.)

APPROACHING LORDSBURG
At the junction of Rte. 181 and with Rte. 80, head north on **Rte. 80** toward **I-10,** 27 mi. away. When you get there, aptly named **Road Forks** offers the choice between east or west on the freeway and some very inexpensive gas. Grab the gas and head east 14 mi. to Lordsburg. The freeway passes a true dust bowl, where high winds can reduce visibility to almost zero. Use extreme caution when driving through dust storms and never stop in the travel lanes. To enter Lordsburg, turn off I-10 onto **Motel Dr.**

Welcome To NEW MEXICO

Apr.-Oct., you pass into the Mountain Time Zone, where it is 1hr. later. Nov.-Mar. there is no change here.

LORDSBURG

Dozens of empty gas stations and motels create the eerie feeling that Lordsburg is nothing but a ghost town. Commercial life struggles on, in the form of a few businesses and still-operating gas stations. Across the highway and down a 3 mi. dirt road stands the real ghost town of **Shakespeare,** which, ironically, is Lordsburg's only attraction. You can tour this defunct mining town, but only on irregularly scheduled days. (☎505-542-9034. Tours $3.) As for Lordsburg, if things continue to degrade, it'll only be a few years before you pay to enter the "Lordsburg ghost town, home of a thousand abandoned gas stations and motels." The **Holiday Motel,** 600 E. Motel Dr., has clean beds and bathrooms, and the price is right. (☎505-542-3535. Singles $22.50; doubles $28.)

APPROACHING SILVER CITY
From Lordsburg it is an uneventful 44 mi. drive northeast on **U.S. 90** to Silver City. The only excitement on this road is cresting the **continental divide,** which at 6300 ft., consists of the region's foothills.

SILVER CITY

In its heyday, Silver City was a rough and wild place that spawned the infamous outlaw Billy the Kid. Brown historical markers strewn about town point out the sites of his home, his school, his first bank robbery, his first jailbreak, and other typical landmarks of a Wild West childhood. Today, a different kind of wild attracts people to the quiet mountain town. The Gila National Forest, a designated natural wilderness, surrounds the town with 559,065 acres of rugged beauty.

GETTING AROUND. Hudson St. (U.S. 90) and Silver Heights Blvd. (U.S. 180) are the major routes through town, running north-south and east-west, respectively. Around the center of town, **College Ave.** bisects Hudson St. and leads to the **University of Western New Mexico.** Most of the action in Silver City can be found along **Bullard St.,** which runs parallel to Hudson St. and is accessible via going west on **Broadway.**

VITAL STATS

Population: 10,500

Visitor Info: 201 N. Hudson St. (☎505-538-3785), near the intersection with Broadway. Open M-Sa 9am-5pm.

Internet Access: Lordsburg Public Library, 515 W. College Ave. (☎505-538-3672). Free. 1hr. max.; sign up in advance. Open M and Th 9am-8pm, Tu-W 9am-6pm, F 9am-5pm, Sa 9am-10pm.

Post Office: 500 N. Hudson St. Open M-F 8:30am-5pm, Sa 10am-noon. **Postal Code:** 88061.

SIGHTS & OUTDOORS. Silver City contains the main **Forestry Station** of the Gila National Forest at 3005 E. Camino del Bosque. The station provides excellent maps of the forest and its wilderness areas, as well as info on various outdoor activities in the region. (On the 32nd Bypass Rd. off U.S. 180, east of town. ☎505-388-8201. Open M-F 8am-4:30pm.) Rent mountain bikes and cross-country skis for exploring Gila and the surrounding foothills at the **Gila Hike and Bike Shop,** 103 E. College Ave. They also repair bikes, sell outdoor equipment, and provide maps of the area. (☎505-388-3222. Bikes 1st day $20, 2nd day $15, 3rd day $10, each additional day $5. Cross-country skis $12 per day. Open M-F 9am-5:30pm, Sa 9am-5pm, Su 10am-4pm.) For a real view of the Wild West, try walking the **Billy the Kid Historical Walk.** The tour starts at the corner of Hudson St. and Broadway; follow the arrows to take the stroll. Art enthusiasts will find an impressive collection of **galleries** on Yankie St., one block north of Broadway at Bullard St.

FOOD. Southwestern artwork hangs for sale on the walls of the home-style dining room in the **Olde World Bakery and Cafe,** at the corner of Bullard St. and Broadway. Pastries are baked fresh every day, and the sandwiches (whole $5.25, half $3) and salads are unbelievable. Try the chicken fajita salad ($6.75) or relax in the comfortable chairs with a game of checkers. (☎505-534-9372. Open M-Sa 7am-5pm.) At the **Jalisco Cafe,** 100 S. Bullard St., the chefs really put the famous New Mexican chili pepper to good use. The unique jalapeño guacamole is delicious (in a masochistic sort of way); the menu warns people to ask for samples of their specialty red and green chili ($5.50) before ordering because many guests just can't take the heat. (☎505-388-2060. Entrees $7-9. Open M-Sa 11am-8:30pm.) **The Pinon Cafe and Bakery,** 603

N. Bullard St., has tasty continental cuisine and an extensive beer and wine menu. (☎505-534-9168. Lunch $5-8. Dinner $11-15. Open M-Th 8am-9pm, F-Sa 8am-11pm, Su 8am-8pm.)

⌂ ACCOMMODATIONS. A night at the ◪**Palace Hotel,** located at the corner of Broadway and Bullard St., is yet another way to experience the history of this mining community. Established in 1882, this charming hotel echoes the grandeur of years gone by. Most of the tiny rooms open onto the spacious sky-lit common room, where guests mingle for breakfast each morning. (☎505-288-1811; www.zianet.com/palacehotel. Singles $35; doubles $47; suites $57.) **The Drifter Motel and Cocktail Lounge,** 711 Silver Heights Blvd., is another solid budget option that comes with the added bonus of live music on weekends. (☎800-853-2916, lounge 505-538-2916. Live music F-Sa. Lounge open daily 5pm-1:30am. Rooms $38-52.)

THE ROAD TO GILA NATIONAL FOREST

From Silver City, a dirt road runs north toward the wilderness of the Gila National Forest. The forest's most famous attraction, the **Gila Cliff Dwellings National Monument,** lies at the end of this road, and is the logical place to begin your exploration of the forest. The cliff dwellings are reached by driving 44 mi. north on **Forest Rd. 15** through Pinos Altos. The road is narrow and winding, and requires about 2 hr. for safe passage.

To follow our route, take **Ranch Club Rd.** or **32nd St.** north from Silver City to **Forest Rd. 15.** This highway will take you to Pinos Altos,

FROM THE ROAD

LITTLE NOISES

"Tink!" It's one sound the roadtripper doesn't want to hear. Although more discrete than the *"thump!"* or *"crunch"* that emanates from that hapless pulverizing of some foreign object on the roadway, and not as insidious as the *"pop"* and *"tsssttt"* of a leaking hose or tire, the *"tink"* is no less menacing.

I heard the *"tink"* somewhere in the midst of the Gila Wilderness on my way to the ancient Cliff Dwellings. Dire explanations for the sound began choking out other thoughts; I was somewhere between the snapping of a break cable and the ejection a Taiwanese widget that would take four weeks to ship and replace, when I heard it again.

Hail. I was relieved. Sure, a mid-summer hail storm seemed a little out of place, especially since I had been sweltering in the Arizona desert the day before. But, oh well, I thought, at least this would clear away some of the mud that had taken up residence on my hood. The *"tinks"* grew in intensity until their furious attacks on my jeep reached an ear splitting din, and a ghostly layer of bouncing ice obscured my path. This was my first monsoon, but I was determined to reach the Cliff Dwellings that I sought.

The storm let up just enough for me to dash up the canyon walls and into the ancient structures that had once protected families within the cliffs. And as I pondered why anyone would choose to live in such a remote place so high above the ground, outside, the storm really got bad. Not just *"tinks,"* but *"booms"* and *"bangs"* of nearby thunder. The temperature dropped as the storm intensified, and I realized I was trapped.

Or was I safe? I was dry, warm, and protected. In the valley below, I would not have been able to see a thing amidst the dime-sized hail that was currently pitting my windshield. And who knows what sound it makes when lightning hits your jeep. The dwellings were my sanctuary. With each *crash*, the cave echoed with the stories of a forgotten people whose only occupation was to live life, not to worry about their jeep.

The clouds finally broke; I climbed down. On the drive back to civilization I listened, not for the little noises to which my ears were attuned, but for those I had ignored.

—Devin Lyons-Quirk

where it degrades into a road so narrow that only one car can pass at a time. The road crosses a few picturesque woodland campgrounds as it meanders its way on a path so twisty that within any given minute the compass has touched every cardinal direction. After 17 mi. of narrow road, the path opens back up again into two lanes at the intersection with **Forest Rd. 35.**

From here, the road climbs to a peak above the Gila River, where pine-covered red rocks extend into endless vistas. After whizzing through the infinitesimal hamlet of **Gila Hot Springs,** where supplies are available at **Doc Campbell's Post Vacation Center,** the road arrives at the national monument.

> Drive carefully, as it is difficult to see through the thick pine groves. Road conditions can be impassable in winter; pay close attention to the weather and road surface.

GILA NATIONAL FOREST

The Gila National Forest encompasses hundreds of miles of hiking trails through mountains, canyons, and forests. This area includes more wilderness than any other national forest in the Southwest; if that's not enough, it abuts Apache-Sitgreaves National Forests in Arizona. Rugged, mountainous terrain makes it ideal for extended and intense **backpacking** trips. Many outdoors pursuits, including **mountain biking** and **rock climbing,** await those willing to traverse this vast and little-traveled area. A variety of **hot springs** are also in the area for more relaxing agendas.

The mysterious ☐**Gila Cliff Dwellings National Monument** preserves over 40 stone and timber rooms which were carved into the cliff's natural caves by the Mogollon tribe during the late 1200s. Around a dozen families lived here for about 20 years, farming on the mesa top and along the river. During the early 14th century, the Mogollon abandoned their homes for reasons unknown, leaving the ruins as their only trace. The fact that these incredible structures have withstood the test of time speaks to the ingenuity of the people.

The trail from the parking lot enters the dwellings and allows visitors to climb replica ladders to maneuver about. Mogollon ruins are scattered throughout the area, and rangers can direct you

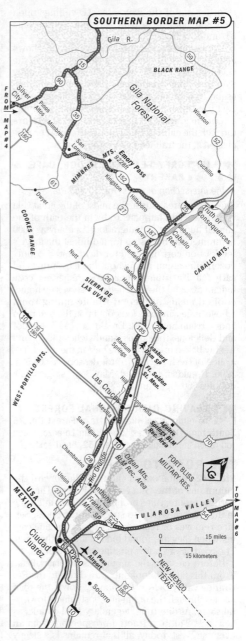

SOUTHERN BORDER MAP #5

to other out-of-the-way sites. (Dwellings open daily 8am-6pm; off-season 9am-4pm. Entrance fee $3, under 12 free.)

The **Visitors Center,** at the end of Rte. 15, shows an informative film and sells various maps of the Gila National Forest. (☎505-536-9461. Open daily 8am-6pm; off-season 8am-4:30pm.) The picturesque 1 mi. round-trip **hike** to the dwellings begins past the Upper Scorpion Campground, and rangers occasionally give short interpretive tours through the cliffs. A trail guide ($0.50) can be purchased at the trailhead or Visitors Center.

GREY FEATHERS LODGE, CAFE, & BAKERY

At the intersection of Forest Rd. 15 and Rte. 35.

This quiet retreat sits in the midst of the great Gila wilderness and happens to be in the path of the annual hummingbird migration. As many as 5000 hummingbirds may stop for a drink at the lodge's feeders on certain summer days, and a couple dozen hum about throughout the late spring and early fall. The rooms themselves are perfect, cozy hideaways, and the attached cafe serves up home-cooked meals in a comfortable dining room whose large windows look out upon the bird patio and surrounding forest. Breakfasts ($3-5) are hot and delicious; the soups, sandwiches ($5-7), and freshly baked breads are the best in the forest. Try a slice of fresh pie ($2.75) for dessert. (☎505-536-3206. Breakfast included. May-Sept. singles $40; doubles $50. Oct.-Apr. $35/$45.)

LEAVING GILA NATIONAL FOREST

To return to civilization, take **Forest Rd. 35 South** through Mimbres toward San Lorenzo. When you reach the junction with **Rte. 152,** head **east.**

THE ROAD TO T OR C

Rte. 152 climbs out of the foothills toward the mountains of the Gila National Forest. This wilderness is pure; rules prohibiting human influence in the wilderness are so strict that the Forest Service removes or tears down historic logging cabins when they are found hidden amidst the trees. The road passes a few pristine campgrounds.

Before cresting the mountains at **Emory Peak.** From this 8000 ft. lookout, gaze down to the Río Grande valley below. On its way down, the road passes through the boom-and-bust mining town of **Hillsboro.** At one time, legendary gold chunks as heavy as 240 lb. attracted prospectors from all over the West; today, all that remains is a sleepy

little downtown that could be straight out of the Andy Griffith Show. From Hillsboro, drive 17 mi. northeast along **Rte. 152** and then 11 mi. north on **I-25** to Truth or Consequences.

TRUTH OR CONSEQUENCES

In 1950, Ralph Edwards's popular radio game show "Truth or Consequences" celebrated its 10th anniversary by naming this small town, formerly Hot Springs, in its honor. Every year on the first weekend of May, residents celebrate the rechristening with a fiesta. Events include parades, rodeos, country music, high-energy drum circles, and canoe races. Day-to-day life in T or C (pronounced "TEE-er-SEE") is as quirky as one would expect from a place willing to change its name for a publicity stunt. Before the days of game shows, Geronimo and other Apaches traveled to this sacred ground, known then as "the seven Apache springs." The truth is that the area's hot mineral waters attract an eclectic sort, and an ex-drifter-turned-down-home spirit is its consequence.

(VITAL STATS)

Population: 7300

Visitor Info: Chamber of Commerce, 201 S. Foch St. (☎505-894-3536 or 800-831-9487). Open M-F 9am-5pm, Sa 9am-1pm.

Internet Access: Truth or Consequences Public Library, 325 Library Ln. (☎505-894-3027). Follow the signs from Main or 2nd St. north onto Foch St., then take a right at 3rd Ave.; the library is on the left. Open M-F 9am-7pm.

Post Office: 300 Main St. (☎505-894-0876). Open M-F 9am-3pm. **Postal Code:** 87901.

GETTING AROUND

Taking the first exit off I-25 North into T or C puts you on **Broadway.** This road becomes **Main St.** as it passes through the center of town and continues north. Downtown, Main St. runs north one-way, while the southbound traffic is diverted onto T or C's other main drag, **2nd Ave.**

SIGHTS & OUTDOORS

T or C's mineral baths are the town's main attraction; locals claim that they heal virtually everything. The only outdoor tubs are located at the

SOUTHERN BORDER

Riverbend Hostel (see p. 795), where four co-ed tubs (bathing suits required) abut the Río Grande. (Open 10am-7pm. $6 per hr. Free for hostel guests 7-10am and 7-10pm.) The **Geronimo Springs Museum** showcases exhibits on Native American history, military history, 1950s television history, and much more. The highlight of the museum is the Native American pottery collection, which is bursting with intricately designed pots in pristine condition. Another exhibit describes the different cowboy hats of the West and those who wear them. (☎505-894-6600. Open M-Sa 9am-5pm. $2, children $1.)

Five miles north of T or C, **Elephant Butte Lake State Park** features New Mexico's largest lake. A public works project dammed up the Río Grande in 1916 after the resolution of a major water rights dispute between the US and Mexico. The resulting lake is named after the elephantine rock formation at its southern end. The park offers sandy beaches for swimming and a marina for boating. There is a **Visitors Center** at the entrance of the park with a small museum on the natural history of the area. (Take Date St. north until a sign for Elephant Butte; turn right onto Rte. 181, and follow the signs. ☎877-664-7787. Open M-F 7:30am-4pm, Sa-Su 7:30am-10pm. Entrance fee $4 per vehicle.) An easy 1½ mi. **nature trail** begins in the nearby parking lot.

🍴🍽 FOOD & NIGHTLIFE

Nearly all of T or C's restaurants are as easy on the wallet as the baths are on the body. For groceries, try **Bullock's,** at the corner of Broadway and Post St. (Open M-Sa 7:30am-8pm, Su 8am-7pm.) The best non-greasy spoon in town, **Hot Springs Bakery and Cafe,** 213 Broadway, serves up excellent sub sandwiches ($5-6) and awesome salads ($5). The shaded patio seating in of the cactus garden is a peaceful place to relax with a meal or cup of coffee. (☎505-894-5555. Open Tu-Sa 8am-3pm.) John Wayne covers the walls of **La Cocina,** 1 Lake Way Dr., which features delicious New Mexican fare. Try the *chimichanga* stuffed with steak, grilled peppers, and onions. (Take Broadway all the way to the north end of town and look for the "Hot Stuff" sign. ☎505-894-6499. Entrees $7. Open daily 10:30am-10pm.) **La Hacienda,** 1615 S. Broadway, is well worth the short drive out of the center of town. *Arroz con pollo* (rice with

chicken; $7), and breakfast *chorizo con huevos* (sausage with eggs; $5) are some of the best Mexican food around. (Open Su and Tu-Sa 11am-9pm.)

Raymond's Lounge, 912 N. Date St., next to the Circle K, is T or C's rock 'n' roll bar and one of the more comfortable dives in town. (☎505-894-4057. Drafts $1.50. Free pool Th night. Open M-Sa 11am-2am, Su noon-midnight.) The **Pine Knot Saloon,** 700 E. 3rd Ave., just past the curve on 3rd St. toward Elephant Butte, is a vintage Western saloon adorned with photos of John Wayne. (☎505-894-2714. Karaoke Th night. Live music on weekends.) **The Dam Site,** just past the Elephant Butte Dam on Rte. 51, is a bar and grille with an outdoor patio, offering spectacular views of the lake and surrounding mountains. (☎505-894-2073. Entrees $7-19. Drafts $3. Live music Sa afternoon. Open Su-Th 11am-9pm, F-Sa 11am-10pm. Bar open F-Sa until midnight.)

🏠 ACCOMMODATIONS

The mineral baths in T or C add a touch of luxury to accommodations, particularly at the 🌟**Riverbend Hot Springs Hostel (HI-AYH),** 100 Austin St. How many places in the world can you live in a teepee on the banks of Río Grande and spend your days soaking in an outdoor mineral bath that overflows into the river? Riverbend is reason enough to stop in T or C, and many travelers wind up staying much longer than expected, perhaps due to daily discounts that increase with time ($2 off each night until the 3rd night). Use of the on-site mineral baths and a riverside meditation cove is free for guests. (From I-25, take Exit 79, turn right, and continue 1½ mi. to a traffic light. Turn left at the light, then immediately right onto Cedar St. and follow it down to the river and the blue building at the road's bend. ☎505-894-6183; www.nmhotsprings.com. Reception 8am-10pm. Teepees and dorms $14, nonmembers $16; private rooms $30-48; tent sites $10, nonmembers $12.)

The standard **Charles Motel and Spa,** 601 Broadway, has simple and clean accommodations, plus the bonus of free mineral baths on the premises. The large rooms have kitchenettes and A/C. (☎505-894-7154 or 800-317-4518; www.charlesspa.com. Singles $39; doubles $45.) Campsites at the **Elephant Butte Lake State Park** have access to restrooms and cold showers. (☎505-744-5421 or 877-664-7787. Sites $8-14.)

THE ROAD TO LAS CRUCES

Follow **I-25 South** out of town past the Caballo Reservoir, and exit the interstate at the **Arrey/Rte. 187** exit, one stop after the Hillsboro exit. The **Rte. 187 Scenic Byway,** which shadows I-25 South from T or C to Las Cruces, is a testament to the fertility of the Río Grande Valley; the soil provides prime farmland for all kinds of produce. The road meanders through orchards, green fields, and cropland devoted to the most famous of all New Mexico exports: the chili. During the right season, these farms offer freshly picked chilies to passersby.

HATCH. Thirty-three miles after leaving the interstate are the "village limits" of Hatch, New Mexico: **Chili Capital of the World.** Every Labor Day weekend the town celebrates its status with the **annual chili festival,** complete with two queens: one for red chilies and one for green. Aside from all the spicy revelry, Hatch provides a necessary rest stop. The **BBB Restaurant,** 316 E. Hall St., serves meals to suit every taste, from steaks to seafood, BBQ to Mexican. And, yes, they have chili. (☎ 505-267-4040. Entrees $6-8. Open Su-Tu and Th-Sa 11:30am-9pm.) After Hatch, the road changes names to Rte. 185, but the scenery stays the same.

RADIUM SPRINGS. After snaking along the Río Grande through scenic canyons, the road reaches the town of **Radium Springs,** 21 mi. from Hatch. While you'll be hard pressed to find any radium or springs here, you can find intriguing ruins at the old **Fort Selden State Monument.** The fort marks the beginning of the *jornada del muerto* (journey of death), where the era's longest highway, El Camino Real, curved away from the Río Grande and into the New Mexican desert. The fort was commissioned to protect this area in 1865 and was in operation until just before the turn of the century. Today, it features a small but excellent collection of historic military artifacts. (Open Su and Tu-Sa 8am-5pm. Period military reenactment 2nd Sa of each month. $3.) The **Leasburg Dam State Park** is right next door to the monument and offers comfortable camping. (☎ 505-534-4068. Gates locked sunset-7am; contact ranger or camp host for gate combo. Sites $8-14.)

APPROACHING LAS CRUCES

To be relieved from the "Jornada del Muerto," continue south on **Rte. 185** for 15 mi. into Las Cruces.

LAS CRUCES

Commercialized, suburban Las Cruces was probably named for the many crosses marking the graves of early pioneers to the area. Today, the major cross is formed by the intersection of I-25 and I-10. To make the most of your visit, bypass the car dealerships, strip malls, and chain motels that make up the city in favor of the historic, slightly touristy, cultural epicenter of Mesilla.

> ### VITAL STATS
>
> **Population:** 74,000
>
> **Visitor Info: Las Cruces Convention and Visitors Bureau,** 211 N. Water St. (☎ 505-541-2444). Open M-F 8am-5pm.
>
> **Internet Access: Thomas Branigan Memorial Library,** 200 E. Picacho Ave. (☎ 505-528-4000). Open M-Th 10am-9pm, F-Sa 10am-6pm, Su 1-5pm; June-July closed Su.
>
> **Post Office:** 201 E. Las Cruces Ave. **Postal Code:** 88001.

GETTING AROUND

Las Cruces is framed by **I-25** to the east and **I-10** to the south. East to west, the major north-south streets are **Telshor Blvd. (I-25), Main St.,** and **Valley Dr. Lohman Ave.** runs east-west through the city, while **University Ave.** forms the southern boundary. This road leads east to the Organ Mountains, and is the easiest route to the Mesilla plaza.

SIGHTS & OUTDOORS

Though Las Cruces is the demographic center of the area, **Mesilla,** only 3 mi. away, is the cultural center. When the US acquired the land in 1854 with the Gadsden Purchase, Mesilla became an important stop for traders and travelers en route between San Antonio and San Francisco. By the 1880s, the town was as wild as any other in the West; it was in Mesilla that Billy the Kid was tried for murder and sentenced to hang in 1881. Today, Mesilla looks much the same as it did in the 1880s, and most of the adobe buildings around the central plaza date back 150 years. While the shops are on the touristy side, the adobe-ringed plaza, presided over by the majestic **San Albino Church** (originally built in 1855), overflows with Mexican food and Old West history. (Turn right off Rte. 185 onto Avenida de Mesilla. This becomes Rte. 28 and goes under the freeway to Mesilla.)

Mary Alexander, the great-granddaughter of Billy the Kid's public defender, takes visitors on a tour of local history at the **Gadsden Museum,** on Boutz Rd. across Rte. 28 from the plaza. Exhibits include a jail cell Billy the Kid once escaped from and some objects belonging to the mysterious "hermit of La Cueva." (☎505-526-6293. Open M-Sa 9-11am and 1-5pm, Su 1-5pm. $2.)

Las Cruces has its own roadside oddity in the form of a ▧**giant roadrunner made from trash,** perched high on hillside rest stop. From the 20 ft. roadrunner, you can see the entire Las Cruces/Río Grande Valley; no wonder this was once voted New Mexico's rest stop of the year. (Take I-10 west out of Las Cruces for 5 mi. The bird can be seen from the westbound lanes, but take the next exit and turn around onto the eastbound lanes to visit the rest stop at mile marker 135.)

Las Cruces provides decent mountain biking opportunities. The **"A" Mountain Trail** is a moderately difficult ride around the base of the hill at the east end of New Mexico State University's campus. The trail takes its name from the "A" formed by the white stones that adorn the mountain's east face, which is visible from most of Las Cruces. The longer, more difficult **Sierra Vista Trail** rises into the Organ Mountains. Check with the bike shop **Outdoor Adventures,** 1424 Missouri Ave., for more info on these and other trails. (☎505-521-1922. Open M-F 10am-6pm, Sa 10am-5pm.)

▧ FOOD

Culinary options in Las Cruces revolve around fast-food and chain restaurants, but there are a number of interesting places to dine in nearby Mesilla. **La Posta,** 2410 Calle de San Albino, is in the plaza on the right as you enter Mesilla. This ancient adobe structure once housed and fed road-weary travelers from the Butterfield Trail, including such characters as Billy the Kid, Kit Carson, and Pancho Villa. You might have a harder time finding lodging these days, but La Posta still serves the finest Mexican cuisine. It doesn't get more authentic or delicious. (☎505-524-3524. Entrees $7. Open Su-Th 11am-9pm, F-Sa 11am-9:30pm.) Nearby, **El Comedor,** 2190 Avenida de Mesilla, is an understated little restaurant that serves up heaping Mexican speciality plates. Try the Doña Ana Fajitas or the Tacos al Pastor. (☎505-524-7002. Entrees $5-7. Open M-Th 8am-8pm, F-Sa 8am-9pm, Su 9am-3pm.)

If you can't make it to Mesilla to eat, **International Delights,** 1245 El Paseo, in the corner of the Albertson's shopping center, is your best bet for dining within Las Cruces. With a relaxed atmosphere, long hours, and a full selection of coffee drinks ($1-3) and sandwiches (falafel $4.50), it provides a comfortable haven away from the city's suburban sprawl. (☎505-647-5956. Open M-Th 7am-6pm, F-Sa 7am-midnight, Su 7am-10pm.)

▧ ACCOMMODATIONS

Cheap motels line **Picacho Ave.** to the west of Valley Dr. This area is not very safe at night, so be careful when walking alone. Other motels cluster around the I-10 and I-25 exits. Located in a beautifully decorated, 100-year-old adobe mansion one block west of Main St., the **Lundeen Inn of the Arts Bed and Breakfast,** 618 S. Alameda Blvd., serves as both a guest house and an art gallery, and is worth the premium price. The spacious rooms are named after area artists, and each has a private bath and A/C. (☎505-526-3327 or 888-526-3326; www.innofthearts.com. Reception 8am-10pm. Reservations required. Singles $58-64; doubles $77-85; suites with kitchen $125. AAA, AARP, and student discounts.) For a cheaper room, **Day's End Lodge,** 755 N. Valley Dr., offers accommodations with A/C, just a couple blocks from the bus station. (☎505-524-7753. Singles $25; doubles $28-33.)

▧ LEAVING LAS CRUCES

Leaving Las Cruces, **Rte. 28** picks up where Rte. 185 left off, in the dusty farm towns along the Río Grande.

▧ DETOUR: ORGAN MOUNTAINS

Drive east on U.S. 70 for 15 mi., then turn left on Aguirre Spring Rd.

East of Las Cruces, great opportunities for hiking, mountain biking, and rock climbing abound. On the western slope of the Organ Mountains, **Dripping Springs** and **La Cueva Trails,** both easy 1 mi. hikes, are accessible via Dripping Springs Rd. For more info, check at the **A.B. Cox Visitors Center.** (☎505-522-1219. Open daily until 5pm.) On the eastern slope of the Organ Mountains, Aguirre Springs is farther from Las Cruces with more challenging hiking. The **Aguirre Spring National Recre-**

ation Area is an idyllic place to pitch your tent. (☎505-525-4300. Entrance gate open daily mid-Apr. to mid-Oct. 8am-7pm; mid-Oct. to mid-Apr. 8am-6pm. Vault toilets. Water available at campground host's site. $3 per vehicle.)

THE ROAD TO EL PASO. Not far outside Mesilla, the road enters the shady glens of massive pecan orchards. Stop at **Stahmann's Country Store** to pick up some fresh pecans. (Open M-Sa 9am-6pm, Su 11am-5pm.) From here, it's just more groves and pepper fields until the highway quietly slips across the Texas border and ends at a junction with **Rte. 20.** Take Rte. 20 South through the suburbs of El Paso until it merges onto **I-85 East.** The interstate hugs barbed wire fences on the US side of the Río Grande, then becomes **Paisano St.** and travels into the heart of downtown El Paso.

Texas is in the Central Time Zone, where it is 1hr. later.

EL PASO

It's all in the name. Since it was first established in the 17th century, this Texas city has always been "the pass." Today, together with its Mexican sister, Ciudad Juárez, it provides a gateway to Mexico. Situated at the southernmost end of the Rocky Mountains, it further serves as the pass to the Río Grande, the western deserts, and the eastern Texas rangeland. Hundreds of years of passersby have left behind a city teeming with diversity. The citizens proudly promote the city's reputation as "third safest city in the US," and, whether it be a Texas t-bone steak or *carne asada* that you crave, it's a safe bet you'll like the flavor of El Paso.

▣ GETTING AROUND

While El Paso and Ciudad Juárez sprawl across the valley floor, the downtown districts of both cities are relatively small and easily navigable. **San**

Jacinto Plaza, at the corner of Main and Oregon St., is the heart of El Paso. **I-10** runs east-west through the city and intersects with north-south **U.S. 54** just east of downtown in a mess of tangled concrete fondly dubbed "the spaghetti bowl." Rte. 85 becomes **Paisano St.** as it enters downtown, and along with **San Antonio Ave.,** is the city's major east-west artery. **Santa Fe Ave., Stanton St.,** and **El Paso St.** run north-south, with El Paso St. continuing to the border crossing. Although El Paso is ranked as one of the safest cities in the US, tourists should be wary of the streets between San Antonio and the border late at night.

Parking abounds in downtown El Paso; try the Convention Center parking lot, underneath the Visitors Center. (Open daily 8am-5pm. $3.)

> **◖VITAL STATS◗**
>
> **Population:** 560,000
>
> **Visitor Info: El Paso Convention and Visitors Bureau,** 1 Civic Center Plaza (☎915-544-0062; www.visitelpaso.com), at Santa Fe and Mills Ave. in the small round building.
>
> **Mexican Consulate:** 910 E. San Antonio Ave. (☎915-533-3644), at the corner of Virginia St. Dispenses tourist cards. Open M-F 8:15am-4pm.
>
> **Currency Exchange: Valuta,** 301 E. Paisano St. (☎915-544-1152), at Mesa St. Open 24hr.
>
> **Internet Access: El Paso Public Library,** 501 N. Oregon St. (☎915-543-5433). Open M-Th 8:30am-8:30pm, F-Sa 8:30am-5:30pm, Su 1-5pm.
>
> **Post Office:** 219 E. Mills Ave., between Mesa and Stanton St. Open M-F 8:30am-5pm, Sa 8:30am-noon. **Postal Code:** 79901.

◉ ◪ SIGHTS & OUTDOORS

The **El Paso Museum of Art,** 1 Arts Festival Plaza, is one of the largest art museums in the Southwest, with over 5000 works of art inside a recently renovated building. Particularly impressive are the collections of 19th- and 20th-century Southwestern art and Mexican colonial art. (☎915-532-1707. Open Su noon-5pm, Tu-Sa 9am-5pm. Free.) Get your adrenaline rush by wandering among the 29 aircraft on display at the **War Eagles Air Museum,** on Rte. 28 at a small airport in Santa Teresa, New Mexico. Most of the planes are veterans of WWII and the Korean War. (16 mi. west of El Paso off I-10. ☎505-589-2000. Open Su and Tu-Sa 10am-4pm. $5, seniors $4, students and children free.)

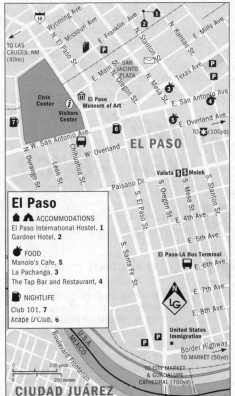

El Paso

🏠 🏕 ACCOMMODATIONS
El Paso International Hostel, **1**
Gardner Hotel, **2**

🍴 FOOD
Manolo's Cafe, **5**
La Pachanga, **3**
The Tap Bar and Restaurant, **4**

🍸 NIGHTLIFE
Club 101, **7**
Xcape D'Club, **6**

North of downtown El Paso, the **Franklin Mountains State Park** covers 24,000 acres, making it the largest urban wilderness park in the US. Flora include Yucca, Pincushion Cactus, and Barrel Cactus. Mule deer and mountain lions are among the park's diverse fauna. The park's **Visitors Center** is located in McKelligon Canyon on the east side of the Franklin Mountains. (From downtown, take Scenic Dr. east and turn left onto Alabama St. The canyon and Visitors Center are a couple of miles down on the left. Visitors Center open in summer M-F 8am-8pm. Park open June-Sept. daily 8am-8pm; Oct.-May 8am-5pm. Park entrance $3.)

The **Wyler Aerial Tramway** takes visitors to the top of Ranger Peak (5632 ft.). The third tramway of its kind in the US, it was built in 1960 to service TV and radio antennas. On a clear day, you can see 7000 sq. mi. from the top—all the way to the Guadalupe Mountains and Ruidoso, New Mexico. (On

the corner of Alabama St. and McKinley Ave. ☎915-562-9899. Open M and Th noon-6pm, F-Su noon-9pm; Last admission 1hr. before close. $7, children $4.)

There are many **hiking** routes throughout the park. Beginning from Sneed's Cory, **West Cottonwood Spring** is a 1½ mi. round-trip hike leading to a spring with an amazing view of the valley. Also from Sneed's Cory, the **North Mt. Franklin Trail** (9 mi.) is a difficult round-trip to the top of 7200 ft. Mt. Franklin. The **Aztec Caves Trail** (1¼ mi.) is a steep, 2hr. workout. (To reach the trailhead, take the 2nd right after the fee station.) One of the easier hikes in the park is **Upper Sunset** (1¼ mi.), which runs along the western edge of the mountain. The trail begins just after the fee station on the left side of the road.

The Tom Mays section of the park is a perfect setting for hiking, mountain biking, and rock climbing, and is accessible only from the west side of the Franklin Mountains.

 Some of the south's larger border crossings see hundreds of senior citizens daily making a run for the border. What do they come for? In short, the drugs. Mexican border towns often have discount pharmacies, where regular prescription drugs are not heavily taxed and are much cheaper than in the US.

🍴 FOOD

There's no shortage of good Mexican food in downtown El Paso, and prices are generally cheap. El Paso's fast-food joints cluster around **Stanton St.** and **Texas St.** Be aware that many downtown restaurants close on the weekends. Don't be scared by the dim lighting and mirrored walls at **The Tap Bar and Restaurant,** 408 E. San Antonio Ave.; this place serves excellent Mexican meals. The burritos ($1.75-4), enchiladas ($4.25), and grilled shrimp in garlic ($9) are delicious. (☎915-532-1848. Open M-Sa 7am-2am, Su noon-2am.) For cheap food in a spartan setting, try **Manolo's Cafe,** 122 S. Mesa St., between Overland and San Antonio Ave. *Menudo* ($2), burritos ($1), and generous lunch specials ($4) are standard fare. (☎915-532-7661. Open M-Sa 7am-5pm, Su 7:30am-3pm.) **La Pachanga,** 222 Texas Ave., between and Stanton St., sells fine sandwiches and excellent fruit smoothies for $2-3. (☎915-544-4454. Open M-Sa 8am-5pm.)

ACCOMMODATIONS

El Paso offers safer, more appealing places to stay than Ciudad Juárez. Several good budget hotels can be found downtown, near Main St. and San Jacinto Sq. Built in the 1920s, the **Gardner Hotel,** 311 E. Franklin, between Stanton and Kansas St., is the oldest continually operating hotel in El Paso. Since 1922, this small, classy joint has housed weary travelers in the center of downtown; John Dillinger stayed here in 1934. Make calls from a wooden phone booth and take the cage elevator up from the ornate lobby. (☎915-532-3661; www.gardnerhotel.com. Singles $20; doubles $30; rooms with private baths from $40.) Located inside the hotel, the **El Paso International Hostel,** 311 E. Franklin, is the best budget accommodation in El Paso. The hostel takes great pride in meeting the needs of backpackers, offering clean, four-bed, single-sex rooms with a full kitchen and a large lounge. (☎915-532-3661. HI, HA, ISIC, student ID, or teacher ID required. Laundry. Linen $2. Towels $0.50. Check-out 10am. Dorms $14, nonmembers $15.)

Camping is available in the **Franklin Mountains State Park.** Due to the campground's proximity to the city, campers should guard belongings and take safety precautions. (☎915-566-6441. Reservations recommended. Primitive tent sites $8.)

NIGHTLIFE

Most nightlife seekers follow the younger drinking age across the border to Ciudad Juárez. Still, there remain several viable options north of the Río Grande. **Club 101,** 500 San Francisco, is El Paso's oldest club, drawing a vibrant crowd with its three dance floors and party scene. (☎915-544-2101. W-F 18+, Sa 21+. Cover $5. Open W-Sa 9pm-3am.) **Xcape D'club,** 209 S. El Paso St., sits downtown in a beautifully restored theater and caters to a chic crowd. (☎915-542-3800. Open F-Sa 9pm-2am.)

LEAVING EL PASO
From El Paso, head north on **U.S. 54** to return to New Mexico.

THE ROAD TO ALAMOGORDO

The lonely 87 mi. stretch from El Paso to Alamogordo remains as untamed, uncivilized, and unbelievably empty as it was in the days of cowboys.

The only break in the flat monotony of the road is the busted mining town of **Orogrande,** existing today only as a gas station strategically placed to save the lives of those who forgot to fill up in El Paso. Nearing Alamogordo, the highway hugs the giant cliffs of the **Sacramento Mountains,** which stand like a stratospheric wall at the desert's edge.

 Back in New Mexico, you're back in the Mountain Time Zone, where it is 1hr. earlier than in Texas.

OLIVER LEE MEMORIAL STATE PARK
10 mi. south of Alamogordo on U.S. 54.

Perched at the mouth of a vast canyon at the edge of the Sacramento Mountains, the Oliver Lee Memorial State Park provides a panoramic view of the canyon and the desert below. Those up for a challenge should think about trekking at least a half-mile up the mountain's face on the ludicrously steep **Dog Canyon Trail** (5½ mi. round-trip) to behold an astonishing vista of the Tularosa Basin all the way to the White Sand dunes. The park has excellent camping facilities with clean showers. (☎505-437-8284. Visitors Center open daily 9am-4pm. Tent sites $10. Hookup $14.)

ALAMOGORDO

Alamogordo is Spanish for "fat poplar," a fitting description for this moderately sized community at the crossroads of many of the region's attractions. Just as the area's poplar trees suck up water flowing down from the nearby Sacramento Mountains, Alamogordo gorges itself on funds from the region's military bases and passing tourists. U.S. 70 passes straight through downtown with the name of **White Sands Blvd.** fast-food and budget motels abound along this main drag.

A down-home Mexican restaurant, **Ramona's,** 2913 N. White Sands Blvd., is a local place where many patrons order "the usual." Ramona's is worth the visit just for the fresh chips and fiery ground jalapeño salsa. Try the *carne asada* ($10) or the *chimichanga* plate for $6.50. (☎505-432-7616. Breakfast $4. Lunch and dinner $6-10. Open M-Sa 6am-10pm, Su 7am-10pm.) **Pepper's Grill,** 3200 N. White Sands Blvd., defies classification, with a menu that ranges from bruschetta to nachos to *escargot*. Their salads are excellent. (☎505-437-9717. Lunch $6. Dinner $12. Open M-Sa 11am-2pm and 5-9pm.) **Maximinos,** 2300 N. White Sands Blvd., has breakfast burritos for $2.50; their popular chicken *mole* goes for $6. (☎505-443-6102. Open Tu-Sa 8am-2pm and 5-9pm, Su 8am-3pm.) Affordable lodging is rare—due to the steady influx of tourists, hotels in the area are able to get away with charging more than their rooms are worth. Of the slew of motels, the **Western Motel,** 1101 S. White Sands Blvd., is standard and the most conveniently located. (On the east side of the road as you enter Alamogordo on U.S. 70 North. ☎505-437-2922. Rooms $40-65; in low season $32-38.) The plain rooms of the **Alamo Inn,** 1450 N. White Sands Blvd., have A/C. (☎505-437-1000. Outdoor pool. Singles $26; doubles $35.) For more information, consult the **Alamogordo Chamber of Commerce,** 1301 N. White Sands Blvd. (☎505-437-6120. Open daily 9am-5pm.) **The Lincoln National Forest Office,** 1101 New York Ave. (☎505-434-7200), provides info on hiking or camping trips in the Sacramento Mountains. (Open M-F 7:30am-4:30pm.) **Outdoor Adventures,** 1516 10th St. (☎505-434-1920), rents bikes and offers advice on where to ride in the area. (Bikes $20-25 per day. Open M-F 10am-6pm, Sa 10am-5pm.)

LEAVING ALAMOGORDO
From White Sands Blvd., head west on **U.S. 82/ 70.** The entrance to the monument will be on your right.

WHITE SANDS NATIONAL PARK & MONUMENT

Perhaps the world's greatest beach, minus the water, the white gypsum sands of the White Sands National Monument evoke awe both for their purity and for their bleakness. The Tularosa Basin, bordered by the Sacramento and San Andres Mountains, lacks any outlet to the sea, so rainwater collects at the low point, known as Lake Lucero. As the desert heat evaporates the lake, gypsum crystals collect on the dry bed, and are swept away by the wind, transforming into blindingly white sand that collects as dunes. In these forboding and treacherous conditions only a few highly adaptive species can survive. The translucent white lizards and super-fast-growing plants are nearly as astounding as the dunes themselves.

GETTING AROUND. The **Dunes Drive** is the best way to enjoy the park. Beginning at the Visitors Center, the scenic road (16 mi. round-trip) winds from the edge of the dunes to the **Heart of the Sands.** Exhibits along the way provide information about geology and natural history.

OUTDOOR ACTIVITIES. Not to be outdone by more aqueous beaches, the most popular activity at White Sands is **sand surfing** (though careening down the incredibly steep sides of 25 ft. dunes via sled is more akin to tobogganing than surfing).

THE LOCAL STORY

STARS AND WARS

This region of the country is known for its pivotal role in the development of weapons of mass destruction. Sixty-five miles northwest of Alamogordo, the Trinity Site was the location of the world's first atomic bomb detonation on July 16, 1945. The heat of the explosion caused the desert sand to melt and form a green glass dubbed Trinitite. The Alamogordo Chamber of Commerce (☎800-826-0294) organizes two tours of the area annually. You can see a collection of the still-radioactive Trinitite at the New Mexico Museum of Space History, 3198 Rte. 2001, which has exhibits about the atomic history of the area as well as an outstanding collection of space memorabilia. The building's architecture is as otherworldly as its exhibits—the giant five-story golden cube situated on the hillside provides an excellent view of the Tularosa Basin, where the White Sands Missile Base continues to be the premier facility for top-secret flight and weapons testing.

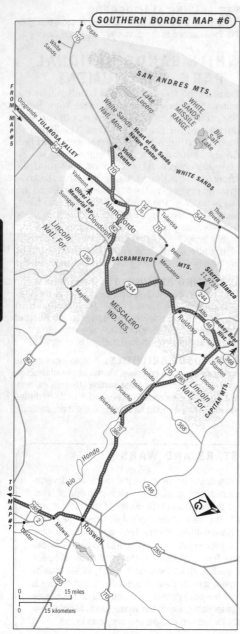

SOUTHERN BORDER MAP #6

Roadies who left their sleds at the chalet might be interested in monthly **auto caravans** across the open dunes to Lake Lucero. (Advance reservations required; contact the Visitors Center for more information.) The **Interdune Boardwalk** (¼ mi.) carves an easy route above the sands, while the strenuous **Alkali Flat Trail** (4½ mi.) loops from the **Heart of the Sands** to the edge of the salty lakebed of Lake Otero. Off-trail hiking is permitted anywhere along the eastern edge of the park. On **full moon nights** in the summer, the park stays open late (until 11pm; last entrance 10pm). During the **Perseid Meteor Shower** (usually the 2nd week of Aug.), the park remains open until midnight.

> ### VITAL STATS
>
> **Area:** 144,000 acres
>
> **Visitor Info: Visitors Center** (☎ 505-479-6124; www.nps.gov/whsa), on U.S. 82/70, 15 mi. from Alamogordo. Distributes sought-after camping permits. Visitors Center open June-Aug. daily 8am-7pm; Sept.-May 8am-5pm. Park open daily June-Aug. 7am-10pm; Sept.-May 7am-sunset.
>
> **Gateway town:** Point of Sands.
>
> **Fees:** Entrance $3, under 16 free.

⚑ CAMPING. There are no established campgrounds available in the park, but 10 daily permits to camp at the primitive backcountry campsites are available on a first-come, first-served basis ($3 per person). The sites have no water or toilet facilities and are not accessible by road, requiring up to a 2 mi. hike through the sand dunes. Campers must register in person at the Visitors Center and be in their sites before dark. Sleeping amidst the white dunes can be a rewarding experience, but plan ahead, as sites fill up early on full moon nights. Camping, like the rest of the park, is subject to closure during the frequent missile tests on the White Sands Missile Range.

⚐ LEAVING WHITE SANDS NATIONAL PARK

From the park, head east on **U.S. 82/70.** Pass back through Alamogordo and head off to Cloudcroft.

THE ROAD TO CLOUDCROFT

After leaving the outskirts of Alamogordo and passing eclectic establishments like a pistachio farm and a rattlesnake kennel, the road begins the 16 mi. ascent toward the town of Cloudcroft. The twisty-turny road winds its way up 4312 ft. in these 16 mi., so be extra careful and turn your lights to be safe. Halfway up the mountain, the road passes through **New Mexico's only tunnel.** Stop just before this subterranean corridor at the tunnel vista turnout to enjoy an excellent view and discover a local secret; at the bottom of the steep hike down the canyon wall are rope swings and **seasonal swimming holes.**

Entering Cloudcroft, notice the old tressels in the gorges; these are remnants of the 19th-century tourist railroad that transported the summer's overheated Texans from El Paso to Cloudcroft along one of the steepest railroads in the world. The railways are accessible via the trails that stem from the highways (look for the signs).

CLOUDCROFT

Perched above 9000 ft., this mountaintop village is in a drastically different environment than the desert valley below. The "playland of the four seasons" lures visitors with a climate ranging from snowy flurries to breezy summer days.

In the pricey **Lodge Hotel** (☎800-395-6343), **Rebecca's** is named for the hotel's ghost, who must be sticking around for the food. The stately dining room serves affordable five-star meals, with excellent fish and steak selection. (Take the first right entering Cloudcroft on U.S. 82 East. ☎505-682-2526. Breakfast $6. Lunch $7-10. Dinner $20. Open daily 7-10:30am, 11am-2:30pm, 5:30-9pm.) The premier budget accommodation in town is the **Cloudcroft Mountain Park Hostel,** 1049 U.S. 82. This relatively new hostel stands on 27 acres adjacent to the Lincoln National Forest and has a living room, kitchen, and large front porch. (5 mi. west of town between mile markers 10 and 11. ☎505-682-0555. Dorms $17; private rooms $34.) The **Aspen Motel,** 1315 U.S. 82, features recently remodeled rooms nestled into the woodland hillside. (On the right leaving Cloudcroft on U.S. 82 East. ☎505-682-2526. Singles $55; doubles $60.) Camping opportunities abound among the majestic pines of the Lincoln National Forest. The **Apache Campground** is 3 mi. northeast of Cloudcroft along Rte. 244, and offers developed sites with hot showers and many cross-country ski trails. (Sites $11.) On private land just down the road, the **Silverlake Campground** boasts developed camping, flush toilets, hot showers on the shores of a pretty pond, and fishing. (Sites $10. Fishing permit $10.)

LEAVING CLOUDCROFT
The junction with **Rte. 244** is 1 mi. east of Cloudcroft. Rte. 244 wanders northeast through pine groves and open meadows, eventually intersecting with U.S. 70. To get to Ruidoso, head east along **U.S. 70** until it intersects with Rte. 48. Take **Rte. 48 West** into town.

MESCALERO INDIAN RESERVATION
Just outside Lincoln National Forest, south of Ruidoso on U.S. 70.

In addition to a large casino just outside of Ruidoso, the Mescalero Apache tribe runs a premier quarter horse racetrack and a world-class ski resort. The tribe's heritage includes famous warriors Geronimo and Cochise, and the Mescalero proudly celebrate their legacy. The tribe generously welcomes visitors during the traditional dances and feasts of the annual **Apache Maiden Puberty Rites Celebration,** (July 4). While the celebrations are extraordinary, they are not intended merely as entertainment, so before going contact the **Mescalero Cultural Center** (☎505-464-4494) regarding proper behavior.

APPROACHING RUIDOSO
The first part of Rte. 48 is called **Sudderth Dr.** and runs east-west splitting off from U.S. 70. About a mile down Sudderth Dr., Rte. 48 turns onto **Mechem Dr.,** which runs north-south through downtown Ruidoso.

RUIDOSO

During the summer months and ski season, West Texas twangs fill the streets of Ruidoso, the premier summer and winter resort destination in southern New Mexico, turning this mountain hideaway into a bustling tourist hub. Towering at 12,000 ft., the peak of Sierra Blanca looms over Ruidoso's sprawl of expensive hotels and cabins. Whatever you do, do not leave town without taking the scenic drive up ▧**Sierra Blanca.** The 12 mi., 11,000 ft. ascent offers views that only birds wouldn't envy. Switchbacks snake their way through pine forests and aspen groves up to the Windy Point Vista, where you can stare hundreds of miles eastward. Those fit enough to handle a very demanding uphill climb through thin air should take the **Lincoln National Forest Scenic Trail,** which departs from just outside the Ski Apache valley and connects with the crest trail; it takes you above the tree line to wildflower meadows at the mountain's summit. After 3 mi., hikers are rewarded with a 360°

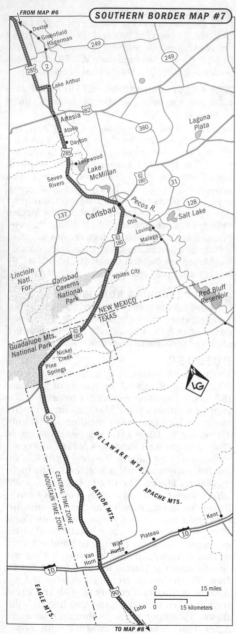

panorama that encompasses everything from Mexico to White Sands to Texas. It's the best view on the trip. (Follow the signs for skiing and recreation that point you up a mountain road just outside Ruidoso on Rte. 48.)

Weber's Grill at Pub 48, 441 Mechem Dr., serves up Italian specialities as well as steaks and chops in a mountain lodge atmosphere, complete with roaring hearth. They hand-craft their own brews to go with the wood-fired pizzas. (☎505-257-9559. 10in. pizza $6.50. Entrees $6-16. Open Su-M and W-Sa 11am-9pm.) A lively twenty-something crowd enjoys pool, video games, and 16 beers on tap at **Farley's,** 1200 Mechem Dr. By day, Farley's is a family restaurant serving burgers, hot dogs, chicken strips, and fajitas. By night it becomes a happening bar where the beer selection is only rivaled by the huge tequila list. (☎505-258-5676. Entrees around $8. Open M-Th 11:30am-midnight, F-Sa 11:30am-1am, Su 11am-11:30pm.) During the peak summer and winter seasons, it is difficult to find an affordable room in town. A few budget motels can be found along U.S. 70, but most of the action is on Rte. 48. **The Arrowhead Motel,** 616 U.S. 70, west of town, has standard conveniently located rooms. The prices are at the low end for Ruidoso—it's up, up, and away from there. (☎888-547-6652; www.ruidoso.net/arrowhead. Singles $49; doubles $59.)

BILLY THE KID SCENIC BYWAY. Continuing northeast down **Rte. 48,** the road maneuvers its way out of the lush pine slopes and into less vegetated foothills. Eighteen miles outside of Ruidoso sits the tiny hamlet of **Capitan.** From here, the route continues with a right onto **U.S. 380 East.**

SMOKEY THE BEAR STATE PARK
To the left of the U.S. 380 junction with Rte. 48.

The quaint log cabin at the Smokey the Bear State Park displays a large collection of Smokey memorabilia from throughout the ages. The original Smokey the Bear is actually buried on the grounds, within view of the mountain where he was found in May of 1950, orphaned by a raging fire in the Lincoln National Forest. After the badly burnt black bear cub healed, he was sent to the National Zoo in Washington, D.C., where he became the spokes-bear for preventing forest fires. (☎505-354-2748. Open daily 9am-5pm. $1, children $0.50.)

LINCOLN. U.S. 380 winds its way southeast through the canyons and valleys that were once the home of the historic Lincoln cattle empire and the setting of a tumultuous history. The town of Lincoln, first settled in the 1850s after US forces quieted Apache raiders, put the wild in Wild West. Its inhabitants, including the infamous William H. Bonney (a.k.a. Billy the Kid), were so lawless that from 1876 to 1879 the area erupted in intra-county combat known as the "Lincoln County War." As a result, many of the outlaws and vigilantes lie in the cemetery on the east side of town. The town's buildings have been maintained in close-to-original state, and historical placards tell a bit of each site's story. Five of the buildings are open to the public and feature museum-quality exhibits preserving the Lincoln of yore. (Open daily 8am-4:30pm. $3.50; combination ticket $6.) There is also a **Visitors Center** on the far side of town with a comprehensive museum. (☎ 505-653-4025. Open daily 8:30am-4pm.)

APPROACHING ROSWELL
Ten miles southeast along **U.S. 380**, the road merges with **U.S. 70 East.** The 47 mi. drive to Roswell meanders down into open rangeland that is so flat, empty, and endless that it leaves you missing even the humble cacti of the deserts.

ROSWELL

With flying saucers atop fast-food joints, street lamps peering over cars with painted-on eyes, and extra-terrestrial fever burning in the crowds of visitors, it seems that aliens *have* invaded Roswell. As the story goes, in July of 1947, a rancher on the outskirts of town found debris from an unidentified source on his property. The military got wind of the find, investigated, and reported in an official Army press release that a "flying saucer" had crash-landed in Roswell, only to retract this statement the next day and claim that the mysterious wreckage was really a weather balloon. Since then, there have been stories involving alien autopsies, whisperings of elaborate cover-ups, and even a formal denial by the military that anything out of the ordinary happened in this dusty New Mexican town. Aside from the few otherworldly blocks of downtown, life in Roswell is surprisingly sleepy. Aliens do not land on every corner, and there is disappointingly little spacecraft debris littering the highways into town.

VITAL STATS

Population: 45,000

Visitor Info: Roswell Chamber of Commerce, 131 W. 2nd St. (☎ 877-849-7679; www.roswellnm.org). Open M-F 8am-5pm.

Internet Access: Roswell Public Library, 301 N. Pennsylvania Ave. (☎ 505-622-7101). Open M-Tu 9am-9pm, W-Sa 9am-6pm, Su 2-6pm.

Post Office: 5904 South Main St. (☎ 505-347-2262). **Postal Code:** 88203

GETTING AROUND. U.S. 70/U.S. 380 runs through the middle of town, with main intersections at **Sycamore Ave., Union Ave., Main St. (U.S. 285),** and **Atkinson Ave. (Rte. 93).** The main streets parallel to the highway are **Country Club Rd., College Blvd.,** and **8th St.** to the north, and **McGaffey St., Poe St.,** and **Brasher Rd.** to the south. Numbered streets begin a bit south of the highway and ascend heading north. Roswell boasts some close encounters of the natural kind, with a large park and trail system that runs parallel to **2nd St.**

SIGHTS. If you're convinced that the truth *is* out there, start looking at the **International UFO Museum,** 114 N. Main St., at the corner of 2nd St. This museum is the centerpiece of Roswell's UFO-oriented downtown. Surprisingly no-nonsense, it displays timelines, photographs, signed affidavits, and newspaper clippings from the historic incident. (☎ 505-625-9495. Open daily 9am-5pm. Free.) Across the street at 204 N. Main St., the **Internation UFO Research Center's** owner Roger Florey greets visitors with evidence on the transmutational properties of spacecraft, details on cattle mutilations, stories of unmarked choppers, and good old-fashioned government conspiracies. (☎ 505-623-2565. Usually open daily 7am-3pm. Free.)

FOOD. The space-themed **Crash Down Diner,** 106 W. 4th St., serves up galactic goodies at down-to-earth prices. A "hungry alien" sub ($3-5) will satisfy any starving species, while the "unidentified burger" ($4) screams "take me to your stomach." (On the other side of the parking lot from the UFO museum, next to Starchilds. ☎ 505-627-5533. Open daily 8:30am-6pm.) **Cattle Baron,** 1112 N. Main St., is famous across New Mexico for its steaks ($14-20). The pasta, chicken, and fish are superb as well. (☎ 505-622-2465. Open M-Th 11am-9:30pm, F-Sa 11am-10pm, Su 11am-9pm.)

SOUTHERN BORDER

ACCOMMODATIONS. Definitely the best place to "crash" in Roswell, the recently remodeled rooms in the **Budget Inn West,** 2200 W. 2nd St., all come with refrigerators and access to the pool and hot tub. (On the right as you enter town from U.S. 70 East. ☎800-806-7030. Singles $25-37; doubles $31-45.) Nearby, the **Belmont Hotel,** 2100 W. 2nd St., may be a little run-down, but it is definitely the cheapest place to stay in Roswell. Though the rooms are not spotless, the sheets and bathrooms are clean and each room comes with refrigerator and microwave. (☎505-623-4522. Singles $20-27; doubles $30-39.) The **Bottomless Lakes State Park,** Union Ave., boasts camping along the edges of seven pristine lakes that formed when limestone caves collapsed and filled with water. (12 mi. east of Roswell on U.S. 70/U.S. 380; head south on Rte. 409. ☎505-624-6058. Visitors Center open daily June-Aug. 9am-6pm; Sept.-May 8am-5pm. Tent sites $10, full hookups $18.)

LEAVING ROSWELL
Drive south on **Main St.** Just after McGaffey St., merge onto **U.S. 285 South.** This turn is easy to miss; if you end up at the Roswell Industrial Air Park, you've gone too far. U.S. 285 traverses miles of dull, empty flat rangeland. After 27 mi. of nothingness, take a left turn onto **Rte. 557,** heading east toward the microscopic town of Lake Arthur.

THE SHRINE OF THE MIRACLE TORTILLA
Head south on Rte. 2 in town. Take the last possible turn in Lake Arthur off Rte. 2 South onto the unmarked Broadway Rd. The Rubio's pinkish-brown house is the 2nd on the left, across from the Catholic church and near the corner of Kansas St. If you can't find it, try asking for help at the town's general store.

Lake Arthur is famous for the Shrine of the Miracle Tortilla. The miraculous appearance of Jesus Christ's image in 1977 on a flour tortilla in the Rubio household set the standard for miracle sightings. The miniature image of Christ immediately attracted thousands of pilgrims, and prompted the Rubios to build a small shrine for the tortilla in a shed in their backyard. In the years that have followed, the image of Jesus has appeared in unlikely places all over the country. The Shrine of the Miracle Tortilla, however, is the original. While years under the desert sun have baked the image almost beyond recognition, a picture of it in all its glory is mounted nearby.

APPROACHING ARTESIA
Continue down **Rte. 2** and merge back onto **U.S. 285,** heading toward the considerably less holy city of Artesia.

ARTESIA
There is a sizable amount of money in the small city of Artesia. The refineries outside town give away the source of the wealth: oil. Even the name of the town comes from the nearby Artesian oil wells. Artesia has used its petroleum-produced pocket change to revitalize the downtown district. The town has built a fanciful **Heritage Walkway,** where its history is documented via a series of murals and fountains on the 2nd block of Main St.; follow the blue river sidewalk.

NO WORK, ALL PLAY

OUT OF THIS WORLD

Whether or not an aliens landed in the desert outside of Roswell in 1947, the town experiences a real-life invasion each July for the **UFO Festival.** The four-day celebration brings 20,000 people for lectures, alien costume contests, UFO plays, and rocketry classes. Alien experts participate each year, sharing their knowledge with the masses. Celebrities from science-fiction TV shows and movies, often in costume, sign almost as many autographs as the sci-fi authors that are also present. Alien-themed TV pilots and documentaries are also screened. Planetarium shows, telescope viewings, an Alien Chase Run-Walk, and a Close Encounters Night parade round off the entertainment. Some visitors are believers, while others are vehement skeptics, and some are just eager to see what the fuss is about—whatever the motivation, the festival is worth the stop. (Contact the International UFO Museum for more information regarding this year's festival. ☎505-625-9495.)

On the left as you enter town, the **Visitors Center,** 107 N. 1st. St., has info and hosts the **Dairy Museum,** which is dedicated to Artesia's other main export. (☎505-746-2744. Open M-F 9am-5pm.) The **Wellhead Restaurant,** 332 W. Main St., has everything an oil tycoon could want. Its sandwiches, country-fried steak, catfish, and salads are all tasty. Try the homemade brews ($3.50) made at the on-site microbrewery. (☎606-746-0640. Entrees $10-13. Open daily 11am-2pm and 5-9pm. Pub open M-Sa 11am-midnight, Su 11am-10pm.) The **La Fonda Restaurant,** 210 W. Main St., is a local favorite offering Mexican specialties as well as more alternative fare. The large burrito plates ($4.75) are classic options, while Indian tacos ($7.50) and bread bowls filled with apple-almond chicken salad ($5.75) are more exotic. (☎505-746-9377. Open daily 11am-9pm.) On the way out of town, the **Starlite Motel,** 1018 S. 1st St., offers recently remodeled rooms with refrigerators. (☎505-746-9834. Continental breakfast included. Reservations required. Singles $36; doubles $45.)

APPROACHING CARLSBAD
From Artesia, Carlsbad lies 35 mi. south on **Rte. 285,** which is **1st St.** in Artesia. The city of Carlsbad stands at the intersection of U.S. 62/180 and U.S. 285. Pierce St. (U.S. 285) enters town from the north and becomes Canal St. (U.S. 62/180), which becomes National Parks Hwy. as it leaves town to the south.

CARLSBAD

In 1899, townsfolk decided to name their riverside agricultural settlement Carlsbad after the Karlsbad Spa in the modern Czech Republic, hoping to attract tourists to the area's natural springs. In a weird twist of fate, their wish came true when the splendors of ⊠**Carlsbad Caverns** became widely known in the 1920s. Carlsbad is a fairly dull city, but it makes a good base for exploring the area. The Pecos River parallels Canal St. to the east, and the pleasant trails, fishing, and swimming opportunities along the river can be accessed via **Church St.** For more tourist info, contact the **Chamber of Commerce,** 302 S. Canal St. (☎505-887-6516. Open M 9am-5pm, Tu-F 8am-5pm, Sa 9am-4pm.) Info for the Caverns can be found at the **National Park Service Information Center,** 3225 National Parks Hwy. (☎505-885-5554. Open June-Aug. daily 8am-4:30pm; Sept.-May M-F 8am-4:30pm.) For

Internet access, go to the **Carlsbad Public Library,** 101 S. Halagueno St. (☎505-885-6776. Open M-Th 10am-8pm, F-Sa 10am-6pm, Su 2-6pm.)

Rules and helpful hints abound in the **No Whiner Diner,** 1801 S. Canal St., a classic roadside stop. The menu suggests you tell your waitress what kind of bread you want because "she can't read minds," while the sign out front gives civic advice: "bad officials are elected by good citizens who don't vote." Keep from whining, and you'll enjoy huge dinner plates, pastas, or sandwiches. (On the west side of Canal St. in front of the Stagecoach Inn. ☎505-239-2815. Entrees $8.50. Open Tu-Th 11am-2pm and 5-8pm, F-Sa 11am-2pm and 5-9pm.) South of downtown, the budget accommodations at the **Great Western Inn & Suites,** 3804 National Parks Hwy., are Carlsbad's best combination of price and quality. The rooms are large and comfortable, and are located conveniently close to the park. (☎800-987-5535. Singles $31; doubles $41.) The **Driftwood Motel,** 844 S. Canal St., boasts the cheapest respectable accommodations in town. Rooms are a bit cramped, but are neat and clean. (☎505-887-6522. Singles $28-34; doubles $40-45.)

WHITE'S CITY

Twenty miles south of Carlsbad on U.S 62/180, right outside the national park entrance, lies White's City, though the area would be more aptly named "Best Western's Tourist Trap." The hotel chain owns just about everything in "town," including the three hotels, RV park, general store, and museum. White's City has no real populace, aside from the tourists who stay rather than seeking out cheaper digs in Carlsbad or the more serene camping in the Guadalupe Mountains.

The **Million Dollar Museum,** 17 Carlsbad Caverns Hwy., under the grocery store, is a collection of antiques from the 19th and 20th centuries. The highlights are four grotesque skulls and two mummies believed to be of ancient natives. (☎505-785-2291. Open daily 7am-9pm. $3, children $2.)

CARLSBAD CAVERNS NATIONAL PARK

Imagine the surprise of European explorers in southeastern New Mexico at the turn of the century when 250,000 bats appeared at dusk, seemingly out of nowhere. Following the swarm led to the discovery of the Carlsbad Caverns, and by 1923, colonies of tourists competed with the bats for space in the caves. Today, Carlsbad Caverns National Park contains one of the world's largest and oldest known cave systems. Even the most experienced spelunker will be struck by its phenomenal geological formations.

> ### (VITAL STATS)
>
> **Area:** 47,000 acres
>
> **Visitor Info: Visitors Center** (☎505-785-2232 or 800-967-2283; www.nps.gov/cave). Open daily June to mid-Aug. 8am-7pm; late Aug. to May 8am-5:30pm. **Natural entrance** open daily June to mid-Aug. 8:30am-3:30pm; mid-Aug. to May 8:30am-2pm. **Big Room** open daily June to mid-Aug. 8:30am-5pm; mid-Aug. to May 8:30am-3:30pm.
>
> **Gateway town:** Carlsbad (p. 807)
>
> **Fees:** Entrance $6, ages 6-15 $3. Audio tour $3.

⚲ GETTING AROUND. To check out the oft-forgotten topside land in the park, the only way to go is the **Desert Drive** (a.k.a the Walnut Canyon Drive). This is a 9½ mi. one-way auto tour on dirt roads (passable to all vehicles). A road guide is available at the beginning of the road (½ mi. from the Visitors Center). The guide mostly points out plant features and the above-ground geology of the park. The road offers excellent views of the basin below the park, and follows a creek bed back to the main road.

◙ ⚲ SIGHTS & OUTDOORS. The guided **King's Palace Tour** passes through four of the cave's lowest rooms and some of the most awesome anomalies. (1½hr. Tours every hr. 9-11am and 1-3pm. $8, ages 6-15 $4. Reservations required.) Other guided tours in the Big Room include a lantern tour though the Left Hand Tunnel ($7) and a climbing tour of the Lower Cave (M-F; $20). Plan your visit for late afternoon to catch the magnificent **bat flight.** The spectacle, during which an enormous cloud of hungry bats storms out of the cave at a rate of 6000 bats per min., is preceded by a ranger talk. (May-Oct. daily just before sunset.)

Tours of the undeveloped **Slaughter Canyon Cave** offer a more rugged spelunking experience. The parking lot is 23 mi. down Rte. 418, an unpaved road, several miles south of the park's main entrance on U.S. 62/180. The cave entrance is a steep, strenuous half mile from the lot. Ranger-led tours traverse difficult terrain; there are no paved trails or handrails. (2hr. Tours; June-Aug. 2 per day; Sept.-May Sa-Su only. $15, ages 6-15 $7.50.

Call the Visitors Center at least 2 days ahead to reserve. Bring a flashlight.) Tours of **Hall of the White Giant** and **Spider Cave** require crawling and climbing through tight passages. These tours are not for claustrophobes. (4hr. 1 per week. $20. Call at least a month in advance to reserve.)

Backcountry hiking is permitted above ground, but a free permit, a map, and massive quantities of water are required.

⚲ ⚲ ACCOMMODATIONS & CAMPING. **Stage Coach In,** 1819 S. Canal St., in Carlsbad, is the best of the budget motels with an outdoor pool, indoor jacuzzi, and laundry. Comfortable, clean rooms have A/C, and refrigerators. (☎505-887-1148. Singles $40; doubles $47. 15% AAA and AARP discount.)

Backcountry camping is allowed in Carlsbad National Park, but a free permit is required. The best option is to travel 32 mi. south on Hwy. 180 to **Guadalupe Mountains National Park,** where developed sites are available for $8. Alternatively, since Carlsbad Caverns has no established campgrounds, many visitors pay to pitch a tent in the **Carlsbad RV Park and Campground,** 4301 National Parks Hwy., 4 mi. south of town. (☎888-885-6333; www.reservations.nps.gov for reservations. Tent sites $14.50; tepees $22; 2 cabins with a full-size bed, 2 bunk beds, and A/C $30.)

THE TEXAS MOUNTAIN TRAIL

Travel 32 mi. south on **Rte. 180** to reach Guadalupe Mountains National Park. Known on this stretch as the Texas Mountain Trail, Rte. 180 weaves through the shadows of the looming Guadalupe Mountains as it descends to the desert valley below. From a picnic area 4 mi. southwest of the Visitors Center, behold the monolithic El Capitan peak thrusting out from the heart of the mountains like the bow of a colossal ship. The park's most famous feature, this 2000 ft. high cliff was formed by a Permian-aged limestone reef deposit. In fact, it was primarily due to these ancient fossil reefs that the area was designated a national park in 1972. Fossils abound in Texas hill country, and are the source of the area's famous oil supply.

GUADALUPE MOUNTAINS NATIONAL PARK

The Guadalupe Mountains are the highest and most remote of the major west Texas ranges. The peaks are remnants of the ancient Capitan reef that formed 225 million years ago along the edge of a vast inland sea and covered much of what is now western Texas and southeastern New Mexico. After the sea receded, the reef was buried under layers of sediment until major block faulting and erosion excavated and exposed the petrified remains 26 million years ago. Hikers in the high Guadalupes are thus treading on the same rock layer that forms the underground Carlsbad caverns. Guadalupe Mountains National Park accommodates a particularly wide variety of flora and fauna. Drivers can glimpse the park's most dramatic sights from U.S. 62/180: El Capitan, a 2000 ft. high limestone cliff; and Guadalupe Peak, the highest point in Texas at 8749 ft.

VITAL STATS

Area: 86,500 acres.

Visitor Info: Headquarters Visitor Center (☎915-828-3251; www.nps.gov/gumo), in Pine Springs, is accessible by U.S. 62/180 between Carlsbad and El Paso. Open daily 8am-4:30pm.

Gateway town: Pine Springs.

Fees: Weekly entrance pass $3. Park campsites $8. Free permit required for backcountry camping.

DRIVING TOUR. Beautiful roadside vistas notwithstanding, the Guadalupe Mountains National Park isn't car-friendly. The road to McKittrick Canyon Visitors Center **is the only paved road that strays far from U.S. 180. The Williams Ranch Rd.** ventures deepest into the park, but this trail has soft sands and rocky sections that are only passable by 4x4, high-ground-clearance vehicles. The 7¼ mi. journey lies behind two locked gates, the keys to which may be checked out free of charge at the Visitors Center. The desert trail ends in Bone Canyon at the historic Williams Ranchhouse.

HIKING. The path from Pine Springs to the McKittrick Canyon Visitors Center is an arduous 20 mi. hike by the shortest route, but there are any number of possible alternate routes and side trips. One interesting backpacking route (24 mi.) follows the Tejas Trail from Pine Springs all the way to the Dog Canyon Campground and then returns via the Bush Mountain Trail. **Guadalupe Peak** (8½ mi.), at 8749 ft., is the highest mountain in Texas. **Devil's Hall** (4¼ mi.) is a moderate hike; the trail starts at Pine Springs and winds through the Chihuahuan Desert. **Smith Spring Trail** (2¼ mi.) is a

short, easy trail; a good choice for those with limited time in the park. **McKittrick Canyon Trail** (2.3-10.9 mi.) lures hikers with the lush vegetation growing alongside McKittrick Stream. The **Bowl Loop** (9 mi.) grants hikers a chance to see the flora and fauna of the Guadalupe high country.

FOOD. The **Nickel Creek Cafe,** 5 mi. north of Pine Springs, is the only restaurant near the park. The friendly owner serves Mexican food ($3-5), burgers ($4), and beer, and pumps gas. (☎915-828-3295. Open M-Sa 7am-2pm and 6-9pm. Cash only.)

CAMPING. The park's two simple campgrounds, **Pine Springs,** just past park headquarters, and **Dog Canyon,** at the north end of the park, have water and restrooms but no hookups or showers. Wood and charcoal fires are not allowed. (☎915-828-3251. Reservations for groups only. Tent sites $8.) Dog Canyon is accessible via Rte. 137 from Carlsbad, New Mexico (72 mi.), or by a full-day hike from Pine Springs. Free backcountry camping permits are available at the Visitors Center. None of the 10 backcountry sites in the park has water or toilets.

THE ROAD TO VAN HORN. Leaving the park, turn south from **Rte. 180** onto **Rte. 54,** 16 mi. past the Guadalupe Mountains Visitors Center. This incredibly lonely stretch of asphalt makes its way toward Van Horn, 55 mi. away. The dusty valley was once a grassy plain, but overgrazing combined with drought has caused desert shrubs like the mesquite, acacia, and creosote to replace the grasses. The road passes by the **Figure 2 Ranch.** Established in 1890, this cattle empire was one of the first to venture into this land.

Welcome To TEXAS

 As you re-enter Texas, you re-enter the Central Time Zone, where it is 1hr. later.

VAN HORN. This town was originally established as a support center for the ranchers in the area. If you're looking for a bite to eat, and the

SOUTHERN BORDER

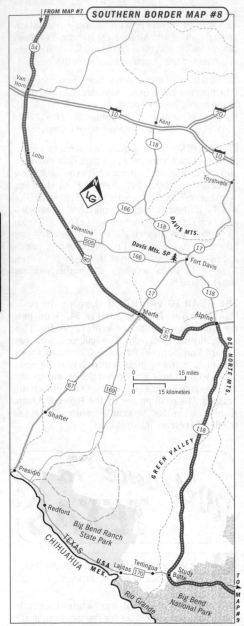

SOUTHERN BORDER MAP #8
FROM MAP #7

plentiful fast-food options aren't up your alley, try **Papa's Pantry,** 515 Van Horn Dr. The little roadside grill, right on U.S. 90 as you leave town, serves up everything from burritos ($2.50) to steak and chicken dinners. (☎432-283-2302. Dinner $6-10. Open M-Sa 7am-9pm.) There are dozens of budget motels along Broadway Ave., the town's main drag. The recently remodeled **Village Inn Motel,** 403 W. Broadway Ave., offers the best value. (☎915-283-7213. Singles $21; doubles $27.)

☎ LEAVING VAN HORN
Leave town via **U.S. 90,** west of where **U.S. 54** entered town.

THE ROAD TO MARFA
The Texas Mountain Trail continues on this highway. Five mi. outside of Van Horn, the road speeds passed a decrepit old ghost town by the name of **Lobo.** An Internet venture, www.lobotexas.com, allows the denizens of cyberspace to buy citizenship into this collection of ramshackle buildings, with promises to turn the "town" into a rewarding vacation site. As of yet, recreational possibilities seem rather limited. Farther down the road, **Valentine's** claim to fame is its name; sweethearts from across the south seek postmarks from this location every February.

Getting to Marfa requires another long stretch of road. The vastness of Texas U.S. 90 humbles drivers; with only the curvature of the earth marring the view, and not so much as a single tree to create some perspective, one really starts to feel small and insignificant.

☎ APPROACHING MARFA
Enter Marfa on **U.S. 90 east (San Antonio St.).** Take a left at the town's only stop sign to visit the prosperous historic district.

MARFA
Billboards on the way to Marfa declare "Marfa is what the West was." If the West was a thriving artist colony, then they hit the nail right on the head. At the end of Highland St. stands the gargantuan peach stucco walls and elaborate dome of the **Presidio County Court House.** The **Marfa & Presidio County Museum,** 110 W. San Antonio St., possesses one of the finer collections of Old West knickknacks and antiques. The museum also supplies excellent advice to tourists and shows a 7min. film on the region's enigma—the spooky Marfa lights. (☎915-729-4140. Open M-F 2-5pm. Free.)

In the marble lobby of the Paisano Hotel, **Jett's Cafe,** 207 N. Highland St., has classy dining at reasonable prices. Try the regional classic, pistachio-crusted fried steak ($10), or the grilled salmon. (☎ 432-729-3838. Open M-F 11am-9pm, F-Sa 8am-10pm, Su 8am-9pm. Reservations often required.) Locals rave about the **Marfa Book Co.,** 105 S. Highland St., which offers a wide variety of coffees, beers, and wines to go with its extensive selection of books. (☎ 915-729-3906. Open daily 9am-9pm.) An old gas-station-turned-pizza-parlor, **The Pizza Foundation,** 100 E. San Antonio St., has a pool table where the garage should be and a nice outdoor patio. (☎ 432-729-3377. Pizza slices $1.50, pies $12. Open M-Tu 11am-2pm, Th-F 11am-11pm, Sa noon-11pm, Su noon-10pm.)

APPROACHING ALPINE
As U.S. 90 climbs out of Marfa, the mountains come alive with green grasses and shrubs. U.S. 90 splits and runs down the town's parallel main streets: **Holland Ave. (U.S. 90 East)** and **Ave. E (U.S. 90. West).**

ALPINE
Twenty-six miles outside of Marfa is the surprisingly lively village of Alpine. High above town on the eastern hills, **Sul Ross State University** is Alpine's main attraction and makes Texas proud with one of the nation's best rodeo teams. Sul Ross also houses the **Museum of the Big Bend,** a small collection of art and artifacts from the Big Bend region of Texas. Exhibits include the history of area Native Americans, Spanish, Mexicans, and cowboys, as well as a cactus garden and a children's center. Every April the museum shows a cowboy art exhibit. (On the 1st fl. of the Lawrence Hall building. Take entrance #2 into Sul Ross. ☎ 915-837-8143. Open Su 1-5pm, Tu-Sa 9am-5pm.)

The Food Basket, 104 N. 2nd St., between Holland Ave. and Ave. E., is the best place to stock up on supplies before heading to Big Bend. (☎ 915-837-3295.) The menu at **Penny's Diner,** 2407 E. Holland Ave., befits the classic 50s diner setting. The sandwiches ($4-5), burgers ($5), and big salads ($5.25) are tasty options, and breakfast is served all day. (☎ 915-837-5711. Open 24hr.) Quietly set against the blossoming foothills, the ◪**Antelope Lodge,** 2310 U.S. 90 West, 1 mi. east of Alpine, is a friendly Texas ranch at a budget motel price. The best lodging in town, each room occupies half a small cottage and opens onto a beautiful courtyard. (☎ 800-880-8106; www.antelopelodge.com.

Rooms from $31.) Near the university, the **Motel Bien Venido,** 809 E. Holland Ave., has the cheapest rooms in town. While it appears a little run-down from the outside, the rooms are in good shape and have A/C. (☎ 915-837-3454. Singles $30; doubles $34.) The **Woodward Ranch** (☎ 915-364-2271), 16 mi. south of Alpine on Rte. 118, has primitive campsites ($10, no bathroom facilities) along a mountain stream, or less scenic sites ($15) with bathrooms and showers.

THE ROAD TO BIG BEND
Rte. 118 south from Alpine runs through green shrublands, grassy foothills, and picturesque mountains. This part of Texas doesn't receive enough water to support tree growth, but the occasional storms bring enough rain for grass to blanket this land. For many miles the road pushes past this lively green desert, an interesting transition zone between environments. Eventually, the dry desert wins out near the dusty town of **Study Butte** and its neighbor **Terlingua,** 80 mi. south of Alpine. From Study Butte, turn left to follow **Rte. 118** east for 25 mi. to Panther Junction, the park's headquarters.

 Always carry at least one gallon of water per person per day in the desert. Many of the park's roads can flood during the "rainy" late summer months.

BIG BEND NATIONAL PARK
Roadrunners, coyotes, wild pigs, mountain lions, and a few black bears make their home in Big Bend National Park, a tract of land about the size of Rhode Island that is cradled by the mighty Río Grande. Spectacular canyons, vast stretches of the Chihuahua Desert, and the airy Chisos Mountains occupy this spot. The high season for tourism is in the early spring—during the summer, the park is excruciatingly hot.

❏ GETTING AROUND.
There are only five paved roads in the park. Of these, the best sightseeing is along the **Ross Maxwell Scenic Drive,** a 30 mi. paved route from the western edge of the Chisos Mountains that leads down to the Río Grande and Santa Eleña Canyon. The 8 mi. drive that winds its way up into the Chisos Basin is also quite rewarding. However, the most spectacular drives in the park are unimproved, only accessible to 4WD jeeps and

VITAL STATS

Area: 800,000 acres.

Visitor Info: Park Headquarters (☎915-477-2251; www.nps.gov/bibe). in Panther Junction, 26 mi. inside the park. Open daily 8am-6pm. Ranger stations located at Río Grande Village, Persimmon Gap, Castolon, and Chisos Basin.

Emergency: ☎915-477-2251 until 5pm, afterwards, call 911.

Gateway town: Panther Junction

Fees: Weekly entrance pass $15 per vehicle; $5 per pedestrian, bike, or motorcycle. Park campgrounds $10; free permit required for backcountry camping.

trucks. **River Road** (51 mi.) skirts along the Río Grande from Castolon to the Río Grande Village. Another good drive is the 26 mi. **Old Ore Road,** which travels along the western edge of the Sierra del Caballo Muerto. Those interested in driving the backroads of Big Bend should purchase the guide to backcountry roads at the Visitors Center ($2).

◪ OUTDOOR ACTIVITIES. Big Bend encompasses several hundred miles of hiking trails, ranging from 30min. nature walks to backpacking trips several days long. Pick up the *Hiker's Guide to Big Bend* pamphlet ($2), available at Panther Junction. The **Lost Mine Trail** (4¾ mi.) leads to an amazing view of the desert and the Sierra de Carmen in Mexico. Also in the Chisos, **Emory Peak** (4½ mi.) requires an intense hike. An easier walk (1¾ mi.) ambles through the **Santa Eleña Canyon** along the Río Grande.

Though upstream damming has markedly decreased the river's flow, rafting is still big fun on the Río Grande. **Far-Flung Adventures,** next to the Starlight Theater Bar and Grill in Terlingua (☎915-371-2633 or 800-839-7238; www.farflung.com/tx), organizes one- to seven-day trips. In Terlingua off Hwy. 170, **Big Bend River Tours** rents canoes and inflatable kayaks. (☎915-371-3033 or 800-545-4240; www.bigbendrivertours.com. Canoes $45 per day. Kayaks $35 per day.)

⚔ FOOD. The **Chisos Mountain Lodge,** in the Chisos Basin, contains the only restaurant in the park, serving three square meals a day. (☎432-477-2291. Breakfast buffet $6.75. Lunch sandwiches $4-8. Dinner entrees $6-15. Open daily 7-10am, 11:30am-4pm, and 5:30-8pm.) **Ms. Tracy's Cafe,** on Rte. 118 in Study Butte, offers eggs, burgers, and

FROM MAP #8

SOUTHERN BORDER MAP #9

TO MAP #10

burritos as well as vegetarian entrees. (☎915-371-2888. Open daily Oct.-May 7am-9:30pm; June 7am-2pm; July-Sept. 7am-5pm.) **Starlight Theater Bar and Grill,** off Rte. 170 in Terlingua, 7 mi. from the park entrance, has healthy portions of Tex-Mex ($3-9) and live music. (☎915-371-2326. Open Su-F 5pm-midnight, Sa 5pm-1am. Kitchen open daily 5:30pm-10pm. Indoor pool: no joke.)

ACCOMMODATIONS AND CAMPING.
The **Chisos Mining Co. Motel,** on Rte. 170, west of the junction with Rte. 118, is the closest budget motel to the park that provides clean rooms with A/C. (☎915-371-2254. Singles $37; doubles $47; 6-person cabins with kitchenettes $60.)

The three developed campsites within the park are run on a first come, first served basis ($10). During Thanksgiving, Christmas, March, and April the campgrounds fill early; call park headquarters to inquire about availability. The **Chisos Basin Campground,** at 5400 ft., has 65 sites with running water and flush toilets and stays cooler than the other campgrounds in the summer. The **Río Grande Village Campground** has 100 sites near the only showers ($0.75) in the park. The RV park at Río Grande Village has 25 full hookups (1-2 people $14.50; $1 per additional person). Backcountry camping in the park is free but requires a permit from one of the area's Visitors Centers.

LEAVING BIG BEND
To leave Big Bend, head north out of Panther Junction along **Rte. 385** for 29 mi. to Persimmon Gap and the northern edge of the park.

THE ROAD THROUGH THE TEXAS FLATLANDS

Sixty-five miles north of Panther Junction on Rte. 385, **Marathon,** the "Gateway to Big Bend," marks your departure from the Big Bend area. This town is a good place to fuel up before heading out into the heart of Texas. As U.S. 90 leaves Marathon, it meanders through the mesa-topped mountain grasslands and then slowly descends toward the desert. It passes the abandoned railroad structures of **Longfellow,** a sparsely populated town that was crushed when diesel locomotives replaced the steam engines that stopped here.

SANDERSON

Fifty miles outside Marathon, U.S. 90 rolls into Sanderson, "Cactus Capital of Texas." Despite the slogan, there are surprisingly few cacti in the area.

Similarly, despite the designation "town," there are surprisingly few people. Like Longfellow, Sanderson was dependent on the railroad. Until recently, trains changed crews in Sanderson, and local businesses housed and fed resting workers. When crews began to switch at Alpine, businesses folded. Only a few diehards remain in this quasi-ghost town. Catch a friendly meal at **Kountry Kitchen,** 290 U.S. 90, decorated with antiques that give it a down-home feel. (☎915-345-2581. Mexican food, salad bar and fresh soups. Burgers and sandwiches $4-5. Open M-Sa 9am-2pm.) The accommodations at the **Outback Oasis Motel,** 800 U.S. 90, are spacious—some are suites, and some have been remodeled in fine Southwestern style. The pool has been converted into a koi pond, and there's a reptile exhibit by the lobby. (☎888-466-8822. Rooms $29-49.) Camping can be found at **Canyons RV Park,** on the right as U.S. 90 leaves town, although sites aren't very private. (☎915-345-2916. Showers and Internet. Sites $15.)

DRYDEN. The empty town of Dryden, where trees grow out of the roofs of burned-out houses, provides only fleeting relief from the monotony of the endless flat horizon. Dryden marks the junction of **U.S. 90** and **Rte. 349;** continue east along U.S. 90 to get to Langtry.

 Be forewarned, there are no services at night for the next 120 mi., and even during the day you'll still have to drive 66 mi. to find anything. This Texas flatland has no trees, very little vegetation, no mountains, no people, and just plain nothing other than the passing yellow stripes in the center of the highway.

LANGTRY. At long last, the arrival of a town—infinitesimal, yet populated Langtry sits 57 mi. from Sanderson. Home of Judge Roy Bean, who embodied "the law west of the Pecos," this town has one of the most colorful histories in the West. From his combination saloon, billiard hall, and courtroom, dubbed the "Jersey Lilly" (after English actress Lilly Langtry, Bean's infatuation), Judge Bean dispensed hard liquor and harsh justice. Since Langtry had no jail, all offenses resulted in fines, payable to Bean. To learn more about this classic Wild West character, stop by the impressive **Judge Roy Bean Visitor Center,** U.S. 90 at W. Loop 25. The center houses both a museum dedicated to Bean and his town and a

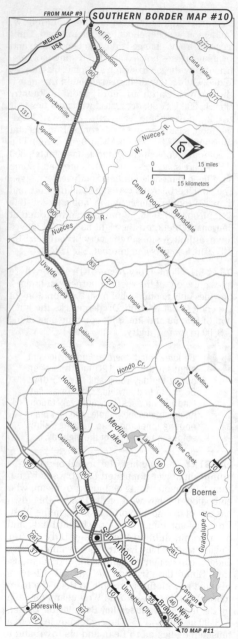

FROM MAP #9

SOUTHERN BORDER MAP #10

first-class Visitors Center run by the state of Texas. The museum features state-of-the-art holographic history exhibits. (Turn right off U.S. 90 at the gas station and into Langtry. ☎915-291-3340. Open daily 8am-6pm. Free.)

PECOS CANYON

The awe-inspiring **Pecos Canyon,** formed by the eponymous river, lies just a few miles down the road on U.S. 90. From the new U.S. 90 bridge over the canyon, it is possible to see the old bridge, high above the water line and washed out from high-water flooding. Picnic facilities and a nature trail are on the east side of the canyon in the Amistad National Recreation Area.

SEMINOLE CANYON STATE PARK & HISTORIC SITE
Off U.S. 90.

Those intrigued by canyons should stop here. The museum features exhibits about the area's history and information on the Native Americans who left pictographs on the canyon walls. The park features 8 mi. of trails, although a guided tour ($3) is required for the canyon trail. (☎915-292-4464. Open daily 9am-5pm. Entrance $2 per person. Cave dwelling and pictograph tour W-Su at 10am and 3pm. Other tours by reservation $10.) Sites with flush toilets and showers are available near the canyon's edge. (Sites $9; hookups $4.)

AMISTAD NATIONAL RECREATION AREA
From U.S. 90 East, Amistad is on the right just after crossing the reservoir bridge.

Amistad ("friendship") is an international recreation area on the US-Mexico border. The reservoir was created by the 6 mi. long dam on the Río Grande, and the water always appears strikingly blue by virtue of the area's limestone rock and water clarity. Run by the Park Service, this area is renowned for its watersports, but it also protects prehistoric pictographs and a diverse animal population. Swimming is allowed along the shoreline, except in harbor areas. Primitive camping is available at many sites throughout the park; the closest sites to U.S. 90 are available at Governor's Landing. (No water, pit toilets. Sites $8.)

APPROACHING DEL RIO

U.S. 90 east enters Del Rio on **Veterans Blvd.** (formerly Ave. F), which is lined with fast-food joints and car dealerships. At the intersection with **Gibbs St.,** a left turn lets you continue on U.S. 90 East, while going straight will take you toward Ciudad Acuna.

DEL RIO

The city of Del Rio caters to recreational visitors, services the Laughlin Air Force Base, and promotes good border relations with its Mexican sister Ciudad Acuna. Many colorful personalities have passed through Del Rio since it was founded in 1883. **The Whitehead Memorial Museum,** 1308 S. Main St., is the burial site of Judge Roy Bean, and houses a collection of 19th- and 20th-century exhibits. (Go straight when U.S. 90 turns at Gibbs St. ☎830-774-7568. Open Su 1-5pm, Tu-Sa 9am-4:30pm. $4.) The nearby **San Felipe Springs** has the distinction of being a watering hole for the US Army Camel Corp, a short-lived pre-Civil War cavalry experiment. The town was also home to Dr. John R. Brinkley, whose inventions included goat-gland implants (to improve the sex lives of men) and autographed pictures of Jesus Christ.

Don Marcelinos, 3510 Veterans Blvd., offers Mexican food in a festive environment. Dinner options include combination plates ($6-8) and steaks ($12-15). A Mexican Buffet ($6) is offered from 11am-4pm. (On the right as you enter Del Rio on U.S. 90 East. ☎830-774-2424. Open M-Sa 11am-10pm, Su 10am-8pm.) The **Desert Hills Motel,** 1912 Veterans Blvd., is on U.S. 90 East in the center of town, and has clean and comfortable budget rooms. (☎830-775-3548. Singles $27; doubles $39.) The **La Siesta Inn,** 200 Veterans Blvd., offers luxurious suites at affordable prices, as well as a pool, a happy hour with complimentary drinks, and a hot breakfast. (☎830-775-6323. Singles $49-55; doubles $59-65.)

BRACKETTVILLE & FT. CLARK SPRINGS

Twenty-eight miles along Rte. 90 outside of Del Rio sit the old white brick buildings of Brackettville. Once the support town of Fort Clark, the town had little left to offer after the army withdrew. An impressive **courthouse** stands in the center of town, accessible by turning north onto Rte. 674, while many of the surrounding buildings have decayed. In contrast, the once-abandoned Ft. Clark base has revitalized itself as a resort community. Civilians have taken up residence in some of the buildings. The best attraction in Brackettville is **John Wayne's Alamo Village,** 7 mi. from U.S. 90 on Rte. 674, a reproduction of the village that was created for the Western epic *Alamo* and has been used for many films since then. (☎830-563-2580. Open daily 9am-5pm.)

Driving tours of the former barracks, parade grounds, guardhouses, and depots are available from the **Visitors Center,** on the right just after passing through the entrance station. (☎830-563-9150. Open Sa-Su 1-4pm. $2 per person, children Free.) The resort boasts a **motel** renovated from cavalry barracks. (☎800-937-1590. Rooms $57-59.) A quick peek around the grounds is fun for anyone interested in seeing a historic army base, but awkward since it is now a gated residential community.

UVALDE

At the intersection of the two longest highways in the continental United States (U.S. 90 and U.S. 83), lie the tree-lined streets of Uvalde. On the east side of town stands the home of the infamous lawman Pat Garret, killer of Billy the Kid, reminding visitors that Wild West blood once coursed through the heart of this town. At the turn of the century, however, Uvalde became as civilized as it once had been wild. Located on the town square, **The Grand Opera House,** 100 W. North St., dates from 1891 and still holds performances. (☎830-278-4184. Open M-F 9am-3pm. Free guided tours.) The town is proudest of its most famous resident, John Nance Garner, two-term vice president who served under Franklin D. Roosevelt. **The Garner Museum,** 333 N. Park St., preserves his home and displays important papers and memorabilia. (From U.S. 90, turn onto Rte. 83 North and drive 2 blocks up, taking a left turn onto W. Mesquite Rd. ☎830-278-5018. Open M-Sa 9am-noon and 1-5pm.)

On the east side of town in a log cabin, **Jack's Steakhouse,** 2500 E. Main St., serves Uvalde's best steaks and chicken. (☎830-278-9955. Entrees $12. Open Su-Th 4:30-9:30pm, F-Sa 4:30-11pm.) The large rooms of the **Amber Sky Motel,** 2005 E. Main St., are slightly overpriced. Still, they are the only reasonable option in Uvalde. (☎830-278-5602. Singles $39; doubles $48.)

THE ROAD TO HONDO

After **U.S. 90** leaves Uvalde, it makes its way through the farmlands and trees that surround the Texas hill country. Many tiny communities dot the roadside. **Knippa's** town sign challenges you to "Go ahead and blink, Knippa is larger than you think." True, but two blinks and you will have missed it. One of the only buildings in town, the **Knippa Homestyle Cafe,** on the south side of U.S. 90., offers cheap breakfasts ($3) and lunches. (☎830-934-2821. Open daily 9am-2pm.)

D'Hanis is another small town where you can find little besides Old West-style trackside brick buildings. Here, **Bill & Rosa's Steak House and Saloon,** 7300 Country Rd. 525, grills fine Texas steaks ($12-18) cut fresh daily from the meat market across the street. Their chicken ($7-12), burgers, and sandwiches ($4-5) can satisfy carnivorous appetites. (From U.S. 90 entering D'Hanis, cross the tracks; the restaurant is on the left. ☎830-863-7230. Open Su-Th 9am-9pm, F-Sa 9am-10pm.)

HONDO. Farther down the road on U.S. 90 sits the larger community of Hondo, where picturesque gas lamps and old brick buildings line the railroad tracks running through town. The impressive **Medina County Courthouse** towers over the center of town. For superb Mexican cuisine, try ▨**El Restaurante Azteca,** 1708 Ave. K. This family-owned restaurant has a no-tip policy—they believe that "good service comes at no extra charge." (From U.S. 90 east, take a left on Ave. K, and cross the tracks. ☎830-426-4511. Combination plates $7. Lunch specials $5. Open M-Sa 10:30am-9pm.) At the **Whitetail Lodge,** 401 U.S. 90 East, you'll find comfortable country living in clean rooms. (☎830-426-3031. Reservations recommended during weekends. Singles midweek $40, weekends $50; doubles $50/$60. AAA discount.)

CASTROVILLE

Just outside San Antonio on the sleepy banks of the Medina River sits the village of Castroville, "the little Alsace of Texas." In the mid-19th century, the town's founder, Henri Castro, a gentleman of French birth, Portuguese ancestry, Jewish faith, and American citizenship, began recruiting settlers from the Rhine Valley and especially from the French province of Alsace. As the French families flocked to their new Texas home, they constructed their houses in the same style as those they had left behind. Many of these quaint French structures still stand, and walking tours around the asymmetrical roof lines of the little cottages begin at the **Chamber of Commerce,** 802 London St. (On the right when you enter town from U.S. 90 East, across from the McDonald's. ☎830-538-3142. Open M-F 9am-noon and 1-3pm.) At the **Castroville Regional Park,** Alsace St., camping, picnicking, and a public pool are available year-round. (The 1st right when you enter town from U.S. 90 East. ☎830-931-4070. Park open M-F 8am-5pm. Sites $10; RVs $18.)

The French denizens of a little Alsatian cottage serve the finest French cuisine this side of Paris at **La Normandie Restaurant,** 1302 Fiorella St. Favorites include the beef medallions Henri IV in béarnaise sauce with artichoke hearts ($17) and the roast duck ($15). Meals of this quality would easily cost four times more in many cities. (☎800-261-1731. Dinner Th-F 5-9pm, Sa-Su 5-10pm. Buffet luncheon Tu-Sa 11am-2:30pm. Champagne brunch Su 11:30am-3pm. Dinner reservations required.) For upscale lodgings, try the **Landmark Inn,** 402 Florence St., where you can stay in an Alsatian home. The inn serves continental breakfast each morning in the 1894 kitchen and loans bikes for exploring the rest of Castroville. For a $1 entry fee, non-guests can tour the small museum and beautiful gardens. (On the right side of U.S. 90 East, a block west of the Medina River Bridge. ☎512-389-8900. Museum open daily 8am-6pm. Reservations required. Rooms $60, with bath $70.)

⛰ APPROACHING SAN ANTONIO

The best way to enter San Antonio is via the **Durango Blvd.** Exit east off the I-10/I-35 freeway just west of downtown. From here it is about ½ mi. drive to **S. Alamo St.** Turn right (north) to drive right by the Alamo into the heart of downtown.

SAN ANTONIO

Though best known as the home of the Alamo—the symbol of Texas's break from Mexico—today, San Antonio is defined by its integration of Anglo and Hispanic cultures. Early Spanish influence can be seen in missions originally built to convert Native Americans to Catholicism; what was once the village settlement of La Villita has been transformed into a workshop for modern artisans, and Mexican culture is constantly on display in Market Square, where weekend revelers enjoy *mariachi* bands and fajita stands. Yet there are enough barbecue joints and 10-gallon hats to remind travelers that they are in the heart of Lone Star country.

🎫 GETTING AROUND

Veering left on **S. Alamo St.** at the **Market St.** intersection will put you onto **Losoya St.,** which becomes **Broadway.** Broadway is the major artery leading out of downtown to the north; it passes under the **I-35** and **I-37** interchange that frames the downtown region and heads north toward the natural beauty of **Brackenridge Park,** the second-largest urban municipal park in the country after New York's Central Park.

Parking lots dot the downtown region and all cost about $5 for the day, but perhaps the best places to park are the lots behind the downtown post office, adjacent to Rte. 246. From here, it is only a short walk to the Alamo, the Riverwalk, the heart of downtown, and the Visitors Center.

(VITAL STATS)

Population: 1.1 million

Visitor Info: 317 Alamo Plaza (☎210-207-6748; www.sanantoniocvb.com), across from the Alamo. Open daily 8:30am-6pm.

Internet Access: San Antonio Public Library, 600 Soledad St. (☎210-207-2534). Open M-Th 9am-9pm, F-Sa 9am-5pm, Su 11am-5pm.

Post Office: 615 E. Houston St., 1 block from the Alamo. Open M-F 8:30am-5:30pm. **Postal Code:** 78205.

👁 SIGHTS

THE ALAMO. Though built as a Spanish mission during the colonization of the New World, the Alamo has come to serve as a touchstone of Lone Star pride, signifying the bravery of those who fought for Texas's independence. For 12 days in 1836, Texan defenders of the Alamo, outnumbered 20 to 1, held their ground against Mexican attackers. The morning of the 13th day saw the end of their defiant stand as the strains of the infamous *deguello* (literally "throat-cutting," the *deguello* is military music that had come to signify annihilation of the enemy in Spanish history) were heard. All 189 men were killed. The massacre served to unite Texans behind the independence movement, and "Remember the Alamo!" became the rallying cry for Sam Houston's ultimately victorious forces. After languishing for decades, the site is presently under the care of the Daughters of the Republic of Texas and is the locus of the city's downtown. *(At the center of Alamo Plaza. ☎210-225-1391. Open M-Sa 9am-5:30pm, Su 10am-6:30pm. Basement under renovations.*

OTHER MISSIONS. The San Antonio Missions National Historical Park preserves the five missions along the river that once formed the soul of San Antonio. Follow the brown-and-white "Mission Trail" signs beginning downtown at S. Saint Mary's St. **Mission San José** ("Queen of the Missions") contains remnants of its own irrigation system, a gorgeous sculpted rose window, and numerous restored buildings. *(Visitors Center located at Mission San José. ☎210-534-8833; www.nps.gov/saan. San José: 6701 San José Dr., off Roosevelt Ave. ☎210-922-0543. Catholic mass Su 7:45, 9, 10:30am, and a noon "Mariachi Mass.")*

Mission Concepción is the oldest unrestored stone church in North America. Traces of the once-colorful frescoes are still visible. *(807 Mission Rd., 4 mi. south of the Alamo off E. Mitchell St. ☎210-534-1540.)*

Mission San Juan Capistrano and **Mission San Francisco de la Espada,** smaller and simpler than the other missions, evoke the isolation of such outposts. Between them lies the Espada Aqueduct, the only remaining waterway built by the Spanish. *(San Juan: 9101 Graf St. ☎210-534-0749. San Francisco: 10040 Espada Rd. ☎210-627-2021. All missions open daily 9am-5pm. Free.)*

PASEO DEL RÍO. The 2½ mi. *Paseo del Río* (Riverwalk) is a series of shaded stone pathways that follow a winding canal built by the WPA in the 1930s. Lined with picturesque gardens, shops, and cafes, the Riverwalk connects most of the major downtown sights and is the hub of San Antonio's nightlife. *(Southwest of the Alamo. Black signs indicate access points.)*

LA VILLITA. A few blocks south of the Riverwalk, this recreated artisans' village contains restaurants, craft shops, and art studios. *(418 Villita. ☎210-207-8610.)*

MARKET SQUARE. On weekends, this lively plaza features the upbeat tunes of *Tejano* bands and the omnipresent buzzing of frozen margarita machines. *(Between San Saba and Santa Rosa St. ☎210-207-8600. Open daily May-Sept. 10am-8pm; Sept.-May 10am-6pm.)*

HEMISFAIR PLAZA. The site of the 1968 World's Fair, HemisFair Plaza still draws tourists with restaurants, museums, and historic houses. *(Plaza located between S. Alamo St., E. Market St., Bowie St., and Durgano Blvd.)* The **Tower of the Americas** rises 750 ft. above the Texas hill country; the view is best at night. *(600 HemisFair Park. ☎210-207-8617. Open Su-Th 9am-10pm, F-Sa 9am-11pm. $3, seniors $2, ages 4-11 $1.)* Inside

SOUTHERN BORDER

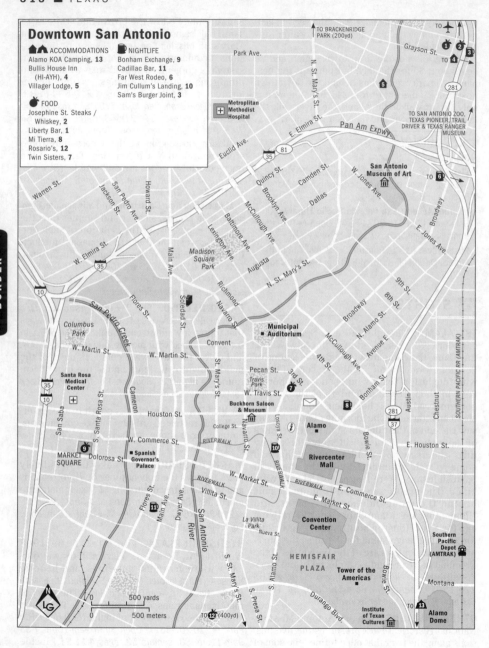

Downtown San Antonio

▲ ACCOMMODATIONS
Alamo KOA Camping, **13**
Bullis House Inn
  (HI-AYH), **4**
Villager Lodge, **5**

NIGHTLIFE
Bonham Exchange, **9**
Cadillac Bar, **11**
Far West Rodeo, **6**
Jim Cullum's Landing, **10**
Sam's Burger Joint, **3**

🍅 FOOD
Josephine St. Steaks /
  Whiskey, **2**
Liberty Bar, **1**
Mi Tierra, **8**
Rosario's, **12**
Twin Sisters, **7**

SOUTHERN BORDER

the park, the **Institute of Texan Cultures** showcases 27 ethnic and cultural groups and their contributions to the history of Texas. (☎ 210-458-2300. *Open Su and Tu-Sa 9am-5pm.*)

BUCKHORN SALOON & MUSEUM. In continuous operation since 1881, this curious saloon and museum displays objects from the Old West. It houses a huge collection of stuffed animals from around the world, an interactive wax museum of Texas history, and exhibits on ranching and on gunfights. Stop in for a drink and a bite at the saloon; while you munch your sandwich ($6), you can peek at the displays visible from the dining room. *(318 Houston St., 2 blocks west of the Alamo, next to the Hyatt Hotel. ☎ 210–247-4000. Museum $11, children 3-11 $8; tickets good for 2 days. Open Memorial Day-Labor Day 10am-6pm; Labor Day-Memorial Day 10am-5pm.)*

SAN ANTONIO MUSEUM OF ART. Housed in the former Lone Star Brewery just north of the city center, this museum showcases an impressive variety of Latin American, Pre-Columbian, Egyptian, Oceanic, Asian, and Islamic folk art. *(200 W. Jones Ave. ☎ 210-978-8100. Open Su noon-5pm, Tu 10am-9pm, W-Sa 10am-5pm. $5, seniors and students with ID $4, ages 4-11 $1.75. Tu 3-9pm free.)*

BRACKENRIDGE PARK. To escape San Antonio's urban congestion, amble down to Brackenridge Park. The 343-acre showground includes playgrounds, a miniature train, and a driving range. The main attraction of the park is a lush, perfumed **Japanese tea garden** with pathways weaving in and out of a pagoda and around a goldfish pond. *(3910 N. Saint Mary's St., 5 mi. north of the Alamo. ☎ 210-223-9534. $2.25, children $1.75. Open daily 5am-11pm. Train daily 9am-6:30pm.)* The park also houses the **San Antonio Zoo.** One of the country's largest zoos, it shelters over 3500 animals in reproductions of their natural settings. The extensive African mammal exhibit is particularly noteworthy. *(3903 N. Saint Mary's St. ☎ 210-734-7184. Open daily June-Aug. 9am-6pm; Sept.-May 9am-5pm. $7, seniors and ages 3-11 $5.)*

TEXAS PIONEER, TRAIL DRIVER, & TEXAS RANGER MUSEUM. This museum displays a splendid collection of cowboy paraphernalia, including artifacts, old guns, documents, and portraits. *(3805 Broadway. ☎ 210-822-9011. Open May-Aug. M-Sa 10am-5pm, Su noon-5pm. $3, seniors $2, ages 6-12 $1.)*

FOOD

Expensive cafes and restaurants surround the **Riverwalk**—breakfast beyond a muffin and coffee can clean out your wallet. North of town, Asian restaurants line **Broadway** across from Brackenridge. On weekends, hundreds of carnival food booths crowd the walkways of **Market Sq.** If you come late in the day, prices drop and vendors are willing to haggle. (☎ 210-207-8600. Open daily May-Sept. 10am-8pm; Sept.-May 10am-6pm.) **Pig Stand** diners offer cheap, decent grub in multiple locations; the two branches near downtown at 801 S. Presa, off S. Alamo, and at 1508 Broadway stay open 24hr.

Mi Tierra, 218 Produce Row (☎ 210-225-1262), in Market Sq. Smiling *mariachi* musicians serenade patrons while they chow down on delicious Mexican fare like chicken enchiladas with chocolate mole sauce ($8.50). Out front, bakers display fresh Mexican pastries. Daily lunch specials provide hearty meals at lower prices (M-F 11am-2pm; $7). Dinner plates $11. Open 24hr.

Rosario's, 910 S. Alamo St. (☎ 210-223-1806), at S. Saint Mary's St. Rosario's is widely acknowledged by locals to be the best eatery in town. Scrumptious chicken quesadillas ($6) uphold the reputation. Live music F-Sa night. Open M 11am-3pm, Tu-Th 11am-10pm, F-Sa 11am-12:30am.

Liberty Bar, 328 E. Josephine St. (☎ 210-227-1187). A friendly local hangout with daily specials and sandwich plates ($7-9). Try the *karkade* (iced hibiscus and mint tea with fresh ginger and white grape juice). Open M-Th 11am-10:30pm, F-Sa 11am-midnight, Su 10:30am-10:30pm.

Josephine St. Steaks/Whiskey, 400 Josephine St. (☎ 210-224-6169), at Ave. A. Josephine St.'s specialty is thick Texan steaks, but they offer a wide array of tasty dishes in a relaxed atmosphere. Entrees $5-12. Lunch specials $5-7. Open M-Th 11am-10pm, F-Sa 11am-11pm.

Twin Sisters, 124 Broadway and 6322 N. New Braunfels (☎ 210-354-1559). Some of the best vegetarian food around. Try tofu quesadillas ($6) or the Caesar salad with eggless tofu ($8). Open M-F 9am-3pm.

ACCOMMODATIONS

For cheap motels, try **Roosevelt Ave.,** a southern extension of Saint Mary's St. and Fredericksburg Rd. Inexpensive motels also line **Broadway**

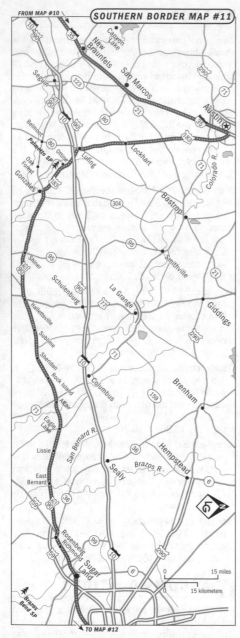

SOUTHERN BORDER MAP #11

FROM MAP #10

TO MAP #12

0 15 miles
0 15 kilometers

between downtown and Brackenridge Park. Follow **I-35 N.** or the **Austin Hwy.** to find cheaper and often safer lodging outside of town.

Bullis House Inn International Hostel (Hi-AYH), 621 Pierce St. (☎210-223-9426). 2 mi. north of downtown on Broadway, turn right on Grayson St., travel ½ mi. east on Grayson, and turn right on Pierce St.; the hostel is on the right. A spacious, ranch-style hostel in a quiet neighborhood next door to the Bullis House mansion. Pool, kitchen, and Internet. Fills quickly in summer. Breakfast $4.50. Linens $2. Key deposit $10. Reception 8am-10pm. Dorms $18, nonmembers $21.

Villager Lodge, 1126 E. Elmira St. (☎800-833-7785). 2 mi. north of downtown. Take Broadway St. north, head left (west) on Grayson St., and turn left (south) on E. Elmira St.; the lodge is on the left. This budget motel provides clean rooms in a quiet neighborhood. Outdoor pool, A/C, and 5 free local calls. Some rooms have fridge and microwave. Small singles $27; large singles and doubles $34. Rates higher on holiday weekends.

Alamo KOA, 602 Gembler Rd. (☎210-224-9296, 800-833-7785). 6 mi. from downtown. From I-10 E., take Exit 580, drive 2 blocks north, then take a left onto Gembler Rd. Well-kept grounds with lots of shade. Each site has a grill and patio. Showers, laundry, pool, and free movies. Reception 7:30am-9:30pm. Sites $28, full hookup $31; $4 per additional person.

NIGHTLIFE

In late April, the 10-day **Fiesta San Antonio** (☎210-227-5191) ushers in spring with concerts, carnivals, and plenty of Tex-Mex celebrations to commemorate Texas' heroes as well as the state's diverse cultural landscape. For excitement after dark any time, in any season, stroll down the Riverwalk.

Cadillac Bar, 212 S. Flores St. (☎210-223-5533). Authentic *Tejano* music, a different band every weeknight. 21+. Open M-Sa 11am-2am.

Sam's Burger Joint, 330 E. Grayson St. (☎210-223-2830). *Puro* Poetry Slam Tu 10pm ($2). Live music. Try the "Big Monster Burger" for $7. Open M-Th 11am-11pm, F-Sa 11-Midnight. Bar closing hours vary.

The Bonham Exchange, 411 Bonham St. (☎210-271-3811), around the corner from the Alamo. San Antonio's biggest gay dance club. W college night. Cover 21+ $3-5, 18-20 $10. Open M-Th 4pm-2am, F 4pm-3am, Sa 8pm-3am.

Jim Cullum's Landing, 123 Losoya St. (☎210-223-7266), in the Hyatt. Traditional jazz, including the legendary Cullum and his jazz band. Cullum band performs M-Sa 8:30pm-1am. Tidy dress. Cover M-Th $3.50, F-Sa $6.50. Open M-Sa 4:30pm-1am, Su noon-1am.

Far West Rodeo, 3030 U.S. 410 NE (☎210-646-9378). Country *and* Western music. Indoor rodeo F-Sa night, a mechanical bull, and 2 dance floors. 18+. Cover $3-6. Open W-Th 7pm-2am, F-Sa 8pm-2am.

◤ APPROACHING AUSTIN

The most direct route from San Antonio to Austin is to take **I-35 North** all the way.

AUSTIN

If the "Lone Star State" still inspires images of rough-and-tumble cattle ranchers riding horses across the plains, then Austin attempts to put the final nails in the coffin of that stereotype. In recent years, 17,000 new millionaires have made their fortunes in Austin and big industry has become increasingly prominent, with Fortune 500 companies and Internet startups seeking to redefine the city's essence. Austin's reputation for musical innovation as the "Live Music Capital of the World" and the 50,000 college students at the University of Texas, make it a vibrant city and a liberal, alternative oasis in a traditional state.

⬢ VITAL STATS

Population: 660,000

Visitor Info: 201 E. 2nd St. (☎512-478-0098 or 800-926-2282). Open M-F 8:30am-5pm, Sa-Su 9am-5pm.

Internet Access: Austin Public Library, 800 Guadalupe St. (☎512-974-7599). Open M-Th 10am-9pm, F-Sa 10am-6pm, Su noon-6pm.

Post Office: 510 Guadalupe, at 6th St. Open M-F 7am-6:30pm, Sa 8am-3pm. **Postal Code:** 78701.

▤ GETTING AROUND

Most of Austin lies between **Mopac Expwy. (Rte. 1)** and **I-35,** both running north-south. University of Texas students inhabit central **Guadalupe St. ("The Drag"),** where music stores and cheap restaurants thrive. The state capitol governs the area a few blocks southeast. South of the capitol dome, **Congress Ave.** has upscale eateries and classy shops. The many bars and clubs of **6th St.** hop at night, though some nightlife has moved to the growing **Warehouse District** around 4th St., west of Congress Ave. Away from the urban sprawl, **Town Lake** offers a haven for joggers, rowers, and cyclists.

◉ SIGHTS

Forming the backbone of city's cultural life, the **University of Texas at Austin (UT)** is both the wealthiest public university in the country, with an annual budget of over a billion dollars, and the largest, with over 50,000 students.

▧ MEXICAN FREE-TAIL BATS. Just before dusk, head underneath the south side of the Congress Ave. Bridge, near the Austin American-Statesman parking lot, and watch the massive swarms of bats emerge from their roosts to feed on the night's mosquitoes. When the bridge was reconstructed in 1980, the engineers unintentionally created crevices that formed ideal homes for the migrating bat colony. The city began exterminating the night-flying creatures until **Bat Conservation International** moved to Austin to educate people about the bats' harmless behavior and the benefits of their presence—the bats eat up to 3000 lb. of insects each night. Today, the bats are among the biggest tourist attractions in Austin. The colony, seen from mid-March to November, peaks in July, when a crop of pups increases the population to around 1.5 million. *(For flight times, or to ask Commissioner Gordon to man the bat signal, call the bat hotline: ☎512-416-5700, ext. 3636.)*

GOVERNMENT BUILDINGS. Not to be outdone, Texans built their **state capitol** 7 ft. higher than the national one. *(At Congress Ave. and 11th St. ☎512-463-0063. Open M-F 7am-10pm, Sa-Su 9am-8pm. 45min. tours every 15min. Tour depart from the capitol steps. Free.)* The **Capitol Visitors Center** is in the southeast corner of the grounds. *(112 E. 11th St. ☎512-305-8400. Open daily 9am-5pm. 2hr. parking on 12th and San Jacinto St.)* Near the capitol, the **Governor's Mansion** runs tours. *(1010 Colorado St. ☎512-463-5516. Free tours M-F every 20min. 10-11:40am.)* The Austin Convention and Visitors Bureau sponsors free **walking tours** from March to November. *(☎512-454-1545. Tours Th-F 9am; Sa-Su 9, 11am, and 2pm.)*

MUSEUMS. The first floor of the **Lyndon B. Johnson Library and Museum** focuses on Texas native LBJ and the history of the American presidency, while the 8th floor features a model of the

Oval Office. *(2313 Red River St. ☎512-916-5137. Open daily 9am-5pm. Free.)* If you've ever wondered about "The Story of Texas," the **Bob Bullock Texas State History Museum** is waiting to tell it to you in three floors of exhibits and two IMAX theaters. The museum traces the history of the state from its Native American legacy and Spanish colonization to statehood and the 20th-century oil boom. *(1800 N. Congress Ave. ☎512-936-8746. Open M-Sa 9am-6pm, Su 1-6pm. $5, seniors $4.25, under 19 free.)* The downtown branch of the **Austin Museum of Art** features American and European masters and an Asian collection. A second branch is housed in a Mediterranean-style villa in a beautiful country setting. *(823 Congress Ave., at the corner of 8th St. ☎512-495-9224. Branch at 3809 W. 35th St. ☎512-458-8191. Open Su noon-5pm, Tu-W and F-Sa 10am-6pm, Th 10am-8pm. Branch grounds open M-Sa 9am-9pm, Su 1-5pm. Free.)*

PARKS. Mt. Bonnell Park offers a sweeping view of Lake Austin and Westlake Hills from the highest point in the city. *(3800 Mt. Bonnell Rd., off W. 35th St.)* On hot afternoons, Austinites come in droves to riverside **Zilker Park,** just south of the Colorado River. *(2201 Barton Springs Rd. ☎512-477-7273. Open daily 5am-10pm. Free.)* Flanked by walnut and pecan trees, **Barton Springs Pool,** a spring-fed swimming hole in Zilker Park, extends 1000 ft. long and 200 ft. wide, and hovers around 68°F. *(☎512-499-6710. Pool open M-W and F-Su 5am-10pm, Th 5-9am and 7-10pm. M-F $2.50, Sa-Su $2.75; ages 12-17 $1; under 12 $0.50. Free daily 5-8am and 9-10pm.)* The **Barton Springs Greenbelt** offers challenging hiking and biking trails.

FOOD

Though a bit removed from downtown, **Barton Springs Rd.** offers a diverse selection of inexpensive restaurants, including Mexican and Texas-style barbecue joints. Prepare your own meals from groceries purchased at the **Wheatsville Food Co-op,** 3101 Guadalupe St., the only food co-op in Texas, selling organic foods and acting as a community gathering place. *(☎512-478-2667. Open daily 9am-11pm.)*

▨ **Ruby's BBQ,** 512 W. 29th St. (☎512-477-1651). Ruby's barbecue is good enough to be served on silver platters, but that just wouldn't seem right in this cow-skull-and-butcher-paper establishment.

The owners only order meat from farm-raised, grass-fed cows. Scrumptious brisket sandwich $4.25. Open daily 11am-midnight.

▨**World Beat Cafe,** 600 Martin Luther King Blvd. (☎512-236-0197). This eclectic cafe has African specialties such as okra vegetable soup ($5) and yam *fu fu* with *egusi,* as well as terrific burger and fries specials on Tu, Th, and Su ($2.75). Open M-Sa 11am-9pm, Su noon-7pm.

Madam Mam's, 2514 Guadalupe St. (☎512-472-8306). This Thai restaurant serves up a wide variety of innovative soups and noodle dishes. Pad thai $6. Open M-F 11am-9pm, Sa-Su noon-9pm.

Hoover's Cooking, 2002 Manor Rd. (☎512-479-5006), ½ mi. east of I-35. Also known as "the good taste place" or "the smoke, fire, and ice house," Hoover's has cooking that is just darn good. Options include the chipotle chicken salad sandwich ($7) or the Cajun ham po'boy ($7). Enjoy salads from the green house (around $7.50) or chicken and ribs (regular or Jamaican jerk style $8-12) from the smoke house. Open M-F 11am-10pm, Sa-Su 9am-10pm.

Hut's Hamburgers, 807 W. 6th St. (☎512-472-0693), near the West Ave. intersection. "God Bless Hut's" has been the motto since 1981, when a great flood destroyed everything in the area but inexplicably spared Hut's. Heavenly burgers, with over 20 different specialty varieties to choose from (all around $4.50). Dark, movie memorabilia-covered walls surround locals who love the place. Open daily 11am-10pm.

The Kerbey Lane Cafe, 3704 Kerbey Ln. (☎512-451-1436). Locations throughout town, including one near UT. An Austin institution. For dinner, try their fajitas ($7.25); for breakfast, order their *migas,* a corn tortilla soufflé ($5.25). Open 24hr.

Magnolia Cafe, 1920 S. Congress Ave. and 2304 Lake Austin Blvd. (☎512-455-0000). A colorful, lively place with a variety of healthy, tasty dishes. Try 2 "Tropical Turkey" tacos for $6.50. Open 24hr.

ACCOMMODATIONS

Chain motels lie along **I-35,** running north and south of Austin. This funkified city, however, is a great place to find cheap options with character. In town, **co-ops** run by the university peddle rooms and meals to hostelers. Guests have access to all co-op facilities, including fully stocked kitchens. (☎512-476-5678. Reservations

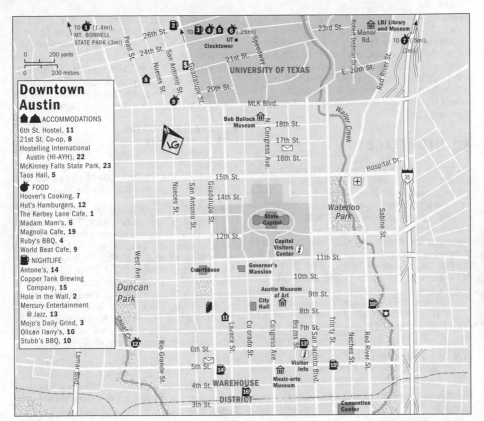

Downtown Austin

▲▲ ACCOMMODATIONS

6th St. Hostel, 11
21st St. Co-op, 8
Hostelling International
  Austin (HI-AYH), 22
McKinney Falls State Park, 23
Taos Hall, 5

🍴 FOOD

Hoover's Cooking, 7
Hut's Hamburgers, 12
The Kerbey Lane Cafe, 1
Madam Mam's, 6
Magnolia Cafe, 19
Ruby's BBQ, 4
World Beat Cafe, 9

NIGHTLIFE

Antone's, 14
Copper Tank Brewing
  Company, 15
Hole in the Wall, 2
Mercury Entertainment
  @ Jazz, 13
Mojo's Daily Grind, 3
Oilcan Harry's, 10
Stubb's BBQ, 10

recommended.) For those interested in camping, only a 10-20min. drive separates Austin from the nearest campgrounds.

■ **Hostelling International Austin (HI-AYH),** 2200 S. Lakeshore Blvd. (☎512-444-2294 or 800-725-2331), about 3 mi. from downtown. From I-35, exit at Riverside, head east, and turn left at Lakeshore Blvd. Beautifully situated, quiet hostel with a 24hr. common room overlooking Town Lake. Live music by local acts M-Sa. 40 dorm-style beds in single-sex rooms. Rents bikes, kayaks, and canoes ($10 each). No alcohol. Reception 8-11am and 5-10pm; arrivals after 10pm must call ahead to check in. Dorms $16, nonmembers $19.

■ **6th St. Hostel,** 604 6th St. (☎512-495-9772 or 866-467-8356). Stay here to be where the action is. Advertises "free earplugs (for those who

sleep)." Free coffee and tea. Small kitchen and game room with pool table. Purchase a hostel wrist band for $5 and get discounts, including free cover at over 20 6th St. hot spots. Reception 24hr. Dorms $18; private rooms $63.

Taos Hall, 2612 Guadalupe St. (☎512-476-5678), at 27th St. The UT co-op where you're most likely to get a private room. Those staying a week or more will be drafted into the chore corps. 3 meals included. Office open M-F 10am-6pm. Open June-Aug. Rooms $20.

21st St. Co-op, 707 W. 21st St. (☎512-476-5678). Treehouse-style building arrangement and hanging plants have residents calling this co-op the "Ewok Village." A bit grungy, but only from all the fun. Suites with A/C, common room on each floor, and kitchen access. 3 meals included. Office open M-F 10am-6pm. Rooms $15.

McKinney Falls State Park, 5808 McKinney Falls Pkwy. (☎512-243-1643, reservations ☎512-389-8900), southeast of the city. Turn right on Burleson off Rte. 71 East, then right on McKinney Falls Pkwy. Caters to RV and tent campers. Swimming permitted in the stream; 7 mi. of hiking trails. Open Su-Th 8am-5pm, F 8am-8pm, Sa 8am-7pm. Primitive sites (accessible only by foot) $9; with water and electricity $12. Day-use $2, under 13 free.

NIGHTLIFE

Austin has replaced Seattle as the nation's underground music hot spot, so keep an eye out for rising indie stars, as well as old blues, folk, country, and rock favorites. On weekends, nighttime swingers seek out dancing on **6th St.,** lined with warehouse nightclubs and fancy bars. More mellow, cigar-smoking night owls gather in the **4th St. Warehouse District.** The bars and clubs along **Red River St.** that have all of the grit of 6th St., but less of the glamour. The Austin coffeehouse scene provides a low-key alternative. The weekly *Austin Chronicle* and *XL-ent* have details on current music performances, shows, and movies. The *Gay Yellow Pages* is free at stands along Guadalupe St.

Mojo's Daily Grind, 2714 Guadalupe St. (☎512-477-6656). Simply "the hub of subculture in Austin." DJs spin music Th-Sa nights. Open 24hr.

Antone's, 213 W. 5th St. (☎512-474-5314). A blues paradise for all ages. Shows at 10pm. Cover $5-25. Open daily 9pm-2am.

Mercury Entertainment @ Jazz, 214 E. 6th St. Caters to hip 20-somethings looking for the latest in jazz, funk, and hip-hop. Cover from $6, ages 18-20 from $9. Open daily 9:30pm-2am.

Stubb's BBQ, 801 Red River St. (☎512-480-8341). Stubb's scrumptious, inexpensive grub includes a fabulous (but pricey) Su gospel brunch with an all-you-can-eat buffet plus live gospel for $15 (reservations recommended; seatings at 11am and 1pm). 18+ club downstairs hosts nightly acts at 10:30pm. All ages welcome for amphitheater shows. Cover $5-25. Open Tu-W 11am-10pm, Th-Sa 11am-11pm, Su 11am-9pm. Nightclub open Tu-Sa 11am-2am.

Oilcan Harry's, 211 W. 4th St. (☎512-320-8823). One of the best gay bars in Austin. Tu and Su strip shows (21+) 10:30pm-1:30am. Cover W $7, ages 18-20 $12. Open Su-Th 2pm-2am, F-Sa 8pm-4am.

Copper Tank Brewing Company, 504 Trinity St. (☎512-478-8444). The city's best microbrewery. W $1 beers, Th $1 drinks, F $2 drinks. 21+. Open Tu-F 5pm-2am, Sa 8pm-2am.

Hole in the Wall, 2538 Guadalupe St. (☎512-472-5599), at 26th St. Mix of punk, alternative, and country-western bands. Music nightly. 21+. Cover Tu-Sa $3-5. Open M-F 11am-2am, Sa-Su noon-2am.

LEAVING AUSTIN
U.S. 183 South is about as Texan as it comes, rolling over grassy hills and through shaded glens where longhorn cattle take their rests. Take **I-35 South** and jump onto **Rte. 71 East.** Take this for a short stint until the intersection with **U.S. 183 South.**

LOCKHART. Twenty-five miles south of Austin, U.S. 183 passes through Lockhart, "BBQ capital of Texas." Don't miss the **county courthouse** in the center of town; its design is sure to bemuse and amaze. **Black's BBQ,** 708 N. Main St., is the self-proclaimed "oldest family BBQ in Texas." That declaration may be as truthful as its claim to be open "8 days a week," but either way, the food is decent and dirt cheap. Try the beef brisket or the pork ribs, both $2.25. (Located 2 blocks west of U.S. 183 on the north side of town. ☎512-398-2712; www.blacksbbq.com. Open daily 10am-8pm.)

LULING. Fourteen miles south of Lockhart sits a town with a different focus—Luling is the name, and watermelons are the game. The last weekend of June, the town hosts the **Luling Watermelon Thump.** Watermelon lovers from all over the state come for the country music, car rally, seed-spitting competitions, and Watermelon Queen pageant. The town dedicates the facade of an old oil drill to the fruit, and private well-heads all over town likewise feature amusing and colorful watermelon-y scenes.

LEAVING LULING
Continuing on **U.S. 183** requires a left turn in the center of Luling. U.S. 183 then crosses the I-10 freeway to head on east toward **Gonzales.**

PALMETTO STATE PARK
From U.S. 183, turn right at the sign 6 mi. out of Luling. Park Headquarters are 2½ mi. down on the right.

This lush tropical oasis in the middle of the Texas grassland feels like the jungle of southern Florida. The dwarf palms of the park's namesake grow abundantly in the underbrush, where armadillos, deer, and other wildlife make their homes. Summer evenings flicker with the light of fireflies, who create a symphony of chirps, calls, and croaks. The San Marcos River and small Oxbow Lake run through the park, perfect for swimming and fishing. The park also features nature trails, picnic areas, a playground, and campsites. (☎512-389-8900. Entrance fee $2. Hot showers and flush toilets. Sites $12, with electricity $14.)

APPROACHING GONZALES
7 mi. past Palmetto State Park, a left onto the **U.S. 183 Bus. Loop** leads to the small town of Gonzales, birthplace of the Texas revolution.

GONZALES
On October 2, 1835, the first shot of the Texas revolution was fired at Mexican troops who were marching into Gonzales demanding that the citizens hand over their cannon. The townsfolk rebelled and defeated the Mexicans, and the famous cannon still sits in the **Gonzales Memorial Museum,** 414 Smith St. The museum complex resembles the Washington Monument's mall and reflecting pool, honoring those who took part in the revolution. It also houses a collection of objects that tell the story of the area's past. (From St. Joseph St. South, take a left on St. Lawrence St. and travel 10 blocks. The museum is on the right. ☎830-672-6532. Open Su 1 5pm, Tu-Sa 10am-noon and 1-5pm. Donations accepted.) The **Gonzales County Jail Museum,** 414 St. Lawrence St., both houses the Visitors Center and showcases the old cell blocks and gallows of the jail, constructed in 1887. Exhibits show the tools of prisons of the past; you'll find balls and chains, weapons, and a dungeon. (Located in the town square off St. Joseph St. ☎888-672-1095. Open M-Sa 8am-5pm, Su noon-4pm.) The **Cafe on the Square,** 511 St. Joseph St., serves soups, salads, sandwiches, steaks, and ice cream. (☎830-672-1871. Open M-Sa 11am-2pm, F 5-9pm.)

 Just outside of town, you'll pass a grove of trees where you can see **Sam Houston's Oak.** Here, the famous Texan General rallied his troops and many volunteers for the march to San Jacinto.

LEAVING GONZALES
To leave downtown Gonzales, drive along St. Joseph St. to **U.S. 90A East.**

SHINER. From Gonzales, it is 16 mi. on U.S. 90A to Shiner, the "cleanest little city in Texas." The "littlest clean city in Texas" would have worked just as well, as the size of Shiner's population of 2100 warrants the title of "hamlet" rather than "city." **Werner's Restaurant,** 317 N. Ave. East, offers excellent steaks, BBQ, burgers and sandwiches. (☎361-594-2928. Entrees $9-$11. Open daily 6-10pm.) The **Shiner Country Inn,** 1016 N. Ave. East, greets visitors with quiet, comfortable beds. These quaint rooms are individually decorated with care and have a ranchhouse feel. (☎361-594-3335; www.shinertx.com. Singles $40; doubles $45.)

HALLETTSVILLE
Just 11 mi. down the road from Shiner, Hallettsville lies at the intersection of Alt. U.S. 90 and Rte. 77. In town, the impressive clock tower of the **Lavaca County Courthouse** looms over the square. The **Hallettsville Chamber of Commerce,** 1614 N. Texana Rd., is located ½ mi. north and provides more info on area attractions. (☎361-798-2662. Open M-Sa 8am-5pm.) **The Smokehouse Restaurant,** at the intersection of Alt. U.S. 90 and Rte. 77, cooks down-home food in a little red barn. Steaks ($8-13) and fried chicken ($7) are beloved across town; order the chicken-fried steak ($7) to get the best of both. (☎800 817-2454. Open Su-Th 7am-9pm, F-Sa 7am-10pm.) The **Hallettsville Inn,** 608 W. Fairwinds Rd., offers the best combination of good rooms and good prices in town. Recently remodeled rooms have refrigerators. (☎361-798-3257. Singles $35; doubles $45.)

EAGLE LAKE. The next stop on Alt. U.S. 90 is the tiny town of Eagle Lake, "Goose Hunting Capital of the World." Hunters find cheap lodging in the **Sportsman's Motel,** 203 Booth Dr. (On the right side of Alt. U.S. 90 as you enter town. ☎979-234-5541. Singles $30; doubles $35.)

APPROACHING HOUSTON
From here, it's 30 mi. to the twin towns of **Rosenberg** and **Richmond,** where the sprawling suburbs of Houston begin. After crossing U.S. 59, **Alt. U.S. 90** turns into **Main St.** and continues all the way into the heart of downtown, passing many sights.

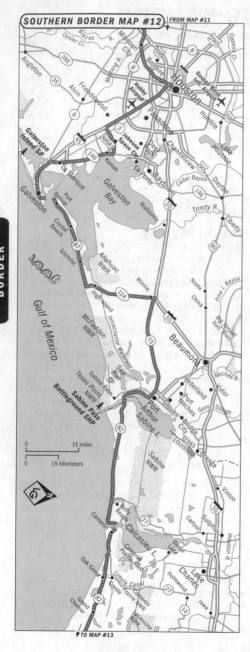

SOUTHERN BORDER

TO MAP #13

HOUSTON

Though often overshadowed by its more famous counterparts, Houston has quietly become America's fourth-largest city. It was named for Sam Houston, the Texan general who won independence for the Lone Star state on a battleground just outside of town, officially establishing it as a city of big men and big deeds. After the Texas-sized accounting disaster of Enron slowed Houston down, other industries have struggled to revive the city's economy. Nevertheless, beyond the glass-and-steel skyscrapers lies a city with one of the country's most impressive collections of world-class restaurants, museums, parks, folk art, and performing arts companies. Southern hospitality and unpretentious attitude in hand, Houston waits for the rest of America to discover it.

◨ GETTING AROUND

Houston's freeway system is a traffic nightmare; the more you avoid it, the happier you'll be. Major interstates **I-45** and **I-10** intersect at the city's downtown and are constantly clogged with angry Texans. The **Sam Houston Tollway** (Beltway 8), an effort to alleviate traffic congestion, wraps around the outer edge of the city. **I-610** forms the same type of belt around the city closer to downtown. **U.S. 59** and **290**, as well as **Rte. 225** and **288**, also turn into large freeways as they approach the city.

Though the flat Texan terrain has sprouted several mini-downtowns, true downtown Houston borders the **Buffalo Bayou** at the intersection of I-10 and I-45. A grid of interlocking one-way streets, downtown centers on **Main St.**, where **parking** is not difficult to find in garages. The museum district sits just southwest of downtown.

From Main St., turning onto **University Blvd.** at the southern end of **Rice** will take you into the **Rice Village** area, which has a happening bar scene. Good eating and shopping abound. University Blvd. intersects **Kirby Dr.**, a main drag dotted with shops and restaurants. Heading north on Kirby Dr., the road winds past the spectacular mansions of the **River Oaks** region on its way to the **Buffalo Bayou.** On the opposite side of the Bayou runs **Memorial Dr.**, next to **Memorial Park.**

VITAL STATS

Population: 1.9 million

Visitor Info: Houston City Hall (☎713-437-5200 or 800-446-8786; www.cityofhouston.gov), at the corner of Walker and Bagby St. Open daily 9am-4pm.

Internet Access: Houston Public Library, 500 McKinney St. (☎713-236-1313), at Bagby St. Open M-Th 9am-9pm, F-Sa 9am-6pm, Su 2-6pm.

Post Office: 701 San Jacinto St. (☎713-223-4402). Open M-F 8am-5pm. **Postal Code:** 77052.

👁 SIGHTS

BUFFALO SOLDIERS NATIONAL MUSEUM. Between the end of the Civil War in 1866 and the integration of the armed forces in 1944, the US Army had several all-black units. During the Indian Wars of the late 1800s, the Cheyenne warriors nicknamed these troops "Buffalo Soldiers," both because of their naturally curly hair and as a sign of respect for their fighting spirit. Learn the history of the Buffalo Soldiers and African-Americans in the military from the Revolutionary War to the present. (*1834 Southmore Blvd. ☎713-942-8920. Open M-F 10am-5pm, Sa 10am-3pm. Free.*)

JOHNSON SPACE CENTER. The city's most popular attraction, the Johnson Space Center is technically not even in Houston but 20 mi. away in Clear Lake, TX. The Mission Control Center is fully operational; when today's astronauts say, "Houston, we have a problem," these are the people who answer. Admission includes tours of the Mission Control Center and other astronaut training facilities. Among the attractions are out-of-this-world harnesses; strap in and bounce around like a real spaceperson. The complex also houses models of the Gemini, Apollo, and Mercury crafts. (*1601 NASA Rd. 1. Take I-45 south to the NASA Rd. exit and head east 3 mi. ☎713-281-244-2100 or 800-972-0369. Open daily June-Aug. 9am-7pm; Sept.-May M-F 10am-5pm, Sa-Su 10am-7pm. $16, seniors $15, ages 4-11 $12. Parking $3.*)

SAN JACINTO STATE PARK. The **San Jacinto Battleground State Historical Park** is the most important monument to Lone Star independence. On this battleground in 1836, Sam Houston's outnumbered Texan Army defeated Santa Anna's Mexican forces, thereby earning Texas its independence from Mexico. The **San Jacinto Monument,** the world's tallest memorial tower, honors all those who fought for Texas's independence. Riding to the top of the 50-story tower yields a stunning view of the area. The museum inside the monument celebrates the state's history with relics like the **Battleship Texas,** the only surviving naval vessel to have served in both World Wars and the last remaining dreadnought. (*Go 21 mi. east on Rte. 225, then 3 mi. north on Rte. 134. ☎281-479-2421. Open daily 9am-6pm. $3, seniors $2.50, under 12 $2. Museum ☎281-479-2431. Open daily 9am-6pm. Free. Battleship ☎281-479-2431. Open daily 10am-5pm. $5, seniors $4, ages 6-18 $3, under 6 free.*)

HERMANN PARK. The 388 beautifully landscaped acres of Hermann Park, near Rice University and the Texas Medical Center, encompass the **Miller Outdoor Theater,** a children's zoo, golf course, sports facilities, a kiddie train, and a Japanese garden. (*Open daily 10am-6pm. Free.*) Near the northern entrance of the park, the **Houston Museum of Natural Science,** offers a six-story glass butterfly center, some formidable looking dinosaurs, and a splendid display of gems and minerals. (*1 Hermann Circle Dr. ☎713-639-4629. Open M-Sa 9am-6pm, Su 11am-6pm. $6, seniors and under 12 $3.50.*) At the southern end of the park, crowds flock to see the gorillas, hippos, and reptiles in the **Houston Zoological Gardens.** (*1513 N. MacGregor St. ☎713-523-5888. Open daily 10am-6pm. $2.50, seniors $2, ages 3-12 $0.50*)

ART ATTRACTIONS. The **Museum of Fine Arts** features paintings of the American West by artists such as Frederic Remington, as well as the largest collection of African gold pieces outside the African continent. Its two large buildings hold Impressionist and post-Impressionist art as well as works from Asia, Africa, and Latin America. The museum's **Sculpture Garden** includes pieces by Matisse and Rodin. (*1001 Bissonet St. ☎713-639-7300. Open Su 12:15-7pm, Tu-W 10am-5pm, Th 10am-9pm, F-Sa 10am-7pm. $5, students and seniors $2.50. Th free. Garden: 5101 Montrose St. Open daily 9am-10pm. Free.*) Across the street, the **Contemporary Arts Museum** frequently rotates exhibits. (*5216 Montrose St. ☎713-284-8250. Open Su noon-5pm, Tu-W and F-Sa 10am-5pm, Th 10am-9pm. Suggested donation $3.*) The Menil Foundation exhibits an array of artwork in four buildings grouped within a block of each other.

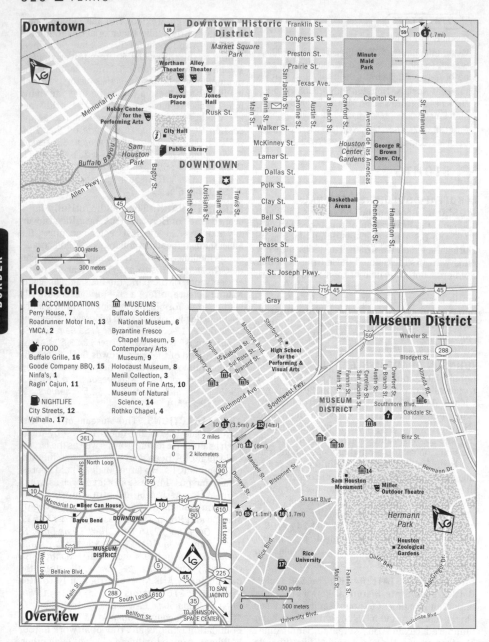

Downtown

Downtown Historic District

Franklin St.
Congress St.
Preston St.
Prairie St.
Texas Ave.
Capitol St.

Market Square Park

Wortham Theater
Alley Theater

Bayou Place
Jones Hall
Rusk St.

Hobby Center for the Performing Arts

City Hall

Public Library

Sam Houston Park

DOWNTOWN

Memorial Dr.

Buffalo Bayou

Allen Pkwy.

Bagby St.

Smith St.

Louisiana St.

Milam St.

Travis St.

Main St.

Fannin St.

San Jacinto St.

Caroline St.

Austin St.

La Branch St.

Crawford St.

Walker St.
McKinney St.
Lamar St.
Dallas St.
Polk St.
Clay St.
Bell St.
Leeland St.
Pease St.
Jefferson St.
St. Joseph Pkwy.

Gray

Minute Maid Park

Houston Center Gardens

George R. Brown Conv. Ctr.

Basketball Arena

Avenida de las Américas

Chenevert St.

Hamilton St.

St. Emanuel

0   300 yards
0   300 meters

SOUTHERN BORDER

Houston

ACCOMMODATIONS
Perry House, 7
Roadrunner Motor Inn, 13
YMCA, 2

FOOD
Buffalo Grille, 16
Goode Company BBQ, 15
Ninfa's, 1
Ragin' Cajun, 11

NIGHTLIFE
City Streets, 12
Valhalla, 17

MUSEUMS
Buffalo Soldiers National Museum, 6
Byzantine Fresco Chapel Museum, 5
Contemporary Arts Museum, 9
Holocaust Museum, 8
Menil Collection, 3
Museum of Fine Arts, 10
Museum of Natural Science, 14
Rothko Chapel, 4

Museum District

Wheeler St.
Blodgett St.

High School for the Performing & Visual Arts

Montrose Blvd.
Stanford St.
Yupon St.
Mulberry St.
W. Alabama St.
Sul Ross St.
Branard St.

Richmond Ave.
Southwest Fwy.

MUSEUM DISTRICT

Fannin St.
Main St.
San Jacinto St.
Caroline St.
Austin St.
La Branch St.
Crawford St.
Almeda Rd.

Southmore St.
Oakdale St.
Binz St.

Sam Houston Monument

Miller Outdoor Theatre

Mandell St.
Dunlavy St.
Bissonnet St.

Sunset Blvd.

Hermann Dr.

Hermann Park

Houston Zoological Gardens

Rice Blvd.
Rice University
Outer Belt
Fannin St.
Main St.
MacGregor Dr.

University Blvd.
Holcombe Blvd.

TO 11 (3.5mi) & 12 (4mi)
TO 13 (6mi)
TO 15 (1.1mi) & 16 (1.7mi)

0   500 yards
0   500 meters

Overview

North Loop
Shepherd Dr.
Memorial Dr.
Beer Can House
Bayou Bend
DOWNTOWN
MUSEUM DISTRICT
Bellaire Blvd.
West Loop
Main St.
South Loop
Bellfort St.

East Loop

TO SAN JACINTO

TO JOHNSON SPACE CENTER

The **Menil Collection** showcases an eclectic assortment of Surrealist paintings and sculptures alongside Byzantine and medieval artifacts and European, American, and African art. A block away, the **Rothko Chapel** houses 14 of the artist's paintings in a non-denominational sanctuary. Worshipful fans of modern art will delight in Rothko's ultra-simplicity; others will wonder where the paintings are. The **Byzantine Fresco Chapel Museum** displays the ornate dome and apse from a 13th-century Byzantine chapel in Cyprus that were rescued in 1983 from thieves before they were sold on the black market. *(Menil Collection: 1515 Sul Ross St. ☎713-525-9400. Open Su and W-Sa 11am-7pm. Free. Rothko Chapel: 3900 Yupon St. ☎713-524-9839. Open daily 10am-6pm. Free. Byzantine Museum: 4011 Yupon St. ☎713-521-3990. Open Su and F-Sa 10am-6pm.)*

BEER CAN HOUSE. Many a Bacchanalian feast must have preceded the construction of the Beer Can House. Adorned with 50,000 beer cans, strings of beer-can tops, and a beer-can fence, the house was built by the late John Mikovisch, an upholsterer from the Southern Pacific Railroad. At $0.05 per can, the tin abode has a market price of $2500. *(222 Malone St., off Washington Ave. Take Memorial Dr. out of downtown and turn left on Wilcox St., which is just before Memorial Park. Turn right on Venice St., then turn left on Malone St; the house is on the right.)*

HOLOCAUST MUSEUM. The chilling architectural style of this building recalls the concentration camps. The museum also has a rotating art gallery and two films about the Holocaust. *(5401 Caroline St. ☎713-942-8000. Open M-F 9am-5pm, Sa-Su noon-5pm. Free.)*

HOUSTON TUNNEL SYSTEM. Earthly pleasures can be found underground the downtown area. Hundreds of shops and restaurants line the 18 mi. Houston Tunnel System, which connects all the major buildings, extending from the Civic Center to the Tenneco Building and the Hyatt Regency. Duck into the air-conditioned passageways via any major building or hotel. Most entrances are closed Saturday and Sunday.

🍴 FOOD

As a city by the sea, Houston has harbored many immigrants, and their cultures are well represented in the city's eclectic, ethnic cuisine.

Along with the more indigenous barbecue and Southern soul food, Mexican, Greek, Cajun, and Asian fare supply travelers with many options. Search for reasonably priced restaurants along the chain-laden streets of **Westheimer** and **Richmond Ave.**, especially where they intersect with **Fountainview Ave.** Houston has two **Chinatowns:** a district south of the George R. Brown Convention Center along Main St. and a newer area on **Bellaire Blvd.** called **DiHo.** Many small Mexican restaurants line the strip malls outside of the downtown region and are usually a good value for an empty stomach. For authentic Mexican fare, try Houston's **East End.**

◪ **Ninfa's,** 2704 Navigation Blvd. (☎713-228-1175). While the restaurant has become a chain around Houston, Mama Ninfa's family still runs this small joint where the legendary eating experience began in 1973. Unbeatable Mexican food. Try the *carne asada* burritos with grilled vegetables ($10) or the fajitas ($8). Wash your meal down with a ninfarita ($5). Open Su-Th 11:30am-10pm, F 11am-11pm, Sa 11:30am-11pm.

Buffalo Grille, 3116 Bissonnet St. (☎713-661-3663. Also at 1201 S. Voss Rd. (☎713-784-3663). From Main St. headed into downtown, take a left off Bissonnet St. at the far end of Hermann Park. Hands down the best breakfast in town. Try the pancakes ($3-4 with fruit), bigger than the plates on which they're served. Breakfast meals like *huevos rancheros* ($5.75) satisfy even the most ferocious appetite. Lunches and dinners are excellent as well. Open M 7am-2pm, Tu-F 7am-9pm, Sa 8am-9pm, Su 8am-2pm.

Goode Company BBQ, 5109 Kirby Dr. (☎713-522-2530), near Bissonnet St. The mesquite-smoked brisket, ribs, and sausage links (all smothered in homemade sauce) will make your mouth water. Sandwiches from $3.75. Open daily 11am-10pm.

Ragin' Cajun, 4302 Richmond Ave. (☎713-623-6321). A local favorite specializing in Cajun-style fish. Indoor picnic tables, Creole music, and a casual atmosphere. Po'boys $6-9. Gumbo $4. Longnecks $2.75. Open M-Th 11am-10pm, F-Sa 11am-11pm.

🏠 ACCOMMODATIONS

Near downtown, **U.S. 59** is rife with budget motels. If you forgo the freeways and approach Houston via Alt. U.S. 90 on **Main St.,** you'll find the south Main St. area also chock full of options, although some stretches may be unsafe at night.

SOUTHERN BORDER

Perry House Houston International Hostel (HI), 5302 Crawford St. (☎713-523-1009). From Main St., take a right (east) on Binz St. and then a left (north) on Crawford St. Just past Hermann Park and near downtown, this beautiful 1920s home is tucked away in a quiet neighborhood. Spacious common area, TV, Internet access ($5 per hr.), and a well-equipped kitchen. Some minor chores may be required. Reception 8-10am and 5-11pm. Lockout 10am-5pm. Dorms $12.50, nonmembers $14.50; singles $21-23; doubles $25-28.

YMCA, 1600 Louisiana Ave. (☎713-659-8501), between Pease and Leeland St. downtown. Small, spartan rooms—all singles—with daily maid service. Some have private baths. Towel deposit $2.50. Key deposit $10. Singles $25-35. Another branch, located at 7903 South Loop East (☎713-643-2804), off the Broadway Exit from I-610, near I-45, is farther out but less expensive. Singles $22.

Roadrunner Motor Inn, 6855 Southwest Fwy. (☎713-771-0641). Exit at Hillcroft Ave./West Park Dr. and take the access road on the east side of the freeway. Slightly cheaper than the Great Western Inn next door, this hotel offers rooms off a fountain-and-jungle filled courtyard. Singles $36; doubles $40.

Brazos Bend State Park, 21901 FM 762 (☎512-389-8900). From Houston, take Rte. 288 to Rosharon. Head west on FM 1462, then north on FM 762. This nature-lover's paradise is less than 1hr. from downtown. Along with a diversity of flora and fauna, visitors are sure to see American alligators, some over 12 ft. long. Sites have water and electricity, and the park offers fishing, picnicking, wildlife observation towers, and 22 mi. of trails. Entrance fee $3. Sites $12.

◧ NIGHTLIFE

City Streets, 5078 Richmond Ave., gives you the opportunity to booty-shake or boot-scoot in its 5 different clubs. (☎713-840-8555. Cover Th ladies free, men $5, F-Sa $5. Open W-F 5pm-2am, Sa 7pm-2am.) For "gods, heroes, mythical beings, and cheap beer," descend to **Valhalla**, 6100 Main St., in the depths of Keck Hall located in the center of the Rice campus. (☎713-348-3258. Lunch $3-4. Beers on tap from $0.85. Open M-F 4pm-2am, Su 7pm-2am. Lunch served M-F 11:30am-1pm.)

▛ LEAVING HOUSTON
To escape Houston, jump on **I-45** and head south toward Galveston. Twenty miles outside of

THE LOCAL STORY

THE GARAGE MAHAL

Is it true that you are what you drive? What if you drive an 8 ft. tall fluffy white rabbit named Rex? Larry Fuente, the Da Vinci of art cars, drives such a vehicle—a 1984 Volkswagen Rabbit mutation—and, like many car artists, he sees his car as an extension of himself.

James Harithas, author of the *Art Car Manifesto,* which the **Art Car Museum** happily distributes, describes the art car movement as a way to subvert materialism and conformity. Garage artists alter their cars to represent adventure and individualism. The art car movement traces its roots back to the first low-riders and hippie vans, which were once as subversive to vehicular norms and conservative tastes as extravagant modern art cars like Rex. Today, the art car movement has taken off. Every year in early May, art cars pull out of the garage, drive onto the freeway, and exit into downtown Houston, where they proudly parade for all to see. Some of the most distinctive cars from this parade make their way into Houston's Art Car Museum. Rex is in good company; an '84 Camero named "Faith" dons a cape, buffalo head, shells, skulls, gems, chrome, pearls, and the Virgin of Guadalupe. She parks next to a Volkswagen bug that resembles a happy canine; it is covered in brown shag carpet and has a giant pink tongue. (The Art Car Museum located at 140 Heights Blvd. From Memorial Dr., turn onto N. Heights Blvd. ☎713-861-3677; www.artcarmuseum.com. Open Su and W-Sa 11am-6pm. Free. See the website for pictures.)

downtown, exit on **Nasa Rd. 1,** which travels east toward the bay. Despite its space age name, passage on Nasa Rd. 1 is much slower than light speed. When the road ends at **Rte. 146,** turn right and cross the bridge into **Kemah.**

KEMAH. This tropical amusement center seems transplanted straight from the resort towns of southern Florida. Caribbean music plays throughout the harbor-side palms as a miniature train tows Texans through the boardwalk attractions. A giant ferris wheel, carousel, boardwalk arcade, and Midway games create an animated carnival atmosphere, and there are many unique (and pricey) restaurants. The Texan favorite, **Joe's Crab Shack,** 5 Kemah Boardwalk, is a funky Christmas light-lit seaside shanty with an awesome view of the harbor. The crabs run $17-21, and other seafood options like fried shrimp ($11) and oysters (dozen $11) are also delicious. (☎281-334-2881. Open Su-Th 11am-10pm, F-Sa 11am-11pm.)

APPROACHING GALVESTON
Continue south on **Rte. 146,** which joins **Rte. 3** after about 18 mi. and then merges onto **I-45,** crossing the bridge onto Galveston Island. On the island, take the first exit (West Beach), which will put you on **61st St.** heading toward the Gulf.

GALVESTON ISLAND

This island made its way into infamy when swashbuckler Jean Lafitte chose it as the base for his pirate fleet. In the 19th century, Galveston was the "Queen of the Gulf," the most prominent port and wealthiest city in Texas. The glamour ended abruptly on September 8, 1900, when a devastating hurricane ripped through the city, claiming 6000 lives. The Galveston hurricane still ranks as one of the worst natural disasters in US history. Now recovered, the city is a beachgoer's paradise and bustling tourist town.

(VITAL STATS)

Population: 57,000

Visitor Info: Galveston Island Visitors Center, 2428 Seawall Blvd. (☎888-425-4753; www.galveston.com). Open daily 8:30am-5pm.

Internet Access: Rosenberg Library, 2310 Sealy Ave. (☎409-763-8854). Open M-Th 9am-9pm, F-Sa 9am-6pm.

Post Office: 601 25th St. (☎409-763-6834). Open M-F 8:30am-5pm. **Postal Code:** 77550.

E GETTING AROUND. 61st St. ends at **Seawall Blvd.,** which hugs the gulf-side beaches of the southern side of the island. Downtown, most establishments, and some beaches are located east along Seawall Blvd., while the western side of the island is more sparsely populated. Nine miles to the west lies **Galveston Island State Park.** On the far eastern edge of the island sits **Apffel Park,** the only beach in Galveston which permits alcoholic beverages. Also on this end of the island, the Galveston Ferry shuttles cars free of charge across to the **Bolivar Peninsula.** Away from the waterfront, Galveston sports a revitalized downtown, known as the **Strand,** with five blocks of gas lamps evoking the 19th-century "Queen of the Gulf" era. **Strand St.** runs east-west along the north side of the island, and is most easily accessible from **Rosenberg St.,** which crosses from Seawall Blvd. to Strand St. north-south. **I-45** ends and becomes **Broadway St.,** which runs east-west through the middle of the island.

◎ SIGHTS. Galveston Island State Park has over 100 campsites with electricity, showers, flush toilets, a park store, fishing, and hiking trails. Those seeking the serenity of the beaches and not the entry fee can use the beach access a quarter mile west of the park, but this requires driving on the sand. (From Seawall Blvd., turn right (west) onto FM 3005 and drive 10 mi. to the park entrance. ☎800-792-1112. Entrance fee $3. Beachfront camping $15-20.) Three giant pyramids are the centerpiece of **Moody Gardens.** One pyramid houses a giant aquarium, another an interactive discovery museum complete with an IMAX theater, and the third a tropical rainforest with butterflies, bats, and exotic flora and fauna. Outside, visitors flock to an artificial white sand beach. The area is packed with shops and restaurants. (Take the West Beach exit onto 61st St. and follow the signs south. ☎800-582-4673. Open summer daily 10am-9pm; winter Su-Th 10am-6pm, F-Sa 10am-9pm. Aquarium $13, seniors $10, ages 4-12 $7. Rainforest $9/$7/$6. IMAX $9/$7/$6. Day pass to all attractions $30; everything half-price after 6pm.)

▟▛ FOOD & ACCOMMODATIONS. Benno's, 1200 Seawall Blvd., serves delicious Cajun seafood, including shrimp, fish, or oyster po'boys ($5.50). Try the Cajun platter (shrimp, oysters, and snapper; $12) with a cup of jambalaya ($3.75), and finish up with key lime pie. (☎409-762-4621. Open Su-Th 11am-10pm, F-Sa 11am-11pm.) **The Original Mexican Cafe,** 1401 Market St., cooks up great Tex-Mex meals with homemade flour tortillas. (Go east from Rosenberg St.; it's on the right. ☎713-762-6001. Lunch specials $6-8. Open M-Th 11am-9:30pm, F 11am-10pm, Sa-Su 8am-10pm.)

On summer weekends, even the shabbiest accommodations can get away with charging upwards of $100, but cheaper deals can be found during the week and in the winter. The beachfront location, large rooms, and pool of the **Sea Horse Inn,** 3404 Seawall Blvd., make it a good place to stop for the night. Although generally affordable, prices change often and are usually higher during summer weekends. (☎407-763-2433. In summer singles M-F $35, Sa-Su $89; doubles $39/$99. In winter singles $29; doubles $33.)

THE ROAD TO PORT ARTHUR

A free 15min. ferry ride from Galveston takes you to the remote Bolivar Peninsula on Rte. 87, an interesting mix of cultures. Homes built high on stilts seem transplanted from the gulf regions of Florida and the rest of the East Coast, while distinctly Texan cattle and oil wells dot the farmlands that extend to the lapping waters and cool sands of the Gulf of Mexico. If you judged by the street signs, you would think the region has a history of lawlessness; signs at the beginning of Rte. 87 remind visitors that "all state and county laws are enforced." A small convenience store near the ferry landing sells supplies and gas to those who forgot to stock up in Galveston. Travelers must merge onto Rte. 124, as Rte. 87 has been permanently washed out by the tremendous storms that batter this coastline. From here, it's a scenic 27 mi. drive through the seaside grasses to the mainland via **High Island,** a bird watcher's paradise.

CRYSTAL BEACH. While the road passes through a few towns, Crystal Beach is the only one with significant services. The **Outrigger Grill,** 1035 Rte. 87, offers all-American meals. Eggs, pancakes, omelettes, and biscuits and gravy run about $2-3. Lunch options ($3-8) include burgers, sandwiches, po'boys, steaks, and chicken. (☎409-684-6212. Open M-Tu and Th-Su 7am-8:30pm, W 7am-2pm, F-Sa 7am-10pm.) If the peninsula particularly strikes your fancy, lodgings can be found at the **Joy Sands Motel,** 1020 Rte. 87. The clean rooms at this coastal dwelling, which is raised high on stilts, all have microfridges. (☎409-684-6152. Summer singles M-F $45, Sa-Su $58; doubles $65/$85. In winter singles $35; doubles $45.)

SOUTHERN BORDER

APPROACHING PORT ARTHUR
Going north on **Rte. 124** takes drivers into the town of **Winnie,** 20 mi. east from High Island. Winnie offers no reason to stop. Instead, jump on **Rte. 73,** which will reach the Memorial Blvd. Exit after about 30 mi. Most of Port Arthur lies down this road, but it is neither convenient nor of much interest. Two exits down off Rte. 73 is **Twin City Hwy.,** a more useful exit.

PORT ARTHUR

The Port Arthur area is a confusing mess of intersecting highways with pockets of smaller cities hiding between them. Perhaps the only thing more confusing than the geography are the miles of pipelines that wind around the endless natural gas and oil refineries that surround the city. This is the heart of the Texas petroleum industry, and natural gas fires burn high into the night.

GETTING AROUND. Rte. 73 enters the Port Arthur area from the south and west. **Rte. 82** defines the southern border of the area, running perpendicular to Rte. 73; a few miles down Rte. 73 is **Memorial Blvd. (U.S. 69),** home to much of downtown Port Arthur. Farther down U.S. 73, **Twin City Hwy. (Rte. 347),** runs parallel to Memorial Blvd. between Port Arthur and Groves; this road is home to many of the area's attractions and services.

VITAL STATS

Population: 58,000

Visitor Info: Port Arthur Convention & Visitors Bureau, 3401 Cultural Center Dr. (☎409-985-7822; www.portarthurtexas.com). Open M-F 8am-noon and 1-5pm.

Internet Access: Public Library, 4615 9th Ave. (☎409-985-8838). Open M-Th 10am-9pm, F 10am-6pm, Sa 10am-5pm, Su 2-5pm; June-Aug. closed Su.

Post Office: 345 Lakeshore Dr. (☎409-983-3423). Open M-F 8am-5pm. **Postal Code:** 77640.

SIGHTS. At the **Museum of the Gulf Coast,** 700 Procter St., Port Arthur demonstrates its pride in some of its many famous residents, including Jimmy Johnson and Janis Joplin. Aside from large exhibits dedicated to football and music, the two-story museum also features excellent displays on the petroleum industry, mariners, and prehistoric animals. (Take Memorial Blvd. all the way to its southeastern end at the intercostal canal. Head right onto Lakeshore Dr., which becomes 4th St. Look for the sign on the left. The museum is hidden on the right, across the street from the police station. ☎ 409-982-7000. Open M-F 9am-5pm, Sa-Su 1-5pm. $3.50, children $1.50.) The **Sabine Pass Battleground State Historical Park,** which offers the nearest camping to Port Arthur, commemorates the Civil War battle in which Texas Confederates defeated Union gunboats, thwarting a Union invasion of Texas. (15 mi. south of Port Arthur on Rte. 87, accessible via Rte. 82. ☎ 512-389-8900. Sites $7, with water and electricity $11. No showers.) Aside from a beautiful coastline, the **Sea Rim State Park** also offers acres of marshland that are accessible via hiking, canoeing, and air boat tours. These wetlands are also home to an impressive diversity of wildlife, including rare birds and alligators. Campsites at the park are on the Gulf's edge and have water, electricity, and showers. (8 mi. south of Sabine Park on Rte. 87. ☎ 512-389-8900. Sites $7, with water $9, with full hookup $12. Day-use $2.)

▉▊ FOOD & ACCOMMODATIONS. The Rib Cage, 4700 Twin City Hwy., offers excellent BBQ sandwiches and po'boys ($3-4), and, of course, ribs. (A few blocks north of Rte. 73 on the right. ☎ 409-962-7427. Open M-Sa 11am-9pm.) The influence of Port Arthur's large Chinese community can be tasted at the **China Inn Restaurant,** 4848 Twin City Hwy. The peaceful setting includes waterfalls and "traditional" furniture. (A few blocks north of Rte. 73. ☎ 409-962-2431. Entrees $8-12. Open daily 11am-2:20pm and 5-9:20pm; F-Sa until 10pm.) By far the best deal for accommodations in Port Arthur, the large, clean rooms at the **Southwinds Inn,** 5101 E. Parkway St., come at the caliber of expensive chains but are even cheaper than the area's budget motels. (☎ 409-962-3000. Pool available for guest use. Continental breakfast included. Singles $36; doubles $39.)

◪ LEAVING PORT ARTHUR
Rte. 87, in the southeast corner of town, is the best way out of Port Arthur, climbing the towering heights of the **Martin Luther King Jr. Bridge.** The bridge connects to **Pleasure Island,** which, despite its name, has little to offer aside from a few large parks. Then take **Rte. 82,** continuing south.

THE ROAD THROUGH LOUISIANA

The moment Rte. 82 bridges Sabine Lake and crosses over into Louisiana, water begins to saturate the ground, changing the terrain into Louisiana swamp and marshland. This entrance into bayou country marks the beginning of the **Creole Nature Trail,** a National Scenic Byway that stretches almost all the way to Pecan Island along Rte. 82. At its beginning here just inside Louisiana, the road veers briefly along the shoreline, as if to say goodbye to the wind-swept white sand beaches that line this part of the gulf. As it wanders eastward, Rte. 82 passes **Holly Beach,** a seaside village with nothing more than a few homes, some rental cabins and an RV park. Eight miles outside Holly Beach, Rte. 82 crosses a shipping channel via the **Calcasieu Ferry.** Service is free and continuous, and while the jump across the canal is only a few hundred yards, the ferry is as slow as it is small—waits can exceed 30min. The ferry lands just outside the small town of **Cameron,** where roadside stands sell the day's catches from the Gulf. The fresh jumbo gulf shrimp are a regional favorite; you eat them right after they catch them.

From here, Rte. 82 cuts a long, 117 mi. path through the marshes and swamps of southern Louisiana. Rural homesteads line most of the highway but offer little more than the occasional picturesque oak grove draped with Spanish moss. Linger as long as you like along this untouristed stretch of backcountry, but if you want to speed through to get to the bright lights of real towns, you can reach them in under 2hr. Fifty miles east of Cameron, the town of **Pecan Island** offers one of the only gas stations in the marsh and a few token pecan trees before the highway disappears into high reeds. Keep your eyes peeled for the elusive American alligators that lurk in these waters.

◪ APPROACHING ABBEVILLE
At the junction with Rte. 35, turn right to stay on **Rte. 82** toward Esther and Abbeville. Rte. 82 continues north through town and joins with **Rte. 14** at Vet-

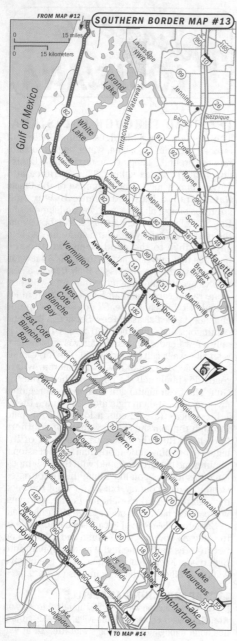

FROM MAP #12
SOUTHERN BORDER MAP #13

erans Dr. Turning right (east) onto Rte. 14 will take you through Abbeville.

ABBEVILLE

Many of the historic buildings that line S. State St. (Rte. 82) in downtown Abbeville date back to the mid-19th century, when the French settled here. Picturesque buildings form the heart of the city and lead up to the Greek Revival columns of the **Vermillion Parish Courthouse.** One-way streets radiate from this impressive structure at the town's center. Just one block to the west on Rte. 74, the older **Magdalen Square** holds the romanesque **St. Mary Magdalen Catholic Church,** built in 1911.

The finer restaurants in town lie along S. State St. before the courthouse. A good bet is the **Coffee Tavern,** 109 S. State St., a cozy cafe that offers excellent sandwiches ($5.50) and salads ($5.25) along with specialty coffees and drinks. (☎337-893-4255. Open M-Sa 7:30am-9:30pm.) On the main drag of Abbeville, the **Sunbelt Lodge,** 1903 Veterans Dr., offers passersby small, clean rooms. (☎866-299-1480. Singles $42-45; doubles $48-50.)

APPROACHING LAFAYETTE
Lafayette lies about 19 mi. north on **U.S. 167** from Abbeville; from U.S. 167, turn left onto **Jefferson Blvd.** to drive through the heart of downtown.

LAFAYETTE

At the center of bayou land, Lafayette is the two-stepping, crawfish-eating, French-speaking heart of Acadiana. While New Orleans may be Louisiana's most popular (and most touristy) city, Lafayette exudes a vibrant and wholesome authenticity that puts the schlocky debauchery of Bourbon Street to shame. Locals here continue to answer their phones with a proud *bonjour*, and invite visitors to share their many takes on crawfish—boiled, fried, in gumbo, and in *etouffee*. At night, they party to fiddles, accordions, and the spoons.

GETTING AROUND

Lafayette is a crossroads at the center of the swamp. **I-10** leads east to New Orleans and west to Lake Charles; **U.S. 90** heads south to New Iberia and the Atchafalaya Basin and north to Alexandria and Shreveport; **U.S. 167/I-49** runs north into central Louisiana. Most of the city is west of the **Evangeline Thwy.** (I-49 in the north, U.S. 90 in the south), where most of the budget motels stand. **Johnston St.** marks the east border of downtown and has many fast-food restaurants.

▼ TO MAP #14

SOUTHERN BORDER

VITAL STATS

Population: 110,000

Visitor Info: Lafayette Convention and Visitors Commission, 1400 N. Evangeline Thwy. (☎337-232-3808; www.lafayettetravel.com). Open M-F 8:30am-5pm, Sa-Su 9am-5pm.

Internet Access: Lafayette Public Library, 301 W. Congress St. (☎337-261-5787). Open M-Th 9am-9pm, F 9am-6pm, Sa 9am-5pm, Su 1-5pm.

Post Office: 1105 Moss St. (☎800-275-8777). Open M-F 8am-5:30pm, Sa 8:30am-noon. **Postal Code:** 70501.

🗝 SIGHTS

The **Acadian Cultural Center,** 501 Fisher Rd., has a dramatic 40min. documentary chronicling the arrival of the Acadians in Louisiana, as well as a film on conservation efforts in the Atchafalaya swamp and terrific bilingual exhibits on Cajun history and culture. (Take Johnston St. to Surrey, then follow the signs. ☎337-232-0789. Open daily 8am-5pm. Shows every hr. 9am-4pm. Free.) Next door, a "living museum" re-creates the Acadian settlement of **Vermilionville,** 1600 Surrey St., with music, crafts, food, actors in costume, and dancing on the Bayou Vermilion banks. (☎337-233-4077 or 800-992-2968. Open Su and Tu-Sa 10am-4pm; last entry 3pm. Live bands Su 1-4pm. Cajun cooking demos daily 10:30am, 12:30, 1:30pm. $8, seniors $6.50, ages 6-18 $5.) **Acadian Village,** 200 Greenleaf Rd., features authentic 19th-century Cajun homes with a fascinating array of artifacts and displays. While at the village, view a small collection of Native American artifacts at the **Native American Museum** or see the collection of 19th-century medical paraphernalia at the **Doctor's House.** (Take Johnston St. to Ridge Rd., then turn left on Broussard; follow the signs. ☎337-981-2489 or 800-962-9133. Open daily 10am-5pm. $7, seniors $6, ages 6-14 $4.) Follow signs to **McGee's Landing,** 1337 Henderson Rd., which sends three 1½hr. boat tours into the Basin each day. (☎337-228-2384. Tours daily 10am, 1, 3pm. Spring and fall sunset tours by reservation. $12, seniors and under 12 $6, under 2 free.)

 Saint John's Cathedral Oak shades an entire lawn with spidery branches reaching from a trunk with a 19 ft. circumference. The largest branch weighs an astonishing 72 tons. (At 914 St. John St.)

🍴 FOOD

It's not hard to find reasonably priced Cajun and Creole cuisine in Lafayette, a city that prides itself on its food. Of course, it also prides itself on music, which can be found live in most of the same restaurants at night.

Dwyer's Cafe, 323 Jefferson St. (☎337-235-9364). Since 1927, this diner has been the best place in town to get breakfast or lunch. They serve a bang-up breakfast special (grits, eggs, ham, biscuits, juice, and coffee; $4). At lunchtime, locals saunter in for a plate of gigantic proportions ($7). Open M-F 5am-4pm, Sa-Su 5am-2pm.

Prejean's, 3480 I-49 North (☎337-896-3247; www.prejeans.com). From I-45 North, take the Gloria St. Exit and head north beside the freeway on the access road. After ½ mi., Prejean's is on the right. Excellent Cajun fare with nightly music as zesty as the food. Try the unique crawfish enchiladas ($9.50) or a BBQ shrimp po'boy ($8). Dinner options include the singing crawfish combo ($18), which features crawfish *etouffee*, salad, and crawfish pie. Live music 7-9:30pm. Open Su-Th 7am-10pm, F-Sa 7am-10pm.

Chris' Po'buys, 631 Jefferson St. (☎337-234-1696; www.chrispoboys.com). From Evangeline Thwy., turn left onto Jefferson St. On the left just after Main St. Chris' holds to the po'boy tradition, offering great sandwiches at great prices. Try the special: roast beef, ham, and swiss with gravy (half $4, whole $6). W nights Cajun music, Th night open mic poetry. Open 11am-8pm daily. Bar open until 10pm.

The Judice Inn, 3134 Johnston St. (☎337-984-5614). A roadside time-warp that serves up great burgers ($2). Open M-Sa 10am-10pm.

🏠 ACCOMMODATIONS

🏨 **Blue Moon Guest House & Saloon,** 215 E. Convent St. (☎337-234-2422; www.bluemoonhostel.com). Driving south on Evangeline Thwy. (U.S. 90), take a left on Johnston St. and a left on Convent St. One of the best lodgings in the south. The marriage of hostel and bar has met with incredible success to the tune of lively Cajun music. Inviting common areas lend themselves to conversation, and the deck and backyard are excellent places to chill out or have a beer. Kitchen, beautiful baths, A/C, and large rooms. Internet access $3 per day. Linen $2. Check-in 5-10pm. Lockout 10am-5pm. Co-ed and single-sex dorms $15; private rooms $40-55.

SOUTHERN BORDER

Travel Host Inn South, 1314 N. Evangeline Thwy. (☎337-233-2090). Clean rooms. Continental breakfast included. Singles $30; doubles $35.

Acadiana Park Campground, 1201 E. Alexander St. (☎337-291-8388), off Louisiana Ave. Close to the center of Lafayette, this campground has 75 sites with access to tennis courts and a soccer field. Reception Su-Th and Sa 8am-5pm, F 8am-8pm. Full hookup $9.

KOA Lafayette, 537 Apollo Rd. (☎337-235-2739), in Scott, 5 mi. west of town on I-10 at Exit 97. This lakeside campground has over 200 sites and offers a store, mini-golf course, and two pools. Reception 7:30am-8:30pm. Sites $19, with water and electricity $24.50, with full hookup $26.

Anyone who thinks couple-dancing went out in the 50s should try a *fais-do-do,* a lengthy, wonderfully energetic traditional dance that got its name from the custom parents had of putting their children to sleep and then running off to dance the night away. (*Fais-do-do* is Cajun baby talk for "to put to bed.")

📭 NIGHTLIFE

To find the best zydeco in town, pick up a copy of *The Times,* free at restaurants and gas stations.

▨ Angelle's Whiskey River Landing, 1365 Henderson Levee Rd. (☎337-228-8567), in Breaux Bridge. Live Cajun music and dancing on the levee next to the swamp. Live music Sa 9pm-1am, Su 1-4pm.

Hamilton's Zydeco Club, 1808 Verot School Rd. (☎337-991-0783). Live Cajun bands and wild dancing. Open daily from 5pm.

Grant St. Dance Hall, 113 Grant St. (☎337-237-8513). Everything from zydeco to metal. 18+. Cover $5-10. Only open days of shows; call ahead.

Blue Moon Saloon, 215 E. Convent St. (☎337-234-2422). Area bands whoop it up in the backyard outdoor bar. W-Th happy hour from 5-7pm with free red beans and rice. Music W-Su nights; ends at 11pm. Cover $5. See **Accommodations,** above.

Randol's, 2320 Kaliste Saloom Rd. (☎337-981-7080). Live Cajun and zydeco music nightly; also a restaurant. Open Su-Th 5-10pm, F-Sa 5-11pm.

El Sid O's Blues and Zydeco, 1523 Martin Luther King Dr. (☎318-235-0647). Here you might catch a glimpse the legendary Buckwheat Zydeco. Open F-Su 7pm-2am.

🚩 APPROACHING NEW IBERIA
From Lafayette, take **U.S. 90** heading south out of the city, then exit left for **Rte. 182,** which becomes **Main St.** in New Iberia.

NEW IBERIA
The "Queen City" of the Bayou Teche, New Iberia was home to many wealthy sugar plantation owners during the Antebellum period. The city's New Orleans-style **Main St.** runs parallel to the bayou, which, as a perfect means of shipping, was the lifeblood of the sugarcane industry. Main St. only runs westward through town, while **St. Peter St.** handles the eastbound traffic one block south. Surrounded by dazzling flower gardens and

SOUTHERN BORDER

THE LOCAL STORY

ACADIANA

Throughout the early 18th century, the English government in Nova Scotia became increasingly resentful of the prosperity of French settlers (Acadians) and deeply offended by their refusal to kneel before the British Crown. During the French and Indian war in 1755, the British rounded up the Acadians and deported them in what came to be called *le Grand Dérangement,* "the Great Upheaval." The settlers found new homes in America's bayous, where "Acadian" was shortened to "Cajun." The Cajuns of St. Martin, Lafayette, and St. Mary parishes are descendants of those settlers. In the 1920s, Louisiana passed laws forcing Acadian schools to teach in English. Later, during the oil boom of the 1970s and 80s, oil executives and developers envisioned the Acadian center of Lafayette as the Houston of Louisiana and threatened to flood the area with mass culture. But the proud people of southern Louisiana have resisted homogenization, and today the state is officially bilingual.

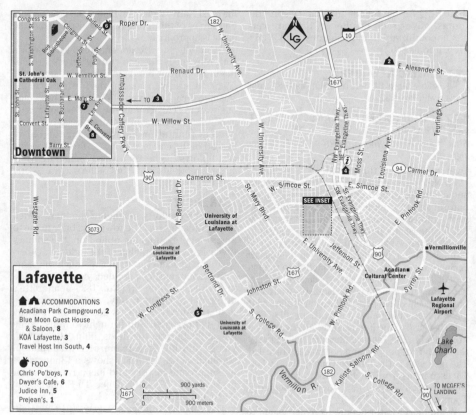

Downtown

Lafayette

🏠🏕 ACCOMMODATIONS
Acadiana Park Campground, **2**
Blue Moon Guest House
& Saloon, **8**
KOA Lafayette, **3**
Travel Host Inn South, **4**

🍎 FOOD
Chris' Po'boys, **7**
Dwyer's Cafe, **6**
Judice Inn, **5**
Prejean's, **1**

shaded by massive live oaks draped in Spanish moss on the banks of the Bayou Teche, **Shadows-on-the-Teche,** 317 E. Main St., is a great Classical Revival planation built by sugarcane planter David Weeks in 1834. It still evokes the aura of an era long gone. (☎337-364-6446. Open daily 9am-4:30pm. 45min. guided tours $7, children $4.)

Center St. is lined with fast food and chain motels, and also has the **Iberia Parish Visitors Bureau,** 2704 Rte. 14. (☎337-365-1540. Open M-F 9am-5pm). **Clementine,** 113 E. Main St., is a gourmet eatery with a Cajun bent. Lunches include seafood gumbo ($5.50), po'boys ($7), and entrees like blackened redfish ($10). Dinners are quite a bit more expensive, but if you're willing to splurge, try the crabmeat *au gratin* ($21.50) or steak ($22). Local artists frequent the dark interior, which is decorated with the

work of the restaurant's namesake, the late folk artist Clementine Hunter. (☎337-560-1007. Open M-Tu 11am-2pm, W-Th 11am-2pm and 6-9pm, F 11am-2pm and 6-10pm, Sa 6-10pm.) Similar to Clementine but a little less expensive, the **Little River Inn,** 833 E. Main St., specializes in Cajun seafood. Try the Cajun shrimp pasta ($13). The restaurant overlooks a giant oak tree, estimated to have been planted in 1640. (☎337-367-7466. Entrees $12-14. Open daily 10am-10pm.) Each room of the 🗺**Teche Motel,** 1829 E. Main St., makes up half of a wooden cabin that sits underneath an oak canopy on the sleepy bayou's edge. Guests have access to the beautiful Bayou Garden, which includes a dock, gazebo, tiki torches, music, rope swing, and even a trampoline. Exceedingly friendly hosts aim to please, and will even lend you the use of their BBQ for bayouside grilling. Despite the rooms' olive-green 60s decor, they are very clean, comfortable, and spacious. (☎337-369-3756. Rooms $40.)

 LEAVING NEW IBERIA
Follow **Main St.** out of town; Main St. soon merges with **Rte. 182.**

DETOUR: AVERY ISLAND, HOME OF TABASCO

6 mi. south of New Iberia on Rte. 329. Follow the signs.

Over 130 years on this island, E. A. McIhenny ("Mr. Ned") planted a crop of capsicum peppers and combined their fiery juices with the island's natural salt to create the now-famous pepper sauce known as Tabasco. Today there is a $0.50 toll for the island, but the charge can quickly be made up in free samples at the Tabasco Country Store, if you can handle the heat. On the **Tabasco Factory Tour,** after a brief introduction to the history of Tabasco, visitors are exposed to 15min. of hard-core pro-Tabasco propaganda (as well as the burning scent of peppers) before being allowed to view the assembly lines and bottlers, all behind glass because of the intense heat. Afterwards, visitors head to the **Tabasco Museum,** where everything Tabasco, pepper, and hot sauce is revealed. The next stop is the **Tabasco Country Store,** where Tabasco items from kitchenware to neckties are for sale. (☎337-365-8173; www.tabasco.com. Tours daily 9am-4pm. Free.)

While most visitors come to Avery Island to view the Tabasco factory, the natural beauty here also rewards explorers. Drivers can take a 4 mi. tour of the beautifully landscaped **Jungle Gardens.** Nature-lovers can relax amid azaleas and camellia fields in season. There is also a bird sanctuary that attracts some 20,000 snowy egrets to platforms in a pond nicknamed **"Bird City."** Just don't picnic too close to the ponds—impolite alligators lurking in the waters are known to take without asking. (Open daily 8am-5pm. $6, ages 6-12 $4.25.)

THE ROAD TO JEANERETTE

The 125 mi. **Bayou Teche,** one of the longest of Louisiana's thousands of swampy waterways, slithers its way from northwest of Lafayette to the Gulf of Mexico at Morgan City. Teche means "snake" in the local Native American dialect, and the serpentine curves of this murky waterway prove that the name is appropriate.

Thankfully, Rte. 182 does not follow the bayou's path religiously, instead cutting across some of the more abrupt bends in favor of a straighter course. It is easy to imagine the frustration of the steamboat captains who often steered these sinuous waters. This commercial waterway was so important that many of the sugar czars built their opulent plantation estates facing the bayou instead of the connecting roads. Rte. 182 heading east follows the bayou toward Jeanerette while sugarcane fields abut the Teche's cypress- and oak-lined banks.

JEANERETTE

Ivy climbs the lofty heights of the lonely brick spire in Jeanerette. The town was once home to a large cypress logging operation; the solitary tower is all that remains of the industry. Otherwise, life in Jeanerette remains much the same as it was a century ago; decaying brick buildings still line Main St. (Rte. 182). Jeanerette's other name is **Sugar City,** and its sugarcane industry survives to this day. In the fall, the cane is harvested and brought to mills, while the stalks burn in the fields, filling the air with sweet smoke. The **Jeanerette Bicentennial Museum,** 500 E. Main St., shows a 13min. video on sugarcane history and has a replica sugar press. (☎337-376-4408. Open Tu-F 10am-5pm, Sa 10am-2pm. $3, students $1.)

The folks at **LeJeune's Bakery,** 1510 W. Main St., bake French bread in their old-fashioned brick oven. Because they primarily ship bread to other places, they don't have a storefront, but they'll gladly sell the bread straight from the kitchen. Enter through the door on the left side of the building and they'll find you a hot loaf. (☎337-276-5690. No set hours.) Opened in 1927 as a Greyhound bus stop, the **Yellow Bowl,** 19478 Rte. 182 West, derives its name from the use of "bowl" as a code word for speakeasy during prohibition. But alcohol is not its claim to fame. A Cajun family acquired it in the 1950s and began serving crawfish, and soon the crustacean was on every menu in the state. For an authentic Cajun delight try a crawfish *etouffee* ($12) or a cup of crawfish bisque ($4). They also have other seafood, steaks ($8-16), and po'boys. (2 mi. east of Jeanerette. ☎318-276-5512. Open Su 11am-2:30pm, Tu-F 11am-9:30pm, Sa 5-9:45pm.)

Cajun legend holds that when the French Acadians left Nova Scotia for Louisiana, the local lobsters grew lonely and swam after them. The long journey left them so exhausted that they shrank to the size of shrimp, becoming the "mud bugs" (a.k.a. crawfish) that inhabit the waters of Louisiana.

FRANKLIN. Seventeen miles outside Jeanerette, Rte. 182 travels by Franklin's antebellum gas lamps, oak canopies, mansions, and graveyard. A town of quintessential Southern beauty, Franklin suggests the elegance and chivalry of years gone by even while its preserved slave quarters stand as constant reminders of the price of such opulence. The clean and comfortable budget rooms at the **Billmar Motel,** on U.S. 90, are cheaper than those found in nearby Morgan City. (On the right just before entering Franklin on Rte. 182. ☎347-828-5130. Singles $31; doubles $41.)

APPROACHING MORGAN CITY
Leaving Franklin, **Rte. 182** merges onto **U.S. 90** and makes its way into Morgan City.

MORGAN CITY
Following the Civil War, Charles Morgan, a steamship and railroad tycoon, dredged the Atchafalaya Bay Channel to make Morgan City a bustling trade center. The halfway point between New Orleans and Lafayette, the city remains an important crossroads of land and water routes at the edge of the swamp. Unfortunately, there isn't much to see or do here. Some may be interested in making the trek to the **International Petroleum Museum and Exposition,** also known as the "Rig Museum" because it's on an abandoned oil rig. Known fondly as "Mr. Charlie," it was the first submersible drilling rig used in offshore production. (☎504-384-3744. Open M-F 8:30am-5pm. 1½ hr. tours 10am and 2pm.)

For a food stop, check out **Manny's Restaurant,** 725 Rte. 90. Traditional hearty American breakfasts (pork chops and eggs $7, pancakes $2.60), roast beef dinners ($7), and a lunch buffet ($8) mean no one goes home hungry. (On U.S. 90 East, on the left just after the underpass. ☎985-384-2359. Open M-Sa 6am-8:30pm, Su 7am-2pm. Buffet 11am-2pm.)

APPROACHING HOUMA
To leave Morgan City, head east onto **U.S. 90,** which crosses a treetop-level bridge that avoids the sinking marshes by traveling above them. Take Exit 182 at Beouf and go left on **Bus. U.S. 90.** Turn left again onto **Rte. 182.** On the way into Houma, the road skirts the aptly named **Black Bayou,** where murky, brackish waters conjure up images of creatures from B-rated horror films. At the fork in the road, stay right. Entering downtown on **Barrow St.,** Rte. 182 turns right for a block at **Main St.**

HOUMA
Houma is at the confluence of seven bayous, so fishing boats line the waterways. Don't be surprised if one of them glides alongside as you meander down one of the bayou-hugging streets. Alligators, wandering from their bayou homes, often approach humans on the sidewalks, making the Houma Alligator Patrol a full time business. In the winter, when cold weather sends alligators into hibernation, an eerie fog often spills forth from the warm bayou waters.

In a comfortable family kitchen atmosphere, **A-Bear's Cafe,** 809 Black Bayou Dr., serves up hearty home-style meals that would make mama proud, provided mama was a full-blood Cajun. The red beans and rice with sausage ($4.75) are wholesome eatin', while the Catfish A-Bear Platter made with a fresh catch is a classic favorite ($11). Don't miss the daily homemade pies. (At the corner of Rte. 182, across from the Civic Center. ☎504-872-6306. Live Cajun music F nights. Open M-Th 10:30am-3pm, F 10:30am-3pm and 5:30-9:30pm, Sa 11am-2pm.) Down the street, the residents of Houma two-step to the rhythms of Cajun and zydeco music at the **Jolly Inn Dance Hall,** 1507 Barrow St. (☎985-872-6114. Cafe open M-F 10:30am-2pm. Dance hall open F 6-10pm, Sa 3-7pm. $3, under 12 free.) Budget accommodations line New Orleans Blvd. On the right of Rte. 182, a half-mile east of downtown, is **A-Bear's Motel,** 342 New Orleans Blvd., which has small rooms with cable TV and A/C. (☎985-872-4528. No non-smoking rooms. Singles $33; doubles $40.)

SOUTHERN BORDER

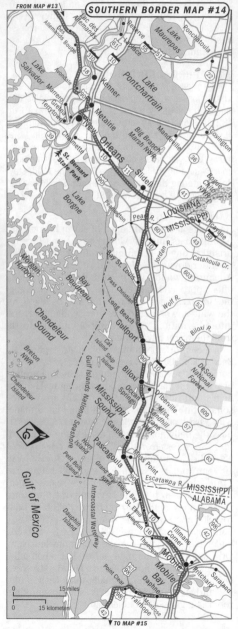

FROM MAP #13

SOUTHERN BORDER MAP #14

SOUTHERN BORDER

▼ TO MAP #15

APPROACHING NEW ORLEANS

From Main St., leave Houma by turning left on **New Orleans Blvd.** From here, **Rte. 182** travels 8 mi. north and then merges onto **U.S. 90,** which passes uneventfully into the suburbs of New Orleans. Nearing the city, avoid the freeway and its hassles by staying on U.S. 90. When U.S. 90 splits into Bus. Rte. 90, stay left on regular U.S. 90, which crosses the great river via the towering **Huey Long Bridge** (free). U.S. 90 becomes **Jefferson Rte.** and then **S. Clairborne Ave.** From S. Clairborne Ave. head right (south) on **Jefferson Ave.** to **St. Charles Ave.,** which is the heart of the Garden District. Following St. Charles Ave. east will take you to downtown and the French Quarter.

NEW ORLEANS

First explored by the French, *La Nouvelle Orléans* was secretly ceded to the Spanish in 1762; the citizens didn't find out until 1766. Spain returned the city to France just in time for the United States to grab it in the Louisiana Purchase of 1803. Centuries of cultural cross-pollination have resulted in a vast melange of Spanish courtyards, Victorian verandas, Cajun jambalaya, Creole gumbo, and French *beignets.* The city's nickname, "the Big Easy," reflects the carefree attitude characteristic of this fun-loving place, where food and music are the two ruling passions. New Orleans has its own style of cooking, speaking, and making music—at the start of the 20th century, its musicians invented the musical style that came to be known as jazz. While New York may claim to be "the city that never sleeps," N'awlins holds the title for "the city that won't stop partying." The only thing that stifles this vivacity is the heavy, humid summer air that slows folks to a near standstill. But when the day's heat retreats into the night, the city drinks and dances into the early morning. Come late February, there's no escaping the month-long celebration of Mardi Gras, the peak of the city's festive mood.

GETTING AROUND

Most sights in New Orleans are located within a central area. The city's main streets follow the curve of the **Mississippi River,** hence the nickname "the Crescent City." Directions from locals reflect bodies of water—lakeside means north, referring to Lake Ponchartrain, and "riverside" means south. Uptown lies west,

(VITAL STATS)

Population: 480,000

Visitor Info: Metropolitan Convention and Visitors Bureau, 529 St. Ann St. (☎504-568-5661 or 800 672-6124; www.neworleanscvb.com), by Jackson Sq. in the French Quarter. Open daily 9am-5pm.

Internet Access: New Orleans Public Library, 219 Loyola Ave. (☎504-529-7323), west of Canal St. Open M-Th 10am-6pm, F-Sa 10am-5pm.

Post Office: 701 Loyola Ave. (☎800-275-8777). Open M-F 7am-8pm, Sa 8am-5pm, Su noon-5pm. **Postal Code:** 70113.

upriver; downtown is downriver. The city is concentrated on the east bank of the Mississippi, but "The East" refers only to the easternmost part of the city.

Tourists flock to the small **French Quarter (Vieux Carré),** bounded by the Mississippi River, **Canal St., Rampart St.,** and **Esplanade Ave.** Streets in the Quarter follow a grid pattern, making travel easy. Just northeast of the Quarter, across Esplanade Ave., **Faubourg Marigny** is a residential neighborhood that has recently developed trendy nightclubs, bars, and cafes. Northwest of the Quarter, across Rampart St., the little-publicized black neighborhood of **Tremé** has a storied history, but has been marred by the encroaching highway overpass and the housing projects lining its Canal St. border. Be careful in Tremé at night. Uptown, the residential **Garden District,** bordered by **St. Charles Ave.** to the north and **Magazine St.** to the south, is distinguished by its elegant homes.

Parking in New Orleans is relatively easy (☎337-299-3700 for parking info). Throughout the French Quarter (and in most other residential neighborhoods), signs along the streets designate "2hr. parking residential" areas. Many streets throughout the city have meters (free M-F after 6pm and on weekends and holidays). Parking lots along Rampart St. sell day-long spaces ($5-12), but many lots within the French Quarter charge upwards of $15 for anything over 3hr. Another viable option is to park for free in the Garden District and take the St. Charles Streetcar along St. Charles Ave. into downtown and the French Quarter. ($1.25.) Of course, during Mardi Gras, most of the free spots will be taken. As a general rule, avoid parking on deserted streets at night. After sunset, it's often best to take a cab or the St. Charles Streetcar.

◎ SIGHTS

The scenic **St. Charles Streetcar route,** easily picked up at Canal St. and Carondelet St., passes through parts of the **Central Business District** ("CBD" or "downtown"), the Garden District, and the **Uptown** and **Carrollton** neighborhoods along **S. Carrollton Ave.** and past **Tulane** and **Loyola Universities.**

The **Jean Lafitte National Historical Park and Preserve Visitors Center,** 419 Decatur St., conducts free walking tours through the French Quarter. (☎504-589-2636. Office open daily 9am-5pm. 1½hr. tour daily 9:30am. Come early; only 25 people per tour. Daily presentations on regional topics 3pm.) On the **Gay Heritage Tour,** Robert Batson, "history laureate" of New Orleans gives perhaps the best possible introduction to New Orleans for anyone, gay or straight. (Leaves from Alternatives, 909 Bourbon St. ☎504-945-6789. 2½hr. tours W and Sa 2pm. $20 per person. Reservations required.)

FRENCH QUARTER. Allow *at least* a full day in the Quarter. The oldest section of the city is famous for its ornate wrought-iron balconies—French, Spanish, and uniquely New Orleans architecture—and raucous atmosphere. Known as the **Vieux Carré** (view ca-RAY), or Old Square, the historic district of New Orleans offers dusty used bookstores, voodoo shops, museums, art galleries, bars, and tourist traps. **Bourbon St.** is packed with touristy bars, strip clubs, and panhandlers disguised as clowns. **Decatur St.** has more mellow coffeehouses and bars; if you're searching for some *bona fide* New Orleans tunes, head just northeast of the Quarter to **Frenchmen St.,** where a block of bars is what some locals say is what Bourbon St. was like 20 years ago. A streetcar named "Desire" once rolled down **Royal St.,** one of the French Quarter's most aesthetically pleasing avenues. Pick up the *French Quarter Self-Guided Walking Tour* from the Visitors Center on St. Ann St. to begin an informed jaunt past balconies of wrought-iron oak leaves and acorns, as well as Louisiana's oldest commercial and government buildings. During the day, much activity in the French Quarter centers around **Jackson Sq.,** a park dedicated to General Andrew Jackson, victor of the Battle of New Orleans. The square swarms with artists, mimes, musicians, psychics, magicians, and con artists. Catch a horse-drawn tour of the Quarter here for $10; wait on the Decatur St. side. The oldest Catholic cathedral in the US, **St. Louis Cathedral** possesses a simple beauty, and has been fully operational since 1718. *(615 Père Antoine's Alley. ☎504-525-9585. Open daily 6:30am-6:30pm. Tours every 15-20min. Free.)* Behind the cathedral lies **Cathedral Garden,** also known as **St. Anthony's Garden,** bordered by **Pirate's Alley** and **Père Antoine's Alley.** Legend has it that the former was the site of covert meetings between pirate Jean Lafitte and Andrew Jackson as they conspired to plan the Battle of New Orleans. In reality, the alley wasn't even built until 16 years later. Pirate's Alley is also home to **Faulkner House Books,** where the late American author wrote his first novel, *Soldier's Pay. (624 Pirate's Alley. ☎504-524-2940. Open daily 10am-6pm.)* The **French Market** takes up several city blocks just east of Jackson Sq., toward the water along N. Peters St. *(☎504-522-2621. Shops open daily 9am-8pm.)* The market begins at the famous **Café du Monde** (see p. 845). Down by Gov. Nicholls St., the market becomes the outdoor **Farmers Market,** which never closes (though they're only really active from dawn to dusk), selling "most anything that grows" since 1791. Beyond the Farmers Market is the **Flea Market,** where vendors sell everything from feather boas to woodcarvings.

WATERFRONT. For an up-close view of the Mississippi River and a unique New Orleans district, take the free **Canal Street Ferry** to **Algiers Point.** The Algiers of old was home to many of New Orleans's African-Americans and was the birthplace of many of the city's famous jazz musicians. Once called "The Brooklyn of the South," it is now a quiet, beautiful neighborhood to explore by foot. Stop at the **Dry Dock Cafe,** just off the ferry landing, to pick up a map of the area. At night, the ferry's outdoor observation deck affords a panoramic view of the city's sights. *(Departs from the end of Canal St. daily every 30min. 5:45am-midnight. Cars $1 round-trip.)*

WAREHOUSE ARTS DISTRICT. Relatively new to the downtown area, the Warehouse Arts District, centered roughly on at the intersection of Julia St. and Camp St., contains several contemporary art galleries in revitalized warehouse buildings, as well as many of the city's museums. The galleries feature widely attended exhibition openings the first Saturday of every month. On **White Linen Night,** the first Saturday in August, thousands take to the streets donning their fanciest white finery. *(☎504-522-1999.)* In an old brick building with a modern glass-and-chrome facade, the **Contemporary Arts Center** mounts exhibits ranging from puzzling to positively cryptic. *(900 Camp St. ☎504-528-3805; www.cacno.org. Open Su and Tu-Sa 11am-5pm. $5, students and seniors $3, under 12 free. Th free.)* In the rear studio of the **New Orleans School of Glassworks and Printmaking,** observe students and instructors transforming molten glass into vases and sculptures. *(727 Magazine St. ☎504-529-7277. Open winter M-Sa 10am-6pm; summer M-F 10am-5:30pm. Free.)* The **Jonathan Ferrara Gallery** hosts all sorts of local and regional artists. *(841 Carondelet St. ☎504-522-5471. Open Tu-Sa noon-6pm. Free.)* Just west of the Warehouse District, the **Zeitgeist Multi-Disciplinary Arts Center** offers films, theatrical and musical performances, and art exhibitions. *(1724 Oretha Castle Haley Blvd., 4 blocks north of St. Charles St. ☎504-525-2767.)* A few blocks farther west on St. Charles St., in **Lee Circle,** stands a bronze Confederate Gen. Robert E. Lee, continuing to stare down the Yankees; he faces due North.

Being dead in New Orleans has always been a problem. Because the city lies 4-6 ft. below sea level, a 6 ft. hole in the earth fills up with 5 ft. of water. At one time coffins literally floated in the graves, while cemetery workers pushed them down with long wooden poles. One early solution was to bore holes in the coffins allowing them to sink. Unfortunately, the sight of a drowning coffin coupled with the awful gargling sound of its immersion proved too much for the families of the departed. Burial soon became passé, and stiffs were laid to rest in beautiful raised stone tombs. Miles and miles of these ghastly structures now fill the city's graveyards and ghost stories.

PLANTATION RIVER ROAD. Across from downtown New Orleans, River Rd. curves along the Mississippi River, accessing several plantations preserved from the 19th century. *Great River Road Plantation Parade: A River of Riches,* available at the New

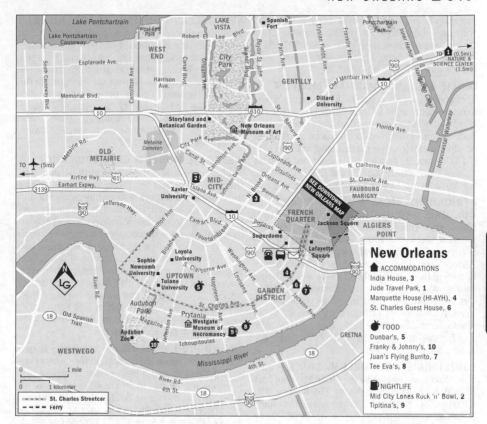

New Orleans

▲ ACCOMMODATIONS
India House, **3**
Jude Travel Park, **1**
Marquette House (HI-AYH), **4**
St. Charles Guest House, **6**

🍴 FOOD
Dunbar's, **5**
Franky & Johnny's, **10**
Juan's Flying Burrito, **7**
Tee Eva's, **8**

🎵 NIGHTLIFE
Mid City Lanes Rock 'n' Bowl, **2**
Tipitina's, **9**

Orleans Visitors Center, contains a good map and descriptions of the houses. Pick carefully, since tours of all the privately owned plantations are quite expensive. The **Hermann-Grimm Historic House** exemplifies French style and volunteers demonstrate period cooking in an 1830s Creole kitchen. The **San Francisco Plantation House** is an example of Creole style with a bright blue, peach, and green exterior. *(820 St. Louis St. On Rte. 44, 2 mi. northwest of Reserve, 42 mi. from New Orleans on the east bank of the Mississippi. Exit 206 off I-10.)* The name **Oak Alley** refers to the magnificent lawn-alley bordered by 28 evenly spaced oaks corresponding to the 28 columns surrounding the Greek Revival house. The Greeks wouldn't have approved, though: the mansion is bright pink. *(3645 Rte. 18., between St. James and Vacherie St.)*

🏛 MUSEUMS

🖼 LAURA: A CREOLE PLANTATION. Unlike the others on the riverbank, Laura was owned and operated by slave-owning Creoles who lived apart from white antebellum planters. Br'er Rabbit hopped into his first briar patch here, the site of the first recorded "Compair Lapin" West African stories. Tours provide an entirely unique look at plantation life. *(2247 Rte. 18/River Rd. At the intersection of Rte. 20 in Vacherie. ☎ 225-265-7690 or 888-799-7690. Tours daily 9:30am-4pm. $10.)*

🖼 NATIONAL D-DAY MUSEUM. This museum lives up to its hype. An engaging, exhaustive, and moving study of World War II in its entirety is a rare find, but one that confronts the lesser-known, Pacific battles and the ugly issues of race and propaganda is remarkable, especially when done with such unbiased scrutiny. *(945 Magazine St. At the corner of Andrew Higgins Dr.* ☎ *504-527-6012. Open daily 9am-5pm. $10; students, seniors, and military with ID $6; ages 5-17 $5.)*

▓ NEW ORLEANS PHARMACY MUSEUM.

This apothecary shop was built by America's first licensed pharmacist in 1823. On display in the old house are 19th-century "miracle drugs" like cocaine and opium, voodoo powders, a collection of old spectacles, the garden, and live leeches. *(514 Chartres St., between St. Louis St. and Toulouse St.* ☎ *504-565-8027. Open Su and Tu-Sa 10am-5pm. $2, students and seniors $1, under 12 free.)*

AFRICAN-AMERICAN MUSEUM OF ART, CULTURE, AND HISTORY.

Housed in an 1829 Creole-style villa rescued from blight in 1991, this museum displays a wide variety of changing and permanent exhibits showcasing local and national African-American artists, along with important historical themes. Slightly off the beaten path and well worth the trek, the museum reveals a different New Orleans than the showy one of the French Quarter. *(1418 Governor Nicholls St., 4 blocks north of Rampart St. in Tremé.* ☎ *504-565-7497. Open M-F 10am-5pm, Sa 10am-2pm. $5, seniors $3, ages 4-17 $2.)*

LOUISIANA STATE MUSEUM.

Eight separate museums are overseen by the "State Museum," six of which are in New Orleans. The **Cabildo,** 701 Chartres St., portrays the history of Louisiana from Indian times to the present, and holds Napoleon's death mask. The **Arsenal,** 615 St. Peter St. (enter through the Cabildo), studies the history of the Mississippi River and New Orleans as a port city. The **Presbytère,** 751 Chartres St., features a gigantic and very interactive exhibit about the history of Mardi Gras. The **1850 House,** 523 St. Ann St., on Jackson Sq., is—you guessed it—a re-created house from the time period. **Mme. John's Legacy,** 632 Dumaine St., showcases a rare example of Creole architecture as well as an exhibit on self-taught Louisiana artists. The **Old US Mint,** 400 Esplanade, not only focuses on currency, but also has an exhibit on jazz. *(☎ 800-568-6968; http://lsm.crt.state.la.us. All open Tu-Su 9am-5pm. Old US Mint, Cabildo, Presbytère $5; students, seniors, and active military $4. 1850 House, Mme. John's Legacy $3/$2. Under 12 free for all museums. 20% discount on tickets to 2 or more museums.)*

NEW ORLEANS MUSEUM OF ART (NOMA).

This magnificent museum houses art from North and South America, one of the best glass collections in existence, works by the jeweler Fabergé, a strong collection of French paintings, and some of the best African and Japanese collections in the country. Be sure to check out the sculpture garden. *(In City Park, at the City Park/Metairie Exit off I-10.* ☎ *504-488-2631; www.noma.org. Open Su and Tu-Sa 10am-5pm. Call for tickets to special exhibits. $6, seniors $5, ages 3-17 $3.)*

WESTGATE MUSEUM OF NECROMANCY.

Skulls, reapers, and despair greet the casual visitor with grim and terrifying seriousness; the museum is not a touristy farce like many voodoo shops in the French Quarter. The literature section displays tomes that contain spells and conjurings that allow the necromancer to harness "death energy" or animate a golem. As if any more bad omens were necessary in "the house of death," the resident black cat will undoubtedly cross your path during your visit. *(5219 Magazine St. Heading west on St. Charles St., take a left on Napoleon Ave., then a left on Magazine St.* ☎ *504-899-3077; www.westgatenecromantic.com. Open Tu-Su 9am-5pm and by appointment. Free.)*

THE VOODOO MUSEUM.

At this quirky haunt, learn why all those dusty shops in the Quarter are selling gris-gris and alligator parts. A priest or a priestess will be glad to do a reading or a ritual for a fee, or visitors can just walk through the rooms full of portraits and artifacts for the basic entrance fee. *(724 Dumaine St.* ☎ *504-523-7685. Open daily 10am-7:30pm. $7; students, seniors, and military $5.50; high-school students $4.50; under 12 $3.50.)*

♬ ENTERTAINMENT

Uptown tends to house authentic Cajun dance halls and popular university hangouts, while the **Marigny** is home to New Orleans' alternative/local music scene. Check out *Off Beat,* free in many local restaurants, *Where Y'At,* another free entertainment weekly, or the Friday *Times-Picayune* to find out who's playing where.

Le Petit Théâtre du Vieux Carré, 616 St. Peters St. (☎ 504-522-9958). One of the city's most beloved historic theaters. The oldest continuously operating community theater in the US, the 1789 building replicates the early 18th-century abode of Joseph de Pontalba,

Louisiana's last Spanish governor. About 5 musicals and plays go up each year, as well as 3 fun productions in the "Children's Corner." Box office open M-Sa 10:30am-5:30pm, Su noon-5pm. Tickets $20-26.

Preservation Hall, 726 St. Peters St. (daytime ☎504-522-2841, after 8pm 504-523-8939). Traditional New Orleans jazz was born at the turn of the century, and it is in its most fundamental element here. With only 2 small ceiling fans trying to move the air around, most people can only stay for one set, so you can usually expect to find a place. Cover $5. Doors open at 8pm; music 8:30pm-midnight.

📇 FOOD

If the eats in the Quarter prove too trendy, touristy, or tough on the budget, there are plenty of options on **Magazine St.** and in the Tulane area.

▧ **Clover Grill,** 900 Bourbon St. (☎504-598-1010). Open 'round the clock since 1950, serving greasy and delicious burgers (from $4) grilled under an American-made hubcap. Breakfast all day $2-3. The only place in New Orleans where bacon comes with a side of sexual innuendo. Open 24hr.

▧ **Coop's Place,** 1109 Decatur St. (☎504-525-9053). Some of the Quarter's best Southern cooking. The gumbo is thick and spicy ($4.35 per bowl), the beer-battered alligator bits ($8) have won awards, and the jambalaya ($8) has a unique flavor found nowhere else. A cozy neighborhood bar to boot. Open daily 11am-2am.

▧ **Juan's Flying Burrito,** 2018 Magazine St. (☎504-569-0000). The best burritos on the planet—that are somehow crunchy. For $5.75, get the "gutter punk" burrito, a meal the size of your head, and wash it down with some Mexican beer. Open M-Sa 11am-11pm, Su noon-10pm.

▧ **Franky and Johnny's,** 321 Arabella St. (☎504-899-9146), southwest of downtown at the corner of Tchoupitoulas St. A noisy and popular local hangout where you can sample alligator soup ($3 per cup) or crawfish pie ($4). Open Su-Th 11am-10pm, F-Sa 11am 'til the cows come home.

Johnny's Po' boys, 511 St. Louis St. (☎504-524-8129), near the Decatur St. corner. This French Quarter institution, with 40 varieties of the classic sandwich, is the place to try a po'boy ($4-7.50). Creole fare is also on the menu. Jambalaya $4.25. Open M-F 8am-4:30pm, Sa-Su 9am-4pm.

Acme Oyster House, 724 Iberville St. (☎504-522-5973). Patrons slurp oysters (6 for $4, 12 for $6.50) shucked before their eyes by Hollywood, the senior shucker. Open Su-Th 11am-10pm, F-Sa 11am-11pm.

Croissant d'Or, 617 Ursuline St. (☎504-524-4663). Well-priced and delicious French pastries, sandwiches, and quiches are served to the crowd that comes here to read the morning paper. Croissants $1.60. Chocolate delights $2. Open M-Sa 7am-5pm.

Mama Rosa's, 616 N. Rampart St. (☎504-523-5546). Locals adore this Italian ristorante, and with good reason; served in a cozy neighborhood setting, Mama Rosa's pizza is some of the best you'll ever eat. Large pie $9. The "outrageous muffuletta" $6.50 per half. Open Su-Th 11am-10pm, F-Sa 11am-11pm.

Café du Monde, 813 Decatur St. (☎504-587-0833 or 800-772-2927), at the tip of the French Market. This consummate people-watching paradise, open since 1862, only does 2 things—hot café au lait and scrumptious *beignets* (each $1.25)—and it does them well. Open 24hr.

Dunbar's, 4927 Freret St. (☎504-899-0734), at the corner of Robert St. Take St. Charles Ave. west, turn right on Jackson St., then left onto Freret St. Residents call it the best place to get mama-just-cooked-it soul food better, they'll tell you, than any in the Quarter. Gumbo meal $5.50. Open M-Sa 7am-9pm.

Tee Eva's, 4430 Magazine St. (☎504-899-8350). Eva sells bayou cooking from her bright yellow storefront window. Soul food lunches ($4-6) change daily. Creole pralines $2. 9 oz. snow balls (flavored shaved ice) for $1.50. Crawfish pie $3. Sweet potato and pecan pie $2. Open daily 11am-7pm.

Mother's Restaurant, 401 Poydras St. (☎504-523-9656), at the corner of Tchoupitoulas St., 4 blocks southwest of Bourbon St. Claims to serve the "world's best baked ham," as the long line outside at lunch seems to testify. Their signature baked ham po'boy is $8. Open M-Sa 6:30am-10pm, Su 7am-10pm.

🔒 ACCOMMODATIONS

Finding inexpensive yet decent rooms in the **French Quarter** can be as difficult as staying sober during Mardi Gras. Luckily, other parts of the city compensate for the absence of cheap lodging downtown. Several hostels cater to the young and almost penniless, as do guesthouses near the **Garden District.** Accommodations for Mardi Gras and the Jazz Festival get booked up to a year in

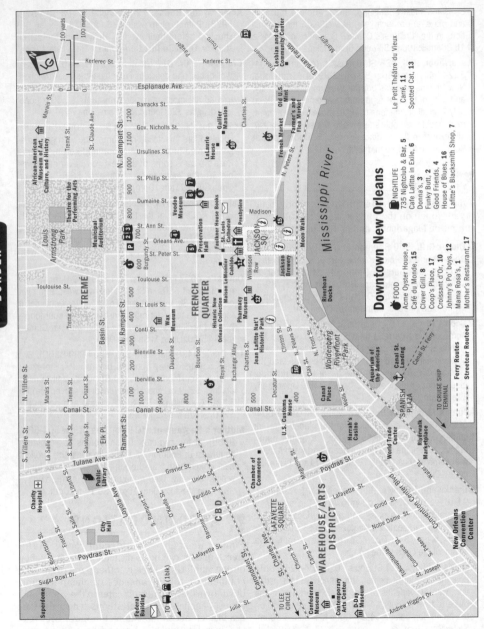

SOUTHERN BORDER

Downtown New Orleans

🍴 FOOD
Acme Oyster House, **9**
Café du Monde, **15**
Clover Grill, **8**
Coop's Place, **17**
Croissant d'Or, **10**
Johnny's Po' boys, **12**
Mama Rosa's, **1**
Mother's Restaurant, **17**

🍷 NIGHTLIFE
735 Nightclub & Bar, **5**
Cafe Lafitte in Exile, **6**
Donna's, **3**
Funky Butt, **2**
Good Friends, **4**
House of Blues, **16**
Lafitte's Blacksmith Shop, **7**

Le Petit Théâtre du Vieux
Carré, **11**
Spotted Cat, **13**

advance. During peak times, proprietors will rent out any extra space—be sure you know what you're paying for. Rates tend to sink in the off season (June to early Sept.) when business is slow, and negotiation can pay off.

■ **St. Charles Guest House,** 1748 Prytania St. (☎505-523-6556; www.stcharlesguesthouse.com), off Jackson St. Located in the heart of the beautiful Garden District, this large 19th-century home is luxury without the hefty price tag. Caring and quirky owner Dennis Hilton is the traveler's personal encyclopedia of all things New Orleans, Louisiana, and the South. Large courtyard, beautiful pool, and continental breakfast. No phones or TVs. Dorms $30-35; singles with A/C $55; doubles $65-95 depending on season. During JazzFest and Mardi Gras all rooms $100-150.

■ **India House,** 124 S. Lopez St. (☎504-821-1904), at Canal St. This bohemian haunt has lots of character. Communal eating (and, on busier nights, sleeping), comfy couches, and backyard patio complete the setting of this beautiful house, once a full-time brothel. Kitchen, pool, turtle pond out back, laundry, Internet, A/C, and lounge areas. Linen deposit $5. Dorms $15-18; private rooms $35, with A/C $40. Weekly rooms $90.

Marquette House New Orleans International Hostel (HI-AYH), 2249 Carondelet St. (☎504-523-3014), in the Garden District. A relaxing hosteling experience due to its no-alcohol policy, cleanliness, and modicum of strictness. 162 beds, A/C, kitchen, study rooms, Internet access ($0.10 per min.) and basic food supplies for cheap. Linen $2.50. Key deposit $5. Dorms $17, nonmembers $20; large, semi-rustic private rooms with queen-size bed and pull-out sofa $50/$53. $10 per additional person.

Jude Travel Park and Guest House, 7400 Chef Menteur Hwy./U.S. 90 (☎504-241-0632 or 800-523-2196), at Exit 240B. 46 sites. Pool and hot tub, showers, laundry, 24hr. security, and shuttle to French Quarter. Sites $20; 5-room guest house $75-120 per person.

St. Bernard State Park, 501 St. Bernard Pkwy. (☎504-682-2101), 18 mi. southeast of New Orleans; take I-10 Exit 246A, turn left onto Rte. 46, travel for 7 mi., then go right on Rte. 39 South for 1 mi. 51 sites with water and electricity, as well as swimming pools and walking trails. Reception 7am-9pm. Sites $12.

 NIGHTLIFE

Life in New Orleans is and always will be a party. On any night of the week, at any time of the year, the masses converge on **Bourbon St.** to drift in and out of bars and strip joints. Ask any local what to do on a weekend, and they'll probably tell you to avoid Bourbon at all costs; the street has become increasingly touristy of late. Where tons of independent, hole-in-the-wall bars, music clubs, and "gentlemen's clubs" used to create an air of classy indulgence, now chain bars repeat themselves over and over down the strip. To experience what the Quarter was like before the tourist traps took over, get off Bourbon and explore the less-traveled side streets. Go up around **Rampart St.** or northeast toward **Esplanade Ave.** Of course, don't do this alone at night. **Marigny,** an up-and-coming nightclub district northeast of the Quarter, offers some swank bars and clubs, particularly on Frenchmen St. **Decatur St.,** near the French market, is a quieter, slightly touristy nightlife area.

While the Quarter offers countless bars and jazz, blues, and brass venues, be assured that there's more to New Orleans entertainment. Head uptown toward the bars and clubs of **Tulane University** to sample the collegiate culture.

 French Quarter shops sell beads for $1-5, but why buy them when you can *earn* them? The best bead bartering locations are along the 700th block of Bourbon St., especially near the balconies above the Cat's Meow and Tricou House. Women (and even men) who flash body parts on the street are compensated with beads. Only in New Orleans is exposing oneself so colorfully rewarded.

BARS

Bars in New Orleans stay open late, and few keep a strict schedule; in general, they open around 11am and close around 3am, but many go all night when there's a crowd or a party. Most blocks feature at least one establishment with cheap draft beer and **Hurricanes** (sweet juice-and-rum drinks). All establishments are 21+ unless otherwise noted.

■ **Lafitte's Blacksmith Shop,** 941 Bourbon St. (☎504-522-9377), at Phillip St. Appropriately,

▨ one of New Orleans's oldest standing structures is a bar—one of the oldest bars in the US. Built in the 1730s, the building is still lit by candlelight after sunset. Named for the scheming hero of the Battle of New Orleans, it offers shaded relief from the elements of the city and a dim hiding place for celebrities. Beer $4-5. Live piano 8pm-late. Open daily 10 or 11am to 4 or 5am.

▨ **Funky Butt,** 714 N. Rampart St. (☎504-558-0872). An awesome hideout where you can hear live jazz and marvel at the wonder of the *derrière*. Walk in to face a gigantic, languorous nude painting and stay to sip a funkybuttjuice ($6) and sit with a select group in the tiny space alongside the band. House band plays at 7pm. Sets nightly 10pm and midnight. Cover $5-10. Open daily 7pm-2am.

Donna's, 800 N. Rampart St. (☎504-596-6914). As one fan says about this restaurant-bar, this is "the place where you can sit and watch New Orleans roll by." On the edge of the French Quarter, where the gay bars face the projects and the extremes of the city swirl together. Brass bands play inside, the smell of ribs and chicken wafts out, and customers sit on the sidewalk and take it all in. Open M and Th-Su 8:30pm-1:30am.

The Spotted Cat, 623 Frenchmen St. (☎504-943-3887), is what you might have imagined most New Orleans bars would be like: cheap beer ($2-4), a place to sit and chill, and passion-filled trumpet and piano solos that pour out the front door onto the sidewalk. "Early" band 6:30pm, "late" band 10pm. Never a cover, just a 1-drink min. Open M-F 2pm-late, Sa-Su noon-late.

DANCE CLUBS

▨ **Tipitina's,** 501 Napoleon Ave. (☎504-895-8477). The best local bands and some big national names—such as the Neville Brothers and Harry Connick, Jr.—play so close you can almost touch them. Cajun *fais-do-dos* Su 5-9pm. 18+. Cover $7-25. Music usually W-Su 9pm-3am; call ahead for times and prices.

House of Blues, 225 Decatur St. (☎504-529-2624). A sprawling complex with a large music/dance hall and a balcony and bar overlooking the action. Check out the gospel brunch on Su. Concerts nightly 9:15pm. 18+. Cover usually $5-10; up to $30. Restaurant open Su-Th 11am-11pm, F-Sa 11am-midnight.

735 Nightclub and Bar, 735 Bourbon St. (☎504-581-6740). Dance music and a hip mixed-age crowd keep this club energized well into the night. Techno, progressive house, and trance play downstairs, with 80s music on the back patio every Th. 18+. Cover $5, under 21 $10 Th-Sa only. Open M-W 2pm-midnight, Th-Su 2pm-4am.

Mid City Lanes Rock 'n' Bowl, 4133 S. Carrollton Ave. (☎504-482-3133), in the mini-mall at Tulane Ave. Since 1941, this place has attracted multi-tasking partiers to its rockin' lanes. The "home of Rock 'n' Bowl" is a bowling alley by day and traditional dance club by night (you can bowl at night, too). Drinks $2.50-3.50. Lanes $15 per hr. plus $1 for shoes. Live music Tu-W 8:30pm. Local zydeco Th 9:30pm, F-Sa 10pm. 18+ at night when the bar gets hopping. Cover $3-10. Open daily noon-1am or later.

GLBT NIGHTLIFE

The New Orleans gay scene is more inclusive than other urban centers and many straight people visit gay venues because the drinks are cheaper and stronger—and because you are less likely to get into a fight. You'll find the majority of gay establishments toward the northeast end of **Bourbon St.** ("downriver"), and along St. Ann St., known to some as the **"Lavender Line."** A good point of reference is where St. Ann St. and Bourbon cross—**Oz** is to the riverside and **Bourbon Pub** is to the lakeside. These are the two biggest gay dance clubs and principal gay institutions in the city. To find the real lowdown of gay nightlife, get a copy of *The Whiz Magazine*, a locally produced guide; there's always a copy on top of the radiator in Cafe Lafitte in Exile.

Cafe Lafitte in Exile, 901 Bourbon St. (☎504-522-8397). Exiled from Laffite's Blacksmith Shop in 1953 when the shop came under new management, the ousted gay patrons trooped up the street to found the oldest gay bar in America. On the opening night, surrounded by patrons dressed as their favorite exile, Cafe Lafitte in Exile lit an "eternal flame" (it still burns today) that aptly represents the soul of the gay community in New Orleans. Today, though Cafe Lafitte has video screens, occasional live music, pageants, and shows, it's still the same old neighborhood gathering place at heart. Open 24hr.

Good Friends, 740 Dauphine St. (☎504-566-7191). This is a gay "Cheers" episode. A cozy, friendly neighborhood bar full of locals happy to welcome in a refugee from Bourbon St. Don't miss sing-a-long Su afternoon. Open 24hr.

LEAVING NEW ORLEANS

Escaping the Big Easy is easiest on **I-10** east, which makes its getaway via a lengthy bridge across Lake Pontchartrain. 27 mi. outside downtown, take **Rte. 607 East** to **U.S. 90** and head east.

THE ROAD TO BAY ST. LOUIS. After crossing over many bayous, the land begins become more solid as the road enters Mississippi, perhaps the deepest state of the "deep south." With a history of extravagant plantations and slavery, this region whispers cultural lessons of several lifetimes to visitors with open ears. Louisiana's swampy bayous give way to the piney woods as you cross the state line from Louisiana to Mississippi. Nineteen miles after the turn onto U.S. 90, the forest clears to reveal the city of Bay St. Louis.

BAY ST. LOUIS

Just over a decade ago, in an effort to increase state revenue, Mississippi legalized gambling, allowing one-armed bandits to march into and take over many cities. **Casino Magic** (follow the signs) manages to attract big-name stars for occasional shows, and boasts more than 1200 slots and 40 gaming tables. Those not interested in testing their luck enjoy the shops of **Old Bay St. Louis.** The seaside district is home to white beaches as well as the city's best eating and shopping.

Decorated with Dalmation spots and fire hydrants, the seaside **Fire Dog,** 120 Beach Blvd., is a favorite local haunt and is popular with tourists. Burgers and colossal sandwiches ($7) can be enjoyed at the bar, at a table, or around a game of pool. (½ mi. south of U.S. 90 on Beach Blvd. On the right. ☎228-467-8257. Open Su-Tu 11am-4am, W-Sa 11am-6am.) Designed to lure gamblers to stay at the slots for weeks on end, the **Economy Inn,** 810 U.S. 90, is a great deal. The rooms are a bit cramped and hardly decorated, but the price is right. Shuttle service to Casino Magic. (☎228-467-8441. Singles $30; doubles $35.)

PASS CHRISTIAN. Fabulous antebellum mansions line the seashore interspersed with abode of modern opulence, all of which are visible from the aptly named **Scenic Dr.,** a lovely street worth cruising. The **Dixie White House,** an 1851 Southern estate with a history as rich as its price tag, is just one of the many historic homes that line the road. A local favorite, the **Harbor View Cafe,** 105 W. Beach Blvd. (U.S. 90), is a cheap and tasty haunt, serving fresh salads, po'boys, soup, pastas, desserts and gourmet coffees. (☎228-452-3901. Open M and W-F 7am-9pm, Su 7am-4pm.)

LEAVING PASS CHRISTIAN

Stay on **U.S. 90** heading east toward Biloxi.

BILOXI & GULF PORT

Biloxi and its neighboring cities are tourist towns; quirky amusement parks line smooth white sand beaches, beach bums rent jet skis to thrill-seekers, resort casinos spring up on prime real estate, and visitors can step inside a three-story great white shark's mouth to buy t-shirts. Although casinos now overshadow older landmarks such as the 1847 Biloxi Lighthouse on Beach Blvd., Biloxi still holds a few interesting remnants of its past.

VITAL STATS

Population: 50,000

Visitor Info: Biloxi Visitors Center, 710 Beach Blvd. (☎228-374-3105; www.biloxi.ms.us), at Main St. Open Apr.-Oct. M-F 8am-4:30pm, Sa 9am-5pm, Su noon-5pm.

Internet Access: Public Library, 139 Lameuse St. (☎228-374-0330). Open M-Th 9am-9pm, F-Sa 9am-5pm.

Post Office: 135 Main St. (☎228-374-4103). Open M-F 8:30am-5pm, Sa 10am-noon. **Postal Code:** 39530.

GETTING AROUND

Nearly all of the city's excitement can be found along **U.S. 90,** which runs right along the shoreline as **Beach Blvd.** Some residential services line **Pass Rd.,** which parallels Beach Blvd. one block inland and is most easily accessible by turning on **Beauvoir Rd.,** next to the Coliseum in central Biloxi.

👁 SIGHTS

CASINOS. Biloxi's brand-new casinos are its main attraction. Biloxi and Gulf Port sport over a dozen major gambling facilities, most of which have been Disneyfied in Las Vegas fashion. The **Treasure Bay Casino Resort** has the most interesting theme; shaped as a pirate ship, it seems to float off Biloxi's coast. *(1980 Beach Blvd. ☎800-747-2839; www.treasurebay.com. Open 24hr.)* Meanwhile, the **Beau Rivage Resort and Casino** is Biloxi's most upscale, with classy white and gold decor and tropical plants. *(875 Beach Blvd. ☎888-595-2534; www.beaurivage.com. Open 24hr.)*

SHIP ISLAND. The marvelous white sand beaches of this large island are as pure as they were when the Spanish discovered them in the 1500s, and remain untarnished by the casinos and rowdy tourists that plague Biloxi. Maintained by the National Park Service as part of the Gulf Islands National Seashore, Ship Island houses the Civil War-era Fort Massachusetts, an impressive monument to the strategic importance of the island. *(Located 12 mi. off the coast of Biloxi, accessible via a 1hr. boat ride. Ferries depart from the Gulfport Yacht Harbor, adjacent to the U.S. 90 and Rte. 49 intersection. ☎866-466-7386; www.msshipisland.com. Tours mid-May to mid-Aug. M-F 9am and noon, Sa-Su 9, 10:30am, noon, 2:30pm; Mar. to early May and late Aug. to late Oct. M-F 9am, Sa-Su 9am and noon. Round-trip $18, ages 3-10 $9.)*

MARITIME & SEAFOOD INDUSTRY MUSEUM. See how shrimp make it to the dinner table with examples of fishing vessels, nets, peeling machines, and pressure cookers. The museum also features an interesting exhibit on the hurricanes that often batter the Biloxi shores. *(115 1st St., on the very eastern tip of Biloxi. Turn onto Myrtle St., and take an immediate right onto 1st St. ☎228-435-6320; www.maritimemuseum.org. $3. Open M-Sa 9am-4:30pm, Su noon-4pm.)*

OHR-O'KEEFE MUSEUM OF ART. The museum houses many of the works of the "Mad Potter of Biloxi," George E. Ohr. This man was the first abstract artist in the US, creating fabulous works of clay that went largely unrecognized until nearly 50 years after his death in 1918. Today, the quirky artist once known only for his buffoonery and 18 in. moustache is now considered a pioneer in the modern art movement. The museum also

houses works in many media by local artists and traveling exhibits. *(136 G.E. Ohr St., behind the Biloxi Public Library. From U.S. 90 turn onto G.E. Ohr St., 2 blocks west of the Main St. stoplight. ☎228-374-5547; www.georgeohr.org. Open M-Sa 9am-6pm. $6, students free.)*

BEAUVOIR, THE JEFFERSON DAVIS HOME & PRESIDENTIAL LIBRARY. This stunning antebellum mansion and its lush grounds were once the home of the only president of the Confederate States of America. The beachfront home was also the site of the Mississippi Confederate Soldier's Home, which cared for hundreds of Southern Civil War veterans. The grounds include the house, the Presidential Library containing Davis's memoirs, a Civil War museum, a cemetery, the Tomb of the Unknown Soldier, and nature trails through the live oak groves. *(2244 Beach Blvd. In central Biloxi, next to the Coliseum. ☎228-388-9074 or 800-570-3818; www.beauvoir.org. Open daily Mar.-Oct. 9am-5pm; Nov.-Feb. 9am-4pm. $7.50; seniors, active military, and AAA members $6.75; students $4.50; under 6 free.)*

SHRIMPING TOURS. Shrimping trawlers still pull through the Biloxi harbor as a reminder of what life was like before the casino empires, though nowadays the boats are known for the tours they give rather than the food they supply. The **Sailfish** takes guests on 70min. tours departing from the Main St. Harbor. *(☎800-289-7908. Tours Feb.-Nov. Times vary; call ahead. $11, ages 4-12 $7.)*

🍴 FOOD

Hidden on the backroads of Biloxi, 📷**Mr. Greek,** 1670 Pass Rd., offers some of the area's best meals. Large portions and excellent lunch specials are accompanied by festive Greek music and murals of warriors and goddesses on the walls. (Located in the K-Plaza strip mall on Pass Rd., about 1 mi. east of Beauvoir Rd., just outside Keesler Air Force Base. ☎228-432-7888. Gyro plate $10.25. Salads and sandwiches $5. Open M-Th 10:30am-9pm, F-Sa 10:30am-10pm, Su 11am-3pm.) The ultra-chic **Mary Mahoney's Old French House Restaurant,** 116 Rue Magnolia, drives budget travelers running and screaming away from its swanky menu, which doesn't even list prices, to the attached **Mary Mahoney's Le Cafe,** which offers similarly upscale food without the first-class price tag. Breakfast, served anytime, includes the traditional short stack of hotcakes ($2.50), omelettes ($5), and *beignets* ($2.25), while the lunch menu is summed up in the Biloxi Special ($8): half a po'boy sandwich, a cup of soup, and a salad or cup of gumbo. (From U.S. 90 East, on the left just after the Beau Rivage Casino. ☎ 228-436-6000. Open 24hr.)

♫ ACCOMMODATIONS

As in any resort town, accommodations in Biloxi do not come cheaply. During summer weekends all hotels jack up prices to well over $65 for a single, so those looking to avoid this heavy hit might want to stay farther away in towns like Bay St. Louis or Pascagoula. The **Diamond Inn,** 100 Brady Dr., is only a few yards from the shore and has clean rooms with refrigerators and access to the pool and laundry machines. (From eastbound U.S. 90, on the right beyond Beauvoir, next to Denny's. ☎ 228-388-7321. Continental breakfast included. Rooms in summer $34-75; winter $29-55.)

☐ APPROACHING OCEAN SPRINGS
Take **Beach Blvd. (U.S. 90 East)** out of Biloxi. Entering Ocean Springs on U.S. 90 East, take a right at the first stoplight onto **Washington Ave.**

OCEAN SPRINGS

While the bridge over Biloxi Bay separating Biloxi and Ocean Springs is only 1 mi. long, the two cities are worlds apart. No casinos, buffets, or beach-crazed tourists overrun the oak-lined streets of Ocean Springs. Instead, residents have quietly made a name for the town as a beachside artist colony. The essence of the village is captured on peaceful Washington Ave., where crafts and cafes line the lazy lane. Life may pass at a slower pace, but price tags still run high. Visitors can experience the bohemian flavor of the town at the **Walter Anderson Museum of Art,** 510 Washington Ave. The permanent collection features the synthesis of visual arts and storytelling created by Walter Anderson. The masterpieces of the museum are the murals that line the walls of the attached community center, which Anderson created in 1951 and gave to the community for $1. (☎ 228-872-3164; www.walterandersonmuseum.org. Open M-Sa 9:30am-5pm, Su 12:30-5pm; Oct.-Apr. 4:30pm. $6, students $4, ages 6-18 $3.) A great place to find a piece of Ocean Springs artistry to

bring home is **Shearwater Pottery,** 102 Shearwater Dr. Here the Anderson family and other artists sell glazewear and watercolor prints in a little wooden shack in the coastal woods. (Take a right at the 3rd stop sign on Washington Ave. and follow the signs over backroads and dirt paths. ☎ 228-875-7320. Open M-Sa 9am-5:30pm, Su 1-5:30pm.) Like every other business in town, the **Visitors Center,** 100 Washington Ave., has some artist's wares for sale. (☎ 228-875-4424. Open M-F 9am-5pm, Sa 9am-4pm.)

Bayview Gourmet, 1010 Robinson St., vends artsy, cafe-style food for the town's artsy, cafe-style residents, serving breakfasts from smoked salmon to omelettes ($7-10). For lunch, gourmet sandwiches feature fillings like portabella mushrooms and grouper ($7-9). Seafood, pasta, and chicken ($14-18) round out the dinner plates. (Across from the Visitors Center, near the corner of Washington Ave. ☎ 228-875-4252. Live music W night. Open Su and W-Sa 7am-9pm, Tu 7am-3pm.)

☐ LEAVING OCEAN SPRINGS.
Outside of Ocean Springs, **U.S. 90** will take you to Mobile through the Davis Bayou.

☐ GULF ISLANDS NATIONAL SEASHORE
3 mi. east of Ocean Springs on U.S. 90.

Protected piney woods, palmetto groves, and grassy bayous make up the Davis Bayou segment of the Gulf Islands National Seashore: Mississippi District. The quiet 2 mi. drive through a thick seaside jungle is a worthwhile trip, even if you don't have time for anything else. Those interested in staying for a while can enjoy a few miles of nature trails, fishing, picnicking, and camping. The small **Visitors Center** gives out park info on the wildlife and the geographic features of the area. (☎ 228-875-0821, campground 228-875-3962. Park open 8am-dusk. Sites $14, with electricity $16.) Despite the Davis Bayou area's natural beauty, at only a few square miles it is a small fraction of the entire park. **Horn Island** and **Petit Bois Island** are designated wilderness areas, and as such remain as untouched by human interference as they were when Native Americans left their sands centuries ago. Primitive camping is allowed on Horn, Petit Bois, and East Ship Islands. It is up to visitors to arrange their own transportation to these islands.

SOUTHERN BORDER

SHEPARD STATE PARK

About 14 mi. east of Ocean Springs. From U.S. 90 East, turn right on Ladnier Rd. Follow the signs 4 mi. to the park.

Shepard Park is nestled in the Singing River area, where legend has it that members of the Pascagoula Indian Nation linked hands and walked into the Pascagoula River rather than be captured. The mournful death chant they sang as they made this final walk gives the Pascagoula River its nickname "Singing River." Aside from ancient tales, the park also offers camping, hiking trails, and an 18-hole frisbee golf course scattered throughout the woods. (☎228-497-2244. Park open 8am-8pm. Entrance fee $2. Sites $9, with electricity $13.)

PASCAGOULA. Pascagoula is a mess of oil rigs and shipping ports, but it's got inexpensive rooms. The **King's Inn Motel,** 2303 Denny Ave., offers clean rooms, many recently remodeled, with refrigerators and satellite TV. (From U.S. 90 East, on the right in the center of town just before the underpass. ☎228-762-8110. No non-smoking rooms. Singles $25-37; doubles from $30.)

THE ROAD TO MOBILE

Eleven miles outside Pascagoula, **U.S. 90** passes uneventfully into Alabama, "the Heart of Dixie." Known also as the "Cradle of the Confederacy," Alabama is often remembered for its controversial role in the Civil Rights movement of the 1960s. Today the state is peppered with monuments to the tumult of the 1960s, as well as homages to the less contentious legacies of the Native American, colonial, and environmental forces that have shaped the state. Driving into Mobile on U.S. 90 confirms the lighter stereotypes: sweet home to some, Alabama can have striking blue skies, and speedways and farm equipment stores line its highways.

MOBILE

French, Spanish, English, Sovereign Alabama, Confederate, and American flags have all flown over Mobile (mo-BEEL) since its founding in 1702. This rich history is revealed in local architecture as well as in the local population; antebellum mansions, Spanish and French forts, and Victorian homes line the streets. Early spring is the time to be in Mobile, when azaleas bloom in a pink line beginning at the Visitors Center, marking the 27 mi. Azalea Trail. The site of the very first Mardi Gras, the city still holds a thrilling three-week-long Fat Tuesday celebration—without the hordes that plague its Cajun counterpart in New Orleans.

VITAL STATS

Population: 200,000

Visitor Info: Mobile Visitors Center, 150 S. Royal St. (☎251-208-7304), in a reconstructed French fort near Government St. Open daily 8am-5pm.

Internet Access: Mobile Public Library, 701 Government St. (☎251-208-7073), at Washington St. Open M-Tu 9am-9pm, W-Sa 9am-6pm.

Post Office: 168 Bay Shore Ave. (☎800-275-8777). Open M-F 9am-4:30pm. **Postal Code:** 36607.

GETTING AROUND

U.S. 90 enters Mobile as **Government Blvd.,** which becomes **Government St.** as it nears downtown. At the **Broad St.** and Government St. intersection, U.S. 90 heads south on Broad St., and Government St. becomes **U.S. 98** as it enters the heart of the city. U.S. 98 continues through town, goes under the **Mobile River** in the **Bankhead Tunnel,** and merges with Alt. 90 near **I-10.** Most of the action lies along **Dauphin St.,** which runs one-way west, two blocks north of Government St. Along with Government St., **Airport Blvd., Springhill Rd.,** and **Old Shell Rd.** are the major east-west routes, and Broad St. is the major north-south byway. Most of the chain stores, supermarkets, and fast-food lie along Airport Blvd., west of downtown and accessible via its intersection with Government St.

👁 SIGHTS

USS ALABAMA. The USS *Alabama* earned nine stars in WWII. Open passageways let civilians explore the ship's depths. The park around the ship houses airplanes and the USS *Drum* submarine. *(In Battleship Park 2½ mi. east of town; accessible from I-10 and the Bankhead Tunnel. ☎ 251-433-2703. Open Apr.-Sept. daily 8am-7pm. $10, ages 6-11 $5, under 6 Free. $2 AAA discount. Parking $2.)*

BIENVILLE SQUARE. With its oaks, white gazebo, and cast-iron fountain, Bienville Square is the central park downtown and a picture of Southern charm. Eight historical districts, marked by signs downtown, display the evidence of the city's varied architectural and cultural influences. *(At the intersection of Dauphin and Conception St.)*

THE MUSEUM OF MOBILE. This museum celebrates and documents Mobilian history in all its glory. Exhibits cover the founding of Mobile and the fate of the slave ship *Clotilda* as well as the wealth of prominent Mobile families. *(111 S. Royal St. ☎ 251-208-7569. Open M-Sa 9am-5pm, Su 1-5pm. $5, students $3, seniors $4, families $20.)*

AFRICAN-AMERICAN ARCHIVES MUSEUM. Housed in what was the first African-American Library are portraits, biographies, books, carvings, and other artifacts that represent the lives of African Americans from the Mobile area and abroad. *(564 Dr. Martin Luther King, Jr. Ave. Adjacent to the Historical DeTonti District. ☎ 251-433-8511. Open M-F 8am-4pm, Sa 10am-2pm. Free.)*

OAKLEIGH HISTORICAL COMPLEX. This complex contains the Oakleigh House Museum, the Cox-Deasy House Museum, and the Mardi Gras Cottage Museum. The houses portray the lives of various classes of Mobilians in the 1800s. *(350 Oakleigh Pl., 2½ blocks south of Government St. at George St. ☎ 251-432-1281. Open M-Sa 9am-3pm. Tours every 30min.; last tour 3:30pm. $10, seniors $9, ages 6-11 $5. $1 AAA discount.)*

BELLINGRATH GARDENS. In bloom year-round, these gardens were voted one of America's top five formal gardens for their rose and oriental displays, boardwalk, and 900-acre setting. Visitors can also tour the Bellingrath Museum Home or take a cruise on the *Southern Belle* riverboat.

(12401 Bellingrath Gardens Rd. Exit 15A off I-10 in Theodore. ☎ 800-247-8420. Open daily 8am-dusk; ticket office closes 5pm. $9, ages 5-11 $5.25.)

🍽 FOOD

Mobile's location on the shores of the Gulf means seafood, while, true to its Southern roots, it also offers abundant barbecue and good, old-fashioned Southern cookin'. The resulting cuisine is fresh, hearty, and quite delicious.

Wintzell's Oyster House, 605 Dauphin St. (☎ 251-432-4605; www.wintzellsoysterhouse.com), at Dearborn St. Wintzell's oysters are often ranked as the best in the country, served "fried, stewed, or nude" in rooms decorated with signs that range from the highly profound to the nearly profane. Beat the 1hr. oyster-eating record of 21½ dozen (held by Heather Andrews; men haven't broken 20 dozen) and gain fame and a free meal. Happy hour M-F 4-7pm with $0.25 raw oysters. Lunch specials daily 11am-4pm $7. Open M-Sa 11am-10pm, Su noon-8pm.

Dreamland, 3314 Old Shell Rd. (☎ 251-479-9898). Hickory ribs, cooked over an open fire in the dining room, will stick to yours. Half rack $9. Half chicken $6.50. Open M-Sa 10am-10pm, Su 11am-9pm.

Dew Drop Inn, 1808 Old Shell Rd. (☎ 251-273-7872). Mobile's oldest restaurant offers many options, but you can decide as you sip your coke ("co-cola") from its classic bottle ($1.30). Hamburgers $2.25. Hot dogs $2.25. Fried chicken $7. Veggie plates $5.75. Open M-F 11am-8pm, Sa 11am-3pm.

A&M Peanut Shop, 209 Dauphin St. (☎ 251-438-9374), at Jackson St. across from the square. A local landmark, this candy shop is solely responsible for the obesity of adjacent Bienville Square Park's squirrels. Of the numerous people who buy hot peanuts ($1.25) fresh from the 100-year-old roast, undoubtedly many of them lend a nut or two to the furry creatures. Open M-Sa 9am-6pm.

Carpe Diem, 4072 Old Shell Rd. (☎ 251-304-0448), slightly west of I-65. For a quieter experience, savor the last moments of your day here. Because this colorful and locally beloved coffee house has its own roaster, the grounds used to make the coffee (from $1.70) are never be more than 2 weeks old. Open M-F 6am-11pm, Sa 7am-11pm, Su 8am-10pm.

SOUTHERN BORDER

ACCOMMODATIONS

Few accommodation options exist in the historical part of downtown Mobile. A modest drive from downtown, affordable motels line I-65 on Beltline, from Exit 5A (Spring Hill Rd.) to Exit 1 (Government Blvd.), and U.S. 90 west of downtown.

Olsson's Motel, 4137 Government Blvd. (☎251-661-5331). Exit 1B off I-65, 2 mi. west on the left-hand side. Though farther from downtown than many lodgings, Olsson's has some perks that make it worthwhile: recliners and mini-fridges, wooden furniture and four-poster beds, a homey layout, and exceptional cleanliness. Singles $35; doubles $39.

Family Inn, 980 S. Beltline Rd. (☎251-344-5500). Exit 3 off I-65 at Airport Blvd., then left onto the southern branch of I-65 Access Rd. West. The best of the chain lodgings. Firm beds and continental breakfast. Rooms $30-49. AAA and AARP discounts.

Mobile's I-10 Kampground, 6430 Theodore Dawes Rd. (☎251-653-9816 or 800-272-1263), 7½ mi. west on I-10, south off Exit 13. A shady and relatively quiet spot, disturbed occasionally by RVs, which typically outnumber tent campers. 150 mostly shady sites, pool, and laundry facilities. Sites $15; RV hookups $21. $1 per additional person.

Meaher State Park, 5 mi. outside Mobile. Across the bay, follow U.S. 98 right as it toward Daphne. Nestled in the pines leading right up to the water. Sites with electricity and water $20. Day use $2 per person.

NIGHTLIFE

Mobile's late-night scene is a bit one-dimensional—downtown, pool is the name of the game. The **Lower Dauphin Street Entertainment District** houses a block of bars, each of which on any given night has a couple of pool tables, 20 or more youngish locals, and drinks for under $5. Most places close around 2 or 3am. Outside of downtown, the **Bubble Lounge,** 5546 Old Shell Rd., serves top-shelf martinis in a funky, dimly lit atmosphere. (☎251-341-5556. Open daily 6pm-2am or later.) **Solomon's,** 5753 Old Shell Rd., at University Rd., has a warehouse-sized space with 18 pool tables, darts, and video games. (☎251-344-0380. Happy hour 11am-7pm. Open 24hr.)

LEAVING MOBILE
From **Government St.,** take the **Bankhead Tunnel** under the bay, turning right on **U.S. 90/U.S. 98 East.** Just across the bay, follow **U.S. 98** toward Daphne.

FAIRHOPE. Fifteen miles outside Mobile, U.S. 98 enters the quiet, artsy village of Fairhope. Founded in 1894 by a group of Midwesterners seeking utopia, Fairhope still maintains its status as the largest "single-tax colony" in the country. Downtown's second stoplight is **Fairhope Ave.,** and a right here takes you down to a panoramic view of the Mobile Bay from the Fairhope municipal pier. For more area info, try the **Eastern Shore Chamber of Commerce,** 327 Fairhope Ave. (☎251-928-6287), one block after the stoplight. The **Down By the Bay Cafe,** 4 Beach Rd., offers salads, seafood, pasta, and sandwiches. The view through large bay windows is a good place to look for whales with polka-dotted tails—or at least that's what my mother would say. (☎251-928-4363. Entrees $8-13. Open M-F 11am-3pm and 5-8pm, Sa-Su 11am-3pm.)

THE ROAD TO FLORIDA

Continue down scenic **U.S. 98A,** which eventually turns left at a stop sign and makes its way along the standard **U.S. 98.** This countryside is a beautiful cross-section of Americana. With open meadows, bayous, windmills, forests, beaches, and a down-home feel, it offers the best of the Deep South. The road rolls into eastern **Foley,** where there is an antique store on every corner. Don't be fooled by these few blocks of quaint turn-of-the-century atmosphere—just after this town the area takes on a blaring highway attitude, complete with strip malls and fast-food chains galore. To avoid the Big Macs, go to **Gumbolaya's & Kathy's BBQ,** 1500 U.S. 59 South, where weekday lunches (11am-2pm) consist of a BBQ buffet ($6) with all the fixin's. The unique "Texas-Cajun" entrees ($12-13) are cooled down a little by the homemade ice cream. (☎257-943-7427. Open M-Sa 11am-9pm, Su 11am-4pm.)

APPROACHING GULF SHORES
Take **U.S. 59** out of Foley; it's about 12 mi. south along U.S. 59 to Gulf Shores.

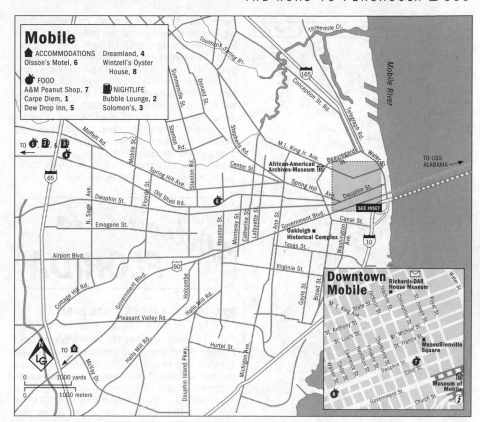

Mobile

▲ ACCOMMODATIONS
Olsson's Motel, **6**

Dreamland, **4**
Wintzell's Oyster
House, **8**

🍴 FOOD
A&M Peanut Shop, **7**
Carpe Diem, **1**
Dew Drop Inn, **5**

🎵 NIGHTLIFE
Bubble Lounge, **2**
Solomon's, **3**

Downtown Mobile

GULF SHORES. A good way to describe this area is "the worst of Florida in Alabama." Here, dozens of B-rated amusement parks, waterslides, jet-ski rentals, and white sand beaches are the summer destination for the masses. Quite possibly the putt-putt and go-cart capital of the world, Gulf Shores offers bountiful goofy entertainment options.

DETOUR: FORT MORGAN HISTORIC SITE
From Gulf Shores, take Rte. 180 22 mi. west to the fort.

The land finally runs out at the Fort Morgan Historic Site, a giant star-shaped fortress that guards the entrance to scenic Mobile Bay. Self-guided tours of the cannons, bunkers and impenetrable brick walls of the fort are avail-

able. (☎ 251-540-7127. Open daily Nov.-Feb. 8am-5pm; Mar.-Apr. 8am-6pm; May-Oct. 8am-7pm. $3.)

THE ROAD TO PENSACOLA

Escape Gulf Shores by traveling east on **Rte. 182.** The development disappears, leaving beautiful white sand dunes and quiet lagoons as you enter **Gulf State Park.** The park offers campsites nestled on the lagoon's edge with electricity, showers, and flush toilets. (☎ 251-948-4853 or 800-544-4853. Sites $14-17.) Outside the park, the condos, chain restaurants and the occasional pink lawn flamingo return to the side of the road. Rte. 182 crosses into Florida about 30 mi. from Gulf Shores. Welcome to the Sunshine State! Florida is a fitting place to end a cross-country roadtrip. Ponce de Leon

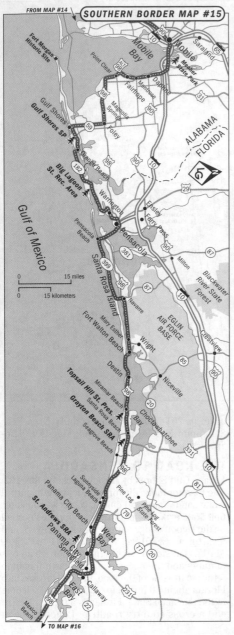

SOUTHERN BORDER MAP #15

SOUTHERN BORDER

Gulf of Mexico

0   15 miles

0   15 kilometers

▼ TO MAP #16

ended his exhausting journey of discovery by landing on the shores of this peninsula in 1513, and ever since then, millions have flocked to this land in search of respite, relaxation, and endless youth. Many of them are roadtrippers; cars, buses, pickup trucks, and Winnebagos have carried roadies from all over the country to warmwater beaches, endless sunshine, Spring Break debauchery, and retirement homes. Florida greets tired drivers with open arms and endless roadside tackiness, though along the back roads it still preserves many serene beaches, shaded woods, and lazy rivers that have escaped the ambitious tide of the tourism industry.

Welcome To FLORIDA

THE BIG LAGOON STATE PARK
1 mi. off of Rte. 182, just west of Pensacola.
This is a place to enjoy the true wilderness of Florida. Sandpine scrub grows on dunes while gnarled and twisted underbrush testifies to the harsh coastal environment. As its name suggests, trails and campsites are situated alongside the quite waters of lake off the Pensacola Bay. Visitors often spot foxes, raccoons, and great blue herons. (☎850-492-1595. *Park open daily 8am-dusk. Entrance fee $3.25. Sites $12, with electricity $14.)*

PENSACOLA
Pensacola's military population and reputation for conservatism have been a part of the city's composition since before the Civil War, when three forts on the shores of Pensacola formed a triangular defense to guard the deep-water ports. Most visitors, however, will be drawn to the area for its sugar-white beaches and the secluded, emerald waters along the Gulf Island National Seashore.

▣ GETTING AROUND. Entering Pensacola, **Rte. 182** becomes **Rte. 292,** and continues into downtown, changing names from Sorrento Rd. to

(**VITAL STATS**)

Population: 56,000

Visitor Info: Pensacola Visitors Center, 1401 E. Gregory St. (☎800-874-1234; www.visitpensacola.com), near the Pensacola Bay Bridge. Open daily 8am-5pm.

Internet Access: Pensacola Public Library, 200 W. Gregory St. (☎850-436-5060). Open Su 2-7pm, Tu-Th 9am-8pm, F-Sa 9am-5pm.

Post Office: 101 S. Palafox St. (☎800-275-8777). Open M-F 8am-5pm. **Postal Code:** 32501.

Gulf Beach Hwy. to Barrancas Ave., and finally into **Garden St.** as it runs east-west through downtown. A few blocks north is **Cervantes St.,** Pensacola's other main east-west artery, while **Palafox St.** and **Alcaniz St.** hold most of the interesting businesses in the north-south direction. Government St., Gregory St., and **Main St.** run east-west. Main St. becomes **Bayfront Pkwy.** along the edge of the bay and runs over the **Pensacola Bay Bridge.** On the other side, **Pensacola Beach Rd.** leads to Santa Rosa Island and Pensacola Beach.

Traveling east, Cervantes St. changes into the aptly named **Scenic Hwy. (U.S. 90),** which hugs the coast of Pensacola Bay. The 11 mi. drive, high on some of the Gulf Coast's only bluffs, provides unforgettable views through lush forests to the quiet bay below.

◪ **SIGHTS.** In the 1980s, millionaire junk collector T.T. Wentworth offered to donate his wacky collection if the city of Pensacola would just continue to display it. The city took the deal, renovated the old downtown city hall, and opened the **T.T. Wentworth Museum,** 830 S. Jefferson St. Unfortunately, only one exhibit hall is dedicated to the strange Wentworth collection, which includes oddities from a petrified cat to a shrunken head to the gigantic shoe of the world's tallest man (who stood at 8' 8½"). The rest of the museum includes exhibits on the area's shipwrecks, Spanish explorers, model trains, sports, and African-American history. (☎850-595-5990. Open M-Sa 10am-4pm. $6, ages 4-16 $2.50. AAA discount.) A drive-through relic from a forgotten time, the **Crystal Ice House,** at the corner of Davis Rte. and Jordan St., is a sparkling white concrete structure that appears to be a house made of ice, complete with icicles and a polar bear. Built in 1932, the building once served as a drive-up ice distributor; a sign remains instructing would-be patrons on the proper hand signals for obtaining ice. The old prices are still listed: hold up one finger for 100 lb. of ice for $0.35. For those seeking solace from sunburn, the **National Museum of US Naval Aviation,** home of the Blue Angels, provides ample diversion. More than 130 planes will have pilot wannabes soaring on natural highs. (Inside the Naval Air Station, at Exit 2 off I-10. ☎850-452-3604. Open daily 9am-5pm. 1½hr. tours daily 9:30, 11am, 1, 2:30pm. Free.) For more peaceful fun, escape to the relaxing paths that meander through a forest at the **Naval Live Oaks Area,** 1801 Gulf Breeze Pkwy. John Quincy Adams established this as the first and only naval tree reservation in the US. Its live oaks were used to make warships. (Head across the 3 mi. Pensacola Bay Bridge and past the chintzy motels. ☎850-934-2600. Open daily 8am-5:30pm. Free.)

The 3 mi. **World's Longest Fishing Pier** shadows the Pensacola Bay Bridge.

▓▛ **FOOD & ACCOMMODATIONS.** ▓Hopkins House, 900 Spring St., is legendary for its all-you-can-eat family-style dinners ($8) every Tuesday and Friday evening, and regular lunch and breakfast specials ($3.50), such as biscuits, grits, and omelettes. (☎850-438-3979. Open Su and Tu-Sa 7-9:30am and 11:15am-2pm.; Tu and F also 5:15-7:30pm.) The owner of **King's BBQ,** 2120 N. Palafox St., built the drive-up stand with his own hands. (½ mi. north of Cervantes St., at Maxwell Rd. ☎850-433-4479. Rib sandwiches $5.50. Dinner $8.50. Open M-F 10:30am-6:30pm, Sa 10:30am-3pm.) A roadside grill, **Jerry's Drive-In,** 2815 E. Cervantes St., serves greasy fare, including sandwiches and barbecue. (☎850-433-9910. Sandwiches and burgers $2-4. Dinner plates $5-6. Open daily 7am-10pm.)

Hotels along the beach cost at least $65 and get significantly more expensive in summer. Cheaper options lie inland, north of downtown off the interstates. One good choice near downtown is the **Civic Inn,** 200 N. Palafox St., which supplies clean and well-furnished rooms. (☎850-432-3441. Singles Su-Th $40, F-Sa $48; doubles $48/$58. Senior and military discounts.)

LEAVING PENSACOLA
U.S. 98 crosses the expansive bay via the Pensacola Bay Bridge, just west of the fishing pier. After traveling for about 1 mi. through the city of **Gulf Breeze,** turn right (south) onto **Rte. 399.** For a $1 toll, Rte. 399 bridges to Santa Rosa Island.

On the left 1 mi. after the bridge is the famed **UFO house,** standing complete with alien cut-outs in the windows.

SANTA ROSA ISLAND

This barrier island, only a matter of yards wide, is unquestionably one of Florida's most scenic areas. Rte. 399 runs down the center, and the quiet shores of the Santa Rosa Sound are alive with sea oaks scrub pines to the north, while the shifting snow-white sand dunes and clear warm waters of the Gulf of Mexico spread out to the south. With much of the park protected from human disturbance, the 8 mi. expanse provides a glimpse of the days before condos trampled the beaches. Picnicking and lifeguarded swimming are available at **Opal Beach,** near the park's center. Santa Rosa is also home to a hodgepodge of military bunkers from different wars. ◢**Fort Pickens** is where Apache leader Geronimo was once imprisoned in the late 1800s. An $8 fee lets visitors explore the ruins and sunbathe on the secluded seashore. (Park open daily 7am-10pm. Visitors Center open daily Mar.-Oct. 9:30am-5pm; Nov.-Feb. 8:30am-4pm.) Sites at the **Fort Pickens Campground** are within walking distance of gorgeous beaches. (☎850-934-2622, reservations 800-326-2622. Sites $15, with electricity $21.) A quiet beachfront town, Navarre offers little in the way of sights. On eastern edge of town, the **Navarre Beach Campground** caters mostly to RV users, but also has a few comfortable campsites and cabins available. The grounds feature beach access to the Santa Rosa Sound, a hot tub, laundry, showers, and electricity. (☎850-939-2188. Sites $26; 1-room cabins $49-69; 2 rooms $79-119. AAA discount.) After passing through Navarre, **Rte. 399** crosses over the sound and merges again with U.S. 98. To continue on to Fort Walton, head right (east) on **U.S. 98,** through the town of Navarre.

FORT WALTON BEACH

The Fort Walton area was first settled around 12,000 BC by prehistoric Indian peoples, who left their mark on the shores in the form of large mounds and middens. The area's bays and bayous were also home to many a pirate schooner recuperating from raiding and plundering. Tales of the notorious Billy Bowlegs are among the area's most famous pirate legends, and are celebrated by the city's annual Billy Bowlegs Festival in June.

◙ **SIGHTS.** Explore the **Indian Temple Mound Museum,** 139 Miracle Strip Pkwy. (U.S. 98), which has a reconstruction of the Chief's Temple, the ancient political and ceremonial center of the area. The museum holds one of the nations's finest collections of southeastern Native American ceramics and artifacts. (On the right side of U.S. 98 East, after Rte. 85. ☎850-833-9595. Open June-Aug. M-Sa 9am-4pm, Su 12:30-4:30pm; Sept.-May M-F 11am-4pm, Sa 9am-4pm. $2, ages 6-17 $1.)

Dolphin stars Princess and Delilah perform daily comedic soccer games and 18 ft. skyward leaps at the **Gulfarium,** 1010 Miracle Strip Pkwy. In their shadow, sea lions, scuba divers, and multi-species acts also perform daily. The grounds feature many aquariums, a shark moat, stingray pool, gators, and penguins. (On the right side of U.S. 98 East, just after the bridge. ☎850-243-9046; www.gulfarium.com. Shows 10am. Open in summer 9am-8pm, last entry 6pm; open in winter 9am-6pm, last entry 4pm. $17, ages 4-11 $10.)

▰ȵ **FOOD & ACCOMMODATIONS.** For food, check out **The Magnolia Grill,** 157 Brooks St. Inside this beautiful, century-old white-washed home, the friendly staff serves up excellent and affordable lunches. (From U.S. 98 East, take a right onto Brooks St. immediately after the Rte. 85 turn off. ☎850-302-0266; www.magnoliagrill-fwb.com. Lunch $6-8. Entrees $11-18. Open M-Th 11am-2pm and 5-8pm, F 11am-2pm and 5-9pm, Sa 5-9pm.) For a cheaper meal, try BBQ sandwiches ($3), huge BBQ dinners ($6-9), or hamburgers ($4.75) at **Brooks Bridge BBQ and Cafe,** 240 Miracle Strip Pkwy. Take out beef, pork, ribs, sausage, or chicken by the pound and throw your own barbecue on the beach. (On the right side of U.S. 98 East, just before crossing the Brooks Bridge. ☎850-244-3003. Open M-Sa 11am-8pm.)

Despite the entirely teal exterior, the budget accommodations at the **Dolphin Inn,** 207 Miracle Strip Pkwy., in the center of Fort Walton Beach, are extremely clean, comfortable, and less than 1 mi. from the warm waters and beautiful sands. (☎850-244-2443. Reservations recommended. Rooms in summer $45-55; winter $35-45.)

THE ROAD TO PANAMA CITY BEACH

U.S. 98 weaves east through the stoplights and beachfront houses of **Destin**. 20 mi. outside Fort Walton Beach, take scenic **Rte. 30A** toward the Gulf. There are a number of parks and recreation areas on the way. The hidden entrance to **Topsail Hill State Preserve** is on the right side of U.S. 98 East, just outside Destin. At this secluded beach area, roadtrippers can take a short dirt-road drive through scrub pines to a quiet, isolated white sand dunes, completely unaffected by the condos and tourists that plague this area. The main entrance to Topsail Hill allows RV camping. (Entrees fee $2.) At the **Grayton Beach State Recreation Area,** off Rte. 30A., camping is available in the woods on the shores of Western Lake, only a short walk from the beaches. Showers, electricity, flush toilets, water, and grills are all available. (☎800-326-3521; www.reserveamerica.com. Park open daily dawn-dusk. Entrance fee $3.25. Sites Mar.-Sept. $14; Oct.-Feb. $8.)

ELMO'S GRILL 6931 Rte. 30A
On the right side of Rte. 30A East, 2 mi. past the U.S. 90 merge.
With screened porch and patio, the entirely outdoor ▧Elmo's Grill is a local hangout and a true taste of Florida. Sitting at the open-air bar beneath the tiki lamps, you might hear a fish story or two, but Elmo's seafood sandwiches and salads ($6-8) are more filling than tales of the one that got away. (☎850-267-2299. Open Su and Tu-Sa 11am-10 pm.)

APPROACHING PANAMA CITY BEACH
Rte. 30A continues along the seaside until merging with U.S. 98, shortly before U.S. 98 again splits into U.S. 98 and U.S. 98A. Take **U.S. 98** to bypass all the beachfront clutter and head straight into Panama City.

PANAMA CITY BEACH

Regardless of whether you're in college or not, the PCB experience is the pinnacle of a Spring Break rampage. As the heart of the "Redneck Riviera," there is no pretension or high culture here—just 27 mi. of sand obscured by thousands of tourists, miles of parties, and loud, thumping bass. Warm-as-a-bath turquoise water, roller coasters, surf shops, and water parks round out the entertainment possibilities. At night, many restaurants on the Strip turn into bars and clubs, most with live bands. Everything gets more crowded around

VITAL STATS

Population: 8000

Visitor Info: Panama City Visitors Center, 17001 Panama City Beach Pkwy. (☎800-722-3224; www.pcbeach.com), at the corner of U.S. 98 (PCB Pkwy.) and Rte. 79. Open daily 8am-5pm.

Internet Access: Bay County Public Library, 25 W. Government St. (☎850-747-5748), in Panama City. Open M-W 9am-8pm, Th-Sa 9am-5pm, Su 1-5pm.

Post Office: 420 Churchwell Dr. (☎800-275-8777). Open M-F 8:30am-5pm, Sa 9am-12:30pm. **Postal Code:** 32401.

 GETTING AROUND. After crossing **Hatha-way Bridge** from the east, **Thomas Dr.** and **Front Beach Rd. (Alt. U.S. 98)** fork off from U.S. 98 and run along the gulf. This becomes that glorious, tourist-crammed beachfront also known as the **"Miracle Strip,"** the main drag of PCB. Beware the sunset and late-night rush; this two-lane road grinds to a standstill at busy times. **U.S. 98** becomes **Panama Beach Pkwy.** and runs parallel to Front Beach Rd. and Thomas Dr. inland, and is the less-trafficked "express route" around the strip.

 SIGHTS & ENTERTAINMENT. Nearly a dozen submarines of various sizes are parked outside the **Museum of Man in the Sea,** 17314 Back Beach Rd. (U.S. 98), making this roadside attraction is hard to miss. Inside, colorful displays are dedicated to the mysteries of the ocean and those who explore them. The museum also houses displays on the treasures of the Gulf's many shipwrecks, an exhibit allowing visitors to crawl inside the small scientific submarine Beave MK IV, and a touch pool with sealife from the gulf. (On the left side of U.S. 98 East, ½ mi. before Rte. 79. ☎850-235-4101. Open daily 9am-5pm. $5, ages 6-16 $2.50.) The **Treasure Island Marina,** 3605 Thomas Dr., is the home base of many a fun and schlocky tourist excursion. The **Glass Bottom Boat** leaves from here to take visitors on dolphin-watching excursions to Shell Island. (☎850-234-8944. 3hr. Departs 9am, 1, and 4:30pm. $15, seniors $14, under 12 $8.) The "world's largest speed boat," the **Sea Screamer,** also casts away from here to cruise the Grand Lagoon. (☎850-233-9107. In summer 4 cruises per day; spring and fall departures vary, call for times. $14, ages 4-12 $8.)

 FOOD & NIGHTLIFE. Buffets fill the Strip and Thomas Dr. "Early bird" specials, usually offered 4-6pm, get you the same food at about

SOUTHERN BORDER

half the price. While food on the strip tends to be of low quality, **Scampy's**, 4933 Thomas Dr., is a notable exception, serving seafood in a smaller, less harried atmosphere than the mega-troughs. This place is obviously the local favorite and might be the only place in town that actually cooks, rather than reheating, scooping, or squirting. (☎ 850-235-4209. 18 different lunch specials $4-7.50. Seafood salad $9. Entrees $11-20. Open Su-Th 11am-10pm, F-Sa 11am-11pm.) Cool off with a Hurricane or a Sharkbite specialty drink ($5.25) at **Sharky's**, 15201 Front Beach Rd. More adventurous spirits will savor "shark bites" (fried shark cubes; $7), Sharky's signature appetizer. (☎ 850-235-2420. Raw oysters $2 per dozen daily 4-6pm. Live performers on the beach deck most nights. Cover $8. Kitchen open daily 11:30am-11pm. Club open until 2am.)

The largest club in the US (capacity 8000) and MTV's former Spring Break headquarters, the behemoth **Club LaVela**, 8813 Thomas Dr., has eight sub-clubs and 48 bar stations under one jammin' roof. Live bands work the Rock Pavilion every night. Wet t-shirt, bikini, and hardbody contests fill the weekends and every night during Spring Break. (☎ 850-234-3866. 18+. No daytime cover; nightly cover varies. Open daily 10am-4am.)

ACCOMMODATIONS. Finding an affordable hotel in PCB is no day at the beach. High season (end of Apr. through early Sept.) typically means $100+ rooms. Call well in advance for summer reservations. Cheap motels can be found in Panama City proper on U.S. 98, just over the bridge from PCB. Though these rooms are rarely worth the $35 they average, they are in a relatively safe neighborhood and are, in comparison, a bargain. Far and away the best deal on the beach is the **South Pacific Motel**, 16701 Front Beach Rd., thanks to a secret treasure: two cheap motel rooms right on the beach. The rest of the rooms at South Pacific are also relatively cheap, even in summer, and the family-owned ambience makes a nice contrast to the impersonal, touristy gaudiness of the rest of the strip. A pool and a private beach are open for guest use. (☎ 850-234-2703 or 800-966-9439. In summer "hidden" singles $45; doubles $75; 2-bedroom apartments $95.) At the **St. Andrews State Recreation Area**, 4607 State Park Ln., you can camp on the beach in a park with over 1000 acres of gators, nature trails, and beaches. Call up to 11 months in advance for res-

ervations at this extremely popular campground. All 176 sites are beneath the pines and on or close to the water. (At the east end of Thomas Dr. ☎ 850-233-5140, reservations 800-326-3521. Open daily 8am-dusk. Sites in summer $17, with electricity or waterside $19; winter $10/$12. $2 per additional person. Entrance fee $3-4.)

FLORIDA'S FORGOTTEN COAST

Panama City, dense with traffic lights, takes a good while to push through, but as soon as **U.S. 98** makes its escape, the road begins a scenic journey along forgotten regions of the Florida coast. This is an area refreshingly free of tourists in tank tops and pink lawn flamingos. Instead, there are breezy islands, shady forests, drowsy alligators, playful waterfowl, and the glittering waters of the Gulf. All these elements meld together under golden sunshine to create the tropical paradise of Florida's fame. The first 26 mi. of the drive wander through the remote coastline and forests that surround **Tyndall Air Force Base**, after which U.S. 98 enters the coastal community of Mexico Beach.

MEXICO BEACH. An offbeat crowd looking for a small-town experience opts to come to this town, which is close enough to the panhandle's resort meccas to attract curious visitors. The locals put up with the modest summer hordes in good spirits and will share the coastline for swimming, shelling, or watching the area's dolphins play at sunset. Locals enjoy cheap meals at **Sharon's Cafe**, 1100 U.S. 98, which include traditional breakfasts like waffles and pancakes, steak and eggs, or deluxe omelettes. Sharon's also cooks up tasty lunches and dinners of sandwiches, burgers, and salads. (☎ 850-648-8634. Meals $2-6. Open daily 6am-2pm.)

 A few miles past Mexico Beach, U.S. 98 enters the Eastern Time Zone, where it is 1hr. later.

PORT ST. JOE. Port St. Joe, 12 mi. down U.S. 98 from Mexico Beach, is a very small coastal village, mostly residential and thankfully undiscovered. **Reld Ave.** is the town's main drag, and its short half mile stretch lies one block inland from U.S. 98. **Russo's Cafe**, 226 Reld Ave., offers a small selection of excellent salads ($5-6) and deli sandwiches ($6-8) in a renovated old flour mill. The cafe's full bakery concocts every sort of sweet treat your heart desires. (☎850-229-6050. Open M-Sa 11am-10pm.)

◣ DETOUR: ST. JOSEPH PENINSULA STATE PARK

Take a right off Rte 30A at the Gulf of Mexico onto Rte. 30 East to reach the tip of the St. Joseph Peninsula.

Here on the edge of the world sits the astoundingly beautiful St. Joseph Peninsula State Park. Miles of white sand beaches stretch out, breezes rustle sea-oat-covered dunes, and a heavily forested interior provides an incredible backdrop for campers, beachgoers, snorkelers, hikers, shellers, and fishermen. Nearly two-thirds of the park toward the tip of the peninsula are dedicated wilderness, sanctuary to brown pelicans, horseshoe crabs, sea turtles, migratory peregrine falcons, and monarch butterflies. (☎850-227-1327 or 800-326-3521; www.reserveamerica.com. Open 8am-dusk. Entrance fee $3. Mar.-Sept. sites $15; remote cabins $70. Oct.-Feb. $8/$55.)

APALACHICOLA. The next stop, 23 mi. down U.S. 98/319 from Port St. Joe, is Apalachicola, a romantic little fishing port on the shores of a peaceful bay. A tranquil seafaring atmosphere distinguishes the red-brick downtown, where little has changed since its construction. Apalachicola is known for its oysters, harvested fresh from Apalachicola Bay; for the best fried oysters in town, visit 100-year-old **Apalchicola Seafood Grill,** 100 Market St. (☎850-653-9510. Open M-Sa 11:30am-8pm.) The **Rancho Inn,** 240 U.S. 98 West, has high-quality, large rooms for decent rates considering their coastal location. (☎850-653-9435. Summer singles $60-70; doubles $65-75. Winter singles $50-60/$55-65.)

The town of Apalachicola was once home to one of Florida's heroes. It was here that Dr. John Gorrie, in a desperate attempt to keep his yellow fever patients cool, invented the world's first mechanical icemaker in the 1840s. This laid the groundwork for the artificial cooling of air, which, with the coming of air-conditioning, has turned Florida from mostly inhospitable swampy wasteland to a first-rate tourist destination.

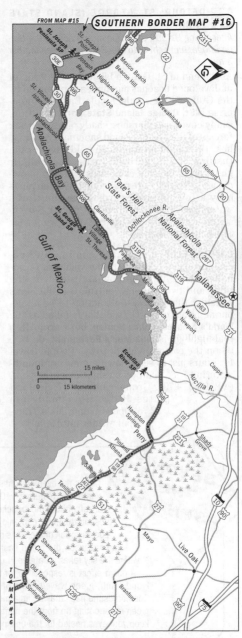

FROM MAP #15

SOUTHERN BORDER MAP #16

SOUTHERN BORDER

0 — 15 miles
0 — 15 kilometers

◢ DETOUR: ST. GEORGE ISLAND STATE PARK

After taking U.S. 98 to Eastpoint and across the Gorrie Bridge, turn right onto Rte. 300 and travel another 3 mi.

At the end of St. George Island sit the 9 mi. of undeveloped beaches and dunes surrounded by the Gulf and the Apalachicola Bay, that comprise ◢**St. George Island State Park.** Amid the sandy coves, salt marshes, shady pines, and oak forests of the pristine island sanctuary, you may hear the call of an American bald eagle or the rustling of a loggerhead turtle, raccoon, or ghost crab. Bayside campsites with hot showers and electricity are nestled in the scrub pines only a few hundred yards from the Gulf's waters. (☎850-927-2111 or 800-326-3521. Sites in summer $14, with electricity $16; in winter $8/ $10. Entrance fee $4.)

CARRABELLE. U.S. 98/319 continues 22 mi. east through thick pines to the village of Carrabelle, where life is as slow and steady as the tides and twice as uneventful. Carrabellians consider their greatest attraction to be a telephone booth off of U.S. 98 that is billed as the **World's Smallest Police Station,** but Carrabelle's real highlight is **Julia Mae's Restaurant,** on U.S. 98 on the eastern edge of town. People travel for hours just to scarf down mounds of mouthwatering fried seafood straight from the Gulf. (☎850-697-3791. Grouper burger $7. Seafood plates $9-15. Homemade pie $2.75. Open Su and Tu-Sa 11am-10pm; winter until 9pm.)

THE ROAD TO PERRY

Outside Carrabelle, the road weaves in and out of Gulf shores and into the ominously named **Tate's Hell State Forest.** Many backroads will take you remote camping areas within the forest for a change from the Gulf-side driving. Take **U.S. 319** as it splits off from **U.S. 98,** and follow it as it passes through the small hamlet of **Sopchoppy** and merges back with U.S. 98. U.S. 98 embarks on a 54 mi. trek, slicing straight through dark woods that loom like giant walls on either side of the highway, blocking out all light but a slim ribbon of sky. Assuming the forest beasties don't get you, you'll reach **Perry** at the crossroads with **U.S. 19.**

PERRY

Quite possibly the dead center of nowhere, the city of Perry, which sits at the crossroads of U.S. routes 98, 19, 27, and 221, exists mostly as a traveler's oasis. Here you can find a slew of budget motels and an ample number of diners to match. The turn-of-the-century **Cracker Homestead** preserves a log cabin, picket fence, kitchen, barn, and many other characteristic artifacts from a Florida settlement. The term "cracker" refers to the settlers who lived in the rural areas, and may have been derived from the early Floridians who cracked their whips to drive their cattle and oxen. (☎850-584-3227. Open M and Th-Su 9am-5pm.)

Next door, **Pouncey's Restaurant,** 2186 U.S. 19 South, has been a local favorite for diner food since the mid-50s. Here you can find huge home-cooked breakfasts like biscuit sandwiches ($1-2) served all day. Order from a ency-

---

BEYOND THE ASPHALT

THE GREEN FLASH

As the evening light steals across the Florida coast, the day's colors retreat into the western sky. Orange, pink, red and purple fill the horizon, reflecting off of white sand beaches. But the pastels aren't the only colors of sunset; those in the know can enjoy an exciting grand finale to this daily show.

Locals speak of the sun's most impressive trick, know as the "green flash." As its name suggests, the green flash is a momentary change in the color of the sunset, where the sky takes on a green hue for a few seconds before the sun sets.

A prism effect is responsible for the sunset's colors, and in large flat regions, like the Florida Gulf, green wavelengths of light can actually by refracted by the atmosphere. Sometimes the flash may be little more than a green dot, while other times it can be giant green ray shooting up from the horizon. So as you enjoy the last moments of fading light, keep your eyes peeled for the unexpected appearance of emerald rays from the sun.

clopedic list of sandwiches ($2-6) from egg salad to BLT to corned beef. (About 1 mi. south of the U.S. 98/U.S. 19 intersection, on the left. ☎850-584-9942. Open daily 6am-10pm.) Among the budget accommodations available, the **Chaparral Inn**, 2159 U.S. 19 South, while not the cheapest in town, stands out as the best with its large, spotless rooms. (☎850-584-2441. Singles $30. $5 per additional person.)

LEAVING PERRY

Take **U.S. 19** out of Perry. U.S. 19 makes its way south along the Gulf, 10 mi. to the west. After 43 mi. of swamps and forest, the next town is Cross City.

CROSS CITY. While it's the seat of tiny Dixie County, there is really nothing to the village aside from a combination hotel and restaurant known as the **Carriage Inn**. (☎352-498-3910. Singles $37; doubles $43. $5 per additional person. AAA discount.) The restaurant serves a hearty country buffet and offers equally hearty breakfasts. (☎352-498-0888. Breakfasts $5-8. Open daily 7am-10pm.)

OLD TOWN. Ten miles down U.S. 19, the village of Old Town sits way down along the **Suwannee River**, where the lazy flow of the dark, wide waterway creates an air of tranquility along its banks. For vacationers looking to enjoy the lingering afternoons and warm peaceful evenings along the old Suwannee, the **Suwannee Gables Motel**, 27659 SE U.S. 19, is an excellent stop. Each room in the tiny motel has a great river view and access to the gorgeous wooded backyard above the Suwannee's banks. A large boat dock serves as the launching point for many a day floating on the river and has a patio for enjoying the scenery. (☎352-542-7752; www.suwanneegables.com. Large cabin rooms available, sleeping six or more. Rooms from $65; cabins $149.)

MANATEE SPRINGS STATE PARK

Entering the town of Chiefland, turn right on Rte. 320 and drive 3 mi.

This giant spring gushes forth crystal clear water at a rate of 50 to 150 million gallons per day, providing refreshing swimming on hot summer afternoons. Rent a canoe and paddle up the spring or down the river to see the gentle mammal for which the park is named. (☎352-493-6072 or 800-326-3521. Sites $11, with electricity $13.)

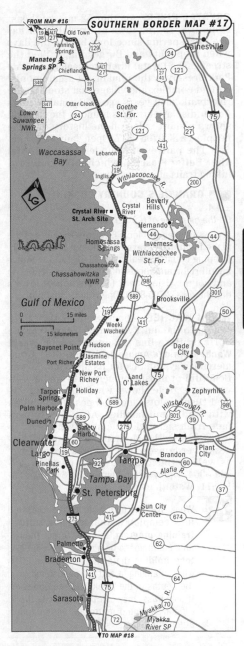

SOUTHERN BORDER

CRYSTAL RIVER. Another 52 mi. southeast along U.S. 19, the town of Crystal River has been prospering since long before the days when stoplights and Burger Kings filled the streets. The **Crystal River Archaeological State Park** preserves the remains of a ceremonial mound complex and village that stood on the riverbank 2500 years ago. The small **Visitors Center** displays artifacts found at the site and shows a short video on the history of these people. (☎352-795-3817. Open daily 9am-5pm. $2.) The park is surrounded by the **Crystal River Buffer Preserve,** which offers miles of hiking trails along the river.

 GRANNIE'S COUNTRY COOKIN'

712 U.S. 19

On the right side of U.S. 19 South

A classic diner and local favorite, Grannie's is the place for hungry travelers who are low on cash. Heaping country breakfasts ($2-5) start the morning off right, and meals like hamburger steak ($4) and country fried steak ($5) are a meat-lover's delight. (☎352-795-8884. Open daily 5am-9pm.)

WEEKI WACHEE. About 28 mi. south, U.S. 19 rolls into the quirky town of Weeki Wachee Springs. Here lies the one-of-a-kind **Weeki Wachee Springs Amusement Park,** 6131 Commercial Way, famous for its Mermaid Shows. Beautiful professional mermaids hold underwater spectacle shows, which are often recycled Disney plots, and then pose for pictures with landbound families. After the flippers fade from sight with the show's finale, visitors flock to the Mermaid Museum, wilderness river cruises, bird and creatures shows, as well as the attached water park. (☎877-469-3354. Open daily 10am-4pm. $14, ages 3-10 $11. Water park $5/$4.)

 Weeki Wachee mermaids must successfully complete a year-long **mermaid training program.** In order to get their fins, mermaids-to-be must pass the final test: holding their breath for 2½min. while changing in and out of costume in the depths of the Weeki Wachee Spring. If they pass, they can proudly recite the official mermaid motto as full-fledged aqua-entertainers.

APPROACHING TARPON SPRINGS
From **U.S. 19,** turn onto the quiet seaside alternative, **U.S. 19A.** A few blocks down, turn right onto **Dodecanese Blvd.** to reach the waterfront of Tarpon Springs.

TARPON SPRINGS. In the 1880s, rich sponge beds were discovered off the coast of Tarpon Springs. Sponge harvesters used hooks to pull the sponges off the sea floor until 1905, when Greek immigrant John Corcoris introduced the sponge diving technology that had long been used by Greeks in the Mediterranean. Corcoris also brought 500 Greek divers to Tarpon Springs, and the sponge harvesting industry took off. Tarpon Springs subsequently emerged as a piece of Greece in Florida, a fact that remains true to this day. Around Christmas, the bayou just south of the docks on Tarpon Ave. hosts a traditional festival in which young Greek Orthodox children dive into the chilly waters to retrieve a ceremonial cross. Some of the best Greek food in town awaits at **Mama's Greek Cuisine,** 735 Dodecanese Blvd. (☎727-944-2888. Gyros $5. Broiled octopus $10. Open daily 7am-10pm.)

APPROACHING CLEARWATER & ST. PETERSBURG
Keep driving on **U.S. 19** to enter both cities.

CLEARWATER & ST. PETERSBURG

Just across the bay from the bustling metropolis of Tampa lies the stretch of white sand beaches between Clearwater and St. Petersburg, where glistening waters are warmed by sunshine about 361 days per year. These sandy stretches cater to beach bums and city folks alike. While the outdoor scenery draws the crowds, indoor activities are equally captivating—museum exhibits on Salvador Dalí and JFK rival even the nicest sunset.

GETTING AROUND

In St. Petersburg, **Central Ave.** parallels numbered avenues, running east-west in the downtown area. **34th St. (U.S. 19), I-275,** and **4th St.** are major north-south thoroughfares. The beaches line a strip of barrier islands on the far west side of town facing the Gulf. Several cause-

(VITAL STATS)

Population: 109,000 / 250,000

Visitor Info: St. Petersburg Visitors Center, 100 2nd Ave. N. (☎ 727-821-4069; www.stpete.com). Open M-F 8am-5pm, Sa 10am-5pm, Su noon-5pm. Several downtown kiosks also provide maps.

Internet Access: St. Petersburg Main Library, 3745 9th Ave. North (☎ 727-893-7724). Open M-Th 9am-9pm, F-Sa 9am-6pm, Su 10am-6pm.

Post Office: 3135 1st Ave. North (☎ 800-275-8777), at 31st St. Open M-F 8am-6pm, Sa 8am-12:30pm. **Postal Code:** 37370.

ways, including the **Clearwater Memorial Causeway (Rte. 60),** access the beaches from St. Pete. Clearwater sits at the far north of the strip. **Gulf Blvd.** runs down the coastline. The beaches past the huge pink Don Cesar Hotel—St. Pete Beach and the Pass-a-Grille Beach—have the best sand, as well as less traffic.

👁 SIGHTS

Grab a copy of *See St. Pete* or the *St. Petersburg Official Visitor's Guide* for the low-down on area events, discounts, and useful maps. Downtown St. Pete is cluttered with museums and galleries that make it worth the effort to leave the beach.

▨ FLORIDA INTERNATIONAL MUSEUM.
The Florida International Museum is an incredible historical experience. The "Cuban Missile Crisis: When the Cold War Got Hot" exhibit allows visitors to relive the terrifying tense Cuban Missile Crisis day-by-day. "John F. Kennedy: The Exhibition" provides a comprehensive look at JFK's personal and political life. (*100 2nd St. North. Parking on Central Ave. between 2nd St. and 1st St.* ☎ 727-822-3693, 800-777-9882; *www.floridamuseum.org. Open M-Sa 10am-5pm, Su noon-5pm; ticket office closes 4pm. $12, seniors $11, students $6.*)

▨ SALVADOR DALÍ MUSEUM. The highlight
of St. Petersburg is the exhaustive Salvador Dalí Museum, which houses the largest private collection of the Surrealist's work in the world. The South's most visited museum houses 95 of Dalí's oil paintings and provides exceptional tours offering fascinating views into the life and works of the enigmatic artist. (*1000 3rd St. South.* ☎ 800-442-3254; *www.salvadordalimuseum.org. Open M-W and F-Sa 9:30am-5:30pm, Th 9:30am-8pm, Su noon-5:30pm. Free tours daily 12:15, 1:30, 2:30, 3:45pm. $10, students $5, seniors $7, under 10 free.*)

BEACHES. Beaches are the most worth-while—but not the only—attraction along the coastline. The nicest beach may be **Pass-a-Grille Beach,** but its parking meters eat quarters by the bucketful. Check out **Clearwater Beach,** at the northern end of the Gulf Blvd. strand, where mainstream beach culture lounges in a decidedly fantastic white sand beach setting. The **Sunsets at Pier 60 Festival** brings arts and entertainment to Clearwater Beach. (☎ 727-449-1036; *www.sunsetsatpier60.com. Festival daily 2hr. before sundown until 2hr. after.*)

🍴 FOOD

St. Petersburg's cheap, health-conscious restaurants cater to its retired population, and generally close by 8 or 9pm.

▨ **Frenchy's Cafe,** 41 Baymont St. (☎ 727-446-3607). After crossing the Clearwater Memorial Causeway (Rte. 60), turn right onto Mandalay Ave. About ¼ mi. north, turn left. This tiny restaurant and bar just off Clearwater Beach is a local favorite. The house specialty, boiled shrimp ($13), comes dusted in secret seasonings. Frenchy's is so popular that 2 other branches of the restaurant have opened within blocks of this original location. Open M-Th 11:30am-11pm, F-Sa 11:30am-midnight, Su noon-11pm.

Molly Goodheads, 400 Orange St. (☎ 727-786-6255; www.mollygoodheads.com). From U.S. 19A, turn right on Tampa Rd., 5 mi. south of Tarpon Springs, and then right on Orange St. This lively quasi-biker bar and family restaurant serves awesome seafood meals. Salads ($6-7), hamburgers ($5-6), fried grouper ($7), and seafood platters ($8-10) are all excellent. Open Su-Th 11am-10pm, F-Sa 11am-11pm.

Dockside Dave's, 13203 Gulf Blvd. South (☎ 727-392-9399), in Madeira Beach. One of the best-kept secrets on the islands. The ½ grouper sandwich (market price, around $8) is simply sublime. Open M-Sa 11am-10pm, Su noon-10pm.

Beach Nutts, 9600 W. Gulf Blvd. (☎ 727-367-7427), on Treasure Island. Fresh grouper ($10) and decent burgers ($6). Spectacular porchside view of the beach; nightly bands. Open daily 11am-2am.

Tangelo's Bar and Grille, 226 1st Ave. North (☎727-894-1695). A superb Cuban restaurant. Their imported sauce spices up a Oaxacan *mole* chicken breast sandwich ($5.50). Open M 11am-6pm, Tu-Th 11am-8pm, F-Sa 11am-9pm.

Fourth Street Shrimp Store, 1006 4th St. North (☎727-822-0325). Purveyor of all things shrimp. Try the filling shrimp taco salad ($7). Open Su-Th 11am-9pm, F-Sa 11am-9:30pm.

ACCOMMODATIONS

St. Petersburg and Clearwater offer two hostels, and many cheap motels line **4th St. North** and **U.S. 19** in St. Pete. Some establishments advertise singles for as little as $25, but these tend to be very worn-down. To avoid the worst neighborhoods, stay on the north end of 4th St. and the south end of U.S. 19. Several inexpensive motels cluster on the beaches along **Gulf Blvd.**

Clearwater Beach International Hostel (HI-AYH), 606 Bay Esplanade Ave. (☎727-443-1211), off Mandalay Ave., at the Sands Motel in Clearwater Beach. Tucked away off the sandy Clearwater shore, this hostel feels more like a country club than budget lodging. Internet $1 per 8min. Linen and key deposit $5. Reception 9am-noon and 5-9pm. Dorms $13, nonmembers $14; private rooms $30-40. Surcharge for credit card payments.

St. Petersburg Youth Hostel, 326 1st Ave. North (☎727-822-4141). Parking at meters on 1st Ave. A quirky beachfront inn in the downtown Kelly Hotel. Call ahead to make sure there is room in the hostel, which consists of 4-person rooms with private baths. Common room, TV, and A/C. Youth hostel card or student ID required. Dorms $20; private rooms $43.

Treasure Island Motel, 10315 Gulf Blvd. (☎727-367-3055). Across the street from the beach, this hotel has big rooms with A/C, fridge, color TV, pull-out couch, and use of a beautiful pool. Catch dinner off a pier in back. Singles and doubles from $40.

Fort De Soto County Park, 3500 Pinellas Bayway S. (☎727-464-3347 or 727-582-2267). Composed of 5 islands and among the best state parks in Florida. Reservations must be made in person either at the Park Office, 501 1st Ave. North, Ste. A116 (☎727-582-

7738), or at the Parks Dept., 631 Chestnut St. in Clearwater. Park Office Open daily 8am-4:30pm. 2-night min. stay. Front gate locked 9pm. Curfew 10pm. Sites Aug.-Dec. $23; Jan.-July $33.)

⚑ LEAVING ST. PETERSBURG

Leaving St. Petersburg requires jumping on **I-275** and crossing the **Sunshine Skyway Bridge** ($1 toll). After crossing Tampa Bay, exit the freeway onto **U.S. 41 South.** Merge right onto the business loop to Bradenton.

🏛 SOUTH FLORIDA MUSEUM   201 10th St.
Off U.S. 41; after crossing the bridge into Bradenton, the museum will be on your right.

This museum chronicles southwestern Florida's natural and cultural history from the Pleistocene to the present with exceptional, life-size dioramas and dramatic exhibits of its anthropological artifacts and biological specimens. The attached **Parker Manatee Aquarium** houses Manatee County's official mascot, Snooty the manatee. (☎941-746-4131; www.southfloridamuseum.org. Open Jan.-Apr. M-Sa 10am-5pm, Su noon-5pm. May-Dec. closed M. $9.50, students with ID $6, ages 5-12 $5.)

THE ROAD TO SARASOTA. From downtown Bradenton follow the signs to stay on **U.S. 41 South;** take a right on **8th Ave.,** then a left on **14th St.** On the 9 mi. stop-and-go drive to **Sarasota,** U.S. 41 passes a wide assortment of budget motels, many of which rent rooms for under $30.

🏛 SARASOTA CLASSIC CAR MUSEUM
5500 N. Tamiami Trail
At the corner of University Ave.

The 🚗**Sarasota Classic Car Museum** has a world-class collection of nearly 100 classic cars that spans the entirety of automotive history. From Model-T Fords to the '74 Bentley Formula Racer and everything in between, cars here demand a look from the avid car enthusiast or the curious roadtripper. The collection is as amusing as is it is astounding, with the original caped crusader's Batmobile, John Lennon's '65 Mercedes Roadster, Paul McCartney's humble Mini, and the '82 Delorean of *Back to the Future* fame. Bring your nickels and dimes for the room dedicated to arcade games from the 50s through the 80s. (☎941-355-6228; www.sarasotacarmuseum.org. Open daily 9am-6pm. $8.50.)

🏛 RINGLING MUSEUM OF ART
5401 Bayshore Rd.

From U.S. 41, turn right just past University Ave. onto Bayshore Rd. Across the street from the car museum.

The Ringling brothers amassed an impressive collection of Baroque and Renaissance art and built one of the finest art museums in Florida on the grounds of their estate to display it. Also on-site is the **Circus Museum,** dedicated to the three traveling rings that made the Ringling name famous, which shows colorful relics—everything from costumes to wagons. Perhaps the best feature of the beautiful grounds is the **Ca d'Zan** mansion, the one-time Ringling home. Evoking the Ringlings' fondness for Venetian-Gothic palaces, the Ca d'Zan sports golden and marble pillars, cathedral ceilings with hand-crafted artwork, and other over-the-top opulence. (☎941-351-1660; www.ringling.org. Open daily 10am-5:30pm. M $10; Tu-Su $15; out of state students $7; in-state students and teachers free.)

🦪 PHILLIPPI CREEK VILLAGE OYSTER BAR
5353 S. Tamiami Tr.

On the left of U.S. 41 South, 5 mi. south of downtown Sarasota at the Phillippi Island Rd. Intersection.

Seafood steams and sizzles in a great atmosphere with dockside open-air seating over Phillippi Creek. Try the soft-shell crab sandwich or the blackened grouper—but don't skip out on oysters on the half shell. (☎941-925-4444. Oysters $6 per dozen. Sandwiches $6.75. Entrees $13-15. Open Su-Th 11am-10pm, F-Sa 11am-10:30pm.)

🏕 OSCAR SCHERER STATE PARK
1843 S. Tamiami Tr.

6 mi. south of Sarasota on U.S. 41

Oscar Scherer State Park offers beautiful creek-side camping, fishing, swimming, and canoeing.(☎800-326-3521; www.reserveamerica.com. Canoes $5 per hr., $25 per day. Sites June-Oct. $11, with electricity $13; Nov.-May $16.50/$18.50.)

🧭 APPROACHING FORT MYERS BEACH
From **U.S. 41,** turn right on **Rte. 865 West,** then turn left on **Rte. 869 West** and left again onto **Rte. 865 South.** All of the turns are well labeled with signs for Fort Myers Beach. Rte. 865 South crosses the bridge over the San Carlos Bay as **Estero Blvd.**

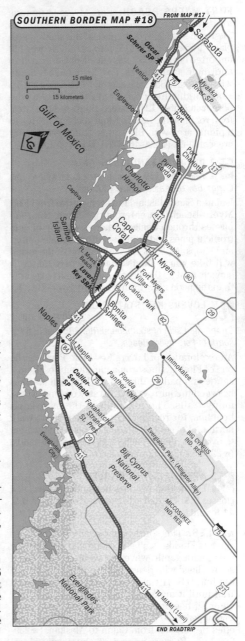

SOUTHERN BORDER MAP #18

FROM MAP #17

END ROADTRIP

SOUTHERN BORDER

FORT MYERS BEACH. Fort Myers is famous for its lively beach scene. Just over the bridge is the town square, where most of the action takes place. **Dusseldorf's,** 1113 Estero Blvd., has over 140 imported beers and serves excellent German grub and huge sandwiches. (☎ 239-463-5251. Sandwiches $5.50. Sausage sampler $11. Open Su-Th 11am-midnight, F-Sa 11am-2am.) Stay at the ■**Beacon Motel,** 1240 Estero Blvd., the best deal for a room on the beach. Some kitchens, access to a picnic area with BBQ grills, and guest laundry are available. (☎ 239-463-5264. Rooms from $45.)

⬛ **DETOUR: SANIBEL ISLAND**
Take Rte. 869 heading west to cross the San Carlos Bay over a causeway ($3 toll).

Isolated Sanibel Island is a scenic drive from Fort Myers Beach. On entering the island, the road passes through **Sanibel,** where a canopy of subtropical pines and palms shades fairy-tale homes and shops. A 15 mi. drive to the end of the island will take you to **Captiva Beach,** where fabulous sunsets light up the sky more softly and pleasantly than the neon glow from busy Fort Myers Beach.

⬛ **LOVERS KEY STATE PARK**
8700 Estero Blvd.
On the right side of southbound Rte. 865, about 5 mi. south of Fort Myers Beach.

An exploration of Lovers Key State Park can be one of Florida's most romantic adventures. Rent a canoe and paddle through the brackish streams between the narrow keys, or stay on land on the many trails. The highlight of the park is its beaches; for real seclusion, take a short walk north on Lovers Key, wading through Gulf waters to avoid the dense thickets, to reach white sands. (☎ 239-463-4588. Entrance fee $4.)

⬛ **APPROACHING NAPLES**
Estero Blvd. becomes **Bonita Beach Blvd.** and crosses **U.S. 41.** Turn right and travel south down **U.S. 41** toward Naples.

NAPLES. The southernmost city on the west coast of Florida, Naples goes through life at a slow pace, with gentle waves on white sand tropical shores lined with dense palms and the occasional tiki hut. U.S. 41 travels through town as **Tamiami Trail** until it makes an eastern turn at **5th Ave.,** where it becomes downtown's ritzy main drag. **Lindburger's,** 330 Tamiami Tr. South, grills 50 varieties of burgers, from Cajun to Alaskan. (☎ 239-262-1127. Burgers around $6. Open daily 11am-

9pm.) **The Tamiami Motel,** 2164 Tamiami Tr. East, is a great deal less than 2 mi. from the beach. (☎ 239-774-4626. Rooms from $42.)

THE ROAD TO THE EVERGLADES

After passing Naples, U.S. 41 heads east into the heart of one of the world's largest swamps: the Everglades. Sixteen miles outside Naples, the swamp takes over all civilization, and the road enters **Collier-Seminole State Park.** Those daring enough to camp in the heart of the swamp can also enjoy fishing and canoeing in the many waterways that surround it. (☎ 239-394-3397 or 800-326-3521. Entrance fee $3. Canoes $5 per hr., $25 per day. Sites Dec.-May $13; May-Nov. $8. Electricity $2.) Collier-Seminole State Park marks the start of the 55 mi. **Tamiami Trail Scenic Byway,** which takes **U.S. 41** east into the heart of the Everglades National Park. Fifteen miles outside the park, turn south onto **Rte. 29** to visit the last bit of civilization in western Florida, Everglades City.

EVERGLADES CITY. Everglades City is a waterlogged town that the rest of civilization has forgotten. In town is the main eastern visitors center for the Everglades, the **Gulf Coast Visitors Center.** (☎ 239-695-3311. Open daily summer 8:30am-5pm; winter 7:30am-5pm.) For a bite to eat in town, try **Susie's Station Restaurant,** a family-run diner that serves up cheap food in a fun atmosphere full of old gas station memorabilia. (☎ 239-695-0704. Sandwich baskets $5-8. Seafood baskets $9-11. Homemade key lime pie $3.25. Open M-Th 10am-5pm, F-Su 10am-9pm.) Stay at the ■**Everglades City Motel,** 310 Collier Ave. (Rte. 29), where extras like tile floors, wicker furniture, and kitchens make for a comfortable sleep. (☎ 800-695-8353. Reservations recommended. Rooms $55-65.)

THE EVERGLADES

The Everglades National Park makes a spectacular end to your trip; encompassing the entire tip of Florida and spearing into Florida Bay, the park spans 1.6 million acres of one of the world's most fragile ecosystems. Vast prairies of sawgrass range through broad expanses of shallow water, creating the famed "river of grass," while tangled mazes of mangrove swamps wind up and down the western coast. To the south, delicate coral reefs lie below the shimmering blue waters of the bay. Species found nowhere else in the world inhabits these lands and waters: American alligators, dolphins, sea turtles, and various birds and fish, as well as the endangered Florida panther, Florida manatee, and American crocodile.

VITAL STATS

Area: 1.6 million acres

Visitor Info: Ernest Coe Visitors Center, 40001 Rte. 9366 (☎305-242-7700; www.nps.gov/ever/), just inside the eastern edge of the Everglades. Open daily 9am-5pm. **Flamingo Visitors Center** (☎239-695-2945), on Rte. 9366, 40 mi. into the park. Open daily summer 8am-5pm; winter 7:30am-5pm. For other area information on lodgings and local discounts, check out the **Tropical Everglades Visitors Center** (☎305-245-9180 or 800-388-9669), on U.S. 1 in Florida City. Open daily 9am-5pm.

Gateway Towns: Everglades City (p. 868), Florida City.

Fees: Entrance fees vary, depending on the area of the park. Gulf Coast free. Ernest Coe $10 per vehicle per day, Shark Valley $8.

GETTING AROUND

The Everglades National Park stretches across the entire southern end of Florida; **Everglades City** lies on the very western edge of the park some distance from other towns. Visitors Centers are scattered throughout the park, but **U.S. 41,** also known as the **Tamiami Trail,** is the only way to get from west to east. To reach the sights, food, and accommodations in **Florida City** and **Homestead,** take **U.S. 41** west to **Rte. 997.** Homestead lies about 20 mi. south along Rte. 997. Florida City is just southwest of Homestead; continue south on Rte. 997 and then take **Rte. 9336** west. The main entrance to the park, **Ernest Coe Visitors Center,** sits near Florida City just inside the eastern edge of the Everglades. From here, Rte. 9366 cuts 40 mi. through the park past campgrounds, trailheads, and waterways to the **Flamingo Visitors Center** and the heavily developed **Flamingo Outpost Resort.**

SIGHTS

For a truly bizarre time, head up U.S. 1 to the **Coral Castle,** 28655 S. Dixie Hwy., in Homestead. Over 20 years, Latvian immigrant Ed Leedskalnin turned hundreds of tons of dense coral rock into a garden of magnificent sculptures. The sight has since been studied by anthropologists who thought it might explain how humans built the Egyptian pyramids. (☎305-248-6344; www.coralcastle.com. Open M-Th 9am-6pm, F-Su 9am-7pm. Tours daily. $7.75, ages 7-12 $5, seniors $6.50. Discounts at Visitors Center.)

View gators, crocs, and snakes at the **Everglades Alligator Farm,** 40351 SW 192 Ave., 4 mi. south of Palm Dr. Though ultra-touristy, this is the best place to see thousands of gators. (☎305-247-2628 or 800-644-9711; http://everglades.com. Open May-Sept. daily 9am-6pm. Wildlife shows 11am, 2, 5pm. $11.50, ages 4-11 $6.50.)

OUTDOOR ACTIVITIES

The park is swamped with fishing, hiking, canoeing, biking, and wildlife-watching opportunities. Forget swimming; alligators, sharks, and barracuda patrol the waters. From November through April, the park sponsors amphitheater programs, canoe trips, and ranger-guided Slough Slogs (swamp tours). Summer visitors can expect mosquitoes aplenty. Stay away from swampy areas during sunrise and sunset. The best time to visit is winter or spring when heat, humidity, storms, and bugs are at a minimum and wildlife congregate in shrinking pools of evaporating water. Wear long sleeves and bring insect repellent.

HIKING

The Everglades are accessible through a series of well-developed short trails. A good choice is the **Pa-hay-okee Overlook,** 13 mi. from the main entrance off Rte. 9336. It rewards its visitors with a stunning view of the park after only a quarter mile hike. One of the best hiking trails, the famous **Anhinga Trail** begins at the Royal Palm Visitors Center, 4 mi. inside the park from the main entrance. Moderately difficult, this trail grants explorers up-close encounters with alligators, anhinga birds, and turtles and is best traversed December to March. For a more difficult trail, head over to Long Pine Key (6 mi. from the main entrance), where the **Long Pine Key Trail** ventures through 10 mi. of slash pine forests. Another arduous hike is the **Mahogany Hammock Trail,** 20 mi. from the main entrance. Though this trail offers incredible routes through freshwater prairie and pineland, mosquitoes swarm during summer, making it most enjoyable in winter months.

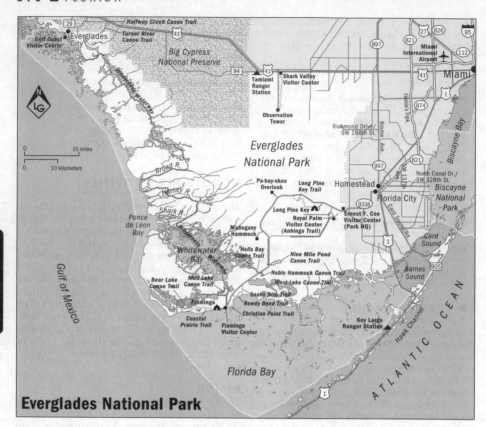

Everglades National Park

BOATING

If you really want to experience the Everglades, start paddling. The 99 mi. **Wilderness Waterway** winds its way from the northwest entrance to the Flamingo Visitors Center in the far south. **Everglades National Park Boat Tours**, at the Gulf Coast Visitors Center, rents canoes ($24) and is the best option for guided boat tours. The **Ten Thousand Island Cruise** ($16) is a 1½hr. tour through the Everglades' myriad tiny islands, and patrons often see bald eagles, dolphins, and manatees. The **Mangrove Wilderness Cruise** is a 2hr. cruise through the inland swamps that brings its six passengers face-to-face with alligators. (☎239-695-2591 or 800-445-7724. Tours every 30min. $25.) For those who would rather do their own paddling, **Hell's Bay Canoe Trail,** located about 29 mi. from the

entrance, is the best spot. For more information on navigating the park's waterways, consult the rangers at the Flamingo Visitors Center.

BIKING

While the Everglades mostly caters to those with walking sticks and canoe paddles, it does offer some excellent biking. The best route can be found at the **Shark Valley Visitors Center,** where a 15 mi. loop awaits. The trail peaks at an incredible observation tower that offers views of the park's rivers of grass, alligators, and the occasional fawn. (☎305-221-8776. Open daily 8:30am-6pm. Tram tours May-Nov. daily 9:30, 11am, 1, 3pm; Dec.-Apr. every hr. 9am-4pm. $10, seniors $9, under 12 $5.50. Reservations recommended. Bike rental daily 8:30am-3pm. $5.25 per hr., including helmets.)

FOOD

Rosita's, 199 Palm Dr., across the street from the hostel in Florida City, has the best Mexican food in the area. Relax with some great *chiles rellenos* or cheese enchiladas. (☎305-246-3114. Open daily 8:30am-9pm.) The pinnacle of eateries in Homestead, the vegan-friendly **Main St. Cafe,** 128 N. Krome Ave., serves up great sandwiches ($4-6) and soups in a deli-style restaurant that doubles as a comedy club on the weekends. (☎305-245-7575. Th open mic 8-midnight. F and Sa folk and acoustic rock 8pm-midnight. Open Tu-W 11am-4pm, Th-Sa 11am-midnight.) At the southern end of Homestead, **Farmers' Market Restaurant,** 300 N. Krome Ave., delivers "good home cooking." Enjoy hearty portions of a traditional, all-American breakfast ($4-6), lunch ($5-8) or dinner ($8-13). (☎305-242-0008. Open daily 5:30am-9pm. Customers save 5% with a copy of the menu available at the local Visitors Center.)

ACCOMMODATIONS

Outside the eastern entrance to the park, Florida City offers cheap motels along U.S. 1. The ☒**Everglades International Hostel (HI-AYH),** 20 SW 2nd Ave., off Rte. 9336 (Palm Dr.), presents a far better option, with modern rooms and friendly staff. After venturing into the Everglades on a hostel-guided tour ($25-30), hang out with fellow travelers in the gazebo, gardens, or kitchen house, which has a large-screen TV and free video collection. (☎305-248-1122 or 800-372-3874; www.evergladeshostel.com. Free Internet. Laundry. Bike rental $5. Canoe rental $20. Linen $2. Dorms $13-14, nonmembers $17-18; private rooms $33-35/$36-38.) The only option for lodging inside the park, **Flamingo Lodge,** 1 Flamingo Lodge Hwy., has large rooms with A/C, TV, private baths, and a great view of the Florida Bay. (☎800-600-3813. Continental breakfast included in summer. Reservations recommended. Rooms Jan.-Mar. $95; May-Oct. $65; Nov.-Dec. and Apr. $79.) A few **campgrounds** line Rte. 9336. All sites have drinking water, grills, dump sites, and restrooms, but none have hookups. (☎800-365-2267. Reservations required Nov.-Apr. Sites $14.) **Backcountry camping** inside the park is accessible primarily by boat. Required **permits** are available on a first come, first served basis at the Flamingo and Gulf Coast Visitors Centers. Camping reservations must be made in person, at least a day in advance, at the Visitors Centers. ($10 permit plus $2 per person for backcountry camping; free in summer. Applications must be made in person at least 24hr. in advance.)

THE PACIFIC COAST

Crashing waves, sheer coastal bluffs, monumental redwoods, expansive ocean sunsets—exhilaration doesn't begin to describe the way it feels to be poised on the western edge of the country, with better times and wilder sights in the cliff-hugging turns ahead, and the past receding in your rearview mirror. Our route takes you the entire length of the Pacific Coast, from **San Diego** (p. 874), the southernmost of California's major cities, all the way to Seattle, on the foggy edge of Puget Sound.

From San Diego, you'll cruise through California beach culture; beach communities begin in earnest (and by earnest, we mean casual lethargy) near San Diego and dot the coast all the way to San Francisco. You'll pass by (or stop and surf) the mythical swells of **Huntington Beach** (p. 885) before reaching laid-back **Hermosa,** carnival-esque **Venice,** and legendary **Santa Monica,** all which bow year-round to the gods of sun and surf. Of course, you'll have to venture into **Los Angeles** (p. 887); visit the Getty Museum, see the silver-screen sights in Hollywood, and party on **Sunset Strip** before heading through **Zuma Beach** (p. 902), which has the best surfing and softest sand.

Continuing north, the 400 mi. stretch of coast between L.A. and San Francisco embodies all that is this route—rolling surf, a seaside highway built for cruising, and dramatic bluffs topped by weathered pines. You'll pass through **Santa Barbara** (p. 904), home to stunning sunsets and Spanish architecture before reaching **Big Sur** (p. 912), where the magnificence that inspired John Steinbeck's novels and Jack Kerouac's musings lives on, and clear skies, dense forests, and old seafaring towns beckon. The landmarks along the way—**Hearst Castle** (p. 913), the **Monterey Bay Aquarium** (p. 920), the **historic missions**—are well worth visiting, but the highlight of this stretch is the road itself.

Give yourself ample time to explore **San Francisco** (p. 930)—wander the streets and watch the sun set beyond the **Golden Gate Bridge** (p. 936) before continuing north. Windswept and larger than life, the coast then winds from the Bay Area to the Oregon border. Redwoods tower over undiscovered black sand beaches, and otters frolic next to jutting rock formations—the

untouched wilderness is simply stunning. From the **Marin Headlands** (p. 947), the road snakes along craggy cliffs between pounding surf and monolithic redwoods. You'll drive along the **Avenue of the Giants,** home of the redwoods that make the region famous, and back to the coast where more redwoods tower, protected within the long strips of **Redwood National Park** (p. 959).

From there, it's on to **Oregon,** where a string of touristy resort towns and small, unspoiled fishing villages line the route. The road winds through the scenic **Oregon Dunes National Recreation Area** (p. 963), and—for those brave enough for the bone-chilling waves—some of the most pristine beaches along the entire coast. Finally, you'll cross into **Washington;** here, the road loops around the **Olympic Peninsula,** skirting the vast, lush, forests of **Olympic National Park** (p. 977), before reaching the end in **Seattle**—the Emerald City, where skyscrapers tower, the streets are nearly spotless, and every hilltop offers impressive views of the surrounding mountains and the glinting waters of the Puget Sound. Try the **coffee.**

The Pacific Coast is no ordinary roadtrip; it's neither lonely nor especially kitschy. You'll probably end up eating more avocado sandwiches than burgers (although the **In-and-Out Burgers** of Southern California are hands-down the best roadfood ever), but you'll return to wherever you came from relaxed, refreshed, and significantly tanner, having experienced the sand, the surf, and all that America's western shore has to offer.

ROUTE STATS

Miles: c. 1500

Route: San Diego, CA to Seattle, WA.

States: 3; California, Oregon, and Washington.

Driving Time: At least 1 week; allow 2-3 weeks to take in the coast at a more leisurely pace (and build up a nice tan).

When To Go: California is pleasant year-round; but a summer roadtrip will find warm days and decreased precipitation in the perpetually rainy Northwest.

Crossroads: The Southern Border, in San Diego, CA (p. 758); **Route 66,** in Santa Monica, CA (p. 537); **The National Road,** in San Francisco, CA (p. 432).

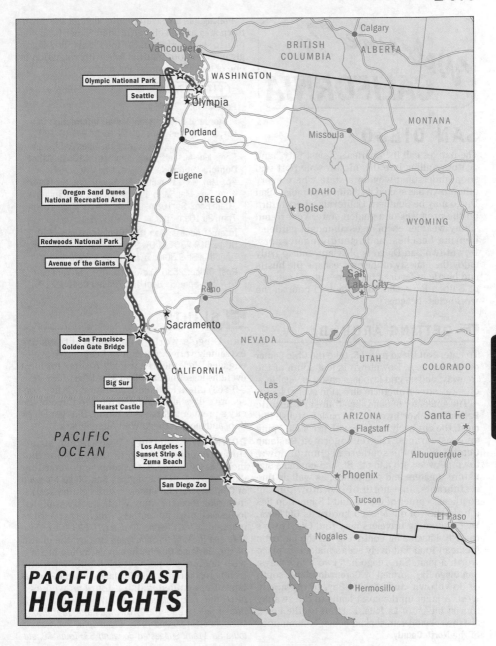

Calgary

BRITISH
COLUMBIA

ALBERTA

Vancouver

Olympic National Park

WASHINGTON

Seattle

★ Olympia

MONTANA

Portland

Missoula

Eugene

IDAHO

OREGON

★ Boise

WYOMING

Oregon Sand Dunes
National Recreation Area

Redwoods National Park

Salt
Lake City

Avenue of the Giants

Reno

Sacramento

NEVADA

UTAH

COLORADO

San Francisco-
Golden Gate Bridge

CALIFORNIA

Big Sur

Las
Vegas

Santa Fe

Hearst Castle

ARIZONA

Flagstaff

*PACIFIC
OCEAN*

Los Angeles -
Sunset Strip &
Zuma Beach

Albuquerque

★ Phoenix

San Diego Zoo

Tucson

El Paso

Nogales

Hermosillo

**PACIFIC COAST
HIGHLIGHTS**

PACIFIC COAST

Welcome To CALIFORNIA

SAN DIEGO

The natives call it "America's Finest City," and visitors pulling into this picturesque port will soon understand why. In a state where every other town has staked its claim as paradise, San Diego may be Southern California's best return on the promises of a golden state. Year-round sunny weather encourages abundant gardens, inviting beaches, and friendly demeanors. Downtown San Diego is pleasant, but to truly enjoy the majesty of the city, escape the hustle and bustle in favor of the more natural settings of Balboa Park, Old Town, and, of course, the world-class beaches.

▐ GETTING AROUND

To enter San Diego from **I-5**, take the **Civic Center** or **4th Ave.** exit. Downtown is just south of the freeway, and its grid layout is easily navigable—one-way streets alternate direction every block.

The epicenter of San Diego tourism is historic **Balboa Park.** Northwest of the park is stylish **Hillcrest,** the city's gay enclave with great shopping and restaurants. The reinvigorated **Gaslamp Quarter** sits in the southern section of downtown between 4th and 6th St. and contains signature theaters and nightclubs, as well as fine restaurants. Just north of downtown in the southeast corner of the I-5 and I-8 junction lies a little slice of old Mexico known as **Old Town.** Discriminating travelers may find Old Town's touristy kitsch a bit contrived, but the fantastic Mexican food and lively scene make this place worth a visit. San Diego has two major bays: **San Diego Bay,** formed by **Coronado Island,** south of downtown, and **Mission Bay,** to the northwest. A jaunt up the coast leads to the swanky tourist haven of **La Jolla.** Farther up the coast are the relaxed, sun-soaked beach communities of the **North County.**

Parking lots are scattered throughout the downtown area and all charge around $5 per hr. If you plan to shop, parking at Horton Plaza (San Diego's gigantic outdoor mall) is free with validation in one of the mall's stores (3hr. max.).

(**VITAL STATS**)

Population: 1.2 million

Visitor Info: International Visitor Information Center, 1040 West Broadway (☎619-236-1212; www.sandiego.org), at Harbor Dr. Open M-Sa 9am-5pm; June-Aug. also Su 10am-5pm. **La Jolla Visitor Center,** 7966 Herschel Ave. Open Sept.-Oct. and Apr.-May M-F 11am-5pm, Sa 10am-6pm, Su 10am-4pm; Nov.-Mar. M-Th 11am-4pm, F 11am-5pm, Sa 10am-6pm, Su 10am-4pm; June-Aug. M-Sa 10am-7pm, Su 10am-7pm.

Internet Access: San Diego Public Library, 820 E St. (☎619-236-5800). Open M and W noon-8pm, Tu and Th-Sa 9:30am-5:30pm, Su 1-5pm.

Post Office: 2535 Midway Dr. Open M 7am-5pm, Tu-F 8am-5pm, Sa 8am-4pm. **Postal Code:** 92186.

◉ SIGHTS

San Diego's world-famous attractions are extremely varied, enough to keep any traveler engaged. Pick the free weekly *Reader* for local event listings. The **San Diego 3-for-1 Pass** ($89, ages 3-9 $63) offers unlimited admission for five consecutive days at discounted rates to three of the city's premier sights—Sea World, the San Diego Zoo, and the San Diego Wild Animal Park.

DOWNTOWN. San Diego's downtown attractions are concentrated in the corridor that includes its business, Gaslamp, and waterfront districts. The steel-and-glass **San Diego Museum of Contemporary Art** encases 20th-century works, including those of Andy Warhol and a wall that looks as though it breathes, which is as weird as it sounds. *(1001 Kettner Blvd. ☎619-234-1001. Open M-Tu and Th-Su 11am-5pm. Free.)* By day, the charm of the **Gaslamp Quarter** lies in its fading history, with antique shops, Victorian buildings, and trendy restaurants. The **Gaslamp Quarter Foundation** offers guided walking tours as well as a museum. *(410 Island Ave., at William Heath Davis House. ☎619-233-4692; www.gaslampquarter.org. Museum open Su and Tu-Sa 11am-3pm. 2hr. walking tours Sa 11am. Suggested donation $3. Tours $8, stu-*

TO OLD TOWN

TO 1 & HILLCREST

San Diego Zoo

Spanish Village Art Center

Museum of Art

Museum of Man
Timkin Gallery

San Diego Intl. Airport

2

Visitor Info Center

El Prado

Maple St.

House of Pacific Relations

Spreckels Organ Pavilion

Ruben H. Fleet Space Center

Laurel St.

163

Curlew St.
Brant St.
Albatross St.
Front St.

Laurel St.

Kalmia St.

8th Avenue E.

Automotive Museum

Casa de Balboa Museums

Balboa Park Gardens

TO OCEAN BEACH

Juniper St.

Pacific Hwy.

India St.
Union St.
Kettner Blvd.

5

San Diego Fwy.

Ivy St.

Hawthorn St.

Grape St.

Fir St.

Cabrillo Fwy.

Pan-American E.

Aerospace Museum

Presidents Way
Park Blvd.

Balboa Dr.
6th Ave.

Balboa Park

U.S. Naval Medical Center

LITTLE ITALY

Elm St.

Date St.

Medea
Berkeley
Maritime Museum

Cedar St.

1st St.
2nd St.
3rd St.
4th St.
5th Ave.
6th Ave.
7th Ave.
8th Ave.
9th Ave.
10th Ave.
11th Ave.

Balboa Stadium

Harbor Dr.

Beech St.

Star of India

Ash St.

Russ Blvd.

San Diego City College

B Street Pier

Pacific Hwy.

Santa Fe Amtrak Depot

A St.

Copley Symphony Hall

12th Ave.

5

Museum of Contemporary Art

B St.

City Hall

163

Broadway Pier

C St.

163

C St.

Navy Pier

Harbor Excursions

International Visitor Information Center

Greyhound

Broadway

E St.

13th St.
14th St.
15th St.
16th St.
17th St.

94

Tuna Harbor Park

Pantoja Park

State St.
Union St.

Horton Plaza Center

F St.

G St.

3

GASLAMP QUARTER

163

Market St.

SEE INSET

Island Ave.

Tuna Harbor

Seaport Village

San Diego Convention Center

8th Ave.

J St.

K St.

L St.

Embarcadero Marina Park

Harbor Dr.

Imperial Ave.

San Diego Harbor

Horton Plaza Center

E St.

4

F St.

5

G St.

3rd Ave.
4th Ave.
5th Ave.
6th Ave.
7th Ave.

Market St.

Coronado Island

GASLAMP QUARTER

6

Bike Tours

Island Ave.

0 200 yards
0 200 meters

San Diego

🏠 **ACCOMMODATIONS**
San Diego Downtown Hostel-HI, **6**
USA Hostels San Diego, **5**

🍴 **FOOD**
The Corvette Diner, **1**
Kansas City Barbecue, **3**

🌙 **NIGHTLIFE**
The Casbah, **2**
Croce's Top Hat Bar and Grill
& Croce's Jazz Bar, **4**

TO CORONADO ISLAND

75

PACIFIC COAST

dents and seniors $6, under 12 free. Self-guided tour maps $2.) Like most old buildings in San Diego, the **Horton Grand Hotel** is supposedly haunted. Believers may catch a glimpse of Wild West lawman Wyatt Earp. (311 Island Ave. ☎ 619-544-1886. Tours W at 3pm. Free.) Spanish for "dock," the **Embarcadero** has boardwalk shops and museums that face moored windjammers, cruise ships, and the occasional naval destroyer. The jewel of San Diego's redevelopment **Horton Plaza,** at Broadway and 4th Ave., a pastel, open-air, multi-level shopping center.

BALBOA PARK. It would take several days to see all of Balboa Park's museums. Most of them reside within the resplendent Spanish colonial-style buildings that line El Prado St. These ornate structures, several of which were designed for exhibits in 1916 or 1936, were originally intended to last two years. The **Balboa Park Visitors Center** sells park maps and the **Passport to Balboa Park,** which allows admission into 13 of the park's attractions. (1549 El Prado St. From I-5, merge onto Rte. 163 North and take the Balboa Park Exit. ☎ 619-239-0512; www.balboapark.org. Maps $0.50. Passport $30. Open daily summer 9am-4:30pm; winter 9am-4pm.) Creationists beware: the **Museum of Man** dedicates an entire floor to the 98.4% of DNA we share with chimpanzees. The real treat, however, is on the outside: the gleaming Spanish mosaic tiles of the museum's much-photographed tower and dome. (On the west end of the park. ☎ 619-239-2001; www.museumofman.org. Open daily 10am-4:30pm. $6, seniors $5, ages 6-17 $3. 3rd Tu of each month free. Special exhibits $8.) At the east end of Balboa Park, the **Natural History Museum** exhibits stuffed mammals and birds. Live insects and arthropods enhance the displays of standard fossils. (☎ 619-232-3821; http://www.sdnhm.org. $9, seniors $6, ages 6-17 $5. 1st Tu of each month free.) The **Aerospace Museum** displays 24 full-scale replicas and 44 original planes, as well as information on aviation history and the International Space Station project. (2001 Pan American Plaza. ☎ 619-234-8291; www.aerospacemuseum.org. Open daily 10am-4:30pm; extended summer hours. $8, seniors $6, ages 6-17 $3. 4th Tu of each month free.) The **Reuben H. Fleet Space Theater and Science Center** houses interactive exhibits and the world's first hemispheric Omnimax theater. (1875 El Prado Way. ☎ 619-238-1233; www.rhfleet.org. Open daily 9:30am-8pm. $6.75, with Omnimax show $11.50; seniors $6/$8.50; ages

3-12 $5.50/$9.50. 1st Tu of each month free.) The small, ultra-modern **Museum of Photographic Arts (MOPA)** features contemporary photography. Its film program ranges from cult classic film festivals to more serious cinematic works. (☎ 619-238-7559; www.mopa.org. Open M-W and F-Su 10am-5pm, Th 10am-9pm. $6, students $4. 2nd Tu of each month free. Films $5/$4.50.) The **San Diego Museum of Art** has a collection ranging from ancient Asian to contemporary Californian works. (☎ 619-232-7931; www.sdmart.org. Open Su and Tu-Sa 10am-6pm, Th 10am-9pm. $8, seniors and students $6, ages 6-17 $3. Special exhibits $2-20.) The fragrant **Botanical Building** looks like a giant, wooden birdcage. The orchid collection is particularly striking among the murmuring fountains. (2200 Park Blvd. ☎ 619-235-1100, tour info 235-1121. Open M-W and F-Su 10am-4pm. Free.) Constructed in 1937, the **Old Globe Theater** is the oldest professional theater in California. (☎ 619-239-2255; www.theoldglobe.org.)

■ **SAN DIEGO ZOO.** With over 100 acres of exquisite fenceless habitats, this zoo deserves its reputation as one of the finest in the world. Its unique "bioclimatic" exhibits group animals and plants by habitat. The legendary panda exhibit is the most timeless feature of the park, and the zoo invests over one million dollars a year on panda habitat preservation in China. The educational 40min. double-decker bus tour covers about 75% of the zoo. Although seats on the upper deck are popular, trees can obstruct views and the seats are in the sun; the lower deck is a better choice. (2920 Zoo Dr., in Balboa Park. ☎ 619-234-3153; www.sandiegozoo.org. Open daily late June to early Sept. 9am-10pm; early Sept. to late June 9am-dusk. $20, with 35min. bus tour and 2 tickets for the aerial tramway $32; ages 3-11 $12/$20.)

OLD TOWN. In 1769, Father Serra, supported by Spanish infantry, established the first of 21 missions that would line the California coast in the area now known as Old Town. The remnants of this early settlement have become a tourist mainstay. (To reach Old Town, take the Old Town Exit from I-5 North.) The most popular of the area's attractions, the **State Park's** early 19th-century buildings contain museums, shops, and restaurants. **Seely Stable** houses a huge museum of 19th-century transportation, namely of the horse and carriage variety. (☎ 619-220-5427. Open daily 10am-5pm. Tours every hr. 11am-2pm.) The **Whaley House** stands on the site of San Diego's first gallows and is one of two **official haunted houses** recognized by the State of California. *(2482 San Diego Ave. ☎619-298-2482, tours 619-293-0117. Open daily 10am-4:30pm; last entry 4pm. $5, seniors $4, ages 3-12 $2.)* Across the street is **Heritage Park,** a group of 150-year-old Victorian buildings. Four are open to the public. (☎858-565-3600.) The adobe walls of the **Serra Museum** were raised at the site of the original fort and mission in 1929. *(In Presidio Park. ☎619-279-3258. Open June-Aug. Su and Tu-Sa 10am-4:30pm; Sept.-May F-Su 10am-4:30pm. $5, seniors and students $4, ages 6-17 $2.)*

CORONADO ISLAND. A slender 7 mi. strip of hauled sand known as the "Silver Strand" tethers the lovely peninsula of Coronado Island to the mainland down near Imperial Beach. The area is perfect for strolling and browsing. Beach babes frolic in the waves that break along the southern shore, while outdoor lovers jog and bike along paved trails. The birthplace of American naval aviation, the **North Island Naval Air Station** comprises the northern chunk of the island. Also among the island's many military enterprises is the training area of the elite **Navy SEAL** (sea, air, and land) special forces teams. Coronado's most famed sight is its Victorian-style **Hotel Del Coronado,** one of America's largest wooden buildings. The long white verandas and the vermilion spires of the "Del" were built in 1888. It has since become one of the world's great hotels (rooms start at $270 per night), hosting 10 presidents and one blonde bombshell—Marilyn Monroe's 1959 *Some Like it Hot* was filmed here. Built in 1969, the graceful **Coronado Bridge** guides cars to Coronado along I-5.

SEA WORLD. Since the 190 acre park opened on March 21, 1964, Sea World has welcomed more than 100 million guests. The A-list star here is the behemoth killer whale Shamu, whose signature move is a cannonball splash that soaks anyone in the first 20 rows. The original Shamu died long ago, but each of his 10 successors has proudly borne the moniker. In addition, there are animals from all walks of sea life in their natural habitats, including penguins, polar bears, and sharks. Try the ray petting pool and Shipwreck Rapids, Sea World's first-ever adventure ride. *(From I-5, take the Sea World Dr. Exit and turn west toward the park. ☎619-226-3901. Open daily summer 9am-11pm; winter 10am to varying closing hours. $50, ages 3-9 $40. Parking $7, RVs $9.)*

BEACHES. San Diego's younger population flocks to these communities by the surf for the hopping nightlife. It is said that home-grown and earthy **Ocean Beach (O.B.)** is what the world would be like if the hippies had lasted past the 70s. Anglers can cast from the Western Hemisphere's longest fishing pier. Farther north, at the corner of W. Mission Bay Dr. and Mission Blvd., **Mission Beach** is a people-watcher's paradise. Belmont Park, a combination amusement park and shopping center, draws a youthful crowd. **Pacific Beach** and its boisterous Garnet Ave. is home to the best nightlife. Ocean Front Walk is packed with joggers, cyclists, and the usual beachfront shops.

MISSION BASILICA SAN DIEGO DE ALCALÁ. In 1774 Father Serra moved his mission, California's first church, some 6 mi. away from the settlement of rough and unholy soldiers to its current location. The mission is still an active parish church and contains gardens, a small museum, and a reconstruction of Serra's living quarters. *(Take bus #43 or I-8 east to the Mission Gorge Rd. exit. Go north and turn left on Twain Ave.; the mission will be 2 blocks ahead on the right. ☎281-8449. Visitors center open daily 9am-4:45pm. Mass held daily at 7am and 5:30pm; visitors welcome. $3, students and seniors $2, under 12 $1. 45min. tote-a-tape guided tours $2.)*

POINT LOMA. Although the US government own the outer two-thirds of this peninsula most of it remains open to citizens and visitors. The **Cabrillo National Monument,** at the tip of Point Loma, is dedicated to the Portuguese explorer Juan Rodríguez Cabrillo, the first European to land in California, but is best known for its views of downtown San Diego and migrating whales. The **visitors center** offers hourly videos or slide presentations as well as information about the monument. *(☎575-5450; www.nps.gov/cabr/. Visitors center open daily 9am-5:15pm. 7-day pass $5 per vehicle, $3 per person on foot or bike. Golden Eagle Passport accepted.)* **Whale-watching** season runs from mid-December to February. The **Bayside Trail** (2 mi.) has stations that explain native vegetation and historic military installations and offer magnificent views of the bay and Coronado Island. Point Loma's oceanfront is rife with tide pools; turn right off Rte. 209 onto Cabrillo Rd. and drive down to the parking lot t the bottom of the hill. At the highest point of the peninsula sits the interesting museum at **Old Point Loma Lighthouse.** *(Open daily 9am-5:15pm.)*

ESCONDIDO. Escondido (pop. 125,000) lies 30 mi. north of San Diego amid rolling, semi-arid hills that blossom with wildflowers in the spring. A look at the free-roaming endangered species of the 2100-acre **San Diego Wild Animal Park** is an essential part of any trip to San Diego. The highlight of the park is the large enclosures where many species roam freely. Rhinos, giraffes, gazelles, and tigers can all be found on the park plains. The open-air Wgasa Bush Line Railway, a 1hr. monorail safari, travels through four created habitat areas; sit on the right if possible. *(From I-15, take the Via Rancho Pkwy. ☎619-747-8702; www.wildanimalpark.org. Open daily from 9am; closing times vary by season. Rail tours June-Aug. 9:30am-9pm; Sept.-May 9:30am-4pm. $26.50, ages 3-11 $19.50. Parking $6.)*

🍴 FOOD

With its large Hispanic population and proximity to Mexico, San Diego is renowned for its exemplary Mexican cuisine. **Old Town** serves some of the best authentic Mexican food in the state. San Diego also offers a spectacular assortment of ethnic and more traditional eateries. Good restaurants cluster downtown along **C St., Broadway Blvd.**, and in historic **Gaslamp Quarter.** The best food near Balboa Park and the zoo is in nearby **Hillcrest** and **University Heights.**

🍽 **La Especial Norte,** 664 N. Rte. 101 (☎760-942-1040), in the center of Leucadia. In a town of excellent Mexican cuisine, this is quite possibly the best. The food is so good that the San Diego Coast lifeguards rent the restaurant for their annual banquet. Try the Mexican shrimp cocktail or the tortilla soup. Entrees $6-8. Open daily 10am-10pm.

🍽 **Casa de Bandini,** 2754 Calhoun St. (☎619-297-8211). An Old Town institution set in a Spanish-style architectural landmark built in 1829. Superb food and boisterous music. The colossal combo plates ($5-8) and heavyweight margaritas ($4-7) are the stuff of legend. Open M-Th 11am-9:30pm, F-Sa 11am-10pm, Su 10am-9:30pm.

🍽 **The Corvette Diner,** 3946 5th Ave. (☎619-542-1001), in Hillcrest. The ultimate flashback to the days of nickel milkshakes, this 50s-style diner has more chrome than Detroit and more neon than Las Vegas. Greasy-spoon classics and unique creations like the Rory Burger (peanut butter and bacon burger; $7). A DJ spins oldies every night (6-9pm) while costumed waitresses give as much lip as service. Open Su-Th 11am-10pm, F-Sa 11am-midnight.

🍽 **Pizza Port,** 135 N. Rte. 101 (☎858-481-7332), in the center of Solana Beach. This surf-themed pizza parlor and microbrewery offers some of the coast's best grub and grog. After the sun sets, the bar fills up with laid-back surfer types discussing the finer points of the day's swell. Open daily 7am-2am.

🍽 **Kansas City Barbecue,** 610 W. Market St. (☎619-231-9680), near Seaport Village. The location of *Top Gun's* Great Balls of Fire bar scene. While the wooden piano remains, all that's left of Goose and Maverick is an abundance of autographed posters and neon signs. Vegetarians will find themselves in the Danger Zone in this barbecue-slathered meatfest. Entrees $9-16. Open daily 11am-2am. Kitchen closes 1am.

🏠 ACCOMMODATIONS

Rates predictably rise on weekends and during the summer season. Reservations are recommended. There is a popular cluster known as **Hotel Circle** (2-3 mi. east of I-5 along I-8), where summer prices begin at $60 for a single and $70 for a double during the week. Several beaches in North County, as well as one on Coronado, are state parks and allow camping.

🏠 **USA Hostels San Diego,** 726 5th Ave. (☎619-232-3100 or 800-438-8622; www.usahostels.com), between F and G St. This colorful Euro-style fun house fits in well with the rocking atmosphere of the Gaslamp district. Hosts frequent parties and pub crawls ($4). Pancake breakfast included. Dinner $4. Linen, lockers, and coin-op laundry. International passport or student ID required. Dorms $19-21; private rooms $46-50.

🏠 **San Diego Downtown Hostel (HI-AYH),** 521 Market St. (☎619-525-1531; www.sandiegohostels.org), at 5th Ave., in the heart of Gaslamp. Quiet, impeccably clean, and close to popular attractions and clubs. Airy common room with kitchen and pool table and communal bathrooms. 4- to 6-bed dorms $20, nonmembers $23; doubles $45-50/$48-43.

International House at the 2nd Floor, 4502 Cass St. (☎858-274-4325), in Pacific Beach and 3204 Mission Bay Dr. (☎858-539-0043), in Mission Beach. Excellent service, clean and bright rooms, comfortable beds, and 2 great beach locations. Internet. Out-of-state ID or international passport required. Breakfast included. 28-day max. stay. Dorms $20, with student ID $18. Weekly rooms $110.

Ocean Beach International (OBI), 4961 Newport Ave. (☎619-223-7873 or 800-339-7263). Clean rooms near the beach. Proof of international travel in the last 6 months required. Pancake breakfast included. Free BBQ Tu and F night. 29-day max. stay. 4- to 6-bed dorms $18-20; doubles $40-43.

San Elijo Beach State Park (☎760-753-5091), off Rte. 101, south of Cardiff-by-the-Sea. Over 170 sites (23 with RV hookups) on seaside cliffs. Laundry and showers. Tent sites; $12 RVs $18.

◎ NIGHTLIFE

Nightlife in San Diego is scattered across distinct pockets of action. Posh locals and party-seeking tourists flock to the **Gaslamp Quarter.** The **Hillcrest,** next to Balboa Park, draws a young, largely gay crowd to its clubs and eateries. Away from downtown, the beach areas (especially **Garnet Ave.** in Pacific Beach) are loaded with clubs, bars, and cheap eateries. The definitive source of entertainment info is the free *Reader,* found in shops, coffeehouses, and Visitors Centers. Listings can also be found in the *San Diego Union-Tribune's* Thursday "Night and Day" section. You can spend a more sedate evening at one of San Diego's excellent theaters, such as the **Balboa Theatre,** 225 Broadway Ave. (☎609-544-1000), and the **Horton Grand Theatre,** 444 4th Ave. (☎619-234-9583), both downtown. The **La Jolla Playhouse,** 2910 La Jolla Village Dr., presents shows on the UCSD campus. (☎858-550-1010; www.lajollaplayhouse.com.)

▓ **Croce's Top Hat Bar and Grille** and **Croce's Jazz Bar,** 802 5th Ave. (☎619-233-4355), at F St. in the Gaslamp. Ingrid Croce, widow of singer Jim Croce, created this rock/blues bar and jazz bar side-by-side on the 1st fl. of the Keating building. Live music nightly from 8:30pm. Cover $5-10; includes 2 live shows. Top Hat open F-Sa 7pm-1:30am. Jazz bar open daily 5:30pm-12:30am.

Pacific Beach Bar and Grill and **Club Tremors,** 860 Garnet Ave. (☎858-483-9227), one of the only dance clubs in Pacific Beach. Live DJ packs the 2-level dance floor with a young and oh-so-hip crowd. The Bar and Grill has respectable food, more than 20 beers on tap,

and live music on Su. Cover $5 if you enter through Club Tremors, but the same club is accessible through the Grill for free. Club open Tu-Sa 9pm-1:30am; bar open 11am-1:30am; kitchen closes midnight.

Canes Bar and Grill, 3105 Ocean front Walk (☎858-488-1780 or 858-488-9690), in Mission Beach. One of the best live music venues in the city, this beachside bar has unbeatable sunset views from the terrace. DJ and dancing every night. Open daily 11am-2am.

The Casbah, 2501 Kettner Blvd. (☎619-232-4355; www.casbahmusic.com). Eddie Vedder of the alternative rock legend Pearl Jam owns this intimate nightspot. Cover varies. 21+. Call ahead or check online for a schedule, as sometimes tickets sell out.

◤▼ LEAVING SAN DIEGO
Take **9th Ave** north., turn right onto **Broadway,** then left onto **11th Ave.** Merge onto **I-5 North.** Take Exit 26A for the **La Jolla Pkwy.,** which becomes **Torrey Pines Rd.** Turn right onto **Prospect Pl.** and turn left onto **Herschel Ave.**

LA JOLLA

Pronounced *la-HOY-a,* this affluent seaside locality houses few budget accommodation options, but offers some of the finest public beaches in the San Diego area. **La Jolla Cove** is popular with scuba divers, snorkelers, and brilliantly colored Garibaldi goldfish. Wander south along the cliffs to a striking semi-circular inlet known as **The Children's Pool,** whose inhabitants are a famously thriving community of sea lions. Some of the best breaks in the county can be found at **Tourmaline Beach** and **Wind 'n Sea Beach.** However, these are notoriously territorial spots, so outsiders might be advised to surf elsewhere. **La Jolla Shores** has gentle swells ideal for new surfers, boogie boarders, and swimmers. Nearby, the ▓**Birch Aquarium at the Scripps Institute of Oceanography,** 2300 Expedition Way, has great educational exhibits including a tank of oozing jellyfish, a large collection of seahorses, and a 70,000-gallon kelp and shark tank. (☎858-534-3474; http://aquarium.ucsd.edu. Open daily 9am-5pm. $9.50, students $6.50, ages 3-17 $6. Parking $3.) The visually stunning **San Diego Museum of Contemporary Art,** 700 Prospect St., shares its rotating collection of pop, minimalist, and conceptualist art from the 1950s with the downtown branch. (☎858-454-3541. Open M-Tu and F-Su 11am-5pm, Th 11am-7pm. $6; students, seniors, and ages 12-18 $2. 1st Su and 3rd Tu of each

PACIFIC COAST

month free.) Be sure to check out the terraces and buttresses of **Geisel Library** at the **University of California San Diego (UCSD),** a space-age structure endowed by resident Theodore Geisel, better known by his middle name as the beloved children's books author, Dr. Seuss. (☎ 858-534-2208. Open M-F 7am-9pm, Sa-Su 7am-5:30pm.)

▐◤ LEAVING LA JOLLA
Go north on **Herschel Ave.** toward **Prospect St.** and turn right onto Prospect St. Turn left onto **Torrey Pines Rd.**

▐◤ TORREY PINES STATE PARK
On Torrey Pines Rd. Look for the entrance at 12600 off N. Torrey Pines Rd. about ½ mi. south of Del Mar Village.

The closest taste of nature near San Diego, Torrey Pines is often crowded but the hiking trails and 5 mi. beach—from which you can frequently see frolicking dolphins—are lovely. It's home to the nation's rarest pine tree and Snowy Plover bird. (☎ 858-755-2063; www.torreypine.org. Open 8am-sunset. $4 per vehicle.) The **Torrey Pines Lodge,** at the top of the hill on the entrance road, provides info on activities and hiking trails, as well as an exhibit on why the torrey pines are so unique. (Open daily 9am-5:30pm.)

▐◤ APPROACHING DEL MAR
Torrey Pines Rd. becomes **Camino Del Mar** north of the park and heads into Del Mar.

DEL MAR
North of La Jolla is the affluent suburb of Del Mar, home to racehorses and famous fairgrounds. Small boutiques and good eats line Camino Del Mar. During June and early July, Del Mar hosts the **San Diego County Fair,** one of the largest fairs in California. Solana Beach to the north boasts the **Cedros Design District,** full of warehouses converted to artist studios. The celebrity-studded **Del Mar Thoroughbred Club,** at the corner of Via de la Valle and Jimmy Durante Blvd., fills with racing fans from late July to the week after Labor Day. Founded in 1937 by Bing Crosby and Pat O'Brien, the racetrack is one of the most beautiful in the world. (☎ 858-755-1141 or 795-5533; www.delmarracing.com. M and W-F 8 races per day, Sa 10 per day, Su 9 per day. Post time 2pm.)

CALIFORNIA'S TOP 10 BEACHES

[10] Mystical Fern Canyon leads to the warm dunes of **Gold Bluffs Beach,** in Redwood National Park.

[9] The steep trail down to hip, secluded **Black's Beach,** in La Jolla, makes the warm sand, marine life, and strong surf all the more welcome.

[8] Surfers meet Shakespeare at **Stinson Beach,** in Marin County.

[7] Fit, beautiful Angelenos play frisbee and lounge on the perfect sands of **Zuma Beach,** Malibu, before hitting the killer waves.

[6] **Point Lobos,** in Carmel, offers great views of otters, whales, and sea birds.

[5] Lively **Cowell Beach** fills with college students playing volleyball and leads to the delightfully kitschy Santa Cruz Beach Boardwalk.

[4] **Ocean Beach,** at the far western edge of Golden Gate Park, is unsafe to swim in due to rip tides, but offers an incredible view.

[3] For the classic surfing experience, head to **Huntington Beach.**

[2] The warm waters of **Pirate's Cove,** in San Luis Obispo, are popular with skinnydippers.

[1] A reef-break at **Del Mar,** in San Diego, makes for consistent swells, while newlyweds and families congregate on the palm-shaded sand.

Surf-weathered locals favor **Board and Brew,** 1212 Camino Del Mar, for its cheap beer ($2-2.50) and delicious sandwiches such as the California Delight ($4.50), full of turkey, cream cheese, and sunflower seeds. (☎858-481-1021. Open daily 10am-7pm.) One block away, a little taste of Europe can be found at **Le Cafe Bleu,** 1140 Camino Del Mar, which specializes in delicious French pastries and $5 gourmet lunch specials such as quiches or crepes. (☎858-350-1432. Open M-Sa 6am-6pm, Su 7am-6pm.) For some awesome deep-dish pizza and "grog," head to **Pizza Port,** 135 N. U.S. 101, in Solana Beach. Expect a wait; the place is usually packed. (☎858-481-7332; www.pizzaport.com. Pizzas from $6. Pints from $3. Open daily 11am-11pm.)

◤ APPROACHING CARLSBAD
Camino Del Mar becomes **Old U.S. 101** and then **Carlsbad Blvd.** as it heads north along the coast. Turn right onto **Carlsbad Village Dr.**

CARLSBAD

Farther up the coast is the charming lagoon hideaway of Carlsbad, where U.S. 101, known here as Carlsbad Blvd., winds past silky sands and shingled homes adorned with wild rosebushes.

(VITAL STATS)

Population: 78,000

Visitor Info: Carlsbad Convention and Visitors Center, 400 Carlsbad Village Dr. (☎760-434-6093; www.carlsbadca.org). Open M-F 9am-5pm, Sa 10am-4pm, Su 10am-3pm.

Internet Access: Georgina Cole Library, 1250 Carlsbad Village Dr., near downtown (☎760-434-2870). Open M-Th 9am-9pm, F-Sa 9am-5pm.

Post Office: 2772 Roosevelt St. (☎760-729-1244). Open 7:30am-5pm, Sa 9am-12:30pm.

Postal Code: 92008.

◪ GETTING AROUND.
Ocean St., Carlsbad Blvd. (U.S. 101), and **Washington St.** are major north-south routes. **Carlsbad Village Dr.,** runs inland toward **I-5.**

◪ ✿ SIGHTS & FESTIVALS.
Legoland, 1 Legoland Dr., is a fun, goofball tribute to the interlocking kiddie blocks that have inspired countless junior architects. (South of town, head east on Canyon Rd. ☎760-918-5346. Open spring Su-M and Th 10am-5pm, F-Sa 10am-6pm; summer daily 10am-8pm; fall M and Th-Su 10am-5pm. $40, ages 3-16 $34. Parking $7.) Shake, rattle, and roll at the extensive **Museum of Making Music,** 5790 Armada Dr., where over 450 vintage musical instruments survey of 20th-century American music. (☎877-551-9976; www.museumofmakingmusic.org. Open Su and Tu-Sa 10am-5pm. $5; seniors, students, military, and ages 4-18 $3.)

The California state park system maintains a number of beautiful beaches. **Carlsbad State Beach** is long and attractive, marred slightly by the mammoth power plant which occupies the coast to the south. **Offshore Surf Shop,** 3179 Carlsbad Blvd., rents boogie boards and 6-8 ft. "soft" surfboards. (☎760-729-4934. Boogie boards $3 per hr., $10 per day. Surfboards $5/$25. Use a credit card for rentals; otherwise, a deposit of $50 for boogie board and $300 for surfboard is required. Open daily 9am-7:30pm.) On the first Sunday in May and November, the famous biannual **Carlsbad Village Street Faire,** the largest one-day fair in California, attracts over 900 vendors and 80,000 people.

◪◪ FOOD & ACCOMMODATIONS.
There is a variety of great beachfront restaurants along Pacific Coast Hwy. (Old U.S. 101). Locals and tourists cram the intimate dining area at ✦**Trattoria I Trulli,** 830 S. Coast Hwy., for good reason: the food is delicious. (☎760-943-6800. Dinner entrees from $10. Open Su-Th 11:30am-2:30pm and 5-10pm, F-Sa 11:30am-2:30pm and 5-10:30pm.) Life is sweet at **Honey's Bistro and Bakery,** 632 S. Coast Hwy., in Encinitas, where they serve large, fresh salads ($6), sandwiches ($5), and soups ($4), as well as mouth-watering baked goods. (☎760-942-5433. Open daily 5:30am-3:30pm.) At the **Miracles Cafe,** 1953 San Elijo Ave., in Encinitas, $6 will get you banana Belgian waffles or a Supreme Scream sandwich. (☎760-943-7924. Open M-Th 6am-10pm, F-Sa 6am-11pm, Su 7am-9pm.)

Inexpensive lodging is difficult to find. **Surf Motel,** 3136 Carlsbad Blvd., is a decent value with large rooms across the street from the beach and a block from Carlsbad Village. (☎760-729-7961. Rooms $109-149; in winter $55-69.) A cheaper, reliable alternative is **Motel 6,** 1006 Carlsbad Village Dr., just east of Carlsbad Village. (☎760-434-7135. Singles $50-58; doubles $56-64.) Camping near the beach is allowed at **South Carlsbad State Park** or at **San Elijo State Park.** The beaches below both campgrounds are beautiful, but sites offer little privacy. Reserva-

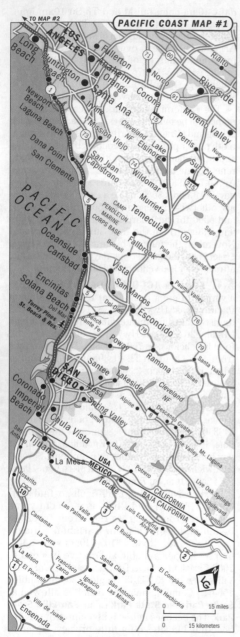

PACIFIC COAST MAP #1

tions for both campgrounds can be made seven months in advance by calling ☎800-444-7275 or via www.reserveamerica.com. (South Carlsbad: ☎760-438-3143. San Elijo: ☎760-753-5091. Water, restrooms, showers, general stores, picnic tables, BBQ stands, and fire pits. Summer reservations essential. Oceanside sites $20, inland $16. Call for availability of RV sites.)

APPROACHING OCEANSIDE
Carlsbad Blvd. become **Coast Hwy.** as it heads north toward Oceanside.

OCEANSIDE

Oceanside is the largest and least glamorous of San Diego's coastal resort towns. Home to Camp Pendleton, a Marine Corps base, as well as one of the world's greatest surfing beaches at Oceanside Harbor, Oceanside is part military order, part surfer-chill. The pier gets crowded during the **World Body Surfing Championships** in mid-August. Call the Oceanside Special Events Office (☎760-435-5540) for info. Oceanside is the perfect place for the ◪**California Surf Museum,** 223 N. Coast Hwy. (☎760-721-6876. Open M and Th-Su 10am-4pm. Free.) You can catch your dinner by renting gear at **Helgren's Sportfishing Trips,** 315 Harbor Dr. South. (☎760-722-2133. 1-day license $7.25. Surface fishing rod $10; deep fishing rod $12. Half-day trips on the fishing boat $29, full-day $55. Nonfishing harbor cruise daily $10, ages 5-12 $5. Times vary with the seasons.) **Mission San Luis Rey de Francia,** 4050 Mission Ave., was founded in 1798, but the only original building still standing is the church built in 1807. (Follow Mission Ave. east from N. Coast Hwy. for 4 mi. ☎760-757-3651. Museum open daily 10am-4:30pm. $4, students and seniors $3, ages 8-14 $1. Cemetery free.)

Power up before hitting the waves at **The Longboarder,** 228 N. Coast Hwy., which serves burgers ($5-6) and heaping omelettes ($6) to surfers. (☎760-721-6776. Open M-F 7am-2pm, Sa-Su 7am-3pm.) Unlike its ritzier neighbors, Oceanside offers inexpensive lodgings. Motels line U.S. 101 through town, though not all are reputable.

LEAVING OCEANSIDE
Take **Mission Ave.** east to **I-5 North.** Follow I-5 North through the Camp Pendleton Marine Base.

THE ROAD THROUGH ORANGE COUNTY

Directly south of L.A. County lies Orange County (pop. 2.9 million). Composed of 34 cities, it is a microcosm of Southern California: dazzling sandy shoreline, bronzed beach bums, oversized shopping malls, homogenous suburban neighborhoods, and frustrating traffic snarls. One of California's staunchest Republican enclaves, Orange County (and no, they don't actually call it "The O.C.") supports big business, and has the economy and the multi-million-dollar hillside mansions oozing luxury cars and disaffected teens to prove it. Disneyland, the stronghold of the Disney empire, is the premier inland attraction. The coast runs the gamut from the budget- and party-friendly surf burg of Huntington Beach to the opulent excess of Newport Beach and the artistic vibe of Laguna. Farther south lies the quiet mission of San Juan Capistrano, set amid rolling hills that spill onto the laid-back beaches of Dana Point and San Clemente. Orange County's beach communities have cleaner sand, better surf, and less madness than their L.A. County counterparts; it is here that L.A. residents seek refuge.

SAN CLEMENTE & DANA POINT. San Clemente, a "small Spanish village by the sea," provides the waves of bigger beach towns minus the noise and antics. Its downtown is known as an antiques mecca, where unrivaled shops and historic buildings are reminiscent of the Revolutionary days. Just south of town is **San Onofre State Beach** and its "Trestles" area, a breakpoint and thus a prime surfing zone for experienced thrill-seekers. Neighboring Dana Point's spectacular bluffs were popularized in namesake Richard Henry Dana's 1841 account of Southern California's sailing culture, *Two Years Before the Mast*. The harbor holds 2500 yachts and also serves as a point of departure for Catalina Island. Dana Point's **swimming beach** lies at Salt Creek and the Strands.

DETOUR: SAN JUAN CAPISTRANO
From San Clemente or Dana Point, take I-5 North to Exit 82. Turn left onto the Ortega Hwy.
The **Mission San Juan Capistrano** was founded in the same year as the United States of America, 1776, and is the birthplace of Orange County. Full of romance and beauty, the mission stands as a monument to Native American, Mexican, and European cultures. Established by Father Junípero Serra, it is considered the "jewel of the missions." Although most of the original structure collapsed in an 1812 earthquake, this is the only standing site where Serra himself is known to have given mass, and the oldest building still in use in California. The crumbling walls of the beautiful **Serra Chapel** are warmed by a 17th-century Spanish altar and Native American designs. Gregorian chants evoke the spiritualism that Serra once envisioned. On March 19th each year, the city of San Juan Capistrano gathers here for the famous **"Return of the Swallows,"** a celebration of the birds that always return to the mission. (☎949-234-1300; www.missionsjc.com. Open daily 8:30am-5pm. $6, seniors $5, ages 3-12 $4)

The **Swallows Inn,** 31786 Camino Capistrano (☎949-493-3188) has been a local favorite in San Juan for over 50 years. It is home to one of the country's largest chili cook-offs and is the best place to catch the **Swallows Day Parade** in March.

APPROACHING LAGUNA BEACH
From the **PCH (Rte. 1)** turn right onto **Forest Ave.** and right onto **Glenneyre St.**

LAGUNA BEACH

A sign at the corner of Forest and Ocean Ave. sums up the industry-less pleasantness of Laguna with the message: "This Gate Hangs Well and Hinders None, Refresh and Rest, Then Travel On." Punctuated by rocky cliffs, coves, and lush hillside vegetation, Laguna is a delightful artistic village in the conservative Orange County. Much of the town's charm is visible along the coastal highway, including dozens of displays of public art.

(VITAL STATS)

Population: 24,000

Visitor Info: 252 Broadway (☎800-877-1115; www.laguna ceachinfo.org). Open daily 9am-5pm.

Internet Access: Laguna Beach Library, 363 Geneyre St. (☎949-497-1733), 1 block south of Forest Ave. Open M-W 10am-8pm, Th 10am-6pm, F-Sa 10am-5pm.

Post Office: 24001 Calle de la Magdalena (☎949-837-1848). Open M-F 8:30am-5pm, Sa 9am-3pm. **Postal Code:** 92654.

PACIFIC COAST

GETTING AROUND. Ocean Ave., at the Pacific Coast Hwy., and **Main Beach** are the prime parading areas. **Westry Beach,** which spreads south of Laguna just below Aliso Beach Park, and **Camel Point,** between Westry and Aliso, form the hub of the local gay community. You'll know you've come to the center of town when you reach the seaside Main Park; the main drags of **Forest Ave.** and **Ocean Ave.** run perpendicular to it. **Parking** downtown can be a problem; meters gobble quarters for 15min. of legality (8am-6pm). For beach access, park on residential streets to the east and look for "Public Access" signs between private properties. If you can find a spot, there is a good parking lot ($1 per hr.) half a block inland from Beach St. between Ocean and Forest Ave.

SIGHTS. The one-name native of Laguna Beach, **Wyland** has distinguished himself as an artist through public expression of the enchantment of whales and other underwater life. Wyland aims to paint 100 murals worldwide, all on a voluntary basis; 90 have been completed so far. You can see one, in tiles, next to the **Wyland Gallery,** 509 S. Coast Hwy. **Friends of Marine Mammal Center,** 20612 Laguna Canyon Rd., rescues sick sea lions and friends, whom you can visit. (☎949-494-3050; www.fslmmc.org. Open daily 10am-4pm.) A **Thousand Steps Beach** may be missing 800 of the steps it claims, but the beauty of the bougainvillea-arched descent is enough to make you lean towards poetic exaggeration. The inconspicuous entrance is one block south of the medical center on 9th St.; park your car inland.

FOOD & ACCOMMODATIONS. The **Orange Inn,** 703 S. Coast Hwy, is a small roadside diner dating from 1931 serving sandwiches ($5-6.50), smoothies ($3.75), and soy bars. Check out the pictures of old Laguna Beach in the back. (☎949-494-6085. Open daily 6am-around 5pm.) **Ho Sum Bistro,** 3112 Newport Blvd., at 32nd St., is a quintessentially Southern Californian mix of healthy Asian-influenced food and neon-lit white decor. The small Ho Sum chicken salad ($4.79) will fill you up. (☎949-675-0896. Open Su-Th 11am-10pm, F-Sa 11pm.) Across the street from the park, upscale American food with a touch of elegance that won't break the bank is available at **The White House,** 340 S. Coast Hwy. The restaurant is a classic that's been around since the early days of 1918. Spinach mango chicken salad is a wonderful lunch ($8). The "twilight dinner" (Su-Th 4-6:30pm,

F-Sa 4-6pm) is a deal, at $12 for a two-course meal with choices such as seafood pasta or peppered steak. (☎949-494-8088. Open Su-Th 11am-10pm, F-Sa 9am-11pm.) **Laguna Village Market and Cafe,** 577 S. Coast Hwy., is atop a cliff and housed in an open-air gazebo. Its oceanfront terrace is the main draw. (☎949-494-6344. Open daily 8:30am-dark.)

Laguna Beach doesn't offer much in the way of budget accommodations; your best bet is probably the hostel in Huntington or camping. The best value in town is the **Seacliff Laguna Inn,** 1661 S. Coast Hwy., a cut above the average motel with some rooms overlooking the ocean (over other roofs) and a heated pool. (☎949-497-1031; www.seaclifflaguna.com. Rooms from $65.)

LEAVING LAGUNA BEACH
Continue up **Rte. 1 North.**

CRYSTAL COVE STATE PARK 8471 Rte. 1
3 mi. north of Laguna Beach.

Covering the San Joaquin Hills, Crystal Cove is a beautiful nature preserve with a rocky shoreline. **El Moro Canyon** extends up the hills east of Rte. 1, offering hikes with coastal views. From the many trails, choose among the best hikes: a comfortable 3 mi. loop around No Dogs Rd., Poles Rd., and El Moro Canyon Rd. or the strenuous 10½ mi. ascent up Moro Ridge Rd. across Missing Link Trail and down the other ridge. (☎949-494-3539. Open daily 6am-sunset. $5.)

NEWPORT BEACH

Multi-million-dollar homes, the world's largest leisure-craft harbor, and Balboa Peninsula are all packed closely enough on the Newport Beach oceanfront to make even New Yorkers feel claustrophobic. The young hedonists partying on the sand are a solid mix of locals and out-of-towners. Surfing and beach volleyball are popular, as is strolling the residential streets of Balboa Peninsula. The Newport Pier is an extension of 22nd St. at W. Balboa Blvd. Newport's **Harbor Nautical Museum,** 151 E. Pacific Coast Hwy., aboard the 190 ft. *Pride of Newport,* displays maritime history and model ships. (☎949-675-8915: www.nhnm.org. Open Su and Tu-Sa 10am-5pm. Free.) Get a dose of O.C. style at **Fashion Island,** just inland from the Pacific Coast Hwy., between MacArthur Blvd. and Jamboree Rd. Divided into seven courts, this outdoor mall has the amenities of a regular mall and lets you get a tan while shopping. The sands of Newport Beach run south onto the two- to-four-block wide **Balboa Peninsula,** separated from the mainland by Newport Bay. **Ocean Front Walk,** which extends the length of the peninsula, lined with neat rows of cottages, is the best place to stroll. The **Balboa Pier,** flanked by beautiful sands, is at Main St. and E. Balboa Blvd.

Joe's Crabshack, 2607 Pacific Coast Hwy., has brightly colored chairs, neon beer lights on the walls, and a fantastic view of the harbor. (☎949-650-1818; www.joescrabshack.com. Appetizers from $6. Entrees from $10. Open M-F 11am-10pm, Sa-Su 11am-11pm.) The **Balboa Inn,** 105 Main St., is a recently renovated landmark that offers rooms with ocean or bay views. Relax in the pool or hot tub. (☎949-675-3412; www.balboainn.com. Continental breakfast, fans, cable TV, and fridge included. Rooms from $139. Parking $8.)

HUNTINGTON BEACH

The prototypical Surf City, USA, Huntington Beach is a beach bum playground. This town has surf lore galore, and the proof is on the **Surfing Walk of Fame** (the sidewalk along PCH at Main St.) and in the **International Surfing Museum,** 411 Olive St. (☎714-960-3483. Open daily noon-5pm. $2, students $1.) Join the wave-riding for about $40 per hr. for an instructor, board, and wetsuit. Inquire at local surf shops or make an appointment with the lifeguard-staffed **Huntington Beach Surfing Instruction** (☎714-962-3515). The pier is the best place to watch the cavalcade of official surfing contests.

Turn off Rte. 1 onto Main St. for six blocks and on your left you'll find **Jan's Health Bar,** 510 Main St. This hold-over from the 60s is a wholesome shop selling fresh

and tasty sandwiches ($4-6), salads, and smoothies. (☎714-536-4856. Open M-Sa 8am-7pm, Su 8am-6pm.) **Ruby's** (☎714-969-7829), at the end of the Huntington Beach Pier, is a flashy white and neon-red 50s-style diner with great burgers ($8) and a fabulous ocean view. Cheap lodging is available at ⌖**Huntington Beach Colonial Inn Youth Hostel,** 421 8th St., four blocks inland at Pecan Ave. This large, early 20th-century yellow and blue house was once a brothel, but things have quieted down since (quiet hours after 10pm). (From PCH, turn onto 8th St. ☎714-536-3315. Common bath, large kitchen, reading/TV room, coin-op laundry, Internet access, deck, and shed with surfboards, boogie boards, and bikes. Linen and breakfast included. Key deposit $5. Check-in 8am-10pm. Reserve 2 days in advance for summer weekends. 3- to 4-person dorms $18; doubles $48.)

⟋ DETOUR: ANAHEIM ATTRACTIONS

From Huntington Beach, take Beach Blvd. (Rte. 39) north 11 mi. For Disneyland, turn right on Ball Rd. and continue 4 mi. For Knott's, stay on Rte. 39 1 mi. longer.

Disneyland calls itself the "Happiest Place on Earth," and a little bit of everyone agrees. After a full day there, your wallet may not. Weekday and low-season visitors will be the happiest, but the clever can wait for parades to distract families from the epic lines or utilize the line-busting Fast-Pass program. New "California Adventure Park" lets you see recreated movie backlots, California sights, a beach boardwalk, eight-acre mini-wilderness, a citrus grove, a winery, and a replica of San Francisco, all without leaving the state of Califor-

---

NO WORK, ALL PLAY

PAGEANT OF THE MASTERS

For years, artists have sought to imitate life upon canvas. The Pageant of the Masters in Laguna Beach does the opposite; it uses life to immortalize some of the most famous works of art. During the 2hr. extravaganza, volunteers from around the world create living replicas of famous works, from Normon Rockwell prints to Da Vinci's *Last Supper* (the perennial finale). The actors, heavily made-up and costumed, step into a painted background as the piece is framed in front of the audience. The lights dim, and when the picture is revealed, the actors, aided by advanced lighting techniques, seemingly disappear into a two-dimensional canvas. In addition to paintings, the Pageant also replicates statues and sculptures, brilliantly imitating marble, stone, gold, and countless other mediums. In all, more than 30 works, encompassing everything from Renaissance to contemporary art, are re-created each year. (July-Aug. ☎949-494-1145; www.foapom.com. Tickets $16.)

nia! (☎714-781-4565; www.disneyland.com. Open Su-Th 8am-11pm, F-Sa 8am-midnight; hours may vary. Disneyland passport $50, ages 3-9 $40, under 3 free; allows repeated single-day entrance. 2- and 3-day passes also available. California Adventure passport prices are the same as Disneyland's. Combination ticket $70, ages 3-9 $60.)

Knott's Berry Farm has long since given up on being the happiest place on Earth—it settles on being "the friendliest place in the West." Highlights include roller coasters like Montezooma's Revenge, Boomerang, and Ghostrider. The latest addition is Xcelerator. (☎714-220-5200. Open Su-Th 9am-10pm, F-Sa 9am-midnight; hours may vary. $43, ages 3-11 $13, under 3 free; after 4pm all tickets half-price. Parking under 3hr. free, each additional hr. $2; all-day parking $8.) Neighboring Soak City USA is Knott's 13-acre effort to make a splash in the drenched water park scene. (☎714-220-5200. Open Su-Th 10am-6pm, F-Sa 10am-8pm; hours may vary. $25, ages 3-11 $13, under 3 free.)

⚔ APPROACHING LONG BEACH

Take the **PCH (Rte. 1)** north. In Long Beach, turn left on **Alamitos Ave.** to head for the shore.

LONG BEACH

Long Beach is an industrial shipping center, massive, hulking and impersonal. There are two main attractions on the coast, the Queen Mary luxury liner and a spiffy Aquarium. Every April, Long Beach hosts a Grand Prix, and world-class racecar drivers and celebrities alike come to career around the downtown track.

> ### (VITAL STATS)
>
> **Population:** 430,000
>
> **Visitor Information: Long Beach Visitors Bureau,** 1 World Trade Ctr., #300 (☎800-452-7829), at Ocean Blvd. Open M-F 8am-5pm.
>
> **Internet Access: Long Beach Library,** 101 Pacific Ave. (☎562-570-7500). Open M and Th 10am-8pm, Tu-W and F-Sa 10am-5:30 pm.
>
> **Post Office:** 300 N. Long Beach Blvd. (☎562-628-1303). Open M-F 8:30am-5pm, Sa 9am-2pm. **Postal Code:** 90802.

▤ GETTING AROUND.

Long Beach's main tourist attractions lie by the bay. **Pine Ave.,** the backbone of downtown, runs north from the bay and **Ocean Blvd.** runs west to the boutiques of Belmont Shores. Be cautious in the inland areas of industrial Long Beach.

◙ SIGHTS.

At the end of Queen's Way Dr., the legendary 1934 Cunard luxury liner **Queen Mary** has been transformed into a hotel with art exhibits, historical displays, and upscale bars. During WWII, the "Grey Ghost" (as she was known) carried the greatest number of passengers of any floating vessel: 15,740 troops and 943 crew. The ship was so crucial to the Allied war effort that Hitler offered highest honors to anyone who sank her. A tour is worthwhile; you won't be able to see more than the engine room, deck, and gift shops otherwise. (☎562-435-3511; www.queenmary.com. Open daily 10am-6pm. $25, seniors and military $23, children $13. Tours $5, ages 5-11 $3.)

A $117 million, 156,735 sq. ft. celebration of the world's largest and most diverse body of water, the **Long Beach Aquarium of the Pacific,** 100 Aquarium Way, is situated atop one of the world's busiest and most polluted harbors. Meet the dazzling creatures of the deep that struggle to coexist with Long Beach's flotsam, jetsam, and effluvium. Among the most striking of the 12,000 displaced inhabitants are unborn sharks floating about in semi-transparent embryos. The seals, sea lions, otters, sharks, and jellyfish are also sure to please. (☎562-590-3100; www.aquariumofpacific.org. Open daily 9am-6pm. $19, seniors $15, ages 3-11 $10.) Just south of Ocean Blvd. and east of the Convention and Entertainment Center is an **enormous mural of life-sized whales,** cited by locals as the largest in the world.

▤🔧 FOOD & ACCOMMODATIONS.

Wicker beach furniture adds to a comfy diner setting at **The Shorehouse Cafe,** 5271 E. 2nd St., in Belmont Shores, where you can order "anything at any time." (☎562-433-2266. Huge burgers $7-8. Open 24hr.) "Good food prepared with your health in mind," brags the organic-egg-in-sunglasses menu logo at **The Omelette Inn,** 108 W. 3rd. St. For the health-conscious, there are egg white omelettes, brown rice, and veggie bacon strips. (☎562-437-5625. Open daily 7am-2:30pm.)

Cheap accommodations are few, but the **Beach Inn Motel,** 823 E. 3rd St., right off the water, is not wholly unreasonable. Basic rooms have fridge, satellite TV, and A/C. (☎562-437-3464. Free parking. Doubles $50, with jacuzzi $70.) If money is not on your mind, try the **Beach Plaza Hotel,** 2010 E.

Ocean Blvd., at Cherry Ave., whose turquoise exterior matches the ocean. Spacious rooms have A/C, cable TV, and fridges. (☎562-437-0771. Pool and beach access. Reserve ahead. Doubles $80-130, with ocean view and kitchenette $150-180.)

APPROACHING LOS ANGELES
Take **Atlantic Ave.** north to **I-405 North.**

LOS ANGELES

In a city where nothing seems to be more than 30 years old, the latest trends demand more respect than the venerable. Many come to this historical vacuum to make (or re-make) themselves. And what better place? Without the tiresome duty of bowing to the gods of an established high culture, Angelenos indulge in a style of their own creation. Cruise through and watch the sun set over the Pacific in Santa Monica or stay to see the sights and the stars; either way, it's one hell of a show.

VITAL STATS

Population: 16 million

Visitor Info: L.A. Convention and Visitor Bureau, 685 S. Figueroa St. (☎213-689-8822; www.visitlanow.com), between Wilshire Blvd. and 7th St. in the Financial District. Open M-F 8am 5:30pm.

Internet Access: Los Angeles Public Library, Central Library, 630 W. 5th St. (☎213-228-7000). Open M-Th 10am-8pm, F-Sa 10am-6pm, Su 1-5pm.

Post Office: 7101 S. Central Ave. (☎800-275-8777). Open M-F 7am-7pm, Sa 7am-3pm. **Postal Code:** 90001.

GETTING AROUND

Five major freeways connect California's vainest city to the rest of the state: **I-5 (Golden State Fwy.), U.S. 101 (Hollywood Fwy.),** the **Pacific Coast Hwy. (PCH or Rte. 1), I-10,** and **I-15. I-5, I-405 (San Diego Fwy.), I-110 (Harbor Fwy.), U.S. 101,** and **Pacific Coast Hwy.** all run north-south. **I-10 (Santa Monica Fwy.)** is the most popular freeway for east-west drivers. I-5 intersects I-10 just east of Downtown and serves as one of the two major north-south thruways. I-405, which goes from **Orange County** in the south all the way through L.A., parallels I-5 closer to the coast, and separates **Santa Monica** and **Malibu** from the L.A. **Westside.**

Roadtrippers will feel at home in L.A.; sometimes it seems like all 16 million residents are flooding I-405 and I-101 all at once. No matter how jammed the freeways are, they are almost always quicker and safer than surface streets. Unless you are "in the know" with inside knowledge of local surface streets in the city, plan to spend quality time in your car. Heavy traffic moves toward downtown from 7 to 10am on weekdays and streams outbound from 4 to 7pm.

DOWNTOWN. A legitimate **Downtown L.A.** exists, but few go there except to work. The heart of downtown is relatively safe on weekdays, but avoid walking there after dark and on weekends. **Monterey Park** is one of the few cities in the US with a predominantly Asian-American population. The **University of Southern California (USC), Exposition Park,** and the mostly African-American districts of **Inglewood, Watts,** and **Compton** stretch south of downtown. **South Central,** the name of this area, suffered the brunt of the 1992 riots, is known for rampant crime, and holds few attractions for tourists. The predominantly Latino section of the city is found east of downtown in **Boyle Heights, East L.A.,** and **Montebello.**

HOLLYWOOD & WESTSIDE. Nowhere is the myth/reality divide more dramatic in Los Angeles than in the sharp contrast between the movieland glamour associated with **Hollywood** and its unromantic modern incarnation. **Sunset Blvd.** presents a cross-section of virtually everything L.A. has to offer. The **Sunset Strip,** hot seat of L.A.'s best nightlife, is the West Hollywood section of Sunset Blvd. closest to Beverly Hills. The region known as **The Westside** encompasses prestigious **West Hollywood, Westwood, Bel Air, Brentwood,** and **Beverly Hills, Pacific Palisades, Santa Monica,** and **Venice.** A good portion of the city's gay community resides in West Hollywood, while Beverly Hills and Bel Air are home to the rich and famous. Westside's attractions include the **University of California at Los Angeles (UCLA)** in Westwood and the trendy **Melrose Ave. West L.A.** is a municipal distinction that refers to Westwood and the no-man's land including Century City. The area west of downtown and south of West Hollywood is known as the **Wilshire District.**

OUTSIDE L.A. Eighty miles of beaches line L.A.'s **coastal region. Long Beach** is the southernmost. North across the Palos Verdes Peninsula is

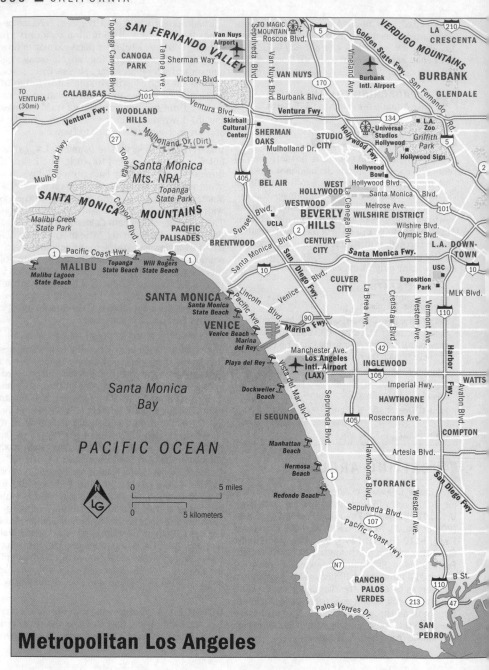

Metropolitan Los Angeles

SAN FERNANDO VALLEY

TO VENTURA (30mi)

Topanga Canyon Blvd.

CANOGA PARK

Tampa Ave.

Sherman Way

Victory Blvd.

Van Nuys Airport

TO MAGIC MOUNTAIN
Roscoe Blvd.

Sepulveda Blvd.

VAN NUYS

Van Nuys Blvd.

170

Burbank Blvd.

Vineland Ave.

Golden State Fwy.

San Fernando Rd.

VERDUGO MOUNTAINS

LA CRESCENTA

210

BURBANK

Burbank Intl. Airport

GLENDALE

CALABASAS

101

Ventura Blvd.

Ventura Fwy.

Ventura Fwy.

134

L.A. Zoo

Griffith Park

5

2

WOODLAND HILLS

27

Mulholland Dr. (Dirt)

Skirball Cultural Center

SHERMAN OAKS

Mulholland Dr.

STUDIO CITY

Hollywood Fwy.

Universal Studios Hollywood

Hollywood Sign

Mulholland Hwy.

Santa Monica Mts. NRA

Topanga State Park

405

BEL AIR

WEST HOLLYWOOD

Hollywood Bowl

Hollywood Blvd.

Santa Monica Blvd.

101

SANTA MONICA

Malibu Creek State Park

MOUNTAINS

WESTWOOD

BEVERLY HILLS

La Cienega Blvd.

Melrose Ave.

WILSHIRE DISTRICT

Wilshire Blvd.

Olympic Blvd.

PACIFIC PALISADES

Sunset Blvd.

UCLA

2

CENTURY CITY

Santa Monica Fwy.

L.A. DOWN-TOWN

BRENTWOOD

USC

10

1

Pacific Coast Hwy.

MALIBU

Malibu Lagoon State Beach

Topanga State Beach

Will Rogers State Beach

1

Santa Monica Blvd.

San Diego Fwy.

10

Venice Blvd.

CULVER CITY

La Brea Ave.

Crenshaw Blvd.

Western Ave.

Vermont Ave.

Exposition Park

MLK Blvd.

110

SANTA MONICA

Santa Monica State Beach

Lincoln Blvd.

Pacific Ave.

VENICE

Venice Beach

Marina del Rey

90

Marina Fwy.

42

INGLEWOOD

105

Harbor Fwy.

WATTS

Avalon Blvd.

Playa del Rey

Manchester Ave.

Los Angeles Intl. Airport (LAX)

Imperial Hwy.

HAWTHORNE

Rosecrans Ave.

COMPTON

Dockweiler Beach

Vista del Mar Blvd.

Sepulveda Blvd.

EL SEGUNDO

405

Hawthorne Blvd.

Artesia Blvd.

San Diego Fwy.

Santa Monica Bay

PACIFIC OCEAN

Manhattan Beach

Hermosa Beach

1

Redondo Beach

Sepulveda Blvd.

107

Pacific Coast Hwy.

Western Ave.

TORRANCE

213

B St.

110

47

N7

RANCHO PALOS VERDES

Palos Verdes Dr.

SAN PEDRO

N

LG

0   5 miles

0   5 kilometers

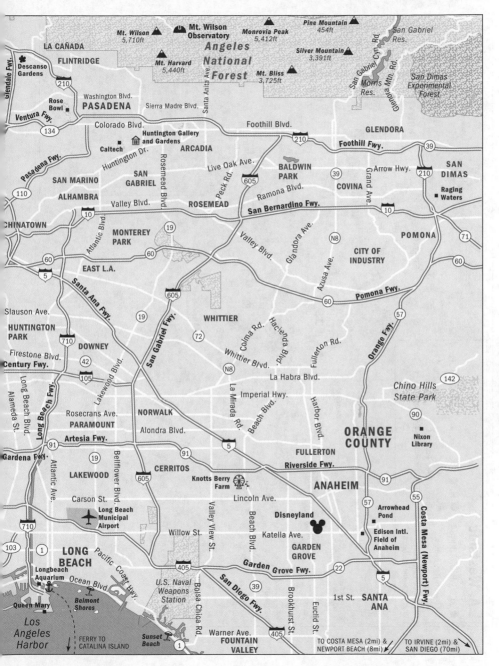

Mt. Wilson
5,710ft
Mt. Wilson
Observatory
Monrovia Peak
5,412ft
Pine Mountain
454ft
San Gabriel
Res.

LA CAÑADA
Angeles
National
Forest
Silver Mountain
3,391ft
San Gabriel Cyn. Rd.

Descanso
Gardens
FLINTRIDGE
Mt. Harvard
5,440ft
Mt. Bliss
3,725ft
Morris
Res.
San Dimas
Experimental
Forest

Glendale Fwy.
210
Washington Blvd.
Santa Anita Ave.
Glendora Mtn. Rd.

Rose
Bowl
PASADENA
Sierra Madre Blvd.
Foothill Blvd.
GLENDORA

Ventura Fwy.
134
Colorado Blvd.
210
Foothill Fwy.
39

Pasadena Fwy.
Huntington Gallery
and Gardens
ARCADIA
BALDWIN
PARK
Arrow Hwy.
210
SAN
DIMAS

Caltech
Huntington Dr.
Live Oak Ave.
Peck Rd.
605
39
Grand Ave.
Raging
Waters

SAN MARINO
SAN
GABRIEL
Rosemead Blvd.
Ramona Blvd.
COVINA
10

ALHAMBRA
Valley Blvd.
ROSEMEAD
San Bernardino Fwy.
10
POMONA
71

110
CHINATOWN
10
MONTEREY
PARK
19
Valley Blvd.
Glandora Ave.
N8
CITY OF
INDUSTRY
60

60
5
EAST L.A.
60
605
Azusa Ave.
Pomona Fwy.
60

Santa Ana Fwy.
19
WHITTIER
72
Fullerton Rd.
Orange Fwy.
57
142

Slauson Ave.
San Gabriel Fwy.
Colma Rd.
Hacienda Blvd.
Chino Hills
State Park

HUNTINGTON
PARK
710
DOWNEY
42
Whittier Blvd.
N8
La Habra Blvd.
90
Nixon
Library

Firestone Blvd.
Century Fwy.
105
Lakewood Blvd.
NORWALK
La Mirada Rd.
Imperial Hwy.
Beach Blvd.
Harbor Blvd.
ORANGE
COUNTY

Long Beach Blvd.
Alameda St.
Rosecrans Ave.
PARAMOUNT
Alondra Blvd.
5
FULLERTON

91
Artesia Fwy.
19
91
Riverside Fwy.
91

Gardena Fwy.
Atlantic Ave.
Bellflower Blvd.
LAKEWOOD
605
CERRITOS
Knotts Berry
Farm
ANAHEIM
57
55

710
Carson St.
Long Beach
Municipal
Airport
Willow St.
Lincoln Ave.
Disneyland
Arrowhead
Pond
Costa Mesa (Newport) Fwy.

103
1
LONG
BEACH
Pacific Coast Hwy.
405
Valley View St.
Beach Blvd.
Katella Ave.
GARDEN
GROVE
Edison Intl.
Field of
Anaheim

Longbeach
Aquarium
Ocean Blvd.
U.S. Naval
Weapons
Station
Bolsa Chica Rd.
San Diego Fwy.
Garden Grove Fwy.
22
5

Queen Mary
Belmont
Shores
405
39
Brookhurst St.
Euclid St.
1st St.
SANTA
ANA

Los
Angeles
Harbor
FERRY TO
CATALINA ISLAND
Sunset
Beach
1
Warner Ave.
FOUNTAIN
VALLEY
405
TO COSTA MESA (2mi) &
NEWPORT BEACH (8mi)
TO IRVINE (2mi) &
SAN DIEGO (70mi)

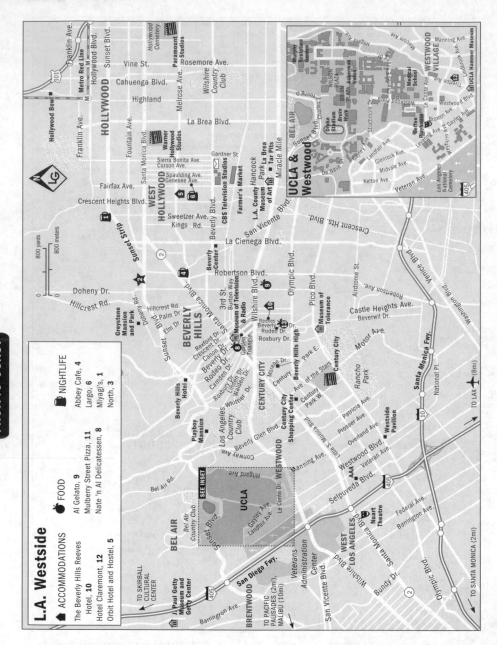

L.A. Westside

▲ ACCOMMODATIONS

The Beverly Hills Reeves
Hotel, **10**
Hotel Claremont, **12**
Orbit Hotel and Hostel, **5**

● FOOD

Al Gelato, **9**
Mulberry Street Pizza, **11**
Nate 'n Al Delicatessen, **8**

■ NIGHTLIFE

Abbey Cafe, **4**
Largo, **6**
Miyagi's, **1**
North, **3**

Map labels:

Franklin Ave.
Metro Red Line
Hollywood Blvd.
Sunset Blvd.
Vine St.
Rosemore Ave.
Cahuenga Blvd.
Highland
HOLLYWOOD
Paramount Studios
Hollywood Cemetery
Melrose Ave.
Wilshire Country Club
Hollywood Bowl
Franklin Ave.
Fountain Ave.
Warner Hollywood Studios
La Brea Blvd.
Santa Monica Blvd.
WEST HOLLYWOOD
Sierra Bonita Ave.
Curson Ave.
Spaulding Ave.
Genesee Ave.
Gardner St
CBS Television Studios
Farmer's Market
Fairfax Ave.
Crescent Heights Blvd.
Sweetzer Ave.
Kings Rd.
Beverly Blvd.
La Cienega Blvd.
Sunset Strip
L.A. County Museum of Art
Hancock Park La Brea Tar Pits
Miracle Mile
San Vicente Blvd.
BEL AIR
Crescent Hts. Blvd.
Venice Blvd.
Beverly Center
Robertson Blvd.
Olympic Blvd.
3rd St.
Burton Way
Museum of Television & Radio
Reeves Dr.
Beverly Dr.
Rodeo Dr.
Roxbury Dr.
Museum of Tolerance
Pico Blvd.
Airdrome St.
Robertson Ave.
Washington Blvd.
Santa Monica Fwy.
Castle Heights Ave.
Beverwil Dr.
Motor Ave.
Century City
Doheny Dr.
Hillcrest Rd.
Greystone Mansion and Park
Hillcrest Rd.
Palm Dr.
Elm Dr.
BEVERLY HILLS
Rexford Dr.
Crescent Dr.
Canon Dr.
Golden Triangle
Century Park E.
Ave. of the Stars
Century Park W.
Rancho Park
National Pl.
TO LAX (8mi)
Beverly Hills Hotel
Camden Dr.
Linden Dr.
Maple Dr.
Beverly Hills High
CENTURY CITY
Moreno Dr.
Century City Shopping Center
Patricia Ave.
Prosser Ave.
Overland Ave.
Westside Pavilion
Roxbury Dr.
Whittier Dr.
Beverly Hills Country Club
Playboy Mansion
Beverly Glen Blvd.
Conway Ave.
Manning Ave.
WESTWOOD
Westwood Blvd.
Veteran Ave.
Little Santa Monica Blvd.
Bel Air Rd.
Bel Air Country Club
BEL AIR
SEE INSET
Hilgard Ave.
UCLA
Gayley Ave.
Landfair Ave.
Le Conte Dr.
Selpuveda Blvd.
405
AAA
Federal Ave.
Barrington Ave.
TO SKIRBALL CULTURAL CENTER
J. Paul Getty Museum and Getty Center
San Diego Fwy.
BRENTWOOD
Sunset Blvd.
Veterans Administration Center
WEST LOS ANGELES
Wilshire Blvd.
Nuart Theatre
Santa Monica Blvd.
Bundy Dr.
Barrington Ave.
San Vicente Blvd.
Olympic Blvd.
TO PACIFIC PALISADES (2mi), MALIBU (10mi)
TO SANTA MONICA (2mi)
Olympic Blvd.

UCLA & Westwood inset:

Murphy Sculpture Garden
WESTWOOD VILLAGE
Manning Ave.
Hilgard Ave.
WILSON PLAZA
Ackerman Union
Medical School
UCLA Hammer Museum
Brain Walk
Drake Stadium
De Neve Dr.
Strathmore Dr.
Westwood Blvd.
Westwood Plaza
Geffen Playhouse
Gayley Ave.
Le Conte Ave.
Landfair Ave.
Glenrock Ave.
Midvale Ave.
Kelton Ave.
Veteran Ave.
Los Angeles National Cemetery
405
Weyburn Ave.
Gayley Ave.
Broxton Ave.
Westwood Ave.
Tiverton Ave.
Lindbrook Ave.

Venice, followed by **Santa Monica, Malibu,** and **Zuma Beach.** The **San Fernando Valley** sprawls north of the Hollywood Hills and the Santa Monica Mountains. The basin is bounded to the north and west by the Santa Susana Mountains and Rte. 118 (Ronald Reagan Fwy.), to the south by Rte. 134 (Ventura Blvd.), and to the east by I-5 (Golden State Fwy.). The **San Bernardino Valley,** also home to about two million, stretches eastward from LL.A. A south of the San Gabriel Mountains. In between these two valleys lie the affluent foothills of **Pasadena** and its famed Rose Parade.

SIGHTS

HOLLYWOOD

Exploring the Hollywood area takes a pair of sunglasses, a camera, cash, and a whole lot of attitude. Running east-west at the foot of the Hollywood Hills, **Hollywood Blvd.** is the center of L.A.'s tourist madness, home to the Walk of Fame, famous theaters, souvenir shops, and museums.

HOLLYWOOD SIGN. Those 50 ft. high, 30 ft. wide, slightly erratic letters perched on Mt. Lee in Griffith Park stand as a universally recognized symbol of the city. The original 1923 sign read HOLLYWOODLAND and was an advertisement for a new subdivision in the Hollywood Hills. The sign has been a target of many college pranks, which have made it read everything from "Hollyweird" to "Ollywood" (after the infamous Lt. Col. Oliver North). A fence keeps you at a distance of 40 ft. *(To get as close to the sign as possible requires a strenuous 2½ mi. hike. Take the Bronson Canyon entrance to Griffith Park and follow Canyon Dr. to its end, where parking is free. The Brush Canyon Trail starts where Canyon Dr. becomes unpaved. At the top of the hill, follow the road to your left. For those satisfied with driving, go north on Vine St., take a right on Franklin Ave. and a left on Beachwood, and drive up until you are forced to drive down.)*

GRAUMAN'S CHINESE THEATRE. Known formerly as Mann's Chinese Theatre, this 75-year-old theater is back to its original name thanks to efforts to establish historical culture. Loosely modeled on a Chinese temple, the theater is a hot spot for movie premieres. The exterior columns—known as "Heaven Dogs"—were imported from China, where they once supported a Ming Dynasty temple and were believed to ward off evil spirits.

In front of the theater are the footprints of more than 200 celebrities, encased in cement. Whoopi Goldberg's dreadlocks and R2D2's wheels are also here. *(6925 Hollywood Blvd., between Highland and Orange St. ☎ 323-461-3331. Tours 4-5 times a day; call ahead. $7.50, under 6 free.)*

WALK OF FAME. Pedestrian traffic along Hollywood Blvd. mimics L.A. freeways as tourists stop midstride to gawk at the sidewalk's over 2000 bronze-inlaid stars, which are inscribed with the names of the famous, the infamous, and the downright obscure. Stars are awarded for achievements in one of five categories—movies, radio, TV, recording, and live performance; only Gene Autry has all five stars. To catch today's stars in person, call the Chamber of Commerce for info on star-unveiling ceremonies. *(☎ 323-469-8311; www.hollywoodchamber.net. Free.)*

OTHER SIGHTS. The hillside **Hollywood Bowl** is synonymous with picnic dining and classy summer entertainment. All are welcome to listen to the L.A. Philharmonic at rehearsals on Mondays, Tuesdays, Thursdays, and Fridays. *(2301 N. Highland Ave. ☎ 323-850-2058, concert line 323-850-2000; www.hollywoodbowl.org. Open July-Sept. Tu-Sa 10am-8pm; Sept.-June Tu-Sa 10am-4:30pm. Free.)* The sizable complex of the **Hollywood & Highland Mall** centers on two monstrous elephant sculptures, and contains ritzy brand name stores, restaurants, and the $94 million **Kodak Theater,** built specifically to be the home of the Academy Awards. *(6801 Hollywood Blvd. Box office ☎ 323-308-6363. Open non-show days 10am-6pm, show days 10am-9pm. Tours daily every 30min., 10:30am-2:30pm. $15, under 12 $10.)*

VENICE & SOUTH BAY

Ocean Front Walk, Venice's main beachfront drag, is a seaside circus of fringe culture. Street people converge on benches, evangelists drown out off-color comedians, and bodybuilders pump iron at **Muscle Beach,** 1800 Ocean Front Walk, closest to 18th St. and Pacific Ave. Fire-juggling cyclists, sand sculptors, bards in Birkenstocks, and "skateboard grandmas" define the bohemian spirit of this playground population. Vendors of jewelry, henna body art, snacks, and beach paraphernalia overwhelm the boardwalk.

About 20 mi. southwest of downtown L.A., PCH passes through the heart of the beach scene at **Redondo Beach, Hermosa Beach,** and

Manhattan Beach. Most visit Redondo Beach for its harbor, pier, and seafood-rich boardwalk. Hermosa Beach, the most popular urban beach in L.A. county, has a reputation for cleanliness. Manhattan Beach, also one of the cleanest, is favored for surfing. Both Manhattan and Hermosa beaches host elite beach volleyball and surf competitions (☎323-426-8000; www.avp.com or www.surffestival.org). **The Strand** is a concrete bike path crowded with bikers and in-line skaters that runs right on the beach from Santa Monica (where it's called Ocean Front Walk) to Hermosa Beach.

BEVERLY HILLS

Conspicuous displays of wealth border on the vulgar in this storied center of extravagance. Residential ritz reaches its peak along **Beverly Dr.**

RODEO DRIVE. The heart of the city, known for its clothing boutiques and jewelry shops, is in the **Golden Triangle,** a wedge formed by Beverly Dr., Wilshire Blvd., and Santa Monica Blvd. Built like an old English manor house, Polo Ralph Lauren stands out from the white marble of the other stores. *(444 N. Rodeo Dr.)* The triple-whammy of Cartier *(370 N. Rodeo Dr.),* Gucci *(347 N. Rodeo Dr.),* and Chanel *(400 N. Rodeo Dr.)* sits on some prime real estate, where rents approach $40,000 per month. At the south end of Rodeo Dr. (closest to Wilshire Blvd.) is the all-pedestrian shopping of **2 Rodeo Drive,** a.k.a. **Via Rodeo,** which contains Dior, Tiffany, and salons of the stars. Across the way is the **Beverly Wilshire Hotel,** featured in *Pretty Woman.* (9500 Wilshire Blvd. ☎ 310-275-5200.)

WEST HOLLYWOOD

Bring your walking shoes and spend a day on the 3 mi. strip of **Melrose Avenue** from Highland Ave. west to the intersection of Doheny Dr. and Santa Monica Blvd. This strip began to develop its funky flair in the late 1980s when art galleries, designer stores, lounge-like coffee shops, used clothing and music stores, and restaurants began to take over. Now it is home to the hip, with the choicest stretch lying between La Brea and Fairfax Ave. While much sold here is used ("vintage"), none of it is really cheap. North of the Beverly Center is the **Pacific Design Center,** a sea-green glass complex nicknamed the Blue Whale and constructed in the shape of a rippin' wave. (8687 Melrose Ave. ☎ 310-657-0800; www.pacificdesigncenter.com.)

DOWNTOWN

Downtown, park in a secure lot, rather than on the street. Due to expensive short-term lot parking ($3 per 20min.) and exorbitant meter prices ($0.25 per 10min.), it's best to park in a public lot ($5-10 per day) and walk. The **L.A. Visitors Center,** 685 S. Figueroa St., can answer your travel queries. (Open M-F 8am-4pm, Sa 8:30am-5pm.)

EL PUEBLO HISTORIC PARK. The historic birthplace of L.A. is now known as **El Pueblo de Los Angeles Historical Monument,** bordered by Cesar Chavez Ave., Alameda St., Hollywood Fwy., and Spring St. In 1781, 44 settlers started a pueblo and farming community here; today, 27 buildings from the eras of Spanish and Mexican rule are preserved. Established in 1825, the **Plaza** is the center of El Pueblo, and hosts festivals including the Mexican Independence celebration (Sept. 16), *Dia de los Muertos* celebrations (Nov. 1-2), and *Cinco de Mayo* (May 5). Treat yourself to the cheapest churros around (2 for $1) as you walk down historic **Olvera St.,** which resembles a colorful Mexican marketplace, and bargain at *puestos* (vendor stalls) selling everything from Mexican crafts and food to personalized t-shirts. The **Avila Adobe** (circa 1818) is the "oldest" house in the city. *(10 E. Olvera St. Open daily 9am-3pm.)*

MUSIC CENTER. The Music Center is an enormous complex that includes **The Dorothy Chandler Pavilion,** home of the L.A. Opera and former site of the Academy Awards. (☎213-972-8001; www.laopera.org.) Across the street rise the silver slices of the Frank Gehry-designed **Walt Disney Concert Hall.** This gleaming 2265-seat structure is the new home of the L.A. Phil and the L.A. Master Chorale. *(151 S. Grand Ave. ☎213-972-7211; www.disneyhall.org.)* Also part of the Music Center are the **Mark Taper Forum** and the **Ahmanson Theatre,** known for world-class shows. (☎213-628-2772; www.taperahmanson.com. Tours of the 3-theater complex M-F 11:30am, 12:30, 1:30pm, as performance schedules permit. Go to the outdoor info booth in the large courtyard between the theaters.)

OTHER SIGHTS. One of the best-known buildings in the Southland, **City Hall,** "has starred in more movies than most actors." *(200 N. Spring St.)* Bargain hounds can haggle to their hearts' delight in the **Fashion District,** which is bordered by 6th and 9th St. along Los Angeles St. The **Library Tower** has a distinctive glass crown and is the tallest building between Chicago and Hong Kong at 1017 ft. *(633 W. 5th St.)* The **Westin Bonaventure Hotel** is composed of five squat but sleek cylinders sheathed in black glass, and has appeared in *Rain Man, In the Line of Fire,* and *Heat. (404 S. Figueroa St.)* The historic **Biltmore Hotel** is a $10 million, 683-room hotel designed by Schultze and Weaver, best known for New York's Waldorf-Astoria. *(506 S. Grand Ave.)*

NEAR DOWNTOWN

UNIVERSITY OF SOUTHERN CALIFORNIA

(USC). North of Exposition Park, USC's 30,000 students bring a youthful character to downtown. The alma mater of celebrities such as astronaut Neil Armstrong, the school has had a gold-medal winning athlete in every summer Olympics since 1912. L.A. sports fans salivate when the burnished USC Trojans clash with the blue-and-gold UCLA Bruins in annual football and basketball classics. *(From downtown, take Figueroa St. south and turn right into campus on 35th St., or exit I-110 on Exposition Blvd. ☎ 213-740-2311; www.usc.edu. Campus tours M-F every hr. 10am-3pm.)*

GRIFFITH PARK & GLENDALE. For fresh air and a respite from city life, take to the slopes of Griffith Park, the nation's largest municipal park, nestled between U.S. 101, I-5, and Rte. 134. A stark contrast to the concrete of downtown and the star-studded streets of Hollywood, the park is a refuge from the city and the site of outdoor diversions. Fifty-two miles of hiking and horseback trails, three golf courses, a planetarium, an enormous zoo, several museums, and the 6000-person Greek Theatre are contained within its rolling 4107 acres. *(Visitors Center and Ranger Headquarters doles out trail info at 4730 Crystal Spring Dr. ☎ 323-913-4688, emergency 323-913-7390. Park open daily 5am-10pm.)* The park has numerous equestrian trails and places to saddle up, such as **J.P. Stables.** No experience necessary; guides are provided. *(1914 Maripose St., in Burbank. ☎ 818-843-9890. Open daily 8am-6pm. No reservations. $18 for 1hr., $12 per additional hr. Cash only.)*

SAN FERNANDO VALLEY

TV and movie studios redeem the Valley (somewhat) from its bland warehouses, blonde Valley Girls, and faceless strip malls. Passing Burbank on Rte. 134, you might catch glimpses of the Valley's most lucrative trademark studios: **Universal, Warner Bros., NBC,** and **Disney.** To best experience the industry, attend a **free TV show taping** or take one of the tours offered by most studios.

■**UNIVERSAL STUDIOS.** A movie and television studio that happens to have the world's first and largest movie-themed amusement park attached, Universal Studios Hollywood is the most popular tourist spot in Tinseltown. North of Hollywood in its own municipality of Universal City (complete with police and fire station), the park began as a tour of the studios in 1964. *(Take U.S. 101 to the Universal Center Dr. Exits. ☎ 800-UNIVERSAL/864-8377; www.universalstudios.com. Open July-Aug. M-F 9am-8pm, Sa-Su 9am-9pm; Sept.-June M-F 10am-6pm, Sa-Su 10am-7pm. Last tram leaves M-F 5:15pm, Sa-Su 6:15pm; low-season 4:15pm. $47, under 48 in. $37, under 3 free. Parking $8.)*

MISSION SAN FERNANDO REY DE ESPAÑA. Founded in 1797, the **San Fernando Mission** is rich with history and is the largest adobe structure in California. The grounds, with museum and gift shop, are beautifully kept and definitely worth a visit. *(15101 San Fernando Mission Blvd. ☎ 818-361-0186. Open daily 9am-4:30pm. Mass M-Tu and Th-Sa 7:25am, Su 9 and 10:30am. $4, seniors and ages 7-15 $3, under 7 free.)*

PASADENA

The excellent **Convention and Visitors Bureau,** 171 S. Los Robles Ave., is a useful first stop in Pasadena, with numerous promotional materials and guides to regional events. *(☎ 626-795-9311; www.pasadenacal.com. Open M-F 8am-5pm, Sa 10am-4pm.)*

ROSE BOWL. In the gorge that forms the city's western boundary stands Pasadena's most famous landmark. The sand-colored, 90,000-seat stadium is home to "the granddaddy of them all," the annual college football clash on January 1st between the champions of the Big Ten and Pac 10 conferences. The Bowl Championship Series comes every four years, and the UCLA Bruins play regular-season home games here as well. *(1001 Rose Bowl Dr. ☎ 626-577-3100; www.rosebowlstadium.com. Bruins info: ☎ 310-825-29469; www.cto.ucla.edu.)* The bowl also hosts a monthly **flea market** that attracts 2000 vendors, selling nearly one million items. *(☎ 323-560-7469. 2nd Su of each month 9am-4:30pm. Admission $7.)*

SCIENCES. Some of the world's greatest scientific minds do their work at the **California Institute of Technology (Caltech).** Founded in 1891, Caltech has amassed a faculty that includes several Nobel laureates and a student body that prides itself both on its staggering collective intellect and its loony practical jokes. *(1201 E. California Blvd., about 2½ mi. southeast of Old Town. Take I-110 N until it becomes the Arroyo Pkwy. Turn right on California Blvd. and go 1¼ mi. Turn left on Hill Ave., left on San Pasqual St., and right on Holliston Ave. Proceed to 370 S. Holliston Ave. to register your car. ☎ 626-395-6327. Tours M-F 2pm.)* **NASA's Jet Propulsion Laboratory,** about 5 mi. north of Old Town, executed the journey of the Mars Pathfinder. Ask to see pictures of the face of Mars. *(4800 Oak Grove Dr. ☎ 818-354-9314. Free tours by appointment.)*

🏛 MUSEUMS

🎨 **J. Paul Getty Center & Museum,** 1200 Getty Center Dr. (☎ 310-440-7300; www.getty.edu), Exit I-405 (San Diego Fwy.) at Getty Center Dr. Above Bel Air and Brentwood in the Santa Monica Mountains shines a modern Coliseum, "The Getty." Wedding classical materials to modern designs, renowned architect Richard Meier designed the stunning $1 billion complex, which opened in 1997. The museum consists of five pavilions overlooking the Robert Irwin-designed Central Garden. The pavilions contain the Getty collection of Impressionist paintings. Headset audio guides $3. Open Su and Tu-Th 10am-6pm, F-Sa 10am-9pm. Parking reservations required Tu-F before 4pm ($5 per car); no reservations needed for college students or Sa-Su. Free.

🎨 **Los Angeles County Museum of Art (LACMA),** 5905 Wilshire Blvd. (☎ 323-857-6000; www.lacma.org). Opened in 1965, the LACMA is the largest museum on the West Coast. The Steve Martin Gallery holds the comedian's collection of Dada and Surrealist works. (This explains how Steve was able to rollerskate LACMA's halls in the film *L.A. Story.*) Open M-Tu and Th noon-8pm, F noon-9pm, Sa-Su 11am-8pm. $9, students and seniors $5, under 18 free; free 2nd Tu of each month. Free jazz F 5:30-8:30pm, chamber music Su 6-7pm. Film tickets $8, seniors and students $6. Parking $5, after 7pm free.

🎨 **Norton Simon Museum of Art,** 411 W. Colorado Blvd. (☎ 626-449-6840; www.nortonsimon.org). Rivaling the much larger Getty in quality, this private collection chronicles Western art from Italian Gothic to 20th-century abstract. The Impressionist and Post-Impressionist hall, the Southeast Asian sculptures, and the 79,000 sq. ft. sculpture garden by Nancy Goslee Power are particularly impressive. Open M, W-Th, Sa-Su noon-6pm; F noon-9pm. $6, seniors $3, students with ID and under 18 free. Free parking.

🎨 **UCLA Hammer Museum of Art,** 10899 Wilshire Blvd. (☎ 310-443-7000; www.hammer.ucla.edu). The museum houses the world's largest collection of works by 19th-century French satirist Honoré Daumier. The gem of the collection is Van Gogh's *Hospital at Saint Rémy.* Open Su, Tu, Sa noon-7pm; W-F noon-9pm. Free tours of permanent collection Su 2pm; of traveling exhibits Th 6pm, Sa-Su 1pm. Summer jazz concerts F 6:30-8pm. $5, seniors $3, under 17 free. Th free. 3hr. parking $2.75, $1.50 per additional 20min.

Autry Museum of Western Heritage, 4700 Western Heritage Way (☎ 323-667-2000), in Griffith Park. City slickers and lone rangers may discover that the West is not what they thought—the museum insists that the real should not be confused with the reel, drawing the line between Old West fact and fiction. Open Su, Tu-W, and F-Sa 10am-5pm, Th 10am-8pm. $7.50, students and seniors $5, ages 2-12 $3. Th after 4pm free.

Petersen Automotive Museum (PAM), 6060 Wilshire Blvd. (☎ 323-930-2277; www.petersen.org), at Fairfax. The world's largest car museum, showcasing over 150 classic cars, hot rods, motorcycles, and movie and celebrity cars, not to mention the 1920s service station, 50s body shop, and 60s suburban garage. Open Su and Tu-Sa 10am-6pm; Discovery Center closes 5pm. Call to set up a tour. $7, students and seniors $5, ages 5-12 $3, under 5 free. Parking $6.

🎵 ENTERTAINMENT

There are many ways to sample the silver screen glitz created and peddled by the entertainment capital of the world. Shopping is a major pastime in the L.A. area, crafted by its devotees into performance art. For after-hours fun, L.A. features some of the trendiest, celeb-frenzied nightlife imaginable. For amusement parks, check out nearby giants like **Disneyland, Knott's Berry Farm, Magic Mountain,** and **Universal Studios.**

TELEVISION STUDIOS

A visit to the world's entertainment capital isn't complete without exposure to the actual business of making a movie or TV show. Fortunately, most production companies oblige. **Paramount** (☎ 323-

956-5000), **NBC** (☎818-840-3537), and **Warner Bros.** (☎818-954-1744) offer 2hr. guided tours that take you onto sets and through backlots. Tickets to a taping are free but studios tend to overbook, so holding a ticket doesn't guarantee you'll get in; show up early. **NBC,** 3000 W. Alameda Ave., at W. Olive Ave. in Burbank, is your best bet. Show up at the ticket office on a weekday at 8am for passes to Jay Leno's **Tonight Show,** filmed at 5pm the same evening (2 tickets per person; must be 16 or older). Studio tours run on the hour. (☎818-840-3537. M-F 9am-3pm. $7.50, ages 5-12 $4.) Many of NBC's other shows are taped at **Warner Bros.,** 4000 Warner Blvd. (☎818-954-6000), in Burbank.

A **CBS box office,** 7800 Beverly Blvd., next to the Farmer's Market in West Hollywood, hands out free tickets to *The Price is Right* (taped M-Th) up to one week in advance. Audience members must be over 18. (☎323-575-2458. Open M-F 9am-5pm.) You can request up to ten tickets by sending a self-addressed, stamped envelope to *The Price is Right* Tickets, 7800 Beverly Blvd., Los Angeles, CA 90036, four to six weeks in advance. If all else fails, **Audiences Unlimited, Inc.** (☎818-506-0067; www.tvtickets.com), is a great resource.

MOVIES

L.A.'s movie palaces show films the way they were meant to be seen: on a big screen, in plush seats, and with top-quality sound and air-conditioning. It would be a cinematic crime not to partake of the city's moviegoing experiences. The gargantuan theaters at **Universal City,** as well as those in **Westwood Village** near UCLA, are incredibly popular. In **Santa Monica,** there are 22 screens within the three blocks of Third St. Promenade. To ogle the stars as they walk the red carpet, drop in on the four premiere hounds: **Grauman's Chinese** (about 2 per month), **El Capitan** (Disney films only), **Mann's Village,** and **Bruin.** For info on what's playing in L.A., call ☎323-777-3456 or read the daily *Calendar* section of the *L.A. Times.* Devotees of second-run, foreign-language, and experimental films can get their fix at the eight **Laemmle Theaters** in Beverly Hills (☎310-274-6869), West Hollywood (☎323-848-3500), Santa Monica (☎310-394-9741), and Pasadena (☎626-844-6500).

■ **Arclight Cinerama Dome,** 6360 Sunset Blvd. (☎323-466-3401), in Hollywood, near Vine St. The ultimate cineplex for the serious moviegoer. 14 movie screens surround a gigantic dome that seats 820 people and displays a screen that

expands from 80 to 180 ft. A spectacular sound system. Recent movies only. Don't be late—doors close 7min. after movies begin. Tickets $7.75-14.

■ **Grauman's Chinese Theatre,** 6925 Hollywood Blvd. (☎323-464-8111), between Highland and La Brea Ave. in Hollywood. Hype to the hilt. For details, see **Hollywood Sights,** p. 891. Tickets $10, seniors and ages 3-12 $7; 1st show of the day $7.50.

LIVE THEATER & MUSIC

L.A.'s live theater scene does not hold the weight of New York's Broadway, but its 115 "equity waiver theaters" (under 100 seats) offer dizzying, eclectic choices for theatergoers, who can also view small productions in art galleries, universities, parks, and even garages. Browse listings in the *L.A. Weekly* to find out what's hot. L.A.'s music venues range from small clubs to massive amphitheaters. The **Wiltern Theater** (☎213-380-5005) shows alterna-rock/folk acts. The **Hollywood Palladium** (☎323-962-7600) is of comparable size with 3500 seats. Mid-sized acts head for the **Universal Amphitheater** (☎818-777-3931). Huge indoor sports arenas, such as the **Great Western Forum** (☎310-330-7300) and the newer **Staples Center** (☎213-742-7100), double as concert halls for big acts. Few dare to play at the 100,000-seat **Los Angeles Memorial Coliseum and Sports Arena;** only U2, Depeche Mode, Guns 'n' Roses, and the Warped Tour have filled the stands in recent years. Call Ticketmaster (☎213-480-3232) to purchase tickets for any of these venues.

■ **Hollywood Bowl,** 2301 N. Highland Ave. (☎323-850-2000), in Hollywood. The premier outdoor music venue in L.A. Free open house rehearsals by the Philharmonic and visiting performers usually Tu and Th at 10:30am. Parking at the Bowl is limited and pricey at $11. It's better to park at one of the lots away from the Bowl and take a shuttle (parking $5, shuttle $2.50; departs every 10-20min. starting 1½hr. before showtime).

Pasadena Playhouse, 39 S. El Molino Ave. (☎626-356-7529; www.pasadenaplayhouse.org), in Pasadena. California's premier theater and historical landmark has spawned Broadway careers and productions. Shows Su 2 and 7pm, Tu-F 8pm, Sa 5 and 9pm. Tickets $35-60. Call for rush tickets.

Geffen Playhouse, 10886 LeConte Ave. (☎310-208-5454), in Westwood. Off-Broadway and Tony award-winning shows. Tickets $34-46. Student rush tickets ($10) 1hr. before shows.

SPORTS

Exposition Park and the often dangerous city of **Inglewood,** southwest of the park, are home to many sports teams. The **USC Trojans** play football at the **L.A. Memorial Coliseum,** 3911 S. Figueroa St. (☎213-740-4672), which seats over 100,000 spectators. It is the only stadium in the world to have hosted the Olympic Games twice. Basketball's doormat, the **L.A. Clippers** (☎213-742-7500), and the dazzling 2000-02 NBA Champion **L.A. Lakers** (☎310-426-6000) play at the new **Staples Center,** 1111 S. Figueroa St. (☎213-742-7100, box office 213-742-7340), along with the **L.A. Kings** hockey team (☎888-546-4752) and the city's women's basketball team, the **L.A. Sparks** (☎310-330-3939). Call Ticketmaster (☎213-480-3232) for tickets. **Elysian Park,** about 3 mi. northeast of downtown, curves around the northern portion of Chavez Ravine, home of **Dodger Stadium** and the popular **L.A. Dodgers** baseball team. Single-game tickets ($6-21) are a hot commodity during the April-October season, especially if the Dodgers are playing well. Call ☎323-224-1448 for more ticketing info.

SHOPPING

In L.A., shopping isn't just a practical necessity; it's a way of life. Many Southland shopping complexes are open-air. The hub of the shop-'til-you-drop spots is the Westside. **图Book Soup,** 8818 Sunset Blvd., in West Hollywood, has a maze of new books, with especially strong film, architecture, poetry, and travel sections. The **Addendum** next door is a gem for bargain-shopping book lovers, featuring discounts of up to 50%. (☎310-659-3110; www.booksoup.com. Main store open daily 9am-11pm. Addendum open daily noon-8pm.) **图Samuel French Bookshop,** 7623 Sunset Blvd., in Hollywood, can prep you for your audition at this haven for entertainment industry wisdom, filled with acting directories, TV and film reference books, trade papers, and a vast selection of plays and screenplays. (☎323-876-0570. Open M-F 10am-6pm, Sa 10am-5pm.) Independent record store **图Amoeba Music,** 6400 Sunset Blvd. in Hollywood, carries all genres and titles, including a lot of underground music. Take advantage of daily $1 clearance sales. (☎323-245-6400; www.amoebamusic.com. Open M-Sa 10:30am-11pm, Su 11am-9pm.) For novelties, **图Dudley Doo-Right Emporium,** 8200 Sunset Blvd.,

in West Hollywood, is cluttered with Rocky and Bullwinkle memorabilia. (☎323-656-6550. Open Tu, Th, Sa 11am-5pm. No credit cards.)

FOOD

Los Angeles elevates chain restaurants to heights unknown. For the supreme burger-and-fries experience, try the beloved **图In-N-Out Burger.** The current craze is lard- and cholesterol-free "healthy Mexican"—**Baja Fresh** leads the pack. If you're looking to cook, **图Trader Joe's** specializes in budget gourmet food. (☎800-SHOP-TJS/746-7857 for locations. Most open daily 9am-9pm.) The **图Farmer's Market,** 6333 W. 3rd St. at Fairfax Ave., attracts 3 million people every year and has over 160 produce stalls, as well as international food booths, handicraft shops, and a juice bar.

HOLLYWOOD

图 The Griddle Cafe, 7916 Sunset Blvd. (☎323-874-0377), in West Hollywood. A popular brunch spot, the Griddle prides itself on breakfast creativity. Especially popular are the "Apple Cobbler French Toast" ($7) and "Black Magic" (Oreo crumb-filled flapjacks; $7). A 45min. wait is not uncommon on weekends. Open M-F 7am-3pm, Sa-Su 8am-3pm.

图 Duke's Coffee Shop, 8909 Sunset Blvd. (☎310-652-3100), in West Hollywood. Legendary Duke's is the best place to see hungry, hungover rockers slumped over tables. The walls are plastered with autographed album covers. Try "Sandy's Favorite" (green peppers, potatoes, and scrambled eggs; $7.25). Entrees $5-11. Attendant parking $1. Open M-F 7:30am-8:30pm, Sa-Su 8am-3:30pm.

Roscoe's House of Chicken and Waffles, 1514 Gower St. (☎323-466-7453), at the corner of Sunset Blvd. Additional location at 5006 W. Pico Blvd. The down-home feel make this a popular spot. Try "1 succulent chicken breast and 1 delicious waffle" ($7). Be prepared to wait (30min.-1hr.) on weekends. Open Su-Th 8:30am-midnight, F-Sa 8:30am-4am.

Pink's Hot Dog Stand, 709 N. La Brea Ave. (☎323-931-4223; www.pinkshollywood.com), at Melrose Ave. An institution since 1939, Pink's serves up chili-slathered goodness in a bun. The aroma of chili and freshly cooked dogs draws crowds far into the night. Try the special "Ozzy Osbourne Spicy Dog" for $5. Chili dogs $2.40; chili fries $2.20. Open Su-Th 9:30am-2am, F-Sa 9:30am-3am. Cash only.

VENICE & THE SOUTH BAY

▨ **Rose Cafe and Market,** 220 Rose Ave. (☎310-399-0711), at Main St. Gigantic walls painted with roses, local art, industrial architecture, and a gift shop might make you think this is a museum, but the colorful cuisine is the main display. Healthy deli specials, including sandwiches ($6-8) and salads ($6-8) available from 11:30am. Limited menu after 3pm. Open M-F 7am-5:30pm, Sa 8am-6pm, Su 8am-5pm.

▨ **Aunt Kizzy's Back Porch,** 4325 Glencoe Ave. (☎310-578-1005), in a huge strip mall at Mindanao Way in Marina Del Rey. A little slice of Southern heaven, offering smothered pork chops with cornbread and veggies. Save room for sweet potato pie ($3). Dinner $12-13. Brunch buffet Su 11am-3pm ($13). Open Su-Th 11am-9pm, F-Sa 11am-11pm.

▨ **Wahoo's Fish Tacos,** 1129 Manhattan Ave. (☎310-796-1044), in Manhattan Beach. A small but quality chain, each Wahoo's pays homage to surfing. Famous for cheap, flavorful Mexican grub. Many swear by the teriyaki steak Maui Bowl ($7). 25 SoCal locations. Open M-Sa 11am-10pm, Su 11am-9pm.

BEVERLY HILLS

▨ **Al Gelato,** 806 S. Robertson Blvd. (☎310-659-8069), between Wilshire and Olympic St. Popular among the theater crowd, this homemade gelato spot also does pasta with a delicious basil tomato sauce. For desert, stick to the gelato ($3.75-5.75) and made-to-order cannoli ($4.50). Open Su, Tu, Th 10am-midnight, F-Sa 10am-1am. No credit cards.

Nate 'n Al Delicatessen, 414 N. Beverly Dr. (☎310-274-0101; www.natenal.com), near Little Santa Monica Blvd. For 55 years, this delicatessen has been serving up hand-pressed latkes ($8.75), blintzes ($9), and Reubens ($11.50). Open daily 7am-9pm.

Mulberry Street Pizzeria, 240 S. Beverly Dr. (☎310-247-8100) and 347 N. Canon Dr., in Beverly Hills. Great pizza by the slice; the wide, flat pizza is among the best anywhere. Slice $2.50-4, whole pies $15-26. Open Su-W 11am-11pm, Th-Sa 11am-midnight.

WESTWOOD & THE WILSHIRE DISTRICT

▨ **Sandbag's Gourmet Sandwiches,** 1134 Westwood Blvd. (☎310-208-1133), in Westwood. Additional locations at 11640 San Vicente Blvd. (☎310-207-4888), in Brentwood and 9497 Santa Monica Blvd. (☎310-786-7878), in Beverly Hills. A healthy, cheap lunch comes with a chocolate cookie. Try the "Sund-

owner" (turkey, herb stuffing, lettuce, and cranberries). Sandwiches $5.75. Open daily 9am-4pm.

Gypsy Cafe, 940 Broxton Ave. (☎310-824-2119), next to Diddie Riese. Modeled after a sister spot in Paris, this cafe's fare is more Italian than French (penne cacciatore $8.25), and its mood is more Turkish than Italian (hookahs $10 per hr.). The tomato soup ($5) is famous throughout Westwood. Open Su-Th 7am-2am, F-Sa 7am-3am.

DOWNTOWN

▨ **Philippe, The Original,** 1001 N. Alameda St. (☎213-628-3781; www.philippes.com), 2 blocks north of Union Station. A long-time fixture of downtown, Philippe's is a popular lunch eatery. Choose pork, beef, ham, turkey, or lamb ($4.70-4.70). Top it off with pie ($2.65) and coffee ($0.09—no, that's not a typo). Free parking. Open daily 6am-10pm.

▨ **The Pantry,** 877 S. Figueroa St. (☎213-972-9279). Since 1924, it hasn't closed once—not for the earthquakes, not for the 1992 riots (when it served as a National Guard outpost), and not even when a taxicab punched through the front wall. There aren't even locks on the doors. Owned by former L.A. mayor Richard Riordan. Known for its large portions, free cole slaw, and fresh sourdough bread. Giant breakfast specials $6. Open 24hr. No credit cards.

PASADENA

Eateries line **Colorado Blvd.** from Los Robles Ave. to Orange Grove Blvd. in Old Town. The concentration of restaurants and sights around Colorado Blvd. make it Pasadena's answer to Santa Monica's Third St. Promenade. From Downtown, take I-110 North (Pasadena Fwy). In Pasadena, I-110 turns into the Arroyo Pkwy. Continue north and take a right onto Colorado Blvd.

▨ **Fair Oaks Pharmacy and Soda Fountain,** 1516 Mission St. (☎626-799-1414), at Fair Oaks Ave. in South Pasadena. From Colorado Blvd., go south 1 mi. on Fair Oaks Ave. to Mission St. This old-fashioned drug store, with soda fountain and lunch counter, has been serving travelers on Rte. 66 since 1915; now, a bit of Pasadena's upscale boutique flavor has crept in. Hand-dipped shakes and malts $4.25. Deli sandwiches $5.50. Patty melts $6. Soda fountain open M-F 9am-9pm, Sa 9am-10pm, Su 11am-8pm. Lunch counter open M-F 11am-9pm, Sa 11am-10pm, Su 11am-8pm.

PACIFIC COAST

Pita! Pita!, 927 E. Colorado Blvd. (☎626-356-0106), 1 block east of Lake Ave. Never has the pita deserved so many exclamation points. Free appetizers of green olives, yellow pepper, and tasty toasted pita. Spicy chicken pita $6. Lamb kebab $6. Open Su-Th 11am-9pm, F-Sa 11am-10pm.

ACCOMMODATIONS

In choosing where to stay, the first consideration should be location. Those looking for a tan should choose lodgings in Venice, Santa Monica or the South Bay. Sightseers will be better off in Hollywood or the more expensive (but nicer) Westside. Listed prices do not include L.A.'s **14% hotel tax.**

HOLLYWOOD

■ **Hollywood Bungalows International Youth Hostel,** 2775 W. Cahuenga Blvd. (☎888-259-9990; www.hollywoodbungalows.com), just north of the Hollywood Bowl in the Hollywood Hills. This recently renovated hostel cultivates a wacky summer camp atmosphere. Spacious rooms and nightly jam sessions. Outdoor pool, billiards, weight room, big screen TV, and mini-diner. Cable in some rooms. Internet $2 per 10min. Breakfast $3.50. Dinner $10. Lockers $0.25. Linen and parking included. Laundry (wash $1.25, dry $0.75). Check-in 24hr. 6- to 10-bed co-ed dorms $15-19; private doubles $59.

■ **USA Hostels Hollywood,** 1624 Schrader Blvd. (☎323-462-3777 or 800-524-6783; www.usahostels.com), south of Hollywood Blvd., west of Cahuenga Blvd. Crawling with young travelers, this lime-green and blue-dotted chain hostel is filled with energy and organized fun. Special events nightly. Passport or proof of travel required. To use lockers, bring your own lock or buy one for $0.50. Linen and all-you-can-eat pancakes included. Free street parking or parking lot $4.50 per day. Dinner $4. 6- to 8-bed dorms with private bath $15-21; private rooms for 2-4 people $39-52.

Flamingo Hotel, 1921 N. Highland Ave. (☎323-876-6544), just north of Hollywood Blvd. A peaceful 8-story maze of rooms offering access to sights. Private rooms well-furnished and large. Lounge with free billiards, TV, and video games. Internet $1 per 10min. Laundry (wash $1, dry $0.75). 4-bed dorms $15-19; private rooms $40-80.

BEVERLY HILLS & WESTWOOD

■ **Orbit Hotel and Hostel,** 7950 Melrose Ave. (☎323-655-1510 or 877-672-4887; www.orbithotel.com), 1 block west of Fairfax Ave. in West Hollywood. Opened by 2 young L.A. locals several years ago,

Orbit sets new standards for swank budget living. Fashion-conscious furniture, spacious retro kitchen, big-screen TV lounge, small courtyard, and late-night party room. Dorms only accept international students with passport. Breakfast and lockers included. Free TV show tickets. 6-bed dorms $20; private rooms for up to 4 from $55.

Hotel Claremont, 1044 Tiverton Ave. (☎310-208-5957 or 800-266-5957), in Westwood Village near UCLA. Pleasant and inexpensive. Still owned by the same family that built it 60 years ago. Clean rooms, ceiling fans, and private baths. Fridge and microwave next to a pleasant Victorian-style TV lounge. Reservations recommended, especially in June. Singles $50; doubles $56; rooms with 2 beds for up to 4 $65.

The Beverly Hills Reeves Hotel, 120 S. Reeves Dr. (☎310-271-3006; www.bhreeves.com). Cheap stays are hard to come by in Beverly Hills, but this recently renovated mansion near Rodeo Dr. offers budget and beauty. Rooms with A/C, TV, microwave, and fridge. Continental breakfast included. Parking $6. Rooms $50, with bath $69. Weekly rooms $250/$349.

VENICE & THE SOUTH BAY

■ **Los Angeles Surf City Hostel,** 26 Pier Ave. (☎310-798-2323), in Hermosa Beach's Pier Plaza. Young, mostly international clientele. Downstairs is the Beach Club, a popular bar and nightclub. Showers, Internet, kitchen, TV lounge, and downstairs bar. Includes boogie boards, breakfast, and linen. Passport or driver's license required for all guests. Laundry. Key deposit $10. 28-night max. stay; 3-day max. stay for U.S. citizens. No parking. Reservations recommended. 4-bunk dorms May-Nov. $19; Dec.-Apr. $15.50. Private rooms $48.

Venice Beach Hostel, 1515 Pacific Ave. (☎310-452-3052; www.caprica.com/venice-beach-hostel), just north of Windward Ave. in Venice. Central location, friendly staff, and lively atmosphere make this a popular hostel. A full kitchen, 2 enormous lounges, and 10 super-comfy couches encourage mingling. Lockers, storage rooms, and linen included. Laundry (wash $1, dry $0.75). Security deposit $25-100. Internet $1 per 10min. 4- to 10-bed dorms $19-22; singles and doubles $55. Weekly discounts available.

NIGHTLIFE

LATE-NIGHT RESTAURANTS

Given the extremely short shelf-life and unpredictability of the L.A. club scene, late-night restaurants have become reliable hangouts.

■ **Canter's,** 419 N. Fairfax Ave. (☎323-651-2030), in **Fairfax,** north of Beverly Blvd. An L.A. institution and the soul of historically Jewish Fairfax since 1931. Grapefruit-sized matzoh ball in chicken broth $4.50. Sandwiches $8-9. Visit the Kibbitz Room for nightly free rock, blues, jazz, and a chance to spot Lenny Kravitz in the audience. Beer $2.50. Open 24hr.

■ **Fred 62,** 1850 N. Vermont Ave. (☎323-667-0062), in **Los Feliz.** "Eat now, dine later." Look for a booth with headrests. Hip, edgy East L.A. crowd's jukebox selections rock the house. The apple waffles ($4.62—all prices end in .62 and .97) are divine. Open 24hr.

■ **The Rainbow Bar and Grill,** 9015 Sunset Blvd. (☎310-278-4232; http://rainbowbarandgrill.com), in **West Hollywood,** next to the Roxy. Dark red vinyl booths, dim lighting, loud music, and colorful characters set the scene. Marilyn Monroe met Joe DiMaggio on a blind (and apparently, rather silent) date here. Brooklyn-quality pizza $6. Calamari $8. Open M-F 11am-2am, Sa-Su 5pm-2am.

Jerry's Famous Deli has multiple locations, including 8701 Beverly Blvd. (☎310-289-1811), at corner of San Vicente Ave. in **West Hollywood;** 10925 Weyburn Ave. (☎310-208-3354), in **Westwood;** and 12655 Ventura Blvd. (☎818-980-4245), in **Studio City.** An L.A. deli with red leather and sky-high prices. Note the menu's height—Jerry reportedly wanted "the longest menu possible while still maintaining structural integrity." Something here is bound to satisfy your 4am craving. Entrees $13-15. Open 24hr.

BARS

The 1996 film *Swingers* has had a homogenizing effect on L.A.'s hipsters. Grab your retro-70s polyester shirts, sunglasses, and throwback Cadillac convertibles, 'cause if you can't beat them, you have to swing with them, daddy-o. Unless otherwise specified, bars in California are 21+.

■ **North,** 8029 Sunset Blvd. (☎323-654-1313), between Laurel Ave. and Crescent Heights Ave. in **West Hollywood.** A classic L.A. undercover bar where the entrance is hard to find and you need to be "in the know" to know about it. Good-looking people buy good-looking drinks and dance until late. Drinks $6. DJ spins hip-hop and house Th-Sa nights. Open daily 6pm-1am.

■ **Miyagi's,** 8225 Sunset Blvd. (☎323-650-3524), on Sunset Strip. With 3 levels, 7 sushi bars ($5-7), 6 liquor bars, and indoor waterfalls and streams, this Japanese restaurant, bar, lounge, and hip-hop dance club is a Strip hot spot. "*Sake* bomb, *sake* bomb, *sake* bomb" $4.50. Open daily 5:30pm-2am.

■ **3 of Clubs,** 1123 N. Vine St. (☎323-462-6441), at the corner of Santa Monica Blvd. in **Hollywood.** In a small strip mall beneath a "Bargain Clown Mart" sign, this bar is famous for appearing in *Swingers.* Live bands Th, DJ F-Sa. Open daily 7pm-2am.

Beauty Bar, 1638 Cahuenga Blvd. (☎323-464-7676), in **Hollywood.** Where else can you get a manicure and henna tattoo while sipping a cocktail and schmoozing? It's like getting ready for the prom again, except that the drinking starts before. Drinks like "Perm" are $8. DJ nightly 10pm. Open Su-W 9pm-2am, Th-Sa 6pm-2am.

CLUBS

With the highest number of bands per capita in the world and more streaming in every day, L.A. is famous for its (often expensive) club scene. Coupons in *L.A. Weekly* and those handed out by the clubs can save you a bundle. To enter the club scene, it's best to be at least 21 (and/or beautiful) to avoid a cover charge for a less desirable venue. All clubs are 21+ unless otherwise noted.

■ **The Derby,** 4500 Los Feliz Blvd. (☎323-663-8979; www.the-derby.com), at the corner of Hillhurst Ave. in **Los Feliz.** Still jumpin' and jivin' with the kings of swing. Ladies, grab your snoods; many dress the 40s part. Italian fare from Louise's Trattoria next door. Full bar. Free swing lessons Sa 8, 9pm. Cover $5-12. Open daily 7:30-2am.

■ **Largo,** 432 N. Fairfax Ave. (☎323-852-1073), between Melrose Ave. and Beverly Blvd. in **West Hollywood.** Intimate sit-down (or, if you get there late, leanback) club. Rock, pop, and folk, and comedy acts. Cover $2-12. Open M-Sa 8:30pm-2am.

Roxy, 9009 Sunset Blvd. (☎310-278-9457), on **Sunset Strip.** Known as the "Sizzling Showcase," it's one of the best-known Sunset Strip clubs. Bruce Springsteen got his start here. Live rock, blues, alternative, and occasional hip-hop. Many big tour acts. All ages. Cover varies. Opens 8pm.

GAY & LESBIAN NIGHTLIFE

While the Sunset Strip features all the nightlife any Jack and Jill could desire, gay men and lesbians may find life more interesting a short tumble down the hill on **Santa Monica Blvd.** Still, many ostensibly straight clubs have gay nights; check *L.A. Weekly* or contact the Gay and Lesbian Community Services Center. Free weekly magazine *fab!* lists happenings in the gay and lesbian community. **Motherload,** 8499 Santa Monica Blvd. (☎310-659-9700), and **Trunks,** 8809 Santa Monica

Blvd. (☎310-652-1015), are two of the friendliest bars. Neither has a cover and both are open until 2am. All clubs are 21+ unless otherwise noted.

▨ **Abbey Cafe,** 692 N. Robertson Blvd. (☎310-289-8410), at Santa Monica Blvd. in **West Hollywood.** 6 candlelit rooms, 2 huge bars, a large outdoor patio, and a hall of private booths make this beautiful lounge and dance club the best place around. Open daily 8am-2am.

Micky's, 8857 Santa Monica Blvd. (☎310-657-1176), in **West Hollywood.** Huge dance floor of delectable men. When other bars close, head to Micky's for another 2hr. of grooving. Music is mostly electronic dance. M night drag shows. Happy hour M-F 5-9pm. Cover $3-5. Open Su-Th noon-2am, F-Sa noon-4am.

🔼 LEAVING L.A.
Hop on **I-10 West,** which drops off in Santa Monica at **Rte. 1.**

SANTA MONICA

The most striking characteristic of Santa Monica is its efficiency. It is safe, clean, and unpretentious—and you can usually find a parking spot. Its residential areas, once populated by screen superstars, are just blocks away from its main districts. The Third Street Promenade is the city's most popular spot to shop by day and schmooze by night, and the nearby beaches are always packed. But Santa Monica is known as much for its shoreside scene as its shore; the promenade and the pier themselves are popular destinations.

┌─────────────────────────┐
│ **VITAL STATS**
│
│ **Population:** 87,000
│
│ **Visitor Info: Santa Monica Visitors Center,** 395 Santa Monica Pl. (☎310-393-7593), 2nd fl. Open daily 10am-6pm.
│
│ **Internet Access: Santa Monica Public Library,** 1234 5th St. (☎310-451-8859). Temporary location; main branch under renovation until 2006. Open M-Th 10am-9pm, F-Sa 10am-5:30pm.
│
│ **Post Office:** 1248 5th St. (☎310-576-6786), at Arizona Blvd. Open M-F 9am-6pm, Sa 9am-3pm.
│ **Postal Code:** 90401.
└─────────────────────────┘

🔳 GETTING AROUND

Rte. 66 enters Santa Monica from the east on **Santa Monica Blvd.** Just north of the boulevard, the **Santa Monica Freeway (I-10)** runs west from L.A. to the **Pacific Coast Hwy.** Car-free **Third St. Promenade** heads north from **Broadway** to **Wilshire Blvd.** Much of Santa Monica is best seen by foot or bike, **park** in one of the lots near the Third St. Promenade; most are free for 2hr. and then $1 each additional 30min. The **Santa Monica Place Mall** has free parking for up to 3hr. ($3 flat fee after 5pm). Downtown streets have meters ($0.50 per hr.), and all-day beach parking is usually available ($6-10).

◉ SIGHTS

Filled with gawkers and hawkers, the area on and around the carnival pier is the hub of tourist activity. The fun spills over to lively **Third St. Promenade.** Farther inland, along Main St. and beyond, are galleries, design shops, and museums.

THIRD STREET PROMENADE. Cars are prohibited on this ultra-popular three-block stretch of mosaic art tiles, fashionable stores, movie theaters, and lively restaurants. The Promenade truly heats up when the sun sets, the ocean breeze kicks in, and the ivy-mesh dinosaur sculptures. On Wednesday and Saturday mornings, the area becomes a **Farmers Market** selling flowers and produce, with Saturdays featuring exclusively organic products. *(Between Broadway and Wilshire in downtown Santa Monica. Exit off 4th St. from I-10.)*

SANTA MONICA PIER & PACIFIC PARK. The famed pier is the heart of Santa Monica Beach and home to the carnivalesque Pacific Park. Adrenaline addicts over 4 ft. tall can twist and turn on the five-story West Coaster or soar 100 ft. above the ocean in the first solar-powered Ferris wheel. *(☎310-458-8900; http://santamonicapier.org. Pier open 24hr. Park open summer Su-Th 11am-11pm, F-Sa 11am-12:30am; in winter hours vary, so call ahead.)*

🍴 FOOD

Giant, colorful table umbrellas sprouting from sidewalk patios along Third St. Promenade and Ocean Ave. punctuate Santa Monica's upscale eating scene. Menus nod to (deep-pocketed) health buffs, offering organic and vegetarian choices.

▨ **Fritto Misto,** 601 Colorado Ave. (☎310-458-2829), at 6th St. "Neighborhood Italian Cafe" with cheery waitstaff lets you create your own pasta (from $6). Vegetarian entrees $8-12. Open M-Th 11:30am-10pm, F-Sa 11:30am-10:30pm, Su 11:30am-9:30pm.

Big Dean's "Muscle-In" Cafe, 1615 Ocean Front Walk (☎310-393-2666). You don't need to venture far for the "burger that made Santa Monica famous" ($7). Veggie burgers $5. Happy hour M-F 4-8pm. Open M-F 10am-dark, Sa-Su 10:30am-dark.

Mariasol, 401 Santa Monica Pier (☎310-917-5050). Prime sunset views accompany your meal. Friendly *mariachi* band. Locals recommend the *campechana* ($12), a combination of shrimp, octopus calamari, and ceviche. Appetizers $6-14. Entrees $9-15. Open Su-Th 10am-10pm, F-Sa 10am-11pm. Reservations recommended for 2nd fl. dining room.

Bread & Porridge, 2315 Wilshire Blvd. (☎310-453-4941). Prides itself on exceptional service and an egalitarian division of labor—dishwashers, busboys, servers, cashiers, and cooks all rotate jobs and share tips. Pancakes $6-8. Omelettes $10. Sandwiches and entrees $8-13. Open M-F 7am-2pm, Sa-Su 7am-3pm.

ACCOMMODATIONS

Accommodations in Santa Monica range from cheap oceanfront hostels to expensive oceanfront hotels. The closer you stay to the beach, the more you dish out. Depending on the hostel/hotel, the tax on your room may be 8.5% or 14%. The best budget option in Santa Monica is the new and airy **Los Angeles/Santa Monica Hostel,** 1436 2nd St., which has prime access to the beach and Santa Monica hot spots. The hostel sponsors tours and activities, and has Internet access, video games, nightly movie showings, library, self-service kitchen, laundry, and a travel store. (☎310-393-9913. Check-in 2pm-midnight. Dorms $27, nonmembers $30; private rooms from $60.) The rooms of the **Pacific Sands Motel,** 1515 Ocean Ave., are at the epicenter of what's happening. (☎310-395-6133. Rooms from $105.) Similarly pleasant rooms are available at the **Ocean Lodge Hotel,** 1667 Ocean Ave., just a block from the beach. (☎310-451-4146. Singles from $150; doubles from $175.)

APPROACHING MALIBU
From **Rte. 1** turn right onto **Malibu Canyon Rd.**

MALIBU

North of Santa Monica along PCH, the cityscape gives way to appealing stretches of sandy, sewage-free shoreline. Stop along the coast and you may see dolphin pods swimming close to shore, or at least pods of surfers trying to catch a wave.

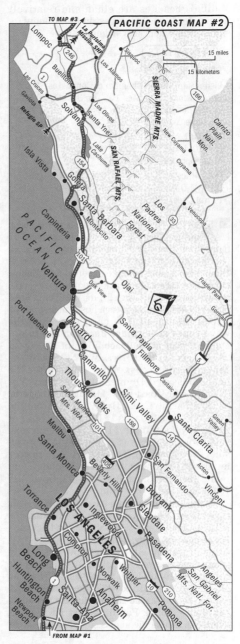

PACIFIC COAST

Malibu's beaches are clean and relatively uncrowded— easily the best in L.A. County for surfers, sunbathers, and swimmers alike.

(VITAL STATS)

Population: 12,500

Visitor Info: Malibu Chamber of Commerce, 23805 Stuart Ranch Rd., Ste. 100. (☎310-456-9025; www.ci.malibu.ca.us). Follow signs to City Hall; it's in the same complex of buildings.

Internet Access: 23519 W. Civic Center Way (☎310-456-6438). Open M-Tu 10am-8pm, W-Th 10am-6pm, F-Sa 10am-5pm.

Post Office: 23648 Pacific Coast Hwy. (☎310-317-0328). Open M-F 9am-5pm, 9:30am-1:30pm.

Postal Code: 90265

◨ **SIGHTS.** The prime spot in Malibu is **Zuma,** L.A. County's largest beach, with immaculate bathrooms. (Parking $2; on an off day, check for free parking on the shore just south at Point Dume.) For a more intimate experience of Malibu, check out **Escondido Beach**—look for the small brown coastal access sign 2½ mi. north of Pepperdine. **Will Rogers State Beach** hosts an annual volleyball tournament. You can jet through the wave tubes at **Surfrider Beach,** a section of **Malibu Lagoon State Beach** north of the pier at 23000 Pacific Coast Hwy.. Walk there via the **Zonker Harris Access Way** (named after the beach-obsessed Doonesbury character) at 22700 Pacific Coast Hwy. **Malibu Ocean Sports,** 22935½ Pacific Coast Hwy., across from the pier, rents surfboards ($10 per hr., $25 per day), kayaks (single $15/$35; tandem $20/$50), boogie boards ($12 per day), and wetsuits ($10 per day). The store offers surfing lessons ($100 for 2hr. lesson and full-day gear rental) and tours. (☎310-456-6302. Open M-F 10am-6pm, Sa-Su 9am-6pm.)

Hike at **Leo Carrillo State Park,** 35000 W. Pacific Coast Hwy., which has some beautiful trails on hills above the ocean (☎818-880-0350. $4-day use). **Pepperdine University,** 24255 Pacific Coast Hwy. (www.pepperdine.edu), rising above the coast in sunny conservative glory, offers free tours of the campus (☎310-506-4000) as well as the Weisman Museum of Art (☎310-506-4851; free). The sprawling, red-roofed **Malibu Lagoon Museum and Adamson House,** 23852 Pacific Coast Hwy. #342, overlooks the Pacific in classic Californian style.

The historic home, now owned by the state, serves as a museum and is open for public tours. (☎310-456-8432. Open W-Sa 11am-3pm; last tour 2pm. $3, under 17 free.)

◨◨ **FOOD & ACCOMMODATIONS.** Cheap eats are hard to come by at Malibu's shoreside restaurants, which charge as much for their view as for their food. **Malibu Chicken,** 22935 Pacific Coast Hwy., downstairs from Malibu Ocean Sports (see p. 902), has sandwiches named after old beach-movie idols, like "Gidget" (grilled chicken breast; $8) and "Big Kahuna" (chicken breast, eggplant, and feta; $8). (☎310-456-0365. Open daily 11:30am-9pm.) A roadside shack feeding barefoot surfers, **Neptune's Net Seafood,** 42505 Pacific Coast Hwy., offers baskets of fried seafood ($10). The indoor tables get dingy but you can cross the street and eat overlooking the sea. Lori Petty from *Point Break* sometimes waitresses here. (☎310-457-3095. Open daily 10:30am-11pm.)

Motels in Malibu pay the same prices for real estate as the multi-million dollar stars, so the best budget option is to head to L.A. or to camp. **Leo Carrillo** has 135 sites in a lot across the highway from the beach. A better option is **Sycamore Canyon,** on the beach 19 mi. northwest of Malibu in Point Magu State Park. (☎805-488-5223. Sites $12.)

↱ **LEAVING MALIBU**
Once again, leaving town is as simple as getting on **Rte. 1 North.**

OXNARD. A sanctuary of sand awaits at **Oxnard State Beach Park,** about 5 mi. south of Ventura, which is quiet and peaceful except on weekends. Oxnard celebrates its farming roots and 6600 berry acres each May with a delightful **Strawberry Festival** (www.strawberry-fest.org; ☎888-288-9242). A great pit stop is 24hr. **USA Gasoline,** 2251 Oxnard Blvd. (☎805-988-3933), with ultra-cheap fuel, an ATM, and clean restrooms.

↱ **APPROACHING VENTURA**
Rte. 1 and **U.S. 101** merge heading into Ventura. Exit and turn right onto **S. California St.,** following it 3 blocks to **Main St.**

VENTURA
The Central Coast's southernmost city, Ventura is blessed with great weather and easygoing charm. Visitors to "California's Rising Star" flock to the recently revitalized downtown,

now home to numerous restaurants, shops, museums, galleries, and an abundance of thrift stores. A cultural district for performers of all genres is emerging, though most of the culture goes inside after dark. Ventura Harbor, a bustling center of activity with over 30 restaurants and shops, concerts, and festivals, lies 10min. from downtown by car. To locate all that Ventura has to offer, pick up the historic walking tour map from the Visitors Bureau.

⌐ GETTING AROUND. Ventura lies 30 mi. south of Santa Barbara and 70 mi. north of L.A. off U.S. 101. **Main St.** runs east-west in the historic downtown area on the east side of town, intersecting with **California St.,** which runs to the pier. **Ventura Harbor** lies south along the coast; from downtown, take Harbor Blvd. to **Spinnaker Dr.**

◉◪ SIGHTS AND BEACHES. Billed as California's "Gold Coast," the clean beaches near Ventura roar with fantastic surf. **Emma Wood State Beach,** on Main St. (take State Beaches exit off U.S. 101), and **Oxnard State Beach Park,** about 5 mi. south of Ventura, are quiet and peaceful except on weekends. On the other hand, **San Buenaventura State Park,** at the end of

---

⌐ VITAL STATS

Population: 102,000

Visitors Info: Ventura Visitors Bureau, 89 S. California St. (☎805-648-2075 or 800-333-2989; www.ventura-usa.com). Open M-F 8:30am-5pm, Sa 9am-5pm, Su 10am-4pm.

Internet Access: E.P. Foster Library, 651 E. Main St. (☎805-648-2716). Open M-Th 10am-8pm, F-Sa 10am-5pm.

Post Office: 675 E. Santa Clara St. (☎800-275-8777). **Postal Code:** 93001

San Pedro St., entertains families and casual beach-goers with its volleyball courts and nearby restaurants. **Surfer's Point,** at the end of Figueroa St., has the best waves around, but novices should start at **McGrath State Beach,** about 1 mi. south of Ventura down Harbor Blvd. Be forewarned that the surfers tend to be territorial. Pick up insider surfing tips and Patagonia outlet gear at **Real Cheap Sports,** 36 W. Santa Clara St. (From Main St., go 1 block south on Ventura Ave. and turn right onto Santa Clara St. ☎805-650-1213. Open M-Sa 10am-6pm, Su 10am-5pm.) For info on surf sessions, call ☎805-648-2662 or check out www.surfclass.com.

SURF'S UP!

FROM THE ROAD

As a proud Michigander, I am always quick to assert that the Great Lakes *do* have beaches, but after surfing on the Pacific coast I must admit Lake Michigan's ripples simply don't count as waves.

I was a little intimidated as I approached my first surfing lesson and my instructor, Corey. It didn't help that he was a sculpted, bronze Adonis and I was a pasty, pudgy Casper. Nevertheless, I signed my life away on a release form and grabbed a 7 ft. board marked with the nicks and dents of novice surfers and, for all I knew, shark bites.

With the rush that comes only from jumping full-force into 55°F water, I paddled out into the oncoming waves. After a number of failed attempts, I was ready to conquer what would be the last wave of the day. I was shooting fast on a wall of water, clutching my board for dear life, until it dawned on me to attempt standing up and maybe even some kind of neat backflip that would make the girls swoon. I was crouched and ready to join the ranks of surfing legends. I was nearly standing. I was exhilarated. I was...quickly head over heels in the swirl of the ocean.

I emerged (eventually) from the arms of the sea, exhausted and physically drained, but filled with a respect for surfers and a desire to hit the waves again—if only to win back my self-respect.

—*Brian J. Emeott*

Inland from Ventura Harbor on Olivas Park Dr. is the **Olivas Adobe.** The restored 1847 home sits on almost 5000 acres of land that the Mexican army gave to Raymundo Olivas for services rendered. The house is decorated in period furnishings and is a tribute to the early rancho period of Ventura's history. Olivias was not only one of the richest ranchers in California, but also an early host to the budget traveler; next to visitors' beds, Raymundo placed bowls of coins from which guests could draw some pocket change. (From U.S. 101, take the Telephone Ave. Exit south to Olivas Park Ave. and turn right. ☎805-644-4346. Open Sa-Su noon-4pm. Free.) **Mission San Buenaventura,** 211 E. Main St., still functions as a parish church, although it also houses a tiny museum of treasures from Father Junípero Serra's order. (☎805-643-4318. Open M-F 10am-5pm, Sa 9am-5pm, Su 10am-4pm. Suggested donation $1.) Across the street is the **Museum of History and Art,** 100 E. Main St., which has one permanent and two rotating exhibits. Among the stellar works are over 200 George Stuart Historical Figures, an acclaimed collection of small-scale sculptures of people from world history that George Stuart, a historian, created to accompany his lectures. (☎805-653-0323; www.vcmha.org. Open Su and Tu-Sa 10am-5pm. $4, seniors $3, ages 5-17 $1, under 5 free.)

⚑ FOOD. Affordable restaurants cluster along **Main St.** in the heart of historic downtown. **Franky's,** 456 E. Main St., between California and Oak St., is a Ventura institution, showcasing local art on the walls and offering healthy, delectable pita pockets ($7.50) and turkey burgers ($6.40) to wash down with jam jars of soda. (☎805-648-6282; www.frankysplace.com. Open daily 7am-3pm.) **Top Hat,** 299 E. Main St., at Palm St., is a roadside shack serving chili cheeseburgers ($2.15), hot dogs ($1), and fries ($1) to a local crowd. (☎805-643-9696. Open Tu-Sa 10am-6pm.) **Jonathan's at Peirano's,** 204 E. Main St., is a popular Mediterranean spot. Its beautiful patio is adjacent to a well-manicured park and large fountain. (☎805-648-4853; www.jonathansatpeiranos.com. Lunch entrees $9-15. Dinner entrees $12-25. Open Su 5:30-9pm, Tu-Th 11:30am-2:30pm and 5:30-9:30pm, F-Sa 11:30am-2:30pm and 5:30-10pm.) If the desire for pasta strikes, try warm **Capriccio Restaurant,** 298 Main St., at the corner of Palm St. Patio seating is available. (☎805-643-7115. Lunch entrees $7-10. Dinner entrees $8-15. Open M-Th 11:30am-8:45pm, F-Sa 11:30am-10pm, Su noon-8:45pm.)

⚑ ACCOMMODATIONS. Prior to its rejuvenation, Ventura was exclusively as a stopover point along the coastal routes. As a result, the city has a number of budget motels, particularly along **E. Thompson Ave.,** though many are decades old and in need of renovation. A good bet is the **Mission Bell Motel,** 3237 E. Main St., near Pacific View Mall. (☎805-642-6831. Rooms with queen-size or double beds $55.) For something fancier, try the **Clocktower Inn,** 181 E. Santa Clara St. Once a firehouse, the inn is near the heart of the city, and offers an outdoor jacuzzi. (From Main St., go south 1 block on California St. and turn right on Santa Clara. ☎805-652-0141. Some rooms have balconies and fireplaces. Rooms $73-160; in low season $69-120.)

Beach camping is in no short supply, but conditions lean toward the primitive. Make reservations through ReserveAmerica (☎800-444-7275) months in advance. **McGrath State Beach Campground,** south of town in Oxnard, has 174 campsites ($22).

◤ APPROACHING SANTA BARBARA
From Ventura, take **U.S. 101 North** (also known as **Ventura Fwy.**) for about 27 mi; exit at **Garden St.** to access downtown Santa Barbara.

SANTA BARBARA

Santa Barbara epitomizes worry-free living. The town is an enclave of wealth and privilege, true to its soap opera image, but in a less aggressive and flashy way than its SoCal counterparts. Spanish Revival architecture decorates hills that rise over the pedestrian district. Santa Barbara's golden beaches, museums, missions, and scenic drives make it a weekend escape for the rich and famous, and an attractive destination for surfers, artists, and backpackers alike.

▣ GETTING AROUND

Santa Barbara is 92 mi. northwest of L.A. and 27 mi. from Ventura on **Ventura Fwy. (U.S. 101).** Since the town is built along an east-west traverse of shoreline, its street grid is skewed. The beach lies at the south end of the city, and **State St.,** the main drag, runs northwest from the waterfront. All streets are designated east and west from State St. The major east-west

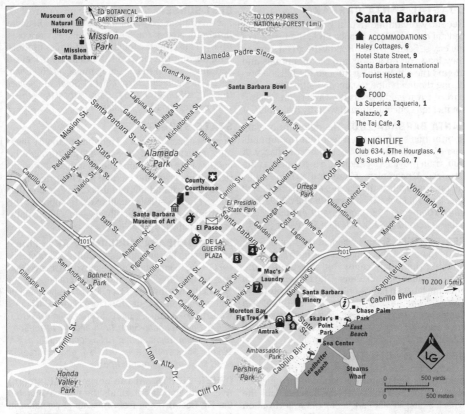

Santa Barbara

🛏 **ACCOMMODATIONS**
Haley Cottages, **6**
Hotel State Street, **9**
Santa Barbara International
   Tourist Hostel, **8**

🍴 **FOOD**
La Superica Taqueria, **1**
Palazzio, **2**
The Taj Cafe, **3**

🍺 **NIGHTLIFE**
Club 634, **5** The Hourglass, **4**
Q's Sushi A-Go-Go, **7**

VITAL STATS

Population: 92,500

Visitor Info: Santa Barbara Visitor Information Center, 1 Garden St. (☎805-965-3021; www.santabarbaraca.com), at Cabrillo Blvd. across from the beach. Open July-Aug. M-Sa 9am-6pm, Su 10am-6pm; Sept.-Nov. and Feb.-June M-Sa 9am-5pm, Su 10am-5pm; Dec.-Jan. M-Sa 9am-4pm, Su 10am-4pm. Outdoor 24hr. computer kiosk.

Internet Access: Santa Barbara Public Library, 40 E. Anapamu St. (☎805-962-7653). Open M-Th 10am-9pm, F-Sa 10am-5:30pm, Su 1-5pm.

Post Office: 836 Anacapa St. (☎800-275-8777), 1 block east of State St. Open M-F 8am-6pm, Sa 9am-5pm. **Postal Code:** 93102.

arteries are U.S. 101 and **Cabrillo Blvd.;** U.S. 101, normally north-south, runs east-west between **Castillo St.** and **Hot Springs Rd.**

Parking is a problem in Santa Barbara. Although there is free street parking (except State St.), you'll more likely find a spot in one of the lots that are off State St. in both directions: the first 75min. (90min. farther from State) are free and then you pay $1 per hr. (Su free.)

🔄 SIGHTS

Santa Barbara is best explored in three sections—the beach and coast, swingin' State St., and the mountains. Essential to discovering local events and goings-on is the *Independent*, published every Thursday and available at city newsstands.

COASTAL SANTA BARBARA

Recently revamped, Santa Barbara's supreme coastal drive is along **Cabrillo Blvd.**, the first leg of the city's "Scenic Drive." Follow the green signs as they lead you on a loop into the mountains and around the city, winding through the hillside bordering the town along Alameda Padre Serra. This part of town is known as the "American Riviera" for its high concentration of wealthy residents.

SANTA BARBARA ZOO. The delightfully leafy habitat has such an open feel that the animals seem kept in captivity only by sheer lethargy. A mini-train provides a park tour. There's also a miniaturized African plain where giraffes stroll lazily, silhouetted against the Pacific. *(500 Niños Dr., off Cabrillo Blvd. from U.S. 101. ☎805-962-5339. Open daily 10am-5pm. $8, seniors and ages 2-12 $6, under 2 free. Train $1.50, children $1. Parking $2.)*

SEA CENTER. **Stearns Wharf,** at the foot of State St., is the oldest working pier on the West Coast, housing the newly renovated Sea Center and some restaurants and shops. The center is now a working lab with hands-on exhibits for visitors. *(At State St. and Cabrillo Blvd. ☎805-962-0885. Sea Center open daily 10am-5pm. Touch tank open daily noon-5pm. $4, seniors and ages 13-17 $3, ages 3-12 $2. First 1½hr. parking free on wharf.)*

BEACHES & ACTIVITIES. Santa Barbara's beaches are breathtaking, lined by flourishing palm trees and countless sailboats around the local harbor. **East** and **Leadbetter Beaches** flank the wharf. **Skater's Point Park,** along the waterfront on Cabrillo Blvd., south of Stearns Wharf, is a free park for skateboarders. Helmets and gear are required. **Beach Rentals** will rent beachgoers a **retro surrey:** a covered, Flintstone-esque bicycle. You and up to eight friends can cruise in style. *(22 State St. ☎805-966-6733. Surreys $15-28 per 2hr., depending on number of riders. Open daily 8am-8pm.)* **Beach House** rents surfboards and body boards plus all the necessary equipment. *(10 State St. ☎805-963-1281. Surfboards $7-35; body boards $4-16. Wetsuits $3-16. Credit card required.)* **Paddle Sports** offers kayak rentals and lessons. *(10 State St. ☎805-899-4925. Rentals $20-40 per 2hr., $40-60 per day. Open summer daily 7am-6pm; winter Su and Sa 10am-5pm, Tu-F noon-6pm.)* Across the street from the Visitors Center is idyllic **Chase Palm Park,** complete with a vintage 1916 Spillman carousel. *(Carousel operates daily 10am-6pm. $2.)*

BEST SUNSET. For the best sunset around, have a drink at the bar at the **Four Seasons Biltmore Hotel.** Appetizers run $9-100 (Beluga caviar costs $100). This five-star lodging is off-limits to most budgets, but the view of the Pacific is priceless and there's often free evening music. *(1260 Channel Dr., in Montecito. Take U.S. 101 South to Channel Dr. Exit. ☎805-969-2261. Park across the street; valet parking runs $50 including tip.)*

STATE STREET

State St., Santa Barbara's monument to city planning, runs a straight, tree-lined 2 mi. through the center of the city. Among the countless shops and restaurants are some cultural and historical landmarks that should not be missed. Everything that doesn't move—malls, mailboxes, telephones, the restrooms at the public library—has been slathered in Spanish tile.

SANTA BARBARA MUSEUM OF ART. This art museum has an impressive collection of classical Greek, Asian, and European works spans 3000 years. The 20th-century and Hindu collections are especially worthwhile. Over 90% of the permanent collection consists of gifts from Santa Barbara's wealthy residents. *(1130 State St. ☎805-963-4364. Open Su noon-5pm, Tu-Th and Sa 11am-5pm, F 11am-9pm. Tours Su and Tu-Sa noon and 2pm. $7, seniors $5, students ages 6-17 $4, under 6 free. Th and 1st Su of each month free.)*

OTHER SIGHTS. At the corner of Montecito Ave. and Chapala St. stands the notable **Moreton Bay Fig Tree.** Brought from Australia by a sailor in 1877, the tree's gnarled branches now span 160 ft.; it can provide shade for more than 1000 people at once. If you'd rather drink than stand in the shade with 999 other people, sample award-winning wine at the **Santa Barbara Winery.** *(202 Anacapa St. ☎805-963-3646. Open daily 10am-5pm. Tours daily 11:30am and 3:30pm. Tastings $4 for 6 wines.)*

THE MOUNTAINS

Up in the northern part of town, things are considerably more pastoral. The awe-inspiring, rugged mountain terrain is artfully balanced by the well-manicured lawns and carefully trimmed hedgerows of the area's multi-million-dollar homes.

MISSION SANTA BARBARA. Praised as the "Queen of Missions" in 1786, the mission was restored after the 1812 earthquake and assumed its present incarnation in 1820. Towers containing splayed Moorish windows stand around a Greco-Roman temple and facade while a Moorish fountain bubbles outside. The museum contains items from the mission archives. The main chapel is colorful and solemn; visitors may attend mass. The mission is also an infirmary and Franciscan friary. *(At the end of Las Olivas St. ☎ 805-682-4149. Open daily 9am-5pm. Self-guided museum tour starts at the gift shop. Mass M-F 7:30am; Sa 4pm; Su 7:30, 9, 10:30am, noon. $4, under 12 free.)*

SANTA BARBARA MUSEUM OF NATURAL HISTORY.
Unlike the typical museum, the only way to get from one exhibit to the next here is to go outside. The founder's wishes to establish a museum of comparative oology (no, not zoology) were overturned by a Board of Trustees who thought devoting the space to the study of eggs was silly. So they hatched the current exhibitions, which include the largest collection of Chumash artifacts in the West, a natural history gallery, and a planetarium. *(2559 Puesta del Sol Rd. Follow signs to parking lot. ☎ 805-682-4711 Open daily 10am-5pm. Planetarium shows in summer daily 1, 2, 3pm; in winter W 3pm, Sa-Su 1, 2, 3pm. $6, seniors and ages 13-17 $6, under 12 $4. Planetarium $2.)*

SANTA BARBARA BOTANICAL GARDEN.
Far from town but close to Mission Santa Barbara and the Museum of Natural History, the botanical garden offers non-native vegetation along easy, meandering paths. Five miles of hiking trails wind through 65 acres of native Californian trees, wildflowers, and cacti. The garden's water system was built by the Chumash and is now one of the last vestiges of the region's native heritage. *(1212 Mission Canyon Rd. ☎ 805-682-4726. Open Mar.-Oct. M-F 9am-5pm, Sa-Su 9am-6pm; Nov.-Feb. M-F 9am-4pm, Sa-Su 9am-5pm. Tours M-Th 10:30am and 2pm, Sa 2pm, Su 10:30am. Special demonstrations Su and F 2pm, Sa 10:30am. $5; students, seniors, and ages 13-19 $3; ages 5-12 $1.)*

HIKING.
Very popular **Inspiration Point** is a 3½ mi. round-trip hike that climbs 800 ft. Half of the hike is an easy walk on a paved road. The other half is a series of mountainside switchbacks. The reward on a clear day is an extensive view of the city, the ocean, and the Channel Islands. Following the creek upstream will lead to **Seven Falls**. *(From Mission Santa Barbara, drive toward the mountains and turn right onto Foothill Rd. Turn left onto Mission Canyon Rd. and continue 1 mi. Bear left onto Tunnel Rd.*

and drive 1¼ mi. to its end.) **Rattlesnake Canyon Trail** is a moderate 3½ mi. round-trip hike to Tunnel Trail junction with a 1000 ft. gain. It passes waterfalls, pools, and secluded spots, but is highly popular—expect company. *(From Mission Santa Barbara, drive toward the mountains and turn right onto Foothill Rd. Turn left onto Mission Canyon Rd. and continue for ½ mi, then make a sharp right onto Las Conas Rd. and travel 1¼ mi.; look for a large sign on the left side of the road.)* The treks from the **Cold Springs Trail** to **Montecito Peak** (7¼ mi. round-trip, 2462 ft. elevation gain) or to **Camino Cielo** (9 mi. round-trip, 2675 ft. elevation gain) are considerably more strenuous but offer great views. *(From U.S. 101 South, take Hot Springs Rd. Exit and turn left. Travel 2½ mi. to Mountain Dr. Turn left, drive 1¼ mi., and stop by the creek crossing.)* For a more extensive listing of trails, try the Botanical Garden gift shop or the Visitors Center in town. Another option is to join the local **Sierra Club** on their group hikes. *(For more information, call ☎ 805-564-7892. Led by expert hikers. Social hike at Mission Santa Barbara 6:15pm. Strenuous hike at Hope Ave. by the Bank of America Sa-Su 9am. Free.)*

UNIVERSITY OF CALIFORNIA AT SANTA BARBARA (UCSB).
This beautiful outpost of the UC system is stuck in Goleta, a shapeless mass of suburbs, gas stations, and coffee shops, but the beachside dorms and gorgeous student body more than make up for the town. The excellent **art museum** is worth visiting. It houses the Sedgwick Collection of 15th- to 17th-century European paintings. *(Museum off U.S. 101. ☎ 805-893-2951. Open Su 1-5pm, Tu-Sa 10am-4pm. Free.)*

🔥 FOOD

Santa Barbara may well have more restaurants per capita than anywhere else in America, so finding a place to eat is not exactly a problem. State and Milpas St. are especially diner-friendly; **State St.** is hipper while **Milpas St.** is cheaper.

Palazzio, 1026 State St. (☎ 805-564-1985). Their reproduction of the Sistine Chapel ceiling is as impressive as the enormous pasta dishes ($17-18, $12-14 for half-portion) and the serve-yourself wine bar. Open Su-Th 11:30am-3pm and 5:30-11pm, F-Sa 11:30am-3pm and 5:30pm-midnight.

La Superica Taqueria, 622 Milpas St. (☎ 805-963-4940). Rumored to have been Julia Child's favorite for

Mexican. The freshest tortillas around (made while you watch), tamales, and excellent *pozole*. Entrees under $10. Be prepared to wait. Open daily 11am-9:30pm.

The Taj Cafe, 905 State St. (☎805-564-8280). Enjoy village-style Indian cooking with natural ingredients. Taj offers tandoori chicken in a sweet, tangy mango sauce ($10). Lunch specials $5.50-7.50. Many vegetarian entrees ($6.50-8). Open M-Th 11:30am-3pm and 5-10pm, F-Sa 11:30am-3pm and 5-11pm.

ACCOMMODATIONS

A 10min. drive north or south on U.S. 101 will reward you with cheaper lodging than that in Santa Barbara proper. Trusty **Motel 6** is always an option. In fact, Santa Barbara is where this glorious chain of budget-friendly motels originated. There are two locations: at the beach at 443 Corona del Mar Dr. (☎805-564-1392), and north of the main drag at 3505 State St. (☎805-687-5400). Prices are more expensive by the beach ($76-86; based on 2-person occupancy). The State St. location starts at $68-80 in the summer and $55 in the winter. All Santa Barbara accommodations are more expensive on the weekends (peaking July-Aug. and on holidays). Camping is also an option; to reach **Carpinteria Beach State Park,** 12 mi. south of Santa Barbara, follow signs from U.S. 101 (entrance is at the end of Palm Ave.) It has 261 developed sites with hot showers. (☎805-684-2811. Sites $12; with hookup $18. Day-use $2.)

Hotel State Street, 121 State St. (☎805-966-6586), 1 block from the beach. Welcoming, comfortable, and meticulously clean, this European-style inn offers a good and relatively cheap night's sleep. Common bathrooms are pristine. Rooms have sinks and cable TV; a few have skylights. Reservations recommended. Rooms $50-70. $5-10 more July-Aug.

Haley Cottages, 227 E. Haley St. (☎805-963-3586; www.haleycottages.com), at Garden St. Run by the same folks as the International Hostel, the spirit of budget funk—for better and for worse—pervades the 14 private cottages. Each cottage has its own kitchen and bathroom and is a 5min. walk from the beach in a formerly dodgy area that's now starting to undergo gentrification. Rooms in summer $54-75; in winter $49-65.

Santa Barbara International Tourist Hostel, 134 Chapala St. (☎905-963-0154; sbres@bananabungalow.com). Great location near the beach and State St. Bike and surfboard rentals. Laundry. Internet $1 per 20min. Dorm rooms sleep 6-8; private rooms have 1 double bed. Dorms $18-20; private rooms $45-55.

NIGHTLIFE

Every night of the week, the clubs on **State St.,** mostly between Haley St. and Canon Perdido St., are packed. This town is full of those who love to eat, drink, and be drunk. Consult the *Independent* to see who's playing on any given night. Bars on State St. charge $4 for beer fairly uniformly.

The Hourglass, 213 W. Cota St. (☎805-963-1436). Soak in an intimate indoor bath or watch the stars from a private outdoor tub; there are 9 spas that you can choose from. No alcohol. Towels $1. 2 people $25 per hr.; each additional person $7. $2 student discount; children free with parent. Open Su and Th-Sa 5pm-midnight.

Q's Sushi A-Go-Go, 409 State St. (☎805-966-9177). A tri-level bar, 8 pool tables, and dancing. Enjoy the sushi ($3.50-13.50) and accompany with *sake* ($3.50). Happy hour M-Sa 4-7pm includes 20% off sushi plates and half-price drinks and appetizers. M Brazilian night. W karaoke. Cover $5 F-Sa after 9pm. Open daily 4pm-2am.

Club 634, 634 State St. (☎805-564-1069). Cocktails, dancing, and 2 large patios. Live bands and DJs. Su and W karaoke, Th Red Bull and vodkas $3, F 5-8pm select beers $1.50. Occasional cover. Open M-F 2pm-2am, Sa-Su noon-2am.

APPROACHING CACHUMA COUNTRY PARK
From U.S. 101, take **Rte. 154** toward Cachuma Lake.

LAKE CACHUMA COUNTRY PARK
Northwest of Santa Barbara along Rte. 154.

Lake Cachuma's clean deep blue waters placidly filling the crooks of the Santa Ynez Mountains are so stunning as to seem almost unreal; and they do in fact come from a man-made dam. The lake is nonetheless an unbelievably beautiful spot for hiking, boating (rentals from $30 per hr., $65-95 per day), fishing, wildlife observation, and camping. No swimming is allowed. Campers enjoy 510 first come, first served sites with a general store, gas station, nature center, pool and marina. (☎805-686-5055; www.cachuma.com. Sites $16; yurts $35-55.)

THE ROAD TO SOLVANG

To the northwest of Santa Barbara along Rte. 154 lies the lovely **Santa Ynez Valley,** home to thousands of acres of vineyards, hundreds of ostriches, and Michael Jackson's **Wonderland**

Ranch, named after Lewis Carroll's fantasy world. The free *Santa Barbara County Wineries Touring Map*, available at the Santa Barbara Visitors Center, provides comprehensive listings. One of the prettiest vineyards is **Gainey Vineyard,** 3950 E. Rte. 246, at Rte. 154. (☎805-688-0558. Open daily 10am-5pm. Tours 11am, 1, 2, 3pm. Tastings $5; includes 9 tastes and logo glass.)

APPROACHING SOLVANG
Take **Rte. 154** to **Rte. 246 West** to Solvang.

SOLVANG
"Something's rotten in Denmark..." So said the group of Midwesterners who moved to this sunny field ("sol vang") in 1911 and established a Danish colony. The town still trumpets its Danish heritage—every shop and motel has a watered-down pitch related to Copenhagen or Hans Christian Anderson. The Danish population has dwindled to a minority, even as the town's Danish thrust has become more concerted. For all its attempts at old-world charm, Solvang retains an *ersatz* and forced Disney-ish feeling; the architecture seems newly contrived instead of charmingly quaint. In a formerly Mexican territory, supplanted with Anglo culture, this Danish pocket holds interest simply for its novelty value. Activity centers on Mission Dr., the town's main drag in town, neighboring **Copenhagen Dr.,** and the intersecting **Alisol Rd.,** which features a turning windmill.

Stroll around the theme streets with their Scandanavian design—a thatched roof is at 1st St. and Copenhagen Dr.—and enjoy the cutesy storefronts, wine-tasting shops, and bakeries. **Elverhoj Museum,** 1624 Elverhoy Way, off 3rd St., has displays and artifacts from Danish-American pioneer life. (☎805-686-1211; www.elverhoj.org. Open W-Su; call for hours.) **The Book Loft,** 1680 Mission Dr., pays homage to Hans Christian Anderson, the children's author of such tales as *The Ugly Duckling, The Emperor's New Clothes* and *The Little Mermaid* with a modest display of his valuable books as well as his paper cutouts. Buffs of the bike will enjoy the **Vintage Motorcycle Museum,** 320 Alisal Rd. (☎805-686-9522; www.motosolvang.com. Open Sa-Su 11am-5pm.) **Mission Santa Inés,** not the brightest jewel in the crown of missions but the very first one, provides an alternative to Denmark, U.S.A. A **Farmer's market** occurs every Wednesday.

At **Olsen's Village Bakery and Coffee Shop,** 1529 Mission Dr., the most authentic Danish bakery in town, the goods are delivered fresh every day by a third-generation Dane. The Kringle is particularly recommended. The Danish breakfast includes bread, cheese, pastry, coffee, and orange juice for $5. (☎805-688-6314; www.olsendanishbakery.com. Open summer M-F 7am-7pm, Sa-Su 7am-8pm; winter M-F 7am-6pm, Sa-Su 7am-8pm.) The **Viking Motel,** 1506 Mission Dr. (☎805-688-1337), chimes in with the lowest price in town at $49 on winter weekdays, though on summer weekends, the cost can skyrocket up to $150.

THE ROAD TO GUADALUPE
Continue west along Rte. 246 toward Lompoc. At the intersection of Rte. 246 and U.S. 101 is the town of **Buellton,** home of **Pea Soup Andersen's,** where the split pea soup has been sold thick, hot, and fresh since 1924. (☎805-688-5581. Soup $3.50. All-you-can-eat soup plus a thick milkshake $7. Open daily 7am-10pm.)

The nation's largest producer of flower seed, **Lompoc** consists of every chain convenience you could imagine, alongside flower fields and a mission. The acres upon acres of blooms, which peak near the end of June, are both a visual and olfactory explosion. Lompoc holds a **flower festival** (☎805-735-8511) at the season's peak, usually the last weekend in June.

LA PURISIMA MISSION STATE PARK
2295 Purisima Rd.
Follow Rte. 246; the entrance is off Mission Rd.

Ten buildings stand in **La Purisima Mission State Park,** the most fully restored of Father Serra's missions, complete with Mexican blankets and horses and goats in the pastures. The park also includes 12 mi. of maintained trails, enjoyable for stretching the legs. (☎805-733-3713; www.lapurisimamission.org. Open daily 9am-5pm. $5)

APPROACHING GUADALUPE
Go west on **Rte. 246** to **Rte. 1 North.**

GUADALUPE. A farming outpost of about 5000, Guadalupe is a town most tourists pass by and herein lies its appeal: a dose of gritty reality, inhabited by people who actually live and work here. To get a taste for this aspect of Guadalupe you can stop at **El Tapatio's,** 914 Guadalupe St. (Rte. 1), a countertop and brown booth diner playing aging Mexican pop on the

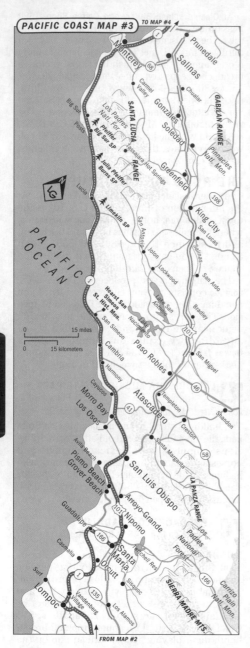

PACIFIC COAST MAP #3

TO MAP #4

Prunedale

Monterey

Salinas

Carmel Valley

Chualar

Gonzales

SANTA LUCIA

Los Padres Nat'l. For.

Big Sur

Posts

Tassajara Hot Springs

Pfeiffer Big Sur SP

Soledad

Greenfield

GABILAN RANGE

Julia Pfeiffer Burns SP

RANGE

Pinnacles Nat'l. Mon.

Lucia

Limekiln SP

King City

San Lucas

198

San Antonio

Jolon

Lockwood

San Ardo

PACIFIC OCEAN

Hearst San Simeon St. Hist. Mon.

San Simeon

Lake San Antonio

Nacimiento

Bradley

San Antonio

101

Cambria

Paso Robles

San Miguel

Harmony

Templeton

46

Cayucos

Atascadero

41

Shandon

Morro Bay

Los Osos

Creston

Avila Beach

Santa Margarita

Pismo Beach

Grover Beach

San Luis Obispo

58

LA PANZA RANGE

Guadalupe

Arroyo Grande

Nipomo

101

Los Padres National Forest

Casmalia

166

Santa Maria

Nitchell Resd.

166

Surf

Orcutt

Sisquoc

Carrizo Plain Nat'l. Mon.

Lompoc

Vandenberg Village

135

Los Alamos

SIERRA MADRE MTS.

0   15 miles
0   15 kilometers

FROM MAP #2

jukebox. Order the house specialty of *chile verde* or *colorado* for $6.75. (☎805-343-2359. Burritos $1.50-3. Open daily 6am-10pm.) Or you can turn the corner to the **Ninth St. Barbershop,** 898 D. Guadalupe St. Even if you don't need a $9 trim, you might be able to chat with the owners about life in area. (Open Tu-F 10am-6pm, Sa 9aMm-noon.) A **historic jail** at the end of Guadalupe St. is open the last Sunday of every month (1-3pm).

APPROACHING PISMO BEACH
Follow **Rte. 1 North** to Pismo Beach.

PISMO BEACH

Pismo Beach is a honky-tonk town situated around one of California's longest and widest beaches. At the **Pismo Dunes,** the loveliness of the broad white sand is spoiled by the all-terrain (ATV) vehicles that cruise around like insects on a picnic spread. (Open 6am-11pm. $4.) Rent ATV equipment from **Steve's ATV,** 1206 W. Grand Ave., in Grover Beach. (☎805-474-6431; www.steve-satv.com. 1hr. ATV rental including helmet $25-75. Hummer beach tours $35, under 12 $15. Open daily 8am-6pm.) Those surpassing the speed limit of 15 mph risk a hefty fine and their lives, as careless, fast driving on the dunes can be deadly. For more information, head to the **Pismo Beach Chamber of Commerce,** 581 Dolliver St. (☎805-773-4382; www.classiccalifornia.com).

Pismo SB North Beach Campground, on Dolliver St. on Rte. 1, has the nicest campsites in Pismo, although even these are still in a parking lot. (☎800-444-7275. No hookups. Sites $13.) Another option is **Pismo Beach State Park,** on Rte. 1, just south of scenic Pismo Beach. The huge campground is split into two areas; **North Beach** has 103 tent sites with water, showers, and restrooms, while **Oceano** has 40 tent sites and 42 RV hookups with water, flush toilets, and showers. North Beach sites are larger and closer to the beach. (☎805-489-1869. Call for reservations. Sites $16; RVs $20.) For indoor accommodations near the dunes, head to **Bill's Home Hostel,** 1040 Cielo Ln., in Nipomo. (Take U.S. 101 South to Tefft St., turn right on Tefft St., left on Orchard Ave., and a right on Primavera Ln.; Cielo Ln. is on the left. (☎805-929-3647. Check-in by 9pm. Bugle wake-up call 8am. Donation of $14 can be replaced with 2½hr. of farm work. Required chore, musical performance, or $4.)

LEAVING PISMO BEACH
Follow **Rte. 1 North** to San Luis Obispo.

SAN LUIS OBISPO

Amid sprawling green hills close to the rocky coast, San Luis Obispo (san-LEW-is oh-BIS-boh; frequently condensed to SLO; pronounced "slow") is a town that lives up to its nickname but by no means stands still. While the mission has reigned as the center of local life since 1772, this area only became a full-fledged town after the Southern Pacific Railroad laid tracks here in 1894. Ranchers and oil refinery employees comprise a large percentage of today's population, and California Polytechnic State University (Cal Poly) students add a young, energetic component to the mix. Along the main roads in downtown, hip students mingle with laid-back locals in outdoor eateries, trendy shops, and music-filled bars.

VITAL STATS

Population: 44,360

Visitor Info: Visitors Center for the Chamber of Commerce, 1039 Chorro St. (☎805-781-2777). Watch for signs on U.S. 101. Open Su-M 10am-5pm, Tu-W 8am-5pm, Th-F 8am-8pm, Sa 10am-8pm. **State Parks Office,** 3220 S. Higuera St., #311 (☎805-549-3312). Open M-F 8am-5pm.

Internet Access: San Luis Obispo Branch Library, 995 Palm St. (☎805-781-5989). Open M-W 10am-8pm, Th-Sa 10am-5pm.

Post Office: 893 Marsh St. (☎805-543-3062). Open M-F 8:30am-5:30pm, Sa 9am-5pm. **Postal Code:** 93405.

GETTING AROUND. Downtown, **Monterey** and **Higuera St.** (north-south) and **Broad** and **Garden St.** (east-west), are the main drags. Walking here is easy and there is plenty of cheap **parking.**

SIGHTS. San Luis Obispo grew around the **Mission San Luis Obispo de Tolosa,** and the city continues to hold celebrations and general lunchtime socializing around its front steps. Founded in 1772, the mission was once covered in white clapboards and crowned with a steeple in the New England style. In the late 1800s, however, the town began reviving the mission's Spanish origins; by the 1930s it was fully restored. It still serves as the Catholic parish church for SLO. The mission also houses a small museum, which displays objects from the early days of the mission and a small collection of Chumash artifacts. (☎805-543-6850. Open daily early Apr. to late Oct. 9am-5pm; late Oct. to early Apr. 9am-4pm. Suggested donation $2.) The mission faces beautiful **Mission Plaza,** where Father Serra held the area's first mass.

A gurgling 14 ft. waterwheel and shady deck await visitors at the **Apple Farm Mill,** 2015 Monterey St. Alternately churning ice cream and flour, the mill provides free samples of cider from a local farm and complimentary tea, popcorn, and chocolates on the deck. Also home to a restaurant, bakery, gift shop, and inn, the mill is a great way to spend a pleasant afternoon. (☎805-544-2040. Open Su-Th 7am-9pm, F-Sa 7am-10pm.)

One million dollars of city money have transformed the old public library into the **SLO Historical Society Museum,** 696 Monterey St. Dioramas and interactive displays depict eras of San Luis Obispo's history, catering to younger audiences. (☎805-543-0638. Open Su and W-Sa 10am-4pm.)

FOOD & NIGHTLIFE. Higuera St. and its cross streets are lined with restaurants and cafes. Voted "Best Restaurant in SLO" and winner of many awards, **Big Sky Cafe,** 1121 Broad St., delivers vegetarian-friendly food under the stars or under the tiled ceiling. (☎805-545-5401. Sandwiches $6.50-10. Open M-Sa 7am-10pm, Su 8am-9pm.) Lavish surroundings and belly dancers enhance the Mediterranean and Moroccan cuisine at **Oasis,** 675 Higuera St. The Oasis feast (appetizer, soup or salad, entree, baklava or cup of mint tea; $24) satisfies even the most weary desert traveler. (☎805-543-1155. Lunch $7-15. Belly dancing F-Sa 7-9pm. Open daily 11am-10pm.)

Woodstock's Pizza Parlour, 1000 Higuera St., is a local hangout that invariably sweeps annual "best pizza" awards. Young crowds keep it lively into the night. Lunch specials include all-you-can-eat pizza and bottomless soda for $6.50. (☎805-541-4420. Single slices $1.75. Open Su-Th 11am-midnight, F-Sa 11am-1am.) **Mother's Tavern,** 725 Higuera St., is a Yukon-inspired bar and restaurant with mounted animal heads that draws mostly Cal Poly students. (☎805-541-8733. Cover $1-5. Open daily 11:30am-1:30am. Kitchen closes 9pm.)

ACCOMMODATIONS. The **San Luis Obispo (HI-AYH),** 1617 Santa Rosa St. is conveniently located three blocks from downtown. Free homemade sourdough pancakes are served

PACIFIC COAST

daily at 7:30am. (☎805-544-4678; www.hostelo-bispo.com. Linen provided; towel $0.50. Laundry $2. Reception 7:30-10am and 4:30-10pm. Lockout 10am-4:30pm. Dorms $18, nonmembers $20; private family room for 2-4 adults $50-80; F-Sa in summer add $5 for private room. No credit cards.) Pitch at tent at **Montaña de Oro State Park,** on Pecho Rd., 4 mi. south of Los Osos, 12 mi. from SLO via Los Osos Valley Rd., which features 50 primitive sites in a gorgeous, secluded park. Gray whales, seals, otters, dolphins, and the occasional orca frequent **Montana de Oro State Park,** whose 8000 acres and 7 mi. of shoreline remain relatively secluded. **Spooner's Cove,** across from the campground three-quarters of a mile north of Coralina Cove, has tide pools and whale-watching spots at Bluff's Trailhead. (☎805-528-0513. Outhouses and cold running water; bring your own drinking water. Reserve weeks in advance June-Sept. Sites $10.)

 LEAVING SAN LUIS OBISPO
Follow **Rte. 1 North** to Morro Bay.

MORRO BAY

The Seven Sisters, a chain of small ex-volcanoes, are remnants of a time when SLO County was highly volcanically active. The lava that once flowed here formed the dramatic shorelines along Rte. 1 from Morro Rock to SLO. The northernmost sister, Morro Rock, and three large smokestacks from an electric company shadow the tiny burg of Morro Bay, just north of its namesake park. **Morro Bay State Park** is home to coastal cypresses that are visited by Monarch butterflies from November to early February. The park's modern, hands-on **Museum of Natural History** flexes its curatorial muscle on the aquatic environment and wildlife of the coastal headlands. A bulletin board near the entrance lists free nature walks led by park docents. Reserve campsites for the park year-round. (☎805-772-2694. Open daily 10am-5pm. $2, under 17 free. Sites $15-20.) South Bay Blvd., which links the town and the park, winds through the new **Morro Bay National Estuary,** a sanctuary for great blue herons, egrets, and sea otters. Take the trail or rent a kayak or canoe to explore. Pack a basket and paddle out to the sand dunes for a picnic lunch. Check for tides to avoid (or take advantage of) numerous sandbars. **Kayak Horizons,** 551 Embarcadero, rents kayaks and offers instruction. (☎805-772-6444; www.kayakhorizons.com. $8-16 per hr. Open daily 9am-5pm.)

Along the beach, the **Embarcadero** is the locus of Morro Bay activity and fish 'n' chips bargains. The modest **Morro Bay Aquarium,** 595 Embarcadero, is a rehabilitation center for distressed marine animals and has over 100 ocean critters. The seal-feeding station is a rare opportunity to see these animals only feet away. (☎805-772-7647. Open daily 9am-6:30pm; in winter 9:30am-5:30pm. $2, ages 5-11 $1, under 5 free.) Morro Bay's pride and joy is the **Giant Chessboard,** 800 Embarcadero, in Centennial Park across from Southern Port Traders. The board is 256 sq. ft., with 18-20 lb. carved redwood pieces. (Call the Morro Bay Recreation office at ☎805-772-6278 to set up a game or watch for free M-F 8am-5pm. $38 per game.)

 LEAVING MORRO BAY
Follow **Rte. 1 North** to Cambria.

CAMBRIA & SAN SIMEON

The original Anglo-Saxon settlers of the southern end of the Big Sur coast were awestruck by the stunning pastoral views and rugged shoreline, reminiscent of the eastern coast of England. In homage to the natural beauty of their homeland, they named this equally impressive New World area Cambria, the ancient Roman name for Wales. Ten miles north of Cambria, neighboring New San Simeon is a strip town along Rte. 1 with few roads and many motels near spectacular beaches. Old San Simeon is north of New San Simeon and consists only of a 150-year-old store, **Sebastian Store,** and the homes of Hearst Corporation ranchers.

 GETTING AROUND. For a quick stop, turn off Rte. 1 at the Burton Dr. exit which takes you straight to **Main St.** There, (after passing the wonderful Robin's restaurant) in a one-block radius you'll find an **ATM,** old-timer **Soto's Market & Deli** (open M-Sa 7am-8pm, Su 8am-6pm), the French bakery, and a gas station. There is plenty of free **parking** on the street.

 SIGHTS & BEACHES. San Simeon marks the beginning of Big Sur's dramatic coastline. Sea otters, once near extinction, live in the kelp beds of **Moonstone Beach,** on Moonstone Dr. off Rte. 1 toward San Simeon. Along this stretch of coast, surfers are occasionally nudged off their boards by playful seals (and, far more rarely, by not-so-playful great white sharks). Scenic **Leffing-**

VITAL STATS

Population: 6232

Visitor Information: Cambria Chamber of Commerce, 767 Main St. (☎805-927-3524). Open daily 9am-5pm. **San Simeon Chamber of Commerce,** 250 San Simeon Dr. (☎805-927-3500 or 800-342-5613), on the west side of Rte. 1; look for tourist info signs. Open Apr.-Oct. M-Sa 9am-5pm; Nov.-Mar. 10am-2pm.

Library and Internet Access: Cambria Branch Library, 900 Main St. (☎805-927-4336), in Cambria. Open Tu-F 11am-5pm, Sa noon-4pm.

Post Offices: Cambria, 4100 Bridge St. (☎805-927-8610). Open M-F 9am-5pm. **Postal Code:** 93428. **San Simeon** (☎805-927-4156), on Rte. 1, in the back of Sebastian's General store. Take the road opposite the entrance to Hearst Castle. Open M-F 8:30am-noon and 1-5pm. **Postal Code:** 93452.

well's Landing is the best spot for **whale-watching.** (Open Apr.-Dec. daily 8am-sunset.) Call **Virg's Landing** for info. (☎805-927-4676.) In addition to providing the best swimming for miles, **San Simeon** and **Hearst State Beaches,** just across from Hearst Castle (see p. 913), are ideal for cliff climbing and beachcombing.

FOOD & ACCOMMODATIONS. Food is more plentiful in Cambria than in San Simeon. Many San Luis Obsipo residents consider **Robin's,** 4095 Burton Dr., the only reason to drive the 30 mi. to Cambria. Eclectic international cuisine is served in a Craftsman-style bungalow with outdoor gardens. (☎805-927-5007. Entrees $12-19. Open daily 11am-9pm or later. Reservations recommended for evenings.) Locals frequent **Creekside Gardens Cafe,** 2114 Main St., at the Redwood Shopping Center, for hearty "California country cookin'." (☎805-927-8646. Su brunch 10am-2:30pm. Open daily 11:30am-2:30pm and 5-9pm. No credit cards.)

Cambria has lovely but pricey B&Bs. Budget travelers will have better luck in San Simeon. The arrival of the national chain Motel 6 set off a pricing war that has led to wildly fluctuating rates, so it is always a good idea to call ahead. Beware of skyrocketing prices in summer. **San Simeon State Beach Campground** (☎805-927-2053), is just north of Cambria on Rte. 1. San Simeon Creek has showers at its 134 developed sites near the beach. Neighboring Washburn sits on a breezy hill overlooking the ocean and has primitive camping, pit toilets, and cold running water. (Reservations ☎800-444-7275. Sites $16. Day-use $3.) Originally built in the 1890s for the preacher of the church next door, **Bridge Street Inn,** 4314 Bridge St., in Cambria, includes sunny and sparklingly clean rooms with sturdy bunks. (☎805-927-7653. Continental breakfast and linen included. Reception 5-9pm. Dorms $20; private rooms $40-70.)

APPROACHING BIG SUR
Follow **Rte. 1 North** to Big Sur. Big Sur is the stretch of highway that was basically left for wilderness, and you need to make preparations in advance. That means getting all your supplies beforehand in San Simeon: food, camping equipment, and gas before you hit the *Sur Grande*. There are a few services in Big Sur and the ones that do exist are priced exorbitantly. Pick up a free copy of the newspaper leaflet *El Sur Grande* which includes a good map of the stretch (www.bigsurcalifornia.org).

HEARST CASTLE
On Rte. 1, 3 mi. north of San Simeon and 9 mi. north of Cambria.

Newspaper magnate and multi-millionaire owner William Randolph Hearst casually referred to it as "the ranch," or in his more romantic moments, "La Cuesta Encantada" (Spanish for the Enchanted Hill). The hilltop estate is an indescribably decadent dreamland of limestone castle, shaded cottages, pools almost too exquisite to swim in, fragrant gardens, and Mediterranean *esprit*. While traveling in Europe with his mother, young Hearst caught a bad case of art collecting fever at age 10. He spent the rest of his life gathering Renaissance sculpture, tapestries, and ceilings, and telling his architect to incorporate them into his castle's design. Scores of celebrities and luminaries such as Greta Garbo, Charlie Chaplin, Charles Lindbergh, and Winston Churchill drove to the castle (by invitation only) to bask in Hearst's legendary hospitality. While countless memorable cast parties were held on these grounds, the only things ever filmed here were 30 seconds of *Spartacus* and the end of a Kodak Funsaver commercial. Hearst Castle is also famous for what was not filmed here—Orson Welles's masterpiece, *Citizen Kane*, which bears more than a passing resemblance to Hearst's life (Hearst reportedly tried to prevent the film from ever seeing the light of a film projector).

Before going to see the castle, your experience will be enhanced by stopping by the **Visitors Center** at the base of the hill, which features a surprisingly frank portrait of Hearst's failed days at Harvard University, his central role in yellow journalism, and the scandals of his life. At one point, Hearst's mistress, Marion Davies, had to sell her jewels so that construction of her indebted lover's mansion could continue without interruption. Five different tours are run by the State Parks Department and are a strictly hands-off experience. Tour 1 is recommended for first-time visitors, and includes a viewing of a National Geographic documentary on the architectural wonder. The banisters or staircases are the only things you may touch in the castle, but there's plenty to occupy your eyes. Tour 5 is available on most weekend evenings during the spring and fall, featuring costumed docents acting out the castle's legendary Hollywood history. (☎805-927-2020, reservations 800-444-4445. Call in advance, as tours often sell out. 4 different types of daytime tours leave frequently. Tour 1: 1¾hr.; $18, ages 6-12 $9, under 6 free. Tours 2, 3, or 4: 1¾hr.; $12/$7/free. Tour 5: 2hr.; $24/$12/free. Each tour involves climbing 150-370 staircase steps. Theater: ☎805-927-6811. Films show daily every hr. 9:30am-5:30pm. $7, under 12 $5; included in Tour 1 pass.)

BIG SUR

Monterey's Spanish settlers called the entire region below their town *El Sur Grande*—the Big South. Today, Big Sur is a more explicitly defined 90 mi. coastal stretch, bordered on the south by San Simeon and on the north by Carmel. Cutting the road into the cliff, whose wending ways and tremendous views make a spectacular driving experience, was quite a lot of work: the entire 139 mi. highway, completed in 1937, took 18 years to build and ended up costing $71,000 per mile—about ten times what was expected. More of a region than a precise destination, the area draws a curious mixture of hippies, rich folk and outdoor enthusiasts who come for it's enchanting wilderness. power. In reality, though, there's not much to do in Big Sur—the water's too cold for swimming and recreation centers camping and hiking. No signs tell you that you are actually in the town of Big Sur, which hosts a handful of pricey restaurants and campsites booked up months in advance.

┌─ **VITAL STATS** ─┐

Visitor Info: Big Sur Chamber of Commerce, mailing address P.O. Box 87, Big Sur, CA 93920 (☎831-667-2100; www.bigsurcalifornia.org). Open M, W, F 9am-1pm. **Big Sur Station** (☎831-667-2315), ½ mi. south of Pfeiffer Big Sur entrance on Rte. 1. Multi-agency station includes the State Park Office, the US Forest Service (USFS) Office, and the CalTrans Office. Provides permits, maps, and info on hikes and campfires. Open daily June-Sept. 8am-6pm; Oct.-May 8am-4:30pm.

Road Conditions: ☎800-427-7623. **Highway Patrol:** ☎805-549-3261.

Post Office: 47500 Rte. 1 (☎831-667-2305), next to the Center Deli in Big Sur Center. Open M-F 8:30am-5pm. **Postal Code:** 93920.

▐ GETTING AROUND

Rte. 1 in Big Sur wraps itself around the curves of the mountain at the third-highest sheer drop in the world. Don't feel pressured to drive faster because it's a one-lane road and someone is tailing you; just pull over into one of the many turnouts to let them pass. Besides, you're here for the views, why rush it? If you are driving through, it takes 6hr. from Monterey to Morro Bay.

⊙ SIGHTS

The water is generally too cold for swimming, although brave souls can bear it best in the summer months of June through August. If you're driving through in one day, the best hikes to hit are the three waterfalls; they give you a taste of the area in various breathtaking incarnations throughout its length. The **McWay Waterfall Trail,** in Julia Pfeiffer Burns State Park, holds the only waterfall that spills directly into the great Pacific, an elegant plume feeding a limitless ocean just south of Carmel; look for the sign.

Big Sur's most jealously guarded treasure is the USFS-operated **Pfeiffer Beach** (day use $5), roughly 10½ mi. north of Julia Pfeiffer Burns State Park. Turn off Rte. 1 at the stop sign just past the bridge by Loma Vista. Follow the road 2 mi. to the parking area, where a path leads to the beach. An offshore rock formation protects sea caves and seagulls from the pounding ocean waves. Other beaches can be found at **Andrew Molera State Park** (5 mi. north of Big Sur station; day use $2), **Sand**

Dollar Beach (33 mi. south of the Big Sur station near Kirk and Plasket Creek campsites; day use $5), and **Jade Cove** (36 mi. south of Big Sur station; free). Roughly at the midpoint of the Big Sur coast lies **Julia Pfeiffer Burns State Park,** where picnickers find refuge in the redwood forest and sea otters in McWay Cove. (Backcountry camping permits at Big Sur Station. No dogs.) At the point where McWay Creek flows into the ocean is a spectacular 80 ft. waterfall, visible from a semi-paved path a quarter-mile from the park entrance.

The inhospitality of dark, rocky **Jade Cove** is perhaps what makes it so enthralling. Although it's illegal and inconsiderate, people reportedly go jade hunting on the beach, and over the years $50 million dollars of jade have been removed. The stone is distinguished by its soapy texture, dark green color and hardness—if you smack it against the other rocks it won't break.

One can also spend some time learning about one of the area's most celebrated former residents—Henry Miller. The **Henry Miller Memorial Library,** just south of Nepenthe and Cafe Kevah, displays books and artwork by the famous author. Miller's casual reminiscences and prophetic ecstasies introduced his readers to Big Sur. Many readers of his more explicit works came to Big Sur seeking a nonexistent sex cult that he purportedly led. While the sex cult is no longer a tourism draw, the cult of history suffices nicely. (☎ 831-667-2574; www.henrymiller.org. Open Su and W-Sa 11am-6pm and by special arrangement.) The library sells books and hosts concerts like the **Big Sur Jazz Festival** and readings such as the **West Coast Championship Poetry Slam.** There is also an interesting sculpture garden featuring a computer-and-wire crucifix and mammoth cocoon.

◤ HIKING

Big Sur's state parks and Los Padres National Forest beckon outdoor enthusiasts of all types. Their hiking trails penetrate redwood forests and cross low chaparral, offering even grander views of Big Sur than those available from Rte. 1. The northern end of Los Padres National Forest, accessible from Pfeiffer Big Sur, has been designated the **Ventana Wilderness** and contains the popular **Pine Ridge Trail,** which runs 12 mi. through primitive sites and the Sikes Hot Springs. The Forest Service ranger station supplies maps and permits for the wilderness area. Within **Pfeiffer Big Sur State**

Park are eight trails ($1 map available at park entrance). **Pfeiffer Falls** (1½ mi. round-trip) and **Valley View** (2 mi. round-trip) are short, easy hikes. Pfeiffer Falls is a scenic hike through redwoods along Pfeiffer Big Sur Creek to a 60 ft. waterfall. The Valley View Trail, from Pfeiffer Falls, offers views of Pt. Sur and Big Sur Valley. **Oak Grove Trail** is a bit more challenging, at 3 mi. round-trip from the Big Sur Lodge, and intersects with the Pfeiffer Falls trail. It features redwood groves, oak woodlands and dry chaparral. The strenuous **Mt. Manuel Trail** (8 mi. round-trip) begins at the Oak Grove Trail and is a steep, dry climb to the 3379 ft. Manuel Peak. **Buzzard's Roost Trail** is a rugged 2hr. hike up torturous switchbacks, but at its peak are views of the Santa Lucia Mountains, Big Sur Valley, and the Pacific Ocean. **Pfeiffer Falls Trail,** Julia Pfeiffer Falls State Park, an easy 1.4 mi. round-trip along Pfeiffer Big Sur Creek, winds through redwoods that end in a 60-foot waterfall. ($4 day use.) At **Limekiln State Park,** 56 mi. south of Carmel, 2 mi. south of Lucia (☎ 831-667-2403), a 30min. round-trip to a waterfall will take you through redwoods and the giant metal namesakes on this less trodden southern stretch of the coast. **Ewoldsen Trail** (4½ mi. round-trip) starts in redwoods at McWay Creek, follows McWay Canyon, and climbs upwards, sometimes steeply. **Tan Bark Trail** starts east of Rte. 1 at Partington Cove. The 5½ mi. round-trip hike traverses oaks and redwoods to the Tin House and has excellent views. To shorten the trip, take the road at the end of the trail. It leads back to Rte. 1, a mile south of the trailhead.

◤ FOOD

Grocery stores are at Big Sur Lodge (in Pfeiffer Big Sur State Park), Pacific Valley, and Gorda, and some packaged food is sold in Lucia and at Ragged Point, but it's better to arrive prepared because prices in Big Sur are generally high. Listings are ordered from south to north along Rte. 1.

◪ **Big Sur Restaurant and Bakery** (☎ 831-667-0520, bakery 831-667-0524), just south of the post office, by the Shell gas station and the Garden Gallery. Serves 12 in. woodfire pizzas ($10-16) and entrees using free range meats and fresh local vegetables ($16-19) in a garden setting. The bakery specializes in organic breads and pastries. Beer and wine available. Open daily 8am-8pm, until 9pm if busy.

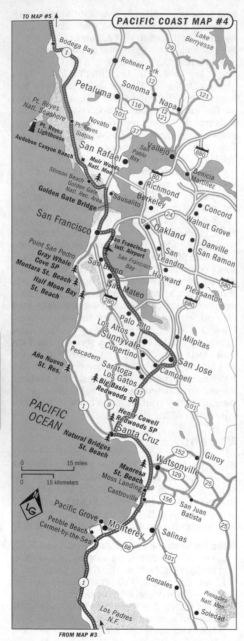

PACIFIC COAST MAP #4

Center Deli and General Store (☎831-667-2225), 1 mi. south of Big Sur Station, beside the post office. This is where you will find the most reasonably priced goods in the area. $3.25-5 sandwiches include veggie options like avocado and egg salad. Pasta salads $5 per lb. Open daily 7:30am-8pm.

Fernwood Bar and Grill (☎831-667-2422), on Rte. 1, 2 mi. north of the post office. Highly popular outdoor patio under redwood canopy. Chicken breasts, veggie burritos, and hamburgers from $6.50. BBQ specials, often with live music ($8-10). Open daily 11am-10pm. Bar open Su-Th 11am-12:30am, F-Sa 11am-2am. Grocery store open daily 8am-10pm.

The Roadhouse (☎831-667-2264), off Rte. 1, about 19 mi. south of Carmel, just south of Riverside Camp. A lively, intimate atmosphere and flavorful food, like sweet corn risotto with grilled vegetable salad ($15). Soups and salads $7-15. Entrees $12-22. Open M and W-Su 5:30-9pm.

ACCOMMODATIONS

Camping in Big Sur is heavenly; in choosing your site, decided whether you'd prefer to be close to the beach (Andrew Molera, Kirk Creek, Limekiln) or in the redwoods, darker and more protected from coastal winds. Low site availability reflects the high demand for camping in the area, so reserve well in advance by calling ReserveAmerica (☎800-444-7275; $7.50 fee). If all sites below are booked, check with the **US Forest Service.** Camping is free in the **Ventana Wilderness,** a backpack-only site at the northern end of Los Padres National Forest (permits at Big Sur Station). Detailed trail maps are necessary for this kind of backcountry camping; ask Big Sur rangers for essential information on current conditions. Listings are ordered from south to north along Rte. 1.

Ventana Big Sur (☎831-667-2712; www.ventanawildernesscampground.com), on Rte. 1, about 24 mi. south of Carmel. 80 shady sites in a gorgeous redwood canyon with picnic tables, fire rings, flush toilets and water faucets. Hot showers. Sites for 2 people and 2 vehicles $27-35. $5 per additional person; 5-person max.

Pfeiffer Big Sur State Park (☎831-667-2315), on Rte. 1, about 22 mi. south of Carmel, just south of Fernwood Resort and Campground. The diverse wildlife and terrain, the beautiful Big Sur River, and several hiking trails ensure that all 218 bustling campsites are always filled. Fire pits, picnic tables, softball field, flush toilets, and hot showers. As one ranger put it, "Your grandma can camp here." Trail maps $1. Sites Feb.-Oct. $20-35. Day use $8.

Fernwood Resort and Campground (☎831-667-2422), on Rte. 1, about 19 mi. south of Carmel. 60 small but well-situated campsites and 2 swimming holes in a redwood forest on the Big Sur River. Several state park trails start from the campground. Hot showers. Reservations recommended. Sites with hookup $29; $5 per additional person. Day-use $5.

Big Sur Campground and Cabins (☎831-667-2322), on Rte. 1, about 18 mi. south of Carmel on the Big Sur River. Hot showers and laundry. Reservations recommended. Sites for 2 people $27, $4 per additional person. 5-person max. Hookup $4. Tent cabins for 2 people $57, 3rd person or dogs $12. Cabins $121-258. Low-season day use $10.

Riverside Camp (☎831-667-2414), next to the Big Sur Campground. Slightly dustier sites. Reservations $4. 2 people and 1 vehicle $28; $4 per additional person. Electricity and water hookup $4. 2 cabins ($130) and 5 rooms ($75-130) are also available.

Andrew Molera State Park (☎831-667-2315), on Rte. 1, about 15 mi. south of Carmel next to a horseback riding facility. A level ½ mi. trail leads to hike-in, tent-only campgrounds near the beach. 24 sites. Ornithology center, picnic tables, fire rings, drinking water, and flush toilets. No showers. 7-night max. stay. Sites $9. Day use $8. No pets.

APPROACHING CARMEL
Go northwest on **Rte. 1** toward Carmel.

POINT LOBOS RESERVE
On Rte. 1, 3 mi. south of Carmel. Park on Rte. 1 before the tollbooth and walk or bike in for free.

This extraordinary 550-acre, state-run wildlife sanctuary is popular with skin divers and day hikers. Bring binoculars to view otters, sea lions, seals, brown pelicans, gulls, or migrating whales from the paths along the cliffs. At the water, Point Lobos offers tide pools and scuba access. (☎831-624-4909. Open daily Apr.-Oct. 9am-7pm; Nov.-Mar. 9am-5pm. Free daily nature tours; call for times. Entrance fee $8 per vehicle. Map $1. Day-use free for campers registered with the state parks. Divers must call ☎831-624-8413 or email ptlobos@mbay.net for reservations. Dive fee $7.)

CARMEL

Moneyed Californians migrate to Carmel (officially Carmel-by-the-Sea; pop. 4400) to live out their fantasies of small-town life. Carmel has beautiful beaches, a main street lined with boutiques and art galleries, and a carefully manufactured aura of quaintness. Local ordinances forbid address numbers, parking meters (though police chalk tires to keep track of how long cars have been parked), live music in bars, billboards, and, at one time, eating ice-cream cones outside—all considered undesirable symbols of urbanization.

(VITAL STATS)

Visitor Information: Carmel-by-the-Sea Chamber of Commerce and Visitor Information Center (☎831-624-2522 or 800-550-4333; www.carmelcalifornia.org), in the Eastwood Bldg. on San Carlos St. between 5th and 6th St. Free city maps. Open M-F 9am-5pm, Sa 11am-5pm.

Internet Access: Mail Mart (☎831-624-4900), at Dolores Ave. and 5th St. $3 per 15 min. Open M-F 8:30am-5:30pm, Sa 9am-3pm.

Post Office: (☎831-624-3630), on 5th Ave. between San Carlos St. and Dolores Ave. Open M-F 9am-4:30pm, Sa 10am-2pm. **Postal Code:** 93921.

⌐ GETTING AROUND. Carmel lies at the southern end of the Monterey Peninsula off **Rte. 1,** 126 mi. south of San Francisco. The town's main street, **Ocean Ave.,** cuts west from the freeway to (surprise) the ocean. All other east-west avenues are numbered; numbers ascend toward the south. **Junípero Ave.** crosses Ocean Ave. downtown and leads south to the mission at **Rio Rd.** Free town maps are available at most hotels and the visitors center. A public lot on the corner of Junípero Ave. and 3rd St. has **free all-day parking.**

◙ SIGHTS. Established at its present site in 1771 by Father Junípero Serra, "the great conquistador of the cross," the ▨**Mission Basilica San Carlos Borromeo del Río Carmelo (Carmel Mission),** 3080 Rio Rd., at Lasuen Dr., off Rte. 1, converted 4000 Native Americans before it was abandoned in 1836. Fastidiously restored in 1931, the mission's marvels continue to astound. Complete with a stone courtyard, bell tower, lavish gardens, and a daily mass, the mission is one of the most extensive in California. Buried here are Father Serra and over 2300 Native Americans. The three museums display the original silver altar furnishings, handsome vestments, and a library. (☎ 831-624-1271. Open M-Sa 9:30am-4:30pm, Su 10:30am-4:30pm. $4, ages 6-17 $1, under 6 free.) The Sunset Cultural Center, which once housed Ansel Adams and Edward Weston's Friends Photography, is now home to the **Center for Photographic Art,** on San Carlos St. between 8th and 9th Ave. The Center exhibits top-notch work by local and international artists. Recently shows included Dennis Hopper, Linda McCartney, and Rodney Smith. (☎ 831-625-5181; www.photography.org. Open Su and Tu-Sa 1-5pm. Free.)

The northern Big Sur coast begins at the end of Ocean Ave., at **Carmel City Beach,** a white, sandy crescent framing a cove of chilly waters. The beach ends abruptly at the base of red cliffs, which make a fine grandstand for sunsets. **Carmel River State Beach,** just south of City Beach, is windier and colder than Carmel City Beach, but it is blessed with better surf and parking and smaller crowds. Bring a jacket or sweater, even in summer. (To get to Carmel River State Beach, walk about 1 mi. along Scenic Rd., or drive to the end of Carmelo St. off Santa Lucía. Parking lot closes at dusk.)

▓▊ FOOD & ACCOMMODATIONS. Food, like everything else in Carmel, is overpriced. It is, however, occasionally good enough to justify the expense. **Em Le's**, on Dolores Ave between 5th and 6th Ave., is known for its fabulous breakfasts, including omelettes with potatoes or cottage cheese and toast ($8-12), and unique French toast ($9). For dinner, early birds (4:30-7pm) can get an entree with soup or salad for $10. (☎ 831-625-6780. Open daily 7am-3pm and 4:30-10pm.) **The Forge in the Forest,** at the southwest corner of 5th Ave. and Junipero St., has been voted best outdoor dining in Monterey County for the last 13 years. The popular restaurant serves pasta, seafood, and grill items ($15-28), and gourmet pizza (roasted duck and caramelized onion $13) on a gorgeous garden patio complete with open-fire forge. (☎ 831-624-2233. Open Su-Th 11:30am-9pm, F-Sa 11:30am-10pm.) Housed in a historic building dating from 1927, **The Tuck Box English Tea Room,** on Dolores Ave. between Ocean and 7th Ave., is famous for scones ($4.25), preserves, and a fairy tale-esque facade. (☎ 831-624-6365. Salads $4.50-10. Omelettes $8-10. Open daily 7:30am-2:50pm.)

The expensive inns and lodges in Carmel usually offer only double-occupancy rooms (which fall below $90 only midweek or in winter) and usually include full breakfasts. A 15min. drive to Monterey will yield lower rates at places with less charm. The upscale **Carmel Sands Lodge,** on San Carlos St. between 4th and 5th Ave., is one of the least expensive options downtown. All rooms have cable TV, phone, and private bath. Some have fireplace, wet bar, or lanai balcony. (☎ 831-624-1255 or 800-252-1255. Free off-street parking and pool. Rooms in high season $85-189; in low season $68-145. AAA and AARP discount.)

▐▌ APPROACHING MONTEREY
Follow **Rte. 1 North** to Monterey.

▞▞ 17 MILE DRIVE
The 17 Mile Dive meanders along the coast from Pacific Grove through Pebble Beach and the forests around Carmel. For the Carmel entrance, take Ocean Ave. down toward the beach and turn right down San Antonio. From Rte. 1 North, take the Pebble Beach/Pacific Grove Hwy. 68 West Exit and turn left at the 1st stoplight. Follow signs for Pebble Beach.

Once owned by Del Monte Foods, Pebble Beach has become the playground of the fabulously well-to-do. Its enormous, manicured golf courses creep up almost to the shore's edge in bizarre contrast to the dramatically jagged cliffs and turbulent surf. The drive is rolling, looping, and often spectacular, though plagued by slow-driving tourists and a hefty $7.50 entrance fee. To drive in and out as you please in one day, present your receipt to the guard and have him record your license plate number. Save money by biking it (bicyclists and pedestrians are allowed in for free) or drive along Sunset Dr. instead (see p. 920). Along 17 Mile Drive, make sure to stop at **Fanshell Overlook** to where massive harbor seals and their pups rest up on the shore, and at the **Lone Cypress,** an old, gnarled tree growing on a rock promontory, valiantly resisting the onslaught of determined, jostling photographers. An image of this tree is now the official logo of the Pebble Beach community.

MONTEREY

Monterey makes good on its public claim to have preserved more of its heritage than any other Californian city. Although luxury hotels and tourist shops abound and the *Cannery Row* of Steinbeck fame has all but vanished, a number of important sites testify to the city's colorful past. The "Path of History," marked by yellow medallions embedded in the sidewalks, passes such landmarks as Colton Hall, the site of the California Constitutional Convention in 1849, and the Robert Louis Stevenson House, where the author found shelter in 1879. Most of this heritage owes its preservation to Monterey's other distinguishing feature: abundant wealth. Multi-million-dollar homes and golf courses line the rocky shoreline, and luxury cars cruise the city streets

⬛ GETTING AROUND

The Monterey Peninsula, 116 mi. south of San Francisco, consists of **Monterey**, residential **Pacific Grove**, and **Pebble Beach**, a nest of mansions and golf courses. **Alvarado St.** runs north-south through

Old Monterey and hosts most nightlife. Parallel to it is **Pacific St.** At its northern end stand luxury hotels and the giant DoubleTree Conference Center; beyond the plaza lies a parking lot, the marina, and Fisherman's Wharf. Perpendicular to Alvarado St., **Del Monte Ave.** runs northeast to the coast; on the other side, **Lighthouse Ave.** leads northwest through Pacific Grove, where it becomes **Central Ave.** and veers back to Lighthouse Ave., ending at Point Piños Lighthouse.

(VITAL STATS)

Population: 33,000

Visitor Information: Monterey Peninsula Visitor and Convention Bureau, 150 Olivier St. (☎831-657-6400, 831-649-1770, or 888-221-1010; www.montereyinfo.org). Open M-Sa 10am-6pm, Su 10am-5pm.

Internet Access: Monterey Public Library, 625 Pacific St. (☎831-646-3930), diagonally across from City Hall. Open M-W 10am-9pm, Th-F 10am-6pm, Sa 10am-5pm, Su 1-5pm.

Post Office: 565 Hartnell St. (☎831-372-4003). Open M-F 8:30am-5:00pm, Sa 10am-2pm. **Postal Code:** 93940.

IN THE PASSENGER SEAT

SURFER SPEAK

Brian, a 19-year-old surfer dude from San Jose, was spotted with his longboard and wetsuit at Carmel City Beach.

LG: How long have you been surfing?

A: 'Bout 12 years.

LG: And exactly how long did it take you to actually stand up on the board and "catch a wave"—is that the proper terminology nowadays?

A: That's fine, some people still say that....it took me a good year until I could ride a wave.

LG: But how long did it take you to even stand up on the board? [It took our researcher 2hr.]

A: I think just about anyone could do it in a day with some instruction.

LG: [Feeling validated—he said *day*] What are the big rules of surfing?

A: The biggest one is that up-wave surfers have the right of way. So, like, if someone is on a wave before you then it is his and you can't get in his way.

LG: Now getting back to the issue of jargon or slang, you said that some people will say "catch a wave." What are some other examples of contemporary surfing parlance?

A: Um, like, what do you mean?

LG: I mean, what words would you use to describe a fantastic surfing expedition? "Gnarly," "rad," "wicked"? And does anyone say "hang ten"?

A: [Pensive] I guess I say "killer" a lot and call going out to surf a "sesh" [short for session]. "Hang ten" is not something I hear.

◉ SIGHTS

⬛ MONTEREY BAY AQUARIUM. The largest of Monterey's attractions, this extraordinary aquarium benefits from the area's superb marine ecology. Gaze through the **world's largest window** at an enormous marine habitat containing green sea turtles, giant ocean sunfish, large sharks, and yellow- and blue-fin tuna in one million gallons of water. Don't miss the provocative exhibit connecting the shape, movement, and beauty of jellyfish to various art forms, or the new exhibit exploring the myth and mystery of sharks. Kids and adults love watching the **sea otters** during feeding time, walking through the **shorebird aviary,** perusing the living kelp forest housed in a two-story glass aquarium, and checking out the petting pool of damp bay creatures (stingrays included). Be patient; the lines for tickets, admission, viewing, and food can be unbelievably long. Save 20-40min. by picking up tickets the day before. *(886 Cannery Row.* ☎ *831-648-4888 or 800-756-3737; www.montereybayaquarium.org. Open daily June to early Sept. and holidays 9:30am-6pm; early Sept. to late May 10am-6pm. $20, seniors $18; students and ages 13-17 $16; ages 3-12 $9.)*

CANNERY ROW. Lying along the waterfront east of the aquarium, Cannery Row was once a dilapidated street crammed with languishing sardine-packing plants. The three-quarter-mile row has since been converted into a different commercial venture of tourist-packed mini-malls, bars, and a pint-sized carnival complex. All that remains of the earthiness and gruff camaraderie celebrated by John Steinbeck in *Cannery Row* and *Sweet Thursday* are a few building facades: 835 Cannery Row was the Wing Chong Market, the bright yellow building next door is where *Sweet Thursday* took place, and Doc Rickett's lab, 800 Cannery Row, is now closed to the public. Take a peek at the **Great Cannery Row Mural;** local artists have covered 400 ft. of a construction-site barrier on the 700 block with depictions of 1930s Monterey and what "The Row" was like in its heyday. The "Taste of Monterey" **Wine Visitors Center** on the second floor of the 700 building offers a sampling of the county's wine industry with well-priced bottles and winery maps. *(700 Cannery Row.* ☎ *888-646-5446. Open daily 11am-6pm. 6 tastings $5; fee can go toward wine purchases.)*

SUNSET DRIVE. West of Monterey in Pacific Grove, Sunset Dr. provides a free, 6 mi. scenic alternative to 17 Mile Drive. Appropriately, Sunset Dr. is the best place in the area to watch the sun go down. People arrive a full 2hr. before sunset in order to secure front-row seats along the road, also known as Ocean Blvd. At the western tip of the peninsula stands **Point Piños Lighthouse,** the oldest continuously running Pacific Coast lighthouse, which houses exhibits on Coast Guard history. *(☎ 831-648-3116. Open Th-Su 1-4pm. Free.)*

PACIFIC GROVE. Pacific Grove took root as a Methodist enclave over 100 years ago, and many of the Victorian houses are still in excellent condition. This unpretentious town (which falls eerily quiet at night) has a beautiful coastline, numerous lunch counters, and lots of antique and artsy home furnishing stores. Browse second-hand clothing, book, and music stores along Lighthouse Ave., or outlet-shop-'til-you-drop at the **American Tin Cannery,** on Ocean View Blvd. near New Monterey. Thousands of **monarch butterflies** winter in Pacific Grove from October to March. Look, but don't touch; bothering the butterflies is a $1000 offense. The **Pacific Grove Museum of Natural History,** at Forest and Central Ave. one block north of Lighthouse Ave., has exhibits on monarchs and local wildlife. The stuffed birds are top-notch. *(☎ 831-648-5716. Open Tu-Sa 10am-5pm. Free.)*

MARITIME MUSEUM OF MONTEREY. This haven for sea buffs illustrates the maritime history of Monterey with ship models, photos, navigation tools, logs, and a free 14 min. film. The museum's centerpiece is the original Fresnel lens of Point Sur Lighthouse. The lens is a two-story structure of gear-works and cut glass later replaced by the electric lighthouse. *(5 Custom House Plaza, across from Fisherman's Wharf in downtown Monterey.* ☎ *831-374-2608. Open daily 10am-5pm. $8, ages 13-17 $3, seniors and military $6, under 12 free.)*

PATH OF HISTORY WALKING TOUR. The early days of Monterey spawned a unique architectural trend that combined flourishes from the South, like wraparound porches, with Mexican adobe features, like 3 ft. thick walls and exterior staircases. The Path of History, marked by yellow sidewalk medallions, snakes through Monterey State Historic Park in downtown, passing numerous historic buildings including the Royal Presidio Chapel, built in 1794, and the Larkin House, home to the US consul to Mexico during the 1840s. Use the visitors center brochure to walk the path unguided, or join a free tour led by state park guides. (☎831-649-7118. Houses open daily 10am-5pm; in winter 10am-4pm. Tour times and starting locations vary; call for details.)

⚠ OUTDOOR ACTIVITIES

Companies on Fisherman's Wharf offer critter-spotting boat trips around Monterey Bay. The best time to go is during gray whale migration season (Nov.-Mar.), but the trips are hit-or-miss year-round. **Chris's Fishing Trips,** 48 Fisherman's Wharf, offers daily whale watching tours and fishing boat charters. (☎831-375-5951. Open daily 4am-5pm. 2-3hr. whale watching tours May-Nov. 11am and 2pm. $25, under 13 $20. 2hr. gray whale migration tours Dec.-Apr. $18, under 13 $12. Boat charters for tuna, salmon, rock cod, halibut, and sea bass also available.) Sea kayaking above kelp forests and among otters can be a heady experience. **Monterey Bay Kayaks,** 693 Del Monte Ave., also provides rentals and tours. (☎831-373-5357 or 800-649-5357. Call for lesson info. Rentals $30 per person; includes gear, wetsuit, and instruction. 3hr. beach tours by a biologist $55. Open daily 9am-6pm; in summer Su-Th 9am-6pm, F-Sa 9am-8pm.)

There are several bike paths in the area. The best is the **Monterey Peninsula Recreation Trail,** which follows the coast for approximately 20 mi. from Castroville to Asilomar St. in Pacific Grove. Bikers can then continue through Pacific Grove to Pebble Beach along famous 17 Mile Drive.

🔱🎸 FOOD & NIGHTLIFE

Once a hot spot for the sardine industry (hence "Cannery Row"), Monterey Bay now yields crab, red snapper, and salmon. Seafood is often expensive; look for free chowder samples or early-bird specials (usually 4-6pm). Monterey's culinary wealth extends beyond the sea; artichokes and strawberries abound. Nibble on free samples at the **Old Monterey Market Place,** on Alvarado St. between Pearl St. and Del Monte Ave. (☎831-655-2607. Open Tu 4-7pm; in summer 4-8pm.)

Monterey knows how to cut loose at night, but some areas of the peninsula quiet down early. The main action is downtown along **Alvarado St.;** there are also a few **Lighthouse Ave.** bars. Those under 21 have few options.

🍴 **Thai Bistro II,** 159 Central Ave. (☎831-372-8700), in Pacific Grove. Graced with a flower-encircled patio, this bistro offers top-quality Thai cuisine in a comfy atmosphere. Mixed vegetable curry and tofu $8. Lunch combos ($7-9) come with soup, salad, egg roll, and rice. Extensive vegetarian menu. Open daily 11:30am-3pm and 5-9:30pm.

🍴 **Tillie Gort's,** 111 Central Ave. (☎831-373-0335), in Pacific Grove. This vegetarian restaurant has been in the business for over 30 years. Large portions of dishes like Mexican fiesta salad ($8.25), eggplant francese ($8.50), or spinach ravioli ($10.50), and sweet treats like berry cheesecake or chocolate vegan cake ($4.50) please even carnivores. Beer and wine. Open June-Oct. M-F 10am-10pm, Sa-Su 8am-10pm; Nov.-May M-F 11am-10pm.

🍴 **Mucky Duck British Pub,** 479 Alvarado St. (☎831-655-3031). Parking lot in back. Empty front window booths might fool you—many patrons are in the back beer garden, listening to music, having a smoke, or staying warm around a coal-burning fire. Monterey locals have voted the pub's beer the city's best for 7 years in a row. Come early to avoid waits. Live music, karaoke, or DJ from around 9pm; some live music during the day. Salads, sandwiches, and appetizers $4.25-10.25. Open daily 11:30am-2am.

Kalisa's, 851 Cannery Row, across from the Monterey Bay Aquarium. This simple yellow structure was the inspiration for La Ida Cafe in Steinbeck's *Cannery Row.* Hearty, healthy, inexpensive sandwiches and salads from $5. Lappert's ice cream from Hawaii ($2.50-4.50) and fresh coconuts drilled for drinking ($3) add a tropical flair. F night belly dancing show from 9pm (cover $5). Sa "Bohemian Night" from 8pm (cover $5-10). Open Su-Th 9am-6:30pm, F-Sa 9am-2am; in summer Su-Th 6:30-9pm.

Club Octane, 321-D Alvarado St. (☎831-646-9244; www.cluboctane.com), on the 2nd floor at Del Monte Ave. Parking structure adjacent. Strobe lights and heavy smoke machines throb like teenage hormones. 3 bars and 4 dance floors with different DJs. Pool tables and a smoking deck. Male and female burlesque M 9:45pm. Live music W. No hats, tennis shoes, or beach flip-flops. Cover M $7, W $5-25, F $5, Sa $10-15. Open daily 9pm-1:45am.

▐ ACCOMMODATIONS

Inexpensive hotels line the 2000 block of **Fremont St.** in Monterey. Others cluster along **Munras Ave.** between downtown Monterey and Rte.

1. The cheapest hotels in the area are in the less appealing towns of Seaside and Marina, just north of Monterey. Prices fluctuate depending on the season, day of the week, and events. In Monterey, camping is an excellent option for the budget traveler. Call **Monterey Parks** (☎831-755-4895) for camping info and ReserveAmerica (☎800-444-7275) for reservations.

Monterey Carpenter's Hall Hostel (HI-AYH), 778 Hawthorne St. (☎831-649-0375), 1 block west of Lighthouse Ave. This 45-bed hostel is fairly new and perfectly located. Modern facilities and a large, comfy living room with a piano, library, and games. Make-your-own pancake breakfast with tea, hot chocolate, and coffee (small donation appreciated). Parking included. Limited shower time: visitors get 2 tokens per day, each good for 3min. of hot water. Towels $0.50. No sleeping bags; linens provided. Lockout 10:30am-5pm. Curfew 11pm. Reservations essential June-Sept. Dorms $22, nonmembers $25, ages 7-17 with adult $17; private rooms for 2-5 people $60-74.

Del Monte Beach Inn, 1110 Del Monte Blvd. (☎831-649-4410), near downtown, across from the beach. Cute, Victorian-style inn with pleasant rooms. Near a fairly loud road. One room has kitchenette. Continental breakfast and tea in sunny main room. Check-in 2-8pm. Reservations recommended. Rooms $55-88; with bath $88-99.

Veterans Memorial Park Campground (☎831-646-3865), 1½ mi. from downtown. From Rte. 68, turn left onto Skyline Dr. From downtown, go south on Pacific St., turn right on Jefferson St., and follow the signs. Located on a hill with a view of the bay. Playground, BBQ pits, and hot showers. 40 sites. 3-night max. stay. No reservations; arrive before 3pm in summer and on weekends. Sites $20.

 LEAVING MONTEREY
Take **Rte. 1 North** toward Santa Cruz.

 DETOUR: SAN JUAN BAUTISTA
Take Rte. 1 North to Rte. 156 East.

A historic **mission** town founded in 1797, centering on a peaceful grassy plaza among green hills, San Juan Bautista has retained the tranquillity of a bygone era by pursuing policies of slow growth and forbidding development by chain commerce. The area around the square—the mission, cemetery, garden, hotel, town hall and stable—have been preserved in an historical park and function like a museum (open daily 9:30am-4:45pm; suggested donation $2), although the mission still holds daily mass (M-F 8am, Sa 5pm, Su 8:30am, 10am and noon in Spanish). The building of San Juan Bautista stands as the largest of the missions built by Spanish friars to bring the salvation of Catholicism to the "savage natives." At the end of the green lies a portion of the **El Camino Real** ("the royal road"), the path that connected the 21 missions from San Diego to San Francisco, each a day's journey on horseback from the next mission in the chain. The first Saturday of every month San Juan Bautista hosts a "living history celebration" with displays of spinning, weaving candle making, and dancing. Pick up an events calendar at the mission or around town for other festivals.

THE ROAD TO SANTA CRUZ

Rte. 1 passes through a number of small towns on it's way north to Santa Cruz. **Castroville** distinguishes itself as "the artichoke center of the world" and hosts an artichoke festival in May. For a taste, head to the **Giant Artichoke Restaurant,** 11261 Merritt St. (☎831-633-3501), with a statue of the world's largest artichoke outside, and try the deep fried artichoke hearts ($4.38 for a small).

Moss Landing is a quaint oceanside town. The last Sunday of July, it hosts one of California's biggest **antique fairs,** where vendors display everything from glassware to rare first editions. (Call ☎831-633-4501 for more info.) **Sanctuary Cruises** (☎831-917-1042) and **Tom's Sportfishing** (☎831-633-2464) offer whale-watching cruises along the harbor. The less aquatically-minded should enjoy strolling or horseback-riding the scenic shores.

Feel free to cruise past **Watsonville,** an eminently skippable chain-store center. The only site of interest is the **Sunset State Beach,** 201 Sunset Beach Rd., which can be reached by taking the San Andreas Rd. Exit and turning right onto Sunset Beach Rd. Wind through eucalyptus-lined roads and end up by a stunning beach. (☎831-763-7063. Food lockers, picnic tables, and coin showers. 90 sites with fire rings. Reservations highly recommended in summer. Sites $16. Day-use $5.)

SANTA CRUZ

One of the few places where the 1960s catchphrase "do your own thing" still applies, Santa Cruz embraces sculpted surfers, aging hippies, freethinking students, and same-sex couples. The atmosphere here is fun-loving but far from hedonistic, intellectual but nowhere near stuffy. This small city exudes both Northern California cool and Southern California fun, whether gobbling cotton candy on the Boardwalk or sipping wheatgrass at poetry readings.

Along the beach, tourism and surf culture reign supreme. Nearby Pacific Ave. teems with independent bookstores, cool bars, trendy cafes, and pricey boutiques. On the inland side of Mission St., the University of California at Santa Cruz (UCSC) sprawls across miles of rolling forests and grasslands filled with prime biking routes and wild students. Restaurants offer avocado sandwiches and industrial coffee, while merchants hawk UCSC paraphernalia. Be careful about visiting on Saturday or Sunday, since the town's population virtually doubles on summer weekends, clogging area highways as daytrippers make their way to and from the Bay Area.

(VITAL STATS)

Population: 56,000

Visitor Infor: Santa Cruz County Conference and Visitor Council, 1211 Ocean St. (☎831-425-1234 or 800-833-3494; www.santacruz.org). Extremely helpful staff. Publishes the free *Santa Cruz County Traveler's Guide*, which has tourist info and discounts. Open M-Sa 9am-5pm, Su 10am-4pm. **Downtown Info Center,** 1126 Pacific Ave. (☎831-459-9486). Open daily noon-6pm. An **information kiosk** (☎831-421-9552) sits to the left of the Santa Cruz Wharf. Open June-Aug. daily 10am-5pm. **California Parks and Recreation Department** (☎831-429-2850). Info on camping and beach facilities in Santa Cruz; for reservations. Open M-F 8am-5pm.

Internet Access: Public Library, 224 Church St. (☎831-420-5730). $5 per hr. Open M-Th 10am-8pm, F 10am-5pm, Sa 10am-5pm, Su 1-5pm.

Post Office: 850 Front St. (☎831-426-8184). Open M-F 9am-5pm. **Postal Code:** 95060.

▐ GETTING AROUND

Santa Cruz is on the northern tip of Monterey Bay, 65 mi. south of San Francisco. Through west Santa Cruz, Rte. 1 becomes **Mission St.** The **University of California at Santa Cruz (UCSC)** blankets the hills inland from Mission St. Southeast of Mission

St. lies the waterfront and the downtown. Down by the ocean, **Beach St.** runs roughly east-west. The narrow **San Lorenzo River** runs north-south, dividing the Boardwalk scene from quiet, affluent residences. **Pacific Ave.** is the main street downtown. Along with **Cedar St.,** Pacific Ave. carves out a nightlife niche accessible from the beach motels. Resident-traffic-only zones, one-way streets, and dead-ends can make Santa Cruz frustrating to navigate by car. It's cheapest to park at a motel or in free 2hr. public lots off Pacific Ave.

⊙ SIGHTS

SANTA CRUZ BEACH BOARDWALK. The beach is great at Santa Cruz, but the water is frigid. Casual beachgoers catch their thrills on the Boardwalk, a three-block strip of over 25 amusement park rides, shooting galleries, and corn-dog vendors. It's a gloriously tacky throwback to 50s-era beach culture, providing a loud, lively diversion. Highly recommended is the **Giant Dipper,** a 1924 wooden roller coaster, where Dirty Harry met his enemy in 1983's *Sudden Impact. (Boardwalk open daily June-Sept. 6, plus many off-season weekends and holidays. $30 per 60 tickets, with most rides 4 or 5 tickets; all-day pass $25 per person. Some height restrictions. Miniature golf $4.)*

UNIVERSITY OF CALIFORNIA AT SANTA CRUZ (UCSC). Five miles northwest of downtown sprawls this 2000-acre campus. Governor Ronald Reagan's plan to make UCSC a "riot-proof campus" (free of a central point where radicals could inflame a crowd) had a beneficial side effect: the university's decentralized and forested layout. Although the campus appears tranquil, amidst rolling hills and redwood groves, UCSC is famous (or infamous) for its leftist politics and conspicuous drug culture. If driving, make sure you have a parking permit on weekdays, available at the kiosk inside the main campus entrance, the police station, or the parking office. *(For UCSC campus tours call ☎831-429-2231 M-F 8am-5pm. Arboretum open daily 9am-5pm. Free. Seymour Marine Discovery Center, 100 Shaffer Rd. ☎831-459-3799. $5; students, seniors, and ages 6-16 $3. 1st Tu of every month free. Parking permit $4.)*

SANTA CRUZ WHARF. Jutting off Beach St. is the longest car-accessible pier on the West Coast. Seafood restaurants and souvenir shops will try to distract you from the expansive views of the ocean. Munch on candy from local favorite **Marini's** while watching sea lions hang out on rafters beneath the end of the pier. (☎ *831-423-7258. Parking $1 per hr., under 30min. free. Disabled patrons free.*)

MISIÓN DE EXALTACIÓN DE LA SANTA CRUZ.
This peaceful adobe church and fragrant garden offer contemplative quiet. (*126 High St. Turn north on Emmet St. off Mission St.* ☎ *831-426-5686. Open Su 10am-2pm, Tu-Sa 10am-4pm. Donation requested.*)

🌊 BEACHES

The **Santa Cruz Beach** (officially named Cowell Beach) is broad, reasonably clean, and packed with volleyball players. If you're seeking solitude, you'll have to venture farther afield. Away from the main drag, beach access points line Rte. 1. Railroad tracks, farmlands, and dune vegetation make several of these access points somewhat difficult to reach, but the beaches are correspondingly less crowded. Folks who want to **bare everything** head north on Rte. 1 to the **Red, White, and Blue Beach,** down Scaroni Rd. Look for a piece of wood painted in patriotic colors that marks the elusive turn-off to the beach. Sunbathers must be 18 or accompanied by a parent. (Beach open Feb.-Oct. daily 10am-6pm. $10, after 3pm $15.)

The best vantage points for **watching surfers** are along W. Cliff Dr. To learn more about the activity, stop in at **Steamer's Lane,** the deep water off the point where surfers have flocked since Hawaiian "Duke" Kahanamoku kick-started California's surf culture here 100 years ago. Surfers also gather at the more remote "Hook" along **Pleasure Point,** north of Santa Cruz in Live Oak. For surfing lessons, contact **Richard Schmidt Surf School,** 236 San Jose Ave., or ask for him at the beach. Schmidt is much respected by locals, who say he can get anyone surfing. (☎ 831-423-0928; www.richardschmidt.com. 1hr. private lesson $65; 2hr. group lesson $70. Lessons include equipment.)

Around the point at the end of W. Cliff Dr. is **Natural Bridges State Beach.** Only one natural bridge remains standing, but the park offers a pristine beach, awe-inspiring tidepools, and tours during **monarch butterfly** season (Oct.-Mar.). In November and December, thousands of the stunning butter-

flies swarm along the beach and cover the nearby groves with their orange hues. (☎ 831-423-4609. Open daily 8am-dusk. Parking $3.)

Outdoor sports enthusiasts will find ample activities in Santa Cruz. Parasailing and other pricey pastimes are popular on the wharf. **Kayak Connection,** 413 Lake Ave., offers tours of the Elkhorn Slough (9:30am or 1:30pm; $40) and the Santa Cruz Harbor ($40-45), and rents ocean-going kayaks at decent rates. (☎ 831-479-1121. Open-deck single $33 per day; closed-deck single $37. Paddle, life jacket, brief instruction, and wetsuit included. Open M-F 10am-5pm, Sa-Su 9am-6pm.) Beware of cheaper rental agencies that don't include instruction sessions; closed-deck ocean kayaking can be dangerous. You must provide ACA certification for a closed-deck kayak unless you go to **Elkhorn Slough,** a beautiful estuary where it is safe for inexperienced kayakers. This incredible spot has an amazing array of wildlife.

🍴 FOOD

Santa Cruz offers an astounding number of budget eateries. The healthful restaurant community goes out of its way to embrace vegans—**tofu** can be substituted for just about anything.

■ **Zoccoli's,** 1534 Pacific Ave. (☎ 831-423-1711). This phenomenal deli makes sandwiches for $4-5. Daily pasta specials ($6.75) come with salad, bread, cheese, and salami. Uses only fresh ingredients. Open M-Sa 10am-6pm, Su 11am-5pm.

■ **Malabar,** 1116 Soquel Ave. (☎ 831-423-7906), at Seabright Ave. Healthy, vegetarian Sri Lankan cuisine. Incredible flatbread served by candlelight with ghee and garlic ($2.50). Hefty entrees are reasonably priced ($5-9). Open M-Th 11am-2:30pm and 5:30-9pm, F 11am-2:30pm and 5:30-10pm, Sa 5:30-10pm. No credit cards.

Zachary's, 819 Pacific Ave. (☎ 831-427-0646). With savory potatoes, fresh bread, and enormous omelettes, earthy Zachary's will give you reason to laze about for the rest of the day. Basic breakfast (2 eggs, oatmeal-molasses toast, and hash browns) for under $5. Beware of crowds; eat at the counter to avoid the wait. Open Su and Tu-Sa 7am-2:30pm.

Saturn Cafe, 145 Laurel St. (☎ 831-429-8505), at Pacific Ave. At this planetary-punk themed restaurant, the hard-working waitstaff does its best to keep your table clean and your coffee fresh. Veggie breakfast

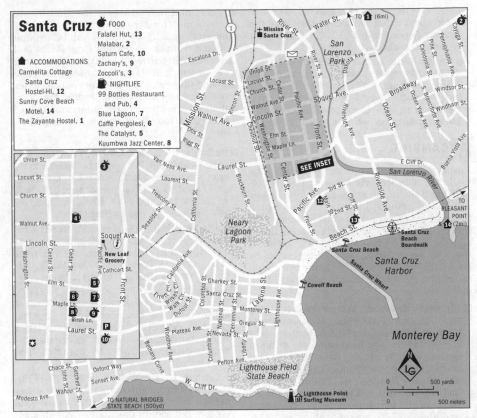

Santa Cruz

ACCOMMODATIONS
Carmelita Cottage
Santa Cruz
Hostel-HI, **12**
Sunny Cove Beach
Motel, **14**
The Zayante Hostel, **1**

FOOD
Falafel Hut, **13**
Malabar, **2**
Saturn Cafe, **10**
Zachary's, **9**
Zoccoli's, **3**

NIGHTLIFE
99 Bottles Restaurant
and Pub, **4**
Blue Lagoon, **7**
Caffe Pergolesi, **6**
The Catalyst, **5**
Kuumbwa Jazz Center, **8**

plates like tofu scramble with fakin' bacon or veggie sausage and pancakes (can be made vegan) $6. Open Su-Th 11:30am-3pm, F-Sa 11:30am-4pm.

Falafel Hut, 309 Beach St. (☎831-423-0567), across the street from the Boardwalk. A good place for a quick late-night snack, it serves Middle Eastern and American dishes. The Lebanese owners pride themselves on their falafel sandwiches ($4.25), but the chicken ($5) is hard to beat. Open daily 11am-11pm.

ACCOMMODATIONS

Santa Cruz gets jam-packed during the summer, especially on weekends. Room rates skyrocket and availability plummets. Surprisingly, the nicer motels tend to have the more reasonable summer weekend rates, but more expensive rates at other times. Reservations are always recommended. Shop around—price fluctuation can be outrageous. Camping may be the best budget option.

Carmelita Cottage Santa Cruz Hostel (HI-AYH), 321 Main St. (☎831-423-8304), 4 blocks from the Greyhound stop and 2 blocks from the beach. Centrally located in a quiet neighborhood, this 40-bed Victorian has a young staff. Chores requested. Linen provided; towels $0.50. Overnight parking free, day permits $1.25. July-Aug. 3-night max. stay. Reception 8-10am and 5-10pm. Lockout 10am-5pm. Strict curfew 11pm. Call for reservations, but no refunds after 48hr. prior to reservation date. Dorms $20, members $17, ages 12-17 $15, ages 4-11 $10, ages 3 and under free.

Sunny Cove Beach Motel, 1610 E. Cliff Dr. (☎831-475-1741), near Schwan Lagoon. Far from downtown, but pleasant, well-kept suites have kitchens and cable TV. Outdoor pool. Market and beach 1 block away. Pets allowed. Rooms Su-Th $60-100, F-Sa $80-130. Weekly rates available.

The Zayante Hostel, on East Zayante Rd. (☎831-335-4265), across the street from the market, near Felton. A former hippie and folk-rock nightclub. Cabins have beds underneath makeshift skylights, with vines creeping through the walls. Linens provided, but it's not a bad idea to bring your own. Dorms $16. Cash only.

CAMPING

Reservations for state campgrounds can be made through ReserveAmerica (☎800-444-7275) and should be made early. Sites below are listed geographically, moving north toward Santa Cruz and then past Santa Cruz into the mountains. New Brighton State Beach and Big Basin Redwoods State Park, two of the more scenic spots, are both accessible by public transportation. As with any other kind of lodging in Santa Cruz, campgrounds fill up quick and early.

Big Basin Redwoods State Park, 21600 Big Basin Way (☎831-338-8860), in Boulder Creek, 23 mi. northwest of Santa Cruz. Go north on Rte. 9 to Rte. 236 through Boulder Creek. Although removed from the city, Big Basin offers the best camping in the region. 80 mi. of cool, breezy trails, including the 2-day, 30 mi. **Skyline-to-the-Sea Trail** (trailhead parking $5). To reserve one of the 145 campsites with showers, call ReserveAmerica (☎800-444-7275, for tent cabins 800-874-8368). $5 non-refundable reservation fee. Reservations for all options required well in advance during the summer. Sites $16; backcountry sites including parking $5. Day use $5 per car.

Manresa Uplands State Beach Park, 205 Manresa Rd. (☎831-761-1795), in La Selva Beach, 13 mi. south of Santa Cruz. Take Rte. 1 and exit at San Andreas Rd. Veer right and follow San Andreas Rd. for 4 mi., then turn right on Sand Dollar Rd. 64 walk-in, tent-only sites $16. Day use $5 per car, seniors $4.

NIGHTLIFE

There are comprehensive weekly events listings in the free local publications *Good Times* and *Metro Santa Cruz*, and also in *Spotlight* in Friday's *Sentinel* (all available

at cafes and bookstores). The Boardwalk bandstand offers free summertime Friday concerts, usually by oldies bands, around 6:30 and 8:30pm. The Santa Cruz Parks and Recreation Department publishes info in the free *Summer Activity Guide*. Underage kids and those asking for spare change gather downtown, especially along **Pacific Ave.** Nevertheless, this strip is also home to a host of bustling coffee shops and a few laid-back bars.

99 Bottles Restaurant and Pub, 110 Walnut Ave. (☎831-459-9999). This modest but lively bar in the heart of downtown offers standard bar meals (burgers $7) and 99 different types of beer. Open M-Th 11:30am-1:30am, F-Sa 11:30am-2am, Su 11:30am-midnight. Kitchen closes 10pm.

Caffe Pergolesi, 418A Cedar St. (☎831-426-1775). Chill coffeehouse/bar with small rooms and a roomy patio for reading or socializing. Four types of hot chocolate. Open M-Th 6:30am-11:30pm, F-Sa 7:30am-midnight, Su 7:30am-11:30pm.

Blue Lagoon, 923 Pacific Ave. (☎831-423-7117). Mega-popular gay-straight club has won all kinds of lawards from "best bartender" to "best place you can't take your parents." Bar in front, 3 pool tables in back, and dancing everywhere. Stronger-than-the-bouncer drinks $3-4. Cover $2-5. Open daily 4pm-1:30am.

The Catalyst, 1011 Pacific Ave. (☎831-423-1338). The town's primary music/dance venue draws national, college, and local bands. Pool and darts upstairs, deli and bar downstairs. Sandwiches $4-8. Cover and age restrictions vary widely with show ($5-30; as young as 16+). Adjacent bar area strictly 21+. Shows W-Sa. Open M-Sa 9am-2am, Su 9am-5pm. Food served Su-Tu 9am-3pm, W-Sa 9am-10pm.

Kuumbwa Jazz Center, 320 Cedar St. (☎831-427-2227; www.kuumbwajazz.org). Known throughout the region for great jazz and innovative off-night programs. Those under 21 are welcome in this small and low-key setting. The big names play here on M; locals have their turn on F. Tickets ($12-23) sold through **Logos Books and Music,** 1117 Pacific Ave. (☎831-427-5100), as well as at www.ticketweb.com. M shows 7 and 9pm; F 8pm.

LEAVING SANTA CRUZ
Follow **Rte. 1 North** from town.

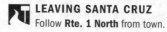

AÑO NEUVO STATE RESERVE
20 mi. north of Santa Cruz.

This wildlife reserve has several hiking trails that offer views of **Año Nuevo Island,** the site of an abandoned lighthouse now taken over by birds, seals, and sea lions. Free hiking permits are available at the ranger station by the entrance and at the Visitors Center (though seal-viewing permits are only issued up until 3:30pm). The Visitors Center also features real-time videos displaying the animal adventures on the island. From mid-December to late March, the reserve is the mating place of the 15 ft., 4500 lb. elephant seal. Thousands of fat seals crowd the shore and, like frat boys looking to score, the males fight each other for dominance over a herd of females. Before mid-August, you can still see the last of the "molters" and the young who have yet to find their sea legs. Don't get too close—if they don't get you, the cops might; the law requires staying 25 ft. away. (☎831-879-0227. No pets. Open daily 8am-sunset. Visitors Center open daily 8:30am-3:30pm. Parking $2, seniors $1.)

PESCADERO. Pescadero, a tiny horse town a couple of miles east of Rte. 1, 33 mi. north of Santa Cruz, is the place to come for awesome **artichoke soup** ($5.50) and a slice of homemade pie. Turn off for Pescadero and take a left at the red flashing light to **Duarte's,** 202 Stage Rd., a simple wooden restaurant and tavern run by the Duarte family since 1984. (☎831-879-0406. Open daily 7am-9:30pm.)

APPROACHING SAN JOSE
Take **Rte 1. North** to **Rte. 92 East.** Follow Rte. 92 East to **I-280 South,** toward San Jose. Take the **Rte. 87/Guadalupe Pkwy.** exit on the left.

SAN JOSE

Founded in 1777 in a bucolic valley of fruit and walnut orchards, San Jose was California's first civilian settlement. The area's primary business was agriculture until the middle of the 20th century, when the technology sector began to develop. In 1939, the first computer company, Hewlett-Packard, had its modest beginnings here—in Dave Packard's garage. By the early 1970s, many of San Jose's orchards had been replaced by offices, and the moniker "Silicon Valley" began to take hold.

For several decades, San Jose has been the country's center of technological innovation, with its residents boasting the second-highest average disposable incomes of any US city. Because of shifting economic conditions in recent years, however, San Jose residents have broadened their one-track focus on the high-tech to include other industries. Museums, restaurants, hotels, and vineyards have all sprouted up around the city as part of an effort to expand San Jose beyond the world of microchips and barefoot office techies.

⊙ VITAL STATS

Population: 894,943

Visitor Information: Visitor Information and Business Center, 150 W. San Carlos St. (☎408-726-5673 or 888-726-56731; www.sanjose.org), at Market and San Carlos St. in the San Jose McEnerny Convention Center. Free maps. Open M-F 9am-5pm, Sa 11am-5pm.

Internet Access: Martin Luther King, Jr. Public Library (☎408-808-2000; www.sjlibrary.org), at the intersection of E. San Fernando St. and 4th St. Open M-W 8am-8pm, Th-Sa 9am-6pm, Su 1-5pm, with expanded hours during the school year.

Post Office: 105 N. 1st St. (☎408-292-0487). Open M-F 8:30am-5pm, Sa 7am-noon. **Postal Code:** 95113.

GETTING AROUND

San Jose is centered around the convention-hosting malls and plazas near the intersection of east-west **San Carlos St.** and north-south **Market St.** Bars, restaurants, and clubs crowd around 1st St. in the so-called **SoFA District.** The **Transit Mall,** the center of San Jose's bus and trolley system, runs north-south along 1st and 2nd St. in the downtown area. **San Jose State University (SJSU)** has grassy grounds that span several blocks between S. 4th and S. 10th St.

SIGHTS

In San Jose proper, a few well-funded museums are the only real diversions.

TECH MUSEUM OF INNOVATION. Curious kids and their parents love the hands-on, cutting-edge science exhibits and IMAX theater at this tourist-savvy attraction. The museum is underwritten by high-tech firms and housed in a sleek geometric building. *(201 S. Market St. ☎408-795-6224; www.thetech.org. Open daily 10am-5pm; Oct.-Mar. closed M. $9, seniors $8, ages 3-12 $7. Exhibits and IMAX film $16/$15/$13.)*

WINCHESTER MYSTERY HOUSE. This odd Victorian house is little more than that, but will amuse those with a penchant for the unusual. Sarah Winchester was the eccentric heir to the Winchester rifle fortune. After the death of her daughter and husband, she was convinced by an occultist that the spirits of all the men ever killed by her family's guns would seek revenge if construction on her home ever ceased. Work on the mansion continued 24hr. a day for over 38 years. A 160-room maze of doors, windows, and stairs elaborately designed to "confuse the spirits" is the end result. *(525 S. Winchester Blvd. Near the intersection of I-880 and I-280, west of town. ☎408-247-2101. Open mid-Oct. to Aug. daily 9am-7pm; Sept. to mid-Oct. Su-Th 9am-5pm, F-Sa 9am-7pm. $20, ages 6-12 $14, under 6 free.)*

ROSICRUCIAN EGYPTIAN MUSEUM AND PLANETARIUM. Rising out of the suburbs, this grand structure houses the largest exhibit of Egyptian artifacts in the western US, with over 4000 ancient Egyptian artifacts, including a walk-in tomb and spooky animal mummies. This collection belongs to the ancient and mystical Rosicrucian Order, whose past members include Amenhotep IV, Pythagoras, Sir Francis Bacon, Rene Descartes, Benjamin Franklin, and Isaac Newton. *(1660 Park Ave., at Naglee Ave. ☎408-947-3635; www.egyptianmuseum.org. Open Tu-F 10am-5pm, Sa-Su 11am-6pm. Planetarium shows Tu-F 2pm, Sa-Su 3:30pm. $9, students and seniors $7, ages 5-10 $5, under 5 free.)*

THE SAN JOSE MUSEUM OF ART. Neighbor to the Tech, this modern museum not only features contemporary art but is itself progressive in design and mission. Admission is free to encourage public awareness of 20th- and 21st-century art, and the museum offers a wide range of exhibits, lectures, programs, and hands-on events for adults and children. *(110 S. Market St. ☎408-294-2787; www.sjma.com. Open Tu-Su 11am-5pm. Free.)*

MISSION SANTA CLARA AND SANTA CLARA UNIVERSITY. The first California mission to honor a woman—Clare of Assisi—as its patron saint, Mission Santa Clara was established on the Guadalupe River in 1777, moving to its present site in 1825. *(Mass M-F noon, Su 10am.)* **Santa Clara University,** built around the mission, was established in 1851, making it California's oldest institution of higher learning. Subsequent restorations have refitted the structures to match the beauty and bliss of the surrounding rose gardens and 180-year-old olive trees. *(500 El Camino Real, 5 mi. northwest of downtown San Jose off The Alameda. ☎408-554-4000; www.scu.edu.)*

AMUSEMENT PARKS. Paramount's Great America theme park is a jungle of roller coasters, log rides, and fiendish contraptions designed to spin you, flip you, drop you, and generally separate you from your stomach. *(☎408-988-1776; www.pgathrills.com. Off U.S. 101 at Great America Pkwy. in Santa Clara, 8 mi. northwest of downtown San Jose. Open June-Aug. Su-F 10am-9pm, Sa 10am-10pm; Sept.-Oct. and Mar.-May Sa 10am-10pm, Su 10am-9pm. $48, ages 3-6 or under 48 in. $34, under 3 free. Parking $10.)* The area's best collection of waterslides, Paramount's **Raging Waters,** is great on a hot day, but don't expect to be the only one seeking a soaking. *(☎408-654-5450; www.rwsplash.com. Off U.S. 101 at the Tully Rd. exit, about 5 mi. east of downtown San Jose. Open June-Aug. daily 10am-6pm; May and Sept. Sa-Su 10am-6pm. $26, under 48 in. $20, seniors $16. After 3pm $19/$14.)*

🍴 FOOD

Familiar fast-food franchises and pizzerias surround SJSU. More international cheap eats lie along **S. 1st St.** or near **San Pedro Sq.,** at St. John and San Pedro St. **House of Siam,** 55 S. Market St., with a bigger branch at 151 S. 2nd St., features excellent Thai entrees (some meatless) for $8-15. (☎408-279-5668. Market St. location open M-F 11am-2:30pm and 5-9:30pm, Sa-Su 5-9:30pm. S. 2nd St. location open M-F 11am-3pm and 5-10pm, Sa-Su noon-10pm.) **Bella Mia,** 58 S. 1st St., serves regional Italian-American cuisine (entrees $13-26) in an inviting atmosphere. The lasagna ($15) and chicken foresta ($15) are especially popular. (☎408-280-1993. Open M-F 11:30am-3pm and 5-9:30pm, Sa 5-9:30pm, Su 11am-3pm and 5-9pm.)

🏠 ACCOMMODATIONS

County parks with campgrounds surround the city, as do chain motels. **Mount Madonna County Park,** on Pole Line Rd. off Hecker Pass Hwy., has 117 sites in a beautiful setting, available by reservation or on a first-come, first-camp basis. (☎408-842-2341 or 842-6761, reservations 355-2201. Sites $15; RVs $25.) The area around **Saratoga**, on Rte. 85, 14 mi. southwest of San Jose, has a number of campsites, as well as miles of horse and hiking trails in **Sanborn-Skyline County Park**. From Rte. 17 South, take Rte. 9 to Big Basin Way and turn left onto Sanborn Rd. (☎408-867-9959, reservations 355-2201. Open late Mar. to mid-Oct. for walk-in camping. Open for day use year-round from 8am to sunset. Sites $8; RVs $25.). Those looking for peace and quiet will be happy to find **Sanborn Park Hostel (HI-AYH)**, 15808 Sanborn Rd., in Sanborn-Skyline County Park, 20 mi. west of downtown San Jose. (☎408-741-0166. Clean rooms and 39 beds. Linen $0.50; towels $0.25. Reception 5-10:30pm. Check-out 9am. 11pm curfew. Dorms $12, nonmembers $14, under 18 $6.)

⚔ LEAVING SAN JOSE

Take **Rte. 87 North** to **U.S. 101 North**, toward Palo Alto.

PALO ALTO

Dominated by the beautiful 8000-acre Stanford University campus, Palo Alto looks like "Collegeland" at a Disney theme park. Stanford's perfectly groomed grounds, sparkling lake, and Spanish mission-style buildings have a manufactured quality that suits the university's speedy rise to international acclaim. The city that Stanford calls home is equally manicured, with a tidy downtown strip of restaurants, bookstores, and boutiques. Its nightlife caters to students and suburbanites, while weekday happy hours help singles wind down.

☐ GETTING AROUND. The pristine lawns of residential Palo Alto are not easily distinguished from the manicured campus of Stanford University. Despite its name, **University Ave.**, the main thoroughfare off U.S. 101, belongs much more to the town than to the college. Cars coming off U.S. 101 onto University Ave. pass very briefly through **East Palo Alto**, a community incorporated in 1983 after Palo Alto and Menlo Park had already annexed most of their revenue-producing districts. East Palo Alto once had one of the highest violent crime rates in the nation. The town has cleaned up its act and grown safer in recent years, but you'll find that the contrast with the immaculate tree-lined lawns of Palo Alto is still striking. **Stanford University** spreads out from the west end

VITAL STATS

Population: 59,000

Visitor Information: Palo Alto Chamber of Commerce, 122 Hamilton Ave. (☎650-324-3121), between Hude and Alta St. Open M-F 9am-5pm. **Stanford University Information Booth** (☎650-723-2560), across from Hoover Tower in Memorial Auditorium. Open daily 8am-5pm.

Internet Access: Palo Alto Main Library, 1213 Newell Rd. (☎650-329-2436). Open M-F 10am-9pm, Sa 10am-6pm, Su 1-5pm. **Downtown branch,** 270 Forest Ave. (☎650-329-2641). Open Tu-F 11am-6pm. Free.

Post Office: Main Office, 2085 E. Bayshore Rd. (☎800-275-8777). Open M-F 8am-5pm. **Postal Code:** 94303. **Hamilton Station,** 380 Hamilton Ave. (☎650-323-2650). **Postal Code:** 94301.

of University Ave. Abutting University Ave. and running northwest-southeast through town is **El Camino Real** (part of Rte. 82). From there, University Ave. turns into Palm Dr., which accesses the heart of Stanford's campus, the **Main Quad.**

◪ SIGHTS. Undoubtedly Palo Alto's main tourist attraction, the secular, co-educational **Stanford University** was founded in 1885 by Jane and Leland Stanford to honor their son who died of typhoid. The Stanfords loved Spanish colonial mission architecture and collaborated with **Frederick Law Olmsted,** designer of New York City's Central Park, to create a red-tiled campus of uncompromising beauty. The school has produced such eminent conservatives as Chief Justice William Rehnquist, and the campus has been called "a hotbed of social rest." The oldest part of campus is the **Main Quadrangle,** on Serra St., the site of most undergraduate classes. The walkways are dotted with diamond-shaped, gold-numbered stone tiles that mark the locations of time capsules put together by each year's graduating class. (Free tours at 11:15am and 3:15pm depart from Information Booth in Memorial Auditorium.) Just south of the Main Quad, at Escondid Mall and Duena, **Memorial Church** is a non-denominational gold shrine with stained glass windows and glittering mosaic walls like those of an Eastern Orthodox church. (☎650-723-3469. Open M-F 8am-5pm. Free tours F 2pm.) The **Hoover** tower's observation deck has views of campus, the East Bay, and San Francisco. (☎650-723-2053. Open daily 10am-4:30pm; closed during finals and academic breaks.

PACIFIC COAST

$2, seniors and under 13 $1.) The **Visual Arts Center,** 328 Lomita Dr., at Museum Way off Palm Dr., displays its eclectic collection of painting and sculpture for free. (☎650-723-4177. Open W and F-Su 11am-5pm, Th 11am-8pm.) The extensive **Rodin Sculpture Garden,** at Museum Way and Lomita Dr., contains a stunning bronze cast of *Gates of Hell,* among other larger figures. It's an ideal spot to enjoy a picnic lunch. (☎650-723-4177. Free tours Sa-Su 2pm.)

▓▐ FOOD & NIGHTLIFE. Dining in Palo Alto is centered around posh restaurants downtown around University and California avenues. Those watching wallets should stay on University Ave. **▓Café Borrone,** 1010 El Camino Real, is a bustling, brasserie-style cafe that spills onto a large patio. Borrone serves freshly baked bread, sinful gateaux ($2-4), coffee drinks, Italian sodas, wine ($5-6 per glass), and beers ($3.75 per pint). Check the chalkboard for specials or choose from a wide range of salads, sandwiches, and quiches for $4-10. (☎650-327-0830. Open M-Th 8am-11pm, F-Sa 8am-midnight, Su 8am-5pm.) One block east of University Ave., **Mango Café,** 435 Hamilton Ave., offers reggae music and Caribbean cuisine. Seriously spicy Jamaican "jerked joints" ($6), tropical smoothies ($3.50), veggie options are available. (☎650-325-3229. Delicious bread pudding $3. Open M-Sa 11:30am-2:30pm and 6-10pm.)

Though Palo Alto can't compete with San Francisco's wild nightlife, it still has a couple of hot spots and bars perfect for sitting back and having a few beers. Visitors mix easily with Stanford students and Silicon Valley geeks. There is a fiesta everyday in the vibrant, super-popular bar at **Nola,** 535 Ramona St. Colorful strings of lights and patio windows open onto a cool courtyard dining area. The late-night New Orleans-themed menu offers Cajun quesadillas ($8-9), Creole prawns ($17), and gumbo ($7) to accompany cocktails. (☎650-328-2722. Open M-F 11:30am-2am, Sa-Sun 5:30pm-2am. Kitchen closes M-Th 10pm, F-Sa 11pm, Su 9pm.) Locals and students loosen up at **Oasis Burgers and Pizza,** 241 El Camino Real, affectionately known as "The O." Burgers ($5.25) and pizza ($18-23) are served amidst tables and walls crudely carved by patrons past. (☎650-326-8896; www.theoasisbeergarden.com. Open daily 11am-2am.)

▐ ACCOMMODATIONS. Motels are plentiful along **El Camino Real,** but rates can be steep. Generally, rooms are cheaper farther away from Stanford. More reasonably priced accommodations may be found farther north toward Redwood City. Many Palo Alto motels cater to business travelers and are actually busier on weekdays than on weekends. One of the few cheap options is **Hidden Villa Ranch Hostel (HI-AYH),** 26870 Moody Rd., about 10 mi. southwest of Palo Alto in the Los Altos Hills. The first hostel on the Pacific Coast (opened in 1937), it functions as a working ranch and farm in a wilderness preserve. Recent renovations have completely rebuilt dorms and extended living, kitchen, and dining rooms. (☎650-949-8648. Reception 8am-noon and 4-9:30pm. Reservations required for weekends and groups. Open Sept.-May. Dorms $15, nonmembers $18, children $7.50; private cabins $30-42.)

▐┓ LEAVING PALO ALTO
Follow **U.S. 101 North** along the bay to downtown San Francisco.

SAN FRANCISCO

If California is a state of mind, then San Francisco is euphoria. Welcome to the city that will take you to new highs, leaving your mind spinning, your tastebuds tingling, and your calves aching. The dazzling views, daunting hills, one-of-a-kind neighborhoods, and laid-back, friendly people fascinate visitors. Though smaller than most "big" cities, the city manages to pack an incredible amount of vitality into its 47 sq. mi., from its thriving art communities and bustling shops to the pulsing beats in some of the country's hippest nightclubs and bars. For more coverage of the City by the Bay, see *▓Let's Go: San Francisco.*

┌─────────────────────────
◖ VITAL STATS ◗

Population: 777,000

Visitor Info: California Welcome Center (☎415-956-3493; www.sfvisitor.org), on Pier 39 at the Great San Francisco Adventure. Open Su-Th 9am-9pm, F-Sa 9am-10pm.

Internet Access: At the California Welcome Center (see above). For complete listings of Internet cafes in SF, check www.surfandsip.com.

Post Office: 170 O'Farrell St. (☎415-956-0131), at Stockton St., in the basement of Macy's. Open M-Sa 10am-5:30pm, Su 11am-5pm. **Postal Code:** 94108.

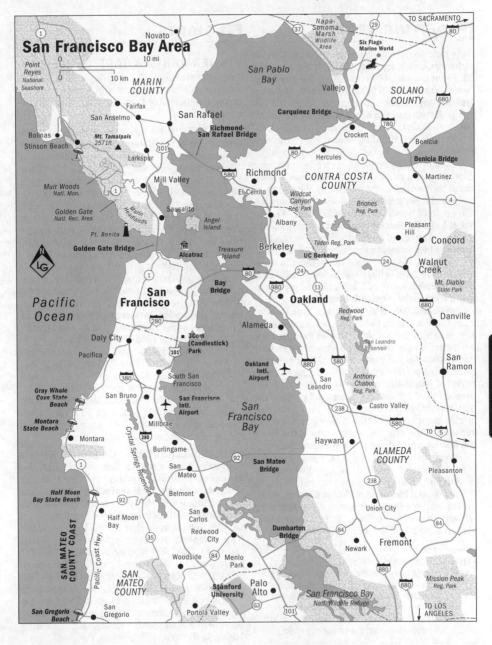

San Francisco Bay Area

TO SACRAMENTO

Napa-Sonoma Marsh Wildlife Area

Six Flags Marine World

Point Reyes National Seashore

Novato

0   10 mi
0   10 km

MARIN COUNTY

San Pablo Bay

SOLANO COUNTY

Vallejo

Fairfax

San Anselmo

San Rafael

Carquinez Bridge

Richmond-San Rafael Bridge

Crockett

Benicia

Bolinas
Stinson Beach

Mt. Tamalpais
2571ft

Larkspur

Hercules

Benicia Bridge

Muir Woods Natl. Mon.

Mill Valley

Richmond

CONTRA COSTA COUNTY

Martinez

Golden Gate Natl. Rec. Area

El Cerrito

Wildcat Canyon Reg. Park

Briones Reg. Park

Pleasant Hill

Marin Headlands

Sausalito

Albany

Concord

Pt. Bonita

Angel Island

Berkeley

Tilden Reg. Park

Walnut Creek

Golden Gate Bridge

Alcatraz

Treasure Island

UC Berkeley

Mt. Diablo State Park

Pacific Ocean

San Francisco

Bay Bridge

Oakland

Redwood Reg. Park

Danville

Daly City

3Com (Candlestick) Park

Alameda

San Leandro Reservoir

San Ramon

Pacifica

Gray Whale Cove State Beach

South San Francisco

Oakland Intl. Airport

Anthony Chabot Reg. Park

Montara State Beach

San Bruno

San Francisco Intl. Airport

San Leandro

Castro Valley

Montara

Millbrae

San Francisco Bay

Burlingame

Hayward

ALAMEDA COUNTY

Crystal Springs Reservoir

San Mateo

San Mateo Bridge

Pleasanton

Half Moon Bay State Beach

Belmont

Half Moon Bay

San Carlos

Union City

Redwood City

Dumbarton Bridge

Fremont

SAN MATEO COUNTY COAST

Pacific Coast Hwy.

Woodside

Menlo Park

Newark

SAN MATEO COUNTY

Stanford University

Palo Alto

San Gregorio

San Francisco Bay Natl. Wildlife Refuge

Mission Peak Reg. Park

San Gregorio Beach

Portola Valley

TO LOS ANGELES

TO SACRAMENTO

TO 5

GETTING AROUND

San Francisco sits at the junction of several major highways, including **I-280, U.S. 101, Hwy. 1,** and **I-80.** From the east, **I-80** runs across the **Bay Bridge** (westbound-only toll $3) into the **South of Market Area (SoMa)** and then connects with U.S. 101 just before it runs into **Van Ness Ave. Market St.,** one of the city's main thoroughfares, runs on a diagonal from the Ferry Building near the bay through downtown and to the Castro in the southwest.

Neighborhood boundaries get a bit confusing; a good map is a must. Touristy **Fisherman's Wharf** sits at the northeast edge of the city. Just south of the wharf is **North Beach,** a historically Italian area, and south of North Beach lies **Chinatown.** Wealthy **Nob Hill** and **Russian Hill** round out the northeast of the city. Municipal buildings cluster in the **Civic Center,** which lines Market St. and is bounded on the west by wide Van Ness Ave. On the other side of Van Ness Ave. is hip **Hayes Valley.** Retail-heavy **Union Square** is north of Market St. and gives way in the west to the rougher **Tenderloin.**

The **Golden Gate Bridge** stretches over the Bay from the **Presidio** in the city's northwest corner. Just south of the Presidio, **Lincoln Park** reaches westward to the ocean, while vast **Golden Gate Park** dominates the western half of the peninsula. Near Golden Gate Park sits the former hippie haven of **Haight-Ashbury.** The trendy **Mission** takes over south of 14th St. The diners and cafes of the "gay mecca" of the **Castro** dazzle on Castro and Market St., northwest of the Mission. On the opposite side of the city, the skyscrapers of the **Financial District** crowd down to the **Embarcadero.**

Parking in San Francisco is rare and expensive even where legal, and zealous cops dole out tickets mercilessly. You can stow your car all day in the residential **Richmond** or **Sunset Districts,** south of Golden Gate Park, but watch signs indicating weekly street-cleaning times. To park near a popular area, your best bet may be a parking garage.

> **TIP** When parking facing uphill, turn front wheels away from the curb, and, if driving a standard, leave the car in first gear. If your car starts to roll, it will stop when the tires hit the curb. When facing downhill, turn the wheels toward the curb and leave the car in reverse. *Always* set the emergency brake.

SIGHTS

FISHERMAN'S WHARF & THE BAY

Piers 39 through 45 provide access to San Francisco's most famous and touristy attractions. Easily visible from the waterfront is Alcatraz Island.

ALCATRAZ. In its 29 years as a maximum-security federal penitentiary, **Alcatraz** harbored a menacing cast of characters, including Al "Scarface" Capone and George "Machine Gun" Kelly. There were 14 separate escape attempts. Only one man is known to have survived crossing the Bay; he was recaptured. On the rock, the cell-house audio tour immerses visitors in the infamous days of Alcatraz. A **Park Ranger tour** can take you around the island and through its 200 years of occupation, from a hunting and fishing ground for Native Americans to a Civil War outpost to a military prison, a federal prison, and finally a birthplace of the Native American civil rights movement. Now part of the **Golden Gate National Recreation Area,** Alcatraz is home to diverse plants and birdlife. *(Take the Blue and Gold Fleet from Pier 41. ☎415-773-1188, tickets 415-705-5555. Ferries 9:30am and every 30min. 10:15am-4:15pm; arrive 20min. early. $9.25, seniors $7.50, ages 5-11 $6. Reservations recommended. Audio tours $4, ages 5-11 $2. Park Ranger tours free. "Alcatraz After Dark" $20.75, seniors and ages 12-17 $18, ages 5-11 $11.50; call for times and availability. Other boating companies run shorter boats around the island for $10.)*

GHIRARDELLI SQUARE. Ghirardelli Sq. is a mall in what used to be a chocolate factory. No golden ticket is required to gawk at the **Ghirardelli Chocolate Manufactory's** vast selection of goodies, or the **Ghirardelli Chocolate Shop and Caffe,** with drinks, frozen yogurt, and a smaller selection of chocolates. Both hand out **free samples,** but the Caffe is usually less crowded. *(Mall 900 N. Point St. ☎415-775-5500. Stores open M-Sa 10am-9pm, Su 10am-6pm. Ghirardelli Chocolate Manufactory ☎415-771-4903. Open Su-Th 10am-11pm, F-Sa 10am-midnight. Soda fountain open Su-Th 10am-11pm, F-Sa 10am-midnight. Chocolate Shop and Caffe ☎415-474-1414. Open M-Th 8:30am-9pm, F 8:30am-10pm, Sa 9am-10pm, Su 9am-9pm.)*

MARINA & FORT MASON

PALACE OF FINE ARTS. With its open-air domed structure and curving colonnades, the Palace of Fine Arts was originally built to commemorate the opening of the Panama Canal, testifying to San Francisco's recovery from the 1906 earthquake. *(On Baker St., between Jefferson and Bay St. next to the Exploratorium. Open daily 6am-9pm. Free.)* The **Palace of Fine Arts Theater,** located directly behind the rotunda, hosts dance and theater performances and film festivals. *(☎ 415-563-6504; www.palaceoffinearts.com.)*

FORT MASON. Fort Mason Center is home to some of the most innovative and impressive cultural museums and resources in San Francisco. The array of outstanding attractions seem to remain unknown to both tourists and locals, making it a quiet waterfront counterpart to the tourist blitz of nearby Fisherman's Wharf. On the first Wednesday of every month all museums are free and open until 7pm. The grounds are also the headquarters of the **Golden Gate National Recreation Area.** *(The park is at the eastern portion of Fort Mason, near Gashouse Cove. ☎ 415-441-3400, ext. 3; www.fortmason.org.)*

NORTH BEACH

WASHINGTON SQUARE. Washington Sq., bordered by Union, Filbert, Stockton, and Powell St., is North Beach's *piazza*, a pretty, not-quite-square, tree-lined lawn. The wedding site of Marilyn Monroe and Joe DiMaggio, the park fills every morning with *tai chi* practitioners. By noon, sunbathers, picnickers, and bocce-ball players take over. **St. Peter and St. Paul Catholic Church,** beckons sightseers to take refuge in its dark nave. *(666 Filbert St.)* Turn-of-the-century San Francisco philanthropist and party-girl Lillie Hitchcock Coit donated the **Volunteer Firemen Memorial** in the middle of the square.

COIT TOWER. Also built by Lillie Hitchcock Coit, the Coit Tower stands 210 ft. high and commands a spectacular view of the city and the Bay. During the Depression, the government's Works Progress Administration employed artists to paint the colorful and subversive murals in the lobby. *(☎ 415-362-0808. Open daily 10am-7pm. Elevator $3.75, seniors $2.50, ages 6-12 $1.50, under 6 free.)*

CITY LIGHTS BOOKSTORE. Beat writers came to national attention when Lawrence Ferlinghetti's City Lights Bookstore (est. 1953) published Allen Ginsberg's *Howl*, which was banned in 1956 and then subjected to an extended trial at the end of which a judge found the poem "not obscene." City Lights has expanded since its Beat days and now stocks wide selection of fiction and poetry, but it remains committed to publishing young poets and writers under its own label. *(2261 Columbus Ave. ☎ 415-362-8193. Open daily 10am-midnight.)*

CHINATOWN

WAVERLY PLACE. Find this little alley and you'll want to spend all day gazing at the incredible architecture. *(Between Sacramento and Washington St. and between Stockton St. and Grant Ave.)* The fire escapes are painted in pinks and greens and held together by railings cast in intricate Chinese patterns. **Tien Hou Temple** is the oldest Chinese temple in the US. *(125 Waverly Pl.)*

ROSS ALLEY. Once lined with brothels and opium dens, today's **Ross Alley** has the look of old Chinatown. The narrow street has stood in for the Orient in such films as *Big Trouble in Little China, Karate Kid II,* and *Indiana Jones and the Temple of Doom.* Squeeze into a doorway to see fortune cookies being shaped at the **Golden Gate Cookie Company.** *(56 Ross Alley. ☎ 415-781-3956. Bag of cookies $3, with "funny," "sexy," or "lucky" fortunes $5. Open daily 10am 8pm.)*

NOB HILL & RUSSIAN HILL

THE CROOKEDEST STREET IN THE WORLD. The famous curves of **Lombard St.**—installed in the 1920s so that horse-drawn carriages could negotiate the extremely steep hill—serve as an icon of SF. From the top, pedestrians and passengers enjoy the view of city and harbor. The view north along Hyde St. isn't too shabby either. *(Between Hyde and Leavenworth St. at the top of Russian Hill.)*

GRACE CATHEDRAL & HUNTINGTON PARK. The largest Gothic edifice west of the Mississippi, **Grace Cathedral** is Nob Hill's stained-glass studded crown. Inside, modern murals mix San Franciscan and national historical events with saintly scenes. The altar of the AIDS Interfaith Memorial Chapel celebrates the church's "inclusive community of love." *(1100 California St.,*

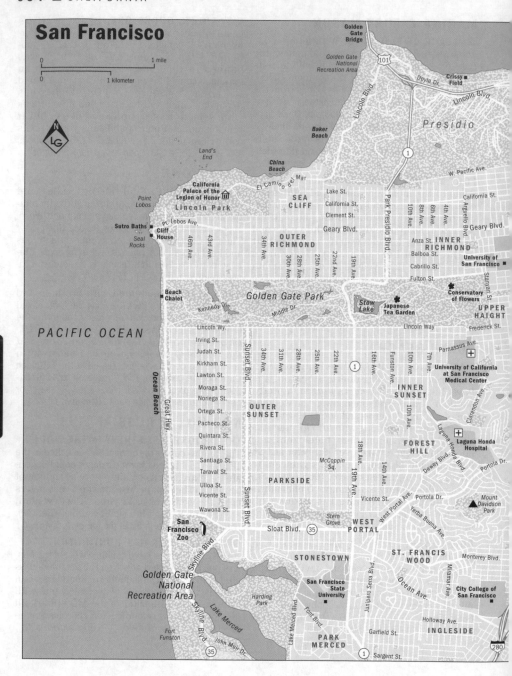

San Francisco

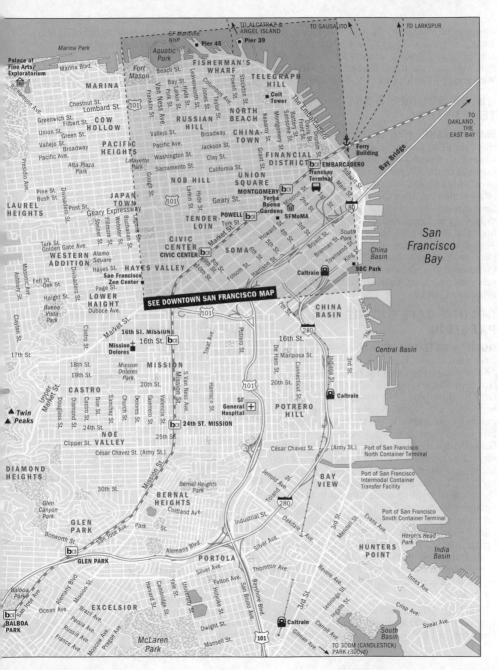

between Jones and Taylor St. ☎ 415-749-6300; www.gracecathedral.org. Open Su-F 7am-6pm, Sa 8am-6pm. Tours M-F 1-3pm, Sa 11:30am-1:30pm, Su 1:30-2pm. Suggested donation $3.) Outside, the building looks onto the turf and trees of **Huntington Park,** equipped with a park and playground.

UNION SQUARE & THE TENDERLOIN

MAIDEN LANE. When the Barbary Coast (now the Financial District) was down and dirty, Union Sq.'s **Morton Alley** was dirtier. Around 1900, murders on the Alley averaged one per week and prostitutes waved to customers from second-story windows. After the 1906 earthquake and fires destroyed most of the brothels, merchants moved in and renamed the area **Maiden Ln.** in hopes of changing the street's image. It worked. Today, the pedestrian-only street that extends two blocks from Union Sq.'s eastern side is as virtuous as they come and makes a pleasant place to stroll or sip espresso while sporting your new Gucci shades.

GOLDEN GATE BRIDGE & THE PRESIDIO

GOLDEN GATE BRIDGE. When Captain John Fremont coined the term "Golden Gate" in 1846, he meant to name the harbor entrance to the San Francisco Bay after the mythical Golden Horn port of Constantinople. In 1937, however, the colorful name became permanently associated with Joseph Strauss's copper-hued engineering masterpiece—the Golden Gate Bridge. Built for $35 million, the bridge stretches across 1¼ mi. of ocean, its towers looming 65 stories above the Bay. It can sway up to 27 ft. in each direction during high winds. On sunny days, hundreds of people take the 30min. walk across. The views from the bridge are amazing, as well as from the Vista Point in Marin County just after the bridge. To see the bridge itself, it's best to get a bit farther away; Fort Point and Fort Baker in the Presidio, Land's End in Lincoln Park, and Mt. Livermore on Angel Island all offer spectacular views on clear days.

PRESIDIO. When Spanish settlers forged their way up the San Francisco peninsula from Baja California in 1769, they established *presidios,* or military outposts, as they went. San Francisco's Presidio, the northernmost point of Spanish territory in North America, was dedicated in 1776.

LINCOLN PARK & OCEAN BEACH

COASTAL TRAIL. The Coastal Trail loops around the interior of Lincoln Park for a scenic and sometimes hardcore coastal hike. The entrance to the trail is not well marked, so be careful not to mistakenly tackle a much more difficult cliffside jaunt. The path leads first into **Fort Miley,** a former army post. Near the picnic tables rests the **USS San Francisco Memorial.** The USS *SF* sustained 45 direct hits in the battle of Guadalcanal on November 12-13, 1942. Nearly 100 men died in the clash, but the ship went on to fight in ten more battles. *(Trail begins at Pt. Lobos and 48th Ave. Free.)* The Coastal Trail continues for a 3 mi. hike into **Land's End,** famous for its views of both the Golden Gate Bridge and the "sunken ships" that signal treacherous waters below. Biking is permitted on the trail, although parts contain stairs and bumpy terrain better suited to mountain bikes. From Land's End, onlookers have the option to hike an extra 6 mi. into the Presidio and on to the arches of Golden Gate Bridge. For hikers and bikers who aren't so inclined, the walk along **El Camino Del Mar** originates close to the Coastal Trail but runs farther in from the shore. Enjoy the forested views the **Palace of the Legion of Honor** before finishing "The Path of the Sea" at **China Beach.** *(Begins at Pt. Lobos and Sea Rock Dr.)*

BEACHES. Swimming is permitted but dangerous at scenic **China Beach** at the end of Seacliff Ave. on the eastern edge of Lincoln Park. Adolph Sutro's 1896 **bathhouse** lies in ruins on the cliffs. Cooled by ocean water, the baths were capable of packing in 25,000 occupants at a time. **Ocean Beach,** the largest and most popular of San Francisco's beaches, begins south of Point Lobos and extends down the northwestern edge of the city's coastline. The undertow along the point is dangerous, but die-hard surfers brave the treacherous currents and the ice-cold water anyway.

GOLDEN GATE PARK

Take your time to enjoy this park. Museums (see p. 941) and cultural events pick up where the lush flora and fauna leave off, and athletic opportunities abound. The park has a municipal golf course, equestrian center, sports fields, tennis courts, and

PACIFIC COAST

stadium. On Sundays, park roads close to traffic, and bicycles and in-line skates come out in full force. The **Visitors Center** is in the Beach Chalet on the western edge of the park. (☎415-751-2766. Open daily 9am-7pm.) **Surrey Bikes and Blades,** 50 Stow Lake Dr., in Golden Gate Park, rents equipment. (☎415-668-6699. Bikes from $6 per hr., $21 per day. Skates $7/$20. Open daily 10am-dusk.)

GARDENS. The **Garden of Fragrance** is designed especially for the visually impaired; all labels are in Braille and the plants are chosen specifically for their textures and scents. Near the Music Concourse off South Dr., the **Shakespeare Garden** contains almost every flower and plant ever mentioned by the Bard. *(Open daily dawn-dusk; in winter closed M. Free.)* The **Japanese Cherry Orchard,** at Lincoln Way and South Dr., blooms intoxicatingly the first week in April. Created for the 1894 Mid-Winter Exposition, the elegant **Japanese Tea Garden** is a serene collection of wooden buildings, small pools, graceful footbridges, carefully pruned trees, and lush plants. *(☎415-752-4227. Open daily summer 8:30am-6pm; winter 8:30am-5pm. $3.50, seniors and ages 6-12 $1.25. Free summer 8:30-9:30am and 5-6pm; winter 8:30-9:30am and 4-5pm.)*

FINANCIAL DISTRICT

TRANSAMERICA PYRAMID. Certain areas of the Financial District's architectural landscape rescue it from the otherwise banal functionalism of the business area. The leading lady of the city's skyline, the Transamerica Pyramid, is, according to new-age sources, directly centered on the telluric currents of the Golden Dragon Ley line between Easter Island and Stonehenge. Planned as an architect's joke and co-opted by one of the leading architectural firms in the country, the building has earned disdain from purists and reverence from city planners. *(600 Montgomery St., between Clay and Washington St.)*

JUSTIN HERMAN PLAZA. When not overrun by skateboarders, the Plaza is home to bands and rallyists who sometimes provide lunch-hour entertainment. U2 rock star Bono was arrested here in 1987 for spray painting "Stop the Traffic—Rock and Roll" on the fountain. Recently, the plaza has been the starting point for Critical Mass, a pro-bicyclist ride that takes place after 5pm on the last Friday of every month. If you happen to be around on a rare hot day, walk through the inviting mist of the **Vaillancourt Fountain** to cool off.

JAPANTOWN & PACIFIC HEIGHTS

SAINT DOMINIC'S ROMAN CATHOLIC CHURCH. Churchgoers and architecture buffs appreciate Saint Dominic's towering altar, carved in the shape of Jesus and the 12 apostles. With its imposing stone and Gothic feel, St. Dominic's is a must see, especially its renowned shrine of **Saint Jude,** skirted by candles and intricately carved oak. *(2390 Bush St., at Steiner St. Open M-Sa 6:30am-5:30pm, Su 7:30am-9pm. Mass M-F 6:30, 8am, 5:30pm; Sa 8am and 5:30pm; Su 7:30, 9:30, 11:30am, 1:30, 5:30, 9pm candlelight service.)*

FUJI SHIATSU & KABUKI SPRINGS. After a rigorous day hiking the hills, reward your weary muscles with an authentic massage at **Fuji Shiatsu.** *(1721 Buchanan Mall, between Post and Sutter St. ☎415-346-4484. $41-44.)* Alternatively, head to the bathhouse at **Kabuki Hot Springs** to relax in the sauna and steam-room, or enjoy the *Reiki* treatment to heal, rejuvenate and restore energy balance. *(1750 Geary Blvd. ☎415-922-6000; www.kabukisprings.com. Open daily 10am-10pm. M-F before 5pm $15, after 5pm and Sa-Su $18. Men only M, Th, Sa; women only Su, W, F; co-ed Tu.)*

CIVIC CENTER

ARCHITECTURE. Referred to as "The Crown Jewel" of American Classical architecture, **City Hall** reigns supreme over the Civic Center, with a dome to rival St. Paul's cathedral and an area of over 500,000 sq. ft. *(1 Dr. Carlton B. Goodlett Pl., at Van Ness Ave. ☎415-554-4000. Open M-F 8am-8pm, Sa-Su noon-4pm.)* The seating in the $33 million glass-and-brass **Louise M. Davies Symphony Hall** was designed to give audience members a close-up view of performers. Its **San Francisco Symphony** is highly esteemed. *(201 Van Ness Ave. ☎415-552-8000; tickets ☎415-431-5400. Open M-F 10am-6pm, Sa noon-6pm.)* The recently renovated **War Memorial Opera House** hosts the **San Francisco Opera Company** and the **San Francisco Ballet.** *(301 Van Ness Ave., between Grove and McAllister St. Box office at 199 Grove St. ☎415-864-3330. Open M-Sa 10am-6pm and 2hr. before each show.)*

PACIFIC COAST

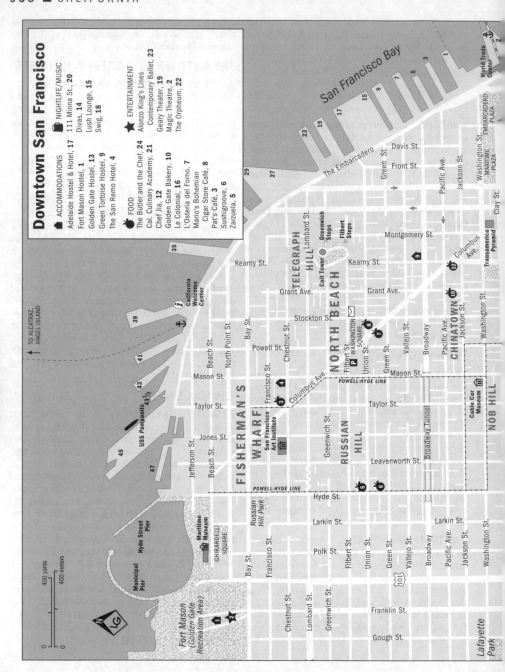

PACIFIC COAST

Downtown San Francisco

▲ ACCOMMODATIONS
Adelaide Hostel & Hotel, **17**
Fort Mason Hostel, **1**
Golden Gate Hostel, **13**
Green Tortoise Hostel, **9**
The San Remo Hotel, **4**

● FOOD
The Butler and the Chef, **24**
Cal. Culinary Academy, **21**
Chef Jia, **12**
Golden Gate Bakery, **10**
Le Colonial, **16**
L'Osteria del Forno, **7**
Mario's Bohemian
 Cigar Store Café, **8**
Pat's Café, **3**
Sushigroove, **6**
Zarzuela, **5**

■ NIGHTLIFE/MUSIC
111 Minna St., **20**
Divas, **14**
Lush Lounge, **15**
Swig, **18**

★ ENTERTAINMENT
Alonzo King's Lines
Contemporary Ballet, **23**
Geary Theater, **19**
Magic Theatre, **2**
The Orpheum, **22**

FINANCIAL
DISTRICT

Ferry
Building

The Embarcadero

JUSTIN
HERMAN
PLAZA

Drumm
St.

Steuart St.

Spear St.

Howard St.

Main St.

Beale St.

The Embarcadero

Folsom St.

San Francisco-
Oakland Bay Bridge

Bryant St.

Harrison St.

Essex St.

Folsom St.

1st St.

2nd St.

3rd St.

4th St.

King St.

Berry St.

Townsend St.

SBC
Park

Caltrain
Depot

280

280

80

80

EMBARCADERO
Embarcadero
Center

California St.

Battery
St.

Sansome St.

Montgomery St.

Kearny St.

Grant Ave.

MONTGOMERY

Market St.

BART/MUNI

Fremont St.

Beale St.

1st St.

2nd St.

Mission St.

Transbay
Terminal

MONTGOMERY

20

South
Park

23

Branman St.

3rd St.

4th St.

Brannan St.

6th St.

Maiden Ln.

San Francisco
Museum of
Modern Art

Moscone
Center

3rd St.

Yerba Buena
Gardens

Zeum

4th St.

Harrison St.

CALIFORNIA STREET LINE

UNION
SQUARE

Pine St.

Bush St.

Stockton St.

Geary St.

Sony
Metreon

POWELL

San Francisco
Shopping Center

5th St.

Folsom St.

Harrison St.

7th St.

Bryant St.

UNION
SQUARE

Powell St.

POWELL-HYDE LINE

i

5th St.

6th St.

Howard St.

SOUTH
OF
MARKET

8th St.

80

POWELL-HYDE LINE

Grace
Cathedral

Sacramento St.

13

Hang
Gallery

Mason St.

19

Ellis St.

Taylor St.

Turk St.

6th St.

Mission St.

7th St.

9th St.

Folsom St.

8th St.

Sutter St.

Post St.

16

17

18

Jones St.

Eddy

St.

Market St.

BART/MUNI

CIVIC CENTER

8th St.

9th St.

Howard St.

10th St.

11th St.

CALIFORNIA STREET LINE

Leavenworth St.

O'Farrell St.

TENDERLOIN

Golden Gate Ave.

22

9th St.

Sacramento St.

Pine St.

Bush St.

Sutter St.

Post St.

14

15

Geary St.

Polk St.

21

Larkin St.

Hyde St.

Van Ness Ave.

CIVIC
CENTER

Grove St.

Hayes St.

12th St.

101

Clay St.

California St.

Sacramento St.

Van Ness Ave.

Van Ness Ave.

City
Hall

101

Van Ness Ave.

St. Mary's
Cathedral

Ellis St.

Eddy St.

Turk St.

Turk St.

Franklin St.

McAllister St.

Fulton St.

Gough St.

Gough St.

JEFFERSON
SQUARE

Franklin St.

HAYES VALLEY

Fell St.

Oak St.

Page St.

Haight St.

Otis St.

Mission St.

MISSION

MISSION DOLORES. Founded in 1776, the **Mission Dolores** is thought to be the city's oldest building. Bougainvillea, poppies, and birds-of-paradise bloom in its cemetery, which was featured in Hitchcock's *Vertigo*. *(3321 16th St., at Dolores St. ☎415-621-8203. Open May-Oct. daily 9am-4:30pm; Nov.-Apr. 9am-4pm. Adults $3, ages 5-12 $2.)*

MISSION MURALS. A walk east or west along 24th St., weaving in and out of the side streets, reveals magnificent murals. Continuing the Mexican mural tradition made famous by Diego Rivera and Jose Orozco, the murals have been a source of pride for Chicano artists and community members since the 1980s. Standouts include the political murals of **Balmy Alley,** off 24th St. between Harrison and Folsom St., a three-building tribute to guitar god **Carlos Santana** at 22nd St. and Van Ness Ave., the face of **St. Peter's Church** at 24th and Florida St., and the **urban living center** on 19th St. between Valencia and Guerrero St.

CASTRO & NEARBY

THE CASTRO. Stores throughout the area cater to gay-mecca pilgrims, with everything from rainbow flags and pride-wear to the latest in BGLT books, dance music, and trinkets of the unmentionable variety. Many local shops, especially on colorful **Castro St.,** also double as novelty galleries. Discover just how anatomically correct Gay Billy is at **Does Your Father Know?,** a one-stop kitsch-and-camp overdose. To read up on gay history and culture, try at **A Different Light Bookstore.**

WALKING TOURS. For a tour of the Castro that includes sights other than biceps and abs, check out **Cruisin' the Castro.** Trevor Hailey, a resident since 1972, is consistently recognized as one of SF's top tour leaders. Her 4hr. walking tours cover Castro life and history from the Gold Rush to today. *(☎415-550-8110; www.webcastro.com/castrotour. Tours Tu-Sa 10am. $40; lunch included. Reservations required.)*

HAIGHT-ASHBURY

FORMER CRIBS. The former homes of counterculture legends still attract visitors. From the corner of Haight and Ashbury St., walk just south of Waller St. to check out the house occupied by the **Grateful Dead** when they were still the Warlocks. *(710 Ashbury St.)* Look across the street for the **Hell's Angels** house. If you walk back to Haight St., go right three blocks, and make a left on Lyon St., you can check out **Janis Joplin's** abode. *(122 Lyon St., between Page and Oak St.)* Cross the Panhandle, continue three blocks to Fulton St., turn right, and wander seven blocks toward the park to see where the Manson "family" planned murder and mayhem at the **Charles Manson** mansion. *(2400 Fulton St., at Willard St.)*

SAN FRANCISCO ZEN CENTER. Appropriately removed from the havoc of the Haight, the **San Francisco Zen Center** offers a peaceful retreat. The temple is called Beginner's Mind Temple, so don't worry if you don't know where to begin looking for your *chi*. The best option for most is the Saturday morning program, which includes a mediation lecture at 8:45am followed by activities and lunch. *(300 Page St., at Laguna St. ☎415-863-3136. Office open M-F 9:30am-12:30pm and 1:30-5pm, Sa 9am-noon. Sa morning program $6.)*

⅏ MUSEUMS & GALLERIES

MARINA

Exploratorium, 3601 Lyon St. (☎415-563-7337 or 415-561-0360; www.exploratorium.edu). The Exploratorium can hold over 4000 people, and when admission is free usually does. Over 650 displays—including miniature tornadoes, computer planet-managing, and giant bubble-makers—explain the wonders of the world. On the 2nd W of each month Nov.-Mar., the Exploratorium hosts avant-garde **art cocktail nights** that feature Bay Area artists, a DJ, and bar. Open June-Aug. daily 10am-6pm; Sept.-May Su and Tu-Sa 10am-5pm. $12; students, seniors, disabled, and ages 9-17 $9.50; ages 4-8 $8. 1st W of each month free. Tactile Dome $15; includes general admission.

FORT MASON

Museum of Craft and Folk Art, Bldg. A. (☎415-775-0990; www.mocfa.org). The MOCFA brings together crafts and functional art from past and present, showcasing everything from 19th-century Chinese children's hats to war-time commentary made through lightbulbs. Open Su and Tu-F 11am-5pm, Sa 10am-5pm.

$4, students and seniors $3, under 18 free. Free Sa 10am-noon and 1st W of each month 11am-7pm.

African-American Historical and Cultural Society Museum, Bldg. C, (☎415-441-0640). Displays historic artifacts and artwork, modern works, and a permanent collection by local artists. Open Su and W-Sa noon-5pm. $3, seniors and students 12 $1, under 12 free. 1st W of each month free.

SF Museum of Modern Artists Gallery, Bldg. A., 1st fl. (☎415-441-4777). Over 1200 Bay Area artists show, rent, and sell work here. Monthly curated exhibits are downstairs, while most other pieces are sold upstairs. Every May, the gallery hosts a benefit sale—all works half-price. Open Tu-Sa 11:30am-5:30pm. Free.

NOB HILL & RUSSIAN HILL

San Francisco Art Institute, 800 Chestnut St. (☎415-771-7020 or 800-345-7324; www.sfai.edu). The oldest art school west of the Mississippi, the Institute is lodged in a converted mission and has produced a number of American greats including Mark Rothko, Ansel Adams, Imogen Cunningham, Dorothea Lange, and James Weeks. To the left as you enter is the **Diego Rivera Gallery,** 1 wall of which is covered by a huge 1931 Rivera mural. Open daily June-Aug. 9am-8pm; Sept.-May 9am-9pm.

Cable Car Powerhouse and Museum, 1201 Mason St. (☎415-474-1887). After the steep journey up Nob Hill, you'll understand the development of the vehicles celebrated here. The modest building is the working center of San Fran's cable car system. Look down on 57,300 ft. of cable whizzing by or learn about the cars, some of which date back to 1873. Open daily Apr.-Oct. 10am-6pm; Nov.-Mar. 10am-5pm. Free.

UNION SQUARE

Martin Lawrence Gallery, 366 Geary St. (☎415-956-0345). Displays works by pop artists like Warhol and Haring, who once distributed his work for free to New York commuters in the form of graffiti; it now commands upwards of $13,000 in print form. Also houses studies by Picasso and America's largest collection of work by Marc Chagall. Open Su 10am-7pm, M-Th 9am-8pm, F-Sa 9am-10pm. Free.

Hang, 556 Sutter St. (☎415-434-4264; www.hangart.com). Works hang from the exposed ceiling beams of this chrome warehouse. An annex recently opened directly across the street. Open Su M-Sa 10am-6pm, Su noon-5pm. Free.

TENDERLOIN

509 Cultural Center/Luggage Store, 1007 Market St. (☎415-255-5971) and 1172 Market St. (☎415-865-0198). Presents performing arts, exhibitions, and education initiatives. The often-graphic art exhibits probably won't be grandma's favorites. Regular events include comedy open mic (Tu 8pm), improv music concerts (Th 8pm), and a theater festival each June. (Suggested donation $6-10 each.) Next door to 509, the **Cohen Alley** houses a third venue for the area's creative talent; the alley is leased to the Luggage Store, which has made it an artistic showcase.

LINCOLN PARK

California Palace of the Legion of Honor (☎415-863-3330; www.legionofhonor.org), in the middle of Lincoln Park. A copy of Rodin's *Thinker* beckons visitors into the grand courtyard, where a little glass pyramid recalls another Paris treasure, the Louvre. A thorough catalogue of masters, from medieval to modern, hangs inside. Just outside the Palace, a **Holocaust memorial** depicts a single, hopeful survivor looking out through a barbed-wire fence to the beauty of the Pacific. Open Su and Tu-Sa 9:30am-5pm. $8, seniors $6, ages 12-17 $5, under 12 free. Tu free.

GOLDEN GATE PARK

▨ **California Academy of Sciences,** 55 Concourse Dr. (☎415-750-7145; www.calacademy.org), on the east side of the park at 9th Ave. Houses several museums specializing in different fields of science. The **Steinhart Aquarium,** home to over 600 aquatic species, is livelier than the natural history exhibits. Shark feedings M-W and F-Su 10:30am, 12:30, 2:30, 4:30pm. Open ocean fish feedings daily 1:30pm. Penguin feedings daily 11:30am and 4pm. At the **Natural History Museum,** the Earthquake Theater shakes visitors. Open June-Aug. daily 9am-6pm; Sept.-May 10am-5pm. Combined admission $8.50; seniors, students, and ages 12-17 $5.50; ages 4-11 $2. 1st W each month free (open until 8:45pm). The **Morrison Planetarium** re-creates the heavens with sky shows M-F 2pm. $2.50/$1.25.

SOMA

▨ **San Francisco Museum of Modern Art (SFMOMA),** 151 3rd St. (☎415-357-4000; www.sfmoma.org), between Mission and Howard St. Holds 5 floors of art, with an emphasis on design, and is home to the largest selection of 20th-century American and European art this side of New

York. Open Sept.-May M-Tu and F-Su 11am-5:45pm, Th 11am-8:45pm; June-Aug. M-Tu and F-Su 10am-6pm, Th 10am-9pm. 4 free gallery tours per day. $10, seniors $7, students $6, under 13 free. Th 6-9pm half-price. 1st Tu of each month free.

Yerba Buena Center for the Arts, 701 Mission St. (☎415-978-2787; www.yerbabuenaarts.org). The center runs an excellent theater and gallery space, with programs emphasizing performance, film, viewer involvement, and local work. It is surrounded by the **Yerba Buena Rooftop Gardens,** a vast expanse of concrete, fountains, and foliage. Open Su and Tu-Sa 11am-6pm. $6, students and seniors $3. Th free.

🎵 ENTERTAINMENT

MUSIC

The distinction between bars, clubs, and live music venues is hazy in San Francisco. Almost all bars will occasionally have bands, and small venues have rock and hip-hop shows. Look for the latest live music listings in *S.F. Weekly* and *The Guardian*. Hard-core audiophiles might snag a copy of *Bay Area Music (BAM)*.

Café du Nord, 2170 Market St. (☎415-861-5016), between Church and Sanchez St. in the **Castro.** Live music nightly—from pop and groove to garage rock. M Night Hoot showcases local singing and songwriting. Happy hour 6-7:30pm; martinis and cosmos $2.50. 21+. Cover $5-10 after 8:30pm. Open Su-Tu 6pm-2am, W-Sa 4pm-2am.

Justice League, 628 Divisadero St. (☎415-440-0409; www.ticketweb.com), at Hayes St. in the **Lower Haight.** Live hip-hop is hard to find in San Francisco, but the Justice League fights ever onward for a good beat. M reggae and dub, W soul night. 21+. Cover $5-25. Open daily 9pm-2am.

Bottom of the Hill, 1233 17th St. (☎415-626-4455; www.bottomofthehill.com), between Missouri and Texas St. in **Potrero Hill.** Intimate rock club with tiny stage is the last best place to see up-and-comers before they move to bigger venues. Most Su afternoons feature local bands and all-you-can-eat barbecue. 21+. Cover $5-10. Open M-Th 8:30pm-2am, F 3pm-2am, Sa 8:30pm-2am, Su hours vary.

The Fillmore, 1805 Geary Blvd. (☎415-346-6000; www.thefillmore.com), at Fillmore St. in **Japantown.** Bands that pack stadiums often play at the legendary Fillmore, the foundation of San Francisco's 1960s music scene. Tickets $15-40.

DANCE

Alonzo King's Lines Contemporary Ballet (☎415-863-3360; www.linesballet.org), in **Hayes Valley.** Dancers combine elegant classical moves with athletic flair to the music of great living jazz and world music composers. Tickets $15-25.

Oberlin Dance Company, 3153 17th St. (☎415-863-9834; www.odctheater.org), between South Van Ness and Folsom St. in the **Mission.** Mainly dance, but occasional theater space with gallery attached. Box office open W-Sa 2-5pm.

California Contemporary Dancers, 530 Moraga St. (☎415-753-6066; www.ccdancers.org), in the **Sunset.** The all-woman modern dance company brings together the best of widely diverse dance and musical traditions to create exciting, innovative performances.

THEATER

Downtown, **Mason St.** and **Geary St.** constitute **"Theater Row,"** the city's center for theatrical entertainment. **TIX Bay Area,** located in a kiosk in Union Sq. at the corner of Geary and Powell St., is a Ticketmaster outlet. (☎415-433-7827; www.theaterbayarea.org. Open Su 11am-3pm, Tu-Th 11am-6pm, F-Sa 11am-7pm.)

Magic Theatre (☎415-441-8822; www.magictheatre.org), in Fort Mason Center, stages international and American premieres. A famous landmark, **The Orpheum,** 1192 Market St. (☎415-512-7770), at Hyde St. near the Civic Center hosts big Broadway shows. **Geary Theater,** 415 Geary St. (☎415-749-2228; www.act-sfbay.org), at Mason St. in Union Sq. is home to the renowned **American Conservatory Theater,** the jewel in SF's theatrical crown. The **Castro Theatre,** 429 Castro St. (☎415-621-6350; www.thecastrotheatre.com), near Market St., shows eclectic films, festivals, and double features, some featuring live organ music.

SPORTS

Home to the five-time Super Bowl champion **49ers** (☎415-468-2249, tickets 415-656-4900; www.sf49ers.com), 3COM Park, also known as **Candlestick Park,** sits right on the ocean, resulting in trademark gusts that led to one of the lowest homerun averages in baseball back when the Giants played there. The **Giants** play at the **Pacific Bell Park,** 24 Willie Mays Plaza (☎415-972-2000 or 888-464-2468; www.sfgiants.com), in SoMa.

✾ FESTIVALS

If you can't find a festival going on in San Francisco, well, you just aren't trying hard enough. Cultural, ethnic, and queer special events take place year-round. For two consecutive weekends in April, the Japanese **Cherry Blossom Festival** (☎415-563-2313) lights up the streets of Japantown with hundreds of performers. The oldest film festival in North America, the **San Francisco International Film Festival** shows more than 100 international films of all genres over two weeks. (☎415-561-5022; www.sffs.org. Most $9.) If film's your thing, you may also want to check out the **San Francisco International Gay and Lesbian Film Festival** (☎415-703-8650; www.frameline.org), California's second-largest film festival and the world's largest gay and lesbian media event. The $6-15 tickets go fast. It takes place during the 11 days leading up to **Pride Day** (☎415-864-3733; www.sfpride.org). The High Holy Day of the queer calendar, Pride Day celebrates with a parade and events downtown starting at 10:30am.

For a bit of high culture, consider the free **San Francisco Shakespeare Festival,** every Saturday and Sunday in September in Golden Gate Park. (☎415-865-4434. Shows 1:30pm, but arrive at noon for a seat.) You'll find guilt-free chocolate heaven at the **Ghirardelli Square Chocolate Festival** (☎415-775-5500; www.ghirardellisq.com) in early September, when proceeds go to Project Open Hand. The oldest in America, **San Francisco Blues Festival** attracts some of the biggest names in the business. (☎415-979-5588; 3rd weekend in Sept. in Fort Mason.) Finally, the leather-and-chains gang lets it all hang out at the **Folsom Street Fair,** Pride Day's raunchier, rowdier little brother. (☎415-861-3247; www.folsomstreetfair.com; on Folsom St. between 7th and 11th St.)

◢ FOOD

Strolling and sampling the food in each neighborhood is an excellent way to get a taste for the city's diversity. For the most up-to-date listings of restaurants, try the *Examiner* and the *S.F. Bay Guardian*. The glossy *Bay Area Vegetarian* can also suggest places to graze.

Pier 39 and **Fisherman's Wharf** overflow with eateries that charge high rates for average food. Tourists may feel compelled to try some clam chowder and sourdough bread.

San Francisco's **Chinese cuisine** is widely held to be unsurpassed outside of Asia, but it can be difficult to distinguish the excellent restaurants from the mediocre. **Chinatown** is filled with cheap restaurants whose sheer number can baffle even the savviest of travelers. Some locals claim that Chinese restaurants in the **Richmond** are better than those in Chinatown. **Clement St.,** between 2nd and 12th Ave., has the widest variety.

In **North Beach's** tourist-friendly restaurants, California cuisine merges with the bold palate of Italy, inspiring *delicioso* dishes that blend tradition and innovation. In the **Financial District,** corner cafes vend Mediterranean grub at rock-bottom prices. Pedestrian side streets are packed with outdoor bistros. The dominance of Mexican specialties and gigantic burritos is undeniable in the **Mission,** but the area also houses homey diners, quirky vegan-friendly cafes (along **Valencia St.**), and Middle Eastern, Italian, and Thai cuisine. Campy diners and posh cafes dominate the nearby **Castro's** culinary offerings, where little is as cheap as in the Mission.

FISHERMAN'S WHARF

Pat's Café, 2330 Taylor St. (☎415-776-8735), between Chestnut and Francisco St. With playful yellow swirls on the building's facade, Pat's bright decor welcomes diners to a hearty home-cooked meal like mom would make. Burgers, sandwiches, and big breakfasts $5-10. Open M and Th-Su 5:30-9pm, Tu-W 7:30am-3pm.

CHINATOWN

▧ **Chef Jia,** 925 Kearny St. (☎415-398-1626), at Pacific St. Insanely cheap and delicious food. A local crowd comes for lunch and dinner specials ($4.80) or the celebrated signature dishes, such as rolling lettuce chicken with pine nuts ($9). Open M-F 11:30am-10pm, Sa-Su 5-10pm. No credit cards.

Golden Gate Bakery, 1029 Grant Ave. (☎415-781-2627), in Chinatown. This tiny bakery's moon cakes, noodle puffs, and vanilla cream buns (all $0.75-1.50) draw long lines. Open daily 8am-8pm.

NORTH BEACH

L'Osteria del Forno, 519 Columbus Ave. (☎415-982-1124), between Green and Union St. Acclaimed Italian roasted and cold foods, plus homemade breads. Terrific thin-crust pizzas (slices $2.50-3.75) and focaccia sandwiches ($5-6.50). Open Su-M and W-Th 11:30am-10pm, F-Sa 11:30am-10:30pm.

Mario's Bohemian Cigar Store Café, 566 Columbus Ave. (☎415-362-0536), at the corner of Washington Sq. The Beats frequented this laid-back cafe, which still serves first-rate grub. Hot focaccia sandwiches ($7-8.50). Open daily 10am-11pm.

NOB HILL & RUSSIAN HILL

Zarzuela, 2000 Hyde St. (☎415-346-0800), at Union St. in Russian Hill. Spanish homestyle cooking and a festively upscale setting make *chorizo al vino* ($4-7) the highlight of the evening. Entrees $8-14. Open Tu-Th 5:30-10pm, F-Sa 5:30-10:30pm.

Sushigroove, 1916 Hyde St. (☎415-440-1905), between Union and Green St. Without a full kitchen, this chic, inexpensive sushi-*sake* joint (most sushi and *maki* $3-7) serves up a lot of rolls (many vegetarian) but noth-ing that has seen the inside of an oven. Open Su-Th 6-10pm, F-Sa 6-10:30pm.

UNION SQUARE & THE TENDERLOIN

Le Colonial, 20 Cosmo Pl. (☎415-931-3600; www.lecolonialsf.com), off Post St. between Taylor and Jones St. Exquisite French-Vietnamese cuisine in a stunning French-inspired building. The veranda, with its high white adobe walls, ivy-clad lattice, and overhead heating lamps, offers the best opportunity to revel in the architecture and down signature moji-tos ($8). Entrees $20-33. Open Su-W 5:30-10pm, Th-Sa 5:30-11pm. Lounge open from 4:30pm.

The California Culinary Academy, 625 Polk St. (☎415-216-4329), between Turk and Eddy St. Academy students cook behind a window visible from the high-ceilinged Carême dining room. The Tu-W *prix-fixe* 3-course lunch ($16) or dinner ($24) indulges patrons with ambitious and extremely successful culinary combinations. Wine pairings with each course are a steal at $5 total. The Th-F grand buffet lunch ($22) or dinner ($38) draws large crowds; reserve 1 week ahead. Open Tu-F 11:30am-1pm and 6-8pm.

ROAD FOOD

GIMME SOME DIM SUM

Dim sum, meaning "little bits of the heart," are the foods traditionally eaten at a Cantonese or Southern Chinese *yum cha* ("tea lunch"). This heavenly dining experience involves many small dishes eaten in the morn-ing or early afternoon, typically on Sundays, in mass quantities. Waiters and waitresses push carts laden with all sorts of Chinese "finger foods," from dump-lings and buns to chicken feet. When they stop at your table, point to whatever looks good or use the handy mini-menu below. The waiter will stamp a card to charge you by the dish. Dim sum is sure to steal your heart one piece at a time.

Cha Siu Bao: Steamed barbecue pork buns.

Haar Gao: Steamed shrimp dumplings.

Dan Taat: Tiny tart shells filled with sweet egg custard.

Siu Mai: Shrimp and pork in a fancy dumpling "basket."

Woltei: Lovingly wrapped pork pot stickers.

Jiaozi: The classic steamed pork dumplings.

Dou Sha Bao: Steamed buns filled with sweet red bean paste.

Loh Bak Goh: A fried mashed turnip patty. Don't knock it until you've tried it.

Fun Gwor: Chicken and mushroom dumplings.

Yuebing: A flaky, frosted pastry with red bean paste filling.

SOUTH OF MARKET AREA (SOMA)

▓ **The Butler and the Chef Cafe,** 155A S. Park Ave. (☎415-896-2075; www.thebutlerandthechef.com), between Bryant, Brannan, 2nd, and 3rd St. Advertising itself as San Francisco's only authentic French bistro, this stellar reproduction of a Parisian street cafe serves breakfast crepes ($4-10) and baguette sandwiches ($7). Open Tu-Sa 8am-4:30pm.

HAIGHT-ASHBURY

▓ **Pork Store Cafe,** 1451 Haight St. (☎415-864-6981), between Masonic Ave. and Ashbury St. A breakfast place that charges itself very seriously with the mission to fatten you up—they proudly stock only whole milk. The 2 delicious healthy options ("Tim's Healthy Thursdays" and "Mike's Low Carb Special"; each $7) pack enough spinach, avocado, and salsa to hold their own against the Piggy Special ($7). Open M-F 7am-3:30pm, Sa-Su 8am-4pm.

Kate's Kitchen, 471 Haight St. (☎415-626-3984), near Fillmore St. Start your day off right with one of the best breakfasts in the neighborhood (served all day), like the "Farmer's Breakfast" or the "French Toast Orgy" (with fruit, yogurt, granola, and honey; $7.50). It's often packed, so sign up on a waiting list outside. Open M 9am-2:45pm, Tu-F 8am-2:45pm, Sa-Su 8:30am-3:45pm. No credit cards.

MISSION & THE CASTRO

▓ **Taquería Cancún,** 2288 Mission St. (☎415-252-9560), at 19th St. Additional locations: 3211 Mission St. (☎415-550-1414) and 1003 Market (☎415-864-6773). Delicious burritos (grilled chicken upon request; $4) and scrumptious egg dishes served with chips and salsa, small tortillas, and choice of sausage, ham, or salsa ($5). Open Su-Th 9am-1:45am, F-Sa 9am-3am.

▓ **Mitchell's Ice Cream,** 688 San Jose Ave. (☎415-648-2300), at 29th St. This takeout parlor gets so busy that you have to take a number at the door. With a list of awards almost as long as the list of flavors (from caramel praline to Thai iced tea), Mitchell's will chocolate dip any scoop. Cone $2.10. Pint $5.10. Open daily 11am-11pm.

Nirvana, 544 Castro St. (☎415-861-2226), between 18th and 19th St. Playfully concocted cocktails such as "nirvana colada" and "phat margarita" ($8-9) complement Burmese cuisine with a twist (from $8). Open M-Th 4:30-9:30pm, F-Sa noon-10:30pm, Su noon-9:30pm.

🏠 ACCOMMODATIONS

For those who don't mind sharing a room with strangers, many San Francisco hostels are homier and cheaper than budget hotels. Book in advance if at all possible, but since many don't take reservations for summer, you might have to just show up or call early on your day of arrival. B&Bs are often the most comfortable and friendly, albeit expensive, option. Beware that some of the cheapest budget hotels may be located in areas requiring extra caution at night.

HOSTELS

▓ **San Francisco International Guesthouse,** 2976 23rd St. (☎415-641-1411), in the **Mission.** Look for the blue Victorian with yellow trim near the corner of Harrison St. With hardwood floors, wall tapestries, and comfortable common areas, this hostel feels like the well-designed (but totally clean) room of your tree-hugger college roommate. Passport with international stamps "required." Free Internet. 5-night min. stay. No reservations, but chronically filled to capacity. All you can do is try calling a few days ahead of time. Dorms $16; doubles $32.

▓ **Adelaide Hostel and Hotel,** 5 Isadora Duncan (☎877-359-1915; www.adelaidehostel.com), at the end of a little alley off Taylor St. between Geary and Post St. in **Union Square.** The bottom 2 floors, recently renovated with fresh paint and new furniture, entice a congenial international crowd. Try to avoid the top 2 floors until they undergo renovations. 4-day max. stay. Check-out 11am. Reserve online or by phone. Dorms $22; rooms from $65.

▓ **Green Tortoise Hostel,** 494 Broadway (☎415-834-1000; www.greentortoise.com), off Columbus Ave. at Kearny St. in **North Beach.** A ballroom preceded this super-mellow and friendly pad, allowing today's laid-back, fun-seeking young travelers to hang out amid abandoned finery in the spacious common room. Free sauna. Breakfast and dinner (M, W, F) included. Key deposit $20. 10-day max. stay. Reception 24hr. Check-out 11am. Reservations recommended. Dorms $19-22; private rooms $48-60. No credit cards.

Fort Mason Hostel (HI-AYH), Bldg. #240 (☎415-771-7277; sfhostel@norcalhostels.org), in **Fort Mason.** The hostel is at the corner of Funston and Pope St. past the administrative buildings. Beautiful surrounding forest and wooden bunks provide a campground feel. Not a place for partiers—strictly enforced quiet hours (11pm) and no smoking or alcohol. Movies, walking tours, dining room, and parking. Laundry (wash $1, dry $1). Check-in 2:30pm. Reserve weeks in advance. Dorms $22.50-29, under 13 $15-17.

HOTELS & GUESTHOUSES

🏨 **The San Remo Hotel,** 2237 Mason St. (☎415-776-8688; www.sanremohotel.com), between Chestnut and Francisco St. in **Russian Hill.** Built in 1906, this pension-style hotel features small but elegantly furnished rooms with antique armoires, bedposts, lamps, and complimentary backscratchers. Shared bathrooms with brass pull-chain toilets. Check-out 11am. Reservations recommended. Rooms $50-70.

🏨 **Hayes Valley Inn,** 417 Gough St. (☎415-431-9131, reservations 800-930-7999; www.hayesvalley-inn.com), just north of Hayes St. in **Hayes Valley.** European-style B&B with small, clean rooms, shared bath, and lace curtains. Bedrooms range from charming singles with daybeds to extravagant turret rooms with wraparound windows and queen-size beds. All rooms have cable TV, phone, and private sink. Breakfast included. Check-in 3pm. Check-out 11am. Singles $47; doubles $53-66; turret rooms $63-71.

🏨 **The Red Victorian Bed, Breakfast, and Art,** 1665 Haight St. (☎415-864-1978; www.redvic.com), west of Belvedere St. in the **Upper Haight.** Inspired by the 1967 "Summer of Love," proprietress Sami Sunchild nurtures guests. Reception 8am-9pm. Check-in 2-5pm or by appointment. Check-out 11am. Reservations strongly recommended, especially if you desire a specific room. Rooms $86-200.

San Francisco Zen Center, 300 Page St. (☎415-863-3136; www.sfzc.org), near Laguna St. in the **Lower Haight.** Even if rigorous soul-searching is not for you, the Zen Center offers breezy, unadorned rooms whose courtyard views instill a meditative peace of mind. All meals included in the discounted weekly (10% off) or monthly (25% off) rates. Rooms $66-120.

Golden Gate Hotel, 775 Bush St. (☎415-392-3702 or 800-835-1118; www.goldengatehotel.com), between Mason and Powell St. in **Union Square.** A positively charming B&B, with a staff as kind and solicitous as the rooms are plush and inviting. Continental breakfast and afternoon tea (4-7pm) included. Reservations recommended. Doubles $85, with bath $115.

🎭 NIGHTLIFE

Nightlife in San Francisco is as varied as the city's personal ads. Everyone from the "shy first-timer" to the "bearded strap daddy" can find places to go on a Saturday (or Tuesday) night. The spots listed below are divided into bars and clubs, but the lines get blurred in SF after dark, and even cafes hop at night. Check out the nightlife listings in the *S.F. Weekly, S.F. Bay Guardian,* and *Metropolitan.* All clubs listed are 21+. San Francisco is not a particularly friendly city to underagers.

Politics aside, nightlife alone is enough to earn San Francisco the title of "gay mecca." Generally, the boys hang in the **Castro** neighborhood, while the girls gravitate to the **Mission** (on and off Valencia St.); all frolic along **Polk St.** (several blocks north of Geary Blvd.), and in **SoMa.** Polk St. can seem seedy and SoMa barren, so keep a watchful eye. Most clubs and bars below are gay-friendly.

BARS & LOUNGES

🍸 **Noc Noc,** 5574 Haight St. (☎415-861-5811), near Fillmore St. in the **Lower Haight.** This lounge, creatively outfitted as a modern cavern, seems like the only happening place before 10pm—neo-hippies mingle at high-backed bar stools, or relax on the padded floor cushions. Open daily 5pm-2am.

🍸 **111 Minna St.** (☎415-974-1719), at 2nd St. in **SoMa.** A funky gallery by day, hipster groove-spot by night. The bar turns club W 5-10pm for a crowded night of progressive house music. Cover $5-15. Gallery open M-F noon-5pm. Bar open Tu 5-9pm, W 5-11pm, Th-F 5pm-2am, Sa 10pm-2am.

Lush Lounge, 1092 Post St. (☎415-771-2022; www.thelushlounge.com), at Polk St. in **Nob Hill.** Oh-so-lush, with ample vegetation and sassy classic Hollywood throwback decor. Kick back as the best in 80s nostalgia, from ABBA to Madonna, streams through the speakers. Open daily 4pm-2am; in summer M-Tu from 5pm. No credit cards.

Swig, 561 Geary St. (☎415-931-7292; www.swig-bar.com), between Taylor and Jones St., in **Union Square.** With an artful, intimate back room and an upstairs smoking lounge this recently opened bar has already entertained Eminem, D12, and the Wallflowers. Open daily 5pm-2am.

CLUBS

🎶 **El Rio,** 3158 Mission St. (☎415-282-3325), between César Chavez and Valencia St. in the **Mission.** Each area in this sprawling club has its own bar, but the patio is center stage for the young urbanites who play cards and smoke cigars. Diverse queer and straight crowd. W and Sa live Bay area bands. Th "Arabian Nights," F world music. Su live salsa (mainly GLBT) 3-8pm; salsa lessons 3-4pm.

Cover M $2, Th after 10pm $5, Su $7. Open M 5pm-1am, Tu-Sa 5pm-2am, Su 3pm-midnight. No credit cards.

Pink, 2925 16th St. (☎415-431-8889), at S. Van Ness Ave. in the **Mission.** With new French owners, this venue plays it chic. Pink satin and gossamer draperies lend a lounge feel weekdays but expect clubbers F-Sa. DJs spin a mix of world music, soulful house, Cuban jazz, and Afro beats. Cover $5, F-Sa $10. Open Su and Tu-Th 9:30pm-2am, F-Sa 9:30pm-3am.

GLBT NIGHTLIFE

◙ **Divas,** 1081 Post St. (☎415-928-6006; www.divassf.com), at Polk St. in the **Tenderloin.** With a starlet at the door and a savvy pin-striped madam working the bar, this transgender nightclub is simply fabulous. Tu Talent night. F-Sa drag show. Cover $7-10. Open daily 6am-2am. No credit cards.

◙ **The Bar on Castro,** 456 Castro St. (☎415-626-7220), between Market and 18th St. An urbane **Castro** staple with padded walls and dark plush couches perfect for eyeing the stylish young crowd, or scoping the techno-raging dance floor. Open M-F 4pm-2am, Sa-Su noon-2am. No credit cards.

◙ **SF Badlands,** 4121 18th St. (☎415-626-0138), near Castro St. in the **Castro.** Strutting past the sea of boys at the bar, cruise a circular dance floor where the latest Top 40 divas shake their thangs. Cover F-Sa $2. Open daily 2pm-2am. No credit cards.

Wild Side West, 424 Cortland Ave. (☎415-647-3099), at Wool St., in **Bernal Heights.** The oldest lesbian bar in SF is a favorite for women and men. The backyard jungle has benches, fountains, and statues by patrons. Open daily 1pm-2am. No credit cards.

▟ APPROACHING THE MARIN HEADLANDS

From San Francisco, follow **U.S. 101 North** across the Golden Gate Bridge. Take the first exit (Alexander Ave.) off 101, veer right off the ramp onto **Alexander Ave.** and then left on **Bunker Rd.** through a tunnel. For the most scenic drive and best view of the city, take your first left onto **McCullough Rd.** and turn right along Conzelman. For the Visitors Center, from Bunker Rd., take a left onto **Field Rd.**

MARIN HEADLANDS

The fog-shrouded hills just west of the Golden Gate Bridge constitute the Marin Headlands. These windswept ridges, precipitous cliffs, and hidden sandy beaches offer superb hiking and biking minutes from downtown. For instant gratifica-

tion, drive up to any of the look-out spots and pose for your own postcard-perfect shot of the Golden Gate Bridge and the city skyline, or take a short walk out to Point Bonita. If you intend to do more serious hiking or biking, choose one of the coastal trails that provide easy access to dark sand beaches and dramatic cliffs of basalt greenstone. Either way, bring a jacket in case of sudden wind, rain, or fog.

One of the best short hikes is to the lighthouse at **Point Bonita,** a prime spot for seeing sunbathing California sea lions in summer and migrating gray whales in the cooler months. The lighthouse at the end of the point really doesn't seem up to the job of guarding the whole San Francisco Bay, but has done so valiantly since 1855; in fact, its original glass lens is still in operation. At the end of a narrow, knife-like ridge lined with purple wildflowers, the lighthouse is reached by a short tunnel through the rock and a miniature suspension bridge. Even when the lighthouse is closed, the short walk (1 mi. from the Visitors Center, a half-mile from the nearest parking) provides gorgeous views on sunny days. (Lighthouse: 1 mi. from Visitors Center, ½ mi. from nearest parking. Open M and Sa-Su 12:30-3:30pm. Guided walks M and Sa-Su 12:30pm. Free. No dogs or bikes through tunnel.)

Formerly a military installation charged with defending the San Francisco harbor, the Headlands are dotted with machine gun nests, missile sites, and soldiers' quarters dating from the Spanish-American War to the 1950s. **Battery Spencer,** on Conzelman Rd. immediately west of U.S. 101, offers one of the best views of the city skyline and the Golden Gate Bridge, especially around sunset on the (rare) clear day. Farther into the park is the **NIKE Missile Site** on Field Rd., at Fort Berry and Fort Cronkite. (NIKE Missile Site ☎415-331-1453. Open W-F and 1st Su of each month 12:30-3:30pm.)

For more info, contact the **Marin Headlands Visitors Center,** Bldg. 948, Fort Barry (☎415-331-1540), at Bunker and Field Rd. Talk to the helpful staff about hiking and biking in the park and pick up maps, trail advice, and permits for free campsites. The center is also a museum and a store with artifacts. Open daily 9:30am-4:30pm. To get to the **Marin Headlands Hostel (HI),** follow the signs to the hostel from the Visitors Center. This solidly good hostel offers a kitchen, large room offers a kitchen, large common room with multiple couches, piano, fireplace and picnic tables as well as a basement game room with pool, foosball and ping-pong tables. (☎415-331-2777; www.norcalhostels.org. Linal rental $1. Closed 10am-3:30pm. $18, children $9; private room $54.) Accessible by car, **Kirby Cove,** off Conzelman Rd. west of the Golden Gate Bridge, consists of four campsites in a grove of cypress and eucalyptus trees on the shore, with fire rings and pit toilets. Kirby Cove is designed for larger groups. (☎800-365-2267. Bring your own water. No pets. 3-day max. stay. 1 weekend reservation per group per year. Open Apr.-Nov. Sites $25.)

⚠ APPROACHING SAUSALITO
Sausalito is a few miles north of the Bay Bridge on **U.S. 101.**

SAUSALITO
Originally a fishing center full of bars and bordellos, the city at Marin's extreme southeastern tip has long since traded its sea-dog days for retail boutiques and overpriced seafood restaurants. The palm trees and 14 ft. elephant statues of Plaza de Vina del Mar Park look out over a wonderful view of San Francisco Bay, making for a sunny, self-consciously Mediterranean-esque excursion. The sheer number and variety of quality art galleries in the small town make it worth checking out, regardless of the touristy feel. Half a mile north of the town center is the **Bay Model and Marinship Museum,** 2100 Bridgeway, a massive working model of San Francisco Bay. Built in the 1950s to test proposals to dam the bay, the water-filled model recreates tides and currents in great detail. (☎415-332-1851. Open Tu-Sa 9am-4pm. Free.)

Those tired of Rice-A-Roni should venture to the **Venice Gourmet Delicatessen,** 625 Bridgeway, which serves sharable sandwiches ($6) and side dishes ($3-5) in a Mediterranean-style marketplace with water-side seating. (☎415-332-3544; www.venicegourmet.com. Open daily in summer 9am-7pm; in winter 9am-6pm.)

⚠ LEAVING SAUSALITO
Take **U.S. 101 North,** switching to **Rte. 1 North.** 3¼ mi. after the turn-off onto Rte. 1, you can choose to go to Muir Woods or Mt. Tamalpais.

⚠ MUIR WOODS
5 mi. west of U.S. 101 on Rte. 1.

At the center of Mt. Tamalpais State Park is **Muir Woods National Monument,** a 560-acre stand of old coastal redwoods. Spared from logging by the steep sides of Redwood Canyon, these massive, centuries-old redwoods are shrouded in silence. The level, paved trails along the canyon floor are lined with wooden fences, but a hike up the canyon's sides will soon take you away from the tourists and face-to-face with wildlife. (☎415-388-2595. Open 9am-6pm. $2.) Avoid the fee by hiking in 2 mi. from the Pan Toll Ranger Station. It's worth the 5min. detour to check out the **Muir Beach Overlook.** Even with the wind, these picnic tables beckon.

STINSON BEACH. A younger, rowdier, and better-looking surfer crowd is attracted to Stinson Beach, although cold and windy conditions often leave them languishing on dry land. The Bard visits Stinson Beach from July to October during **Shakespeare at Stinson.** (☎415-868-1115; www.shakespeareatstinson.org. Stinson Beach open dawn-dusk.) Turn west at the only stop sign in town to reach the **Parkside Cafe,** where a light interior and garden patio complement an American menu that edges towards gourmet (lunch $9) and an extensive wine list. (☎415-868-1272; www.parksidecafe.com. Tu $5 spaghetti night, W $5 soup and salad. Sa live jazz, Su Brazilian bossa nova. Open M-F 7:30am-4pm and 5-9:30pm, Sa-Su 8am-4pm and 5-9:30pm.)

THE ROAD TO BOLINAS
Continuing a few miles northwest from Stinson Beach along Rte. 1, you'll find the **Audubon Canyon Ranch.** Dedicated to preserving the surrounding lands as well as other areas in Marin and Sonoma counties, the ranch provides educational programs and conducts several research projects. Come watch great blue herons and great egrets nest, or go for a hike on the 8 mi. of trails. From Rte. 1, exit onto **Olema Bolinas Rd.,** traveling south to the city.

BOLINAS
Bolinas—a tiny colony of hippies, artists, and writers—is perhaps the most mellow place on earth. Many of the tiny art galleries and eateries that dot the town have no set hours, and watching three generations of hippies walk side-by-side down the street emphasizes the village's strong

atemporal vibe. Eccentric Bolinas residents have included authors Richard Brautigan (*Trout Fishing in America*) and Jim Carroll (*The Basketball Diaries*). For years, locals have hoped to discourage tourist traffic by tearing down any and all signs marking the Bolinas-Olema road. Press coverage of the "sign war" won the people of Bolinas exactly the publicity they wanted to avoid, but for now, at least, the town remains unspoiled in ways that Sausalito is not—and they intend to keep it that way, so don't expect to feel welcomed. But who needs signs anyway?

To graze while you gaze, try Northern California cuisine at **Coast Cafe,** open for breakfast, lunch, and dinner, but don't tell them we sent you. (☎415-868-2298. Lunch $9. Dinner $14. Open 7:30am-2pm and 5-8pm.) At the end of Olema-Bolinas Rd. there's a small **art museum.** (Open F 1-5pm, Sa-Su noon-5pm. Suggested donation.) Turn right and you can see the convergence of the lagoon with the ocean. Take the next-to-last right off Olema-Bolinas Rd. to reach **The Grand Hotel,** 15 Brighton Ave., which has two cozy rooms each with a double and twin bed above a second-hand shop run by an old-timer. Share the bathroom and kitchen downstairs. (☎415-868-1757. Rooms $49.50.)

APPROACHING POINT REYES
Follow **Rte. 1 North** for about 11 mi. Continue onto **Mesa Rd.,** which ends at Point Reyes Station.

POINT REYES

A near-island surrounded by nearly 100 mi. of isolated coastline, the Point Reyes National Seashore is a wilderness of pine forests, chaparral ridges, and grassy flatlands. Five million years ago, this outcropping was a suburb of L.A., but it hitched a ride on the submerged Pacific Plate and has been creeping northward along the San Andreas Fault ever since. In summer, colorful wildflowers attract crowds of gawking tourists, but with hundreds of miles of amazing trails, it's quite possible to gawk alone.

SIGHTS. The **Earthquake Trail** is a three-quarter-mile walk along the infamous San Andreas Fault Line that starts right at Bear Valley. Lovely **Limantour Beach** sits at the end of Limantour Rd., 8 mi. west of the Visitors Center, which runs a free shuttle bus to the beach in summer. Both Limantour and Point Reyes

VITAL STATS

Population: 818

Visitor Info: Point Reyes National Seashore Headquarters (also referred to as Bear Valley Visitor Center; ☎415-464-5100; www.nps.gov/pore), on Bear Valley Rd., ½ mi. west of Olema. Rangers distribute camping permits, maps, and sage advice on trails, tides, and weather conditions, and lead guided hikes. Excellent exhibits on the cultural and natural history of Pt. Reyes. Open M-F 9am-5pm, Sa-Su and holidays 8am-5pm.

Post Office: 10155 Rte. 1 (☎415-663-1761), in Olema. Open M-F 8am-1pm and 2-4:30pm. **Postal Code:** 94950.

Beaches have high, grassy dunes and long stretches of sand, but strong ocean currents along the point make swimming very dangerous. Swimming is safest at **Hearts Desire Beach,** north of the Visitors Center on sheltered **Tomales Bay.** To reach the dramatic **Point Reyes Lighthouse** at the very tip of the point, follow Sir Francis Drake Blvd. to its end (20 mi. from the Visitors Center) and head right along the stairway to Sea Lion Overlook. From December until February, migrating gray whales can be spotted from the overlook. (Lighthouse Visitors Center ☎415-669-1534. Open Th-M 10am-4:30pm.) To hike from the Coast Trail to **Bass Lake Swimming Hole,** take the unmarked Olema-Bolinas Rd. 2½ mi. north of Stinson immediately after the Lagoon and before the Olema sign. Take a left at the fork and then a right onto Mesa Rd. which will curve around for several miles, past the bird observatory (pick up a map of Point Reyes), to the Palomarin trailhead. The hike will take you along the cliffs of the Pacific into the rocky cliffs, through trees and finally to a truly secret swimming spot. Bring a picnic and take a dip, with or without a suit. To reach **Goat Rock Beach,** 2 mi. south of the Russian River, turn west for Goat Rock Beach where late May to early September you can see newborn baby seals; harbor seals and elephant seals are currently in a silent war over the territory.

FOOD & ACCOMMODATIONS. Across the street from an ATM in the town of Point Ryes, **Bovine Bakery,** 11315 Rte. 1, proffers caffeinated drinks and vegan-friendly gooey treats like the morning bun ($1.85). Sandwiches are $5 when fresh (Tu and F) and

$2.50 other days. (☎415-663-9420. Open M-F 6:30am-5pm, Sa-Su 7am-5pm.) A much acclaimed area favorite, **The Station House Café**, 11180 State Rte. 1, serves classic American food that's perfectly prepared. Don't miss the heavenly bread pudding dessert for $5.25. (☎415-663-1515. Open Su-Tu and Th 8am-9pm, F-Sa 8am-10pm.) On the south side of the Russian River, **Sizzling Tandoor**, 9960 Rte. 1, serves Indian food on a beautifully situated isolated perch above the Russian River. (☎707-864-0000. Entrees $7-15.)

The ◪**Point Reyes Hostel (HI-AYH)** is just off Limatour Rd., 2 mi. from Limatour Beach. Miles from civilization, this excellent hostel provides shelter and solace for a stay in the wilderness. The surrounding landscape is still scarred by a major forest fire that torched the region in 1995. (☎415-663-8811; www.norcal-hostels.org. Linen $1; sleeping bags encouraged. Towels $1. Check-in 4:30-9:30pm. Check-out 10am. Lockout 10am-4:30pm. Dorms $16, under 17 $10.) Lodging is also available at **Doran Beach Campground**, 1 mi. south of Bodega Bay and 31 mi. north of Point Reyes, a beautiful campground on a strip of land between Bodega Bay and Harbor. The spot has limited hiking access but it's excellent for bird-watching and if you can stand the frigid water it's one of the only Sonoma beaches safe for swimming. Whales can also sometimes be spotted. (☎707-875-3540; www.sonoma-county.org/camping. No hookups. Sites $16. Day use $2.)

◪ **DINUCCI'S ITALIAN DINNERS**
≡◖ 14485 Valley Ford Rd.
In Valley Ford, 23 mi. north of Point Reyes on Rte. 1.
Stop in Valley Ford if only to go to ◪**Dinucci's Italian Dinners**, an old-school, family-oriented and totally unpretentious restaurant with brown-checked cloths on the table. Don't expect any delicate olive oil on the table here. Hearty five-course meals of spaghetti, lasagna, or ravioli come with antipasto, fabulous minestrone, and salad all for under $13. (☎707-876-3260. Open M and Th-Sa from 4pm, Su from noon.)

◪ **APPROACHING BODEGA BAY**
Follow **Rte. 1/Shoreline Hwy.** for about 8 mi., turn right onto **Bodega Hwy.**, then right onto **Bodega Ln.**

BODEGA BAY

The small town of Bodega Bay displays its seafaring roots in the incredibly fresh salmon and crab at oceanside restaurants. The **Bodega Bay Visitors Center**, 850 Rte. 1, has info on the North Coast. (☎707-875-3866; www.bodegabay.com. Open M-Th 10am-6pm, F-Sa noon-8pm, Su 11am-7pm.) Both the towns of Bodega Bay and Bodega, 1½ mi. away, were featured in Alfred Hitchcock's 1963 film *The Birds*. See pictures at the Visitors Center. On the Sonoma coast west of Bodega Bay, the **Bodega Head Loop** is a short coastal hike with pristine beach and ocean views. To reach the 1½ mi. trail from the town, turn left on E. Shore Rd., turn west on Bay Flat Rd., and continue around the bay past Spud Point Marina to Bedge Head parking, the trailhead's location.

Sonoma Coast State Beach begins just north of Bodega Bay off Rte. 1. The 5000 acres of land offer 16 mi. of beach, spectacular views, and places to picnic, hike, and camp. However, unpredictable currents make these beaches dangerous (see **Sleeper Waves**, p. 955). The most popular coastal campgrounds are **Bodega Dunes** (hot showers; sites $16) and **Wright's Beach** (sites $20). Call ReserveAmerica for reservations at ☎800-444-7275. If the campsites are full, the clean rooms with TV and private bath at **Bodega Harbor Inn**, 1345 Bodega Ave., off Rte. 1 in Bodega Bay, are your cheapest bet. (☎707-875-3594; www.bodega-harborinn.com. Rooms $60-82.)

THE ROAD TO GUALALA

Heading north from Bodega Bay, Rte. 1 hits **Jenner** at the mouth of the Russian River. Jenner's **Goat Rock Beach**, with its astounding waves and coast, is the site of a famous harbor seal rookery. **Reef Campground**, 10 mi. north of Jenner, is part of **Fort Ross State Historic Park**, providing 20 sites in a wooded gulch, a 5min. walk from a rocky secluded beach. (☎707-847-3286. No showers. Sites $10.)

Salt Point State Park, 20 mi. north of Jenner, is a 6000-acre park for the hiker or horseback rider with an inland campsite, **Woodside Creek**, and a coastside campsite, **Gerstle Cove**, on a bluff among scattered pines overlooking the sea. There are 109 sites with fire pits and picnic tables. (☎707-847-3221, reservations 800-444-7275. No showers. Drinking water and toilets.

Open for day use sunrise-sunset. Sites $10-12. Day-use $4.)

APPROACHING GUALALA
From Bodega, follow **Rte. 1** for 53 mi. and then turn right onto **Old State Hwy.**

GUALALA. Pass through Gualala but if you must stay, try **Gualala Hotel.** The hotel has served as the central establishment in town for over 100 years and its age shows, for better and for worse (although they are embarking on a project of extensive renovations). Rooms lack TVs and phones and some joint bathrooms have old-fashioned clawed tubs. Downstairs is a good restaurant and **saloon** with pool tables, offering the only nightlife around. While it might be a bit rough around the edges, it's still the cheapest roof around. (☎707-884-3441; www.thegualalahotel.com. Rooms $65, with ocean view and bath $85; 2-room suites $120.)

APPROACHING POINT ARENA
Turn right onto **Rte. 1/Shoreline Hwy.** and continue for 14 mi. Turn right onto **Mill St.** and left onto **Center St.**

POINT ARENA
Point Arena's center attraction is the **Point Arena Lighthouse,** 2 mi. north of town. The 115 ft. lighthouse, the tallest that the public can access in America, is vintage 1906, built after the San Francisco earthquake demolished the 1870 original. Although no longer in commission, it contains a Fresnel lens, an intricate array of prisms and magnifying glass worth $3.5 million—an optician's paradise. The downstairs exhibit includes a whale-watching information room. (☎707-882-2777; www.pointarenalighthouse.com. Open daily 10am-4:30pm; winter until 3pm. $4, under 12 $1.) Point Arena Lighthouse also has vacation **rental homes** with three bedrooms and two full baths at the foot of the lighthouse. (☎877-725-4448. Rental homes in summer $190; in winter $175.) A restored vaudeville **theater** shows independent films and sells organic hot chocolate at the counter. (☎707-882-3456; www.arenacinema.com. Films $1.50.) **CityArt** (☎707-882-3616; www.cityart.ws), a non-profit community arts gallery

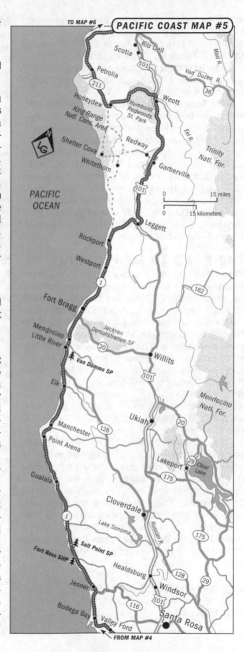

PACIFIC COAST MAP #5

in the former home of a teacher who murdered her lover, shows interesting changing exhibits of the local artists and hosts a poetry reading the third Thursday of every month at 7:30pm. Surfers like **the cove** (take the coastal access sign from Rte. 1) although it's an inferior notch for coastal beauty.

◪**The Record,** a cafe and natural gourmet market, is the best place to meet the town locals—mostly artists whose work decorates the walls. (☎707-882-3663. Sandwiches $5.75. Open summer M-Sa 7am-8pm, Su 9am-5pm; winter M-Sa 7am-6pm, Su 9am-5pm.) All organic, high-quality Mexican fare awaits at **El Burrito.** The namesake is $6, quesadillas are $4.50-5.50. Their commitment to organic make them a borderline non-profit. Take $0.25 off when you bring your own plate or utensils. (☎707-882-2910. Open M-F 8am-7pm, Sa-Su 11:30am-7pm.)

THE ROAD TO MENDOCINO

From Point Arena, it is roughly a 35 mi. drive north on Rte 1 to Mendocino. In **Manchester,** 6 mi. north of Point Arena, the **Manchester Beach KOA** is a hyper-organized "kamping" franchise with pool, hot tub, and playground hailed for cleanliness that makes it clear how "camp" is a cousin of kitsch. The neat wooden "Kabins" sleep four to six people with an outdoor shower and restroom (bring your own bedding), while the cozy "kottages" with bath and kitchen sleep four. (☎707-882-2375, reservations 800-562-4188; www.manchesterbeachkoa.com. Tents sites $30-33; RVs $38-52; "Kabins" $53-67; "Kottages" $138-145.)

Fans of **Jack London** should stop in **Elk,** where the famed author liked to visit and write in one of the town's hotel rooms overlooking the ocean. **Navarro Head** is little more than a charming rest stop with a quaint inns and a few walking trails. Poor drainage, thin soil, and ocean winds have created an unusual bonsai garden 3 mi. south of Mendocino at the **Pygmy Forest** in **Van Damme State Park** (camping $16; day-use $4). The forest, off Rte. 1 past the park free to hikers.

◤ APPROACHING MENDOCINO
To enter Mendocino from **Rte. 1,** turn left onto **Little Lake Rd.**

MENDOCINO

Teetering on bluffs over the ocean, isolated Mendocino is a charming coastal community of art galleries, craft shops, bakeries, and B&Bs. The town's weathered shingles, white picket fences, and clustered homes seem out of place on the West Coast; maybe that's why Mendocino was able to masquerade for years as the fictional Maine village of Cabot Cove in the TV series *Murder, She Wrote.*

VITAL STATS

Population: 1100

Visitor Info: Fort-Bragg-Mendocino Coast Chamber of Commerce (☎707-961-6300 or 800-726-2780), in Fort Bragg (see p. 953).

Post Office: 10500 Ford St. (☎707-937-5282). Open M-F 7:30am-4:30pm. **Postal Code:** 95460.

◧ **GETTING AROUND.** Mendocino sits on Rte. 1, right on the Pacific Coast, 30 mi. west of U.S. 101 and 12 mi. south of Fort Bragg. Once in Mendocino, exploring is best done on foot.

◙ **SIGHTS.** Mendocino's greatest natural feature lies 900 ft. to its west, where the earth comes to a halt and falls off into the Pacific, forming the impressive coastline of the ◪**Mendocino Headlands.** The windy quarter-mile stretch of land that separates the town from the rocky shore remains an undeveloped meadow of tall grass and wildflowers, despite its obvious value as a site for even more multi-million dollar vacation homes. The **ecological staircase** at **Jug Handle State Park,** 5 mi. north of town, is a terrace of five different ecosystems formed by a combination of erosion and tectonic uplift, with each ecosystem roughly 100,000 years older than the one below it.

An abundance of hot springs in the Mendocino area proves once and for all that the region is a natural paradise. **Orr Hot Springs,** 13201 Orr Springs Rd., an hour's drive east of Mendocino, in Ukiah, off U.S. 101. Sauna, steam room, and gardens make the world disappear at this clothing-optional resort. (☎707-462-6277. 18+. Open daily 10am-10pm. Day-use $20.) In July, enjoy the **Mendocino Music Festival,** a two-week melee of classical music, opera, and cultural dance. Tickets for some events go quickly. (☎707-937-2044; www.mendocinomusic.com. Tickets $15-40.)

FOOD. All of Mendocino's breads are freshly baked, all vegetables locally grown, all wheat unmilled, and almost all prices inflated. Restaurants in Mendocino often close unusually early. **Lipinski's Juice Joint,** on Ukiah St. east of Lansing St., has a relaxed hippie vibe, free Internet upstairs and the best value breakfasts around (waffles with fruit or syrup $3). Lunch options include Middle Eastern fare (falafel $4.25) or the Hawgenfedda sandwich, which packs in meats, cheeses, and veggies for $5.25. (☎707-937-4033. F-Su live music, Sa open mic with occasional performances by the legendary folksinger Wolf. Open M-Th 6:30am-7pm, F-Su 6:30am-10:30pm.)

Picnicking on the Mendocino Headlands is the cheapest option and should be preceded by a trip to **Mendosa's Market,** 10501 Lansing St., the closest thing in Mendocino to a real supermarket. (☎707-937-5879. Open daily 8am-9pm.) **Tote Fête,** 10450 Lansing St., has delicious tote-out food. An asiago, pesto, and artichoke heart sandwich ($4.75) hits the spot. The bakery in the back has a flower garden and a small fountain. (☎707-937-3383. Open M-Sa 10:30am-7pm, Su 10:30am-4pm. Bakery open daily 7:30am-4pm.) **Lu's Kitchen,** 45013 Ukiah St., west of Lansing St., is a local favorite. It serves leafy vegetarian cuisine in an informal, outdoor atmosphere. (☎707-937-4939. Meals $5-10. Open daily 11:30am-5:30pm; closed Jan.-Mar. and on very rainy days.)

ACCOMMODATIONS. The **Jug Handle Creek Farm,** 5 mi. north of Mendocino off Rte. 1, across the street from the Jug Handle State Reserve, is a beautiful 133-year-old house sitting on 40 acres of gardens, with campsites and small rustic cabins. One hour of chores (or $5) is required per night. (☎707-964-4630. 30 beds. No linen. Reservations recommended in summer; walk-ins welcome. Dorms $22, students $16, children $9; cabins $23-30 per person; sites $11.) If you're arriving after 10pm you can crash "late night" at the **Sweetwater Spa & Inn,** 44840 Main St. (☎707-937-4076 or 800-300-4140) where for $70, you'll get and free exclusive use of the hot tub and sauna all night. Less expensive and less eye-pleasing accommodations can be found in Fort Bragg.

APPROACHING FORT BRAGG
Continue on **Rte. 1 North/Shoreline Hwy.** for 10 mi. Turn right onto **E. Laurel St.** and left onto **N. Rankline St.**

FORT BRAGG

Fort Bragg is noticeably a little rougher around the edges than its genteel sibling Mendocino, but the town's major industry, the lumber mill, was shut down in August 2002 and the town is slowly turning to rely on tourism, as well as smaller fishing and logging operations.

VITAL STATS

Population: 8000

Visitor Info: Fort-Bragg-Mendocino Coast Chamber of Commerce, 332 N. Main St. (☎707-961-6300 or 800-726-2780). Open daily 9am-5pm.

Internet Access: Regional Branch Library of Mendocino, 499 Laurel St., at the corner of N. Whipple St. Open Tu-W 11am-7:45pm, Th-F 11am-5:45pm, Sa 10am-4:45pm.

Post Office: 203 N. Franklin St. (☎717-964-2302). Open M-F 8:30am-5pm. **Postal Code:** 95437.

SIGHTS. The much-accoladed **North Coast Brewing Company,** 44 N. Main St., makes 13 of their own brews on the block; the excellent Old Rasputin (9.6% alcohol) or Old Stock (a whopping 11.9% alcohol) will get you tipsy faster than you'll realize—at the bar they'll only serve you two. The food is good too, with salad and burger lunch options ($7) and New American pasta, seafood and the like for dinner ($14). Across the street you can peek in at the enormous brewing vats behind the store or take a free tour. (☎707-964-3400; www.northcoastbrewing.com. Open daily 11:30am-11pm. Tours Sa 12:30pm.) The California Western Railroad, also called the **Skunk Train,** at Rte. 1 and Laurel St., offers a jolly, child-friendly diversion through its Redwood Route, and has since 1885. A steam engine, diesel locomotive, and vintage motorcar take turns running between Fort Bragg and Northspur. (☎707-964-6371 or 800-777-5865; www.skunktrain.com. 3hr. round-trip. Departs Fort Bragg daily at 10am and 2:15 pm. $35, ages 5-11 $17, under 5 free. Reservations recommended.)

PACIFIC COAST

⚑ FOOD & ACCOMMODATIONS. Egg-heads offers omelettes stuffed with the likes of cheese, bacon, and Dungeness crab along with other cheery diner favorites. (☎ 707-964-5505. Open Th-Tu 7am-2pm.) The most budget-friendly option for lodgings is **Colombi Motel,** 647 Oak St., five blocks east of Main St. It has clean single and double units with cable TV, phone, and private bath; some units also have a full kitchen. (☎ 707-964-5773. Motel office inside market. Check-out 11am. Singles $45; doubles $55. $5 less in winter.) **MacKerricher State Park campground,** 2½ mi. north of Fort Bragg, has excellent views of tidepool life, passing seals, sea lions, and migratory whales, as well as 9 mi. of beaches and a murky lake for trout fishing. Around this lake is **Lake Cleone Trail** (1 mi.)—a short, easy hike that features thick cypress trees and a pretty marsh. Access the trail from Cleone Camp or Surfwood Camp. (☎ 707-937-5804. Showers, bathrooms, and potable water. Reservations necessary in summer. Sites $16. Day-use free.)

⚑ APPROACHING WESTPORT
Continue on **Rte. 1/Shoreline Hwy.** for about 16 mi.

WESTPORT. Blink and you'll miss Westport (pop. 200), a town with only a general store (gas available) and a couple of inns; despite its size it still manages to display a lot of tie-dye. If this kind of seclusion appeals to you, try the lovely **De Haven Valley Farm,** housed in an 1875 Victorian ranch house, 1¾ mi. north of town on Rte. 1. The owners plan on turning the old barn into an artists' co-operative. A private chef serves a nightly four-course dinner $29. (☎ 707-961-1660; www.dehaven-valley-farm.com. Rooms $89-144; cottages $134-144.)

THE ROAD TO GARBERVILLE

The road north of Westport becomes exceedingly curvy and therefore slow. North of **Rockport** it turns inland to **Leggett;** there is no possible way to continue along the coast here. Road-builders decided to circumvent the formidable King Range, abandoning this portion of land, the mysterious **Lost Coast** to, as it turns out, the wiles of marijuana farmers.

Where Rte. 1 turns inland and snakes around the Lost Coast, stay on smoothly paved, speedy U.S. 101 toward Garberville and the Avenue of the Giants for some of the most beautiful redwoods in the world.

GARBERVILLE

Garberville is a good jumping-off point for Humboldt State Park. The **Garberville-Redway Chamber of Commerce,** 773 Redway Dr., in Jacob Garber Sq., offers information on local events and attractions. (☎ 800-923-2613. Open M-F 10am-5pm.) **Sentry Market,** on Redwood Dr., is the largest supermarket for miles. (☎ 707-923-2279. Open daily 7am-10pm.) Locals highly recommend **Calico's Cafe,** on Redwood Dr. next to Sherwood Forest Motel, for its homemade pastas, salads, and burgers as well. Try the garlicky fettucine gorgonzola ($9) made from scratch. (☎ 707-923-2253. Open M-Th 8am-9pm, F-Sa 8am-10pm, Su 11am-9pm.) **Nacho Mama's,** at Redwood Dr. and Sprowl Creek Rd., is an organic Mexican fast-food stand with healthy burritos, dolphin-free albacore tacos, and refreshing soy wildberry or peach frosties. (☎ 707-923-4060. Entrees $3-9. Open M-Sa 11am-7pm.)

HUMBOLDT REDWOODS STATE PARK

About 10 mi. north of Garberville on U.S. 101 in the Humboldt Redwoods State Park, the Avenue of the Giants (the actual name of the road) splits off the highway and winds its way through 31 mi. of redwoods, the world's largest living organisms above ground level. Hiking, swimming, fishing, biking, and rafting opportunities abound in this rugged area. Garberville is the main town along the Avenue and is connected to its smaller neighbor, Redway, by Redwood Dr., the main street in both towns. Moving north up the Avenue, drivers encounter the tiny towns of Phillipsville, Miranda, Myers Flat, Weott, Redcrest, and Pepperwood.

The **Humboldt Redwoods State Park Visitors Center,** just south of Weott on the Avenue of the Giants, has a very knowledgeable staff that can highlight the Avenue's groves, facilities and trails, while providing safety tips on camping. The center also has hands-on displays for kids about area wildlife. (☎ 707-946-2263. Open Apr.-Oct. daily 9am-5pm; Oct.-Apr. Su and Th-Sa

10am-3pm.) The park's camping options are plentiful. Each developed **campsite** offers coin-op showers, flush toilets, and fire rings. (☎707-946-2409. Sites $15.) The most remote site, wildlife-filled **Albee Creek,** on Mattole Rd. 5 mi. west of U.S. 101, near Rockefeller Forest, has access to biking and hiking trails and is open year-round. (Sites $15.) **Hidden Springs,** near Myers Flat, is situated on a hillside in a mixed forest and has 154 semi-secluded sites with hot showers. Few hiking trails start directly at the campsite, but the South Fork of Eel River is a short hike away. (Open mid-May through mid-Oct. Sites $15.

APPROACHING PETROLIA
From **Rte. 254/Redwood Hwy./Avenue of the Giants**, turn left onto **Mattole Rd.** and continue on Mattole Rd. for 35 mi. to reach Petrolia.

PETROLIA. Named for being the site of the first oil drilling in California, **Petrolia** is now one of the few town outposts for the furtive dwellers of the region. Stop for a bite at the cosy, authentic **Hideaway,** 1 mi. southeast of Petrolia General Store. Yes, it is somewhat hidden away from the road; immediately north of the Lindley Bridge take a right off Mattole Rd. The burgers are your best bet, while other options include Philly cheesesteaks and clam chowder. (☎707-629-3533. Open daily 9am-9pm. Beer and wine bar open until 10:30pm.) After Petrolia, the road passes by a stretch of the coast which is made all the sweeter by its remoteness. Chances are you'll be one of the few cars on this beautiful outpost on the globe, with only the wildflowers, dark sea rocks, and grazing cows for company.

SLEEPER WAVES.
Sleeper waves are overpowering waves that crash ashore and then forcefully pull back whatever or whomever they happen upon. Many beaches have posted warnings about such dangerous currents, and it is safest to simply stay out of treacherous waters. However, if a sleeper wave yanks you into the surf, do not swim toward shore. Doing so will only tire you out in a futile battle against the current. Instead, swim parallel to the beach until you're out of the wave's clutches.

100 MILE RADIUS

THE LOST COAST

Northeast of Garberville lie the mysterious, rugged shores of the Lost Coast, a region known for its undeveloped beaches, hiking trails, and marijuana farmers. The town of **Shelter Cove** is the tamest part of the Lost Coast; located over 20 mi. west of Garberville, this tiny community of fishermen now welcomes vacationers with a small assortment of restaurants and hotels.

Stretching 24 mi. along the coast between Shelter Cove and Petrolia, the **King Range National Conservation Area** is home to excellent primitive camping, an abandoned lighthouse, and one of North America's most unstable mountain ranges, which sits on a fault line between three tectonic plates. **King Peak Rd.** travels through the center of the conservation area, leading to many trailheads and campsites.

The windy, flat beach in King Range is framed by steep grass-covered mountains and rolling dunes. Here visitors can enjoy the **Mattole River Estuary,** a nursery for young salmon and a refuge for egrets and pelicans, or take off on the three-day **Lost Coast Trail** (25 mi. one-way), which offers ever-changing vistas of mountains and coastline, and occasional encounters with sea lions, shore birds, and black-tailed deer.

To reach Shelter Cove from Garberville, take Briceland Rd. west, then turn right on Shelter Cove Rd. Roads in the area are poorly maintained; 4WD vehicles are recommended. Contact the **King Range BLM** office, on Shelter Cove Rd., 9 mi from Shelter Cove, for info on camping and fire permits. (☎707-986-5400. Open M-Sa 8am-4:30pm.)

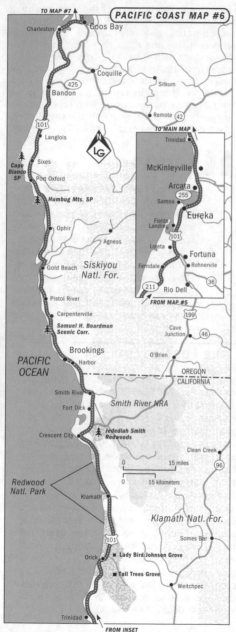

PACIFIC COAST

APPROACHING FERNDALE
From Petrolia, follow **Mattole Rd. (Rte. 211)** for about 30 mi. to reach Ferndale.

FERNDALE

A dairy community since the 1800s, Ferndale (pop. 1320) feeds the Humboldt Creamery, a giant plant churning out milk and ice cream (pick some up at the Red Front Store) that you'll see as you pass the northern edge of town. The town has preserved all its Victorian architecture—the entire village is a designated State Historical Landmark—and the result is small-town perfection: not a franchise in sight, and an atmosphere honest and friendly enough to allow for an unattended jam shop, **Jackie Jett Jam,** with a box for payments (the $6 jams are delicious, too).

The amphitheater-like **cemeteries** near **Russ Park** on Ocean Ave. give a sense of the town's history and provide a breathtaking view of the Victorian town with its grazing dairy cattle. One of Ferndale's oddest features, the annual Arcata Kinetic Sculpture Race, ends at the studio of the event's founder, **Hobart Galleries,** 393 Main St., at Brown St. See kooky contraptions from past races in the form of a raccoon, dragon, bumblebee, flying saucer, and purple crayon at the **Ferndale Kinetic Sculpture Museum,** inside the **Arts and Cultural Center,** 580 Main St., at Shaw Ave. The **Ferndale Museum,** around the corner from Main St. on Shaw Ave., is worth a stop for its exhibits on local history. (☎707-786-5483. Open W-Sa 11am-4pm, Su 1-4pm.) **Ferndale Repertory Theatre,** on Main St., hosts live performances (F-Sa 2 and 8pm) and has an art gallery showcasing local work.

The accommodations here are mainly exorbitantly priced B&Bs, but if you have been saving for a splurge, this is the place. One option is California's oldest B&B, the **Shaw House,** 703 Main St. Founded in 1860, the Carpenter Gothic Revival-style home offers seven rooms, a sit-down hot breakfast, and afternoon tea. (☎707-786-9958; www.shawhouse.com. Check-in 4-6pm. Checkout 11am. Rooms in summer $85-165; in winter $75-165.) For a cheaper rest, **Ruriko's Motel and Laundromat** (☎707-786-9471), at Main St. and Shaw Ave., offers two rooms with two beds and a kitchenette for $49.

■**Village Baking and Catering,** 472 Main St., is worth a stop off the highway. Try the incredible Special Turkey Sandwich with homemade artichoke relish ($4.25), sip coffee drinks ($1-2.25), or delight in gooey sticky buns for under $2. (☎707-786-9440. Open M-Sa 7am-3pm, Su 7am-1:30pm.).

 The films *The Majestic* and *Outbreak* were filmed in Ferndale.

APPROACHING EUREKA
Follow **Rte. 211** out of Ferndale for about 5 mi., then merge onto **U.S. 101 North** and continue 14 mi. to Eureka.

EUREKA

Eureka (pop. 27,218) was born out of the demands of mid-19th-century gold prospectors who wanted a more convenient alternative to the tedious overland route from Sacramento. The Humboldt Bay provided a landing spot, and Eureka was founded as its port. The decline of the region's gold mining and lumber businesses has led Eureka to shift from a reliance on natural resources to fishing and tourism. While the town is less attractive than its northern neighbors, Old Town Eureka offers some historical appeal. Victorian buildings clustered next to the harbor contain a series of shops, restaurants, and art galleries. Don't judge Eureka solely on the basis of a drive through town on U.S. 101; the city's perimeter may appear a bit gritty, but the center of Eureka retains a pleasant, old-town charm.

VITAL STATS

Population: 27,218

Visitor Info: Eureka/Humboldt Visitors Bureau, 1034 2nd St. (☎707-443-5097 or 800-346-3482), will answer specific questions. Open M-F 9am-5pm. **Chamber of Commerce,** 2112 Broadway (☎707-442-3738). Information and brochures. Open M-F 8:30am-5pm; extended summer hours.

Post Office: 337 W. Clark St. (☎707-442-1768), near Broadway St. Open M-F 8:30am-5pm and Sa noon-3pm. **Postal Code:** 95501.

GETTING AROUND. Eureka straddles **U.S. 101,** 7 mi. south of Arcata and 280 mi. north of San Francisco. To the south, U.S. 101 is referred to as **Broadway.** In town, U.S. 101 is called **4th St.** (heading south) and **5th St.** (heading north).

◙ SIGHTS. Eureka is very proud of its bevy of restored **Victorian homes,** a few of which are worth driving past. Self-guided tour maps are available at the Chamber of Commerce. Some of the more handsome houses are now expensive B&Bs. If you drive by, don't miss the much-photographed, dramatically stark **Carson Mansion,** which belonged to a prominent logger in the 1850s.

Art galleries, Eureka's main claim to fame, cluster downtown. Check out **First Street Gallery,** 422 1st St. (☎707-443-6363), **The Ink People Gallery,** 411 12th St. (☎707-442-8413), and the **Morris Graves Museum of Art,** 636 F St. (☎707-442-0278) for their interesting collections. Ask the Chamber of Commerce about current exhibits.

◨ᴦ FOOD & ACCOMMODATIONS.
Ramone's Bakery and Cafe, 209 E St., between 2nd and 3rd St., specializes in homemade truffles, fresh-baked pies, and the ever-popular "Chocolate Sin"—a chocolate and liqueur torte. Sandwiches ($4), soups ($3), and salads ($4) are also available. (☎707-445-2923. Open M-Sa 7am-6pm, Su 7am-4pm.) **Saffire Rose Cafe,** 525 2nd St., is located in the historic Vance Hotel. Dine inside an old-fashioned brass elevator and listen to live jazz at night. Grilled panini sandwiches ($6-9) and salads ($6-10) are offered for both lunch and dinner, and there is a dinner buffet special on weekend nights. (☎707-441-0805. Call for jazz details. Open daily 9am for coffee, breads, and pastries; Su-Th 11am-9pm; F-Sa 11am-midnight.) Another notable choice is **Los Bagels,** 403 2nd St., a vibrant spot that combines Mexican and Jewish baking traditions with tasty results. (☎707-442-8525. Open M-Sa 7am-5pm, Su 8am-4pm). **Cafe Marina,** 601 Startare Dr., is off U.S. 101 at the Samoa Bridge Exit (Rte. 255). From there, take the Woodley Island Exit north of town. Outdoor dining on the marina is the perfect way to enjoy their fresh seafood, like the spicy blackened snapper. The polished bar is a night spot for local fishermen. (☎707-443-2233. Sandwiches $6-13. Entrees $10-16. Open daily summer 7am-10pm; off season 7am-9pm.)

Travelers will find many budget motels off U.S. 101, but most are unappealing; be selective. Walking around alone at night, especially along Broadway, is not recommended. Old Town Eureka is more suitable for evening dinners and strolls. **Motel 6,** 1934 Broadway, lies south of town off U.S. 101 and offers satellite TV. (☎707-445-9631.

PACIFIC COAST

Singles $44; doubles $46. $3 per additional person. Rates may vary in July and Aug.) **Big Lagoon County Park,** 20 mi. north of Eureka on U.S. 101, is a favorite. The park has 32 sites with flush toilets, drinking water, and a big lagoon for swimming, canoeing, and kayaking. (☎707-445-7652. No hookups. Sites $12. Day-use $2; arrive early to beat the rush.)

DETOUR: SAMOA
From U.S. 101 take Rte. 255 over the Samoa Bridge to the end, turn left on Samoa Blvd., then take first left turn.

The **dunes recreation area** in Samoa was once a thriving dune ecosystem. Now, this peninsula offers beach access and dune hiking. Opened in 1893 to feed the lumberjacks of the mill company that owned the town, the **Samoa Cookhouse** opened to the public in the 60s and remains a place to roll up your sleeves and pack down some solid food. One set meal (no menu) is served for breakfast (7-11am; $9), lunch (11am-3:30pm; $10) and dinner (5-9pm; $14). At oil cloths on picnic-style tables, people chow down on the likes of pot roast and baked ham. Vegetarians will have to skip the main course (which leaves soup, salad, potato, dessert and coffee). Seconds are served for free. The building houses a logging exhibit also. (☎707-442-1659; www.humboldtdining.com/cookhouse).

APPROACHING ARCATA
Follow **U.S. 101 North** for 6¾ mi. and take the **Rte. 255/Samora Blvd.** exit toward Arcata.

ARCATA

Arcata (ar-KAY-ta) is like a transplanted slice of Berkeley in the remote northern corner of California. At the intersection of U.S. 101 and Rte. 299, Arcata typifies the laid-back existence that characterizes the state's northern coast. Check out the town's many murals, Victorian homes, and characters living "alternative" lifestyles. Arcata's neighbor, Humboldt State University, focuses on forestry and marine biology (Earth First! was founded here). All over Humboldt County, students get baked in the sun—and on the county's number-one cash crop.

SIGHTS.
Experience Arcata by taking a short stroll around the **Arcata Plaza,** in the center of town near the intersection of 8th and H St. The

VITAL STATS

Population: 16,500

Visitor Info: Arcata Chamber of Commerce, 1635 Heindon Rd. (☎707-822-3619). Open daily 9am-5pm.

Post Office: 799 H St. (☎707-822-3570). Open M-F 8:30am-5pm. **Postal Code:** 95521.

plaza hosts folk music on the weekends and an annual **Summer Solstice Festival** on the weekend nearest the summer solstice. The **Natural History Museum,** at 13th and G St., is a brief walk from the plaza and home to a modest collection of prehistoric fossils and whale skulls. (Open Tu-Sa 10am-5pm. Suggested donation $2.) Nearby **Redwood Park,** at 14th and Union St., contains lots of nooks for picnicking among giant trees. Behind the park lies **Arcata Community Forest,** which has picnic spaces, meadows, redwoods, and hiking trails.

A former "sanitary" landfill, the 75-acre **Arcata Marsh and Wildlife Sanctuary** lies at the foot of I St., across from Samoa Blvd. Visitors can take a tour to see how this saltwater marsh/converted sewer system works with treated waste, or wander the trails around the lake. The **Sanctuary Trail** (2 mi., 1hr.) along the Humboldt Bay offers great bird-watching opportunities. (☎707-826-2359. Tours Sa 8:30am, meet at the foot of I St., and at 2pm, meet at the info center on S. G St. Open daily 9am-5pm.)

The 36-year-old **Kinetic Sculpture Race,** held annually over Memorial Day weekend, is Humboldt County's oddest festival. A few dozen insane and artsy adventurers attempt to pilot unwieldy homemade vehicles (like the squash-shaped "Gourd of the Rings") on a grueling three-day, 42 mi. trek from Arcata to Ferndale over road, sand, and water. Vehicles from previous competitions are on display in Ferndale (see p. 956).

FOOD.
■**Live From New York Pizza,** 1504 G St., has incredible slices of pizza. Plain cheese is $1.55 but try something more exciting like the Godfather with ricotta, fresh tomatoes, sun-dried tomatoes, pesto and mozzarella. (Open M-Th 11am-9pm, F-Sa 11am-10pm, Su 2-9pm.) A popular breakfast venue, **Golden Harvest Cafe,** 1062 G St., has menu options for vegetarians and vegans. (☎707-822-8962. All dishes $4-10. Open M-F 6:30am-3pm, Sa-Su 7:30am-3pm.) **Crosswinds,** 860 10th St., offers a number of hearty breakfast and lunch variations in a beautifully restored Victorian home. Vegan substitutes are available for all meat

used in the Mexican, Italian, and Californian specialties, which cost $5-13. (☎707-826-2133. Open Su and Tu-Sa 7:30am-2pm.) A **farmer's market,** offering tie-dyed dresses, candles, and the usual fresh produce, livens up the Arcata Plaza on Saturdays from April to November (9am-1pm). Several local bands playing at full volume make the affair a weekly party.

ⱪ ACCOMMODATIONS. Arcata has many budget motels off U.S. 101 at the Giuntoli Exit. **Motel 6,** 4755 Valley West Blvd., is clean and quiet, and offers cable TV, a pool, and A/C. (☎707-822-7061. Singles $40, under 17 free; $3-6 per additional person. AARP discount.) Popular **Clam Beach County Park,** on U.S. 101, 7½ mi. north of Arcata, has dunes and a huge beach with seasonal clam digging; call ahead. (☎707-445-7651. Campsites with water and pit toilets $8. Entrance fee $3.) **Patrick's Point State Park,** 15 mi. north of Arcata, is an excellent spot for **watching-whales** and seals. The 124 sites feature terrific ocean views, lush vegetation, and treasure-hunting in the beach's tidepools. (☎707-677-3570, reservations ☎800-444-7275. Showers and flush toilets. No dumpsite. Reservations recommended. Sites $12 per vehicle; no hookups. Day-use $2.)

⚆ LEAVING ARCATA
Continue on **U.S. 101 North** and take the exit toward Trinidad. Turn left onto **Westhaven Dr./Main St.** and continue to follow Main St.

THE ROAD TO ORICK

In **Trinidad** (14 mi. north of Eureka), originally founded as a port during the gold rush era, a beach unofficially named **College Cove** provides sandy shores for the clothed to the north and the nudies to the south. (From the Trinidad exit, follow signs for the Trinidad Beach on Stagecoach Rd., then take the second left onto a gravel road at the Elk Head Park sign.)

Patrick's Point State Park, 5 mi. north of Trinidad, is worth a stop for the 2 mi. walk along the Rim Trail which sweeps by Agate Beach, Mussel Rocks, Patrick's Point and ▧**Wedding Rock,** a giant boulder still attached to land which you can climb out on. On the beach you can hunt for the semi-precious soapy soft stones. Sharing the 640-acre park is also a model **Yurok village** for visitors (day use $4) and a nice **campground** with water and coin-operated showers. (☎707-677-3570. Sites $15.)

⚆ APPROACHING ORICK
Continue on **U.S. 101 North/Redwood Hwy.** and then right onto **Lowell St.**

ORICK. Orick (pop. 650) is a somewhat desolate town overrun with souvenir stores selling burl sculptures (over-crafted and expensive wood carvings) and cows (which outnumber the people). However, it also has a post office and a market for campfire groceries. The **Visitors Center** lies on U.S. 101, just 1 mi. south of Orick and half a mile south of the Shoreline Deli (the Greyhound bus stop). A popular sight is the **Tall Trees Grove,** accessible by car to those with permits (free from the Visitors Center) when the road is open. Allow at least 3-4hr. for the trip. From the trailhead at the end of Tall Trees Access Rd., off Bald Hills Rd. from U.S. 101 north of Orick, it's a 1¼ mi. hike down (about 30min.) to some of the tallest trees in the world. The return hike up is steep—allow 1hr. The **Palm Cafe** is famous for its for Paul Bunyan rolls ($6), enormous cinnamon rolls that will feed five, or if you're really hungry just one. (☎707-488-3381. Meals $7.)

REDWOOD NATIONAL PARK

Rising up hundreds of feet above the ground, the lofty trees in Redwood National Park have towered in lush profusion for 150 million years. Native Americans called them "the eternal spirit" because of their 2000-year life span, ability to adapt to climatic changes, and resistance to insects, fire, and even lightning. The redwoods were indeed almost invincible—until the era of logging. With money on their minds (1 tree builds 22 houses) and saws in their hands, loggers cleared 96% of the virgin coast redwoods in one century. Despite the economic boom that the logging industry brought to the area's small towns, conservationists fought to maintain the forest ecology. Concerned citizens began buying redwood plots from loggers in the 1920s, and in 1968 the Redwood National Park was formed by the federal government, preserving these silent giants for the next few hundred generations. Present-day activists insist that the Pacific Lumber Co., which still harvests the trees outside of national park areas, must stop their programs entirely. In order to get their point across, Earth First! volunteers stage "tree sits," sometimes spending months in tents suspended from the trees, 180 ft. above the ground.

The **Redwood National Park Headquarters and Information Center,** 1111 2nd St., in Crescent City, is the headquarters of the entire national park, although ranger stations are just as well informed. (☎707-464-6101, ext. 5064. Open daily 9am-5pm; in winter closed Su.) Depending on whether you like to camp on the beach or in the redwoods, there are two excellent options. **Gold Bluffs Beach Campground** (see directions for Fern Canyon below) sits among tall yellow grass on a sandy shore that is surprisingly sheltered from the wind. This former port for gold miners is now one of the best spots for beach camping along the coast. (Sites $12.) If you prefer to sleep in the woods, you can nestle in among old-growth redwoods at the **Jedediah Smith Redwoods State Park** campground. (☎707-464-6101. Shower, water, RV hookups. Sites $12.)

Even if you don't stay at Gold Bluffs, rest your head at ◪**Fern Canyon.** Turn west on Davison Rd., 3 mi. north of Orick, pass Elk Meadows (where you'll see the wild beasts grazing—don't get out of your car here) to the pocked dirt road (read: huge holes in the road) to Gold Bluffs. Follow the road around to the end, or if it terminates at Gold Bluffs take the short walk farther up the coast to Fern Canyon, an enchanted slice of primordial beauty. Unfortunately, the path is unsigned. (Day-use $4.)

◪ APPROACHING KLAMATH
Continue on **U.S. 101/Redwood Hwy.** for 16½ mi. to reach Klamath.

KLAMATH

The Klamath Area to the north occupies a thin stretch of parkland connecting Prairie Creek with Del Norte State Park. The town itself consists of a few stores stretched over 4 mi., so the main attraction here is the spectacular coastline. The **Klamath Overlook,** where Requa Rd. meets the steep **Coastal Trail** (8 mi.), is an excellent **whale-watching** site with a fantastic view (provided the fog doesn't obscure it), though the overlook can be crowded by North Coast standards.

The mouth of the **Klamath River** is a popular commercial fishing spot in fall and spring, when salmon spawn, and in winter, when steelhead trout do the same. (Permit required; contact the Redwood Visitors Info Center, ☎541-464-6101, ext. 5064.) In spring and summer, sea lions and harbor seals congregate along Coastal Dr., which

passes by the remains of the **Douglas Memorial Bridge** and continues along the ocean for 8 mi. of incredible views.

◪ TREES OF MYSTERY 15500 U.S. 101 North
North of Klamath on U.S. 101.
Kitsch meets high-tech at Trees of Mystery, a three-quarter-mile walk through a maze of curiously shaped trees and elaborate chainsaw sculptures that talk and play music. There is also a small, free Native American museum that displays ornate costumes, baskets, and tapestries. The tourist trap's latest addition, the **Sky Trail,** is a multi-million-dollar gondola snaking up the hill to offer an exclusive bird's eye view of the towering trees. A 200 ft. tall Paul Bunyan and his blue ox Babe mark the entrance to the sight. (☎541-482-2251 or 800-638-3389. Trail open daily 8am-6:30pm. Gift shop and museum open 8am-7:30pm. $15, seniors $12, children $8. Parties of 5 or more get a 20% discount, as do those who pick up a discount card at the Crescent City Chamber of Commerce, ☎800-343-8300.) The **Del Norte Coast Redwoods State Park** offers magnificent ocean views and inland camping at **Mill Creek Campground,** right off U.S. 101.

◪ APPROACHING CRESCENT CITY
Continue on **U.S. 101 North/Redwood Hwy.** and merge onto **U.S. 199 North/Redwood Hwy.** toward **I-5/Grants Pass.**

CRESCENT CITY

An outstanding location from which to explore the parks, Crescent City calls itself the city "where the redwoods meet the sea." The **Battery Point Lighthouse** is on a causeway jutting out from Front St.; turn left onto A St. at the top of Front St. The lighthouse contains a museum open only during low tide. (☎707-464-3089. Open Apr.-Sept. W-Su 10am-4pm, tide permitting. $2, children $0.50.) From June through August, the national park offers **tidepool walks,** which leave from the Enderts Beach parking lot. The trailhead is at the **Crescent Beach Overlook** on Enderts Beach Rd., just off U.S. 101. (Turn-off 4 mi. south of Crescent City. Call ☎707-464-6101, ext. 5064 for schedules.) A scenic drive from Crescent City along **Pebble Beach Drive** to **Point Saint George** snakes past coastline that looks transplanted from New England; craggy cliffs, lush prairies, and an old lighthouse add to the atmosphere.

Annual highlights include the **World Championship Crab Races,** featuring races and crab feasts on the third Sunday in February. The **Sea Cruise,** a parade of over 500 classic cars, happens over three days on the first or second weekend in October. Call the Crescent City/Del Norte County Chamber of Commerce (☎ 800-343-8300) for information regarding any of these events.

North of Crescent City, the **Smith River,** the state's last major undammed river, rushes through the rocky gorges on its way from the mountains to the coast. This area offers the best salmon, trout, and steelhead fishing around, and excellent camping awaits on the riverbanks. There are also numerous hiking trails throughout the forest.

Available accommodations include **Nickel Creek Campground,** at the end of Enderts Beach Rd. outside Crescent City, which has ocean access and toilets, but no showers or water. **Hiouchi Motel,** 2097 Rte. 199, 8 mi. east of Crescent City, offers basic motel amenities in the redwoods. (Singles $33; doubles $55-60. $5 per additional person.)

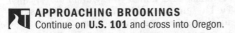 APPROACHING BROOKINGS
Continue on **U.S. 101** and cross into Oregon.

BROOKINGS
In Brookings, one of the few coastal towns that remains relatively tourist-free, hardware stores are easier to find than trinket shops, and the beaches are among Oregon's least spoiled. The city also sits in Oregon's "banana belt" (a.k.a. California's "arctic circle"); warm weather is not rare in January, and some Brookings backyards even boast scraggly palm trees.

Brookings is known statewide for its flowers. In downtown's **Azalea Park,** azaleas encircle pristine lawns and bloom from April to June, at intervals: don't visit for the blooms without calling ahead to make sure the flowers are out. The pride of Brookings is its **Azalea Festival** (☎ 541-469-3181), held in Azalea Park over Memorial

Day weekend. South Beach is just north of town and offers haunting vistas of angular volcanic rocks strewn about the sea, plus sand that's soft on bare feet. It is also designated a "marine garden." Harris Beach, a bit farther north, has an equally excellent view of the rock diaspora, and has less developed views.

A half-sandwich and a cup of soup or chili goes for $4.50 at the **Homeport Bagel Shop,** 1011 Chetco Ave. (☎ 541-469-6611. Open M-F 7am-5pm.) A number of seafood spots can be found near the harbor. The locals' favorite is **Oceanside Diner,** 16403 Lower Harbor Rd. (☎ 541-469-7971. Open daily 4am-3pm.) **The Bonn Motel,** 1216 U.S. 101, has a heated indoor pool and cable TV. (☎ 541-469-2161. Singles $40; doubles $45. $10 less in winter.) **Harris Beach State Park Campground,** at the north edge of Brookings, has 63 good tent sites set back in the trees. (☎ 541-469-2021 or 800-452-5687. Sites $17; full RV sites $20; yurts $28; hiker/biker sites $4. Free showers.) For campsites off the beaten path, travel 15 mi. east of Brookings on N. Bank Rd. to the charming **Little Redwood Campground,** alongside a salamander-filled creek. (12 sites. Drinking water and pit toilet. Sites $10.) **Redwood Bar,** across the way with drinking water, charges $5. Contact the Chetco Ranger Station for info (☎ 541-469-2196).

SAMUEL BOARDMAN STATE PARK
From Brookings, follow U.S. 101 North.

Explore 15 mi. of countless trails, some leading to beaches covered in volcanic rocks. Don't be surprised if an exploratory hike unexpectedly ends at an intimate seaside cove.

GOLD BEACH. Thirty miles north of Brookings, in Gold Beach, you can ride a jet boat up the Rogue River. **Mail Boat Hydro-Jets,** 94294 Rogue River Rd., offers 6-7hr. whitewater daytrips. Longer trips get more whitewater; all trips offer many wildlife viewing opportunities. (☎ 541-247-7033 or 800-458-3511. May-Oct. $30-75.)

HUMBUG MOUNTAIN STATE PARK
6 mi. south of Port Orford along U.S. 101.

Humbug Mountain State Park surrounds the heavily forested mountain. A 3 mi., moderate trail ascends to the 1700 ft. peak with amazing views on top and lush ferns on the trail up. The trail is accessible from a campground at the foot of the mountain, which has 101 tightly packed sites with toilets. (☎541-332-6774. Tents $16; hiker/biker sites $4. Showers $2 for non-campers.)

◪ CAPE BLANCO STATE PARK
North of Port Orford.

Cape Blanco State Park offers a long stretch of empty beach; it is the farthest point west on the Oregon Coast and its **lighthouse** is the coast's oldest, with miles of views north and south. Take a tour of the lighthouse and its mesmerizing lens, located at the end of the road leading into the park. (Open Apr.-Oct. M and Th-Su 10am-3:30pm.) Few stop at the **campground** a few miles back from the lighthouse; it offers exceptional seclusion between hedges, plus access to a beautiful but isolated beach. (Toilets and showers. RV sites $18; hiker/biker sites $4.)

◪ APPROACHING BANDON-BY-THE-SEA
Continue on **U.S. 101/Oregon Coast Hwy.** Bandon is 27 mi. north of Port Orford.

BANDON-BY-THE-SEA

Bandon (pop. 2833) is a quaint harbor town with chipper greeting banners and sweet shops that sell the various products of the bright red cranberries they grow. The color of the crop makes Bandon the prime area for juice berries, pumping over $10 million into the economy. No longer supported by the logging and fishing industries, Bandon now also relies on your tourist dollars, although a degree of authenticity persists. In September they hold an annual **Cranberry Festival** (☎541-347-9616; www.bandon.com).

The **Old Town** actually just dates from 1936 when a giant fire swept through and destroyed all the living quarters, but not the industry, in Bandon. People were living in tents and hurried to put up "temporary" buildings, many of which are still standing today (Lloyd's and the museum are just a couple). At the traffic light turn onto Hwy. 42S for 1½ mi. and then right on Morrison Rd. for 1 mi., to reach the cranberry bog at **Faber Farms,** 54982 Morrison Rd., which offers interesting free tours. In October see the floating berries bob on the water as they're harvested. (☎866-347-1166; www.faberfarms.com. Open M-Sa 10am-4pm.) A visit to **Bandon's Coquille River Museum**, 270 Fillmore, at U.S. 101, is like leafing through a grandmother's scrap-

book filled with the area's Native American, industrial, maritime, and pioneer heritage. If Edgar Capps is around, ask him to take you through the collections. (☎541-347-2164; www.bandonhistoricalmuseum.org. Open M-Sa 10am-4pm. $2, under 12 free.)

At **Bandon Dunes** (5 mi. north of town), one of the best public golf courses in the world is available for play at $140 (less if you stay at the lodge or are a resident of Oregon). Two miles north of town and across the bridge, **Bullard's Beach State Park** houses the **Coquille River Lighthouse,** built in 1896. The park's 185 sites have little privacy. (☎541-347-2209. Sites $19; yurts $27; hiker/biker sites $4 per person. Showers $2 for non-campers.)

At **Bandon Baking Co. and Deli,** 160 2nd St., offers soups and breads like pumpkin-raisin-walnut and, of course, cranberry-nut. (☎541-347-9440; www.bandonbakingco.com. Open daily 7am-4pm.) The **Sea Star Cafe,** 375 2nd St., serves excellent gyros and other "world food" in a mellow atmosphere. (☎541-347-8204. Breakfast $4-6. Lunch $5-7. Dinner $9-15. Open Tu-Th 7am-8pm, F-Sa 7am-9pm.) The small adjoining **Sea Star Guest House** contains the remains of a once-thriving hostel as well as several elegant guesthouse rooms overlooking the marina. (www.seastarbandon.com. Dorms $20; private hostel rooms $35-39; guesthouse rooms with living room and kitchen $50-130.)

◪ APPROACHING CHARLESTON
Go north on **U.S. 101/Oregon Coast Hwy.** about 9 mi., then turn left onto **Seven Devils Rd.** and continue toward the coast for about 6 mi.

CHARLESTON

Tiny Charleston sits peacefully on the coast. This is one of the few places on the Pacific where life slows down as you near the shore, with a string of state parks along the coastline and a pristine estuary near its bay. Four miles south of Charleston up Seven Devils Rd., the **⬛South Slough National Estuarine Research Reserve** ("Slough" is pronounced "Slew") is one of the most fascinating and under-appreciated venues on the central coast. Spreading out from a small interpretive center, almost 7 sq. mi. of salt- and freshwater estuaries nurture all kinds of wildlife, from sand shrimp to blue herons to deer.

Head to the interpretive center first to check if there are any guided hikes or paddles going out (free), or to begin one of the short trails leading from the center. A great way to observe wildlife close-up by canoe or kayak is to start from the **Charleston Marina** (near the Charleston Bridge) at low tide. Paddle into the estuary with the tide and out as it subsides; much of the interior is miserable mud flats at low tide. (☎541-888-5558; www.southsloughestuary.com. Open June-Aug. daily 8:30am-4:30pm; Sept.-May M-F 8:30am-4:30pm. Trails open year-round dawn-dusk.)

▲1 APPROACHING COOS BAY
From Charleston, go 5 mi. on **Cape Arago Hwy.**, then follow **Empire Coos Bay Hwy.** into town.

COOS BAY

The largest city on the Oregon Coast, Coos Bay still has the feel of a down-to-earth working town. For two weeks in mid-July, Coos Bay plays host to the **Oregon Coast Music Festival,** the most popular summer music event on the coast. A week of jazz, blues, and folk is followed by a week of performances by the renowned festival orchestra. Art exhibits and a free classical concert in Mingus Park spice up the festival even for the ticketless. (☎541-267-0938. Festival concerts $6-10; orchestra concerts $12-17.)

At the **Blue Heron Bistro,** 100 Commercial Ave., at the corner of Broadway, German cuisine complements the WWII memorabilia on the walls. (☎541-267-3933. Sandwiches $8. Dinner $9-13. Open M-Sa 11am-10pm, Su 5-10pm.) **Cranberry Sweets,** 1005 Newmark St., near the corner of Ocean Blvd., is a far-from-average candy factory with numerous original offerings such as beer squares and cheddar cheese fudge. Cheapskates can exploit the free samples. (☎541-888-9824. Open M-Sa 9am-6pm, Su 11am-4pm.)

Akin to camping in a well-landscaped parking lot, **Sunset Bay State Park,** 89814 Cape Arago Hwy., 12 mi. south of Coos Bay and 3½ mi. west of Charleston, has 138 sites. The **loop B** sites have a bit more seclusion. (☎541-888-4902, reservations 800-452-5687. Sites $16; RV sites $19; yurts $27; hiker/biker sites $4.) Three miles north of North Bend off U.S. 101 lies the **Bluebill Campground,** which offers 18 sites among sandy scrub half a mile from the ocean.

(Follow the signs to the Horsfall Beach area, then continue down the road. ☎541-271-3611. Closed in winter. Sites $15.)

◤ DETOUR: GOLDEN AND SILVER FALLS STATE PARK
24 mi. inland from Coos Bay. Take the Eastside-Allegany Exit from U.S. 101 and continue east along a narrow, gravel road.

At Golden and Silver Falls State Park, three trails lead to the awesome Golden Falls, a 210 ft. drop into the abyss, and the beautiful Silver Falls, thin sheets of water cascading down a rock face.

THE ROAD ALONG THE OREGON DUNES

Nature's ever-changing sculpture, the **Oregon Dunes National Recreation Area,** presents sand in shapes and sizes unequaled in the Northwest. Formed by millennia of wind and wave action, the dunes shift constantly and the sand sweeps over footprints, tire marks, and—in years past—entire forests. Perhaps the only hotbed of "reverse conservation," the dunes are actually greening rapidly as European beachgrass, planted in the 1920s, spreads its tenacious roots and sparks concerns that the dunes may disappear in as few as 100 years. Get them while they're hot: the dunes have something for everyone, from the hard-partying buggy or ATV rider to the hiker seeking solitude in the endless expanses of windblown sand. The dunes stretch from Coos Bay to Florence, broken only where the Umpqua and Smith Rivers empty into Winchester Bay. Depending on where you see them, the dunes will leave widely varying impressions. Regions that allow off-road vehicles will probably seem like mazes of madcap buggy riders, but other hiker-only areas offer timeless dreamscapes with nothing but sand, shrubs, and footprints vanishing in the wind. For an unmuffled and undeniably thrilling dune experience, venture out on wheels. While there are no accurately defined buggy trails through the dunes, simply following other riders can yield the best action in the sand. Plenty of shops on U.S. 101 between Coos Bay and Florence rent and offer tours, and most either transport ATVs to the dunes or are located on them; the Visitors Center in Reedsport (see p. 965) also offers a list of places that rent.

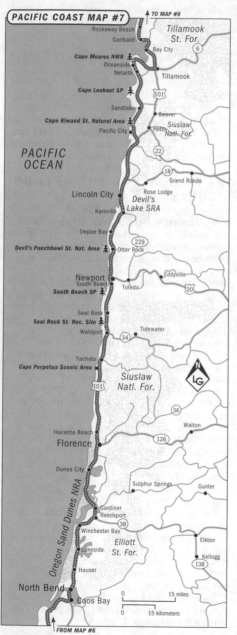

PACIFIC COAST MAP #7

▲ TO MAP #8

PACIFIC COAST

FROM MAP #6

APPROACHING WINCHESTER BAY
Continue on **U.S. 101 North/Oregon Coast Hwy.** for 22½ mi.

WINCHESTER BAY

The vast stretches of sand south of Winchester Bay and around Eel Creek represent Oregon Dunes at their most primal. The experience of any **day hike** is heightened by solitude: go early or late to avoid other tourists. With little to guide you besides an occasional marking pole, the **Umpqua Dunes Trail** (2½ mi.) wanders through unparalleled beauty in the sand slopes, wind cornices and rippled surfaces of the dunes. Access the trailhead off U.S. 101, a quarter-mile south of the sandy **Eel Creek Campground** (toilets; water; sites $15). The area is ATV-free, and you'll probably find yourself wandering along the ridgetops of the dunes while exploring an occasional patch of vegetation and being enraptured by the beauty and solitude of the area. The views are best when the sun is low in the sky and the shadows highlight the precise transitions between slopes and other wind-sculptured features. Walk as long as you like; the trail goes 2 mi. to the ocean over progressively softer sand, requiring several hours of hiking.

This coastal city is also home to an excellent surf spot on the coast. Rent crab traps to try and capture the elusive creatures; even if you can't get one, cheap meal options abound here. The **Bayfront Bar and Bistro,** 208 Bayfront Loop, is a classy but casual choice on the waterfront. For lunch, a salmon burger is $6.25, and grilled oysters are $9.25. Dinner is pricey ($9-16), but tasty. (☎541-271-9463. Open Tu-Su 11am-9pm.) The **Harbor View Motel,** 540 Beach Blvd., is so close to the marina that there are boats in the parking lot. A robotic frog welcomes guests to the office. Rooms are comfortable and clean, with striking color schemes. (☎541-271-3352. Rooms with queen-size bed $39; double occupancy $46. Kitchens $2 more.)

For less private, but still well-sheltered campsites, **William M. Tugman State Park,** 8 mi. south of Reedsport on U.S. 101, is close to gorgeous Eel Lake. Hike-in sites ($4) afford the most privacy. (☎541-759-3604, reservations 800-452-5687. 115 sites. Water and electricity. Sites $15; yurts $27. Non-camper showers $2.)

◤ APPROACHING REEDSPORT
Follow **U.S. 101/Oregon Coast Hwy.** for 4 mi, then turn right to follow **Rte. 38** into Reedsport.

REEDSPORT
A popular stopover by the dunes, Reedsport has excellent camping and is a great place to rest between runs on the sand. **Bird-watching** is popular around town; lists of species and their seasons are available at the **Oregon Dunes National Recreation Area Visitor Center,** 855 U.S. 101, at Rte. 38, just south of the Umpqua River Bridge. The center also includes displays, a 10min. video on dune ecology, and essential info on fees, regulations, hiking, and camping. (☎541-271-3611. Maps $4-6. Open June-Oct. daily 8am-4:30pm; Nov.-May M-F 8am-4:30pm, Sa 10am-4pm.) Most tourists content themselves with stopping at the **Oregon Dunes Overlook,** between Reedsport and Florence. Here, they peer out at a smallish stretch of oblique dunes whose lines of shrub stretch to the ocean. Several 1½-3hr. walks depart from the overlook and are far more satisfying, featuring a wider variety of dunes to explore amidst the constant barrage of bird calls from the cover of the shrubs.

Carter Lake Campground, 12 mi. north of Reedsport on U.S. 101, has boat access to the lake; some sites are lakeside. The well-screened spots are about as quiet as it gets out here. (23 sites. No ATVs. Nice bathrooms. Open May-Sept. Sites $15.) **Harbor Lights Family Restaurant,** at U.S. 101 and Rte. 38, offers dependable American food in a diner with zero pretension, with options like chef salad or fried chicken for $8.25. (☎541-271-3848. Open daily 8am-9pm.)

FLORENCE. Florence (pop. 7000) is home of the "most photographed" lighthouse in the US as well as a cormorant rookery. The **Siuslaw Pioneer Museum** is worth a gander. (☎541-997-7884. Open Tu-Su noon-4pm. $2, children free.) Nearby, the picturesque red-topped **Heceta Lighthouse,** built in 1894, is another worthy a photo op. (☎541-547-3416. Tours Memorial Day-Labor Day 11am-5pm; hours vary the rest of the year. $3.)

◥ DETOUR: ALPHA FARM
Drive 14 mi. east of Florence, a long strip of fast-food joints and expensive motels, to the tiny community of Mapleton. Press on 30min. farther along Rte. 36 and then 7 mi. up Deadwood Creek Rd.

Alpha Farm offers a communal alternative to the coast's bourgeois tourism. Members farm and produce giftshop-type items to support the communal purse. Anyone willing to lend a hand with the chores is welcome to camp out or stay in the beautiful, simple bedrooms. Visitors can stay up to three days; afterward, a long-term commitment to the farm is required. The **Alpha Bit Cafe,** in Mapleton on Rte. 126, is owned and staffed by the very chill and very dreadlocked members of Alpha Farm. (Farm ☎541-964-5102. Cafe ☎541-268-4311. Cafe open Sa-Th 10am-6pm, F 10am-9pm.)

◐ SEA LION CAVES   91560 U.S. 101
On U.S. 101, 11 mi. north of Florence.

In the fall and winter hundreds of boisterous sea lions make their home here in the **world's largest sea cave** (which accounts for the smell). In spring and summer months they prefer to sun themselves just outside on the rookery. This is the perfect place to catch a glimpse of their flippered antics. (☎541-547-3111; www.sealioncaves.com. Open daily 9am-6pm. $7, ages 6-15 $4.50.)

◤ APPROACHING CAPE PERPETUA
Continue on U.S. **101/Oregon Coast Hwy.** for 21½ mi. and end at **Cape Perpetua Scenic Area.**

CAPE PERPETUA
Cape Perpetua is the highest point on the coast (803 ft.) and arguably its high point for scenic beauty. Even if you're only passing through, drive to the top of the **Cape Perpetua Viewpoint** (2 mi.) and walk the quarter-mile loop at the top. Gaze out at the ocean, as well as the headlands to the north and south. Those looking for a more challenging hike can take the difficult 1¼ mi. **St. Perpetua Trail** up to the same viewpoint. The trail departs from **Cape Perpetua Interpretive Center,** 2400 U.S. 101, just south of the viewpoint turn-off, which has informative exhibits about the surrounding area and hilarious rangers. (☎541-547-3289. Open May-Nov. M-Sa 9am-5pm, Su noon-5pm; also during whale week, Christmas-Jan. 1.) At high tide, witness an orgy of thundering spray in the **Devil's Churn** (¼ mi. north of the interpretive center down Restless Water Trail) and **Spouting Horn** (¼ mi. south down Captain Cook Trail). The two sites, as well as the tidal pools, are connected; the tidal pools can also be reached from the inter-

pretive center. The **Cape Perpetua campground** is an excellent place to sleep. Located at the viewpoint turn-off, it has 37 sites alongside a tiny, fern-banked creek. (Reservations ☎ 877-444-6777. Water, toilets. Firewood $5. Sites $15.) **The Rock Creek Campground,** 8 mi. farther south, has 16 sites under mossy spruces a half-mile from the sea. (Drinking water, toilets. Sites $14.)

APPROACHING YACHATS

From Cape Perpetua, follow **U.S. 101/Oregon Coast Hwy.** for 3½ mi. toward **Cummins Peak Rd.**

YACHATS

Billing itself as the "Gem of the Oregon Coast," Yachats (YAH-hots) comes from the Native American word meaning "dark water between timbered hills." A small resort town (pop. 620), there's not much to do but stroll around and enjoy. The **Visitors Center,** 241 U.S. 101, next to the supermarket, is extremely helpful for information on local attractions. (☎ 800-929-0477; www.yachats.org. Open daily 10am-4pm.)

The cozy **Town Center Cafe,** on U.S. 101 at 4th St., is an excellent place to stop for a warm drink, omelette ($7) or sandwich ($6) on the balcony. (☎ 541-547-4242. Open Th-Tu 8am-3pm.) A number of resort restuarants offer pricer meals in elegant settings, some with panoramic views of the ocean. Live music goes on nightly around 6:30pm at the **Drift Inn** pub, 124 U.S. 101 (☎ 541-547-4477), a local favorite. **Silver Surf Motel,** 3767 U.S. 101, at the north end of town, features sliding glass doors looking onto a grass lawn that rolls 120 ft. to the sea. (☎ 800-281-5723 or 541-547-3175; silversurf@harborside.com. Central indoor pool and hot tub. All rooms have full kitchenettes. Rooms in summer $89-99; winter $64-89.)

LEAVING YACHATS

Continue north on **U.S. 101/Oregon Coast Hwy.**

THE ROAD TO NEWPORT

There are several worthy stops along the road to Newport. In **Waldport,** just south of a beautiful bridge, the **Alsea Bay Bridge Interpretive Center** offers interactive exhibits on all you ever wanted to know about how Oregonians have managed to get across their bodies of water. (☎ 541-563-2002. Open Tu-Sa 9am-

4pm.) The **Waldport Ranger Station,** 1049 Pacific Hwy. SW, has information on hiking in **Siuslaw National Forest,** a patchwork of three wilderness areas along the Oregon Coast. The station sells detailed maps and offers advice on the area's campgrounds. (☎ 541-563-3211. Open M-F 8am-4pm.)

Seal Rock is 5 mi. north of Waldport on U.S. 101 and home to the yellow stone cliffs of the Seal Rock State Park. The **Triad Art Gallery,** at milepost 153 on U.S. 101 (look for the blue neon horse out front) shows work a cut above the usual. (☎ 541-563-5442; www.triadgallery.com. Open daily 10am-5pm.) Yuzen, right on 101 in Seal Rock, has some of the finest sushi around ($15).

Farther north, **South Beach** offers haunting vistas of angular volcanic rocks strewn about the sea, plus sand that's soft on bare feet. It is also a designated "marine garden." **South Beach State Park,** 5580 S. Coast Hwy., is 2 mi. south of town. The campground has sparse conifers which offer little shelter and no privacy. Ask about the kayak tours from nearby Ona Beach. (☎ 541-867-4715. RV sites $20; yurts $29; hiker/biker sites $4.50. Showers $2 for non-campers.)

APPROACHING NEWPORT

From South Beach, take **U.S. 101/S. Coast Hwy.** to enter Newport.

NEWPORT

After the miles of malls along U.S. 101, Newport's renovated waterfront area of pleasantly kitschy restaurants and shops is a delight. Newport's claim to fame, however, is the world-class Oregon Coast Aquarium. Best known as the former home of Keiko the Orca of *Free Willy,* the aquarium offers several interesting exhibits. This, in addition to the Mark Hatfield Marine Science Center and loads of inexpensive seafood, make Newport a marine lover's starred attraction.

GETTING AROUND. Newport is bordered on the west by the foggy Pacific Ocean and on the south by Yaquina Bay. U.S. 101, known in town as the **Coast Hwy.,** divides east and west Newport. U.S. 20, known as **Olive St.** in town, bisects the north and south sides of town. Just north of the bridge, **Bay Blvd.** (accessible via Herbert St., on the north side of the bay bridge) circles the bay and runs through the heart of the

PACIFIC COAST

(VITAL STATS)

Population: 9500

Visitor Info: Chamber of Commerce, 555 SW Coast Hwy. (☎541-265-8801 or 800-262-7844; www.discovernewport.com). 24hr. info board outside. Open M-F 8:30am-5pm; summer also Sa-Su 10am-4pm.

Internet Access: Newport Public Library: 35 Nye St. NW (☎541-265-2153), at Olive St. Open M-Th 10am-9pm, F-Sa 10am-6pm, Su 1-4pm.

Post Office: 310 2nd St. SW (☎800-275-8777). Open M-F 8:30am-5pm, Sa 10:30am-1:30pm. **Postal Code:** 97365.

port. Historic **Nye Beach,** bustling with tiny shops, is on the northwest side of town in between 3rd and 6th St.

◪ **SIGHTS.** The 🖾**Mark O. Jatfield Marine Science Center,** at the south end of the bridge on Marine Science Dr., is the hub of Oregon State University's coastal research. The 300 scientists working here ensure rigorous intellectual standards for the exhibits, which explore fascinating topics ranging from chaos—demonstrated by a paddle wheel/waterclock—to climatic change and a behavioral analysis of Wile E. Coyote's causality. While the live octopus can't be played with, a garden of sea anemones, slugs, and bottom-dwelling fish awaits your curiousity in the touch tanks. (☎541-867-0100. Open daily 10am-5pm; in winter M and Th-Su 10am-4pm. Donations accepted.)

More famous, less serious, and much more expensive than the Science Center is the **Oregon Coast Aquarium,** 2820 Ferry Slip Rd. SE, at the south end of the bridge. This world-class aquarium housed Keiko, the much-loved *Free Willy* Orca during his rehabilitation before he returned to his childhood waters near Iceland (he passed away in 2003). The Passages of the Deep exhibit features a 200 ft. undersea tunnel; experience being surrounded by sharks, rays, and fish. (☎541-867-3474; www.aquarium.org. Open daily June-Sept. 9am-6pm; Sept.-June 10am-5pm. $10.25, seniors $9.25, ages 4-13 $6.25.)

The **Rogue Ale Brewery,** 2320 Oregon State University Dr. SE, has won more awards than you can shake a pint at. Cross the bay bridge, follow the signs to the aquarium, and you'll see it. Twenty brews, including Oregon Golden, Shakespeare

Stout, and Dead Guy Ale, are available upstairs at **Brewers by the Bay,** where taster trays of four beers cost $4.50. (Brewers by the Bay ☎541-867-3664. Brewery ☎541-867-3660. Open Su-Th 11am-9pm, F-Sa 11am-10pm. Free tours of the brewery leave daily at 4pm, depending on demand.)

📷🍴 **FOOD & ACCOMMODATIONS.** Food in Newport is surprisingly varied, but seafood is the dining option of choice. **Mo's Restaurant,** 622 Bay Blvd. SW, is just about always filled to the gills. This is the original location of what is now a regional franchise. Go for the clam chowder ($7) or fish and chips for $9. (☎541-265-2979. Open daily 11am-10pm.) **April's,** 749 3rd St. NW, down by Nye Beach, is the pinnacle of local dining. The serene ocean view and good food are worth every penny. Tables fill early, especially on weekends; call ahead. (☎541-265-6855. Dinners $12-19; daily specials are pricier. Towering chocolate eclairs $4. Open Tu-Su dinner from 5pm. Reservations recommended.)

For lodgings, the 🖾**Sylvia Beach Hotel** is by far the best choice (see feature, p. 7). Other options include **Beverly Beach State Park,** 198 123rd St. NE, 7 mi. north of Newport and just south of Devil's Punch Bowl. Beverly Beach is a year-round campground of gargantuan proportions. (☎541-265-9278; reservations 800-452-5687. Sites $17-21; yurts $29; hiker/biker sites $4.25. Non-camper showers $2.) Opposite the Visitors Center stands **City Center Motel,** 538 Coast Hwy. SW, which has spacious but oddly empty rooms. (☎541-265-7381 or 800-627-9099. Singles $30; doubles $45.)

🔼 **APPROACHING OTTER ROCK**
Continue on **U.S. 101/Oregon Coast Hwy.** for 7 mi. Make a slight left onto **Otter Crest Loop.**

OTTER ROCK. Just south of Depoe Bay, detour from U.S. 101 on the renowned **Otter Crest Loop,** a twisting 4 mi. excursion high above the shore that affords spectacular vistas at every bend and includes views of **Otter Rock** and the **Marine Gardens.** A lookout over the aptly named **Cape Foulweather** has telescopes ($0.25) for spotting sea lions lazing on the rocks. **The Devil's Punch Bowl,** formed when the roof of a seaside cave collapsed, is also accessible off the loop. It becomes a frothing cauldron during high tide when ocean water crashes through an opening in the side of the bowl. **Otter Rocks**

Beach is known as a great place to learn to surf; beginners can partake of the smaller breaks close to shore.

⚑ APPROACHING DEPOE BAY
Follow **U.S. 101 North/Oregon Coast Hwy.** for about 5 mi.

DEPOE BAY. Diminutive Depoe Bay boasts gray whale viewing along the town's low seawall, at the **Depoe Bay State Park Wayside** and the **Observatory Lookout,** 4½ mi. to the south. Go early in the morning on a cloudy day during the annual migration (Dec.-May) for your best chance of spotting the giants. **Tradewinds Charters** (☎541-765-2345 or 800-445-8730) has 6hr. fishing and crabbing trips ($70), and 1-2hr. whale-watching trips ($15-20). **Dockside Charters** offers similar trips; head east at the only traffic light in Depoe Bay. They're next to the Coast Guard. (☎541-765-2545 or 800-733-8915. Fishing trips $55. Whale-watching trips $15, ages 13-17 $11, ages 4-12 $7.)

⚑ APPROACHING LINCOLN CITY
Follow **U.S. 101/N. Oregon Coast Hwy.** for 12 mi.

LINCOLN CITY

Lincoln City is actually five towns wrapped around a 7 mi. strip of ocean-front motels, gas stations, and souvenir shops along U.S. 101. Most budget travelers, and this travel guide, will tell you that the Three Capes area to the north is far superior as a destination. As one of the largest "cities" on the North Coast, Lincoln City can, however, be used as a gateway to better points north and south. Four miles north of Lincoln City in Kernville, Life-long Oregon resident and author Ken Kesey *(One Flew Over a Cuckoo's Nest; Sometimes a Great Notion)* is memorialized in the "Sometimes a Great Notion" house on the Siletz River.

Dory Cove, 5819 Logan Rd., at the far north of town, is the locals' unanimous choice for affordable seafood. Dinners start at $10 a plate. (☎541-994-5180. Open summer M-Sa 11:30am-8pm, Su noon-8pm; winter M-Th 11:30am-8pm, F-Sa 11:30am-9pm, Su noon-8pm.) Beautiful, small rooms await at the **Captain Cook Inn,** 2626 U.S. 101 NE. (☎541-994-2522 or 800-994-2522. Singles $48; doubles $52.)

⚑ APPROACHING PACIFIC CITY
Follow **U.S. 101/S. Oregon Coast Hwy.** for 22½ mi. and turn left onto **Brooten Rd.**

PACIFIC CITY. The nearest town to Cape Kiwanda, Pacific City is a hidden gem that most travelers on U.S. 101 never even see. The town hides away some surprisingly good restaurants. At the **Grateful Bread Bakery,** 34805 Brooten (BRAW-ten) Rd., enjoy vegetarian stuffed focaccia ($7) or sample one of the many excellent omelettes. (☎541-965-7337. Open summer Th-Tu 8am-8:30pm; winter Th-M 8am-8:30pm.) If you plan to stay overnight, the **Anchorage Motel,** 6585 Pacific Ave., offers homey rooms. (☎541-965-6773 or 800-941-6250. Rooms from $45; off season from $37.) Camping on beaches in Oregon is illegal, but local youth have been known to camp near the beach, or on more secluded beaches north of Cape Kiwanda.

THE ROAD TO TILLAMOOK

Between Lincoln City and Tillamook, U.S. 101 wanders east into wooded land, leaving the coast. The **Three Capes Loop** is a 35 mi. circle that connects a trio of spectacular promontories—Cape Meares, Cape Lookout, and Cape Kiwanda State Parks—that will almost certainly make you linger longer than you expect; plan accordingly. The loop leaves U.S. 101 10 mi. north of Lincoln City and rejoins at Tillamook. Unless time is of the utmost importance, taking the loop is a far better choice than driving straight up U.S. 101.

◤ CAPE KIWANDA STATE PARK
Along the Three Capes Loop, North of Lincoln City.

Cape Kiwanda State Park (☎800-551-6949), is the jewel of the Three Capes Loop's triple crown. This sheltered cape draws beachcombers, kite-flyers, volleyball players, surfers, and windsurfers, not to mention the odd snowboarder out to ride a giant sand hill. A walk up the sculptured sandstone on the north side (wear shoes with good grips) reveals a ▓**hypnotic view** of swells rising over the rocks, forming crests, and smashing into the cliffs. If the surf is up, head to **South County Surf,** 33310 Cape Kiwanda Dr., a little ways of the beach, where the walls are lined with shots of wipeouts and the Northwest's biggest surfing days. (☎503-

965-7505. Surfboard rental $20; boogieboards $10. Wetsuits $15. Open Su and Tu-F 10am-5pm, Sa 9am-5pm.)

◤ CAPE LOOKOUT STATE PARK
12 mi. southwest of Cape Meares.

Cape Lookout State Park offers a small, rocky beach with incredible views of the surrounding sights. It also has some fine camping near the dunes and the forests behind them. (☎503-842-4981 or 800-551-6949. Sites $16. Day-use $3.) From here, the 2½ mi. **Cape Trail** heads past the 1943 crash site of a military plane to the end of the lookout, where a spectacular 360° view featuring **Haystack Rock** awaits. The **Cape Lookout Campground** offers fine camping near the dunes and the forests behind them, although sites with better privacy tend to go far in advance. (☎503-842-4981 or 800-551-6949. 216 sites. Tents $16; hookups $20. Oct.-Apr. $4 less. Yurts $27. Non-camper showers $2.)

OCEANSIDE & NETARTS. The towns of Oceanside and Netarts lie a couple miles south of Cape Meares, and offer overpriced gas, a market, and a few places to stay that tend to fill up fast. **The Terimore,** 5103 Crab Ave., in Netarts, has the least expensive rooms in the two towns, some with ocean views. (☎541-842-4623 or 800-635-1821. Rooms $45-60, with views $60-70.) The **Whiskey Creek Cafe,** 6060 Whiskey Creek Rd., in Neharts, is popular for its oysters and fresh from the bay; halibut and chips costs $9.25. (☎541-842-5117. Open Su-Th 11am-9pm, F-Sa 11am-10pm.)

◤ CAPE MEARES STATE PARK
At the tip of the promontory jutting out from Tillamook.

Cape Meares State Park protects one of the few remaining old-growth forests on the Oregon Coast. The mind-blowing **Octopus Tree,** a gnarled Sitka spruce with six candelabra trunks, looks like the imaginative doodlings of an eight-year-old. The **Cape Meares Lighthouse** operates as an illuminating on-site interpretive center. (Open May-Sept. daily 11am-4pm; Oct. and Mar.-Apr. F-Sa 11am-4pm. Free.) If you walk down to the lighthouse, bring binoculars or use the $0.25 viewer to look at the amazing seabird colony on the giant volcanic rock. As you drive south of Cape Meares, a break in the trees reveals a beach between two cliffs; this is a beautiful place to pull off the road and explore.

TILLAMOOK
Although the word Tillamook (TILL-uh-muk) translates to "land of many waters," to the Northwest it is synonymous with cheese. Tourists come by the hundreds to gaze at blocks of cheese being cut into smaller blocks on a conveyor belt at the **Tillamook Cheese Factory,** 4175 U.S. 101 North. (☎800-542-7290; www.tillamookcheese.com. Open daily summer 8am-8pm; winter 8am-6pm.) Plane buffs and all who celebrate mechanical marvels will appreciate the impressive **Tillamook Naval Air Station Museum,** 2 mi. south of town. This hulking seven-acre former blimp hangar is the largest wooden clear-span structure in the world.

THE LOCAL STORY

A WRITERS' RETREAT

The **Sylvia Beach Hotel** sits on the edge of a bluff overlooking historic Nye Beach. The theme of the establishment is books, with each of the 20 rooms named after a famous author (the Edgar Allen Poe room is not for the faint of heart: a swinging blade hangs above the bed). Each room is decorated to match the tone of the writer—from the whimsical Dr. Seuss room to the Agatha Christie room, which contains clues from all her classic mysteries hidden throughout. Packed with books and littered with board games and half-finished puzzles, the B&B's communal feel is matched at meals, served family style at the restaurant *Tables of Content.* Breakfast is included for all guests; dinner is a four-course affair and offers a choice of several entrees. All guests have access to the common room, where comfy chairs invite curling up with one of the library's books. (267 NW Cliff St. ☎541-265-5428; www.sylviabeachhotel.com. Dorms $28. Singles $88-123; off season $68-94.)

The airy cavern is home to over 34 fully functional war planes, including WWII beauties like the P-38 Lightning and a PBY-5A Catalina. (☎503-842-1130. Open daily 10am-5pm. $9.50, ages 13-17 $5.50, under 13 $2.) Downtown, the **Tillamook County Pioneer Museum,** 2106 2nd St., features exceptionally thorough collections of WWII medals, rifles, and collectibles. (☎503-842-4553. Open M-Sa 8am-5pm, Su 11am-5pm. $2, ages 12-17 $0.50, under 12 free.)

Find a list of campsites and hiking trails at the **Tillamook Chamber of Commerce,** 3705 U.S. 101 North, in the big red barn near the Tillamook Cheese Factory, 1½ mi. north of town. (☎503-842-7525. Open summer M-Sa 9am-5pm, Su 10am-4pm; winter M-F 9am-5pm, Sa 10am-3pm.)

Tillamook may be a cheese-lover's paradise, but other food choices in town are lacking. The **Blue Heron French Cheese Company,** 2001 Blue Heron Dr., 1 mi. south of the Tillamook Cheese factory, has tasty deli sandwiches. Although the sheer quantity of items for sale is almost overwhelming, sandwiches stand out at $6.25. (☎503-842-8281. Open daily summer 8am-8pm; winter 9am-5pm. Deli open daily 11:30am-4pm.) Motel prices in Tillamook are steep (and aren't helped by the 7% city lodging tax), but the camping is some of the area's finest. **Kilchis River Park,** 6 mi. northeast of town at the end of Kilchis River Rd., which leaves U.S. 101 roughly 1 mi. north of the factory, has 35 sites between a mossy forest and the Kilchis River. The campground itself is mostly geared towards families, with a baseball field, volleyball court, horseshoes, and swimming. ☎503-842-6694. Water, toilets. Open May-Oct. Tent sites $10; walk-in sites $3.) To sleep on the sand, try the **campgrounds** on the Three Capes Loop.

LEAVING TILLAMOOK
Continue on **U.S. 101/Oregon Coast Hwy.**

GARIBALDI. Garibaldi sits on Tillamook Bay and has excellent marine facilities and RV parks. The **Parkside Coffee House,** 235 Garibaldi Ave. (☎503-322-0357), offers no-frills sandwiches (home-style meatloaf; turkey and swiss) for reasonable prices. Come May Garibaldi hosts the **Pacific NW Champion Crab Races** (☎503-322-0301).

ROCKAWAY BEACH. A soulless tourist development complex has sprung up along Rockaway's narrow black sand beach, 5 mi. north of Garibaldi.

The public bathrooms, however, are nice. The **Sea Breeze Motel,** with generic decor including TV, distinguishes itself only by its location and views 10m from the beach (☎503-359-3903. Rooms with queen-size bed $55-66; 2 double beds $60.50-71.50.)

NEHALEM. Ten miles north of Rockaway Beach, a cluster of made-in-Oregon-type shops clustered along U.S. 101 make up Nehalem. The **Nehalem Bay Winery,** 34965 Rte. 53, 3 mi. south of town, has free tastings of local cranberry and blackberry vintages. The backpacker-friendly winery sponsors performances in a small theater and an annual reggae and bluegrass festival, providing a forum for general bacchanalian revelry. (☎503-368-9463. Open daily summer 9am-6pm; winter 10am-5pm.) Outside of town, **Nehalem Bay State Park** has plentiful camping options.

◤ OSWALD WEST STATE PARK
Located off of U.S. 101.

Oswald West State Park is a tiny headland rainforest of hefty spruce and cedars. Local surfers call the sheltered beach here **Short Sands Beach,** or Shorty's; with a first-rate break and camping so close by, the beach is a premier surf destination. The beach and woodsy campsites are only accessible by a quarter-mile trail off U.S. 101, but the park provides wheelbarrows for transporting gear from the parking lot to the 29 sites. The campground fills quickly; call ahead. (Open Mar.-Nov. Sites $15.) From the south side of the park, a segment of the Oregon Coast Trail leads over the headland to 1661 ft. **Neahkahnie Mountain.**

HUG POINT. The **tidal caves,** Hug Point's main claim to fame, are accessible only at low tide. The beach is framed by tall cliffs, and secluded picnic tables dot the headlands near the parking lot. The point is about 2 mi. south of Cannon Beach.

◤ APPROACHING CANNON BEACH
Go north on **U.S. 101/Oregon Coast Hwy.** for about 8 mi. The four exits into town from U.S. 101 all lead to **Hemlock St.**

CANNON BEACH
Many moons ago, a rusty cannon from a shipwrecked schooner washed ashore at Arch Cape, giving this town its name. Today, home to a verita-

ble army of boutiques, bakeries, and galleries, Cannon Beach is a more refined alternative to nearby Seaside's crass commercialism. Arguably the most desirable location on the entire Oregon Coast because of its amazing ocean views and interesting shops, Cannon Beach is always crowded with Portlanders and other tourists. Still, it's well worth the stop to take in the view.

VITAL STATS

Population: 1600

Visitor Info: Cannon Beach Chamber of Commerce and Visitor Info, 207 N. Spruce St. (☎503-436-2623), at 2nd St. Open M-F 9:30am-5pm. Visitor Info open M-Sa 10am-5pm, Su 11am-4pm.

Internet Access: Cannon Beach Library, 131 N. Hemlock St. (☎503-436-1391). $6 per hr. Open M-W and F 1-5pm, Th 1-7pm.

Post Office: 163 N. Hemlock St., 97110 (☎503-436-2822). Open M-F 9am-5pm. **Postal Code:** 97110.

⌐ GETTING AROUND. Cannon Beach lies 8 mi. south of Seaside and 42 mi. north of Tillamook on U.S. 101. Lovely **Ecola** and **Oswald State Parks** lie just to the north and a few miles south of the town, respectively. **Hemlock St.** is lined with galleries and restaurants.

◙ SIGHTS. Cannon Beach has expensive, sporadically elegant galleries and gift shops. A stroll along the 7 mi. stretch of flat, bluff-framed beach suits many better. **Coaster Theater,** 108 N. Hemlock St., is a small playhouse that stages theater productions, concerts, dance performances, comedy, and musical revues year-round. (☎503-436-1242; www.coastertheater.com. Box office open W-Sa 1-8pm. Tickets $12-15.)

The best place to enjoy the dramatic volcanic coastline of Cannon Beach is at **Ecola State Park,** which attracts picnickers, hikers, and surfers alike. Have a look at Ecola Point's views of hulking **Haystack Rock,** which is spotted with (and by) seagulls, puffins, barnacles, anemones, and the occasional sea lion. (To reach the park, follow signs from U.S. 101. Entrance fee $3.) **Indian Beach** is a gorgeous surfing destination; catch waves between volcanic rock walls, with a freshwater stream running down the beach to rinse the salt off after you're done. To surf, rent

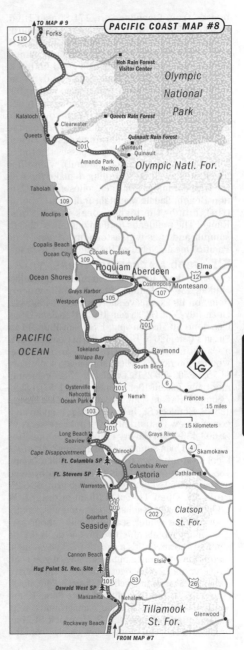

PACIFIC COAST MAP #8

boards from **Cleanline Surf,** 171 Sunset Blvd. (☎503-436-9726. Surfboards and boogieboards $15 per day. Wetsuits $20 per day. Open M-F 10am-6pm, Sa 9am-7pm, Su 10am-6pm; winter daily 10am-5pm.) There is also good hiking in the area. **Indian Beach Trail** (2 mi.) leads to the Indian Beach tide pools, which teem with colorful sea life. Follow signs to "Ecola" to reach trailhead. **Tillamook Head Trail** (12 mi. round-trip) leaves from Indian Beach, and hugs the coast to the mini-cape that separates Seaside Beach from Cannon Beach. The trail passes the top of Tillamook head (2 mi. up the trail), where five hiker sites await those willing to make the trek for free camping. Fourteen miles east of Cannon Beach, **Saddle Mountain Trail** (5 mi. round-trip), climbs the highest peak in the Coast Range. The trail leads to the mountain's 3283 ft. summit and ends with astounding views of the Pacific Ocean, Nehalem Bay, and the Cascades.

▓▌ FOOD & ACCOMMODATIONS. The deals are down **Hemlock St.** in mid-town. **Mariner Market,** 139 N. Hemlock St., holds 7439 grocery items on its expansive shelves. (☎503-436-2442. Open July-Sept. Su-Th 8am-10pm, F-Sa 8am-11pm; Oct.-June Su-Th 8am-9pm, F-Sa 8am-10pm.) **Lazy Susan's Cafe,** 126 N. Hemlock St., in Coaster Sq., is a Cannon Beach favorite with an intimate, woodsy interior. Excellent homemade scones are $1.75. (☎503-436-2816. Omelettes $7-8. Open summer daily 7:30am-10pm; winter M and W-Th 8am-2:30pm, F-Sa 8am-8pm, Su 8am-5pm.) **Cafe Mango,** 1235 S. Hemlock St., in Haystack Sq., is an up-and-coming new restaurant with first-rate service. (☎503-436-2393. Savory crepes $5-7. Omelettes about $9. Open summer Th-M 7:30am-2:30pm.) A local spot for down-to-earth eatin', **Bill's Tavern,** 188 N. Hemlock St., has beer on tap brewed upstairs. (☎503-436-2202. Basic pub grub $3-8.25. Pints $3. Open Th-Tu 11:30am-midnight, W 4:30pm-midnight. Kitchen closes around 9:30pm.)

During the winter season, inquire about specials; many motels offer two-for-one deals. In the summer, however, it's a seller's market, so most motels have two-night minimum stays if you want a reservation. Real budget deals are a short drive away: the **Seaside International Hostel** is 7 mi. north (see p. 973), and **Oswald West State Park,** 10 mi. south of town, has a stunning campground (see p. 970). **McBee Cottages,** 888 S. Hemlock St., has bright and cheerful rooms a few blocks from the beach. The office is in the **Sandtrap Inn** at 539 S. Hemlock St. (☎503-436-2569. Some kitchen units and cottages available. Rooms $60; in winter $45.) Tree-shaded sites make **Wright's for Camping,** 334 Reservoir Rd., off U.S. 101, relaxing retreat from RV mini-cities. (☎503-436-2347. Showers, toilets. Reservations advised in summer. Sites $17.)

▞▌ APPROACHING SEASIDE
Continue to follow **U.S. 101** for 8 mi.

SEASIDE

In the winter of 1805-1806, explorers Lewis and Clark made their westernmost camp near Seaside. While the amenities were few and far between at the time, after the development of a resort in 1870 the situation improved and visitors began to pour in. The tourism industry, replete with indoor mini-golf and barrels of saltwater taffy, has transformed Seaside from a remote coastal outpost to a bustling beachfront. For those uninterested in video arcades, Seaside still has merit as a base for exploring the beautiful Oregon Coast. Seaside is also less expensive than nearby Cannon Beach, and its hostel is one of the best in the Northwest.

> **◖VITAL STATS◗**
>
> **Population:** 5900
>
> **Visitor Info: Chamber of Commerce,** 7 N. Roosevelt Dr. (☎503-738-6391 or 800-444-6740), on U.S. 101 and Broadway. **Seaside Visitor Bureau** (☎503-738-3097 or 888-306-2326; www.seasideor.com), in the same building. Open June-Aug. daily 8am-5pm; Oct.-May M-F 9am-5pm, Sa-Su 10am-4pm.
>
> **Internet Access: Seaside Library:** 60 N. Roosevelt Dr. (☎503-738-6742). Open Tu-Th 9am-8pm, F-Sa 9am-5pm, Su 1-5pm.
>
> **Post Office:** 300 Ave. A (☎800-275-8777), off Columbia Ave. Open M-F 8:30am-5pm, Sa 8:30-10:30am. **Postal Code:** 97138.

▛ GETTING AROUND. Seaside lies 17 mi. south of Astoria and 8 mi. north of Cannon Beach along **U.S. 101.** The Necanicum River runs north-south through Seaside, two blocks from the coastline. In town, U.S. 101 becomes **Roosevelt Dr.,** and another major road, **Holladay Dr.,** splits off from it. **Broadway** runs perpendicular to the two, and is the town's main street and a tourist-dollar black hole. Streets north of Broadway are numbered, and those south of Broadway are lettered. The **Prome-nade** (or "Prom") is a paved foot-path that hugs the beach for the length of town.

◪ SIGHTS. Seaside's tourist population (which often outnumbers that of true locals) swarms around **Broadway,** a garish strip of arcades and shops running the half-mile from Roosevelt (U.S. 101) to the beach. "The Arcade," as it is called, is the focal point of downtown and attracts a youthful crowd. Bumper cars, basket-ball games, and other methods of fleecing visitors abound. The turnaround at the end of Broadway signals the end of the **Lewis and Clark Trail.** If it's a bright day, you might want to take a stroll down the beach, or bike or skate along the wooden walkway, **The Prom.** Get into the spirit by renting a beach bike (one of those small roofed contraptions that you pedal) yourself, tossing back you hair and then eating an ice-cream cone in the sand. The **Salt Cairns** (next to the beach 8 blocks south of Broadway; follow the signs) are also worth a gander. Pots in a pile of stones are traditionally none too exciting but then, those other pots weren't on the spot where members of Lewis and Clark's party boiled sea water for two months, supplying the explorers with the essential salt to preserve their food.

Seaside's beachfront is sometimes crowded despite bone-chilling water and strong under-tows that more or less preclude swimming. For a slightly quieter beach, head to **Gearhart,** 2 mi. north of downtown off U.S. 101, where long stretches of dunes await exploration.

The Seaside Aquarium, 200 N. Promenade, is smaller than its companion in Newport, but makes up for its small size by giving visitors the chance to feed playful harbor seals. (☎ 503-738-6211. Open Mar.-June daily 9am-5pm; July-Dec. Su-Th 9am-6pm, F-Sa 9am-8pm; Jan.-Feb. generally W-Su 9am-5pm but days open may change, so call ahead. $6, seniors $4.75, ages 6-13 $3, under 6 free, families as large as 6 $19. Seal feeding $0.75.)

Perhaps the US's premier recreational road race, the **Hood to Coast Relay** is the ultimate team running event. Held annually at the end of August, runners tear up the trails between Mt. Hood and Seaside (195 mi.) to the cheers of 50,000 spectators. About 750 12-person teams run three 5 mi. shifts in this one- to two-day relay race. For more info, call ☎ 503-292-2626 or 800-444-6749.

🍴🛏 FOOD & ACCOMMODATIONS. Prices on Broadway, especially toward the beach, are outrageous. At **Morning Star Cafe,** 280 S. Roosevelt Dr., comfy beat-up couches and aging board games will remind you of your old basement rec room. Enjoy a sandwich ($3-4) or quiche ($3.50) with a mocha. (☎ 503-717-8188. Breakfast panini $3.50. Open daily 7am-7pm.) **The Stand,** 101 N. Holladay Dr., serves the cheapest Mexican meals around to a local crowd. (☎ 503-738-6592. Burritos $2.25-4. Open daily 11am-8pm.)

Seaside's expensive motels are hardly an issue for the budget traveler thanks to the large hostel on the south side of town. Motel prices are directly proportional to their proximity to the beach and start at $50 (less during the off-season). The **◪Seaside International Hostel (HI),** 930 N. Holladay Dr., offers free nightly movies, a well-equipped kitchen, an espresso bar, and a grassy yard along the river. (☎ 503-738-7911. Kayak and canoe rental. Reception 8am-11pm. Call well ahead for weekends. Dorms $16, nonmembers $19; private rooms with bath and cable TV $36-42/$39-65.) The closest state parks are **Fort Stevens** (☎ 503-861-1671; see p. 973), 21 mi. north, and **Saddle Mountain** (☎ 800-551-6949), 10 mi. east, off U.S. 26 after it splits with U.S. 101. Drive 8 mi. northeast of Necanicum Junction, then another 7 mi. up a winding road to the base camp. (Drinking water. Sites Oct.-Apr. $7; May-Sept. $10.) Sleeping on the beach in Seaside is illegal, as it is in all of Oregon.

◪ FORT CLATSOP NATIONAL MEMORIAL
Continue north on U.S. 101 and follow the signs to the memorial.

This memorial reconstructs Lewis and Clark's winter headquarters from journal descriptions. The fort has been completely restored and contains exhibits about the explorers' quest for the Pacific Ocean. In summer, rangers in feathers and buckskin demonstrate quill writing, moccasin sewing, and musket firing. (☎ 503-861-2471. Open daily June-Labor Day 8am-6pm; Labor Day-May 8am-5pm. $2, under 17 free.)

◪ FORT STEVENS STATE PARK
About 10 mi. north of Seaside, follow Fort Stevens Hwy. north to the park.

Fort Stevens was constructed in 1863 to prevent attack by Confederate naval raiders and was significantly upgraded in 1897 with the addition of eight concrete artillery batteries. Several of these remaining batteries are the focus of a self-guided walking tour (about 2hr.) that begins up the road from the campground area. Great places to board- or kayak-surf await at the South Jetty, near the northern tip of the peninsula in the park. Waves get big when the wave refraction off the jetty kicks in. Everyone loves catching a wave in front of the **Wreck of the Peter Iredale** that sticks out of the sand, even though the breaks are nothing special. (☎503-861-2000. Get a map and pass from the camp registration. Entrance fee $3.) Rugged, empty beaches and hiking and bike trails surround the **campground.** (☎503-861-1671, reservations 800-452-5687. Toilets, water. Reservations recommended; $6 fee. Sites $18; full RV sites $21; hiker/biker sites $4.25 per person; yurts $29.)

◤ APPROACHING ASTORIA
Follow **Fort Stevens Hwy. (Alt. U.S. 101)** out of the park, and turn left to follow **U.S. 101** into Astoria.

ASTORIA

Established in 1811 by John Jacob Astor's trading party, Astoria is the oldest US city west of the Rocky Mountains. Originally built as a fort to guard the mouth of the Columbia River, it quickly became a port city for ships heading to Portland and Longview, WA. A much more pleasant and less expensive destination than the overrun resort cities to the south, Astoria offers the same beautiful views of the Pacific Ocean from nearby Ft. Stevens State Park. Its Victorian homes, bustling waterfront, rolling hills, and persistent fog suggest a smaller-scale San Francisco. Differentiating it from that metropolis is a microclimate with wicked winter storms; hurricane-force winds aren't uncommon, and many come to watch storms roll into the Columbia River outlet.

⬛ GETTING AROUND. Astoria is a peninsula that extends into the Columbia River, approximately 7 mi. from the ocean beaches in both Fort Stevens and nearby Washington. All streets parallel to the water are named in alphabetical order, except for the first one.

◉ SIGHTS. On the rare clear day, ⬛**Astoria Column** grants its climbers a stupendous view of Astoria cradled between **Saddle Mountain** to the south and the **Columbia River Estuary** to the north. Completed in 1926, the column on Coxcomb Hill

PACIFIC COAST

⬛ VITAL STATS

Population: 9800

Visitor Info: Astoria-Warrenton Area Chamber of Commerce, 111 W. Marine Dr. (☎503-325-6311), just east of Astoria Bridge. Open June-Sept. M-F 8am-6pm, Sa 9am-6pm, Su 9am-5pm; Oct.-May M-F 8am-5pm, Sa-Su 11am-4pm.

Internet Access: Astoria Library, 450 10th St. (☎503-325-7323). For 1hr. of free Internet access sign up a day in advance, or get 15min. walk-up (ID required). Open Tu-Th 10am-7pm, F-Sa 10am-5pm.

Post Office: 748 Commercial St. Open M-F 8:30am-5pm. **Postal Code:** 97103.

Rd. encloses a dizzying 164 steps past newly repainted friezes depicting local history; picture something like an exceptionally well-decorated barber's pole jutting into the sky, albeit one that (luckily) doesn't spin. (Follow signs from 16th Ave. and Commercial St. Open dawn-10pm. Parking $1.) The cavernous, wave-shaped **Columbia River Maritime Museum,** 1792 Marine Dr., on the waterfront, is packed with marine lore, including displays on the salmon fisheries that once dominated Astoria. Among the model boats is the 1792 vessel that Robert Grey first steered into the mouth of the Columbia River. (☎503-325-2323. Open daily 9:30am-5pm. $5, seniors $4, ages 6-17 $2, under 6 free.) The annual **Astoria-Warrenton Crab and Seafood Festival** is a misnomer for a large assembly of Oregon winemakers, brewers, and restaurants. ($5 general admission. Call the Chamber of Commerce, ☎800-875-6807, for more info.)

⬛ FOOD. A small but growing **farmer's market** convenes each summer Sunday downtown at 12th St. ⬛**Columbian Cafe,** 1114 Marine Dr., offers local banter, wines by the glass, and fantastic pasta and seafood (lunch $5-8; dinner $10-15). Try "Seafood" or "Vegetarian Mercy"—name the heat your mouth can stand and the chef will design a meal for you. (☎503-325-2233. Open M-Tu 8am-2pm, W-Sa 8am-9pm, Su 9am-2pm.) At the ⬛**Home Spirit Bakery and Cafe,** 1585 Exchange St., you can enjoy a tasty, inexpensive meal in a restored Victorian home just a block away from the Shallon Winery. (☎503-325-6846. Open for lunch Tu-Sa 11am-2pm; dinner Th-Sa 5:30-8pm. Call ahead.) In addition to the normal delicious Italian fare ($5-14), **Someplace Else,** 965 Commercial St., serves a popular dish from a different country every night. (☎503-325-3500. Open W-Su 11:30am-2pm and 4-9pm.)

☐ ACCOMMODATIONS. Motel rooms can be expensive and elusive during summer. U.S. 101, both north and south of Astoria, is littered with clean and scenic campgrounds. **Grandview B&B,** 1574 Grand Ave., has intimate, cheery, and luxurious rooms. (☎503-325-0000 or 325-5555. Delicious breakfast included. Rooms $45, with bath from $71. Off-season 2nd night is $36.) **Lamplighter Motel,** 131 W. Marine Dr., is located between the Pig 'n' Pancake diner and the Visitors Center. Spotlessly clean, well-lit rooms with cable TV and phones include large bathrooms and refrigerators. (☎503-325-4051 or 800-845-8847. Rooms $49-55. Less in winter.)

☒ NIGHTLIFE. The nightlife in Astoria has recently begun to come into its own. The **▨Voodoo Room,** adjacent to Columbian Cafe, is the new hot venue for live music, known by many as the artists' hang. Egyptian sarcophagi complete the scene. (☎503-325-2233. F-Sa funk, jazz, and every other kind of music; Su bluegrass. Cover F Sa $3-5. Open daily 5-10pm or later.) Youthful crowds flock to **Wet Dog Cafe & Pacific Rim Brewing Co.,** 144 11th St., for hip-hop and top-40 music on weekends. (☎503-325-6975. Burgers $5.50-8. Occasional live music. Game room. DJ Th-F. 21+ after 9pm. Opens daily at 11am, closes Su-W 10pm, Th 1am, F-Sa 1:30am.)

☒ APPROACHING CHINOOK
Follow the **U.S. 101/Oregon Coast Hwy.** out of Oregon and into Washington state.

CHINOOK. As you stop in the Country Store for some candy or a bottle of juice, look up and check out the photographs of how Chinook looked in days of yore—the dirt streets,

the horses pulling in the fishing catch, and the **Sanctuary Restaurant** when it was still a church. Today, the restaurant offers quite a treat, if a pricey way to salvation. The menu includes rack of lamb $18, or you can opt for the Swedish pea soup and crepes with ligonberry appetizer for $8.50. (☎360-777-8380. Open Th-Sa from 5pm.) One of the few intact coastal defense sites in the US, **Ft. Colombia** is now a state park offering 5 mi. of hiking trails, a museum, and wildlife viewing. (Open daily summer 6:30am-9:30pm; winter 8am-5pm. No camping. Parking permit $5.)

▨ CAPE DISAPPOINTMENT STATE PARK
West of Chinook on U.S. 101, just south of Ilwaco.

The best thing to do once you've set foot on the beautiful, wet state of Washington is traipse around its southernmost tip, **▨Cape Disappointment.** The confluence of the Columbia and Pacific is breathtaking, and along the way you'll stumble over some unexpected beaches tucked into the jetty. The cape was named for that 'aw, shucks' feeling that the British explorer Captain John Meares felt in 1788 when he missed the passage over the bar. The bar, where the river deposits its silt in the ocean, is betrayed by lackadaisical whitecaps which you can see from the lighthouse. Follow the signs to the **Lewis and Clark Interpretive Center,** park your car, and wander; you can't go too far without coming to the water's edge. A three-quarter-mile trail leads to the **Cape Disappointment Lighthouse,** the oldest operating lighthouse on the West Coast. If the weather turns on you, which is a frequent occurrence in Washington, you can pop into the Interpretive Center, which has excellent displays about the famous trio's journey, as well as maritime and Native American history.

☒ APPROACHING LONG BEACH PENINSULA
From Ilwaco, outside Cape Disappointment, continue north on **U.S. 101.** Ilwaco is the first of several tiny hamlets lining the road through the Long Beach Peninsula.

 The **world's largest frying pan** makes its home in Long Beach.

LONG BEACH PENINSULA

The 28 mi. of unbroken sand that is Long Beach Peninsula is a frenzy of kitsch and souvenir shops sporadically broken up by calm forests and beautiful ocean views. Just don't let the looks deceive you into taking a dip—the water is very cold and carries lethal riptide currents. Accessible by U.S. 101 and Rte. 103, every town has a clearly marked beach access road (unmarked roads end in private property). Fishing, boating, and kite-flying are how residents recuperate from pounding winter storms. Clamming season lasts from October to mid-March (but beware red tide). **Short Stop,** in the Shell Station across from the Visitors Center, sells non-resident licenses (2-day license $8) along with tips and tide tables.

Like most other towns along the bay, **Ilwaco** was nearly devastated when depleted salmon stocks required a shutdown of the fishery for several years. Salmon steaks are plentiful along the waterfront, where the industry is beginning to recover (barring a ban on fishing). **Pacific Salmon Charters** leads 8hr. fishing tours. (☎503-642-3466 or 800-831-2695. From $70. Open daily at 5:30am.)

The **Long Beach Peninsula Visitors Bureau** is 5min. south of Long Beach on U.S. 101. (☎503-642-2400 or 800-451-2542; www.funbeach.com. Open M-Sa 9am-5pm, Su 9am-4pm. Call for winter hours.) During the last week in August, flyers from Thailand, China, Japan, and Australia compete in the spectacular **International Kite Festival.**

Among the cheap places to hit the hay on the Peninsula is the **Sand-Lo-Motel,** 1910 N. Pacific Hwy. (☎503-642-2600. Rooms from $50; rates drop in winter.) **My Mom's Pie Kitchen,** 1113 S. Pacific Hwy., is a delicious respite from steak houses and greasy spoons. (☎503-642-2342. Open W-Sa 11am-6pm.) For the best meal around, head up Rte. 103 in Ocean Park to historic **Oysterville.** The star draw of this tiny, whitewashed town is **Oysterville Sea Farms,** at 1st and Clark, which raises and dishes out its namesake mollusk. (☎503-665-6585. Open daily 10am-5pm.) For some entertainment, head to **Marsh's Free Museum,** 409 S. Pacific Way, home to a mechanical fortune teller, Jake the petrified alligator-man, and honky-tonk souvenirs. (☎503-642-2188. Open, ironically, whenever tourists bring money.)

LEAVING LONG BEACH PENINSULA
Follow **U.S. 101** as it heads off of the peninsula and north toward Nemah.

WILLAPA BAY
Willapa Bay stretches between the Long Beach Peninsula and the Washington mainland just north of the Washington-Oregon border and the mouth of the Columbia River.

Home to the last unpolluted estuary in the nation, the Willapa Bay is an excellent place to watch birdlife, especially in late spring and early fall. From the north, stop at the headquarters of the **Willapa National Wildlife Refuge,** just off U.S. 101 on the left, 12 mi. north Chinook. The headquarters offers info on Canada geese, loons, grebes, cormorants, and trumpeter swans. (☎503-484-3482. Open M-F 7:30am-4pm.)

THE ROAD TO ABERDEEN

Located off U.S. 101, **South Bend** grew into a township as the location of the Northern Pacific railroad terminus. As you drive through, pull over into the harbor for a closer view of the wooden statues dedicated to fishermen and women. Don't miss the beautiful 1910 **courthouse** (one block east of U.S. 101, and signed) set into landscaped gardens. Visit during opening hours and take a look up at the kaleidoscopic colored glass dome. (Open M-F 8:30am-5pm.)

Continue on U.S. 101 to Raymond, and follow Rte. 105 out of Raymond along the coast; it's worth it to take the little extra time to loop around the coastal route of Rte. 105, instead of staying inland on boring U.S. 101. Be careful of the low speed limits here, especially the 25 mph of the **Shoalwater Reservation,** which are enforced with particular diligence. A stop in Tokeland is worth it for the **Tokeland Hotel.** Isolated on the Willapa Bay, the gracious 1889 hotel has pretty whitewashed rooms with quilts and shared bathrooms. The downstairs living room and restaurant are open from 7:30am to 8pm. (From Rte. 105 take the Tokeland exit and it will be on your left after 2 mi. ☎360-267-7006. Reservations required. Doubles $65; $10 per additional person.)

Fourteen more miles along Rte. 105, **Westport** is a pleasant fishing town with not much going on but plenty of motels for the weary traveler. The highlight is the beautiful **West-**

haven State Beach ($5 parking) where there is a 1½ mi. trail along the coast to the lighthouse. Charter a fishing boat or surf the cove; you can rent board and wetsuit ($25 per 24hr.) from **Steepwater,** 1200 N. Montesano St. (Open M and W-F 10am-4pm, Sa-Su 9am-5pm.)

APPROACHING ABERDEEN
Continue on **Rte. 105** for about 18 mi., then turn left to approach Aberdeen on **U.S. 101 North.**

ABERDEEN
Aberdeen is the gritty, rough and tumble Washington town (pop. 16,467) where **Kurt Cobain** grew up. Across the street from the tourist office, which is well signed from U.S. 101, is a muffler repair shop at 208 Sumner where, tucked behind a curtain in the corner, a statue and small homemade shrine to Cobain stand. The sculptor Randy is married to the mechanic who runs the shop. (☎360-533-1957. Open M-F 8am-5pm, Sa-Su 10am-2pm.) The town has a fraught relationship with honoring its most famous resident and it has been controversial whether the statue will be allowed to be displayed publicly, as many residents have reservations about honoring a heroin addict who committed suicide. Unless you're a big Nirvana fan, Aberdeen is not a wonderful place to linger, although it's not a terrible one either. The Historic Seaport, now slightly obscured behind a gigantic Wal-Mart, occasionally harbors the **Lady Washington,** which was launched in 1789 as the first American ship to round Cape Horn and dock in the Northwest. The ship had been a privateer during the American revolution and then set out to trade iron, axe heads, chisels and sheet copper. The Lady Washington also broke records for being the first American vessel to reach Hawaii and Japan. The boat that exists today is a 1989 remodel of the historic brig, and is most recently famous for its appearance in Disney's *Pirates of the Caribbean.* When she's in port—usually May and September—the boat is open to the public. The Lady Washington also takes people out for 3hr. tours in three programs: a sunset sail, a "sailing adventure" where you can pull the ropes and navigate yourself, or the most exciting—a 18th-century sea battle. (☎800-200-5239 or 360-532-8611; www.ladywashington.org. Open M-F 4-6pm, Sa-Su 10am-1pm. $3, students and seniors $2, children $1. Trips $30-45.) The **Visitors Center** is at 506 Duffy St. (☎360-532-1924; www.graysharbor.org).

Billy's, 322 E. Heron at G St., crosses a rugged Old West saloon (it's named for a sailor who used to keep the men's money in his safe and then, when they came back after a few drinks to take it out, would pull a trap door on them and sink them into the ocean) with Howard Johnson's (mass produced booth coverings that fail at art). Hearty entrees like yak burgers average $8-11. (☎360-533-7144. Open Su-Th 8am-11pm, F-Sa 8am-midnight.)

Accommodations can be found at **Olympic Inn Motel,** 616 W. Heron St. (☎800-562-8681 or 360-533-4200) on U.S. 101 North. You'll recognize it by the flashing neon torch on the sign out front. (Rooms in high season $56-65; in low season $46-54.) More tourist attraction than reasonable lodging, **Hoquiam's Castle**, 515 Chenault Ave., is not a castle at all, but a cloyingly cute 1897 Victorian Inn with five rooms built by the lumber baron who started the town (the town name is Quinault for "hungry for wood"). Dolls crowd the windowsill in the Princess room and some bathrooms have vanity tables and clawfoot tubs. (☎877-542-2785 or 360-533-2005; www.hoquiamscastle.com. Rooms June-Sept. $115-150; Oct.-May $80-125.)

DETOUR: OCEAN SHORES
Follow U.S. 101 out of Aberdeen, then turn left onto Rte. 109. About 16 mi. later, turn left on Rte. 115.

Declared "the richest little city in America" in 1969 because of its lucrative real estate, Ocean Shores remains an enviable destination for its antiquing, boating, and gambling facilities. Grab your shillelagh and head to **Galway Bay Irish Pub**, 880 Point Brown Ave. NE, for live music every Friday and Saturday nights. (☎360-289-2300. Open M-Th 11am-11pm, F-Sa 11am-2am, Su 11am-10pm.)

LEAVING ABERDEEN
Continue north on **U.S. 101,** through Amanda Park and Queets.

OLYMPIC PENINSULA
North of Aberdeen, U.S. 101 loops around the Olympic Peninsula, a remote backpacking paradise, before heading back south toward Seattle. Olympic National Park dominates much of the peninsula, and it prevents the

area's ferocious timber industry from threatening the glacier-capped mountains and temperate rainforests. To the west, the Pacific Ocean stretches to a distant horizon; to the north, the Strait of Juan de Fuca separates the Olympic Peninsula from Vancouver Island; and to the east, Hood Canal and the Kitsap Peninsula isolate this sparsely inhabited wilderness from the ever-spreading sprawl of Seattle. Roads lead to many corners of Olympic National Park, but they only hint at the depths of its wilderness. A dive into the backcountry leaves summer tourists behind and reveals the richness and diversity of the park's many faces.

> ### (VITAL STATS)
>
> **Area:** 869,000 acres
>
> **Visitor Info: Olympic National Park Visitors Center,** 3002 Mt. Angeles Rd. (☎ 306-565-3130), off Race St. in Port Angeles. Open daily summer 9am-5:30pm; winter 9am-4pm.
>
> **Gateway Towns:** Forks, Port Angeles, Port Townsend.
>
> **Fees:** $10 per vehicle.

▐ GETTING AROUND

U.S. 101 encircles the park in the shape of an upside-down U. Farthest south is **Forks,** a gateway to the park's rainforested **western rim.** Separate from the rest of the park, much of the Pacific coastline comprises a gorgeous **coastal zone.** The much-visited **northern rim** extends eastward to **Port Angeles,** the major gateway to the park and home to many food and lodging options. The park is huge, and U.S. 101 passes through far more than you could experience in one roadtrip; don't be in any hurry to get to Seattle.

COASTAL ZONE

North of Queets, U.S. 101 joins the ocean again and there are a series of delightful beach turn-offs. Pullover into one of the turnouts and hop out to the beautiful, long, deserted shore if only for a moment to stretch your legs. There are two campgrounds here that are both lovely: **South Bend Campground,** 3 mi. south of the ranger station, is open so everywhere has a view of the ocean even though it can get quite windy. (No potable water. $8.) **Kalaloch Campground,** north of the station, is more sheltered in the trees near the beach. (Sites $12.) Fourteen miles north of Queets is **Ruby Beach,** the northernmost plot of the serene strip along U.S. 101. Ruby Beach is a magical spot where lovers and photographers tend to congregate. Twenty miles south of Forks on U.S. 101, between Hoh Rain Forest and Kalaloch, you'll find the **Rainforest Hostel,** 169312 U.S. 101. To get there, follow hostel signs off U.S. 101, 4 mi. north of Ruby Beach. Family rooms and dorms are available, as are outside trailers for couples or people allergic to the resident dog and cat.

ROAD FOOD

CLAMMING UP

Food on the Olympic Peninsula often seems limited to, at best, picnic munchies. Luckily, there is a more exciting option; visitors to the peninsula's beaches can dig up razor clams. The Long Beach Peninsula, from Oysterville to Leadbetter Point, is known as the best digging spot. Check with the Department of Fish and Wildlife for rules and regulations.

Head to the beach at least 2hr. before low tide. The clams hide just inches below the surface of the sand; when they sense trouble, they retract their necks, leaving "shows" on the beach. Stomping on the sand will force the clams to show. After spotting a clam, the key is to dig it up before it burrows deep into the sand. Beginners should use a clam gun, a 3 ft. tube with a small hole and a handle. Push it into the sand and place a thumb over the hole, then pull it out of the sand, hopefully with a tube full of sand and a clam. Before cooking, clams should be dipped in boiling water, and the siphon and shell removed. (Department of Fish and Wildlife ☎ 360-586-6129; wdfw.wa.gov.)

(☎360-374-2270. Morning chore required. Beds $12; family rooms $1 plus $12 per adult, $6 per child.)

FORKS

Between ONP's northern and western rims lies the logging town of Forks. Once the king timber town in the region, Forks both embraces and mourns its historic legacy. If you're passing through town or grabbing a bite to eat, take time to visit the **Forks Logging Museum.** (☎360-374-2531. Open M-Su 10am-4pm. Logging and mill tours M, W, F 9am.) Check out forestry research in action at the **Olympic Natural Resources Center,** just south of the Logging Museum. Students and faculty from the University of Washington (and beyond) use this research facility to experiment with forest management techniques. Forks lies 2hr. west of Port Angeles and offers the widest selection of services in the western peninsula. Visit during the dry season (summer) if possible; Forks gets more rain than any other city or town in Washington.

The **Raindrop Cafe,** 111 E. A St., at S. Forks Ave., serves breakfast until 11am and names its burgers after clouds. (☎360-374-6612. Seriously delicious salads $7. Open summer M-Sa 6am-9pm, Su 6am 8pm; winter daily 6am-8pm.) In Forks you'll also find a row of motels offering budget prices. The **Town Motel,** 1080 S. Forks Ave., has a beautiful garden and comfortable rooms. (☎360-374-6231. Singles $37-45; doubles $47-55.)

NORTHERN RIM

A massive body of water located in the north-central region of the peninsula, just off U.S. 101, **Lake Crescent** is often ignored by travelers. The lake offers brisk swimming, blissful picnicking, and frequent sunshine. **Storm King Ranger Station** is on a small peninsula in the center of the lake and offers all of the regular services. (☎360-928-3380. Open summer daily 10am-5pm.) At the west end of the lake, just past the Fairholm General Store, there is a small road that heads to **Fairholm Campground,** which has wheelchair access, beautiful moss-covered trees, picnic areas, and some sites right on the lakeshore. (☎360-928-3380. Sites $10.) Several strenuous hikes head out from the lake up the steep slopes. The **Lake Crescent Lodge,** next to the Storm King Station, rents rowboats to help in summertime seduction. (☎360-928-3211. Rentals 7am-8pm. $8.50 per hr., $20 per half-day.)

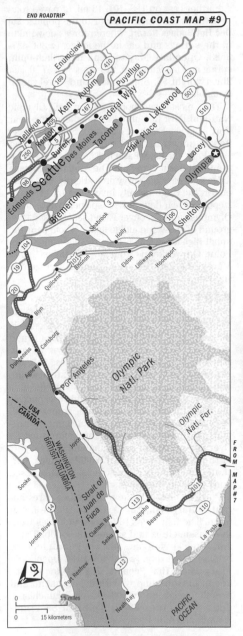

PACIFIC COAST MAP #9

END ROADTRIP

PACIFIC COAST

Farther east on U.S. 101, 13 mi. of paved road penetrates the park's interior to the popular **Sol Duc Hot Springs Resort,** where retirees de-wrinkle in the springs and eat in the lodge. (☎360-327-3583. Open late May to Sept. daily 9am-9pm; spring and fall 9am-7pm. $10, ages 4-12 $7.50; last 2hr. twilight $7. Suit, locker, and towel rental available.)

The most developed section of Olympic National Park lies along its northern rim, near Port Angeles. Farthest east off U.S. 101 lies **Deer Park,** where trails tend to be uncrowded. Past Deer Park, the **Royal Basin Trail** meanders 6¼ mi. to the **Royal Basin Waterfall.** The road up **Hurricane Ridge** is an easy but curvy drive. Before July, walking on the ridge usually involves a bit of snow-stepping. Clear days provide splendid views of Mt. Olympus and Vancouver Island set against a foreground of snow and indigo lupine. From here, the uphill **High Ridge Trail** is a short walk from Sunset Point. On weekends from late December to late March, the Park Service organizes free guided snowshoe walks atop the ridge.

PORT ANGELES

Port Angeles is the "gateway" to the Olympic National Park. The main draw of Port Angeles is the park itself, which looms behind the town in the form of Mt. Angeles. Near town, a 5 mi. (2hr.) trail leads out on the **Dungeness Spit,** the world's longest natural sand spit, extends 6 mi. into the Strait of Juan de Fuca. The trail winds all the way to **New Dungeness Lighthouse,** once at the tip of the spit, now a half-mile from the end. (☎ 603-683-9166; www.newdungenesslighthouse.com. Open 9am until 2hr. before sunset.) Over 200 species of birds inhabit this area, part of the **Dungeness National Wildlife Refuge.** Offshore, indigenous crabs, clams, seals, and sea lions populate the waters.

Port Angeles is home to a number of restaurants. **Crazy Fish,** 229 W. 1st St. is the hit in town. The fish tacos (2 for $6) and sides from the classic chips and salsa to the oddball mac and cheese wedges ($4) are guaranteed to brighten your day. (☎603-457-1944. Open M-Sa 11am-2am.) **Thai Peppers,** 222 N. Lincoln St., keeps patrons happy with a Thai menu and excellent seafood. (☎603-452-4995. Lunch specials $6. Dinner $8-10. Open M-Sa 11am-2:30pm and 4:30-9pm.)

The least expensive of the many motels in town line U.S. 101 west of town. **Thor Town Hostel,** 316 N. Race St., is a friendly refuge located in a renovated house. (☎603-452-0931; www.thortown.com. Laundry $1. Bike rental $8 per day. Dorms $12; private rooms $28.)

▲ APPROACHING SEATTLE
Leave Port Angeles on **U.S. 101;** continue east and then south. 35 mi. beyond Port Angeles, bear right onto **Rte. 104,** and follow south. 25 mi. later, take the ferry to Edmonds, leaving the Olympic Peninsula, and take I-5 South into Seattle. Get to **downtown** (including Pioneer Square, Pike Place Market, and the waterfront) from I-5 by taking any of the exits from James St. to Stewart St. For the **Seattle Center,** take the Mercer St./Fairview Ave. Exit; follow signs from there. The Denny Way Exit leads to **Capitol Hill,** and, farther north, the 45th St. Exit heads toward the **University District (U District).**

SEATTLE

Seattle's mix of mountain views, clean streets, espresso stands, and rainy weather proved to be the magic formula of the 90s, attracting transplants from across the US. The droves of newcomers provide an interesting contrast to the older residents who remember Seattle as a city-town, not a thriving metropolis bubbling over with young millionaires. Computer and coffee money have helped drive rents sky-high in some areas, but the grungy, punk-loving street culture still prevails in others. In the end, there is a nook or cranny for almost anyone in Seattle. Every hilltop offers an impressive view of Mt. Olympus, Mt. Baker, and Mt. Rainier. The city is shrouded in cloud cover 200 days a year, but when the skies clear, Seatleites rejoice that "the mountain is out" and head for the country.

▐ GETTING AROUND

Seattle stretches from north to south on an isthmus between **Puget Sound** to the west and **Lake Washington** to the east. The city is easily accessible by car via **I-5,** which runs north-south through the city, and **I-90** from the east, which ends at I-5 southeast of downtown. The less crowded **Route 99** (also called **Aurora Avenue** and Aurora Hwy.) runs parallel to I-5 and skirts the western side of

PACIFIC COAST

VITAL STATS

Population: 563,374

Visitor Info: Seattle's Convention and Visitors Bureau (☎206-461-5840; www.seeseattle.org), at 8th and Pike St. Helpful staff doles out maps, brochures, newspapers, and Metro and ferry schedules. Open M-F 9am-4pm.

Internet Access: Seattle Public Library, 1000 4th Ave. (☎206-386-4636), at Madison. One-time visitors can use Internet for free with photo ID. Open M-W 10am-8pm, Th-Sa 10am-6pm, Su 1-5pm. Schedule may change; call for current hours.

Post Office: 301 Union St. (☎206-748-5417 or 800-275-8777), at 3rd Ave. downtown. Open M-F 8am-5:30pm, Sa 8am-noon. General delivery window M-F 9-11:20am and noon-3pm. **Postal Code:** 98101.

downtown, with great views from the Alaskan Way Viaduct. Rte. 99 is often the better choice driving downtown or to **Queen Anne, Fremont, Green Lake,** and the northwestern part of the city.

Even the most road-weary drivers can learn their way around the Emerald City. Street parking creates many blind pull-outs in Seattle, so be extra careful when turning onto cross roads. Downtown, **avenues** run northwest to southeast and **streets** run southwest to northeast. Outside downtown, everything is simplified: with few exceptions, avenues run north-south and streets east-west. The city is in **quadrants:** 1000 1st Ave. NW is a far walk from 1000 1st Ave. SE.

When driving in Seattle, **yield to pedestrians.** They will not look, so make sure you do. Locals drive slowly, calmly, and politely; police ticket frequently. Downtown driving can be nightmarish: parking is expensive, hills are steep, and one-way streets are ubiquitous. Read the street signs carefully, as many areas have time and hour restrictions; ticketers know them by heart. **Parking** is reasonable, plentiful, and well lit at **Pacific Place Parking** between 6th and 7th Ave. and Olive and Pine St., with hourly rates comparable to the meters and at **Seattle Center,** near the Space Needle. (☎206-652-0416. 24hr. $2 per hr.; $19 per day.) Park at the Needle and take the monorail to the convenient **Westlake Center** downtown. If you are driving in Seattle, prepare yourself for heavy traffic, especially on I-5, at almost any hour of the day.

👁 SIGHTS

It takes only three frenetic days to get a decent look at most of the city's major sights. Seattle taxpayers spend more per capita on the arts than any other Americans, and the investment pays off in unparalleled public art installations throughout the city and plentiful galleries. The investments of Seattle-based millionaires have brought startlingly new and bold architecture in the Experience Music Project and International Fountain. Self-guided tours begin at the Visitors Center. Outside cosmopolitan downtown, Seattle boasts over 300 areas of well-watered greenery.

DOWNTOWN & THE WATERFRONT

The **Pike Place Hillclimb** descends from the south end of Pike Place Market past chic shops and ethnic restaurants to the Alaskan Way and waterfront. You will not be lonely in the harbor; the waterfront is lined with vendors.

SEATTLE ART MUSEUM (SAM). Housed in a grandiose building designed by Philadelphia architect and father of postmodernism Robert Venturi, the Seattle Art Museum balances special exhibits with the region's largest collection of African, Native American, and Asian art and an eclectic bunch of contemporary western painting and sculpture. Call for info on special musical shows, films, and lectures. Admission is also good for the Seattle Asian Art Museum (see p. 985) for a week. *(100 University St., near 1st Ave. ☎206-654-3100. Open Tu-W and F-Su 10am-5pm, Th 10am-9pm. $7, students and seniors $5, under 12 free. 1st Th of each month free.)*

🖼THE SEATTLE AQUARIUM. The star attraction of the Seattle Aquarium is a huge underwater dome, and the harbor seals, fur seals, otters, and endless supply of fish won't disappoint. Touch tanks and costumes delight kids, while a million-dollar salmon exhibit and ladder teaches about the state's favorite fish. Feedings occur throughout the day. Next door, the **IMAX Dome** shows films, many focusing on natural events or habitats. *(Pier 59, near Union St. ☎206-386-4320, TDD ☎206-386-4322. Open daily summer 9:30am-8pm; fall and winter 10am-6pm; spring 9:30am-6pm. Last admission 1hr. before closing. $11, ages 6-12 $7, ages 3-5 $5. IMAX Dome: 206-*

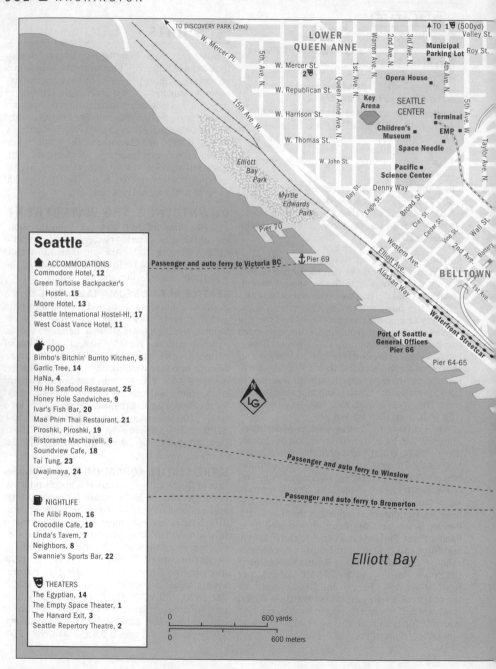

TO DISCOVERY PARK (2mi)

W. Mercer Pl.

5th. Ave. N.

15th Ave. W.

W. Mercer St.

W. Republican St.

W. Harrison St.

W. Thomas St.

W. John St.

Warren Ave. N.

1st. Ave. N.

Queen Anne Ave. N.

2nd Ave. N.

3rd Ave. N.

4th Ave. N.

5th Ave. N.

Taylor Ave. N.

LOWER QUEEN ANNE

Municipal Parking Lot

TO 1 (500yd)

Valley St.

Roy St.

Opera House

2

Key Arena

SEATTLE CENTER

Children's Museum

Space Needle

Terminal

EMP

5th Ave. W.

Pacific Science Center

Denny Way

Bay St.

Eagle St.

Broad St.

Clay St.

Cedar St.

Vine St.

2nd Ave.

Battery

Wall St.

1st. Ave.

Elliott Bay Park

Myrtle Edwards Park

Pier 70

Western Ave.

Elliott Ave.

Alaskan Way

BELLTOWN

Passenger and auto ferry to Victoria BC

Pier 69

Port of Seattle General Offices Pier 66

Pier 64-65

Waterfront Streetcar

Seattle

🏠 **ACCOMMODATIONS**
Commodore Hotel, **12**
Green Tortoise Backpacker's Hostel, **15**
Moore Hotel, **13**
Seattle International Hostel-HI, **17**
West Coast Vance Hotel, **11**

🍎 **FOOD**
Bimbo's Bitchin' Burrito Kitchen, **5**
Garlic Tree, **14**
HaNa, **4**
Ho Ho Seafood Restaurant, **25**
Honey Hole Sandwiches, **9**
Ivar's Fish Bar, **20**
Mae Phim Thai Restaurant, **21**
Piroshki, Piroshki, **19**
Ristorante Machiavelli, **6**
Soundview Cafe, **18**
Tai Tung, **23**
Uwajimaya, **24**

🍸 **NIGHTLIFE**
The Alibi Room, **16**
Crocodile Cafe, **10**
Linda's Tavern, **7**
Neighbors, **8**
Swannie's Sports Bar, **22**

🎭 **THEATERS**
The Egyptian, **14**
The Empty Space Theater, **1**
The Harvard Exit, **3**
Seattle Repertory Theatre, **2**

Passenger and auto ferry to Winslow

Passenger and auto ferry to Bremerton

Elliott Bay

N

LG

0   600 yards

0   600 meters

TO VOLUNTEER PARK (.5mi), LAKE
UNION & UNIVERSITY DISTRICT (3mi)

E Roy St.

Mercer St.
Republican St.
Harrison St.

Fairview Ave. N.
Boren Ave. N.
Terry Ave. N.

Westlake Ave. N.
9th Ave. N.
8th Ave. N.

Dexter Ave. N.
Aurora Ave. N.

Eastlake Ave. E.
Melrose Ave. E.
Bellevue Ave. E.
Summit Ave. E.
Belmont Ave. E.
Boylston Ave. E.
Harvard Ave. E.
Broadway East
10th Ave. E.
11th Ave. E.
12th Ave. E.
13th Ave. E.
14th Ave. E.
Malden Ave. E.

CAPITOL HILL

E. Harrison St.

E. Thomas St.

John St.
Denny Wy.

Denny
Park

REI/National
Park Information

Yale St.

E. Olive Way
E. Denny Wy.

E. John St.

13th Ave. E.
14th Ave. E.
15th Ave. E.

E. Howell St.
E. Howell St.

E. Olive St.
E. Olive St.

Broadway
Playfield

Virginia St.
Stewart St.
Howell St.

Bellevue Ave.

E. Pine St.
E. Pine St.

9th Ave.
7th Ave.

Blanchard St.

Bell

Monorail

Greyhound

Olive Way
Pine St.

Lenora St.
5th Ave.
4th Ave.

E. Pike St
E. Union St.
E. Union St.

Seattle
Public Library 14
State Convention
and Trade Center

Terminal

Boren Ave.
Minor Ave.

Hubbell St.

Terry Ave.

Seneca St.

FIRST
HILL

Madison St.

SEATTLE
UNIVERSITY

E. Spring St.
E. Marion St.

Freeway
Park

9th Ave.
8th Ave.
7th Ave.
6th Ave.

Virginia Mason
Medical Center

Swedish Medical
Center

E. Columbia St.
F. Cherry St

Pike St.

Pike
Place
Market

Union St.
University St.

Seattle
Art Museum

Madison St.

Marion St.

Columbia St.

Cherry St.

Broadway

E. Jefferson St.

Seattle
Aquarium &
IMAX Dome

Spring St.

Water-
front
Park

99

Marion St.

3rd Ave.
2nd Ave.
1st Ave.

Post St.
Western Ave.

Columbia Tower

James St.

Jefferson St.
Terry Ave.

E. Terrace St.

Alder St.

Pier 56
Pier 54

Harborview
Medical
Center

E. Spruce St.
E. Fir St.

Boren Ave.

Pier 52

Washington
State Ferry
Terminal

Alaskan Way S.

Underground
Tours

PIONEER
SQUARE

5th Ave.
4th Ave.

Smith
Tower

Yesler Way

6th Ave. S.

E. Yesler Way

Klondike Gold Rush
National History Museum

Eliott Bay
Books

S. Washington St.
S. Main St.

King Street
Station

Union
Station

Maynard St.

7th Ave. S.
8th Ave. S.

Wing Luke
Asian American Museum

S. Jackson St.

Pier 48

Pier 46

E. Marginal Way S.

1st Ave. S.
Occidental Ave.

4th Ave. S.

INTERNATIONAL
DISTRICT

S. King St.
S. Weller St.
S. Dearborn St.

5

S. King St.
S. Weller St.
S. Lane St.

12th Ave. S.

90

TO
MERCER
ISLAND

Charles St.

S. Dearborn St.

Seattle Overview

622-1868. Films daily 10am-10pm. $7, ages 6-12 $6. Aquarium and IMAX Dome combo ticket $16.50, ages 6-12 $11.75, ages 3-5 $5.)

THE SEATTLE CENTER

The 1962 World's Fair demanded a Seattle Center to herald the city of the future. Now the Center houses everything from carnival rides to ballet. The center is bordered by Denny Way, W. Mercer St., 1st Ave., and 5th Ave. and has eight gates, each with a model of the center and a map of its facilities. It is accessible via a **monorail** which departs from the third floor of the Westlake Center. The anchor point is the **Center House,** which holds a food court, stage, and **Info Desk.** (☎ 206-684-8582. Monorail every 15min. M-F 7:30am-11pm, Sa-Su 9am-11pm. $1.50, seniors and "juniors" $0.75. Info Desk open daily 11am-6pm.)

EXPERIENCE MUSIC PROJECT. Undoubtedly the biggest and best attraction at the Seattle Center is the new, futuristic, abstract, and technologically brilliant Experience Music Project (EMP). The museum is the brainchild of Seattle billionaire Paul Allen, who originally wanted to create a shrine to worship his music idol Jimi Hendrix. Splash together the technological sophistication and foresight of Microsoft, dozens of ethnomusicologists and multimedia specialists, a collection of musical artifacts topping 80,000, the world-renowned architect Frank Gehry, and enough money to make the national debt appear small (fine, it was only $350 million), and you have the rock 'n' roll museum of the future. The building alone—consisting of sheet metal molded into abstract curves and then acid-dyed gold, silver, purple, light-blue, and red—is enough to make the average person gasp for breath. Walk in and strap on a personal computer guide (MEG) that allows you to interact with the exhibits. Hear clips from Hendrix's famous "Star Spangled Banner" while looking at the remnants of the guitar he smashed on a London stage. Move into the Sound Lab and test your own skills on guitars, drums, and keyboards linked to computer teaching devices and cushioned in state-of-the art sound rooms. When you are ready, step over to On Stage, a first-class karaoke-gone-haywire, and blast your tunes in front of a virtual audience. (*325 5th St., at Seattle Center. From I-5, take Exit 167 and follow signs to Seattle Center. ☎ 206-367-5483 or 877-367-5483. Open summer Su-Th 9am-6pm, F-Sa 9am-9pm; fall Su-Th 10am-5pm, F-Sa 10am-9pm. $20; seniors, military, and ages 13-17 $16; ages 7-12 $15; under 7 free. Free live music Tu-Sa in the lounge; national acts perform F-Sa in the Sky Church.*)

SPACE NEEDLE. Until the EMP came to town, the **Space Needle** appeared to be something from another time—now it matches quite well with its futuristic neighbor. On a clear day, the Needle provides a great view and an invaluable landmark for the disoriented. The elevator ride itself is a show, and operators are hired for their unique talents. The Needle houses an observation tower and a high-end 360° rotating restaurant. (*☎ 206-905-2100. $12.50, seniors $11, ages 4-10 $5.*)

THE INTERNATIONAL DISTRICT/ CHINATOWN

■ **SEATTLE ASIAN ART MUSEUM.** What do you do when you have too much good art to exhibit all at once? Open a second museum. This is just what SAM did, creating a wonderful stand-on-its-own attraction. The museum displays a particularly strong collection of Chinese art. (*In Volunteer Park just beyond the water tower. ☎ 206-654-3100. Open Tu-Su 10am-5pm, Th 10am-9pm. Suggested donation $3, under 12 free. Free with SAM ticket from the previous 7 days; SAAM ticket good for $3 discount at SAM.*)

■ **ARBORETUM.** The **University of Washington Arboretum** nurtures over 4000 species of trees, shrubs, and flowers, and maintains superb trails. Tours depart the **Graham Visitor Center,** at the southern end of the arboretum. (*10 blocks east of Volunteer Park. Visitors Center on Arboretum Dr. East, off Lake Washington Blvd. ☎ 206-543-8800. Open daily sunrise-sunset. Visitors Center open 10am-4pm. Free tours 1st Su of the month.*)

JAPANESE TEA GARDEN. The tranquil 3½ acre park is a retreat of sculpted gardens, fruit trees, a reflecting pool, and a traditional tea house. (*At the south end of the UW Arboretum, entrance on Lake Washington Blvd. ☎ 206-684-4725. Open Mar.-Nov. daily 10am-dusk. $3; students, seniors, and ages 6-18 $2; under 6 free.*)

▶ ENTERTAINMENT

Seattle has one of the world's most notorious underground music scenes and the third-largest theater community in the US. The city supports performances in all sorts of venues, from bars to bakeries. In summer the free **Out to Lunch** series (☎ 206-623-0340) brings everything from reggae to folk dancing into parks, squares, and office buildings. Check cheeky free weekly *The Stranger* for event listings.

MUSIC

The **Seattle Opera** performs favorites from August to May. Buffs should reserve well in advance, although rush tickets are sometimes available. (☎ 206-389-7676; www.seattleopera.com. Box office open M-F 9am-5pm. Tickets from $35. Students and seniors can get half-price tickets 1½hr. before the performance.) From September to June, the **Seattle Symphony** performs in the new **Benaroya Hall,** 200 University St., at 3rd Ave. (☎ 206-215-4747; www.seattlesymphony.org. Box office open M-F 10am-6pm, Sa 1-6pm. Tickets from $15-39, seniors half-price. Same-day student tickets $10.)

THEATER & CINEMA

The city hosts an exciting array of first-run plays and alternative works, particularly by many talented amateur groups. Rush tickets are often available at nearly half-price on the day of the show from **Ticket/Ticket.** (☎ 206-324-2744. Cash only.) ■**The Empty Space Theatre,** 3509 Fremont Ave. N, one and a half blocks north of the Fremont Bridge, presents comedies from October to early July. (☎ 206-547-7500. Tickets $10-40. Half-price tickets 30min. before curtain.) **Seattle Repertory**

Theater, 155 Mercer St., at the wonderful Bagley Wright Theater in the Seattle Center, presents contemporary and classic winter productions. (☎206-443-2222; www.seattlerep.org. $15-45, seniors $32, under 25 $10. Rush tickets 30min. before curtain.)

Seattle is a cinephiles paradise. Most of the theaters that screen non-Hollywood films are on Capitol Hill and in the University District. On summer Saturdays, outdoor cinema in Fremont begins at dusk at 670 N. 34th St., in the U-Park lot by the bridge, behind the Red Door Alehouse. (☎206-781-4230. Entrance 7pm; live music 8pm. $5.) **TCI Outdoor Cinema** shows everything from classics to cartoons at the Gasworks Park. (Live music 7pm to dusk. Free.) Unless otherwise specified, the theaters below charge $5.50 for matinees and $8.50 for features. **The Egyptian,** 801 E. Pine St.

(☎206-323-4978), at Harvard Ave. on Capitol Hill, is an Art Deco art house best known for hosting the **Seattle International Film Festival** in the last week of May and first week of June. **The Harvard Exit,** 807 E. Roy St., on Capitol Hill near the north end of the Broadway business district, has its own ghost, an enormous antique projector, and offers quality classic and foreign films. (☎206-323-8986. $9, seniors and under 12 $6.) **Grand Illusion Cinema,** 1403 50th St. NE, in the U District at University Way, is one of the last independent theaters in Seattle and often shows old classics and hard-to-find films. (☎206-523-3935. $7, seniors and children $5.)

SPORTS

The **Mariners,** or "M's" are now playing baseball in the half-billion-dollar, hangar-like **Safeco Field,** at 1st Ave. South and Royal Brougham Way

DE LIBERTAS QUIRKAS

Of all the corners of Seattle, Fremont has undeniably set itself furthest apart; its motto is "De Libertas Quirkas," or "freedom to be peculiar." Here are the top 10 things that make Fremont, well, Fremont:

10 History House. This house preserves Fremont's past with handmade exhibits. (790 N. 34th St. ☎206-675-8875; www.historyhouse.org. Open Su and W-Sa noon-5pm.)

9 Fremont Drawbridge. This bright blue and red contraption is *the* way to enter town.

8 Rocket Monument. For unknown reasons, Fremonters believe the 53 ft. rocket perched at N. 34th St. and Evanston Ave. marks the Center of the Universe.

7 Fremont Fair. Fremont celebrates the summer Solstice with a costume and float parade, topped by a costume-less (nude) bicycle ride. (www.fremontfair.com.)

6 Outdoor movies. Fremont boasts two outdoor movie locations. Cinema Dali, at N. 34th St., shows cult films in costume. Saturday, the party moves to 35th St. and Phinney Ave., where it's BYOC—bring your own couch. (☎206-781-4230; www.outdoorcinema.net/seattle.com.)

5 Oktoberfest. Beer. Lederhosen. (www.fremontoktoberfest.com. 3rd weekend in Sept.)

4 Dinosaur topiary. Maintained by a local artist, Dino's Dinos, as they're fondly called, pose for portraits on the corner of Canal and N. 34th St.

3 Waiting for the Interurban. At the neighborhood center, five people, a baby, and a dog forever wait for the public transportation that will never come.

2 Statue of Lenin. If there are any doubts about Fremont's political leanings, this 7-ton Soviet leader looming over the corner of N. 36th and N. Fremont Pl. should clear things up.

1 Fremont Troll. Underneath the Aurora Bridge lives Fremont's most famous resident: the enormous car-munching troll. The result of a public art competition, he has his own holiday: Trolloween, on Oct. 31.

South, under an enormous retractable roof. (☎206-622-4487. Tickets from $10.) Seattle's football team, the **Seahawks,** are stuck playing in UW's Husky Stadium until construction on their new stadium is finished. (☎206-628-0888. Tickets from $10.) On the other side of town, the sleek **Key Arena,** in the Seattle Center, hosts Seattle's NBA basketball team, the **Supersonics.** (☎206-628-0888. Tickets from $9.) The **University of Washington Huskies** football team has contended in the PAC-10 for years and doesn't plan to let up. Call the Athletic Ticket Office (☎206-543-2200) for schedules and prices.

FOOD

Although Seattleites appear to subsist solely on espresso and steamed milk, they do occasionally eat. When they do, they seek out healthy cuisine, especially seafood. **Puget Sound Consumer Coops (PCCs)** are local health food markets at 7504 Aurora Ave. North (☎206-525-3586), in Green Lake, and 6514 40th St. NE (☎206-526-7661), in the Ravenna District north of the university. Capitol Hill, the U District, and Fremont close main thoroughfares on summer Saturdays for **Farmers Markets.**

PIKE PLACE MARKET & DOWNTOWN

In 1907, angry citizens demanded the elimination of the middle-man and local farmers began selling produce by the waterfront, creating the **Pike Place Market.** Business thrived until an enormous fire burned the building in 1941. Today, thousands of tourists mob the market daily to watch flying fish. (Open M-Sa 9am-6pm, Su 11am-5pm. Produce and fish open earlier; restaurants and lounges close later.) In the **Main Arcade,** on the west side of Pike St., fishmongers compete for audiences as they hurl fish from shelves to scales.

Piroshki, Piroshki, 1908 Pike Pl. (☎206-441-6068). The Russian *piroshki* is a croissant-like dough baked around sausages, mushrooms, cheeses, salmon, or apples doused in cinnamon ($3-4). Watch the *piroshki* process in progress. Open daily 8am-7pm.

Soundview Cafe (☎206-623-5700), on the mezzanine in the Pike Place Main Arcade. The sandwich-and-salad bar is a good place to brown-bag a moment of

solace. Breakfast and lunch $3-6. Open M-F 8am-5pm, Sa 8am-5:30pm, Su 8am-5pm.

Garlic Tree, 94 Stewart St. (☎206-441-5681), 1 block up from Pike Place Market. This smell will drag you in. Loads of fabulous veggie, chicken, and seafood stir-fries ($7-9). Open M-Sa 11am-8pm.

THE WATERFRONT

Budget eaters, steer clear of Pioneer Sq. Instead, take a picnic to **Waterfall Garden,** on the corner of S. Main St. and 2nd Ave. South. The garden sports tables and chairs and a man-made waterfall that masks traffic outside. (Open daily dawn to dusk.)

Mae Phim Thai Restaurant, 94 Columbia St. (☎206-624-2979), a few blocks north of Pioneer Sq. between 1st Ave. and Alaskan Way. Slews of pad thai junkies crowd in for cheap, delicious Thai cuisine. All dishes $6. Open M-Sa 11am-7pm.

Ivar's Fish Bar, Pier 54 (☎206-467-8063), north of the square. A fast-food window that serves the definitive Seattle clam chowder ($2). Clam and chips $5. Open M-Th and Su 10am-midnight, F-Sa 10am-2am.

INTERNATIONAL DISTRICT

Along King and Jackson St., between 5th and 8th Ave. east of the Kingdome, Seattle's International District is packed with great eateries.

▨ **Uwajimaya,** 600 5th Ave. South (☎206-624-6248). The Uwajimaya Center—the largest Japanese department store in the Northwest—is a full city block of groceries, gifts, videos, and CDs. There is even a food court, plying Korean BBQ and Taiwanese-style baked goods. Pork dumpling $7. Open M-Sa 9am-11pm, Su 9am-10pm.

Tai Tung, 655 S. King St. (☎206-622-7372). Select authentic Mandarin cuisine from a comprehensive menu. Entrees $5-12. Open Su-Th 10am-11pm, F-Sa 10am-1:30am.

Ho Ho Seafood Restaurant, 653 S. Weller St. (☎206-382-9671). Generous portions of tank-fresh seafood. Stuffed fish hang from the ceilings. Lunch $5-7. Dinner $7-12. Open Su-Th 11am-1am, F-Sa 11am-3am.

CAPITOL HILL

With bronze dance-steps emblazoned on the sidewalks and neon storefronts, **Broadway Ave.** is a land of espresso houses, imaginative shops, elegant clubs, and good eats.

▨ **Bimbo's Bitchin' Burrito Kitchen,** 506 E. Pine St. (☎206-329-9978). The name explains it, and the decorations (fake palm trees and lots of plastic) prove it. Walk right on through the door to the **Cha Cha,** a similarly decorated bar (tequila shots $3.50). Spicy Bimbo's burrito $4.25. Dining room open M-Th noon-10pm, F-Sa noon-1am, Su 2-9pm.

Ristorante Machiavelli, 1215 Pine St. (☎206-621-7941), across the street from Bauhaus. A small Italian place that locals swear by. Pasta $8-10. Open M-Sa 5-11pm.

HaNa, 219 Broadway Ave. East (☎206-328-1187). Packed quarters testify to the popularity of the sushi here. Lunch sushi combo platter with rice and soup $7.25. Dinner $9-10. Open M-Sa 11am-10pm, Su 4-10pm.

Honey Hole Sandwiches, 703 E. Pike St. (☎206-709-1399). The primary colors and veggie-filled sandwiches make you feel healthy and happy. Try the hummus-loaded "Daytripper" ($5.50). Lunch menu available until 5pm. Open daily 10am-2am.

UNIVERSITY DISTRICT

The neighborhood around the immense **University of Washington** ("U-Dub"), north of downtown between Union and Portage Bay, supports funky shops, international restaurants, and coffeehouses. The best of each lies within a few blocks of **University Way,** known as "the Ave."

Flowers, 4247 University Way NE (☎206-633-1903). This 1920s landmark was once a flower shop; now, the mirrored ceiling tastefully reflects an all-you-can-eat vegetarian buffet ($7.50). Great daily drink specials. Open M-Sa 11am-2am, Su 11am-midnight.

Neelam's, 4735 University Way NE (☎206-523-5275). The best authentic Indian cuisine in the University District, and the price is right. Lunch buffet $6. Brunch $7. Open daily 11:30am-3pm and 5-10pm.

Araya's Vegan Thai Cuisine, 4732 University Way NE (☎206-524-4332). Consistently among the top vegan restaurants in Seattle, Araya's will satisfy any meatless desire. Lunch buffet $6.55. Open M-Th 11:30am-9pm, F-Sa 11:30am-9:30pm, Su 5-9pm.

ACCOMMODATIONS

Seattle's hostel scene is not amazing, but there are plenty of choices and establishments to fit all types of personalities. **Pacific Reservation Service**

(☎800-684-2932) arranges B&B singles for $50-65. For inexpensive motels farther from downtown, drive north on **Aurora Ave.**

Seattle International Hostel (HI), 84 Union St. (☎206-622-5443 or 888-622-5443), at Western Ave., by the waterfront. Take Union St. from downtown; follow signs down the stairs under the "Pike Pub & Brewery." Great location, laundry, and Internet access. 7-night max. stay in summer. Reception 24hr. Reservations recommended. 199 beds. Dorms $22, nonmembers $25; private rooms for 2-4 $54/$60.

Green Tortoise Backpacker's Hostel, 1525 2nd Ave. (☎206-340-1222), between Pike and Pine St. A young party hostel downtown. Laundry, kitchen, Internet access. Key deposit $20 cash. Blanket $1. Free breakfast (7-9:30am) and dinner (M, W, F). Reception 24hr. Dorms $18-20.

Moore Hotel, 1926 2nd Ave. (☎206-448-4851 or 800-421-5508), at Virginia St. 1 block from Pike Place Market. Open lobby, cavernous halls, and attentive service. Singles $39, with bath $59 (double occupancy $10 extra). Doubles $49/$68.

Commodore Hotel, 2013 2nd Ave. (☎206-448-8868), at Virginia St. Pleasant decor only a few blocks from the waterfront. Reception 24hr.; no visitors past 8pm. Singles $59, with bath $69; doubles with bath $79.

West Coast Vance Hotel, 620 Steward St. (☎206-441-4200). Built in 1926, the West Coast Vance has charming rooms from $95. The hotel is located within walking distance from Pike Place Market and the 5th Ave. shopping district.

NIGHTLIFE

Seattle has moved beyond beer to a new nightlife frontier: the cafe-bar. The popularity of espresso bars in Seattle might lead one to conclude that caffeine is more intoxicating than alcohol, but often an establishment that poses as a diner by day brings on a band, breaks out the disco ball, and pumps out the microbrews by night. Many locals tell tourists that the best spot to go for guaranteed good beer, live music, and big crowds is **Pioneer Square,** where UW students from frat row dominate the bar stools. You may prefer to go to **Capitol Hill,** or up Rte. 99 to **Fremont,** where the atmosphere is usually more laid-back than in the Square. Wherever

PACIFIC COAST

you go, but especially downtown, do stay alert—Seattle is big city, and has the homelessness, crime, and dark alleys that come with size.

DOWNTOWN

🏴 **The Alibi Room,** 85 Pike St. (☎206-623-3180), across from the Market Cinema in the Post Alley in Pike Place. A remarkably friendly local indie filmmaker hangout. Bar with music. Downstairs dance floor F-Sa. Brunch Sa-Su. No cover. Open daily 11am-3pm and 5pm-2am.

Crocodile Cafe, 2200 2nd Ave. (☎206-448-2114), at Blanchard St. in Belltown. Cooks from scratch by day, and features live music by night (Tu-Sa). Shows usually start 9pm; some require advance ticket purchase. 21+ after 9pm. Cover $6-22. Open Tu-F 11am-11pm, Sa 8am-11pm, Su 9am-3pm.

PIONEER SQUARE

Pioneer Square provides a happening scene, dominated by twenty-somethings, frat kids, and cover bands. Most bars participate in a joint cover (Su-Th $5, F-Sa $10) that will let you wander from bar to bar to sample the bands. The larger venues are listed below. Two smaller venues, **Larry's,** 209 1st Ave. S. (☎206-624-7665), and **New Orleans,** 114 1st Ave. S. (☎206-622-2563), feature great blues and jazz nightly. Most clubs close at 2am weekends and midnight weekdays.

🏴 **Bohemian Cafe,** 111 Yesler Way (☎206-447-1514). Reggae pumps every night through 3 sections—a cafe, bar, and stage—all adorned with art from Jamaica. Live shows, often national acts on

weekends. Happy hour 4-7pm. Joint cover Th-Sa. Open M-Th and Sa 4pm-2am, F 3pm-2am.

Central Tavern, 207 1st Ave. S. (☎206-622-0209). One of the early venues for grunge has now become a favorite for bikers. Live rock M and W-Su 9:30pm. Tu open mic. Joint cover. Open daily 11:30am-2am. Kitchen closes 8pm.

Last Supper Club, 124 S. Washington St. (☎206-748-9975), at Occidental. 2 dance floors, DJed with everything from 70s disco to funky house, drum 'n' bass, and trance. Cover varies. Open W-Su 5pm-2am.

Swannie's Sports Bar, 222 S. Main St. (☎206-622-9353). Share drink specials with pro ballplayers who stop by post-game. Any Seattle sports junkie will swear this is the place to be. Drink specials change daily. Open daily 11:30am-2am.

CAPITOL HILL

East off Broadway, find your atmosphere and acclimatize in a cool lounge on **Pine St.** West off Broadway, **Pike St.** has the clubs that push the limits (gay, punk, industrial, fetish, dance) and break the sound barrier.

🏴 **Linda's Tavern,** 707 Pine St. East (☎206-325-1220). A very chill post-gig scene for Seattle rockers. On Tu night a live DJ plays jazz and old rock. Expanded menu, liquor, and breakfast on weekends. W movie night. No cover. Open daily 4pm-2am.

Neighbors, 1509 Broadway Ave. (☎206-324-5358). Enter from the alley on Pike St. A gay dance club for 20 years, Neighbors prides itself on techno slickness. Open 7 nights a week with drag nights and special events.

APPENDIX

MEASUREMENT CONVERSIONS

1 inch (in.) = 25.4 millimeters (mm)	1 millimeter (mm) = 0.039 in.
1 foot (ft.) = 0.30 m	1 meter (m) = 3.28 ft.
1 yard (yd.) = 0.914m	1 meter (m) = 1.09 yd.
1 mile = 1.61km	1 kilometer (km) = 0.62 mi.
1 ounce (oz.) = 28.35g	1 gram (g) = 0.035 oz.
1 pound (lb.) = 0.454kg	1 kilogram (kg) = 2.202 lb.
1 fluid ounce (fl. oz.) = 29.57ml	1 milliliter (ml) = 0.034 fl. oz.
1 gallon (gal.) = 3.785L	1 liter (L) = 0.264 gal.
1 acre (ac.) = 0.405ha	1 hectare (ha) = 2.47 ac.
1 square mile (sq. mi.) = 2.59 sq. km	1 square kilometer (sq. km) = 0.386 sq. mi.

DISTANCE CONVERSION SCALE

Miles	1	2	3	4	5	10	20	30	40	50	60	70	80	90	100	250	500	1000
Kilometers	1.6	3.2	4.8	6.4	8	16	32	48	64	81	97	113	115	145	161	402	805	1609
Kilometers	1	2	3	4	5	10	20	30	40	50	60	70	80	90	100	250	500	1000
Miles	.62	1.3	1.9	2.5	3.1	6.2	12.4	18.6	25	31	37	43	50	56	62	155	310	620

TEMPERATURE CONVERSION SCALE

Degrees Celsius	-20	-15	-10	-5	0	5	10	15	20	25	30	35	40	45
Degrees Fahrenheit	-4	5	14	23	32	41	50	59	68	77	86	95	104	113

LANGUAGE BASICS

FRENCH QUICK REFERENCE

Both English and French are official languages in Canada. Roadtrippers should have no trouble getting around in English, but a basic familiarity with French is helpful, especially in Quebec, where attempts to use French words will be much appreciated.

ENGLISH	FRENCH	PRONOUNCIATION
	BASIC FRENCH	
Hello/Good day	Bonjour	bohn-ZJHOOR
Good evening	Bonsoir	bohn-SWAH
Hi!	Salut!	SAH-LU
Goodbye	Au revoir	oh ruh-VWAHR
Good night	Bonne nuit	bonn NWEE
yes/no/maybe	oui/non/peut-être	wee/nohn/puh-TET-ruh
Please	S'il vous plait	see voo PLAY

Thank you	Merci	mehr-SEE
You're welcome	De rien	duh rhee-EHN
Pardon me!	Excusez-moi!	ex-KU-zay-MWAH
Go away!	Allez-vous en!	ah-lay vooz ON!
Where is...?	Où se trouve...?	oo s'TRHOOV...?
What time do you open/close?	Vous ouvrez/fermez à quelle heure?	vooz oo-VRAY/ferh-MAY ah kel-UHR?
Help!	Au secours!	oh-skOOR
I'm lost	Je suis perdu(e)	zh'SWEE pehr-DU
I'm sorry	Je suis désolé(e)	zh'SWEE day-zoh-LAY
Do you speak English?	Parlez-vous anglais?	PAR-lay-voo ahn-GLAY

SPANISH QUICK REFERENCE

Although English is fairly common in Mexico City and in larger tourist destinations, roadtrippers may have to manage in Spanish in the smaller towns dotting their route. Even when English is spoken, many Mexicans appreciate an attempt to use even the most basic Spanish in greeting.

PRONUNCIATION

Each **vowel** has only one pronunciation: *A* ("ah" in father); *E* ("eh" in pet); *I* ("ee" in eat); *O* ("oh" in oat); *U* ("oo" in boot); *Y*, by itself, is pronounced the same as Spanish *I*. Most **consonants** are pronounced the same as in English. Important exceptions are: *J*, pronounced like the English "h" in "hello"; *LL*, pronounced like the English "y" in "yes"; *Ñ*, pronounced like the "gn" in "cognac." *R* at the beginning of a word or *RR* anywhere in a word is trilled. *H* is always silent. *G* before *E* or *I* is pronounced like the "ch" in "chutzpah"; elsewhere it is pronounced like the "g" in "gate." Because it became used as a placeholder by Spaniards transcribing native languages, *X* has a variety of pronunciations: depending on dialect and word position it can sound like English "h," "s," "sh," or "x." *Tl*, another placeholder, is pronounced with the tongue at the teeth, as if to make the "t" in toy; the air is expelled out the sides of the mouth, without releasing the tongue. Spanish words receive **stress** on the syllable marked with an **accent** (´). In the absence of an accent mark, words that end in vowels, "n," or "s" receive stress on the second to last syllable. For words ending in all other consonants, stress falls on the last syllable. The Spanish language has masculine and feminine nouns, and gives a **gender** to all adjectives. Masculine words generally end with an "o": *él es un tonto* (he is a fool). Feminine words generally end with an "a": *ella es bella* (she is beautiful). Pay close attention—slight changes in word ending can have drastic changes in meaning. For instance, when receiving directions, mind the distinction between *derecho* (straight) and *derecha* (right).

ENGLISH	SPANISH	ENGLISH	SPANISH
		Essential Phrases	
Yes/No	Sí/No	Hello/Goodbye	Hola/Adíos
Go on!/Come on!/Hurry up!	¡Ándale!	Until later	Hasta luego/Nos vemos
Please	Por favor	I'm sick/fine	Estoy enfermo(a)/bien
Thank you	Gracias	Could you speak more slowly?	¿Podría hablar más despacio?
You're welcome	De nada	I don't speak Spanish	No hablo español
Excuse me	Perdón/Disculpe	Sorry	Lo siento
How do you say it in Spanish?	¿Cómo se dice en español?	It doesn't matter	No importa

ENGLISH	SPANISH	ENGLISH	SPANISH
We'll see	Vamos a ver	Perhaps	Tal vez/Puede ser
Who knows?	¿Quién sabe?	Of course	Claro que sí
I forgot	Se me olvidó.	That's the way it is	Así es
Do you speak English?	¿Habla inglés?	How are you?	¿Cómo está?/¿Qué pasa?
What?	¿Cómo?/¿Qué?/¿Mande?	Where is (the center)?	¿Dónde está (el centro)?
How do you say (ice cream) in Spanish?	¿Cómo se dice (ice cream) en español?	Good morning (Good afternoon/night)	Buenos días (Buenas tardes/noches)
What is your name?	¿Cómo se llama?	My name is (Inigo Montoya)	Me llamo (Inigo Montoya)
You killed my father...	Mató a mi padre...	Prepare to die.	Prepárese para morir.
I don't understand	No entiendo	Why (are you staring at me)?	¿Por qué (me mira)?
I am hot/cold	Tengo calor/frio	Whoa! Geez!	¡Híjole!
How much does it cost?	¿Cuánto cuesta?	I want/would like...	Quiero/Me gustaría...
Closed/Open	Cerrado(a)/Abierto(a)	That is cheap/expensive	Es barato/caro

Your Arrival

ENGLISH	SPANISH	ENGLISH	SPANISH
I am from the US/Europe.	Soy de los Estados Unidos/de Europa	I will be here for less than 6 months	Estaré aquí por menos de seis meses
Here is my passport	Aquí está mi pasaporte	I lost my passport	Se me perdió mi pasaporte
I have nothing to declare	No tengo nada que declarar	Please do not detain me	Por favor no me detenga

Getting Around

ENGLISH	SPANISH	ENGLISH	SPANISH
How long does the trip take?	¿Cuánto tiempo dura el viaje?	How do you get there?	¿Cómo se puede llegar?
I am in a hurry	Estoy de prisa	Is it near/far?	¿Está cerca/lejos de aquí?
Freeway (no toll)	Autopista/vía libre	Toll road	Carretera de cuota
Turn right/left	Doble a la derecha/izquierda	Continue straight	Siga derecho
I would like to rent (a car)	Quisiera rentar (un coche)	Please let me off at...	Por favor, déjeme en...

Accommodations

ENGLISH	SPANISH	ENGLISH	SPANISH
How much does it cost per day/week?	¿Cuánto cuesta por día/semana?	I am going to stay for (four) days	Me voy a quedar (cuatro) días
Is there a cheap hotel around here?	¿Hay un hotel económico por aquí?	Are there rooms with windows?	¿Hay habitaciones con ventanas?
Do you have rooms available?	¿Tiene habitaciones libres?	Does it have air-conditioning?	¿Tiene aire acondicionado?
I would like to reserve a room	Quisiera reservar una habitación	Are there cheaper rooms?	¿Hay habitaciones más baratas?
Do you have any singles/doubles?	¿Tiene habitaciones sencillas/dobles?	Do they come with private bath?	¿Vienen con baño privado?
Can I see a room?	¿Puedo ver una habitación?	I'll take it	Lo acepto
There are cockroaches in my room	Hay cucarachas en mi habitación	Dance, cockroaches, dance!	¡Bailen, cucarachas, bailen!

Eating Out

ENGLISH	SPANISH	ENGLISH	SPANISH
I am hungry/thirsty	Tengo hambre/sed	Do you have hot sauce?	¿Tiene salsa picante?
Where is a good restaurant?	¿Dónde hay un restaurante bueno?	Table for (one), please	Mesa para (uno), por favor
Can I see the menu?	¿Puedo ver la carta?	Delicious!	¡Qué rico!/¡Delicioso!

ENGLISH	SPANISH	ENGLISH	SPANISH
I would like...	Quisiera...	Check, please!	¡La cuenta, por favor!
Do you have anything without meat?	¿Hay algún plato sin carne?	Do you take credit cards?	¿Aceptan tarjetas de crédito?

Emergency			
Help!	¡Auxilio!/¡Ayúdame!	Call the police!	Llame a la policía!
I am hurt	Estoy herido(a)	Leave me alone!	¡Déjame en paz!
It's an emergency!	¡Es una emergencia!	I have been robbed!	¡Me han robado!
Fire!	¡Fuego!/¡Incendio!	They went that-a-way!	¡Se fueron por allá!
My car broke down	Mi coche está averiado	Can you fix it?	Puede repararlo?
I locked my keys in my car.	He cerrado las llaves en mi coche.	It won't start	No arranca
My car has a flat tire	Mi coche tiene una llanta desinflata	Is there a mechanic shop nearby?	¿Hay un taller mecánico por aquí?
Call a clinic/ambulance/doctor/priest!	¡Llame a una clínica/una ambulancia/un médico/un padre!	How can we solve this problem?	¿Cómo podemos resolverlo?
I need to contact my embassy	Necesito comunicar con mi embajada	I will only speak in the presence of a lawyer	Sólo hablaré en presencia de un(a) abogado(a)

Medical			
I feel bad/better/worse	Me siento mal/mejor/peor	I have a cold/a fever/diarrhea/nausea	Tengo gripe/un fiebre/diarrea/náusea
I have a headache	Tengo dolor de cabeza	I have a stomach ache	Tengo dolor de estómago
I'm sick/ill	Estoy enfermo(a)	It hurts here	Me duele aquí
I'm allergic to...	Soy alérgico(a) a...	Here is my prescription	Aquí está mi receta médica
What is this medicine for?	¿Para qué es esta medicina?	I think i'm going to vomit	Pienso que voy a vomitar
Where is the nearest hospital/doctor?	¿Donde está el hospital/doctor más cercano?	I haven't been able to go to the bathroom in (four) days	No he podido ir al baño en (cuatro) días

(Informal) Personal Relationships			
What's up?/What's shakin'?	¿Qué tal?/¿Qué hay?	Pleased to meet you	Encantado(a)/Mucho gusto
Where are you from?	¿De dónde eres?	He/she/it seems cool	Me cae bien
It's my first time in Mexico.	Es mi primera vez en México.	I'm (twenty) years old	Tengo (veinte) anos
Do you have a light?	¿Tienes fuego?	I have a boyfriend/girlfriend	Tengo novio/novia.
What happened to you?	¿Qué te pasó?	I'm married.	Soy casado/casada.
Will you go out with me?	¿Quieres salir conmigo?	I love you.	Te quiero.

Numbers and Days			
0	cero	14	catorce
1	uno	15	quince
2	dos	16	dieciseis
3	tres	17	diecisiete
4	cuatro	18	dieciocho
5	cinco	19	diecinueve
6	seis	20	veinte
7	siete	21	veintiuno
8	ocho	30	treinta
9	nueve	80	ochenta
10	diez	90	noventa
11	once	100	cien

APPENDIX

ENGLISH	SPANISH	ENGLISH	SPANISH
12	doce	1000	mil
13	trece	1 million	un millón
Sunday	domingo	Saturday	sábado
Monday	lunes	tomorrow	mañana
Tuesday	martes	today	hoy
Wednesday	miércoles	tomorrow	mañana
Thursday	jueves	day before yesterday	antes de ayer/anteayer
Friday	viernes	weekend	fin de semana

GLOSSARY OF SPANISH TERMS

aduana: customs
agua (purificada): water (purified)
al gusto: as you wish
albergue: accommodation
almuerzo: lunch
amigo/a: friend
antojito: appetizer
arroz: rice
artesanía: artisanry, crafts
autopista: freeway
avenida: avenue
azulejo: glazed tile
bahía: bay
balneario: public pool; spa
baño: bathroom
barato: cheap
barranca: canyon
basílica: basilica, church
biblioteca: library
bistec/bistek: beefsteak
bonito/a: pretty
borracho/a: drunk
bosque: forest; park
buena suerte: good luck
burro: donkey
caballero: gentleman
café: coffee; cafe
cajero automático: ATM
caldo: soup, broth, or stew
calle: street
camarero: waiter
camarón: shrimp
cambio: change
camión: bus; commercial truck
campo: countryside; field
cantina: saloon, bar
carne (asada): (roast) meat
carnitas: pork
caro: expensive
casa: house
casa de cambio: currency exchange booth
cascada: waterfall
catedral: cathedral
cena: supper
centro: center (of town)
cerro: hill

cerveza: beer
colonia: neighborhood
combi: small local bus
comedor: small diner
comida: food; afternoon main meal
comida corrida: fixed menu
consulado: consulate
correo (registrado): (registered) mail
corrida: bullfight; race
cuarto: room
cuenta: bill/check
cucaracha: cockroach
cuota: toll
chico/a: child; small
chicle: chewing gum
chicharrón: pieces of fried pork rind
chilaquiles: fried tortilla casserole
chimichanga: fried, filled tortilla
chuleta de chancho: pork chop
dama: lady
deporte: sport
desayuno: breakfast
dinero: money
discoteca: dance club
disputa: argument
dulce: sweet
enchilada: baked filled tortilla
entrada: entrance
este: east; this
extranjero: foreigner
farmacia: pharmacy
faro: lighthouse
fiesta: party; holiday
flauta: large fried taco; flute
frijoles: beans
frito: fried
frontera: border
fuente: fountain
fumar: to smoke
fútbol: soccer
gabacho: white American
géiser: geyser
glorieta: traffic circle
gobierno: government
gordo: fat
gracias: thank you

grande: big
grasa: fat (from food)
gratis: free (no charge)
gringo: person from the US
grosero: uncouth
grueso: thick, heavy
gruta: cave
guapo/a: handsome/foxy
helado: ice cream
hombre: man
huevos: eggs
iglesia: church
isla: island
jamón: ham
jardín: garden
jugo: juice
ladrón: thief
lago: lake
lancha: boat
langostina: lobster
lavandería: laundromat
leche: milk
libre: free, independent
loma: hill
maíz: corn
malecón: promenade
mantequilla: butter
mar: ocean; sea
maricón (vulgar): homosexual
mariscos: seafood
mentira: lie, falsehood
mercado: (outdoor) market
mesa: table
mochila: backpack
mirador: viewpoint
mole: chocolate and chile sauce
mollete: refried beans and cheese
mordida: bribe
mujer: woman
museo: museum
niño/a: child
norte (Nte.): north
noticia: news
novio/a: boyfriend/girlfriend;
oeste: west
oriente (Ote.): east
parada: a stop (bus or train)

parque: park
paseo: promenade
pequeño: small
pescado: fish
pesero: small local bus
peligro: danger
picante: spicy
pirámide: pyramid
playa: beach
pollo: chicken
poniente (Pte.): west
posada: inn
postre: dessert
pueblo: town; community
puerta: door
puerto: port
queso: cheese
refresco: soft drink
ropa: clothes
ruinas: ruins
ruta: route; local bus
salida: exit
salud: health
selva: jungle
sierra: mountain range
siesta: afternoon nap
simpático/a: friendly/nice
supermercado: supermarket
sur: south
taberna: tavern, bar
taquería: taco stand
taquilla: ticket booth
tarifa: fee
templo: church; temple
tianguis: *(indígena)* markets
tienda: store
tipo de cambio: exchange rate
toalla: towel
tonto/a: dumb
toro: bull
torre: tower
torta: sandwich
trolebús: electric bus
turista: tourist; diarrhea
zócalo: central square
zona: zone; region

APPENDIX

INDEX

go the distance with

LONG ON WEEKEND. SHORT ON CASH.

The fastest way to the best fare.

MAP INDEX